Customer Support Information

The Almanac of American Employers 2010

Please register your book immediately...

if you did not purchase it directly from Plunkett Research, Ltd. This will enable us to fulfill your replacement request if you have a damaged product, or your requests for assistance. Also it will enable us to notify you of future editions, so that you may purchase them from the source of your choice.

If you are an actual, original purchaser but did not receive a FREE CD-ROM version with your book...*

you may request it by returning this form.

_____ YES, please register me as a purchaser of the book.
I did not buy it directly from Plunkett Research, Ltd.

_____ YES, please send me a free CD-ROM version of the book.
I am an actual purchaser, but I did not receive one with my book. (Proof of purchase may be required.)

Customer Name _____

Title_____

Organization _____

Address _____

City_____State_____Zip_____

Country (if other than USA) _____

Phone_____Fax _____

E-mail _____

Mail or Fax to: **Plunkett Research, Ltd.**
Attn: FREE CD-ROM and/or Registration
P.O. Drawer 541737, Houston, TX 77254-1737 USA
713.932.0000 · Fax 713.932.7080 · www.plunkettresearch.com

* Purchasers of used books are not eligible to register. Use of CD-ROMs is subject to the terms of their end user license agreements.

THE ALMANAC OF AMERICAN EMPLOYERS 2010

The Only Guide to America's Hottest, Fastest-Growing Major Corporations

Jack W. Plunkett

Published by:
Plunkett Research, Ltd., Houston, Texas
www.plunkettresearch.com

THE ALMANAC OF AMERICAN EMPLOYERS 2010

The Only Guide to America's Hottest, Fastest-Growing Major Corporations

Jack W. Plunkett

Published by:
Plunkett Research, Ltd., Houston, Texas
www.plunkettresearch.com

THE ALMANAC OF AMERICAN EMPLOYERS 2010

Editor and Publisher:
Jack W. Plunkett

Executive Editor and Database Manager:
Martha Burgher Plunkett

Senior Editors and Researchers:
Brandon Brison
Addie K. FryeWeaver
Christie Manck

Editors, Researchers and Assistants:
Kalonji Bobb
Elizabeth Braddock
Michelle Dotter
Michael Esterheld
Lindsey Meyn
Andrew Olsen
Jill Steinberg
Kyle Wark
Suzanne Zarosky

E-Commerce Managers:
Mark Cassells
Emily Hurley

Information Technology Manager:
Wenping Guo

Cover Design:
Kim Paxson, Just Graphics
Junction, TX

Special Thanks to:
U.S. Department of Labor
Bureau of Labor Statistics
U.S. Department of Commerce
*Bureau of Economic Analysis, National Technical
Information Service*

Plunkett Research, Ltd.
P. O. Drawer 541737, Houston, Texas 77254 USA
Phone: 713.932.0000 Fax: 713.932.7080
www.plunkettresearch.com

Published by:

Plunkett Research, Ltd.
P. O. Drawer 541737
Houston, Texas 77254-1737

Phone: 713.932.0000
Fax: 713.932.7080
Internet: www.plunkettresearch.com

ISBN13 # 978-1-59392-153-8

Disclaimer of liability
for use and results of use:

The editors and publishers assume no responsibility for your own success in making an investment or business decision, in seeking or keeping any job, in succeeding at any firm or in obtaining any amount or type of benefits or wages. Your own results and the job stability or financial stability of any company depend on influences outside of our control. All risks are assumed by the reader. Investigate any potential employer or business relationship carefully and carefully verify past and present finances, present business conditions and the level of compensation and benefits currently paid. Each company's details are taken from sources deemed reliable; however, their accuracy is not guaranteed. The editors and publishers assume no liability, beyond the actual payment received from a reader, for any direct, indirect, incidental or consequential, special or exemplary damages, and they do not guarantee, warrant nor make any representation regarding the use of this material. Trademarks or tradenames are used without symbols and only in a descriptive sense, and this use is not authorized by, associated with or sponsored by the trademarks' owners. Ranks and ratings are presented as an introductory and general glance at corporations, based on our research and our knowledge of businesses and the industries in which they operate. The reader should use caution.

THE ALMANAC OF AMERICAN EMPLOYERS 2010

CONTENTS

Continued on the next page

INTRODUCTION

THE ALMANAC OF AMERICAN EMPLOYERS is an easy-to-use solution to what would otherwise be a complicated problem: How can you tell, among America's giant companies, which firms are most likely to be hiring? Among those firms, which are the best to work for? No other source provides this book's easy-to-understand comparisons of growth, treatment of employees, salaries, benefits, pension plans, profit sharing and many other items of great importance to job seekers.

Especially helpful is the way in which THE ALMANAC OF AMERICAN EMPLOYERS enables readers with no business background to readily compare the growth potential and benefit plans of large employers. You'll see the mid-term financial record of each firm, along with the impact of earnings, sales and growth plans on each company's potential to provide employment opportunities.

Information is presented in a way that addresses the differing interests of individual employees. You'll find separate listings for dozens of categories of data that you may want to consider. While this book is aimed primarily at job seekers, it will also be of tremendous value to researchers, marketing executives and personnel professionals. THE ALMANAC OF AMERICAN EMPLOYERS is the premier guide to the most successful employers in the nation, their policies and their performance.

THE ALMANAC OF AMERICAN EMPLOYERS is your opportunity to gain valuable knowledge in a matter of minutes. Five hundred of the biggest, most successful corporate employers in America are analyzed in this book. Tens of thousands of pieces of information, gathered from a wide variety of sources, have been researched for these corporations and are presented here in a form that can be easily understood by job seekers of all types.

Thanks to THE ALMANAC OF AMERICAN EMPLOYERS' exclusive data system, potentially confusing considerations have been reduced to simple groups of focused data. By scanning the data groups and the long list of unique indexes, you can find the right employers to fit your personal needs.

The AMERICAN EMPLOYERS 500 are among the best major growth companies to work for in America. Which companies offer the best benefits, are the biggest employers or earn the most profits? Where are these companies operating? All of these things and more are made easy for the reader to determine.

Thousands of observations are made that will be of great interest to prospective employees. For many of the firms, you'll find comments about such items as plans for growth, increases or decreases in the number of employees and charitable programs. You'll also find notes about corporate culture and special programs for the convenience of employees, such as health and recreation facilities, on-site child care, job training or career paths. Finally, you'll find basic information on each company, including the home office address and telephone number; regional, national and international locations; a description of the business; and a list of selected subsidiaries and trade names. In addition, you will find fax numbers and Internet addresses.

Whether you are currently employed by one of these corporate giants or are considering applying for a job with one, you will be able to see how each company compares with the others, even if you don't have the slightest understanding of accounting, finance or employee benefits.

Whatever your purpose for researching corporate employers, you'll find this book to be an indispensable guide. Nonetheless, as is true with all resources, this volume has limitations that the reader should be aware of:

- Financial data and other corporate information can change quickly. A book of this type can be no more current than the data that was available as of the time of editing. Consequently, the financial picture, management and ownership of the firm(s) you are studying may have changed since the date of this book. For example, this almanac includes the most up-to-date sales figures and profits available to the editors as of mid-2009. This means that we have typically used corporate financial data as of the end of 2008.

- Corporate mergers, changes in corporate financial ratings or stability, acquisitions and downsizing are occurring at a very rapid rate. Such events may have created significant change, subsequent to the publishing of this book, within a company you are studying.

- Some of the companies in THE AMERICAN EMPLOYERS 500 are so large in scope and in variety of business endeavors conducted within a parent organization that we have been unable to completely list all subsidiaries, affiliations, divisions and activities within a firm's corporate structure.

- This volume is intended to be a general guide to major employers in numerous industries. That means that researchers should look to this book

for an overview and, when conducting in-depth research, should contact the specific corporations and related industry associations in question for the very latest changes and data. Where possible, we have listed contact information, telephone numbers and Internet addresses for pertinent companies, government agencies and industry associations so that the reader may get further details without unnecessary delay.

- We have used exhaustive efforts to locate and fairly present accurate and complete data. However, when using this book or any other source for business and industry information, the reader should use caution and due diligence by conducting further research where it seems appropriate. We wish you success in your endeavors, and we trust that your experience with this book will be both satisfactory and productive.

- To obtain the best results and to best understand the fields in the company profiles, you should first read the chapter titled "How to Use This Book."

Good luck in your job search. Be patient, do your research and use this book as an important start in the right direction.

Jack W. Plunkett
Houston, Texas
September 2009

HOW TO USE THIS BOOK

Dozens of excellent books already exist to help you choose a career, write a resume, apply for a job and so on. That is not the purpose of THE ALMANAC OF AMERICAN EMPLOYERS. Instead, this book's job is to help you sort through America's giant corporate employers to determine which may be the best for you, or to see how your current employer compares to others. Whether you are entering the job market and looking for your first position, or you are thinking about switching companies in mid-career to find more promising vistas, this book will be a valuable guide.

The two primary sections of the book are devoted first to general information for job seekers (trends analysis and advice on conducting employer research, along with resources, statistics and contacts), followed by the "Individual Data Listings" for THE AMERICAN EMPLOYERS 500. If time permits, you should begin your research in the front chapters of this book. Also, you will find lengthy indexes in Chapter 5 and in the back of the book.

GENERAL INFORMATION FOR JOB SEEKERS

Chapter 1: Major Trends Affecting Job Seekers. This chapter presents an encapsulated view of the major trends in business and the economy that are creating rapid changes in the employment picture at large corporations.

Chapter 2: Statistics. This chapter presents in-depth statistics on employment by education level, sex and race, along with unemployment rates, the fastest-growing occupations and more.

Chapter 3: Research–7 Keys for Job Seekers. This chapter provides a definitive list of items that job seekers should look for when conducting research into major corporate employers.

Chapter 4: Important Contacts for Job Seekers. This chapter covers contacts for important government agencies, professional societies, industry associations, job banks, reference sources and more. Included are Internet sites and contact addresses for a wide variety of job search uses.

THE AMERICAN EMPLOYERS 500

Chapter 5: THE AMERICAN EMPLOYERS 500: Who They Are and How They Were Chosen.
The companies compared in this book were chosen from nearly all industries, on a nationwide basis. They were individually chosen from the largest U.S. employers, based on selected types of business and industry sectors. For a complete description, see Chapter 5.

Individual Data Listings:
Look at one of the companies in THE AMERICAN EMPLOYERS 500's Individual Data Listings. You'll find the following information fields:

Company Name:

The company profiles are in alphabetical order by company name. If you don't find the company you are seeking, it may be a subsidiary or division of one of the firms covered in this book. Try looking it up in the Index by Subsidiaries, Brand Names and Selected Affiliations in the back of the book.

Ranks:

Industry Group Code: An NAIC code used to group companies within like segments. (See Chapter 5 for a list of codes.)

Ranks Within This Company's Industry Group: Ranks, within this firm's segment only, for annual sales and annual profits, with 1 being the highest rank.

Suggested Career Paths:

A grid arranged into six major career categories and several sub-categories. A "Y" indicates that the firm is suggested for certain types of employees, by job discipline.

Types of Business:

A listing of the primary types of business specialties conducted by the firm.

Brands/Divisions/Affiliations:

Brand names, operating divisions or subsidiaries of the firm, as well as major corporate affiliations—such as another firm that owns a significant portion of the company's stock. A complete Index by Subsidiaries, Brand Names and Selected Affiliations is in the back of the book.

Contacts:

The names and titles up to 27 top officers of the company are listed, including human resources contacts.

Address:

The firm's full headquarters address, the headquarters telephone, plus toll-free and fax numbers where available. Also provided is the Internet site address.

Financials:

Annual Sales (2008 or the latest fiscal year available to the editors, plus up to four previous years): These are stated in thousands of dollars (add three zeros if you want the full number). This figure represents consolidated worldwide sales from all operations. 2008 figures may be estimates.

Annual Profits (2008 or the latest fiscal year available to the editors, plus up to four previous years): These are stated in thousands of dollars (add three zeros if you want the full number). This figure represents consolidated, after-tax net profit from all operations. 2008 figures may be estimates.

Stock Ticker/Parent Company: When available, the unique stock market symbol used to identify this firm's common stock for trading and tracking purposes is indicated. Where appropriate, this field may contain "private" or "subsidiary" rather than a ticker symbol. If the firm is a subsidiary, its parent company is listed.

Total Number of Employees: The approximate total number of employees, worldwide, as of the end of 2008 (or the latest data available to the editors).

Apparent Salaries/Benefits:

(The following descriptions generally apply to U.S. employers only.)

A "Y" in appropriate fields indicates "Yes."

Due to wide variations in the manner in which corporations report benefits to the U.S. Government's regulatory bodies, not all plans will have been uncovered or correctly evaluated during our effort to research this data. Also, the availability to employees of such plans will vary according to the qualifications that employees must meet to become eligible. For example, some benefit plans may be available only to salaried workers—others only to employees who work more than 1,000 hours yearly. Benefits that are available to employees of the main or parent company may not be available to employees of the subsidiaries. In addition, employers frequently alter the nature and terms of plans offered.

NOTE: Generally, employees covered by wealth-building benefit plans do not *fully* own ("vest in") funds contributed on their behalf by the employer until as many as five years of service with that employer have passed. All pension plans are voluntary—that is, employers are not obligated to offer pensions.

Pension Plan: The firm offers a pension plan to qualified employees. In this case, in order for a "Y" to appear, the editors believe that the employer offers a defined benefit or cash balance pension plan (see discussions below). The type and generosity of these plans vary widely from firm to firm. Caution: Some employers refer to plans as "pension" or "retirement" plans when they are actually 401(k) savings plans that require a contribution by the employee.

- Defined Benefit Pension Plans: Pension plans that do not require a contribution from the employee are infrequently offered. However, a few companies, particularly larger employers in high-profit-margin industries, offer defined benefit pension plans where the employee is guaranteed to receive a set pension benefit upon retirement. The amount of the benefit is determined by the years of service with the company and the employee's salary during the later years of employment. The longer a person works for the employer, the higher the retirement benefit. These defined benefit plans are funded entirely by the employer. The benefits, up to a reasonable limit, are guaranteed by the Federal Government's Pension Benefit Guaranty Corporation. These plans are not portable—if you leave the company, you cannot transfer your benefits into a different plan. Instead, upon retirement you will receive the benefits that vested during your service with the company. If your employer offers a pension plan, it must give you a summary plan description within 90 days of the date you join the plan. You can also request a summary annual report of the plan, and once every 12 months you may request an individual benefit statement accounting of your interest in the plan.

- Defined Contribution Plans: These are quite different. They do not guarantee a certain amount of pension benefit. Instead, they set out circumstances under which the employer will make a contribution to a plan on your behalf. The most common example is the 401(k) savings plan. Pension benefits are not guaranteed under these plans.

- Cash Balance Pension Plans: These plans were recently invented. These are hybrid plans—part defined benefit and part defined contribution. Many employers have converted their older defined benefit plans into cash balance plans. The employer makes deposits (or credits a given amount of money) on the employee's behalf, usually based on a percentage of pay. Employee accounts grow based on a predetermined interest benchmark, such as the interest rate on Treasury Bonds. There are some advantages to these plans, particularly for younger workers: a) The benefits, up to a reasonable limit, are guaranteed by the Pension Benefit Guaranty Corporation. b) Benefits are portable—they can be moved to another plan when the employee changes companies. c) Younger workers and those who spend a shorter number of years with an employer may receive higher benefits than they would under a traditional defined benefit plan.

ESOP Stock Plan (Employees' Stock Ownership Plan): This type of plan is in wide use. Typically, the plan borrows money from a bank and uses those funds to purchase a large block of the corporation's stock. The corporation makes contributions to the plan over a period of time, and the stock purchase loan is eventually paid off. The value of the plan grows significantly as long as the market price of the stock holds up. Qualified employees are allocated a share of the plan based on their length of service and their level of salary. Under federal regulations, participants in ESOPs are allowed to diversify their account holdings in set percentages that rise as the employee ages and gains years of service with the company. In this manner, not all of the employee's assets are tied up in the employer's stock.

Savings Plan, 401(k): Under this type of plan, employees make a tax-deferred deposit into an account. In the best plans, the company makes annual matching donations to the employees' accounts, typically in some proportion to deposits made by the employees themselves. A good plan will match one-half of employee deposits of up to 6% of wages. For example, an employee earning $30,000 yearly might deposit $1,800 (6%) into the plan. The company will match one-half of the employee's deposit, or $900. The plan grows on a tax-deferred basis, similar to an IRA. A very generous plan will match 100% of employee deposits. However, some plans do not call for the employer to make a matching deposit at all. Other plans call for a matching contribution to be made at the discretion of the firm's board of directors. Actual terms of these plans vary widely from firm to firm. Generally, these savings plans allow employees to deposit as much as 15% of salary into the plan on a tax-deferred basis. However, the portion that the company uses to calculate its matching deposit is generally limited to a maximum of 6%. Employees should take care to diversify the holdings in their 401(k) accounts, and most people should seek professional guidance or investment management for their accounts.

Stock Purchase Plan: Qualified employees may purchase the company's common stock at a price below its market value under a specific plan. Typically, the employee is limited to investing a small percentage of wages in this plan. The discount may range from 5 to 15%. Some of these plans allow for deposits to be made through regular monthly payroll deductions. However, new accounting rules for corporations, along with other factors, are leading many companies to curtail these plans—dropping the discount allowed, cutting the maximum yearly stock purchase or otherwise making the plans less generous or appealing.

Profit Sharing: Qualified employees are awarded an annual amount equal to some portion of a company's profits. In a very generous plan, the pool of money awarded to employees would be 15% of profits. Typically, this money is deposited into a long-term retirement account. Caution: Some employers refer to plans as "profit sharing" when they are actually 401(k) savings plans. True profit sharing plans are rarely offered.

Highest Executive Salary: The highest executive salary paid, typically a 2008 amount (or the latest year available to the editors) and typically paid to the Chief Executive Officer.

Highest Executive Bonus: The apparent bonus, if any, paid to the above person.

Second Highest Executive Salary: The next-highest executive salary paid, typically a 2008 amount (or the latest year available to the editors) and typically paid to the President or Chief Operating Officer.

Second Highest Executive Bonus: The apparent bonus, if any, paid to the above person.

Other Thoughts:

Apparent Women Officers or Directors: It is difficult to obtain this information on an exact basis, and employers generally do not disclose the data in a public way. However, we have indicated what our best efforts reveal to be the apparent number of women who either are in the posts of corporate officers or sit on the board of directors. There is a wide variance from company to company.

Hot Spot for Advancement for Women/Minorities: A "Y" in appropriate fields indicates "Yes." These are firms that appear either to have posted a substantial number of women and/or minorities to high posts or that appear to have a good record of going out of their way to recruit, train, promote and retain women or minorities. (See the Index of Hot Spots For Women and Minorities in the back of the book.) This information may change frequently and can be difficult to obtain and verify. Consequently, the reader should use caution and conduct further investigation where appropriate.

Growth Plans/ Special Features:

Listed here are observations regarding the firm's strategy, hiring plans, plans for growth and product development, along with general information regarding a company's business and prospects.

Locations:

A "Y" in the appropriate field indicates "Yes."

Primary locations outside of the headquarters, categorized by regions of the United States and by international locations. A complete index by locations is also in the front of this chapter.

Chapter 1

MAJOR TRENDS AFFECTING JOB SEEKERS

Major trends sweeping through business and the economy that affect job seekers of all types:

1) U.S. Job Market Overview
2) Cost Control is a Major Concern at Employers/ Downsizing and Consolidation Through Mergers Continue
3) Unemployment Will Remain High
4) Consumers Spend Less, Save More, Affecting a Wide Variety of Companies
5) Technology Continues to Create Sweeping Changes in the Workplace
6) Continued Growth in Outsourcing, Including Supply Chain and Logistics Services
7) Millions Working as Temps
8) Offshoring and the Globalization of Business
9) Older Americans Will Delay Retirement and Work Longer/Many Employers Find Older Employees Desirable
10) Employment Sectors that Will Offer an Above-Average Number of Job Opportunities in 2010

- Batteries—Advanced Battery Technologies
- Biotechnology
- Construction and Engineering Services for Infrastructure and Government Projects
- Consulting—Selected Fields where Consultants May Be Able to Effect Cost-Savings for Clients
- Consumer Products Manufacturers
- Cosmetics Manufacturers
- Data Processing Services Providers
- Defense Contractors—Selected Firms
- Education
- Elder Care, Home Health Care, Nursing Homes and Assisted Living Communities
- Electronic Games, Games for Cell Phones
- Energy Conservation Products and Services
- Food Processing
- Guard Services, Investigation and Surveillance
- Health Care Services
- Health Care Products
- Health Care Technology, Including Computerized Patient Records
- Health Foods, Organic Foods, Enhanced Foods
- Insurance Providers
- Internet Service Providers
- Nanotechnology and MEMS
- Online Search Services with Advertising Revenues
- Online-based Business and Consumer Services
- Outsourcing, Including Outsourced Business and Computer Services
- Pharmaceuticals—Generics
- Radio Frequency ID Tags (RFID)
- Renewable Energy, Especially Solar and Wind Power
- Retailing—Basic, Including Drugstores and Supermarkets
- Retailing—Discount and Warehouse Clubs
- Supply Chain Services That Offer Cost-Savings to Clients
- Water Filtration and Conservation Equipment
- Wireless and Cellular Communications

1)   U.S. Job Market Overview

Job seekers in 2010 will continue to face a difficult job market, although conditions may improve a bit by the end of the year. Many types of employers are restructuring and downsizing thanks to the deep financial crisis of 2007-2009. Job seekers who want good positions will be forced to be better prepared and to do better research than in the boom years of the recent past. They will also have to work harder to find a good job.

Job seekers in 2010 should be prepared for the fact that nearly all industry sectors have suffered ill effects from economic and financial market problems that originated when the housing bubble finally popped in mid-2007 and the financial meltdown accelerated in 2008. America's unemployment grew steadily through 2009, and unemployment will remain very high in 2010.

The good news is that a select set of employers and growth companies will offer good job opportunities during 2010. In this period of challenges, a few companies will enjoy booming business. Sectors such as hi-tech batteries, education and health care are growing. Many companies with exciting new technologies or cost-saving services will see terrific growth.

Other firms will hire only limited numbers of employees, while some will downsize. Most firms that specialize in the manufacture or sale of luxury items, along with those that sell discretionary personal services, will find business to be very slow. Many companies will continue to wrestle with challenges such as intense competition and tight credit. The number of firms taking bankruptcy will remain high.

Growing numbers of consumers will prefer to buy from firms that sell goods and services online, offering savings of time, money and car travel. This boosts companies like Amazon.com that offer low prices combined with deep selections and great customer service.

The travel industry will continue to suffer as both business and leisure travel have been cut dramatically. Travel firms that do best will be those that have everyday low prices, such as Southwest Airlines, along with those that offer all-inclusive prices that seem like bargains, such as popular cruise lines.

The automobile sector will face continued tough times. Many consumers will be more likely to fix up their old cars than buy new ones. While this is hard on new car dealers, auto parts stores and car repair firms are enjoying booming business. Likewise, homeowners may make repairs or do light remodeling rather than move up to larger homes.

Americans who find themselves in the market for a job will need to understand the changes surging through the economy in order to determine which companies to pursue and which to avoid. The U.S. employment market is evolving quickly, and job seekers must be both knowledgeable and nimble in order to position themselves to find promising careers.

In order to create a robust job market, corporate investment, profits, productivity and revenues must align themselves correctly. These economic indicators were positive during the 2003 to mid-2007 period, and millions of new American jobs were created. As 2007 was winding down, the residential real estate crash, high levels of debt and difficult credit markets were combining to restrain the economy and put a damper on the creation of new jobs. Unfortunately, 2008-2009 saw these problems spread throughout most U.S. business sectors and throughout the global economy as well. Eventually, a major global meltdown at banks and investment firms occurred.

During 2010, chief executives will continue to find themselves under intense pressure to maintain profitability while keeping their staffs and investment needs lean. The uncertainty created by the financial crisis will make corporate executives extremely cautious. New grads will find it difficult to land their dream jobs. Nonetheless, there will still be job opportunities for those who are diligent in seeking good employers in stronger business sectors.

Some employees will find their work hours cut, face temporary furloughs, or have their pay or benefits cut. Many people who would prefer to be hired as permanent employees will find work as temps instead. Other employees will find that their jobs have been eliminated because work has been outsourced to another firm.

Hiring at federal government offices was very high in 2009 and will most likely continue in 2010. On the other hand, most city and state governments are facing major budget crises, and the job market in those sectors may be grim.

Economic Factors Affecting the Job Market

Business Productivity: Productivity has been rising at desirable rates in recent years. That is, more business can be produced—whether it is goods or services—by utilizing fewer workers than before. This will be extremely beneficial to the U.S. economy in the long run, but it can hurt the job market over the short term. Productivity is boosted by new technologies, improved management methods and other factors. It can also receive a quick boost from restrained corporate hiring. If rising productivity occurs along with rapidly rising sales and profits, then the job market will improve.

Corporate Sales: For 2010, many sectors, particularly retailing, will find revenue growth hard to come by. This will make many employers much less likely to hire new people.

Corporate Profits: When profits increase sharply, companies are inclined to increase both business investment and hiring. Fortunately, 2004 through 2007 saw steady growth in corporate profits as the economy rebounded. As a result, large numbers of new jobs were created, and the national unemployment rate was extremely low. Profitability took a deep downturn in 2008. Many employers were able to post reasonable profits during 2009, but this was generally a result of deep cuts in spending and hiring. The jobs market has suffered as a result. Hiring will rebound when corporate sales, and accompanying profits, show significant growth. This is not likely to occur in 2010.

In order to compete effectively in today's job market, one of the most important things you can do is arm yourself with knowledge. It is vital for the knowledgeable job seeker to use the best reference tools possible in order to seek out employers that offer a reasonable balance of financial stability, opportunities for advancement and good pay. Excellent job opportunities always exist if you know where to look. Many of America's most successful firms currently need large numbers of new employees.

For example, the health care sector continues to grow. Leading companies in biotechnology, renewable energy, online services and education will greatly expand their businesses over the mid term. Thousands of companies, in technical and non-technical sectors, will need large numbers of new hires. In particular, companies that offer products or services that save time and/or money will prosper—for example, many types of discount retailers, along with companies that offer services that help businesses operate more efficiently, will be hiring. Meanwhile, large companies that are not increasing their overall numbers of employees will be hiring on a regular basis due to normal attrition—that is, the loss of employees due to retirement, relocation or other personal circumstances. For example, a company the size of Walgreen's typically needs to hire tens of thousands of workers yearly due to normal attrition.

2) Cost Control is a Major Concern at Employers/Downsizing and Consolidation Through Mergers Continue

Since growth is not easy for most firms during the current, difficult economic environment, many employers are focusing on cost control as a means to maintain profits and financial stability. Throughout the world of business and industry, expenses of virtually all types have been cut, from travel budgets to advertising to investments in equipment. Employee costs have been targeted as well. This means that hiring has been restrained at best, since the economic crisis began in late 2007, while many companies have announced big layoffs. Others have cut work hours or even cut pay rates.

Often, companies have merged with others in order to seek operating efficiencies or gain access to needed capital. Employers have been struggling to earn profits and preserve cash, and some see mergers as their best strategy. Large mergers have been taking place in nearly all types of industries. Although this activity slowed during the recent financial crisis, mergers were picking up speed by mid-2009. A consolidation of companies via a merger may enable the firms to combine customer bases, administrative staff, sales offices and production facilities, while cutting employees who hold duplicated jobs, in hopes of thereby creating more efficient, more profitable firms. These employee reductions often number in the thousands. Mergers may be spurred by economic difficulties and falling profits, or they may involve large firms seeking to acquire companies that have the potential to boost growth and accelerate profits. For example, extreme duress in the home construction market in 2007-2009 instigated the merger of two massive construction firms, Centex and Pulte. On the other hand, prosperous software giant Oracle has been on a buying spree,

acquiring companies that it feels will boost Oracle's own growth. Most recently, it agreed to acquire Sun Microsystems.

Because they face tough, global competition, manufacturing firms are frequently involved in such mergers. Good jobs in the U.S. manufacturing sector can still be found, despite intense competition from Chinese manufacturers. Factories are running with fewer people thanks to immense investments in technology. Output per employee is up spectacularly—to the extent that millions of manufacturing jobs were cut due to the rise in productivity. In addition, fewer employees are needed to manage non-production functions, such as engineering, logistics, administration and marketing. Of course, some American manufacturing industries are in deep decline, particularly the automobile industry.

Meanwhile, some of the loss in manufacturing employment has been exaggerated by the fact that firms now outsource a good deal of their non-manufacturing operations to services companies. For example, many computer departments, company cafeterias, distribution centers and engineering needs are outsourced to outside companies that specialize in such work, thus reducing the number of in-house jobs at manufacturing companies.

Another extremely important factor in the loss of U.S. manufacturing jobs is the movement of production to foreign nations where costs are often much lower.

Companies in both manufacturing and service sectors have caught on to management by teams, vastly enhanced supply chain technology (such as the use of the Internet for ordering and tracking components), along with networked management, distribution and manufacturing systems, which all add up to the fact that fewer mid-management, white-collar types are needed to communicate with the people doing the day-to-day work. Production workers have been encouraged to communicate among themselves. In many cases, workers are taking on unprecedented responsibilities, setting their own goals and schedules, tracking costs and output and boosting profits. Historically, these were the tasks of middle managers. Today, vast numbers of those management jobs have been eliminated.

Businesses without factories are also undergoing re-engineering and leaps in productivity. For example, by upgrading software and linking desktop computers to central databases, a major U.S. insurance firm was able to go from 3,000 employees issuing new policies to only 700. At the same time, it was able to reduce the time necessary to write a new policy from 15 days to only five. Today's corporations are searching hard for innovative ways to get more work done with fewer people.

3) Unemployment Will Remain High

If you are looking for a job, it's time to face the fact that 2010's employment market will be very challenging. Employers will be cautious about hiring new people or investing in new facilities. Layoffs may slow from the fast pace of 2008-2009, but will be a problem nonetheless.

The U.S. unemployment rate in August 2007 was down to 4.6%. By August 2008, the unemployment rate shot up to 6.1%, and it reached 7.6% in early 2009. By August 2009, unemployment had soared to 9.7%, and more than 6 million jobs had been eliminated. Unemployment may go higher in 2010. In any event, the job market will take a significant amount of time to recover. Nonetheless, many job seekers will be able to find satisfying jobs if they apply themselves to the job hunt, make sure their resumes and self-marketing skills are in superb shape, network effectively and do thorough research. The number of people applying for each job opening is very high. Consequently, it is vital for a job seeker to understand how to best apply for a job online, how to conduct research that will help him or her to shine during an interview and how to create an effective list of prospective employers.

Large layoffs have become commonplace. Corporate restructuring, mergers and re-engineering are driving vast changes in businesses of all types. Even during an upturn in the economy, major job cuts are announced as corporate mergers and restructuring continue. Today's challenging economy will continue to force many firms to restructure and downsize.

4) Consumers Spend Less, Save More, Affecting a Wide Variety of Companies

After piling on debt, running up their credit cards, signing mortgages and buying new cars at a soaring rate from 2002 through 2007, consumers have now reversed course. Personal savings rates are soaring. Credit card use has plummeted. House sales are dismal, and millions of people are facing foreclosure on home mortgages. Saving money is in; spending money is out. Welcome to a new era of reduced personal circumstances, increased frugality and worried consumers. Even people with high, steady incomes are spending less. The financial crisis of 2007-2009, resulting unemployment and a high level of uncertainty have put the brakes on conspicuous consumption.

While increased personal savings and lower debt levels will be very good for America over the long run, it is a difficult adjustment for the nation to make, and, for 2010 at least, it puts a damper on the job market. Worst-hit are employers in industries that create or sell discretionary or luxury items. For example, sales in 2008 and 2009 at retailers such as Neiman Marcus and Saks Fifth Avenue were absolutely dismal. Jewelry, apparel, vacations, luxury automobiles, home furnishings and many, many other categories of goods have seen greatly reduced demand. Even firms that make essential day-to-day consumer items, like paper products, household cleansers and basic food items, have seen a drastic change in their business. Consumers have switched to cheaper, generic store-brands where possible, and have reduced purchases of high-end food.

These changes have been tough on manufacturers, distributors, transport providers and retailers. In sum, this means that many employers have not only been unable to hire new people, they have cut both work hours and total staff counts.

Smart job seekers will be aware that this is not a short-term change. It is going to take years for consumers to pay down debts and rebuild personal savings. The most successful employers will be those that provide lasting value, low prices, good service, cost-saving strategies and innovative technologies. Excellent examples are Wal-Mart (low prices), Costco (good service and low prices), NetFlix and Amazon (innovative use of technology to provide convenience and cost-savings), travel firms like JetBlue and Carnival Cruise Lines (good service, low prices, high value) and car makers like Honda, Kia and Hundai (lasting value, low prices).

5) Technology Continues to Create Sweeping Changes in the Workplace

Technology has introduced vast changes throughout industries of all types, greatly boosting productivity and reallocating (or eliminating) workers. A major cause of change for employees, and therefore job seekers, is the tidal wave of new technologies revolutionizing the workplace at all levels. Prospering companies are using new technologies to communicate with customers, automate back-office tasks and industrial operations, and push ahead with research and development. There is a never-ending stream of technological innovation. For example, major companies have already harnessed the power of networked computers. Today, they are rapidly adopting the use of Internet-based telephone systems and video conferencing technologies.

The trend of using new practices and technologies while cutting layers of management is largely about communication. This is true whether it is communication between the top offices and the factory floor, communication with customers, communication between the computers in one corporate office with those in another, or communication from desk-to-desk in massive service businesses.

These new technologies mean continuous retraining for much of the workforce. Job seekers who want the best posts must have the training and skills that will let them utilize new technologies effectively. Jobs are remaining unfilled at many companies because of a shortage of technically qualified people. Workforce development is a critical need nationwide.

Jobs in America are shifting to new categories of work based on technologies that didn't exist 20 years ago. For example, the job title "webmaster" was coined in the 1990s to describe the employee in charge of a firm's Internet sites and intranet operations. Services firms, as well as manufacturers, are placing more and more employees in recently created technical and service positions, while many of the tasks once performed in-house are now provided by outsourced services providers. For example, in the telecommunications industry, digital technology has completely changed the list of job titles while enabling phone service providers to reduce the ratio of employees to customers. In the meantime, tens of thousands of jobs have been created at cellular telephone companies. Now, Internet-based telephony (Voice Over Internet Protocol, or VOIP), competition from cable providers, fiber to the premises and wireless networks such as Wi-Fi and WiMax continue to force telecommunications firms to evolve.

Another excellent example: Retailing, shipping and warehousing are about to see a technology revolution due to the introduction of Radio Frequency Identification Tags (RFID). This breakthrough in inventory management is based on the placement of microchips in product packaging, combined with the use of special sensors in stores and warehouses that alert a central inventory management system of product purchases and the need to restock inventory. From loading docks to shelves to cash registers to parking lots, radio frequency readers will track the movement of each pallet or individual item. Many bar codes will eventually be replaced by RFIDs, with electronic product codes stored on these microchips. The chips even eliminate the need to scan each item at checkout. Checkout stations will be equipped with readers that automatically calculate purchases. Benefits include less shoplifting and no inventory errors. Another benefit is that manufacturers will be able to reduce overall inventory thanks to greater efficiency.

As online ordering, tracking and inventory management continue to become more sophisticated and cost-effective, purchasing executives at firms of all types and sizes will accelerate the use of Internet-based systems for management of their supply chains. There are significant opportunities here for e-commerce services and software companies. Likewise, there is great promise for third-party logistics (3PL) companies that combine the power of Internet-based information with strategically located warehouses to fulfill the inventory needs of manufacturers.

6) Continued Growth in Outsourcing, Including Supply Chain and Logistics Services

Part of the re-engineering process at employers has been a boom in "outsourcing," or the use of outside specialty firms to do chores that firms formerly performed through in-house departments. For example, Pitney Bowes takes over the mailrooms, desktop printers and copiers at major corporations. As part of this turnkey service, Pitney Bowes supplies its own copiers and desktop printers, and then buys toner and paper by the truckload at the best possible price. It trains its employees to keep track of every single copy so its clients can control costs. Copy department employees are transferred from the client firm to Pitney Bowes, the outsourcing firm. There, these employees learn that the head of a Pitney Bowes' copy department can rise to be a regional manager, a vice president or an even higher position within the company. The client firm's costs are lowered and its profits increase.

The outsourcing provider makes a tidy profit through its focused expertise.

The greatest area of outsourcing growth has long been in computer departments. IBM, Accenture and Hewlett-Packard (HP) are among the global leaders in this field. However, several other business functions are commonly outsourced. For example, ServiceMaster takes over janitorial tasks, building management and maintenance functions for giant corporate office campuses and industrial facilities. Another company outsources all of the food warehousing and distribution for nationwide restaurant chains. Why? Because it can run trucks and warehouses more efficiently while its clients concentrate on running restaurants.

While the 1960s, '70s and '80s saw many firms frantically trying to do all tasks in-house, recent trends are quite different. As a decade noted for rising productivity and efficiency, the '90s was an era of specialization and focus. Companies may do a better job by focusing on their core tasks, while allowing outside firms to provide support and maintenance needs. That trend continues today. Outsourcing, which rapidly gained popularity, will persist in leading the way to higher efficiency and profits. Many outsourced services companies continue to grow, and they will create (and displace) large numbers of jobs.

Some companies combine outsourcing services with temporary workers. For example, Spherion, a major temporary help firm and one of America's largest employers, is also a leading outsourcing company. Spherion's outsourcing division takes over all human resources administration functions for large clients. This means that Spherion's employees do all of the recruiting, employee records management, benefits management and so on for its client companies. This is a logical extension of Spherion's human resources expertise and good cross-marketing to its roster of corporate clients.

One of the fastest-growing fields in outsourcing has been supply chain and logistics management. Companies offering services in this field include giant transportation companies like UPS. "Supply chain" refers to the entire set of providers of supplies and services that are involved in creating and delivering a component or end product. For example, for an automobile manufacturer like Ford, the supply chain includes companies that make tires, batteries, interior components and engine parts, as well as the trucks and trains that ship these parts and the warehouses that hold them. This supply chain supports Ford's own manufacturing and assembly plants. At the end of Ford's business chain lie the automobile dealers that receive completed cars and deliver them to the end customers. Another example: For a clothing store chain like The Gap, the supply chain includes clothing designers, clothing manufacturers and the warehouses and transportation systems that deliver completed clothes to the stores. The Gap's supply chain is located across dozens of nations.

Logistics is the art of moving goods through the supply chain. Supply chains are so complex and so critical to a company's operations that there are countless ways to automate, improve efficiencies and cut costs. Many manufacturers and retailers are outsourcing all or part of their logistics needs to firms that specialize in creating efficiencies and saving costs. Logistics and supply chain companies have been growing rapidly over the past several years, and creating large numbers of jobs. A concept you should be familiar with is Third Party Logistics ("3PL"), a system whereby a specialist firm in logistics provides a variety of transportation, warehousing and logistics-related services to its clients. These tasks were previously performed in-house by the client. When 3PL services are provided within the client's own facilities, it can also be referred to as "Insourcing." In other words, you might find yourself working for UPS at a site within a distribution company that has no other ties to UPS.

7) Millions Working as Temps

More and more, major firms are using temporary workers to fill short-term needs, thereby cutting overall employment costs, since temps usually do not receive extensive benefits, bonuses or training. In addition to employees who are placed in temporary jobs by agencies, there are millions of people employed as "independent contractors" and "contract workers." Temporary staffing companies operate offices throughout the U.S., in cities small and large. To a growing extent, they hire and place workers via their sophisticated Internet sites.

The largest temporary help agencies tend to have vast global operations. For example, Adecco is a Swiss firm with extensive operations in the U.S., Europe and elsewhere, employing hundreds of thousands of people. Manpower, based in the U.S., does a major part of its business in dozens of nations worldwide.

Demand for temporary workers slows dramatically during economic downturns. The use of temps enables employers to increase the workforce quickly when orders from customers increase, and reduce the workforce rapidly when revenues decrease. Temporary workers are also an extremely efficient way to meet needs for one-time projects, fill the slots of permanent employees who are on leave and screen potential candidates for full-time positions by first hiring them on a temporary basis.

In addition, some Americans prefer to work as temporary employees, feeling that this gives them more flexibility in their working lives. Unfortunately, many other people who end up working in temporary positions would greatly prefer to be employed full-time. Many of these workers hold significant skills as well as college degrees.

A large percentage of temps work in professional specialties, such as law, finance, engineering or accounting. Interestingly, the number of information technology temps has increased dramatically in the past several years. As shortages of certain types of IT workers occurred, many highly skilled workers were able to demand very lucrative pay for temporary or contract assignments. Some temporary workers have gotten the

most out of the system by moving readily from shrinking industries to those that are expanding as the economy evolves. Others found excellent permanent work when they were introduced to new companies as temps.

> ***Internet Research Tip:***
> For data on the temporary staffing industry and the temporary workforce in the U.S., see the American Staffing Association (www.americanstaffing.net).

8) Offshoring and the Globalization of Business

Competition from workers in such nations as Mexico, Indonesia, Thailand, South Korea and, in particular, China, means that fewer pure manufacturing jobs will be available in the U.S., where pay is high and employee benefit costs are immense compared to those of competing nations. In fact, the costs of Social Security taxes, Medicare taxes, employer-sponsored health care, vacations, holidays, retirement plans and other benefits have risen so high (an amount typically equal to 38% to 45% of wages) that they provide considerable incentive for firms to hold down the number of employees working in U.S. locations. Instead, companies are utilizing workers in other nations. Depending on their experience and job title, a typical factory worker in China may earn $150 to $300 monthly for long hours of hard work. These employees often receive dormitory-style housing and cafeteria meals as well. Otherwise, employee benefit costs are nominal.

"Offshoring" is the word now used to describe the movement of jobs of all types away from industrialized nations, like America, to less developed countries, like India, the Philippines, Indonesia and China. For example, U.S. financial services companies are sending hundreds of thousands of jobs overseas, in such areas as call centers and financial analysis. Moving jobs to countries such as India, China and the Philippines poses serious job displacement problems in the U.S. (At the same time, there is a positive factor to the growth of these emerging economies: Increased exports to these nations of U.S. goods and services of all types are creating jobs and profits in America.)

Globalization has a profound effect on Americans— consumer prices become lower, while the U.S. job market changes considerably. Consumer goods are quite inexpensive due to the vast variety of items the U.S. imports from other nations, and prices for many categories of these goods have declined dramatically. For example, Americans can purchase consumer electronics like DVD players and color televisions at extremely low prices, and the price of many types of apparel is much lower thanks to globalization. For example, 90% of the shoes sold in America are manufactured in China.

More than ever before, the world is one vast marketplace. Globalization of business supply chains is a strong trend today and will grow even stronger in the future. For example, consider the rapid globalization of the automobile industry. The entire global automobile sector is dominated by only a handful of companies, including Toyota, GM, Ford, Daimler, Honda, Volkswagen and Nissan, as well as the increasingly successful Korean automakers Kia and Hyundai. Car manufacturers in China, such as BYD and Geeley, are growing more dominant as well. Car manufacturers commonly have engineering teams collaborating from offices in multiple nations, while parts and components may be imported from a wide variety of suppliers in various countries to undergo final assembly at home.

American companies in many industry sectors have been merging and consolidating on a global basis at a rapid clip. That consolidation will continue. One benefit is that U.S. firms can enter into foreign markets through international acquisitions.

Trade is not necessarily always stable. While global economies are undeniably linked, they do not march hand-in-hand. For example, the nose-dive taken by many Asian economies in the late 1990s occurred during one of the biggest economic booms in U.S. history. The strength of America as a consumer market was a platform that helped to stabilize and regenerate Asian businesses that were having difficulties. Likewise, China's economic stimulus during the economic crisis of 2007-2009 helped to boost business in many nations that were undergoing difficult national recessions.

U.S. firms hold leadership positions in several key product and service sectors vital to the rest of the world, including health technology, computers, e-commerce, software and entertainment of all types. The message is clear: global trade and export markets are extremely vital to the health of American business and industry. A study of 2006 results showed that a U.S. corporation listed in the Standard & Poor's 500 created, on average, 49% of its revenues from foreign nations, up from 30% in 2001.

A growing middle class in India and China has been creating demand for goods exported from the U.S., including consumer products bearing desirable brands, as well as luxury automobiles. Also, U.S.-based firms have been enjoying great success in franchising and licensing their methods to startup businesses in China and India, in everything from hotels to fast food to services.

Meanwhile, the U.S. is also exporting its newfound expertise in the booming superstore and discount retailing sectors. For instance, hundreds of Wal-Mart's stores are in foreign locations such as Argentina, Brazil, Canada, China, Korea, Mexico, Puerto Rico and the U.K. Eventually, Wal-Mart may bring its brand of retailing to virtually all of the world's major markets.

9) Older Americans Will Delay Retirement and Work Longer/Many Employers Find Older Employees Desirable

Certain large employers, particularly national retail chains, have discovered that older workers are a terrific pool of potential employees. This may be positive for older workers, but to younger job seekers it means more competition for work.

While 2006 marked the year that the first Baby Boomers turned 60, many members of this generation are no longer planning to retire any time soon. The job market has been made more difficult by the fact that many of America's workers who want to retire will be reluctant (or unable) to do so because the value of their investments in real estate, stocks, bonds and/or pension plans is down considerably, and they lost confidence in financial markets at the same time that they lost retirement dollars. Some would-be retirees will be working much later in life than they had planned.

Baby boomer generally refers to the 78 million people born from 1946 to 1964. The term evolved to describe the children of soldiers and war industry workers who were involved in World War II. When those veterans and workers returned to civilian life, they started or added to families in large numbers. As a result, this generation is one of the largest demographic segments in the U.S. Baby Boomers make up about 24% of the U.S. population. .

By 2011, millions will begin turning traditional retirement age (65), resulting in extremely rapid growth in the senior portion of the population. Many Baby Boomers will leave their traditional, long-term jobs and turn to part-time work. Others will continue in their full-time jobs as long as possible.

A survey released in June 2009 by the AARP found that 20% of the group's members said they were likely to work until they were in their 70s. 40% of couples surveyed said that one or both spouses will work part-time in retirement. In the first part of 2008, a Bureau of Labor Statistics survey found that 30% of people between the ages of 65 and 69 were either employed or seeking work. This number will grow over the near term.

By the early 2000s, many employers were already developing human resources strategies aimed at hiring or retaining older workers. On the lower end of the scale, retailers like Home Depot, a firm that has been known to need tens of thousands of new hires in one year, have found older people to be ideal employees. They have knowledge that is extremely useful for providing advice and service to shoppers. They are experienced workers who understand the need to show up on time. Wal-Mart reported in 2005 that it had 220,000 employees who were age 55 or older. This trend is powerful enough that the AARP has advised members who are seeking work to consider a list of eager employers that includes Pitney Bowes, MetLife, Borders, Principal Financial and Walgreens.

On the higher end of the employment scale, older workers with long-term experience in scientific and engineering tasks will be vital in keeping the gears of business and industry turning. For example, during the 2000s boom, when the airline industry saw good growth, rules were altered in the U.S. to enable commercial airline pilots to keep flying until age 65, instead of facing forced retirement at age 60 as they had in the past. A serious shortage of experienced pilots was averted. (Granted, airlines soon went into a tailspin during the Great

Recession, along with the rest of the travel industry, and they mothballed a lot of airplanes while cutting the number of routes and flights. Nonetheless, older, experienced pilots will eventually be in high demand.) Heavy industry is an even better example. The National Science Foundation estimated that 38% of America's scientists and engineers were 50+ years old as of 2006. These older workers may not be good at creating the latest electronic games, but they are undeniably the people who have the experience and the knowledge necessary to successfully operate the laboratories, factories, refineries and legacy systems that keep industry humming. They are going to be extremely difficult to replace in America, because younger generations have been shunning degrees in science and engineering for softer disciplines. Energy industry firms like ExxonMobil, Halliburton and Schlumberger, and chemicals firms like global giant BASF, are dealing with this challenge along two lines: First, how to document and pass along the immense treasure of work-related knowledge that these employees have, and second, how to keep these employees interested in working later into their lives. BASF, a firm with about $90 billion in annual revenues and an employee base of 90,000 scattered around the world, estimates that by 2020, 50% or more of its employees will be 50 to 65 years old. It has implemented measures ranging from making the workplace more comfortable and safe for older workers, to an intense knowledge transfer program where older workers mentor younger staff members.

10) Employment Sectors that Will Offer an Above-Average Number of Job Opportunities in 2010

Job seekers should remain aware of the fact that certain industries will have an above-average likelihood to offer job openings during 2010. This is due to a number of circumstances, including shifts in consumer tastes and requirements, normal employee turnover and attrition, structural changes within industries, global economic conditions and national policies and priorities.

Below is a list of the industries on which job seekers should concentrate their efforts.

Employment Sectors that Will Offer an Above-Average Number of Job Opportunities in 2010:

- Batteries—Advanced Battery Technologies
- Biotechnology
- Construction and Engineering Services for Infrastructure and Government Projects
- Consulting—Selected Fields where Consultants May Be Able to Effect Cost-Savings for Clients
- Consumer Products Manufacturers
- Cosmetics Manufacturers
- Data Processing Services Providers
- Defense Contractors—Selected Firms
- Education
- Elder Care, Home Health Care, Nursing Homes and Assisted Living Communities
- Electronic Games, Games for Cell Phones
- Energy Conservation Products and Services
- Food Processing
- Guard Services, Investigation and Surveillance
- Health Care Services
- Health Care Products
- Health Care Technology, Including Computerized Patient Records
- Health Foods, Organic Foods, Enhanced Foods
- Insurance Providers
- Internet Service Providers
- Nanotechnology and MEMS
- Online Search Services with Advertising Revenues
- Online-based Business and Consumer Services
- Outsourcing, Including Outsourced Business and Computer Services
- Pharmaceuticals—Generics
- Radio Frequency ID Tags (RFID)
- Renewable Energy, Especially Solar and Wind Power
- Retailing—Basic, Including Drugstores and Supermarkets
- Retailing—Discount and Warehouse Clubs
- Supply Chain Services That Offer Cost-Savings to Clients
- Water Filtration and Conservation Equipment
- Wireless and Cellular Communications

Chapter 2

STATISTICS

Contents:

U.S. Employment Overview: 2008-2009

(Labor Counts In Thousands)

	Aug-08	Jan-09	Aug-09
Civilian Labor Force, Total	154,853	153,716	154,577
Employed	145,477	142,099	139,649
Unemployed	9,376	11,616	14,928
Persons 16 Years of Age and Over, Not in Labor Force	79,253	81,203	81,509
Unemployment Rate, All Workers	6.1%	7.6%	9.7%
Adult Men	5.6%	7.6%	10.1%
Adult Women	5.3%	6.2%	7.6%
Teenagers	18.9%	20.8%	25.5%
White	5.4%	6.9%	8.9%
Black or African American	10.6%	12.6%	15.1%
Hispanic or Latino	8.0%	9.7%	13.0%
Average Hourly Earnings, Private Industry[P]	$18.14	$18.46	$18.65
Weekly Earnings, Private Industry[P]	$611.32	$614.72	$617.32
Average Work Week, Private Industry (Hours)[P]	33.7	33.3	33.1
Nonfarm Employment[P]	137,423	134,580	131,223
Goods-Producing	21,367	20,245	18,571
Construction	7,153	6,742	6,093
Manufacturing	13,426	12,713	11,771
Service-Providing	116,056	114,335	112,652
Retail Trade	15,275	14,998	14,739
Professional & Business Services	17,854	17,261	16,600
Education & Health Services	18,997	19,143	19,321
Leisure & Hospitality	13,639	13,285	13,156
Government	22,514	22,539	22,487

P = Preliminary figures (for August 2009).

Source: U.S. Bureau of Labor Statistics
Plunkett Research, Ltd.
www.plunkettresearch.com

U.S. Civilian Labor Force:
1997-August 2009

(Persons 16 & Older; In Thousands)

Year	Civilian Workforce Level
1997	136,297
1998	137,673
1999	139,368
2000	142,583
2001	143,734
2002	144,863
2003	146,510
2004	147,401
2005	149,320
2006	151,428
2007	153,124
2008	154,287
2009*	154,577

* As of August; seasonally adjusted.

Note: The labor force includes all persons classified as employed or unemployed. Employed persons include people 16 years and over in the civilian noninstitutional population who, during a reference week, (a) did any work at all (at least 1 hour) as paid employees, worked in their own business, profession, or on their own farm, or worked 15 hours or more as unpaid workers in an enterprise operated by a member of the family, and (b) all those who were not working but who had jobs or businesses from which they were temporarily absent because of vacation, illness, bad weather, childcare problems, maternity or paternity leave, labor-management dispute, job training, or other family or personal reasons, whether or not they were paid for the time off or were seeking other jobs. Each employed person is counted only once, even if he or she holds more than one job. Excluded are persons whose only activity consisted of work around their own house (painting, repairing, or own home housework) or volunteer work for religious, charitable, and other organizations.

Source: U.S. Bureau of Labor Statistics

Plunkett Research, Ltd.

www.plunkettresearch.com

Number of People Employed and Unemployed, U.S.:
August 2008 vs. August 2009

(Persons 16 & Older; In Thousands; Not Seasonally Adjusted)

Occupation	Employed		Unemployed		Unemp. Rates	
	Aug-08	Aug-09	Aug-08	Aug-09	Aug-08	Aug-09
All workers*	**145,909**	**140,074**	**9,479**	**14,823**	**6.1**	**9.6**
Management, professional & related	52,626	51,724	1,779	2,925	3.3	5.4
Management, business & financial	22,314	21,849	645	1,141	2.8	5.0
Professional & related	30,312	29,875	1,135	1,785	3.6	5.6
Service	25,185	25,115	1,898	2,797	7.0	10.0
Sales & office	35,156	34,132	2,218	3,252	5.9	8.7
Sales & related	16,114	15,902	1,089	1,511	6.3	8.7
Office & administrative support	19,042	18,230	1,129	1,741	5.6	8.7
Natural resources, construction & maintenance	15,141	13,561	1,186	2,176	7.3	13.8
Farming, fishing & forestry	1,082	984	93	182	7.9	15.6
Construction & extraction	8,927	7,613	856	1,555	8.7	17.0
Installation, maintenance & repair	5,132	4,964	237	439	4.4	8.1
Production, transportation & material moving	17,801	15,542	1,466	2,421	7.6	13.5
Production	8,917	7,691	771	1,366	8.0	15.1
Transportation & material moving	8,883	7,852	695	1,055	7.3	11.8

* Persons with no previous work experience and persons whose last job was in the Armed Forces are included in the unemployed total. Updated population controls are introduced annually with the release of January data.

Source: U.S. Bureau of Labor Statistics

Plunkett Research, Ltd.

www.plunkettresearch.com

Unemployed Jobseekers by Sex, Reason for Unemployment & Active Job Search Methods Used: 2008

Sex and reason	(Thousands of persons)		Methods used as a percent of total jobseekers							Average number of methods used
	Total unem- ployed	Total job- seekers	Emp- loyer directly	Sent out resumes or filled out app- lications	Placed or ans- wered ads	Friends or relatives	Public employ- ment agency	Private employ- ment agency	Other	
Total, 16 years and over	**8,924**	**7,749**	**56.9**	**52.3**	**17.1**	**23.8**	**18.9**	**8.0**	**14.1**	**1.92**
Job losers and persons who completed temporary jobs*	4,789	3,614	59.5	51.4	20.1	28.0	24.3	10.6	15.2	2.10
Job leavers	896	896	58.7	54.8	18.3	22.5	16.9	7.8	13.2	1.93
Reentrants	2,472	2,472	53.3	51.7	14.0	19.5	14.6	5.9	14.0	1.73
New entrants	766	766	54.5	55.1	11.2	19.3	9.9	3.4	10.8	1.64
Men, 16 years and over	**5,033**	**4,234**	**58.7**	**49.8**	**17.1**	**26.1**	**19.3**	**8.1**	**14.2**	**1.94**
Job losers and persons who completed temporary jobs*	3,055	2,255	61.0	48.7	19.5	29.9	23.7	10.2	15.0	2.08
Job leavers	458	458	59.2	52.6	17.9	24.2	16.9	7.2	13.2	1.92
Reentrants	1,128	1,128	55.1	49.1	14.0	21.0	14.9	6.0	14.1	1.75
New entrants	393	393	55.9	54.9	11.8	21.4	9.5	3.0	10.8	1.67
Women, 16 years and over	**3,891**	**3,515**	**54.7**	**55.3**	**17.0**	**21.0**	**18.4**	**8.0**	**14.1**	**1.89**
Job losers and persons who completed temporary jobs*	1,735	1,359	57.1	56.0	21.1	24.9	25.2	11.2	15.6	2.12
Job leavers	438	438	58.1	57.1	18.8	20.7	17.0	8.5	13.2	1.94
Reentrants	1,345	1,345	51.8	54.0	14.0	18.3	14.2	5.8	13.9	1.73
New entrants	374	374	53.1	55.2	10.5	17.1	10.3	3.7	10.7	1.61

Note: The jobseekers total is less than the total unemployed because it does not include persons on temporary layoff. The percent using each method will always total more than 100 because many jobseekers use more than one method.

* Data on the number of jobseekers and the jobsearch methods used exclude persons on temporary layoff.

Source: U.S. Bureau of Labor Statistics

Plunkett Research, Ltd.

www.plunkettresearch.com

U.S. Labor Force Ages 16 to 24 Years Old by School Enrollment, Educational Attainment, Sex, Race & Ethnicity: October 2008

(Numbers in Thousands, Latest Year Available)	Civilian non-institutional population	Total in Labor Force	Percent of Populace	Employed		Unemployed		Not in Labor Force
				Total	Percent of Populace	Number	Rate (%)	
Total, 16 to 24 years	37,569	21,931	58.4	19,020	50.6	2,911	13.3	15,637
Educational Attainment								
Enrolled in school	21,348	8,974	42.0	7,907	37.0	1,067	11.9	12,374
Enrolled in high school[1]	9,677	2,661	27.5	2,099	21.7	562	21.1	7,016
Men	4,991	1,272	25.5	960	19.2	311	24.5	3,720
Women	4,686	1,389	29.6	1,139	24.3	251	18.0	3,297
White	7,274	2,153	29.6	1,729	23.8	424	19.7	5,120
Black or African American	1,604	339	21.2	236	14.7	104	30.5	1,264
Asian	349	66	18.9	57	16.4	9	[2]	283
Hispanic or Latino ethnicity	1,804	365	20.2	238	13.2	127	34.8	1,439
Enrolled in college	11,671	6,313	54.1	5,809	49.8	505	8.0	5,358
Enrolled in 2-year college	3,521	2,229	63.3	2,035	57.8	194	8.7	1,292
Enrolled in 4-year college	8,150	4,084	50.1	3,773	46.3	311	7.6	4,065
Full-time students	10,148	5,010	49.4	4,599	45.3	412	8.2	5,137
Part-time students	1,523	1,303	85.5	1,210	79.4	93	7.1	220
Men	5,492	2,814	51.2	2,522	45.9	293	10.4	2,678
Women	6,179	3,499	56.6	3,287	53.2	212	6.1	2,680
White	9,283	5,289	57.0	4,900	52.8	389	7.4	3,994
Black or African American	1,381	630	45.6	540	39.1	90	14.3	751
Asian	680	238	35.1	223	32.7	16	6.6	441
Hispanic or Latino ethnicity	1,385	775	55.9	682	49.2	93	12.0	610
Not enrolled in school	16,220	12,957	79.9	11,113	68.5	1,845	14.2	3,263
16 to 19 years	3,301	2,253	68.3	1,719	52.1	534	23.7	1,048
20 to 24 years	12,920	10,704	82.9	9,394	72.7	1,310	12.2	2,216
Sex								
Men	8,465	7,229	85.4	6,028	71.2	1,201	16.6	1,236
Less than a high school diploma	1,606	1,204	74.9	887	55.2	317	26.3	403
High school graduates, no college[3]	4,121	3,487	84.6	2,874	69.7	613	17.6	634
Some college or associate degree	1,859	1,696	91.3	1,498	80.6	198	11.7	162
Bachelor's degree and higher[4]	879	842	95.8	769	87.5	73	8.7	37
Women	7,756	5,728	73.9	5,084	65.6	644	11.2	2,028
Less than a high school diploma	1,403	697	49.6	523	37.2	174	25.0	707
High school graduates, no college[3]	3,200	2,274	71.1	1,982	61.9	292	12.8	926
Some college or associate degree	1,953	1,629	83.4	1,525	78.1	104	6.4	324
Bachelor's degree and higher[4]	1,200	1,128	94.1	1,054	87.9	74	6.6	71
Race								
White	12,485	10,244	82.0	8,971	71.8	1,273	12.4	2,242
Black or African American	2,630	1,878	71.4	1,433	54.5	446	23.7	752
Asian	435	320	73.7	297	68.3	23	7.3	114
Hispanic or Latino ethnicity	3,531	2,684	76.0	2,279	64.5	405	15.1	848

Note: Detail for the above race groups do not sum to totals because data are not presented for all races. Persons whose ethnicity is identified as Hispanic or Latino may be of any race. Because of rounding, sums of individual items may not equal totals.

[1] Includes a small number of persons who are in grades below high school.

[2] Data not shown where base is less than 75,000.

[3] Includes persons with a high school diploma or equivalent.

[4] Includes persons with a bachelor's, master's, professional, and doctoral degrees.

Source: U.S. Bureau of Labor Statistics

Plunkett Research, Ltd.

www.plunkettresearch.com

Mean Hourly Earnings & Weekly Hours, Private Industry & State & Local Government: 2008

(By Worker & Establishment Characteristics, Latest Year Available)	Civilian		Private Industry		State & Local Gov't	
	Hourly Earnings[1]	Weekly Hours[2]	Hourly Earnings[1]	Weekly Hours[2]	Hourly Earnings[1]	Weekly Hours[2]
Total	**$20.62**	**35.5**	**$19.92**	**35.4**	**$25.08**	**36.2**
Worker Characteristics[3,4]						
Management, professional & related	33.56	37.0	34.13	37.4	31.83	35.9
Management, business & financial	37.57	39.6	38.17	39.9	34.08	37.5
Professional & related	31.67	35.9	31.82	36.0	31.30	35.6
Service	11.68	31.2	10.29	30.3	18.46	36.5
Sales & office	16.31	34.9	16.27	34.7	16.76	36.4
Sales & related	17.34	32.6	17.35	32.6	16.26	34.2
Office & administrative support	15.74	36.2	15.60	36.2	16.78	36.5
Natural resources, construction & maintenance	20.81	39.2	20.88	39.3	20.11	38.8
Construction & extraction	20.91	39.2	21.05	39.3	19.38	38.6
Installation, maintenance & repair	20.84	39.3	20.82	39.4	21.04	39.2
Production, transportation & material moving	15.53	37.4	15.43	37.5	18.59	34.4
Production	15.92	38.8	15.85	38.8	20.62	39.0
Transportation & material moving	15.11	35.9	14.97	36.0	17.95	33.2
Full time	21.90	39.6	21.25	39.7	25.72	38.9
Part time	11.76	20.6	11.43	20.8	15.99	18.5
Union	24.74	36.7	22.44	36.6	28.18	37.0
Nonunion	19.89	35.3	19.62	35.2	22.59	35.6
Time	20.32	35.3	19.53	35.2	25.06	36.2
Incentive	25.93	38.1	25.89	38.1	111.64	26.7
Establishment Characteristics						
Goods producing	(5)	(5)	21.58	39.5	(5)	(5)
Service Producing	(5)	(5)	19.44	34.3	(5)	(5)
1 to 49 workers	17.42	34.0	17.38	34.1	18.90	32.9
50 to 99 workers	18.77	34.9	18.68	34.8	20.26	35.9
100 to 499 workers	20.18	36.2	19.79	36.2	23.23	36.0
500 workers or more	25.79	37.0	25.35	37.2	26.69	36.7

Note: The survey covers all 50 states and the District of Columbia. Data were collected between December 2007 and January 2009. The average month of reference was July 2008.

[1] Earnings are the straight-time hourly wages or salaries paid to employees. They include incentive pay, cost-of-living adjustments and hazard pay. Excluded are premium pay for overtime, vacations, holidays, nonproduction bonuses and tips. The mean is computed by totaling the pay of all workers and dividing by the number of workers, weighted by hours.

[2] Mean weekly hours are the hours an employee is scheduled to work in a week, exclusive of overtime.

[3] Employees are classified as working either a full-time or a part-time schedule based on the definition used by each establishment. Union workers are those whose wages are determined through collective bargaining. Wages of time workers are based solely on hourly rate or salary; incentive workers are those whose wages are at least partially based on productivity payments such as piece rates, commissions, and production bonuses.

[4] A classification system including about 800 individual occupations is used to cover all workers in the civilian economy.

[5] Estimates for goods-producing and service-providing industries are published for private industry only. Industries are determined by the 2007 North American Industry Classification System (NAICS).

Source: U.S. Bureau of Labor Statistics
Plunkett Research, Ltd.
www.plunkettresearch.com

Medical Care Benefits in the U.S.: Access, Participation and Take-Up Rates, March 2009

(All workers = 100 percent)

Characteristics	Private Industry			State/Local Government		
	Access	Particip-ation	Take-up Rate[1]	Access	Particip-ation	Take-up Rate[1]
All workers	71%	52%	74%	88%	73%	84%
Worker Characteristics						
Management, professional and related	86%	67%	78%	90%	74%	82%
Service	46%	29%	63%	81%	69%	85%
Sales and office	72%	51%	70%	88%	75%	84%
Natural resources, construction and maintenance	77%	61%	80%	95%	83%	88%
Production, transportation and material moving	77%	58%	76%	83%	70%	84%
Full time	86%	65%	75%	99%	83%	84%
Part time	24%	13%	56%	27%	19%	71%
Union	90%	76%	85%	95%	80%	84%
Nonunion	69%	49%	72%	81%	68%	83%
Wage percentiles[2]						
Lowest 10 percent	25%	13%	50%	51%	40%	78%
Lowest 25 percent	38%	22%	57%	68%	56%	81%
Second 25 percent	77%	54%	71%	91%	79%	86%
Third 25 percent	86%	67%	78%	95%	79%	84%
Highest 25 percent	89%	72%	81%	97%	80%	83%
Highest 10 percent	90%	73%	80%	97%	80%	83%
Establishment Characteristics						
1 to 99 workers	59%	42%	72%	75%	64%	86%
1 to 49 workers	55%	39%	71%	69%	59%	86%
50 to 99 workers	71%	51%	72%	85%	73%	85%
100 workers or more	84%	63%	75%	89%	74%	83%
100 to 499 workers	81%	59%	73%	84%	72%	86%
500 workers or more	88%	69%	78%	91%	75%	82%

Note: For this table, a worker with access to medical care benefits is defined as having an employer-provided medical plan available for use, regardless of the worker's decision to enroll or participate in the plan. Farm and private household workers, the self-employed and Federal government workers are excluded from the survey.

[1] The take-up rate is a rounded estimate of the percentage of workers with access to a plan who participate in the plan.

[2] The percentile groupings are based on the average wage for each occupation surveyed, which may include workers both above and below the threshold. The percentile values are based on the estimates published in the "National Compensation Survey: Occupational Earnings in the United States, 2008."

Source: U.S. Bureau of Labor Statistics

Plunkett Research, Ltd.

www.plunkettresearch.com

Retirement Benefits in the U.S.: Access, Participation and Take-Up Rates, March 2009

(All workers = 100 percent)

Characteristics	Private Industry			State/Local Government		
	Access	Particip-ation	Take-up Rate[1]	Access	Particip-ation	Take-up Rate[1]
All workers	67%	51%	77%	90%	86%	95%
Worker Characteristics						
Management, professional and related	80%	69%	87%	92%	87%	95%
Service	45%	26%	57%	84%	79%	95%
Sales and office	71%	54%	75%	90%	87%	96%
Natural resources, construction and maintenance	68%	53%	79%	94%	91%	97%
Production, transportation and material moving	69%	53%	77%	88%	85%	97%
Full time	76%	61%	80%	99%	95%	96%
Part time	39%	22%	55%	41%	37%	89%
Union	87%	82%	94%	97%	94%	96%
Nonunion	65%	48%	74%	84%	79%	95%
Wage percentiles[2]						
Lowest 10 percent	35%	15%	43%	58%	54%	92%
Lowest 25 percent	43%	23%	52%	74%	69%	94%
Second 25 percent	69%	50%	73%	94%	89%	95%
Third 25 percent	76%	63%	83%	95%	91%	96%
Highest 25 percent	84%	75%	89%	97%	94%	96%
Highest 10 percent	86%	78%	90%	97%	94%	96%
Establishment Characteristics						
1 to 99 workers	53%	36%	69%	78%	75%	96%
1 to 49 workers	48%	33%	69%	72%	68%	95%
50 to 99 workers	66%	46%	69%	88%	85%	97%
100 workers or more	83%	68%	82%	91%	87%	95%
100 to 499 workers	79%	61%	77%	87%	83%	95%
500 workers or more	88%	77%	88%	93%	89%	95%

Note: Benefits may include defined benefit pension plans as well as defined contribution retirement plans. Workers are considered as having access or as participating if they have access to or participate in at least one of these plan types. Farm and private household workers, the self-employed and Federal government workers are excluded from the survey.

[1] The take-up rate is a rounded estimate of the percentage of workers with access to a plan who participate in the plan.

[2] The percentile groupings are based on the average wage for each occupation surveyed, which may include workers both above and below the threshold. The percentile values are based on the estimates published in the "National Compensation Survey: Occupational Earnings in the United States, 2008."

Source: U.S. Bureau of Labor Statistics

Plunkett Research, Ltd.

www.plunkettresearch.com

Top 25 U.S. Occupations by Percent Change in Job Growth: 2006-2016

(Employment in Thousands)

Occupation	Employment		Change		Training*
	2006	2016	Number	Percent	
Network systems & data communications analysts	262	402	140	53.4	Bachelor's degree
Personal & home care aides	767	1,156	389	50.6	Short-term on-the-job training
Home health aids	787	1,171	384	48.7	Short-term on-the-job training
Computer software engineers, applications	507	733	226	44.6	Bachelor's degree
Veterinary technologists & technicians	71	100	29	41.0	Associate degree
Personal financial advisors	176	248	72	41.0	Bachelor's degree
Makeup artists, theatrical & performance	2	3	1	39.8	Postsecondary vocational award
Medical assistants	417	565	148	35.4	Moderate-term on-the-job training
Veterinarians	62	84	22	35.0	First professional degree
Substance abuse & behavioral disorder counselors	83	112	29	34.3	Bachelor's degree
Skin care specialists	38	51	13	34.3	Postsecondary vocational award
Financial analysts	221	295	75	33.8	Bachelor's degree
Social & human service assistants	339	453	114	33.6	Moderate-term on-the-job training
Gaming surveillance officers & gaming investigators	9	12	3	33.6	Moderate-term on-the-job training
Physical therapist assistants	60	80	20	32.4	Associate degree
Pharmacy technicians	285	376	91	32.0	Moderate-term on-the-job training
Forensic science technicians	13	17	4	30.7	Bachelor's degree
Dental hygienists	167	217	50	30.1	Associate degree
Mental health counselors	100	130	30	30.0	Master's degree
Mental health & substance abuse social workers	122	159	37	29.9	Master's degree
Marriage and family therapists	25	32	7	29.8	Master's degree
Dental assistants	280	362	82	29.2	Moderate-term on-the-job training
Computer systems analysts	504	650	146	29.0	Bachelor's degree
Database administrators	119	154	35	28.6	Bachelor's degree
Computer software engineers, systems software	350	449	99	28.2	Bachelor's degree

* An occupation is placed into 1 of 11 categories that best describes the postsecondary education or training needed by most workers to become fully qualified in that occupation. For more information about the categories, see Occupational Projections and Training Data, 2006-07 edition, Bulletin 2602 (Bureau of Labor Statistics, February 2006) and Occupational Projections and Training Data, 2008-09 edition, Bulletin 2702 (Bureau of Labor Statistics, forthcoming).

Source: U.S. Bureau of Labor Statistics

Plunkett Research, Ltd.

www.plunkettresearch.com

Top 25 U.S. Occupations by Numerical Change in Job Growth: 2006-2016

(By Thousands of Employees)

Occupation	Employment		Change		Training*
	2006	2016	Number	Percent	
Registered nurses	2,505	3,092	587	23.5	Associate degree
Retail salespersons	4,477	5,034	557	12.4	Short-term on-the-job training
Customer service representatives	2,202	2,747	545	24.8	Moderate-term on-the-job training
Combined food preparation & serving workers, including fast food	2,503	2,955	452	18.1	Short-term on-the-job training
Office clerks, general	3,200	3,604	404	12.6	Short-term on-the-job training
Personal & home care aides	767	1,156	389	50.6	Short-term on-the-job training
Home health aides	787	1,171	384	48.7	Short-term on-the-job training
Postsecondary teachers	1,672	2,054	382	22.9	Doctoral degree
Janitors & cleaners, except maids & housekeeping cleaners	2,387	2,732	345	14.5	Short-term on-the-job training
Nursing aides, orderlies & attendants	1,447	1,711	264	18.2	Postsecondary vocational award
Bookkeeping, accounting & auditing clerks	2,114	2,377	264	12.5	Moderate-term on-the-job training
Waiters & waitresses	2,361	2,615	255	10.8	Short-term on-the-job training
Child care workers	1,388	1,636	248	17.8	Short-term on-the-job training
Executive secretaries & administrative assistants	1,618	1,857	239	14.8	Work experience in a related occupation
Computer software engineers, applications	507	733	226	44.6	Bachelor's degree
Accountants & auditors	1,274	1,500	226	17.7	Bachelor's degree
Landscaping & groundskeeping workers	1,220	1,441	221	18.1	Short-term on-the-job training
Elementary school teachers, except special education	1,540	1,749	209	13.6	Bachelor's degree
Receptionists & information clerks	1,173	1,375	202	17.2	Short-term on-the-job training
Truck drivers, heavy & tractor-trailer	1,860	2,053	193	10.4	Moderate-term on-the-job training
Maids and housekeeping cleaners	1,470	1,656	186	12.7	Short-term on-the-job training
Security guards	1,040	1,216	176	16.9	Short-term on-the-job training
Carpenters	1,462	1,612	150	10.3	Long-term on-the-job training
Management analysts	678	827	149	22.0	Bachelor's or higher degree, plus work experience
Medical assistants	417	565	148	35.5	Moderate-term on-the-job training

* An occupation is placed into 1 of 11 categories that best describes the postsecondary education or training needed by most workers to become fully qualified in that occupation. For more information about the categories, see Occupational Projections and Training Data, 2006-07 edition, Bulletin 2602 (Bureau of Labor Statistics, February 2006) and Occupational Projections and Training Data, 2008-09 edition, Bulletin 2702 (Bureau of Labor Statistics, forthcoming).

Source: U.S. Bureau of Labor Statistics

Plunkett Research, Ltd.

www.plunkettresearch.com

Jobs with the Largest Expected Employment Increases, U.S.: 2006-2016

(By Increase in Number Employed, in Thousands)

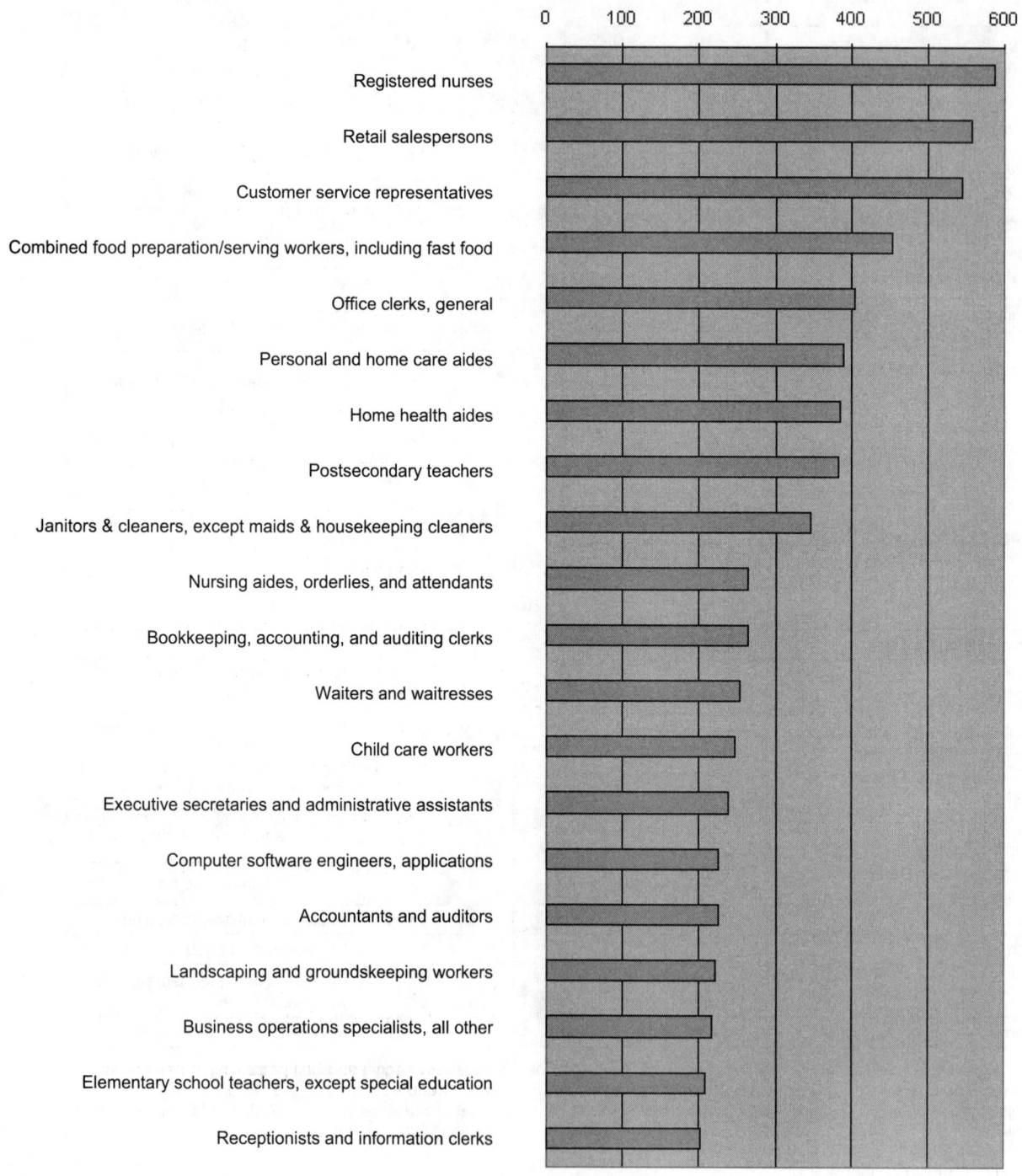

Source: U.S. Bureau of Labor Statistics
Plunkett Research, Ltd.
www.plunkettresearch.com

Jobs with the Largest Expected Employment Decreases, U.S.: 2006-2016

(By Decrease in Number Employed)

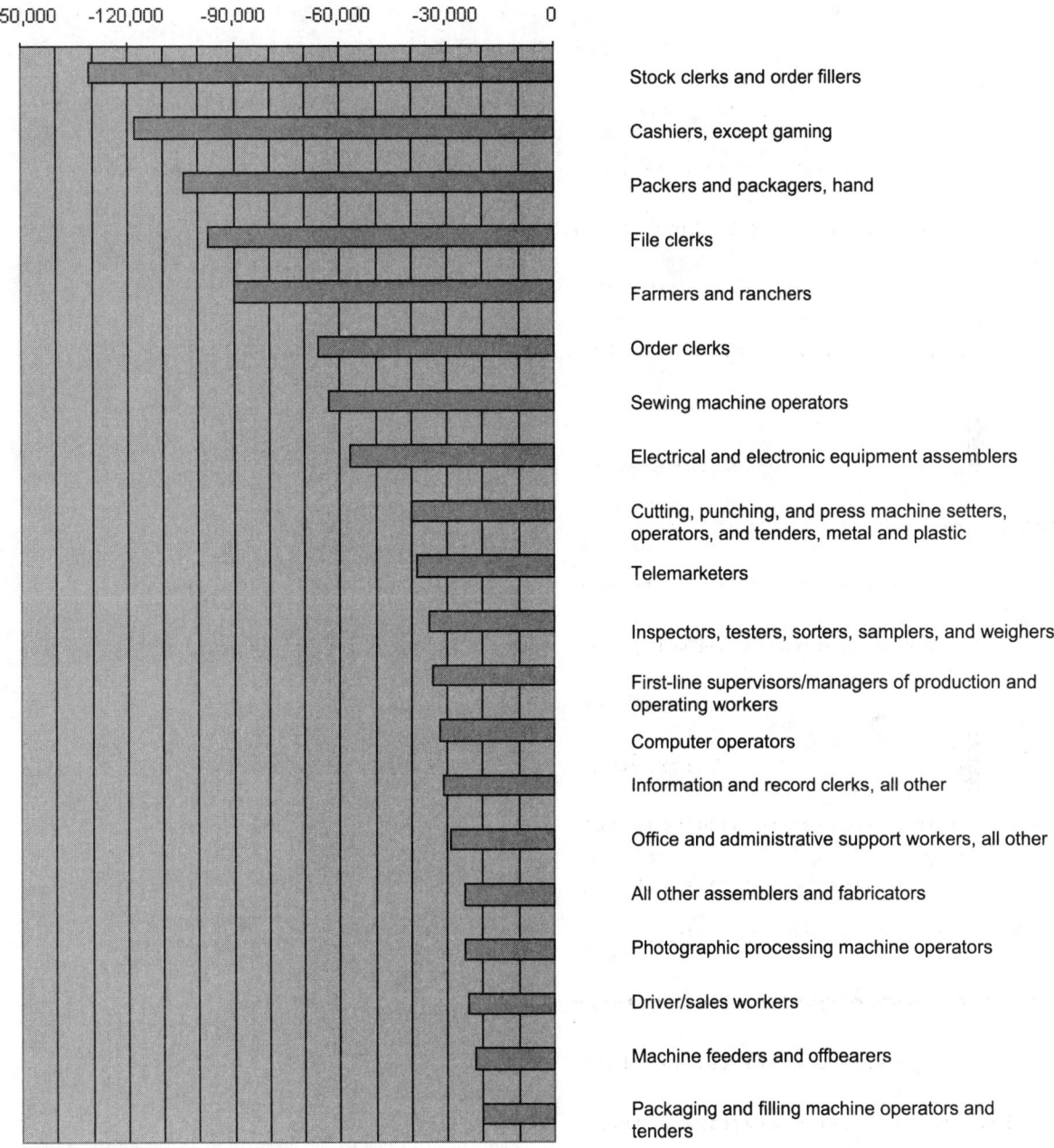

Source: U.S. Bureau of Labor Statistics

Plunkett Research, Ltd.

www.plunkettresearch.com

Chapter 3

RESEARCH: 7 KEYS FOR JOB SEEKERS

**How to use your library, college placement office, the Internet and other resources
to become well-informed about a company and its industry
<u>before</u> you ask for an interview**

Research is the key to finding appropriate job openings, targeting the best possible employers and performing well when you go to job interviews. Learn what's unique about a company compared to other firms in its industry. Learn why it's prospering–or why it isn't. Where is this company going? Is it favored by stock investors? Is it privately-owned by a family, or has it been acquired by private equity investors who plan to resell it over the mid-term? What are its hottest-selling products and services? Is it investing in research and new facilities so that it may prosper in the future? Also, as many people who have been laid off from failing startup firms have learned the hard way, determining a company's level of financial stability can be one of the most important factors in making a career decision.

The more you're willing to dig deep at the library or your college's career planning office, and the more adept you are at using the Internet for research, the better your chances of success in a job search. If you are willing to ask questions of businesspeople and of employees who currently work for your target employers, you will enhance your job search even further. The two secrets to successful job research are tenacity and focus. Know what to look for and where to find it.

Once you've landed an interview, you should research both the prospective employer and its industry even further. In this manner, you'll know what questions to ask before you agree to take the job, and you'll present yourself as a knowledgeable potential hire who is truly interested in the company and its business.

Here are the seven keys for research that can lead you to a great employer:

1) Financial Stability
Check bond ratings, credit ratings, debt level, growth in sales and growth in profits, along with the views of stock analysts and business journalists.

2) Growth Plans
Look for new plants, stores or offices to be opened; new technologies, products or divisions to be launched; or plans for strategic acquisitions. (See 3, 4 and 5 below.)

3) Research and Development Programs
How much does the firm invest in R&D? Is this research and development budget growing? For many types of companies, research is a vital investment in the future.

4) Product Launch and Production
Does the company have the ability to successfully launch new products and services (see 5 below) or to invest in and utilize cutting-edge technologies needed to maintain a competitive edge?

5) Marketing and Distribution Methods
Does the firm utilize an in-house sales force? Does it work through outside dealers and distribution partners? What are its advertising methods? Is it increasing its market share, or are competitors taking customers away? Is the company growing its international sales? Is it adept at using the Internet as a powerful sales tool? Is it successful at selling into growing international markets, such as China and India?

6) Employee Benefits
Are wealth-building benefit plans offered? Will the company match all or part of your deposits to a 401(k) savings plan? Check for tuition reimbursement, pension plans, profit sharing, ESOP stock ownership plans, discount stock purchase plans, stock options or performance-based bonuses.

7) Quality-of-Work Factors

Does the company offer continual training, wellness programs, child care, elder care support, promote-from-within policies, flexible work schedules, performance reviews, product discounts or on-site health clubs? Is it a corporate culture that fits your lifestyle?

As a serious job seeker, you should conduct in-depth research and make detailed notes about these seven key factors for each firm you are considering. Then compare each company's finances, plans and programs to others in the same industry. You'll begin to see what makes some firms outstanding and why those outstanding companies are the best places to make a career investment. For example, if you compare two discount store giants, Wal-Mart and Costco, you will find that Wal-Mart is by far the larger firm, but Costco has an outstanding record of providing superior employee pay and benefits.

Your research goal should be twofold: First, determine whether this is a firm you want to work for. Are the salaries and benefits appealing? Are layoffs likely? Is it a company with solid growth plans? A growing company will offer opportunities for you to advance when it launches new locations, services, technologies or product lines. Second, develop a personal understanding of the company and its industry so you can better sell yourself as a potential employee.

Other Considerations:

Women and Minorities:

Certain industries have a greater tendency to offer advancement opportunities for women or minorities. Historically, the banking and insurance segments have tended to promote both women and minorities, as have retailing, electric utilities, publishing and major telephone companies.

Major employers in many other industries are making serious efforts to hire, develop and promote women and minorities for top officers' positions. An August 2009 study released by Catalyst, a New York-based research group that focuses on women's issues in the workplace found that 3% of the *Fortune 500* firms had female CEOs, up from 1% in 2001. Some technology companies have been terrific places for women who want to advance, and many tech companies, such as Xerox and eBay, have posted women to CEO spots.

Catalyst reports that 15.2% of members of boards of directors in the *Fortune 500* firms were women in 2009, up from 9.6% in 1995. (You can access the results of Catalyst studies at www.catalyst.org.) Obviously, women are making slow progress in gaining representation in the highest ranks of corporate America, and they fall far short of parity with men in that regard. The *Fortune 1000* companies recently included 23 female CEOs, according to an August 2008 study by Catalyst.

Black Enterprise magazine publishes an annual list of the "Most Powerful African Americans in Corporate America," (see www.blackenterprise.com). Meanwhile, the Executive Leadership Council, www.elcinfo.com, a Washington, D.C.-based nonprofit group that conducts programs aimed at filling more executive posts with African-Americans, has a unique statistic to report. Its membership is composed of senior-level black executives who have jobs that are no more than three levels below the CEO spot at Fortune 500 companies. When the group was founded in 1986, it had only a handful of members. Today, its membership is about 380 people employed in high-level executive jobs at major corporations.

The Hispanic Association on Corporate Responsibility (www.hacr.org) promotes Hispanic advancement in the areas of employment, procurement, philanthropy and governance. Another nonprofit agency, National Hispanic Corporate Achievers (hispanicachievers.org), provides an educational forum for Hispanics working for *Fortune 1000* companies.

Tips on Using Business Magazines, Newspapers and Trade Journals to Find Job Leads and Do Employer Research

Many job seekers overlook the tremendous advantages of using industry magazines (called "trade journals") and other publications to do research.

Industry-specific trade journals frequently have classified ads in the back that list job openings. An example of a great magazine to study is *American Banker,* which can be found at major libraries. Additional information is available at www.americanbanker.com.

Journalists at trade journals and business newspapers continuously interview industry-leading executives regarding their companies' growth plans. New projects and company expansion plans described in these articles provide terrific job leads.

You can also get great contact information from these publications. Read the latest business stories about companies and industries that interest you and you will learn vital information. Best of all, you can glean from stories and interviews the names and titles of executives who lead projects, divisions and subsidiaries.

There are literally hundreds of these trade journals—at least one for each industry sector and sometimes dozens covering the largest industries.

Other great resources include local business newspapers such as the *Dallas/Ft. Worth Business Journal, The Wall Street Journal*, the business pages of major newspapers like *The New York Times* and publications written for major investors like *Investor's Business Daily*. At www.bizjournals.com, you can gain access to news stories from business journals from all over the U.S.

Quality-of-Life Benefits:

Many companies offer benefits that help employees balance their personal and professional lives. The concept is that employees who are healthy and comfortable with their personal and family lives make better, more productive employees. To that end, many companies include fitness programs and family services such as extended maternity leaves and child care or elder care, whether on-site or off-site in the form of referral services. Other popular family-friendly benefits include flextime, flexible benefits spending accounts, adoption assistance and telecommuting. In many cases, benefits are listed on employers' web sites.

Work-Life has become a popular phrase for family-friendly benefits and programs among major employers such as Intel, Abbott Laboratories, Baxter International and Aramark. For additional information, you can study such organizations as the Alliance for Work-Life Progress at www.awlp.org.

Growth Potential and Job Stability:

A firm's growth potential should be among your top priorities. Companies are always trying to maintain or increase productivity, or the ratio of sales per employee. If a company's sales are sliding, or if it is running out of cash, the job picture starts to collapse. A little extra research into a company's finances and true potential for growth might save you from a future layoff.

Of course, employers sometimes have to resort to layoffs due to conditions outside of their control. For example, travel industry companies worldwide cut hundreds of thousands of jobs in the revenue slump following the September 11, 2001 attacks on New York City and Washington, D.C.

As a job seeker, you're forced to look out for your own best interests while you sort through thousands of potential employers in dozens of industries. This means that good research is vital. For example, if you put salary at the top of your list, you may have the wrong priorities. From time to time, some of the highest-paying firms have been among those cutting the largest numbers of employees. If you are looking for job stability, your biggest challenge is to pick companies that are more likely to hire now and less likely to have layoffs in the future. That's why a firm's growth outlook should be one of your guiding lights.

However, the goal is *internal* growth caused by expanding sales. Generally less appealing are firms that post a quick spike in growth through big mergers. (In many cases, merged companies lay off people who suddenly find themselves filling jobs duplicated in newly consolidated offices. Also, companies that grow excessively through acquisitions may be taking on loads of debt that can become hard to handle later. However, there are occasional exceptions to this rule, where firms are enjoying soaring demand for products or services and find it difficult to hire quickly enough to keep up.) Companies that are growing rapidly through internal expansion include those opening new stores, distribution centers or offices, developing exciting new products, moving into new markets (including international markets) and creating hot new technologies, retail formats or services. Those types of expansion frequently mean great career opportunities, including the chance for rapid job promotion.

Where can you look for growth companies? If you're tenacious, you can find opportunities where others will find only rejection. Identifying real prospects for growth takes more than a quick glance.

Here's an extremely important point for you to remember: You should look for opportunities in growing divisions that serve special niches, even when the company as a whole is cutting jobs.

Additional key factors for strong corporate growth, and thereby the best job prospects, include:

1) Companies or divisions with a growing share of a promising market.

Management's ability to anticipate or create change in the marketplace makes for a growing company with great prospects. For example, Sam Walton revolutionized the department store business by realizing that consumers want everyday low prices on name-brand merchandise. He created Wal-Mart, while competitor Sears suffered by maintaining an old-fashioned policy of special sales events on private-label goods. Wal-Mart rapidly became one of the largest creators of new jobs in the private sector. Sears was forced to slash its ranks.

Microsoft made its way to the top with unique products serving a soaring market when it developed highly functional software for personal computers. The software giant created thousands of millionaire employees through the immense increase in the value of its stock plans. HEB, an innovative grocer in Texas, has evolved continually over the decades, constantly introducing improvements to store layouts, and even creating an exciting new HEB Marketplace concept that is a retail industry leader. HEB has large numbers of job openings of many types on a continuous basis.

The point to these stories is that you shouldn't invest your career in a company with mediocre prospects. With perseverance, you can target your own list of employers that are posting growth due to competitive advantages or growing market demand. Your best bets are companies taking reasonable risks in order to move ahead. Those risks may include investments in advertising, research and development, new technology, improved techniques on the manufacturing floor, testing of new products and the opening of new retail store formats. For example, Chico's FAS stores scored a hit by filling a niche in the women's apparel market, and Genentech became a leader in the biotechnology field by risking vast amounts on research. Also, don't overlook the potential of the export market—many American firms find much of their growth by creating products and services that enjoy demand overseas as well as in the U.S.

2) Sales and profits: past and present.

The companies most likely to move along at a good clip are those with an exciting mid-term history. Firms with an average annual growth in sales of 10% to 15% or more over the last three to five years are generally very promising. Many small and mid-size firms grow at much faster rates and find themselves hiring continuously.

3) Beware of fads.

Unfortunately, a few companies post meteoric growth in businesses that turn out to be mere fads. The restaurant industry suffers from this problem on a regular basis. In recent years, companies selling bagels, frozen yogurt, rotisserie chicken and the like enjoyed impressive, nationwide growth only to collapse like a house of cards a couple of years later. Here's another example: the 1990s produced a rash of new dotcoms that were fueled by fad investors. Many of the biggest web-based busts were companies that planned to steal market share from traditional retail stores by selling items like pet food and living room furniture over the Internet. Most of these fad-based firms wasted valuable years in the careers of employees in addition to billions of dollars of venture capital—only a handful truly succeeded.

How to Find and Use Expert Opinions:

Superior sources used by sophisticated job researchers include reports written by: 1) stock analysts; 2) professional market research firms; and 3) journalists at business magazines and industry "trade magazines." Many major libraries have large collections of industry-specific trade magazines that can give you clues that competing job seekers will overlook. For example, *Retail Traffic Magazine*, www.retailtrafficmag.com, publishes lists of the fastest-growing retail chains. Virtually every other industry is covered by one or two trade magazines that will give you leads to growing companies. Many articles in these magazines contain the names of executives you may want to contact. Also, most industry trade magazines publish help-wanted ads in the back. The *Gale Directory of Publications and Broadcast Media* is a good index to magazines, organized by industry. You can find this directory in major libraries.

Next, move on to reports from experts. Marketing and investment professionals are looking for some of the same clues you should use as a job seeker, and reports written by full-time analysts who cover specific companies or industries can help you find firms that are growing and hiring. Reuters, www.reuters.com, is the best source for stock analysts' reports. Here, you'll find the latest business news as well as online access to industry and company coverage written by the nation's best analysts. Most of the reports have a cost, but many are free of charge, and others have prices as low as $5 to $25. Learn to use the stock research and "analyst research" features at Reuters to find exactly what you want.

Professionally written market research can be found at Marketresearch.com, www.marketresearch.com. This market research broker charges varying fees for access to the reports. However, many of the reports are reasonably priced, and the insight you gain into industries, markets and leading companies can be extremely helpful. Web sites such as this offer the ability to search for reports by a wide variety of criteria, including company name and industry.

Other Basic Resources:

Annual Reports/10-Ks/S-1s: Companies that sell their stocks to the public, including most of the firms covered in this book, publish annual reports that contain a wealth of information. Annual reports and 10-Ks cover yearly results, financial statements, management practices and other vital information for publicly held firms. S-1s provide the same type of information on companies that are selling stock to the public for the first time. You can find copies of these reports at large libraries. Online, the best place to acquire this information is at the site of the U.S. Securities and Exchange Commission. They have a user-friendly service that enables you to search for companies and access their financial reports at www.sec.gov. Look especially at the five-year "summary financial statement" in the back of these reports. Also, look for growth in sales and earnings. If these are falling, dig deeper to find out why. Faltering sales or profits can lead to layoffs or to a merger with another firm (which could result in deep job cuts).

Also, you can find a wealth of financial information on publicly-traded firms at Yahoo! Finance, http://finance.yahoo.com.

See Chapter 4, "Important Contacts for Job Seekers," for additional places to get basic corporate data.

Tips on Utilizing Financial Documents Filed by Publicly Held Firms

(Access these documents at the Securities Exchange Commission, www.sec.gov.)

10-K (also called Annual Report on Form 10-K):
This is an annual filing required by federal law. It follows a standard format. Information includes a complete description of the business, risk factors, historical financial data and much more. It is vital reading for job seekers. You will find that these documents are written in dry, legal language, but they contain a wealth of information.

DEF 14A Proxy Statement:
This is an annual document that gives shareholders certain options to consider at their annual meeting. It names the firm's board of directors and top management. It also gives the dollar value and description of salaries, bonuses, pension plans, stock options and other benefits enjoyed by the company's five highest-paid officers. Job seekers can learn a great deal about a firm's management, pay and benefits from this document. Included is a list of the people or organizations that own more than 5% of the company's stock.

S-1:
This is a new registration document for companies that are going public for the first time. In other words, they are creating an IPO (initial public offering). The information includes all of the data found in the 10-K and proxy statement filed annually by companies that have been public for more than one year.

10-Q:
This is a quarterly report detailing a company's latest sales, profits and balance sheet.

More Ways to Research an Employer's Financial Stability and Growth Plans:

1) Check out its bond rating.
There's no sense in trying to become a financial analyst on your own. Instead, go to your library and turn to the *Bond Guide* published by Standard & Poor's (New York, NY). This monthly booklet rates thousands of corporate bonds, based on a company's ability to pay principal and interest when due. If you're considering a major corporation with a bond rating of less than BB (an indicator that a company's debt is riskier than "investment grade"), you should do a lot more investigating before you continue chasing a job at that company.

2) Talk to vendors and current employees.
Talk to employees who work for the employer, or talk to people who do business with it. No one knows what's really going on better than people who are on the scene. If there are problems that are not yet known by the media, or if there are exciting new developments that have not yet been announced, you may find out a lot just by asking around. While you're at it, ask about corporate culture—how well are employees treated?

Popular Job-Search Internet Sites

HotJobs	http://hotjobs.yahoo.com/
CareerBuilder	www.careerbuilder.com
Monster	www.monster.com

Tips on Finding Information on Privately Held Employers

Study back-issue indexes and archives to major newspapers to see what journalists are reporting about a prospective private employer. Many libraries have back issues of *The Wall Street Journal, The New York Times* and other important newspapers on microfilm. At major public and university libraries, you may be able to access online databases like ProQuest and InfoTrac. These databases have excellent search engines that lead you into online archives of the best publications, including *The Wall Street Journal*, as well as many trade and local publications.

For smaller firms, go online and try American Journalism Review at www.newslink.org, where you'll be able to search news sites including hometown newspapers across the nation. Likewise, search local business newspapers at www.bizjournals.com, where you'll find links to dozens of major business weeklies like the *Houston Business Journal*.

Finally, invest in a credit report. If you really want reassurance, go to Experian SmartBusinessReports, www.smartbusinessreports.com. You can use its links to order a credit report on the employer. These reports are reasonably priced from about $20 to $45, and they can help you determine whether the company is paying its bills on time or has other problems. This could be vital in helping you determine whether to accept a job at a privately-held firm.

3) Use Internet search engines.
Look up your firm and industry in an Internet search engine such as Google or a portal such as Yahoo Finance, http://finance.yahoo.com. There, you may find unusual articles that were recently written about a company's product breakthroughs, treatment of women or minorities, human interest stories, training programs or stories written from other unique slants.

4) Study other business books and guides.

Search at a library or at an online bookseller like Amazon.com for recent books regarding major companies. For example, if you want to apply to biotech leader Genentech for a job, don't fail to read *The Billion Dollar Molecule: One Company's Quest for the Perfect Drug.* With a little research, you can turn up many other excellent books about specific companies, from banks like Bank of America to publishers like Gannett.

Great Places for Industry Research

Plunkett Research, www.plunkettresearch.com. Go to the specific industry of your choice to see an overview of trends and statistics. At our subscription service, www.plunkettresearchonline.com, subscribers have access to thousands of pages of industry analysis, statistics, contacts and company profiles, along with multiple search and export tools.

Quintessentialcareers.com, www.quintessentialcareers.com. Offers a "Career Resources Toolkit."

Wetfeet.com, www.wetfeet.com. Publishes snapshots of hundreds of employers.

Vault.com, www.vault.com. This site publishes insights about careers with hundreds of leading firms.

---

5) Explore industry-specific web sites.

See Chapter 4, "Important Contacts for Job Seekers," for hundreds of sites from dozens of different industry sectors. In particular, study the industry associations for the sector you want to work in.

6) Research benefits and pension plans.

For additional information about corporate pension plans, start with the government agency charged with protecting and regulating pensions: the Pension Benefit Guaranty Corporation, 1200 K St. NW, Washington, D.C. 20005-4026, 202-326-4000, www.pbgc.gov. They can answer certain questions over the telephone.

The U.S. Department of Labor publishes a useful book titled "Protect your Pension." They can be contacted at: U.S. Department of Labor, Employee Benefits Security Administration, 200 Constitution Ave. NW, Room N5635, Washington, D.C. 20210, 866-444-3272 or 202-219-8776, www.dol.gov/ebsa/publications/main.html.

The Social Security Administration, 800-772-1213, www.ssa.gov, can provide you with information regarding your potential Social Security benefits.

NOTE: Generally, employees covered by wealth-building benefit plans do not fully own ("vest in") funds contributed on their behalf by the employer until as many as five years of service with that employer have passed. All pension plans are voluntary—that is, employers are not obligated to offer pensions.

Pension Plans: The type and generosity of these plans vary widely from firm to firm. Caution: Some employers refer to plans as "pension" or "retirement" plans when they are actually 401(k) savings plans that require a contribution by the employee.

Defined Benefit Pension Plans: Pension plans that do not require a contribution from the employee are infrequently offered. However, a few companies, particularly larger employers in high-profit-margin industries, offer defined benefit pension plans where the employee is guaranteed to receive a set pension benefit upon retirement. The amount of the benefit is determined by the years of service with the company and the employee's salary during the later years of employment. The longer a person works for the employer, the higher the retirement benefit. These defined benefit plans are funded entirely by the employer. The benefits, up to a reasonable limit, are guaranteed by the Federal Government's Pension Benefit Guaranty Corporation. These plans are not portable—if you leave the company, you cannot transfer your benefits into a different plan. Instead, upon retirement you will receive the benefits that vested during your service with the company. If your employer offers a pension plan, it must give you a "summary plan description" within 90 days of the date you join the plan. You can also request a "summary annual report" of the plan, and once every 12 months you may request an "individual benefit statement" accounting of your interest in the plan.

Defined Contribution Plans: These are quite different. They do not guarantee a certain amount of pension benefit. Instead, they set out circumstances under which the employer will make a contribution to a plan on your behalf. The most common example is the 401(k) savings plan. Pension benefits are not guaranteed under these plans.

Cash Balance Pension Plans: These plans were recently invented. They are hybrid plans—part defined benefit and part defined contribution. Many employers have converted their older defined benefit plans into cash balance plans. The employer makes deposits (or credits a given amount of money) on the employee's behalf, usually based on a percentage of pay. Employee accounts grow based on a predetermined interest benchmark, such as the interest rate on Treasury Bonds. There are some advantages to these plans, particularly for younger workers: a) The benefits, up to a reasonable limit, are guaranteed by the Pension Benefit Guaranty Corporation. b) Benefits are portable—they can be moved to another plan when the employee changes companies. c) Younger workers and those who spend a shorter number of years with an employer may receive higher benefits than they would under a traditional defined benefit plan.

ESOP Stock Plan (Employees' Stock Ownership Plan): This type of plan is in wide use. Typically, the plan borrows money from a bank and uses those funds to purchase a large block of the corporation's stock. The corporation makes contributions to the plan over a period of time, and the stock purchase loan is eventually paid off. The value of the plan grows significantly as long as the market price of the stock holds up. Qualified employees are allocated a share of the plan based on their length of service and their level of salary. Under federal regulations, participants in ESOPs are allowed to diversify their account holdings in set percentages that rise as the employee ages and gains years of service with the company. In this manner, not all of the employee's assets are tied up in the employer's stock.

Savings Plan, 401(k): Under this type of plan, employees make a tax-deferred deposit into an account. In the best plans, the company makes annual matching donations to the employees' accounts, typically in some proportion to deposits made by the employees themselves. A good plan will match one-half of employee deposits of up to 6% of wages. For example, an employee earning $30,000 yearly might deposit $1,800 (6%) into the plan. The company will match one-half of the employee's deposit, or $900. The plan grows on a tax-deferred basis, similar to an IRA. A very generous plan will match 100% of employee deposits. However, some plans do not call for the employer to make a matching deposit at all. Other plans call for a matching contribution to be made at the discretion of the firm's board of directors. Actual terms of these plans vary widely from firm to firm. Generally, these savings plans allow employees to deposit as much as 15% of salary into the plan on a tax-deferred basis. However, the portion that the company uses to calculate its matching deposit is generally limited to a maximum of 6%. Employees should take care to diversify the holdings in their 401(k) accounts, and most people should seek professional guidance or investment management for their accounts. (Note: when profits are down, many employers exercise their right to suspend their contributions to 401(k)s. Employees may continue to make contributions, but they will not be matched by the employer in these cases.)

Stock Purchase Plan: Qualified employees may purchase the company's common stock at a price below its market value under a specific plan. Typically, the employee is limited to investing a small percentage of wages in this plan. The discount may range from 5% to 15%. Some of these plans allow for deposits to be made through regular monthly payroll deductions. However, new accounting rules for corporations, along with other factors, are leading many companies to curtail these plans—dropping the discount allowed, cutting the maximum yearly stock purchase or otherwise making the plans less generous or appealing.

Profit Sharing: Qualified employees are awarded an annual amount equal to some portion of a company's profits. In a very generous plan, the pool of money awarded to employees would be 15% of profits. Typically, this money is deposited into a long-term retirement account. Caution: Some employers refer to plans as "profit sharing" when they are actually 401(k) savings plans. True profit sharing plans are rarely offered.

Plunkett Research Online and Plunkett's Industry Reference Books:

1) Internet-Based Services: Plunkett Research Online is a reference service that is subscribed to by the nation's leading university placement offices, libraries and information offices. You can use it to filter prospective employers by location, industry, size and more. You can then export contact information for those companies into spreadsheets or text files. In addition, you can use the site to research the latest editions of our industry analysis. Many additional tools for job seekers are included. For an extensive online tour, see www.plunkettresearch.com.

2) Printed Almanacs: Plunkett Research also publishes industry-specific almanacs for the most important industries. These are top-notch resources for job seekers.

Industry-Specific Books from Plunkett Research:

- Plunkett's Advertising & Branding Industry Almanac
- Plunkett's Airline, Hotel & Travel Industry Almanac
- Plunkett's Almanac of Middle Market Companies
- Plunkett's Apparel & Textiles Industry Almanac
- Plunkett's Automobile Industry Almanac
- Plunkett's Banking, Mortgages & Credit Industry Almanac
- Plunkett's Biotech & Genetics Industry Almanac
- Plunkett's Chemicals, Coatings & Plastics Industry Almanac
- Plunkett's Consulting Industry Almanac
- Plunkett's E-Commerce & Internet Business Almanac
- Plunkett's Energy Industry Almanac
- Plunkett's Engineering & Research Industry Almanac
- Plunkett's Entertainment & Media Industry Almanac
- Plunkett's Food Industry Almanac
- Plunkett's Health Care Industry Almanac
- Plunkett's Insurance Industry Almanac
- Plunkett's InfoTech Industry Almanac
- Plunkett's Investment & Securities Industry Almanac
- Plunkett's Nanotechnology & MEMS Industry Almanac
- Plunkett's Outsourcing & Offshoring Industry Almanac
- Plunkett's Real Estate & Construction Industry Almanac
- Plunkett's Renewable, Alternative & Hydrogen Energy Industry Almanac
- Plunkett's Retail Industry Almanac
- Plunkett's Sports Industry Almanac
- Plunkett's Telecommunications Industry Almanac

- Plunkett's Transportation, Supply Chain & Logistics Industry Almanac
- Plunkett's Wireless & Cellular Telephone Industry Almanac

Publications from Plunkett Research Written Especially for Job Seekers:

- The Almanac of American Employers
- Plunkett's Companion to the Almanac of American Employers

Our books will give you in-depth coverage of specific industries and the leading firms in those industries, along with trends and developments in technology and services. You will find these books in public and academic libraries, college placement offices, human resources offices, corporate libraries and government agency libraries. For sample chapters and additional details, you can preview as well as purchase these books at www.plunkettresearch.com.

Plunkett's Companion to The Almanac of American Employers is our book that provides profiles on 500 additional, rapidly growing corporate employers. This companion book covers smaller firms than those in the main volume of *The Almanac of American Employers*.

Chapter 4

IMPORTANT CONTACTS
FOR JOB SEEKERS

I. Accountants & CPAs Associations

American Institute of CPAs (AICPA)
1211 Ave. of the Americas
New York, NY 10036-8775 US
Phone: 212-596-6200
Fax: 1-800-362-5066
Toll Free: 888-777-7077
E-mail Address: *service@aicpa.org*
Web Address: www.aicpa.org
American Institute of CPAs (AICPA) provides information and news for CPAs, news from the organization and a search for accounting firms on its web site.

Council of Petroleum Accountants Societies, Inc. (COPAS)
3900 E. Mexico Ave., Ste. 602
Denver, CO 80210 US
Phone: 303-300-1131
Fax: 303-300-3733
Toll Free: 877-992-6727
E-mail Address: *Execdir@copas.org*
Web Address: www.copas.org
The Council of Petroleum Accountants Societies, Inc. (COPAS) provides a forum for discussing and solving the variety of problems related to accounting for oil and gas. COPAS also provides valuable educational materials related to oil and gas accounting.

International Accounting Standards Board (IASB)
30 Cannon St.
London, EC4M 6XH UK
Phone: 44-20-7246-6410
Fax: 44-20-7246-6411
E-mail Address: *iasb@iasb.org.uk*
Web Address: www.iasb.org
The International Accounting Standards Board (IASB) website hosts an electronic subscription service to the International Financial Reporting (IFRS) Standards as well access to IFRS summaries.

II. Advertising/Marketing Associations

4A's (American Association of Advertising Agencies)
405 Lexington Ave., 18th Fl.
New York, NY 10174-1801 US
Phone: 212-682-2500
Fax: 212-682-8391
E-mail Address: *nhill@aaaa.org*
Web Address: www.aaaa.org
The 4A's, formerly the American Association of Advertising Agencies, is the national trade association representing the advertising agency industry in the United States. The association announced in 2009 that it would go by the name 4A's to better reflect its international business and leadership efforts.

Advertising Women of New York (AWNY)
25 W. 45th St., Ste. 403
New York, NY 10036 US
Phone: 212-221-7969
Fax: 212-221-8296
E-mail Address: *awny@awny.org*
Web Address: www.awny.org
Advertising Women of New York (AWNY) provides a forum for personal and professional growth, serves as a catalyst for the advancement of women in the communications field and promotes and supports philanthropic endeavors through the AWNY Foundation. The web site also provides content from Women Executives in Public Relations (WERP), such as its a dynamic job board.

American Institute of Graphic Arts (AIGA)
164 5th Ave.
New York, NY 10010 US
Phone: 212-807-1990
Fax: 212-807-1799
E-mail Address:
steve_rogenstein@aiga.org
Web Address: www.aiga.org
The American Institute of Graphic Arts (AIGA) strives to further excellence in communication design, both as a strategic tool for business and as a cultural force.

American Marketing Association (AMA)
311 S. Wacker Dr., Ste. 5800
Chicago, IL 60606 US
Phone: 312-542-9000
Fax: 312-542-9001
Toll Free: 800-262-1150
E-mail Address: *info@ama.org*
Web Address:
www.marketingpower.com
The American Marketing Association (AMA) serves marketing professionals in both business and education and serves all levels of marketing practitioners, educators and students.

Cable & Telecommunications Association for Marketing (CTAM)
201 N. Union St., Ste. 440
Alexandria, VA 22314 US
Phone: 703-549-4200
E-mail Address: *info@ctam.com*
Web Address:
www.ctamnetforum.com/eweb
The Cable & Telecommunications Association for Marketing (CTAM) is

dedicated to the discipline and development of consumer marketing excellence in cable television, new media and telecommunications services.

Direct Marketing Association (DMA)
1120 Ave. of the Americas
New York, NY 10036-6700 US
Phone: 212-768-7277
Fax: 212-302-6714
E-mail Address: *customerservice@the-dma.org*
Web Address: www.the-dma.org
The Direct Marketing Association (DMA) is the oldest and largest trade association for users and suppliers in the direct, database and interactive marketing fields.

III. Aerospace & Defense Industry Associations

American Institute of Aeronautics and Astronautics (AIAA)
1801 Alexander Bell Dr., Ste. 500
Reston, VA 20191-4344 US
Phone: 703-264-7500
Fax: 703-264-7551
Toll Free: 800-639-2422
E-mail Address: *klausd@aiaa.org*
Web Address: www.aiaa.org
The American Institute of Aeronautics and Astronautics (AIAA) is a nonprofit society aimed at advancing the arts, sciences and technology of aeronautics and astronautics. The institute represents the U.S. in the International Astronautical Federation and the International Council on the Aeronautical Sciences.

IV. Airline & Air Cargo Industry Associations

International Air Transport Association (IATA)
800 Place Victoria
P.O. Box 113
Montreal, QC H4Z 1M1 Canada
Phone: 514-874-0202
Fax: 514-874-9632
E-mail Address: *corpcomms@iata.org*
Web Address: www.iata.org
The International Air Transport Association (IATA) represents about 260 airlines in order to offer the

highest standards of passenger and cargo service.

V. Alternative Energy-Ethanol

Renewable Fuels Association (RFA)
1 Massachusetts Ave. NW, Ste. 820
Washington, DC 20001 US
Phone: 202-289-3835
E-mail Address: *info@ethanolrfa.org*
Web Address: www.ethanolrfa.org
The Renewable Fuels Association (RFA) is a trade organization representing the ethanol industry. It publishes a wealth of useful information, including a listing of biorefineries and monthly U.S. fuel ethanol production and demand.

VI. Alternative Energy-Solar

Solar Energy Industries Association (SEIA)
805 15th St. NW, Ste. 510
Washington, DC 20005 US
Phone: 202-682-0556
Fax: 202-682-7779
E-mail Address: *info@seia.org*
Web Address: www.seia.org
Solar Energy Industries Association (SEIA) operates a web site that provides news for the solar energy industry, links to related products and companies and solar energy statistics.

VII. Alternative Energy-Wind

American Wind Energy Association (AWEA)
1501 M St. NW, Ste. 1000
Washington, DC 20005 US
Phone: 202-383-2500
Fax: 202-383-2505
E-mail Address: *windmail@awea.org*
Web Address: www.awea.org
The American Wind Energy Association (AWEA) promotes wind energy as a clean source of electricity worldwide. Its website provides excellent resources for research, including an online library, discussions of legislation, and descriptions of wind technologies.

VIII. Banking Industry Associations

American Bankers Association (ABA)
1120 Connecticut Ave. NW
Washington, DC 20036 US
Fax: 202-663-7578
Toll Free: 800-226-5377
E-mail Address: *smarshall@aba.com*
Web Address: www.aba.com
The American Bankers Association (ABA) represents banks of all sizes on issues of national importance for financial institutions and their customers. The site offers financial information and solutions, financial news and member access to further advice and content.

IX. Biotechnology and Biological Industry Associations

BioIndustry Association
14/15 Belgrave Sq.
London, SW1X 8PS UK
Phone: 44-20-7565-7190
Fax: 44-20-7565-7191
E-mail Address: *admin@bioindustry.org*
Web Address: www.bioindustry.org
The BioIndustry Association promotes bioscience development in the U.K. The organization operates a public affairs program, a conference and seminar program, trade missions and publications for internal and external audiences.

Biotechnology Industry Organization (BIO)
1201 Maryland Ave. SW, Ste. 900
Washington, DC 20024 US
Phone: 202-962-9200
Fax: 202-488-6301
E-mail Address: *info@bio.org*
Web Address: www.bio.org
The Biotechnology Industry Organization (BIO) is involved in the research and development of health care, agricultural, industrial and environmental biotechnology products. BIO has both small and large member organizations.

X. Booksellers Associations

American Booksellers Association, Inc.
200 White Plains Rd., Ste. 600
Tarrytown, NY 10591 US
Fax: 914-591-2720
Toll Free: 800-637-0037
E-mail Address: *info@bookweb.org*
Web Address: www.bookweb.org
The American Booksellers Association is a nonprofit association representing independent bookstores in the United States.

XI. Broadcasting, Cable, Radio & TV Associations

Academy of Television Arts and Sciences
5220 Lankershim Blvd.
North Hollywood, CA 91601-3109
Phone: 818-754-2800
Fax: 818-761-2827
E-mail Address: *support@emmys.org*
Web Address: www.emmys.org
The Academy of Television Arts and Sciences is a nonprofit corporation devoted to the advancement of telecommunications arts and sciences and to fostering creative leadership in the telecommunications industry. It is one of three organizations that administer the Emmy Awards. It is responsible for prime time Emmys.

American Federation of Television and Radio Artists (AFTRA)
260 Madison Ave., 7th Fl.
New York, NY 10016-2401 US
Phone: 212-532-0800
Fax: 212-532-2242
E-mail Address: *info@aftra.org*
Web Address: www.aftra.org
The American Federation of Television and Radio Artists (AFTRA) represents actors and other professional performers and broadcasters in television, radio, sound recordings, non-broadcast/industrial programming and new technologies such as interactive programming and CD-ROMs.

American Women in Radio and Television, Inc. (AWRT)
1760 Old Meadow Rd., Ste. 500
McLean, VA 22102 US
Phone: 703-506-3290
Fax: 703-506-3266
E-mail Address: *info@awrt.org*
Web Address: www.awrt.org
American Women in Radio and Television (AWRT), founded in 1951, is a national nonprofit organization dedicated to advancing the role of women in electronic media and related fields.

Association of America's Public Television Stations (APTS)
2100 Crystal Dr., Ste. 700
Arlington, VA 22202 US
Phone: 202-654-4200
Fax: 202-654-4236
E-mail Address: *jeffrey@apts.org*
Web Address: www.apts.org
The Association of America's Public Television Stations (APTS) is a nonprofit membership organization formed to support the continued growth and development of strong and financially sound noncommercial television service for the American public.

Broadcast Education Association (BEA)
1771 N St. NW
Washington, DC 20036-2891 US
Phone: 202-429-3935
E-mail Address: *tbailey@nab.org*
Web Address: www.beaweb.org
The Broadcast Education Association (BEA) is the professional association for professors, industry professionals and graduate students interested in teaching and research related to electronic media and multimedia enterprises.

National Academy of Television Arts and Sciences
111 W. 57th St., Ste. 600
New York, NY 10019 US
Phone: 212-586-8424
Fax: 212-246-8129
E-mail Address: *info@emmyonline.tv*
Web Address: www.emmyonline.org
The National Academy of Television Arts and Sciences is dedicated to the advancement of the arts and sciences of television and the promotion of creative leadership for artistic, educational and technical achievements within the television industry. It is responsible for awarding the Emmy Awards.

National Association of Broadcasters (NAB)
1771 N St. NW
Washington, DC 20036 US
Phone: 202-429-5300
Fax: 202-429-4199
E-mail Address: *nab@nab.org*
Web Address: www.nab.org
The National Association of Broadcasters (NAB) represents broadcasters for radio and television. The organization also provides benefits to employees of member companies and to individuals and companies that provide products and services to the electronic media industries.

National Association of Television Program Executives (NATPE)
5757 Wilshire Blvd.
Penthouse 10
Los Angeles, CA 90036-3681 US
Phone: 310-453-4440
Fax: 310-453-5258
E-mail Address: *info@natpe.org*
Web Address: www.natpe.org
The National Association of Television Program Executives (NATPE) is the leading association for content professionals in the global television industry.

National Cable and Telecommunications Association (NCTA)
25 Massachusetts Ave. NW, Ste. 100
Washington, DC 20001 US
Phone: 202-222-2300
Fax: 202-222-2514
E-mail Address: *webmaster@ncta.com*
Web Address: www.ncta.com
The National Cable and Telecommunications Association (NCTA) is the principal trade association of the cable television industry in the United States.

Radio Television News Directors Association (RTNDA)
1025 F St. NW, 7th Fl.
Washington, DC 20004 US
Phone: 202-659-6510
Fax: 202-223-4007
Toll Free: 800-807-8632
E-mail Address: *stefanib@rtnda.org*

Web Address: www.rtnda.org
The Radio Television News Directors
Association (RTNDA) is the world's
largest professional organization
exclusively committed to professionals
in electronic journalism.

**Syndication Network Television
Association (SNTA)**
1 Penn Plz., Ste. 5310
New York, NY 10119 US
Phone: 212-259-3740
Fax: 212-259-3770
E-mail Address: *mburg@snta.com*
Web Address: www.snta.com
The Syndication Network Television
Association (SNTA) is an organization
of national and independent television
stations that syndicate television
shows.

**Women in Cable &
Telecommunications (WICT)**
14555 Avion Pkwy., Ste. 250
Chantilly, VA 20151 US
Phone: 703-234-9810
Fax: 703-817-1595
E-mail Address: *lvega@wict.org*
Web Address: www.wict.org
Women in Cable &
Telecommunications (WICT) exists to
advance the position and influence of
women in media through leadership
programs and services at both the
national and local level.

XII.   Careers-Airlines/Flying

Aviation/Aerospace Jobs Page
NationJob, Inc.
601 SW 9th St., Stes. J&K
Des Moines, IA 50309 US
Fax: 515-283-1223
Toll Free: 888-526-5967
E-mail Address:
customerservice@nationjob.com
Web Address:
www.nationjob.com/aviation
The Aviation/Aerospace Jobs Page, a
division of NationJob, Inc., features
detailed aviation and aerospace job
listings and company profiles.

aviationjobsearch.com
London Rd. Sayers Common
West Sussex, BN6 9HS UK
Phone: 01273-837538

Web Address:
www.aviationjobsearch.com
The aviationjobsearch.com lists jobs
related to the airline industry.

Avjobs, Inc.
P.O. Box 630830
Littleton, CO 80163 US
Phone: 303-683-2322
Fax: 888-624-8691
E-mail Address: *info@avjobs.com*
Web Address: www.avjobs.com
Avjobs, Inc. is a group of employers
dedicated to helping individuals obtain
aviation, airline, aerospace and airport
careers.

Flightdeck Recruitment Ltd.
82c E. Hill
Colchester, Essex CO1 2QW UK
Phone: 44-1206-383730
Web Address:
www.flightdeckrecruitment.com
Flightdeck Recruitment Ltd. provides a
link between aviation recruiters who
are looking for flight deck crew and
pilots or flight engineers who are
seeking employment.

XIII.   Careers-Apparel

24 Seven Fashion Recruitment
120 Wooster St., 4th Fl.
New York, NY 10012 US
Phone: 212-966-4426
Fax: 212-966-2313
Web Address: www.24seveninc.com
24 Seven Fashion Recruitment is an
employment agency serving the
fashion, beauty, entertainment,
advertising, marketing and retail
industries.

Fashion Career Center
E-mail Address:
fashioncc@fashioncareercenter.com
Web Address:
www.fashioncareercenter.com
The Fashion Career Center site
provides employees and employers
with a place to meet and access
information about employment in the
fashion industry. The
FashionCareerCenter.com web site
offers links to fashion jobs and fashion
schools, as well as offering fashion
career advice.

XIV.   Careers-Banking

**National Banking & Financial
Service Network (NBFSN)**
3075 Brickhouse Ct.
Virginia Beach, VA 23452-6860
Phone: 757-463-5766
Fax: 757-340-0826
E-mail Address: *susan@nbn-jobs.com*
Web Address: www.banking-
financejobs.com
The National Banking & Financial
Service Network (NBFSN) is made up
of recruiting firms in the banking and
financial services marketplace. The
web site provides job listings.

XV.   Careers-Biotech

Biotechemployment.com
Phone: 561-630-5201
E-mail Address:
jobs@Biotechemployment.com
Web Address:
www.biotechemployment.com
Biotechemployment.com is an online
resource for job seekers in
biotechnology. The site's features
includes resume posting, job search
agents and employer profiles. It is part
of the eJobstores.com, Inc., which
includes the Health Care Job Store
sites.

Chase Group (The)
10955 Lowell Ave., Ste. 500
Overland Park, KS 66210 US
Phone: 913-663-3100
Fax: 913-663-3131
E-mail Address:
chase@chasegroup.com
Web Address: www.chasegroup.com
The Chase Group is an executive
search firm specializing in biomedical
and pharmaceutical placement.

XVI.   Careers-Coatings

CoatingsJobs.com
Phone: 480-857-7400
Web Address: www.coatingsjobs.com
CoatingsJobs.com connects coatings
industry job seekers and employers.
The website offers job postings,
resume postings, information for job
seekers and an employment newsletter.

XVII. Careers-Computers/ Technology

Computerjobs.com, Inc.
280 Interstate N. Cir. SE, Ste. 300
Atlanta, GA 30339-2411 US
Toll Free: 800-850-0045
E-mail Address:
michael@marketingmax.com
Web Address: www.computerjobs.com
Computerjobs.com, Inc. is an
employment web site that offers users
a link to computer-related job
opportunities organized by skill and
market.

Dice
4101 NW Urbandale Dr.
Urbandale, IA 50322 US
Phone: 515-280-1144
Fax: 515-280-1452
Toll Free: 877-386-3323
Web Address: www.dice.com
Dice provides free employment
services for IT jobs. The site includes
advanced job searches by geographic
location and category, availability
announcements and resume postings,
as well as employer profiles, a
recruiter's page and career links. Dice
is owned by Dice Holdings, Inc., a
publicly traded company.

**Institute for Electrical and
Electronics Engineers (IEEE) Job
Site**
IEEE
445 Hoes Ln.
Piscataway, NJ 08855-1331 US
Phone: 732-981-0060
Toll Free: 800-678-4333
E-mail Address:
candidatejobsite@ieee.org
Web Address: www.careers.ieee.org
The Institute for Electrical and
Electronics Engineers (IEEE) Job Site
provides a host of employment
services for technical professionals,
employers and recruiters. The site
offers job listings by geographic area, a
resume bank and links to employment
services.

Pencom Systems, Inc.
152 Remsen St.
New York, NY 11201 US
Phone: 718-923-1111
Fax: 718-923-6066

E-mail Address: *tom@pencom.com*
Web Address: www.pencom.com
Pencom Systems, Inc., an open
systems recruiting company, offers a
web site geared toward high-
technology and scientific professionals,
featuring an interactive salary survey,
career advisor, job listings and
technology resources.

XVIII. Careers-Contract and Free Lance

Guru.com
5001 Baum Blvd., Ste. 760
Pittsburgh, PA 15213 US
Fax: 412-687-4466
Toll Free: 888-678-0136
E-mail Address: *pr@guru.com*
Web Address: www.guru.com
Guru.com is an excellent site for
freelancers and contract workers, in
fields ranging from interior design to
architecture, marketing, web design
and much more. Employers can post
projects, and freelancers can bid on the
work. Many excellent tools are
provided to enable freelancers to be
completely informed about the scope
of the work needed.

XIX. Careers-First Time Jobs/New Grads

**Alumni-Network Recruitment
Corporation**
Phone: 905-465-2547
E-mail Address: *karen@alumni-
network.com*
Web Address: www.alumni-
network.com
Alumni-Network Recruitment
Corporation is a professional search
and recruiting firm, specializing in
ERP, E-Commerce and Engineering.

Black Collegian Online (The)
140 Carondelet St.
New Orleans, LA 70130 US
Phone: 504-523-0154
Web Address: www.black-
collegian.com
The Black Collegian Online features
listings for job and internship
opportunities, as well as other tools for
students of color; it is the web site of
The Black Collegian Magazine,
published by IMDiversity, Inc. The site

includes a list of the top 100 minority
corporate employers and an assessment
of job opportunities.

Collegegrad.com, Inc.
234 E. College Ave., Ste. 200
State College, PA 16801 US
Phone: 262-375-6700
Toll Free: 1-800-991-4642
Web Address: www.collegegrad.com
Collegegrad.com, Inc. offers in-depth
resources for college students and
recent grads seeking entry-level jobs.

Job Web
Nat'l Association of Colleges &
Employers (NACE)
62 Highland Ave.
Bethlehem, PA 18017-9085 US
Phone: 610-868-1421
Fax: 610-868-0208
Toll Free: 800-544-5272
E-mail Address: *editors@jobweb.com*
Web Address: www.jobweb.com
Job Web, owned and sponsored by
National Association of Colleges and
Employers (NACE), displays job
openings and employer descriptions.
The site also offers a database of career
fairs, searchable by state or keyword,
with contact information.

MBAjobs.net
Fax: 413-556-8849
E-mail Address: *contact@mbajobs.net*
Web Address: www.mbajobs.net
MBAjobs.net is a unique international
service for MBA students and
graduates, employers, recruiters and
business schools. The MBAjobs.net
service is provided by WebInfoCo.

MonsterTRAK
11845 W. Olympic Blvd., Ste. 500
Los Angeles, CA 90064 US
Toll Free: 800-999-8725
E-mail Address:
trakstudent@monster.com
Web Address:
www.monstertrak.monster.com
MonsterTRAK provides information
about internships and entry-level jobs.

**National Association of Colleges and
Employers (NACE)**
62 Highland Ave.
Bethlehem, PA 18017-9085 US
Phone: 610-868-1421

Fax: 610-868-0208
Toll Free: 800-544-5272
E-mail Address:
mcollins@naceweb.org
Web Address: www.naceweb.org
The National Association of Colleges and Employers (NACE) is a premier U.S. organization representing college placement offices and corporate recruiters who focus on hiring new grads.

XX. Careers-General Job Listings

6FigureJobs
25 3rd St., Ste. 230
Stamford, CT 06905 US
Toll Free: 800-605-5154
Web Address: www.6figurejobs.com
6FigureJobs offers executives a database of high-level positions. Membership is free for qualified individuals.

Career Exposure, Inc.
805 SW Broadway, Ste. 2250
Portland, OR 97205 US
Phone: 503-221-7779
Fax: 503-221-7780
E-mail Address: *lisam@mackenzie-marketing.com*
Web Address:
www.careerexposure.com
Career Exposure, Inc. is an online career center and job placement service, with resources for employers, recruiters and job seekers.

CareerBuilder, Inc.
200 N. LaSalle St., Ste. 1100
Chicago, IL 60601 US
Phone: 773-527-3600
Toll Free: 800-638-4212
Web Address: www.careerbuilder.com
CareerBuilder, Inc. focuses on the needs of companies and also provides a database of job openings. The site has 1.5 million jobs posted by 300,000 employers, and receives an average 23 million unique visitors monthly. The company also operates online career centers for 150 newspapers, 1,000 partners and other online portals such as America Online. Resumes are sent directly to the company, and applicants can set up a special e-mail account for job-seeking purposes. CareerBuilder is primarily a joint venture between three newspaper giants: The McClatchy Company (which recently acquired former partner Knight Ridder), Gannett Co., Inc. and Tribune Company. In 2007, Microsoft acquired a minority interest in CareerBuilder, allowing the site to ally itself with MSN.

CareerOneStop
Toll Free: 877-348-0502
E-mail Address:
info@careeronestop.org
Web Address: www.careeronestop.org
CareerOneStop is operated by the employment commissions of various state agencies. It contains job listings in both the private sector and in government. CareerOneStop is sponsored by the U.S. Department of Labor. It includes a wide variety of useful career resources and workforce information.

Careers Organization (The)
E-mail Address: *info@Careers.Org*
Web Address: www.careers.org
The Career Organization is a job resource center with links to jobs and pointers to other career-related web sites as well as links to associations, franchising opportunities and library resources.

Collegerecruiter.com
3109 W. 50 St., Ste. 121
Minneapolis, MN 55410-2102 US
Phone: 952-848-2211
Fax: 702-537-2227
Toll Free: 800-835-4989
E-mail Address:
Steven@CollegeRecruiter.com
Web Address:
www.collegerecruiter.com
Collegerecruiter.com provides college students with internship, part-time and summer job listings. Recent graduates can search for career opportunities by category and location. The site also provides information about student loans and loan consolidation.

ContractJobHunter
C. E. Publications, Inc.
P.O. Box 3006
Bothell, WA 98041-3006 US
Phone: 425-806-5200
Fax: 425-806-5585
E-mail Address: *staff@cjhunter.com*
Web Address: www.ceweekly.wa.com
ContractJobHunter is a web-based version of the magazine Contract Employment Weekly Online. It posts job listings and links to contract firms. Libraries for reference materials and resume writing guidelines are also offered. The site is a service of C. E. Publications, Inc.

EmploymentGuide
150 Granby St.
Norfolk, VA 23510 US
Toll Free: 877-876-4039
Web Address:
www.employmentguide.com
EmploymentGuide offers general career resources along with lists of position openings, company profiles and a resume database. It also circulates a free print publication.

EscapeArtist.com Inc.
832-1245 World Trade Ctr.
Panama, WTC-0832 Republic of Panama
Fax: 786-513-3702
Web Address: www.escapeartist.com
EscapeArtist.com Inc.'s web site provides job searches for overseas positions, as well as international working condition resources and immigration information.

ExecuNet, Inc.
295 Westport Ave.
Norwalk, CT 06851 US
Toll Free: 800-637-3126
E-mail Address:
member.services@execunet.com
Web Address: www.execunet.com
ExecuNet, Inc. is an executive career management information and contact service.

Executiveagent.com
Kennedy Information, Inc.
1 Phoenix Mill Ln., 3rd Fl.
Peterborough, NH 03458 US
Phone: 603-924-1006
Fax: 603-924-4034
Toll Free: 800-531-0007
Web Address:
www.executiveagent.com
Executiveagent.com allows senior-level professionals to have their resumes sent to executive placement

firms for a fee. The site is owned by Kennedy Information, Inc.

Higheredjobs.com
328 Innovation Blvd., Ste. 300
State College, PA 16803 US
Phone: 814-861-3080
Fax: 814-861-3082
E-mail Address:
sales@HigherEdJobs.com
Web Address: www.higheredjobs.com
Higheredjobs.com lists job vacancies in colleges and universities.

IMDiversity, Inc.
140 Carondelet St.
New Orleans, LA 70130 US
Phone: 504-523-0154
Fax: 504-523-9271
Web Address: www.imdiversity.com
IMDiversity, Inc. provides job listings and career development information. The web site also has divisions for particular minority groups.

Indeed.com
Stamford, CT US
Web Address: www.indeed.com
Indeed.com provides extensive lists of jobs of all types, with links directly to the employers. It covers the U.S., Canada, India, Mexico and other nations. Job search forums are available. Employers may post jobs. Job seekers may use several criteria in their searches, including geographic location.

Job Search USA
E-mail Address:
info@jobsearchusa.org
Web Address: www.jobsearchusa.org
Job Search USA is a major job posting site that contains job opportunities classified by a variety of keywords.

JobCentral
DirectEmployers Association, Inc.
9002 N. Purdue Rd., Quad III, Ste. 100
Indianapolis, IN 46268 US
Phone: 317-874-9000
Fax: 317-874-9100
Toll Free: 866-268-6206
E-mail Address: *info@jobcentral.com*
Web Address: www.jobcentral.com
JobCentral, operated by the nonprofit DirectEmployers Association, Inc., links users directly to hundreds of

thousands of job opportunities posted on the sites of participating employers, thus bypassing the usual job search sites. This saves employers money and allows job seekers to access many more job opportunities.

Jobs in Logistics
Toll Free: 877-562-7678
E-mail Address:
cs@jobsinlogistics.com
Web Address:
www.jobsinlogistics.com
Jobs in Logistics provides contacts for job seekers in the transportation and logistics fields.

Jobsinthemoney.com
4101 NW Urbandale Dr.
Urbandale, IA 50322 US
Phone: 515-280-1144
Fax: 515-280-1452
Toll Free: 800-979-3423
E-mail Address:
cs@jobsinthemoney.com
Web Address:
www.jobsinthemoney.com
Jobsinthemoney.com provides employment listings in the finance industry as well as job tools, such as salary surveys, resume writing assistance and industry news. It is owned by Dice, a part of Dice Holdings, Inc.

LaborMarketInfo
Employment Dev. Dept., Labor Market Info. Div.
800 Capitol Mall, MIC 83
Sacramento, CA 95814 US
Phone: 916-262-2162
Fax: 916-262-2352
Toll Free: 800-480-3287
Web Address:
www.labormarketinfo.edd.ca.gov
LaborMarketInfo, formerly the California Cooperative Occupational Information System, is geared to providing job seekers and employers a wide range of resources, namely the ability to find, access and use labor market information and services. It provides demographical statistics for employment on both a local and regional level, as well as career searching tools for California residents. The web site is sponsored by

California's Employment Development Office.

Mediabistro.com
475 Park Ave. S., 4th Fl.
New York, NY 10016 US
Phone: 212-389-2000
Fax: 212-966-8984
E-mail Address:
laurelT@mediabistro.com
Web Address: www.mediabistro.com
Mediabistro.com offers an array of employment resources, including job listings in the media industry.

Monster Worldwide, Inc.
622 Third Ave., 39th Fl.
New York, NY 10017 US
Phone: 212-351-7000
Fax: 646-658-0541
Toll Free: 800-666-7837
Web Address: www.monster.com
Monster Worldwide, Inc., parent company of Monster.com, provides online career and personnel services. The firm operates in 36 countries.

NationJob, Inc.
601 SW 9th St., Ste. J&K
Des Moines, IA 50309 US
Fax: 515-283-1223
Toll Free: 888-526-5967
E-mail Address:
customerservice@nationjob.com
Web Address: www.nationjob.com
NationJob, Inc.'s web site allows users can develop a profile of the ideal job based on the criterion of location, industry, salary; and, if they provide an e-mail address, wait for appropriate listings to be sent to them through the firm's PJScout feature.

NETSHARE, Inc.
83 Hamilton Dr., Ste. 202
Novato, CA 94949 US
Toll Free: 800-241-5642
E-mail Address:
netshare@netshare.com
Web Address: www.netshare.com
Netshare provides access to exclusive listings of executive jobs that pay $70,000 and up. Job seekers pay either $37.50/month or $395/year for the service.

Net-Temps, Inc.
55 Middlesex St., Ste. 220

North Chelmsford, MA 01863 US
Fax: 978-251-7250
Toll Free: 800-307-0062
E-mail Address: *service@net-temps.com*
Web Address: www.net-temps.com
Net-Temps, Inc. offers a web site, operated by professional career consultants, that features job listings and job seeking tips.

Recruiters Online Network
947 Essex Ln.
Medina, OH 44256 US
Phone: 888-364-4667
Fax: 888-237-8686
E-mail Address: *info@recruitersonline.com*
Web Address: www.recruitersonline.com
The Recruiters Online Network provides job postings from thousands of recruiters, Careers Online Magazine, a resume database, as well as other career resources.

True Careers, Inc.
Web Address: www.truecareers.com
True Careers, Inc. offers job listings and provides an array of career resources. The company also offers a search of over 2 million scholarships. It is partnered with CareerBuilder.com, which powers its career information and resume posting functions.

USAJOBS
U.S. Office of Personnel Management
1900 E St. NW
Washington, DC 20415 US
Phone: 202-606-1800
Web Address: usajobs.opm.gov
USAJOBS, a program of the U.S. Office of Personnel Management, is the official job site for the U.S. Federal Government. It provides a comprehensive list of U.S. government jobs, allowing users to search for employment by location; agency; type of work, using the Federal Government's numerical identification code, the General Schedule (GS) Series; or by senior executive positions. It also has a special veterans' employment section; an information center, offering resume and interview tips and other useful information such as hiring trends and a glossary of

Federal terms; and allows users to create a profile and post a resume.

Wall Street Journal - CareerJournal
Wall Street Journal
200 Liberty St.
New York, NY 10281 US
Phone: 212-416-2000
Toll Free: 800-568-7625
E-mail Address: *onelinejournal@wsj.com*
Web Address: www.online.wsj.com/careers
The Wall Street Journal's CareerJournal, an executive career site, features a job database with thousands of available positions; career news and employment related articles; and advice regarding resume writing, interviews, networking, office life and job hunting.

Yahoo! HotJobs
45 W. 18th St., 6th Fl.
New York, NY 10011 US
Phone: 646-351-5300
Web Address: www.hotjobs.yahoo.com
Yahoo! HotJobs, designed for experienced professionals, employers and job seekers, is a Yahoo-owned site that provides company profiles, a resume posting service and a resume workshop. The site allows posters to block resumes from being viewed by certain companies and provides a notification service of new jobs.

XXI. Careers-Health Care

Health Care Source
8 Winchester Pl.
Winchester, MA 01890 US
Phone: 781-368-1033
Fax: 800-829-6600
Toll Free: 800-869-5200
E-mail Address: *info@healthcaresource.com*
Web Address: www.healthcaresource.com
Health Care Source offers career-related information and job finding tools for health care professionals.

Medicalworkers.com
191 University Blvd., Ste. 252
Denver, CO 80206 US
Phone: 720-227-9364

E-mail Address: *cs@medicalworkers.com*
Web Address: www.medicalworkers.com
Medicalworkers.com is an employment site for medical and health care professionals.

Medjump.com
7119 E. Shea Blvd.
Stes. 109-535
Scottsdale, AZ 85254 US
E-mail Address: *info@medjump.net*
Web Address: www.medjump.com
Medjump.com is dedicated to empowering health care and medical-related professionals with the necessary tools to market their abilities and skills.

Medzilla, Inc.
P.O. Box 1710
Marysville, WA 98270 US
Phone: 360-657-5681
Fax: 775-514-9440
E-mail Address: *mgroutage@medzilla.com*
Web Address: www.medzilla.com
Medzilla, Inc.'s web site offers job searches, salary surveys, a search agent and information on health care employment.

Monster Career Advice-Healthcare
Monster Worldwide, Inc.
622 3rd Ave.
New York, NY 10017 US
Phone: 212-351-7000
Toll Free: 800-666-7837
Web Address: career-advice.monster.com/get-the-job/healthcare/home.aspx
Monster Career Advice-Healthcare, a service of Monster Worldwide, Inc., provides job listings, job searches and search agents for the medical field.

NationJob Network-Medical and Health Care Jobs Page
601 SW 9th St., Suites H&J
Des Moines, IA 50309 US
Fax: 515-243-5384
Toll Free: 800-292-7731
E-mail Address: *customerservice@nationjob.com*
Web Address: www.nationjob.com/medical

The NationJob Network-Medical and Health Care Jobs Page offers information and listings for health care employment.

Nurse-Recruiter.com
36 Washington St., Ste. 170
Wellesley, MA 02481 US
Toll Free: 877-562-7966
E-mail Address:
support@nurserecruiter.com
Web Address: www.nurse-recruiter.com
Nurse-Recruiter.com is a nurse-owned, web-centric company devoted to bringing health care employers and the nursing community together.

PracticeLink
P.O. Box 100
415 2nd Ave.
Hinton, WV 25951 US
Toll Free: 800-776-8383
Web Address: www.practicelink.com
PracticeLink is one of the largest physician employment web sites. It is a free service used by more than 18,000 practice-seeking physicians annually to quickly search and locate potential physician practice opportunities. PracticeLink is financially supported by more than 700 hospitals, medical groups, private practices and health care systems that advertise more than 5,000 opportunities.

RPh on the Go USA, Inc.
5510 Howard St.
Skokie, IL 60077-2620 US
Phone: 847-588-7170
Fax: 847-588-7060
Toll Free: 800-553-7359
E-mail Address:
lbalaguer@rphonthego.com
Web Address: www.rphonthego.com
RPh on the Go USA, Inc. places temporary and permanent qualified professionals in the pharmacy community.

XXII. Careers-Interviewing with Consulting Firms

McKinsey & Company Interviewing Tips
55 E. 52nd St
New York, NY 10022 US
Phone: 212-446-7000

Fax: 212-446-8575
Web Address:
www.mckinsey.com/careers/how_do_i
_apply/the_application_process.aspx
The McKinsey & Company Interviewing Tips site is an excellent resource for preparing for a consulting interview.

XXIII. Careers-Job Listings for Seniors

Dinosaur Exchange
Dino-X Ltd., P.O. Box 100
Sydney Vane House Admiral Park
St. Peter Port, Guernsey GY1 3EL
Channel Islands
E-mail Address:
CustomerSupport@dinosaur-exchange.com
Web Address: www.dinosaur-exchange.com
Dinosaur Exchange, opened in 2003, is a job forum for the elderly, which allows seniors to post resumes and be contacted by employers. Dino-X Ltd. owns and operates the web site.

Employment Network for Retired Government Experts (ENRGE)
Zavala, Inc.
P.O. Box 1532
N. Falmouth, MA 02556 US
Phone: 508-564-4140
Web Address: www.enrge.us
The Employment Network for Retired Government Experts (ENRGE) helps government employees to remain active in their professions after retirement. ENERGE is the business name of Zavala, Inc.

Senior Job Bank
NHC Group, Inc.
P.O. Box 508
Marlborough, MA 01752 US
Toll Free: 888-501-0804
Web Address: www.seniorjobbank.org
The Senior Job Bank web site offers an easy, effective and free method for senior citizens to find occasional, part-time, flexible, temporary or full-time jobs. The site is owned and managed by NHC Group, Inc.

Seniors4Hire.org
The Forward Group, OBO
Seniors4Hire.org

7071 Warner Ave. F466
Huntington Beach, CA 92647 US
Phone: 714-848-0996
Fax: 714-848-5445
E-mail Address:
info@seniors4hire.org
Web Address: www.seniors4hire.org
Seniors4Hire.org is an online career center with job postings, employment resources and information on community service employment programs for older workers, retirees and senior citizens. The site is owned and operated by The Forward Group.

YourEncore
20 N. Meridian St., Ste. 800
Indianapolis, IN 46204 US
Phone: 317-226-9301
Fax: 317-226-9312
E-mail Address:
General.Information@yourencore.com
Web Address: www.yourencore.com
YourEncore is a program that seeks to employ retirees by matching them with member companies. The web site utilizes retirees mainly in the areas of engineering, science and product development.

XXIV. Careers-Job Reference Tools

CareerXroads (CXR)
Mark Mehler
P.O. Box 253
Kendall Park, NJ 08824 US
Phone: 732-821-6652
E-mail Address:
mmc@careerxroads.com
Web Address: www.careerxroads.com
CareerXroads (CXR) publishes an annual guide on job and resume web sites. It was cofounded by Gerry Crispin and Mark Mehler.

Job-Hunt.org
NETability, Inc.
186 Main St.
Marlborough, MA 01752 US
Phone: 508-624-6261
E-mail Address: *info@job-hunt.org*
Web Address: www.job-hunt.org
Job-Hunt.org, rather than collecting resumes or posting job vacancies, offers a vast list of job listing web sites and links to helpful job search tools. It is owned by NETability, Inc.

JobStar
E-mail Address:
electrajobstar@earthlink.net
Web Address: www.jobstar.org
JobStar has a salary info link to over
300 different salary information and
salary survey sites. It also contains job
listings focused on the California
market.

Joyce Lain Kennedy's Careers
Sun Features Inc.
P.O. Box 368
Cardiff, CA 92007 US
Web Address: www.sunfeatures.com
Provides links to recommended
employment sites, as well as links to
Joyce Lain Kennedy's books and
booklets and her well-respected career
tips.

MBA Career Services Council (CSC)
E-mail Address:
kip.harrell@thunderbird.edu.
Web Address: www.mbacsc.org
The MBA Career Services Council
(CSC) is a global professional
association for individuals in the field
of MBA career services and those that
recruit directly from graduate
management programs.

NewsVoyager
4401 Wilson Blvd., Ste. 900
Arlington, VA 22203-1867 US
Phone: 571-366-1000
Fax: 571-366-1195
E-mail Address: *sally.clarke@naa.org*
Web Address: www.newsvoyager.com
NewsVoyager, a service of the
Newspaper Association of America
(NAA), links individuals to local,
national and international newspapers.
Job seekers can search through
thousands of classified sections.

Quintessential Careers (QC)
EmpoweringSties.com
DeLand, Fl 32720 US
Phone: 386-740-8872
Fax: 386-740-9764
E-mail Address:
randall@quintcareers.com
Web Address: www.quintcareers.com
Quintessential Careers (QC) provides a
large collection of data and links for
job seekers, including advice, tools and
job postings; it also offers a guide to

researching companies. QC is a
subsidiary of EmpoweringSites.com.

Vault.com, Inc.
75 Varick St., 8th Fl.
New York, NY 10013 US
Phone: 212-366-4212
E-mail Address:
feedback@staff.vault.com
Web Address: www.vault.com
Vault.com, Inc. is a comprehensive
career web site for employers and
employees, with job postings and
valuable information on a wide variety
of industries. Vault gears many of its
features toward MBAs. The site has
been recognized by Forbes and Fortune
Magazines.

Wetfeet.com
101 Howard St., Ste. 300
San Francisco, CA 94105 US
Phone: 415-284-7900
Fax: 415-284-7910
E-mail Address: *info@wetfeet.com*
Web Address: www.wetfeet.com
Wetfeet.com provides an excellent
combination of links and resources for
job seekers.

What Color is Your Parachute?
E-mail Address:
rnbolles@jobhuntersbible.com
Web Address:
www.jobhuntersbible.com
The What Color is Your Parachute?
official web site is based on the "Job-
Hunting on the Internet" chapter of
Richard (Dick) Bolle's best-selling
book. Designed to aid job hunters and
career changers who want to use the
Internet as part of their job search, the
site provides links to job listing,
resume, career counseling, contacts
and research sites.

XXV.   Careers-Nanotechnology

Working in Nanotechnology
Phone: 64-9-3020-977
Fax: 64-9-3020-976
E-mail Address: *webteam@workingin-nanotechnology.com*
Web Address: www.workingin-nanotechnology.com
Working in Nanotechnology provides a
global listing of job openings sortable
by education, technology type,

industry, and scientific field.
Applicants may apply for jobs online.

XXVI.   Careers-Restaurants

Foodservice.com
Phone: 678-256-8014
Toll Free: 800-896-4442
E-mail Address:
customercare@Foodservice.com
Web Address: www.foodservice.com
Foodservice.com, managed and run by
Food Service Interactive, LLC, offers
web site design and job search services
for the food service industry.

Resources in Food, Inc. (RIF)
1007 N. Main St.
Columbia, IL 62236 US
Phone: 618-281-3100
Fax: 866-281-7374
Toll Free: 877-743-1100
E-mail Address:
rifchicago@rifood.com
Web Address: www.rifood.com
Resources in Food (RIF) provides
professional management placement
for the hospitality industry.

XXVII.   Careers-Science

Chem Jobs
ChemIndustry.com
730 E. Cypress Ave.
Monrovia, CA 91016 US
Phone: 626-930-0808
Fax: 626-930-0102
E-mail Address:
info@chemindustry.com
Web Address: www.chemjobs.net
Chem Jobs is a leading Internet site for
job seekers in chemistry and related
fields, aimed at chemists, biochemists,
pharmaceutical scientists and chemical
engineers looking for work. The web
site is powered by Chemindustry.com.

New Scientist Jobs
New Scientist, Lacon House
84 Theobald's Rd.
London, WC1X 8NS UK
Phone: 44-20-7611-1200
Fax: 44-20-7611-1250
E-mail Address:
nssales@elsevier.com.
Web Address:
www.newscientistjobs.com

New Scientist Jobs is a web site produced by the publishers of New Scientist Magazine, which helps jobseekers and employers in the bioscience fields find each other. The site includes a job search engine and a free-of-charge e-mail job alert service. New Scientist Jobs is owned by Reed Business Information Ltd.

Science Jobs

E-mail Address: *help@science-jobs.org*
Web Address: www.science-jobs.org/index.htm
Science Jobs is a web site that contains many useful categories of links, including employment newsgroups, scientific journals and placement agencies. It also links to sites containing information regarding internship and fellowship opportunities for high school students and undergrads.

XXVIII.   Careers-Sports

Jobs in Sports

2038 N. Clark St., Ste. 107
Chicago, IL 60614-4713 US
E-mail Address:
comments@jobsinsports.com
Web Address: www.jobsinsports.com
Jobs in Sports is an employment web site that provides job listings in areas including sports marketing, sports media, sales, health and fitness, computers and administration, as well as other job resources.

National Sports Employment News

Web Address:
www.sportsemploymentnews.com
National Sports Employment News is an employment resources site for the sports industry.

Sports Careers

2990 E. Northern Ave., Ste. B101
Phoenix, AZ 85028 US
Phone: 602-485-5555
Fax: 480-467-0196
E-mail Address:
info@sportscareers.com
Web Address: www.sportscareers.com
Sports Careers offers a range of services to help individuals and employers in the sports industry,

including job listings, a resume bank, industry contacts and salary information.

Sports Job Board

E-mail Address:
info@sportsjobboard.com
Web Address:
www.sportsjobboard.com
The Sports Job Board is an employment website for the sports industry.

SportsCastingJobs.com

Phone: 303-623-5565
E-mail Address:
comments@sportscastingjobs.com
Web Address:
www.sportscastingjobs.com
SportsCastingJobs.com is an online employment site for sportscasters. The site was created by veteran sportscaster Dave Benz in 1999.

Women Sports Jobs

Women's Sport Services, LLC
P.O. Box 11
Huntington Beach, CA 92648 US
Phone: 714-848-1201
Fax: 714-848-5111
E-mail Address:
Feedback@WSServices.com
Web Address:
www.womensportsjobs.com
Women Sports Jobs is an employment web site specializing in jobs for women in the sports industry. The site is offered by Women's Sport Services, LLC.

Work in Sports, LLC

7335 E. Acoma Dr., Ste. 200
Scottsdale, AZ 85260 US
Phone: 480-905-7221
Fax: 480-905-7231
E-mail Address:
info@workinsports.com
Web Address: www.workinsports.com
Work in Sports, LLC is an online employment resource for the sports industry that posts hundreds of jobs on its web site.

XXIX.   Careers-Telecommunications

Call Center Careers

6525 Gunpark Dr., Ste. 570, PMB 127

Boulder, CO 80301 US
Phone: 303-527-1440
Fax: 303-530-0154
Toll Free: 877-562-8588
E-mail Address:
sales@callcentercareers.com
Web Address:
www.callcentercareers.com
Call Center Careers provides recruiting and staffing services to the call center industry.

XXX.   Chemicals Industry Associations

American Chemical Society (ACS)

1155 16th St. NW
Washington, DC 20036 US
Phone: 202-872-4600
Fax: 202-776-8258
Toll Free: 800-227-5558
E-mail Address: *help@acs.org*
Web Address:
portal.acs.org/portal/acs/corg/content
The American Chemical Society (ACS) is a nonprofit organization aimed at promoting the understanding of chemistry and chemical sciences. It represents a wide range of disciplines including chemistry, chemical engineering and other technical fields.

XXXI.   Communications Professional Associations

Association for Women In Communications (AWC)

3337 Duke St.
Alexandria, VA 22314 US
Phone: 703-370-7436
Fax: 703-370-7437
E-mail Address: *info@womcom.org*
Web Address: www.womcom.org
The Association for Women In Communications (AWC) is a professional organization that works for the advancement of women across all communications disciplines by recognizing excellence, promoting leadership and positioning its members at the forefront of the communications industry.

Health and Science Communications Association (HeSCA)

39 Wedgewood Dr., Ste. A
Jewett City, CT 06351 US
Phone: 860-376-5915

Fax: 860-376-6621
E-mail Address: *hesca@hesca.org*
Web Address: www.hesca.org
The Health and Science
Communications Association (HeSCA)
is an association of communications
professionals committed to sharing
knowledge and resources in the health
sciences arena.

Health Industry Business Communications Council (HIBCC)
2525 E. Arizona Biltmore Cir., Ste.
127
Phoenix, AZ 85016 US
Phone: 602-381-1091
Fax: 602-381-1093
E-mail Address: *info@hibcc.org*
Web Address: www.hibcc.org
The Health Industry Business
Communications Council (HIBCC)
seeks to facilitate electronic
communications by developing
appropriate standards for information
exchange among all health care trading
partners.

International Association of Business Communicators (IABC)
1 Hallidie Plz., Ste. 600
San Francisco, CA 94102 US
Phone: 415-544-4700
Fax: 415-544-4747
Toll Free: 800-776-4222
E-mail Address: *jugalde@iabc.com*
Web Address: www.iabc.com
The International Association of
Business Communicators (IABC) is
the leading resource for effective
business communication practices.

XXXII. Computer & Electronics Industry Associations

AeA
5201 Great America Pkwy., Ste. 400
Santa Clara, CA 95054 US
Phone: 408-987-4200
Fax: 408-987-4298
Toll Free: 800-284-4232
E-mail Address: *csc@aeanet.org*
Web Address: www.aeanet.org
AeA, formerly the American
Electronics Association, is a trade
association which represents thousands
of U.S. electronics firms, including
electronic systems and component
manufacturers, suppliers and end users.

It also publishes the annual AeA
Directory with geographic and product
indexes.

Electronics Technicians Association (ETA)
5 Depot St.
Greencastle, IN 46135 US
Phone: 765-653-8262
Fax: 765-653-4287
Toll Free: 800-288-3824
E-mail Address: *eta@eta-i.org*
Web Address: www.eta-i.org
The Electronics Technicians
Association (ETA) is a nonprofit
professional association for electronics
technicians. The firm provides
recognized professional credentials for
electronics technicians.

Semiconductor Industry Association (SIA)
181 Metro Dr., Ste. 450
San Jose, CA 95110 US
Phone: 408-436-6600
Fax: 408-436-6646
E-mail Address: *mailbox@sia-online.org*
Web Address: www.sia-online.org
The Semiconductor Industry
Association (SIA) is a trade association
representing the semiconductor
industry in the U.S. Through its
coalition of 95 companies, SIA
represents more than 85% of
semiconductor production in the U.S.
The coalition aims to advance the
competitiveness of the chip industry
and shape public policy on issues
particular to the industry.

XXXIII. Consulting Industry Associations

American Association of Healthcare Consultants (AAHC)
5938 N. Drake Ave.
Chicago, IL 60659 US
Fax: 773-463-3552
Toll Free: 888-350-2242
E-mail Address: *info@aahcmail.org*
Web Address: www.aahc.net
The American Association of
Healthcare Consultants (AAHC) is a
professional society for credentialed
consultants practicing in health care
organization and delivery.

XXXIV. Corporate Information Resources

---

bizjournals.com
120 W. Morehead St., Ste. 400
Charlotte, NC 28202 US
Web Address: www.bizjournals.com
Bizjournals.com is the online media
division of American City Business
Journals, the publisher of dozens of
leading city business journals
nationwide. It provides access to
research into the latest news regarding
companies small and large.

Business Wire
44 Montgomery St., 39th Fl.
San Francisco, CA 94104 US
Phone: 415-986-4422
Fax: 415-788-5335
Toll Free: 800-227-0845
Web Address: www.businesswire.com
Business Wire offers news releases,
industry- and company-specific news,
top headlines, conference calls, IPOs
on the Internet, media services and
access to tradeshownews.com and BW
Connect On-line through its
informative and continuously updated
web site.

Edgar Online, Inc.
50 Washington St., 11th Fl.
Norwalk, CT 06854 US
Phone: 203-852-5666
Fax: 203-852-5667
Toll Free: 800-416-6651
Web Address: www.edgar-online.com
Edgar Online, Inc. is a gateway and
search tool for viewing corporate
documents, such as annual reports on
Form 10-K, filed with the U.S.
Securities and Exchange Commission.

PR Newswire Association LLC
810 7th Ave., 32nd Fl.
New York, NY 10019 US
Phone: 201-360-6700
Toll Free: 800-832-5522
E-mail Address:
information@prnewswire.com
Web Address: www.prnewswire.com
PR Newswire Association LLC
provides comprehensive
communications services for public
relations and investor relations
professionals ranging from information
distribution and market intelligence to

the creation of online multimedia content and investor relations web sites. Users can also view recent corporate press releases. The Association is owned by United Business Media plc.

Silicon Investor
100 W. Main
P.O. Box 29
Freeman, MO 64746 US
E-mail Address:
admin_dave@techstocks.com
Web Address:
www.siliconinvestor.advfn.com
Silicon Investor is focused on providing information about technology companies. The company's web site serves as a financial discussion forum and offers quotes, profiles and charts.

XXXV. Disabling Conditions

Job Accommodation Network (JAN)
P.O. Box 6080
Morgantown, WV 26506-6080 US
Phone: 304-293-7186
Fax: 304-293-5407
Toll Free: 800-526-7234
E-mail Address: *jan@jan.wvu.edu*
Web Address: janweb.icdi.wvu.edu
The Job Accommodation Network (JAN) is a free consulting service that provides information about job accommodations, the Americans with Disabilities Act and the employability of people with disabilities.

XXXVI. Economic Data & Research

STAT-USA/Internet
STAT-USA, HCHB, U.S. Dept. of Commerce, Rm. 4885
Washington, DC 20230 US
Phone: 202-482-1986
Fax: 202-482-2164
Toll Free: 800-782-8872
E-mail Address: *statmail@esa.doc.gov*
Web Address: www.stat-usa.gov
STAT-USA/Internet offers daily economic news, statistical releases and databases relating to export and trade, as well as the domestic economy. It is provided by STAT-USA, which is an agency in the Economics & Statistics Administration of the U.S. Department

of Commerce. The site mainly consists of two main databases, the State of the Nation (SOTN), which focuses on the current state of the U.S. economy; and the Global Business Opportunities (GLOBUS) & the National Trade Data Bank (NTDB), which deals with U.S. export opportunities, global political/socio-economic conditions and other world economic issues.

XXXVII. Electrical Engineering Industry Associations

International Society for Optical Engineering (SPIE)
1000 20th St.
Bellingham, WA 98225-6705 US
Phone: 360-676-3290
Fax: 360-647-1445
Toll Free: 888-504-8171
E-mail Address:
CustomerService@SPIE.org
Web Address: www.spie.org
The International Society for Optical Engineering (SPIE) is a nonprofit technical society aimed at the advancement and dissemination of knowledge in optics, photonics and imaging.

XXXVIII. Electronic Health Records/Continuity of Care Records

American Health Information Management Association (AHIMA)
233 N. Michigan Ave., 21st Fl.
Chicago, IL 60601-5800 US
Phone: 312-233-1100
Fax: 312-233-1090
E-mail Address: *info@ahima.org*
Web Address: www.ahima.org
The American Health Information Management Association (AHIMA) is a professional association that consists health information management professionals who work throughout the health care industry.

American Medical Informatics Association (AMIA)
4915 St. Elmo Ave., Ste. 401
Bethesda, MD 20814 US
Phone: 301-657-1291
Fax: 301-657-1296
E-mail Address: *mail@amia.org*

Web Address: www.amia.org
The American Medical Informatics Association (AMIA) is a membership organization of individuals, institutions and corporations dedicated to developing and using information technologies to improve health care.

College of Healthcare Information Management Executives (CHIME)
3300 Washtenaw Ave., Ste. 225
Ann Arbor, MI 48104 US
Phone: 734-665-0000
Fax: 734-665-4922
E-mail Address: *staff@cio-chime.org*
Web Address: www.cio-chime.org
College of Healthcare Information Management Executives (CHIME) was formed with the dual objective of serving the professional development needs of health care CIOs and advocating the more effective use of information management within health care.

Healthcare Information and Management Systems Society (HIMSS)
230 E. Ohio St., Ste. 500
Chicago, IL 60611-3270 US
Phone: 312-664-4467
Fax: 312-664-6143
E-mail Address: *himss@himss.org*
Web Address: www.himss.org
The Healthcare Information and Management Systems Society (HIMSS) provides leadership in the optimal use of technology, information and management systems for the betterment of health care.

XXXIX. Energy Associations- Electric Power

American Public Power Association (APPA)
1875 Connecticut Ave. NW, Ste. 1200
Washington, DC 20009-5715 US
Phone: 202-467-2900
Fax: 202-467-2910
E-mail Address: *mrufe@appanet.org*
Web Address: www.appanet.org
The American Public Power Association (APPA) is a nonprofit service organization for the country's community-owned electric utilities, dedicated to advancing the public

policy interests of its members and their consumers.

Edison Electric Institute (EEI)
701 Pennsylvania Ave. NW
Washington, DC 20004-2696 US
Phone: 202-508-5000
E-mail Address: *feedback@eei.org*
Web Address: www.eei.org
The Edison Electric Institute (EEI) is an association of U.S. shareholder-owned electric companies as well as worldwide affiliates and industry associates. Its web site provides energy news and a link to Electric Perspectives magazine.

Women's International Network of Utility Professionals (WINUP)
P.O. Box 817
Fergus Falls, MN 56538-0817 US
Phone: 218-731-1659
E-mail Address: *tdrexler@otpco.com*
Web Address: www.winup.org
The Women's International Network of Utility Professionals (WINUP) provides networking and support for women in the utility industry.

XL. Energy Associations-Natural Gas

American Gas Association (AGA)
400 N. Capitol St. NW, Ste. 450
Washington, DC 20001 US
Phone: 202-824-7000
E-mail Address: *rshelby@aga.org*
Web Address: www.aga.org
The American Gas Association (AGA) represents a large number of natural gas providers, advocating for these companies and providing a broad range of programs and services for members.

XLI. Energy Associations-Other

American Association of Blacks in Energy
1625 K St. NW, Ste. 450
Washington, DC 20006 US
Phone: 202-371-9530
Fax: 202-371-9218
E-mail Address: *info@aabe.org*
Web Address: www.aabe.org
The American Association of Blacks in Energy is dedicated to ensuring the input of African Americans and other minorities in discussions and

developments of energy policies, regulations, research and development technologies and environmental issues.

XLII. Energy Associations-Petroleum, Exploration, Production, etc.

American Association of Professional Landmen (AAPL)
4100 Fossil Creek Blvd.
Fort Worth, TX 76137 US
Phone: 817-847-7700
Fax: 817-847-7704
E-mail Address: *aapl@landman.org*
Web Address: www.landman.org
The American Association of Professional Landmen (AAPL) promotes the highest standards of performance for all land professionals and seeks to advance their stature and to encourage sound stewardship of energy and mineral resources.

American Petroleum Institute (API)
1220 L St. NW
Washington, DC 20005-4070 US
Phone: 202-682-8000
Web Address: www.api.org
American Petroleum Institute (API) represents U.S. oil and gas industries and its web site includes in-depth sections for energy consumers and energy professionals.

Independent Petroleum Association of America (IPAA)
1201 15th St. NW, Ste. 300
Washington, DC 20005 US
Phone: 202-857-4722
Fax: 202-857-4799
E-mail Address: *rcarter@ipaa.org*
Web Address: www.ipaa.org
The Independent Petroleum Association of America (IPAA) provides a forum for the exploration and production segment of the independent oil and natural gas business. It also provides information on the domestic exploration and production industry.

International Association of Drilling Contractors (IADC)
10370 Richmond Ave., Ste. 760
Houston, TX 77042 US
Phone: 713-292-1945
Fax: 713-292-1946

E-mail Address: *info@iadc.org*
Web Address: www.iadc.org
The International Association of Drilling Contractors (IADC) represents the worldwide oil and gas drilling industry and promotes commitment to safety, preservation of the environment and advances in drilling technology.

American Association of Petroleum Geologists (AAPG)
1444 S. Boulder Ave.
Tulsa, OK 74119 US
Phone: 918-584-2555
Fax: 918-560-2665
Toll Free: 800-364-2274
E-mail Address: *lnation@aapg.org*
Web Address: www.aapg.org
The American Association of Petroleum Geologists (AAPG) is an international geological organization that supports educational and scientific programs and projects related to geosciences.

XLIII. Engineering, Research & Scientific Associations

American Institute of Chemical Engineers (AIChE)
3 Park Ave.
New York, NY 10016-5991 US
Phone: 203-702-7660
Fax: 203-775-5177
Toll Free: 800-242-4363
E-mail Address: *xpress@aiche.org*
Web Address: www.aiche.org
The American Institute of Chemical Engineers (AIChE) provides leadership in advancing the chemical engineering profession. The organization, which is comprised of 40,000 members from 93 countries, provides informational resources to chemical engineers.

American Society for Healthcare Engineering (ASHE)
1 N. Franklin, 28th Fl.
Chicago, IL 60606 US
Phone: 312-422-3800
Fax: 312-422-4571
E-mail Address: *ashe@aha.org*
Web Address: www.ashe.org
The American Society for Healthcare Engineering (ASHE) is the advocate and resource for continuous improvement in the health care

engineering and facilities management professions.

American Society of Agricultural and Biological Engineers (ASABE)
2950 Niles Rd.
St. Joseph, MI 49085 US
Phone: 269-429-0300
Fax: 269-429-3852
E-mail Address: *hq@asabe.org*
Web Address: www.asabe.org
The American Society of Agricultural and Biological Engineers (ASABE) is a nonprofit professional and technical organization interested in engineering knowledge and technology for food and agriculture and associated industries.

American Society of Civil Engineers (ASCE)
1801 Alexander Bell Dr.
Reston, VA 20191-4400 US
Phone: 703-295-6300
Fax: 703-295-6222
Toll Free: 800-548-2723
Web Address: www.asce.org
The American Society of Civil Engineers (ASCE) is a leading professional organization serving civil engineers. It ensures safer buildings, water systems and other civil engineering works by developing technical codes and standards.

American Society of Safety Engineers (ASSE)
Customer Service
1800 E. Oakton St.
Des Plaines, IL 60018 US
Phone: 847-699-2929
Fax: 847-768-3434
E-mail Address:
customerservice@asse.org
Web Address: www.asse.org
The American Society of Safety Engineers (ASSE) is the world's oldest and largest professional safety organization. It manages, supervises and consults on safety, health and environmental issues in industry, insurance, government and education.

Association of Federal Communications Consulting Engineers (AFCCE)
P.O. Box 19333
Washington, DC 20036 US

Web Address: www.afcce.org
The Association of Federal Communications Consulting Engineers (AFCCE) is a professional organization of individuals who regularly assist clients on technical issues before the Federal Communications Commission (FCC).

Institute of Industrial Engineers (IIE)
3577 Parkway Ln., Ste. 200
Norcross, GA 30092 US
Phone: 770-449-0460
Fax: 770-441-3295
Toll Free: 800-494-0460
E-mail Address: *execoffice@iienet.org*
Web Address: www.iienet.org
The Institute of Industrial Engineers (IIE) is dedicated to the professional needs of industrial engineers.

Institute of Structural Engineers (IStructE)
11 Upper Belgrave St.
London, SW1X 8BH UK
Phone: 44-(0)20-7235-4535
Fax: 44-(0)20-7235-4294
Web Address: www.istructe.org.uk
The Institute of Structural Engineers (IStructE) is a professional organization, headquartered in the U.K., that sets and maintains standards for professional structural engineers.

National Society of Professional Engineers (NSPE)
1420 King St.
Alexandria, VA 22314-2794 US
Phone: 703-684-2800
Fax: 703-836-4875
Toll Free: 888-285-6773
E-mail Address: *memserv@nspe.org*
Web Address: www.nspe.org
The National Society of Professional Engineers (NSPE) represents individual engineering professionals and licensed engineers across all disciplines. NSPE serves approximately 45,000 members and has more than 500 chapters.

Society of Automotive Engineers (SAE)
755 W. Big Beaver, Ste. 1600
Troy, MA 48084 US
Phone: 248-273-2455
Fax: 248-273-2494

Toll Free: 877-606-7323
E-mail Address:
automotive_hq@sae.org
Web Address: www.sae.org
The Society of Automotive Engineers (SAE) is a resource for technical information and expertise used in designing, building, maintaining and operating self-propelled vehicles for use on land, sea, air or space.

Society of Broadcast Engineers, Inc. (SBE)
9102 N. Meridian St., Ste. 150
Indianapolis, IN 46260 US
Phone: 317-846-9000
Fax: 317-846-9120
E-mail Address: *mclappe@sbe.org*
Web Address: www.sbe.org
The Society of Broadcast Engineers (SBE) exists to increase knowledge of broadcast engineering and promote its interests, as well as to continue the education of professionals in the industry.

Society of Cable Telecommunications Engineers (SCTE)
140 Philips Rd.
Exton, PA 19341-1318 US
Phone: 610-363-6888
Fax: 610-363-5898
Toll Free: 800-542-5040
E-mail Address: *scte@scte.org*
Web Address: www.scte.org
The Society of Cable Telecommunications Engineers (SCTE) is a nonprofit professional association dedicated to advancing the careers and serving the industry of telecommunications professionals by providing technical training, certification and standards.

Society of Hispanic Professional Engineers (SHPE)
5400 E. Olympic Blvd., Ste. 210
Los Angeles, CA 90022 US
Phone: 323-725-3970
Fax: 323-725-0316
E-mail Address:
shpenational@shpe.org
Web Address: oneshpe.shpe.org
The Society of Hispanic Professional Engineers (SHPE) is a national nonprofit organization that promotes

Hispanics in science, engineering and math.

Society of Manufacturing Engineers (SME)
1 SME Dr.
Dearborn, MI 48121 US
Phone: 313-425-3000
Fax: 313-425-3412
Toll Free: 800-733-4763
E-mail Address:
communications@sme.org
Web Address: www.sme.org
The Society of Manufacturing Engineers (SME) a leading professional organization serving engineers in the manufacturing industries.

Society of Motion Picture and Television Engineers (SMPTE)
3 Barker Ave.
5th Fl.
White Plains, NY 10601 US
Phone: 914-761-1100
Fax: 914-761-3115
Web Address: www.smpte.org
The Society of Motion Picture and Television Engineers (SMPTE) is the leading technical society for the motion imaging industry. The firm publishes recommended practice and engineering guidelines, as well the SMPTE Journal.

Society of Women Engineers (SWE)
230 E. Ohio St., Ste. 400
Chicago, IL 60611 US
Phone: 312-596-5223
Toll Free: 877-793-4636
E-mail Address: *hq@swe.org*
Web Address: www.swe.org
The Society of Women Engineers (SWE) is a nonprofit educational and service organization of female engineers.

XLIV. Entertainment & Amusement Associations

International Association of Amusement Parks and Attractions (IAAPA)
1448 Duke St.
Alexandria, VA 22314 US
Phone: 703-836-4800
Fax: 703-836-6742
E-mail Address: *dmandt@iaapa.org*

Web Address: www.iaapa.org
The International Association of Amusement Parks and Attractions (IAAPA) is dedicated to the preservation and prosperity of the amusement industry.

International Special Events Society (ISES)
401 N. Michigan Ave.
Chicago, IL 60611-4267 US
Phone: 312-321-6853
Fax: 312-673-6953
Toll Free: 800-688-4737
E-mail Address: *info@ises.com*
Web Address: www.ises.com
The International Special Events Society (ISES) is a society of special events professionals representing the industry's diverse disciplines.

XLV. Film & Television Resources

SCREENSite
P.O. Box 870152
Tuscaloosa, AL 35487 US
Phone: 205-348-6350
E-mail Address: *jbutler@ua.edu*
Web Address: www.screensite.org
SCREENSite is a resource center for film and TV scholarship with an archive of course syllabi, e-mail listings of media scholars, conference information, school listings and job list.

XLVI. Film & Theater Associations

Academy of Motion Picture Arts and Sciences (AMPAS)
8949 Wilshire Blvd.
Beverly Hills, CA 90211-1972 US
Phone: 310-247-3000
Fax: 310-859-9619
Web Address: www.oscars.org
The Academy of Motion Picture Arts and Sciences (AMPAS) is a professional honorary organization, founded to advance the arts and sciences of motion pictures. Besides hosting the Academy Awards and selecting the winners of the Oscars, AMPAS organizes smaller events highlighting the art of filmmaking, including lectures and seminars, and is

currently building the Academy Museum of Motion Pictures.

Alliance of Motion Picture and Television Producers (AMPTP)
15301 Ventura Blvd.
Encino, CA 91403 US
Toll Free: 818-995-3600
Web Address: www.amptp.org
The Alliance of Motion Picture and Television Producers (AMPTP) is the primary trade association with respect to labor issues in the motion picture and television industry.

American Cinema Editors, Inc. (ACE)
100 Universal City Plz.
Verna Fields Bldg. 2282, Rm. 190
Universal City, CA 91608 US
Phone: 818-777-2900
Fax: 818-733-5023
E-mail Address:
amercinema@earthlink.net
Web Address: www.ace-filmeditors.org
American Cinema Editors (ACE) is an honorary society of motion picture editors that seeks to advance the art and science of the editing profession.

American Society of Cinematographers (ASC)
1782 N. Orange Dr.
Hollywood, CA 90028 US
Phone: 323-969-4333
Fax: 323-882-6391
Toll Free: 800-448-0145
E-mail Address: *office@theasc.com*
Web Address: www.theasc.com
The American Society of Cinematographers (ASC) is a trade association for cinematographers in the motion picture industry.

Art Directors Guild (ADG)
11969 Ventura Blvd.
2nd Fl.
Studio City, CA 91604 US
Phone: 818-762-9995
Fax: 818-762-9997
E-mail Address: *nick@artdirectors.org*
Web Address: www.artdirectors.org
The Art Directors Guild (ADG) represents the creative talents that conceive and manage the background and settings for most films and television projects.

Association of Cinema and Video Laboratories (ACVL)
630 9th Ave.
Chip Wilkinson, Pres., ACVL
New York, NY 10036 US
Phone: 212-586-4822
Fax: 212-582-3744
E-mail Address: *cfw2447@rcn.com*
Web Address: www.acvl.org
The Association of Cinema and Video Laboratories (ACVL) is an international organization whose members are pledged to the highest possible standards of service to the film and video industries.

Independent Film & Television Alliance (IFTA)
10850 Wilshire Blvd., 9th Fl.
Los Angeles, CA 90024-4321 US
Phone: 310-446-1000
Fax: 310-446-1600
E-mail Address: *info@ifta-online.org*
Web Address: www.ifta-online.org
The Independent Film & Television Alliance (IFTA), formerly the American Film Marketing Association (AFMA), is a trade association whose mission is to provide the independent film and television industry with high-quality, market-oriented services and worldwide representation.

International Alliance of Theatrical Stage Employees (IATSE)
1430 Broadway
20th Fl.
New York, NY 10018 US
Phone: 212-730-1770
Fax: 212-921-7699
E-mail Address: *webmaster@iatse-intl.org*
Web Address: www.iatse-intl.org
The International Alliance of Theatrical Stage Employees (IATSE) is the labor union representing technicians, artisans and crafts workers in the entertainment industry, including live theater, film and television production and trade shows.

International Animated Film Society (ASIFA-Hollywood)
2114 W. Burbank Blvd.
Burbank, CA 91506 US
Phone: 818-842-4691
E-mail Address: *info@asifa-hollywood.org*

Web Address: www.asifa-hollywood.org
International Animated Film Society (ASIFA-Hollywood) is a nonprofit organization dedicated to the advancement of the art of animation.

International Documentary Association (IDA)
1201 W. 5th St., Ste. M270
Los Angeles, CA 90017 US
Phone: 213-534-3600
Fax: 213-534-3610
E-mail Address: *amina@documentary.org*
Web Address: www.documentary.org
The International Documentary Association (IDA) is a nonprofit member service organization, providing publications, benefits and a public forum to its members for issues regarding nonfiction film, video and multimedia.

Motion Picture Association of America (MPAA)
15301 Ventura Blvd.
Bldg. E
Sherman Oaks, CA 91403 US
Phone: 818-995-6600
Fax: 818-285-4403
Web Address: www.mpaa.org
The Motion Picture Association of America (MPAA) serves as the voice and advocate of the U.S. motion picture, home video and television industries.

Motion Picture Editors Guild (MPEG)
7715 Sunset Blvd., Ste. 200
Hollywood, CA 90046 US
Phone: 323-876-4770
Fax: 323-876-0861
Toll Free: 800-705-8700
E-mail Address: *mail@editorsguild.com*
Web Address: www.editorsguild.com
The Motion Picture Editors Guild's (MPEG) web site provides an online directory of editors, a discussion forum and links to related magazines and other organizations that serve the motion picture industry.

Producers Guild of America, Inc. (PGA)
8530 Wilshire Blvd., Ste. 450

Beverly Hills, CA 90211 US
Phone: 310-358-9020
Fax: 310-358-9520
E-mail Address: *info@producersguild.org*
Web Address: www.producersguild.org
The Producers Guild of America, Inc. (PGA) is a nonprofit organization for career professionals who initiate, create, coordinate, supervise and control all aspects of the motion picture and television production processes.

Screen Actors Guild (SAG)
5757 Wilshire Blvd.
7th Fl.
Los Angeles, CA 90036-3600 US
Phone: 323-954-1600
Fax: 323-549-6603
Toll Free: 800-724-0767
E-mail Address: *saginfo@sag.org*
Web Address: www.sag.org
The Screen Actors Guild (SAG) represents its members through negotiation and enforcement of collective bargaining agreements that establish equitable levels of compensation, benefits and working conditions for performers. Established in 1933, the guild has 20 branches that represent 120,000 actors nationwide.

Women In Film (WIF)
8857 W. Olympic Blvd., Ste. 201
Beverly Hills, CA 90211-3605 US
Phone: 310-657-5144
Fax: 310-657-5154
E-mail Address: *info@wif.org*
Web Address: www.wif.org
Women In Film (WIF) strives to empower, promote and mentor women in the entertainment, communication and media industries through a network of contacts, educational programs and events.

XLVII. Fitness

American Fitness Professionals and Associates (AFPA)
P.O. Box 214
Ship Bottom, NJ 08008 US
Phone: 609-978-7583
Fax: 609-978-7582
E-mail Address: *afpa@afpafitness.com*
Web Address: www.afpafitness.com

American Fitness Professionals and Associates (AFPA) offers health and fitness professionals certification programs, continuing education courses, home correspondence courses and regional conventions.

XLVIII. Food Industry Associations, General

Institute of Food Technologies (IFT)
525 W. Van Buren, Ste. 1000
Chicago, IL 60607 US
Phone: 312-782-8424
Fax: 312-782-8348
Toll Free: 800-438-3663
E-mail Address: *info@ift.org*
Web Address: www.ift.org
The Institute of Food Technologies (IFT) is devoted to the advancement of the science and technology of food through the exchange of knowledge. The site also provides information and resources for job seekers in the food industry. Members work in food science, food technology and related professions in industry, academia and government.

XLIX. Food Processor Industry Associations

Grocery Manufacturers Association (GMA)
1350 I St. NW, Ste. 300
Washington, DC 20005 US
Phone: 202-639-5900
Fax: 202-639-5932
E-mail Address: *info@gmaonline.org*
Web Address: www.gmaonline.org
The Grocery Manufacturers Association (GMA), formerly the National Food Products Association (NFPA), is the voice of the food, beverage and consumer products industry on scientific and public policy issues involving food safety, food security, nutrition, technical and regulatory matters and consumer affairs.

L. Grocery Industry Associations

Food Marketing Institute (FMI)
2345 Crystal Dr., Ste. 800
Arlington, VA 22202 US
Phone: 202-452-8444

Fax: 202-429-4519
E-mail Address: *fmi@fmi.org*
Web Address: www.fmi.org
The Food Marketing Institute (FMI) is a nonprofit association conducting programs in research, education, industry relations and public affairs on behalf of its 1,500 members.

LI. Health & Nutrition Associations

American Dietetic Association (ADA)
120 S. Riverside Plz., Ste. 2000
Chicago, IL 60606-6995 US
Fax: 312-899-4899
Toll Free: 800-877-1600
E-mail Address:
foundation@eatright.org
Web Address: www.eatright.org
The American Dietetic Association (ADA) is the world's largest organization of food and nutrition professionals, with nearly 65,000 members. In addition to services for its professional members, this organization's web site offers consumers a Nutrition Knowledge Center and a Healthy Lifestyle Center.

LII. Health Associations-International

Regulatory Affairs Professionals Society (RAPS)
5635 Fishers Ln., Ste. 550
Rockville, MD 20852 US
Phone: 301-770-2920
Fax: 301-770-2924
E-mail Address: *raps@raps.org*
Web Address: www.raps.org
The Regulatory Affairs Professionals Society (RAPS) is an international professional society representing the health care regulatory affairs profession and individual professionals worldwide.

LIII. Health Care Business & Professional Associations

Advanced Medical Technology Association (AdvaMed)
701 Pennsylvania Ave. NW, Ste. 800
Washington, DC 20004-2654 US
Phone: 202-783-8700

Fax: 202-783-8750
E-mail Address: *info@advamed.org*
Web Address: www.advamed.org
The Advanced Medical Technology Association (AdvaMed) strives to be the advocate for a legal, regulatory and economic climate that advances global health care by assuring worldwide access to the benefits of medical technology.

American Academy of Medical Administrators (AAMA)
701 Lee St., Ste. 600
Des Plaines, IL 60016-4516 US
Phone: 847-759-8601
Fax: 847-759-8602
E-mail Address: *info@aameda.org*
Web Address: www.aameda.org
The American Academy of Medical Administrators (AAMA) is an association for health care leaders to enhance their profession and community health.

American Academy of Nursing (AAN)
888 17th St. NW, Ste. 800
Washington, DC 20006 US
Phone: 202-777-1170
Fax: 202-777-0107
E-mail Address: *info@aannet.org*
Web Address: www.aannet.org
The American Academy of Nursing (AAN) works to help nursing leaders transform the health care system in order to optimize public well-being.

American Association of Medical Assistants (AAMA)
20 N. Wacker Dr., Ste. 1575
Chicago, IL 60606 US
Phone: 312-899-1500
Fax: 312-899-1259
Web Address: www.aama-ntl.org
The American Association of Medical Assistants (AAMA) seeks to promote the professional identity and stature of its members and the medical assisting profession through education and credentialing.

American College of Health Care Administrators (ACHCA)
12100 Sunset Hills Rd., Ste. 130
Reston, VA 20190 US
Phone: 703-739-7900
Fax: 866-874-1585

E-mail Address:
kbgallagher@achca.org
Web Address: www.achca.org
The American College of Health Care
Administrators (ACHCA) offers
educational programming and career
development for health care
administrators.

**American College of Healthcare
Executives (ACHE)**
1 N. Franklin, Ste. 1700
Chicago, IL 60606-3529 US
Phone: 312-424-2800
Fax: 312-424-0023
E-mail Address: *geninfo@ache.org*
Web Address: www.ache.org
The American College of Healthcare
Executives (ACHE) is an international
professional society of health care
executives that offers certification and
educational programs.

American Dental Association (ADA)
211 E. Chicago Ave.
Chicago, IL 60611-2678 US
Phone: 312-440-2500
E-mail Address: *online@ada.org*
Web Address: www.ada.org
The American Dental Association
(ADA) is a professional association of
dentists committed to the public's oral
health, ethics, science and professional
advancement.

**American Medical Technologists
(AMT)**
10700 W. Higgins Rd., Ste. 150
Rosemont, IL 60018 US
Phone: 847-823-5169
Fax: 847-823-0458
Toll Free: 800-275-1268
E-mail Address:
membership@amt1.com
Web Address: www.amt1.com
American Medical Technologists
(AMT) is a nonprofit certification
agency and professional membership
association representing individuals in
health care.

**American Medical Women's
Association (AMWA)**
100 N. 200th St., 4th Fl.
Philadelphia, PA 19103 US
Phone: 215-320-3716
Fax: 215-564-2175
Toll Free: 866-564-2483

E-mail Address: *info@amwa-doc.org*
Web Address: www.amwa-doc.org
The American Medical Women's
Association (AMWA) is an
organization of women physicians and
medical students dedicated to serving
as the unique voice for women's health
and the advancement of women in
medicine.

**American Occupational Therapy
Association, Inc. (AOTA)**
4720 Montgomery Ln.
P.O. Box 31220
Bethesda, MD 20824-1220 US
Phone: 301-652-2682
Fax: 301-652-7711
Web Address: www.aota.org
The American Occupational Therapy
Association, Inc. (AOTA) advances the
quality, availability, use and support of
occupational therapy through standard-
setting, advocacy, education and
research on behalf of its members and
the public.

**American Organization of Nurse
Executives (AONE)**
325 7th St. NW
Liberty Pl.
Washington, DC 20004 US
Phone: 202-626-2240
Fax: 202-638-5499
E-mail Address: *aone@aha.org*
Web Address: www.aone.org
The American Organization of Nurse
Executives (AONE) is a national
organization of nurses who design,
facilitate and manage health care.

**American Public Health Association
(APHA)**
800 I St. NW
Washington, DC 20001-3710 US
Phone: 202-777-2742
Fax: 202-777-2534
E-mail Address: *comments@apha.org*
Web Address: www.apha.org
The American Public Health
Association (APHA) is an association
of individuals and organizations
working to improve the public's health
and to achieve equity in health status
for all.

**American School Health Association
(ASHA)**
7263 State Rte. 43

P.O. Box 708
Kent, OH 44240 US
Phone: 330-678-1601
Fax: 330-678-4526
E-mail Address: *asha@ashaweb.org*
Web Address: www.ashaweb.org
The American School Health
Association (ASHA) advocates high-
quality school health instruction, health
services and a healthy school
environment.

Dental Trade Alliance (DTA)
2300 Clarendon Blvd., Ste. 1003
Arlington, VA 22201 US
Phone: 703-379-7755
Fax: 703-931-9429
E-mail Address:
info@dentaltradealliance.org
Web Address:
www.dentaltradealliance.org
The Dental Trade Alliance (DTA)
represents dental manufacturers, dental
dealers and dental laboratories.

**Health Industry Distributors
Association (HIDA)**
310 Montgomery St.
Alexandria, VA 22314-1516 US
Phone: 703-549-4432
Fax: 703-549-6495
E-mail Address: *sandler@hida.org*
Web Address: www.hida.org
The Health Industry Distributors
Association (HIDA) is the international
trade association representing medical
products distributors.

**Healthcare Financial Management
Association (HFMA)**
2 Westbrook Corporate Ctr., Ste. 700
Westchester, IL 60154 US
Phone: 708-531-9600
Fax: 708-531-0032
Toll Free: 800-252-4362
Web Address: www.hfma.org
The Healthcare Financial Management
Association (HFMA) is one of the
nation's leading personal membership
organizations for health care financial
management executives and leaders.

**Medical Device Manufacturers
Association (MDMA)**
1350 I St. NW, Ste. 540
Washington, DC 20005 US
Phone: 202-354-7171

Web Address:
www.medicaldevices.org
The Medical Device Manufacturers
Association (MDMA) is a national
trade association that represents
independent manufacturers of medical
devices, diagnostic products and health
care information systems.

**Medical Group Management
Association (MGMA)**
104 Inverness Ter. E.
Englewood, CO 80112-5306 US
Phone: 303-799-1111
Fax: 303-643-4439
Toll Free: 877-275-6462
E-mail Address: *service@mgma.com*
Web Address: www.mgma.com
Medical Group Management
Association (MGMA) is one of the
nation's principal voices for medical
group practice.

**National Association of Health
Services Executives (NAHSE)**
1140 Connecticut Ave. NW, Ste. 505
Washington, DC 20036 US
Phone: 202-429-6060
Fax: 301-429-6767
E-mail Address: *nahsehq@nahse.org*
Web Address: www.nahse.org
The National Association of Health
Services Executives (NAHSE) is a
nonprofit association of black health
care executives who promote the
advancement and development of
black health care leaders and elevate
the quality of health care services
rendered to minority and underserved
communities.

LIV.   Hearing & Speech

**Hearing Industries Association
(HIA)**
1444 I St. NW, Ste. 700
Washington, DC 20005 US
Phone: 202-449-1090
Fax: 202-216-9646
E-mail Address:
mspangler@bostrom.com
Web Address: www.hearing.org
The Hearing Industries Association
(HIA) represents and unifies the many
aspects of the hearing industry.

LV.   Hotel/Lodging Associations

**American Hotel and Lodging
Association**
1201 New York Ave. NW, Ste. 600
Washington, DC 20005-3931 US
Phone: 202-289-3100
Fax: 202-289-3199
E-mail Address:
informationcenter@ahla.com
Web Address: www.ahla.com
The American Hotel and Lodging
Association is a federation of state
lodging associations throughout the
U.S.

LVI.   Human Resources Industry Associations

**Society of Human Resource
Management (SHRM)**
1800 Duke St.
Alexandria, VA 22314 US
Phone: 703-548-3440
Fax: 703-535-6490
Toll Free: 800-283-7476
E-mail Address: *shrm@shrm.org*
Web Address: www.shrm.org
The Society of Human Resource
Management (SHRM) addresses the
interests and needs of HR professionals
through its resource materials.

LVII.   Industry Research/Market Research

Forrester Research
400 Technology Sq.
Cambridge, MA 02139 US
Phone: 617-613-6000
Fax: 617-613-5200
Toll Free: 866-367-7378
Web Address: www.forrester.com
Forrester Research identifies and
analyzes emerging trends in
technology and their impact on
business. Among the firm's specialties
are the financial services, retail, health
care, entertainment, automotive and
information technology industries.

Marketresearch.com
11200 Rockville Pike, Ste. 504
Rockville, MD 20852 US
Phone: 240-747-3000
Fax: 240-747-3004
Toll Free: 800-298-5699

E-mail Address:
customerservice@marketresearch.com
Web Address:
www.marketresearch.com
Marketresearch.com is a leading
broker for professional market research
and industry analysis. Users are able to
search the company's database of
research publications including data on
global industries, companies, products
and trends.

Plunkett Research, Ltd.
P.O. Drawer 541737
Houston, TX 77254-1737 US
Phone: 713-932-0000
Fax: 713-932-7080
E-mail Address:
*customersupport@plunkettresearch.co
m*
Web Address:
www.plunkettresearch.com
Plunkett Research, Ltd. is a leading
provider of market research, industry
trends analysis and business statistics.
Since 1985, it has served clients
worldwide, including corporations,
universities, libraries, consultants and
government agencies. At the firm's
web site, visitors can view product
information and pricing and access a
great deal of basic market information
on industries such as financial services,
infotech, e-commerce, health care and
biotech.

LVIII.   Insurance Industry Associations

**American Insurance Association
(AIA)**
1130 Connecticut Ave. NW, Ste. 1000
Washington, DC 20036 US
Phone: 202-828-7100
Fax: 202-293-1219
E-mail Address: *info@aiadc.org*
Web Address: www.aiadc.org
The American Insurance Association
(AIA) is a leading property and
casualty insurance trade organization,
representing companies that offer all
types of property and casualty
insurance.

LIX. Insurance Industry Associations-Agents & Brokers

Council of Insurance Agents & Brokers (CIAB)
701 Pennsylvania Ave. NW, Ste. 750
Washington, DC 20004 US
Phone: 202-783-4400
Fax: 202-783-4410
E-mail Address: *ciab@ciab.com*
Web Address: www.ciab.com
The Council of Insurance Agents & Brokers (CIAB) is an association for commercial insurance and employee benefits intermediaries in the U.S. and abroad.

Independent Insurance Agents & Brokers of America, Inc. (IIABA)
127 S. Peyton St.
Alexandria, VA 22314 US
Fax: 703-683-7556
Toll Free: 800-221-7917
E-mail Address: *info@iiaba.org*
Web Address:
www.independentagent.com
Independent Insurance Agents & Brokers of America (IIABA) represents its over 300,000 members who are independent insurance agents and brokers.

Professional Insurance Agents (PIA)
25 Chamberlain St.
P.O. Box 997
Glenmont, NY 12077-0997 US
Fax: 888-225-6935
Toll Free: 800-424-4244
E-mail Address: *pia@pia.org*
Web Address: www.piaonline.org
Professional Insurance Agents (PIA) is a group of voluntary, membership-based trade associations representing professional, independent property and casualty insurance agents.

LX. Insurance-Health Associations

America's Health Insurance Plans (AHIP)
601 Pennsylvania Ave. NW, Ste. 500
Washington, DC 20004 US
Phone: 202-778-3200
Fax: 202-331-7487
E-mail Address: *ahip@ahip.org*
Web Address: www.ahip.org

America's Health Insurance Plans (AHIP) is a prominent trade association representing the private health care insurance system.

LXI. Magazines, Business & Financial

BusinessWeek Online
P.O. Box 8418
Red Oak, IA 51591-1418 US
Fax: 712-623-5229
Toll Free: 800-635-1200
E-mail Address:
bwzcustserv@cdsfulfillment.com
Web Address: www.businessweek.com
Business Week Online offers an investor service, global business advice, technology news, small business guides, career information, business school advice, daily news briefs and more.

Forbes Online
90 5th Ave.
New York, NY 10011 US
Phone: 212-366-8900
E-mail Address: *dweathers@forbes.net*
Web Address: www.forbes.com
Forbes Online offers varied stock information, news and commentary on business, technology and personal finance, as well as financial calculators and advice.

Fortune
Time & Life Bldg.
Rockefeller Ctr.
New York, NY 10020-1393 US
Phone: 212-522-6724
Fax: 212-522-6412
Toll Free: 800-777-1444
E-mail Address:
Katy_Reitz@timeinc.com
Web Address:
money.cnn.com/magazines/fortune
Fortune, one of the world's premiere business magazines, contains news, business profiles and information on investing, careers, small business, technology and other details of U.S. and international business. Fortune is a publication of Cable News Network (CNN), a Time Warner company.

Investor's Business Daily (IBD)
12655 Beatrice St.
Los Angeles, CA 90066 US

Phone: 310-448-6600
Toll Free: 800-831-2525
E-mail Address:
ibdnews@investors.com
Web Address: www.investors.com
Investor's Business Daily (IBD) offers subscribers information and articles on the stock market, educational resources, advice from analyst William O'Neil, personal portfolios and updates on events and workshops.

Wall Street Journal Online (The)
200 Liberty St.
New York, NY 10281 US
Phone: 212-416-2000
Toll Free: 800-568-7625
E-mail Address:
onlinejournal@wsj.com
Web Address: www.wsj.com
The outstanding resources of The Wall Street Journal are available online for a nominal fee.

LXII. MBA Resources

MBA Depot
Phone: 512-499-8728
Web Address: www.mbadepot.com
MBA Depot is an online community for MBA professionals.

LXIII. Online Recruiting & Employment ASPs & Solutions

Authoria, Inc.
300 5th Ave.
Waltham, MA 02451 US
Phone: 781-530-2000
Fax: 781-530-2001
Toll Free: 877-422-1114
E-mail Address: *info@authoria.com*
Web Address: www.authoria.com
Authoria, Inc.'s web site offers companies and job seekers a variety of human resources content. The site includes recruiting management, performance management, incentive management, compensation management, succession planning and benefit and policy communication services.

Insala
1331 Airport Fwy., Ste. 313
Euless, TX 76040 US
Phone: 817-355-0939

Fax: 817-355-0746
E-mail Address: *info@insala.com*
Web Address: www.insala.com
Insala provides job search software solutions for the outplacement industry.

Kenexa
650 E. Swedesford Rd.
2nd Fl.
Wayne, PA 19087 US
Phone: 877-971-9171
Fax: 610-971-9181
Toll Free: 800-391-9557
E-mail Address:
contactus@kenexa.com
Web Address: www.kenexa.com
Kenexa is a back-end recruiting and job-posting service that is used by many companies in building a workforce. Products and services include recruitment software solutions, talent consulting and recruitment process management.

Workstream
2600 Lake Lucien Dr., Ste. 410
Maitland, FL 32751 US
Phone: 407-475-5500
Fax: 407-475-5502
Toll Free: 866-953-8800
E-mail Address:
info@workstreaminc.com
Web Address:
www.workstreaminc.com
Workstream creates workforce management solutions through a combination of technology and services designed to integrate an organization.

LXIV.   Outsourcing Industry Associations

International Association of Outsourcing Professionals (IAOP)
2600 South Rd., Ste. 44-240
Poughkeepsie, NY 12601 US
Phone: 845-452-0600
Fax: 845-452-6988
E-mail Address:
*memberservices@outsourcingprofessio
nal.org*
Web Address:
www.outsourcingprofessional.org
The International Association of Outsourcing Professionals (IAOP) represents outsourcing leaders and

experts representing companies of all sizes and industries around the world.

LXV.   Pensions, Benefits & 401(k)s Associations

Profit Sharing/401(k) Council of America (PSCA)
20 N. Wacker Dr., Ste. 3700
Chicago, IL 60606 US
Phone: 312-419-1863
Fax: 312-419-1864
E-mail Address: *psca@psca.org*
Web Address: www.psca.org
The Profit Sharing/401(k) Council of America (PSCA) is a national nonprofit association of 1,200 companies and their 6 million employees. The group expresses its members' interests to federal policymakers and offers practical, cost-effective assistance with profit sharing and 401(k) plan design, administration, investment, compliance and communication. Its web site offers a thorough glossary, statistics and educational material.

LXVI.   Pensions, Benefits & 401(k)s Resources

Employee Benefits Security Administration (EBSA)
200 Constitution Ave. NW
Washington, DC 20210 US
Phone: 202-693-8700
Fax: 202-693-8736
Toll Free: 866-444-3272
Web Address: www.dol.gov/ebsa
The Employee Benefits Security Administration (EBSA) is a division of the U.S. Department of Labor, whose web site features a wealth of benefits information for both employers and employees. Included are the answers to such questions as to how a company's bankruptcy will affect its employees and what one should know about pension rights.

Pension Benefit Guarantee Corporation (PBGC)
1200 K St. NW
Washington, DC 20005-4026 US
Phone: 202-326-4000
Fax: 202-326-4344
Toll Free: 800-400-7242

E-mail Address:
participant.pro@pbgc.gov
Web Address: www.pbgc.gov
The Pension Benefit Guarantee Corporation (PBGC) is a U.S. Government agency that guarantees a portion of the retirement incomes of about 44 million American workers in about 30,000 private defined benefit pension plans. Its web site contains information regarding this guarantee, along with information on retirement planning and links to several related organizations.

LXVII.   Pharmaceutical Industry Associations (Drug Industry)

American Pharmaceutical Association (APhA)
1100 15th St. NW, Ste. 400
Washington, DC 20005-1707 US
Phone: 202-628-4410
Fax: 202-783-2351
Toll Free: 800-237-2742
E-mail Address:
infocenter@aphanet.org
Web Address: www.aphanet.org
American Pharmaceutical Association (APhA) is a national professional society that provides news and information to pharmacists.

Pharmaceutical Research and Manufacturers of America (PhRMA)
950 F St. NW, Ste. 300
Washington, DC 20004 US
Phone: 202-835-3400
Fax: 202-835-3414
Web Address: www.phrma.org
Pharmaceutical Research and Manufacturers of America (PhRMA) represents the nation's leading research-based pharmaceutical and biotechnology companies.

LXVIII.   Pilots Associations

Airline Pilots Association (ALPA)
1625 Massachusetts Ave NW
Washington, DC 20036 US
Phone: 703-689-2270
Web Address: www.alpa.org
ALPA is an association for professional airline pilots in the United States, in Canada and internationally.

LXIX. Printers & Publishers Associations

International Publishing Management Association (IPMA)
710 Regency Dr., Ste. 6
Kearney, MO 64060 US
Phone: 816-902-4762
Fax: 816-902-4766
E-mail Address: *ipmainfo@ipma.org*
Web Address: www.ipma.org
The International Publishing Management Association (IPMA) is an exclusive not-for-profit organization dedicated to assisting in-house corporate publishing and distribution professionals.

Magazine Publishers of America, Inc.
810 7th Ave., 24th Fl.
New York, NY 10019 US
Phone: 212-872-3700
E-mail Address: *mpa@magazine.org*
Web Address: www.magazine.org
Magazine Publishers of America, Inc. is the industry association for consumer magazines.

National Association of Printers & Lithographers (NAPL)
75 W. Century Rd., Ste. 100
Paramus, NJ 07652 US
Phone: 201-634-9600
Fax: 201-634-0234
Toll Free: 800-642-6275
E-mail Address: *dlospaluto@napl.org*
Web Address: www.napl.org
The National Association of Printers & Lithographers (NAPL) focuses on helping graphic arts professionals increase their expertise.

Newspaper Association of America (NAA)
4401 Wilson Blvd., Ste. 900
Arlington, VA 22203-1867 US
Phone: 571-366-1000
Fax: 571-366-1195
E-mail Address:
Jeff.Sigmund@naa.org
Web Address: www.naa.org
The Newspaper Association of America (NAA) is a nonprofit organization representing the newspaper industry.

LXX. Real Estate Industry Associations

Institute of Real Estate Management (IREM)
430 N. Michigan Ave.
Chicago, IL 60611 US
Fax: 800-338-4736
Toll Free: 800-837-0706
E-mail Address: *custserv@irem.org*
Web Address: www.irem.org
The Institute of Real Estate Management (IREM) seeks to educate real estate managers, certify their competence and professionalism, serve as an advocate on issues affecting the real estate management industry and enhance its members' professional competence so they can better identify and meet the needs of those who use their services.

National Association of Real Estate Brokers (NAREB)
9831 Greenbelt Rd., Ste. 309
Lanham, MD 20706 US
Phone: 301-552-9340
Fax: 301-552-9216
E-mail Address:
NAREB3@comcast.net
Web Address: www.nareb.com
The National Association of Real Estate Brokers (NAREB) is a national trade organization dedicated to bringing together the nation's minority professionals in the real estate industry.

National Association of Real Estate Companies (NAREC)
216 W. Jackson Blvd., Ste. 625
Chicago, IL 60606 US
Phone: 312-263-1755
Fax: 312-750-1203
E-mail Address: *info@narec.org*
Web Address: www.narec.org
The National Association of Real Estate Companies (NAREC) is composed of representatives of publicly and privately owned real estate companies, significant subsidiaries of publicly owned companies and public accounting firms.

National Association of Realtors (NAR)
430 N. Michigan Ave.
Chicago, IL 60611-4087 US
Phone: 202-383-1176
Toll Free: 800-874-6500
E-mail Address: *lsalvant@realtors.org*
Web Address: www.realtor.org
The National Association of Realtors (NAR) is composed of realtors involved in residential and commercial real estate as brokers, salespeople, property managers, appraisers and counselors and in other areas of the industry. NAR also sponsors Realtor.com, operated by Move, Inc.

Women's Council of Realtors (WCR)
430 N. Michigan Ave.
Chicago, IL 60611 US
Toll Free: 800-245-8512
E-mail Address: *wcr@wcr.org*
Web Address: www.wcr.org
The Women's Council of Realtors (WCR) is a community of female real estate professionals.

LXXI. Recording & Music Associations

American Federation of Musicians (AFM)
1501 Broadway, Ste. 600
New York, NY 10036 US
Phone: 212-869-1330
Fax: 212-764-6134
E-mail Address: *sam@afm.org*
Web Address: www.afm.org
The American Federation of Musicians (AFM) is the largest union in the world for music professionals.

American Society of Composers, Authors & Publishers (ASCAP)
1 Lincoln Plz.
New York, NY 10023 US
Phone: 212-621-6000
Fax: 212-724-9064
E-mail Address: *info@ascap.com*
Web Address: www.ascap.com
American Society of Composers, Authors & Publishers (ASCAP) is a membership association of U.S. composers, songwriters and publishers of every kind of music with hundreds of thousands of members worldwide.

Content Delivery & Storage Association (CDSA)
182 Nassau St., Ste. 204
Princeton, NJ 08542-7005 US

Phone: 609-279-1700
Fax: 609-279-1999
E-mail Address:
mbevel@contentdeliveryandstorage.org
Web Address:
www.contentdeliveryandstorage.org
The Content Delivery & Storage
Association (CDSA), formerly the
International Recording Media
Association, is a worldwide trade
association encompassing
organizations involved in every facet
of recording media, including
entertainment, information and
software content storage.

**International Association of Audio
Information Services (IAAIS)**
3920 Willshire Dr.
Lawrence, KS 66049 US
Toll Free: 800-280-5325
E-mail Address:
Stuart.Holland@state.mn.us
Web Address: www.iaais.org
International Association of Audio
Information Services (IAAIS) is an
organization that provides audio access
to information for people who are
print-disabled.

**Music Publisher's Association of the
United States (MPA)**
243 5th Ave., Ste. 236
New York, NY 10016 US
Phone: 212-327-4044
E-mail Address: *admin@mpa.org*
Web Address: mpa.org
The Music Publisher's Association of
the United States (MPA) serves as a
forum for publishers to deal with the
music industry's vital issues and is
actively involved in supporting and
advancing compliance with copyright
law, combating copyright infringement
and exploring the need for further
reform.

**Recording Industry Association of
America (RIAA)**
1025 F St. NW, 10th Fl.
Washington, DC 20004 US
Phone: 202-775-0101
Web Address: www.riaa.com
The Recording Industry Association of
America (RIAA) is the trade group that
represents the U.S. recording industry.

**Society of Professional Audio
Recording Services (SPARS)**
9 Music Sq. S., Ste. 222
Nashville, TN 37203 US
Fax: 615-296-0386
Toll Free: 800-771-7727
E-mail Address: *spars@spars.com*
Web Address: www.spars.com
The Society of Professional Audio
Recording Services (SPARS) is an
organization for members of the
recording industry to share practical
business information about audio and
multimedia facility ownership,
management and operations.

Songwriters Guild of America
209 10th Ave. S., Ste. 321
Nashville, TN 37203 US
Phone: 615-742-9945
Fax: 615-742-9948
E-mail Address:
corporate@songwritersguild.com
Web Address:
www.songwritersguild.com
The Songwriters Guild of America is
the nation's largest and oldest
songwriters' organization, serving its
members with information and
programs to further their careers and
understanding of the music industry.

**LXXII.   Satellite-Related
          Professional
          Organizations**

**Satellite Broadcasting &
Communications Association of
America (SBCA)**
1730 M St. NW, Ste. 600
Washington, DC 20036 US
Phone: 202-349-3620
Fax: 202-349-3621
Toll Free: 800-541-5981
E-mail Address: *info@sbca.org*
Web Address: www.sbca.com
The Satellite Broadcasting &
Communications Association of
America (SBCA) is the national trade
organization representing all segments
of the satellite consumer services
industry.

**Society of Satellite Professionals
International (SSPI)**
The New York Information
Technology Ctr.
55 Broad St., 14th Fl.

New York, NY 10004 US
Phone: 212-809-5199
Fax: 212-825-0075
E-mail Address: *rbell@sspi.org*
Web Address: www.sspi.org
The Society of Satellite Professionals
International (SSPI) is a nonprofit
member-benefit society that serves
satellite professionals worldwide
throughout the span of their careers.

**LXXIII.   Securities Industry
            Associations**

**North American Securities
Administrators Association, Inc.
(NASAA)**
750 1st St. NE, Ste. 1140
Washington, DC 20002 US
Phone: 202-737-0900
Fax: 202-783-3571
E-mail Address: *bw@nasaa.org*
Web Address: www.nasaa.org
The North American Securities
Administrators Association (NASAA)
is the oldest international organization
committed to investor protection. Its
web site provides information on
franchising and raising capital, as well
as state blue sky securities laws and
resources for small investment
advisors.

**Securities Industry and Financial
Markets Association (SIFMA)**
120 Broadway, 35th Fl.
New York, NY 10271-0080 US
Phone: 212-313-1200
Fax: 212-313-1301
E-mail Address: *inquiries@sifma.org*
Web Address: www.sifma.org
The Securities Industry and Financial
Markets Association (SIFMA), formed
by the recent merger of the Securities
Industry Association (SIA) and the
Bond Market Association, brings
together the shared interests of more
than 650 securities and bond industry
firms to accomplish common goals.

**LXXIV.   Software Industry
            Associations**

Business Software Alliance (BSA)
1150 18th St. NW, Ste. 700
Washington, DC 20036 US
Phone: 202-872-5500
Fax: 202-872-5501

E-mail Address: *software@bsa.org*
Web Address: www.bsa.org
The Business Software Alliance (BSA) is a leading global software industry association. BSA educates consumers regarding software management, copyright protection, cyber security, trade, e-commerce and other Internet-related issues.

Colorado Software & Internet Association (CSIA)
1625 Broadway, Ste. 950
Denver, CO 80202 US
Phone: 303-592-4070
E-mail Address:
info@coloradotechnology.org
Web Address:
www.coloradosoftware.org
The Colorado Software & Internet Association (CSIA) promotes the software industry in Colorado through networking and organization.

Entertainment Software Association (ESA)
575 7th St. NW, Ste. 300
Washington, DC 20004 US
E-mail Address: *esa@theesa.com*
Web Address: www.theesa.com
The Entertainment Software Association (ESA) serves the business and public affairs needs of companies that publish video and computer games for consoles, personal computers and the Internet. The ESA owns the E3 Media & Business Summit, a major invitation-only annual trade show for the video game industry.

International Game Developers Association (IGDA)
19 Mantua Rd.
Mt. Royal, NJ 08061 US
Phone: 856-423-2990
Fax: 856-423-3420
E-mail Address: *contact@igda.org*
Web Address: www.igda.org
The International Game Developers Association (IGDA) represents members who produce video games. The firm promotes professional development and advocates issues which affect the game developer community.

New Mexico Technology Council
P.O. Box 31278

Santa Fe, NM 87594-1278 US
Phone: 505-830-8414
E-mail Address:
heather.lovato@tig.com
Web Address: www.nmtechcouncil.org
The New Mexico Technology Council represents the interests of the software industry in New Mexico.

Software & Information Industry Association (SIIA)
1090 Vermont Ave. NW, 6th Fl.
Washington, DC 20005-4095 US
Phone: 202-289-7442
Fax: 202-289-7097
Web Address: www.siia.net
The Software & Information Industry Association (SIIA) is a principal trade association for the software and digital content industry.

Software Association of Oregon (SAO)
111 SW 5th Ave.
US Bank Twr., Ste. 120
Portland, OR 97204 US
Phone: 503-228-5401
Fax: 503-228-5411
E-mail Address: *info@sao.org*
Web Address: www.sao.org
The Software Association of Oregon (SAO) promotes the growth of Oregon's software industry.

Washington Software Association (WSA)
2200 Alaskan Way, Ste. 390
Seattle, WA 98121 US
Phone: 206-448-3033
E-mail Address:
info@washingtontechnology.org
Web Address: www.wsa.org
The Washington Software Association (WSA) promotes and helps coordinate the software industry in the state of Washington.

LXXV.   Stocks and Financial Markets Data

MSN Money Central
Web Address: moneycentral.msn.com
MSN Money Central features daily announcements, special reports, highlights from financial providers and a wealth of links and other financial information.

Reuters.com
Thompson Reuters Headquarters
3 Times Sq.
New York, NY 10036 US
Phone: 646-223-4000
Toll Free: 800-738-8377
Web Address: www.reuters.com
Reuters.com, a service of Thompson Reuters, offers information on business and world markets, political and international news and company-specific stock information.

Yahoo! Finance
Yahoo! Inc.
701 1st Ave.
Sunnyvale, CA 94089 US
Phone: 408-349-5070
Web Address: finance.yahoo.com
Yahoo! Finance provides a wealth of links and a supreme search guide. Users can find just about any financial information concerning both U.S. and world markets. Tax, insurance information, financial news and community research can be conducted through this site, as can searches for other aspects of the financial world.

LXXVI.   Telecommunications Industry Associations

National Association of Telecommunications Officers and Advisors (NATOA)
1800 Diagonal Rd., Ste. 495
Alexandria, VA 22314 US
Phone: 703-519-8035
Fax: 703-519-8036
E-mail Address: *info@natoa.org*
Web Address: www.natoa.org
The National Association of Telecommunications Officers and Advisors (NATOA) works to support and serve the telecommunications interests and needs of local governments.

LXXVII.   Temporary Staffing Firms

Adecco
Saegereistrasse 10
Glattbrugg, CH-8152 Switzerland
Phone: 41-44-878-88-88
Fax: 41-44-829-89-24
E-mail Address:
investor.relations@adecco.com

Web Address: www.adecco.com
Adecco maintains human resources and staffing services offices in 70 countries. It provides temporary and permanent personnel.

Allegis Group
7301 Parkway Dr.
Hanover, MD 21076 US
Phone: 410-579-4800
Fax: 410-540-7556
Toll Free: 877-388-3823
Web Address: www.allegisgroup.com
The Allegis Group provides technical, professional and industrial recruiting and staffing services. Allegis specializes in information technology staffing services. The firm operates in the United Kingdom, Germany and The Netherlands as Aerotek and TEKsystems, and in India as Allegis Group India. Aerotek provides staffing solutions for aviation, engineering, automotive and scientific personnel markets.

CDI Corporation
1717 Arch St.
35th Fl.
Philadelphia, PA 19103-2768 US
Phone: 215-569-2200
Fax: 215-569-1300
Toll Free: 800-996-7566
Web Address: www.cdicorp.com
CDI Corporation specializes in engineering and information technology staffing services. Company segments include CDI IT Solutions, specializing in information technology; CDI Engineering Solutions, specializing in engineering outsourcing services; AndersElite Limited, operating in the United Kingdom and Australia; and MRINetwork, specializing in executive recruitment.

Express Personnel Services
Int'l Headquarters
8516 NW Expy.
Oklahoma, OK 73162 US
Phone: 405-840-5000
Toll Free: 800-222-4057
E-mail Address:
OnlineInfo@expresspros.com
Web Address: www.expresspros.com
Express Personnel Services operates through a network of over 600 locations in the United States, Canada,

South Africa and Australia. Services include temporary and flexible staffing, evaluation and direct hire, professional and contract staffing, human resource services and online payroll processing (U.S. only).

Glotel Inc.
30 S. Wacker Dr., Ste. 2800
Chicago, IL 60606 US
Phone: 312-612-7480
Fax: 312-715-0756
E-mail Address:
chicago@glotelinc.com
Web Address: www.usa.glotel.com
Glotel is a global technology staffing and managed projects solutions company specializing in the placement of contract and permanent personnel within all areas of technology. Glotel has a network of 19 offices throughout Europe, the U.S. and Asia-Pacific.

Harvey Nash
1680 Rte. 23 N, Ste. 300
Wayne, NJ 07470 US
Phone: 973-646-2100
Fax: 973-696-3985
E-mail Address: *info@harveynash.com*
Web Address: www.harveynash.com
Harvey Nash provides professional recruitment, interim executive leadership services and outsourcing services. The firm specializes in information technology staffing on a permanent and contract basis in US, UK and Europe. It also offers outsourcing services including offshore software development services, information technology systems management, workforce risk management and managed services for network administration.

Hays plc
141 Moorgate
London, EC2M 6TX UK
Phone: 0800-716026
E-mail Address:
customerservice@hays.com
Web Address: www.hays.com
Hays is a global leader in specialist recruitment, placing professional candidates in permanent, temporary and interim positions with over 8,900 staff in 390 offices across 27 countries.

Hudson Highland Group, Inc.
560 Lexington Ave.
4th & 5th Fl.
New York, NY 10022 US
Phone: 212-351-7400
Fax: 917-256-8592
Web Address: www.hudson.com
Hudson Highland Group, Inc. provides permanent recruitment, contract and human resources consulting and inclusion solutions. Services range from single placements to total outsourced solutions. The company employs more than 3,300 professionals serving clients and candidates in more than 20 countries.

Kelly Services, Inc.
999 W. Big Beaver Rd.
Troy, MI 48084-4782 US
Phone: 248-362-4444
E-mail Address:
kfirst@kellyservices.com
Web Address: www.kellyservices.com
Kelly Services is a staffing solutions company providing approximately 700,000 employees to more than 150,000 client companies in 26 countries.

Kforce, Inc.
1001 E. Palm Ave.
Tampa, FL 33605 US
Phone: 813-552-5000
Toll Free: 877-453-6723
Web Address: www.kforce.com
Kforce, Inc. is one of America's largest temporary placement firms, with more than 70 offices in 44 cities across the U.S. It specializes in employees for the following types of jobs: finance and accounting, scientific, technology, health care, clinical research, mortgages, title insurance and real estate.

Labor Ready, Inc.
P.O. Box 2910
Tacoma, WA 98401-2910 US
Phone: 253-383-9101
Fax: 877-733-0399
Toll Free: 877-733-0430
Web Address: www.laborready.com
Labor Ready, Inc. specializes in temporary staffing in construction, manufacturing, hospitality services, transportation, landscaping, warehousing, retail and more with

almost 700 branches throughout the U.S., Canada and Puerto Rico.

Manpower, Inc.
100 Manpower Pl.
Milwaukee, WI 53212 US
Phone: 414-961-1000
Web Address: www.manpower.com
One of the largest temporary staffing providers in the world, Manpower places approximately 2 million workers annually in a variety of positions around the world.

Michael Page International plc
Page House, 1 Dashwood Lang Rd.
Addlestone, Weybridge
Surrey, KT15 2QW UK
Phone: 44-1932-264-144
Fax: 44-1932-264-297
Web Address:
www.michaelpage.co.uk
Michael Page is one of the world's leading professional recruitment consultancies specializing in the placement of candidates in permanent, contract, temporary and interim positions. The Group has operations in the US, UK, Continental Europe, Asia-Pacific and a regional presence in France and Australia. In the US, the firm's focus is on the areas of financial services, supply chain, executive searches, marketing, legal and administrative support.

MPS Group, Inc.
1 Independent Dr.
Jacksonville, FL 32202 US
Phone: 904-360-2000
Fax: 904-360-2972
Web Address: www.mpsgroup.com
MPS Group is a leading provider of staffing, consulting, and human resource solutions with offices throughout the United States, Canada, the United Kingdom and continental Europe. Primary brands include Accounting Principals, Badenoch, Entegee Engineering Technical Group, Soliant Health and Modis International IT solutions.

Pasona Group Inc. (Japan)
Chiyoda-ku
Otemachi-Nomura Bldg. 2-1-1
Otemachi
Tokyo, 100-0004 Japan

Phone: 03-6734-1100
Web Address: www.pasonagroup.co.jp
Pasona Inc. provides personnel services. Services offered range from temporary staffing/contracting, placement/recruiting, outplacement, to outsourcing and training.

Proffice
P.O. Box 70368
Stockholm, SE-107 24 Sweden
Phone: 46-8-787-17-00
E-mail Address: *info@proffice.se*
Web Address: www.proffice.com
Proffice is one of the leading flexible staffing companies in Denmark, Finland, Norway and Sweden. The firm provides temporary staffing, recruitment services and career development programs.

Radia Holdings, Inc.
6-10-1 Roppongi, Minato-ku
Roppongi Hills Mori Twr. 35F
Tokyo, 106-6135 Japan
Phone: 81-03-3405-9228
Fax: 81-03-3405-9449
Web Address: www.radiaholdings.com
Radia Holdings, Inc., provides integrated human resources services under multiple brands in Asia, North America, Europe and Australia. Radia is one of the largest staffing providers in Japan. Some brands in the United States and Canada include Technical Aid Corporation (TAC), Talent Tree, Inc., Willstaff, Inc., and Advantage Human Resourcing Inc. European brands include TAC Europe, Advantage and FSS. Japanese brands include Ctec, HiTec, CSI and Premier Staff. Asia brands include TechnoPro and TAC China.

Randstad USA
2015 S. Park Pl. SE
Atlanta, GA 30339 US
Phone: 770-937-7000
Fax: 770-937-7001
Toll Free: 877-922-2468
Web Address: www.us.randstad.com
Randstad provides staffing services in the office, industrial, technical, creative and professional markets. It specializes in temporary and permanent staffing; recruitment and consultant services; and human resource services. It operates in 83

countries, primarily in Europe, Asia and the U.S. Brands include Capac, Yacht, and Tempo-Team.

Robert Half International Inc. (RHI)
2884 Sand Hill Rd.
Menlo Park, CA 94025 US
Phone: 650-234-6000
E-mail Address: *webmaster@rhi.com*
Web Address: www.rhi.com
Robert Half International Inc. (RHI) specializes in accounting and finance positions. It also places workers in administrative, information technology, legal, advertising and marketing positions on temporary or permanent bases.

Robert Walters PLC
55 Strand
London, WC2N 5WR UK
Phone: 44 (0) 20 7379 3333
Fax: 44 (0) 20 7509 8714
E-mail Address:
london@robertwalters.com
Web Address: www.robertwalters.com
Robert Walters PLC is a professional recruitment specialist, outsourcing and human resource consultant. The firm provides services for the temporary, contract and permanent placement of individuals in the sectors of finance, operations, legal, information technology, marketing and administration support. It has offices in 17 countries including the US.

Spherion Corporation
2050 Spectrum Blvd.
Fort Lauderdale, FL 33309 US
Phone: 954-308-7600
E-mail Address:
kiphavel@spherion.com
Web Address: www.spherion.com
Spherion, which was Interim Services, provides temporary staffing, recruitment and employee consulting. The company has more than 900 offices throughout the world.

Synergie SA (France)
11 Ave. de Colonel Bonnet
Paris, 75016 France
Phone: 33-1-44-14-90-20
Web Address: www.synergie.fr
Synergie provides human resource management services which include temporary placement, consulting and

training. The firm operates primarily in France, but also operates through a network of 550 agencies in 12 European countries, UK and Canada.

Tempstaff Co., Ltd (Japan)
Shinjuku Maynds Twr. 2-1-1
Yoyogi, Shibuya-ku
Tokyo, 151-0053 Japan
Phone: 03-5350-1212
Fax: 03-3597-6160
Web Address: www.tempstaff.co.jp
Tempstaff Co., Ltd provides temporary and permanent placement and recruiting and outsourcing services. It has 264 offices in Japan and ten overseas offices including Los Angeles, Shanghai, Suzhou, Guangzhou, Hong Kong, Taiwan, Korea, Singapore and Indonesia.

United Services Group
Landdrostdreef 124
Postbus 1, 1300 AA
Almere, 1314 SK The Netherlands
Phone: 31 (0)36 529 95 00
Fax: 31 (0)36 529 95 09
E-mail Address: *info@usgpeople.com*
Web Address: www.usgpeople.com
United Services Group is active in The Netherlands, Belgium, Germany, Italy and Spain, and its subsidiary Solvus N.V. also offers services in various European countries. United Services Group is a provider of temporary employment services.

Volt Information Sciences, Inc.
560 Lexington Ave.
15th Fl.
New York, NY 10022 US
Phone: 212-704-2400
Web Address: www.volt.com
Volt Information Sciences, Inc. maintains 300 temporary staffing offices in North America and in the U.K.

LXXVIII.   Testing Resources

CPP, Inc.
1055 Joaquin Rd., 2nd Fl.
Mountain View, CA 94043 US
Phone: 650-969-8901
Fax: 650-969-8608
Toll Free: 800-624-1765
E-mail Address: *custserv@cpp.com*
Web Address: www.cpp.com

CPP, Inc. (formerly known as Consulting Psychologists Press) publishes the Meyers-Briggs Type Indicator, Strong Inventory Test and other psychological assessment-related products. CPP also provides information about the tests and, through division Davies-Black Publishing, offers business-related books and services, including those covering career management and leadership development.

LXXIX.   Textile & Fabric Associations

International Textile and Apparel Association (ITAA)
6060 Sunrise Vista Dr., Ste. 1300
Citrus Heights, CA 95610 US
Phone: 916-723-1628
Fax: 719-722-8149
E-mail Address: *info@itaaonline.org*
Web Address: www.itaaonline.org
The International Textile and Apparel Association (ITAA) is a nonprofit educational and scientific corporation dedicated to providing opportunities to scholars in the retail, textile and apparel industries.

LXXX.   Trade Associations-General

United States Council for International Business (USCIB)
1212 Ave. of the Americas
New York, NY 10036 US
Phone: 212-354-4480
Fax: 212-575-0327
E-mail Address:
membership@uscib.org
Web Address: www.uscib.org
The United States Council for International Business has promoted an open system of world trade and investment with its unique global network. Standard USCIB membership are corporations, law firms, consulting firms and industry associations. Limited membership options are available for chambers of commerce and sole legal practitioners.

LXXXI.   Travel Business & Professional Associations

American Society of Travel Agents (ASTA)
1101 King St., Ste. 200
Alexandria, VA 22314 US
Fax: 703-739-3268
Toll Free: 800-275-2782
E-mail Address: *askasta@astahq.com*
Web Address: www.astanet.com
The American Society of Travel Agents (ASTA) is one of the world's largest associations of travel professionals.

Association of Corporate Travel Executives (ACTE)
515 King St., Ste. 440
Alexandria, VA 22314 US
Phone: 703-683-5322
Fax: 703-683-2720
E-mail Address: *info@acte.org*
Web Address: www.acte.org
The Association of Corporate Travel Executives (ACTE) serves the specialized travel interests of corporate purchasers and travel service suppliers from nearly 50 countries.

Association of Retail Travel Agents (ARTA)
c/o Travel Destinations, Inc.
4320 North Miller Rd.
Scottsdale, AZ 85251 US
Fax: 615-985-0600
Toll Free: 800-969-6069
E-mail Address: *info@artaonline.com*
Web Address: www.artaonline.com
The Association of Retail Travel Agents (ARTA) is one of the largest nonprofit associations in North America to exclusively represent travel agents.

Association of Travel Marketing Executives (ATME)
P.O. Box 3176
West Tisbury, MA 02575 US
Phone: 508-693-0550
Fax: 508-693-0115
E-mail Address: *admin@atme.org*
Web Address: www.atme.org
The Association of Travel Marketing Executives (ATME) is a global professional association of senior-level travel marketing executives dedicated

to providing cutting-edge information, education and opportunities for meaningful networking with peers.

National Society of Minorities in Hospitality

107 S. West St.
PMB 119
Alexandria, VA 22314 US
Phone: 703-549-9899
Fax: 703-997-7795
E-mail Address: *hq@nsmh.org*
Web Address: www.nsmh.org
The National Society of Minorities in Hospitality strives to establish a working relationship between the hospitality industry and minority students.

Network of Executive Women in Hospitality, Inc. (NEWH)

P.O. Box 322
Shawano, WI 54166 US
Fax: 800-693-6394
Toll Free: 800-593-6394
Web Address: www.newh.org
The Network of Executive Women in Hospitality, Inc. (NEWH) brings together professionals from all facets of the hospitality industry by providing opportunities for education, professional development and networking. Although primarily a U.S.-based organization, NEWH does have international chapters in Toronto and London.

Society of Incentive and Travel Executives

401 N. Michigan Ave.
Chicago, IL 60611 US
Phone: 312-321-5148
Fax: 312-527-6783
E-mail Address: *Marcie_Valerio@site-intl.org*
Web Address: www.site-intl.org
The Society of Incentive and Travel Executives is a worldwide organization of business professionals dedicated to the recognition and development of motivational and performance improvement strategies in the travel industry.

LXXXII. Travel Industry Associations

Destination Marketing Association International

2025 M St. NW, Ste. 500
Washington, DC 20036 US
Phone: 202-296-7888
Fax: 202-296-7889
Toll Free: 888-275-3140
E-mail Address:
info@destinationmarketing.org
Web Address:
www.destinationmarketing.org
The Destination Marketing Association International, formerly the International Association of Convention & Visitor Bureaus, strives to enhance the professionalism, effectiveness and image of destination management organizations worldwide.

International Association of Conference Centers (IACC)

243 N. Lindbergh Blvd.
St. Louis, MO 63141 US
Phone: 314-993-8575
Fax: 314-993-8919
E-mail Address: *info@iacconline.org*
Web Address: www.iacconline.com
The International Association of Conference Centers (IACC) is a nonprofit, facilities-based organization founded to promote a greater awareness and understanding of the unique features of conference centers around the world.

National Tour Association (NTA)

546 E. Main St.
Lexington, KY 40508 US
Phone: 859-226-4444
Fax: 859-226-4414
Toll Free: 800-682-8886
E-mail Address:
questions@ntastaff.com
Web Address: www.ntaonline.com
The National Tour Association (NTA) is an association for travel professionals who have an interest in the packaged travel sector of the industry.

U.S. Travel Association

1100 New York Ave. NW, Ste. 450
Washington, DC 20005-3934 US
Phone: 202-408-8422
Fax: 202-408-1255
E-mail Address: *feedback@tia.org*
Web Address: www.tia.org
The U.S. Travel Association is the result of a merger between the Travel Industry Association (TIA) and the Travel Business Roundtable. It is a nonprofit association that represents and speaks for the common interests and concerns of all components of the U.S. travel industry.

LXXXIII. U.S. Government Agencies

Bureau of Economic Analysis (BEA)

1441 L St. NW
Washington, DC 20230 US
Phone: 202-606-9900
E-mail Address:
customerservice@bea.gov
Web Address: www.bea.gov
The Bureau of Economic Analysis (BEA), an agency of the U.S. Department of Commerce, is the nation's economic accountant, preparing estimates that illuminate key national, international and regional aspects of the U.S. economy.

Bureau of Labor Statistics (BLS)

2 Massachusetts Ave. NE
Washington, DC 20212-0001 US
Phone: 202-691-5200
Web Address: stats.bls.gov
The Bureau of Labor Statistics (BLS) is the principal fact-finding agency for the Federal Government in the field of labor economics and statistics. It is an independent national statistical agency that collects, processes, analyzes and disseminates statistical data to the American public, U.S. Congress, other federal agencies, state and local governments, business and labor. The BLS also serves as a statistical resource to the Department of Labor.

Equal Employment Opportunity Commission (EEOC)

1801 L St. NW
Washington, DC 20507 US
Phone: 202-663-4900
Toll Free: 800-669-4000
E-mail Address: *info@eeoc.gov*
Web Address: www.eeoc.gov
The Equal Employment Opportunity Commission (EEOC) is a Federal Government agency focused on

practices and programs that foster equal opportunity at work and elsewhere. Its web site features details about various protective laws regarding employment. It also provides information on how to file a discrimination claim.

FedStats
Web Address: www.fedstats.gov
FedStats compiles information for statistics from over 100 U.S. federal agencies. Visitors can sort the information by agency, geography and topic, as well as perform searches.

Government Printing Office (GPO)
732 N. Capitol St. NW
Washington, DC 20401 US
Phone: 202-512-0000
Fax: 202-512-2104
Toll Free: 866.512.1800
E-mail Address:
contactcenter@gpo.gov
Web Address: www.gpo.gov
The U.S. Government Printing Office (GPO) is the primary information source concerning the activities of Federal agencies. GPO gathers, catalogues, produces, provides, authenticates and preserves published information.

National Labor Relations Board (NLRB)
1099 14th St. NW
Washington, DC 20570-0001 US
Phone: 202-208-3000
Fax: 202-208-3013
Toll Free: 866-667-6572
Web Address: www.nlrb.gov
The National Labor Relations Board (NLRB) provides case reports on labor disputes, searchable by company or union.

U.S. Census Bureau
4600 Silver Hill Rd.
Washington, DC 20233-8800 US
Phone: 301-763-4636
Fax: 301-457-3670
Toll Free: 800-923-8282
E-mail Address: *pio@census.gov*
Web Address: www.census.gov
The U.S. Census Bureau is the official collector of data about the people and economy of the U.S. Founded in 1790,

it provides official social, demographic and economic information.

U.S. Department of Commerce (DOC)
1401 Constitution Ave. NW
Washington, DC 20230 US
Phone: 202-482-2000
E-mail Address: *cgutierrez@doc.gov*
Web Address: www.doc.gov
The U.S. Department of Commerce (DOC) regulates trade and provides valuable economic analysis of the economy.

U.S. Department of Labor (DOL)
Frances Perkins Bldg.
200 Constitution Ave. NW
Washington, DC 20210 US
Toll Free: 866-487-2365
Web Address: www.dol.gov
The U.S. Department of Labor (DOL) is the government agency responsible for labor regulations. This site provides tools to help citizens find out whether companies are complying with family and medical-leave requirements.

U.S. Securities and Exchange Commission (SEC)
100 F St. NE
Washington, DC 20549 US
Phone: 202-551-6000
Toll Free: 888-732-6585
E-mail Address: *publicinfo@sec.gov*
Web Address: www.sec.gov
The U.S. Securities and Exchange Commission (SEC) is a nonpartisan, quasi-judicial regulatory agency responsible for administering federal securities laws. These laws are designed to protect investors in securities markets and ensure that they have access to disclosure of all material information concerning publicly traded securities. Visitors to the web site can access the EDGAR database of corporate financial and business information.

LXXXIV. Waste Industry Associations

Air & Waste Management Association
420 Fort Duquesne Blvd.
1 Gateway Ctr., 3rd Fl.
Pittsburgh, PA 15222-1435 US

Phone: 412-232-3444
Fax: 412-232-3450
Toll Free: 800-270-3444
E-mail Address: *info@awma.org*
Web Address: www.awma.org
The Air & Waste Management Association provides training, information and networking opportunities to environmental professionals worldwide.

LXXXV. Water Resources Associations

American Water Resources Association (AWRA)
P.O. Box 1626
Middleburg, VA 20118 US
Phone: 540-687-8390
Fax: 540-687-8395
E-mail Address: *info@awra.org*
Web Address: www.awra.org
The American Water Resources Association (AWRA) represents the interests of professionals involved in water resources.

LXXXVI. Writers, Photographers & Editors Associations

American Society of Journalists and Authors, Inc. (ASJA)
1501 Broadway, Ste. 302
New York, NY 10036 US
Phone: 212-997-0947
Fax: 212-937-2315
E-mail Address: *director@asja.org*
Web Address: www.asja.org
The American Society of Journalists and Authors (ASJA) is of the nation's leading organizations of independent nonfiction writers.

American Society of Magazine Editors (ASME)
Magazine Publishers of America (MPA)
810 7th Ave., 24th Fl.
New York, NY 10019 US
Phone: 212-872-3736
E-mail Address: *asme@magazine.org*
Web Address:
www.magazine.org/asme
The American Society of Magazine Editors (ASME) is a professional organization for editors of print and online magazines. ASME is part of the

Magazine Publishers of America (MPA).

American Society of Newspaper Editors (ASNE)
11690B Sunrise Valley Dr.
Reston, VA 20191-1409 US
Phone: 703-453-1122
Fax: 703-453-1133
E-mail Address: *asne@asne.org*
Web Address: www.asne.org
The American Society of Newspaper Editors (ASNE) is an association that brings together editors of daily newspapers and people directly involved with developing content for daily newspapers.

International Women's Writing Guild (IWWG)
P.O. Box 810
Gracie Station
New York, NY 10028-0082 US
Phone: 212-737-7536
Fax: 212-737-9469
E-mail Address: *dirhahn@iwwg.org*
Web Address: www.iwwg.com
The International Women's Writing Guild (IWWG) is a network for the personal and professional empowerment of women through writing.

Media Communications Association International (MCAI)
2810 Crossroads Dr., Ste. 3800
Madison, WI 53718 US
Phone: 608-443-2464
Fax: 608-443-2474
E-mail Address: *execdirect@mca-i.org*
Web Address: www.mca-i.org
The Media Communications Association International (MCAI) is the leading global community for media communications professionals seeking to drive the convergence of communications and technology for the growth of the profession.

National Association of Hispanic Journalists (NAHJ)
529 14th St. NW
1000 National Press Bldg.
Washington, DC 20045-2001 US
Phone: 202-662-7145
Fax: 202-662-7144
Toll Free: 888-346-6245
E-mail Address: *nahj@nahj.org*

Web Address: www.nahj.org
The National Association of Hispanic Journalists (NAHJ) is dedicated to the recognition and professional advancement of Hispanics in the news industry.

National Association of Science Writers, Inc. (NASW)
P.O. Box 890
Hedgesville, WV 25427 US
Phone: 304-754-5077
Fax: 304-754-5076
E-mail Address: *director@nasw.org*
Web Address: www.nasw.org
The National Association of Science Writers (NASW) exists to foster the dissemination of accurate information regarding science through all media devoted to informing the public.

National Conference of Editorial Writers (NCEW)
3899 N. Front St.
Harrisburg, PA 17110 US
Phone: 717-703-3015
Fax: 717-703-3014
E-mail Address: *ncew@pa-news.org*
Web Address: www.ncew.org
The National Conference of Editorial Writers (NCEW) strives to stimulate the conscience and quality of editorial writing.

National Federation of Press Women (NFPW)
P.O. Box 5556
Arlington, VA 22205 US
Fax: 703-812-4555
Toll Free: 800-780-2715
E-mail Address: *presswomen@aol.com*
Web Address: www.nfpw.org
The National Federation of Press Women (NFPW) is an organization of professional journalists and communicators.

National Writers Union (NWU)
113 University Pl., 6th Fl.
New York, NY 10003 US
Phone: 212-254-0279
Fax: 212-254-0673
E-mail Address: *nwu@nwu.org*
Web Address: www.nwu.org
The National Writers Union (NWU) is a labor union that represents freelance writers in all genres, formats and media. It is committed to improving

the economic and working conditions of freelance writers.

Society of Children's Book Writers and Illustrators (SCBWI)
8271 Beverly Blvd.
Los Angeles, CA 90048 US
Phone: 323-782-1010
Fax: 323-782-1892
E-mail Address: *scbwi@scbwi.org*
Web Address: www.scbwi.org
The Society of Children's Book Writers and Illustrators (SCBWI) serves people who write, illustrate or share a vital interest in children's literature, including publishers, librarians, booksellers and agents.

Chapter 5

THE AMERICAN EMPLOYERS 500:
WHO THEY ARE AND
HOW THEY WERE CHOSEN

Note: financial data given for each of the AMERICAN EMPLOYERS 500 firms is for the year ended December 31, 2008, a fiscal year ended in 2008 or the latest figures available to the editors. Telephone numbers, addresses, contact names, Internet addresses and other vital facts were collected in the summer of 2009.

The companies chosen to be listed in THE ALMANAC OF AMERICAN EMPLOYERS are not the same as the "Fortune 500" or any other list of corporations. The AMERICAN EMPLOYERS 500 were chosen specifically for their likelihood to provide new job openings to the greatest number of employees. Complete information about each firm can be found in the "Individual Data Listings," beginning about the middle of this book. They are in alphabetical order.

THE AMERICAN EMPLOYERS 500 includes companies from all parts of the United States and from nearly all industry segments: selected banks, retailers, service companies, wholesalers and distributors, insurance companies and others, as well as industrial companies, technology firms and manufacturers.

Simply stated, the list contains 500 of the largest, most successful employers in the United States today. In particular, the list contains companies that we have hand-selected to have qualities that we feel will be of greatest interest to job seekers of today who are

looking for opportunities to obtain employment with major corporations.

Job seekers in America will face a tough market in 2010. Many industry sectors are undergoing structural changes that will be long lasting and will reduce their number of job openings. Virtually all business sectors continue to endure challenges due to the global financial crisis. Unemployment will remain high, although it may begin to show improvement before 2010 is over.

For the past several years, in order to make this reference guide as useful as possible, we have altered the company selection criteria that were used in early editions. Rather than focusing largely on mid-term growth histories, we are instead focusing more on type of business, industry sector served and competitive advantage. This is because some sectors may not offer good career prospects today. Consequently, we have deleted some well known companies due to the state of their particular markets.

Fortunately, in the prior 2008 and 2009 editions of this book, we had already eliminated most employers that were deeply involved in residential construction and support activities, because we were predicting a significant correction in the housing market. Likewise, we have long avoided listing America's Big Three automakers in this book, and we have been avoiding most airlines for years. However, JetBlue and Southwest Airlines are included in the 2010 edition. This edition lists only a handful of banking and investment firms. Although we expect 2010 to be a difficult year for retailers and for hotel companies, we do list a select group of employers in these sectors that we feel will tend to have an above-average number of job openings.

However, job seekers should always bear in mind the fact that firms of many types will continue to restrain hiring. In addition, frequent layoffs have become standard in corporate America. (See Chapter 1 "Major Trends Affecting Job Seekers" for further thoughts about layoffs and other trends.)

To be included in our list, the firms were selected based on the following criteria:

1) U.S.-based companies. (However, a small number of companies may be subsidiaries of foreign-based firms. Also, four firms are major U.S. employers that utilize headquarters addresses in other nations.)

2) 2,500 employees or more.

3) These are almost exclusively for-profit companies. However, a small number are major, non-profit health care companies.

4) Selected Type of Business and/or Industry Sector. Companies were chosen based on our analysis of the business potential of their products, services and industrial sectors in light of today's economy.

The companies were chosen in this manner for the following reasons:

500 COMPANIES so there is a broad base among which to make comparisons and from which you can study potential employers.

LARGER EMPLOYERS (2,500 or more employees) so the information can pertain to as many employees as reasonably possible, and so the companies ranked will tend to create large numbers of job openings. Also, large companies historically have offered significantly higher wages, better benefits and better training than small employers.

FOR-PROFIT so that job seekers using THE ALMANAC OF AMERICAN EMPLOYERS can choose positions in the profit-seeking, private sector, where incentive plans are available to motivate and reward them, such as profit sharing, stock ownership, bonuses, stock options and the high pay and prestige of top executive posts.

COMPANIES THAT OPERATE IN PROMISING BUSINESS SECTORS because:

1) Companies that are stable or enjoying growing business are much more likely to have job openings. Corporate stability is more important to job seekers today than ever before due to the wave of layoffs and downsizing that continues to sweep through the U.S. business world. (See Chapter 1, "Major Trends Affecting Job Seekers.")

2) These companies are much more likely to offer advancement opportunities. Current employees will benefit from promote-from-within policies when new plants, new stores, new product lines or new offices are opened.

Obviously, some companies are better to work for than others, depending on what you value. Creating this annual list is an arduous task. Generally, our results are very good, but we do occasionally select a company that soon develops problems or announces a layoff. The world of business constantly goes through major changes, and unforeseen events often occur. Nonetheless, it is not easy for a firm to be selected for the AMERICAN EMPLOYERS 500, and the mere presence of a company on the list can be taken as evidence that it has excelled in many ways. To start with, it has to have generated enough business to employ thousands of people–never a simple task Also, many of these firms are among the dominant companies in their industries.

20 Largest Employers of the American Employers 500, By Number of Employees

Company	City	State	No. of Employees	Primary Line of Business
WAL-MART STORES INC	Bentonville	AR	2,100,000	Discount Department Stores
KELLY SERVICES INC	Troy	MI	650,000	Staffing & Temporary Help
UNITED PARCEL SERVICE INC (UPS)	Atlanta	GA	426,000	Express Delivery Service
MCDONALD'S CORP	Oak Brook	IL	400,000	Fast Food Restaurants
INTERNATIONAL BUSINESS MACHINES CORP (IBM)	Armonk	NY	395,000	Computer Hardware
TARGET CORPORATION	Minneapolis	MN	351,000	Discount Department Stores
YUM! BRANDS INC	Louisville	KY	336,000	Fast Food Restaurants
KROGER CO (THE)	Cincinnati	OH	326,000	Grocery Stores
GENERAL ELECTRIC CO (GE)	Fairfield	CT	323,000	Business Leasing & Finance
HOME DEPOT INC	Atlanta	GA	322,000	Home Centers, Retail
AT&T INC	San Antonio	TX	301,000	Local Telephone Service
WELLS FARGO & CO	San Francisco	CA	281,000	Banking
ARAMARK CORPORATION	Philadelphia	PA	260,000	Food Service Contractor
BERKSHIRE HATHAWAY INC	Omaha	NE	246,000	Direct Property & Casualty Insurance & Reinsurance
BANK OF AMERICA CORP	Charlotte	NC	243,075	Banking
WALGREEN CO	Deerfield	IL	237,000	Drug Stores
LOWE'S COMPANIES INC	Mooresville	NC	229,000	Home Centers, Retail
JP MORGAN CHASE & CO INC	New York	NY	224,961	Banking
VERIZON COMMUNICATIONS	New York	NY	223,900	Local Telephone Service
UNITED TECHNOLOGIES CORPORATION	Hartford	CT	223,100	Aerospace Technology

20 Largest Employers of the American Employers 500, By Revenues

Company	City	State	2008 Sales (in thousands of dollars)	Primary Line of Business
EXXON MOBIL CORPORATION (EXXONMOBIL)	Irving	TX	$459,579,000	Oil & Gas Exploration & Production
WAL-MART STORES INC	Bentonville	AR	$374,526,000	Discount Department Stores
CHEVRON CORPORATION	San Ramon	CA	$273,005,000	Oil & Gas Exploration & Production
CONOCOPHILLIPS COMPANY	Houston	TX	$240,842,000	Oil & Gas Exploration & Production
GENERAL ELECTRIC CO (GE)	Fairfield	CT	$182,515,000	Business Leasing & Finance
AT&T INC	San Antonio	TX	$124,028,000	Local Telephone Service
CARGILL INC	Wayzata	MN	$120,439,000	Crop Production, Milling and Distribution
VALERO ENERGY CORP	San Antonio	TX	$119,114,000	Petroleum Refineries & Retail Marketing
BANK OF AMERICA CORP	Charlotte	NC	$113,106,000	Banking
BERKSHIRE HATHAWAY INC	Omaha	NE	$107,786,000	Direct Property & Casualty Insurance & Reinsurance
INTERNATIONAL BUSINESS MACHINES CORP (IBM)	Armonk	NY	$103,600,000	Computer Hardware
MCKESSON CORPORATION	San Francisco	CA	$101,703,000	Pharmaceutical Distribution
JP MORGAN CHASE & CO INC	New York	NY	$101,491,000	Banking
SHELL OIL CO	Houston	TX	$100,818,000	Oil & Gas Exploration & Production
KOCH INDUSTRIES INC	Wichita	KS	$100,000,000	Petroleum Refining
VERIZON COMMUNICATIONS	New York	NY	$97,354,000	Local Telephone Service
CARDINAL HEALTH INC	Dublin	OH	$90,975,500	Healthcare Products & Services
CVS CAREMARK CORPORATION	Woonsocket	RI	$87,471,900	Drug Stores
PROCTER & GAMBLE CO	Cincinnati	OH	$81,748,000	Household Products Manufacturing
UNITEDHEALTH GROUP INC	Minnetonka	MN	$81,186,000	Medical Insurance

20 Largest Employers of the American Employers 500, By Profits

Company	City	State	2008 Profits (in thousands of dollars)	Primary Line of Business
EXXON MOBIL CORPORATION (EXXONMOBIL)	Irving	TX	$45,220,000	Oil & Gas Exploration & Production
CHEVRON CORPORATION	San Ramon	CA	$23,931,000	Oil & Gas Exploration & Production
MICROSOFT CORP	Redmond	WA	$17,681,000	Computer Software
GENERAL ELECTRIC CO (GE)	Fairfield	CT	$17,410,000	Business Leasing & Finance
JOHNSON & JOHNSON	New Brunswick	NJ	$12,949,000	Personal Health Care & Hygiene Products
AT&T INC	San Antonio	TX	$12,867,000	Local Telephone Service
WAL-MART STORES INC	Bentonville	AR	$12,731,000	Discount Department Stores
INTERNATIONAL BUSINESS MACHINES CORP (IBM)	Armonk	NY	$12,300,000	Computer Hardware
PROCTER & GAMBLE CO	Cincinnati	OH	$12,075,000	Household Products Manufacturing
PFIZER INC	New York	NY	$8,104,000	Pharmaceutical Drugs
CISCO SYSTEMS INC	San Jose	CA	$8,052,000	Computer Networking Equipment
MERCK & CO INC	Whitehouse Station	NJ	$7,808,400	Pharmaceuticals Development & Manufacturing
PEPSICO INC	Purchase	NY	$6,935,000	Soft Drink Manufacturing
OCCIDENTAL PETROLEUM CORP	Los Angeles	CA	$6,857,000	Oil & Natural Gas Exploration & Production
VERIZON COMMUNICATIONS	New York	NY	$6,428,000	Local Telephone Service
T-MOBILE USA	Bellevue	WA	$6,123,000	PCS Cellular Telephone Service
COCA-COLA COMPANY (THE)	Atlanta	GA	$5,807,000	Soft Drink Manufacturing
JP MORGAN CHASE & CO INC	New York	NY	$5,605,000	Banking
ORACLE CORP	Redwood Shores	CA	$5,521,000	Computer Software-Database Management
SCHLUMBERGER LIMITED	Houston	TX	$5,435,000	Oil & Gas Drilling Support Services

INDUSTRY LIST, WITH CODES

This book refers to the following list of unique industry codes, based on the 2007 NAIC code system (NAIC is used by many analysts as a replacement for older SIC codes because NAIC is more specific to today's industry sectors, see www.census.gov/NAICS). Companies profiled in this book are given a primary NAIC code, reflecting the main line of business of each firm.

Agriculture

Agriculture
11511	Agricultural Crop Production Support, Seeds, Fertilizers

Farming
311612	Meat Production
311615	Poultry Production

Apparel

Apparel & Shoe Manufacturing
315	Apparel Manufacturing-General
315211	Apparel Manufacturing-Athletic
316213	Shoe Manufacturing-Men's
316219	Shoe Manufacturing-Athletic Shoes & Misc. Shoes, Incl. Children's

Automotive

Automotive Manufacturing
3363	Automobile Parts Manufacturing

Automotive Distribution
441120	Automobile, Used Car Distribution

Automotive Services
5321	Automobile, Rental/Leasing
8111	Automotive Repair & Maintenance

Energy

Fuel Mining & Extraction
211111	Oil & Natural Gas Exploration & Production
21211	Coal Mining
213111	Petroleum-Drilling Oil & Gas Wells Support
213112	Oil Field Services

Utilities
221	Utilities-Electric & Gas
2211	Utilities-Electric

Petroleum-Refining & Manufacturing
324110	Petroleum Refineries
325110	Petrochemicals Manufacturing
325120	Industrial Gas Manufacturing

Manufacturing, Electrical
33591	Battery Manufacturing

Entertainment

Toys, Sporting Goods & Miscellaneous Manufacturing
339932	Toys, Manufacturing

Publishing
511140	Databases & Directories, Publishing

Broadcasting
515120	Television Broadcasting
515210	Cable TV Networks
517110	Cable & Satellite TV & Data Service

Gambling & Recreation
329999	Gambling Equipment
713940	Fitness Centers/Health Clubs

Hotels & Accommodations
721110	Hotels/Resorts/Motels
721120	Casino Resorts

Financial Services

Banking, Credit & Finance
522110	Commercial Banking
522210	Banking, Credit Cards
52222	Financing--Automobiles
522298	Pawn Shops
522320	Payment & Transaction Processing Services
522320A	Payment & Transaction Processing--Benefits Management

Stocks & Investments
523110	Investment Banking
523920	Investment Management/Mutual Funds/Pension Funds

Insurance
524113	Insurance-Life
524114	Insurance-Health, HMO's & PPO's
524126	Insurance--Property & Casualty, Specialty, Surety
524210	Insurance Brokerage, Agencies & Exchanges

Professional Services, Financial
5412	Accounting Services

Credit Bureaus
561450	Credit Bureaus

Food & Restaurants

Food Service
722110	Restaurants
722310	Food Service Contractors

Health Care

Health Products, Manufacturing
325412	Drugs (Pharmaceuticals), Discovery & Manufacturing
325413	Diagnostic Services and Substances Manufacturing

33911	Medical/Dental/Surgical Equipment & Supplies, Manufacturing

Health Products, Wholesale Distribution

423450	Medical/Dental/Surgical Equipment & Supplies, Distribution
424210	Drugs (Pharmaceuticals), Distribution

Health Care-Clinics, Labs and Organizations

524298	Disease Management & Utilization Management
6214	Clinics--Outpatient Clinics & Surgery
6215	Laboratories & Diagnostic Services--Medical
6216	Home Health Care

Hospitals

622110	Hospitals/Clinics--General & Specialty Hospitals
622210	Hospitals/Clinics--Psychiatric Clinics

Nursing

623110	Long-Term Health Care & Assisted Living

Veterinary Care

541940	Veterinary Clinics

InfoTech

Computers & Electronics Manufacturing

33411	Computer Networking & Related Equipment, Manufacturing
334111	Computer Hardware, Manufacturing
334112	Computer Storage Equipment & Misc Parts, Manufacturing
334119	Computer Accessories, Monitors, Printers Manufacturing
33441	Semiconductors (Microchips)/Integrated Circuits/Components, Manufacturing
334419	Contract Electronics Manufacturing
3345	Instrument Manufacturing, including Measurement, Control, Test & Navigational

Electrical Equipment & Wire, Manufacturing

335921	Fiber Optic Cable & Electrical Wire

Computers & Electronics, Distribution

423430	Computer & Telecommunications Equipment Distribution

Software

511210	Computer Software, Publisher
511210E	Computer Software, Security & Anti-Virus
511210F	Computer Software, Multimedia, Graphics & Publishing
511210G	Computer Software, Games & Entertainment
511210H	Computer Software, Business Management & ERP
511210I	Computer Software, Operating Systems, Languages & Development Tools
511210K	Computer Software, Sales & Customer Relationship Management
511210N	Computer Software, Product Lifecycle, Engineering, Design & CAD

Information & Data Processing Services

518210	Data Processing Services

Information Services-Professional

541512	Consulting--Computer, Telecommunications & Internet
541513	Computer Programming & Software Design

Internet

519130	Internet Publishing & Web Search Portals

Manufacturing

Food Products Manufacturing

311	Food Products, Manufacturing
3112	Grain Distribution, Milling & Oilseed Processing
311230	Breakfast Cereal Manufacturing
311320	Chocolate & Confectionery Manufacturing
31142	Fruit & Vegetable Growing & Processing
3115	Dairy Products, Manufacturing
3118	Bakeries & Tortilla Manufacturing

Beverage & Tobacco Manufacturing

3121	Beverages--Soft Drinks & Juices Manufacturing
312140	Beverages--Distilleries
3122	Tobacco Products, Manufacturing

Paper Products/Forest Products

322	Forest Products/Paper, Manufacturing
3222	Packaging, Manufacturing

Printing Services

323	Printing

Chemicals

325	Chemicals, Manufacturing
325510	Paints & Coatings, Manufacturing
3256	Soaps, Cleaners, Cosmetics & Toiletries, Manufacturing
325611	Soap & Cleaning Compound Manufacturing

Fabricated Metals

336510	Railroad Car Manufacturing

Machinery & Manufacturing Equipment

333	Machinery, Manufacturing
33313	Machinery-Mining & Oil & Gas Field, Manufacturing
333313	Business Machines, Manufacturing
33351	Machine Tools, Manufacturing

Electrical Equipment, Appliances, Tools

335	Electrical Equipment, Manufacturing

Jewelry, Watch & Other Manufacturing

334518	Watch & Clock Manufacturing

Real Estate

Real Estate

531120	Real Estate Investment Trusts - Nonresidential

Retailing

Automobiles & Parts Stores
441110	Auto Dealers, Retail
441310	Auto Parts Stores
441320	Tire Stores

Furniture & Home Furnishings Stores
442299	Linens/Housewares/Art/Framing Stores

Computers & Electronics Stores
44311	Electronics, Audio & Appliance Stores

Building Materials & Garden Supplies Stores
444110	Home Centers, Retail
444120	Paint & Wallpaper Stores

Food & Beverage Stores
445110	Grocery Stores/Supermarkets
445120	Convenience Stores

Drug Stores, Beauty Supply & Health Items Stores
446110	Pharmacies & Drug Stores

Apparel & Accessories Stores
448	Apparel Stores, General
448110	Apparel Stores, Men's
448120	Apparel Stores, Women's
448210	Shoes & Accessories Stores
448310	Jewelry Stores

Sporting Goods, Hobbies, Books & Music Stores
451110	Sporting Goods Stores
451120	Toys/Hobbies/Games/Crafts Stores
451211	Book Stores
451211E	Book Stores-Online
451220	Music Stores
451220E	Music Stores-Online

Department & Discount Stores
452111	Department Stores
452112	Discount Stores

Miscellaneous Retailers
453210	Office Supplies Stores
453910	Pets/Pet Supplies Stores
454112	Auctions, Retail-Online

Nonstore Retailers
454113	Mail Order and Non-Store Selling, Incl. TV Shopping

Rental & Leasing Outlets
5322	Rental Stores, Consumer Goods

Personal Services & Salons
446199	Other Health & Personal Care Stores/Weight Management
81211	Hair, Nail & Skin Care Salons

Services

Construction
237	Construction, Heavy & Civil Engineering
237130	Construction, Power & Communication Line

Real Estate
5311	Real Estate Operations & Development--General

Consulting & Professional Services
541330	Engineering Services
54161	Consulting--Management & Business
541612	Consulting-Human Resources
541613	Consulting--Marketing
541712	Research & Development-Physical, Engineering & Life Sciences
5418	Marketing Agencies & Related Services
541810	Advertising Services/Agencies
541910	Market Research

Management
55111	Management of Companies & Enterprises

Personnel, Administrative & Support Services
561	Staffing or Outsourcing
561320	Temporary Help/Staffing
812331	Linen/Uniform Supply

Call Centers
56142	Call Centers and Support Services Outsourcing

Travel Agencies
5615E	Travel Services-Online

Waste Management
562	Waste Disposal, Waste Management

Educational
611410	Business Training, Distance Learning

Security Services
5616	Security, Protection, Armored Car & Investigation Services

Telecommunications

Telecommunications Equipment
3342	Communications Equipment, Manufacturing
334210	Telecommunications Equipment Manufacturing

Telecommunications
5172	Telecommunications Service Cellular, U.S. & Non-U.S.

Transportation

Aerospace
33641	Aerospace & Aircraft Related Manufacturing

Air
481111	Air Transportation

Ships
483111	Shipping-Deep Sea
483112	Cruise Lines

Truck
4885	Freight Forwarding & Support Services
4921	Courier/Express Delivery Service

Wholesale Distribution-Other

Distribution-Durable Goods
4238 Machinery, Equipment & Supplies,
Distribution
Distribution-Nondurable Goods
4244 Food Distribution
486 Petroleum Products (except Bulk
Stations/Terminals) Distribution & Pipelines

INDEX OF RANKINGS WITHIN INDUSTRY GROUPS

Company	Industry Code	2008 Sales (U.S. $ thousands)	Sales Rank	2008 Profits (U.S. $ thousands)	Profits Rank
Accounting Services					
BDO SEIDMAN LLP	5412	659,000	6		
DELOITTE & TOUCHE USA LLP	5412	10,980,000	3		
ERNST & YOUNG LLP	5412	24,500,000	2		
GRANT THORNTON LLP	5412	1,220,000	5		
KPMG LLP	5412	7,000,000	4		
PRICEWATERHOUSECOOPERS	5412	28,185,000	1		
Advertising Services/Agencies					
OMNICOM GROUP INC	541810	13,359,900	1	1,000,300	1
Aerospace & Aircraft Related Manufacturing					
BOEING COMPANY	33641	60,909,000	1	2,672,000	4
CUBIC CORP	33641	881,135	9	36,854	8
GENERAL DYNAMICS CORP	33641	29,300,000	6	2,459,000	5
HONEYWELL INTERNATIONAL	33641	36,556,000	4	2,792,000	3
LOCKHEED MARTIN CORP	33641	42,731,000	3	3,217,000	2
NORTHROP GRUMMAN CORP	33641	33,887,000	5	-1,281,000	9
RAYTHEON CO	33641	23,174,000	7	1,672,000	6
TELEDYNE TECHNOLOGIES INC	33641	1,893,000	8	111,300	7
UNITED TECHNOLOGIES CORP	33641	58,681,000	2	4,689,000	1
Agricultural Crop Production Support, Seeds, Fertilizers					
MONSANTO CO	11511	11,365,000	1	2,024,000	1
SCOTTS MIRACLE GROW CO	11511	2,981,800	2	-10,900	2
Air Transportation					
JETBLUE AIRWAYS CORP	481111	3,388,000	2	-76,000	2
SOUTHWEST AIRLINES CO	481111	11,023,000	1	178,000	1
Apparel Manufacturing & Design-General					
POLO RALPH LAUREN CORP	315	4,880,100	1	419,800	1
Apparel Manufacturing-Athletic					
QUIKSILVER INC	315211	2,264,636	1	-226,265	1
Apparel Stores, General					
BUCKLE INC	448	619,888	4	75,247	4
GUESS? INC	448	1,749,916	3	186,472	3
ROSS STORES INC	448	5,975,212	2	261,051	2
TJX COMPANIES INC	448	18,336,726	1	771,750	1
Apparel Stores, Men's					
MEN'S WEARHOUSE INC	448110	2,112,558	1	147,041	1
Apparel Stores, Women's					
ANNTAYLOR STORES CORP	448120	2,396,510	4	97,235	2
BEBE STORES INC	448120	687,622	8	63,080	5
CHARLOTTE RUSSE HOLDING	448120	823,252	7	18,166	6
CHARMING SHOPPES INC	448120	2,722,462	3	-83,413	8
CHICO'S FAS INC	448120	1,714,326	5	88,875	3
CHRISTOPHER & BANKS CORP	448120	560,912	9	17,018	7
DRESS BARN INC	448120	1,444,165	6	74,088	4
LIMITED BRANDS INC	448120	10,134,000	1	718,000	1

Company	Industry Code	2008 Sales (U.S. $ thousands)	Sales Rank	2008 Profits (U.S. $ thousands)	Profits Rank
VICTORIAS SECRET	448120	5,601,046	2		
Auctions, Retail-Online					
EBAY INC	454112	8,541,261	1	1,779,474	1
Auto Dealers, Retail					
CARMAX GROUP	441110	8,199,571	1	182,025	1
Auto Parts Stores					
ADVANCE AUTO PARTS INC	441310	5,142,255	2	238,038	2
AUTOZONE INC	441310	6,522,706	1	641,606	1
O'REILLY AUTOMOTIVE INC	441310	3,576,553	3	186,232	3
Automobile Parts Manufacturing					
CUMMINS INC	3363	14,342,000	3	755,000	3
EATON CORP	3363	15,376,000	2	1,058,000	1
JOHNSON CONTROLS INC	3363	38,062,000	1	979,000	2
LKQ CORP	3363	1,937,301	4	99,899	4
Automobile, Rental/Leasing					
AVIS BUDGET GROUP INC	5321	5,984,000	3	-1,124,000	2
DOLLAR THRIFTY AUTOMOTIVE GROUP INC	5321	1,697,993	4	340,422	1
ENTERPRISE RENT-A-CAR	5321	10,100,000	1		
HERTZ GLOBAL HOLDINGS INC	5321	8,525,100	2	-1,206,700	3
Automobile, Used Car Distribution					
ADESA INC	441120	1,123,400	1		
Automotive Repair & Maintenance					
MONRO MUFFLER BRAKE INC	8111	439,389	1	21,921	1
Bakeries & Tortilla Manufacturing					
SARA LEE CORP	3118	13,212,000	1	-79,000	1
Banking, Credit Cards					
VISA INC	522210	6,263,000	1	804,000	1
Battery Manufacturing					
AMERICAN POWER CONVERSION (APC)	33591				
Beverages--Distilleries					
FORTUNE BRANDS INC	312140	7,608,900	1	317,100	1
Beverages--Soft Drinks, Bottled Water & Juices Manufacturing					
COCA-COLA COMPANY	3121	31,944,000	2	5,807,000	2
COCA-COLA ENTERPRISES INC	3121	21,807,000	3	-4,394,000	4
PEPSI BOTTLING GROUP INC	3121	13,796,000	4	162,000	3
PEPSICO INC	3121	43,251,000	1	6,935,000	1
Book Stores					
BARNES & NOBLE INC	451211	5,410,828	1	135,799	1
Book Stores-Online					
AMAZON.COM INC	451211E	19,166,000	1	645,000	1
Breakfast Cereal Manufacturing					
GENERAL MILLS INC	311230	13,652,100	1	1,294,700	2
KELLOGG CO	311230	12,822,000	2	1,953,000	1
Business Machines, Manufacturing					
PITNEY BOWES INC	333313	6,262,305	2	419,793	1
XEROX CORP	333313	17,608,000	1	230,000	2

Company	Industry Code	2008 Sales (U.S. $ thousands)	Sales Rank	2008 Profits (U.S. $ thousands)	Profits Rank
Business Training, Distance Learning					
APOLLO GROUP INC	611410	3,140,931	1	476,525	1
DEVRY INC	611410	1,091,833	2	125,532	2
Cable TV Networks					
VIACOM INC	515210	14,625,000	2	1,251,000	2
WALT DISNEY COMPANY	515210	37,843,000	1	4,427,000	1
Call Centers and Support Services Outsourcing					
SYKES ENTERPRISES INC	56142	819,190	3	60,561	2
TELETECH HOLDINGS INC	56142	1,400,147	2	73,747	1
WEST CORPORATION	56142	2,247,434	1	19,507	3
Casino Resorts					
HARRAH'S ENTERTAINMENT INC	721120	10,127,000	1	-5,197,200	4
LAS VEGAS SANDS CORP (THE VENETIAN)	721120	4,735,126	3	-163,558	2
MGM MIRAGE	721120	7,208,767	2	-855,286	3
WYNN RESORTS LIMITED	721120	2,987,324	4	210,206	1
Chemicals, Manufacturing					
E I DU PONT DE NEMOURS & CO (DUPONT)	325	30,529,000	1	2,007,000	1
GEORGIA GULF CORPORATION	325	2,916,477	2	-257,643	4
SENSIENT TECHNOLOGIES	325	1,252,620	4	90,861	3
SIGMA-ALDRICH CORP	325	2,200,700	3	341,500	2
Chocolate & Confectionery Manufacturing					
MARS INC	311320	22,000,000	1		
Clinics--Outpatient Clinics & Surgery					
DAVITA INC	6214	5,660,173	1	374,160	1
UNIVERSAL HEALTH SERVICES	6214	5,022,417	2	192,941	2
Coal Mining					
CONSOL ENERGY INC	21211	4,652,445	2	442,470	2
MASSEY ENERGY COMPANY	21211	2,989,789	3	56,248	3
PEABODY ENERGY CORP	21211	6,593,400	1	953,500	1
Commercial Banking					
BANK OF AMERICA CORP	522110	113,106,000	1	4,008,000	2
JP MORGAN CHASE & CO INC	522110	101,491,000	2	5,605,000	1
WELLS FARGO & CO	522110	51,652,000	3	2,655,000	3
Communications Equipment, Manufacturing					
HARRIS CORPORATION	3342	4,596,100	2	444,200	2
L-3 COMMUNICATIONS HOLDINGS INC	3342	14,901,000	1	949,000	1
Computer & Telecommunications Equipment Distribution					
ARROW ELECTRONICS INC	423430	16,761,009	4	-613,739	4
AVNET INC	423430	17,952,700	3	499,100	1
CDW CORPORATION	423430	8,071,000	5		
INGRAM MICRO INC	423430	34,362,152	1	-394,921	3
TECH DATA CORP	423430	23,423,078	2	108,269	2
Computer Accessories, Monitors, Printers Manufacturing					
LEXMARK INTERNATIONAL INC	334119	4,528,400	1	240,200	1

Company	Industry Code	2008 Sales (U.S. $ thousands)	Sales Rank	2008 Profits (U.S. $ thousands)	Profits Rank
Computer Hardware, Manufacturing					
APPLE INC	334111	32,479,000	1	4,834,000	1
DIEBOLD INC	334111	3,170,080	2	88,583	2
Computer Networking & Related Equipment, Manufacturing					
CISCO SYSTEMS INC	33411	39,540,000	1	8,052,000	1
JUNIPER NETWORKS INC	33411	3,572,376	2	511,749	2
Computer Programming & Software Design					
ACCENTURE LTD	541513	25,313,826	3	1,691,751	2
AFFILIATED COMPUTER SERVICES INC	541513	6,160,550	5	329,010	5
CIBER INC	541513	1,191,567	10	29,956	11
COGNIZANT TECHNOLOGY SOLUTIONS CORP	541513	2,816,304	6	430,845	3
IBM GLOBAL SERVICES	541513	58,892,000	2		
IGATE CORPORATION	541513	218,798	13	30,904	10
INTERNATIONAL BUSINESS MACHINES CORP (IBM)	541513	103,600,000	1	12,300,000	1
KEANE INC	541513	1,200,000	9		
PEROT SYSTEMS CORP	541513	2,779,000	7	117,000	6
SAIC INC	541513	8,926,000	4	416,000	4
SAPIENT CORPORATION	541513	687,488	11	62,476	9
SRA INTERNATIONAL INC	541513	1,506,933	8	73,264	8
SYNTEL INC	541513	410,426	12	86,681	7
Computer Software Publisher					
INTUIT INC	511210	3,070,974	2	476,762	1
SUNGARD DATA SYSTEMS INC	511210	5,596,000	1	470,000	2
Computer Software, Business Management & ERP					
ORACLE CORP	511210H	22,430,000	1	5,521,000	1
SAS INSTITUTE INC	511210H	2,260,000	2		
Computer Software, Electronic Games & Entertainment					
ACTIVISION BLIZZARD INC	511210G	3,026,000	2	-233,000	1
ELECTRONIC ARTS INC	511210G	3,665,000	1	-454,000	2
Computer Software, Multimedia, Graphics & Publishing					
ADOBE SYSTEMS INC	511210F	3,579,889	1	871,814	1
Computer Software, Operating Systems, Languages & Development Tools					
MICROSOFT CORP	511210I	60,420,000	1	17,681,000	1
Computer Software, Product Lifecycle, Engineering, Design & CAD					
PARAMETRIC TECHNOLOGY	511210N	1,070,330	2	79,702	2
SYNOPSYS INC	511210N	1,336,951	1	189,978	1
Computer Software, Sales & Customer Relationship Management					
ACXIOM CORP	511210K	1,384,079	1	-7,780	1
Computer Software, Security & Anti-Virus					
MCAFEE INC	511210E	1,600,065	2	172,209	2
SYMANTEC CORP	511210E	5,874,419	1	463,850	1
VERISIGN INC	511210E	961,735	3	-374,692	3
Computer Storage Equipment & Misc. Parts, Manufacturing					
EMC CORP	334112	14,880,000	1	2,160,000	1
NETAPP INC	334112	3,303,167	3	309,738	3

Company	Industry Code	2008 Sales (U.S. $ thousands)	Sales Rank	2008 Profits (U.S. $ thousands)	Profits Rank
WESTERN DIGITAL CORP	334112	8,074,000	2	867,000	2
Construction, Heavy & Civil Engineering					
AECOM TECHNOLOGY CORP	237	5,194,482	6	147,226	4
BECHTEL GROUP INC	237	31,400,000	1		
FLUOR CORP	237	22,325,900	2	720,500	1
FOSTER WHEELER AG	237	6,854,290	5	526,620	2
JACOBS ENGINEERING GROUP	237	11,252,159	3	420,742	3
PARSONS BRINCKERHOFF INC	237	2,343,117	7	73,882	6
SHAW GROUP INC	237	6,998,011	4	140,717	5
Construction, Power & Communication Line					
DYCOM INDUSTRIES INC	237130	1,229,956	2	21,678	2
QUANTA SERVICES INC	237130	3,780,213	1	176,790	1
Consulting--Computer, Telecommunications & Internet					
CACI INTERNATIONAL INC	541512	2,420,537	1	83,323	1
Consulting-Human Resources					
HEWITT ASSOCIATES	541612	3,227,648	2	188,142	1
MERCER INC	541612	3,642,000	1		
TOWERS PERRIN	541612	2,500,000	3		
WATSON WYATT WORLDWIDE	541612	1,760,055	4	155,441	2
Consulting--Management & Business					
BOOZ ALLEN HAMILTON	54161	3,680,000	3		
DELOITTE CONSULTING LLP	54161	6,300,000	1		
FTI CONSULTING INC	54161	1,293,145	4	125,435	1
MCKINSEY & COMPANY INC	54161	4,800,000	2		
Consulting--Marketing					
INVENTIV HEALTH INC	541613	1,119,812	1	-128,021	1
Convenience Stores					
7-ELEVEN INC.	445120				
PANTRY INC	445120	8,995,626	1	31,783	1
Cosmetics Manufacturing					
AVON PRODUCTS INC	325620	10,690,100	1	875,300	1
ESTEE LAUDER COMPANIES	325620	7,910,800	2	473,800	2
MARY KAY INC	325620	2,600,000	3		
Courier/Express Delivery Service					
FEDEX CORPORATION	4921	37,953,000	2	2,075,000	2
UNITED PARCEL SERVICE INC (UPS)	4921	51,486,000	1	3,003,000	1
Credit Bureaus					
EXPERIAN AMERICAS	561450	2,000,000	1		
FIRST ADVANTAGE CORP	561450	727,276	2	34,857	1
Cruise Lines					
CARNIVAL CORPORATION	483112	14,646,000	1	2,330,000	1
ROYAL CARIBBEAN CRUISES	483112	6,532,525	2	573,722	2
Dairy Products, Manufacturing					
DEAN FOODS CO	3115	12,454,613	1	183,770	1
Data Processing, Hosting & Related Services					
AUTOMATIC DATA PROCESSING	518210	8,776,500	1	1,161,700	1
PAYCHEX INC	518210	2,066,323	2	576,145	2

Company	Industry Code	2008 Sales (U.S. $ thousands)	Sales Rank	2008 Profits (U.S. $ thousands)	Profits Rank
Databases & Directories, Publishing					
INFOGROUP INC	511140	738,270	1	4,360	1
Department Stores					
J C PENNEY COMPANY INC	452111	19,860,000	2	1,111,000	1
MACY'S INC	452111	26,313,000	1	893,000	2
Diagnostic Services & Substances Manufacturing					
IDEXX LABORATORIES INC	325413	1,024,030	1	116,169	1
Discount Stores					
BJ'S WHOLESALE CLUB INC	452112	8,791,618	7	122,861	7
COSTCO WHOLESALE CORP	452112	70,977,484	2	1,282,725	4
DOLLAR GENERAL CORP	452112	9,495,300	6	-12,800	10
FAMILY DOLLAR STORES INC	452112	6,983,628	8	233,073	6
FRED'S INC	452112	1,780,923	9	10,718	9
KOHL'S CORP	452112	16,473,734	5	1,083,851	5
PRICESMART INC	452112	1,119,876	10	38,106	8
SAM'S CLUB	452112	44,357,000	4	1,618,000	3
TARGET CORPORATION	452112	63,367,000	3	2,849,000	2
WAL-MART STORES INC	452112	374,526,000	1	12,731,000	1
Disease Management & Utilization Management					
HEALTHWAYS INC	524298	736,243	1	54,815	1
Drugs (Pharmaceuticals), Discovery & Manufacturing					
ABBOTT LABORATORIES	325412	29,527,600	3	4,880,700	4
ALLERGAN INC	325412	4,339,700	12	578,600	11
AMGEN INC	325412	15,003,000	8	4,196,000	6
CELGENE CORP	325412	2,254,781	15	-1,533,653	17
CEPHALON INC	325412	1,974,554	16	222,548	13
ELI LILLY & COMPANY	325412	20,378,000	6	-2,071,900	18
FOREST LABORATORIES INC	325412	3,501,802	13	967,933	10
GENENTECH INC	325412	13,418,000	9	3,427,000	7
GILEAD SCIENCES INC	325412	5,335,750	10	2,011,154	8
JOHNSON & JOHNSON	325412	63,747,000	1	12,949,000	1
KENDLE INTERNATIONAL INC	325412	678,581	18	29,397	15
MERCK & CO INC	325412	23,850,300	4	7,808,400	3
MYLAN INC	325412	5,137,585	11	-181,215	16
PERRIGO CO	325412	1,729,921	17	135,773	14
PFIZER INC	325412	48,296,000	2	8,104,000	2
SCHERING-PLOUGH CORP	325412	18,502,000	7	1,903,000	9
WATSON PHARMACEUTICALS	325412	2,535,501	14	238,379	12
WYETH	325412	22,833,908	5	4,417,833	5
Drugs (Pharmaceuticals), Distribution					
AMERISOURCEBERGEN CORP	424210	70,189,733	3	250,559	3
CARDINAL HEALTH INC	424210	90,975,500	2	1,300,600	1
MCKESSON CORPORATION	424210	101,703,000	1	990,000	2
Electrical Equipment, Manufacturing					
BLACK & DECKER CORP	335	6,086,100	2	293,600	2
DANAHER CORP	335	12,697,456	1	1,317,631	1
Electronic Component Manufacturing/Contract Manufacturing					
BENCHMARK ELECTRONICS	334419	2,590,167	2	-135,632	4

Company	Industry Code	2008 Sales (U.S. $ thousands)	Sales Rank	2008 Profits (U.S. $ thousands)	Profits Rank
CTS CORP	334419	691,707	4	29,886	3
JABIL CIRCUIT INC	334419	12,779,703	1	133,892	1
PLEXUS CORP	334419	1,841,622	3	84,144	2
Electronics, Audio & Appliance Stores					
BEST BUY CO INC	44311	40,023,000	1	1,407,000	1
Engineering Services					
CH2M HILL COMPANIES LTD	541330	5,589,900	3	32,100	3
MCDERMOTT INTERNATIONAL	541330	6,572,423	2	429,302	1
URS CORPORATION	541330	10,086,289	1	219,791	2
Fiber Optic Cable & Electrical Wire					
GENERAL CABLE CORP	335921	6,230,100	1	217,200	1
Financing--Automobiles					
GENERAL ELECTRIC CO (GE)	52222	182,515,000	1	17,410,000	1
Fitness Centers/Health Clubs					
HEALTH FITNESS CORP	713940	77,676	1	2,722	1
Food Distribution					
CHS INC	4244	32,167,461	2	803,045	2
SYSCO CORP	4244	37,522,111	1	1,106,151	1
UNITED NATURAL FOODS INC	4244	3,365,857	3	48,479	3
Food Products, Manufacturing					
CONAGRA FOODS INC	311	11,563,500	2	930,600	2
JM SMUCKER CO	311	2,524,774	4	170,379	3
KRAFT FOODS INC	311	42,201,000	1	2,901,000	1
RALCORP HOLDINGS INC	311	2,824,400	3	167,800	4
TREEHOUSE FOODS INC	311	1,500,650	5	28,224	5
Food Service Contractors					
ARAMARK CORPORATION	722310	13,470,200	1	39,500	1
Forest Products/Paper, Manufacturing					
KIMBERLY-CLARK CORP	322	19,415,000	1	1,690,000	1
Freight Forwarding & Support Services					
CH ROBINSON WORLDWIDE	4885	8,578,614	1	359,177	1
Fruit & Vegetable Growing & Processing					
DOLE FOOD COMPANY INC	31142	7,620,000	1	409,000	1
Gambling Equipment					
SCIENTIFIC GAMES CORP	329999	1,118,829	1	8,488	1
Golf Courses & Country Clubs					
CLUBCORP INC	713910	1,000,000	1		
Grain Distribution, Milling & Oilseed Processing					
ARCHER DANIELS MIDLAND CO	3112	69,816,000	2	1,802,000	2
BUNGE LTD	3112	52,574,000	3	1,064,000	3
CARGILL INC	3112	120,439,000	1	3,951,000	1
Grocery Stores/Supermarkets					
HE BUTT GROCERY CO (HEB)	445110	15,000,000	5		
KROGER CO	445110	70,235,000	1	1,181,000	1
MEIJER INC	445110	13,700,000	6		
PUBLIX SUPER MARKETS INC	445110	23,929,064	4	1,089,770	2
SAFEWAY INC	445110	44,104,000	2	965,300	3

Company	Industry Code	2008 Sales (U.S. $ thousands)	Sales Rank	2008 Profits (U.S. $ thousands)	Profits Rank
SUPERVALU INC	445110	44,048,000	3	593,000	4
WHOLE FOODS MARKET INC	445110	7,953,912	7	114,524	5
Hair, Nail & Skin Care Salons					
REGIS CORPORATION	81211	2,481,391	1	85,204	1
Home Centers, Retail					
HOME DEPOT INC	444110	77,349,000	1	4,395,000	1
LOWE'S COMPANIES INC	444110	48,283,000	2	2,809,000	2
Home Health Care					
AMEDISYS INC	6216	1,187,415	2	86,682	2
CHEMED CORPORATION	6216	1,148,941	3	71,017	3
LINCARE HOLDINGS INC	6216	1,664,580	1	237,205	1
METHODIST HEALTH CARE SYSTEM	6216				
ODYSSEY HEALTHCARE INC	6216	616,050	4	14,426	4
Hospitals/Clinics--General & Specialty Hospitals					
ASCENSION HEALTH	622110	13,489,000	3	351,000	2
CATHOLIC HEALTH INITIATIVES	622110	8,244,600	5	123,058	5
COMMUNITY HEALTH SYSTEMS	622110	10,840,098	4	218,304	4
HCA INC	622110	28,374,000	2	673,000	1
HEALTH MANAGEMENT ASSOCIATES INC	622110	4,451,611	7	223,302	3
KAISER PERMANENTE	622110	40,300,000	1		
MAYO FOUNDATION FOR MEDICAL EDUCATION AND RESEARCH	622110	7,221,800	6	0	
SELECT MEDICAL	622110	2,153,362	9	43,373	7
SISTERS OF MERCY HEALTH SYSTEMS	622110	3,747,805	8	54,900	6
Hospitals/Clinics--Psychiatric Clinics					
PSYCHIATRIC SOLUTIONS INC	622210	1,765,977	1	104,953	1
RES CARE INC	622210	1,543,583	2	36,560	2
Hotels/Resorts/Motels					
GLOBAL HYATT CORPORATION	721110	3,900,000	5		
HILTON HOTELS CORP	721110	8,250,000	2		
LODGIAN INC	721110	240,428	6	-11,984	3
MARRIOTT INTERNATIONAL INC	721110	12,879,000	1	359,000	1
RITZ-CARLTON HOTEL COMPANY LLC	721110				
STARWOOD HOTELS & RESORTS WORLDWIDE INC	721110	5,907,000	3	329,000	2
WYNDHAM WORLDWIDE	721110	4,281,000	4	-1,074,000	4
Industrial Gas Manufacturing					
AIR PRODUCTS & CHEMICALS	325120	10,415,000	2	910,000	2
PRAXAIR INC	325120	10,796,000	1	1,211,000	1
Instrument Manufacturing, including Measurement, Control, Test & Navigational					
AGILENT TECHNOLOGIES INC	3345	5,774,000	2	693,000	2
EMERSON ELECTRIC CO	3345	24,807,000	1	2,412,000	1
MILLIPORE CORP	3345	1,602,138	3	145,801	3
TEKTRONIX INC	3345				

Company	Industry Code	2008 Sales (U.S. $ thousands)	Sales Rank	2008 Profits (U.S. $ thousands)	Profits Rank
Insurance Brokerages, Agencies & Exchanges					
ARTHUR J GALLAGHER & CO	524210	1,645,000	2	77,300	2
BROWN & BROWN INC	524210	977,554	3	166,124	1
MARSH & MCLENNAN COMPANIES INC	524210	11,587,000	1	-73,000	3
Insurance--Health, HMO's & PPO's					
AETNA INC	524114	30,950,700	3	1,384,100	3
AFLAC INC	524114	16,554,000	6	1,254,000	4
CIGNA CORP	524114	19,101,000	5	292,000	8
COVENTRY HEALTH CARE INC	524114	11,913,646	9	381,895	7
HEALTH CARE SERVICE CORP	524114	16,024,600	7	742,600	5
HEALTH NET INC	524114	15,366,589	8	95,003	9
HUMANA INC	524114	28,946,372	4	647,154	6
UNITEDHEALTH GROUP INC	524114	81,186,000	1	2,977,000	1
WELLPOINT INC	524114	61,251,000	2	2,491,000	2
Insurance--Life					
AXA FINANCIAL INC	524113				
GENWORTH FINANCIAL INC	524113	9,948,000	3	-572,000	4
HARTFORD FINANCIAL SERVICES GROUP INC	524113	9,219,000	6	-2,749,000	6
LINCOLN NATIONAL CORP	524113	9,883,000	5	57,000	3
METLIFE INC	524113	55,085,000	1	3,209,000	1
PRINCIPAL FINANCIAL GROUP	524113	9,935,900	4	458,100	2
PRUDENTIAL FINANCIAL INC	524113	29,275,000	2	-1,073,000	5
Insurance--Property & Casualty, Specialty, Surety					
ALLSTATE CORPORATION	524126	29,394,000	1	-1,679,000	8
CHUBB CORPORATION	524126	13,221,000	5	1,804,000	3
LIBERTY MUTUAL GROUP INC	524126	28,855,000	2	1,140,000	4
LOEWS CORPORATION	524126	14,543,000	4	4,530,000	1
PROGRESSIVE CORPORATION	524126	12,840,100	7	-70,000	7
SAFECO INSURANCE COMPANY OF AMERICA	524126				
TRAVELERS COMPANIES INC	524126	24,477,000	3	2,924,000	2
USAA	524126	12,912,000	6	423,000	5
W R BERKLEY CORPORATION	524126	4,033,899	8	281,141	6
Internet Publishing & Web Search Portals					
BLOOMBERG LP	519130	6,100,000	3		
GOOGLE INC	519130	21,795,550	1	4,226,858	1
IAC/INTERACTIVECORP	519130	1,445,100	4	-156,200	3
YAHOO! INC	519130	7,208,502	2	424,298	2
Investment Banking					
GOLDMAN SACHS GROUP INC	523110	53,579,000	1	2,322,000	1
STIFEL FINANCIAL CORP	523110	888,847	2	55,502	2
Investment Management/Mutual Funds/Pension Funds					
BLACKROCK INC	523920	5,064,000	1	786,000	1
Jewelry Stores					
TIFFANY & CO	448310	2,938,771	1	323,478	1

Company	Industry Code	2008 Sales (U.S. $ thousands)	Sales Rank	2008 Profits (U.S. $ thousands)	Profits Rank
Laboratories & Diagnostic Services--Medical					
LABORATORY CORP OF AMERICA HOLDINGS	6215	4,505,200	2	464,500	2
QUEST DIAGNOSTICS INC	6215	7,249,447	1	581,490	1
Linens/Uniform Supply					
CINTAS CORP	812331	3,937,900	1	335,405	1
Linens/Housewares/Art/Framing Stores					
BED BATH & BEYOND INC	442299	7,048,942	1	562,808	1
CONTAINER STORE	442299	600,000	2		
Long-Term Health Care & Assisted Living					
CAPITAL SENIOR LIVING CORP	623110	193,274	6	3,724	3
EMERITUS CORP	623110	769,429	5	-104,751	4
KINDRED HEALTHCARE INC	623110	4,151,396	1	36,285	2
MANOR CARE INC	623110	3,850,000	2		
SUN HEALTHCARE GROUP	623110	1,824,184	3	109,287	1
SUNRISE SENIOR LIVING	623110	1,701,643	4	-439,179	5
Machine Tools, Manufacturing					
PRECISION CASTPARTS CORP	33351	6,749,800	1	987,300	1
Machinery, Equipment & Supplies, Distribution					
WW GRAINGER INC	4238	6,850,032	1	475,355	1
Machinery, Manufacturing					
CATERPILLAR INC	333	51,324,000	1	3,557,000	1
DEERE & CO	333	28,438,000	2	2,053,000	2
Machinery, Mining & Oil & Gas Field, Manufacturing					
BUCYRUS INTERNATIONAL INC	33313	2,505,838	2	233,315	2
CAMERON INTERNATIONAL	33313	5,848,877	1	593,726	1
Mail Order and Non-Store Selling, Incl. TV Shopping					
COLDWATER CREEK INC	454113	1,151,472	1	-2,488	1
Management of Companies & Enterprises					
BERKSHIRE HATHAWAY INC	55111	107,786,000	1	4,994,000	1
Market Research					
IMS HEALTH INC	541910	2,329,528	1	311,250	1
Marketing Agencies & Related Services					
ICT GROUP INC	5418	428,177	1	-23,285	1
Meat Production					
SMITHFIELD FOODS INC	311612	11,351,200	1	128,900	1
Medical/Dental/Surgical Equipment & Supplies, Distribution					
HENRY SCHEIN INC	423450	6,394,874	3	243,143	2
OWENS & MINOR INC	423450	7,243,237	2	93,327	4
PATTERSON COMPANIES INC	423450	2,998,729	4	224,858	3
THERMO FISHER SCIENTIFIC	423450	10,498,000	1	994,200	1
Medical/Dental/Surgical Equipment & Supplies, Manufacturing					
3M COMPANY	33911	25,269,000	1	3,460,000	1
BAXTER INTERNATIONAL INC	33911	12,348,000	3	2,014,000	3
BECKMAN COULTER INC	33911	3,098,900	9	194,000	11
BECTON DICKINSON & CO	33911	7,155,910	5	1,127,000	5
BIO RAD LABORATORIES INC	33911	1,764,365	12	89,510	12
BOSTON SCIENTIFIC CORP	33911	8,050,000	4	-2,036,000	15

Company	Industry Code	2008 Sales (U.S. $ thousands)	Sales Rank	2008 Profits (U.S. $ thousands)	Profits Rank
COOPER COMPANIES INC	33911	1,063,176	15	65,476	14
CR BARD INC	33911	2,452,100	10	416,500	7
MEDTRONIC INC	33911	13,515,000	2	2,231,000	2
ST JUDE MEDICAL INC	33911	4,363,251	7	384,327	8
STERIS CORP	33911	1,265,090	13	77,106	13
STRYKER CORP	33911	6,718,200	6	1,147,800	4
VARIAN MEDICAL SYSTEMS	33911	2,069,700	11	279,500	10
WATERS CORP	33911	1,139,886	14	322,479	9
ZIMMER HOLDINGS INC	33911	4,121,100	8	848,600	6
Office Supplies Stores					
OFFICE DEPOT INC	453210	14,495,544	2	-1,478,938	2
STAPLES INC	453210	19,372,682	1	995,670	1
Oil & Natural Gas Exploration & Production					
ANADARKO PETROLEUM CORP	211111	14,640,000	9	3,260,000	4
APACHE CORP	211111	12,389,750	11	711,954	8
CHEVRON CORPORATION	211111	273,005,000	2	23,931,000	2
CONOCOPHILLIPS COMPANY	211111	240,842,000	3	-16,998,000	12
DEVON ENERGY CORP	211111	15,211,000	8	-2,148,000	11
EXXON MOBIL CORPORATION (EXXONMOBIL)	211111	459,579,000	1	45,220,000	1
HELMERICH & PAYNE INC	211111	2,036,543	13	461,738	9
HESS CORPORATION	211111	41,165,000	5	2,360,000	5
MURPHY OIL CORPORATION	211111	27,440,834	6	1,739,986	6
OCCIDENTAL PETROLEUM	211111	24,217,000	7	6,857,000	3
SHELL OIL CO	211111	100,818,000	4		
TRANSOCEAN INC	211111	12,674,000	10	4,202	10
WILLIAMS COMPANIES INC	211111	12,352,000	12	1,418,000	7
Oil Field Support Services					
HALLIBURTON COMPANY	213112	18,279,000	2	1,538,000	4
NATIONAL OILWELL VARCO INC	213112	1,343,140	9	1,952,000	2
NOBLE CORPORATION	213112	3,446,501	5	1,560,995	3
OCEANEERING INTERNATIONAL	213112	1,977,421	8	317,558	8
OIL STATES INTERNATIONAL	213112	2,948,457	6	222,710	9
PATTERSON-UTI ENERGY INC	213112	2,209,126	7	347,069	7
SCHLUMBERGER LIMITED	213112	27,163,000	1	5,435,000	1
SMITH INTERNATIONAL INC	213112	10,770,838	3	767,284	6
TEAM INC	213112	478,475	10	23,623	10
WEATHERFORD INTERNATIONAL LTD	213112	9,600,564	4	1,353,903	5
Other Health & Personal Care Stores/Weight Management					
WEIGHT WATCHERS INTERNATIONAL INC	446199	1,535,812	1	204,331	1
Packaging, Manufacturing					
WEST PHARMACEUTICAL SERVICES INC	3222	1,051,100	1	86,000	1
Paint & Wallpaper Stores					
SHERWIN WILLIAMS COMPANY	444120	7,980,000	1	477,000	1

Company	Industry Code	2008 Sales (U.S. $ thousands)	Sales Rank	2008 Profits (U.S. $ thousands)	Profits Rank
Paints & Coatings, Manufacturing					
VALSPAR CORPORATION	325510	3,482,378	1	150,766	1
Pawn Shops					
CASH AMERICA INTERNATIONAL	522298	1,030,794	1	81,140	1
Payment & Transaction Processing Services					
ALLIANCE DATA SYSTEMS CORP	522320	2,025,300	3	217,400	2
CONVERGYS CORPORATION	522320	2,785,800	2	-92,900	4
FIRST DATA CORP	522320	8,811,300	1	-3,800,000	5
GLOBAL PAYMENTS INC	522320	1,274,229	5	162,754	3
TOTAL SYSTEM SERVICES INC (TSYS)	522320	1,938,608	4	250,100	1
Payment & Transaction Processing--Benefits Management					
EXPRESS SCRIPTS INC	522320A	21,978,000	2	776,100	2
MEDCO HEALTH SOLUTIONS	522320A	51,258,000	1	1,102,900	1
Petrochemicals Manufacturing					
CHEVRON PHILLIPS CHEMICAL COMPANY LLC	325110	12,646,000	2	276,000	2
EXXONMOBIL CHEMICAL	325110	55,000,000	1	2,957,000	1
Petroleum Products (except Bulk Stations/Terminals) Distribution & Pipelines					
ENTERPRISE PRODUCTS PARTNERS LP	486	21,905,656	1	954,021	1
Petroleum Refineries					
KOCH INDUSTRIES INC	324110	100,000,000	2		
SUNOCO INC	324110	54,052,000	3	776,000	1
TESORO CORP	324110	23,309,000	4	278,000	2
VALERO ENERGY CORP	324110	119,114,000	1	-1,131,000	3
Petroleum--Drilling Oil & Gas Wells Support					
BAKER HUGHES INC	213111	11,864,000	1	1,635,000	1
DIAMOND OFFSHORE DRILLING	213111	3,544,057	3	1,311,020	2
PRIDE INTERNATIONAL INC	213111	2,310,400	2	852,100	3
Pets/Pet Supplies Stores					
PETCO ANIMAL SUPPLIES INC	453910	2,600,000	2		
PETSMART INC	453910	4,672,656	1	258,684	1
Pharmacies & Drug Stores					
CVS CAREMARK CORP	446110	87,471,900	1	3,212,100	1
OMNICARE INC	446110	6,310,607	4	156,108	3
RITE AID CORPORATION	446110	24,326,846	3	-1,078,990	4
WALGREEN CO	446110	59,034,000	2	2,157,000	2
Poultry Production					
TYSON FOODS INC	311615	26,862,000	1	86,000	1
Printing					
AVERY DENNISON CORP	323	6,710,400	2	266,100	1
R R DONNELLEY & SONS CO	323	11,581,600	1	-189,900	2
Railroad Car Manufacturing					
WABTEC CORP	336510	1,575,000	1	130,550	1
Real Estate Investment Trusts - Nonresidential					
PUBLIC STORAGE INC	531120	1,745,607	1	935,176	1

Company	Industry Code	2008 Sales (U.S. $ thousands)	Sales Rank	2008 Profits (U.S. $ thousands)	Profits Rank
Real Estate Rental, Leasing, Development & Management					
ABM INDUSTRIES INC	5311	3,623,590	1	45,434	1
Rental Stores, Consumer Goods					
AARON'S INC	5322	1,592,608	2	90,189	2
RENT-A-CENTER INC	5322	2,884,172	1	139,624	1
Research & Development--Physical, Engineering & Life Sciences					
COVANCE INC	541712	1,827,067	1	196,760	1
PAREXEL INTERNATIONAL	541712	964,283	3	64,640	3
PHARMACEUTICAL PRODUCT DEVELOPMENT INC	541712	1,569,901	2	187,519	2
Restaurants					
BRINKER INTERNATIONAL INC	722110	4,235,223	4	51,722	8
BUFFALO WILD WINGS INC	722110	422,417	13	24,435	9
BURGER KING HOLDINGS INC	722110	2,454,700	7	189,600	4
CHIPOTLE MEXICAN GRILL INC	722110	1,331,968	11	78,202	6
CRACKER BARREL OLD COUNTRY STORE INC	722110	2,384,521	8	65,553	7
DARDEN RESTAURANTS INC	722110	6,626,500	3	377,200	3
DENNY'S CORPORATION	722110	760,271	12	14,662	10
DINEEQUITY INC	722110	1,613,628	10	-154,459	11
JACK IN THE BOX INC	722110	2,539,561	6	119,279	5
MCDONALD'S CORP	722110	23,522,400	1	4,313,200	1
OSI RESTAURANT PARTNERS	722110	3,962,854	5	-739,409	13
WENDY'S/ARBY'S GROUP INC	722110	1,662,291	9	-479,741	12
YUM! BRANDS INC	722110	11,279,000	2	964,000	2
Security, Protection, Armored Car & Investigation Services					
BRINKS COMPANY	5616	3,163,500	1	183,300	1
GEO GROUP INC	5616	1,043,006	2	58,902	2
Semiconductors (Microchips)/Integrated Circuits/Components, Manufacturing					
ADVANCED MICRO DEVICES INC (AMD)	33441	5,808,000	4	-3,098,000	8
ANALOG DEVICES INC	33441	2,582,931	6	786,284	3
BROADCOM CORP	33441	4,658,125	5	214,794	6
INTEL CORP	33441	37,586,000	1	5,292,000	1
MAXIM INTEGRATED PRODUCTS	33441	2,052,783	7	317,725	4
MICROCHIP TECHNOLOGY INC	33441	1,035,737	8	297,748	5
MICRON TECHNOLOGY INC	33441	5,841,000	3	-1,619,000	7
QUALCOMM INC	33441	11,142,000	2	3,160,000	2
Shipping-Deep Sea					
SEACOR HOLDINGS INC	483111	1,655,956	1	223,688	1
Shoe Manufacturing-Athletic Shoes & Misc. Shoes, Incl. Children's					
NIKE INC	316219	18,627,000	1	1,883,400	1
Shoe Manufacturing-Men's					
GENESCO INC	316213	1,502,119	1	6,885	1
Shoes & Accessories Stores					
COACH INC	448210	3,180,757	1	783,055	1
FINISH LINE INC	448210	1,277,162	2	-48,502	2

Company	Industry Code	2008 Sales (U.S. $ thousands)	Sales Rank	2008 Profits (U.S. $ thousands)	Profits Rank
Soap & Cleaning Compound Manufacturing					
COLGATE PALMOLIVE CO	325611	15,329,900	1	1,957,200	1
Soap, Cleaning Compound, & Toilet Prep Mfg.					
PROCTER & GAMBLE CO	3256	81,748,000	1	12,075,000	1
Sporting Goods Stores					
ACADEMY SPORTS & OUTDOORS LTD	451110	2,000,000	4		
BASS PRO SHOPS INC	451110	3,000,000	2		
CABELA'S INC	451110	2,552,721	3	76,404	2
DICK'S SPORTING GOODS INC	451110	3,888,422	1	155,036	1
HIBBETT SPORTS INC	451110	520,720	5	30,329	3
Staffing or Outsourcing					
STARTEK INC	561	272,890	1	-9,901	1
Telecommunications Equipment Manufacturing					
ADC TELECOMMUNICATIONS	334210	1,456,400	1	-41,900	1
Telecommunications Service Cellular, U.S. & Non-U.S.					
CELLCO PARTNERSHIP (VERIZON WIRELESS)	5172	58,600,000	1		
NII HOLDINGS INC	5172	2,371,340	4	294,490	2
T-MOBILE USA	5172	21,885,000	2	6,123,000	1
UNITED STATES CELLULAR	5172	4,243,185	3	32,990	3
Telecommunications Service Wired, Satellite or Cable					
AT&T INC	517110	124,028,000	1	12,867,000	1
CABLEVISION SYSTEMS CORP	517110	7,230,116	8	-227,576	9
COMCAST CORP	517110	34,256,000	4	2,547,000	3
COX COMMUNICATIONS INC	517110	8,500,000	7		
DIRECTV GROUP INC	517110	19,693,000	5	1,515,000	4
EMBARQ CORP	517110	6,124,000	9	769,000	5
FRONTIER COMMUNICATIONS	517110	2,237,018	12	182,660	6
LEVEL 3 COMMUNICATIONS INC	517110	4,301,000	11	-290,000	10
LIBERTY GLOBAL INC	517110	10,561,100	6	-788,900	11
TELEPHONE AND DATA SYSTEMS INC (TDS)	517110	5,092,000	10	93,500	7
TIME WARNER INC	517110	46,984,000	3	-13,402,000	12
TW TELECOM INC	517110	1,159,019	13	8,525	8
VERIZON COMMUNICATIONS	517110	97,354,000	2	6,428,000	2
Television Broadcasting					
FOX ENTERTAINMENT GROUP	515120				
NEWS CORP	515120	32,996,000	1	5,381,000	1
UNIVISION COMMUNICATIONS	515120				
Temporary Help/Staffing					
KELLY SERVICES INC	561320	5,517,290	2	-82,239	4
MANPOWER INC	561320	21,552,800	1	218,900	2
ROBERT HALF INTERNATIONAL	561320	4,600,554	3	250,181	1
VOLT INFORMATION SCIENCES	561320	2,427,318	4	-40,648	3
Tire Stores					
TBC CORPORATION	441320				

Company	Industry Code	2008 Sales (U.S. $ thousands)	Sales Rank	2008 Profits (U.S. $ thousands)	Profits Rank
Tobacco, Manufacturing					
ALTRIA GROUP INC	3122	19,356,000	1	4,930,000	1
Toys, Manufacturing					
MATTEL INC	339932	5,918,002	1	379,636	1
Toys/Hobbies/Games/Crafts Stores					
GAMESTOP CORP	451120	7,093,962	1	288,291	1
Travel Services-Online					
SABRE HOLDINGS CORP	5615E	3,000,000	1		
Trucks, RVs & Misc. Automotive, Manufacturing					
OSHKOSH CORPORATION	336120	7,138,300	1	79,300	1
Utilities-Electric					
AMERICAN ELECTRIC POWER COMPANY INC (AEP)	2211	14,440,000	3	1,380,000	3
EDISON INTERNATIONAL	2211	11,248,000	6	1,215,000	6
ENTERGY CORP	2211	13,093,756	5	1,220,566	5
FIRSTENERGY CORP	2211	13,627,000	4	1,342,000	4
FPL GROUP INC	2211	16,410,000	2	1,639,000	2
HAWAIIAN ELECTRIC INDUSTRIES INC	2211	3,218,920	7	-90,278	7
SOUTHERN CALIFORNIA EDISON COMPANY	2211				
SOUTHERN COMPANY	2211	17,127,000	1	1,742,000	1
Utilities-Electric & Gas					
AES CORPORATION	221	16,070,000	2	1,234,000	4
BALTIMORE GAS AND ELECTRIC COMPANY	221	2,680,000	12		
CONSOLIDATED EDISON INC	221	13,583,000	4	1,196,000	5
DTE ENERGY COMPANY	221	9,329,000	9	546,000	7
DUKE ENERGY CORP	221	13,207,000	5	1,362,000	3
EXELON CORPORATION	221	18,859,000	1	2,737,000	1
MIDAMERICAN ENERGY HOLDINGS CO	221	12,700,000	6		
NRG ENERGY INC	221	6,885,000	10		
PG&E CORPORATION	221	14,628,000	3	2,261,000	2
RRI ENERGY INC	221	12,600,000	7	-739,700	9
SCANA CORPORATION	221	5,319,000	11	346,000	8
SEMPRA ENERGY	221	10,758,000	8	1,113,000	6
Veterinary Clinics					
VCA ANTECH INC	541940	1,277,470	1	132,984	1
Waste Disposal, Waste Management					
WASTE MANAGEMENT INC	562	13,388,000	1	1,087,000	1
Watch & Clock Manufacturing					
FOSSIL INC	334518	1,583,242	1	138,097	1

ALPHABETICAL INDEX

ENTERPRISE RENT-A-CAR
ERNST & YOUNG LLP
ESTEE LAUDER COMPANIES INC (THE)
EXELON CORPORATION
EXPERIAN AMERICAS
EXPRESS SCRIPTS INC
EXXON MOBIL CORPORATION (EXXONMOBIL)
EXXONMOBIL CHEMICAL
FAMILY DOLLAR STORES INC
FEDEX CORPORATION
FINISH LINE INC (THE)
FIRST ADVANTAGE CORPORATION
FIRST DATA CORP
FIRSTENERGY CORP
FLUOR CORP
FOREST LABORATORIES INC
FORTUNE BRANDS INC
FOSSIL INC
FOSTER WHEELER AG
FOX ENTERTAINMENT GROUP INC
FPL GROUP INC
FRED'S INC
FRONTIER COMMUNICATIONS CORPORATION
FTI CONSULTING INC
GAMESTOP CORP
GENENTECH INC
GENERAL CABLE CORP
GENERAL DYNAMICS CORP
GENERAL ELECTRIC CO (GE)
GENERAL MILLS INC
GENESCO INC
GENWORTH FINANCIAL INC
GEO GROUP INC
GEORGIA GULF CORPORATION
GILEAD SCIENCES INC
GLOBAL HYATT CORPORATION
GLOBAL PAYMENTS INC
GOLDMAN SACHS GROUP INC
GOOGLE INC
GRANT THORNTON LLP
GUESS? INC
HALLIBURTON COMPANY
HARRAH'S ENTERTAINMENT INC
HARRIS CORPORATION
HARTFORD FINANCIAL SERVICES GROUP INC (THE)
HAWAIIAN ELECTRIC INDUSTRIES INC
HCA INC
HE BUTT GROCERY COMPANY (HEB)
HEALTH CARE SERVICE CORPORATION
HEALTH FITNESS CORP
HEALTH MANAGEMENT ASSOCIATES INC
HEALTH NET INC
HEALTHWAYS INC
HELMERICH & PAYNE INC
HENRY SCHEIN INC
HERTZ GLOBAL HOLDINGS INC
HESS CORPORATION
HEWITT ASSOCIATES

HIBBETT SPORTS INC
HILTON HOTELS CORP
HOME DEPOT INC
HONEYWELL INTERNATIONAL INC
HUMANA INC
IAC/INTERACTIVECORP
IBM GLOBAL SERVICES
ICT GROUP INC
IDEXX LABORATORIES INC
IGATE CORPORATION
IMS HEALTH INC
INFOGROUP INC
INGRAM MICRO INC
INTEL CORP
INTERNATIONAL BUSINESS MACHINES CORP (IBM)
INTUIT INC
INVENTIV HEALTH INC
J C PENNEY COMPANY INC
JABIL CIRCUIT INC
JACK IN THE BOX INC
JACOBS ENGINEERING GROUP INC
JETBLUE AIRWAYS CORPORATION
JM SMUCKER CO
JOHNSON & JOHNSON
JOHNSON CONTROLS INC
JP MORGAN CHASE & CO INC
JUNIPER NETWORKS INC
KAISER PERMANENTE
KEANE INC
KELLOGG CO
KELLY SERVICES INC
KENDLE INTERNATIONAL INC
KIMBERLY-CLARK CORP
KINDRED HEALTHCARE INC
KOCH INDUSTRIES INC
KOHL'S CORP
KPMG LLP
KRAFT FOODS INC
KROGER CO (THE)
L-3 COMMUNICATIONS HOLDINGS INC
LABORATORY CORP OF AMERICA HOLDINGS
LAS VEGAS SANDS CORP (THE VENETIAN)
LEVEL 3 COMMUNICATIONS INC
LEXMARK INTERNATIONAL INC
LIBERTY GLOBAL INC
LIBERTY MUTUAL GROUP INC
LIMITED BRANDS INC
LINCARE HOLDINGS INC
LINCOLN NATIONAL CORPORATION
LKQ CORP
LOCKHEED MARTIN CORP
LODGIAN INC
LOEWS CORPORATION
LOWE'S COMPANIES INC
MACY'S INC
MANOR CARE INC
MANPOWER INC
MARRIOTT INTERNATIONAL INC
MARS INC
MARSH & MCLENNAN COMPANIES INC

MARY KAY INC
MASSEY ENERGY COMPANY
MATTEL INC
MAXIM INTEGRATED PRODUCTS INC
MAYO FOUNDATION FOR MEDICAL EDUCATION AND RESEARCH
MCAFEE INC
MCDERMOTT INTERNATIONAL INC
MCDONALD'S CORP
MCKESSON CORPORATION
MCKINSEY & COMPANY INC
MEDCO HEALTH SOLUTIONS
MEDTRONIC INC
MEIJER INC
MEN'S WEARHOUSE INC (THE)
MERCER INC
MERCK & CO INC
METHODIST HEALTH CARE SYSTEM
METLIFE INC
MGM MIRAGE
MICROCHIP TECHNOLOGY INC
MICRON TECHNOLOGY INC
MICROSOFT CORP
MIDAMERICAN ENERGY HOLDINGS CO
MILLIPORE CORP
MONRO MUFFLER BRAKE INC
MONSANTO CO
MURPHY OIL CORPORATION
MYLAN INC
NATIONAL OILWELL VARCO INC
NETAPP INC
NEWS CORP
NII HOLDINGS INC
NIKE INC
NOBLE CORPORATION
NORTHROP GRUMMAN CORP
NRG ENERGY INC
OCCIDENTAL PETROLEUM CORP
OCEANEERING INTERNATIONAL INC
ODYSSEY HEALTHCARE INC
OFFICE DEPOT INC
OIL STATES INTERNATIONAL INC
OMNICARE INC
OMNICOM GROUP INC
ORACLE CORP
O'REILLY AUTOMOTIVE INC
OSHKOSH CORPORATION
OSI RESTAURANT PARTNERS LLC
OWENS & MINOR INC
PANTRY INC (THE)
PARAMETRIC TECHNOLOGY CORP
PAREXEL INTERNATIONAL CORP
PARSONS BRINCKERHOFF INC
PATTERSON COMPANIES INC
PATTERSON-UTI ENERGY INC
PAYCHEX INC
PEABODY ENERGY CORP
PEPSI BOTTLING GROUP INC
PEPSICO INC
PEROT SYSTEMS CORP
PERRIGO CO
PETCO ANIMAL SUPPLIES INC
PETSMART INC
PFIZER INC

PG&E CORPORATION
PHARMACEUTICAL PRODUCT
DEVELOPMENT INC
PITNEY BOWES INC
PLEXUS CORP
POLO RALPH LAUREN CORP
PRAXAIR INC
PRECISION CASTPARTS CORP
PRICESMART INC
PRICEWATERHOUSECOOPERS
PRIDE INTERNATIONAL INC
PRINCIPAL FINANCIAL GROUP (THE)
PROCTER & GAMBLE CO
PROGRESSIVE CORPORATION (THE)
PRUDENTIAL FINANCIAL INC
PSYCHIATRIC SOLUTIONS INC
PUBLIC STORAGE INC
PUBLIX SUPER MARKETS INC
QUALCOMM INC
QUANTA SERVICES INC
QUEST DIAGNOSTICS INC
QUIKSILVER INC
R R DONNELLEY & SONS CO
RALCORP HOLDINGS INC
RAYTHEON CO
REGIS CORPORATION
RENT-A-CENTER INC
RES CARE INC
RITE AID CORPORATION
RITZ-CARLTON HOTEL COMPANY
LLC (THE)
ROBERT HALF INTERNATIONAL INC
ROSS STORES INC
ROYAL CARIBBEAN CRUISES LTD
RRI ENERGY INC
SABRE HOLDINGS CORP
SAFECO INSURANCE COMPANY OF
AMERICA
SAFEWAY INC
SAIC INC
SAM'S CLUB
SAPIENT CORPORATION
SARA LEE CORP
SAS INSTITUTE INC
SCANA CORPORATION
SCHERING-PLOUGH CORP
SCHLUMBERGER LIMITED
SCIENTIFIC GAMES CORPORATION
SCOTTS MIRACLE GROW CO
SEACOR HOLDINGS INC
SELECT MEDICAL
SEMPRA ENERGY
SENSIENT TECHNOLOGIES
CORPORATION
SHAW GROUP INC (THE)
SHELL OIL CO
SHERWIN WILLIAMS COMPANY
(THE)
SIGMA-ALDRICH CORP
SISTERS OF MERCY HEALTH
SYSTEMS
SMITH INTERNATIONAL INC
SMITHFIELD FOODS INC
SOUTHERN CALIFORNIA EDISON
COMPANY

SOUTHERN COMPANY (THE)
SOUTHWEST AIRLINES CO
SRA INTERNATIONAL INC
ST JUDE MEDICAL INC
STAPLES INC
STARTEK INC
STARWOOD HOTELS & RESORTS
WORLDWIDE INC
STERIS CORP
STIFEL FINANCIAL CORP
STRYKER CORP
SUN HEALTHCARE GROUP
SUNGARD DATA SYSTEMS INC
SUNOCO INC
SUNRISE SENIOR LIVING
SUPERVALU INC
SYKES ENTERPRISES INC
SYMANTEC CORP
SYNOPSYS INC
SYNTEL INC
SYSCO CORP
TARGET CORPORATION
TBC CORPORATION
TEAM INC
TECH DATA CORP
TEKTRONIX INC
TELEDYNE TECHNOLOGIES
INCORPORATED
TELEPHONE AND DATA SYSTEMS
INC (TDS)
TELETECH HOLDINGS INC
TESORO CORP
THERMO FISHER SCIENTIFIC INC
TIFFANY & CO
TIME WARNER INC
TJX COMPANIES INC (THE)
T-MOBILE USA
TOTAL SYSTEM SERVICES INC
(TSYS)
TOWERS PERRIN
TRANSOCEAN INC
TRAVELERS COMPANIES INC (THE)
TREEHOUSE FOODS INC
TW TELECOM INC
TYSON FOODS INC
UNITED NATURAL FOODS INC
UNITED PARCEL SERVICE INC (UPS)
UNITED STATES CELLULAR CORP
UNITED TECHNOLOGIES
CORPORATION
UNITEDHEALTH GROUP INC
UNIVERSAL HEALTH SERVICES INC
UNIVISION COMMUNICATIONS INC
URS CORPORATION
USAA
VALERO ENERGY CORP
VALSPAR CORPORATION (THE)
VARIAN MEDICAL SYSTEMS INC
VCA ANTECH INC
VERISIGN INC
VERIZON COMMUNICATIONS
VIACOM INC
VICTORIAS SECRET
VISA INC
VOLT INFORMATION SCIENCES INC

W R BERKLEY CORPORATION
WABTEC CORP
WALGREEN CO
WAL-MART STORES INC
WALT DISNEY COMPANY (THE)
WASTE MANAGEMENT INC
WATERS CORP
WATSON PHARMACEUTICALS INC
WATSON WYATT WORLDWIDE INC
WEATHERFORD INTERNATIONAL
LTD
WEIGHT WATCHERS
INTERNATIONAL INC
WELLPOINT INC
WELLS FARGO & CO
WENDY'S/ARBY'S GROUP INC
WEST CORPORATION
WEST PHARMACEUTICAL SERVICES
INC
WESTERN DIGITAL CORP
WHOLE FOODS MARKET INC
WILLIAMS COMPANIES INC (THE)
WW GRAINGER INC
WYETH
WYNDHAM WORLDWIDE
WYNN RESORTS LIMITED
XEROX CORP
YAHOO! INC
YUM! BRANDS INC
ZIMMER HOLDINGS INC

INDEX OF U.S. HEADQUARTERS LOCATION BY STATE

To help you locate members of THE AMERICAN EMPLOYERS 500 geographically, the city and state of the headquarters of each company are in the following index.

ALABAMA
HIBBETT SPORTS INC; Birmingham

ARIZONA
APOLLO GROUP INC; Phoenix
AVNET INC; Phoenix
MICROCHIP TECHNOLOGY INC; Chandler
PETSMART INC; Phoenix

ARKANSAS
ACXIOM CORP; Little Rock
MURPHY OIL CORPORATION; El Dorado
SAM'S CLUB; Bentonville
TYSON FOODS INC; Springdale
WAL-MART STORES INC; Bentonville

CALIFORNIA
ACTIVISION BLIZZARD INC; Santa Monica
ADOBE SYSTEMS INC; San Jose
ADVANCED MICRO DEVICES INC (AMD); Sunnyvale
AECOM TECHNOLOGY CORPORATION; Los Angeles
AGILENT TECHNOLOGIES INC; Santa Clara
ALLERGAN INC; Irvine
AMGEN INC; Thousand Oaks
APPLE INC; Cupertino
AVERY DENNISON CORP; Pasadena
BEBE STORES INC; Brisbane
BECHTEL GROUP INC; San Francisco
BECKMAN COULTER INC; Fullerton
BIO RAD LABORATORIES INC; Hercules
BROADCOM CORP; Irvine
CHARLOTTE RUSSE HOLDING; San Diego
CHEVRON CORPORATION; San Ramon
CISCO SYSTEMS INC; San Jose
COOPER COMPANIES INC; Pleasanton
CUBIC CORP; San Diego
DAVITA INC; El Segundo
DINEEQUITY INC; Glendale
DIRECTV GROUP INC (THE); El Segundo
DOLE FOOD COMPANY INC; Westlake Village
EBAY INC; San Jose
EDISON INTERNATIONAL; Rosemead
ELECTRONIC ARTS INC; Redwood City

EXPERIAN AMERICAS; Costa Mesa
FIRST ADVANTAGE CORPORATION; Poway
FOX ENTERTAINMENT GROUP INC; Los Angeles
GENENTECH INC; South San Francisco
GILEAD SCIENCES INC; Foster City
GOOGLE INC; Mountain View
GUESS? INC; Los Angeles
HEALTH NET INC; Woodland Hills
HILTON HOTELS CORP; Beverly Hills
INGRAM MICRO INC; Santa Ana
INTEL CORP; Santa Clara
INTUIT INC; Mountain View
JACK IN THE BOX INC; San Diego
JACOBS ENGINEERING GROUP INC; Pasadena
JUNIPER NETWORKS INC; Sunnyvale
KAISER PERMANENTE; Oakland
KEANE INC; San Ramon
MATTEL INC; El Segundo
MAXIM INTEGRATED PRODUCTS INC; Sunnyvale
MCAFEE INC; Santa Clara
MCKESSON CORPORATION; San Francisco
NETAPP INC; Sunnyvale
NORTHROP GRUMMAN CORP; Los Angeles
OCCIDENTAL PETROLEUM CORP; Los Angeles
ORACLE CORP; Redwood Shores
PETCO ANIMAL SUPPLIES INC; San Diego
PG&E CORPORATION; San Francisco
PRICESMART INC; San Diego
PUBLIC STORAGE INC; Glendale
QUALCOMM INC; San Diego
QUIKSILVER INC; Huntington Beach
ROBERT HALF INTERNATIONAL INC; Menlo Park
ROSS STORES INC; Pleasanton
SAFEWAY INC; Pleasanton
SAIC INC; San Diego
SEMPRA ENERGY; San Diego
SOUTHERN CALIFORNIA EDISON COMPANY; Rosemead
SUN HEALTHCARE GROUP; Irvine
SYMANTEC CORP; Cupertino
SYNOPSYS INC; Mountain View
TELEDYNE TECHNOLOGIES INCORPORATED; Thousand Oaks
URS CORPORATION; San Francisco
VARIAN MEDICAL SYSTEMS INC; Palo Alto
VCA ANTECH INC; Los Angeles
VERISIGN INC; Mountain View
VISA INC; San Francisco
WALT DISNEY COMPANY (THE); Burbank
WATSON PHARMACEUTICALS INC; Corona
WELLS FARGO & CO; San Francisco
WESTERN DIGITAL CORP; Lake Forest
YAHOO! INC; Sunnyvale

COLORADO
CATHOLIC HEALTH INITIATIVES; Denver
CH2M HILL COMPANIES LTD; Englewood
CHIPOTLE MEXICAN GRILL INC; Denver
CIBER INC; Greenwood Village
FIRST DATA CORP; Greenwood Village
LEVEL 3 COMMUNICATIONS INC; Broomfield
LIBERTY GLOBAL INC; Englewood
STARTEK INC; Denver
TELETECH HOLDINGS INC; Englewood
TW TELECOM INC; Littleton

CONNECTICUT
AETNA INC; Hartford
FRONTIER COMMUNICATIONS CORPORATION; Stamford
GENERAL ELECTRIC CO (GE); Fairfield
HARTFORD FINANCIAL SERVICES GROUP INC (THE); Hartford
IMS HEALTH INC; Norwalk
PITNEY BOWES INC; Stamford
PRAXAIR INC; Danbury
TOWERS PERRIN; Stamford
UNITED NATURAL FOODS INC; Dayville
UNITED TECHNOLOGIES CORPORATION; Hartford
W R BERKLEY CORPORATION; Greenwich
XEROX CORP; Norwalk

DELAWARE
E I DU PONT DE NEMOURS & CO (DUPONT); Wilmington

DISTRICT OF COLUMBIA
DANAHER CORP; Washington

FLORIDA
BROWN & BROWN INC; Daytona Beach
BURGER KING HOLDINGS INC; Miami
CARNIVAL CORPORATION; Miami
CHICO'S FAS INC; Fort Myers
DARDEN RESTAURANTS INC; Orlando
DYCOM INDUSTRIES INC; Palm Beach Gardens
FPL GROUP INC; Juno Beach
GEO GROUP INC; Boca Raton
HARRIS CORPORATION; Melbourne
HEALTH MANAGEMENT ASSOCIATES INC; Naples
JABIL CIRCUIT INC; St. Petersburg
LINCARE HOLDINGS INC; Clearwater
OFFICE DEPOT INC; Boca Raton
OSI RESTAURANT PARTNERS LLC; Tampa
PUBLIX SUPER MARKETS INC; Lakeland
ROYAL CARIBBEAN CRUISES LTD; Miami

SEACOR HOLDINGS INC; Ft. Lauderdale
SYKES ENTERPRISES INC; Tampa
TBC CORPORATION; Palm Beach Gardens
TECH DATA CORP; Clearwater

GEORGIA
AARON'S INC; Atlanta
AFLAC INC; Columbus
COCA-COLA COMPANY (THE); Atlanta
COCA-COLA ENTERPRISES INC; Atlanta
COX COMMUNICATIONS INC; Atlanta
GEORGIA GULF CORPORATION; Atlanta
GLOBAL PAYMENTS INC; Atlanta
HOME DEPOT INC; Atlanta
LODGIAN INC; Atlanta
SOUTHERN COMPANY (THE); Atlanta
TOTAL SYSTEM SERVICES INC (TSYS); Columbus
UNITED PARCEL SERVICE INC (UPS); Atlanta
WENDY'S/ARBY'S GROUP INC; Atlanta

HAWAII
HAWAIIAN ELECTRIC INDUSTRIES INC; Honolulu

IDAHO
COLDWATER CREEK INC; Sandpoint
MICRON TECHNOLOGY INC; Boise

ILLINOIS
ABBOTT LABORATORIES; Abbott Park
ALLSTATE CORPORATION (THE); Northbrook
ARCHER DANIELS MIDLAND CO; Decatur
ARTHUR J GALLAGHER & CO; Itasca
BAXTER INTERNATIONAL INC; Deerfield
BDO SEIDMAN LLP; Chicago
BOEING COMPANY (THE); Chicago
CATERPILLAR INC; Peoria
CDW CORPORATION; Vernon Hills
DEERE & CO; Moline
DEVRY INC; Oakbrook Terrace
EXELON CORPORATION; Chicago
FORTUNE BRANDS INC; Deerfield
GLOBAL HYATT CORPORATION; Chicago
GRANT THORNTON LLP; Chicago
HEALTH CARE SERVICE CORPORATION; Chicago
HEWITT ASSOCIATES; Lincolnshire
KRAFT FOODS INC; Northfield
LKQ CORP; Chicago
MCDONALD'S CORP; Oak Brook
R R DONNELLEY & SONS CO; Chicago
SARA LEE CORP; Downers Grove
TELEPHONE AND DATA SYSTEMS INC (TDS); Chicago
TREEHOUSE FOODS INC; Westchester

UNITED STATES CELLULAR CORP; Chicago
WALGREEN CO; Deerfield
WW GRAINGER INC; Lake Forest

INDIANA
ADESA INC; Carmel
CTS CORP; Elkhart
CUMMINS INC; Columbus
ELI LILLY & COMPANY; Indianapolis
FINISH LINE INC (THE); Indianapolis
WELLPOINT INC; Indianapolis
ZIMMER HOLDINGS INC; Warsaw

IOWA
MIDAMERICAN ENERGY HOLDINGS CO; Des Moines
PRINCIPAL FINANCIAL GROUP (THE); Des Moines

KANSAS
EMBARQ CORP; Overland Park
KOCH INDUSTRIES INC; Wichita

KENTUCKY
GENERAL CABLE CORP; Highland Heights
HUMANA INC; Louisville
KINDRED HEALTHCARE INC; Louisville
LEXMARK INTERNATIONAL INC; Lexington
OMNICARE INC; Covington
RES CARE INC; Louisville
YUM! BRANDS INC; Louisville

LOUISIANA
AMEDISYS INC; Baton Rouge
ENTERGY CORP; New Orleans
SHAW GROUP INC (THE); Baton Rouge

MAINE
IDEXX LABORATORIES INC; Westbrook

MARYLAND
BALTIMORE GAS AND ELECTRIC COMPANY; Baltimore
BLACK & DECKER CORP; Towson
COVENTRY HEALTH CARE INC; Bethesda
FTI CONSULTING INC; Baltimore
LOCKHEED MARTIN CORP; Bethesda
MARRIOTT INTERNATIONAL INC; Bethesda
RITZ-CARLTON HOTEL COMPANY LLC (THE); Chevy Chase

MASSACHUSETTS
ANALOG DEVICES INC; Norwood
BJ'S WHOLESALE CLUB INC; Natick
BOSTON SCIENTIFIC CORP; Natick
EMC CORP; Hopkinton
LIBERTY MUTUAL GROUP INC; Boston

MILLIPORE CORP; Billerica
PARAMETRIC TECHNOLOGY CORP; Needham
PAREXEL INTERNATIONAL CORP; Waltham
RAYTHEON CO; Waltham
SAPIENT CORPORATION; Boston
STAPLES INC; Framingham
THERMO FISHER SCIENTIFIC INC; Waltham
TJX COMPANIES INC (THE); Framingham
WATERS CORP; Milford

MICHIGAN
DTE ENERGY COMPANY; Detroit
KELLOGG CO; Battle Creek
KELLY SERVICES INC; Troy
MEIJER INC; Grand Rapids
PERRIGO CO; Allegan
STRYKER CORP; Kalamazoo
SYNTEL INC; Troy

MINNESOTA
3M COMPANY; St. Paul
ADC TELECOMMUNICATIONS INC; Eden Prairie
BEST BUY CO INC; Richfield
BUFFALO WILD WINGS INC; Minneapolis
CARGILL INC; Wayzata
CH ROBINSON WORLDWIDE INC; Eden Prairie
CHRISTOPHER & BANKS CORP; Plymouth
CHS INC; Inver Grove Heights
GENERAL MILLS INC; Minneapolis
HEALTH FITNESS CORP; Minneapolis
MAYO FOUNDATION FOR MEDICAL EDUCATION AND RESEARCH; Rochester
MEDTRONIC INC; Minneapolis
PATTERSON COMPANIES INC; St. Paul
REGIS CORPORATION; Edina
ST JUDE MEDICAL INC; St. Paul
SUPERVALU INC; Eden Prairie
TARGET CORPORATION; Minneapolis
UNITEDHEALTH GROUP INC; Minnetonka
VALSPAR CORPORATION (THE); Minneapolis

MISSOURI
ASCENSION HEALTH; St. Louis
BASS PRO SHOPS INC; Springfield
EMERSON ELECTRIC CO; St. Louis
ENTERPRISE RENT-A-CAR; St. Louis
EXPRESS SCRIPTS INC; St. Louis
MONSANTO CO; St. Louis
O'REILLY AUTOMOTIVE INC; Springfield
PEABODY ENERGY CORP; St. Louis
RALCORP HOLDINGS INC; St. Louis
SIGMA-ALDRICH CORP; St. Louis

SISTERS OF MERCY HEALTH
SYSTEMS; Chesterfield
STIFEL FINANCIAL CORP; St. Louis

NEBRASKA
BERKSHIRE HATHAWAY INC; Omaha
BUCKLE INC (THE); Kearney
CABELA'S INC; Sidney
CONAGRA FOODS INC; Omaha
INFOGROUP INC; Omaha
WEST CORPORATION; Omaha

NEVADA
HARRAH'S ENTERTAINMENT INC; Las
Vegas
LAS VEGAS SANDS CORP (THE
VENETIAN); Las Vegas
MGM MIRAGE; Las Vegas
WYNN RESORTS LIMITED; Las Vegas

NEW JERSEY
AUTOMATIC DATA PROCESSING
INC; Roseland
AVIS BUDGET GROUP INC; Parsippany
BECTON DICKINSON & CO; Franklin
Lakes
BED BATH & BEYOND INC; Union
CELGENE CORP; Summit
CELLCO PARTNERSHIP (VERIZON
WIRELESS); Basking Ridge
CHUBB CORPORATION (THE); Warren
COGNIZANT TECHNOLOGY
SOLUTIONS CORP; Teaneck
COVANCE INC; Princeton
CR BARD INC; Murray Hill
FOSTER WHEELER AG; Clinton
HERTZ GLOBAL HOLDINGS INC; Park
Ridge
HONEYWELL INTERNATIONAL INC;
Morristown
INVENTIV HEALTH INC; Somerset
JOHNSON & JOHNSON; New Brunswick
MEDCO HEALTH SOLUTIONS; Franklin
Lakes
MERCK & CO INC; Whitehouse Station
NRG ENERGY INC; Princeton
PRUDENTIAL FINANCIAL INC; Newark
QUEST DIAGNOSTICS INC; Madison
SCHERING-PLOUGH CORP; Kenilworth
WYETH; Madison
WYNDHAM WORLDWIDE; Parsippany

NEW YORK
ABM INDUSTRIES INC; New York
ANNTAYLOR STORES CORP; New
York
ARROW ELECTRONICS INC; Melville
AVON PRODUCTS INC; New York
AXA FINANCIAL INC; New York
BARNES & NOBLE INC; New York
BLACKROCK INC; New York
BLOOMBERG LP; New York
BUNGE LTD; White Plains
CABLEVISION SYSTEMS CORP;
Bethpage

COACH INC; New York
COLGATE PALMOLIVE CO; New York
CONSOLIDATED EDISON INC; New
York
DELOITTE & TOUCHE USA LLP; New
York
DELOITTE CONSULTING LLP; New
York
DRESS BARN INC (THE); Suffern
ERNST & YOUNG LLP; New York
ESTEE LAUDER COMPANIES INC
(THE); New York
FOREST LABORATORIES INC; New
York
GOLDMAN SACHS GROUP INC; New
York
HENRY SCHEIN INC; Melville
HESS CORPORATION; New York
IAC/INTERACTIVECORP; New York
IBM GLOBAL SERVICES; Armonk
INTERNATIONAL BUSINESS
MACHINES CORP (IBM); Armonk
JETBLUE AIRWAYS CORPORATION;
Forest Hills
JP MORGAN CHASE & CO INC; New
York
KPMG LLP; New York
L-3 COMMUNICATIONS HOLDINGS
INC; New York
LOEWS CORPORATION; New York
MARSH & MCLENNAN COMPANIES
INC; New York
MCKINSEY & COMPANY INC; New
York
MERCER INC; New York
METLIFE INC; New York
MONRO MUFFLER BRAKE INC;
Rochester
NEWS CORP; New York
OMNICOM GROUP INC; New York
PARSONS BRINCKERHOFF INC; New
York
PAYCHEX INC; Rochester
PEPSI BOTTLING GROUP INC; Somers
PEPSICO INC; Purchase
PFIZER INC; New York
POLO RALPH LAUREN CORP; New
York
PRICEWATERHOUSECOOPERS; New
York
SCIENTIFIC GAMES CORPORATION;
New York
STARWOOD HOTELS & RESORTS
WORLDWIDE INC; White Plains
TIFFANY & CO; New York
TIME WARNER INC; New York
TRAVELERS COMPANIES INC (THE);
New York
UNIVISION COMMUNICATIONS INC;
New York
VERIZON COMMUNICATIONS; New
York
VIACOM INC; New York
VOLT INFORMATION SCIENCES INC;
Westbury

WEIGHT WATCHERS
INTERNATIONAL INC; New York

NORTH CAROLINA
BANK OF AMERICA CORP; Charlotte
DUKE ENERGY CORP; Charlotte
FAMILY DOLLAR STORES INC;
Charlotte
LABORATORY CORP OF AMERICA
HOLDINGS; Burlington
LOWE'S COMPANIES INC; Mooresville
PANTRY INC (THE); Sanford
PHARMACEUTICAL PRODUCT
DEVELOPMENT INC; Wilmington
SAS INSTITUTE INC; Cary

OHIO
AMERICAN ELECTRIC POWER
COMPANY INC (AEP); Columbus
CARDINAL HEALTH INC; Dublin
CHEMED CORPORATION; Cincinnati
CINTAS CORP; Cincinnati
CONVERGYS CORPORATION;
Cincinnati
DIEBOLD INC; North Canton
EATON CORP; Cleveland
FIRSTENERGY CORP; Akron
JM SMUCKER CO; Orrville
KENDLE INTERNATIONAL INC;
Cincinnati
KROGER CO (THE); Cincinnati
LIMITED BRANDS INC; Columbus
MACY'S INC; Cincinnati
MANOR CARE INC; Toledo
PROCTER & GAMBLE CO; Cincinnati
PROGRESSIVE CORPORATION (THE);
Mayfield Village
SCOTTS MIRACLE GROW CO;
Marysville
SHERWIN WILLIAMS COMPANY
(THE); Cleveland
STERIS CORP; Mentor
VICTORIAS SECRET; Reynoldsburg

OKLAHOMA
DEVON ENERGY CORPORATION;
Oklahoma City
DOLLAR THRIFTY AUTOMOTIVE
GROUP INC; Tulsa
HELMERICH & PAYNE INC; Tulsa
WILLIAMS COMPANIES INC (THE);
Tulsa

OREGON
NIKE INC; Beaverton
PRECISION CASTPARTS CORP;
Portland
TEKTRONIX INC; Beaverton

PENNSYLVANIA
AIR PRODUCTS & CHEMICALS INC;
Allentown
AMERISOURCEBERGEN CORP;
Chesterbrook

ARAMARK CORPORATION;
Philadelphia
CEPHALON INC; Frazer
CHARMING SHOPPES INC; Bensalem
CIGNA CORP; Philadelphia
COMCAST CORP; Philadelphia
CONSOL ENERGY INC; Canonsburg
DICK'S SPORTING GOODS INC;
Pittsburgh
ICT GROUP INC; Newtown
IGATE CORPORATION; Pittsburgh
LINCOLN NATIONAL CORPORATION;
Radnor
MYLAN INC; Canonsburg
RITE AID CORPORATION; Camp Hill
SELECT MEDICAL; Mechanicsburg
SUNGARD DATA SYSTEMS INC;
Wayne
SUNOCO INC; Philadelphia
UNIVERSAL HEALTH SERVICES INC;
King of Prussia
WABTEC CORP; Wilmerding
WEST PHARMACEUTICAL SERVICES
INC; Lionville

RHODE ISLAND
AMERICAN POWER CONVERSION
(APC); West Kingston
CVS CAREMARK CORPORATION;
Woonsocket

SOUTH CAROLINA
DENNY'S CORPORATION; Spartanburg
SCANA CORPORATION; Columbia

TENNESSEE
AUTOZONE INC; Memphis
COMMUNITY HEALTH SYSTEMS INC;
Franklin
CRACKER BARREL OLD COUNTRY
STORE INC; Lebanon
DOLLAR GENERAL CORPORATION;
Goodlettsville
FEDEX CORPORATION; Memphis
FRED'S INC; Memphis
GENESCO INC; Nashville
HCA INC; Nashville
HEALTHWAYS INC; Franklin
PSYCHIATRIC SOLUTIONS INC;
Franklin

TEXAS
7-ELEVEN INC; Dallas
ACADEMY SPORTS & OUTDOORS
LTD; Katy
AFFILIATED COMPUTER SERVICES
INC; Dallas
ALLIANCE DATA SYSTEMS
CORPORATION; Dallas
ANADARKO PETROLEUM
CORPORATION; The Woodlands
APACHE CORP; Houston
AT&T INC; San Antonio
BAKER HUGHES INC; Houston

BENCHMARK ELECTRONICS INC;
Angleton
BRINKER INTERNATIONAL INC;
Dallas
CAMERON INTERNATIONAL
CORPORATION; Houston
CAPITAL SENIOR LIVING CORP;
Dallas
CASH AMERICA INTERNATIONAL
INC; Fort Worth
CHEVRON PHILLIPS CHEMICAL
COMPANY LLC; The Woodlands
CLUBCORP INC; Dallas
CONOCOPHILLIPS COMPANY;
Houston
CONTAINER STORE (THE); Coppell
DEAN FOODS CO; Dallas
DIAMOND OFFSHORE DRILLING INC;
Houston
ENTERPRISE PRODUCTS PARTNERS
LP; Houston
EXXON MOBIL CORPORATION
(EXXONMOBIL); Irving
EXXONMOBIL CHEMICAL; Houston
FLUOR CORP; Irving
FOSSIL INC; Richardson
GAMESTOP CORP; Grapevine
HALLIBURTON COMPANY; Houston
HE BUTT GROCERY COMPANY
(HEB); San Antonio
J C PENNEY COMPANY INC; Plano
KIMBERLY-CLARK CORP; Dallas
MARY KAY INC; Dallas
MCDERMOTT INTERNATIONAL INC;
Houston
MEN'S WEARHOUSE INC (THE);
Houston
METHODIST HEALTH CARE SYSTEM;
Houston
NATIONAL OILWELL VARCO INC;
Houston
OCEANEERING INTERNATIONAL
INC; Houston
ODYSSEY HEALTHCARE INC; Dallas
OIL STATES INTERNATIONAL INC;
Houston
PATTERSON-UTI ENERGY INC;
Houston
PEROT SYSTEMS CORP; Plano
PRIDE INTERNATIONAL INC; Houston
QUANTA SERVICES INC; Houston
RENT-A-CENTER INC; Plano
RRI ENERGY INC; Houston
SABRE HOLDINGS CORP; Southlake
SCHLUMBERGER LIMITED; Houston
SHELL OIL CO; Houston
SMITH INTERNATIONAL INC; Houston
SOUTHWEST AIRLINES CO; Dallas
SYSCO CORP; Houston
TEAM INC; Alvin
TESORO CORP; San Antonio
USAA; San Antonio
VALERO ENERGY CORP; San Antonio
WASTE MANAGEMENT INC; Houston
WHOLE FOODS MARKET INC; Austin

VIRGINIA
ADVANCE AUTO PARTS INC; Roanoke
AES CORPORATION (THE); Arlington
ALTRIA GROUP INC; Richmond
BOOZ ALLEN HAMILTON; McLean
BRINKS COMPANY (THE); Richmond
CACI INTERNATIONAL INC; Arlington
CARMAX GROUP; Richmond
GENERAL DYNAMICS CORP; Falls
Church
GENWORTH FINANCIAL INC;
Richmond
MARS INC; McLean
MASSEY ENERGY COMPANY;
Richmond
NII HOLDINGS INC; Reston
OWENS & MINOR INC; Mechanicsville
SMITHFIELD FOODS INC; Smithfield
SRA INTERNATIONAL INC; Fairfax
SUNRISE SENIOR LIVING; McLean
WATSON WYATT WORLDWIDE INC;
Arlington

WASHINGTON
AMAZON.COM INC; Seattle
COSTCO WHOLESALE CORP; Issaquah
EMERITUS CORP; Seattle
MICROSOFT CORP; Redmond
SAFECO INSURANCE COMPANY OF
AMERICA; Seattle
T-MOBILE USA; Bellevue

WISCONSIN
BUCYRUS INTERNATIONAL INC;
South Milwaukee
JOHNSON CONTROLS INC; Milwaukee
KOHL'S CORP; Menomonee Falls
MANPOWER INC; Milwaukee
OSHKOSH CORPORATION; Oshkosh
PLEXUS CORP; Neenah
SENSIENT TECHNOLOGIES
CORPORATION; Milwaukee

OTHER
ACCENTURE LTD; Hamilton, Bermuda
NOBLE CORPORATION; Geneva,
Switzerland
TRANSOCEAN INC; Vernier, Switzerland
WEATHERFORD INTERNATIONAL
LTD; Geneva, Switzerland

INDEX BY REGIONS OF THE U.S. WHERE THE FIRMS HAVE LOCATIONS

WEST

3M COMPANY
7-ELEVEN INC
AARON'S INC
ABBOTT LABORATORIES
ABM INDUSTRIES INC
ACCENTURE LTD
ACTIVISION BLIZZARD INC
ACXIOM CORP
ADESA INC
ADOBE SYSTEMS INC
ADVANCED MICRO DEVICES INC
(AMD)
AECOM TECHNOLOGY
CORPORATION
AES CORPORATION (THE)
AETNA INC
AFFILIATED COMPUTER SERVICES
INC
AFLAC INC
AGILENT TECHNOLOGIES INC
AIR PRODUCTS & CHEMICALS INC
ALLERGAN INC
ALLSTATE CORPORATION (THE)
ALTRIA GROUP INC
AMAZON.COM INC
AMEDISYS INC
AMERISOURCEBERGEN CORP
AMGEN INC
ANADARKO PETROLEUM
CORPORATION
ANALOG DEVICES INC
ANNTAYLOR STORES CORP
APOLLO GROUP INC
APPLE INC
ARAMARK CORPORATION
ARCHER DANIELS MIDLAND CO
ARROW ELECTRONICS INC
ARTHUR J GALLAGHER & CO
ASCENSION HEALTH
AT&T INC
AUTOMATIC DATA PROCESSING INC
AUTOZONE INC
AVERY DENNISON CORP
AVIS BUDGET GROUP INC
AVNET INC
AVON PRODUCTS INC
AXA FINANCIAL INC
BAKER HUGHES INC
BANK OF AMERICA CORP
BARNES & NOBLE INC
BASS PRO SHOPS INC
BAXTER INTERNATIONAL INC
BDO SEIDMAN LLP
BEBE STORES INC
BECHTEL GROUP INC
BECKMAN COULTER INC
BECTON DICKINSON & CO
BED BATH & BEYOND INC

BENCHMARK ELECTRONICS INC
BERKSHIRE HATHAWAY INC
BEST BUY CO INC
BIO RAD LABORATORIES INC
BLACK & DECKER CORP
BLACKROCK INC
BLOOMBERG LP
BOEING COMPANY (THE)
BOOZ ALLEN HAMILTON
BOSTON SCIENTIFIC CORP
BRINKER INTERNATIONAL INC
BRINKS COMPANY (THE)
BROADCOM CORP
BROWN & BROWN INC
BUCKLE INC (THE)
BUFFALO WILD WINGS INC
BURGER KING HOLDINGS INC
CABELA'S INC
CACI INTERNATIONAL INC
CAMERON INTERNATIONAL
CORPORATION
CAPITAL SENIOR LIVING CORP
CARDINAL HEALTH INC
CARGILL INC
CARMAX GROUP
CARNIVAL CORPORATION
CASH AMERICA INTERNATIONAL
INC
CATERPILLAR INC
CATHOLIC HEALTH INITIATIVES
CELLCO PARTNERSHIP (VERIZON
WIRELESS)
CEPHALON INC
CH ROBINSON WORLDWIDE INC
CH2M HILL COMPANIES LTD
CHARLOTTE RUSSE HOLDING
CHARMING SHOPPES INC
CHEMED CORPORATION
CHEVRON CORPORATION
CHEVRON PHILLIPS CHEMICAL
COMPANY LLC
CHICO'S FAS INC
CHIPOTLE MEXICAN GRILL INC
CHRISTOPHER & BANKS CORP
CHS INC
CHUBB CORPORATION (THE)
CIBER INC
CIGNA CORP
CINTAS CORP
CISCO SYSTEMS INC
CLUBCORP INC
COACH INC
COCA-COLA COMPANY (THE)
COCA-COLA ENTERPRISES INC
COGNIZANT TECHNOLOGY
SOLUTIONS CORP
COLDWATER CREEK INC
COLGATE PALMOLIVE CO
COMCAST CORP
COMMUNITY HEALTH SYSTEMS INC
CONAGRA FOODS INC
CONOCOPHILLIPS COMPANY
CONSOL ENERGY INC
CONTAINER STORE (THE)
CONVERGYS CORPORATION

COOPER COMPANIES INC
COSTCO WHOLESALE CORP
COVANCE INC
COX COMMUNICATIONS INC
CR BARD INC
CRACKER BARREL OLD COUNTRY
STORE INC
CTS CORP
CUBIC CORP
CUMMINS INC
CVS CAREMARK CORPORATION
DANAHER CORP
DARDEN RESTAURANTS INC
DAVITA INC
DEAN FOODS CO
DEERE & CO
DELOITTE & TOUCHE USA LLP
DELOITTE CONSULTING LLP
DENNY'S CORPORATION
DEVRY INC
DICK'S SPORTING GOODS INC
DIEBOLD INC
DINEEQUITY INC
DIRECTV GROUP INC (THE)
DOLE FOOD COMPANY INC
DOLLAR THRIFTY AUTOMOTIVE
GROUP INC
DRESS BARN INC (THE)
DYCOM INDUSTRIES INC
E I DU PONT DE NEMOURS & CO
(DUPONT)
EATON CORP
EBAY INC
EDISON INTERNATIONAL
ELECTRONIC ARTS INC
ELI LILLY & COMPANY
EMC CORP
EMERITUS CORP
EMERSON ELECTRIC CO
ENTERPRISE PRODUCTS PARTNERS
LP
ENTERPRISE RENT-A-CAR
ERNST & YOUNG LLP
EXPERIAN AMERICAS
EXPRESS SCRIPTS INC
EXXON MOBIL CORPORATION
(EXXONMOBIL)
FAMILY DOLLAR STORES INC
FEDEX CORPORATION
FINISH LINE INC (THE)
FIRST ADVANTAGE CORPORATION
FIRST DATA CORP
FLUOR CORP
FOSSIL INC
FOSTER WHEELER AG
FOX ENTERTAINMENT GROUP INC
FPL GROUP INC
FRONTIER COMMUNICATIONS
CORPORATION
FTI CONSULTING INC
GAMESTOP CORP
GENENTECH INC
GENERAL CABLE CORP
GENERAL DYNAMICS CORP
GENERAL ELECTRIC CO (GE)

GENERAL MILLS INC
GENESCO INC
GENWORTH FINANCIAL INC
GEO GROUP INC
GEORGIA GULF CORPORATION
GILEAD SCIENCES INC
GLOBAL HYATT CORPORATION
GLOBAL PAYMENTS INC
GOLDMAN SACHS GROUP INC
GOOGLE INC
GRANT THORNTON LLP
GUESS? INC
HALLIBURTON COMPANY
HARRAH'S ENTERTAINMENT INC
HARRIS CORPORATION
HARTFORD FINANCIAL SERVICES
GROUP INC (THE)
HAWAIIAN ELECTRIC INDUSTRIES
INC
HCA INC
HEALTH CARE SERVICE
CORPORATION
HEALTH FITNESS CORP
HEALTH MANAGEMENT
ASSOCIATES INC
HEALTH NET INC
HEALTHWAYS INC
HELMERICH & PAYNE INC
HENRY SCHEIN INC
HERTZ GLOBAL HOLDINGS INC
HESS CORPORATION
HEWITT ASSOCIATES
HILTON HOTELS CORP
HOME DEPOT INC
HONEYWELL INTERNATIONAL INC
HUMANA INC
IAC/INTERACTIVECORP
ICT GROUP INC
IDEXX LABORATORIES INC
IGATE CORPORATION
IMS HEALTH INC
INGRAM MICRO INC
INTEL CORP
INTERNATIONAL BUSINESS
MACHINES CORP (IBM)
INTUIT INC
INVENTIV HEALTH INC
J C PENNEY COMPANY INC
JABIL CIRCUIT INC
JACK IN THE BOX INC
JACOBS ENGINEERING GROUP INC
JETBLUE AIRWAYS CORPORATION
JM SMUCKER CO
JOHNSON & JOHNSON
JOHNSON CONTROLS INC
JP MORGAN CHASE & CO INC
JUNIPER NETWORKS INC
KAISER PERMANENTE
KEANE INC
KELLOGG CO
KELLY SERVICES INC
KENDLE INTERNATIONAL INC
KIMBERLY-CLARK CORP
KINDRED HEALTHCARE INC
KOCH INDUSTRIES INC

KOHL'S CORP
KPMG LLP
KRAFT FOODS INC
KROGER CO (THE)
L-3 COMMUNICATIONS HOLDINGS
INC
LABORATORY CORP OF AMERICA
HOLDINGS
LAS VEGAS SANDS CORP (THE
VENETIAN)
LEVEL 3 COMMUNICATIONS INC
LEXMARK INTERNATIONAL INC
LIBERTY GLOBAL INC
LIBERTY MUTUAL GROUP INC
LIMITED BRANDS INC
LINCARE HOLDINGS INC
LINCOLN NATIONAL CORPORATION
LKQ CORP
LOCKHEED MARTIN CORP
LODGIAN INC
LOEWS CORPORATION
LOWE'S COMPANIES INC
MACY'S INC
MANOR CARE INC
MANPOWER INC
MARRIOTT INTERNATIONAL INC
MARS INC
MARSH & MCLENNAN COMPANIES
INC
MARY KAY INC
MATTEL INC
MAXIM INTEGRATED PRODUCTS INC
MCAFEE INC
MCDERMOTT INTERNATIONAL INC
MCDONALD'S CORP
MCKESSON CORPORATION
MCKINSEY & COMPANY INC
MEDCO HEALTH SOLUTIONS
MEDTRONIC INC
MEN'S WEARHOUSE INC (THE)
MERCER INC
MERCK & CO INC
METLIFE INC
MGM MIRAGE
MICROCHIP TECHNOLOGY INC
MICRON TECHNOLOGY INC
MICROSOFT CORP
MIDAMERICAN ENERGY HOLDINGS
CO
MILLIPORE CORP
MONSANTO CO
MURPHY OIL CORPORATION
NATIONAL OILWELL VARCO INC
NETAPP INC
NEWS CORP
NIKE INC
NORTHROP GRUMMAN CORP
NRG ENERGY INC
OCCIDENTAL PETROLEUM CORP
OCEANEERING INTERNATIONAL INC
ODYSSEY HEALTHCARE INC
OFFICE DEPOT INC
OIL STATES INTERNATIONAL INC
OMNICARE INC
OMNICOM GROUP INC

ORACLE CORP
O'REILLY AUTOMOTIVE INC
OSHKOSH CORPORATION
OSI RESTAURANT PARTNERS LLC
OWENS & MINOR INC
PARAMETRIC TECHNOLOGY CORP
PAREXEL INTERNATIONAL CORP
PARSONS BRINCKERHOFF INC
PATTERSON COMPANIES INC
PATTERSON-UTI ENERGY INC
PAYCHEX INC
PEABODY ENERGY CORP
PEPSI BOTTLING GROUP INC
PEPSICO INC
PEROT SYSTEMS CORP
PETCO ANIMAL SUPPLIES INC
PETSMART INC
PFIZER INC
PG&E CORPORATION
PHARMACEUTICAL PRODUCT
DEVELOPMENT INC
PITNEY BOWES INC
PLEXUS CORP
POLO RALPH LAUREN CORP
PRECISION CASTPARTS CORP
PRICESMART INC
PRICEWATERHOUSECOOPERS
PRINCIPAL FINANCIAL GROUP (THE)
PROCTER & GAMBLE CO
PROGRESSIVE CORPORATION (THE)
PRUDENTIAL FINANCIAL INC
PSYCHIATRIC SOLUTIONS INC
PUBLIC STORAGE INC
QUALCOMM INC
QUANTA SERVICES INC
QUEST DIAGNOSTICS INC
QUIKSILVER INC
R R DONNELLEY & SONS CO
RALCORP HOLDINGS INC
RAYTHEON CO
REGIS CORPORATION
RENT-A-CENTER INC
RES CARE INC
RITE AID CORPORATION
RITZ-CARLTON HOTEL COMPANY
LLC (THE)
ROBERT HALF INTERNATIONAL INC
ROSS STORES INC
ROYAL CARIBBEAN CRUISES LTD
RRI ENERGY INC
SAFECO INSURANCE COMPANY OF
AMERICA
SAFEWAY INC
SAIC INC
SAM'S CLUB
SAPIENT CORPORATION
SARA LEE CORP
SAS INSTITUTE INC
SCHERING-PLOUGH CORP
SCHLUMBERGER LIMITED
SCIENTIFIC GAMES CORPORATION
SCOTTS MIRACLE GROW CO
SEACOR HOLDINGS INC
SELECT MEDICAL
SEMPRA ENERGY

SENSIENT TECHNOLOGIES
CORPORATION
SHAW GROUP INC (THE)
SHELL OIL CO
SHERWIN WILLIAMS COMPANY
(THE)
SIGMA-ALDRICH CORP
SMITH INTERNATIONAL INC
SOUTHERN CALIFORNIA EDISON
COMPANY
SRA INTERNATIONAL INC
ST JUDE MEDICAL INC
STAPLES INC
STARTEK INC
STARWOOD HOTELS & RESORTS
WORLDWIDE INC
STERIS CORP
STIFEL FINANCIAL CORP
STRYKER CORP
SUN HEALTHCARE GROUP
SUNGARD DATA SYSTEMS INC
SUNOCO INC
SUNRISE SENIOR LIVING
SUPERVALU INC
SYKES ENTERPRISES INC
SYMANTEC CORP
SYNOPSYS INC
SYNTEL INC
SYSCO CORP
TARGET CORPORATION
TBC CORPORATION
TEAM INC
TECH DATA CORP
TEKTRONIX INC
TELEDYNE TECHNOLOGIES
INCORPORATED
TELEPHONE AND DATA SYSTEMS
INC (TDS)
TELETECH HOLDINGS INC
TESORO CORP
THERMO FISHER SCIENTIFIC INC
TIME WARNER INC
TJX COMPANIES INC (THE)
T-MOBILE USA
TOTAL SYSTEM SERVICES INC
(TSYS)
TOWERS PERRIN
TRAVELERS COMPANIES INC (THE)
TW TELECOM INC
TYSON FOODS INC
UNITED NATURAL FOODS INC
UNITED PARCEL SERVICE INC (UPS)
UNITED STATES CELLULAR CORP
UNITED TECHNOLOGIES
CORPORATION
UNITEDHEALTH GROUP INC
UNIVERSAL HEALTH SERVICES INC
UNIVISION COMMUNICATIONS INC
URS CORPORATION
USAA
VALERO ENERGY CORP
VALSPAR CORPORATION (THE)
VARIAN MEDICAL SYSTEMS INC
VCA ANTECH INC
VERISIGN INC

VERIZON COMMUNICATIONS
VIACOM INC
VICTORIAS SECRET
VISA INC
VOLT INFORMATION SCIENCES INC
W R BERKLEY CORPORATION
WABTEC CORP
WALGREEN CO
WAL-MART STORES INC
WALT DISNEY COMPANY (THE)
WASTE MANAGEMENT INC
WATERS CORP
WATSON PHARMACEUTICALS INC
WATSON WYATT WORLDWIDE INC
WEATHERFORD INTERNATIONAL
LTD
WEIGHT WATCHERS
INTERNATIONAL INC
WELLPOINT INC
WELLS FARGO & CO
WENDY'S/ARBY'S GROUP INC
WEST CORPORATION
WESTERN DIGITAL CORP
WHOLE FOODS MARKET INC
WILLIAMS COMPANIES INC (THE)
WW GRAINGER INC
WYETH
WYNDHAM WORLDWIDE
WYNN RESORTS LIMITED
XEROX CORP
YAHOO! INC
YUM! BRANDS INC
ZIMMER HOLDINGS INC

SOUTHWEST
3M COMPANY
7-ELEVEN INC
AARON'S INC
ABBOTT LABORATORIES
ABM INDUSTRIES INC
ACADEMY SPORTS & OUTDOORS
LTD
ACCENTURE LTD
ACTIVISION BLIZZARD INC
ACXIOM CORP
ADESA INC
ADVANCE AUTO PARTS INC
ADVANCED MICRO DEVICES INC
(AMD)
AECOM TECHNOLOGY
CORPORATION
AES CORPORATION (THE)
AETNA INC
AFFILIATED COMPUTER SERVICES
INC
AFLAC INC
AIR PRODUCTS & CHEMICALS INC
ALLIANCE DATA SYSTEMS
CORPORATION
ALLSTATE CORPORATION (THE)
ALTRIA GROUP INC
AMAZON.COM INC
AMEDISYS INC

AMERICAN ELECTRIC POWER
COMPANY INC (AEP)
AMERICAN POWER CONVERSION
(APC)
AMERISOURCEBERGEN CORP
ANADARKO PETROLEUM
CORPORATION
ANALOG DEVICES INC
ANNTAYLOR STORES CORP
APACHE CORP
APOLLO GROUP INC
APPLE INC
ARAMARK CORPORATION
ARCHER DANIELS MIDLAND CO
ARROW ELECTRONICS INC
ARTHUR J GALLAGHER & CO
ASCENSION HEALTH
AT&T INC
AUTOMATIC DATA PROCESSING INC
AUTOZONE INC
AVERY DENNISON CORP
AVIS BUDGET GROUP INC
AVNET INC
AXA FINANCIAL INC
BAKER HUGHES INC
BANK OF AMERICA CORP
BARNES & NOBLE INC
BASS PRO SHOPS INC
BAXTER INTERNATIONAL INC
BDO SEIDMAN LLP
BEBE STORES INC
BECHTEL GROUP INC
BECTON DICKINSON & CO
BED BATH & BEYOND INC
BENCHMARK ELECTRONICS INC
BERKSHIRE HATHAWAY INC
BEST BUY CO INC
BIO RAD LABORATORIES INC
BLOOMBERG LP
BOEING COMPANY (THE)
BOOZ ALLEN HAMILTON
BOSTON SCIENTIFIC CORP
BRINKER INTERNATIONAL INC
BRINKS COMPANY (THE)
BROADCOM CORP
BROWN & BROWN INC
BUCKLE INC (THE)
BUFFALO WILD WINGS INC
BURGER KING HOLDINGS INC
CABELA'S INC
CACI INTERNATIONAL INC
CAMERON INTERNATIONAL
CORPORATION
CAPITAL SENIOR LIVING CORP
CARDINAL HEALTH INC
CARGILL INC
CARMAX GROUP
CASH AMERICA INTERNATIONAL
INC
CATERPILLAR INC
CATHOLIC HEALTH INITIATIVES
CELLCO PARTNERSHIP (VERIZON
WIRELESS)
CH ROBINSON WORLDWIDE INC
CH2M HILL COMPANIES LTD

CHARLOTTE RUSSE HOLDING
CHARMING SHOPPES INC
CHEMED CORPORATION
CHEVRON CORPORATION
CHEVRON PHILLIPS CHEMICAL
COMPANY LLC
CHICO'S FAS INC
CHIPOTLE MEXICAN GRILL INC
CHRISTOPHER & BANKS CORP
CHS INC
CHUBB CORPORATION (THE)
CIBER INC
CIGNA CORP
CINTAS CORP
CISCO SYSTEMS INC
CLUBCORP INC
COACH INC
COCA-COLA COMPANY (THE)
COCA-COLA ENTERPRISES INC
COGNIZANT TECHNOLOGY
SOLUTIONS CORP
COLDWATER CREEK INC
COLGATE PALMOLIVE CO
COMCAST CORP
COMMUNITY HEALTH SYSTEMS INC
CONAGRA FOODS INC
CONOCOPHILLIPS COMPANY
CONSOLIDATED EDISON INC
CONTAINER STORE (THE)
CONVERGYS CORPORATION
COOPER COMPANIES INC
COSTCO WHOLESALE CORP
COVANCE INC
COX COMMUNICATIONS INC
CR BARD INC
CRACKER BARREL OLD COUNTRY
STORE INC
CTS CORP
CUMMINS INC
CVS CAREMARK CORPORATION
DANAHER CORP
DARDEN RESTAURANTS INC
DAVITA INC
DEAN FOODS CO
DEERE & CO
DELOITTE & TOUCHE USA LLP
DELOITTE CONSULTING LLP
DENNY'S CORPORATION
DEVON ENERGY CORPORATION
DEVRY INC
DIAMOND OFFSHORE DRILLING INC
DICK'S SPORTING GOODS INC
DIEBOLD INC
DINEEQUITY INC
DIRECTV GROUP INC (THE)
DOLE FOOD COMPANY INC
DOLLAR GENERAL CORPORATION
DOLLAR THRIFTY AUTOMOTIVE
GROUP INC
DRESS BARN INC (THE)
DYCOM INDUSTRIES INC
E I DU PONT DE NEMOURS & CO
(DUPONT)
EATON CORP
EBAY INC

EDISON INTERNATIONAL
ELECTRONIC ARTS INC
ELI LILLY & COMPANY
EMERITUS CORP
EMERSON ELECTRIC CO
ENTERGY CORP
ENTERPRISE PRODUCTS PARTNERS
LP
ENTERPRISE RENT-A-CAR
ERNST & YOUNG LLP
EXELON CORPORATION
EXPERIAN AMERICAS
EXPRESS SCRIPTS INC
EXXON MOBIL CORPORATION
(EXXONMOBIL)
EXXONMOBIL CHEMICAL
FAMILY DOLLAR STORES INC
FEDEX CORPORATION
FINISH LINE INC (THE)
FIRST ADVANTAGE CORPORATION
FIRST DATA CORP
FLUOR CORP
FOSSIL INC
FOSTER WHEELER AG
FPL GROUP INC
FRED'S INC
FRONTIER COMMUNICATIONS
CORPORATION
FTI CONSULTING INC
GAMESTOP CORP
GENERAL CABLE CORP
GENERAL DYNAMICS CORP
GENERAL ELECTRIC CO (GE)
GENERAL MILLS INC
GENESCO INC
GENWORTH FINANCIAL INC
GEO GROUP INC
GEORGIA GULF CORPORATION
GLOBAL HYATT CORPORATION
GLOBAL PAYMENTS INC
GOLDMAN SACHS GROUP INC
GOOGLE INC
GRANT THORNTON LLP
GUESS? INC
HALLIBURTON COMPANY
HARRAH'S ENTERTAINMENT INC
HARRIS CORPORATION
HARTFORD FINANCIAL SERVICES
GROUP INC (THE)
HCA INC
HE BUTT GROCERY COMPANY (HEB)
HEALTH CARE SERVICE
CORPORATION
HEALTH FITNESS CORP
HEALTH MANAGEMENT
ASSOCIATES INC
HEALTH NET INC
HEALTHWAYS INC
HELMERICH & PAYNE INC
HENRY SCHEIN INC
HERTZ GLOBAL HOLDINGS INC
HESS CORPORATION
HEWITT ASSOCIATES
HIBBETT SPORTS INC
HILTON HOTELS CORP

HOME DEPOT INC
HONEYWELL INTERNATIONAL INC
HUMANA INC
IAC/INTERACTIVECORP
ICT GROUP INC
IDEXX LABORATORIES INC
IGATE CORPORATION
INGRAM MICRO INC
INTEL CORP
INTERNATIONAL BUSINESS
MACHINES CORP (IBM)
INTUIT INC
INVENTIV HEALTH INC
J C PENNEY COMPANY INC
JACK IN THE BOX INC
JACOBS ENGINEERING GROUP INC
JETBLUE AIRWAYS CORPORATION
JOHNSON & JOHNSON
JOHNSON CONTROLS INC
JP MORGAN CHASE & CO INC
JUNIPER NETWORKS INC
KELLOGG CO
KELLY SERVICES INC
KIMBERLY-CLARK CORP
KINDRED HEALTHCARE INC
KOCH INDUSTRIES INC
KOHL'S CORP
KPMG LLP
KRAFT FOODS INC
KROGER CO (THE)
L-3 COMMUNICATIONS HOLDINGS
INC
LABORATORY CORP OF AMERICA
HOLDINGS
LEVEL 3 COMMUNICATIONS INC
LIBERTY MUTUAL GROUP INC
LIMITED BRANDS INC
LINCARE HOLDINGS INC
LINCOLN NATIONAL CORPORATION
LKQ CORP
LOCKHEED MARTIN CORP
LODGIAN INC
LOEWS CORPORATION
LOWE'S COMPANIES INC
MACY'S INC
MANOR CARE INC
MANPOWER INC
MARRIOTT INTERNATIONAL INC
MARS INC
MARSH & MCLENNAN COMPANIES
INC
MARY KAY INC
MATTEL INC
MAXIM INTEGRATED PRODUCTS INC
MAYO FOUNDATION FOR MEDICAL
EDUCATION AND RESEARCH
MCAFEE INC
MCDERMOTT INTERNATIONAL INC
MCDONALD'S CORP
MCKESSON CORPORATION
MCKINSEY & COMPANY INC
MEDCO HEALTH SOLUTIONS
MEDTRONIC INC
MEN'S WEARHOUSE INC (THE)
MERCER INC

MERCK & CO INC
METHODIST HEALTH CARE SYSTEM
METLIFE INC
MICROCHIP TECHNOLOGY INC
MICRON TECHNOLOGY INC
MICROSOFT CORP
MIDAMERICAN ENERGY HOLDINGS
CO
MILLIPORE CORP
MONSANTO CO
MURPHY OIL CORPORATION
MYLAN INC
NATIONAL OILWELL VARCO INC
NEWS CORP
NIKE INC
NOBLE CORPORATION
NORTHROP GRUMMAN CORP
NRG ENERGY INC
OCCIDENTAL PETROLEUM CORP
OCEANEERING INTERNATIONAL INC
ODYSSEY HEALTHCARE INC
OFFICE DEPOT INC
OIL STATES INTERNATIONAL INC
OMNICARE INC
OMNICOM GROUP INC
ORACLE CORP
O'REILLY AUTOMOTIVE INC
OSHKOSH CORPORATION
OSI RESTAURANT PARTNERS LLC
OWENS & MINOR INC
PARAMETRIC TECHNOLOGY CORP
PARSONS BRINCKERHOFF INC
PATTERSON COMPANIES INC
PATTERSON-UTI ENERGY INC
PAYCHEX INC
PEPSI BOTTLING GROUP INC
PEPSICO INC
PEROT SYSTEMS CORP
PETCO ANIMAL SUPPLIES INC
PETSMART INC
PFIZER INC
PHARMACEUTICAL PRODUCT
DEVELOPMENT INC
PITNEY BOWES INC
POLO RALPH LAUREN CORP
PRECISION CASTPARTS CORP
PRICEWATERHOUSECOOPERS
PRIDE INTERNATIONAL INC
PRINCIPAL FINANCIAL GROUP (THE)
PROCTER & GAMBLE CO
PROGRESSIVE CORPORATION (THE)
PRUDENTIAL FINANCIAL INC
PSYCHIATRIC SOLUTIONS INC
PUBLIC STORAGE INC
QUALCOMM INC
QUANTA SERVICES INC
QUEST DIAGNOSTICS INC
R R DONNELLEY & SONS CO
RALCORP HOLDINGS INC
RAYTHEON CO
REGIS CORPORATION
RENT-A-CENTER INC
RES CARE INC
RITE AID CORPORATION

RITZ-CARLTON HOTEL COMPANY
LLC (THE)
ROBERT HALF INTERNATIONAL INC
ROSS STORES INC
SABRE HOLDINGS CORP
SAFECO INSURANCE COMPANY OF
AMERICA
SAFEWAY INC
SAIC INC
SAM'S CLUB
SAPIENT CORPORATION
SARA LEE CORP
SAS INSTITUTE INC
SCHERING-PLOUGH CORP
SCHLUMBERGER LIMITED
SCIENTIFIC GAMES CORPORATION
SCOTTS MIRACLE GROW CO
SEACOR HOLDINGS INC
SELECT MEDICAL
SEMPRA ENERGY
SHAW GROUP INC (THE)
SHELL OIL CO
SHERWIN WILLIAMS COMPANY
(THE)
SIGMA-ALDRICH CORP
SISTERS OF MERCY HEALTH
SYSTEMS
SMITH INTERNATIONAL INC
SMITHFIELD FOODS INC
SOUTHERN CALIFORNIA EDISON
COMPANY
SOUTHWEST AIRLINES CO
SRA INTERNATIONAL INC
ST JUDE MEDICAL INC
STAPLES INC
STARTEK INC
STARWOOD HOTELS & RESORTS
WORLDWIDE INC
STERIS CORP
STIFEL FINANCIAL CORP
STRYKER CORP
SUN HEALTHCARE GROUP
SUNGARD DATA SYSTEMS INC
SUNOCO INC
SUNRISE SENIOR LIVING
SUPERVALU INC
SYKES ENTERPRISES INC
SYMANTEC CORP
SYNOPSYS INC
SYNTEL INC
SYSCO CORP
TARGET CORPORATION
TBC CORPORATION
TEAM INC
TECH DATA CORP
TEKTRONIX INC
TELEDYNE TECHNOLOGIES
INCORPORATED
TELEPHONE AND DATA SYSTEMS
INC (TDS)
TELETECH HOLDINGS INC
TESORO CORP
TIME WARNER INC
TJX COMPANIES INC (THE)
T-MOBILE USA

TOTAL SYSTEM SERVICES INC
(TSYS)
TOWERS PERRIN
TRANSOCEAN INC
TRAVELERS COMPANIES INC (THE)
TW TELECOM INC
TYSON FOODS INC
UNITED PARCEL SERVICE INC (UPS)
UNITED STATES CELLULAR CORP
UNITED TECHNOLOGIES
CORPORATION
UNITEDHEALTH GROUP INC
UNIVERSAL HEALTH SERVICES INC
UNIVISION COMMUNICATIONS INC
URS CORPORATION
USAA
VALERO ENERGY CORP
VALSPAR CORPORATION (THE)
VCA ANTECH INC
VERISIGN INC
VERIZON COMMUNICATIONS
VICTORIAS SECRET
VISA INC
W R BERKLEY CORPORATION
WABTEC CORP
WALGREEN CO
WAL-MART STORES INC
WALT DISNEY COMPANY (THE)
WASTE MANAGEMENT INC
WATERS CORP
WATSON WYATT WORLDWIDE INC
WEATHERFORD INTERNATIONAL
LTD
WEIGHT WATCHERS
INTERNATIONAL INC
WELLPOINT INC
WELLS FARGO & CO
WENDY'S/ARBY'S GROUP INC
WEST CORPORATION
WEST PHARMACEUTICAL SERVICES
INC
WHOLE FOODS MARKET INC
WILLIAMS COMPANIES INC (THE)
WW GRAINGER INC
WYETH
WYNDHAM WORLDWIDE
XEROX CORP
YUM! BRANDS INC
ZIMMER HOLDINGS INC

MIDWEST
3M COMPANY
7-ELEVEN INC
AARON'S INC
ABBOTT LABORATORIES
ABM INDUSTRIES INC
ACADEMY SPORTS & OUTDOORS
LTD
ACCENTURE LTD
ACTIVISION BLIZZARD INC
ACXIOM CORP
ADC TELECOMMUNICATIONS INC
ADESA INC
ADVANCE AUTO PARTS INC

ADVANCED MICRO DEVICES INC (AMD)
AECOM TECHNOLOGY CORPORATION
AES CORPORATION (THE)
AETNA INC
AFFILIATED COMPUTER SERVICES INC
AFLAC INC
AIR PRODUCTS & CHEMICALS INC
ALLIANCE DATA SYSTEMS CORPORATION
ALLSTATE CORPORATION (THE)
ALTRIA GROUP INC
AMAZON.COM INC
AMEDISYS INC
AMERICAN ELECTRIC POWER COMPANY INC (AEP)
AMERICAN POWER CONVERSION (APC)
AMERISOURCEBERGEN CORP
ANALOG DEVICES INC
ANNTAYLOR STORES CORP
APOLLO GROUP INC
APPLE INC
ARAMARK CORPORATION
ARCHER DANIELS MIDLAND CO
ARROW ELECTRONICS INC
ARTHUR J GALLAGHER & CO
ASCENSION HEALTH
AT&T INC
AUTOMATIC DATA PROCESSING INC
AUTOZONE INC
AVERY DENNISON CORP
AVIS BUDGET GROUP INC
AVNET INC
AVON PRODUCTS INC
AXA FINANCIAL INC
BAKER HUGHES INC
BANK OF AMERICA CORP
BARNES & NOBLE INC
BASS PRO SHOPS INC
BAXTER INTERNATIONAL INC
BDO SEIDMAN LLP
BEBE STORES INC
BECHTEL GROUP INC
BECTON DICKINSON & CO
BED BATH & BEYOND INC
BENCHMARK ELECTRONICS INC
BERKSHIRE HATHAWAY INC
BEST BUY CO INC
BJ'S WHOLESALE CLUB INC
BLACKROCK INC
BLOOMBERG LP
BOEING COMPANY (THE)
BOOZ ALLEN HAMILTON
BOSTON SCIENTIFIC CORP
BRINKER INTERNATIONAL INC
BRINKS COMPANY (THE)
BROADCOM CORP
BROWN & BROWN INC
BUCKLE INC (THE)
BUCYRUS INTERNATIONAL INC
BUFFALO WILD WINGS INC
BUNGE LTD

BURGER KING HOLDINGS INC
CABELA'S INC
CACI INTERNATIONAL INC
CAMERON INTERNATIONAL CORPORATION
CAPITAL SENIOR LIVING CORP
CARDINAL HEALTH INC
CARGILL INC
CARMAX GROUP
CASH AMERICA INTERNATIONAL INC
CATERPILLAR INC
CATHOLIC HEALTH INITIATIVES
CDW CORPORATION
CELLCO PARTNERSHIP (VERIZON WIRELESS)
CEPHALON INC
CH ROBINSON WORLDWIDE INC
CH2M HILL COMPANIES LTD
CHARLOTTE RUSSE HOLDING
CHARMING SHOPPES INC
CHEMED CORPORATION
CHEVRON CORPORATION
CHEVRON PHILLIPS CHEMICAL COMPANY LLC
CHICO'S FAS INC
CHIPOTLE MEXICAN GRILL INC
CHRISTOPHER & BANKS CORP
CHS INC
CHUBB CORPORATION (THE)
CIBER INC
CIGNA CORP
CINTAS CORP
CISCO SYSTEMS INC
CLUBCORP INC
COACH INC
COCA-COLA COMPANY (THE)
COCA-COLA ENTERPRISES INC
COGNIZANT TECHNOLOGY SOLUTIONS CORP
COLDWATER CREEK INC
COLGATE PALMOLIVE CO
COMCAST CORP
COMMUNITY HEALTH SYSTEMS INC
CONAGRA FOODS INC
CONOCOPHILLIPS COMPANY
CONSOLIDATED EDISON INC
CONTAINER STORE (THE)
CONVERGYS CORPORATION
COSTCO WHOLESALE CORP
COVANCE INC
COX COMMUNICATIONS INC
CR BARD INC
CRACKER BARREL OLD COUNTRY STORE INC
CTS CORP
CUBIC CORP
CUMMINS INC
CVS CAREMARK CORPORATION
DANAHER CORP
DARDEN RESTAURANTS INC
DAVITA INC
DEAN FOODS CO
DEERE & CO
DELOITTE & TOUCHE USA LLP

DELOITTE CONSULTING LLP
DENNY'S CORPORATION
DEVRY INC
DICK'S SPORTING GOODS INC
DIEBOLD INC
DINEEQUITY INC
DIRECTV GROUP INC (THE)
DOLE FOOD COMPANY INC
DOLLAR GENERAL CORPORATION
DOLLAR THRIFTY AUTOMOTIVE GROUP INC
DRESS BARN INC (THE)
DTE ENERGY COMPANY
DUKE ENERGY CORP
DYCOM INDUSTRIES INC
E I DU PONT DE NEMOURS & CO (DUPONT)
EATON CORP
EBAY INC
EDISON INTERNATIONAL
ELECTRONIC ARTS INC
ELI LILLY & COMPANY
EMBARQ CORP
EMERITUS CORP
EMERSON ELECTRIC CO
ENTERPRISE PRODUCTS PARTNERS LP
ENTERPRISE RENT-A-CAR
ERNST & YOUNG LLP
ESTEE LAUDER COMPANIES INC (THE)
EXELON CORPORATION
EXPERIAN AMERICAS
EXPRESS SCRIPTS INC
EXXON MOBIL CORPORATION (EXXONMOBIL)
FAMILY DOLLAR STORES INC
FEDEX CORPORATION
FINISH LINE INC (THE)
FIRST ADVANTAGE CORPORATION
FIRST DATA CORP
FIRSTENERGY CORP
FLUOR CORP
FOREST LABORATORIES INC
FORTUNE BRANDS INC
FOSSIL INC
FOSTER WHEELER AG
FPL GROUP INC
FRED'S INC
FRONTIER COMMUNICATIONS CORPORATION
FTI CONSULTING INC
GAMESTOP CORP
GENERAL CABLE CORP
GENERAL DYNAMICS CORP
GENERAL ELECTRIC CO (GE)
GENERAL MILLS INC
GENESCO INC
GENWORTH FINANCIAL INC
GEO GROUP INC
GEORGIA GULF CORPORATION
GLOBAL HYATT CORPORATION
GLOBAL PAYMENTS INC
GOLDMAN SACHS GROUP INC
GRANT THORNTON LLP

GUESS? INC
HARRAH'S ENTERTAINMENT INC
HARRIS CORPORATION
HARTFORD FINANCIAL SERVICES
GROUP INC (THE)
HCA INC
HEALTH CARE SERVICE
CORPORATION
HEALTH FITNESS CORP
HEALTH MANAGEMENT
ASSOCIATES INC
HEALTHWAYS INC
HELMERICH & PAYNE INC
HENRY SCHEIN INC
HERTZ GLOBAL HOLDINGS INC
HESS CORPORATION
HEWITT ASSOCIATES
HIBBETT SPORTS INC
HILTON HOTELS CORP
HOME DEPOT INC
HONEYWELL INTERNATIONAL INC
HUMANA INC
IAC/INTERACTIVECORP
ICT GROUP INC
IDEXX LABORATORIES INC
IGATE CORPORATION
INFOGROUP INC
INGRAM MICRO INC
INTEL CORP
INTERNATIONAL BUSINESS
MACHINES CORP (IBM)
INTUIT INC
INVENTIV HEALTH INC
J C PENNEY COMPANY INC
JABIL CIRCUIT INC
JACK IN THE BOX INC
JACOBS ENGINEERING GROUP INC
JETBLUE AIRWAYS CORPORATION
JM SMUCKER CO
JOHNSON & JOHNSON
JOHNSON CONTROLS INC
JP MORGAN CHASE & CO INC
JUNIPER NETWORKS INC
KAISER PERMANENTE
KELLOGG CO
KELLY SERVICES INC
KENDLE INTERNATIONAL INC
KIMBERLY-CLARK CORP
KINDRED HEALTHCARE INC
KOCH INDUSTRIES INC
KOHL'S CORP
KPMG LLP
KRAFT FOODS INC
KROGER CO (THE)
L-3 COMMUNICATIONS HOLDINGS
INC
LABORATORY CORP OF AMERICA
HOLDINGS
LEXMARK INTERNATIONAL INC
LIBERTY MUTUAL GROUP INC
LIMITED BRANDS INC
LINCARE HOLDINGS INC
LINCOLN NATIONAL CORPORATION
LKQ CORP
LOCKHEED MARTIN CORP

LODGIAN INC
LOEWS CORPORATION
LOWE'S COMPANIES INC
MACY'S INC
MANOR CARE INC
MANPOWER INC
MARRIOTT INTERNATIONAL INC
MARS INC
MARSH & MCLENNAN COMPANIES
INC
MARY KAY INC
MATTEL INC
MAXIM INTEGRATED PRODUCTS INC
MAYO FOUNDATION FOR MEDICAL
EDUCATION AND RESEARCH
MCAFEE INC
MCDERMOTT INTERNATIONAL INC
MCDONALD'S CORP
MCKESSON CORPORATION
MCKINSEY & COMPANY INC
MEDCO HEALTH SOLUTIONS
MEDTRONIC INC
MEIJER INC
MEN'S WEARHOUSE INC (THE)
MERCER INC
MERCK & CO INC
METLIFE INC
MGM MIRAGE
MICROCHIP TECHNOLOGY INC
MICRON TECHNOLOGY INC
MICROSOFT CORP
MIDAMERICAN ENERGY HOLDINGS
CO
MILLIPORE CORP
MONRO MUFFLER BRAKE INC
MONSANTO CO
MURPHY OIL CORPORATION
MYLAN INC
NATIONAL OILWELL VARCO INC
NEWS CORP
NIKE INC
NORTHROP GRUMMAN CORP
NRG ENERGY INC
OCCIDENTAL PETROLEUM CORP
ODYSSEY HEALTHCARE INC
OFFICE DEPOT INC
OIL STATES INTERNATIONAL INC
OMNICARE INC
OMNICOM GROUP INC
ORACLE CORP
O'REILLY AUTOMOTIVE INC
OSHKOSH CORPORATION
OSI RESTAURANT PARTNERS LLC
OWENS & MINOR INC
PANTRY INC (THE)
PARAMETRIC TECHNOLOGY CORP
PARSONS BRINCKERHOFF INC
PATTERSON COMPANIES INC
PATTERSON-UTI ENERGY INC
PAYCHEX INC
PEABODY ENERGY CORP
PEPSI BOTTLING GROUP INC
PEPSICO INC
PEROT SYSTEMS CORP
PETCO ANIMAL SUPPLIES INC

PETSMART INC
PFIZER INC
PHARMACEUTICAL PRODUCT
DEVELOPMENT INC
PITNEY BOWES INC
PLEXUS CORP
POLO RALPH LAUREN CORP
PRECISION CASTPARTS CORP
PRICEWATERHOUSECOOPERS
PRINCIPAL FINANCIAL GROUP (THE)
PROCTER & GAMBLE CO
PROGRESSIVE CORPORATION (THE)
PRUDENTIAL FINANCIAL INC
PSYCHIATRIC SOLUTIONS INC
PUBLIC STORAGE INC
QUALCOMM INC
QUANTA SERVICES INC
QUEST DIAGNOSTICS INC
R R DONNELLEY & SONS CO
RALCORP HOLDINGS INC
RAYTHEON CO
REGIS CORPORATION
RENT-A-CENTER INC
RES CARE INC
RITE AID CORPORATION
RITZ-CARLTON HOTEL COMPANY
LLC (THE)
ROBERT HALF INTERNATIONAL INC
ROYAL CARIBBEAN CRUISES LTD
RRI ENERGY INC
SAFECO INSURANCE COMPANY OF
AMERICA
SAFEWAY INC
SAIC INC
SAM'S CLUB
SAPIENT CORPORATION
SARA LEE CORP
SAS INSTITUTE INC
SCHERING-PLOUGH CORP
SCHLUMBERGER LIMITED
SCIENTIFIC GAMES CORPORATION
SCOTTS MIRACLE GROW CO
SEACOR HOLDINGS INC
SELECT MEDICAL
SENSIENT TECHNOLOGIES
CORPORATION
SHAW GROUP INC (THE)
SHELL OIL CO
SHERWIN WILLIAMS COMPANY
(THE)
SIGMA-ALDRICH CORP
SISTERS OF MERCY HEALTH
SYSTEMS
SMITH INTERNATIONAL INC
SMITHFIELD FOODS INC
SOUTHWEST AIRLINES CO
SRA INTERNATIONAL INC
ST JUDE MEDICAL INC
STAPLES INC
STARTEK INC
STARWOOD HOTELS & RESORTS
WORLDWIDE INC
STERIS CORP
STIFEL FINANCIAL CORP
STRYKER CORP

SUN HEALTHCARE GROUP
SUNGARD DATA SYSTEMS INC
SUNOCO INC
SUNRISE SENIOR LIVING
SUPERVALU INC
SYKES ENTERPRISES INC
SYMANTEC CORP
SYNOPSYS INC
SYNTEL INC
SYSCO CORP
TARGET CORPORATION
TEAM INC
TECH DATA CORP
TELEDYNE TECHNOLOGIES
INCORPORATED
TELEPHONE AND DATA SYSTEMS
INC (TDS)
TELETECH HOLDINGS INC
TESORO CORP
THERMO FISHER SCIENTIFIC INC
TIME WARNER INC
TJX COMPANIES INC (THE)
T-MOBILE USA
TOTAL SYSTEM SERVICES INC
(TSYS)
TOWERS PERRIN
TRAVELERS COMPANIES INC (THE)
TREEHOUSE FOODS INC
TW TELECOM INC
TYSON FOODS INC
UNITED NATURAL FOODS INC
UNITED PARCEL SERVICE INC (UPS)
UNITED STATES CELLULAR CORP
UNITED TECHNOLOGIES
CORPORATION
UNITEDHEALTH GROUP INC
UNIVERSAL HEALTH SERVICES INC
UNIVISION COMMUNICATIONS INC
URS CORPORATION
VALERO ENERGY CORP
VALSPAR CORPORATION (THE)
VARIAN MEDICAL SYSTEMS INC
VCA ANTECH INC
VERISIGN INC
VERIZON COMMUNICATIONS
VIACOM INC
VICTORIAS SECRET
VISA INC
W R BERKLEY CORPORATION
WABTEC CORP
WALGREEN CO
WAL-MART STORES INC
WALT DISNEY COMPANY (THE)
WASTE MANAGEMENT INC
WATERS CORP
WATSON PHARMACEUTICALS INC
WATSON WYATT WORLDWIDE INC
WEATHERFORD INTERNATIONAL
LTD
WEIGHT WATCHERS
INTERNATIONAL INC
WELLPOINT INC
WELLS FARGO & CO
WENDY'S/ARBY'S GROUP INC
WEST CORPORATION

WEST PHARMACEUTICAL SERVICES
INC
WHOLE FOODS MARKET INC
WILLIAMS COMPANIES INC (THE)
WW GRAINGER INC
WYETH
WYNDHAM WORLDWIDE
XEROX CORP
YUM! BRANDS INC
ZIMMER HOLDINGS INC

SOUTHEAST
3M COMPANY
7-ELEVEN INC
AARON'S INC
ABM INDUSTRIES INC
ACADEMY SPORTS & OUTDOORS
LTD
ACCENTURE LTD
ACTIVISION BLIZZARD INC
ACXIOM CORP
ADESA INC
ADVANCE AUTO PARTS INC
ADVANCED MICRO DEVICES INC
(AMD)
AECOM TECHNOLOGY
CORPORATION
AETNA INC
AFFILIATED COMPUTER SERVICES
INC
AFLAC INC
AIR PRODUCTS & CHEMICALS INC
ALLSTATE CORPORATION (THE)
ALTRIA GROUP INC
AMEDISYS INC
AMERICAN ELECTRIC POWER
COMPANY INC (AEP)
AMERICAN POWER CONVERSION
(APC)
AMERISOURCEBERGEN CORP
AMGEN INC
ANADARKO PETROLEUM
CORPORATION
ANALOG DEVICES INC
ANNTAYLOR STORES CORP
APACHE CORP
APOLLO GROUP INC
APPLE INC
ARAMARK CORPORATION
ARCHER DANIELS MIDLAND CO
ARROW ELECTRONICS INC
ARTHUR J GALLAGHER & CO
ASCENSION HEALTH
AT&T INC
AUTOMATIC DATA PROCESSING INC
AUTOZONE INC
AVERY DENNISON CORP
AVIS BUDGET GROUP INC
AVNET INC
AVON PRODUCTS INC
AXA FINANCIAL INC
BAKER HUGHES INC
BANK OF AMERICA CORP
BARNES & NOBLE INC

BASS PRO SHOPS INC
BAXTER INTERNATIONAL INC
BDO SEIDMAN LLP
BEBE STORES INC
BECHTEL GROUP INC
BECKMAN COULTER INC
BECTON DICKINSON & CO
BED BATH & BEYOND INC
BENCHMARK ELECTRONICS INC
BERKSHIRE HATHAWAY INC
BEST BUY CO INC
BJ'S WHOLESALE CLUB INC
BLACK & DECKER CORP
BLOOMBERG LP
BOEING COMPANY (THE)
BOOZ ALLEN HAMILTON
BOSTON SCIENTIFIC CORP
BRINKER INTERNATIONAL INC
BRINKS COMPANY (THE)
BROADCOM CORP
BROWN & BROWN INC
BUCKLE INC (THE)
BUFFALO WILD WINGS INC
BURGER KING HOLDINGS INC
CACI INTERNATIONAL INC
CAMERON INTERNATIONAL
CORPORATION
CAPITAL SENIOR LIVING CORP
CARDINAL HEALTH INC
CARGILL INC
CARMAX GROUP
CARNIVAL CORPORATION
CASH AMERICA INTERNATIONAL
INC
CATERPILLAR INC
CATHOLIC HEALTH INITIATIVES
CELLCO PARTNERSHIP (VERIZON
WIRELESS)
CH ROBINSON WORLDWIDE INC
CH2M HILL COMPANIES LTD
CHARLOTTE RUSSE HOLDING
CHARMING SHOPPES INC
CHEMED CORPORATION
CHEVRON CORPORATION
CHEVRON PHILLIPS CHEMICAL
COMPANY LLC
CHICO'S FAS INC
CHIPOTLE MEXICAN GRILL INC
CHRISTOPHER & BANKS CORP
CHS INC
CHUBB CORPORATION (THE)
CIBER INC
CIGNA CORP
CINTAS CORP
CISCO SYSTEMS INC
CLUBCORP INC
COACH INC
COCA-COLA COMPANY (THE)
COCA-COLA ENTERPRISES INC
COLDWATER CREEK INC
COLGATE PALMOLIVE CO
COMCAST CORP
COMMUNITY HEALTH SYSTEMS INC
CONAGRA FOODS INC
CONOCOPHILLIPS COMPANY

CONTAINER STORE (THE)
CONVERGYS CORPORATION
COSTCO WHOLESALE CORP
COVANCE INC
COX COMMUNICATIONS INC
CR BARD INC
CRACKER BARREL OLD COUNTRY
STORE INC
CUBIC CORP
CUMMINS INC
CVS CAREMARK CORPORATION
DANAHER CORP
DARDEN RESTAURANTS INC
DAVITA INC
DEAN FOODS CO
DEERE & CO
DELOITTE & TOUCHE USA LLP
DELOITTE CONSULTING LLP
DENNY'S CORPORATION
DEVRY INC
DIAMOND OFFSHORE DRILLING INC
DICK'S SPORTING GOODS INC
DIEBOLD INC
DINEEQUITY INC
DIRECTV GROUP INC (THE)
DOLE FOOD COMPANY INC
DOLLAR GENERAL CORPORATION
DOLLAR THRIFTY AUTOMOTIVE
GROUP INC
DRESS BARN INC (THE)
DUKE ENERGY CORP
DYCOM INDUSTRIES INC
E I DU PONT DE NEMOURS & CO
(DUPONT)
EATON CORP
EDISON INTERNATIONAL
ELECTRONIC ARTS INC
ELI LILLY & COMPANY
EMERITUS CORP
EMERSON ELECTRIC CO
ENTERGY CORP
ENTERPRISE PRODUCTS PARTNERS
LP
ENTERPRISE RENT-A-CAR
ERNST & YOUNG LLP
EXPERIAN AMERICAS
EXPRESS SCRIPTS INC
EXXON MOBIL CORPORATION
(EXXONMOBIL)
FAMILY DOLLAR STORES INC
FEDEX CORPORATION
FINISH LINE INC (THE)
FIRST ADVANTAGE CORPORATION
FIRST DATA CORP
FLUOR CORP
FOSSIL INC
FOSTER WHEELER AG
FPL GROUP INC
FRED'S INC
FRONTIER COMMUNICATIONS
CORPORATION
FTI CONSULTING INC
GAMESTOP CORP
GENERAL CABLE CORP
GENERAL DYNAMICS CORP

GENERAL ELECTRIC CO (GE)
GENERAL MILLS INC
GENESCO INC
GENWORTH FINANCIAL INC
GEO GROUP INC
GEORGIA GULF CORPORATION
GLOBAL HYATT CORPORATION
GLOBAL PAYMENTS INC
GOLDMAN SACHS GROUP INC
GRANT THORNTON LLP
GUESS? INC
HALLIBURTON COMPANY
HARRAH'S ENTERTAINMENT INC
HARRIS CORPORATION
HARTFORD FINANCIAL SERVICES
GROUP INC (THE)
HCA INC
HEALTH FITNESS CORP
HEALTH MANAGEMENT
ASSOCIATES INC
HEALTHWAYS INC
HELMERICH & PAYNE INC
HENRY SCHEIN INC
HERTZ GLOBAL HOLDINGS INC
HESS CORPORATION
HEWITT ASSOCIATES
HIBBETT SPORTS INC
HILTON HOTELS CORP
HOME DEPOT INC
HONEYWELL INTERNATIONAL INC
HUMANA INC
IAC/INTERACTIVECORP
ICT GROUP INC
IDEXX LABORATORIES INC
IGATE CORPORATION
INGRAM MICRO INC
INTEL CORP
INTERNATIONAL BUSINESS
MACHINES CORP (IBM)
INTUIT INC
INVENTIV HEALTH INC
J C PENNEY COMPANY INC
JABIL CIRCUIT INC
JACK IN THE BOX INC
JACOBS ENGINEERING GROUP INC
JETBLUE AIRWAYS CORPORATION
JM SMUCKER CO
JOHNSON & JOHNSON
JOHNSON CONTROLS INC
JP MORGAN CHASE & CO INC
JUNIPER NETWORKS INC
KAISER PERMANENTE
KELLOGG CO
KELLY SERVICES INC
KIMBERLY-CLARK CORP
KINDRED HEALTHCARE INC
KOCH INDUSTRIES INC
KOHL'S CORP
KPMG LLP
KRAFT FOODS INC
KROGER CO (THE)
L-3 COMMUNICATIONS HOLDINGS
INC
LABORATORY CORP OF AMERICA
HOLDINGS

LEVEL 3 COMMUNICATIONS INC
LIBERTY MUTUAL GROUP INC
LIMITED BRANDS INC
LINCARE HOLDINGS INC
LINCOLN NATIONAL CORPORATION
LKQ CORP
LOCKHEED MARTIN CORP
LODGIAN INC
LOEWS CORPORATION
LOWE'S COMPANIES INC
MACY'S INC
MANOR CARE INC
MANPOWER INC
MARRIOTT INTERNATIONAL INC
MARS INC
MARY KAY INC
MATTEL INC
MAXIM INTEGRATED PRODUCTS INC
MAYO FOUNDATION FOR MEDICAL
EDUCATION AND RESEARCH
MCAFEE INC
MCDERMOTT INTERNATIONAL INC
MCDONALD'S CORP
MCKESSON CORPORATION
MCKINSEY & COMPANY INC
MEDCO HEALTH SOLUTIONS
MEDTRONIC INC
MEN'S WEARHOUSE INC (THE)
MERCER INC
MERCK & CO INC
METLIFE INC
MGM MIRAGE
MICROCHIP TECHNOLOGY INC
MICRON TECHNOLOGY INC
MICROSOFT CORP
MIDAMERICAN ENERGY HOLDINGS
CO
MILLIPORE CORP
MONSANTO CO
MURPHY OIL CORPORATION
NATIONAL OILWELL VARCO INC
NEWS CORP
NIKE INC
NOBLE CORPORATION
NORTHROP GRUMMAN CORP
NRG ENERGY INC
OCCIDENTAL PETROLEUM CORP
OCEANEERING INTERNATIONAL INC
ODYSSEY HEALTHCARE INC
OFFICE DEPOT INC
OIL STATES INTERNATIONAL INC
OMNICARE INC
OMNICOM GROUP INC
ORACLE CORP
O'REILLY AUTOMOTIVE INC
OSHKOSH CORPORATION
OSI RESTAURANT PARTNERS LLC
OWENS & MINOR INC
PANTRY INC (THE)
PARAMETRIC TECHNOLOGY CORP
PARSONS BRINCKERHOFF INC
PATTERSON COMPANIES INC
PATTERSON-UTI ENERGY INC
PAYCHEX INC
PEPSI BOTTLING GROUP INC

PEPSICO INC
PEROT SYSTEMS CORP
PETCO ANIMAL SUPPLIES INC
PETSMART INC
PFIZER INC
PHARMACEUTICAL PRODUCT
DEVELOPMENT INC
PITNEY BOWES INC
PLEXUS CORP
POLO RALPH LAUREN CORP
PRECISION CASTPARTS CORP
PRICEWATERHOUSECOOPERS
PRIDE INTERNATIONAL INC
PRINCIPAL FINANCIAL GROUP (THE)
PROCTER & GAMBLE CO
PROGRESSIVE CORPORATION (THE)
PRUDENTIAL FINANCIAL INC
PSYCHIATRIC SOLUTIONS INC
PUBLIC STORAGE INC
PUBLIX SUPER MARKETS INC
QUALCOMM INC
QUANTA SERVICES INC
QUEST DIAGNOSTICS INC
R R DONNELLEY & SONS CO
RALCORP HOLDINGS INC
RAYTHEON CO
REGIS CORPORATION
RENT-A-CENTER INC
RES CARE INC
RITE AID CORPORATION
RITZ-CARLTON HOTEL COMPANY
LLC (THE)
ROBERT HALF INTERNATIONAL INC
ROSS STORES INC
ROYAL CARIBBEAN CRUISES LTD
RRI ENERGY INC
SAFECO INSURANCE COMPANY OF
AMERICA
SAIC INC
SAM'S CLUB
SAPIENT CORPORATION
SARA LEE CORP
SAS INSTITUTE INC
SCANA CORPORATION
SCHERING-PLOUGH CORP
SCIENTIFIC GAMES CORPORATION
SCOTTS MIRACLE GROW CO
SEACOR HOLDINGS INC
SELECT MEDICAL
SEMPRA ENERGY
SHAW GROUP INC (THE)
SHELL OIL CO
SHERWIN WILLIAMS COMPANY
(THE)
SIGMA-ALDRICH CORP
SISTERS OF MERCY HEALTH
SYSTEMS
SMITH INTERNATIONAL INC
SMITHFIELD FOODS INC
SOUTHERN COMPANY (THE)
SRA INTERNATIONAL INC
ST JUDE MEDICAL INC
STAPLES INC
STARTEK INC

STARWOOD HOTELS & RESORTS
WORLDWIDE INC
STERIS CORP
STIFEL FINANCIAL CORP
STRYKER CORP
SUN HEALTHCARE GROUP
SUNGARD DATA SYSTEMS INC
SUNOCO INC
SUNRISE SENIOR LIVING
SUPERVALU INC
SYKES ENTERPRISES INC
SYMANTEC CORP
SYNOPSYS INC
SYSCO CORP
TARGET CORPORATION
TBC CORPORATION
TEAM INC
TECH DATA CORP
TELEDYNE TECHNOLOGIES
INCORPORATED
TELEPHONE AND DATA SYSTEMS
INC (TDS)
TELETECH HOLDINGS INC
THERMO FISHER SCIENTIFIC INC
TIME WARNER INC
TJX COMPANIES INC (THE)
T-MOBILE USA
TOTAL SYSTEM SERVICES INC
(TSYS)
TOWERS PERRIN
TRAVELERS COMPANIES INC (THE)
TW TELECOM INC
TYSON FOODS INC
UNITED NATURAL FOODS INC
UNITED PARCEL SERVICE INC (UPS)
UNITED STATES CELLULAR CORP
UNITED TECHNOLOGIES
CORPORATION
UNITEDHEALTH GROUP INC
UNIVERSAL HEALTH SERVICES INC
UNIVISION COMMUNICATIONS INC
URS CORPORATION
USAA
VALERO ENERGY CORP
VALSPAR CORPORATION (THE)
VARIAN MEDICAL SYSTEMS INC
VCA ANTECH INC
VERISIGN INC
VERIZON COMMUNICATIONS
VICTORIAS SECRET
VISA INC
W R BERKLEY CORPORATION
WABTEC CORP
WALGREEN CO
WAL-MART STORES INC
WALT DISNEY COMPANY (THE)
WASTE MANAGEMENT INC
WATERS CORP
WATSON PHARMACEUTICALS INC
WATSON WYATT WORLDWIDE INC
WEATHERFORD INTERNATIONAL
LTD
WEIGHT WATCHERS
INTERNATIONAL INC
WELLPOINT INC

WELLS FARGO & CO
WENDY'S/ARBY'S GROUP INC
WEST CORPORATION
WEST PHARMACEUTICAL SERVICES
INC
WHOLE FOODS MARKET INC
WILLIAMS COMPANIES INC (THE)
WW GRAINGER INC
WYETH
WYNDHAM WORLDWIDE
XEROX CORP
YUM! BRANDS INC
ZIMMER HOLDINGS INC

NORTHEAST
3M COMPANY
7-ELEVEN INC
AARON'S INC
ABBOTT LABORATORIES
ABM INDUSTRIES INC
ACCENTURE LTD
ACTIVISION BLIZZARD INC
ADESA INC
ADOBE SYSTEMS INC
ADVANCE AUTO PARTS INC
ADVANCED MICRO DEVICES INC
(AMD)
AECOM TECHNOLOGY
CORPORATION
AES CORPORATION (THE)
AETNA INC
AFFILIATED COMPUTER SERVICES
INC
AFLAC INC
AGILENT TECHNOLOGIES INC
AIR PRODUCTS & CHEMICALS INC
ALLIANCE DATA SYSTEMS
CORPORATION
ALLSTATE CORPORATION (THE)
ALTRIA GROUP INC
AMAZON.COM INC
AMEDISYS INC
AMERICAN ELECTRIC POWER
COMPANY INC (AEP)
AMERICAN POWER CONVERSION
(APC)
AMERISOURCEBERGEN CORP
AMGEN INC
ANALOG DEVICES INC
ANNTAYLOR STORES CORP
APOLLO GROUP INC
APPLE INC
ARAMARK CORPORATION
ARCHER DANIELS MIDLAND CO
ARROW ELECTRONICS INC
ARTHUR J GALLAGHER & CO
ASCENSION HEALTH
AT&T INC
AUTOMATIC DATA PROCESSING INC
AUTOZONE INC
AVERY DENNISON CORP
AVIS BUDGET GROUP INC
AVNET INC
AVON PRODUCTS INC

AXA FINANCIAL INC
BAKER HUGHES INC
BALTIMORE GAS AND ELECTRIC
COMPANY
BANK OF AMERICA CORP
BARNES & NOBLE INC
BASS PRO SHOPS INC
BAXTER INTERNATIONAL INC
BDO SEIDMAN LLP
BEBE STORES INC
BECHTEL GROUP INC
BECTON DICKINSON & CO
BED BATH & BEYOND INC
BENCHMARK ELECTRONICS INC
BERKSHIRE HATHAWAY INC
BEST BUY CO INC
BIO RAD LABORATORIES INC
BJ'S WHOLESALE CLUB INC
BLACK & DECKER CORP
BLACKROCK INC
BLOOMBERG LP
BOEING COMPANY (THE)
BOOZ ALLEN HAMILTON
BOSTON SCIENTIFIC CORP
BRINKER INTERNATIONAL INC
BRINKS COMPANY (THE)
BROADCOM CORP
BROWN & BROWN INC
BUCKLE INC (THE)
BUFFALO WILD WINGS INC
BUNGE LTD
BURGER KING HOLDINGS INC
CABELA'S INC
CABLEVISION SYSTEMS CORP
CACI INTERNATIONAL INC
CAMERON INTERNATIONAL
CORPORATION
CAPITAL SENIOR LIVING CORP
CARDINAL HEALTH INC
CARMAX GROUP
CASH AMERICA INTERNATIONAL
INC
CATERPILLAR INC
CATHOLIC HEALTH INITIATIVES
CELGENE CORP
CELLCO PARTNERSHIP (VERIZON
WIRELESS)
CEPHALON INC
CH ROBINSON WORLDWIDE INC
CH2M HILL COMPANIES LTD
CHARLOTTE RUSSE HOLDING
CHARMING SHOPPES INC
CHEMED CORPORATION
CHEVRON CORPORATION
CHEVRON PHILLIPS CHEMICAL
COMPANY LLC
CHICO'S FAS INC
CHIPOTLE MEXICAN GRILL INC
CHRISTOPHER & BANKS CORP
CHS INC
CHUBB CORPORATION (THE)
CIBER INC
CIGNA CORP
CINTAS CORP
CISCO SYSTEMS INC

CLUBCORP INC
COACH INC
COCA-COLA COMPANY (THE)
COCA-COLA ENTERPRISES INC
COGNIZANT TECHNOLOGY
SOLUTIONS CORP
COLDWATER CREEK INC
COLGATE PALMOLIVE CO
COMCAST CORP
COMMUNITY HEALTH SYSTEMS INC
CONAGRA FOODS INC
CONOCOPHILLIPS COMPANY
CONSOL ENERGY INC
CONSOLIDATED EDISON INC
CONTAINER STORE (THE)
CONVERGYS CORPORATION
COOPER COMPANIES INC
COSTCO WHOLESALE CORP
COVANCE INC
COVENTRY HEALTH CARE INC
COX COMMUNICATIONS INC
CR BARD INC
CRACKER BARREL OLD COUNTRY
STORE INC
CTS CORP
CUBIC CORP
CUMMINS INC
CVS CAREMARK CORPORATION
DANAHER CORP
DARDEN RESTAURANTS INC
DAVITA INC
DEAN FOODS CO
DEERE & CO
DELOITTE & TOUCHE USA LLP
DELOITTE CONSULTING LLP
DENNY'S CORPORATION
DEVRY INC
DICK'S SPORTING GOODS INC
DIEBOLD INC
DINEEQUITY INC
DIRECTV GROUP INC (THE)
DOLE FOOD COMPANY INC
DOLLAR GENERAL CORPORATION
DOLLAR THRIFTY AUTOMOTIVE
GROUP INC
DRESS BARN INC (THE)
DYCOM INDUSTRIES INC
E I DU PONT DE NEMOURS & CO
(DUPONT)
EATON CORP
EBAY INC
EDISON INTERNATIONAL
ELECTRONIC ARTS INC
ELI LILLY & COMPANY
EMC CORP
EMERITUS CORP
EMERSON ELECTRIC CO
ENTERPRISE RENT-A-CAR
ERNST & YOUNG LLP
ESTEE LAUDER COMPANIES INC
(THE)
EXELON CORPORATION
EXPERIAN AMERICAS
EXPRESS SCRIPTS INC

EXXON MOBIL CORPORATION
(EXXONMOBIL)
FAMILY DOLLAR STORES INC
FEDEX CORPORATION
FINISH LINE INC (THE)
FIRST ADVANTAGE CORPORATION
FIRST DATA CORP
FIRSTENERGY CORP
FLUOR CORP
FOREST LABORATORIES INC
FOSSIL INC
FOSTER WHEELER AG
FPL GROUP INC
FRED'S INC
FRONTIER COMMUNICATIONS
CORPORATION
FTI CONSULTING INC
GAMESTOP CORP
GENERAL CABLE CORP
GENERAL DYNAMICS CORP
GENERAL ELECTRIC CO (GE)
GENERAL MILLS INC
GENESCO INC
GENWORTH FINANCIAL INC
GEO GROUP INC
GEORGIA GULF CORPORATION
GILEAD SCIENCES INC
GLOBAL HYATT CORPORATION
GLOBAL PAYMENTS INC
GOLDMAN SACHS GROUP INC
GOOGLE INC
GRANT THORNTON LLP
GUESS? INC
HARRAH'S ENTERTAINMENT INC
HARRIS CORPORATION
HARTFORD FINANCIAL SERVICES
GROUP INC (THE)
HCA INC
HEALTH CARE SERVICE
CORPORATION
HEALTH FITNESS CORP
HEALTH MANAGEMENT
ASSOCIATES INC
HEALTH NET INC
HEALTHWAYS INC
HENRY SCHEIN INC
HERTZ GLOBAL HOLDINGS INC
HESS CORPORATION
HEWITT ASSOCIATES
HIBBETT SPORTS INC
HILTON HOTELS CORP
HOME DEPOT INC
HONEYWELL INTERNATIONAL INC
HUMANA INC
IAC/INTERACTIVECORP
IBM GLOBAL SERVICES
ICT GROUP INC
IDEXX LABORATORIES INC
IGATE CORPORATION
IMS HEALTH INC
INGRAM MICRO INC
INTEL CORP
INTERNATIONAL BUSINESS
MACHINES CORP (IBM)
INTUIT INC

INVENTIV HEALTH INC
J C PENNEY COMPANY INC
JABIL CIRCUIT INC
JACK IN THE BOX INC
JACOBS ENGINEERING GROUP INC
JETBLUE AIRWAYS CORPORATION
JM SMUCKER CO
JOHNSON & JOHNSON
JOHNSON CONTROLS INC
JP MORGAN CHASE & CO INC
JUNIPER NETWORKS INC
KAISER PERMANENTE
KEANE INC
KELLOGG CO
KELLY SERVICES INC
KENDLE INTERNATIONAL INC
KIMBERLY-CLARK CORP
KINDRED HEALTHCARE INC
KOCH INDUSTRIES INC
KOHL'S CORP
KPMG LLP
KRAFT FOODS INC
KROGER CO (THE)
L-3 COMMUNICATIONS HOLDINGS
INC
LABORATORY CORP OF AMERICA
HOLDINGS
LAS VEGAS SANDS CORP (THE
VENETIAN)
LEVEL 3 COMMUNICATIONS INC
LIBERTY MUTUAL GROUP INC
LIMITED BRANDS INC
LINCARE HOLDINGS INC
LINCOLN NATIONAL CORPORATION
LKQ CORP
LOCKHEED MARTIN CORP
LODGIAN INC
LOEWS CORPORATION
LOWE'S COMPANIES INC
MACY'S INC
MANOR CARE INC
MANPOWER INC
MARRIOTT INTERNATIONAL INC
MARS INC
MARSH & MCLENNAN COMPANIES
INC
MARY KAY INC
MASSEY ENERGY COMPANY
MATTEL INC
MAXIM INTEGRATED PRODUCTS INC
MCAFEE INC
MCDERMOTT INTERNATIONAL INC
MCDONALD'S CORP
MCKESSON CORPORATION
MCKINSEY & COMPANY INC
MEDCO HEALTH SOLUTIONS
MEDTRONIC INC
MEN'S WEARHOUSE INC (THE)
MERCER INC
MERCK & CO INC
METLIFE INC
MGM MIRAGE
MICROCHIP TECHNOLOGY INC
MICRON TECHNOLOGY INC
MICROSOFT CORP

MIDAMERICAN ENERGY HOLDINGS
CO
MILLIPORE CORP
MONRO MUFFLER BRAKE INC
MONSANTO CO
MURPHY OIL CORPORATION
MYLAN INC
NATIONAL OILWELL VARCO INC
NETAPP INC
NEWS CORP
NII HOLDINGS INC
NIKE INC
NORTHROP GRUMMAN CORP
NRG ENERGY INC
OCCIDENTAL PETROLEUM CORP
OCEANEERING INTERNATIONAL INC
ODYSSEY HEALTHCARE INC
OFFICE DEPOT INC
OMNICARE INC
OMNICOM GROUP INC
ORACLE CORP
O'REILLY AUTOMOTIVE INC
OSHKOSH CORPORATION
OSI RESTAURANT PARTNERS LLC
OWENS & MINOR INC
PANTRY INC (THE)
PARAMETRIC TECHNOLOGY CORP
PAREXEL INTERNATIONAL CORP
PARSONS BRINCKERHOFF INC
PATTERSON COMPANIES INC
PATTERSON-UTI ENERGY INC
PAYCHEX INC
PEPSI BOTTLING GROUP INC
PEPSICO INC
PEROT SYSTEMS CORP
PERRIGO CO
PETCO ANIMAL SUPPLIES INC
PETSMART INC
PFIZER INC
PG&E CORPORATION
PHARMACEUTICAL PRODUCT
DEVELOPMENT INC
PITNEY BOWES INC
PLEXUS CORP
POLO RALPH LAUREN CORP
PRAXAIR INC
PRECISION CASTPARTS CORP
PRICEWATERHOUSECOOPERS
PRINCIPAL FINANCIAL GROUP (THE)
PROCTER & GAMBLE CO
PROGRESSIVE CORPORATION (THE)
PRUDENTIAL FINANCIAL INC
PSYCHIATRIC SOLUTIONS INC
PUBLIC STORAGE INC
QUALCOMM INC
QUANTA SERVICES INC
QUEST DIAGNOSTICS INC
R R DONNELLEY & SONS CO
RALCORP HOLDINGS INC
RAYTHEON CO
REGIS CORPORATION
RENT-A-CENTER INC
RES CARE INC
RITE AID CORPORATION

RITZ-CARLTON HOTEL COMPANY
LLC (THE)
ROBERT HALF INTERNATIONAL INC
ROSS STORES INC
RRI ENERGY INC
SAFECO INSURANCE COMPANY OF
AMERICA
SAFEWAY INC
SAIC INC
SAM'S CLUB
SAPIENT CORPORATION
SARA LEE CORP
SAS INSTITUTE INC
SCANA CORPORATION
SCHERING-PLOUGH CORP
SCHLUMBERGER LIMITED
SCIENTIFIC GAMES CORPORATION
SCOTTS MIRACLE GROW CO
SEACOR HOLDINGS INC
SELECT MEDICAL
SENSIENT TECHNOLOGIES
CORPORATION
SHAW GROUP INC (THE)
SHELL OIL CO
SHERWIN WILLIAMS COMPANY
(THE)
SIGMA-ALDRICH CORP
SMITH INTERNATIONAL INC
SMITHFIELD FOODS INC
SOUTHWEST AIRLINES CO
SRA INTERNATIONAL INC
ST JUDE MEDICAL INC
STAPLES INC
STARTEK INC
STARWOOD HOTELS & RESORTS
WORLDWIDE INC
STERIS CORP
STIFEL FINANCIAL CORP
STRYKER CORP
SUN HEALTHCARE GROUP
SUNGARD DATA SYSTEMS INC
SUNOCO INC
SUNRISE SENIOR LIVING
SUPERVALU INC
SYKES ENTERPRISES INC
SYMANTEC CORP
SYNOPSYS INC
SYNTEL INC
SYSCO CORP
TARGET CORPORATION
TEAM INC
TECH DATA CORP
TEKTRONIX INC
TELEDYNE TECHNOLOGIES
INCORPORATED
TELEPHONE AND DATA SYSTEMS
INC (TDS)
TELETECH HOLDINGS INC
THERMO FISHER SCIENTIFIC INC
TIFFANY & CO
TIME WARNER INC
TJX COMPANIES INC (THE)
T-MOBILE USA
TOTAL SYSTEM SERVICES INC
(TSYS)

TOWERS PERRIN
TRAVELERS COMPANIES INC (THE)
TW TELECOM INC
TYSON FOODS INC
UNITED NATURAL FOODS INC
UNITED PARCEL SERVICE INC (UPS)
UNITED STATES CELLULAR CORP
UNITED TECHNOLOGIES CORPORATION
UNITEDHEALTH GROUP INC
UNIVERSAL HEALTH SERVICES INC
UNIVISION COMMUNICATIONS INC
URS CORPORATION
USAA
VALERO ENERGY CORP
VALSPAR CORPORATION (THE)
VARIAN MEDICAL SYSTEMS INC
VCA ANTECH INC
VERISIGN INC
VERIZON COMMUNICATIONS
VIACOM INC
VICTORIAS SECRET
VISA INC
VOLT INFORMATION SCIENCES INC
W R BERKLEY CORPORATION
WABTEC CORP
WALGREEN CO
WAL-MART STORES INC
WALT DISNEY COMPANY (THE)
WASTE MANAGEMENT INC
WATERS CORP
WATSON PHARMACEUTICALS INC
WATSON WYATT WORLDWIDE INC
WEATHERFORD INTERNATIONAL LTD
WEIGHT WATCHERS INTERNATIONAL INC
WELLPOINT INC
WELLS FARGO & CO
WENDY'S/ARBY'S GROUP INC
WEST CORPORATION
WEST PHARMACEUTICAL SERVICES INC
WHOLE FOODS MARKET INC
WILLIAMS COMPANIES INC (THE)
WW GRAINGER INC
WYETH
WYNDHAM WORLDWIDE
XEROX CORP
YUM! BRANDS INC
ZIMMER HOLDINGS INC

INDEX OF FIRMS WITH INTERNATIONAL OPERATIONS

3M COMPANY
7-ELEVEN INC
AARON'S INC
ABBOTT LABORATORIES
ABM INDUSTRIES INC
ACCENTURE LTD
ACTIVISION BLIZZARD INC
ACXIOM CORP
ADC TELECOMMUNICATIONS INC
ADESA INC
ADOBE SYSTEMS INC
ADVANCE AUTO PARTS INC
ADVANCED MICRO DEVICES INC (AMD)
AECOM TECHNOLOGY CORPORATION
AES CORPORATION (THE)
AFFILIATED COMPUTER SERVICES INC
AFLAC INC
AGILENT TECHNOLOGIES INC
AIR PRODUCTS & CHEMICALS INC
ALLERGAN INC
ALLIANCE DATA SYSTEMS CORPORATION
ALLSTATE CORPORATION (THE)
ALTRIA GROUP INC
AMAZON.COM INC
AMERICAN POWER CONVERSION (APC)
AMGEN INC
ANADARKO PETROLEUM CORPORATION
ANALOG DEVICES INC
ANNTAYLOR STORES CORP
APACHE CORP
APOLLO GROUP INC
APPLE INC
ARAMARK CORPORATION
ARCHER DANIELS MIDLAND CO
ARROW ELECTRONICS INC
ARTHUR J GALLAGHER & CO
AT&T INC
AUTOMATIC DATA PROCESSING INC
AUTOZONE INC
AVERY DENNISON CORP
AVIS BUDGET GROUP INC
AVNET INC
AVON PRODUCTS INC
AXA FINANCIAL INC
BAKER HUGHES INC
BANK OF AMERICA CORP
BASS PRO SHOPS INC
BAXTER INTERNATIONAL INC
BDO SEIDMAN LLP
BEBE STORES INC
BECHTEL GROUP INC
BECKMAN COULTER INC
BECTON DICKINSON & CO

BED BATH & BEYOND INC
BENCHMARK ELECTRONICS INC
BERKSHIRE HATHAWAY INC
BEST BUY CO INC
BIO RAD LABORATORIES INC
BLACK & DECKER CORP
BLACKROCK INC
BLOOMBERG LP
BOEING COMPANY (THE)
BOOZ ALLEN HAMILTON
BOSTON SCIENTIFIC CORP
BRINKER INTERNATIONAL INC
BRINKS COMPANY (THE)
BROADCOM CORP
BROWN & BROWN INC
BUNGE LTD
BURGER KING HOLDINGS INC
CABELA'S INC
CACI INTERNATIONAL INC
CAMERON INTERNATIONAL CORPORATION
CARDINAL HEALTH INC
CARGILL INC
CARNIVAL CORPORATION
CASH AMERICA INTERNATIONAL INC
CATERPILLAR INC
CDW CORPORATION
CELGENE CORP
CEPHALON INC
CH ROBINSON WORLDWIDE INC
CH2M HILL COMPANIES LTD
CHARLOTTE RUSSE HOLDING
CHARMING SHOPPES INC
CHEMED CORPORATION
CHEVRON CORPORATION
CHEVRON PHILLIPS CHEMICAL COMPANY LLC
CHICO'S FAS INC
CHIPOTLE MEXICAN GRILL INC
CHUBB CORPORATION (THE)
CIBER INC
CIGNA CORP
CINTAS CORP
CISCO SYSTEMS INC
CLUBCORP INC
COACH INC
COCA-COLA COMPANY (THE)
COCA-COLA ENTERPRISES INC
COGNIZANT TECHNOLOGY SOLUTIONS CORP
COLGATE PALMOLIVE CO
COMCAST CORP
CONAGRA FOODS INC
CONOCOPHILLIPS COMPANY
CONSOL ENERGY INC
CONVERGYS CORPORATION
COOPER COMPANIES INC
COSTCO WHOLESALE CORP
COVANCE INC
CR BARD INC
CTS CORP
CUBIC CORP
CUMMINS INC
DANAHER CORP

DARDEN RESTAURANTS INC
DEAN FOODS CO
DEERE & CO
DELOITTE & TOUCHE USA LLP
DELOITTE CONSULTING LLP
DENNY'S CORPORATION
DEVON ENERGY CORPORATION
DEVRY INC
DIAMOND OFFSHORE DRILLING INC
DIEBOLD INC
DINEEQUITY INC
DIRECTV GROUP INC (THE)
DOLE FOOD COMPANY INC
DOLLAR THRIFTY AUTOMOTIVE
GROUP INC
DUKE ENERGY CORP
E I DU PONT DE NEMOURS & CO
(DUPONT)
EATON CORP
EBAY INC
EDISON INTERNATIONAL
ELECTRONIC ARTS INC
ELI LILLY & COMPANY
EMC CORP
EMERSON ELECTRIC CO
ENTERPRISE RENT-A-CAR
ERNST & YOUNG LLP
ESTEE LAUDER COMPANIES INC
(THE)
EXPRESS SCRIPTS INC
EXXON MOBIL CORPORATION
(EXXONMOBIL)
EXXONMOBIL CHEMICAL
FEDEX CORPORATION
FIRST ADVANTAGE CORPORATION
FIRST DATA CORP
FLUOR CORP
FOREST LABORATORIES INC
FORTUNE BRANDS INC
FOSSIL INC
FOSTER WHEELER AG
FTI CONSULTING INC
GAMESTOP CORP
GENENTECH INC
GENERAL CABLE CORP
GENERAL DYNAMICS CORP
GENERAL ELECTRIC CO (GE)
GENERAL MILLS INC
GENWORTH FINANCIAL INC
GEO GROUP INC
GEORGIA GULF CORPORATION
GILEAD SCIENCES INC
GLOBAL HYATT CORPORATION
GLOBAL PAYMENTS INC
GOLDMAN SACHS GROUP INC
GOOGLE INC
GUESS? INC
HALLIBURTON COMPANY
HARRAH'S ENTERTAINMENT INC
HARRIS CORPORATION
HARTFORD FINANCIAL SERVICES
GROUP INC (THE)
HCA INC
HE BUTT GROCERY COMPANY (HEB)
HEALTH FITNESS CORP

HEALTHWAYS INC
HELMERICH & PAYNE INC
HENRY SCHEIN INC
HERTZ GLOBAL HOLDINGS INC
HESS CORPORATION
HEWITT ASSOCIATES
HILTON HOTELS CORP
HOME DEPOT INC
HONEYWELL INTERNATIONAL INC
HUMANA INC
IAC/INTERACTIVECORP
IBM GLOBAL SERVICES
ICT GROUP INC
IDEXX LABORATORIES INC
IGATE CORPORATION
IMS HEALTH INC
INFOGROUP INC
INGRAM MICRO INC
INTEL CORP
INTERNATIONAL BUSINESS
MACHINES CORP (IBM)
INTUIT INC
J C PENNEY COMPANY INC
JABIL CIRCUIT INC
JACOBS ENGINEERING GROUP INC
JETBLUE AIRWAYS CORPORATION
JM SMUCKER CO
JOHNSON & JOHNSON
JOHNSON CONTROLS INC
JP MORGAN CHASE & CO INC
JUNIPER NETWORKS INC
KEANE INC
KELLOGG CO
KELLY SERVICES INC
KENDLE INTERNATIONAL INC
KIMBERLY-CLARK CORP
KOCH INDUSTRIES INC
KPMG LLP
KRAFT FOODS INC
L-3 COMMUNICATIONS HOLDINGS
INC
LABORATORY CORP OF AMERICA
HOLDINGS
LAS VEGAS SANDS CORP (THE
VENETIAN)
LEVEL 3 COMMUNICATIONS INC
LEXMARK INTERNATIONAL INC
LIBERTY GLOBAL INC
LIBERTY MUTUAL GROUP INC
LIMITED BRANDS INC
LINCOLN NATIONAL CORPORATION
LOCKHEED MARTIN CORP
LODGIAN INC
LOEWS CORPORATION
LOWE'S COMPANIES INC
MACY'S INC
MANPOWER INC
MARRIOTT INTERNATIONAL INC
MARS INC
MARSH & MCLENNAN COMPANIES
INC
MARY KAY INC
MATTEL INC
MAXIM INTEGRATED PRODUCTS INC
MCAFEE INC

MCDERMOTT INTERNATIONAL INC
MCDONALD'S CORP
MCKESSON CORPORATION
MCKINSEY & COMPANY INC
MEDTRONIC INC
MEN'S WEARHOUSE INC (THE)
MERCER INC
MERCK & CO INC
METLIFE INC
MGM MIRAGE
MICROCHIP TECHNOLOGY INC
MICRON TECHNOLOGY INC
MICROSOFT CORP
MIDAMERICAN ENERGY HOLDINGS
CO
MILLIPORE CORP
MONSANTO CO
MURPHY OIL CORPORATION
MYLAN INC
NATIONAL OILWELL VARCO INC
NETAPP INC
NEWS CORP
NII HOLDINGS INC
NIKE INC
NOBLE CORPORATION
NORTHROP GRUMMAN CORP
NRG ENERGY INC
OCCIDENTAL PETROLEUM CORP
OCEANEERING INTERNATIONAL INC
OFFICE DEPOT INC
OIL STATES INTERNATIONAL INC
OMNICARE INC
OMNICOM GROUP INC
ORACLE CORP
OSHKOSH CORPORATION
OSI RESTAURANT PARTNERS LLC
PARAMETRIC TECHNOLOGY CORP
PAREXEL INTERNATIONAL CORP
PARSONS BRINCKERHOFF INC
PATTERSON COMPANIES INC
PATTERSON-UTI ENERGY INC
PAYCHEX INC
PEABODY ENERGY CORP
PEPSI BOTTLING GROUP INC
PEPSICO INC
PEROT SYSTEMS CORP
PERRIGO CO
PETSMART INC
PFIZER INC
PHARMACEUTICAL PRODUCT
DEVELOPMENT INC
PITNEY BOWES INC
PLEXUS CORP
POLO RALPH LAUREN CORP
PRAXAIR INC
PRECISION CASTPARTS CORP
PRICESMART INC
PRICEWATERHOUSECOOPERS
PRIDE INTERNATIONAL INC
PRINCIPAL FINANCIAL GROUP (THE)
PROCTER & GAMBLE CO
PRUDENTIAL FINANCIAL INC
PSYCHIATRIC SOLUTIONS INC
QUALCOMM INC
QUANTA SERVICES INC

QUEST DIAGNOSTICS INC
QUIKSILVER INC
R R DONNELLEY & SONS CO
RALCORP HOLDINGS INC
RAYTHEON CO
REGIS CORPORATION
RENT-A-CENTER INC
RES CARE INC
RITZ-CARLTON HOTEL COMPANY
LLC (THE)
ROBERT HALF INTERNATIONAL INC
ROSS STORES INC
ROYAL CARIBBEAN CRUISES LTD
SABRE HOLDINGS CORP
SAFEWAY INC
SAIC INC
SAM'S CLUB
SAPIENT CORPORATION
SARA LEE CORP
SAS INSTITUTE INC
SCHERING-PLOUGH CORP
SCHLUMBERGER LIMITED
SCIENTIFIC GAMES CORPORATION
SCOTTS MIRACLE GROW CO
SEACOR HOLDINGS INC
SEMPRA ENERGY
SENSIENT TECHNOLOGIES
CORPORATION
SHAW GROUP INC (THE)
SHELL OIL CO
SHERWIN WILLIAMS COMPANY
(THE)
SIGMA-ALDRICH CORP
SISTERS OF MERCY HEALTH
SYSTEMS
SMITH INTERNATIONAL INC
SMITHFIELD FOODS INC
ST JUDE MEDICAL INC
STAPLES INC

STARTEK INC
STARWOOD HOTELS & RESORTS
WORLDWIDE INC
STERIS CORP
STIFEL FINANCIAL CORP
STRYKER CORP
SUNGARD DATA SYSTEMS INC
SUNOCO INC
SUNRISE SENIOR LIVING
SYKES ENTERPRISES INC
SYMANTEC CORP
SYNOPSYS INC
SYNTEL INC
SYSCO CORP
TARGET CORPORATION
TEAM INC
TECH DATA CORP
TEKTRONIX INC
TELEDYNE TECHNOLOGIES
INCORPORATED
TELETECH HOLDINGS INC
TESORO CORP
THERMO FISHER SCIENTIFIC INC
TIME WARNER INC
TJX COMPANIES INC (THE)
TOTAL SYSTEM SERVICES INC
(TSYS)
TOWERS PERRIN
TRANSOCEAN INC
TRAVELERS COMPANIES INC (THE)
TYSON FOODS INC
UNITED PARCEL SERVICE INC (UPS)
UNITED TECHNOLOGIES
CORPORATION
UNITEDHEALTH GROUP INC
UNIVISION COMMUNICATIONS INC
URS CORPORATION
USAA
VALERO ENERGY CORP

VALSPAR CORPORATION (THE)
VARIAN MEDICAL SYSTEMS INC
VERISIGN INC
VERIZON COMMUNICATIONS
VIACOM INC
VICTORIAS SECRET
VISA INC
VOLT INFORMATION SCIENCES INC
W R BERKLEY CORPORATION
WABTEC CORP
WALGREEN CO
WAL-MART STORES INC
WALT DISNEY COMPANY (THE)
WATERS CORP
WATSON WYATT WORLDWIDE INC
WEATHERFORD INTERNATIONAL
LTD
WEIGHT WATCHERS
INTERNATIONAL INC
WELLS FARGO & CO
WENDY'S/ARBY'S GROUP INC
WEST CORPORATION
WEST PHARMACEUTICAL SERVICES
INC
WESTERN DIGITAL CORP
WHOLE FOODS MARKET INC
WILLIAMS COMPANIES INC (THE)
WW GRAINGER INC
WYETH
WYNDHAM WORLDWIDE
WYNN RESORTS LIMITED
XEROX CORP
YAHOO! INC
YUM! BRANDS INC
ZIMMER HOLDINGS INC

Individual Data
Profiles
On Each Of
The AMERICAN EMPLOYERS 500

3M COMPANY

www.mmm.com

Industry Group Code: 33911 **Ranks within this company's industry group:** Sales: 1 Profits: 1

Management:		Sales/Marketing:		Liberal Arts:		Information Systems:		Professionals:		Tech./Scientific:	
Management Trainees:	Y	Marketing Pros.:	Y	Gen. Writing/Editing:	Y	Info. Management:	Y	Finance/Acct.:	Y	Engineers, Electrical:	Y
Experienced Mngmt.:	Y	Retail Sales:		Technical Writing:	Y	Software Dev.:	Y	Law:	Y	Engineers, Other:	Y
International Business:	Y	Commercial/Industrial:	Y	Graphic Arts/Photog.:	Y	Hardware Dev.:		HR/Other:	Y	Health/Lab:	Y
MBA Grads:	Y	Sales Trainees:	Y	Music:		Consulting/Other:		Training:	Y	Scientists/Research:	Y
		Advertising Pros.:	Y	Broadcasting:				Health Care:	Y	Petroleum/Chemicals:	
				Other:	Y			Consulting:		Math/Other:	Y

TYPES OF BUSINESS:

Health Care Products
Specialty Materials & Textiles
Industrial Products
Safety, Security & Protection Products
Display & Graphics Products
Consumer & Office Products
Electronics & Communications Products
Fuel-Cell Technology

BRANDS/DIVISIONS/AFFILIATES:

Aearo Technologies Inc
Les Entreprieses Solumed Inc
Quest Technologies Inc
ABRASIVOS SA
Financiere Burgienne
3M eStore

CONTACTS: *Note: Officers with more than one job title may be intentionally listed here more than once.*

George W. Buckley, CEO
George W. Buckley, Pres.
Patrick D. Campbell, CFO/Sr. VP
Robert D. MacDonald, Sr. VP-Mktg. & Sales
Angela S. Lalor, Sr. VP-Human Resources
Frederick J. Palensky, Exec. VP-R&D
Frederick J. Palensky, CTO
Marschall I. Smith, General Counsel/Sr. VP-Legal Affairs
Brad T. Sauer, Exec. VP-Health Care Bus.
H.C. Shin, Exec. VP-Industrial & Transportation Bus.
Joe E. Harlan, Exec. VP-Electro & Comm. Bus.
Moe S. Nozari, Exec. VP-Consumer & Office Bus.
George W. Buckley, Chmn.
Inge Thulin, Exec. VP-Int'l Oper.
John K. Woodworth, Sr. VP-Corp. Supply Chain Oper.

Phone: 651-733-1110	**Fax:** 651-733-9973
Toll-Free: 800-364-3577	
Address: 3M Center, Bldg. 220-11W-02, St. Paul, MN 55144-1000 US	

GROWTH PLANS/SPECIAL FEATURES:

3M Company is involved in the research, manufacturing and marketing of a variety of products. The firm is organized into six segments: health care; consumer and office; display and graphics; electronics and communications; industrial and transportation; and safety, security and protection. The health care segment's products include medical and surgical supplies, skin infection prevention products, pharmaceuticals, drug delivery systems, orthodontic products, health information systems and microbiology products. The consumer and office segment includes office supply, stationery, construction, home improvement, protective material and visual systems products. The display and graphics segment's products include optical film and lenses for electronic displays; touch screens and monitors; screen filters; reflective sheeting; and commercial graphics systems. The electronics and communications segment's products include packaging and interconnection devices (used in circuits); fluids used in computer chips; high-temperature and display tapes; pressure-sensitive tapes and resins; and products for telecommunications systems. The industrial and transportation segment's products include vinyl, polyester, tapes, a variety of non-woven abrasives, adhesives, specialty materials, supply chain execution software, filtration systems, paint finishing products, engineering fluids and components for catalytic converters. The safety, security and protection services segment provides products for personal protection, safety and security, energy control, commercial cleaning and protection, passports and secure cards. The company also maintains a 3M eStore, providing easy access to its line of industrial products. Recent acquisitions include Aearo Technologies Inc.; Les Entreprieses Solumed Inc.; Quest Technologies Inc.; ABRASIVOS S.A.; and Financiere Burgienne.

Employees are offered medical and dental insurance; health and dependent care reimbursement accounts; disability benefits; life insurance; domestic partner benefits; profit sharing; a management stock ownership program; a discount stock purchase plan; a 401(k) plan; tuition reimbursement; an employee assistance program; adoption assistance; group auto and home insurance; and discounts on company products.

FINANCIALS: Sales and profits are in thousands of dollars—add 000 to get the full amount. 2008 Note: Financial information for 2008 was not available for all companies at press time.

2008 Sales: $25,269,000	2008 Profits: $3,460,000	**U.S. Stock Ticker:** MMM
2007 Sales: $24,462,000	2007 Profits: $4,096,000	**Int'l Ticker:** Int'l Exchange:
2006 Sales: $22,923,000	2006 Profits: $3,851,000	Employees: 79,183
2005 Sales: $21,167,000	2005 Profits: $3,111,000	Fiscal Year Ends: 12/31
2004 Sales: $20,011,000	2004 Profits: $2,841,000	Parent Company:

SALARIES/BENEFITS:

Pension Plan:	ESOP Stock Plan: Y	Profit Sharing: Y	Top Exec. Salary: $1,720,000	Bonus: $2,844,074
Savings Plan: Y	Stock Purch. Plan: Y		Second Exec. Salary: $757,050	Bonus: $551,873

OTHER THOUGHTS:

Apparent Women Officers or Directors: 3
Hot Spot for Advancement for Women/Minorities: Y

LOCATIONS: ("Y" = Yes)

West:	Southwest:	Midwest:	Southeast:	Northeast:	International:
Y	Y	Y	Y	Y	Y

Note: Financial information, benefits and other data can change quickly and may vary from those stated here.

7-ELEVEN INC

www.7-eleven.com

Industry Group Code: 445120 Ranks within this company's industry group: Sales: Profits:

Management:		Sales/Marketing:		Liberal Arts:		Information Systems:		Professionals:		Tech./Scientific:	
Management Trainees:	Y	Marketing Pros.:	Y	Gen. Writing/Editing:	Y	Info. Management:	Y	Finance/Acct.:	Y	Engineers, Electrical:	
Experienced Mngmt.:	Y	Retail Sales:	Y	Technical Writing:		Software Dev.:	Y	Law:	Y	Engineers, Other:	
International Business:	Y	Commercial/Industrial:		Graphic Arts/Photog.:	Y	Hardware Dev.:		HR/Other:	Y	Health/Lab:	
MBA Grads:	Y	Sales Trainees:	Y	Music:		Consulting/Other:		Training:	Y	Scientists/Research:	
		Advertising Pros.:	Y	Broadcasting:				Health Care:		Petroleum/Chemicals:	
				Other:	Y			Consulting:		Math/Other:	

TYPES OF BUSINESS:
Convenience Stores
Gas Stations

BRANDS/DIVISIONS/AFFILIATES:
Seven & I Holdings Co Ltd
Cafe Select
Big Gulp
Big Bite
Go-Go Taquitos
World Ovens Bakery
Slurpee
White Hen Pantry, Inc.

CONTACTS: Note: Officers with more than one job title may be intentionally listed here more than once.
Joseph DePinto, CEO
Darren Rebelez, COO/Exec. VP
Joseph DePinto, Pres.
Stanley Reynolds, CFO/Exec. VP
Kevin Elliott, Sr. VP-Mktg.
Krystin Mitchell, Sr. VP-Human Resources
Wes Hargrove, CIO/Sr. VP
Kevin Elliott, Sr. VP-Merch.
Dave Fenton, General Counsel/Sr. VP/Corp. Sec.
Brad Jenkins, Sr. VP-Store Oper.
Carole Davidson, Sr. VP-Strategic Planning
Don Thomas, Chief Acct. Officer/VP/Controller
Jeffrey Schenck, Sr. VP-National Franchise
Shiro Ozeki, VP/Treas.
David Seltzer, VP-Bus. Dev.
Mark Wise, VP-New Store Dev.
Bob Jenkins, VP-Int'l & Domestic Licensing
Kevin Elliott, Sr. VP-Logistics

Phone: 214-828-7011	Fax: 214-828-7848
Toll-Free:	
Address: 2711 N. Haskell Ave., Dallas, TX 75204-2906 US	

GROWTH PLANS/SPECIAL FEATURES:

7-Eleven, Inc., the North American subsidiary for Seven & I Holdings Co, Ltd., franchises and licenses a total of 6,850 7-Eleven convenience stores throughout the U.S. and Canada. The company's convenience stores are extended-hour retail stores, emphasizing convenience and providing beverages, candy, fresh take-out foods, groceries, tobacco items, beer, wine, self-serve gasoline, magazines, specialty items, lottery tickets and certain financial services. 7-Eleven, Inc. also operates a number of additional store chains, including Garb-Ko, Inc. and White Hen Pantry, Inc. in the Midwest, Handee Marts, Inc. in Pennsylvania and Ohio, Resort Retailers in Utah, Prima Marketing in West Virginia and Southwest Convenience Stores, Inc. in Texas and New Mexico. The company continues to focus on its point-of-sale automated retail information system, the first of its kind in use in a major convenience store chain. With regard to merchandising programs, 7-Eleven offers Vcom kiosks in many of its locations. These computerized, interactive kiosks offer self service financial transactions including wire transfers, money orders and check cashing, in addition to standard ATM services. Through a partnership with Citibank, the company also offers free ATM access to Citibank customers in more than 5,500 of its stores. In January 2009, the company opened an environmentally friendly Commissary and Combined Distribution Center in Bohemia, Long Island. Also in January 2009, the firm began carrying the Redbox $1 per night DVD rental kiosks. In April 2009, the firm entered into a Master Franchise agreement with PT. Modern Putraindonesia of Jakarta, Indonesia as part of its plan to expand its business into Indonesia. In July 2009, the company announced they will add 100 new stores across Southern California over the next three years as part of an aggressive growth plan.

The firm offers its employees a benefits package that includes a stock purchase plan, 401(k) program, an employee assistance program, tuition reimbursement, adoption assistance, same-sex domestic partner benefits and a company vehicle or car allowance for field consultants.

FINANCIALS: Sales and profits are in thousands of dollars—add 000 to get the full amount. 2008 Note: Financial information for 2008 was not available for all companies at press time.

2008 Sales: $	2008 Profits: $	**U.S. Stock Ticker:** Subsidiary
2007 Sales: $15,797,590	2007 Profits: $133,694	**Int'l Ticker:** Int'l Exchange:
2006 Sales: $15,373,770	2006 Profits: $130,200	Employees: 27,748
2005 Sales: $14,000,000	2005 Profits: $110,000	Fiscal Year Ends: 2/28
2004 Sales: $12,121,000	2004 Profits: $96,500	Parent Company: SEVEN & I HOLDINGS CO LTD

SALARIES/BENEFITS:

Pension Plan:	ESOP Stock Plan:	Profit Sharing:	Top Exec. Salary: $	Bonus: $870,422
Savings Plan: Y	Stock Purch. Plan:		Second Exec. Salary: $	Bonus: $

OTHER THOUGHTS:
Apparent Women Officers or Directors: 6
Hot Spot for Advancement for Women/Minorities: Y

LOCATIONS: ("Y" = Yes)

West:	Southwest:	Midwest:	Southeast:	Northeast:	International:
Y	Y	Y	Y	Y	Y

Note: Financial information, benefits and other data can change quickly and may vary from those stated here.

AARON'S INC

www.aaronrents.com

Industry Group Code: 5322 Ranks within this company's industry group: Sales: 2 Profits: 2

Management:		Sales/Marketing:		Liberal Arts:		Information Systems:		Professionals:		Tech./Scientific:	
Management Trainees:	Y	Marketing Pros.:	Y	Gen. Writing/Editing:	Y	Info. Management:	Y	Finance/Acct.:	Y	Engineers, Electrical:	
Experienced Mngmt.:	Y	Retail Sales:	Y	Technical Writing:		Software Dev.:	Y	Law:	Y	Engineers, Other:	
International Business:	Y	Commercial/Industrial:		Graphic Arts/Photog.:	Y	Hardware Dev.:		HR/Other:	Y	Health/Lab:	
MBA Grads:	Y	Sales Trainees:	Y	Music:		Consulting/Other:		Training:	Y	Scientists/Research:	
		Advertising Pros.:	Y	Broadcasting:				Health Care:		Petroleum/Chemicals:	
				Other:				Consulting:		Math/Other:	

TYPES OF BUSINESS:

Furniture Stores, Rental
Home & Office Accessories Rental
Consumer Electronics Rental
Household Appliances Rental
Business Equipment Rental
Furniture Manufacturing
Rent-to-Own Contracts

BRANDS/DIVISIONS/AFFILIATES:

MacTavish Furniture Industries
Cleek's Lease or Own
Rosey Rentals, L. P.
Kelly's Sales & Leasing

CONTACTS: *Note: Officers with more than one job title may be intentionally listed here more than once.*

Robert C. Loudermilk, Jr., CEO
William K. Butler, COO
Robert C. Loudermilk, Jr., Pres.
Gilbert L. Danielson, CFO/Exec. VP
B. Lee Landers, Jr., CIO/VP
Mitchell S. Paull, Sr. VP-Merch.
Elizabeth L. Gibbs, General Counsel/VP
Robert P. Sinclair, Jr., Controller/VP
James L. Cates, Sr. VP/Corp. Sec.
Paul A. Doize, VP-Real Estate, Sales & Lease Ownership Div.
K. Todd Evans, VP-Franchising, Sales & Lease Ownership Div.
R. Charles Loudermilk, Sr., Chmn.
Mitchell S. Paull, Sr. VP-Logistics

Phone: 404-231-0011	Fax: 404-240-6584
Toll-Free:	
Address: 309 E. Paces Ferry Rd., NE, Atlanta, GA 30305-2377 US	

GROWTH PLANS/SPECIAL FEATURES:

Aaron's, Inc., formerly Aaron Rents, Inc., operates in the lease ownership, rental and specialty retailing businesses. The firm has two major operating divisions: the sales and lease ownership division and the MacTavish Furniture Industries division. Aaron's sales and lease ownership division has approximately 1,022 company-operated sales and lease ownership stores in 32 states and Canada; and 539 franchised stores in 48 states and Canada. This division provides household goods such as furniture, household appliances, electronics and accessories for consumers with limited or no access to traditional credit sources. The company offers monthly and semi-monthly payments, as well as a rent-to-own option that leads to ownership within one year. Its rental products are serviced or replaced free of charge. A typical sales & lease ownership store combines a showroom and warehouse, averages 9,000 square feet and is often located in working class neighborhoods and communities. The MacTavish Furniture Industries division manufactures more than half of the furniture for the company's rental purchase stores. It operates seven furniture manufacturing plants and five bedding facilities. Aaron's is one of the only rental companies in the U.S. that manufactures its own furniture. The company's stores carry brand names such as Dell, Philips, Microsoft, Maytag, Sony, HP, Compaq, Mitsubishi and JVC. In November 2008, Aaron's sold its corporate furnishings division, which rented residential and office furniture to businesses in 16 states, to CORT Business Services Corporation for approximately $76.4 million. In December 2008, the firm acquired rental retail chain Cleek's Lease or Own; and all 35 of the stores of Rosey Rentals, L. P. In February 2009, Kelly's Sales & Leasing agreed to convert 18 of its stores in Virginia and North Carolina to franchised Aaron's locations. In April 2009, the firm changed its name from Aaron Rents, Inc., to Aaron's, Inc.

FINANCIALS: Sales and profits are in thousands of dollars—add 000 to get the full amount. 2008 Note: Financial information for 2008 was not available for all companies at press time.

2008 Sales: $1,592,608	2008 Profits: $90,189	U.S. Stock Ticker: AAN
2007 Sales: $1,394,939	2007 Profits: $80,275	Int'l Ticker: Int'l Exchange:
2006 Sales: $1,326,592	2006 Profits: $78,635	Employees: 9,600
2005 Sales: $1,125,505	2005 Profits: $57,993	Fiscal Year Ends: 12/31
2004 Sales: $946,480	2004 Profits: $52,616	Parent Company:

SALARIES/BENEFITS:

Pension Plan:	ESOP Stock Plan:	Profit Sharing:	Top Exec. Salary: $800,000	Bonus: $1,034,545
Savings Plan: Y	Stock Purch. Plan:		Second Exec. Salary: $500,000	Bonus: $309,339

OTHER THOUGHTS:

Apparent Women Officers or Directors: 1
Hot Spot for Advancement for Women/Minorities:

LOCATIONS: ("Y" = Yes)

West:	Southwest:	Midwest:	Southeast:	Northeast:	International:
Y	Y	Y	Y	Y	Y

ABBOTT LABORATORIES

www.abbott.com

Industry Group Code: 325412 Ranks within this company's industry group: Sales: 3   Profits: 4

Management:		Sales/Marketing:		Liberal Arts:		Information Systems:		Professionals:		Tech./Scientific:	
Management Trainees:	Y	Marketing Pros.:	Y	Gen. Writing/Editing:	Y	Info. Management:	Y	Finance/Acct.:	Y	Engineers, Electrical:	Y
Experienced Mngmt.:	Y	Retail Sales:		Technical Writing:	Y	Software Dev.:	Y	Law:	Y	Engineers, Other:	Y
International Business:	Y	Commercial/Industrial:	Y	Graphic Arts/Photog.:	Y	Hardware Dev.:		HR/Other:	Y	Health/Lab:	Y
MBA Grads:	Y	Sales Trainees:	Y	Music:		Consulting/Other:		Training:	Y	Scientists/Research:	Y
		Advertising Pros.:	Y	Broadcasting:				Health Care:	Y	Petroleum/Chemicals:	Y
				Other:				Consulting:		Math/Other:	Y

TYPES OF BUSINESS:

Pharmaceuticals Manufacturing
Nutritional Products
Diagnostics
Consumer Health Products
Medical & Surgical Devices
Pharmaceutical Products
Animal Health

BRANDS/DIVISIONS/AFFILIATES:

Abbott Medical Optics Inc
Prevacid
Lupix
Trilipix
Humira
Simcor
Glucerna
Ensure

CONTACTS: *Note: Officers with more than one job title may be intentionally listed here more than once.*

Miles D. White, CEO
Thomas C. Freyman, CFO
Stephen R. Fussell, Sr. VP-Human Resources
John M. Leonard, Sr. VP-R&D
John C. Landgraf, Sr. VP-Global Pharmaceutical Mgmt. & Supply
Laura J. Schumacher, General Counsel/Exec. VP/Corp. Sec.
Richard W. Ashley, Exec. VP-Corp. Dev.
Melissa Brotz, VP-External Comm.
Thomas C. Freyman, Exec. VP-Finance
James L. Tyree, Exec. VP-Pharmaceutical Products Group
Holger Liepmann, Exec. VP-Global Nutrition
John M. Capek, Exec. VP-Medical Devices
Michael J. Warmuth, Sr. VP-Diagnostics
Miles D. White, Chmn.
Olivier Bohuon, Sr. VP-Int'l Oper.

Phone: 847-937-6100	Fax: 847-937-9555
Toll-Free:	
Address: 100 Abbott Park Rd., Abbott Park, IL 60064-3500 US	

GROWTH PLANS/SPECIAL FEATURES:

Abbott Laboratories develops, manufactures and sells health care products and technologies ranging from pharmaceuticals to medical devices. The firm markets its products in more than 130 countries. The pharmaceutical segment deals with adult and pediatric conditions such as rheumatoid arthritis, HIV, epilepsy and manic depression. The diagnostic instruments and test segment deals with a range of medical tests to diagnose infectious diseases, cancer, diabetes and genetic conditions. Products include Humira for arthritis, Prevacid (Ogastro), a proton pump inhibitor for the short-term treatment of gastroesophageal reflux disease and Lupix for prostate cancer. The nutritional products segment offers consumer products such as Similac, Ensure, Glucerna and AdvantEdge, as well as medical nutritional products and feeding devices. The diagnostic products segment includes diagnostic systems and tests such as immunoassay, chemistry and hematology systems, which are manufactured, marketed and sold to blood banks, hospitals, commercial laboratories, physicians' offices and plasma protein therapeutic companies. The vascular products segment consists of coronary, endovascular and vessel closure devices, used in the treatment of vascular disease. These products are generally marketed and sold directly to hospitals from Abbot-owned distribution centers and public warehouses. The firm also produces a line of animal products such as anesthetics, wound care products and intravenous fluid therapy for the veterinary market. The company operates internationally in Europe, Asia, Africa, Latin and South America and the Middle East. In December 2008, Abbott received FDA approval for Trilipix, a cholesterol management medication. In February 2009, the company acquired Advanced Medical Optics which has been renamed Abbott Medical Optics Inc.

Employees are offered medical, dental and vision insurance; flexible spending accounts; child care solutions; an employee assistance program; legal referral services; a pension plan; a 401(k) plan; profit sharing; tuition assistance; travel accident insurance; long-term care insurance; and life insurance.

FINANCIALS: Sales and profits are in thousands of dollars—add 000 to get the full amount. 2008 Note: Financial information for 2008 was not available for all companies at press time.

2008 Sales: $29,527,600	2008 Profits: $4,880,700	**U.S. Stock Ticker: ABT**
2007 Sales: $25,914,200	2007 Profits: $3,606,300	**Int'l Ticker:** Int'l Exchange:
2006 Sales: $22,476,322	2006 Profits: $1,716,755	Employees: 69,000
2005 Sales: $22,337,808	2005 Profits: $3,372,065	Fiscal Year Ends: 12/31
2004 Sales: $19,680,016	2004 Profits: $3,235,851	Parent Company:

SALARIES/BENEFITS:

Pension Plan: Y	ESOP Stock Plan:	Profit Sharing: Y	Top Exec. Salary: $1,795,471	Bonus: $4,200,000
Savings Plan: Y	Stock Purch. Plan:		Second Exec. Salary: $886,363	Bonus: $1,232,500

OTHER THOUGHTS:

Apparent Women Officers or Directors: 5
Hot Spot for Advancement for Women/Minorities: Y

LOCATIONS: ("Y" = Yes)

West:	Southwest:	Midwest:	Southeast:	Northeast:	International:
Y	Y	Y		Y	Y

Note: Financial information, benefits and other data can change quickly and may vary from those stated here.

ABM INDUSTRIES INC

www.abm.com

Industry Group Code: 5311 Ranks within this company's industry group: Sales: 1 Profits: 1

Management:		Sales/Marketing:		Liberal Arts:		Information Systems:		Professionals:		Tech./Scientific:	
Management Trainees:	Y	Marketing Pros.:	Y	Gen. Writing/Editing:	Y	Info. Management:	Y	Finance/Acct.:	Y	Engineers, Electrical:	
Experienced Mngmt.:	Y	Retail Sales:		Technical Writing:		Software Dev.:		Law:	Y	Engineers, Other:	
International Business:	Y	Commercial/Industrial:	Y	Graphic Arts/Photog.:		Hardware Dev.:		HR/Other:	Y	Health/Lab:	
MBA Grads:	Y	Sales Trainees:	Y	Music:		Consulting/Other:		Training:	Y	Scientists/Research:	
		Advertising Pros.:	Y	Broadcasting:				Health Care:		Petroleum/Chemicals:	
				Other:				Consulting:		Math/Other:	

TYPES OF BUSINESS:

Janitorial Services
Parking Facilities
Maintenance Personnel
Security Services
Lighting Services
Billing & Accounting Services
Supplier Management
Call Center Services

BRANDS/DIVISIONS/AFFILIATES:

ABM Janitorial Services
American Building Maintenance
ABM Security Services
Security Services of America
Silverhawk Security Specialists
Elite Protection Services
ABM Engineering Services
Amtech Lighting Services

CONTACTS: Note: Officers with more than one job title may be intentionally listed here more than once.

Henrik C. Slipsager, CEO
Henrik C. Slipsager, Pres.
James Lusk, CFO/Exec. VP
Gary R. Wallace, Chief Mktg. Officer
Erin M. Andre, Sr. VP-Human Resources
Sarah Hlavinka McConnell, General Counsel/Sr. VP/Corp. Sec.
Gary R. Wallace, Sr. VP-Bus. Dev.
Joe Yospe, Chief Acct. Officer/Controller/Sr. VP
James P. McClure, Exec. VP/Pres., ABM Janitorial Svcs.
Steven M. Zaccagnini, Exec. VP/Pres., ABM Facility Svcs.
David L. Farwell, Sr. VP/Chief of Staff
Maryellen C. Herringer, Chmn.

Phone: 212-297-0200	**Fax:** 415-733-7333
Toll-Free:	
Address: 551 5th Ave., Ste. 300, New York, NY 10176 US	

GROWTH PLANS/SPECIAL FEATURES:

ABM Industries, Inc. is one of the country's largest facility services providers. Founded in California in 1909 as a one-man window cleaning business, today the firm provides janitorial, parking, engineering, security, lighting and mechanical services to commercial, industrial, institutional and retail facilities throughout the U.S. and Canada. ABM operates through a number of subsidiaries, which are grouped into four segments: janitorial, parking, security and engineering. The company's janitorial services companies include ABM Janitorial Services and American Building Maintenance. Services provided include floor cleaning and finishing; window washing; furniture polishing; and carpet cleaning and dusting. ABM's security services subsidiaries include ABM Security Services, SSA Security, Security Services of America, Silverhawk Security Specialists and Elite Protection Services. Security services offered by these subsidiaries include security officers; investigative services; electronic monitoring of fire, life safety systems and access control devices; and security consulting. ABM Engineering Services is the company's primary engineering subsidiary, offering on-site engineers to operate and maintain mechanical, electrical and plumbing systems at such facilities as high-rise office buildings, schools, computer centers, shopping malls, manufacturing facilities, museums and universities. The engineering segment also provides facility services through ABM Facility Services, which provides streamlined, centralized control and coordination of multiple facility service needs. In January 2008, AMB acquired the remaining 50% stake in Southern Management Company, a Tennessee-based facilities services company acquired by ABM with OneSource, for $24 million. In October 2008, ABM completed the sale of substantially all of the assets of the company's lighting division to Sylvania Lighting Services Corp.

ABM offers its employees a tuition reimbursement program, credit union membership, an employee assistance program and medical, dental, vision, life, AD&D and disability insurance.

FINANCIALS: Sales and profits are in thousands of dollars—add 000 to get the full amount. 2008 Note: Financial information for 2008 was not available for all companies at press time.

2008 Sales: $3,623,590	2008 Profits: $45,434	**U.S. Stock Ticker: ABM**
2007 Sales: $2,706,105	2007 Profits: $52,440	**Int'l Ticker:** Int'l Exchange:
2006 Sales: $2,579,351	2006 Profits: $93,205	Employees: 100,000
2005 Sales: $2,587,761	2005 Profits: $57,941	Fiscal Year Ends: 10/31
2004 Sales: $2,375,149	2004 Profits: $30,473	Parent Company:

SALARIES/BENEFITS:

Pension Plan:	ESOP Stock Plan:	Profit Sharing:	Top Exec. Salary: $765,000	Bonus: $1,040,000
Savings Plan: Y	Stock Purch. Plan:		Second Exec. Salary: $550,000	Bonus: $449,708

OTHER THOUGHTS:

Apparent Women Officers or Directors: 4
Hot Spot for Advancement for Women/Minorities: Y

LOCATIONS: ("Y" = Yes)

West:	Southwest:	Midwest:	Southeast:	Northeast:	International:
Y	Y	Y	Y	Y	Y

ACADEMY SPORTS & OUTDOORS LTD   www.academy.com

Industry Group Code: 451110 Ranks within this company's industry group: Sales: 4   Profits:

Management:		Sales/Marketing:		Liberal Arts:		Information Systems:		Professionals:		Tech./Scientific:	
Management Trainees:	Y	Marketing Pros.:	Y	Gen. Writing/Editing:	Y	Info. Management:	Y	Finance/Acct.:	Y	Engineers, Electrical:	
Experienced Mngmt.:	Y	Retail Sales:	Y	Technical Writing:		Software Dev.:	Y	Law:	Y	Engineers, Other:	
International Business:		Commercial/Industrial:		Graphic Arts/Photog.:	Y	Hardware Dev.:		HR/Other:	Y	Health/Lab:	
MBA Grads:	Y	Sales Trainees:	Y	Music:		Consulting/Other:		Training:	Y	Scientists/Research:	
		Advertising Pros.:	Y	Broadcasting:				Health Care:		Petroleum/Chemicals:	
				Other:	Y			Consulting:		Math/Other:	

TYPES OF BUSINESS:

Sporting Goods Stores
Apparel
Footwear
Outdoor Sports Gear
Hunting Licenses

BRANDS/DIVISIONS/AFFILIATES:

CONTACTS: *Note: Officers with more than one job title may be intentionally listed here more than once.*

David Gochman, CEO
Rodney Faldyn, Pres.
Rodney Faldyn, CFO
Robert Frennea, Exec. VP/Mgr.-Gen. Merch.
Michelle McKinney, Exec. VP-Corp. Dev.
David Gochman, Chmn.

Phone: 281-646-5200	Fax: 281-646-5000
Toll-Free: 888-922-2336	
Address: 1800 N. Mason Rd., Katy, TX 77449 US	

GROWTH PLANS/SPECIAL FEATURES:

Academy Sports & Outdoors, Ltd. is one of the largest sporting goods retailers in the U.S. The company operates over 112 stores throughout 11 states including Alabama, Arkansas, Florida, Georgia, Louisiana, Mississippi, Missouri, Oklahoma, South Carolina; Tennessee and Texas. Additionally, the firm plans to further expand its business by opening stores in the southern and southeastern U.S. in the near future. Academy Sports offers a broad selection of sporting equipment, apparel and footwear. The stores, which range in size from 50,000 to 80,000 square feet, are laid out in a racetrack format with athletic, casual and seasonal apparel on the inside and camping, hunting, fishing, marine, golf, fitness, team sports and footwear products on the outside. Academy Sports has experienced steady sales growth over the past decade at an average of 17% a year. The company supplies its stores through a 1 million square foot distribution center out of Katy, Texas. The center utilizes radio frequency devices (RFD), automated inventory and replenishment systems and a state-of-the-art warehouse management system to smoothly operate its large processing and inventory space.

The company offers its employees a 401(k) plan; medical, dental and vision insurance; life insurance; short- and long-term disability benefits; tuition reimbursement; merchandise discounts; bereavement leave; continuing education benefits; and business travel accident insurance.

FINANCIALS: Sales and profits are in thousands of dollars—add 000 to get the full amount. 2008 Note: Financial information for 2008 was not available for all companies at press time.

2008 Sales: $2,000,000	2008 Profits: $	U.S. Stock Ticker: Private
2007 Sales: $2,060,000	2007 Profits: $	Int'l Ticker: Int'l Exchange:
2006 Sales: $1,840,000	2006 Profits: $	Employees: 13,000
2005 Sales: $1,215,100	2005 Profits: $65,000	Fiscal Year Ends: 1/31
2004 Sales: $1,059,000	2004 Profits: $	Parent Company:

SALARIES/BENEFITS:

Pension Plan:	ESOP Stock Plan:	Profit Sharing:	Top Exec. Salary: $	Bonus: $
Savings Plan: Y	Stock Purch. Plan:		Second Exec. Salary: $	Bonus: $

OTHER THOUGHTS:

Apparent Women Officers or Directors: 1
Hot Spot for Advancement for Women/Minorities:

LOCATIONS: ("Y" = Yes)

West:	Southwest:	Midwest:	Southeast:	Northeast:	International:
	Y	Y	Y		

ACCENTURE LTD

www.accenture.com

Industry Group Code: 541513 **Ranks within this company's industry group:** Sales: 3 Profits: 2

Management:		Sales/Marketing:		Liberal Arts:		Information Systems:		Professionals:		Tech./Scientific:	
Management Trainees:	Y	Marketing Pros.:	Y	Gen. Writing/Editing:	Y	Info. Management:	Y	Finance/Acct.:	Y	Engineers, Electrical:	Y
Experienced Mngmt.:	Y	Retail Sales:		Technical Writing:	Y	Software Dev.:	Y	Law:	Y	Engineers, Other:	Y
International Business:	Y	Commercial/Industrial:	Y	Graphic Arts/Photog.:	Y	Hardware Dev.:	Y	HR/Other:	Y	Health/Lab:	
MBA Grads:	Y	Sales Trainees:		Music:		Consulting/Other:	Y	Training:	Y	Scientists/Research:	
		Advertising Pros.:	Y	Broadcasting:				Health Care:		Petroleum/Chemicals:	
				Other:	Y			Consulting:	Y	Math/Other:	

TYPES OF BUSINESS:

Technology Consulting Services
Computer Operations Outsourcing
Supply Chain Management
Technology Research
Software Development
Human Resources Consulting
Management Consulting
Research & Development

BRANDS/DIVISIONS/AFFILIATES:

Gestalt, LLC
Maxamine
SOPIA Corporation
AddVal Technology
ATAN
Accenture Mobility Operated Services

CONTACTS: Note: Officers with more than one job title may be intentionally listed here more than once.

William D. Green, CEO
Stephen J. Rohleder, COO
Pamela J. Craig, CFO
Roxanne Taylor, Chief Mktg. Officer
Jill B. Smart, Chief Human Resources Officer
Gianfranco Casati, Group CEO-Prod.
Douglas G. Scrivner, General Counsel/Corp. Sec./Compliance Officer
David C. Thomlinson, Sr. Managing Dir.-Geographic Strategy & Oper.
R. Timothy Breene, Chief Strategy & Corp. Dev. Officer
Roxanne Taylor, Chief Comm. Officer
David P. Rowland, Sr. VP-Finance
Karl-Heinz Floether, Group CEO-Systems Integration, Tech. & Delivery
Martin I. Cole, Group CEO-Comm. & High Tech.
Kevin M. Campbell, Group CEO-Outsourcing
Mark Foster, Group CEO-Mgmt. Consulting & Integrated Markets
William D. Green, Chmn.
Diego Visconti, Chmn.-Int'l, Strategic Countries
Basilio Rueda, Sr. Managing Dir.-Global Delivery Network

Phone: 441-296-8262	Fax: 441-296-4245
Toll-Free:	
Address: Canon's Ct., 22 Victoria St., Hamilton, HM12 Bermuda	

GROWTH PLANS/SPECIAL FEATURES:

Accenture, Ltd. is a leading provider of management consulting, technology and outsourcing services, with operations in over 200 cities in 52 countries. The firm delivers services through five operating groups, which together comprise 17 industry groups. The operating groups are communications and high-tech; financial services; products; resources; and public services. Accenture's communications and high-tech group offers technology, consulting and systems integration to the electronics, communications and media industries. Its financial services group provides consulting and outsourcing strategies to the insurance, capital markets and banking industries. Accenture's products group serves the automotive; health and life sciences; consumer goods; industrial equipment; retail; and transportation and travel services industries. The company's resources group works with the chemicals; energy; forest products; metals and mining; and utilities industries. Finally, its public service group works with local, state, provincial and national governments in the areas of defense; revenue; human services; health; justice; and postal and education authorities. Accenture offers management consulting services including customer relationship management; supply chain management; human performance; finance and performance management; and strategy. The firm's systems integration and technology services include enterprise resource planning; service-oriented architecture; mobility solutions; Microsoft solutions; IT strategy and transformation services; enterprise architecture; infrastructure consulting services; research and development services; and e-commerce solutions. Accenture also offers outsourcing for business processes, applications and infrastructure needs. Clients include AT&T; Microsoft; Sony; Bank of America; and the U.S. Department of Commerce. During 2008, Accenture acquired defense consulting firm Gestalt, LLC; testing and optimization services provider Maxamine; consulting and IT solutions company SOPIA Corporation; shipment management services provider AddVal Technology; and Brazilian IT and automation solutions provider ATAN. In February 2009, the firm launched Accenture Mobility Operated Services.

Accenture offers its employees flexible work arrangements and ongoing training and development resources.

FINANCIALS: Sales and profits are in thousands of dollars—add 000 to get the full amount. 2008 Note: Financial information for 2008 was not available for all companies at press time.

2008 Sales: $25,313,826	2008 Profits: $1,691,751	**U.S. Stock Ticker: ACN**	
2007 Sales: $21,452,747	2007 Profits: $1,243,148	**Int'l Ticker:** Int'l Exchange:	
2006 Sales: $18,228,366	2006 Profits: $973,329	Employees: 186,000	
2005 Sales: $17,094,400	2005 Profits: $940,500	Fiscal Year Ends: 8/31	
2004 Sales: $15,113,582	2004 Profits: $690,828	Parent Company:	

SALARIES/BENEFITS:

Pension Plan:	ESOP Stock Plan:	Profit Sharing:	Top Exec. Salary: $1,237,121	Bonus: $1,939,526
Savings Plan:	Stock Purch. Plan: Y		Second Exec. Salary: $1,133,640	Bonus: $3,010,000

OTHER THOUGHTS:

Apparent Women Officers or Directors: 7
Hot Spot for Advancement for Women/Minorities: Y

LOCATIONS: ("Y" = Yes)

West:	Southwest:	Midwest:	Southeast:	Northeast:	International:
Y	Y	Y	Y	Y	Y

Note: Financial information, benefits and other data can change quickly and may vary from those stated here.

ACTIVISION BLIZZARD INC

www.activisionblizzard.com

Industry Group Code: 511210G Ranks within this company's industry group: Sales: 2 Profits: 1

Management:		Sales/Marketing:		Liberal Arts:		Information Systems:		Professionals:		Tech./Scientific:	
Management Trainees:	Y	Marketing Pros.:	Y	Gen. Writing/Editing:	Y	Info. Management:	Y	Finance/Acct.:	Y	Engineers, Electrical:	Y
Experienced Mngmt.:	Y	Retail Sales:		Technical Writing:	Y	Software Dev.:	Y	Law:	Y	Engineers, Other:	
International Business:	Y	Commercial/Industrial:		Graphic Arts/Photog.:	Y	Hardware Dev.:		HR/Other:	Y	Health/Lab:	
MBA Grads:	Y	Sales Trainees:		Music:	Y	Consulting/Other:		Training:	Y	Scientists/Research:	
		Advertising Pros.:	Y	Broadcasting:				Health Care:		Petroleum/Chemicals:	
				Other:	Y			Consulting:		Math/Other:	

TYPES OF BUSINESS:

Video Games
Logistics Services

BRANDS/DIVISIONS/AFFILIATES:

Activision Publishing, Inc.
Blizzard Entertainment, Inc.
Vivendi Games
Bizarre Creations, Ltd.
FreeStyleGames
Budcat Creations
World of Warcraft
Guitar Hero

CONTACTS: *Note: Officers with more than one job title may be intentionally listed here more than once.*

Robert A. Kotick, CEO
Thomas Tippl, CFO
Brian Hodous, Chief Customer Officer
Ann Weiser, Chief Human Resources Officer
George Rose, Chief Legal Officer
Michael Griffith, CEO/Pres., Activision Publishing Inc.
Michael Morhaime, CEO/Pres., Blizzard Entertainment
Bruce Hack, Vice-Chmn./Chief Corp. Officer
Brian Kelly, Co-Chmn.
Rene Pennison, Co-Chmn.

Phone: 310-255-2000	**Fax:**
Toll-Free:	
Address: 3100 Ocean Park Blvd., Santa Monica, CA 90405 US	

GROWTH PLANS/SPECIAL FEATURES:

Activision Blizzard, Inc., formerly Activision, Inc., is a leading international publisher and distributor of interactive entertainment software and peripherals for a variety of game genres, operating through subsidiaries Activision Publishing and Blizzard Entertainment. The firm operates in four segments: Blizzard Entertainment, Inc. and its subsidiaries, which publish traditional games and online subscription-based games in the massively multiplayer online game (MMOG) category; Activision Publishing, which publishes interactive entertainment software and peripherals, including certain studios, assets and titles previously included in Vivendi Games' Sierra Entertainment; Activision Blizzard Distribution, which handles the distribution of interactive entertainment software and hardware products; and non-core exit operations. Activision Blizzard offers products that operate primarily on the Sony PlayStation 2, Sony PlayStation 3, Nintendo Wii, and Microsoft Xbox 360 console systems, Sony PlayStation Portable and Nintendo Dual Screen handheld devices, as well as PCs. Some of its most popular products include Guitar Hero, Call of Duty and Tony Hawk, as well as Spider-Man, James Bond, TRANSFORMERS, StarCraft, Diablo, and Warcraft franchise games, including World of Warcraft. Activision Blizzard maintains operations worldwide throughout North America, Europe and Asia. In September 2007, the company acquired video game developer Bizarre Creations Ltd. In July 2008, the company completed its merger with Vivendi Games and renaming as Activision Blizzard, Inc. Following this merger, the company restructured to operate through two subsidiaries, Activision Publishing and Blizzard Entertainment, formerly a subsidiary of Vivendi. In September 2008, Activision Blizzard acquired FreeStyleGames, a video game developer specializing in music-based games. In November 2008, the firm acquired Budcat Creations, a development studio focused on games for the Nintendo Wii and Nintendo DS systems.

The company offers its employees medical, dental and vision insurance, a college savings plan, tuition reimbursement, identity theft protection, home and auto insurance and group legal insurance, as well as company store discounts.

FINANCIALS: Sales and profits are in thousands of dollars—add 000 to get the full amount. 2008 Note: Financial information for 2008 was not available for all companies at press time.

2008 Sales: $3,026,000	2008 Profits: $-233,000	**U.S. Stock Ticker:** ATVI
2007 Sales: $1,349,000	2007 Profits: $179,000	**Int'l Ticker:** Int'l Exchange:
2006 Sales: $1,018,000	2006 Profits: $121,000	Employees: 7,000
2005 Sales: $1,405,857	2005 Profits: $135,057	Fiscal Year Ends: 12/31
2004 Sales: $947,656	2004 Profits: $77,715	Parent Company:

SALARIES/BENEFITS:

Pension Plan:	ESOP Stock Plan:	Profit Sharing:	Top Exec. Salary: $899,560	Bonus: $5,000,000
Savings Plan: Y	Stock Purch. Plan: Y		Second Exec. Salary: $875,387	Bonus: $5,000,000

OTHER THOUGHTS:

Apparent Women Officers or Directors: 2
Hot Spot for Advancement for Women/Minorities: Y

LOCATIONS: ("Y" = Yes)

West:	Southwest:	Midwest:	Southeast:	Northeast:	International:
Y	Y	Y	Y	Y	Y

Note: Financial information, benefits and other data can change quickly and may vary from those stated here.

ACXIOM CORP

www.acxiom.com

Industry Group Code: 511210K **Ranks within this company's industry group:** Sales: 1 Profits: 1

Management:		Sales/Marketing:		Liberal Arts:		Information Systems:		Professionals:		Tech./Scientific:	
Management Trainees:	Y	Marketing Pros.:	Y	Gen. Writing/Editing:	Y	Info. Management:	Y	Finance/Acct.:	Y	Engineers, Electrical:	Y
Experienced Mngmt.:	Y	Retail Sales:		Technical Writing:	Y	Software Dev.:	Y	Law:	Y	Engineers, Other:	
International Business:	Y	Commercial/Industrial:	Y	Graphic Arts/Photog.:		Hardware Dev.:		HR/Other:	Y	Health/Lab:	
MBA Grads:	Y	Sales Trainees:		Music:		Consulting/Other:		Training:	Y	Scientists/Research:	
		Advertising Pros.:		Broadcasting:				Health Care:		Petroleum/Chemicals:	
				Other:				Consulting:		Math/Other:	

TYPES OF BUSINESS:

Consumer Data Management
Consumer Databases
Consulting and Analytics
Risk Mitigation Services
CDI Technology
Consumer Privacy Solutions

BRANDS/DIVISIONS/AFFILIATES:

PersonicX
InfoBase-X
Acxiom Access-X Express
InsightIdentify
Acxiom Information Security Services (AISS)
Quinetix LLC
Acxiom Digital
Mktg Services

CONTACTS: Note: Officers with more than one job title may be intentionally listed here more than once.

John A. Meyer, CEO
John A. Adams, COO/Exec. VP
John A. Meyer, Pres.
Christopher W. Wolf, CFO
Richard K. Howe, Sr. VP-Mktg.
Cindy K. Childers, Sr. VP-Human Resources
David R. Guzman, Sr. VP-IT Svcs.
Jerry C. Jones, Chief Legal Officer/Sr. VP
Cindy K. Childers, Corp. Comm.
Martin D. Sunde, Sr. VP
Michael Durham, Chmn.

Phone: 501-342-1000	Fax: 501-342-3913
Toll-Free: 800-322-9466	
Address: 1 Information Way, Little Rock, AR 72202 US	

GROWTH PLANS/SPECIAL FEATURES:

Acxiom Corp. is a customer information management firm offering 11 core products and services. Customer data integration (CDI) solutions include analyzing, optimizing, expanding and protecting a client's existing customer data. Data products include InfoBase-X, a database of U.S. telephone and consumer data; products that customize InfoBase-X such as PersonicX, which divides InfoBase into 70 segments based on demographics and consumer behavior; Acxiom Access-X Express, an data management tool for InfoBase; and others. Consulting and analytics solutions include diagnostic software, analytic consulting and other professional services to support existing customer information. Privacy services consist of privacy policy and compliance consultations. IT services include IT outsourcing, network management and other services, such as IT security. Direct marketing agency solutions include campaign and database management; direct mail and e-mail services; creative consultations; and CDI and analytics. Risk mitigation solutions include identification products to assist banks, investigators and credit unions prevent fraud loss and meet U.S.A. P.A.T.R.I.O.T. Act regulations, and investigation tools, as for debt collection or law enforcement agencies. Acxiom Information Security Services (AISS) provides criminal, civil and driving record background searches. Government solutions provides products that identify, locate and evaluates individuals for government service roles. Marketing-database solutions analyzes prospects and customers, designs, plans and manages campaigns and tracks results. Online Marketing Services assists clients in improving business through e-mail, search marketing and personalizing websites. Acxiom's clients are mostly of Fortune 1000 finance, insurance, information services, direct marketing, publishing, retail and telecommunications companies. Acquisitions of 2008 include the database marketing solutions division from ChoicePoint Inc; the direct marketing technology unit of Alvion, LLC; and Quinetix, LLC.

Employees are offered health, dental and vision insurance; a health savings account; a flexible spending account; an employee assistance program; short-and long-term disability; life insurance; pet insurance; education reimbursement assistance; adoption reimbursement assistance; and credit union.

FINANCIALS: Sales and profits are in thousands of dollars—add 000 to get the full amount. 2008 Note: Financial information for 2008 was not available for all companies at press time.

2008 Sales: $1,384,079	2008 Profits: $-7,780	**U.S. Stock Ticker:** ACXM
2007 Sales: $1,390,511	2007 Profits: $67,873	**Int'l Ticker:** Int'l Exchange:
2006 Sales: $1,328,773	2006 Profits: $61,775	Employees: 6,400
2005 Sales: $1,220,139	2005 Profits: $67,918	Fiscal Year Ends: 3/31
2004 Sales: $1,010,822	2004 Profits: $58,344	Parent Company:

SALARIES/BENEFITS:

Pension Plan:	ESOP Stock Plan:	Profit Sharing:	Top Exec. Salary: $715,998	Bonus: $700,000
Savings Plan: Y	Stock Purch. Plan: Y		Second Exec. Salary: $490,000	Bonus: $224,475

OTHER THOUGHTS:

Apparent Women Officers or Directors: 3
Hot Spot for Advancement for Women/Minorities: Y

LOCATIONS: ("Y" = Yes)

West:	Southwest:	Midwest:	Southeast:	Northeast:	International:
Y	Y	Y	Y		Y

ADC TELECOMMUNICATIONS INC

www.adc.com

Industry Group Code: 334210 Ranks within this company's industry group: Sales: 1 Profits: 1

Management:		Sales/Marketing:		Liberal Arts:		Information Systems:		Professionals:		Tech./Scientific:	
Management Trainees:	Y	Marketing Pros.:	Y	Gen. Writing/Editing:		Info. Management:	Y	Finance/Acct.:	Y	Engineers, Electrical:	Y
Experienced Mngmt.:	Y	Retail Sales:		Technical Writing:	Y	Software Dev.:	Y	Law:	Y	Engineers, Other:	
International Business:	Y	Commercial/Industrial:	Y	Graphic Arts/Photog.:	Y	Hardware Dev.:	Y	HR/Other:	Y	Health/Lab:	
MBA Grads:	Y	Sales Trainees:		Music:		Consulting/Other:		Training:	Y	Scientists/Research:	Y
		Advertising Pros.:	Y	Broadcasting:				Health Care:		Petroleum/Chemicals:	
				Other:				Consulting:		Math/Other:	

TYPES OF BUSINESS:

Telecommunications Equipment
Networking Systems
Broadband Connectivity Products
Equipment Services
Systems Integration

BRANDS/DIVISIONS/AFFILIATES:

OmniReach FTTX Infrastructure Solutions
Fiber Guide Raceway
Century Man Communication
RF Worx
DSX1/3
ADC Krone
LGC Wireless

CONTACTS: *Note: Officers with more than one job title may be intentionally listed here more than once.*

Robert E. Switz, CEO
Robert E. Switz, Pres.
James G. Mathews, CFO/VP
Hubert Shanne, VP-EMEA, Mktg. & Customer Service
Laura N. Owen, VP-Human Resources
Christopher Jurasek, CIO
Mike Day, CTO
Laura N. Owen, Chief Admin. Officer/VP
Jeffery D. Pflaum, General Counsel/Sec./VP
Mike Day, VP-Strategy
Mike Smith, Dir.-Corp. Comm.
Mark P. Borman, VP-Investor Rel./Treas.
Bradley V. Crary, VP-Tax
Kimberly Hartwell, VP-Americas Sales, Mktg. & Customer Service
Richard B. Parran, VP/Pres., Network Solutions
Patrick D. O'Brien, Pres., Connectivity Solutions
Steven G. Nemitz, VP/Controller
Robert E. Switz, Chmn.

Phone: 952-938-8080	Fax: 952-917-1717
Toll-Free: 800-366-3889	
Address: 13625 Technology Dr., Eden Prairie, MN 55344 US	

GROWTH PLANS/SPECIAL FEATURES:

ADC Telecommunications, Inc. is a provider of global network infrastructure products and services that enable the delivery of high-speed Internet, data, video and voice services to consumers and businesses worldwide. The company operates in three business segments: connectivity, network solutions and professional services. Connectivity is by far its largest segment, accounting for 77.2% of ADC's sales. ADC's connectivity devices are used in copper, coaxial, fiber-optic, wireless and broadcast communications networks. These products provide the physical interconnections between network components or access points into networks. These devices include DSX and DDF products, FTTX products, fiber distribution panels and frames, radio frequency digital management products, power distribution and protection panels, modular fiber-optic cable systems, structured cabling products and broadcast and entertainment products. ADC's network solutions services cover both in-building and outdoor services, and its wireline products (principally Soneplex and HiGain) enable communications service providers to deliver high capacity voice and data services over copper or optical facilities in the last mile/kilometer of communications networks. The company's professional services department helps operators plan, deploy and maintain networks, including cable, wireless and wireline networks. ADC serves markets such as broadcast and entertainment, global and local carriers, global original equipment manufacturers, government and wireless. ADC subsidiary ADC Krone is a global supplier of copper- and fiber-based connectivity solutions. In January 2008, the company completed its acquisition of Century Man Communication, a provider of communication distribution frame products in China. In July 2008, ADC announced a new version of its InterReach Fusion in-building cellular system designated for use by Canadian cellular providers.

FINANCIALS: Sales and profits are in thousands of dollars—add 000 to get the full amount. 2008 Note: Financial information for 2008 was not available for all companies at press time.

2008 Sales: $1,456,400	2008 Profits: $-41,900	**U.S. Stock Ticker:** ADCT
2007 Sales: $1,276,700	2007 Profits: $106,300	**Int'l Ticker:** Int'l Exchange:
2006 Sales: $1,231,900	2006 Profits: $65,700	Employees: 10,600
2005 Sales: $1,128,900	2005 Profits: $98,800	Fiscal Year Ends: 10/31
2004 Sales: $733,900	2004 Profits: $16,400	Parent Company:

SALARIES/BENEFITS:

Pension Plan:	ESOP Stock Plan:	Profit Sharing:	Top Exec. Salary: $742,415	Bonus: $673,205
Savings Plan:	Stock Purch. Plan:		Second Exec. Salary: $329,231	Bonus: $208,001

OTHER THOUGHTS:

Apparent Women Officers or Directors: 2
Hot Spot for Advancement for Women/Minorities: Y

LOCATIONS: ("Y" = Yes)

West:	Southwest:	Midwest:	Southeast:	Northeast:	International:
		Y			Y

Note: Financial information, benefits and other data can change quickly and may vary from those stated here.

ADESA INC

www.adesainc.com

Industry Group Code: 441120 **Ranks within this company's industry group:** Sales: 1 Profits:

Management:		Sales/Marketing:		Liberal Arts:		Information Systems:		Professionals:		Tech./Scientific:	
Management Trainees:	Y	Marketing Pros.:	Y	Gen. Writing/Editing:	Y	Info. Management:	Y	Finance/Acct.:	Y	Engineers, Electrical:	
Experienced Mngmt.:	Y	Retail Sales:		Technical Writing:		Software Dev.:		Law:	Y	Engineers, Other:	
International Business:	Y	Commercial/Industrial:	Y	Graphic Arts/Photog.:		Hardware Dev.:		HR/Other:	Y	Health/Lab:	
MBA Grads:	Y	Sales Trainees:	Y	Music:		Consulting/Other:		Training:	Y	Scientists/Research:	
		Advertising Pros.:		Broadcasting:				Health Care:		Petroleum/Chemicals:	
				Other:				Consulting:		Math/Other:	

TYPES OF BUSINESS:

Vehicle Auctions-Wholesale
Salvage Vehicle Auctions
Automobile Transportation
Automobile Reconditioning
Automotive Market Analysis

BRANDS/DIVISIONS/AFFILIATES:

ADESA LiveBlock
ADESA DealerBlock
ADESA Run Lists
ADESA Market Guide
ADESA Virtual Inventory
ADESA Notify Me
Kontos Kommentary

CONTACTS: *Note: Officers with more than one job title may be intentionally listed here more than once.*

James P. Hallett, CEO
Tom Caruso, COO
James P. Hallett, Pres.
Bob Rauschenberg, Exec. VP-Mktg. & Sales
Michelle Mallon, VP-Legal
Paul Lips, Exec. VP-Oper.
Warren Byrd, VP-Corp. Dev.
Jason Ferreri, VP-e-Bus. Sales & Oper.
Paul Lips, Exec. VP-Finance
Jeff Bescher, VP-Commercial Sales & Oper.
Mike Caggiano, Regional VP-Eastern Region
Tim DeBerry, Regional VP-Western Region
Tom Kontos, Exec. VP-Customer Strategies & Analytics
Benjamin Skuy, Exec. VP-Int'l Markets
David Vignes, Exec. VP-Logistics & Strategic Improvements

Phone: 317-815-1100	**Fax:** 317-249-4651
Toll-Free: 800-923-3725	
Address: 13085 Hamilton Crossing Blvd., Carmel, IN 46032 US	

GROWTH PLANS/SPECIAL FEATURES:

ADESA, Inc., a wholly-owned subsidiary of KAR Holdings, Inc., is primarily engaged in automotive auctions, transportation and cosmetic and mechanical reconditioning. The firm operates 61 used-vehicle auction sites across the U.S. and serves two main client types, institutional buyers and dealers. The firm's institutional customers include vehicle manufacturers; banks, credit unions and other financial institutions; vehicle finance companies; vehicle rental companies; and insurance companies. Dealers buying from ADESA include both licensed franchises and independent wholesale dealers. ADESA's online auction tools include ADESA LiveBlock, an online real-time bidding tool; ADESA Run Lists, a summary of consigned vehicles offered for auction sale; and ADESA DealerBlock, a bulletin board type online auction platform. The firm also offers ADESA Market Guide, a summary of wholesale auction prices, auction sales results, market data and condition reports; ADESA Virtual Inventory, a subscription-based service that allows dealers to embed ADESA Search technology into their web sites; and ADESA Notify Me, an e-mail notification service for dealers looking for particular vehicles. The firm also offers analytical services via monthly, semi-annual and annual market analysis publications including Kontos Kommentary, Pulse and Global Vehicle Remarketing. ADESA was recently acquired by KAR Holdings, Inc.

ADESA offers its employees medical, dental and vision coverage; flexible spending accounts; short- and long-term disability; life and AD&D insurance; a 401(k) plan; and an employee assistance program.

FINANCIALS: Sales and profits are in thousands of dollars—add 000 to get the full amount. 2008 Note: Financial information for 2008 was not available for all companies at press time.

2008 Sales: $1,123,400	2008 Profits: $	**U.S. Stock Ticker:** Private
2007 Sales: $	2007 Profits: $	**Int'l Ticker:** Int'l Exchange:
2006 Sales: $1,103,900	2006 Profits: $126,300	Employees:
2005 Sales: $968,800	2005 Profits: $125,500	Fiscal Year Ends: 12/31
2004 Sales: $931,600	2004 Profits: $105,300	Parent Company: KAR HOLDINGS INC

SALARIES/BENEFITS:

Pension Plan:	ESOP Stock Plan:	Profit Sharing:	Top Exec. Salary: $	Bonus: $
Savings Plan: Y	Stock Purch. Plan: Y		Second Exec. Salary: $	Bonus: $

OTHER THOUGHTS:

Apparent Women Officers or Directors: 3
Hot Spot for Advancement for Women/Minorities: Y

LOCATIONS: ("Y" = Yes)

West:	Southwest:	Midwest:	Southeast:	Northeast:	International:
Y	Y	Y	Y	Y	Y

ADOBE SYSTEMS INC

www.adobe.com

Industry Group Code: 511210F Ranks within this company's industry group: Sales: 1 Profits: 1

Management:		Sales/Marketing:		Liberal Arts:		Information Systems:		Professionals:		Tech./Scientific:	
Management Trainees:	Y	Marketing Pros.:	Y	Gen. Writing/Editing:	Y	Info. Management:	Y	Finance/Acct.:	Y	Engineers, Electrical:	Y
Experienced Mngmt.:	Y	Retail Sales:		Technical Writing:	Y	Software Dev.:	Y	Law:	Y	Engineers, Other:	
International Business:	Y	Commercial/Industrial:	Y	Graphic Arts/Photog.:	Y	Hardware Dev.:		HR/Other:	Y	Health/Lab:	
MBA Grads:	Y	Sales Trainees:	Y	Music:		Consulting/Other:	Y	Training:	Y	Scientists/Research:	
		Advertising Pros.:	Y	Broadcasting:				Health Care:		Petroleum/Chemicals:	
				Other:	Y			Consulting:		Math/Other:	

TYPES OF BUSINESS:

Computer Software-Desktop & Publishing
Document Management Software
Photo Editing & Management Software
Graphic Design Software

BRANDS/DIVISIONS/AFFILIATES:

Adobe Acrobat
Adobe Flash Player
Adobe Photoshop
Adobe Creative Suite
Macromedia Flash SDK
Adobe Reader LE
Macromedia ColdFusion
Scene7 Inc

CONTACTS: Note: Officers with more than one job title may be intentionally listed here more than once.

Shantanu Narayen, CEO
Shantanu Narayen, Pres.
Mark Garrett, CFO/Exec. VP
Ann Lewnes, Sr. VP-Corp. Mktg. & Comm.
Donna Morris, Sr. VP-Human Resources
Naresh Gupta, Managing Dir.-R&D, India
Gerri Martin-Flickinger, CIO/Sr. VP
Kevin Lynch, CTO
Digby Horner, Sr. VP-Eng. Tech. Group
Karen Cottle, General Counsel/Corp. Sec./Sr. VP
Matt Thompson, Sr. VP-Worldwide Field Oper.
Paul Weiskopf, Sr. VP-Corp. Dev.
Kevin Burr, VP-Corp. Affairs & Comm.
Mike Saviage, VP-Investor Rel.
John E. Warnock, Co-Chmn.
Naresh Gupta, Sr. VP-Print & Classic Publishing Solutions Unit
John Loiacono, Sr. VP-Creative Solutions Bus. Unit
Charles M. Geschke, Co-Chmn.

Phone: 408-536-6000	Fax: 408-537-6000
Toll-Free: 800-833-6687	
Address: 345 Park Ave., San Jose, CA 95110 US	

GROWTH PLANS/SPECIAL FEATURES:

Adobe Systems, Inc. is one of the largest software companies in the world. It offers a line of creative, business and mobile software and services used by creative professionals, designers, knowledge workers, high-end consumers, original equipment manufacturers, developers and enterprises for creating, managing, delivering and engaging with content and experiences across multiple operating systems, devices and media. The company operates in five segments: creative solutions; knowledge worker solutions (KWS); enterprise and developer solutions (EDS); mobile and device solutions (MDS); and other. Creative Solutions focuses primarily on professional creative clients such as graphic designers, production artists, writers and photographers. Products include Adobe After Effects Professional; Adobe Audition; Adobe Photoshop; and Adobe Ultra. The KWS segment focuses on knowledge clients such as accountants, architects, educators, insurance underwriters and stock analysts. Products include Adobe Document Center and Adobe Acrobat Professional. The EDS segment works with corporate clients to make business processes more efficient and web applications more engaging for these firms. Products include Adobe LiveCycle Data Services ES and Adobe Output Designer. The MDS segment, though the continued relationships with organizations such as Verizon, Nokia and Sony/Ericsson, focuses on mobile devices. Products include Adobe Reader LE and Adobe Flash Lite. The other segment contains products and services that address market opportunities ranging from publishing to printing. In September 2008, the firm acquired YaWah ApS, a European imaging software provider. In September 2009, the company agreed to acquire web analytics company, Omniture Inc. for $1.8 billion.

Employees of the firm (based in the U.S.) are offered medical, dental and vision coverage; dependent and health care reimbursement accounts; home, auto and pet insurance; back-up child care; adoption assistance; commuter program; educational assistance program; employee discounts; a fitness program; and an employee assistance program.

FINANCIALS: Sales and profits are in thousands of dollars—add 000 to get the full amount. 2008 Note: Financial information for 2008 was not available for all companies at press time.

2008 Sales: $3,579,889	2008 Profits: $871,814	**U.S. Stock Ticker: ADBE**
2007 Sales: $3,157,881	2007 Profits: $723,807	Int'l Ticker: Int'l Exchange:
2006 Sales: $2,575,300	2006 Profits: $505,809	Employees: 7,335
2005 Sales: $1,966,321	2005 Profits: $602,839	Fiscal Year Ends: 11/30
2004 Sales: $1,666,581	2004 Profits: $450,398	Parent Company:

SALARIES/BENEFITS:

Pension Plan:	ESOP Stock Plan:	Profit Sharing: Y	Top Exec. Salary: $875,000	Bonus: $1,257,812
Savings Plan: Y	Stock Purch. Plan: Y		Second Exec. Salary: $504,167	Bonus: $492,823

OTHER THOUGHTS:

Apparent Women Officers or Directors: 5
Hot Spot for Advancement for Women/Minorities: Y

LOCATIONS: ("Y" = Yes)

West:	Southwest:	Midwest:	Southeast:	Northeast:	International:
Y				Y	Y

Note: Financial information, benefits and other data can change quickly and may vary from those stated here.

ADVANCE AUTO PARTS INC

www.advanceautoparts.com

Industry Group Code: 441310 Ranks within this company's industry group: Sales: 2   Profits: 2

Management:		Sales/Marketing:		Liberal Arts:		Information Systems:		Professionals:		Tech./Scientific:	
Management Trainees:	Y	Marketing Pros.:	Y	Gen. Writing/Editing:	Y	Info. Management:	Y	Finance/Acct.:	Y	Engineers, Electrical:	
Experienced Mngmt.:	Y	Retail Sales:	Y	Technical Writing:		Software Dev.:	Y	Law:	Y	Engineers, Other:	
International Business:	Y	Commercial/Industrial:	Y	Graphic Arts/Photog.:	Y	Hardware Dev.:		HR/Other:	Y	Health/Lab:	
MBA Grads:	Y	Sales Trainees:	Y	Music:		Consulting/Other:		Training:	Y	Scientists/Research:	
		Advertising Pros.:	Y	Broadcasting:				Health Care:		Petroleum/Chemicals:	
				Other:				Consulting:		Math/Other:	

TYPES OF BUSINESS:
Auto Parts & Accessories Stores
Online Sales

BRANDS/DIVISIONS/AFFILIATES:
Western Auto
Advance Discount Auto Parts

CONTACTS: Note: Officers with more than one job title may be intentionally listed here more than once.
Darren R. Jackson, CEO
Darren R. Jackson, Pres.
Mike Norona, CFO/Exec. VP
Donna Broome, Sr. VP-Commercial Sales
Keith A. Oreson, Sr. VP-Human Resources
Rick Coro, CIO/Sr. VP-IT
Elwyn G. Murray III, Exec. VP-Tech.
Kevin Freeland, Exec. VP-Merch. & IT
Eric M. Margolin, General Counsel/Sr. VP/Sec.
Carl Hauch, Sr. VP-Oper., West
Jim L. Wade, Exec. VP-Bus. Dev.
Jill A. Livesay, Controller/Sr. VP
Jim Wade, Exec. VP/Customer Dev. Officer, Commercial
Elwyn G. Murray, Exec. VP/Customer Dev. Officer, DIY
Ken Wirth, Sr. VP/Customer Experience Officer
Mike Marolt, Sr. VP/Customer Oper. Excellence Officer
John Brouillard, Interim Chmn.
Kevin Freeland, Exec. VP-Supply Chain

Phone: 540-362-4911	Fax: 540-561-1448
Toll-Free: 877-238-2623	
Address: 5008 Airport Rd., Roanoke, VA 24012 US	

GROWTH PLANS/SPECIAL FEATURES:

Advance Auto Parts, Inc. primarily operates within the automotive aftermarket industry, which includes replacement parts (excluding tires), accessories, maintenance items, batteries and automotive chemicals for cars and light trucks (pickup trucks, vans, minivans and sport utility vehicles). The company is the second largest specialty retailer of automotive parts, accessories and maintenance items to do-it-yourself (DIY) and do-it-for-me customers in the U.S. The firm operates in two segments: Advance Auto Parts (AAP) and Autopart International (AI). The AAP segment operates roughly 3,300 stores within the 40 U.S. states, Puerto Rico and the Virgin Islands under the Advance Auto Parts trade name (Advance Discount Auto Parts in Florida), which offers a broad selection of brand name and proprietary automotive replacement parts, accessories and maintenance items for domestic and imported cars and light trucks. In addition, the firm operates about 30 stores under the Western Auto and Advance Auto Parts trade names, located primarily in Puerto Rico and the Virgin Islands, which offer automotive tires and service in addition to automotive parts, accessories and maintenance items. Replacement parts sold at the firm's stores include automotive filters, radiators, brake pads, fan belts, radiator hoses, starters, alternators, batteries, shock absorbers, engines and transmissions. The AI segment, which includes 125 stores throughout New England and New York, a distribution center and a wholesale distribution business, primarily serves the commercial market from its store locations.

The company offers its employee medical, dental and vision insurance; life insurance; short- and long-term disability insurance; a 401(k) plan; and flexible spending accounts.

FINANCIALS: Sales and profits are in thousands of dollars—add 000 to get the full amount. 2008 Note: Financial information for 2008 was not available for all companies at press time.

2008 Sales: $5,142,255	2008 Profits: $238,038	U.S. Stock Ticker: AAP
2007 Sales: $4,844,404	2007 Profits: $238,317	Int'l Ticker: Int'l Exchange:
2006 Sales: $4,616,503	2006 Profits: $231,318	Employees: 47,582
2005 Sales: $4,264,971	2005 Profits: $234,725	Fiscal Year Ends: 12/31
2004 Sales: $3,770,297	2004 Profits: $187,988	Parent Company:

SALARIES/BENEFITS:

Pension Plan:	ESOP Stock Plan:	Profit Sharing:	Top Exec. Salary: $800,000	Bonus: $1,959,884
Savings Plan: Y	Stock Purch. Plan: Y		Second Exec. Salary: $509,627	Bonus: $352,308

OTHER THOUGHTS:
Apparent Women Officers or Directors: 3
Hot Spot for Advancement for Women/Minorities: Y

LOCATIONS: ("Y" = Yes)

West:	Southwest:	Midwest:	Southeast:	Northeast:	International:
	Y	Y	Y	Y	Y

Note: Financial information, benefits and other data can change quickly and may vary from those stated here.

ADVANCED MICRO DEVICES INC (AMD)

www.amd.com

Industry Group Code: 33441 Ranks within this company's industry group: Sales: 4   Profits: 8

Management:		Sales/Marketing:		Liberal Arts:		Information Systems:		Professionals:		Tech./Scientific:	
Management Trainees:	Y	Marketing Pros.:	Y	Gen. Writing/Editing:		Info. Management:	Y	Finance/Acct.:	Y	Engineers, Electrical:	Y
Experienced Mngmt.:	Y	Retail Sales:		Technical Writing:	Y	Software Dev.:	Y	Law:	Y	Engineers, Other:	
International Business:	Y	Commercial/Industrial:	Y	Graphic Arts/Photog.:	Y	Hardware Dev.:	Y	HR/Other:	Y	Health/Lab:	
MBA Grads:	Y	Sales Trainees:		Music:		Consulting/Other:		Training:	Y	Scientists/Research:	Y
		Advertising Pros.:	Y	Broadcasting:				Health Care:		Petroleum/Chemicals:	
				Other:				Consulting:		Math/Other:	Y

TYPES OF BUSINESS:

Microprocessors
Semiconductors
Chipsets
Wafer Manufacturing
Multimedia Graphics

BRANDS/DIVISIONS/AFFILIATES:

GLOBALFOUNDRIES, Inc.
Advanced Technology Investment Company
West Coast Hitech L.P.
Broadcom Corp.
Qualcomm, Inc.
ATI Technologies Inc.

CONTACTS: *Note: Officers with more than one job title may be intentionally listed here more than once.*

Dirk Meyer, CEO
Robert J. Rivet, COO
Dirk Meyer, Pres.
Nigel Dessau, Chief Mktg. Officer/Sr. VP
Allen Sockwell, Sr. VP-Human Resources/Chief Talent Officer
Amhed Mahamoud, CIO/Sr. VP
Chekib Akrout, Gen. Mgr.-Tech. Group
Richard Bergman, Sr. VP/Gen. Mgr.-Prod. Div.
Robert J. Rivet, Chief Admin. Officer
Thomas M. McCoy, Exec. VP-Legal Affairs
Thomas M. McCoy, Exec. VP-Corp. & Public Affairs
Ben Bar-Haim, VP-Software
Emilio Ghilardi, Chief Sales Officer/Sr. VP
Bruce L. Claflin, Exec. Chmn.
Ben Bar-Haim, Gen. Mgr.-AMD Canada
Douglas Grose, Sr. VP-Supply Chain

Phone: 408-749-4000	Fax:
Toll-Free:	
Address: 1 AMD Pl., Sunnyvale, CA 94088-3453 US	

GROWTH PLANS/SPECIAL FEATURES:

Advanced Micro Devices, Inc. (AMD) is a global semiconductor company that provides processing solutions for the computing, graphics and consumer electronics markets. It supplies microprocessors for the commercial and consumer markets; embedded microprocessors for commercial, commercial client and consumer markets; chipsets for desktop and notebook PCs, professional workstations and servers; and graphics, video and multimedia products for desktop and notebook computers, including home media PCs and professional workstations, servers and technology for game consoles. AMD has operations across the U.S., Canada, South and Central America, Europe, Africa, the Middle East and the Asia Pacific region. The company operates through three segments: Computing Solutions; Graphics; and Foundry. AMD's Computing Solutions segment encompasses microprocessors, chipsets and embedded processors. The Graphics segment consists of graphics, video and multimedia products, as well as royalties from the sale of game consoles that incorporate the firm's graphics technology. The Foundry segment consists of the operations of GLOBALFOUNDRIES, Inc., a manufacturing joint venture whose operations include front end wafer manufacturing and related activities. In 2008, AMD sold its digital TV assets to Broadcom Corporation. In October 2008, the firm announced its intent to spin off its computer chip factories, with Advanced Technology Investment Company (ATIC) agreeing to contribute more than $8 billion in initial funding in exchange for a 55.6% stake in the new company. In January 2009, AMD sold its handheld graphics and multimedia business to Qualcomm, Inc. In March 2009, the company, in cooperation with ATIC and West Coast Hitech L.P., formed GLOBALFOUNDRIES, Inc., a wafer manufacturing joint venture based in the Cayman Islands.

Employees are offered health and dental insurance; disability plans; life insurance; business travel accident insurance; an educational assistance program; fitness centers; and discounted tickets to movie theaters, sporting events and amusement parks.

FINANCIALS: Sales and profits are in thousands of dollars—add 000 to get the full amount. 2008 Note: Financial information for 2008 was not available for all companies at press time.

2008 Sales: $5,808,000	2008 Profits: $-3,098,000	**U.S. Stock Ticker: AMD**
2007 Sales: $5,858,000	2007 Profits: $-3,379,000	Int'l Ticker: Int'l Exchange:
2006 Sales: $5,627,000	2006 Profits: $-166,000	Employees: 14,700
2005 Sales: $4,973,000	2005 Profits: $165,000	Fiscal Year Ends: 12/31
2004 Sales: $3,924,000	2004 Profits: $91,000	Parent Company:

SALARIES/BENEFITS:

Pension Plan:	ESOP Stock Plan:	Profit Sharing:	Top Exec. Salary: $1,123,990	Bonus: $
Savings Plan:	Stock Purch. Plan:		Second Exec. Salary: $856,732	Bonus: $

OTHER THOUGHTS:

Apparent Women Officers or Directors:
Hot Spot for Advancement for Women/Minorities:

LOCATIONS: ("Y" = Yes)

West:	Southwest:	Midwest:	Southeast:	Northeast:	International:
Y	Y	Y	Y	Y	Y

Note: Financial information, benefits and other data can change quickly and may vary from those stated here.

AECOM TECHNOLOGY CORPORATION

www.aecom.com

Industry Group Code: 237 Ranks within this company's industry group: Sales: 6   Profits: 4

Management:		Sales/Marketing:		Liberal Arts:		Information Systems:		Professionals:		Tech./Scientific:	
Management Trainees:	Y	Marketing Pros.:	Y	Gen. Writing/Editing:		Info. Management:	Y	Finance/Acct.:	Y	Engineers, Electrical:	Y
Experienced Mngmt.:	Y	Retail Sales:		Technical Writing:	Y	Software Dev.:	Y	Law:	Y	Engineers, Other:	Y
International Business:	Y	Commercial/Industrial:	Y	Graphic Arts/Photog.:	Y	Hardware Dev.:		HR/Other:	Y	Health/Lab:	
MBA Grads:	Y	Sales Trainees:		Music:		Consulting/Other:	Y	Training:	Y	Scientists/Research:	
		Advertising Pros.:		Broadcasting:				Health Care:		Petroleum/Chemicals:	
				Other:				Consulting:	Y	Math/Other:	

TYPES OF BUSINESS:

Engineering & Design Services
Transportation Projects
Environmental Projects
Power & Mining Support
Consulting
Economic Development Consulting

BRANDS/DIVISIONS/AFFILIATES:

AGS
CTE
DMJM Aviation
Faber Maunsell
Tecsult, Inc
Boyle Engineering
Totten Sims Hubicki Associates
Earth Tech Inc

CONTACTS: *Note: Officers with more than one job title may be intentionally listed here more than once.*

John M. Dionisio, CEO
James R. Royer, COO/Exec. VP
John M. Dionisio, Pres.
Michael S. Burke, CFO/Sr. VP
Robert Kelleher, Chief Human Capital Officer
Raul Cruz, CIO/Sr. VP
Stephanie Hunter, Chief Admin. Officer
Eric Chen, General Counsel
Robert L. Costello, Exec. VP-Global Oper.
Jane Chmielinski, CEO-Corp. Dev.
Paul J. Gennaro, Jr., Chief Comm. Officer
Paul J. Gennaro, Jr., Sr. VP-Investor Rel.
Eric Chen, Sr. VP-Finance
John L. Kinley, CEO-Canada
Glenn R. Robson, Chief Strategy Officer/Sr. VP-Finance
Frederick W. Werner, CEO-U.S.
Jane Chmielinski, CEO-Corp. Dev.
Richard G. Newman, Chmn.
Anthony C. K. Shum, CEO-Hong Kong, China & Asia

Phone: 213-593-8000	Fax: 213-593-8730
Toll-Free:	
Address: 555 S. Flower St., Ste. 3700, Los Angeles, CA 90071-2300 US	

GROWTH PLANS/SPECIAL FEATURES:

AECOM Technology Corporation is a global engineering and design company engaged in facility, transportation, environment and specialty engineering projects for corporate, institutional and government clients. Certain specialized services are available in mining, power, international development, and operations and maintenance. The firm's facility design and construction projects encompass land development assignments and a wide variety of building projects. Transportation services include feasibility studies, planning, design, engineering, construction management and asset management for transit and rail, highway, bridge, port, harbor and airport projects. AECOM offers water resource, wastewater, wet weather, hazardous waste management and other environmental engineering services. The power sector offers design, construction management and commissioning services. The company operates largely through a network of subsidiaries, including AGS, AECOM's government services arm; CTE, an infrastructure engineering firm (with a wastewater treatment plant in Antarctica); DMJM Aviation, the firm's flagship aviation design and construction management company; Faber Maunsell, a European engineering consultancy firm; Metcalf & Eddy, an environmental engineering group; UMA, a Canadian division; Hayes, Seay, Mattern & Mattern, Inc., an architectural and engineering firm that merged into AECOM in January 2007; and PADCO, a firm that promotes sustainable economic development in more than 100 countries. AECOM Austin, another subsidiary, is devoted to serving engineering and development clients in a variety of sectors, including pharmaceutical, industrial and aviation companies. Recent acquisitions include Earth Tech, Inc., a business unit of Tyco International Ltd; Totten Sims Hubicki Associates, a Canadian engineering firm; Boyle Engineering, a company that specializes in the water sector; and Tecsult, Inc. an international engineering firm based in Quebec.

Employees are offered health, life and disability insurance, as well as retirement benefits.

FINANCIALS: Sales and profits are in thousands of dollars—add 000 to get the full amount. 2008 Note: Financial information for 2008 was not available for all companies at press time.

2008 Sales: $5,194,482	2008 Profits: $147,226	**U.S. Stock Ticker:** ACM
2007 Sales: $4,237,270	2007 Profits: $100,297	**Int'l Ticker:** Int'l Exchange:
2006 Sales: $3,421,492	2006 Profits: $53,686	Employees: 43,000
2005 Sales: $2,395,340	2005 Profits: $53,814	Fiscal Year Ends: 9/30
2004 Sales: $2,012,000	2004 Profits: $50,400	Parent Company:

SALARIES/BENEFITS:

Pension Plan: Y	ESOP Stock Plan:	Profit Sharing:	Top Exec. Salary: $956,543	Bonus: $2,000,000
Savings Plan: Y	Stock Purch. Plan: Y		Second Exec. Salary: $918,090	Bonus: $1,700,000

OTHER THOUGHTS:

Apparent Women Officers or Directors: 2
Hot Spot for Advancement for Women/Minorities: Y

LOCATIONS: ("Y" = Yes)

West:	Southwest:	Midwest:	Southeast:	Northeast:	International:
Y	Y	Y	Y	Y	Y

Note: Financial information, benefits and other data can change quickly and may vary from those stated here.

AES CORPORATION (THE)

www.aes.com

Industry Group Code: 221 Ranks within this company's industry group: Sales: 2 Profits: 4

Management:		Sales/Marketing:		Liberal Arts:		Information Systems:		Professionals:		Tech./Scientific:	
Management Trainees:	Y	Marketing Pros.:	Y	Gen. Writing/Editing:	Y	Info. Management:	Y	Finance/Acct.:	Y	Engineers, Electrical:	Y
Experienced Mngmt.:	Y	Retail Sales:		Technical Writing:	Y	Software Dev.:	Y	Law:	Y	Engineers, Other:	Y
International Business:	Y	Commercial/Industrial:	Y	Graphic Arts/Photog.:	Y	Hardware Dev.:		HR/Other:	Y	Health/Lab:	
MBA Grads:	Y	Sales Trainees:		Music:		Consulting/Other:		Training:	Y	Scientists/Research:	
		Advertising Pros.:	Y	Broadcasting:				Health Care:		Petroleum/Chemicals:	
				Other:				Consulting:		Math/Other:	

TYPES OF BUSINESS:

Utilities-Electricity
Wind Generation
Contract Power Generation

BRANDS/DIVISIONS/AFFILIATES:

Indianapolis Power & Light
AES Wind Generation
AES Solar Energy LLC
Greenhouse Gas Services, LLC
Sonel
AES Eletropaulo
AES Kievoblenergo
AES Rivneenergo

CONTACTS: Note: Officers with more than one job title may be intentionally listed here more than once.

Paul T. Hanrahan, CEO
Andres Gluski, COO/Exec. VP
Paul T. Hanrahan, Pres.
Victoria Harker, CFO/Exec. VP
Rita Trehan, VP-Human Resources & Internal Comm.
Elizabeth Hackenson, CIO/Sr. VP
Scott Kicker, VP-Eng. & Construction
Brian Miller, General Counsel/Exec. VP/Corp. Sec.
Mark Woodruff, Managing Dir.-Bus. Dev.
Meghan Dotter, Dir.-External Comm.
Ahmed Pasha, VP-Investor Rel.
Chip Hoagland, Treas./VP
Andrew M. Vesey, Exec. VP/Pres., Latin America & Africa
Ned Hall, Exec. VP/Pres., North America
Richard Santoroski, VP-Global Risk & Commodity Organization
Mary Wood, VP/Controller
Philip Odeen, Chmn.
John McLaren, Pres., Asia, Europe & Middle East /Exec. VP

Phone: 703-522-1315	Fax: 703-528-4510
Toll-Free:	
Address: 4300 Wilson Blvd., 11th Fl., Arlington, VA 22203 US	

GROWTH PLANS/SPECIAL FEATURES:

The AES Corporation, through its subsidiaries, operates in the global power industry in 29 countries on five continents. AES operates two primary business lines: power generation and utilities. Utilities operations consist of 14 distribution companies in seven countries that serve over 11 million customers. The segment has integrated utilities in the U.S. through Indianapolis Power & Light and in Cameroon through Sonel; additionally, it has distribution companies in Brazil through AES Eletropaulo and AES Sul; in Chile through AES Gener; in El Salvador through Compañia de Alumbrado Eléctrico de San Salvador, S.A.; and in the Ukraine through AES Kievoblenergo and AES Rivneenergo. AES's generation business generates and sells electricity to wholesale customers through 93 power generation plants in 26 countries. AES Corp. is focused on expanding its wind, solar and other alternative energy operations. Currently, the firm's wind power business, AES Wind Generation, has 16 facilities in three countries with a total capacity of over 1,200 megawatts (MW). The company also maintains a recently formed joint venture, AES Solar Energy LLC (with Riverstone Holdings, LLC), which has eight plants in Spain with an output capacity of 24 MW of solar power. Greenhouse Gas Services, LLC, a joint venture with GE Energy Financial Services, was formed to create verifiable emission offsets in the U.S. In May 2008, AES Corp. sold a Kazakhi power plant and coal mine for $1.1 billion. In July 2008, the company acquired 49% of the Guohua Hulunbeier Wind Farm in China. In September 2008, the firm's 170 MW wind farm in Texas began commercial operations. In December 2008, majority-owned subsidiary AES Geo Energy agreed to build and operate a 156 MW wind farm in Bulgaria; and wholly-owned subsidiary Wind Energy (North Rhins), Limited, agreed to build and operate a 22 MW wind farm in Scotland.

FINANCIALS: Sales and profits are in thousands of dollars—add 000 to get the full amount. 2008 Note: Financial information for 2008 was not available for all companies at press time.

2008 Sales: $16,070,000	2008 Profits: $1,234,000	U.S. Stock Ticker: AES
2007 Sales: $13,516,000	2007 Profits: $-95,000	Int'l Ticker: Int'l Exchange:
2006 Sales: $11,509,000	2006 Profits: $247,000	Employees: 25,000
2005 Sales: $11,021,000	2005 Profits: $605,000	Fiscal Year Ends: 12/31
2004 Sales: $9,392,000	2004 Profits: $300,000	Parent Company:

SALARIES/BENEFITS:

Pension Plan: Y	ESOP Stock Plan:	Profit Sharing: Y	Top Exec. Salary: $999,000	Bonus: $4,063,800
Savings Plan: Y	Stock Purch. Plan:		Second Exec. Salary: $660,000	Bonus: $1,407,956

OTHER THOUGHTS:

Apparent Women Officers or Directors: 11
Hot Spot for Advancement for Women/Minorities: Y

LOCATIONS: ("Y" = Yes)

West:	Southwest:	Midwest:	Southeast:	Northeast:	International:
Y	Y	Y		Y	Y

Note: Financial information, benefits and other data can change quickly and may vary from those stated here.

AETNA INC

www.aetna.com

Industry Group Code: 524114 **Ranks within this company's industry group:** Sales: 3   Profits: 3

Management:		Sales/Marketing:		Liberal Arts:		Information Systems:		Professionals:		Tech./Scientific:	
Management Trainees:	Y	Marketing Pros.:	Y	Gen. Writing/Editing:	Y	Info. Management:	Y	Finance/Acct.:	Y	Engineers, Electrical:	
Experienced Mngmt.:	Y	Retail Sales:		Technical Writing:	Y	Software Dev.:	Y	Law:	Y	Engineers, Other:	
International Business:		Commercial/Industrial:	Y	Graphic Arts/Photog.:	Y	Hardware Dev.:		HR/Other:	Y	Health/Lab:	
MBA Grads:	Y	Sales Trainees:	Y	Music:		Consulting/Other:		Training:	Y	Scientists/Research:	
		Advertising Pros.:	Y	Broadcasting:				Health Care:	Y	Petroleum/Chemicals:	
				Other:	Y			Consulting:		Math/Other:	

TYPES OF BUSINESS:

Insurance-Medical & Health
Long-Term Care Insurance
Group Insurance
Pension Products
Dental Insurance
Disability Insurance
Life Insurance

BRANDS/DIVISIONS/AFFILIATES:

Schaller Anderson, Inc.
Goodhealth Worldwide
Aetna Global Benefits
i.Choose
Direct2You

CONTACTS: *Note: Officers with more than one job title may be intentionally listed here more than once.*

Ronald A. Williams, CEO
Mark T. Bertolini, Pres.
Joseph M. Zubretsky, CFO/Exec. VP
Robert M. Mead, Sr. VP-Strategic Mktg.
Elease E. Wright, Sr. VP-Human Resources
Lonny Reisman, Chief Medical Officer
Meg McCarthy, CIO
William J. Casazza, General Counsel/Sr. VP
Gery J. Barry, Chief Strategy Officer
Robert M. Mead, Sr. VP-Comm.
Rajan Parmeswar, Chief Acct. Officer/Controller/VP
Ronald A. Williams, Chmn.
Meg McCarthy, Sr. VP-Procurement & Real Estate

Phone: 860-273-0123	**Fax:** 860-273-3971
Toll-Free: 800-872-3862	
Address: 151 Farmington Ave., Hartford, CT 06156 US	

GROWTH PLANS/SPECIAL FEATURES:

Aetna, Inc. is a diversified healthcare benefits company, offering a broad range of traditional and consumer-directed health insurance products and related services, including medical, pharmacy, dental, behavioral health, group life, long-term care and disability plans and medical management capabilities. The firm operates in three segments: health care, group insurance and large case pensions. The health care segment's products consist of medical, pharmacy, benefits management, dental and vision plans offered on both a risk basis and an employee-funded basis. Medical products also include point of service, health maintenance organization, preferred provider organization and indemnity benefit plans. The group insurance segment's products consist primarily of life insurance products, including renewable life insurance; disability insurance products, which provide employee income replacement benefits for both short- and long-term disability; and long-term care insurance products, which provide befits to cover the cost of care in private home settings, adult day care, assisted living or nursing facilities. The large case pensions segment manages retirement products primarily for tax qualified pension plans. Customers include employer groups; individuals; college students; part-time and hourly workers; health plans; and government-sponsored plans. The company's subsidiaries include Schaller Anderson, Inc., a provider of healthcare management services and Goodhealth Worldwide, a managing general underwriter for international private medical insurance. The firm's international division is Aetna Global Benefits. In November 2008, the company introduced i.Choose, a voluntary personal benefits plan that covers any contribution percentage from employees and includes dental, life, accident and disability insurance. In March 2009, Aetna launched Direct2You, a worksite health and wellness services product suite which includes cholesterol and blood pressure screenings, as well as counseling about preventative care and prescription drug consultations.

Employees are offered medical, dental and vision insurance; flexible spending accounts; short- and long-term disability coverage; a 401(k) plan; pension plan; a stock purchase program; and tuition assistance.

FINANCIALS: Sales and profits are in thousands of dollars—add 000 to get the full amount. 2008 Note: Financial information for 2008 was not available for all companies at press time.

2008 Sales: $30,950,700	2008 Profits: $1,384,100	**U.S. Stock Ticker:** AET
2007 Sales: $27,599,600	2007 Profits: $1,831,000	**Int'l Ticker:** Int'l Exchange:
2006 Sales: $25,145,700	2006 Profits: $1,701,700	Employees: 35,500
2005 Sales: $22,491,900	2005 Profits: $1,634,500	Fiscal Year Ends: 12/31
2004 Sales: $19,904,100	2004 Profits: $2,245,100	Parent Company:

SALARIES/BENEFITS:

Pension Plan: Y	ESOP Stock Plan:	Profit Sharing:	Top Exec. Salary: $1,091,764	Bonus: $1,950,000
Savings Plan: Y	Stock Purch. Plan: Y		Second Exec. Salary: $919,368	Bonus: $1,390,500

OTHER THOUGHTS:

Apparent Women Officers or Directors: 6
Hot Spot for Advancement for Women/Minorities: Y

LOCATIONS: ("Y" = Yes)

West:	Southwest:	Midwest:	Southeast:	Northeast:	International:
Y	Y	Y	Y	Y	

Note: Financial information, benefits and other data can change quickly and may vary from those stated here.

AFFILIATED COMPUTER SERVICES INC

www.acs-inc.com

Industry Group Code: 541513 **Ranks within this company's industry group:** Sales: 5 Profits: 5

Management:		Sales/Marketing:		Liberal Arts:		Information Systems:		Professionals:		Tech./Scientific:	
Management Trainees:	Y	Marketing Pros.:	Y	Gen. Writing/Editing:	Y	Info. Management:	Y	Finance/Acct.:	Y	Engineers, Electrical:	Y
Experienced Mngmt.:	Y	Retail Sales:		Technical Writing:	Y	Software Dev.:	Y	Law:	Y	Engineers, Other:	
International Business:	Y	Commercial/Industrial:	Y	Graphic Arts/Photog.:	Y	Hardware Dev.:	Y	HR/Other:	Y	Health/Lab:	
MBA Grads:	Y	Sales Trainees:		Music:		Consulting/Other:	Y	Training:	Y	Scientists/Research:	
		Advertising Pros.:		Broadcasting:				Health Care:		Petroleum/Chemicals:	
				Other:	Y			Consulting:	Y	Math/Other:	

TYPES OF BUSINESS:

IT Consulting
Loan Processing Services
Systems Integration
Human Resources Services
IT Outsourcing
Business Process Outsourcing

BRANDS/DIVISIONS/AFFILIATES:

Grupo Multivoice

CONTACTS: Note: Officers with more than one job title may be intentionally listed here more than once.

Lynn Blodgett, CEO
Tom Burlin, COO/Exec. VP
Lynn Blodgett, Pres.
Kevin Kyser, CFO/Exec. VP
Lora Villarreal, Chief People Officer/Exec. VP
Tasos Tsolakis, CIO
Skip Stitt, Chief Admin. Officer
Tas Panos, General Counsel/Exec. VP
John Rexford, Exec. VP-Corp. Dev.
Ann Vezina, Exec. VP/Pres., Commercial Solutions
Tom Blodgett, Exec. VP/Pres., Bus. Process Solutions
Derrell James, Exec. VP/Pres., ITO Svcs.
Michael Huerta, Exec. VP/Pres., Transportation Solutions
Darwin Deason, Chmn.

Phone: 214-841-6111	Fax: 214-823-9369
Toll-Free:	
Address: 2828 N. Haskell Ave., Bldg. 1, Dallas, TX 75204 US	

GROWTH PLANS/SPECIAL FEATURES:

Affiliated Computer Services, Inc. (ACS) is a provider of business process outsourcing and IT (information technology) services to commercial and government clients. The company operates in two segments: government and commercial. Through the commercial segment, which generates approximately 60% of its revenues, ACS provides business process outsourcing, systems integration services and consulting services to a variety of commercial clients. The commercial segment is focused on markets including communications and consumer goods; healthcare; transportation; consumer goods and services; and financial services, which includes education services. ACS' solutions for the commercial segment include IT services; human capital management; finance and accounting; customer care; transaction processing; payment services; and commercial education. Services in the government market, which represents approximately 40% of the company's revenues, include technology and business process based services with a focus on transaction processing, child support payment processing, electronic toll collection, traffic violations processing, program management services (such as Medicaid fiscal agent services) and student loan processing services. While ACS serves customers in over 100 countries, approximately 92% of its revenue for 2008 was derived from domestic clients. In December 2008, the company acquired Grupo Multivoice, an Argentina based provider of customer care services.

ACS offers its employees medical, dental, vision, life and disability insurance.

FINANCIALS: Sales and profits are in thousands of dollars—add 000 to get the full amount. 2008 Note: Financial information for 2008 was not available for all companies at press time.

2008 Sales: $6,160,550	2008 Profits: $329,010	**U.S. Stock Ticker:** ACS
2007 Sales: $5,772,479	2007 Profits: $253,090	**Int'l Ticker:** Int'l Exchange:
2006 Sales: $5,353,661	2006 Profits: $358,806	Employees: 74,000
2005 Sales: $4,351,159	2005 Profits: $409,569	Fiscal Year Ends: 6/30
2004 Sales: $4,106,393	2004 Profits: $521,728	Parent Company:

SALARIES/BENEFITS:

Pension Plan:	ESOP Stock Plan:	Profit Sharing:	Top Exec. Salary: $923,911	Bonus: $1,772,856
Savings Plan: Y	Stock Purch. Plan:		Second Exec. Salary: $750,000	Bonus: $1,127,025

OTHER THOUGHTS:

Apparent Women Officers or Directors: 3
Hot Spot for Advancement for Women/Minorities: Y

LOCATIONS: ("Y" = Yes)

West:	Southwest:	Midwest:	Southeast:	Northeast:	International:
Y	Y	Y	Y	Y	Y

Note: Financial information, benefits and other data can change quickly and may vary from those stated here.

AFLAC INC

www.aflac.com

Industry Group Code: 524114 **Ranks within this company's industry group:** Sales: 6 Profits: 4

Management:		Sales/Marketing:		Liberal Arts:		Information Systems:		Professionals:		Tech./Scientific:	
Management Trainees:	Y	Marketing Pros.:	Y	Gen. Writing/Editing:	Y	Info. Management:	Y	Finance/Acct.:	Y	Engineers, Electrical:	
Experienced Mngmt.:	Y	Retail Sales:		Technical Writing:	Y	Software Dev.:	Y	Law:	Y	Engineers, Other:	
International Business:	Y	Commercial/Industrial:	Y	Graphic Arts/Photog.:	Y	Hardware Dev.:		HR/Other:	Y	Health/Lab:	
MBA Grads:	Y	Sales Trainees:	Y	Music:		Consulting/Other:		Training:	Y	Scientists/Research:	
		Advertising Pros.:	Y	Broadcasting:				Health Care:	Y	Petroleum/Chemicals:	
				Other:	Y			Consulting:		Math/Other:	

TYPES OF BUSINESS:

Insurance-Supplemental & Specialty Health
Life Insurance
Cancer Insurance
Medicare Supplement Insurance
Accident & Disability Insurance
Long-Term Care Insurance
Dental Plans

BRANDS/DIVISIONS/AFFILIATES:

AFLAC Japan
AFLAC U.S.
American Family Life Assurance Company of Columbus
Ever

CONTACTS: Note: Officers with more than one job title may be intentionally listed here more than once.

Daniel P. Amos, CEO
Paul S. Amos, II, COO
Kriss Cloninger, III, Pres.
Kriss Cloninger, III, CFO
Jeff Charney, Chief Mktg. Officer/Sr. VP
Gerald Shields, CIO/Sr. VP
Teresa L. White, Chief Admin. Officer/Exec. VP
Joey M. Loudermilk, General Counsel/Exec. VP/Corp. Sec.
Kenneth S. Janke, Jr., Sr. VP-Investor Rel.
Ralph A. Rogers, Chief Acct. Officer/Sr. VP-Financial Svcs.
Janet Baker, Sr. VP-Corp. Learning
Paul S. Amos, II, Pres./COO-Aflac U.S.
Audrey B. Tillman, Exec. VP-Corp. Svcs.
Phillip J. Friou, Sr. VP/Dir.-Gov't Rel.
Daniel P. Amos, Chmn.
Charles D. Lake II, Chmn.-Aflac Japan

Phone: 706-323-3431	Fax: 706-324-6330
Toll-Free: 800-992-3522	
Address: 1932 Wynnton Rd., Columbus, GA 31999 US	

GROWTH PLANS/SPECIAL FEATURES:

AFLAC, Inc. is a holding company whose principle subsidiary, AFLAC (American Family Life Assurance Company of Columbus), insures more than 40 million people worldwide. The subsidiary is a leading writer of supplemental insurance marketed to employers in the U.S., offering policies for 427,700 payroll accounts through more than 74,300 licensed agents. AFLAC U.S. sells cancer plans and various types of health insurance, including accident and disability, fixed-benefit dental, personal sickness and hospital indemnity, hospital intensive care, long-term care, ordinary life and short-term disability plans. In addition, AFLAC offers specified health event coverage for major medical crises such as heart attack and stroke, among others. U.S. insurance products are designed to provide supplemental coverage to individuals who already have major medical or primary insurance coverage. Another subsidiary, AFLAC Japan, is one of the largest foreign-based insurerers in that country, insuring roughly one in four households. AFLAC Japan's insurance products are designed to help consumers pay for medical and non-medical costs that are not reimbursed under Japan's national health insurance system. EVER, a whole life medical insurance policy sold in Japan, hit the 500,000 policy sales mark the year it was introduced. AFLAC Japan sells cancer plans, care plans, general medical expense plans, medical/sickness riders to its cancer plan, a living benefit life plan, ordinary life insurance plans and annuities. AFLAC Japan accounted for 72% of AFLAC's insurance earnings in 2008.

Employees are offered medical and dental insurance; disability coverage; life insurance; flexible spending accounts; an employee assistance program; a pension plan; a 401(k) plan; a stock purchase program; profit sharing; on-site child-care facilities; a health clinic; onsite fitness centers; health screenings; employee discount programs; and educational scholarships.

FINANCIALS: Sales and profits are in thousands of dollars—add 000 to get the full amount. 2008 Note: Financial information for 2008 was not available for all companies at press time.

2008 Sales: $16,554,000	2008 Profits: $1,254,000	**U.S. Stock Ticker:** AFL
2007 Sales: $15,393,000	2007 Profits: $1,634,000	**Int'l Ticker:** Int'l Exchange:
2006 Sales: $14,616,000	2006 Profits: $1,483,000	Employees: 7,949
2005 Sales: $14,363,000	2005 Profits: $1,483,000	Fiscal Year Ends: 12/31
2004 Sales: $13,281,000	2004 Profits: $1,266,000	Parent Company:

SALARIES/BENEFITS:

Pension Plan: Y	ESOP Stock Plan:	Profit Sharing: Y	Top Exec. Salary: $1,338,200	Bonus: $
Savings Plan: Y	Stock Purch. Plan: Y		Second Exec. Salary: $857,700	Bonus: $

OTHER THOUGHTS:

Apparent Women Officers or Directors: 7
Hot Spot for Advancement for Women/Minorities: Y

LOCATIONS: ("Y" = Yes)

West:	Southwest:	Midwest:	Southeast:	Northeast:	International:
Y	Y	Y	Y	Y	Y

AGILENT TECHNOLOGIES INC

www.agilent.com

Industry Group Code: 3345 Ranks within this company's industry group: Sales: 2 Profits: 2

Management:		Sales/Marketing:		Liberal Arts:		Information Systems:		Professionals:		Tech./Scientific:	
Management Trainees:	Y	Marketing Pros.:	Y	Gen. Writing/Editing:	Y	Info. Management:	Y	Finance/Acct.:	Y	Engineers, Electrical:	Y
Experienced Mngmt.:	Y	Retail Sales:		Technical Writing:	Y	Software Dev.:	Y	Law:	Y	Engineers, Other:	
International Business:	Y	Commercial/Industrial:	Y	Graphic Arts/Photog.:	Y	Hardware Dev.:	Y	HR/Other:	Y	Health/Lab:	
MBA Grads:	Y	Sales Trainees:		Music:		Consulting/Other:	Y	Training:	Y	Scientists/Research:	Y
		Advertising Pros.:	Y	Broadcasting:				Health Care:		Petroleum/Chemicals:	
				Other:				Consulting:		Math/Other:	Y

TYPES OF BUSINESS:

Test Equipment
Communications Test Equipment
Integrated Circuits Test Equipment
Optoelectronics Test Equipment
Image Sensors
Bioinstrumentation
Software Products
Informatics Products

BRANDS/DIVISIONS/AFFILIATES:

Agilent Technologies Laboratories
Particle Sizing Systems
RVM Scientific Inc
TILL Photonics GmbH
Stratagene Corp.

CONTACTS: *Note: Officers with more than one job title may be intentionally listed here more than once.*

William P. Sullivan, CEO
William P. Sullivan, Pres.
Adrian T. Dillon, CFO
Jean M. Halloran, Sr. VP-Human Resources
Darlene J. S. Solomon, VP-Agilent Laboratories
Darlene J. S. Solomon, CTO
Adrian T. Dillon, Exec. VP-Admin.
D. Craig Nordlund, General Counsel/Sec./Sr. VP
Amy Flores, Mgr.-Public Rel.
Rodney Gonsalves, Dir.-Investor Rel.
Adrian T. Dillon, Exec. VP-Finance
Gooi Soon Chai, VP/Gen. Mgr.-Electronic Instruments
Ron Nersesian, VP/Gen. Mgr.-Wireless
Nick Roelofs, VP/Gen. Mgr.-Life Sciences Solutions
David Churchill, VP/Gen. Mgr.-Network & Digital Solutions
James G. Cullen, Chmn.

Phone: 408-345-8886	Fax: 408-345-8474
Toll-Free: 877-424-4536	
Address: 5301 Stevens Creek Blvd., Santa Clara, CA 95051 US	

GROWTH PLANS/SPECIAL FEATURES:

Agilent Technologies, Inc. is a diversified technology company with two main business segments: Electronic Measurement and Bio-analytical Measurement. The Electronic Measurement business operates in two markets. Its products for the communications testing market include testing equipment for fiber optic networks; broadband and data networks; and wireless communications and microwave networks. It also assists in installing, activating and maintaining optical, wireless, wireline and large-company networks. Supplying the aerospace, defense, computer and semiconductor industries, its offerings for the general purpose testing market include general purpose instruments, including voltmeters and signal generators; modular instruments and test software; digital design products; high-frequency electronic design automation software tools used to construct computer simulations; parametric test instruments and systems for semiconductor wafers; and electronic manufacturing test products such as automated x-ray inspection and in-circuit testing products. The Bio-analytical Measurement business serves two main life sciences markets: Pharmaceuticals, biotech, contract research and contract manufacturing; and academic and government institutions. It also serves five main chemical analysis markets: petroleum and chemicals; the environment; forensics and homeland security; bio-agriculture and food safety; and materials science. Its main product categories are gas chromatography, liquid chromatography, mass spectrometry, microfluidics, microarrays, atomic force microscopy, PCR (Polymerase Chain Reaction) instrumentation, software and informatics. It also supplies consumables and related bioagents. Agilent conducts centralized research for both segments through Agilent Technologies Laboratories, based in Santa Clara, California. In 2008, the company acquired Particle Sizing Systems, a particle measuring instruments manufacturer; RVM Scientific Inc, a manufacturer of direct heating/cooling systems for gas chromatography capillary columns; and TILL Photonics GmbH, a developer and manufacturer of microscopy products.

Employees are offered medical, dental and vision insurance; life insurance; disability coverage; an employee and family assistance plan; and adoption assistance.

FINANCIALS: Sales and profits are in thousands of dollars—add 000 to get the full amount. 2008 Note: Financial information for 2008 was not available for all companies at press time.

2008 Sales: $5,774,000	2008 Profits: $693,000	**U.S. Stock Ticker: A**
2007 Sales: $5,420,000	2007 Profits: $638,000	**Int'l Ticker:** Int'l Exchange:
2006 Sales: $4,973,000	2006 Profits: $3,307,000	Employees: 19,600
2005 Sales: $4,685,000	2005 Profits: $327,000	Fiscal Year Ends: 10/31
2004 Sales: $4,556,000	2004 Profits: $369,000	Parent Company:

SALARIES/BENEFITS:

Pension Plan: Y	ESOP Stock Plan:	Profit Sharing:	Top Exec. Salary: $986,667	Bonus: $1,305,563
Savings Plan: Y	Stock Purch. Plan: Y		Second Exec. Salary: $699,996	Bonus: $627,775

OTHER THOUGHTS:

Apparent Women Officers or Directors: 3
Hot Spot for Advancement for Women/Minorities: Y

LOCATIONS: ("Y" = Yes)

West:	Southwest:	Midwest:	Southeast:	Northeast:	International:
Y				Y	Y

Note: Financial information, benefits and other data can change quickly and may vary from those stated here.

AIR PRODUCTS & CHEMICALS INC

www.airproducts.com

Industry Group Code: 325120 Ranks within this company's industry group: Sales: 2   Profits: 2

Management:		Sales/Marketing:		Liberal Arts:		Information Systems:		Professionals:		Tech./Scientific:	
Management Trainees:	Y	Marketing Pros.:	Y	Gen. Writing/Editing:	Y	Info. Management:	Y	Finance/Acct.:	Y	Engineers, Electrical:	Y
Experienced Mngmt.:	Y	Retail Sales:		Technical Writing:	Y	Software Dev.:	Y	Law:	Y	Engineers, Other:	Y
International Business:	Y	Commercial/Industrial:	Y	Graphic Arts/Photog.:		Hardware Dev.:		HR/Other:	Y	Health/Lab:	
MBA Grads:	Y	Sales Trainees:		Music:		Consulting/Other:		Training:	Y	Scientists/Research:	Y
		Advertising Pros.:		Broadcasting:				Health Care:		Petroleum/Chemicals:	Y
				Other:				Consulting:		Math/Other:	

TYPES OF BUSINESS:

Industrial Gases & Chemicals
Respiratory Therapy & Home Medical Equipment
Specialty Resins
Hydrogen Refinery
Natural Gas Liquefaction
Semiconductor Materials

BRANDS/DIVISIONS/AFFILIATES:

Air Products Asia
Air Products Europe
Air Products Japan
Harvest Energy Technology Inc
Goar Allison & Associates Inc
CryoService Limited

CONTACTS: *Note: Officers with more than one job title may be intentionally listed here more than once.*

John McGlade, CEO
John McGlade, Pres.
Paul Huck, CFO/Sr. VP
Lynn Minella, Sr. VP-Human Resources & Comm.
Stephen Jones, General Counsel/Corp. Sec./Sr. VP
Nelson Squires, Dir.-Investor Rel.
Michael Crocco, Controller/VP
Scott Sherman, VP-Tonnage Gases, Equipment & Energy
Robert Dixon, Sr. VP/Gen Mgr.-Merchant Gasses
Patricia A. Mattimore, VP/Gen. Mgr.-Performance Materials
John Marsland, VP-Bus. Svcs.
John McGlade, Chmn.

Phone: 610-481-4911	Fax: 610-481-5900
Toll-Free:	
Address: 7201 Hamilton Blvd., Allentown, PA 18195-1501 US	

GROWTH PLANS/SPECIAL FEATURES:

Air Products & Chemicals, Inc. serves global technology, energy, industrial and healthcare customers. Products and services include atmospheric gases; process and specialty gases; performance materials; and equipment and services. The company is one of the world's largest suppliers of hydrogen and helium and has built leading positions in growth markets such as semiconductor materials, refinery hydrogen, natural gas liquefaction, and advanced coatings and adhesives. The firm conducts business under four segments: merchant gasses; tonnage gases; electronics and performance materials; and equipment. The merchant gasses segment sells industrial gases such as oxygen, nitrogen, argon, hydrogen and helium, as well as certain medical and specialty gases. The segment also includes healthcare products such as respiratory therapies, home medical equipment and infusion services. These products are provided to patients in their homes, primarily in Europe. Tonnage gases provides hydrogen, carbon monoxide, nitrogen, oxygen and syngas, primarily to the petroleum refining, chemical and metallurgical industries worldwide. Electronics and performance materials provides solutions to a broad range of global industries through chemical synthesis, analytical technology, process engineering and surface science. The equipment and energy segment designs and manufactures cryogenic and gas processing equipment for air separation; hydrocarbon recovery; and purification, natural gas liquefaction and helium distribution. The company has majority or wholly-owned foreign subsidiaries that operate in Canada, 17 European countries, 10 Asian countries and four Latin American countries. International subsidiaries include Air Products Asia, Air Products Europe and Air Products Japan. Recent acquisitions include Harvest Energy Technology, Inc. a developer of hydrogen generation technology; Goar, Allison & Associates Inc, a process engineering company, and a majority interest in CryoService Limited.

Employees are offered medical and dental coverage; life insurance; disability insurance; educational assistance; flexible spending accounts; access to an onsite fitness center; credit union membership; discounts on personal purchases; and an onsite health unit.

FINANCIALS: Sales and profits are in thousands of dollars—add 000 to get the full amount. 2008 Note: Financial information for 2008 was not available for all companies at press time.

2008 Sales: $10,415,000	2008 Profits: $910,000	**U.S. Stock Ticker: APD**
2007 Sales: $9,148,000	2007 Profits: $1,036,000	**Int'l Ticker:** Int'l Exchange:
2006 Sales: $7,885,000	2006 Profits: $723,400	Employees: 21,100
2005 Sales: $7,673,000	2005 Profits: $711,700	Fiscal Year Ends: 9/30
2004 Sales: $7,031,900	2004 Profits: $604,100	Parent Company:

SALARIES/BENEFITS:

Pension Plan: Y	ESOP Stock Plan:	Profit Sharing: Y	Top Exec. Salary: $1,000,000	Bonus: $2,002,000
Savings Plan: Y	Stock Purch. Plan:		Second Exec. Salary: $575,000	Bonus: $696,000

OTHER THOUGHTS:

Apparent Women Officers or Directors: 5
Hot Spot for Advancement for Women/Minorities: Y

LOCATIONS: ("Y" = Yes)

West:	Southwest:	Midwest:	Southeast:	Northeast:	International:
Y	Y	Y	Y	Y	Y

Note: Financial information, benefits and other data can change quickly and may vary from those stated here.

ALLERGAN INC

www.allergan.com

Industry Group Code: 325412 Ranks within this company's industry group: Sales: 12   Profits: 11

Management:		Sales/Marketing:		Liberal Arts:		Information Systems:		Professionals:		Tech./Scientific:	
Management Trainees:	Y	Marketing Pros.:	Y	Gen. Writing/Editing:	Y	Info. Management:	Y	Finance/Acct.:	Y	Engineers, Electrical:	Y
Experienced Mngmt.:	Y	Retail Sales:		Technical Writing:	Y	Software Dev.:	Y	Law:	Y	Engineers, Other:	Y
International Business:	Y	Commercial/Industrial:	Y	Graphic Arts/Photog.:	Y	Hardware Dev.:		HR/Other:	Y	Health/Lab:	Y
MBA Grads:	Y	Sales Trainees:		Music:		Consulting/Other:		Training:	Y	Scientists/Research:	Y
		Advertising Pros.:	Y	Broadcasting:				Health Care:	Y	Petroleum/Chemicals:	Y
				Other:				Consulting:		Math/Other:	Y

TYPES OF BUSINESS:

Pharmaceutical Development
Eye Care Supplies
Dermatological Products
Neuromodulator Products
Obesity Intervention Products
Urologic Products
Medical Aesthetics

BRANDS/DIVISIONS/AFFILIATES:

Restasis
Lumigan
Optive
Latisse
Botox
Sanctura XR
Aczone
Spectrum Pharmaceuticals, Inc.

CONTACTS: *Note: Officers with more than one job title may be intentionally listed here more than once.*

David Pyott, CEO
F. Michael Ball, Pres.
Jeffrey L. Edwards, CFO
Dianne Dyer-Bruggeman, Exec. VP-Human Resources
Scott M. Whitcup, Exec. VP-R&D
Raymond H. Diradoorian, Exec. VP-Global Tech. Oper.
Douglas S. Ingram, Chief Admin. Officer/Chief Ethics Officer
Douglas S. Ingram, General Counsel/Corp. Sec./Exec. VP
Jeffrey L. Edwards, Exec. VP-Bus. Dev.
Jeffrey L. Edwards, Exec. VP-Finance
David Pyott, Chmn.

Phone: 714-246-4500	**Fax:** 714-246-6987
Toll-Free: 800-433-8871	
Address: 2525 Dupont Dr., Irvine, CA 92612 US	

GROWTH PLANS/SPECIAL FEATURES:

Allergan, Inc. is a technology-driven global health care company that develops and commercializes specialty pharmaceutical products, biologics and medical devices for the ophthalmic, neurological, medical aesthetics, medical dermatology, breast aesthetics, obesity intervention, urological and other specialty markets in more than 100 countries. The company focuses on treatments for chronic dry eye, glaucoma, retinal disease, psoriasis, acne, movement disorders, neuropathic pain and genitourinary diseases. The company operates in two segments: specialty pharmaceuticals and medical devices. The specialty pharmaceuticals segment includes eye care products, such as Restasis ophthalmic emulsion, Lumigan ophthalmic solution, Optive lubricant eye drops and the Refresh line of artificial tears; Botox, used in the treatment of neuromuscular disorders, pain management, the temporary improvement of wrinkles and for certain other therapeutic and aesthetic indications; skin care products, principally tazarotene products in cream and gel formulations for the treatment of acne, facial wrinkles and psoriasis, marketed under the name Tazorac; eyelash growth products; and urologics products, including Sanctura XR, a medication for overactive bladder. The medical devices segment includes breast implants for augmentation, revision and reconstructive surgery; obesity intervention products, including the Lap-Band, an adjustable gastric banding system, and the Orbera intragastric balloon system; and facial aesthetics products, including the Juvederm line of dermal filler products. In July 2008, the company completed the acquisition of the Aczone Gel 5% product, a topical treatment for acne vulgaris, from QLT, Inc. In January 2009, the firm launched Latisse, the first and only FDA-approved prescription treatment designed for eyelash growth.

The firm offers employees benefits including a 401(k) plan; a defined benefit retirement contribution; adoption assistance; education assistance; before-tax flex dollars and flexible spending accounts; backup child care; an employee credit union; an employee assistance program; dependent scholarship awards; and U.S. savings bond deductions.

FINANCIALS: Sales and profits are in thousands of dollars—add 000 to get the full amount. 2008 Note: Financial information for 2008 was not available for all companies at press time.

2008 Sales: $4,339,700	2008 Profits: $578,600	**U.S. Stock Ticker: AGN**
2007 Sales: $3,879,000	2007 Profits: $499,300	**Int'l Ticker:** Int'l Exchange:
2006 Sales: $3,010,100	2006 Profits: $-127,400	Employees: 8,740
2005 Sales: $2,319,200	2005 Profits: $403,900	Fiscal Year Ends: 12/31
2004 Sales: $2,045,600	2004 Profits: $377,100	Parent Company:

SALARIES/BENEFITS:

Pension Plan: Y	ESOP Stock Plan:	Profit Sharing:	Top Exec. Salary: $1,350,000	Bonus: $1,212,100
Savings Plan: Y	Stock Purch. Plan:		Second Exec. Salary: $683,308	Bonus: $324,100

OTHER THOUGHTS:

Apparent Women Officers or Directors: 3
Hot Spot for Advancement for Women/Minorities: Y

LOCATIONS: ("Y" = Yes)

West:	Southwest:	Midwest:	Southeast:	Northeast:	International:
Y					Y

Note: Financial information, benefits and other data can change quickly and may vary from those stated here.

ALLIANCE DATA SYSTEMS CORPORATION

www.alliancedata.com

Industry Group Code: 522320 Ranks within this company's industry group: Sales: 3 Profits: 2

Management:		Sales/Marketing:		Liberal Arts:		Information Systems:		Professionals:		Tech./Scientific:	
Management Trainees:	Y	Marketing Pros.:	Y	Gen. Writing/Editing:	Y	Info. Management:	Y	Finance/Acct.:	Y	Engineers, Electrical:	
Experienced Mngmt.:	Y	Retail Sales:		Technical Writing:		Software Dev.:	Y	Law:	Y	Engineers, Other:	
International Business:	Y	Commercial/Industrial:	Y	Graphic Arts/Photog.:	Y	Hardware Dev.:		HR/Other:	Y	Health/Lab:	
MBA Grads:	Y	Sales Trainees:		Music:		Consulting/Other:		Training:	Y	Scientists/Research:	
		Advertising Pros.:	Y	Broadcasting:				Health Care:		Petroleum/Chemicals:	
				Other:				Consulting:		Math/Other:	

TYPES OF BUSINESS:

Marketing Services
Credit Services
Transaction Services

BRANDS/DIVISIONS/AFFILIATES:

Epsilon
AIR MILES
LoyaltyOne Consulting
Precima
COLLOQUY

CONTACTS: Note: Officers with more than one job title may be intentionally listed here more than once.

Michael Parks, CEO
John Scullion, COO
John Scullion, Pres.
Edward Heffernan, CFO/Exec. VP
Dwayne Tucker, Exec. VP-Human Resources & Transaction Svcs.
Alan Utay, Chief Admin. Officer
Alan Utay, General Counsel/Exec. VP/Corp. Sec.
Bryan A. Pearson, Exec. VP/Pres., Loyalty Svcs.
Ivan Szeftel, Exec. VP/Pres., Retail Credit Svcs.
Brian Kennedy, Exec. VP/Pres., Epsilon Mktg. Svcs.
Michael Parks, Chmn.

Phone: 972-348-5100	Fax: 972-348-5335
Toll-Free:	
Address: 17655 Waterview Pkwy., Dallas, TX 75252 US	

GROWTH PLANS/SPECIAL FEATURES:

Alliance Data Systems Corp. (ADS) is a provider of data-driven and transaction-based marketing and customer loyalty solutions. It partners with clients to develop unique insight into consumer behavior, and then uses that insight to create and manage customized solutions that helps its clients strengthen their relationship with their customers. The company operates in four segments: loyalty services, Epsilon marketing services, private label services and private label credit. The loyalty services segment, which includes the Canadian AIR MILES Reward Program, the firm provides loyalty marketing services, including consumer data, customer-centric retail strategies, direct-to-consumer marketing and loyalty consulting services. Other aspects of this segment include LoyaltyOne Consulting; Precima, a strategic analytics firm; Direct Antidote, a loyalty marketing agency; and COLLOQUY, a collection of resources pertaining to the global loyalty-marketing industry. The Epsilon marketing services provides integrated direct marketing solutions that combine database marketing technology and analytics with a broad range of direct marketing services through subsidiary Epsilon. The operations of the private label services segment include transaction processing, customer care and collections services for the company's private label and other retail card programs; the private label credit segment provides risk management solutions, account origination and funding services for the same programs. ADS' client base mainly serves the retail, financial services, hospitality, telecommunications and healthcare markets. In April 2008, ADS announced that it had terminated its May 2007 merger agreement with the Blackstone Group. In May 2008, the company sold its merchant services business to Heartland Payment Systems, Inc. for approximately $77.5 million. In July 2008, ADS also sold the majority of its utility services business to VTX Holdings, Ltd.

The company offers its employees medical, dental and vision insurance; flexible spending accounts; a 401(k) plan; tuition reimbursement; adoption assistance; and an employee assistance program.

FINANCIALS: Sales and profits are in thousands of dollars—add 000 to get the full amount. 2008 Note: Financial information for 2008 was not available for all companies at press time.

2008 Sales: $2,025,300	2008 Profits: $217,400	**U.S. Stock Ticker:** ADS
2007 Sales: $1,962,200	2007 Profits: $164,061	**Int'l Ticker:** Int'l Exchange:
2006 Sales: $1,998,742	2006 Profits: $189,605	Employees: 7,400
2005 Sales: $1,552,437	2005 Profits: $138,745	Fiscal Year Ends: 12/31
2004 Sales: $1,257,438	2004 Profits: $120,371	Parent Company:

SALARIES/BENEFITS:

Pension Plan:	ESOP Stock Plan:	Profit Sharing:	Top Exec. Salary: $936,000	Bonus: $1,414,670
Savings Plan: Y	Stock Purch. Plan:		Second Exec. Salary: $674,291	Bonus: $878,222

OTHER THOUGHTS:

Apparent Women Officers or Directors:
Hot Spot for Advancement for Women/Minorities:

LOCATIONS: ("Y" = Yes)

West:	Southwest:	Midwest:	Southeast:	Northeast:	International:
	Y	Y		Y	Y

Note: Financial information, benefits and other data can change quickly and may vary from those stated here.

ALLSTATE CORPORATION (THE)   www.allstate.com

Industry Group Code: 524126 Ranks within this company's industry group: Sales: 1 Profits: 8

Management:		Sales/Marketing:		Liberal Arts:		Information Systems:		Professionals:		Tech./Scientific:	
Management Trainees:	Y	Marketing Pros.:	Y	Gen. Writing/Editing:	Y	Info. Management:	Y	Finance/Acct.:	Y	Engineers, Electrical:	
Experienced Mngmt.:	Y	Retail Sales:		Technical Writing:	Y	Software Dev.:	Y	Law:	Y	Engineers, Other:	
International Business:	Y	Commercial/Industrial:	Y	Graphic Arts/Photog.:	Y	Hardware Dev.:		HR/Other:	Y	Health/Lab:	
MBA Grads:	Y	Sales Trainees:	Y	Music:		Consulting/Other:		Training:	Y	Scientists/Research:	
		Advertising Pros.:	Y	Broadcasting:				Health Care:		Petroleum/Chemicals:	
				Other:	Y			Consulting:		Math/Other:	Y

TYPES OF BUSINESS:

Insurance, Direct Property & Casualty
Auto Insurance
Homeowners Insurance
Life Insurance
Business Insurance

BRANDS/DIVISIONS/AFFILIATES:

Allstate Insurance Co.
Allstate Life Insurance Co.
Allstate Motor Club, Inc.
Deerbrook
Encompass
Allstate
Partnership Marketing Group

CONTACTS: Note: Officers with more than one job title may be intentionally listed here more than once.

Tom Wilson, CEO
Tom Wilson, Pres.
Don Civgin, CFO/Sr. VP
Joan H. Walker, Interim Chief Mktg. Officer
Jim D. DeVries, Sr. VP-Human Resources
Catherine S. Brune, CIO/Sr. VP
Michele Coleman Mayes, General Counsel/VP
Steven P. Sorenson, Sr. VP-Prod. Oper.
Joan H. Walker, Sr. VP-Corp. Rel.
George E. Ruebenson, Pres., Allstate Protection
Judy Greffin, Chief Investment Officer/Sr. VP
George E. Ruebenson, Interim CEO/Pres., Allstate Financial
Thomas J. Wilson, Chmn.

Phone: 847-402-5000	Fax: 847-402-2351
Toll-Free: 800-255-7828	
Address: 2775 Sanders Rd., Northbrook, IL 60062 US	

GROWTH PLANS/SPECIAL FEATURES:

The Allstate Corp. is a holding company for Allstate Insurance Co., through which it principally conducts its business. The firm is primarily engaged in the personal property and casualty insurance business; and the life insurance, retirement and investment products business. Allstate provides insurance products to more than 17 million households through a distribution network that utilizes a total of over 14,000 exclusive agencies and exclusive financial specialists in the U.S. and Canada. The company conducts its business through four business segments: Allstate Protection; Allstate Financial; discounted lines and coverages; and corporate/other. Allstate Protection, which accounts for approximately 93% of the firm's consolidated insurance premiums and contract charges, sells primarily private passenger auto and homeowners insurance (principally through agencies), under the Allstate, Encompass and Deerbrook brand names. The segment also sells a wide range of personal property and casualty insurance products; these products are for renters, condominiums, residential fire, manufactured housing, boat owners, loan protection and selected commercial property. In addition, it operates the Allstate Motor Club, Inc., which provides emergency road service. Allstate Financial provides life insurance; retirement and investment products; and supplemental accident and health insurance to individual and institutional customers. The discontinued lines and coverages segment includes results from insurance coverage that the company no longer writes and results for certain commercial and other business in run-off. The corporate/other division is comprised of holding company activities and certain non-insurance operations. In June 2008, Allstate acquired Partnership Marketing Group, a roadside assistance service provider, from General Electric Money.

The company offers its employees medical, dental, vision and life insurance; AD&D and disability insurance; flexible spending accounts; a retirement plan; a profit sharing fund with 401(k) options; tuition reimbursement; and childcare discounts.

FINANCIALS: Sales and profits are in thousands of dollars—add 000 to get the full amount. 2008 Note: Financial information for 2008 was not available for all companies at press time.

2008 Sales: $29,394,000	2008 Profits: $-1,679,000	U.S. Stock Ticker: ALL
2007 Sales: $36,769,000	2007 Profits: $4,636,000	Int'l Ticker: Int'l Exchange:
2006 Sales: $35,796,000	2006 Profits: $4,993,000	Employees: 38,900
2005 Sales: $35,383,000	2005 Profits: $1,765,000	Fiscal Year Ends: 12/31
2004 Sales: $33,936,000	2004 Profits: $3,181,000	Parent Company:

SALARIES/BENEFITS:

Pension Plan: Y	ESOP Stock Plan:	Profit Sharing: Y	Top Exec. Salary: $1,040,769	Bonus: $736,261
Savings Plan: Y	Stock Purch. Plan:		Second Exec. Salary: $655,556	Bonus: $461,763

OTHER THOUGHTS:

Apparent Women Officers or Directors: 5
Hot Spot for Advancement for Women/Minorities: Y

LOCATIONS: ("Y" = Yes)

West:	Southwest:	Midwest:	Southeast:	Northeast:	International:
Y	Y	Y	Y	Y	Y

Note: Financial information, benefits and other data can change quickly and may vary from those stated here.

ALTRIA GROUP INC

www.altria.com

Industry Group Code: 3122 Ranks within this company's industry group: Sales: 1 Profits: 1

Management:		Sales/Marketing:		Liberal Arts:		Information Systems:		Professionals:		Tech./Scientific:	
Management Trainees:	Y	Marketing Pros.:		Gen. Writing/Editing:	Y	Info. Management:	Y	Finance/Acct.:	Y	Engineers, Electrical:	
Experienced Mngmt.:	Y	Retail Sales:		Technical Writing:		Software Dev.:	Y	Law:	Y	Engineers, Other:	
International Business:	Y	Commercial/Industrial:	Y	Graphic Arts/Photog.:	Y	Hardware Dev.:		HR/Other:	Y	Health/Lab:	
MBA Grads:	Y	Sales Trainees:	Y	Music:		Consulting/Other:		Training:	Y	Scientists/Research:	
		Advertising Pros.:	Y	Broadcasting:				Health Care:		Petroleum/Chemicals:	
				Other:				Consulting:		Math/Other:	

TYPES OF BUSINESS:

Tobacco Products
Wine

BRANDS/DIVISIONS/AFFILIATES:

UST Inc
US Smokeless Tobacco Company
John Middleton Co
Ste. Michelle Wine Estates Ltd
SABMiller plc

CONTACTS: *Note: Officers with more than one job title may be intentionally listed here more than once.*

Michael E. Szymanczyk, CEO
David R. Beran, CFO/Exec. VP
Nancy B. Lund, Sr. VP-Mktg., Altria Client Services, Inc.
John R. Nelson, Exec. VP/CTO
Martin J. Barrington, Exec. VP/Chief Admin. & Compliance Officer
Denise F. Keane, General Counsel/Exec. VP
Howard A. Willard III, Exec. VP-Strategy & Bus. Dev.
Theodor P. Baseler, Pres./CEO-Ste. Michelle Wine Estates Ltd.
Daniel W. Butler, Pres., U.S. Smokeless Tobacco Company
Murray Garnick, Sr. VP-Litigation, Altria Client Services, Inc.
Craig A. Johnson, Pres., Philip Morris USA, Inc.
Michael E. Szymanczyk, Chmn.

Phone: 804-274-2200	Fax:
Toll-Free:	
Address: 6601 West Broad St., Richmond, VA 23230 US	

GROWTH PLANS/SPECIAL FEATURES:

Altria Group, Inc. is a consumer goods company whose products include cigarettes, cigars, smokeless tobacco and alcoholic beverages. The group's operating units include domestic tobacco, wine and financial services. The domestic tobacco unit includes the operations of wholly-owned subsidiaries, U.S. Smokeless Tobacco Company and John Middleton Co. U.S. Smokeless Tobacco Company is a leading producer and marketer of moist smokeless tobacco, with brands such as Copenhagen, Skoal, Red Seal and Husky. John Middleton Co. is a manufacturer of machine-made large cigars including its Black & Mild brand, as well as pipe tobaccos such as Prince Albert, Carter Hall, Middleton's and Kentucky Club. The wine unit includes the operations of wholly-owned subsidiary Ste. Michelle Wine Estates Ltd., which produces wines in Washington, Oregon and California under such labels as Chateau Ste. Michelle, Columbia Crest, Stag's Leap Wine Cellars, Conn Creek and Villa Mt. Eden. The financial services unit includes the operations of wholly-owned subsidiary Philip Morris Capital Corporation, which manages a portfolio consisting primarily of leveraged and direct finance leases. In addition, Altria Group holds a 28.5% share in SABMiller plc, one of the largest brewers in the world. SABMiller owns and operates the Miller Brewing Company in the U.S. and is one of the largest bottlers and distributors of Coca-Cola products internationally. In March 2008, Altria Group completed the spin-off of 100% of the shares of Philip Morris International to Altria's shareholders. In January 2009, the company completed its acquisition of UST, Inc. and premium wines, through Ste. Michelle Wine Estates.

FINANCIALS: Sales and profits are in thousands of dollars—add 000 to get the full amount. 2008 Note: Financial information for 2008 was not available for all companies at press time.

2008 Sales: $19,356,000	2008 Profits: $4,930,000	**U.S. Stock Ticker: MO**
2007 Sales: $73,801,000	2007 Profits: $9,786,000	**Int'l Ticker:** Int'l Exchange:
2006 Sales: $67,051,000	2006 Profits: $12,022,000	Employees: 10,000
2005 Sales: $97,854,000	2005 Profits: $10,435,000	Fiscal Year Ends: 12/31
2004 Sales: $89,610,000	2004 Profits: $9,416,000	Parent Company:

SALARIES/BENEFITS:

Pension Plan:	ESOP Stock Plan:	Profit Sharing:	Top Exec. Salary: $1,200,000	Bonus: $
Savings Plan:	Stock Purch. Plan:		Second Exec. Salary: $770,000	Bonus: $

OTHER THOUGHTS:

Apparent Women Officers or Directors: 3
Hot Spot for Advancement for Women/Minorities: Y

LOCATIONS: ("Y" = Yes)

West:	Southwest:	Midwest:	Southeast:	Northeast:	International:
Y	Y	Y	Y	Y	Y

Note: Financial information, benefits and other data can change quickly and may vary from those stated here.

AMAZON.COM INC

www.amazon.com

Industry Group Code: 451211E **Ranks within this company's industry group:** Sales: 1   Profits: 1

Management:		Sales/Marketing:		Liberal Arts:		Information Systems:		Professionals:		Tech./Scientific:	
Management Trainees:	Y	Marketing Pros.:	Y	Gen. Writing/Editing:	Y	Info. Management:	Y	Finance/Acct.:	Y	Engineers, Electrical:	
Experienced Mngmt.:	Y	Retail Sales:	Y	Technical Writing:	Y	Software Dev.:	Y	Law:	Y	Engineers, Other:	
International Business:	Y	Commercial/Industrial:		Graphic Arts/Photog.:	Y	Hardware Dev.:		HR/Other:	Y	Health/Lab:	
MBA Grads:	Y	Sales Trainees:	Y	Music:		Consulting/Other:		Training:	Y	Scientists/Research:	
		Advertising Pros.:	Y	Broadcasting:				Health Care:		Petroleum/Chemicals:	
				Other:	Y			Consulting:		Math/Other:	

TYPES OF BUSINESS:

Online Retail
Online Books & Music Retail
Online Videos/DVDs Retail
Online Electronics Retail
Online Auctions
Online Household Goods Retail
Online Auto & Industrial Retail
E-Commerce Support & Hosting

BRANDS/DIVISIONS/AFFILIATES:

Amazon Marketplace
Merchants@
IMDb.com
AbeBooks
Fabric.com
Advanced Book Exchange, Inc.
Audible, Inc.

CONTACTS: *Note: Officers with more than one job title may be intentionally listed here more than once.*

Jeffrey P. Bezos, CEO
Jeffrey P. Bezos, Pres.
Thomas J. Szkutak, CFO/Sr. VP
L. Michelle Wilson, General Counsel/Sr. VP/Sec.
Marc A. Onetto, Sr. VP-Worldwide Oper.
Jeffrey Blackburn, Sr. VP-Bus. Dev.
H. Brian Valentine, Sr. VP-e-commerce
Shelley L. Reynolds, Worldwide Controller/Principal Acct. Officer/VP
Sebastian J. Gunningham, Sr. VP-Seller Svcs.
Andrew Jassy, Sr. VP-Web Svcs.
Steven Kessel, Sr. VP-Worldwide Digital Media
Jeff Wilke, Sr. VP-North American Retail
Jeffrey P. Bezos, Chmn.
Diego Piacentini, Sr. VP-Int'l Retail

Phone: 206-266-1000	Fax:
Toll-Free:	
Address: 1200 12th Ave. S., Ste. 1200, Seattle, WA 98144 US	

GROWTH PLANS/SPECIAL FEATURES:

Amazon.com, Inc. is an Internet consumer-shopping site which offers millions of new, used, refurbished and collectible items in categories such as books, movies, music and games, electronics and computers, home and garden, toys, children's goods, grocery, apparel and jewelry, health and beauty, sports, outdoors, digital downloads, tools and auto and industrial. The company operates in two primary segments: North America and International. In line with this division, the firm operates several international web sites serving the U.K., Germany, Canada, Japan, China and France. Amazon also maintains more than 25 fulfillment centers around the world, comprising more than 12 million total square feet. The Amazon Marketplace and Merchants@ programs allow third parties to integrate their products on Amazon web sites, as well as providing related fulfillment and advertising services to third-party merchants; allow customers to shop for products owned by third parties using Amazon's features and technologies; and allow customers to complete transactions that include multiple sellers in a single checkout process. The firm also offers services such as Amazon Web Services, co-branded credit cards and miscellaneous marketing and promotional offers, such as online advertising. The firm operates IMDB.com, an international movie database offering film reviews and other information. During 2008, Amazon made a number of acquisitions, including: AbeBooks, an online bookseller; Fabric.com, an online fabric store; and Audible, Inc., a provider of audio information and entertainment. In July 2009, Amazon agreed to acquire online shoe seller Zappos.com in a transaction valued at approximately $847 million, the largest in Amazon's history. Also in July 2009, the firm launched an online outdoor recreation store for the sale of outdoor gear and apparel.

Amazon.com offers employees medical, dental and vision plans, an employee assistance program, relocation assistance and discount programs. Full-time employees also receive units of restricted stock.

FINANCIALS: Sales and profits are in thousands of dollars—add 000 to get the full amount. 2008 Note: Financial information for 2008 was not available for all companies at press time.

			U.S. Stock Ticker: AMZN
2008 Sales: $19,166,000	2008 Profits: $645,000		**Int'l Ticker:** Int'l Exchange:
2007 Sales: $14,835,000	2007 Profits: $476,000		Employees: 20,700
2006 Sales: $10,711,000	2006 Profits: $190,000		Fiscal Year Ends: 12/31
2005 Sales: $8,490,000	2005 Profits: $359,000		Parent Company:
2004 Sales: $6,921,124	2004 Profits: $588,000		

SALARIES/BENEFITS:

Pension Plan:	ESOP Stock Plan:	Profit Sharing:	Top Exec. Salary: $157,500	Bonus: $733,333
Savings Plan: Y	Stock Purch. Plan: Y		Second Exec. Salary: $81,840	Bonus: $

OTHER THOUGHTS:

Apparent Women Officers or Directors: 3
Hot Spot for Advancement for Women/Minorities: Y

LOCATIONS: ("Y" = Yes)

West:	Southwest:	Midwest:	Southeast:	Northeast:	International:
Y	Y	Y		Y	Y

Note: Financial information, benefits and other data can change quickly and may vary from those stated here.

AMEDISYS INC

www.amedisys.com

Industry Group Code: 6216 Ranks within this company's industry group: Sales: 2 Profits: 2

Management:		Sales/Marketing:		Liberal Arts:		Information Systems:		Professionals:		Tech./Scientific:	
Management Trainees:	Y	Marketing Pros.:	Y	Gen. Writing/Editing:	Y	Info. Management:	Y	Finance/Acct.:	Y	Engineers, Electrical:	
Experienced Mngmt.:	Y	Retail Sales:		Technical Writing:	Y	Software Dev.:		Law:	Y	Engineers, Other:	
International Business:		Commercial/Industrial:	Y	Graphic Arts/Photog.:	Y	Hardware Dev.:		HR/Other:	Y	Health/Lab:	Y
MBA Grads:	Y	Sales Trainees:		Music:		Consulting/Other:		Training:	Y	Scientists/Research:	
		Advertising Pros.:		Broadcasting:				Health Care:	Y	Petroleum/Chemicals:	
				Other:				Consulting:		Math/Other:	

TYPES OF BUSINESS:

Home Health Care
Home Health Care
Hospice Care

BRANDS/DIVISIONS/AFFILIATES:

Surgery Recovery @ Home
Heart @ Home
Diabetes @ Home
Rehab @ Home
Dysphagia @ Home
Chronic Kidney Disease @ Home
TLC Health Care Services, Inc.
Okanogan Regional Home Health and Hospice

CONTACTS: *Note: Officers with more than one job title may be intentionally listed here more than once.*

William F. Borne, CEO
Larry R. Graham, COO
Larry R. Graham, Pres.
Dale E. Redman, CFO
Patty Graham, Sr. VP-Mktg.
Cindy Phillips, Sr. VP-Human Resources
Michael Fleming, Chief Medical Officer
Alice Ann Schwartz, CIO
David R. Bucey, General Counsel/Sr. VP/Sec.
Jill Cannon, Sr. VP-Oper.
John R. Nugent, Chief Dev. Officer
Tom Dolan, Sr. VP-Finance
Beth Boulet, Sr. VP-Audit
Janet Britt, Sr. VP-Billing & Collections
Thomas Fisher, Sr. VP-MIS
Scott Ginn, Controller/Sr. VP
William F. Borne, Chmn.
Francis Mayer, Sr. VP-Contracting

Phone: 225-292-2031	Fax: 225-295-9624
Toll-Free: 800-467-2662	
Address: 5959 South Sherwood Forest Blvd., Baton Rouge, LA 70816 US	

GROWTH PLANS/SPECIAL FEATURES:

Amedisys, Inc., provides home health and hospice services to 37 U.S. states, Washington D.C. and Puerto Rico. The firm owns and operates approximately 480 Medicare-certified home health agencies, 48 Medicare-certified hospice agencies. The company also manages the operations of four Medicare-certified home health and two Medicare-certified hospice agencies. Approximately 87% of the firm's revenue derived from Medicare. Amedisys' services include skilled nursing; home health aides; physical, occupational and speech therapy; medical social workers; oncology; and psychiatric services. In addition, the firm offers several at-home recovery and rehabilitation programs created to meet specific patient needs; these include the Heart @ Home cardiac program; Diabetes @ Home; Surgery Recovery @ Home; Rehab @ Home; Chronic Kidney Disease @ Home; and Dysphagia @ Home. In March 2008, the firm acquired TLC Health Care Services, Inc., a provider of home nursing and hospice services with 93 home health and 11 hospice agencies located in 22 states and Washington, D.C., for $395 million. In June 2008, the firm acquired five home health locations from Health Management Associates, Inc. In October 2008, Amedisys acquired six home health agencies in Pennsylvania, Delaware and Maryland from Home Health Corporation of America, Inc. Also in October 2008, the firm acquired Okanogan Regional Home Health and Hospice in Washington. In February 2009, Amedisys acquired Yuma Home Care and Arizona Home Rehabilitation & Health Care, both located in Arizona. In March 2009, the company purchased a hospice agency and three home health agencies from White River Health System; and agreed to acquire a home health and hospice agency from Upper Chesapeake Health System and St. Joseph Medical Center in Maryland.

Amedisys offers employees benefits including a 401(K) plan; medical, dental and vision insurance; supplemental life and cancer coverage; flexible spending accounts; a stock purchase plan; tuition reimbursement; and an assistance program.

FINANCIALS: Sales and profits are in thousands of dollars—add 000 to get the full amount. 2008 Note: Financial information for 2008 was not available for all companies at press time.

2008 Sales: $1,187,415	2008 Profits: $86,682	**U.S. Stock Ticker:** AMED
2007 Sales: $697,934	2007 Profits: $65,113	**Int'l Ticker:** Int'l Exchange:
2006 Sales: $541,148	2006 Profits: $38,255	Employees: 14,800
2005 Sales: $381,558	2005 Profits: $30,102	Fiscal Year Ends: 12/31
2004 Sales: $227,100	2004 Profits: $20,500	Parent Company:

SALARIES/BENEFITS:

Pension Plan:	ESOP Stock Plan:	Profit Sharing:	Top Exec. Salary: $723,077	Bonus: $1,125,000
Savings Plan: Y	Stock Purch. Plan: Y		Second Exec. Salary: $529,808	Bonus: $618,750

OTHER THOUGHTS:

Apparent Women Officers or Directors: 8
Hot Spot for Advancement for Women/Minorities: Y

LOCATIONS: ("Y" = Yes)

West:	Southwest:	Midwest:	Southeast:	Northeast:	International:
Y	Y	Y	Y	Y	

Note: Financial information, benefits and other data can change quickly and may vary from those stated here.

AMERICAN ELECTRIC POWER COMPANY INC (AEP) www.aep.com

Industry Group Code: 2211 Ranks within this company's industry group: Sales: 3 Profits: 3

Management:		Sales/Marketing:		Liberal Arts:		Information Systems:		Professionals:		Tech./Scientific:	
Management Trainees:	Y	Marketing Pros.:	Y	Gen. Writing/Editing:	Y	Info. Management:	Y	Finance/Acct.:	Y	Engineers, Electrical:	Y
Experienced Mngmt.:	Y	Retail Sales:		Technical Writing:	Y	Software Dev.:	Y	Law:	Y	Engineers, Other:	Y
International Business:	Y	Commercial/Industrial:	Y	Graphic Arts/Photog.:	Y	Hardware Dev.:		HR/Other:	Y	Health/Lab:	
MBA Grads:	Y	Sales Trainees:		Music:		Consulting/Other:		Training:	Y	Scientists/Research:	
		Advertising Pros.:	Y	Broadcasting:				Health Care:		Petroleum/Chemicals:	
				Other:				Consulting:		Math/Other:	

TYPES OF BUSINESS:

Utilities-Electricity
Natural Gas Power Generation
Nuclear Power Generation
Coal Transport-Barge & Rail
Energy Trading
Coal Power Generation
Solar Power Generation

BRANDS/DIVISIONS/AFFILIATES:

AEP Ohio
AEP Texas
Appalachian Power
Indiana Michigan Power
Kentucky Power
Public Service Company of Oklahoma
Southwestern Electric Power Company
MEMCO Barge Line, Inc.

CONTACTS: Note: Officers with more than one job title may be intentionally listed here more than once.

Michael G. Morris, CEO
Carl English, COO
Michael G. Morris, Pres.
Holly Koeppel, CFO/Exec. VP
Kevin Walker, CIO
Barbara Radous, Sr. VP-Commercial Oper.
Pat D. Hemlepp, Dir.-Corp. Media Rel.
Julie Sherwood, Dir.-Investor Rel.
Charles E. Zebula, Treas./Sr. VP
Robert Powers, Pres., AEP Utilities
Susan Tomasky, Pres., AEP Transmission
Venita McCellon-Allen, Exec. VP-AEP Utilities West
Brian X. Tierney, Exec. VP-AEP Utilities East
Michael G. Morris, Chmn.

Phone: 614-716-1000	Fax: 614-716-1823
Toll-Free:	
Address: 1 Riverside Plz., Columbus, OH 43215-2372 US	

GROWTH PLANS/SPECIAL FEATURES:

American Electric Power Company, Inc. (AEP) is a holding company based in Ohio. The firm serves 5 million customers through thirteen utility subsidiaries: AEP Ohio; AEP Texas; Appalachian Power; Indiana Michigan Power; Kentucky Power; Kingsport Power Company; CSPCo; TCC; TNC; AEGCo; WPCo; Public Service Company of Oklahoma; and Southwestern Electric Power Company. AEP's generating and transmission facilities comprise a 39,000-mile network spanning 11 states. The company's transmission system serves roughly 10% of the electrical demand in the Eastern Interconnection in the U.S. and eastern Canada; and approximately 11% of the electrical demand for Electric Reliability Council of Texas. AEP owns approximately 80 generating stations in the U.S., with 73% based on coal, 16% natural gas and 8% nuclear. These generating stations have a power capacity of approximately 38,000 megawatts. Through MEMCO Barge Line, Inc., the company transports coal by rail car, barge and tugboat. The company owns approximately 2,850 barges, 75 towboats and 7,500 rail cars. AEP owns interest in two terminal facilities: the Cook Coal Terminal on the Ohio River and the International Marine Terminal in New Orleans. These terminals have a combined 32 million tons per year transfer capability. Operations in Ohio account for the largest percentage of the firm's revenue (approximately 32%). In August 2008, the firm formed a joint venture with Duke Energy to build new electric transmission assets. In April 2009, Southwestern Electric Power Company agreed to purchase 50% interest of the Oxbow Mine lignite reserves in Louisiana. In June 2009, AEP agreed to purchase all of the output of a 10.08-megawatt (MW) solar energy facility scheduled to be built in Ohio.

FINANCIALS: Sales and profits are in thousands of dollars—add 000 to get the full amount. 2008 Note: Financial information for 2008 was not available for all companies at press time.

2008 Sales: $14,440,000	2008 Profits: $1,380,000	**U.S. Stock Ticker: AEP**	
2007 Sales: $13,380,000	2007 Profits: $1,089,000	**Int'l Ticker:**	Int'l Exchange:
2006 Sales: $12,622,000	2006 Profits: $1,002,000	Employees: 21,912	
2005 Sales: $12,111,000	2005 Profits: $814,000	Fiscal Year Ends: 12/31	
2004 Sales: $14,245,000	2004 Profits: $1,089,000	Parent Company:	

SALARIES/BENEFITS:

Pension Plan:	ESOP Stock Plan:	Profit Sharing:	Top Exec. Salary: $1,259,615	Bonus: $1,654,071
Savings Plan: Y	Stock Purch. Plan:		Second Exec. Salary: $554,231	Bonus: $450,000

OTHER THOUGHTS:

Apparent Women Officers or Directors: 7
Hot Spot for Advancement for Women/Minorities: Y

LOCATIONS: ("Y" = Yes)

West:	Southwest:	Midwest:	Southeast:	Northeast:	International:
	Y	Y	Y	Y	

Note: Financial information, benefits and other data can change quickly and may vary from those stated here.

AMERICAN POWER CONVERSION (APC)

www.apcc.com

Industry Group Code: 33591 Ranks within this company's industry group: Sales: Profits:

Management:		Sales/Marketing:		Liberal Arts:		Information Systems:		Professionals:		Tech./Scientific:	
Management Trainees:	Y	Marketing Pros.:	Y	Gen. Writing/Editing:	Y	Info. Management:	Y	Finance/Acct.:	Y	Engineers, Electrical:	Y
Experienced Mngmt.:	Y	Retail Sales:		Technical Writing:	Y	Software Dev.:	Y	Law:	Y	Engineers, Other:	Y
International Business:	Y	Commercial/Industrial:	Y	Graphic Arts/Photog.:	Y	Hardware Dev.:	Y	HR/Other:	Y	Health/Lab:	
MBA Grads:	Y	Sales Trainees:	Y	Music:		Consulting/Other:		Training:	Y	Scientists/Research:	
		Advertising Pros.:	Y	Broadcasting:				Health Care:		Petroleum/Chemicals:	
				Other:				Consulting:		Math/Other:	

TYPES OF BUSINESS:

Back-Up Power Supplies
Power Protection & Management Products
Consulting Services
PC Accessories
Power Management Software
Fuel Cell-Based Power Backup

BRANDS/DIVISIONS/AFFILIATES:

InfraStruXure
Mobile Power Pack
Smart-UPS
SureArrest
PowerChute
NetworkAIR
Silcon UPS
Schneider Electric SA

CONTACTS: *Note: Officers with more than one job title may be intentionally listed here more than once.*

Laurent Vernerey, CEO
Laurent Vernerey, Pres.
Herve Coureil, CFO
Aaron Davis, Chief Mktg. Officer
Kevin Roche, Sr. VP-Human Resources
Jim Simonelli, CTO
Ed Machala, Sr. VP-Mfg.
Nei Rasmussen, Chief Innovation Officer
Chun Lauener, Pres., Greater China
Jean-Marc Lang, Sr. VP-Customer Care, Quality & Bus. Processes
Dave Guidette, Sr. VP-Enterprise Sys. & Svc.
Daniel Doimo, Pres., EMEA & Latin America
Ed Machala, Sr. VP-Supply Chain & Purchasing

Phone: 401-789-5735	Fax: 401-789-3710
Toll-Free: 800-788-2208	
Address: 132 Fairgrounds Rd., West Kingston, RI 02892 US	

GROWTH PLANS/SPECIAL FEATURES:

American Power Conversion (APC), a subsidiary of Schneider Electric SA, designs, develops, manufactures and markets power protection and management solutions for computer, communications and electronic applications worldwide. The company's products include uninterruptible power supply products, commonly known as UPSs; electrical surge protection devices; power distribution products; precision cooling equipment; power management software and accessories; racks and enclosures; and various desktop and notebook personal computer accessories. These products are primarily used with sensitive electronic devices which rely on electric utility power, such as home electronics, PCs, high-performance computer workstations, servers, networking equipment, communications equipment, Internet equipment, data centers, mainframe computers and facilities. APC's UPS products regulate the flow of utility power to the protected equipment and provide seamless back-up power during utility power interruptions. The back-up power lasts for enough time to continue computer operations, conduct an orderly shutdown, preserve data, work through short power outages or, in some cases, continue operating for several hours or longer. The company's security and environmental appliances and accessories protect against environmental or human threats and monitor valuable systems with sensors, cameras and accessories. APC's precision cooling equipment regulates temperature and humidity. In addition, the company provides power management software, consulting services and notebook and PC accessories. In 2008, APC introduced its Fuel Cell Extended Run (FCXR) product that provides hydrogen-based power backup for the firm's InfraStruXure power, cooling, environmental monitoring and management data center for modular and mobile configurations. The firm also launched an AV In-Wall Power Filter and Connection Kit designed to protect home theater components such as wall mounted TVs and ceiling mounted projectors.

APC offers employees comprehensive health coverage as well as other benefits, including flexible spending accounts, tuition assistance and a relocation program.

FINANCIALS: Sales and profits are in thousands of dollars—add 000 to get the full amount. 2008 Note: Financial information for 2008 was not available for all companies at press time.

2008 Sales: $	2008 Profits: $	U.S. Stock Ticker: Subsidiary
2007 Sales: $	2007 Profits: $	Int'l Ticker: Int'l Exchange:
2006 Sales: $	2006 Profits: $	Employees: 7,900
2005 Sales: $1,979,532	2005 Profits: $144,081	Fiscal Year Ends: 12/31
2004 Sales: $1,699,900	2004 Profits: $181,500	Parent Company: SCHNEIDER ELECTRIC SA

SALARIES/BENEFITS:

Pension Plan:	ESOP Stock Plan:	Profit Sharing:	Top Exec. Salary: $	Bonus: $230,019
Savings Plan: Y	Stock Purch. Plan: Y		Second Exec. Salary: $	Bonus: $

OTHER THOUGHTS:

Apparent Women Officers or Directors: 1
Hot Spot for Advancement for Women/Minorities:

LOCATIONS: ("Y" = Yes)

West:	Southwest:	Midwest:	Southeast:	Northeast:	International:
	Y	Y	Y	Y	Y

AMERISOURCEBERGEN CORP

www.amerisourcebergen.com

Industry Group Code: 424210 **Ranks within this company's industry group:** Sales: 3 Profits: 3

Management:		Sales/Marketing:		Liberal Arts:		Information Systems:		Professionals:		Tech./Scientific:	
Management Trainees:	Y	Marketing Pros.:	Y	Gen. Writing/Editing:	Y	Info. Management:	Y	Finance/Acct.:	Y	Engineers, Electrical:	
Experienced Mngmt.:	Y	Retail Sales:		Technical Writing:	Y	Software Dev.:	Y	Law:	Y	Engineers, Other:	
International Business:	Y	Commercial/Industrial:	Y	Graphic Arts/Photog.:	Y	Hardware Dev.:		HR/Other:	Y	Health/Lab:	
MBA Grads:	Y	Sales Trainees:	Y	Music:		Consulting/Other:		Training:	Y	Scientists/Research:	
		Advertising Pros.:	Y	Broadcasting:				Health Care:		Petroleum/Chemicals:	
				Other:				Consulting:		Math/Other:	

TYPES OF BUSINESS:

Drug Distribution
Pharmacy Management & Consulting Services
Packaging Solutions
Information Technology
Healthcare Equipment

BRANDS/DIVISIONS/AFFILIATES:

AmerisourceBergen Drug Corp.
AmerisourceBergen Specialty Group
AmerisourceBergen Packaging Group
American Health Packaging
Anderson Packaging
Brecon Pharmaceutical, Ltd.

CONTACTS: *Note: Officers with more than one job title may be intentionally listed here more than once.*

R. David Yost, CEO
R. David Yost, Pres.
Michael D. DiCandilo, CFO/Exec. VP
David W. Neu, Sr. VP-Retail Sales & Mktg.
Jeanne Fisher, Sr. VP-Human Resources
Thomas H. Murphy, CIO/Sr. VP
John G. Chou, General Counsel/Sr. VP/Sec.
Denise Shane, Sr. VP-Oper.
David M. Senior, Sr. VP-Strategy & Corp. Dev.
Michael Kilpatric, VP-Corp & Investor Rel.
J.F. Quinn, Treas./VP
Steven H. Collis, Exec. VP/Pres., AmerisourceBergen Specialty Group
John Palumbo, Sr. VP-Health Systems Solutions
Tim G. Guttman, Corp. Controller/VP
Richard C. Gozon, Chmn.
Antonia Pera, Sr. VP-Supply Chain Mgmt.

Phone: 610-727-7000	Fax: 610-727-3600
Toll-Free: 800-829-3132	
Address: 1300 Morris Dr., Ste. 100, Chesterbrook, PA 19087 US	

GROWTH PLANS/SPECIAL FEATURES:

AmerisourceBergen Corp is one of the largest wholesale distributors of pharmaceutical products and services to a wide variety of healthcare providers and pharmacies. The firm offers brand name and generic pharmaceuticals, supplies and equipment and serves the U.S., Canada and selected global markets. After the recent divesture of its long-term care and workers compensation segment, operations have been consolidated into one reportable segment: Pharmaceutical Distribution. The Pharmaceutical Distribution segment comprises three operating segments, which includes the operations of the AmerisourceBergen Drug Corporation (ABDC), the AmerisourceBergen Specialty Group (ABSG) and the AmerisourceBergen Packaging Group (ABPG). Servicing both healthcare providers and pharmaceutical manufacturers in the pharmaceutical supply channel, the Pharmaceutical Distribution segment's operations provide drug distribution and related services designed to reduce healthcare costs and improve patient outcomes. ABDC provides pharmacy management, staffing and other consulting services, scalable automated pharmacy dispensing equipment, medication and supply dispensing cabinets, and supply management software to a variety of retail and institutional healthcare providers. ABSG provides drug commercialization services, group purchasing, reimbursement consulting, data analytics and physician education. ABPG consists of American Health Packaging, a deliverer of unit dose, punch card and other packaging solutions to institutional and retail health providers; Anderson Packaging, a provider of contract packaging services for pharmaceutical manufacturers; and Brecon Pharmaceuticals Limited, a U.K.-based provider of contract packaging and clinical trials materials services for pharmaceutical manufacturers. In June 2009, the company acquired Innomar Strategies Inc., a specialty pharmaceuticals services company for $13.8 million.

Employees are offered medical, dental and vision insurance; life insurance; travel accident insurance; short- and long-term disability insurance; domestic partner benefits; a 401(k) plan; an employee stock purchase plan; tuition reimbursement; and an employee assistance program.

FINANCIALS: Sales and profits are in thousands of dollars—add 000 to get the full amount. 2008 Note: Financial information for 2008 was not available for all companies at press time.

2008 Sales: $70,189,733	2008 Profits: $250,559	**U.S. Stock Ticker:** ABC
2007 Sales: $65,672,072	2007 Profits: $469,167	**Int'l Ticker:** Int'l Exchange:
2006 Sales: $56,282,216	2006 Profits: $467,714	Employees: 10,900
2005 Sales: $54,577,300	2005 Profits: $264,645	Fiscal Year Ends: 9/30
2004 Sales: $53,178,954	2004 Profits: $468,390	Parent Company:

SALARIES/BENEFITS:

Pension Plan:	ESOP Stock Plan:	Profit Sharing:	Top Exec. Salary: $1,182,060	Bonus: $2,719,537
Savings Plan: Y	Stock Purch. Plan: Y		Second Exec. Salary: $619,231	Bonus: $632,572

OTHER THOUGHTS:

Apparent Women Officers or Directors: 3
Hot Spot for Advancement for Women/Minorities: Y

LOCATIONS: ("Y" = Yes)

West:	Southwest:	Midwest:	Southeast:	Northeast:	International:
Y	Y	Y	Y	Y	

Note: Financial information, benefits and other data can change quickly and may vary from those stated here.

AMGEN INC

www.amgen.com

Industry Group Code: 325412 **Ranks within this company's industry group:** Sales: 8 Profits: 6

Management:		Sales/Marketing:		Liberal Arts:		Information Systems:		Professionals:		Tech./Scientific:	
Management Trainees:	Y	Marketing Pros.:	Y	Gen. Writing/Editing:	Y	Info. Management:	Y	Finance/Acct.:	Y	Engineers, Electrical:	Y
Experienced Mngmt.:	Y	Retail Sales:		Technical Writing:	Y	Software Dev.:	Y	Law:	Y	Engineers, Other:	Y
International Business:	Y	Commercial/Industrial:	Y	Graphic Arts/Photog.:	Y	Hardware Dev.:		HR/Other:	Y	Health/Lab:	Y
MBA Grads:	Y	Sales Trainees:	Y	Music:		Consulting/Other:		Training:	Y	Scientists/Research:	Y
		Advertising Pros.:		Broadcasting:				Health Care:	Y	Petroleum/Chemicals:	Y
				Other:				Consulting:		Math/Other:	Y

TYPES OF BUSINESS:

Drugs-Diversified
Oncology Drugs
Nephrology Drugs
Inflammation Drugs
Neurology Drugs
Metabolic Drugs

BRANDS/DIVISIONS/AFFILIATES:

Aranesp
EPOGEN
Neulasta
NEUPOGEN
Enbrel

CONTACTS: *Note: Officers with more than one job title may be intentionally listed here more than once.*

Kevin W. Sharer, CEO
Kevin W. Sharer, Pres.
Robert A. Bradway, CFO/Exec. VP
Brian McNamee, Sr. VP-Human Resources
Roger M. Perlmutter, Exec. VP-R&D
Thomas J. (Tom) Flanagan, CIO/Sr. VP
David J. Scott, General Counsel/Sr. VP/Corp. Sec.
Fabrizio Bonanni, Exec. VP-Oper.
David Beier, Sr. VP-Corp. Affairs & Global Gov't
Anna Richo, Sr. VP/Chief Compliance Officer
Kevin W. Sharer, Chmn.
George J. Morrow, Exec. VP-Global Commercial Oper.

Phone: 805-447-1000	Fax: 805-447-1010
Toll-Free:	
Address: 1 Amgen Center Dr., Thousand Oaks, CA 91320-1799 US	

GROWTH PLANS/SPECIAL FEATURES:

Amgen, Inc. is a global biotechnology company that develops, manufactures and markets human therapeutics based on cellular and molecular biology. Its products are used for treatment in the fields of supportive cancer care, nephrology and inflammation. Amgen's primary products include Aranesp, EPOGEN, Neulasta, NEUPOGEN and Enbrel, which together represent 94% of the company's sales. Aranesp and EPOGEN stimulate the production of red blood cells to treat anemia and belong to a class of drugs referred to as erythropoiesis-stimulating agents. Aranesp is used for the treatment of anemia both in supportive cancer care and in nephrology. EPOGEN is used to treat anemia associated with chronic renal failure. Neulasta and NEUPOGEN selectively stimulate the production of neutrophils, one type of white blood cell that helps the body fight infections. ENBREL inhibits tumor necrosis factor (TNF), a substance induced in response to inflammatory and immunological responses, such as rheumatoid arthritis and psoriasis. Amgen maintains sales and marketing forces primarily in the U.S., Europe and Canada, and markets its products to healthcare providers including physicians, dialysis centers, hospitals and pharmacies. Amgen focuses its research and development efforts in the core areas of oncology, inflammation, bone, metabolic disorders and neuroscience, taking a modality-independent approach to drug discovery by choosing the best possible approach to block a specific disease process before considering the type of drug that may be required to pursue that approach. In September 2008, Biovitrum AB acquired the marketed biologic therapeutic products Kepivance and Stemgen from Amgen and obtained a worldwide exclusive license from the firm for Kineret.

Amgen offers its employees an education reimbursement plan, a Long Term Incentive program and medical, prescription, vision and dental benefits.

FINANCIALS: Sales and profits are in thousands of dollars—add 000 to get the full amount. 2008 Note: Financial information for 2008 was not available for all companies at press time.

2008 Sales: $15,003,000	2008 Profits: $4,196,000	**U.S. Stock Ticker: AMGN**
2007 Sales: $14,771,000	2007 Profits: $3,166,000	**Int'l Ticker:** Int'l Exchange:
2006 Sales: $14,268,000	2006 Profits: $2,950,000	Employees: 16,900
2005 Sales: $12,430,000	2005 Profits: $3,674,000	Fiscal Year Ends: 12/31
2004 Sales: $10,550,000	2004 Profits: $2,363,000	Parent Company:

SALARIES/BENEFITS:

Pension Plan:	ESOP Stock Plan:	Profit Sharing:	Top Exec. Salary: $1,561,923	Bonus: $3,875,000
Savings Plan: Y	Stock Purch. Plan: Y		Second Exec. Salary: $970,408	Bonus: $1,290,000

OTHER THOUGHTS:

Apparent Women Officers or Directors: 2
Hot Spot for Advancement for Women/Minorities: Y

LOCATIONS: ("Y" = Yes)

West:	Southwest:	Midwest:	Southeast:	Northeast:	International:
Y			Y	Y	Y

ANADARKO PETROLEUM CORPORATION   www.anadarko.com

Industry Group Code: 211111 Ranks within this company's industry group: Sales: 9 Profits: 4

Management:		Sales/Marketing:		Liberal Arts:		Information Systems:		Professionals:		Tech./Scientific:	
Management Trainees:	Y	Marketing Pros.:	Y	Gen. Writing/Editing:	Y	Info. Management:	Y	Finance/Acct.:	Y	Engineers, Electrical:	Y
Experienced Mngmt.:	Y	Retail Sales:		Technical Writing:	Y	Software Dev.:	Y	Law:	Y	Engineers, Other:	Y
International Business:	Y	Commercial/Industrial:		Graphic Arts/Photog.:	Y	Hardware Dev.:		HR/Other:	Y	Health/Lab:	
MBA Grads:	Y	Sales Trainees:		Music:		Consulting/Other:		Training:	Y	Scientists/Research:	
		Advertising Pros.:		Broadcasting:				Health Care:		Petroleum/Chemicals:	Y
				Other:				Consulting:		Math/Other:	

TYPES OF BUSINESS:
Oil & Gas Exploration & Production
Field Services
Drilling Technology
Mineral Exploration
Coal-Bed Methane Production

BRANDS/DIVISIONS/AFFILIATES:
Anadarko Energy Services Company
Anadarko Algeria Company LLC
Kerr-McGee Corporation
Western Gas Resources, Inc.

CONTACTS: *Note: Officers with more than one job title may be intentionally listed here more than once.*
James T. Hackett, CEO
R.A. Walker, COO
James T. Hackett, Pres.
Robert G. Gwin, CFO/Sr. VP-Finance
David C. Bretches, VP-Mktg. & Minerals
Julia A. Struble, VP-Human Resources
Mario M. Coll, III, CIO/VP-IT
Robert K. Reeves, Chief Admin. Officer/Sr. VP
Robert K. Reeves, General Counsel
Charles A. Meloy, Sr. VP-Worldwide Oper.
Katie Jackson, VP-Corp. Dev.
John M. Colglazier, VP-Comm.
John M. Colglazier, VP-Investor Rel.
M. Cathy Douglas, Chief Acct. Officer/VP
Danny J. Rea, VP-Midstream
Robert D. Abendschein, VP-Exploration & Production
Gregory M. Pensabene, VP-Gov't Rel.
James T. Hackett, Chmn.
Robert P. Daniels, Sr. VP-Worldwide Exploration

Phone: 832-636-1000	Fax: 832-636-8220
Toll-Free: 800-800-1101	
Address: 1201 Lake Robbins Dr., The Woodlands, TX 77380 US	

GROWTH PLANS/SPECIAL FEATURES:
Anadarko Petroleum Corporation is one of the world's largest independent oil and gas exploration and production companies, holding approximately 2.28 billion barrels of oil equivalent (BOE) of proved reserves, consisting of 8.1 trillion cubic feet of natural gas and 0.9 billion barrels of crude oil, condensate and natural gas liquids (NGL). The company operates has 2,645 natural gas wells, 149 oil wells and 19 dry holes. The company's production activities are located primarily in Louisiana, Texas, the U.S. mid-continent area, Alaska, Canada and offshore in the Gulf of Mexico. The company is also active in Venezuela, Algeria, Qatar, Tunisia, West Africa, the North Atlantic Margin and the Black Sea. The firm's domestic and international operations lie in field services, producer services, market services and financial services. The midstream segment includes gathering, compression and processing operations. The company actively markets natural gas, oil and natural gas liquids and owns and operates gas-gathering systems in its core producing areas. In addition to traditional drilling, the company is engaged in carbon-dioxide-enhanced oil recovery, as well as coal-bed methane production and the production of minerals including coal and soda ash. The company has several subsidiaries, including Anadarko Energy Services Company; Anadarko Algeria Company, LLC; Western Gas Holdings LLC; Kerr-McGee Oil and Western Gas Resources, Inc.

Employees are offered medical, dental and vision insurance; an employee assistance program; life insurance; business travel accident insurance; disability coverage; flexible spending accounts; a retirement plan; a 401(k) plan; adoption assistance; and educational assistance.

FINANCIALS: Sales and profits are in thousands of dollars—add 000 to get the full amount. 2008 Note: Financial information for 2008 was not available for all companies at press time.

2008 Sales: $14,640,000	2008 Profits: $3,260,000	U.S. Stock Ticker: APC
2007 Sales: $11,132,000	2007 Profits: $3,778,000	Int'l Ticker: Int'l Exchange:
2006 Sales: $10,116,000	2006 Profits: $4,746,000	Employees: 4,300
2005 Sales: $7,100,000	2005 Profits: $2,466,000	Fiscal Year Ends: 12/31
2004 Sales: $6,079,000	2004 Profits: $1,601,000	Parent Company:

SALARIES/BENEFITS:
Pension Plan: Y	ESOP Stock Plan:	Profit Sharing:	Top Exec. Salary: $1,510,385	Bonus: $3,416,491
Savings Plan: Y	Stock Purch. Plan:		Second Exec. Salary: $655,000	Bonus: $1,139,700

OTHER THOUGHTS:
Apparent Women Officers or Directors: 4
Hot Spot for Advancement for Women/Minorities: Y

LOCATIONS: ("Y" = Yes)
West:	Southwest:	Midwest:	Southeast:	Northeast:	International:
Y	Y		Y		Y

ANALOG DEVICES INC

www.analog.com

Industry Group Code: 33441 Ranks within this company's industry group: Sales: 6   Profits: 3

Management:		Sales/Marketing:		Liberal Arts:		Information Systems:		Professionals:		Tech./Scientific:	
Management Trainees:	Y	Marketing Pros.:	Y	Gen. Writing/Editing:		Info. Management:	Y	Finance/Acct.:	Y	Engineers, Electrical:	Y
Experienced Mngmt.:	Y	Retail Sales:		Technical Writing:	Y	Software Dev.:	Y	Law:	Y	Engineers, Other:	
International Business:	Y	Commercial/Industrial:	Y	Graphic Arts/Photog.:	Y	Hardware Dev.:	Y	HR/Other:	Y	Health/Lab:	
MBA Grads:	Y	Sales Trainees:		Music:		Consulting/Other:		Training:	Y	Scientists/Research:	Y
		Advertising Pros.:	Y	Broadcasting:				Health Care:		Petroleum/Chemicals:	
				Other:				Consulting:		Math/Other:	Y

TYPES OF BUSINESS:

Integrated Circuits-Analog & Digital
MEMS Products
DSP Products
Accelerometers & Gyroscopes

BRANDS/DIVISIONS/AFFILIATES:

CONTACTS: *Note: Officers with more than one job title may be intentionally listed here more than once.*

Jerald G. Fishman, CEO
Jerald G. Fishman, Pres.
Joseph E. McDonough, CFO/VP-Finance
Vincent Roche, VP-Worldwide Sales
William Matson, VP-Human Resources
Samuel H. Fuller, VP-R&D
Robert R. Marshall, VP-Worldwide Mfg.
Margaret K. Seif, General Counsel/VP/Sec.
Keith Rutherford, VP-Comm. Bus. Dev.
Mindy Kohl, Dir.-Investor Rel.
William A. Martin, Treas./Dir.-Mergers & Acquisitions
Thomas Wessel, VP-European Sales & Mktg.
Dennis Dempsey, VP/Gen. Mgr.-Limerick Mfg.
Mark Norton, VP/Gen. Mgr.-Mfg.
Alex Glass, VP-Global Acct.
Ray Stata, Chmn.
Howard Cheng, VP-Asia
Gerry Dundon, VP-Planning & Supply Chain Logistics

Phone: 781-329-4700	Fax: 781-461-4482
Toll-Free: 800-262-5643	
Address: 1 Technology Way, P.O. Box 9106, Norwood, MA 02062 US	

GROWTH PLANS/SPECIAL FEATURES:

Analog Devices, Inc. (ADI) designs, manufactures and markets a broad line of high-performance analog, mixed-signal and digital signal processing (DSP) integrated circuits (ICs). Its principal products are used in a wide variety of electronic equipment, including industrial process control, factory automation systems, smart munitions, base stations, central office equipment, wireless telephones, computers, cars, CAT scanners, digital cameras and DVD players. The company's product portfolio includes several thousand analog ICs, with as many as several hundred customers per design. ADI's analog technology base also includes an advanced IC technology known in the industry as surface micromachining, which is used to produce micro-electromechanical systems (MEMS) semiconductor products. The firm's MEMS product portfolio includes accelerometers used to sense acceleration and gyroscopes used to sense position. The majority of the ADI's current revenue from micromachined products comes from accelerometers used by automotive manufacturers in airbag applications. These accelerometers are also used in the IBM ThinkPad to protect the hard drives from drops and falls. The company offers both general-purpose and application-specific DSP products. Its application-specific DSP products typically include analog and DSP technology, with the DSPs preprogrammed to execute software for applications such as wireless telecommunications or image processing. ADI's customers include Dell, Alcatel, Lucent, Ericsson, Siemens, Sony, Philips, Ford and Volkswagen. The firm has manufacturing facilities in the U.S., Ireland and the Philippines. The company has approximately 1,300 U.S. patents and nearly 550 non-provisional pending U.S. patent applications. In 2008, Analog Devices sold its cellular handset radio and baseband chipset operations to MediaTek, Inc. for $350 million. Additionally, the firm sold its CPU voltage regulation and PC thermal monitoring business to ON Semiconductor Corporation for $184 million.

The company offers its employees medical, dental and vision coverage; life insurance; dependant and health care spending accounts; a retirement plan; and an education assistance plan.

FINANCIALS: Sales and profits are in thousands of dollars—add 000 to get the full amount. 2008 Note: Financial information for 2008 was not available for all companies at press time.

2008 Sales: $2,582,931	2008 Profits: $786,284	**U.S. Stock Ticker:** ADI
2007 Sales: $2,464,721	2007 Profits: $496,907	**Int'l Ticker:** Int'l Exchange:
2006 Sales: $2,250,100	2006 Profits: $549,482	Employees: 9,000
2005 Sales: $2,037,154	2005 Profits: $414,787	Fiscal Year Ends: 10/31
2004 Sales: $2,633,800	2004 Profits: $570,738	Parent Company:

SALARIES/BENEFITS:

Pension Plan: Y	ESOP Stock Plan:	Profit Sharing:	Top Exec. Salary: $930,935	Bonus: $1,812,030
Savings Plan:	Stock Purch. Plan:		Second Exec. Salary: $407,357	Bonus: $372,487

OTHER THOUGHTS:

Apparent Women Officers or Directors: 1
Hot Spot for Advancement for Women/Minorities:

LOCATIONS: ("Y" = Yes)

West:	Southwest:	Midwest:	Southeast:	Northeast:	International:
Y	Y	Y	Y	Y	Y

ANNTAYLOR STORES CORP

www.anntaylor.com

Industry Group Code: 448120 Ranks within this company's industry group: Sales: 4 Profits: 2

Management:		Sales/Marketing:		Liberal Arts:		Information Systems:		Professionals:		Tech./Scientific:	
Management Trainees:	Y	Marketing Pros.:	Y	Gen. Writing/Editing:	Y	Info. Management:	Y	Finance/Acct.:	Y	Engineers, Electrical:	
Experienced Mngmt.:	Y	Retail Sales:	Y	Technical Writing:		Software Dev.:	Y	Law:	Y	Engineers, Other:	
International Business:	Y	Commercial/Industrial:		Graphic Arts/Photog.:	Y	Hardware Dev.:		HR/Other:	Y	Health/Lab:	
MBA Grads:	Y	Sales Trainees:	Y	Music:		Consulting/Other:		Training:	Y	Scientists/Research:	
		Advertising Pros.:	Y	Broadcasting:				Health Care:		Petroleum/Chemicals:	
				Other:	Y			Consulting:		Math/Other:	

TYPES OF BUSINESS:

Women's Apparel, Retail
Clothing & Accessories
Shoes
Online & Catalog Sales
Ann Taylor University
Accelerated Leadership Program

BRANDS/DIVISIONS/AFFILIATES:

Ann Taylor
Ann Taylor LOFT
Ann Taylor Factory Store

CONTACTS: *Note: Officers with more than one job title may be intentionally listed here more than once.*

Kay Krill, CEO
Kay Krill, Pres.
Michael J. Nicholson, CFO/Exec. VP
Barbara K. Eisenberg, General Counsel/Exec. VP/Corp. Sec.
Brian E. Lynch, Pres., Corp. Oper.
Judith Pirro, Dir.-Investor Rel.
Christine M. Beauchamp, Pres., Ann Taylor Stores

Phone: 212-541-3300	Fax: 212-541-3379
Toll-Free: 800-342-5266	
Address: 7 Times Square, 15th Fl., New York, NY 10036 US	

GROWTH PLANS/SPECIAL FEATURES:

AnnTaylor Stores Corporation is a leading national specialty retailer of high-quality women's apparel, shoes and accessories. Its stores offer a full range of career and casual separates, weekend wear, dresses, tops, accessories and shoes, coordinated as part of a total wardrobe strategy. All of the company's merchandise is developed and designed exclusively for its own stores. The company's line is marketed in 935 stores in 46 states, Washington, D.C. and Puerto Rico, of which 320 are Ann Taylor stores, 510 are LOFT stores, 91 are Ann Taylor Factory stores and 14 are LOFT Outlet stores. Ann Taylor stores represent the firm's core merchandise line and compete in the higher-priced market. The stores are located primarily in regional malls and upscale specialty retail centers, these stores cater primarily to affluent, fashion-conscious, professional women with limited time from the ages of 25-55. Ann Taylor Loft is the firm's more moderately priced operation. Loft is marketed toward more price-conscious women with a more relaxed lifestyle and work environment. The Loft stores have enjoyed terrific success recently due to consumer response to stylish designs at reasonable prices. Through the Ann Taylor Factory stores, the firm offers clearance merchandise from the other two store formats. In 2008, the firm announced plans to close 117 stores due to the slowing economy. It also delayed plans to test a new store concept aimed at Baby Boomer women. The company announced restructuring plans in early 2009.

AnnTaylor employees receive benefits including medical, dental and vision insurance, flexible spending accounts, a transportation reimbursement incentive program, tuition assistance, an adoption assistance program, an employee assistance program, discounted merchandise, a pension plan and a 401(k) savings plan.

FINANCIALS: Sales and profits are in thousands of dollars—add 000 to get the full amount. 2008 Note: Financial information for 2008 was not available for all companies at press time.

2008 Sales: $2,396,510	2008 Profits: $97,235	**U.S. Stock Ticker:** ANN
2007 Sales: $2,342,907	2007 Profits: $142,982	**Int'l Ticker:** Int'l Exchange:
2006 Sales: $2,073,146	2006 Profits: $81,872	Employees: 18,400
2005 Sales: $1,853,583	2005 Profits: $63,276	Fiscal Year Ends: 1/31
2004 Sales: $1,587,700	2004 Profits: $100,900	Parent Company:

SALARIES/BENEFITS:

Pension Plan: Y	ESOP Stock Plan:	Profit Sharing:	Top Exec. Salary: $1,183,333	Bonus: $1,888,961
Savings Plan: Y	Stock Purch. Plan: Y		Second Exec. Salary: $657,084	Bonus: $683,030

OTHER THOUGHTS:

Apparent Women Officers or Directors: 4
Hot Spot for Advancement for Women/Minorities: Y

LOCATIONS: ("Y" = Yes)

West:	Southwest:	Midwest:	Southeast:	Northeast:	International:
Y	Y	Y	Y	Y	Y

Note: Financial information, benefits and other data can change quickly and may vary from those stated here.

APACHE CORP

www.apachecorp.com

Industry Group Code: 211111　**Ranks within this company's industry group:**　Sales: 11　　Profits: 8

Management:		Sales/Marketing:		Liberal Arts:		Information Systems:		Professionals:		Tech./Scientific:	
Management Trainees:	Y	Marketing Pros.:	Y	Gen. Writing/Editing:	Y	Info. Management:	Y	Finance/Acct.:	Y	Engineers, Electrical:	Y
Experienced Mngmt.:	Y	Retail Sales:		Technical Writing:	Y	Software Dev.:	Y	Law:	Y	Engineers, Other:	Y
International Business:	Y	Commercial/Industrial:		Graphic Arts/Photog.:		Hardware Dev.:		HR/Other:	Y	Health/Lab:	
MBA Grads:	Y	Sales Trainees:		Music:		Consulting/Other:		Training:	Y	Scientists/Research:	
		Advertising Pros.:		Broadcasting:				Health Care:		Petroleum/Chemicals:	Y
				Other:				Consulting:		Math/Other:	

TYPES OF BUSINESS:

Oil & Gas Exploration & Production

BRANDS/DIVISIONS/AFFILIATES:

Apache Canada Ltd.
DEK Energy Company
Apache Energy Ltd.
Apache North America, Inc.
Apache Overseas, Inc.

CONTACTS: *Note: Officers with more than one job title may be intentionally listed here more than once.*

G. Steven Farris, CEO
John A. Crum, Co-COO
Roger B. Plank, Pres.
Janine J. McArdle, VP-Oil & Gas Mktg.
Margery M. Harris, VP-Human Resources
Michael S. Bahorich, Exec. VP-Exploration & Prod. Tech.
Kregg Olson, Sr. VP-Corp. Reservoir Eng.
P. Anthony Lannie, General Counsel/Sr. VP
John J. Christmann, IV, VP-Bus. Dev.
Anthony Lentini, Jr., VP-Public & Int'l Affairs
Robert J. Dye, VP-Investor Rel.
Matthew W. Dundrea, Treas./VP
John A. Crum, Pres., North America
Jon A. Jeppesen, Sr. VP-Gulf Coast Region
Rodney J. Eichler, Exec. VP/Gen. Mgr.-Apache Egypt Companies
G. Steven Farris, Chmn.
Rodney J. Eichler, Pres., Int'l
Scott Byrd, Mgr.-Global Sourcing & Special Projects

Phone: 713-296-6000	**Fax:** 713-296-6496
Toll-Free: 800-272-2434	
Address: 2000 Post Oak Blvd., Ste. 100, Houston, TX 77056-4400 US	

GROWTH PLANS/SPECIAL FEATURES:

Apache Corp. is an independent energy company that explores, develops and produces natural gas, crude oil and natural gas liquids in North America, Argentina, the U.K., Egypt and Australia. In North America, Apache's exploration and production interests are focused on the Gulf of Mexico; the Anadarko Basin of western Oklahoma; the Permian Basin of western Texas and New Mexico; the Texas-Louisiana Gulf Coast; East Texas; and the Western Sedimentary basin of Canada. Internationally, Apache has exploration and production interests in Egypt, Australia, Argentina and the U.K. sector of the North Sea. In 2008, crude oil and liquids provided 50% of the firm's production and 68% of its revenue. Natural gas accounted for the remaining 50% of production and 32% of revenues. Apache's estimated proved reserves were balanced at 55% natural gas and 45% crude oil and liquids. Although the company treats all operations as one line of business, interests in many of its properties are through subsidiaries, such as Apache Canada Ltd.; DEK Energy Company; Apache Energy Ltd.; Apache North America, Inc.; and Apache Overseas, Inc. Apache's Canadian natural gas operations have been growing significantly in recent years due to several acquisitions and discoveries. Growth strategies in the U.S. focus on exploiting and expanding established areas, while growth abroad is a mix of exploration and exploitation.

Employees of Apache receive education assistance, a gift matching program, compressed work-week options, tax-free day care spending accounts and an employee assistance plan.

FINANCIALS: Sales and profits are in thousands of dollars—add 000 to get the full amount. 2008 Note: Financial information for 2008 was not available for all companies at press time.

2008 Sales: $12,389,750	2008 Profits: $711,954	**U.S. Stock Ticker:** APA
2007 Sales: $9,999,752	2007 Profits: $2,806,678	**Int'l Ticker:**　　Int'l Exchange:
2006 Sales: $8,309,131	2006 Profits: $2,546,771	**Employees:** 3,639
2005 Sales: $7,584,244	2005 Profits: $2,623,730	**Fiscal Year Ends:** 12/31
2004 Sales: $5,332,900	2004 Profits: $1,668,800	**Parent Company:**

SALARIES/BENEFITS:

Pension Plan: Y	ESOP Stock Plan:	Profit Sharing:	Top Exec. Salary: $1,493,750	Bonus: $500,000
Savings Plan: Y	Stock Purch. Plan:		Second Exec. Salary: $1,493,750	Bonus: $500,000

OTHER THOUGHTS:

Apparent Women Officers or Directors: 5
Hot Spot for Advancement for Women/Minorities: Y

LOCATIONS: ("Y" = Yes)

West:	Southwest:	Midwest:	Southeast:	Northeast:	International:
	Y		Y		Y

APOLLO GROUP INC

www.apollogrp.edu

Industry Group Code: 611410 Ranks within this company's industry group: Sales: 1 Profits: 1

Management:		Sales/Marketing:		Liberal Arts:		Information Systems:		Professionals:		Tech./Scientific:	
Management Trainees:	Y	Marketing Pros.:	Y	Gen. Writing/Editing:	Y	Info. Management:	Y	Finance/Acct.:	Y	Engineers, Electrical:	
Experienced Mngmt.:	Y	Retail Sales:		Technical Writing:		Software Dev.:	Y	Law:	Y	Engineers, Other:	
International Business:	Y	Commercial/Industrial:		Graphic Arts/Photog.:	Y	Hardware Dev.:		HR/Other:	Y	Health/Lab:	
MBA Grads:	Y	Sales Trainees:		Music:		Consulting/Other:		Training:	Y	Scientists/Research:	
		Advertising Pros.:	Y	Broadcasting:				Health Care:		Petroleum/Chemicals:	
				Other:	Y			Consulting:		Math/Other:	

TYPES OF BUSINESS:

University-Level Education
Continuing Education
Online University Courses
Adult Education

BRANDS/DIVISIONS/AFFILIATES:

University of Phoenix, Inc. (The)
University of Phoenix Online
Institute for Professional Development
College for Financial Planning, Inc.
Western International University, Inc.
Insight Schools, Inc.
Apollo Global, Inc.
BPP Holdings plc.

CONTACTS: *Note: Officers with more than one job title may be intentionally listed here more than once.*

Charles B. Edelstein, Co-CEO
Joseph L. D'Amico, COO
Joseph L. D'Amico, Pres.
Brian L. Swartz, CFO/Sr. VP/Treas.
Robert W. Wrubel, Sr. VP-Mktg. & Prod. Strategy
Frederick J. Newton, Sr. VP-Human Resources
Joseph N. Mildenhall, CIO
P. Robert Moya, General Counsel/Exec. VP/Sec
Allyson Pooley, Investor Rel. Contact
Gregory J. Iverson, Chief Acct. Officer/Controller/VP
Gregory W. Cappelli, Co-CEO
William J. Pepicello, Pres., University of Phoenix
Terri C. Bishop, Exec. VP-External Affairs
Jay Goin, Exec. VP-University of Phoenix
John G. Sperling, Chmn.

Phone: 480-966-5394	Fax: 480-379-3503
Toll-Free: 800-990-2765	
Address: 4025 S. Riverpoint Pkwy., Phoenix, AZ 85040 US	

GROWTH PLANS/SPECIAL FEATURES:

Apollo Group, Inc., through its subsidiaries, is a provider of higher education programs for working adults. Its subsidiaries include the University of Phoenix, Inc.; University of Phoenix Online; the Institute for Professional Development; the College for Financial Planning; Western International University, Inc; and Insight Schools, Inc. The consolidated enrollment in the company's educational programs is approximately 362,000 students, over 80% of whom work full-time. Apollo offers its programs and services at campuses and learning centers in 39 states, D.C., Puerto Rico, Mexico, Canada and the Netherlands. The University of Phoenix Online has the distinction of being the leading private, accredited university in the U.S. with undergraduate and graduate degree programs. The Institute for Professional Development, Inc. (IPD) enables private, small to medium-sized accredited colleges and universities to provide viable degree programs for working adults. IPD offers its clients services such as degree program design, curriculum development, market research, student recruitment, accounting and administrative services. The College for Financial Planning provides financial planning education, including the Certified Financial Planner Professional Education Program. Western International University offers undergraduate and graduate degree programs at campuses in Arizona and, through joint ventures, in China and India. Insight Schools, Inc offers curriculum and administrative services to public schools to operate full-time online high school programs serving students in 10 states. It also provides students with a laptop computer and a printer, an online curriculum with over 120 available course offerings, and the instruction of state certified teachers and online mentors. In July 2009, subsidiary, Apollo Global, Inc. acquired UK company, BPP Holdings plc.

Employees are offered medical, dental and vision insurance; flexible spending accounts; life insurance; business travel accident insurance; a 401(k) plan; a stock purchase plan; disability coverage; an education tuition program; and a college savings plan.

FINANCIALS: Sales and profits are in thousands of dollars—add 000 to get the full amount. 2008 Note: Financial information for 2008 was not available for all companies at press time.

2008 Sales: $3,140,931	2008 Profits: $476,525	U.S. Stock Ticker: APOL
2007 Sales: $2,723,793	2007 Profits: $408,810	Int'l Ticker: Int'l Exchange:
2006 Sales: $2,477,533	2006 Profits: $414,833	Employees: 44,647
2005 Sales: $2,251,472	2005 Profits: $444,731	Fiscal Year Ends: 8/31
2004 Sales: $1,798,423	2004 Profits: $277,774	Parent Company:

SALARIES/BENEFITS:

Pension Plan:	ESOP Stock Plan:	Profit Sharing:	Top Exec. Salary: $850,000	Bonus: $1,700,000
Savings Plan: Y	Stock Purch. Plan: Y		Second Exec. Salary: $500,000	Bonus: $1,000,000

OTHER THOUGHTS:

Apparent Women Officers or Directors: 5
Hot Spot for Advancement for Women/Minorities: Y

LOCATIONS: ("Y" = Yes)

West:	Southwest:	Midwest:	Southeast:	Northeast:	International:
Y	Y	Y	Y	Y	Y

APPLE INC

www.apple.com

Industry Group Code: 334111 Ranks within this company's industry group: Sales: 1 Profits: 1

Management:		Sales/Marketing:		Liberal Arts:		Information Systems:		Professionals:		Tech./Scientific:	
Management Trainees:	Y	Marketing Pros.:	Y	Gen. Writing/Editing:	Y	Info. Management:	Y	Finance/Acct.:	Y	Engineers, Electrical:	Y
Experienced Mngmt.:	Y	Retail Sales:	Y	Technical Writing:	Y	Software Dev.:	Y	Law:	Y	Engineers, Other:	
International Business:	Y	Commercial/Industrial:	Y	Graphic Arts/Photog.:	Y	Hardware Dev.:	Y	HR/Other:	Y	Health/Lab:	
MBA Grads:	Y	Sales Trainees:	Y	Music:	Y	Consulting/Other:	Y	Training:	Y	Scientists/Research:	Y
		Advertising Pros.:	Y	Broadcasting:	Y			Health Care:		Petroleum/Chemicals:	
				Other:	Y			Consulting:		Math/Other:	Y

TYPES OF BUSINESS:

Computer Hardware-PCs
Software
Computer Accessories
Retail Stores
Portable Music Players
Online Music Sales
Cellular Phones
Home Entertainment Software & Systems

BRANDS/DIVISIONS/AFFILIATES:

iLife
MacBook Pro
Xserve
Mac OS X
MacBook Air
iPod
iPhone
Safari

CONTACTS: *Note: Officers with more than one job title may be intentionally listed here more than once.*

Steve P. Jobs, CEO
Timothy D. Cook, COO
Peter Oppenheimer, CFO/Sr. VP
Philip W. Schiller, Sr. VP-Worldwide Prod. Mktg.
Bertrand Serlet, Sr. VP-Software Eng.
Daniel Cooperman, General Counsel/Sr. VP/Sec.
Ronald B. Johnson, Sr. VP-Retail
Jonathan Ive, Sr. VP-Industrial Design
Sina Tamaddon, Sr. VP-Applications
Scott Forstall, Sr. VP-iPhone Software
Bill Campbell, Chmn.

Phone: 408-996-1010	Fax: 408-974-2113
Toll-Free: 800-692-7753	
Address: 1 Infinite Loop, Cupertino, CA 95014 US	

GROWTH PLANS/SPECIAL FEATURES:

Apple, Inc. designs, manufactures and markets personal computers, portable digital music players and mobile communication devices; and sells a variety of related software, services, peripherals and networking solutions. The company's hardware products include the MacBook, MacBook Air and MacBook Pro notebook computers; Mac Pro and iMac desktop computers; Mac minis; and Xserve servers and Xserve RAID Storage Systems. The firm's Mac products feature Intel microprocessors, Mac OS X Leopard operating systems and iLife software. Software products include Mac OS X; iLife '09; iWork '09; Logic Studio; and FileMaker Pro. Additional products include the iSight digital video cameras; the iPod line of portable digital music players and accessories; the iPhone, with touch controls, phone, iPod, and Internet services; Final Cut Studio, a high-definition video production suite of applications; and the iTunes digital entertainment management software for MP3 music files, television shows and movies. The iPhone is available in over 80 countries through individual carrier distribution deals. Peripheral products include printers, storage devices, memory, widescreen flat panel displays and Apple TV, which plays iTunes content wirelessly. The firm operates over 258 retail stores in Canada, China, Japan, the U.K., the U.S., Australia and Italy. The company recently released upgrades for its desktop computer line as well as new editions of the iPod Nano, Touch and Shuffle. In June 2009, Apple release the new iPhone 3GS, which has a longer battery life and a better camera than the previous iPhone; new editions of the MacBook Pro with a longer lasting integrated battery; a new version of Mac OS X called Snow leopard, along with its Server counterpart; and Safari 4, a new edition of the firm's browser. In August 2009, the company launched its iTunes store in Mexico.

FINANCIALS: Sales and profits are in thousands of dollars—add 000 to get the full amount. 2008 Note: Financial information for 2008 was not available for all companies at press time.

2008 Sales: $32,479,000	2008 Profits: $4,834,000	**U.S. Stock Ticker:** AAPL
2007 Sales: $24,006,000	2007 Profits: $3,496,000	**Int'l Ticker:** Int'l Exchange:
2006 Sales: $19,315,000	2006 Profits: $1,989,000	Employees: 35,100
2005 Sales: $13,931,000	2005 Profits: $1,328,000	Fiscal Year Ends: 9/30
2004 Sales: $8,279,000	2004 Profits: $266,000	Parent Company:

SALARIES/BENEFITS:

Pension Plan:	ESOP Stock Plan:	Profit Sharing:	Top Exec. Salary: $718,860	Bonus: $700,000
Savings Plan: Y	Stock Purch. Plan: Y		Second Exec. Salary: $600,012	Bonus: $600,000

OTHER THOUGHTS:

Apparent Women Officers or Directors:
Hot Spot for Advancement for Women/Minorities:

LOCATIONS: ("Y" = Yes)

West:	Southwest:	Midwest:	Southeast:	Northeast:	International:
Y	Y	Y	Y	Y	Y

ARAMARK CORPORATION

www.aramark.com

Industry Group Code: 722310 Ranks within this company's industry group: Sales: 1 Profits: 1

Management:		Sales/Marketing:		Liberal Arts:		Information Systems:		Professionals:		Tech./Scientific:	
Management Trainees:	Y	Marketing Pros.:	Y	Gen. Writing/Editing:	Y	Info. Management:	Y	Finance/Acct.:	Y	Engineers, Electrical:	
Experienced Mngmt.:	Y	Retail Sales:		Technical Writing:	Y	Software Dev.:	Y	Law:	Y	Engineers, Other:	
International Business:	Y	Commercial/Industrial:	Y	Graphic Arts/Photog.:	Y	Hardware Dev.:		HR/Other:	Y	Health/Lab:	
MBA Grads:	Y	Sales Trainees:	Y	Music:		Consulting/Other:		Training:	Y	Scientists/Research:	
		Advertising Pros.:	Y	Broadcasting:				Health Care:		Petroleum/Chemicals:	
				Other:				Consulting:		Math/Other:	

TYPES OF BUSINESS:

Food Service Contractor
Facilities Management
Uniforms & Career Apparel Rental
Parks & Resorts Concessions & Facilities
Health Care Support Services
Apparel Manufacturing
Clinical Equipment Maintenance

BRANDS/DIVISIONS/AFFILIATES:

Galls
GS Capital Partners
CCMP Capital Advisors
J.P. Morgan Partners
Thomas H. Lee Partners
Warburg Pincus LLC

CONTACTS: Note: Officers with more than one job title may be intentionally listed here more than once.

Joseph Neubauer, CEO
L. Frederick (Fred) Sutherland, CFO/Exec. VP
Lynn B. McKee, Exec. VP-Human Resources
Bart J. Colli, General Counsel/Sec./Exec. VP
Debbie Albert, External Comm.
Joseph (Joe) Munnelly, Chief Acct. Officer/Controller/Sr. VP
Andrew C. Kerin, Exec. VP/Pres., North America Food & Support Svcs.
Thomas J. Vozzo, Exec. VP/Pres., ARAMARK Uniform & Career Apparel
Robert W. Wilson, Pres., ARAMARK Refreshment Svcs.
Ira Cohn, Pres., Bus. & Industry Group
Joseph Neubauer, Chmn.
Ravi K. Saligram, Exec. VP/Pres., ARAMARK Int'l

Phone: 215-238-3000	Fax: 215-238-3333
Toll-Free: 800-272-6275	
Address: ARAMARK Tower, 1101 Market St., Philadelphia, PA 19107-2988 US	

GROWTH PLANS/SPECIAL FEATURES:

ARAMARK Corporation is a leading in the food, hospitality and facilities services company, serving business, educational, healthcare and governmental institutions as well as sports, recreational and entertainment facilities. Serving clients in 22 countries, ARAMARK has three operating segments: North America Food and Support Services, which generated 66% of 2008 sales; International Food and Support Services, 21%; and Uniform and Career Apparel, 13%. Operating in the U.S. and Canada, the North America Food and Support Services segment provides food and facility services to business and industrial clients, 80 professional and college sports teams, 36 convention and civic centers, 15 state and national parks, over 1,200 healthcare and senior living facilities, 600 correctional facilities and 1,000 colleges, universities, school districts and private schools. The International Food Service and Support Services segment serves the same types of clients as the North America segment, and operates in 20 foreign countries, with its largest operations in the U.K., Germany, Chile, Ireland, Spain and Belgium. Food services provided by these segments include dining halls, on-site restaurants, convenience stores, concessions stands, banquet halls, catering and executive dining rooms. ARAMARK's facilities management services include laundry, housekeeping, facilities maintenance, plant operations, landscaping, transportation, clinical equipment maintenance, grounds keeping, custodial services and construction management. The Uniform and Career Apparel segment provides both rental and direct marketing services to customers in the manufacturing, transportation, construction, restaurant, hotel, public safety and health care industries, including gear and clothing for emergency response and law enforcement under the Galls brand. The firm operates a fabric cutting plant in Georgia and sewing plants in Puerto Rico and Mexico. ARAMARK is owned by an investor group led by Chairman and CEO Joseph Neubauer and investment funds managed by GS Capital Partners, CCMP Capital Advisors and J.P. Morgan Partners, Thomas H. Lee Partners and Warburg Pincus LLC.

FINANCIALS: Sales and profits are in thousands of dollars—add 000 to get the full amount. 2008 Note: Financial information for 2008 was not available for all companies at press time.

2008 Sales: $13,470,200	2008 Profits: $39,500	U.S. Stock Ticker: Private
2007 Sales: $12,384,300	2007 Profits: $30,900	Int'l Ticker: Int'l Exchange:
2006 Sales: $11,621,173	2006 Profits: $261,098	Employees: 260,000
2005 Sales: $10,963,360	2005 Profits: $288,475	Fiscal Year Ends: 9/30
2004 Sales: $10,192,200	2004 Profits: $263,100	Parent Company:

SALARIES/BENEFITS:

Pension Plan: Y	ESOP Stock Plan:	Profit Sharing:	Top Exec. Salary: $1,250,000	Bonus: $2,100,000
Savings Plan:	Stock Purch. Plan:		Second Exec. Salary: $680,577	Bonus: $500,000

OTHER THOUGHTS:

Apparent Women Officers or Directors: 1
Hot Spot for Advancement for Women/Minorities:

LOCATIONS: ("Y" = Yes)

West:	Southwest:	Midwest:	Southeast:	Northeast:	International:
Y	Y	Y	Y	Y	Y

ARCHER DANIELS MIDLAND CO
www.admworld.com
Industry Group Code: 3112 Ranks within this company's industry group: Sales: 2   Profits: 2

Management:		Sales/Marketing:		Liberal Arts:		Information Systems:		Professionals:		Tech./Scientific:	
Management Trainees:	Y	Marketing Pros.:	Y	Gen. Writing/Editing:	Y	Info. Management:	Y	Finance/Acct.:	Y	Engineers, Electrical:	
Experienced Mngmt.:	Y	Retail Sales:		Technical Writing:	Y	Software Dev.:	Y	Law:	Y	Engineers, Other:	Y
International Business:	Y	Commercial/Industrial:	Y	Graphic Arts/Photog.:	Y	Hardware Dev.:		HR/Other:	Y	Health/Lab:	
MBA Grads:	Y	Sales Trainees:		Music:		Consulting/Other:		Training:	Y	Scientists/Research:	Y
		Advertising Pros.:	Y	Broadcasting:				Health Care:		Petroleum/Chemicals:	Y
				Other:				Consulting:		Math/Other:	

TYPES OF BUSINESS:
Food Processing-Oilseeds, Corn & Wheat
Agricultural Services
Nutraceuticals
Transportation Services
Biodiesel
Natural Plastics
Chocolate

BRANDS/DIVISIONS/AFFILIATES:
ADM Cocoa
ADM Milling Co.
Schokinag-Schokolade-Industrie Herrmann GMBH
Wilmar International Limited

CONTACTS: Note: Officers with more than one job title may be intentionally listed here more than once.
Patricia A. Woertz, CEO
Patricia A. Woertz, Pres.
Steven R. Mills, CFO/Exec. VP
John D. Rice, Exec. VP-Global Mktg. & Risk Mgmt.
Michael D'Ambrose, Sr. VP-Human Resources
John D. Rice, Exec. VP-Commercial & Prod.
David J. Smith, General Counsel/Exec. VP/Sec.
Ismael Roig, VP-Planning & Bus. Dev.
Victoria A. Podesta, VP-Corp. Comm.
Vikram Luthar, Treas./VP
Shannon S. Herzfeld, Sr. VP-Gov't Rel.
Edward A. Harjehausen, Sr. VP-Global Corn
Mark J. Cheviron, VP-Security & Corp. Svcs.
Mark A. Bemis, VP-Cocoa & Milling.
Patricia A. Woertz, Chmn.

Phone: 217-424-5200	Fax: 217-424-6196
Toll-Free: 800-637-5843	
Address: 4666 Faries Pkwy., Decatur, IL 62525 US	

GROWTH PLANS/SPECIAL FEATURES:
Archer Daniels Midland Co. (ADM) is an agricultural processor that produces and sells oils and corn-based sweeteners. It procures, transports, stores, processes and markets oils and protein meals from soy, canola, sunflower seeds, palm, cotton, peanut and other oilseeds. The company also uses corn to develop sweeteners, such as high fructose corn syrup, citric acid, feed additives and biofuels like ethanol. It produces a variety of other food and feed ingredients, including cocoa, wheat flour, oats, bulgur, starch, soy concentrates, nutraceuticals and industrial flour used to make wallboard. These materials are processed and stored in over 230 processing plants, as well as grain elevators in the U.S. and abroad. ADM offers sourcing and distribution services for third parties, making use of the company's network of 20,900 railcars, 1,350 tractor trailers, 2,150 barges, 58 tow boats and 29 lines boats, also used for its own goods. It owns a 16.1% controlling interest in Singapore-based company, Wilmar International Limited, which operates palm and other plantations. ADM also has a number of corn milling plants. In October 2008, the firm formed a joint venture with ACH Food Companies called Stratas Foods, LLC, which manufactures and distributes packaged oil products to the U.S. and Canada. In May 2009, the company acquired the German chocolate producer, Schokinag-Schokolade-Industrie Herrmann GMBH & Co. KG.

Employees are offered medical, dental and vision insurance; flexible spending accounts; health screenings; fitness reimbursements; financial planning services; pension and retirement plans; a 401(k) plan; an employee stock purchase plan; life and disability insurance; college funds; tuition reimbursement; adoption assistance; a transportation reimbursement plan; a group legal plan; and auto, home and property insurance.

FINANCIALS: Sales and profits are in thousands of dollars—add 000 to get the full amount. 2008 Note: Financial information for 2008 was not available for all companies at press time.

2008 Sales: $69,816,000	2008 Profits: $1,802,000	**U.S. Stock Ticker: ADM**
2007 Sales: $44,018,000	2007 Profits: $2,162,000	**Int'l Ticker:** Int'l Exchange:
2006 Sales: $36,596,111	2006 Profits: $1,312,070	Employees: 28,200
2005 Sales: $35,943,810	2005 Profits: $1,044,385	Fiscal Year Ends: 6/30
2004 Sales: $36,151,394	2004 Profits: $494,710	Parent Company:

SALARIES/BENEFITS:
Pension Plan: Y	ESOP Stock Plan:	Profit Sharing:	Top Exec. Salary: $1,291,867	Bonus: $3,042,000
Savings Plan: Y	Stock Purch. Plan: Y		Second Exec. Salary: $901,600	Bonus: $826,800

OTHER THOUGHTS:
Apparent Women Officers or Directors: 5
Hot Spot for Advancement for Women/Minorities: Y

LOCATIONS: ("Y" = Yes)
West:	Southwest:	Midwest:	Southeast:	Northeast:	International:
Y	Y	Y	Y	Y	Y

ARROW ELECTRONICS INC

www.arrow.com

Industry Group Code: 423430 Ranks within this company's industry group: Sales: 4 Profits: 4

Management:		Sales/Marketing:		Liberal Arts:		Information Systems:		Professionals:		Tech./Scientific:	
Management Trainees:	Y	Marketing Pros.:	Y	Gen. Writing/Editing:	Y	Info. Management:	Y	Finance/Acct.:	Y	Engineers, Electrical:	
Experienced Mngmt.:	Y	Retail Sales:		Technical Writing:	Y	Software Dev.:	Y	Law:	Y	Engineers, Other:	
International Business:	Y	Commercial/Industrial:	Y	Graphic Arts/Photog.:	Y	Hardware Dev.:		HR/Other:	Y	Health/Lab:	
MBA Grads:	Y	Sales Trainees:	Y	Music:		Consulting/Other:		Training:	Y	Scientists/Research:	
		Advertising Pros.:	Y	Broadcasting:				Health Care:		Petroleum/Chemicals:	
				Other:				Consulting:		Math/Other:	

TYPES OF BUSINESS:

Electronic Components-Distributor
Computer Products-Distributor
Technical Support Services
Supply Chain Services
Design Services
Materials Planning
Assembly Services
Inventory Management

BRANDS/DIVISIONS/AFFILIATES:

Agilysys Keylink Systems Group
Arrow Asia Pacific
Adilam Pty Ltd
LOGIX SA
Achieva Limited
Excel Tech Inc
Eteq Components Pte Ltd

CONTACTS: Note: Officers with more than one job title may be intentionally listed here more than once.

William E. Mitchell, CEO
Michael J. Long, COO
Michael J. Long, Pres.
Paul J. Reilly, CFO/Sr. VP
Vincent Vellucci, Sr. VP-Sales, North American Components
John P. McMahon, Sr. VP-Human Resources
Vincent Melvin, CIO/VP
Peter S. Brown, General Counsel/Corp. Sec./Sr. VP
M. Catherine Morris, Chief Strategy Officer/Sr. VP
Brian P. McNally, VP/Pres., EMEASA
Andrew S. Bryant, Pres., Enterprise Computing Solutions
Kurt Colehower, VP/Pres., North American Components
William E. Mitchell, Chmn.
Peter T. Kong, VP/Pres., Arrow Asia Pacific

Phone: 631-847-2000	Fax: 631-847-2222
Toll-Free: 877-237-8621	
Address: 50 Marcus Dr., Melville, NY 11747-4210 US	

GROWTH PLANS/SPECIAL FEATURES:

Arrow Electronics, Inc. is a global provider of products, services, and solutions to industrial and commercial users of electronic components and enterprise computing solutions. It also offers services including materials planning, programming and assembly services, online supply chain tools and design services to the electronics industry. The company's distribution network spans the three dominant electronics markets: North America, Europe and the Asia/Pacific region. Arrow serves as a supply channel partner for over 700 suppliers and 140,000 original equipment manufacturers, contract manufacturers and commercial customers through a global network of over 260 locations in 50 countries and territories. Approximately 70% of the company's sales consist of electronic components, while enterprise computing solutions make up 30% of sales. In order to provide an avenue for growth, the company is focusing on providing additional services for its clients, such as procurement and inventory management. These services are designed to reduce inventory problems, cut delivery times and save component costs for clients. In 2007, Arrow completed the acquisition of Agilysys Keylink Systems Group for $485 million in cash. Soon after, Arrow Asia Pacific purchased the component distribution business of Adilam Pty. Ltd, a leading component distributor in Australia and New Zealand. In June 2008, Arrow acquired LOGIX SA, a subsidiary of Groupe OPEN, for $205.5 million. In July 2008, the company completed its acquisition of the components distribution business of Achieva Limited. In November 2008, Arrow announced that it had entered into agreements to acquire Excel Tech, Inc., a Korean company, and Eteq Components Pte Ltd, both of which serve as semiconductor distributors in the Asia and Pacific markets.

The company offers employees a stock ownership plan, health and welfare insurance, a domestic partners program and education assistance, among other benefits.

FINANCIALS: Sales and profits are in thousands of dollars—add 000 to get the full amount. 2008 Note: Financial information for 2008 was not available for all companies at press time.

2008 Sales: $16,761,009	2008 Profits: $-613,739	U.S. Stock Ticker: ARW	
2007 Sales: $15,984,992	2007 Profits: $407,792	Int'l Ticker:	Int'l Exchange:
2006 Sales: $13,577,112	2006 Profits: $388,331	Employees: 12,700	
2005 Sales: $11,164,196	2005 Profits: $253,600	Fiscal Year Ends: 12/31	
2004 Sales: $10,646,113	2004 Profits: $207,500	Parent Company:	

SALARIES/BENEFITS:

Pension Plan:	ESOP Stock Plan:	Profit Sharing:	Top Exec. Salary: $1,100,000	Bonus: $975,000
Savings Plan: Y	Stock Purch. Plan:		Second Exec. Salary: $575,000	Bonus: $520,000

OTHER THOUGHTS:

Apparent Women Officers or Directors: 5
Hot Spot for Advancement for Women/Minorities: Y

LOCATIONS: ("Y" = Yes)

West:	Southwest:	Midwest:	Southeast:	Northeast:	International:
Y	Y	Y	Y	Y	Y

Note: Financial information, benefits and other data can change quickly and may vary from those stated here.

ARTHUR J GALLAGHER & CO

www.ajg.com

Industry Group Code: 524210   **Ranks within this company's industry group:** Sales: 2   Profits: 2

Management:		Sales/Marketing:		Liberal Arts:		Information Systems:		Professionals:		Tech./Scientific:	
Management Trainees:	Y	Marketing Pros.:	Y	Gen. Writing/Editing:	Y	Info. Management:	Y	Finance/Acct.:	Y	Engineers, Electrical:	
Experienced Mngmt.:	Y	Retail Sales:		Technical Writing:	Y	Software Dev.:	Y	Law:	Y	Engineers, Other:	
International Business:	Y	Commercial/Industrial:	Y	Graphic Arts/Photog.:	Y	Hardware Dev.:		HR/Other:	Y	Health/Lab:	
MBA Grads:	Y	Sales Trainees:		Music:		Consulting/Other:		Training:	Y	Scientists/Research:	
		Advertising Pros.:	Y	Broadcasting:				Health Care:		Petroleum/Chemicals:	
				Other:				Consulting:		Math/Other:	

TYPES OF BUSINESS:

Insurance Brokerage & Management
Risk Management Services
Employee Benefit Services
Investment Operations
Claims Management
Information Management
Insurance Software
Reinsurance

BRANDS/DIVISIONS/AFFILIATES:

Arthur J. Gallagher Latin America, LLC
Arthur J. Gallagher & Co. (Canada) Ltd.
Arthur J. Gallagher & Co. (Bermuda) Limited
Gallagher Holdings (UK) Limited
Arthur J. Gallagher Australasia Holdings Pty Ltd.
Nourse Insurance Brokers, Inc.
PartnerSource, Inc.
Sellers Group, LLC

CONTACTS: *Note: Officers with more than one job title may be intentionally listed here more than once.*

J. Patrick Gallagher, Jr., CEO
J. Patrick Gallagher, Jr., Pres.
Douglas K. Howell, CFO/VP
Susan E. McGrath, VP/Chief Human Resources Officer
Walter D. Bay, General Counsel/VP/Corp. Sec.
James W. Durkin, Jr., VP/Pres., Employee Benefit Consulting & Brokerage
James S. Gault, VP/Pres., Property & Casualty Brokerage
J. Patrick Gallagher, Jr., Chmn.
David E. McGurn, Jr., VP/Pres., Wholesale & Int'l Brokerage

Phone: 630-773-3800	Fax: 630-285-4000
Toll-Free:	
Address: 2 Pierce Pl., Itasca, IL 60143-3141 US	

GROWTH PLANS/SPECIAL FEATURES:

Arthur J. Gallagher & Co. (Gallagher) and its subsidiaries provide insurance brokerage and third-party claims settlement and administration services to clients in the U.S. and abroad, with Gallagher's brokers, agents and administrators acting as intermediaries between insurers and their customers. The firm operates in three business segments: brokerage; risk management; and financial services and corporate. The brokerage segment, which accounted for 72% of the company's 2008 revenues, is composed of retail and wholesale brokerage operations. The retail segment focuses on property/casualty, employer-provided health and welfare insurance and retirement planning on behalf of middle market commercial, industrial, public, religious and not-for-profit clients, while wholesale brokers assist the retail brokers and other non-Gallagher brokers in placing specialized and hard-to-place insurance coverage. The risk management segment, which accounted for 28% of the company's 2008 revenues, provides contract claim settlement and administration services for clients that self-insure some or all of their property/casualty coverage and for insurance companies choosing to outsource some or all of their property/casualty claims departments. Gallagher markets its risk management services primarily to Fortune 1000 companies, larger middle market companies, not-for-profit organizations and public entities. The financial services and corporate segment manages Gallagher's interests in a number of clean energy and tax-advantaged investments and venture capital funds. The company's revenues are generated primarily in the U.S., with only about 13% resulting from operations in Canada, the U.K., Australia, New Zealand and Bermuda. Acquisitions in the first half of 2009 included PartnerSource, Inc., in Dallas, Texas; Sellers Group, LLC, in The Woodlands, Texas; Nourse Insurance Brokers, Inc., in Walnut Creek, California; the Walker Taylor Agency of Wilmington, North Carolina; and certain policy renewal rights acquired from Liberty Mutual's commercial property/casualty business.

Gallagher offers employees medical and dental coverage; life insurance; educational expense reimbursement; an employee assistance program; and flexible work hours.

FINANCIALS: Sales and profits are in thousands of dollars—add 000 to get the full amount. 2008 Note: Financial information for 2008 was not available for all companies at press time.

2008 Sales: $1,645,000	2008 Profits: $77,300	**U.S. Stock Ticker:** AJG
2007 Sales: $1,623,300	2007 Profits: $138,800	**Int'l Ticker:** Int'l Exchange:
2006 Sales: $1,470,100	2006 Profits: $128,500	Employees: 9,900
2005 Sales: $1,483,900	2005 Profits: $30,800	Fiscal Year Ends: 12/31
2004 Sales: $1,437,000	2004 Profits: $188,500	Parent Company:

SALARIES/BENEFITS:

Pension Plan:	ESOP Stock Plan:	Profit Sharing:	Top Exec. Salary: $1,000,000	Bonus: $500,000
Savings Plan: Y	Stock Purch. Plan: Y		Second Exec. Salary: $700,000	Bonus: $350,000

OTHER THOUGHTS:

Apparent Women Officers or Directors: 3
Hot Spot for Advancement for Women/Minorities: Y

LOCATIONS: ("Y" = Yes)

West:	Southwest:	Midwest:	Southeast:	Northeast:	International:
Y	Y	Y	Y	Y	Y

Note: Financial information, benefits and other data can change quickly and may vary from those stated here.

ASCENSION HEALTH

www.ascensionhealth.org

Industry Group Code: 622110 Ranks within this company's industry group: Sales: 3 Profits: 2

Management:		Sales/Marketing:		Liberal Arts:		Information Systems:		Professionals:		Tech./Scientific:	
Management Trainees:	Y	Marketing Pros.:		Gen. Writing/Editing:	Y	Info. Management:	Y	Finance/Acct.:	Y	Engineers, Electrical:	
Experienced Mngmt.:	Y	Retail Sales:		Technical Writing:	Y	Software Dev.:	Y	Law:	Y	Engineers, Other:	
International Business:		Commercial/Industrial:		Graphic Arts/Photog.:	Y	Hardware Dev.:		HR/Other:	Y	Health/Lab:	Y
MBA Grads:	Y	Sales Trainees:		Music:		Consulting/Other:		Training:	Y	Scientists/Research:	
		Advertising Pros.:	Y	Broadcasting:				Health Care:	Y	Petroleum/Chemicals:	
				Other:	Y			Consulting:		Math/Other:	

TYPES OF BUSINESS:

Hospitals
Acute Care Hospitals
Rehabilitation Hospitals
Psychiatric Hospitals

BRANDS/DIVISIONS/AFFILIATES:

Daughters of Charity National Health System
Sisters of St. Joseph Health System
Sisters of St. Joseph of Carondelet
Ascension Health Ventures
Impulse Monitoring
Interventional Spine
Isto Technologies
Haven Behavioral Healthcare

CONTACTS: *Note: Officers with more than one job title may be intentionally listed here more than once.*

Anthony R. Tersigni, CEO
Robert J. Henkel, COO
Anthony R. Tersigni, Pres.
Anthony J. Speranzo, CFO/Sr. VP
Hyung T. Kim, VP-Research
Mark D. Barner, Sr. VP/CIO
Joseph R. Impicciche, General Counsel/Sr. VP-Legal Svcs.
John D. Doyle, Chief Strategy Officer
Stephen D. LeResche, VP-Comm.
James K. Beckmann, Jr., Sr. VP-System Support Svcs.
Leo Brideau, Pres./CEO-Columbia St. Mary's
Charles Barnett, Pres./CEO-Seton Family of Hospitals
Ruth Brinkley, Pres./CEO-Carondelet Health Network
Kathleen Kelly, Chmn.
Scott Caldwell, Chief Supply Chain Officer

Phone: 314-733-8000	Fax: 314-733-8013
Toll-Free:	
Address: 4600 Edmundson Rd., St. Louis, MO 63134 US	

GROWTH PLANS/SPECIAL FEATURES:

Ascension Health is a leading not-for-profit health system in the U.S., with roughly 67 general acute care hospitals in 20 states, two long-term acute care hospitals, three rehabilitation hospitals and four psychiatric hospitals. The Catholic organization was formed in 1999 through the union of the Daughters of Charity National Health System, based in St. Louis, Missouri, and the Sisters of St. Joseph Health System, based in Ann Arbor, Michigan. In 2002, Ascension Health added the hospitals and health facilities of the Sisters of St. Joseph of Carondelet, also based in St. Louis, Missouri. Ascension Health Ventures (AHV), the organization's investment subsidiary, identifies and supports companies that offer potential breakthroughs in health-care-related products, services and technologies. AHV invested in a number of companies during 2008, including Impulse Monitoring, which provides intraoperative neurophysiological monitoring; Interventional Spine, which is an early stage developer of a spinal device platform enabling percutaneous approaches for spinal fusion; Isto Technologies, which is an early stage developer of orthobiologic products for sports medicine and spinal therapy applications; Millennium Pharmacy Systems, which provides pharmaceutical management services to the long-term care industry; and United Surgical Partners, which operates ambulatory and short-stay surgical facilities in the U.S. and owns private hospitals in Europe. Ascension Health is committed to assisting uninsured and underinsured patients as part of its hope to move U.S. health care toward a more compassionate system. As part of this effort, Ascension Health offers an online resource center that provides information about programs for the uninsured. In June 2008, AHV invested Haven Behavioral Healthcare, a provider of specialty behavioral health services in Arizona, Colorado, Oklahoma and Virginia.

Ascension Health offers employee benefits such as medical, dental, vision and life insurance; health care and dependent care reimbursement accounts; a retirement savings program and a pension plan; tuition reimbursement; and an employee assistance program.

FINANCIALS: Sales and profits are in thousands of dollars—add 000 to get the full amount. 2008 Note: Financial information for 2008 was not available for all companies at press time.

2008 Sales: $13,489,000	2008 Profits: $351,000	**U.S. Stock Ticker: Nonprofit**
2007 Sales: $12,304,000	2007 Profits: $1,223,000	**Int'l Ticker:** Int'l Exchange:
2006 Sales: $11,405,552	2006 Profits: $802,965	Employees: 107,000
2005 Sales: $10,770,887	2005 Profits: $651,245	Fiscal Year Ends: 6/30
2004 Sales: $10,046,370	2004 Profits: $469,694	Parent Company:

SALARIES/BENEFITS:

Pension Plan:	ESOP Stock Plan:	Profit Sharing:	Top Exec. Salary: $	Bonus: $
Savings Plan: Y	Stock Purch. Plan:		Second Exec. Salary: $	Bonus: $

OTHER THOUGHTS:

Apparent Women Officers or Directors: 14
Hot Spot for Advancement for Women/Minorities: Y

LOCATIONS: ("Y" = Yes)

West:	Southwest:	Midwest:	Southeast:	Northeast:	International:
Y	Y	Y	Y	Y	

Note: Financial information, benefits and other data can change quickly and may vary from those stated here.

AT&T INC

www.att.com

Industry Group Code: 517110 **Ranks within this company's industry group:** Sales: 1 Profits: 1

Management:		Sales/Marketing:		Liberal Arts:		Information Systems:		Professionals:		Tech./Scientific:	
Management Trainees:	Y	Marketing Pros.:	Y	Gen. Writing/Editing:	Y	Info. Management:	Y	Finance/Acct.:	Y	Engineers, Electrical:	Y
Experienced Mngmt.:	Y	Retail Sales:	Y	Technical Writing:	Y	Software Dev.:	Y	Law:	Y	Engineers, Other:	Y
International Business:	Y	Commercial/Industrial:	Y	Graphic Arts/Photog.:	Y	Hardware Dev.:		HR/Other:	Y	Health/Lab:	
MBA Grads:	Y	Sales Trainees:	Y	Music:		Consulting/Other:		Training:	Y	Scientists/Research:	
		Advertising Pros.:	Y	Broadcasting:				Health Care:		Petroleum/Chemicals:	
				Other:	Y			Consulting:		Math/Other:	

TYPES OF BUSINESS:

Local Telephone Service
Wireless Telecommunications
Long-Distance Telephone Service
Corporate Telecom, Backbone & Wholesale Services
Directory Publishing
Entertainment & Television via Internet
International Telephone Services
Internet Access via DSL

BRANDS/DIVISIONS/AFFILIATES:

Edge Wireless
Ingenio
AT&T Mobility
Centennial Communications Corp.
Wayport, Inc.
Berry Company (The)
Sterling Commerce Inc.
Berry Network Inc.

CONTACTS: *Note: Officers with more than one job title may be intentionally listed here more than once.*

Randall L. Stephenson, CEO
Randall L. Stephenson, Pres.
Richard G. Lindner, CFO/Sr. Exec. VP
Catherine M. Coughlin, Global Mktg. Officer/Sr. Exec. VP
William A. Blase Jr., Sr. Exec. VP-Human Resources
John Donovan, CTO
Wayne Watts, General Counsel/Sr. Exec. VP
James W. Callaway, Sr. Exec. VP-Exec. Oper.
Forest Miller, Group Pres., Corp. Strategy & Dev.
Ronald E. Spears, Pres./CEO-AT&T Bus. Solutions
John T. Stankey, Pres./CEO-AT&T Operations, Inc.
Ralph de la Vega, Pres./CEO-AT&T Mobility/Consumer Markets
Rayford Wilkins, Jr., Group Pres., AT&T Diversified Bus.
Randall L. Stephenson, Chmn.

Phone: 210-821-4105	Fax:
Toll-Free:	
Address: 208 S. Akard St., San Antonio, TX 75202 US	

GROWTH PLANS/SPECIAL FEATURES:

AT&T, Inc. is one of the world's largest providers of diversified telecommunications services. The company and its subsidiaries deliver a portfolio of wireless communications; local exchange services; long-distance services; data and broadband and Internet services; video services; telecommunications equipment; managed networking; wholesale services; and directory advertising and publishing services. The company operates through four segments: wireless, wireline, advertising and publishing and other. The wireless segment operates through subsidiary AT&T Mobility and primarily provides wireless voice communications services to business and consumer customers. The wireline segment provides retail and wholesale communication services, including voice and data services, domestically and internationally. This segment also includes AT&T's Virtual Private Network (VPN) and Voice over IP (VoIP) services. The advertising and publishing segment Yellow and White Pages directories and sell directory advertising and Internet-based advertising, Operations of the other segment include managed web hosting, application management, security and integration services, outsourcing, government-related services and satellite video services, as well as the company's U-Verse high-speed broadband and TV services. The firm is one of the nation's largest wireless carriers, serving 77 million customers, with service spanning more than 200 countries worldwide. AT&T is the exclusive retailer for the Apple iPhone. In 2008, the company's acquisitions included Edge Wireless, a wireless communications services company; Ingenio, a Pay Per Call technology provider; Centennial Communications Corp., a regional communications services provider; Wayport, Inc., a Wi-Fi services provider; certain assets of Easterbrooke Cellular Corporation; and spectrum licenses covering 196 million people from a subsidiary of Aloha Partners, L.P.

AT&T offers its employees medical, dental and vision insurance, tuition reimbursement, company discounts, flexible spending accounts and a 401(k) savings and pension plan.

FINANCIALS: Sales and profits are in thousands of dollars—add 000 to get the full amount. 2008 Note: Financial information for 2008 was not available for all companies at press time.

2008 Sales: $124,028,000	2008 Profits: $12,867,000	**U.S. Stock Ticker:** T
2007 Sales: $118,928,000	2007 Profits: $11,951,000	**Int'l Ticker:** Int'l Exchange:
2006 Sales: $63,055,000	2006 Profits: $7,356,000	Employees: 301,000
2005 Sales: $43,764,000	2005 Profits: $4,786,000	Fiscal Year Ends: 12/31
2004 Sales: $40,733,000	2004 Profits: $5,887,000	Parent Company:

SALARIES/BENEFITS:

Pension Plan: Y	ESOP Stock Plan:	Profit Sharing:	Top Exec. Salary: $1,420,833	Bonus: $
Savings Plan: Y	Stock Purch. Plan:		Second Exec. Salary: $825,000	Bonus: $260,000

OTHER THOUGHTS:

Apparent Women Officers or Directors: 6
Hot Spot for Advancement for Women/Minorities: Y

LOCATIONS: ("Y" = Yes)

West:	Southwest:	Midwest:	Southeast:	Northeast:	International:
Y	Y	Y	Y	Y	Y

AUTOMATIC DATA PROCESSING INC

www.adp.com

Industry Group Code: 518210 Ranks within this company's industry group: Sales: 1 Profits: 1

Management:		Sales/Marketing:		Liberal Arts:		Information Systems:		Professionals:		Tech./Scientific:	
Management Trainees:	Y	Marketing Pros.:	Y	Gen. Writing/Editing:	Y	Info. Management:	Y	Finance/Acct.:	Y	Engineers, Electrical:	Y
Experienced Mngmt.:	Y	Retail Sales:		Technical Writing:	Y	Software Dev.:	Y	Law:	Y	Engineers, Other:	
International Business:	Y	Commercial/Industrial:	Y	Graphic Arts/Photog.:	Y	Hardware Dev.:		HR/Other:	Y	Health/Lab:	
MBA Grads:	Y	Sales Trainees:	Y	Music:		Consulting/Other:	Y	Training:	Y	Scientists/Research:	
		Advertising Pros.:	Y	Broadcasting:				Health Care:		Petroleum/Chemicals:	
				Other:				Consulting:		Math/Other:	

TYPES OF BUSINESS:

Data Processing Services
Business Outsourcing Solutions
Information Services
Payroll Processing
Automobile Dealer Services

BRANDS/DIVISIONS/AFFILIATES:

ADP TotalSource
ADP Employer Services
ADP Leave Administration Service
ADP Access
ADP Business Services (Shanghai) Co., Ltd.
ChinaLink

CONTACTS: Note: Officers with more than one job title may be intentionally listed here more than once.

Gary C. Butler, CEO
S. Michael Martone, COO
Gary C. Butler, Pres.
Christopher R. Reidy, CFO
Benito Cachinero, VP-Human Resources
Michael L. Capone, CIO/VP
James B. Benson, General Counsel/VP/Sec.
Terry Corallo, Sr. Dir.-Public Rel. & Advertising
Raymond L. Colotti, VP/Treas.
Steven J. Anenen, Pres., Dealer Svcs.
Campbell B. Langdon, Pres., Employer Svcs., Major Accounts Div.
Regina R. Lee, Pres., Employer Svcs.-National Acct. Div.
Carlos Rodriguez, Pres., Employer Svcs.-Small Bus. Svcs. Div.
Leslie A. Brun, Chmn.
Lisa Bao, Mgr.-Mktg., ADP China

Phone: 973-974-5000	Fax: 973-974-5390
Toll-Free: 800-225-5237	
Address: 1 ADP Blvd., Roseland, NJ 07068 US	

GROWTH PLANS/SPECIAL FEATURES:

Automatic Data Processing, Inc. (ADP) is one of the world's largest providers of business outsourcing solutions. The company offers a wide range of human resources, payroll, tax and benefits administration solutions from a single source. The firm also provides integrated computing solutions to automotive, heavy truck, motorcycle, marine and recreational vehicle dealers throughout the world. ADP operates in three segments: ADP Employer Services, professional employer organization (PEO) services and dealer services. ADP Employer Services offers a range of human resources information, payroll processing, tax and benefits administration products and services, including traditional and web-based outsourcing solutions. The segment assists roughly 560,000 employers in the U.S., Canada, Europe, South America, Australia and Asia to staff, manage, pay and retain their employees. The PEO services segment, which operates as ADP TotalSource, provides small and medium sized businesses with comprehensive employment administration outsourcing solutions (through a co-employment relationship), including payroll; payroll tax filing; human resources guidance; 401(k) plan administration; benefits administration; compliance services; health and workers' compensation coverage; and other supplemental benefits for employees. ADP TotalSouce has approximately 46 offices in 19 states; the businesses it serves have a combined 188,000 employees. The dealer services division provides integrated dealer management systems and business solutions to over 25,000 automotive, heavy truck and powersports vehicle retailers in approximately 60 countries. In October 2008, the firm launched ADP Leave Administration Service, a program supported by NexTrak Leave Administration platform that manages and simplifies the process associated with employee leave. In March 2009, ADP Employer Services released ADP Access, a new retirement program. In April 2009, part of the employer services division, ADP Business Services (Shanghai) Co., Ltd., acquired majority ownership of ChinaLink.

The company offers its employees benefits including life, AD&D, home, medical, dental and vision insurance; a pension plan; a 401(k) plan; and tuition reimbursement.

FINANCIALS: Sales and profits are in thousands of dollars—add 000 to get the full amount. 2008 Note: Financial information for 2008 was not available for all companies at press time.

2008 Sales: $8,776,500	2008 Profits: $1,161,700	**U.S. Stock Ticker: ADP**
2007 Sales: $7,800,000	2007 Profits: $1,021,200	**Int'l Ticker:** Int'l Exchange:
2006 Sales: $6,835,600	2006 Profits: $1,554,000	Employees: 45,000
2005 Sales: $6,131,300	2005 Profits: $1,055,400	Fiscal Year Ends: 6/30
2004 Sales: $7,279,400	2004 Profits: $935,600	Parent Company:

SALARIES/BENEFITS:

Pension Plan: Y	ESOP Stock Plan:	Profit Sharing:	Top Exec. Salary: $900,000	Bonus: $2,579,405
Savings Plan: Y	Stock Purch. Plan: Y		Second Exec. Salary: $750,000	Bonus: $1,085,950

OTHER THOUGHTS:

Apparent Women Officers or Directors: 8
Hot Spot for Advancement for Women/Minorities: Y

LOCATIONS: ("Y" = Yes)

West:	Southwest:	Midwest:	Southeast:	Northeast:	International:
Y	Y	Y	Y	Y	Y

Note: Financial information, benefits and other data can change quickly and may vary from those stated here.

AUTOZONE INC

www.autozone.com

Industry Group Code: 441310 Ranks within this company's industry group: Sales: 1 Profits: 1

Management:		Sales/Marketing:		Liberal Arts:		Information Systems:		Professionals:		Tech./Scientific:	
Management Trainees:	Y	Marketing Pros.:	Y	Gen. Writing/Editing:	Y	Info. Management:	Y	Finance/Acct.:	Y	Engineers, Electrical:	
Experienced Mngmt.:	Y	Retail Sales:	Y	Technical Writing:		Software Dev.:	Y	Law:	Y	Engineers, Other:	
International Business:	Y	Commercial/Industrial:	Y	Graphic Arts/Photog.:	Y	Hardware Dev.:		HR/Other:	Y	Health/Lab:	
MBA Grads:	Y	Sales Trainees:	Y	Music:		Consulting/Other:		Training:	Y	Scientists/Research:	
		Advertising Pros.:	Y	Broadcasting:				Health Care:		Petroleum/Chemicals:	
				Other:				Consulting:		Math/Other:	

TYPES OF BUSINESS:

Auto Parts, Retail
Automotive Software
Online Sales
General Automotive Service

BRANDS/DIVISIONS/AFFILIATES:

Autozone.com
ALLDATA
Loan-a-Tool

CONTACTS: *Note: Officers with more than one job title may be intentionally listed here more than once.*

William C. Rhodes, III, CEO
William C. Rhodes, III, Pres.
William T. Giles, CFO/Exec. VP-Finance
James A. Shea, Exec. VP-Mktg., Merch. & Supply Chain
Timothy W. Briggs, Sr. VP-Human Resources
Jon A. Bascom, CIO/Sr. VP
Mark A. Finestone, Exec. VP-Merch.
Harry L. Goldsmith, General Counsel/Exec. VP/Corp. Sec.
Robert D. Olsen, Exec. VP-Retail & Commercial Oper.
Charlie Pleas, III, Sr. VP/Controller
William T. Giles, Exec. VP-Store Dev. & IT
Thomas B. Newbern, Sr. VP-Store Oper.
Lisa R. Kranc, Sr. VP-Mktg.
William C. Rhodes, III, Chmn.
Robert D. Olsen, Sr. VP-Mexico
James A. Shea, Exec. VP-Supply Chain

Phone: 901-495-6500	Fax: 901-495-8300
Toll-Free: 800-288-6966	
Address: 123 S. Front St., Memphis, TN 38103 US	

GROWTH PLANS/SPECIAL FEATURES:

AutoZone, Inc. is a leading specialty retailer of automotive parts and accessories, targeting do-it-yourself (DIY) customers. With over 4,172 stores in the U.S. and Puerto Rico and 168 in Mexico, each AutoZone store carries an extensive product line for cars, sport utility vehicles, vans and light trucks, including new and remanufactured automotive parts, maintenance items, accessories and non-automotive products. Many AutoZone stores have a commercial sales program that provides commercial credit and prompt delivery of parts and other products to local, regional and national repair garages, dealers and service stations. The company has over 800,000 stock keeping units (SKU). Although each of the company's stores carry the same basic product lines, the company does tailor each store's parts inventory to the makes and models of the vehicles in their trade areas. Parts not kept in stock can be ordered and delivered to the store within a few days, or they can be ordered online. AutoZone allows parts ordered online to be returned at any store location. The company also has a Loan-a-Tool program, through which customers can borrow a specialty tool, such as a steering wheel puller, for which they would have little or no use other than for a single job. AutoZone also provides other free services, including check engine light readings; battery charging and installation assistance; fluid recycling; and testing of starters, alternators, batteries, sensors and actuators. The company also offers automotive diagnostic software and repair through its ALLDATA subsidiary.

Employees are offered medical, dental and vision insurance; disability coverage; life insurance; a 401(k); store discounts; tuition reimbursement; adoption assistance; credit union; and a stock purchase plan.

FINANCIALS: Sales and profits are in thousands of dollars—add 000 to get the full amount. 2008 Note: Financial information for 2008 was not available for all companies at press time.

2008 Sales: $6,522,706	2008 Profits: $641,606	U.S. Stock Ticker: AZO
2007 Sales: $6,169,804	2007 Profits: $595,672	Int'l Ticker: Int'l Exchange:
2006 Sales: $5,948,355	2006 Profits: $569,275	Employees: 57,000
2005 Sales: $5,710,900	2005 Profits: $571,000	Fiscal Year Ends: 8/31
2004 Sales: $5,637,025	2004 Profits: $566,202	Parent Company:

SALARIES/BENEFITS:

Pension Plan:	ESOP Stock Plan:	Profit Sharing:	Top Exec. Salary: $706,019	Bonus: $779,446
Savings Plan: Y	Stock Purch. Plan: Y		Second Exec. Salary: $455,865	Bonus: $301,966

OTHER THOUGHTS:

Apparent Women Officers or Directors: 2
Hot Spot for Advancement for Women/Minorities: Y

LOCATIONS: ("Y" = Yes)

West:	Southwest:	Midwest:	Southeast:	Northeast:	International:
Y	Y	Y	Y	Y	Y

AVERY DENNISON CORP

www.averydennison.com

Industry Group Code: 323 Ranks within this company's industry group: Sales: 2 Profits: 1

Management:		Sales/Marketing:		Liberal Arts:		Information Systems:		Professionals:		Tech./Scientific:	
Management Trainees:	Y	Marketing Pros.:	Y	Gen. Writing/Editing:	Y	Info. Management:	Y	Finance/Acct.:	Y	Engineers, Electrical:	
Experienced Mngmt.:	Y	Retail Sales:		Technical Writing:	Y	Software Dev.:	Y	Law:	Y	Engineers, Other:	Y
International Business:	Y	Commercial/Industrial:	Y	Graphic Arts/Photog.:	Y	Hardware Dev.:		HR/Other:	Y	Health/Lab:	
MBA Grads:	Y	Sales Trainees:	Y	Music:		Consulting/Other:		Training:	Y	Scientists/Research:	
		Advertising Pros.:	Y	Broadcasting:				Health Care:		Petroleum/Chemicals:	
				Other:	Y			Consulting:		Math/Other:	

TYPES OF BUSINESS:

Printing-Adhesive Labels
Office Products
Labeling Systems
Adhesive Materials
Highway Safety Products
Specialty Chemicals

BRANDS/DIVISIONS/AFFILIATES:

Avery
Fasson
Marks-A-Lot
HI-LITER
JAC
Paxar Corp
DM Label Group

CONTACTS: Note: Officers with more than one job title may be intentionally listed here more than once.

Dean A. Scarborough, CEO
Dean A. Scarborough, Pres.
Daniel R. O'Bryant, CFO/Exec. VP-Finance
Anne Hill, Sr. VP/Chief Human Resources Officer
Richard W. Hoffman, CIO/Sr. VP
David N. Edwards, CTO/VP
Susan C. Miller, General Counsel/Sr. VP/Corp. Sec.
Robert M. Malchione, Sr. VP-Corp. Strategy & Tech.
Diane B. Dixon, Sr. VP-Corp. Comm. & Advertising
Mitchell R. Butier, Corp. VP-Global Finance
Timothy S. Clyde, Group VP-Specialty Materials & Converting
Donald A. Nolan, Group VP-Roll Materials
R. Shawn Neville, Group VP-Retail Info. Systems
Timothy G. Bond, Group VP-Office Prod.
Kent Kresa, Chmn.
Greg E. Temple, VP-Global Oper.
Greg E. Temple, VP-Supply Chain

Phone: 626-304-2000	Fax: 626-792-7312
Toll-Free:	
Address: 150 N. Orange Grove Blvd., Pasadena, CA 91103 US	

GROWTH PLANS/SPECIAL FEATURES:

Avery Dennison Corporation, with over 200 manufacturing and distribution facilities in more than 60 countries, is a global leader in pressure-sensitive technology and self-adhesive materials for use in consumer products, labels and graphic imaging. The company manufactures and markets a wide range of products for consumer and industrial markets, including Avery-brand office products, Fasson-brand self-adhesive materials, peel-and-stick postage stamps, battery labels, reflective highway safety products, automated retail tag and labeling systems and specialty tapes and chemicals. Its reporting segments include pressure-sensitive materials; office and consumer products; and retail information services. Pressure-sensitive materials generated about 54% of the firm's total 2008 sales and specializes in making papers, films and foils coated with adhesive and sold in rolls to printers under the Avery Dennison, JAC and Fasson brands. Avery's office and consumer supplies segment manufactures and sells products for office, school and home use such as printer products, filing and presentation products and ink-jet and laser printer cards. In addition, it makes notebooks, three-ring binders, markers, fasteners, business forms, tickets, tags and imprinting equipment, marketed under the brand names Avery, Marks-A-Lot and HI-LITER. Finally, the retail information services segment designs, manufactures and sells price marking and brand identification products for retailers, apparel manufacturers, distributors and industrial customers. Avery also has several businesses that produce specialty tapes and engineered labels that include radio frequency identification (RFID) inlays and other converted products. International business accounted for 65% of 2008 sales, with a concentration in Asia, Latin America and Eastern Europe. In April 2008, the company acquired DM Label Group, a manufacturer of labels, tags and tickets for retail and apparel applications.

Avery Dennison offers its employees leadership development programs; healthcare coverage; domestic partner benefits; life and disability insurance; a 401(k) plan; a stock purchase plan; and tuition reimbursement for job-related coursework.

FINANCIALS: Sales and profits are in thousands of dollars—add 000 to get the full amount. 2008 Note: Financial information for 2008 was not available for all companies at press time.

2008 Sales: $6,710,400	2008 Profits: $266,100	U.S. Stock Ticker: AVY
2007 Sales: $6,307,800	2007 Profits: $303,500	Int'l Ticker: Int'l Exchange:
2006 Sales: $5,575,900	2006 Profits: $373,200	Employees: 35,700
2005 Sales: $5,743,500	2005 Profits: $226,400	Fiscal Year Ends: 12/31
2004 Sales: $5,317,000	2004 Profits: $279,700	Parent Company:

SALARIES/BENEFITS:

Pension Plan:	ESOP Stock Plan:	Profit Sharing:	Top Exec. Salary: $945,000	Bonus: $1,325,650
Savings Plan: Y	Stock Purch. Plan: Y		Second Exec. Salary: $581,900	Bonus: $611,058

OTHER THOUGHTS:

Apparent Women Officers or Directors: 5
Hot Spot for Advancement for Women/Minorities: Y

LOCATIONS: ("Y" = Yes)

West:	Southwest:	Midwest:	Southeast:	Northeast:	International:
Y	Y	Y	Y	Y	Y

Note: Financial information, benefits and other data can change quickly and may vary from those stated here.

AVIS BUDGET GROUP INC

www.avisbudgetgroup.com

Industry Group Code: 5321 Ranks within this company's industry group: Sales: 3 Profits: 2

Management:		Sales/Marketing:		Liberal Arts:		Information Systems:		Professionals:		Tech./Scientific:	
Management Trainees:	Y	Marketing Pros.:	Y	Gen. Writing/Editing:	Y	Info. Management:	Y	Finance/Acct.:	Y	Engineers, Electrical:	
Experienced Mngmt.:	Y	Retail Sales:	Y	Technical Writing:		Software Dev.:	Y	Law:	Y	Engineers, Other:	
International Business:	Y	Commercial/Industrial:	Y	Graphic Arts/Photog.:	Y	Hardware Dev.:		HR/Other:	Y	Health/Lab:	
MBA Grads:	Y	Sales Trainees:	Y	Music:		Consulting/Other:		Training:	Y	Scientists/Research:	
		Advertising Pros.:	Y	Broadcasting:				Health Care:		Petroleum/Chemicals:	
				Other:	Y			Consulting:		Math/Other:	

TYPES OF BUSINESS:

Automobile Rental
Franchising
Truck Rental

BRANDS/DIVISIONS/AFFILIATES:

Avis
Budget
Budget Truck

CONTACTS: *Note: Officers with more than one job title may be intentionally listed here more than once.*

Ronald L. Nelson, CEO
F. Robert Salerno, COO
F. Robert Salerno, Pres.
David B. Wyshner, CFO/Exec. VP
Thomas M. Gartland, Exec. VP-Mktg. & Sales
Mark J. Servodidio, Chief Human Resources Officer/Exec. VP
Karen Sclafani, General Counsel/Exec. VP
Larry De Shon, Exec. VP-Oper.
Scott Deaver, Exec. VP-Strategy
Brett Weinblatt, Sr. VP/Chief Acct. Officer
Kaye E. Ceille, Sr. VP-Global Travel & Partnership Sales
Bob Lambert, Sr. VP-Commercial Sales
Edward Gitlitz, Sr. VP-Fleet Svcs.
Becky Alseth, Sr. VP-Mktg.
Ronald L. Nelson, Chmn.
Patric Siniscalchi, Exec. VP-Int'l Oper.

Phone: 973-496-3500	Fax: 888-304-2315
Toll-Free:	
Address: 6 Sylvan Way, Parsippany, NJ 07054 US	

GROWTH PLANS/SPECIAL FEATURES:

Avis Budget Group, Inc. (ABG) operates in the global vehicle rental industry through Avis and Budget. Avis is a rental car supplier to the premium commercial and leisure segments of the travel industry and Budget is a rental car supplier to the price-conscious. Its car rental operations share the same fleet, maintenance facilities, technology and administrative infrastructure. The company operates in three segments: domestic car rental, international car rental and truck rental. The Avis, Budget and Budget Truck brands accounted for approximately 62%, 32% and 6% of ABG's vehicle rental revenue, respectively, in 2008. ABG's operations include approximately 7,000 car and truck rental locations in the U.S., Canada, Australia, New Zealand, Latin America, the Caribbean and the Pacific region. It completed more than 27 million vehicle rental transactions worldwide in 2008. Domestically, ABG derived approximately 75% of its car rental revenue from on-airport locations in 2008 and the remainder from off-airport locations, referred to as the local rental segment. In 2008, ABG expanded its presence in the local segment. ABG rents its fleet of approximately 29,700 Budget trucks through a network of approximately 2,500 dealer-operated, 300 company-operated and 75 franchise-operated locations throughout the continental U.S. ABG also licenses the use of the Avis and Budget trademarks to multiple licensees in areas where the company does not operate. The Avis and/or Budget vehicle rental systems in Europe, Africa, the Middle East and parts of Asia are operated at approximately 3,800 locations by subsidiaries and sub-licensees of an independent third party. In 2008, the firm opened 90 new off-airport locations. In December 2008, the company announced layoffs of 2,200 employees.

FINANCIALS: Sales and profits are in thousands of dollars—add 000 to get the full amount. 2008 Note: Financial information for 2008 was not available for all companies at press time.

		U.S. Stock Ticker: CAR
2008 Sales: $5,984,000	2008 Profits: $-1,124,000	Int'l Ticker: Int'l Exchange:
2007 Sales: $5,986,000	2007 Profits: $-916,000	Employees: 26,000
2006 Sales: $5,689,000	2006 Profits: $-1,994,000	Fiscal Year Ends: 12/31
2005 Sales: $5,400,000	2005 Profits: $1,618,000	Parent Company:
2004 Sales: $4,820,000	2004 Profits: $2,091,000	

SALARIES/BENEFITS:

Pension Plan:	ESOP Stock Plan:	Profit Sharing:	Top Exec. Salary: $1,000,000	Bonus: $
Savings Plan: Y	Stock Purch. Plan:		Second Exec. Salary: $700,000	Bonus: $

OTHER THOUGHTS:

Apparent Women Officers or Directors: 5
Hot Spot for Advancement for Women/Minorities: Y

LOCATIONS: ("Y" = Yes)

West:	Southwest:	Midwest:	Southeast:	Northeast:	International:
Y	Y	Y	Y	Y	Y

Note: Financial information, benefits and other data can change quickly and may vary from those stated here.

AVNET INC

www.avnet.com

Industry Group Code: 423430 **Ranks within this company's industry group:** Sales: 3 Profits: 1

Management:		Sales/Marketing:		Liberal Arts:		Information Systems:		Professionals:		Tech./Scientific:	
Management Trainees:	Y	Marketing Pros.:	Y	Gen. Writing/Editing:		Info. Management:	Y	Finance/Acct.:	Y	Engineers, Electrical:	
Experienced Mngmt.:	Y	Retail Sales:		Technical Writing:	Y	Software Dev.:		Law:	Y	Engineers, Other:	
International Business:	Y	Commercial/Industrial:	Y	Graphic Arts/Photog.:	Y	Hardware Dev.:		HR/Other:	Y	Health/Lab:	
MBA Grads:	Y	Sales Trainees:		Music:		Consulting/Other:		Training:	Y	Scientists/Research:	
		Advertising Pros.:		Broadcasting:				Health Care:		Petroleum/Chemicals:	
				Other:				Consulting:		Math/Other:	

TYPES OF BUSINESS:

Components-Distributor
Marketing Services
Supply Chain Advisory Services

BRANDS/DIVISIONS/AFFILIATES:

Avnet Technology Solutions
Avnet Electronics Marketing
Avnet Managed Technologies
Avnet Memec
Avnet Time
Avnet Japan
Azzurri Technology Ltd
Nippon Denso Industry of Japan

CONTACTS: *Note: Officers with more than one job title may be intentionally listed here more than once.*

Roy Vallee, CEO
Rick Hamada, COO
Ray Sadowski, CFO
Harley Feldberg, Pres., Avnet Electronics Mktg. Global
Steve Church, Chief Human Resources Dev. Officer
Steve Phillips, CIO/Sr. VP
David Birk, General Counsel/Sr. VP
Al Maag, Chief Comm. Officer
Michelle Gorel, VP-Public Rel.
John Paget, Global Pres., Tech. Solutions
Jim Smith, Pres., Avnet Logistics
Roy Vallee, Chmn.

Phone: 480-643-2000	Fax: 480-643-7370
Toll-Free: 800-408-8353	
Address: 2211 S. 47th St., Phoenix, AZ 85034 US	

GROWTH PLANS/SPECIAL FEATURES:

Avnet, Inc. is one of the world's largest value-added distributors of semiconductors, connectors, passive and electromechanical components, RF and microwave devices, enterprise networking and computer equipment and embedded subsystems. The company operates through two divisions, Technology Solutions and Electronics Marketing, which together operate more than 300 locations in 70 countries. The company connects more than 300 suppliers to over 100,000 original equipment manufacturers (OEMs) electronic manufacturing services (EMS) providers, original design manufacturers (ODMs) and value-added resellers (VARs) that design and build the electronic equipment for end-market use, as well as to other industrial customers. Additionally, the firm provides engineering design, materials management and logistics services, system integration and configuration and supply chain advisory services. The Electronics Marketing division markets and sells semiconductors and interconnect, passive and electromechanical devices to a customer base whose end-markets include automotive, communications, computer hardware and peripheral, industrial and manufacturing, medical equipment, military and aerospace. The Technology Solutions division markets and sells servers, data storage, software and networking solutions and other services to resellers and mid- to high-end users, as well as focusing on the worldwide OEM market. In 2008, the company acquired Horizon Technology Group plc, a technical distributor of information technology products in the U.K. and Ireland and Azzurri Technology Ltd, a U.K.-based high technology semiconductors and embedded systems products distributors. In December 2008, the company agreed to acquire Nippon Denso Industry of Japan through its subsidiary, Avnet Japan.

Employees are offered medical, dental and vision insurance; life and AD&D insurance; travel accident insurance; a pension plan; a 401(k) savings plan; an employee stock purchase plan; short- and long-term disability; tuition reimbursement; computer loans; financial planning services; adoption assistance; on-site health screenings; employee assistance programs; discounted pet and car insurance; discounted movie tickets; and traveler's emergency assistance.

FINANCIALS: Sales and profits are in thousands of dollars—add 000 to get the full amount. 2008 Note: Financial information for 2008 was not available for all companies at press time.

2008 Sales: $17,952,700	2008 Profits: $499,100	**U.S. Stock Ticker:** AVT
2007 Sales: $15,681,100	2007 Profits: $393,100	**Int'l Ticker:** Int'l Exchange:
2006 Sales: $14,253,630	2006 Profits: $204,547	Employees: 12,800
2005 Sales: $11,066,816	2005 Profits: $168,239	Fiscal Year Ends: 6/30
2004 Sales: $10,244,741	2004 Profits: $72,897	Parent Company:

SALARIES/BENEFITS:

Pension Plan: Y	ESOP Stock Plan: Y	Profit Sharing:	Top Exec. Salary: $995,000	Bonus: $889,715
Savings Plan: Y	Stock Purch. Plan:		Second Exec. Salary: $590,000	Bonus: $430,997

OTHER THOUGHTS:

Apparent Women Officers or Directors: 3
Hot Spot for Advancement for Women/Minorities: Y

LOCATIONS: ("Y" = Yes)

West:	Southwest:	Midwest:	Southeast:	Northeast:	International:
Y	Y	Y	Y	Y	Y

Note: Financial information, benefits and other data can change quickly and may vary from those stated here.

AVON PRODUCTS INC

www.avoncompany.com

Industry Group Code: 325620 **Ranks within this company's industry group:** Sales: 1 Profits: 1

Management:		Sales/Marketing:		Liberal Arts:		Information Systems:		Professionals:		Tech./Scientific:	
Management Trainees:	Y	Marketing Pros.:	Y	Gen. Writing/Editing:	Y	Info. Management:	Y	Finance/Acct.:	Y	Engineers, Electrical:	
Experienced Mngmt.:	Y	Retail Sales:	Y	Technical Writing:		Software Dev.:	Y	Law:	Y	Engineers, Other:	
International Business:	Y	Commercial/Industrial:		Graphic Arts/Photog.:	Y	Hardware Dev.:		HR/Other:	Y	Health/Lab:	
MBA Grads:	Y	Sales Trainees:	Y	Music:		Consulting/Other:		Training:	Y	Scientists/Research:	
		Advertising Pros.:	Y	Broadcasting:				Health Care:		Petroleum/Chemicals:	Y
				Other:	Y			Consulting:		Math/Other:	

TYPES OF BUSINESS:

Cosmetics & Beauty Supplies, Direct Selling
Fragrances & Toiletries
Gift & Decorative Items
Apparel & Accessories
Fashion Jewelry
Health & Fitness Products
Online Sales

BRANDS/DIVISIONS/AFFILIATES:

Avon Color
Beyond Color
Anew
Avon Skin-So-Soft
Naturals
Mark
M-The Catalog for Men
Advance Techniques

CONTACTS: *Note: Officers with more than one job title may be intentionally listed here more than once.*

Andrea Jung, CEO
Gina R. Boswell, COO
Elizabeth A. Smith, Pres.
Charles Cramb, CFO/Vice. Chmn.
Lucien Alziari, Sr. VP-Human Resources
Donagh Herlihy, CIO/Sr. VP
Jeri B. Finard, Sr. VP/Pres., Global Brand
Kim Rucker, General Counsel/Sr. VP
Charles Cramb, Chief Strategy Officer
Nancy Glaser, Sr. VP-Global Comm.
Charles M. Herington, Sr. VP-Latin America, Central & Eastern Europe
John P. Higson, Sr. VP-Direct Selling Bus. & Bus. Innovation
Geralyn B. Breig, Sr. VP/Pres., North America
Andrea Jung, Chmn.
Bennett R. Gallina, Sr. VP-Asia Pacific, China & EMEA
John F. Owen, Sr. VP-Global Supply Chain

Phone: 212-282-5000	Fax:
Toll-Free:	
Address: 1345 Ave. of the Americas, New York, NY 10020 US	

GROWTH PLANS/SPECIAL FEATURES:

Avon Products, Inc. is a global manufacturer and marketer of beauty and related products. The firm groups these products into three categories: Beauty, consisting of cosmetics, fragrances, skin care and toiletries, which accounted for 72% of sales in 2008; Fashion, which consists of fashion jewelry, watches, apparel, footwear and accessories and accounted for 18% of 2008 sales; and Home, which consists of gift and decorative products, housewares, entertainment and leisure products, children's products and nutritional products and accounted for 10% of sales. The company sells makeup under the Avon Color and Beyond Color brands; skincare products under Anew and Avon Solutions; bath and body products under Avon Skin-So-Soft and Naturals; hair care products under Advance Techniques; health and fitness products under Avon Wellness; and fragrance products under a variety of brands, including Crystal Aura, Derek Jeter Driven, U by Ungaro and Today, Tomorrow, Always. Additionally, Avon has launched a global business targeting teenage girls through the Mark brand name, and a portfolio of products for men offered in a publication called M-The Men's Catalog. The company sells products primarily through direct selling and marketing by more than 5.8 million independent representatives in over 110 countries in North America, Latin America, Asia Pacific, Africa and Europe. Approximately 80% of the firm's 2008 revenue was derived from operations outside the U.S. Avon also sells products online. In January 2008, the company announced plans to realign certain Latin America distribution and manufacturing operations, including plans to build a new distribution center in Brazil by 2010 and phase out its distribution center in Sao Paulo by 2011. In September 2008, the firm selected Cabrueva, Brazil, for the site of the new distribution center. In February 2009, Avon announced a new restructuring program focused on the efficiency of its global supply chain operations.

FINANCIALS: Sales and profits are in thousands of dollars—add 000 to get the full amount. 2008 Note: Financial information for 2008 was not available for all companies at press time.

2008 Sales: $10,690,100	2008 Profits: $875,300	U.S. Stock Ticker: AVP
2007 Sales: $9,938,700	2007 Profits: $530,700	Int'l Ticker: Int'l Exchange:
2006 Sales: $8,763,900	2006 Profits: $477,600	Employees: 42,000
2005 Sales: $8,149,600	2005 Profits: $847,600	Fiscal Year Ends: 12/31
2004 Sales: $7,747,800	2004 Profits: $846,100	Parent Company:

SALARIES/BENEFITS:

Pension Plan:	ESOP Stock Plan:	Profit Sharing:	Top Exec. Salary: $1,375,000	Bonus: $1,689,428
Savings Plan:	Stock Purch. Plan:		Second Exec. Salary: $750,000	Bonus: $526,575

OTHER THOUGHTS:

Apparent Women Officers or Directors: 9
Hot Spot for Advancement for Women/Minorities: Y

LOCATIONS: ("Y" = Yes)

West:	Southwest:	Midwest:	Southeast:	Northeast:	International:
Y		Y	Y	Y	Y

Note: Financial information, benefits and other data can change quickly and may vary from those stated here.

AXA FINANCIAL INC

www.axa-equitable.com

Industry Group Code: 524113 **Ranks within this company's industry group:** Sales: Profits:

Management:		Sales/Marketing:		Liberal Arts:		Information Systems:		Professionals:		Tech./Scientific:	
Management Trainees:	Y	Marketing Pros.:	Y	Gen. Writing/Editing:	Y	Info. Management:	Y	Finance/Acct.:	Y	Engineers, Electrical:	
Experienced Mngmt.:	Y	Retail Sales:		Technical Writing:		Software Dev.:	Y	Law:	Y	Engineers, Other:	
International Business:	Y	Commercial/Industrial:	Y	Graphic Arts/Photog.:	Y	Hardware Dev.:		HR/Other:	Y	Health/Lab:	
MBA Grads:	Y	Sales Trainees:	Y	Music:		Consulting/Other:		Training:	Y	Scientists/Research:	
		Advertising Pros.:	Y	Broadcasting:				Health Care:		Petroleum/Chemicals:	
				Other:	Y			Consulting:		Math/Other:	Y

TYPES OF BUSINESS:

Investment Management
Mutual Funds & Pension Funds
Stock Brokerage
Investment Banking
Securities Underwriting
Annuities
Asset Management
Life Insurance

BRANDS/DIVISIONS/AFFILIATES:

AXA Advisors LLC
AXA Equitable Life Insurance Company
AXA Distributors
AllianceBernstein LP
MONY Group
MONY Life Insurance Company
MONY Life Insurance Company of America
AXA Group

CONTACTS: *Note: Officers with more than one job title may be intentionally listed here more than once.*

Christopher M. (Kip) Condron, CEO
Christopher M. (Kip) Condron, Pres.
Richard S. Dziadzio, CFO
Barbara Goodstein, Exec. VP-Mktg./Chief Innovation Officer
Jennifer L. Blevins, Exec. VP-Human Resources
Kevin E. Murray, CIO/Exec. VP
Barbara Goodstein, Exec. VP/Dir.-Prod. Dev.
Richard V. Silver, General Counsel/Exec. VP
Michael Arcaro, VP-External Affairs
William Whitesell, VP-Underwriting & New Bus. Admin.
Charles Marino, Sr. VP/Chief Actuary
Christine Nigro, Pres., AXA Advisors
Kevin Molloy, Sr. VP-Distribution Finance, AXA Equitable Life
Christopher M. (Kip) Condron, Chmn.

Phone: 212-554-1234	Fax: 212-314-4480
Toll-Free: 888-292-4492	
Address: 1290 Ave. of the Americas, New York, NY 10104 US	

GROWTH PLANS/SPECIAL FEATURES:

AXA Financial, Inc., a wholly-owned subsidiary of AXA Group, is a diversified financial services organization offering a broad spectrum of insurance, investment banking and asset management services. The company's main operating subsidiaries are AXA Advisors, AXA Equitable, AXA Distributors, AllianceBernstein and The MONY Group. AXA Advisors provides financial, retirement and estate planning; life insurance; annuities; and mutual funds to individuals and small businesses. AXA Equitable Life Insurance Company offers a variety of traditional variable and interest-sensitive life insurance products, variable and fixed-interest annuity products, mutual funds and other investment products to individuals, small groups, small and medium-size corporations, state and local governments and not-for-profit organizations. AXA Distributors, another of AXA Financial's main operating subsidiaries, distributes managed investment products and services including whole and variable life insurance and fixed and variable annuities, as well as mutual funds to affiliated and independent professional financial intermediaries like brokerages, banks and independent financial planners. AXA Distributors comprises approximately 400 firms and represents over 17,000 individual producers. AllianceBernstein, L.P. provides investment management services and is one of the largest mutual fund sponsors, with approximately $800 billion in assets under management. The MONY Group is a financial services organization that originates and distributes protection, asset accumulation and retail brokerage products and services to individuals, corporations and institutions through advisory and wholesale distribution channels. MONY companies include MONY Life Insurance Company and MONY Life Insurance Company of America.

The company offers performance-based compensation including short- and long-term incentive compensation. Employees can build healthcare based on their own specifications, in addition, the company offers dental, vision and retirement plans.

FINANCIALS: Sales and profits are in thousands of dollars—add 000 to get the full amount. 2008 Note: Financial information for 2008 was not available for all companies at press time.

2008 Sales: $	2008 Profits: $	**U.S. Stock Ticker: Subsidiary**
2007 Sales: $	2007 Profits: $	**Int'l Ticker:** Int'l Exchange:
2006 Sales: $	2006 Profits: $	Employees: 11,350
2005 Sales: $10,964,800	2005 Profits: $553,200	Fiscal Year Ends: 12/31
2004 Sales: $9,644,500	2004 Profits: $944,900	Parent Company: AXA GROUP

SALARIES/BENEFITS:

Pension Plan:	ESOP Stock Plan:	Profit Sharing:	Top Exec. Salary: $	Bonus: $
Savings Plan:	Stock Purch. Plan:		Second Exec. Salary: $	Bonus: $

OTHER THOUGHTS:

Apparent Women Officers or Directors: 3
Hot Spot for Advancement for Women/Minorities: Y

LOCATIONS: ("Y" = Yes)

West:	Southwest:	Midwest:	Southeast:	Northeast:	International:
Y	Y	Y	Y	Y	Y

Note: Financial information, benefits and other data can change quickly and may vary from those stated here.

BAKER HUGHES INC

www.bakerhughes.com

Industry Group Code: 213111 **Ranks within this company's industry group:** Sales: 1 Profits: 1

Management:		Sales/Marketing:		Liberal Arts:		Information Systems:		Professionals:		Tech./Scientific:	
Management Trainees:	Y	Marketing Pros.:	Y	Gen. Writing/Editing:	Y	Info. Management:	Y	Finance/Acct.:	Y	Engineers, Electrical:	Y
Experienced Mngmt.:	Y	Retail Sales:		Technical Writing:	Y	Software Dev.:	Y	Law:	Y	Engineers, Other:	Y
International Business:	Y	Commercial/Industrial:	Y	Graphic Arts/Photog.:	Y	Hardware Dev.:		HR/Other:	Y	Health/Lab:	
MBA Grads:	Y	Sales Trainees:		Music:		Consulting/Other:		Training:	Y	Scientists/Research:	
		Advertising Pros.:		Broadcasting:				Health Care:		Petroleum/Chemicals:	Y
				Other:				Consulting:		Math/Other:	

TYPES OF BUSINESS:

Oil & Gas Drilling Support Services
Specialty Chemicals
Process Equipment
Geophysical Services
Drilling Fluids
Drill Bits
Data Management

BRANDS/DIVISIONS/AFFILIATES:

Baker Atlas
Baker Hughes INTEQ
Baker Hughes Drilling Fluids
Hughes Christensen
Tricone
Baker Oil Tools
Baker Petrolite
Centrilift

CONTACTS: *Note: Officers with more than one job title may be intentionally listed here more than once.*

Chad C. Deaton, CEO
Martin S. Craighead, COO/Sr. VP
Chad C. Deaton, Pres.
Peter A. Ragauss, CFO/Sr. VP
Maria Claudia Borras, VP-Global Mktg.
Didier Charreton, VP-Human Resources
Clifton Triplett, CIO/VP
Derek Mathieson, Pres., Tech.
Derek Mathieson, Pres., Prod.
Alan R. Crain, General Counsel/Sr. VP
Rusty McNicoll, Pres., Integrated Oper.
David E. Emerson, VP-Corp. Dev.
Gary R. Flaharty, Dir.-Investor Rel.
Alan J. Keifer, Controller/VP
John A. O'Donnell, Pres., Western Hemisphere
Sandra E. Alford, Corp. Sec.
Bob Bennett, Pres., Baker Oil Tools
Patrick Marfone, Pres., Baker Petrolite
Chad C. Deaton, Chmn.
Belgacem Chariag, Pres., Eastern Hemisphere Oper./VP
Arthur Soucy, VP-Supply Chain

Phone: 713-439-8600	Fax: 713-439-8699
Toll-Free:	
Address: 2929 Allen Pkwy., Ste. 2100, Houston, TX 77019-2118 US	

GROWTH PLANS/SPECIAL FEATURES:

Baker Hughes, Inc. is a major supplier of wellbore-related products and technology services and a provider of drilling, formation evaluation, completion and production products and services to the oil and natural gas industry. The firm operates through two main segments: drilling and evaluation, and completion and production. The drilling and evaluation segment provides products and services used to drill and evaluate oil and natural gas wells, as well as consulting services for the analysis of oil and gas reservoirs. This segment includes subsidiary Baker Atlas, a provider of wireline formation evaluation and wireline completion services, which also provides data management, processing and analysis services. Baker Hughes INTEQ, another subsidiary, is a major supplier of real-time drilling, measurement-while-drilling and logging-while-drilling services. Baker Hughes Drilling Fluids provides drilling and completion fluids and related services. Hughes Christensen is a leading provider of Tricone roller cone drill bits and ream-while-drilling and casing drilling technology. The completion and production segment provides equipment and services used through the productive life of oil and natural gas wells. Baker Hughes' completion and production segment includes Baker Oil Tools, a provider of workover, fishing and completion equipment; Baker Petrolite, which provides oilfield specialty chemicals and chemical technology solutions for petroleum production, transportation and refining; and Centrilift, a provider of electric submersible pumps and progressing cavity pumps. Baker Hughes operates roughly 2,007 rigs worldwide and maintains more than 1,000 service locations in 70 countries. In April 2008, the firm acquired Gaffney, Cline & Associates and GeoMechanics International, two reservoir consulting firms. In December 2008, Baker Hughes Drilling Fluids acquired the assets of North East Mud Services Company LLC, a provider of drilling fluids and solids control equipment. In August 2009, the company completed the construction of new full-service completion fluids plants in Fourchon, Louisiana, and Galveston, Texas, and it agreed to acquire BJ Services in a deal valued at $5.5 billion.

FINANCIALS: Sales and profits are in thousands of dollars—add 000 to get the full amount. 2008 Note: Financial information for 2008 was not available for all companies at press time.

2008 Sales: $11,864,000	2008 Profits: $1,635,000	**U.S. Stock Ticker: BHI**
2007 Sales: $10,428,200	2007 Profits: $1,513,900	**Int'l Ticker:** Int'l Exchange:
2006 Sales: $9,027,400	2006 Profits: $2,419,000	Employees: 39,800
2005 Sales: $7,185,500	2005 Profits: $878,400	Fiscal Year Ends: 12/31
2004 Sales: $6,079,600	2004 Profits: $528,600	Parent Company:

SALARIES/BENEFITS:

Pension Plan:	ESOP Stock Plan:	Profit Sharing:	Top Exec. Salary: $1,155,000	Bonus: $6,383,399
Savings Plan:	Stock Purch. Plan:		Second Exec. Salary: $568,000	Bonus: $2,091,601

OTHER THOUGHTS:

Apparent Women Officers or Directors: 4
Hot Spot for Advancement for Women/Minorities: Y

LOCATIONS: ("Y" = Yes)

West:	Southwest:	Midwest:	Southeast:	Northeast:	International:
Y	Y	Y	Y	Y	Y

BALTIMORE GAS AND ELECTRIC COMPANY

www.bge.com

Industry Group Code: 221 Ranks within this company's industry group: Sales: 12 Profits:

Management:		Sales/Marketing:		Liberal Arts:		Information Systems:		Professionals:		Tech./Scientific:	
Management Trainees:	Y	Marketing Pros.:	Y	Gen. Writing/Editing:	Y	Info. Management:	Y	Finance/Acct.:	Y	Engineers, Electrical:	Y
Experienced Mngmt.:	Y	Retail Sales:		Technical Writing:	Y	Software Dev.:	Y	Law:	Y	Engineers, Other:	Y
International Business:		Commercial/Industrial:	Y	Graphic Arts/Photog.:	Y	Hardware Dev.:		HR/Other:	Y	Health/Lab:	
MBA Grads:	Y	Sales Trainees:		Music:		Consulting/Other:		Training:	Y	Scientists/Research:	
		Advertising Pros.:	Y	Broadcasting:				Health Care:		Petroleum/Chemicals:	Y
				Other:				Consulting:		Math/Other:	

TYPES OF BUSINESS:

Utilities-Electricity & Natural Gas
Distribution & Transmission Lines

BRANDS/DIVISIONS/AFFILIATES:

Constellation Energy Group
PJM Interconnection, LLC

CONTACTS: Note: Officers with more than one job title may be intentionally listed here more than once.

Kenneth W. DeFontes, Jr., CEO
Kenneth W. DeFontes, Jr., Pres.
Kevin Hadlock, CFO
David Vosvick, VP-Human Resources
Stephen Woerner, Sr. VP-Gas & Electric Oper.
Malinda Small, VP-Corp. Comm.
Anne A. Hahn, Mgr.-Finance & Acct.
Jeannette Mills, Sr. VP-Customer Rel. & Account Svcs.
A. Christopher Burton, Sr. VP-Asset Mgmt. Svcs.
Mark Case, Sr. VP-Strategy & Regulatory Affairs
Thomas Valenti, Sr. VP-Logistics Mgmt. Svcs.

Phone: 410-685-0123	Fax: 410-712-9323
Toll-Free: 800-685-0123	
Address: 39 W. Lexington St., Baltimore, MD 21201 US	

GROWTH PLANS/SPECIAL FEATURES:

Baltimore Gas and Electric Company (BGE), a subsidiary of Constellation Energy, is a regulated electric and gas public utility serving Baltimore City and 10 central Maryland counties. It transmits and distributes electricity to over 1.2 million business and residential customers and distributes natural gas to more than 630,000 customers. Overall, the firm's electric service spans more than 2,300 square miles, and its natural gas service covers 800 square miles. The company only delivers energy produced by neighboring utility systems. The company maintains approximately 248 substations and more than 1,269 circuit miles of electrical transmission lines and over 22,500 circuit miles of overhead and underground distribution lines. Under the PJM Tariff and various agreements, BGE and other market participants can use regional transmission facilities for energy, capacity, and ancillary services transactions including emergency assistance. In addition to providing its residential natural gas customers with storage, distribution and livery services, BGE also provides customers with meter reading, billing, emergency response, regular maintenance and balancing services. The firm delivers gas through contracts with Columbia Transmission Corporation, Transcontinental Gas Pipe Line Corporation and Dominion Transmission, Inc. The company is a member of PJM Interconnection, LLC; the independent system operator in Maryland, Pennsylvania, New Jersey and Delaware. BGE also has large volumes of propane under contract for the operation of its propane air facility and is capable of liquefying sufficient volumes of natural gas during the summer months for operations of its liquefied natural gas facility during peak winter periods

The company offers its employees flexible spending accounts and educational assistance. Employees also have access to auto and home insurance discounts, adoption assistance, a travel reimbursement incentive program, alternate work schedules and onsite medical facilities.

FINANCIALS: Sales and profits are in thousands of dollars—add 000 to get the full amount. 2008 Note: Financial information for 2008 was not available for all companies at press time.

2008 Sales: $2,680,000	2008 Profits: $	U.S. Stock Ticker: Subsidiary
2007 Sales: $3,418,500	2007 Profits: $139,800	Int'l Ticker: Int'l Exchange:
2006 Sales: $3,015,400	2006 Profits: $170,300	Employees:
2005 Sales: $3,009,300	2005 Profits: $189,000	Fiscal Year Ends: 12/31
2004 Sales: $2,724,700	2004 Profits: $166,300	Parent Company: CONSTELLATION ENERGY GROUP

SALARIES/BENEFITS:

Pension Plan: Y	ESOP Stock Plan:	Profit Sharing:	Top Exec. Salary: $	Bonus: $475,780
Savings Plan:	Stock Purch. Plan:		Second Exec. Salary: $	Bonus: $

OTHER THOUGHTS:

Apparent Women Officers or Directors: 2
Hot Spot for Advancement for Women/Minorities: Y

LOCATIONS: ("Y" = Yes)

West:	Southwest:	Midwest:	Southeast:	Northeast:	International:
				Y	

Note: Financial information, benefits and other data can change quickly and may vary from those stated here.

BANK OF AMERICA CORP

www.bankofamerica.com

Industry Group Code: 522110 Ranks within this company's industry group: Sales: 1 Profits: 2

Management:		Sales/Marketing:		Liberal Arts:		Information Systems:		Professionals:		Tech./Scientific:	
Management Trainees:	Y	Marketing Pros.:	Y	Gen. Writing/Editing:	Y	Info. Management:	Y	Finance/Acct.:	Y	Engineers, Electrical:	
Experienced Mngmt.:	Y	Retail Sales:		Technical Writing:		Software Dev.:	Y	Law:	Y	Engineers, Other:	
International Business:	Y	Commercial/Industrial:	Y	Graphic Arts/Photog.:	Y	Hardware Dev.:		HR/Other:	Y	Health/Lab:	
MBA Grads:	Y	Sales Trainees:		Music:		Consulting/Other:		Training:	Y	Scientists/Research:	
		Advertising Pros.:	Y	Broadcasting:				Health Care:		Petroleum/Chemicals:	
				Other:	Y			Consulting:		Math/Other:	

TYPES OF BUSINESS:

Banking
Commercial Real Estate
Investment & Brokerage Services
Insurance
Mutual Funds
Venture Capital
Mortgages
Credit Cards

BRANDS/DIVISIONS/AFFILIATES:

Barnett Banks, Inc.
FleetBoston
Merrill Lynch & Co.
MBNA Corp.
China Construction Bank
Countrywide Financial Corp
LaSalle Bank Corp
U.S. Trust

CONTACTS: *Note: Officers with more than one job title may be intentionally listed here more than once.*

Kenneth D. Lewis, CEO
Kenneth D. Lewis, Pres.
Joe L. Price, CFO
Anne Finucane, Chief Mktg. Officer
J. Steele Alphin, Chief Admin. Officer
Edward P. O'Keefe, General Counsel
Amy Woods Brinkley, Exec.-Global Risk
Neil A. Cotty, Chief Acct. Officer
Walter J. Muller, Chief Investment Officer
Barbara J. Desoer, Pres., Home Loans & Insurance
Tom Montag, Pres., Global Markets & Corp. Banking
Brian Moynihan, Pres., Consumer & Small Bus. Bank
Walter E. Massey, Chmn.
Sallie Krawcheck, Head-Global Wealth & Investment Mgmt.

Phone: 704-386-8486	Fax: 704-386-6699
Toll-Free: 800-432-1000	
Address: 100 N. Tryon St., 18th Fl., Charlotte, NC 28255 US	

GROWTH PLANS/SPECIAL FEATURES:

Bank of America Corp. is a global provider of a diversified range of banking and financial services. In banking, the company operates through three business segments: global consumer and small business banking; global corporate and investment banking; and global wealth and investment management. The firm's global consumer and small business banking division maintains nearly 6,100 banking centers worldwide with over 19,000 ATMs serving 59 million customers. Over 24 million customers use Bank of America's online banking service. The global consumer and small business banking division offers a variety of services including checking and savings accounts, CDs, IRAs, debit cards, credit cards, mortgage and home equity products. The global corporate and investment banking division provides services in three areas: business lending; capital markets and advisory services; and treasury services. The global wealth and investment banking segment includes Premier Banking and Investments, which provides banking, credit, investment services to clients with less than $3 million in assets, The Private Bank for clients with greater than $3 million in assets; Columbia Management Group for intuitional customers. Bank of America's credit card business is the result of the $35 billion acquisition of MBNA. As one of America's strongest financial institutions, the company was able to grow substantially during the 2008 global financial crisis, by agreeing to acquire both Countrywide Financial and Merrill Lynch & Co. The January 2009 Merrill Lynch acquisition increased Bank of America's financial advisor ranks to more than 20,000, making it the largest stock brokerage in the world in that regard, and boosted the total amount of client assets under management to $2.5 trillion. This acquisition includes a 50% ownership in asset management firm BlackRock. In July 2008, Bank of America acquired Countrywide Financial, Corp., one of the largest mortgage lenders in the U.S., immediately providing Bank of America with a massive network of mortgage offices and millions of additional mortgage customers.

The company offers its employees educational partnerships, health care and dependent care flexible spending accounts.

FINANCIALS: Sales and profits are in thousands of dollars—add 000 to get the full amount. 2008 Note: Financial information for 2008 was not available for all companies at press time.

		U.S. Stock Ticker: BAC
2008 Sales: $113,106,000	2008 Profits: $4,008,000	Int'l Ticker: Int'l Exchange:
2007 Sales: $124,321,000	2007 Profits: $14,982,000	Employees: 243,075
2006 Sales: $117,017,000	2006 Profits: $21,133,000	Fiscal Year Ends: 12/31
2005 Sales: $83,980,000	2005 Profits: $16,465,000	Parent Company:
2004 Sales: $48,965,000	2004 Profits: $14,143,000	

SALARIES/BENEFITS:

Pension Plan: Y	ESOP Stock Plan:	Profit Sharing:	Top Exec. Salary: $1,500,000	Bonus: $
Savings Plan: Y	Stock Purch. Plan:		Second Exec. Salary: $800,000	Bonus: $

OTHER THOUGHTS:

Apparent Women Officers or Directors: 5
Hot Spot for Advancement for Women/Minorities: Y

LOCATIONS: ("Y" = Yes)

West:	Southwest:	Midwest:	Southeast:	Northeast:	International:
Y	Y	Y	Y	Y	Y

Note: Financial information, benefits and other data can change quickly and may vary from those stated here.

BARNES & NOBLE INC

www.barnesandnobleinc.com

Industry Group Code: 451211 Ranks within this company's industry group: Sales: 1 Profits: 1

Management:		Sales/Marketing:		Liberal Arts:		Information Systems:		Professionals:		Tech./Scientific:	
Management Trainees:	Y	Marketing Pros.:	Y	Gen. Writing/Editing:	Y	Info. Management:	Y	Finance/Acct.:	Y	Engineers, Electrical:	
Experienced Mngmt.:	Y	Retail Sales:	Y	Technical Writing:		Software Dev.:	Y	Law:	Y	Engineers, Other:	
International Business:		Commercial/Industrial:		Graphic Arts/Photog.:	Y	Hardware Dev.:		HR/Other:	Y	Health/Lab:	
MBA Grads:	Y	Sales Trainees:	Y	Music:		Consulting/Other:		Training:	Y	Scientists/Research:	
		Advertising Pros.:	Y	Broadcasting:				Health Care:		Petroleum/Chemicals:	
				Other:	Y			Consulting:		Math/Other:	

TYPES OF BUSINESS:

Book Stores
Music & Software Sales
In-Store Cafes
Online Sales
Book Publishing
Book Distribution

BRANDS/DIVISIONS/AFFILIATES:

B. Dalton Bookseller
Barnes & Noble Bookseller
Sterling Publishing Co., Inc.
BarnesAndNoble.com, Inc.
Quamut.com
Fictionwise

CONTACTS: Note: Officers with more than one job title may be intentionally listed here more than once.

Stephen Riggio, CEO
Mitchell S. Klipper, COO
Joseph Lombardi, CFO
Michelle Smith, VP-Human Resources
Chris Troia, CIO
Jaime Carey, Chief Merch. Officer
Jennifer Daniels, General Counsel/VP/Sec.
David Deason, VP-Dev.
William J. Lynch, Jr., Pres., BarnesAndNoble.com
Mary Ellen Keating, Sr. VP-Corp. Comm. & Public Affairs
Andy Milevoj, Mgr.-Investor Rel.
Allen W. Lindstrom, Corp. Controller/VP
Mark Bottini, VP/Dir.-Stores
J. Alan Kahn, Pres., Publishing Group
Kevin Frain, Exec. VP-E-Commerce Oper.
Marcus E. Leaver, Pres., Sterling Publishing
Leonard Riggio, Chmn.
William F. Duffy, Exec. VP-Logistics & Dist.

Phone: 212-633-3300	Fax: 212-352-3660
Toll-Free: 800-422-7717	
Address: 122 5th Ave., New York, NY 10011 US	

GROWTH PLANS/SPECIAL FEATURES:

Barnes & Noble, Inc. (B&N) is one of the largest booksellers in the U.S., operating over 777 book stores in all 50 states, operating under the Barnes & Nobles Bookseller and B. Dalton Bookseller trade names. The company conducts the online part of its business through BarnesAndNoble.com. The firm is also a general trade book publisher, offering many series of books with the label Barnes and Noble Classics. This is enabled in part through the firm's acquisition of Sterling Publishing, a non-fiction trade publisher. Sterling is now a subsidiary of the firm. B&N's principal business is the sale of trade books (generally hardcover and paperback consumer titles, excluding educational textbooks and specialized religious titles), mass market paperbacks (such as mystery, romance, science fiction and other popular fiction), children's books, bargain books, magazines, music and movies direct to customers. Many B&N stores feature additional amenities such as a cafe serving sandwiches and Starbucks coffee; a children's area; and music, DVD, books, video and game sections. In-store music departments provide over 40,000 titles in classical music, opera, jazz, blues and pop rock. While stores average 25,000 square feet each, the largest are 60,000-square-foot giants stocking up to 200,000 titles. Typical stores stock approximately 60,000 core titles within a variety of popular subject categories reflecting local interests, which are supplemented by new releases and bestsellers. In March 2009, the company acquired e-book retailer Fictionwise for roughly $15.7 million. In August 2009, the company announced plans to acquire privately-held Barnes & Noble College Booksellers, Inc., which operates about 624 bookstores on U.S. college campuses, for approximately $596 million.

The company offers its employees medical, vision and dental insurance; life insurance; business travel insurance; short- and long-term disability; a 401(k) plan; tuition assistance; a book loan program; and merchandise discounts.

FINANCIALS: Sales and profits are in thousands of dollars—add 000 to get the full amount. 2008 Note: Financial information for 2008 was not available for all companies at press time.

2008 Sales: $5,410,828	2008 Profits: $135,799	U.S. Stock Ticker: BKS
2007 Sales: $5,261,254	2007 Profits: $150,527	Int'l Ticker: Int'l Exchange:
2006 Sales: $5,103,004	2006 Profits: $146,681	Employees: 37,000
2005 Sales: $4,873,595	2005 Profits: $143,376	Fiscal Year Ends: 1/31
2004 Sales: $4,372,177	2004 Profits: $151,775	Parent Company:

SALARIES/BENEFITS:

Pension Plan:	ESOP Stock Plan:	Profit Sharing:	Top Exec. Salary: $800,000	Bonus: $1,961,507
Savings Plan: Y	Stock Purch. Plan:		Second Exec. Salary: $800,000	Bonus: $1,557,611

OTHER THOUGHTS:

Apparent Women Officers or Directors: 4
Hot Spot for Advancement for Women/Minorities: Y

LOCATIONS: ("Y" = Yes)

West:	Southwest:	Midwest:	Southeast:	Northeast:	International:
Y	Y	Y	Y	Y	

Note: Financial information, benefits and other data can change quickly and may vary from those stated here.

BASS PRO SHOPS INC

www.basspro.com

Industry Group Code: 451110 Ranks within this company's industry group: Sales: 2   Profits:

Management:		Sales/Marketing:		Liberal Arts:		Information Systems:		Professionals:		Tech./Scientific:	
Management Trainees:	Y	Marketing Pros.:	Y	Gen. Writing/Editing:	Y	Info. Management:	Y	Finance/Acct.:	Y	Engineers, Electrical:	
Experienced Mngmt.:	Y	Retail Sales:	Y	Technical Writing:		Software Dev.:	Y	Law:	Y	Engineers, Other:	
International Business:	Y	Commercial/Industrial:		Graphic Arts/Photog.:	Y	Hardware Dev.:		HR/Other:	Y	Health/Lab:	
MBA Grads:	Y	Sales Trainees:	Y	Music:		Consulting/Other:		Training:	Y	Scientists/Research:	
		Advertising Pros.:	Y	Broadcasting:				Health Care:		Petroleum/Chemicals:	
				Other:				Consulting:		Math/Other:	

TYPES OF BUSINESS:

Sporting Goods, Retail
Sport Boats
Hunting & Fishing Equipment
Catalog & Online Sales
Outdoor Apparel
Resort Operations
Television Production

BRANDS/DIVISIONS/AFFILIATES:

Outdoor World
RedHead
Offshore Angler
White River Fly Shops
Tracker Marine
American Rod & Gun
Big Cedar Lodge
Dogwood Canyon

CONTACTS: *Note: Officers with more than one job title may be intentionally listed here more than once.*

James Hagale, COO
James Hagale, Pres.
Toni Miller, CFO/VP
Katie A. Mitchell, Specialist-Comm.
Martin G. MacDonald, Dir.-Public Rel. & Conservation
Jenna M. Kendall, Coordinator-Media Info.
John L. Morris, Chmn.

Phone: 417-873-5000	Fax: 417-873-5060
Toll-Free: 800-227-7776	
Address: 2500 E. Kearney St., Springfield, MO 65898 US	

GROWTH PLANS/SPECIAL FEATURES:

Bass Pro Shops, Inc. is a leader in sporting goods retail. The company markets its products through 49 sports superstores across the United States and Canada, a mail-order catalog and through Internet sites. The firm is dedicated to providing outdoor recreational products, including specialty apparel, and also aims to model and inspire environmental conservation among its customers. The sporting goods superstores operate under the Bass Pro Shop and Outdoor World brand names and range from 100,000 to 600,000 square feet. Products include boats and campers, as well as myriads of fishing, hunting, camping, automobile and marine supplies. Many of these stores sport a variety of unique features and attractions to draw more customers, including restaurants, snack bars, archery ranges, indoor fish tanks, waterfalls and video arcades. In addition to its stores, the company sells goods over the Internet and through more than 34 million mail-order catalogs under the Bass Pro Shops, RedHead, Offshore Angler and White River Fly Shops brand names. On the wholesale side, the firm owns and operates Tracker Marine, a leader in sport boat manufacturing, and American Rod & Gun, one of the largest wholesale hunting and fishing distributors in the country. In addition to offering a variety of hunting and fishing trips and contests, the Bass Pro runs Big Cedar Lodge, an outdoors-themed vacation spot in Missouri, located near the company's own nature park, Dogwood Canyon; and produces two weekly television programs on The Outdoor Channel.

FINANCIALS: Sales and profits are in thousands of dollars—add 000 to get the full amount. 2008 Note: Financial information for 2008 was not available for all companies at press time.

2008 Sales: $3,000,000	2008 Profits: $	U.S. Stock Ticker: Private
2007 Sales: $3,000,000	2007 Profits: $	Int'l Ticker: Int'l Exchange:
2006 Sales: $2,660,000	2006 Profits: $	Employees: 15,000
2005 Sales: $1,915,000	2005 Profits: $	Fiscal Year Ends: 12/31
2004 Sales: $2,050,000	2004 Profits: $	Parent Company:

SALARIES/BENEFITS:

Pension Plan:	ESOP Stock Plan:	Profit Sharing:	Top Exec. Salary: $	Bonus: $
Savings Plan:	Stock Purch. Plan:		Second Exec. Salary: $	Bonus: $

OTHER THOUGHTS:

Apparent Women Officers or Directors: 3
Hot Spot for Advancement for Women/Minorities: Y

LOCATIONS: ("Y" = Yes)

West:	Southwest:	Midwest:	Southeast:	Northeast:	International:
Y	Y	Y	Y	Y	Y

BAXTER INTERNATIONAL INC

www.baxter.com

Industry Group Code: 33911 Ranks within this company's industry group: Sales: 3 Profits: 3

Management:		Sales/Marketing:		Liberal Arts:		Information Systems:		Professionals:		Tech./Scientific:	
Management Trainees:	Y	Marketing Pros.:	Y	Gen. Writing/Editing:	Y	Info. Management:	Y	Finance/Acct.:	Y	Engineers, Electrical:	Y
Experienced Mngmt.:	Y	Retail Sales:		Technical Writing:	Y	Software Dev.:	Y	Law:	Y	Engineers, Other:	Y
International Business:	Y	Commercial/Industrial:	Y	Graphic Arts/Photog.:	Y	Hardware Dev.:		HR/Other:	Y	Health/Lab:	Y
MBA Grads:	Y	Sales Trainees:	Y	Music:		Consulting/Other:		Training:	Y	Scientists/Research:	Y
		Advertising Pros.:	Y	Broadcasting:				Health Care:	Y	Petroleum/Chemicals:	
				Other:				Consulting:		Math/Other:	

TYPES OF BUSINESS:

Medical Equipment Manufacturing
Supplies-Intravenous & Renal Dialysis Systems
Medication Delivery Products & IV Fluids
Biopharmaceutical Products
Plasma Collection & Processing
Vaccines
Software
Contract Research

BRANDS/DIVISIONS/AFFILIATES:

Medication Delivery
BioScience
Renal
Colleague CX
Enlightened
ADVATE
RenalSoft HD
ARTISS

CONTACTS: *Note: Officers with more than one job title may be intentionally listed here more than once.*

Robert L. Parkinson, Jr., CEO
Robert L. Parkinson, Jr., Pres.
Robert M. Davis, CFO/VP
Jeanne K. Mason, VP-Human Resources
Norbert G. Riedel, Chief Scientific Officer/VP
Karenann Terrell, CIO/VP
J. Michael Gatling, VP-Mfg.
Susan R. Lichtenstein, General Counsel/VP
Michael J. Baughman, Controller/VP
Joy A. Amundson, VP/Pres., Bioscience
Bruce McGillivray, VP/Pres., Renal
Peter J. Arduini, Pres., Medication Delivery/VP
Gerald Lema, VP/Pres., Asia Pacific
Robert L. Parkinson, Jr., Chmn.
John J. Greisch, VP/Pres., Int'l

Phone: 847-948-2000	Fax: 847-948-3642
Toll-Free: 800-422-9837	
Address: 1 Baxter Pkwy., Deerfield, IL 60015-4625 US	

GROWTH PLANS/SPECIAL FEATURES:

Baxter International, Inc. manufactures and markets products for the treatment of hemophilia, immune disorders, cancer, infectious diseases, kidney disease, trauma and other chronic and acute medical conditions, offering expertise in medical devices, pharmaceuticals and biotechnology. Baxter markets its offerings to hospitals; clinical and medical research labs; blood and blood dialysis centers; rehab facilities; nursing homes; doctor's offices; and patients undergoing supervised home care. The firm has manufacturing facilities in 26 countries and offers products and services in 100 countries. Baxter operates in three segments: Medication Delivery, its largest sector, which provides a range of intravenous solutions and specialty products that are used in combination for fluid replenishment, nutrition therapy, pain management, antibiotic therapy and chemotherapy; BioScience, which develops biopharmaceuticals, biosurgery products, vaccines, blood collection, processing and storage products and technologies; and Renal, which develops products and provides services to treat end-stage kidney disease. Products include the Colleague CX infusion pump; the Enlightened bar-coding system for flexible IV containers; ADVATE, a coagulant for hemophilia patients; and RenalSoft HD, a software module for the management of prescription, therapy and monitoring information relating to patients suffering from kidney failure. In addition, the company provides the following services: BioLife Plasma Services, a plasma collection and processing business; BioPharma Solutions, biotechnology; Global Technical Services, providing instrument service and support for devices manufactured and marketed by Baxter; Renal Clinical Helpline; Renal Services, an education and research operation; and Training and Education, a portfolio of interactive clinical web sites. In March 2008, the company received FDA approval of ARTISS, a slow-setting fibrin sealant for the use of adhering skin grafts in burn patients.

Employees are offered medical and dental insurance; vision care discounts; health and dependent care reimbursement accounts; an educational assistance program; credit union membership; adoption reimbursement; an employee assistance program; a 401(k) plan; and a stock purchase plan.

FINANCIALS: Sales and profits are in thousands of dollars—add 000 to get the full amount. 2008 Note: Financial information for 2008 was not available for all companies at press time.

2008 Sales: $12,348,000	2008 Profits: $2,014,000	U.S. Stock Ticker: BAX
2007 Sales: $11,263,000	2007 Profits: $1,707,000	Int'l Ticker: Int'l Exchange:
2006 Sales: $10,378,000	2006 Profits: $1,397,000	Employees: 48,500
2005 Sales: $9,849,000	2005 Profits: $956,000	Fiscal Year Ends: 12/31
2004 Sales: $9,509,000	2004 Profits: $388,000	Parent Company:

SALARIES/BENEFITS:

Pension Plan:	ESOP Stock Plan:	Profit Sharing:	Top Exec. Salary: $1,339,339	Bonus: $2,708,940
Savings Plan: Y	Stock Purch. Plan:		Second Exec. Salary: $613,462	Bonus: $937,950

OTHER THOUGHTS:

Apparent Women Officers or Directors: 6
Hot Spot for Advancement for Women/Minorities: Y

LOCATIONS: ("Y" = Yes)

West:	Southwest:	Midwest:	Southeast:	Northeast:	International:
Y	Y	Y	Y	Y	Y

Note: Financial information, benefits and other data can change quickly and may vary from those stated here.

BDO SEIDMAN LLP

www.bdo.com

Industry Group Code: 5412 Ranks within this company's industry group: Sales: 6 Profits:

Management:		Sales/Marketing:		Liberal Arts:		Information Systems:		Professionals:		Tech./Scientific:	
Management Trainees:	Y	Marketing Pros.:	Y	Gen. Writing/Editing:	Y	Info. Management:	Y	Finance/Acct.:	Y	Engineers, Electrical:	
Experienced Mngmt.:	Y	Retail Sales:		Technical Writing:	Y	Software Dev.:	Y	Law:	Y	Engineers, Other:	
International Business:	Y	Commercial/Industrial:	Y	Graphic Arts/Photog.:	Y	Hardware Dev.:		HR/Other:	Y	Health/Lab:	
MBA Grads:	Y	Sales Trainees:		Music:		Consulting/Other:	Y	Training:	Y	Scientists/Research:	
		Advertising Pros.:	Y	Broadcasting:				Health Care:		Petroleum/Chemicals:	
		Other:		Other:	Y			Consulting:	Y	Math/Other:	

TYPES OF BUSINESS:

Accounting Services
Financial Regulatory Assurance
Tax Services
Financial Consulting
Business Consulting
Insurance & Insurance Consulting
Securities Brokerage Services

BRANDS/DIVISIONS/AFFILIATES:

Seidman Private Advisors, LLC
Seidman Private Securities, LLC
Seidman Insurance Consultants, LLC
BDO Consulting Services
Trenwith Group, LLC
BDO Seidman Alliance
BDO Business Resource Network
BDO International

CONTACTS: *Note: Officers with more than one job title may be intentionally listed here more than once.*

Jack Weisbaum, CEO
Howard B. Allenberg, CFO
Ben Neuhausen, Dir.-Acct.
Carl W. Pergola, Exec. Dir.-BDO Consulting
Timothy L. Mohr, Dir.-Employee Misconduct Investigations
Stephanie Giammarco, Dir.-Computer Forensics & E-Discovery
Lee Dewey, Dir.-Corporate Investigations
Wayne Kolins, Chmn.

Phone: 312-240-1236	**Fax:** 312-240-3311
Toll-Free:	
Address: 130 E. Randolph, Ste. 2800, 1 Prudential Pl., Chicago, IL 60601 US	

GROWTH PLANS/SPECIAL FEATURES:

BDO Seidman, LLP is a financial, tax advisory, assurance, consulting and accounting firm. Its main service branches cover assurance, taxes, private client wealth management and corporate real estate. Assurance services cover regulatory compliance, financial statement audits and access to capital markets to name a few. Tax services include property, sales and international tax; mergers and acquisitions; and cost segregation among others. Private client wealth management services are offered through Seidman Private Advisors, LLC, which offers financial planning, investment management and investment advisory services; Seidman Private Securities, LLC for clients securities brokerage services; and Seidman Insurance Consultants, LLC for insurance consulting services and long-term care, disability and life insurance products. Corporate real estate services include lease audits, lease consulting and analysis of and consultations regarding utilities fees. The firm also runs BDO Consulting Services, offering litigation, risk advisory, restructuring and investigations services; along with investment banking and business valuation services through Trenwith Group, LLC. Additionally, the BDO Seidman Alliance is a network of independent businesses that share resources with BDO and with each other. It includes the BDO Business Resource Network, which focuses on IT related issues, and various industry groups, mainly serving construction, governmental, healthcare, nonprofit, manufacturing, energy, dealership or financial institution clients. BDO has 37 offices of its own in the U.S., and through its alliances offers an additional 400 independent locations nationwide. It is also the U.S. member of BDO International, which has 1,095 member firm offices in 110 countries. BDO Seidman is able to offers its clients the varied services offered by BDO International's global network. In 2008, the firm expanded its footprint with two new offices, one in Las Vegas, Nevada and the other Austin, Texas.

Employees receive comprehensive medical benefits; paid time off; flexible spending accounts; continuing education and tuition reimbursement; and legal assistance.

FINANCIALS: Sales and profits are in thousands of dollars—add 000 to get the full amount. 2008 Note: Financial information for 2008 was not available for all companies at press time.

2008 Sales: $659,000	2008 Profits: $	**U.S. Stock Ticker:** Private	
2007 Sales: $589,000	2007 Profits: $	**Int'l Ticker:**　Int'l Exchange:	
2006 Sales: $558,000	2006 Profits: $	Employees: 3,020	
2005 Sales: $440,000	2005 Profits: $	Fiscal Year Ends: 6/30	
2004 Sales: $365,000	2004 Profits: $	Parent Company:	

SALARIES/BENEFITS:

Pension Plan:	ESOP Stock Plan:	Profit Sharing:	Top Exec. Salary: $	Bonus: $
Savings Plan: Y	Stock Purch. Plan:		Second Exec. Salary: $	Bonus: $

OTHER THOUGHTS:

Apparent Women Officers or Directors: 1
Hot Spot for Advancement for Women/Minorities:

LOCATIONS: ("Y" = Yes)

West:	Southwest:	Midwest:	Southeast:	Northeast:	International:
Y	Y	Y	Y	Y	Y

BEBE STORES INC

www.bebe.com

Industry Group Code: 448120 Ranks within this company's industry group: Sales: 8   Profits: 5

Management:		Sales/Marketing:		Liberal Arts:		Information Systems:		Professionals:		Tech./Scientific:	
Management Trainees:	Y	Marketing Pros.:	Y	Gen. Writing/Editing:	Y	Info. Management:	Y	Finance/Acct.:	Y	Engineers, Electrical:	
Experienced Mngmt.:	Y	Retail Sales:	Y	Technical Writing:		Software Dev.:	Y	Law:	Y	Engineers, Other:	
International Business:	Y	Commercial/Industrial:		Graphic Arts/Photog.:	Y	Hardware Dev.:		HR/Other:	Y	Health/Lab:	
MBA Grads:	Y	Sales Trainees:	Y	Music:		Consulting/Other:		Training:	Y	Scientists/Research:	
		Advertising Pros.:	Y	Broadcasting:				Health Care:		Petroleum/Chemicals:	
				Other:	Y			Consulting:		Math/Other:	

TYPES OF BUSINESS:

Young Women's Apparel, Retail
Accessories
Shoes
Online Sales

BRANDS/DIVISIONS/AFFILIATES:

bebe
BEBE SPORT
bebe.com
2b bebe
Bebe Stores (Canada), Inc.

CONTACTS: Note: Officers with more than one job title may be intentionally listed here more than once.

Manny Mashouf, CEO
Walter Parks, COO
Walter Parks, CFO
Kathy Lee, Chief Merch. Officer
Barbara Wambach, Chief Admin. Officer
Lawrence Smith, General Counsel/VP
Amy Nichelini, Controller/Principal Acct. Officer
Susan Powers, Sr. VP-Stores
Tara Poseley, Pres., Bebe Sport
Manny Mashouf, Chmn.

Phone: 415-715-3900	**Fax:** 415-715-3939
Toll-Free: 877-232-3777	
Address: 400 Valley Dr., Brisbane, CA 94005 US	

GROWTH PLANS/SPECIAL FEATURES:

Bebe Stores, Inc. designs, develops and produces a line of contemporary women's apparel and accessories, marketed under the bebe; COLLECTION bebe; BEBE SPORT; bbsp; bebe O; and 2b bebe brand names. The company operates approximately 308 retail stores located in 35 states, Puerto Rico, the U.S. Virgin Islands and Canada. Of these stores, 213 are bebe stores, 62 are BEBE SPORT stores and 33 are bebe outlet stores operated under the 2b bebe banner. In addition, the firm operates an online store at www.bebe.com and holds 21 international stores through licensees in Singapore, Indonesia, Israel, Thailand, the United Arab Emirates, Turkey, Malaysia, Egypt, Russia and Mexico. The company targets female customers between the ages of 21-35, with offerings including suits, tops, skirts, dresses, pants, active wear, outerwear and handbags, shoes, jewelry and other accessories. Most of its merchandise is designed and developed in-house and manufactured in conjunction with third parties. The company has pursued growth through new store openings and the introduction of new product categories, including denim, leather, lingerie, swimwear and footwear. Bebe stores average 4,000 square feet and are primarily located in regional shopping malls and freestanding street locations. The firm opened its first Russian store, in Moscow, during late 2008. In July 2009, the company announced a licensing partnership with Titan Industries, Inc. for the design and development of women's non-casual footwear to be sold primarily in bebe stores in the U.S. and Canada, as well as in select department and specialty stores worldwide.

Bebe offers its employees medical, dental and vision coverage; flexible spending accounts; life and disability insurance; a 401(k) plan; a stock purchase plan; an employee assistance program; and discounts on bebe merchandise, among other benefits.

FINANCIALS: Sales and profits are in thousands of dollars—add 000 to get the full amount. 2008 Note: Financial information for 2008 was not available for all companies at press time.

2008 Sales: $687,622	2008 Profits: $63,080	**U.S. Stock Ticker: BEBE**
2007 Sales: $670,912	2007 Profits: $77,278	**Int'l Ticker:** Int'l Exchange:
2006 Sales: $579,073	2006 Profits: $73,807	Employees: 4,433
2005 Sales: $509,527	2005 Profits: $66,332	Fiscal Year Ends: 6/30
2004 Sales: $372,257	2004 Profits: $33,770	Parent Company:

SALARIES/BENEFITS:

Pension Plan:	ESOP Stock Plan:	Profit Sharing:	Top Exec. Salary: $600,000	Bonus: $
Savings Plan: Y	Stock Purch. Plan: Y		Second Exec. Salary: $387,000	Bonus: $

OTHER THOUGHTS:

Apparent Women Officers or Directors: 7
Hot Spot for Advancement for Women/Minorities: Y

LOCATIONS: ("Y" = Yes)

West:	Southwest:	Midwest:	Southeast:	Northeast:	International:
Y	Y	Y	Y	Y	Y

BECHTEL GROUP INC

www.bechtel.com

Industry Group Code: 237   Ranks within this company's industry group: Sales: 1   Profits:

Management:		Sales/Marketing:		Liberal Arts:		Information Systems:		Professionals:		Tech./Scientific:	
Management Trainees:	Y	Marketing Pros.:	Y	Gen. Writing/Editing:	Y	Info. Management:	Y	Finance/Acct.:	Y	Engineers, Electrical:	Y
Experienced Mngmt.:	Y	Retail Sales:		Technical Writing:	Y	Software Dev.:	Y	Law:	Y	Engineers, Other:	Y
International Business:	Y	Commercial/Industrial:	Y	Graphic Arts/Photog.:	Y	Hardware Dev.:		HR/Other:	Y	Health/Lab:	
MBA Grads:	Y	Sales Trainees:	Y	Music:		Consulting/Other:	Y	Training:	Y	Scientists/Research:	
		Advertising Pros.:		Broadcasting:				Health Care:		Petroleum/Chemicals:	Y
				Other:				Consulting:	Y	Math/Other:	Y

TYPES OF BUSINESS:

Engineering, Construction & Project Management Services
Civic Engineering
Outsourcing
Financial Services
Atomic Propulsion Systems Engineering
Airport Construction
Electric Power Plant Construction
Nuclear Power Plant Construction

BRANDS/DIVISIONS/AFFILIATES:

Bechtel Systems & Infrastructure, Inc.
Bechtel Power Corp.

CONTACTS: *Note: Officers with more than one job title may be intentionally listed here more than once.*

Riley P. Bechtel, CEO
Bill Dudley, COO
Bill Dudley, Pres.
Peter Dawson, CFO
John MacDonald, Dir.-Human Resources
Geir Ramleth, Dir.-Info. Systems
Geir Ramleth, Dir.-Tech.
Tom Patterson, Mgr.-Eng.
Judith Miller, General Counsel
Jim Jackson, Pres., Oil, Gas & Chemicals
Mike Adams, Pres., Civil
Scott Ogilvie, Pres., Bechtel Systems & Infrastructure, Inc.
Andy Greig, Pres., Mining & Metals
Riley P. Bechtel, Chmn.
Eli Smith, Mgr.-Contracts & Procurement

Phone: 415-768-1234	Fax: 415-768-9038
Toll-Free:	
Address: 50 Beale St., San Francisco, CA 94105-1895 US	

GROWTH PLANS/SPECIAL FEATURES:

Bechtel Group, Inc., founded in 1906 by Warren A. Bechtel, is one of the world's largest engineering companies. The privately-owned firm offers engineering, construction and project management services, with a broad project portfolio including road and rail systems, airports and seaports, nuclear power plants, petrochemical facilities, mines, defense and aerospace facilities, environmental cleanup projects, telecommunication networks, pipelines and oil fields development. The firm has participated in such notable endeavors as the construction of the Hoover Dam, the creation of the Bay Area Rapid Transit system in San Francisco, the massive James Bay Hydroelectric Project in Quebec and the quelling of oil field fires in Kuwait following the Persian Gulf War. Bechtel also constructed the Trans-Alaska Oil Pipeline, covering 800 miles between the Prudhoe Bay oil field and Valdez. In recent years, Bechtel has been awarded two multi-million dollar contracts by the U.S. Agency for International Development for the repair and reconstruction of Iraq's infrastructure. Bechtel has also been contracted to develop the New Doha International Airport in Qatar. An 11-year, multi-billion-dollar project, the new airport will be designed to accommodate six Airbus A380-800's, the largest passenger aircraft in the world. In February 2008, the company began construction of a 5.2 million-metric-ton-per-year liquified natural gas (LNG) train, with marine loading facilities and storage for LNG, liquefied petroleum gas in Angola; In July 2008, the firm signed a $200 million construction, engineering, and procurement agreement with Rio Tinto Alcan in Kitimat, British Columbia for the Kitmat Smelter modernization project. In December 2008, the company entered a $40 million front end engineering design (FEED) for the downstream components of Gladstone LNG in Queensland, Australia. In January 2009, the firm and American Municipal Power-Ohio, Inc are collaborating to construct an electric generation facility in Meigs County, Ohio.

FINANCIALS: Sales and profits are in thousands of dollars—add 000 to get the full amount. 2008 Note: Financial information for 2008 was not available for all companies at press time.

2008 Sales: $31,400,000	2008 Profits: $	**U.S. Stock Ticker: Private**
2007 Sales: $27,000,000	2007 Profits: $	**Int'l Ticker:** Int'l Exchange:
2006 Sales: $20,500,000	2006 Profits: $	Employees: 44,000
2005 Sales: $18,600,000	2005 Profits: $	Fiscal Year Ends: 12/31
2004 Sales: $17,400,000	2004 Profits: $	Parent Company:

SALARIES/BENEFITS:

Pension Plan:	ESOP Stock Plan:	Profit Sharing:	Top Exec. Salary: $	Bonus: $
Savings Plan:	Stock Purch. Plan:		Second Exec. Salary: $	Bonus: $

OTHER THOUGHTS:

Apparent Women Officers or Directors: 2
Hot Spot for Advancement for Women/Minorities: Y

LOCATIONS: ("Y" = Yes)

West:	Southwest:	Midwest:	Southeast:	Northeast:	International:
Y	Y	Y	Y	Y	Y

Note: Financial information, benefits and other data can change quickly and may vary from those stated here.

BECKMAN COULTER INC

www.beckmancoulter.com

Industry Group Code: 33911 Ranks within this company's industry group: Sales: 9   Profits: 11

Management:		Sales/Marketing:		Liberal Arts:		Information Systems:		Professionals:		Tech./Scientific:	
Management Trainees:	Y	Marketing Pros.:	Y	Gen. Writing/Editing:	Y	Info. Management:	Y	Finance/Acct.:	Y	Engineers, Electrical:	Y
Experienced Mngmt.:	Y	Retail Sales:		Technical Writing:	Y	Software Dev.:	Y	Law:	Y	Engineers, Other:	Y
International Business:	Y	Commercial/Industrial:	Y	Graphic Arts/Photog.:	Y	Hardware Dev.:	Y	HR/Other:	Y	Health/Lab:	Y
MBA Grads:	Y	Sales Trainees:		Music:		Consulting/Other:		Training:	Y	Scientists/Research:	Y
		Advertising Pros.:	Y	Broadcasting:				Health Care:	Y	Petroleum/Chemicals:	
				Other:				Consulting:		Math/Other:	Y

TYPES OF BUSINESS:

Equipment-Laboratory Instruments
Chemistry Systems
Genetic Analysis/Nucleic Acid Testing
Biomedical Research Supplies
Immunoassay Systems
Cellular Systems
Discovery & Automation Systems

BRANDS/DIVISIONS/AFFILIATES:

Nephromics, LLC
Cogenics

CONTACTS: Note: Officers with more than one job title may be intentionally listed here more than once.

Scott Garrett, CEO
Scott Garrett, Pres.
Charlie Slacik, CFO/Sr. VP
Bob Hurley, Sr. VP-Human Resources
Scott Atkin, Group VP-Chemistry, Discovery & Automation
Arnie Pinkston, General Counsel/Sr. VP/Corp. Sec.
Bob Kleinert, Exec. VP-Worldwide Commercial Oper.
Paul Glyer, Sr. VP-Strategy & Bus. Dev.
Paul Glyer, Sr. VP-Comm.
Paul Glyer, Sr. VP-Investor Rel.
Melina Cimler, Sr. VP-Quality & Regulatory Affairs
Cynthia Collins, Group VP-Cellular Bus. Group
Richard Creager, Group VP-High Sensitivity Testing Group
Scott Garrett, Chmn.
Pam Miller, Sr. VP-Supply Chain Mgmt.

Phone: 714-871-4848	Fax: 714-773-8613
Toll-Free: 800-742-2345	
Address: 4300 N. Harbor Blvd., Fullerton, CA 92834-3100 US	

GROWTH PLANS/SPECIAL FEATURES:

Beckman Coulter, Inc. develops, manufactures and markets biomedical testing instrument systems, tests and supplies that automate complex biomedical tests. Spanning the biomedical testing continuum, from medical research and clinical trials to laboratory diagnostics and point-of-care testing, the company-installed base of over 200,000 systems provides essential biomedical information to enhance health care around the world. The firm's predominate customer base includes hospital clinical laboratories, physicians' offices, group practices, commercial reference laboratories, universities, medical research laboratories, pharmaceutical companies and biotechnology firms. Based on profitability, the company has four focus segments: chemistry systems; immunoassay systems; cellular systems; and discovery and automation systems. The firm's revenue is about evenly divided between sales inside and outside the U.S. Sales to clinical laboratories represent approximately 80% of its total revenue, with the balance coming from the life science research market. About 78% of the company's total revenue is generated by the recurring sale of consumable supplies, test kits, services and operating-type lease payments. Central laboratories of mid- to large-size hospitals represent Beckman Coulter's most significant customer group. In August 2008, Beckman Coulter acquired the worldwide diagnostics assets of Nephromics, LLC. In April 2009, the company acquired Cogenics, the genomics services division of Clinical Data, Inc. with operations in the U.S., the U.K., Germany and France, for approximately $17 million.

Beckman Coulter offers its employees health and other insurance benefits, paid vacations and holidays, tuition assistance and retirement savings plans.

FINANCIALS: Sales and profits are in thousands of dollars—add 000 to get the full amount. 2008 Note: Financial information for 2008 was not available for all companies at press time.

2008 Sales: $3,098,900	2008 Profits: $194,000	**U.S. Stock Ticker: BEC**
2007 Sales: $2,761,300	2007 Profits: $211,300	**Int'l Ticker:** Int'l Exchange:
2006 Sales: $2,528,500	2006 Profits: $186,900	Employees: 11,000
2005 Sales: $2,443,800	2005 Profits: $150,600	Fiscal Year Ends: 12/31
2004 Sales: $2,408,300	2004 Profits: $210,900	Parent Company:

SALARIES/BENEFITS:

Pension Plan: Y	ESOP Stock Plan:	Profit Sharing:	Top Exec. Salary: $915,569	Bonus: $690,000
Savings Plan: Y	Stock Purch. Plan:		Second Exec. Salary: $498,568	Bonus: $274,936

OTHER THOUGHTS:

Apparent Women Officers or Directors: 5
Hot Spot for Advancement for Women/Minorities: Y

LOCATIONS: ("Y" = Yes)

West:	Southwest:	Midwest:	Southeast:	Northeast:	International:
Y			Y		Y

Note: Financial information, benefits and other data can change quickly and may vary from those stated here.

BECTON DICKINSON & CO

www.bd.com

Industry Group Code: 33911 Ranks within this company's industry group: Sales: 5   Profits: 5

Management:		Sales/Marketing:		Liberal Arts:		Information Systems:		Professionals:		Tech./Scientific:	
Management Trainees:	Y	Marketing Pros.:	Y	Gen. Writing/Editing:	Y	Info. Management:	Y	Finance/Acct.:	Y	Engineers, Electrical:	Y
Experienced Mngmt.:	Y	Retail Sales:		Technical Writing:	Y	Software Dev.:	Y	Law:	Y	Engineers, Other:	Y
International Business:	Y	Commercial/Industrial:	Y	Graphic Arts/Photog.:	Y	Hardware Dev.:		HR/Other:	Y	Health/Lab:	Y
MBA Grads:	Y	Sales Trainees:		Music:		Consulting/Other:		Training:	Y	Scientists/Research:	Y
		Advertising Pros.:	Y	Broadcasting:				Health Care:	Y	Petroleum/Chemicals:	
				Other:				Consulting:		Math/Other:	

TYPES OF BUSINESS:

Medical Equipment-Injection/Infusion
Drug Delivery Systems
Infusion Therapy Products
Diabetes Care Products
Surgical Products
Microbiology Products
Diagnostic Products
Consulting Services

BRANDS/DIVISIONS/AFFILIATES:

Becton Dickinson Medical
Becton Dickinson Biosciences
Becton Dickinson Diagnostics
Vacutainer
Hypak
Cytopeia
BD BACTEC FX Blood Culture System

CONTACTS: *Note: Officers with more than one job title may be intentionally listed here more than once.*

Edward J. Ludwig, CEO
Vincent A. Forlenza, Pres.
David V. Elkins, CFO/Exec. VP
Donna M. Boles, Sr. VP-Human Resources
Scott P. Bruder, CTO/Sr. VP
Jeffrey S. Sherman, General Counsel/Sr. VP
Richard K. Berman, Treas./VP
Gary M. Cohen, Exec. VP
William A. Kozy, Exec. VP
A. John Hanson, Exec. VP
Mark H. Borofsky, VP-Taxes
Edward J. Ludwig, Chmn.

Phone: 201-847-6800	Fax: 201-847-6475
Toll-Free: 800-284-6845	
Address: 1 Becton Dr., Franklin Lakes, NJ 07417-1880 US	

GROWTH PLANS/SPECIAL FEATURES:

Becton, Dickinson & Co. (BD) manufactures and sells a broad line of medical supplies, devices and diagnostic systems used by health care professionals, medical research institutions and the general public. The company operates in three segments: medical, biosciences and diagnostics. The medical segment offers hypodermic products, specially designed devices for diabetes care; prefillable drug delivery systems; and infusion therapy products. It also offers anesthesia and surgical products; ophthalmic surgery devices; critical care systems; elastic support products; and thermometers. The biosciences segment offers industrial microbiology products; cellular analysis systems; research; and clinical reagents for cellular and nucleic acid analysis; cell culture labware and growth media; hematology instruments; and other diagnostic systems, including immunodiagnostic test kits. The diagnostics segment offers specimen collection products and services, consulting services and customized, automated barcode systems for patient identification and point-of-care data capture. Two of BD's most popular products are Hypak prefillable syringes and Vacutainer blood-collection products. Outside of the U.S., BD's products are manufactured and sold in Europe, Japan, Mexico, Asia Pacific, Canada and Brazil. In May 2008, the company acquired Cytopeia, a developer and marketer of advanced flow cytometry cell sorting instrument. In June 2008, the firm launched the BD BACTEC FX Blood Culture System for detecting infections in the bloodstream.

FINANCIALS: Sales and profits are in thousands of dollars—add 000 to get the full amount. 2008 Note: Financial information for 2008 was not available for all companies at press time.

2008 Sales: $7,155,910	2008 Profits: $1,127,000	**U.S. Stock Ticker: BDX**	
2007 Sales: $6,359,700	2007 Profits: $890,000	Int'l Ticker:	Int'l Exchange:
2006 Sales: $5,738,000	2006 Profits: $752,300	Employees: 28,300	
2005 Sales: $5,340,800	2005 Profits: $722,300	Fiscal Year Ends: 9/30	
2004 Sales: $4,934,745	2004 Profits: $467,402	Parent Company:	

SALARIES/BENEFITS:

Pension Plan: Y	ESOP Stock Plan:	Profit Sharing:	Top Exec. Salary: $1,059,846	Bonus: $1,526,179
Savings Plan: Y	Stock Purch. Plan:		Second Exec. Salary: $667,162	Bonus: $675,000

OTHER THOUGHTS:

Apparent Women Officers or Directors: 6
Hot Spot for Advancement for Women/Minorities: Y

LOCATIONS: ("Y" = Yes)

West:	Southwest:	Midwest:	Southeast:	Northeast:	International:
Y	Y	Y	Y	Y	Y

Note: Financial information, benefits and other data can change quickly and may vary from those stated here.

BED BATH & BEYOND INC

www.bedbathandbeyond.com

Industry Group Code: 442299 Ranks within this company's industry group: Sales: 1 Profits: 1

Management:		Sales/Marketing:		Liberal Arts:		Information Systems:		Professionals:		Tech./Scientific:	
Management Trainees:	Y	Marketing Pros.:	Y	Gen. Writing/Editing:	Y	Info. Management:	Y	Finance/Acct.:	Y	Engineers, Electrical:	
Experienced Mngmt.:	Y	Retail Sales:	Y	Technical Writing:		Software Dev.:	Y	Law:	Y	Engineers, Other:	
International Business:	Y	Commercial/Industrial:	Y	Graphic Arts/Photog.:	Y	Hardware Dev.:		HR/Other:	Y	Health/Lab:	
MBA Grads:	Y	Sales Trainees:	Y	Music:		Consulting/Other:		Training:	Y	Scientists/Research:	
		Advertising Pros.:	Y	Broadcasting:				Health Care:		Petroleum/Chemicals:	
				Other:				Consulting:		Math/Other:	

TYPES OF BUSINESS:

Linens & Housewares, Retail
Small Appliances
Home Accessories
Health & Beauty Care
Baby & Toddler Merchandise

BRANDS/DIVISIONS/AFFILIATES:

Bed Bath & Beyond Superstores
Harmon Stores, Inc.
Christmas Tree Shops
buybuy BABY
Home & More

CONTACTS: Note: Officers with more than one job title may be intentionally listed here more than once.

Steven H. Temares, CEO
Arthur Stark, Pres.
Eugene A. Castagna, CFO/Treas./Pres., Buy Buy Baby, Inc.
Rita Little, VP-Mktg.
Concetta Van Dyke, VP-Human Resources
Kevin R. Murphy, CIO/VP
Kevin Wanner, VP-Tech. & Oper.
Arthur Stark, Chief Merch. Officer
Allan N. Rauch, General Counsel/VP-Legal
Richard McMahon, VP-Corp. Oper.
Richard McMahon, Chief Strategy Officer
Joseph P. Rowland, VP-e-Service Oper.
Ronald Curwin, Sr. VP-Investor Rel.
Susan E. Lattmann, VP-Finance
Matthew Fiorilli, Sr. VP-Stores
Chuck Bilezikian, CEO-Christmas Tree Shops, Inc.
G. William Waltzinger, Jr., Pres., Harmon Stores, Inc.
Leonard Feinstein, Co-Chmn.
Warren Eisenberg, Co-Chmn.
Teresa A. Miller, VP-Purchasing

Phone: 908-688-0888	Fax: 908-688-6483
Toll-Free: 800-462-3966	
Address: 650 Liberty Ave., Union, NJ 07083 US	

GROWTH PLANS/SPECIAL FEATURES:

Bed Bath & Beyond, Inc. (BBB) is one of the nation's largest operators of domestic superstores, with more 1,044 stores in 49 states, as well as Washington D.C., Canada and Puerto Rico. BBB operates four retail entities: Bed Bath and Beyond; Harmon; buybuy BABY; and Christmas Tree Shops. Bed Bath and Beyond, with 935 stores, offers a full line of domestic merchandise and home furnishings. The firm's domestic merchandise line includes items such as bed linens, bath accessories and kitchen tiles, while its home furnishings line includes a variety of cookware, dinnerware and glassware. Harmon and Harmon Face Values stores sell beauty care products in 40 stores in New York, New Jersey and Connecticut. Buybuy BABY is a retailer of infant and toddler merchandise, with 18 stores in Florida, Georgia, Illinois, Indiana, Maryland, Michigan, New Jersey, New York, Ohio, Texas and Virginia. Christmas Tree Shops offer giftware, household items and furnishings in 53 stores in 14 states. Additionally, the company operates two stores in Mexico under the name Home & More. BBB relies on paid advertising and uses circulars and mailing pieces as its primary vehicles. In addition, the company only has three central distribution centers, since the majority of merchandise is shipped to each store from the firm's vendors. The company is engaged in an ongoing expansion program involving the opening of new stores in both existing and new markets, as well as the expansion or replacement of existing stores with larger ones. Local store managers have significant influence over the merchandise they carry.

Employees are offered health insurance; a retirement plan and a 401(k) plan.

FINANCIALS: Sales and profits are in thousands of dollars—add 000 to get the full amount. 2008 Note: Financial information for 2008 was not available for all companies at press time.

2008 Sales: $7,048,942	2008 Profits: $562,808	U.S. Stock Ticker: BBBY
2007 Sales: $6,617,429	2007 Profits: $594,244	Int'l Ticker: Int'l Exchange:
2006 Sales: $5,809,562	2006 Profits: $572,847	Employees: 37,000
2005 Sales: $5,147,678	2005 Profits: $504,964	Fiscal Year Ends: 2/28
2004 Sales: $4,477,981	2004 Profits: $399,470	Parent Company:

SALARIES/BENEFITS:

Pension Plan: Y	ESOP Stock Plan:	Profit Sharing:	Top Exec. Salary: $1,468,269	Bonus: $
Savings Plan: Y	Stock Purch. Plan:		Second Exec. Salary: $1,100,000	Bonus: $

OTHER THOUGHTS:

Apparent Women Officers or Directors: 10
Hot Spot for Advancement for Women/Minorities: Y

LOCATIONS: ("Y" = Yes)

West:	Southwest:	Midwest:	Southeast:	Northeast:	International:
Y	Y	Y	Y	Y	Y

Note: Financial information, benefits and other data can change quickly and may vary from those stated here.

BENCHMARK ELECTRONICS INC

www.bench.com

Industry Group Code: 334419 **Ranks within this company's industry group:** Sales: 2   Profits: 4

Management:		Sales/Marketing:		Liberal Arts:		Information Systems:		Professionals:		Tech./Scientific:	
Management Trainees:	Y	Marketing Pros.:	Y	Gen. Writing/Editing:		Info. Management:	Y	Finance/Acct.:	Y	Engineers, Electrical:	Y
Experienced Mngmt.:	Y	Retail Sales:		Technical Writing:	Y	Software Dev.:	Y	Law:	Y	Engineers, Other:	Y
International Business:	Y	Commercial/Industrial:	Y	Graphic Arts/Photog.:	Y	Hardware Dev.:	Y	HR/Other:	Y	Health/Lab:	
MBA Grads:	Y	Sales Trainees:		Music:		Consulting/Other:	Y	Training:	Y	Scientists/Research:	
		Advertising Pros.:	Y	Broadcasting:				Health Care:		Petroleum/Chemicals:	
				Other:				Consulting:		Math/Other:	

TYPES OF BUSINESS:

Contract Manufacturing-Printed Circuit Boards
Design & Engineering

BRANDS/DIVISIONS/AFFILIATES:

Pemstar, Inc.

CONTACTS: *Note: Officers with more than one job title may be intentionally listed here more than once.*

Cary T. Fu, CEO
Gayla J. Delly, Pres.
Donald F. Adam, CFO
Kenneth S. Barrow, Sec.

Phone: 979-849-6550	**Fax:** 979-848-5270
Toll-Free:	
Address: 3000 Technology Dr., Angleton, TX 77515 US	

GROWTH PLANS/SPECIAL FEATURES:

Benchmark Electronics, Inc. provides contract-manufacturing services for complex printed circuit boards and related electronics systems and subsystems. Benchmark primarily serves original equipment manufacturers (OEMs) of computers and related products for business enterprises, medical devices, industrial control equipment, testing and instrumentation products, and telecommunications equipment. The firm provides comprehensive and integrated design and manufacturing services, from initial product design to volume production and direct order fulfillment. In addition, the company offers specialized engineering services including product design, printed circuit board layout, prototyping and test development. Substantially all of Benchmark's manufacturing services are provided on a turnkey basis (though some are provided on consignment), whereby it purchases customer-specified components from its suppliers, assembles the components on finished printed circuit boards, performs post-production testing and provides production process and testing documentation. Benchmark offers flexible, just-in-time delivery programs allowing product shipments to be closely coordinated with customer inventory requirements. In addition to traditional manufacturing technologies, the company also provides its customers with a comprehensive set of advanced solutions, including pin-through-hole, surface mount, chip-on-board, fine pitch and ball grid array. The firm has 20 manufacturing facilities worldwide, operating a total of 144 surface mount production lines, where electrical components are soldered directly onto printed circuit boards. Benchmark operates domestic facilities in Alabama, Minnesota, New Hampshire, North Dakota, Oregon and Texas, totaling approximately 1.4 million square feet. Operations outside the U.S., totaling 1.3 million square feet, include Brazil, China, Ireland, Malaysia, Mexico, the Netherlands, Romania, Singapore and Thailand, providing international customers with a combination of strategic regional locations and global procurement capabilities. In 2007, the firm acquired Pemstar, Inc., a provider of engineering, design and manufacturing services, for $300 million. In 2008, Benchmark partnered with Silicon Graphics, Inc., to help create NASA's new Pleiades supercomputer system.

FINANCIALS: Sales and profits are in thousands of dollars—add 000 to get the full amount. 2008 Note: Financial information for 2008 was not available for all companies at press time.

2008 Sales: $2,590,167	2008 Profits: $-135,632	**U.S. Stock Ticker:** BHE
2007 Sales: $2,915,919	2007 Profits: $93,282	**Int'l Ticker:** Int'l Exchange:
2006 Sales: $2,907,304	2006 Profits: $111,677	Employees: 10,522
2005 Sales: $2,257,225	2005 Profits: $80,589	Fiscal Year Ends: 12/31
2004 Sales: $2,001,340	2004 Profits: $70,991	Parent Company:

SALARIES/BENEFITS:

Pension Plan:	ESOP Stock Plan:	Profit Sharing:	Top Exec. Salary: $671,154	Bonus: $112,083
Savings Plan:	Stock Purch. Plan:		Second Exec. Salary: $470,096	Bonus: $58,762

OTHER THOUGHTS:

Apparent Women Officers or Directors: 1
Hot Spot for Advancement for Women/Minorities:

LOCATIONS: ("Y" = Yes)

West:	Southwest:	Midwest:	Southeast:	Northeast:	International:
Y	Y	Y	Y	Y	Y

BERKSHIRE HATHAWAY INC

www.berkshirehathaway.com

Industry Group Code: 55111 Ranks within this company's industry group: Sales: 1 Profits: 1

Management:		Sales/Marketing:		Liberal Arts:		Information Systems:		Professionals:		Tech./Scientific:	
Management Trainees:	Y	Marketing Pros.:	Y	Gen. Writing/Editing:	Y	Info. Management:	Y	Finance/Acct.:	Y	Engineers, Electrical:	Y
Experienced Mngmt.:	Y	Retail Sales:	Y	Technical Writing:	Y	Software Dev.:	Y	Law:	Y	Engineers, Other:	
International Business:	Y	Commercial/Industrial:	Y	Graphic Arts/Photog.:	Y	Hardware Dev.:		HR/Other:	Y	Health/Lab:	
MBA Grads:	Y	Sales Trainees:	Y	Music:		Consulting/Other:		Training:	Y	Scientists/Research:	
		Advertising Pros.:	Y	Broadcasting:				Health Care:		Petroleum/Chemicals:	
				Other:	Y			Consulting:		Math/Other:	Y

TYPES OF BUSINESS:

Direct Property & Casualty Insurance & Reinsurance
Retail Operations
Foodservice Operations
Building Products & Services
Apparel & Footwear
Technology Training
Manufactured Housing & RVs
Business Jet Flexible Ownership Services

BRANDS/DIVISIONS/AFFILIATES:

General Re Corporation
GEICO Corporation
International Dairy Queen
Benjamin Moore & Co
Netjets Inc
Cort Business Services Corporation
Clayton Homes Inc
Borsheim Jewelry Company, Inc.

CONTACTS: Note: Officers with more than one job title may be intentionally listed here more than once.

Warren Buffet, CEO
Marc D. Hamburg, CFO/Sr. VP
Forrest N. Krutter, Sec.
Charles Munger, Vice Chmn.
Warren Buffet, Chmn.

Phone: 402-346-1400	Fax: 402-346-3375
Toll-Free:	
Address: 3555 Farnam St., Ste. 1440, Omaha, NE 68131 US	

GROWTH PLANS/SPECIAL FEATURES:

Berkshire Hathaway, Inc. is a holding company that owns subsidiaries engaged in diverse business activities, most importantly insurance and reinsurance. Berkshire provides property and casualty insurance and reinsurance, as well as life accident and health reinsurance, through approximately 60 U.S. and foreign businesses. General Re Corp., through its subsidiaries, conducts global reinsurance business in 55 cities and provides reinsurance worldwide. GEICO mainly provides private passenger auto insurance to individuals in 49 states in the U.S. and Washington, D.C. The company's financial subsidiaries include Clayton Homes, a manufactured housing company; XTRA Corporation, a provider of transportation equipment leases; and furniture rental company CORT Business Services Corp. Berkshire's apparel and footwear businesses include Fruit of the Loom; Garan; Fechheimer Brothers; H.H. Brown Shoe Group; and Justin Brands. The firm manufactures and distributes building products through Acme Building Brands; Benjamin Moore & Co.; Johns Manville; and MiTek. Subsidiary FlightSafety provides training to aircraft and ship pilots, while NetJets, Inc. offers fractional ownership programs for aircraft. In addition, subsidiary International Dairy Queen services approximately 5,700 Dairy Queen, Orange Julius and Karmelkorn stores. Marmon Holdings, Inc. consists of approximately 130 manufacturing and service businesses. Borsheim Jewelry Company, Inc. is a retailer of fine jewelry, watches, crystal, china, stemware, flatware, gifts and collectibles. Other non-insurance operations include grocery and foodservice distribution, furniture retail, carpet manufacturing, utilities and energy, newspapers, cleaning products, confectioneries, agricultural equipment, kitchen tools and recreational vehicles. In September 2008, Berkshire invested $5 billion in banking firm Goldman Sachs, retaining the option to invest up to $10 billion total over the next five years.

FINANCIALS: Sales and profits are in thousands of dollars—add 000 to get the full amount. 2008 Note: Financial information for 2008 was not available for all companies at press time.

2008 Sales: $107,786,000	2008 Profits: $4,994,000	**U.S. Stock Ticker: BRK.A**
2007 Sales: $118,245,000	2007 Profits: $13,213,000	**Int'l Ticker:** Int'l Exchange:
2006 Sales: $98,539,000	2006 Profits: $11,015,000	Employees: 246,000
2005 Sales: $81,663,000	2005 Profits: $8,528,000	Fiscal Year Ends: 12/31
2004 Sales: $74,382,000	2004 Profits: $7,308,000	Parent Company:

SALARIES/BENEFITS:

Pension Plan: Y	ESOP Stock Plan:	Profit Sharing:	Top Exec. Salary: $775,000	Bonus: $
Savings Plan:	Stock Purch. Plan:		Second Exec. Salary: $100,000	Bonus: $

OTHER THOUGHTS:

Apparent Women Officers or Directors: 2
Hot Spot for Advancement for Women/Minorities: Y

LOCATIONS: ("Y" = Yes)

West:	Southwest:	Midwest:	Southeast:	Northeast:	International:
Y	Y	Y	Y	Y	Y

Note: Financial information, benefits and other data can change quickly and may vary from those stated here.

BEST BUY CO INC

www.bestbuy.com

Industry Group Code: 44311 Ranks within this company's industry group: Sales: 1   Profits: 1

Management:		Sales/Marketing:		Liberal Arts:		Information Systems:		Professionals:		Tech./Scientific:	
Management Trainees:	Y	Marketing Pros.:	Y	Gen. Writing/Editing:	Y	Info. Management:	Y	Finance/Acct.:	Y	Engineers, Electrical:	
Experienced Mngmt.:	Y	Retail Sales:	Y	Technical Writing:		Software Dev.:	Y	Law:	Y	Engineers, Other:	
International Business:	Y	Commercial/Industrial:	Y	Graphic Arts/Photog.:	Y	Hardware Dev.:		HR/Other:	Y	Health/Lab:	
MBA Grads:	Y	Sales Trainees:	Y	Music:		Consulting/Other:		Training:	Y	Scientists/Research:	
		Advertising Pros.:	Y	Broadcasting:				Health Care:		Petroleum/Chemicals:	
				Other:	Y			Consulting:		Math/Other:	

TYPES OF BUSINESS:

Consumer Electronics Stores
Retail Music & Video Sales
Personal Computers
Office Supplies
Cell Phones and Accessories
Appliances
Cameras
Consumer Electronics Installation & Service

BRANDS/DIVISIONS/AFFILIATES:

Geek Squad
Best Buy Mobile
Napster
Insignia
Pacific Sales
Speakeasy, Inc.
Phone House (The)
Carphone Warehouse (The)

CONTACTS: *Note: Officers with more than one job title may be intentionally listed here more than once.*

Brian J. Dunn, CEO
James L. Muehlbauer, CFO/Exec. VP-Finance
Barry J. Judge, Chief Mktg. Officer
John E. Pershing, Exec. VP-Human Capital
Robert A. Willett, CIO
Joseph M. Joyce, General Counsel/Sr. VP
Susan S. Grafton, Chief Acct. Officer/Controller/VP
Shari L. Ballard, Exec. VP-Retail Channel Mgmt.
Michael J. Pratt, Pres., Best Buy Canada
Scott Wheway, CEO-Best Buy Europe
Kalendu Patel, Exec. VP-Emerging Bus.
Richard M. Schulze, Chmn.
Robert A. Willett, CEO-Best Buy Int'l

Phone: 612-291-1000	Fax: 612-292-4001
Toll-Free: 888-237-8289	
Address: 7601 Penn Ave. S., Richfield, MN 55423 US	

GROWTH PLANS/SPECIAL FEATURES:

Best Buy Co., Inc. is a retailer of name-brand consumer electronics, entertainment software and appliances. The company conducts business in the domestic and international markets. The domestic market includes Best Buy; Best Buy Mobile; Geek Squad, a provider of computer repair services; Magnolia Audio Video; Pacific Sales Kitchen and Bath Centers; Napster, an online provider of digital music; and Speakeasy, a provider of broadband, voice and data services to small business. The international segment, in Canada and China, includes Best Buy; Geek Squad; Future Shop, an electronics retailer; and Five Star, an appliance retailer. The company's products include home office equipment; cameras; computer and audio/video equipment furniture; computer upgrades; and car audio and security system installation. In Europe, the firm focuses mainly on mobile products and operates under the brand names The Carphone Warehouse, The Phone House and Geek Squad. Best Buy operates 1,023 retail stores in the U.S., 58 Best Buy stores in Canada, five Best Buy Stores in China, one Best Buy Store in Mexico, 38 U.S. Best Buy mobile stand-alone stores, 34 Pacific Sales stores, 897 The Carphone Warehouse stores, 1,568 The Phone House stores, 164 Five Star Stores six Magnolia Audio Video Stores and 139 Future Shop stores. Best Buy is rolling out a chain of smaller stores and kiosks that sell cell phones, calling plans and accessories. It hopes to eventually capture a 15% share of the handset market. In October 2008, the company acquired Napster, Inc.

Employees are offered medical, dental, vision and life insurance; disability coverage; 401(k) plans; an employee stock purchase plan; bonus/incentive program; tuition assistance; adoption assistance; and employee discount.

FINANCIALS: Sales and profits are in thousands of dollars—add 000 to get the full amount. 2008 Note: Financial information for 2008 was not available for all companies at press time.

2008 Sales: $40,023,000	2008 Profits: $1,407,000	U.S. Stock Ticker: BBY
2007 Sales: $35,934,000	2007 Profits: $1,377,000	Int'l Ticker: Int'l Exchange:
2006 Sales: $30,848,000	2006 Profits: $1,140,000	Employees: 155,000
2005 Sales: $27,433,000	2005 Profits: $984,000	Fiscal Year Ends: 2/28
2004 Sales: $24,547,000	2004 Profits: $704,000	Parent Company:

SALARIES/BENEFITS:

Pension Plan:	ESOP Stock Plan:	Profit Sharing:	Top Exec. Salary: $1,247,311	Bonus: $
Savings Plan: Y	Stock Purch. Plan: Y		Second Exec. Salary: $792,393	Bonus: $1,808,134

OTHER THOUGHTS:

Apparent Women Officers or Directors: 3
Hot Spot for Advancement for Women/Minorities: Y

LOCATIONS: ("Y" = Yes)

West:	Southwest:	Midwest:	Southeast:	Northeast:	International:
Y	Y	Y	Y	Y	Y

Note: Financial information, benefits and other data can change quickly and may vary from those stated here.

BIO RAD LABORATORIES INC

www.bio-rad.com

Industry Group Code: 33911 **Ranks within this company's industry group:** Sales: 12 Profits: 12

Management:		Sales/Marketing:		Liberal Arts:		Information Systems:		Professionals:		Tech./Scientific:	
Management Trainees:	Y	Marketing Pros.:	Y	Gen. Writing/Editing:	Y	Info. Management:	Y	Finance/Acct.:	Y	Engineers, Electrical:	Y
Experienced Mngmt.:	Y	Retail Sales:		Technical Writing:	Y	Software Dev.:	Y	Law:	Y	Engineers, Other:	Y
International Business:	Y	Commercial/Industrial:	Y	Graphic Arts/Photog.:	Y	Hardware Dev.:		HR/Other:	Y	Health/Lab:	Y
MBA Grads:	Y	Sales Trainees:		Music:		Consulting/Other:		Training:	Y	Scientists/Research:	Y
		Advertising Pros.:	Y	Broadcasting:				Health Care:	Y	Petroleum/Chemicals:	
				Other:				Consulting:		Math/Other:	

TYPES OF BUSINESS:

Equipment-Life Sciences Research
Clinical Diagnostics Products
Analytical Instruments
Laboratory Devices
Biomaterials
Imaging Products
Assays
Software

BRANDS/DIVISIONS/AFFILIATES:

DiaMed Holding AG
BioPlex 2200
iScript
ProteOn XPR36

CONTACTS: *Note: Officers with more than one job title may be intentionally listed here more than once.*

Norman Schwartz, CEO
Norman Schwartz, Pres.
Christine Tsingos, CFO/VP
Colleen Corey, Dir.-Corp. Human Resources
Sanford S. Wadler, General Counsel/VP/Sec.
Tina Cuccia, Mgr.-Corp. Comm.
James R. Stark, Corp. Controller
Ronald W. Hutton, Treas.
Brad Crutchfield, VP/Group Mgr.-Life Science
John Goetz, VP/Group Mgr.-Clinical Diagnostics
David Schwartz, Chmn.
Giovanni Magni, VP/Mgr.-Int'l Sales

Phone: 510-724-7000	**Fax:** 510-741-5815
Toll-Free: 800-424-6723	
Address: 1000 Alfred Nobel Dr., Hercules, CA 94547 US	

GROWTH PLANS/SPECIAL FEATURES:

Bio-Rad Laboratories, Inc., supplies the life science research, health care and analytical chemistry markets with a broad range of products and systems. These are used to separate complex chemical and biological materials and to identify, analyze and purify components. The company operates in two industry segments: life science and clinical diagnostics. The firm's life science division develops products for applications including electrophoresis, image analysis, molecular detection, chromatography, gene transfer, sample preparation and amplification. Products include a range of laboratory instruments, apparatus and consumables used for research in genomics, proteomics and food safety. The Bio-Rad life science division provides its services to universities; medical schools; pharmaceutical manufacturers; industrial research organizations; food testing laboratories; government agencies; and biotechnology researchers. The clinical diagnostics division encompasses an array of technologies incorporated into a variety of tests used to detect, identify and quantify substances in blood or other body fluids and tissues. The test results are used as aids for medical diagnosis, detection, evaluation, monitoring and treatment of diseases and other conditions. This division is known for diabetes monitoring products, quality control systems, blood virus testing, blood typing, toxicology, genetic disorders products, molecular pathology and Internet-based software. Bio-Rad is also an international provider of bovine spongiform encephalopathy (mad cow disease) tests. Bio-Rad's brand name systems include the BioPlex 2200 multiplex testing platform; iScript, reverse transcription reagent kits; and ProteOn XPR36, a protein interaction array system. In 2008, Bio-Rad acquired additional shares of DiaMed Holding AG, which develops and markets products used in blood typing/screening; the firm now owns 93.46% of DiaMed Holdings. In March 2009, the firm signed an exclusive marketing and development agreement with Bruker Corporation, a manufacturer of mass spectrometry instruments; the companies will work together to develop new products to identify intact peptides and proteins under 30 kilodaltons.

FINANCIALS: Sales and profits are in thousands of dollars—add 000 to get the full amount. 2008 Note: Financial information for 2008 was not available for all companies at press time.

2008 Sales: $1,764,365	2008 Profits: $89,510	**U.S. Stock Ticker: BIO**
2007 Sales: $1,461,052	2007 Profits: $92,994	**Int'l Ticker:** Int'l Exchange:
2006 Sales: $1,273,930	2006 Profits: $103,263	Employees: 6,600
2005 Sales: $1,180,985	2005 Profits: $81,553	Fiscal Year Ends: 12/31
2004 Sales: $1,090,012	2004 Profits: $68,242	Parent Company:

SALARIES/BENEFITS:

Pension Plan:	ESOP Stock Plan:	Profit Sharing:	Top Exec. Salary: $690,450	Bonus: $559,212
Savings Plan: Y	Stock Purch. Plan:		Second Exec. Salary: $520,065	Bonus: $208,000

OTHER THOUGHTS:

Apparent Women Officers or Directors: 3
Hot Spot for Advancement for Women/Minorities: Y

LOCATIONS: ("Y" = Yes)

West:	Southwest:	Midwest:	Southeast:	Northeast:	International:
Y	Y			Y	Y

Note: Financial information, benefits and other data can change quickly and may vary from those stated here.

BJ'S WHOLESALE CLUB INC

www.bjs.com

Industry Group Code: 452112   **Ranks within this company's industry group:**   Sales: 7   Profits: 7

Management:		Sales/Marketing:		Liberal Arts:		Information Systems:		Professionals:		Tech./Scientific:	
Management Trainees:	Y	Marketing Pros.:	Y	Gen. Writing/Editing:	Y	Info. Management:	Y	Finance/Acct.:	Y	Engineers, Electrical:	
Experienced Mngmt.:	Y	Retail Sales:	Y	Technical Writing:		Software Dev.:	Y	Law:	Y	Engineers, Other:	
International Business:		Commercial/Industrial:		Graphic Arts/Photog.:	Y	Hardware Dev.:		HR/Other:	Y	Health/Lab:	
MBA Grads:	Y	Sales Trainees:	Y	Music:		Consulting/Other:		Training:	Y	Scientists/Research:	
		Advertising Pros.:	Y	Broadcasting:				Health Care:		Petroleum/Chemicals:	
				Other:	Y			Consulting:		Math/Other:	

TYPES OF BUSINESS:

Warehouse Clubs, Retail
Gas Stations
Optical Stores
Photo Labs
Travel Services
Pharmacies
Restaurant Supply

BRANDS/DIVISIONS/AFFILIATES:

Inner Circle
Executive Choice
Berkley and Jensen

CONTACTS:
Note: Officers with more than one job title may be intentionally listed here more than once.
Laura Sen, CEO
Laura Sen, Pres.
Frank D. Forward, CFO/Exec. VP
Allison G. Corcoran, Exec. VP-Mktg.
Thomas F. Gallagher, Exec. VP-Store Oper.
Cathy Maloney, VP-Investor Rel.
Herbert J. Zarkin, Chmn.

Phone: 508-651-7400	Fax: 508-651-6114
Toll-Free:	
Address: 1 Mercer Rd., Natick, MA 01760 US	

GROWTH PLANS/SPECIAL FEATURES:

BJ's Wholesale Club, Inc. introduced the warehouse club concept to New England in 1984 and has since expanded to become a leading warehouse club operator in the Eastern U.S. As of January 2009, BJ's operated 180 warehouse clubs in 15 states and sells nearly 7,300 brand-name general merchandise items and food products, with food accounting for approximately 60% of sales. General merchandise items include office supplies, electronics, media, auto accessories, jewelry, books, apparel, toys, personal care items and seasonal items. Food categories include frozen foods, canned goods, fresh produce, dairy products, fresh meat and dry grocery items. Prices are generally lower than those of typical wholesalers and supermarkets. Food accounted for approximately 64% of sales and the remaining 36% consisted of a wide variety of general merchandise items. BJ's offers two types of membership, small business and individual household (also known as the Inner Circle), the latter of which targets home owners with above-average incomes. Both memberships are generally $45 per year, which includes one free supplemental membership, with additional supplemental memberships for $20 each. In addition, the company has its own private labels: Executive Choice for products marketed to business members and Berkley and Jensen for products marketed to Inner Circle members. BJ's also offers its members a number of specialty services, including full-service optical stores, one-hour photo services, travel services, including member discounts on rental cars, food courts, a selection of garden sheds and gazebos, a propane tank filling service and muffler and brake services. BJ's has 102 gas stations currently located at its various clubs. The company attracts potential customers by being the only major warehouse club operator that accepts manufacturers' coupons and several major credit cards.

FINANCIALS:
Sales and profits are in thousands of dollars—add 000 to get the full amount. 2008 Note: Financial information for 2008 was not available for all companies at press time.

2008 Sales: $8,791,618	2008 Profits: $122,861	**U.S. Stock Ticker: BJ**
2007 Sales: $8,280,379	2007 Profits: $72,016	**Int'l Ticker:** Int'l Exchange:
2006 Sales: $7,748,184	2006 Profits: $128,533	Employees: 22,000
2005 Sales: $7,375,300	2005 Profits: $114,400	Fiscal Year Ends: 1/31
2004 Sales: $6,724,219	2004 Profits: $102,866	Parent Company:

SALARIES/BENEFITS:

Pension Plan: Y	ESOP Stock Plan:	Profit Sharing:	Top Exec. Salary: $975,000	Bonus: $
Savings Plan: Y	Stock Purch. Plan:		Second Exec. Salary: $675,000	Bonus: $506,493

OTHER THOUGHTS:

Apparent Women Officers or Directors: 3
Hot Spot for Advancement for Women/Minorities: Y

LOCATIONS: ("Y" = Yes)

West:	Southwest:	Midwest:	Southeast:	Northeast:	International:
		Y	Y	Y	

BLACK & DECKER CORP

www.bdk.com

Industry Group Code: 335   **Ranks within this company's industry group: Sales: 2   Profits: 2**

Management:		Sales/Marketing:		Liberal Arts:		Information Systems:		Professionals:		Tech./Scientific:	
Management Trainees:	Y	Marketing Pros.:	Y	Gen. Writing/Editing:	Y	Info. Management:	Y	Finance/Acct.:	Y	Engineers, Electrical:	Y
Experienced Mngmt.:	Y	Retail Sales:		Technical Writing:	Y	Software Dev.:	Y	Law:	Y	Engineers, Other:	Y
International Business:	Y	Commercial/Industrial:	Y	Graphic Arts/Photog.:	Y	Hardware Dev.:	Y	HR/Other:	Y	Health/Lab:	
MBA Grads:	Y	Sales Trainees:	Y	Music:		Consulting/Other:		Training:	Y	Scientists/Research:	
		Advertising Pros.:	Y	Broadcasting:				Health Care:		Petroleum/Chemicals:	
				Other:	Y			Consulting:		Math/Other:	

TYPES OF BUSINESS:

Power Tools & Accessories Manufacturer
Residential Security Hardware
Household Appliances
Home Improvement Products
Fastening & Assembly Systems
Plumbing Products

BRANDS/DIVISIONS/AFFILIATES:

DeWALT
Dustbuster
Price Pfister
Kwikset
SnakeLight
Delta Machinery
Porter-Cable
Emhart Teknologies

CONTACTS: *Note: Officers with more than one job title may be intentionally listed here more than once.*

Nolan D. Archibald, CEO
Nolan D. Archibald, Pres.
Stephen F. Reeves, CFO/Sr. VP
Paul F. McBride, Sr. VP-Human Resources & Corp. Initiatives
Charles E. Fenton, General Counsel/Sr. VP
James R. Raskin, VP-Bus. Dev.
Mark M. Rothleitner, VP-Investor Rel./Treas.
Christina M. McMullen, Controller/VP
James T. Caudill, VP/Pres., Hardware & Home Improvement Group
Bruce W. Brooks, VP/Pres., Consumer Prod. Group
Natalie A. Shields, VP/Corp. Sec.
Michael A. Tyll, VP/Pres., Fastening & Assembly Systems Group
Nolan D. Archibald, Chmn.

Phone: 410-716-3900	**Fax:** 410-716-2933
Toll-Free: 800-544-6986	
Address: 701 E. Joppa Rd., Towson, MD 21286 US	

GROWTH PLANS/SPECIAL FEATURES:

The Black & Decker Corp. is a global manufacturer and marketer of power tools and accessories; hardware and home improvement products; and technology-based fastening systems. The firm is also a global supplier of engineered fastening and assembly systems. The company's products and services are marketed in over 100 countries in hardware and home improvement stores around the globe. Black & Decker operates in three business segments: power tools and accessories; hardware and home improvement; and fastening and assembly systems. These business segments comprise approximately 73%, 15%, and 12%, respectively, of the corporation's sales. The power tools and accessories segment includes consumer and industrial power tools and accessories; lawn and garden tools; electric cleaning; automotive; lightning products; and product services. In addition, the power pools and accessories segment has responsibility for the sale of security hardware to customers in Mexico, Central America, the Caribbean and South America; for the sale of plumbing products to customers outside of the U.S. and Canada; and for sales of household products, principally in Europe and Brazil. The hardware and home improvement segment includes security hardware such as locksets, keying systems and exit devices; general hardware products including hinges, door stops and kick plates; decorative hardware such as cabinet hardware, switchplates and door pulls; and plumbing products. This section of the company is also responsible for producing faucets. The fastening and assembly systems group manufactures and sells an array of metal and plastic fasteners and engineered fastening systems for commercial applications. The company's product names include DeWALT, Porter-Cable, Delta Machinery and Black and Decker, as well as Price Pfister plumbing products, Kwikset security hardware, Emhart fastening systems, Dustbuster vacuum cleaners and SnakeLight flashlights. The company maintains manufacturing operations in 11 countries.

FINANCIALS: Sales and profits are in thousands of dollars—add 000 to get the full amount. 2008 Note: Financial information for 2008 was not available for all companies at press time.

2008 Sales: $6,086,100	2008 Profits: $293,600	**U.S. Stock Ticker: BDK**
2007 Sales: $6,563,200	2007 Profits: $518,100	**Int'l Ticker:** Int'l Exchange:
2006 Sales: $6,447,300	2006 Profits: $486,100	Employees: 22,100
2005 Sales: $6,523,700	2005 Profits: $5,352,100	Fiscal Year Ends: 12/31
2004 Sales: $5,398,400	2004 Profits: $445,600	Parent Company:

SALARIES/BENEFITS:

Pension Plan:	ESOP Stock Plan:	Profit Sharing:	Top Exec. Salary: $1,500,000	Bonus: $1,875,000
Savings Plan:	Stock Purch. Plan:		Second Exec. Salary: $657,500	Bonus: $630,000

OTHER THOUGHTS:

Apparent Women Officers or Directors: 4
Hot Spot for Advancement for Women/Minorities: Y

LOCATIONS: ("Y" = Yes)

West:	Southwest:	Midwest:	Southeast:	Northeast:	International:
Y			Y	Y	Y

BLACKROCK INC

www.blackrock.com

Industry Group Code: 523920 Ranks within this company's industry group: Sales: 1 Profits: 1

Management:		Sales/Marketing:		Liberal Arts:		Information Systems:		Professionals:		Tech./Scientific:	
Management Trainees:	Y	Marketing Pros.:	Y	Gen. Writing/Editing:	Y	Info. Management:	Y	Finance/Acct.:	Y	Engineers, Electrical:	
Experienced Mngmt.:	Y	Retail Sales:		Technical Writing:		Software Dev.:	Y	Law:	Y	Engineers, Other:	
International Business:	Y	Commercial/Industrial:		Graphic Arts/Photog.:		Hardware Dev.:		HR/Other:	Y	Health/Lab:	
MBA Grads:	Y	Sales Trainees:		Music:		Consulting/Other:		Training:	Y	Scientists/Research:	
		Advertising Pros.:		Broadcasting:				Health Care:		Petroleum/Chemicals:	
				Other:				Consulting:		Math/Other:	

TYPES OF BUSINESS:

Investment Management
Risk Management Services
Investment System Services

BRANDS/DIVISIONS/AFFILIATES:

PNC Financial Services Group, Inc.
BlackRock Solutions
Quellos Group LLC
BlackRock Alternative Advisors
Merrill Lynch
Merrill Lynch Investment Managers
Bank of America

CONTACTS: Note: Officers with more than one job title may be intentionally listed here more than once.

Laurence D. Fink, CEO
Susan Wagner, COO
Ralph L. Schlosstein, Pres.
Paul L. Audet, Acting CFO
Kieth T. Anderson, CIO-Fixed Income
Robert P. Connolly, General Counsel/Managing Dir.
Steven E. Buller, Controller/Head-Global Acct. Policy
Ann Marie Petach, Managing Dir./Head-Bus. Finance
Robert S. Kapito, Vice Chmn./Head-Portfolio Management
Charles S. Hallac, Vice Chmn./Head-Blackrock Solutions
Barbara G. Novick, Vice Chmn./Head-Account Management
Laurence D. Fink, Chmn.
Robert Fairbairn, Vice Chmn./Chmn.-EMEA & Australia

Phone: 212-810-5300	Fax: 212-935-1370
Toll-Free:	
Address: 40 E. 52nd St., New York, NY 10022 US	

GROWTH PLANS/SPECIAL FEATURES:

BlackRock, Inc. and its subsidiaries form one of the largest investment management firms in the US, with $1.26 trillion worth of assets under management on behalf of institutional and individual investors worldwide, through a variety of fixed income, cash management, equity and balanced and alternative investment separate accounts and funds. The company also provides risk management, investment system outsourcing and financial advisory services. Its clients include a diverse group of institutional and retail investors globally. Institutional clients include pension funds, official institutions, foundations, endowments and charities, insurance companies, banks, sub-advisory relationships and private banks in more than 60 countries. The firm also offers risk management and investment system services through its BlackRock Solutions product line. Headquartered in New York, the company maintains offices in 19 countries around the world. Of the firm's total assets under management in 2007, fixed income products represented approximately 38%, equity and balanced products approximately 34%, cash management products approximately 23% and alternative investment products approximately 5%. Approximately 69% of assets were managed for institutions and approximately 31% for retail and high net worth investors. Over one-third of the company's assets are managed on behalf of non-US investors, and nearly one-third of its employees live and work outside the US. In 2007 the company acquired the fund-of-funds business of Quellos Group LLC, resulting in the formation of BlackRock Alternative Advisors. The PNC Financial Services Group holds an interest of approximately 34% in BlackRock, while Merrill Lynch holds approximately 49%, which it acquired in exchange for its Merrill Lynch Investment Managers business, which BlackRock acquired in 2006. Bank of America will take over Merrill Lynch's position as a result of the 2009 merger of Bank of America and Merrill Lynch. In June 2009, BlackRock announced that it would acquire Barclays Global Investors, with more than $1 trillion in assets, from Barclays PLC for approximately $13.5 billion.

The company provides its employees with tuition reimbursement, flexible healthcare and financial services and retirement benefits.

FINANCIALS: Sales and profits are in thousands of dollars—add 000 to get the full amount. 2008 Note: Financial information for 2008 was not available for all companies at press time.

2008 Sales: $5,064,000	2008 Profits: $786,000	**U.S. Stock Ticker: BLK**
2007 Sales: $4,844,655	2007 Profits: $995,272	**Int'l Ticker:** Int'l Exchange:
2006 Sales: $2,097,976	2006 Profits: $322,602	Employees: 5,341
2005 Sales: $1,191,386	2005 Profits: $233,908	Fiscal Year Ends: 12/31
2004 Sales: $725,311	2004 Profits: $143,141	Parent Company:

SALARIES/BENEFITS:

Pension Plan: Y	ESOP Stock Plan:	Profit Sharing:	Top Exec. Salary: $500,000	Bonus: $11,372,500
Savings Plan:	Stock Purch. Plan:		Second Exec. Salary: $400,000	Bonus: $8,720,760

OTHER THOUGHTS:

Apparent Women Officers or Directors: 3
Hot Spot for Advancement for Women/Minorities: Y

LOCATIONS: ("Y" = Yes)

West:	Southwest:	Midwest:	Southeast:	Northeast:	International:
Y		Y		Y	Y

BLOOMBERG LP

www.bloomberg.com

Industry Group Code: 519130 **Ranks within this company's industry group:** Sales: 3 Profits:

Management:		Sales/Marketing:		Liberal Arts:		Information Systems:		Professionals:		Tech./Scientific:	
Management Trainees:	Y	Marketing Pros.:	Y	Gen. Writing/Editing:	Y	Info. Management:	Y	Finance/Acct.:	Y	Engineers, Electrical:	Y
Experienced Mngmt.:	Y	Retail Sales:		Technical Writing:	Y	Software Dev.:	Y	Law:	Y	Engineers, Other:	
International Business:	Y	Commercial/Industrial:	Y	Graphic Arts/Photog.:	Y	Hardware Dev.:	Y	HR/Other:	Y	Health/Lab:	
MBA Grads:	Y	Sales Trainees:	Y	Music:		Consulting/Other:		Training:	Y	Scientists/Research:	
		Advertising Pros.:	Y	Broadcasting:				Health Care:		Petroleum/Chemicals:	
				Other:	Y			Consulting:		Math/Other:	

TYPES OF BUSINESS:

Financial Data Publishing-Print & Online
Magazine Publishing
Management Software
Multimedia Presentation Services
Broadcast Television
Radio Broadcasting
Electronic Exchange Systems
Software

BRANDS/DIVISIONS/AFFILIATES:

Bloomberg Professional
Bloomberg Terminals
Bloomberg Tradebook
Bloomberg Electronic Trading Systems
Bloomberg Roadshows
Bloomberg Television
Bloomberg Magazine
Bloomberg News

CONTACTS: *Note: Officers with more than one job title may be intentionally listed here more than once.*

Lex Fenwick, CEO
Daniel L. Doctoroff, Pres.
Thomas Secunda, CTO
Peter T. Grauer, Treas.
Norman Pearlstine, Chief Content Officer
Kathleen Campion, Exec. VP
Peter T. Grauer, Chmn.

Phone: 212-318-2000	Fax: 917-369-5000
Toll-Free:	
Address: 731 Lexington Ave., New York, NY 10022 US	

GROWTH PLANS/SPECIAL FEATURES:

Bloomberg LP is an information services, news and media company, serving the financial services industry; government offices and agencies; corporations; and news organizations in 160 countries. The firm's core business, the Bloomberg Professional service, is delivered online to Bloomberg Terminals rented by subscribers. The terminals provide traders and asset managers real-time, around-the-clock financial news, market data, analysis, electronic trading, multimedia report capabilities and e-mail on a single platform at an average monthly fee of about $1,500 per terminal. There are four primary services included with Bloomberg Professional. Bloomberg Tradebook allows customers to trade on 65 markets in 54 countries. Bloomberg Electronic Trading Systems allows the firm's professional services to work in conjunction with outside infrastructure and includes a global risk-management software solution and a portfolio management system. Bloomberg Data License provides access to the Bloomberg financial database and to more than 4 million financial instruments. Finally, Bloomberg Roadshows is a multimedia presentation service featuring synchronized slides, audio, streaming video and live video technology. The company also offers Bloomberg Television, broadcasting in seven languages across 10 networks into 200 million homes; Bloomberg Radio, providing business news to 750 affiliates worldwide; Bloomberg.com, offering financial news and information; and Bloomberg Magazine, specially edited for Bloomberg Professional subscribers. Bloomberg Law provides legal research tools. Finally, Bloomberg News, staffed with 1,500 reporters and editors in 145 bureaus worldwide, files over 6,000 news stories daily. In July 2008, Merrill Lynch sold its 20% interest in the company to a blind trust owned by Michael Bloomberg.

Bloomberg offers its employees tuition reimbursement; adoption assistance; back-up childcare services; short- and long-term disability insurance; medical, dental and vision care benefits; onsite medical services; commuter expense saving programs; and flexible spending accounts.

FINANCIALS: Sales and profits are in thousands of dollars—add 000 to get the full amount. 2008 Note: Financial information for 2008 was not available for all companies at press time.

2008 Sales: $6,100,000	2008 Profits: $	**U.S. Stock Ticker: Private**
2007 Sales: $5,400,000	2007 Profits: $	**Int'l Ticker:** Int'l Exchange:
2006 Sales: $4,700,000	2006 Profits: $1,500,000	Employees: 10,000
2005 Sales: $4,100,000	2005 Profits: $	Fiscal Year Ends: 12/31
2004 Sales: $3,100,000	2004 Profits: $	Parent Company:

SALARIES/BENEFITS:

Pension Plan:	ESOP Stock Plan:	Profit Sharing:	Top Exec. Salary: $	Bonus: $
Savings Plan: Y	Stock Purch. Plan:		Second Exec. Salary: $	Bonus: $

OTHER THOUGHTS:

Apparent Women Officers or Directors: 2
Hot Spot for Advancement for Women/Minorities: Y

LOCATIONS: ("Y" = Yes)

West:	Southwest:	Midwest:	Southeast:	Northeast:	International:
Y	Y	Y	Y	Y	Y

BOEING COMPANY (THE)

www.boeing.com

Industry Group Code: 33641 **Ranks within this company's industry group:** Sales: 1 Profits: 4

Management:		Sales/Marketing:		Liberal Arts:		Information Systems:		Professionals:		Tech./Scientific:	
Management Trainees:	Y	Marketing Pros.:	Y	Gen. Writing/Editing:	Y	Info. Management:	Y	Finance/Acct.:	Y	Engineers, Electrical:	Y
Experienced Mngmt.:	Y	Retail Sales:		Technical Writing:	Y	Software Dev.:	Y	Law:	Y	Engineers, Other:	Y
International Business:	Y	Commercial/Industrial:	Y	Graphic Arts/Photog.:	Y	Hardware Dev.:	Y	HR/Other:	Y	Health/Lab:	
MBA Grads:	Y	Sales Trainees:		Music:		Consulting/Other:	Y	Training:	Y	Scientists/Research:	Y
		Advertising Pros.:	Y	Broadcasting:				Health Care:		Petroleum/Chemicals:	
				Other:	Y			Consulting:		Math/Other:	Y

TYPES OF BUSINESS:

Commercial Aircraft Manufacturing
Aerospace Technology & Manufacturing
Military Aircraft
Satellite Manufacturing
Communications Products & Services
Air Traffic Management Technology
Financing Services
Research & Development

BRANDS/DIVISIONS/AFFILIATES:

Boeing Business Jets
787 Dreamliner
Integrated Defense Systems
Boeing Capital
Phantom Works
AH-64D Apache
Spectrolab Inc
Aviall Inc

CONTACTS: *Note: Officers with more than one job title may be intentionally listed here more than once.*

W. James McNerney, Jr., CEO
W. James McNerney, Jr., Pres.
James A. Bell, CFO/Exec. VP
Richard Stephens, Sr. VP-Human Resources
John J. Tracy, CTO/Sr. VP-Eng. & Oper. Bus. Unit
Richard Stephens, Sr. VP-Admin.
J. Michael Luttig, General Counsel/Sr. VP
Michael J. Cave, Sr. VP-Bus. Dev. & Strategy
Thomas J. Downey, Sr. VP-Comm.
James F. Albaugh, CEO/Pres., Integrated Defense Systems/Exec. VP
Scott E. Carson, CEO/Pres., Commercial Airplanes/Exec. VP
Timothy Keating, Sr. VP-Public Policy
Wanda K. Denson-Low, Sr. VP-Office of Internal Governance
W. James McNerney, Jr., Chmn.
Shephard W. Hill, Pres., Boeing Int'l

Phone: 312-544-2000	**Fax:** 312-544-2082
Toll-Free:	
Address: 100 N. Riverside, Chicago, IL 60606 US	

GROWTH PLANS/SPECIAL FEATURES:

The Boeing Company is one of the world's major aerospace firms. The company operates in three segments: commercial airplanes (CA); integrated defense systems, which is comprised of precision engagement and mobility systems (PE&MS), network and space systems (N&SS) and support systems; and Boeing Capital Corp. CA develops, produces and markets commercial jet aircraft and provides related support services. The family of jet aircraft includes the 737 Next-Generation narrow-body model and the 747, 767, 777 and the new 787 Dreamliner wide-body models. The division also offers aviation support, aircraft modifications, training, maintenance documents and technical advice to commercial customers worldwide. The integrated defense systems segment researches, develops, produces, modifies and supports products and related systems and services such as military aircraft, including fighters, transports, tankers and helicopters; missiles; space systems; missile defense systems; satellites and satellite launch vehicles; and communications, information and battle management systems. The PE&MS subdivision oversees precision engagement and mobility products and services. The N&SS subdivision provides products and services to assist customers in transforming operations through network integration, intelligence and surveillance systems, communications and space exploration. The support systems subdivision is engaged in operations, maintenance, and logistics support functions for military platforms. Boeing Capital Corp. provides financing to CA customers. Boeing's other businesses include Connection by Boeing, a high speed broadband communications business; and Engineering, Operations and Technology, a research and development organization. The 787 Dreamliner is Boeing's exciting, new-generation aircraft. It is manufactured of extremely light components that, combined with advanced technology jet engines, will enable the aircraft to enjoy very high fuel efficiency. It will seat 210-250 passengers, with a maximum range of 9,266 miles. Unfortunately, the aircraft's launch date has been delayed several times, making it nearly two years late. A trial flight scheduled for June 2009 was postponed.

The company offers its employees health, disability and life insurance; and an employee assistance program.

FINANCIALS: Sales and profits are in thousands of dollars—add 000 to get the full amount. 2008 Note: Financial information for 2008 was not available for all companies at press time.

2008 Sales: $60,909,000	2008 Profits: $2,672,000	**U.S. Stock Ticker: BA**
2007 Sales: $66,387,000	2007 Profits: $4,074,000	**Int'l Ticker:** Int'l Exchange:
2006 Sales: $61,530,000	2006 Profits: $2,215,000	Employees: 162,200
2005 Sales: $53,621,000	2005 Profits: $2,572,000	Fiscal Year Ends: 12/31
2004 Sales: $51,400,000	2004 Profits: $1,872,000	Parent Company:

SALARIES/BENEFITS:

Pension Plan: Y	ESOP Stock Plan:	Profit Sharing:	Top Exec. Salary: $1,915,288	Bonus: $6,089,625
Savings Plan: Y	Stock Purch. Plan:		Second Exec. Salary: $930,269	Bonus: $2,381,468

OTHER THOUGHTS:

Apparent Women Officers or Directors: 3
Hot Spot for Advancement for Women/Minorities: Y

LOCATIONS: ("Y" = Yes)

West:	Southwest:	Midwest:	Southeast:	Northeast:	International:
Y	Y	Y	Y	Y	Y

Note: Financial information, benefits and other data can change quickly and may vary from those stated here.

BOOZ ALLEN HAMILTON   www.boozallen.com

Industry Group Code: 54161 **Ranks within this company's industry group:** Sales: 3   Profits:

Management:		Sales/Marketing:		Liberal Arts:		Information Systems:		Professionals:		Tech./Scientific:	
Management Trainees:	Y	Marketing Pros.:	Y	Gen. Writing/Editing:	Y	Info. Management:	Y	Finance/Acct.:	Y	Engineers, Electrical:	
Experienced Mngmt.:	Y	Retail Sales:		Technical Writing:	Y	Software Dev.:	Y	Law:	Y	Engineers, Other:	
International Business:	Y	Commercial/Industrial:	Y	Graphic Arts/Photog.:	Y	Hardware Dev.:		HR/Other:	Y	Health/Lab:	
MBA Grads:	Y	Sales Trainees:		Music:		Consulting/Other:	Y	Training:	Y	Scientists/Research:	
		Advertising Pros.:	Y	Broadcasting:				Health Care:		Petroleum/Chemicals:	
				Other:	Y			Consulting:	Y	Math/Other:	Y

TYPES OF BUSINESS:

Strategy Consulting
Engineering & IT Consulting
Supply Chain Management
Industry Research & Publications
War Gaming & Strategic Simulation

BRANDS/DIVISIONS/AFFILIATES:

Carlyle Group (The)

CONTACTS: Note: Officers with more than one job title may be intentionally listed here more than once.

Ralph W. Shrader, CEO
Samuel R. Strickland, CFO/Sr. VP
Horacio D. Rozanski, VP/Chief Personnel Officer
Samuel R. Strickland, Chief Admin. Officer/Sr. VP
C. G. Appleby, Chief Legal Officer
Francis J. Henry, Sr. VP-Finance
Dennis O. Doughty, Pres., US Gov't Bus.
Joseph E. Garner, Sr. VP-Defense Market Bus.
Lloyd Howell, Jr., Sr. VP-Organization & Strategy Bus.
John M. (Mike) McConnell, Sr. VP-National Security Bus.
Ralph W. Shrader, Chmn.

Phone: 703-902-5000	Fax: 703-902-3333
Toll-Free:	
Address: 8283 Greensboro Dr., McLean, VA 22102 US	

GROWTH PLANS/SPECIAL FEATURES:

Booz Allen Hamilton, founded in 1914, is a global strategy and technology consulting firm with operations on six continents. Booz Allen's major areas of expertise include corporate finance and business analysis; information technology; marketing and sales; mergers and restructuring; operations and logistics; organization and change; product and service innovation; public sector mission effectiveness; strategy and leadership; and systems engineering and integration. The company serves such market sectors as aerospace, automotive, chemicals, defense, energy, environment, financial services, government departments, health, homeland security, media, non-profits, oil, retail, technology, telecommunications and transportation. Some of Booz Allen's commercial clients have included Aetna, Boeing, BP, MTV, Pfizer, RJ Reynolds and Vodafone. The company's work with national governments around the world has included projects to enhance national security, economic well-being and the health and safety of citizens. Some of Booz Allen's largest clients have included the U.S. Department of Defense; the Air Force, Army, Navy and Marine Corps; the U.S. Departments of Energy, Health, Human Services, Homeland Security, Justice, Labor, Transportation and Treasury; NASA; the U.S. Centers for Disease Control and Prevention; the U.S. Environmental Protection Agency; the U.S. General Services Administration; and the U.S. Internal Revenue Service. The company's work for other governments includes assignments with the U.K. Department for Work and Pensions as well as government institutions in Abu Dhabi, Australia, Germany, Italy, Jordan and New Zealand. The company also publishes books, reports and studies on industry subjects ranging from information technology to leadership. In July 2008, the firm completed the spin-off of all business units that do not provide consulting to the U.S. government into a new company called Booz & Company. It also sold a majority stake in its U.S. Government business (Booz Allen Hamilton) to The Carlyle Group for approximately $2.54 billion.

FINANCIALS: Sales and profits are in thousands of dollars—add 000 to get the full amount. 2008 Note: Financial information for 2008 was not available for all companies at press time.

2008 Sales: $3,680,000	2008 Profits: $	**U.S. Stock Ticker:** Private
2007 Sales: $3,147,000	2007 Profits: $	**Int'l Ticker:** Int'l Exchange:
2006 Sales: $2,846,000	2006 Profits: $	Employees: 20,000
2005 Sales: $3,500,000	2005 Profits: $	Fiscal Year Ends: 3/31
2004 Sales: $3,300,000	2004 Profits: $	Parent Company:

SALARIES/BENEFITS:

Pension Plan:	ESOP Stock Plan:	Profit Sharing: Y	Top Exec. Salary: $	Bonus: $
Savings Plan: Y	Stock Purch. Plan:		Second Exec. Salary: $	Bonus: $

OTHER THOUGHTS:

Apparent Women Officers or Directors:
Hot Spot for Advancement for Women/Minorities:

LOCATIONS: ("Y" = Yes)

West:	Southwest:	Midwest:	Southeast:	Northeast:	International:
Y	Y	Y	Y	Y	Y

Note: Financial information, benefits and other data can change quickly and may vary from those stated here.

BOSTON SCIENTIFIC CORP

www.bostonscientific.com

Industry Group Code: 33911 Ranks within this company's industry group: Sales: 4 Profits: 15

Management:		Sales/Marketing:		Liberal Arts:		Information Systems:		Professionals:		Tech./Scientific:	
Management Trainees:	Y	Marketing Pros.:	Y	Gen. Writing/Editing:	Y	Info. Management:	Y	Finance/Acct.:	Y	Engineers, Electrical:	
Experienced Mngmt.:	Y	Retail Sales:		Technical Writing:	Y	Software Dev.:	Y	Law:	Y	Engineers, Other:	Y
International Business:	Y	Commercial/Industrial:	Y	Graphic Arts/Photog.:	Y	Hardware Dev.:		HR/Other:	Y	Health/Lab:	Y
MBA Grads:	Y	Sales Trainees:		Music:		Consulting/Other:		Training:	Y	Scientists/Research:	Y
		Advertising Pros.:	Y	Broadcasting:				Health Care:	Y	Petroleum/Chemicals:	
				Other:				Consulting:		Math/Other:	

TYPES OF BUSINESS:

Supplies-Surgery
Interventional Medical Products
Catheters
Guide wires
Stents
Oncology Research

BRANDS/DIVISIONS/AFFILIATES:

LATITUDE Patient Management
Synchro2 Guidewires
Afocus Steerable Diagnostic Catheter
Inquiry H-Curve Steerable Diagnostic Catheter
EndoVive
LeVeen Needle Electrode
ALTRUA
PROENCY

CONTACTS: *Note: Officers with more than one job title may be intentionally listed here more than once.*

Ray Elliott, CEO
Paul A. LaViolette, COO
Ray Elliott, Pres.
Samuel R. Leno, CFO/Exec. VP-Finance
William F. McConnell, Jr., VP-Sales, Mktg. & Bus. Strategy
Lucia Luce Quinn, Exec. VP-Human Resources
Donald S. Baim, Chief Medical & Scientific Officer/Exec. VP
Samuel R. Leno, Exec. VP-Info. Systems
Timothy Pratt, General Counsel/Sec./Exec. VP
Kenneth J. Pucel, Exec. VP-Oper.
Jim Gilbert, Exec. VP-Strategy & Bus. Dev.
Paul Donovan, Sr. VP-Corp. Comm.
Jeffrey D. Capello, Controller/Chief Acct. Officer/Sr, VP
Stephen F. Moreci, Sr. VP/Group Pres., Endosurgery
Fredericus A. Colen, Exec. VP/Group Pres., CRM
William H. Kucheman, Sr. VP/Group Pres., Cardiovascular
Michael Onuscheck, Sr. VP/Group Pres., Neuromodulation
Peter M. Nicholas, Chmn.
David McFaul, Sr. VP-Int'l

Phone: 508-650-8000	Fax: 508-650-8923
Toll-Free: 888-272-1001	
Address: 1 Boston Scientific Pl., Natick, MA 01760-1537 US	

GROWTH PLANS/SPECIAL FEATURES:

Boston Scientific Corp., with operations in over 45 countries, manufactures minimally invasive medical devices intended as an alternative to major surgical procedures that reduces risk, trauma, cost, procedure time and the need for aftercare. The company's products are used in a wide range of interventional medical applications, including cardiology; oncology; gastroenterology; vascular surgery; neurovascular therapy; radiology; urology; and pain management. Products include AFocus and Inquiry H-Curve Steerable Diagnostic Catheters; LIVIAN Cardiac Resynchronization Therapy Defibrillator; ALTRUA pacemakers; EndoVive feeding tubes; WallFlex stents; TLC retractor; Synchro2 Guidewires; and LeVeen Needle Electrode. Stents account for 20% of sales. Recent product developments include drug-eluting stents, which have been proven more effective than bare metal stents; the LATITUDE Patient Management system which allows clinicians to store information from a patient's implanted cardiac device into GE Healthcare's Centricity Electronic Medical Record. In January 2008, the firm sold its auditory business and drug pump development program to previous shareholders of Boston Scientific's subsidiary, Advanced Bionics; it also sold its Vascular and Cardiac Surgery businesses to Getinge Group for $750 million. In February 2008, Boston Scientific launched PROENCY European registry to compare different coronary stents, and sold its Venous Access and Fluid Management businesses to Avista Capital Partners. In March 2008, the company sold subsidiary Boston Scientific Santa Rosa Corp. to TV2 Holding Company for $30 million. In April 2008, the firm signed a licensing agreement with Surgi-Vision, Inc., to develop/market MRI-safe cardiac devices. In May 2008, Boston Scientific acquired CryoCor, Inc., for approximately $17.6 million. In June 2008, the company agreed to sell various venture fund and company investments to secondary investment firms Saints Capital and Paul Capital Partners. In January 2009, Boston Scientific acquired Labcoat Ltd., a drug-eluting stent developer. In March 2009, the company released TAXUS Liberte, a drug-eluding stent, in Japan.

FINANCIALS: Sales and profits are in thousands of dollars—add 000 to get the full amount. 2008 Note: Financial information for 2008 was not available for all companies at press time.

2008 Sales: $8,050,000	2008 Profits: $-2,036,000	**U.S. Stock Ticker: BSX**
2007 Sales: $8,357,000	2007 Profits: $-495,000	**Int'l Ticker:** Int'l Exchange:
2006 Sales: $7,821,000	2006 Profits: $-3,577,000	Employees: 24,800
2005 Sales: $6,283,000	2005 Profits: $628,000	Fiscal Year Ends: 12/31
2004 Sales: $5,624,000	2004 Profits: $1,062,000	Parent Company:

SALARIES/BENEFITS:

Pension Plan:	ESOP Stock Plan: Y	Profit Sharing:	Top Exec. Salary: $989,572	Bonus: $885,664
Savings Plan: Y	Stock Purch. Plan:		Second Exec. Salary: $746,721	Bonus: $675,000

OTHER THOUGHTS:

Apparent Women Officers or Directors: 5
Hot Spot for Advancement for Women/Minorities: Y

LOCATIONS: ("Y" = Yes)

West:	Southwest:	Midwest:	Southeast:	Northeast:	International:
Y	Y	Y	Y	Y	Y

Note: Financial information, benefits and other data can change quickly and may vary from those stated here.

BRINKER INTERNATIONAL INC

www.brinker.com

Industry Group Code: 722110   Ranks within this company's industry group: Sales: 4   Profits: 8

Management:		Sales/Marketing:		Liberal Arts:		Information Systems:		Professionals:		Tech./Scientific:	
Management Trainees:	Y	Marketing Pros.:	Y	Gen. Writing/Editing:	Y	Info. Management:	Y	Finance/Acct.:	Y	Engineers, Electrical:	
Experienced Mngmt.:	Y	Retail Sales:		Technical Writing:		Software Dev.:	Y	Law:	Y	Engineers, Other:	
International Business:	Y	Commercial/Industrial:		Graphic Arts/Photog.:	Y	Hardware Dev.:		HR/Other:	Y	Health/Lab:	
MBA Grads:	Y	Sales Trainees:		Music:		Consulting/Other:		Training:	Y	Scientists/Research:	
		Advertising Pros.:	Y	Broadcasting:				Health Care:		Petroleum/Chemicals:	
				Other:	Y			Consulting:		Math/Other:	

TYPES OF BUSINESS:

Casual Dining Restaurants
Cafes

BRANDS/DIVISIONS/AFFILIATES:

Chili's Grill and Bar
Romano's Macaroni Grill
On the Border Mexican Grill and Cantina
Maggiano's Little Italy

CONTACTS: *Note: Officers with more than one job title may be intentionally listed here more than once.*

Douglas H. Brooks, CEO
Douglas H. Brooks, Pres.
Charles M. Sonsteby, CFO/Exec. VP
Michael B. Webberman, Exec. VP-Brand Solutions
Valerie L. Davisson, Exec. VP-PeopleWorks
Roger F. Thomson, Chief Admin. Officer/Exec. VP
Roger F. Thomson, General Counsel/Sec.
Todd E. Diener, Pres., Chili's Grill & Bar
Wyman T. Roberts, Pres., Maggiano's Little Italy
Michael B. Webberman, Exec. VP-Brand Solutions
Douglas H. Brooks, Chmn.
Greg Walther, Pres., Global Bus. Dev.

Phone: 972-980-9917	Fax:
Toll-Free:	
Address: 6820 LBJ Fwy., Dallas, TX 75240 US	

GROWTH PLANS/SPECIAL FEATURES:

Brinker International, Inc. owns, operates, develops and franchises approximately 1,700 casual dining restaurant chains in 29 countries. Chili's Grill & Bar serves lunch and dinner, also offering a To-Go menu. Entree selections for Chili's range in price from approximately $6 to $18. On The Border is a Mexican restaurant known for its fajitas and margaritas. On The Border also offers a To-Go entrance and a catering service. Entrees for On The Border range in price from approximately $8-14. Maggiano's Little Italy is a classic Italian-American restaurant, featuring individual and family style menus and extensive banquet facilities. Entrée selections for Maggiano's range in price from approximately $8-39. The firm also has a minority stake in Romano's Macaroni Grill is an Italian restaurant featuring brick ovens, festive string lights and a selection of wines. Entrée selections for Macaroni Grill range in price from approximately $9-20. Brinker also grows through franchises and joint ventures, most revolving around Chili's Grill and Bar. The company plans to open 500 new restaurants outside the U.S. from 2009 through 2014. In 2009, it opened its first locations in El Salvador, Turkey, Singapore and India (where it will feature an 80% vegetarian menu). In August 2009, the firm signed an agreement with Trio's Group Ltd. to expand Chili's to Russia. It plants to open 25 restaurants in Russia by 2017.

Employees are offered medical, dental and vision insurance; life insurance; disability coverage; health and dependent care flexible spending accounts; and reimbursement programs.

FINANCIALS: Sales and profits are in thousands of dollars—add 000 to get the full amount. 2008 Note: Financial information for 2008 was not available for all companies at press time.

2008 Sales: $4,235,223	2008 Profits: $51,722	**U.S. Stock Ticker: EAT**	
2007 Sales: $4,376,904	2007 Profits: $230,049	**Int'l Ticker:** Int'l Exchange:	
2006 Sales: $4,151,291	2006 Profits: $212,395	Employees: 77,100	
2005 Sales: $3,749,291	2005 Profits: $160,219	Fiscal Year Ends: 6/30	
2004 Sales: $3,541,005	2004 Profits: $150,918	Parent Company:	

SALARIES/BENEFITS:

Pension Plan:	ESOP Stock Plan:	Profit Sharing:	Top Exec. Salary: $900,000	Bonus: $333,333
Savings Plan:	Stock Purch. Plan:		Second Exec. Salary: $628,852	Bonus: $146,898

OTHER THOUGHTS:

Apparent Women Officers or Directors: 3
Hot Spot for Advancement for Women/Minorities: Y

LOCATIONS: ("Y" = Yes)

West:	Southwest:	Midwest:	Southeast:	Northeast:	International:
Y	Y	Y	Y	Y	Y

Note: Financial information, benefits and other data can change quickly and may vary from those stated here.

BRINKS COMPANY (THE)

www.brinkscompany.com

Industry Group Code: 5616 **Ranks within this company's industry group:** Sales: 1 Profits: 1

Management:		Sales/Marketing:		Liberal Arts:		Information Systems:		Professionals:		Tech./Scientific:	
Management Trainees:	Y	Marketing Pros.:	Y	Gen. Writing/Editing:	Y	Info. Management:	Y	Finance/Acct.:	Y	Engineers, Electrical:	
Experienced Mngmt.:	Y	Retail Sales:		Technical Writing:		Software Dev.:	Y	Law:	Y	Engineers, Other:	
International Business:	Y	Commercial/Industrial:	Y	Graphic Arts/Photog.:	Y	Hardware Dev.:		HR/Other:	Y	Health/Lab:	
MBA Grads:	Y	Sales Trainees:	Y	Music:		Consulting/Other:		Training:	Y	Scientists/Research:	
		Advertising Pros.:	Y	Broadcasting:				Health Care:		Petroleum/Chemicals:	
				Other:				Consulting:		Math/Other:	

TYPES OF BUSINESS:

Security Services
Armored Car Transport
Document Shredding Services
ATM Servicing
Safe Services
Currency & Deposit Processing
Residential Security Systems & Electronics

BRANDS/DIVISIONS/AFFILIATES:

Brink's, Inc.
CompuSafe
SCS Technology
Secure Data Solutions
Brink's-Seguranca e Transporte de Valores Ltda

CONTACTS: Note: Officers with more than one job title may be intentionally listed here more than once.

Michael T. Dan, CEO
Michael T. Dan, Pres.
Michael J. Cazer, CFO/VP
Frank T. Lennon, Chief Admin. Officer/VP
McAlister C. Marshall, General Counsel/VP/Sec.
Jonathan Leon, Treas.
Arthur E. Wheatley, VP-Risk Mgmt. & Insurance
Matthew A.P. Schumacher, Controller
Michael T. Dan, Chmn.

Phone: 804-289-9600	**Fax:** 804-289-9770
Toll-Free:	
Address: 1801 Bayberry Ct., Richmond, VA 23226-1800 US	

GROWTH PLANS/SPECIAL FEATURES:

The Brink's Company conducts business in the security industry through Brink's, Inc.
Based in Richmond, Virginia the company has operations in roughly 50 countries. North American operations include 182 branches in the U.S. and 55 branches in Canada. Brink's, Inc. provides armored-car transportation; automated teller machine (ATM) services; currency and deposit processing; coin sorting; check and cash processing services; guarding services, including airport security; and secure air transportation of valuable property, including its patented CompuSafe service. CompuSafe is utilized by a number of the firm's cash-intensive retail customers, including convenience stores, gas stations and restaurants. The service includes installing a specialized safe in the retail establishment that holds safeguarded cassettes. The customer's employees deposit currency into the cassettes, which can only be removed by Brink's armored car personnel. Brinks, Inc. also provides secure document destruction services through its SCS Technology, an advanced size-based shredding system, as well as Secure Data Solutions, which provides customers with domestic and international solutions for transferring, storing and destroying sensitive information. In November 2008, the company completed the spin-off of its home security business, Brink's Home Security Holdings, Inc. The same year, the firm sold certain coal assets to Massey Energy Company for $9.4 million. In January 2009, the company's Brazil-based subsidiary, Brink's-Seguranca e Transporte de Valores Ltda. acquired Brazilian security companies, Seival-Seguranca Bancaria Industrial e Valores Ltda. and Setal Servicos Especializados, Technicos e Auxiliares Ltda. for approximately $50 million.

FINANCIALS: Sales and profits are in thousands of dollars—add 000 to get the full amount. 2008 Note: Financial information for 2008 was not available for all companies at press time.

2008 Sales: $3,163,500	2008 Profits: $183,300	**U.S. Stock Ticker:** BCO
2007 Sales: $2,734,600	2007 Profits: $137,300	**Int'l Ticker:**　Int'l Exchange:
2006 Sales: $2,354,300	2006 Profits: $587,200	Employees: 56,900
2005 Sales: $2,505,400	2005 Profits: $142,400	Fiscal Year Ends: 12/31
2004 Sales: $2,277,500	2004 Profits: $121,500	Parent Company:

SALARIES/BENEFITS:

Pension Plan: Y	ESOP Stock Plan:	Profit Sharing:	Top Exec. Salary: $1,101,875	Bonus: $3,309,600
Savings Plan: Y	Stock Purch. Plan:		Second Exec. Salary: $409,167	Bonus: $661,920

OTHER THOUGHTS:

Apparent Women Officers or Directors: 1
Hot Spot for Advancement for Women/Minorities:

LOCATIONS: ("Y" = Yes)

West:	Southwest:	Midwest:	Southeast:	Northeast:	International:
Y	Y	Y	Y	Y	Y

BROADCOM CORP

www.broadcom.com

Industry Group Code: 33441 Ranks within this company's industry group: Sales: 5 Profits: 6

Management:		Sales/Marketing:		Liberal Arts:		Information Systems:		Professionals:		Tech./Scientific:	
Management Trainees:	Y	Marketing Pros.:	Y	Gen. Writing/Editing:		Info. Management:	Y	Finance/Acct.:	Y	Engineers, Electrical:	Y
Experienced Mngmt.:	Y	Retail Sales:		Technical Writing:	Y	Software Dev.:	Y	Law:	Y	Engineers, Other:	
International Business:	Y	Commercial/Industrial:	Y	Graphic Arts/Photog.:	Y	Hardware Dev.:	Y	HR/Other:	Y	Health/Lab:	
MBA Grads:	Y	Sales Trainees:		Music:		Consulting/Other:		Training:	Y	Scientists/Research:	
		Advertising Pros.:	Y	Broadcasting:				Health Care:		Petroleum/Chemicals:	
				Other:				Consulting:		Math/Other:	

TYPES OF BUSINESS:

Integrated Circuits-Broadband Transmission
Communications Products

BRANDS/DIVISIONS/AFFILIATES:

Sunext Design, Inc.

CONTACTS: Note: Officers with more than one job title may be intentionally listed here more than once.

Scott A. McGregor, CEO
Scott A. McGregor, Pres.
Eric K. Brandt, CFO/Sr. VP
Kenneth E. Venner, CIO/Sr. VP
Neil Y. Kim, Sr. VP-Central Eng.
Arthur Chong, General Counsel/Sec./Sr. VP
Robert L. Tirva, Corp. Controller/Principal Acct. Officer/VP
Scott A. Bibaud, Sr. VP/Gen. Mgr.-Mobile Platforms Group
Daniel A. Marotta, Sr. VP/Gen. Mgr.-Broadband Comm. Group
Robert A. Rango, Sr. VP/Gen. Mgr.-Wireless Connectivity Group
Nariman Yousefi, Sr. VP/Gen. Mgr.-Enterprise Networking Group
Thomas F. Lagatta, Sr. VP-Worldwide Sales

Phone: 949-926-5000	Fax: 949-926-5203
Toll-Free:	
Address: 5300 California Ave., Irvine, CA 92617-3038 US	

GROWTH PLANS/SPECIAL FEATURES:

Broadcom Corp. is a developer of semiconductors for wired and wireless communications. The company's products enable the delivery of voice, data and multimedia to and throughout the home, office and mobile environment. Broadcom produces highly integrated silicon chips and software solutions to manufacturers of computing and networking equipment, digital entertainment products, broadband access products and mobile devices. The firm's products target the broadband communications, enterprise networking and mobile and wireless markets. In the broadband communications market, products incorporating Broadcom's solutions include broadband cable modems and residential gateways; cable modem termination systems and central office DSL applications; cable, satellite and IP set-top boxes, media servers and digital converters; high-definition digital televisions; high-definition Blu-ray Disc players and recorders; and personal video recorders. In the enterprise networking markets, products incorporating the firm's solutions include servers; workstations; desktop and notebook computers; service provider metro equipment; switches, hubs and routers; network interface cards; and virtual private networks and security appliances. In the mobile and wireless market, products incorporating Broadcom's solutions include wireless-enabled laptop and desktop computers; home broadband gateways; printers; Voice over Internet Protocol (VoIP) phones; handheld media devices; personal navigation devices; and home gaming and entertainment systems. In March 2008, Broadcom acquired Sunext Design, Inc., which will contribute technology for the development of a Blu-ray DVD disk platform. In October 2008, the firm acquired AMD's digital television business.

Broadcom offers its employees tuition reimbursement, credit union membership, an employee assistance program, flexible spending accounts, health care benefits, disability programs and dental and vision care plans.

FINANCIALS: Sales and profits are in thousands of dollars—add 000 to get the full amount. 2008 Note: Financial information for 2008 was not available for all companies at press time.

2008 Sales: $4,658,125	2008 Profits: $214,794	**U.S. Stock Ticker:** BRCM	
2007 Sales: $3,776,395	2007 Profits: $213,342	**Int'l Ticker:** Int'l Exchange:	
2006 Sales: $3,667,818	2006 Profits: $379,041	Employees: 7,402	
2005 Sales: $2,670,788	2005 Profits: $367,089	Fiscal Year Ends: 12/31	
2004 Sales: $2,400,610	2004 Profits: $173,185	Parent Company:	

SALARIES/BENEFITS:

Pension Plan:	ESOP Stock Plan:	Profit Sharing:	Top Exec. Salary: $679,250	Bonus: $615,000
Savings Plan: Y	Stock Purch. Plan: Y		Second Exec. Salary: $360,154	Bonus: $300,000

OTHER THOUGHTS:

Apparent Women Officers or Directors: 1
Hot Spot for Advancement for Women/Minorities:

LOCATIONS: ("Y" = Yes)

West:	Southwest:	Midwest:	Southeast:	Northeast:	International:
Y	Y	Y	Y	Y	Y

Note: Financial information, benefits and other data can change quickly and may vary from those stated here.

BROWN & BROWN INC

www.bbinsurance.com

Industry Group Code: 524210 Ranks within this company's industry group: Sales: 3 Profits: 1

Management:		Sales/Marketing:		Liberal Arts:		Information Systems:		Professionals:		Tech./Scientific:	
Management Trainees:	Y	Marketing Pros.:	Y	Gen. Writing/Editing:	Y	Info. Management:	Y	Finance/Acct.:	Y	Engineers, Electrical:	
Experienced Mngmt.:	Y	Retail Sales:		Technical Writing:	Y	Software Dev.:	Y	Law:	Y	Engineers, Other:	
International Business:	Y	Commercial/Industrial:	Y	Graphic Arts/Photog.:	Y	Hardware Dev.:		HR/Other:	Y	Health/Lab:	
MBA Grads:	Y	Sales Trainees:		Music:		Consulting/Other:		Training:	Y	Scientists/Research:	
		Advertising Pros.:	Y	Broadcasting:				Health Care:		Petroleum/Chemicals:	
				Other:	Y			Consulting:		Math/Other:	

TYPES OF BUSINESS:

Insurance-Property & Casualty
Risk Management Services
Professional Liability Insurance
Third-Party Administration & Consulting
Managed Care & Utilization Management Services
Reinsurance
Life Insurance
Health Insurance

BRANDS/DIVISIONS/AFFILIATES:

One Source Insurance, Inc.
W. R. Reed & Co.
Irving Weber Associates, Inc.

CONTACTS: *Note: Officers with more than one job title may be intentionally listed here more than once.*

J. Powell Brown, CEO
Jim W. Henderson, COO/Vice Chmn.
J. Powell Brown, Pres.
Cory T. Walker, CFO/Sr. VP
Laurel L. Grammig, Chief Corp. Counsel/VP/Sec.
Richard Freebourn, Sr., VP-Internal Oper.
Cory T. Walker, Treas.
Kenneth Kirk, Regional Pres.
Thomas Riley, Regional Pres.
Linda S. Downs, Exec. VP-Leadership Dev.
C. Roy Bridges, Regional Exec. VP
J. Hyatt Brown, Chmn.

Phone: 386-252-9601	Fax: 386-239-5729
Toll-Free:	
Address: 220 S. Ridgewood Ave., Daytona Beach, FL 32114 US	

GROWTH PLANS/SPECIAL FEATURES:

Brown & Brown, Inc. is a diversified insurance agency, wholesale brokerage, insurance programs and service organization. The firm markets and sells insurance products and services, primarily in the property, casualty and employee benefit areas. The company is compensated for its services primarily by commissions paid by insurance companies and by fees paid by customers for certain services. As an agent and broker, Brown & Brown does not assume underwriting risks. The company operates through 219 locations in 37 states and one location in London. It operates through four segments: retail, wholesale brokerage, national programs and services. The retail segment provides a range of insurance products and services to commercial, public entity, professional and individual customers. The wholesale brokerage division markets and sells excess and surplus commercial and personal insurance and reinsurance, primarily through independent agents and brokers. The national programs division consists of two units: professional programs, which provides professional liability and related package products for certain professionals; and special programs, which markets targeted products and services designated for specific industries, trade groups, public entities and market niches. The services division provides clients with third-party claims administration, consulting for the workers' compensation insurance markets, comprehensive medical utilization management services and Medicare Secondary Payer statute compliance-related services. The retail division generated the majority (60.7%) of the company's 2008 revenue, followed by the national programs division (18.4%), the wholesale brokerage division (17.5%), the services division (3.3%) and other operations (0.1%). During 2008, Brown & Brown acquired 43 insurance intermediary operations, including customer accounts. Recent acquisitions include One Source Insurance, Inc. in March 2009; W. R. Reed & Co. in April 2009; and Irving Weber Associates, Inc. in May 2009.

FINANCIALS: Sales and profits are in thousands of dollars—add 000 to get the full amount. 2008 Note: Financial information for 2008 was not available for all companies at press time.

2008 Sales: $977,554	2008 Profits: $166,124	**U.S. Stock Ticker: BRO**
2007 Sales: $959,667	2007 Profits: $190,959	**Int'l Ticker:** Int'l Exchange:
2006 Sales: $878,004	2006 Profits: $172,350	Employees: 5,398
2005 Sales: $785,807	2005 Profits: $150,551	Fiscal Year Ends: 12/31
2004 Sales: $646,934	2004 Profits: $128,843	Parent Company:

SALARIES/BENEFITS:

Pension Plan:	ESOP Stock Plan:	Profit Sharing:	Top Exec. Salary: $658,406	Bonus: $879,752
Savings Plan: Y	Stock Purch. Plan:		Second Exec. Salary: $470,837	Bonus: $781,134

OTHER THOUGHTS:

Apparent Women Officers or Directors: 4
Hot Spot for Advancement for Women/Minorities: Y

LOCATIONS: ("Y" = Yes)

West:	Southwest:	Midwest:	Southeast:	Northeast:	International:
Y	Y	Y	Y	Y	Y

Note: Financial information, benefits and other data can change quickly and may vary from those stated here.

BUCKLE INC (THE)

www.buckle.com

Industry Group Code: 448 Ranks within this company's industry group: Sales: 4 Profits: 4

Management:		Sales/Marketing:		Liberal Arts:		Information Systems:		Professionals:		Tech./Scientific:	
Management Trainees:	Y	Marketing Pros.:	Y	Gen. Writing/Editing:	Y	Info. Management:	Y	Finance/Acct.:	Y	Engineers, Electrical:	
Experienced Mngmt.:	Y	Retail Sales:	Y	Technical Writing:		Software Dev.:	Y	Law:	Y	Engineers, Other:	
International Business:		Commercial/Industrial:		Graphic Arts/Photog.:	Y	Hardware Dev.:		HR/Other:	Y	Health/Lab:	
MBA Grads:	Y	Sales Trainees:	Y	Music:		Consulting/Other:		Training:	Y	Scientists/Research:	
		Advertising Pros.:	Y	Broadcasting:				Health Care:		Petroleum/Chemicals:	
				Other:	Y			Consulting:		Math/Other:	

TYPES OF BUSINESS:

Teen Apparel, Retail
Children's Apparel
Online Sales
Promotional Merchandise

BRANDS/DIVISIONS/AFFILIATES:

Buckle
Buckle [The]
Buckle Screenprinting
buckle.com

CONTACTS: *Note: Officers with more than one job title may be intentionally listed here more than once.*

Dennis Nelson, CEO
Dennis Nelson, Pres.
Karen Rhoads, CFO
Kari Smith, VP-Sales
Patricia Whisler, VP-Women's Merch.
Kyle Hanson, General Counsel
Karen Rhoads, VP-Finance/Treas.
Brett Milkie, VP-Leasing
Robert Carlberg, VP-Men's Merch.
Daniel Hirschfeld, Chmn.

Phone: 308-236-8491	Fax: 308-236-4493
Toll-Free: 800-626-1255	
Address: 2407 W. 24th St., Kearney, NE 68845 US	

GROWTH PLANS/SPECIAL FEATURES:

The Buckle, Inc. is a retailer of medium- to high-priced casual apparel, footwear and accessories primarily for young men and women ages 12-24. The company currently operates more than 390 stores in 40 states throughout the central, northwest, southwest and southeast U.S. These stores operate under the names Buckle and The Buckle. The majority of the stores are located in regional shopping malls, although some are located in strip centers, downtown areas and lifestyle centers. Buckle markets mostly brand-name casual apparel including denims, tops, sportswear, outerwear, accessories and footwear. Brand names such as Lucky Brand Dungarees, Big Star, Silver, Hurley, Affliction, Fossil, MEK, Billabong, Guess, Quiksilver/Roxy, 7 Diamonds, OBEY and Manchester constitute about 72% of overall sales. The remaining merchandise consists of items manufactured to the company's specifications by private labels. The firm emphasizes personalized attention to its customers by providing free alterations, free gift-wrapping and a frequent shopper program. Buckle Screenprinting offers promotional merchandising to outside athletic teams, organizations, clubs and individuals. The company tailors individual store inventories to reflect differences in customer buying patterns by shipping new merchandise daily to most stores through its transfer program. This assures that popular merchandise is in stock and reduces the need to lower the price of low-selling merchandise at a particular location.

Employees are offered medical and dental insurance; disability coverage; life insurance; performance bonuses; an employee assistance program; a 40% merchandise discount; a 401(k) plan; and flexible spending accounts.

FINANCIALS: Sales and profits are in thousands of dollars—add 000 to get the full amount. 2008 Note: Financial information for 2008 was not available for all companies at press time.

2008 Sales: $619,888	2008 Profits: $75,247	**U.S. Stock Ticker:** BKE	
2007 Sales: $530,074	2007 Profits: $55,726	**Int'l Ticker:** Int'l Exchange:	
2006 Sales: $501,101	2006 Profits: $51,906	Employees: 8,225	
2005 Sales: $470,937	2005 Profits: $43,229	Fiscal Year Ends: 1/31	
2004 Sales: $422,820	2004 Profits: $33,745	Parent Company:	

SALARIES/BENEFITS:

Pension Plan:	ESOP Stock Plan:	Profit Sharing:	Top Exec. Salary: $862,000	Bonus: $5,613,503
Savings Plan: Y	Stock Purch. Plan:		Second Exec. Salary: $387,083	Bonus: $2,161,199

OTHER THOUGHTS:

Apparent Women Officers or Directors: 3
Hot Spot for Advancement for Women/Minorities: Y

LOCATIONS: ("Y" = Yes)

West:	Southwest:	Midwest:	Southeast:	Northeast:	International:
Y	Y	Y	Y	Y	

BUCYRUS INTERNATIONAL INC

www.bucyrus.com

Industry Group Code: 33313 Ranks within this company's industry group: Sales: 2 Profits: 2

Management:		Sales/Marketing:		Liberal Arts:		Information Systems:		Professionals:		Tech./Scientific:	
Management Trainees:	Y	Marketing Pros.:	Y	Gen. Writing/Editing:		Info. Management:	Y	Finance/Acct.:	Y	Engineers, Electrical:	Y
Experienced Mngmt.:	Y	Retail Sales:		Technical Writing:	Y	Software Dev.:		Law:	Y	Engineers, Other:	Y
International Business:		Commercial/Industrial:	Y	Graphic Arts/Photog.:	Y	Hardware Dev.:	Y	HR/Other:	Y	Health/Lab:	
MBA Grads:	Y	Sales Trainees:		Music:		Consulting/Other:		Training:	Y	Scientists/Research:	
		Advertising Pros.:		Broadcasting:				Health Care:		Petroleum/Chemicals:	
				Other:				Consulting:		Math/Other:	

TYPES OF BUSINESS:

Mining Equipment Manufacturing

BRANDS/DIVISIONS/AFFILIATES:

OKD, Bastro a.s.
Appalachian Mine Sales, Inc.
DBT GmbH

CONTACTS: *Note: Officers with more than one job title may be intentionally listed here more than once.*

Timothy W. Sullivan, CEO
Kenneth W. Krueger,
Timothy W. Sullivan, Pres.
Craig R. Mackus, CFO
Craig R. Mackus, Corp. Sec.
John F. Bosbous, Treas.
William S. Tate, Exec. VP
Kenneth W. Krueger, COO-Surface
Luis de Leon, COO-Underground
Theodore C. Rogers, Chmn.

Phone: 414-768-4000	Fax: 414-768-4474
Toll-Free:	
Address: 1100 Milwaukee Ave., South Milwaukee, WI 53172 US	

GROWTH PLANS/SPECIAL FEATURES:

Bucyrus International, Inc. is a designer and manufacturer of mining equipment for the extraction of coal, copper, oil sands, iron ore and other minerals in major mining centers throughout the world. In addition to the manufacture of mining equipment, the company also provides aftermarket replacement parts and service for this equipment. Bucyrus operates in two business segments: surface mining and underground mining. The surface mining segment designs, manufactures and markets draglines, electric mining shovels and rotary blasthole drills used for surface mining. The underground mining segment, created following the acquisition of DBT GmbH, manufactures and distributes equipment for coal mining such as hydraulic roof supports and electro-hydraulic controls, automated plow systems, shearers and armored face conveyors, including entry conveyors with a built-in crusher. Additional underground mining products include continuous miners, feeder breakers, battery- and diesel-powered underground utility vehicles, continuous haulage systems, roof bolters and belt systems. All of the firm's products and services are marketed under the Bucyrus name. Bucyrus has manufacturing facilities in Australia, China, Germany, Poland and the U.S., as well as service and sales centers in Australia, Brazil, Canada, Chile, China, the Czech Republic, the U.K., India, Mexico, Peru, Russia, South Africa and the U.S. In October 2008, the company acquired Appalachian Mine Sales, Inc., a belt conveyor manufacturer with a presence in the Appalachia coals fields region. In December 2008, the firm acquired OKD, Bastro a.s., an engineering services and manufacturing support company located in the Czech Republic.

FINANCIALS: Sales and profits are in thousands of dollars—add 000 to get the full amount. 2008 Note: Financial information for 2008 was not available for all companies at press time.

2008 Sales: $2,505,838	2008 Profits: $233,315	**U.S. Stock Ticker: BUCY**
2007 Sales: $1,613,391	2007 Profits: $136,134	**Int'l Ticker:** Int'l Exchange:
2006 Sales: $738,050	2006 Profits: $70,344	Employees: 7,200
2005 Sales: $	2005 Profits: $	Fiscal Year Ends: 12/31
2004 Sales: $	2004 Profits: $	Parent Company:

SALARIES/BENEFITS:

Pension Plan:	ESOP Stock Plan:	Profit Sharing:	Top Exec. Salary: $843,250	Bonus: $1,724,361
Savings Plan:	Stock Purch. Plan:		Second Exec. Salary: $432,634	Bonus: $530,339

OTHER THOUGHTS:

Apparent Women Officers or Directors:
Hot Spot for Advancement for Women/Minorities:

LOCATIONS: ("Y" = Yes)

West:	Southwest:	Midwest:	Southeast:	Northeast:	International:
		Y			

Note: Financial information, benefits and other data can change quickly and may vary from those stated here.

BUFFALO WILD WINGS INC
www.buffalowildwings.com

Industry Group Code: 722110 Ranks within this company's industry group: Sales: 13 Profits: 9

Management:		Sales/Marketing:		Liberal Arts:		Information Systems:		Professionals:		Tech./Scientific:	
Management Trainees:	Y	Marketing Pros.:	Y	Gen. Writing/Editing:	Y	Info. Management:	Y	Finance/Acct.:	Y	Engineers, Electrical:	
Experienced Mngmt.:	Y	Retail Sales:		Technical Writing:		Software Dev.:	Y	Law:	Y	Engineers, Other:	
International Business:		Commercial/Industrial:		Graphic Arts/Photog.:	Y	Hardware Dev.:		HR/Other:	Y	Health/Lab:	
MBA Grads:	Y	Sales Trainees:		Music:		Consulting/Other:		Training:	Y	Scientists/Research:	
		Advertising Pros.:	Y	Broadcasting:				Health Care:		Petroleum/Chemicals:	
				Other:	Y			Consulting:		Math/Other:	

TYPES OF BUSINESS:
Restaurants

BRANDS/DIVISIONS/AFFILIATES:
Buffalo Wild Wings
Wild Flatbreads
Buffalito
Buzztime

CONTACTS: *Note: Officers with more than one job title may be intentionally listed here more than once.*
Sally J. Smith, CEO
Sally J. Smith, Pres.
Mary J. Twinem, CFO/Exec. VP
Kathleen M. Benning, Sr. VP-Mktg. & Brand Dev.
Linda G. Traylor, Sr. VP-Human Resources
James M. Schmidt, General Counsel/Exec. VP
Judith A. Shoulak, Sr. VP-Oper.
Mary J. Twinem, Treas.
Mounir N. Sawda, Sr. VP-Franchise and Dev.
James M. Damian, Chmn.

Phone: 952-593-9943	Fax: 952-593-9787
Toll-Free: 800-499-9586	
Address: 5500 Wayzata Blvd., Ste. 1600, Minneapolis, MN 55416 US	

GROWTH PLANS/SPECIAL FEATURES:

Buffalo Wild Wings, Inc. founded in 1982, is the operator of Buffalo Wild Wings restaurants. The company operates over 600 restaurants in 41 states, of which approximately 215 are company-owned and 385 are franchised. The restaurants serve chicken wings in the Buffalo, New York-style spun in 14 signature sauces. The menu also features chicken tenders, salads, Wild Flatbreads, popcorn shrimp, specialty hamburgers and sandwiches, wraps, Buffalito soft tacos and appetizers, which are made to order and are available for dine-in and take-out. The restaurants are geared toward both sports fans and families and feature a full bar, 13 projection screens where sporting events are shown, as well as 40 additional television sets where customers can play Buzztime trivia and video games. Sales at company-owned restaurants represented 90% of the company's total revenue in 2008. Food and nonalcoholic beverages accounted for 74% of restaurant sales, with 26% from alcoholic beverages. The menu item with the highest sales volume is chicken wings, which account for 20% of total restaurant sales.

Employees are offered medical and dental insurance; vision coverage; short -and long-term disability protection; a bonus plan; an employee stock purchase plan; a 401(k) plan; and an employee assistance program.

FINANCIALS: Sales and profits are in thousands of dollars—add 000 to get the full amount. 2008 Note: Financial information for 2008 was not available for all companies at press time.

2008 Sales: $422,417	2008 Profits: $24,435	U.S. Stock Ticker: BWLD
2007 Sales: $329,652	2007 Profits: $19,654	Int'l Ticker: Int'l Exchange:
2006 Sales: $278,183	2006 Profits: $16,273	Employees: 12,000
2005 Sales: $	2005 Profits: $	Fiscal Year Ends: 12/31
2004 Sales: $	2004 Profits: $	Parent Company:

SALARIES/BENEFITS:

Pension Plan:	ESOP Stock Plan:	Profit Sharing:	Top Exec. Salary: $535,000	Bonus: $454,212
Savings Plan: Y	Stock Purch. Plan: Y		Second Exec. Salary: $335,000	Bonus: $284,419

OTHER THOUGHTS:
Apparent Women Officers or Directors: 5
Hot Spot for Advancement for Women/Minorities: Y

LOCATIONS: ("Y" = Yes)

West:	Southwest:	Midwest:	Southeast:	Northeast:	International:
Y	Y	Y	Y	Y	

BUNGE LTD

www.bunge.com

Industry Group Code: 3112 Ranks within this company's industry group: Sales: 3 Profits: 3

Management:		Sales/Marketing:		Liberal Arts:		Information Systems:		Professionals:		Tech./Scientific:	
Management Trainees:	Y	Marketing Pros.:	Y	Gen. Writing/Editing:		Info. Management:	Y	Finance/Acct.:	Y	Engineers, Electrical:	
Experienced Mngmt.:	Y	Retail Sales:		Technical Writing:		Software Dev.:		Law:	Y	Engineers, Other:	Y
International Business:	Y	Commercial/Industrial:	Y	Graphic Arts/Photog.:	Y	Hardware Dev.:		HR/Other:	Y	Health/Lab:	
MBA Grads:	Y	Sales Trainees:		Music:		Consulting/Other:		Training:	Y	Scientists/Research:	Y
		Advertising Pros.:		Broadcasting:				Health Care:		Petroleum/Chemicals:	
				Other:				Consulting:		Math/Other:	

TYPES OF BUSINESS:

Crop Production, Soybeans
Oils & Shortening
Oilseed Processing
Ingredients & Prepared Foods
Fertilizer
Milling

BRANDS/DIVISIONS/AFFILIATES:

Serrana
Manah
Ouro Verde
IAP
Tate & Lyle plc

CONTACTS: Note: Officers with more than one job title may be intentionally listed here more than once.

Alberto Weisser, CEO
Jacqualyn A. Fouse, CFO
Vicente C. Teixeira, Chief Personnel Officer
Fernando Kfouri, Managing Dir.-Food Products
Sergio Roberto Waldrich, CEO-Bunge Alimentos
Mario A. Barbosa Neto, CEO-Bunge Fertilizantes
Drew Burke, Co-CEO-Bunge Global Agribusiness
Carl L. Hausmann, CEO-Bunge North America
Alberto Weisser, Chmn.
Jean-Louis Gourbin, CEO-Bunge Europe

Phone: 914-684-2800	Fax: 914-684-3499
Toll-Free:	
Address: 50 Main St., 6th Fl., White Plains, NY 10606 US	

GROWTH PLANS/SPECIAL FEATURES:

Bunge, Ltd., founded in 1818, is a Bermuda-based agribusiness and food company with operations in oilseed processing; fertilizer production and supply; and edible oil products supply. Through its facilities in North and South America, the company manufactures fertilizer and animal feed for farmers; transporting oilseeds and grains to markets worldwide; processing oilseeds to produce meal for the livestock industry and oil for the food processing, food service and biofuel industries; produces bottled oils, mayonnaise, margarines and other food products for consumers; and mills wheat and corn for food processors, bakeries, brewers and other commercial customers. The company divides its operations into four segments: agribusiness, fertilizer, edible oil products and milling products. The agribusiness division includes grain and oilseed origination, oilseed processing and international marketing. This segment also offers financial, risk management and identity preservation services. The company's main focus is soybeans, but it also processes and sells rapeseed, sunseed, corn, wheat and other crops and derivative products. The fertilizer division is engaged in all stages of the fertilizer business, from raw material mining and mixing fertilizer components to product marketing, with activities located primarily in Brazil. Bunge markets its fertilizers under the Serrana, Manah, Ouro Verde and IAP brand names. Bunge's edible oil products segment involves the manufacturing and marketing of products derived from vegetable oils. The edible oil products segment has operations in the U.S., Canada, Brazil, India and numerous European countries. The milling products segment involves the manufacturing and marketing of products derived primarily from wheat and corn. In July 2008, Bunge acquired the sugar trading and marketing division of Tate & Lyle plc, an acquisition meant to strengthen the company's position in the sugar value chain. In October 2008, the firm acquired a 50% stake in a Vietnamese port operating company.

FINANCIALS: Sales and profits are in thousands of dollars—add 000 to get the full amount. 2008 Note: Financial information for 2008 was not available for all companies at press time.

2008 Sales: $52,574,000	2008 Profits: $1,064,000	U.S. Stock Ticker: BG
2007 Sales: $37,842,000	2007 Profits: $778,000	Int'l Ticker: Int'l Exchange:
2006 Sales: $26,274,000	2006 Profits: $521,000	Employees: 25,000
2005 Sales: $24,377,000	2005 Profits: $530,000	Fiscal Year Ends: 12/31
2004 Sales: $25,168,000	2004 Profits: $469,000	Parent Company:

SALARIES/BENEFITS:

Pension Plan:	ESOP Stock Plan:	Profit Sharing:	Top Exec. Salary: $1,200,000	Bonus: $3,200,000
Savings Plan:	Stock Purch. Plan:		Second Exec. Salary: $686,667	Bonus: $1,300,000

OTHER THOUGHTS:

Apparent Women Officers or Directors: 1
Hot Spot for Advancement for Women/Minorities:

LOCATIONS: ("Y" = Yes)

West:	Southwest:	Midwest:	Southeast:	Northeast:	International:
		Y		Y	Y

BURGER KING HOLDINGS INC

www.burgerking.com

Industry Group Code: 722110 Ranks within this company's industry group: Sales: 7 Profits: 4

Management:		Sales/Marketing:		Liberal Arts:		Information Systems:		Professionals:		Tech./Scientific:	
Management Trainees:	Y	Marketing Pros.:	Y	Gen. Writing/Editing:	Y	Info. Management:	Y	Finance/Acct.:	Y	Engineers, Electrical:	
Experienced Mngmt.:	Y	Retail Sales:		Technical Writing:		Software Dev.:	Y	Law:	Y	Engineers, Other:	
International Business:	Y	Commercial/Industrial:		Graphic Arts/Photog.:	Y	Hardware Dev.:		HR/Other:	Y	Health/Lab:	
MBA Grads:	Y	Sales Trainees:		Music:		Consulting/Other:		Training:	Y	Scientists/Research:	
		Advertising Pros.:	Y	Broadcasting:				Health Care:		Petroleum/Chemicals:	
				Other:	Y			Consulting:		Math/Other:	

TYPES OF BUSINESS:

Fast Food Restaurants
Franchising

BRANDS/DIVISIONS/AFFILIATES:

Whopper
BK Fish Filet
BK Veggie Burger
Croissan'wich
Fresh Apple Fries
Burger King Europe GmbH

CONTACTS: Note: Officers with more than one job title may be intentionally listed here more than once.

John W. Chidsey, CEO
Ben K. Wells, CFO
Russell B. Klein, Pres., Global Mktg. Strategy & Innovation
Peter C. Smith, Chief Human Resources Officer
Raj Rawal, CIO/Sr. VP
Anne Chwat, General Counsel/Corp. Sec.
Julio Ramirez, Exec. VP-Global Oper.
Amy E. Wagner, Sr. VP-Global Comm.
Amy E. Wagner, Sr. VP-Investor Rel.
Ben K. Wells, Treas.
Chuck Fallon, Pres., North America
Peter Tan, Pres., Asia Pacific
Armando Jacomino, Pres., Latin America
John W. Chidsey, Chmn.
Peter Robinson, VP/Pres., EMEA

Phone: 305-378-3000	**Fax:** 305-378-7262
Toll-Free:	
Address: 5505 Blue Lagoon Dr., Miami, FL 33126 US	

GROWTH PLANS/SPECIAL FEATURES:

Burger King Holdings, Inc., one of the largest fast food restaurant chains in the world, operates approximately 11,800 restaurants in 74 countries and all 50 U.S. states and serves about nearly 12 million customers daily. Approximately 90% of Burger King restaurants are owned and operated by independent franchisees. The company's products include hamburgers, chicken sandwiches and tenders, fish sandwiches, french fries, onion rings and shakes, as well as breakfast items including croissant and sourdough sandwiches, french toast sticks and hash browns. Brand names include the Whopper, BK Fish Filet, BK Veggie Burger and Croissan'wich. In an effort to provide healthier food choices, the firm has added a line of salads to its menu, low-fat versions of existing menu items and Fresh Apple Fries, red apples skinned and sliced to look like french fries. Burger King has also begun to transition to using only trans-fat-free oil. Burger King restaurants typically offer counter service, a dining room and drive-through service. Many franchises offer regional favorites in addition to standard menu items. These offerings include breakfast burritos in the southwestern U.S., garlic-flavored pork Bulgogi Burgers in Korea, Churrasquito steak sandwiches in Argentina and fried Green Tea Pies in Thailand. In November 2008, the company's European subsidiary, Burger King Europe GmbH, announced the opening of the first Burger King in the Czech Republic. In January 2009, the company introduced the Angry WHOPPER sandwich to the menu, which features spicy sauce, crispy onions, jalapenos, pepper jack cheese and bacon. In March 2009, the firm opened the first WHOPPER Bar at Universal CityWalk at Universal Orlando Resort in Florida, which specializes in made-to-order sandwiches and features a topping bar for customers to choose from.

Employees are offered medical, dental and life insurance, as well as a 401(k) plan.

FINANCIALS: Sales and profits are in thousands of dollars—add 000 to get the full amount. 2008 Note: Financial information for 2008 was not available for all companies at press time.

2008 Sales: $2,454,700	2008 Profits: $189,600	**U.S. Stock Ticker:** BKC
2007 Sales: $2,233,700	2007 Profits: $148,100	**Int'l Ticker:** Int'l Exchange:
2006 Sales: $2,048,000	2006 Profits: $27,000	Employees: 41,320
2005 Sales: $1,940,000	2005 Profits: $47,000	Fiscal Year Ends: 6/30
2004 Sales: $1,754,000	2004 Profits: $5,000	Parent Company:

SALARIES/BENEFITS:

Pension Plan:	ESOP Stock Plan:	Profit Sharing:	Top Exec. Salary: $1,012,500	Bonus: $1,306,125
Savings Plan: Y	Stock Purch. Plan:		Second Exec. Salary: $500,000	Bonus: $516,000

OTHER THOUGHTS:

Apparent Women Officers or Directors: 3
Hot Spot for Advancement for Women/Minorities: Y

LOCATIONS: ("Y" = Yes)

West:	Southwest:	Midwest:	Southeast:	Northeast:	International:
Y	Y	Y	Y	Y	Y

Note: Financial information, benefits and other data can change quickly and may vary from those stated here.

CABELA'S INC

www.cabelas.com

Industry Group Code: 451110 **Ranks within this company's industry group: Sales: 3 Profits: 2**

Management:		Sales/Marketing:		Liberal Arts:		Information Systems:		Professionals:		Tech./Scientific:	
Management Trainees:	Y	Marketing Pros.:	Y	Gen. Writing/Editing:	Y	Info. Management:	Y	Finance/Acct.:	Y	Engineers, Electrical:	
Experienced Mngmt.:	Y	Retail Sales:	Y	Technical Writing:		Software Dev.:	Y	Law:	Y	Engineers, Other:	
International Business:	Y	Commercial/Industrial:		Graphic Arts/Photog.:	Y	Hardware Dev.:		HR/Other:	Y	Health/Lab:	
MBA Grads:	Y	Sales Trainees:	Y	Music:		Consulting/Other:		Training:	Y	Scientists/Research:	
		Advertising Pros.:	Y	Broadcasting:				Health Care:		Petroleum/Chemicals:	
				Other:	Y			Consulting:		Math/Other:	

TYPES OF BUSINESS:

Sporting Goods Stores
Hunting & Fishing Supplies
Antique & Collectible Furniture
Outdoor Apparel
Catalog & Online Sales
Credit Cards

BRANDS/DIVISIONS/AFFILIATES:

World's Foremost Bank
Cabela's Club
SIR Warehouse Sports Store
Bargain Cave
Dunn's
VanDyke's
Wild Wings
Club Visa Signature

CONTACTS: *Note: Officers with more than one job title may be intentionally listed here more than once.*

Dennis Highby, CEO
Dennis Highby, Pres.
Ralph W. Castner, CFO/VP
Patrick A. Snyder, Sr. VP-Mktg.
Charles Baldwin, Chief Human Resources Officer/VP
Patrick A. Snyder, Sr. VP-Merch. & Retail Oper.
Brian J. Linneman, Sr. VP-Oper.
Joe Arterburn, Media Contact
Chris Gay, Investor Rel. Contact
Ralph W. Castner, Chmn.-World's Foremost Bank
James W. Cabela, Vice Chmn.
Joseph M. Friebe, CEO/VP-World's Foremost Bank
Richard N. Cabela, Chmn.
Brian J. Linneman, Sr. VP-Global Supply Chain

Phone: 308-254-5505	Fax: 308-254-4800
Toll-Free:	
Address: 1 Cabela Dr., Sidney, NE 69160 US	

GROWTH PLANS/SPECIAL FEATURES:

Cabela's, Inc. is a leading outdoor and hunting supply store, which mails over 140 million catalogs yearly to all 50 states and to more than 170 countries. Through its web site, mail-order catalogs and retail stores, the company supplies hunting, marine, automobile, ATV, fishing, camping equipment and clothing. Cabela's also has a line of brand-name casual clothing and hunting and outdoors gear in a variety of camouflage and safety patterns. The company had 28 retail stores as of late 2008, in states such as Arizona, Idaho, Nebraska, Minnesota, Wisconsin, Michigan, Pennsylvania, West Virginia, South Dakota, Kansas, Utah, Washington, Nevada and Texas and one store in Canada. The stores, which are considered tourist attractions, receive as many as 6 million visitors per year. They are designed to communicate an outdoor lifestyle environment characterized by the outdoor feel of the lighting, wood or tile flooring, cedar wood beams, open ceilings and lodge-style atmosphere. The large-format stores contain a mountain and pond with museum-quality taxidermy and native game fish; gun libraries featuring high-quality firearms; archery training systems; virtual shooting arcades; museums or educational centers; and restaurants and banquet and meeting facilities. Additionally, the firm owns the World's Foremost Bank, a wholly-owned subsidiary managing store-branded Visa credit cards. The company also owns Canadian outdoors equipment retailer S.I.R. Warehouse Sports Store. In late 2008, the firm announced a reduction of its workforce by 10%. In January 2009, World's Foremost Bank introduced the Club Visa Signature card which allows cardholders a minimum annual spending amount of $25,000 and the opportunity to earn free Cabela's merchandise.

Employees are offered health and dental insurance; a 401(k) plan; and product discounts.

FINANCIALS: Sales and profits are in thousands of dollars—add 000 to get the full amount. 2008 Note: Financial information for 2008 was not available for all companies at press time.

2008 Sales: $2,552,721	2008 Profits: $76,404	**U.S. Stock Ticker: CAB**
2007 Sales: $2,349,599	2007 Profits: $87,879	**Int'l Ticker:** Int'l Exchange:
2006 Sales: $2,063,524	2006 Profits: $85,785	Employees: 14,700
2005 Sales: $1,799,661	2005 Profits: $72,569	Fiscal Year Ends: 12/31
2004 Sales: $1,555,974	2004 Profits: $64,996	Parent Company:

SALARIES/BENEFITS:

Pension Plan:	ESOP Stock Plan:	Profit Sharing:	Top Exec. Salary: $716,290	Bonus: $
Savings Plan: Y	Stock Purch. Plan:		Second Exec. Salary: $464,605	Bonus: $

OTHER THOUGHTS:

Apparent Women Officers or Directors:
Hot Spot for Advancement for Women/Minorities:

LOCATIONS: ("Y" = Yes)

West:	Southwest:	Midwest:	Southeast:	Northeast:	International:
Y	Y	Y		Y	Y

CABLEVISION SYSTEMS CORP

www.cablevision.com

Industry Group Code: 517110 Ranks within this company's industry group: Sales: 8 Profits: 9

Management:		Sales/Marketing:		Liberal Arts:		Information Systems:		Professionals:		Tech./Scientific:	
Management Trainees:	Y	Marketing Pros.:	Y	Gen. Writing/Editing:	Y	Info. Management:	Y	Finance/Acct.:	Y	Engineers, Electrical:	Y
Experienced Mngmt.:	Y	Retail Sales:		Technical Writing:	Y	Software Dev.:	Y	Law:	Y	Engineers, Other:	Y
International Business:		Commercial/Industrial:	Y	Graphic Arts/Photog.:	Y	Hardware Dev.:		HR/Other:	Y	Health/Lab:	
MBA Grads:	Y	Sales Trainees:	Y	Music:		Consulting/Other:		Training:	Y	Scientists/Research:	
		Advertising Pros.:	Y	Broadcasting:	Y			Health Care:		Petroleum/Chemicals:	
				Other:	Y			Consulting:		Math/Other:	

TYPES OF BUSINESS:

Cable Television Service
Professional Sports Teams
Television Programming
Communications Services
Sports & Music Venues
Voice Over Internet Protocol
High-Speed Internet

BRANDS/DIVISIONS/AFFILIATES:

Rainbow Media Holdings LLC
Lightpath, Inc.
New York Rangers
New York Knickerbockers
Hartford Wolf Pack
MSG Entertainment
Madison Square Garden
Newsday Media Group

CONTACTS: *Note: Officers with more than one job title may be intentionally listed here more than once.*

James L. Dolan, CEO
Tom Rutledge, COO
James L. Dolan, Pres.
Michael Huseby, CFO/Exec. VP
Wilt Hildenbrand, Sr. Advisor-Tech.
Wilt Hildenbrand, Sr. Advisor-Eng.
Jonathan D. Schwartz, General Counsel/Exec. VP
John Bickman, Pres., Cable & Comm.
Patricia Armstrong, Sr. VP-Investor Rel.
Joshua Sapan, Pres./CEO-Rainbow Media Holdings LLC
James L. Dolan, Chmn.-MSG
Hank J. Ratner, Vice Chmn.
Gregg Seibert, Exec. VP
Charles F. Dolan, Chmn.

Phone: 516-803-2300	Fax: 516-803-3134
Toll-Free:	
Address: 1111 Stewart Ave., Bethpage, NY 11714 US	

GROWTH PLANS/SPECIAL FEATURES:

Cablevision Systems Corp. is engaged in cable programming networks, entertainment businesses and telecommunications companies. It serves about 4.7 million basic video subscribers in and around the New York City metropolitan area, and operates solely through cable operator subsidiary CSC Holdings. Through wholly-owned subsidiary Rainbow Media Holdings, LLC, the company owns interests in and manages numerous national and regional programming networks, the Madison Square Garden sports and entertainment businesses and cable television advertising sales companies. Through another subsidiary, Lightpath, Inc., the firm provides telephone services and high-speed Internet access to the business market. CSC operates in four segments: telecommunications services, Rainbow, Madison Square Garden and Newsday. The telecommunications services segment oversees the cable television business, including its video, high-speed data and voice over Internet protocol (VoIP) and the operations of the telephone and high-speed data services provided by Lightpath. The Rainbow segment consists principally of interests in national programming services (AMC, WE tv, IFC and fuse) and regional news programming businesses held by Rainbow Media Holdings. The division also includes a local advertising sales representation business. The Madison Square Garden segment owns and operates the Madison Square Garden Arena and the adjoining WaMu Theater at Madison Square Garden; the New York Knickerbockers professional basketball team; the New York Rangers professional hockey team; the New York Liberty professional women's basketball team; the Hartford Wolf Pack professional hockey team; the regional sports programming networks Madison Square Garden Network and Fox Sports Net New York; and MSG Entertainment. The Newsday segment includes the Newsday daily newspaper, amNew York, Star Community Publishing Group and online web sites such as Newsday.com and explore LI.com. In May 2008, Cablevision purchased the Sundance Channel, a cable network founded by Robert Redford, for about $500 million. In July 2008, the company acquired 97% of Newsday Media Group. In July 2009, the firm announced plans to spin off its Madison Square Garden operations, including its sports assets, into a separately-traded company.

FINANCIALS: Sales and profits are in thousands of dollars—add 000 to get the full amount. 2008 Note: Financial information for 2008 was not available for all companies at press time.

2008 Sales: $7,230,116	2008 Profits: $-227,576	U.S. Stock Ticker: CVC
2007 Sales: $6,484,481	2007 Profits: $218,456	Int'l Ticker: Int'l Exchange:
2006 Sales: $5,828,493	2006 Profits: $-126,465	Employees: 20,105
2005 Sales: $5,082,045	2005 Profits: $89,320	Fiscal Year Ends: 12/31
2004 Sales: $4,750,037	2004 Profits: $-676,092	Parent Company:

SALARIES/BENEFITS:

Pension Plan:	ESOP Stock Plan:	Profit Sharing:	Top Exec. Salary: $1,800,000	Bonus: $6,567,600
Savings Plan: Y	Stock Purch. Plan:		Second Exec. Salary: $1,600,000	Bonus: $5,582,800

OTHER THOUGHTS:

Apparent Women Officers or Directors: 4
Hot Spot for Advancement for Women/Minorities: Y

LOCATIONS: ("Y" = Yes)

West:	Southwest:	Midwest:	Southeast:	Northeast:	International:
				Y	

Note: Financial information, benefits and other data can change quickly and may vary from those stated here.

CACI INTERNATIONAL INC

www.caci.com

Industry Group Code: 541512 Ranks within this company's industry group: Sales: 1 Profits: 1

Management:		Sales/Marketing:		Liberal Arts:		Information Systems:		Professionals:		Tech./Scientific:	
Management Trainees:	Y	Marketing Pros.:	Y	Gen. Writing/Editing:	Y	Info. Management:	Y	Finance/Acct.:	Y	Engineers, Electrical:	Y
Experienced Mngmt.:	Y	Retail Sales:		Technical Writing:	Y	Software Dev.:	Y	Law:	Y	Engineers, Other:	
International Business:	Y	Commercial/Industrial:	Y	Graphic Arts/Photog.:	Y	Hardware Dev.:	Y	HR/Other:	Y	Health/Lab:	
MBA Grads:	Y	Sales Trainees:		Music:		Consulting/Other:	Y	Training:	Y	Scientists/Research:	
		Advertising Pros.:		Broadcasting:				Health Care:		Petroleum/Chemicals:	
				Other:				Consulting:	Y	Math/Other:	

TYPES OF BUSINESS:

Consulting-InfoTech Related
Engineering Simulation Software
Custom Software Engineering
Managed Network Services
Information Management Tools
Marketing Systems Software
C4ISR
Radio Frequency Identification

BRANDS/DIVISIONS/AFFILIATES:

CACI Limited
Institute for Quality Management, Inc.
Wexford Group International
Athena Innovative Solutions, Inc.
Dragon Development Corp.
Wide Area Workflow
Oracle Contract Lifecycle Management
CACI Research and Development Labs

CONTACTS: *Note: Officers with more than one job title may be intentionally listed here more than once.*

Paul M. Cofoni, CEO
Paul M. Cofoni, Pres.
Thomas A. Mutryn, CFO/Exec. VP
H. Robert Boehm, Chief Human Resources Officer/Exec. VP
Deborah B. Dunie, CTO/Exec. VP
Steven H. Weiss, Exec. VP-Gov't Bus. Oper.
Ronald Schneider, Exec. VP-Bus. Dev.
Jody A. Brown, Exec. VP-Public Rel. & Bus. Comm.
David Dragics, Sr. VP-Investor Rel.
Thomas A. Mutryn, Treas.
William M. Fairl, Pres., U.S. Oper.
Randall C. Fuerst, COO-US Oper.
Gregory R. Bradford, CEO-CACI Ltd.
J.P. London, Chmn.
Gregory R. Bradford, Pres., U.K. Oper.

Phone: 703-841-7800	**Fax:** 703-841-7882
Toll-Free:	
Address: 1100 N. Glebe Rd., Arlington, VA 22201 US	

GROWTH PLANS/SPECIAL FEATURES:

CACI International, Inc. is an information technology (IT) company that provides IT and network services to defense, intelligence and e-government departments. The firm specializes in four areas: systems integration; engineering and logistics; managed network services; and knowledge management. CACI's domestic operations work through several joint ventures and subsidiaries, providing data, information and knowledge management programs such as HighView Document Exploitation; business systems like the Wide Area Workflow solution; command, control, communications, computers, intelligence, surveillance and reconnaissance (C4ISR) programs such as Rapid Deployment Communications; and information assurance and cyber security; logistics information systems which utilize Radio Frequency Identification (RFID). International operations are conducted through subsidiary CACI Ltd., which is based in the U.K. and accounts for over 90% of the company's commercial revenue. The subsidiary focuses on business systems solutions; data, information and knowledge management; and enterprise IT and network services. The company also operates the CACI Vision & Solution Center, where customers can test IT solutions before installing them. Recent acquisitions include Institute for Quality Management, Inc.; Wexford Group International; Athena Innovative Solutions, Inc; and Dragon Development Corp. In October 2008, CACI agreed to partner with Oracle to develop Oracle Contract Lifecycle Management, which aids federal organizations in the creation and management of procurement contracts. In December 2008, the company partnered with Guidance Software, Inc., to develop a new eDiscovery program (which automatically collects and centralizes electronically stored information) for federal agencies such as the U.S. Department of Justice. Also in December 2008, CACI opened CACI Research and Development Labs on the U.S. Army's Aberdeen Proving Ground in Maryland.

Employee benefits include medical, dental and vision insurance; life and AD&D insurance; disability insurance; tuition reimbursement; and an employee assistance program.

FINANCIALS: Sales and profits are in thousands of dollars—add 000 to get the full amount. 2008 Note: Financial information for 2008 was not available for all companies at press time.

2008 Sales: $2,420,537	2008 Profits: $83,323	**U.S. Stock Ticker: CAI**
2007 Sales: $1,937,972	2007 Profits: $78,532	**Int'l Ticker:** Int'l Exchange:
2006 Sales: $1,755,324	2006 Profits: $84,840	Employees: 12,400
2005 Sales: $1,623,062	2005 Profits: $79,725	Fiscal Year Ends: 6/30
2004 Sales: $1,145,785	2004 Profits: $57,714	Parent Company:

SALARIES/BENEFITS:

Pension Plan:	ESOP Stock Plan:	Profit Sharing:	Top Exec. Salary: $675,000	Bonus: $1,414,335
Savings Plan: Y	Stock Purch. Plan: Y		Second Exec. Salary: $425,000	Bonus: $907,814

OTHER THOUGHTS:

Apparent Women Officers or Directors: 2
Hot Spot for Advancement for Women/Minorities: Y

LOCATIONS: ("Y" = Yes)

West:	Southwest:	Midwest:	Southeast:	Northeast:	International:
Y	Y	Y	Y	Y	Y

CAMERON INTERNATIONAL CORPORATION

www.c-a-m.com

Industry Group Code: 33313 Ranks within this company's industry group: Sales: 1 Profits: 1

Management:		Sales/Marketing:		Liberal Arts:		Information Systems:		Professionals:		Tech./Scientific:	
Management Trainees:	Y	Marketing Pros.:	Y	Gen. Writing/Editing:		Info. Management:	Y	Finance/Acct.:	Y	Engineers, Electrical:	Y
Experienced Mngmt.:	Y	Retail Sales:		Technical Writing:	Y	Software Dev.:	Y	Law:	Y	Engineers, Other:	Y
International Business:	Y	Commercial/Industrial:	Y	Graphic Arts/Photog.:	Y	Hardware Dev.:	Y	HR/Other:	Y	Health/Lab:	
MBA Grads:	Y	Sales Trainees:		Music:		Consulting/Other:		Training:	Y	Scientists/Research:	
		Advertising Pros.:		Broadcasting:				Health Care:		Petroleum/Chemicals:	
				Other:				Consulting:		Math/Other:	

TYPES OF BUSINESS:

Oil Field Machinery
Gas Turbines, Compressors & Engines
Oil Field Services
Pressure & Flow Control Equipment

BRANDS/DIVISIONS/AFFILIATES:

Cooper Cameron Corporation
Petreco Processing Systems
Cameron Drilling & Production Systems
Cameron Valves & Measurement
Cameron Compression
KB Industries
Willis
NATCO Group, Inc.

CONTACTS: *Note: Officers with more than one job title may be intentionally listed here more than once.*

Jack B. Moore, CEO
Jack B. Moore, Pres.
Charles M. Sledge, CFO/VP
Joseph H. Mongrain, VP-Human Resources
John Bartos, VP-Tech. & Dev.
William C. Lemmer, General Counsel/VP
Stephen P. Tomlinson, VP-Oper. Support
Scott Amann, VP-Investor Rel.
Christopher A. Krummel, Chief Acct. Officer/Controller/VP
Robert J. Rajeski, VP/Pres., Cameron Compression Systems
Jim E. Wright, VP/Pres., Valves & Measurement
John Carne, Sr. VP/Pres., Cameron Drilling & Prod. Systems
Grace B. Holmes, Corp. Sec.
Sheldon R. Erikson, Chmn.

Phone: 713-513-3300	Fax: 713-513-3456
Toll-Free:	
Address: 1333 West Loop S., Ste. 1700, Houston, TX 77027 US	

GROWTH PLANS/SPECIAL FEATURES:

Cameron International Corporation, formerly Cooper Cameron Corporation, is an international provider of flow equipment products, systems and services to oil, gas and processing industries. The firm is also a leading manufacturer of centrifugal air compressors, integral and separable gas compressors and turbochargers. The company has 300 locations all over the world and is divided into three business segments: drilling and production systems; valves and measurement; and compression systems. The drilling and production systems products include surface and subsea production systems, blowout preventers (BOPs), drilling and production control systems, oil and gas separation equipment, gate valves, actuators, chokes, wellheads, drilling riser and aftermarket parts and services. Subsidiary, Petreco Processing Systems provides custom-engineered process packages to operators worldwide for separation and treatment of oil, gas, water and solids. The division's products are marketed under the brand names Cameron, W-K-M, McEvoy and Willis. The valves and measurement segment's products include ball valves, butterfly valves, Orbit valves, double block and bleed valves, globe valves and aftermarket parts and services. The segment markets its products under various brand names, including WKM, Demco, Nutron, TBV, TexSteam and Wheatley. The compression systems segment produces reciprocating and integrally geared centrifugal compression equipment and aftermarket parts and services, and markets under various brand names, including Ajax, Superior, Compression Specialties and Turbine Specialties. In 2008, the firm acquired KB Industries, a blowout preventers manufacturer. In June 2009, the company agreed to acquire NATCO Group Inc., a process equipment provider.

FINANCIALS: Sales and profits are in thousands of dollars—add 000 to get the full amount. 2008 Note: Financial information for 2008 was not available for all companies at press time.

		U.S. Stock Ticker: CAM
2008 Sales: $5,848,877	2008 Profits: $593,726	Int'l Ticker: Int'l Exchange:
2007 Sales: $4,666,368	2007 Profits: $500,860	Employees: 17,100
2006 Sales: $3,742,907	2006 Profits: $317,816	Fiscal Year Ends: 12/31
2005 Sales: $2,517,847	2005 Profits: $171,130	Parent Company:
2004 Sales: $2,092,845	2004 Profits: $94,415	

SALARIES/BENEFITS:

Pension Plan:	ESOP Stock Plan:	Profit Sharing:	Top Exec. Salary: $1,025,000	Bonus: $1,645,433
Savings Plan:	Stock Purch. Plan:		Second Exec. Salary: $745,385	Bonus: $902,981

OTHER THOUGHTS:

Apparent Women Officers or Directors: 1
Hot Spot for Advancement for Women/Minorities:

LOCATIONS: ("Y" = Yes)

West:	Southwest:	Midwest:	Southeast:	Northeast:	International:
Y	Y	Y	Y	Y	Y

Note: Financial information, benefits and other data can change quickly and may vary from those stated here.

CAPITAL SENIOR LIVING CORP

www.capitalsenior.com

Industry Group Code: 623110 **Ranks within this company's industry group: Sales: 6   Profits: 3**

Management:		Sales/Marketing:		Liberal Arts:		Information Systems:		Professionals:		Tech./Scientific:	
Management Trainees:	Y	Marketing Pros.:	Y	Gen. Writing/Editing:	Y	Info. Management:	Y	Finance/Acct.:	Y	Engineers, Electrical:	
Experienced Mngmt.:	Y	Retail Sales:		Technical Writing:	Y	Software Dev.:		Law:	Y	Engineers, Other:	
International Business:		Commercial/Industrial:		Graphic Arts/Photog.:	Y	Hardware Dev.:		HR/Other:	Y	Health/Lab:	
MBA Grads:	Y	Sales Trainees:		Music:		Consulting/Other:		Training:	Y	Scientists/Research:	
		Advertising Pros.:	Y	Broadcasting:				Health Care:	Y	Petroleum/Chemicals:	
				Other:	Y			Consulting:		Math/Other:	

TYPES OF BUSINESS:

Long-Term Health Care
Nursing Homes
Assisted Living Services
Home Care Services

BRANDS/DIVISIONS/AFFILIATES:

Capital Senior Living ILM-B, Inc.
Triad Senior Living I, LP
Quality Home Care, Inc.
Capital Senior Living Acquisition, LLC
Capital Senior Living, Inc.
Capital Senior Development, Inc.
Capital Senior Management AC, Inc.

CONTACTS: *Note: Officers with more than one job title may be intentionally listed here more than once.*

Lawrence A. Cohen, CEO
Keith N. Johannessen, COO
Keith N. Johannessen, Pres.
Ralph A. Beattie, CFO/Exec. VP
David R. Brickman, General Counsel
James A. Stroud, Chmn.

Phone: 972-770-5600	Fax: 972-770-5666
Toll-Free:	
Address: 14160 Dallas Pkwy., Ste. 300, Dallas, TX 75254 US	

GROWTH PLANS/SPECIAL FEATURES:

Capital Senior Living Corporation (CSL) is one of the nation's largest operators and developers of residential communities for seniors. The firm operates 64 communities: one managed for a third party; 25 which are leased; and 38 in which it maintains at least partial ownership. CSL offers its senior living services in 23 states. Its combined facilities can support approximately 9,500 residents. 95% of the company's revenue is generated through private pay parties at these communities. The firm provides senior living services to the elderly, including independent living, assisted living, skilled nursing and home care services. Many of CSL's communities offer a continuum of care to meet its residents' needs as they change over time. This continuum of care, which integrates independent living, assisted living and home care through independent home care agencies or the company's home care agency, sustains residents' autonomy and independence based on their physical and mental abilities. Currently, 69% of the firm's clients are in independent living, 24% in assisted living and 7% require continuing home care. Each Capital community features social and recreational programs, maid service, restaurant-quality meals and complimentary laundry rooms. The company also operates through approximately 50 subsidiaries, including: Capital Senior Living ILM-B, Inc.; Triad Senior Living I, LP; Quality Home Care, Inc.; Capital Senior Living Acquisition, LLC; Capital Senior Living, Inc.; Capital Senior Development, Inc.; and Capital Senior Management AC, Inc. In August 2008, CSL opened a new senior community in Miami Township, Ohio, through a joint venture with Prudential Real Estate Investors. As part of the venture, two more facilities are scheduled to be opened in 2009 near Toledo, Ohio (Richmond Heights and Levis Commons). In December 2008, CSL announced that this deal will be the company's last development project until general business conditions improve.

FINANCIALS: Sales and profits are in thousands of dollars—add 000 to get the full amount. 2008 Note: Financial information for 2008 was not available for all companies at press time.

2008 Sales: $193,274	2008 Profits: $3,724	**U.S. Stock Ticker: CSU**	
2007 Sales: $189,052	2007 Profits: $4,360	Int'l Ticker: Int'l Exchange:	
2006 Sales: $159,070	2006 Profits: $-2,600	Employees: 3,871	
2005 Sales: $126,404	2005 Profits: $-5,354	Fiscal Year Ends: 12/31	
2004 Sales: $108,935	2004 Profits: $-6,758	Parent Company:	

SALARIES/BENEFITS:

Pension Plan:	ESOP Stock Plan:	Profit Sharing:	Top Exec. Salary: $422,173	Bonus: $189,053
Savings Plan: Y	Stock Purch. Plan:		Second Exec. Salary: $351,811	Bonus: $118,742

OTHER THOUGHTS:

Apparent Women Officers or Directors: 1
Hot Spot for Advancement for Women/Minorities:

LOCATIONS: ("Y" = Yes)

West:	Southwest:	Midwest:	Southeast:	Northeast:	International:
Y	Y	Y	Y	Y	

CARDINAL HEALTH INC
www.cardinal.com

Industry Group Code: 424210 Ranks within this company's industry group: Sales: 2 Profits: 1

Management:		Sales/Marketing:		Liberal Arts:		Information Systems:		Professionals:		Tech./Scientific:	
Management Trainees:	Y	Marketing Pros.:	Y	Gen. Writing/Editing:	Y	Info. Management:	Y	Finance/Acct.:	Y	Engineers, Electrical:	
Experienced Mngmt.:	Y	Retail Sales:		Technical Writing:	Y	Software Dev.:	Y	Law:	Y	Engineers, Other:	
International Business:	Y	Commercial/Industrial:	Y	Graphic Arts/Photog.:	Y	Hardware Dev.:		HR/Other:	Y	Health/Lab:	
MBA Grads:	Y	Sales Trainees:	Y	Music:		Consulting/Other:		Training:	Y	Scientists/Research:	
		Advertising Pros.:	Y	Broadcasting:				Health Care:		Petroleum/Chemicals:	
				Other:				Consulting:		Math/Other:	

TYPES OF BUSINESS:
Healthcare Products & Services
Supply Chain Services
Medical Products

BRANDS/DIVISIONS/AFFILIATES:
Alaris
Pyxis
ChloraPrep
Viasys Healthcare, Inc.
CareFusion
Pyxsis MedStation 4000
Monoject
Pyxis Infant Care Verification

CONTACTS: *Note: Officers with more than one job title may be intentionally listed here more than once.*
George Barrett, CEO
Jeff Henderson, CFO
Carole Watkins, Chief Human Resources Officer
Patricia B. Morrison, CIO/Exec. VP
Steve Falk, General Counsel/Exec. VP/Corp. Sec.
Craig Morford, Chief Legal & Compliance Officer
John Giacomin, Exec. VP-Oper., Pharmaceuticals Segment
Mike Duffy, Exec. VP-Oper., Medical Segment
Mike Lynch, CEO-Medical Segment
George Barrett, Chmn.

Phone: 614-757-5000	Fax: 614-757-8871
Toll-Free: 800-234-8701	
Address: 7000 Cardinal Pl., Dublin, OH 43017 US	

GROWTH PLANS/SPECIAL FEATURES:
Cardinal Health, Inc. is a provider of products and services that improve the safety and productivity of healthcare. The company operates two businesses: healthcare supply chain services; and clinical and medical products. The healthcare supply chain segment provides comprehensive financial inventory and marketing services as well as specialized nuclear pharmaceuticals to hospitals and outpatient centers. Recently launched products include the Pyxsis MedStation 4000, an automated medication dispensing system; the Monoject 35 mL syringe, which is designed for easier storing; and Pyxis Infant Care Verification, which tracks and identifies breast milk in the hospital by scanning barcode information on breast milk packaging. The company spun-off CareFusion as a separate, publicly-held firm in 2009.

Employees are offered medical, dental and vision insurance; a 401(k) savings plan; an employee stock purchase plan; flexible spending accounts; short- and long-term disability coverage; life insurance; business travel insurance; an employee assistance program; adoption assistance; and tuition reimbursement.

FINANCIALS: Sales and profits are in thousands of dollars—add 000 to get the full amount. 2008 Note: Financial information for 2008 was not available for all companies at press time.

2008 Sales: $90,975,500	2008 Profits: $1,300,600	**U.S. Stock Ticker: CAH**
2007 Sales: $86,755,000	2007 Profits: $1,931,100	**Int'l Ticker:** Int'l Exchange:
2006 Sales: $79,664,200	2006 Profits: $1,000,100	Employees: 46,500
2005 Sales: $72,666,000	2005 Profits: $1,050,700	Fiscal Year Ends: 6/30
2004 Sales: $63,043,100	2004 Profits: $1,474,500	Parent Company:

SALARIES/BENEFITS:
Pension Plan:	ESOP Stock Plan:	Profit Sharing:	Top Exec. Salary: $1,441,257	Bonus: $691,804
Savings Plan: Y	Stock Purch. Plan: Y		Second Exec. Salary: $926,404	Bonus: $416,883

OTHER THOUGHTS:
Apparent Women Officers or Directors: 4
Hot Spot for Advancement for Women/Minorities: Y

LOCATIONS: ("Y" = Yes)
West:	Southwest:	Midwest:	Southeast:	Northeast:	International:
Y	Y	Y	Y	Y	Y

Note: Financial information, benefits and other data can change quickly and may vary from those stated here.

CARGILL INC

Industry Group Code: 3112 **Ranks within this company's industry group:** Sales: 1 Profits: 1

www.cargill.com

Management:		Sales/Marketing:		Liberal Arts:		Information Systems:		Professionals:		Tech./Scientific:	
Management Trainees:	Y	Marketing Pros.:	Y	Gen. Writing/Editing:	Y	Info. Management:	Y	Finance/Acct.:	Y	Engineers, Electrical:	
Experienced Mngmt.:	Y	Retail Sales:		Technical Writing:	Y	Software Dev.:	Y	Law:	Y	Engineers, Other:	Y
International Business:	Y	Commercial/Industrial:	Y	Graphic Arts/Photog.:	Y	Hardware Dev.:		HR/Other:	Y	Health/Lab:	
MBA Grads:	Y	Sales Trainees:		Music:		Consulting/Other:		Training:	Y	Scientists/Research:	Y
		Advertising Pros.:	Y	Broadcasting:				Health Care:		Petroleum/Chemicals:	Y
				Other:				Consulting:		Math/Other:	

TYPES OF BUSINESS:

Crop Production, Milling and Distribution
Meat Processing
Food Ingredients
Fertilizers
Steel
Money Markets & Commodity Trading
Supply Chain Solutions
Risk Management & Financial Services

BRANDS/DIVISIONS/AFFILIATES:

Cargill AgHorizons U.S.
Emerald Renewable Energy LLC
Renessen Feed & Processing
Cerestar Sweeteners Europe
Black River Asset Management
Duckworth Flavors
Cargill Animal Nutrition
Truvia

CONTACTS: *Note: Officers with more than one job title may be intentionally listed here more than once.*

Gregory R. Page, CEO
David MacLennan, CFO/Sr. VP
Peter Vrijsen, VP-Human Resources
Christopher P. Mallett, VP-R&D
Rita J. Heise, VP-IT
Ronald L. Christenson, CTO/VP
Steven C. Euller, General Counsel/VP/Corp. Sec.
Bonnie E. Raquet, VP-Corp. Affairs
Galen G. Johnson, Controller/VP
Gert Jan Vandenakker, Pres., Ocean Transportation
Jayme D. Olson, Treas./VP
Scott Portnoy, VP-Biofuels & Bioproducts Bus.
Gregory R. Page, Chmn.

Phone: 952-742-7575	**Fax:** 952-742-7393
Toll-Free: 800-277-4455	
Address: 15407 McGinty Rd. W., Wayzata, MN 55391 US	

GROWTH PLANS/SPECIAL FEATURES:

Cargill, Inc. is a provider of food, agricultural and risk management products/services. It operates in five sectors: agriculture services; industrial; food ingredients/applications; origination/processing; and risk management/financial. The company provides customized farm services and products and operates worldwide through its five agricultural services companies: Banks Cargill Agriculture; Cargill AgHorizons Canada; Cargill AgHorizons U.S.; Cargill Animal Nutrition; and Renessen Feed & Processing. The company's food sector serves food manufacturers, service companies and retailers with food and beverage ingredients and meat/poultry products. Cargill's food ingredient subsidiaries include Cargill Dressings, Cerestar Sweeteners Europe and Cargill Kitchens. In the industrial sector, Cargill supplies customers worldwide with fertilizer through The Mosaic Co.; steel products/services through North Star Steel; and industrial applications for agricultural feedstocks through NatureWorks LLC. The origination and processing unit connects producers and users of grain, oilseeds and other agricultural commodities through its three subsidiaries, Cargill Cotton; Cargill Grain & Oilseed Supply Chain; and Cargill Sugar. Cargill provides risk management and financial solutions through several firms, including Black River Asset Management LLC and Cargill Investor Services. In 2008, Cargill introduced Truvia, a zero-calorie sweetener; HemiForce, which increases the strength of paper products; and Gerkens organic cocoa powders. Also in 2008, the firm opened new plants/facilities in France and Ghana; ceased plant operations in Missouri, Arkansas and Indonesia; and agreed to acquire the grain elevators of Madison Energy LLC and joint-venture Terminal 22. In May 2008, the company opened new centers in Minneapolis. In July 2008, the firm opened a BiOH brand plyols manufacturing plant in Chicago, Illinois. In 2009, the company decided to cease operations at plants in Connecticut and Ontario. In January 2009, Cargill acquired a ground beef processing facility and 80 acres from Carneco Foods LLC. In April 2009, Cargill agreed to sell its Saskatchewan crop input facility to Horizon Fertilizers, Ltd.

FINANCIALS: Sales and profits are in thousands of dollars—add 000 to get the full amount. 2008 Note: Financial information for 2008 was not available for all companies at press time.

2008 Sales: $120,439,000	2008 Profits: $3,951,000	**U.S. Stock Ticker:** Private
2007 Sales: $88,266,000	2007 Profits: $2,343,000	**Int'l Ticker:** Int'l Exchange:
2006 Sales: $75,208,000	2006 Profits: $1,537,000	Employees: 159,000
2005 Sales: $71,066,000	2005 Profits: $2,103,000	Fiscal Year Ends: 5/31
2004 Sales: $62,907,000	2004 Profits: $1,331,000	Parent Company:

SALARIES/BENEFITS:

Pension Plan:	ESOP Stock Plan:	Profit Sharing:	Top Exec. Salary: $	Bonus: $
Savings Plan:	Stock Purch. Plan:		Second Exec. Salary: $	Bonus: $

OTHER THOUGHTS:

Apparent Women Officers or Directors: 2
Hot Spot for Advancement for Women/Minorities: Y

LOCATIONS: ("Y" = Yes)

West:	Southwest:	Midwest:	Southeast:	Northeast:	International:
Y	Y	Y	Y		Y

CARMAX GROUP

www.carmax.com

Industry Group Code: 441110 Ranks within this company's industry group: Sales: 1 Profits: 1

Management:		Sales/Marketing:		Liberal Arts:		Information Systems:		Professionals:		Tech./Scientific:	
Management Trainees:	Y	Marketing Pros.:	Y	Gen. Writing/Editing:	Y	Info. Management:	Y	Finance/Acct.:	Y	Engineers, Electrical:	
Experienced Mngmt.:	Y	Retail Sales:	Y	Technical Writing:		Software Dev.:	Y	Law:	Y	Engineers, Other:	
International Business:		Commercial/Industrial:	Y	Graphic Arts/Photog.:	Y	Hardware Dev.:		HR/Other:	Y	Health/Lab:	
MBA Grads:	Y	Sales Trainees:	Y	Music:		Consulting/Other:		Training:	Y	Scientists/Research:	
		Advertising Pros.:	Y	Broadcasting:				Health Care:		Petroleum/Chemicals:	
				Other:				Consulting:		Math/Other:	

TYPES OF BUSINESS:

Used Auto Dealers, Retail
New Auto Dealers
Online Sales
Vehicle Repair Services
Financial Services

BRANDS/DIVISIONS/AFFILIATES:

CarMax Foundation (The)

CONTACTS: *Note: Officers with more than one job title may be intentionally listed here more than once.*

Thomas J. Folliard, CEO
Thomas J. Folliard, Pres.
Keith D. Browning, CFO/Exec. VP
Joseph S. Kunkel, Sr. VP-Mktg. & Strategy
Roberta Douma, VP-Human Resource Dev.
Richard M. Smith, CIO/Sr. VP
Bill Nash, VP-Merch.
Michael K. Dolan, Chief Admin. Officer/Exec. VP
Eric Margolin, General Counsel/Sr. VP/Corp. Sec.
Lynn Mussatt, VP-Bus. Oper.
Anu Agarwal, VP-Bus. Strategy
John Montegari, Asst. VP-Media
Katharine Kenny, Asst. VP-Investor Rel.
Thomas W. Reedy, Jr., VP/Treas.
Laura Donahue, VP-Advertising
Angela S. Chattin, VP-CarMax Auto Finance
Dave Banks, VP-IT
Kim Orcutt, VP/Controller
William R. Tiefel, Chmn.
Mark Adams, Asst. VP-Logistics

Phone: 804-747-0422	Fax: 804-967-2918
Toll-Free: 800-519-1511	
Address: 12800 Tuckahoe Creek Pkwy., Richmond, VA 23238 US	

GROWTH PLANS/SPECIAL FEATURES:

CarMax Group is one of the nation's largest retailers of used cars. The firm purchases, reconditions and sells used vehicles through its 100 used car superstores in 46 metropolitan markets across the U.S. 85% of the company's used vehicle inventory are between one and six years old and have less than 60,000 miles. Vehicles that do not meet retail standards are sold in closed wholesale auctions. CarMax also sells new vehicles at five of its locations under franchise agreements with four new car manufacturers. The company offers a wide selection of makes and models of both domestic and imported vehicles to appeal to diverse consumer preferences and budgets, including popular brands from manufacturers such as Daimler, Chrysler, Ford, General Motors, Honda, Mitsubishi, Subaru, Toyota and Volkswagen. Vehicles purchased through the company's in-store appraisal process that fall short of retail standards are sold at on-site wholesale auctions restricted to licensed automobile dealers. All store locations provide vehicle repair service and used-car warranty service. In addition, through the company's web site, customers can search new and used cars as well as find information on Kelley Blue Book figures, car buying tips, rebates and incentives and more. CarMax has finance operations through CarMax Auto Finance that offer revolving credit and automobile installment loans. The company also works through The CarMax Foundation, which supports community service and philanthropic endeavors. The firm sold approximately 345,000 used vehicles retailed in 2008.

CarMax offers its employees a benefits package including educational assistance, a daycare savings account, life insurance, adoption assistance, an associate discount program and an employee assistance program. CarMax has been named by Fortune magazine as one of its 2009 100 Best Companies to Work For.

FINANCIALS: Sales and profits are in thousands of dollars—add 000 to get the full amount. 2008 Note: Financial information for 2008 was not available for all companies at press time.

2008 Sales: $8,199,571	2008 Profits: $182,025	**U.S. Stock Ticker: KMX**
2007 Sales: $7,465,656	2007 Profits: $198,597	**Int'l Ticker:** Int'l Exchange:
2006 Sales: $6,259,967	2006 Profits: $134,220	Employees: 13,035
2005 Sales: $5,260,300	2005 Profits: $112,900	Fiscal Year Ends: 2/28
2004 Sales: $4,597,691	2004 Profits: $116,450	Parent Company:

SALARIES/BENEFITS:

Pension Plan: Y	ESOP Stock Plan:	Profit Sharing:	Top Exec. Salary: $846,154	Bonus: $
Savings Plan: Y	Stock Purch. Plan: Y		Second Exec. Salary: $614,233	Bonus: $

OTHER THOUGHTS:

Apparent Women Officers or Directors: 13
Hot Spot for Advancement for Women/Minorities: Y

LOCATIONS: ("Y" = Yes)

West:	Southwest:	Midwest:	Southeast:	Northeast:	International:
Y	Y	Y	Y	Y	

Note: Financial information, benefits and other data can change quickly and may vary from those stated here.

CARNIVAL CORPORATION
www.carnivalcorp.com

Industry Group Code: 483112 Ranks within this company's industry group: Sales: 1 Profits: 1

Management:		Sales/Marketing:		Liberal Arts:		Information Systems:		Professionals:		Tech./Scientific:	
Management Trainees:	Y	Marketing Pros.:	Y	Gen. Writing/Editing:	Y	Info. Management:	Y	Finance/Acct.:	Y	Engineers, Electrical:	
Experienced Mngmt.:	Y	Retail Sales:		Technical Writing:	Y	Software Dev.:	Y	Law:	Y	Engineers, Other:	Y
International Business:	Y	Commercial/Industrial:	Y	Graphic Arts/Photog.:	Y	Hardware Dev.:		HR/Other:	Y	Health/Lab:	
MBA Grads:	Y	Sales Trainees:	Y	Music:	Y	Consulting/Other:		Training:	Y	Scientists/Research:	
		Advertising Pros.:	Y	Broadcasting:				Health Care:		Petroleum/Chemicals:	
				Other:	Y			Consulting:		Math/Other:	

TYPES OF BUSINESS:
Cruise Line
On-Board Casinos
Tours
Resort Hotels

BRANDS/DIVISIONS/AFFILIATES:
Carnival Cruise Lines
Holland America Line
P&O Cruises Australia
Seabourn Cruise Line
Princess Cruises
Costa Cruises
Cunard Line
P&O Cruises

CONTACTS: *Note: Officers with more than one job title may be intentionally listed here more than once.*
Micky Arison, CEO
Howard S. Frank, COO/Vice Chmn.
David Bernstein, CFO/Sr. VP
Arnaldo Perez, General Counsel/Sr. VP/Corp. Sec.
Larry Freedman, Chief Acct. Officer/VP/Controller
Richard D. Ames, Sr. VP-Shared Svcs.
Michael Thamm, Pres., AIDA Cruises
Gerald R. Cahill, CEO/Pres., Carnival Cruise Lines
Ann Sherry, CEO-Carnival Australia
Micky Arison, Chmn.
Alan B. Buckelew, CEO-P&O Princess Cruises Int'l

Phone: 305-599-2600	Fax: 305-406-4700
Toll-Free:	
Address: 3655 NW 87th Ave., Miami, FL 33178-2428 US	

GROWTH PLANS/SPECIAL FEATURES:

Carnival Corporation provides cruises and tours to vacation destinations worldwide. Its cruise brands include Carnival Cruise Lines, Princess Cruises, Costa Cruises, Holland America Line, P&O Cruises, Cunard, AIDA, Ibero Cruises, Seabourn Cruise Line and Ocean Village. In total, the company operates 89 ships with a capacity for over 171,000 passengers. Carnival Cruise Lines operates 22 ships and is based in North America. Princess is a global cruise and tour company operating 17 ships. Costa Crociere is the leading cruise company in Europe and South America, operating a modern fleet of 12 ships. Holland America Line serves the industry's premium segment, with 14 ships sailing to all seven continents. P&O Cruises offers passengers destinations including the Caribbean, South America, Scandinavia, the Mediterranean, Atlantic Islands and Round the World cruises. Cunard operates the Queen Mary 2 and Queen Victoria. AIDA Cruises operates in the German-speaking cruise market and Ibero Cruises caters to the Spanish-speaking cruise market in Southern Europe. Seabourn Cruise Line offers luxury cruises on its combined three yachts, with three more scheduled to be added by 2011. Ocean Village operates informal and discovery cruises for younger, more active passengers, though it is due to be phased out starting in November 2009, with its remaining ships transferred to P&O Cruises Australia. The company also owns Holland America Tours and Princess Tours, which are tour operators in Alaska and the Canadian Yukon. These companies offer lodging, chartered motorcoaches, rail cars, luxury day boats and sightseeing packages. The firm has over 17 cruise ships scheduled to enter service between March 2009 and June 2012. Carnival has announced plans to expand its Australia and New Zealand services by expanding the fleet sizes of P&O Australia and Princess Cruises' Australian services.

FINANCIALS: Sales and profits are in thousands of dollars—add 000 to get the full amount. 2008 Note: Financial information for 2008 was not available for all companies at press time.

2008 Sales: $14,646,000	2008 Profits: $2,330,000	U.S. Stock Ticker: CCL
2007 Sales: $13,033,000	2007 Profits: $2,408,000	Int'l Ticker: Int'l Exchange:
2006 Sales: $11,839,000	2006 Profits: $2,279,000	Employees: 85,900
2005 Sales: $11,094,000	2005 Profits: $2,253,000	Fiscal Year Ends: 11/30
2004 Sales: $9,727,000	2004 Profits: $1,809,000	Parent Company:

SALARIES/BENEFITS:

Pension Plan:	ESOP Stock Plan:	Profit Sharing:	Top Exec. Salary: $1,415,500	Bonus: $800,441
Savings Plan: Y	Stock Purch. Plan: Y		Second Exec. Salary: $880,000	Bonus: $

OTHER THOUGHTS:
Apparent Women Officers or Directors: 4
Hot Spot for Advancement for Women/Minorities: Y

LOCATIONS: ("Y" = Yes)

West:	Southwest:	Midwest:	Southeast:	Northeast:	International:
Y			Y		Y

CASH AMERICA INTERNATIONAL INC

www.cashamerica.com

Industry Group Code: 522298 Ranks within this company's industry group: Sales: 1 Profits: 1

Management:		Sales/Marketing:		Liberal Arts:		Information Systems:		Professionals:		Tech./Scientific:	
Management Trainees:	Y	Marketing Pros.:	Y	Gen. Writing/Editing:	Y	Info. Management:	Y	Finance/Acct.:	Y	Engineers, Electrical:	
Experienced Mngmt.:	Y	Retail Sales:	Y	Technical Writing:		Software Dev.:	Y	Law:	Y	Engineers, Other:	
International Business:	Y	Commercial/Industrial:	Y	Graphic Arts/Photog.:	Y	Hardware Dev.:		HR/Other:	Y	Health/Lab:	
MBA Grads:	Y	Sales Trainees:	Y	Music:		Consulting/Other:		Training:	Y	Scientists/Research:	
		Advertising Pros.:	Y	Broadcasting:				Health Care:		Petroleum/Chemicals:	
				Other:				Consulting:		Math/Other:	

TYPES OF BUSINESS:

Pawn Shops
Check Cashing
Payday Loans
Money Orders
Money Transfers
Stored Value Cards

BRANDS/DIVISIONS/AFFILIATES:

Mr. Payroll Corp.
SuperPawn
Cashland Financial Services, Inc.
Cash America Payday Advance
Prenda Facil
CashNetUSA.com
QuickQuid.co.uk
DollarsDirect.com.au

CONTACTS: Note: Officers with more than one job title may be intentionally listed here more than once.

Daniel R. Feehan, CEO
Daniel R. Feehan, Pres.
Thomas A. Bessant, Jr., CFO/Exec. VP
Timothy Ho, Pres., Internet Svcs.
Robert D. Brockman, Exec. VP-Admin.
J. Curtis Linscott, General Counsel/Exec. VP/Corp. Sec.
Jerry D. Finn, Exec. VP-Domestic Pawn Oper.
Michael D. Gaston, Exec. VP-Corp. Dev.
John A. McDorman, Pres., Shared Svcs. Div.
Dennis J. Weese, COO/Pres., Retail Services Div.
Jerry A. Wackerhagen, Pres., Stores Div.
Jack R. Daugherty, Chmn.

Phone: 817-335-1100	Fax: 817-570-1225
Toll-Free:	
Address: 1600 W. 7th St., Fort Worth, TX 76102 US	

GROWTH PLANS/SPECIAL FEATURES:

Cash America International, Inc. provides pawn loans, short-term cash advances, check cashing services and other specialty financial services. The company also sells merchandise in its pawnshops, primarily personal property that has been forfeited in connection with its pawn lending operations. The firm provides its specialty financial services via its 1,000+ locations, including 501 pawnshops in 22 states (including 15 pawnshops that are franchises), as well as via the Internet. Most of Cash American's pawnshops operate under the Cash America trade name; 43 pawnshops (located in Arizona, California, Nevada and Washington) operate under the SuperPawn trade name. The company offers unsecured cash advances to individuals through most of its pawnshops, 74 stand-alone Cash America Payday Advance locations and 174 locations operated by wholly-owned subsidiary Cashland Financial Services, Inc. Cash America also offers short-term loans over the Internet in the U.S. via its CashNetUSA.com web site and in the U.K. via the QuickQuid.co.uk web site. Through Mr. Payroll Corp., it offers check cashing services through 128 franchised and five company-owned check cashing centers. Many of Cash America's pawn and cash advance locations also offer check cashing services and other retail financial services such as stored value cards, money orders and money transfers. In July 2008, the company, through a wholly-owned subsidiary, Primary Cash Holdings, LLC (now known as Primary Innovations, LLC), purchased the assets of Primary Business Services, Inc.; Primary Finance, Inc.; Primary Processing, Inc.; and Primary Members Insurance Services, Inc., a group of companies engaged in providing loan processing services for a bank-issued line of credit. In 2008, Cash America purchased majority ownership in Prenda Facil, a Mexican chain of pawn shops. Following this acquisition, in 2009, the company opened its 1,000th worldwide location in Mexico and expanded online lending into Australia with DollarsDirect.com.au.

FINANCIALS: Sales and profits are in thousands of dollars—add 000 to get the full amount. 2008 Note: Financial information for 2008 was not available for all companies at press time.

2008 Sales: $1,030,794	2008 Profits: $81,140	U.S. Stock Ticker: CSH
2007 Sales: $929,394	2007 Profits: $79,346	Int'l Ticker: Int'l Exchange:
2006 Sales: $694,514	2006 Profits: $60,940	Employees: 5,587
2005 Sales: $594,346	2005 Profits: $45,018	Fiscal Year Ends: 12/31
2004 Sales: $469,478	2004 Profits: $56,835	Parent Company:

SALARIES/BENEFITS:

Pension Plan:	ESOP Stock Plan:	Profit Sharing:	Top Exec. Salary: $726,000	Bonus: $700,000
Savings Plan: Y	Stock Purch. Plan:		Second Exec. Salary: $375,436	Bonus: $169,202

OTHER THOUGHTS:

Apparent Women Officers or Directors:
Hot Spot for Advancement for Women/Minorities:

LOCATIONS: ("Y" = Yes)

West:	Southwest:	Midwest:	Southeast:	Northeast:	International:
Y	Y	Y	Y	Y	Y

Note: Financial information, benefits and other data can change quickly and may vary from those stated here.

CATERPILLAR INC

www.cat.com

Industry Group Code: 333 Ranks within this company's industry group: Sales: 1   Profits: 1

Management:		Sales/Marketing:		Liberal Arts:		Information Systems:		Professionals:		Tech./Scientific:	
Management Trainees:	Y	Marketing Pros.:	Y	Gen. Writing/Editing:	Y	Info. Management:	Y	Finance/Acct.:	Y	Engineers, Electrical:	Y
Experienced Mngmt.:	Y	Retail Sales:		Technical Writing:	Y	Software Dev.:	Y	Law:	Y	Engineers, Other:	Y
International Business:	Y	Commercial/Industrial:	Y	Graphic Arts/Photog.:	Y	Hardware Dev.:	Y	HR/Other:	Y	Health/Lab:	
MBA Grads:	Y	Sales Trainees:		Music:		Consulting/Other:		Training:	Y	Scientists/Research:	
		Advertising Pros.:	Y	Broadcasting:				Health Care:		Petroleum/Chemicals:	
				Other:				Consulting:		Math/Other:	

TYPES OF BUSINESS:

Machinery-Earth Moving & Agricultural
Engines
Financing
Fuel Cell Manufacturing
Turbine Engines
Engine & Equipment Remanufacturing
Supply Chain Services

BRANDS/DIVISIONS/AFFILIATES:

Progress Rail Services, Inc.
Navistar International Corp.

CONTACTS: *Note: Officers with more than one job title may be intentionally listed here more than once.*

James W. Owens, CEO
David B. Burritt, CFO/VP
W. F. Springer, VP-Mktg. & Sales
Sidney C. Banwart, VP-Human Svcs.
John S. Heller, CIO/VP
Tana L. Utley, CTO/VP
James B. Buda, General Counsel/VP/Corp. Sec.
Robert T. Williams, VP-Americas Oper.
Kevin E. Colgan, Treas.
Jiming Zhu, VP-China Div.
Thomas A. Gales, VP-Latin America Div.
Steven L. Fisher, VP-Remanufacturing Div.
James W. Owens, Chmn.
Cristiano V. Schena, VP-EMEA
Daniel M. Murphy, VP-Global Purchasing

Phone: 309-675-1000	Fax: 309-675-4332
Toll-Free:	
Address: 100 NE Adams St., Peoria, IL 61629 US	

GROWTH PLANS/SPECIAL FEATURES:

Caterpillar, Inc. manufactures construction equipment. The company's three principal lines of business are machinery, engines and financial products. The machinery segment designs, manufactures and markets construction, mining, agricultural and forestry machinery, including track and wheel tractors, track and wheel loaders, pipe layers, motor graders, wheel tractor-scrapers, track and wheel excavators, backhoe loaders, mining shovels, log skidders, log loaders, off-highway trucks, articulated trucks, paving products, telescopic handlers, skid steer loaders and parts. The engines segment designs, manufactures and markets engines for Caterpillar machinery; electric power generation systems; on-highway vehicles and locomotives; marine, petroleum, construction, industrial, agricultural and other applications; and related parts. Caterpillar also manufactures fuel cells, designed to incorporate ethanol, methanol, natural gas, propane, methane, hydrogen and biomass fuels. The firm's Solar Turbines subsidiary is a world leader in industrial gas turbine power system engines. The financial products segment provides financing to customers and dealers for the purchase and lease of Caterpillar and other equipment, financing approximately 60% of equipment sold. Caterpillar has a network 52 U.S. dealers and 128 outside of the U.S. Worldwide, these dealers serve 182 countries and operate 3,537 places of business, including rental outlets. More than half of the company's sales are to overseas customers. Caterpillar's logistics business provides supply chain services to Caterpillar and over 55 other companies worldwide. The company has targeted China as an area for potentially explosive growth. Caterpillar also holds Progress Rail Services, a remanufacturer of locomotives and railcars. In April 2009, Caterpillar and Navistar International Corp. signed a deal to produce Caterpillar trucks and form a 50/50 joint venture to develop international commercial opportunities.

FINANCIALS: Sales and profits are in thousands of dollars—add 000 to get the full amount. 2008 Note: Financial information for 2008 was not available for all companies at press time.

2008 Sales: $51,324,000	2008 Profits: $3,557,000	**U.S. Stock Ticker: CAT**
2007 Sales: $44,958,000	2007 Profits: $3,541,000	**Int'l Ticker:** Int'l Exchange:
2006 Sales: $41,517,000	2006 Profits: $3,537,000	Employees: 112,887
2005 Sales: $36,339,000	2005 Profits: $2,854,000	Fiscal Year Ends: 12/31
2004 Sales: $30,306,000	2004 Profits: $2,035,000	Parent Company:

SALARIES/BENEFITS:

Pension Plan: Y	ESOP Stock Plan:	Profit Sharing:	Top Exec. Salary: $1,550,004	Bonus: $4,353,227
Savings Plan: Y	Stock Purch. Plan:		Second Exec. Salary: $880,993	Bonus: $1,755,385

OTHER THOUGHTS:

Apparent Women Officers or Directors: 6
Hot Spot for Advancement for Women/Minorities: Y

LOCATIONS: ("Y" = Yes)

West:	Southwest:	Midwest:	Southeast:	Northeast:	International:
Y	Y	Y	Y	Y	Y

Note: Financial information, benefits and other data can change quickly and may vary from those stated here.

CATHOLIC HEALTH INITIATIVES

www.catholichealthinit.org

Industry Group Code: 622110 **Ranks within this company's industry group:** Sales: 5 Profits: 5

Management:		Sales/Marketing:		Liberal Arts:		Information Systems:		Professionals:		Tech./Scientific:	
Management Trainees:	Y	Marketing Pros.:	Y	Gen. Writing/Editing:	Y	Info. Management:	Y	Finance/Acct.:	Y	Engineers, Electrical:	
Experienced Mngmt.:	Y	Retail Sales:		Technical Writing:	Y	Software Dev.:	Y	Law:	Y	Engineers, Other:	
International Business:		Commercial/Industrial:		Graphic Arts/Photog.:	Y	Hardware Dev.:		HR/Other:	Y	Health/Lab:	Y
MBA Grads:	Y	Sales Trainees:		Music:		Consulting/Other:		Training:	Y	Scientists/Research:	
		Advertising Pros.:	Y	Broadcasting:				Health Care:	Y	Petroleum/Chemicals:	
				Other:	Y			Consulting:		Math/Other:	

TYPES OF BUSINESS:

Hospitals
Long-Term Care
Assisted & Independent Living Facilities
Community Health Organizations
Home Care Services
Occupational Health Clinic
Cancer Prevention Institute

BRANDS/DIVISIONS/AFFILIATES:

Centura Health
Franciscan Health System
Alegant Health
Good Samaritan Health Systems
Premier Health Partners

CONTACTS: Note: Officers with more than one job title may be intentionally listed here more than once.

Kevin E. Lofton, CEO
Michael T. Rowan, COO/Exec. VP
Kevin E. Lofton, Pres.
Colleen M. Blye, CFO
Herbert J. Vallier, Chief Human Resource Officer/Sr. VP
Kathleen D. Sanford, Interim Chief Medical Officer
Michael O'Rourke, CIO/Sr. VP
John E. Newton, VP-Legal Svcs.
John F. DiCola, Sr. VP-Strategy & Bus. Dev.
Joyce M. Ross, Sr. VP-Comm.
Colleen M. Blye, Exec. VP-Finance & Integrated Svcs.
A. Michelle Cooper, VP-Corp. Responsibility
Paul W. Edgett, III, Sr. VP-National Bus. Lines
Susan M. Peach, Sr. VP-Performance Mgmt.
Kathleen D. Sanford, Chief Nursing Officer
Phyllis Hughes, Chmn.
Phillip W. Mears, Sr. VP-Supply Chain

Phone: 303-298-9100	**Fax:** 303-298-9296
Toll-Free:	
Address: 1999 Broadway, Ste. 4000, Denver, CO 80202 US	

GROWTH PLANS/SPECIAL FEATURES:

Catholic Health Initiatives (CHI) is a national nonprofit health care organization focused on strengthening and advancing the Catholic health ministry. The organization encompasses approximately 78 hospitals; more than 40 long-term care, assisted and independent living residential facilities; and two community health organizations, serving approximately 69 urban and rural communities across 20 states. The group's major affiliates include Centura Health, Alegent Health, Good Samaritan Health Systems, Premier Health Partners and Franciscan Health System. Altogether, CHI has over 14,000 beds, and is among the largest Catholic health systems in the U.S. Centura Health, jointly operated by CHI and PorterCare Adventist Health Care, has 12 hospitals and seven senior residences and home care and hospice services. Alegent Health, jointly operated with Immanuel Healthcare System, is made up of nine acute care hospitals with 1,800 beds, two long-term care facilities and a primary care physician network. Good Samaritan Health Systems is a network of hospitals and services serving more than 350,000 customers in the Midwest. Premier Health Partners, jointly operated with MedAmerica Health Systems, includes four hospitals, one assisted living community, a home health care service and a cancer prevention institute. Franciscan Health System includes a number of full-service hospitals, a long-term care facility, a women's health center and midwife service and an occupational health clinic, among other services. In April 2008, Good Samaritan Hospital in Dayton, Ohio, acquired the assets of Dayton Heart Hospital for $55 million and assumed control of Dayton Heart's operations in May 2008. In April 2009, subsidiary St. Joseph Medical Center in Reading, Pennsylvania announced an affiliation with Penn State Hershey Medical Center to provide additional services and treatment options to oncology patients. In March 2009, Franciscan Health System opened a new hospital, St. Anthony's, in Gig Harbor, Washington; the 80-bed facility is the fifth in the Franciscan Health System network.

FINANCIALS: Sales and profits are in thousands of dollars—add 000 to get the full amount. 2008 Note: Financial information for 2008 was not available for all companies at press time.

2008 Sales: $8,244,600	2008 Profits: $123,058	**U.S. Stock Ticker: Nonprofit**	
2007 Sales: $7,731,500	2007 Profits: $	**Int'l Ticker:** Int'l Exchange:	
2006 Sales: $7,636,233	2006 Profits: $693,701	Employees: 57,859	
2005 Sales: $7,091,448	2005 Profits: $498,374	Fiscal Year Ends: 6/30	
2004 Sales: $6,659,711	2004 Profits: $538,295	Parent Company:	

SALARIES/BENEFITS:

Pension Plan:	ESOP Stock Plan:	Profit Sharing:	Top Exec. Salary: $	Bonus: $
Savings Plan:	Stock Purch. Plan:		Second Exec. Salary: $	Bonus: $

OTHER THOUGHTS:

Apparent Women Officers or Directors: 9
Hot Spot for Advancement for Women/Minorities: Y

LOCATIONS: ("Y" = Yes)

West:	Southwest:	Midwest:	Southeast:	Northeast:	International:
Y	Y	Y	Y	Y	

Note: Financial information, benefits and other data can change quickly and may vary from those stated here.

CDW CORPORATION

www.cdw.com

Industry Group Code: 423430 **Ranks within this company's industry group:** Sales: 5   Profits:

Management:		Sales/Marketing:		Liberal Arts:		Information Systems:		Professionals:		Tech./Scientific:	
Management Trainees:	Y	Marketing Pros.:	Y	Gen. Writing/Editing:	Y	Info. Management:	Y	Finance/Acct.:	Y	Engineers, Electrical:	
Experienced Mngmt.:	Y	Retail Sales:		Technical Writing:	Y	Software Dev.:	Y	Law:	Y	Engineers, Other:	
International Business:	Y	Commercial/Industrial:	Y	Graphic Arts/Photog.:	Y	Hardware Dev.:		HR/Other:	Y	Health/Lab:	
MBA Grads:	Y	Sales Trainees:	Y	Music:		Consulting/Other:		Training:	Y	Scientists/Research:	
		Advertising Pros.:	Y	Broadcasting:				Health Care:		Petroleum/Chemicals:	
				Other:				Consulting:		Math/Other:	

TYPES OF BUSINESS:

Computer Products, Direct Selling
Catalog Sales
Online Sales
Retail Showrooms
Support Services

BRANDS/DIVISIONS/AFFILIATES:

CDW Government Inc
CDW Canada Inc
Berbee Information Networks Corp
Madison Dearborn Partners LLC
Providence Equity Partners

CONTACTS: *Note: Officers with more than one job title may be intentionally listed here more than once.*

John A. Edwardson, CEO
Ann E. Ziegler, CFO/Sr. VP
Mark J. Gambill, Chief Mktg. Officer/VP
Dennis G. Berger, Sr. VP/Chief Coworker Svcs. Officer
Jonathan J. Stevens, CIO/Sr. VP
Terry L. Swanson, VP-Advanced Tech.
Christine A. Leahy, General Counsel/Sr. VP/Sec.
Douglas E. Eckrote, Sr. VP-Oper.
Gary Ross, Sr. Mgr.-Corp. Comm.
Cindy Thorson Klimstra, VP-Investor Rel.
Virginia L. Seggerman, Controller/VP
Christina V. Rother, Pres., CDW Government, Inc.
James J. Lillis, VP-Svcs.
Maria M. Sullivan, VP-Small Bus.
John A. Edwardson, Chmn.

Phone: 847-465-6000	Fax: 847-465-6800
Toll-Free: 800-750-4239	
Address: 200 N. Milwaukee Ave., Vernon Hills, IL 60061 US	

GROWTH PLANS/SPECIAL FEATURES:

CDW Corp., owned by private equity firms Madison Dearborn Partners, LLC and Providence Equity Partners, Inc., is a provider of multi-branded information technology products and services to business, government and education customers in the U.S. and Canada. The company operates in three segments, corporate sector, public sector and Berbee. The firm offers more than 80,000 microcomputer products include hardware and peripherals; software; accessories; and other products. CDW offers customers a broad range of technology products from brands such as Acer, Adobe, APS, Apple, Cisco, Fujitsu, Hewlett-Packard, IBM, Lenovo, Microsoft, Panasonic, Quantum, Samsung, Sony, Symantec and ViewSonic, among others. The company manages its inventory with a proprietary information technology system combined with a 450,000-square-foot distribution center, shipping approximately 15,000 items daily. The firm focuses on selling to small and medium-sized businesses through catalogs, direct mailings, advertisements in trade magazines, web sites and various other web advertising vehicles. Additionally, it promotes the CDW brand nationally through its branding campaign, which includes television, print media and other activities. CDW offers customers free access to over 140 support technicians with over 400 manufacturer certifications, in addition to direct links to manufacturers' tech support web sites. CDW Government, Inc. subsidiary provides specialized product offerings and services to federal, state and local governments, as well as the educational sector. CDW Canada, Inc. serves business and public sector customers in Canada.

The company offers its employees medical, dental and vision insurance; a 401(k) plan; a profit sharing plan; an employee stock purchase plan; life and AD&D insurance; short- and long-term disability insurance; and an employee assistance program.

FINANCIALS: Sales and profits are in thousands of dollars—add 000 to get the full amount. 2008 Note: Financial information for 2008 was not available for all companies at press time.

2008 Sales: $8,071,000	2008 Profits: $	**U.S. Stock Ticker:** Private
2007 Sales: $8,145,000	2007 Profits: $	**Int'l Ticker:** Int'l Exchange:
2006 Sales: $6,785,473	2006 Profits: $266,080	Employees: 6,850
2005 Sales: $6,291,845	2005 Profits: $272,092	Fiscal Year Ends: 12/31
2004 Sales: $5,737,800	2004 Profits: $241,400	Parent Company: MADISON DEARBORN PARTNERS LLC

SALARIES/BENEFITS:

Pension Plan:	ESOP Stock Plan: Y	Profit Sharing: Y	Top Exec. Salary: $	Bonus: $1,055,629
Savings Plan: Y	Stock Purch. Plan:		Second Exec. Salary: $	Bonus: $

OTHER THOUGHTS:

Apparent Women Officers or Directors: 6
Hot Spot for Advancement for Women/Minorities: Y

LOCATIONS: ("Y" = Yes)

West:	Southwest:	Midwest:	Southeast:	Northeast:	International:
		Y			Y

Note: Financial information, benefits and other data can change quickly and may vary from those stated here.

CELGENE CORP

www.celgene.com

Industry Group Code: 325412 **Ranks within this company's industry group:** Sales: 15 Profits: 17

Management:		Sales/Marketing:		Liberal Arts:		Information Systems:		Professionals:		Tech./Scientific:	
Management Trainees:	Y	Marketing Pros.:	Y	Gen. Writing/Editing:		Info. Management:	Y	Finance/Acct.:	Y	Engineers, Electrical:	Y
Experienced Mngmt.:	Y	Retail Sales:		Technical Writing:	Y	Software Dev.:	Y	Law:	Y	Engineers, Other:	Y
International Business:	Y	Commercial/Industrial:	Y	Graphic Arts/Photog.:	Y	Hardware Dev.:		HR/Other:	Y	Health/Lab:	Y
MBA Grads:	Y	Sales Trainees:		Music:		Consulting/Other:		Training:	Y	Scientists/Research:	Y
		Advertising Pros.:		Broadcasting:				Health Care:	Y	Petroleum/Chemicals:	Y
				Other:				Consulting:		Math/Other:	Y

TYPES OF BUSINESS:

Cancer & Immune-Inflammatory Related Diseases Drugs

BRANDS/DIVISIONS/AFFILIATES:

REVLIMID
THALOMID
ALKERAN
FOCALIN
FOCALIN XR
RITALIN
VIDAZA
Pharmion Corp

CONTACTS: Note: Officers with more than one job title may be intentionally listed here more than once.

Sol J. Barer, CEO
Robert J. Hugin, COO
Robert J. Hugin, Pres.
David W. Gryska, CFO/Sr. VP
Graham Burton, Sr. VP-Regulatory Affairs & Pharmacovigilance
Sol J. Barer, Chmn.
Aart Brouwer, Pres., Int'l

Phone: 908-673-9000	Fax: 732-271-4184
Toll-Free:	
Address: 86 Morris Ave., Summit, NJ 07901 US	

GROWTH PLANS/SPECIAL FEATURES:

Celgene Corp. is a global integrated biopharmaceutical company primarily engaged in the discovery, development and commercialization of therapies designed to treat cancer and immune-inflammatory related diseases. The company's commercial stage products are Revlimid, Thalomid and Vidaza. Revlimid has been approved by the U.S. FDA, the European Commission (EC), the Swiss Agency for Therapeutic Products (Swissmedic) and the Australian Therapeutic Goods Administration for treatment in combination with dexamethasone for multiple myeloma patients who have received at least one prior therapy. In addition, Revlimid has been approved by the FDA and the Canadian Therapeutics Directorate for treatment of patients with transfusion-dependent anemia due to low- or intermediate-1-risk myelodysplastic syndromes (MDS) associated with a deletion 5q cytogenetic abnormality with or without additional cytogenetic abnormalities. Thalomid has been approved by the FDA for treatment in combination with dexamethasone of patients with newly diagnosed multiple myeloma and is also approved for the treatment and suppression of cutaneous manifestations of erythema nodosum leprosum (ENL), an inflammatory complication of leprosy. Vidaza, which was integrated into the Celgene lineup after their 2008 acquisition of Pharmion Corp., is approved for treatment in patients with various myelodysplastic syndrome subtypes. Celgene also sells Alkeran, which it obtains through a supply and distribution agreement with GlaxoSmithKline (GSK), and Focalin, which it sells exclusively to Novartis Pharma AG. Other sources of revenue include royalties which the company receives primarily from Novartis on its sales of the entire family of Ritalin drugs and Focalin XR, in addition to revenues from collaborative agreements and licensing fees. Its portfolio of drug candidates includes IMiDs compounds, which are proprietary to the firm and have demonstrated certain immunomodulatory and other biologically important properties.

Celgene offers its employees educational assistance; travel assistance; and medical, dental, vision, life, AD&D, business travel accident and disability insurance.

FINANCIALS: Sales and profits are in thousands of dollars—add 000 to get the full amount. 2008 Note: Financial information for 2008 was not available for all companies at press time.

2008 Sales: $2,254,781	2008 Profits: $-1,533,653	**U.S. Stock Ticker:** CELG	
2007 Sales: $1,405,820	2007 Profits: $226,433	**Int'l Ticker:** Int'l Exchange:	
2006 Sales: $898,873	2006 Profits: $68,981	Employees: 2,550	
2005 Sales: $536,941	2005 Profits: $63,656	Fiscal Year Ends: 12/31	
2004 Sales: $377,502	2004 Profits: $52,756	Parent Company:	

SALARIES/BENEFITS:

Pension Plan:	ESOP Stock Plan:	Profit Sharing:	Top Exec. Salary: $939,000	Bonus: $2,166,955
Savings Plan: Y	Stock Purch. Plan:		Second Exec. Salary: $733,333	Bonus: $1,571,730

OTHER THOUGHTS:

Apparent Women Officers or Directors: 1
Hot Spot for Advancement for Women/Minorities:

LOCATIONS: ("Y" = Yes)

West:	Southwest:	Midwest:	Southeast:	Northeast:	International:
				Y	Y

Note: Financial information, benefits and other data can change quickly and may vary from those stated here.

CELLCO PARTNERSHIP (VERIZON WIRELESS)

www.verizonwireless.com
Industry Group Code: 5172 Ranks within this company's industry group: Sales: 1   Profits:

Management:		Sales/Marketing:		Liberal Arts:		Information Systems:		Professionals:		Tech./Scientific:	
Management Trainees:	Y	Marketing Pros.:	Y	Gen. Writing/Editing:	Y	Info. Management:	Y	Finance/Acct.:	Y	Engineers, Electrical:	Y
Experienced Mngmt.:	Y	Retail Sales:	Y	Technical Writing:	Y	Software Dev.:	Y	Law:	Y	Engineers, Other:	Y
International Business:		Commercial/Industrial:	Y	Graphic Arts/Photog.:	Y	Hardware Dev.:		HR/Other:	Y	Health/Lab:	
MBA Grads:	Y	Sales Trainees:	Y	Music:		Consulting/Other:		Training:	Y	Scientists/Research:	
		Advertising Pros.:	Y	Broadcasting:				Health Care:		Petroleum/Chemicals:	
				Other:	Y			Consulting:		Math/Other:	

TYPES OF BUSINESS:

Cellular Phone Service
Retail Sales
Wireless Internet
Media & Ringtones

BRANDS/DIVISIONS/AFFILIATES:

Verizon Wireless
Verizon Communications Inc
Vodafone Group PLC
SureWest Communications
Rural Cellular Corp
Ramcell
LiMo Foundation
Alltel Corporation

CONTACTS: *Note: Officers with more than one job title may be intentionally listed here more than once.*

Lowell McAdam, CEO
Jack Plating, COO/Exec. VP
Lowell McAdam, Pres.
John Townsend, CFO/VP
Mike Lanman, Chief Mktg. Officer/VP
Martha Delehanty, VP-Human Resources
Ajay Waghray, CIO
Anthony Melone, CTO/Sr. VP
Steve Zipperstein, VP-Legal & External Affairs
Margaret Feldman, VP-Bus. Dev.
Jim Gerace, VP-Corp. Comm.
Mark Harris, VP-Gov't Sales & Oper.
Charlie Falco, VP-Customer Svc. Oper.
Rose M. Kirk, VP-Enterprise Sales & Distribution
Anthony A. Lewis, VP-Open Dev.

Phone: 908-559-7000	Fax:
Toll-Free: 800-922-0204	
Address: 1 Verizon Way, Basking Ridge, NJ 07920 US	

GROWTH PLANS/SPECIAL FEATURES:

Cellco Partnership, doing business as Verizon Wireless, is a joint venture between Verizon Communications and Vodafone; the former owns 55% of Cellco, while the latter owns 45%. Verizon Wireless was formed in 2000 when Vodafone and Bell Atlantic merged their U.S. wireless holdings. The company then acquired the U.S. wireless assets of GTE, when Bell Atlantic bought GTE to create Verizon Communications. The firm operates over 2,000 company stores and kiosks; and 175 switching centers. The company offers BroadbandAccess and NationalAccess for coast-to-coast laptop, personal digital assistants (PDAs) and handset connectivity; VCAST Music service for downloading music, music videos, VCAST video clips, 3D games and other multimedia services; and Get It Now for text and picture messaging, downloading ringtones, ringback tones, games and news alerts on a mobile handset. In May 2008, Verizon Wireless signed a five-year agreement with Qwest Communications International Inc. for Qwest to market and sell Verizon service. Also in May, the company purchased the wireless assets of SureWest Communications in the Sacramento, California area. In May 2008, the firm joined the LiMo Foundation, a global alliance based around open handset platform development.   In August 2008, the company acquired Rural Cellular Corp. In January 2009, the company acquired Alltel Corporation from Atlantis Holdings LLC, increasing its network coverage to 290 million people, and making Verizon the largest wireless carriers in the country with 83.7 million customers.

The company provides its employees with medical and dental insurance; vision care; life insurance; prescription drug benefits; adoption assistance; health and dependant care spending accounts; phone discounts; childcare discounts; and tuition assistance.

FINANCIALS: Sales and profits are in thousands of dollars—add 000 to get the full amount. 2008 Note: Financial information for 2008 was not available for all companies at press time.

2008 Sales: $58,600,000	2008 Profits: $	U.S. Stock Ticker: Joint Venture
2007 Sales: $43,900,000	2007 Profits: $	Int'l Ticker: Int'l Exchange:
2006 Sales: $38,000,000	2006 Profits: $	Employees: 86,000
2005 Sales: $32,300,000	2005 Profits: $6,152,000	Fiscal Year Ends: 12/31
2004 Sales: $27,662,000	2004 Profits: $4,698,000	Parent Company:

SALARIES/BENEFITS:

Pension Plan:	ESOP Stock Plan:	Profit Sharing: Y	Top Exec. Salary: $	Bonus: $4,252,500
Savings Plan: Y	Stock Purch. Plan:		Second Exec. Salary: $	Bonus: $

OTHER THOUGHTS:

Apparent Women Officers or Directors: 7
Hot Spot for Advancement for Women/Minorities: Y

LOCATIONS: ("Y" = Yes)

West:	Southwest:	Midwest:	Southeast:	Northeast:	International:
Y	Y	Y	Y	Y	

CEPHALON INC

www.cephalon.com

Industry Group Code: 325412 Ranks within this company's industry group: Sales: 16   Profits: 13

Management:		Sales/Marketing:		Liberal Arts:		Information Systems:		Professionals:		Tech./Scientific:	
Management Trainees:	Y	Marketing Pros.:	Y	Gen. Writing/Editing:		Info. Management:	Y	Finance/Acct.:	Y	Engineers, Electrical:	Y
Experienced Mngmt.:	Y	Retail Sales:		Technical Writing:	Y	Software Dev.:	Y	Law:	Y	Engineers, Other:	Y
International Business:	Y	Commercial/Industrial:	Y	Graphic Arts/Photog.:	Y	Hardware Dev.:		HR/Other:	Y	Health/Lab:	Y
MBA Grads:	Y	Sales Trainees:		Music:		Consulting/Other:		Training:	Y	Scientists/Research:	Y
		Advertising Pros.:		Broadcasting:				Health Care:	Y	Petroleum/Chemicals:	Y
				Other:				Consulting:		Math/Other:	Y

TYPES OF BUSINESS:

Pharmaceutical Discovery & Development
Neurological Disorder Treatments
Cancer Treatments
Pain Medications
Addiction Treatment

BRANDS/DIVISIONS/AFFILIATES:

Provigil
Actiq
Fentora
Trisenox
Vivitrol
Nuvigil
Treanda
AMRIX

CONTACTS: *Note: Officers with more than one job title may be intentionally listed here more than once.*

Frank Baldino, Jr., CEO
J. Kevin Buchi, CFO/Exec. VP
Jeffry L. Vaught, Chief Science Officer/Exec. VP-R&D
Peter E. Grebow, Sr. VP-Worldwide Tech. Oper.
Carl A. Savini, Chief Admin. Officer/Exec. VP
Gerald J. Pappert, General Counsel/Exec. VP
Lesley Russell, Exec. VP-Worldwide Medical & Regulatory Oper.
Valli F. Baldassano, Chief Compliance Officer/Exec. VP
Frank Baldino, Jr., Chmn.
Robert P. Roche, Jr., Sr. VP-Worldwide Pharmaceutical Oper.

Phone: 610-344-0200	Fax: 610-738-6590
Toll-Free:	
Address: 41 Moores Rd., Frazer, PA 19355 US	

GROWTH PLANS/SPECIAL FEATURES:

Cephalon, Inc. is a biopharmaceutical company focused on the discovery, development and marketing of products in four core areas: Central nervous system (CNS) disorders, pain, oncology and addiction. It conducts research and development as well as marketing its products in the U.S. and Europe. Cephalon's technology principally focuses on understanding the class of enzymes known as kinases and the role they play in cellular survival and proliferation. The company's CNS products include its most significant product, Provigil which is designed to treat extreme sleepiness associated with narcolepsy and other sleep disorders. The firm's other CNS medication is Gabitril, designed for partial seizures in epileptic patients. The firm's two pain management products, Actiq and Fentora, are designed for patients who are opiod-tolerant. Cephalon's oncology products include Trisenox (an arsenic salt), which is marketed in the U.S. and Europe to treat patients with relapsed acute promyelocytic leukemia (APL). Other products include Amrix, a muscle relaxant (obtained from E. Claiborne Robins Co., Inc.) designed to relieve spasms due to musculoskeletal conditions; Treanda, a chemotherapy drug used for chronic lymphocytic leukemia; and Nuvigil, a treatment similar to Provigil. Cephalon also has a number of products in development, including treatments for Alzheimer's Disease, pain management, tumors, leukemia, multiple myeloma, lymphoma and lupus. In January 2009, the company acquired Ception Therapeutics, a private biopharmaceutical company developing drugs to treat pediatric eosinophilic esophagitis and adult eosinophilic asthma. In February 2009, the firm obtained a majority stake in the Australian biopharmaceutical company Arana, which develops and licenses anti-inflammatory treatments.

Cephalon's benefits include medical, prescription drug, dental and disability coverage; life insurance; a 401(k) profit sharing plan; flexible spending accounts; educational reimbursements; and health advocacy services.

FINANCIALS: Sales and profits are in thousands of dollars—add 000 to get the full amount. 2008 Note: Financial information for 2008 was not available for all companies at press time.

2008 Sales: $1,974,554	2008 Profits: $222,548	**U.S. Stock Ticker: CEPH**
2007 Sales: $1,772,638	2007 Profits: $-191,704	**Int'l Ticker:** Int'l Exchange:
2006 Sales: $1,764,069	2006 Profits: $144,816	Employees: 2,780
2005 Sales: $1,211,892	2005 Profits: $-174,954	Fiscal Year Ends: 12/31
2004 Sales: $1,015,400	2004 Profits: $-73,800	Parent Company:

SALARIES/BENEFITS:

Pension Plan:	ESOP Stock Plan:	Profit Sharing: Y	Top Exec. Salary: $1,244,600	Bonus: $1,779,800
Savings Plan: Y	Stock Purch. Plan:		Second Exec. Salary: $567,600	Bonus: $380,300

OTHER THOUGHTS:

Apparent Women Officers or Directors: 1
Hot Spot for Advancement for Women/Minorities:

LOCATIONS: ("Y" = Yes)

West:	Southwest:	Midwest:	Southeast:	Northeast:	International:
Y		Y		Y	Y

Note: Financial information, benefits and other data can change quickly and may vary from those stated here.

CH ROBINSON WORLDWIDE INC

www.chrobinson.com

Industry Group Code: 4885 Ranks within this company's industry group: Sales: 1 Profits: 1

Management:		Sales/Marketing:		Liberal Arts:		Information Systems:		Professionals:		Tech./Scientific:	
Management Trainees:	Y	Marketing Pros.:	Y	Gen. Writing/Editing:	Y	Info. Management:	Y	Finance/Acct.:	Y	Engineers, Electrical:	
Experienced Mngmt.:	Y	Retail Sales:		Technical Writing:	Y	Software Dev.:	Y	Law:	Y	Engineers, Other:	
International Business:	Y	Commercial/Industrial:	Y	Graphic Arts/Photog.:		Hardware Dev.:		HR/Other:	Y	Health/Lab:	
MBA Grads:	Y	Sales Trainees:		Music:		Consulting/Other:		Training:	Y	Scientists/Research:	
		Advertising Pros.:	Y	Broadcasting:				Health Care:		Petroleum/Chemicals:	
				Other:				Consulting:		Math/Other:	

TYPES OF BUSINESS:

Freight Logistics
Produce Sourcing
Expedited Services
Fuel Purchasing Management Services
3PL Third Party Logistics
Warehouse & Distribution Services

BRANDS/DIVISIONS/AFFILIATES:

CHREX
T-Check Systems, Inc.
Fresh 1 (The)
OurWorld

CONTACTS: *Note: Officers with more than one job title may be intentionally listed here more than once.*

John P. Wiehoff, CEO
Chad M. Lindbloom, CFO/Sr. VP
Laura Gillund, VP-Human Resources
Thomas K. Mahlke, CIO/VP
Ben Campbell, General Counsel/VP/Sec.
Angie Freeman, VP-Public Rel.
Angie Freeman, VP-Investor Rel.
Troy A. Renner, Treas.
Jim Butts, Sr. VP
Mark A. Walker, Sr. VP
Jim Lemke, Sr. VP-Produce
Timothy P. Manning, VP
John P. Wiehoff, Chmn.

Phone: 952-937-8500	Fax: 952-937-6714
Toll-Free:	
Address: 14701 Charlson Rd., Eden Prairie, MN 55347-5076 US	

GROWTH PLANS/SPECIAL FEATURES:

C.H. Robinson Worldwide, Inc. (CHRW) is one of North America's largest third-party logistics (3PL) providers and a global provider of multimodal transportation services. It operates through 224 offices in the U.S., Canada, Mexico, Europe, South America and Asia. CHRW operates in three sectors: multimodal transportation services, which account for 88% of the firm's gross profits; fresh produce sourcing, 8%; and information services, 4%. In the multimodal transportation services sector, the company (which does not own any of its own equipment) maintains one of the largest networks of motor carrier capacity in the world through contracts with approximately 48,000 carriers. CHRW serves more than 29,000 customers and handles approximately 6.5 million shipments annually. Subsidiary CHREX provides expedited services and is one of the largest capacity providers in the expedited market. The group also contracts air carriers and specialty motor carriers that provide temperature-controlled and less-than-truckload services. The sourcing sector focuses on procuring fresh produce for retailers, wholesalers and foodservice operators nationwide. CHRW has its own brands of produce called The Fresh 1 and Ourworld which is sourced through various growers and packed through contract agreements with other packaging firms. The information services segment operates primarily through subsidiary T-Check Systems, Inc., which offers fuel purchasing management services for motor carriers. In August 2008, the company acquired certain operating subsidiaries of Canada-based firm, Transera International Holdings Ltd.

Employees are offered Medical, dental and vision insurance; life insurance; short-and long-term disability coverage; flexible spending accounts; a 401(k) plan; profit sharing; a discount stock purchase plan; and an employee assistance program.

FINANCIALS: Sales and profits are in thousands of dollars—add 000 to get the full amount. 2008 Note: Financial information for 2008 was not available for all companies at press time.

2008 Sales: $8,578,614	2008 Profits: $359,177	**U.S. Stock Ticker: CHRW**	
2007 Sales: $7,316,223	2007 Profits: $324,261	**Int'l Ticker:** Int'l Exchange:	
2006 Sales: $6,556,194	2006 Profits: $266,925	Employees: 7,961	
2005 Sales: $5,688,948	2005 Profits: $203,358	Fiscal Year Ends: 12/31	
2004 Sales: $4,341,500	2004 Profits: $137,300	Parent Company:	

SALARIES/BENEFITS:

Pension Plan:	ESOP Stock Plan:	Profit Sharing: Y	Top Exec. Salary: $400,000	Bonus: $1,314,197
Savings Plan: Y	Stock Purch. Plan: Y		Second Exec. Salary: $260,000	Bonus: $372,099

OTHER THOUGHTS:

Apparent Women Officers or Directors: 4
Hot Spot for Advancement for Women/Minorities: Y

LOCATIONS: ("Y" = Yes)

West:	Southwest:	Midwest:	Southeast:	Northeast:	International:
Y	Y	Y	Y	Y	Y

CH2M HILL COMPANIES LTD

www.ch2m.com

Industry Group Code: 541330 Ranks within this company's industry group: Sales: 3 Profits: 3

Management:		Sales/Marketing:		Liberal Arts:		Information Systems:		Professionals:		Tech./Scientific:	
Management Trainees:	Y	Marketing Pros.:	Y	Gen. Writing/Editing:	Y	Info. Management:	Y	Finance/Acct.:	Y	Engineers, Electrical:	Y
Experienced Mngmt.:	Y	Retail Sales:		Technical Writing:	Y	Software Dev.:	Y	Law:	Y	Engineers, Other:	Y
International Business:	Y	Commercial/Industrial:	Y	Graphic Arts/Photog.:	Y	Hardware Dev.:		HR/Other:	Y	Health/Lab:	
MBA Grads:	Y	Sales Trainees:		Music:		Consulting/Other:	Y	Training:	Y	Scientists/Research:	
		Advertising Pros.:		Broadcasting:				Health Care:		Petroleum/Chemicals:	
				Other:				Consulting:	Y	Math/Other:	

TYPES OF BUSINESS:

Engineering Services-Consultation
Environmental Engineering & Consulting
Nuclear Management Services
Water & Electrical Utility Services
Decommissioning & Decontamination
Facilities Design & Construction
Project Financing & Procurement
Nanotechnology Research

BRANDS/DIVISIONS/AFFILIATES:

Operations Management International
CH2M HILL Canada, Ltd.
Lockwood Greene
Industrial Design and Construction
CH2M-IDC China
Wade & Assoicates, Inc.
Goldston Engineering, Inc.
VECO

CONTACTS: Note: Officers with more than one job title may be intentionally listed here more than once.

Lee A. McIntire, CEO
Catherine Santee, CFO
Donald S. Evans, Chief Mktg. Officer
Bob Allen, Chief Human Resources Officer/Sr. VP
John Corsi, Dir.-Corp. Comm.
Gary Higdem, Pres., CH2M HILL Energy & Chemicals
Mike McKelvy, Pres., CH2M HILL Industrial
Robert G. Card, Pres., CH2M HILL Government, Environment, Nuclear
Ralph R. Peterson, Chmn.
Thomas G. Searle, Pres., CH2M HILL Int'l

Phone: 303-771-0900	**Fax:** 720-286-9250
Toll-Free: 888-242-6445	
Address: 9191 S. Jamaica St., Englewood, CO 80112 US	

GROWTH PLANS/SPECIAL FEATURES:

CH2M HILL Companies, Ltd. is an employee-owned firm that offers engineering, consulting, design, construction, procurement, operations, maintenance and program and project management services to clients in the public and private sectors. CH2M HILL conducts business in more than 80 countries. The company's environmental services division offers its clients ecological and natural resource damage assessments, environmental consulting for remediation projects and treatment systems for properties that have been contaminated by toxic or radioactive waste. The nuclear services segment manages the decontamination and demolition of weapons production facilities and designs nuclear waste treatment and handling facilities. CH2M HILL's Operations Management International subsidiary provides water, wastewater and electrical utility services to private and public clients. CH2M HILL Canada, Ltd. is the Canadian division of the company. Lockwood Greene is a major engineering and construction firm focused on national and multinational industrial and power clients worldwide. Industrial Design and Construction (IDC) is a high-technology facilities design, construction, maintenance and operations company serving process-intensive technology clients. IDC also has interests in nanotechnology research and manufacturing. CH2M-IDC China provides full-service solution to manufacturing companies that are building or have plants in China. In March 2008, the company acquired Goldston Engineering, Inc., a Texas based engineering solutions provider w. Details of the transaction were not disclosed.

In 2009, CH2M HILL was ranked 84 on FORTUNE Magazine's 12th annual list of the100 Best Companies to Work For.

FINANCIALS: Sales and profits are in thousands of dollars—add 000 to get the full amount. 2008 Note: Financial information for 2008 was not available for all companies at press time.

2008 Sales: $5,589,900	2008 Profits: $32,100	**U.S. Stock Ticker:** Private
2007 Sales: $4,376,200	2007 Profits: $	**Int'l Ticker:** Int'l Exchange:
2006 Sales: $4,000,000	2006 Profits: $	Employees:
2005 Sales: $3,152,200	2005 Profits: $81,600	Fiscal Year Ends: 12/31
2004 Sales: $2,715,400	2004 Profits: $32,300	Parent Company:

SALARIES/BENEFITS:

Pension Plan:	ESOP Stock Plan:	Profit Sharing:	Top Exec. Salary: $	Bonus: $
Savings Plan:	Stock Purch. Plan:		Second Exec. Salary: $	Bonus: $

OTHER THOUGHTS:

Apparent Women Officers or Directors: 4
Hot Spot for Advancement for Women/Minorities: Y

LOCATIONS: ("Y" = Yes)

West:	Southwest:	Midwest:	Southeast:	Northeast:	International:
Y	Y	Y	Y	Y	Y

CHARLOTTE RUSSE HOLDING

www.charlotte-russe.com

Industry Group Code: 448120 Ranks within this company's industry group: Sales: 7 Profits: 6

Management:		Sales/Marketing:		Liberal Arts:		Information Systems:		Professionals:		Tech./Scientific:	
Management Trainees:	Y	Marketing Pros.:	Y	Gen. Writing/Editing:	Y	Info. Management:	Y	Finance/Acct.:	Y	Engineers, Electrical:	
Experienced Mngmt.:	Y	Retail Sales:	Y	Technical Writing:		Software Dev.:	Y	Law:	Y	Engineers, Other:	
International Business:	Y	Commercial/Industrial:		Graphic Arts/Photog.:	Y	Hardware Dev.:		HR/Other:	Y	Health/Lab:	
MBA Grads:	Y	Sales Trainees:	Y	Music:		Consulting/Other:		Training:	Y	Scientists/Research:	
		Advertising Pros.:	Y	Broadcasting:				Health Care:		Petroleum/Chemicals:	
				Other:	Y			Consulting:		Math/Other:	

TYPES OF BUSINESS:

Women's Apparel, Retail

BRANDS/DIVISIONS/AFFILIATES:

Charlotte Russe
blu chic
Refuge

CONTACTS:
Note: Officers with more than one job title may be intentionally listed here more than once.

John D. Goodman, CEO
Edward Wong, COO
Frederick G. Silny, CFO/Exec. VP
Emilia Fabricant, Chief Merch. Officer
Frederick G. Silny, Corp. Sec.
Sandra Tillett, Exec. VP-Store Oper.
Frederick G. Silny, Treas.
Edward Wong, Chief Supply Chain Officer/Exec. VP

Phone: 858-587-1500	Fax: 858-587-0902
Toll-Free: 877-266-9327	
Address: 4645 Morena Blvd., San Diego, CA 92117 US	

GROWTH PLANS/SPECIAL FEATURES:

Charlotte Russe Holding, Inc. is a mall-based specialty retailer of fashionable, value-priced apparel and accessories targeting young women between ages 15-35. The stores offer a broad assortment of merchandise centered on styles that are affordable and feminine and reflect the latest fashion trends. There are approximately 487 Charlotte Russe stores located in 45 states and Puerto Rico. These stores reflect established fashion trends and rely on exciting in-store graphics and window displays to convey a fashion-forward orientation, and offer ready-to-wear apparel such as tops, dresses, shorts, pants and skirts, as well as seasonal items such as prom dresses and outerwear. The majority of merchandise sold at the Charlotte Russe stores is under the company's proprietary labels, which has the symbols of a heart, moon and star, and includes Charlotte Russe, Refuge and blu Chic. The company markets this merchandise to both younger career women and to teenagers, building brand awareness through a national print marketing campaign. Charlotte Russe stores are located predominantly in high-visibility, center court mall locations in spaces that average 7,100 square feet. The company maintains a 265,000-square-foot distribution center in Ontario, California. In 2008, the company opened 57 new stores and closed two. In August 2009, the firm agreed to be acquired by private equity company, Advent International Corporation, for roughly $380 million.

Employees are offered medical, dental and vision insurance; disability coverage; a 401(k) plan; an employee stock purchase plan; life insurance; an employee assistance program; tuition reimbursement and employee discounts on store merchandise.

FINANCIALS:
Sales and profits are in thousands of dollars—add 000 to get the full amount. 2008 Note: Financial information for 2008 was not available for all companies at press time.

2008 Sales: $823,252	2008 Profits: $18,166	**U.S. Stock Ticker:** CHIC	
2007 Sales: $740,939	2007 Profits: $36,304	**Int'l Ticker:** Int'l Exchange:	
2006 Sales: $681,504	2006 Profits: $25,138	**Employees:** 10,545	
2005 Sales: $511,259	2005 Profits: $10,801	**Fiscal Year Ends:** 9/30	
2004 Sales: $449,035	2004 Profits: $15,084	**Parent Company:**	

SALARIES/BENEFITS:

Pension Plan:	ESOP Stock Plan:	Profit Sharing:	Top Exec. Salary: $871,057	Bonus: $
Savings Plan: Y	Stock Purch. Plan: Y		Second Exec. Salary: $390,953	Bonus: $

OTHER THOUGHTS:

Apparent Women Officers or Directors: 2
Hot Spot for Advancement for Women/Minorities: Y

LOCATIONS: ("Y" = Yes)

West:	Southwest:	Midwest:	Southeast:	Northeast:	International:
Y	Y	Y	Y	Y	Y

CHARMING SHOPPES INC

www.charmingshoppes.com

Industry Group Code: 448120 Ranks within this company's industry group: Sales: 3 Profits: 8

Management:		Sales/Marketing:		Liberal Arts:		Information Systems:		Professionals:		Tech./Scientific:	
Management Trainees:	Y	Marketing Pros.:	Y	Gen. Writing/Editing:	Y	Info. Management:	Y	Finance/Acct.:	Y	Engineers, Electrical:	
Experienced Mngmt.:	Y	Retail Sales:	Y	Technical Writing:		Software Dev.:	Y	Law:	Y	Engineers, Other:	
International Business:	Y	Commercial/Industrial:		Graphic Arts/Photog.:	Y	Hardware Dev.:		HR/Other:	Y	Health/Lab:	
MBA Grads:	Y	Sales Trainees:	Y	Music:		Consulting/Other:		Training:	Y	Scientists/Research:	
		Advertising Pros.:	Y	Broadcasting:				Health Care:		Petroleum/Chemicals:	
				Other:	Y			Consulting:		Math/Other:	

TYPES OF BUSINESS:

Women's Apparel, Retail
Plus-Size Women's Apparel
Fashion Accessories
Food & Gifts

BRANDS/DIVISIONS/AFFILIATES:

Lane Bryant
Venezia
Cacique
Lane Bryant Outlet
Petite Sophisticate Outlet
Fashion Bug
Catherine's Plus Sizes
Figi's

CONTACTS: Note: Officers with more than one job title may be intentionally listed here more than once.

Alan Rosskamm, CEO
Joseph M. Baron, COO/Exec. VP
Dorrit J. Bern, Pres.
Eric M. Specter, CFO/Exec. VP
Tim M. White, Chief Mktg. Officer/Exec. VP
Gale H. Varma, Exec. VP-Human Resources
James G. Bloise, VP-Tech. & Bus. Svcs.
Colin D. Stern, General Counsel/Exec. VP/Sec.
Lori Twomey, Pres., Direct-to-Consumer
Anthony A. DeSabato, Exec. VP-Corp. & Labor Rel.
Gayle M. Coolick, VP-Investor Rel.
John J. Sullivan, Corp. Controller/VP
Michel Bourlon, Exec. VP-Sourcing
Alan Rosskamm, Chmn.
James G. Bloise, Exec. VP-Supply Chain

Phone: 215-245-9100	Fax: 215-633-4640
Toll-Free:	
Address: 450 Winks Ln., Bensalem, PA 19020 US	

GROWTH PLANS/SPECIAL FEATURES:

Charming Shoppes, Inc. operates women's plus size specialty apparel stores, including Lane Bryant, Fashion Bug and Catherines. Charming Shoppes maintains 795 Lane Bryant stores, catering to women ages 25-45, in 46 states and averaging about 5,800 square feet. Through private labels, such as Venezia, Cacique, and Lane Bryant, the company offers fashionable and sophisticated apparel in sizes 14-28, including intimate apparel, wear-to-work, and casual sportswear, as well as accessories. Lane Bryant Outlet operates 101 stores in 35 states, and is the only national chain offering women's plus-size apparel in the outlet sales channel. The 52 Petite Sophisticate Outlet stores, averaging 2,700 square feet, target women 35-55 years-old, offering traditional, updated classic and contemporary apparel, sizes 0-14, in casual and career assortments, tailored to petite women. The company's 989 Fashion Bug and Fashion stores specialize in selling a wide variety of plus size, misses and junior apparel, accessories, intimate apparel, and footwear. It targets customers 20-49 years old who shop in the low-to-moderate price range. Fashion Bug's stores are located in 44 states, primarily in strip shopping centers, and average approximately 8,800 square feet. The firm's 468 Catherine's stores, catering primarily to women ages 40-65, specialize in plus-sized classic apparel and accessories for career and casual lifestyles. The chain is well known for its extended sizes (over size 28) and its petite plus-sizes. Located in 44 states, the stores, averaging approximately 4,100 square feet, are primarily in strip shopping centers in the Southeast, Mid-Atlantic, and Eastern Central U.S. Some of Charming Shoppes' products are sold online or through catalogues. Its Figi's catalog offers food and gifts. In August 2008, the company agreed to sell its non-core misses apparel catalogs (collectively, Crosstown Traders) to Orchard Brands, a portfolio company of Golden Gate Capital, for $35 million.

The company offers employees a 40% discount on company merchandise; medical, dental and vision insurance; on-site childcare at headquarters; dependant care spending account; membership in a credit union and fitness centers; adoption assistance; prescription drug coverage; parenting education resources; and tuition reimbursement.

FINANCIALS: Sales and profits are in thousands of dollars—add 000 to get the full amount. 2008 Note: Financial information for 2008 was not available for all companies at press time.

2008 Sales: $2,722,462	2008 Profits: $-83,413	**U.S. Stock Ticker:** CHRS
2007 Sales: $2,751,845	2007 Profits: $108,923	**Int'l Ticker:** Int'l Exchange:
2006 Sales: $2,755,725	2006 Profits: $99,391	Employees: 30,200
2005 Sales: $2,332,334	2005 Profits: $64,526	Fiscal Year Ends: 1/31
2004 Sales: $2,285,680	2004 Profits: $40,639	Parent Company:

SALARIES/BENEFITS:

Pension Plan:	ESOP Stock Plan:	Profit Sharing: Y	Top Exec. Salary: $1,250,000	Bonus: $
Savings Plan: Y	Stock Purch. Plan: Y		Second Exec. Salary: $532,172	Bonus: $

OTHER THOUGHTS:

Apparent Women Officers or Directors: 1
Hot Spot for Advancement for Women/Minorities: Y

LOCATIONS: ("Y" = Yes)

West:	Southwest:	Midwest:	Southeast:	Northeast:	International:
Y	Y	Y	Y	Y	Y

CHEMED CORPORATION

www.chemed.com

Industry Group Code: 6216 Ranks within this company's industry group: Sales: 3 Profits: 3

Management:		Sales/Marketing:		Liberal Arts:		Information Systems:		Professionals:		Tech./Scientific:	
Management Trainees:	Y	Marketing Pros.:	Y	Gen. Writing/Editing:	Y	Info. Management:	Y	Finance/Acct.:	Y	Engineers, Electrical:	
Experienced Mngmt.:	Y	Retail Sales:		Technical Writing:	Y	Software Dev.:		Law:	Y	Engineers, Other:	
International Business:	Y	Commercial/Industrial:	Y	Graphic Arts/Photog.:	Y	Hardware Dev.:		HR/Other:	Y	Health/Lab:	Y
MBA Grads:	Y	Sales Trainees:	Y	Music:		Consulting/Other:		Training:	Y	Scientists/Research:	
		Advertising Pros.:		Broadcasting:				Health Care:	Y	Petroleum/Chemicals:	
				Other:	Y			Consulting:		Math/Other:	

TYPES OF BUSINESS:

Hospice & Home Health Care Services
Plumbing Services

BRANDS/DIVISIONS/AFFILIATES:

Vitas Healthcare Corporation
Roto-Rooter Corporation

CONTACTS: *Note: Officers with more than one job title may be intentionally listed here more than once.*

Kevin J. McNamara, CEO
Kevin J. McNamara, Pres.
David P. Williams, CFO/Exec. VP
Lisa A. Reinhard, Chief Admin. Officer
Naomi C. Dallob, Sec./VP
Arthur V. Tucker, Jr., Controller/VP
Tim S. O'Toole, Exec. VP
Spencer S. Lee, Exec. VP
Thomas C. Hutton, VP
Thomas J. Reilly, VP
George J. Walsh, III, Chmn.

Phone: 513-762-6900	Fax: 513-762-6919
Toll-Free:	
Address: 255 E. 5th St., 2600 Chemed Ctr., Cincinnati, OH 45202-4726 US	

GROWTH PLANS/SPECIAL FEATURES:

Chemed Corporation, through its VITAS and Roto-Rooter groups, offers hospice care and plumbing services, respectively. Headquartered in Miami, Florida, subsidiary VITAS Healthcare Corporation, which generated over 70% of Chemed's 2008 service revenues and sales, is one of the largest national providers of hospice care and end-of-life services. It cares for more than 12,000 patients daily either in their own home or through the subsidiary's 45 hospice programs at 95 leased facilities in 15 states and Washington, D.C. In all, VITAS provided over 4.3 million days of care in 2008. Of this group's revenues, the largest share (72.5%) was generated by routine homecare services, followed by continuous care (15.4%) and general inpatient services (12.1%). More than 90% of VITAS's revenues consist of payments from the Medicare and Medicaid programs. Founded in 1935, subsidiary Roto-Rooter Corporation, generating the remaining 30% of 2008 service revenues and sales, supports the maintenance needs of the residential, industrial, commercial and municipal markets by providing plumbing, sewer, drain and pipe cleaning products and services, as well as pipe rehabilitation and drain cleaning products and services. One of the largest businesses of its type in North America, Roto-Rooter runs businesses in more than 110 company-owned branch and independent contractors as well as approximately 500 franchisees in 27 U.S. states and Canada, which combined grant it access to almost 90% of the U.S. population and 40% of the Canadian population. Additionally, the subsidiary operates franchises in Mexico, the U.K., Japan, China, Hong Kong, the Philippines, Indonesia and Singapore. Roto-Rooter shares its corporate headquarters with Chemed. Of this group's revenues, the largest share (42.9%) was generated by sewer and drain cleaning, followed by plumbing repair and maintenance (42.8%), independent contractors (6.5%), HVAC (heating, ventilation and air conditioning) repair and maintenance (1.2%) and other products and services (6.6%).

FINANCIALS: Sales and profits are in thousands of dollars—add 000 to get the full amount. 2008 Note: Financial information for 2008 was not available for all companies at press time.

2008 Sales: $1,148,941	2008 Profits: $71,017	**U.S. Stock Ticker:** CHE
2007 Sales: $1,100,058	2007 Profits: $63,976	**Int'l Ticker:** Int'l Exchange:
2006 Sales: $1,018,587	2006 Profits: $50,651	Employees: 11,884
2005 Sales: $915,970	2005 Profits: $35,817	Fiscal Year Ends: 12/31
2004 Sales: $734,877	2004 Profits: $27,512	Parent Company:

SALARIES/BENEFITS:

Pension Plan: Y	ESOP Stock Plan:	Profit Sharing:	Top Exec. Salary: $713,333	Bonus: $1,450,000
Savings Plan: Y	Stock Purch. Plan:		Second Exec. Salary: $529,167	Bonus: $365,000

OTHER THOUGHTS:

Apparent Women Officers or Directors: 4
Hot Spot for Advancement for Women/Minorities: Y

LOCATIONS: ("Y" = Yes)

West:	Southwest:	Midwest:	Southeast:	Northeast:	International:
Y	Y	Y	Y	Y	Y

CHEVRON CORPORATION

www.chevron.com

Industry Group Code: 211111 Ranks within this company's industry group: Sales: 2 Profits: 2

Management:		Sales/Marketing:		Liberal Arts:		Information Systems:		Professionals:		Tech./Scientific:	
Management Trainees:	Y	Marketing Pros.:	Y	Gen. Writing/Editing:	Y	Info. Management:	Y	Finance/Acct.:	Y	Engineers, Electrical:	Y
Experienced Mngmt.:	Y	Retail Sales:		Technical Writing:	Y	Software Dev.:	Y	Law:	Y	Engineers, Other:	Y
International Business:	Y	Commercial/Industrial:	Y	Graphic Arts/Photog.:	Y	Hardware Dev.:		HR/Other:	Y	Health/Lab:	
MBA Grads:	Y	Sales Trainees:	Y	Music:		Consulting/Other:		Training:	Y	Scientists/Research:	Y
		Advertising Pros.:	Y	Broadcasting:				Health Care:		Petroleum/Chemicals:	Y
				Other:				Consulting:		Math/Other:	Y

TYPES OF BUSINESS:

Oil & Gas Exploration & Production
Power Generation
Petrochemicals
Gasoline Retailing
Coal Mining
Fuel & Oil Additives
Convenience Stores
Pipelines

BRANDS/DIVISIONS/AFFILIATES:

Texaco
Youngs Creek Mining Company LLC
Chevron Phillips Chemical Company
Caltex

CONTACTS: Note: Officers with more than one job title may be intentionally listed here more than once.

David J. O'Reilly, CEO
Patricia E. Yarrington, CFO/VP
Joe W. Laymon, VP-Human Resources
John E. Bethancourt, Exec. VP-Tech. & Svcs.
Charles A. James, General Counsel/VP
John S. Watson, Exec. VP-Strategy & Dev.
Jim Aleveras, Gen. Mgr.-Corp. Investor Rel.
Mark A. Humphrey, Comptroller/VP
Michael (Mike) K. Wirth, Exec. VP-Global Downstream
George L. Kirkland, Exec. VP-Global Upstream & Gas
John D. Gass, VP/Pres., Global Gas
Charles A. Taylor, VP-Health, Environment & Safety
David J. O'Reilly, Chmn.

Phone: 925-842-1000	Fax: 925-842-3530
Toll-Free:	
Address: 6001 Bollinger Canyon Rd., San Ramon, CA 94583 US	

GROWTH PLANS/SPECIAL FEATURES:

Chevron Corp. is an integrated energy company that conducts refining, marketing and transportation operations and, to a lesser degree, chemical operations, mining operations and power generation. The company conducts business activities in the U.S. and approximately 180 other countries. Refining operations maintains a refining network capable of processing 2.1 million barrels of crude oil per day. Marketing operations operates primarily under the brands Chevron, Texaco and Caltex. In the U.S., the company markets under the Chevron and Texaco brands. The company supplies directly or through retailers and marketers approximately 9,700 Chevron- and Texaco-branded motor vehicle retail outlets. Outside the U.S., the firm supplies approximately 15,300 branded service stations, including affiliates. Transportation operations maintains the Chevron owned and operated system of crude oil, refined products, chemicals, natural gas liquids and natural gas pipelines in the U.S. The company also has direct or indirect interests in other U.S. and international pipelines. Chemical operations include the manufacturing and marketing of fuel and lubricating oil additives and commodity petrochemicals through Chevron Phillips Chemical Company (CPChem), a joint venture company. CPChem operates manufacturing and research facilities in eight countries. Mining operations produces and markets coal and molybdenum. The firm owns three coal mines and controls a 50% interest in Youngs Creek Mining Company LLC. The power generation business develops and operates commercial power projects and has interests in 13 power assets through joint ventures in the U.S. and Asia. The company manages the production of more than 2,300 megawatts (MW) of electricity at 11 facilities it owns through joint ventures. Additionally, Chevron operates gas-fired cogeneration facilities that use waste heat recovery to produce additional electricity or to support industrial thermal hosts.

Chevron offers employees medical and dental insurance; domestic partner benefits; a retirement plan; tuition reimbursement; flexible work schedules; and fitness centers and/or memberships.

FINANCIALS: Sales and profits are in thousands of dollars—add 000 to get the full amount. 2008 Note: Financial information for 2008 was not available for all companies at press time.

2008 Sales: $273,005,000	2008 Profits: $23,931,000	**U.S. Stock Ticker: CVX**
2007 Sales: $220,904,000	2007 Profits: $18,688,000	**Int'l Ticker:** Int'l Exchange:
2006 Sales: $210,118,000	2006 Profits: $17,138,000	Employees: 67,000
2005 Sales: $198,200,000	2005 Profits: $14,099,000	Fiscal Year Ends: 12/31
2004 Sales: $155,300,000	2004 Profits: $13,328,000	Parent Company:

SALARIES/BENEFITS:

Pension Plan: Y	ESOP Stock Plan:	Profit Sharing:	Top Exec. Salary: $1,650,000	Bonus: $3,220,000
Savings Plan: Y	Stock Purch. Plan:		Second Exec. Salary: $1,035,417	Bonus: $1,350,000

OTHER THOUGHTS:

Apparent Women Officers or Directors: 3
Hot Spot for Advancement for Women/Minorities: Y

LOCATIONS: ("Y" = Yes)

West:	Southwest:	Midwest:	Southeast:	Northeast:	International:
Y	Y	Y	Y	Y	Y

CHEVRON PHILLIPS CHEMICAL COMPANY LLC　www.cpchem.com

Industry Group Code: 325110　Ranks within this company's industry group: Sales: 2　Profits: 2

Management:		Sales/Marketing:		Liberal Arts:		Information Systems:		Professionals:		Tech./Scientific:	
Management Trainees:	Y	Marketing Pros.:	Y	Gen. Writing/Editing:	Y	Info. Management:	Y	Finance/Acct.:	Y	Engineers, Electrical:	Y
Experienced Mngmt.:	Y	Retail Sales:		Technical Writing:	Y	Software Dev.:	Y	Law:	Y	Engineers, Other:	Y
International Business:	Y	Commercial/Industrial:	Y	Graphic Arts/Photog.:		Hardware Dev.:		HR/Other:	Y	Health/Lab:	
MBA Grads:	Y	Sales Trainees:		Music:		Consulting/Other:		Training:	Y	Scientists/Research:	Y
		Advertising Pros.:		Broadcasting:				Health Care:		Petroleum/Chemicals:	Y
				Other:				Consulting:		Math/Other:	

TYPES OF BUSINESS:

Petrochemical & Plastics Manufacturing
Olefins & Polyolefins
Aromatics & Styrenics
Specialty Chemicals

BRANDS/DIVISIONS/AFFILIATES:

K-Resin
Aromax
Ryton
TrackTek
Soltex
Marlex
Arabian Chevron Phillips Petrochemical Company Ltd
Jubail Chevron Phillips Company

CONTACTS: *Note: Officers with more than one job title may be intentionally listed here more than once.*

Greg Garland, CEO
Greg Garland, Pres.
Greg Maxwell, CFO/Sr. VP/Controller
Chantal Veevaete, VP-Human Resources
Peggy Colsman, CIO
Mary Jane Hagenson, VP-Tech.
Rick Roberts, Sr. VP-Mfg.
Craig Glidden, General Counsel/Sr. VP/Corp. Sec.
Mark Lashier, VP-Corp. Planning & Dev.
Trevor Roberts, Treas.
Mark Haney, Sr. VP-Specialties, Aromatics & Styrenics
Tim Taylor, Sr. VP-Olefins & Polyolefins
Charleen Dickson, VP-Environment, Health & Safety
Dave S. Smith, VP-Polyethylene
Bob Patel, Mgr.-Asia Region

Phone: 832-813-4100	Fax:
Toll-Free: 800-231-1212	
Address: 10001 Six Pines Dr., The Woodlands, TX 77380 US	

GROWTH PLANS/SPECIAL FEATURES:

Chevron Phillips Chemical Company LLC (CPChem) is the combined petrochemical businesses of Chevron Corporation and ConocoPhillips, both 50% owners. With 36 production and research centers in nine countries, CPChem is an international producer of olefins and polyolefins and is also a supplier of aromatics, alpha olefins, styrenics, specialty chemicals, polyethylene pipe and proprietary plastics. The company manufactures chemical products that are vital in the various production processes of 70,000 consumer and industrial products. Its mix of petrochemical and plastics businesses is segmented into two divisions: olefins and polyolefins; and aromatics, styrenics specialty products. Products in the olefins and polyolefins family consist of ethylene, propylene and their polymer derivatives; olefins and polyalpha olefins; and high-density polyethylene pipe, conduit and pipe fitting. These products are sold as building blocks for other chemicals and as ingredients for use in a variety of end-products including motor oils, lubricants, plastics, coatings, textiles and packaging. CPChem's aromatics and styrenics include cyclohexane, paraxylene, benzene, styrene, polystyrene and K-Resin SBC, a unique type of copolymer. Aromax is the company's proprietary benzene production process. The aromatics and styrenics are used in the manufacturing of insulation products, housewares, food packaging, electronic parts and media enclosures. Its specialty chemicals are used in various applications, including electronics, automobiles, oil and gas well drilling, appliances, agriculture and pharmaceuticals. This division sells TrackTek brand racing fuels and Soltex drill mud additive. Olefins and polyolefins account for 72% of sales while specialties, aromatics and styrenics for accounted for 28%. In August 2008, subsidiary, Arabian Chevron Phillips Petrochemical Company Ltd.'s joint venture, Jubail Chevron Phillips Company (JCP), began operations in Al-Jubail, Saudi Arabia.

Employees are offered medical, dental and vision benefits; educational assistance; life insurance; and employee assistance program and behavioral health plan; discounts on computers, office supply, cars, books and music, educational scholarships for dependents; and relocation assistance.

FINANCIALS: Sales and profits are in thousands of dollars—add 000 to get the full amount. 2008 Note: Financial information for 2008 was not available for all companies at press time.

2008 Sales: $12,646,000	2008 Profits: $276,000	**U.S. Stock Ticker:** Joint Venture
2007 Sales: $12,534,000	2007 Profits: $719,000	**Int'l Ticker:**　Int'l Exchange:
2006 Sales: $11,839,000	2006 Profits: $1,349,000	Employees: 5,000
2005 Sales: $11,038,000	2005 Profits: $853,000	Fiscal Year Ends: 12/31
2004 Sales: $9,558,000	2004 Profits: $605,000	Parent Company:

SALARIES/BENEFITS:

Pension Plan:	ESOP Stock Plan:	Profit Sharing: Y	Top Exec. Salary: $	Bonus: $
Savings Plan: Y	Stock Purch. Plan:		Second Exec. Salary: $	Bonus: $

OTHER THOUGHTS:

Apparent Women Officers or Directors: 4
Hot Spot for Advancement for Women/Minorities: Y

LOCATIONS: ("Y" = Yes)

West:	Southwest:	Midwest:	Southeast:	Northeast:	International:
Y	Y	Y	Y	Y	Y

CHICO'S FAS INC

www.chicos.com

Industry Group Code: 448120 **Ranks within this company's industry group:** Sales: 5 Profits: 3

Management:		Sales/Marketing:		Liberal Arts:		Information Systems:		Professionals:		Tech./Scientific:	
Management Trainees:	Y	Marketing Pros.:	Y	Gen. Writing/Editing:	Y	Info. Management:	Y	Finance/Acct.:	Y	Engineers, Electrical:	
Experienced Mngmt.:	Y	Retail Sales:	Y	Technical Writing:		Software Dev.:	Y	Law:	Y	Engineers, Other:	
International Business:	Y	Commercial/Industrial:		Graphic Arts/Photog.:	Y	Hardware Dev.:		HR/Other:	Y	Health/Lab:	
MBA Grads:	Y	Sales Trainees:	Y	Music:		Consulting/Other:		Training:	Y	Scientists/Research:	
		Advertising Pros.:	Y	Broadcasting:				Health Care:		Petroleum/Chemicals:	
				Other:	Y			Consulting:		Math/Other:	

TYPES OF BUSINESS:

Women's Apparel, Retail
Online & Catalog Sales
Franchising

BRANDS/DIVISIONS/AFFILIATES:

Chico's
White House/Black Market
Soma by Chico's
Fitigues
Passport Club
Chico's Outlet

CONTACTS: *Note: Officers with more than one job title may be intentionally listed here more than once.*

David F. Dyer, CEO
Chuck Nesbit, COO/Exec. VP
Kent Kleeberger, CFO/Treas./Exec. VP
Judd Harner, Chief Mktg. Officer/Sr. VP-Chico's brand
Manuel Jessup, Chief Human Resources Officer/Exec. VP
Elaine Boltz, Sr. VP-Consumer Research
Gary King, CIO/Exec. VP
Linda Costello, Sr. VP-Prod. Dev.
Sandy Rhodes, General Counsel/Corp. Sec./Sr. VP
Elaine Boltz, Sr. VP-Strategy
Michael Kincaid, Chief Acct. Officer/Sr. VP-Finance
Sher Canada, Sr. VP-Chico's Stores
Mike Elleman, Sr. VP-Real Estate
Mori MacKenzie, Chief Stores Officer/Exec. VP

Phone: 239-277-6200	**Fax:** 239-277-5237
Toll-Free: 888-550-5559	
Address: 11215 Metro Pkwy., Fort Myers, FL 33966 US	

GROWTH PLANS/SPECIAL FEATURES:

Chico's FAS, Inc. retails exclusively designed, private label, sophisticated, casual-to-dressy clothing, complementary accessories and gift items under the Chico's, White House/Black Market and Soma by Chico's. Chico's currently operates 1,045 retail stores in 49 states, Washington, D.C., the U.S. Virgin Islands and Puerto Rico. The Chico's brand primarily targets women aged 35 and over with moderate and high income levels. All of Chico's products are designed and developed by its Product Development Team, headquartered in Fort Myers, Florida. Chico's mails a monthly catalog. To increase its customer base, the company advertises in national fashion and home and garden magazines such as Martha Stewart Living, Vogue and Vanity Fair. The company offers Passport Club membership to women who have spent at least $500 over time, allowing them perks, such as a permanent 5% discount on future purchases. There are 606 Chico's front-line stores and 37 Chico's outlet stores. Chico's also operates the White House/Black Market chain of 313 women's clothing stores and 19 outlet locations that focuses on women aged 25 and older who lead active work and social lives with moderate to high income levels. White House/Black Market offers clothes in shades of white and black, although the stores do offer a line of denim jeans as well. The Soma intimate wear line currently consists of 69 boutique-style stores and one outlet location. Soma by Chico's offers foundation products in intimate apparel, sleepwear, bodywear and active wear that the firm hopes could ultimately appeal to a broader customer base than Chico's.

Chico's employee benefits include merchandise discounts, a retirement savings plan and a stock purchase plan.

FINANCIALS: Sales and profits are in thousands of dollars—add 000 to get the full amount. 2008 Note: Financial information for 2008 was not available for all companies at press time.

2008 Sales: $1,714,326	2008 Profits: $88,875	**U.S. Stock Ticker:** CHS	
2007 Sales: $1,640,927	2007 Profits: $166,636	**Int'l Ticker:**	**Int'l Exchange:**
2006 Sales: $1,404,575	2006 Profits: $193,981	Employees: 14,460	
2005 Sales: $1,066,882	2005 Profits: $141,206	Fiscal Year Ends: 1/31	
2004 Sales: $768,499	2004 Profits: $100,230	Parent Company:	

SALARIES/BENEFITS:

Pension Plan:	ESOP Stock Plan:	Profit Sharing:	Top Exec. Salary: $1,094,000	Bonus: $
Savings Plan: Y	Stock Purch. Plan: Y		Second Exec. Salary: $725,000	Bonus: $

OTHER THOUGHTS:

Apparent Women Officers or Directors: 12
Hot Spot for Advancement for Women/Minorities: Y

LOCATIONS: ("Y" = Yes)

West:	Southwest:	Midwest:	Southeast:	Northeast:	International:
Y	Y	Y	Y	Y	Y

CHIPOTLE MEXICAN GRILL INC

www.chipotle.com

Industry Group Code: 722110 Ranks within this company's industry group: Sales: 11   Profits: 6

Management:		Sales/Marketing:		Liberal Arts:		Information Systems:		Professionals:		Tech./Scientific:	
Management Trainees:	Y	Marketing Pros.:	Y	Gen. Writing/Editing:	Y	Info. Management:	Y	Finance/Acct.:	Y	Engineers, Electrical:	
Experienced Mngmt.:	Y	Retail Sales:		Technical Writing:		Software Dev.:	Y	Law:	Y	Engineers, Other:	
International Business:	Y	Commercial/Industrial:		Graphic Arts/Photog.:	Y	Hardware Dev.:		HR/Other:	Y	Health/Lab:	
MBA Grads:	Y	Sales Trainees:		Music:		Consulting/Other:		Training:	Y	Scientists/Research:	
		Advertising Pros.:	Y	Broadcasting:				Health Care:		Petroleum/Chemicals:	
				Other:	Y			Consulting:		Math/Other:	

TYPES OF BUSINESS:

Restaurants

BRANDS/DIVISIONS/AFFILIATES:

CONTACTS: Note: Officers with more than one job title may be intentionally listed here more than once.

Steve Ells, Co-CEO
Montgomery F. Moran, Co-CEO
John R. Hartung, CFO
Mark Crumpacker, Chief Mktg. Officer
Rex Jones, Chief Dev. Officer
Robert N. Blessing, Jr., Restaurant Support Officer
Steve Ells, Chmn.

Phone: 303-595-4000	Fax:
Toll-Free:	
Address: 1401 Wynkoop St., Ste. 500, Denver, CO 80202 US	

GROWTH PLANS/SPECIAL FEATURES:

Chipotle Mexican Grill, Inc. operates Mexican food restaurants serving a relatively focused menu of burritos, tacos, burrito bowls (burrito ingredients without the tortilla) and salads, with an emphasis on fresh and naturally-sourced meats and produce. Chipotle was majority-owned by McDonald's Corporation from 2001 to 2006, when the firm was spun-off and completed its initial public offering. The company operates approximately 886 restaurants located across 34 U.S. states, Washington D.C. and Ontario, Canada. Basic Chipotle ingredients include marinated chicken and steak, carnitas (seasoned and braised pork), barbacoa (spicy shredded beef) and pinto and vegetarian black beans. Customers can customize their food with rice (tossed with lime juice and chopped cilantro), as well as shredded cheese, sour cream, lettuce, peppers and onions. Chipotle also provide a variety of extras such as guacamole, salsas and tortilla chips. In addition to sodas and fruit drinks, most locations also offer a selection of beer and margaritas. Chipotle has used its limited list of ingredients as an opportunity to carefully source the food it serves, part of the company's ongoing Food with Integrity strategy that has helped boost brand image as the chain has grown larger. At its U.S. locations, all the chicken and pork served is naturally raised, from animals on vegetarian diets raised in open pastures or deeply bedded pens without the use of antibiotics and growth hormones. Currently, approximately 60% of the beef served in Chipotle's U.S. restaurants is also naturally raised, while 35% of the beans it buys are organically grown; the company has also committed to purchasing some local produce from small and midsize farms in the regions near its restaurants. Chipotle opened 50 new restaurants during the first half of 2009, with plans to open roughly 120 more by year's end. The company's first overseas location, in London, U.K., is slated for a 2010 opening.

Chipotle offers benefits such as a 401(k) plan and medical insurance.

FINANCIALS: Sales and profits are in thousands of dollars—add 000 to get the full amount. 2008 Note: Financial information for 2008 was not available for all companies at press time.

2008 Sales: $1,331,968	2008 Profits: $78,202	U.S. Stock Ticker: CMG
2007 Sales: $1,085,782	2007 Profits: $70,563	Int'l Ticker: Int'l Exchange:
2006 Sales: $822,930	2006 Profits: $41,423	Employees: 20,400
2005 Sales: $	2005 Profits: $	Fiscal Year Ends: 12/31
2004 Sales: $	2004 Profits: $	Parent Company:

SALARIES/BENEFITS:

Pension Plan:	ESOP Stock Plan:	Profit Sharing:	Top Exec. Salary: $938,462	Bonus: $777,700
Savings Plan: Y	Stock Purch. Plan:		Second Exec. Salary: $576,923	Bonus: $396,627

OTHER THOUGHTS:

Apparent Women Officers or Directors: 1
Hot Spot for Advancement for Women/Minorities:

LOCATIONS: ("Y" = Yes)

West:	Southwest:	Midwest:	Southeast:	Northeast:	International:
Y	Y	Y	Y	Y	Y

CHRISTOPHER & BANKS CORP

www.christopherandbanks.com

Industry Group Code: 448120 Ranks within this company's industry group: Sales: 9 Profits: 7

Management:		Sales/Marketing:		Liberal Arts:		Information Systems:		Professionals:		Tech./Scientific:	
Management Trainees:	Y	Marketing Pros.:	Y	Gen. Writing/Editing:	Y	Info. Management:	Y	Finance/Acct.:	Y	Engineers, Electrical:	
Experienced Mngmt.:	Y	Retail Sales:	Y	Technical Writing:		Software Dev.:	Y	Law:	Y	Engineers, Other:	
International Business:		Commercial/Industrial:		Graphic Arts/Photog.:	Y	Hardware Dev.:		HR/Other:	Y	Health/Lab:	
MBA Grads:	Y	Sales Trainees:	Y	Music:		Consulting/Other:		Training:	Y	Scientists/Research:	
		Advertising Pros.:	Y	Broadcasting:				Health Care:		Petroleum/Chemicals:	
				Other:	Y			Consulting:		Math/Other:	

TYPES OF BUSINESS:

Women's Business Apparel, Retail
Private-Label Merchandise
Accessories

BRANDS/DIVISIONS/AFFILIATES:

C.J. Banks

CONTACTS: Note: Officers with more than one job title may be intentionally listed here more than once.

Lorna Nagler, CEO
Lorna Nagler, Pres.
Rodney Carter, CFO/Exec. VP
Susan Connell, Chief Merch. Officer
Luke R. Komarek, General Counsel/Sr. VP/Corp. Sec.
Gary Thompson, Sr. VP-Store Oper.
Monica L. Dahl, Sr. VP-Planning & Allocation
Monica L. Dahl, Sr. VP-e-Commerce
Michael Lyftogt, VP-Finance
Dustin Henry, Mktg. Coordinator
Larry Barenbaum, Chmn.

Phone: 763-551-5000	Fax: 763-551-5198
Toll-Free:	
Address: 2400 Xenium Ln. N., Plymouth, MN 55441 US	

GROWTH PLANS/SPECIAL FEATURES:

Christopher & Banks Corporation (C&B) is a Minnesota-based specialty retailer of women's specialty apparel. The company operates 814 stores in 46 states under the names Christopher & Banks (545 stores) and C.J. Banks (269). The stores are generally mall-based and located in small to mid-sized markets. Sportswear and sweaters account for the bulk of the company's sales, though the firm has been shifting merchandise focus away from sweaters and expanding its offering of novelty jackets and fashion-knit tops. Sweaters comprised 20% of the company's sales in 2009. The principal store concept, Christopher & Banks, emphasizes style, quality and value in casual sportswear and sweaters exclusively designed for working women ages 40-60. The company's plus size store concept, C.J. Banks, offers similar apparel in sizes 14-24, and is often paired with an existing C&B store. C&B uses carefully designed front-of-store displays to attract customers. To keep its fashions fresh, it introduces a new color palette from month to month. The company is also upgrading customer service, offering merchandise on wooden hangers, receipts placed in envelopes and purchases wrapped in tissue and placed in drawstring bags. In September 2008, the firm launched a petite line of women's clothing available at 300 Christopher and Banks locations. In December of the same year, the company completed the closing of its Acorn stores.

FINANCIALS: Sales and profits are in thousands of dollars—add 000 to get the full amount. 2008 Note: Financial information for 2008 was not available for all companies at press time.

2008 Sales: $560,912	2008 Profits: $17,018	U.S. Stock Ticker: CBK
2007 Sales: $533,156	2007 Profits: $33,686	Int'l Ticker: Int'l Exchange:
2006 Sales: $490,508	2006 Profits: $30,413	Employees: 8,300
2005 Sales: $438,862	2005 Profits: $27,015	Fiscal Year Ends: 2/28
2004 Sales: $390,723	2004 Profits: $39,340	Parent Company:

SALARIES/BENEFITS:

Pension Plan:	ESOP Stock Plan:	Profit Sharing:	Top Exec. Salary: $854,000	Bonus: $60,000
Savings Plan: Y	Stock Purch. Plan:		Second Exec. Salary: $387,500	Bonus: $

OTHER THOUGHTS:

Apparent Women Officers or Directors: 4
Hot Spot for Advancement for Women/Minorities: Y

LOCATIONS: ("Y" = Yes)

West:	Southwest:	Midwest:	Southeast:	Northeast:	International:
Y	Y	Y	Y	Y	

Note: Financial information, benefits and other data can change quickly and may vary from those stated here.

CHS INC

www.chsinc.com

Industry Group Code: 4244 **Ranks within this company's industry group:** Sales: 2 Profits: 2

Management:		Sales/Marketing:		Liberal Arts:		Information Systems:		Professionals:		Tech./Scientific:	
Management Trainees:	Y	Marketing Pros.:	Y	Gen. Writing/Editing:	Y	Info. Management:	Y	Finance/Acct.:	Y	Engineers, Electrical:	
Experienced Mngmt.:	Y	Retail Sales:		Technical Writing:		Software Dev.:		Law:	Y	Engineers, Other:	
International Business:		Commercial/Industrial:	Y	Graphic Arts/Photog.:	Y	Hardware Dev.:		HR/Other:	Y	Health/Lab:	
MBA Grads:	Y	Sales Trainees:		Music:		Consulting/Other:		Training:	Y	Scientists/Research:	
		Advertising Pros.:		Broadcasting:				Health Care:		Petroleum/Chemicals:	
				Other:				Consulting:		Math/Other:	

TYPES OF BUSINESS:

Food Distribution
Energy Products & Services
Grain Marketing
Convenience Stores

BRANDS/DIVISIONS/AFFILIATES:

Cenex
Ampride

CONTACTS: *Note: Officers with more than one job title may be intentionally listed here more than once.*

John D. Johnson, CEO
John D. Johnson, Pres.
John Schmitz, CFO/Exec. VP
Jay Debertin, Exec. VP/COO-Processing
Patrick Kluempke, Exec. VP-Sharesd Svcs.
Thomas Larson, Exec. VP-Bus. Solutions
Mark Palmquist, Exec. VP/COO-AG Bus.
Michael Toelle, Chmn.

Phone: 651-355-6000	Fax:
Toll-Free: 800-232-3639	
Address: 5500 Cenex Dr., Inver Grove Heights, MN 55077 US	

GROWTH PLANS/SPECIAL FEATURES:

CHS, Inc. is an agricultural company and cooperative owned by farmers and ranchers and their local cooperatives across the U.S. The company operates in three segments: Energy, Ag business and processing. The energy segment's operations include petroleum refining and pipelines; the supply, marketing (including ethanol and biodiesel) and distribution of refined fuels (gasoline, diesel and other energy products); the blending, sale and distribution of lubricants; and the wholesale supply of propane. The division processes crude oil into refined petroleum products at refineries in Montana and Kansas; and sells those products under the Cenex brand to member cooperatives and others through a network of roughly 1,650 independent retail sites, the majority of which operate Cenex/Ampride convenience stores. The Ag business segment includes agronomy, country operations and grain marketing. The agronomy operations comprise the wholesale crop nutrients business, which sells roughly 6.7 million tons of fertilizer annually. The fertilizer is either delivered directly to the customer from the manufacturer or through 15 inland or river warehouse terminals and other non-owned storage facilities located throughout the country. The country operations business purchases a variety of grains and provides cooperative members and producers with access to products and services such as farm supplies and programs for crop and livestock production. Country operations operate at 376 locations, which include three sunflower plants. The grain marketing operations purchase grain, which is typically contracted for sale for future delivery at a specified location, and bear responsibility for handling the grain and arranging for its transportation to that location. The processing segment converts raw agricultural commodities into ingredients for finished food products or into finished consumer food products.

Employees are offered medical, dental, vision and hearing coverage; life and dependent life insurance; short-and long-term disability; flexible spending accounts; and a travel assistance program.

FINANCIALS: Sales and profits are in thousands of dollars—add 000 to get the full amount. 2008 Note: Financial information for 2008 was not available for all companies at press time.

2008 Sales: $32,167,461	2008 Profits: $803,045	**U.S. Stock Ticker:** CHSCP
2007 Sales: $17,215,992	2007 Profits: $756,723	**Int'l Ticker:** Int'l Exchange:
2006 Sales: $14,383,835	2006 Profits: $505,391	Employees: 8,099
2005 Sales: $11,926,962	2005 Profits: $250,016	Fiscal Year Ends: 8/31
2004 Sales: $10,969,081	2004 Profits: $221,332	Parent Company:

SALARIES/BENEFITS:

Pension Plan:	ESOP Stock Plan:	Profit Sharing:	Top Exec. Salary: $900,000	Bonus: $3,557,000
Savings Plan: Y	Stock Purch. Plan:		Second Exec. Salary: $570,700	Bonus: $1,576,074

OTHER THOUGHTS:

Apparent Women Officers or Directors:
Hot Spot for Advancement for Women/Minorities:

LOCATIONS: ("Y" = Yes)

West:	Southwest:	Midwest:	Southeast:	Northeast:	International:
Y	Y	Y	Y	Y	

Note: Financial information, benefits and other data can change quickly and may vary from those stated here.

CHUBB CORPORATION (THE)

www.chubb.com

Industry Group Code: 524126 Ranks within this company's industry group: Sales: 5 Profits: 3

Management:		Sales/Marketing:		Liberal Arts:		Information Systems:		Professionals:		Tech./Scientific:	
Management Trainees:	Y	Marketing Pros.:	Y	Gen. Writing/Editing:	Y	Info. Management:	Y	Finance/Acct.:	Y	Engineers, Electrical:	
Experienced Mngmt.:	Y	Retail Sales:		Technical Writing:	Y	Software Dev.:	Y	Law:	Y	Engineers, Other:	
International Business:	Y	Commercial/Industrial:	Y	Graphic Arts/Photog.:	Y	Hardware Dev.:		HR/Other:	Y	Health/Lab:	
MBA Grads:	Y	Sales Trainees:	Y	Music:		Consulting/Other:		Training:	Y	Scientists/Research:	
		Advertising Pros.:	Y	Broadcasting:				Health Care:		Petroleum/Chemicals:	
				Other:	Y			Consulting:		Math/Other:	Y

TYPES OF BUSINESS:

Insurance, Direct Property & Casualty
Reinsurance Services
Consulting Services
Claims Administration Services
Real Estate
Computer Training & Staffing
Luxury Items Insurance

BRANDS/DIVISIONS/AFFILIATES:

Chubb Commercial Insurance
Chubb Specialty Insurance
Chubb Personal Insurance
Federal Insurance Company
Pacific Indemnity Company
Vigilant Insurance Company
Chubb Custom Insurance Company
Executive Risk Indemnity, Inc

CONTACTS: Note: Officers with more than one job title may be intentionally listed here more than once.

John D. Finnegan, CEO
John J. Degnan, COO/Vice Chmn.
John D. Finnegan, Pres.
Richard G. Spiro, CFO/Exec. VP
James P. Knight, CIO/Exec. VP-Chubb & Son
Dino E. Robusto, Chief Admin. Officer/Exec. VP
Maureen Brundage, General Counsel/Exec. VP
Paul J. Krump, Exec. VP/Chief Underwriting Officer
Robert C. Cox, Exec. VP-Chubb & Son/COO-Chubb Specialty Insurance
Andrew A. McElwee, Jr., Exec. VP-Chubb & Son/COO-Chubb Personal Insurance
Janice M. Tomlinson, Exec. VP/Int'l Field Oper. Mgr.-Chubb & Son
John D. Finnegan, Chmn.
Harold L. Morrison, Jr., Chief Global Field Officer/Exec. VP

Phone: 908-903-2000	Fax: 908-903-2027
Toll-Free:	
Address: 15 Mountain View Rd., Warren, NJ 07059 US	

GROWTH PLANS/SPECIAL FEATURES:

The Chubb Corporation is a holding company whose subsidiaries provide property and casualty insurance in the U.S., Canada, Europe, Australia and parts of Latin America and Asia. Headquartered in New Jersey, the firm has $48 billion in assets and more than 120 offices in 27 countries internationally. The firm's property and casualty group is divided into three units: Chubb Commercial Insurance, which offers a range of commercial insurance products; Chubb Specialty Insurance, which offers a variety of specialized professional liability products for privately and publicly owned companies, financial institutions, professional firms and healthcare organizations; and Chubb Personal Insurance, which offers products for individuals who require more coverage choices and higher limits than standard insurance policies. The firm's property and casualty insurance group includes, among others, Federal Insurance Company; Pacific Indemnity Company; Vigilant Insurance Company; Chubb Custom Insurance Company; and Executive Risk Indemnity, Inc. The group underwrites mostly lines of property and casualty insurance and writes non-participating policies. Several members also write participating policies, particularly in the workers' compensation class of business. The firm's other operations include commercial real estate development activities, primarily in New Jersey; residential development activities, primarily in central Florida; consulting and claims administration services; computer training and staffing; and reinsurance services. Chubb offers insurance for primary vacation homes and contents; city homes; valuable possessions including much of the world's individually owned precious jewelry, automobiles and watercraft; and personal liability for some of the wealthiest individuals in the U.S. In recent years, the company introduced My Loss Scenarios, which provides over 150 professional and management liability loss scenarios through an online library.

Chubb offers its employees flexible spending accounts and medical, dental, vision, life, business travel and disability insurance.

FINANCIALS: Sales and profits are in thousands of dollars—add 000 to get the full amount. 2008 Note: Financial information for 2008 was not available for all companies at press time.

		U.S. Stock Ticker: CB
2008 Sales: $13,221,000	2008 Profits: $1,804,000	Int'l Ticker: Int'l Exchange:
2007 Sales: $14,107,000	2007 Profits: $2,807,000	Employees: 10,400
2006 Sales: $14,003,000	2006 Profits: $2,528,000	Fiscal Year Ends: 12/31
2005 Sales: $14,082,300	2005 Profits: $1,825,900	Parent Company:
2004 Sales: $13,177,200	2004 Profits: $1,548,400	

SALARIES/BENEFITS:

Pension Plan:	ESOP Stock Plan:	Profit Sharing:	Top Exec. Salary: $1,275,000	Bonus: $3,357,800
Savings Plan:	Stock Purch. Plan:		Second Exec. Salary: $759,588	Bonus: $1,765,300

OTHER THOUGHTS:

Apparent Women Officers or Directors: 6
Hot Spot for Advancement for Women/Minorities: Y

LOCATIONS: ("Y" = Yes)

West:	Southwest:	Midwest:	Southeast:	Northeast:	International:
Y	Y	Y	Y	Y	Y

Note: Financial information, benefits and other data can change quickly and may vary from those stated here.

CIBER INC

www.ciber.com

Industry Group Code: 541513 Ranks within this company's industry group: Sales: 10 Profits: 11

Management:		Sales/Marketing:		Liberal Arts:		Information Systems:		Professionals:		Tech./Scientific:	
Management Trainees:	Y	Marketing Pros.:	Y	Gen. Writing/Editing:	Y	Info. Management:	Y	Finance/Acct.:	Y	Engineers, Electrical:	Y
Experienced Mngmt.:	Y	Retail Sales:		Technical Writing:	Y	Software Dev.:	Y	Law:	Y	Engineers, Other:	
International Business:	Y	Commercial/Industrial:	Y	Graphic Arts/Photog.:	Y	Hardware Dev.:	Y	HR/Other:	Y	Health/Lab:	
MBA Grads:	Y	Sales Trainees:		Music:		Consulting/Other:	Y	Training:	Y	Scientists/Research:	
		Advertising Pros.:		Broadcasting:				Health Care:		Petroleum/Chemicals:	
				Other:				Consulting:	Y	Math/Other:	

TYPES OF BUSINESS:
IT Consulting
Equipment Reselling
Application Development
Enterprise Integrations
Application Management Outsourcing
Global Security Solutions

BRANDS/DIVISIONS/AFFILIATES:
CIBER Europe
Metamor Enterprise Solutions, LLC
Condevor AB
Iteamic Pvt. Ltd.

CONTACTS: *Note: Officers with more than one job title may be intentionally listed here more than once.*
Mac J. Slingerlend, CEO
Mac J. Slingerlend, Pres.
Peter H. Cheesbrough, CFO/Exec. VP
Robin Caputo, VP-Mktg.
Susan Keesen, General Counsel/VP
Robin Caputo, VP-Public Rel.
Jennifer J. Matuschek, VP-Investor Rel.
Chris Loffredo, Chief Acct. Officer/VP
Russ Wheeler, Pres., CIBER Enterprise Solutions
Joe Mancuso, Sr. VP-U.S. Commercial Oper.
Ed Burns, Pres., State Gov't Solutions
Tony Kelsey, VP-Creative Svcs.
Bobby G. Stevenson, Chmn.
Terje Laugerund, CEO-Ciber Europe

Phone: 303-220-0100	Fax: 303-220-7100
Toll-Free: 800-242-3799	
Address: 5251 DTC Pkwy., Ste. 1400, Greenwood Village, CO 80111 US	

GROWTH PLANS/SPECIAL FEATURES:
CIBER, Inc. provides information technology (IT) system integration consulting and other IT services. To a small extent, it also resells certain IT hardware and software products. The company operates in five segments: commercial solutions; federal government solutions; state and local solutions; U.S. package solutions; and European operations. The commercial, federal government and state and local solutions segments offer services including application development, enterprise integrations, application management outsourcing and global security. Application development services provide analysis, design, development, testing, implementation and maintenance of business applications. The enterprise integration services integrate data and applications for companies and organizations to deliver functional business solutions. The application management outsourcing service assumes responsibility for a client's specific IT operation and provides ongoing application support. The U.S. package solutions segment operates as the CIBER Enterprise Solutions (CES) division. CES provides consulting services to support software from enterprise solutions vendors including Oracle, SAP and Lawson, as well as several supply chain and higher education management products. Services include package software assessment, selection, planning and implementation. The European operations segment provides a broad range of business and technical consulting services that include package implementation, application development, systems integration and support services, as well as the firm's own Customer Relationship Management software products. CIBER Europe has 25 offices in more than 10 European countries. The firm also operates seven offices in Asia and the Pacific. Partner relationships in Europe include SAP, Sage, Microsoft and Oracle. In September 2007, CIBER acquired the SAP Practice of Headstrong Corp. from Metamor Enterprise Solutions, LLC. In October 2007, the company acquired Condevor AB, a SAP consultancy. In September 2008, the firm agreed to acquire Iteamic Pvt. Ltd. to expand business into India.

The company offer its employees medical, dental and vision insurance; disability insurance; life insurance; and tuition assistance.

FINANCIALS: Sales and profits are in thousands of dollars—add 000 to get the full amount. 2008 Note: Financial information for 2008 was not available for all companies at press time.

2008 Sales: $1,191,567	2008 Profits: $29,956	U.S. Stock Ticker: CBR
2007 Sales: $1,081,975	2007 Profits: $29,026	Int'l Ticker: Int'l Exchange:
2006 Sales: $995,837	2006 Profits: $24,735	Employees: 8,300
2005 Sales: $956,009	2005 Profits: $24,707	Fiscal Year Ends: 12/31
2004 Sales: $843,021	2004 Profits: $29,701	Parent Company:

SALARIES/BENEFITS:

Pension Plan:	ESOP Stock Plan:	Profit Sharing:	Top Exec. Salary: $329,308	Bonus: $355,400
Savings Plan: Y	Stock Purch. Plan: Y		Second Exec. Salary: $414,000	Bonus: $665,000

OTHER THOUGHTS:
Apparent Women Officers or Directors: 6
Hot Spot for Advancement for Women/Minorities: Y

LOCATIONS: ("Y" = Yes)

West:	Southwest:	Midwest:	Southeast:	Northeast:	International:
Y	Y	Y	Y	Y	Y

CIGNA CORP

www.cigna.com

Industry Group Code: 524114 **Ranks within this company's industry group:** Sales: 5 Profits: 8

Management:		Sales/Marketing:		Liberal Arts:		Information Systems:		Professionals:		Tech./Scientific:	
Management Trainees:	Y	Marketing Pros.:	Y	Gen. Writing/Editing:	Y	Info. Management:	Y	Finance/Acct.:	Y	Engineers, Electrical:	
Experienced Mngmt.:	Y	Retail Sales:		Technical Writing:	Y	Software Dev.:	Y	Law:	Y	Engineers, Other:	
International Business:	Y	Commercial/Industrial:	Y	Graphic Arts/Photog.:	Y	Hardware Dev.:		HR/Other:	Y	Health/Lab:	
MBA Grads:	Y	Sales Trainees:		Music:		Consulting/Other:		Training:	Y	Scientists/Research:	
		Advertising Pros.:	Y	Broadcasting:				Health Care:	Y	Petroleum/Chemicals:	
				Other:	Y			Consulting:		Math/Other:	

TYPES OF BUSINESS:

Insurance-Medical & Health, HMOs & PPOs
Indemnity Insurance
Investment Management Services
Group Life, Accident & Disability

BRANDS/DIVISIONS/AFFILIATES:

CIGNA International
CIGNA Group Insurance
CIGNA HealthCare
CIGNATURE
CareAllies
Star HRG
Cigna Behavioral Health
Cigna Cost of Care Estimator

CONTACTS: Note: Officers with more than one job title may be intentionally listed here more than once.

H. Edward Hanway, CEO
David M. Cordani, COO
David M. Cordani, Pres.
Annmarie Hagan, CFO/Exec. VP
Benjamin Karsch, Chief Mktg. Officer/Sr. VP
John M. Murabito, Exec. VP-Human Resources & Svcs.
Jeffrey Kang, Chief Medical Officer
Michael D. Woeller, CIO/Exec. VP
Carol Ann Petren, General Counsel/Exec. VP
Ted Detrick, VP-Investor Rel.
Mary Hoeltzel, Chief Acct. Officer/VP
David M. Cordani, Pres., CIGNA Health Care
Karen S. Rohan, Pres., CIGNA Dental & Vision Care
Karen S. Rohan, Pres., CIGNA Group Insurance
Jeffrey L. Kang, Chief Medical Officer
H. Edward Hanway, Chmn.
William Atwell, Pres., CIGNA Int'l

Phone: 215-761-1000	Fax: 215-761-5515
Toll-Free:	
Address: 2 Liberty Pl., 1650 Chestnut St., Philadelphia, PA 19192 US	

GROWTH PLANS/SPECIAL FEATURES:

CIGNA Corporation and its subsidiaries constitute one of the largest investor-owned employee benefits organizations in the U.S. The group is a major provider of employee benefits, including health care products and services, group life, accident and disability insurance, retirement products and services and investment management. CIGNA HealthCare offers a wide range of medical insurance plans, including consumer-directed health plans, health maintenance organizations (HMOs), network-only and point-of-services (POS) medical plans, preferred provider plans (PPOs) and traditional medical indemnity coverage. The Star HRG business unit offers medical plan for hourly employees who lack benefits. CIGNA offers a modular product portfolio, including CIGNATURE, CareAllies and CIGNA Choice Fund solutions, which offer a choice of benefit, participating provider network, funding, medical management, consumerism and health advocacy options for employers and consumers. CIGNA Group Insurance markets benefits packages to employers that include life insurance, accident insurance, disability insurance and specialty programs. CIGNA International services clients in Asia, Europe and the Americas. The firm also maintains online coaching capabilities such as Cigna Behavioral Health, which arranges for the provision of behavioral health care services to individuals through its network of participating behavioral health care providers and also offers employee assistance programs and work/life programs to employer sponsored benefit plans, HMOs, governmental entities and disability insurers. Other online coaching resources include Cigna Dental Health, Cigna Vision and Cigna Pharmacy. In 2009, the company introduced the Cigna Cost of Care Estimator, which informs patients and doctors the cost of medical services based on a person's particular Cigna plan.

Employees are offered medical, dental, disability and life insurance; mental health coverage; a 401(k) plan; long-term care insurance; flexible work arrangements; adoption assistance; educational reimbursement; wellness and fitness programs; employee retail discount programs; lactation centers; and an employee assistance program.

FINANCIALS: Sales and profits are in thousands of dollars—add 000 to get the full amount. 2008 Note: Financial information for 2008 was not available for all companies at press time.

2008 Sales: $19,101,000	2008 Profits: $292,000	**U.S. Stock Ticker: CI**
2007 Sales: $17,623,000	2007 Profits: $1,115,000	**Int'l Ticker:** Int'l Exchange:
2006 Sales: $16,547,000	2006 Profits: $1,155,000	Employees: 30,300
2005 Sales: $16,684,000	2005 Profits: $1,625,000	Fiscal Year Ends: 12/31
2004 Sales: $18,176,000	2004 Profits: $1,438,000	Parent Company:

SALARIES/BENEFITS:

Pension Plan:	ESOP Stock Plan:	Profit Sharing:	Top Exec. Salary: $1,142,885	Bonus: $6,650,000
Savings Plan: Y	Stock Purch. Plan:		Second Exec. Salary: $701,500	Bonus: $1,583,960

OTHER THOUGHTS:

Apparent Women Officers or Directors: 7
Hot Spot for Advancement for Women/Minorities: Y

LOCATIONS: ("Y" = Yes)

West:	Southwest:	Midwest:	Southeast:	Northeast:	International:
Y	Y	Y	Y	Y	Y

Note: Financial information, benefits and other data can change quickly and may vary from those stated here.

CINTAS CORP

www.cintas.com

Industry Group Code: 812331 **Ranks within this company's industry group:** Sales: 1 Profits: 1

Management:		Sales/Marketing:		Liberal Arts:		Information Systems:		Professionals:		Tech./Scientific:	
Management Trainees:	Y	Marketing Pros.:	Y	Gen. Writing/Editing:	Y	Info. Management:	Y	Finance/Acct.:	Y	Engineers, Electrical:	
Experienced Mngmt.:	Y	Retail Sales:		Technical Writing:		Software Dev.:	Y	Law:	Y	Engineers, Other:	
International Business:	Y	Commercial/Industrial:	Y	Graphic Arts/Photog.:	Y	Hardware Dev.:		HR/Other:	Y	Health/Lab:	
MBA Grads:	Y	Sales Trainees:	Y	Music:		Consulting/Other:		Training:	Y	Scientists/Research:	
		Advertising Pros.:	Y	Broadcasting:				Health Care:		Petroleum/Chemicals:	
				Other:				Consulting:		Math/Other:	

TYPES OF BUSINESS:

Linen & Uniform Supply
Uniform Rental, Sales & Cleaning
Uniform Design & Manufacturing
Outsourcing Services
Dust Control Services
Restroom Cleaning Services
Document Shredding & Management
First Aid & Safety Products

BRANDS/DIVISIONS/AFFILIATES:

CONTACTS: *Note: Officers with more than one job title may be intentionally listed here more than once.*

Scott D. Farmer, CEO
J. Phillip Holloman, COO
J. Phillip Holloman, Pres.
William C. Gale, CFO/Sr. VP
Thomas Frooman, General Counsel/VP/Corp. Sec.
Michael L. Thompson, Treas./VP
Richard T. Farmer, Chmn.

Phone: 513-459-1200	Fax: 513-573-4130
Toll-Free:	
Address: 6800 Cintas Blvd., Cincinnati, OH 45262-5737 US	

GROWTH PLANS/SPECIAL FEATURES:

Cintas Corp. is a leading uniform supplier in the U.S. that designs, manufactures and implements corporate identity uniform programs. The company's products include entrance mats, restroom supplies, hygiene service supplies, first aid and safety products, fire protection products, document shredding and storage, cleanroom resources and flame resistant clothing. Cintas supplies products and services to approximately 800,000 businesses. The company's products and services are designed to enhance its customers' images and brand identification as well as provide a safe and efficient workplace. The firm operates through two segments: Rental Uniforms and Ancillary Products; and Other Services. The Rentals segment and Ancillary Products segment, accounting for approximately 72% of the company's revenue, reflects the rental and servicing of uniforms and other garments, mats, mops, shop towels and restroom and hygiene products and services. Rental services include the cleaning of uniforms as well as providing on-going uniform replacements as required to each customer. The Other services unit, accounting for approximately 28% of the company's revenue, consists of the direct sale of uniforms and related items, first aid, safety and fire protection products and services, document management services and branded promotional products. The company also has specialized services tailored to the requirements of a number of additional industries, including automotive, casino, food processing, healthcare, lawn and garden, lodging, pest control, restaurant, supermarket and veterinary. The firm operates 11 manufacturing plants and eight distribution centers across North America, as well as more than 400 other facilities. Cintas provides its products and services through a distribution network and approximately 7,300 local delivery routes. In June 2008, following the opening of service offices in Hong Kong and Macau, the company announced plans to launch services in various other international markets, led by Cintas' new Global Accounts and Strategic Markets Division.

FINANCIALS: Sales and profits are in thousands of dollars—add 000 to get the full amount. 2008 Note: Financial information for 2008 was not available for all companies at press time.

2008 Sales: $3,937,900	2008 Profits: $335,405	**U.S. Stock Ticker: CTAS**
2007 Sales: $3,706,900	2007 Profits: $334,538	**Int'l Ticker:** Int'l Exchange:
2006 Sales: $3,403,608	2006 Profits: $323,382	Employees: 31,000
2005 Sales: $3,067,283	2005 Profits: $292,547	Fiscal Year Ends: 5/31
2004 Sales: $2,814,059	2004 Profits: $300,518	Parent Company:

SALARIES/BENEFITS:

Pension Plan:	ESOP Stock Plan: Y	Profit Sharing: Y	Top Exec. Salary: $700,000	Bonus: $
Savings Plan: Y	Stock Purch. Plan:		Second Exec. Salary: $427,330	Bonus: $

OTHER THOUGHTS:

Apparent Women Officers or Directors:
Hot Spot for Advancement for Women/Minorities:

LOCATIONS: ("Y" = Yes)

West:	Southwest:	Midwest:	Southeast:	Northeast:	International:
Y	Y	Y	Y	Y	Y

Note: Financial information, benefits and other data can change quickly and may vary from those stated here.

CISCO SYSTEMS INC

www.cisco.com

Industry Group Code: 33411 Ranks within this company's industry group: Sales: 1 Profits: 1

Management:		Sales/Marketing:		Liberal Arts:		Information Systems:		Professionals:		Tech./Scientific:	
Management Trainees:	Y	Marketing Pros.:	Y	Gen. Writing/Editing:	Y	Info. Management:	Y	Finance/Acct.:	Y	Engineers, Electrical:	Y
Experienced Mngmt.:	Y	Retail Sales:		Technical Writing:	Y	Software Dev.:	Y	Law:	Y	Engineers, Other:	
International Business:	Y	Commercial/Industrial:	Y	Graphic Arts/Photog.:	Y	Hardware Dev.:	Y	HR/Other:	Y	Health/Lab:	
MBA Grads:	Y	Sales Trainees:	Y	Music:		Consulting/Other:	Y	Training:	Y	Scientists/Research:	Y
		Advertising Pros.:	Y	Broadcasting:				Health Care:		Petroleum/Chemicals:	
				Other:				Consulting:		Math/Other:	Y

TYPES OF BUSINESS:

Computer Networking Equipment
Routers & Switches
Real-Time Conferencing Technology
Server Virtualization Software
Data Storage Products
Security Products
Servers
Unified Communications Systems

BRANDS/DIVISIONS/AFFILIATES:

Scientific Atlanta Inc
Jabber, Inc.
PostPath, Inc.
Pure Networks
Webex Communications Inc
Tidal Software, Inc.
Pure Digital Technologies, Inc.
Cisco CapitalSM (Dubai), Ltd.

CONTACTS: *Note: Officers with more than one job title may be intentionally listed here more than once.*

John T. Chambers, CEO
Frank Calderoni, CFO/Exec. VP
Bill LePage, Sr. VP-Global Sales Oper.
Brian Schipper, Sr. VP-Human Resources
Gregory Akers, Sr. VP-R&D
Rebecca J. Jacoby, CIO/Sr. VP
Padmasree Warrior, CTO
Mark Chandler, General Counsel/Sr. VP/Sec.
Robert Lloyd, Exec. VP-Worldwide Oper.
Ned Hooper, Sr. VP-Corp. Dev./Chief Strategy Officer
Blair Christie, Sr. VP-Corp. Comm.
Jonathan Chadwick, Principal Acct. Officer/Corp. Controller/Sr. VP
Keith Goodwin, Sr. VP-Worldwide Channels
Marilyn Mersereau, Sr. VP-Corp. Mktg.
David K. Holland, Treas./Sr. VP
Randy Pond, Exec. VP-Oper., Processes & Systems
John T. Chambers, Chmn.
Chris Dedicoat, Pres., European Markets

Phone: 408-526-4000	Fax:
Toll-Free: 800-553-6387	
Address: 170 W. Tasman Dr., San Jose, CA 95134 US	

GROWTH PLANS/SPECIAL FEATURES:

Cisco Systems, Inc. designs, develops, manufactures and markets Internet protocol (IP)-based networking and other products related to the communications and information technology industries, and provides services associated with these products. The firm's products, which include routers, switches and advanced technologies, are installed at large enterprises, public institutions, telecommunications companies, commercial businesses and personal residences. Cisco divides its products into five categories. Network systems products include routers, switches, interfaces and modules, optical networking, network management solutions and infrastructure software. The collaboration, voice and video group includes voice and unified communications, WebEx and TelePresence real-time conference technology, video, cable and content delivery, service exchange, universal gateways and access server products. Security products include network security, physical and building security, virtual private networks (VPN), firewall and security management solutions. The data center group includes unified computing, data center switches, storage networking, blade switches and applications networking services. Finally, the mobility and wireless group offers wireless, access point, outdoor wireless, mobility services, wireless local-area network (LAN) controller and service exchange products. In addition to its product offerings, Cisco provides a range of product support services. Cisco's strategic push is now focused on Unified Computing Systems, which bundle server, storage and networking systems into one new product. Each of Cisco's new servers is capable of running hundreds of virtual servers by utilizing virtualization software. The firm's business is divided by region into five segments: the U.S. and Canada, European Markets, Emerging Markets, Asia Pacific and Japan. In 2008, Cisco acquired Jabber, Inc.; PostPath, Inc; Pure Networks; the remaining 20% stake of Nuova Systems; and agreed to acquire DiviTech A/S. Cisco's acquisitions in 2009 included Richards-Zeta Building Intelligence, Inc.; Tidal Software, Inc.; and Pure Digital Technologies, Inc. In July 2009, the company launched Cisco CapitalSM (Dubai), Ltd., a financing solutions provider, in Dubai, United Arab Emirates.

FINANCIALS: Sales and profits are in thousands of dollars—add 000 to get the full amount. 2008 Note: Financial information for 2008 was not available for all companies at press time.

2008 Sales: $39,540,000	2008 Profits: $8,052,000	**U.S. Stock Ticker:** CSCO
2007 Sales: $34,922,000	2007 Profits: $7,333,000	**Int'l Ticker:** Int'l Exchange:
2006 Sales: $28,484,000	2006 Profits: $5,580,000	Employees: 65,545
2005 Sales: $24,801,000	2005 Profits: $5,741,000	Fiscal Year Ends: 7/31
2004 Sales: $22,045,000	2004 Profits: $4,401,000	Parent Company:

SALARIES/BENEFITS:

Pension Plan:	ESOP Stock Plan:	Profit Sharing:	Top Exec. Salary: $750,000	Bonus: $1,484,700
Savings Plan:	Stock Purch. Plan:		Second Exec. Salary: $575,000	Bonus: $1,138,270

OTHER THOUGHTS:

Apparent Women Officers or Directors: 11
Hot Spot for Advancement for Women/Minorities: Y

LOCATIONS: ("Y" = Yes)

West:	Southwest:	Midwest:	Southeast:	Northeast:	International:
Y	Y	Y	Y	Y	Y

Note: Financial information, benefits and other data can change quickly and may vary from those stated here.

CLUBCORP INC

www.clubcorp.com

Industry Group Code: 713910 **Ranks within this company's industry group:** Sales: 1 Profits:

Management:		Sales/Marketing:		Liberal Arts:		Information Systems:		Professionals:		Tech./Scientific:	
Management Trainees:	Y	Marketing Pros.:	Y	Gen. Writing/Editing:	Y	Info. Management:	Y	Finance/Acct.:	Y	Engineers, Electrical:	
Experienced Mngmt.:	Y	Retail Sales:		Technical Writing:		Software Dev.:	Y	Law:	Y	Engineers, Other:	
International Business:	Y	Commercial/Industrial:	Y	Graphic Arts/Photog.:	Y	Hardware Dev.:		HR/Other:	Y	Health/Lab:	
MBA Grads:	Y	Sales Trainees:		Music:		Consulting/Other:		Training:	Y	Scientists/Research:	
		Advertising Pros.:		Broadcasting:				Health Care:		Petroleum/Chemicals:	
				Other:	Y			Consulting:		Math/Other:	

TYPES OF BUSINESS:

Golf Courses & Country Clubs
Business/Sports Clubs
Resorts

BRANDS/DIVISIONS/AFFILIATES:

KSL Capital LLC
Firestone Country Club
Metropolitan Club
Homestead (The)
Boston College Club
Seville Golf and Country Club
Private Clubs
Tower Club

CONTACTS: *Note: Officers with more than one job title may be intentionally listed here more than once.*

Eric L. Affeldt, CEO
Eric L. Affeldt, Pres.
Curt McClellan, CFO
Jamie Walters, Exec. VP-Sales & Mktg.
Ingrid Keiser, Exec. VP-People Strategy
Daniel T. Tilley, CIO/Exec. VP
Ingrid Keiser, Chief Legal Officer/Corp. Sec.
Mark Murphy, Sr. VP-Strategic Alliances
Mark Burnett, Exec. VP-Golf & Country Club Div.
Mark Murphy, Sr. VP-Global Sales
David B. Woodyard, Exec. VP-New Bus. Dev.
John H. Longstreet, Exec. VP-Oper., ClubCorp USA Inc.
William T. Walden, Sr. VP-Purchasing

Phone: 972-243-6191	**Fax:** 972-406-7856
Toll-Free:	
Address: 3030 LBJ Freeway, Ste. 600, Dallas, TX 75234 US	

GROWTH PLANS/SPECIAL FEATURES:

ClubCorp, Inc. is an owner and operator of nearly 160 golf courses, country clubs, private clubs, golf resorts and resorts in the U.S., with additional operations in Australia, Europe and Asia. The company has approximately 175,000 memberships and 170 operations in 26 states and Washington, D.C., as well as internationally, including 74 private country clubs, eight semi-private golf clubs, eight public golf facilities, six resorts (including Firestone Country Club, the Homestead and Barton Creek Resort and Spa), four international clubs and more than 60 business/sports clubs (including 35 business clubs, 10 business/sports clubs and three sports clubs). The firm's operations include nationally recognized golf courses and country clubs such as the Firestone Country Club in Akron, Ohio; The Homestead in Hot Springs, Virginia, the oldest resort in America; and the Mission Hills Country Club in Rancho Mirage, California. Additionally, the company's business and sports clubs can be found in major metropolitan areas, including the Boston College Club; City Club on Bunker Hill in Los Angeles; Citrus Club in Orlando, Florida; Columbia Tower Club in Seattle; Metropolitan Club in Chicago; Tower Club in Dallas; and the City Club of Washington, D.C. Some of the company's unique programs include Ace Adventures, a golf tournament vacation package; Club Tournaments 101, a series of complimentary tournament education classes; and Signature Gold, a benefit program offering complimentary golf and dining, discounts and VIP services to members. ClubCorp maintains partnerships with Acura, E-Z-Go/Textron, Titleist and ESPN, among others. The firm is owned by Denver-based KSL Capital, a private-equity investor. In January 2008, ClubCorp acquired Seville Golf and Country Club in Gilbert, Arizona, from Shea Homes. In August 2008, the firm announced the relaunch of Private Clubs, its luxury lifestyle magazine. In January 2009, Tower Club, a ClubCorp property, completed its $3.8 million renovation project.

FINANCIALS: Sales and profits are in thousands of dollars—add 000 to get the full amount. 2008 Note: Financial information for 2008 was not available for all companies at press time.

2008 Sales: $1,000,000	2008 Profits: $	**U.S. Stock Ticker:** Private
2007 Sales: $1,000,000	2007 Profits: $	**Int'l Ticker:** Int'l Exchange:
2006 Sales: $1,020,000	2006 Profits: $	Employees: 15,000
2005 Sales: $1,028,088	2005 Profits: $70,754	Fiscal Year Ends: 12/31
2004 Sales: $938,802	2004 Profits: $-6,242	Parent Company:

SALARIES/BENEFITS:

Pension Plan:	ESOP Stock Plan:	Profit Sharing:	Top Exec. Salary: $	Bonus: $281,250
Savings Plan:	Stock Purch. Plan:		Second Exec. Salary: $	Bonus: $

OTHER THOUGHTS:

Apparent Women Officers or Directors: 1
Hot Spot for Advancement for Women/Minorities: Y

LOCATIONS: ("Y" = Yes)

West:	Southwest:	Midwest:	Southeast:	Northeast:	International:
Y	Y	Y	Y	Y	Y

Note: Financial information, benefits and other data can change quickly and may vary from those stated here.

COACH INC

www.coach.com

Industry Group Code: 448210 **Ranks within this company's industry group:** Sales: 1 Profits: 1

Management:		Sales/Marketing:		Liberal Arts:		Information Systems:		Professionals:		Tech./Scientific:	
Management Trainees:	Y	Marketing Pros.:	Y	Gen. Writing/Editing:	Y	Info. Management:	Y	Finance/Acct.:	Y	Engineers, Electrical:	
Experienced Mngmt.:	Y	Retail Sales:	Y	Technical Writing:		Software Dev.:	Y	Law:	Y	Engineers, Other:	
International Business:	Y	Commercial/Industrial:	Y	Graphic Arts/Photog.:	Y	Hardware Dev.:		HR/Other:	Y	Health/Lab:	
MBA Grads:	Y	Sales Trainees:	Y	Music:		Consulting/Other:		Training:	Y	Scientists/Research:	
		Advertising Pros.:	Y	Broadcasting:				Health Care:		Petroleum/Chemicals:	
				Other:	Y			Consulting:		Math/Other:	

TYPES OF BUSINESS:

Leather Accessories-Retail
Online & Catalog Sales
Outlet Stores

BRANDS/DIVISIONS/AFFILIATES:

Coach.com
Coach Japan, Inc.
Coach Legacy
ImagineX
Jamilco

CONTACTS: Note: Officers with more than one job title may be intentionally listed here more than once.

Lew Frankfort, CEO
Jerry Stritzke, COO/Pres.
Reed Krakoff, Pres./Exec. Creative Dir.
Micheal F. Devine, III, CFO/Exec. VP
Sarah Dunn, Sr. VP-Human Resources
Todd Kahn, General Counsel/Sr. VP/Sec.
Michael Tucci, Pres., North American Retail
Lew Frankfort, Chmn.

Phone: 212-594-1850	**Fax:** 212-594-1682
Toll-Free: 888-262-6224	
Address: 516 W. 34th St., New York, NY 10001-1394 US	

GROWTH PLANS/SPECIAL FEATURES:

Coach, Inc. is a designer, producer and marketer of fine accessories and gifts for men and women, including handbags, women's and men's accessories, footwear, outerwear, business luggage and travel accessories, cases, eyewear, watches, jewelry and fragrance. The firm also licenses its name for watches, shoes and eyewear. The company sells its products through a number of direct channels, accounting for approximately 80% of its sales. The Coach brand is available at over 850 department store locations in the U.S., 140 international department stores, retail store and duty-free shop locations in 21 countries. The company operates approximately 624 stores, including 330 North American retail stores, 111 North American outlet stores, 155 Coach Japan locations and 28 Coach China locations. Approximately 62% of the company's sales come from handbags, roughly 29% come from accessories (wristlets, cosmetic cases, money pieces, etc.) and the final 9% of sales derive from all other products (sunglasses, watches, fragrance, etc.). Over the last several years, Coach has successfully transformed itself from a manufacturer of classic leather products to a marketer of more modern, fashionable handbags and accessories, using a broader range of fabrics and materials. In January 2008, the firm announced plans to enter the Russian market through an agreement with Jamilco, a domestic distributor. Coach plans to open 15 locations in Russia over a five year time frame. In May 2008, the company acquired the Coach domestic retail businesses in Hong Kong, Macau and mainland China from its current distributor, ImagineX group. The firm recently opened a new flagship store in Hong Kong. Future growth plans include 200 new stores in the U.S. over several years. In addition, Coach hopes to add 50 stores in China.

FINANCIALS: Sales and profits are in thousands of dollars—add 000 to get the full amount. 2008 Note: Financial information for 2008 was not available for all companies at press time.

2008 Sales: $3,180,757	2008 Profits: $783,055	**U.S. Stock Ticker:** COH	
2007 Sales: $2,612,456	2007 Profits: $663,665	**Int'l Ticker:** Int'l Exchange:	
2006 Sales: $2,035,085	2006 Profits: $494,277	Employees: 12,000	
2005 Sales: $1,651,704	2005 Profits: $358,612	Fiscal Year Ends: 6/30	
2004 Sales: $1,316,300	2004 Profits: $261,700	Parent Company:	

SALARIES/BENEFITS:

Pension Plan:	ESOP Stock Plan:	Profit Sharing:	Top Exec. Salary: $2,299,167	Bonus: $9,128,432
Savings Plan:	Stock Purch. Plan:		Second Exec. Salary: $1,159,917	Bonus: $1,609,964

OTHER THOUGHTS:

Apparent Women Officers or Directors: 1
Hot Spot for Advancement for Women/Minorities: Y

LOCATIONS: ("Y" = Yes)

West:	Southwest:	Midwest:	Southeast:	Northeast:	International:
Y	Y	Y	Y	Y	Y

Note: Financial information, benefits and other data can change quickly and may vary from those stated here.

COCA-COLA COMPANY (THE)

www.coca-cola.com

Industry Group Code: 3121 Ranks within this company's industry group: Sales: 2 Profits: 2

Management:		Sales/Marketing:		Liberal Arts:		Information Systems:		Professionals:		Tech./Scientific:	
Management Trainees:	Y	Marketing Pros.:	Y	Gen. Writing/Editing:	Y	Info. Management:	Y	Finance/Acct.:	Y	Engineers, Electrical:	
Experienced Mngmt.:	Y	Retail Sales:		Technical Writing:	Y	Software Dev.:	Y	Law:	Y	Engineers, Other:	Y
International Business:	Y	Commercial/Industrial:	Y	Graphic Arts/Photog.:	Y	Hardware Dev.:		HR/Other:	Y	Health/Lab:	
MBA Grads:	Y	Sales Trainees:	Y	Music:		Consulting/Other:		Training:	Y	Scientists/Research:	
		Advertising Pros.:	Y	Broadcasting:				Health Care:		Petroleum/Chemicals:	
				Other:	Y			Consulting:		Math/Other:	

TYPES OF BUSINESS:

Soft Drink Manufacturing
Concentrates & Syrups
Sports Drinks
Bottled Water
Fruit Juices

BRANDS/DIVISIONS/AFFILIATES:

Dasani
Odwalla
Powerade
Sprite
Evian
Multon
Beverage Partners Worldwide
Ilko Coffee International

CONTACTS: *Note: Officers with more than one job title may be intentionally listed here more than once.*

Muhtar Kent, CEO
Muhtar Kent, Pres.
Gary P. Fayard, CFO/Exec. VP
Joseph V. Tripodi, Chief Mktg. & Commercial Officer/Sr. VP
Cynthia P. McCague, Sr. VP/Dir.-Human Resources
Eddie R. Hays, VP-Science
Jean-Michel R. Ares, CIO/Sr. VP
Bilal Kaafarani, Sr. VP-Research & Innovation
Alexander B. Cummings, Chief Admin. Officer/Exec. VP
Geoffrey J. Kelly, General Counsel/Sr. VP
John M. Farrell, VP-Strategic Planning
Clyde C. Tuggle, Sr. VP-Corp. Affairs & Productivity
Ingrid Saunders Jones, Sr. VP-Global Community Connections
Robert P. Leechman, Chief Customer & Commercial Officer
Jane Ann Westpheling, Pres., Global Bus. Svcs.
Dominique Reiniche, Pres., Europe Group
Muhtar Kent, Chmn.
Ahmet C. Bozer, Pres., Eurasia & Africa Group
Rick Frazier, VP-Supply Chain

Phone: 404-676-2121	Fax: 404-676-6792
Toll-Free:	
Address: 1 Coca-Cola Plz., Atlanta, GA 30313 US	

GROWTH PLANS/SPECIAL FEATURES:

The Coca-Cola Company, founded in 1892, manufactures, distributes and markets nonalcoholic beverages, beverage concentrates and beverage syrups in over 200 countries. The company sells its beverage concentrates and syrups to bottling and canning operations; fountain wholesalers; and some fountain retailers. It also sells finished beverages, primarily to distributors. Coca-Cola owns or licenses more than 450 brands, including diet and light beverages; waters; enhanced waters; juices and juice drinks; teas; coffees; and energy and sports drinks. In addition, the firm has ownership interests in numerous beverage joint ventures, bottling operations and canning operations, although most of these operations are independently owned and managed. The company operates through six regional segments in addition to its corporate and bottling segments. Coca-Cola's carbonated products include Coca-Cola Classic, Fanta, Sprite, Fresca, Barq's, Powerade, Dasani, Canada Dry, Dr. Pepper and Crush. The firm also produces, distributes and markets juice and juice-drink products including Minute Maid, Simply, Odwalla, Five Alive, Bacardi mixers concentrate and Hi-C. Coca-Cola also has a license to manufacture and sell concentrates for Seagram's mixers, a line of sparkling drinks. The company is the exclusive master distributor of Evian bottled water in North America and of Rockstar, an energy drink. Multon, a Russian juice business operated as a joint venture with Coca-Cola Hellenic Bottling Company S.A., markets juice products in Russia, Ukraine and Belarus. Beverage Partners Worldwide, a joint venture with Nestlé S.A., markets tea products under trademarks including Enviga, Gold Peak, Nestea and Frestea; and coffee products under Nescafé, Taster's Choice and Georgia Club. In March 2008, the company formed Ilko Coffee International, a joint venture with illycaffe SpA. In September 2008, Coca-Cola offered to acquire China Huiyuan Juice Group Limited. In October 2008, the firm announced plans to place calorie information on the front of all packages for its U.S. beverage portfolio.

FINANCIALS: Sales and profits are in thousands of dollars—add 000 to get the full amount. 2008 Note: Financial information for 2008 was not available for all companies at press time.

2008 Sales: $31,944,000	2008 Profits: $5,807,000	**U.S. Stock Ticker: KO**
2007 Sales: $28,857,000	2007 Profits: $5,981,000	**Int'l Ticker:** Int'l Exchange:
2006 Sales: $24,088,000	2006 Profits: $5,080,000	Employees: 92,400
2005 Sales: $23,104,000	2005 Profits: $4,872,000	Fiscal Year Ends: 12/31
2004 Sales: $21,962,000	2004 Profits: $4,847,000	Parent Company:

SALARIES/BENEFITS:

Pension Plan:	ESOP Stock Plan:	Profit Sharing:	Top Exec. Salary: $1,650,000	Bonus: $4,500,000
Savings Plan: Y	Stock Purch. Plan:		Second Exec. Salary: $1,100,000	Bonus: $4,500,000

OTHER THOUGHTS:

Apparent Women Officers or Directors: 7
Hot Spot for Advancement for Women/Minorities: Y

LOCATIONS: ("Y" = Yes)

West:	Southwest:	Midwest:	Southeast:	Northeast:	International:
Y	Y	Y	Y	Y	Y

Note: Financial information, benefits and other data can change quickly and may vary from those stated here.

COCA-COLA ENTERPRISES INC

www.cokecce.com

Industry Group Code: 3121 Ranks within this company's industry group: Sales: 3 Profits: 4

Management:		Sales/Marketing:		Liberal Arts:		Information Systems:		Professionals:		Tech./Scientific:	
Management Trainees:	Y	Marketing Pros.:	Y	Gen. Writing/Editing:	Y	Info. Management:	Y	Finance/Acct.:	Y	Engineers, Electrical:	
Experienced Mngmt.:	Y	Retail Sales:		Technical Writing:	Y	Software Dev.:	Y	Law:	Y	Engineers, Other:	Y
International Business:	Y	Commercial/Industrial:	Y	Graphic Arts/Photog.:	Y	Hardware Dev.:		HR/Other:	Y	Health/Lab:	
MBA Grads:	Y	Sales Trainees:	Y	Music:		Consulting/Other:		Training:	Y	Scientists/Research:	
		Advertising Pros.:	Y	Broadcasting:				Health Care:		Petroleum/Chemicals:	
				Other:				Consulting:		Math/Other:	

TYPES OF BUSINESS:

Soft Drink Bottling
Production, Marketing & Distribution-Coca-Cola Products
Vending Machines

BRANDS/DIVISIONS/AFFILIATES:

Coca Cola Co
Monster Energy

CONTACTS: Note: Officers with more than one job title may be intentionally listed here more than once.

John F. Brock, CEO
John F. Brock, Pres.
William W. Douglas III, CFO/Sr. VP
Greg A. Lee, Sr. VP-Human Resources
Esat Sezer, CIO/Sr. VP
John J. Culhane, General Counsel/Exec. VP
Brian E. Wynne, VP-Bus. Dev. & Revenue Growth Mgmt.
John H. Downs, Jr., Sr. VP-Public Affairs & Comm.
Joseph D. Heinrich, Chief Acct. Officer/Controller/VP
Steve Cahillane, Exec. VP/Pres., North American Group
Scott Anthony, CFO/VP-North American Group
Joyce King-Lavinder, Treas./VP
William T. Plybon, Corp. Sec./VP
Lowry F. Kline, Chmn.
Steve Cahillane, Exec. VP/Pres., European Group
Edward L. Sutter, VP-Supply Chain

Phone: 770-989-3000	Fax: 770-989-3788
Toll-Free:	
Address: 2500 Windy Ridge Pkwy., Atlanta, GA 30339 US	

GROWTH PLANS/SPECIAL FEATURES:

Coca-Cola Enterprises, Inc. (CCE) is one of the largest marketers, distributors and producers of bottled and canned non-alcoholic beverages in the world. CCE serves a market of approximately 414 million consumers in North America, Great Britain, France, Belgium, the Netherlands, Luxembourg and Monaco, selling around 42 billion bottles and cans in its territories. It is also the largest marketer, producer and distributor of Coca-Cola products, representing approximately 18% of Coca-Cola product volume worldwide. The Coca-Cola Company in turn owns 35% of CCE. The firm sells 80% of The Coca-Cola Company's bottle and can volumes in North America and has operations in 46 U.S. states and all 10 provinces in Canada. The firm also distributes Dr Pepper, Sprite, A&W, Canada Dry, Nestea, Fanta, Schweppes, bottled water, juices, coffee-based drinks and sports drinks. Products are manufactured from syrups and concentrates purchased from The Coca-Cola Company and other licensors. The firm delivers most of its products directly to retailers, but some drink brands, in some territories, are distributed through wholesalers who then deliver to retailers. About 54% of the company's North American bottle and can volume and 43% of its European bottle and can volume are sold through in supermarkets. CCE has 431 facilities, 55,000 vehicles and 2.4 million vending machines, beverage dispensers and coolers in operation. Approximately 94% of company sales are Coca-Cola products. In October 2008, the company entered into an agreement with Hansen Natural Corporation to distribute Monster Energy drinks in six European countries, Canada and selected areas in the U.S.

The company offers its employees a 401(k) plan, a pension plan, life insurance, an employee assistance program and educational assistance.

FINANCIALS: Sales and profits are in thousands of dollars—add 000 to get the full amount. 2008 Note: Financial information for 2008 was not available for all companies at press time.

2008 Sales: $21,807,000	2008 Profits: $-4,394,000	U.S. Stock Ticker: CCE
2007 Sales: $20,936,000	2007 Profits: $711,000	Int'l Ticker: Int'l Exchange:
2006 Sales: $19,804,000	2006 Profits: $-1,143,000	Employees: 72,000
2005 Sales: $18,743,000	2005 Profits: $514,000	Fiscal Year Ends: 12/31
2004 Sales: $18,158,000	2004 Profits: $596,000	Parent Company:

SALARIES/BENEFITS:

Pension Plan: Y	ESOP Stock Plan:	Profit Sharing:	Top Exec. Salary: $1,144,039	Bonus: $147,344
Savings Plan: Y	Stock Purch. Plan:		Second Exec. Salary: $602,311	Bonus: $565,959

OTHER THOUGHTS:

Apparent Women Officers or Directors: 6
Hot Spot for Advancement for Women/Minorities: Y

LOCATIONS: ("Y" = Yes)

West:	Southwest:	Midwest:	Southeast:	Northeast:	International:
Y	Y	Y	Y	Y	Y

Note: Financial information, benefits and other data can change quickly and may vary from those stated here.

COGNIZANT TECHNOLOGY SOLUTIONS CORP   www.cognizant.com

Industry Group Code: 541513   Ranks within this company's industry group: Sales: 6   Profits: 3

Management:		Sales/Marketing:		Liberal Arts:		Information Systems:		Professionals:		Tech./Scientific:	
Management Trainees:	Y	Marketing Pros.:		Gen. Writing/Editing:	Y	Info. Management:	Y	Finance/Acct.:	Y	Engineers, Electrical:	Y
Experienced Mngmt.:	Y	Retail Sales:		Technical Writing:	Y	Software Dev.:	Y	Law:	Y	Engineers, Other:	
International Business:	Y	Commercial/Industrial:	Y	Graphic Arts/Photog.:	Y	Hardware Dev.:	Y	HR/Other:	Y	Health/Lab:	
MBA Grads:	Y	Sales Trainees:		Music:		Consulting/Other:	Y	Training:	Y	Scientists/Research:	
		Advertising Pros.:		Broadcasting:				Health Care:		Petroleum/Chemicals:	
				Other:	Y			Consulting:	Y	Math/Other:	

TYPES OF BUSINESS:
Consulting-IT & Systems
Outsourcing Services
Software Engineering

BRANDS/DIVISIONS/AFFILIATES:
Q*VIEW
Strategic Vision Consulting

CONTACTS: Note: Officers with more than one job title may be intentionally listed here more than once.
Fransisco D'Souza, CEO
Gordon Coburn, COO
Fransisco D'Souza, Pres.
Gordon Coburn, CFO
Steven Schwartz, General Counsel/Sr. VP/Sec.
Chandra Sekaran, Pres./Managing Dir.-Global Delivery
Rajeev Mehta, COO-Global Client Svcs.
John E. Klein, Chmn.

Phone: 201-801-0233	Fax: 201-801-0243
Toll-Free: 888-937-3277	
Address: 500 Frank W. Burr Blvd., Teaneck, NJ 07666 US	

GROWTH PLANS/SPECIAL FEATURES:

Cognizant Technology Solutions Corporation is a leading provider of custom IT design, development, integration and maintenance services, primarily for Global 2000 companies located in the U.S., Europe and Asia. The company's core competencies include Technology Strategy Consulting, Complex Systems Development, Enterprise Software Package Implementation and Maintenance, Data Warehousing & Business Intelligence, Application Testing, Application Maintenance, Infrastructure Management and Vertically-Oriented Business Process Outsourcing (V-BPO). Cognizant provides its IT services using an integrated on-site/offshore business model. This business model combines technical and account management teams located on-site at the customer location and offshore at dedicated development centers located primarily in India. Cognizant operates in four business segments: financial services, which provides services to customers in the capital markets; banking and insurance industries; healthcare, which provides services to healthcare and life science industries; manufacturing, retail and logistics, which provides services to those industries; and other, which covers telecommunications, information services, media and high technology. The firm has developed proprietary methodologies for integrating on-site and offshore teams, including Cognizant's Q*VIEW software engineering process, which is available to all on-site and offshore programmers. For most projects, Q*VIEW is used as part of an initial assessment that allows the firm to define the scope and risks of the project and subdivide the project into smaller phases with frequent deliverables and feedback from customers. The company also uses its Q*VIEW process to detect, mitigate and correct possible quality defects and to establish appropriate contingencies for each project. Cognizant has offices in the U.S., Canada, and throughout Asia and Europe. In June 2008, the company acquired Strategic Vision Consulting, a management and technology consulting firm serving the entertainment industry.

Employees are offered medical, dental and vision insurance; life insurance; and short-and long-term disability coverage.

FINANCIALS: Sales and profits are in thousands of dollars—add 000 to get the full amount. 2008 Note: Financial information for 2008 was not available for all companies at press time.

2008 Sales: $2,816,304	2008 Profits: $430,845	**U.S. Stock Ticker: CTSH**
2007 Sales: $2,135,577	2007 Profits: $350,133	**Int'l Ticker:** Int'l Exchange:
2006 Sales: $1,424,267	2006 Profits: $232,795	Employees: 61,700
2005 Sales: $885,830	2005 Profits: $166,266	Fiscal Year Ends: 12/31
2004 Sales: $586,673	2004 Profits: $100,243	Parent Company:

SALARIES/BENEFITS:
Pension Plan:	ESOP Stock Plan: Y	Profit Sharing:	Top Exec. Salary: $518,400	Bonus: $260,387
Savings Plan: Y	Stock Purch. Plan: Y		Second Exec. Salary: $466,560	Bonus: $234,348

OTHER THOUGHTS:
Apparent Women Officers or Directors:
Hot Spot for Advancement for Women/Minorities:

LOCATIONS: ("Y" = Yes)
West:	Southwest:	Midwest:	Southeast:	Northeast:	International:
Y	Y	Y		Y	Y

COLDWATER CREEK INC

www.coldwatercreek.com

Industry Group Code: 454113 Ranks within this company's industry group: Sales: 1 Profits: 1

Management:		Sales/Marketing:		Liberal Arts:		Information Systems:		Professionals:		Tech./Scientific:	
Management Trainees:	Y	Marketing Pros.:	Y	Gen. Writing/Editing:	Y	Info. Management:	Y	Finance/Acct.:	Y	Engineers, Electrical:	
Experienced Mngmt.:	Y	Retail Sales:	Y	Technical Writing:		Software Dev.:	Y	Law:	Y	Engineers, Other:	
International Business:		Commercial/Industrial:		Graphic Arts/Photog.:	Y	Hardware Dev.:		HR/Other:	Y	Health/Lab:	
MBA Grads:	Y	Sales Trainees:	Y	Music:		Consulting/Other:		Training:	Y	Scientists/Research:	
		Advertising Pros.:	Y	Broadcasting:				Health Care:		Petroleum/Chemicals:	
				Other:	Y			Consulting:		Math/Other:	

TYPES OF BUSINESS:

Upscale Apparel-Women's
Catalog Sales
Gifts, Jewelry & Accessories
Retail & Outlet Stores
Online Sales

BRANDS/DIVISIONS/AFFILIATES:

Coldwatercreek.com
Gifts-To-Go
Northcountry
Spirit

CONTACTS: *Note: Officers with more than one job title may be intentionally listed here more than once.*

Daniel Griesemer, CEO/Pres.
Georgia Shonk-Simmons, Pres.
Tim Martin, CFO/Sr. VP
Dan Moen, Sr. VP-Mktg.
Karen Horejs, VP-Human Resources
Dan Moen, CIO/Sr. VP
Georgia Shonk-Simmons, Chief Merch. Officer
Jeffrey Parisian, Sr. VP-Admin.
John E. Hayes, III, General Counsel/Sr. VP
Gerard El Chaar, Sr. VP-Oper.
Lyn Walter, VP-Investor Rel.
Joe Gravitt, VP-Retail Oper.
Arthur (Skip) Jones, VP-Outlets
Kathy McConnell, Sr. VP-Prod. Dev.
Peter Prandato, VP-Creative
Dennis C. Pence, Chmn.

Phone: 208-263-2266	Fax: 208-263-1582
Toll-Free: 800-510-2808	
Address: 1 Coldwater Creek Dr., Sandpoint, ID 83864 US	

GROWTH PLANS/SPECIAL FEATURES:

Coldwater Creek, Inc. retails women's apparel, jewelry, footwear, gift items and home merchandise through three sales channels: a traditional catalog business, an e-commerce web site business and retail stores. The company targets professional women who are 35 years of age and older, with household incomes in excess of $75,000. The firm's primary catalog titles and merchandise lines are Northcountry and Spirit. Northcountry is the firm's most established and popular line, offering a broad selection of casual merchandise. Spirit offers a more upscale assortment of apparel, including dresses, jackets and sportswear appropriate for office wear. The Coldwater Creek catalog exclusively features merchandise available in the company's stores and is designed to encourage customers to shop in store. Coldwater Creek also sends periodic specialty mailings, such as the Gifts-To-Go holiday catalog. The firm's web site features its entire full-priced, first-line merchandise collection. Coldwater Creek's fastest-growing segment is its retail store business, for which it opened 42 additional stores in fiscal 2008. The company currently has 348 full-line stores and 35 merchandise clearance outlet stores across the U.S. To remove customers' reluctance about buying online or through a catalog, the company has an all-inclusive return policy. Coldwater Creek also maintains a customer contact and technical center in Coeur d'Alene, Idaho, spanning 60,000 square feet, and a 960,000-square-foot customer contact and distribution center in Parkersburg, Virginia. The firm's long-range plan is to have as many as 550 stores by 2011.

Employees are offered medical, dental and life insurance; a 401(k) plan; an employee stock purchase plan; and discounts on Coldwater Creek products.

FINANCIALS: Sales and profits are in thousands of dollars—add 000 to get the full amount. 2008 Note: Financial information for 2008 was not available for all companies at press time.

2008 Sales: $1,151,472	2008 Profits: $-2,488	**U.S. Stock Ticker: CWTR**
2007 Sales: $1,054,611	2007 Profits: $55,372	**Int'l Ticker:** Int'l Exchange:
2006 Sales: $779,663	2006 Profits: $41,570	Employees: 11,200
2005 Sales: $590,310	2005 Profits: $29,130	Fiscal Year Ends: 1/31
2004 Sales: $518,800	2004 Profits: $12,500	Parent Company:

SALARIES/BENEFITS:

Pension Plan:	ESOP Stock Plan:	Profit Sharing:	Top Exec. Salary: $725,000	Bonus: $154,063
Savings Plan: Y	Stock Purch. Plan: Y		Second Exec. Salary: $600,000	Bonus: $118,125

OTHER THOUGHTS:

Apparent Women Officers or Directors: 6
Hot Spot for Advancement for Women/Minorities: Y

LOCATIONS: ("Y" = Yes)

West:	Southwest:	Midwest:	Southeast:	Northeast:	International:
Y	Y	Y	Y	Y	

Note: Financial information, benefits and other data can change quickly and may vary from those stated here.

COLGATE PALMOLIVE CO

www.colgate.com

Industry Group Code: 325611 **Ranks within this company's industry group: Sales: 1   Profits: 1**

Management:		Sales/Marketing:		Liberal Arts:		Information Systems:		Professionals:		Tech./Scientific:	
Management Trainees:	Y	Marketing Pros.:	Y	Gen. Writing/Editing:	Y	Info. Management:	Y	Finance/Acct.:	Y	Engineers, Electrical:	
Experienced Mngmt.:	Y	Retail Sales:		Technical Writing:	Y	Software Dev.:	Y	Law:	Y	Engineers, Other:	Y
International Business:	Y	Commercial/Industrial:	Y	Graphic Arts/Photog.:	Y	Hardware Dev.:		HR/Other:	Y	Health/Lab:	Y
MBA Grads:	Y	Sales Trainees:	Y	Music:		Consulting/Other:		Training:	Y	Scientists/Research:	Y
		Advertising Pros.:	Y	Broadcasting:				Health Care:		Petroleum/Chemicals:	Y
				Other:	Y			Consulting:		Math/Other:	

TYPES OF BUSINESS:

Toothpaste & Oral Care Products Manufacturer
Household Cleaning Products
Soap Products
Baby Care Products
Pet Food
Hair Products
Shaving Products

BRANDS/DIVISIONS/AFFILIATES:

Softsoap
Palmolive
Ajax
Irish Spring
Tom's of Maine
Lady Speed Stick
Hill's Pet Nutrition
Science Diet

CONTACTS: *Note: Officers with more than one job title may be intentionally listed here more than once.*

Ian M. Cook, CEO
Ian M. Cook, Pres.
Stephen C. Patrick, CFO
Stephen J. Fogarty, VP-Worldwide Shopper Mktg.
Daniel B. Marsili, VP-Global Human Resources
Constantina Christopoulou, VP-Global R&D
Tom Greene, CIO/VP
Derrick E. M. Samuel, Pres., Global Tech.
Andrew D. Hendry, General Counsel/Sr. VP/Sec.
Franck J. Moison, Pres., Global Bus. Dev. & Tech.
Jack J. Haber, VP-e-bus. & Global Advertising
Jan Guifarro, VP-Corp. Comm.
Bina H. Thompson, VP-Investor Rel.
Edward J. Filusch, Corp. Treas./VP
Nigel B. Burton, Pres., Global Oral Care
Hector I. Erezuma, VP-Taxation
Thomas M. Chappell, CEO-Tom's of Maine
Robert C. Wheeler, CEO-Hill's Pet Nutrition
Reuben Mark, Chmn.
Michael J. Tangney, COO-Colgate-Europe, Greater Asia & Africa
David R. Groener, VP-Global Supply Chain

Phone: 212-310-2000	Fax: 212-310-2475
Toll-Free: 800-468-6502	
Address: 300 Park Ave., New York, NY 10022 US	

GROWTH PLANS/SPECIAL FEATURES:

Colgate-Palmolive Co. (Colgate), founded in 1806, is a consumer products company whose products are marketed in over 200 countries and territories throughout the world. The company manages its business in two product segments: oral, personal and home care; and pet nutrition. Colgate oral care products include toothbrushes, toothpaste, tooth whitener, mouth rinses, dental floss and pharmaceutical products for dentists and other oral health professionals. The segment also markets bar and liquid hand soaps; shower gels, shampoos; conditioners; deodorants; antiperspirants; and shave products. The firm's Softsoap and Palmolive brands are two U.S. market leaders in liquid soaps. Other major products include household care products such as Ajax and Palmolive dishwashing liquids, Murphy's Oil Soap and Fabuloso laundry detergent. Additional oral, personal and home care brands include Mennen, Irish Spring, Tom's of Maine and Lady Speed Stick. Colgate also supplies specialty pet nutrition products for dogs and cats through subsidiary Hill's Pet Nutrition, with products marketed in over 90 countries. Pet foods are marketed primarily under the Science Diet and Prescription Diet trademarks. Science Diet is sold by authorized pet supply retailers, breeders and veterinarians for everyday nutritional needs, while Prescription Diet includes a range of therapeutic products sold by veterinarians to help nutritionally manage disease conditions in dogs and cats.

Colgate offers its employees tuition assistance, relocation assistance, back-up childcare centers, flexible spending accounts and medical, dental, disability and life insurance.

FINANCIALS: Sales and profits are in thousands of dollars—add 000 to get the full amount. 2008 Note: Financial information for 2008 was not available for all companies at press time.

2008 Sales: $15,329,900	2008 Profits: $1,957,200	**U.S. Stock Ticker: CL**
2007 Sales: $13,789,700	2007 Profits: $1,737,400	**Int'l Ticker:** Int'l Exchange:
2006 Sales: $12,237,700	2006 Profits: $1,353,400	Employees: 36,000
2005 Sales: $11,396,900	2005 Profits: $1,351,400	Fiscal Year Ends: 12/31
2004 Sales: $10,584,200	2004 Profits: $1,327,100	Parent Company:

SALARIES/BENEFITS:

Pension Plan: Y	ESOP Stock Plan:	Profit Sharing: Y	Top Exec. Salary: $1,075,000	Bonus: $3,162,500
Savings Plan: Y	Stock Purch. Plan:		Second Exec. Salary: $808,667	Bonus: $610,790

OTHER THOUGHTS:

Apparent Women Officers or Directors: 36
Hot Spot for Advancement for Women/Minorities: Y

LOCATIONS: ("Y" = Yes)

West:	Southwest:	Midwest:	Southeast:	Northeast:	International:
Y	Y	Y	Y	Y	Y

COMCAST CORP

Industry Group Code: 517110 **Ranks within this company's industry group:** Sales: 4 Profits: 3

Management:		Sales/Marketing:		Liberal Arts:		Information Systems:		Professionals:		Tech./Scientific:	
Management Trainees:	Y	Marketing Pros.:	Y	Gen. Writing/Editing:	Y	Info. Management:	Y	Finance/Acct.:	Y	Engineers, Electrical:	Y
Experienced Mngmt.:	Y	Retail Sales:		Technical Writing:	Y	Software Dev.:	Y	Law:	Y	Engineers, Other:	Y
International Business:	Y	Commercial/Industrial:	Y	Graphic Arts/Photog.:	Y	Hardware Dev.:		HR/Other:	Y	Health/Lab:	
MBA Grads:	Y	Sales Trainees:	Y	Music:		Consulting/Other:		Training:	Y	Scientists/Research:	
		Advertising Pros.:	Y	Broadcasting:	Y			Health Care:		Petroleum/Chemicals:	
				Other:	Y			Consulting:		Math/Other:	

TYPES OF BUSINESS:

Cable Television
VoIP Service
Cable Network Programming
High-Speed Internet Service
Video-on-Demand
Advertising Services
Interactive Program Schedules
Wireless Services

BRANDS/DIVISIONS/AFFILIATES:

Fandango Inc
Philadelphia Flyers
Philadelphia 76ers
Fandango Inc
E! Channel
Golf Channel (The)
Comcast Interactive Media
Clearwire Corporation

CONTACTS: *Note: Officers with more than one job title may be intentionally listed here more than once.*

Brian L. Roberts, CEO
Stephen B. Burke, COO
Michael J. Angelakis, CFO
Karen D. Buchholz, VP-Admin.
Arthur R. Block, General Counsel/Sr. VP/Corp. Sec.
Mark A. Coblitz, Sr. VP-Strategic Planning
D'Arcy F. Rudnay, Sr. VP-Corp. Comm.
Marlene S. Dooner, Sr. VP-Investor Rel.
Lawrence J. Salva, Chief Acct. Officer/Controller/Sr. VP
Stephen B. Burke, Pres., Comcast Cable Comm.
David L. Cohen, Exec. VP
Amy L. Banse, Sr. VP/Pres., Comcast Interactive Media
Robert S. Pick, Sr. VP-Corp. Dev.
Brian L. Roberts, Chmn.

Phone: 215-665-1700	**Fax:**
Toll-Free: 800-266-2278	
Address: 1 Comcast Ctr., Philadelphia, PA 19103 US	

GROWTH PLANS/SPECIAL FEATURES:

Comcast Corp. is one of the largest cable operators in the U.S. and offers a variety of entertainment, information and communications services to residential and commercial customers. The firm's cable systems serve roughly 24.2 million video subscribers, 14.9 million high-speed Internet subscribers and 6.5 million telephone subscribers and pass over 50.6 million homes in 39 states and Washington, D.C. The company operates in two segments, cable and programming. The cable segment, which generates approximately 95% of revenue, manages and operates the firm's cable systems, including video, high-speed Internet and phone services, as well as the regional sports networks. The programming segment consists primarily of consolidated national programming networks, including E!, The Golf Channel, VERSUS, G4 and Style. Comcast's other business interests include Comcast Spectacor and Comcast Interactive Media. Comcast Spectacor owns the Philadelphia Flyers, the Philadelphia 76ers and the Philadelphia Phantoms and two large, multipurpose arenas in Philadelphia, in addition to managing other facilities for sporting events, concerts and other events. Comcast Interactive Media develops and operates the company's Internet businesses focused on entertainment, information and communication, including comcast.net, Fancast, thePlatform, Fandango, Plaxo and DailyCandy. Recent acquisitions include cable systems serving Illinois and Indiana due to the dissolution of Insight Midwest, LP. In July 2008, the firm's cable division management structure was reorganized from five divisions to four. In December 2008, the company combined its WiMAX business with that of Sprint Nextel to create a 4G mobile Internet company. The joint venture will operate as Clearwire Corporation. In March 2009, the company and Sony Electronics, Inc. announced the opening of Sony Style Comcast Labs, a co-branded retail store in the Comcast Center.

The company offers its employees health and life insurance; disability benefits; an employee assistance program; adoption assistance; educational assistance; a 401(k) plan; and an employee stock purchase plan.

FINANCIALS: Sales and profits are in thousands of dollars—add 000 to get the full amount. 2008 Note: Financial information for 2008 was not available for all companies at press time.

2008 Sales: $34,256,000	2008 Profits: $2,547,000	**U.S. Stock Ticker:** CMCSA
2007 Sales: $30,895,000	2007 Profits: $2,587,000	**Int'l Ticker:** Int'l Exchange:
2006 Sales: $24,966,000	2006 Profits: $2,533,000	Employees: 100,000
2005 Sales: $23,556,000	2005 Profits: $928,000	Fiscal Year Ends: 12/31
2004 Sales: $20,307,000	2004 Profits: $970,000	Parent Company:

SALARIES/BENEFITS:

Pension Plan:	ESOP Stock Plan:	Profit Sharing:	Top Exec. Salary: $2,769,365	Bonus: $881,027
Savings Plan: Y	Stock Purch. Plan: Y		Second Exec. Salary: $2,218,117	Bonus: $5,922,372

OTHER THOUGHTS:

Apparent Women Officers or Directors: 6
Hot Spot for Advancement for Women/Minorities: Y

LOCATIONS: ("Y" = Yes)

West:	Southwest:	Midwest:	Southeast:	Northeast:	International:
Y	Y	Y	Y	Y	Y

Note: Financial information, benefits and other data can change quickly and may vary from those stated here.

COMMUNITY HEALTH SYSTEMS INC

www.chs.net

Industry Group Code: 622110 Ranks within this company's industry group: Sales: 4 Profits: 4

Management:		Sales/Marketing:		Liberal Arts:		Information Systems:		Professionals:		Tech./Scientific:	
Management Trainees:	Y	Marketing Pros.:	Y	Gen. Writing/Editing:	Y	Info. Management:	Y	Finance/Acct.:	Y	Engineers, Electrical:	
Experienced Mngmt.:	Y	Retail Sales:		Technical Writing:	Y	Software Dev.:	Y	Law:	Y	Engineers, Other:	
International Business:		Commercial/Industrial:		Graphic Arts/Photog.:	Y	Hardware Dev.:		HR/Other:	Y	Health/Lab:	Y
MBA Grads:	Y	Sales Trainees:		Music:		Consulting/Other:		Training:	Y	Scientists/Research:	
		Advertising Pros.:	Y	Broadcasting:				Health Care:	Y	Petroleum/Chemicals:	
				Other:	Y			Consulting:		Math/Other:	

TYPES OF BUSINESS:

Hospitals
Surgical & Emergency Services
Acute Care Services
Internal Medicine
Obstetrics
Emergency Room Services
Diagnostic Services
Ambulatory Surgery Centers

BRANDS/DIVISIONS/AFFILIATES:

Quorum Health Resources, LLC (QHR)
Siloam Springs Memorial Hospital

CONTACTS: *Note: Officers with more than one job title may be intentionally listed here more than once.*

Wayne Smith, CEO
Wayne Smith, Pres.
W. Larry Cash, CFO/Exec. VP
Debra S. Landers, Chief Mktg. Officer/VP
Robert A. Horrar, VP-Human Resources
Barbara R. Paul, Chief Medical Officer/Sr. VP
J. Gary Seay, CIO/Sr. VP
Robert A. Horrar, VP-Admin.
Rachel A. Seifert, General Counsel/Sr. VP/Sec.
Martin G. Schweinhart, Sr. VP-Oper.
Kenneth D. Hawkins, Sr. VP-Acquisitions & Dev.
Tomi Galin, VP-Corp. Comm.
Lizbeth R. Schuler, VP-Investor Rel.
T. Mark Buford, Chief Acct. Officer/VP/Corp. Controller
Carolyn Lipp, Sr. VP-Quality & Resource Mgmt.
Larry M. Carlton, VP-Revenue Mgmt.
James W. Doucette, Treas/VP
Robert O. Horrar, VP-Bus. Dev.
Wayne Smith, Chmn.
Tim G. Marlette, Chief Purchasing Officer/Sr. VP

Phone: 615-465-7000	Fax:
Toll-Free:	
Address: 4000 Meridian Blvd., Franklin, TN 37067 US	

GROWTH PLANS/SPECIAL FEATURES:

Community Health Systems, Inc. is one of the largest operators of hospitals in the U.S. The company owns, leases and operates 122 hospitals in 29 states. The firm generates revenue by providing a broad range of hospital healthcare services including general acute care services, emergency room services, surgery, critical care, internal medicine, obstetrics and diagnostic services. As part of providing these services, the company also owns, either outright or through partnerships with physicians, imaging centers, physician practices and ambulatory surgery centers. Through the company's subsidiary, Quorum Health Resources, LLC (QHR), it also provides management and consulting services to non-affiliated general acute care hospitals. The company's strategy for future growth is acquisition. It targets hospitals in growing, non-urban and select urban healthcare markets for acquisition because of their favorable demographic and economic trends and competitive conditions. In 2009, the company acquired the 74-bed acute care hospital in Arkansas, Siloam Springs Memorial Hospital; the assets of Wyoming Valley Health Care System in Pennsylvania; and a joint venture minority interest in Massillon Community Health System, LLC.

Employees are offered health, dental, vision and life insurance; long-term disability coverage; and a 401(k) plan.

FINANCIALS: Sales and profits are in thousands of dollars—add 000 to get the full amount. 2008 Note: Financial information for 2008 was not available for all companies at press time.

2008 Sales: $10,840,098	2008 Profits: $218,304	**U.S. Stock Ticker: CYH**
2007 Sales: $7,063,775	2007 Profits: $30,289	**Int'l Ticker:** Int'l Exchange:
2006 Sales: $4,180,136	2006 Profits: $168,263	Employees: 78,334
2005 Sales: $3,738,320	2005 Profits: $167,544	Fiscal Year Ends: 12/31
2004 Sales: $3,203,507	2004 Profits: $151,433	Parent Company:

SALARIES/BENEFITS:

Pension Plan:	ESOP Stock Plan:	Profit Sharing:	Top Exec. Salary: $1,080,000	Bonus: $2,071,440
Savings Plan: Y	Stock Purch. Plan:		Second Exec. Salary: $664,000	Bonus: $958,152

OTHER THOUGHTS:

Apparent Women Officers or Directors: 18
Hot Spot for Advancement for Women/Minorities: Y

LOCATIONS: ("Y" = Yes)

West:	Southwest:	Midwest:	Southeast:	Northeast:	International:
Y	Y	Y	Y	Y	

Note: Financial information, benefits and other data can change quickly and may vary from those stated here.

CONAGRA FOODS INC

www.conagrafoods.com

Industry Group Code: 311 Ranks within this company's industry group: Sales: 2 Profits: 2

Management:		Sales/Marketing:		Liberal Arts:		Information Systems:		Professionals:		Tech./Scientific:	
Management Trainees:	Y	Marketing Pros.:	Y	Gen. Writing/Editing:	Y	Info. Management:	Y	Finance/Acct.:	Y	Engineers, Electrical:	
Experienced Mngmt.:	Y	Retail Sales:		Technical Writing:	Y	Software Dev.:	Y	Law:	Y	Engineers, Other:	Y
International Business:	Y	Commercial/Industrial:	Y	Graphic Arts/Photog.:	Y	Hardware Dev.:		HR/Other:	Y	Health/Lab:	
MBA Grads:	Y	Sales Trainees:		Music:		Consulting/Other:		Training:	Y	Scientists/Research:	
		Advertising Pros.:	Y	Broadcasting:				Health Care:		Petroleum/Chemicals:	
				Other:				Consulting:		Math/Other:	

TYPES OF BUSINESS:

Food Products Manufacturing
Food Ingredients
Meat Processing
Foodservice Supply

BRANDS/DIVISIONS/AFFILIATES:

Marie Callender's
Healthy Choice
Hunt's
Chef Boyardee
Peter Pan
Slim Jim
Lamb Weston
Watts Brothers

CONTACTS: Note: Officers with more than one job title may be intentionally listed here more than once.

Gary Rodkin, CEO
Andre Hawaux, CFO/Exec. VP
Joan K. Chow, Chief Mktg. Officer/Exec. VP
Peter Perez, Exec. VP-Human Resources
Al Bolles, Exec. VP-Research, Quality & Innovation
Rob Sharpe, Jr., Exec. VP-Legal & External Affairs
Doug Knudsen, Pres., ConAgra Food Sales
Steven F. Goldstone, Chmn.
Greg Smith, Exec. VP-Supply Chain

Phone: 402-595-4000	Fax: 402-595-4707
Toll-Free:	
Address: 1 ConAgra Dr., Omaha, NE 68102 US	

GROWTH PLANS/SPECIAL FEATURES:

ConAgra Foods, Inc. is a packaged food company serving grocery retailers, as well as restaurants and other food service establishments. It operates in two segments: consumer foods and commercial products. The consumer foods segment includes branded, private label and customized food products that are sold in various retail and foodservice channels in the United States and internationally. Products include a variety of categories (meals, entrees, condiments, sides, snacks and desserts) across frozen, refrigerated and shelf-stable temperature classes. Brands include Chef Boyardee, Healthy Choice, Marie Callender's, Orville Redenbacher's, Slim Jim, Hebrew National, Kid Cuisine, Reddi-Wip, VanCamp, Libby's, LaChoy, The Max, David's, Angela Mia, Wesson, Swiss Miss, Egg Beaters, Blue Bonnet and Rosarita. The commercial products division, also known as the food and ingredients segment includes commercially branded foods and ingredients such as Lamb Weston, a provider of frozen potato products, ConAgra Mills, a producer of multi-use flours, and Gilroy Foods and Flavors, an industrial seasons supplier, offering vegetables, garlic, onions and capsicum ingredients. In February 2008, the company acquired Watts Brothers, a private vegetable processing company to strengthen its Lamb Weston brand. In May of the same year, ConAgra sold its Knotts Berry Farm food brand to the J.M. Smucker Company.

Employees are offered health, dental and vision insurance; life and disability insurance; and a 401(k) plan.

FINANCIALS: Sales and profits are in thousands of dollars—add 000 to get the full amount. 2008 Note: Financial information for 2008 was not available for all companies at press time.

2008 Sales: $11,563,500	2008 Profits: $930,600	U.S. Stock Ticker: CAG
2007 Sales: $10,489,500	2007 Profits: $764,600	Int'l Ticker: Int'l Exchange:
2006 Sales: $10,251,400	2006 Profits: $533,800	Employees: 25,600
2005 Sales: $11,383,800	2005 Profits: $641,500	Fiscal Year Ends: 5/31
2004 Sales: $10,926,300	2004 Profits: $811,300	Parent Company:

SALARIES/BENEFITS:

Pension Plan:	ESOP Stock Plan:	Profit Sharing:	Top Exec. Salary: $1,000,000	Bonus: $1,800,000
Savings Plan: Y	Stock Purch. Plan:		Second Exec. Salary: $662,019	Bonus: $725,000

OTHER THOUGHTS:

Apparent Women Officers or Directors: 2
Hot Spot for Advancement for Women/Minorities: Y

LOCATIONS: ("Y" = Yes)

West:	Southwest:	Midwest:	Southeast:	Northeast:	International:
Y	Y	Y	Y	Y	Y

Note: Financial information, benefits and other data can change quickly and may vary from those stated here.

CONOCOPHILLIPS COMPANY

www.conocophillips.com

Industry Group Code: 211111 Ranks within this company's industry group: Sales: 3   Profits: 12

Management:		Sales/Marketing:		Liberal Arts:		Information Systems:		Professionals:		Tech./Scientific:	
Management Trainees:	Y	Marketing Pros.:	Y	Gen. Writing/Editing:	Y	Info. Management:	Y	Finance/Acct.:	Y	Engineers, Electrical:	Y
Experienced Mngmt.:	Y	Retail Sales:		Technical Writing:	Y	Software Dev.:	Y	Law:	Y	Engineers, Other:	Y
International Business:	Y	Commercial/Industrial:	Y	Graphic Arts/Photog.:	Y	Hardware Dev.:		HR/Other:	Y	Health/Lab:	
MBA Grads:	Y	Sales Trainees:	Y	Music:		Consulting/Other:		Training:	Y	Scientists/Research:	Y
		Advertising Pros.:	Y	Broadcasting:				Health Care:		Petroleum/Chemicals:	Y
				Other:				Consulting:		Math/Other:	Y

TYPES OF BUSINESS:

Oil & Gas Exploration & Production
Natural Gas Distribution
Refining
Pipelines
Oil Sands Operations
Chemical Production
Technology Investment
Gasoline Retail

BRANDS/DIVISIONS/AFFILIATES:

LUKOIL (OAO)
Conoco
Phillips 66
DCP Midstream LLC
Chevron Phillips Chemical Company LLC
Alaska Gas Pipe
Origin Energy
JET

CONTACTS: *Note: Officers with more than one job title may be intentionally listed here more than once.*

James J. Mulva, CEO
John A. Carrig, COO
John A. Carrig, Pres.
Sigmund L. Cornelius, CFO
W.C.W Chiang, Sr. VP-Mktg.
Carin S. Knickel, VP-Human Resources
Gene L. Batchelder, CIO/Sr. VP-Svcs.
Stephen R. Brand, Sr. VP-Tech.
Luc J. Messier, Sr. VP-Project Dev.
Janet Langford Kelly, General Counsel/Corp. Sec./Sr. VP-Legal
Jeff Sheets, Sr. VP-Planning & Strategy
Red Cavaney, Sr. VP-Public Affairs
Sigmund L. Cornelius, Sr. VP-Finance
Robert A. Ridge, VP-Health, Safety & Environment
Kevin Meyers, Sr. VP-Exploration & Prod., Americas
W.C.W Chiang, Sr. VP-Refining & Transportation
Gregory Goff, Sr. VP-Commercial
James J. Mulva, Chmn.
Ryan M. Lance, Sr. VP-Exploration & Prod., Int'l

Phone: 281-293-1000	Fax:
Toll-Free:	
Address: 600 N. Dairy Ashford Rd., Houston, TX 77079-1175 US	

GROWTH PLANS/SPECIAL FEATURES:

ConocoPhillips Company is an integrated global energy company. Its six business segments are exploration and production, midstream, refining and marketing, LUKOIL Investment, chemicals and emerging businesses. The exploration and production segment explores for, produces, transports and markets crude oil, natural gas and natural gas liquids worldwide. It also mines oil sands to extract bitumen, which it upgrades into synthetic crude oil. The midstream division gathers, processes and markets natural gas produced by the company and others, and also fractionates and markets natural gas liquids. This segment includes the firm's 50% equity investment in DCP Midstream, LLC. The refining and marketing segment purchases, refines, markets and transports crude oil and petroleum products, mainly in the U.S., Europe and Asia. The LUKOIL Investment segment consists of ConocoPhillips' 20% equity interest in OAO LUKOIL, an integrated oil and gas company headquartered in Russia. The chemicals group, including the company's 50% equity investment in Chevron Phillips Chemical Company LLC, manufactures and markets petrochemicals and plastics worldwide. The emerging businesses segment oversees businesses such as technologies related to hydrocarbon recovery (including heavy oil), refining, alternative energy, biofuels and the environment. In 2008, the company acquired 50% ownership interest in Transcanada's Keystone Oil Pipeline, a project capable of producing 590,000 barrels of crude oil per day, scheduled to begin deliveries in 2009. In April 2008, the company combined resources with BP to begin the Alaska Gas Pipe, a pipeline with the capacity to move 4 billion cubic feet of natural gas per day to markets in Canada and the U.S. In September 2008, ConocoPhillips and Origin Energy announced plans to create a long-term Australasian natural gas business focused on coal bed methane production and liquefied natural gas.

ConocoPhillips' employees receive benefits including spending accounts, insurance, a retirement plan, paid time off, scholarships and tuition reimbursement.

FINANCIALS: Sales and profits are in thousands of dollars—add 000 to get the full amount. 2008 Note: Financial information for 2008 was not available for all companies at press time.

2008 Sales: $240,842,000	2008 Profits: $-16,998,000	**U.S. Stock Ticker: COP**
2007 Sales: $187,437,000	2007 Profits: $11,891,000	**Int'l Ticker:** Int'l Exchange:
2006 Sales: $183,650,000	2006 Profits: $15,550,000	Employees: 33,800
2005 Sales: $179,442,000	2005 Profits: $13,529,000	Fiscal Year Ends: 12/31
2004 Sales: $135,076,000	2004 Profits: $8,129,000	Parent Company:

SALARIES/BENEFITS:

Pension Plan: Y	ESOP Stock Plan: Y	Profit Sharing:	Top Exec. Salary: $1,500,000	Bonus: $1,417,500
Savings Plan: Y	Stock Purch. Plan:		Second Exec. Salary: $967,333	Bonus: $1,054,944

OTHER THOUGHTS:

Apparent Women Officers or Directors: 5
Hot Spot for Advancement for Women/Minorities: Y

LOCATIONS: ("Y" = Yes)

West:	Southwest:	Midwest:	Southeast:	Northeast:	International:
Y	Y	Y	Y	Y	Y

Note: Financial information, benefits and other data can change quickly and may vary from those stated here.

CONSOL ENERGY INC

www.consolenergy.com

Industry Group Code: 21211 Ranks within this company's industry group: Sales: 2 Profits: 2

Management:		Sales/Marketing:		Liberal Arts:		Information Systems:		Professionals:		Tech./Scientific:	
Management Trainees:	Y	Marketing Pros.:	Y	Gen. Writing/Editing:		Info. Management:	Y	Finance/Acct.:	Y	Engineers, Electrical:	
Experienced Mngmt.:	Y	Retail Sales:		Technical Writing:	Y	Software Dev.:		Law:	Y	Engineers, Other:	Y
International Business:	Y	Commercial/Industrial:	Y	Graphic Arts/Photog.:		Hardware Dev.:		HR/Other:	Y	Health/Lab:	
MBA Grads:	Y	Sales Trainees:		Music:		Consulting/Other:		Training:	Y	Scientists/Research:	
		Advertising Pros.:		Broadcasting:				Health Care:		Petroleum/Chemicals:	Y
				Other:				Consulting:		Math/Other:	

TYPES OF BUSINESS:

Coal Mining
Energy Services
Gas Exploration & Production

BRANDS/DIVISIONS/AFFILIATES:

CNX Gas Corporation
CNX Land Resources Inc

CONTACTS: *Note: Officers with more than one job title may be intentionally listed here more than once.*

J. Brett Harvey, CEO
Nicholas J. Deluliis, COO/Exec. VP
J. Brett Harvey, Pres.
William J. Lyons, CFO/Exec. VP
Robert Pusateri, Exec. VP-Energy Sales
Michael D. McLean, VP-Human Resources
P. Jerome Richey, Chief Legal Officer/Sec./Exec. VP-Corp. Affairs
Thomas F. Hoffman, Sr. VP-External Affairs
Joseph Cerenzia, Dir.-Public Rel.
Nicholas J. Deluliis, CEO/Chmn.-CNX Gas Corp.
John Whitmire, Chmn.

Phone: 724-485-4000	Fax: 724-485-4833
Toll-Free:	

Address: CNX Center, 1000 Consol Energy Dr., Canonsburg, PA 15317-6506 US

GROWTH PLANS/SPECIAL FEATURES:

CONSOL Energy, Inc. is a multi-fuel energy producer and energy services provider, primarily serving the U.S. electric power generation industry. It produces high-BTU bituminous coal from 16 mining complexes in the U.S., as well as pipeline-quality coalbed methane gas from coal properties in Pennsylvania, Virginia and West Virginia, and conventional gas from Tennessee and Virginia. The company's mining complexes contain an approximate reserve base of 4.5 billion tons of coal. CONSOL is one of the largest producers of bituminous coal in the U.S., as well as one of the largest coal producers from underground mines, one of the largest coal producers east of the Mississippi River and one of the largest coal exporters. The company operates 26 towboats and a fleet of more than 700 barges. It employs transportation specialists who negotiate freight and equipment agreements with railroads, barge lines, terminal operators, ocean vessel brokers and trucking companies. CONSOL's gas operations involve producing coalbed methane and natural gas. The company owns over 2,600 wells and has estimated proved reserves of approximately 1.4 trillion cubic feet of oil equivalent. Through its subsidiary, CNX Land Resources, Inc., the firm has timber and farming operations, as well as commercial development ventures. CNX Gas Corp., a wholly-owned subsidiary, produces pipeline-quality coalbed methane gas from coal properties in the Northern and Central Appalachian basin. In addition, the firm provides industrial supply services, terminal services, river and dock services and coal waste disposal services. In December 2008, the company's Consol Energy Center became the home for the Pittsburgh Penguins. The firm also acquired the naming rights to the arena for 21 years.

FINANCIALS: Sales and profits are in thousands of dollars—add 000 to get the full amount. 2008 Note: Financial information for 2008 was not available for all companies at press time.

2008 Sales: $4,652,445	2008 Profits: $442,470	U.S. Stock Ticker: CNX
2007 Sales: $3,762,197	2007 Profits: $267,782	Int'l Ticker: Int'l Exchange:
2006 Sales: $3,715,171	2006 Profits: $408,882	Employees: 8,176
2005 Sales: $3,810,449	2005 Profits: $580,861	Fiscal Year Ends: 12/31
2004 Sales: $2,776,749	2004 Profits: $198,582	Parent Company:

SALARIES/BENEFITS:

Pension Plan: Y	ESOP Stock Plan:	Profit Sharing:	Top Exec. Salary: $1,000,000	Bonus: $1,832,400
Savings Plan: Y	Stock Purch. Plan:		Second Exec. Salary: $598,806	Bonus: $

OTHER THOUGHTS:

Apparent Women Officers or Directors: 1
Hot Spot for Advancement for Women/Minorities: Y

LOCATIONS: ("Y" = Yes)

West:	Southwest:	Midwest:	Southeast:	Northeast:	International:
Y				Y	Y

Note: Financial information, benefits and other data can change quickly and may vary from those stated here.

CONSOLIDATED EDISON INC

www.conedison.com

Industry Group Code: 221 Ranks within this company's industry group: Sales: 4   Profits: 5

Management:		Sales/Marketing:		Liberal Arts:		Information Systems:		Professionals:		Tech./Scientific:	
Management Trainees:	Y	Marketing Pros.:	Y	Gen. Writing/Editing:	Y	Info. Management:	Y	Finance/Acct.:	Y	Engineers, Electrical:	Y
Experienced Mngmt.:	Y	Retail Sales:		Technical Writing:	Y	Software Dev.:	Y	Law:	Y	Engineers, Other:	Y
International Business:	Y	Commercial/Industrial:	Y	Graphic Arts/Photog.:	Y	Hardware Dev.:		HR/Other:	Y	Health/Lab:	
MBA Grads:	Y	Sales Trainees:		Music:		Consulting/Other:		Training:	Y	Scientists/Research:	
		Advertising Pros.:	Y	Broadcasting:				Health Care:		Petroleum/Chemicals:	Y
				Other:				Consulting:		Math/Other:	

TYPES OF BUSINESS:

Utilities-Electricity & Natural Gas
Steam Utility
Electric Generation
Energy Consulting
Energy Marketing

BRANDS/DIVISIONS/AFFILIATES:

Orange and Rockland Utilities, Inc.
Consolidated Edison Company of New York, Inc.
Consolidated Edison Development
Consolidated Edison Solutions
Consolidated Edison Energy
Smart Grid Pilot Program

CONTACTS: *Note: Officers with more than one job title may be intentionally listed here more than once.*

Kevin Burke, CEO
Kevin Burke, Pres.
Robert N. Hoglund, CFO/Sr. VP
Charles E. McTiernan, Jr., General Counsel
Gurudatta Nadkarni, VP-Strategic Planning
Jan C. Childress, Dir.-Investor Rel.
Robert Muccilo, Chief Acct. Officer/Controller/VP
James P. O'Brien, Treas./VP
Carole Sobin, Sec.
Louis L. Rana, COO/Pres., Consolidated Energy Co. of NY, Inc.
William G. Longhi, CEO/Pres., Orange & Rockland Utilities, Inc.
Kevin Burke, Chmn.

Phone: 212-460-4600	Fax: 212-982-7816
Toll-Free:	
Address: 4 Irving Pl., New York, NY 10003 US	

GROWTH PLANS/SPECIAL FEATURES:

Consolidated Edison, Inc. (Con Edison) principally operates through the regulated electric, gas and steam utility segments of its two main subsidiaries, Consolidated Edison Company of New York, Inc. and Orange and Rockland Utilities, Inc. (O&R). Con Edison of New York provides electric services to New York City and most of Westchester County, a service area covering approximately 660 square miles with a population of more than 9 million. The company provides gas services in Manhattan, the Bronx and parts of Queens and Westchester, and steam services in parts of Manhattan. The firm purchases all its electricity and gas from other suppliers. O&R and its subsidiaries provide electricity to southeastern New York, northern New Jersey and eastern Pennsylvania, an approximately 1,350-square-mile service area. The firm's non-utilities subsidiaries include Consolidated Edison Energy, Inc.; Consolidated Edison Development; and Consolidated Edison Solutions. Consolidated Edison Energy supplies wholesale energy and specialized energy supply services to customers in the electric and gas markets in the Northeast and Mid-Atlantic regions. Consolidated Edison Development owns, leases or operates energy and infrastructure projects, principally in the U.S., and sells capacity and energy in wholesale markets administered by independent system operators in New England and New York and to other utilities through Consolidated Edison Energy. The segment currently owns the equivalent of approximately 1,706 megawatts (MW) of capacity. Consolidated Edison Solutions is a leading non-residential retail energy and services provider, primarily selling electricity to industrial and large commercial customer and also to residential customers in approximately 11 states, serving nearly 48,300 customers. In May 2009, the firm announced plans to invest $1.5 billion, over a five year period, to upgrade its electric delivery system. In August 2009, the firm launched its Smart Grid Pilot Program, conducted in Queens, New York, which will test how various technologies support electronic grid modernization efforts.

FINANCIALS: Sales and profits are in thousands of dollars—add 000 to get the full amount. 2008 Note: Financial information for 2008 was not available for all companies at press time.

2008 Sales: $13,583,000	2008 Profits: $1,196,000	**U.S. Stock Ticker: ED**
2007 Sales: $13,120,000	2007 Profits: $929,000	**Int'l Ticker:** Int'l Exchange:
2006 Sales: $11,962,000	2006 Profits: $737,000	Employees: 14,299
2005 Sales: $11,641,000	2005 Profits: $719,000	Fiscal Year Ends: 12/31
2004 Sales: $9,730,000	2004 Profits: $537,000	Parent Company:

SALARIES/BENEFITS:

Pension Plan:	ESOP Stock Plan:	Profit Sharing:	Top Exec. Salary: $1,102,500	Bonus: $1,066,100
Savings Plan:	Stock Purch. Plan:		Second Exec. Salary: $722,500	Bonus: $595,300

OTHER THOUGHTS:

Apparent Women Officers or Directors: 4
Hot Spot for Advancement for Women/Minorities: Y

LOCATIONS: ("Y" = Yes)

West:	Southwest:	Midwest:	Southeast:	Northeast:	International:
	Y	Y		Y	

Note: Financial information, benefits and other data can change quickly and may vary from those stated here.

CONTAINER STORE (THE)

www.containerstore.com

Industry Group Code: 442299 **Ranks within this company's industry group:** Sales: 2 Profits:

Management:		Sales/Marketing:		Liberal Arts:		Information Systems:		Professionals:		Tech./Scientific:	
Management Trainees:	Y	Marketing Pros.:	Y	Gen. Writing/Editing:	Y	Info. Management:	Y	Finance/Acct.:	Y	Engineers, Electrical:	
Experienced Mngmt.:	Y	Retail Sales:	Y	Technical Writing:		Software Dev.:	Y	Law:	Y	Engineers, Other:	
International Business:		Commercial/Industrial:	Y	Graphic Arts/Photog.:	Y	Hardware Dev.:		HR/Other:	Y	Health/Lab:	
MBA Grads:	Y	Sales Trainees:	Y	Music:		Consulting/Other:		Training:	Y	Scientists/Research:	
		Advertising Pros.:	Y	Broadcasting:				Health Care:		Petroleum/Chemicals:	
				Other:	Y			Consulting:		Math/Other:	

TYPES OF BUSINESS:

Home Organization Products, Retail
Luggage
Packing Materials
Specialty Boxes
Online Sales

BRANDS/DIVISIONS/AFFILIATES:

Elfa
Leonard Green & Partners

CONTACTS: Note: Officers with more than one job title may be intentionally listed here more than once.

Kip Tindell, CEO
Melissa Reiff, Pres.
Garrett Boone, Co-Chmn.
Kip Tindell, Chmn.

Phone: 972-538-6000	**Fax:** 972-538-7623
Toll-Free: 800-733-3532	
Address: 500 Freeport Pkwy., Coppell, TX 75019 US	

GROWTH PLANS/SPECIAL FEATURES:

The Container Store is a national retailer known for its unique organizational and storage products and its commitment to customer service. The company sells drawer and cabinet organizers, luggage, tool racks, packing materials, specialty and shipping boxes and locker organizers, among many other household objects designed to manage space efficiently. Store interiors have an open layout, which is divided into sections with brightly colored banners such as Closet, Kitchen, Closet and Laundry. The firm's stores average 25,000 square feet and carry more than 10,000 items, with the company's Elfa brand of wire shelving making up nearly one-fifth of sales. The majority of the Container Store's 40 stores are located in large cities, including locations in Atlanta, Chicago, Houston, Miami, New York and San Diego. The Container Store processes and ships its entire product line from its 725,000-square-foot distribution center near Dallas, Texas. The distribution center uses state-of-the-art warehouse and inventory systems to increase profitability and response time. The company's web site allows customers to view and order store products, plan organizational and storage projects and receive free customized assistance from in-store space planning experts. In recent years, the company was acquired by Leonard Green & Partners, a private investment firm.

The company offers its employees a benefits package that includes a 40% discount on merchandise, flexible spending plans, a 401(k) savings plan and special schedules for employees with children. Each full-time employee receives about 240 hours of training during his or her first year and almost one-half of new hires come from employee recommendations.

FINANCIALS: Sales and profits are in thousands of dollars—add 000 to get the full amount. 2008 Note: Financial information for 2008 was not available for all companies at press time.

2008 Sales: $600,000	2008 Profits: $	**U.S. Stock Ticker:** Private
2007 Sales: $500,000	2007 Profits: $	**Int'l Ticker:** Int'l Exchange:
2006 Sales: $491,000	2006 Profits: $	Employees: 3,994
2005 Sales: $425,000	2005 Profits: $	Fiscal Year Ends: 3/31
2004 Sales: $350,000	2004 Profits: $	Parent Company: LEONARD GREEN & PARTNERS

SALARIES/BENEFITS:

Pension Plan:	ESOP Stock Plan:	Profit Sharing:	Top Exec. Salary: $	Bonus: $
Savings Plan: Y	Stock Purch. Plan:		Second Exec. Salary: $	Bonus: $

OTHER THOUGHTS:

Apparent Women Officers or Directors: 1
Hot Spot for Advancement for Women/Minorities:

LOCATIONS: ("Y" = Yes)

West:	Southwest:	Midwest:	Southeast:	Northeast:	International:
Y	Y	Y	Y	Y	

CONVERGYS CORPORATION

www.convergys.com

Industry Group Code: 522320 Ranks within this company's industry group: Sales: 2 Profits: 4

Management:		Sales/Marketing:		Liberal Arts:		Information Systems:		Professionals:		Tech./Scientific:	
Management Trainees:	Y	Marketing Pros.:	Y	Gen. Writing/Editing:	Y	Info. Management:	Y	Finance/Acct.:	Y	Engineers, Electrical:	
Experienced Mngmt.:	Y	Retail Sales:		Technical Writing:		Software Dev.:	Y	Law:	Y	Engineers, Other:	
International Business:	Y	Commercial/Industrial:	Y	Graphic Arts/Photog.:	Y	Hardware Dev.:		HR/Other:	Y	Health/Lab:	
MBA Grads:	Y	Sales Trainees:		Music:		Consulting/Other:		Training:	Y	Scientists/Research:	
		Advertising Pros.:	Y	Broadcasting:				Health Care:		Petroleum/Chemicals:	
				Other:				Consulting:		Math/Other:	

TYPES OF BUSINESS:

Outsourced Customer Care Services
Professional & Consulting Services
Information Management Solutions & Software
Human Resource Business Process Outsourcing Solutions

BRANDS/DIVISIONS/AFFILIATES:

Intervoice, Inc.
Ceon Corporation

CONTACTS: *Note: Officers with more than one job title may be intentionally listed here more than once.*

David F. Dougherty, CEO
David F. Dougherty, Pres.
Earl C. Shanks, CFO
Clark D. Handy, Sr. VP-Human Resources
Karen R. Bowman, General Counsel/Corp. Sec.

Phone: 513-723-7000	Fax:
Toll-Free: 888-284-9900	
Address: 201 E. 4th St., Cincinnati, OH 45202 US	

GROWTH PLANS/SPECIAL FEATURES:

Convergys Corp. is a global provider of customer care, billing and human resources services. It operates through three segments: customer care, information management and Human Resource (HR) resources. The customer care segment provides outsourced agent-assisted and self-service customer care solutions, as well as consulting and technology solutions to the in-house customer care market. Phone and web-based agent-assisted service channels provide customers with assistance across the entire customer lifecycle. The company delivers these services using a variety of tools, including computer telephony integration, interactive voice response, advanced speech recognition, knowledge-based management and the Internet through agent-assisted and self-service channel. The information management segment serves clients principally by providing business and operating support system solutions for the global communications industry that address all segments of the communications industry. The division provides its software products through licensed, outsourced or build-operate-transfer (BOT) delivery modes, allowing customers to perform billing internally or for Convergys to provide billing services from one of its data centers. The HR management segment provides human resource business process outsourcing solutions, talent management and learning solutions. Services include benefits administration, compensation, human resource administration, learning, payroll administration, performance management, recruiting and sourcing services. Convergys primarily services companies in the automotive, communications, financial services, government, healthcare, manufacturing, retail, technology and transportation sectors. In May 2008, the company announced plans to expand its Philippine operations with the addition of five integrated contact centers throughout the country. In September 2008, Convergys acquired Intervoice, Inc. for $335 million. In October 2008, the company acquired Ceon Corporation, a product lifecycle management firm.

The company offers its employees medical, dental and vision insurance; life and AD&D insurance; disability insurance; tuition reimbursement; a 401(k) plan; a pension plan; and an employee stock purchase plan.

FINANCIALS: Sales and profits are in thousands of dollars—add 000 to get the full amount. 2008 Note: Financial information for 2008 was not available for all companies at press time.

2008 Sales: $2,785,800	2008 Profits: $-92,900	U.S. Stock Ticker: CVG
2007 Sales: $2,844,300	2007 Profits: $169,500	Int'l Ticker: Int'l Exchange:
2006 Sales: $2,789,800	2006 Profits: $166,200	Employees: 75,000
2005 Sales: $2,582,100	2005 Profits: $122,600	Fiscal Year Ends: 12/31
2004 Sales: $2,487,700	2004 Profits: $111,500	Parent Company:

SALARIES/BENEFITS:

Pension Plan: Y	ESOP Stock Plan:	Profit Sharing:	Top Exec. Salary: $777,780	Bonus: $
Savings Plan: Y	Stock Purch. Plan: Y		Second Exec. Salary: $497,780	Bonus: $

OTHER THOUGHTS:

Apparent Women Officers or Directors: 1
Hot Spot for Advancement for Women/Minorities:

LOCATIONS: ("Y" = Yes)

West:	Southwest:	Midwest:	Southeast:	Northeast:	International:
Y	Y	Y	Y	Y	Y

Note: Financial information, benefits and other data can change quickly and may vary from those stated here.

COOPER COMPANIES INC

www.coopercos.com

Industry Group Code: 33911 Ranks within this company's industry group: Sales: 15 Profits: 14

Management:		Sales/Marketing:		Liberal Arts:		Information Systems:		Professionals:		Tech./Scientific:	
Management Trainees:	Y	Marketing Pros.:	Y	Gen. Writing/Editing:		Info. Management:	Y	Finance/Acct.:	Y	Engineers, Electrical:	
Experienced Mngmt.:	Y	Retail Sales:		Technical Writing:	Y	Software Dev.:	Y	Law:	Y	Engineers, Other:	Y
International Business:	Y	Commercial/Industrial:	Y	Graphic Arts/Photog.:	Y	Hardware Dev.:		HR/Other:	Y	Health/Lab:	Y
MBA Grads:	Y	Sales Trainees:		Music:		Consulting/Other:		Training:	Y	Scientists/Research:	
		Advertising Pros.:	Y	Broadcasting:				Health Care:	Y	Petroleum/Chemicals:	
				Other:				Consulting:		Math/Other:	

TYPES OF BUSINESS:

Medical Devices
Contact Lenses
Gynecological Instruments
Diagnostic Products

BRANDS/DIVISIONS/AFFILIATES:

CooperVision, Inc.
CooperSurgical, Inc.
Biofinity
Avaira
Proclear
Phosphorylcholine (PC) Technology

CONTACTS: Note: Officers with more than one job title may be intentionally listed here more than once.

Robert S. Weiss, CEO
Robert S. Weiss, Pres.
Eugene J. Midlock, CFO/Sr. VP
Carol R. Kaufman, Chief Admin. Officer/Sr. VP-Legal Affairs/Sec.
Daniel G. McBride, General Counsel/VP
Jeffrey A. McLean, Exec. VP-Commercial Strategies, CooperVision, Inc.
Albert G. White, III, VP-Investor Rel./Treas.
Rodney E. Folden, Controller
Nicholas J. Pichotta, CEO-CooperSurgical, Inc.
Paul L. Remmell, COO/Pres., CooperSurigical, Inc.
John A. Weber, Pres., CooperVision
Dennis J. Murphy, Pres., Americas, CooperVision, Inc.
A. Thomas Bender, Chmn.
Andrew Sedgwick, Pres., EMEA, CooperVision, Inc.

Phone: 925-460-3600	**Fax:** 925-460-3649

Toll-Free: 800-538-7850

Address: 6140 Stoneridge Mall Rd., Ste. 590, Pleasanton, CA 94588 US

GROWTH PLANS/SPECIAL FEATURES:

Cooper Companies, Inc. develops, manufactures and markets healthcare products, primarily medical devices. The company operates through two business units: CooperVision, Inc. and CooperSurgical, Inc. CooperVision develops, manufactures and markets a broad range of contact lenses for the worldwide vision correction market. It uses three different manufacturing processes to produce its lenses: Lathing, cast molding and FIPS, a combination of lathing and molding. The subsidiary's core product lines include disposable spherical and specialty contact lenses. It is a leading manufacturer of toric lenses, which correct astigmatism; multifocal lenses for presbyopia, the blurring of vision due to advancing age; and spherical lenses, including hydrogel lenses, which correct the most common visual defects. Silicone hydrogel lenses are sold under the Biofinity and Avaira brands. Cooper's Proclear line of spherical, toric and multifocal lenses are manufactured with omafilcon A, a material that incorporates its proprietary Phosphorylcholine (PC) Technology to enhance tissue-device compatibility. CooperVision's products are primarily manufactured at its domestic facilities in Norfolk, Virginia and Scottsville, New York, as well as its international facilities in the U.K. and Puerto Rico. It distributes its products out of Rochester, New York; the U.K.; Liege, Belgium; and various smaller international distribution facilities. CooperSurgical develops, manufactures and markets medical devices, diagnostic products and surgical instruments and accessories used primarily by gynecologists and obstetricians. The subsidiary primarily manufactures and distributes its products at its facilities in Trumbull, Connecticut and Stafford, Texas. During 2008, CooperVision represented 87% and CooperSurgical represented 13% of the company's total expenditures for research and development.

FINANCIALS: Sales and profits are in thousands of dollars—add 000 to get the full amount. 2008 Note: Financial information for 2008 was not available for all companies at press time.

2008 Sales: $1,063,176	2008 Profits: $65,476	**U.S. Stock Ticker:** COO
2007 Sales: $950,641	2007 Profits: $-11,192	**Int'l Ticker:** Int'l Exchange:
2006 Sales: $858,960	2006 Profits: $66,234	Employees: 7,400
2005 Sales: $806,617	2005 Profits: $91,722	Fiscal Year Ends: 10/31
2004 Sales: $490,176	2004 Profits: $92,825	Parent Company:

SALARIES/BENEFITS:

Pension Plan:	ESOP Stock Plan:	Profit Sharing:	Top Exec. Salary: $600,000	Bonus: $222,000
Savings Plan:	Stock Purch. Plan:		Second Exec. Salary: $371,696	Bonus: $78,932

OTHER THOUGHTS:

Apparent Women Officers or Directors: 2
Hot Spot for Advancement for Women/Minorities: Y

LOCATIONS: ("Y" = Yes)

West:	Southwest:	Midwest:	Southeast:	Northeast:	International:
Y	Y			Y	Y

COSTCO WHOLESALE CORP

www.costco.com

Industry Group Code: 452112 Ranks within this company's industry group: Sales: 2   Profits: 4

Management:		Sales/Marketing:		Liberal Arts:		Information Systems:		Professionals:		Tech./Scientific:	
Management Trainees:	Y	Marketing Pros.:	Y	Gen. Writing/Editing:	Y	Info. Management:	Y	Finance/Acct.:	Y	Engineers, Electrical:	
Experienced Mngmt.:	Y	Retail Sales:	Y	Technical Writing:		Software Dev.:	Y	Law:	Y	Engineers, Other:	
International Business:	Y	Commercial/Industrial:		Graphic Arts/Photog.:	Y	Hardware Dev.:		HR/Other:	Y	Health/Lab:	
MBA Grads:	Y	Sales Trainees:	Y	Music:		Consulting/Other:		Training:	Y	Scientists/Research:	
		Advertising Pros.:	Y	Broadcasting:				Health Care:		Petroleum/Chemicals:	
				Other:	Y			Consulting:		Math/Other:	

TYPES OF BUSINESS:

Warehouse Clubs, Retail
Food
Health & Beauty Products
Electronics
Furniture
Apparel
Automotive Supplies
Gasoline Sales

BRANDS/DIVISIONS/AFFILIATES:

Costco Wholesale Industries
Costco Mexico

CONTACTS: *Note: Officers with more than one job title may be intentionally listed here more than once.*

James D. Sinegal, CEO
W. Craig Jelinek, COO
James D. Sinegal, Pres.
Richard A. Galanti, CFO/Exec. VP
John Matthews, Sr. VP-Human Resources
Don Burdick, Sr. VP-Info. Systems
W. Craig Jelinek, Exec. VP-Merch.
Joel Benoliel, Sr. VP-Admin.
Joel Benoliel, Chief Legal Officer
Richard D. DiCerchio, COO-Global Oper.
Richard C. Chavez, Sr. VP-Bus. Dev.
Ginnie M. Roeglin, Sr. VP-e-Commerce & Publishing
David S. Petterson, Corp. Controller/Sr. VP
John Thelan, Sr. VP-Depot Oper.
Charles V. Burnett, Sr. VP-Pharmacy
Dennis Knapp, Sr. VP-Non-Foods
Ali Moayeri, Sr. VP-Construction
Jeffrey H. Brotman, Chmn.
James P. Murphy, Sr. VP-Int'l Oper.

Phone: 425-313-8100	**Fax:** 425-313-8103
Toll-Free: 800-774-2678	
Address: 999 Lake Dr., Issaquah, WA 98027 US	

GROWTH PLANS/SPECIAL FEATURES:

Costco Wholesale Corp. operates membership warehouses based on the concept that offering members very low prices on a limited selection of branded and private-label products will produce high sales volumes and rapid inventory turnover. This rapid turnover, combined with volume purchasing, efficient distribution and reduced handling of merchandise in self-service warehouse facilities, allows the firm to operate at significantly lower margins than traditional discount retailers. Costco buys the majority of its merchandise directly from manufacturers for shipment to warehouses or to consolidation points, minimizing freight and handling costs. Products include health and beauty aids, cleaning supplies, foods, alcohol, appliances, electronics, tools, office supplies, furniture, automotive supplies, apparel, cameras, house wares and books. Stores contain other features, including pharmacies, print shops, photo labs and gas stations. Memberships are designed to build customer loyalty and cost between $40-100 per year. Costco has approximately 5.6 million business members and approximately 20.2 million Gold Star (individual) members. The firm operates 554 membership warehouses in the U.S., U.K., Canada, Korea, Mexico, Taiwan and Japan, including 31 controlled by the company's joint venture Costco Mexico. The stores average approximately 140,000 square feet and stock around 4,000 distinct products, including upscale items such as jewelry and wines. Costco Wholesale Industries, a division of the company, operates manufacturing businesses, including special food packaging, optical laboratories, meat processing and jewelry distribution. In April 2009, the company ended its experimental two-store Costco Home format, which was designed to exclusively sell home furnishes.

Costco offers its employees health care, dental, vision and prescription coverage; a 401(k) plan; employee assistance plans; care networks; short- and long-term disability; life insurance; an employee stock purchase plan; health care reimbursement; and long-term care insurance.

FINANCIALS: Sales and profits are in thousands of dollars—add 000 to get the full amount. 2008 Note: Financial information for 2008 was not available for all companies at press time.

2008 Sales: $70,977,484	2008 Profits: $1,282,725	**U.S. Stock Ticker: COST**
2007 Sales: $63,087,601	2007 Profits: $1,082,772	**Int'l Ticker:** Int'l Exchange:
2006 Sales: $58,963,180	2006 Profits: $1,103,215	Employees: 137,000
2005 Sales: $51,789,080	2005 Profits: $1,063,092	Fiscal Year Ends: 8/31
2004 Sales: $47,148,627	2004 Profits: $882,393	Parent Company:

SALARIES/BENEFITS:

Pension Plan:	ESOP Stock Plan:	Profit Sharing:	Top Exec. Salary: $575,000	Bonus: $42,063
Savings Plan: Y	Stock Purch. Plan: Y		Second Exec. Salary: $570,000	Bonus: $42,063

OTHER THOUGHTS:

Apparent Women Officers or Directors: 3
Hot Spot for Advancement for Women/Minorities: Y

LOCATIONS: ("Y" = Yes)

West:	Southwest:	Midwest:	Southeast:	Northeast:	International:
Y	Y	Y	Y	Y	Y

Note: Financial information, benefits and other data can change quickly and may vary from those stated here.

COVANCE INC

www.covance.com

Industry Group Code: 541712 Ranks within this company's industry group: Sales: 1 Profits: 1

Management:		Sales/Marketing:		Liberal Arts:		Information Systems:		Professionals:		Tech./Scientific:	
Management Trainees:	Y	Marketing Pros.:	Y	Gen. Writing/Editing:		Info. Management:	Y	Finance/Acct.:	Y	Engineers, Electrical:	
Experienced Mngmt.:	Y	Retail Sales:		Technical Writing:	Y	Software Dev.:	Y	Law:	Y	Engineers, Other:	
International Business:	Y	Commercial/Industrial:	Y	Graphic Arts/Photog.:	Y	Hardware Dev.:		HR/Other:	Y	Health/Lab:	Y
MBA Grads:	Y	Sales Trainees:		Music:		Consulting/Other:	Y	Training:	Y	Scientists/Research:	Y
		Advertising Pros.:	Y	Broadcasting:				Health Care:	Y	Petroleum/Chemicals:	
				Other:				Consulting:	Y	Math/Other:	

TYPES OF BUSINESS:

Pharmaceutical Research & Development
Drug Preclinical/Clinical Trials
Laboratory Testing & Analysis
Approval Assistance
Health Economics & Outcomes Services
Online Tools

BRANDS/DIVISIONS/AFFILIATES:

LabLink
Study Tracker
Trial Tracker

CONTACTS: Note: Officers with more than one job title may be intentionally listed here more than once.

Joseph L. Herring, CEO
Wendel Barr, COO/Exec. VP
William Klitgaard, CFO/Sr. VP
James W. Lovett, General Counsel/Sr. VP
Richard F. Cimino, Pres., Late Stage Dev.
Joseph L. Herring, Chmn.
Anthony Cork, Pres., Early Dev. Europe

Phone: 609-452-4440	Fax:
Toll-Free: 888-268-2623	
Address: 210 Carnegie Ctr., Princeton, NJ 08540 US	

GROWTH PLANS/SPECIAL FEATURES:

Covance, Inc. is a leading drug development services company and contract research organization. It provides a wide range of product development services to pharmaceutical, biotechnology and medical device industries across the globe. The company also provides laboratory testing services for clients in the chemical, agrochemical and food businesses. The firm operates two business segments: early development services and late-stage development services. Covance's early development services include preclinical services (such as toxicology, pharmaceutical development, research products and a bioanalytical testing service) and Phase I clinical services. Its late-stage development services cover clinical development and support; clinical trials; periapproval and market access; and central laboratory operations. Covance has also introduced several Internet-based products: Study Tracker, an Internet-based client access product, which permits customers of toxicology services to review study data and schedules on a near real-time basis; LabLink, a client access program that allows customers of central laboratory services to review and query lab data; and Trial Tracker, a web-enabled clinical trial project management and tracking tool intended to allow both employees and customers of its late-stage clinical business to review and manage all aspects of clinical-trial projects. In October 2008, Covance purchased an early drug development facility in Greenfield, Indiana from Eli Lilly and Company. In addition, Covance upgraded several research facilities and in June 2008 opened a 50,000 square foot research clinic in Evansville, Indiana. In September 2008 , the firm announced plans to build a preclinical facility in China, and announced in 2009 that it plans to open clinical development offices in Ukraine, Slovakia and Israel. In December 2008, Covance purchased a minority stake in Caprion Proteomics, a provider of proteomics based services to the pharmaceutical industry.

Covance offers its employees benefits such as medical, dental and vision plans; a range of insurance benefits; employee assistance; financial planning services; and tuition reimbursement.

FINANCIALS: Sales and profits are in thousands of dollars—add 000 to get the full amount. 2008 Note: Financial information for 2008 was not available for all companies at press time.

2008 Sales: $1,827,067	2008 Profits: $196,760	**U.S. Stock Ticker: CVD**
2007 Sales: $1,631,516	2007 Profits: $175,929	**Int'l Ticker:** Int'l Exchange:
2006 Sales: $1,406,058	2006 Profits: $144,998	Employees: 9,600
2005 Sales: $1,250,400	2005 Profits: $119,600	Fiscal Year Ends: 12/31
2004 Sales: $1,056,397	2004 Profits: $97,947	Parent Company:

SALARIES/BENEFITS:

Pension Plan:	ESOP Stock Plan:	Profit Sharing:	Top Exec. Salary: $729,167	Bonus: $850,000
Savings Plan: Y	Stock Purch. Plan: Y		Second Exec. Salary: $415,000	Bonus: $255,000

OTHER THOUGHTS:

Apparent Women Officers or Directors: 2
Hot Spot for Advancement for Women/Minorities: Y

LOCATIONS: ("Y" = Yes)

West:	Southwest:	Midwest:	Southeast:	Northeast:	International:
Y	Y	Y	Y	Y	Y

Note: Financial information, benefits and other data can change quickly and may vary from those stated here.

COVENTRY HEALTH CARE INC

www.coventryhealth.com

Industry Group Code: 524114 Ranks within this company's industry group: Sales: 9 Profits: 7

Management:		Sales/Marketing:		Liberal Arts:		Information Systems:		Professionals:		Tech./Scientific:	
Management Trainees:	Y	Marketing Pros.:	Y	Gen. Writing/Editing:	Y	Info. Management:	Y	Finance/Acct.:	Y	Engineers, Electrical:	
Experienced Mngmt.:	Y	Retail Sales:		Technical Writing:	Y	Software Dev.:	Y	Law:	Y	Engineers, Other:	
International Business:		Commercial/Industrial:	Y	Graphic Arts/Photog.:	Y	Hardware Dev.:		HR/Other:	Y	Health/Lab:	
MBA Grads:	Y	Sales Trainees:		Music:		Consulting/Other:		Training:	Y	Scientists/Research:	
		Advertising Pros.:	Y	Broadcasting:				Health Care:	Y	Petroleum/Chemicals:	
				Other:	Y			Consulting:		Math/Other:	

TYPES OF BUSINESS:

Health Plans
Insurance
Managed Care Products

BRANDS/DIVISIONS/AFFILIATES:

Altius Health Plans
Carelink Health Plans
HealthAmerica
HealthAssurance
OmniCare
PersonalCare
WellPath
Southern Health

CONTACTS: *Note: Officers with more than one job title may be intentionally listed here more than once.*

Allen F. Wise, CEO
Shawn M. Guertin, CFO/Exec. VP
Patrisha L. Davis, Chief Human Resources Officer/Sr. VP
Maria Fitzpatrick, CIO/Sr. VP
Thomas C. Zielinski, General Counsel/Exec. VP
James E. McGarry, Sr. VP-Customer Service Oper.
John J. Ruhlmann, Sr. VP
Allen F. Wise, Chmn.

Phone: 301-581-0600	Fax: 301-493-0742
Toll-Free:	
Address: 6705 Rockledge Dr., Ste. 900, Bethesda, MD 20817 US	

GROWTH PLANS/SPECIAL FEATURES:

Coventry Healthcare, Inc. is a diversified national managed healthcare company operating health plans, insurance companies, network rental and workers' compensation services companies. The firm provides a range of risk and fee-based managed care products and services to individuals; employer- and government-funded groups; government agencies; and other insurance carriers and administrators. Coventry operates through three divisions: commercial business; individual consumer and government; and specialty business divisions. The commercial business division provides products to employer groups of all sizes, including health maintenance organization (HMO), preferred provider organization (PPO) and point of service products. Coventry also offers commercial management services products on a self-funded basis where it performs administrative services for a fee and the customer assumes the risk for medical costs. Within these products, it also offers consumer-directed benefit options, including health reimbursement accounts and health savings accounts. The individual consumer & government division provides comprehensive health benefits to members participating in the Medicare Advantage HMO, Medicare Advantage PPO, Medicare Advantage Private-Fee-For-Service, Medicare Prescription Drug and Medicaid programs and receives premium payments from federal and state governments. The specialty business division provides workers' compensation managed care services on a fee-based basis, with products including access to its provider network, pharmacy benefits management, field case management, telephonic case management and independent medical exam and bill review capabilities. Its health plans are operated under the names Altius Health Plans; Carelink Health Plans; Coventry Health Care; Coventry Health and Life; Group Health Plan; HealthAmerica; HealthAssurance; Healthcare USA; OmniCare; PersonalCare; Southern Health; Vista; and WellPath. In June 2009, Coventry agreed to sell subsidiary First Health Services Corporation to Magellan Health Services, Inc. for approximately $110 million.

Coventry offers its employees tuition assistance, an employee assistance plan, a community service program, a business casual environment, flexible spending accounts and medical, dental, vision, life and disability insurance.

FINANCIALS: Sales and profits are in thousands of dollars—add 000 to get the full amount. 2008 Note: Financial information for 2008 was not available for all companies at press time.

2008 Sales: $11,913,646	2008 Profits: $381,895	**U.S. Stock Ticker: CVH**
2007 Sales: $9,879,531	2007 Profits: $626,094	**Int'l Ticker:** Int'l Exchange:
2006 Sales: $7,733,756	2006 Profits: $560,045	Employees: 15,800
2005 Sales: $6,611,246	2005 Profits: $501,639	Fiscal Year Ends: 12/31
2004 Sales: $5,311,969	2004 Profits: $337,117	Parent Company:

SALARIES/BENEFITS:

Pension Plan:	ESOP Stock Plan:	Profit Sharing:	Top Exec. Salary: $965,000	Bonus: $
Savings Plan: Y	Stock Purch. Plan:		Second Exec. Salary: $600,000	Bonus: $

OTHER THOUGHTS:

Apparent Women Officers or Directors: 3
Hot Spot for Advancement for Women/Minorities: Y

LOCATIONS: ("Y" = Yes)

West:	Southwest:	Midwest:	Southeast:	Northeast:	International:
				Y	

Note: Financial information, benefits and other data can change quickly and may vary from those stated here.

COX COMMUNICATIONS INC

ww2.cox.com

Industry Group Code: 517110 Ranks within this company's industry group: Sales: 7 Profits:

Management:		Sales/Marketing:		Liberal Arts:		Information Systems:		Professionals:		Tech./Scientific:	
Management Trainees:	Y	Marketing Pros.:	Y	Gen. Writing/Editing:	Y	Info. Management:	Y	Finance/Acct.:	Y	Engineers, Electrical:	Y
Experienced Mngmt.:	Y	Retail Sales:		Technical Writing:	Y	Software Dev.:	Y	Law:	Y	Engineers, Other:	Y
International Business:	Y	Commercial/Industrial:	Y	Graphic Arts/Photog.:	Y	Hardware Dev.:		HR/Other:	Y	Health/Lab:	
MBA Grads:	Y	Sales Trainees:	Y	Music:		Consulting/Other:		Training:	Y	Scientists/Research:	
		Advertising Pros.:	Y	Broadcasting:	Y			Health Care:		Petroleum/Chemicals:	
				Other:	Y			Consulting:		Math/Other:	

TYPES OF BUSINESS:

Cable TV Service
Digital Cable TV Service
Cable-Based Internet Access
Local & Long-Distance Phone Service
Commercial Telecommunications Services
Data & Video Transport Services

BRANDS/DIVISIONS/AFFILIATES:

Cox Enterprises, Inc.
Cox Media
Cox Newspapers
Cox Television
AutoTrader.com
Cox Business Services
Travel Channel (The)
Cox Radio, Inc.

CONTACTS: *Note: Officers with more than one job title may be intentionally listed here more than once.*

Leo W. Brennan, COO
Patrick J. Esser, Pres.
Mark F. Bowser, CFO/Sr. VP
Joseph J. Rooney, Chief Mktg. Officer
Mae A. Douglas, Chief People Officer/Sr. VP
Thomas G. Guthrie, VP-IT Oper.
Scott A. Hatfield, Sr. VP-Tech.
Christopher J. Bowick, Sr. VP-Eng.
James A. Hatcher, Sr. VP-Law & Policy
Jill Campbell, Sr. VP-Oper.
Dallas S. Clement, Sr. VP-Strategy & Prod. Mgmt.
Steve M. Gorman, VP-Online Strategy & Interactive Media
David Grabert, Dir.-Media Rel.
William J. Fitzsimmons, Chief Acct. Officer/VP-Acct. & Financial Planning
David Pugliese, Sr. VP-Mktg. & Prod. Mgmt.
Stephen Bye, VP-Wireless
Susan W. Coker, Treas./VP
Sheila Hicks, VP-Sales & Dist.
James Cox Kennedy, Chmn.
George Richter, VP-Supply Chain Mgmt.

Phone: 404-843-5000	Fax:
Toll-Free: 888-566-7751	
Address: 1400 Lake Hearn Dr., Atlanta, GA 30319 US	

GROWTH PLANS/SPECIAL FEATURES:

Cox Communications, Inc., owned by Cox Enterprises, Inc., is a multi-service broadband communications and entertainment company serving more than 6 million customers throughout the U.S. Cox offers advanced digital video, analog cable television and high-definition television, high-speed Internet and local and long distance telephone services over its own nationwide IP network. Cox Business Services provides communications solutions for commercial customers, offering high-speed Internet, voice and long distance services, as well as data and video transport services, for businesses. Cox Media offers national and local cable advertising in traditional spot and new media formats, along with promotional opportunities and production services. The company also maintains Cox Newspapers; Cox Television; Cox Radio; Manheim; Cox Reps; AutoTrader.com; and the Travel Channel. The firm invests in telecommunications companies such as Sprint PCS. Following the dissolution, in late 2008, of a joint venture with Time Warner, Comcast and others aimed at providing mobile phone services through a partnership with Sprint. In March 2009, Cox announced plans to acquire the outstanding minority interest in Cox Radio, Inc. Cox announced in April 2009 that it was working to build its own cellular network in order to offer its customers bundled packages including cell phone services and wireless broadband access for laptop computers. In June 2009, the company announced that it is considering selling the Travel Channel.

Employees are offered medical and dental coverage; life and business travel insurance; health and dependent care spending accounts; tuition reimbursement; an employee assistance program; a pension plan; a 401(k) plan; adoption assistance; discounted Cox services such as cable, telephone and internet where available; and employee discounts with Dell, Sprint, Ford, GM and others. The firm also operates Cox University, which offers over 150 free online courses.

FINANCIALS: Sales and profits are in thousands of dollars—add 000 to get the full amount. 2008 Note: Financial information for 2008 was not available for all companies at press time.

2008 Sales: $8,500,000	2008 Profits: $	**U.S. Stock Ticker:** Subsidiary
2007 Sales: $8,300,000	2007 Profits: $	**Int'l Ticker:** Int'l Exchange:
2006 Sales: $7,300,000	2006 Profits: $	Employees: 22,000
2005 Sales: $7,054,300	2005 Profits: $-230,700	Fiscal Year Ends: 12/31
2004 Sales: $6,106,100	2004 Profits: $-2,375,300	Parent Company: COX ENTERPRISES INC

SALARIES/BENEFITS:

Pension Plan: Y	ESOP Stock Plan:	Profit Sharing:	Top Exec. Salary: $	Bonus: $1,166,798
Savings Plan: Y	Stock Purch. Plan:		Second Exec. Salary: $	Bonus: $

OTHER THOUGHTS:

Apparent Women Officers or Directors: 14
Hot Spot for Advancement for Women/Minorities: Y

LOCATIONS: ("Y" = Yes)

West:	Southwest:	Midwest:	Southeast:	Northeast:	International:
Y	Y	Y	Y	Y	

Note: Financial information, benefits and other data can change quickly and may vary from those stated here.

CR BARD INC

www.crbard.com

Industry Group Code: 33911 **Ranks within this company's industry group:** Sales: 10 Profits: 7

Management:		Sales/Marketing:		Liberal Arts:		Information Systems:		Professionals:		Tech./Scientific:	
Management Trainees:	Y	Marketing Pros.:	Y	Gen. Writing/Editing:	Y	Info. Management:	Y	Finance/Acct.:	Y	Engineers, Electrical:	
Experienced Mngmt.:	Y	Retail Sales:		Technical Writing:	Y	Software Dev.:	Y	Law:	Y	Engineers, Other:	Y
International Business:	Y	Commercial/Industrial:	Y	Graphic Arts/Photog.:	Y	Hardware Dev.:		HR/Other:	Y	Health/Lab:	Y
MBA Grads:	Y	Sales Trainees:		Music:		Consulting/Other:		Training:	Y	Scientists/Research:	Y
		Advertising Pros.:	Y	Broadcasting:				Health Care:	Y	Petroleum/Chemicals:	
				Other:				Consulting:		Math/Other:	

TYPES OF BUSINESS:

Equipment-Urological Catheters
Diagnostic and Interventional Products
Minimally Invasive Vascular Products
Surgical Specialty Products
Supply Chain and Business Services
Oncology Products
Urology Products

BRANDS/DIVISIONS/AFFILIATES:

PerFix
Ventralex
Collamend
Ventrio
Sepra
Allomax
Permasorb
Statlock

CONTACTS: *Note: Officers with more than one job title may be intentionally listed here more than once.*

Timothy M. Ring, CEO
John H. Weiland, COO
John H. Weiland, Pres.
Todd C. Schermerhorn, CFO/Sr. VP
Bronwen K. Kelly, VP-Human Resources
John A. DeFord, VP-Science, Tech. & Clinical Affairs
Vincent J. Gurnari, Jr., VP-IT
Stephen J. Long, General Counsel/Sec./VP
Robert L. Mellen, VP-Bus. Dev. & Strategic Planning
Frank Lupisella Jr., Controller/VP
Gary D. Dolch, Sr. VP-Quality & Regulatory Affairs
Patricia Chirstian, VP-Regulatory Affairs
Christopher D. Ganser, VP-Quality, Environmental Sciences & Safety
James M. Howard, VP-Regulatory & Quality Systems Excellence
Timothy M. Ring, Chmn.

Phone: 908-277-8000	Fax: 908-277-8240
Toll-Free: 800-367-2273	
Address: 730 Central Ave., Murray Hill, NJ 07974 US	

GROWTH PLANS/SPECIAL FEATURES:

C.R. Bard, Inc. designs, manufactures, packages, distributes and sells medical, surgical and diagnostic devices. The company's line of minimally invasive vascular products include percutaneous transluminal angioplasty catheters; guidewires; introducers and accessories; peripheral vascular stents and stent grafts; vena cava filters; and biopsy devices. Additional products include cardiac mapping and electrophysiology laboratory systems, as well as diagnostic and temporary pacing electrode catheters; fabrics and meshes; and implantable blood vessel replacements. The firm's surgical specialty products include meshes for vessel and hernia repair; irrigation devices for orthopedic, laparoscopic and gynecological procedures; and products for topical hemostasis. These products include the PerFix plug; Ventralex, Collamend, Ventrio, Sepra and Allomax hernia patches; and the Permasorb fixation device, which attaches hernia patches top host tissue. Hernia operations using these products can be done in an outpatient setting in as little as 20 minutes. The urology segment markets products which include the Foley catheter, the Agento IC infection control tube and the Statlock catheter stabilization line. C.R. Bard's oncology products eliminate the need for unnecessary additional catheters; products include the PowerPICC and PowerPort devices. The company's products are distributed in the U.S. directly to hospitals and other health care institutions, as well as through numerous hospital/surgical supply and other medical specialty distributors. About 75% of C.R. Bard's international sales are products manufactured in the U.S., Puerto Rico or Mexico. The company recently received FDA approval for its Flair endovascular stent graft, the E*Luminexx vascular stent the Lifestent vascular stent.

C.R. Bard offers its employees medical, prescription drug, dental and vision coverage; life insurance and accidental death and dismemberment plans; short- and long-term disability; flexible spending accounts; a 401(k) plan; and retirement pensions.

FINANCIALS: Sales and profits are in thousands of dollars—add 000 to get the full amount. 2008 Note: Financial information for 2008 was not available for all companies at press time.

2008 Sales: $2,452,100	2008 Profits: $416,500	**U.S. Stock Ticker: BCR**
2007 Sales: $2,202,000	2007 Profits: $406,400	**Int'l Ticker:** Int'l Exchange:
2006 Sales: $1,979,600	2006 Profits: $272,100	Employees: 11,000
2005 Sales: $1,771,300	2005 Profits: $337,100	Fiscal Year Ends: 12/31
2004 Sales: $1,656,100	2004 Profits: $302,800	Parent Company:

SALARIES/BENEFITS:

Pension Plan: Y	ESOP Stock Plan:	Profit Sharing:	Top Exec. Salary: $991,667	Bonus: $1,377,500
Savings Plan: Y	Stock Purch. Plan:		Second Exec. Salary: $805,750	Bonus: $895,044

OTHER THOUGHTS:

Apparent Women Officers or Directors: 4
Hot Spot for Advancement for Women/Minorities: Y

LOCATIONS: ("Y" = Yes)

West:	Southwest:	Midwest:	Southeast:	Northeast:	International:
Y	Y	Y	Y	Y	Y

CRACKER BARREL OLD COUNTRY STORE INC

www.crackerbarrel.com

Industry Group Code: 722110 Ranks within this company's industry group: Sales: 8 Profits: 7

Management:		Sales/Marketing:		Liberal Arts:		Information Systems:		Professionals:		Tech./Scientific:	
Management Trainees:	Y	Marketing Pros.:	Y	Gen. Writing/Editing:	Y	Info. Management:	Y	Finance/Acct.:	Y	Engineers, Electrical:	
Experienced Mngmt.:	Y	Retail Sales:		Technical Writing:		Software Dev.:	Y	Law:	Y	Engineers, Other:	
International Business:		Commercial/Industrial:		Graphic Arts/Photog.:	Y	Hardware Dev.:		HR/Other:	Y	Health/Lab:	
MBA Grads:	Y	Sales Trainees:	Y	Music:		Consulting/Other:		Training:	Y	Scientists/Research:	
		Advertising Pros.:	Y	Broadcasting:				Health Care:		Petroleum/Chemicals:	
				Other:	Y			Consulting:		Math/Other:	

TYPES OF BUSINESS:

Restaurants-Country Cooking, Food Service
Retail Gifts and Food Products

BRANDS/DIVISIONS/AFFILIATES:

Cracker Barrel Old Country Store

CONTACTS: Note: Officers with more than one job title may be intentionally listed here more than once.

Michael A. Woodhouse, CEO
Doug Barber, COO/Exec. VP
Michael A. Woodhouse, Pres.
Sandra Brophy Cochran, CFO/Exec. VP
Robert J. Harig, Sr. VP-Human Resources
N. B. Forrest Shoaf, Chief Legal Officer/Sec./Sr. VP
Edward A. Greene, Sr. VP-Strategic Initiatives
Diana S. Wynne, Sr. VP-Corp. Affairs
Patrick A. Scruggs, Chief Acct. Officer/ VP-Acct. & Tax
Terry Maxwell, Sr. VP-Retail
Michael A. Woodhouse, Chmn.

Phone: 615-444-5533	Fax: 615-443-9818
Toll-Free:	
Address: 305 Hartmann Dr., Lebanon, TN 37087 US	

GROWTH PLANS/SPECIAL FEATURES:

Cracker Barrel Old Country Store, Inc., formerly CBRL Group, Inc. is primarily a restaurant chain operator, with 579 Cracker Barrel Old Country Store restaurants in 41 states. In 1999, CBRL Group underwent restructuring, transforming itself into a holding company in order to accommodate plans to expand into new business areas. Cracker Barrel Old Country Store restaurants resemble turn-of-the-century country stores and are famous throughout the southern portion of the U.S. for country cooking and early 20th century decor. Restaurants also feature small retail areas where customers can purchase various products reminiscent of turn-of-the century goods typically found at old-fashioned general stores, such as rocking chairs, seasonal gifts, apparel, toys, music CDs, cookware, old-fashioned-looking ceramics, figurines, a book-on-audio sale-and-exchange program and various other gift items, as well as various candies, preserves, syrups and other food items. Cracker Barrel's Books-on-Audio program allows customers to purchase an audio book at any location, listen to it and then return it for full price minus a small exchange fee. The company's restaurant operations generated approximately 79% of total revenue in 2008. The retail operations generated approximately 21% of Cracker Barrel's total revenue.

FINANCIALS: Sales and profits are in thousands of dollars—add 000 to get the full amount. 2008 Note: Financial information for 2008 was not available for all companies at press time.

2008 Sales: $2,384,521	2008 Profits: $65,553	U.S. Stock Ticker: CBRL
2007 Sales: $2,351,576	2007 Profits: $162,065	Int'l Ticker: Int'l Exchange:
2006 Sales: $2,219,475	2006 Profits: $116,291	Employees: 65,000
2005 Sales: $2,190,866	2005 Profits: $126,640	Fiscal Year Ends: 7/31
2004 Sales: $1,595,244	2004 Profits: $113,262	Parent Company:

SALARIES/BENEFITS:

Pension Plan:	ESOP Stock Plan:	Profit Sharing:	Top Exec. Salary: $1,000,000	Bonus: $
Savings Plan: Y	Stock Purch. Plan: Y		Second Exec. Salary: $383,778	Bonus: $

OTHER THOUGHTS:

Apparent Women Officers or Directors: 4
Hot Spot for Advancement for Women/Minorities: Y

LOCATIONS: ("Y" = Yes)

West:	Southwest:	Midwest:	Southeast:	Northeast:	International:
Y	Y	Y	Y	Y	

CTS CORP

www.ctscorp.com

Industry Group Code: 334419 **Ranks within this company's industry group:** Sales: 4 Profits: 3

Management:		Sales/Marketing:		Liberal Arts:		Information Systems:		Professionals:		Tech./Scientific:	
Management Trainees:	Y	Marketing Pros.:	Y	Gen. Writing/Editing:		Info. Management:	Y	Finance/Acct.:	Y	Engineers, Electrical:	Y
Experienced Mngmt.:	Y	Retail Sales:		Technical Writing:	Y	Software Dev.:	Y	Law:	Y	Engineers, Other:	
International Business:	Y	Commercial/Industrial:	Y	Graphic Arts/Photog.:	Y	Hardware Dev.:	Y	HR/Other:	Y	Health/Lab:	
MBA Grads:	Y	Sales Trainees:		Music:		Consulting/Other:		Training:	Y	Scientists/Research:	
		Advertising Pros.:		Broadcasting:				Health Care:		Petroleum/Chemicals:	
				Other:				Consulting:		Math/Other:	

TYPES OF BUSINESS:

Electronic Components
Components & Sensors
Manufacturing & Assembly Services
Interconnect Systems
Supply Chain Services
Electronics Manufacturing Services

BRANDS/DIVISIONS/AFFILIATES:

CTS Electronics Manufacturing Solutions
Alpha Ceramics Inc
Tusonix Inc
Orion Manufacturing Inc

CONTACTS: *Note: Officers with more than one job title may be intentionally listed here more than once.*

Vinod M. Khilnani, CEO
Vinod M. Khilnani, Pres.
Matthew W. Long, Interim CFO/Treas.
Tony Corscadden, Sr. VP-Global Oper.
Matthew Long, Treas.
Donald R. Schroeder, Exec. VP/Pres., CTS Electronics Mfg. Solutions
H. Tyler Buchanan, Sr. VP
Roger R. Hemminghaus, Chmn.

Phone: 574-293-7511	Fax: 574-293-6146
Toll-Free:	
Address: 905 West Blvd. N., Elkhart, IN 46514 US	

GROWTH PLANS/SPECIAL FEATURES:

CTS Corp. designs, manufactures and sells electronic components and custom electronic assemblies for the automotive, computer, communications, medical, industrial, defense and aerospace markets. The company operates manufacturing facilities throughout North America, Asia and Europe. Its product lines serve major markets worldwide, focused primarily on the needs of original equipment manufacturers. The company operates through two business segments: Components and Sensors; and Electronics Manufacturing Services (EMS). Components and sensors division consists of products which perform specific electronic functions for a given product family and are intended for use in customer assemblies. Components and sensors consist principally of automotive sensors and actuators used in commercial or consumer vehicles; electronic components used in communications infrastructure and computer markets; components used in computer and other high-speed applications, switches, resistor networks, and potentiometers used to serve multiple markets and fabricated piezoelectric materials and substrates used primarily in medical, industrial and defense and aerospace markets. Products from the Components and Sensors segment are principally sold in three major original equipment manufacturer (OEM) markets: automotive; communications; and computer. EMS includes the higher level assembly of electronic and mechanical components into a finished subassembly or assembly performed under a contract manufacturing agreement with an OEM or other contract manufacturer. Additionally, for some customers, the firm provides full turnkey manufacturing and completion including design, bill-of-material management, logistics and repair. Products from the EMS segment are principally sold in the communications, computer, medical, industrial, and defense and aerospace OEM markets. In January 2008, the company acquired Tusonix, Inc. for approximately $15 million. In March 2008, the firm acquired Orion Manufacturing, Inc. for $10 million.

Employees are offered medical and dental coverage; life insurance; a 401(k) plan; health and dependent care reimbursement accounts; and tuition reimbursement.

FINANCIALS: Sales and profits are in thousands of dollars—add 000 to get the full amount. 2008 Note: Financial information for 2008 was not available for all companies at press time.

2008 Sales: $691,707	2008 Profits: $29,886	**U.S. Stock Ticker: CTS**
2007 Sales: $685,945	2007 Profits: $25,412	**Int'l Ticker:** Int'l Exchange:
2006 Sales: $655,614	2006 Profits: $24,197	Employees: 5,044
2005 Sales: $617,484	2005 Profits: $20,756	Fiscal Year Ends: 12/31
2004 Sales: $531,316	2004 Profits: $19,956	Parent Company:

SALARIES/BENEFITS:

Pension Plan:	ESOP Stock Plan:	Profit Sharing:	Top Exec. Salary: $528,846	Bonus: $402,249
Savings Plan: Y	Stock Purch. Plan:		Second Exec. Salary: $337,644	Bonus: $163,887

OTHER THOUGHTS:

Apparent Women Officers or Directors:
Hot Spot for Advancement for Women/Minorities:

LOCATIONS: ("Y" = Yes)

West:	Southwest:	Midwest:	Southeast:	Northeast:	International:
Y	Y	Y		Y	Y

Note: Financial information, benefits and other data can change quickly and may vary from those stated here.

CUBIC CORP

www.cubic.com

Industry Group Code: 33641 Ranks within this company's industry group: Sales: 9   Profits: 8

Management:		Sales/Marketing:		Liberal Arts:		Information Systems:		Professionals:		Tech./Scientific:	
Management Trainees:	Y	Marketing Pros.:	Y	Gen. Writing/Editing:		Info. Management:	Y	Finance/Acct.:	Y	Engineers, Electrical:	Y
Experienced Mngmt.:	Y	Retail Sales:		Technical Writing:	Y	Software Dev.:	Y	Law:	Y	Engineers, Other:	Y
International Business:	Y	Commercial/Industrial:	Y	Graphic Arts/Photog.:	Y	Hardware Dev.:	Y	HR/Other:	Y	Health/Lab:	
MBA Grads:	Y	Sales Trainees:		Music:		Consulting/Other:		Training:	Y	Scientists/Research:	Y
		Advertising Pros.:		Broadcasting:				Health Care:		Petroleum/Chemicals:	
				Other:				Consulting:		Math/Other:	

TYPES OF BUSINESS:

Communications & Surveillance Systems
Military Training Systems
Automated Ticketing Systems

BRANDS/DIVISIONS/AFFILIATES:

Cubic Transportation Systems,Ltd.
Cubic Defense Applications, Inc.
Cubic Applications, Inc.

CONTACTS: Note: Officers with more than one job title may be intentionally listed here more than once.

Walter J. Zable, CEO
Walter J. Zable, Pres.
William W. Boyle, CFO
Bernard A. Kulchin, VP-Human Resources
John A. Minteer, VP-IT
William L. Hoesee, General Counsel/VP/Corp. Sec.
John D. Thomas, VP-Corp. Dev. & Finance
Mark A. Harrison, Corp. Controller/VP
Bradley H. Feldmann, Pres., Cubic Defense Applications, Inc.
Steve Shewmaker, Pres., Worldwide Cubic Transportation Systems
Jimmie L. Balentine, Pres./CEO-Cubic Applications, Inc.
Kenneth A. Kopf, Chief Legal Officer/VP
Walter J. Zable, Chmn.

Phone: 858-277-6780	**Fax:** 858-277-1878
Toll-Free: 800-818-8303	
Address: 9333 Balboa Ave., San Diego, CA 92123 US	

GROWTH PLANS/SPECIAL FEATURES:

Cubic Corporation designs, develops, manufactures and installs products for military defense and mass transit networks. The company has two primary segments: Defense and Transportation Systems. The Defense segment has three main business units: Training Systems; Mission Support Services; and Communications and Electronics. The company's products include customized military range instrumentation systems, tactical engagement simulation systems, firearm simulation systems, communications and surveillance systems, surveillance receivers, power amplifiers and avionics systems. Services offered within the Defense segment include training mission support, computer simulation training, distributed interactive simulation, development of military training doctrine and field operations and maintenance. The firm markets its capabilities directly to various U.S. government departments and agencies and foreign governments. The company also frequently contracts or teams with other defense suppliers. The Transportation Systems segment designs, produces, installs and services electronic revenue collection systems for mass transit projects, including bus, bus rapid transit, light rail, commuter rail, heavy rail, ferry and parking markets. Its products include contactless smart cards, magnetic stripe cards, device software, central computer systems, passenger gates, card readers and ticket vending machines. The company's transportation segment has been awarded over 400 projects in 40 major markets on 5 continents. Active projects include London; the New York region; the Washington, D.C. region; the Los Angeles region; the San Diego region; San Francisco; Minneapolis/St. Paul; Chicago; Atlanta; Brisbane, Australia; and Sweden. Subsidiaries include Cubic Transportation Systems, Ltd.; Cubic Defense Applications, Inc.; and Cubic Applications, Inc. In 2008, the company sold its 50% interest in C4 Advanced Tactical Systems LLC, a joint venture formed in 2004 with the Israeli defense company Rafael Armament Development Authority, Ltd.

FINANCIALS: Sales and profits are in thousands of dollars—add 000 to get the full amount. 2008 Note: Financial information for 2008 was not available for all companies at press time.

2008 Sales: $881,135	2008 Profits: $36,854	**U.S. Stock Ticker:** CUB	
2007 Sales: $889,870	2007 Profits: $41,586	**Int'l Ticker:** Int'l Exchange:	
2006 Sales: $821,386	2006 Profits: $24,133	Employees: 5,000	
2005 Sales: $804,372	2005 Profits: $11,628	Fiscal Year Ends: 9/30	
2004 Sales: $722,012	2004 Profits: $36,911	Parent Company:	

SALARIES/BENEFITS:

Pension Plan: Y	ESOP Stock Plan:	Profit Sharing: Y	Top Exec. Salary: $686,400	Bonus: $250,000
Savings Plan:	Stock Purch. Plan:		Second Exec. Salary: $520,000	Bonus: $170,000

OTHER THOUGHTS:

Apparent Women Officers or Directors:
Hot Spot for Advancement for Women/Minorities:

LOCATIONS: ("Y" = Yes)

West:	Southwest:	Midwest:	Southeast:	Northeast:	International:
Y		Y	Y	Y	Y

Note: Financial information, benefits and other data can change quickly and may vary from those stated here.

CUMMINS INC

www.cummins.com

Industry Group Code: 3363   Ranks within this company's industry group: Sales: 3   Profits: 3

Management:		Sales/Marketing:		Liberal Arts:		Information Systems:		Professionals:		Tech./Scientific:	
Management Trainees:	Y	Marketing Pros.:	Y	Gen. Writing/Editing:	Y	Info. Management:	Y	Finance/Acct.:	Y	Engineers, Electrical:	Y
Experienced Mngmt.:	Y	Retail Sales:		Technical Writing:	Y	Software Dev.:	Y	Law:	Y	Engineers, Other:	Y
International Business:	Y	Commercial/Industrial:	Y	Graphic Arts/Photog.:	Y	Hardware Dev.:	Y	HR/Other:	Y	Health/Lab:	
MBA Grads:	Y	Sales Trainees:		Music:		Consulting/Other:		Training:	Y	Scientists/Research:	
		Advertising Pros.:	Y	Broadcasting:				Health Care:		Petroleum/Chemicals:	
				Other:				Consulting:		Math/Other:	

TYPES OF BUSINESS:

Automotive Products, Motors & Parts Manufacturing
Engines
Filtration Systems
Power Generation Systems
Alternators
Air Handling Systems
Filtration & Emissions Solutions
Fuel Systems

BRANDS/DIVISIONS/AFFILIATES:

Cummins Power Generation
Onan

CONTACTS: *Note: Officers with more than one job title may be intentionally listed here more than once.*

Theodore M. Solso, CEO
Tom Linebarger, COO
Tom Linebarger, Pres.
Pat Ward, CFO/VP
John C. Wall, CTO/VP
Mark Gerstle, Chief Admin. Officer/VP
Marya M. Rose, General Counsel/VP/Sec.
Richard J. Freeland
Tony Satterthwaite, VP/Pres., Components Group
J. D. Kelly, VP/Pres., Engine Bus.
Steven M. Chapman, VP-Emerging Markets & Bus.
Theodore M. Solso, Chmn.

Phone: 812-377-5000	Fax: 812-377-3334
Toll-Free:	
Address: 500 Jackson St., Columbus, IN 47202 US	

GROWTH PLANS/SPECIAL FEATURES:

Cummins, Inc. designs, manufactures, distributes and services diesel and natural gas engines; electric power generation systems; and engine-related component products, including filtration and emissions solutions, fuel systems, controls and air handling systems. The engine segment, which generated 50% of 2008 sales, manufactures and markets diesel and natural gas-powered engines, parts, and services under the Cummins brand name for the heavy- and medium-duty truck, bus, recreational vehicle, light-duty automotive, agricultural, construction, mining, marine, oil and gas, rail and governmental equipment markets. The power generation segment generated 20% of 2008 revenue, and designs and manufactures components of power generation systems, including engines, controls, alternators, transfer switches and switchgear. Products are marketed principally under the Cummins Power Generation and Onan brands and include diesel and alternative-fuel electrical generator sets for commercial, institutional and consumer applications, such as office buildings, hospitals, factories, municipalities, utilities, universities, boats and homes. The components segment, which accounted for 18% of 2008 net sales, produces filters, silencers and intake and exhaust systems and commercial turbochargers. The distribution segment, producing 12% of revenue, consists of 18 company-owned and 18 joint ventures that distribute the company's products and services in over 70 countries and territories. Cummins serves customers through a network of more than 500 company-owned and independent distributor locations and roughly 5,200 dealer locations in more than 190 countries and territories. In December 2008 and January 2009, the company laid off 1,400 workers, or about 10% of its workforce. In June 2009, Chrysler cancelled plans to use Cummins diesel engines in its Dodge Ram 1500 line, halting the reopening of a plant to manufacture those engines.

Cummins offers its employees medical, dental and life insurance; a 401(k) plan; a profit sharing plan; pension plans; an employee stock purchase plan; and disability plans.

FINANCIALS: Sales and profits are in thousands of dollars—add 000 to get the full amount. 2008 Note: Financial information for 2008 was not available for all companies at press time.

2008 Sales: $14,342,000	2008 Profits: $755,000	**U.S. Stock Ticker: CMI**
2007 Sales: $13,048,000	2007 Profits: $739,000	**Int'l Ticker:** Int'l Exchange:
2006 Sales: $11,362,000	2006 Profits: $715,000	Employees: 39,800
2005 Sales: $9,918,000	2005 Profits: $550,000	Fiscal Year Ends: 12/31
2004 Sales: $8,438,000	2004 Profits: $350,000	Parent Company:

SALARIES/BENEFITS:

Pension Plan:	ESOP Stock Plan: Y	Profit Sharing: Y	Top Exec. Salary: $1,210,000	Bonus: $5,390,800
Savings Plan: Y	Stock Purch. Plan: Y		Second Exec. Salary: $887,500	Bonus: $2,424,500

OTHER THOUGHTS:

Apparent Women Officers or Directors: 2
Hot Spot for Advancement for Women/Minorities: Y

LOCATIONS: ("Y" = Yes)

West:	Southwest:	Midwest:	Southeast:	Northeast:	International:
Y	Y	Y	Y	Y	Y

CVS CAREMARK CORPORATION

info.cvscaremark.com

Industry Group Code: 446110 Ranks within this company's industry group: Sales: 1 Profits: 1

Management:		Sales/Marketing:		Liberal Arts:		Information Systems:		Professionals:		Tech./Scientific:	
Management Trainees:	Y	Marketing Pros.:	Y	Gen. Writing/Editing:	Y	Info. Management:	Y	Finance/Acct.:	Y	Engineers, Electrical:	
Experienced Mngmt.:	Y	Retail Sales:	Y	Technical Writing:		Software Dev.:	Y	Law:	Y	Engineers, Other:	
International Business:		Commercial/Industrial:		Graphic Arts/Photog.:	Y	Hardware Dev.:		HR/Other:	Y	Health/Lab:	
MBA Grads:	Y	Sales Trainees:	Y	Music:		Consulting/Other:		Training:	Y	Scientists/Research:	
		Advertising Pros.:	Y	Broadcasting:				Health Care:	Y	Petroleum/Chemicals:	
				Other:	Y			Consulting:		Math/Other:	

TYPES OF BUSINESS:

Drug Stores
Pharmacy Benefits Management
Online Pharmacy Services

BRANDS/DIVISIONS/AFFILIATES:

MinuteClinic
Caremark Rx., Inc.
CVS Corp.
Longs Drug Stores Corp.
PharmaCare Pharmacy
CVS/pharmacy
Accendo Insurance Company
SilverScript Insurance Company

CONTACTS: *Note: Officers with more than one job title may be intentionally listed here more than once.*

Thomas M. Ryan, CEO
Thomas M. Ryan, Pres.
David B. Rickard, CFO/Exec. VP
Helena B. Foulkes, Chief Mktg. Officer/Exec. VP
V. Michael Ferdinandi, Sr. VP-Human Resources
Troyen A. Brennan, Chief Medical Officer/Exec. VP
Stuart M. McGuigan, CIO/Sr. VP
David B. Rickard, Chief Admin. Officer
Douglas A. Sgarro, Chief Legal Officer/Exec. VP/Pres., CVS Realty Co.
V. Michael Ferdinandi, Sr. VP-Corp. Comm.
Nancy R. Christal, Sr. VP-Investor Rel.
David M. Denton, Chief Acct. Officer/Controller/Sr. VP
Jonathan C. Roberts, Exec. VP-Pricing & Network Rel.
Larry J. Merlo, Exec. VP/Pres., CVS/pharmacy
Howard A. McLure, Pres., Caremark Pharmacy Svcs./Exec. VP
Thomas M. Ryan, Chmn.
Jonathan C. Roberts, Exec. VP-RX Purchasing

Phone: 401-765-1500	Fax: 401-762-2137
Toll-Free: 888-746-7287	
Address: 1 CVS Dr., Woonsocket, RI 02895 US	

GROWTH PLANS/SPECIAL FEATURES:

CVS Caremark Corp. is one of the largest providers of prescription and related healthcare services in the U.S., filling more than 1 billion prescriptions annually. It operates in two segments: retail pharmacy and pharmacy services. The retail pharmacy segment includes over 6,900 retail drugstores, of which approximately 6,800 operate a pharmacy; an online retail web site; and retail healthcare clinics. The retail drugstores are located in 41 states and Washington, D.C., operating under the CVS/pharmacy and Longs Drugs names. The firm's drugstores sell prescription drugs and a wide assortment of general merchandise, including over-the-counter drugs, beauty products and cosmetics, photo finishing, seasonal merchandise, greeting cards and convenience foods. The division operates over 570 retail healthcare clinics in 27 states under the MinuteClinic name, of which about 534 are located within CVS retail drug stores. The clinics diagnose and treat minor health conditions and are staffed by board-certified nurse practitioners and physician assistants. The pharmacy services segment provides a full range of prescription benefit management services, including mail order pharmacy services, specialty pharmacy services, plan design and administration, formulary management and claims processing. It also offers health management programs. Through subsidiaries SilverScript Insurance Company and Accendo Insurance Company, the division is a national provider of drug benefits. The segment operates a national retail pharmacy network with over 60,000 participating pharmacies; 58 retail specialty pharmacy stores; 19 specialty mail order pharmacies; and seven mail services pharmacies located in 26 states, Puerto Rico and Washington, D.C. Specialty pharmacy stores average 2,000 square feet in size. In October 2008, the firm acquired Longs Drug Stores, with 521 stores located primarily in California and Hawaii, for about $2.6 billion.

FINANCIALS: Sales and profits are in thousands of dollars—add 000 to get the full amount. 2008 Note: Financial information for 2008 was not available for all companies at press time.

2008 Sales: $87,471,900	2008 Profits: $3,212,100	**U.S. Stock Ticker:** CVS
2007 Sales: $76,329,500	2007 Profits: $2,637,000	**Int'l Ticker:** Int'l Exchange:
2006 Sales: $43,821,400	2006 Profits: $1,368,900	Employees: 215,000
2005 Sales: $37,006,200	2005 Profits: $1,224,700	Fiscal Year Ends: 12/31
2004 Sales: $30,594,300	2004 Profits: $918,800	Parent Company:

SALARIES/BENEFITS:

Pension Plan:	ESOP Stock Plan:	Profit Sharing:	Top Exec. Salary: $1,400,000	Bonus: $4,568,503
Savings Plan:	Stock Purch. Plan:		Second Exec. Salary: $781,154	Bonus: $600,000

OTHER THOUGHTS:

Apparent Women Officers or Directors: 5
Hot Spot for Advancement for Women/Minorities: Y

LOCATIONS: ("Y" = Yes)

West:	Southwest:	Midwest:	Southeast:	Northeast:	International:
Y	Y	Y	Y	Y	

Note: Financial information, benefits and other data can change quickly and may vary from those stated here.

DANAHER CORP

www.danaher.com

Industry Group Code: 335 Ranks within this company's industry group: Sales: 1 Profits: 1

Management:		Sales/Marketing:		Liberal Arts:		Information Systems:		Professionals:		Tech./Scientific:	
Management Trainees:	Y	Marketing Pros.:	Y	Gen. Writing/Editing:	Y	Info. Management:	Y	Finance/Acct.:	Y	Engineers, Electrical:	Y
Experienced Mngmt.:	Y	Retail Sales:		Technical Writing:	Y	Software Dev.:	Y	Law:	Y	Engineers, Other:	Y
International Business:	Y	Commercial/Industrial:	Y	Graphic Arts/Photog.:	Y	Hardware Dev.:	Y	HR/Other:	Y	Health/Lab:	
MBA Grads:	Y	Sales Trainees:	Y	Music:		Consulting/Other:		Training:	Y	Scientists/Research:	
		Advertising Pros.:	Y	Broadcasting:				Health Care:		Petroleum/Chemicals:	
				Other:				Consulting:		Math/Other:	

TYPES OF BUSINESS:

Power Tools Manufacturing
Environmental Management Products
Test & Calibration Equipment
Medical Tools & Equipment
Motors & Drives
Bar Code Equipment
Security & Defense Products
Automotive Components & Repair Equipment

BRANDS/DIVISIONS/AFFILIATES:

Delta Consolidated Industries
Hennessy Industries
Jacobs Chuck Manufacturing Company
Jacobs Vehicle Systems
Craftsman

CONTACTS: *Note: Officers with more than one job title may be intentionally listed here more than once.*

H. Lawrence Culp, Jr., CEO
H. Lawrence Culp, Jr., Pres.
Daniel L. Comas, CFO/Exec. VP
Jonathan P. Graham, General Counsel/Sr. VP
Daniel A. Raskas, VP-Corp. Dev.
Robert S. Lutz, Chief Acct. Officer/VP
Mitchell P. Rales, Chmn.-Exec. Committee
Thomas P. Joyce, Exec. VP
Phillip W. Knisely, Exec. VP
William K. Daniel, II, Exec. VP
Steven M. Rales, Chmn.

Phone: 202-828-0850	Fax: 202-828-0860
Toll-Free:	
Address: 2099 Pennsylvania Ave., NW, Washington, DC 20006-1813 US	

GROWTH PLANS/SPECIAL FEATURES:

Danaher Corp., through its 790 subsidiaries, designs, manufactures and markets products typically characterized by strong brand names, proprietary technology and major market positions. It operates four business segments: Professional Instrumentation, generating 38% of 2008 revenue; Medical Technologies, 26%; Industrial Technologies, 26%; and Tools & Components, 10%. The Professional Instrumentation segment offers professional and technical customers products and services encompassing two main product areas: environmental products, such as water purification systems, and test and measurement products, typically used to calibrate equipment. The Medical Technologies segment offers four main product categories: dental, acute care, pathology and life sciences research. Specific products include dental implants, dentists' tools, blood gas monitors, DNA detection products and laser scanning microscopes. The Industrial Technologies segment manufactures products and sub-systems generally incorporated into other products by customers including systems integrators and original equipment manufacturers. It encompasses two strategic business lines: motion and product identification; and two niche businesses: aerospace and defense and sensors and controls. Specific products include motors, bar code printers and readers, electronic security systems, submarine periscopes and monitoring equipment for electrical grids. Lastly, the Tools & Components segment comprises a strategic business line, mechanics' hand tools, and four niche businesses: Delta Consolidated Industries, a truck box and gang box manufacturer; Hennessy Industries, a wheel service equipment manufacturer; Jacobs Chuck Manufacturing Company, a manufacturer of chucks and work holding devices for portable power tools; and Jacobs Vehicle Systems, a supplier of supplemental braking systems for commercial vehicles. The mechanics' hand tools business is the principal manufacturer of Sears' Craftsman line of hand tools. By geographic area, North America generated the largest share (50%) of 2008 sales, followed by Europe (31%), Asia/Australia (14%) and other regions (5%).

Employees of Danaher receive benefits including medical, dental, vision, disability, AD&D and life insurance, as well as flexible spending plans.

FINANCIALS: Sales and profits are in thousands of dollars—add 000 to get the full amount. 2008 Note: Financial information for 2008 was not available for all companies at press time.

2008 Sales: $12,697,456	2008 Profits: $1,317,631	U.S. Stock Ticker: DHR
2007 Sales: $11,025,917	2007 Profits: $1,369,904	Int'l Ticker: Int'l Exchange:
2006 Sales: $9,466,056	2006 Profits: $1,122,029	Employees: 50,300
2005 Sales: $7,984,704	2005 Profits: $897,800	Fiscal Year Ends: 12/31
2004 Sales: $6,889,301	2004 Profits: $746,000	Parent Company:

SALARIES/BENEFITS:

Pension Plan:	ESOP Stock Plan:	Profit Sharing:	Top Exec. Salary: $1,100,000	Bonus: $3,267,250
Savings Plan: Y	Stock Purch. Plan:		Second Exec. Salary: $675,000	Bonus: $725,000

OTHER THOUGHTS:

Apparent Women Officers or Directors: 1
Hot Spot for Advancement for Women/Minorities:

LOCATIONS: ("Y" = Yes)

West:	Southwest:	Midwest:	Southeast:	Northeast:	International:
Y	Y	Y	Y	Y	Y

DARDEN RESTAURANTS INC

www.dardenrestaurants.com

Industry Group Code: 722110 Ranks within this company's industry group: Sales: 3 Profits: 3

Management:		Sales/Marketing:		Liberal Arts:		Information Systems:		Professionals:		Tech./Scientific:	
Management Trainees:	Y	Marketing Pros.:	Y	Gen. Writing/Editing:	Y	Info. Management:	Y	Finance/Acct.:	Y	Engineers, Electrical:	
Experienced Mngmt.:	Y	Retail Sales:		Technical Writing:		Software Dev.:	Y	Law:	Y	Engineers, Other:	
International Business:	Y	Commercial/Industrial:		Graphic Arts/Photog.:	Y	Hardware Dev.:		HR/Other:	Y	Health/Lab:	
MBA Grads:	Y	Sales Trainees:		Music:		Consulting/Other:		Training:	Y	Scientists/Research:	
		Advertising Pros.:	Y	Broadcasting:				Health Care:		Petroleum/Chemicals:	
				Other:	Y			Consulting:		Math/Other:	

TYPES OF BUSINESS:

Restaurants-Casual Dining

BRANDS/DIVISIONS/AFFILIATES:

Red Lobster
Olive Garden
Capital Grille (The)
Bahama Breeze
LongHorn Steakhouse
Seasons 52
Hemenway's Seafood Grille & Oyster Bar
Old Grist Mill Tavern (The)

CONTACTS: Note: Officers with more than one job title may be intentionally listed here more than once.

Clarence Otis, Jr., CEO
Andrew H. Madsen, COO
Andrew H. Madsen, Pres.
Brad Richmond, CFO/Sr. VP
Ronald Bojalad, Sr. VP-Group Human Resources
Paula J. Shives, General Counsel/Sr. VP/Sec.
J.J. Buettgen, Sr. VP-Bus. Dev.
Valerie K. Collins, Corp. Controller/Sr. VP
David T. Pickens, Sr. VP/Pres., Olive Garden
Dave George, Pres., LongHorn Steakhouse
Kim A. Lopdrup, Sr. VP/Pres., Red Lobster
Gene Lee, Pres., Specialty Restaurants Group
Clarence Otis, Jr., Chmn.
Barry B. Moullet, Sr. VP-Supply Chain & Dev.

Phone: 407-245-4000	Fax:
Toll-Free:	
Address: 5900 Lake Ellenor Dr., Orlando, FL 32809 US	

GROWTH PLANS/SPECIAL FEATURES:

Darden Restaurants, Inc. is one of the largest publicly held casual dining companies in the U.S. It owns and operates over 1,770 restaurants throughout the U.S. and Canada. Darden operates six restaurant chains: Red Lobster, Olive Garden, LongHorn Steakhouse, The Capital Grille, Bahama Breeze and Seasons 52. Red Lobster, with 690 restaurants, is a seafood-specialty restaurant in the U.S. and Canada. Its menu features fresh fish, shrimp, crab, lobster, scallops and other seafood, as well as non-seafood entrees, appetizers and desserts. Olive Garden, with 691 restaurants, is a casual dining Italian restaurant in the U.S. and Canada. Its menu includes a variety of Italian foods, including antipasti; soups, salad and garlic breadsticks; baked pastas; sauteed chicken, seafood and vegetables; grilled meats; and a variety of desserts. It also offers an expanded wine list that includes a broad selection of imported Italian wines, as well as coffee imported from Italy for its espresso and cappuccino. LongHorn Steakhouse restaurants, with 321 locations, are full service establishments serving both lunch and dinner in establishments decorated to evoke the American West. The Capital Grille chain dry-ages its steaks on the premises and flies in fresh seafood daily to its 37 locations, as well as featuring a 350-selection wine list. Bahama Breeze, which has 24 restaurants, is a Caribbean-themed restaurant that offers guests an island dining experience with a menu featuring Caribbean-style beef, chicken and seafood. Seasons 52, with eight restaurants, is a fresh grill and wine bar with seasonally inspired menus, offering nutritionally balanced meals lower in calories than comparable restaurant meals. Darden also operates two standalone restaurants: Hemenway's Seafood Grille & Oyster Bar and The Old Grist Mill Tavern. Additionally, the firm operates five franchised LongHorn Steakhouse restaurants in Puerto Rico and 25 franchised Red Lobster restaurants in Japan through unaffiliated companies.

FINANCIALS: Sales and profits are in thousands of dollars—add 000 to get the full amount. 2008 Note: Financial information for 2008 was not available for all companies at press time.

2008 Sales: $6,626,500	2008 Profits: $377,200	**U.S. Stock Ticker: DRI**	
2007 Sales: $5,567,100	2007 Profits: $201,400	**Int'l Ticker:** Int'l Exchange:	
2006 Sales: $5,353,600	2006 Profits: $338,194	Employees: 178,692	
2005 Sales: $4,977,600	2005 Profits: $290,606	Fiscal Year Ends: 5/31	
2004 Sales: $5,003,355	2004 Profits: $231,462	Parent Company:	

SALARIES/BENEFITS:

Pension Plan:	ESOP Stock Plan:	Profit Sharing:	Top Exec. Salary: $992,146	Bonus: $498,100
Savings Plan:	Stock Purch. Plan:		Second Exec. Salary: $731,362	Bonus: $742,800

OTHER THOUGHTS:

Apparent Women Officers or Directors: 4
Hot Spot for Advancement for Women/Minorities: Y

LOCATIONS: ("Y" = Yes)

West:	Southwest:	Midwest:	Southeast:	Northeast:	International:
Y	Y	Y	Y	Y	Y

Note: Financial information, benefits and other data can change quickly and may vary from those stated here.

DAVITA INC

www.davita.com

Industry Group Code: 6214 Ranks within this company's industry group: Sales: 1 Profits: 1

Management:		Sales/Marketing:		Liberal Arts:		Information Systems:		Professionals:		Tech./Scientific:	
Management Trainees:	Y	Marketing Pros.:	Y	Gen. Writing/Editing:	Y	Info. Management:	Y	Finance/Acct.:	Y	Engineers, Electrical:	
Experienced Mngmt.:	Y	Retail Sales:		Technical Writing:	Y	Software Dev.:	Y	Law:	Y	Engineers, Other:	
International Business:		Commercial/Industrial:	Y	Graphic Arts/Photog.:		Hardware Dev.:		HR/Other:	Y	Health/Lab:	Y
MBA Grads:	Y	Sales Trainees:		Music:		Consulting/Other:		Training:	Y	Scientists/Research:	Y
		Advertising Pros.:		Broadcasting:				Health Care:	Y	Petroleum/Chemicals:	
				Other:				Consulting:		Math/Other:	

TYPES OF BUSINESS:

Renal Care Services
Clinical Research

BRANDS/DIVISIONS/AFFILIATES:

DaVita Rx
DaVita Clinical Research

CONTACTS: *Note: Officers with more than one job title may be intentionally listed here more than once.*

Kent J. Thiry, CEO
Dennis Kogod, COO
Richard K. Whitney, CFO
Laura Mildenberger, Chief People Officer
LeAnne Zumwalt, VP-Investor Rel.
Thomas O. Usilton, Sr. VP
Allen R. Nissenson, Chief Medical Officer
Javier Rodriguez, Sr. VP
Kent J. Thiry, Chmn.

Phone: 310-536-2400	Fax:
Toll-Free: 800-244-0680	
Address: 601 Hawaii St., El Segundo, CA 90245 US	

GROWTH PLANS/SPECIAL FEATURES:

DaVita, Inc. is a provider of dialysis services in the U.S. for patients suffering from chronic kidney failure, also known as end stage renal disease, or ESRD. The company operates or provides administrative services to roughly 1,500 outpatient dialysis centers located in 43 states and Washington, D.C., serving approximately 114,000 patients. The firm also provides acute inpatient dialysis services in approximately 700 hospitals and related laboratory services. The firm's dialysis services include hemodialysis, peritoneal dialysis and pre-ESRD education. In addition, the company provides certain patients the option of home-based hemodialysis. The firm owns two licensed clinical laboratories, located in Florida, which specialize in ERSD patient testing. These specialized laboratories provide routine laboratory tests covered by the Medicare composite payment rate for dialysis and other physician-prescribed laboratory tests for ESRD patients. Dialysis and related lab services business accounts for approximately 96% of the company's revenue. DaVita Rx is a wholly-owned pharmacy that provides oral medications to DaVita's patients with chronic kidney disease and ERSD. DaVita Clinical Research conducts research trials with dialysis patients and provides administrative support for research conducted by DaVita-affiliated nephrology practices. Other ancillary services provided by DaVita include infusion therapy services, pharmacy services, vascular access services, physician services, disease management services and full-service special need plans, as well as clinical research programs. In November 2008, the firm launched a resource web site for physicians who treat chronic kidney disease. In May 2009, DaVita announced its intention to relocate its corporate headquarters to Denver, Colorado.

The company provides its employees medical, dental and vision insurance; short- and long-term disability insurance; flexible spending accounts; life insurance; a 401(k) plan; a stock purchase program; an employee assistance program; and tuition reimbursement.

FINANCIALS: Sales and profits are in thousands of dollars—add 000 to get the full amount. 2008 Note: Financial information for 2008 was not available for all companies at press time.

2008 Sales: $5,660,173	2008 Profits: $374,160	**U.S. Stock Ticker: DVA**
2007 Sales: $5,264,151	2007 Profits: $381,778	**Int'l Ticker:** Int'l Exchange:
2006 Sales: $4,880,662	2006 Profits: $289,691	Employees: 32,500
2005 Sales: $2,973,918	2005 Profits: $228,643	Fiscal Year Ends: 12/31
2004 Sales: $2,177,330	2004 Profits: $222,254	Parent Company:

SALARIES/BENEFITS:

Pension Plan:	ESOP Stock Plan:	Profit Sharing:	Top Exec. Salary: $1,023,076	Bonus: $2,000,000
Savings Plan: Y	Stock Purch. Plan: Y		Second Exec. Salary: $773,077	Bonus: $150,000

OTHER THOUGHTS:

Apparent Women Officers or Directors: 3
Hot Spot for Advancement for Women/Minorities: Y

LOCATIONS: ("Y" = Yes)

West:	Southwest:	Midwest:	Southeast:	Northeast:	International:
Y	Y	Y	Y	Y	

Note: Financial information, benefits and other data can change quickly and may vary from those stated here.

DEAN FOODS CO

www.deanfoods.com

Industry Group Code: 3115 Ranks within this company's industry group: Sales: 1 Profits: 1

Management:		Sales/Marketing:		Liberal Arts:		Information Systems:		Professionals:		Tech./Scientific:	
Management Trainees:	Y	Marketing Pros.:	Y	Gen. Writing/Editing:	Y	Info. Management:	Y	Finance/Acct.:	Y	Engineers, Electrical:	
Experienced Mngmt.:	Y	Retail Sales:		Technical Writing:		Software Dev.:		Law:	Y	Engineers, Other:	Y
International Business:	Y	Commercial/Industrial:	Y	Graphic Arts/Photog.:	Y	Hardware Dev.:		HR/Other:	Y	Health/Lab:	
MBA Grads:	Y	Sales Trainees:	Y	Music:		Consulting/Other:		Training:	Y	Scientists/Research:	
		Advertising Pros.:	Y	Broadcasting:				Health Care:		Petroleum/Chemicals:	
				Other:				Consulting:		Math/Other:	

TYPES OF BUSINESS:

Dairy Products, Manufacturing
Milk Processing & Distribution
Organic Dairy Products
Soy-Based Products
Juices
Coffee Creamers
Powdered Ingredients

BRANDS/DIVISIONS/AFFILIATES:

WhiteWave Foods Company
Creamland
Hershey's
LAND O'LAKES
Silk
Horizon Organic
International Delight
Rachel's Organic

CONTACTS: Note: Officers with more than one job title may be intentionally listed here more than once.

Gregg L. Engles, CEO
Jack F. Callahan, Jr., CFO/Exec. VP
Paul T. Moskowitz, Exec. VP-Human Resources
Kelly Duffin-Maxwell, Exec. VP-R&D
Steven J. Kemps, General Counsel/Exec. VP/Corp. Sec
Gregory A. McKelvey, Chief Strategy & Transformation Officer/Exec. VP
Deborah B. Carosella, Sr. VP-Innovation
Joseph E. Scalzo, CEO/Pres., WhiteWave Foods
Rick Fehr, Sr. VP-Business Optimization
Gregg L. Engles, Chmn.
Gregg A. Tanner, Chief Supply Chain Officer/Exec. VP

Phone: 214-303-3400	Fax: 214-303-2850
Toll-Free: 800-431-9214	
Address: 2515 McKinney Ave. LB 30, Ste. 1200, Dallas, TX 75201 US	

GROWTH PLANS/SPECIAL FEATURES:

Dean Foods Co. is a leading food and beverage company. The firm operates through two business segments, the dairy group and WhiteWave Foods. Generating approximately 88% of the company's net sales, Dean's dairy group manufactures, markets and distributes a variety of branded and private-label dairy-case products to retailers, distributors, foodservice outlets, schools and government entities across the U.S., with 100 manufacturing facilities in 36 states. Products sold by the dairy group include fresh milk, ice cream, flavored milks, buttermilk, half-and-half, whipping cream, coffee creamers, yogurt, cottage cheese, sour cream and dairy based dips, under its more than 50 proprietary and licensed brands, including Berkeley Farms, Brown Cow, Chug, Country Charm, Creamland, Dairy Fresh, Dean's, Hershey's, LAND O'LAKES, Meadow Brook, Mountain High, Nature's Pride, Oak Farms, Shenandoah's Pride and Swiss Pride. Dean purchases its raw milk primarily from farmers' cooperatives. Generating approximately 12% of Dean's net sales, subsidiary White Wave Foods Company develops, manufactures, markets and sells a variety of nationally branded soy, dairy and dairy-related products, such as Silk soymilk and cultured soy products; Horizon Organic dairy products; International Delight coffee creamers; Rachel's Organic dairy products; The Organic Cow organic dairy products; White Wave and Tofu Town branded tofu; and Hershey's milks and milkshakes. Roughly 30% of White Wave's products are manufactured by third-party manufacturers under processing agreements. It purchases organic raw milk from a network of over 400 dairy farmers across the U.S., as well as producing certain of its own organic raw milk in at two organic farms that it owns and one organic farm that it leases and manages. WhiteWave Foods sells its products to a variety of customers, including grocery stores, club stores, natural foods stores, mass merchandisers, convenience stores and foodservice outlets. The segment's largest customer is Wal-Mart and its subsidiary, Sam's Club.

FINANCIALS: Sales and profits are in thousands of dollars—add 000 to get the full amount. 2008 Note: Financial information for 2008 was not available for all companies at press time.

2008 Sales: $12,454,613	2008 Profits: $183,770	U.S. Stock Ticker: DF
2007 Sales: $11,821,903	2007 Profits: $131,353	Int'l Ticker: Int'l Exchange:
2006 Sales: $10,098,555	2006 Profits: $225,414	Employees: 25,820
2005 Sales: $10,174,718	2005 Profits: $308,654	Fiscal Year Ends: 12/31
2004 Sales: $10,822,300	2004 Profits: $324,100	Parent Company:

SALARIES/BENEFITS:

Pension Plan:	ESOP Stock Plan:	Profit Sharing:	Top Exec. Salary: $1,300,000	Bonus: $2,350,900
Savings Plan: Y	Stock Purch. Plan:		Second Exec. Salary: $700,000	Bonus: $784,900

OTHER THOUGHTS:

Apparent Women Officers or Directors: 3
Hot Spot for Advancement for Women/Minorities: Y

LOCATIONS: ("Y" = Yes)

West:	Southwest:	Midwest:	Southeast:	Northeast:	International:
Y	Y	Y	Y	Y	Y

Note: Financial information, benefits and other data can change quickly and may vary from those stated here.

DEERE & CO

www.deere.com

Industry Group Code: 333 **Ranks within this company's industry group:** Sales: 2　Profits: 2

Management:		Sales/Marketing:		Liberal Arts:		Information Systems:		Professionals:		Tech./Scientific:	
Management Trainees:	Y	Marketing Pros.:	Y	Gen. Writing/Editing:	Y	Info. Management:	Y	Finance/Acct.:	Y	Engineers, Electrical:	Y
Experienced Mngmt.:	Y	Retail Sales:		Technical Writing:	Y	Software Dev.:	Y	Law:	Y	Engineers, Other:	Y
International Business:	Y	Commercial/Industrial:	Y	Graphic Arts/Photog.:	Y	Hardware Dev.:	Y	HR/Other:	Y	Health/Lab:	
MBA Grads:	Y	Sales Trainees:		Music:		Consulting/Other:		Training:	Y	Scientists/Research:	
		Advertising Pros.:	Y	Broadcasting:				Health Care:		Petroleum/Chemicals:	
				Other:				Consulting:		Math/Other:	

TYPES OF BUSINESS:

Construction & Agricultural Equipment
Commercial & Consumer Equipment
Forestry Equipment
Financing

BRANDS/DIVISIONS/AFFILIATES:

John Deere

CONTACTS: *Note: Officers with more than one job title may be intentionally listed here more than once.*

Robert W. Lane, CEO
Samuel R. Allen, COO
Samuel R. Allen, Pres.
James M. Field, CFO/Sr. VP
Metroe B. Hornbuckle, VP-Human Resources
James R. Jabanoski, VP-IT
Klaus G. Hoehn, VP-Advanced Tech.
Klaus G. Hoehn, VP-Eng.
James R. Jenkins, General Counsel/Sr. VP
Ganesh Jayaram, VP-Corp. Bus. Dev.
H.J. Markley, VP-Corp. Comm.
Marie Z. Ziegler, VP-Investor Rel.
James A. Davlin, Treas./VP
Kenneth C. Huhn, VP-Labor Rel.
Michael J. Mack, Jr., Pres., Worldwide Construction & Forestry Equipment
Dennis R. Schwartz, VP-Pension Fund & Investments
Linda E. Newborn, Chief Compliance Officer/VP
Robert W. Lane, Chmn.
Markwart von Pentz, Pres., Agriculture-Europe, Africa & South America
H.J. Markley, Exec. VP-Global Supply Mgmt. & Logistics

Phone: 309-765-8000	Fax: 309-765-5671
Toll-Free:	
Address: 1 John Deere Pl., Moline, IL 61265-8098 US	

GROWTH PLANS/SPECIAL FEATURES:

Deere & Co., better known by its John Deere brand name, conducts business in three divisions: agricultural and turf equipment; construction and forestry; and credit. The agricultural and turf segment manufactures and distributes farm, lawn and garden equipment including tractors; combines and harvesters; tillage, seeding and soil preparation machinery; sprayers; hay and forage equipment; material handling equipment; integrated agricultural management systems technology; mowers; golf course equipment; utility vehicles; landscape and irrigation equipment; and other outdoor power products. In May 2009, the segment consolidated two previously separate divisions: Agricultural and Consumer/Commercial. The construction and forestry offers equipment and service parts used in construction, earthmoving, material handling and timber harvesting, including backhoe loaders; crawler dozers and loaders; four-wheel-drive loaders; excavators; and more. The credit segment provides financing services for products offered by the agricultural and turf and construction/forestry segments. Sales are generally conducted through the largely independently-owned 2,752 dealer locations, 1,567 of which sell agricultural equipment. The firm has locations throughout the world in over 100 different countries. Deere & Co. also offers the John Deere University, an online training resource that provides lessons and courses on basic and advanced technology. The company owns and operates 22 factories, 13 of which are used to produce agricultural equipment. In August 2008, Deere & Co. announced it would be investing $80 million into manufacturing and parts distribution capabilities in South America. In September 2008, the company revealed plans to build a technology and innovation center in Germany in order to engineer and produce better region-specific products.

Deere offers its employees medical, prescription, vision, and dental coverage; flexible spending accounts; a stock purchase plan; salary continuance; long-term disability; life insurance; a pension plan; a 401(k) plan; and tuition reimbursement.

FINANCIALS: Sales and profits are in thousands of dollars—add 000 to get the full amount. 2008 Note: Financial information for 2008 was not available for all companies at press time.

2008 Sales: $28,438,000	2008 Profits: $2,053,000	**U.S. Stock Ticker: DE**
2007 Sales: $24,082,200	2007 Profits: $1,821,700	**Int'l Ticker:**　Int'l Exchange:
2006 Sales: $22,147,800	2006 Profits: $1,693,800	Employees: 56,700
2005 Sales: $21,190,800	2005 Profits: $1,446,800	Fiscal Year Ends: 10/31
2004 Sales: $19,204,200	2004 Profits: $1,406,100	Parent Company:

SALARIES/BENEFITS:

Pension Plan: Y	ESOP Stock Plan:	Profit Sharing:	Top Exec. Salary: $1,435,545	Bonus: $6,930,421
Savings Plan: Y	Stock Purch. Plan: Y		Second Exec. Salary: $590,115	Bonus: $2,008,179

OTHER THOUGHTS:

Apparent Women Officers or Directors: 4
Hot Spot for Advancement for Women/Minorities: Y

LOCATIONS: ("Y" = Yes)

West:	Southwest:	Midwest:	Southeast:	Northeast:	International:
Y	Y	Y	Y	Y	Y

DELOITTE & TOUCHE USA LLP

www.deloitte.com

Industry Group Code: 5412 Ranks within this company's industry group: Sales: 3 Profits:

Management:		Sales/Marketing:		Liberal Arts:		Information Systems:		Professionals:		Tech./Scientific:	
Management Trainees:	Y	Marketing Pros.:	Y	Gen. Writing/Editing:	Y	Info. Management:	Y	Finance/Acct.:	Y	Engineers, Electrical:	
Experienced Mngmt.:	Y	Retail Sales:		Technical Writing:	Y	Software Dev.:	Y	Law:	Y	Engineers, Other:	
International Business:	Y	Commercial/Industrial:	Y	Graphic Arts/Photog.:	Y	Hardware Dev.:		HR/Other:	Y	Health/Lab:	
MBA Grads:	Y	Sales Trainees:		Music:		Consulting/Other:	Y	Training:	Y	Scientists/Research:	
		Advertising Pros.:	Y	Broadcasting:				Health Care:		Petroleum/Chemicals:	
				Other:	Y			Consulting:	Y	Math/Other:	

TYPES OF BUSINESS:

Accounting Services
Management Consulting
Risk Management Services
Financial Advisory Services
Outsourcing Services
Legal & Compliance Advisory Services

BRANDS/DIVISIONS/AFFILIATES:

Deloitte Tax LLP
Deloitte & Touche LLP
Deloitte Consulting LLP
Deloitte Financial Advisory Services LLP
Deloitte Foundation
Solbourne Computer Inc
Recombinant Capital Inc
Deloitte & Touche Tohmatsu

CONTACTS: Note: Officers with more than one job title may be intentionally listed here more than once.

Barry Salzberg, CEO
Jeff Rohr, CFO
Sharon Allen, Chmn.

Phone: 212-489-1600	Fax: 212-489-1687
Toll-Free:	
Address: 1633 Broadway, New York, NY 10019-6754 US	

GROWTH PLANS/SPECIAL FEATURES:

Deloitte & Touche USA LLP (D&T), the U.S. division of global accounting firm Deloitte Touche Tohmatsu, offers a variety of financial and consulting services. The firm operates through several subsidiaries, including Deloitte & Touche LLP; Deloitte Consulting LLP; Deloitte Financial Advisory Services LLP; and Deloitte Tax LLP. The largest portion of the firm's revenue, approximately 40% in 2008, comes from audit and enterprise risk services. Deloitte also offers consulting, tax and other financial advisory services. Additionally, the firm has expertise in offering complementary services such as legal and compliance advisory services involving litigation, ethics, management and disclosure issues. Industries served by D&T include aerospace and defense; automotive; banking and securities; consumer products; healthcare; insurance; life sciences; media and entertainment; oil and gas; power and utilities; private equity; industrial products; real estate; retail; technology; telecom; tourism, hospitality and leisure; and federal, state and local government. The firm also funds the Deloitte Foundation, created 80 years ago and dedicated to supporting accounting, business and related fields of study in the U.S. The foundation funds the Deloitte Doctoral Fellowship Program and Trueblood Seminars for Professors, among other higher education initiatives. Deloitte also conducts and publishes research concerning consumer spending patterns and economic growth. The company maintains offices in more than 80 U.S. cities. During 2008, Deloitte acquired Solbourne Computer, Inc. a systems integration firm, as well as Recombinant Capital, Inc., a life sciences subscription database and advisory services firm.

Employees of the firm are offered child care and adoption assistance; flexible work arrangements; medical plans; and a tuition assistance program. In 2009, for the tenth year, Deloitte & Touche was named to Fortune Magazine's list of 100 Best Companies to Work For; in 2008, the firm was named to Working Mother magazine's list of Best Companies for Multicultural Women.

FINANCIALS: Sales and profits are in thousands of dollars—add 000 to get the full amount. 2008 Note: Financial information for 2008 was not available for all companies at press time.

2008 Sales: $10,980,000	2008 Profits: $	U.S. Stock Ticker: Subsidiary	
2007 Sales: $9,850,000	2007 Profits: $	Int'l Ticker:	Int'l Exchange:
2006 Sales: $8,769,000	2006 Profits: $	Employees: 41,500	
2005 Sales: $7,814,000	2005 Profits: $	Fiscal Year Ends: 5/31	
2004 Sales: $6,876,000	2004 Profits: $	Parent Company: DELOITTE TOUCHE TOHMATSU	

SALARIES/BENEFITS:

Pension Plan: Y	ESOP Stock Plan:	Profit Sharing:	Top Exec. Salary: $	Bonus: $
Savings Plan: Y	Stock Purch. Plan:		Second Exec. Salary: $	Bonus: $

OTHER THOUGHTS:

Apparent Women Officers or Directors: 1
Hot Spot for Advancement for Women/Minorities:

LOCATIONS: ("Y" = Yes)

West:	Southwest:	Midwest:	Southeast:	Northeast:	International:
Y	Y	Y	Y	Y	Y

DELOITTE CONSULTING LLP

www.deloitte.com

Industry Group Code: 54161 **Ranks within this company's industry group:** Sales: 1   Profits:

Management:		Sales/Marketing:		Liberal Arts:		Information Systems:		Professionals:		Tech./Scientific:	
Management Trainees:	Y	Marketing Pros.:		Gen. Writing/Editing:	Y	Info. Management:	Y	Finance/Acct.:	Y	Engineers, Electrical:	
Experienced Mngmt.:	Y	Retail Sales:		Technical Writing:	Y	Software Dev.:	Y	Law:	Y	Engineers, Other:	
International Business:	Y	Commercial/Industrial:	Y	Graphic Arts/Photog.:	Y	Hardware Dev.:		HR/Other:	Y	Health/Lab:	
MBA Grads:	Y	Sales Trainees:		Music:		Consulting/Other:	Y	Training:	Y	Scientists/Research:	
		Advertising Pros.:	Y	Broadcasting:				Health Care:		Petroleum/Chemicals:	
				Other:	Y			Consulting:	Y	Math/Other:	Y

TYPES OF BUSINESS:

Management Consulting
Technology Integration Consulting
Human Resources Consulting
Business Strategy Consulting
Outsourcing Services
Strategic Consulting
Software

BRANDS/DIVISIONS/AFFILIATES:

Deloitte Touche Tohmatsu
J.D. Edwards
Oracle Corp
PeopleSoft
SAP AG
Xcelicor, Inc.
Oracle Human Capital Management

CONTACTS: *Note: Officers with more than one job title may be intentionally listed here more than once.*

Ainar D. Aijala Jr., Global Managing Partner
John Kocjan, National Managing Dir.-Financial Svcs.
Bruce Westbrook, National Managing Dir.-Consumer Bus.
Douglas J. Lattner, Chmn.

Phone: 212-618-4000	Fax: 212-618-4500
Toll-Free:	
Address: 25 Broadway, New York, NY 10004 US	

GROWTH PLANS/SPECIAL FEATURES:

Deloitte Consulting LLC, the largest subsidiary of Deloitte Touche Tohmatsu, offers a range of expert consulting services from offices in 40 countries worldwide. It operates five main service categories: enterprise applications; human capital; outsourcing; strategy and operations; and technology integration. Enterprise applications are software tools that help companies coordinate information, talk with business partners and utilize customer data better. The company maintains partnerships with business software developers (including J.D. Edwards, Oracle, PeopleSoft and SAP) that give Deloitte Consulting's consultants the information necessary to help customers implement technological and organizational changes. The firm's human capital expertise provides ways to measure and manage employee productivity, change organizational structure, improve human resource functions and manage isolated groups of employees. Deloitte Consulting's outsourcing services help companies make outsourcing decisions in IT and noncore business functions. The company also analyzes and revises its clients' customer strategies, merger and acquisition strategies, supply chain operations, investment priorities and IT strategies. Lastly, Deloitte Consulting provides technology integration. Since businesses are beginning to integrate desktop and laptop PCs, the firm's consultants help its clients to figure out the how to use their computerized assets.

Deloitte Consulting offers its employees tuition assistance; flexible work arrangements; an employee assistance program; adoption assistance and reimbursement; emergency backup daycare; a lactation support program; flexible spending accounts; medical, dental, prescription and vision plans; and a professional development program.

FINANCIALS: Sales and profits are in thousands of dollars—add 000 to get the full amount. 2008 Note: Financial information for 2008 was not available for all companies at press time.

2008 Sales: $6,300,000	2008 Profits: $	**U.S. Stock Ticker:** Subsidiary
2007 Sales: $5,200,000	2007 Profits: $	**Int'l Ticker:** Int'l Exchange:
2006 Sales: $4,500,000	2006 Profits: $	Employees: 27,000
2005 Sales: $4,300,000	2005 Profits: $	Fiscal Year Ends: 5/31
2004 Sales: $3,900,000	2004 Profits: $	Parent Company: DELOITTE TOUCHE TOHMATSU

SALARIES/BENEFITS:

Pension Plan: Y	ESOP Stock Plan:	Profit Sharing:	Top Exec. Salary: $	Bonus: $
Savings Plan: Y	Stock Purch. Plan:		Second Exec. Salary: $	Bonus: $

OTHER THOUGHTS:

Apparent Women Officers or Directors:
Hot Spot for Advancement for Women/Minorities:

LOCATIONS: ("Y" = Yes)

West:	Southwest:	Midwest:	Southeast:	Northeast:	International:
Y	Y	Y	Y	Y	Y

DENNY'S CORPORATION

www.dennys.com

Industry Group Code: 722110 **Ranks within this company's industry group:** Sales: 12   Profits: 10

Management:		Sales/Marketing:		Liberal Arts:		Information Systems:		Professionals:		Tech./Scientific:	
Management Trainees:	Y	Marketing Pros.:	Y	Gen. Writing/Editing:	Y	Info. Management:	Y	Finance/Acct.:	Y	Engineers, Electrical:	
Experienced Mngmt.:	Y	Retail Sales:		Technical Writing:		Software Dev.:	Y	Law:	Y	Engineers, Other:	
International Business:	Y	Commercial/Industrial:		Graphic Arts/Photog.:	Y	Hardware Dev.:		HR/Other:	Y	Health/Lab:	
MBA Grads:	Y	Sales Trainees:		Music:		Consulting/Other:		Training:	Y	Scientists/Research:	
		Advertising Pros.:	Y	Broadcasting:				Health Care:		Petroleum/Chemicals:	
				Other:	Y			Consulting:		Math/Other:	

TYPES OF BUSINESS:
Restaurants-Casual Dining

BRANDS/DIVISIONS/AFFILIATES:
Denny's, Inc.
Denny's Holdings, Inc.
Meat Lover's Breakfast
Original Grand Slam
Meadowbrook Meat Company

CONTACTS: *Note: Officers with more than one job title may be intentionally listed here more than once.*
Nelson J. Marchioli, CEO
Janis S. Emplit, COO/Exec. VP
Nelson J. Marchioli, Pres.
F. Mark Wolfinger, CFO/Exec. VP
Mark E. Chmiel, Chief Mktg. & Innovation Officer/Exec. VP
Jill A. Van Pelt, VP-Human Resources
F. Mark Wolfinger, Chief Admin. Officer
Timothy E. Flemming, Chief Legal Officer/General Counsel/VP
Susan L. Mirdamadi, VP-Oper.
Stephen C. Dunn, VP-Dev.
S. Alex Lewis, VP-Investor Rel./Treas.
Jay C. Gilmore, Chief Acct. Officer/VP/Controller
John W. Dillon, VP-Mktg.
William H. Ruby, VP-Sales
Enrique Mayor-Mora, VP-Planning & Analysis
Ross B. Nell, VP-Tax
Debra Smithart-Oglesby, Chmn.
R. Gregory Linford, VP-Procurement & Dist.

Phone: 864-597-8000	Fax: 864-597-8780
Toll-Free: 800-733-6697	
Address: 203 E. Main St., Spartanburg, SC 29319 US	

GROWTH PLANS/SPECIAL FEATURES:

Denny's Corporation, through its wholly-owned subsidiaries Denny's Holdings, Inc. and Denny's, Inc., owns and operates the Denny's restaurant brand, one of America's largest family-style restaurant chains. The company consists of approximately 1,546 restaurants, 394 of which are company-owned and operated and 1,152 of which are franchised/licensed restaurants. Denny's restaurants operate in 49 states, Washington, D.C., two U.S. territories and five foreign countries. California makes up 26% of total restaurants; Florida, 10%; and Texas, 10%. The company offers traditional American-style food, and is known for serving breakfast around the clock, including its Meat Lover's Breakfast and Original Grand Slam. Denny's restaurants are open 24-hours-a-day, seven-days-a-week. Customers over age 55 are offered a special menu with lower prices and children under age 10 are also offered lower priced selections. Denny's employs both unit managers and regional/area managers to ensure brand consistency in all of its company restaurants. A network of regional franchise operations managers provides the same function for franchised restaurants. Denny's franchise system requires franchisees to meet minimum liquidity and net worth requirements and to have appropriate operational experience. The initial fee for a single 20-year Denny's franchise agreement is $40,000 and the royalty payment is 4% of gross sales. Franchisees are also required to contribute up to 4% of gross sales for advertising. The company uses a centralized purchasing program that is designed to ensure uniform product quality as well as to minimize food, beverage and supply costs. The majority of Denny's products are purchased and distributed through the Meadowbrook Meat Company under a long-term distribution contract.

Employees are offered medical, dental and vision insurance; employee, spousal and children's life insurance plan; personal accident insurance; short-and long-term disability coverage; a 401(k) plan; an employee assistance plan; and tuition reimbursement.

FINANCIALS: Sales and profits are in thousands of dollars—add 000 to get the full amount. 2008 Note: Financial information for 2008 was not available for all companies at press time.

2008 Sales: $760,271	2008 Profits: $14,662	**U.S. Stock Ticker:** DENN	
2007 Sales: $939,368	2007 Profits: $34,713	**Int'l Ticker:** Int'l Exchange:	
2006 Sales: $994,044	2006 Profits: $30,338	Employees: 15,000	
2005 Sales: $978,725	2005 Profits: $-7,328	Fiscal Year Ends: 12/31	
2004 Sales: $960,006	2004 Profits: $-37,675	Parent Company:	

SALARIES/BENEFITS:

Pension Plan:	ESOP Stock Plan:	Profit Sharing:	Top Exec. Salary: $810,000	Bonus: $468,000
Savings Plan: Y	Stock Purch. Plan:		Second Exec. Salary: $505,462	Bonus: $292,800

OTHER THOUGHTS:
Apparent Women Officers or Directors: 6
Hot Spot for Advancement for Women/Minorities: Y

LOCATIONS: ("Y" = Yes)

West:	Southwest:	Midwest:	Southeast:	Northeast:	International:
Y	Y	Y	Y	Y	Y

Note: Financial information, benefits and other data can change quickly and may vary from those stated here.

DEVON ENERGY CORPORATION

www.devonenergy.com

Industry Group Code: 211111 Ranks within this company's industry group: Sales: 8 Profits: 11

Management:		Sales/Marketing:		Liberal Arts:		Information Systems:		Professionals:		Tech./Scientific:	
Management Trainees:	Y	Marketing Pros.:	Y	Gen. Writing/Editing:	Y	Info. Management:	Y	Finance/Acct.:	Y	Engineers, Electrical:	Y
Experienced Mngmt.:	Y	Retail Sales:		Technical Writing:	Y	Software Dev.:	Y	Law:	Y	Engineers, Other:	Y
International Business:	Y	Commercial/Industrial:		Graphic Arts/Photog.:		Hardware Dev.:		HR/Other:	Y	Health/Lab:	
MBA Grads:	Y	Sales Trainees:		Music:		Consulting/Other:		Training:	Y	Scientists/Research:	
		Advertising Pros.:		Broadcasting:				Health Care:		Petroleum/Chemicals:	Y
				Other:				Consulting:		Math/Other:	

TYPES OF BUSINESS:

Oil & Gas Exploration & Production
Pipelines
Gas Storage & Processing

BRANDS/DIVISIONS/AFFILIATES:

Dana Petroleum plc
Afren plc
Oranje-Nassau Energie B.V.
GEPetrol
Jackfish
Barnett Shale

CONTACTS: *Note: Officers with more than one job title may be intentionally listed here more than once.*

J. Larry Nichols, CEO
John Richels, Pres.
Darryl G. Smette, Sr. VP-Mktg. & Midstream
Frank W. Rudolph, Sr. VP-Human Resources
R. Alan Marcum, Sr. VP-Admin.
Lyndon C. Taylor, General Counsel/Sr. VP
K. Earl Reynolds, VP-Strategic Planning
Chip Minty, Supervisor-External Comm.
Vincent W. White, VP-Investor Rel.
Jeff A. Agosta, VP-Corp. Finance/Treas.
Don D. DeCarlo, VP/Gen. Mgr.-Western Div.
Janice A. Dobbs, Mgr.-Corp. Governance/Corp. Sec.
Bradley A. Foster, VP/Gen. Mgr.-Central Div.
Stephen J. Hadden, Sr. VP-Exploration & Production
J. Larry Nichols, Chmn.
Joseph P. Ash, VP/Gen. Mgr.-Int'l Div.

Phone: 405-235-3611	Fax: 405-552-4550
Toll-Free:	
Address: 20 N. Broadway, Oklahoma City, OK 73102-8260 US	

GROWTH PLANS/SPECIAL FEATURES:

Devon Energy Corporation is an independent energy company engaged primarily in oil and gas exploration, development and production; the transportation of oil, gas and natural gas liquids (NGL); and the processing of natural gas. In addition to its oil and gas operations, the company has marketing and midstream operations primarily in North America. Devon's U.S. onshore operations include the Barnett Shale in north Texas; the Carthage, Groesbeck and Permian Basin areas in Texas; the Washakie area in southern Wyoming; and the Permian Basin in New Mexico. Barnett Shale is Devon's largest property, consisting of 727,000 net acres. The company's U.S. offshore operations include deepwater productions in the Gulf of Mexico, deepwater development and deepwater exploration. Deepwater production properties include Magnolia, Merganser, Nansen and Red Hawk, totaling approximately 46,000 net acres. Devon's Canadian operations include its wholly-owned Jackfish thermal heavy oil project in central Alberta; its Deep Basin properties in Alberta and British Columbia; its Lloydminster properties in Alberta and Saskatchewan; its Peace River Arch properties in Alberta; and its northeast British Columbia properties. The company's international operations include its Azeri-Chirag-Gunashli (ACG) oil field offshore Azerbaijan; its Panyu field in the South China Sea; and its Polvo field offshore Brazil. In March 2008, the company agreed to sell its Cote d'Ivoire oil and gas business to Afren plc. In May 2008, Devon completed the sale of its Gabon operations to Oranje-Nassau Energie B.V., and in June 2008 completed the sale of its Equatorial Guinea oil and gas business to GEPetrol for $2.2 billion.

Devon Energy offers its U.S. employees a flexible spending account; an employee assistance program; a tuition reimbursement program; business travel insurance; and medical, dental and vision insurance.

FINANCIALS: Sales and profits are in thousands of dollars—add 000 to get the full amount. 2008 Note: Financial information for 2008 was not available for all companies at press time.

2008 Sales: $15,211,000	2008 Profits: $-2,148,000	U.S. Stock Ticker: DVN
2007 Sales: $11,362,000	2007 Profits: $3,606,000	Int'l Ticker: Int'l Exchange:
2006 Sales: $9,767,000	2006 Profits: $2,846,000	Employees: 5,500
2005 Sales: $10,741,000	2005 Profits: $2,920,000	Fiscal Year Ends: 12/31
2004 Sales: $9,189,000	2004 Profits: $2,176,000	Parent Company:

SALARIES/BENEFITS:

Pension Plan: Y	ESOP Stock Plan:	Profit Sharing:	Top Exec. Salary: $1,400,000	Bonus: $3,000,600
Savings Plan: Y	Stock Purch. Plan:		Second Exec. Salary: $1,150,000	Bonus: $2,000,600

OTHER THOUGHTS:

Apparent Women Officers or Directors: 3
Hot Spot for Advancement for Women/Minorities: Y

LOCATIONS: ("Y" = Yes)

West:	Southwest:	Midwest:	Southeast:	Northeast:	International:
	Y				Y

DEVRY INC

www.devryinc.com

Industry Group Code: 611410 Ranks within this company's industry group: Sales: 2   Profits: 2

Management:		Sales/Marketing:		Liberal Arts:		Information Systems:		Professionals:		Tech./Scientific:	
Management Trainees:	Y	Marketing Pros.:	Y	Gen. Writing/Editing:	Y	Info. Management:	Y	Finance/Acct.:	Y	Engineers, Electrical:	
Experienced Mngmt.:	Y	Retail Sales:		Technical Writing:		Software Dev.:	Y	Law:	Y	Engineers, Other:	
International Business:	Y	Commercial/Industrial:		Graphic Arts/Photog.:	Y	Hardware Dev.:		HR/Other:	Y	Health/Lab:	
MBA Grads:	Y	Sales Trainees:		Music:		Consulting/Other:		Training:	Y	Scientists/Research:	
		Advertising Pros.:	Y	Broadcasting:				Health Care:		Petroleum/Chemicals:	
				Other:	Y			Consulting:		Math/Other:	

TYPES OF BUSINESS:

Higher Education
Online Education
Medical School
Nursing School
Veterinary School
Accounting School

BRANDS/DIVISIONS/AFFILIATES:

DeVry University
Ross University
Keller Graduate School of Management
Becker Professional Review
Chamberlain College of Nursing
Stalla Review
Fanor
U.S. Education Corporation

CONTACTS: Note: Officers with more than one job title may be intentionally listed here more than once.

Daniel Hamburger, CEO
Daniel Hamburger, Pres.
Richard M. Gunst, CFO/Sr. VP
Donna N. Jennings, Sr. VP-Human Resources
Eric Dirst, CIO/Sr. VP
Gregory S. Davis, General Counsel/Sr. VP/Sec.
John P. Roselli, VP-Corp. Dev. & Planning
Steven P. Riehs, Pres., DeVry University Online
Richard M. Gunst, Treas.
David J. Pauldine, Exec. VP/Pres., DeVry University
Thomas C. Shepherd, Exec. VP/Pres., Ross University
Thomas J. Vucinic, Pres., Becker Professional Review
Sharon Thomas Parrott, Chief Compliance Office/Sr. VP-Gov't & Reg.
Harold T. Shapiro, Chmn.

Phone: 630-571-7700	Fax:
Toll-Free: 800-733-3879	
Address: 1 Tower Ln., Oakbrook Terrace, IL 60181 US	

GROWTH PLANS/SPECIAL FEATURES:

DeVry, Inc. is a publicly held higher-education company in North America, operating DeVry University, Advanced Academics, Ross University, Chamberlain College of Nursing and Becker Professional Review. DeVry University provides career-oriented, business- and technology-based education to students and graduates at 91 locations in the U.S. and Canada, both in traditional classrooms and online. The university offers associate, bachelor's and master's degree programs in technology, healthcare technology, business and management, with the latter offered through the university's Keller Graduate School of Management. Advanced Academics, which provides online secondary education, is part of the DeVry University segment. Ross University operates two schools: the Ross University School of Medicine, which confers the Doctor of Medicine (MD) degree; and The Ross University School of Veterinary Medicine, which confers the Doctor of Veterinary Medicine (DVM) degree. Over 6,500 graduates have received MD degrees and over 2,000 have received DVM degrees since the university's inception. The Chamberlain College of Nursing offers programs in nursing education. The Becker Professional Review is a provider of professional education and training, serving the accounting and finance professions. Becker served more than 50,000 students in 2008 through locations in more than 27 countries. In February 2008, DeVry University announced a sale and leaseback of its 98,000-square-foot Houston campus. DeVry will leaseback approximately 60% of the original space. In September 2008, the company acquired U.S. Education Corporation, the parent company of Apollo College and Western Career College. These two colleges operate 17 campus locations in the U.S. and serve 8,700 healthcare students. Also in 2008, Becker announced an exclusive provider agreement between its Stalla Review and the CFA Society of the U.K. to provide Chartered Financial Analyst review courses. In April 2009, the company acquired a majority stake in Fanor, a provider of private post-secondary education in Brazil.

FINANCIALS: Sales and profits are in thousands of dollars—add 000 to get the full amount. 2008 Note: Financial information for 2008 was not available for all companies at press time.

2008 Sales: $1,091,833	2008 Profits: $125,532	U.S. Stock Ticker: DV
2007 Sales: $933,473	2007 Profits: $76,188	Int'l Ticker: Int'l Exchange:
2006 Sales: $839,513	2006 Profits: $43,053	Employees: 10,200
2005 Sales: $780,662	2005 Profits: $18,011	Fiscal Year Ends: 6/30
2004 Sales: $784,885	2004 Profits: $58,061	Parent Company:

SALARIES/BENEFITS:

Pension Plan:	ESOP Stock Plan:	Profit Sharing:	Top Exec. Salary: $675,322	Bonus: $991,749
Savings Plan:	Stock Purch. Plan:		Second Exec. Salary: $402,231	Bonus: $

OTHER THOUGHTS:

Apparent Women Officers or Directors: 5
Hot Spot for Advancement for Women/Minorities: Y

LOCATIONS: ("Y" = Yes)

West:	Southwest:	Midwest:	Southeast:	Northeast:	International:
Y	Y	Y	Y	Y	Y

Note: Financial information, benefits and other data can change quickly and may vary from those stated here.

DIAMOND OFFSHORE DRILLING INC

www.diamondoffshore.com

Industry Group Code: 213111 Ranks within this company's industry group: Sales: 3 Profits: 2

Management:		Sales/Marketing:		Liberal Arts:		Information Systems:		Professionals:		Tech./Scientific:	
Management Trainees:	Y	Marketing Pros.:	Y	Gen. Writing/Editing:		Info. Management:	Y	Finance/Acct.:	Y	Engineers, Electrical:	Y
Experienced Mngmt.:	Y	Retail Sales:		Technical Writing:	Y	Software Dev.:	Y	Law:	Y	Engineers, Other:	Y
International Business:	Y	Commercial/Industrial:	Y	Graphic Arts/Photog.:		Hardware Dev.:		HR/Other:	Y	Health/Lab:	
MBA Grads:	Y	Sales Trainees:		Music:		Consulting/Other:		Training:	Y	Scientists/Research:	
		Advertising Pros.:		Broadcasting:				Health Care:		Petroleum/Chemicals:	Y
				Other:				Consulting:		Math/Other:	

TYPES OF BUSINESS:

Oil & Gas Drilling
Contract Drilling

BRANDS/DIVISIONS/AFFILIATES:

CONTACTS: *Note: Officers with more than one job title may be intentionally listed here more than once.*

Lawrence Dickerson, CEO
Lawrence Dickerson, Pres.
Gary Krenek, CFO/Sr. VP
Robert Blair, Sr. VP-Mktg. & Contracts
R. Lynn Charles, VP-Human Resources
John Vecchio, Sr. VP-Tech. Svcs.
Karl S. Sellers, VP-Eng.
Mark Baudoin, Sr. VP-Admin.
William Long, General Counsel/Sr. VP/Sec.
Lyndol Dew, Sr. VP-Worldwide Oper.
Beth Gordon, Chief Acct. Officer/Controller
James S. Tisch, Chmn.

Phone: 281-492-5300	Fax: 281-492-5316
Toll-Free: 800-848-1980	
Address: 15415 Katy Fwy., Ste. 100, Houston, TX 77094-1810 US	

GROWTH PLANS/SPECIAL FEATURES:

Diamond Offshore Drilling, Inc. is a leading deepwater drilling contractor. Diamond operates one of the world's largest fleets of offshore drilling units, consisting of 31 semi-submersibles, 14 jack-ups and one drill ship. Its semi-submersible rigs float with their lower hulls between 55 and 90 feet below the water line and are held in position partly with anchors and partly through a special hull characteristic known as wave transparency; three of the rigs also have a special computer-controlled thruster system known as dynamic-positioning. Eleven of Diamond's 30 semi-submersibles are high-specification, which means that they are capable of drilling in harsh environments and water depths greater than 4,000 feet; and the other 19 rigs may only work in depths up to 4,000 feet. The company operates in many geographic areas, including the Gulf of Mexico, including the U.S. and Mexico; Europe, principally in the U.K. and Norway; the Mediterranean Basin, including Egypt, Libya, Tunisia and other parts of Africa; South America, principally in Brazil; Australia and Asia, including Malaysia, Indonesia and Vietnam; and the Middle East, including Kuwait, Qatar and Saudi Arabia. In June 2009, the company acquired the PetroRig I from Jurong Shipyard Pte Ltd. for $460 million. The rig will consequently be renamed Ocean Courage.

Employees are offered medical, vision and dental insurance; life insurance; disability coverage; an employee assistance plan; flexible spending accounts; a 401(k) plan; and profit sharing.

FINANCIALS: Sales and profits are in thousands of dollars—add 000 to get the full amount. 2008 Note: Financial information for 2008 was not available for all companies at press time.

2008 Sales: $3,544,057	2008 Profits: $1,311,020	U.S. Stock Ticker: DO
2007 Sales: $2,567,723	2007 Profits: $846,541	Int'l Ticker: Int'l Exchange:
2006 Sales: $2,052,572	2006 Profits: $706,847	Employees: 5,700
2005 Sales: $1,221,002	2005 Profits: $260,337	Fiscal Year Ends: 12/31
2004 Sales: $814,662	2004 Profits: $-7,243	Parent Company:

SALARIES/BENEFITS:

Pension Plan:	ESOP Stock Plan:	Profit Sharing: Y	Top Exec. Salary: $732,500	Bonus: $555,000
Savings Plan: Y	Stock Purch. Plan:		Second Exec. Salary: $431,625	Bonus: $310,000

OTHER THOUGHTS:

Apparent Women Officers or Directors: 1
Hot Spot for Advancement for Women/Minorities:

LOCATIONS: ("Y" = Yes)

West:	Southwest:	Midwest:	Southeast:	Northeast:	International:
	Y		Y		Y

Note: Financial information, benefits and other data can change quickly and may vary from those stated here.

DICK'S SPORTING GOODS INC

www.dickssportinggoods.com

Industry Group Code: 451110 **Ranks within this company's industry group:** Sales: 1 Profits: 1

Management:		Sales/Marketing:		Liberal Arts:		Information Systems:		Professionals:		Tech./Scientific:	
Management Trainees:	Y	Marketing Pros.:	Y	Gen. Writing/Editing:	Y	Info. Management:	Y	Finance/Acct.:	Y	Engineers, Electrical:	
Experienced Mngmt.:	Y	Retail Sales:	Y	Technical Writing:		Software Dev.:	Y	Law:	Y	Engineers, Other:	
International Business:		Commercial/Industrial:		Graphic Arts/Photog.:	Y	Hardware Dev.:		HR/Other:	Y	Health/Lab:	
MBA Grads:	Y	Sales Trainees:	Y	Music:		Consulting/Other:		Training:	Y	Scientists/Research:	
		Advertising Pros.:	Y	Broadcasting:				Health Care:		Petroleum/Chemicals:	
				Other:	Y			Consulting:		Math/Other:	

TYPES OF BUSINESS:

Sporting Goods Stores
Outdoor Apparel
Footwear
Hunting & Fishing Supplies
Golf Supplies
Bicycles
Online Sales

BRANDS/DIVISIONS/AFFILIATES:

Golf Galaxy Inc
Chick's Sporting Goods

CONTACTS: *Note: Officers with more than one job title may be intentionally listed here more than once.*

Edward W. Stack, CEO
Joseph H. Schmidt, COO
Joseph H. Schmidt, Pres.
Timothy E. Kullman, CFO
Jeffrey R. Hennion, Chief Mktg. Officer/Exec. VP
Kathy Sutter, Sr. VP-Human Resources
Matthew J. Lynch, CIO/Sr. VP
Gwen Manto, Chief Merch. Officer/Exec. VP
Timothy E. Kullman, Exec. VP-Admin.
Timothy E. Kullman, Exec. VP-Finance
David G. Stanchak, Sr. VP-Real Estate
Edward W. Stack, Chmn.
Lee Belitsky, Sr. VP-Dist. & Transportation

Phone: 724-273-3400	Fax:
Toll-Free:	
Address: 300 Industry Dr., RIDC Park W., Pittsburgh, PA 15275 US	

GROWTH PLANS/SPECIAL FEATURES:

Dick's Sporting Goods, Inc. is a retail sporting goods chain with 483 stores in 41 states, including 384 Dick's Sporting Goods stores, 85 Golf Galaxy stores and 14 Chick's Sporting Goods stores. The firm's stores are primarily in the eastern half of the U.S. The company offers a broad assortment of sporting goods equipment, footwear and apparel under national and private-brand labels, including its own Ativa, Power Bolt, Walter Hagen, Fitness Gear and Acuity brands. Each Dick's Sporting Goods location typically contains five store-within-a-store specialty stores. The company seeks to create a distinct look and feel for each specialty department to heighten the customer's interest in the products offered. A typical facility has the following in-store specialty shops: the Pro Shop, a golf shop with a putting green and hitting area and video monitors featuring golf tournaments and instruction on the Golf Channel or other sources; the Footwear Center, featuring hardwood floors, a track for testing athletic shoes and a bank of video monitors playing sporting events; the Cycle Shop, designed to sell and service bikes, complete with a mechanics' work area and equipment on the sales floor; the Sportsman's Lodge for the hunting and fishing customer, designed to have the look of an authentic bait and tackle shop; and Total Sports, seasonal sports area displaying sports equipment and athletic apparel associated with specific seasonal sports, such as football and baseball. Dick's stores offer a variety of maintenance, repair and support services in all departments, as well as an e-commerce site. Galaxy Golf stores are designed for an interactive shopping environment, which includes an artificial bent grass putting green and golf simulators. Chick's Sporting Goods stores are located in southern California.

FINANCIALS: Sales and profits are in thousands of dollars—add 000 to get the full amount. 2008 Note: Financial information for 2008 was not available for all companies at press time.

2008 Sales: $3,888,422	2008 Profits: $155,036	**U.S. Stock Ticker: DKS**
2007 Sales: $3,114,162	2007 Profits: $112,611	**Int'l Ticker:** Int'l Exchange:
2006 Sales: $2,624,987	2006 Profits: $72,980	Employees: 23,000
2005 Sales: $2,109,400	2005 Profits: $68,905	Fiscal Year Ends: 1/31
2004 Sales: $1,470,800	2004 Profits: $52,408	Parent Company:

SALARIES/BENEFITS:

Pension Plan:	ESOP Stock Plan:	Profit Sharing:	Top Exec. Salary: $662,500	Bonus: $2,650,000
Savings Plan:	Stock Purch. Plan:		Second Exec. Salary: $625,000	Bonus: $215,074

OTHER THOUGHTS:

Apparent Women Officers or Directors: 2
Hot Spot for Advancement for Women/Minorities: Y

LOCATIONS: ("Y" = Yes)

West:	Southwest:	Midwest:	Southeast:	Northeast:	International:
Y	Y	Y	Y	Y	

Note: Financial information, benefits and other data can change quickly and may vary from those stated here.

DIEBOLD INC

www.diebold.com

Industry Group Code: 334111 Ranks within this company's industry group: Sales: 2 Profits: 2

Management:		Sales/Marketing:		Liberal Arts:		Information Systems:		Professionals:		Tech./Scientific:	
Management Trainees:	Y	Marketing Pros.:	Y	Gen. Writing/Editing:	Y	Info. Management:	Y	Finance/Acct.:	Y	Engineers, Electrical:	Y
Experienced Mngmt.:	Y	Retail Sales:		Technical Writing:	Y	Software Dev.:	Y	Law:	Y	Engineers, Other:	
International Business:	Y	Commercial/Industrial:	Y	Graphic Arts/Photog.:	Y	Hardware Dev.:	Y	HR/Other:	Y	Health/Lab:	
MBA Grads:	Y	Sales Trainees:	Y	Music:		Consulting/Other:	Y	Training:	Y	Scientists/Research:	Y
		Advertising Pros.:	Y	Broadcasting:				Health Care:		Petroleum/Chemicals:	
				Other:	Y			Consulting:		Math/Other:	Y

TYPES OF BUSINESS:

Computer Hardware-Automated Teller Machines
Self-Service Terminals
Security Systems
Technical Services
Software
Electronic Voting Machines

BRANDS/DIVISIONS/AFFILIATES:

Premier Election Solutions
Procomp Industria Electronica S.A.
LINX Predator EliteGateMaster
Electronic Vault Attendant Elite

CONTACTS: *Note: Officers with more than one job title may be intentionally listed here more than once.*

Thomas W. Swidarski, CEO
Thomas W. Swidarski, Pres.
Leslie A. Pierce, Interim CFO/VP/Corp. Controller
Sheila M. Rutt, Chief Human Resources Officer/VP
Sean F. Forrester, CIO/VP
Warren W. Dettinger, General Counsel/VP
George S. Mayes, Jr., Exec. VP-Global Oper.
Robert J. Warren, VP-Corp. Dev. & Finance
John D. Kristoff, Chief Comm. Officer/VP
Timothy J. McDannold, VP/Treas.
David Bucci, Sr. VP-Customer Solutions Group
M. Scott Hunter, Chief Tax Officer/VP
Bradley J. Stephenson, VP-Security Div.
Leslie A. Pierce, VP/Controller
John N. Lauer, Chmn.
James L.M. Chen, Sr. VP-EMEA & Asia Pacific Divisions
Linda M. Parcher, Chief Procurement Officer/VP

Phone: 330-490-4000	Fax: 330-490-3794
Toll-Free: 800-999-3600	
Address: 5995 Mayfair Rd., North Canton, OH 44720-8077 US	

GROWTH PLANS/SPECIAL FEATURES:

Diebold, Inc., incorporated in 1876, develops, manufactures, sells and services self-service transaction systems; electronic and physical security systems; software; and various products used to equip bank facilities and electronic voting terminals. The company's primary customers include banks and financial institutions, as well as public libraries, government agencies, utilities and various retail outlets in over 90 countries. The company operates in three segments: Self-service, security and election systems. The self-service segment primarily serves the banking industry by supplying automated teller machines (ATMs). Diebold provides the hardware, software and customer support for these systems. The security unit specializes in protecting customer assets. This division serves financial, retail, commercial and government customers with both physical and electronic systems. The physical products include vaults, safes, depositories, bullet-resistive items and other similar safety measures. The electronic applications include alarms, remote monitoring and identity confirmation measures like card verifiers and biometrics. The company's election systems business provides equipment, software, training, support and installation services for ballot casting equipment. In this area, Diebold works through its wholly-owned subsidiaries Premier Election Solutions and the Brazil-based Procomp Industria Eletronica S.A. In May 2009, the company launched its LINX Predator EliteGateMaster, a security system designed to protect government sites. In July 2009, the firm unveiled its Electronic Vault Attendant Elite, a dual-controlled vault and safe deposit box marketed towards banks.

Diebold offers its employees medical, dental, vision and prescription drug coverage; a 401(k) plan; an employee stock purchase plan; educational assistance; long-term disability; flexible spending accounts; an employee assistance program; adoption assistance and a college scholarship program.

FINANCIALS: Sales and profits are in thousands of dollars—add 000 to get the full amount. 2008 Note: Financial information for 2008 was not available for all companies at press time.

2008 Sales: $3,170,080	2008 Profits: $88,583	**U.S. Stock Ticker:** DBD
2007 Sales: $2,947,481	2007 Profits: $39,541	**Int'l Ticker:** Int'l Exchange:
2006 Sales: $2,920,974	2006 Profits: $104,552	Employees: 16,658
2005 Sales: $2,587,049	2005 Profits: $96,746	Fiscal Year Ends: 12/31
2004 Sales: $2,357,108	2004 Profits: $183,797	Parent Company:

SALARIES/BENEFITS:

Pension Plan:	ESOP Stock Plan:	Profit Sharing:	Top Exec. Salary: $750,000	Bonus: $1,500,000
Savings Plan: Y	Stock Purch. Plan: Y		Second Exec. Salary: $377,805	Bonus: $680,049

OTHER THOUGHTS:

Apparent Women Officers or Directors: 3
Hot Spot for Advancement for Women/Minorities: Y

LOCATIONS: ("Y" = Yes)

West:	Southwest:	Midwest:	Southeast:	Northeast:	International:
Y	Y	Y	Y	Y	Y

DINEEQUITY INC

www.dineequity.com

Industry Group Code: 722110 Ranks within this company's industry group: Sales: 10 Profits: 11

Management:		Sales/Marketing:		Liberal Arts:		Information Systems:		Professionals:		Tech./Scientific:	
Management Trainees:	Y	Marketing Pros.:	Y	Gen. Writing/Editing:	Y	Info. Management:	Y	Finance/Acct.:	Y	Engineers, Electrical:	
Experienced Mngmt.:	Y	Retail Sales:		Technical Writing:		Software Dev.:	Y	Law:	Y	Engineers, Other:	
International Business:	Y	Commercial/Industrial:		Graphic Arts/Photog.:	Y	Hardware Dev.:		HR/Other:	Y	Health/Lab:	
MBA Grads:	Y	Sales Trainees:		Music:		Consulting/Other:		Training:	Y	Scientists/Research:	
		Advertising Pros.:	Y	Broadcasting:				Health Care:		Petroleum/Chemicals:	
				Other:	Y			Consulting:		Math/Other:	

TYPES OF BUSINESS:

Restaurants

BRANDS/DIVISIONS/AFFILIATES:

International House of Pancakes
Applebee's International Inc

CONTACTS: Note: Officers with more than one job title may be intentionally listed here more than once.

Julia A. Stewart, CEO
John F. Tierney, CFO
John Jakubek, Sr. VP-Human Resources
Randi Val Morrison, General Counsel/Sr. VP-Legal/Corp. Sec.
Greggory Kalvin, Corp. Controller/VP
Richard C. Celio, Chief Restaurant Support Officer
Jean M. Birch, Pres., IHOP Restaurants
Michael J. Archer, Pres., Applebee's International, Inc.
Julia A. Stewart, Chmn.

Phone: 818-240-6055	**Fax:** 818-637-3131
Toll-Free: 866-955-3463	
Address: 450 N. Brand Blvd., 7th Fl., Glendale, CA 91203-4415 US	

GROWTH PLANS/SPECIAL FEATURES:

DineEquity, Inc., formerly IHOP Corp., owns and operates two restaurant concepts in the casual dining and family dining niches: Applebee's Neighborhood Grill and Bar, or Applebee's, and International House of Pancakes, or IHOP. The company develops, franchises and operates roughly 1,350 IHOP restaurants in North America. IHOP restaurants offer a selection of pancakes, omelets and other breakfast items, as well as lunch, dinner and snack items. Most of the restaurants additionally offer special items for children and seniors at reduced prices. In recognition of local tastes, IHOP restaurants typically offer regional specialties that complement the IHOP core menu. Applebee's restaurants operate in the bar and grill segment of the casual dining industry. DineEquity currently controls approximately 1,900 Applebee's restaurants across the U.S. The company operates in four categories: franchise operations, rental operations, company restaurant operations and financing operations. The franchise operations segment consists of restaurant operated by the firm's franchisees and area licensees in the U.S. and Canada, with revenue consisting primarily of royalty revenues, sales of proprietary products, advertising fees and the portion of the franchise fees allocated to the company's intellectual property. Rental operations revenue consists of revenue from operating leases and interest income from direct financing leases. The company restaurant operations segment consists of company-operated restaurants. Financing operations revenue consists of the portion of franchise fees not allocated to DineEquity's intellectual property and sales of equipment.

FINANCIALS: Sales and profits are in thousands of dollars—add 000 to get the full amount. 2008 Note: Financial information for 2008 was not available for all companies at press time.

2008 Sales: $1,613,628	2008 Profits: $-154,459	**U.S. Stock Ticker:** DIN
2007 Sales: $484,559	2007 Profits: $- 480	**Int'l Ticker:** Int'l Exchange:
2006 Sales: $349,560	2006 Profits: $44,553	Employees: 25,248
2005 Sales: $348,023	2005 Profits: $43,937	Fiscal Year Ends: 12/31
2004 Sales: $	2004 Profits: $	Parent Company:

SALARIES/BENEFITS:

Pension Plan:	ESOP Stock Plan:	Profit Sharing:	Top Exec. Salary: $885,090	Bonus: $312,106
Savings Plan: Y	Stock Purch. Plan:		Second Exec. Salary: $407,500	Bonus: $498,690

OTHER THOUGHTS:

Apparent Women Officers or Directors: 4
Hot Spot for Advancement for Women/Minorities: Y

LOCATIONS: ("Y" = Yes)

West:	Southwest:	Midwest:	Southeast:	Northeast:	International:
Y	Y	Y	Y	Y	Y

Note: Financial information, benefits and other data can change quickly and may vary from those stated here.

DIRECTV GROUP INC (THE)

www.directv.com

Industry Group Code: 517110 Ranks within this company's industry group: Sales: 5 Profits: 4

Management:		Sales/Marketing:		Liberal Arts:		Information Systems:		Professionals:		Tech./Scientific:	
Management Trainees:	Y	Marketing Pros.:	Y	Gen. Writing/Editing:	Y	Info. Management:	Y	Finance/Acct.:	Y	Engineers, Electrical:	Y
Experienced Mngmt.:	Y	Retail Sales:		Technical Writing:	Y	Software Dev.:	Y	Law:	Y	Engineers, Other:	Y
International Business:	Y	Commercial/Industrial:		Graphic Arts/Photog.:	Y	Hardware Dev.:	Y	HR/Other:	Y	Health/Lab:	
MBA Grads:	Y	Sales Trainees:	Y	Music:		Consulting/Other:		Training:	Y	Scientists/Research:	
		Advertising Pros.:	Y	Broadcasting:	Y			Health Care:		Petroleum/Chemicals:	
				Other:	Y			Consulting:		Math/Other:	

TYPES OF BUSINESS:

Satellite Broadcasting
Commercial Satellite Fleet
Satellite-Based Internet Services
Digital Television

BRANDS/DIVISIONS/AFFILIATES:

Liberty Media Corp
DIRECTV U.S.
DIRECTV Latin America
PanAmericana
Sky Brasil Servicos Ltda.
Innova, S. de R.L. de C.V.
Sat-Go

CONTACTS: *Note: Officers with more than one job title may be intentionally listed here more than once.*

Larry D. Hunter, Interim CEO
Patrick T. Doyle, CFO/Exec. VP
Romulo G. Pontual, CTO/Exec. VP
Larry D. Hunter, General Counsel/Corp. Sec./Exec. VP
Michael W. Palkovic, Exec. VP-Oper.
J. William Little, Sr. VP-Bus. Dev./Treas.
Robert Mercer, Press Contact
John Murphy, Chief Acct. Officer/Controller/Sr. VP
J. William Little, Treas./Sr. VP
John C. Malone, Chmn.
Bruce B. Churchill, Exec. VP/Pres., DIRECTV Latin America

Phone: 212-462-5200	Fax: 310-535-5225
Toll-Free:	
Address: 2230 E. Imperial Hwy., El Segundo, CA 90245-0956 US	

GROWTH PLANS/SPECIAL FEATURES:

The DIRECTV Group, Inc. is one of the world's top providers of digital television entertainment and wireless systems. The company's two business segments, DIRECTV U.S. and DIRECTV Latin America (DTVLA), are engaged in digital entertainment programming via satellite for residential and commercial subscribers. DIRECTV U.S. is the one of the largest providers of direct-to-home digital television services, with over 17.6 million U.S. subscribers and approximately 2,000 digital video and audio channels, including about 200 basic and music channels, 40 premium movie channels, more than 50 regional and specialty sports networks and over 125 Spanish and other foreign language channels. There are also dozens of pay-per-view movie and event choices, and about 130 national high-definition television channels. DTVLA is comprised of PanAmericana, which provides services in Venezuela, Argentina, Chile, Colombia, Puerto Rico and certain other countries through wholly-owned subsidiary DIRECTV Latin America, LLC. PanAmericana also operates through 74%-owned subsidiary Sky Brasil Servicos Ltda. (Sky Brazil); and 41%-owned subsidiary Innova, S. de R.L. de C.V. (Sky Mexico). PanAmericana has approximately 2.2 million subscribers; Sky Brazil, 1.6 million; and Sky Mexico, 1.8 million. The firm is considering the launch of a massive, wireless voice and data network, probably based on WiMAX, which would offer bundled services including TV, phone and Internet access. The company is 54%-owned by Liberty Media Corporation. In May 2009, Liberty Media and DIRECTV announced plans to merge DIRECTV with Liberty Entertainment, Inc., a newly created subsidiary of Liberty Media, with Liberty Entertainment to be ultimately spun off from Liberty Media. The spin-off company, which will benefit from a simplified ownership structure, will also control certain regional sports and programming assets formerly held by Liberty Media.

Employees of the firm are offered medical, dental and vision coverage; flexible spending accounts; wellness and employee assistance programs; education assistance; and adoption benefits.

FINANCIALS: Sales and profits are in thousands of dollars—add 000 to get the full amount. 2008 Note: Financial information for 2008 was not available for all companies at press time.

2008 Sales: $19,693,000	2008 Profits: $1,515,000	**U.S. Stock Ticker: DTV**
2007 Sales: $17,246,000	2007 Profits: $1,451,000	**Int'l Ticker:** Int'l Exchange:
2006 Sales: $14,755,500	2006 Profits: $1,420,100	Employees: 13,000
2005 Sales: $13,164,500	2005 Profits: $335,900	Fiscal Year Ends: 12/31
2004 Sales: $11,360,000	2004 Profits: $-1,944,000	Parent Company:

SALARIES/BENEFITS:

Pension Plan: Y	ESOP Stock Plan:	Profit Sharing:	Top Exec. Salary: $2,291,620	Bonus: $3,500,000
Savings Plan: Y	Stock Purch. Plan:		Second Exec. Salary: $1,136,188	Bonus: $1,256,000

OTHER THOUGHTS:

Apparent Women Officers or Directors:
Hot Spot for Advancement for Women/Minorities:

LOCATIONS: ("Y" = Yes)

West:	Southwest:	Midwest:	Southeast:	Northeast:	International:
Y	Y	Y	Y	Y	Y

Note: Financial information, benefits and other data can change quickly and may vary from those stated here.

DOLE FOOD COMPANY INC

www.dole.com

Industry Group Code: 31142 Ranks within this company's industry group: Sales: 1 Profits: 1

Management:		Sales/Marketing:		Liberal Arts:		Information Systems:		Professionals:		Tech./Scientific:	
Management Trainees:	Y	Marketing Pros.:	Y	Gen. Writing/Editing:	Y	Info. Management:	Y	Finance/Acct.:	Y	Engineers, Electrical:	
Experienced Mngmt.:	Y	Retail Sales:		Technical Writing:		Software Dev.:	Y	Law:	Y	Engineers, Other:	
International Business:	Y	Commercial/Industrial:	Y	Graphic Arts/Photog.:	Y	Hardware Dev.:		HR/Other:	Y	Health/Lab:	
MBA Grads:	Y	Sales Trainees:	Y	Music:		Consulting/Other:		Training:	Y	Scientists/Research:	
		Advertising Pros.:	Y	Broadcasting:				Health Care:		Petroleum/Chemicals:	
				Other:				Consulting:		Math/Other:	

TYPES OF BUSINESS:

Fruit Farming
Fresh-Cut Flowers
Fresh Produce
Packaged Foods
Imports

BRANDS/DIVISIONS/AFFILIATES:

DHM Holding Company
JP Fruit Distributors Ltd.
5 A Day for Better Health
Dolefil

CONTACTS: Note: Officers with more than one job title may be intentionally listed here more than once.

David DeLorenzo, CEO
David DeLorenzo, Pres.
Brad C. Bartlett, Sr. VP-Mktg. & Sales
Scott A. Griswold, Exec. VP-Corp. Dev.
Kevin Davis, Managing Dir.-Dolefil
Jonathan Bass, Pres., Dole Latin America
Kevin Fiori, Sr. VP-Agriculture Oper.
David H. Murdock, Chmn.
Jean-Christophe Juilliard, Pres., Dole Europe

Phone: 818-879-6600	**Fax:** 818-879-6615
Toll-Free: 800-356-3111	
Address: 1 Dole Dr., Westlake Village, CA 91362 US	

GROWTH PLANS/SPECIAL FEATURES:

Dole Food Company, Inc. is engaged in the sourcing, growing, processing, packaging, distribution and marketing of fresh produce, packaged foods and fresh-cut flowers. The firm is one of the world's leading producers of bananas and pineapples, as well as an importer of fresh-cut flowers in the U.S. These flowers are grown on Dole-owned land in Latin America and subsequently imported to the U.S. where they are distributed to retail flower stores and grocery chains. Dole has offices worldwide that sell its products to the wholesale, retail and institutional markets. The company operates 11 packing and cold storage facilities, a corrugated box plant and a wooden box plant in Chile, as well as corrugated box plants in Colombia, Costa Rica, Ecuador and Honduras. In Japan, Dole operates 18 fresh-cut fruit and vegetable distribution centers; in China, the firm operates two processing and distribution centers. Within Europe, Dole operates nine banana ripening, produce and flower distribution centers in Sweden; nine in France; five in Spain; four in Italy; one in Belgium; one in Turkey; one in Austria; and three in Germany. DHM Holding Company, a company entirely owned by David Murdoch, owns all of Dole's stock. In November 2008, the firm sold JP Fresh and Dole France to the Compagnie Fruitere Group as part of the three phase flowers division sale. In September 2008, Dole announced plans to sell its flowers division in a three phase transaction. In July 2008, the firm sold 2,000 acres of land located in Oahu, Hawaii, the flowers division headquarters in Miami and approximately 4,300 acres of California orchards.

The company offers its employees medical, dental and vision coverage; life and AD&D insurance; business travel accident and long-term disability insurance; flexible spending accounts; a 401(k) plan; and an employee assistance program.

FINANCIALS: Sales and profits are in thousands of dollars—add 000 to get the full amount. 2008 Note: Financial information for 2008 was not available for all companies at press time.

2008 Sales: $7,620,000	2008 Profits: $409,000	**U.S. Stock Ticker:** Private
2007 Sales: $6,931,000	2007 Profits: $309,000	**Int'l Ticker:** Int'l Exchange:
2006 Sales: $6,171,500	2006 Profits: $89,000	Employees: 75,800
2005 Sales: $5,870,600	2005 Profits: $	Fiscal Year Ends: 12/31
2004 Sales: $5,316,200	2004 Profits: $134,400	Parent Company:

SALARIES/BENEFITS:

Pension Plan:	ESOP Stock Plan:	Profit Sharing:	Top Exec. Salary: $	Bonus: $285,000
Savings Plan: Y	Stock Purch. Plan:		Second Exec. Salary: $	Bonus: $

OTHER THOUGHTS:

Apparent Women Officers or Directors:
Hot Spot for Advancement for Women/Minorities:

LOCATIONS: ("Y" = Yes)

West:	Southwest:	Midwest:	Southeast:	Northeast:	International:
Y	Y	Y	Y	Y	Y

DOLLAR GENERAL CORPORATION

www.dollargeneral.com

Industry Group Code: 452112 Ranks within this company's industry group: Sales: 6   Profits: 10

Management:		Sales/Marketing:		Liberal Arts:		Information Systems:		Professionals:		Tech./Scientific:	
Management Trainees:	Y	Marketing Pros.:	Y	Gen. Writing/Editing:	Y	Info. Management:	Y	Finance/Acct.:	Y	Engineers, Electrical:	
Experienced Mngmt.:	Y	Retail Sales:	Y	Technical Writing:		Software Dev.:	Y	Law:	Y	Engineers, Other:	
International Business:		Commercial/Industrial:		Graphic Arts/Photog.:	Y	Hardware Dev.:		HR/Other:	Y	Health/Lab:	
MBA Grads:	Y	Sales Trainees:	Y	Music:		Consulting/Other:		Training:	Y	Scientists/Research:	
		Advertising Pros.:	Y	Broadcasting:				Health Care:		Petroleum/Chemicals:	
				Other:	Y			Consulting:		Math/Other:	

TYPES OF BUSINESS:
Discount Stores
Dollar Stores

BRANDS/DIVISIONS/AFFILIATES:
KKR & Co LP (Kohlberg Kravis Roberts & Co)

CONTACTS: *Note: Officers with more than one job title may be intentionally listed here more than once.*
Richard W. Dreiling, CEO
David L. Bere, Pres.
David M. Tehle, CFO/Exec. VP
Bob Ravener, Chief People Officer/Sr. VP
Todd Vasos, Chief Merch. Officer/Div. Pres.
Susan S. Lanigan, General Counsel/Exec. VP
Kathleen R. Guion, Pres., Store Oper. & Dev.
David L. Bere, Chief Strategy Officer
Anita Elliott, Controller/Sr. VP
Richard W. Dreiling, Chmn.

Phone: 615-855-4000	Fax: 615-855-5252
Toll-Free:	
Address: 100 Mission Ridge, Goodlettsville, TN 37072 US	

GROWTH PLANS/SPECIAL FEATURES:
Dollar General Corporation, owned by private equity firm KKR & Co., owns and operates more than 8,400 discount merchandise stores in 35 states, serving primarily low- and fixed-income families. Additionally, the firm operates nine distribution centers located in several states including: Oklahoma, Virginia, Ohio, South Carolina, Mississippi, Kentucky, Missouri, Florida and Indiana. The traditional Dollar General store has, on average, approximately 7,000 square feet of selling space, which is attractive to the company's target customers who live within five miles of the store. Roughly half of the company's stores serve communities with populations of 20,000 or less. Dollar General stores offer such products as health and beauty aids; packaged food and refrigerated products; home cleaning supplies; house wares; stationery; seasonal goods; basic apparel; and domestics; as well as approximately 7,300 core items from some of the most trusted manufacturers in America. The majority of Dollar General's products are priced at $10 or less, with nearly a third of the products priced at $1 or less. The most expensive items generally cost $20. In August 2009, the firm, through the Dollar General Literacy Foundation, issued $4.9 million in grants to various schools and nonprofit organizations that support literacy and education initiatives.

Employees of the firm are offered a 401(k) plan; a retirement plan; medical, dental, vision and prescription plans; flexible spending accounts; short and long term disability; wellness programs; home and education financing assistance; employee, spouse and dependent life insurance; business travel accident insurance; benefits for part-time employees; and rewards programs.

FINANCIALS: Sales and profits are in thousands of dollars—add 000 to get the full amount. 2008 Note: Financial information for 2008 was not available for all companies at press time.

2008 Sales: $9,495,300	2008 Profits: $-12,800	**U.S. Stock Ticker:** Private
2007 Sales: $9,169,800	2007 Profits: $137,900	**Int'l Ticker:** Int'l Exchange:
2006 Sales: $8,582,237	2006 Profits: $350,155	Employees: 72,500
2005 Sales: $7,660,927	2005 Profits: $344,190	Fiscal Year Ends: 1/31
2004 Sales: $6,871,992	2004 Profits: $301,000	Parent Company: KKR & CO LP (KOHLBERG KRAVIS ROBERTS & CO)

SALARIES/BENEFITS:
Pension Plan: Y	ESOP Stock Plan:	Profit Sharing:	Top Exec. Salary: $	Bonus: $
Savings Plan: Y	Stock Purch. Plan:		Second Exec. Salary: $	Bonus: $

OTHER THOUGHTS:
Apparent Women Officers or Directors: 3
Hot Spot for Advancement for Women/Minorities: Y

LOCATIONS: ("Y" = Yes)
West:	Southwest:	Midwest:	Southeast:	Northeast:	International:
	Y	Y	Y	Y	

Note: Financial information, benefits and other data can change quickly and may vary from those stated here.

DOLLAR THRIFTY AUTOMOTIVE GROUP INC

www.dtag.com

Industry Group Code: 5321 Ranks within this company's industry group: Sales: 4 Profits: 1

Management:		Sales/Marketing:		Liberal Arts:		Information Systems:		Professionals:		Tech./Scientific:	
Management Trainees:	Y	Marketing Pros.:	Y	Gen. Writing/Editing:	Y	Info. Management:	Y	Finance/Acct.:	Y	Engineers, Electrical:	
Experienced Mngmt.:	Y	Retail Sales:	Y	Technical Writing:		Software Dev.:	Y	Law:	Y	Engineers, Other:	
International Business:	Y	Commercial/Industrial:	Y	Graphic Arts/Photog.:	Y	Hardware Dev.:		HR/Other:	Y	Health/Lab:	
MBA Grads:	Y	Sales Trainees:	Y	Music:		Consulting/Other:		Training:	Y	Scientists/Research:	
		Advertising Pros.:	Y	Broadcasting:				Health Care:		Petroleum/Chemicals:	
				Other:	Y			Consulting:		Math/Other:	

TYPES OF BUSINESS:

Automobile Rental
Used Car Sales
Financial Services

BRANDS/DIVISIONS/AFFILIATES:

Dollar Rent A Car, Inc.
Thrifty, Inc.
Thrifty Car Sales, Inc.
Thrifty Canada, Ltd.
Rental Car Finance Corp.
Dollar Thrifty Funding Corp.
Thrifty Rent-A-Car System, Inc.
DTG Operations, Inc.

CONTACTS: Note: Officers with more than one job title may be intentionally listed here more than once.

Scott L. Thompson, CEO
Scott L. Thompson, Pres.
H. Clifford Buster, CFO/Exec. VP
Scott Anderson, Sr. Exec. VP-Global Mktg. & Sales
Rick Morris, CIO/Exec. VP
Vicki Vaniman, General Counsel/Sec./Exec. VP
Scott Anderson, Sr. Exec. VP-Corp. & Franchise Oper.
James F. Duffy, Exec. VP-Corp. Oper.
Thomas P. Capo, Chmn.

Phone: 918-660-7700	Fax: 918-669-2934
Toll-Free:	
Address: 5330 E. 31st St., Tulsa, OK 74135 US	

GROWTH PLANS/SPECIAL FEATURES:

Dollar Thrifty Automotive Group, Inc. (DTG) is involved in many aspects of renting and selling vehicles. The firm owns DTG Operations, Inc.; Dollar Rent A Car, Inc. (Dollar); and Thrifty, Inc. (Thrifty). Thrifty owns Thrifty Car Sales, Inc., which operates a franchised retail used car sales network, and Thrifty Rent-A-Car System, Inc., which owns Dollar Thrifty Automotive Group Canada, Inc. DTG Operations operates company-owned stores under the Dollar and Thrifty brands; provides vehicle leasing to franchisees; and operates reservation centers for both brands. Thrifty Rent-A-Car System, Inc. and Dollar Rent A Car, Inc. conduct franchising, sales and marketing activities for their respective brands. The group has two additional subsidiaries, Rental Car Finance Corp. and Dollar Thrifty Funding Corp., which are special purpose financing companies. Dollar, Thrifty and their respective independent franchisees operate the Dollar and Thrifty vehicle rental systems. The Dollar and Thrifty brands are primarily utilized by leisure customers, including foreign tourists, and to small businesses, government business and independent business travelers. The Dollar brand's serves the airport and retail market, with most locations either at or near an airport. The brands have 280 in-terminal locations in the U.S., and 741 total locations in the U.S. and Canada. The Thrifty brand serves both the airport, with 80% of revenue derived, and local markets, with 20% of revenue. In 2008, Chrysler vehicles represented approximately 76% of the total U.S. fleet purchases by DTG Operations. In October 2008, the company completed a workforce reduction, including layoffs of 30% of its executive staff, 15% of its headquarters staff and 5% of its field staff.

DTG offers its employees medical, dental and vision coverage; flexible spending accounts; short- and long-term disability; profit sharing; life, AD&D and business travel insurance; a 401(k) plan; tuition reimbursement; and discount programs.

FINANCIALS: Sales and profits are in thousands of dollars—add 000 to get the full amount. 2008 Note: Financial information for 2008 was not available for all companies at press time.

2008 Sales: $1,697,993	2008 Profits: $340,422	**U.S. Stock Ticker: DTG**	
2007 Sales: $1,760,791	2007 Profits: $1,215	**Int'l Ticker:** Int'l Exchange:	
2006 Sales: $1,660,677	2006 Profits: $51,692	Employees: 6,800	
2005 Sales: $1,507,554	2005 Profits: $76,355	Fiscal Year Ends: 12/31	
2004 Sales: $1,403,847	2004 Profits: $66,473	Parent Company:	

SALARIES/BENEFITS:

Pension Plan:	ESOP Stock Plan:	Profit Sharing: Y	Top Exec. Salary: $700,000	Bonus: $
Savings Plan: Y	Stock Purch. Plan:		Second Exec. Salary: $379,082	Bonus: $

OTHER THOUGHTS:

Apparent Women Officers or Directors: 2
Hot Spot for Advancement for Women/Minorities: Y

LOCATIONS: ("Y" = Yes)

West:	Southwest:	Midwest:	Southeast:	Northeast:	International:
Y	Y	Y	Y	Y	Y

Note: Financial information, benefits and other data can change quickly and may vary from those stated here.

DRESS BARN INC (THE)

www.dressbarn.com

Industry Group Code: 448120 Ranks within this company's industry group: Sales: 6   Profits: 4

Management:		Sales/Marketing:		Liberal Arts:		Information Systems:		Professionals:		Tech./Scientific:	
Management Trainees:	Y	Marketing Pros.:	Y	Gen. Writing/Editing:	Y	Info. Management:	Y	Finance/Acct.:	Y	Engineers, Electrical:	
Experienced Mngmt.:	Y	Retail Sales:	Y	Technical Writing:		Software Dev.:	Y	Law:	Y	Engineers, Other:	
International Business:		Commercial/Industrial:		Graphic Arts/Photog.:	Y	Hardware Dev.:		HR/Other:	Y	Health/Lab:	
MBA Grads:	Y	Sales Trainees:	Y	Music:		Consulting/Other:		Training:	Y	Scientists/Research:	
		Advertising Pros.:	Y	Broadcasting:				Health Care:		Petroleum/Chemicals:	
				Other:	Y			Consulting:		Math/Other:	

TYPES OF BUSINESS:

Women's Apparel, Retail
Teen Fashion Stores
Fashion Accessories
Private-Label Credit Cards

BRANDS/DIVISIONS/AFFILIATES:

Maurice's
Atrium
Westport, Ltd.
Princeton Club
SBX
Dress Barn Woman
Studio Y
Industrial Exchange

CONTACTS: *Note: Officers with more than one job title may be intentionally listed here more than once.*

David R. Jaffe, CEO
David R. Jaffe, Pres.
Armand Correia, CFO/Sr. VP
Vivian Behrens, Chief Mktg. Officer/Sr. VP
Gene L. Wexler, General Counsel/Sr. VP
Elliot S. Jaffe, Chmn.

Phone: 845-369-4500	Fax: 845-369-4829
Toll-Free: 800-373-7722	
Address: 30 Dunnigan Dr., Suffern, NY 10901 US	

GROWTH PLANS/SPECIAL FEATURES:

The Dress Barn, Inc. operates a national chain, primarily located in strip malls, of value-priced specialty stores offering in-season, moderate- to better-quality career apparel and accessories, primarily to working women in their mid-30's to mid-50's. The company has three store formats; dressbarn stores, which carry junior and misses sizes; dressbarn woman stores, which feature larger sizes; and combination stores, which carry both. The combination stores are more prevalent, though the company does have some locations that are only either dressbarn or dressbarn women. Dress Barn's subsidiary, maurices, offers moderately priced, up-to-date fashions designed to appeal to a younger female consumer than the dressbarn and dressbarn woman brands. From its Duluth, Minnesota headquarters, maurices operates primarily within smaller cities of 25,000 to 100,000 in population. Maurice's merchandise is sold under three brand names, maurices, Studio Y and Industrial Exchange. Dress Barn operates 821 Dress Barn stores in 48 states and Washington, D.C. and 607 maurices stores in 42 states. The company offers a dressbarn credit card operated by World Financial Network National Bank, as well as personal and corporate gift cards in a variety of values. Holders of the dressbarn credit card receive targeted promotions including directed mailings and special coupons.

The company offers its employees short term disability, life and accidental death and dismemberment insurance, paid time off, 30% merchandise discount, career training, merchandise discounts, tuition reimbursement and medical, dental and vision coverage.

FINANCIALS: Sales and profits are in thousands of dollars—add 000 to get the full amount. 2008 Note: Financial information for 2008 was not available for all companies at press time.

2008 Sales: $1,444,165	2008 Profits: $74,088	U.S. Stock Ticker: DBRN
2007 Sales: $1,426,607	2007 Profits: $101,182	Int'l Ticker: Int'l Exchange:
2006 Sales: $1,300,277	2006 Profits: $78,954	Employees: 13,700
2005 Sales: $1,000,264	2005 Profits: $52,560	Fiscal Year Ends: 7/31
2004 Sales: $754,903	2004 Profits: $30,141	Parent Company:

SALARIES/BENEFITS:

Pension Plan:	ESOP Stock Plan:	Profit Sharing:	Top Exec. Salary: $850,000	Bonus: $
Savings Plan: Y	Stock Purch. Plan: Y		Second Exec. Salary: $358,800	Bonus: $

OTHER THOUGHTS:

Apparent Women Officers or Directors: 4
Hot Spot for Advancement for Women/Minorities: Y

LOCATIONS: ("Y" = Yes)

West:	Southwest:	Midwest:	Southeast:	Northeast:	International:
Y	Y	Y	Y	Y	

Note: Financial information, benefits and other data can change quickly and may vary from those stated here.

DTE ENERGY COMPANY
www.dteenergy.com

Industry Group Code: 221 Ranks within this company's industry group: Sales: 9   Profits: 7

Management:		Sales/Marketing:		Liberal Arts:		Information Systems:		Professionals:		Tech./Scientific:	
Management Trainees:	Y	Marketing Pros.:	Y	Gen. Writing/Editing:	Y	Info. Management:	Y	Finance/Acct.:	Y	Engineers, Electrical:	Y
Experienced Mngmt.:	Y	Retail Sales:		Technical Writing:	Y	Software Dev.:	Y	Law:	Y	Engineers, Other:	Y
International Business:		Commercial/Industrial:	Y	Graphic Arts/Photog.:	Y	Hardware Dev.:		HR/Other:	Y	Health/Lab:	
MBA Grads:	Y	Sales Trainees:		Music:		Consulting/Other:		Training:	Y	Scientists/Research:	
		Advertising Pros.:	Y	Broadcasting:				Health Care:		Petroleum/Chemicals:	Y
				Other:				Consulting:		Math/Other:	

TYPES OF BUSINESS:
Utilities-Electricity & Natural Gas
Energy Management
Wholesale Energy Trading
Fuel Supply Services
Hydroelectric Power
Nuclear Power
Coal Shipping-Rail & Boat
Consulting Services

BRANDS/DIVISIONS/AFFILIATES:
Detroit Edison Company (The)
Michigan Consolidated Gas Company
Citizen's Gas Fuel Corp.
DTE Biomass Energy
DTE Coal Services
DTE Energy Services

CONTACTS: Note: Officers with more than one job title may be intentionally listed here more than once.
Anthony F. Earley, Jr., CEO
Gerard M. Anderson, COO
Gerard M. Anderson, Pres.
David E. Meador, CFO/Exec. VP
Trevor F. Lauer, VP-Retail Mktg.
Larry Steward, VP-Human Resources
Lynne Ellyn, CIO/Sr. VP
Sandra Ennis, Chief of Staff/Corp. Sec.
Bruce Peterson, General Counsel/Sr. VP
Paul Hillegonds, Sr. VP-Corp. Affairs
Peter Oleksiak, Controller/VP
Steven E. Kurmas, Pres./COO-Detroit Edison
Jerry Norcia, Pres./COO-MichCon
Ron A. May, Sr. VP
Michael Porter, VP-Corp. Comm.
Anthony F. Earley, Jr., Chmn.

Phone: 313-235-4000	Fax: 313-235-6743
Toll-Free: 866-966-5555	
Address: 1 Energy Plz., Detroit, MI 48226 US	

GROWTH PLANS/SPECIAL FEATURES:

DTE Energy Company is a diversified energy and energy technology company that develops merchant power and industrial energy projects and works in energy trading, selling electricity, natural gas, coal, chilled water, landfill gas and steam.   DTE is one of the nation's largest purchasers, transporters and marketers of coal. The company's principal operating segments include its Electric Utility division, which consists of The Detroit Edison Company, an electric utility in southeastern Michigan that has a generating capacity of 11,000 megawatts (MW) and serves 2.2 million customers, and its Gas Utilities division, represented by Michigan Consolidated Gas (MichCon), which distributes natural gas to 1.2 million customers. The firm's Non-Utility Operations segments include Coal and Gas Midstream, encompassing DTE's gas pipelines, its marketing and transportation of coal, its rail management services and its storage services; Power and Industrial Projects, primarily consisting of on-site energy services, steel-related projects and power generation; Unconventional Gas Production, primarily consisting of unconventional gas project development and production; DTE Energy Trading, which buys, sells and trades electricity, coal and natural gas and provides risk management services consisting of energy marketing and trading operations; and DTE Energy Ventures, which invests in start-up companies focused on alternative/renewable energy and advanced energy storage technologies.   During 2008, the firm completed the sale of certain gas properties near Dallas, Texas, as well as the acquisition of the E.J. Stoneman Power Plant in Cassville, Wisconsin, which DTE planned to convert to burn wood waste. In August 2009, DTE completed construction of a $61-million, 15-mile gas pipeline to serve one of its Michigan facilities.

The company offers benefits to its employees that include medical, dental and vision coverage; flexible spending accounts; wellness programs; pension and 401(k) plans; training and development programs; life and disability insurance; an employee assistance program; and flex time.

FINANCIALS: Sales and profits are in thousands of dollars—add 000 to get the full amount. 2008 Note: Financial information for 2008 was not available for all companies at press time.

2008 Sales: $9,329,000	2008 Profits: $546,000	**U.S. Stock Ticker: DTE**
2007 Sales: $8,506,000	2007 Profits: $971,000	**Int'l Ticker:** Int'l Exchange:
2006 Sales: $8,159,000	2006 Profits: $433,000	Employees: 10,471
2005 Sales: $9,021,000	2005 Profits: $537,000	Fiscal Year Ends: 12/31
2004 Sales: $7,071,000	2004 Profits: $431,000	Parent Company:

SALARIES/BENEFITS:

Pension Plan: Y	ESOP Stock Plan:	Profit Sharing:	Top Exec. Salary: $1,186,538	Bonus: $1,500,000
Savings Plan: Y	Stock Purch. Plan:		Second Exec. Salary: $807,885	Bonus: $759,500

OTHER THOUGHTS:
Apparent Women Officers or Directors: 7
Hot Spot for Advancement for Women/Minorities: Y

LOCATIONS: ("Y" = Yes)

West:	Southwest:	Midwest:	Southeast:	Northeast:	International:
		Y			

DUKE ENERGY CORP

www.duke-energy.com

Industry Group Code: 221 Ranks within this company's industry group: Sales: 5 Profits: 3

Management:		Sales/Marketing:		Liberal Arts:		Information Systems:		Professionals:		Tech./Scientific:	
Management Trainees:	Y	Marketing Pros.:	Y	Gen. Writing/Editing:	Y	Info. Management:	Y	Finance/Acct.:	Y	Engineers, Electrical:	Y
Experienced Mngmt.:	Y	Retail Sales:		Technical Writing:	Y	Software Dev.:	Y	Law:	Y	Engineers, Other:	Y
International Business:	Y	Commercial/Industrial:	Y	Graphic Arts/Photog.:	Y	Hardware Dev.:		HR/Other:	Y	Health/Lab:	
MBA Grads:	Y	Sales Trainees:		Music:		Consulting/Other:		Training:	Y	Scientists/Research:	
		Advertising Pros.:	Y	Broadcasting:				Health Care:		Petroleum/Chemicals:	Y
				Other:				Consulting:		Math/Other:	

TYPES OF BUSINESS:

Utilities-Electricity & Natural Gas
Merchant Power Generation
Natural Gas Transportation & Storage
Electricity Transmission
Energy Marketing
Real Estate
Telecommunications
Facility & Plant Services

BRANDS/DIVISIONS/AFFILIATES:

Franchised Electric & Gas Service
Crescent Resources, LLC
Duke Energy Generation Services
Duke Energy International, LLC
National Methanol Company
Attiki Gas Supply S.A.

CONTACTS: *Note: Officers with more than one job title may be intentionally listed here more than once.*

James E. Rogers, CEO
James E. Rogers, Pres.
David L. Hauser, CFO/Group Exec.
Christopher Rolfe, VP-Human Resources
David W. Mohler, CTO/VP
Christopher C. Rolfe, Chief Admin. Officer/Group Exec.
Marc Manly, Chief Legal Officer/Group Exec.
B. Keith Trent, Chief Strategy, Policy & Regulatory. Officer
Cathy S. Roche, Chief Comm. Officer/Sr. VP
R. Sean Trauschke, VP-Investor Rel.
Stephen D. De May, Treas./VP
James L. Turner, COO/Pres., U.S. Franchised Electric & Gas
Ellen T. Ruff, Pres., Duke Energy Carolinas
Dhiaa M. Jamil, Chief Nuclear Officer/Group Exec.
Julia S. Janson, Sr. VP-Ethics & Compliance/Corp. Sec.
James E. Rogers, Chmn.

Phone: 704-594-6200	Fax: 704-382-3814
Toll-Free: 800-873-3853	
Address: 526 S. Church St., Charlotte, NC 28202-1802 US	

GROWTH PLANS/SPECIAL FEATURES:

Duke Energy Corp. is an integrated energy and energy services provider that offers delivery and management of electricity and natural gas throughout the U.S. The company operates four principle business segments: U.S. franchised electric & gas service; commercial power; international energy; and the company's 50% interest in the Crescent Resources joint venture. The franchised electric & gas service segment can generate 32,000 megawatts of electricity, has 4 million customers, including 515,000 retail gas customers, and has locations in Ohio, Indiana, Kentucky and the Carolinas, covering approximately 47,000 square miles. This segment operates three nuclear power plants; 15 coal-fire plants; 31 hydroelectric stations; 15 combustion turbines that burn natural gas, oil or other fuels; and two combine cycle stations that burn natural or synthetic gas. The commercial power segment owns, operates and manages non-regulated power plants and engages in the marketing and procurement of electric power, fuel and emissions allowances related to the plants. Its plants utilize a variety of fuels such as natural gas, waste coal and wood, and can generate approximately 8,020 megawatts of power primarily in the Midwestern U.S. Duke Energy International, LLC, operates power generation plants primarily in Latin America. It also has investments in National Methanol Company, a regional producer of methanol in Saudi Arabia; and Attiki Gas Supply S.A., a natural gas distributor located in Athens, Greece. The Crescent Resources joint venture develops and manages commercial, residential and multi-family real estate projects, and manages land holdings, primarily in the Southeastern and Southwestern U.S. The venture owns 900,000 square feet of real estate, with an additional 500,000 under construction. In September 2008, the company announced plans to begin installing solar electric panels at 850 locations in North Carolina, capable of generating 16 megawatts of electricity, enough to power 2,600 homes for one year.

FINANCIALS: Sales and profits are in thousands of dollars—add 000 to get the full amount. 2008 Note: Financial information for 2008 was not available for all companies at press time.

2008 Sales: $13,207,000	2008 Profits: $1,362,000	**U.S. Stock Ticker: DUK**
2007 Sales: $12,720,000	2007 Profits: $1,500,000	**Int'l Ticker:** Int'l Exchange:
2006 Sales: $10,607,000	2006 Profits: $1,863,000	Employees: 18,250
2005 Sales: $16,297,000	2005 Profits: $1,824,000	Fiscal Year Ends: 12/31
2004 Sales: $19,596,000	2004 Profits: $1,490,000	Parent Company:

SALARIES/BENEFITS:

Pension Plan: Y	ESOP Stock Plan:	Profit Sharing:	Top Exec. Salary: $650,004	Bonus: $900,000
Savings Plan: Y	Stock Purch. Plan:		Second Exec. Salary: $600,000	Bonus: $1,000,000

OTHER THOUGHTS:

Apparent Women Officers or Directors: 4
Hot Spot for Advancement for Women/Minorities: Y

LOCATIONS: ("Y" = Yes)

West:	Southwest:	Midwest:	Southeast:	Northeast:	International:
		Y	Y		Y

Note: Financial information, benefits and other data can change quickly and may vary from those stated here.

DYCOM INDUSTRIES INC

www.dycomind.com

Industry Group Code: 237130 Ranks within this company's industry group: Sales: 2 Profits: 2

Management:		Sales/Marketing:		Liberal Arts:		Information Systems:		Professionals:		Tech./Scientific:	
Management Trainees:	Y	Marketing Pros.:	Y	Gen. Writing/Editing:		Info. Management:	Y	Finance/Acct.:	Y	Engineers, Electrical:	Y
Experienced Mngmt.:	Y	Retail Sales:		Technical Writing:	Y	Software Dev.:		Law:	Y	Engineers, Other:	Y
International Business:		Commercial/Industrial:	Y	Graphic Arts/Photog.:	Y	Hardware Dev.:		HR/Other:	Y	Health/Lab:	
MBA Grads:	Y	Sales Trainees:		Music:		Consulting/Other:		Training:	Y	Scientists/Research:	
		Advertising Pros.:		Broadcasting:				Health Care:		Petroleum/Chemicals:	
				Other:				Consulting:		Math/Other:	

TYPES OF BUSINESS:

Construction, Maintenance & Installation Services
Engineering Services
Utility Maintenance Services

BRANDS/DIVISIONS/AFFILIATES:

CONTACTS: *Note: Officers with more than one job title may be intentionally listed here more than once.*

Steven E. Nielsen, CEO
Timothy R. Estes, COO/Exec. VP
Steven E. Nielsen, Pres.
H. Andrew DeFerrari, CFO/Sr. VP
Richard B. Vilsoet, General Counsel/VP/Corp. Sec.
Steven E. Nielsen, Chmn.

Phone: 561-627-7171	Fax: 561-627-7709
Toll-Free:	
Address: 11770 U.S. Highway 1, Ste. 101, Palm Beach Gardens, FL 33408 US	

GROWTH PLANS/SPECIAL FEATURES:

Dycom Industries, Inc. is a leading provider of specialty contracting services. Dycom provides services throughout the U.S. and on a limited basis in Canada, including engineering, construction, maintenance and installation services to telecommunications providers; underground locating services to various utilities including telecommunications providers; and other construction and maintenance services to electric utilities and others. During 2008, the company generated approximately 76.2% of its total revenue from specialty contracting services related to the telecommunications industry; approximately 17.7% from underground utility locating; and approximately 6.1% from electric and other construction and maintenance services to electric utilities and others. Dycom provides outside plant engineers and drafters to telecommunication providers, who design aerial, underground and buried optic, copper and coaxial cable systems that extend from the telephone company central office, or cable operator headend, to the consumer's home or business. Engineering services the company provides to telephone companies include fiber cable routing and design; the design of service area concept boxes, terminals, drops and transmission and central office equipment; and the proper administration of feeder and distribution cable pairs. For cable television multiple system operators, Dycom performs make-ready studies, strand mapping, field walk-out, computer-aided radio frequency design and fiber cable routing and design. The firm's construction, maintenance and installation services include placing and splicing fiber, copper and coaxial cables; excavating trenches in which to place cables; placing related structures such as poles, anchors, conduits, manholes, cabinets and closures; placing drop lines from main distribution lines to the consumer's home or business; and maintaining and removing these facilities. It also provides premise wiring services to various corporations and state and local governments, predominantly limited to the installation, repair and maintenance of telecommunications infrastructure within improved structures. Dycom's top five customers generated approximately 64% of its 2008 revenue.

FINANCIALS: Sales and profits are in thousands of dollars—add 000 to get the full amount. 2008 Note: Financial information for 2008 was not available for all companies at press time.

2008 Sales: $1,229,956	2008 Profits: $21,678	U.S. Stock Ticker: DY
2007 Sales: $1,137,812	2007 Profits: $41,884	Int'l Ticker: Int'l Exchange:
2006 Sales: $1,023,673	2006 Profits: $18,180	Employees: 10,746
2005 Sales: $986,627	2005 Profits: $24,314	Fiscal Year Ends: 7/31
2004 Sales: $872,700	2004 Profits: $58,600	Parent Company:

SALARIES/BENEFITS:

Pension Plan:	ESOP Stock Plan:	Profit Sharing:	Top Exec. Salary: $705,000	Bonus: $207,251
Savings Plan:	Stock Purch. Plan:		Second Exec. Salary: $480,000	Bonus: $138,193

OTHER THOUGHTS:

Apparent Women Officers or Directors: 1
Hot Spot for Advancement for Women/Minorities:

LOCATIONS: ("Y" = Yes)

West:	Southwest:	Midwest:	Southeast:	Northeast:	International:
Y	Y	Y	Y	Y	

E I DU PONT DE NEMOURS & CO (DUPONT)   www2.dupont.com

Industry Group Code: 325 Ranks within this company's industry group: Sales: 1 Profits: 1

Management:		Sales/Marketing:		Liberal Arts:		Information Systems:		Professionals:		Tech./Scientific:	
Management Trainees:	Y	Marketing Pros.:	Y	Gen. Writing/Editing:	Y	Info. Management:	Y	Finance/Acct.:	Y	Engineers, Electrical:	Y
Experienced Mngmt.:	Y	Retail Sales:		Technical Writing:	Y	Software Dev.:	Y	Law:	Y	Engineers, Other:	Y
International Business:	Y	Commercial/Industrial:	Y	Graphic Arts/Photog.:		Hardware Dev.:		HR/Other:	Y	Health/Lab:	Y
MBA Grads:	Y	Sales Trainees:		Music:		Consulting/Other:		Training:	Y	Scientists/Research:	Y
		Advertising Pros.:		Broadcasting:				Health Care:		Petroleum/Chemicals:	Y
				Other:				Consulting:		Math/Other:	

TYPES OF BUSINESS:

Chemicals Manufacturing
Polymers
Performance Coatings
Nutrition & Health Products
Electronics Materials
Agricultural Seeds
Fuel-Cell, Biofuels & Solar Panel Technology
Contract Research & Development

BRANDS/DIVISIONS/AFFILIATES:

Pioneer
Teflon
Corian
Kevlar
Tyvek
Coastal Training Technologies Corporation
MapShots, Inc.

CONTACTS: *Note: Officers with more than one job title may be intentionally listed here more than once.*

Ellen J. Kullman, CEO
Richard R. Goodmanson, COO/Exec. VP
Jeffrey L. Keefer, CFO/Exec. VP
David G. Bills, Chief Mktg. & Sales Officer
W. Donald Johnson, Sr. VP-DuPont Human Resources
John Bedbrook, VP-R&D, Agriculture & Nutrition
Phuong Tram, CIO/VP-DuPont IT
Uma Chowdhry, CTO/Chief Science Officer/Sr. VP
Thomas M. Connelly, Jr., Chief Innovation Officer/Exec. VP
Mathieu Vrijsen, Sr. VP-DuPont Eng.
Thomas L. Sager, General Counsel/Sr. VP-DuPont Legal
Mathieu Vrijsen, Sr. VP-DuPont Oper.
Peter C. Hemken, VP-Strategic Dir. & Bus. Dev., Pioneer Hi-Bred
Karen A. Fletcher, VP-DuPont Investor Rel.
Susan M. Stalnecker, VP-Finance/Treas.
Criag F. Binetti, Sr. VP-DuPont Nutrition & Health
Diane H. Gulyas, Group VP-DuPont Performance Materials
Terry Caloghiris, Group VP-DuPont Coatings & Color Tech.
Nicholas C. Fanandakis, Group VP-DuPont Applied BioSciences
Charles O. Holliday, Jr., Chmn.
Don Wirth, VP-Global Oper.
Jeffrey A. Coe, Sr. VP-DuPont Sourcing & Logistics

Phone: 302-774-1000	Fax: 302-773-2631
Toll-Free: 800-441-7515	
Address: 1007 Market St., Wilmington, DE 19898 US	

GROWTH PLANS/SPECIAL FEATURES:

E. I. du Pont de Nemours & Co. (DuPont), founded in 1802, develops and manufactures products in the biotechnology, electronics, materials science, synthetic fibers and safety and security sectors. DuPont operates in five segments: Agriculture and Nutrition (A&N); Coatings and Color Technologies (C&CT); Electronic and Communication Technologies (E&C); Performance Materials (PM); and Safety and Protection (S&P). A&N delivers Pioneer brand seed products, insecticides, fungicides, herbicides, soy-based food ingredients, food quality diagnostic testing equipment and liquid food packaging systems. The C&CT segment supplies automotive coatings, titanium dioxide white pigments and pigment and dye-based inks for ink-jet digital printing. E&C provides a range of advanced materials for the electronics industry, flexographic printing, color communication systems and a range of fluoropolymer and fluorochemical products. PM manufactures polymer-based materials, which include engineered polymers, specialized resins and films for use in food packaging, sealants, adhesives, sporting goods and laminated safety glass. The S&P segment provides protective materials and safety consulting services. Significant brands include Teflon fluoropolymers, films, fabric protectors, fibers and dispersions; Corian surfaces; Kevlar high strength material; and Tyvek protective material. Recent acquisitions include Chemtura Corporation's fluorine chemicals business in February 2008; the Industrial Apparel line of Cardinal Health's Scientific and Production Products business in April 2008; Coastal Training Technologies Corporation, a producer and marketer of training programs, in October 2008; and MapShots, Inc., an agricultural data management company, in December 2008. Recent divestitures include DuPont Super Boll and FreeFall brand cotton products in February 2008; and its 8th Continent soy milk joint venture with General Mills in February 2008. Also in 2008, DuPont opened new offices in Abu Dhabi, U.A.E. and Hyderabad, India.

DuPont offers its employees tuition assistance, ongoing training programs, flexible work practices, adoption assistance, an employee resource program, an emergency backup childcare resource and dependent care spending accounts.

FINANCIALS: Sales and profits are in thousands of dollars—add 000 to get the full amount. 2008 Note: Financial information for 2008 was not available for all companies at press time.

2008 Sales: $30,529,000	2008 Profits: $2,007,000	**U.S. Stock Ticker: DD**
2007 Sales: $29,378,000	2007 Profits: $2,988,000	**Int'l Ticker:** Int'l Exchange:
2006 Sales: $27,421,000	2006 Profits: $3,148,000	Employees: 60,000
2005 Sales: $26,639,000	2005 Profits: $2,053,000	Fiscal Year Ends: 12/31
2004 Sales: $27,340,000	2004 Profits: $1,780,000	Parent Company:

SALARIES/BENEFITS:

Pension Plan: Y	ESOP Stock Plan:	Profit Sharing:	Top Exec. Salary: $1,369,500	Bonus: $1,932,000
Savings Plan: Y	Stock Purch. Plan:		Second Exec. Salary: $865,992	Bonus: $763,000

OTHER THOUGHTS:

Apparent Women Officers or Directors: 17
Hot Spot for Advancement for Women/Minorities: Y

LOCATIONS: ("Y" = Yes)

West:	Southwest:	Midwest:	Southeast:	Northeast:	International:
Y	Y	Y	Y	Y	Y

Note: Financial information, benefits and other data can change quickly and may vary from those stated here.

EATON CORP

www.eaton.com

Industry Group Code: 3363 **Ranks within this company's industry group:** Sales: 2 Profits: 1

Management:		Sales/Marketing:		Liberal Arts:		Information Systems:		Professionals:		Tech./Scientific:	
Management Trainees:	Y	Marketing Pros.:	Y	Gen. Writing/Editing:		Info. Management:	Y	Finance/Acct.:	Y	Engineers, Electrical:	Y
Experienced Mngmt.:	Y	Retail Sales:		Technical Writing:	Y	Software Dev.:	Y	Law:	Y	Engineers, Other:	Y
International Business:	Y	Commercial/Industrial:	Y	Graphic Arts/Photog.:	Y	Hardware Dev.:		HR/Other:	Y	Health/Lab:	
MBA Grads:	Y	Sales Trainees:		Music:		Consulting/Other:		Training:	Y	Scientists/Research:	Y
		Advertising Pros.:	Y	Broadcasting:				Health Care:		Petroleum/Chemicals:	
				Other:				Consulting:		Math/Other:	

TYPES OF BUSINESS:

Hydraulic Products
Electrical Power Distribution & Control Equipment
Truck Transmissions & Axles
Engine Components
Aerospace & Military Components

BRANDS/DIVISIONS/AFFILIATES:

Moeller Group (The)
Phoenixtec Power Company Ltd.
Integ Holdings Limited
Integrated Hydraulics Ltd.
Marina Power Lighting

CONTACTS: *Note: Officers with more than one job title may be intentionally listed here more than once.*

Alexander M. Cutler, CEO
Alexander M. Cutler, Pres.
Richard H. Fearon, CFO/Chief Planning Officer
Jeffrey M. Krakowiak, Sr. VP-Mktg. & Sales
Susan J. Cook, Exec. VP-Human Resources
William W. Blausey, Jr., CIO/VP
Yannis P. Tsavalas, CTO/Sr. VP
Mark M. McGuire, General Counsel/Exec. VP
Kurt B. McMaken, Sr. VP-Corp. Dev. & Treasury
William B. Doggett, Sr. VP-Comm. & Public Affairs
William C. Hartman, Sr. VP-Investor Rel.
Billie K. Rawot, Sr. VP/Controller
Joseph P. Palchak, Pres., Automotive
James E. Sweetnam, Pres., Truck Group
Craig Arnold, COO-Industrial
Thomas S. Gross, COO-Electrical
Alexander M. Cutler, Chmn.
Yannis P. Tsavalas, Pres., EMEA
Craig Reed, Sr. VP-Supply Chain Mgmt.

Phone: 216-523-5000	**Fax:** 216-523-4787
Toll-Free: 800-386-1911	
Address: 1111 Superior Ave., Cleveland, OH 44114-2584 US	

GROWTH PLANS/SPECIAL FEATURES:

Eaton Corporation is a global designer, manufacturer and marketer of electrical systems and components. The firm operates in two business segments: industrial and electrical. The industrial sector is made up of four divisions: hydraulics, aerospace, automotive and truck. The hydraulics segment develops and sells fluid power products to industrial, mobile equipment and aerospace customers worldwide. The aerospace business unit serves commercial/military aviation, space, military weapon, marine and off-road applications. The automotive unit focuses on the powertrain and specialized sensor and actuator areas of passenger cars and light trucks. Its primary products include engine air management systems such as superchargers, cylinder head modules, engine valves and lifters. The truck segment features drivetrain systems and components for medium-duty and heavy-duty commercial vehicles. Its products include manual and automatic transmissions; clutches; driveshafts; drive and trailer axles; brakes; chassis control systems; and collision warning systems. The electrical sector distributes electrical power and control equipment for industrial, commercial and residential markets. The company sells its products to customers in over 150 countries. In the first half of 2008, the firm acquired the engine valves business of Kirloskar Oil Engines Ltd.; The Moeller Group; and Phoenixtec Power Company Ltd. In August 2008, Eaton agreed to a joint-venture with Nittan Valve Co. Ltd. for engine valve products in Japan and Korea. In October 2008, the company acquired Integ Holdings Limited, the parent firm of U.K.-based screw-in cartridge valve manufacturer Integrated Hydraulics Ltd. In November 2008, Eaton purchased a new regional headquarters building in Shanghai, China. In January 2009, the firm sold its Vehicle On-Board Radar (VORAD) system to Bendix Commercial Vehicle Systems LLC.

Eaton offers employees benefits including medical, dental, vision and disability insurance; flexible spending accounts; a personal investment plan; employee assistance; tuition reimbursement; and adoption assistance.

FINANCIALS: Sales and profits are in thousands of dollars—add 000 to get the full amount. 2008 Note: Financial information for 2008 was not available for all companies at press time.

2008 Sales: $15,376,000	2008 Profits: $1,058,000	**U.S. Stock Ticker:** ETN
2007 Sales: $13,033,000	2007 Profits: $994,000	**Int'l Ticker:** Int'l Exchange:
2006 Sales: $12,232,000	2006 Profits: $950,000	Employees: 75,000
2005 Sales: $10,874,000	2005 Profits: $805,000	Fiscal Year Ends: 12/31
2004 Sales: $9,712,000	2004 Profits: $648,000	Parent Company:

SALARIES/BENEFITS:

Pension Plan: Y	ESOP Stock Plan:	Profit Sharing:	Top Exec. Salary: $1,132,500	Bonus: $3,987,500
Savings Plan: Y	Stock Purch. Plan:		Second Exec. Salary: $596,730	Bonus: $1,193,860

OTHER THOUGHTS:

Apparent Women Officers or Directors: 2
Hot Spot for Advancement for Women/Minorities: Y

LOCATIONS: ("Y" = Yes)

West:	Southwest:	Midwest:	Southeast:	Northeast:	International:
Y	Y	Y	Y	Y	Y

Note: Financial information, benefits and other data can change quickly and may vary from those stated here.

EBAY INC

www.ebay.com

Industry Group Code: 454112 Ranks within this company's industry group: Sales: 1   Profits: 1

Management:		Sales/Marketing:		Liberal Arts:		Information Systems:		Professionals:		Tech./Scientific:	
Management Trainees:	Y	Marketing Pros.:	Y	Gen. Writing/Editing:	Y	Info. Management:	Y	Finance/Acct.:	Y	Engineers, Electrical:	Y
Experienced Mngmt.:	Y	Retail Sales:		Technical Writing:	Y	Software Dev.:	Y	Law:	Y	Engineers, Other:	
International Business:	Y	Commercial/Industrial:		Graphic Arts/Photog.:	Y	Hardware Dev.:		HR/Other:	Y	Health/Lab:	
MBA Grads:	Y	Sales Trainees:		Music:		Consulting/Other:		Training:	Y	Scientists/Research:	
		Advertising Pros.:	Y	Broadcasting:				Health Care:		Petroleum/Chemicals:	
				Other:	Y			Consulting:		Math/Other:	

TYPES OF BUSINESS:

Online Retail-Auctions
Online Payment Processing
Memorabilia & Collectibles
E-Commerce Services

BRANDS/DIVISIONS/AFFILIATES:

eBay Express
Bill Me Later
PayPal
Rent.com
Gmarket, Inc.
bilbasen.dk
dba.dk

CONTACTS: *Note: Officers with more than one job title may be intentionally listed here more than once.*

John Donahoe, CEO
John Donahoe, Pres.
Bob Swan, CFO
Elizabeth Axelrod, Sr. VP-Human Resources
Michael Jacobson, General Counsel/Sr. VP
Michael van Swaaij, Chief Strategy Officer
Lorrie Norrington,, Pres., eBay Marketplaces
Alan Marks, Sr. VP-Corp. Comm.
Bob Swan, Sr. VP-Finance
Scott Thompson, Pres., PayPal
Pierre M. Omidyar, Chmn.

Phone: 408-376-7400	Fax: 408-376-7401
Toll-Free:	
Address: 2145 Hamilton Ave., San Jose, CA 95125 US	

GROWTH PLANS/SPECIAL FEATURES:

eBay, Inc. is an online auction venue that brings together millions of buyers and sellers every day locally, nationally and internationally through its array of web sites. eBay provides online marketplaces for the sale of goods and services, online payments services and online communication offerings. It currently has three primary businesses: marketplaces, payments and communications. The marketplaces segment enables online commerce through a variety of platforms, including the traditional eBay.com platform and the company's other online platforms, such as its classifieds websites, as well as Half.com, Rent.com, Shopping.com and StubHub. The wide array of web sites that comprise the firms' marketplaces segment brings together millions of buyers and sellers every day on a local, national and international basis. The payments segment consists of PayPal, which enables individuals and businesses to securely, easily and quickly send and receive payments online in approximately 190 markets worldwide, and Bill Me Later, which enables online U.S. merchants to offer customers transactional credit. Bill Me Later was acquired in November 2008. In October 2008, the company announced its intent to cut roughly 10% of jobs. eBay also announced plans to acquire online payments firm Bill Me Later and two Danish web sites dba.dk and bilbasen.dk. In June 2009, the company acquired Gmarket, Inc., owner of a Korean e-commerce web site.

eBay offers its employees adoption assistance, a pet insurance plan, tuition reimbursement, employee training courses, referral bonuses and on-site services such as dry cleaning and chiropractic care. The firm also provides a wide range of insurance benefits such as medical, dental, vision, life and accidental death and dismemberment, short and long term disability and business travel accident insurance.

FINANCIALS: Sales and profits are in thousands of dollars—add 000 to get the full amount. 2008 Note: Financial information for 2008 was not available for all companies at press time.

2008 Sales: $8,541,261	2008 Profits: $1,779,474	**U.S. Stock Ticker: EBAY**
2007 Sales: $7,672,329	2007 Profits: $348,251	**Int'l Ticker:** Int'l Exchange:
2006 Sales: $5,969,741	2006 Profits: $1,125,639	Employees: 16,200
2005 Sales: $4,552,401	2005 Profits: $1,082,043	Fiscal Year Ends: 12/31
2004 Sales: $3,271,309	2004 Profits: $778,223	Parent Company:

SALARIES/BENEFITS:

Pension Plan:	ESOP Stock Plan:	Profit Sharing:	Top Exec. Salary: $879,808	Bonus: $500,000
Savings Plan: Y	Stock Purch. Plan: Y		Second Exec. Salary: $713,947	Bonus: $

OTHER THOUGHTS:

Apparent Women Officers or Directors: 4
Hot Spot for Advancement for Women/Minorities: Y

LOCATIONS: ("Y" = Yes)

West:	Southwest:	Midwest:	Southeast:	Northeast:	International:
Y	Y	Y		Y	Y

EDISON INTERNATIONAL

www.edison.com

Industry Group Code: 2211 Ranks within this company's industry group: Sales: 6 Profits: 6

Management:		Sales/Marketing:		Liberal Arts:		Information Systems:		Professionals:		Tech./Scientific:	
Management Trainees:	Y	Marketing Pros.:	Y	Gen. Writing/Editing:	Y	Info. Management:	Y	Finance/Acct.:	Y	Engineers, Electrical:	Y
Experienced Mngmt.:	Y	Retail Sales:		Technical Writing:	Y	Software Dev.:	Y	Law:	Y	Engineers, Other:	Y
International Business:	Y	Commercial/Industrial:	Y	Graphic Arts/Photog.:	Y	Hardware Dev.:		HR/Other:	Y	Health/Lab:	
MBA Grads:	Y	Sales Trainees:		Music:		Consulting/Other:		Training:	Y	Scientists/Research:	
		Advertising Pros.:	Y	Broadcasting:				Health Care:		Petroleum/Chemicals:	Y
				Other:				Consulting:		Math/Other:	

TYPES OF BUSINESS:

Utilities-Electricity & Natural Gas
Financial Services
Operations Services
Energy Trading

BRANDS/DIVISIONS/AFFILIATES:

Southern California Edison Company
Edison Mission Energy
Edison Capital

CONTACTS: Note: Officers with more than one job title may be intentionally listed here more than once.

Theodore F. Craver Jr., CEO
Theodore F. Craver Jr., Pres.
Jim Scilacci, CFO/Exec. VP/Treas.
Daryl David, Sr. VP-Human Resources
Robert L. Adler, General Counsel/Exec. VP
Andrew J. Hertneky, VP-Strategy
Barbara J. Parsky, Sr. VP-Corp. Comm.
Scott Cunningham, VP-Investor Rel.
Mark Clarke, Controller/VP
Polly Gault, Exec. VP-Public Affairs
Jeff Barnett, VP-Tax
Barbara E. Matthews, Chief Governance Officer/VP/Corp. Sec.
Kenneth S. Stewart, Chief Ethics & Compliance Officer/VP
Theodore F. Craver Jr., Chmn.

Phone: 626-302-2222	Fax: 626-302-2517
Toll-Free: 800-655-4555	
Address: 2244 Walnut Grove Ave., Rosemead, CA 91770 US	

GROWTH PLANS/SPECIAL FEATURES:

Edison International is a California-based holding company with subsidiaries operating primarily in the U.S., with some investments abroad. Major subsidiaries include Southern California Edison Company (SCE), a utility corporation, and non-utility companies Edison Mission Energy (EME) and Edison Capital. SCE is one of the nation's largest electric utilities, providing electric service to a 50,000-square-mile area of California, including over 180 cities and communities, serving over 14 million customers. The energy provided is developed from a range of different kinds of power plants including coal-burning, nuclear, hydroelectric and diesel-burning facilities. SCE also owns over 71,500 circuit miles of overhead lines and about 40,000 circuit miles of underground lines. SCE has assets of over $32.6 billion. EME is an independent power producer engaged in the business of developing, acquiring, owning or leasing, operating and selling energy and capacity from independent power production facilities. These operations consist in owning or leasing interests in 37 domestic operating power plants with a capacity of 11,019 megawatts. EME also conducts price risk management and energy trading activities in power markets open to competition. Edison Capital invests in energy and infrastructure projects, including power generation; electric transmission and distribution; transportation; affordable housing; and telecommunications. In December 2008, SCE completed its first solar photovoltaic installation on a 600,000 square-foot warehouse roof. Composed of 33,700 advanced thin-film solar panels, the installation has the ability to power 1,300 homes.

Employers are offered medical, dental and vision insurance; a 401(k) plan; disability benefits; an employee assistance program; life insurance; a pension plan; educational reimbursement; credit union membership; and business travel accident insurance.

FINANCIALS: Sales and profits are in thousands of dollars—add 000 to get the full amount. 2008 Note: Financial information for 2008 was not available for all companies at press time.

2008 Sales: $11,248,000	2008 Profits: $1,215,000	U.S. Stock Ticker: EIX
2007 Sales: $13,113,000	2007 Profits: $1,098,000	Int'l Ticker: Int'l Exchange:
2006 Sales: $12,622,000	2006 Profits: $1,181,000	Employees: 18,291
2005 Sales: $11,852,000	2005 Profits: $1,137,000	Fiscal Year Ends: 12/31
2004 Sales: $10,199,000	2004 Profits: $916,000	Parent Company:

SALARIES/BENEFITS:

Pension Plan: Y	ESOP Stock Plan:	Profit Sharing:	Top Exec. Salary: $892,485	Bonus: $1,050,000
Savings Plan: Y	Stock Purch. Plan:		Second Exec. Salary: $768,308	Bonus: $3,099,404

OTHER THOUGHTS:

Apparent Women Officers or Directors: 6
Hot Spot for Advancement for Women/Minorities: Y

LOCATIONS: ("Y" = Yes)

West:	Southwest:	Midwest:	Southeast:	Northeast:	International:
Y	Y	Y	Y	Y	Y

Note: Financial information, benefits and other data can change quickly and may vary from those stated here.

ELECTRONIC ARTS INC

www.ea.com

Industry Group Code: 511210G Ranks within this company's industry group: Sales: 1   Profits: 2

Management:		Sales/Marketing:		Liberal Arts:		Information Systems:		Professionals:		Tech./Scientific:	
Management Trainees:	Y	Marketing Pros.:	Y	Gen. Writing/Editing:	Y	Info. Management:	Y	Finance/Acct.:	Y	Engineers, Electrical:	Y
Experienced Mngmt.:	Y	Retail Sales:		Technical Writing:	Y	Software Dev.:	Y	Law:	Y	Engineers, Other:	
International Business:	Y	Commercial/Industrial:	Y	Graphic Arts/Photog.:	Y	Hardware Dev.:		HR/Other:	Y	Health/Lab:	
MBA Grads:	Y	Sales Trainees:	Y	Music:	Y	Consulting/Other:		Training:	Y	Scientists/Research:	
		Advertising Pros.:	Y	Broadcasting:				Health Care:		Petroleum/Chemicals:	
				Other:	Y			Consulting:		Math/Other:	

TYPES OF BUSINESS:

Computer Software-Video Games
Online Interactive Games
E-Commerce Sales
Mobile Games

BRANDS/DIVISIONS/AFFILIATES:

EA Games
EA Sports
EA Casual Entertainment
Bioware Corp
Madden NFL
Pogo.com
ThreeSF Inc
J2MSoft Inc

CONTACTS: *Note: Officers with more than one job title may be intentionally listed here more than once.*

John S. Riccitiello, CEO
John Pleasants, COO/Pres., Global Publishing
Eric Brown, CFO/Exec. VP
Gabrielle Toledano, Exec. VP-Human Resources
Stephen G. Bene, General Counsel/Sec./Sr. VP
Joel Linzner, Exec. VP-Bus. & Legal Affairs
Tammy Schachter, Sr. Dir.-Public Rel.
Ken Barker, Chief Acct. Officer/Sr. VP
Peter Moore, Pres., EA Sports Label
Frank Gibeau, Pres., EA Games Label
Gerhard Florin, Exec. VP-Publishing
Lawrence F. Probst, III, Chmn.

Phone: 650-628-1500	Fax: 650-628-1415
Toll-Free:	
Address: 209 Redwood Shores Pkwy., Redwood City, CA 94065-1175 US	

GROWTH PLANS/SPECIAL FEATURES:

Electronic Arts, Inc. (EA) develops, markets, publishes and distributes video game software. The company designs products for a number of platforms, including video game consoles, such as the Sony PlayStation 3, Microsoft Xbox 360 and Nintendo Wii; handheld game systems, including PlayStation Portable (PSP), Nintendo DS and Apple iPod; personal computers (PCs); and mobile phones. The company operates in four segments, or labels: EA Games, EA Sports, The Sims and EA Casual Entertainment. The EA Games label encompasses the largest percentage of the company's studios and development staff, focused on producing a diverse portfolio of action-adventure, role playing, racing and combat games, as well as massively-multiplayer online role-playing games (MMORPG) such as Warhammer Online. The EA Sports label produces a variety of sports-based video games, including the Madden NFL, FIFA Soccer and Tiger Woods PGA TOUR franchises. EA's The Sims label develops life simulation games and online communities, such as The Sims 2, which offers an online community of over 4 million unique monthly users. The EA Casual Entertainment label develops games that are intended to be quick to learn and play, making them easily accessible for a wide audience. Pogo, an online service with over 1.6 million subscribers, offers a variety of card, puzzle and word games. Through EA Mobile, the firm publishes games and related content for mobile phones. The company distributes games in over 35 countries worldwide. In June 2008, EA acquired ThreeSF, Inc., a gaming-based social network. In December 2008, the company acquired J2MSoft Inc., a Korean-based developer of PC online games. Also in December 2008, Electronic Arts announced plans to cut its worldwide workforce by approximately 10% and to consolidate or close at least nine of its studio and publishing locations.

EA offers its employees discounts on game systems; education reimbursement; medical insurance; a bonus plan; and an employee assistance program.

FINANCIALS: Sales and profits are in thousands of dollars—add 000 to get the full amount. 2008 Note: Financial information for 2008 was not available for all companies at press time.

2008 Sales: $3,665,000	2008 Profits: $-454,000	**U.S. Stock Ticker: ERTS**
2007 Sales: $3,091,000	2007 Profits: $76,000	**Int'l Ticker:** Int'l Exchange:
2006 Sales: $2,951,000	2006 Profits: $236,000	Employees: 9,100
2005 Sales: $3,129,000	2005 Profits: $504,000	Fiscal Year Ends: 3/31
2004 Sales: $2,957,141	2004 Profits: $577,292	Parent Company:

SALARIES/BENEFITS:

Pension Plan:	ESOP Stock Plan:	Profit Sharing:	Top Exec. Salary: $752,599	Bonus: $349,358
Savings Plan: Y	Stock Purch. Plan: Y		Second Exec. Salary: $750,000	Bonus: $625,350

OTHER THOUGHTS:

Apparent Women Officers or Directors: 3
Hot Spot for Advancement for Women/Minorities: Y

LOCATIONS: ("Y" = Yes)

West:	Southwest:	Midwest:	Southeast:	Northeast:	International:
Y	Y	Y	Y	Y	Y

ELI LILLY & COMPANY

www.lilly.com

Industry Group Code: 325412 **Ranks within this company's industry group:** Sales: 6 Profits: 18

Management:		Sales/Marketing:		Liberal Arts:		Information Systems:		Professionals:		Tech./Scientific:	
Management Trainees:	Y	Marketing Pros.:	Y	Gen. Writing/Editing:	Y	Info. Management:	Y	Finance/Acct.:	Y	Engineers, Electrical:	Y
Experienced Mngmt.:	Y	Retail Sales:		Technical Writing:	Y	Software Dev.:	Y	Law:	Y	Engineers, Other:	Y
International Business:	Y	Commercial/Industrial:	Y	Graphic Arts/Photog.:	Y	Hardware Dev.:		HR/Other:	Y	Health/Lab:	Y
MBA Grads:	Y	Sales Trainees:	Y	Music:		Consulting/Other:		Training:	Y	Scientists/Research:	Y
		Advertising Pros.:	Y	Broadcasting:				Health Care:	Y	Petroleum/Chemicals:	Y
				Other:				Consulting:		Math/Other:	Y

TYPES OF BUSINESS:

Pharmaceuticals Discovery & Development
Veterinary Products

BRANDS/DIVISIONS/AFFILIATES:

Zyprexa
Prozac
Humalog
Gemzar
Coban
Applied Molecular Evolution Inc
Icos Corporation
ImClone Systems Inc.

CONTACTS: Note: Officers with more than one job title may be intentionally listed here more than once.

John Lechleiter, CEO
John Lechleiter, Pres.
Derica Rice, CFO/Sr. VP
Bryce D. Carmine, Exec. VP-Global Mktg. & Sales
Steven M. Paul, Exec. VP-Science
Michael Heim, CIO/VP-IT
Steven M. Paul, Exec. VP-Tech.
Thomas Verhoeven, Pres., Global Prod. Dev.
W. Darin Moody, VP-Corp. Eng. & Continuous Improvement
Frank Deane, Pres., Mfg.
Robert A. Armitage, Co-General Counsel/Sr. VP
Gino Santini, Exec. Dir.-Corp. Strategy & Policy
Alex M. Azar II, Sr. VP-Corp. Affairs & Comm.
Thomas W. Grein, Treas./VP
Enrique Conterno, Pres., Lilly USA
Alfonso Zulueta, Pres./Gen. Mgr.-Lilly Japan
Alecia A. DeCoudreaux, Co-General Counsel/VP
Tim Garnett, Chief Medical Officer/VP-Medical
John Lechleiter, Chmn.
Karim Bitar, Pres., European Oper.

Phone: 317-276-2000	Fax:
Toll-Free: 800-545-5979	
Address: Lilly Corporate Ctr., Indianapolis, IN 46285 US	

GROWTH PLANS/SPECIAL FEATURES:

Eli Lilly & Co. researches, develops, manufactures and sells pharmaceuticals designed to treat a variety of conditions. Most of Eli Lilly's products are developed by its in-house research staff, which primarily directs its research efforts towards the search for products to prevent and treat cancer and diseases of the central nervous, endocrine and cardiovascular systems. The firm's other research lies in anti-infectives and products to treat animal diseases. Major brands include neuroscience products Zyprexa, Strattera, Prozac, Cymbalta and Permax; endocrine products Humalog, Humulin and Actos; oncology products Gemzar and Alimta; animal health products Tylan, Rumensin and Coban; cardiovascular products ReoPro and Xigris; anti-infectives Ceclor and Vancocin; and Cialis, for erectile dysfunction. In the U.S., the company distributes pharmaceuticals primarily through independent wholesale distributors. The company manufactures and distributes its products through facilities in the U.S., Puerto Rico and 25 other countries, which are then sold to markets in 135 countries throughout the world. In 2008, the firm owned 15 production and distribution facilities in the U.S. and Puerto Rico. Major research and development facilities abroad are located in the U.K., Canada, Singapore and Spain. In April 2008, the firm acquired Hypnion, Inc., a neuroscience drug discovery company focused on sleep disorder research. In October 2008, the company agreed to acquire ImClone Systems, Inc. for $6.5 billion.

Eli Lilly offers its employees domestic partner benefits and an employee assistance program, as well as up to 10 weeks of paid maternity leave. The firm also offers an on-site fitness center, flexible hours or telecommuting, parenting and dependant care leaves, adoption assistance and tuition reimbursement.

FINANCIALS: Sales and profits are in thousands of dollars—add 000 to get the full amount. 2008 Note: Financial information for 2008 was not available for all companies at press time.

		U.S. Stock Ticker: LLY
2008 Sales: $20,378,000	2008 Profits: $-2,071,900	**Int'l Ticker:** Int'l Exchange:
2007 Sales: $18,633,500	2007 Profits: $2,953,000	Employees: 40,500
2006 Sales: $15,691,000	2006 Profits: $2,662,700	Fiscal Year Ends: 12/31
2005 Sales: $14,645,300	2005 Profits: $1,979,600	Parent Company:
2004 Sales: $13,857,900	2004 Profits: $1,810,100	

SALARIES/BENEFITS:

Pension Plan: Y	ESOP Stock Plan:	Profit Sharing:	Top Exec. Salary: $1,339,125	Bonus: $2,709,053
Savings Plan: Y	Stock Purch. Plan:		Second Exec. Salary: $1,000,250	Bonus: $1,309,327

OTHER THOUGHTS:

Apparent Women Officers or Directors: 4
Hot Spot for Advancement for Women/Minorities: Y

LOCATIONS: ("Y" = Yes)

West:	Southwest:	Midwest:	Southeast:	Northeast:	International:
Y	Y	Y	Y	Y	Y

EMBARQ CORP

www.embarq.com

Industry Group Code: 517110 **Ranks within this company's industry group:** Sales: 9 Profits: 5

Management:		Sales/Marketing:		Liberal Arts:		Information Systems:		Professionals:		Tech./Scientific:	
Management Trainees:	Y	Marketing Pros.:	Y	Gen. Writing/Editing:	Y	Info. Management:	Y	Finance/Acct.:	Y	Engineers, Electrical:	Y
Experienced Mngmt.:	Y	Retail Sales:		Technical Writing:	Y	Software Dev.:	Y	Law:	Y	Engineers, Other:	Y
International Business:		Commercial/Industrial:	Y	Graphic Arts/Photog.:	Y	Hardware Dev.:		HR/Other:	Y	Health/Lab:	
MBA Grads:	Y	Sales Trainees:	Y	Music:		Consulting/Other:		Training:	Y	Scientists/Research:	
		Advertising Pros.:	Y	Broadcasting:				Health Care:		Petroleum/Chemicals:	
				Other:				Consulting:		Math/Other:	

TYPES OF BUSINESS:

Local & Long-Distance Phone Services
High-Speed Internet Access
Satellite Video Services
Wireless Services

BRANDS/DIVISIONS/AFFILIATES:

Sprint Nextel Corp

CONTACTS: *Note: Officers with more than one job title may be intentionally listed here more than once.*

Thomas A. Gerke, CEO
Thomas A. Gerke, Pres.
Gene M. Betts, CFO
E.J. Holland, Jr., Sr. VP-Human Resources
Vercie L. Lark, CIO
Dennis G. Huber, CTO
Claudia S. Toussaint, General Counsel/Corp. Sec.
E.J. Holland, Jr., Sr. VP-Comm.
Les Meredith, Treas.
William E. (Bill) Cheek, Pres., Wholesale Markets
Harrison S. Campbell, Pres., Consumer Markets
Thomas J. McEvoy, Pres., Bus. Markets
James C. Mayfield, Pres., Embarq Logistics
William A. Owens, Chmn.

Phone: 913-323-4637	Fax: 913-523-9120
Toll-Free: 866-404-4637	
Address: 5454 W. 110th St., Overland Park, KS 66211 US	

GROWTH PLANS/SPECIAL FEATURES:

Embarq Corporation is a provider of local and long-distance voice, data, high-speed Internet, satellite, video, wireless and other communication-related products and services to consumer and business customers in 18 states. It also provides access to its local network and other wholesale communications services for customers, including other carriers. Through its Logistics segment, the firm provides wholesale product distribution, logistics and configuration services. Embarq has a significant presence in Florida, North Carolina, Nevada and Ohio, which together represent approximately 66% of all its access lines. The company offers six general categories of products and services through its Telecommunications segment: voice, data, high-speed Internet, wireless, product and other. As of December 2008, Embarq had approximately 3.8 million local service consumer access lines and 1.8 million business access lines. It offers long-distance voice and data services through a wholesale agreement with Sprint Nextel. The company's most significant data service is special access, which consists of dedicated circuits used to connect the customer's business sites or network to its network; to connect the customer's networks directly to their customers' locations, or, in the case of wireless carriers, to connect their cell sites with their mobile switching centers. Embarq provided high-speed Internet access to approximately 1.4 million subscribers. The company offers wireless services through a wholesale arrangement involving a mobile virtual network operator relationship with Sprint Nextel. Embarq sells and services a range of customer premises equipment and wireless handsets and sells video services through its sales agency relationship with DISH Network Corporation and DIRECTV. In October 2008, Embarq agreed to be acquired by CenturyTel for $5.8 billion. In March 2009, the company sold its supply chain subsidiary, Embarq Logistics to KGP Telecommunications, Inc.

Employees are offered medical, dental and vision insurance; a 401(k) plan; pension plans; an employee assistance program; and a tuition assistance program.

FINANCIALS: Sales and profits are in thousands of dollars—add 000 to get the full amount. 2008 Note: Financial information for 2008 was not available for all companies at press time.

2008 Sales: $6,124,000	2008 Profits: $769,000	U.S. Stock Ticker: EQ
2007 Sales: $6,365,000	2007 Profits: $683,000	Int'l Ticker: Int'l Exchange:
2006 Sales: $6,363,000	2006 Profits: $784,000	Employees: 16,000
2005 Sales: $6,254,000	2005 Profits: $878,000	Fiscal Year Ends: 12/31
2004 Sales: $6,139,000	2004 Profits: $917,000	Parent Company:

SALARIES/BENEFITS:

Pension Plan: Y	ESOP Stock Plan:	Profit Sharing:	Top Exec. Salary: $834,292	Bonus: $852,045
Savings Plan: Y	Stock Purch. Plan: Y		Second Exec. Salary: $532,644	Bonus: $466,400

OTHER THOUGHTS:

Apparent Women Officers or Directors: 3
Hot Spot for Advancement for Women/Minorities: Y

LOCATIONS: ("Y" = Yes)

West:	Southwest:	Midwest:	Southeast:	Northeast:	International:
		Y			

EMC CORP

www.emc.com

Industry Group Code: 334112 Ranks within this company's industry group: Sales: 1 Profits: 1

Management:		Sales/Marketing:		Liberal Arts:		Information Systems:		Professionals:		Tech./Scientific:	
Management Trainees:	Y	Marketing Pros.:	Y	Gen. Writing/Editing:		Info. Management:	Y	Finance/Acct.:	Y	Engineers, Electrical:	Y
Experienced Mngmt.:	Y	Retail Sales:		Technical Writing:	Y	Software Dev.:	Y	Law:	Y	Engineers, Other:	
International Business:	Y	Commercial/Industrial:	Y	Graphic Arts/Photog.:	Y	Hardware Dev.:	Y	HR/Other:	Y	Health/Lab:	
MBA Grads:	Y	Sales Trainees:		Music:		Consulting/Other:		Training:	Y	Scientists/Research:	Y
		Advertising Pros.:	Y	Broadcasting:				Health Care:		Petroleum/Chemicals:	
				Other:				Consulting:		Math/Other:	Y

TYPES OF BUSINESS:

Computer Storage Equipment-Mainframe Disk Memory
Network Storage Systems
Management Protection Software
Consulting Services
Storage Management Services

BRANDS/DIVISIONS/AFFILIATES:

Iomega Corp
RSA Security Inc
Captiva Software Corporation
Document Sciences Corporation
Infra Corporation Pty Limited
Decho Corporation
VMware, Inc.
Symmetrix

CONTACTS: Note: Officers with more than one job title may be intentionally listed here more than once.

Joseph M. Tucci, CEO
Joseph M. Tucci, Pres.
David I. Goulden, CFO/Exec. VP
Frank M. Hauck, Exec. VP-Global Mktg. & Customer Quality
John T. (Jack) Mollen, Exec. VP-Human Resources
Jeffrey M. Nick, CTO/Sr. VP
Paul T. Dacier, General Counsel/Exec. VP
Irina Simmons, Treas./Sr. VP
William J. Teuber, Jr., Vice Chmn.
Arthur W. Coviello, Jr., Pres., RSA Security Div.
David A. Donatelli, Pres., Storage Div.
Mark S. Lewis, Pres., Content Mgmt. & Archiving
Joseph M. Tucci, Chmn.
Rainer Erlat, Pres., EMEA

Phone: 508-435-1000	Fax: 508-497-6912
Toll-Free:	
Address: 176 South St., Hopkinton, MA 01748-9103 US	

GROWTH PLANS/SPECIAL FEATURES:

EMC Corporation, along with its subsidiaries, develops, delivers and supports systems, software and services for the storage, management and protection of electronic information. EMC operates in four segments: information storage; content management and archiving; RSA information security; and VMware virtual infrastructure. The information storage segment is composed of networked information storage systems, multi-platform software and services to support information lifecycle management strategies. EMC's storage systems can be deployed in a storage area network, network attached storage, content addressed storage or direct attached storage environment. Product lines include the Symmetrix, CLARiiON, Celera, Centera and Connectrix systems. EMC's content management and archiving software includes the Documentum and Captiva families. The RSA information security segment includes Smart Application Discovery Manager software. Subsidiary VMware, Inc. provides virtual infrastructure solutions and services for server consolidation; disaster recovery and business continuity; capacity planning and development; enterprise desktop hosting; test optimization; and software distribution. VMware's products include Infrastructure 3, Virtual Desktop Infrastructure, VMware Lab Manager, VMware Converter 3, VMware Server and the Virtual Appliance Marketplace. In February 2008, EMC agreed to acquire Pi Corporation, a developer of personal information management software and services. In March 2008, the firm acquired Document Sciences Corporation, a provider of document output management and customer communications management software. Also in March 2008, EMC acquired Infra Corporation Pty Limited, a provider of IT service management software. In April 2008, the company agreed to acquire Conchango plc, a technology consulting firm. In June 2008, the firm acquired Iomega Corporation, a data storage and protection company. In November 2008, EMC established Decho Corporation, a combination of its Mozy, Inc. and Pi Corp. subsidiaries that is focused on personal information management.

EMC offers its employees tuition assistance; credit union membership; a group legal plan; behavioral health benefits; flexible spending accounts; and medical, dental, prescription and vision insurance.

FINANCIALS: Sales and profits are in thousands of dollars—add 000 to get the full amount. 2008 Note: Financial information for 2008 was not available for all companies at press time.

2008 Sales: $14,880,000	2008 Profits: $2,160,000	U.S. Stock Ticker: EMC
2007 Sales: $13,230,205	2007 Profits: $1,665,668	Int'l Ticker: Int'l Exchange:
2006 Sales: $11,155,090	2006 Profits: $1,227,601	Employees: 42,100
2005 Sales: $9,663,955	2005 Profits: $1,133,165	Fiscal Year Ends: 12/31
2004 Sales: $8,229,488	2004 Profits: $871,189	Parent Company:

SALARIES/BENEFITS:

Pension Plan:	ESOP Stock Plan:	Profit Sharing:	Top Exec. Salary: $1,000,000	Bonus: $1,388,628
Savings Plan: Y	Stock Purch. Plan: Y		Second Exec. Salary: $700,000	Bonus: $652,329

OTHER THOUGHTS:

Apparent Women Officers or Directors: 1
Hot Spot for Advancement for Women/Minorities: Y

LOCATIONS: ("Y" = Yes)

West:	Southwest:	Midwest:	Southeast:	Northeast:	International:
Y				Y	Y

Note: Financial information, benefits and other data can change quickly and may vary from those stated here.

EMERITUS CORP

www.emeritus.com

Industry Group Code: 623110 **Ranks within this company's industry group:** Sales: 5 Profits: 4

Management:		Sales/Marketing:		Liberal Arts:		Information Systems:		Professionals:		Tech./Scientific:	
Management Trainees:	Y	Marketing Pros.:	Y	Gen. Writing/Editing:	Y	Info. Management:	Y	Finance/Acct.:	Y	Engineers, Electrical:	
Experienced Mngmt.:	Y	Retail Sales:		Technical Writing:	Y	Software Dev.:		Law:	Y	Engineers, Other:	
International Business:	Y	Commercial/Industrial:		Graphic Arts/Photog.:	Y	Hardware Dev.:		HR/Other:	Y	Health/Lab:	
MBA Grads:	Y	Sales Trainees:		Music:		Consulting/Other:		Training:	Y	Scientists/Research:	
		Advertising Pros.:	Y	Broadcasting:				Health Care:	Y	Petroleum/Chemicals:	
				Other:	Y			Consulting:		Math/Other:	

TYPES OF BUSINESS:

Long-Term Health Care
Assisted Living Communities

BRANDS/DIVISIONS/AFFILIATES:

Arbor Place at Silverlake

CONTACTS: *Note: Officers with more than one job title may be intentionally listed here more than once.*

Daniel R. Baty, Co-CEO
Granger Cobb, Pres./Co-CEO
Raymond R. Brandstrom, CFO/Exec. VP-Finance
Jayne Sallerson, Sr. VP-Mktg.
Melanie Werdel, Exec. VP-Admin.
Raymond R. Brandstrom, Corp. Sec.
Eric Mendelsohn, Sr. VP-Corp. Dev.
Jim L. Hanson, Sr. VP-Financial Svcs./Controller
Budgie Amparo, Sr. VP-Quality & Risk Mgmt.
Martin D. Roffe, Sr. VP-Financial Planning
John Cincotta, Sr. VP-Sales
Leo Watterson, VP-Corp. Acct.
Daniel R. Baty, Chmn.

Phone: 206-298-2909	Fax: 206-301-4500
Toll-Free: 800-429-4828	
Address: 3131 Elliott Ave., Ste. 500, Seattle, WA 98121 US	

GROWTH PLANS/SPECIAL FEATURES:

Emeritus Corp. operates assisted living residential communities in the U.S. It operates or has an interest in 307 communities across 36 states, totaling approximately 27,000 units with a capacity for roughly 32,100 residents. These communities cater to senior citizens who need help with daily living, but do not require the intensive care provided in skilled nursing facilities. Assisted living generally provides housing and 24-hour personal support services. Seniors reside in a private or semi-private residential unit for a monthly fee based on each resident's individual service needs. Emeritus's specialty is in Alzheimer's and dementia related care, for which the company has developed a program that links memory training, familiar environments and personalized care services. Accessing the market for Alzheimer's care is one of the firm's key business strategies. In its other assisted living programs, Emeritus business strategy calls for customer service that addresses both physical and social health. The firm's target customers are middle to upper-middle income seniors, 75 and older, living in smaller cities (50,000 to 150,000 persons). Emeritus attempts to generate growth through increases in residential occupancy rates and revenue per occupied unit as well as through investments in IT infrastructure and through the selective acquisition of assisted living communities. In recent years, the company has sought to increase the number of communities it owns and decrease the number it merely manages.

Employees are offers health insurance; a 401(k) plan; a stock purchase plan; and tuition assistance.

FINANCIALS: Sales and profits are in thousands of dollars—add 000 to get the full amount. 2008 Note: Financial information for 2008 was not available for all companies at press time.

2008 Sales: $769,429	2008 Profits: $-104,751	**U.S. Stock Ticker: ESC**
2007 Sales: $534,679	2007 Profits: $-48,741	**Int'l Ticker:** Int'l Exchange:
2006 Sales: $411,375	2006 Profits: $-14,618	Employees: 18,671
2005 Sales: $387,732	2005 Profits: $11,703	Fiscal Year Ends: 12/31
2004 Sales: $316,866	2004 Profits: $-40,540	Parent Company:

SALARIES/BENEFITS:

Pension Plan:	ESOP Stock Plan:	Profit Sharing:	Top Exec. Salary: $608,748	Bonus: $460,000
Savings Plan: Y	Stock Purch. Plan: Y		Second Exec. Salary: $579,688	Bonus: $460,000

OTHER THOUGHTS:

Apparent Women Officers or Directors: 2
Hot Spot for Advancement for Women/Minorities: Y

LOCATIONS: ("Y" = Yes)

West:	Southwest:	Midwest:	Southeast:	Northeast:	International:
Y	Y	Y	Y	Y	

EMERSON ELECTRIC CO

www.gotoemerson.com

Industry Group Code: 3345 Ranks within this company's industry group: Sales: 1 Profits: 1

Management:		Sales/Marketing:		Liberal Arts:		Information Systems:		Professionals:		Tech./Scientific:	
Management Trainees:	Y	Marketing Pros.:	Y	Gen. Writing/Editing:		Info. Management:	Y	Finance/Acct.:	Y	Engineers, Electrical:	Y
Experienced Mngmt.:	Y	Retail Sales:		Technical Writing:	Y	Software Dev.:	Y	Law:	Y	Engineers, Other:	Y
International Business:	Y	Commercial/Industrial:	Y	Graphic Arts/Photog.:	Y	Hardware Dev.:	Y	HR/Other:	Y	Health/Lab:	
MBA Grads:	Y	Sales Trainees:		Music:		Consulting/Other:		Training:	Y	Scientists/Research:	Y
		Advertising Pros.:	Y	Broadcasting:				Health Care:		Petroleum/Chemicals:	
				Other:				Consulting:		Math/Other:	Y

TYPES OF BUSINESS:

Engineering & Technology Products & Services
Industrial Automation Products
Power Products
Air Conditioning & Refrigeration Products
Appliances & Tools

BRANDS/DIVISIONS/AFFILIATES:

PlantWeb Digital Plant Architecture
Process Management
Industrial Automation
Network Power
Climate Technologies
Appliances & Tools
Damcos Holding A/S
Lionville Systems, Inc.

CONTACTS: Note: Officers with more than one job title may be intentionally listed here more than once.

David N. Farr, CEO
Edward L. Monser, COO
David N. Farr, Pres.
Walter J. Galvin, CFO/Sr. Exec. VP
Frank L. Steeves, General Counsel/Sec.
Craig W. Ashmore, Sr. VP-Planning & Dev.
Charles A. Peters, Sr. Exec. VP
Steven A. Sonnenberg, Exec. VP-Emerson Process Mgmt.
Edgar M. Purvis, Jr., Exec. VP-Emerson Climate Tech.
Ed Feeney, Exec. VP-Emerson Network Power
David N. Farr, Chmn.

Phone: 314-553-2000	**Fax:** 314-553-3527
Toll-Free:	
Address: 8000 W. Florissant Ave., P.O. Box 4100, St. Louis, MO 63136 US	

GROWTH PLANS/SPECIAL FEATURES:

Emerson Electric Co. designs and supplies technology products and engineering services, serving a wide range of industrial, commercial and consumer markets worldwide. The company is organized into five business segments. The Process Management segment, accounting for 26% of sales, provides measurement, control and diagnostic capabilities for automated industrial processes producing items such as foods, medicines, power and fuels. As part of this segment, Emerson offers PlantWeb Digital Plant Architecture, a platform designed to open communication between industrial plant devices and, with its accompanying software, collect and analyze information concerning plant assets and processes. These capabilities give customers the ability to predict changes in equipment and process performance and the impact they can have on plant operations. The Industrial Automation segment, accounting for 19%, assists clients in automating production lines. Products for this group include motors, transmissions, alternators, fluid controls and materials joining equipment. The Network Power segment, accounting for 25%, provides power and environmental conditioning systems to help ensure telecommunication systems, data networks and critical business applications operate continuously. The Climate Technologies segment, accounting for 15%, primarily focuses on household and commercial air-conditioning and refrigeration technologies for comfort and food safety. The Appliances and Tools segment, accounting for 15%, provides motors for a broad range of applications, appliances and integrated appliance solutions; tools for homeowners and professionals; and home and commercial storage systems. Emerson operates approximately 265 manufacturing locations in the U.S. and 165 overseas, evenly divided between Europe, Asia and other locations. In January 2009, the company opened a new regional headquarters facility in Dubai.

Employees are offered medical and life insurance, as well as disability coverage.

FINANCIALS: Sales and profits are in thousands of dollars—add 000 to get the full amount. 2008 Note: Financial information for 2008 was not available for all companies at press time.

2008 Sales: $24,807,000	2008 Profits: $2,412,000	**U.S. Stock Ticker: EMR**
2007 Sales: $22,131,000	2007 Profits: $2,136,000	**Int'l Ticker:** Int'l Exchange:
2006 Sales: $19,734,000	2006 Profits: $1,845,000	Employees: 140,700
2005 Sales: $17,305,000	2005 Profits: $1,422,000	Fiscal Year Ends: 9/30
2004 Sales: $15,615,000	2004 Profits: $1,257,000	Parent Company:

SALARIES/BENEFITS:

Pension Plan: Y	ESOP Stock Plan:	Profit Sharing: Y	Top Exec. Salary: $1,200,000	Bonus: $3,000,000
Savings Plan: Y	Stock Purch. Plan:		Second Exec. Salary: $710,000	Bonus: $1,175,000

OTHER THOUGHTS:

Apparent Women Officers or Directors: 2
Hot Spot for Advancement for Women/Minorities: Y

LOCATIONS: ("Y" = Yes)

West:	Southwest:	Midwest:	Southeast:	Northeast:	International:
Y	Y	Y	Y	Y	Y

ENTERGY CORP

www.entergy.com

Industry Group Code: 2211   **Ranks within this company's industry group:** Sales: 5   Profits: 5

Management:		Sales/Marketing:		Liberal Arts:		Information Systems:		Professionals:		Tech./Scientific:	
Management Trainees:	Y	Marketing Pros.:	Y	Gen. Writing/Editing:	Y	Info. Management:	Y	Finance/Acct.:	Y	Engineers, Electrical:	Y
Experienced Mngmt.:	Y	Retail Sales:		Technical Writing:	Y	Software Dev.:	Y	Law:	Y	Engineers, Other:	Y
International Business:	Y	Commercial/Industrial:	Y	Graphic Arts/Photog.:	Y	Hardware Dev.:		HR/Other:	Y	Health/Lab:	
MBA Grads:	Y	Sales Trainees:		Music:		Consulting/Other:		Training:	Y	Scientists/Research:	
		Advertising Pros.:	Y	Broadcasting:				Health Care:		Petroleum/Chemicals:	
				Other:				Consulting:		Math/Other:	

TYPES OF BUSINESS:

Utilities-Electric
Energy Management
Energy Trading
Nuclear Generation
Hydroelectric Generation
Wind Generation

BRANDS/DIVISIONS/AFFILIATES:

Entergy Arkansas, Inc.
Entergy Louisiana LLC
Entergy Mississipi, Inc.
Entergy Texas, Inc.
Entergy New Orleans, Inc.
Entergy Gulf States Louisiana, LLC
Entergy Nuclear, Inc.

CONTACTS: *Note: Officers with more than one job title may be intentionally listed here more than once.*

J. Wayne Leonard, CEO
Richard Smith, COO
Richard Smith, Pres.
Leo Denault, CFO/Exec. VP
Terry Seamons, Sr. VP-Human Resources
Terry Seamons, Sr. VP-Admin.
Robert Sloan, General Counsel/Exec. VP
Mark T. Savoff, Exec. VP-Oper.
Michele Lopiccolo, Sr. VP-Investor Rel.
Curt L. Hebert, Jr., Exec. VP-External Affairs
Gary Taylor, Pres., Utility Oper.
Michael D. Bakewell, Sr. VP-Fossil Oper.
J. Wayne Leonard, Chmn.

Phone: 504-576-4000	**Fax:** 504-576-4428
Toll-Free:	
Address: 639 Loyola Ave., New Orleans, LA 70113 US	

GROWTH PLANS/SPECIAL FEATURES:

Entergy Corp. is an integrated energy company engaged primarily in the electric power production and retail electric distribution operations. The company owns and operates power plants with roughly 30,000 megawatts (MW) of electric general capacity, making it one of the largest nuclear power generators in the U.S. The firm operates in two primary segments, utility and non-utility nuclear. The utility segment, which generated 79% of revenue in 2008, generates, transmits, distributes and sells electric power to 2.7 million customers in a four-state service territory that includes portions of Arkansas, Mississippi, Texas and Louisiana, including New Orleans. The division also operates a small natural gas distribution system. The non-utility nuclear segment, responsible for 19% of revenue in 2008, owns and operates six nuclear power plants located in the northeastern U.S. and sells the electric power produced by those plants primarily to wholesale customers. The division also provides services to other nuclear power plant owners. Nuclear operations are carried out by subsidiary, Entergy Nuclear, Inc. In addition to these two segments, Entergy also operates a non-nuclear wholesale assets business, which sells to wholesale customers the electric power produced by power plants that it owns while it focuses on improving performance and exploring sales or restructuring opportunities for its power plants. The firm has six main regional subsidiaries, all falling under the U.S. utility segment: Entergy Arkansas; Entergy Gulf States of Louisiana; Entergy Louisiana; Entergy Mississippi; Entergy New Orleans; and Entergy Texas.

Employees are offered medical, dental and vision insurance; life insurance; flexible spending accounts; disability coverage; a 401(k) plan; a retirement plan; an employee assistance program; a relocation assistance program; and education reimbursement.

FINANCIALS: Sales and profits are in thousands of dollars—add 000 to get the full amount. 2008 Note: Financial information for 2008 was not available for all companies at press time.

2008 Sales: $13,093,756	2008 Profits: $1,220,566	**U.S. Stock Ticker:** ETR
2007 Sales: $11,484,398	2007 Profits: $1,134,849	**Int'l Ticker:** Int'l Exchange:
2006 Sales: $10,932,158	2006 Profits: $1,132,602	Employees: 14,669
2005 Sales: $10,106,247	2005 Profits: $923,758	Fiscal Year Ends: 12/31
2004 Sales: $9,685,521	2004 Profits: $933,049	Parent Company:

SALARIES/BENEFITS:

Pension Plan: Y	ESOP Stock Plan:	Profit Sharing:	Top Exec. Salary: $1,273,523	Bonus: $2,169,720
Savings Plan: Y	Stock Purch. Plan:		Second Exec. Salary: $638,394	Bonus: $632,100

OTHER THOUGHTS:

Apparent Women Officers or Directors: 3
Hot Spot for Advancement for Women/Minorities: Y

LOCATIONS: ("Y" = Yes)

West:	Southwest:	Midwest:	Southeast:	Northeast:	International:
	Y		Y		

ENTERPRISE PRODUCTS PARTNERS LP

www.epplp.com

Industry Group Code: 486 Ranks within this company's industry group: Sales: 1 Profits: 1

Management:		Sales/Marketing:		Liberal Arts:		Information Systems:		Professionals:		Tech./Scientific:	
Management Trainees:	Y	Marketing Pros.:	Y	Gen. Writing/Editing:		Info. Management:	Y	Finance/Acct.:	Y	Engineers, Electrical:	
Experienced Mngmt.:	Y	Retail Sales:		Technical Writing:	Y	Software Dev.:	Y	Law:	Y	Engineers, Other:	Y
International Business:		Commercial/Industrial:	Y	Graphic Arts/Photog.:		Hardware Dev.:		HR/Other:	Y	Health/Lab:	
MBA Grads:	Y	Sales Trainees:		Music:		Consulting/Other:		Training:	Y	Scientists/Research:	
		Advertising Pros.:		Broadcasting:				Health Care:		Petroleum/Chemicals:	Y
				Other:				Consulting:		Math/Other:	

TYPES OF BUSINESS:

Pipelines-Natural Gas
Natural Gas Transportation, Processing & Storage
Natural Gas Liquid Fractionation & Processing
Import/Export Terminals

BRANDS/DIVISIONS/AFFILIATES:

TEPPCO Partners L.P.
Jonah Gas Gathering Company
Piceance Creek Pipeline
EnCana Corporation
Dixie Pipeline Company
Dixie Terminals and Storage Company

CONTACTS: *Note: Officers with more than one job title may be intentionally listed here more than once.*

Michael A. Creel, CEO
William Ordemann, COO/Exec. VP
Michael A. Creel, Pres.
W. Randall Fowler, CFO/Exec. VP
Lynn L. Bourdon, III, Sr. VP-Mktg. & Supply
Charles M. Brabson, Sr. VP-Eng.
Richard H. Bachmann, Sec./Chief Legal Officer/Exec. VP
John R. Burkhalter, VP-Investor Rel.
Michael J. Knesek, Principal Acct. Officer/Controller/Sr. VP
Bryan F. Bulawa, Treas./VP
Gil H. Radtke, Sr. VP-Natural Gas Processing
A. J. Teague, Exec. VP/Chief Commercial Officer
G.R. Jerry Cardillo, VP-Petrochemical Svcs.
Dan L. Duncan, Chmn.

Phone: 713-381-6500	**Fax:** 713-880-6668
Toll-Free: 866-230-0745	
Address: 1100 Louisiana St., 10th Fl., Houston, TX 77002 US	

GROWTH PLANS/SPECIAL FEATURES:

Enterprise Products Partners, LP (EPP) provides natural gas processing, natural gas liquids (NGL) fractionation and transportation and storage services to producers and consumers of NGL products. The company is divided into four business segments. The offshore pipelines and services segment manages assets that the company has interest in or owns in the Gulf of Mexico. Under a 20-year agreement with Shell Oil, the firm processes Shell's current and future Gulf of Mexico production. The onshore natural gas pipelines and services segment oversees approximately 18,890 miles of pipeline systems, transporting gas in Alabama, Louisiana, Mississippi, Texas, New Mexico, Colorado and Wyoming. Enterprise works in the Greater Green River Basin of southwestern Wyoming through a joint venture with TEPPCO Partners L.P. called the Jonah Gas Gathering Company. This segment also owns or leases three salt domes and other natural gas storage facilities. The NGL pipelines and services segment includes about 13,295 miles of pipelines, 23 natural gas processing plants, seven fractionation plants and storage facilities with a capacity of 162 million barrels. The petrochemical services segment includes four propylene fractionation facilities, an isometrization complex and an octane additive production facility, as well as 679 miles of petrochemical pipeline systems. In August 2008, EPP partners announced they will build a pipeline to transport new supplies of natural gas produced from the Barnett Shale to the Sherman Extension pipeline. Also in August 2008, EPP, TEPPCO Partners, L.P., and Oiltanking Holding Americas, Inc. formed a joint venture to build a new Texas offshore crude oil port and pipeline system for delivery of crude oil to refining centers along the upper Texas Gulf Coast. Also in August 2008, the company's subsidiary Enterprise Products Operating LLC acquired 25.8% interest in Dixie Pipeline Company and Dixie Terminals and Storage Company, the company now wholly-owns Dixie.

FINANCIALS: Sales and profits are in thousands of dollars—add 000 to get the full amount. 2008 Note: Financial information for 2008 was not available for all companies at press time.

2008 Sales: $21,905,656	2008 Profits: $954,021	**U.S. Stock Ticker:** EPD
2007 Sales: $16,950,125	2007 Profits: $533,674	**Int'l Ticker:** Int'l Exchange:
2006 Sales: $13,990,969	2006 Profits: $601,155	Employees: 3,500
2005 Sales: $12,256,959	2005 Profits: $419,508	Fiscal Year Ends: 12/31
2004 Sales: $8,321,202	2004 Profits: $268,261	Parent Company:

SALARIES/BENEFITS:

Pension Plan:	ESOP Stock Plan:	Profit Sharing:	Top Exec. Salary: $563,200	Bonus: $552,000
Savings Plan: Y	Stock Purch. Plan:		Second Exec. Salary: $558,333	Bonus: $500,000

OTHER THOUGHTS:

Apparent Women Officers or Directors:
Hot Spot for Advancement for Women/Minorities:

LOCATIONS: ("Y" = Yes)

West:	Southwest:	Midwest:	Southeast:	Northeast:	International:
Y	Y	Y	Y		

Note: Financial information, benefits and other data can change quickly and may vary from those stated here.

ENTERPRISE RENT-A-CAR   www.enterprise.com

Industry Group Code: 5321   Ranks within this company's industry group: Sales: 1   Profits:

Management:		Sales/Marketing:		Liberal Arts:		Information Systems:		Professionals:		Tech./Scientific:	
Management Trainees:	Y	Marketing Pros.:	Y	Gen. Writing/Editing:	Y	Info. Management:	Y	Finance/Acct.:	Y	Engineers, Electrical:	
Experienced Mngmt.:	Y	Retail Sales:	Y	Technical Writing:		Software Dev.:	Y	Law:	Y	Engineers, Other:	
International Business:	Y	Commercial/Industrial:	Y	Graphic Arts/Photog.:	Y	Hardware Dev.:		HR/Other:	Y	Health/Lab:	
MBA Grads:	Y	Sales Trainees:	Y	Music:		Consulting/Other:		Training:	Y	Scientists/Research:	
		Advertising Pros.:	Y	Broadcasting:				Health Care:		Petroleum/Chemicals:	
				Other:	Y			Consulting:		Math/Other:	

TYPES OF BUSINESS:

Automobile Rental
Fleet Management Services
Used Vehicle Sales
Commuter Services

BRANDS/DIVISIONS/AFFILIATES:

Enterprise Rent-a-Car
Enterprise Car Sales
Enterprise Fleet Services
Enterprise Rent-a-Truck
Vanguard Car Rental USA Inc
National Car Rental
Alamo Rental

CONTACTS: *Note: Officers with more than one job title may be intentionally listed here more than once.*

Andrew C. Taylor, CEO
Pamela M. Nicholson, COO
Pamela M. Nicholson, Pres
William W. Snyder, CFO/Exec. VP
Edward Adams, Sr. VP-Human Resources
Craig Kennedy, CIO/Sr. VP
Lee Kaplan, Sr. VP/Chief Admin. Officer
Rose Langhorst, Treas./VP
Matthew G. Darrah, Sr. VP-North American Oper.
Jim Runnels, Sr. VP-Rental
Andrew C. Taylor, Chmn.

Phone: 314-512-5000	Fax: 314-512-4706
Toll-Free:	
Address: 600 Corporate Park Dr., St. Louis, MO 63105 US	

GROWTH PLANS/SPECIAL FEATURES:

Enterprise Rent-A-Car is a car rental company with over 728,000 rental and fleet vehicles through more than 7,000 locations in the U.S. and 900 in Canada, Germany, Ireland and the U.K. The firm markets to visitors from other cities, and people whose cars are in repair shops or who want luxury cars or convertibles for special occasions. The company serves the most-traveled airports in the U.S. and several of the largest airports in Canada and the U.K. Enterprise's services also include fleet management, used car sales, the California Vanpool Services and Rent-A-Truck. Enterprise Fleet Services (EFS) provides a number of services, including acquisition, insurance services, registration, funding, fuel management, maintenance and disposal. Enterprise Car Sales (ECS) sells used vehicles directly to local franchised dealers, independent used car dealers and auto auctions. Customers are offered an inventory of over 120 makes and models, most of which are low-mileage cars. The Enterprise Rideshare division, also known as the California Vanpool Service, operates over 700 vehicles, which are used to transport commuters in Northern and Southern California. Enterprise Rent-a-Truck has over 90 locations across the nation specializing in commercial truck rentals. In 2008, Enterprise initiated various environmentally friendly efforts, including E85/flexfuel locations, increased hybrid and fuel-efficient vehicles, carbon offset programs and car sharing services. In September 2008, the company expanded its WeCar, a car-sharing program, nationwide. In February 2009, the firm added 5,000 hybrids to its nationwide fleet and established nearly 80 Hybrid Branch rental locations. In May 2009, the Enterprise Commercial Trucks division began offering consumer rentals at more than 125 locations nationwide.

Employee benefits include adoption assistance and employee discounts.

FINANCIALS: Sales and profits are in thousands of dollars—add 000 to get the full amount. 2008 Note: Financial information for 2008 was not available for all companies at press time.

2008 Sales: $10,100,000	2008 Profits: $	**U.S. Stock Ticker: Private**
2007 Sales: $9,500,000	2007 Profits: $	Int'l Ticker: Int'l Exchange:
2006 Sales: $9,000,000	2006 Profits: $	Employees: 65,000
2005 Sales: $8,230,000	2005 Profits: $	Fiscal Year Ends: 7/31
2004 Sales: $7,400,000	2004 Profits: $	Parent Company:

SALARIES/BENEFITS:

Pension Plan:	ESOP Stock Plan:	Profit Sharing: Y	Top Exec. Salary: $	Bonus: $
Savings Plan: Y	Stock Purch. Plan:		Second Exec. Salary: $	Bonus: $

OTHER THOUGHTS:

Apparent Women Officers or Directors: 3
Hot Spot for Advancement for Women/Minorities: Y

LOCATIONS: ("Y" = Yes)

West:	Southwest:	Midwest:	Southeast:	Northeast:	International:
Y	Y	Y	Y	Y	Y

ERNST & YOUNG LLP

www.ey.com

Industry Group Code: 5412 **Ranks within this company's industry group:** Sales: 2 Profits:

Management:		Sales/Marketing:		Liberal Arts:		Information Systems:		Professionals:		Tech./Scientific:	
Management Trainees:	Y	Marketing Pros.:	Y	Gen. Writing/Editing:	Y	Info. Management:	Y	Finance/Acct.:	Y	Engineers, Electrical:	
Experienced Mngmt.:	Y	Retail Sales:		Technical Writing:	Y	Software Dev.:	Y	Law:	Y	Engineers, Other:	
International Business:	Y	Commercial/Industrial:	Y	Graphic Arts/Photog.:	Y	Hardware Dev.:		HR/Other:	Y	Health/Lab:	
MBA Grads:	Y	Sales Trainees:		Music:		Consulting/Other:	Y	Training:	Y	Scientists/Research:	
		Advertising Pros.:	Y	Broadcasting:				Health Care:		Petroleum/Chemicals:	
				Other:	Y			Consulting:		Math/Other:	

TYPES OF BUSINESS:

Accounting
Risk Management
Tax Preparation Services
Human Resources Management
IT Services
Transaction Support Services
Industry Publications

BRANDS/DIVISIONS/AFFILIATES:

Entrepreneur of the Year Award
Ernst & Young Online
Ernst & Young International

CONTACTS: *Note: Officers with more than one job title may be intentionally listed here more than once.*

Steve Howe, Area Managing Partner-Americas
James Turley, Chmn.-Ernst & Young International

Phone: 212-773-3000	**Fax:** 212-773-6350
Toll-Free:	
Address: 5 Times Square, New York, NY 10036 US	

GROWTH PLANS/SPECIAL FEATURES:

Ernst & Young, LLP, the U.S. branch of the global accounting firm Ernst & Young International, is a provider of audit, tax, transaction and risk-related services. The firm has offices throughout the U.S. and Puerto Rico. In addition to providing accounting advisory and tax preparation services, the firm offers a number of complementary services such as human resource programs and online/IT services. Ernst & Young serves companies in a number of industry sectors, including the financial services, automotive, consumer products, oil and gas, health care, technology, mining and metals, real estate, retail, communications and entertainment industries. In addition, the company publishes a variety of industry-specific publications and studies providing expertise in quickly-changing markets. Ernst & Young Online is a personalized client portal that provides news and information relating to specific customer needs, a reference library and links to other web resources, as well as access to Ernst & Young staff for answers to direct questions. Additionally, the company oversees the Entrepreneur of the Year Award, a prestigious award given each year for exceptional business acumen and ability. Clients of the firm include Best Buy, British Petroleum, Coca-Cola, FedEx, Google, Lockheed Martin, McDonald's, Target Corporation and Whole Foods Markets, among others.

Ernst & Young offers its employees benefits including medical, vision and dental plans; tax-free day care and healthcare reimbursement accounts; an adoption assistance program; a 401(k) plan and a 529 college savings plan; a mortgage referral program; flexible work arrangements; bereavement benefits; life, disability and AD&D insurance; and reimbursement for certification expenses.

FINANCIALS: Sales and profits are in thousands of dollars—add 000 to get the full amount. 2008 Note: Financial information for 2008 was not available for all companies at press time.

2008 Sales: $24,500,000	2008 Profits: $	**U.S. Stock Ticker: Subsidiary**
2007 Sales: $21,100,000	2007 Profits: $	**Int'l Ticker:** Int'l Exchange:
2006 Sales: $	2006 Profits: $	Employees: 135,730
2005 Sales: $	2005 Profits: $	Fiscal Year Ends: 6/30
2004 Sales: $	2004 Profits: $	Parent Company: ERNST & YOUNG INTERNATIONAL

SALARIES/BENEFITS:

Pension Plan:	ESOP Stock Plan:	Profit Sharing:	Top Exec. Salary: $	Bonus: $
Savings Plan:	Stock Purch. Plan:		Second Exec. Salary: $	Bonus: $

OTHER THOUGHTS:

Apparent Women Officers or Directors:
Hot Spot for Advancement for Women/Minorities:

LOCATIONS: ("Y" = Yes)

West:	Southwest:	Midwest:	Southeast:	Northeast:	International:
Y	Y	Y	Y	Y	Y

Note: Financial information, benefits and other data can change quickly and may vary from those stated here.

ESTEE LAUDER COMPANIES INC (THE)

www.elcompanies.com

Industry Group Code: 325620 Ranks within this company's industry group: Sales: 2 Profits: 2

Management:		Sales/Marketing:		Liberal Arts:		Information Systems:		Professionals:		Tech./Scientific:	
Management Trainees:	Y	Marketing Pros.:	Y	Gen. Writing/Editing:	Y	Info. Management:	Y	Finance/Acct.:	Y	Engineers, Electrical:	
Experienced Mngmt.:	Y	Retail Sales:	Y	Technical Writing:	Y	Software Dev.:	Y	Law:	Y	Engineers, Other:	Y
International Business:	Y	Commercial/Industrial:	Y	Graphic Arts/Photog.:	Y	Hardware Dev.:		HR/Other:	Y	Health/Lab:	
MBA Grads:	Y	Sales Trainees:	Y	Music:		Consulting/Other:		Training:	Y	Scientists/Research:	Y
		Advertising Pros.:	Y	Broadcasting:				Health Care:		Petroleum/Chemicals:	Y
				Other:	Y			Consulting:		Math/Other:	

TYPES OF BUSINESS:

Cosmetics & Toiletries Manufacturing
Cosmetic & Fragrance Sales
Retail Cosmetics Stores
Hair Care Products

BRANDS/DIVISIONS/AFFILIATES:

Aveda
La Mer
Clinique
Prescriptivees
Bobbie Brown
M.A.C
Origins
Aramis

CONTACTS: *Note: Officers with more than one job title may be intentionally listed here more than once.*

Fabrizio Freda, CEO
Fabrizio Freda, Pres.
Richard W. Kunes, CFO/Exec. VP
Amy DiGeso, Exec. VP-Global Human Resources
Harvey Gedeon, Exec. VP-Global R&D
Sara E. Moss, General Counsel/Exec. VP
Alexandra C. Trower, Exec. VP-Global Comm.
John Demsey, Group Pres.
Harvey Gedeon, Exec. VP-Prod. Innovation
Evelyn H. Lauder, Sr. Corp. VP
Leonard A. Lauder, Chmn.
Cedric Prouve, Group Pres., Int'l
Gregory Polcer, Exec. VP-Global Supply Chain

Phone: 212-572-4200	Fax: 212-572-3941
Toll-Free:	
Address: 767 Fifth Ave., New York, NY 10153 US	

GROWTH PLANS/SPECIAL FEATURES:

The Estee Lauder Companies, Inc. is a global manufacturer and marketer of skin care, cosmetics, fragrance and hair care products. The company's products are sold in over 140 countries and territories under 29 brand names such as Estee Lauder, Aramis, Clinique, Prescriptives, Lab Series, Origins, M.A.C., Bobbi Brown, La Mer, Aveda, Jo Malone, Bumble and bumble, Darphin, American Beauty, Flirt!, Good Skin and Grassroots. The firm is also the global licensee for fragrances and cosmetics sold under the Tommy Hilfiger, Donna Karan, Michael Kors, Sean John, Missoni, Coach, Daisy Fuentes and Tom Ford brand names. Estee Lauder sells its products principally through 30,000 points of sale including upscale department stores, .specialty retailers, upscale perfumeries and pharmacies and prestige salons and spas, as well as freestanding company-owned stores and spas, authorized retailer web sites, stores on cruise ships, television direct marketing, in-flight and duty-free shops and self-select outlets. Estee Lauder has 14 manufacturing factories in five countries and six principle facilities research and development facilities. The founding Lauder family still controls 87.6% of the company's voting shares. The company operates on a global basis, with approximately 59% of its 2008 sales generated outside the U.S. Skin care products currently account for 39% of the company's sales; makeup products, also 39% and fragrance products, 16%. In October 2008, the Estee Lauder brand introduced Time Zone line and wrinkle reducing moisturizers.

FINANCIALS: Sales and profits are in thousands of dollars—add 000 to get the full amount. 2008 Note: Financial information for 2008 was not available for all companies at press time.

2008 Sales: $7,910,800	2008 Profits: $473,800	**U.S. Stock Ticker: EL**
2007 Sales: $7,037,500	2007 Profits: $449,200	**Int'l Ticker:** Int'l Exchange:
2006 Sales: $6,463,800	2006 Profits: $244,200	Employees: 31,300
2005 Sales: $6,336,300	2005 Profits: $406,100	Fiscal Year Ends: 6/30
2004 Sales: $5,790,400	2004 Profits: $342,100	Parent Company:

SALARIES/BENEFITS:

Pension Plan:	ESOP Stock Plan:	Profit Sharing:	Top Exec. Salary: $1,500,000	Bonus: $3,074,500
Savings Plan:	Stock Purch. Plan:		Second Exec. Salary: $1,250,000	Bonus: $2,305,900

OTHER THOUGHTS:

Apparent Women Officers or Directors: 9
Hot Spot for Advancement for Women/Minorities: Y

LOCATIONS: ("Y" = Yes)

West:	Southwest:	Midwest:	Southeast:	Northeast:	International:
		Y		Y	Y

Note: Financial information, benefits and other data can change quickly and may vary from those stated here.

EXELON CORPORATION

www.exeloncorp.com

Industry Group Code: 221 Ranks within this company's industry group: Sales: 1 Profits: 1

Management:		Sales/Marketing:		Liberal Arts:		Information Systems:		Professionals:		Tech./Scientific:	
Management Trainees:	Y	Marketing Pros.:	Y	Gen. Writing/Editing:	Y	Info. Management:	Y	Finance/Acct.:	Y	Engineers, Electrical:	Y
Experienced Mngmt.:	Y	Retail Sales:		Technical Writing:	Y	Software Dev.:	Y	Law:	Y	Engineers, Other:	Y
International Business:		Commercial/Industrial:	Y	Graphic Arts/Photog.:	Y	Hardware Dev.:		HR/Other:	Y	Health/Lab:	
MBA Grads:	Y	Sales Trainees:		Music:		Consulting/Other:		Training:	Y	Scientists/Research:	
		Advertising Pros.:	Y	Broadcasting:				Health Care:		Petroleum/Chemicals:	Y
				Other:				Consulting:		Math/Other:	

TYPES OF BUSINESS:

Utilities-Electricity & Natural Gas
Nuclear Generation
Energy Marketing

BRANDS/DIVISIONS/AFFILIATES:

Commonwealth Edison Company
PECO Energy Company
Exelon Generation Company LLC
Exelon Business Services Company
SunPower Corporation

CONTACTS: *Note: Officers with more than one job title may be intentionally listed here more than once.*

John W. Rowe, CEO
Christopher M. Crane, COO
Christopher M. Crane, Pres.
Matthew F. Helzinger, CFO/Sr. VP
Ruth Ann M. Gillis, Chief Diversity Officer
Andrea I. Zopp, General Counsel/Exec. VP
Ian P. McLean, Exec. VP-Dev.
Elizabeth A. Moler, Exec. VP-Gov't & Environmental Affairs
Katie Anderson, VP-Investor Rel.
William A. Von Hoene, Jr., Exec. VP-Finance & Legal
Frank M. Clark, Chmn./CEO-ComEd
Denis P. O'Brien, Pres./CEO-PECO Energy
Christopher M. Crane, COO-Exelon Generation
Ruth Ann M. Gillis, Exec. VP/Pres., Exelon Bus. Svcs. Co.
John W. Rowe, Chmn.

Phone: 312-394-7398	Fax:
Toll-Free: 800-483-3220	
Address: 10 S. Dearborn St., 48th Fl., Chicago, IL 60680-5398 US	

GROWTH PLANS/SPECIAL FEATURES:

Exelon Corporation is a utility services company that operates through subsidiaries Exelon Generation Company LLC; Commonwealth Edison Company (ComEd); and PECO Energy Company. Exelon Generation's business consists of its owned and contracted electric generating facilities; its wholesale energy marketing operations; and its competitive retail supply operations. The subsidiary owns generation assets, which include nuclear, fossil, renewable and hydropower, with an aggregate net capacity of nearly 25,000 megawatts (MW), including over 16,900 MW of nuclear capacity. Additionally, Generation controls almost 6,500 MW of capacity through long-term contracts. ComEd's energy delivery business consists of the purchase and regulated retail sale of electricity and the provision of distribution and transmission services to over 3.8 million retail, commercial and industrial customers in northern Illinois. The subsidiary's retail service territory has an area of roughly 11,300 square miles and an estimated population of 8 million. PECO's energy delivery business consists of the purchase and regulated retail sale of electricity; and the provision of distribution and transmission services to retail customers in southeastern Pennsylvania, including Philadelphia, as well as surrounding counties. The subsidiary's retail service territory has an area of about 2,100 square miles and an estimated population of 3.9 million. PECO delivers electricity to roughly 1.6 million customers and natural gas to approximately 485,000 customers. In addition to its primary segments, Exelon Business Services Company provides financial, human resource, legal, IT, supply management and corporate governance services to Exelon and its subsidiaries. In April 2009, the firm signed an agreement with SunPower Corp. for the development of a 10 MW solar photovoltaic (PV) facility in Chicago, Illinois, the largest urban solar power plant in the U.S.

The company offers its employees health, life and disability insurance; a 401(k) plan and stock purchase plan; flexible spending accounts; and tuition reimbursement.

FINANCIALS: Sales and profits are in thousands of dollars—add 000 to get the full amount. 2008 Note: Financial information for 2008 was not available for all companies at press time.

			U.S. Stock Ticker: EXC
2008 Sales: $18,859,000	2008 Profits: $2,737,000		**Int'l Ticker:** Int'l Exchange:
2007 Sales: $18,916,000	2007 Profits: $2,736,000		Employees: 19,610
2006 Sales: $15,655,000	2006 Profits: $1,592,000		Fiscal Year Ends: 12/31
2005 Sales: $15,357,000	2005 Profits: $923,000		Parent Company:
2004 Sales: $14,515,000	2004 Profits: $1,864,000		

SALARIES/BENEFITS:

Pension Plan: Y	ESOP Stock Plan:	Profit Sharing:	Top Exec. Salary: $1,474,423	Bonus: $1,835,166
Savings Plan: Y	Stock Purch. Plan: Y		Second Exec. Salary: $694,230	Bonus: $750,000

OTHER THOUGHTS:

Apparent Women Officers or Directors: 7
Hot Spot for Advancement for Women/Minorities: Y

LOCATIONS: ("Y" = Yes)

West:	Southwest:	Midwest:	Southeast:	Northeast:	International:
	Y	Y		Y	

EXPERIAN AMERICAS

www.experian.com

Industry Group Code: 561450 Ranks within this company's industry group: Sales: 1   Profits:

Management:		Sales/Marketing:		Liberal Arts:		Information Systems:		Professionals:		Tech./Scientific:	
Management Trainees:	Y	Marketing Pros.:	Y	Gen. Writing/Editing:	Y	Info. Management:	Y	Finance/Acct.:	Y	Engineers, Electrical:	
Experienced Mngmt.:	Y	Retail Sales:		Technical Writing:	Y	Software Dev.:	Y	Law:	Y	Engineers, Other:	
International Business:		Commercial/Industrial:	Y	Graphic Arts/Photog.:	Y	Hardware Dev.:		HR/Other:	Y	Health/Lab:	
MBA Grads:	Y	Sales Trainees:	Y	Music:		Consulting/Other:		Training:	Y	Scientists/Research:	
		Advertising Pros.:	Y	Broadcasting:				Health Care:		Petroleum/Chemicals:	
				Other:	Y			Consulting:		Math/Other:	Y

TYPES OF BUSINESS:

Credit Bureau
Customer Relationship Software & Solutions
Marketing Software & Solutions
Business & Consumer Internet Sites
Online Services
Risk Management Services, Automotive

BRANDS/DIVISIONS/AFFILIATES:

Experian Information Solutions, Inc.
Prospect Navigator
Credit Migration Solutions
Experian Group
Red Flag Rules
BankruptcyPredict
FreeCreditReport.com
LowerMyBills.com

CONTACTS: *Note: Officers with more than one job title may be intentionally listed here more than once.*

Michael DeVico, Exec. VP-Experian North America
Don Robert, CEO-Experian plc
Kerry Williams, Pres., Credit Svcs. & Decisions Analytics
Paul Brooks, CFO-Experian plc

Phone: 714-830-7000	Fax:
Toll-Free:	
Address: 475 Anton Blvd., Costa Mesa, CA 92626 US	

GROWTH PLANS/SPECIAL FEATURES:

Experian Americas, formerly Experian Information Solutions, Inc., is a subsidiary of Experian plc, formerly Experian Group Limited.   Experian Americas is a leading credit-reporting agency in the U.S. It also helps organizations find, develop and manage customer relationships by providing information, decision-making solutions and processing services. Experian operates through four segments: credit services, decision analytics, marketing services and interactive. The credit services unit, which accounted for 35% of Experian Americas' 2009 revenue, provides clients with solutions that optimize processes in acquiring new customers (Prospect Navigator), maximize customer relationships (Credit Migration Solutions), improve collections (Credit Profile Report), prevent fraud losses (Red Flag Rules), analyze critical data (BankruptcyPredict) and improve business-to-business results (business credit reports). The decision analytics unit, 6% of revenue, is closely related to the credit services segment and provides analytical software and services to help clients optimize their lending strategies. The marketing services unit, 17% of revenue, provides customer acquisition, retention and growth and marketing strategy services to the advertising and media, automotive, banking, catalog, retail, financial services, consumer products and travel and hospitality markets.   Finally, the interactive segment, 42% of 2009 revenue, offers consumers access to their credit histories through various web tools, including CreditExpert, FreeCreditReport.com and LowerMyBills.com. Experian Americas also offers risk management, customer acquisition and market reporting services tailored to the automotive industry. North American operations accounted for 55% of Experian plc's total revenue in fiscal 2009. In May 2008, Experian plc launched Account Monitoring Service, a credit monitoring system for businesses, with credit-based alerts.

Experian offers its employees health, dental and vision care plans, flexible spending accounts, education assistance, credit union membership, employee assistance, referral bonuses, employee discounts, adoption assistance and fitness reimbursement.

FINANCIALS: Sales and profits are in thousands of dollars—add 000 to get the full amount. 2008 Note: Financial information for 2008 was not available for all companies at press time.

2008 Sales: $2,000,000	2008 Profits: $	**U.S. Stock Ticker:** Subsidiary	
2007 Sales: $1,994,000	2007 Profits: $	**Int'l Ticker:** Int'l Exchange:	
2006 Sales: $1,804,000	2006 Profits: $	Employees: 5,500	
2005 Sales: $	2005 Profits: $	Fiscal Year Ends: 3/31	
2004 Sales: $	2004 Profits: $	Parent Company: EXPERIAN PLC	

SALARIES/BENEFITS:

Pension Plan:	ESOP Stock Plan:	Profit Sharing:	Top Exec. Salary: $	Bonus: $
Savings Plan: Y	Stock Purch. Plan: Y		Second Exec. Salary: $	Bonus: $

OTHER THOUGHTS:

Apparent Women Officers or Directors:
Hot Spot for Advancement for Women/Minorities:

LOCATIONS: ("Y" = Yes)

West:	Southwest:	Midwest:	Southeast:	Northeast:	International:
Y	Y	Y	Y	Y	

EXPRESS SCRIPTS INC

www.express-scripts.com

Industry Group Code: 522320A Ranks within this company's industry group: Sales: 2 Profits: 2

Management:		Sales/Marketing:		Liberal Arts:		Information Systems:		Professionals:		Tech./Scientific:	
Management Trainees:	Y	Marketing Pros.:	Y	Gen. Writing/Editing:	Y	Info. Management:	Y	Finance/Acct.:	Y	Engineers, Electrical:	
Experienced Mngmt.:	Y	Retail Sales:		Technical Writing:	Y	Software Dev.:	Y	Law:	Y	Engineers, Other:	
International Business:	Y	Commercial/Industrial:	Y	Graphic Arts/Photog.:	Y	Hardware Dev.:		HR/Other:	Y	Health/Lab:	
MBA Grads:	Y	Sales Trainees:		Music:		Consulting/Other:		Training:	Y	Scientists/Research:	
		Advertising Pros.:	Y	Broadcasting:				Health Care:	Y	Petroleum/Chemicals:	
				Other:				Consulting:		Math/Other:	

TYPES OF BUSINESS:

Pharmacy Benefits Management
Mail & Internet Pharmacies
Formulary Management
Integrated Drug & Medical Data Analysis
Market Research Programs
Medical Information Management
Workers' Compensation Programs
Informed-Decision Counseling

BRANDS/DIVISIONS/AFFILIATES:

CuraScrit Inc
Phoenix Marketing Group LLC

CONTACTS: *Note: Officers with more than one job title may be intentionally listed here more than once.*

George Paz, CEO
George Paz, Pres.
Jeffrey Hall, CFO/Exec. VP
Edward Ignaczak, Exec. VP-Sales & Mktg.
Michael Holmes, Exec. VP-Human Capital
Patrick McNamee, Exec. VP-Tech.
Keith Ebling, General Counsel/Exec. VP/Sec.
Patrick McNamee, Exec. VP-Oper.
Michael Holmes, Exec. VP-Strategy & Emerging Markets
Kelley Elliott, Chief Acct. Officer/Controller/VP
George Paz, Chmn.
Agnes Rey-Giraud, Pres., Int'l Oper.

Phone: 314-996-0900	Fax: 314-770-0303
Toll-Free:	
Address: 1 Express Way, St. Louis, MO 63121 US	

GROWTH PLANS/SPECIAL FEATURES:

Express Scripts, Inc. is one of the largest independent pharmacy benefit managers in the U.S., providing pharmacy service and pharmacy benefit plan design consultation for clients including HMOs, unions and government health care plans. The company's core services include pharmacy network management, mail and Internet pharmacies, formulary management, targeted clinical programs, integrated drug and medical data analysis, market research programs, medical information management, workers' compensation programs and informed-decision counseling. Express Scripts provides progressive health care management by leveraging expertise in pharmacy benefit management (PBM) in order to positively impact clients' total health care benefits. The firm combines pharmacy and medical claims data to develop new strategies for decreasing total health care spending and improving health outcomes. The PBM business provides managed prescription drug services to members in the U.S. and Canada. Services from the specialty and ancillary services segment, which consists of the specialty operations of CuraScript, Inc., and the specialty distribution services and Phoenix Marketing Group LLC lines of business, include delivery of injectible biopharmaceutical products to patients' homes, physician offices and certain associated patient care services; third party logistics services for contracted pharma clients; distribution of sample units to physicians and verification of practitioner licensure; and biopharma services. Through pharmacy network management, the firm contracts with retail pharmacies to provide prescription drugs to members of the pharmacy benefit plans it manages. Express Scripts also provides a number of Internet-based services, including disease tracking, consumer prescription drug information and electronic claims processing. In July 2008, the company acquired the worker's PBM business of Medical Services Company from the private equity investment firm, Monitor Clipper Partners. In April 2009, Express Scripts agreed to buy Wellpoint's pharmacy benefits management unit for $4.7 billion.

Employees are offered health and dental insurance; a 401(k) plan; disability coverage; life insurance; a stock purchase plan; tuition assistance; adoption assistance; employee assistance programs; and health club discounts.

FINANCIALS: Sales and profits are in thousands of dollars—add 000 to get the full amount. 2008 Note: Financial information for 2008 was not available for all companies at press time.

2008 Sales: $21,978,000	2008 Profits: $776,100	U.S. Stock Ticker: ESRX
2007 Sales: $21,824,000	2007 Profits: $567,800	Int'l Ticker: Int'l Exchange:
2006 Sales: $21,562,600	2006 Profits: $474,400	Employees: 10,820
2005 Sales: $16,212,000	2005 Profits: $400,100	Fiscal Year Ends: 12/31
2004 Sales: $15,114,700	2004 Profits: $278,200	Parent Company:

SALARIES/BENEFITS:

Pension Plan:	ESOP Stock Plan:	Profit Sharing:	Top Exec. Salary: $941,808	Bonus: $2,450,500
Savings Plan: Y	Stock Purch. Plan: Y		Second Exec. Salary: $490,442	Bonus: $725,850

OTHER THOUGHTS:

Apparent Women Officers or Directors: 3
Hot Spot for Advancement for Women/Minorities: Y

LOCATIONS: ("Y" = Yes)

West:	Southwest:	Midwest:	Southeast:	Northeast:	International:
Y	Y	Y	Y	Y	Y

Note: Financial information, benefits and other data can change quickly and may vary from those stated here.

EXXON MOBIL CORPORATION (EXXONMOBIL) www.exxonmobil.com

Industry Group Code: 211111　Ranks within this company's industry group: Sales: 1　Profits: 1

Management:		Sales/Marketing:		Liberal Arts:		Information Systems:		Professionals:		Tech./Scientific:	
Management Trainees:	Y	Marketing Pros.:	Y	Gen. Writing/Editing:	Y	Info. Management:	Y	Finance/Acct.:	Y	Engineers, Electrical:	Y
Experienced Mngmt.:	Y	Retail Sales:		Technical Writing:	Y	Software Dev.:	Y	Law:	Y	Engineers, Other:	Y
International Business:	Y	Commercial/Industrial:	Y	Graphic Arts/Photog.:	Y	Hardware Dev.:		HR/Other:	Y	Health/Lab:	
MBA Grads:	Y	Sales Trainees:	Y	Music:		Consulting/Other:		Training:	Y	Scientists/Research:	Y
		Advertising Pros.:	Y	Broadcasting:				Health Care:		Petroleum/Chemicals:	Y
				Other:				Consulting:		Math/Other:	Y

TYPES OF BUSINESS:

Oil & Gas Exploration & Production
Gas Refining & Supply
Fuel Marketing
Power Generation
Coal & Mineral Exploration
Chemicals
Fuel Cell Research
Convenience Stores

BRANDS/DIVISIONS/AFFILIATES:

ExxonMobil Chemical
Exxon Neftegas Limited

CONTACTS: *Note: Officers with more than one job title may be intentionally listed here more than once.*

Rex W. Tillerson, CEO
Lucille J. Cavanaugh, VP-Human Resources
C. W. Matthews, General Counsel/VP
W. M. Colton, VP-Strategic Planning
K.P. Cohen, VP-Public Affairs
D. S. Rosenthal, VP-Investor Rel./Sec.
Donald D. Humphreys, Treas./Sr. VP
P. T. Mulva, Controller/VP
S. R. LaSala, VP/General Tax Counsel
J. Stephen Simon, Sr. VP
A.Tim Cejka, Sr. VP
Rex W. Tillerson, Chmn.

Phone: 972-444-1000	Fax: 972-444-1350
Toll-Free:	
Address: 5959 Las Colinas Blvd., Irving, TX 75039 US	

GROWTH PLANS/SPECIAL FEATURES:

Exxon Mobil Corporation (ExxonMobil) is one of the largest global petroleum and natural gas exploration and production companies in the world. ExxonMobil's various divisions and affiliated companies operate and market products in the U.S. and about 200 other countries and territories. Its principal business is energy, involving exploration and production crude oil and natural gas; manufacture of petroleum products; and transportation and sale of crude oil, natural gas and petroleum products. The company has a resource base of exploration and production acreage in 36 countries and production operations in 24 countries, producing more than 4.2 million oil equivalent barrels of oil and gas each day. The firm is also a major manufacturer and marketer of commodity petrochemicals, including olefins, aromatics, polyethylene and polypropylene plastics and a wide variety of specialty products. In addition, Exxon Mobil has interests in electric power generation facilities. Moreover, the firm has a chemical company and a coal and minerals company. The company has several divisions and hundreds of affiliates, many with names that include ExxonMobil, Exxon or Mobil. Overall, the firm has 11 separate global business units. The five global upstream businesses undertake exploration, development, production, gas marketing and upstream research. The four global downstream businesses carry out refining and supply, fuels marketing, lubricants and petroleum technology operations. Exxon Mobil spends more than $700 million annually towards research in new technologies, including developments in synthetic lubricants, catalyst research, nanotechnology, biomedical services and hydro-carbon-based fuel cells.

ExxonMobil's 2008 corporate and professional training expenditures totaled more than $69 million for 48,000 participants. The company plans to train 50,000 staff members in 2009.

FINANCIALS: Sales and profits are in thousands of dollars—add 000 to get the full amount. 2008 Note: Financial information for 2008 was not available for all companies at press time.

2008 Sales: $459,579,000	2008 Profits: $45,220,000	**U.S. Stock Ticker: XOM**
2007 Sales: $390,328,000	2007 Profits: $40,610,000	**Int'l Ticker:**　　Int'l Exchange:
2006 Sales: $365,467,000	2006 Profits: $39,500,000	Employees: 79,900
2005 Sales: $358,955,000	2005 Profits: $36,130,000	Fiscal Year Ends: 12/31
2004 Sales: $291,252,000	2004 Profits: $25,330,000	Parent Company:

SALARIES/BENEFITS:

Pension Plan: Y	ESOP Stock Plan:	Profit Sharing:	Top Exec. Salary: $1,870,000	Bonus: $4,000,000
Savings Plan:	Stock Purch. Plan:		Second Exec. Salary: $910,000	Bonus: $2,364,000

OTHER THOUGHTS:

Apparent Women Officers or Directors: 2
Hot Spot for Advancement for Women/Minorities: Y

LOCATIONS: ("Y" = Yes)

West:	Southwest:	Midwest:	Southeast:	Northeast:	International:
Y	Y	Y	Y	Y	Y

EXXONMOBIL CHEMICAL

www.exxonmobilchemical.com

Industry Group Code: 325110 Ranks within this company's industry group: Sales: 1 Profits: 1

Management:		Sales/Marketing:		Liberal Arts:		Information Systems:		Professionals:		Tech./Scientific:	
Management Trainees:	Y	Marketing Pros.:	Y	Gen. Writing/Editing:	Y	Info. Management:	Y	Finance/Acct.:	Y	Engineers, Electrical:	Y
Experienced Mngmt.:	Y	Retail Sales:		Technical Writing:	Y	Software Dev.:	Y	Law:	Y	Engineers, Other:	Y
International Business:	Y	Commercial/Industrial:	Y	Graphic Arts/Photog.:		Hardware Dev.:		HR/Other:	Y	Health/Lab:	
MBA Grads:	Y	Sales Trainees:		Music:		Consulting/Other:		Training:	Y	Scientists/Research:	Y
		Advertising Pros.:		Broadcasting:				Health Care:		Petroleum/Chemicals:	Y
				Other:				Consulting:		Math/Other:	

TYPES OF BUSINESS:

Plastics & Rubber Manufacturing
Petrochemicals
Catalyst Technology
Polypropylene

BRANDS/DIVISIONS/AFFILIATES:

Univation Technologies, LLC
Label-Lyte
XyMax
PxMax
Exxon Mobil Corporation (ExxonMobil)
Dow Chemical Company (The)

CONTACTS: Note: Officers with more than one job title may be intentionally listed here more than once.

Rex W. Tillerson, CEO
Donald D. Humphreys, Treas./Sr. VP
J. Stephen Simon, Sr. VP
Mark W. Albers, Sr. VP
Rex W. Tillerson, Chmn.

Phone: 281-870-6000	Fax: 281-870-6661
Toll-Free:	
Address: 13501 Katy Freeway, Houston, TX 77079 US	

GROWTH PLANS/SPECIAL FEATURES:

ExxonMobil Chemical, a division of ExxonMobil Corp., is one of the world's largest petrochemical companies, manufacturing and marketing olefins, aromatics, fluids, synthetic rubber, polyethylene, polypropylene, oriented polypropylene packaging films, plasticizers, synthetic lubricant base-stocks, additives for fuels and lubricants, zeolite catalysts and other petrochemical products. The division has manufacturing locations in more than 20 countries and markets products in more than 150 countries. ExxonMobil Chemical is the only major olefins producer with proprietary pyrolysis-reactor technology, which delivers the highest olefin yields in the industry. The unit's XyMax and PxMax aromatics utilize proprietary zeolite shape-selective catalyst technology. This technology increases conversion and reduces losses versus other technologies in the production of higher olefins. Univation Technologies, LLC, a joint venture company owned by ExxonMobil Chemical and Dow Chemical Co., has developed the Prodigy catalyst technology that allows the production of resins at substantially lower cost than traditional staged processes. This technology is used in a broad range of applications such as pipes, films and blow molding. In 2008, the firm completed and started a new compound facility to supply polymers to the automotive, appliance and specialty consumer products industries.

FINANCIALS: Sales and profits are in thousands of dollars—add 000 to get the full amount. 2008 Note: Financial information for 2008 was not available for all companies at press time.

2008 Sales: $55,000,000	2008 Profits: $2,957,000	U.S. Stock Ticker: Subsidiary
2007 Sales: $53,000,000	2007 Profits: $4,563,000	Int'l Ticker: Int'l Exchange:
2006 Sales: $49,000,000	2006 Profits: $4,382,000	Employees:
2005 Sales: $26,777,000	2005 Profits: $3,943,000	Fiscal Year Ends: 12/31
2004 Sales: $27,788,000	2004 Profits: $3,428,000	Parent Company: EXXON MOBIL CORPORATION (EXXONMOBIL)

SALARIES/BENEFITS:

Pension Plan:	ESOP Stock Plan:	Profit Sharing:	Top Exec. Salary: $	Bonus: $
Savings Plan:	Stock Purch. Plan:		Second Exec. Salary: $	Bonus: $

OTHER THOUGHTS:

Apparent Women Officers or Directors:
Hot Spot for Advancement for Women/Minorities:

LOCATIONS: ("Y" = Yes)

West:	Southwest:	Midwest:	Southeast:	Northeast:	International:
	Y				Y

Note: Financial information, benefits and other data can change quickly and may vary from those stated here.

FAMILY DOLLAR STORES INC

www.familydollar.com

Industry Group Code: 452112 **Ranks within this company's industry group:** Sales: 8 Profits: 6

Management:		Sales/Marketing:		Liberal Arts:		Information Systems:		Professionals:		Tech./Scientific:	
Management Trainees:	Y	Marketing Pros.:	Y	Gen. Writing/Editing:	Y	Info. Management:	Y	Finance/Acct.:	Y	Engineers, Electrical:	
Experienced Mngmt.:	Y	Retail Sales:	Y	Technical Writing:		Software Dev.:	Y	Law:	Y	Engineers, Other:	
International Business:		Commercial/Industrial:		Graphic Arts/Photog.:	Y	Hardware Dev.:		HR/Other:	Y	Health/Lab:	
MBA Grads:	Y	Sales Trainees:	Y	Music:		Consulting/Other:		Training:	Y	Scientists/Research:	
		Advertising Pros.:	Y	Broadcasting:				Health Care:		Petroleum/Chemicals:	
				Other:	Y			Consulting:		Math/Other:	

TYPES OF BUSINESS:
Discount Stores
Dollar Stores

BRANDS/DIVISIONS/AFFILIATES:

CONTACTS: *Note: Officers with more than one job title may be intentionally listed here more than once.*
Howard R. Levine, CEO
R. James Kelly, COO
R. James Kelly, Pres.
Kenneth T. Smith, CFO/Sr. VP
Bryan Venberg, Sr. VP-Human Resources
Joshua R. Jewett, CIO/Sr. VP-IT & Procurement
Robert George, Chief Merch. Officer/Exec. VP
James C. Snyder, General Counsel/Corp. Sec./Sr. VP
Barry Sullivan, Sr. VP-Store Oper.
Bryan P. Causey, Sr. VP-Planning, Allocation & Replenishment
C. Martin Sowers, Sr. VP-Finance
Thomas M. Nash, Sr. VP-Real Estate Dev.
Keith M. Gehl, Sr. VP-Real Estate & Facilities
Howard R. Levine, Chmn.
Kevin Boyanowski, Sr. VP-Global Sourcing
Charles S. Gibson, Jr., Exec. VP-Supply Chain

Phone: 704-847-6961	Fax: 704-847-5534
Toll-Free:	
Address: 10401 Old Monroe Rd., Charlotte, NC 28201-1017 US	

GROWTH PLANS/SPECIAL FEATURES:

Family Dollar Stores, Inc. operates a chain of more than 6,700 general merchandise retail discount stores across 44 states, primarily serving low to lower-middle income consumers. The goods offered by Family Dollar generally have price points that range from under $1 to $10 and include apparel, food, cleaning products, paper products, home decor, beauty products, health aids, toys, pet products, automotive products, domestics, seasonal goods and electronics. Approximately 49% of its products are manufactured in the U.S., and substantially all such merchandise is purchased directly from the manufacturer. Family Dollar owns and operates nine distribution centers. Nationally advertised brand name merchandise accounts for approximately 44% of Family Dollar's sales, with the company's closeout merchandise accounting for approximately 2%. The company supplements its basic assortment of merchandise with the purchase of certain Treasure Hunt items designed to create more excitement in stores and attract customers throughout the year, with particular emphasis on the holiday seasons. Approximately 5,600 stores include refrigerated coolers for a perishable food section. In 2008, consumables, such as household chemicals, paper products, food, health and beauty items, hardware, automotive supplies and pet supplies accounted for 61% of sales; followed by home products; apparel and accessories; and seasonal and electronics with 14.4%, 13.1% and 11.5% respectively.

Family Dollar Stores offers its employees medical, vision, dental and prescription drug benefits; life insurance; short- and long-term disability; flexible spending accounts; a 401(k) plan; and an employee stock purchase plan.

FINANCIALS: Sales and profits are in thousands of dollars—add 000 to get the full amount. 2008 Note: Financial information for 2008 was not available for all companies at press time.

2008 Sales: $6,983,628	2008 Profits: $233,073	**U.S. Stock Ticker:** FDO	
2007 Sales: $6,834,305	2007 Profits: $242,854	**Int'l Ticker:**	Int'l Exchange:
2006 Sales: $6,394,772	2006 Profits: $195,111	Employees: 44,000	
2005 Sales: $5,824,808	2005 Profits: $217,509	Fiscal Year Ends: 8/31	
2004 Sales: $5,281,888	2004 Profits: $262,685	Parent Company:	

SALARIES/BENEFITS:

Pension Plan:	ESOP Stock Plan:	Profit Sharing:	Top Exec. Salary: $878,462	Bonus: $533,170
Savings Plan: Y	Stock Purch. Plan: Y		Second Exec. Salary: $649,038	Bonus: $295,524

OTHER THOUGHTS:
Apparent Women Officers or Directors: 3
Hot Spot for Advancement for Women/Minorities: Y

LOCATIONS: ("Y" = Yes)

West:	Southwest:	Midwest:	Southeast:	Northeast:	International:
Y	Y	Y	Y	Y	

Note: Financial information, benefits and other data can change quickly and may vary from those stated here.

FEDEX CORPORATION

www.fedex.com

Industry Group Code: 4921 Ranks within this company's industry group: Sales: 2   Profits: 2

Management:		Sales/Marketing:		Liberal Arts:		Information Systems:		Professionals:		Tech./Scientific:	
Management Trainees:	Y	Marketing Pros.:	Y	Gen. Writing/Editing:	Y	Info. Management:	Y	Finance/Acct.:	Y	Engineers, Electrical:	Y
Experienced Mngmt.:	Y	Retail Sales:		Technical Writing:	Y	Software Dev.:	Y	Law:	Y	Engineers, Other:	
International Business:	Y	Commercial/Industrial:	Y	Graphic Arts/Photog.:	Y	Hardware Dev.:		HR/Other:	Y	Health/Lab:	
MBA Grads:	Y	Sales Trainees:	Y	Music:		Consulting/Other:		Training:	Y	Scientists/Research:	
		Advertising Pros.:	Y	Broadcasting:				Health Care:		Petroleum/Chemicals:	
				Other:	Y			Consulting:		Math/Other:	Y

TYPES OF BUSINESS:

Express Delivery Services
Ground Delivery Services
Freight Services
Document Solutions & Business Services
International Trade Services

BRANDS/DIVISIONS/AFFILIATES:

FedEx Ground Package System Inc
FedEx Freight Corp
FedEx Express Corp
FedEx Custom Critical Inc
FedEx Trade Networks Inc
FedEx Home Delivery
FedEx Kinkos Office And Print Services Inc
Fedex Supply Chain Services Inc

CONTACTS: Note: Officers with more than one job title may be intentionally listed here more than once.

Frederick W. Smith, CEO
Frederick W. Smith, Pres.
Alan B. Graf, Jr., CFO/Exec. VP
Robert B. Carter, CIO/Exec. VP-Info. Svcs.
Christine P. Richards, General Counsel/Exec. VP/Corp. Sec.
T. Michael Glenn, Exec. VP-Corp. Comm. & Market Dev.
David J. Bronczek, CEO/Pres., FedEx Express
David F. Rebholz, CEO/Pres., FedEx Ground
Brian Philips, CEO/Pres., FedEx Office
Douglas G. Duncan, CEO/Pres., FedEx Freight
Frederick W. Smith, Chmn.
Michael L. Ducker, Pres., FedEx Express Int'l

Phone: 901-818-7500	Fax: 901-395-2000
Toll-Free:	
Address: 942 S. Shady Grove Rd., Memphis, TN 38120 US	

GROWTH PLANS/SPECIAL FEATURES:

FedEx Corporation provides transportation, e-commerce and business services and operates through Federal Express Corp. (FedEx Express); FedEx Ground Package System, Inc. (FedEx Ground); FedEx Freight Corp. (FedEx Freight); and FedEx Kinko's Office & Print Services, Inc. (FedEx Kinko's). FedEx Express is an express transportation company, offering time-certain delivery within one to three business days. The division also includes FedEx Trade Networks, Inc., which provides international trade services, specializing in custom brokerage and global cargo distribution. FedEx Ground offers small-package ground delivery service. It provides service to almost every business address in the U.S., Canada and Puerto Rico, as well as residential delivery to nearly 100% of U.S. residents through FedEx Home Delivery. The segment also includes FedEx SmartPost, Inc., which specializes in the consolidation and delivery of high volumes of low-weight, less time-sensitive business-to-consumer packages using the U.S. Postal Service for final delivery to residences. FedEx Freight provides less-than-truckload (LTL) freight services through the FedEx Freight business (regional next-day and second-day and interregional LTL freight services) and the FedEx National LTL business (long-haul LTL freight services). The division also includes FedEx Custom Critical, Inc., a time-specific, critical shipment carrier; and Caribbean Transportation Services, Inc., a provider of airfreight forwarding services between the U.S. and Puerto Rico. FedEx Kinko's offers business services, including access to technology for copying and printing, professional finishing, document creation, Internet access, computer rentals, videoconferencing, signs and graphics, direct mail, web-based printing and the full range of FedEx day-definite ground shipping and time-definite global express shipping services, in addition to a variety of other retail services and products. In August 2008, FedEx Express introduced domestic service in Mexico by opening FedEx Express Nacional.

Employees are offered medical, dental and vision insurance; short-and long-term disability coverage; life insurance; a pension plan; a 401(k); tuition assistance; a stock purchase plan; and reduced rate shipping.

FINANCIALS: Sales and profits are in thousands of dollars—add 000 to get the full amount. 2008 Note: Financial information for 2008 was not available for all companies at press time.

2008 Sales: $37,953,000	2008 Profits: $2,075,000	U.S. Stock Ticker: FDX
2007 Sales: $35,214,000	2007 Profits: $3,276,000	Int'l Ticker: Int'l Exchange:
2006 Sales: $32,294,000	2006 Profits: $3,014,000	Employees: 140,000
2005 Sales: $29,363,000	2005 Profits: $1,449,000	Fiscal Year Ends: 5/31
2004 Sales: $24,710,000	2004 Profits: $838,000	Parent Company:

SALARIES/BENEFITS:

Pension Plan: Y	ESOP Stock Plan:	Profit Sharing:	Top Exec. Salary: $1,430,466	Bonus: $2,705,000
Savings Plan: Y	Stock Purch. Plan: Y		Second Exec. Salary: $940,096	Bonus: $1,336,544

OTHER THOUGHTS:

Apparent Women Officers or Directors: 2
Hot Spot for Advancement for Women/Minorities: Y

LOCATIONS: ("Y" = Yes)

West:	Southwest:	Midwest:	Southeast:	Northeast:	International:
Y	Y	Y	Y	Y	Y

Note: Financial information, benefits and other data can change quickly and may vary from those stated here.

FINISH LINE INC (THE)

Industry Group Code: 448210 **Ranks within this company's industry group:** Sales: 2 Profits: 2

www.finishline.com

Management:		Sales/Marketing:		Liberal Arts:		Information Systems:		Professionals:		Tech./Scientific:	
Management Trainees:	Y	Marketing Pros.:	Y	Gen. Writing/Editing:	Y	Info. Management:	Y	Finance/Acct.:	Y	Engineers, Electrical:	
Experienced Mngmt.:	Y	Retail Sales:	Y	Technical Writing:		Software Dev.:	Y	Law:	Y	Engineers, Other:	
International Business:		Commercial/Industrial:		Graphic Arts/Photog.:	Y	Hardware Dev.:		HR/Other:	Y	Health/Lab:	
MBA Grads:	Y	Sales Trainees:	Y	Music:		Consulting/Other:		Training:	Y	Scientists/Research:	
		Advertising Pros.:	Y	Broadcasting:				Health Care:		Petroleum/Chemicals:	
				Other:	Y			Consulting:		Math/Other:	

TYPES OF BUSINESS:

Athletic Shoes, Retail
Activewear
Athletic Accessories

BRANDS/DIVISIONS/AFFILIATES:

Finish Line
Finish Line Man Alive, Inc. (The)
Man Alive
Genesco, Inc.

CONTACTS: *Note: Officers with more than one job title may be intentionally listed here more than once.*

Glenn S. Lyon, CEO
Steven J. Schneider, COO
Steven J. Schneider, Pres.
Edward W. Wilhelm, CFO/Exec. VP
Kevin G. Flynn, Sr. VP-Mktg.
Donald E. Courtney, CIO/Exec. VP
Samuel M. Sato, Chief Merch. Officer/Exec. VP
Gary D. Cohen, Chief Admin. Officer
Gary D. Cohen, Corp. Sec.
Michael L. Marchetti, Exec. VP-Store Oper.
George S. Sanders, Exec. VP-Store Dev. & Real Estate
Michael J. Smith, Sr. VP-Loss Prevention
Roger C. Underwood, Sr. VP-Info. Systems
Alan H. Cohen, Chmn.
Robert A. Edwards, Sr. VP-Dist.

Phone: 317-899-1022	**Fax:**
Toll-Free: 888-777-3949	
Address: 3308 N. Mitthoeffer Rd., Indianapolis, IN 46235 US	

GROWTH PLANS/SPECIAL FEATURES:

Finish Line, Inc. is a mall-based specialty retailer of men's, women's and children's brand-name athletic, outdoor and casual footwear, activewear and accessories in the U.S. The company owns and operates 687 Finish Line stores in 47 states, which average approximately 5,437 square feet. Brand names offered by these stores include Nike, adidas, Puma, New Balance, Asics, Converse, Lacoste, K-Swiss, Reebok and Under Armour. Footwear products are categorized into sections by application, including basketball, running, sport style, fitness and outdoor. Most categories are available in men's, women's and children's styles. Softgoods account for approximately 15% of the store's net sales. The company purchases products from approximately 286 suppliers and manufacturers, the largest of which, Nike, accounted for approximately 59% of Finish Line's total purchases in 2008. In March 2008, Finish Line announced that its pending merger with Genesco had been terminated. In July 2009, the company divested its The Finish Line Man Alive, Inc. subsidiary, a street fashion retailer offering men's and women's name brand fashions, to Man Alive Acquisition LLC, an entity controlled by the ownership of Jimmy Jazz stores.

The Finish Line offers its employees an education reimbursement plan, employee discounts, basic life insurance and medical, dental, vision and prescription drug coverage plans.

FINANCIALS: Sales and profits are in thousands of dollars—add 000 to get the full amount. 2008 Note: Financial information for 2008 was not available for all companies at press time.

2008 Sales: $1,277,162	2008 Profits: $-48,502	**U.S. Stock Ticker:** FINL
2007 Sales: $1,331,959	2007 Profits: $40,264	**Int'l Ticker:** Int'l Exchange:
2006 Sales: $1,306,045	2006 Profits: $61,049	Employees: 12,300
2005 Sales: $1,166,767	2005 Profits: $61,263	Fiscal Year Ends: 2/28
2004 Sales: $985,891	2004 Profits: $47,270	Parent Company:

SALARIES/BENEFITS:

Pension Plan:	ESOP Stock Plan:	Profit Sharing: Y	Top Exec. Salary: $518,750	Bonus: $60,000
Savings Plan: Y	Stock Purch. Plan:		Second Exec. Salary: $468,000	Bonus: $177,950

OTHER THOUGHTS:

Apparent Women Officers or Directors: 2
Hot Spot for Advancement for Women/Minorities: Y

LOCATIONS: ("Y" = Yes)

West:	Southwest:	Midwest:	Southeast:	Northeast:	International:
Y	Y	Y	Y	Y	

Note: Financial information, benefits and other data can change quickly and may vary from those stated here.

FIRST ADVANTAGE CORPORATION

www.fadv.com

Industry Group Code: 561450 Ranks within this company's industry group: Sales: 2 Profits: 1

Management:		Sales/Marketing:		Liberal Arts:		Information Systems:		Professionals:		Tech./Scientific:	
Management Trainees:	Y	Marketing Pros.:	Y	Gen. Writing/Editing:	Y	Info. Management:	Y	Finance/Acct.:	Y	Engineers, Electrical:	
Experienced Mngmt.:	Y	Retail Sales:		Technical Writing:	Y	Software Dev.:	Y	Law:	Y	Engineers, Other:	
International Business:	Y	Commercial/Industrial:	Y	Graphic Arts/Photog.:	Y	Hardware Dev.:		HR/Other:	Y	Health/Lab:	
MBA Grads:	Y	Sales Trainees:	Y	Music:		Consulting/Other:		Training:	Y	Scientists/Research:	
		Advertising Pros.:		Broadcasting:				Health Care:		Petroleum/Chemicals:	
				Other:				Consulting:		Math/Other:	

TYPES OF BUSINESS:

Credit Reports
Computer Forensics
Legal & Criminal Records Investigation
Tax Consulting
Credit Information
Supply Chain Services
Employee Screening

BRANDS/DIVISIONS/AFFILIATES:

First American Corp
Verify Limited

CONTACTS: Note: Officers with more than one job title may be intentionally listed here more than once.

Anand K. Nallathambi, CEO
Anand K. Nallathambi, Pres.
John Lamson, CFO/Exec. VP
Anita Tefft, VP-Human Resources
Bret Jardine, Acting General Counsel/VP/Corp. Sec.
Todd Mavis, Exec. VP-Oper.
Andrew MacDonald, Sr. VP-Corp. Dev.
Thomas Milligan, Treas./VP
Isabell Theisen, Chief Security Officer
Akshaya Mehta, Exec. VP-Corp. Infrastructure
Lisa Steinbach, Controller/VP
Parker S. Kennedy, Chmn.

Phone: 619-938-7500	Fax:
Toll-Free:	
Address: 12395 First American Way, Poway, CA 92064 US	

GROWTH PLANS/SPECIAL FEATURES:

First Advantage Corporation is a provider of risk mitigation products and services marketed primarily to business customers. The company operates through six segments: Lender Services, Data Services, Dealer Services, Employer Services, Multifamily Services, and Investigative and Litigation Support Services. Lender Services, generating roughly 18% of the company's revenue, provides specialized credit reports for mortgage lenders. Data Services, generating about 20% of First Advantage's revenue, offers motor vehicle records; transportation industry credit reporting; supply chain theft and damage mitigation consulting; consumer location; criminal records reselling; subprime credit reporting; consumer credit reporting services; and lead generation. Dealer Services, accounting for approximately 12% of the company's revenue, provides specialized credit reports, credit automation software and lead generation services to auto dealers and lenders. First Advantage's Employer Services segment, generating roughly 29% of the company's revenue, helps companies manage risk with its employment screening, occupational health, tax incentive and services hiring products. The Multifamily Services segment, generating approximately 10% of the company's revenue, provides resident screening services, including information about a prospective renter's eviction record, lease and payment performance history. Investigative and Litigation Support Services, generating roughly 11% of the company's revenue, provides corporate litigation and investigative services, including computer forensics, electronic discovery, due diligence reports and other related services. Business information provider First American Corporation holds a substantial interest in First Advantage. In February 2008, the company acquired Verify Limited, an employment screening company serving clients in the Asia Pacific region, with offices in Malaysia, India, Hong Kong, Japan and Mainland China. In February 2009, the firm opened a new litigation consulting office in Munich, Germany.

First Advantage offers its employees tuition reimbursement; e-learning programs; banking discounts; an employee assistance program; flexible spending accounts; and medical, dental, vision, prescription, life and disability insurance, among other benefits.

FINANCIALS: Sales and profits are in thousands of dollars—add 000 to get the full amount. 2008 Note: Financial information for 2008 was not available for all companies at press time.

2008 Sales: $727,276	2008 Profits: $34,857	**U.S. Stock Ticker: FADV**	
2007 Sales: $770,165	2007 Profits: $138,107	**Int'l Ticker:** Int'l Exchange:	
2006 Sales: $797,801	2006 Profits: $66,161	Employees: 4,000	
2005 Sales: $643,749	2005 Profits: $58,426	Fiscal Year Ends: 12/31	
2004 Sales: $516,741	2004 Profits: $42,333	Parent Company:	

SALARIES/BENEFITS:

Pension Plan:	ESOP Stock Plan:	Profit Sharing:	Top Exec. Salary: $700,000	Bonus: $444,500
Savings Plan: Y	Stock Purch. Plan: Y		Second Exec. Salary: $395,533	Bonus: $238,125

OTHER THOUGHTS:

Apparent Women Officers or Directors: 4
Hot Spot for Advancement for Women/Minorities: Y

LOCATIONS: ("Y" = Yes)

West:	Southwest:	Midwest:	Southeast:	Northeast:	International:
Y	Y	Y	Y	Y	Y

Note: Financial information, benefits and other data can change quickly and may vary from those stated here.

FIRST DATA CORP

www.firstdatacorp.com

Industry Group Code: 522320 **Ranks within this company's industry group:** Sales: 1   Profits: 5

Management:		Sales/Marketing:		Liberal Arts:		Information Systems:		Professionals:		Tech./Scientific:	
Management Trainees:	Y	Marketing Pros.:	Y	Gen. Writing/Editing:	Y	Info. Management:	Y	Finance/Acct.:	Y	Engineers, Electrical:	
Experienced Mngmt.:	Y	Retail Sales:		Technical Writing:		Software Dev.:	Y	Law:	Y	Engineers, Other:	
International Business:	Y	Commercial/Industrial:	Y	Graphic Arts/Photog.:	Y	Hardware Dev.:		HR/Other:	Y	Health/Lab:	
MBA Grads:	Y	Sales Trainees:	Y	Music:		Consulting/Other:		Training:	Y	Scientists/Research:	
		Advertising Pros.:	Y	Broadcasting:				Health Care:		Petroleum/Chemicals:	
				Other:				Consulting:		Math/Other:	

TYPES OF BUSINESS:

Credit Card Processing
Electronic Payment Processing
Check Verification
Prepaid Card Services
Private-Label Credit Card Services
ATMs
Terminals
eCommerce

BRANDS/DIVISIONS/AFFILIATES:

Kohlberg Kravis Roberts & Co.
First Data Loyalty Solution
AccessNet
GO-Tag
Virtual Terminal
Merchant Solutions
First Merchant Solutions
AIB Merchant Services

CONTACTS: *Note: Officers with more than one job title may be intentionally listed here more than once.*

Michael D. Capellas, CEO
Phil Wall, CFO
Grace Chen Trent, Exec. VP-Mktg.
Peter Boucher, Exec. VP-Human Resources
Robert P. DeRodes, Exec. VP-Tech.
David Money, General Counsel/Exec. VP
Bob DeRodes, Exec. VP-Oper.
Thomas R. Bell, Jr., Chief Strategy Officer/Exec. VP
Grace Chen Trent, Exec. VP-Corp. Comm.
David Yates, Pres., First Data Int'l
Ed Labry, Pres., Retail & Alliance Services
Michael D. Capellas, Chmn.
Vincent Roland, Regional Head-EMEA

Phone: 303-967-8000	Fax: 303-967-6701
Toll-Free: 800-735-3362	
Address: 6200 S. Quebec St., Greenwood Village, CO 80111 US	

GROWTH PLANS/SPECIAL FEATURES:

First Data Corp. is a payment services company that processes and safeguards electronic payments using credit cards, debit cards, stored-value cards and electronic checks. It also develops, implements and manages prepaid stored-value card services for retailers (i.e., gift cards); general use credit cards; and private-label credit cards for businesses. Additional credit card services include account maintenance, transaction authorization, and fraud/risk management services. The firm offers First Data Loyalty Solution, which provides merchants with credit and debit card transaction processing services, guarantee services and customer spending patterns; and offers financial institutions customer management solutions. Additional programs include AccessNet, an automated services platform; the GO-Tag solution for mobile transactions; Virtual Terminal, which allows fast and secure access to credit card information; and Global Merchant Acquiring Solution, which connects international currency payments in one interface. The firm is owned by affiliates of Kohlberg Kravis Roberts & Co. In recent years, First Data Corp. and Standard Chartered PLC launched Merchant Solutions, which provides acquiring services to merchants across Asia. In January 2008, the company partnered with Allied Irish Banks p.l.c. (AIB) and the Republic of Ireland to establish AIB Merchant Services to offer card acquiring services in Europe. In October 2008, the company partnered with Cardinal Commerce Corporation to offer merchants all major alternative payment brands and a complete eCommerce solution; in the same month, the firm opened a new office in Karachi, Pakistan. In November 2008, First Data partnered with two German companies: PLUS Finanzservice, to offer German customers the option to sign up for a credit card through a merchant and receive one instantly; and Bankverein Werther AG, to release a new prepaid card branded by MasterCard. In January 2009, the company and WestLB agreed to start a new company, First Merchant Solutions, to provide card approval services to European retailers.

FINANCIALS: Sales and profits are in thousands of dollars—add 000 to get the full amount. 2008 Note: Financial information for 2008 was not available for all companies at press time.

2008 Sales: $8,811,300	2008 Profits: $-3,800,000	**U.S. Stock Ticker:** Private
2007 Sales: $8,051,400	2007 Profits: $-907,200	**Int'l Ticker:** Int'l Exchange:
2006 Sales: $7,076,400	2006 Profits: $1,513,400	Employees: 26,600
2005 Sales: $6,526,100	2005 Profits: $1,717,400	Fiscal Year Ends: 12/31
2004 Sales: $6,633,400	2004 Profits: $1,908,300	Parent Company: KKR & CO LP (KOHLBERG KRAVIS ROBERTS & CO)

SALARIES/BENEFITS:

Pension Plan:	ESOP Stock Plan:	Profit Sharing:	Top Exec. Salary: $	Bonus: $655,000
Savings Plan: Y	Stock Purch. Plan: Y		Second Exec. Salary: $	Bonus: $

OTHER THOUGHTS:

Apparent Women Officers or Directors: 1
Hot Spot for Advancement for Women/Minorities:

LOCATIONS: ("Y" = Yes)

West:	Southwest:	Midwest:	Southeast:	Northeast:	International:
Y	Y	Y	Y	Y	Y

FIRSTENERGY CORP

www.firstenergycorp.com

Industry Group Code: 2211 **Ranks within this company's industry group:** Sales: 4 Profits: 4

Management:		Sales/Marketing:		Liberal Arts:		Information Systems:		Professionals:		Tech./Scientific:	
Management Trainees:	Y	Marketing Pros.:	Y	Gen. Writing/Editing:	Y	Info. Management:	Y	Finance/Acct.:	Y	Engineers, Electrical:	Y
Experienced Mngmt.:	Y	Retail Sales:		Technical Writing:	Y	Software Dev.:	Y	Law:	Y	Engineers, Other:	Y
International Business:		Commercial/Industrial:	Y	Graphic Arts/Photog.:	Y	Hardware Dev.:		HR/Other:	Y	Health/Lab:	
MBA Grads:	Y	Sales Trainees:		Music:		Consulting/Other:		Training:	Y	Scientists/Research:	
		Advertising Pros.:	Y	Broadcasting:				Health Care:		Petroleum/Chemicals:	Y
				Other:				Consulting:		Math/Other:	

TYPES OF BUSINESS:

Utilities-Electricity & Natural Gas
Power Generation
Energy Management
Telecommunications

BRANDS/DIVISIONS/AFFILIATES:

Ohio Edison Co.
Cleveland Electric Illuminating Co. (The)
Toledo Edison Co. (The)
Pennsylvania Electric Co.
American Transmission Systems, Inc.
Jersey Central Power & Light Co.
Metropolitan Edison Co.
Pennsylvania Power Co.

CONTACTS: *Note: Officers with more than one job title may be intentionally listed here more than once.*

Anthony J. Alexander, CEO
Anthony J. Alexander, Pres.
Mark T. Clark, CFO/Exec. VP
Arthur W. Yuan, VP-Mktg. & Sales, FirstEnergy Solutions Corp.
Lynn M. Cavalier, Sr. VP-Human Resources, FirstEnergy Service Co
Bennett L. Gaines, CIO-FirstEnergy Service Co.
Bennett L. Gaines, VP-Admin., FirstEnergy Service Co.
Leila L. Vespoli, General Counsel/Exec. VP
Tony C. Banks, VP-Bus. Dev., FirstEnergy Service Co.
Michael J. Dowling, VP-Comm., FirstEnergy Service Co.
Ronald E. Seeholzer, VP-Investor Rel., FirstEnergy Service Co.
James F. Pearson, Treas./VP
Richard R. Grigg, Exec. VP/Pres., FirstEnergy Utilities
Gary R. Leidich, Exec. VP/Pres., FirstEnergy Generation
Harvey L. Wagner, Controller/Chief Acct. Officer/VP
Rhonda S. Ferguson, Corp. Sec./Chief Ethics Officer
George M. Smart, Chmn.

Phone: 330-761-4245	Fax: 330-384-3545
Toll-Free: 800-736-3402	
Address: 76 S. Main St., Akron, OH 44308 US	

GROWTH PLANS/SPECIAL FEATURES:

FirstEnergy Corporation is a diversified energy services holding company involved in the generation, transmission and distribution of electricity, energy management and other energy-related services. The firm operates eight principal electric utility subsidiaries: Ohio Edison Co.; The Cleveland Electric Illuminating Co.; The Toledo Edison Co.; Pennsylvania Electric Co.; American Transmission Systems, Inc.; Jersey Central Power & Light Co.; Metropolitan Edison Co.; and Pennsylvania Power Co. FirstEnergy is one of the largest investor-owned electric systems, serving 4.5 million customers in a service area that ranges over 36,100 square miles of Ohio, Pennsylvania and New Jersey. It has more than 14,173 megawatts (MW) of generating capacity. Generation is conducted through a variety of methods including coal, nuclear power, gas and oil and hydroelectric generation. FirstEnergy also has subsidiaries in the telecommunications market. In addition, FirstEnergy holds all of the outstanding common stock of other direct subsidiaries including FirstEnergy Ventures Corp.; FirstEnergy Properties, Inc.; GPU Diversified Holdings, LLC; GPU Telecom Services, Inc.; GPU Nuclear, Inc.; FENOC; FirstEnergy Securities Transfer Company; and FESC. In July 2008, the firm entered into a joint venture with the Boich Companies to acquire a majority stake in the Bull Mountain Mine Operations near Roundup, Montana. In February 2009, FirstEnergy Solutions Corp. expanded its service territory to include Illinois. In August 2009, the firm agreed to consolidate its transmission operations and assets into PJM Interconnection LLC, a wholesale electric coordinator that operates in 13 states and Washington, D.C.

FINANCIALS: Sales and profits are in thousands of dollars—add 000 to get the full amount. 2008 Note: Financial information for 2008 was not available for all companies at press time.

2008 Sales: $13,627,000	2008 Profits: $1,342,000	**U.S. Stock Ticker:** FE
2007 Sales: $12,802,000	2007 Profits: $1,309,000	**Int'l Ticker:** Int'l Exchange:
2006 Sales: $11,501,000	2006 Profits: $1,254,000	Employees: 14,698
2005 Sales: $11,358,000	2005 Profits: $861,000	Fiscal Year Ends: 12/31
2004 Sales: $11,600,000	2004 Profits: $878,200	Parent Company:

SALARIES/BENEFITS:

Pension Plan:	ESOP Stock Plan:	Profit Sharing:	Top Exec. Salary: $1,329,423	Bonus: $2,305,403
Savings Plan: Y	Stock Purch. Plan:		Second Exec. Salary: $759,615	Bonus: $799,801

OTHER THOUGHTS:

Apparent Women Officers or Directors: 7
Hot Spot for Advancement for Women/Minorities: Y

LOCATIONS: ("Y" = Yes)

West:	Southwest:	Midwest:	Southeast:	Northeast:	International:
		Y		Y	

Note: Financial information, benefits and other data can change quickly and may vary from those stated here.

FLUOR CORP

www.fluor.com

Industry Group Code: 237 **Ranks within this company's industry group:** Sales: 2 Profits: 1

Management:		Sales/Marketing:		Liberal Arts:		Information Systems:		Professionals:		Tech./Scientific:	
Management Trainees:	Y	Marketing Pros.:	Y	Gen. Writing/Editing:	Y	Info. Management:	Y	Finance/Acct.:	Y	Engineers, Electrical:	Y
Experienced Mngmt.:	Y	Retail Sales:		Technical Writing:	Y	Software Dev.:	Y	Law:	Y	Engineers, Other:	Y
International Business:	Y	Commercial/Industrial:	Y	Graphic Arts/Photog.:	Y	Hardware Dev.:		HR/Other:	Y	Health/Lab:	
MBA Grads:	Y	Sales Trainees:	Y	Music:		Consulting/Other:	Y	Training:	Y	Scientists/Research:	
		Advertising Pros.:	Y	Broadcasting:				Health Care:		Petroleum/Chemicals:	Y
				Other:				Consulting:	Y	Math/Other:	Y

TYPES OF BUSINESS:

Construction, Heavy & Civil Engineering
Power Plant Construction and Management
Facilities Management
Procurement Services
Consulting Services
Project Management
Asset Management
Staffing Services

BRANDS/DIVISIONS/AFFILIATES:

Fluor Construction Company
Department of Energy
Department of Homeland Security
Department of Defense
Kuwait Oil Company
LDK Solar Co
UNEC Engineering NV
Fluor Canada

CONTACTS: *Note: Officers with more than one job title may be intentionally listed here more than once.*

Alan L. Boeckmann, CEO
D. Michael Steuert, CFO/Sr. VP
Glenn Gilkey, Sr. VP-Human Resources
Ray F. Barnard, CIO/VP
Glenn Gilkey, Sr. VP-Admin.
Carlos M. Hernandez, Chief Legal Officer/Corp. Sec.
Lee Tashjian, VP-Corp. Comm.
Kenneth H. Lockwood, VP-Investor Rel. & Corp. Finance
Gary Smalley, Controller/VP
Dwayne Wilson, Pres., Industrial & Infrastructure
David T. Seaton, Pres., Energy & Chemicals
David E. Constable, Pres., Power
Richard P. Carter, Pres., Fluor Constructors International, Inc.
Alan L. Boeckmann, Chmn.
Kirk D. Grimes, Pres., Global Svcs.

Phone: 469-398-7000	Fax: 469-398-7255
Toll-Free:	
Address: 6700 Las Colinas Blvd., Irving, TX 75039 US	

GROWTH PLANS/SPECIAL FEATURES:

Fluor Corp., founded in 1912 as Fluor Construction Company, is a privately-held, global provider of engineering, procurement, construction and maintenance services. As well as being a primary service provider to the U.S. federal government, Fluor serves a diverse set of industries including oil and gas; chemical and petrochemicals; transportation; mining and metals; power; life sciences; and manufacturing. Fluor operates in five business segments: oil and gas; industrial and infrastructure; government; global services; and power. The oil and gas segment offers design, engineering, procurement, construction and project management services to energy-related industries. The industrial and infrastructure segment provides design, engineering and construction services to the transportation, mining, life sciences, telecommunications, manufacturing, microelectronics and healthcare sectors. The government segment provides project management services, including environmental restoration, engineering, construction, site operations and maintenance, to the U.S. government, particularly to the Department of Energy, the Department of Homeland Security and the Department of Defense. The global services segment provides operations, maintenance and construction services, as well as industrial fleet outsourcing, plant turnaround services, temporary staffing, procurement services and construction-related support. The power segment provides such services as engineering, procurement, construction, program management, start-up, commissioning and maintenance to the gas fueled, solid fueled, renewable and nuclear marketplaces. In January 2008, the company was awarded a $334 million consultancy services contract to provide overall program management for the Kuwait Oil Company. In April 2008, Fluor was awarded an engineering, procurement and construction management contract by LDK Solar Co., Ltd. for a poly-silicon facility in China. In November 2008, the company acquired two private engineering firms in Europe: UNEC Engineering NV in Antwerp, Belgium, and Europea de Ingenieria Y Asesoramiento of Tarragona, Spain.

Fluor offers its employees education assistance; an employee assistance program; and medical, dental, life and disability insurance.

FINANCIALS: Sales and profits are in thousands of dollars—add 000 to get the full amount. 2008 Note: Financial information for 2008 was not available for all companies at press time.

2008 Sales: $22,325,900	2008 Profits: $720,500	**U.S. Stock Ticker: FLR**
2007 Sales: $16,691,000	2007 Profits: $533,300	**Int'l Ticker:** Int'l Exchange:
2006 Sales: $14,078,500	2006 Profits: $263,500	Employees: 42,119
2005 Sales: $13,161,100	2005 Profits: $227,300	Fiscal Year Ends: 12/31
2004 Sales: $9,380,300	2004 Profits: $186,700	Parent Company:

SALARIES/BENEFITS:

Pension Plan: Y	ESOP Stock Plan:	Profit Sharing:	Top Exec. Salary: $1,232,270	Bonus: $6,873,200
Savings Plan: Y	Stock Purch. Plan:		Second Exec. Salary: $781,871	Bonus: $2,563,000

OTHER THOUGHTS:

Apparent Women Officers or Directors: 4
Hot Spot for Advancement for Women/Minorities: Y

LOCATIONS: ("Y" = Yes)

West:	Southwest:	Midwest:	Southeast:	Northeast:	International:
Y	Y	Y	Y	Y	Y

Note: Financial information, benefits and other data can change quickly and may vary from those stated here.

FOREST LABORATORIES INC

www.frx.com

Industry Group Code: 325412 Ranks within this company's industry group: Sales: 13 Profits: 10

Management:		Sales/Marketing:		Liberal Arts:		Information Systems:		Professionals:		Tech./Scientific:	
Management Trainees:	Y	Marketing Pros.:	Y	Gen. Writing/Editing:	Y	Info. Management:	Y	Finance/Acct.:	Y	Engineers, Electrical:	Y
Experienced Mngmt.:	Y	Retail Sales:		Technical Writing:	Y	Software Dev.:	Y	Law:	Y	Engineers, Other:	Y
International Business:	Y	Commercial/Industrial:	Y	Graphic Arts/Photog.:	Y	Hardware Dev.:		HR/Other:	Y	Health/Lab:	Y
MBA Grads:	Y	Sales Trainees:		Music:		Consulting/Other:		Training:	Y	Scientists/Research:	Y
		Advertising Pros.:		Broadcasting:				Health Care:	Y	Petroleum/Chemicals:	Y
				Other:				Consulting:		Math/Other:	Y

TYPES OF BUSINESS:

Drugs, Manufacturing
Over-the-Counter Pharmaceuticals
Generic Pharmaceuticals
Antidepressants
Asthma Medications
Cardiovascular Products
OB/Gyn Products
Endocrinology

BRANDS/DIVISIONS/AFFILIATES:

Lexapro
Namenda
Benicar
Forest Research Institute
Forest Pharmaceuticals, Inc.
Forest Laboratories Europe
Inwood Laboratories
Cerexa, Inc.

CONTACTS: Note: Officers with more than one job title may be intentionally listed here more than once.

Howard Solomon, CEO
Lawrence S. Olanoff, COO
Lawrence S. Olanoff, Pres.
Francis I. Perier, Jr., CFO
Elaine Hochberg, Sr. VP-Mktg./Chief Commercial Officer
William J. Candee III, Sec.
Frank Murdolo, VP-Investor Rel.
Francis I. Perier, Jr., Sr. VP-Finance
Howard Solomon, Chmn.

Phone: 212-421-7850	Fax:
Toll-Free: 800-947-5227	
Address: 909 3rd Ave., New York, NY 10022 US	

GROWTH PLANS/SPECIAL FEATURES:

Forest Laboratories, Inc. develops, delivers and sells pharmaceutical products. It currently covers six therapeutic areas, developing treatments for respiratory, pain management, ob/gyn, endocrinology, central nervous system and cardiovascular conditions. Forest's four principal brands are Lexapro, an antidepressant; Benicar, a hypertension treatment; Namenda, a therapy for moderate or severe Alzheimer's disease; and Campral, which helps reduce withdrawals for those seeking to eliminate alcohol dependence. Other products include Aerobid, an asthma medication; AeroChamber Plus, an inhalant delivery system for asthma medications; Infasurf, used to prevent respiratory distress syndrome (RDS), a condition caused by a lack of surfactant, found mainly in premature infants; Armour Thyroid, Levothroid and Thyrolar, for treating hypothyroidism; Celexa, an antidepressant; Cervidil, used to prepare the cervix before inducing labor; and Combunox, a pain medication combining both opioids and non-steroidal anti-inflammatory drugs. Forest markets directly to physicians who have the most potential for growth and are agreeable to the introduction of new products, as well as to pharmacies, hospitals, managed care and other healthcare organizations. Forest Research Institute, Forest's scientific division, maintains labs on Long Island and in New Jersey. Subsidiary Forest Pharmaceuticals, Inc. manufactures and distributes Forest's branded prescription products in the U.S. Subsidiary Forest Laboratories Europe has two manufacturing sites in Dublin, Ireland and one in Bexley, Kent, and distributes prescription and over-the-counter drugs in Europe, the Middle East, Australia and Asia. Subsidiary Inwood Laboratories manufactures and supplies generic versions of Forest's medications. Cerexa, Inc., acquired in 2007, develops and commercializes treatments for life-threatening infections. In January 2009, the company's Savella, a selective serotonin and norepinephrine inhibitor, was approved by the FDA for the management of fibromyalgia, a chronic pain condition.

Employees at Forest receive financial assistance for adoption and fertility treatments; medical, dental and life insurance; flexible spending accounts; child-care resources; and a commuter benefit program.

FINANCIALS: Sales and profits are in thousands of dollars—add 000 to get the full amount. 2008 Note: Financial information for 2008 was not available for all companies at press time.

2008 Sales: $3,501,802	2008 Profits: $967,933	**U.S. Stock Ticker: FRX**
2007 Sales: $3,183,324	2007 Profits: $454,103	**Int'l Ticker:** Int'l Exchange:
2006 Sales: $2,793,934	2006 Profits: $708,514	Employees: 5,225
2005 Sales: $3,052,408	2005 Profits: $838,805	Fiscal Year Ends: 3/31
2004 Sales: $2,650,432	2004 Profits: $735,874	Parent Company:

SALARIES/BENEFITS:

Pension Plan:	ESOP Stock Plan:	Profit Sharing: Y	Top Exec. Salary: $1,162,500	Bonus: $635,000
Savings Plan: Y	Stock Purch. Plan:		Second Exec. Salary: $758,750	Bonus: $400,000

OTHER THOUGHTS:

Apparent Women Officers or Directors: 1
Hot Spot for Advancement for Women/Minorities: Y

LOCATIONS: ("Y" = Yes)

West:	Southwest:	Midwest:	Southeast:	Northeast:	International:
		Y		Y	Y

Note: Financial information, benefits and other data can change quickly and may vary from those stated here.

FORTUNE BRANDS INC

www.fortunebrands.com

Industry Group Code: 312140 Ranks within this company's industry group: Sales: 1   Profits: 1

Management:		Sales/Marketing:		Liberal Arts:		Information Systems:		Professionals:		Tech./Scientific:	
Management Trainees:	Y	Marketing Pros.:		Gen. Writing/Editing:	Y	Info. Management:	Y	Finance/Acct.:	Y	Engineers, Electrical:	
Experienced Mngmt.:	Y	Retail Sales:		Technical Writing:	Y	Software Dev.:	Y	Law:	Y	Engineers, Other:	Y
International Business:	Y	Commercial/Industrial:	Y	Graphic Arts/Photog.:	Y	Hardware Dev.:		HR/Other:	Y	Health/Lab:	
MBA Grads:	Y	Sales Trainees:	Y	Music:		Consulting/Other:		Training:	Y	Scientists/Research:	
		Advertising Pros.:	Y	Broadcasting:				Health Care:		Petroleum/Chemicals:	
				Other:				Consulting:		Math/Other:	

TYPES OF BUSINESS:

Home & Hardware Products
Spirits & Wine
Golf Products

BRANDS/DIVISIONS/AFFILIATES:

MasterBrand Cabinets, Inc.
Moen, Inc.
Simonton Holdings, Inc.
Beam Global Spirits & Wine, Inc.
Acushnet Co.
Aristokraft
Omega
Cruzan

CONTACTS: Note: Officers with more than one job title may be intentionally listed here more than once.

Bruce A. Carbonari, CEO
Bruce A. Carbonari, Pres.
Craig P. Omtvedt, CFO/Sr. VP
Elizabeth R. Lane, VP-Human Resources
Mark A. Roche, General Counsel/Sr. VP/Sec.
Christopher J. Klein, Sr. VP-Strategy & Corp. Dev.
C. Clarkson Hine, VP-Corp. Comm. & Public Affairs
Anthony J. Diaz, VP-Investor Rel.
Mark Hausberg, Sr. VP-Finance/Treas.
Matt Stanton, VP-Public Affairs
Charlie Ryan, VP-Taxes
Allan J. Snape, VP-Bus. Dev.
Edward Wiertel, Controller/VP
Bruce A. Carbonari, Chmn.

Phone: 847-484-4400	Fax: 847-478-0073
Toll-Free:	
Address: 520 Lake Cook Rd., Deerfield, IL 60015 US	

GROWTH PLANS/SPECIAL FEATURES:

Fortune Brands, Inc. is a holding company with subsidiaries engaged in the manufacture, production and sale of home and hardware products, premium spirits, and golf products. Home and hardware subsidiaries include MasterBrand Cabinets, Inc., which manufactures custom, semi-custom, stock and ready-to-assemble cabinetry for the kitchen, bath and home sold under brands including Aristokraft, Omega, Kitchen Craft, Schrock, Diamond, Decora and Kemper; Moen, Inc., which manufactures faucets, bath furnishings, accessories, parts and kitchen sinks in North America and China; Therma-Thru Corp., which manufactures fiberglass and steel residential entry door and patio door systems; Simonton Holdings, Inc., whose brands include Simonton Windows, a vinyl-framed windows and patio doors brand; and Fortune Brands Storage and Security, LLC, which manufactures tool storage products and safety and security devices. The premium spirits business operates through holding company Beam Global Spirits & Wine, Inc., whose subsidiaries include Jim Beam Brands Co.; Future Brands, LLC; Jim Brands Australia Pty. Ltd.; Beam Global Espanol S.A.; Beam Global Spirits & Wine (U.K.) Ltd.; Tequila Sauza S.A. de C.F.; Canadian Club Canada, Inc.; Maker's Mark Distillery, Inc.; Courvoisier S.A.S.; and Beam Wine Estates, Inc. The company has significant positions in categories including tequila, cognac, Scotch whisky and Canadian whisky. Brands include Courvosier, Maker's Mark, Cruzan, Sauza, Canadian Club and Laphoaig. It also has significant business in regional and national spirits categories such as German liqueurs and Spanish brandies; and an agency relationship for the importation and marketing of New Zealand and Australian wines of the Lion Nathan Wine Group. The golf business operates through Acushnet Co., a manufacturer and marketer of golf balls, clubs, shoes and gloves. Other products include golf bags, outwear and accessories. Brands include Titleist, Pinnacle, Scotty Cameron, Vokey and FootJoy. In August 2008, the company acquired the Cruzan Rum brand.

FINANCIALS: Sales and profits are in thousands of dollars—add 000 to get the full amount. 2008 Note: Financial information for 2008 was not available for all companies at press time.

2008 Sales: $7,608,900	2008 Profits: $317,100	U.S. Stock Ticker: FO
2007 Sales: $8,563,100	2007 Profits: $762,600	Int'l Ticker: Int'l Exchange:
2006 Sales: $8,769,000	2006 Profits: $830,100	Employees: 37,100
2005 Sales: $7,061,200	2005 Profits: $621,100	Fiscal Year Ends: 12/31
2004 Sales: $7,320,900	2004 Profits: $783,800	Parent Company:

SALARIES/BENEFITS:

Pension Plan:	ESOP Stock Plan:	Profit Sharing:	Top Exec. Salary: $1,100,000	Bonus: $
Savings Plan:	Stock Purch. Plan:		Second Exec. Salary: $937,500	Bonus: $

OTHER THOUGHTS:

Apparent Women Officers or Directors: 4
Hot Spot for Advancement for Women/Minorities: Y

LOCATIONS: ("Y" = Yes)

West:	Southwest:	Midwest:	Southeast:	Northeast:	International:
		Y			Y

FOSSIL INC

www.fossil.com

Industry Group Code: 334518 **Ranks within this company's industry group:** Sales: 1 Profits: 1

Management:		Sales/Marketing:		Liberal Arts:		Information Systems:		Professionals:		Tech./Scientific:	
Management Trainees:	Y	Marketing Pros.:	Y	Gen. Writing/Editing:	Y	Info. Management:	Y	Finance/Acct.:	Y	Engineers, Electrical:	Y
Experienced Mngmt.:	Y	Retail Sales:	Y	Technical Writing:	Y	Software Dev.:	Y	Law:	Y	Engineers, Other:	
International Business:	Y	Commercial/Industrial:	Y	Graphic Arts/Photog.:	Y	Hardware Dev.:		HR/Other:	Y	Health/Lab:	
MBA Grads:	Y	Sales Trainees:	Y	Music:		Consulting/Other:		Training:	Y	Scientists/Research:	
		Advertising Pros.:	Y	Broadcasting:				Health Care:		Petroleum/Chemicals:	
				Other:	Y			Consulting:		Math/Other:	

TYPES OF BUSINESS:

Watch Manufacturing
Accessories
Online Sales
Leather Goods
Belts
Handbags
Jewelry
Retail Stores

BRANDS/DIVISIONS/AFFILIATES:

Fossil
Relic
Zodiac
Abacus
MW
MW Michele
Big Tic
Fifty-Four by Fossil

CONTACTS: *Note: Officers with more than one job title may be intentionally listed here more than once.*

Kosta N. Kartsotis, CEO
Michael W. Barnes, COO
Michael W. Barnes, Pres.
Mike L. Kovar, CFO/Sr. VP
Mike L. Kovar, Treas.
Livio Galanti, Exec. VP
Mark D. Quick, Vice Chmn.
Jennifer Pritchard, Pres., Retail Div.
Tom Kartsotis, Chmn.

Phone: 972-234-2525	Fax: 972-234-4669
Toll-Free:	
Address: 2280 N. Greenville Ave., Richardson, TX 75082 US	

GROWTH PLANS/SPECIAL FEATURES:

Fossil, Inc. designs, develops, markets and distributes fashion accessories. The company's principal offerings include a line of men's and women's watches and jewelry sold under proprietary and licensed brands, handbags, leather goods, sunglasses, and apparel. In the watch and jewelry product category, Fossil has a diverse portfolio of globally recognized brands such as Fossil, Relic, MW, MW Michele, Abacus Wrist Net, Abacus Wrist PDA and Zodiac. Also, through license agreements, the company utilizes prestigious brand names such as Burberry, DKNY, Michael Kors, Marc Jacobs, Jacobs and Emporio Armani. The company distributes products through various channels including wholesale, export and direct to the consumer. Domestically, the company sells its products through a distribution network that includes Neiman Marcus, Nordstrom, Macy's, Dillard's, JCPenney, Kohl's, Sears, Wal-Mart and Target. The firm also sells its products through a network of company-owned stores, which includes 125 retail and 74 outlet stores. Additionally, the company offers an extensive collection of Fossil brand products through its catalog and website as well as proprietary and licensed watch and jewelry brands through other managed and affiliate websites. Internationally, products are sold to department stores and specialty stores in over 100 countries through 23 company-owned foreign sales subsidiaries and through approximately 59 independent distributors. Fossil products are offered on airlines, cruise ships and in international company-owned retail stores, which included 104 accessory retail stores, 13 multi-brand stores and 8 outlet stores in select international markets. In 2008, the firm announced plans to open 80-85 stores, concentrating on the full price accessory concept with equal distribution between U.S. and international locations.

FINANCIALS: Sales and profits are in thousands of dollars—add 000 to get the full amount. 2008 Note: Financial information for 2008 was not available for all companies at press time.

2008 Sales: $1,583,242	2008 Profits: $138,097	**U.S. Stock Ticker:** FOSL
2007 Sales: $1,432,984	2007 Profits: $123,261	**Int'l Ticker:** Int'l Exchange:
2006 Sales: $1,213,965	2006 Profits: $77,582	Employees: 7,355
2005 Sales: $1,043,120	2005 Profits: $75,670	Fiscal Year Ends: 12/31
2004 Sales: $957,309	2004 Profits: $89,545	Parent Company:

SALARIES/BENEFITS:

Pension Plan:	ESOP Stock Plan:	Profit Sharing:	Top Exec. Salary: $629,808	Bonus: $300,000
Savings Plan:	Stock Purch. Plan:		Second Exec. Salary: $536,923	Bonus: $260,000

OTHER THOUGHTS:

Apparent Women Officers or Directors: 3
Hot Spot for Advancement for Women/Minorities: Y

LOCATIONS: ("Y" = Yes)

West:	Southwest:	Midwest:	Southeast:	Northeast:	International:
Y	Y	Y	Y	Y	Y

FOSTER WHEELER AG

www.fwc.com

Industry Group Code: 237 Ranks within this company's industry group: Sales: 5 Profits: 2

Management:		Sales/Marketing:		Liberal Arts:		Information Systems:		Professionals:		Tech./Scientific:	
Management Trainees:	Y	Marketing Pros.:	Y	Gen. Writing/Editing:	Y	Info. Management:	Y	Finance/Acct.:	Y	Engineers, Electrical:	Y
Experienced Mngmt.:	Y	Retail Sales:		Technical Writing:	Y	Software Dev.:	Y	Law:	Y	Engineers, Other:	Y
International Business:	Y	Commercial/Industrial:	Y	Graphic Arts/Photog.:	Y	Hardware Dev.:		HR/Other:	Y	Health/Lab:	
MBA Grads:	Y	Sales Trainees:	Y	Music:		Consulting/Other:	Y	Training:	Y	Scientists/Research:	
		Advertising Pros.:		Broadcasting:				Health Care:		Petroleum/Chemicals:	Y
				Other:				Consulting:	Y	Math/Other:	Y

TYPES OF BUSINESS:

Engineering & Construction
Industrial Plant Design & Development
Energy Equipment
Power Systems Manufacturer
Steam Generation Equipment
Renewable Energy Technology

BRANDS/DIVISIONS/AFFILIATES:

Foster Wheeler, Ltd.
Foster Wheeler International Corp.
Foster Wheeler Energy, Ltd.
Foster Wheeler Constructors
Foster Wheeler Power Machinery Co., Ltd.
Foster Wheeler Power Systems, Inc.
Quotient Engineering, Inc.
Foster Wheeler USA Corp.

CONTACTS: *Note: Officers with more than one job title may be intentionally listed here more than once.*

Raymond J. Milchovich, CEO
Umberto della Sala, COO
Umberto della Sala, Pres.
Franco Baseotto, CFO/Exec. VP/Treas.
Peter J. Ganz, General Counsel/Exec. VP
Lisa Z. Wood, VP/Controller
Umberto della Sala, CEO-Global E&C Group
Gary Nedelka, Acting CEO-Global Power Group
Raymond J. Milchovich, Chmn.

Phone: 908-730-4000	Fax: 908-713-3245
Toll-Free:	
Address: Perryville Corp. Park, Clinton, NJ 08809-4000 US	

GROWTH PLANS/SPECIAL FEATURES:

Foster Wheeler AG, formerly Foster Wheeler, Ltd., provides services in the oil and gas, oil refining, chemical/petrochemical, pharmaceutical, environmental, power generation and power plant operation and maintenance industries through offices in more than 28 countries. The company operates through its numerous subsidiaries, including Foster Wheeler Power Machinery Co., Ltd.; Foster Wheeler International Corp.; Foster Wheeler Energy, Ltd.; Foster Wheeler Constructors; Foster Wheeler Power Systems, Inc.; and Foster Wheeler Facilities Management, Inc. The firm's engineering services include industrial plant construction, water treatment plant engineering, and petroleum, chemical and alternative fuel facilities construction. Foster Wheeler operates under two business groups: the Global Engineering and Construction (E&C) Group, which designs, engineers and constructs onshore and offshore upstream oil and gas processing facilities, natural gas liquefaction facilities and receiving terminals, gas-to-liquids facilities, oil refining, chemical and petrochemical, pharmaceutical and biotechnology facilities and related infrastructure; and the Global Power Group, which designs, manufactures and erects steam generating and auxiliary equipment for electric power generating stations and industrial facilities worldwide. Other services include the design, manufacture and installation of auxiliary equipment, which includes steam generators for solar thermal power plants, feedwater heaters, steam condensers and heat-recovery equipment. The company has engineered and built process, power and industrial facilities in over 125 countries. In February 2008, the company strengthened its foothold in the biotech and pharmaceutical markets with the acquisition of Biokinetics Inc., a leading U.S. biopharmaceutical process design company, from MPA Holdings LP. In July 2008, the company's operating unit Foster Wheeler USA Corporation acquired the assets of Quotient Engineering, Inc., a full-service engineering and design company. In February 2009, Foster Wheeler completed its redomestication to change the place of incorporation of its group holding company from Bermuda to Switzerland. The firm also reregistered its company as Foster Wheeler AG.

FINANCIALS: Sales and profits are in thousands of dollars—add 000 to get the full amount. 2008 Note: Financial information for 2008 was not available for all companies at press time.

2008 Sales: $6,854,290	2008 Profits: $526,620	U.S. Stock Ticker: FWLT
2007 Sales: $5,107,243	2007 Profits: $393,874	Int'l Ticker: Int'l Exchange:
2006 Sales: $3,495,048	2006 Profits: $261,984	Employees: 14,729
2005 Sales: $2,199,955	2005 Profits: $-109,749	Fiscal Year Ends: 12/31
2004 Sales: $2,661,324	2004 Profits: $-285,294	Parent Company:

SALARIES/BENEFITS:

Pension Plan:	ESOP Stock Plan:	Profit Sharing:	Top Exec. Salary: $1,031,940	Bonus: $2,063,900
Savings Plan:	Stock Purch. Plan:		Second Exec. Salary: $800,068	Bonus: $1,048,961

OTHER THOUGHTS:

Apparent Women Officers or Directors: 3
Hot Spot for Advancement for Women/Minorities: Y

LOCATIONS: ("Y" = Yes)

West:	Southwest:	Midwest:	Southeast:	Northeast:	International:
Y	Y	Y	Y	Y	Y

FOX ENTERTAINMENT GROUP INC

www.fox.com

Industry Group Code: 515120 Ranks within this company's industry group: Sales: Profits:

Management:		Sales/Marketing:		Liberal Arts:		Information Systems:		Professionals:		Tech./Scientific:	
Management Trainees:	Y	Marketing Pros.:	Y	Gen. Writing/Editing:	Y	Info. Management:	Y	Finance/Acct.:	Y	Engineers, Electrical:	Y
Experienced Mngmt.:	Y	Retail Sales:		Technical Writing:		Software Dev.:	Y	Law:	Y	Engineers, Other:	
International Business:	Y	Commercial/Industrial:	Y	Graphic Arts/Photog.:	Y	Hardware Dev.:		HR/Other:	Y	Health/Lab:	
MBA Grads:	Y	Sales Trainees:		Music:	Y	Consulting/Other:		Training:	Y	Scientists/Research:	
		Advertising Pros.:	Y	Broadcasting:	Y			Health Care:		Petroleum/Chemicals:	
				Other:	Y			Consulting:		Math/Other:	

TYPES OF BUSINESS:

Broadcast Television
Film Distribution and Production
Television Programming
Online Communities and Game Sites
Professional Sports
Electronic Games
Cable TV Programming
Online Entertainment

BRANDS/DIVISIONS/AFFILIATES:

News Corp
Fox Filmed Entertainment
Twentieth Century Fox Television
Fox Television Studios
Fox Interactive Media
National Geographic Channel

CONTACTS: *Note: Officers with more than one job title may be intentionally listed here more than once.*

Rupert Murdoch, CEO
Chase Carey, COO
Chase Carey, Pres.
David DeVoe, CFO/Sr. Exec. VP
K. Rupert Murdoch, Chmn.

Phone: 310-369-1000	**Fax:** 310-969-3300
Toll-Free:	
Address: 10201 W. Pico Blvd., Bldg. 100, Ste. 3220, Los Angeles, CA 90035 US	

GROWTH PLANS/SPECIAL FEATURES:

Fox Entertainment Group, Inc., a wholly-owned subsidiary of The News Corporation, is an entertainment conglomerate that operates through four business segments: filmed entertainment, television stations, television broadcast network and cable network programming. The company engages in feature film and television production and distribution principally through the following businesses: Fox Filmed Entertainment, a leading producer and distributor of feature films; Twentieth Century Fox Television, a producer of network television programming; Fox Television Studios, a leading producer of U.S. broadcast, cable and international programming; and Fox Interactive Media, a network of integrated Internet sites including Myspace.com, which has more than 60 million users worldwide. Twentieth Century Fox Home Entertainment, Inc. distributes motion pictures and other programming produced by units of Fox Entertainment and its affiliates in all home media formats, including digital media available for download from Apple's iTunes Music Store. The company's motion picture and television library consists of varying rights to well over 3,000 previously released motion pictures and many television programs. In television, Fox Television Stations owns and operates 27 located in nine of the 10 largest designated market areas. Its television broadcast network consists of approximately 200 affiliated stations, including the full-power stations that are owned by subsidiaries of Fox. The company produces television programs through Twentieth Century Fox Television, Fox Television Studios, Fox News Channel, Fox Sports Networks, FX Network, SPEED Channel, FUEL TV, Fox College Sports, Fox Movie Channel, Fox Sports International, National Geographic Channel, Fox Movie Channel and several foreign subsidiaries. The company also owns a 14.6% limited partnership interest in the Colorado Rockies, the baseball franchise in Denver, Colorado. In recent years, the firm began distributing movies in the Blu-ray high definition disk format.

FINANCIALS: Sales and profits are in thousands of dollars—add 000 to get the full amount. 2008 Note: Financial information for 2008 was not available for all companies at press time.

2008 Sales: $	2008 Profits: $	**U.S. Stock Ticker: Subsidiary**
2007 Sales: $	2007 Profits: $	**Int'l Ticker:** Int'l Exchange:
2006 Sales: $	2006 Profits: $	Employees:
2005 Sales: $	2005 Profits: $	Fiscal Year Ends: 6/30
2004 Sales: $12,175,000	2004 Profits: $1,353,000	Parent Company: NEWS CORP

SALARIES/BENEFITS:

Pension Plan:	ESOP Stock Plan:	Profit Sharing:	Top Exec. Salary: $	Bonus: $21,175,000
Savings Plan:	Stock Purch. Plan:		Second Exec. Salary: $	Bonus: $

OTHER THOUGHTS:

Apparent Women Officers or Directors:
Hot Spot for Advancement for Women/Minorities:

LOCATIONS: ("Y" = Yes)

West:	Southwest:	Midwest:	Southeast:	Northeast:	International:
Y					

FPL GROUP INC

www.fplgroup.com

Industry Group Code: 2211 Ranks within this company's industry group: Sales: 2 Profits: 2

Management:		Sales/Marketing:		Liberal Arts:		Information Systems:		Professionals:		Tech./Scientific:	
Management Trainees:	Y	Marketing Pros.:	Y	Gen. Writing/Editing:	Y	Info. Management:	Y	Finance/Acct.:	Y	Engineers, Electrical:	Y
Experienced Mngmt.:	Y	Retail Sales:		Technical Writing:	Y	Software Dev.:	Y	Law:	Y	Engineers, Other:	Y
International Business:		Commercial/Industrial:	Y	Graphic Arts/Photog.:	Y	Hardware Dev.:		HR/Other:	Y	Health/Lab:	
MBA Grads:	Y	Sales Trainees:		Music:		Consulting/Other:		Training:	Y	Scientists/Research:	
		Advertising Pros.:	Y	Broadcasting:				Health Care:		Petroleum/Chemicals:	Y
				Other:				Consulting:		Math/Other:	

TYPES OF BUSINESS:

Utilities-Electricity & Natural Gas
Fiber-Optic Services
Financial Services
Nuclear Power
Energy Trading & Marketing
Wind Power
Solar Power

BRANDS/DIVISIONS/AFFILIATES:

Florida Power & Light Company
NextEra Energy Resources
FPL FiberNet, LLC
FPL Group Capitol
NextEra Energy Power Marketing LLC

CONTACTS: *Note: Officers with more than one job title may be intentionally listed here more than once.*

Lewis Hay, III, CEO
James L. Robo, COO
James L. Robo, Pres.
Armando Pimentel, Jr., CFO/Exec. VP-Finance
James W. Poppell, Exec. VP-Human Resources
Robert L. McGrath, VP-Eng., Construction & Corp. Svcs.
Charles E. Sieving, General Counsel/Exec. VP
Christopher A. Bennett, Chief Strategy, Policy & Bus. Officer/Exec. VP
K. Michael Davis, Chief Acct. Officer/Controller
Carmen Perez, Pres., FPL FiberNet LLC
F. Mitchell Davidson, CEO/Pres., NextEra Energy Resources
Armando J. Olivera, CEO/Pres., Florida Power & Light Company
Antonio Rodriguez, Exec. VP-Power Generation Div.
Lewis Hay, III, Chmn.

Phone: 561-694-4000	Fax:
Toll-Free:	
Address: 700 Universe Blvd., Juno Beach, FL 33408 US	

GROWTH PLANS/SPECIAL FEATURES:

FPL Group, Inc. is a public utility holding company. Its primary subsidiary, Florida Power & Light Company (FPL), generates, transmits, distributes, buys and sells electricity. FPL supplies electric service to over 8.7 million people throughout the east and lower west coasts of Florida, and has 4.5 million customer accounts. Approximately 53% of its 2008 sales were from residential customers, 40% from commercial customers, 3% from industrial customers and 4% from others. Approximately 53% of the company's 2008 power was produced by natural gas fueled plants, 22% by nuclear plants, 5% by oil plants, 6% by coal plants and 14% was purchased from other companies. In all, FPL operates 83 plants that burn natural gas, oil or a combination of both; three coal plants; and four nuclear plants. FPL also has three solar generation facilities under construction. Besides FPL, the group operates NextEra Energy Resources, formerly FPL Energy LLC, and FPL FiberNet LLC, both of which are owned by subsidiary FPL Group Capitol. NextEra Energy Resources has a capacity of nearly 17,000 megawatts (MW), utilizing 39% natural gas, 38% wind, 15% nuclear, 5% oil, 2% hydro and 1% other energy sources. NextEra Energy Power Marketing LLC, a subsidiary of NextEra Energy Resources, buys and sells wholesale energy commodities, such as natural gas, oil and electricity, and manages the fuel needs of NextEra Energy Resources' power generation fleet. FPL FiberNet leases wholesale fiber-optic network capacity and dark fiber to various clients. In March 2008, FPL Energy LLC applied to build a 250 MW solar plant in California's Mojave Desert. In July 2008, FPL was approved to construct three new solar projects in Florida for 110 MW of total power.

FPL offers medical, dental and vision benefits; flexible spending plans; life insurance and dependant life insurance; and education and adoption assistance.

FINANCIALS: Sales and profits are in thousands of dollars—add 000 to get the full amount. 2008 Note: Financial information for 2008 was not available for all companies at press time.

2008 Sales: $16,410,000	2008 Profits: $1,639,000	**U.S. Stock Ticker: FPL**
2007 Sales: $15,263,000	2007 Profits: $1,312,000	Int'l Ticker: Int'l Exchange:
2006 Sales: $15,710,000	2006 Profits: $1,281,000	Employees: 10,700
2005 Sales: $11,846,000	2005 Profits: $901,000	Fiscal Year Ends: 12/31
2004 Sales: $10,522,000	2004 Profits: $896,000	Parent Company:

SALARIES/BENEFITS:

Pension Plan: Y	ESOP Stock Plan:	Profit Sharing:	Top Exec. Salary: $1,255,800	Bonus: $2,400,000
Savings Plan: Y	Stock Purch. Plan:		Second Exec. Salary: $756,000	Bonus: $1,082,592

OTHER THOUGHTS:

Apparent Women Officers or Directors: 5
Hot Spot for Advancement for Women/Minorities: Y

LOCATIONS: ("Y" = Yes)

West:	Southwest:	Midwest:	Southeast:	Northeast:	International:
Y	Y	Y	Y	Y	

FRED'S INC

www.fredsinc.com

Industry Group Code: 452112 **Ranks within this company's industry group:** Sales: 9 Profits: 9

Management:		Sales/Marketing:		Liberal Arts:		Information Systems:		Professionals:		Tech./Scientific:	
Management Trainees:	Y	Marketing Pros.:	Y	Gen. Writing/Editing:	Y	Info. Management:	Y	Finance/Acct.:	Y	Engineers, Electrical:	
Experienced Mngmt.:	Y	Retail Sales:	Y	Technical Writing:		Software Dev.:	Y	Law:	Y	Engineers, Other:	
International Business:		Commercial/Industrial:		Graphic Arts/Photog.:	Y	Hardware Dev.:		HR/Other:	Y	Health/Lab:	
MBA Grads:	Y	Sales Trainees:	Y	Music:		Consulting/Other:		Training:	Y	Scientists/Research:	
		Advertising Pros.:	Y	Broadcasting:				Health Care:		Petroleum/Chemicals:	
				Other:	Y			Consulting:		Math/Other:	

TYPES OF BUSINESS:

Discount Stores
Pharmacies
Photo Processing
General Merchandise

BRANDS/DIVISIONS/AFFILIATES:

Fred's
Fred's Pharmacies

CONTACTS: *Note: Officers with more than one job title may be intentionally listed here more than once.*

Bruce A. Efird, CEO
Bruce A. Efird, Pres.
Jerry A. Shore, CFO/Exec. VP
Dennis K. Curtis, Exec. VP/Gen. Merch. Mgr.
Jerry A. Shore, Chief Admin. Officer
Charles S. Vail, General Counsel/Corp. Sec./Sr. VP-Legal Svcs.
Earl Taylor, Exec. VP-Store Oper.
John A. Casey, Exec. VP-Pharmacy Acquisitions
Rick A. Chambers, Exec. VP-Pharmacy Oper.
Michael J. Hayes, Chmn.
Reggie Jacobs, Exec. VP-Dist. & Corp. Svcs.

Phone: 901-365-8880	Fax:
Toll-Free:	
Address: 4300 New Getwell Rd., Memphis, TN 38118 US	

GROWTH PLANS/SPECIAL FEATURES:

Fred's, Inc., operates approximately 639 discount general merchandise and pharmacy stores throughout the southeastern U.S. Approximately 82% of Fred's stores are in markets with populations of 15,000 or fewer people. Of these locations, 284 contain full-service pharmacies. The firm also markets goods and services to 24 franchised Fred's stores. Fred's stores feature over 12,000 items, including national brand names, off-brands and Fred's private label. About half of Fred's stores' merchandise is received through its distribution centers in Georgia and Tennessee, while the remaining stock is shipped directly from suppliers. The Fred's sales mix is divided into seven categories: pharmaceuticals (31.7% of sales); household goods (24.8%); food and tobacco (15.5%); paper and cleaning supplies (9.2%); apparel and linens (8.6%); health and beauty aids (8%); and sales to franchised Fred's stores (2.2%). The company's strategy for obtaining customers for new pharmacies is through the acquisition of prescription files from independent pharmacies. These acquisitions provide an immediate sales benefit, and in many cases, the independent pharmacist will move to Fred's. In 2008, Fred's opened 21 stores and closed 74 stores. The majority of the new stores opened were located in Mississippi, Alabama, Georgia and South Carolina. The company's new store prototype has 16,000 square feet of space. Opening a new store currently costs between $450,000 and $600,000 for inventory, furniture, fixtures, equipment and leasehold improvements. Also in 2008, the company added 11 new pharmacies and closed 23 pharmacies. Approximately 44% of Fred's stores, as of January 2009, contain a pharmacy and sell prescription drugs. In 2009, the company plans to continue its conservative expansion approach and intends to open approximately 12 to 16 stores and 10 to 14 pharmacies.

FINANCIALS: Sales and profits are in thousands of dollars—add 000 to get the full amount. 2008 Note: Financial information for 2008 was not available for all companies at press time.

2008 Sales: $1,780,923	2008 Profits: $10,718	**U.S. Stock Ticker: FRED**
2007 Sales: $1,767,239	2007 Profits: $26,746	**Int'l Ticker:** Int'l Exchange:
2006 Sales: $1,589,342	2006 Profits: $26,094	Employees: 9,979
2005 Sales: $1,441,781	2005 Profits: $27,952	Fiscal Year Ends: 1/31
2004 Sales: $1,302,700	2004 Profits: $33,700	Parent Company:

SALARIES/BENEFITS:

Pension Plan:	ESOP Stock Plan:	Profit Sharing:	Top Exec. Salary: $595,000	Bonus: $
Savings Plan:	Stock Purch. Plan:		Second Exec. Salary: $250,000	Bonus: $

OTHER THOUGHTS:

Apparent Women Officers or Directors:	**LOCATIONS:** ("Y" = Yes)					
Hot Spot for Advancement for Women/Minorities:	West:	Southwest:	Midwest:	Southeast:	Northeast:	International:
		Y	Y	Y	Y	

FRONTIER COMMUNICATIONS CORPORATION   www.frontier.com

Industry Group Code: 517110 **Ranks within this company's industry group:** Sales: 12   Profits: 6

Management:		Sales/Marketing:		Liberal Arts:		Information Systems:		Professionals:		Tech./Scientific:	
Management Trainees:	Y	Marketing Pros.:	Y	Gen. Writing/Editing:	Y	Info. Management:	Y	Finance/Acct.:	Y	Engineers, Electrical:	Y
Experienced Mngmt.:	Y	Retail Sales:		Technical Writing:	Y	Software Dev.:	Y	Law:	Y	Engineers, Other:	Y
International Business:		Commercial/Industrial:	Y	Graphic Arts/Photog.:	Y	Hardware Dev.:		HR/Other:	Y	Health/Lab:	
MBA Grads:	Y	Sales Trainees:		Music:		Consulting/Other:		Training:	Y	Scientists/Research:	
		Advertising Pros.:	Y	Broadcasting:				Health Care:		Petroleum/Chemicals:	
				Other:				Consulting:		Math/Other:	

TYPES OF BUSINESS:

Telecommunications
Internet Services
Long-Distance Phone Services
Directory Service
Access Services

BRANDS/DIVISIONS/AFFILIATES:

Frontier Pages
GVN Services
Commonwealth Telephone Enterprises, Inc.
Global Valley Networks

CONTACTS: Note: Officers with more than one job title may be intentionally listed here more than once.

Maggie Wilderotter, CEO
Daniel McCarthy, COO/Exec. VP
Maggie Wilderotter, Pres.
Donald R. Shassian, CFO/Exec. VP
Peter B. Hayes, Exec. VP-Mktg. & Sales
Cecilia K. McKenney, Exec. VP-Human Resources
Hilary E. Glassman, General Counsel/Sr. VP/Sec.
Peter B. Hayes, Exec. VP-Bus. Dev.
Melinda White, Gen. Mgr./Sr. VP-Mktg. & New Bus. Oper.
Cecilia K. McKenney, Exec. VP-Call Center Sales & Svcs.
Ken Arndt, Sr. VP/Gen. Mgr.-Southeast Region
Denise Baumbach, Sr. VP/Gen. Mgr.-West Region
Maggie Wilderotter, Chmn.

Phone: 203-614-5600	Fax: 203-614-4602
Toll-Free: 800-921-8102	
Address: 3 High Ridge Pk., Stamford, CT 06905 US	

GROWTH PLANS/SPECIAL FEATURES:

Frontier Communications Corporation, formerly Citizens Communications, provides communication services to homes and business, primarily in rural areas. The firm operates as an incumbent local exchange carrier in 24 states. The company provides access, local, long distance, data/Internet, directory, television and wireless services. The firm has approximately 2.83 million access lines and Internet subscribers. Access services allow other carriers the use of Frontier facilities for long distance voice and data transmissions. Local services include basic telephone wireline services, as well as call forwarding, conference calling, caller identification, voicemail and call waiting. Long distance services use external interexchange carrier facilities. Data and Internet services include Internet access via high-speed or dial up connections, frame relay, Metro Ethernet and asynchronous transfer mode (ATM) switching services, as well as data transmission services to other carriers and commercial customers with dedicated high-capacity circuits. Directory services include white and yellow page directories of residential and business listings; and the Frontier Pages, an online directory service. Television services are offered in partnership with Echostar's DISH Network, including access to local channels, digital television channels and high-definition programming. Wireless services include wireless data WIFI networks in 18 municipalities, four colleges/universities and over 120 businesses. In recent years, Frontier Communications acquired Commonwealth Telephone Enterprises, Inc., Global Valley Networks, Inc., and GVN Services for approximately $1.16 billion. In July 2008, the firm changed its name to Frontier Communications Corporation; Frontier was previously the firm's service brand. In May 2009, Frontier announced that it would acquire roughly 4.8 million access lines, primarily in rural locations and small towns, from Verizon Communications, in a transaction valued at approximately $8.6 billion. Frontier will also inherit some 11,000 Verizon employees in the acquisition.

Frontier employee benefits include medical, dental and vision coverage; flexible spending accounts; life, disability and accident insurance; and tuition reimbursement.

FINANCIALS: Sales and profits are in thousands of dollars—add 000 to get the full amount. 2008 Note: Financial information for 2008 was not available for all companies at press time.

2008 Sales: $2,237,018	2008 Profits: $182,660	**U.S. Stock Ticker:** FTR
2007 Sales: $2,288,015	2007 Profits: $214,654	**Int'l Ticker:** Int'l Exchange:
2006 Sales: $2,025,367	2006 Profits: $344,555	Employees: 5,671
2005 Sales: $2,017,041	2005 Profits: $202,375	Fiscal Year Ends: 12/31
2004 Sales: $2,168,422	2004 Profits: $72,150	Parent Company:

SALARIES/BENEFITS:

Pension Plan:	ESOP Stock Plan:	Profit Sharing:	Top Exec. Salary: $920,833	Bonus: $878,611
Savings Plan:	Stock Purch. Plan:		Second Exec. Salary: $448,000	Bonus: $428,290

OTHER THOUGHTS:

Apparent Women Officers or Directors: 9
Hot Spot for Advancement for Women/Minorities: Y

LOCATIONS: ("Y" = Yes)

West:	Southwest:	Midwest:	Southeast:	Northeast:	International:
Y	Y	Y	Y	Y	

Note: Financial information, benefits and other data can change quickly and may vary from those stated here.

FTI CONSULTING INC

www.fticonsulting.com

Industry Group Code: 54161 Ranks within this company's industry group: Sales: 4 Profits: 1

Management:		Sales/Marketing:		Liberal Arts:		Information Systems:		Professionals:		Tech./Scientific:	
Management Trainees:	Y	Marketing Pros.:	Y	Gen. Writing/Editing:	Y	Info. Management:	Y	Finance/Acct.:	Y	Engineers, Electrical:	
Experienced Mngmt.:	Y	Retail Sales:		Technical Writing:	Y	Software Dev.:	Y	Law:	Y	Engineers, Other:	
International Business:	Y	Commercial/Industrial:	Y	Graphic Arts/Photog.:	Y	Hardware Dev.:		HR/Other:	Y	Health/Lab:	
MBA Grads:	Y	Sales Trainees:		Music:		Consulting/Other:	Y	Training:	Y	Scientists/Research:	
		Advertising Pros.:		Broadcasting:				Health Care:		Petroleum/Chemicals:	
				Other:	Y			Consulting:	Y	Math/Other:	

TYPES OF BUSINESS:

Bankruptcy & Restructuring Consulting
Interim Management Staffing
Corporate Recovery Services
Litigation Assistance
Forensic Accounting
Data Mining
Technology Consulting
Software Development

BRANDS/DIVISIONS/AFFILIATES:

FTI Palladium Partners
Compass Lexecon
Network Industries Strategies
Ringtail
Attenex Corporation
FD Kinesis
CXO LLC
Element Agency (The)

CONTACTS: Note: Officers with more than one job title may be intentionally listed here more than once.

Jack B. Dunn, IV, CEO
Dominic DiNapoli, COO/Exec. VP
Jack B. Dunn, IV, Pres.
Jorge A. Celaya, CFO/Exec. VP
Roger Carlile, Chief Human Resources Officer/Exec. VP
David G. Bannister, Chief Admin. Officer/Exec. VP
Eric Miller, General Counsel/Exec. VP
David C. Bannister, Chief Dev. Officer
Catherine Freeman, Chief Acct. Officer/Controller/Sr. VP
John MacColl, Chief Risk Mgmt. Officer/Exec. VP
Declan Kelly, Chief Integration Officer/Exec. VP
Joanne Catanese, Sec./Associate General Counsel
Dennis J. Shaugnessy, Chmn.

Phone: 410-951-4800	Fax: 410-951-4895
Toll-Free: 800-334-5701	
Address: 500 E. Pratt St., Ste. 1400, Baltimore, MD 21202 US	

GROWTH PLANS/SPECIAL FEATURES:

FTI Consulting, Inc. is a global consulting firm that provides turnaround, restructuring, bankruptcy and other related consulting services. The firm's professionals address critical legal, financial and reputation issues in areas such as fraud, damages, anti-trust, contract disputes, patent infringement, purchase price disputes, fraudulent conveyance and trademark and copyright infringements. The firm works in 12 industries ranging from retail to insurance and from media and entertainment to energy and utilities, operating in 37 U.S. states and 26 foreign countries, including the U.K., Russia, the U.A.E, Japan and China. The firm operates in five segments. Forensic and Litigation Consulting includes reconstructing events from incomplete and corrupt data; business intelligence and investigations; and trial services. Corporate Finance/Restructuring consists of turnaround and restructuring services; interim key executive staffing, through FTI Palladium Partners; and mergers and acquisitions services. Economic Consulting, offered through Compass Lexecon and Network Industries Strategies, includes analyses of complex economic issues in legal and regulatory proceedings. The Technology segment includes FTI's proprietary Ringtail on-premise, on-demand data and document management services; and general technology consultations, including litigation readiness, computer forensics and compiling so-called Second Requests, an in-depth report for the government regarding a company's operations before the consummations of mergers and acquisitions. Strategic Consulting, offered through subsidiary Financial Dynamics, includes financial and brand communications, public affairs and business consulting. In 2008, the company acquired Attenex Corporation, a provider of eDiscovery software, and Kinesis Marketing, an online communications firm, which is subsequently known as FD Kinesis. In 2009, the firm acquired CXO, L.L.C., an interim and turnaround management services company, and The Element Agency, a Canadian communications consultancy.

Employees are offered medical, dental and vision insurance; health and dependent care flexible spending accounts; a 401(k) plan; life and AD&D insurance; short-and long-term disability coverage; and an employee assistance program.

FINANCIALS: Sales and profits are in thousands of dollars—add 000 to get the full amount. 2008 Note: Financial information for 2008 was not available for all companies at press time.

2008 Sales: $1,293,145	2008 Profits: $125,435	**U.S. Stock Ticker: FCN**
2007 Sales: $1,001,270	2007 Profits: $92,121	**Int'l Ticker:** Int'l Exchange:
2006 Sales: $707,933	2006 Profits: $42,024	Employees: 3,378
2005 Sales: $539,545	2005 Profits: $56,368	Fiscal Year Ends: 12/31
2004 Sales: $427,005	2004 Profits: $42,878	Parent Company:

SALARIES/BENEFITS:

Pension Plan:	ESOP Stock Plan:	Profit Sharing:	Top Exec. Salary: $1,434,616	Bonus: $1,100,000
Savings Plan: Y	Stock Purch. Plan:		Second Exec. Salary: $2,000,000	Bonus: $600,000

OTHER THOUGHTS:

Apparent Women Officers or Directors: 3
Hot Spot for Advancement for Women/Minorities: Y

LOCATIONS: ("Y" = Yes)

West:	Southwest:	Midwest:	Southeast:	Northeast:	International:
Y	Y	Y	Y	Y	Y

Note: Financial information, benefits and other data can change quickly and may vary from those stated here.

GAMESTOP CORP

www.gamestop.com

Industry Group Code: 451120 Ranks within this company's industry group: Sales: 1 Profits: 1

Management:		Sales/Marketing:		Liberal Arts:		Information Systems:		Professionals:		Tech./Scientific:	
Management Trainees:	Y	Marketing Pros.:	Y	Gen. Writing/Editing:	Y	Info. Management:	Y	Finance/Acct.:	Y	Engineers, Electrical:	
Experienced Mngmt.:	Y	Retail Sales:	Y	Technical Writing:		Software Dev.:	Y	Law:	Y	Engineers, Other:	
International Business:	Y	Commercial/Industrial:		Graphic Arts/Photog.:	Y	Hardware Dev.:		HR/Other:	Y	Health/Lab:	
MBA Grads:	Y	Sales Trainees:	Y	Music:		Consulting/Other:		Training:	Y	Scientists/Research:	
		Advertising Pros.:	Y	Broadcasting:				Health Care:		Petroleum/Chemicals:	
				Other:	Y			Consulting:		Math/Other:	

TYPES OF BUSINESS:

Video Games-Retail
PC Software Sales
Game Accessories
Online Sales
Magazine Publication

BRANDS/DIVISIONS/AFFILIATES:

EB Games
GameStop.com
EBGames.com
Game Informer Magazine
SFMI Micromania SAS
Casual Digital Store

CONTACTS: *Note: Officers with more than one job title may be intentionally listed here more than once.*

Daniel A. DeMatteo, CEO
J. Paul Raines, COO
Steven R. Morgan, Pres.
David W. Carlson, CFO/Exec. VP
Tony D. Bartel, Exec. VP-Mktg.
Tony D. Bartel, Exec. VP-Merch.
Michael N. Rosen, Sec.
Matt Hodges, Dir.-Investor Rel.
Robert A. Lloyd, Chief Acct. Officer/Sr. VP
Daniel A. DeMatteo, Vice Chmn.
Chris Petrovic, Gen. Mgr.-Digital Media
R. Richard Fontaine, Chmn.

Phone: 817-424-2000	Fax: 817-424-2002
Toll-Free: 800-883-8895	
Address: 625 Westport Pkwy., Grapevine, TX 76051 US	

GROWTH PLANS/SPECIAL FEATURES:

GameStop Corp. is a retailer of video games and PC games. The company operates 6,207 retail stores throughout U.S., Canada, Australia and Europe under the names Gamestop and EB Games. Approximately 4,331 stores are included in the U.S. segment with 325 stores in Canada, 350 in Australia and 1,201 in the European segment. The firm's retail outlets offer new and used video game products. By purchasing used products, the company provides its customers with an opportunity to trade in used video games and peripherals for store credits and apply those credits towards other merchandise, which increases sales. Stores also typically feature several video game sampling areas, which provide its customers the opportunity to play games before purchase, as well as equipment to play video game clips. Additionally, GameStop operates two e-commerce web sites, GameStop.com and EBGames.com, as well as publishing Game Informer, one of the largest multi-platform video game magazines in the U.S., based on its 2.7 million subscribers. Paid Game Informer subscribers receive a GameStop loyalty card, which offers discounts on selected merchandise in the company's stores. In November 2008, the company acquired SFMI Micromania SAS, a France-based retailer of video games which operates 332 locations in the country. In July 2009, the firm launched the Casual Digital Store, and online game download service powered by RealNetworks, Inc. that allows users to download PC games directly. Gamestop reported excellent results for its quarter ending January 31, 2009, despite the economic slowdown. The firm also announced plans to build 400 new stores during 2009.

Gamestop offers its employees medical, dental, vision and prescription drug coverage; paid holidays and vacation; flexible spending account; short- and long-term disability; a 401(k) plan; tuition reimbursement; and employee discounts of 15% in-store and up to 30% in Barnes & Noble and B. Dalton Bookstores.

FINANCIALS: Sales and profits are in thousands of dollars—add 000 to get the full amount. 2008 Note: Financial information for 2008 was not available for all companies at press time.

2008 Sales: $7,093,962	2008 Profits: $288,291	**U.S. Stock Ticker:** GME	
2007 Sales: $5,318,900	2007 Profits: $158,250	**Int'l Ticker:** Int'l Exchange:	
2006 Sales: $3,091,783	2006 Profits: $100,784	**Employees:** 56,000	
2005 Sales: $1,842,806	2005 Profits: $60,926	**Fiscal Year Ends:** 1/31	
2004 Sales: $1,578,838	2004 Profits: $63,467	**Parent Company:**	

SALARIES/BENEFITS:

Pension Plan:	ESOP Stock Plan:	Profit Sharing:	Top Exec. Salary: $1,184,615	Bonus: $2,400,000
Savings Plan: Y	Stock Purch. Plan:		Second Exec. Salary: $1,035,385	Bonus: $2,400,000

OTHER THOUGHTS:

Apparent Women Officers or Directors: 1
Hot Spot for Advancement for Women/Minorities:

LOCATIONS: ("Y" = Yes)

West:	Southwest:	Midwest:	Southeast:	Northeast:	International:
Y	Y	Y	Y	Y	Y

GENENTECH INC

www.gene.com

Industry Group Code: 325412 Ranks within this company's industry group: Sales: 9 Profits: 7

Management:		Sales/Marketing:		Liberal Arts:		Information Systems:		Professionals:		Tech./Scientific:	
Management Trainees:	Y	Marketing Pros.:	Y	Gen. Writing/Editing:	Y	Info. Management:	Y	Finance/Acct.:	Y	Engineers, Electrical:	Y
Experienced Mngmt.:	Y	Retail Sales:		Technical Writing:	Y	Software Dev.:	Y	Law:	Y	Engineers, Other:	Y
International Business:	Y	Commercial/Industrial:	Y	Graphic Arts/Photog.:	Y	Hardware Dev.:		HR/Other:	Y	Health/Lab:	Y
MBA Grads:	Y	Sales Trainees:	Y	Music:		Consulting/Other:		Training:	Y	Scientists/Research:	Y
		Advertising Pros.:	Y	Broadcasting:				Health Care:	Y	Petroleum/Chemicals:	Y
				Other:				Consulting:		Math/Other:	Y

TYPES OF BUSINESS:

Drug Development & Manufacturing
Genetically Engineered Drugs

BRANDS/DIVISIONS/AFFILIATES:

Avastin
TNKase
Herceptin
Rituxan
Activase
Pulmozyme
Nutropin

CONTACTS: Note: Officers with more than one job title may be intentionally listed here more than once.

Arthur D. Levinson, CEO
David A. Ebersman, CFO/Exec. VP
Richard H. Scheller, Exec. VP-Research
Susan Desmond-Hellmann, Pres., Prod. Dev.
Stephen G. Juelsgaard, Exec. VP/Corp. Sec.
Ian T. Clark, Exec. VP-Comm. Oper.
Robert E. Andreatta, Chief Acct. Officer/Controller
Stephen G. Juelsgaard, Chief Compliance Officer
Patrick Y. Yang, Exec. VP-Prod. Oper.
Arthur D. Levinson, Chmn.

Phone: 650-225-1000	Fax: 650-225-6000
Toll-Free:	
Address: 1 DNA Way, South San Francisco, CA 94080 US	

GROWTH PLANS/SPECIAL FEATURES:

Genentech, Inc. makes medicines by splicing genes into fast-growing bacteria that then produce therapeutic proteins and combat diseases on a molecular level. Genentech uses cutting-edge technologies such as computer visualization of molecules, micro arrays and sensitive assaying techniques to develop, manufacture and market pharmaceuticals for unmet medical needs. Genentech's research is directed toward the oncology, immunology and vascular biology fields. The company's products consist of a variety of cardio-centric medications, as well as cancer, growth hormone deficiency (GHD) and cystic fibrosis treatments. Biotechnology products offered by Genentech include Herceptin, used to treat metastatic breast cancers; Avastin, used to inhibit angiogenesis of solid-tumor cancers; Nutropin, a growth hormone for the treatment of GHD in children and adults; TNKase, for the treatment of acute myocardial infarction; and Pulmozyme, for the treatment of cystic fibrosis. The company also produces the Rituxan antibody, used for the treatment of patients with non-Hodgkin's lymphoma. Through its long-standing Genentech Access to Care Foundation, Genentech assists those without sufficient health insurance to receive its medicines. In 2008, sales to Genentech's three major distributors, AmerisourceBergen, McKesson and Cardinal Health, represented 86% of its total U.S. net product sales. There are three manufacturing sites in California, with an additional facility planned for 2010 licensure in Hillsboro, Oregon. In addition, it expects FDA licensure of a bulk drug substance manufacturing site in Singapore in 2010. The firm recently completed the acquisition of Tanox, a firm that focuses on monoclonal antibody technology and development partner for its Xolair asthma product. In March 2009, Roche Group completed its acquisition of the company.

For the last ten years, the company has been named to Fortune Magazine's 100 Best Companies to Work For. Every Friday evening, Genentech hosts socials called Ho-Hos, providing free food, beverages and a chance to socialize with co-workers.

FINANCIALS: Sales and profits are in thousands of dollars—add 000 to get the full amount. 2008 Note: Financial information for 2008 was not available for all companies at press time.

2008 Sales: $13,418,000	2008 Profits: $3,427,000	U.S. Stock Ticker: Subsidiary
2007 Sales: $11,724,000	2007 Profits: $2,769,000	Int'l Ticker: Int'l Exchange:
2006 Sales: $9,284,000	2006 Profits: $2,113,000	Employees: 11,186
2005 Sales: $6,633,372	2005 Profits: $1,278,991	Fiscal Year Ends: 12/31
2004 Sales: $4,621,157	2004 Profits: $784,816	Parent Company: ROCHE GROUP

SALARIES/BENEFITS:

Pension Plan:	ESOP Stock Plan:	Profit Sharing:	Top Exec. Salary: $	Bonus: $2,725,000
Savings Plan: Y	Stock Purch. Plan: Y		Second Exec. Salary: $	Bonus: $

OTHER THOUGHTS:

Apparent Women Officers or Directors: 2
Hot Spot for Advancement for Women/Minorities: Y

LOCATIONS: ("Y" = Yes)

West:	Southwest:	Midwest:	Southeast:	Northeast:	International:
Y					Y

Note: Financial information, benefits and other data can change quickly and may vary from those stated here.

GENERAL CABLE CORP

www.generalcable.com

Industry Group Code: 335921 Ranks within this company's industry group: Sales: 1 Profits: 1

Management:		Sales/Marketing:		Liberal Arts:		Information Systems:		Professionals:		Tech./Scientific:	
Management Trainees:	Y	Marketing Pros.:	Y	Gen. Writing/Editing:		Info. Management:	Y	Finance/Acct.:	Y	Engineers, Electrical:	Y
Experienced Mngmt.:	Y	Retail Sales:		Technical Writing:	Y	Software Dev.:		Law:	Y	Engineers, Other:	Y
International Business:	Y	Commercial/Industrial:	Y	Graphic Arts/Photog.:	Y	Hardware Dev.:		HR/Other:	Y	Health/Lab:	
MBA Grads:	Y	Sales Trainees:		Music:		Consulting/Other:		Training:	Y	Scientists/Research:	
		Advertising Pros.:		Broadcasting:				Health Care:		Petroleum/Chemicals:	
				Other:				Consulting:		Math/Other:	

TYPES OF BUSINESS:

Copper, Aluminum & Fiber Optic Cable

BRANDS/DIVISIONS/AFFILIATES:

Gepco International, Inc.
Isotec, Inc.
Silec
BICC
PowrServ
Empowr
Carol
GenSPEED

CONTACTS: *Note: Officers with more than one job title may be intentionally listed here more than once.*

Gregory B. Kenny, CEO
Gregory B. Kenny, Pres.
Brian J. Robinson, CFO/Exec. VP/Treas.
Roderick Macdonald, Exec. VP-Global Sales
Stephen Roush, VP-North American Human Resources
Robert J. Siverd, General Counsel/Exec. VP/Sec.
Roderick Macdonald, Exec. VP-Bus. Dev.
Michael P. Dickerson, VP-Investor Rel.
Michael P. Dickerson, VP-Finance
Gregory J. Lampert, CEO/Pres./Exec. VP-North America
Mathias Sandoval, CEO/Exec. VP-Latin America & Mideast/Asia-Pacific
Michael P. Dickerson, VP-Corp. Dev.
Lance G. Bates, VP-U.S. Sales
John E. Welsh, III, Chmn.
Domingo Goenaga, Exec. VP/CEO/Pres., Europe and North Africa

Phone: 859-572-8000	**Fax:** 859-572-8458
Toll-Free:	
Address: 4 Tesseneer Dr., Highland Heights, KY 41076-9753 US	

GROWTH PLANS/SPECIAL FEATURES:

General Cable Corporation is a leading developer and manufacturer or copper, aluminum and fiber optic wire, as well as cable products. The company operates 46 manufacturing locations in 23 countries. The company is divided into three segments organized by location: North America, Europe and North Africa and Rest of World (ROW), which consists of operations in Latin America, Sub-Saharan Africa, Middle East and Asia Pacific. The North America segment, accounting for 35% of 2008 revenues, provides products to the U.S. and Canada, primarily to domestic customers for use in the electric utility, electrical infrastructure and communications industries. The Europe and North Africa segment, accounting for 35% of revenue, designs, manufactures and distributes copper, aluminum and fiber optic cables originating in Spain, Portugal, France, Germany and Algeria and services markets throughout Europe and North Africa. The ROW segment, accounting for 30% of sales, consists of sales and manufacturing facilities in Latin America, Africa, Middle East and Asia Pacific. The firm's products are organized into five product categories. Electrical Utility products include low- and medium- voltage distribution cable; high- and extra-high voltage power transmission cable products and installation; and bare overhead aluminum conductor. Electrical Infrastructure products consist of portable cord products, transportation products and industrial harnesses. Construction products include construction cables, building wire and flexible cords. Communication products include wire and cable products that transmit low-voltage signals for voice and data applications. Rod Mill products, produced and sold only by the ROW segment, include continuous cast copper and aluminum rod, which is sold to other wire and cable manufacturers. Company brands include Silec, BICC, PowrServ, Empowr, Carol, GenSPEED, NextGen, Brand Rex and Anaconda. In August 2009, the firm acquired Gepco International, Inc. and Isotec, Inc., which manufacture cabling products for the broadcasting and entertainment industry.

FINANCIALS: Sales and profits are in thousands of dollars—add 000 to get the full amount. 2008 Note: Financial information for 2008 was not available for all companies at press time.

2008 Sales: $6,230,100	2008 Profits: $217,200	**U.S. Stock Ticker:** BGC
2007 Sales: $4,614,800	2007 Profits: $208,600	**Int'l Ticker:** Int'l Exchange:
2006 Sales: $3,665,100	2006 Profits: $135,300	Employees: 13,000
2005 Sales: $	2005 Profits: $	Fiscal Year Ends: 12/31
2004 Sales: $	2004 Profits: $	Parent Company:

SALARIES/BENEFITS:

Pension Plan: Y	ESOP Stock Plan:	Profit Sharing:	Top Exec. Salary: $823,270	Bonus: $843,975
Savings Plan: Y	Stock Purch. Plan:		Second Exec. Salary: $376,913	Bonus: $228,000

OTHER THOUGHTS:

Apparent Women Officers or Directors:
Hot Spot for Advancement for Women/Minorities:

LOCATIONS: ("Y" = Yes)

West:	Southwest:	Midwest:	Southeast:	Northeast:	International:
Y	Y	Y	Y	Y	Y

GENERAL DYNAMICS CORP

www.generaldynamics.com

Industry Group Code: 33641 Ranks within this company's industry group: Sales: 6 Profits: 5

Management:		Sales/Marketing:		Liberal Arts:		Information Systems:		Professionals:		Tech./Scientific:	
Management Trainees:	Y	Marketing Pros.:	Y	Gen. Writing/Editing:	Y	Info. Management:	Y	Finance/Acct.:	Y	Engineers, Electrical:	Y
Experienced Mngmt.:	Y	Retail Sales:		Technical Writing:	Y	Software Dev.:	Y	Law:	Y	Engineers, Other:	Y
International Business:	Y	Commercial/Industrial:	Y	Graphic Arts/Photog.:	Y	Hardware Dev.:	Y	HR/Other:	Y	Health/Lab:	
MBA Grads:	Y	Sales Trainees:		Music:		Consulting/Other:	Y	Training:	Y	Scientists/Research:	Y
		Advertising Pros.:	Y	Broadcasting:				Health Care:		Petroleum/Chemicals:	
				Other:				Consulting:		Math/Other:	Y

TYPES OF BUSINESS:

Aerospace Products & Services
Combat Vehicles & Systems
Telecommunications Systems
Naval Vessels & Submarines
Ship Management Services
Information Systems & Technology
Defense Systems & Services
Business Jets

BRANDS/DIVISIONS/AFFILIATES:

Gulfstream Aerospace
General Dynamics Advanced Information Systems
M1A1 Abrams Tank
Abrams Integrated Management
SNC Technologies, Inc.
ViPS Inc
Jet Aviation
AxleTech International

CONTACTS: Note: Officers with more than one job title may be intentionally listed here more than once.

Nicholas D. Chabraja, CEO
L. Hugh Redd, CFO/Sr. VP
Walter M. Oliver, Sr. VP-Human Resources
Tommy R. Augustsson, VP-IT
Gerard J. DeMuro, Exec. VP-Info. Systems & Tech.
Walter M. Oliver, Sr. VP-Admin.
David A. Savner, General Counsel/Sec./Sr. VP
Phebe N. Novakovic, Sr. VP-Planning & Dev.
Kendell Pease, VP-Gov't Rel. & Comm.
John W. Schwartz, Controller/VP
Jeffrey Kudlac, VP-Real Estate
John P. Casey, VP/Pres., Electric Boat
Lewis F. von Thaer, VP/Pres., Advanced Info. Systems
Charles M. Hall, Exec. VP-Combat Systems
Nicholas D. Chabraja, Chmn.
William O. Schmieder, VP-Int'l

Phone: 703-876-3000	Fax: 703-876-3125
Toll-Free:	
Address: 2941 Fairview Park Dr., Ste. 100, Falls Church, VA 22042-4513 US	

GROWTH PLANS/SPECIAL FEATURES:

General Dynamics Corp. (GDC) is one of the world's largest aerospace and defense contractors. Its customers include the U.S. military, other government organizations, the armed forces of allied nations and a diverse base of corporate and industrial buyers. The firm's operations are divided into four segments: Information systems and technology (IST), marine systems, combat systems and aerospace. The IST group provides defense and commercial customers with infrastructure and systems integration skills required to process, communicate and manage information effectively. The group has market-leading positions in the design, deployment and maintenance of wireline and wireless voice and data networks, telecommunications system security, encryption and fiber optics. The marine systems division provides the U.S. Navy with combat vessels, including nuclear submarines, surface combatants and auxiliary ships. The segment also provides ship management services for the U.S. government and builds commercial ships. The combat systems group provides systems integration, design, development, production and support for armored vehicles, armaments, munitions and components, with product lines including unmanned systems, medium-caliber guns, space propulsion systems, reactive armor and suspensions, engines and transmissions. It is the leading builder of armored vehicles and makes products such as the M1A1 Abrams Tank. The aerospace group designs, develops, manufactures and provides services for technologically advanced business jet aircraft under the Gulfstream name. Recent acquisitions include ViPS, Inc, a healthcare technology solutions provider; Jet Aviation; a Switzerland-based aviation services company; and AxleTech International, a private equity firm based in Washington, D.C.

FINANCIALS: Sales and profits are in thousands of dollars—add 000 to get the full amount. 2008 Note: Financial information for 2008 was not available for all companies at press time.

2008 Sales: $29,300,000	2008 Profits: $2,459,000	U.S. Stock Ticker: GD
2007 Sales: $27,240,000	2007 Profits: $2,072,000	Int'l Ticker: Int'l Exchange:
2006 Sales: $24,063,000	2006 Profits: $1,856,000	Employees: 92,300
2005 Sales: $20,975,000	2005 Profits: $1,461,000	Fiscal Year Ends: 12/31
2004 Sales: $18,868,000	2004 Profits: $1,227,000	Parent Company:

SALARIES/BENEFITS:

Pension Plan:	ESOP Stock Plan:	Profit Sharing:	Top Exec. Salary: $1,375,000	Bonus: $4,500,000
Savings Plan:	Stock Purch. Plan:		Second Exec. Salary: $618,750	Bonus: $1,000,000

OTHER THOUGHTS:

Apparent Women Officers or Directors: 3
Hot Spot for Advancement for Women/Minorities: Y

LOCATIONS: ("Y" = Yes)

West:	Southwest:	Midwest:	Southeast:	Northeast:	International:
Y	Y	Y	Y	Y	Y

Note: Financial information, benefits and other data can change quickly and may vary from those stated here.

GENERAL ELECTRIC CO (GE)

www.ge.com

Industry Group Code: 52222   Ranks within this company's industry group: Sales: 1   Profits: 1

Management:		Sales/Marketing:		Liberal Arts:		Information Systems:		Professionals:		Tech./Scientific:	
Management Trainees:	Y	Marketing Pros.:	Y	Gen. Writing/Editing:	Y	Info. Management:	Y	Finance/Acct.:	Y	Engineers, Electrical:	Y
Experienced Mngmt.:	Y	Retail Sales:		Technical Writing:	Y	Software Dev.:	Y	Law:	Y	Engineers, Other:	
International Business:	Y	Commercial/Industrial:	Y	Graphic Arts/Photog.:	Y	Hardware Dev.:		HR/Other:	Y	Health/Lab:	
MBA Grads:	Y	Sales Trainees:		Music:		Consulting/Other:		Training:	Y	Scientists/Research:	Y
		Advertising Pros.:	Y	Broadcasting:				Health Care:		Petroleum/Chemicals:	
				Other:	Y			Consulting:		Math/Other:	Y

TYPES OF BUSINESS:

Business Leasing & Finance
Energy Systems & Consulting
Financial Services
Industrial & Electrical Equipment & Consumer Products
Television & Film Production & Distribution
Real Estate Investments & Finance
Medical Equipment
Transportation, Aircraft Engines, Rail Systems & Truck Fleet Management

BRANDS/DIVISIONS/AFFILIATES:

GE Energy Infrastructure
GE Technology Infrastructure
GE Capital
NBC Universal
GE Money
GE Aviation
GE Healthcare
GE Global Research

CONTACTS:
Note: Officers with more than one job title may be intentionally listed here more than once.

Jeffrey R. Immelt, CEO
Keith S. Sherin, CFO
Beth Comstock, Chief Mktg. Officer/Sr. VP
John Lynch, Sr. VP-Corp. Human Resources
Mark M. Little, Sr. VP/Dir.-Global Research
Gary M. Reiner, CIO/Sr. VP
Brackett B. Denniston, III, General Counsel/Sr. VP
Wayne Hewett, VP-Oper.
Pamela Daley, Sr. VP-Corp. Bus. Dev.
Trevor Schauenberg, Corp. Investor Comm.
Kathryn A. Cassidy, Treas./VP
John Krenicki, Jr., CEO/Pres., GE Energy Infrastructure
Michael A Neal, CEO/Pres., GE Capital
John G. Rice, CEO/Pres., GE Technology Infrastructure
Mark M. Little, Sr. VP/Dir.-GE Global Research
Jeffrey R. Immelt, Chmn.
Ferdinando Beccalli-Falco, CEO/Pres., Int'l
Wayne Hewett, VP-Supply Chain

Phone: 203-373-2211	Fax: 203-373-3131
Toll-Free:	
Address: 3135 Easton Turnpike, Fairfield, CT 06828-0001 US	

GROWTH PLANS/SPECIAL FEATURES:

General Electric Co. (GE) is one of the largest and most diversified technology, media, and financial services corporations in the world. The company's products, which range from aircraft engines, power generation, water processing, and security technology to medical imaging, business and consumer financing, media content and industrial products, are designed and manufactured by GE's five operating division: Energy Infrastructure, Technology Infrastructure, NBC Universal, Capital and Consumer & Industrial. The Energy Infrastructure division, which accounted for 21.1% of 2008 revenues, serves power generation, industrial, government and other customers worldwide with products and services related to energy production, distribution and management. Products produced by this segment include wind and gas turbines; oil and gas equipment; and water treatment technologies. The Technology Infrastructure division, which accounted for 25.4% of 2008 revenues, comprises the firm's aviation, enterprise solutions, healthcare technology and transportation technology operations. NBC Universal, 80%-owned by GE with the remaining 20% owned by Vivendi S.A., consolidates GE's media operations, and is engaged in the production and distribution of film and television programming; the operation of cable/satellite television networks around the world; the broadcast of network television; and investment and programming activities in digital media and the Internet. NBC Universal accounted for 9.3% of GE's 2008 revenues. The Capital division manages all of the firm's lending and financial services units, as well as its real estate activities, and accounted for 36.7% of GE's 2008 revenues. GE's Consumer & Industrial division, 6.4% of 2008 revenues, manufactures, sells and services major home appliances including refrigerators, freezers, electric and gas ranges, cooktops, dishwashers, clothes washers and dryers, microwave ovens, room air conditioners, and residential water systems for filtration, softening and heating. The company underwent a major restructuring in 2008, discontinuing several operations and consolidating its former six divisions into the current five.

FINANCIALS:
Sales and profits are in thousands of dollars—add 000 to get the full amount. 2008 Note: Financial information for 2008 was not available for all companies at press time.

2008 Sales: $182,515,000	2008 Profits: $17,410,000	**U.S. Stock Ticker: GE**
2007 Sales: $172,488,000	2007 Profits: $22,208,000	**Int'l Ticker:** Int'l Exchange:
2006 Sales: $151,568,000	2006 Profits: $20,742,000	Employees: 323,000
2005 Sales: $136,580,000	2005 Profits: $16,720,000	Fiscal Year Ends: 12/31
2004 Sales: $134,481,000	2004 Profits: $16,285,000	Parent Company:

SALARIES/BENEFITS:

Pension Plan:	ESOP Stock Plan:	Profit Sharing:	Top Exec. Salary: $3,300,000	Bonus: $
Savings Plan: Y	Stock Purch. Plan:		Second Exec. Salary: $1,650,000	Bonus: $2,900,000

OTHER THOUGHTS:

Apparent Women Officers or Directors: 10
Hot Spot for Advancement for Women/Minorities: Y

LOCATIONS: ("Y" = Yes)

West:	Southwest:	Midwest:	Southeast:	Northeast:	International:
Y	Y	Y	Y	Y	Y

GENERAL MILLS INC

www.generalmills.com

Industry Group Code: 311230 Ranks within this company's industry group: Sales: 1 Profits: 2

Management:		Sales/Marketing:		Liberal Arts:		Information Systems:		Professionals:		Tech./Scientific:	
Management Trainees:	Y	Marketing Pros.:	Y	Gen. Writing/Editing:	Y	Info. Management:	Y	Finance/Acct.:	Y	Engineers, Electrical:	
Experienced Mngmt.:	Y	Retail Sales:		Technical Writing:	Y	Software Dev.:	Y	Law:	Y	Engineers, Other:	Y
International Business:	Y	Commercial/Industrial:	Y	Graphic Arts/Photog.:	Y	Hardware Dev.:		HR/Other:	Y	Health/Lab:	
MBA Grads:	Y	Sales Trainees:	Y	Music:		Consulting/Other:		Training:	Y	Scientists/Research:	
		Advertising Pros.:	Y	Broadcasting:				Health Care:		Petroleum/Chemicals:	
				Other:				Consulting:		Math/Other:	

TYPES OF BUSINESS:

Cereal Manufacturing
Snack Foods
Frozen Foods
Baking Products
Yogurt
Organic Foods
Convenience Meal Products
Canned and Frozen Vegetables

BRANDS/DIVISIONS/AFFILIATES:

Big G Cereals
Cheerios
Betty Crocker
Progresso
Pillsbury
Yoplait
Bisquick
Cascadian Farm

CONTACTS: Note: Officers with more than one job title may be intentionally listed here more than once.

Kendall J. Powell, CEO
Kendall J. Powell, Pres.
Donal L. Mulligan, CFO/Exec. VP
Jeffrey J. Rotsch, Exec. VP-Worldwide Sales & Channel Dev.
Michael L. Davis, Sr. VP-Global Human Resources
Randy G. Darcy, CTO/Exec. VP-Tech.
Michael A. Peel, Exec. VP-Admin. Svcs.
Roderick A. Palmore, General Counsel/Chief Corp. & Risk Officer
Randy G. Darcy, Exec. VP-Worldwide Oper.
Christina L. Shea, Sr. VP-External Rel./Pres., Community Action
Richard O. Lund, VP/Controller
Ian R. Friendly, COO-U.S. Retail/Exec. VP
Peter J. Capell, Sr. VP-Int'l Mktg. & Sales
Gary Chu, Pres., Greater China
Robert F. Waldron, Pres., Yoplait /Sr. VP
Kendall J. Powell, Chmn.
Christopher D. O'Leary, Exec. VP/COO-Int'l
John R. Church, VP-Supply Chain

Phone: 763-764-7600	Fax: 763-764-7384
Toll-Free:	
Address: 1 General Mills Blvd., Minneapolis, MN 55426 US	

GROWTH PLANS/SPECIAL FEATURES:

General Mills, Inc. is a leading global producer of packaged consumer foods. The company markets its products in over 100 countries and manufactures its products in 16 countries, according to three divisions: U.S. retail, generating approximately 66.5% of net sales; bakeries and food service, generating 14.8%; and international, generating 18.7%. The U.S. retail division consists of seven segments: Big G Cereals, which controls Cheerios, Chex and Lucky Charms; meals, with products such as Betty Crocker, Hamburger Helper and Progresso; Pillsbury, including frozen dough products and frozen breakfast products; Yogurt, including Yoplait Light, Go-GURT and Yoplait Kids; snacks, which includes Fruit Roll-Ups and Bugles; baking products, including Bisquick baking mix and Warm Delights microwaveable desserts; and organics, featuring Cascadian Farm and Muir Glen brands. The bakeries and food service segment consists of products marketed to retail and wholesale bakeries; and offered to commercial and noncommercial food service sectors, such as restaurants and school cafeterias, throughout the U.S. and Canada, under the Pillsbury and Gold Medal trademarks. The international segment is made up of retail and food services businesses outside the U.S. and Canada, with major product categories including super-premium ice cream; grain snacks; shelf-stable and frozen vegetables; refrigerated and frozen dough products; and dry dinners. The firm owns 50% of Haagen-Dazs ice cream, as well as 50% interest in Seretram, a joint venture with Co-op de Pau for the production of Green Giant corn in France. In September 2008, the company sold its Pop Secret popcorn business to Diamond Foods, Inc.

Employees are offered medical and dental benefits; flexible spending accounts; life, legal, auto and homeowners insurance; short-and long-term disability coverage; relocation benefits; educational assistance; and domestic partner benefits.

FINANCIALS: Sales and profits are in thousands of dollars—add 000 to get the full amount. 2008 Note: Financial information for 2008 was not available for all companies at press time.

2008 Sales: $13,652,100	2008 Profits: $1,294,700	**U.S. Stock Ticker: GIS**
2007 Sales: $12,442,000	2007 Profits: $1,143,900	**Int'l Ticker:** Int'l Exchange:
2006 Sales: $11,712,000	2006 Profits: $1,090,300	Employees: 30,000
2005 Sales: $11,308,000	2005 Profits: $1,900,000	Fiscal Year Ends: 5/31
2004 Sales: $11,070,000	2004 Profits: $1,055,000	Parent Company:

SALARIES/BENEFITS:

Pension Plan:	ESOP Stock Plan: Y	Profit Sharing:	Top Exec. Salary: $1,257,330	Bonus: $3,539,190
Savings Plan: Y	Stock Purch. Plan:		Second Exec. Salary: $843,333	Bonus: $1,674,900

OTHER THOUGHTS:

Apparent Women Officers or Directors: 13
Hot Spot for Advancement for Women/Minorities: Y

LOCATIONS: ("Y" = Yes)

West:	Southwest:	Midwest:	Southeast:	Northeast:	International:
Y	Y	Y	Y	Y	Y

Note: Financial information, benefits and other data can change quickly and may vary from those stated here.

GENESCO INC

www.genesco.com

Industry Group Code: 316213 **Ranks within this company's industry group:** Sales: 1   Profits: 1

Management:		Sales/Marketing:		Liberal Arts:		Information Systems:		Professionals:		Tech./Scientific:	
Management Trainees:	Y	Marketing Pros.:	Y	Gen. Writing/Editing:	Y	Info. Management:	Y	Finance/Acct.:	Y	Engineers, Electrical:	
Experienced Mngmt.:	Y	Retail Sales:	Y	Technical Writing:		Software Dev.:	Y	Law:	Y	Engineers, Other:	
International Business:	Y	Commercial/Industrial:	Y	Graphic Arts/Photog.:	Y	Hardware Dev.:		HR/Other:	Y	Health/Lab:	
MBA Grads:	Y	Sales Trainees:	Y	Music:		Consulting/Other:		Training:	Y	Scientists/Research:	
		Advertising Pros.:	Y	Broadcasting:				Health Care:		Petroleum/Chemicals:	
				Other:	Y			Consulting:		Math/Other:	

TYPES OF BUSINESS:

Shoes, Retail
Retail Stores
Men's Accessories
Wholesale Operations
Hats, Retail
Catalog & Online Operations
Athletic Team Products

BRANDS/DIVISIONS/AFFILIATES:

Johnston & Murphy
Journeys
Underground Station
Journeys Kidz
Hat World Corporation
Dockers
Lids
Impact Sports

CONTACTS: *Note: Officers with more than one job title may be intentionally listed here more than once.*

Robert J. Dennis, CEO
Robert J. Dennis, Pres.
James S. Gulmi, CFO/Sr. VP-Finance
Roger G. Sisson, General Counsel/Corp. Sec./Sr. VP
Mimi E. Vaughn, Sr. VP-Strategy & Shared Svcs.
Claire S. McCall, Dir.-Investor Rel.
Paul D. Williams, Chief Acct. Officer/VP
Kenneth J. Kocher, Sr. VP/Pres., Hat World
James C. Estepa, Sr. VP/CEO/Pres., Genesco Retail
Jonathan D. Caplan, Sr. VP/CEO-Genesco Branded Group
Jonathan D. Caplan, Pres., Johnston & Murphy
Hal N. Pennington, Chmn.

Phone: 615-367-7000	Fax: 615-367-8579
Toll-Free:	
Address: 1415 Murfreesboro Rd., Nashville, TN 37217-2895 US	

GROWTH PLANS/SPECIAL FEATURES:

Genesco is a leading specialty retailer of footwear, headwear and accessories through 2,236 retail stores in the U.S., Canada and Puerto Rico. The company operates five business segments: Journeys Group, accounting for 49% of the firm's sales; Underground Station Group, 7% of sales; Hat World Group, 26%; Johnston & Murphy Group, 12%; and Licensed Brands, 6%. The Journey's Group segment operates 1,012 stores, including Journeys, Journeys Kidz and Shi by Journeys, and markets products through a catalog and journeys.com. Journeys stores target customers in the 13-22 year age group through youth-oriented decor and music videos. The Underground Station Group segment operates 180 stores, including Underground Station and Jarman. The Hat World Group segment operates 885 stores, including Hat World, Lids, Hat Shack, Hat Zone, Head Quarters, Cap Connection, Lids Kids and Lids Locker Room, and also markets products through the Internet and the Impact Sports athletic team products business. The segment's major stores, located in malls, airports, street level stores and factory outlet stores, target customers in the early-teen to mid-20s age group. The Johnston & Murphy Group segment operates 157 retail and factory stores, as well as johnstonmurphy.com, and sells footwear, luggage and accessories primarily for men, targeting business and professional customers. Retail prices for Johnston & Murphy footwear generally range from $110-250. The Licensed Brands segment is comprised primarily of Dockers footwear, marketed under a license from Levi Strauss & Company. In November 2008, Hat World acquired Impact Sports, a branded athletic and team products dealer for college and high school teams.

Genesco offers its employees educational assistance, flexible spending accounts, adoption assistance, scholarships, healthcare and dental plans, company discounts, an employee credit association, child care alternatives, fitness classes and Weight Watchers at Work.

FINANCIALS: Sales and profits are in thousands of dollars—add 000 to get the full amount. 2008 Note: Financial information for 2008 was not available for all companies at press time.

2008 Sales: $1,502,119	2008 Profits: $6,885	**U.S. Stock Ticker: GCO**	
2007 Sales: $1,460,478	2007 Profits: $67,646	**Int'l Ticker:** Int'l Exchange:	
2006 Sales: $1,283,876	2006 Profits: $62,686	Employees: 14,125	
2005 Sales: $1,112,681	2005 Profits: $48,249	Fiscal Year Ends: 1/31	
2004 Sales: $837,379	2004 Profits: $28,730	Parent Company:	

SALARIES/BENEFITS:

Pension Plan:	ESOP Stock Plan:	Profit Sharing:	Top Exec. Salary: $768,333	Bonus: $227,524
Savings Plan: Y	Stock Purch. Plan: Y		Second Exec. Salary: $575,000	Bonus: $

OTHER THOUGHTS:

Apparent Women Officers or Directors: 2
Hot Spot for Advancement for Women/Minorities: Y

LOCATIONS: ("Y" = Yes)

West:	Southwest:	Midwest:	Southeast:	Northeast:	International:
Y	Y	Y	Y	Y	

GENWORTH FINANCIAL INC

www.genworth.com

Industry Group Code: 524113 Ranks within this company's industry group: Sales: 3 Profits: 4

Management:		Sales/Marketing:		Liberal Arts:		Information Systems:		Professionals:		Tech./Scientific:	
Management Trainees:	Y	Marketing Pros.:	Y	Gen. Writing/Editing:	Y	Info. Management:	Y	Finance/Acct.:	Y	Engineers, Electrical:	
Experienced Mngmt.:	Y	Retail Sales:		Technical Writing:	Y	Software Dev.:	Y	Law:	Y	Engineers, Other:	
International Business:	Y	Commercial/Industrial:	Y	Graphic Arts/Photog.:	Y	Hardware Dev.:		HR/Other:	Y	Health/Lab:	
MBA Grads:	Y	Sales Trainees:	Y	Music:		Consulting/Other:		Training:	Y	Scientists/Research:	
		Advertising Pros.:	Y	Broadcasting:				Health Care:	Y	Petroleum/Chemicals:	
				Other:	Y			Consulting:		Math/Other:	Y

TYPES OF BUSINESS:

Life Insurance
Annuities
Group Health, Life, Dental & Disability Insurance
Payment Protection Insurance
Mortgage Insurance
Retirement Income & Investment Products & Services
Long-Term Care Insurance

BRANDS/DIVISIONS/AFFILIATES:

Genworth Seguros Mexico, S.A de C.V.

CONTACTS: Note: Officers with more than one job title may be intentionally listed here more than once.

Michael D. Fraizer, CEO
Michael D. Fraizer, Pres.
Patrick B. Kelleher, CFO/Sr. VP
Michael S. Laming, Sr. VP-Human Resources
Scott J. McKay, CIO
Leon E. Roday, General Counsel/Sr. VP/Sec.
Joseph J. Pehota, Sr. VP-Corp. Dev.
Michel Perreault, Chief Risk Officer/Sr. VP
Kevin Schneider, Pres., US Mortgage Insurance
Ronald Joelson, Chief Investment Officer/Sr. VP
Pamela Schutz, Exec. VP-Retirement & Protection
Michael D. Fraizer, Chmn.
Thomas Mann, Exec. VP-Int'l

Phone: 804-281-6000	Fax: 804-662-2414
Toll-Free: 888-436-9678	
Address: 6620 W. Broad St., Richmond, VA 23230 US	

GROWTH PLANS/SPECIAL FEATURES:

Genworth Financial, Inc. is a financial security company focused on developing solutions that help the investment, protection, homeownership, retirement and independent lifestyle needs of more than 15 million customers with a presence in more than 25 countries. The company operates in three segments: retirement and protection; international; and U.S. mortgage insurance. The retirement and protection segment provides protection, wealth accumulation, retirement income and institutional products, such as: life insurance; long-term care insurance; a linked-benefits product that combines long-term care insurance with universal life insurance; Medicare supplement insurance; wellness and care coordination services for its long-term care policyholders; fixed and variable deferred and immediate individual annuities; group variable annuities offered through retirement plans; a variety of managed account programs, financial planning services and mutual funds; funding agreements; funding agreements backing notes; and guaranteed investment contracts. The international division provides structured, or bulk, mortgage insurance products as well as analytical tools and technology in Canada, Australia, New Zealand, Mexico and various European countries. This division also provides payment protection in North America and Europe. The U.S. mortgage insurance segment offers flow, or prime-based, individually underwritten residential mortgage loans. Genworth Financial also has corporate and other activities, which consist primarily of unallocated corporate income and expenses, results of a small, non-core business and most interest and other financing expenses. In January 2009, the company agreed to sell Genworth Seguros Mexico, S.A de C.V., which consists of automobile, property, casualty, life and personal accident insurance in order to focus on mortgage and lifestyle protection insurance in Mexico.

Employees are offered medical, dental and vision insurance; life insurance; disability coverage; flexible spending accounts; child care subsidies; pension; 401(k) plans; an employee discount program; and tuition reimbursement.

FINANCIALS: Sales and profits are in thousands of dollars—add 000 to get the full amount. 2008 Note: Financial information for 2008 was not available for all companies at press time.

2008 Sales: $9,948,000	2008 Profits: $-572,000	**U.S. Stock Ticker:** GNW
2007 Sales: $11,125,000	2007 Profits: $1,154,000	**Int'l Ticker:** Int'l Exchange:
2006 Sales: $10,285,000	2006 Profits: $1,283,000	Employees: 6,000
2005 Sales: $10,504,000	2005 Profits: $1,221,000	Fiscal Year Ends: 12/31
2004 Sales: $11,057,000	2004 Profits: $1,157,000	Parent Company:

SALARIES/BENEFITS:

Pension Plan: Y	ESOP Stock Plan:	Profit Sharing:	Top Exec. Salary: $1,121,403	Bonus: $
Savings Plan: Y	Stock Purch. Plan:		Second Exec. Salary: $647,922	Bonus: $

OTHER THOUGHTS:

Apparent Women Officers or Directors: 3
Hot Spot for Advancement for Women/Minorities: Y

LOCATIONS: ("Y" = Yes)

West:	Southwest:	Midwest:	Southeast:	Northeast:	International:
Y	Y	Y	Y	Y	Y

GEO GROUP INC

Industry Group Code: 5616 Ranks within this company's industry group: Sales: 2   Profits: 2

Management:		Sales/Marketing:		Liberal Arts:		Information Systems:		Professionals:		Tech./Scientific:	
Management Trainees:	Y	Marketing Pros.:		Gen. Writing/Editing:	Y	Info. Management:	Y	Finance/Acct.:	Y	Engineers, Electrical:	
Experienced Mngmt.:	Y	Retail Sales:		Technical Writing:		Software Dev.:	Y	Law:	Y	Engineers, Other:	
International Business:	Y	Commercial/Industrial:	Y	Graphic Arts/Photog.:		Hardware Dev.:		HR/Other:	Y	Health/Lab:	
MBA Grads:	Y	Sales Trainees:		Music:		Consulting/Other:		Training:	Y	Scientists/Research:	
		Advertising Pros.:		Broadcasting:				Health Care:		Petroleum/Chemicals:	
				Other:				Consulting:		Math/Other:	

TYPES OF BUSINESS:

Prison Management
Institutional Facilities Management
Facilities Maintenance
Facilities Design
Support Services

BRANDS/DIVISIONS/AFFILIATES:

GEO Care, Inc.
CentraCore Properties Trust

CONTACTS: *Note: Officers with more than one job title may be intentionally listed here more than once.*

George C. Zoley, CEO
Wayne H. Calabrese, COO
Wayne H. Calabrese, Pres.
John G. O'Rourke, CFO/Sr. VP
John J. Bulfin, General Counsel/Sr. VP/Corp. Sec.
Jorge A. Dominicis, Sr. VP-Residential Treatment/Pres., Geo Care, Inc.
John M. Hurley, Sr. VP/Pres., U.S. Corrections
Thomas M. Wierdsma, Sr. VP-Project Dev.
George C. Zoley, Chmn.
Mark H. Underwood, Sr. VP/Pres., Int'l Svcs.

Phone: 561-893-0101	**Fax:** 561-999-7635
Toll-Free: 866-301-4436	
Address: 1 Park Plz., 621 NW 53rd St., Ste. 700, Boca Raton, FL 33487 US	

GROWTH PLANS/SPECIAL FEATURES:

GEO Group, Inc. is a provider of government-outsourced services specializing in the management of correctional, detention and mental health and residential treatment facilities in the U.S., Canada, Australia, South Africa and the U.K. It operates a broad range of correctional and detention facilities including maximum, medium and minimum security prisons; immigration detention centers; minimum security detention centers; and mental health and residential treatment facilities. The company operates in four segments: U.S. corrections; international services; GEO Care; and facility construction and design. The U.S. correction segment primarily encompasses the U.S.-based privatized corrections and detention business. The international services segment primarily consists of privatized corrections and detention operations in South Africa, Australia and the U.K. This division review opportunities to further diversify into related foreign-based governmental-outsourced services on an ongoing basis. The GEO Care segment, which is operated by wholly-owned subsidiary GEO Care, Inc., comprises the privatized mental health and residential treatment services business, all of which is currently conducted in the U.S. The facility construction and design segment primarily consists of contracts with various state, local and federal agencies for the design and construction of facilities for which the firm has management contracts. At its correctional and detention facilities, GEO Group offers services that include a wide array of in-facility rehabilitative and educational programs such as basic education through academic programs designed to improve literacy levels and enhance the opportunity to acquire skills planning programs. The company manages 59 facilities totaling roughly 50,400 beds worldwide and has an additional 6,800 beds under development at 10 facilities, including the expansion of five facilities it currently operates and five new facilities under construction. The firm also has about 730 additional inactive beds available to meet customers' potential future demand for bed space.

FINANCIALS: Sales and profits are in thousands of dollars—add 000 to get the full amount. 2008 Note: Financial information for 2008 was not available for all companies at press time.

2008 Sales: $1,043,006	2008 Profits: $58,902	**U.S. Stock Ticker:** GEO
2007 Sales: $976,299	2007 Profits: $41,845	**Int'l Ticker:** Int'l Exchange:
2006 Sales: $818,439	2006 Profits: $30,031	Employees: 12,378
2005 Sales: $612,900	2005 Profits: $7,006	Fiscal Year Ends: 12/31
2004 Sales: $593,994	2004 Profits: $16,815	Parent Company:

SALARIES/BENEFITS:

Pension Plan:	ESOP Stock Plan:	Profit Sharing:	Top Exec. Salary: $932,692	Bonus: $1,408,110
Savings Plan:	Stock Purch. Plan:		Second Exec. Salary: $648,654	Bonus: $783,120

OTHER THOUGHTS:

Apparent Women Officers or Directors: 1
Hot Spot for Advancement for Women/Minorities:

LOCATIONS: ("Y" = Yes)

West:	Southwest:	Midwest:	Southeast:	Northeast:	International:
Y	Y	Y	Y	Y	Y

GEORGIA GULF CORPORATION

www.ggc.com

Industry Group Code: 325 Ranks within this company's industry group: Sales: 2 Profits: 4

Management:		Sales/Marketing:		Liberal Arts:		Information Systems:		Professionals:		Tech./Scientific:	
Management Trainees:	Y	Marketing Pros.:	Y	Gen. Writing/Editing:		Info. Management:	Y	Finance/Acct.:	Y	Engineers, Electrical:	
Experienced Mngmt.:	Y	Retail Sales:		Technical Writing:	Y	Software Dev.:	Y	Law:	Y	Engineers, Other:	Y
International Business:	Y	Commercial/Industrial:	Y	Graphic Arts/Photog.:		Hardware Dev.:		HR/Other:	Y	Health/Lab:	
MBA Grads:	Y	Sales Trainees:		Music:		Consulting/Other:		Training:	Y	Scientists/Research:	Y
		Advertising Pros.:		Broadcasting:				Health Care:		Petroleum/Chemicals:	Y
				Other:				Consulting:		Math/Other:	

TYPES OF BUSINESS:

Basic Chemicals
Building & Home Improvement Products
Outdoor Building Products

BRANDS/DIVISIONS/AFFILIATES:

Royal Group Inc
Colorscapes
Journeymen Select
Royal DuraPlank
Crown Select

CONTACTS: *Note: Officers with more than one job title may be intentionally listed here more than once.*

Paul D. Carrico, CEO
Paul D. Carrico, Pres.
Gregory C. Thompson, CFO
James Worrell, VP-Human Resources
Joel I. Beerman, General Counsel/VP/Sec.
Mark Buckis, Corp. Controller/VP
Mark J. Seal, VP-Aromatics & Additives
William H. Doherty, VP-PVC Compounds
Mark J. Orcutt, Exec. VP-Building Prod.
Patrick J. Fleming, Chmn.
C. Douglas Shannon, VP-Procurement

Phone: 770-395-4500	**Fax:** 770-395-4529
Toll-Free:	
Address: 115 Perimeter Center Pl., Ste. 460, Atlanta, GA 30346 US	

GROWTH PLANS/SPECIAL FEATURES:

Georgia Gulf Corporation manufactures and markets two integrated chemical product lines, chlorovinyls and aromatics. The company operates in four segments: chlorovinyls; window and door profiles and mouldings products; outdoor building products; and aromatics. The chlorovinyls segment sells a chain of products, which includes chlorine, caustic soda, ethylene dichloride (EDC), vinyl chloride monomer (VCM), vinyl resins and compounds. In North America, Georgia Gulf is one of the largest producers of VCM, vinyl resins and vinyl compounds. These chlorovinyls are sold to customers in the electrical, insulation, piping, siding, windows, chemical, pulp, paper and alumina industries. The window and door profiles and mouldings segment consists of extruded vinyl window and door profiles as well as interior and exterior mouldings. The segment operates 13 manufacturing facilities located in Canada and the U.S, as well as a number of distribution centers. The outdoor building products segment, operating 11 manufacturing facilities, produces siding; pipe and pipe fittings; and deck, fence and rail structures. Siding is sold under brand names such as Colorscapes, Journeymen Select, Crown Select and Royal DuraPlank, which is designed to offer a look and feel similar to real wood combined with the convenience of vinyl. The aromatics segment produces cumene and the co-products phenol and acetone. The company is among the largest worldwide producers of cumene. The firm markets its vinyl-based building and home improvement products primarily through its Royal Group subsidiary. In 2008, Georgia Gulf sold its outdoor storage buildings business for $13 million; sold and leased buildings in Ontario for $13.5 million; and utilized the money to pay down debt. In December 2008, the company closed its polyvinyl chloride (PVC) plant in Oklahoma City.

The company offers its employees health and welfare benefits; life insurance; short and long-term disability coverage; and a 401(k) plan.

FINANCIALS: Sales and profits are in thousands of dollars—add 000 to get the full amount. 2008 Note: Financial information for 2008 was not available for all companies at press time.

2008 Sales: $2,916,477	2008 Profits: $-257,643	**U.S. Stock Ticker: GGC**
2007 Sales: $3,157,270	2007 Profits: $-266,027	**Int'l Ticker:** Int'l Exchange:
2006 Sales: $2,427,843	2006 Profits: $48,539	Employees: 4,463
2005 Sales: $2,273,719	2005 Profits: $95,503	Fiscal Year Ends: 12/31
2004 Sales: $2,206,239	2004 Profits: $105,892	Parent Company:

SALARIES/BENEFITS:

Pension Plan: Y	ESOP Stock Plan:	Profit Sharing:	Top Exec. Salary: $663,247	Bonus: $
Savings Plan: Y	Stock Purch. Plan:		Second Exec. Salary: $570,769	Bonus: $

OTHER THOUGHTS:

Apparent Women Officers or Directors:
Hot Spot for Advancement for Women/Minorities:

LOCATIONS: ("Y" = Yes)

West:	Southwest:	Midwest:	Southeast:	Northeast:	International:
Y	Y	Y	Y	Y	Y

GILEAD SCIENCES INC

www.gilead.com

Industry Group Code: 325412 **Ranks within this company's industry group:** Sales: 10   Profits: 8

Management:		Sales/Marketing:		Liberal Arts:		Information Systems:		Professionals:		Tech./Scientific:	
Management Trainees:	Y	Marketing Pros.:	Y	Gen. Writing/Editing:		Info. Management:	Y	Finance/Acct.:	Y	Engineers, Electrical:	Y
Experienced Mngmt.:	Y	Retail Sales:		Technical Writing:	Y	Software Dev.:	Y	Law:	Y	Engineers, Other:	Y
International Business:	Y	Commercial/Industrial:	Y	Graphic Arts/Photog.:	Y	Hardware Dev.:		HR/Other:	Y	Health/Lab:	Y
MBA Grads:	Y	Sales Trainees:		Music:		Consulting/Other:		Training:	Y	Scientists/Research:	Y
		Advertising Pros.:		Broadcasting:				Health Care:	Y	Petroleum/Chemicals:	Y
				Other:				Consulting:		Math/Other:	Y

TYPES OF BUSINESS:

Viral & Bacterial Infections Drugs
Respiratory & Cardiopulmonary Diseases Drugs

BRANDS/DIVISIONS/AFFILIATES:

Vistide
Truvada
Emtriva
Atripla
Hepsera
Viread
Lexiscan
Ranexa

CONTACTS: *Note: Officers with more than one job title may be intentionally listed here more than once.*

John C. Martin, CEO
John F. Milligan, COO
John F. Milligan, Pres.
Robin Washington, CFO/Sr. VP
Kristen M. Metza, Sr. VP-Human Resources
Norbert W. Bischofberger, Chief Scientific Officer/Exec. VP-R&D
Anthony D. Caracciolo, Sr. VP-Mfg.
Gregg H. Alton, General Counsel/Sr. VP
Anthony D. Caracciolo, Sr. VP-Oper.
John Toole, Sr. VP-Corp. Dev.
Kevin Young, Exec. VP-Commercial Oper.
A. Bruce Montgomery, Sr. VP/Head-Respiratory Therapeutics
Seigo Izump, Sr. VP-Cardiovascular Therapeutics
William A. Lee, Sr. VP-Research
John C. Martin, Chmn.
Paul Carter, Sr. VP-Int'l Commercial Oper.

Phone: 650-574-3000	Fax: 650-578-9264
Toll-Free: 800-445-3235	
Address: 333 Lakeside Dr., Foster City, CA 94404 US	

GROWTH PLANS/SPECIAL FEATURES:

Gilead Sciences, Inc. is a biopharmaceutical company that discovers, develops and commercializes therapeutics for the treatment of life-threatening diseases such as viral and bacterial infections. The company expanded its efforts to include respiratory and cardiopulmonary diseases. The firm maintains research, development, manufacturing, sales and marketing facilities in the U.S., Europe and Australia and operates marketing subsidiaries in another 12 countries. Gilead currently has 12 products on the market: Viread, Truvada and Emtriva, which are oral medicines used as part of a combination therapy to treat HIV; Atripla, an oral formulation for treatment of HIV; Hespera, an oral medication used for treatment of Hepatitis B; AmBisome, an antifungal agent to treat serious invasive fungal infections; Vistide, an antiviral medication for the treatment of cytomegalovirus retinitis in patients with AIDS; Ranexa, a treatment for chronic angina; Letairis, for the treatment of pulmonary arterial hypertension; and Lexiscan, which is used as a pharmacologic stress agent. The firm also has a number of products in development, including treatments for cystic fibrosis, hypertension, heart failure, hepatitis C, HIV/AIDS, and others. The company also derives revenues from licensing agreements for Macugen, a macular degeneration treatment developed by OSI Pharmaceuticals, Inc.; and Tamiflu, an influenza medication sold by F. Hoffman-LaRoche. In August 2008, Gilead entered into an agreement with Merck & Co., Inc. to distribute Atripla in 12 countries, mostly in Latin America and Asia. Also in August 2008, the FDA approved Viread for treatment of chronic hepatitis B in adults. In April 2009, the firm acquired CV Therapeutics.

The company offers its employees medical, vision, dental, life and AD&D insurance; short- and long-term disability coverage; a 401(k) plan; a stock purchase plan; an employee assistance plan; and tuition reimbursement.

FINANCIALS: Sales and profits are in thousands of dollars—add 000 to get the full amount. 2008 Note: Financial information for 2008 was not available for all companies at press time.

2008 Sales: $5,335,750	2008 Profits: $2,011,154	**U.S. Stock Ticker:** GILD
2007 Sales: $4,230,045	2007 Profits: $1,615,298	**Int'l Ticker:** Int'l Exchange:
2006 Sales: $3,026,139	2006 Profits: $-1,189,957	Employees: 3,441
2005 Sales: $2,028,400	2005 Profits: $813,914	Fiscal Year Ends: 12/31
2004 Sales: $1,324,621	2004 Profits: $449,371	Parent Company:

SALARIES/BENEFITS:

Pension Plan:	ESOP Stock Plan:	Profit Sharing:	Top Exec. Salary: $1,146,261	Bonus: $1,651,650
Savings Plan: Y	Stock Purch. Plan: Y		Second Exec. Salary: $727,988	Bonus: $693,589

OTHER THOUGHTS:

Apparent Women Officers or Directors: 4
Hot Spot for Advancement for Women/Minorities: Y

LOCATIONS: ("Y" = Yes)

West:	Southwest:	Midwest:	Southeast:	Northeast:	International:
Y				Y	Y

GLOBAL HYATT CORPORATION
www.hyatt.com

Industry Group Code: 721110 **Ranks within this company's industry group:** Sales: 5 Profits:

Management:		Sales/Marketing:		Liberal Arts:		Information Systems:		Professionals:		Tech./Scientific:	
Management Trainees:	Y	Marketing Pros.:	Y	Gen. Writing/Editing:	Y	Info. Management:	Y	Finance/Acct.:	Y	Engineers, Electrical:	
Experienced Mngmt.:	Y	Retail Sales:		Technical Writing:		Software Dev.:	Y	Law:	Y	Engineers, Other:	
International Business:	Y	Commercial/Industrial:	Y	Graphic Arts/Photog.:	Y	Hardware Dev.:		HR/Other:	Y	Health/Lab:	
MBA Grads:	Y	Sales Trainees:	Y	Music:		Consulting/Other:		Training:	Y	Scientists/Research:	
		Advertising Pros.:	Y	Broadcasting:				Health Care:		Petroleum/Chemicals:	
				Other:	Y			Consulting:		Math/Other:	

TYPES OF BUSINESS:
Hotel Ownership & Management
Timeshares
Golf Courses
Gaming
Retirement Communities
Motels & Inns
Hotel Franchising

BRANDS/DIVISIONS/AFFILIATES:
Hyatt Regency
Grand Hyatt
Hyatt Resorts
Hyatt Summerfield Suites
U.S. Franchise Systems, Inc.
Hyatt Vacation Ownership, Inc.
Hyatt Gold Passport
Andaz

CONTACTS: *Note: Officers with more than one job title may be intentionally listed here more than once.*
Mark S. Hoplamazian, CEO
Mark S. Hoplamazian, Pres.
Katie Meyer, VP-Corp. Comm.
Steve Sokal, Sr. VP-Global Asset Mgmt.
Steve Haggerty, Exec. VP-Real Estate Dev.
Jill Johnson, VP-Asset Mgmt.
Thomas J. Pritzker, Chmn.

Phone: 312-750-1234	Fax: 312-750-8550
Toll-Free:	
Address: 71 S. Wacker Dr., 16th Fl., Chicago, IL 60606 US	

GROWTH PLANS/SPECIAL FEATURES:
Global Hyatt Corporation (Hyatt) owns and operates full-service luxury hotels. With its subsidiaries, Hyatt has approximately 370 resorts and hotels across 44 countries and 37 U.S. states. Its best known brand, Hyatt Regency, caters mainly to corporate travel clients. Grand Hyatt hotels cater to leisure and business travelers and include accommodations for banquets and conferences. Hyatt Resorts often feature professional, PGA golf courses; adventure travel opportunities, such as scuba diving, biking, hot air balloon trips or horseback riding; Hyatt Pure spas; and activities for kids and families. Hyatt Summerfield Suites, an all-suites hotel concept designed to feel more like home, offers 32-inch HDTVs, a full kitchen and complementary shopping service for its outdoor BBQ-pits. Recently introduced Hyatt Place hotels feature high-tech amenities such as 42-inch HDTVs in every room, free Wi-Fi Internet access and a 24-hour, touch-screen room service ordering system. Lastly, Park Hyatt hotels are smaller, full-service luxury hotels that offer unique services including limited time specials and Pamper at the Park, which includes breakfast and spa time. Subsidiary Hyatt Vacation Ownership, Inc. offers vacation ownership and vacation rental opportunities, offering members timeshare or points-based resort vacation opportunities. Hyatt hotel services include Hyatt Gold Passport, a frequent-traveler rewards program; and some properties feature casinos. Recently, the firm launched its newest brand, Andaz, which has one hotel in London, with three more under development in New York and Texas. Hyatt's newest locations include the Hyatt Regency Toronto in Toronto, Canada; and the Hyatt Regency Hong Kong, Sha Tin, in Hong Kong. In 2008, Hyatt sold, to Wyndham Worldwide, U.S. Franchise Systems, Inc., which franchises Hawthorn Suites and Microtel Inns and Suites.

Employees of Hyatt receive complementary hotel rooms; medical, dental, vision and prescription drug coverage; and life insurance.

FINANCIALS: Sales and profits are in thousands of dollars—add 000 to get the full amount. 2008 Note: Financial information for 2008 was not available for all companies at press time.
2008 Sales: $3,900,000	2008 Profits: $	U.S. Stock Ticker: Private
2007 Sales: $3,750,000	2007 Profits: $	Int'l Ticker: Int'l Exchange:
2006 Sales: $3,500,000	2006 Profits: $	Employees: 125,000
2005 Sales: $7,266,000	2005 Profits: $	Fiscal Year Ends: 1/31
2004 Sales: $5,500,000	2004 Profits: $	Parent Company:

SALARIES/BENEFITS:
Pension Plan:	ESOP Stock Plan:	Profit Sharing:	Top Exec. Salary: $	Bonus: $
Savings Plan: Y	Stock Purch. Plan:		Second Exec. Salary: $	Bonus: $

OTHER THOUGHTS:
Apparent Women Officers or Directors: 2
Hot Spot for Advancement for Women/Minorities: Y

LOCATIONS: ("Y" = Yes)
West:	Southwest:	Midwest:	Southeast:	Northeast:	International:
Y	Y	Y	Y	Y	Y

Note: Financial information, benefits and other data can change quickly and may vary from those stated here.

GLOBAL PAYMENTS INC
www.globalpaymentsinc.com

Industry Group Code: 522320 Ranks within this company's industry group: Sales: 5   Profits: 3

Management:		Sales/Marketing:		Liberal Arts:		Information Systems:		Professionals:		Tech./Scientific:	
Management Trainees:	Y	Marketing Pros.:	Y	Gen. Writing/Editing:	Y	Info. Management:	Y	Finance/Acct.:	Y	Engineers, Electrical:	
Experienced Mngmt.:	Y	Retail Sales:		Technical Writing:		Software Dev.:	Y	Law:	Y	Engineers, Other:	
International Business:	Y	Commercial/Industrial:	Y	Graphic Arts/Photog.:	Y	Hardware Dev.:		HR/Other:	Y	Health/Lab:	
MBA Grads:	Y	Sales Trainees:	Y	Music:		Consulting/Other:		Training:	Y	Scientists/Research:	
		Advertising Pros.:	Y	Broadcasting:				Health Care:		Petroleum/Chemicals:	
				Other:				Consulting:		Math/Other:	

TYPES OF BUSINESS:
Electronic Payment Processing
Credit & Debit Card Processing
Funds Transfer Services
Check Guarantee Services
Merchant Services

BRANDS/DIVISIONS/AFFILIATES:
Global Payments Europe
DolEx
HSBC Merchant Services

CONTACTS: Note: Officers with more than one job title may be intentionally listed here more than once.
Paul R. Garcia, CEO
James G. Kelly, COO
James G. Kelly, Pres.
David Mangum, CFO/Exec. VP
Morgan M. (Mac) Schuessler, Exec. VP-Mktg.
Morgan M. (Mac) Schuessler, Exec. VP-Human Resources
Morgan M. (Mac) Schuessler, Chief Admin. Officer
Suellyn P. Tornay, General Counsel/Exec. VP
Morgan M. (Mac) Schuessler, Exec. VP-Corp. Comm.
Carl Williams, Pres., World-Wide Payment Processing
Paul R. Garcia, Chmn.
Joseph C. Hyde, Pres., Int'l

Phone: 770-829-8000	Fax: 770-829-8267
Toll-Free: 800-560-2960	
Address: 10 Glenlake Pkwy. NE, N. Tower, Atlanta, GA 30328 US	

GROWTH PLANS/SPECIAL FEATURES:

Global Payments, Inc. is a leading payment processing and consumer money transfer company enabling merchants, multinational corporations, financial institutions, consumers, government agencies and other profit and non-profit business enterprises to facilitate payments or further other economic goals. Global Payments markets its products and services throughout the U.S., Canada, Europe and the Asia-Pacific region. It operates in two business segments: merchant services and money transfer. It operates 793 originating retail branch locations in the U.S. and 90 in Europe. Global Payments has settlement arrangements with over 12,000 bank, exchange house and retail locations worldwide. The company's offerings in its merchant services segment provide merchants, independent sales organizations (ISOs) and financial institutions with credit and debit card transaction processing and check-related services. Global Payments also offers sales, installation and servicing of ATM and point of sale terminals and selected card issuing services through its Czech Republic-based Global Payments Europe subsidiary. The company markets its merchant services both directly, using a salaried and commissioned sales force, ISOs and independent sales representatives to sell its products directly to merchants; and indirectly, providing its products and services primarily to financial institutions and a limited number of ISOs on an unbundled basis, which in turn resell its products and services to merchants. It receives referrals from 1,600 bank branches in Canada. Global Payments Europe provides the company's indirect merchant services in Europe. The company's money transfer segment provides consumer money transfer services primarily marketed through its DolEx brand electronic money transfer services targeting first and second generation Latin Americans living in the U.S. In June 2008, the company created HSBC Merchant Services, a joint venture with HSBC Bank plc, to provide payment processing services to U.K merchants.

Employees are offered health, dental and vision insurance; life insurance; disability coverage; flexible spending accounts; an employee assistance program; and an educational assistance program.

FINANCIALS: Sales and profits are in thousands of dollars—add 000 to get the full amount. 2008 Note: Financial information for 2008 was not available for all companies at press time.

2008 Sales: $1,274,229	2008 Profits: $162,754	**U.S. Stock Ticker: GPN**	
2007 Sales: $1,061,523	2007 Profits: $142,985	**Int'l Ticker:**	Int'l Exchange:
2006 Sales: $908,056	2006 Profits: $125,524	Employees: 5,844	
2005 Sales: $784,331	2005 Profits: $92,896	Fiscal Year Ends: 5/31	
2004 Sales: $629,320	2004 Profits: $62,443	Parent Company:	

SALARIES/BENEFITS:

Pension Plan:	ESOP Stock Plan:	Profit Sharing:	Top Exec. Salary: $850,000	Bonus: $873,000
Savings Plan: Y	Stock Purch. Plan: Y		Second Exec. Salary: $500,000	Bonus: $361,000

OTHER THOUGHTS:
Apparent Women Officers or Directors: 2
Hot Spot for Advancement for Women/Minorities: Y

LOCATIONS: ("Y" = Yes)

West:	Southwest:	Midwest:	Southeast:	Northeast:	International:
Y	Y	Y	Y	Y	Y

Note: Financial information, benefits and other data can change quickly and may vary from those stated here.

GOLDMAN SACHS GROUP INC

www2.goldmansachs.com

Industry Group Code: 523110 Ranks within this company's industry group: Sales: 1 Profits: 1

Management:		Sales/Marketing:		Liberal Arts:		Information Systems:		Professionals:		Tech./Scientific:	
Management Trainees:	Y	Marketing Pros.:	Y	Gen. Writing/Editing:	Y	Info. Management:	Y	Finance/Acct.:	Y	Engineers, Electrical:	
Experienced Mngmt.:	Y	Retail Sales:		Technical Writing:		Software Dev.:	Y	Law:	Y	Engineers, Other:	
International Business:	Y	Commercial/Industrial:	Y	Graphic Arts/Photog.:	Y	Hardware Dev.:		HR/Other:	Y	Health/Lab:	
MBA Grads:	Y	Sales Trainees:		Music:		Consulting/Other:		Training:	Y	Scientists/Research:	
		Advertising Pros.:	Y	Broadcasting:				Health Care:		Petroleum/Chemicals:	
				Other:	Y			Consulting:		Math/Other:	Y

TYPES OF BUSINESS:

Investment Banking
Securities & Investment Management
Financial Services
Asset Management
Bank Holding Company

BRANDS/DIVISIONS/AFFILIATES:

PrimeAccess
Institutional Portal
USI Holdings Corporation

CONTACTS: Note: Officers with more than one job title may be intentionally listed here more than once.

Lloyd C. Blankfein, CEO
Gary Cohn, COO
Gary Cohn, Pres.
David A. Viniar, CFO/Exec. VP
Gregory K. Palm, Co-General Counsel/Exec. VP/Sec.
Esta E. Stecher, Co-General Counsel/Exec. VP/Sec.
Alan M. Cohen, Exec. VP/Global Head-Compliance
Lloyd C. Blankfein, Chmn.

Phone: 212-902-1000	Fax: 212-902-3000
Toll-Free:	
Address: 85 Broad St., New York, NY 10004 US	

GROWTH PLANS/SPECIAL FEATURES:

Goldman Sachs Group, Inc. is an investment banking, securities and investment management firm operating in over 30 countries. The firm has three main business divisions: investment banking; trading and principal investments; and asset management and securities services. The investment banking division, which accounted for 23% of net revenues in 2008, handles financial advisory and underwriting. Trading and principal investments segment, which accounted for 41%, is divided into three segments: fixed income, currency and commodities; equities; and principal investments. The asset management and securities services division, responsible for 36%, offers asset management, which includes advisory services and investments products across all major asset classes such as money markets, fixed income, equities and alternative investments; and securities services, which include prime brokerage, financing services and securities lending. The Goldman Sachs PrimeAccess program in Europe and the U.S. delivers investment research, products and execution services to brokerage firms. Goldman Sachs' Institutional Portal gives clients access to a range of market insights and intelligence including research reports, company information, business opportunities and trading data. Clients include corporations, financial institutions, governments and high-net-worth individuals. In recent news, the firm has opened offices in Mumbai, Moscow, Sao Paulo, Dubai, Qatar and Tel Aviv; opened banks in Brazil and Ireland; and entered into the asset management business in South Korea. In September 2008, the firm elected to become a bank holding company. It will transition to a business model that it more regulated, uses less leverage and may attract more retail deposits. In January 2009, the company was selected by the U.S. Federal Reserve to buy mortgage-backed securities that were backed by Fannie Mae, Freddie Mac and Ginnie Mae.

Employees are offered medical, dental and vision insurance; tuition reimbursement; an employee discounts and services program; discounted banking, loans and mortgages; an employee investing services.

FINANCIALS: Sales and profits are in thousands of dollars—add 000 to get the full amount. 2008 Note: Financial information for 2008 was not available for all companies at press time.

2008 Sales: $53,579,000	2008 Profits: $2,322,000	U.S. Stock Ticker: GS
2007 Sales: $87,968,000	2007 Profits: $11,599,000	Int'l Ticker: Int'l Exchange:
2006 Sales: $69,353,000	2006 Profits: $9,537,000	Employees: 30,067
2005 Sales: $43,391,000	2005 Profits: $5,626,000	Fiscal Year Ends: 11/30
2004 Sales: $29,839,000	2004 Profits: $4,553,000	Parent Company:

SALARIES/BENEFITS:

Pension Plan:	ESOP Stock Plan:	Profit Sharing:	Top Exec. Salary: $600,000	Bonus: $
Savings Plan: Y	Stock Purch. Plan:		Second Exec. Salary: $600,000	Bonus: $

OTHER THOUGHTS:

Apparent Women Officers or Directors: 3
Hot Spot for Advancement for Women/Minorities: Y

LOCATIONS: ("Y" = Yes)

West:	Southwest:	Midwest:	Southeast:	Northeast:	International:
Y	Y	Y	Y	Y	Y

Note: Financial information, benefits and other data can change quickly and may vary from those stated here.

GOOGLE INC

www.google.com

Industry Group Code: 519130 Ranks within this company's industry group: Sales: 1 Profits: 1

Management:		Sales/Marketing:		Liberal Arts:		Information Systems:		Professionals:		Tech./Scientific:	
Management Trainees:	Y	Marketing Pros.:	Y	Gen. Writing/Editing:	Y	Info. Management:	Y	Finance/Acct.:	Y	Engineers, Electrical:	Y
Experienced Mngmt.:	Y	Retail Sales:		Technical Writing:	Y	Software Dev.:	Y	Law:	Y	Engineers, Other:	
International Business:	Y	Commercial/Industrial:	Y	Graphic Arts/Photog.:	Y	Hardware Dev.:	Y	HR/Other:	Y	Health/Lab:	
MBA Grads:	Y	Sales Trainees:		Music:		Consulting/Other:		Training:	Y	Scientists/Research:	
		Advertising Pros.:	Y	Broadcasting:				Health Care:		Petroleum/Chemicals:	
				Other:	Y			Consulting:		Math/Other:	

TYPES OF BUSINESS:

Search Engine-Internet
Paid Search Listing Advertising Services
News Site Search Service
Catalog Search Service
Shopping Site
Web Log Tool
Search and Advertising on Cell Phones

BRANDS/DIVISIONS/AFFILIATES:

Google AdSense
Google Finance
Google News
Gmail
YouTube
Picasa
Chrome
Android

CONTACTS: *Note: Officers with more than one job title may be intentionally listed here more than once.*

Eric Schmidt, CEO
Patrick Pichette, CFO/Sr. VP
Omid Kordestani, Sr. VP-Worldwide Sales & Bus. Dev.
Laszlo Bock, VP-People Oper.
Alan Eustace, Sr. VP-Research & Eng.
Ben Fried, CIO
Sergey Brin, Pres., Tech./Co-Founder
Larry Page, Pres., Prod./Co-Founder
W.M. Coughran, Jr., Sr. VP-Eng.
David C. Drummond, Chief Legal Officer
Urs Holzle, Sr. VP-Oper./Google Fellow
David C. Drummond, VP-Corp. Dev.
Vinton G. Cerf., Chief Internet Evangelist/VP
Rachel Whetstone, VP-Public Policy & Comm.
Mark Fuchs, Chief Acct. Officer/VP-Finance
Shona Brown, Sr. VP-Bus. Oper.
Jeff Huber, Sr. VP-Eng.
Jonathan Rosenberg, Sr. VP-Prod. Mgmt.
Susan Wojcicki, VP-Product Mgmt.
Eric Schmidt, Chmn.
Nikesh Arora, Pres., Global Sales Oper. & Bus. Dev.

Phone: 650-623-4000	Fax: 650-253-0001
Toll-Free:	
Address: 1600 Amphitheatre Pkwy., Mountain View, CA 94043 US	

GROWTH PLANS/SPECIAL FEATURES:

Google, Inc. operates Google.com, one of the worlds largest and most used search engines, which indexes the content of billions of Internet pages. While Google charges nothing for its search engine, it charges fees to other sites that use its search technology, and has a lucrative program that enables business clients to bid for ad space. Its AdSense program delivers ads that are relevant to search results. Google provides its services in 120 different languages, with more than 50% of its searches coming from outside the U.S. The company's technology employs a unique, distributed-computing system utilizing thousands of low-end servers rather than a small number of high-powered computers. In addition to the Google search engine, the firm offers dozens of additional web sites, applications and services including Google Finance, Google News, Gmail, YouTube, Picasa, Google Earth and Google Maps. In March 2008, Google acquired marketing firm DoubleClick Inc. for $3.1 billion. Google hopes to dominate search-generated advertising on cellphones. It was instrumental in developing Android, an open source platform for cellphone handsets. In July 2008, the company announced that it has signed an agreement with Rambler Media to acquire ZAO Begun, a Russian context advertising service. In August 2008, Google released a beta version of its open source Internet browser called Chrome.

Employee benefits include medical, dental and vision insurance; 401(k); 18 weeks maternity leave; flexible spending accounts; college savings plan; adoption assistance; tuition reimbursement; free on-site lunches and dinners; paid vacation that increases with years of service;. Google also provides recreation facilities, financial planning classes and on-site dry cleaning, oil change and car wash facilities.

FINANCIALS: Sales and profits are in thousands of dollars—add 000 to get the full amount. 2008 Note: Financial information for 2008 was not available for all companies at press time.

2008 Sales: $21,795,550	2008 Profits: $4,226,858	**U.S. Stock Ticker:** GOOG
2007 Sales: $16,593,986	2007 Profits: $4,203,720	**Int'l Ticker:** Int'l Exchange:
2006 Sales: $10,604,917	2006 Profits: $3,077,446	Employees: 20,222
2005 Sales: $6,138,560	2005 Profits: $1,465,397	Fiscal Year Ends: 12/31
2004 Sales: $3,189,223	2004 Profits: $399,119	Parent Company:

SALARIES/BENEFITS:

Pension Plan: Y	ESOP Stock Plan:	Profit Sharing:	Top Exec. Salary: $450,000	Bonus: $1,638,063
Savings Plan: Y	Stock Purch. Plan:		Second Exec. Salary: $450,000	Bonus: $1,376,251

OTHER THOUGHTS:

Apparent Women Officers or Directors: 9
Hot Spot for Advancement for Women/Minorities: Y

LOCATIONS: ("Y" = Yes)

West:	Southwest:	Midwest:	Southeast:	Northeast:	International:
Y	Y			Y	Y

Note: Financial information, benefits and other data can change quickly and may vary from those stated here.

GRANT THORNTON LLP

www.grantthornton.com

Industry Group Code: 5412 Ranks within this company's industry group: Sales: 5 Profits:

Management:		Sales/Marketing:		Liberal Arts:		Information Systems:		Professionals:		Tech./Scientific:	
Management Trainees:	Y	Marketing Pros.:	Y	Gen. Writing/Editing:	Y	Info. Management:	Y	Finance/Acct.:	Y	Engineers, Electrical:	
Experienced Mngmt.:	Y	Retail Sales:		Technical Writing:	Y	Software Dev.:	Y	Law:	Y	Engineers, Other:	
International Business:		Commercial/Industrial:	Y	Graphic Arts/Photog.:	Y	Hardware Dev.:		HR/Other:	Y	Health/Lab:	
MBA Grads:	Y	Sales Trainees:		Music:		Consulting/Other:	Y	Training:	Y	Scientists/Research:	
		Advertising Pros.:	Y	Broadcasting:				Health Care:		Petroleum/Chemicals:	
				Other:	Y			Consulting:	Y	Math/Other:	

TYPES OF BUSINESS:

Accounting & Auditing Services
Financial Services
Administration Consulting

BRANDS/DIVISIONS/AFFILIATES:

Grant Thornton International
On The Horizon

CONTACTS: Note: Officers with more than one job title may be intentionally listed here more than once.

Edward E. Nusbaum, CEO
Shelley S. Stein, COO
Fred K. Walz, CFO
Brad B. Wilson, Chief Admin. Officer
Peggy M. Zagel, Managing Partner-Regulatory & Legal Affairs
Joel B. Anik, Regional Managing Partner-West
Martin E. Cooperman, Regional Managing Partner-Northeast
Lou J. Grabowsky, Regional Managing Partner-Central
Mike C. Hall, Regional Managing Partner-Midwest

Phone: 312-856-0200	Fax: 312-602-8099
Toll-Free:	
Address: 175 W. Jackson Blvd., 20th Fl., Chicago, IL 60604 US	

GROWTH PLANS/SPECIAL FEATURES:

Grant Thornton LLP is the U.S. arm of Grant Thornton International, a global accounting, tax and business advisory organization with over 50 offices across the country. The company seeks to become a leading accounting firm in the U.S., as a provider of specialist financial, tax and advisory services to both public and privately held clients. Some of its key audit and assurance services include integrated auditing, benefits management and public finance. The company's investment banking services involve sell side advisory, buy side advisory, management buyouts, restructurings and capital raising. It also offers more general administrative consulting services, such as Sarbanes-Oxley compliance; services for Chief Information Officers and Chief Financial Officers; project management office strategies; and performance improvement. Grant Thornton serves customers in the construction, real estate, consumer products, food and beverage, health care, energy, technology, manufacturing, retail, transportation, non-profit and financial services industries. Grant Thornton offers audit and assurance services tailored to particular needs, as well as providing the public with a series of publications, including On the Horizon, which publishes weekly news on developments in the accounting world. With support from Grant Thornton International's investment banking teams in London, Paris, Hamburg and Hong Kong, as well as other offices in the organization, Grant Thornton LLP can assist international clients with cross-border merger and acquisition activities. The company also provides expatriate services, international tax services and transfer pricing. In February 2008, the company unveiled a new brand identity, logo and web site. The new brand identity will be adopted by all member firms, domestic and international. In May 2008, the firm created a new Advisory Services practice to oversee its various financial advisory service lines.

Grant Thornton's employee benefits include medical and dental plans; domestic partner benefits; reimbursement accounts; a 401(k) plan; a variety of insurance offerings; an employee assistance program; and legal services.

FINANCIALS: Sales and profits are in thousands of dollars—add 000 to get the full amount. 2008 Note: Financial information for 2008 was not available for all companies at press time.

2008 Sales: $1,220,000	2008 Profits: $	U.S. Stock Ticker: Private
2007 Sales: $1,075,000	2007 Profits: $	Int'l Ticker: Int'l Exchange:
2006 Sales: $886,000	2006 Profits: $	Employees: 5,000
2005 Sales: $795,000	2005 Profits: $	Fiscal Year Ends: 7/31
2004 Sales: $635,000	2004 Profits: $	Parent Company:

SALARIES/BENEFITS:

Pension Plan:	ESOP Stock Plan:	Profit Sharing:	Top Exec. Salary: $	Bonus: $
Savings Plan: Y	Stock Purch. Plan:		Second Exec. Salary: $	Bonus: $

OTHER THOUGHTS:

Apparent Women Officers or Directors: 2
Hot Spot for Advancement for Women/Minorities: Y

LOCATIONS: ("Y" = Yes)

West:	Southwest:	Midwest:	Southeast:	Northeast:	International:
Y	Y	Y	Y	Y	

Note: Financial information, benefits and other data can change quickly and may vary from those stated here.

GUESS? INC

Industry Group Code: 448 **Ranks within this company's industry group: Sales: 3 Profits: 3**

Management:		Sales/Marketing:		Liberal Arts:		Information Systems:		Professionals:		Tech./Scientific:	
Management Trainees:	Y	Marketing Pros.:	Y	Gen. Writing/Editing:	Y	Info. Management:	Y	Finance/Acct.:	Y	Engineers, Electrical:	
Experienced Mngmt.:	Y	Retail Sales:	Y	Technical Writing:		Software Dev.:	Y	Law:	Y	Engineers, Other:	
International Business:	Y	Commercial/Industrial:		Graphic Arts/Photog.:	Y	Hardware Dev.:		HR/Other:	Y	Health/Lab:	
MBA Grads:	Y	Sales Trainees:	Y	Music:		Consulting/Other:		Training:	Y	Scientists/Research:	
		Advertising Pros.:	Y	Broadcasting:				Health Care:		Petroleum/Chemicals:	
				Other:	Y			Consulting:		Math/Other:	

TYPES OF BUSINESS:

Casual Clothing Stores
Accessories
Fragrances
Footwear
Online Sales
Jeans

BRANDS/DIVISIONS/AFFILIATES:

Baby GUESS
Guess? Jeans
Triangle Design
Question Mark
GUESS by MARCIANO
Brand G
Baby GUESS
Focus Europe, S.r.l.

CONTACTS: *Note: Officers with more than one job title may be intentionally listed here more than once.*

Paul Marciano, CEO
Carlos Alberini, COO
Carlos Alberini, Pres.
Dennis Secor, CFO/Sr. VP
Michael Relich, CIO/Sr. VP
Joseph Teklits, Integrated Corp. Rel.
Dennis Secor, Principal Financial & Acct. Officer
Maurice Marciano, Chmn.
Massimo Macchi, Pres., Guess Europe

Phone: 213-765-3100	Fax:
Toll-Free: 800-224-8377	
Address: 1444 S. Alameda St., Los Angeles, CA 90021 US	

GROWTH PLANS/SPECIAL FEATURES:

Guess?, Inc. designs, markets, distributes and licenses lifestyle collections of contemporary apparel and accessories for men, women and children that reflect the American lifestyle and European fashion sensibilities. The company's apparel is marketed under trademarks including GUESS, GUESS?, GUESS U.S.A., GUESS Jeans, Triangle Design, Question Mark, Brand G, a stylized G, GUESS Kids, Baby GUESS, YES and GUESS by Marciano. The lines include full collections of denim and cotton clothing, including jeans, pants, overalls, skirts, dresses, shorts, blouses, shirts, jackets and knitwear. The firm also grants licenses to manufacture and distribute a broad range of products that complement its apparel lines, including eyewear, watches, handbags, footwear, infants' and children's apparel, leather apparel, fragrance, jewelry and other fashion accessories. Guess products are sold through three primary distribution channels, its own stores in the U.S. and Canada, a network of wholesale accounts in the U.S. and via the Internet. The company operates 425 stores in U.S. and Canada, consisting of 192 full-price retail stores, 104 factory outlet stores, 43 G by GUESS stores, 52 GUESS by MARCIANO stores and 34 Guess Accessories stores. Guess also directly operates 61 stores in Europe, 24 stores in Asia and 11 stores in Mexico. The firm's European headquarters is located in Lugano, Switzerland. The company opened 57 new stores in the U.S. and Canada during 2009.

Guess offers its employees medical, dental and vision insurance; flexible spending accounts; an employee assistance program; life and AD&D insurance; short- and long-term disability; a 401(k) plan; an employee stock purchase plan; a corporate wellness program; access to a credit union; and tuition reimbursement.

FINANCIALS: Sales and profits are in thousands of dollars—add 000 to get the full amount. 2008 Note: Financial information for 2008 was not available for all companies at press time.

2008 Sales: $1,749,916	2008 Profits: $186,472	**U.S. Stock Ticker: GES**
2007 Sales: $1,252,664	2007 Profits: $131,172	**Int'l Ticker:** Int'l Exchange:
2006 Sales: $1,185,184	2006 Profits: $123,168	Employees: 9,900
2005 Sales: $936,092	2005 Profits: $58,813	Fiscal Year Ends: 12/31
2004 Sales: $729,262	2004 Profits: $29,566	Parent Company:

SALARIES/BENEFITS:

Pension Plan:	ESOP Stock Plan:	Profit Sharing:	Top Exec. Salary: $1,000,000	Bonus: $1,821,237
Savings Plan: Y	Stock Purch. Plan:		Second Exec. Salary: $1,000,000	Bonus: $2,207,500

OTHER THOUGHTS:

Apparent Women Officers or Directors: 3
Hot Spot for Advancement for Women/Minorities: Y

LOCATIONS: ("Y" = Yes)

West:	Southwest:	Midwest:	Southeast:	Northeast:	International:
Y	Y	Y	Y	Y	Y

HALLIBURTON COMPANY

www.halliburton.com

Industry Group Code: 213112 Ranks within this company's industry group: Sales: 2 Profits: 4

Management:		Sales/Marketing:		Liberal Arts:		Information Systems:		Professionals:		Tech./Scientific:	
Management Trainees:	Y	Marketing Pros.:	Y	Gen. Writing/Editing:	Y	Info. Management:	Y	Finance/Acct.:	Y	Engineers, Electrical:	Y
Experienced Mngmt.:	Y	Retail Sales:		Technical Writing:	Y	Software Dev.:	Y	Law:	Y	Engineers, Other:	Y
International Business:	Y	Commercial/Industrial:	Y	Graphic Arts/Photog.:	Y	Hardware Dev.:		HR/Other:	Y	Health/Lab:	
MBA Grads:	Y	Sales Trainees:		Music:		Consulting/Other:		Training:	Y	Scientists/Research:	Y
		Advertising Pros.:	Y	Broadcasting:				Health Care:		Petroleum/Chemicals:	Y
				Other:				Consulting:		Math/Other:	

TYPES OF BUSINESS:

Oil & Gas Drilling Support Services
Software Information Systems

BRANDS/DIVISIONS/AFFILIATES:

Landmark
Security DBS Drill Bits
Sperry Drilling Services
Easywell
Protech Centerform
Pinnacle Technologies
WellDynamics
OOO Burservice

CONTACTS: Note: Officers with more than one job title may be intentionally listed here more than once.

David J. Lesar, CEO
Andrew Lane, COO/Exec. VP
David J. Lesar, Pres.
Mark A. McCollum, CFO/Exec. VP
Lawrence Pope, Chief Human Resources Officer
Lawrence Pope, VP-Admin.
Bert Cornelison, General Counsel/Exec. VP
Tim Probert, Exec. VP-Strategy & Corp. Dev.
Christian Garcia, VP-Investor Rel.
Craig Nunez, Treas./Sr. VP
Sherry Williams, Corp. Sec./VP
Tim Probert, Pres., Halliburton's Drilling & Evaluation Div.
Evelyn Angelle, Corp. Controller/Principal Acct. Officer/VP
James S. Brown, Pres., Western Hemisphere
David J. Lesar, Chmn.
Ahmed H.M. Lotfy, Pres., Eastern Hemisphere

Phone: 713-759-2605	Fax: 713-759-2635
Toll-Free: 888-669-3920	
Address: 5 Houston Center, 1401 McKinney, Ste. 2400, Houston, TX 77010 US	

GROWTH PLANS/SPECIAL FEATURES:

Halliburton Company is a provider of products and services to the energy industry. The firm serves major, national, and independent oil and gas companies around the world, operating in approximately 70 countries. The company has two business segments through which it operates: Drilling and Evaluation; and Completion and Production. The Drilling and Evaluation segment provides field and reservoir modeling, drilling, evaluation, and precise well-bore placement solutions that enable customers to model, measure, and optimize their well construction activities. This segment consists of Baroid Fluid Services; Sperry Drilling Services; Security DBS Drill Bits; wireline and perforating services; Landmark; and project management. The Completion and Production segment delivers cementing, stimulation, intervention, and completion services. This segment consists of production enhancement services, completion tools and services, and cementing services. Production enhancement services include stimulation services, pipeline process services, sand control services, and well intervention services. Completion tools and services include subsurface safety valves and flow control equipment, surface safety systems, packers and specialty completion equipment, intelligent completion systems, expandable liner hanger systems, sand control systems, well servicing tools, and reservoir performance services. Cementing services involve bonding the well and well casing while isolating fluid zones and maximizing wellbore stability. Halliburton recently acquired Protech Centerform, which provide casing centralization; WellDynamics, a provider of well completion technology; and Pinnacle Technologies, a microseismic mapping service. In June 2009, the company released its GEM Elemental Analysis Tool, which allows evaluation of complex reservoirs.

FINANCIALS: Sales and profits are in thousands of dollars—add 000 to get the full amount. 2008 Note: Financial information for 2008 was not available for all companies at press time.

2008 Sales: $18,279,000	2008 Profits: $1,538,000	U.S. Stock Ticker: HAL
2007 Sales: $15,264,000	2007 Profits: $3,499,000	Int'l Ticker: Int'l Exchange:
2006 Sales: $12,955,000	2006 Profits: $2,348,000	Employees: 57,000
2005 Sales: $10,100,000	2005 Profits: $2,358,000	Fiscal Year Ends: 12/31
2004 Sales: $19,878,000	2004 Profits: $-979,000	Parent Company:

SALARIES/BENEFITS:

Pension Plan:	ESOP Stock Plan:	Profit Sharing:	Top Exec. Salary: $1,300,000	Bonus: $8,120,000
Savings Plan: Y	Stock Purch. Plan: Y		Second Exec. Salary: $650,000	Bonus: $2,304,983

OTHER THOUGHTS:

Apparent Women Officers or Directors: 3
Hot Spot for Advancement for Women/Minorities: Y

LOCATIONS: ("Y" = Yes)

West:	Southwest:	Midwest:	Southeast:	Northeast:	International:
Y	Y		Y		Y

HARRAH'S ENTERTAINMENT INC

www.harrahs.com

Industry Group Code: 721120 Ranks within this company's industry group: Sales: 1 Profits: 4

Management:		Sales/Marketing:		Liberal Arts:		Information Systems:		Professionals:		Tech./Scientific:	
Management Trainees:	Y	Marketing Pros.:	Y	Gen. Writing/Editing:	Y	Info. Management:	Y	Finance/Acct.:	Y	Engineers, Electrical:	
Experienced Mngmt.:	Y	Retail Sales:		Technical Writing:		Software Dev.:	Y	Law:	Y	Engineers, Other:	
International Business:	Y	Commercial/Industrial:	Y	Graphic Arts/Photog.:	Y	Hardware Dev.:		HR/Other:	Y	Health/Lab:	
MBA Grads:	Y	Sales Trainees:	Y	Music:	Y	Consulting/Other:		Training:	Y	Scientists/Research:	
		Advertising Pros.:	Y	Broadcasting:				Health Care:		Petroleum/Chemicals:	
				Other:	Y			Consulting:		Math/Other:	

TYPES OF BUSINESS:

Casino Hotels
Dockside & Riverboat Casinos
Racing Venues
Casino Management
Golf Facility

BRANDS/DIVISIONS/AFFILIATES:

Harrah's Operating Company Inc
Flamingo
Caesars
Horseshoe
Total Rewards
Paris
Rio
Apollo Management LP

CONTACTS: Note: Officers with more than one job title may be intentionally listed here more than once.

Gary Loveman, CEO
Gary W. Loveman, Pres.
Jonathan S. Halkyard, CFO/Sr. VP/Treas.
David Norton, Chief Mktg. Officer/Sr. VP
Mary Thomas, Sr. VP-Human Resources
Steve Brammell, General Counsel/Sr. VP
Jan Jones, Sr. VP-Comm. & Gov't Rel.
Anthony D. McDuffie, Chief Acct. Officer/Controller/Sr. VP
Tom M. Jenkin, Pres., Western Div.
John Payne, Pres., Central Div.
J. Carlos Tolosa, Pres., Eastern Div.
Gary Loveman, Chmn.

Phone: 702-407-6000	Fax: 702-407-6037
Toll-Free: 800-318-0047	
Address: 1 Caesars Palace Dr., Las Vegas, NV 89109 US	

GROWTH PLANS/SPECIAL FEATURES:

Harrah's Entertainment, Inc. is one of the largest gaming companies in the world. The firm owns or manages approximately 40 casinos throughout the world. Harrah's also earns fees from managing three casinos for Indian tribes: Harrah's Phoenix Ak-Chin, located near Phoenix, Arizona; Harrah's Rincon Casino and Resort, near San Diego, California; and Harrah's Cherokee Casino and Hotel, in Cherokee, North Carolina. These contracts expire in 2011. Additional brands operated and/or owned by Harrah's, Caesars; Horseshoe; Bally's; Flamingo; Grand Biloxi; Harveys; Imperial Palace; Paris; Rio; and Showboat. The firm offers casino entertainment facilities primarily under the Harrah's, Caesars and Horseshoe brands in the U.S., including land-based casinos; riverboat or dockside casinos; casino clubs; and three racing venues. Besides casinos, the firm's properties generally include hotel and convention space; restaurants; and non-gaming entertainment facilities. Harrah's properties total approximately 3 million square feet of gaming space and 38,000 hotel rooms. For returning customers in the U.S., the firm offers the Total Rewards card plan, allowing holders to earn reward credits for prizes such as vacations, event tickets and cars; Total Rewards currently has over 40 million members. The company owns and operates the World Series of Poker tournament and brand. In January 2008, Harrah's was acquired by Hamlet Holdings LLC, an affiliate of TGP Capital, LP and Apollo Management, L.P., for $29.7 billion dollars, and subsequently taken private.

Employees of Harrah's receive medical, dental and vision plans; educational assistance; a health and wellness programs such as the Healthy Pregnancy Program and employee assistance programs.

FINANCIALS: Sales and profits are in thousands of dollars—add 000 to get the full amount. 2008 Note: Financial information for 2008 was not available for all companies at press time.

2008 Sales: $10,127,000	2008 Profits: $-5,197,200	U.S. Stock Ticker: Private
2007 Sales: $10,825,200	2007 Profits: $619,400	Int'l Ticker: Int'l Exchange:
2006 Sales: $9,673,900	2006 Profits: $535,800	Employees: 84,000
2005 Sales: $7,010,000	2005 Profits: $236,400	Fiscal Year Ends: 12/31
2004 Sales: $4,396,800	2004 Profits: $367,709	Parent Company: HAMLET HOLDINGS LLC

SALARIES/BENEFITS:

Pension Plan:	ESOP Stock Plan:	Profit Sharing:	Top Exec. Salary: $	Bonus: $
Savings Plan: Y	Stock Purch. Plan:		Second Exec. Salary: $	Bonus: $

OTHER THOUGHTS:

Apparent Women Officers or Directors: 2
Hot Spot for Advancement for Women/Minorities: Y

LOCATIONS: ("Y" = Yes)

West:	Southwest:	Midwest:	Southeast:	Northeast:	International:
Y	Y	Y	Y	Y	Y

Note: Financial information, benefits and other data can change quickly and may vary from those stated here.

HARRIS CORPORATION

www.harris.com

Industry Group Code: 3342 Ranks within this company's industry group: Sales: 2 Profits: 2

Management:		Sales/Marketing:		Liberal Arts:		Information Systems:		Professionals:		Tech./Scientific:	
Management Trainees:		Marketing Pros.:	Y	Gen. Writing/Editing:	Y	Info. Management:	Y	Finance/Acct.:	Y	Engineers, Electrical:	Y
Experienced Mngmt.:	Y	Retail Sales:		Technical Writing:	Y	Software Dev.:	Y	Law:	Y	Engineers, Other:	
International Business:	Y	Commercial/Industrial:	Y	Graphic Arts/Photog.:	Y	Hardware Dev.:	Y	HR/Other:	Y	Health/Lab:	
MBA Grads:	Y	Sales Trainees:		Music:		Consulting/Other:	Y	Training:	Y	Scientists/Research:	Y
		Advertising Pros.:	Y	Broadcasting:				Health Care:		Petroleum/Chemicals:	
				Other:				Consulting:		Math/Other:	Y

TYPES OF BUSINESS:

Communications Equipment Manufacturing
Wireless Communications Equipment
Broadcasting Equipment
Microwave Equipment

BRANDS/DIVISIONS/AFFILIATES:

Zandar Technologies
DESKTOPBOX
Harris Stratex

CONTACTS: *Note: Officers with more than one job title may be intentionally listed here more than once.*

Howard L. Lance, CEO
Robert K. Henry, COO/Exec. VP
Howard L. Lance, Pres.
Gary L. McArthur, CFO/Sr. VP
Jeffrey S. Shuman, VP-Human Resources & Corp. Rel.
William H. Miller, Jr., CIO/VP-Info. Svcs.
R. Kent Buchanan, CTO
R. Kent Buchanan, VP-Eng.
Eugene S. Cavallucci, General Counsel/VP
Leon V. Shivamber, VP-Oper.
Ricardo A. Navarro, VP-Corp. Dev.
Pamela Padgett, VP-Corp. Comm.
Pamela Padgett, VP-Investor Rel.
Lewis A. Schwartz, Principal Acct. Officer/VP
Daniel R. Pearson, Pres., Gov't Comm. Systems Div.
Wesley B. Covell, Pres., Defense Programs
Timothy Thorsteinson, Pres., Broadcast Comm.
Peter Challan, VP-Gov't Rel.
Howard L. Lance, Chmn.
Leon V. Shivamber, VP-Supply Chain Mgmt.

Phone: 321-727-9100	Fax:
Toll-Free: 800-442-7747	
Address: 1025 W. NASA Blvd., Melbourne, FL 32919-0001 US	

GROWTH PLANS/SPECIAL FEATURES:

Harris Corporation, along with its subsidiaries, is an international communications and information technology company that provides sales and services to government and commercial markets in more than 150 countries. Harris operates through four divisions: RF Communications, Government Communications Systems, Broadcast Communications and Harris Stratex Networks. The RF Communications segment is a global supplier of secure radio communications products and systems for defense and government operations; and also performs advanced research, primarily for the U.S. Department of Defense and for international customers in government, defense and peacekeeping organizations. The Government Communications Systems segment designs, develops and supplies communications and information networks and equipment; develops integrated intelligence, surveillance and reconnaissance solutions; develops, designs and supports information systems for image and other data collection, processing, analysis, interpretation, display, storage and retrieval; offers enterprise IT and communications engineering, operations and support services; and conducts advanced research studies, primarily for various agencies of the U.S. government and other aerospace and defense companies. The Broadcast Communications segment serves the global digital and analog media markets, providing infrastructure and networking products and solutions, media and workflow solutions, and television and radio transmission equipment and systems. The Harris Stratex Networks segment offers reliable, flexible, scalable and cost-efficient wireless transmission network solutions, including microwave radio systems and network management software, which are backed by comprehensive services and support, primarily to mobile and fixed telephone service providers, private network operators, government agencies, transportation and utility companies, public safety agencies and broadcast system operators. In 2008, Harris acquired Zandar Technologies, a privately held developer and provider of high-quality multi-image display processors for television broadcast and professional video markets; and the assets of DESKTOPBOX, a technology firm offering an Internet broadcasting platform that synchronizes a television or radio broadcast and an automatic web page broadcast.

FINANCIALS: Sales and profits are in thousands of dollars—add 000 to get the full amount. 2008 Note: Financial information for 2008 was not available for all companies at press time.

2008 Sales: $4,596,100	2008 Profits: $444,200	**U.S. Stock Ticker: HRS**
2007 Sales: $3,737,900	2007 Profits: $480,400	**Int'l Ticker:** Int'l Exchange:
2006 Sales: $3,474,800	2006 Profits: $237,900	Employees: 15,400
2005 Sales: $3,000,600	2005 Profits: $202,200	Fiscal Year Ends: 6/30
2004 Sales: $2,518,600	2004 Profits: $132,800	Parent Company:

SALARIES/BENEFITS:

Pension Plan:	ESOP Stock Plan:	Profit Sharing:	Top Exec. Salary: $972,115	Bonus: $1,422,777
Savings Plan: Y	Stock Purch. Plan:		Second Exec. Salary: $549,989	Bonus: $247,417

OTHER THOUGHTS:

Apparent Women Officers or Directors: 4
Hot Spot for Advancement for Women/Minorities: Y

LOCATIONS: ("Y" = Yes)

West:	Southwest:	Midwest:	Southeast:	Northeast:	International:
Y	Y	Y	Y	Y	Y

Note: Financial information, benefits and other data can change quickly and may vary from those stated here.

HARTFORD FINANCIAL SERVICES GROUP INC (THE)

www.thehartford.com
Industry Group Code: 524113 Ranks within this company's industry group: Sales: 6   Profits: 6

Management:		Sales/Marketing:		Liberal Arts:		Information Systems:		Professionals:		Tech./Scientific:	
Management Trainees:	Y	Marketing Pros.:	Y	Gen. Writing/Editing:	Y	Info. Management:	Y	Finance/Acct.:	Y	Engineers, Electrical:	
Experienced Mngmt.:	Y	Retail Sales:		Technical Writing:	Y	Software Dev.:	Y	Law:	Y	Engineers, Other:	
International Business:	Y	Commercial/Industrial:	Y	Graphic Arts/Photog.:	Y	Hardware Dev.:		HR/Other:	Y	Health/Lab:	
MBA Grads:	Y	Sales Trainees:	Y	Music:		Consulting/Other:		Training:	Y	Scientists/Research:	
		Advertising Pros.:	Y	Broadcasting:				Health Care:	Y	Petroleum/Chemicals:	
				Other:	Y			Consulting:		Math/Other:	Y

TYPES OF BUSINESS:

Life Insurance
Mutual Funds
Property & Casualty Insurance
Group Life & Accident Insurance
Reinsurance
Employee Benefits Administration
Asset Management
Bank Holding Company

BRANDS/DIVISIONS/AFFILIATES:

Allianz SE
Princeton Retirement Group
Hartford Life and Accident
Hartford Life Group Insurance Company
Hartford Life and Annuity
Hartford Investment Financial Services, LLC
Hartford International Management Services Company
Hartford Mutual Funds, Inc. (The)

CONTACTS: Note: Officers with more than one job title may be intentionally listed here more than once.

Ramani Ayer, CEO
Lizabeth H. Zlatkus, CFO/Exec. VP
Connie Weaver, Sr. VP-Mktg.
Eileen Whelley, Exec. VP-Human Resources
Alan J. Kreczko, General Counsel/Exec. VP
Connie Weaver, Sr. VP-Comm.
Beth A. Bombara, Controller/Sr. VP
Greg McGreevey, Chief Investment Officer/Exec. VP
Juan Andrade, Pres./COO-Property & Casualty Oper.
John C. Walters, Pres./COO-Hartford Life, Inc.
Ramani Ayer, Chmn.
Marc Lieberman, Pres./CEO-Hartford Life, Ltd., Europe

Phone: 860-547-5000	Fax: 860-547-2680
Toll-Free:	
Address: 690 Asylum Ave., 1 Hartford Plaza, Hartford, CT 06115-1900 US	

GROWTH PLANS/SPECIAL FEATURES:

The Hartford Financial Services Group is a diversified insurance and financial services company that offers insurance and investment products. Through its many subsidiaries, it is among the largest providers of investment products, individual life, group life and group disability insurance products and property and casualty insurance products in the U.S. and Canada. The company also operates in Brazil, Japan, England and Ireland serving millions worldwide through independent agents and brokers, financial institutions and online. Products and services for individuals and families include annuities; mutual funds; college savings plans; and auto, flood, home and life insurance. Business offerings include property and casualty, group benefits, retirement, reinsurance and investment management products and services. Subsidiary Hartford Investment Management Co., offers a range of investment products including multi-sector fixed income, specialty fixed income, cash and enhanced cash and passive investing. Hartford is organized into two major divisions: life and property/casualty. The life division is involved with segments of investment products, individual life, group benefits and corporate-owned life insurance. The property and casualty operations include North American underwriting segments of business insurance, affinity personal lines, personal insurance, specialty commercial and reinsurance. Hartford recently announced its launching of a new target retirement fund, The Hartford Target Retirement Funds, to help baby boomers plan for retirement needs. In October 2008, German insurance company Allianz SE invested $2.5 billion in the firm. In November 2008, the firm purchased a small savings and loan firm, and then received approval to become a bank holding company. This maneuver qualified Hartford for federal bank bailout funds. In July 2009, the company acquired Federal Trust Corporation for $10 million

Hartford employees receive a benefits package including adoption and tuition assistance; degree development, on-site fitness center; employee discounts; and health coverage. Qualified employees enjoy the opportunity for additional rewards when Hartford meets or exceeds business objectives.

FINANCIALS: Sales and profits are in thousands of dollars—add 000 to get the full amount. 2008 Note: Financial information for 2008 was not available for all companies at press time.

2008 Sales: $9,219,000	2008 Profits: $-2,749,000	U.S. Stock Ticker: HIG
2007 Sales: $25,916,000	2007 Profits: $2,949,000	Int'l Ticker: Int'l Exchange:
2006 Sales: $26,500,000	2006 Profits: $2,745,000	Employees: 31,000
2005 Sales: $27,083,000	2005 Profits: $2,274,000	Fiscal Year Ends: 12/31
2004 Sales: $22,693,000	2004 Profits: $2,115,000	Parent Company:

SALARIES/BENEFITS:

Pension Plan: Y	ESOP Stock Plan:	Profit Sharing:	Top Exec. Salary: $1,150,000	Bonus: $
Savings Plan: Y	Stock Purch. Plan: Y		Second Exec. Salary: $990,000	Bonus: $

OTHER THOUGHTS:

Apparent Women Officers or Directors: 3
Hot Spot for Advancement for Women/Minorities: Y

LOCATIONS: ("Y" = Yes)

West:	Southwest:	Midwest:	Southeast:	Northeast:	International:
Y	Y	Y	Y	Y	Y

Note: Financial information, benefits and other data can change quickly and may vary from those stated here.

HAWAIIAN ELECTRIC INDUSTRIES INC

www.hei.com

Industry Group Code: 2211 Ranks within this company's industry group: Sales: 7 Profits: 7

Management:		Sales/Marketing:		Liberal Arts:		Information Systems:		Professionals:		Tech./Scientific:	
Management Trainees:	Y	Marketing Pros.:	Y	Gen. Writing/Editing:	Y	Info. Management:	Y	Finance/Acct.:	Y	Engineers, Electrical:	Y
Experienced Mngmt.:	Y	Retail Sales:		Technical Writing:	Y	Software Dev.:	Y	Law:	Y	Engineers, Other:	Y
International Business:		Commercial/Industrial:	Y	Graphic Arts/Photog.:	Y	Hardware Dev.:		HR/Other:	Y	Health/Lab:	
MBA Grads:	Y	Sales Trainees:		Music:		Consulting/Other:		Training:	Y	Scientists/Research:	
		Advertising Pros.:	Y	Broadcasting:				Health Care:		Petroleum/Chemicals:	
				Other:				Consulting:		Math/Other:	

TYPES OF BUSINESS:

Utilities-Electricity
Savings Bank
Renewable Energy
Biofuels

BRANDS/DIVISIONS/AFFILIATES:

Hawaiian Electric Company
Hawaiian Electric Light Company
Maui Electric Company, Limited
Renewable Hawaii, Inc.
American Savings Bank, F.S.B.
HEI Diversified
Pacific Energy Conservation Services, Inc.
Uluwehiokama Biofuels Corp.

CONTACTS: Note: Officers with more than one job title may be intentionally listed here more than once.

Constance H. Lau, CEO
Constance H. Lau, Pres.
James A. Ajello, CFO/Sr. Financial VP/Treas.
Karl E. Stahlkopf, CTO/Sr. VP-Energy Solutions, Hawaiian Electric Co.
Chet A. Richardson, Chief Admin. Officer
Chet A. Richardson, General Counsel/Sr. VP
Andrew I. T. Chang, VP-External Affairs
Curtis Y. Harada, Chief Acct. Officer/VP/Controller
Richard M. Rosenblum, CEO/Pres., Hawaiian Electric Company Inc.
Jay M. Ignacio, Pres., Hawaii Electric Light Company, Inc.
Timothy K. Schools, Pres., American Savings Bank, F.S.B.
Edward L. Reinhardt, Pres., Maui Electric Company, Ltd.
Jeffrey N. Watanabe, Chmn.

Phone: 808-543-5662	Fax: 808-543-7966
Toll-Free:	
Address: 900 Richards St., Honolulu, HI 96813 US	

GROWTH PLANS/SPECIAL FEATURES:

Hawaiian Electric Industries, Inc. (HEI) is a diversified holding company engaged in independent power and utility services and the operation of a savings bank. HEI's Hawaiian Electric Company (HECO) subsidiary, founded in 1891, is a regulated electric public utility company, along with its subsidiaries Hawaiian Electric Light Company (HELCO) and Maui Electric Company, Limited (MECO). HECO's Renewable Hawaii, Inc. subsidiary invests in renewable energy projects while Uluwehiokama Biofuels Corp. invests in a Maui-based biofuel refining plant. Additional subsidiaries of HEI include HEI Diversified (HEIDI), a holding company; Pacific Energy Conservation Services, Inc. (PECS), a contract services company; HEI Properties, Inc. (HEIPI); HEI Investments, Inc.; Hawaiian Electric Industries Capital Trusts II and III; and The Old Oahu Tug Service, Inc. (TOOTS). HEIDI's American Savings Bank, F.S.B. subsidiary is a leading financial institution in Hawaii, with more than 60 branch offices offering investment products, financial planning services, insurance, deposit accounts and consumer loans. HECO, HELCO and MELCO are regulated operating electric public utilities engaged in the production, purchase, transmission, distribution and sale of electricity on the islands of Oahu, Maui, Lanai, Molokai and Hawaii. HEI's electric utility operations generate approximately 89% of its revenues. The islands of Oahu, Maui, Lanai, Molokai and Hawaii have a combined population of approximately 1.2 million, or approximately 95% of the Hawaii population, and comprise a service area of 5,766 square miles. The principle communities served include Honolulu on Oahu; Wailuku and Kahului on Maui; and Hilo and Kona on Hawaii. Each island has its own generation and transmission system that is not connected to any other grid, which results in the company maintaining a larger amount of surplus capacity than most utilities.

FINANCIALS: Sales and profits are in thousands of dollars—add 000 to get the full amount. 2008 Note: Financial information for 2008 was not available for all companies at press time.

2008 Sales: $3,218,920	2008 Profits: $-90,278	**U.S. Stock Ticker:** HE
2007 Sales: $2,536,400	2007 Profits: $84,779	**Int'l Ticker:** Int'l Exchange:
2006 Sales: $2,460,904	2006 Profits: $108,001	Employees: 3,560
2005 Sales: $2,215,564	2005 Profits: $126,689	Fiscal Year Ends: 12/31
2004 Sales: $1,924,057	2004 Profits: $109,652	Parent Company:

SALARIES/BENEFITS:

Pension Plan: Y	ESOP Stock Plan:	Profit Sharing:	Top Exec. Salary: $763,200	Bonus: $1,363,695
Savings Plan:	Stock Purch. Plan:		Second Exec. Salary: $609,933	Bonus: $551,807

OTHER THOUGHTS:

Apparent Women Officers or Directors: 8
Hot Spot for Advancement for Women/Minorities: Y

LOCATIONS: ("Y" = Yes)

West:	Southwest:	Midwest:	Southeast:	Northeast:	International:
Y					

Note: Financial information, benefits and other data can change quickly and may vary from those stated here.

HCA INC

www.hcahealthcare.com

Industry Group Code: 622110 Ranks within this company's industry group: Sales: 2 Profits: 1

Management:		Sales/Marketing:		Liberal Arts:		Information Systems:		Professionals:		Tech./Scientific:	
Management Trainees:	Y	Marketing Pros.:	Y	Gen. Writing/Editing:	Y	Info. Management:	Y	Finance/Acct.:	Y	Engineers, Electrical:	
Experienced Mngmt.:	Y	Retail Sales:		Technical Writing:	Y	Software Dev.:	Y	Law:	Y	Engineers, Other:	
International Business:	Y	Commercial/Industrial:		Graphic Arts/Photog.:	Y	Hardware Dev.:		HR/Other:	Y	Health/Lab:	Y
MBA Grads:	Y	Sales Trainees:		Music:		Consulting/Other:		Training:	Y	Scientists/Research:	
		Advertising Pros.:	Y	Broadcasting:				Health Care:	Y	Petroleum/Chemicals:	
				Other:	Y			Consulting:		Math/Other:	

TYPES OF BUSINESS:

Hospitals-General
Outpatient Surgery Centers
Sub-Acute Care
Psychiatric Hospitals
Rehabilitation Services
Hospital Management Services

BRANDS/DIVISIONS/AFFILIATES:

Bain Capital LLC
KKR & Co LP (Kohlberg Kravis Roberts & Co)
Merrill Lynch & Co Inc

CONTACTS: Note: Officers with more than one job title may be intentionally listed here more than once.

Richard M. Bracken, CEO
Richard M. Bracken, Pres.
R. Milton Johnson, CFO/Exec. VP
John M. Steele, Sr. VP-Human Resources
Noel B. Williams, CIO/Sr. VP
Robert A. Waterman, General Counsel/Sr. VP
V. Carl George, VP-Dev.
David G. Anderson, Sr. VP-Finance/Treas.
Chuck J. Hall, Pres., Eastern Group
Jonathan B. Perlin, Chief Medical Officer/Sr. VP-Quality
Victor L. Campbell, Sr. VP
Paul Rutledge, Pres., Central Group
Jack O. Bovender, Jr., Chmn.

Phone: 615-344-2068	Fax:
Toll-Free:	
Address: 1 Park Plaza, Nashville, TN 37203 US	

GROWTH PLANS/SPECIAL FEATURES:

HCA, Inc., formerly known as HCA Healthcare Co., owns and operates approximately 163 hospitals and approximately 105 outpatient surgery centers in 20 states and the U.K. The company's acute care hospitals provide a full range of services, including internal medicine, general surgery, neurosurgery, orthopedics, obstetrics, cardiac care, diagnostic and emergency services, radiology, respiratory therapy, cardiology and physical therapy. The psychiatric hospitals provide therapeutic programs including child, adolescent and adult psychiatric care and adult and adolescent alcohol and drug abuse treatment and counseling. The outpatient health care facilities operated by HCA include surgery centers, diagnostic and imaging centers, comprehensive outpatient rehabilitation and physical therapy centers. The company's hospitals do not engage in extensive medical research and education programs; however, some facilities are affiliated with medical schools and may participate in the clinical rotation of medical interns and residents. In addition, HCA provides a variety of management services to health care facilities such as patient safety programs; ethics and compliance programs; national supply contracts; equipment purchasing and leasing contracts; and accounting, financial and clinical systems. Other services include governmental reimbursement assistance; construction planning and coordination; information technology systems; legal counsel; human resource services; and internal audit. The firm is owned by a group of private equity companies, including KKR & Co., Merrill Lynch and Bain Capital.

HCA offers its employees a day care flexible spending account; child care center discounts; an adoption assistance program; a ConSern student loan program; laser surgery discounts at LaserVision; a healthcare flexible spending account; and medical, dental and vision coverage.

FINANCIALS: Sales and profits are in thousands of dollars—add 000 to get the full amount. 2008 Note: Financial information for 2008 was not available for all companies at press time.

2008 Sales: $28,374,000	2008 Profits: $673,000	**U.S. Stock Ticker: Private**
2007 Sales: $26,900,000	2007 Profits: $	Int'l Ticker: Int'l Exchange:
2006 Sales: $25,477,000	2006 Profits: $1,036,000	Employees: 160,000
2005 Sales: $24,455,000	2005 Profits: $1,424,000	Fiscal Year Ends: 12/31
2004 Sales: $23,502,000	2004 Profits: $1,246,000	Parent Company: BAIN CAPITAL LLC

SALARIES/BENEFITS:

Pension Plan: Y	ESOP Stock Plan:	Profit Sharing:	Top Exec. Salary: $	Bonus: $
Savings Plan: Y	Stock Purch. Plan:		Second Exec. Salary: $	Bonus: $

OTHER THOUGHTS:

Apparent Women Officers or Directors: 3
Hot Spot for Advancement for Women/Minorities: Y

LOCATIONS: ("Y" = Yes)

West:	Southwest:	Midwest:	Southeast:	Northeast:	International:
Y	Y	Y	Y	Y	Y

HE BUTT GROCERY COMPANY (HEB)

www.heb.com

Industry Group Code: 445110 Ranks within this company's industry group: Sales: 5 Profits:

Management:		Sales/Marketing:		Liberal Arts:		Information Systems:		Professionals:		Tech./Scientific:	
Management Trainees:	Y	Marketing Pros.:	Y	Gen. Writing/Editing:	Y	Info. Management:	Y	Finance/Acct.:	Y	Engineers, Electrical:	
Experienced Mngmt.:	Y	Retail Sales:	Y	Technical Writing:		Software Dev.:	Y	Law:	Y	Engineers, Other:	
International Business:	Y	Commercial/Industrial:		Graphic Arts/Photog.:	Y	Hardware Dev.:		HR/Other:	Y	Health/Lab:	
MBA Grads:	Y	Sales Trainees:	Y	Music:		Consulting/Other:		Training:	Y	Scientists/Research:	
		Advertising Pros.:	Y	Broadcasting:				Health Care:		Petroleum/Chemicals:	
				Other:	Y			Consulting:		Math/Other:	

TYPES OF BUSINESS:

Supermarkets
Grocery Stores
Gourmet Food Stores
Dairy Processing
Bakery
Pharmacy Services

BRANDS/DIVISIONS/AFFILIATES:

H-E-B
Central Market
H-E-B plus!
H-E-B Insurance Agency
H-E-B Wireless

CONTACTS: Note: Officers with more than one job title may be intentionally listed here more than once.

Charles C. Butt, CEO
Robert Loeffler, Pres.
Cory Basso, VP-Mktg. & Advertising
Tina James, VP-Human Resources
Winell Herron, VP-Public Affairs
Kathy Durbin, Dir.-Benefits
Winell Herron, VP-Diversity
Bill Reynolds, VP-Facility Alliance

Phone: 210-938-8357	Fax: 210-938-8169
Toll-Free: 800-432-3113	
Address: 646 S. Main Ave., San Antonio, TX 78204 US	

GROWTH PLANS/SPECIAL FEATURES:

H.E. Butt Grocery Company (H-E-B) is one of the largest regional food retailers in the southwestern U.S. and Mexico. It operates over 300 grocery stores in 150 communities in Texas and Mexico under H-E-B brand names. The firm owns one of the largest milk plants in Texas, as well as a large bread bakery, a meat plant, a pastry bakery, an ice cream plant, a chip plant and a photo processing lab. The stores carry a wide variety of merchandise, including a line of products under the H-E-B brand name. H-E-B also operates the Central Market stores, with single locations in Houston, Dallas, Forth Worth, Plano, San Antonio and Southlake, as well as two locations in Austin. H-E-B Central Markets are gourmet specialty stores featuring large prepared foods-to-go areas, eat-in areas, comprehensive wine departments, specialty butcher and fish counters, a European bakery, a deli with meats, a large selection of cheeses from around the globe and a juice and ice cream bar. H-E-B plus! stores offer additional departments including Do-It-Yourself, Bed & Bath, Cook & Grill and Card & Party. H-E-B Insurance Agency offers automobile, life, health, travel, homeowners and renters insurance with locations in six Texas cities. H-E-B Wireless, with approximately 39 in-store locations, offers cell phone plans in partnership with providers such as Sprint and T-Mobile. To better serve its Mexican markets, the company owns and operates a $30-million retail support center in Monterrey, Mexico. In August 2008, the firm opened its fourth H-E-B plus! store in San Antonio at McCreless Market, a redeveloped city landmark. In October 2008, the company opened H-E-B Kids' Market, a permanent interactive exhibit at the San Antonio Children's Museum.

H-E-B offers its employees health insurance, life and disability insurance; a leadership development program; a scholarship program; flexible spending accounts; and credit union membership, as well as discounts on groceries and other benefits.

FINANCIALS: Sales and profits are in thousands of dollars—add 000 to get the full amount. 2008 Note: Financial information for 2008 was not available for all companies at press time.

2008 Sales: $15,000,000	2008 Profits: $	U.S. Stock Ticker: Private
2007 Sales: $13,500,000	2007 Profits: $	Int'l Ticker: Int'l Exchange:
2006 Sales: $13,500,000	2006 Profits: $	Employees: 68,000
2005 Sales: $11,500,000	2005 Profits: $	Fiscal Year Ends: 10/31
2004 Sales: $10,500,000	2004 Profits: $	Parent Company:

SALARIES/BENEFITS:

Pension Plan: Y	ESOP Stock Plan:	Profit Sharing:	Top Exec. Salary: $	Bonus: $
Savings Plan: Y	Stock Purch. Plan:		Second Exec. Salary: $	Bonus: $

OTHER THOUGHTS:

Apparent Women Officers or Directors: 2
Hot Spot for Advancement for Women/Minorities: Y

LOCATIONS: ("Y" = Yes)

West:	Southwest:	Midwest:	Southeast:	Northeast:	International:
	Y				Y

Note: Financial information, benefits and other data can change quickly and may vary from those stated here.

HEALTH CARE SERVICE CORPORATION

www.hcsc.net

Industry Group Code: 524114 Ranks within this company's industry group: Sales: 7 Profits: 5

Management:		Sales/Marketing:		Liberal Arts:		Information Systems:		Professionals:		Tech./Scientific:	
Management Trainees:	Y	Marketing Pros.:	Y	Gen. Writing/Editing:	Y	Info. Management:	Y	Finance/Acct.:	Y	Engineers, Electrical:	
Experienced Mngmt.:	Y	Retail Sales:		Technical Writing:	Y	Software Dev.:	Y	Law:	Y	Engineers, Other:	
International Business:		Commercial/Industrial:	Y	Graphic Arts/Photog.:	Y	Hardware Dev.:		HR/Other:	Y	Health/Lab:	
MBA Grads:	Y	Sales Trainees:		Music:		Consulting/Other:		Training:	Y	Scientists/Research:	
		Advertising Pros.:		Broadcasting:				Health Care:	Y	Petroleum/Chemicals:	
				Other:	Y			Consulting:		Math/Other:	

TYPES OF BUSINESS:

Insurance-Medical & Health, HMOs & PPOs
Traditional Indemnity Plans
Medicare Supplemental Health
Life Insurance
Dental & Vision Insurance
Electronic Claims & Information Network
Workers' Compensation
Retirement Services

BRANDS/DIVISIONS/AFFILIATES:

Blue Cross and Blue Shield of Illinois
Blue Cross and Blue Shield of Texas
Blue Cross and Blue Shield of New Mexico
Blue Cross and Blue Shield of Oklahoma
Preferred Financial Group
Colorado Bankers Life Insurance Company
Dental Network of America, Inc.
TMG Health

CONTACTS: *Note: Officers with more than one job title may be intentionally listed here more than once.*

Patricia A. Hemingway Hall, CEO
Colleen Reitan, COO/Exec. VP
Patricia A. Hemingway Hall, Pres.
Denise A. Bujak, CFO/Sr. VP
Carolyn H. Clift, Chief Diversity Officer/Sr. VP
Paul B. Handel, Chief Medical Officer/Sr. VP
Brian Hedberg, CIO/Sr. VP
Deborah Dorman-Rodriguez, Chief Legal Officer/Sr. VP
Martin G. Foster, Exec. VP/Pres., Plan Oper.
Tara Dowd Gurber, Exec. VP-Corp. Svcs.
Kenneth S. Avner, Chief Actuary/Sr. VP
Milton Carroll, Chmn.

Phone: 312-653-6000	Fax: 312-819-1220
Toll-Free:	
Address: 300 E. Randolph St., Chicago, IL 60601-5099 US	

GROWTH PLANS/SPECIAL FEATURES:

Health Care Service Corporation (HCSC) is a non-investor-owned mutual insurance company that operates through its Blue Cross and Blue Shield divisions in Illinois, Texas, New Mexico and Oklahoma. It also has several subsidiaries that offer a variety of health and life insurance products and related services to employers and individuals. It provides PPOs, HMOs, POS plans, traditional indemnity and Medicare supplemental health plans to approximately 12.4 million members through Blue Cross and Blue Shield of Illinois (BCBSI), Blue Cross and Blue Shield of Oklahoma (BCBSO), Blue Cross and Blue Shield of Texas (BCBST) and Blue Cross and Blue Shield of New Mexico (BCBSNM). Through its non-Blue Cross and Blue Shield subsidiaries, the company offers prescription drug plans; Medicare supplemental insurance; dental and vision coverage; life and disability insurance; workers' compensation; retirement services; and medical financial services. One such subsidiary, Preferred Financial Group, is made up of HSCS's various life insurance subsidiaries, including Fort Dearborn Life Insurance Company of Illinois (FDL) and Colorado Bankers Life Insurance Company. Another subsidiary, Dental Network of America, Inc., functions as a third-party administrator for all company dental programs and is registered in every state except Florida. It also offers a dental discount card program. MedConnect, LLC is an online resource for medical professionals. Hallmark Services Corporation provides administration and claim adjudication services for individual policies to the direct markets divisions of BCBSI and BCBST. Availity, L.L.C., a partially-owned subsidiary, operates a health care clearinghouse and provides Internet-based health information services. In November 2008, the company acquired TMG Health, which offers business process outsourcing (BPO) for Medicare and Medicaid.

HCSC offers its employees educational assistance, a transportation reimbursement account, an employee assistance program, a wellness program, flextime, credit union membership, a savings bond program, adoption assistance, flexible spending accounts and medical, vision, life and disability insurance.

FINANCIALS: Sales and profits are in thousands of dollars—add 000 to get the full amount. 2008 Note: Financial information for 2008 was not available for all companies at press time.

2008 Sales: $16,024,600	2008 Profits: $742,600	U.S. Stock Ticker: Mutual Company
2007 Sales: $14,348,400	2007 Profits: $	Int'l Ticker: Int'l Exchange:
2006 Sales: $12,971,600	2006 Profits: $1,115,400	Employees: 17,500
2005 Sales: $11,713,900	2005 Profits: $1,145,600	Fiscal Year Ends: 12/31
2004 Sales: $10,629,100	2004 Profits: $1,049,400	Parent Company:

SALARIES/BENEFITS:

Pension Plan: Y	ESOP Stock Plan:	Profit Sharing:	Top Exec. Salary: $	Bonus: $
Savings Plan: Y	Stock Purch. Plan:		Second Exec. Salary: $	Bonus: $

OTHER THOUGHTS:

Apparent Women Officers or Directors: 6
Hot Spot for Advancement for Women/Minorities: Y

LOCATIONS: ("Y" = Yes)

West:	Southwest:	Midwest:	Southeast:	Northeast:	International:
Y	Y	Y		Y	

Note: Financial information, benefits and other data can change quickly and may vary from those stated here.

HEALTH FITNESS CORP

www.hfit.com

Industry Group Code: 713940 Ranks within this company's industry group: Sales: 1   Profits: 1

Management:		Sales/Marketing:		Liberal Arts:		Information Systems:		Professionals:		Tech./Scientific:	
Management Trainees:	Y	Marketing Pros.:	Y	Gen. Writing/Editing:	Y	Info. Management:	Y	Finance/Acct.:	Y	Engineers, Electrical:	
Experienced Mngmt.:	Y	Retail Sales:		Technical Writing:		Software Dev.:		Law:	Y	Engineers, Other:	
International Business:	Y	Commercial/Industrial:	Y	Graphic Arts/Photog.:	Y	Hardware Dev.:		HR/Other:	Y	Health/Lab:	
MBA Grads:	Y	Sales Trainees:	Y	Music:		Consulting/Other:		Training:	Y	Scientists/Research:	
		Advertising Pros.:	Y	Broadcasting:				Health Care:		Petroleum/Chemicals:	
				Other:	Y			Consulting:		Math/Other:	

TYPES OF BUSINESS:

Fitness Center Management
Consulting Services
Corporate & Hospital-Based Fitness Centers
Fitness Center Design
Wellness Programs
Health & Fitness Assessment
On-Site Physical Therapy Services

BRANDS/DIVISIONS/AFFILIATES:

INSIGHT Health Risk Assessment
HFC Wellness Programs
HFC Fitness Programs
JumpStart
Science Advisory Board
INSIGHT Health Risk Assessment
EMPOWERED Health Coaching
Partner Program

CONTACTS: *Note: Officers with more than one job title may be intentionally listed here more than once.*

Greg Lehman, CEO
John Griffin, COO
Greg Lehman, Pres.
Wesley Winnekins, CFO
Debra Marshall, VP-Mktg.
Jeanne Crawford, Chief Human Resources Officer
Jim Reynolds, Chief Medical Officer
John Ellis, CIO
J.Mark McConnell, Sr. VP-Bus. & Corp. Dev.
David Hurt, VP-Fitness Mgmt. Account Svcs.
Katherine Meacham, VP-Health Mgmt. Account Svcs.
Brian Gagne, Sr. VP-Account Management
Mark W. Sheffert, Chmn.

Phone: 952-831-6830	Fax: 952-897-5173

Toll-Free: 800-639-7913

Address: 1650 W. 82nd St., Ste. 1100, Minneapolis, MN 55431 US

GROWTH PLANS/SPECIAL FEATURES:

HealthFitness Corp. (HFC) and its subsidiaries provide fitness and wellness management services and programs to corporations, hospitals, communities and universities in the U.S. and Canada. The firm also provides injury prevention programs and on-site physical therapy services. Currently, HFC is under contract to manage approximately 400 sites, including 215 corporate, hospital, community and university fitness centers; 166 corporate health management sites; and 99 unstaffed health management locations. Through its two business segments, Fitness Management Services and Health Management Services, the company provides a full range of development, management, marketing and consulting services, including demographic analysis; interior/floor plan and fitness program design; and occupational health consulting services. HFC programs include INSIGHT Health Risk Assessment, a full range of tools to assess the health and well-being of individuals; JumpStart, a six-week weight loss program; HFC Wellness Programs, a menu of lifestyle programs addressing the specific needs of a company's workforce, including weight loss and stress management; and HFC Fitness Programs, customized exercise-based programs including personal training and specialty group classes. In recent years, HFC formed a Science Advisory Board to review HFC's research programs and the quality of HFC's products and services. In April 2008, the company agreed to partner with Pfizer Health Solutions to develop Senior Risk Reduction Demonstration, a project aimed at helping senior citizens prevent chronic diseases/conditions. In November 2008, HFC launched Partner Program, which offers small employers a health package that combines eHealth portal, INSIGHT Health Risk Assessment and EMPOWERED Health Coaching solutions. In April 2009, the firm agreed to partner with Nebraska to develop and implement an inclusive health management program for over 17,000 of the state's employees.

HFC offers employees medical, dental, long-term disability and vision insurance; flexible spending accounts; life and AD&D insurance; employee assistance; a 401(k) plan; and an employee stock purchase plan.

FINANCIALS: Sales and profits are in thousands of dollars—add 000 to get the full amount. 2008 Note: Financial information for 2008 was not available for all companies at press time.

2008 Sales: $77,676	2008 Profits: $2,722	**U.S. Stock Ticker:** FIT	
2007 Sales: $69,958	2007 Profits: $ 910	**Int'l Ticker:** Int'l Exchange:	
2006 Sales: $63,578	2006 Profits: $1,352	Employees: 3,472	
2005 Sales: $54,942	2005 Profits: $1,204	Fiscal Year Ends: 12/31	
2004 Sales: $52,455	2004 Profits: $1,588	Parent Company:	

SALARIES/BENEFITS:

Pension Plan:	ESOP Stock Plan:	Profit Sharing:	Top Exec. Salary: $319,431	Bonus: $95,031
Savings Plan: Y	Stock Purch. Plan: Y		Second Exec. Salary: $217,308	Bonus: $36,250

OTHER THOUGHTS:

Apparent Women Officers or Directors: 4

Hot Spot for Advancement for Women/Minorities: Y

LOCATIONS: ("Y" = Yes)

West:	Southwest:	Midwest:	Southeast:	Northeast:	International:
Y	Y	Y	Y	Y	Y

Note: Financial information, benefits and other data can change quickly and may vary from those stated here.

HEALTH MANAGEMENT ASSOCIATES INC

www.hma.com

Industry Group Code: 622110 Ranks within this company's industry group: Sales: 7   Profits: 3

Management:		Sales/Marketing:		Liberal Arts:		Information Systems:		Professionals:		Tech./Scientific:	
Management Trainees:	Y	Marketing Pros.:	Y	Gen. Writing/Editing:	Y	Info. Management:	Y	Finance/Acct.:	Y	Engineers, Electrical:	
Experienced Mngmt.:	Y	Retail Sales:		Technical Writing:	Y	Software Dev.:	Y	Law:	Y	Engineers, Other:	
International Business:		Commercial/Industrial:		Graphic Arts/Photog.:	Y	Hardware Dev.:		HR/Other:	Y	Health/Lab:	Y
MBA Grads:	Y	Sales Trainees:		Music:		Consulting/Other:		Training:	Y	Scientists/Research:	
		Advertising Pros.:	Y	Broadcasting:				Health Care:	Y	Petroleum/Chemicals:	
				Other:	Y			Consulting:		Math/Other:	

TYPES OF BUSINESS:
Acute Care Hospitals

BRANDS/DIVISIONS/AFFILIATES:
Brooksville Regional Hospital
Barrow Regional Medical Center
Natchez Community Hospital
Twin Rivers Regional Medical Center
Lancaster Regional Medical Center
Williamson Memorial Hospital

CONTACTS: Note: Officers with more than one job title may be intentionally listed here more than once.
Gary D. Newsome, CEO
Gary D. Newsome, Pres.
Robert E. Farnham, CFO/Sr. VP
Frederick L. Drow, Sr. VP-Human Resources
Jim L. Jordan, Sr. VP-MIS
Randel J. Holly, Sr., VP-Corp. Eng.
Kelly E. Curry, Chief Admin. Officer/Exec. VP
Timothy R. Parry, General Counsel/Sr. VP/Corp. Sec.
Stanley D. McLemore, Sr. VP-Oper.
Peter M. Lawson, Exec. VP-Dev.
John C. Merriwether, VP-Financial Rel.
Joseph C. Meek, Treas./VP
Kenneth M. Koopman, Sr. VP-Reimbursement
Johnny A. Owenby, Sr. VP-Support Svcs.
Lisa Gore, Sr. VP-Clinical Affairs
Vicki Romero Briggs, Sr. VP/Div. CEO-North & South Carolina Hospitals
William J. Schoen, Chmn.

Phone: 239-598-3131	Fax: 239-598-2705
Toll-Free:	
Address: 5811 Pelican Bay Blvd., Ste. 500, Naples, FL 34108 US	

GROWTH PLANS/SPECIAL FEATURES:
Health Management Associates, Inc. (HMA) owns and operates acute care hospitals in non-urban communities. The company operates approximately 56 hospitals, with a total of 8,019 licensed beds. The firm operates facilities in Alabama, Arkansas, Florida, Georgia, Kentucky, Mississippi, Missouri, North Carolina, Oklahoma, Pennsylvania, South Carolina, Tennessee, Texas, Washington and West Virginia. These hospitals offer services such as general surgery; internal medicine; obstetrics; radiology; oncology; and emergency room, diagnostic, coronary and pediatric care. HMA also provides outpatient services which include cardiology, one-day surgery, respiratory therapy, laboratory, x-ray and physical therapy. In addition, certain HMA hospitals provide specialty services in areas like cardiology (e.g. open-heart surgery), oncology, magnetic resonance imaging, radiation therapy, neurosurgery, computer-assisted tomography scanning, lithotripsy and full-service obstetrics. The facilities benefit from centralized corporate resources such as finance and control systems; purchasing; physicians recruitment services; administrative personnel management; information technology; legal services; facilities planning; marketing; and public relations. Some of the company's hospitals provide services to retired and certain other military personnel and their families, pursuant to the Civilian Health and Medical Program of Uniformed Services (CHAMPUS). HMA hospitals include Brooksville Regional Hospital; Barrow Regional Medical Center; Natchez Community Hospital; Twin Rivers Regional Medical Center; Lancaster Regional Medical Center; and Williamson Memorial Hospital. HMA also operates approximately 90 clinics in 11 states. In August 2008, the firm sold Southwest Regional Medical Center, a 79-bed hospital located in Arkansas, to Baptist Health.

The company offers its employees medical, dental and vision coverage; flexible spending accounts; a 401(k) plan; and life, disability and critical illness insurance.

FINANCIALS: Sales and profits are in thousands of dollars—add 000 to get the full amount. 2008 Note: Financial information for 2008 was not available for all companies at press time.

2008 Sales: $4,451,611	2008 Profits: $223,302	U.S. Stock Ticker: HMA
2007 Sales: $4,392,086	2007 Profits: $119,879	Int'l Ticker: Int'l Exchange:
2006 Sales: $4,050,425	2006 Profits: $182,749	Employees: 32,700
2005 Sales: $3,479,568	2005 Profits: $353,077	Fiscal Year Ends: 12/31
2004 Sales: $3,092,547	2004 Profits: $325,099	Parent Company:

SALARIES/BENEFITS:

Pension Plan:	ESOP Stock Plan:	Profit Sharing:	Top Exec. Salary: $675,000	Bonus: $431,719
Savings Plan: Y	Stock Purch. Plan:		Second Exec. Salary: $566,667	Bonus: $

OTHER THOUGHTS:
Apparent Women Officers or Directors: 3
Hot Spot for Advancement for Women/Minorities: Y

LOCATIONS: ("Y" = Yes)

West	Southwest	Midwest	Southeast	Northeast	International
Y	Y	Y	Y	Y	

Note: Financial information, benefits and other data can change quickly and may vary from those stated here.

HEALTH NET INC

www.healthnet.com

Industry Group Code: 524114 Ranks within this company's industry group: Sales: 8   Profits: 9

Management:		Sales/Marketing:		Liberal Arts:		Information Systems:		Professionals:		Tech./Scientific:	
Management Trainees:	Y	Marketing Pros.:	Y	Gen. Writing/Editing:	Y	Info. Management:	Y	Finance/Acct.:	Y	Engineers, Electrical:	
Experienced Mngmt.:	Y	Retail Sales:		Technical Writing:	Y	Software Dev.:	Y	Law:	Y	Engineers, Other:	
International Business:		Commercial/Industrial:	Y	Graphic Arts/Photog.:	Y	Hardware Dev.:		HR/Other:	Y	Health/Lab:	
MBA Grads:	Y	Sales Trainees:		Music:		Consulting/Other:		Training:	Y	Scientists/Research:	
		Advertising Pros.:	Y	Broadcasting:				Health Care:	Y	Petroleum/Chemicals:	
				Other:	Y			Consulting:		Math/Other:	

TYPES OF BUSINESS:

Insurance-Medical & Health, HMOs & PPOs
Utilization Management
Health Care Services Management
Administrative Services
Health Insurance Underwriting
Life Insurance Underwriting

BRANDS/DIVISIONS/AFFILIATES:

Decision Power
It's Your Life Wellsite
Salud Con Health Net
Managed Health Network, Inc.

CONTACTS: Note: Officers with more than one job title may be intentionally listed here more than once.

Jay M. Gellert, CEO
James E. Woys, COO
Jay M. Gellert, Pres.
Joseph C. Capezza, CFO
Jonathan H. Scheff, Chief Medical Officer
Linda V. Tiano, General Counsel/Sr. VP/Sec.
Patricia T. Clarey, Chief Regulatory & External Rel. Officer/Sr. VP
Jonathan Rollins, Treas./VP
John P. Sivori, Sr. VP/Pres., Health Net Pharmaceutical Svcs.
Paul S. Lambdin, Pres., Health Net of the Northeast, Inc.
Steven Sell, Pres., Health Net of California, Inc.
Steven D. Tough, Pres., Health Net Federal Services, LLC
Roger F. Greaves, Chmn.

Phone: 818-676-6000	Fax: 818-676-8591
Toll-Free: 800-291-6911	
Address: 21650 Oxnard St., Woodland Hills, CA 91367 US	

GROWTH PLANS/SPECIAL FEATURES:

Health Net, Inc. is an integrated managed care organization that delivers managed health care services through health plans and government sponsored managed care plans. The firm's subsidiaries offer products related to prescription drugs; managed health care product coordination for multi-region employers; and administrative services for medical groups and self-funded benefits programs. HealthNet's managed health care providers include a network of health maintenance organizations (HMOs), insured preferred provider organizations (PPOs) and point-of-service (POS) plans to approximately 6.6 million individuals. These operations extend through group, individual, Medicare, Medicaid, TRICARE and Veterans Affairs programs. HealthNet's HMOs and PPOs contract approximately 70,265 primary care physicians and 238,371 specialist physicians. Health Net's behavioral health subsidiary, Managed Health Network, Inc. (MHN), provides mental health benefits to approximately 6.7 million individuals. The company owns insurance companies licensed to sell exclusive provider organization (EPO), PPO, POS and indemnity products, as well as auxiliary non-health products such as life and accidental death and dismemberment, dental, vision, behavioral health and disability insurance. In 2008, approximately 54% of the company's commercial members were covered by HMOs; 42% were covered by POS and PPO products; and 4% by EPO and fee-for-service products including consumer-directed health plans. The firm provides the Decision Power series of programs designed to directly involve patients in their health care decisions; the It's Your Life Wellsite, similar to the Decision Power programs, but targeted at Medicare members; the Salud Con Health Net, a project of its Californian branch designed to help uninsured Latino immigrants meet their health care needs; Medicare stores in Phoenix, Arizona and Meriden, Connecticut; and community enrollment and customer service centers in Los Angeles and Modesto, California. In August 2008, the firm disbursed over $5 million in no-interest loans to 12 Central Valley Californian health clinics to keep them open during budget negotiations.

FINANCIALS: Sales and profits are in thousands of dollars—add 000 to get the full amount. 2008 Note: Financial information for 2008 was not available for all companies at press time.

2008 Sales: $15,366,589	2008 Profits: $95,003	**U.S. Stock Ticker:** HNT
2007 Sales: $14,108,271	2007 Profits: $193,697	**Int'l Ticker:** Int'l Exchange:
2006 Sales: $12,908,350	2006 Profits: $329,313	Employees: 9,396
2005 Sales: $11,940,533	2005 Profits: $229,785	Fiscal Year Ends: 12/31
2004 Sales: $11,646,393	2004 Profits: $42,604	Parent Company:

SALARIES/BENEFITS:

Pension Plan:	ESOP Stock Plan:	Profit Sharing:	Top Exec. Salary: $1,204,615	Bonus: $
Savings Plan: Y	Stock Purch. Plan:		Second Exec. Salary: $705,385	Bonus: $

OTHER THOUGHTS:

Apparent Women Officers or Directors: 5
Hot Spot for Advancement for Women/Minorities: Y

LOCATIONS: ("Y" = Yes)

West:	Southwest:	Midwest:	Southeast:	Northeast:	International:
Y	Y			Y	

Note: Financial information, benefits and other data can change quickly and may vary from those stated here.

HEALTHWAYS INC

www.americanhealthways.com

Industry Group Code: 524298 Ranks within this company's industry group: Sales: 1   Profits: 1

Management:		Sales/Marketing:		Liberal Arts:		Information Systems:		Professionals:		Tech./Scientific:	
Management Trainees:	Y	Marketing Pros.:	Y	Gen. Writing/Editing:	Y	Info. Management:	Y	Finance/Acct.:	Y	Engineers, Electrical:	
Experienced Mngmt.:	Y	Retail Sales:		Technical Writing:	Y	Software Dev.:	Y	Law:	Y	Engineers, Other:	
International Business:	Y	Commercial/Industrial:	Y	Graphic Arts/Photog.:	Y	Hardware Dev.:		HR/Other:	Y	Health/Lab:	Y
MBA Grads:	Y	Sales Trainees:		Music:		Consulting/Other:		Training:	Y	Scientists/Research:	
		Advertising Pros.:	Y	Broadcasting:				Health Care:	Y	Petroleum/Chemicals:	
				Other:				Consulting:		Math/Other:	

TYPES OF BUSINESS:

Disease Management Programs
Ambulatory Surgery Centers
Arthritis Care
Osteoporosis Care
Cardiac Disease Management Services
Respiratory Disease Management Services
Online Disease Management
Outsourced Diabetes Treatment Programs

BRANDS/DIVISIONS/AFFILIATES:

SilverSneakers
Cardiac Healthways
Respiratory Healthways
Diabetes Healthways
MyHealthways

CONTACTS: *Note: Officers with more than one job title may be intentionally listed here more than once.*

Ben R. Leedle, Jr., CEO
Stefen F. Brueckner, COO
Stefen F. Brueckner, Pres.
Mary A. Chaput, CFO/Exec. VP
Anne Wilkins, Chief Mktg. Officer/Exec. VP
Chris Cigarran, Sr. VP-Human Resources & Organization Dev.
James Pope, Chief Science Officer/Exec. VP
Anne Wilkins, Chief Strategy Officer
Robert E. Stone, Exec. VP
John Harris, Chief Wellness Officer/Sr. VP
Thomas G. Cigarran, Chmn.
Matthew E. Kelliher, Exec. VP-Int'l Bus.

Phone: 615-614-4929	Fax:
Toll-Free: 800-327-3822	
Address: 701 Cool Springs Blvd., Franklin, TN 37067 US	

GROWTH PLANS/SPECIAL FEATURES:

Healthways, Inc., formerly American Healthways, Inc., provides specialized, comprehensive care enhancement and disease management services to health plans, physicians and hospitals in all 50 states, Washington, D.C., Puerto Rico and Guam. Through its educational programs and life-coaching services, the firm helps customers understand and follow doctors' orders; become aware of and recognize early warning signs associated with a major health episode; and set achievable goals for themselves, such as to exercise more, lose weight, quit smoking or otherwise improve their current health status. The firm also offers specialized support for people with diabetes, coronary artery disease, heart failure, asthma, chronic obstructive pulmonary disease, end-stage renal disease, cancer, chronic kidney disease, acid-related stomach disorders, hepatitis C, inflammatory bowel disease, irritable bowel syndrome, lower-back pain, osteoarthritis, osteoporosis, urinary incontinence and high-risk population management. Healthways also features MyHealthways, a web-based application that allows physicians, patients and care coordinators to actively monitor a chronic disease, receive customized plans of action or identify at-risk individuals through predictive modeling technology. The SilverSneakers program is an exercise program designed specifically for senior citizens. In early 2009, the program was brought to 6,500 Curves (a gym for women) locations across the U.S.

Employees are offered medical, dental and vision insurance; short-and long-term disability coverage; life insurance; a flexible spending plan; a 401(k) plan; tuition reimbursement; and an employee assistance program.

FINANCIALS: Sales and profits are in thousands of dollars—add 000 to get the full amount. 2008 Note: Financial information for 2008 was not available for all companies at press time.

2008 Sales: $736,243	2008 Profits: $54,815	**U.S. Stock Ticker: HWAY**
2007 Sales: $615,586	2007 Profits: $45,121	**Int'l Ticker:** Int'l Exchange:
2006 Sales: $412,308	2006 Profits: $37,151	Employees: 3,500
2005 Sales: $312,504	2005 Profits: $33,084	Fiscal Year Ends: 8/31
2004 Sales: $245,410	2004 Profits: $26,058	Parent Company:

SALARIES/BENEFITS:

Pension Plan:	ESOP Stock Plan:	Profit Sharing:	Top Exec. Salary: $685,000	Bonus: $318,167
Savings Plan: Y	Stock Purch. Plan:		Second Exec. Salary: $404,400	Bonus: $92,243

OTHER THOUGHTS:

Apparent Women Officers or Directors: 4
Hot Spot for Advancement for Women/Minorities: Y

LOCATIONS: ("Y" = Yes)

West:	Southwest:	Midwest:	Southeast:	Northeast:	International:
Y	Y	Y	Y	Y	Y

Note: Financial information, benefits and other data can change quickly and may vary from those stated here.

HELMERICH & PAYNE INC

www.hpinc.com

Industry Group Code: 211111 Ranks within this company's industry group: Sales: 13   Profits: 9

Management:		Sales/Marketing:		Liberal Arts:		Information Systems:		Professionals:		Tech./Scientific:	
Management Trainees:	Y	Marketing Pros.:	Y	Gen. Writing/Editing:		Info. Management:	Y	Finance/Acct.:	Y	Engineers, Electrical:	Y
Experienced Mngmt.:	Y	Retail Sales:		Technical Writing:	Y	Software Dev.:		Law:	Y	Engineers, Other:	Y
International Business:	Y	Commercial/Industrial:	Y	Graphic Arts/Photog.:		Hardware Dev.:		HR/Other:	Y	Health/Lab:	
MBA Grads:	Y	Sales Trainees:		Music:		Consulting/Other:		Training:	Y	Scientists/Research:	
		Advertising Pros.:		Broadcasting:				Health Care:		Petroleum/Chemicals:	Y
				Other:				Consulting:		Math/Other:	

TYPES OF BUSINESS:

Oil & Gas Exploration & Production
Contract Drilling Services
Drilling Technology Development
Commercial Real Estate

BRANDS/DIVISIONS/AFFILIATES:

FlexRigs
FlexRig3
FlexRig4

CONTACTS: Note: Officers with more than one job title may be intentionally listed here more than once.

Hans Helmerich, CEO
Hans Helmerich, Pres.
Douglas E. Fears, CFO/Exec. VP
M. Alan Orr, Exec. VP-Eng. & Dev., Int'l Drilling Co.
Steven R. Mackey, General Counsel/Exec. VP/Corp. Sec.
W. H. Helmerich, III, Chmn.
John W. Lindsay, Exec. VP-US & Int'l Oper., Int'l Drilling Co.

Phone: 918-742-5531	Fax: 918-742-0237
Toll-Free:	
Address: 1437 S. Boulder Ave., Tulsa, OK 74119 US	

GROWTH PLANS/SPECIAL FEATURES:

Helmerich and Payne, Inc. (HP) operates both on and offshore rigs under contract with oil and gas companies. The firm offers clients drilling rigs, equipment, personnel and camps on a contract basis. These drilling rigs include a number of the newest generation of FlexRigs, which allow a greater depth and flexibility of between 8,000 to 18,000 feet, and provide greater operating efficiency. The company has completed design and manufacturing work on the FlexRig3 and FlexRig4, now available to U.S. and international drilling companies. Drilling rigs consist of engines, drawworks, a mast, pumps, blowout preventers, a drillstring and related equipment. HP has 185 land rigs available for work in the U.S., nine offshore platform rigs in the Gulf of Mexico and 26 international rigs. HP's contract drilling business is composed of three reportable business segments: U.S. land drilling, U.S. offshore platform drilling and international drilling. The firm's U.S. land drilling is conducted primarily in Oklahoma, California, Texas, Wyoming, Colorado, Louisiana, Mississippi, Alabama, Arkansas, Utah, New Mexico and North Dakota. The company's offshore platform operations are conducted in the Gulf of Mexico, California, Trinidad and Equatorial Guinea. It also operates land rigs in five international locations, including Venezuela, Ecuador, Colombia, Argentina, and Tunisia. In addition to its oil rig business, HP has real estate operations that are conducted within the metropolitan area of Tulsa, Oklahoma. Its major holdings include a shopping center containing roughly 441,000 leasable square feet, multi-tenant industrial warehouse properties containing 990 leasable square feet and 210 acres of undeveloped real estate.

Employees are offered medical, dental, vision and life insurance; long-term disability coverage; flexible spending accounts; and a 401(k).

FINANCIALS: Sales and profits are in thousands of dollars—add 000 to get the full amount. 2008 Note: Financial information for 2008 was not available for all companies at press time.

2008 Sales: $2,036,543	2008 Profits: $461,738	U.S. Stock Ticker: HP
2007 Sales: $1,629,658	2007 Profits: $449,261	Int'l Ticker: Int'l Exchange:
2006 Sales: $1,224,813	2006 Profits: $293,858	Employees: 6,198
2005 Sales: $800,726	2005 Profits: $127,606	Fiscal Year Ends: 9/30
2004 Sales: $589,056	2004 Profits: $4,359	Parent Company:

SALARIES/BENEFITS:

Pension Plan:	ESOP Stock Plan:	Profit Sharing:	Top Exec. Salary: $601,425	Bonus: $1,112,000
Savings Plan: Y	Stock Purch. Plan:		Second Exec. Salary: $370,453	Bonus: $546,500

OTHER THOUGHTS:

Apparent Women Officers or Directors: 1
Hot Spot for Advancement for Women/Minorities:

LOCATIONS: ("Y" = Yes)

West:	Southwest:	Midwest:	Southeast:	Northeast:	International:
Y	Y	Y	Y		Y

Note: Financial information, benefits and other data can change quickly and may vary from those stated here.

HENRY SCHEIN INC

www.henryschein.com

Industry Group Code: 423450 Ranks within this company's industry group: Sales: 3 Profits: 2

Management:		Sales/Marketing:		Liberal Arts:		Information Systems:		Professionals:		Tech./Scientific:	
Management Trainees:	Y	Marketing Pros.:	Y	Gen. Writing/Editing:	Y	Info. Management:	Y	Finance/Acct.:	Y	Engineers, Electrical:	
Experienced Mngmt.:	Y	Retail Sales:		Technical Writing:	Y	Software Dev.:	Y	Law:	Y	Engineers, Other:	
International Business:	Y	Commercial/Industrial:	Y	Graphic Arts/Photog.:	Y	Hardware Dev.:		HR/Other:	Y	Health/Lab:	
MBA Grads:	Y	Sales Trainees:	Y	Music:		Consulting/Other:		Training:	Y	Scientists/Research:	
		Advertising Pros.:	Y	Broadcasting:				Health Care:	Y	Petroleum/Chemicals:	
				Other:				Consulting:		Math/Other:	

TYPES OF BUSINESS:

Health Care Products Distribution
Dental Supplies Distribution
Veterinary Products Distribution
Electronic Catalogs

BRANDS/DIVISIONS/AFFILIATES:

AVImark
DENTRIX
Easy Dental
MicroMD
EXACT
Oasis
Ortho Organizers

CONTACTS: *Note: Officers with more than one job title may be intentionally listed here more than once.*

Stanley M. Bergman, CEO
James P. Breslawski, COO
James P. Breslawski, Pres.
Steven Paladino, CFO/Exec. VP
James A. Harding, CTO/Sr. VP
Michael Racioppi, Chief Merch. Officer/Sr. VP
Gerald A. Benjamin, Chief Admin. Officer/Exec. VP
Mark E. Mlotek, Exec. VP-Corp. Bus. Dev.
Susan Vassallo, VP-Corp. Comm.
Leonard A. David, Chief Compliance Officer/Corp. Sr. VP
Stanley Komaroff, Sr. Advisor
Stanley M. Bergman, Chmn.
Michael Zack, Pres., Int'l Group

Phone: 631-843-5500	Fax: 631-843-5658
Toll-Free:	
Address: 135 Duryea Rd., Melville, NY 11747 US	

GROWTH PLANS/SPECIAL FEATURES:

Henry Schein, Inc. distributes products and services to office-based healthcare practitioners in North America and Europe. The firm has over 575,000 customers in more than 200 countries, including dental practitioners and laboratories; physician practices; government institutions; and animal health clinics. The company operates in two segments: healthcare distribution and technology. The healthcare distribution segment aggregates the dental, medical (including animal health) and international operating segments. This segment distributes branded and generic pharmaceuticals; small equipment; laboratory products; large dental equipment; consumable products; infection-control products; vaccines; diagnostic tests; surgical products; and vitamins. The technology segment provides software, technology and other value-added services to healthcare practitioners, primarily in the U.S. and Canada. Value-added solutions include practice-management software systems for dental and medical practitioners and animal health clinics. The lead practice-management software solutions include Oasis, DENTRIX, EXACT and Easy Dental for dental practices; AVImark for veterinary clinics; and MicroMD for physician usage. The technology group also provides financial services and continuing education for practitioners. Henry Schein offers more than 190,000 branded and Henry Schein private-brand products. The firm currently distributes approximately 28 million pieces of direct marketing material through its electronic catalog and ordering system. Henry Schein's web site provides an array of value-added features including instant customer registration and improved customer service and supply procurement capabilities. In November 2008, the firm agreed to discontinue its wholesale ultrasound distribution operations. In January 2009, Henry Schein acquired DNA Anthos Impianti, Noviko and Medka, distributors to the European dental, veterinary and medical industries, respectfully. In March 2009, the company acquired orthodontic product manufacturer and distributor Ortho Organizers.

The company offers its employees medical, dental, vision, life, AD&D and disability insurance; flexible spending accounts; a 401(k); tuition assistance; a college savings plan; and on-site wellness programs.

FINANCIALS: Sales and profits are in thousands of dollars—add 000 to get the full amount. 2008 Note: Financial information for 2008 was not available for all companies at press time.

2008 Sales: $6,394,874	2008 Profits: $243,143	**U.S. Stock Ticker: HSIC**
2007 Sales: $5,920,190	2007 Profits: $215,173	Int'l Ticker: Int'l Exchange:
2006 Sales: $5,048,191	2006 Profits: $163,759	Employees: 12,500
2005 Sales: $4,635,929	2005 Profits: $139,759	Fiscal Year Ends: 12/31
2004 Sales: $3,898,485	2004 Profits: $114,274	Parent Company:

SALARIES/BENEFITS:

Pension Plan:	ESOP Stock Plan:	Profit Sharing:	Top Exec. Salary: $1,123,462	Bonus: $1,400,000
Savings Plan: Y	Stock Purch. Plan:		Second Exec. Salary: $585,141	Bonus: $444,813

OTHER THOUGHTS:

Apparent Women Officers or Directors: 2
Hot Spot for Advancement for Women/Minorities: Y

LOCATIONS: ("Y" = Yes)

West:	Southwest:	Midwest:	Southeast:	Northeast:	International:
Y	Y	Y	Y	Y	Y

HERTZ GLOBAL HOLDINGS INC

www.hertz.com

Industry Group Code: 5321 Ranks within this company's industry group: Sales: 2 Profits: 3

Management:		Sales/Marketing:		Liberal Arts:		Information Systems:		Professionals:		Tech./Scientific:	
Management Trainees:	Y	Marketing Pros.:	Y	Gen. Writing/Editing:	Y	Info. Management:	Y	Finance/Acct.:	Y	Engineers, Electrical:	
Experienced Mngmt.:	Y	Retail Sales:	Y	Technical Writing:		Software Dev.:	Y	Law:	Y	Engineers, Other:	
International Business:	Y	Commercial/Industrial:	Y	Graphic Arts/Photog.:	Y	Hardware Dev.:		HR/Other:	Y	Health/Lab:	
MBA Grads:	Y	Sales Trainees:	Y	Music:		Consulting/Other:		Training:	Y	Scientists/Research:	
		Advertising Pros.:	Y	Broadcasting:				Health Care:		Petroleum/Chemicals:	
				Other:	Y			Consulting:		Math/Other:	

TYPES OF BUSINESS:

Automobile Rental
Truck Rental
Claims Management
Heavy Equipment Rental
Used Automobile Sales
Leasing
Actuarial Services
Franchising

BRANDS/DIVISIONS/AFFILIATES:

Hertz Local Edition
Hertz Car Sales
Hertz Equipment Rental Corp.
Hertz Rent A Car
Hertz Leasing

CONTACTS: Note: Officers with more than one job title may be intentionally listed here more than once.

Mark Frissora, CEO
Elyse Douglas, CFO/Exec. VP
Michael P. Senackerib, Chief Mktg. Officer/Sr. VP
LeighAnne Baker, Sr. VP/Chief Human Resources Officer
Joseph F. Eckroth, CIO/Sr. VP
Jeffrey Zimmerman, General Counsel/Sr. VP/Sec.
Jatindar Kapur, Corp. Controller/Sr. VP-Finance
Joseph R. Nothwang, Exec. VP/Pres., Vehicle Renting & Leasing
Gerald A. Plescia, Exec. VP/Pres., Hertz Equipment Rental Corp.
Lois Boyd, Sr. VP-Process Improvement & Project Mgmt.
Robert J. Stuart, Sr. VP-Global Sales
Mark Frissora, Chmn.
Michael Taride, Exec. VP/Pres., Hertz Europe Ltd.
John A. Thomas, Exec. VP-Supply Chain Mgmt.

Phone: 201-307-2000	Fax: 201-307-2644
Toll-Free: 800-654-3131	
Address: 225 Brae Blvd., Park Ridge, NJ 07656-0713 US	

GROWTH PLANS/SPECIAL FEATURES:

Hertz Global Holdings, Inc. comprises a family of companies preceded by the name Hertz: Local Edition, which can be found at many airports, specializes in local rentals at affordable rates; Equipment Rental, which rents and sells heavy equipment and tools for construction and industrial applications; Car Sales, which sells one-year-old vehicles from Hertz' rental car fleet; Claim Management, which provides claim management services for liability exposures; Truck & Van Rental, which rents trucks and vans to facilitate customers' moves and large deliveries; and Lease, which offers leasing and fleet management services throughout its franchise network in Europe, the Middle East and Africa. Hertz is best known for its car rental activities, both in the U.S. market and internationally. Hertz and its independent licensees and associates accept reservations for car rentals at approximately 8,100 locations in approximately 145 countries. About 80% of the company's 2008 revenues came from car rentals, with equipment rentals making up most of the remaining portion. Approximately 65% of the revenues were derived from U.S. operations, with the remaining 35% coming from international sources. Within the U.S., the vast majority of 2008 business was conducted within airports, with about 78% of revenue coming from in-terminal locations. In 2008, the company introduced its Connect by Hertz services, which allows customers to rent cars by the hour in select locations. In January 2009, the company announced it will reduce its workforce by about 4,000 employees. In April 2009, the company acquired Advantage Rent A Car for about $33 million. Also in April 2009, the firm acquired the Spanish power generation company Rent One, which provides rental power generation and climate equipment.

FINANCIALS: Sales and profits are in thousands of dollars—add 000 to get the full amount. 2008 Note: Financial information for 2008 was not available for all companies at press time.

2008 Sales: $8,525,100	2008 Profits: $-1,206,700	U.S. Stock Ticker: HTZ
2007 Sales: $8,685,600	2007 Profits: $264,500	Int'l Ticker: Int'l Exchange:
2006 Sales: $8,058,400	2006 Profits: $115,900	Employees: 24,900
2005 Sales: $7,314,700	2005 Profits: $371,300	Fiscal Year Ends: 12/31
2004 Sales: $6,676,000	2004 Profits: $365,500	Parent Company:

SALARIES/BENEFITS:

Pension Plan: Y	ESOP Stock Plan:	Profit Sharing:	Top Exec. Salary: $1,094,712	Bonus: $600,925
Savings Plan: Y	Stock Purch. Plan:		Second Exec. Salary: $661,731	Bonus: $880,000

OTHER THOUGHTS:

Apparent Women Officers or Directors: 3
Hot Spot for Advancement for Women/Minorities: Y

LOCATIONS: ("Y" = Yes)

West:	Southwest:	Midwest:	Southeast:	Northeast:	International:
Y	Y	Y	Y	Y	Y

Note: Financial information, benefits and other data can change quickly and may vary from those stated here.

HESS CORPORATION

www.hess.com

Industry Group Code: 211111 **Ranks within this company's industry group:** Sales: 5   Profits: 5

Management:		Sales/Marketing:		Liberal Arts:		Information Systems:		Professionals:		Tech./Scientific:	
Management Trainees:	Y	Marketing Pros.:	Y	Gen. Writing/Editing:		Info. Management:	Y	Finance/Acct.:	Y	Engineers, Electrical:	Y
Experienced Mngmt.:	Y	Retail Sales:		Technical Writing:	Y	Software Dev.:	Y	Law:	Y	Engineers, Other:	Y
International Business:	Y	Commercial/Industrial:		Graphic Arts/Photog.:		Hardware Dev.:		HR/Other:	Y	Health/Lab:	
MBA Grads:	Y	Sales Trainees:		Music:		Consulting/Other:		Training:	Y	Scientists/Research:	
		Advertising Pros.:		Broadcasting:				Health Care:		Petroleum/Chemicals:	Y
				Other:				Consulting:		Math/Other:	

TYPES OF BUSINESS:

Oil & Gas Exploration & Production
Natural Gas
Refining
Energy Marketing

BRANDS/DIVISIONS/AFFILIATES:

CONTACTS: *Note: Officers with more than one job title may be intentionally listed here more than once.*

John B. Hess, CEO
John P. Reilly, CFO/Sr. VP
F. Borden Walker, Exec. VP/Pres., Mktg. & Refining
B. J. Bohling, Sr. VP-Human Resources
Jeffery L. Steinhorn, CIO/VP
Timothy B. Goodell, General Counsel/Sr. VP
Howard Paver, Sr. VP-Bus. Dev.
Jay R. Wilson, VP-Investor Rel.
John J. Scelfo, Sr. VP-Finance
Gregory P. Hill, Exec. VP/Pres., Worldwide Exploration & Prod.
John A. Gartman, Sr. VP-Energy Mktg.
Scott M. Heck, Sr. VP-Global Prod. & Tech.
Lori J. Ryerkerk, Sr. VP-Terminals & Refining
John B. Hess, Chmn.
Lawrence H. Ornstein, Sr. VP-Supply

Phone: 212-997-8500	Fax: 212-536-8590
Toll-Free:	
Address: 1185 Ave. of the Americas, New York, NY 10036 US	

GROWTH PLANS/SPECIAL FEATURES:

Hess Corporation is a globally integrated energy company that operates in two segments: exploration and production; and marketing and refining. The exploration and production segment explores for, develops, produces, purchases, transports and sells crude oil and natural gas. These exploration and production activities take place in the U.S., the U.K., Norway, Denmark, Equatorial Guinea, Algeria, Malaysia, Thailand, Russia, Gabon, Azerbaijan, Indonesia, Libya, Egypt and other countries. The manufacturing and refining segment manufactures, purchases, transports, trades and markets refined petroleum products, natural gas and electricity. The company also owns 50% of a refinery joint venture with Petroleos de Venezuela in the U.S. Virgin Islands. Other assets of the company include an additional refining facility, as well as various terminals and retail gasoline stations, most of which include convenience stores, located on the east coast of the U.S. In 2008, the company had 970 million barrels of proven reserves of crude oil and natural gas liquids and over 2,700 billions of thousands of cubic feet of natural gas. The company markets refined petroleum products in the U.S. to the motoring public; wholesale distributors; industrial and commercial users; other petroleum companies; governmental agencies; and public utilities. The firm operates approximately 1,366 HESS retail facilities from Massachusetts to Florida. In 2008, 19% of the company's total proved reserves were located in the U.S.; 31% were located in Europe; 23% were in Africa; and 27% were in Asia and other regions. In 2008, the company began developing fields in the Gulf of Mexico, Malaysia and Thailand; exploration efforts also went into effect in areas including the Gulf of Mexico, Australia, Libya and Egypt.

FINANCIALS: Sales and profits are in thousands of dollars—add 000 to get the full amount. 2008 Note: Financial information for 2008 was not available for all companies at press time.

2008 Sales: $41,165,000	2008 Profits: $2,360,000	U.S. Stock Ticker: HES
2007 Sales: $31,647,000	2007 Profits: $1,832,000	Int'l Ticker: Int'l Exchange:
2006 Sales: $28,067,000	2006 Profits: $1,916,000	Employees: 13,500
2005 Sales: $22,747,000	2005 Profits: $1,242,000	Fiscal Year Ends: 12/31
2004 Sales: $16,733,000	2004 Profits: $977,000	Parent Company:

SALARIES/BENEFITS:

Pension Plan:	ESOP Stock Plan:	Profit Sharing:	Top Exec. Salary: $1,500,000	Bonus: $3,500,000
Savings Plan:	Stock Purch. Plan:		Second Exec. Salary: $1,350,000	Bonus: $2,350,000

OTHER THOUGHTS:

Apparent Women Officers or Directors: 3
Hot Spot for Advancement for Women/Minorities: Y

LOCATIONS: ("Y" = Yes)

West:	Southwest:	Midwest:	Southeast:	Northeast:	International:
Y	Y	Y	Y	Y	Y

HEWITT ASSOCIATES

www.hewitt.com

Industry Group Code: 541612 Ranks within this company's industry group: Sales: 2 Profits: 1

Management:		Sales/Marketing:		Liberal Arts:		Information Systems:		Professionals:		Tech./Scientific:	
Management Trainees:	Y	Marketing Pros.:	Y	Gen. Writing/Editing:	Y	Info. Management:	Y	Finance/Acct.:	Y	Engineers, Electrical:	
Experienced Mngmt.:	Y	Retail Sales:		Technical Writing:	Y	Software Dev.:	Y	Law:	Y	Engineers, Other:	
International Business:	Y	Commercial/Industrial:	Y	Graphic Arts/Photog.:	Y	Hardware Dev.:		HR/Other:	Y	Health/Lab:	
MBA Grads:	Y	Sales Trainees:		Music:		Consulting/Other:	Y	Training:	Y	Scientists/Research:	
		Advertising Pros.:	Y	Broadcasting:				Health Care:		Petroleum/Chemicals:	
				Other:	Y			Consulting:	Y	Math/Other:	

TYPES OF BUSINESS:

Human Resources Consulting
Human Resources Outsourcing
Actuarial Services
Payroll & Benefits Consulting

BRANDS/DIVISIONS/AFFILIATES:

HeptaCon
RealLife HR
Global Risk Services
Vista Equity Partners
New Bridge Street Consultants
Csi-The Remuneration Specialists
LewisCo Group

CONTACTS: Note: Officers with more than one job title may be intentionally listed here more than once.

Russell Fradin, CEO
John Park, CFO
Tracy Keogh, Sr. VP-Human Resources
David Baruch, CIO
Vincent Coppola, Sr. VP-Tech. & Global Bus. Svcs.
Steven Kyono, General Counsel/Sr. VP/Corp. Sec.
Matthew Levin, Sr. VP-Corp. Dev. & Strategy
Kristi Savacool, Sr. VP-Benefits Outsourcing
Julie Gordon, Pres., Client & Market Leadership
Eric Fiedler, Pres., Consulting
Jay Rising, Pres., HR Outsourcing
Russell Fradin, Chmn.

Phone: 847-295-5000	Fax: 847-295-7634
Toll-Free:	
Address: 100 Half Day Rd., Lincolnshire, IL 60069-3342 US	

GROWTH PLANS/SPECIAL FEATURES:

Hewitt Associates, Inc. is a human resources benefits, outsourcing and consulting services provider with offices in 33 countries. The company operates in three segments: Benefits Outsourcing, Human Resource Business Process Outsourcing (HR BPO) and Consulting. The Benefits Outsourcing sector of Hewitt provides integrated, single-system administration with the flexibility of multiple access channels (call centers, interactive voice response and the Internet) for employees to execute transactions and manage benefit programs for both defined contribution, such as a 401(k), and defined benefit (pension) plans, as well as health and welfare programs. The company offers its outsourcing services primarily to large companies with complex benefit programs. In the HR BPO segment, the firm helps more than 300 client companies manage employee data, administer benefits, payroll and other human resources processes, and record and manage transactions across talent management, workforce management and core process management. In the Consulting segment, Hewitt helps more than 3,000 client companies create effective strategies and programs in human resources, retirement plans, compensation, health care, benefits and payroll through its three sectors: retirement and financial management consulting; health care consulting; and talent and organization consulting. Global Risk Services is a risk management organization for retirement plan sponsors. In March 2008, the company acquired New Bridge Street Consultants, a compensation consultancy in the U.K. In September of the same year, the firm acquired CSi, The Remuneration Specialists, a compensation consulting company based in Australia and LewisCo Group, a provider of integrated disability and leave and absence-management solutions.

Employees are offered medical, dental and vision insurance; health and dependent care flexible spending accounts; a retirement plan; profit sharing plans; a 401(k) plan; short-and long-term disability coverage; life and AD&D insurance; an associate assistance program; tuition reimbursement; group legal plans; entertainment and retail discounts; adoption assistance; overnight care for dependents and pets; and interest-free computer loans.

FINANCIALS: Sales and profits are in thousands of dollars—add 000 to get the full amount. 2008 Note: Financial information for 2008 was not available for all companies at press time.

2008 Sales: $3,227,648	2008 Profits: $188,142	U.S. Stock Ticker: HEW
2007 Sales: $2,990,326	2007 Profits: $-175,080	Int'l Ticker: Int'l Exchange:
2006 Sales: $2,857,161	2006 Profits: $-115,938	Employees: 23,000
2005 Sales: $2,889,650	2005 Profits: $134,732	Fiscal Year Ends: 9/30
2004 Sales: $2,257,400	2004 Profits: $122,844	Parent Company:

SALARIES/BENEFITS:

Pension Plan: Y	ESOP Stock Plan:	Profit Sharing: Y	Top Exec. Salary: $900,000	Bonus: $1,647,641
Savings Plan: Y	Stock Purch. Plan:		Second Exec. Salary: $520,000	Bonus: $642,260

OTHER THOUGHTS:

Apparent Women Officers or Directors: 7
Hot Spot for Advancement for Women/Minorities: Y

LOCATIONS: ("Y" = Yes)

West:	Southwest:	Midwest:	Southeast:	Northeast:	International:
Y	Y	Y	Y	Y	Y

Note: Financial information, benefits and other data can change quickly and may vary from those stated here.

HIBBETT SPORTS INC

www.hibbett.com

Industry Group Code: 451110 **Ranks within this company's industry group:** Sales: 5   Profits: 3

Management:		Sales/Marketing:		Liberal Arts:		Information Systems:		Professionals:		Tech./Scientific:	
Management Trainees:	Y	Marketing Pros.:	Y	Gen. Writing/Editing:	Y	Info. Management:	Y	Finance/Acct.:	Y	Engineers, Electrical:	
Experienced Mngmt.:	Y	Retail Sales:	Y	Technical Writing:		Software Dev.:	Y	Law:	Y	Engineers, Other:	
International Business:		Commercial/Industrial:		Graphic Arts/Photog.:	Y	Hardware Dev.:		HR/Other:	Y	Health/Lab:	
MBA Grads:	Y	Sales Trainees:	Y	Music:		Consulting/Other:		Training:	Y	Scientists/Research:	
		Advertising Pros.:	Y	Broadcasting:				Health Care:		Petroleum/Chemicals:	
				Other:				Consulting:		Math/Other:	

TYPES OF BUSINESS:

Sporting Goods Stores
Sports Apparel
Athletic Shoes
Training Equipment

BRANDS/DIVISIONS/AFFILIATES:

Hibbett Sports
Sports & Co.
Sports Additions
Hibbett Team Sales, Inc.

CONTACTS: *Note: Officers with more than one job title may be intentionally listed here more than once.*

Michael J. Newsome, CEO
Jeffry O. Rosenthal, COO
Jeffry O. Rosenthal, Pres.
Gary A. Smith, CFO/VP
David Benck, General Counsel/VP
Cathy E. Pryor, VP-Store Oper.
Jeff Gray, VP-Real Estate
Michael J. Newsome, Chmn.

Phone: 205-942-4292	Fax: 205-912-7290
Toll-Free:	
Address: 451 Industrial Ln., Birmingham, AL 35211 US	

GROWTH PLANS/SPECIAL FEATURES:

Hibbett Sports, Inc. is an operator of sporting goods stores in small to mid-sized markets predominantly in the Sunbelt, Mid-Atlantic and Midwest. Its stores offer a broad assortment of athletic equipment, footwear and apparel. The company's merchandise assortment features a broad selection of brand name merchandise emphasizing team sports complemented by localized apparel and accessories designed to appeal to a wide range of customers. The firm's primary retail format is Hibbett Sports, a 5,000 square foot store located in enclosed malls or in strip centers that are generally the center of commerce within an area and that are usually anchored by a Wal-Mart store. The Hibbett Sports stores strive to respond quickly to major sporting events of local interests. The Sports Additions stores are small, mall-based stores averaging 2,500 square feet with roughly 90% of merchandise consisting of athletic footwear and the remainder consisting of caps and a limited assortment of apparel. Sports Additions stores offer a broader assortment of athletic footwear, with a greater emphasis on fashion than the athletic footwear assortment offered by Hibbett Sports stores. The Sports & Co. superstores average 25,000 square feet and offer a broader assortment of athletic footwear, apparel and equipment than the Hibbett Sports stores. Hibbett Sports operates over 650 stores in 23 states. Subsidiary Hibbett Team Sales, Inc. supplies customized athletic apparel, equipment and footwear to school, athletic and youth programs primarily in Alabama. It sells its merchandise directly to educational institutions and youth associations.

Employees are offered medical and dental insurance; life insurance; short-and long-term disability coverage; a vision care plan; a stock purchase plan; a 401(k) plan; employee discounts; and a 529 college savings plan.

FINANCIALS: Sales and profits are in thousands of dollars—add 000 to get the full amount. 2008 Note: Financial information for 2008 was not available for all companies at press time.

2008 Sales: $520,720	2008 Profits: $30,329	**U.S. Stock Ticker: HIBB**
2007 Sales: $512,094	2007 Profits: $38,073	**Int'l Ticker:** Int'l Exchange:
2006 Sales: $440,269	2006 Profits: $33,624	Employees: 5,500
2005 Sales: $377,534	2005 Profits: $25,147	Fiscal Year Ends: 1/31
2004 Sales: $320,964	2004 Profits: $20,348	Parent Company:

SALARIES/BENEFITS:

Pension Plan:	ESOP Stock Plan:	Profit Sharing:	Top Exec. Salary: $465,000	Bonus: $12,730
Savings Plan: Y	Stock Purch. Plan: Y		Second Exec. Salary: $265,000	Bonus: $6,100

OTHER THOUGHTS:

Apparent Women Officers or Directors: 1
Hot Spot for Advancement for Women/Minorities:

LOCATIONS: ("Y" = Yes)

West:	Southwest:	Midwest:	Southeast:	Northeast:	International:
	Y	Y	Y	Y	

HILTON HOTELS CORP

www.hiltonworldwide.com

Industry Group Code: 721110 **Ranks within this company's industry group:** Sales: 2 Profits:

Management:		Sales/Marketing:		Liberal Arts:		Information Systems:		Professionals:		Tech./Scientific:	
Management Trainees:	Y	Marketing Pros.:	Y	Gen. Writing/Editing:	Y	Info. Management:	Y	Finance/Acct.:	Y	Engineers, Electrical:	
Experienced Mngmt.:	Y	Retail Sales:		Technical Writing:		Software Dev.:	Y	Law:	Y	Engineers, Other:	
International Business:	Y	Commercial/Industrial:	Y	Graphic Arts/Photog.:	Y	Hardware Dev.:		HR/Other:	Y	Health/Lab:	
MBA Grads:	Y	Sales Trainees:	Y	Music:		Consulting/Other:		Training:	Y	Scientists/Research:	
		Advertising Pros.:	Y	Broadcasting:				Health Care:		Petroleum/Chemicals:	
				Other:	Y			Consulting:		Math/Other:	

TYPES OF BUSINESS:

Hotels & Resorts
Timeshare Properties
Conference Centers
Franchising
Management Services
Online Reservations

BRANDS/DIVISIONS/AFFILIATES:

Blackstone Group LP
Hilton Group plc
Hampton Inn
Conrad Hotels and Resorts
Waldorf=Astoria Collection
Embassy Suits
Hilton Garden Vacations Company LLC
Hhonors

CONTACTS: *Note: Officers with more than one job title may be intentionally listed here more than once.*

Christopher J. Nassetta, CEO
Christopher J. Nassetta, Pres.
Robert M. La Forgia, CFO/Exec. VP
Kenneth Smith, Pres., Sales & Revenue Mgmt.
Molly McKenzie-Swarts, Exec. VP-Human Resources & Diversity
Tim Harvey, CIO/Exec. VP-Shared Svcs.
Molly McKenzie-Swarts, Exec. VP-Admin.
Rich Lucas, General Counsel/Exec. VP
Ian R. Carter, Pres., Global Oper.
Kevin Jacobs, Sr. VP-Corp. Strategy
Ellen Gonda, Sr. VP-Global Comm. & Public Rel.
Atish Shah, VP-Investor Rel.
Thomas L. Keltner, Exec. VP/CEO-Americas & Global Brands
Mark Wang, Pres., Hilton Grand Vacations
Steven Goldman, Pres., Global Department & Real Estate
Paul J. Brown, Pres., Global Brands & Svcs.
Ian R. Carter, Pres., Int'l Oper.

Phone: 310-278-4321	Fax: 310-205-7678
Toll-Free: 800-445-8667	
Address: 9336 Civic Center Dr., Beverly Hills, CA 90210 US	

GROWTH PLANS/SPECIAL FEATURES:

Hilton Hotels Corp. (HHC), founded in 1919, owns, manages and develops hotels, resorts and timeshare properties; and franchises lodging properties. HHC consists of nine hotel brands and more than 3,200 hotels in over 77 countries around the world. Its hotel brands include Hilton, Hilton Garden Inn, Doubletree, Embassy Suites, Homewood, Hampton Inn, Conrad Hotels and Resorts and The Waldorf=Astoria Collection. HHC owns the worldwide rights to develop and market Hilton and Conrad brands. Although the majority of the company's hotels are located within the U.S., the company also operates luxury lodgings in locations such as Thailand, Ireland, Singapore, Uruguay, Indonesia and Egypt. Hilton Worldwide Resorts offers approximately 50 self-contained resorts in the Middle East, Asia Pacific, Europe, the Americas, the Indian Ocean and the Caribbean. Through Hilton Garden Vacations Company, LLC, the firm also owns and manages approximately 33 vacation timeshare properties. HHonors, the firm's loyalty enrollment program for returning customers, has over 17 million members. The firm is investing in innovative technologies such as check-in kiosks to facilitate an easier and faster check-in process for its customers. HHC, in separate deals with three real estate groups, is developing over 55 properties in Russia, the U.K. and Central America, all planned to be completed by 2012. Over the next decade, the firm plans to open 300 new hotels in Asia, including properties in India and China.

Employees are offered medical, dental and vision coverage; flexible spending accounts; employee assistance programs; tuition reimbursements; discounted home and auto insurance options; credit union/banking options; and legal assistance.

FINANCIALS: Sales and profits are in thousands of dollars—add 000 to get the full amount. 2008 Note: Financial information for 2008 was not available for all companies at press time.

2008 Sales: $8,250,000	2008 Profits: $	**U.S. Stock Ticker:** Private
2007 Sales: $8,090,000	2007 Profits: $121,000	**Int'l Ticker:** Int'l Exchange:
2006 Sales: $7,438,000	2006 Profits: $572,000	Employees: 130,000
2005 Sales: $3,218,000	2005 Profits: $460,000	Fiscal Year Ends: 12/31
2004 Sales: $4,146,000	2004 Profits: $238,000	Parent Company: BLACKSTONE GROUP LP (THE)

SALARIES/BENEFITS:

Pension Plan:	ESOP Stock Plan:	Profit Sharing:	Top Exec. Salary: $	Bonus: $
Savings Plan: Y	Stock Purch. Plan:		Second Exec. Salary: $	Bonus: $

OTHER THOUGHTS:

Apparent Women Officers or Directors: 2
Hot Spot for Advancement for Women/Minorities: Y

LOCATIONS: ("Y" = Yes)

West:	Southwest:	Midwest:	Southeast:	Northeast:	International:
Y	Y	Y	Y	Y	Y

HOME DEPOT INC

www.homedepot.com

Industry Group Code: 444110   Ranks within this company's industry group: Sales: 1   Profits: 1

Management:		Sales/Marketing:		Liberal Arts:		Information Systems:		Professionals:		Tech./Scientific:	
Management Trainees:	Y	Marketing Pros.:	Y	Gen. Writing/Editing:	Y	Info. Management:	Y	Finance/Acct.:	Y	Engineers, Electrical:	
Experienced Mngmt.:	Y	Retail Sales:	Y	Technical Writing:		Software Dev.:	Y	Law:	Y	Engineers, Other:	
International Business:	Y	Commercial/Industrial:	Y	Graphic Arts/Photog.:	Y	Hardware Dev.:		HR/Other:	Y	Health/Lab:	
MBA Grads:	Y	Sales Trainees:	Y	Music:		Consulting/Other:		Training:	Y	Scientists/Research:	
		Advertising Pros.:	Y	Broadcasting:				Health Care:		Petroleum/Chemicals:	
				Other:	Y			Consulting:		Math/Other:	

TYPES OF BUSINESS:

Home Centers, Retail
Home Improvement Products
Building Materials
Lawn & Garden Products
Online & Catalog Sales
Tool & Truck Rental
Installation & Design Services

BRANDS/DIVISIONS/AFFILIATES:

THD Design Center
EXPO Design Centers
Yardbirds

CONTACTS: *Note: Officers with more than one job title may be intentionally listed here more than once.*

Francis S. Blake, CEO
Carol B. Tome, CFO
Frank Bifulco, Sr. VP/Chief Mktg. Officer
Timothy M. Crow, Exec. VP-Human Resources
Cara Kinzey, Sr. VP-IT
Craig A. Menear, Exec. VP-Merch.
Jack A. VanWoerkom, General Counsel/Exec. VP/Corp. Sec.
Mark Powers, Sr. VP-Oper.
Carol B. Tome, Exec. VP-Corp. Svcs.
Brad Shaw, Sr. VP-Corp Comm. & External Affairs
Dianne Dayhoff, Sr. VP-Investor Rel.
Ted Decker, Sr. VP-Retail Finance
Kelly Barrett, Sr. VP-Enterprise Program Mgmt.
Ricardo E. Saldivar, Pres., The Home Depot Mexico
Anne-Marie Campbell, Pres., Southern Div.
Marvin R. Ellison, Exec. VP-U.S. Stores
Francis S. Blake, Chmn.
Annette M. Verschuren, Pres., The Home Depot Canada & Asia
Mark Holifield, Sr. VP-Supply Chain

Phone: 770-433-8211	Fax: 770-384-2356
Toll-Free: 800-533-3199	
Address: 2455 Paces Ferry Rd., Atlanta, GA 30339 US	

GROWTH PLANS/SPECIAL FEATURES:

Home Depot, Inc. is one of the world's largest home improvement retailers. The company operates 2,233 Home Depot stores throughout the U.S., Canada, China, Puerto Rico, the Virgin Islands and Mexico. A typical store encompasses 105,000 square feet of enclosed space with a 24,000 square foot outdoor garden center; these locations usually stock between 35,000 and 45,000 items. These stores sell an assortment of building materials, plumbing materials, electrical materials, kitchen products, hardware, seasonal items, paint, flooring and wall coverings. Home Depot markets its products primarily to three types of customers: professional customers, such as remodelers, contractors, repairmen and small business owners; do-it-for-me shoppers, who are homeowners that personally purchase Home Depot products but hire third party individuals for installation and/or project completion; and do-it-yourself customers, who are homeowners that both shop for and personally install and/or utilize the firm's materials. In early 2009, the firm announced plans to close its five Yardbirds stores, two THD Design Center stores and 34 full-service interior design and home furnishing EXPO Design Centers. The nationwide real estate slowdown of 2007-2009 hurt Home Depot's business. In mid 2008, the firm canceled plans for about 50 new store openings, and announced that it was closing 15 underperforming stores. In 2009, sales per square foot of store space were averaging $300. Home Depot is focusing on improvements to existing stores rather than expansion.

The company offers its employees medical, dental, vision, life, AD&D and disability insurance; a 401(k) plan; a stock purchase plan; adoption, education and relocation assistance; flexible spending accounts; a legal services plan; auto and homeowners insurance; and veterinary coverage.

FINANCIALS: Sales and profits are in thousands of dollars—add 000 to get the full amount. 2008 Note: Financial information for 2008 was not available for all companies at press time.

2008 Sales: $77,349,000	2008 Profits: $4,395,000	U.S. Stock Ticker: HD
2007 Sales: $79,022,000	2007 Profits: $5,761,000	Int'l Ticker: Int'l Exchange:
2006 Sales: $77,019,000	2006 Profits: $5,838,000	Employees: 322,000
2005 Sales: $73,094,000	2005 Profits: $5,001,000	Fiscal Year Ends: 1/31
2004 Sales: $64,816,000	2004 Profits: $4,304,000	Parent Company:

SALARIES/BENEFITS:

Pension Plan:	ESOP Stock Plan:	Profit Sharing:	Top Exec. Salary: $1,013,461	Bonus: $
Savings Plan: Y	Stock Purch. Plan: Y		Second Exec. Salary: $901,923	Bonus: $666,346

OTHER THOUGHTS:

Apparent Women Officers or Directors: 6
Hot Spot for Advancement for Women/Minorities: Y

LOCATIONS: ("Y" = Yes)

West:	Southwest:	Midwest:	Southeast:	Northeast:	International:
Y	Y	Y	Y	Y	Y

HONEYWELL INTERNATIONAL INC

www.honeywell.com

Industry Group Code: 33641 Ranks within this company's industry group: Sales: 4   Profits: 3

Management:		Sales/Marketing:		Liberal Arts:		Information Systems:		Professionals:		Tech./Scientific:	
Management Trainees:	Y	Marketing Pros.:	Y	Gen. Writing/Editing:	Y	Info. Management:	Y	Finance/Acct.:	Y	Engineers, Electrical:	Y
Experienced Mngmt.:	Y	Retail Sales:		Technical Writing:	Y	Software Dev.:	Y	Law:	Y	Engineers, Other:	Y
International Business:	Y	Commercial/Industrial:	Y	Graphic Arts/Photog.:	Y	Hardware Dev.:	Y	HR/Other:	Y	Health/Lab:	
MBA Grads:	Y	Sales Trainees:		Music:		Consulting/Other:	Y	Training:	Y	Scientists/Research:	Y
		Advertising Pros.:	Y	Broadcasting:				Health Care:		Petroleum/Chemicals:	
				Other:				Consulting:		Math/Other:	Y

TYPES OF BUSINESS:

Aerospace & Defense Products
Automation & Control Systems
Turboprop Engines
Performance Polymers
Specialty Chemicals
Nuclear Services
Life Sciences
Nanotechnology & MEMS Research

BRANDS/DIVISIONS/AFFILIATES:

Honeywell Aerospace Solutions
Prestone
FRAM
Enraf Holdings B.V.
UOP LLC
Dimensions International
Metrologic Instruments Inc
Sentinel

CONTACTS: *Note: Officers with more than one job title may be intentionally listed here more than once.*

David M. Cote, CEO
David J. Anderson, CFO/Sr. VP
Mark James, Sr. VP-Human Resources
Larry E. Kittelberger, Sr. VP-Tech.
Peter M. Kreindler, General Counsel/Sr. VP
Larry E. Kittelberger, Sr. VP-Oper.
Rhonda Germany, VP-Strategy & Bus. Dev.
Mark James, Sr. VP-Comm.
Murray Grainger, VP-Investor Rel.
Rob Gillette, CEO/Pres., Aerospace
Andreas Kramvis, CEO/Pres., Specialty Materials
Roger Fradin, CEO/Pres., Automation & Control Solutions
Adriane M. Brown, CEO/Pres., Transportation Systems
David M. Cote, Chmn.

Phone: 973-455-2000	Fax: 973-455-4807
Toll-Free: 800-328-5111	
Address: 101 Columbia Rd., Morristown, NJ 07962 US	

GROWTH PLANS/SPECIAL FEATURES:

Honeywell International, Inc. is a leading producer of high-tech control systems, including turboprop engines for airplanes, specialty chemicals for heavy equipment, polymers for electronics, sensing and security technologies for buildings, homes and industry and process technology for refining and petrochemicals. The company is divided into four sectors: Aerospace solutions; automation and control solutions; specialty materials; transportation systems; and intellectual properties. The aerospace unit is associated with engines, electronic systems, integrated avionics systems and service solutions. It is Honeywell's largest segment, earning 35% of sales. The automation and control solutions division focuses on control products such as heating and air conditioning for homes and buildings, water controls and electronic systems for burners, broilers and furnaces, along with security and fire products and services. The specialty materials segment is involved in nylon products and services, fluorocarbons, specialty fibers, nuclear services and customized research chemicals for use in segments such as telecommunications, ballistic protection, pharmaceutical packaging and counterfeit avoidance. The transportation and power systems division includes charge air systems and thermal systems, as well as consumer car care products (under the Prestone, FRAM and Autolite brands). The firm is engaged in manufacturing, sales and research and development mainly in the U.S., Europe, Canada, Asia and Latin America. The Company recently acquired Maxon Corporation, an industrial combustion controls business. In February 2009, the company's Sentinel helicopter avionics system, which includes flight safety information, became available for use in the U.S.

Employees are offered medical, dental and life insurance; disability coverage; a pension plan; and a 401(k).

FINANCIALS: Sales and profits are in thousands of dollars—add 000 to get the full amount. 2008 Note: Financial information for 2008 was not available for all companies at press time.

2008 Sales: $36,556,000	2008 Profits: $2,792,000	**U.S. Stock Ticker:** HON	
2007 Sales: $34,589,000	2007 Profits: $2,444,000	**Int'l Ticker:** Int'l Exchange:	
2006 Sales: $31,367,000	2006 Profits: $2,083,000	Employees: 128,000	
2005 Sales: $27,652,000	2005 Profits: $1,638,000	Fiscal Year Ends: 12/31	
2004 Sales: $25,593,000	2004 Profits: $1,246,000	Parent Company:	

SALARIES/BENEFITS:

Pension Plan: Y	ESOP Stock Plan:	Profit Sharing:	Top Exec. Salary: $1,825,962	Bonus: $17,500,000
Savings Plan: Y	Stock Purch. Plan:		Second Exec. Salary: $1,075,962	Bonus: $4,650,000

OTHER THOUGHTS:

Apparent Women Officers or Directors: 3
Hot Spot for Advancement for Women/Minorities: Y

LOCATIONS: ("Y" = Yes)

West:	Southwest:	Midwest:	Southeast:	Northeast:	International:
Y	Y	Y	Y	Y	Y

HUMANA INC

www.humana.com

Industry Group Code: 524114　**Ranks within this company's industry group:** Sales: 4　Profits: 6

Management:		Sales/Marketing:		Liberal Arts:		Information Systems:		Professionals:		Tech./Scientific:	
Management Trainees:	Y	Marketing Pros.:	Y	Gen. Writing/Editing:	Y	Info. Management:	Y	Finance/Acct.:	Y	Engineers, Electrical:	
Experienced Mngmt.:	Y	Retail Sales:		Technical Writing:	Y	Software Dev.:	Y	Law:	Y	Engineers, Other:	
International Business:	Y	Commercial/Industrial:	Y	Graphic Arts/Photog.:	Y	Hardware Dev.:		HR/Other:	Y	Health/Lab:	
MBA Grads:	Y	Sales Trainees:		Music:		Consulting/Other:		Training:	Y	Scientists/Research:	
		Advertising Pros.:	Y	Broadcasting:				Health Care:	Y	Petroleum/Chemicals:	
				Other:	Y			Consulting:		Math/Other:	

TYPES OF BUSINESS:

Insurance-Medical & Health, HMOs & PPOs
Insurance-Dental
Employee Benefit Plans
Insurance-Group Life
Wellness Programs

BRANDS/DIVISIONS/AFFILIATES:

HumanaDental
HumanaOne
Humana Ventures
Humana Medicare
OSF HealthPlans, Inc.
Metcare Health Plans, Inc.
PHP Companies
Cariten Healthcare

CONTACTS: *Note: Officers with more than one job title may be intentionally listed here more than once.*

Michael B. McCallister, CEO
James E. Murray, COO/Sr. VP
Michael B. McCallister, Pres.
James H. Bloem, CFO/Sr. VP/Treas.
Raja Rajamannar, Chief Innovation & Mktg. Officer/Sr. VP
Bonnita C. Hathcock, Chief Human Resources Officer/Sr. VP
Bruce J. Goodman, Chief Svc. & Info. Officer/Sr. VP
Thomas J. Liston, Sr. VP-Senior Prod.
Christopher M. Todoroff, General Counsel/Sr. VP
Paul B. Kusserow, Chief Strategy Officer/Sr. VP
Steven E. McCulley, Controller/Principal Acct. Officer/VP
Heidi S. Margulis, Sr. VP-Gov't Rel.
David A. Jones, Jr., Chmn.

Phone: 502-580-1000	**Fax:** 502-580-3639
Toll-Free:	
Address: 500 W. Main St., Louisville, KY 40202 US	

GROWTH PLANS/SPECIAL FEATURES:

Humana, Inc. is a leading health benefits company in the U.S., serving approximately 11.6 million medical benefit plan members and 6.8 million specialty products members in the U.S. and Puerto Rico. It operates in two segments: Government and Commercial. The Government segment consists of beneficiaries of government benefit programs and includes three lines of business: Medicare, Military and Medicaid. The company offers at least one type of Medicare plan in all 50 states. Humana's commercial operations, which are offered to both employer groups and individuals, consist of medical and specialty services. HumanaDental covers 2.6 million customers, making it one of the largest dental carries in the U.S. HumanaOne offers insurance coverage to individuals. Humana Ventures is a capital investing branch of Humana. Finally, Humana Medicare offers plans for Medicare patients to help them with drug and medical coverage. The company also offers a wide variety of services to employers, such as workers' compensation, dental plans, group life plans and an administrative-services-only plan. Humana provides health benefits and related services to companies ranging from fewer than 10 to over 10,000 employees. Many of its products are offered through HMOs (health maintenance organizations), Private Fee-For-Service (PFFS) and preferred provider organizations (PPOs). In May 2008, Humana acquired UnitedHealth Group's Medicare Advantage business for approximately $185 million. In May 2008, the firm acquired OSF HealthPlans, Inc., a managed care company. In September 2008, the company acquired Metcare Health Plans, Inc., a healthcare organization in Florida, for approximately $14 million. In October 2008, Humana acquired PHP Companies (doing business as Cariten Healthcare), a health benefits company operating in the east Tennessee region.

Humana offers its employees tuition reimbursement; a work-life program; adoption assistance; flexible spending accounts; and medical, dental, life and disability insurance.

FINANCIALS: Sales and profits are in thousands of dollars—add 000 to get the full amount. 2008 Note: Financial information for 2008 was not available for all companies at press time.

2008 Sales: $28,946,372	2008 Profits: $647,154	**U.S. Stock Ticker: HUM**
2007 Sales: $25,289,989	2007 Profits: $833,684	**Int'l Ticker:**　Int'l Exchange:
2006 Sales: $21,416,537	2006 Profits: $487,423	Employees: 28,900
2005 Sales: $14,418,127	2005 Profits: $296,730	Fiscal Year Ends: 12/31
2004 Sales: $13,104,325	2004 Profits: $269,947	Parent Company:

SALARIES/BENEFITS:

Pension Plan: Y	ESOP Stock Plan:	Profit Sharing:	Top Exec. Salary: $1,017,308	Bonus: $
Savings Plan: Y	Stock Purch. Plan:		Second Exec. Salary: $663,846	Bonus: $

OTHER THOUGHTS:

Apparent Women Officers or Directors: 4
Hot Spot for Advancement for Women/Minorities: Y

LOCATIONS: ("Y" = Yes)

West:	Southwest:	Midwest:	Southeast:	Northeast:	International:
Y	Y	Y	Y	Y	Y

Note: Financial information, benefits and other data can change quickly and may vary from those stated here.

IAC/INTERACTIVECORP

www.iac.com

Industry Group Code: 519130 **Ranks within this company's industry group:** Sales: 4 Profits: 3

Management:		Sales/Marketing:		Liberal Arts:		Information Systems:		Professionals:		Tech./Scientific:	
Management Trainees:	Y	Marketing Pros.:	Y	Gen. Writing/Editing:	Y	Info. Management:	Y	Finance/Acct.:	Y	Engineers, Electrical:	Y
Experienced Mngmt.:	Y	Retail Sales:		Technical Writing:		Software Dev.:	Y	Law:	Y	Engineers, Other:	
International Business:	Y	Commercial/Industrial:	Y	Graphic Arts/Photog.:	Y	Hardware Dev.:		HR/Other:	Y	Health/Lab:	
MBA Grads:	Y	Sales Trainees:		Music:		Consulting/Other:		Training:	Y	Scientists/Research:	
		Advertising Pros.:	Y	Broadcasting:	Y			Health Care:		Petroleum/Chemicals:	
				Other:	Y			Consulting:		Math/Other:	

TYPES OF BUSINESS:

e-Commerce, Online Advertising & Search Engines
Online Personals & Dating Services
Online Entertainment & Shopping Directories
Service Provider Listings Online

BRANDS/DIVISIONS/AFFILIATES:

Ask.com
Citysearch
Evite
Shoebuy
Pronto
Meetic
Match.com
Excite.com

CONTACTS: *Note: Officers with more than one job title may be intentionally listed here more than once.*

Barry Diller, CEO
Thomas J. McInerney, CFO/Exec. VP
Jason Stewart, Chief Admin. Officer
Gregg Winiarski, General Counsel/Sr. VP
Shana Fisher, Sr. VP-Strategy, Mergers & Acquisitions
Stacy Simpson, VP-Corp. Comm.
Lisa Jaffa, Dir.-Investor Rel.
Joey Levin, Sr. VP-Finance, Mergers & Acquisitions
Victor Kaufman, Vice Chmn.
Joanne Hawkins, Deputy General Counsel/Sr. VP
Greg Blatt, Exec. VP
Greg Morrow, Sr. VP-Tax
Barry Diller, Chmn.
Jane Thompson, Managing Dir.-Int'l

Phone: 212-314-7300	Fax: 212-314-7309
Toll-Free:	
Address: 555 W. 18th St., New York, NY 10011 US	

GROWTH PLANS/SPECIAL FEATURES:

IAC/InterActiveCorp's operating businesses provide various products and services through four segments: Media & Advertising, Match, ServiceMagic and Emerging Businesses. The Media & Advertising segment consists primarily of the firm's search business, which includes Ask.com and other destination search web sites through which the firm provide search and related advertising services, and toolbars and applications through which the company promotes and distributes these services, Citysearch, a leading online local city guide, and Evite, an online social planning web site. The Match segment provides subscription-based online personals services in the U.S. and various international countries, primarily via its Match.com web site. ServiceMagic is a leading online marketplace that connects consumers, by way of various patented and patent-pending proprietary technologies, with home service professionals that are pre-screened and generally customer-rated. The Emerging Businesses segment currently consists of Shoebuy and Pronto. Shoebuy is an Internet retailer of footwear and related apparel and accessories and generally acts as an agent in connection with the purchase of merchandise through its various web sites, passing purchases made by customers through its various web sites on to the relevant vendors for fulfillment and shipping. Pronto owns and operates Pronto.com, a comparison search engine through which consumers can search and compare prices for a range of merchandise offered by online retailers. Additional operations in the Emerging Businesses segment include Gifts.com, Connected Ventures, InstantAction.com, VeryShortList.com, RushmoreDrive.com, Life123.com and The Daily Beast. The firm also operates the following portals: MyWay.com, which provides e-mail services, Excite.com, a portal that aggregates news, sports, weather and entertainment content and iWon.com, which offers a variety of casual games and sweepstakes. In February 2009, Match.com and Meetic, a leading European online dating company based in France, entered into an agreement for Meetic to acquire the European operations of Match.com in exchange for a 27% interest in Meetic and $6.38 million.

FINANCIALS: Sales and profits are in thousands of dollars—add 000 to get the full amount. 2008 Note: Financial information for 2008 was not available for all companies at press time.

2008 Sales: $1,445,100	2008 Profits: $-156,200	**U.S. Stock Ticker:** IACI
2007 Sales: $1,332,600	2007 Profits: $-144,069	**Int'l Ticker:** Int'l Exchange:
2006 Sales: $5,908,902	2006 Profits: $187,065	Employees: 3,220
2005 Sales: $5,024,635	2005 Profits: $869,683	Fiscal Year Ends: 12/31
2004 Sales: $3,911,050	2004 Profits: $151,808	Parent Company:

SALARIES/BENEFITS:

Pension Plan:	ESOP Stock Plan:	Profit Sharing:	Top Exec. Salary: $650,000	Bonus: $2,000,000
Savings Plan: Y	Stock Purch. Plan:		Second Exec. Salary: $650,000	Bonus: $2,000,000

OTHER THOUGHTS:

Apparent Women Officers or Directors: 8
Hot Spot for Advancement for Women/Minorities: Y

LOCATIONS: ("Y" = Yes)

West:	Southwest:	Midwest:	Southeast:	Northeast:	International:
Y	Y	Y	Y	Y	Y

Note: Financial information, benefits and other data can change quickly and may vary from those stated here.

IBM GLOBAL SERVICES

www.ibm.com/services

Industry Group Code: 541513 **Ranks within this company's industry group:** Sales: 2 Profits:

Management:		Sales/Marketing:		Liberal Arts:		Information Systems:		Professionals:		Tech./Scientific:	
Management Trainees:	Y	Marketing Pros.:	Y	Gen. Writing/Editing:	Y	Info. Management:	Y	Finance/Acct.:	Y	Engineers, Electrical:	Y
Experienced Mngmt.:	Y	Retail Sales:		Technical Writing:	Y	Software Dev.:	Y	Law:	Y	Engineers, Other:	Y
International Business:	Y	Commercial/Industrial:	Y	Graphic Arts/Photog.:	Y	Hardware Dev.:	Y	HR/Other:	Y	Health/Lab:	
MBA Grads:	Y	Sales Trainees:		Music:		Consulting/Other:	Y	Training:	Y	Scientists/Research:	
		Advertising Pros.:	Y	Broadcasting:				Health Care:		Petroleum/Chemicals:	
				Other:	Y			Consulting:	Y	Math/Other:	

TYPES OF BUSINESS:

Computer Services & Consulting
IT Services
Computer Operations Outsourcing
Customer Relationship Management
Supply Chain Management
Financial Management
Human Capital Management

BRANDS/DIVISIONS/AFFILIATES:

International Business Machines Corp (IBM)
Global Technology Services
Global Business Services
IMB Daksh Business Process Services PVT Ltd

CONTACTS: *Note: Officers with more than one job title may be intentionally listed here more than once.*

Michael E. Daniels, Sr. VP-Global Tech. Svcs.
Virginia M. Rometty, Sr. VP-Enterprise Bus. Services
Robert W. Moffat, Jr., Sr. VP-Integrated Solutions
Bridget van Kralingen, Managing Partner-Global Bus. Services., NE Europe
Jim Bramante, Managing Partner-Global Bus. Services, Americas
Andrew Stevens, Managing Partner-Global Bus. Svcs., Asia Pacific

Phone: 914-499-1900	Fax: 914-765-7382
Toll-Free: 800-426-4968	
Address: New Orchard Rd., Armonk, NY 10504 US	

GROWTH PLANS/SPECIAL FEATURES:

IBM Global Services, a business segment of IBM Corp., provides consulting services to businesses of all sizes. The subsidiary as it operates today, which generates over half of parent company IBM's revenue, is largely the result of IBM's 2002 acquisition of PwC Consulting from Pricewaterhouse Coopers. The subsidiary operates in two segments: Global Technology Services (GTS) and Global Business Services (GBS). GTS offers strategic outsourcing services, business transformation outsourcing, integrated technology services and maintenance. GBS offers consulting and systems integration and application management services. In a nutshell, IBM Global Services provides clients with strategies on building e-commerce and supply chain management systems, as well as enterprise resource planning, and can then implement and manage those systems. Clients benefit from the company's long history of cutting-edge technology and continuing commitment to research and development. Information technology (IT) services offered include: business continuity and resiliency services; IT strategy and architecture services, integrated communications services, outsourcing, end user and middleware services; server, cabling and site facilities services; and storage and data storage services. While IBM Global Services tends to use IBM software and hardware, it often implements the products of other suppliers, such as Oracle, SAP and Siebel Systems. In November 2008, the firm announced its new program of bundled services, resilient cloud validation services, which utilizes cloud computing, or software as a service, and incorporates the internet to provide a resilient and uninterrupted flow of data and information for clients. These cloud-related validation services are offered in three segments: industry-specific business consulting services; technology consulting, design and implementation services; and cloud security. IBM plans to build a data center in North Carolina in order to deliver its cloud computing technologies to its clients. In addition, during 2008 the firm opened two new global delivery centers in Pune and Noida, India.

FINANCIALS: Sales and profits are in thousands of dollars—add 000 to get the full amount. 2008 Note: Financial information for 2008 was not available for all companies at press time.

2008 Sales: $58,892,000	2008 Profits: $	**U.S. Stock Ticker: Subsidiary**	
2007 Sales: $54,100,000	2007 Profits: $	**Int'l Ticker:** Int'l Exchange:	
2006 Sales: $48,300,000	2006 Profits: $	Employees: 210,000	
2005 Sales: $47,357,000	2005 Profits: $	Fiscal Year Ends: 12/31	
2004 Sales: $46,213,000	2004 Profits: $	Parent Company: INTERNATIONAL BUSINESS MACHINES CORP (IBM)	

SALARIES/BENEFITS:

Pension Plan:	ESOP Stock Plan:	Profit Sharing:	Top Exec. Salary: $	Bonus: $
Savings Plan: Y	Stock Purch. Plan: Y		Second Exec. Salary: $	Bonus: $

OTHER THOUGHTS:

Apparent Women Officers or Directors: 2
Hot Spot for Advancement for Women/Minorities: Y

LOCATIONS: ("Y" = Yes)

West:	Southwest:	Midwest:	Southeast:	Northeast:	International:
				Y	Y

ICT GROUP INC

www.ictgroup.com

Industry Group Code: 5418 Ranks within this company's industry group: Sales: 1   Profits: 1

Management:		Sales/Marketing:		Liberal Arts:		Information Systems:		Professionals:		Tech./Scientific:	
Management Trainees:	Y	Marketing Pros.:	Y	Gen. Writing/Editing:	Y	Info. Management:	Y	Finance/Acct.:	Y	Engineers, Electrical:	
Experienced Mngmt.:	Y	Retail Sales:		Technical Writing:		Software Dev.:	Y	Law:	Y	Engineers, Other:	
International Business:	Y	Commercial/Industrial:	Y	Graphic Arts/Photog.:	Y	Hardware Dev.:		HR/Other:	Y	Health/Lab:	
MBA Grads:	Y	Sales Trainees:		Music:		Consulting/Other:		Training:	Y	Scientists/Research:	
		Advertising Pros.:		Broadcasting:				Health Care:		Petroleum/Chemicals:	
				Other:				Consulting:	Y	Math/Other:	

TYPES OF BUSINESS:

Customer Relationship Management
Database Marketing
Sales Services
CRM Technologies
Financial Marketing Services
Outsourcing

BRANDS/DIVISIONS/AFFILIATES:

CONTACTS: *Note: Officers with more than one job title may be intentionally listed here more than once.*

John J. Brennan, CEO
Vincent A. Paccapaniccia, CFO/Exec. VP
John Duffy Cambell, Exec. VP-Global Sales
Gail M. Lebel, Sr. VP-Global Human Resources
Pamela Goyke, CIO/Sr. VP-Systems & Tech.
Timothy F. Kowalski, Pres./COO-Tech. Svcs.
Jeffrey C. Moore, Sr. VP/Corp. Sec.
Rachel M. Macha, Sr. VP-Planning
Timothy F. Kowalski, Pres./COO-Mktg.
John L. Magee, Pres./COO-North America
Janice A. Jones, Sr. VP-Corp. Svcs.
Rachel M. Macha, Sr. VP-Mktg.
John J. Brennan, Chmn.
Guy T. Gray, Pres./COO-Int'l

Phone: 267-685-5000	**Fax:** 267-685-5705
Toll-Free: 800-201-1085	
Address: 100 Brandywine Blvd., Newtown, PA 18940 US	

GROWTH PLANS/SPECIAL FEATURES:

ICT Group, Inc. is a global provider of outsourced customer management and business process outsourcing solutions. Its sales, service, marketing and technology solutions include customer care/retention; technical support and customer acquisition; cross-selling/upselling; as well as market research, database marketing, data capture/collection, e-mail management, collections and other back-office business processing services. The company also offers a suite of customer relationship management (CRM) technologies, which are available on a hosted basis for use by clients at their own in-house facilities, or on a co-sourced basis in conjunction with a fully integrated, web-enabled contact centers. These technologies include automatic call distribution voice processing; interactive voice response and advanced speech recognition; voice over Internet protocol (VoIP); contact management; automated e-mail management and processing, sales force and marketing automation; alert notification; and web self-help for the delivery of consistent quality customer care across multiple channels. The firm's services are provided through contact centers located across the globe. The technology assets may be located at a different physical location or country than the contact center. Accordingly, many of ICT's contact centers are not limited to performing only one service. Rather, they perform a variety of different services for a number of different customers/programs. The company's domestic sales force is organized by specific vertical industries, which enables the sales personnel to develop in-depth industry and product knowledge. Selected industries targeted include financial services and insurance; telecommunications; health care services; and technology and consumer electronics products and services. In January 2009, the firm announced plans to increase focus on customer care technology and BPO services while limiting the telesales activities and to cease performing market research services.

FINANCIALS: Sales and profits are in thousands of dollars—add 000 to get the full amount. 2008 Note: Financial information for 2008 was not available for all companies at press time.

2008 Sales: $428,177	2008 Profits: $-23,285	**U.S. Stock Ticker:** ICTG
2007 Sales: $453,621	2007 Profits: $-11,809	**Int'l Ticker:** Int'l Exchange:
2006 Sales: $447,912	2006 Profits: $16,811	Employees: 18,000
2005 Sales: $401,300	2005 Profits: $12,200	Fiscal Year Ends: 12/31
2004 Sales: $325,500	2004 Profits: $-2,700	Parent Company:

SALARIES/BENEFITS:

Pension Plan:	ESOP Stock Plan:	Profit Sharing: Y	Top Exec. Salary: $537,548	Bonus: $537,548
Savings Plan: Y	Stock Purch. Plan:		Second Exec. Salary: $365,246	Bonus: $273,935

OTHER THOUGHTS:

Apparent Women Officers or Directors: 4
Hot Spot for Advancement for Women/Minorities: Y

LOCATIONS: ("Y" = Yes)

West:	Southwest:	Midwest:	Southeast:	Northeast:	International:
Y	Y	Y	Y	Y	Y

Note: Financial information, benefits and other data can change quickly and may vary from those stated here.

IDEXX LABORATORIES INC

www.idexx.com

Industry Group Code: 325413 **Ranks within this company's industry group:** Sales: 1   Profits: 1

Management:		Sales/Marketing:		Liberal Arts:		Information Systems:		Professionals:		Tech./Scientific:	
Management Trainees:	Y	Marketing Pros.:	Y	Gen. Writing/Editing:		Info. Management:	Y	Finance/Acct.:	Y	Engineers, Electrical:	Y
Experienced Mngmt.:	Y	Retail Sales:		Technical Writing:	Y	Software Dev.:	Y	Law:	Y	Engineers, Other:	Y
International Business:	Y	Commercial/Industrial:	Y	Graphic Arts/Photog.:		Hardware Dev.:		HR/Other:	Y	Health/Lab:	Y
MBA Grads:	Y	Sales Trainees:		Music:		Consulting/Other:		Training:	Y	Scientists/Research:	Y
		Advertising Pros.:		Broadcasting:				Health Care:	Y	Petroleum/Chemicals:	
				Other:				Consulting:		Math/Other:	

TYPES OF BUSINESS:

Veterinary Laboratory Testing & Consulting
Point-of-Care Diagnostic Products
Veterinary Pharmaceuticals
Information Management Software
Food & Water Testing Products

BRANDS/DIVISIONS/AFFILIATES:

VetTest
VetLyte
VetStat
LaserCyte
SNAPshot DX
Coag Dx
Colisure
Parallux

CONTACTS: *Note: Officers with more than one job title may be intentionally listed here more than once.*

Jonathan W. Ayers, CEO
Jonathan W. Ayers, Pres.
Merilee Raines, CFO/VP
William C. Wallen, Chief Scientific Officer/Sr. VP
S. Sam Fratoni, VP-Computer Systems
William E. Brown, III, VP-Mfg. & Instrument R&D
Conan R. Deady, General Counsel/Sec./VP
Irene C. Kerr, VP-Worldwide Oper.
Merilee Raines, Treas.
James Polewaczyck, VP-Rapid Assay & Digital Radiography
Michael Williams, VP-Instrument Diagnostics
Thomas J. Dupree, VP-Companion Animal Group
Johnny D. Powers, VP-IDEXX Reference Laboratories
Jonathan W. Ayers, Chmn.
Ali Naqui, VP-Int'l

Phone: 207-556-0300	Fax: 207-556-4286
Toll-Free: 800-548-6733	
Address: 1 Idexx Dr., Westbrook, ME 04092-2041 US	

GROWTH PLANS/SPECIAL FEATURES:

IDEXX Laboratories, Inc. develops, manufactures and distributes products and provides services for the veterinary and the food and water testing markets. The company operates in two business segments: The Companion Animal Group, which provides products and services for the veterinary market, and the Production Animal Segment, which provides products for production animal health. The company also operated two smaller segments: Dairy, comprising products for dairy quality, and OPTI Medical, comprising products for the human medical diagnostic market. Its primary business focus is on animal health. IDEXX currently markets an integrated and flexible suite of in-house laboratory analyzers for use in veterinary practices, which is referred to as the VetLab suite of analyzers. The suite includes several instrument systems, as well as associated proprietary consumable products such as VetTest, VetLyte, VetStat, and LaserCyte analyzers, the IDEXX SNAPshot Dx and the Coag Dx Analyzer, among other offerings. In addition, it also provides assay kits, software and instrumentation for accurate assessment of infectious disease in production animals, such as cattle, swine and poultry. The company currently offers commercial veterinary laboratory and consulting services throughout the U.S. The water quality segment's products include Colilert-18 and Colisure tests, which simultaneously detect total coliforms and E. coli in water. IDEXX's two principal products for use in testing for antibiotic residue in milk are the SNAP Beta-lactam test and the Parallux system. In March 2009, IDEXX announced new Vector-Borne Disease Panels, its next-generation in infectious disease testing, which allow for more comprehensive diagnoses.

IDEXX offers its employee health, dental and life insurance; a 401(k) plan; short- and long-term disability programs; flexible spending accounts; an employee stock purchase plan; and employee assistance programs.

FINANCIALS: Sales and profits are in thousands of dollars—add 000 to get the full amount. 2008 Note: Financial information for 2008 was not available for all companies at press time.

2008 Sales: $1,024,030	2008 Profits: $116,169	**U.S. Stock Ticker: IDXX**
2007 Sales: $922,555	2007 Profits: $94,014	**Int'l Ticker:** Int'l Exchange:
2006 Sales: $739,117	2006 Profits: $93,678	Employees: 4,700
2005 Sales: $638,095	2005 Profits: $78,254	Fiscal Year Ends: 12/31
2004 Sales: $549,181	2004 Profits: $78,332	Parent Company:

SALARIES/BENEFITS:

Pension Plan:	ESOP Stock Plan:	Profit Sharing:	Top Exec. Salary: $700,000	Bonus: $675,000
Savings Plan: Y	Stock Purch. Plan: Y		Second Exec. Salary: $375,000	Bonus: $200,000

OTHER THOUGHTS:

Apparent Women Officers or Directors: 2
Hot Spot for Advancement for Women/Minorities: Y

LOCATIONS: ("Y" = Yes)

West:	Southwest:	Midwest:	Southeast:	Northeast:	International:
Y	Y	Y	Y	Y	Y

IGATE CORPORATION

www.igatecorp.com

Industry Group Code: 541513 **Ranks within this company's industry group:** Sales: 13 Profits: 10

Management:		Sales/Marketing:		Liberal Arts:		Information Systems:		Professionals:		Tech./Scientific:	
Management Trainees:	Y	Marketing Pros.:	Y	Gen. Writing/Editing:	Y	Info. Management:	Y	Finance/Acct.:	Y	Engineers, Electrical:	Y
Experienced Mngmt.:	Y	Retail Sales:		Technical Writing:	Y	Software Dev.:	Y	Law:	Y	Engineers, Other:	
International Business:	Y	Commercial/Industrial:	Y	Graphic Arts/Photog.:	Y	Hardware Dev.:	Y	HR/Other:	Y	Health/Lab:	
MBA Grads:	Y	Sales Trainees:		Music:		Consulting/Other:	Y	Training:	Y	Scientists/Research:	
		Advertising Pros.:		Broadcasting:				Health Care:		Petroleum/Chemicals:	
				Other:				Consulting:	Y	Math/Other:	

TYPES OF BUSINESS:

IT Consulting
Data Warehousing
Business Process Outsourcing
Web Integration Services
Software Design Services
Clinical Research

BRANDS/DIVISIONS/AFFILIATES:

iGATE Solutions
iGATE Professional Services
iGATE Global Solutions
iGATE Shared Services
iGATE Global Solutions Ltd.
iGATE Clinical Research International Private Ltd.
Clinical Research International, Inc.
Mastech Holdings, Inc.

CONTACTS: *Note: Officers with more than one job title may be intentionally listed here more than once.*

Phaneesh Murthy, CEO
Phaneesh Murthy, Pres.
Sujit Sircar, CFO
Hari Murthy, Head-Mktg. & Sales
Srinivas Kandula, VP-Human Resources
Amit Goyal, Head-Info. Systems
Mukund Srinath, Corp. Sec./Head-Legal
Salil Ravindran, Dir.-Investor Rel.
Sunil Wadhwani, Co-Chmn.
Elizabeth Koshy, Head-Quality
Ajit Nair, Pres., iGATE IMS Ltd.
Nina Babirad, Head- Insurance Practice
Ashok Trivedi, Co-Chmn.
Osamu Shiraishi, Country Mgr.-Japan

Phone: 412-787-2100	**Fax:** 412-494-9272
Toll-Free: 877-924-4283	
Address: 1000 Commerce Dr., Ste. 200, Pittsburgh, PA 15275 US	

GROWTH PLANS/SPECIAL FEATURES:

iGATE Corporation is a global integrated Technology and Operations (iTOPS) company. Together with its offshore subsidiary, iGATE Global Solutions, the company offers a combination of process investment strategies, technology leverage and business process outsourcing. The company operates in three business segments: iGATE Professional Services, iGATE Solutions and iGATE Shared Services. iGATE Professional Services offers various client-supervised/managed IT staffing services and is exclusively available in the U.S. The iGATE Solutions segment offers outsourcing of IT and BPO services using an onsite/offshore delivery model. IT services include software application development services and maintenance; implementation and support of enterprise application; and data management and integration. BPO services include call center services and transaction processing services, the latter of which are designed for mortgage banking, insurance and capital market industries. iGATE Shared Services consists of two segments: Clinical Research International, Inc. and iGATE Clinical Research International Private Ltd; this division offers Phase II - IV clinical trial support services. In January 2008, iGATE acquired all remaining shares of iGATE Global Solutions, Ltd., and delisted its stock on all Indian stock exchanges. In July 2008, the company sold its clinical business and consolidated iGATE Shared Services into the iGATE Solutions division; in September 2008, the firm divested its iGATE Professional Services segment and turned it into Mastech Holdings, Inc. As a result of these two divestitures, the company's operations are now limited to those of the iGATE Solutions sector, and are currently conducted solely through wholly-owned subsidiary iGATE Global Solutions Ltd. In October 2008, the company opened a new facility in Guadalajara, Mexico. In February 2009, the company partnered with Jaros Technologies Corporation to jointly offer services to Jaros Analytics for Oracle E-Business Suite customers. In March 2009, iGATE agreed to offer iTOPS services to the Japanese clients of CAC Corporation, an IT services firm.

FINANCIALS: Sales and profits are in thousands of dollars—add 000 to get the full amount. 2008 Note: Financial information for 2008 was not available for all companies at press time.

2008 Sales: $218,798	2008 Profits: $30,904	**U.S. Stock Ticker:** IGTE
2007 Sales: $201,734	2007 Profits: $15,585	**Int'l Ticker:** Int'l Exchange:
2006 Sales: $170,414	2006 Profits: $8,704	Employees: 6,658
2005 Sales: $275,992	2005 Profits: $6,969	Fiscal Year Ends: 12/31
2004 Sales: $264,585	2004 Profits: $-18,211	Parent Company:

SALARIES/BENEFITS:

Pension Plan:	ESOP Stock Plan:	Profit Sharing:	Top Exec. Salary: $500,000	Bonus: $347,000
Savings Plan:	Stock Purch. Plan:		Second Exec. Salary: $300,000	Bonus: $93,205

OTHER THOUGHTS:

Apparent Women Officers or Directors: 2
Hot Spot for Advancement for Women/Minorities: Y

LOCATIONS: ("Y" = Yes)

West:	Southwest:	Midwest:	Southeast:	Northeast:	International:
Y	Y	Y	Y	Y	Y

IMS HEALTH INC

www.imshealth.com

Industry Group Code: 541910　Ranks within this company's industry group: Sales: 1　Profits: 1

Management:		Sales/Marketing:		Liberal Arts:		Information Systems:		Professionals:		Tech./Scientific:	
Management Trainees:	Y	Marketing Pros.:	Y	Gen. Writing/Editing:	Y	Info. Management:	Y	Finance/Acct.:	Y	Engineers, Electrical:	Y
Experienced Mngmt.:	Y	Retail Sales:		Technical Writing:	Y	Software Dev.:	Y	Law:	Y	Engineers, Other:	
International Business:	Y	Commercial/Industrial:	Y	Graphic Arts/Photog.:	Y	Hardware Dev.:		HR/Other:	Y	Health/Lab:	Y
MBA Grads:	Y	Sales Trainees:		Music:		Consulting/Other:		Training:	Y	Scientists/Research:	
		Advertising Pros.:	Y	Broadcasting:				Health Care:	Y	Petroleum/Chemicals:	
				Other:	Y			Consulting:	Y	Math/Other:	

TYPES OF BUSINESS:

Market Research - Pharmaceuticals
Pharmaceutical Sales Tracking
Health Care Databases
Software-Sales Management & Market Research
Physician Profiling
Industry Audits
Prescription Tracking Reporting Services

BRANDS/DIVISIONS/AFFILIATES:

MIDAS
Market Research Publications
Pharmaceutical World Review
ValueMedics Research LLC
MIHS Holdings, Inc.
HIS
Health Services Research Network
RMBC

CONTACTS: *Note: Officers with more than one job title may be intentionally listed here more than once.*

David R. Carlucci, CEO
Giles V. J. Pajot, COO
Leslye G. Katz, CFO/Sr. VP
Karla L. Packer, Sr. VP-Human Resources
Robert H. Steinfeld, General Counsel/Sr. VP/Corp. Sec.
John R. Walsh, Sr. VP-Strategy & Bus. Dev.
Jeffrey J. Ford, Treas./VP
Murray L. Aitken, Sr. VP-Healthcare Insight
Tatsuyuki Saeki, Pres., Japan
Kevin Knightly, Sr. VP-Bus Line Mgmt.
William J. Nelligan, Pres., Americas
David R. Carlucci, Chmn.
Adel Al-Saleh, Pres., EMEA

Phone: 203-845-5200	Fax:
Toll-Free:	
Address: 901 Main Ave., Ste. 612, Norwalk, CT 06851-1187 US	

GROWTH PLANS/SPECIAL FEATURES:

IMS Health, Inc. is a leading global provider of market intelligence to the pharmaceutical and health care industries. IMS offers such products and services as portfolio optimization capabilities; launch and brand management solutions; sales force effectiveness innovations; managed markets and consumer health offerings; and consulting and services solutions that improve ROI and the delivery of quality healthcare worldwide. The company's information products use data secured from a worldwide network of suppliers in over 100 countries. The firm's sales force effectiveness products generated roughly 45% of its worldwide revenue in 2008 and include sales territory reporting services; prescription tracking reporting services; and sales and account management services. Portfolio optimization products generated roughly 28% of IMS's revenue, and include pharmaceutical, medical, hospital and prescription audits; MIDAS, its online multinational integrated data analysis tool used to assess global pharmaceutical information and trends; other portfolio optimization reports, including personal care reports, reports of bulk chemical shipments and Market Research Publications such as the Pharmaceutical World Review; and consulting and services. Launch, brand management and other offerings comprised roughly 27% of the company's 2007 revenue. Launch and brand management offerings combine information, analytical tools and consulting and services to address client needs relevant to the management of each stage of the lifecycle of their pharmaceutical brands. Additional products offered by IMS include information to quantify the effects of managed markets on the pharmaceutical and healthcare industries and product movement, market share and pricing information for over-the-counter, personal care, patient care and nutritional products. In April 2008, the company joined with 10 academic researchers in medicine, public health and health economics to establish the Health Services Research Network, a consortium that will address healthcare issues. In August of the same year, the firm acquired RMBC, a Russia-based provider of pharmaceutical market intelligence and analytics.

FINANCIALS: Sales and profits are in thousands of dollars—add 000 to get the full amount. 2008 Note: Financial information for 2008 was not available for all companies at press time.

2008 Sales: $2,329,528	2008 Profits: $311,250	**U.S. Stock Ticker: RX**
2007 Sales: $2,192,571	2007 Profits: $234,040	**Int'l Ticker:**　Int'l Exchange:
2006 Sales: $1,958,588	2006 Profits: $315,511	Employees: 7,500
2005 Sales: $1,754,791	2005 Profits: $284,091	Fiscal Year Ends: 12/31
2004 Sales: $1,569,045	2004 Profits: $285,422	Parent Company:

SALARIES/BENEFITS:

Pension Plan:	ESOP Stock Plan:	Profit Sharing:	Top Exec. Salary: $850,000	Bonus: $567,500
Savings Plan:	Stock Purch. Plan:		Second Exec. Salary: $725,000	Bonus: $364,400

OTHER THOUGHTS:

Apparent Women Officers or Directors: 4
Hot Spot for Advancement for Women/Minorities: Y

LOCATIONS: ("Y" = Yes)

West:	Southwest:	Midwest:	Southeast:	Northeast:	International:
Y				Y	Y

Note: Financial information, benefits and other data can change quickly and may vary from those stated here.

INFOGROUP INC

www.infogroup.com

Industry Group Code: 511140 **Ranks within this company's industry group:** Sales: 1 Profits: 1

Management:		Sales/Marketing:		Liberal Arts:		Information Systems:		Professionals:		Tech./Scientific:	
Management Trainees:	Y	Marketing Pros.:	Y	Gen. Writing/Editing:	Y	Info. Management:	Y	Finance/Acct.:	Y	Engineers, Electrical:	
Experienced Mngmt.:	Y	Retail Sales:		Technical Writing:		Software Dev.:	Y	Law:	Y	Engineers, Other:	
International Business:	Y	Commercial/Industrial:	Y	Graphic Arts/Photog.:	Y	Hardware Dev.:		HR/Other:	Y	Health/Lab:	
MBA Grads:	Y	Sales Trainees:	Y	Music:		Consulting/Other:		Training:	Y	Scientists/Research:	
		Advertising Pros.:	Y	Broadcasting:				Health Care:		Petroleum/Chemicals:	
				Other:				Consulting:		Math/Other:	

TYPES OF BUSINESS:

Online Directories
Sales Leads
Mailing Lists
Direct Marketing
Database Marketing
E-mail Marketing
Market Research Solution

BRANDS/DIVISIONS/AFFILIATES:

Yesmail.com Inc
OneSource Information Services Inc
Opinion Research Corp
Salesgenie.com
MarketZone
Walter Karl
Donnelley Marketing
InfoUSA, Inc.

CONTACTS: *Note: Officers with more than one job title may be intentionally listed here more than once.*

Bill L. Fairfield, CEO
Stormy Dean, CFO
Fred Vakili, Exec. VP-Admin./Chief Admin. Officer
John Longwell, General Counsel/Corp. Sec./Exec. VP-Bus. Conduct
Lisa Olson, Sr. VP-Corp. Rel.
Edward C. Mallin, Pres., Svcs. Group
Gerard Miodus, Pres., Opinion Research Corporation
Greg Mahnke, Pres., Macro International
Mark Israelsen, Pres., SalesGenie.com
Bernard W. Reznicek, Chmn.

Phone: 402-593-4500	Fax:
Toll-Free:	
Address: 5711 S. 86th Cir., Omaha, NE 68127 US	

GROWTH PLANS/SPECIAL FEATURES:

InfoGROUP, Inc., formerly InfoUSA, Inc., is a provider of sales leads, mailing lists, direct marketing, database marketing, e-mail marketing and market research solutions. It operates in three principal segments: data, services and market research. The data group maintains 12 proprietary databases of information relating to U.S. and international businesses and consumers. The division offers business databases, which contain information on nearly 16 million businesses in the U.S. and Canada; and consumer databases, which contain roughly 210 million individuals and 129 million households. Its flagship offerings are Salesgenie.com, a web-based subscription service that helps sales representatives and business owners find new prospective customers; MarketZone, a customer data solution combining lead-generation and database marketing functions with data storage, hygiene and updating; and OneSource, a web-based data service with information about the world's largest companies and their executives. The segment also licenses its data to customers in several industries, including directory assistance, GIS/mapping, navigation, local search, Internet directories, site location analysis, sales leads, marketing, demographic modeling and fraud prevention. The services group consists of subsidiaries providing customer data management and brokerage services; e-mail marketing services; and catalog marketing services. The services group is divided into several divisions: list brokerage and list management, which includes subsidiary Walter Karl; Donnelley Marketing, a provider of data processing services to the catalog direct marketing industry; Triplex, a provider of data processing services for high-profile political and non-profit organizations; and Yesmail, which specializes in providing e-mail solutions for a wide range of industries including retail, travel, entertainment, financial, healthcare and consumer packaged goods. The research group provides customer surveys, opinion polling and other market research services for business, through its Opinion Research division; and for government, through its Macro International division. In January 2008, the company acquired Direct Media, Inc., which subsequently became part of the firm's services group.

FINANCIALS: Sales and profits are in thousands of dollars—add 000 to get the full amount. 2008 Note: Financial information for 2008 was not available for all companies at press time.

2008 Sales: $738,270	2008 Profits: $4,360	**U.S. Stock Ticker:** IUSA
2007 Sales: $688,773	2007 Profits: $40,942	**Int'l Ticker:** Int'l Exchange:
2006 Sales: $434,876	2006 Profits: $33,300	Employees: 4,771
2005 Sales: $383,158	2005 Profits: $31,507	Fiscal Year Ends: 12/31
2004 Sales: $344,859	2004 Profits: $17,838	Parent Company:

SALARIES/BENEFITS:

Pension Plan:	ESOP Stock Plan:	Profit Sharing:	Top Exec. Salary: $694,349	Bonus: $150,000
Savings Plan: Y	Stock Purch. Plan:		Second Exec. Salary: $499,039	Bonus: $

OTHER THOUGHTS:

Apparent Women Officers or Directors: 1
Hot Spot for Advancement for Women/Minorities:

LOCATIONS: ("Y" = Yes)

West:	Southwest:	Midwest:	Southeast:	Northeast:	International:
		Y			Y

Note: Financial information, benefits and other data can change quickly and may vary from those stated here.

INGRAM MICRO INC

www.ingrammicro.com

Industry Group Code: 423430 Ranks within this company's industry group: Sales: 1   Profits: 3

Management:		Sales/Marketing:		Liberal Arts:		Information Systems:		Professionals:		Tech./Scientific:	
Management Trainees:	Y	Marketing Pros.:	Y	Gen. Writing/Editing:	Y	Info. Management:	Y	Finance/Acct.:	Y	Engineers, Electrical:	
Experienced Mngmt.:	Y	Retail Sales:		Technical Writing:	Y	Software Dev.:	Y	Law:	Y	Engineers, Other:	
International Business:	Y	Commercial/Industrial:	Y	Graphic Arts/Photog.:	Y	Hardware Dev.:		HR/Other:	Y	Health/Lab:	
MBA Grads:	Y	Sales Trainees:	Y	Music:		Consulting/Other:		Training:	Y	Scientists/Research:	
		Advertising Pros.:	Y	Broadcasting:				Health Care:		Petroleum/Chemicals:	
				Other:				Consulting:		Math/Other:	

TYPES OF BUSINESS:

Microcomputers, Distribution
Networking Equipment
Software & Accessories Distribution
Supply Chain Management Services
Online Marketing Services

BRANDS/DIVISIONS/AFFILIATES:

Micro Logistics
Ingram Micro Asia Pacific Pte Ltd
Ingram Micro Canada
InGram Micro UK Ltd
Cantechs Group
Eurequat SA
Intertrade A F AG

CONTACTS: *Note: Officers with more than one job title may be intentionally listed here more than once.*

Gregory M.E. Spierkel, CEO
Alain Monie, COO
Alain Monie, Pres.
William D. Humes, CFO/Exec. VP
Carol Kurimsky, Sr. VP-Mktg., North America
Lynn Jolliffe, Sr. VP-Human Resources
Karen Salem, CIO
Larry C. Boyd, General Counsel/Sr. VP/Sec.
Ria M. Carlson, Corp. VP-Strategy
Ria M. Carlson, Corp. VP-Comm.
Shailendra Gupta, Exec. VP/Pres., Ingram Micro Asia-Pacific
Keith W. F. Bradley, Exec. VP/Pres., Ingram Micro North America
Alain Maquet, Sr. VP/Pres., Ingram Micro Latin America
Dale R. Laurance, Chmn.
Jay A. Forbes, Exec. VP/Pres., EMEA

Phone: 714-566-1000	Fax: 714-566-7900
Toll-Free:	
Address: 1600 E. St. Andrew Pl., Santa Ana, CA 92799 US	

GROWTH PLANS/SPECIAL FEATURES:

Ingram Micro is a global distributor of technology products and supply chain management services. The company markets microcomputer hardware, networking equipment and software products to nearly 170,000 resellers in approximately 150 countries. Ingram provides a comprehensive inventory of hundreds of thousands of distinct items from nearly 1,400 suppliers. Networking products include routers, switches, hubs, wireless networks, networking cards, video conferencing, storage area networks and software products such as business application, operating system, entertainment and security software. Systems products include servers, desktops, laptop computers and personal digital assistants. Peripherals include printers, scanners, displays, projectors, monitors, mass storage and tape. In addition, the company offers components, such as processors, motherboards, hard drives and memory; supplies and accessories, including ink and toner supplies, paper, carrying cases and anti-glare screens; and consumer electronic products, such as cell phones, digital cameras, DVD players, game consoles and televisions. Ingram also offers supply chain management services such as sales and marketing, customer care, financial services and logistics to suppliers and resellers. Its Micro Logistics division provides end-to-end order management and fulfillment, retail logistics merchandizing, warehousing and storage, contract manufacturing, distribution center services, product procurement, reverse logistics, transportation management, marketing services and other outsourcing services. Through its web site, Ingram also offers online account management, a vast resource library and advanced marketing tools. Some of the company's supply chain management clients include CompUSA, Intuit, Iomega and Microsoft. In November of 2008, Ingram acquired French-based company, Eurequat SA and German-based Intertrade A.F. AG.

Employees are offered life insurance; disability coverage; flexible spending accounts; educational assistance; health club membership discounts; and onsite dry cleaning and auto detailing.

FINANCIALS: Sales and profits are in thousands of dollars—add 000 to get the full amount. 2008 Note: Financial information for 2008 was not available for all companies at press time.

2008 Sales: $34,362,152	2008 Profits: $-394,921	**U.S. Stock Ticker: IM**	
2007 Sales: $35,047,089	2007 Profits: $275,908	**Int'l Ticker:** Int'l Exchange:	
2006 Sales: $31,357,477	2006 Profits: $265,766	Employees: 14,500	
2005 Sales: $28,808,312	2005 Profits: $216,906	Fiscal Year Ends: 12/31	
2004 Sales: $25,462,071	2004 Profits: $219,901	Parent Company:	

SALARIES/BENEFITS:

Pension Plan:	ESOP Stock Plan:	Profit Sharing:	Top Exec. Salary: $850,000	Bonus: $
Savings Plan: Y	Stock Purch. Plan:		Second Exec. Salary: $542,160	Bonus: $411,857

OTHER THOUGHTS:

Apparent Women Officers or Directors: 7
Hot Spot for Advancement for Women/Minorities: Y

LOCATIONS: ("Y" = Yes)

West:	Southwest:	Midwest:	Southeast:	Northeast:	International:
Y	Y	Y	Y	Y	Y

Note: Financial information, benefits and other data can change quickly and may vary from those stated here.

INTEL CORP

www.intel.com

Industry Group Code: 33441 Ranks within this company's industry group: Sales: 1 Profits: 1

Management:		Sales/Marketing:		Liberal Arts:		Information Systems:		Professionals:		Tech./Scientific:	
Management Trainees:	Y	Marketing Pros.:	Y	Gen. Writing/Editing:	Y	Info. Management:	Y	Finance/Acct.:	Y	Engineers, Electrical:	Y
Experienced Mngmt.:	Y	Retail Sales:		Technical Writing:	Y	Software Dev.:	Y	Law:	Y	Engineers, Other:	
International Business:	Y	Commercial/Industrial:	Y	Graphic Arts/Photog.:	Y	Hardware Dev.:	Y	HR/Other:	Y	Health/Lab:	
MBA Grads:	Y	Sales Trainees:		Music:		Consulting/Other:	Y	Training:	Y	Scientists/Research:	Y
		Advertising Pros.:	Y	Broadcasting:				Health Care:		Petroleum/Chemicals:	
				Other:	Y			Consulting:		Math/Other:	Y

TYPES OF BUSINESS:

Microprocessors
Semiconductors
Circuit Boards
Flash Memory Products
Software Development
Home Network Equipment
Digital Imaging Products
Healthcare Products

BRANDS/DIVISIONS/AFFILIATES:

Pentium
Dual Core
Numonyx B.V.
SpectraWatt Inc
NetEffect Inc.
UQ Communications
Wind River Systems, Inc.
Intel Research Labs

CONTACTS: Note: Officers with more than one job title may be intentionally listed here more than once.

Paul S. Otellini, CEO
Paul S. Otellini, Pres.
Stacy J. Smith, CFO/VP
Sean M. Maloney, Chief Sales & Mktg. Officer/Exec. VP
Patricia Murray, Sr. VP/Dir.-Human Resources
Diane M. Bryant, CIO/VP
Justin R. Rattner, CTO/VP/Dir.-Intel Labs
Robert J. Baker, Sr. VP/Gen. Mgr.-Mfg. & Tech. Group
Andy D. Bryant, Chief Admin. Officer/Exec. VP
D. Bruce Sewell, General Counsel/Sr. VP
Andy D. Bryant, Exec. VP-Finance & Enterprise Svcs.
John N. Johnson, VP/CIO
Arvind Sodhani, Exec. VP/Pres., Intel Capital
William M. Holt, Sr. VP/Gen. Mgr.-Mfg. & Tech. Group
David Perlmutter, Exec. VP/Gen. Mgr.-Mobility Group
Jane E. Shaw, Chmn.
Brain M. Krzanich, VP/Gen. Mgr.-Supply Chain & Mfg.

Phone: 408-765-8080	Fax:
Toll-Free:	
Address: 2200 Mission College Blvd., Santa Clara, CA 95054-1549 US	

GROWTH PLANS/SPECIAL FEATURES:

Intel Corp. is a global semiconductor chip maker that develops advanced integrated digital technology platforms for the computing and communications industries. It operates in seven segments: Digital Enterprise, Mobility, NAND Solutions, Digital Home, Digital Health and Software and Services. The Digital Enterprise Group's products are incorporated into desktop computers, enterprise computing servers and workstations, embedded applications and other products that make up the infrastructure for the Internet. This division produced 55% of the firm's 2008 revenues. The Mobility Group's products, which make up 24% of the firm's revenue, include microprocessors and related chipsets designed for the notebook market, wireless connectivity products and energy-efficient products for the ultra-mobile PC market. The NAND Products Group produces memory products used in solid-state drives. Digital Home offers products for use in PCs and in-home consumer electronics devices. Digital Health offers technology products for healthcare providers and for use in personal healthcare. The Software and Solutions Group promotes Intel architecture as the platform of choice for software applications and operating systems. During 2008, the firm spun off its solar energy technology business into a new company, SpectraWatt, Inc.; sold its RFID business to Impinj, Inc.; divested its NOR flash memory assets in exchange for a 45.1% ownership interest in Numonyx B.V., a joint venture with STMicroelectronics; acquired NetEffect, Inc.; and launched a technology development lab in Egypt. In February 2009, the firm announced plans to invest $7 billion in advanced chip manufacturing facilities in the U.S. In June 2009, the company invested $43 million in Japan-based UQ Communications, a WiMAX mobile services provider. In July 2009, Intel acquired Wind River Systems, Inc., an embedded device software provider, for $884 million.

Employees are offered medical and dental coverage; an employee assistance program; flexible spending accounts; a stock purchase plan; a profit-sharing plan; a pension plan; and a 401(k) plan.

FINANCIALS: Sales and profits are in thousands of dollars—add 000 to get the full amount. 2008 Note: Financial information for 2008 was not available for all companies at press time.

2008 Sales: $37,586,000	2008 Profits: $5,292,000	**U.S. Stock Ticker: INTC**
2007 Sales: $38,334,000	2007 Profits: $6,976,000	**Int'l Ticker:** Int'l Exchange:
2006 Sales: $35,382,000	2006 Profits: $5,044,000	Employees: 83,900
2005 Sales: $38,826,000	2005 Profits: $8,664,000	Fiscal Year Ends: 12/31
2004 Sales: $34,209,000	2004 Profits: $7,516,000	Parent Company:

SALARIES/BENEFITS:

Pension Plan: Y	ESOP Stock Plan:	Profit Sharing: Y	Top Exec. Salary: $1,000,000	Bonus: $3,873,300
Savings Plan: Y	Stock Purch. Plan: Y		Second Exec. Salary: $500,000	Bonus: $1,311,000

OTHER THOUGHTS:

Apparent Women Officers or Directors: 9
Hot Spot for Advancement for Women/Minorities: Y

LOCATIONS: ("Y" = Yes)

West:	Southwest:	Midwest:	Southeast:	Northeast:	International:
Y	Y	Y	Y	Y	Y

Note: Financial information, benefits and other data can change quickly and may vary from those stated here.

INTERNATIONAL BUSINESS MACHINES CORP (IBM) www.ibm.com

Industry Group Code: 541513 Ranks within this company's industry group: Sales: 1 Profits: 1

Management:		Sales/Marketing:		Liberal Arts:		Information Systems:		Professionals:		Tech./Scientific:	
Management Trainees:		Marketing Pros.:	Y	Gen. Writing/Editing:	Y	Info. Management:	Y	Finance/Acct.:	Y	Engineers, Electrical:	Y
Experienced Mngmt.:	Y	Retail Sales:		Technical Writing:	Y	Software Dev.:	Y	Law:	Y	Engineers, Other:	Y
International Business:	Y	Commercial/Industrial:	Y	Graphic Arts/Photog.:	Y	Hardware Dev.:	Y	HR/Other:	Y	Health/Lab:	
MBA Grads:	Y	Sales Trainees:	Y	Music:		Consulting/Other:	Y	Training:	Y	Scientists/Research:	Y
		Advertising Pros.:	Y	Broadcasting:				Health Care:		Petroleum/Chemicals:	
				Other:	Y			Consulting:		Math/Other:	Y

TYPES OF BUSINESS:

Computer Hardware
Supercomputers
Microelectronic Technology
Software Development
Networking Systems
IT Consulting & Outsourcing
Financial Services

BRANDS/DIVISIONS/AFFILIATES:

Rational Software Corp
IBM Global Services
MRO Software Inc
IBM Research
IBM Canada Ltd
IBM India Pvt Ltd
Internet Security Systems Inc
ILOG S.A.

CONTACTS: Note: Officers with more than one job title may be intentionally listed here more than once.

Samuel J. Palmisano, CEO
Samuel J. Palmisano, Pres.
Mark Loughridge, CFO/Sr. VP
Jon C. Iwata, Sr. VP-Mktg.
J. Randall MacDonald, Sr. VP-Human Resources
John E. Kelly, III, Sr. VP/Dir.-IBM Research
Mark J. Hennessy, CIO/VP
Robert W. Moffat, Jr., Sr. VP-Systems & Tech. Group
Rodney C. Adkins, Sr. VP-Dev. & Mfg., IBM Systems & Tech. Group
Robert C. Weber, General Counsel/Sr. VP-Legal & Regulatory Affairs
Jon C. Iwata, Sr. VP-Comm.
Linda S. Sanford, Sr. VP-IT & Enterprise On Demand Transformation
Michael E. Daniels, Sr. VP-Global Tech. Svcs., IBM Global Svcs.
Steven A. Mills, Sr. VP/Group Exec.-IBM Software Group
R. Frankin Kern, Sr. VP-IBM Global Bus. Svcs.
Samuel J. Palmisano, Chmn.
Virginia M Rometty, Sr. VP-IBM Global Sales & Dist.

Phone: 914-499-1900	Fax: 800-314-1092
Toll-Free: 800-426-4968	
Address: 1 New Orchard Rd., Armonk, NY 10504-1722 US	

GROWTH PLANS/SPECIAL FEATURES:

International Business Machines Corporation (IBM) is a global producer of computer hardware and software, with one of the largest technology consulting businesses in the world. It operates in five primary segments: global technology services; global business services; software; systems and technology; and global financing. The global technology services segment primarily includes IT infrastructure services and business process services. The global business services segment primarily reflects professional services and application outsourcing services. Capabilities include consulting, systems integration and application management services. The software segment consists primarily of middleware and operating systems software. Middleware software enables clients to integrate systems, processes and applications across a standard software platform. Offerings include information management software; operating systems; and Tivoli software for infrastructure management, including security and storage management. The systems and technology division provides IBM's clients with business solutions built on advanced computing power and storage capabilities. Offerings include servers and infrastructure storage products; microelectronics for IBM systems and for sale to original equipment manufacturers (OEMs); and retail store solutions, such as network-connected cash registers to improve point-of-sale operations. The global financing division's capabilities include commercial financing, client financing and remarketing. IBM is active in over 170 countries worldwide, with major markets including the U.S., Canada, the U.K., France, Germany, Italy, Japan, Denmark, Sweden, Switzerland, Austria, Belgium, Finland, Greece, Ireland, the Netherlands, Portugal, Cyprus, Norway, Israel, Spain, the Bahamas and the Caribbean region. In May 2009, the company acquired Exeros, a producer of data discovery software. In July 2009, IBM agreed to acquire SPSS, Inc., an analytical software development firm, for approximately $1.2 billion.

The company offers its employees medical, dental and vision coverage including domestic partner benefits; an annual bonus program; life, disability and long-term care insurance; a 401(k) plan; and an employee stock purchase plan, among other benefits.

FINANCIALS: Sales and profits are in thousands of dollars—add 000 to get the full amount. 2008 Note: Financial information for 2008 was not available for all companies at press time.

2008 Sales: $103,600,000	2008 Profits: $12,300,000	U.S. Stock Ticker: IBM
2007 Sales: $98,786,000	2007 Profits: $10,418,000	Int'l Ticker: Int'l Exchange:
2006 Sales: $91,424,000	2006 Profits: $9,492,000	Employees: 395,000
2005 Sales: $91,134,000	2005 Profits: $7,934,000	Fiscal Year Ends: 12/31
2004 Sales: $96,503,000	2004 Profits: $8,430,000	Parent Company:

SALARIES/BENEFITS:

Pension Plan:	ESOP Stock Plan:	Profit Sharing:	Top Exec. Salary: $1,800,000	Bonus: $5,500,000
Savings Plan: Y	Stock Purch. Plan: Y		Second Exec. Salary: $707,500	Bonus: $1,322,500

OTHER THOUGHTS:

Apparent Women Officers or Directors: 6
Hot Spot for Advancement for Women/Minorities: Y

LOCATIONS: ("Y" = Yes)

West:	Southwest:	Midwest:	Southeast:	Northeast:	International:
Y	Y	Y	Y	Y	Y

Note: Financial information, benefits and other data can change quickly and may vary from those stated here.

INTUIT INC

www.intuit.com

Industry Group Code: 511210 **Ranks within this company's industry group:** Sales: 2 Profits: 1

Management:		Sales/Marketing:		Liberal Arts:		Information Systems:		Professionals:		Tech./Scientific:	
Management Trainees:	Y	Marketing Pros.:	Y	Gen. Writing/Editing:	Y	Info. Management:	Y	Finance/Acct.:	Y	Engineers, Electrical:	Y
Experienced Mngmt.:	Y	Retail Sales:		Technical Writing:	Y	Software Dev.:	Y	Law:	Y	Engineers, Other:	
International Business:	Y	Commercial/Industrial:	Y	Graphic Arts/Photog.:	Y	Hardware Dev.:		HR/Other:	Y	Health/Lab:	
MBA Grads:	Y	Sales Trainees:		Music:		Consulting/Other:		Training:	Y	Scientists/Research:	
		Advertising Pros.:	Y	Broadcasting:				Health Care:		Petroleum/Chemicals:	
				Other:				Consulting:		Math/Other:	

TYPES OF BUSINESS:

Computer Software-Financial Management
Business Accounting Software
Consumer Finance Software
Tax Preparation Software
Online Financial Services

BRANDS/DIVISIONS/AFFILIATES:

QuickBooks
QuickBooks Payroll
Innovative Merchant Services
Quicken
Quicken.com
Intuit Real Estate Solutions
TurboTax
PayCycle, Inc.

CONTACTS: *Note: Officers with more than one job title may be intentionally listed here more than once.*

Brad D. Smith, CEO
Brad D. Smith, Pres.
R. Neil Williams, CFO/Sr. VP
Caroline Donahue, VP-Sales
Laura A. Fennell, General Counsel/Sr. VP/Corp. Sec.
Alexander M. Lintner, Sr. VP-Strategy & Corp. Dev.
Jeffrey P. Hank, Controller/VP
Scott D. Cook, Chmn.-Exec. Committee
Kiran Patel, Exec. VP-Small Bus. Ecosystem Div.
Rick W. Jensen, Sr. VP/Gen. Mgr.-Small Bus. Group
Sasan Goodarzi, Sr. VP/Gen. Mgr.-Intuit Financial Institutions
Bill Campbell, Chmn.
Alexander M. Lintner, Pres., Global Bus. Div.

Phone: 650-944-6000	Fax: 650-944-3699
Toll-Free: 800-446-8848	
Address: 2632 Marine Way, Mountain View, CA 94043 US	

GROWTH PLANS/SPECIAL FEATURES:

Intuit, Inc. is a provider of software and web-based services. The firm specializes in providing financial management and tax solutions to consumers; small and medium-sized businesses; financial institutions; and accounting professionals. The company has five business segments: Small Business Ecosystem; Consumer Tax; Accounting Professionals; Financial Institutions; Other Businesses. The Small Business Ecosystem unit was formed in December 2008 when the firm combined its QuickBooks and Payroll/Payments divisions. QuickBooks products include QuickBooks Simple Start, which provides accounting functionality suitable for very small, less complex businesses; QuickBooks Pro, which provides accounting functionality suitable for slightly larger businesses, including those with payroll needs; QuickBooks Pro for Mac; QuickBooks Premier; and QuickBooks Enterprise Solutions. The company also offers QuickBooks Online Edition, suitable for multiple users working in various locations. Payroll and payments services are offered through QuickBooks Payroll, a family of products sold on a subscription basis to small businesses that prepare their own payroll, and the Innovative Merchant Services business, which provides credit card, debit card, electronic benefits, check guarantee and gift card processing services (as well as web-based transaction processing services for online merchants). The Consumer Tax and Accounting Professionals segments offer a variety of software and services for customers whose returns have varying levels of complexity, as well as for accountants and tax preparers in public practice who serve multiple clients. Digital Insight, the firm's Financial Institutions segment, primarily offers outsourced online banking applications and services for banks and credit unions. The Other Businesses segment includes the Quicken software, Quicken.com, Intuit Real Estate Solutions and its global business operations. Intuit's other popular brand names include TurboTax and Lacerte. In July 2009, Intuit acquired online payroll services provider PayCycle, Inc., for approximately $170 million.

FINANCIALS: Sales and profits are in thousands of dollars—add 000 to get the full amount. 2008 Note: Financial information for 2008 was not available for all companies at press time.

2008 Sales: $3,070,974	2008 Profits: $476,762	**U.S. Stock Ticker:** INTU
2007 Sales: $2,672,947	2007 Profits: $440,003	**Int'l Ticker:** Int'l Exchange:
2006 Sales: $2,293,010	2006 Profits: $416,963	Employees: 8,000
2005 Sales: $1,993,102	2005 Profits: $381,627	Fiscal Year Ends: 7/31
2004 Sales: $1,867,663	2004 Profits: $317,030	Parent Company:

SALARIES/BENEFITS:

Pension Plan:	ESOP Stock Plan:	Profit Sharing:	Top Exec. Salary: $761,539	Bonus: $1,700,000
Savings Plan: Y	Stock Purch. Plan: Y		Second Exec. Salary: $700,000	Bonus: $800,000

OTHER THOUGHTS:

Apparent Women Officers or Directors: 5
Hot Spot for Advancement for Women/Minorities: Y

LOCATIONS: ("Y" = Yes)

West:	Southwest:	Midwest:	Southeast:	Northeast:	International:
Y	Y	Y	Y	Y	Y

INVENTIV HEALTH INC

www.ventiv.com

Industry Group Code: 541613 Ranks within this company's industry group: Sales: 1　Profits: 1

Management:		Sales/Marketing:		Liberal Arts:		Information Systems:		Professionals:		Tech./Scientific:	
Management Trainees:	Y	Marketing Pros.:	Y	Gen. Writing/Editing:	Y	Info. Management:	Y	Finance/Acct.:	Y	Engineers, Electrical:	
Experienced Mngmt.:	Y	Retail Sales:		Technical Writing:	Y	Software Dev.:	Y	Law:	Y	Engineers, Other:	
International Business:	Y	Commercial/Industrial:	Y	Graphic Arts/Photog.:	Y	Hardware Dev.:		HR/Other:	Y	Health/Lab:	
MBA Grads:	Y	Sales Trainees:		Music:		Consulting/Other:	Y	Training:	Y	Scientists/Research:	
		Advertising Pros.:		Broadcasting:				Health Care:	Y	Petroleum/Chemicals:	
				Other:	Y			Consulting:	Y	Math/Other:	

TYPES OF BUSINESS:

Marketing-Life Sciences & Pharmaceuticals
Sales & Marketing Outsourcing
Clinical Staffing
Health Care Communications
Advertising Services
Data Services
Sales Force Deployment
Clinical & Statistical Research

BRANDS/DIVISIONS/AFFILIATES:

inVentiv Commercial Services
inVentiv Communications
inVentiv Clinical Services
inVentiv Patient Outcomes
Pharmaceutical Resource Solutions
GSW Worldwide
Stonefly
Gerbig Snell Weisheimer

CONTACTS: *Note: Officers with more than one job title may be intentionally listed here more than once.*

Blane Walter, CEO
Terrell Herring, COO
Terrell Herring, Pres.
David Bassin, CFO
Paul Mignon, inVentiv Commercial
William O'Donnell, COO/Pres., inVentiv Communications
Dan Rubin, Pres., inVentiv Patient Outcomes
Michael Hlinak, Pres., inVentiv Clinical
Eran Broshy, Chmn.

Phone: 732-748-4666	Fax: 732-537-4912
Toll-Free: 800-416-0555	
Address: 200 Cottontail Ln., Vantage Ct. N., Somerset, NJ 08873 US	

GROWTH PLANS/SPECIAL FEATURES:

inVentiv Health, Inc. is a clinical services and marketing services provider for the pharmaceutical and life sciences industry. inVentiv's services include sales and marketing; clinical staffing; planning and analytics; marketing support; professional development and training; and data collection and management. The company is structured into four business units: inVentiv Commercial, inVentiv Communications, inVentiv Clinical and inVentiv Patient Outcomes. inVentiv Commercial Services, formerly inVentiv Pharma Services, oversees most of the firm's services such as sales and marketing teams and recruitment of sales representatives in the commercial services area. Additional subsidiaries and acquisitions of this group include the Franklin Group, Pharmaceutical Resource Solutions and Promotech. inVentiv Communications provides advertising, business communications, branding, medical education and contract marketing services via subsidiaries GSW Worldwide, Palio, Navicor, Stonefly, Ignite, Chamberlain and Jeffrey Simbrow and Associates. inVentiv Clinical Services consists of subsidiaries Smith Hanley Associates, Smith Hanley Consulting Group and MedFocus (collectively Smith Hanley), HHI Clinical & Statistical Research Services and Anova Clinical Resources. This segment provides services related to recruitment, clinical staffing and data collection and management. inVentiv Patient Outcomes provides services related to patient adherence, assistance and reimbursement; clinical educator teams; and medical cost containment and disease management. The segment includes Adheris, Inc., The Franklin Group, The Therapeutics Institute and AWAC. inVentiv's clients include Sanofi-Aventis Group; Bayer Corporation; Bristol-Myers Squibb; and Watson Pharmaceuticals, Inc.

Employees are offered health and life insurance, as well as a 401(k) plan.

FINANCIALS: Sales and profits are in thousands of dollars—add 000 to get the full amount. 2008 Note: Financial information for 2008 was not available for all companies at press time.

2008 Sales: $1,119,812	2008 Profits: $-128,021	**U.S. Stock Ticker: VTIV**	
2007 Sales: $977,300	2007 Profits: $47,484	**Int'l Ticker:** Int'l Exchange:	
2006 Sales: $766,245	2006 Profits: $51,235	Employees: 7,100	
2005 Sales: $556,312	2005 Profits: $43,863	Fiscal Year Ends: 12/31	
2004 Sales: $352,184	2004 Profits: $31,132	Parent Company:	

SALARIES/BENEFITS:

Pension Plan:	ESOP Stock Plan:	Profit Sharing:	Top Exec. Salary: $528,846	Bonus: $362,187
Savings Plan: Y	Stock Purch. Plan:		Second Exec. Salary: $440,654	Bonus: $

OTHER THOUGHTS:

Apparent Women Officers or Directors:
Hot Spot for Advancement for Women/Minorities:

LOCATIONS: ("Y" = Yes)

West:	Southwest:	Midwest:	Southeast:	Northeast:	International:
Y	Y	Y	Y	Y	

J C PENNEY COMPANY INC

www.jcpenney.com

Industry Group Code: 452111 Ranks within this company's industry group: Sales: 2 Profits: 1

Management:		Sales/Marketing:		Liberal Arts:		Information Systems:		Professionals:		Tech./Scientific:	
Management Trainees:	Y	Marketing Pros.:	Y	Gen. Writing/Editing:	Y	Info. Management:	Y	Finance/Acct.:	Y	Engineers, Electrical:	
Experienced Mngmt.:	Y	Retail Sales:	Y	Technical Writing:		Software Dev.:	Y	Law:	Y	Engineers, Other:	
International Business:	Y	Commercial/Industrial:		Graphic Arts/Photog.:	Y	Hardware Dev.:		HR/Other:	Y	Health/Lab:	
MBA Grads:	Y	Sales Trainees:	Y	Music:		Consulting/Other:		Training:	Y	Scientists/Research:	
		Advertising Pros.:	Y	Broadcasting:				Health Care:		Petroleum/Chemicals:	
				Other:	Y			Consulting:		Math/Other:	

TYPES OF BUSINESS:

Department Stores
Online & Catalog Sales
Optometry
Photography Services
Salons
Custom Decorating

BRANDS/DIVISIONS/AFFILIATES:

jcpenney.com
JCPenney Optical Services
JCPenney Portraits
JCPenney Salon
JCPenney Custom Decorating
Original Arizona Jean Company (The)
Worthington
St. John's Bay

CONTACTS: *Note: Officers with more than one job title may be intentionally listed here more than once.*

Myron E. Ullman, III, CEO
Robert B. Cavanaugh, CFO/Exec. VP
Michael J. Boylson, Chief Mktg. Officer/Exec. VP
Michael T. Theilmann, Chief Human Resources Officer/Exec. VP
Thomas Nealon, CIO/Exec. VP
Peter M. McGrath, Exec. VP/Dir.-Prod. Dev. & Sourcing
Michael T. Theilmann, Chief Admin. Officer
Janet L. Dhillon, General Counsel/Exec. VP/Sec.
Clarence Kelley, Exec. VP-Planning & Allocation
Phil Sanchez, Investor Rel.
Thomas A. Clerkin, Sr. VP-Finance
Michael W. Taxter, Exec. VP-JC Penney Stores
Michael P. Dastuge, Sr. VP--Property Dev.
Elizabeth H. Sweney, Exec. VP-Women's Apparel
Steven Lawrence, Exec. VP-Men's Apparel
Myron E. Ullman, III, Chmn.
Marie Lacertosa, Sr. VP-Supply Chain

Phone: 972-431-1000	Fax: 972-431-9140
Toll-Free:	
Address: 6501 Legacy Dr., Plano, TX 75024 US	

GROWTH PLANS/SPECIAL FEATURES:

J.C. Penney Co., Inc. is a holding company for J.C. Penney Corp., Inc., a department store retailer. J.C. Penney provides merchandise and services through department stores, catalogs and the Internet. The company operates 1,106 JCPenney department stores throughout the U.S. and Puerto Rico. The firm's major products include family apparel, jewelry, shoes, accessories and home furnishings. The company operates the nation's largest general catalog businesses, as well as JCPenney.com, one of the largest apparel and home furnishings sites on the Internet. The JCPenney's entire product offering is available online. Local stores receive revenue credit for online and catalog sales made within their regions. Company brands include Every Day Matters, Worthington, St. John's Bay, The Original Arizona Jean Company, and Studio. The direct and retail segments of J.C. Penney's business are fully integrated, making pickups and returns at retail stores possible for direct sales. Other services offered by the company are JCPenney Optical services, JCPenney Portraits, JCPenney Salon and JCPenney Custom Decorating, all of which departments can be found within JCPenney department stores. Additionally, the firm sells beauty products through Sephora stores, housed inside 91 J.C. Penney locations. In July 2009, the company opened its first store in Manhattan.

Employees are offered medical, dental and vision insurance; life insurance; a 401(k) plan; and discounts at JCPenney stores.

FINANCIALS: Sales and profits are in thousands of dollars—add 000 to get the full amount. 2008 Note: Financial information for 2008 was not available for all companies at press time.

2008 Sales: $19,860,000	2008 Profits: $1,111,000	U.S. Stock Ticker: JCP
2007 Sales: $19,903,000	2007 Profits: $1,153,000	Int'l Ticker: Int'l Exchange:
2006 Sales: $18,781,000	2006 Profits: $1,088,000	Employees: 147,000
2005 Sales: $18,424,000	2005 Profits: $524,000	Fiscal Year Ends: 1/31
2004 Sales: $17,786,000	2004 Profits: $-928,000	Parent Company:

SALARIES/BENEFITS:

Pension Plan:	ESOP Stock Plan:	Profit Sharing:	Top Exec. Salary: $1,500,000	Bonus: $1,406,250
Savings Plan: Y	Stock Purch. Plan:		Second Exec. Salary: $885,000	Bonus: $675,000

OTHER THOUGHTS:

Apparent Women Officers or Directors: 6
Hot Spot for Advancement for Women/Minorities: Y

LOCATIONS: ("Y" = Yes)

West:	Southwest:	Midwest:	Southeast:	Northeast:	International:
Y	Y	Y	Y	Y	Y

JABIL CIRCUIT INC

www.jabil.com

Industry Group Code: 334419 Ranks within this company's industry group: Sales: 1   Profits: 1

Management:		Sales/Marketing:		Liberal Arts:		Information Systems:		Professionals:		Tech./Scientific:	
Management Trainees:	Y	Marketing Pros.:	Y	Gen. Writing/Editing:		Info. Management:	Y	Finance/Acct.:	Y	Engineers, Electrical:	Y
Experienced Mngmt.:	Y	Retail Sales:		Technical Writing:	Y	Software Dev.:	Y	Law:	Y	Engineers, Other:	
International Business:	Y	Commercial/Industrial:	Y	Graphic Arts/Photog.:	Y	Hardware Dev.:	Y	HR/Other:	Y	Health/Lab:	
MBA Grads:	Y	Sales Trainees:		Music:		Consulting/Other:		Training:	Y	Scientists/Research:	
		Advertising Pros.:	Y	Broadcasting:				Health Care:		Petroleum/Chemicals:	
				Other:				Consulting:		Math/Other:	

TYPES OF BUSINESS:

Electronic Manufacturing Services & Solutions
Maintenance & Support Services
Custom Design Services

BRANDS/DIVISIONS/AFFILIATES:

CONTACTS: *Note: Officers with more than one job title may be intentionally listed here more than once.*

Timothy L. Main, CEO
Mark T. Mondello, COO
Timothy L. Main, Pres.
Forbes I. J. Alexander, CFO
William E. Peters, Sr. VP-Human Dev.
David Couch, CIO
Robert L. Paver, General Counsel/Corp. Sec.
Donald J. Myers, VP-Corp. Dev.
Beth A. Walters, VP-Comm.
Beth A. Walters, VP-Investor Rel.
Sergio A. Cadavrid, Treas.
John P. Lovato, CEO/Exec. VP-Consumer Div.
William D. Muir, Jr., CEO/Exec. VP-EMS Div.
Meheryar Dastoor, Controller
William D. Morean, Chmn.

Phone: 727-577-9749	Fax: 727-579-8529
Toll-Free:	
Address: 10560 Dr. Martin Luther King Jr. St. N., St. Petersburg, FL 33716 US	

GROWTH PLANS/SPECIAL FEATURES:

Jabil Circuit, Inc., with operations in 22 countries, is a provider of worldwide electronic manufacturing services and solutions. It provides electronics and mechanical design, production, product management and after-market services to companies in the aerospace, automotive, computing, consumer, defense, industrial, instrumentation, medical, networking, peripherals, storage and telecommunications industry. The company's business units are capable of providing customers with varying combinations of the following services: Integrated design and engineering; component selection, sourcing and procurement; automate assembly; design and implementation of product testing; parallel global production; enclosure service; systems assembly, direct-order fulfillment and configure-to-order; and after-market services. The firm conducts its operations in facilities located in Austria, Belgium, Brazil, China, England, France, Germany, Hungary, India, Ireland, Italy, Japan, Malaysia, Mexico, the Netherlands, Poland, Scotland, Singapore, Taiwan, Ukraine, Vietnam and the U.S. The largest customers include Cisco Systems, Inc.; EMC Corp.; Hewlett-Packard Co.; International Business Machines Corp. (IBM); Network Appliance; NEC Corp.; Nokia Corp.; Royal Philips Electronics; Tellabs, Inc.; and Valeo S.A.

FINANCIALS: Sales and profits are in thousands of dollars—add 000 to get the full amount. 2008 Note: Financial information for 2008 was not available for all companies at press time.

2008 Sales: $12,779,703	2008 Profits: $133,892	U.S. Stock Ticker: JBL
2007 Sales: $12,290,592	2007 Profits: $73,236	Int'l Ticker: Int'l Exchange:
2006 Sales: $10,265,447	2006 Profits: $164,518	Employees: 61,000
2005 Sales: $7,524,386	2005 Profits: $203,875	Fiscal Year Ends: 8/31
2004 Sales: $6,252,897	2004 Profits: $166,900	Parent Company:

SALARIES/BENEFITS:

Pension Plan:	ESOP Stock Plan:	Profit Sharing:	Top Exec. Salary: $1,000,000	Bonus: $155,925
Savings Plan:	Stock Purch. Plan:		Second Exec. Salary: $675,000	Bonus: $77,963

OTHER THOUGHTS:

Apparent Women Officers or Directors: 2
Hot Spot for Advancement for Women/Minorities: Y

LOCATIONS: ("Y" = Yes)

West:	Southwest:	Midwest:	Southeast:	Northeast:	International:
Y		Y	Y	Y	Y

JACK IN THE BOX INC

www.jackinthebox.com

Industry Group Code: 722110 **Ranks within this company's industry group:** Sales: 6 Profits: 5

Management:		Sales/Marketing:		Liberal Arts:		Information Systems:		Professionals:		Tech./Scientific:	
Management Trainees:	Y	Marketing Pros.:		Gen. Writing/Editing:	Y	Info. Management:	Y	Finance/Acct.:	Y	Engineers, Electrical:	
Experienced Mngmt.:	Y	Retail Sales:		Technical Writing:		Software Dev.:	Y	Law:		Engineers, Other:	
International Business:		Commercial/Industrial:	Y	Graphic Arts/Photog.:	Y	Hardware Dev.:		HR/Other:	Y	Health/Lab:	
MBA Grads:	Y	Sales Trainees:		Music:		Consulting/Other:		Training:	Y	Scientists/Research:	
		Advertising Pros.:	Y	Broadcasting:				Health Care:		Petroleum/Chemicals:	
				Other:	Y			Consulting:		Math/Other:	

TYPES OF BUSINESS:

Fast Food Restaurants
Convenience Stores

BRANDS/DIVISIONS/AFFILIATES:

Jack in the Box
Qdoba Restaurant Corporation
Qdoba Mexican Grill
Jumbo Jack
Jack's Ultimate Salads
Quick Stuff
Breakfast Jack
Jack in the Box Foundation

CONTACTS: Note: Officers with more than one job title may be intentionally listed here more than once.

Linda A. Lang, CEO
Paul L. Schultz, COO
Paul L. Schultz, Pres.
Jerry P. Rebel, CFO/Exec. VP
Terri F. Graham, Chief Mktg. Officer/Sr. VP
Mark H. Blankenship, VP-Human Resources & Operational Svcs.
Derek Walker, Div. VP-R&D
Phillip H. Rudolph, General Counsel/Sr. VP/Corp. Sec.
Charles E. Watson, Chief Dev. Officer/Sr. VP
Carol A. DiRaimo, VP-Corp. Comm.
Carol A. DiRaimo, VP-Investor Rel.
Gary J. Beisler, CEO-Qdoba Restaurant Corp.
Ann Marie McNamara, Div. VP-Food Safety
Michael Bamrick, VP-Franchising
Linda A. Lang, Chmn.

Phone: 858-571-2121	Fax: 858-571-2101
Toll-Free: 800-955-5225	
Address: 9330 Balboa Ave., San Diego, CA 92123-1516 US	

GROWTH PLANS/SPECIAL FEATURES:

Jack in the Box, Inc. (JB) operates and franchises the Jack in the Box fast food chain and, through its wholly-owned subsidiary Qdoba Restaurant Corporation, which also operates Qdoba Mexican Grill. The Jack in the Box hamburger chain has over 2,158 locations in 18 states, primarily in the Western and Southern U.S. JB is known for being the first fast food chain to introduce drive-through services, breakfast sandwiches and portable salads. The Jack in the Box menu features a variety of hamburgers (Jumbo Jack, Sourdough Jack and Ultimate Cheeseburger), salads (Jack's Ultimate Salads), specialty sandwiches (Ciabatta sandwiches), drinks and side items. Qdoba Mexican Grill, which offers Mexican food in a casual dining atmosphere, has 454 locations in 41 states (111 company-operated and 343 franchised). Qdoba's menu features Mexican spices, fresh flavors and customizable menu creations which cater primarily to adult tastes. JB also operates approximately 61 proprietary convenience stores named Quick Stuff, which include fuel stations and are built adjacent to many Jack in the Box Restaurants. In 2008, the company opened new stores in Colorado Springs, Colorado; Odessa, Texas; and San Angelo, Texas. New menu items include the Homestyle Ranch Chicken Club, Breakfast Homestyle Chicken Biscuit, Pita Snacks and Breakfast Bowls. In October 2008, JB announced plans to sell Quick Stuff convenience stores.

Employees are offered medical, dental and vision insurance; life insurance; short-and long-term disability coverage; flexible spending accounts; company travel accident insurance; an employee assistance program; a 401(k) plan; retirement benefits; tuition reimbursement; and a discount meal card. JB operates the Jack in the Box Foundation, a nonprofit organization which partners primarily with Big Brothers Big Sisters.

FINANCIALS: Sales and profits are in thousands of dollars—add 000 to get the full amount. 2008 Note: Financial information for 2008 was not available for all companies at press time.

2008 Sales: $2,539,561	2008 Profits: $119,279	**U.S. Stock Ticker: JACK**
2007 Sales: $2,513,431	2007 Profits: $125,583	Int'l Ticker: Int'l Exchange:
2006 Sales: $2,381,244	2006 Profits: $107,067	Employees: 42,700
2005 Sales: $2,480,214	2005 Profits: $91,537	Fiscal Year Ends: 10/31
2004 Sales: $2,320,465	2004 Profits: $74,684	Parent Company:

SALARIES/BENEFITS:

Pension Plan: Y	ESOP Stock Plan:	Profit Sharing:	Top Exec. Salary: $849,519	Bonus: $802,729
Savings Plan: Y	Stock Purch. Plan:		Second Exec. Salary: $539,423	Bonus: $378,308

OTHER THOUGHTS:

Apparent Women Officers or Directors: 6
Hot Spot for Advancement for Women/Minorities: Y

LOCATIONS: ("Y" = Yes)

West:	Southwest:	Midwest:	Southeast:	Northeast:	International:
Y	Y	Y	Y	Y	

Note: Financial information, benefits and other data can change quickly and may vary from those stated here.

JACOBS ENGINEERING GROUP INC

www.jacobs.com

Industry Group Code: 237 Ranks within this company's industry group: Sales: 3 Profits: 3

Management:		Sales/Marketing:		Liberal Arts:		Information Systems:		Professionals:		Tech./Scientific:	
Management Trainees:	Y	Marketing Pros.:	Y	Gen. Writing/Editing:	Y	Info. Management:	Y	Finance/Acct.:	Y	Engineers, Electrical:	Y
Experienced Mngmt.:	Y	Retail Sales:		Technical Writing:	Y	Software Dev.:	Y	Law:	Y	Engineers, Other:	Y
International Business:	Y	Commercial/Industrial:	Y	Graphic Arts/Photog.:	Y	Hardware Dev.:		HR/Other:	Y	Health/Lab:	
MBA Grads:	Y	Sales Trainees:	Y	Music:		Consulting/Other:	Y	Training:	Y	Scientists/Research:	
		Advertising Pros.:		Broadcasting:				Health Care:		Petroleum/Chemicals:	Y
				Other:				Consulting:	Y	Math/Other:	

TYPES OF BUSINESS:

Engineering & Design Services
Facility Management
Construction & Field Services
Technical Consulting Services
Environmental Services

BRANDS/DIVISIONS/AFFILIATES:

Edwards and Kelcey
Carter and Burgess
Neste Jacobs Oy of Kilpilahti
Rintekno
Jacobs Technology, Inc.

CONTACTS: Note: Officers with more than one job title may be intentionally listed here more than once.

Craig Martin, CEO
Craig Martin, Pres.
Andrew F. Kremer, Sr. VP-Global Sales
Patricia H. Summers, Sr. VP-Human Resources
Cora Carmody, Sr. VP-IT
John W. Prosser Jr., Exec. VP-Admin.
William C. Markley III, General Counsel/Sec./Sr. VP
Thomas R. Hammond, Exec. VP-Oper.
John McLachlan, Sr. VP-Acquisitions & Strategy
John W. Prosser Jr., Exec. VP-Finance/Treas.
Thomas R. Hammond, Exec. VP
George A. Kunberger, Exec. VP-Oper.
Rogers F. Starr, Pres., Jacobs Technology, Inc.
Nazim Thawerbhoy, Sr. VP/Controller
Noel G. Watson, Chmn.

Phone: 626-578-3500	Fax: 626-568-7144
Toll-Free:	
Address: 1111 S. Arroyo Pkwy., Pasadena, CA 91109-7084 US	

GROWTH PLANS/SPECIAL FEATURES:

Jacobs Engineering Group, Inc. offers technical, professional, and construction services to industrial, commercial and governmental clients throughout North America, Europe, Asia, South America, India, the U.K. and Australia. The company's global network includes more than 160 offices in over 20 countries. The company provides project services, which include engineering, design and architecture; process, scientific, and systems consulting services; operations and maintenance services; and construction services, which include direct-hire construction and management services. Services are offered to selected industry groups such as oil and gas exploration, production, and refining; programs for various federal governments; pharmaceuticals and biotechnology; chemicals and polymers; buildings, which includes projects in the fields of health care and education as well as civic, governmental, and other buildings; infrastructure; technology and manufacturing; and pulp and paper, among others. Jacobs also provides pricing studies, project feasibility reports and automation and control system analysis for U.S. government agencies involved in defense and aerospace programs. In addition, the company is one of the leading providers of environmental engineering and consulting services in the U.S. and abroad, including hazardous and nuclear waste management and site cleanup and closure, providing support in such areas as underground storage tank removal, contaminated soil and water remediation, and long-term groundwater monitoring. Jacobs also designs, builds, installs, operates and maintains various types of soil and groundwater cleanup systems. In 2008, the company acquired a 60% stake in the Saudi Arabian firm, Zamel & Turbag Consulting Engineers. The same year, the company agreed to acquire L.E.S. Engineering Limited, a U.K.-based construction and service works contractor and a one-third stake in AWE Management Limited.

Employees are offered medical, dental and vision insurance; health and dependent care flexible spending accounts; an employee assistance program; disability coverage; life insurance; prepaid legal benefits; home and auto insurance; commuter assistance benefits; tuition reimbursements; and supplier discounts.

FINANCIALS: Sales and profits are in thousands of dollars—add 000 to get the full amount. 2008 Note: Financial information for 2008 was not available for all companies at press time.

2008 Sales: $11,252,159	2008 Profits: $420,742	**U.S. Stock Ticker: JEC**
2007 Sales: $8,473,970	2007 Profits: $287,130	**Int'l Ticker:** Int'l Exchange:
2006 Sales: $7,421,270	2006 Profits: $196,883	Employees: 42,700
2005 Sales: $5,635,001	2005 Profits: $131,608	Fiscal Year Ends: 9/30
2004 Sales: $4,594,235	2004 Profits: $115,574	Parent Company:

SALARIES/BENEFITS:

Pension Plan:	ESOP Stock Plan:	Profit Sharing:	Top Exec. Salary: $1,084,615	Bonus: $1,301,703
Savings Plan: Y	Stock Purch. Plan: Y		Second Exec. Salary: $850,000	Bonus: $1,020,129

OTHER THOUGHTS:

Apparent Women Officers or Directors: 3
Hot Spot for Advancement for Women/Minorities: Y

LOCATIONS: ("Y" = Yes)

West:	Southwest:	Midwest:	Southeast:	Northeast:	International:
Y	Y	Y	Y	Y	Y

Note: Financial information, benefits and other data can change quickly and may vary from those stated here.

JETBLUE AIRWAYS CORPORATION

www.jetblue.com

Industry Group Code: 481111 Ranks within this company's industry group: Sales: 2 Profits: 2

Management:		Sales/Marketing:		Liberal Arts:		Information Systems:		Professionals:		Tech./Scientific:	
Management Trainees:	Y	Marketing Pros.:	Y	Gen. Writing/Editing:	Y	Info. Management:	Y	Finance/Acct.:	Y	Engineers, Electrical:	Y
Experienced Mngmt.:	Y	Retail Sales:		Technical Writing:	Y	Software Dev.:	Y	Law:	Y	Engineers, Other:	Y
International Business:	Y	Commercial/Industrial:		Graphic Arts/Photog.:	Y	Hardware Dev.:		HR/Other:	Y	Health/Lab:	
MBA Grads:	Y	Sales Trainees:		Music:		Consulting/Other:		Training:	Y	Scientists/Research:	
		Advertising Pros.:	Y	Broadcasting:				Health Care:	Y	Petroleum/Chemicals:	
				Other:	Y			Consulting:		Math/Other:	

TYPES OF BUSINESS:
Airline
In-Flight Entertainment

BRANDS/DIVISIONS/AFFILIATES:
Lufthansa

CONTACTS: Note: Officers with more than one job title may be intentionally listed here more than once.
David Barger, CEO
Robert Maruster, COO/Exec. VP
David Barger, Pres.
Ed Barnes, CFO/Exec. VP
Robin Hayes, Chief Commercial Officer/Exec. VP
Joseph Eng, CIO/Exec. VP
James Hnat, General Counsel/Corp. Sec.
James Hnat, Exec. VP-Corp. Affairs
Don Daniels, Chief Acct. Officer
Dennis Corrigan, VP-Revenue Mgmt.
Alex Battaglia, VP-Airports
Joel Peterson, Chmn.

Phone: 718-709-2202	Fax:
Toll-Free: 800-538-2583	
Address: 118-29 Queens Blvd., Forest Hills, NY 11375 US	

GROWTH PLANS/SPECIAL FEATURES:

JetBlue Airways Corporation is a low-fare, low-cost passenger airline. The company's roughly 600 daily flights are single-class, but feature leather seats and seat-back televisions with 36 channels of live DirecTV programming, 100 channels of free XM satellite radio and in-flight pay-per-view movie offerings. JetBlue provides service to 56 destinations in 19 states, Puerto Rico, Mexico and five countries in the Caribbean and Latin America, with most flights originating or arriving at one of their focus cities: Boston, Fort Lauderdale, Long Beach, New York and Orlando. In 2008, the company operated over 600 daily flights with a fleet of 109 Airbus A320 aircraft and 41 EMBRAER 190 aircraft, with an average fleet age of 3.7 years. That year, the firm completed 98.4% of scheduled flights. As part of its low operating cost strategy, the company encourages passengers to purchase tickets through the Internet, selling approximately 77% of its tickets online. The airline flies its planes for an average of 12.1 hours daily, higher than the industry standard. In 2008, German airline Lufthansa acquired an approximately 19% interest in JetBlue. Also in 2008, the firm announced that it was putting off delivery of 21 Airbus planes for up to five years. In early 2009, JetBlue commenced service to Bogota, Colombia and San Jose, Costa Rica, and announced plans to begin service to Kingston, Jamaica and the Caribbean island Saint Lucia. Despite the general travel industry slump in 2009, the firm added nine new airplanes, expanded into new cities and hoped to hire more than 2,000 employees.

JetBlue offers employees prepaid group legal assistance; self-directed accounts; flexible spending accounts; medical, dental and vision insurance; flight benefits; wellness programs; and voluntary discount programs. The firm's highly admired corporate culture is based on its stated goals of safety, integrity, caring, passion and fun.

FINANCIALS: Sales and profits are in thousands of dollars—add 000 to get the full amount. 2008 Note: Financial information for 2008 was not available for all companies at press time.

2008 Sales: $3,388,000	2008 Profits: $-76,000	**U.S. Stock Ticker:** JBLU
2007 Sales: $2,842,000	2007 Profits: $18,000	**Int'l Ticker:** Int'l Exchange:
2006 Sales: $2,363,000	2006 Profits: $-1,000	**Employees:** 11,852
2005 Sales: $1,701,282	2005 Profits: $-20,262	**Fiscal Year Ends:** 12/31
2004 Sales: $1,265,972	2004 Profits: $47,467	**Parent Company:**

SALARIES/BENEFITS:

Pension Plan:	ESOP Stock Plan:	Profit Sharing: Y	Top Exec. Salary: $395,833	Bonus: $200,000
Savings Plan: Y	Stock Purch. Plan: Y		Second Exec. Salary: $372,917	Bonus: $250,000

OTHER THOUGHTS:
Apparent Women Officers or Directors: 2
Hot Spot for Advancement for Women/Minorities: Y

LOCATIONS: ("Y" = Yes)

West:	Southwest:	Midwest:	Southeast:	Northeast:	International:
Y	Y	Y	Y	Y	Y

Note: Financial information, benefits and other data can change quickly and may vary from those stated here.

JM SMUCKER CO

www.smucker.com

Industry Group Code: 311 **Ranks within this company's industry group:** Sales: 4 Profits: 3

Management:		Sales/Marketing:		Liberal Arts:		Information Systems:		Professionals:		Tech./Scientific:	
Management Trainees:	Y	Marketing Pros.:	Y	Gen. Writing/Editing:	Y	Info. Management:	Y	Finance/Acct.:	Y	Engineers, Electrical:	
Experienced Mngmt.:	Y	Retail Sales:		Technical Writing:		Software Dev.:		Law:	Y	Engineers, Other:	Y
International Business:	Y	Commercial/Industrial:	Y	Graphic Arts/Photog.:	Y	Hardware Dev.:		HR/Other:	Y	Health/Lab:	
MBA Grads:	Y	Sales Trainees:	Y	Music:		Consulting/Other:		Training:	Y	Scientists/Research:	
		Advertising Pros.:	Y	Broadcasting:				Health Care:		Petroleum/Chemicals:	
				Other:				Consulting:		Math/Other:	

TYPES OF BUSINESS:

Food Products, Manufacturing
Fruit Spreads
Dessert Toppings
Peanut Butter
Beverages
Shortening and Oils
Baking Mixes
Condiments

BRANDS/DIVISIONS/AFFILIATES:

Smuckers
Jif
Crisco
Uncrustables
Adams
Pillsbury
Knott's Berry Farm
Folgers

CONTACTS: Note: Officers with more than one job title may be intentionally listed here more than once.

Timothy P. Smucker, Co-CEO
Mark R. Belgya, CFO/VP
Christopher P. Resweber, VP-Mktg. Svcs.
Andrew G. Platt, CIO/VP-Info. Svcs.
M. Ann Harlan, General Counsel/VP/Corp. Sec.
Barry C. Dunaway, VP-Corp. Dev.
John W. Denman, VP/Controller
Richard K. Smucker, Co-CEO
Vincent C. Byrd, Sr. VP-Consumer Market
Julia L. Sabin, VP/Gen. Mgr.-Smucker Quality Beverages
Donald D. Hurrle, VP-Sales & Grocery Market
Timothy P. Smucker, Chmn.
Dennis J. Armstrong, VP-Logistics & Oper. Support

Phone: 330-682-3000	**Fax:** 330-684-6410
Toll-Free: 888-550-9555	
Address: 1 Strawberry Ln., Orrville, OH 44667-0280 US	

GROWTH PLANS/SPECIAL FEATURES:

J.M. Smucker Company (Smuckers) manufactures and markets branded food products on a worldwide basis, with the majority of its sales in the U.S. and Canada. Products offered by Smuckers include peanut butter; shortening and oils; flour and baking ingredients; fruit spreads; baking mixes and ready-to-spread frostings; fruit and vegetable juices; beverages; dessert toppings; syrups; frozen sandwiches; pickles and condiments; potato side dishes; and, most recently, canned milk. Products are sold through brokers to food retailers, food wholesalers, club stores, mass merchandisers, discount stores and military commissaries. The company's products are also sold to food service distributors and operators including restaurants, schools and universities; health care operators; and health/natural food stores. The raw fruit materials used by Smuckers in the production of its food products are purchased from independent growers and suppliers. The company's major trademarks include Smuckers, Jif, Crisco, Dutch Girl, White Lily, Hungry Jack, Uncrustables, Adams, Laura Scudder's, Goober, Pet, R. W. Knudsen Family, and Magic Shell. Smuckers also uses the Pillsbury trademark under a royalty-free license. In May 2008, the company acquired the Knott's Berry Farm food brand from ConAgra Foods, Inc. In November of the same year, the firm acquired Folgers coffee business from The Procter & Gamble Company for $3 billion.

Employees are offered medical, dental, life and disability insurance; a pension plan; a 401(k) plan; and an employee stock ownership plan.

FINANCIALS: Sales and profits are in thousands of dollars—add 000 to get the full amount. 2008 Note: Financial information for 2008 was not available for all companies at press time.

2008 Sales: $2,524,774	2008 Profits: $170,379	**U.S. Stock Ticker:** SJM	
2007 Sales: $2,148,017	2007 Profits: $157,219	**Int'l Ticker:** Int'l Exchange:	
2006 Sales: $2,154,726	2006 Profits: $143,354	Employees: 4,700	
2005 Sales: $2,043,877	2005 Profits: $129,073	Fiscal Year Ends: 4/30	
2004 Sales: $1,417,011	2004 Profits: $111,350	Parent Company:	

SALARIES/BENEFITS:

Pension Plan: Y	ESOP Stock Plan: Y	Profit Sharing:	Top Exec. Salary: $730,000	Bonus: $
Savings Plan: Y	Stock Purch. Plan:		Second Exec. Salary: $730,000	Bonus: $

OTHER THOUGHTS:

Apparent Women Officers or Directors: 7
Hot Spot for Advancement for Women/Minorities: Y

LOCATIONS: ("Y" = Yes)

West:	Southwest:	Midwest:	Southeast:	Northeast:	International:
Y		Y	Y	Y	Y

JOHNSON & JOHNSON

www.jnj.com

Industry Group Code: 325412 Ranks within this company's industry group: Sales: 1 Profits: 1

Management:		Sales/Marketing:		Liberal Arts:		Information Systems:		Professionals:		Tech./Scientific:	
Management Trainees:	Y	Marketing Pros.:	Y	Gen. Writing/Editing:	Y	Info. Management:	Y	Finance/Acct.:	Y	Engineers, Electrical:	Y
Experienced Mngmt.:	Y	Retail Sales:		Technical Writing:	Y	Software Dev.:	Y	Law:	Y	Engineers, Other:	Y
International Business:	Y	Commercial/Industrial:	Y	Graphic Arts/Photog.:	Y	Hardware Dev.:		HR/Other:	Y	Health/Lab:	Y
MBA Grads:	Y	Sales Trainees:	Y	Music:		Consulting/Other:		Training:	Y	Scientists/Research:	Y
		Advertising Pros.:	Y	Broadcasting:				Health Care:	Y	Petroleum/Chemicals:	Y
				Other:				Consulting:		Math/Other:	Y

TYPES OF BUSINESS:

Personal Health Care & Hygiene Products
Sterilization Products
Surgical Products
Pharmaceuticals
Skin Care Products
Baby Care Products
Contact Lenses
Medical Equipment

BRANDS/DIVISIONS/AFFILIATES:

Scios Inc
Centocor Inc
Alza Corp
Depuy Inc
Ethicon Inc
Cordis Corp
LifeScan Inc
Omrix Biopharmaceuticals Inc

CONTACTS: Note: Officers with more than one job title may be intentionally listed here more than once.

William C. Weldon, CEO
Dominic J. Caruso, CFO
Kaye Foster-Cheek, VP-Human Resources
Russell C. Deyo, General Counsel/VP/Chief Compliance Officer
Nicholas J. Valeriani, VP-Strategy & Growth
Dominic J. Caruso, VP-Finance
Colleen Goggins, Chmn.-Consumer Group
Sheri S. McCoy, Chmn.-Pharmaceutical Group
Alex Gorsky, Chmn.-Surgical Care Group
Donald M. Casey, Jr., Chmn.-Comprehensive Care Group
William C. Weldon, Chmn.

Phone: 732-524-0400	Fax: 732-214-0332
Toll-Free:	
Address: 1 Johnson & Johnson Plz., New Brunswick, NJ 08933 US	

GROWTH PLANS/SPECIAL FEATURES:

Johnson & Johnson, founded in 1886, is one of the world's most comprehensive and well-known manufacturers of health care products. The firm owns more than 250 companies in over 90 countries and markets its products in almost every country in the world. Johnson & Johnson's worldwide operations are divided into three segments: consumer, pharmaceutical and medical devices and diagnostics. The company's principal consumer goods are personal care and hygiene products, including nonprescription drugs, adult skin and hair care, baby care, oral care, first aid and sanitary protection products. Major consumer brands include Mylanta, Band-Aid, Tylenol, Aveeno and Monistat. The pharmaceutical segment covers a wide spectrum of health fields, including antifungal, anti-infective, cardiovascular, dermatology, immunology, pain management, psychotropic and women's health. Among its pharmaceutical products are Risperdal, an antipsychotic used to treat schizophrenia, and Remicade for the treatment of Crohn's disease and rheumatoid arthritis. In the medical devices and diagnostics segment, Johnson & Johnson makes a number of products including suture and mechanical wound closure products, surgical instruments, disposable contact lenses, joint reconstruction products and intravenous catheters. Subsidiaries of the company include Cordis LLC, DePuy, Inc., Diabetes Diagnostics, Inc., Ethicon Endo-Surgery, Inc., LifeScan, Inc., McNeil Healthcare LLC, Neutrogena Corporation, SurgRx, Inc. and The Tylenol Company. In November 2008, Johnson & Johnson acquired HealthMedia, Inc. In December 2008, the company acquired Omrix Biopharmaceuticals, Inc. for $438 million. In January 2009, the firm completed its acquisition of Mentor Corporation, a producer of medical products for the aesthetic specialties market. In July 2009, Johnson & Johnson announced that it would invest approximately $1.5 billion for an 18.4% stake in Elan Corporation, an Ireland-based biotechnology firm. The transaction will also give the company certain rights related to Elan's Alzheimer's drug development program.

Johnson & Johnson offers its employees benefits that include medical coverage; an employee assistance program; health assessments and health counseling; and on-site fitness centers and fitness classes at certain locations.

FINANCIALS: Sales and profits are in thousands of dollars—add 000 to get the full amount. 2008 Note: Financial information for 2008 was not available for all companies at press time.

2008 Sales: $63,747,000	2008 Profits: $12,949,000	U.S. Stock Ticker: JNJ
2007 Sales: $61,095,000	2007 Profits: $10,576,000	Int'l Ticker: Int'l Exchange:
2006 Sales: $53,324,000	2006 Profits: $11,053,000	Employees: 118,700
2005 Sales: $50,514,000	2005 Profits: $10,060,000	Fiscal Year Ends: 12/31
2004 Sales: $47,348,000	2004 Profits: $8,180,000	Parent Company:

SALARIES/BENEFITS:

Pension Plan:	ESOP Stock Plan:	Profit Sharing:	Top Exec. Salary: $1,792,019	Bonus: $8,972,360
Savings Plan: Y	Stock Purch. Plan:		Second Exec. Salary: $1,042,404	Bonus: $3,721,500

OTHER THOUGHTS:

Apparent Women Officers or Directors: 5
Hot Spot for Advancement for Women/Minorities: Y

LOCATIONS: ("Y" = Yes)

West:	Southwest:	Midwest:	Southeast:	Northeast:	International:
Y	Y	Y	Y	Y	Y

Note: Financial information, benefits and other data can change quickly and may vary from those stated here.

JOHNSON CONTROLS INC

www.johnsoncontrols.com

Industry Group Code: 3363 Ranks within this company's industry group: Sales: 1 Profits: 2

Management:		Sales/Marketing:		Liberal Arts:		Information Systems:		Professionals:		Tech./Scientific:	
Management Trainees:	Y	Marketing Pros.:	Y	Gen. Writing/Editing:	Y	Info. Management:	Y	Finance/Acct.:	Y	Engineers, Electrical:	Y
Experienced Mngmt.:	Y	Retail Sales:		Technical Writing:	Y	Software Dev.:	Y	Law:	Y	Engineers, Other:	Y
International Business:	Y	Commercial/Industrial:	Y	Graphic Arts/Photog.:	Y	Hardware Dev.:	Y	HR/Other:	Y	Health/Lab:	
MBA Grads:	Y	Sales Trainees:		Music:		Consulting/Other:		Training:	Y	Scientists/Research:	Y
		Advertising Pros.:	Y	Broadcasting:				Health Care:		Petroleum/Chemicals:	
				Other:				Consulting:		Math/Other:	Y

TYPES OF BUSINESS:

Automobile Parts & Controls
Automotive Batteries
Facilities Management
Automotive Interior Components
Energy Management Services
Building Security, Lighting & HVAC Systems

BRANDS/DIVISIONS/AFFILIATES:

York International Corp
Johnson Controls-Saft Advanced Power Solutions
Automotive Experience
Optima
Varta
Johnson Controls (Wuhu) Automotive Interiors
Metasys Sustainability Manager
Plastech Engineered Products

CONTACTS: *Note: Officers with more than one job title may be intentionally listed here more than once.*

Stephen A. Roell, CEO
Keith Wandell, COO
Keith Wandell, Pres.
R. Bruce McDonald, CFO/Exec. VP
Susan F. Davis, Exec. VP-Human Resources
Colin Boyd, CIO/VP-IT
Jerome D. Okarma, General Counsel/Sec./VP
Denise Zutz, VP-Strategy
Jacqueline F. Strayer, VP-Corp. Comm.
Jeffrey G. Augustin, VP-Finance
C. David Meyers, VP/Pres., Building Efficiency
Beda Bolzenius, VP/Pres., Automotive Experience
Alex A. Molinaroli, VP/Pres., Power Solutions
Charles A. Harvey, VP-Public Affairs & Diversity
Stephen A. Roell, Chmn.
Jeffrey S. Edwards, VP-Automotive Experience, Japan & Asia Pacific

Phone: 414-524-2363	Fax: 414-524-2070
Toll-Free: 800-524-6220	
Address: 5757 N. Green Bay Ave., P.O. Box 591, Milwaukee, WI 53201 US	

GROWTH PLANS/SPECIAL FEATURES:

Johnson Controls, Inc. is a leader in automotive interiors/batteries, building efficiency and facility management. The firm's Automotive Experience segment designs and manufactures concept cars; complete seat systems; seating components; electronics; instrument panels; overhead, door and cargo management systems; cockpits; and interior trim for manufacturers of cars and light trucks. The firm's Power Solutions division manufactures and replaces automotive batteries, focusing on innovations for hybrid electric vehicles. Its battery brands include Optima, Varta, Heliar (in South America), and LTH (in Mexico). Prominent clients include BMW; DaimlerChrysler; Ford; Toyota; Volkswagen; AutoZone; Interstate Battery System of America; and Wal-Mart. Johnson's Building Efficiency segment operates in 125 countries, supplying systems designed for heating; ventilation; air conditioning; lighting; security; and fire management. The U.S. Department of Defense utilizes Johnson Controls for the Pentagon's energy management and environmental control systems. Global WorkPlace Solutions, part of Building Efficiency, provides companies with a real-estate based approach to shareholder value. The Building Efficiency division also does facility management, using its patented Metasys Building Management System. It handles school districts, hospitals, factories, airports and government facilities. The company has a joint venture with Saft SA, a battery company, called Johnson Controls-Saft Advanced Power Solutions. In January 2008, the company acquired Metro Mechanical, Inc., a mechanical services company. In April 2008, Johnson and Chery Technology Co., Ltd., of Chery Automobile Co., Ltd., formed Johnson Controls (Wuhu) Automotive Interiors Co., Ltd. In July 2008, the firm agreed to acquire 70% interest in formerly bankrupt Plastech Engineered Products. Between July and October 2008 the firm acquired the following companies: PWI Energy, provider of greenhouse gas and energy management; Engineered Equipment and Systems Company, a representative of equipment manufacturers; and software company Gridlogix. In January 2009, Johnson Controls incorporated Gridlogix's technology into its Metasys building management system, launching the new Metasys Sustainability Manager.

FINANCIALS: Sales and profits are in thousands of dollars—add 000 to get the full amount. 2008 Note: Financial information for 2008 was not available for all companies at press time.

2008 Sales: $38,062,000	2008 Profits: $979,000	**U.S. Stock Ticker:** JCI
2007 Sales: $34,624,000	2007 Profits: $1,252,000	**Int'l Ticker:** Int'l Exchange:
2006 Sales: $32,235,000	2006 Profits: $1,028,000	Employees: 140,000
2005 Sales: $27,479,400	2005 Profits: $909,400	Fiscal Year Ends: 9/30
2004 Sales: $26,553,400	2004 Profits: $817,500	Parent Company:

SALARIES/BENEFITS:

Pension Plan: Y	ESOP Stock Plan:	Profit Sharing:	Top Exec. Salary: $1,325,000	Bonus: $5,408,000
Savings Plan: Y	Stock Purch. Plan:		Second Exec. Salary: $919,000	Bonus: $3,072,000

OTHER THOUGHTS:

Apparent Women Officers or Directors: 4
Hot Spot for Advancement for Women/Minorities: Y

LOCATIONS: ("Y" = Yes)

West:	Southwest:	Midwest:	Southeast:	Northeast:	International:
Y	Y	Y	Y	Y	Y

JP MORGAN CHASE & CO INC

www.jpmorganchase.com

Industry Group Code: 522110 Ranks within this company's industry group: Sales: 2 Profits: 1

Management:		Sales/Marketing:		Liberal Arts:		Information Systems:		Professionals:		Tech./Scientific:	
Management Trainees:	Y	Marketing Pros.:	Y	Gen. Writing/Editing:	Y	Info. Management:	Y	Finance/Acct.:	Y	Engineers, Electrical:	
Experienced Mngmt.:	Y	Retail Sales:		Technical Writing:		Software Dev.:	Y	Law:	Y	Engineers, Other:	
International Business:	Y	Commercial/Industrial:	Y	Graphic Arts/Photog.:	Y	Hardware Dev.:		HR/Other:	Y	Health/Lab:	
MBA Grads:	Y	Sales Trainees:		Music:		Consulting/Other:		Training:	Y	Scientists/Research:	
		Advertising Pros.:	Y	Broadcasting:				Health Care:		Petroleum/Chemicals:	
				Other:	Y			Consulting:		Math/Other:	

TYPES OF BUSINESS:

Banking
Mortgages
Investment Banking
Stock Brokerage
Credit Cards
Business Finance
Mutual Funds
Annuities

BRANDS/DIVISIONS/AFFILIATES:

JPMorgan Chase Vastera Inc
Bear Stearns Cos Inc (The)
J.P. Morgan Securities
MorganMarkets
JPMorgan Partners
Washington Mutual (WAMU)
Bank of New York
JP Morgan Commodities Canada Corp.

CONTACTS: Note: Officers with more than one job title may be intentionally listed here more than once.

James Dimon, CEO
Michael J. Cavanagh, Dir.-Finance
John L. Donnelly, Dir.-Human Resources
Guy Chiarello, CIO
Frank J. Bisignano, Chief Admin. Officer
Stephen M. Cutler, General Counsel/Dir.-Legal & Compliance
Jay Mandelbaum, Dir.-Strategy
Joseph M. Evangelisti, Dir.-Corp. Comm.
Heidi Miller, Treas./Dir.-Securities Svcs.
Barry Zubrow, Chief Risk Officer
Paul T. Bateman, Dir.-Investment Mgmt.
Anthony J. Best, Dir.-Investment Bank
Steven D. Black, Dir.-Investment Bank
James Dimon, Chmn.
Andrew D. Crockett, Dir.-JPMorgan Chase Int'l

Phone: 212-270-6000	**Fax:** 212-270-2613
Toll-Free: 877-242-7372	
Address: 270 Park Ave., New York, NY 10017-2070 US	

GROWTH PLANS/SPECIAL FEATURES:

J.P. Morgan Chase & Co., Inc. (JPM) is one of the largest banking institutions in the world, operating in more than 60 nations and controlling more than $2.1 trillion in assets. As one of the strongest financial organizations in America, JPM was able to grow significantly in 2008 by acquiring the assets of two major companies during the global financial crisis. In March 2008, JPM purchased the assets of Bear Stearns & Co., one of America's largest investment banking firms. In September 2008, the firm acquired the assets of Washington Mutual (WAMU), one of the nation's largest savings associations, after federal regulators took control of WAMU due to massive losses in its mortgage portfolio. These acquisitions boosted JPM to $2.03 trillion in assets and 5,410 branches in 23 states. In addition, it grew to 14,272 ATMs and 238,792 employees. JPM provides investment banking; financial services; financial transaction processing; asset and wealth management; and private equity services for consumers and businesses. Among JPM's principal subsidiaries are JPMorgan Chase Bank, a national banking association; Chase Bank USA, the firm's leading provider of credit cards; and J.P. Morgan Securities, an investment banking firm. The company is organized into six segments: investment banking; retail finance; card services; commercial banking; treasury and securities; and asset management. JPM also operates private equity and treasury businesses through its subsidiary, One Equity Partners. In the investment banking sector, JPM provides strategic advice, capital raising and risk management expertise in areas such as healthcare, technology, energy, real estate and transportation. JPM also offers global research in areas such as fixed income/rates, credit, foreign exchange, emerging markets, derivatives, structured finance and bond indices. The firm operates a research data portal, MorganMarkets. In February 2009, JPM purchased UBS Commodities Canada Ltd., renaming the company J.P. Morgan Commodities Canada Corp., and the global agriculture business of UBS AG.

FINANCIALS: Sales and profits are in thousands of dollars—add 000 to get the full amount. 2008 Note: Financial information for 2008 was not available for all companies at press time.

2008 Sales: $101,491,000	2008 Profits: $5,605,000	**U.S. Stock Ticker:** JPM
2007 Sales: $71,372,000	2007 Profits: $15,365,000	**Int'l Ticker:** Int'l Exchange:
2006 Sales: $61,999,000	2006 Profits: $14,444,000	Employees: 224,961
2005 Sales: $54,248,000	2005 Profits: $8,483,000	Fiscal Year Ends: 12/31
2004 Sales: $43,097,000	2004 Profits: $4,466,000	Parent Company:

SALARIES/BENEFITS:

Pension Plan: Y	ESOP Stock Plan:	Profit Sharing:	Top Exec. Salary: $1,000,000	Bonus: $
Savings Plan: Y	Stock Purch. Plan: Y		Second Exec. Salary: $500,000	Bonus: $2,000,000

OTHER THOUGHTS:

Apparent Women Officers or Directors: 11
Hot Spot for Advancement for Women/Minorities: Y

LOCATIONS: ("Y" = Yes)

West:	Southwest:	Midwest:	Southeast:	Northeast:	International:
Y	Y	Y	Y	Y	Y

Note: Financial information, benefits and other data can change quickly and may vary from those stated here.

JUNIPER NETWORKS INC

www.juniper.net

Industry Group Code: 33411 Ranks within this company's industry group: Sales: 2   Profits: 2

Management:		Sales/Marketing:		Liberal Arts:		Information Systems:		Professionals:		Tech./Scientific:	
Management Trainees:	Y	Marketing Pros.:	Y	Gen. Writing/Editing:	Y	Info. Management:	Y	Finance/Acct.:	Y	Engineers, Electrical:	Y
Experienced Mngmt.:	Y	Retail Sales:		Technical Writing:	Y	Software Dev.:	Y	Law:	Y	Engineers, Other:	
International Business:	Y	Commercial/Industrial:	Y	Graphic Arts/Photog.:	Y	Hardware Dev.:	Y	HR/Other:	Y	Health/Lab:	
MBA Grads:	Y	Sales Trainees:	Y	Music:		Consulting/Other:		Training:	Y	Scientists/Research:	Y
		Advertising Pros.:	Y	Broadcasting:				Health Care:		Petroleum/Chemicals:	
				Other:				Consulting:		Math/Other:	Y

TYPES OF BUSINESS:

Networking Equipment
IP Networking Systems
Internet Routers
Network Security Products
Internet Software
Intrusion Prevention
Application Acceleration

BRANDS/DIVISIONS/AFFILIATES:

JUNOS
E-Series
J-Series
M-Series
T-Series
MX-Series
SDX Service Deployment System
SSL VPN

CONTACTS: *Note: Officers with more than one job title may be intentionally listed here more than once.*

Kevin Johnson, CEO
Robyn Denholm, CFO/Exec. VP
Lauren Patricia Flaherty, Chief Mktg. Officer/Exec. VP
Steven Rice, Exec. VP-Human Resources
Mitchell Gaynor, General Counsel
Michael Rose, Exec. VP-Service, Support & Oper.
Gene Zamiska, Chief Acct. Officer
Kim Perdikou, Exec. VP-Infrastructure Products Group
John Morris, Exec. VP-Worldwide Field Oper.
Mark Bauhaus, Exec. VP/Gen. Mgr.-Service Layer Tech. Bus. Group
Hitesh Sheth, Exec. VP/Gen. Mgr.-Ethernet Platforms Bus. Group
Scott Kriens, Chmn.

Phone: 408-745-2000	**Fax:** 408-745-2100
Toll-Free: 888-586-4737	
Address: 1194 N. Mathilda Ave., Sunnyvale, CA 94089-1206 US	

GROWTH PLANS/SPECIAL FEATURES:

Juniper Networks, Inc. is a provider of custom-designed Internet protocol (IP) networking platforms for Internet service providers, enterprises, governments and educational institutions. Operations are organized into two segments: infrastructure and service layer technologies (SLT). The infrastructure segment primarily offers scalable router products used to control and direct network traffic. Product families offered by the firm include the M-Series, T-Series and E-Series. The SLT segment offers services that protect networks as well as maximize existing bandwidth and acceleration of applications across a distributed network. The SLT product families include firewall services, virtual private network (VPN) systems, intrusion detection and prevention (IDP) and application acceleration platforms. The firm outsources manufacturing to companies such as IBM, Toshiba, Celestica and Plexus; these manufacturers create application-specific chips from Juniper's designs. Additionally, the company sells Internet backbone routers, which are offered through a direct sales force to Internet and telecommunication service providers around the world. The firm maintains several strategic alliances with prominent companies including Avaya, Ericsson, Lucent Technologies, Siemens, and more recently, Lockheed Martin, Microsoft and Oracle. Juniper's customers include wireline, wireless and cable ISPs; private enterprises; federal, state and local government agencies; and research and education institutions. The firm maintains international headquarters in the U.K., Hong Kong and Tokyo and sales offices in 40 countries worldwide. Juniper owns 500 technology patents, either issued or pending.

Employees are offered medical, dental and vision insurance; a 401(k) plan; and a stock purchase plan.

FINANCIALS: Sales and profits are in thousands of dollars—add 000 to get the full amount. 2008 Note: Financial information for 2008 was not available for all companies at press time.

2008 Sales: $3,572,376	2008 Profits: $511,749	**U.S. Stock Ticker:** JNPR
2007 Sales: $2,836,100	2007 Profits: $360,800	**Int'l Ticker:** Int'l Exchange:
2006 Sales: $2,303,580	2006 Profits: $-1,001,437	Employees: 7,014
2005 Sales: $2,063,957	2005 Profits: $350,701	Fiscal Year Ends: 12/31
2004 Sales: $1,336,019	2004 Profits: $128,228	Parent Company:

SALARIES/BENEFITS:

Pension Plan:	ESOP Stock Plan:	Profit Sharing:	Top Exec. Salary: $675,000	Bonus: $903,000
Savings Plan: Y	Stock Purch. Plan: Y		Second Exec. Salary: $495,000	Bonus: $430,000

OTHER THOUGHTS:

Apparent Women Officers or Directors: 4
Hot Spot for Advancement for Women/Minorities: Y

LOCATIONS: ("Y" = Yes)

West:	Southwest:	Midwest:	Southeast:	Northeast:	International:
Y	Y	Y	Y	Y	Y

KAISER PERMANENTE

www.kaiserpermanente.org

Industry Group Code: 622110 Ranks within this company's industry group: Sales: 1 Profits:

Management:		Sales/Marketing:		Liberal Arts:		Information Systems:		Professionals:		Tech./Scientific:	
Management Trainees:	Y	Marketing Pros.:	Y	Gen. Writing/Editing:	Y	Info. Management:	Y	Finance/Acct.:	Y	Engineers, Electrical:	
Experienced Mngmt.:	Y	Retail Sales:		Technical Writing:	Y	Software Dev.:	Y	Law:	Y	Engineers, Other:	
International Business:		Commercial/Industrial:	Y	Graphic Arts/Photog.:	Y	Hardware Dev.:		HR/Other:	Y	Health/Lab:	Y
MBA Grads:	Y	Sales Trainees:		Music:		Consulting/Other:		Training:	Y	Scientists/Research:	
		Advertising Pros.:	Y	Broadcasting:				Health Care:	Y	Petroleum/Chemicals:	
				Other:	Y			Consulting:		Math/Other:	

TYPES OF BUSINESS:

Hospitals & Clinics
General & Specialty Hospitals
Outpatient Facilities
HMO
Health Insurance
Integrated Health Care System
Physician Networks

BRANDS/DIVISIONS/AFFILIATES:

Kaiser Foundation Health Plan, Inc.
Kaiser Foundation Hospitals
Permanente Medical Groups
KP HealthConnect
Kaiser Permanente Healthcare Institute

CONTACTS: *Note: Officers with more than one job title may be intentionally listed here more than once.*

George C. Halvorson, CEO
Kathy Lancaster, CFO/Exec. VP
Paul B. Records, Chief Human Resources Officer/Sr. VP
Raymond J. Baxter, Sr. VP-Research
Phil Fasano, CIO/Sr. VP
Steven Zatkin, General Counsel/Sr. VP/Sec.
Arthur M. Southam, Exec. VP-Health Plan Oper.
Diane Gage Lofgren, Sr. VP-Brand Strategy
Diane Gage Lofgren, Sr. VP-Corp. Comm. & Public Rel.
John H. Cochran, Exec. Dir.-Permanente Federation
Raymond J. Baxter, Sr. VP-Community Benefit & Health Policy
Louise L. Liang, Sr. VP-Quality & Clinical Systems Support
Bernard J. Tyson, Exec. VP-Health Plan & Hospital Oper.
George C. Halvorson, Chmn.

Phone: 510-271-5800	Fax: 510-267-7524
Toll-Free:	
Address: 1 Kaiser Plz., Ste. 2600, Oakland, CA 94612-3673 US	

GROWTH PLANS/SPECIAL FEATURES:

Kaiser Permanente is a non-profit company dedicated to providing integrated health care coverage. The firm operates in Washington, D.C. and nine states: California, Colorado, Georgia, Hawaii, Maryland, Ohio, Oregon, Virginia and Washington. It serves almost 8.7 million members, of which over 6.5 million are in California. Kaiser has three main operating divisions: Kaiser Foundation Health Plan, Inc., which contracts with individuals and groups to provide medical coverage; Kaiser Foundation Hospitals and their subsidiaries, operating community hospitals and outpatient facilities in several states; and Permanente Medical Groups, the company's network of physicians providing health care to its members. The company resources include approximately 35 medical centers, including hospitals and outpatient facilities; 431 medical offices; and 14,600 physicians. Kaiser Foundation Hospitals also fund medical and health-related research. The firm, as a participant in the Medicare program, cares for over 880,000 Medicare members, making it one of the largest health plans serving the Medicare program. The KP HealthConnect program integrates clinical records with appointments, registration and billing, thereby significantly improving care delivery and patient satisfaction. In March 2009, Kaiser Permanente and IBM formed a strategic partnership, by which IBM will manage the firm's data center operations.

The company offers its employees paid time off for vacations, designated holidays, sick leave and what it calls life balance days. Kaiser Permanente's employee health care coverage extends to spouses, domestic partners and unmarried children. The firm also offers pensions plans, life insurance and disability benefits.

FINANCIALS: Sales and profits are in thousands of dollars—add 000 to get the full amount. 2008 Note: Financial information for 2008 was not available for all companies at press time.

2008 Sales: $40,300,000	2008 Profits: $	**U.S. Stock Ticker: Nonprofit**
2007 Sales: $37,800,000	2007 Profits: $1,700,000	**Int'l Ticker:** Int'l Exchange:
2006 Sales: $34,600,000	2006 Profits: $	Employees: 167,300
2005 Sales: $31,100,000	2005 Profits: $1,000,000	Fiscal Year Ends: 12/31
2004 Sales: $26,600,000	2004 Profits: $1,600,000	Parent Company:

SALARIES/BENEFITS:

Pension Plan: Y	ESOP Stock Plan:	Profit Sharing:	Top Exec. Salary: $	Bonus: $
Savings Plan: Y	Stock Purch. Plan:		Second Exec. Salary: $	Bonus: $

OTHER THOUGHTS:

Apparent Women Officers or Directors: 13
Hot Spot for Advancement for Women/Minorities: Y

LOCATIONS: ("Y" = Yes)

West:	Southwest:	Midwest:	Southeast:	Northeast:	International:
Y		Y	Y	Y	

KEANE INC

www.keane.com

Industry Group Code: 541513 Ranks within this company's industry group: Sales: 9 Profits:

Management:		Sales/Marketing:		Liberal Arts:		Information Systems:		Professionals:		Tech./Scientific:	
Management Trainees:	Y	Marketing Pros.:		Gen. Writing/Editing:	Y	Info. Management:	Y	Finance/Acct.:	Y	Engineers, Electrical:	Y
Experienced Mngmt.:	Y	Retail Sales:		Technical Writing:	Y	Software Dev.:	Y	Law:	Y	Engineers, Other:	
International Business:	Y	Commercial/Industrial:	Y	Graphic Arts/Photog.:	Y	Hardware Dev.:	Y	HR/Other:	Y	Health/Lab:	
MBA Grads:	Y	Sales Trainees:		Music:		Consulting/Other:	Y	Training:	Y	Scientists/Research:	
		Advertising Pros.:	Y	Broadcasting:				Health Care:		Petroleum/Chemicals:	
				Other:	Y			Consulting:	Y	Math/Other:	

TYPES OF BUSINESS:

IT Consulting
Business Management Software
Software Development & Integration
System Design & Implementation
Applications Outsourcing
Health Care Consulting

BRANDS/DIVISIONS/AFFILIATES:

Caritor, Inc.
Adobe Systems Inc
BMC Software Inc
Business Objects SA
Compuware Corp
International Business Machines Corp (IBM)
Microsoft Corp
BestShores

CONTACTS: *Note: Officers with more than one job title may be intentionally listed here more than once.*

Mani Subramanian, CEO
Jim Puthuff, COO/Exec. VP
Chris Setterington, CFO/Exec. VP
John Riley, Chief Mktg. Officer
Dean Williams, Sr. VP-Global Human Capital
Marv Mouchawar, Exec. VP-Prod. & Corp. Dev.
John M. Dick, General Counsel
Sandeep Bhargava, Exec. VP-Bus. Dev. & Industry Solutions
Srikanth Rao, Exec. VP-Quality/Pres., Keane India
Karen Powell, Sr. VP-Global Client Mgmt.
Krishna Prabhu, Sr. VP-Global Client Mgmt.
Mani Subramanian, Chmn.
Srikanth Rao, Exec VP/Pres., Keane India

Phone: 925-838-8600	Fax: 925-838-7138
Toll-Free:	
Address: 210 Porter Dr., Ste. 315, San Ramon, CA 94583 US	

GROWTH PLANS/SPECIAL FEATURES:

Keane, Inc. is a global services company specializing in enabling the transformation of businesses and IT functions. In June 2007, Keane was acquired by and integrated into Caritor, Inc. for a purchase price of roughly $854 million. The combined company has operations in Australia, Canada, China, France, Germany, India, New Zealand, Switzerland, Singapore, UAE, the U.K. and the U.S., with more than $1 billion in annual revenue. Keane's global delivery approach includes onsite, offsite, nearshore and offshore options. The company has partnerships with Adobe; BMC Software; Business Objects; Cerylion; Compuware; Curam Software; DataCore; Enlighta; ExperSolve; HP Software; IBM; Lombardi Software; Microsoft; Oracle; PlanetSoft; PlanView; SAP; Vertica; and ZC Sterling. Keane provides business services including consulting, process outsourcing, strategy and program and performance management services, and technology services including application, architecture, enterprise application, infrastructure and quality assurance and testing services. The company serves the financial services, insurance, healthcare, manufacturing, public sector, telecom, life sciences, energy and utilities, hospitality; transportation and retail industries. In July 2007, Keane launched a joint-venture named BestShores with ZC Sterling to provide mortgage lenders with business process outsourcing solutions.

Keane offers its employees tuition assistance, an employee assistance program, a 529 College Savings Plan and a variety of healthcare options.

FINANCIALS: Sales and profits are in thousands of dollars—add 000 to get the full amount. 2008 Note: Financial information for 2008 was not available for all companies at press time.

2008 Sales: $1,200,000	2008 Profits: $	U.S. Stock Ticker: Private
2007 Sales: $1,100,000	2007 Profits: $	Int'l Ticker: Int'l Exchange:
2006 Sales: $948,306	2006 Profits: $34,514	Employees: 13,000
2005 Sales: $955,855	2005 Profits: $33,426	Fiscal Year Ends: 12/31
2004 Sales: $911,543	2004 Profits: $32,282	Parent Company:

SALARIES/BENEFITS:

Pension Plan:	ESOP Stock Plan:	Profit Sharing:	Top Exec. Salary: $	Bonus: $309,750
Savings Plan: Y	Stock Purch. Plan:		Second Exec. Salary: $	Bonus: $

OTHER THOUGHTS:

Apparent Women Officers or Directors: 1
Hot Spot for Advancement for Women/Minorities:

LOCATIONS: ("Y" = Yes)

West:	Southwest:	Midwest:	Southeast:	Northeast:	International:
Y				Y	Y

Note: Financial information, benefits and other data can change quickly and may vary from those stated here.

KELLOGG CO

www.kelloggs.com

Industry Group Code: 311230 **Ranks within this company's industry group:** Sales: 2 Profits: 1

Management:		Sales/Marketing:		Liberal Arts:		Information Systems:		Professionals:		Tech./Scientific:	
Management Trainees:	Y	Marketing Pros.:	Y	Gen. Writing/Editing:	Y	Info. Management:	Y	Finance/Acct.:	Y	Engineers, Electrical:	
Experienced Mngmt.:	Y	Retail Sales:		Technical Writing:	Y	Software Dev.:	Y	Law:	Y	Engineers, Other:	Y
International Business:	Y	Commercial/Industrial:	Y	Graphic Arts/Photog.:	Y	Hardware Dev.:		HR/Other:	Y	Health/Lab:	
MBA Grads:	Y	Sales Trainees:	Y	Music:		Consulting/Other:		Training:	Y	Scientists/Research:	
		Advertising Pros.:	Y	Broadcasting:				Health Care:		Petroleum/Chemicals:	
				Other:				Consulting:		Math/Other:	

TYPES OF BUSINESS:

Cereal Manufacturing
Frozen Foods
Snack Foods
Convenience Foods
Processed Foods

BRANDS/DIVISIONS/AFFILIATES:

Keebler
Pop-Tarts
Nutri-Grain
Eggo
Rice Krispies
Kellogg Snacks Division
Nabisco Fruit Sancks
Specialty Cereals Pty Limited

CONTACTS: Note: Officers with more than one job title may be intentionally listed here more than once.

A.D. David Mackay, CEO
A.D. David Mackay, Pres.
John A. Bryant, CFO/Exec. VP
Mark Baynes, Global Chief Mktg. Officer
Kathleen Wilson-Thompson, Sr. VP-Global Human Resources
Ruth E. Bruch, CIO/Sr. VP
Gary H. Pilnick, General Counsel/Corp. Sec.
Gary H. Pilnick, Sr. VP-Corp. Dev.
Alan R. Andrews, VP/Corp. Controller
Donna J. Banks, Sr. VP-Global Innovation/Environmental Officer
Celeste Clark, Sr. VP-Corp. Affairs & Global Nutrition
James M. Jenness, Chmn.
Timothy P. Mobsy, Pres., Kellogg Europe

Phone: 269-961-2000	Fax: 269-961-2871
Toll-Free: 800-962-1413	
Address: 1 Kellogg Sq., Battle Creek, MI 49016 US	

GROWTH PLANS/SPECIAL FEATURES:

Kellogg Company is one of the world's largest producers of cereal and a major producer of convenience foods, including cookies, crackers, toaster pastries, cereal bars, frozen waffles, meat alternatives, pie crusts and ice cream cones. The firm's products are manufactured in 19 countries and marketed in over 180 countries worldwide. Kellogg's two major divisions are U.S. and international, which is further divided into Europe, Latin America, Canada, Australia and Asia. Kellogg owns a number of familiar cereal trademarks including Apple Jacks, Corn Pops, Kellogg's Corn Flakes, Crispix, Froot Loops, Frosted Mini-Wheats, Rice Krispies and Special K. Other Kellogg trademarks and products include Eggo frozen waffles, Rice Krispies Treats, Nutri-Grain convenience foods, Pop-Tarts toaster pastries, Kashi nutritional foods and Morningstar Farms meat and dairy alternatives. Cookie and cracker trademarks include Cheez-It, E.L. Fudge, Famous Amos, Chips Deluxe, Hydrox, Soft Batch, Town House, Vienna Fingers and Zesta. Kellogg also owns Keebler Foods Company and its line of snack food products. Kellogg offers a number of products with a focus on health and wellness. These products include: Smart Start, a cold cereal with ingredients that may help lower blood pressure and cholesterol; Special K Protein Meal and Snack Bars; Special K20 Protein Waters, which each contain five grams of protein and come in three fruit flavors; and Special K Honey Nut Cereal Bars. Kellogg's largest customer is Wal-Mart, which accounted for 19% of consolidated net sales in 2007. In 2008, the company acquired the majority of the assets of Zhenghang Food Company Ltd., a China-based manufacturer of cookies and crackers and the assets of IndyBake Products LLC and Brownie Products Co. The firm also acquired Specialty Cereals Pty Limited, a private Australian manufacturer of cereals and the trademarks and recipes of Mother's Cake and Cookie Co.

Employees are offered medical health benefits; tuition reimbursement an employee assistance programs.

FINANCIALS: Sales and profits are in thousands of dollars—add 000 to get the full amount. 2008 Note: Financial information for 2008 was not available for all companies at press time.

2008 Sales: $12,822,000	2008 Profits: $1,953,000	**U.S. Stock Ticker:** K	
2007 Sales: $11,776,000	2007 Profits: $1,103,000	**Int'l Ticker:** Int'l Exchange:	
2006 Sales: $10,906,700	2006 Profits: $1,004,100	Employees: 32,400	
2005 Sales: $10,177,200	2005 Profits: $980,400	Fiscal Year Ends: 12/31	
2004 Sales: $9,613,900	2004 Profits: $890,600	Parent Company:	

SALARIES/BENEFITS:

Pension Plan:	ESOP Stock Plan:	Profit Sharing:	Top Exec. Salary: $1,136,545	Bonus: $2,601,300
Savings Plan: Y	Stock Purch. Plan: Y		Second Exec. Salary: $697,613	Bonus: $992,000

OTHER THOUGHTS:

Apparent Women Officers or Directors: 6
Hot Spot for Advancement for Women/Minorities: Y

LOCATIONS: ("Y" = Yes)

West:	Southwest:	Midwest:	Southeast:	Northeast:	International:
Y	Y	Y	Y	Y	Y

Note: Financial information, benefits and other data can change quickly and may vary from those stated here.

KELLY SERVICES INC

www.kellyservices.com

Industry Group Code: 561320 Ranks within this company's industry group: Sales: 2 Profits: 4

Management:		Sales/Marketing:		Liberal Arts:		Information Systems:		Professionals:		Tech./Scientific:	
Management Trainees:	Y	Marketing Pros.:	Y	Gen. Writing/Editing:	Y	Info. Management:	Y	Finance/Acct.:	Y	Engineers, Electrical:	
Experienced Mngmt.:	Y	Retail Sales:		Technical Writing:	Y	Software Dev.:	Y	Law:	Y	Engineers, Other:	
International Business:	Y	Commercial/Industrial:	Y	Graphic Arts/Photog.:	Y	Hardware Dev.:		HR/Other:	Y	Health/Lab:	
MBA Grads:	Y	Sales Trainees:	Y	Music:		Consulting/Other:		Training:	Y	Scientists/Research:	
		Advertising Pros.:	Y	Broadcasting:				Health Care:		Petroleum/Chemicals:	
				Other:	Y			Consulting:		Math/Other:	

TYPES OF BUSINESS:

Staffing & Temporary Help
Human Resources Consulting
Outsourcing Solutions
Permanent Hiring Programs
Call Center Services
Benefits & Payroll Outsourcing

BRANDS/DIVISIONS/AFFILIATES:

Kelly Office Services
KellyConnect
KellyDirect
Kelly Scientific Resources
P-Serv
CGR/seven LLC
Kelly Financial Resources
Toner Graham

CONTACTS: *Note: Officers with more than one job title may be intentionally listed here more than once.*

Carl T. Camden, CEO
George S. Corona, COO
Carl T. Camden, Pres.
Patricia Little, CFO
Michael S. Morrow, Sr. VP-Global Mktg.
Nina M. Ramsey, Sr. VP-Human Resources
Joseph Drouin, CIO
Michael L. Durik, Chief Admin. Officer/Exec. VP
Daniel T. Lis, General Counsel/Corp. Sec.
Jonathan D. Means, Gen. Mgr.-Oper.
Michael E. Debs, Controller/Chief Acct. Officer
Michael S. Webster, Gen. Mgr.-Americas
Rolf E. Kleiner, Sr. VP-Outsourcing & Consulting Group
Michael S. Morrow, Sr. VP-Mktg.
James H. Bradley, Sr. VP-Admin.
Terence E. Adderley, Chmn.
Leif Agneus, Sr. VP/Gen. Mgr.-EMEA

Phone: 248-362-4444	Fax: 248-244-4360
Toll-Free:	
Address: 999 W. Big Beaver Rd., Troy, MI 48084 US	

GROWTH PLANS/SPECIAL FEATURES:

Kelly Services, Inc. is a staffing solutions and services company that offers temporary staffing services, staff leasing, outsourcing and full-time placement, serving customers in 36 countries and territories. It operates in four segments: Americas-commercial; Americas-professional, technical and staffing alternatives (Americas-PTSA); international-commercial; and international-professional, technical and staffing alternatives (international-PTSA). The Americas-commercial segment includes Kelly Office Services, an administrative support staff; KellyConnect, which offers staff for contact centers, technical support hotlines and telemarketing units; and KellyDirect, a permanent placement service for people of all business areas. The Americas-PTSA segment includes industry-specific services such as CGR/seven, placing employees in creative services positions; Kelly Financial Resources, serving the needs of corporate accounting firms, finance departments and financial institutions; Kelly Law Registry, placing legal professionals including legal administrators, attorneys and paralegals; and Kelly Scientific Resources, which offers entry-level to PhD professionals to a broad spectrum of scientific and clinical research industries. The international-commercial division offers broad commercial staffing services. The international-PTSA segment provides recruitment and IT, financial engineering, health care, legal and scientific staffing. Recent acquisitions include Asian consulting firm P-Serv and Talents Technology, a permanence placement firm operating in the Czech Republic and Poland. In July 2008, the firm agreed to acquire all of Randstad Holding N.V.'s Portugal subsidiaries. In September 2008, Kelly Services acquired U.K. based financial recruitment and accounting company Toner Graham. In October 2008, the company partnered with inData Corporation, an information management and presentation firm, to jointly offer nationwide courtroom presentation services and trial consultation. In November 2008, Kelly Services partnered with Ariba, Inc., a spend management solutions firm, to offer a new network for temporary labor placement.

FINANCIALS: Sales and profits are in thousands of dollars—add 000 to get the full amount. 2008 Note: Financial information for 2008 was not available for all companies at press time.

2008 Sales: $5,517,290	2008 Profits: $-82,239	**U.S. Stock Ticker: KELYA**	
2007 Sales: $5,667,589	2007 Profits: $61,016	**Int'l Ticker:** Int'l Exchange:	
2006 Sales: $5,546,778	2006 Profits: $63,491	Employees: 650,000	
2005 Sales: $5,186,358	2005 Profits: $39,263	Fiscal Year Ends: 12/31	
2004 Sales: $4,932,650	2004 Profits: $21,211	Parent Company:	

SALARIES/BENEFITS:

Pension Plan:	ESOP Stock Plan:	Profit Sharing:	Top Exec. Salary: $917,500	Bonus: $
Savings Plan:	Stock Purch. Plan:		Second Exec. Salary: $614,583	Bonus: $

OTHER THOUGHTS:

Apparent Women Officers or Directors: 7
Hot Spot for Advancement for Women/Minorities: Y

LOCATIONS: ("Y" = Yes)

West:	Southwest:	Midwest:	Southeast:	Northeast:	International:
Y	Y	Y	Y	Y	Y

KENDLE INTERNATIONAL INC

www.kendle.com

Industry Group Code: 325412 Ranks within this company's industry group: Sales: 18   Profits: 15

Management:		Sales/Marketing:		Liberal Arts:		Information Systems:		Professionals:		Tech./Scientific:	
Management Trainees:	Y	Marketing Pros.:	Y	Gen. Writing/Editing:		Info. Management:	Y	Finance/Acct.:	Y	Engineers, Electrical:	Y
Experienced Mngmt.:	Y	Retail Sales:		Technical Writing:	Y	Software Dev.:	Y	Law:	Y	Engineers, Other:	Y
International Business:	Y	Commercial/Industrial:	Y	Graphic Arts/Photog.:	Y	Hardware Dev.:		HR/Other:	Y	Health/Lab:	Y
MBA Grads:	Y	Sales Trainees:		Music:		Consulting/Other:	Y	Training:	Y	Scientists/Research:	Y
		Advertising Pros.:		Broadcasting:				Health Care:	Y	Petroleum/Chemicals:	Y
				Other:				Consulting:		Math/Other:	Y

TYPES OF BUSINESS:

Pharmaceutical Development-Clinical Trials
Statistical Analysis
Technical Writing
Regulatory Assistance
Consulting Services
Clinical Trial Software
Clinical Data Management
e-Learning

BRANDS/DIVISIONS/AFFILIATES:

eKendleCollege
TrialWare
TrialWeb
TrialBase
TrialView
TriaLine
Early Stage
Late Stage

CONTACTS: Note: Officers with more than one job title may be intentionally listed here more than once.

Candace Kendle, CEO
Christopher C. Bergen, COO
Simon Higginbotham, Pres.
Karl Brenkert, III, CFO/Sr. VP
Alan J. Boyce, Chief Mktg. Officer
Karen L. Crone, VP-Global Human Resources
Gary Wedig, CIO/VP
Karl Brenkert, III, Corp. Sec.
Lori Dorer, Dir.-Corp. Comm.
Michael Lawson, Dir.-Investor Rel.
Anthony L. Forcellini, Treas.
Martha Feller, Sr. VP-Global Clinical Dev.
Melanie A. Bruno, VP-Global Regulatory Affairs, Quality & Safety
Philip J.W. Davies, VP-Phase I
Patricia A. Steigerwald, VP-Global Late Phase
Candace Kendle, Chmn.
Ross J. Horsburgh, VP-Global Clinical Dev., Asia/Pacific

Phone: 513-381-5550	Fax: 513-381-5870
Toll-Free: 800-733-1572	
Address: 441 Vine St., Ste. 1200, Cincinnati, OH 45202 US	

GROWTH PLANS/SPECIAL FEATURES:

Kendle International, Inc. is a global clinical research organization that provides a broad range of Phase I-IV global clinical development services to the biopharmaceutical industry. The company supplements the research and development activities of biopharmaceutical companies by offering clinical research services and information technology designed to reduce the time and expense of drug development. The firm operates in two segments: early stage, which handles all Phase I testing services; and late stage, which handles all Phase II-IV services. Kendle's services include clinical trial management, clinical data management, statistical analysis, technical writing and regulatory consulting/representation. It a state-of-the-art clinical pharmacology unit in the Netherlands, where it offers Phase I clinical trials with drugs under development. The company's therapeutic expertise covers fields such as cardiovascular, dermatological, hematological, metabolic and respiratory health. The firm's proprietary TrialWare product line includes a database management system, TrialBase; a validated medical imaging system, TrialView; an interactive voice response patient randomization systsem, TriaLine; an Internet based collaborative tool, TrialWeb; a global project management system, TrialWatch; and a late phase technology system, Trial4. Additionally, the company operates Kendle College, an online e-learning division that runs seminars and training programs, focusing on the organization of clinical trials. In June 2008, Kendle International acquired Canadian company DecisionLine Clinical Research Corporation, providing Kendle with a new high-end medical facility in Toronto; the new facility has been incorporated into the firm's early stage division. In January 2009, Kendle International opened a new office in Ahmedabad, India.

The company offers its employees medical, dental and vision insurance; flexible spending accounts; life and AD&D insurance; a 401(k) plan; tuition reimbursement; and a profit sharing plan. The firm also offers opportunities for professional and personal development through eKendle College.

FINANCIALS: Sales and profits are in thousands of dollars—add 000 to get the full amount. 2008 Note: Financial information for 2008 was not available for all companies at press time.

2008 Sales: $678,581	2008 Profits: $29,397	**U.S. Stock Ticker:** KNDL
2007 Sales: $568,818	2007 Profits: $18,687	**Int'l Ticker:** Int'l Exchange:
2006 Sales: $373,936	2006 Profits: $8,530	Employees: 4,275
2005 Sales: $250,639	2005 Profits: $10,674	Fiscal Year Ends: 12/31
2004 Sales: $215,868	2004 Profits: $3,572	Parent Company:

SALARIES/BENEFITS:

Pension Plan:	ESOP Stock Plan:	Profit Sharing: Y	Top Exec. Salary: $581,450	Bonus: $84,000
Savings Plan: Y	Stock Purch. Plan:		Second Exec. Salary: $422,050	Bonus: $48,160

OTHER THOUGHTS:

Apparent Women Officers or Directors: 8
Hot Spot for Advancement for Women/Minorities: Y

LOCATIONS: ("Y" = Yes)

West:	Southwest:	Midwest:	Southeast:	Northeast:	International:
Y		Y		Y	Y

Note: Financial information, benefits and other data can change quickly and may vary from those stated here.

KIMBERLY-CLARK CORP

www.kimberly-clark.com

Industry Group Code: 322 Ranks within this company's industry group: Sales: 1 Profits: 1

Management:		Sales/Marketing:		Liberal Arts:		Information Systems:		Professionals:		Tech./Scientific:	
Management Trainees:	Y	Marketing Pros.:	Y	Gen. Writing/Editing:	Y	Info. Management:	Y	Finance/Acct.:	Y	Engineers, Electrical:	
Experienced Mngmt.:	Y	Retail Sales:		Technical Writing:		Software Dev.:	Y	Law:	Y	Engineers, Other:	
International Business:	Y	Commercial/Industrial:	Y	Graphic Arts/Photog.:	Y	Hardware Dev.:		HR/Other:	Y	Health/Lab:	
MBA Grads:	Y	Sales Trainees:	Y	Music:		Consulting/Other:		Training:	Y	Scientists/Research:	
		Advertising Pros.:	Y	Broadcasting:				Health Care:		Petroleum/Chemicals:	
				Other:	Y			Consulting:		Math/Other:	

TYPES OF BUSINESS:

Personal Care Products-Paper
Consumer Tissue Products
Safety Products
Healthcare Products

BRANDS/DIVISIONS/AFFILIATES:

Kleenex
Scott
Huggies
Kotex
Depend
Pull-Ups
Jackson Products, Inc.
Colombiana Kimberly Colpapel S.A.

CONTACTS: *Note: Officers with more than one job title may be intentionally listed here more than once.*

Thomas J. Falk, CEO
Thomas J. Falk, Pres.
Mark A. Buthman, CFO/Sr. VP
Anthony J. Palmer, Chief Mktg. Officer/Sr. VP
Lizanne C. Gottung, Sr. VP-Human Resources
Thomas J. Mielke, Sr. VP-Law/Chief Compliance Officer
Christian A. Brickman, Chief Strategy Officer/Sr. VP
Thomas J. Mielke, Sr. VP-Gov't Affairs
Michael D. Masseth, VP-Investor Rel.
Robert W. Black, Pres., Developing & Emerging Markets
Joanne Bauer, Pres., Healthcare Bus.
Robert. E. Abernathy, Pres., North Atlantic Consumer Prod.
Jan B. Spencer, Pres., Kimberly-Clark Professional
Thomas J. Falk, Chmn.

Phone: 972-281-1200	Fax: 972-281-1490
Toll-Free:	
Address: P.O. Box 619100, Dallas, TX 75261-9100 US	

GROWTH PLANS/SPECIAL FEATURES:

Kimberly-Clark Corp. (KC) is a health and hygiene company that manufactures and markets a wide range of health and hygiene products in 35 countries. KC operates in four segments: KC professional and other; personal care; consumer tissue; and healthcare. The KC professional and other segment manufactures and markets paper towels; napkins; wipers; facial and bathroom tissue; and a range of safety products for the away-from-home marketplace. Brand names in this segment include Kimberly-Clark, Kimtech, Kleenguard, Scott, WypAll, Kleenex and Kimcare. The personal care segment manufactures and markets products such as feminine and incontinence care products; baby wipes; training, youth and swim pants; and disposable diapers. Items in this segment are sold under brand names such as Kotex, Lightdays, Depend, Poise, Little-Swimmers, Pull-Ups, Huggies and GoodNites. The consumer tissue segment manufactures and markets napkins; paper towels; facial and bathroom tissue; and related products for household use. Products in this division are sold under brands such as Scott, Kleenex, Viva, Andrex, Scottex, Cottonelle, Page and Hakle. The healthcare segment manufactures and markets sterilization wrap; drapes; surgical gowns; disposable face masks and exam gloves; respiratory products; infection control products; and other disposable medical items. Products in this division are sold under brand names such as Kimberly-Clark and Ballard. In 2008, sales to Wal-Mart Stores, Inc., accounted for approximately 14% of the company's sales. KC products are sold in over 150 countries. In October 2008, the firm agreed to acquire the remaining 31% interest in Colombiana Kimberly Colpapel S.A., KC's Andean subsidiary, from Compania Colombiana de Inversiones S.A. In April 2009, the company acquired safety products provider Jackson Products, Inc. Also in April 2009, the firm released Scott Naturals, a line of partially recycled napkins, bathroom tissue and paper towels; and the hypoallergenic Huggies Pure & Natural diapers, made from 20% recycled materials.

FINANCIALS: Sales and profits are in thousands of dollars—add 000 to get the full amount. 2008 Note: Financial information for 2008 was not available for all companies at press time.

2008 Sales: $19,415,000	2008 Profits: $1,690,000	U.S. Stock Ticker: KMB
2007 Sales: $18,266,000	2007 Profits: $1,822,900	Int'l Ticker: Int'l Exchange:
2006 Sales: $16,746,900	2006 Profits: $1,499,500	Employees: 53,000
2005 Sales: $15,902,600	2005 Profits: $1,568,300	Fiscal Year Ends: 12/31
2004 Sales: $15,083,200	2004 Profits: $1,800,200	Parent Company:

SALARIES/BENEFITS:

Pension Plan: Y	ESOP Stock Plan:	Profit Sharing:	Top Exec. Salary: $1,224,996	Bonus: $943,247
Savings Plan:	Stock Purch. Plan:		Second Exec. Salary: $645,000	Bonus: $370,260

OTHER THOUGHTS:

Apparent Women Officers or Directors: 4
Hot Spot for Advancement for Women/Minorities: Y

LOCATIONS: ("Y" = Yes)

West:	Southwest:	Midwest:	Southeast:	Northeast:	International:
Y	Y	Y	Y	Y	Y

KINDRED HEALTHCARE INC

www.kindredhealthcare.com

Industry Group Code: 623110 Ranks within this company's industry group: Sales: 1 Profits: 2

Management:		Sales/Marketing:		Liberal Arts:		Information Systems:		Professionals:		Tech./Scientific:	
Management Trainees:	Y	Marketing Pros.:	Y	Gen. Writing/Editing:	Y	Info. Management:	Y	Finance/Acct.:	Y	Engineers, Electrical:	
Experienced Mngmt.:	Y	Retail Sales:		Technical Writing:	Y	Software Dev.:	Y	Law:	Y	Engineers, Other:	
International Business:		Commercial/Industrial:		Graphic Arts/Photog.:	Y	Hardware Dev.:		HR/Other:	Y	Health/Lab:	Y
MBA Grads:	Y	Sales Trainees:		Music:		Consulting/Other:		Training:	Y	Scientists/Research:	
		Advertising Pros.:	Y	Broadcasting:				Health Care:	Y	Petroleum/Chemicals:	
				Other:	Y			Consulting:		Math/Other:	

TYPES OF BUSINESS:

Hospitals
Nursing Centers
Contract Rehabilitation Services

BRANDS/DIVISIONS/AFFILIATES:

Peoplefirst Rehabilitation

CONTACTS: Note: Officers with more than one job title may be intentionally listed here more than once.

Paul J. Diaz, CEO
Frank J. Battafarano, COO
Paul J. Diaz, Pres.
Richard A. Lechleiter, CFO/Exec. VP
Richard E. Chapman, CIO/Exec. VP
Richard E. Chapman, Chief Admin. Officer
M. Suzanne Riedman, General Counsel/Sr. VP
Gregory C. Miller, Sr. VP-Corp. Dev. & Financial Planning
Benjamin A. Breier, Exec. VP/Pres., Hospital Div.
Lane M. Bowen, Exec. VP/Pres., Health Svcs. Div.
William M. Altman, Sr. VP-Strategy & Public Policy
Joseph L. Landenwich, Sr. VP-Corp. Legal Affairs/Corp. Sec.
Edward L. Kuntz, Chmn.

Phone: 502-596-7300	Fax:
Toll-Free: 800-545-0749	
Address: 680 S. 4th St., Louisville, KY 40202 US	

GROWTH PLANS/SPECIAL FEATURES:

Kindred Healthcare, Inc. is a healthcare services company that operates hospitals, nursing centers and a contract rehabilitation services business across the U.S. The company runs three operating divisions. The hospital division operates 82 long-term acute care hospitals with 6,482 licensed beds in 24 states. The firm treats medically complex patients, including the critically ill, suffering from multiple organ system failures, most commonly the cardiovascular, pulmonary, kidney, gastrointestinal and cutaneous systems. A number of hospitals in this division offer skilled nursing, sub-acute and outpatient services, which may include diagnostic services, rehabilitation therapy, CT scanning, one-day surgery and laboratory. More than 62% of patients are over 65 years of age. The health service division operates 228 nursing centers with 28,525 licensed beds in 27 states. Through its nursing centers, Kindred Healthcare provides long-term care services; a full range of pharmacy, medical and clinical services; and routine services, including daily dietary, social and recreational services. A number of nursing centers offer specialized programs for residents suffering from Alzheimer's disease and other dementias. The contract rehabilitation services business provides rehabilitative services under the name Peoplefirst Rehabilitation in 514 nursing centers, 87 hospitals and 54 other locations in 40 states. In addition to standard physical, occupational and speech therapies, the company provides specialized care programs for wound care, pain management, cognitive deficit, neurologic, orthopedic and pulmonary rehabilitation therapies. In February 2008, Kindred reopened the relocated and expanded Indianapolis South in Greenwood, Indiana, and opened the new long term acute care Northwest Phoenix hospital in Peoria, Arizona. In September 2008, the company announced plans to sell two unprofitable hospitals. In October 2008, the firm opened a hospital in Palm Beach County, Florida, and announced plans for another hospital in Melbourne, Florida. In June 2009, Kindred acquired six under-performing nursing centers from Ventas, Inc.

FINANCIALS: Sales and profits are in thousands of dollars—add 000 to get the full amount. 2008 Note: Financial information for 2008 was not available for all companies at press time.

2008 Sales: $4,151,396	2008 Profits: $36,285	**U.S. Stock Ticker:** KND	
2007 Sales: $4,220,266	2007 Profits: $-46,870	**Int'l Ticker:** Int'l Exchange:	
2006 Sales: $4,266,661	2006 Profits: $78,711	Employees: 53,700	
2005 Sales: $3,852,975	2005 Profits: $144,909	Fiscal Year Ends: 12/31	
2004 Sales: $3,421,411	2004 Profits: $70,580	Parent Company:	

SALARIES/BENEFITS:

Pension Plan:	ESOP Stock Plan:	Profit Sharing:	Top Exec. Salary: $998,269	Bonus: $1,083,575
Savings Plan:	Stock Purch. Plan:		Second Exec. Salary: $898,408	Bonus: $

OTHER THOUGHTS:

Apparent Women Officers or Directors: 1
Hot Spot for Advancement for Women/Minorities: Y

LOCATIONS: ("Y" = Yes)

West:	Southwest:	Midwest:	Southeast:	Northeast:	International:
Y	Y	Y	Y	Y	

KOCH INDUSTRIES INC

Industry Group Code: 324110 **Ranks within this company's industry group:** Sales: 2   Profits:

www.kochind.com

Management:		Sales/Marketing:		Liberal Arts:		Information Systems:		Professionals:		Tech./Scientific:	
Management Trainees:		Marketing Pros.:	Y	Gen. Writing/Editing:	Y	Info. Management:	Y	Finance/Acct.:	Y	Engineers, Electrical:	Y
Experienced Mngmt.:	Y	Retail Sales:		Technical Writing:	Y	Software Dev.:	Y	Law:	Y	Engineers, Other:	Y
International Business:	Y	Commercial/Industrial:	Y	Graphic Arts/Photog.:	Y	Hardware Dev.:		HR/Other:	Y	Health/Lab:	
MBA Grads:	Y	Sales Trainees:		Music:		Consulting/Other:		Training:	Y	Scientists/Research:	
		Advertising Pros.:		Broadcasting:				Health Care:		Petroleum/Chemicals:	Y
				Other:				Consulting:		Math/Other:	

TYPES OF BUSINESS:

Petroleum Refining
Chemicals
Textiles
Pipelines
Fertilizer Production
Chemical Equipment
Asphalt & Paving Supplies
Beef Production

BRANDS/DIVISIONS/AFFILIATES:

Flint Hills Resources
Koch Mineral Services
Matador Cattle Company
Koch Pipeline Company
Koch Chemical Technologies Group
Koch Fertilizer LLC
INVISTA
Georgia-Pacific Corp

CONTACTS: *Note: Officers with more than one job title may be intentionally listed here more than once.*

Charles G. Koch, CEO
David L. Robertson, COO
David L. Robertson, Pres.
David H. Koch, Exec. VP
Charles G. Koch, Chmn.

Phone: 316-828-5500	Fax:
Toll-Free:	
Address: 4111 E. 37th St. N., Wichita, KS 67220 US	

GROWTH PLANS/SPECIAL FEATURES:

Koch Industries, Inc. is a diversified group of companies with operations in markets as diverse as refining and chemicals; process and pollution control equipment and technologies; minerals and fertilizers; polymers and fibers; commodity and financial trading and services; and forest and consumer products. It also conducts operations in venture capital investments, municipal finance, capital market investments and business development. Subsidiary Flint Hills Resources operates petroleum refineries in Alaska, Minnesota and Texas, with a combined crude oil processing capacity of more than 800,000 barrels per day. These plants produce aromatics, olefins, polymers and intermediate chemicals. Flint Hills also produces and markets asphalt in the Midwest and owns an interest in a base oil facility in Louisiana. Subsidiary Koch Mineral Services supplies coal and petroleum coke as well as cement, pulp and paper, sulfur and related products internationally. Koch Fertilizer LLC and its affiliates own or have interests in nitrogen fertilizer plants capable of manufacturing more than 9 million metric tons of nitrogen products annually. Koch's ranching subsidiary, Matador Cattle Company, operates three ranches with a total of 15,000 head of cattle. Subsidiary Koch Pipeline Company, LP and its affiliates operate a 4,000-mile network of pipelines. Subsidiary Koch Chemical Technologies Group and its affiliates design, manufacture, sell, install and service process and pollution control equipment. Subsidiary INVISTA is a global producer and marketer of polymers and fibers, primarily for nylon, spandex and polyester applications. Subsidiary Georgia-Pacific manufactures and markets tissue, packaging, paper, building products, related chemicals and fluff, filter and market pulp under such brand names as Quilted Northern, Angel Soft, Brawny and Dixie. In September 2008, Koch Fertilizer acquired certain assets of Usborne Fertiliser Limited, a U.K.-based fertilizer importing and marketing firm.

Koch offers its employees educational assistance, flexible spending accounts and medical, dental, life, AD&D and disability insurance.

FINANCIALS: Sales and profits are in thousands of dollars—add 000 to get the full amount. 2008 Note: Financial information for 2008 was not available for all companies at press time.

2008 Sales: $100,000,000	2008 Profits: $	U.S. Stock Ticker: Private	
2007 Sales: $98,000,000	2007 Profits: $	Int'l Ticker:	Int'l Exchange:
2006 Sales: $90,000,000	2006 Profits: $	Employees: 70,000	
2005 Sales: $80,000,000	2005 Profits: $	Fiscal Year Ends: 12/31	
2004 Sales: $60,000,000	2004 Profits: $	Parent Company:	

SALARIES/BENEFITS:

Pension Plan: Y	ESOP Stock Plan:	Profit Sharing:	Top Exec. Salary: $	Bonus: $
Savings Plan: Y	Stock Purch. Plan:		Second Exec. Salary: $	Bonus: $

OTHER THOUGHTS:

Apparent Women Officers or Directors:
Hot Spot for Advancement for Women/Minorities:

LOCATIONS: ("Y" = Yes)

West:	Southwest:	Midwest:	Southeast:	Northeast:	International:
Y	Y	Y	Y	Y	Y

KOHL'S CORP

www.kohls.com

Industry Group Code: 452112 **Ranks within this company's industry group:** Sales: 5   Profits: 5

Management:		Sales/Marketing:		Liberal Arts:		Information Systems:		Professionals:		Tech./Scientific:	
Management Trainees:	Y	Marketing Pros.:	Y	Gen. Writing/Editing:	Y	Info. Management:	Y	Finance/Acct.:	Y	Engineers, Electrical:	
Experienced Mngmt.:	Y	Retail Sales:	Y	Technical Writing:		Software Dev.:	Y	Law:	Y	Engineers, Other:	
International Business:		Commercial/Industrial:		Graphic Arts/Photog.:	Y	Hardware Dev.:		HR/Other:	Y	Health/Lab:	
MBA Grads:	Y	Sales Trainees:	Y	Music:		Consulting/Other:		Training:	Y	Scientists/Research:	
		Advertising Pros.:	Y	Broadcasting:				Health Care:		Petroleum/Chemicals:	
				Other:	Y			Consulting:		Math/Other:	

TYPES OF BUSINESS:

Discount Department Stores
Online Sales

BRANDS/DIVISIONS/AFFILIATES:

Kohls.com

CONTACTS:
Note: Officers with more than one job title may be intentionally listed here more than once.

Kevin Mansell, CEO
Kevin Mansell, Pres.
Wes McDonald, CFO/Exec. VP
Tom Kingsbury, Sr. Exec. VP-Mktg.
Tom Kingsbury, Sr. Exec. VP-Info. Svcs.
Donald Brennan, Sr. Exec. VP-Merch.
Richard Schepp, General Counsel/Exec. VP/Sec.
Vicki Shamion, VP-Public Rel.
John Worthington, Sr. Exec. VP-Store Oper. & Store Admin.
John Worthington, Sr. Exec. VP-Merch. Presentation & Loss Prevention
Larry Montgomery, Chmn.

Phone: 262-703-7000	Fax:
Toll-Free:	
Address: N56 W17000 Ridgewood Dr., Menomonee Falls, WI 53051 US	

GROWTH PLANS/SPECIAL FEATURES:

Kohl's Corp. operates family-oriented specialty department stores. The company currently operates 1,004 stores in 48 states, with three store formats: prototype, small and urban. Kohl's stores offer merchandise that consists of apparel, shoes and accessories for women, children and men; soft home products, such as sheets and pillows; and other home products such as small electrics and luggage. Kohl's offered brands include Dockers, Lee, Levi's, Jockey, Candie's, Nike, Simply Vera Vera Wang, Dana Buchman Food Network, Vanity Fair and Chaps. Brands introduced in 2009 include Jumping Beans, a children's brand; Bobby Flay, an expansion of the Food Network brand; FILA Sport, performance and leisure apparel, footwear and accessories for men, women and children; ELLE, women's apparel; and Abbey Dawn, a junior's lifestyle brand by singer Avril Lavigne. The company also markets its products online. The company has nine distribution centers and a 940,000-square-foot fulfillment center for its e-commerce site, www.Kohls.com. In June 2008, Kohl's agreed to become exclusive U.S. retailer for the Hang Ten brand, owned by American Brand Holdings. The firm plans to open about 50 new stores during 2009. In March 2009, the company announced Candie's has signed an exclusive partnership with Britney Spears. Spears will appear in print, television, online and in-store marketing and advertising campaigns for 2009; the firm will also be integrated into all of Spear's upcoming promotional activities. In April 2009, the company opened 11 new stores including Kohl's debut in Alaska. The firm plans to open about 50 new stores during 2009.

The company offers its employees medical, dental and vision insurance; long-term disability and life insurance; a 401(k) plan; an employee stock ownership plan; tuition reimbursement; and merchandise discounts.

FINANCIALS:
Sales and profits are in thousands of dollars—add 000 to get the full amount. 2008 Note: Financial information for 2008 was not available for all companies at press time.

2008 Sales: $16,473,734	2008 Profits: $1,083,851	**U.S. Stock Ticker: KSS**
2007 Sales: $15,596,910	2007 Profits: $1,108,681	**Int'l Ticker:** Int'l Exchange:
2006 Sales: $13,402,217	2006 Profits: $841,960	Employees: 126,000
2005 Sales: $11,700,619	2005 Profits: $730,380	Fiscal Year Ends: 1/31
2004 Sales: $10,282,094	2004 Profits: $591,152	Parent Company:

SALARIES/BENEFITS:

Pension Plan:	ESOP Stock Plan: Y	Profit Sharing:	Top Exec. Salary: $1,150,000	Bonus: $
Savings Plan: Y	Stock Purch. Plan:		Second Exec. Salary: $1,067,500	Bonus: $

OTHER THOUGHTS:

Apparent Women Officers or Directors: 1
Hot Spot for Advancement for Women/Minorities: Y

LOCATIONS: ("Y" = Yes)

West:	Southwest:	Midwest:	Southeast:	Northeast:	International:
Y	Y	Y	Y	Y	

KPMG LLP

www.us.kpmg.com

Industry Group Code: 5412 **Ranks within this company's industry group:** Sales: 4   Profits:

Management:		Sales/Marketing:		Liberal Arts:		Information Systems:		Professionals:		Tech./Scientific:	
Management Trainees:	Y	Marketing Pros.:	Y	Gen. Writing/Editing:	Y	Info. Management:	Y	Finance/Acct.:	Y	Engineers, Electrical:	
Experienced Mngmt.:	Y	Retail Sales:		Technical Writing:	Y	Software Dev.:	Y	Law:	Y	Engineers, Other:	
International Business:	Y	Commercial/Industrial:	Y	Graphic Arts/Photog.:	Y	Hardware Dev.:		HR/Other:	Y	Health/Lab:	
MBA Grads:	Y	Sales Trainees:		Music:		Consulting/Other:	Y	Training:	Y	Scientists/Research:	
		Advertising Pros.:	Y	Broadcasting:				Health Care:		Petroleum/Chemicals:	
				Other:	Y			Consulting:	Y	Math/Other:	

TYPES OF BUSINESS:

Accounting Services
Human Resource Advisory Services
Accounting Technology
Publications
Risk Management

BRANDS/DIVISIONS/AFFILIATES:

KPMG International
Audit Committee Institute
KPMG TaxWatch Thought Leadership Series
Japanese Practice
Tax Governance Institute
KPMG Canada
Chartwell International Holdings, Inc.
Chartwell IRM, Inc.

CONTACTS: Note: Officers with more than one job title may be intentionally listed here more than once.

John B. Veihmeyer, CEO
Jack T. Taylor, COO
Richard S. Hiss, Exec. Dir.-Mktg. & Industries
Richard (Dick) K. Anderson, CIO
Jack T. Taylor, Exec. VP-Oper.
Dan Ginsburg, Dir.-Corp. Comm.
Deborah Primano, Sr. Dir.-Tax Comm.
Vicki Gault, Sr. Dir.-Advisory Comm.
George Ledwith, Global Dir.-External Comm.
Patrick (Pat) W. Dolan, Head-Consumer Markets
Timothy P. Flynn, Chmn.

Phone: 212-909-5600	**Fax:** 212-909-5699
Toll-Free:	
Address: 757 3rd Ave., New York, NY 10017 US	

GROWTH PLANS/SPECIAL FEATURES:

KPMG LLP, the U.S. subsidiary of global accounting cooperative KPMG International, is a leading provider of audit, advisory and tax services across the U.S. The firm's audit operations are based on a multidisciplinary approach focused on compliance tools, technological assistance and cultural values central to clients' companies. KPMG founded and maintains the Audit Committee Institute, designed to educate audit committee members about governance, accounting, financial reporting and other audit issues. KPMG's tax services segment provides tax assistance in the following areas: economic and valuation services; exempt organizations tax; federal tax; international corporate tax; international executive services; legislative and regulatory services; mergers and acquisitions; state and local tax; and trade and customs. The company also provides tax-related news through its KPMG TaxWatch Thought Leadership Series and tax-related newsletters and publications. The firm's advisory services division assists its clients in achieving strengthened governance, reporting and internal controls; early identification and assessment of risk and control issues that affect performance; improved efficiency and effectiveness of key business processes; and informed responses to existing and proposed regulatory requirements. With approximately 100 offices across the U.S., KPMG serves companies and organizations in such major industry sectors as financial services; industrial markets; consumer markets; information, communications and entertainment; government; and healthcare. The firm also maintains a special focus group that has industry experience with the issues Japanese companies face in the U.S., as well as both Japanese and American business cultures, practices and standards. In 2009, KPMG Canada announced plans to acquire Chartwell International Holdings, Inc. and subsidiary Chartwell IRM, Inc., a Canadian consulting firm dedicated to Enterprise Architecture and public-sector transformation.

KPMG offers employees alternative work arrangements; a mortgage assistance program; flexible spending accounts; and comprehensive health insurance. The firm was named one of Fortune Magazine's 100 Best Companies to Work For in 2009.

FINANCIALS: Sales and profits are in thousands of dollars—add 000 to get the full amount. 2008 Note: Financial information for 2008 was not available for all companies at press time.

2008 Sales: $7,000,000	2008 Profits: $	**U.S. Stock Ticker: Subsidiary**
2007 Sales: $6,000,000	2007 Profits: $	**Int'l Ticker:** Int'l Exchange:
2006 Sales: $5,000,000	2006 Profits: $	Employees: 30,000
2005 Sales: $4,700,000	2005 Profits: $	Fiscal Year Ends: 9/30
2004 Sales: $4,100,000	2004 Profits: $	Parent Company: KPMG INTERNATIONAL

SALARIES/BENEFITS:

Pension Plan: Y	ESOP Stock Plan:	Profit Sharing:	Top Exec. Salary: $	Bonus: $
Savings Plan: Y	Stock Purch. Plan:		Second Exec. Salary: $	Bonus: $

OTHER THOUGHTS:

Apparent Women Officers or Directors: 2
Hot Spot for Advancement for Women/Minorities: Y

LOCATIONS: ("Y" = Yes)

West:	Southwest:	Midwest:	Southeast:	Northeast:	International:
Y	Y	Y	Y	Y	Y

Note: Financial information, benefits and other data can change quickly and may vary from those stated here.

KRAFT FOODS INC

www.kraft.com

Industry Group Code: 311 Ranks within this company's industry group: Sales: 1 Profits: 1

Management:		Sales/Marketing:		Liberal Arts:		Information Systems:		Professionals:		Tech./Scientific:	
Management Trainees:	Y	Marketing Pros.:	Y	Gen. Writing/Editing:	Y	Info. Management:	Y	Finance/Acct.:	Y	Engineers, Electrical:	
Experienced Mngmt.:	Y	Retail Sales:		Technical Writing:	Y	Software Dev.:	Y	Law:	Y	Engineers, Other:	Y
International Business:	Y	Commercial/Industrial:	Y	Graphic Arts/Photog.:	Y	Hardware Dev.:		HR/Other:	Y	Health/Lab:	
MBA Grads:	Y	Sales Trainees:	Y	Music:		Consulting/Other:		Training:	Y	Scientists/Research:	
		Advertising Pros.:	Y	Broadcasting:				Health Care:		Petroleum/Chemicals:	
				Other:				Consulting:		Math/Other:	

TYPES OF BUSINESS:

Food Manufacturing
Snack Foods
Beverages
Prepared Foods
Convenience Meals
Cheese Products
Energy & Nutrition Products
Processed Meats

BRANDS/DIVISIONS/AFFILIATES:

Altria Group Inc
Jacobs
Maxwell House
Philadelphia
Velveeta
Oscar Mayer
Jell-O
Oreo

CONTACTS: *Note: Officers with more than one job title may be intentionally listed here more than once.*

Irene Rosenfeld, CEO
Timothy R. McLevish, CFO/Exec. VP
Mary Beth West, Chief Mktg. Officer/Exec. VP
Karen May, Exec. VP-Global Human Resources
Jean Spence, Exec. VP-R&D
Marc Firestone, General Counsel/Exec. VP-Legal Affairs/Corp. Sec.
David Brearton, Exec. VP-Oper. & Bus. Svcs.
Michael Osanloo, Exec. VP-Strategy
Richard Searer, Pres., North America/Exec. VP
Gustavo Abelenda, Pres., Kraft Latin America
Maurizio Calenti, Pres., Kraft EMEA/VP
Pradeep Pant, Pres., Kraft Asia Pacific
Irene Rosenfeld, Chmn.
Sanjay Khosla, Pres., Kraft Int'l/Exec. VP
Franz-Josef H. Vogelsang, Exec. VP-Global Supply Chain

Phone: 847-646-2000	Fax: 847-646-6005
Toll-Free:	
Address: 3 Lakes Dr., Northfield, IL 60093 US	

GROWTH PLANS/SPECIAL FEATURES:

Kraft Foods, Inc., formerly part of Altria Group, Inc., is one of the largest food companies in the U.S, which manufactures and markets packaged food products. The company's products consist principally of snacks, generating roughly 31% of its revenues; beverages, generating roughly 22%; cheese and dairy products, generating roughly 19%; convenient meals, generating roughly 15%; and various packaged grocery products; generating roughly 14%. Kraft has operations in more than 70 countries and sells its products in more than 150 countries. The company markets many of the world's leading food brands with more than 50 of which have revenues of $100 million and nine of which have revenues exceeding of $1 billion. Some of its major brands include Jacobs, Maxwell House, Gevalia, Kool-Aid, Tang, Crystal Light and Country Time beverages; Philadelphia, Velveeta, Cheez Whiz, Deli Deluxe and Knudsen cheese products; DiGiorno, Tombstone, Lunchables, Oscar Mayer, Boca and Stove Top convenient meal products; Jell-O, Cool Whip, Handi-Snacks, Miracle Whip, A.1., Bull's-Eye, Grey Poupon and Shake' N Bake grocery products; and Oreo, Chips Ahoy!, Newtons, Nilla, Nutter Butter, SnackWell's, Ritz, Triscuit, Wheat Thins, Cheese Nips, Teddy Grahams, Planters and Toblerone snacks. These products are generally sold to supermarket chains, wholesalers, club stores, mass merchandisers, distributors, convenience stores, gasoline stations and other retail food outlets. In August 2008, the company completed the sale of its Post cereals business to Ralcorp Holdings, Inc.

FINANCIALS: Sales and profits are in thousands of dollars—add 000 to get the full amount. 2008 Note: Financial information for 2008 was not available for all companies at press time.

2008 Sales: $42,201,000	2008 Profits: $2,901,000	**U.S. Stock Ticker: KFT**	
2007 Sales: $37,241,000	2007 Profits: $2,590,000	**Int'l Ticker:** Int'l Exchange:	
2006 Sales: $34,356,000	2006 Profits: $3,060,000	Employees: 98,000	
2005 Sales: $34,113,000	2005 Profits: $2,632,000	Fiscal Year Ends: 12/31	
2004 Sales: $32,168,000	2004 Profits: $2,665,000	Parent Company:	

SALARIES/BENEFITS:

Pension Plan: Y	ESOP Stock Plan:	Profit Sharing:	Top Exec. Salary: $1,452,231	Bonus: $4,070,000
Savings Plan: Y	Stock Purch. Plan:		Second Exec. Salary: $718,654	Bonus: $810,000

OTHER THOUGHTS:

Apparent Women Officers or Directors: 8
Hot Spot for Advancement for Women/Minorities: Y

LOCATIONS: ("Y" = Yes)

West:	Southwest:	Midwest:	Southeast:	Northeast:	International:
Y	Y	Y	Y	Y	Y

KROGER CO (THE)

Industry Group Code: 445110 **Ranks within this company's industry group:** Sales: 1   Profits: 1

Management:		Sales/Marketing:		Liberal Arts:		Information Systems:		Professionals:		Tech./Scientific:	
Management Trainees:	Y	Marketing Pros.:	Y	Gen. Writing/Editing:	Y	Info. Management:	Y	Finance/Acct.:	Y	Engineers, Electrical:	
Experienced Mngmt.:	Y	Retail Sales:	Y	Technical Writing:		Software Dev.:	Y	Law:	Y	Engineers, Other:	
International Business:		Commercial/Industrial:		Graphic Arts/Photog.:	Y	Hardware Dev.:		HR/Other:	Y	Health/Lab:	
MBA Grads:	Y	Sales Trainees:	Y	Music:		Consulting/Other:		Training:	Y	Scientists/Research:	
		Advertising Pros.:	Y	Broadcasting:				Health Care:		Petroleum/Chemicals:	
				Other:	Y			Consulting:		Math/Other:	

TYPES OF BUSINESS:

Grocery Stores
Convenience Stores
Jewelry Stores
Pharmacies
Food Processing
Gas Stations
Department Stores

BRANDS/DIVISIONS/AFFILIATES:

Smith's Food & Drug Centers Inc
Fry's
Barclay
QFC
Ralph's
Smith's
King Soopers
Quik Stop

CONTACTS: *Note: Officers with more than one job title may be intentionally listed here more than once.*

David Dillon, CEO
Rodney W. McMullen, COO
Rodney W. McMullen, Pres.
J. Michael Schlotman, CFO/Sr. VP
Della Wall, VP-Human Resources
Christopher Hjelm, CIO/Sr. VP
Joseph Grieshaber, VP-Merch., Procurement & Perishables
Calvin Kaufman, VP/Pres., Kroger Mfg.
Paul Heldman, General Counsel/Exec. VP/Sec.
Elizabeth M. Van Oflen, Controller/VP
Donald E. Becker, Exec. VP
Carver Johnson, Chief Diversity Officer
R. Pete Williams, Sr. VP
Scott Henderson, Treas./VP
David Dillon, Chmn.
Kevin Dougherty, VP-Logistics

Phone: 513-762-4000	**Fax:** 513-762-1160
Toll-Free: 866-221-4141	
Address: 1014 Vine St., Cincinnati, OH 45202-1100 US	

GROWTH PLANS/SPECIAL FEATURES:

The Kroger Co. is one of the largest supermarket operators in the U.S. The company operates 2,475 supermarkets in 31 states under a variety of names: Kroger; Kroger Fresh Fare; Kroger Marketplace; Ralphs; Food 4 Less; King Soopers; Smith's; Smith's Marketplace; Fry's; Fry's Marketplace; Dillons; Dillons Marketplace; QFC; Baker's; Owen's; Hilander; Scott's; Jay C; Pay Less; Fred Meyer; Foods Co.; and City Market. Of these stores, 798 have fuel centers. Select supermarkets also offer pharmacy services. Kroger's supermarkets operate under one of three store formats: combination food and drug stores, multi-department stores or price-impact warehouse stores. Kroger stores offer one-stop shopping, including whole health sections, pharmacies, pet centers and world-class perishables, such as fresh seafood and organic produce. Kroger also operates 764 convenience stores under the Quik Stop; Loaf N' Jug; Tom Thumb; Turkey Hill; and Kwik Shop names. These stores offer a limited assortment of staple food items and general merchandise, and, in most cases, sell gasoline. The company operates 387 fine jewelry stores under the banners Fred Meyer Jewelers, Littman Jewelers, Barclay Jewelers and Fox's Jewelers. In addition, the firm offers financial services such as credit cards loans, and theft protection under Kroger Personal Finance. The 40 food processing or manufacturing plants operated by Kroger are primarily bakeries and dairies, which supply approximately 40% of the corporate brand units sold in its retail outlets. These plants consisted of 18 dairies, 10 deli or bakery plants, five grocery product plants, three beverage plants, three meat plants and two cheese plants.

Employees are offered medical, dental and vision insurance; life insurance; personal accident insurance; disability coverage a 401(k) plan; flexible spending accounts; legal insurance; home owners and auto insurance; an employee stock purchase plan; an employee assistance plan; credit union membership; a continuing education program; and professional liability coverage.

FINANCIALS: Sales and profits are in thousands of dollars—add 000 to get the full amount. 2008 Note: Financial information for 2008 was not available for all companies at press time.

2008 Sales: $70,235,000	2008 Profits: $1,181,000	**U.S. Stock Ticker:** KR
2007 Sales: $66,111,000	2007 Profits: $1,115,000	**Int'l Ticker:** Int'l Exchange:
2006 Sales: $60,553,000	2006 Profits: $958,000	Employees: 326,000
2005 Sales: $56,434,000	2005 Profits: $-104,000	Fiscal Year Ends: 1/31
2004 Sales: $53,791,000	2004 Profits: $285,000	Parent Company:

SALARIES/BENEFITS:

Pension Plan:	ESOP Stock Plan:	Profit Sharing:	Top Exec. Salary: $1,204,758	Bonus: $1,574,220
Savings Plan: Y	Stock Purch. Plan: Y		Second Exec. Salary: $848,686	Bonus: $1,049,480

OTHER THOUGHTS:

Apparent Women Officers or Directors: 6
Hot Spot for Advancement for Women/Minorities: Y

LOCATIONS: ("Y" = Yes)

West:	Southwest:	Midwest:	Southeast:	Northeast:	International:
Y	Y	Y	Y	Y	

L-3 COMMUNICATIONS HOLDINGS INC

www.l-3com.com

Industry Group Code: 3342 Ranks within this company's industry group: Sales: 1 Profits: 1

Management:		Sales/Marketing:		Liberal Arts:		Information Systems:		Professionals:		Tech./Scientific:	
Management Trainees:	Y	Marketing Pros.:	Y	Gen. Writing/Editing:		Info. Management:	Y	Finance/Acct.:	Y	Engineers, Electrical:	Y
Experienced Mngmt.:	Y	Retail Sales:		Technical Writing:	Y	Software Dev.:	Y	Law:	Y	Engineers, Other:	
International Business:	Y	Commercial/Industrial:	Y	Graphic Arts/Photog.:	Y	Hardware Dev.:	Y	HR/Other:	Y	Health/Lab:	
MBA Grads:	Y	Sales Trainees:		Music:		Consulting/Other:	Y	Training:	Y	Scientists/Research:	
		Advertising Pros.:	Y	Broadcasting:				Health Care:		Petroleum/Chemicals:	
				Other:				Consulting:		Math/Other:	Y

TYPES OF BUSINESS:

Electronic Equipment-Specialized Communications
Intelligence, Surveillance & Reconnaissance Systems
Aviation & Aerospace Products
Telemetry Products
Instrumentation Products
Microwave Components
Security Systems
Signal Intelligence Products

BRANDS/DIVISIONS/AFFILIATES:

L-3 Communications Corporation
Microdyne Outsourcing Inc.
L-3 Titan Group
Northrop Grumman
Chesapeake Sciences Corporation
HAS Systems Pty Limited
International Resources Group Ltd.

CONTACTS: Note: Officers with more than one job title may be intentionally listed here more than once.

Michael T. Strianese, CEO
Michael T. Strianese, Pres.
Ralph G. D'Ambrosio, CFO/VP
John Hill, VP-Human Resources
Paul De Lia, VP-Science & Tech.
Vincent T. Taylor, CIO/VP
A. Michael Andrews II, CTO/VP
Sheila M. Sheridan, VP-Admin.
Steven M. Post, General Counsel/Sr. VP/Corp. Sec.
David T. Butler III, Sr. VP-Bus. Oper.
Curtis Brunson, Sr. VP-Corp. Strategy & Dev.
Karen Tripp, VP-Corp. Comm.
Dan Azmon, Controller/Principal Acct. Officer
Jimmie V. Adams, Sr. VP-Washington Oper.
Robert W. RisCassi, Sr. VP
Lois Bailey, VP-Int'l Licensing
Jill J. Wittels, VP-Bus. Dev.
Michael T. Strianese, Chmn.
Ron Cook, VP-London Oper.
R.L. DeNino, VP-Procurement

Phone: 212-697-1111	Fax: 212-805-5477
Toll-Free:	
Address: 600 3rd Ave., New York, NY 10016 US	

GROWTH PLANS/SPECIAL FEATURES:

L-3 Communications Holdings, Inc., operating through its subsidiary L-3 Communications Corp., is a supplier of products and services used in various aerospace and defense platforms. The company operates through four business segments: Command, Control, Communications, Intelligence, Surveillance and Reconnaissance (C3ISR); Government Services; Aircraft Modernization and Maintenance (AM&M); and Specialized Products. The C3ISR segment specializes in signals intelligence and communications intelligence. Its products and services are used to connect a variety of airborne, space, ground and sea-based communication systems, and in the transmission, processing, recording, monitoring and dissemination functions of these systems. The Government Services division provides training and operational support services; enterprise information technology solutions; intelligence solutions; support, command and control systems and software services; global security; and engineering solutions services. Through the AM&M segment, the company provides modernization, sustainment, maintenance and logistics services for military and various government aircraft. The Specialized Products segment provides aviation; security and detection; microwave RF, SATCOM and antenna; sensor and simulation; and power and control system products. The company's customers include the U.S. Department of Defense, the U.S. Department of Homeland Security, U.S. Government intelligence agencies, aerospace and defense contractors, foreign governments and commercial customers. In March 2008, the company completed its acquisition of HAS Systems Pty Limited, an Australian provider of geospatial, marine and electronic systems for the defense and maritime industries. In April 2008, L-3 acquired Northrop Grumman's Electro-Optical Systems business. In December 2008, the company acquired International Resources Group Ltd., an international professional services firm. In February 2009, the company acquired Chesapeake Sciences Corporation, a developer and producer of anti-submarine warfare (ASW) systems.

L-3 Communications offers its employees medical, dental, vision and prescription drug plans; an employee assistance plan; flexible spending accounts; a 401(k) savings plan; and an employee stock purchase plan.

FINANCIALS: Sales and profits are in thousands of dollars—add 000 to get the full amount. 2008 Note: Financial information for 2008 was not available for all companies at press time.

2008 Sales: $14,901,000	2008 Profits: $949,000	**U.S. Stock Ticker: LLL**
2007 Sales: $13,960,500	2007 Profits: $756,100	**Int'l Ticker:** Int'l Exchange:
2006 Sales: $12,476,900	2006 Profits: $526,100	Employees: 65,000
2005 Sales: $9,444,700	2005 Profits: $508,500	Fiscal Year Ends: 12/31
2004 Sales: $6,897,000	2004 Profits: $381,900	Parent Company:

SALARIES/BENEFITS:

Pension Plan:	ESOP Stock Plan:	Profit Sharing:	Top Exec. Salary: $1,145,385	Bonus: $2,750,000
Savings Plan: Y	Stock Purch. Plan:		Second Exec. Salary: $518,269	Bonus: $1,000,000

OTHER THOUGHTS:

Apparent Women Officers or Directors: 7
Hot Spot for Advancement for Women/Minorities: Y

LOCATIONS: ("Y" = Yes)

West:	Southwest:	Midwest:	Southeast:	Northeast:	International:
Y	Y	Y	Y	Y	Y

Note: Financial information, benefits and other data can change quickly and may vary from those stated here.

LABORATORY CORP OF AMERICA HOLDINGS   www.labcorp.com

Industry Group Code: 6215 Ranks within this company's industry group: Sales: 2 Profits: 2

Management:		Sales/Marketing:		Liberal Arts:		Information Systems:		Professionals:		Tech./Scientific:	
Management Trainees:	Y	Marketing Pros.:	Y	Gen. Writing/Editing:	Y	Info. Management:	Y	Finance/Acct.:	Y	Engineers, Electrical:	
Experienced Mngmt.:	Y	Retail Sales:		Technical Writing:	Y	Software Dev.:	Y	Law:	Y	Engineers, Other:	
International Business:	Y	Commercial/Industrial:	Y	Graphic Arts/Photog.:	Y	Hardware Dev.:		HR/Other:	Y	Health/Lab:	Y
MBA Grads:	Y	Sales Trainees:		Music:		Consulting/Other:		Training:	Y	Scientists/Research:	Y
		Advertising Pros.:		Broadcasting:				Health Care:	Y	Petroleum/Chemicals:	
				Other:				Consulting:		Math/Other:	

TYPES OF BUSINESS:

Clinical Laboratory Testing
Diagnostics
Urinalyses
Blood Cell Counts
Blood Chemistry Analysis
HIV Tests
Genetic Testing
Specialty & Niche Tests

BRANDS/DIVISIONS/AFFILIATES:

Center for Molecular Biology and Pathology (CMBP)
National Genetics Institute, Inc. (NGI)
Viro-Med Laboratories, Inc.
DIANON Systems, Inc.
US LABS
Esoterix
Litholink Corporation
Tandem Labs, Inc.

CONTACTS: *Note: Officers with more than one job title may be intentionally listed here more than once.*

David P. King, CEO
Don M. Hardison, COO/Exec. VP
David P. King, Pres.
William B. Hayes, CFO/Exec. VP
Lidia L. Fonseca, CIO/Sr. VP
F. Samuel Eberts, III, Chief Legal Officer/Sec./Sr. VP
Andrew S. Walton, Exec. VP-Strategic Planning & Corp. Dev.
Bill Bonello, Sr. VP-Investor Rel.
William B. Hayes, Treas.
James T. Boyle, Jr., Sr. VP-Managed Care & Occupational Testing
Mark E. Brecher, Sr. VP/Chief Medical Officer
David P. King, Chmn.

Phone: 336-229-1127	Fax: 336-513-4510
Toll-Free:	
Address: 358 S. Main St., Burlington, NC 27215 US	

GROWTH PLANS/SPECIAL FEATURES:

Laboratory Corporation of America Holdings (LabCorp) is a leading independent clinical laboratory company in the U.S., offering health-related laboratory tests to the medical industry. Its tests are used primarily for routine screening, patient diagnosis and the monitoring and treatment of disease. The company operates a nationwide network of 36 primary testing facilities and over 1,600 service centers, consisting of branches, patient service centers and STAT labs, which can perform routine tests quickly and report results to the physician immediately. LabCorp's testing services include routine testing, specialty testing and new test development. The most frequently requested routine tests offered by the firm include blood chemistry analyses, thyroid tests, urinalyses, blood cell counts, Pap tests, HIV tests, microbiology cultures and substance-abuse tests. Specialty testing businesses in which LabCorp offers testing and related services include infectious diseases, diagnostic genetics, oncology testing, clinical trials testing, identity testing, allergy testing and occupational testing. Its Center for Molecular Biology and Pathology (CMBP) is a leading molecular diagnostics and polymerase chain reaction (PCR) technology firm. The company's National Genetics Institute, Inc. (NGI) subsidiary is a leading developer of PCR assays for Hepatitis C. Subsidiary Viro-Med Laboratories, Inc. provides molecular microbial testing using real time PCR platforms. Additional specialty testing subsidiaries include pathology testing firm DIANON Systems, Inc.; anatomic pathology and oncology testing firm US LABS; specialty reference testing firm Esoterix; and kidney stone analysis laboratory Litholink Corporation. The company processes an average of approximately 3420,000 specimens per day and provides clinical laboratory services in all 50 states, Washington, D.C., Puerto Rico and Canada. In June 2008, LabCorp acquired Tandem Labs, Inc. In August 2009, it acquired Monogram Biosciences, Inc.

LabCorp offers its employees tuition reimbursement, career development programs, an employee assistance program, credit union membership, flexible spending accounts and medical, dental, optical, life and disability insurance.

FINANCIALS: Sales and profits are in thousands of dollars—add 000 to get the full amount. 2008 Note: Financial information for 2008 was not available for all companies at press time.

2008 Sales: $4,505,200	2008 Profits: $464,500	**U.S. Stock Ticker: LH**	
2007 Sales: $4,068,200	2007 Profits: $476,800	**Int'l Ticker:**	Int'l Exchange:
2006 Sales: $3,590,800	2006 Profits: $431,600	Employees: 28,000	
2005 Sales: $3,327,600	2005 Profits: $386,200	Fiscal Year Ends: 12/31	
2004 Sales: $3,084,800	2004 Profits: $363,000	Parent Company:	

SALARIES/BENEFITS:

Pension Plan: Y	ESOP Stock Plan: Y	Profit Sharing:	Top Exec. Salary: $791,667	Bonus: $765,674
Savings Plan: Y	Stock Purch. Plan:		Second Exec. Salary: $558,333	Bonus: $358,294

OTHER THOUGHTS:

Apparent Women Officers or Directors: 3
Hot Spot for Advancement for Women/Minorities: Y

LOCATIONS: ("Y" = Yes)

West:	Southwest:	Midwest:	Southeast:	Northeast:	International:
Y	Y	Y	Y	Y	Y

Note: Financial information, benefits and other data can change quickly and may vary from those stated here.

LAS VEGAS SANDS CORP (THE VENETIAN) www.lasvegassands.com

Industry Group Code: 721120 Ranks within this company's industry group: Sales: 3 Profits: 2

Management:		Sales/Marketing:		Liberal Arts:		Information Systems:		Professionals:		Tech./Scientific:	
Management Trainees:	Y	Marketing Pros.:	Y	Gen. Writing/Editing:	Y	Info. Management:	Y	Finance/Acct.:	Y	Engineers, Electrical:	
Experienced Mngmt.:	Y	Retail Sales:		Technical Writing:		Software Dev.:	Y	Law:	Y	Engineers, Other:	
International Business:	Y	Commercial/Industrial:	Y	Graphic Arts/Photog.:	Y	Hardware Dev.:		HR/Other:	Y	Health/Lab:	
MBA Grads:	Y	Sales Trainees:	Y	Music:	Y	Consulting/Other:		Training:	Y	Scientists/Research:	
		Advertising Pros.:	Y	Broadcasting:				Health Care:		Petroleum/Chemicals:	
				Other:	Y			Consulting:		Math/Other:	

TYPES OF BUSINESS:

Hotel Casinos
Convention & Conference Centers
Shopping Center Development
Casino Property Development

BRANDS/DIVISIONS/AFFILIATES:

Venetian Resort Hotel Casino (The)
Sands Expo and Convention Center (The)
Congress Center (The)
Sands Macao Casino (The)
Palazzo Resort Hotel Casino (The)
Venetian Macao Resort Hotel (The)
Marina Bay Sands
Cotai Strip

CONTACTS: *Note: Officers with more than one job title may be intentionally listed here more than once.*

Sheldon G. Adelson, CEO
Michael A. Leven, COO
Michael A. Leven, Pres.
Kenneth J. Kay, CFO/Sr. VP
Bradley H. Stone, Exec. VP/Pres., Global Oper. & Construction
Scott D. Henry, Sr. VP-Finance
Robert G. Goldstein, Sr. VP/Pres., The Venetian Resort Hotel Casino
Nigel Roberts, Pres., Marina Bay Sands
Mark A. Brown, Pres., Sands Macao & The Venetian Macao
Sheldon G. Adelson, Chmn.
Leonard DeAngelo, Sr. VP-Asia Oper.

Phone: 702-414-1000	Fax: 702-414-4884
Toll-Free:	
Address: 3355 Las Vegas Blvd. S., Las Vegas, NV 89109 US	

GROWTH PLANS/SPECIAL FEATURES:

Las Vegas Sands Corp. (The Venetian) (LVSC) is an international hotel, resort and casino firm. Its flagship property is The Venetian Resort Hotel Casino, which is connected the firm's The Palazzo Resort Hotel Casino. Together, The Venetian and The Palazzo offer 225,000 square feet (sq. ft.) of gaming space with 260 table games and 2,850 slot machines; almost 7,100 hotel suites; and 840,000 square feet of dining, retail and entertainment space, including The Shoppes at The Palazzo. LVSC also runs the 1.2 million square foot convention and trade show facility, The Sands Expo and Convention Center, and supplemental event and conference center The Congress Center, which connect to The Venetian. In China, the firm runs The Sands Macao and The Venetian Macao Resort Hotel, the anchor property on the Cotai Strip development project. Together, these properties feature a 779,000 square foot casino floor with 1,070 table games and 3,240 slot machines; almost 3,190 hotel suites; 1.2 million square feet of meeting, exhibition and convention space; 1 million sq. ft. of retail and dining space; and the 15,000 seat Venetian Arena. The company's two largest development projects are the $4.9 billion Marina Bay Sands resort in Singapore and the $12 billion Cotai Strip, a collection of hotel properties, casinos and entertainment venues in Macao, China. In August 2008, the firm opened The Four Seasons Macao next to The Venetian Macao. It features 360 hotel rooms; a 70,000 square foot casino floor with 120 table games and 200 slot machines; and 211,000 square feet of retail space. In November 2008, due to current economic conditions, LVSC postponed some of its international development projects. The company recently announced it plans to open Sands Casino Resort Bethlehem, featuring 3,000 slot machines and various entertainment options, in May 2009.

FINANCIALS: Sales and profits are in thousands of dollars—add 000 to get the full amount. 2008 Note: Financial information for 2008 was not available for all companies at press time.

2008 Sales: $4,735,126	2008 Profits: $-163,558	**U.S. Stock Ticker: LVS**
2007 Sales: $3,104,422	2007 Profits: $116,688	**Int'l Ticker:** Int'l Exchange:
2006 Sales: $2,340,178	2006 Profits: $442,003	Employees: 28,500
2005 Sales: $1,824,225	2005 Profits: $283,686	Fiscal Year Ends: 12/31
2004 Sales: $1,258,570	2004 Profits: $495,183	Parent Company:

SALARIES/BENEFITS:

Pension Plan:	ESOP Stock Plan:	Profit Sharing:	Top Exec. Salary: $1,000,000	Bonus: $
Savings Plan: Y	Stock Purch. Plan:		Second Exec. Salary: $1,000,000	Bonus: $

OTHER THOUGHTS:

Apparent Women Officers or Directors:
Hot Spot for Advancement for Women/Minorities:

LOCATIONS: ("Y" = Yes)

West:	Southwest:	Midwest:	Southeast:	Northeast:	International:
Y				Y	Y

Note: Financial information, benefits and other data can change quickly and may vary from those stated here.

LEVEL 3 COMMUNICATIONS INC

www.level3.com

Industry Group Code: 517110 Ranks within this company's industry group: Sales: 11 Profits: 10

Management:		Sales/Marketing:		Liberal Arts:		Information Systems:		Professionals:		Tech./Scientific:	
Management Trainees:	Y	Marketing Pros.:	Y	Gen. Writing/Editing:	Y	Info. Management:	Y	Finance/Acct.:	Y	Engineers, Electrical:	Y
Experienced Mngmt.:	Y	Retail Sales:		Technical Writing:	Y	Software Dev.:	Y	Law:	Y	Engineers, Other:	Y
International Business:	Y	Commercial/Industrial:	Y	Graphic Arts/Photog.:	Y	Hardware Dev.:	Y	HR/Other:	Y	Health/Lab:	
MBA Grads:	Y	Sales Trainees:		Music:		Consulting/Other:		Training:	Y	Scientists/Research:	
		Advertising Pros.:	Y	Broadcasting:				Health Care:		Petroleum/Chemicals:	
				Other:				Consulting:		Math/Other:	

TYPES OF BUSINESS:

Private Data Networks-Fiber Optic
Broadband Network Services
Managed Modem Access Services

BRANDS/DIVISIONS/AFFILIATES:

Peter Kiewit Sons, Inc. (PKS)
ICG Communications Inc
Softswitch
Broadwing Communications LLC
Telcove Corp

CONTACTS: *Note: Officers with more than one job title may be intentionally listed here more than once.*

James Q. Crowe, CEO
Jeff K. Storey, COO
Jeff K. Storey, Pres.
Sunit Patel, CFO/Exec. VP
Sureel Choksi, Chief Mktg. Officer
Michele Vion, Group VP-Human Resources
Jack Waters, CTO/Pres., Global Network Svcs.
Thomas C. Stortz, Chief Legal Officer/Exec. VP
Jeff Battcher, Sr. VP-Corp. Comm.
Jennifer Daumler, Sr. Dir.-Investor Analyst Rel.
Robin Grey, Corp. Treas.
Andrew Crouch, Pres., Wholesale Markets
Walter Scott, Jr., Chmn.
James Heard, Pres., European Markets

Phone: 720-888-1000	Fax: 720-888-5085
Toll-Free: 877-253-8353	
Address: 1025 Eldorado Blvd., Broomfield, CO 80021 US	

GROWTH PLANS/SPECIAL FEATURES:

Level 3 Communications, Inc. is a leading provider of integrated communications services. The company's main offering is the firm's broadband networks in the U.S. and Europe. Using these networks, Level 3 supplies a portfolio of services including Internet Protocol (IP) services (Internet access, Ethernet and virtual private network, or VPN), broadband transport, colocation services, and patented Softswitch-based managed modem and voice services, which use a distributed computer system to emulate traditional circuit switches. Level 3 divides these services according to customer base into four segments: wholesale markets group, business markets group, content markets group and the European group. The wholesale group services high bandwidth needs of large communications providers. The business group provides services to enterprises, regional carriers, educational institutions and government agencies. The content group sells services designed for video distribution companies; providers of online gaming and mega-portals; software service providers; social networking providers; and traditional media distribution companies including broadcasters, television networks and sports leagues. Lastly, the European groups supplies communications services in Europe for customers similar to the wholesale and content customers. The firm owns and operates several subsidiaries including Telcove Corp.; Broadwing Corporation, which owns Broadwing Communications, LLC; and ICG Communications, Inc. Originally founded as a part of Peter Kiewit Sons', Inc., a mining, construction and communications company, Level 3 also has holdings in coal mining and other diversified interests. In June 2008, the firm sold its advertising distribution business to DG FastChannel, Inc. In May 2009, the firm launched a new High-Speed Content Upload services available to its content delivery network customers.

The firm offers employees a 401(k) plan; educational assistance; flexible spending accounts; and medical, dental and vision coverage.

FINANCIALS: Sales and profits are in thousands of dollars—add 000 to get the full amount. 2008 Note: Financial information for 2008 was not available for all companies at press time.

2008 Sales: $4,301,000	2008 Profits: $-290,000	U.S. Stock Ticker: LVLT	
2007 Sales: $4,269,000	2007 Profits: $-1,114,000	Int'l Ticker: Int'l Exchange:	
2006 Sales: $3,378,000	2006 Profits: $-744,000	Employees: 5,300	
2005 Sales: $1,719,000	2005 Profits: $-638,000	Fiscal Year Ends: 12/31	
2004 Sales: $1,776,000	2004 Profits: $-458,000	Parent Company:	

SALARIES/BENEFITS:

Pension Plan:	ESOP Stock Plan:	Profit Sharing:	Top Exec. Salary: $812,692	Bonus: $1,800,000
Savings Plan: Y	Stock Purch. Plan:		Second Exec. Salary: $502,692	Bonus: $630,000

OTHER THOUGHTS:

Apparent Women Officers or Directors: 3
Hot Spot for Advancement for Women/Minorities: Y

LOCATIONS: ("Y" = Yes)

West:	Southwest:	Midwest:	Southeast:	Northeast:	International:
Y	Y		Y	Y	Y

LEXMARK INTERNATIONAL INC

www.lexmark.com

Industry Group Code: 334119 Ranks within this company's industry group: Sales: 1 Profits: 1

Management:		Sales/Marketing:		Liberal Arts:		Information Systems:		Professionals:		Tech./Scientific:	
Management Trainees:	Y	Marketing Pros.:	Y	Gen. Writing/Editing:	Y	Info. Management:	Y	Finance/Acct.:	Y	Engineers, Electrical:	Y
Experienced Mngmt.:	Y	Retail Sales:		Technical Writing:	Y	Software Dev.:	Y	Law:	Y	Engineers, Other:	
International Business:	Y	Commercial/Industrial:	Y	Graphic Arts/Photog.:	Y	Hardware Dev.:	Y	HR/Other:	Y	Health/Lab:	
MBA Grads:	Y	Sales Trainees:	Y	Music:		Consulting/Other:		Training:	Y	Scientists/Research:	
		Advertising Pros.:	Y	Broadcasting:				Health Care:		Petroleum/Chemicals:	
				Other:				Consulting:		Math/Other:	

TYPES OF BUSINESS:

Computer Accessories-Printers
Laser & Inkjet Printers
Printer Consumables
Typewriters & Supplies
Connectivity Products
Document Software
Managed Print Services Outsourcing

BRANDS/DIVISIONS/AFFILIATES:

IBM

CONTACTS: Note: Officers with more than one job title may be intentionally listed here more than once.

Paul J. Curlander, CEO
John W. Gamble Jr., CFO/Exec. VP
Jeri Isbell, VP-Human Resources
Robert J. Patton, General Counsel/Sec./VP
Gary D. Stromquist, Corp. Controller/VP
Paul A. Rooke, Exec. VP/Pres., Consumer Printer Div.
Marty Canning, VP/Pres., Printing Solutions & Svcs. Div.
Paul J. Curlander, Chmn.
Ronaldo Foresti, VP-Asia Pacific & Latin America

Phone: 859-232-2000	Fax: 859-232-2403
Toll-Free: 800-539-6275	
Address: 740 W. New Circle Rd., Lexington, KY 40550 US	

GROWTH PLANS/SPECIAL FEATURES:

Lexmark International, Inc., a former subsidiary of International Business Machines Corp. (IBM), is a global developer, manufacturer and supplier of laser and inkjet printers and associated consumable supplies for the office and home markets. Its products are sold in over 150 countries across the Americas, Europe, the Middle East, Africa, Asia, the Pacific Rim and the Caribbean. The firm has six manufacturing sites and approximately 70 sales offices. The company's research and development activity for the past several years has focused on laser and inkjet printers, associated supplies and network connectivity products. In addition to its laser and inkjet printers, Lexmark sells dot matrix printers for printing single and multi-part forms by business users, as well as the consumable supplies used by its large installed base of printers. Because consumable supplies must be replaced on average one to three times a year, depending on type of printer and usage, demand for laser and inkjet print cartridges is increasing at a higher rate than their associated printer shipments. Besides its core printer business, the firm manufactures a broad line of other office imaging products, including supplies for IBM-branded printers; after-market supplies for original equipment manufacturer products; and typewriters and typewriter supplies that are sold under the IBM trademark. International sales, including exports from the U.S., accounted for approximately 57% of the firm's revenue, which was $5 billion at the end of fiscal 2007. Lexmark's offerings include outsourced managed print services, a service where Lexmark takes over ownership and/or operation of a client's printers, copiers and fax machines with the goal of savings substantial operating costs for the client.

Employees are offered a 401(k) plan; a stock purchase plan; and health benefits.

FINANCIALS: Sales and profits are in thousands of dollars—add 000 to get the full amount. 2008 Note: Financial information for 2008 was not available for all companies at press time.

2008 Sales: $4,528,400	2008 Profits: $240,200	**U.S. Stock Ticker:** LXK
2007 Sales: $4,973,900	2007 Profits: $300,800	**Int'l Ticker:** Int'l Exchange:
2006 Sales: $5,108,100	2006 Profits: $338,400	Employees: 14,000
2005 Sales: $5,221,500	2005 Profits: $356,300	Fiscal Year Ends: 12/31
2004 Sales: $5,313,800	2004 Profits: $568,700	Parent Company:

SALARIES/BENEFITS:

Pension Plan:	ESOP Stock Plan:	Profit Sharing:	Top Exec. Salary: $1,007,692	Bonus: $335,880
Savings Plan: Y	Stock Purch. Plan: Y		Second Exec. Salary: $574,385	Bonus: $319,388

OTHER THOUGHTS:

Apparent Women Officers or Directors: 3
Hot Spot for Advancement for Women/Minorities: Y

LOCATIONS: ("Y" = Yes)

West:	Southwest:	Midwest:	Southeast:	Northeast:	International:
Y		Y			Y

Note: Financial information, benefits and other data can change quickly and may vary from those stated here.

LIBERTY GLOBAL INC

Industry Group Code: 517110 Ranks within this company's industry group: Sales: 6 Profits: 11

www.lgi.com

Management:		Sales/Marketing:		Liberal Arts:		Information Systems:		Professionals:		Tech./Scientific:	
Management Trainees:	Y	Marketing Pros.:	Y	Gen. Writing/Editing:	Y	Info. Management:	Y	Finance/Acct.:	Y	Engineers, Electrical:	Y
Experienced Mngmt.:	Y	Retail Sales:		Technical Writing:	Y	Software Dev.:	Y	Law:	Y	Engineers, Other:	Y
International Business:	Y	Commercial/Industrial:	Y	Graphic Arts/Photog.:	Y	Hardware Dev.:		HR/Other:	Y	Health/Lab:	
MBA Grads:	Y	Sales Trainees:		Music:		Consulting/Other:		Training:	Y	Scientists/Research:	
		Advertising Pros.:	Y	Broadcasting:				Health Care:		Petroleum/Chemicals:	
				Other:				Consulting:		Math/Other:	

TYPES OF BUSINESS:

Video, Voice & Broadband Internet Access Services
Telephony Services
VoIP Services
Mobile Telephony Services

BRANDS/DIVISIONS/AFFILIATES:

UPC Broadband Holding BV
UPC Holding BV
VTR Global Com S.A.
Telenet Group Holding NV
Jupiter Telecommunications Co., Ltd.
Austar United Communications Limited
Chellomedia BV

CONTACTS: *Note: Officers with more than one job title may be intentionally listed here more than once.*

Michael T. Fries, CEO
Michael T. Fries, Pres.
Charles H. R. Bracken, Co-CFO/Principal Financial Officer/Sr. VP
Amy M. Blair, Sr. VP-Global Human Resources
Balan Nair, CTO/Sr. VP
Elizabeth M. Markowski, General Counsel/Sec./Sr. VP
Shane O'Neill, Chief Strategy Officer/Sr. VP
Bernard C. Dvorak, Co-CFO/Principle Acct. Officer/Sr. VP
Mauricio Ramos, Pres., Liberty Global Latin America/CEO-VTR Global
W. Gene Musselman, Pres./COO-UPC Broadband Div.
Shane O'Neill, Pres., Chellomedia BV
Bob Leighton, Sr. VP-Programming
John C. Malone, Chmn.
Miranda Curtis, Pres., Liberty Global Japan

Phone: 303-220-6600	Fax: 303-220-6601
Toll-Free:	
Address: 12300 Liberty Blvd., Englewood, CO 80112 US	

GROWTH PLANS/SPECIAL FEATURES:

Liberty Global, Inc. (LGI) is an international provider of video, voice and broadband Internet services, with consolidated broadband communications and/or direct-to-home satellite operations in 15 countries around the world, primarily in Europe, Japan and Chile. LGI has roughly 16.9 million customers and 26.7 million video, voice and/or Internet subscribers. The firm conducts it business operations through various subsidiaries. Through LGI's indirect wholly-owned subsidiary, UPC Holding BV, the firm provides video, voice and broadband Internet services in 10 European countries and in Chile. The European broadband communications operations of UPC Broadband Holding BV, a subsidiary of UPC Holding, are collectively referred to as the UPC Broadband Division. UPC Broadband Holding's broadband communication operations in Chile are provided through VTR Global Com S.A. Through LGI's 50.6% indirect majority ownership interest in Telenet Group Holding NV, the firm provides broadband communications services in Belgium. Through its indirect 37.8% controlling ownership interest in Jupiter Telecommunications Co., Ltd., the firm provides broadband communications services in Japan. Through its 54% indirect majority owned subsidiary, Austar United Communications Limited, the firm provides DTH satellite services in Australia. LGI also has consolidated broadband communications operations in Puerto Rico and consolidated interests in certain programming businesses in Europe, Japan and Argentina. The firm's consolidated programming interests in Europe are primarily held through Chellomedia BV, which owns or manages investments in various businesses, primarily in Europe. Certain of Chellomedia's subsidiaries and affiliates provide programming services to its broadband communications operations, primarily in Europe.

FINANCIALS: Sales and profits are in thousands of dollars—add 000 to get the full amount. 2008 Note: Financial information for 2008 was not available for all companies at press time.

2008 Sales: $10,561,100		2008 Profits: $-788,900		U.S. Stock Ticker: LBTYA	
2007 Sales: $9,003,300		2007 Profits: $-422,600		Int'l Ticker: Int'l Exchange:	
2006 Sales: $6,483,900		2006 Profits: $706,200		Employees: 22,300	
2005 Sales: $5,151,332		2005 Profits: $-80,097		Fiscal Year Ends: 12/31	
2004 Sales: $2,531,889		2004 Profits: $-21,481		Parent Company:	

SALARIES/BENEFITS:

Pension Plan:	ESOP Stock Plan:	Profit Sharing:	Top Exec. Salary: $957,000	Bonus: $1,600,000
Savings Plan:	Stock Purch. Plan:		Second Exec. Salary: $699,890	Bonus: $900,000

OTHER THOUGHTS:

Apparent Women Officers or Directors: 3
Hot Spot for Advancement for Women/Minorities: Y

LOCATIONS: ("Y" = Yes)

West:	Southwest:	Midwest:	Southeast:	Northeast:	International:
Y					Y

LIBERTY MUTUAL GROUP INC

www.libertymutualgroup.com

Industry Group Code: 524126 Ranks within this company's industry group: Sales: 2 Profits: 4

Management:		Sales/Marketing:		Liberal Arts:		Information Systems:		Professionals:		Tech./Scientific:	
Management Trainees:	Y	Marketing Pros.:	Y	Gen. Writing/Editing:	Y	Info. Management:	Y	Finance/Acct.:	Y	Engineers, Electrical:	
Experienced Mngmt.:	Y	Retail Sales:		Technical Writing:	Y	Software Dev.:	Y	Law:	Y	Engineers, Other:	
International Business:	Y	Commercial/Industrial:	Y	Graphic Arts/Photog.:	Y	Hardware Dev.:		HR/Other:	Y	Health/Lab:	
MBA Grads:	Y	Sales Trainees:		Music:		Consulting/Other:		Training:	Y	Scientists/Research:	
		Advertising Pros.:	Y	Broadcasting:				Health Care:		Petroleum/Chemicals:	
				Other:	Y			Consulting:		Math/Other:	

TYPES OF BUSINESS:

Insurance, Direct Property & Casualty
Rehabilitation Services
Disability Care Management
Homeowners' Insurance
Auto Insurance
Group Life Insurance
Asset Management & Investment Products
Workers' Compensation

BRANDS/DIVISIONS/AFFILIATES:

Liberty International
Liberty Mutual Property
Liberty Mutual Reinsurance
Liberty International Underwriters
Research Institute for Safety
Liberty Insurance Company, Ltd.
Ohio Casualty Insurance Company
Safeco Insurance Company of America

CONTACTS: Note: Officers with more than one job title may be intentionally listed here more than once.

Edmund F. Kelly, CEO
Edmund F. Kelly, Pres.
Dennis J. Langwell, CFO/Sr. VP
Helen E.R. Sayles, Sr. VP-Human Resources
James M. McGlennon, CIO/Sr. VP
Helen E.R. Sayles, Sr. VP-Admin.
Christopher C. Mansfield, General Counsel/Sr. VP
Matthew T. Coyle, VP-Investor Rel.
J. Paul Condrin, III, Exec. VP-Commercial Markets
Gary R. Gregg, Exec. VP-Agency Markets
A. Alexander Fontanes, Chief Investment Officer/Exec. VP
Timothy M. Sweeney, Exec. VP-Personal Markets
Edmund F. Kelly, Chmn.
Thomas C. Ramey, Exec. VP-Liberty Int'l

Phone: 617-357-9500	Fax: 617-350-7648
Toll-Free: 800-837-5254	
Address: 175 Berkeley St., Boston, MA 02116 US	

GROWTH PLANS/SPECIAL FEATURES:

Liberty Mutual Group is a group of insurance companies with over 900 offices worldwide and $104.3 billion in assets. Liberty Mutual has four strategic business units: Personal Markets, Commercial Markets, Agency Markets and Liberty International, none of which accounts for more than 30% of annual business. The company's Personal Markets business unit provides private passenger automobile, homeowners, valuable possessions, identity theft and personal liability coverage through more than 400 U.S. offices. This unit also offers traditional and variable life insurance and annuity products through subsidiary Liberty Life Assurance Company of Boston. The company's Commercial Markets business unit provides risk and disability management and risk transfer products and services through six smaller units: National Market, Middle Market, Liberty Mutual Property, Specialty Lines, Group Market and Liberty Mutual Reinsurance. Liberty Mutual's Agency Markets business unit consists of specialty, property and casualty insurance carriers that sell products primarily through independent agents and brokers. The company's Liberty International business unit provides personal and commercial insurance through operations in such locations as China and Hong Kong, Singapore, Portugal, Spain, Turkey, Argentina, Brazil, Colombia and Venezuela. Liberty International Underwriters provides casualty, specialty casualty, marine, energy, engineering and aviation insurance through 36 offices in Asia, Europe, the Middle East, and the Americas. Liberty Mutual also operates the Research Institute for Safety, which conducts original investigations of job-related accidents and publishes its findings in a range of peer-reviewed journals. In June 2008, Liberty Mutual and its partner Dabur GI Invest Corp. announced plans for a new non-life insurance company in India. In September 2008, Liberty Mutual acquired Safeco Corporation for roughly $6.2 billion. In February 2009, the firm opened a branch office in Beijing, China.

Liberty Mutual offers its employees tuition reimbursement; health care and dependent care reimbursement accounts; and medical, dental and vision insurance, among other benefits.

FINANCIALS: Sales and profits are in thousands of dollars—add 000 to get the full amount. 2008 Note: Financial information for 2008 was not available for all companies at press time.

2008 Sales: $28,855,000	2008 Profits: $1,140,000	U.S. Stock Ticker: Mutual Company
2007 Sales: $25,961,000	2007 Profits: $1,518,000	Int'l Ticker: Int'l Exchange:
2006 Sales: $23,520,000	2006 Profits: $1,626,000	Employees: 45,000
2005 Sales: $21,161,000	2005 Profits: $1,027,000	Fiscal Year Ends: 12/31
2004 Sales: $19,641,000	2004 Profits: $1,245,000	Parent Company:

SALARIES/BENEFITS:

Pension Plan: Y	ESOP Stock Plan:	Profit Sharing:	Top Exec. Salary: $	Bonus: $
Savings Plan: Y	Stock Purch. Plan:		Second Exec. Salary: $	Bonus: $

OTHER THOUGHTS:

Apparent Women Officers or Directors: 9
Hot Spot for Advancement for Women/Minorities: Y

LOCATIONS: ("Y" = Yes)

West:	Southwest:	Midwest:	Southeast:	Northeast:	International:
Y	Y	Y	Y	Y	Y

Note: Financial information, benefits and other data can change quickly and may vary from those stated here.

LIMITED BRANDS INC

www.limitedbrands.com

Industry Group Code: 448120 Ranks within this company's industry group: Sales: 1 Profits: 1

Management:		Sales/Marketing:		Liberal Arts:		Information Systems:		Professionals:		Tech./Scientific:	
Management Trainees:	Y	Marketing Pros.:	Y	Gen. Writing/Editing:	Y	Info. Management:	Y	Finance/Acct.:	Y	Engineers, Electrical:	
Experienced Mngmt.:	Y	Retail Sales:	Y	Technical Writing:		Software Dev.:	Y	Law:	Y	Engineers, Other:	
International Business:	Y	Commercial/Industrial:		Graphic Arts/Photog.:	Y	Hardware Dev.:		HR/Other:	Y	Health/Lab:	
MBA Grads:	Y	Sales Trainees:	Y	Music:		Consulting/Other:		Training:	Y	Scientists/Research:	
		Advertising Pros.:	Y	Broadcasting:				Health Care:		Petroleum/Chemicals:	
				Other:	Y			Consulting:		Math/Other:	

TYPES OF BUSINESS:

Apparel, Retail
Contract Manufacturing
Apparel Importing
Catalog & Online Sales
Lingerie
Cosmetics
Fragrances
Candles

BRANDS/DIVISIONS/AFFILIATES:

Limited, Inc. (The)
Victoria's Secret
Victoria's Secret Beauty
Bath & Body Works
White Barn Candle Company
C.O. Bigelow
Mast Industries
La Senza Corporation

CONTACTS: *Note: Officers with more than one job title may be intentionally listed here more than once.*

Leslie H. Wexner, CEO
Stuart Burgdoerfer, CFO/Exec. VP
Jane L. Ramsey, Exec. VP-Human Resources
Martyn R. Redgrave, Chief Admin. Officer/Exec. VP
Sharen J. Turney, CEO/Pres.-Victoria's Secret Megabrand
Diane Neal, CEO-Bath & Body Works
Peter Horvath, Exec. VP-Bus. Integration
Leslie H. Wexner, Chmn.

Phone: 614-415-7000	Fax: 614-415-7094
Toll-Free:	
Address: 3 Limited Pkwy., Columbus, OH 43230 US	

GROWTH PLANS/SPECIAL FEATURES:

Limited Brands, Inc., formerly The Limited, Inc., is an apparel, lingerie, personal care products, accessories and fragrances retailer. The company operates over 2,990 retail stores, mainly in malls and shopping centers throughout the U.S. Victoria's Secret and Victoria's Secret Beauty, with 1,043 stores in the U.S. and 322 in Canada, are specialty retailers of women's intimate apparel, beauty products and related accessories. The direct marketing segment is in charge of the catalog, which is produced at volumes of approximately 390 million copies annually. Bath & Body Works, with 1,638 stores, features personal care products and also operates White Barn Candle Company and C.O. Bigelow. C.O. Bigelow also has brand specific stores in Ohio, Massachusetts, Illinois and New Jersey. Limited Brands retains full ownership of the five Henri Bendel stores located in New York City and Columbus, Ohio. The firm also owns Mast Industries, a contract manufacturer and apparel importer, which supplies merchandise to Victoria's Secret, Express and Limited Stores. Finally, the company operates La Senza, a Canadian lingerie company. La Senza operates 322 stores in Canada and 487 stores in 45 other countries. The company runs three e-commerce sites: VictoriasSecret.com, LaSenza.com and bathandbodyworks.com. In December 2008, Victoria's Secret launched Espanol.VictoriasSectet.com a Spanish language version of its e-commerce website. Also in December 2009, Victoria's Secret introduced a new two-story flagship store in Manhattan, New York.

Limited Brands offers medical, dental and vision insurance; product discounts; tuition assistance; paid time off; and adoption assistance.

FINANCIALS: Sales and profits are in thousands of dollars—add 000 to get the full amount. 2008 Note: Financial information for 2008 was not available for all companies at press time.

2008 Sales: $10,134,000	2008 Profits: $718,000	**U.S. Stock Ticker: LTD**
2007 Sales: $10,671,000	2007 Profits: $675,000	**Int'l Ticker:** Int'l Exchange:
2006 Sales: $9,699,000	2006 Profits: $683,000	Employees: 97,500
2005 Sales: $9,408,000	2005 Profits: $705,000	Fiscal Year Ends: 1/31
2004 Sales: $8,934,000	2004 Profits: $717,000	Parent Company:

SALARIES/BENEFITS:

Pension Plan:	ESOP Stock Plan:	Profit Sharing:	Top Exec. Salary: $1,909,769	Bonus: $1,523,192
Savings Plan: Y	Stock Purch. Plan: Y		Second Exec. Salary: $1,240,385	Bonus: $1,090,500

OTHER THOUGHTS:

Apparent Women Officers or Directors: 3
Hot Spot for Advancement for Women/Minorities: Y

LOCATIONS: ("Y" = Yes)

West:	Southwest:	Midwest:	Southeast:	Northeast:	International:
Y	Y	Y	Y	Y	Y

LINCARE HOLDINGS INC

www.lincare.com

Industry Group Code: 6216 Ranks within this company's industry group: Sales: 1 Profits: 1

Management:		Sales/Marketing:		Liberal Arts:		Information Systems:		Professionals:		Tech./Scientific:	
Management Trainees:	Y	Marketing Pros.:	Y	Gen. Writing/Editing:	Y	Info. Management:	Y	Finance/Acct.:	Y	Engineers, Electrical:	
Experienced Mngmt.:	Y	Retail Sales:		Technical Writing:	Y	Software Dev.:		Law:	Y	Engineers, Other:	
International Business:		Commercial/Industrial:	Y	Graphic Arts/Photog.:	Y	Hardware Dev.:		HR/Other:	Y	Health/Lab:	Y
MBA Grads:	Y	Sales Trainees:		Music:		Consulting/Other:		Training:	Y	Scientists/Research:	
		Advertising Pros.:		Broadcasting:				Health Care:	Y	Petroleum/Chemicals:	Y
				Other:				Consulting:		Math/Other:	

TYPES OF BUSINESS:

Home Health Care-Oxygen & Other Respiratory Therapy Services
Durable Medical Equipment
Home Infusion Therapies

BRANDS/DIVISIONS/AFFILIATES:

CONTACTS: *Note: Officers with more than one job title may be intentionally listed here more than once.*

John P. Byrnes, CEO
Shawn S. Schabel, COO
Shawn S. Schabel, Pres.
Paul G. Gabos, CFO
Paul G. Gabos, Corp. Sec.
John P. Byrnes, Chmn.

Phone: 727-530-7700	Fax: 727-532-9692
Toll-Free:	
Address: 19387 US 19 N., Clearwater, FL 33764 US	

GROWTH PLANS/SPECIAL FEATURES:

Lincare Holdings, Inc. is a provider of oxygen and other respiratory therapy services to in-home patients. The firm serves roughly 700,000 customers in 48 states through 1,056 operating centers. The company also provides durable medical equipment and home infusion therapies in certain geographic markets. The firm's customers typically suffer from chronic obstructive pulmonary diseases (COPD), such as emphysema, chronic bronchitis or asthma, and require supplemental oxygen or other respiratory therapy services in order to alleviate the symptoms and discomfort of respiratory dysfunction. Lincare's home oxygen equipment comes in two variations: oxygen concentrators and liquid oxygen systems. Oxygen concentrators are stationary units that provide a continuous flow of oxygen by filtering ordinary room air and are often supplemented with portable gaseous oxygen cylinders or liquid oxygen systems to meet the ambulatory or emergency needs of the customer. Liquid oxygen systems are thermally insulated containers of liquid oxygen; they generally consist of a stationary unit and a portable unit, and are most commonly used by customers with significant ambulatory requirements. Other respiratory therapy services offered by the company include nebulizers and associated respiratory medications, which provide aerosol therapy for customers suffering from COPD and asthma; non-invasive ventilation, which provides nocturnal ventilatory support for customers with neuromuscular disease and COPD; ventilators, which support respiratory function in severe cases of respiratory failure where the customer can no longer sustain the mechanics of breathing without the assistance of a machine; and continuous positive airway pressure devices, which maintain open airways in customer suffering from obstructive sleep apnea by providing airflow at prescribed pressures during sleep. Lincare's home infusion therapy products and services include chemotherapy; continuous pain management; intravenous antibiotic therapy; parenteral nutrition; dobutamine infusions; enteral nutrition; immunoglobulin therapy; and central catheter management.

FINANCIALS: Sales and profits are in thousands of dollars—add 000 to get the full amount. 2008 Note: Financial information for 2008 was not available for all companies at press time.

2008 Sales: $1,664,580	2008 Profits: $237,205	**U.S. Stock Ticker: LNCR**	
2007 Sales: $1,595,990	2007 Profits: $226,077	Int'l Ticker: Int'l Exchange:	
2006 Sales: $1,409,795	2006 Profits: $212,981	Employees: 9,957	
2005 Sales: $1,266,627	2005 Profits: $213,696	Fiscal Year Ends: 12/31	
2004 Sales: $1,268,531	2004 Profits: $273,428	Parent Company:	

SALARIES/BENEFITS:

Pension Plan:	ESOP Stock Plan:	Profit Sharing:	Top Exec. Salary: $896,816	Bonus: $1,165,860
Savings Plan: Y	Stock Purch. Plan: Y		Second Exec. Salary: $598,177	Bonus: $777,630

OTHER THOUGHTS:

Apparent Women Officers or Directors:
Hot Spot for Advancement for Women/Minorities:

LOCATIONS: ("Y" = Yes)

West:	Southwest:	Midwest:	Southeast:	Northeast:	International:
Y	Y	Y	Y	Y	

Note: Financial information, benefits and other data can change quickly and may vary from those stated here.

LINCOLN NATIONAL CORPORATION

www.lfg.com

Industry Group Code: 524113 **Ranks within this company's industry group:** Sales: 5 Profits: 3

Management:		Sales/Marketing:		Liberal Arts:		Information Systems:		Professionals:		Tech./Scientific:	
Management Trainees:	Y	Marketing Pros.:	Y	Gen. Writing/Editing:	Y	Info. Management:	Y	Finance/Acct.:	Y	Engineers, Electrical:	
Experienced Mngmt.:	Y	Retail Sales:		Technical Writing:	Y	Software Dev.:	Y	Law:	Y	Engineers, Other:	
International Business:	Y	Commercial/Industrial:	Y	Graphic Arts/Photog.:	Y	Hardware Dev.:		HR/Other:	Y	Health/Lab:	
MBA Grads:	Y	Sales Trainees:	Y	Music:		Consulting/Other:		Training:	Y	Scientists/Research:	
		Advertising Pros.:	Y	Broadcasting:				Health Care:	Y	Petroleum/Chemicals:	
				Other:	Y			Consulting:		Math/Other:	Y

TYPES OF BUSINESS:

Life Insurance
Investment Management
Retirement Plans
Mutual Funds
Financial Planning
Annuities

BRANDS/DIVISIONS/AFFILIATES:

Delaware Management Holdings, Inc.
Lincoln UK
Lincoln LifeReserve IUL
Lincoln LifeReserve UL
MoneyGuard

CONTACTS: *Note: Officers with more than one job title may be intentionally listed here more than once.*

Dennis R. Glass, CEO
Dennis R. Glass, Pres.
Frederick J. Crawford, CFO/Exec. VP
Heather Dzielak, Chief Mktg. Officer/Sr. VP
Lisa M. Buckingham, Chief Human Resources Officer/Sr. VP
Charles C. Cornelio, Chief Admin. Officer/Exec. VP
Dennis L. Schoff, General Counsel/Sr. VP
Lauren Sammerson, Comm. & Programs Officer
Jim Sjoreen, VP-Investor Rel.
Robert W. Dineen, Chmn. & CEO-Lincoln Financial Network
Patrick P. Coyne, Pres., Delaware Mgmt. Holdings, Inc.
Mark E. Konen, Pres., Insurance Solutions
C. Suzanne Womack, Sec.
Michael Tallett-Williams, Pres./Managing Dir.-Lincoln U.K.

Phone: 484-583-1400	Fax: 484-583-3962
Toll-Free: 877-275-5462	
Address: 150 N. Radnor Chester Rd., Ste. A305, Radnor, PA 19087 US	

GROWTH PLANS/SPECIAL FEATURES:

Lincoln National Corp. is a holding company operating multiple insurance and investment businesses. The operations of the firm's subsidiaries, collectively known as Lincoln Financial Group, are divided into five business segments: Retirement Solutions, Insurance Solutions, Investment Management, Enterprise Services and Lincoln U.K. The Retirement Solutions business operates in two segments: the annuities segment, which provides tax-deferred growth and lifetime income opportunities for its clients by offering individual fixed annuities; and the defined contribution segment, which provides employer-sponsored fixed/variable annuities and 401(k), 403(b) and 457 mutual fund-based programs. Lincoln's Insurance Solutions division is also divided into two segments: the life insurance segment, which provides wealth protection, transfer opportunities, term insurance and a linked-benefit product called MoneyGuard; and the group protection segment, which offers group term life, disability income and dental insurance primarily to small and mid-sized employers. The Investment Management division provides mutual funds, investment advisory services and retirement plans to both individual and institutional investors through its subsidiary, Delaware Management Holdings, Inc. The company's Enterprise Services group, launched in March 2009, offers customer service centers that specialize in law, compliance, shared services and information technology. Wholly-owned subsidiary Lincoln U.K. primarily offers unit-linked life and pension products throughout the U.K. In December 2008, the firm launched two new accumulation-aimed products for its Insurance Solutions division: Lincoln LifeReserve UL (universal life) and Lincoln LifeReserve IUL (indexed universal life). In June 2009, the company agreed to sell Lincoln U.K. to SLF of Canada UK Limited for approximately $318.3 million. In August 2009, Lincoln National agreed to sell Delaware Management Holdings, Inc., and its subsidiaries to Macquarie Group for approximately $428 million.

Lincoln offers employee benefits including disability, life, AD&D, medical, dental and vision insurance; domestic partner benefits; training programs; tuition reimbursement; educational and adoption assistance; counseling services; and a 401(k).

FINANCIALS: Sales and profits are in thousands of dollars—add 000 to get the full amount. 2008 Note: Financial information for 2008 was not available for all companies at press time.

2008 Sales: $9,883,000	2008 Profits: $57,000	**U.S. Stock Ticker:** LNC
2007 Sales: $10,594,000	2007 Profits: $1,215,000	**Int'l Ticker:** Int'l Exchange:
2006 Sales: $8,962,000	2006 Profits: $1,316,000	Employees: 9,696
2005 Sales: $5,475,000	2005 Profits: $831,055	Fiscal Year Ends: 12/31
2004 Sales: $5,351,000	2004 Profits: $707,009	Parent Company:

SALARIES/BENEFITS:

Pension Plan:	ESOP Stock Plan:	Profit Sharing: Y	Top Exec. Salary: $1,000,000	Bonus: $800,000
Savings Plan: Y	Stock Purch. Plan:		Second Exec. Salary: $509,769	Bonus: $244,400

OTHER THOUGHTS:

Apparent Women Officers or Directors: 4
Hot Spot for Advancement for Women/Minorities: Y

LOCATIONS: ("Y" = Yes)

West:	Southwest:	Midwest:	Southeast:	Northeast:	International:
Y	Y	Y	Y	Y	Y

Note: Financial information, benefits and other data can change quickly and may vary from those stated here.

LKQ CORP

www.lkqcorp.com

Industry Group Code: 3363 Ranks within this company's industry group: Sales: 4 Profits: 4

Management:		Sales/Marketing:		Liberal Arts:		Information Systems:		Professionals:		Tech./Scientific:	
Management Trainees:	Y	Marketing Pros.:	Y	Gen. Writing/Editing:		Info. Management:	Y	Finance/Acct.:	Y	Engineers, Electrical:	
Experienced Mngmt.:	Y	Retail Sales:		Technical Writing:	Y	Software Dev.:		Law:	Y	Engineers, Other:	Y
International Business:		Commercial/Industrial:	Y	Graphic Arts/Photog.:		Hardware Dev.:		HR/Other:	Y	Health/Lab:	
MBA Grads:	Y	Sales Trainees:		Music:		Consulting/Other:		Training:	Y	Scientists/Research:	
		Advertising Pros.:		Broadcasting:				Health Care:		Petroleum/Chemicals:	
				Other:				Consulting:		Math/Other:	

TYPES OF BUSINESS:

Remanufactured OEM Parts
Aftermarket Replacement Parts
Vehicle Salvage
Scrap/Bulk Automotive Parts
Refurbished Aluminum Wheels

BRANDS/DIVISIONS/AFFILIATES:

Pick-Your-Part Auto Wrecking
Automotive Rebuilders Supply Co
Goody's Truck Parts, Inc.

CONTACTS: Note: Officers with more than one job title may be intentionally listed here more than once.

Joseph M. Holsten, CEO
Joseph M. Holsten, Pres.
Mark T. Spears, CFO/Exec. VP
Victor M. Casini, General Counsel/VP/Corp. Sec.
Robert L. Wagman, VP-Insurance Svcs. & Aftermarket Oper.
Walter P. Hanley, VP-Dev./Associate General Counsel/Asst. Sec.
Frank P. Erlain, VP-Finance/Controller
Leonard A. Damron, Sr. VP-Southeast Region
H. Bradley Willen, VP-Midwest Region
Steven H. Jones, VP-Central Region & Core Oper.
Donald F. Flynn, Chmn.

Phone: 312-621-1950	Fax: 312-621-1969
Toll-Free: 877-557-2677	
Address: 120 N. LaSalle St., Ste. 3300, Chicago, IL 60602 US	

GROWTH PLANS/SPECIAL FEATURES:

LKQ Corporation is one of the largest providers of recycled OEM (original equipment manufacturer) automotive parts and related services in the U.S. LKQ operates approximately 280 facilities around the world. In the U.S., the company has a network of 73 locations that supply wholesale recycled OEM parts, 57 of which include a combination of processing, sales and redistribution operations, and 16 of which are primarily redistribution facilities. The firm's aftermarket parts business operates from facilities that serve as sales, warehousing or distribution centers, with a total of 152 facilities in the U.S. and Canada. LKQ also has locations providing self-service retail recycled vehicle products. The company refurbishes bumpers and wheels at 54 locations in the U.S. and Canada and one location in northeast Mexico. It also refurbishes head lamps and tail lamps at a facility in Grand Rapids, Michigan. The firm procures salvage vehicles, primarily at auctions, using its local professionals and centralized purchasing systems, and directly from insurance companies, automobile manufacturers and other suppliers. Once LKQ has received the proper title, assuring that the vehicles have not been stolen, it dismantles it for recycled parts. The firm's customers include collision and mechanical repair shops and, indirectly, insurance companies, including extended-warranty companies. LKQ's most popular products include engines, vehicle front-end assemblies, doors, transmissions, trunk lids, bumper assemblies, wheels, head and tail lamp assemblies, mirrors, fenders and axles. In 2008, the firm acquired Pick-Your-Part Auto Wrecking; Automotive Rebuilders Supply Co., Inc.; and Goody's Truck Parts, Inc.

FINANCIALS: Sales and profits are in thousands of dollars—add 000 to get the full amount. 2008 Note: Financial information for 2008 was not available for all companies at press time.

2008 Sales: $1,937,301	2008 Profits: $99,899	**U.S. Stock Ticker:** LKQX	
2007 Sales: $1,126,825	2007 Profits: $65,901	**Int'l Ticker:** Int'l Exchange:	
2006 Sales: $789,381	2006 Profits: $44,395	Employees: 9,600	
2005 Sales: $547,392	2005 Profits: $30,887	Fiscal Year Ends: 12/31	
2004 Sales: $424,756	2004 Profits: $20,573	Parent Company:	

SALARIES/BENEFITS:

Pension Plan:	ESOP Stock Plan:	Profit Sharing:	Top Exec. Salary: $650,000	Bonus: $515,937
Savings Plan: Y	Stock Purch. Plan:		Second Exec. Salary: $420,000	Bonus: $257,250

OTHER THOUGHTS:

Apparent Women Officers or Directors:
Hot Spot for Advancement for Women/Minorities:

LOCATIONS: ("Y" = Yes)

West:	Southwest:	Midwest:	Southeast:	Northeast:	International:
Y	Y	Y	Y	Y	

Note: Financial information, benefits and other data can change quickly and may vary from those stated here.

LOCKHEED MARTIN CORP

www.lockheedmartin.com

Industry Group Code: 33641 Ranks within this company's industry group: Sales: 3 Profits: 2

Management:		Sales/Marketing:		Liberal Arts:		Information Systems:		Professionals:		Tech./Scientific:	
Management Trainees:	Y	Marketing Pros.:	Y	Gen. Writing/Editing:	Y	Info. Management:	Y	Finance/Acct.:	Y	Engineers, Electrical:	Y
Experienced Mngmt.:	Y	Retail Sales:		Technical Writing:	Y	Software Dev.:	Y	Law:	Y	Engineers, Other:	Y
International Business:	Y	Commercial/Industrial:	Y	Graphic Arts/Photog.:	Y	Hardware Dev.:	Y	HR/Other:	Y	Health/Lab:	
MBA Grads:	Y	Sales Trainees:		Music:		Consulting/Other:	Y	Training:	Y	Scientists/Research:	Y
		Advertising Pros.:	Y	Broadcasting:				Health Care:		Petroleum/Chemicals:	
				Other:				Consulting:		Math/Other:	Y

TYPES OF BUSINESS:

Aerospace & Defense Technology
Military Aircraft
Defense Electronics
Systems Integration & Technology Services
Communications Satellites & Launch Services
Undersea, Shipboard, Land & Airborne Systems & Subsystems

BRANDS/DIVISIONS/AFFILIATES:

Orion
Skunk Works
Management Systens Designers, Inc.
RLM Systems, Ltd.
3Dsolve, Inc.
Aculight Corporation

CONTACTS: *Note: Officers with more than one job title may be intentionally listed here more than once.*

Robert J. Stevens, CEO
Robert J. Stevens, Pres.
Bruce L. Tanner, CFO/Exec. VP
Linda Gooden, Exec. VP-Info. Systems & Global Svcs.
Ralph D. Heath, Exec. VP-Aeronautics
Christopher E. Kubasik, Exec. VP-Electronic Systems
Joanne M. Maguire, Exec. VP-Space Systems
Robert J. Stevens, Chmn.

Phone: 301-897-6000	Fax: 301-897-6704
Toll-Free:	
Address: 6801 Rockledge Dr., Bethesda, MD 20817 US	

GROWTH PLANS/SPECIAL FEATURES:

Lockheed Martin Corp. specializes in developing and servicing advanced technological systems. It serves domestic and international customers with products and services that have defense, civil and commercial applications, with principal customers being agencies of the U.S. government. The company operates in four segments: aeronautics; electronic systems; information systems & global services (IS&GS); and space systems. The aeronautics segment is engaged in the design, research and development, systems integration, production, sustainment, support and upgrade of advanced military aircraft, air vehicles and related technologies. Major products and programs include design, development, production and sustainment of the F-35 stealth multi-role international coalition fighter; the F-16 international multi-role fighter and U-2 high-altitude reconnaissance aircraft. It also produces major components for Japan's F-2 fighter and is a co-developer of the T-50 advanced jet trainer. The Skunk Works advanced development organization provides system solutions using rapid prototyping and advanced technologies. The electronic systems segment designs, researches, develops, integrates, produces and sustains systems and subsystems for undersea, shipboard, land and airborne applications. Major products include tactical missiles and weapon fire control systems; ground combat vehicle integrations; and surveillance and reconnaissance systems. The IS&GS segment provides federal services, IT solutions and technology expertise across a broad spectrum of applications and customers. It provides full life cycle support and highly specialized talent in the areas of software and systems engineering, including capabilities in space, air and ground systems, and also provides logistics, mission operations support, peacekeeping and nation-building services for a wide variety of U.S. defense and civil government agencies in the U.S. and abroad. The space systems segment designs, researches, develops, engineers and produces satellites, strategic and defensive missile systems and space transportation systems. In September 2008, the company acquired Aculight Corporation, a provider of laser-based solutions.

Employees are offered healthcare coverage; a retirement plan; and a 401(k) plan.

FINANCIALS: Sales and profits are in thousands of dollars—add 000 to get the full amount. 2008 Note: Financial information for 2008 was not available for all companies at press time.

2008 Sales: $42,731,000	2008 Profits: $3,217,000	**U.S. Stock Ticker: LMT**
2007 Sales: $41,862,000	2007 Profits: $3,033,000	**Int'l Ticker:** Int'l Exchange:
2006 Sales: $39,620,000	2006 Profits: $2,529,000	Employees: 146,000
2005 Sales: $37,213,000	2005 Profits: $1,825,000	Fiscal Year Ends: 12/31
2004 Sales: $35,526,000	2004 Profits: $1,266,000	Parent Company:

SALARIES/BENEFITS:

Pension Plan: Y	ESOP Stock Plan:	Profit Sharing:	Top Exec. Salary: $1,774,038	Bonus: $12,817,750
Savings Plan: Y	Stock Purch. Plan:		Second Exec. Salary: $916,154	Bonus: $2,709,550

OTHER THOUGHTS:

Apparent Women Officers or Directors: 4
Hot Spot for Advancement for Women/Minorities: Y

LOCATIONS: ("Y" = Yes)

West:	Southwest:	Midwest:	Southeast:	Northeast:	International:
Y	Y	Y	Y	Y	Y

LODGIAN INC

www.lodgian.com

Industry Group Code: 721110 Ranks within this company's industry group: Sales: 6 Profits: 3

Management:		Sales/Marketing:		Liberal Arts:		Information Systems:		Professionals:		Tech./Scientific:	
Management Trainees:	Y	Marketing Pros.:	Y	Gen. Writing/Editing:	Y	Info. Management:	Y	Finance/Acct.:	Y	Engineers, Electrical:	
Experienced Mngmt.:	Y	Retail Sales:		Technical Writing:		Software Dev.:		Law:	Y	Engineers, Other:	
International Business:	Y	Commercial/Industrial:	Y	Graphic Arts/Photog.:	Y	Hardware Dev.:		HR/Other:	Y	Health/Lab:	
MBA Grads:	Y	Sales Trainees:		Music:		Consulting/Other:		Training:	Y	Scientists/Research:	
		Advertising Pros.:	Y	Broadcasting:				Health Care:		Petroleum/Chemicals:	
				Other:				Consulting:		Math/Other:	

TYPES OF BUSINESS:

Hotels

BRANDS/DIVISIONS/AFFILIATES:

InterContinental Hotels Group plc
Marriott International Inc
Hilton Group plc
Wyndham Worldwide
Crowne Plaza
Holiday Inn
Courtyard by Marriott
Residence Inn by Marriott

CONTACTS: *Note: Officers with more than one job title may be intentionally listed here more than once.*

Peter T. Cyrus, Interim CEO
Peter T. Cyrus, Interim Pres.
James A. MacLennan, CFO/Exec. VP
Carol L. Mayne, VP-Human Resources
Johnny A. Green, VP-IT
Daniel E. (Dan) Ellis, General Counsel/Corp. Sec./Sr. VP
Joseph F. Kelly, VP-Oper.
Susan King, VP-Franchise Comm.
Deborah N. (Debi) Ethridge, VP-Investor Rel.
Deborah N. (Debi) Ethridge, VP-Finance
Barbra Beaulieu, VP-Internal Audit & Controls
Kevin B. Richards, VP-Asset Mgmt.
Donna B. Cohen, Controller/VP
Stewart J. Brown, Chmn.

Phone: 404-364-9400	**Fax:** 404-364-0088

Toll-Free:

Address: 3445 Peachtree Rd. NE, Ste. 700, Atlanta, GA 30326 US

GROWTH PLANS/SPECIAL FEATURES:

Lodgian, Inc. is an independent owner and operator of 46 hotels containing 7,448 rooms located in 22 states and Canada. Of its hotels, 35 are held for use and 11 are held for sale. One of the firm's hotels is operated in a joint venture in which a subsidiary serves as the general partner and has a 50% voting interest. Lodgian operates substantially all of its hotels under nationally recognized brands, with 25 operated under franchises obtained from InterContinental Hotels Group, with brands including Crowne Plaza, Holiday Inn, Holiday Inn Select and Holiday Inn Express; 12 operated under franchises from Marriott International, with brands including Marriott, Courtyard by Marriott, Fairfield Inn by Marriott, Residence Inn by Marriott and SpringHill Suites by Marriott; seven operated under other nationally recognized brands, including Hilton and Wyndham; and two non-branded. The company's hotels are primarily full-service properties that offer food and beverage services; meeting and banquet facilities; and compete in the midscale and upscale market segments of the lodging industry. Lodgian operates hotel brands in the Upper Upscale; Upscale; Midscale with Food & Beverage; and Midscale without Food & Beverage segments. Transient revenues, derived from guests staying only for brief periods of time without a long-term contract, generate roughly 69% of the firm's room revenues, while groups generate 24% and contract revenues (such as contracts with airlines for crew rooms) generate 7%.

Employees are offered medical, dental and vision insurance; disability coverage; life insurance; a 401(k) plan; educational assistance; and hotel discounts.

FINANCIALS: Sales and profits are in thousands of dollars—add 000 to get the full amount. 2008 Note: Financial information for 2008 was not available for all companies at press time.

2008 Sales: $240,428	2008 Profits: $-11,984	**U.S. Stock Ticker: LGN**	
2007 Sales: $242,558	2007 Profits: $-8,446	**Int'l Ticker:** Int'l Exchange:	
2006 Sales: $227,635	2006 Profits: $-15,176	Employees: 3,046	
2005 Sales: $222,762	2005 Profits: $12,301	Fiscal Year Ends: 12/31	
2004 Sales: $217,189	2004 Profits: $-31,834	Parent Company:	

SALARIES/BENEFITS:

Pension Plan:	ESOP Stock Plan:	Profit Sharing:	Top Exec. Salary: $324,038	Bonus: $12,000
Savings Plan: Y	Stock Purch. Plan:		Second Exec. Salary: $299,039	Bonus: $12,000

OTHER THOUGHTS:

Apparent Women Officers or Directors: 5
Hot Spot for Advancement for Women/Minorities: Y

LOCATIONS: ("Y" = Yes)

West:	Southwest:	Midwest:	Southeast:	Northeast:	International:
Y	Y	Y	Y	Y	Y

Note: Financial information, benefits and other data can change quickly and may vary from those stated here.

LOEWS CORPORATION

www.loews.com

Industry Group Code: 524126 **Ranks within this company's industry group:** Sales: 4   Profits: 1

Management:		Sales/Marketing:		Liberal Arts:		Information Systems:		Professionals:		Tech./Scientific:	
Management Trainees:	Y	Marketing Pros.:	Y	Gen. Writing/Editing:	Y	Info. Management:	Y	Finance/Acct.:	Y	Engineers, Electrical:	
Experienced Mngmt.:	Y	Retail Sales:		Technical Writing:	Y	Software Dev.:	Y	Law:	Y	Engineers, Other:	
International Business:	Y	Commercial/Industrial:	Y	Graphic Arts/Photog.:	Y	Hardware Dev.:		HR/Other:	Y	Health/Lab:	
MBA Grads:	Y	Sales Trainees:	Y	Music:		Consulting/Other:		Training:	Y	Scientists/Research:	
		Advertising Pros.:	Y	Broadcasting:				Health Care:		Petroleum/Chemicals:	
				Other:	Y			Consulting:		Math/Other:	Y

TYPES OF BUSINESS:

Direct Property & Casualty Insurance
Natural Gas Exploration & Production
Offshore Oil & Gas Drilling
Hotel Operation
Pipelines

BRANDS/DIVISIONS/AFFILIATES:

CNA Financial Corp.
Lorillard Inc
Loews Hotels Holding Corporation
Diamond Offshore Drilling, Inc.
HighMount Exploration & Production, LLC
Boardwalk Pipeline Partners, LP

CONTACTS: *Note: Officers with more than one job title may be intentionally listed here more than once.*

James S. Tisch, CEO
James S. Tisch, Pres.
Peter W. Keegan, CFO/Sr. VP
Alan Momeyer, VP-Human Resources
Robert D. Fields, CIO/VP
Gary W. Sgarson, General Counsel/Sr. VP/Sec.
Jonathan Nathanson, VP-Corp. Dev.
Candace Leeds, VP-Public Rel.
Darren Daugherty, Head-Investor Rel.
John J. Kenny, Treas.
Jonathan M. Tisch, Co-Chmn.
Jonathan M. Tisch, CEO/Chmn.-Loews Hotels
Mark S. Schwartz, Controller
Richard W. Scott, Chief Investment Officer/VP
Andrew H. Tisch, Co-Chmn.

Phone: 212-521-2000	Fax: 212-521-2525
Toll-Free:	
Address: 667 Madison Ave., New York, NY 10065-8087 US	

GROWTH PLANS/SPECIAL FEATURES:

Loews Corp. is a holding firm for companies involved in various industries. The company operates primarily through five subsidiaries: CNA Financial Corp.; Boardwalk Pipeline Partners, LP; Diamond Offshore Drilling, Inc.; Loews Hotels Holdings Corp.; and HighMount Exploration & Production, LLC. CNA Financial, a 90%-owned subsidiary, is an insurance holding company; its property and casualty insurance businesses are conducted by Continental Casualty Co. and The Continental Insurance Co. Boardwalk Pipeline Partners, a 75%-owned subsidiary, specializes in the interstate transportation and storage of natural gas. The subsidiary conducts its operations through three companies: Texas Gas Transmission LLC, which operates roughly 5,950 miles of natural gas pipeline in nine states; Gulf Crossing Pipeline Company LLC, which operates roughly 350 miles of natural gas pipeline in Louisiana and Texas; and Gulf South Pipeline, LP, which operates about 7,700 miles of natural gas pipeline located in five states. Diamond Offshore, a 50.4%-owned subsidiary, owns and operates drilling rigs that are used in the drilling of offshore oil and gas wells by companies that explore and produce hydrocarbons. The subsidiary owns 46 offshore rigs, of which 30 are semi-submersible. Loews Hotels, a wholly-owned subsidiary, operates 18 hotels, including Loews Annapolis; Hard Rock Hotel in Orlando, Florida; The Regency in New York; and Loews Hotel Vogue in Montreal, Canada. HighMount Exploration, another wholly-owned subsidiary, explores and produces natural gas. In 2008, the firm spun off Lorillard, Inc., its cigarettes producing subsidiary.

FINANCIALS: Sales and profits are in thousands of dollars—add 000 to get the full amount. 2008 Note: Financial information for 2008 was not available for all companies at press time.

2008 Sales: $14,543,000	2008 Profits: $4,530,000	**U.S. Stock Ticker: L**
2007 Sales: $18,380,000	2007 Profits: $2,489,000	**Int'l Ticker:** Int'l Exchange:
2006 Sales: $17,702,000	2006 Profits: $2,491,300	Employees: 19,100
2005 Sales: $16,017,800	2005 Profits: $1,211,600	Fiscal Year Ends: 12/31
2004 Sales: $15,236,900	2004 Profits: $1,215,800	Parent Company:

SALARIES/BENEFITS:

Pension Plan:	ESOP Stock Plan:	Profit Sharing:	Top Exec. Salary: $1,100,000	Bonus: $2,500,000
Savings Plan: Y	Stock Purch. Plan:		Second Exec. Salary: $990,000	Bonus: $1,510,000

OTHER THOUGHTS:

Apparent Women Officers or Directors: 5
Hot Spot for Advancement for Women/Minorities: Y

LOCATIONS: ("Y" = Yes)

West:	Southwest:	Midwest:	Southeast:	Northeast:	International:
Y	Y	Y	Y	Y	Y

LOWE'S COMPANIES INC

www.lowes.com

Industry Group Code: 444110 Ranks within this company's industry group: Sales: 2 Profits: 2

Management:		Sales/Marketing:		Liberal Arts:		Information Systems:		Professionals:		Tech./Scientific:	
Management Trainees:	Y	Marketing Pros.:	Y	Gen. Writing/Editing:	Y	Info. Management:	Y	Finance/Acct.:	Y	Engineers, Electrical:	
Experienced Mngmt.:	Y	Retail Sales:	Y	Technical Writing:		Software Dev.:	Y	Law:	Y	Engineers, Other:	
International Business:	Y	Commercial/Industrial:	Y	Graphic Arts/Photog.:	Y	Hardware Dev.:		HR/Other:	Y	Health/Lab:	
MBA Grads:	Y	Sales Trainees:	Y	Music:		Consulting/Other:		Training:	Y	Scientists/Research:	
		Advertising Pros.:	Y	Broadcasting:				Health Care:		Petroleum/Chemicals:	
				Other:	Y			Consulting:		Math/Other:	

TYPES OF BUSINESS:

Home Centers, Retail
Home Improvement Products
Home Installation Services
Special Order Sales

BRANDS/DIVISIONS/AFFILIATES:

Premier Living
Kobalt
Portfolio
Harbor Breeze
Reliabilt
Utilitech
Top Choice Lumber
Lowes.com

CONTACTS: Note: Officers with more than one job title may be intentionally listed here more than once.

Robert A. Niblock, CEO
Larry D. Stone, COO
Larry D. Stone, Pres.
Robert F. Hull, Jr., CFO/Exec. VP
Robert J. Gfeller, Jr., Sr. VP-Mktg. & Advertising
Maureen K. Ausura, Sr. VP-Human Resources
Scott C. Butterfield, Sr. VP-Research & Strategic Planning
Steven M. Stone, CIO/Sr. VP
Charles W. Canter, Jr., Exec. VP-Merch.
Gary E. Wyatt, Sr. VP-Eng., Real Estate & Construction
Gaither M. Keener, Jr., General Counsel/Sr. VP/Corp. Sec.
Michael K. Brown, Exec. VP-Store Oper.
Gregory M. Bridgeford, Exec. VP-Bus. Dev.
N. Brian Peace, Sr. VP-Corp. Affairs
Matthew V. Hollifield, Chief Acct. Officer/Sr. VP
Theresa A. Anderson, Sr. VP/Gen. Merch. Mgr.-Home Decor
Patricia M. Price, Sr. VP/Gen. Merch. Mgr.-Outdoor Living
Marshall A. Croom, Sr. VP-Merch. & Store Support
Clinton T. Davis, Sr. VP/Gen. Merch. Mgr.-Hardlines
Robert A. Niblock, Chmn.
Joseph M. Mabry, Jr., Exec. VP-Logistics & Distribution

Phone: 704-758-1000	**Fax:** 336-6584766
Toll-Free: 800-445-6937	
Address: 1000 Lowe's Blvd., Mooresville, NC 28117 US	

GROWTH PLANS/SPECIAL FEATURES:

Lowe's Companies, Inc., is one of the largest home improvement retailers in the world. The company owns over 1,675 superstores in 50 states and Canada, each carrying approximately 40,000 products. Hundreds of thousands of items are also available through the firm's special order system. Lowe's stores chiefly serve do-it-yourself homeowners and commercial business customers, including contractors, landscapers, electricians, painters and plumbers. Each Lowe's store carries a wide selection of national brand name merchandise such as KitchenAid, Samsung, Whirlpool, Pella, Werner, Kohler, DeWalt, JohnDeere, Troy-Bilt, Jenn-Air and Bosch; and exclusive brand names such as Premier Living, Kobalt, Portfolio, Harbor Breeze, Reliabilt, Utilitech and Top Choice Lumber. The company's website, Lowes.com, facilitates customers researching, comparing and buying Lowe's products and services. Lowe's recently completed the remerchandising of 116 of its earlier format stores to make them more closely resemble its most current store prototypes. The remerchandising efforts focused on moving entire departments, improving adjacencies, replacing or refurbishing the selling centers, adding interior signage and installing self check-out in each of the remerchandised stores. During fiscal 2008, the company opened 115 new stores, five of which are in Canada. For 2009-2014, Lowe's plans to open approximately 35 to 40 new stores yearly.

Lowe's offers its employees benefits such as life, disability, accident, auto, home, health, dental and vision insurance; merchandise discounts; a stock purchase plan; a 401(k); and flexible spending accounts.

FINANCIALS: Sales and profits are in thousands of dollars—add 000 to get the full amount. 2008 Note: Financial information for 2008 was not available for all companies at press time.

2008 Sales: $48,283,000	2008 Profits: $2,809,000	**U.S. Stock Ticker: LOW**
2007 Sales: $46,927,000	2007 Profits: $3,105,000	**Int'l Ticker:** Int'l Exchange:
2006 Sales: $43,243,000	2006 Profits: $2,765,000	Employees: 229,000
2005 Sales: $36,464,000	2005 Profits: $2,167,000	Fiscal Year Ends: 1/31
2004 Sales: $30,838,000	2004 Profits: $877,000	Parent Company:

SALARIES/BENEFITS:

Pension Plan:	ESOP Stock Plan:	Profit Sharing:	Top Exec. Salary: $1,100,000	Bonus: $1,500,763
Savings Plan: Y	Stock Purch. Plan: Y		Second Exec. Salary: $840,000	Bonus: $765,131

OTHER THOUGHTS:

Apparent Women Officers or Directors: 5
Hot Spot for Advancement for Women/Minorities: Y

LOCATIONS: ("Y" = Yes)

West:	Southwest:	Midwest:	Southeast:	Northeast:	International:
Y	Y	Y	Y	Y	Y

Note: Financial information, benefits and other data can change quickly and may vary from those stated here.

MACY'S INC

www.macysinc.com

Industry Group Code: 452111 Ranks within this company's industry group: Sales: 1 Profits: 2

Management:		Sales/Marketing:		Liberal Arts:		Information Systems:		Professionals:		Tech./Scientific:	
Management Trainees:	Y	Marketing Pros.:	Y	Gen. Writing/Editing:	Y	Info. Management:	Y	Finance/Acct.:	Y	Engineers, Electrical:	
Experienced Mngmt.:	Y	Retail Sales:	Y	Technical Writing:		Software Dev.:	Y	Law:	Y	Engineers, Other:	
International Business:	Y	Commercial/Industrial:		Graphic Arts/Photog.:	Y	Hardware Dev.:		HR/Other:	Y	Health/Lab:	
MBA Grads:	Y	Sales Trainees:	Y	Music:		Consulting/Other:		Training:	Y	Scientists/Research:	
		Advertising Pros.:	Y	Broadcasting:				Health Care:		Petroleum/Chemicals:	
				Other:	Y			Consulting:		Math/Other:	

TYPES OF BUSINESS:

Department Stores
Bridal & Formalwear Stores
Direct Marketing
Online Sales
Catalogs
Wedding Planning & Bridal Registries
Credit Services
Furniture Stores

BRANDS/DIVISIONS/AFFILIATES:

Federated Department Stores, Inc.
Bloomingdale's
FDS Bank
Macy's Credit & Customer Service, Inc.
Macy's Systems & Technology, Inc.
Macy's Merchandising Group, Inc.
Macy's Logistics & Operations
Macy's Corporate Marketing

CONTACTS: *Note: Officers with more than one job title may be intentionally listed here more than once.*

Terry J. Lundgren, CEO
Terry J. Lundgren, Pres.
Karen M. Hoguet, CFO/Exec. VP
Peter Sachse, Chief Mktg. Officer
David W. Clark, Sr. VP-Human Resources
Julie Greiner, Chief Merch. Planning Officer
Thomas L. Cole, Chief Admin. Officer
Dennis J. Broderick, General Counsel/Sr. VP/Sec.
James A. Sluzewski, VP-Corp. Comm. & External Affairs
Joel A. Belsky, Controller
Ronald Klein, Chief Stores Officer
Timothy M. Adams, Chief Private Brands Officer
Jeffrey Gennette, Chief Merch. Officer
Mark S. Cosby, Pres., Stores
Terry J. Lundgren, Chmn.

Phone: 513-579-7000	**Fax:** 513-579-7555
Toll-Free: 800-261-5385	
Address: 7 W. 7th St., Cincinnati, OH 45202 US	

GROWTH PLANS/SPECIAL FEATURES:

Macy's, Inc., formerly Federated Department Stores, Inc., is a U.S. operator of full-line department stores with more than 840 stores in 45 states, Washington D.C., Guam and Puerto Rico. Macy's department stores offer men's, women's and children's apparel and accessories; cosmetics; home furnishings; and other consumer goods. Through its Bloomingdale's and Macy's stores, the firm conducts direct-to-customer catalog and e-commerce businesses under the names Bloomingdale's By Mail, bloomingdales.com and macys.com. Additionally, the company offers online bridal registry and gift purchase facilities to customers. Macy's Home Store, LLC, a wholly-owned indirect subsidiary of the firm, is responsible for the overall strategy, merchandising and marketing of home-related merchandise categories of all Macy's stores. Feminine accessories, intimate apparel, shoes and cosmetics generated 36% of revenue in 2008, while feminine apparel; men's and children's; and home and miscellaneous generated 27%, 22% and 15%, respectively. The company conducts many of its support functions through subsidiary firms. These include FDS Bank and Macy's Credit and Customer Service, Inc., which handle credit processing; Macy's Systems and Technology, Inc., which is in charge of information technology; Macy's Merchandising Group, Inc., which is responsible for private label products; Macy's Logistics and Operations, which operates warehouses and distribution services; and Macy's Corporate Marketing, which handles public relations. In September 2008, the company announced that the first Bloomingdale's location outside of the U.S. will open in Dubai in 2010. In early 2009, Macy's announced the closing of 11 stores in nine states.

Macy's offers its employees medical and dental coverage; flexible spending accounts; wellness programs, including health screenings and WeightWatchers; disability protection; a 401(k) plan; a cash account pension plan; life, AD&D and travel insurance; paid time off, and a merchandise discount.

FINANCIALS: Sales and profits are in thousands of dollars—add 000 to get the full amount. 2008 Note: Financial information for 2008 was not available for all companies at press time.

2008 Sales: $26,313,000	2008 Profits: $893,000	**U.S. Stock Ticker: M**
2007 Sales: $26,970,000	2007 Profits: $995,000	**Int'l Ticker:** Int'l Exchange:
2006 Sales: $22,390,000	2006 Profits: $1,406,000	Employees: 167,000
2005 Sales: $15,776,000	2005 Profits: $689,000	Fiscal Year Ends: 1/31
2004 Sales: $15,412,000	2004 Profits: $693,000	Parent Company:

SALARIES/BENEFITS:

Pension Plan: Y	ESOP Stock Plan:	Profit Sharing:	Top Exec. Salary: $1,500,000	Bonus: $900,000
Savings Plan: Y	Stock Purch. Plan:		Second Exec. Salary: $1,100,000	Bonus: $330,000

OTHER THOUGHTS:

Apparent Women Officers or Directors: 10
Hot Spot for Advancement for Women/Minorities: Y

LOCATIONS: ("Y" = Yes)

West:	Southwest:	Midwest:	Southeast:	Northeast:	International:
Y	Y	Y	Y	Y	Y

MANOR CARE INC

www.hcr-manorcare.com

Industry Group Code: 623110 Ranks within this company's industry group: Sales: 2 Profits:

Management:		Sales/Marketing:		Liberal Arts:		Information Systems:		Professionals:		Tech./Scientific:	
Management Trainees:	Y	Marketing Pros.:	Y	Gen. Writing/Editing:	Y	Info. Management:	Y	Finance/Acct.:	Y	Engineers, Electrical:	
Experienced Mngmt.:	Y	Retail Sales:		Technical Writing:	Y	Software Dev.:		Law:	Y	Engineers, Other:	
International Business:	Y	Commercial/Industrial:		Graphic Arts/Photog.:	Y	Hardware Dev.:		HR/Other:	Y	Health/Lab:	
MBA Grads:	Y	Sales Trainees:		Music:		Consulting/Other:		Training:	Y	Scientists/Research:	
		Advertising Pros.:	Y	Broadcasting:				Health Care:	Y	Petroleum/Chemicals:	
				Other:	Y			Consulting:		Math/Other:	

TYPES OF BUSINESS:

Long-Term Health Care/Nursing Homes
Home Health Care
Short-Term Care Facilities
Assisted Living Facilities
Rehabilitation Clinics

BRANDS/DIVISIONS/AFFILIATES:

HCR Manor Care
Heartland
ManorCare Health Services
Arden Courts
Carlyle Group (The)

CONTACTS: Note: Officers with more than one job title may be intentionally listed here more than once.

Paul A. Ormond, CEO
Stephen L. Guillard, COO/Exec. VP
Paul A. Ormond, Pres.
Steven M. Cavanaugh, CFO
Chris Ullman, Dir.-Global Comm.
Paul A. Ormond, Chmn.

Phone: 419-252-5500	Fax: 419-252-6404
Toll-Free:	
Address: 333 N. Summit St., Toledo, OH 43604-2617 US	

GROWTH PLANS/SPECIAL FEATURES:

Manor Care, Inc., doing business as HCR Manor Care, provides a range of health care services, including skilled nursing care, assisted living, post-acute medical care, hospice care, home health care and rehabilitation therapy. Manor Care operates over 500 properties in 32 states, with facilities operating primarily under the Heartland, ManorCare Health Services and Arden Courts names. Manor Care's long-term care services consist of skilled nursing centers, assisted living services, post-acute medical and rehabilitation care and Alzheimer's care. The skilled nursing centers use interdisciplinary teams of experienced medical professionals, including registered nurses, licensed practical nurses and certified nursing assistants, to provide services prescribed by physicians. Other services include the design of Quality of Life programs to give the highest practicable level of functional independence to patients, provide physical, speech, respiratory and occupational therapy and provide quality nutrition services, social services, activities and housekeeping and laundry services. Manor Care's assisted living services provide personal care services and assistance with general activities of daily living such as dressing, bathing, meal preparation and medication management. In recent years, the firm was acquired by private equity firm The Carlyle Group for roughly $6.3 billion.

FINANCIALS: Sales and profits are in thousands of dollars—add 000 to get the full amount. 2008 Note: Financial information for 2008 was not available for all companies at press time.

2008 Sales: $3,850,000	2008 Profits: $	**U.S. Stock Ticker:** Private
2007 Sales: $3,800,000	2007 Profits: $	**Int'l Ticker:** Int'l Exchange:
2006 Sales: $3,613,185	2006 Profits: $169,560	Employees: 60,000
2005 Sales: $3,417,290	2005 Profits: $160,955	Fiscal Year Ends: 12/31
2004 Sales: $3,208,867	2004 Profits: $168,222	Parent Company: CARLYLE GROUP (THE)

SALARIES/BENEFITS:

Pension Plan:	ESOP Stock Plan:	Profit Sharing:	Top Exec. Salary: $	Bonus: $1,429,000
Savings Plan:	Stock Purch. Plan:		Second Exec. Salary: $	Bonus: $

OTHER THOUGHTS:

Apparent Women Officers or Directors:
Hot Spot for Advancement for Women/Minorities:

LOCATIONS: ("Y" = Yes)

West:	Southwest:	Midwest:	Southeast:	Northeast:	International:
Y	Y	Y	Y	Y	

MANPOWER INC

www.manpower.com

Industry Group Code: 561320 Ranks within this company's industry group: Sales: 1 Profits: 2

Management:		Sales/Marketing:		Liberal Arts:		Information Systems:		Professionals:		Tech./Scientific:	
Management Trainees:	Y	Marketing Pros.:	Y	Gen. Writing/Editing:	Y	Info. Management:	Y	Finance/Acct.:	Y	Engineers, Electrical:	
Experienced Mngmt.:	Y	Retail Sales:		Technical Writing:	Y	Software Dev.:	Y	Law:	Y	Engineers, Other:	
International Business:	Y	Commercial/Industrial:	Y	Graphic Arts/Photog.:	Y	Hardware Dev.:		HR/Other:	Y	Health/Lab:	
MBA Grads:	Y	Sales Trainees:	Y	Music:		Consulting/Other:		Training:	Y	Scientists/Research:	
		Advertising Pros.:	Y	Broadcasting:				Health Care:		Petroleum/Chemicals:	
				Other:	Y			Consulting:		Math/Other:	

TYPES OF BUSINESS:

Staffing & Temporary Help
Employee Testing, Training & Development
Internal Audit, Accounting & Tax Services
Organizational Performance Consulting
IT Recruitment & Managed Services
Business Function Outsourcing
Market Research

BRANDS/DIVISIONS/AFFILIATES:

Manpower Professional
Elan
Right Management
Jefferson Wells
Clarendon Parker Middle East FZ LLC
Vitae
Global Learning Center
Gelber Organization (The)

CONTACTS: *Note: Officers with more than one job title may be intentionally listed here more than once.*

Jeffrey A. Joerres, CEO
Jeffrey A. Joerres, Pres.
Mike Van Handel, CFO/Exec. VP
Emma van Rooyen, Chief Mktg. Officer/Sr. VP
Mara Swan, Exec. VP-Global Talent & Strategy
Denis Edwards, Global CIO/VP
Ken C. Hunt, Chief Legal Officer/Sr. VP
Tammy Johns, Sr. VP-Workforce Strategy
David Arkless, Sr. VP-Corp. & Gov't Affairs
Owen J. Sullivan, Exec. VP/CEO-Right Mgmt. & Jefferson Wells
Francoise Gri, Exec. VP/Pres., France
Darryl Green, Exec. VP/Pres., Asia-Pacific
Jonas Prising, Exec. VP/Pres., Americas
Jeffrey A. Joerres, Chmn.
Barbara J. Beck, Exec. VP/Pres., EMEA

Phone: 414-961-1000	Fax: 414-906-7985
Toll-Free:	
Address: 100 Manpower Pl., Milwaukee, WI 53212 US	

GROWTH PLANS/SPECIAL FEATURES:

Manpower, Inc. is a world leader in the employment services industry, with a global network of roughly 4,400 offices in 82 countries and territories. Manpower offers permanent, temporary and contract recruitment; employee assessment and selection; training; outplacement; outsourcing; consulting; and professional services. The company's recruitment services are offered under the Manpower, Manpower Professional and Elan brands. Under its Right Management brand, Manpower provides transition services and organizational consulting services. The company's transition services range from advising employers on severance packages to assisting displaced employees with resume writing, networking and interviewing skills. Its organizational consulting services use customized tools, interventions and workshops to drive organizational effectiveness, employee engagement and alignment of the workforce. The firm's Jefferson Wells brand is an alternative to public accounting firms and other consulting groups, providing project professionals along four primary solution areas: Internal controls, tax, technology risk management and finance and accounting. During 2008, Manpower found permanent and temporary jobs for nearly 5 million people who work to help the company's 400,000 clients. Manpower's largest operations are located in Australia, Japan, Mexico, Argentina and Canada, with additional operations located throughout the Americas, Europe and Asia. The firm primarily supplies workers to the office (representing 45% of recruitment revenues), industrial (42%) and technical (13%) markets. In August 2008, Jefferson Wells acquired The Gelber Organization, a State and Local Tax consulting firm. In February 2009, the company was awarded licensed for permanent employment services in Vietnam but the Hanoi People Committee.

Employees are offered medical and dental insurance; life insurance; an employee stock purchase plan; a 401(k) plan; a profit sharing plan; short-and long-term disability coverage; and tuition reimbursement.

FINANCIALS: Sales and profits are in thousands of dollars—add 000 to get the full amount. 2008 Note: Financial information for 2008 was not available for all companies at press time.

2008 Sales: $21,552,800	2008 Profits: $218,900	**U.S. Stock Ticker: MAN**
2007 Sales: $20,500,300	2007 Profits: $484,700	**Int'l Ticker:** Int'l Exchange:
2006 Sales: $17,562,500	2006 Profits: $398,000	Employees: 33,000
2005 Sales: $15,845,400	2005 Profits: $260,100	Fiscal Year Ends: 12/31
2004 Sales: $14,675,000	2004 Profits: $245,700	Parent Company:

SALARIES/BENEFITS:

Pension Plan:	ESOP Stock Plan:	Profit Sharing: Y	Top Exec. Salary: $100,000	Bonus: $300,000
Savings Plan: Y	Stock Purch. Plan: Y		Second Exec. Salary: $524,880	Bonus: $252,000

OTHER THOUGHTS:

Apparent Women Officers or Directors: 6
Hot Spot for Advancement for Women/Minorities: Y

LOCATIONS: ("Y" = Yes)

West:	Southwest:	Midwest:	Southeast:	Northeast:	International:
Y	Y	Y	Y	Y	Y

MARRIOTT INTERNATIONAL INC

www.marriott.com

Industry Group Code: 721110 Ranks within this company's industry group: Sales: 1 Profits: 1

Management:		Sales/Marketing:		Liberal Arts:		Information Systems:		Professionals:		Tech./Scientific:	
Management Trainees:	Y	Marketing Pros.:	Y	Gen. Writing/Editing:	Y	Info. Management:	Y	Finance/Acct.:	Y	Engineers, Electrical:	
Experienced Mngmt.:	Y	Retail Sales:		Technical Writing:		Software Dev.:	Y	Law:	Y	Engineers, Other:	
International Business:	Y	Commercial/Industrial:	Y	Graphic Arts/Photog.:	Y	Hardware Dev.:		HR/Other:	Y	Health/Lab:	
MBA Grads:	Y	Sales Trainees:	Y	Music:		Consulting/Other:		Training:	Y	Scientists/Research:	
		Advertising Pros.:	Y	Broadcasting:				Health Care:		Petroleum/Chemicals:	
				Other:	Y			Consulting:		Math/Other:	

TYPES OF BUSINESS:

Hotels & Resorts
Hotels and Lodging
Timeshares
Extended Stay Lodging
Resorts
Corporate Apartments
Timeshares

BRANDS/DIVISIONS/AFFILIATES:

Marriott Hotels and Resorts
Ritz-Carlton (The)
Bulgari Hotel and Resort
Renaissance Hotels, Resorts and ClubSport
Courtyard Residence Inn
Fairfield Inn
ExecuStay
TownePlace Suites

CONTACTS: Note: Officers with more than one job title may be intentionally listed here more than once.

J. W. Marriott, Jr., CEO
Arne M. Sorenson, COO
Arne M. Sorenson, Pres.
Carl T. Berquist, CFO/Exec. VP
Amy C. McPherson, Exec. VP-Global Sales & Mktg.
David E. Rodriguez, Exec. VP-Global Human Resources
Carl Wilson, CIO/Exec. VP
Edward A. Ryan, General Counsel/Exec. VP
Kathleen Matthews, Exec. VP-Global Comm. & Public Affairs
Laura E. Paugh, Sr. VP-Investor Rel.
Carl T. Berquist, Chief Acct. Officer
William J. Shaw, Vice Chmn.
James M. Sullivan, Exec. VP-Lodging Dev.
Simon F. Cooper, Pres./COO-Rtiz-Carlton Hotel Co. LLC
Robert J. McCarthy, Pres., North American Lodging Oper.
J. W. Marriott, Jr., Chmn.
Edwin D. Fuller, Pres./Managing Dir.-Marriott Lodging Int'l

Phone: 301-380-3000	Fax: 301-380-3967
Toll-Free: 800-721-7033	
Address: 10400 Fernwood Rd., Bethesda, MD 20817 US	

GROWTH PLANS/SPECIAL FEATURES:

Marriott International, Inc. operates about 3,000 hotels and related lodging facilities in the U.S. and 65 other countries and territories. Though primarily known for the firm's various hotel brands, Marriot also has operations in time shares. The company operates through five segments: North American Full-Service, North American Limited-Service, International, Luxury and Timeshare. Marriott develops, operates and franchises hotels under 14 brand names, including Marriott Hotels and Resorts; JW Marriott Hotels and Resorts; the Ritz-Carlton, featuring luxury hotels and resorts; Bulgari Hotel and Resort; Renaissance Hotels, Resorts and ClubSport; Courtyard; Residence Inn, the firm's extended-stay brand; Fairfield Inn; SpringHill Suites; and TownePlace Suites. The firm also provides furnished corporate housing units in more than 45 major markets through its ExecuStay brand, as well as operating 18 upscale serviced apartments through Marriott Executive Apartments. The company also develops, markets and operates timeshare, fractional ownership and residential properties under four separate brand names in over 50 locations. The resorts are usually adjacent to the firm's hotels, bearing the brand names Marriott Vacation Club International, Horizons by Marriott Vacation Club International, Ritz-Carlton Club and Grand Residences by Marriott. Additionally, Marriott manages approximately 80 golf resorts worldwide. During 2008, the company opened new hotels in Maryland; Florida; Hong Kong, Shanghai and Ningbo, China; and Thailand. Marriott also announced its intention to open new hotels in Puerto Rico, France, Saudi Arabia, Russia and China, as well as plans to open 29 new hotels in Mexico over the next five years.

Marriot offers its employees medical, dental and life insurance, tuition reimbursement, career development programs and hotel room discounts. Marriot was named one of the 100 Best Companies to work for by Working Mother Magazine.

FINANCIALS: Sales and profits are in thousands of dollars—add 000 to get the full amount. 2008 Note: Financial information for 2008 was not available for all companies at press time.

2008 Sales: $12,879,000	2008 Profits: $359,000	U.S. Stock Ticker: MAR
2007 Sales: $12,990,000	2007 Profits: $696,000	Int'l Ticker: Int'l Exchange:
2006 Sales: $11,995,000	2006 Profits: $608,000	Employees: 146,000
2005 Sales: $11,129,000	2005 Profits: $669,000	Fiscal Year Ends: 12/31
2004 Sales: $10,099,000	2004 Profits: $596,000	Parent Company:

SALARIES/BENEFITS:

Pension Plan:	ESOP Stock Plan:	Profit Sharing:	Top Exec. Salary: $1,253,654	Bonus: $904,700
Savings Plan: Y	Stock Purch. Plan:		Second Exec. Salary: $1,019,231	Bonus: $522,891

OTHER THOUGHTS:

Apparent Women Officers or Directors: 7
Hot Spot for Advancement for Women/Minorities: Y

LOCATIONS: ("Y" = Yes)

West:	Southwest:	Midwest:	Southeast:	Northeast:	International:
Y	Y	Y	Y	Y	Y

Note: Financial information, benefits and other data can change quickly and may vary from those stated here.

MARS INC

www.mars.com

Industry Group Code: 311320 Ranks within this company's industry group: Sales: 1 Profits:

Management:		Sales/Marketing:		Liberal Arts:		Information Systems:		Professionals:		Tech./Scientific:	
Management Trainees:	Y	Marketing Pros.:	Y	Gen. Writing/Editing:	Y	Info. Management:	Y	Finance/Acct.:	Y	Engineers, Electrical:	
Experienced Mngmt.:	Y	Retail Sales:		Technical Writing:	Y	Software Dev.:	Y	Law:	Y	Engineers, Other:	Y
International Business:	Y	Commercial/Industrial:	Y	Graphic Arts/Photog.:	Y	Hardware Dev.:		HR/Other:	Y	Health/Lab:	
MBA Grads:	Y	Sales Trainees:	Y	Music:		Consulting/Other:		Training:	Y	Scientists/Research:	
		Advertising Pros.:	Y	Broadcasting:				Health Care:		Petroleum/Chemicals:	
				Other:				Consulting:		Math/Other:	

TYPES OF BUSINESS:

Chocolate & Confectionery Manufacturing
Snack Foods & Candy Bars
Pet Nutrition
Drink Vending Systems
Prepared Foods
Information Technology Services

BRANDS/DIVISIONS/AFFILIATES:

M&Ms
Snickers
Milky Way
Twix
Sheba
Cesar
Uncle Ben's
Wm Wrigley Jr Company

CONTACTS: Note: Officers with more than one job title may be intentionally listed here more than once.

Paul S. Michaels, CEO
Paul S. Michaels, Pres.
Andre Martin, Dir.-Global Leadership Dev.
John Franklyn Mars, Chmn.

Phone: 703-821-4900	Fax: 703-448-9678
Toll-Free: 800-627-7852	
Address: 6885 Elm St., McLean, VA 22101 US	

GROWTH PLANS/SPECIAL FEATURES:

Mars, Inc., founded in 1911, is family-owned company that operates through six business divisions: chocolate; pet care; food; drinks; Symbioscience; and Wrigley Gum and Sugar. One of the world's largest family-owned companies, Mars operates over 150 manufacturing facilities and distributes products to over 79 countries. Approximately 50% of the company's sales are in Europe, 40% are in the Americas and 10% are in Australia and Asia. The company's chocolate segment makes some of the world's most popular and widely available snacks and confectionery products, including M&Ms, Mars, Snickers, Milky Way, Twix, and Dove, Combos snacks, 3 Musketeers and Kudos bars. The pet care unit offers products for cats and dogs include such brands as Sheba, Cesar, Whiskas, Pedigree, Royal Canin, My Dog, Kitekat, Buckeye, Frolic, Chappi, Winergy, Trill, Waltham, Aquarian, Rena and Nutro. In the food division, Mars produces rice, entrees, sauces and condiments under brand names including Uncle Ben's, Dolmio, Suzi-Wan, Seeds of Change and Ebly. The firm's drink's segment distributes Mars' KLIX and FLAVIA drink vending machine systems, which are industry leading products that provide in-cup drinks such as fresh ground coffee, leaf tea and hot chocolate. The Symbioscience unit offers products such as Mars Botanical Cocoapro; Mars Plantcare - Seramis; Mars Veterinary - Wisdom Panel MX; and Mars Sustainable Solutions. The Wrigley Gum and Sugar division offers snacks such as Starburst, Skittles, Juicy Fruit gum, Life savers and Altoids. In addition, the company manufactures nutritional foods, snacks and beverages under the Cocoa Via brand. In October 2008, the company acquired Wm. Wrigley Jr. Company for approximately $23 billion. In January 2008, Mars announced its participation in a European Union forum established to reverse obesity trends through voluntary measures.

The firm offers its employees medical and dental coverage; retirement and savings opportunities; a competitive vacation plan.

FINANCIALS: Sales and profits are in thousands of dollars—add 000 to get the full amount. 2008 Note: Financial information for 2008 was not available for all companies at press time.

2008 Sales: $22,000,000	2008 Profits: $	**U.S. Stock Ticker: Private**
2007 Sales: $27,000,000	2007 Profits: $	**Int'l Ticker:** Int'l Exchange:
2006 Sales: $21,500,000	2006 Profits: $	Employees: 70,000
2005 Sales: $20,000,000	2005 Profits: $	Fiscal Year Ends: 12/31
2004 Sales: $18,000,000	2004 Profits: $	Parent Company:

SALARIES/BENEFITS:

Pension Plan:	ESOP Stock Plan:	Profit Sharing:	Top Exec. Salary: $	Bonus: $
Savings Plan: Y	Stock Purch. Plan:		Second Exec. Salary: $	Bonus: $

OTHER THOUGHTS:

Apparent Women Officers or Directors:
Hot Spot for Advancement for Women/Minorities:

LOCATIONS: ("Y" = Yes)

West:	Southwest:	Midwest:	Southeast:	Northeast:	International:
Y	Y	Y	Y	Y	Y

MARSH & MCLENNAN COMPANIES INC

www.marshmac.com

Industry Group Code: 524210 Ranks within this company's industry group: Sales: 1 Profits: 3

Management:		Sales/Marketing:		Liberal Arts:		Information Systems:		Professionals:		Tech./Scientific:	
Management Trainees:	Y	Marketing Pros.:	Y	Gen. Writing/Editing:	Y	Info. Management:	Y	Finance/Acct.:	Y	Engineers, Electrical:	
Experienced Mngmt.:	Y	Retail Sales:		Technical Writing:	Y	Software Dev.:	Y	Law:	Y	Engineers, Other:	
International Business:	Y	Commercial/Industrial:	Y	Graphic Arts/Photog.:	Y	Hardware Dev.:		HR/Other:	Y	Health/Lab:	
MBA Grads:	Y	Sales Trainees:		Music:		Consulting/Other:		Training:	Y	Scientists/Research:	
		Advertising Pros.:	Y	Broadcasting:				Health Care:		Petroleum/Chemicals:	
				Other:	Y			Consulting:	Y	Math/Other:	

TYPES OF BUSINESS:

Insurance Brokerage
Consulting Services
Risk Management
Benefits Administration
Human Resources Services

BRANDS/DIVISIONS/AFFILIATES:

Marsh, Inc.
Guy Carpenter & Company, LLC
Companias DeLima S.A.
Kroll Inc
Mercer Inc
Oliver Wyman Group
Mercer Specialty Consulting
Putnam LLC

CONTACTS: *Note: Officers with more than one job title may be intentionally listed here more than once.*

Brian Duperreault, CEO
Brian Duperreault, Pres.
Vanessa A. Wittman, CFO/Exec. VP
Peter J. Beshar, General Counsel/Exec. VP
Christine Walton, VP-Public Rel.
M. Michele Burns, Chmn./CEO-Mercer, Inc.
Ben Allen, CEO/Pres., Kroll, Inc.
John Drzik, CEO/Pres., Oliver Wyman Group
Daniel S. Glaser, Chmn./CEO-Marsh, Inc.
Stephen R. Hardis, Chmn.
Mathis Cabiallavetta, Chmn.-MCC Int'l

Phone: 212-345-5000	**Fax:** 212-345-4838
Toll-Free:	
Address: 1166 Ave. of the Americas, New York, NY 10036-2774 US	

GROWTH PLANS/SPECIAL FEATURES:

Marsh and McLennan Companies, Inc. (MMC), is a global professional services firm providing advice and solutions in the areas of risk, strategy and human capital. It is the parent company of a number of leading risk experts and specialty consultants, including: Marsh, the insurance broker, intermediary and risk advisor; Guy Carpenter, the risk and reinsurance specialist; Mercer, the provider of HR and related financial advice and services; Oliver Wyman Group, the management consultancy; and Kroll, the risk consulting firm.   The company operates three segments: Risk and Insurance Services; Risk Consulting and Technology; and Consulting.   The Risk and Insurance segment, which generated 47% of MMC's operating segments revenue, is primarily composed of two companies and their subsidiaries. Marsh, Inc., which operates through approximately 400 offices in 100 countries; and Guy Carpenter & Company. This segment also owns investments in private equity funds and other firms through Marsh & McLennan Risk Capital Holdings. Risk Consulting and Technology, which generated 9% of revenues, consists of Kroll, Inc. and its subsidiaries. Besides technology and consulting services, it provides security as well as corporate advisory and restructuring. Knoll also offers financial consulting services.   The Consulting segment, which generated 43% of revenue, operates through Mercer and Oliver Wyman Group.   This division offers investment services, and specialized management and economic consulting services, as well as human resources consulting and related outsourcing.   In February 2009, MMC acquired the remaining 49% of Companias DeLima S.A., located in Cali, Colombia, thereby making the company wholly owned by MMC.

The company provides an employee gifts matching program; and health and welfare benefit programs.   The firm was named one of the 2009 Best Places to Work by the Human Rights Campaign Foundation.

FINANCIALS: Sales and profits are in thousands of dollars—add 000 to get the full amount. 2008 Note: Financial information for 2008 was not available for all companies at press time.

2008 Sales: $11,587,000	2008 Profits: $-73,000	**U.S. Stock Ticker: MMC**
2007 Sales: $11,350,000	2007 Profits: $2,475,000	**Int'l Ticker:** Int'l Exchange:
2006 Sales: $10,547,000	2006 Profits: $990,000	Employees: 54,000
2005 Sales: $11,578,000	2005 Profits: $404,000	Fiscal Year Ends: 12/31
2004 Sales: $11,727,000	2004 Profits: $176,000	Parent Company:

SALARIES/BENEFITS:

Pension Plan: Y	ESOP Stock Plan:	Profit Sharing:	Top Exec. Salary: $1,000,000	Bonus: $3,000,000
Savings Plan: Y	Stock Purch. Plan: Y		Second Exec. Salary: $927,083	Bonus: $3,000,000

OTHER THOUGHTS:

Apparent Women Officers or Directors: 4
Hot Spot for Advancement for Women/Minorities: Y

LOCATIONS: ("Y" = Yes)

West:	Southwest:	Midwest:	Southeast:	Northeast:	International:
Y	Y	Y		Y	Y

Note: Financial information, benefits and other data can change quickly and may vary from those stated here.

MARY KAY INC

www.marykay.com

Industry Group Code: 325620 Ranks within this company's industry group: Sales: 3 Profits:

Management:		Sales/Marketing:		Liberal Arts:		Information Systems:		Professionals:		Tech./Scientific:	
Management Trainees:	Y	Marketing Pros.:	Y	Gen. Writing/Editing:	Y	Info. Management:	Y	Finance/Acct.:	Y	Engineers, Electrical:	
Experienced Mngmt.:	Y	Retail Sales:	Y	Technical Writing:		Software Dev.:	Y	Law:	Y	Engineers, Other:	
International Business:	Y	Commercial/Industrial:		Graphic Arts/Photog.:	Y	Hardware Dev.:		HR/Other:	Y	Health/Lab:	
MBA Grads:	Y	Sales Trainees:	Y	Music:		Consulting/Other:		Training:	Y	Scientists/Research:	
		Advertising Pros.:	Y	Broadcasting:				Health Care:		Petroleum/Chemicals:	Y
				Other:	Y			Consulting:		Math/Other:	

TYPES OF BUSINESS:

Cosmetics & Beauty Supplies, Direct Selling
Online Retail
Fragrances
Over-the-Counter Drugs
Cosmetics & Beauty Supplies, Manufacturing

BRANDS/DIVISIONS/AFFILIATES:

Embrace
TimeWise
Belara
Domain
Velocity
Journey
Angelfire
Elige

CONTACTS: Note: Officers with more than one job title may be intentionally listed here more than once.

David B. Holl, CEO
David B. Holl, Pres.
Terry Jacks, VP-R&D
Yvette Franco, VP-Brand Dev.
Richard R. Rogers, Chmn.

Phone: 972-687-6300	**Fax:** 972-687-1611
Toll-Free: 800-627-9529	
Address: 16251 Dallas Pkwy., Dallas, TX 75001 US	

GROWTH PLANS/SPECIAL FEATURES:

Mary Kay, Inc. is one of the largest direct sellers of skin care products in the U.S. Mary Kay Ash, the company's founder, launched the company in 1963 along with her son. The company's merchandise includes more than 200 products across several categories, including skin care, color cosmetics, spa and body care and fragrances. Skin care includes anti-aging creams, cleansers, moisturizers, basic skin care for different skin types, products for specific needs such as acne treatment and oil control, and lip and eye care. Color cosmetics products include lip, eyes, cheeks, nails, foundations and powder color enhancers, as well as travel sets and applicators. The Mary Kay fragrance line has specialty scents for both men and women, including Journey, Belara and Elige for women and Domain, MK High Intensity and Velocity for men. Mary Kay develops, tests, manufactures and packages the majority of its products at its own plants. Most inventory is manufactured at the Dallas site, where the company headquarters and the Mary Kay Museum are located. An additional manufacturing facility is located in China. With FDA approval, the company also manufactures and distributes certain products classified as over-the-counter drugs, such as sunscreens and acne treatment products. There are over 1.8 million Mary Kay independent beauty consultants serving customers in more than 30 countries worldwide. Independent beauty consultants may eventually become independent sales directors and/or independent national sales directors. Since its inception, the family of Mary Kay Ash has owned the majority of the company.

Mary Kay's independent sales consultants, who serve as the company's front-line sales force, generally work out of their homes and set their own working schedules.

FINANCIALS: Sales and profits are in thousands of dollars—add 000 to get the full amount. 2008 Note: Financial information for 2008 was not available for all companies at press time.

2008 Sales: $2,600,000	2008 Profits: $	**U.S. Stock Ticker: Private**	
2007 Sales: $2,400,000	2007 Profits: $	**Int'l Ticker:**	Int'l Exchange:
2006 Sales: $2,250,000	2006 Profits: $	Employees: 5,000	
2005 Sales: $2,200,000	2005 Profits: $	Fiscal Year Ends: 12/31	
2004 Sales: $1,800,000	2004 Profits: $	Parent Company:	

SALARIES/BENEFITS:

Pension Plan:	ESOP Stock Plan:	Profit Sharing:	Top Exec. Salary: $	Bonus: $
Savings Plan:	Stock Purch. Plan:		Second Exec. Salary: $	Bonus: $

OTHER THOUGHTS:

Apparent Women Officers or Directors: 2
Hot Spot for Advancement for Women/Minorities: Y

LOCATIONS: ("Y" = Yes)

West:	Southwest:	Midwest:	Southeast:	Northeast:	International:
Y	Y	Y	Y	Y	Y

MASSEY ENERGY COMPANY

www.masseyenergyco.com

Industry Group Code: 21211 Ranks within this company's industry group: Sales: 3 Profits: 3

Management:		Sales/Marketing:		Liberal Arts:		Information Systems:		Professionals:		Tech./Scientific:	
Management Trainees:	Y	Marketing Pros.:	Y	Gen. Writing/Editing:		Info. Management:	Y	Finance/Acct.:	Y	Engineers, Electrical:	
Experienced Mngmt.:	Y	Retail Sales:		Technical Writing:	Y	Software Dev.:		Law:	Y	Engineers, Other:	Y
International Business:		Commercial/Industrial:	Y	Graphic Arts/Photog.:		Hardware Dev.:		HR/Other:	Y	Health/Lab:	
MBA Grads:	Y	Sales Trainees:		Music:		Consulting/Other:		Training:	Y	Scientists/Research:	
		Advertising Pros.:		Broadcasting:				Health Care:		Petroleum/Chemicals:	Y
				Other:				Consulting:		Math/Other:	

TYPES OF BUSINESS:

Coal Mining
Natural Gas Gathering
Synthetic Fuel Manufacturing
Rail Cargo Transport

BRANDS/DIVISIONS/AFFILIATES:

CONTACTS: *Note: Officers with more than one job title may be intentionally listed here more than once.*

Don L. Blankenship, CEO
J. Christopher Adkins, COO/Sr. VP
Baxter F. Phillips, Jr., Pres.
Eric B. Tolbert, CFO/VP
Steve E. Sears, VP-Sales
Jeff Gillenwater, VP-Human Resources
John M. Poma, Chief Admin. Officer/VP
M. Shane Harvey, General Counsel/VP
Mark A. Clemens, Sr. VP-Group Oper.
Michael D. Bauersachs, VP-Planning
Jeffrey Jarosinski, VP-Finance
Richard R. Grinnan, Corp. Sec./VP
Jeffrey Jarosinski, Chief Compliance Officer
Michael K. Snelling, VP-Surface Oper.
David W. Owings, Corp. Controller
Don L. Blankenship, Chmn.

Phone: 804-788-1800	Fax: 804-788-1870
Toll-Free:	
Address: 4 N. 4th St., Richmond, VA 23219 US	

GROWTH PLANS/SPECIAL FEATURES:

Massey Energy Company is a leading coal company in the U.S. and is one of the largest in the Central Appalachian region. The company produces, processes and sells bituminous, low-sulfur coal of steam and metallurgical grades, operating 46 underground and 20 surface mine complexes in West Virginia, Kentucky and Virginia. These complexes blend, process and ship coal that is produced the mines to one of the company's 23 resource groups. Any one of these preparation plants can handle the coal production from as many as 10 distinct underground or surface mines. The mines have been strategically developed in close proximity to the Massey preparation plants and rail shipping facilities in order to cut down transportation costs. Once prepared, the coal is transported to customers by means of railroad cars, trucks or barges, with rail shipments representing approximately 91% of 2008 coal shipments. Massey's steam coal is primarily purchased by utilities and industrial clients as fuel for power plants, and its metallurgical coal is used primarily to make coke for use in the manufacture of steel. Through its subsidiaries, the company also manages a synthetic fuel manufacturing facility in West Virginia; unloading, storage and conveying facilities; and natural gas gathering operations. Massey owns and operates approximately 160 gas wells, 200 miles of gathering line and various small compression facilities, as well as interests in 63 wells operated by others. In October 2008, the firm acquired the Mountaineer #2 Mine in West Virginia, as well as 200,000 tons of metallurgical coal reserves. In July 2009, the company acquired 23 million tons of coal reserves in West Virginia.

Employees are offered health and dental insurance; life insurance; long-term disability coverage; and a 401(k) plan.

FINANCIALS: Sales and profits are in thousands of dollars—add 000 to get the full amount. 2008 Note: Financial information for 2008 was not available for all companies at press time.

2008 Sales: $2,989,789	2008 Profits: $56,248	**U.S. Stock Ticker: MEE**
2007 Sales: $2,413,523	2007 Profits: $94,098	**Int'l Ticker:** Int'l Exchange:
2006 Sales: $2,219,854	2006 Profits: $40,977	Employees: 6,743
2005 Sales: $1,777,700	2005 Profits: $-101,600	Fiscal Year Ends: 12/31
2004 Sales: $1,456,700	2004 Profits: $13,900	Parent Company:

SALARIES/BENEFITS:

Pension Plan:	ESOP Stock Plan:	Profit Sharing:	Top Exec. Salary: $1,000,000	Bonus: $6,322,447
Savings Plan: Y	Stock Purch. Plan:		Second Exec. Salary: $598,798	Bonus: $1,273,414

OTHER THOUGHTS:

Apparent Women Officers or Directors: 1
Hot Spot for Advancement for Women/Minorities: Y

LOCATIONS: ("Y" = Yes)

West:	Southwest:	Midwest:	Southeast:	Northeast:	International:
				Y	

Note: Financial information, benefits and other data can change quickly and may vary from those stated here.

MATTEL INC

www.mattel.com

Industry Group Code: 339932 Ranks within this company's industry group: Sales: 1 Profits: 1

Management:		Sales/Marketing:		Liberal Arts:		Information Systems:		Professionals:		Tech./Scientific:	
Management Trainees:	Y	Marketing Pros.:	Y	Gen. Writing/Editing:	Y	Info. Management:	Y	Finance/Acct.:	Y	Engineers, Electrical:	Y
Experienced Mngmt.:	Y	Retail Sales:		Technical Writing:	Y	Software Dev.:	Y	Law:	Y	Engineers, Other:	
International Business:	Y	Commercial/Industrial:	Y	Graphic Arts/Photog.:	Y	Hardware Dev.:		HR/Other:	Y	Health/Lab:	
MBA Grads:	Y	Sales Trainees:		Music:		Consulting/Other:		Training:	Y	Scientists/Research:	
		Advertising Pros.:	Y	Broadcasting:				Health Care:		Petroleum/Chemicals:	
				Other:	Y			Consulting:		Math/Other:	

TYPES OF BUSINESS:

Toy Manufacturing

BRANDS/DIVISIONS/AFFILIATES:

Fisher-Price
American Girl
Barbie
Polly Pocket!
Disney Classics
Hot Wheels
Matchbox
Sekkoia SAS

CONTACTS: *Note: Officers with more than one job title may be intentionally listed here more than once.*

Robert A. Eckert, CEO
Kevin M. Farr, CFO
Alan Kaye, Sr. VP-Human Resources
Robert (Bob) Normile, General Counsel/Corp. Sec./Sr. VP
Thomas A. Debrowski, Exec. VP-Worldwide Oper.
Neil B. Friedman, Pres., Mattel Brands
Ellen L. Brothers, Pres., American Girl Brands
Geoff Massingberd, Sr. VP-Corp. Responsibility
Robert A. Eckert, Chmn.
Bryan G. Stockton, Pres., Int'l

Phone: 310-252-2000	Fax: 310-252-2179
Toll-Free:	
Address: 333 Continental Blvd., El Segundo, CA 90245-5012 US	

GROWTH PLANS/SPECIAL FEATURES:

Mattel, Inc., designs, manufactures and markets a variety of toy products worldwide. Mattel's product portfolio of brands and products are grouped into three categories; Mattel Girls & Boys Brands; Fisher-Price Brands; and American Girl Brands. The Mattel Girls & Boys Brands include Barbie fashion dolls and accessories; Polly Pocket; Disney Classics; High School Musical; Hot Wheels; Matchbox; Speed Racer; Tyco R/C vehicles and playsets; CARS; Radica; Speed Racer; Batman; Kung Fu Panda; and games and puzzles. Fisher-Price brands include Fisher-Price; LittlePeople; BabyGear; View-Master; Sesame Street; Dora the Explorer; Go-Diego-Go!; Mickey Mouse Clubhouse; Winnie the Pooh; Handy Manny; See 'N Say; and Power Wheels. American Girl Brands include Just Like You; the historical collection; and Bitty Baby. Mattel plans to build on the success of its 2008 launch of Batman: The Dark Knight products with a new line based on the TV series Batman: The Brave and the Bold. The firm's products in the domestic segment are sold directly to retailers, including discount and free-standing toy stores, chain stores, department stores and other retail outlets.   The company's international sales represent approximately 49% of its total sales, of which sales in Europe represent approximately 53%, sales in Latin America represent approximately 31%, sales in Asia Pacific represent approximately 9% and sales in other regions represent approximately 7%. Products marketed internationally are generally the same as those developed and marketed domestically, with the exception of American Girl Brands. During 2008, Wal-Mart, Toys R Us and Target, Mattel's largest customers, accounted for approximately 38% of worldwide net sales. In January 2009, the company acquired Sekkoia SAS, a French toy maker.

Mattel offers its employees medical, dental and prescription drug coverage; life and AD&D insurance; short- and long-term disability; business travel insurance; a 401(k) plan; product discounts; adoption assistance; and an employee stock purchase program.

FINANCIALS: Sales and profits are in thousands of dollars—add 000 to get the full amount. 2008 Note: Financial information for 2008 was not available for all companies at press time.

2008 Sales: $5,918,002	2008 Profits: $379,636	U.S. Stock Ticker: MAT
2007 Sales: $5,970,090	2007 Profits: $599,993	Int'l Ticker:　　Int'l Exchange:
2006 Sales: $5,650,156	2006 Profits: $592,927	Employees: 29,000
2005 Sales: $5,179,016	2005 Profits: $417,019	Fiscal Year Ends: 12/31
2004 Sales: $	2004 Profits: $	Parent Company:

SALARIES/BENEFITS:

Pension Plan: Y	ESOP Stock Plan:	Profit Sharing:	Top Exec. Salary: $1,250,000	Bonus: $
Savings Plan: Y	Stock Purch. Plan: Y		Second Exec. Salary: $1,000,000	Bonus: $

OTHER THOUGHTS:

Apparent Women Officers or Directors: 3
Hot Spot for Advancement for Women/Minorities: Y

LOCATIONS: ("Y" = Yes)

West:	Southwest:	Midwest:	Southeast:	Northeast:	International:
Y	Y	Y	Y	Y	Y

MAXIM INTEGRATED PRODUCTS INC

www.maxim-ic.com

Industry Group Code: 33441 Ranks within this company's industry group: Sales: 7   Profits: 4

Management:		Sales/Marketing:		Liberal Arts:		Information Systems:		Professionals:		Tech./Scientific:	
Management Trainees:	Y	Marketing Pros.:	Y	Gen. Writing/Editing:		Info. Management:	Y	Finance/Acct.:	Y	Engineers, Electrical:	Y
Experienced Mngmt.:	Y	Retail Sales:		Technical Writing:	Y	Software Dev.:	Y	Law:	Y	Engineers, Other:	
International Business:	Y	Commercial/Industrial:	Y	Graphic Arts/Photog.:	Y	Hardware Dev.:	Y	HR/Other:	Y	Health/Lab:	
MBA Grads:	Y	Sales Trainees:		Music:		Consulting/Other:		Training:	Y	Scientists/Research:	Y
		Advertising Pros.:	Y	Broadcasting:				Health Care:		Petroleum/Chemicals:	
				Other:				Consulting:		Math/Other:	

TYPES OF BUSINESS:

Integrated Circuits-Analog & Mixed Signal
High-Frequency Design Processes
Manufacturing Capabilities
Power Conversion Chips

BRANDS/DIVISIONS/AFFILIATES:

Dallas Semiconductor Corp.
Vitesse Semiconductor Corp.

CONTACTS: Note: Officers with more than one job title may be intentionally listed here more than once.

Tunc Doluca, CEO
Tunc Doluca, Pres.
Bruce E. Kiddoo, CFO
Matthew J. Murphy, VP-Worldwide Sales
Charles G. Rigg, Sr. VP-Admin.
Charles G. Rigg, General Counsel
Paresh Maniar, Exec. Dir.-Investor Rel.
Vijay Ullal, Group Pres.
Pirooz Parvarandeh, Group Pres.
Richard Hood, VP
Christopher J. Neil, Div. VP
B. Kipling Hagopian, Chmn.

Phone: 408-737-7600	Fax: 408-737-7194
Toll-Free: 800-998-8800	
Address: 120 San Gabriel Dr., Sunnyvale, CA 94086 US	

GROWTH PLANS/SPECIAL FEATURES:

Maxim Integrated Products, Inc. designs, develops, manufactures and markets analog, mixed-signal, high frequency and digital circuits. Its products are primarily created by wholly-owned subsidiary Dallas Semiconductor Corporation. Maxim's circuits connect the analog and digital world by detecting, measuring, amplifying and converting real-world signals into the digital signals necessary for computer processing. It produces electronic interface products to interact with people, through audio, video, touchpad, key pad and security devices; the physical world, through motion, time, temperature and humidity sensors; power sources, via conversion, charging, supervision and regulation systems; and other digital systems, including wireless, storage and fiber optic systems. Maxim's products serve four major end-markets: industrial, which includes automotive products, automatic test equipment, and military and medical equipment and instruments; communications, including base stations, networking/data communications and telecommunications; consumer products, specifically cell phones, digital cameras, gps, handhelds and media players and home entertainment products; and computing, including notebook and desktop computers, peripherals, servers and workstations and storage. The company also offers the use of its manufacturing capabilities for custom designs. Some of Maxim's newest products include one of the industry's smallest DC/DC converters; one of the first fully integrated switch-mode/linear LED drivers; bidirectional video filters/buffers for portable consumer devices; high-voltage, low-power linear regulators for automotive and industrial applications; dual-band, dual-mode tuners for Japanese digital broadcasts; a programmable high-brightness LED driver for automotive and other lighting applications; and one of the first chips to convert an all-analog power supply to a fully programmable, digital power-management solution. In October 2008, the company agreed to acquire Mobilygen, a private, fables semiconductor company that specializes in H.264 video compression.

Employees are offered health insurance; health club subsidies; preventative wellness screenings; life and AD&D coverage; disability coverage; an educational assistance program; flexible spending accounts; an employee assistance program; and business travel accident insurance.

FINANCIALS: Sales and profits are in thousands of dollars—add 000 to get the full amount. 2008 Note: Financial information for 2008 was not available for all companies at press time.

2008 Sales: $2,052,783	2008 Profits: $317,725	U.S. Stock Ticker: MXIM.PK
2007 Sales: $2,009,124	2007 Profits: $286,227	Int'l Ticker: Int'l Exchange:
2006 Sales: $1,856,945	2006 Profits: $387,701	Employees: 8,765
2005 Sales: $1,617,734	2005 Profits: $462,277	Fiscal Year Ends: 8/31
2004 Sales: $1,439,263	2004 Profits: $419,752	Parent Company:

SALARIES/BENEFITS:

Pension Plan:	ESOP Stock Plan:	Profit Sharing:	Top Exec. Salary: $498,077	Bonus: $2,334,209
Savings Plan: Y	Stock Purch. Plan:		Second Exec. Salary: $400,000	Bonus: $1,902,767

OTHER THOUGHTS:

Apparent Women Officers or Directors:
Hot Spot for Advancement for Women/Minorities:

LOCATIONS: ("Y" = Yes)

West:	Southwest:	Midwest:	Southeast:	Northeast:	International:
Y	Y	Y	Y	Y	Y

Note: Financial information, benefits and other data can change quickly and may vary from those stated here.

MAYO FOUNDATION FOR MEDICAL EDUCATION AND RESEARCH

www.mayo.edu

Industry Group Code: 622110 **Ranks within this company's industry group:** Sales: 6   Profits:

Management:		Sales/Marketing:		Liberal Arts:		Information Systems:		Professionals:		Tech./Scientific:	
Management Trainees:	Y	Marketing Pros.:	Y	Gen. Writing/Editing:	Y	Info. Management:	Y	Finance/Acct.:	Y	Engineers, Electrical:	
Experienced Mngmt.:	Y	Retail Sales:		Technical Writing:	Y	Software Dev.:	Y	Law:	Y	Engineers, Other:	
International Business:		Commercial/Industrial:		Graphic Arts/Photog.:	Y	Hardware Dev.:		HR/Other:	Y	Health/Lab:	Y
MBA Grads:	Y	Sales Trainees:		Music:		Consulting/Other:		Training:	Y	Scientists/Research:	
		Advertising Pros.:	Y	Broadcasting:				Health Care:	Y	Petroleum/Chemicals:	
				Other:	Y			Consulting:		Math/Other:	

TYPES OF BUSINESS:

Hospitals/Clinics-General & Specialty Hospitals
Physician Practice Management
Medical Research
Health Care Education

BRANDS/DIVISIONS/AFFILIATES:

Mayo Clinic
St. Marys Hospital
Rochester Medical Hospital
Mayo Clinic Hospital
Mayo Health System
Mayo Clinic College of Medicine
Dan Abraham Healthy Living
Birdsall Medical Research Building

CONTACTS: *Note: Officers with more than one job title may be intentionally listed here more than once.*

Denis A. Cortese, CEO
Denis A. Cortese, Pres.
Jeffrey W. Bolton, CFO
Abdul Bengali, Chmn.-IT
Shirley A. Weis, Chief Admin. Officer/VP
Jonathan J. Oviatt, Chief Legal Officer/Sec.
Harry N. Hoffman, Treas.
William C. Rupp, VP
Glenn S. Forbes, VP
Nina M. Schwenk, VP
Victor Trastek, VP
James L. Barksdale, Chmn.

Phone: 507-284-2511	Fax: 507-284-0161
Toll-Free:	
Address: 200 First St. S.W., Rochester, MN 55905 US	

GROWTH PLANS/SPECIAL FEATURES:

The Mayo Foundation for Medical Education and Research is a not-for-profit health care organization providing medical treatment, physician management, health care education, research and other specialized medical services through a network of clinics and hospitals in Minnesota, Arizona and Florida.   The three primary clinics, which house physician group practices, are located in Rochester, Minnesota; Jacksonville, Florida; and Scottsdale, Arizona.   The Rochester, Minnesota campus is comprised of the Mayo, Gonda and Plummer buildings, as well as St. Mary's Hospital, with 1,265 beds, and the Rochester Methodist Hospital, with 794 beds.   This facility is a fully integrated medical research and education center. The Dan Abraham Healthy Living Center, located in the Rochester campus, is a four story, 127,000 square feet state-of-the-art wellness and fitness facility. The Jacksonville, Florida campus is centered around the Davis, Mayo and Cannaday buildings, in conjunction with the Birdsall Medical Research Building. This facility focuses on neurological diseases. The Mayo Clinic Hospital, located on the Jacksonville campus, offers 214 beds and 22 operating rooms. The Scottsdale, Arizona campus is centered around a five-story outpatient clinic. The facility contains 244 beds, 18 operating rooms, an outpatient surgery center, a patient education library, a pharmacy, a full service laboratory, an endoscopy suite and a 188-seat auditorium for patients, staff and students.

Benefits offered to Mayo employees vary by location and include flexible spending accounts, tuition assistance, child care services, adoption reimbursement, a scholarship plan, relocation reimbursement and a variety of insurance options. For the sixth consecutive year, in 2009 Mayo made Fortune Magazine's list of The100 Best Companies to Work For.

FINANCIALS: Sales and profits are in thousands of dollars—add 000 to get the full amount. 2008 Note: Financial information for 2008 was not available for all companies at press time.

2008 Sales: $7,221,800	2008 Profits: $	U.S. Stock Ticker: Nonprofit
2007 Sales: $6,897,600	2007 Profits: $198,000	Int'l Ticker: Int'l Exchange:
2006 Sales: $6,291,600	2006 Profits: $117,500	Employees: 57,000
2005 Sales: $5,802,300	2005 Profits: $	Fiscal Year Ends: 12/31
2004 Sales: $5,353,800	2004 Profits: $	Parent Company:

SALARIES/BENEFITS:

Pension Plan: Y	ESOP Stock Plan:	Profit Sharing:	Top Exec. Salary: $	Bonus: $
Savings Plan: Y	Stock Purch. Plan:		Second Exec. Salary: $	Bonus: $

OTHER THOUGHTS:

Apparent Women Officers or Directors: 4
Hot Spot for Advancement for Women/Minorities: Y

LOCATIONS: ("Y" = Yes)

West:	Southwest:	Midwest:	Southeast:	Northeast:	International:
	Y	Y	Y		

MCAFEE INC

www.mcafee.com

Industry Group Code: 511210E Ranks within this company's industry group: Sales: 2   Profits: 2

Management:		Sales/Marketing:		Liberal Arts:		Information Systems:		Professionals:		Tech./Scientific:	
Management Trainees:	Y	Marketing Pros.:	Y	Gen. Writing/Editing:	Y	Info. Management:	Y	Finance/Acct.:	Y	Engineers, Electrical:	Y
Experienced Mngmt.:	Y	Retail Sales:		Technical Writing:	Y	Software Dev.:	Y	Law:	Y	Engineers, Other:	
International Business:	Y	Commercial/Industrial:	Y	Graphic Arts/Photog.:	Y	Hardware Dev.:		HR/Other:	Y	Health/Lab:	
MBA Grads:	Y	Sales Trainees:		Music:		Consulting/Other:	Y	Training:	Y	Scientists/Research:	
		Advertising Pros.:	Y	Broadcasting:				Health Care:		Petroleum/Chemicals:	
				Other:				Consulting:		Math/Other:	

TYPES OF BUSINESS:

Software-Security
Virus Protection Software
Network Management Software

BRANDS/DIVISIONS/AFFILIATES:

McAfee Total Protection
LoJack for Laptops
Registry Power Cleaner
McAfee PCI Certifications Service
McAfee Network DPL Discovery
McAfee OK Mobile
Reconnex
Secure Computing Corporation

CONTACTS: Note: Officers with more than one job title may be intentionally listed here more than once.

David DeWalt, CEO
Albert A. Pimentel, COO
David DeWalt, Pres.
Albert A. Pimentel, CFO
David Milam, Chief Mktg. Officer/Exec. VP
Joseph Gabbert, Exec. VP-Human Resources
Christopher Bolin, CTO/Exec. VP
Mark Cochran, General Counsel/Exec. VP
Gerhard Watzinger, Exec. VP-Corp. Strategy & Bus. Dev.
Keith Krzeminski, Chief Acct. Officer/Sr. VP-Finance
Michael DeCesare, Exec. VP-Worldwide Sales
Todd Gebhart, Exec. VP/Gen. Mgr.-Consumer, Mobile & Small Bus.
Dan Ryan, Exec. VP/Gen. Mgr.-Network Security Bus. Unit
George Kurtz, Sr. VP/Gen. Mgr.-Risk & Compliance Bus. Unit
Charles J. Robel, Chmn.

Phone: 408-988-3832	Fax: 408-970-9727
Toll-Free:	
Address: 3965 Freedom Cir., Santa Clara, CA 95054 US	

GROWTH PLANS/SPECIAL FEATURES:

McAfee, Inc. is a developer and supplier of software-based computer security systems that prevent intrusions on networks and protect computer systems from attacks. It allows home users, businesses, government agencies, service providers and partners to block attacks, prevent disruptions and continuously track and improve their security. The company's products are categorized for Home and Home Office, Small Business, Medium Business and Large Enterprise. Home and Home Office products are geared toward users who work from home on one or multiple computers. Products consist of PC protection software such as McAfee Total Protection, which works as an anti-virus and maintains an enhanced firewall. LoJack for Laptops tracks and recovers lost or stolen computers and is supported by a professional theft recovery team. Registry Power Cleaner software repairs registry errors and protects data with automatic backups. Small Business products are designed for businesses with 10-50 computers. The McAfee PCI Certification Service offers analysis of compliance status, assisting companies in completing PCI DSS requirement. The McAfee Site Advisor reviews the security of web sites and issues safety ratings before the user visits them. Medium Business products are targeted towards businesses with 100-1,000 computers and consist of data protection products such as the McAfee Network DPL Discovery, which protects sensitive data; compliance services, such as McAfee Email Security Service, which blocks viruses carried by e-mail; and network security products such as Total Protection for Secure Businesses. Enterprise products are geared toward companies with hundreds to tens of thousands computers. McAfee OK Mobile and Content Safety inspects content and certification for mobile devices. The McAfee Policy Auditor provides automated manual audit processes. In 2008, the company acquired Reconnex, a data loss prevention (DPL) company for $46 million and Secure Computing Corporation for $418 million.

FINANCIALS: Sales and profits are in thousands of dollars—add 000 to get the full amount. 2008 Note: Financial information for 2008 was not available for all companies at press time.

2008 Sales: $1,600,065	2008 Profits: $172,209	U.S. Stock Ticker: MFE
2007 Sales: $1,308,220	2007 Profits: $166,980	Int'l Ticker: Int'l Exchange:
2006 Sales: $1,142,327	2006 Profits: $137,529	Employees: 5,600
2005 Sales: $987,299	2005 Profits: $138,828	Fiscal Year Ends: 12/31
2004 Sales: $910,542	2004 Profits: $225,065	Parent Company:

SALARIES/BENEFITS:

Pension Plan:	ESOP Stock Plan:	Profit Sharing:	Top Exec. Salary: $950,000	Bonus: $1,000,000
Savings Plan:	Stock Purch. Plan:		Second Exec. Salary: $600,000	Bonus: $592,575

OTHER THOUGHTS:

Apparent Women Officers or Directors:
Hot Spot for Advancement for Women/Minorities:

LOCATIONS: ("Y" = Yes)

West:	Southwest:	Midwest:	Southeast:	Northeast:	International:
Y	Y	Y	Y	Y	Y

Note: Financial information, benefits and other data can change quickly and may vary from those stated here.

MCDERMOTT INTERNATIONAL INC

www.mcdermott.com

Industry Group Code: 541330 Ranks within this company's industry group: Sales: 2 Profits: 1

Management:		Sales/Marketing:		Liberal Arts:		Information Systems:		Professionals:		Tech./Scientific:	
Management Trainees:	Y	Marketing Pros.:	Y	Gen. Writing/Editing:	Y	Info. Management:	Y	Finance/Acct.:	Y	Engineers, Electrical:	Y
Experienced Mngmt.:	Y	Retail Sales:		Technical Writing:	Y	Software Dev.:	Y	Law:	Y	Engineers, Other:	
International Business:	Y	Commercial/Industrial:	Y	Graphic Arts/Photog.:	Y	Hardware Dev.:		HR/Other:	Y	Health/Lab:	
MBA Grads:	Y	Sales Trainees:		Music:		Consulting/Other:	Y	Training:	Y	Scientists/Research:	
		Advertising Pros.:	Y	Broadcasting:				Health Care:		Petroleum/Chemicals:	
				Other:				Consulting:	Y	Math/Other:	

TYPES OF BUSINESS:

Engineering Services
Power Generation Services
Nuclear Fuel Assemblies
Government Services
Marine Construction
Procurement Services
Project Management
Consulting

BRANDS/DIVISIONS/AFFILIATES:

J. Ray McDermott, S.A.
BWX Technologies, Inc.
Y-12 National Security Complex
Pantex Plant
Los Alamos National Laboratory
Babcock & Wilcox Company (The)
Babcock & Wilcox Companies (The)

CONTACTS: *Note: Officers with more than one job title may be intentionally listed here more than once.*

John A. Fees, CEO
John A. Fees, Pres.
Michael S. Taff, CFO/Sr. VP
Preston Johnson, Jr., Sr. VP-Human Resources
John C. Knowles, CIO/VP
John T. Nesser, III, Chief Admin. & Legal Officer/Exec. VP
Liane K. Hinrichs, General Counsel/VP/Corp. Sec.
John D. Krueger, VP-Corp. Dev. & Strategic Planning
John E. Roueche, III, VP-Corp. Comm.
John E. Roueche, III, VP-Investor Rel.
Dennis S. Baldwin, Chief Acct. Officer/VP
James C. Lewis, Treas./VP
J. Timothy Woodard, VP/Chief Risk Officer
Robert A. Deason, CEO/Pres., J. Ray McDermott, S.A.
Thomas A. Henzler, Corp. Compliance Officer
Bruce W. Wilkinson, Chmn.

Phone: 281-870-5901	Fax:
Toll-Free:	
Address: 777 N. Eldridge Pkwy., Houston, TX 77079 US	

GROWTH PLANS/SPECIAL FEATURES:

McDermott International, Inc. is a leading energy services company that operates three main business segments: Offshore oil and gas construction services; government operations; and power generation systems. The offshore construction services are provided through subsidiary J. Ray McDermott, S.A. (JRMSA) and its subsidiaries. JRMSA and its subsidiaries design, engineer, fabricate and install offshore drilling and production facilities, as well as install marine pipelines and subsea production systems. It operates in most major offshore oil and gas producing regions throughout the world, including Mexico, the Gulf of Mexico, the Middle East, the Caspian Sea, India and Asia Pacific. This segment owns, or operates through a joint-venture, one derrick vessel and six combination derrick-pipe laying vessels, equipped with various cranes, welding equipment, pile-driving hammers and other equipment; and tug boats, barges and utility boats to support its operations. The government operations segment, with services performed by subsidiary BWX Technologies, Inc. and its subsidiaries, supplies nuclear components to the U.S. government, as well as processing uranium; offering environmental site restoration services; and managing and operating U.S. government-owned facilities, primarily within the nuclear weapons complex of the U.S. Department of Energy. Facilities served by the segment include the Y-12 National Security Complex, the Pantex Plant and Los Alamos National Laboratory. The power generation systems segment, run by the Babcock & Wilcox Company (B&W) and its subsidiaries, provides a variety of services, equipment and systems to generate steam and electric power at energy facilities worldwide. In June 2008, JRMSA entered a joint venture with a subsidiary of state-owned China Shipbuilding Industry Corporation. In July 2008, the firm purchased the Intech group of companies. In August 2008, B&W entered into a definitive agreement to acquire Nuclear Fuel Services, Inc., a provider of specialty nuclear fuels and related services.

FINANCIALS: Sales and profits are in thousands of dollars—add 000 to get the full amount. 2008 Note: Financial information for 2008 was not available for all companies at press time.

2008 Sales: $6,572,423	2008 Profits: $429,302	**U.S. Stock Ticker: MDR**
2007 Sales: $5,631,610	2007 Profits: $607,828	Int'l Ticker: Int'l Exchange:
2006 Sales: $4,120,141	2006 Profits: $330,515	Employees: 26,400
2005 Sales: $1,856,311	2005 Profits: $205,687	Fiscal Year Ends: 12/31
2004 Sales: $1,923,019	2004 Profits: $61,639	Parent Company:

SALARIES/BENEFITS:

Pension Plan: Y	ESOP Stock Plan:	Profit Sharing:	Top Exec. Salary: $592,500	Bonus: $841,026
Savings Plan: Y	Stock Purch. Plan:		Second Exec. Salary: $562,500	Bonus: $323,550

OTHER THOUGHTS:

Apparent Women Officers or Directors: 2
Hot Spot for Advancement for Women/Minorities: Y

LOCATIONS: ("Y" = Yes)

West:	Southwest:	Midwest:	Southeast:	Northeast:	International:
Y	Y	Y	Y	Y	Y

MCDONALD'S CORP

www.mcdonalds.com

Industry Group Code: 722110 **Ranks within this company's industry group:** Sales: 1 Profits: 1

Management:		Sales/Marketing:		Liberal Arts:		Information Systems:		Professionals:		Tech./Scientific:	
Management Trainees:	Y	Marketing Pros.:	Y	Gen. Writing/Editing:	Y	Info. Management:	Y	Finance/Acct.:	Y	Engineers, Electrical:	
Experienced Mngmt.:	Y	Retail Sales:		Technical Writing:		Software Dev.:	Y	Law:	Y	Engineers, Other:	
International Business:	Y	Commercial/Industrial:		Graphic Arts/Photog.:	Y	Hardware Dev.:		HR/Other:	Y	Health/Lab:	
MBA Grads:	Y	Sales Trainees:		Music:		Consulting/Other:		Training:	Y	Scientists/Research:	
		Advertising Pros.:	Y	Broadcasting:				Health Care:		Petroleum/Chemicals:	
				Other:	Y			Consulting:		Math/Other:	

TYPES OF BUSINESS:

Fast Food Restaurants
Home-Meal Replacement Restaurants
Franchising

BRANDS/DIVISIONS/AFFILIATES:

CONTACTS: *Note: Officers with more than one job title may be intentionally listed here more than once.*

Jim Skinner, CEO
Ralph Alvarez, COO
Ralph Alvarez, Pres.
Peter J. Bensen, CFO/Exec. VP
Mary Dillon, Global Chief Mktg. Officer/Exec. VP
Richard Floersch, Chief Human Resources Officer/Exec. VP
Gloria Santona, General Counsel/Exec. VP/Corp. Sec.
Jose Armario, Pres., McDonald's Latin America
Don Thompson, Pres., McDonald's USA
Denis Hannequin, Pres., Europe
Jeff Stratton, Worldwide Chief Restaurant Officer/Exec. VP
Andrew J. McKenna, Chmn.
Tim Fenton, Pres., McDonald's EMEA

Phone: 630-623-3000	**Fax:** 630-623-5700
Toll-Free: 800-244-6227	
Address: 2111 McDonald's Dr., Oak Brook, IL 60523 US	

GROWTH PLANS/SPECIAL FEATURES:

McDonald's Corp. operates more than 31,158 fast-food restaurants in over 118 countries, serving approximately 48 million customers per day. McDonald's has expanded primarily based on its successful franchising model, whereby independent businessmen and women provide capital by initially investing in equipment, signs, seating and decor of restaurants and personally operating them. The company shares the investment by owning or leasing the land and buildings. Approximately 70% of McDonald's worldwide restaurants are franchises, the rest being operated directly by the company or under joint-venture agreements. The McDonald's menu includes items such as hamburgers, cheeseburgers, fish and chicken sandwiches, chicken nuggets, french fries, salads, milkshakes, desserts and soft drinks. McDonald's restaurants are also open during breakfast hours and offer egg sandwiches, hotcakes, biscuit and bagel sandwiches and muffins. As part of a multi-year beverage business strategy designed to take advantage of the significant and growing beverage category, the company is introducing hot specialty coffee offerings on a market-by-market basis, all of which will serve as a platform for the anticipated future introduction of smoothies, frappes and other beverage options. In 2009, the company announced plans to invest $2.1 billion to open approximately 1,000 new locations through 2010; 240 in Europe, 165 in the U.S. and 600 in Asia. Almost two-thirds of sales are generated outside the U.S.

The firm offers qualified employees medical, dental and vision insurance; short- and long-term disability; profit sharing and very generous savings plans; adoption assistance; vacation and holiday pay; and a child care discount. McDonald's U.S. employees at corporate division and region offices may receive benefits including a bonus program, educational assistance, credit union membership and sabbaticals of eight weeks every 10 years. Hamburger University is McDonald's worldwide management training center located in Illinois.

FINANCIALS: Sales and profits are in thousands of dollars—add 000 to get the full amount. 2008 Note: Financial information for 2008 was not available for all companies at press time.

2008 Sales: $23,522,400	2008 Profits: $4,313,200	**U.S. Stock Ticker: MCD**
2007 Sales: $22,786,600	2007 Profits: $2,395,100	**Int'l Ticker:** Int'l Exchange:
2006 Sales: $20,895,200	2006 Profits: $3,544,200	Employees: 400,000
2005 Sales: $19,832,500	2005 Profits: $2,602,200	Fiscal Year Ends: 12/31
2004 Sales: $19,064,700	2004 Profits: $2,278,500	Parent Company:

SALARIES/BENEFITS:

Pension Plan:	ESOP Stock Plan:	Profit Sharing: Y	Top Exec. Salary: $1,337,500	Bonus: $4,600,000
Savings Plan: Y	Stock Purch. Plan:		Second Exec. Salary: $967,500	Bonus: $2,800,000

OTHER THOUGHTS:

Apparent Women Officers or Directors: 4
Hot Spot for Advancement for Women/Minorities: Y

LOCATIONS: ("Y" = Yes)

West:	Southwest:	Midwest:	Southeast:	Northeast:	International:
Y	Y	Y	Y	Y	Y

MCKESSON CORPORATION

www.mckesson.com

Industry Group Code: 424210 **Ranks within this company's industry group:** Sales: 1   Profits: 2

Management:		Sales/Marketing:		Liberal Arts:		Information Systems:		Professionals:		Tech./Scientific:
Management Trainees:	Y	Marketing Pros.:	Y	Gen. Writing/Editing:	Y	Info. Management:	Y	Finance/Acct.:	Y	Engineers, Electrical:
Experienced Mngmt.:	Y	Retail Sales:		Technical Writing:	Y	Software Dev.:	Y	Law:	Y	Engineers, Other:
International Business:	Y	Commercial/Industrial:	Y	Graphic Arts/Photog.:	Y	Hardware Dev.:		HR/Other:	Y	Health/Lab:
MBA Grads:	Y	Sales Trainees:	Y	Music:		Consulting/Other:	Y	Training:	Y	Scientists/Research:
		Advertising Pros.:	Y	Broadcasting:				Health Care:		Petroleum/Chemicals:
				Other:				Consulting:		Math/Other:

TYPES OF BUSINESS:

Pharmaceutical Distribution
Medical-Surgical Products Distribution
Health Care Management Software
Consulting
Outsourcing

BRANDS/DIVISIONS/AFFILIATES:

McKesson U.S. Pharmaceutical
McKesson Canada
McKesson Health Solutions
McKesson Pharmacy Systems and Automation
InterQual
Moore Medical Corp.
Per-Se Technologies Inc
McKesson International

CONTACTS: *Note: Officers with more than one job title may be intentionally listed here more than once.*

John H. Hammergren, CEO
John H. Hammergren, Pres.
Jeffrey C. Campbell, CFO/Exec. VP
Jorge L. Figueredo, Exec. VP-Human Resources
Randall N. Spratt, CIO/Exec. VP
Randall N. Spratt, CTO/Exec. VP
Laureen E. Seeger, General Counsel/Exec. VP/Sec.
Marc E. Owen, Exec. VP-Corp. Strategy & Bus. Dev.
Paul C. Julian, Exec. VP/ Group Pres., McKesson Corporation
Patrick J. Blake, Exec. VP/Pres., McKesson Technology Solutions
John H. Hammergren, Chmn.

Phone: 415-983-8300	Fax:
Toll-Free:	
Address: 1 Post St., San Francisco, CA 94104 US	

GROWTH PLANS/SPECIAL FEATURES:

McKesson Corp. provides supply, information and care management products and services to the healthcare industry. The company operates in two segments: McKesson distribution solutions and McKesson technology solutions. The McKesson distribution solutions segment distributes ethical and proprietary drugs, medical-surgical supplies and equipment, and health and beauty care products throughout North America. This segment also provides specialty pharmaceutical solutions for biotech and pharmaceutical manufacturers, sells pharmacy software and provides consulting, outsourcing and other services. This segment includes a 49% interest in Nadro, S.A. de C.V., the leading pharmaceutical distributor in Mexico, and a 39% interest in Parata Systems LLC, which sells automated pharmacy and supply management systems and services to retail and institutional outpatient pharmacies. The McKesson technology solutions segment delivers enterprise-wide clinical, patient care, financial, supply chain and strategic management software solutions, as well as pharmacy automation for hospitals and connectivity, outsourcing and other services. The firm's payor group of businesses, which includes InterQual, clinical auditing and compliance and medical management software businesses and care management programs, are also included in this segment. This segment's customers include hospitals, physicians, homecare providers, retail pharmacies and payors from North America, the U.K., other European countries and the Asia Pacific region. The company's subsidiaries include U.S. Pharmaceutical Distribution; McKesson Canada; Medical-Surgical Distribution; McKesson Pharmacy Systems and Automation; Zee Medical; RelayHealth; McKesson Health Solutions; and McKesson International. During 2008, the firm acquired Rosebud Solutions LLC; McQueary Brothers Drug Company, Inc.; Vivalog LLC; EN-Chart Scanning Program LLC; and HTP, Inc. In October 2008, McKesson renamed its specialty pharmaceutical business unit McKesson Specialty Care Solutions. In April 2009, the firm acquired LMS Medical Systems' intellectual property for obstetrics surveillance and archival capabilities. Also in April 2009, the company launched the McKesson Plasma and BioLogics unit for the distribution of plasma and biologics products.

FINANCIALS: Sales and profits are in thousands of dollars—add 000 to get the full amount. 2008 Note: Financial information for 2008 was not available for all companies at press time.

2008 Sales: $101,703,000	2008 Profits: $990,000	**U.S. Stock Ticker:** MCK
2007 Sales: $92,977,000	2007 Profits: $913,000	**Int'l Ticker:** Int'l Exchange:
2006 Sales: $86,983,000	2006 Profits: $751,000	Employees: 32,500
2005 Sales: $79,096,000	2005 Profits: $-157,000	Fiscal Year Ends: 3/31
2004 Sales: $69,210,000	2004 Profits: $646,500	Parent Company:

SALARIES/BENEFITS:

Pension Plan:	ESOP Stock Plan:	Profit Sharing:	Top Exec. Salary: $1,566,154	Bonus: $12,035,000
Savings Plan:	Stock Purch. Plan:		Second Exec. Salary: $894,281	Bonus: $5,059,000

OTHER THOUGHTS:

Apparent Women Officers or Directors: 4
Hot Spot for Advancement for Women/Minorities: Y

LOCATIONS: ("Y" = Yes)

West:	Southwest:	Midwest:	Southeast:	Northeast:	International:
Y	Y	Y	Y	Y	Y

Note: Financial information, benefits and other data can change quickly and may vary from those stated here.

MCKINSEY & COMPANY INC

www.mckinsey.com

Industry Group Code: 54161 Ranks within this company's industry group: Sales: 2 Profits:

Management:		Sales/Marketing:		Liberal Arts:		Information Systems:		Professionals:		Tech./Scientific:	
Management Trainees:	Y	Marketing Pros.:	Y	Gen. Writing/Editing:	Y	Info. Management:	Y	Finance/Acct.:	Y	Engineers, Electrical:	
Experienced Mngmt.:	Y	Retail Sales:		Technical Writing:	Y	Software Dev.:	Y	Law:	Y	Engineers, Other:	
International Business:	Y	Commercial/Industrial:	Y	Graphic Arts/Photog.:	Y	Hardware Dev.:		HR/Other:	Y	Health/Lab:	
MBA Grads:	Y	Sales Trainees:		Music:		Consulting/Other:	Y	Training:	Y	Scientists/Research:	
		Advertising Pros.:	Y	Broadcasting:				Health Care:		Petroleum/Chemicals:	
				Other:	Y			Consulting:	Y	Math/Other:	Y

TYPES OF BUSINESS:

Management Consulting
Strategic & Logistics Consulting
Industry-Specific Consulting
Business Research
Business Publications

BRANDS/DIVISIONS/AFFILIATES:

McKinsey & Co.
McKinsey Global Institute
McKinsey Quarterly (The)

CONTACTS: Note: Officers with more than one job title may be intentionally listed here more than once.

Ian Davis, Managing Dir.
Patricia Welch, Media Contact-Asia
Bill Bradley, Advisor-Non-Profit Practice

Phone: 212-446-7000	Fax: 212-446-8575
Toll-Free:	
Address: 55 E. 52nd St., 21st Fl., New York, NY 10022 US	

GROWTH PLANS/SPECIAL FEATURES:

McKinsey & Company, Inc. is a privately held international business consulting firm that was established in 1926. Headquartered in New York, the firm maintains 94 offices in 52 countries, as well as a cross-functional global business technology office. The firm provides consulting services for companies seeking functional assistance or market insights. Through a variety of leadership and financial consulting services, McKinsey helps clients sustain growth and maximize revenue. McKinsey serves companies within a wide range of industries including banking, insurance, telecom, information services, media/entertainment, industrial, health care, public sector and retail/consumer. The company helps clients achieve functional efficiency with consulting services such as outsourcing, information technology (IT) services, financial strategy, operations strategy, organization and leadership. McKinsey's consultants publish a variety of books and articles with topics ranging from company productivity and structural engineering to accentuating the positive. The firm also publishes The McKinsey Quarterly, a business journal expounding the company's current views about business strategy, finance and management. Through the McKinsey Global Institute (MGI), the company conducts business research and develops points of view relating to the economic issues faced by businesses and governments.

FINANCIALS: Sales and profits are in thousands of dollars—add 000 to get the full amount. 2008 Note: Financial information for 2008 was not available for all companies at press time.

2008 Sales: $4,800,000	2008 Profits: $	U.S. Stock Ticker: Private
2007 Sales: $4,500,000	2007 Profits: $	Int'l Ticker: Int'l Exchange:
2006 Sales: $4,200,000	2006 Profits: $	Employees: 14,500
2005 Sales: $3,900,000	2005 Profits: $	Fiscal Year Ends: 12/31
2004 Sales: $3,700,000	2004 Profits: $	Parent Company:

SALARIES/BENEFITS:

Pension Plan:	ESOP Stock Plan:	Profit Sharing:	Top Exec. Salary: $	Bonus: $
Savings Plan:	Stock Purch. Plan:		Second Exec. Salary: $	Bonus: $

OTHER THOUGHTS:

Apparent Women Officers or Directors: 1
Hot Spot for Advancement for Women/Minorities:

LOCATIONS: ("Y" = Yes)

West:	Southwest:	Midwest:	Southeast:	Northeast:	International:
Y	Y	Y	Y	Y	Y

MEDCO HEALTH SOLUTIONS

www.medco.com

Industry Group Code: 522320A Ranks within this company's industry group: Sales: 1   Profits: 1

Management:		Sales/Marketing:		Liberal Arts:		Information Systems:		Professionals:		Tech./Scientific:	
Management Trainees:	Y	Marketing Pros.:	Y	Gen. Writing/Editing:	Y	Info. Management:	Y	Finance/Acct.:	Y	Engineers, Electrical:	
Experienced Mngmt.:	Y	Retail Sales:		Technical Writing:	Y	Software Dev.:	Y	Law:	Y	Engineers, Other:	
International Business:		Commercial/Industrial:	Y	Graphic Arts/Photog.:	Y	Hardware Dev.:		HR/Other:	Y	Health/Lab:	
MBA Grads:	Y	Sales Trainees:		Music:		Consulting/Other:		Training:	Y	Scientists/Research:	
		Advertising Pros.:	Y	Broadcasting:				Health Care:	Y	Petroleum/Chemicals:	
				Other:				Consulting:		Math/Other:	

TYPES OF BUSINESS:

Pharmacy Benefits Management
Payment & Transaction Processing
Online Services

BRANDS/DIVISIONS/AFFILIATES:

Polymedica Corporation
Critical Care Systems
Accredo Health Group Inc
Optimal Health
RationalMed
Physician Service Center
Europa Apotheek Venlo
Medco Center for Health Action

CONTACTS: *Note: Officers with more than one job title may be intentionally listed here more than once.*

David Snow, CEO
Kenneth Klepper, COO
Kenneth Klepper, Pres.
Richard J. Rubino, CFO/Sr. VP-Finance
Jack Smith, Chief Mktg. Officer/Sr. VP
Karin Princivalle, Sr. VP-Human Resources
Robert Epstein, Chief Medical Officer/Sr. VP-Medical & Analytical
Thomas Moriarty, General Counsel/Corp. Sec./ Sr. VP
Gabriel Cappucci, Chief Acct. Officer/Sr. VP/Controller
Mary Daschner, Group Pres., Retiree Solutions
Timothy Wentworth, Group Pres., Employer Accounts
Brian Griffin, Group Pres., Health Plans
Glenn Taylor, Group Pres., Key Accounts
David Snow, Chmn.

Phone: 201-269-3400	Fax: 201-269-1109
Toll-Free:	
Address: 100 Parsons Pond Dr., Franklin Lakes, NJ 07417-2603 US	

GROWTH PLANS/SPECIAL FEATURES:

Medco Health Solutions, Inc. is a leading national pharmacy benefit manager. Its prescription drug benefit programs are designed to drive down the cost of pharmacy healthcare for private and public employers, health plans, labor unions, government agencies of all sizes and individuals served by the Medicare Part D Prescription Drug Program. Medco collaborates with retail pharmacies, physicians, the Centers for Medicare & Medicaid Services for Medicare and state Medicaid agencies. It provides its services through a national network of retail pharmacies, its mail-order pharmacies and its Specialty Pharmacy segment, Accredo Health Group. The company maintains Medco Therapeutic Resource Centers, staffed with hundreds of pharmacists trained and certified in specific complex and chronic conditions and associated medications. The company's services include benefit plan design services, which take into account formulary, pharmacy management, mail-order initiatives, specialty pharmacy, drug coverage, cost-share options and generic drug utilization initiatives; clinical management services, including utilization management and its RationalMed patient safety program and Optimal Health support solution; pharmacy management services, such as its mail-order service, specialty pharmacy management, retail pharmacy networks, call center pharmacies and reimbursement services; physician services, such as its Physician Service Center, designed to motivate physicians to prescribe more cost-effective medications; and web-based services for members, clients and pharmacists. The firm holds a majority interest in Europa Apotheek Venlo, a provider of clinical health care and mail-order pharmacy services in Germany. In May 2008, the company announced the launch of the Medco Center for Health Action, in collaboration with Healthways. The center will offer support and advocacy services for patients with chronic conditions and health risks. In April 2009, the company announced collaboration with Google health that allows Medco's members create online personal health records and providing a place for the storage of their information.

FINANCIALS: Sales and profits are in thousands of dollars—add 000 to get the full amount. 2008 Note: Financial information for 2008 was not available for all companies at press time.

2008 Sales: $51,258,000	2008 Profits: $1,102,900	**U.S. Stock Ticker:** MHS	
2007 Sales: $44,506,200	2007 Profits: $912,000	**Int'l Ticker:**	Int'l Exchange:
2006 Sales: $42,543,700	2006 Profits: $630,200	Employees: 21,800	
2005 Sales: $37,870,400	2005 Profits: $602,000	Fiscal Year Ends: 12/31	
2004 Sales: $35,351,900	2004 Profits: $481,600	Parent Company:	

SALARIES/BENEFITS:

Pension Plan:	ESOP Stock Plan:	Profit Sharing:	Top Exec. Salary: $1,281,542	Bonus: $3,000,000
Savings Plan:	Stock Purch. Plan:		Second Exec. Salary: $756,724	Bonus: $1,100,000

OTHER THOUGHTS:

Apparent Women Officers or Directors: 5
Hot Spot for Advancement for Women/Minorities: Y

LOCATIONS: ("Y" = Yes)

West:	Southwest:	Midwest:	Southeast:	Northeast:	International:
Y	Y	Y	Y	Y	

MEDTRONIC INC

www.medtronic.com

Industry Group Code: 33911 Ranks within this company's industry group: Sales: 2 Profits: 2

Management:		Sales/Marketing:		Liberal Arts:		Information Systems:		Professionals:		Tech./Scientific:	
Management Trainees:	Y	Marketing Pros.:	Y	Gen. Writing/Editing:	Y	Info. Management:	Y	Finance/Acct.:	Y	Engineers, Electrical:	Y
Experienced Mngmt.:	Y	Retail Sales:		Technical Writing:	Y	Software Dev.:	Y	Law:	Y	Engineers, Other:	Y
International Business:	Y	Commercial/Industrial:	Y	Graphic Arts/Photog.:	Y	Hardware Dev.:	Y	HR/Other:	Y	Health/Lab:	Y
MBA Grads:	Y	Sales Trainees:	Y	Music:		Consulting/Other:		Training:	Y	Scientists/Research:	Y
		Advertising Pros.:	Y	Broadcasting:				Health Care:	Y	Petroleum/Chemicals:	
				Other:				Consulting:		Math/Other:	Y

TYPES OF BUSINESS:

Equipment-Defibrillators & Pacing Products
Neurological Devices
Diabetes Management Devices
Ear, Nose & Throat Surgical Equipment
Pain Management Devices
Catheters & Stents
Cardiac Surgery Equipment

BRANDS/DIVISIONS/AFFILIATES:

Talent Abdominal Stent Graft
Restore Medical Inc
CryoCath Technologies Inc
Ablation Frontiers Inc
Ventor Technologies Inc.
INFUSE Bone Graft
Continuous Glucose Monitoring
Integrated Power Console (IPC)

CONTACTS: Note: Officers with more than one job title may be intentionally listed here more than once.

William A. Hawkins, CEO
William A. Hawkins, Pres.
Gary Ellis, CFO/Sr. VP
Martha Goldberg Aronson, Chief Talent Officer/Sr. VP
Stephen N. Oesterle, Sr. VP-Medicine & Tech.
Terrance Carlson, General Counsel/Corp. Sec./Sr. VP
H. James Dallas, Sr. VP-Quality & Oper.
Catherine Szyman, Sr. VP-Strategy & Innovation
Susan Alpert, Chief Regulatory Officer/Sr. VP
Bob Blankenmeyer, Sr. VP/Pres., Surgical Tech.
Scott R. Ward, Sr. VP/Pres., Cardiovascular
Stephen Mahle, Exec. VP-Healthcare Policy & Regulatory
William A. Hawkins, Chmn.
Jean-Luc Butel, Sr. VP/Pres., Medtronic Int'l

Phone: 763-514-4000	Fax: 763-514-4879
Toll-Free: 800-328-2518	
Address: 710 Medtronic Pkwy., Minneapolis, MN 55432 US	

GROWTH PLANS/SPECIAL FEATURES:

Medtronic, Inc. is a global leader in medical technology, whose professed mission is alleviating pain, restoring health and extending life for millions of people around the world. The firm operates in seven business sectors: cardiac rhythm disease management; surgical technologies; neuromodulation; spinal; cardiovascular; physio-control; and diabetes. Medtronic is one of the world's largest suppliers of medical devices for cardiac rhythm management, including pacemakers and implantable cardiac defibrillators. The surgical technologies division develops products for the treatment of ear, nose and throat (ENT) and neurological diseases, as well as for cranial, spinal, sinus and orthopedic maladies. The neuromodulation division develops, manufactures and markets devices for the treatment of neurological, urological and gastroenterological disorders. The spinal division produces medical devices and implants used in the treatment of spinal conditions. The cardiovascular segment offers minimally invasive products and therapies to treat coronary artery disease, aortic and thoracic aneurysms, and peripheral vascular disease. The physio-control segment produces external defibrillators, including manual defibrillators used by hospitals and emergency response personnel, as well as automated external defibrillators used in public settings. The diabetes unit provides glucose monitors, insulin pumps and other products, as well as informational resources available on the firm's web site. In 2008, the FDA approved the firm's Talent Abdominal Stent Graft for reparing aortic aneurysms. Recent company acquisitions include Restore Medical, Inc; CryoCath Technologies Inc; the Repose product line from InfluENT Medical; Ablation Frontiers, Inc.; and Ventor Technologies Inc. In February 2009, the company agreed to acquire CoreValve, Inc. a developer of aortic valve replacement products. Also in 2009, Medtronic launched the Integrated Power Console (IPC) platform for the use in spinal cranial and ENT surgeries.

Employees are offered medical insurance; disability coverage; retirement plans; stock ownership; and adoption and eldercare assistance.

FINANCIALS: Sales and profits are in thousands of dollars—add 000 to get the full amount. 2008 Note: Financial information for 2008 was not available for all companies at press time.

2008 Sales: $13,515,000	2008 Profits: $2,231,000	**U.S. Stock Ticker: MDT**
2007 Sales: $12,299,000	2007 Profits: $2,802,000	**Int'l Ticker:** Int'l Exchange:
2006 Sales: $11,292,000	2006 Profits: $2,546,700	Employees: 41,158
2005 Sales: $10,054,600	2005 Profits: $1,803,900	Fiscal Year Ends: 4/30
2004 Sales: $9,087,200	2004 Profits: $1,959,300	Parent Company:

SALARIES/BENEFITS:

Pension Plan:	ESOP Stock Plan:	Profit Sharing:	Top Exec. Salary: $1,092,000	Bonus: $987,656
Savings Plan: Y	Stock Purch. Plan:		Second Exec. Salary: $996,000	Bonus: $971,749

OTHER THOUGHTS:

Apparent Women Officers or Directors: 6
Hot Spot for Advancement for Women/Minorities: Y

LOCATIONS: ("Y" = Yes)

West:	Southwest:	Midwest:	Southeast:	Northeast:	International:
Y	Y	Y	Y	Y	Y

Note: Financial information, benefits and other data can change quickly and may vary from those stated here.

MEIJER INC

www.meijer.com

Industry Group Code: 445110 **Ranks within this company's industry group:** Sales: 6   Profits:

Management:		Sales/Marketing:		Liberal Arts:		Information Systems:		Professionals:		Tech./Scientific:	
Management Trainees:	Y	Marketing Pros.:	Y	Gen. Writing/Editing:	Y	Info. Management:	Y	Finance/Acct.:	Y	Engineers, Electrical:	
Experienced Mngmt.:	Y	Retail Sales:	Y	Technical Writing:		Software Dev.:	Y	Law:	Y	Engineers, Other:	
International Business:		Commercial/Industrial:		Graphic Arts/Photog.:	Y	Hardware Dev.:		HR/Other:	Y	Health/Lab:	
MBA Grads:	Y	Sales Trainees:	Y	Music:		Consulting/Other:		Training:	Y	Scientists/Research:	
		Advertising Pros.:	Y	Broadcasting:				Health Care:		Petroleum/Chemicals:	
				Other:	Y			Consulting:		Math/Other:	

TYPES OF BUSINESS:

Grocery Stores
General Merchandise
Hardware
Photo Services
Pharmacies
In-Store Restaurants
Gasoline, Retail
Home Decor

BRANDS/DIVISIONS/AFFILIATES:

Meijer Naturals
Meijer Organics
Meijer Gold

CONTACTS: Note: Officers with more than one job title may be intentionally listed here more than once.

Hendrik G. Meijer, CEO
Mark Murray, Pres.
Bob Mooney, VP-Mfg.
Stacie Behler, VP-Corp. Comm. & Public Rel.
Doug Meijer, Co-Chmn.
Hendrik G. Meijer, Co-Chmn.
Bob Mooney, VP-Distribution Oper.

Phone: 616-453-6711	Fax: 616-791-2572
Toll-Free: 877-363-4537	
Address: 2929 Walker Ave. N.W., Grand Rapids, MI 49544-9424 US	

GROWTH PLANS/SPECIAL FEATURES:

Meijer, Inc. is a leading grocery retailer in the Midwest, with approximately superstores throughout Illinois, Indiana, Kentucky, Michigan and Ohio. The firm's combination grocery and general merchandise stores range in size from 200,000 to 250,000 square feet, which is about four times the size of typical grocery stores. Each Meijer store carries about 120,000 brand-name and private-label products, including bulk foods, fresh produce, frozen items, seafood and meat products. Most stores feature nearly 40 departments, such as electronics, hardware, toys, garden, entertainment, jewelry, photo, banking, pharmacy, books, apparel, automotive and furniture. In addition, some stores offer a discount gas station. Company brands include Meijer Naturals, Meijer Organics and Meijer Gold. The superstores also offer several in-store restaurants, including delis and cafes. Meijer stores are open 24-hours-a-day and close only on Christmas. In addition to its retail stores, the firm operates a web site that features a baby club, wine guides, contests, advertisements, pharmaceutical help and gardening tips. In September 2008, the company announced the construction of a new bakery facility at its Middlebury, Indiana food-service plant. In October of the same year, the firm launched Grocery By The Case, an online shopping feature at Meijer.com that allows customers to purchase groceries in bulk.

Employees are offered medical, dental, vision and life insurance; flexible spending accounts; disability protection; a pension plan; a 401(k) plan; employee discounts; and adoption assistance.

FINANCIALS: Sales and profits are in thousands of dollars—add 000 to get the full amount. 2008 Note: Financial information for 2008 was not available for all companies at press time.

2008 Sales: $13,700,000	2008 Profits: $	U.S. Stock Ticker: Private
2007 Sales: $13,900,000	2007 Profits: $	Int'l Ticker: Int'l Exchange:
2006 Sales: $12,500,000	2006 Profits: $	Employees: 60,000
2005 Sales: $12,000,000	2005 Profits: $	Fiscal Year Ends: 1/31
2004 Sales: $11,900,000	2004 Profits: $	Parent Company:

SALARIES/BENEFITS:

Pension Plan: Y	ESOP Stock Plan:	Profit Sharing:	Top Exec. Salary: $	Bonus: $
Savings Plan: Y	Stock Purch. Plan:		Second Exec. Salary: $	Bonus: $

OTHER THOUGHTS:

Apparent Women Officers or Directors: 1
Hot Spot for Advancement for Women/Minorities:

LOCATIONS: ("Y" = Yes)

West:	Southwest:	Midwest:	Southeast:	Northeast:	International:
		Y			

MEN'S WEARHOUSE INC (THE)

www.menswearhouse.com

Industry Group Code: 448110 **Ranks within this company's industry group:** Sales: 1 Profits: 1

Management:		Sales/Marketing:		Liberal Arts:		Information Systems:		Professionals:		Tech./Scientific:	
Management Trainees:	Y	Marketing Pros.:	Y	Gen. Writing/Editing:	Y	Info. Management:	Y	Finance/Acct.:	Y	Engineers, Electrical:	
Experienced Mngmt.:	Y	Retail Sales:	Y	Technical Writing:		Software Dev.:	Y	Law:	Y	Engineers, Other:	
International Business:	Y	Commercial/Industrial:		Graphic Arts/Photog.:	Y	Hardware Dev.:		HR/Other:	Y	Health/Lab:	
MBA Grads:	Y	Sales Trainees:	Y	Music:		Consulting/Other:		Training:	Y	Scientists/Research:	
		Advertising Pros.:	Y	Broadcasting:				Health Care:		Petroleum/Chemicals:	
				Other:	Y			Consulting:		Math/Other:	

TYPES OF BUSINESS:

Men's Apparel, Retail
Men's Suits
Shoes & Accessories
Business Casual Wear
Sportswear
Shoes & Accessories
Ladies' Career Apparel

BRANDS/DIVISIONS/AFFILIATES:

K&G
Moores Clothing for Men
MW Tux
Perfect Fit
After Hours Formalwear

CONTACTS: *Note: Officers with more than one job title may be intentionally listed here more than once.*

George A. Zimmer, CEO
Douglas S. Ewert, COO
Douglas S. Ewert, Pres.
Neill P. Davis, CFO/Exec. VP
Charles Bresler, Exec. VP-Mktg.
Charles Bresler, Exec. VP-Human Resources
Neill P. Davis, Treas.
David H. Edwab, Vice Chmn.
George A. Zimmer, Chmn.

Phone: 281-776-7000	Fax:
Toll-Free:	
Address: 6380 Rogerdale Rd., Houston, TX 77072-1624 US	

GROWTH PLANS/SPECIAL FEATURES:

The Men's Wearhouse, Inc. is a leading specialty retailer of men's suits and provider of tuxedo rental products in the U.S. and Canada. The company's U.S. operations include more than 805 stores in 46 states and Washington, D.C., primarily operating under the brand names of Men's Wearhouse and K&G. In Canada, operations include 117 retail apparel stores in 10 provinces operating under the brand name of Moores Clothing for Men. Its tuxedo rental stores are operated under the brand name of MW Tux in 35 states. Men's Wearhouse apparel stores target middle and upper-middle income men and offer designer, brand name and private label merchandise at discounted prices through 563 locations. Merchandise offered includes suits, sport coats, slacks, formalwear, business casual, sportswear, outerwear, dress shirts, shoes and accessories. Most of these stores also offer tuxedo rental products in a section branded as MW Tux. The Men's Wearhouse's 108 K&G branded stores target more price sensitive customers and include ladies' career apparel at 93 locations. Under the Moores brand, the company targets middle and upper-middle income men in Canada. During 2008, 54.6% of The Men's Wearhouse's clothing product sales were attributable to tailored clothing and 45.4% were attributable to casual attire, sportswear, shoes, shirts, ties, outerwear and other clothing product revenues. The firm offers a private label credit card as well as a Perfect Fit loyalty program to its customers. In July 2008, the company closed its manufacturing facility in Montreal, Quebec.

The Men's Wearhouse offers its employees a tuition reimbursement program, a sabbatical leave program, a wellness program, merchandise discounts and medical, dental, life and disability insurance.

FINANCIALS: Sales and profits are in thousands of dollars—add 000 to get the full amount. 2008 Note: Financial information for 2008 was not available for all companies at press time.

2008 Sales: $2,112,558	2008 Profits: $147,041	**U.S. Stock Ticker: MW**
2007 Sales: $1,882,064	2007 Profits: $148,575	**Int'l Ticker:** Int'l Exchange:
2006 Sales: $1,724,898	2006 Profits: $103,903	Employees: 16,200
2005 Sales: $1,546,679	2005 Profits: $71,356	Fiscal Year Ends: 1/31
2004 Sales: $1,392,680	2004 Profits: $50,026	Parent Company:

SALARIES/BENEFITS:

Pension Plan:	ESOP Stock Plan: Y	Profit Sharing:	Top Exec. Salary: $1,016,016	Bonus: $34,000
Savings Plan: Y	Stock Purch. Plan: Y		Second Exec. Salary: $486,154	Bonus: $59,500

OTHER THOUGHTS:

Apparent Women Officers or Directors:
Hot Spot for Advancement for Women/Minorities:

LOCATIONS: ("Y" = Yes)

West:	Southwest:	Midwest:	Southeast:	Northeast:	International:
Y	Y	Y	Y	Y	Y

MERCER INC

www.mercer.com

Industry Group Code: 541612 Ranks within this company's industry group: Sales: 1 Profits:

Management:		Sales/Marketing:		Liberal Arts:		Information Systems:		Professionals:		Tech./Scientific:	
Management Trainees:	Y	Marketing Pros.:	Y	Gen. Writing/Editing:	Y	Info. Management:	Y	Finance/Acct.:	Y	Engineers, Electrical:	
Experienced Mngmt.:	Y	Retail Sales:		Technical Writing:	Y	Software Dev.:	Y	Law:	Y	Engineers, Other:	
International Business:	Y	Commercial/Industrial:	Y	Graphic Arts/Photog.:	Y	Hardware Dev.:		HR/Other:	Y	Health/Lab:	
MBA Grads:	Y	Sales Trainees:		Music:		Consulting/Other:	Y	Training:	Y	Scientists/Research:	
		Advertising Pros.:	Y	Broadcasting:				Health Care:		Petroleum/Chemicals:	
				Other:	Y			Consulting:	Y	Math/Other:	

TYPES OF BUSINESS:

Consulting-Human Resources
Investment/Financial Consulting
Health and Benefits Management
Human Capital Consulting
Outsourced Human Resources Services (BPO)
Investment Management
Retirement Plan Administration
Merger/Acquisition Consulting

BRANDS/DIVISIONS/AFFILIATES:

Mercer Sentinel
Mercer Retirement Solutions
MyView
MyView Plus
Global HR Monitor
ePRISM
Shanghai Mercer Insurance Brokers Co., Ltd.
Mercer Tesi

CONTACTS: *Note: Officers with more than one job title may be intentionally listed here more than once.*

M. Michele Burns, CEO
Terry Thompson, COO
Bob Van Pelt, CFO
Larry Woerner, Interim Global Head-Human Resources
Terry Thompson, Head-IT
David Goldenberg, General Counsel
Terry Thompson, Head-Oper.
Terry Thompson, Head-Corp. Strategy
Terry Thompson, Head-Finance
Patricia Milligan, Pres., Human Capital
Phil de Cristo, Pres., Investment Mgmt.
Jeff Miller, Pres., Outsourcing
Larry Woerner, Global Head-Regions
M. Michele Burns, Chmn.
Jeff Crispin, Principal-Sentinel Group (Europe)

Phone: 212-345-7000	Fax: 212-345-7414
Toll-Free:	
Address: 1166 Ave. of the Americas, New York, NY 10036 US	

GROWTH PLANS/SPECIAL FEATURES:

Mercer, Inc., a subsidiary of Marsh & McLennan Companies, Inc., offers a broad range of human resource advice and solutions in 41 countries. The firm has eight lines of business: Consulting; Health and Benefits; Human Capital; Surveys and Products; Mergers/Acquisitions; Investment Management; Workforce Communication; and Outsourcing. The Consulting segment handles retirement, risk, financial and investment issues; programs include Mercer Retirement Solutions and Mercer Sentinel. The Health and Benefits segment offers advice/solutions for health care strategy and funding; pharmacy; and disease and absentee management. The Human Capital business analyzes clients' compensation and performance management systems, including executive and broad-based employee compensation programs, and offers additional compensation administration services. The Surveys and Products division offers human resources tools like ePRISM and Global HR Monitor. The Mergers/Acquisitions unit helps clients through each step of every type of business reorganization and transformation. Mercer's Investment Management team offers its services in the U.S., Europe, Australia and Canada. The Workforce Communication division helps businesses reorganize at every operating level (e.g. benefit packages, mergers/acquisitions, employee retention, executive responsibility, etc.). The Outsourcing segment provides outsourced human resources administration, technology and business process solutions. The majority of the firm's clients are Fortune 1000 and FTSE 100 companies. In August 2008, the company and joint venture Shanghai Mercer Insurance Brokers Co., Ltd., agreed to open branch offices in Guangzhou, Beijing and Shanghai. In October 2008, Mercer's Italian branch of the Human Capital division merged with consulting firm Tesi to form Mercer Tesi, a consulting company focused on international and Italian human capital issues. In November 2008, the firm unveiled its wealth management unit, targeted at private banks, in Singapore. In February 2009, Mercer released MyView and MyView Plus, online retirement planning tools. In March 2009, the company allied with Staffcare Limited, incorporating Staffcare's benefits platform into its own.

FINANCIALS: Sales and profits are in thousands of dollars—add 000 to get the full amount. 2008 Note: Financial information for 2008 was not available for all companies at press time.

		U.S. Stock Ticker: Subsidiary
2008 Sales: $3,642,000	2008 Profits: $	Int'l Ticker: Int'l Exchange:
2007 Sales: $3,368,000	2007 Profits: $	Employees: 18,000
2006 Sales: $3,021,000	2006 Profits: $	Fiscal Year Ends: 12/31
2005 Sales: $2,794,000	2005 Profits: $	Parent Company: MARSH & MCLENNAN COMPANIES INC
2004 Sales: $	2004 Profits: $	

SALARIES/BENEFITS:

Pension Plan:	ESOP Stock Plan:	Profit Sharing:	Top Exec. Salary: $	Bonus: $
Savings Plan:	Stock Purch. Plan:		Second Exec. Salary: $	Bonus: $

OTHER THOUGHTS:

Apparent Women Officers or Directors: 2
Hot Spot for Advancement for Women/Minorities: Y

LOCATIONS: ("Y" = Yes)

West:	Southwest:	Midwest:	Southeast:	Northeast:	International:
Y	Y	Y	Y	Y	Y

Note: Financial information, benefits and other data can change quickly and may vary from those stated here.

MERCK & CO INC

www.merck.com

Industry Group Code: 325412 Ranks within this company's industry group: Sales: 4 Profits: 3

Management:		Sales/Marketing:		Liberal Arts:		Information Systems:		Professionals:		Tech./Scientific:	
Management Trainees:	Y	Marketing Pros.:	Y	Gen. Writing/Editing:	Y	Info. Management:	Y	Finance/Acct.:	Y	Engineers, Electrical:	Y
Experienced Mngmt.:	Y	Retail Sales:		Technical Writing:	Y	Software Dev.:	Y	Law:	Y	Engineers, Other:	Y
International Business:	Y	Commercial/Industrial:	Y	Graphic Arts/Photog.:	Y	Hardware Dev.:		HR/Other:	Y	Health/Lab:	Y
MBA Grads:	Y	Sales Trainees:	Y	Music:		Consulting/Other:		Training:	Y	Scientists/Research:	Y
		Advertising Pros.:	Y	Broadcasting:				Health Care:	Y	Petroleum/Chemicals:	Y
				Other:				Consulting:		Math/Other:	Y

TYPES OF BUSINESS:

Pharmaceuticals Development & Manufacturing
Cholesterol Drugs
Hypertension Drugs
Heart Failure Drugs
Allergy & Asthma Drugs
Animal Health Products
Vaccines
Preventative Drugs

BRANDS/DIVISIONS/AFFILIATES:

Merck Institute for Science Education
Sirna Therapeutics, Inc.
Singulair
Propecia
Merck BioVentures
Fosamax
Gardasil
EMEND

CONTACTS: Note: Officers with more than one job title may be intentionally listed here more than once.

Richard Clark, CEO
Peter N. Kellogg, CFO/Exec. VP
Wendy Yarno, Chief Mktg. Officer
Mirian Graddick-Weir, Exec. VP-Human Resources
Peter S. Kim, Pres., Research Laboratories
J. Chris Scalet, CIO/Exec. VP-Global Svcs.
Willie Deese, Pres., Mfg. Div.
Bruce N. Kuhlik, General Counsel/Exec. VP
Adele Ambrose, Chief Comm. Officer
John Canan, Controller/Sr. VP
Kenneth C. Frazier, Pres., Global Human Health
Margaret McGlynn, Pres., Merck Vaccines & Infectious Diseases
Celia Colbert, Sr. VP/Sec.
Mark McDonough, VP/Treas.
Richard Clark, Chmn.
Stefan Oschmann, Pres., EMEA & Canada

Phone: 908-423-1000	Fax: 908-735-1253
Toll-Free:	
Address: 1 Merck Dr., Whitehouse Station, NJ 08889-0100 US	

GROWTH PLANS/SPECIAL FEATURES:

Merck & Co., Inc. is a leading research-driven pharmaceutical company that manufactures a broad range of products sold in approximately 150 countries. These products include therapeutic and preventative drugs generally sold by prescription and medications used to control and alleviate disease. The company operates in two segments. The Pharmaceutical segment includes human health pharmaceutical products consisting of therapeutic and preventative agents, sold by prescription. Medications include Fosamax, for the prevention of osteoporosis; Zocor, for lowering cholesterol; and Singulair, a seasonal allergy and asthma medication. The Vaccines and Infectious Diseases segment includes preventative vaccines such as Rotateq, designed to prevent gastroenteritis in infants and children; and Gardasil, a vaccine for the prevention of HPV. The segment also produces therapeutic agents for the treatment of infections such as Invanz and Cancidas, an anti-fungal product. The company also manufactures Propecia, a popular treatment for male pattern baldness. Recent FDA approved products include EMEND, a drug that prevents chemotherapy-induced nausea and ISENTRESS (raltegravir) tablets, which treats patients with the HIV-1 infection. In late 2008, Merck established a new unit, Merck BioVentures. This new group will focus on biotech drugs, including generic biotech drugs know as follow-on biologics. Also, the company will continue to focus on growing sales in emerging markets, particularly China and India. In February 2009, Merck agreed to acquire the portfolio of follow-on biologic therapeutic candidates, as well as the commercial manufacturing facilities in Boulder Colorado, of Insmed Inc. In August 2009, the company agreed to merge with Schering-Plough.

Employees are offered medical, vision and dental insurance; health and dependent care accounts; a 401(k) plan; a pension plan; financial planning services; life insurance; business travel accident insurance; credit union membership; educational assistance and scholarship programs; and corporate discounts on cars, travel, entertainment and electronics.

FINANCIALS: Sales and profits are in thousands of dollars—add 000 to get the full amount. 2008 Note: Financial information for 2008 was not available for all companies at press time.

2008 Sales: $23,850,300	2008 Profits: $7,808,400	**U.S. Stock Ticker: MRK**
2007 Sales: $24,197,700	2007 Profits: $3,275,400	**Int'l Ticker:** Int'l Exchange:
2006 Sales: $22,636,000	2006 Profits: $4,433,800	Employees: 55,200
2005 Sales: $22,011,900	2005 Profits: $4,631,300	Fiscal Year Ends: 12/31
2004 Sales: $22,938,600	2004 Profits: $5,813,400	Parent Company:

SALARIES/BENEFITS:

Pension Plan: Y	ESOP Stock Plan:	Profit Sharing:	Top Exec. Salary: $178,334	Bonus: $2,244,510
Savings Plan: Y	Stock Purch. Plan:		Second Exec. Salary: $1,033,338	Bonus: $875,023

OTHER THOUGHTS:

Apparent Women Officers or Directors: 7
Hot Spot for Advancement for Women/Minorities: Y

LOCATIONS: ("Y" = Yes)

West:	Southwest:	Midwest:	Southeast:	Northeast:	International:
Y	Y	Y	Y	Y	Y

Note: Financial information, benefits and other data can change quickly and may vary from those stated here.

METHODIST HEALTH CARE SYSTEM

www.methodisthealth.com

Industry Group Code: 6216 Ranks within this company's industry group: Sales:　Profits:

Management:		Sales/Marketing:		Liberal Arts:		Information Systems:		Professionals:		Tech./Scientific:	
Management Trainees:	Y	Marketing Pros.:		Gen. Writing/Editing:	Y	Info. Management:	Y	Finance/Acct.:	Y	Engineers, Electrical:	
Experienced Mngmt.:	Y	Retail Sales:		Technical Writing:	Y	Software Dev.:	Y	Law:	Y	Engineers, Other:	
International Business:		Commercial/Industrial:		Graphic Arts/Photog.:	Y	Hardware Dev.:		HR/Other:	Y	Health/Lab:	Y
MBA Grads:	Y	Sales Trainees:		Music:		Consulting/Other:		Training:	Y	Scientists/Research:	
		Advertising Pros.:	Y	Broadcasting:				Health Care:	Y	Petroleum/Chemicals:	
				Other:	Y			Consulting:		Math/Other:	

TYPES OF BUSINESS:

Hospitals

BRANDS/DIVISIONS/AFFILIATES:

Methodist Hospital (The)
Methodist Sugar Land Hospital
Methodist Willowbrook Hospital
San Jacinto Methodist Hospital
Weill Medical College of Cornell University
Baylor College of Medicine
Methodist Hospital Physician Organization
Methodist Hospital Foundation (The)

CONTACTS: Note: Officers with more than one job title may be intentionally listed here more than once.

Ronald G. (Ron) Girotto, CEO
Marc L. Boom, COO/Exec. VP
Ronald G. (Ron) Girotto, Pres.
Amelia Ortiz, Mgr.-Bus. Dev., Methodist Int'l
Stefanie Asin, Dir.-Media
Jane Ortega, Mgr.-Financial Oper., Methodist Int'l
Joseph J. Naples, Chmn.-Anesthesiology Dep't
Miguel Quinones, Dir.-Cardiology Dep't
Alan Lumsden, Dir.-Cardiovascular Surgery Dep't
Richard J. Robbins, Dir.-Medicine Dep't
Ewing Werlein, Jr., Chmn.
Valter Aleixo, Mgr.-Oper., Methodist Int'l

Phone: 713-790-3311	Fax: 713-790-2605
Toll-Free:	
Address: 6565 Fannin St., Houston, TX 77030 US	

GROWTH PLANS/SPECIAL FEATURES:

Methodist Health Care System, doing business as The Methodist Hospital, is a not-for-profit health care organization that owns and operates several hospitals located in Houston, Texas. Its hospitals include The Methodist Hospital, Methodist Sugar Land Hospital, Methodist Willowbrook Hospital and San Jacinto Methodist Hospital. Some of The Methodist Hospital's focuses include breast care, heart care, neuroscience, orthopedics and oncology. The hospital is an adult teaching hospital and is affiliated with Weill Medical College of Cornell University. It also maintains joint programs with Baylor College of Medicine. The Methodist Sugar Land Hospital serves the Fort Bend and surrounding communities, providing such medical services as inpatient and outpatient medical care; inpatient and outpatient surgery; cancer treatment services; emergency care; and diagnostic and therapeutic medical imaging. The Methodist Willowbrook Hospital consists of a 139,000-square-foot professional building and a 173,000-square-foot hospital with inpatient and outpatient treatment areas. Services offered by the hospital include a diagnostic center, surgery, a birthing center, a pharmacy, a laboratory, a blood bank, wellness services, pastoral services and an education and conference center. Located in Baytown, The San Jacinto Methodist Hospital is one of the only not-for-profit church-affiliated hospitals in the area. Methodist Health Care System conducts translational and clinical research through its Methodist Hospital Research Institute. The organization also manages the Methodist Hospital Physician Organization, which focuses on engaging physicians in an academic environment while maintaining clinical practice autonomy. The Methodist Health Care System is funded by The Methodist Hospital Foundation.

FINANCIALS: Sales and profits are in thousands of dollars—add 000 to get the full amount. 2008 Note: Financial information for 2008 was not available for all companies at press time.

2008 Sales: $	2008 Profits: $	U.S. Stock Ticker: Private	
2007 Sales: $	2007 Profits: $	Int'l Ticker:	Int'l Exchange:
2006 Sales: $	2006 Profits: $	Employees: 10,535	
2005 Sales: $	2005 Profits: $	Fiscal Year Ends:	
2004 Sales: $	2004 Profits: $	Parent Company:	

SALARIES/BENEFITS:

Pension Plan:	ESOP Stock Plan:	Profit Sharing:	Top Exec. Salary: $	Bonus: $
Savings Plan:	Stock Purch. Plan:		Second Exec. Salary: $	Bonus: $

OTHER THOUGHTS:

Apparent Women Officers or Directors: 3
Hot Spot for Advancement for Women/Minorities: Y

LOCATIONS: ("Y" = Yes)

West:	Southwest:	Midwest:	Southeast:	Northeast:	International:
	Y				

METLIFE INC

www.metlife.com

Industry Group Code: 524113 Ranks within this company's industry group: Sales: 1 Profits: 1

Management:		Sales/Marketing:		Liberal Arts:		Information Systems:		Professionals:		Tech./Scientific:	
Management Trainees:	Y	Marketing Pros.:	Y	Gen. Writing/Editing:	Y	Info. Management:	Y	Finance/Acct.:	Y	Engineers, Electrical:	
Experienced Mngmt.:	Y	Retail Sales:		Technical Writing:	Y	Software Dev.:	Y	Law:	Y	Engineers, Other:	
International Business:	Y	Commercial/Industrial:	Y	Graphic Arts/Photog.:	Y	Hardware Dev.:		HR/Other:	Y	Health/Lab:	
MBA Grads:	Y	Sales Trainees:	Y	Music:		Consulting/Other:		Training:	Y	Scientists/Research:	
		Advertising Pros.:	Y	Broadcasting:				Health Care:	Y	Petroleum/Chemicals:	
				Other:	Y			Consulting:		Math/Other:	Y

TYPES OF BUSINESS:

Insurance
Banking
Investment Products
Mutual Funds
Life Insurance
Property & Casualty Insurance
Auto Insurance

BRANDS/DIVISIONS/AFFILIATES:

MetLife Bank
Simple Solutions Variable Annuity

CONTACTS: *Note: Officers with more than one job title may be intentionally listed here more than once.*

C. Robert Henrikson, CEO
C. Robert Henrikson, Pres.
William J. Wheeler, CFO/Exec. VP
Maria R. Morris, Exec. VP-Tech.
Exec. VP-Tech. & Oper.
James L. Lipscomb, General Counsel/Exec. VP
Maria R. Morris, Exec. VP-Oper.
Steven A. Kandarian, Chief Investment Officer/Exec. VP
William J. Mullaney, Pres., U.S.
Gwenn L. Carr, Sr. VP
C. Robert Henrikson, Chmn.
William J. Toppeta, Pres., Int'l

Phone: 212-578-2211	Fax: 212-578-3320
Toll-Free: 800-638-5433	
Address: 200 Park Ave., New York, NY 10166 US	

GROWTH PLANS/SPECIAL FEATURES:

MetLife, Inc. is a provider of insurance and other financial services with operations throughout the U.S. and regions of Latin America, Europe and Asia Pacific. Through its domestic and international subsidiaries and affiliates, the company offers life insurance; annuities; automobile and homeowners insurance; retail banking; and other financial services to individuals, as well as group insurance; and retirement and savings products and services to corporations and other institutions. The firm operates in five segments. The institutional segment offers group insurance, retirement and savings products and services to corporations and other institutions. The individual segment offers asset protection and accumulation products, primarily life and disability insurance. The auto and home group operates through the Metropolitan Property and Casualty Insurance Company subsidiary and offers personal lines property and casualty insurance including renters', homeowners', car and recreational vehicle insurance. The international segment provides accident and health insurance; credit insurance; annuities; and savings and retirement products to customers within the Latin America, Europe and Asia Pacific regions. The corporate and other segment contains the excess capital not allocated to the business segments; various start-up entities, including MetLife Bank; National Association, and run-off entities and interest expense related to the majority of the company's outstanding debt and expenses associated with certain legal proceedings and income tax audit issues. In 2008, the company split off its majority ownership stake in Reinsurance Group of America. In July 2009, the firm launched Simple

Employees are offered medical and dental insurance; disability coverage; life insurance; flexible spending accounts; prepaid legal services; wellness and fitness programs; adoption assistance; a pension plan; and a 401(k) plan.

FINANCIALS: Sales and profits are in thousands of dollars—add 000 to get the full amount. 2008 Note: Financial information for 2008 was not available for all companies at press time.

2008 Sales: $55,085,000	2008 Profits: $3,209,000	**U.S. Stock Ticker: MET**
2007 Sales: $53,070,000	2007 Profits: $4,317,000	**Int'l Ticker:** Int'l Exchange:
2006 Sales: $48,254,000	2006 Profits: $6,293,000	Employees: 57,000
2005 Sales: $44,683,000	2005 Profits: $4,714,000	Fiscal Year Ends: 12/31
2004 Sales: $38,712,000	2004 Profits: $2,758,000	Parent Company:

SALARIES/BENEFITS:

Pension Plan: Y	ESOP Stock Plan:	Profit Sharing:	Top Exec. Salary: $1,000,000	Bonus: $3,250,000
Savings Plan: Y	Stock Purch. Plan:		Second Exec. Salary: $625,000	Bonus: $800,000

OTHER THOUGHTS:

Apparent Women Officers or Directors: 6
Hot Spot for Advancement for Women/Minorities: Y

LOCATIONS: ("Y" = Yes)

West:	Southwest:	Midwest:	Southeast:	Northeast:	International:
Y	Y	Y	Y	Y	Y

MGM MIRAGE

www.mgmmirage.com

Industry Group Code: 721120 Ranks within this company's industry group: Sales: 2 Profits: 3

Management:		Sales/Marketing:		Liberal Arts:		Information Systems:		Professionals:		Tech./Scientific:	
Management Trainees:	Y	Marketing Pros.:	Y	Gen. Writing/Editing:	Y	Info. Management:	Y	Finance/Acct.:	Y	Engineers, Electrical:	
Experienced Mngmt.:	Y	Retail Sales:		Technical Writing:		Software Dev.:	Y	Law:	Y	Engineers, Other:	
International Business:	Y	Commercial/Industrial:	Y	Graphic Arts/Photog.:	Y	Hardware Dev.:		HR/Other:	Y	Health/Lab:	
MBA Grads:	Y	Sales Trainees:	Y	Music:	Y	Consulting/Other:		Training:	Y	Scientists/Research:	
		Advertising Pros.:	Y	Broadcasting:				Health Care:		Petroleum/Chemicals:	
				Other:	Y			Consulting:		Math/Other:	

TYPES OF BUSINESS:

Casino Hotels & Resorts
Golf Courses
Real Estate Development

BRANDS/DIVISIONS/AFFILIATES:

Bellagio
MGM Grand Las Vegas
Mandalay Bay
Mirage (The)
Luxor
Excalibur
CityCenter
MGM Grand Macau

CONTACTS: *Note: Officers with more than one job title may be intentionally listed here more than once.*

James J. Murren, CEO
Daniel J. (Dan) D'Arrigo, CFO/Exec. VP
Cynthia Kiser Murphey, Sr. VP-Human Resources/Pres./COO-New York
Robert Baldwin, Chief Design & Construction Officer
Aldo Manzini, Chief Admin. Officer/Exec. VP
Gary N. Jacobs, General Counsel/Sec./Exec. VP
Alan M. Feldman, Sr. VP-Public Affairs
Robert C. Selwood, Chief Acct. Officer/Exec. VP
Randy Morton, Pres./COO-Bellagio
Bill Hornbuckle, Pres./COO-Mandalay Bay & MGM Grand Atlantic City
Robert Baldwin, Pres./CEO-CityCenter
Lorenzo Creighton, Pres./COO-MGM Grand Detroit
James J. Murren, Chmn.
Pansy Ho Chiu-king, Managing Dir.-MGM Grand Macau
Teresa Reynolds, Chief Procurement Officer

Phone: 702-693-7120	Fax: 702-693-8626
Toll-Free:	
Address: 3600 Las Vegas Blvd. S., Las Vegas, NV 89109 US	

GROWTH PLANS/SPECIAL FEATURES:

MGM Mirage (MGM) operates casino resorts in Nevada, Mississippi and Michigan, as well as four 50%-owned casino resorts in Nevada, Macau, New Jersey and Illinois. Its Las Vegas Strip casino resorts include Bellagio, MGM Grand Las Vegas, Mandalay Bay, The Mirage, Luxor, New York-New York, Excalibur, Monte Carlo, Slots-A-Fun and Circus Circus Las Vegas. Combined, they feature 37,696 guestrooms, nearly 1.2 million square feet of gaming space, 19,335 slot machines and 994 gaming tables. Its other Nevada properties, including Circus Circus Reno, Silver Legacy (50% owned), Gold Strike and Railroad Pass, offer 4,212 guestrooms, 207,000 square feet of gaming space, 3,477 slot machines and 127 gaming tables. Finally, its other operations include MGM Grand Detroit, Beau Rivage and Gold Strike (in Michigan), all wholly-owned; and MGM Grand Macau, Borgata and Grand Victoria, all 50%-owned. These facilities offer 5,666 guestrooms, 663,000 square feet of gaming space, 13,874 slot machines and 835 gaming tables. MGM's casinos often feature restaurants, bars, spas, salons, retail space, nightclubs and lounges. The firm also owns and operates three championship golf courses: Shadow Creek, in North Las Vegas; Fallen Oak, in Saucier, Mississippi; and Primm Valley Golf Club, in Primm, Nevada, near the California boarder. Almost two-thirds of MGM's revenue is generated by non-gaming activities. In December 2008, the company agreed to sell Treasure Island hotel and casino in Las Vegas to Ruffin Acquisition, LLC for roughly $775 million. The firm has a joint venture agreement with Dubai World, splitting the ownership of the $8 billion Project CityCenter, still under development, located between Bellagio and Monte Carlo. With completion planned by the end of 2009, it will feature a 4,000-room casino resort, two 400-room non-casino hotels, and 425,000 square feet of retail, restaurant and entertainment space; as well as luxury condominiums. As of early 2009, the company had entered into hotel management arrangements with various international developers and was considering several other development opportunities that could put MGM-branded facilities in locations throughout the Middle East and Asia. Specific plans include MGM Grand and Bellagio properties currently under development in China, Vietnam and Egypt.

FINANCIALS: Sales and profits are in thousands of dollars—add 000 to get the full amount. 2008 Note: Financial information for 2008 was not available for all companies at press time.

2008 Sales: $7,208,767	2008 Profits: $-855,286	**U.S. Stock Ticker: MGM**
2007 Sales: $7,691,637	2007 Profits: $1,584,419	**Int'l Ticker:** Int'l Exchange:
2006 Sales: $7,175,956	2006 Profits: $648,264	Employees: 61,000
2005 Sales: $6,128,843	2005 Profits: $443,256	Fiscal Year Ends: 12/31
2004 Sales: $4,001,804	2004 Profits: $412,332	Parent Company:

SALARIES/BENEFITS:

Pension Plan:	ESOP Stock Plan:	Profit Sharing:	Top Exec. Salary: $2,000,000	Bonus: $
Savings Plan: Y	Stock Purch. Plan:		Second Exec. Salary: $1,500,000	Bonus: $

OTHER THOUGHTS:

Apparent Women Officers or Directors: 5
Hot Spot for Advancement for Women/Minorities: Y

LOCATIONS: ("Y" = Yes)

West:	Southwest:	Midwest:	Southeast:	Northeast:	International:
Y		Y	Y	Y	Y

Note: Financial information, benefits and other data can change quickly and may vary from those stated here.

MICROCHIP TECHNOLOGY INC

www.microchip.com

Industry Group Code: 33441 Ranks within this company's industry group: Sales: 8 Profits: 5

Management:		Sales/Marketing:		Liberal Arts:		Information Systems:		Professionals:		Tech./Scientific:	
Management Trainees:	Y	Marketing Pros.:	Y	Gen. Writing/Editing:		Info. Management:	Y	Finance/Acct.:	Y	Engineers, Electrical:	Y
Experienced Mngmt.:	Y	Retail Sales:		Technical Writing:	Y	Software Dev.:	Y	Law:	Y	Engineers, Other:	
International Business:	Y	Commercial/Industrial:	Y	Graphic Arts/Photog.:	Y	Hardware Dev.:	Y	HR/Other:	Y	Health/Lab:	
MBA Grads:	Y	Sales Trainees:		Music:		Consulting/Other:		Training:	Y	Scientists/Research:	Y
		Advertising Pros.:	Y	Broadcasting:				Health Care:		Petroleum/Chemicals:	
				Other:				Consulting:		Math/Other:	

TYPES OF BUSINESS:

Semiconductors-Specialized
Microcontrollers
Battery Management & Interface Devices
Development Tools
Memory Products

BRANDS/DIVISIONS/AFFILIATES:

PIC
dsPIC
Digital Signal Controllers
EEPROM
EPROM Memory
Flash
Hampshire Company Inc

CONTACTS: Note: Officers with more than one job title may be intentionally listed here more than once.

Steve Sanghi, CEO
Steve Sanghi, Pres.
Gordon W. Parnell, CFO/VP
Mitchell R. Little, VP-Worldwide Sales & Applications
Lauren A. Carr, VP-Human Resources
Robert H. Owen, VP-Info. Svcs.
Stephen V. Drehobl, VP-Security, Microcontroller & Tech. Div.
Kenneth N. Pye, VP-Worldwide Applications Eng.
J. Eric Bjornholt, Corp. Sec.
David S. Lambert, VP-Fab Oper.
J. Eric Bjornholt, VP-Finance
Paul R. Breault, VP-Greater China Sales
Randall L. Drwinga, VP-Memory Prod. Div.
Dan L. Termer, VP-Vertical Markets Group
William Yang, VP-Pacific Rim Finance
Steve Sanghi, Chmn.
Gary P. Marsh, VP-European Sales

Phone: 480-792-7200	Fax: 480-899-9210
Toll-Free:	
Address: 2355 W. Chandler Blvd., Chandler, AZ 85224-6199 US	

GROWTH PLANS/SPECIAL FEATURES:

Microchip Technology, Inc. develops and manufactures specialized semiconductor products used for a wide variety of embedded control applications. In addition, the company offers a broad spectrum of high-performance linear, mixed-signal, power management, thermal management, battery management and interface devices. The firm focuses on embedded control solutions, including microcontrollers; development tools; analog and interface products; and memory products. Microchip offers a broad family of microcontroller products featuring the proprietary architecture PIC with a variety of memory technology configurations, low voltage and power and small footprint. The company targets the 8-bit and 16-bit microcontroller markets. Additionally, the scalable product architecture allows it to target both the entry-level of the 32-bit microcontroller markets, as well as the 4-bit microcontroller marketplace. In addition, the firm is able to incorporate non-volatile memory, such as Flash, EEPROM and EPROM Memory, into the microcontroller and offers reprogrammable microcontroller products. The development tools enable system designers to program a PIC microcontroller and dsPIC Digital Signal Controllers for specific applications. Microchip's family of development tools operate in the standard Windows environment on standard PC hardware. These tools range from entry-level systems, which include an assembler and programmer or in-circuit debugging hardware, to fully configured systems that provide in-circuit emulation hardware. Analog and interface products consist of several families with over 500 power management, linear, mixed-signal, thermal management and interface products. Memory products consists primarily of serial electrically erasable programmable read only memory, referred to as Serial EEPROMs. Serial EEPROM products are used for non-volatile program and data storage systems where such data must be either modified frequently or retained for long periods. In 2008, the company announced its intention to acquire Atmel Corp. In October 2008, the company acquired Hampshire Company, Inc.

Employees are offered medical, vision, dental, and life insurance; disability coverage; a group legal plan; a health club reimbursement program; and tuition reimbursement.

FINANCIALS: Sales and profits are in thousands of dollars—add 000 to get the full amount. 2008 Note: Financial information for 2008 was not available for all companies at press time.

2008 Sales: $1,035,737	2008 Profits: $297,748	**U.S. Stock Ticker:** MCHP
2007 Sales: $1,039,671	2007 Profits: $357,029	**Int'l Ticker:** Int'l Exchange:
2006 Sales: $927,893	2006 Profits: $242,369	Employees: 4,895
2005 Sales: $846,936	2005 Profits: $213,785	Fiscal Year Ends: 3/31
2004 Sales: $699,260	2004 Profits: $137,262	Parent Company:

SALARIES/BENEFITS:

Pension Plan:	ESOP Stock Plan:	Profit Sharing: Y	Top Exec. Salary: $532,675	Bonus: $759,209
Savings Plan: Y	Stock Purch. Plan: Y		Second Exec. Salary: $252,625	Bonus: $98,747

OTHER THOUGHTS:

Apparent Women Officers or Directors: 2
Hot Spot for Advancement for Women/Minorities: Y

LOCATIONS: ("Y" = Yes)

West:	Southwest:	Midwest:	Southeast:	Northeast:	International:
Y	Y	Y	Y	Y	Y

Note: Financial information, benefits and other data can change quickly and may vary from those stated here.

MICRON TECHNOLOGY INC

www.micron.com

Industry Group Code: 33441 **Ranks within this company's industry group:** Sales: 3   Profits: 7

Management:		Sales/Marketing:		Liberal Arts:		Information Systems:		Professionals:		Tech./Scientific:	
Management Trainees:	Y	Marketing Pros.:	Y	Gen. Writing/Editing:		Info. Management:	Y	Finance/Acct.:	Y	Engineers, Electrical:	Y
Experienced Mngmt.:	Y	Retail Sales:		Technical Writing:	Y	Software Dev.:	Y	Law:	Y	Engineers, Other:	
International Business:	Y	Commercial/Industrial:	Y	Graphic Arts/Photog.:	Y	Hardware Dev.:	Y	HR/Other:	Y	Health/Lab:	
MBA Grads:	Y	Sales Trainees:		Music:		Consulting/Other:		Training:	Y	Scientists/Research:	Y
		Advertising Pros.:	Y	Broadcasting:				Health Care:		Petroleum/Chemicals:	
				Other:				Consulting:		Math/Other:	

TYPES OF BUSINESS:

Components-Semiconductor Memory
PCs & Peripherals
Flash Memory Devices
CMOS Image Sensors

BRANDS/DIVISIONS/AFFILIATES:

IM Flash Technologies, LLC
Intel Corp
Avago Technologies Ltd.
Aptina Imaging

CONTACTS: *Note: Officers with more than one job title may be intentionally listed here more than once.*

Steven R. Appleton, CEO
D. Mark Durcan, COO
D. Mark Durcan, Pres.
Ronald C. Foster, CFO/VP-Finance
Mark W. Adams, VP-Worldwide Sales
Pat Otte, VP-Human Resources
James E. Mahoney, VP-Info. Systems
Brian J. Shields, VP-Worldwide Wafer Fabrication
Roderic W. Lewis, General Counsel/VP-Legal Affairs/Corp. Sec.
Jay L. Hawkins, VP-Oper.
Kipp A. Bedard, VP-Investor Rel.
Norman L. Schlachter, Treas.
John F. Schreck, DRAM Dev.
Brian M. Shirley, VP-Memory
Dean A. Klein, VP-Memory System Dev.
Frankie F. Roohparvar, VP-NAND Dev.
Steven R. Appleton, Chmn.
Paul C. Mullen, VP-Int'l OEM Sales
Steve Thorsen, VP-Worldwide Procurement

Phone: 208-368-4000	Fax: 208-368-4435
Toll-Free:	
Address: 8000 S. Federal Way, Boise, ID 83707-0006 US	

GROWTH PLANS/SPECIAL FEATURES:

Micron Technology, Inc. and its subsidiaries design, develop, manufacture and market semiconductor memory products and personal computer systems. Its products are used in a range of electronic devices, including personal computers, workstations, servers, cell phones, digital cameras and other consumer and industrial products. The products are sold to computing and consumer, networking, telecommunications and imaging markets. Micron has two segments: Memory, producing dynamic random access memory (DRAM), accounting for 54% of 2008 sales, and NAND flash memory, 35% of sales; and Imaging, producing complementary metal-oxide semiconductor (CMOS) image sensors, 11%. DRAMs are high-density, low-cost-per-bit RAM storage units. Micron offers double data rate (DDR) and DDR2 DRAM, primarily used for the main system memory in computers; and synchronous DRAM (SDRAM), used in networking devices, servers, consumer electronics, communications equipment, computer peripherals and as memory upgrades to older computers. NAND products are re-writable, non-volatile semiconductor devices, meaning they retain memory after power has been shut off. It is used in mobile devices such as digital cameras, MP3 players, USB Flash Drives and cellular phones. IM Flash Technologies, LLC, a joint venture with Intel Corp., produces Micron's NAND products. CMOS image sensors are semiconductor devices that capture and process images into pictures or video for consumer and industrial applications. They are used in digital cameras, automotive systems and other emerging applications. The firm has manufacturing facilities located in the U.S., Italy, Japan, Puerto Rico and Singapore. In March 2008, the company launched Aptina Imaging, a new independent division for the company's CMOS business. In April of the same year, the company agreed to form a DRAM joint venture with Nanya Technology Corporation to be named MeiYa Technology Corporation. In October 2008, the firm announced plans to reduce its global workforce by 15% over the next two years, as part of the restructuring of its memory operations.

Employees are offered medical, dental, vision and life insurance; short-and long-term disability coverage, business travel accident coverage; and educational assistance.

FINANCIALS: Sales and profits are in thousands of dollars—add 000 to get the full amount. 2008 Note: Financial information for 2008 was not available for all companies at press time.

2008 Sales: $5,841,000	2008 Profits: $-1,619,000	**U.S. Stock Ticker:** MU
2007 Sales: $5,688,000	2007 Profits: $-320,000	**Int'l Ticker:** Int'l Exchange:
2006 Sales: $5,272,000	2006 Profits: $408,000	Employees: 22,800
2005 Sales: $4,880,200	2005 Profits: $188,000	Fiscal Year Ends: 8/31
2004 Sales: $4,404,200	2004 Profits: $157,200	Parent Company:

SALARIES/BENEFITS:

Pension Plan:	ESOP Stock Plan:	Profit Sharing:	Top Exec. Salary: $950,000	Bonus: $233,712
Savings Plan: Y	Stock Purch. Plan:		Second Exec. Salary: $600,000	Bonus: $127,080

OTHER THOUGHTS:

Apparent Women Officers or Directors: 1
Hot Spot for Advancement for Women/Minorities: Y

LOCATIONS: ("Y" = Yes)

West:	Southwest:	Midwest:	Southeast:	Northeast:	International:
Y	Y	Y	Y	Y	Y

MICROSOFT CORP

www.microsoft.com

Industry Group Code: 511210I **Ranks within this company's industry group:** Sales: 1 Profits: 1

Management:		Sales/Marketing:		Liberal Arts:		Information Systems:		Professionals:		Tech./Scientific:	
Management Trainees:	Y	Marketing Pros.:	Y	Gen. Writing/Editing:	Y	Info. Management:	Y	Finance/Acct.:	Y	Engineers, Electrical:	Y
Experienced Mngmt.:	Y	Retail Sales:		Technical Writing:	Y	Software Dev.:	Y	Law:	Y	Engineers, Other:	
International Business:	Y	Commercial/Industrial:	Y	Graphic Arts/Photog.:	Y	Hardware Dev.:		HR/Other:	Y	Health/Lab:	
MBA Grads:	Y	Sales Trainees:		Music:	Y	Consulting/Other:	Y	Training:	Y	Scientists/Research:	Y
		Advertising Pros.:	Y	Broadcasting:				Health Care:		Petroleum/Chemicals:	
				Other:	Y			Consulting:		Math/Other:	Y

TYPES OF BUSINESS:

Computer Software
Personal Communications Services
Video Games Systems
Mobile Communications
Voice-Enabled Mobile Search
Internet Search Engine
E-Mail Services
Instant Messaging

BRANDS/DIVISIONS/AFFILIATES:

Windows 7
Tellme Networks
Microsoft Dynamics
Fast Search & Transfer ASA
Xbox
MSN Video
BigPark Inc.
Rosetta Biosoftware

CONTACTS: Note: Officers with more than one job title may be intentionally listed here more than once.

Steve Ballmer, CEO
B. Kevin Turner, COO
Christopher Liddell, CFO
Mich Mathews, Sr. VP-Central Mktg. Group
Lisa Brummel, Sr. VP-Human Resources
Rick Rashid, Sr. VP-Research
David Vaskevitch, CTO/Sr. VP
Brad Smith, General Counsel/Sr. VP-Legal/Sec.
Craig Mundie, Chief Research & Strategy Officer
Qi Lu, Pres., Online Svcs.
Brad Smith, Sr. VP-Corp. Affairs
Robert J. Bach, Pres., Entertainment & Devices Div.
Steven Sinofsky, Pres., Windows Div.
Ray Ozzie, Chief Software Architect
Bob Muglia, Pres., Server & Tools Bus.
Bill Gates, Chmn.
Jean-Philippe Courtois, Pres., Microsoft Int'l

Phone: 425-882-8080	Fax: 425-936-7329
Toll-Free:	
Address: 1 Microsoft Way, Redmond, WA 98052-7329 US	

GROWTH PLANS/SPECIAL FEATURES:

Microsoft Corp. develops, manufactures and supports software for a wide range of computing devices. Microsoft operates in five segments. The client segment provides premium and standard-edition Windows operating systems and manages the company's relationships with personal computer manufacturers. The company's latest operating system, introduced in 2009, is Windows 7. The server and tools segment licenses products, applications, tools, content and services related to Windows server products and operating systems. The division offers Windows Server operating system, Microsoft SQL Server, Microsoft Enterprise Services, Visual Studio and System Center products, among others. The online services business segment consists of an online advertising platform and provides personal services including MSN Video Service and Windows Live Search. The business division offers the Microsoft Office system and Microsoft Dynamics business solutions. The entertainment and devices division is responsible for developing, producing and marketing Xbox and Xbox 360 video game systems, including consoles and accessories; the Zune digital music and entertainment platform; PC software games; the Mediaroom Internet television software; the Surface computing system; and online games and services. During 2008, Microsoft acquired Navic Networks, a provider of television advertising solutions; Komoku, Inc, a security detection company; Rapt, Inc., a provider of advertising yield management solutions; Greenfiled Online Inc., a European price comparison site; and DATAllegro Inc., a provider of data warehouse appliances. In May 2009, Microsoft agreed to acquire BigPark, Inc., an interactive online gaming company. In June 2009, the firm agreed to acquire certain data management software assets from Rosetta Biosoftware. In August 2009, the company announced plans to sell its interactive ad agency, Razorfish, Inc., to Paris-based Publicis Groupe for approximately $530 million.

Microsoft offers its employees health, dental and vision coverage; health club memberships; autism therapy benefits; adoption assistance; a 401(k) plan; a stock purchase plan; charity gift matching; and tuition assistance.

FINANCIALS: Sales and profits are in thousands of dollars—add 000 to get the full amount. 2008 Note: Financial information for 2008 was not available for all companies at press time.

2008 Sales: $60,420,000	2008 Profits: $17,681,000	**U.S. Stock Ticker: MSFT**
2007 Sales: $51,122,000	2007 Profits: $14,065,000	**Int'l Ticker:** Int'l Exchange:
2006 Sales: $44,282,000	2006 Profits: $12,599,000	Employees: 93,000
2005 Sales: $39,788,000	2005 Profits: $12,254,000	Fiscal Year Ends: 6/30
2004 Sales: $36,835,000	2004 Profits: $8,168,000	Parent Company:

SALARIES/BENEFITS:

Pension Plan:	ESOP Stock Plan:	Profit Sharing:	Top Exec. Salary: $640,833	Bonus: $700,000
Savings Plan: Y	Stock Purch. Plan: Y		Second Exec. Salary: $620,833	Bonus: $600,000

OTHER THOUGHTS:

Apparent Women Officers or Directors: 4
Hot Spot for Advancement for Women/Minorities: Y

LOCATIONS: ("Y" = Yes)

West:	Southwest:	Midwest:	Southeast:	Northeast:	International:
Y	Y	Y	Y	Y	Y

MIDAMERICAN ENERGY HOLDINGS CO

www.midamerican.com

Industry Group Code: 221 Ranks within this company's industry group: Sales: 6 Profits:

Management:		Sales/Marketing:		Liberal Arts:		Information Systems:		Professionals:		Tech./Scientific:	
Management Trainees:	Y	Marketing Pros.:	Y	Gen. Writing/Editing:	Y	Info. Management:	Y	Finance/Acct.:	Y	Engineers, Electrical:	Y
Experienced Mngmt.:	Y	Retail Sales:		Technical Writing:	Y	Software Dev.:	Y	Law:	Y	Engineers, Other:	Y
International Business:	Y	Commercial/Industrial:	Y	Graphic Arts/Photog.:	Y	Hardware Dev.:		HR/Other:	Y	Health/Lab:	
MBA Grads:	Y	Sales Trainees:		Music:		Consulting/Other:		Training:	Y	Scientists/Research:	
		Advertising Pros.:		Broadcasting:				Health Care:		Petroleum/Chemicals:	Y
				Other:				Consulting:		Math/Other:	

TYPES OF BUSINESS:

Utilities-Electricity & Natural Gas
Pipelines
Wind Generation
Hydroelectric Generation
Thermal Generation
Real Estate Brokerage

BRANDS/DIVISIONS/AFFILIATES:

Berkshire Hathaway Inc
PacifiCorp
MidAmerican Energy Company
Northern Natural Gas Company
Kern River Gas Transmission Company
CE Electric U.K. Funding Company
CalEnergy Generation
HomeServices of America, Inc.

CONTACTS: Note: Officers with more than one job title may be intentionally listed here more than once.

Gregory E. Abel, CEO
Gregory E. Abel, Pres.
Patrick J. Goodman, CFO/Sr. VP
Maureen Sammon, Sr. VP/Chief Admin. Officer
Douglas L. Anderson, General Counsel/Corp. Sec./Sr. VP
David L. Sokol, Chmn.

Phone: 515-242-4300	Fax:
Toll-Free:	
Address: 666 Grand Ave., Des Moines, IA 50306-0657 US	

GROWTH PLANS/SPECIAL FEATURES:

MidAmerican Energy Holdings Co. (MEHC), with over $39.2 billion in assets, generates, transmits, stores, distributes and supplies energy through its subsidiaries to over 6.9 million customers. It is an 88.2% owned subsidiary of Berkshire Hathaway, Inc. The company is organized into eight distinct platforms. PacifiCorp serves more than 1.7 million customers, operating as Pacific Power on the West Coast; and as Rocky Mountain Power in Wyoming, Utah and Idaho. MidAmerican Funding LLC consists of MidAmerican Energy Company, which generates, transmits and sells electricity to 720,000 customers and supplies natural gas to an additional 702,000 customers. It operates in Iowa, Illinois, Nebraska and South Dakota. Northern Natural Gas Company owns one of the largest interstate natural gas pipeline systems in the U.S. extending from Texas to the upper Midwest. Kern River Gas Transmission Company owns 1,680 miles of interstate pipeline and delivers more than 1.7 billion cubic feet of natural gas per day. CE Electric U.K. Funding Company, a holding company for Northern Electric and Yorkshire Electric, distributes electricity to 3.8 million customers in the U.K. Its transmission network covers approximately 10,000 square miles. CalEnergy Generation is an international leader in the development and production of energy from diversified fuel sources including geothermal, natural gas and hydroelectric. Lastly, HomeServices of America, Inc. is a leading residential real estate brokerage firm in the U.S. HomeServices offers integrated real estate services, including brokerage services, mortgage originations, title and closing services, home warranties, property and casualty insurance, and other related services. MEHC's natural gas pipeline subsidiaries have a delivery capacity of 6.9 billion cubic feet of gas per day. In September 2008, MEHC agreed to acquire Constellation Energy, an industrial electricity supplier.

MEHC offers its employees medical, dental and vision insurance, an employee assistance program, flexible spending accounts, tuition reimbursement and adoption assistance.

FINANCIALS: Sales and profits are in thousands of dollars—add 000 to get the full amount. 2008 Note: Financial information for 2008 was not available for all companies at press time.

2008 Sales: $12,700,000	2008 Profits: $	**U.S. Stock Ticker: Subsidiary**
2007 Sales: $12,376,000	2007 Profits: $	**Int'l Ticker:** Int'l Exchange:
2006 Sales: $10,300,700	2006 Profits: $916,100	Employees:
2005 Sales: $7,115,539	2005 Profits: $562,654	Fiscal Year Ends: 12/31
2004 Sales: $6,553,400	2004 Profits: $170,200	Parent Company: BERKSHIRE HATHAWAY INC

SALARIES/BENEFITS:

Pension Plan: Y	ESOP Stock Plan:	Profit Sharing: Y	Top Exec. Salary: $	Bonus: $2,500,000
Savings Plan: Y	Stock Purch. Plan:		Second Exec. Salary: $	Bonus: $

OTHER THOUGHTS:

Apparent Women Officers or Directors: 1
Hot Spot for Advancement for Women/Minorities:

LOCATIONS: ("Y" = Yes)

West:	Southwest:	Midwest:	Southeast:	Northeast:	International:
Y	Y	Y	Y	Y	Y

Note: Financial information, benefits and other data can change quickly and may vary from those stated here.

MILLIPORE CORP

www.millipore.com

Industry Group Code: 3345 Ranks within this company's industry group: Sales: 3 Profits: 3

Management:		Sales/Marketing:		Liberal Arts:		Information Systems:		Professionals:		Tech./Scientific:	
Management Trainees:	Y	Marketing Pros.:	Y	Gen. Writing/Editing:		Info. Management:	Y	Finance/Acct.:	Y	Engineers, Electrical:	Y
Experienced Mngmt.:	Y	Retail Sales:		Technical Writing:	Y	Software Dev.:	Y	Law:	Y	Engineers, Other:	
International Business:	Y	Commercial/Industrial:	Y	Graphic Arts/Photog.:	Y	Hardware Dev.:	Y	HR/Other:	Y	Health/Lab:	Y
MBA Grads:	Y	Sales Trainees:		Music:		Consulting/Other:		Training:	Y	Scientists/Research:	Y
		Advertising Pros.:	Y	Broadcasting:				Health Care:		Petroleum/Chemicals:	
				Other:				Consulting:		Math/Other:	Y

TYPES OF BUSINESS:

Biotechnology Instruments
Fluid Analysis, Identification & Purification Equipment
Chromatography Technologies

BRANDS/DIVISIONS/AFFILIATES:

Direct-Q 3
Lynx S2S
MicroSafe, B.V.
Newport Bio Systems
Serologicals Corporation
MilliPROBE

CONTACTS: Note: Officers with more than one job title may be intentionally listed here more than once.

Martin D. Madaus, CEO
Martin D. Madaus, Pres.
Charles Wagner, CFO/VP
Bruce Bonnevier, VP-Worldwide Human Resources
Dennis W. Harris, Chief Scientific Officer/VP
Peter C. Kershaw, VP-Worldwide Mfg. Oper.
Jeffrey Rudin, General Counsel/VP/Corp. Sec.
Wei Zhang, VP-Strategic & Corp. Dev.
Karen Marinella Hall, Dir.-Corp. Comm.
Joshua S. Young, Dir.-Investor Rel.
Jon DiVincenzo, VP/Pres., Bioscience Div.
Gregory J. Sam, VP-Quality
Jean-Paul Mangeolle, VP/Pres., Bioprocess Div.
Martin D. Madaus, Chmn.
Geoffrey F. Ide, VP-Millipore Int'l
Peter C. Kershaw, VP-Global Supply Chain

Phone: 978-715-4321	Fax: 800-645-5439
Toll-Free: 800-645-5476	
Address: 290 Concord Rd., Billerica, MA 01821 US	

GROWTH PLANS/SPECIAL FEATURES:

Millipore Corp. is a multinational bioscience company that provides technologies, tools and services for research, development and production. The company's products and services are based on technologies such as filtration, chromatography, cell culture supplements, antibodies and cell lines. The firm's products are offered through its two segments, the Bioscience division and the Bioprocess division. Millipore's Bioscience division, which accounted for 45% of 2008 revenue, is organized around four specific market segments: biotools for the separation, isolation and purification of biological samples; research reagents such as antibodies, dyes and biochemical reagents; drug discovery reagent for the analysis of drug candidates; and laboratory water purification systems that remove contaminants for critical laboratory analysis. The Bioprocess division, which accounted for 55% of 2008 revenue, provides bio-products and technologies for the manufacturing of biologic drugs in mammalian cell cultures; filtration, purification and chromatography technologies to clarify, concentrate, purify and remove viruses; process monitoring tools for the sampling and testing of drugs and intermediate products and advanced manufacturing systems for use in sterile biomanufacturing environments. The firm operates 11 manufacturing sites in Massachusetts, New Hampshire, Missouri, Illinois, California, France and the U.K., and 47 offices worldwide. In 2008, the firm entered into a license agreement with Bayer HeathCare AG. In January 2008, Millipore and Gen-Probe created the MilliPROBE system for real time tests of contaminants in manufacturing. In February 2009, the firm acquired Epitome Biosystems' EpiTag technology as well as Guava Technologies. Also in February, Millipore opened a new biomanufacturing sciences and training facility in Singapore. In June 2009, the firm opened a new bioprocess manufacturing facility in Massachusetts.

Millipore offers employees flexible spending accounts, tuition reimbursement, employee assistance programs and adoption assistance.

FINANCIALS: Sales and profits are in thousands of dollars—add 000 to get the full amount. 2008 Note: Financial information for 2008 was not available for all companies at press time.

2008 Sales: $1,602,138	2008 Profits: $145,801	U.S. Stock Ticker: MIL
2007 Sales: $1,531,555	2007 Profits: $136,472	Int'l Ticker: Int'l Exchange:
2006 Sales: $1,255,371	2006 Profits: $96,984	Employees: 5,900
2005 Sales: $991,031	2005 Profits: $80,168	Fiscal Year Ends: 12/31
2004 Sales: $883,263	2004 Profits: $105,556	Parent Company:

SALARIES/BENEFITS:

Pension Plan:	ESOP Stock Plan:	Profit Sharing:	Top Exec. Salary: $850,962	Bonus: $655,666
Savings Plan: Y	Stock Purch. Plan:		Second Exec. Salary: $375,587	Bonus: $217,096

OTHER THOUGHTS:

Apparent Women Officers or Directors: 3
Hot Spot for Advancement for Women/Minorities: Y

LOCATIONS: ("Y" = Yes)

West:	Southwest:	Midwest:	Southeast:	Northeast:	International:
Y	Y	Y	Y	Y	Y

MONRO MUFFLER BRAKE INC

www.monro.com

Industry Group Code: 8111 **Ranks within this company's industry group:** Sales: 1   Profits: 1

Management:		Sales/Marketing:		Liberal Arts:		Information Systems:		Professionals:		Tech./Scientific:	
Management Trainees:	Y	Marketing Pros.:		Gen. Writing/Editing:	Y	Info. Management:	Y	Finance/Acct.:	Y	Engineers, Electrical:	
Experienced Mngmt.:	Y	Retail Sales:	Y	Technical Writing:	Y	Software Dev.:	Y	Law:	Y	Engineers, Other:	
International Business:		Commercial/Industrial:		Graphic Arts/Photog.:	Y	Hardware Dev.:		HR/Other:	Y	Health/Lab:	
MBA Grads:	Y	Sales Trainees:		Music:		Consulting/Other:		Training:	Y	Scientists/Research:	
		Advertising Pros.:	Y	Broadcasting:				Health Care:		Petroleum/Chemicals:	
				Other:				Consulting:		Math/Other:	

TYPES OF BUSINESS:

Automotive Repair & Maintenance
Under-Car Repair Services
Inspection Services
Tires

BRANDS/DIVISIONS/AFFILIATES:

Monro Muffler Brake & Service
Mr. Tire
Tread Quarters Discount Tire
Monro Service Corporation

CONTACTS: *Note: Officers with more than one job title may be intentionally listed here more than once.*

Robert G. Gross, CEO
John W. Van Heel, Pres.
Catherine D'Amico, CFO
John W. Van Heel, Sec.
Joseph Tomarchio, Jr., Exec. VP-Store Oper.
Catherine D'Amico, Exec. VP-Finance/Treas.
Craig L. Hoyle, Div. VP-Southern Oper.
Christopher R. Hoornbeck, Div. VP-Western Oper.
Robert G. Gross, Chmn.

Phone: 585-647-6400	**Fax:** 585-647-0945
Toll-Free:	
Address: 200 Holleder Pkwy., Rochester, NY 14615 US	

GROWTH PLANS/SPECIAL FEATURES:

Monro Muffler Brake, Inc., based in Rochester, New York, operates through a chain of 710 company-operated stores and 14 dealer-operated stores providing automotive under-car repair and tire services in the U.S. These stores are typically located in high-visibility locations in suburban and small towns in New York, Pennsylvania, Ohio, Connecticut, Massachusetts, West Virginia, Virginia, Maryland, Vermont, New Hampshire, New Jersey, North Carolina, South Carolina, Indiana, Rhode Island, Delaware and Maine. The stores operate under the names Monro Muffler Brake & Service, Tread Quarters Discount Tire and Mr. Tire. During 2009, the firm's stores serviced approximately 3.5 million vehicles. Monro provides a range of services on passenger cars, light trucks and vans for brakes; mufflers and exhaust systems; and steering, drive train, suspension and wheel alignment. Other products and services offered by the company include tires and routine maintenance services, such as state inspections. The company specializes in the repair and replacement of parts that must be periodically replaced due to normal wear and tear. Typically, the firm does not perform under-the-hood repair, except for oil change services, heating and cooling system flush and fill services and some minor tune-ups. Monro operates one subsidiary, Monro Service Corporation, which provides purchasing, distribution, merchandising, advertising, accounting and other store support functions. In 2009, the firm serviced 3.4 million vehicles with sales as follows: 21% brakes, 6% exhaust, 12% steering, 29% tires and 32% maintenance. In June 2009, Monro acquired Autotire Car Care Center, comprising 26 locations in Missouri, for approximately $10 million.

Monro offers its employees ASE certification reimbursement, recreational discounts, an employee assistance program, tool insurance and medical, dental, life and disability insurance.

FINANCIALS: Sales and profits are in thousands of dollars—add 000 to get the full amount. 2008 Note: Financial information for 2008 was not available for all companies at press time.

2008 Sales: $439,389	2008 Profits: $21,921	**U.S. Stock Ticker: MNRO**
2007 Sales: $417,226	2007 Profits: $22,271	**Int'l Ticker:** Int'l Exchange:
2006 Sales: $368,727	2006 Profits: $22,666	Employees: 4,277
2005 Sales: $337,409	2005 Profits: $19,669	Fiscal Year Ends: 3/31
2004 Sales: $279,457	2004 Profits: $17,005	Parent Company:

SALARIES/BENEFITS:

Pension Plan:	ESOP Stock Plan:	Profit Sharing:	Top Exec. Salary: $769,125	Bonus: $150,000
Savings Plan: Y	Stock Purch. Plan: Y		Second Exec. Salary: $360,000	Bonus: $

OTHER THOUGHTS:

Apparent Women Officers or Directors: 1
Hot Spot for Advancement for Women/Minorities:

LOCATIONS: ("Y" = Yes)

West:	Southwest:	Midwest:	Southeast:	Northeast:	International:
		Y		Y	

Note: Financial information, benefits and other data can change quickly and may vary from those stated here.

MONSANTO CO

www.monsanto.com

Industry Group Code: 11511 Ranks within this company's industry group: Sales: 1 Profits: 1

Management:		Sales/Marketing:		Liberal Arts:		Information Systems:		Professionals:		Tech./Scientific:	
Management Trainees:	Y	Marketing Pros.:	Y	Gen. Writing/Editing:	Y	Info. Management:	Y	Finance/Acct.:	Y	Engineers, Electrical:	
Experienced Mngmt.:	Y	Retail Sales:		Technical Writing:	Y	Software Dev.:	Y	Law:	Y	Engineers, Other:	Y
International Business:	Y	Commercial/Industrial:	Y	Graphic Arts/Photog.:	Y	Hardware Dev.:		HR/Other:	Y	Health/Lab:	
MBA Grads:	Y	Sales Trainees:	Y	Music:		Consulting/Other:		Training:	Y	Scientists/Research:	Y
		Advertising Pros.:	Y	Broadcasting:				Health Care:		Petroleum/Chemicals:	Y
				Other:				Consulting:		Math/Other:	Y

TYPES OF BUSINESS:

Agricultural Biotechnology Products & Chemicals Manufacturing
Herbicides
Seeds
Genetic Products
Lawn & Garden Products

BRANDS/DIVISIONS/AFFILIATES:

Asgrow
Roundup Ready
Agroeste Sementes
Delta and Pine Land Company
Seminis
De Ruiter Seeds Group BV
Marmot SA
Aly Participacoes Ltda

CONTACTS: Note: Officers with more than one job title may be intentionally listed here more than once.

Hugh Grant, CEO
Hugh Grant, Pres.
Terrell K. Crews, CFO/Exec. VP
Steven C. Mizell, Exec. VP-Human Resources
Robert T. Fraley, CTO/Exec. VP
Mark J. Leidy, Exec. VP-Mfg.
Janet M. Holloway, Chief of Staff/VP
David F. Snively, General Counsel/Sr. VP/Sec.
Carl M. Casale, Exec. VP-Oper. & Strategy
Cheryl Morley, Sr. VP-Corp. Strategy
Janet M. Holloway, Sr. VP-Comm. Rel.
Scarlett Lee Foster, VP-Investor Rel.
Richard B. Clark, VP/Controller
Robert A. Paley, VP/Treas.
Nicole M. Ringenberg, VP-Finance & Oper./Global Commercial
Terrell K. Crews, CEO-Seminis
Gerald A. Steiner, Exec. VP-Corp. Affairs & Sustainability
Hugh Grant, Chmn.
Kerry J. Preete, Exec. VP-Int'l Commercial

Phone: 314-694-1000	Fax: 314-694-8394
Toll-Free:	
Address: 800 N. Lindbergh Blvd., St. Louis, MO 63167 US	

GROWTH PLANS/SPECIAL FEATURES:

Monsanto Co. is a global provider of agricultural products for farmers. The company operates in two principal business segments: Seeds and Genomics; and Agricultural Productivity. The Seeds and Genomics segment is responsible for producing seed brands and patenting genetic traits that enable seeds to resist insects, disease, drought and weeds. Major seed brands produced by Monsanto include Agroceres, Asgrow, DEKALB, Stoneville, Vistive, Monsoy, Holden's Foundation Seeds, American Seeds, Inc., Seminis, Royal Sluis and Petoseed. The company's genetic trait products include Roundup Ready traits in soybeans, corn, canola and cotton; Bollgard and Bollgard II traits in cotton; and YieldGard Corn Borer and YieldGard Rootworm traits in corn. The Agricultural Productivity segment produces herbicide products. The firm's branded herbicides include Roundup, Harness, Degree, Machete, Maverick, Certainty, Outrider and Monitor. Monsanto market its seeds and commercial herbicides through a variety of channels and directly to farmers. Residential herbicides are marketed through the Scotts Miracle-Gro Company. Subsidiaries include Delta and Pine Land Company, a developer of cotton and soybean seeds; and Agroeste Sementes, a Brazilian corn seed company. In 2008, the company acquired the Dutch holding company, De Ruiter Seeds Group B.V. for $850 million; Marmot, S.A. which operates the private Guatemalan seed company Semillas Cristiani Burkhard; and Aly Participacoes Ltda., which operates sugarcane technology companies, CanaVialis S.A. and Alellyx S.A. Also in 2008, the company sold its POSILAC bovine somatotropin brand and related business to Eli Lilly and Company for $300 million.

Employees are offered medical, dental, and vision insurance; life insurance; disability coverage; a pension plan; a 401(k) plan; a stock purchase plan; long term care insurance; adoption assistance; group auto and home insurance; an employee assistance program; and relocation assistance.

FINANCIALS: Sales and profits are in thousands of dollars—add 000 to get the full amount. 2008 Note: Financial information for 2008 was not available for all companies at press time.

2008 Sales: $11,365,000	2008 Profits: $2,024,000	U.S. Stock Ticker: MON
2007 Sales: $8,563,000	2007 Profits: $993,000	Int'l Ticker: Int'l Exchange:
2006 Sales: $7,294,000	2006 Profits: $689,000	Employees: 21,700
2005 Sales: $6,275,000	2005 Profits: $255,000	Fiscal Year Ends: 8/31
2004 Sales: $5,457,000	2004 Profits: $267,000	Parent Company:

SALARIES/BENEFITS:

Pension Plan: Y	ESOP Stock Plan:	Profit Sharing:	Top Exec. Salary: $1,286,019	Bonus: $3,326,796
Savings Plan: Y	Stock Purch. Plan:		Second Exec. Salary: $566,827	Bonus: $840,000

OTHER THOUGHTS:

Apparent Women Officers or Directors: 5
Hot Spot for Advancement for Women/Minorities: Y

LOCATIONS: ("Y" = Yes)

West:	Southwest:	Midwest:	Southeast:	Northeast:	International:
Y	Y	Y	Y	Y	Y

Note: Financial information, benefits and other data can change quickly and may vary from those stated here.

MURPHY OIL CORPORATION

www.murphyoilcorp.com

Industry Group Code: 211111 Ranks within this company's industry group: Sales: 6 Profits: 6

Management:		Sales/Marketing:		Liberal Arts:		Information Systems:		Professionals:		Tech./Scientific:	
Management Trainees:	Y	Marketing Pros.:		Gen. Writing/Editing:		Info. Management:	Y	Finance/Acct.:	Y	Engineers, Electrical:	Y
Experienced Mngmt.:	Y	Retail Sales:		Technical Writing:	Y	Software Dev.:		Law:	Y	Engineers, Other:	Y
International Business:	Y	Commercial/Industrial:	Y	Graphic Arts/Photog.:		Hardware Dev.:		HR/Other:	Y	Health/Lab:	
MBA Grads:	Y	Sales Trainees:		Music:		Consulting/Other:		Training:	Y	Scientists/Research:	
		Advertising Pros.:		Broadcasting:				Health Care:		Petroleum/Chemicals:	Y
				Other:				Consulting:		Math/Other:	

TYPES OF BUSINESS:

Oil & Gas Exploration & Production
Refining
Pipelines
Retail Gas Stations
Wholesale Marketing
Synthetic Crude

BRANDS/DIVISIONS/AFFILIATES:

Syncrude Canada, Ltd.
Murco Petroleum, Ltd.
Murphy Oil USA, Inc.
SPUR
Murphy USA
Murphy Canada
Murphy Oil Company, Ltd.
Bear Ridge Resources, Ltd.

CONTACTS: Note: Officers with more than one job title may be intentionally listed here more than once.

David Wood, CEO
David Wood, Pres.
Kevin G. Fitzgerald, CFO/Sr. VP
Steven Cosse, General Counsel/Exec. VP
John Eckart, Controller/VP
Bill H. Stobaugh, Sr. VP
Tom McKinlay, VP
Mindy West, Treasurer/VP
Walter Compton, VP/Corp. Sec.
William Nolan, Chmn.

Phone: 870-862-6411	Fax: 870-864-6371
Toll-Free:	
Address: 200 Peach St., El Dorado, AR 71730 US	

GROWTH PLANS/SPECIAL FEATURES:

Murphy Oil Corporation, through its subsidiaries, is a global oil and gas exploration and production company with refining and marketing operations in North America and the U.K. The company's U.S. exploration and production activities are located primarily in the Gulf of Mexico, onshore Louisiana and Alaska. Murphy's Canadian assets include interests in the Hibernia and Terra Nova properties offshore Newfoundland and in Syncrude Canada, Ltd., which produces synthetic crude from bitumen oil sands. Western and offshore eastern Canadian operations are carried out by Murphy Oil Company Ltd. The company's crude oil, condensate and natural gas liquids production averages 118,254 barrels per day from its facilities in the U.S., Canada, Malaysia, Ecuador, the Republic of Congo and the North Sea. Murphy conducts its refining and marketing operations through Murphy Oil USA, Inc. and the U.K. subsidiary Murco Petroleum, Ltd. These companies refine crude oil and feedstock into petroleum products such as gasoline and distillates; buy and sell crude oil and refined products; and transport and market petroleum products. Murphy owns interests in three refineries in Louisiana, Wisconsin and Wales. The company's petroleum products are marketed under the brands SPUR and Murphy USA, with most locations in the parking areas of Wal-Mart stores. The company also has an agreement to market products through Murphy Canada stations at Canadian Wal-Mart stores. Murphy also owns interests in a number of pipelines in North America and the U.K. In November 2008, the firm acquired a 70% interest in, as well as the operatorship of a second Browse Basin exploration permit in Block WA-423-P.

Employees are offered medical, dental and vision insurance; a 401(k) plan; life insurance; long-term disability coverage; a pension plan; and a stock purchase plan.

FINANCIALS: Sales and profits are in thousands of dollars—add 000 to get the full amount. 2008 Note: Financial information for 2008 was not available for all companies at press time.

2008 Sales: $27,440,834	2008 Profits: $1,739,986	U.S. Stock Ticker: MUR
2007 Sales: $18,423,771	2007 Profits: $766,529	Int'l Ticker: Int'l Exchange:
2006 Sales: $14,279,325	2006 Profits: $638,279	Employees: 8,277
2005 Sales: $11,680,079	2005 Profits: $846,452	Fiscal Year Ends: 12/31
2004 Sales: $8,299,147	2004 Profits: $701,315	Parent Company:

SALARIES/BENEFITS:

Pension Plan: Y	ESOP Stock Plan:	Profit Sharing:	Top Exec. Salary: $1,241,667	Bonus: $2,000,000
Savings Plan: Y	Stock Purch. Plan: Y		Second Exec. Salary: $670,833	Bonus: $850,000

OTHER THOUGHTS:

Apparent Women Officers or Directors: 2
Hot Spot for Advancement for Women/Minorities: Y

LOCATIONS: ("Y" = Yes)

West:	Southwest:	Midwest:	Southeast:	Northeast:	International:
Y	Y	Y	Y	Y	Y

Note: Financial information, benefits and other data can change quickly and may vary from those stated here.

MYLAN INC

www.mylan.com

Industry Group Code: 325412 Ranks within this company's industry group: Sales: 11 Profits: 16

Management:		Sales/Marketing:		Liberal Arts:		Information Systems:		Professionals:		Tech./Scientific:	
Management Trainees:	Y	Marketing Pros.:	Y	Gen. Writing/Editing:		Info. Management:	Y	Finance/Acct.:	Y	Engineers, Electrical:	Y
Experienced Mngmt.:	Y	Retail Sales:		Technical Writing:	Y	Software Dev.:	Y	Law:	Y	Engineers, Other:	Y
International Business:	Y	Commercial/Industrial:	Y	Graphic Arts/Photog.:		Hardware Dev.:		HR/Other:	Y	Health/Lab:	Y
MBA Grads:	Y	Sales Trainees:		Music:		Consulting/Other:		Training:	Y	Scientists/Research:	Y
		Advertising Pros.:		Broadcasting:				Health Care:	Y	Petroleum/Chemicals:	Y
				Other:				Consulting:		Math/Other:	Y

TYPES OF BUSINESS:

Drugs-Generic
Generic Pharmaceuticals
Active Pharmaceutical Ingredients

BRANDS/DIVISIONS/AFFILIATES:

UDL Laboratories, Inc.
Mylan Pharmaceuticals, Inc.
Mylan Technologies, Inc.
Matrix Laboratories Limited
Docpharma
Dey
Genpharm ULC
Somerset Pharmaceuticals, Inc.

CONTACTS: Note: Officers with more than one job title may be intentionally listed here more than once.

Robert J. Coury, CEO
Heather Bresch, COO/Exec. VP
Jolene Varney, CFO/Exec. VP
David A. Lillback, Sr. VP/Global Head-Human Resource
Gregory L. Sheldon, Global CIO/Sr. VP
Rajiv Malik, Exec. VP/Head-Global Tech. Oper.
Joseph F. Haggerty, Global General Counsel/Sr. VP
Andrew G. Cuneo, VP-Global Bus. Dev.
Michael Laffin, Sr. VP-Global Public Affairs
Daniel E. Crookshank, VP-Investor Rel.
Daniel C. Rizzo Jr., Controller/Chief Acct. Officer/Sr. VP
Carolyn Meyers, Pres., Specialty
Harry A. Korman, Pres., North America
Brian Byala, Treas./Sr. VP
John Montgomery, Pres., APAC
Robert J. Coury, Chmn.
Didier Barret, Pres., EMEA

Phone: 724-514-1800	Fax: 724-514-1870
Toll-Free:	
Address: 1500 Corporate Dr., Canonsburg, PA 15317 US	

GROWTH PLANS/SPECIAL FEATURES:

Mylan, Inc., formerly Mylan Laboratories, Inc., develops, licenses, manufactures, distributes and markets generic/branded generic pharmaceutical products and active pharmaceutical ingredients (APIs). The company reports as three segments: Generics, Matrix and Specialty. The generics segment operates in the U.S., Canada, Europe, the Middle East, Africa, Australia, Japan and New Zealand. In the U.S., this segment markets over 200 products through four subsidiaries: Mylan Pharmaceuticals Inc. (MPI), which sells solid oral dosage products; UDL Laboratories, Inc., which re-packages and markets products obtained from MPI and third parties; Genpharm ULC, which sells generic prescriptions for all major therapeutic needs; and Mylan Technologies, Inc., which develops and markets transdermal patches. Generic international operations primarily consist of subsidiaries that the firm acquired as part of the Merck Generics acquisition. All together, the generics business derives roughly 31% of its revenues from calcium channel blockers and 29% from narcotic agonist analgesics. Mylan's Matrix segment, operated by its 71.5 %-owned subsidiary Matrix Laboratories Limited, is a leading manufacturer of APIs. Matrix currently has over 200 APIs in the market or under development, including anti-bacterials; central nervous system agents; anti-histamines; cardiovasculars; anti-virals; anti-diabetics; anti-fungals; proton pump inhibitors; pain management drugs; and anti-retrovirals used in the treatment of HIV. These products are used in Mylan pharmaceuticals or sold to third parties. This segment also includes the Docpharma subsidiary, which is a distributor of pharmaceutical products in the Benelux region of Europe. Lastly, the specialty segment is conducted by Dey, which focuses on the respiratory and severe allergy markets. Its principal products are EpiPen, for severe allergic reactions; and Performist Inhalation Solution, a formoterol fumarate inhalation solution. In July 2008, Mylan bought Watson Pharmaceuticals' 50% interest in joint venture Somerset Pharmaceuticals, Inc. (now a wholly-owned subsidiary of Mylan).

FINANCIALS: Sales and profits are in thousands of dollars—add 000 to get the full amount. 2008 Note: Financial information for 2008 was not available for all companies at press time.

2008 Sales: $5,137,585	2008 Profits: $-181,215	U.S. Stock Ticker: MYL
2007 Sales: $1,611,819	2007 Profits: $217,284	Int'l Ticker: Int'l Exchange:
2006 Sales: $1,257,164	2006 Profits: $184,542	Employees: 15,000
2005 Sales: $1,253,374	2005 Profits: $203,592	Fiscal Year Ends: 12/31
2004 Sales: $1,374,617	2004 Profits: $334,609	Parent Company:

SALARIES/BENEFITS:

Pension Plan:	ESOP Stock Plan:	Profit Sharing:	Top Exec. Salary: $1,500,000	Bonus: $3,750,000
Savings Plan: Y	Stock Purch. Plan:		Second Exec. Salary: $500,000	Bonus: $1,000,000

OTHER THOUGHTS:

Apparent Women Officers or Directors: 4
Hot Spot for Advancement for Women/Minorities: Y

LOCATIONS: ("Y" = Yes)

West:	Southwest:	Midwest:	Southeast:	Northeast:	International:
	Y	Y		Y	Y

Note: Financial information, benefits and other data can change quickly and may vary from those stated here.

NATIONAL OILWELL VARCO INC

www.nov.com

Industry Group Code: 213112 Ranks within this company's industry group: Sales: 9 Profits: 2

Management:		Sales/Marketing:		Liberal Arts:		Information Systems:		Professionals:		Tech./Scientific:	
Management Trainees:	Y	Marketing Pros.:	Y	Gen. Writing/Editing:		Info. Management:	Y	Finance/Acct.:	Y	Engineers, Electrical:	Y
Experienced Mngmt.:	Y	Retail Sales:		Technical Writing:	Y	Software Dev.:	Y	Law:	Y	Engineers, Other:	Y
International Business:	Y	Commercial/Industrial:	Y	Graphic Arts/Photog.:		Hardware Dev.:		HR/Other:	Y	Health/Lab:	
MBA Grads:	Y	Sales Trainees:		Music:		Consulting/Other:		Training:	Y	Scientists/Research:	
		Advertising Pros.:		Broadcasting:				Health Care:		Petroleum/Chemicals:	Y
				Other:				Consulting:		Math/Other:	

TYPES OF BUSINESS:
Oil & Gas Drilling Equipment & Systems
Distribution & Logistics Services
IT Services

BRANDS/DIVISIONS/AFFILIATES:
Grant Prideco Inc
ASEP Group Holding B.V.
Anson Limited

CONTACTS: *Note: Officers with more than one job title may be intentionally listed here more than once.*
Merrill (Pete) Miller, Jr., CEO
Merrill (Pete) Miller, Jr., Pres.
Clay C. Williams, CFO/Sr. VP
Hege Kverneland, CTO/VP
Dwight W. Rettig, General Counsel/VP
Robert Blanchard, Chief Acct. Officer/Corp. Controller/VP
Mark Reese, Pres., Rig Tech.
Haynes B. Smith, III, Pres., Svcs.
Merrill (Pete) Miller, Jr., Chmn.

Phone: 713-375-3700	**Fax:**
Toll-Free: 888-262-8645	
Address: 7909 Parkwood Circle Dr., Houston, TX 77036 US	

GROWTH PLANS/SPECIAL FEATURES:
National Oilwell Varco, Inc. designs, manufactures and sells equipment and components used in oil and gas drilling and production operations, and provides oilfield services and supply chain integration services to the upstream oil and gas industry, with operations in over 800 locations across six continents. The company operates through three business segments: rig technology; petroleum services and supplies; and distribution services. The firm's rig technology segment designs, manufactures, sells and services offshore and onshore drilling rigs; derricks; rig instrumentation systems; coiled tubing equipment and pressure pumping units; wireline winches; and cranes. Its operations extend to Canada, Norway, the U.K., India, China and Belarus. The petroleum services and supplies segment manufactures, rents and sells drill pipe, wired drill pipe, transfer pumps, solids control systems, drilling motors, drill bits and mud pump consumables. Its operations extend to Canada, the U.K., China, Kazakhstan, Mexico, Russia, Argentina, India, Bolivia, the Netherlands, Singapore, Malaysia, Vietnam and the United Arab Emirates. The company's distribution services segment provides maintenance, repair and operating supplies and spare parts to drill site and production locations throughout North America, Mexico, the Middle East, Europe, Southeast Asia and South America. Through its information technology platforms and processes, this segment provides complete procurement, inventory management and logistics services to its customers. In February 2008, the firm, in partnership with Fabtech International Limited, created a joint venture for rig up and structural refurbishment services in the Middle East and North African land rig markets. In April 2008, the company acquired Grant Prideco, Inc., a developer of drill stem technology. In November 2008, the firm signed an agreement with Schlumberger for the creation of an intelligent drill pipe joint venture. In April 2009, National Oilwell Varco acquired ASEP Group Holding B.V., a manufacturer of well service equipment; and Anson Limited, a manufacturer of flowline equipment.

FINANCIALS: Sales and profits are in thousands of dollars—add 000 to get the full amount. 2008 Note: Financial information for 2008 was not available for all companies at press time.

2008 Sales: $1,343,140	2008 Profits: $1,952,000	**U.S. Stock Ticker: NOV**
2007 Sales: $9,789,000	2007 Profits: $1,337,100	**Int'l Ticker:**　Int'l Exchange:
2006 Sales: $7,025,800	2006 Profits: $684,000	Employees: 40,205
2005 Sales: $4,644,500	2005 Profits: $286,900	Fiscal Year Ends: 12/31
2004 Sales: $2,318,100	2004 Profits: $115,200	Parent Company:

SALARIES/BENEFITS:

Pension Plan:	ESOP Stock Plan:	Profit Sharing:	Top Exec. Salary: $950,000	Bonus: $1,825,960
Savings Plan: Y	Stock Purch. Plan:		Second Exec. Salary: $550,000	Bonus: $845,708

OTHER THOUGHTS:
Apparent Women Officers or Directors:
Hot Spot for Advancement for Women/Minorities:

LOCATIONS: ("Y" = Yes)

West:	Southwest:	Midwest:	Southeast:	Northeast:	International:
Y	Y	Y	Y	Y	Y

NETAPP INC

www.netapp.com

Industry Group Code: 334112 Ranks within this company's industry group: Sales: 3 Profits: 3

Management:		Sales/Marketing:		Liberal Arts:		Information Systems:		Professionals:		Tech./Scientific:	
Management Trainees:	Y	Marketing Pros.:	Y	Gen. Writing/Editing:	Y	Info. Management:	Y	Finance/Acct.:	Y	Engineers, Electrical:	Y
Experienced Mngmt.:	Y	Retail Sales:		Technical Writing:	Y	Software Dev.:	Y	Law:	Y	Engineers, Other:	
International Business:	Y	Commercial/Industrial:	Y	Graphic Arts/Photog.:		Hardware Dev.:	Y	HR/Other:	Y	Health/Lab:	
MBA Grads:	Y	Sales Trainees:		Music:		Consulting/Other:		Training:	Y	Scientists/Research:	
		Advertising Pros.:	Y	Broadcasting:				Health Care:		Petroleum/Chemicals:	
				Other:				Consulting:		Math/Other:	

TYPES OF BUSINESS:

Data Management Solutions
Storage Solutions
Data Protection Software Products
Data Protection Platform Products
Storage Security Products
Data Retention & Archive Software Products
Storage Management & Application Software
Management Tools

BRANDS/DIVISIONS/AFFILIATES:

Data ONTAP
Network Appliance
NetCache
NetStore
NearStore
Data ONTAP
FlexVol
Onaro Inc

CONTACTS: Note: Officers with more than one job title may be intentionally listed here more than once.

Dan Warmenhoven, CEO
Tom Georgens, COO
Tom Georgens, Pres.
Steve Gomo, CFO/Exec. VP
Jay Kidd, Chief Mktg. Officer
Gwen McDonald, Sr. VP-Human Resources
Steve Kleiman, Chief Scientist/Sr. VP
Marina Levinson, CIO/Sr. VP
Rob Salmon, Exec. VP-Field Oper.
James Lau, Chief Strategy Officer/Exec. VP
Steve Gomo, Exec. VP-Finance
Ed Deenihan, Exec. VP-NetApp Global Svcs.
Mark Jon Bluth, Sr. VP-Oper.
Rich Clifton, Gen. Mgr.-Virtualization & Grid Infrastructures
D. Patrick Linehan, Sr. VP-Worldwide Sales
Dan Warmenhoven, Chmn.

Phone: 408-822-6000	Fax: 408-822-4501
Toll-Free:	
Address: 495 E. Java Dr., Sunnyvale, CA 94089 US	

GROWTH PLANS/SPECIAL FEATURES:

NetApp, Inc. (formerly Network Appliance, Inc.) is a provider of data management solutions. The NetApp enterprise-class storage solutions are interoperable across all platforms. The storage solutions are all based on Data ONTAP, an optimized, scalable and flexible operating system that supports any mix of SAN, NAS and IP SAN environments concurrently. Data ONTAP software platform integrates seamlessly into UNIX, Linux, Windows and Web environments. The Data ONTAP operating system provides the foundation to build storage infrastructure and an enterprise-wide data fabric for business applications. It includes the patented NetApp WAFL (Write Anywhere File Layout) file management system and the RADI-DP (RAID Double Parity), a double-parity software RAID architecture. It supports all of the major industry-standard protocols' storage, as well as a suite of data management, data replication and data protection software products. The firm offers a variety of data management tools and software, including the FlexVol technology, which enables storage architectures to be more efficient and achieve higher utilization using flexible volumes that do not require repartitioning of physical storage space; FlexClone technology, which enables data cloning or the instant replication of data volumes and data sets; Deduplication technology, which provides the ability to eliminate duplicate data within primary and secondary disk storage environments; FlexShare technology, which directs how storage system resources are used to deliver an appropriate level of service for each application; FlexCache technology, which allows the creation of read-writeable replicas of volumes by creating caching volumes on multiple storage controllers; and MultiStore software, which allows for the creation of separate logical partitions in storage systems and network storage resources. In January 2008, NetApp acquired Onaro, a privately owned firm located in Massachusetts.

NetApp offers employees medical, dental and vision insurance; flexible spending account; mass transit/parking account; an employee assistance program; an employee stock purchase plan; paid volunteer days, adoption assistance; and educational assistance.

FINANCIALS: Sales and profits are in thousands of dollars—add 000 to get the full amount. 2008 Note: Financial information for 2008 was not available for all companies at press time.

2008 Sales: $3,303,167	2008 Profits: $309,738	**U.S. Stock Ticker:** NTAP
2007 Sales: $2,804,282	2007 Profits: $297,735	**Int'l Ticker:** Int'l Exchange:
2006 Sales: $2,066,456	2006 Profits: $266,452	Employees: 7,976
2005 Sales: $1,598,131	2005 Profits: $225,754	Fiscal Year Ends: 4/30
2004 Sales: $1,170,310	2004 Profits: $152,087	Parent Company:

SALARIES/BENEFITS:

Pension Plan:	ESOP Stock Plan:	Profit Sharing:	Top Exec. Salary: $786,538	Bonus: $507,160
Savings Plan: Y	Stock Purch. Plan: Y		Second Exec. Salary: $582,500	Bonus: $346,704

OTHER THOUGHTS:

Apparent Women Officers or Directors: 3
Hot Spot for Advancement for Women/Minorities: Y

LOCATIONS: ("Y" = Yes)

West:	Southwest:	Midwest:	Southeast:	Northeast:	International:
Y				Y	Y

Note: Financial information, benefits and other data can change quickly and may vary from those stated here.

NEWS CORP

www.newscorp.com

Industry Group Code: 515120 **Ranks within this company's industry group:** Sales: 1   Profits: 1

Management:		Sales/Marketing:		Liberal Arts:		Information Systems:		Professionals:		Tech./Scientific:	
Management Trainees:	Y	Marketing Pros.:	Y	Gen. Writing/Editing:	Y	Info. Management:	Y	Finance/Acct.:	Y	Engineers, Electrical:	Y
Experienced Mngmt.:	Y	Retail Sales:		Technical Writing:		Software Dev.:	Y	Law:	Y	Engineers, Other:	
International Business:	Y	Commercial/Industrial:	Y	Graphic Arts/Photog.:	Y	Hardware Dev.:		HR/Other:	Y	Health/Lab:	
MBA Grads:	Y	Sales Trainees:		Music:	Y	Consulting/Other:		Training:	Y	Scientists/Research:	
		Advertising Pros.:	Y	Broadcasting:	Y			Health Care:		Petroleum/Chemicals:	
				Other:	Y			Consulting:		Math/Other:	

TYPES OF BUSINESS:

Television Broadcasting & Distribution
Film & Television Production
Newspaper Publishing
Online Media
Advertising Services
Magazine & Book Publishing
Satellite Television

BRANDS/DIVISIONS/AFFILIATES:

MySpace
Intermix Media
Fox Entertainment Group Inc
Fox Broadcasting Company
HarperCollins Publishers Inc
Fox Sports Net Inc
IGN Entertainment
Dow Jones & Co Inc

CONTACTS: *Note: Officers with more than one job title may be intentionally listed here more than once.*

K. Rupert Murdoch, CEO
Chase Carey, COO
Chase Carey, Pres.
David F. DeVoe, CFO/Sr. Exec. VP
Gary Ginsberg, Exec. VP-Global Mktg.
Beryl Cook, Chief Human Resources Officer
Lawrence A. Jacobs, General Counsel/Sr. Exec. VP
Jon Miller, Chief Digital Officer
Gary Ginsberg, Exec. VP-Corp. Affairs
Anthea Disney, Exec. VP-Content
Michael Regan, Exec. VP-Gov't Affairs
Genie Gavenchak, Chief Compliance & Ethics Officer/Sr. VP
Mark Williams, CFO-Europe & Asia
K. Rupert Murdoch, Chmn.
James Murdoch, Chmn./CEO-Europe & Asia

Phone: 212-852-7000	Fax: 212-852-7147
Toll-Free:	
Address: 1211 Ave. of the Americas, 8th Fl., New York, NY 10036 US	

GROWTH PLANS/SPECIAL FEATURES:

News Corp. is an entertainment company operating in: filmed entertainment; television; cable network programming; direct broadcast satellite television; magazines and inserts; newspapers; book publishing; and other. The filmed entertainment segment produces and acquires live-action and animated motion pictures for distribution and licensing in all formats; and produces and licenses television programming worldwide. Subsidiaries include Fox Filmed Entertainment and Twentieth Century Fox Television. The television segment operates broadcast television stations; broadcasts network programming in the U.S.; and develops, produces and broadcasts television programming in Asia. The cable networking programming division produces and licenses news, sports, general entertainment and movie programming for distributors worldwide. The direct broadcast satellite television segment operates through SKY Italia, which currently distributes services via satellite and broadband to subscribers in Italy. The magazines and inserts group engages in marketing operations, primarily the publication of free standing inserts and the provision of in-store marketing products and services; and magazine publishing, such as The Weekly Standard. The newspapers segment publishes newspapers and magazines in the U.K., Ireland, Australia and the U.S., including The Sun, News of the World and the New York Post. The book publishing division operates through HarperCollins Publishers, which primarily publishes fiction and non-fiction for the general consumer. The other segment includes News' Internet businesses, including Myspace.com; interests in various companies; and other operations. In December 2007, News acquired Dow Jones & Co., Inc. In February 2008, Liberty Media Corp. received News' 41% stake in DIRECTV, $625 million in cash and three regional sports networks for Liberty's $10.1 billion stake in News itself. In May 2008, the firm increased its ownership of Premiere AG, a German pay-TV operator, to 25.01% and acquired the remaining 30% interest in TV Riga, a Latvian-Russian broadcaster. In October 2008, the firm acquired the remaining 49% of Jamba from VeriSign, Inc.

FINANCIALS: Sales and profits are in thousands of dollars—add 000 to get the full amount. 2008 Note: Financial information for 2008 was not available for all companies at press time.

2008 Sales: $32,996,000	2008 Profits: $5,381,000	**U.S. Stock Ticker: NWS**
2007 Sales: $28,655,000	2007 Profits: $3,426,000	Int'l Ticker: Int'l Exchange:
2006 Sales: $25,327,000	2006 Profits: $2,314,000	Employees: 55,000
2005 Sales: $23,859,000	2005 Profits: $2,128,000	Fiscal Year Ends: 6/30
2004 Sales: $20,959,000	2004 Profits: $1,647,000	Parent Company:

SALARIES/BENEFITS:

Pension Plan:	ESOP Stock Plan:	Profit Sharing:	Top Exec. Salary: $8,100,000	Bonus: $5,435,000
Savings Plan: Y	Stock Purch. Plan:		Second Exec. Salary: $8,100,000	Bonus: $11,250,000

OTHER THOUGHTS:

Apparent Women Officers or Directors: 3
Hot Spot for Advancement for Women/Minorities: Y

LOCATIONS: ("Y" = Yes)

West:	Southwest:	Midwest:	Southeast:	Northeast:	International:
Y	Y	Y	Y	Y	Y

NII HOLDINGS INC

www.nii.com

Industry Group Code: 5172 Ranks within this company's industry group: Sales: 4 Profits: 2

Management:		Sales/Marketing:		Liberal Arts:		Information Systems:		Professionals:		Tech./Scientific:	
Management Trainees:	Y	Marketing Pros.:	Y	Gen. Writing/Editing:	Y	Info. Management:	Y	Finance/Acct.:	Y	Engineers, Electrical:	Y
Experienced Mngmt.:	Y	Retail Sales:		Technical Writing:	Y	Software Dev.:	Y	Law:	Y	Engineers, Other:	Y
International Business:	Y	Commercial/Industrial:	Y	Graphic Arts/Photog.:	Y	Hardware Dev.:		HR/Other:	Y	Health/Lab:	
MBA Grads:	Y	Sales Trainees:		Music:		Consulting/Other:		Training:	Y	Scientists/Research:	
		Advertising Pros.:	Y	Broadcasting:				Health Care:		Petroleum/Chemicals:	
				Other:				Consulting:		Math/Other:	

TYPES OF BUSINESS:

Cell Phone Service
GPS Technologies
Internet Service

BRANDS/DIVISIONS/AFFILIATES:

Motorola Inc
iDEN
Nextel Direct Connect
International Direct Connect
Nextel Online
BlackBerry Curve 8350i
Sprint Nextel Corp
TELUS Corporation

CONTACTS: Note: Officers with more than one job title may be intentionally listed here more than once.

Steven P. Dussek, CEO
Gokul V. Hemmady, CFO/VP
Gregory J. Santoro, Chief Mktg. Officer
Alfonso Martinez, VP-Human Resources
Alan Strauss, CTO/VP
Alan Strauss, VP-Eng.
Gary Begeman, General Counsel/VP
John M. McMahon, VP-Bus. Oper.
Gregory J. Santoro, Chief Strategy Officer
Claudia E. Restrepo, Dir.-Corp. Comm.
Tim Perrott, Dir.-Investor Rel.
Catherine Neel, Controller/VP
Miguel E. Rivera, Pres., Nextel Peru
Sergio Borges Chaia, CEO/Pres., Nextel Brazil
Ruben Butvilofsky, Pres., Nextel Argentina
Jose Felipe, Pres., Mercosur
Steven M. Shindler, Chmn.
Peter A. Foyo, Pres., Nextel Mexico

GROWTH PLANS/SPECIAL FEATURES:

NII Holdings, Inc., provides digital wireless communication services through operating companies located in selected Latin American markets. Based in Virginia, the firm operates through five major divisions named for their geographic area: Nextel Mexico, Nextel Chile, Nextel Brazil, Nextel Argentina and Nextel Peru. The company uses a transmission technology developed by Motorola, Inc., called integrated digital enhanced network (iDEN), to provide its digital mobile services on 800 MHz spectrum holdings throughout its market area. This technology allows NII to use its spectrum efficiently and to offer multiple wireless services integrated into a variety of handset devices. Services offered by NII include mobile telephone, Nextel Direct Connect, international roaming, International Direct Connect, global positioning system (GPS) technologies, text messaging and e-mail. The company's mobile telephone service includes such features as speakerphone, conference calling, voice mail, call forwarding and additional line service. Nextel Direct Connect is a long-range walkie-talkie service enabling users to set up a conference more quickly than would be possible with a traditional mobile telephone call. International Direct Connect allows subscribers to communicate instantly across national borders with other subscribers in Mexico, Brazil, Argentina, Peru and Chile; any Sprint Nextel Corporation subscriber in the U.S. and TELUS subscriber in Canada using a compatible handset. NII's operating companies have approximately 6.2 million digital handsets in commercial service. In February 2009, the firm, through Nextel Argentina, Nextel Peru, Nextel Mexico and Nextel Brazil, released the BlackBerry Curve 8350i smartphone; the product offers a Push-to-Talk feature and several other multimedia capabilities.

Phone: 703-390-5100	Fax: 703-547-5269
Toll-Free:	
Address: 1875 Explorer St., Ste. 1000, Reston, VA 20190 US	

FINANCIALS: Sales and profits are in thousands of dollars—add 000 to get the full amount. 2008 Note: Financial information for 2008 was not available for all companies at press time.

2008 Sales: $2,371,340	2008 Profits: $294,490	**U.S. Stock Ticker: NIHD**
2007 Sales: $3,296,295	2007 Profits: $378,418	**Int'l Ticker:** Int'l Exchange:
2006 Sales: $2,371,340	2006 Profits: $294,490	Employees: 12,299
2005 Sales: $1,745,839	2005 Profits: $174,781	Fiscal Year Ends: 12/31
2004 Sales: $1,279,908	2004 Profits: $57,289	Parent Company:

SALARIES/BENEFITS:

Pension Plan:	ESOP Stock Plan:	Profit Sharing:	Top Exec. Salary: $720,000	Bonus: $581,760
Savings Plan:	Stock Purch. Plan:		Second Exec. Salary: $648,317	Bonus: $673,670

OTHER THOUGHTS:

Apparent Women Officers or Directors: 3
Hot Spot for Advancement for Women/Minorities: Y

LOCATIONS: ("Y" = Yes)

West:	Southwest:	Midwest:	Southeast:	Northeast:	International:
				Y	Y

NIKE INC
www.nike.com

Industry Group Code: 316219 Ranks within this company's industry group: Sales: 1 Profits: 1

Management:		Sales/Marketing:		Liberal Arts:		Information Systems:		Professionals:		Tech./Scientific:	
Management Trainees:	Y	Marketing Pros.:	Y	Gen. Writing/Editing:	Y	Info. Management:	Y	Finance/Acct.:	Y	Engineers, Electrical:	
Experienced Mngmt.:	Y	Retail Sales:	Y	Technical Writing:		Software Dev.:	Y	Law:	Y	Engineers, Other:	
International Business:	Y	Commercial/Industrial:	Y	Graphic Arts/Photog.:	Y	Hardware Dev.:		HR/Other:	Y	Health/Lab:	
MBA Grads:	Y	Sales Trainees:	Y	Music:		Consulting/Other:		Training:	Y	Scientists/Research:	
		Advertising Pros.:	Y	Broadcasting:				Health Care:		Petroleum/Chemicals:	
				Other:	Y			Consulting:		Math/Other:	

TYPES OF BUSINESS:

Athletic Shoes/Apparel Manufacturing
Athletic Equipment
Sports Accessories
Retail Stores
Sports Apparel
Plastic Products
Hockey Products
Swimwear

BRANDS/DIVISIONS/AFFILIATES:

Cole Haan Holdings, Inc.
Nike Bayer Hockey Corp.
Nike Bauer Hockey U.S.A., Inc
Converse Inc
Hurley International, LLC
Chuck Taylor
Bragano
All Star

CONTACTS: *Note: Officers with more than one job title may be intentionally listed here more than once.*

Mark G. Parker, CEO
Mark G. Parker, Pres.
Donald Blair, CFO/VP
John F. Slusher, VP-Global Sports Mktg.
Ronald D. McCray, Chief Admin. Officer/VP
Gary M. DeStefano, VP/Pres., Global Oper.
Bernard F. Pliska, VP/Corp. Controller
Charlie Denson, Pres., Nike Brand
Trevor A. Edwards, VP-Global Brand & Category Mgmt.
Eric D. Sprunk, VP-Global Footwear
Peter Hudson, VP-Footwear Design
Philip H. Knight, Chmn.
Nick Athanasakos, VP-Global Supply Chain

Phone: 503-671-2500	Fax:
Toll-Free: 800-344-6453	
Address: 1 Bowerman Dr., Beaverton, OR 97005 US	

GROWTH PLANS/SPECIAL FEATURES:

Nike, Inc. designs, develops and markets footwear, apparel, equipment and accessories. It is one of the largest sellers of athletic footwear and athletic apparel in the world. The company's athletic footwear products are designed primarily for specific athletic use, although a large percentage of the products are worn for casual or leisure purposes. Running, training, basketball, soccer, sport-inspired urban shoes and children's shoes are the firm's top-selling product categories. Nike also markets shoes designed for tennis, golf, baseball, football, lacrosse, walking, outdoor activities, skateboarding, bicycling, volleyball, wrestling, cheerleading, aquatic activities and other athletic and recreational uses. The firm maintains several wholly-owned subsidiaries including Cole Haan, a line of casual footwear, apparel and accessories for men and women; Converse, Inc., a line of footwear, apparel and accessories; Hurley International LLC, a collection of action sports apparel; and Umbro Ltd., a line of athletic and casual footwear, apparel and equipment, primarily for soccer. Nike sells its products to retail accounts, through Nike-owned retail stores and through a mix of independent distributors and licensees, in more than 180 countries. Within the U.S., the firm operates 296 Nike Brand and subsidiary retail stores. U.S. sales generate approximately 43% of the firm's total revenues. In the international market, which includes several countries within Europe, Asia, South America, and Africa, the firm maintains 260 retail stores. The international market accounts for 57% of total revenues. In March 2008, the firm acquired Umbro Ltd., a line that designs, distributes, and licenses athletic and casual footwear, apparel and equipment.

The company offers employees medical coverage; life insurance; a profit sharing retirement program; fitness center memberships; a 401(k) plan; employee stock purchase plan; an annual performance sharing plan; scholarships for children of employees; adoption assistance; tuition assistance; employee discounts; and an employee assistance plan.

FINANCIALS: Sales and profits are in thousands of dollars—add 000 to get the full amount. 2008 Note: Financial information for 2008 was not available for all companies at press time.

2008 Sales: $18,627,000	2008 Profits: $1,883,400	**U.S. Stock Ticker: NKE**
2007 Sales: $16,325,900	2007 Profits: $1,491,500	**Int'l Ticker:** Int'l Exchange:
2006 Sales: $14,954,900	2006 Profits: $1,392,000	Employees: 34,300
2005 Sales: $13,739,700	2005 Profits: $1,211,600	Fiscal Year Ends: 5/31
2004 Sales: $12,253,100	2004 Profits: $945,600	Parent Company:

SALARIES/BENEFITS:

Pension Plan:	ESOP Stock Plan:	Profit Sharing: Y	Top Exec. Salary: $1,376,923	Bonus: $2,682,684
Savings Plan: Y	Stock Purch. Plan: Y		Second Exec. Salary: $1,192,308	Bonus: $2,222,727

OTHER THOUGHTS:

Apparent Women Officers or Directors: 14
Hot Spot for Advancement for Women/Minorities: Y

LOCATIONS: ("Y" = Yes)

West:	Southwest:	Midwest:	Southeast:	Northeast:	International:
Y	Y	Y	Y	Y	Y

NOBLE CORPORATION

www.noblecorp.com

Industry Group Code: 213112 Ranks within this company's industry group: Sales: 5 Profits: 3

Management:		Sales/Marketing:		Liberal Arts:		Information Systems:		Professionals:		Tech./Scientific:	
Management Trainees:	Y	Marketing Pros.:	Y	Gen. Writing/Editing:		Info. Management:	Y	Finance/Acct.:	Y	Engineers, Electrical:	Y
Experienced Mngmt.:	Y	Retail Sales:		Technical Writing:	Y	Software Dev.:	Y	Law:	Y	Engineers, Other:	Y
International Business:	Y	Commercial/Industrial:	Y	Graphic Arts/Photog.:		Hardware Dev.:		HR/Other:	Y	Health/Lab:	
MBA Grads:	Y	Sales Trainees:		Music:		Consulting/Other:		Training:	Y	Scientists/Research:	
		Advertising Pros.:		Broadcasting:				Health Care:		Petroleum/Chemicals:	Y
				Other:				Consulting:		Math/Other:	

TYPES OF BUSINESS:

Oil & Gas Services
Drilling Services

BRANDS/DIVISIONS/AFFILIATES:

Noble Drilling Holding LLC

CONTACTS: Note: Officers with more than one job title may be intentionally listed here more than once.

David W. Williams, CEO
David W. Williams, Pres.
Thomas L. Mitchell, CFO/Sr. VP
William E. Turcotte, General Counsel/Sr. VP
Donald Jacobsen, Sr. VP-Oper.
Lee M. Ahlstrom, VP-Planning
Lee M. Ahlstrom, VP-Investor Rel.
Thomas L. Mitchell, Controller/Treas.
Julie J. Robertson, Exec. VP/Corp. Sec.
Brook Wootton, Dir.-Investor Rel.
David W. Williams, Chmn.

Phone: 41-22-560-6035	Fax:
Toll-Free:	
Address: 4-6 Ave. Industrielle, Geneva, CH-1227 Switzerland	

GROWTH PLANS/SPECIAL FEATURES:

Noble Corporation provides contract drilling services for the oil and gas industry through its fleet of 62 mobile offshore drilling units located in key markets worldwide. The fleet includes 43 jackup drilling rigs, 13 semi-submersible rigs, four dynamically positioned drillships and three submersible drilling platforms, with four rigs currently under construction. Approximately 87% of Noble's fleet is deployed in international markets including the Middle East, India, Mexico, the North Sea, Brazil and West Africa; and offshore drilling accounts for approximately 98% of the company's revenue. Contracts with Petroleos Mexicanos (PEMEX), a Mexican oil company, accounted for 20% of 2008 revenue. Unlike other firms in the industry, Noble generally buys only specially contracted rigs, and not those built on speculation. In January 2008, the company sold its North Sea labor contract drilling services business to Seawell Holding UK Limited for approximately $35 million. In September 2008, the firm's indirect subsidiary, Noble Drilling Holding LLC, signed an agreement with STX Heavy Industries Co., Ltd., for the construction of a new ultra-deepwater Globetrotter-class drillship. In March 2009, Noble changed its place of incorporation from the Cayman Islands to Switzerland.

FINANCIALS: Sales and profits are in thousands of dollars—add 000 to get the full amount. 2008 Note: Financial information for 2008 was not available for all companies at press time.

2008 Sales: $3,446,501	2008 Profits: $1,560,995	**U.S. Stock Ticker: NE**
2007 Sales: $2,995,311	2007 Profits: $1,206,011	**Int'l Ticker:** Int'l Exchange:
2006 Sales: $2,100,239	2006 Profits: $731,866	Employees: 6,000
2005 Sales: $1,382,137	2005 Profits: $296,696	Fiscal Year Ends: 12/31
2004 Sales: $1,066,231	2004 Profits: $146,086	Parent Company:

SALARIES/BENEFITS:

Pension Plan:	ESOP Stock Plan:	Profit Sharing:	Top Exec. Salary: $765,001	Bonus: $1,223,750
Savings Plan:	Stock Purch. Plan:		Second Exec. Salary: $452,500	Bonus: $540,000

OTHER THOUGHTS:

Apparent Women Officers or Directors: 4
Hot Spot for Advancement for Women/Minorities: Y

LOCATIONS: ("Y" = Yes)

West:	Southwest:	Midwest:	Southeast:	Northeast:	International:
	Y		Y		Y

NORTHROP GRUMMAN CORP

www.northropgrumman.com

Industry Group Code: 33641 **Ranks within this company's industry group:** Sales: 5 Profits: 9

Management:		Sales/Marketing:		Liberal Arts:		Information Systems:		Professionals:		Tech./Scientific:	
Management Trainees:	Y	Marketing Pros.:	Y	Gen. Writing/Editing:	Y	Info. Management:	Y	Finance/Acct.:	Y	Engineers, Electrical:	Y
Experienced Mngmt.:	Y	Retail Sales:		Technical Writing:	Y	Software Dev.:	Y	Law:	Y	Engineers, Other:	Y
International Business:	Y	Commercial/Industrial:	Y	Graphic Arts/Photog.:	Y	Hardware Dev.:	Y	HR/Other:	Y	Health/Lab:	
MBA Grads:	Y	Sales Trainees:		Music:		Consulting/Other:	Y	Training:	Y	Scientists/Research:	Y
		Advertising Pros.:	Y	Broadcasting:				Health Care:		Petroleum/Chemicals:	
				Other:				Consulting:		Math/Other:	Y

TYPES OF BUSINESS:

Aerospace & Defense Technology
Shipbuilding & Engineering
Aircraft Manufacturing
Electronic Systems & Components
Hardware & Software Manufacturing
Design & Engineering Services
IT Systems & Services
Nuclear-Powered Aircraft Carriers & Submarines

BRANDS/DIVISIONS/AFFILIATES:

F/A-18
F-35
B-2
Multi-Platform Radar Technology Insertion Program
Global Hawk
James Webb Space Telescope
Airborne Laser
EA-6B

CONTACTS: *Note: Officers with more than one job title may be intentionally listed here more than once.*

Ronald D. Sugar, CEO
Wes Bush, COO
Wes Bush, Pres.
James F. Palmer, CFO/Corp. VP
Ian V. Ziskin, Chief Human Resources Officer/Corp. VP
Linda A. Mills, Corp. VP/Pres., Info. Systems
Alexis Livanos, CTO/Corp. VP
Ian V. Ziskin, Chief Admin. Officer
Stephen D. Yslas, General Counsel/Corp. VP
Darryl M. Fraser, Corp. VP-Comm.
Kenneth N. Heintz, Chief Acct. Officer/Controller/Corp. VP
Robert W. Helm, Corp. VP-Gov't Rel.
James F. Pitts, Corp. VP/Pres., Electronic Systems
Mike Petters, Corp. VP/Pres., Shipbuilding
Gary W. Ervin, Corp. VP/Pres., Aerospace Systems
Ronald D. Sugar, Chmn.

Phone: 310-553-6262	**Fax:** 310-553-2076
Toll-Free:	
Address: 1840 Century Park E., Los Angeles, CA 90067-2199 US	

GROWTH PLANS/SPECIAL FEATURES:

Northrop Grumman Corp. is a global aerospace and defense technology company. It has five primary businesses: Information Systems, Aerospace Systems, Electronic Systems, Shipbuilding and Technical Services. Information Systems encompasses two divisions: Mission Systems and Information Technology (IT). Mission Systems offers land forces and global combat support, satellite ground stations and signals intelligence. The IT division offers data analysis; document management; data center, IT security, storage and help desk management; in addition to R&D and test and education centers. Aerospace Systems encompasses Space Technology and Integrated Systems. The Space Technology division's major projects include the James Webb Space Telescope; Space Tracking and Surveillance System; and the Airborne Laser. Integrated Systems has two business areas. Integrated Systems Western Region is focused on the F/A-18, F-35 and B-2 manned aircraft programs; the Multi-Platform Radar Technology Insertion Program (MP-RTIP); and the Global Hawk and Fire Scout unmanned vehicle programs. Integrated Systems Eastern Region produced the E-2C Hawkeye command plane; and developed the EA-6B (Prowler) offensive tactical radar jamming aircraft. Electronic Systems offers missile tracking and warning systems; fire control radars; advanced simulation systems; infrared detection and countermeasures systems; night vision goggles; laser designators; Chemical, Biological, Radiological, Nuclear and Explosive (CBRNE) material detection and alert systems; U.S. Postal Service bio-detection systems; and power generation systems for aircraft carriers. The Shipbuilding business designs, builds, maintains and refuels nuclear-powered aircraft carriers; and designs and constructs amphibious assault ships, Aegis guided missile destroyers, nuclear-powered submarines and oil tankers. Technical Services offers base support, including civil engineering, and support functions, including space launch services, combat vehicle maintenance and protective and emergency services. It also covers training and simulation services. In 2009, the company began planning to sell its consulting and engineering service division, TASC.

FINANCIALS: Sales and profits are in thousands of dollars—add 000 to get the full amount. 2008 Note: Financial information for 2008 was not available for all companies at press time.

2008 Sales: $33,887,000	2008 Profits: $-1,281,000	**U.S. Stock Ticker:** NOC
2007 Sales: $31,828,000	2007 Profits: $1,811,000	**Int'l Ticker:** Int'l Exchange:
2006 Sales: $29,991,000	2006 Profits: $1,593,000	**Employees:** 123,600
2005 Sales: $29,978,000	2005 Profits: $1,400,000	**Fiscal Year Ends:** 12/31
2004 Sales: $29,000,000	2004 Profits: $1,080,000	**Parent Company:**

SALARIES/BENEFITS:

Pension Plan: Y	ESOP Stock Plan:	Profit Sharing:	Top Exec. Salary: $1,525,000	Bonus: $2,775,500
Savings Plan: Y	Stock Purch. Plan:		Second Exec. Salary: $938,462	Bonus: $1,197,000

OTHER THOUGHTS:

Apparent Women Officers or Directors: 3
Hot Spot for Advancement for Women/Minorities: Y

LOCATIONS: ("Y" = Yes)

West:	Southwest:	Midwest:	Southeast:	Northeast:	International:
Y	Y	Y	Y	Y	Y

Note: Financial information, benefits and other data can change quickly and may vary from those stated here.

NRG ENERGY INC

www.nrgenergy.com

Industry Group Code: 221   **Ranks within this company's industry group:** Sales: 10   Profits:

Management:		Sales/Marketing:		Liberal Arts:		Information Systems:		Professionals:		Tech./Scientific:	
Management Trainees:	Y	Marketing Pros.:	Y	Gen. Writing/Editing:	Y	Info. Management:	Y	Finance/Acct.:	Y	Engineers, Electrical:	Y
Experienced Mngmt.:	Y	Retail Sales:		Technical Writing:	Y	Software Dev.:	Y	Law:	Y	Engineers, Other:	Y
International Business:	Y	Commercial/Industrial:	Y	Graphic Arts/Photog.:	Y	Hardware Dev.:		HR/Other:	Y	Health/Lab:	
MBA Grads:	Y	Sales Trainees:		Music:		Consulting/Other:		Training:	Y	Scientists/Research:	
		Advertising Pros.:		Broadcasting:				Health Care:		Petroleum/Chemicals:	
				Other:				Consulting:		Math/Other:	

TYPES OF BUSINESS:

Electricity Generation
Waste Energy
Energy Trading
Hydroelectric Generation
Operating & Maintenance Services
Steam Transmission
Heating & Cooling Systems

BRANDS/DIVISIONS/AFFILIATES:

Nuclear Innovation North America LLC
Wayzata Investment Partners LLC
Red Bluff
Chowchilla II
United Illuminating Company
Toshiba Corporation
South Texas Project
Padoma Wind Power LLC

CONTACTS: Note: Officers with more than one job title may be intentionally listed here more than once.

David Crane, CEO
Robert Flexon, COO/Exec. VP
David Crane, Pres.
Clint Freeland, CFO/Sr. VP
Kevin Howell, Chief Admin. Officer
Drew Murphy, General Counsel/Exec. VP
Mauricio Gutierrez, Sr. VP-Commercial Oper.
Jonathan Bailiff, Exec. VP-Strategy
Meredith Moore, VP-Comm.
James Ingoldsby, Chief Acct. Officer/VP
Kevin Howell, Exec. VP/Regional Pres., NRG Texas
Michael Liebelson, Exec. VP/Chief Dev. Officer, Low-Carbon Tech.
John Ragan, Exec. VP/Regional Pres., Northeast
Jeff Baudier, Sr. VP/Regional Pres., South Central
Howard E. Cosgrove, Chmn.

Phone: 609-524-4500	Fax: 609-524-4501
Toll-Free:	
Address: 211 Carnegie Center, Princeton, NJ 08540-6213 US	

GROWTH PLANS/SPECIAL FEATURES:

NRG Energy, Inc. is an independent wholesale power generation company primarily engaged in the ownership, development, construction and operation of power generation facilities; the transacting in and trading of fuel and transportation services; and the trading of energy, capacity and related products in the U.S. and select international markets. NRG has approximately 191 active operating generation units as 49 power generation plants, with an aggregate generation capacity of approximately 24,115 megawatts and approximately 740 megawatts under construction. Domestically, NRG has approximately 22,880 megawatts of generation capacity in 175 active generation units at 43 plants, primarily located in Texas, with approximately 10,805 megawatts, as well as the Northeast, South Central and Western regions of the U.S., with approximately 115 megawatts from the company's thermal assets. NRG's principal domestic power plants consist of natural gas-fired facilities, representing approximately 46% of its total domestic generation capacity; coal-fired facilities, representing 33%; oil-fired facilities, representing 16%; and nuclear facilities, representing 5%. In addition, 15% of NRG's domestic generating facilities have dual or multiple fuel capacity, which allows a plant to dispatch with the lowest cost fuel option, and consist primarily of baseload, intermediate and peaking power generation facilities, and also include thermal energy production plants. In February 2008, Padoma Wind Power LLC, a subsidiary of NRG, entered into a joint venture with BP Alternative Energy North America Inc. The two organizations will build the first phase of the Sherbino Wind Farm. In March 2008, NRG and Southern California Edison Co. entered into a 10-year power purchase agreement. NRG will provide 550 megawatts of power to over 400,000 homes. In March 2008, NRG formed Nuclear Innovation North America LLC, a company focused on marketing, siting, developing, financing and investing in nuclear projects.

FINANCIALS: Sales and profits are in thousands of dollars—add 000 to get the full amount. 2008 Note: Financial information for 2008 was not available for all companies at press time.

2008 Sales: $6,885,000	2008 Profits: $	**U.S. Stock Ticker:** NRG
2007 Sales: $5,989,000	2007 Profits: $586,000	**Int'l Ticker:** Int'l Exchange:
2006 Sales: $5,585,000	2006 Profits: $621,000	Employees: 3,526
2005 Sales: $2,430,000	2005 Profits: $84,000	Fiscal Year Ends: 12/31
2004 Sales: $2,348,000	2004 Profits: $185,617	Parent Company:

SALARIES/BENEFITS:

Pension Plan:	ESOP Stock Plan:	Profit Sharing:	Top Exec. Salary: $1,097,693	Bonus: $1,923,706
Savings Plan:	Stock Purch. Plan:		Second Exec. Salary: $648,154	Bonus: $908,226

OTHER THOUGHTS:

Apparent Women Officers or Directors: 1
Hot Spot for Advancement for Women/Minorities: Y

LOCATIONS: ("Y" = Yes)

West:	Southwest:	Midwest:	Southeast:	Northeast:	International:
Y	Y	Y	Y	Y	Y

Note: Financial information, benefits and other data can change quickly and may vary from those stated here.

OCCIDENTAL PETROLEUM CORP

www.oxy.com

Industry Group Code: 211111 Ranks within this company's industry group: Sales: 7   Profits: 3

Management:		Sales/Marketing:		Liberal Arts:		Information Systems:		Professionals:		Tech./Scientific:	
Management Trainees:	Y	Marketing Pros.:	Y	Gen. Writing/Editing:	Y	Info. Management:	Y	Finance/Acct.:	Y	Engineers, Electrical:	Y
Experienced Mngmt.:	Y	Retail Sales:		Technical Writing:	Y	Software Dev.:	Y	Law:	Y	Engineers, Other:	Y
International Business:	Y	Commercial/Industrial:		Graphic Arts/Photog.:		Hardware Dev.:		HR/Other:	Y	Health/Lab:	
MBA Grads:	Y	Sales Trainees:		Music:		Consulting/Other:		Training:	Y	Scientists/Research:	
		Advertising Pros.:		Broadcasting:				Health Care:		Petroleum/Chemicals:	Y
				Other:				Consulting:		Math/Other:	

TYPES OF BUSINESS:

Oil & Natural Gas Exploration & Production
Basic Chemicals
Vinyls

BRANDS/DIVISIONS/AFFILIATES:

OxyChem

CONTACTS: Note: Officers with more than one job title may be intentionally listed here more than once.

Ray R. Irani, CEO
Stephen I. Chazen, Pres.
Stephen I. Chazen, CFO
Martin A. Cozyn, Exec. VP-Human Resources
Donald P. de Brier, General Counsel/Exec. VP/Sec.
James M. Lienert, Exec. VP-Planning & Finance
Richard S. Kline, VP-Comm. & Public Affairs
Christopher G. Stavros, VP-Investor Rel.
Roy Pineci, Chief Acct. Officer/VP/Controller
B. Chuck Anderson, Pres., OxyChem
William E. Albrecht, Pres., Oxy Oil & Gas, USA
Anita Powers, VP/Exec. VP-Oxy Oil & Gas, Worldwide Exploration
Ray R. Irani, Chmn.
Edward A. Lowe, Pres., Oxy Oil and Gas, Int'l Prod./VP

Phone: 310-208-8800	Fax: 310-443-6690
Toll-Free:	
Address: 10889 Wilshire Blvd., Los Angeles, CA 90024-4201 US	

GROWTH PLANS/SPECIAL FEATURES:

Occidental Petroleum Corp. (OPC) explores for, develops, produces and markets crude oil and natural gas. The company also manufactures and markets basic chemicals, vinyls and specialty chemicals. The firm operates in two segments: Oil and gas; chemical, and midstream. The oil and gas segment has proven reserves of oil amounting to 2.98 billion barrels and of natural gas amounting to 9,202 billion cubic feet, including the reserves of its consolidated subsidiaries. OPC's primary domestic oil and gas operations are in California; the Hugoton field in Kansas and Oklahoma; and the Permian field in west Texas and New Mexico. International operations are principally located in Colombia, Argentina, Oman, Qatar, Libya and Yemen, with exploration interests in other countries. The firm's chemicals business, run by OxyChem, owns and operates 21 chemical manufacturing plants in the U.S. and three internationally. The segment produces chlorine; caustic soda; potassium chemicals for use in glass, fertilizer, cleaning products and rubber; and other chemicals including chlorinated isocyanurates, resorcinol and sodium silicates for use in pool sanitation, home soaps and detergents. The company is also a leading producer of vinyls for piping, medical, building and automotive products, focusing on polyvinyl chloride (PVC) resins and vinyl chloride monomers (VCM). The midstream segment gathers, treats, processes, and trades crude oil, natural gas, NGLs, condensate and carbon dioxide and generates and markets power. In April 2009, the company, along with Mubadala Development Company, signed an agreement with the National Oil and Gas Authority of Bahrain to develop a field in Bahrain.

OPC offers employees medical and dental insurance, matches contributions to a personal savings account, educational assistance and employee retirement accounts.

FINANCIALS: Sales and profits are in thousands of dollars—add 000 to get the full amount. 2008 Note: Financial information for 2008 was not available for all companies at press time.

2008 Sales: $24,217,000	2008 Profits: $6,857,000	U.S. Stock Ticker: OXY
2007 Sales: $18,784,000	2007 Profits: $5,400,000	Int'l Ticker: Int'l Exchange:
2006 Sales: $17,175,000	2006 Profits: $4,191,000	Employees: 10,400
2005 Sales: $15,208,000	2005 Profits: $5,281,000	Fiscal Year Ends: 12/31
2004 Sales: $11,368,000	2004 Profits: $2,568,000	Parent Company:

SALARIES/BENEFITS:

Pension Plan: Y	ESOP Stock Plan:	Profit Sharing:	Top Exec. Salary: $1,300,000	Bonus: $3,630,000
Savings Plan: Y	Stock Purch. Plan:		Second Exec. Salary: $800,000	Bonus: $1,450,000

OTHER THOUGHTS:

Apparent Women Officers or Directors: 2
Hot Spot for Advancement for Women/Minorities: Y

LOCATIONS: ("Y" = Yes)

West:	Southwest:	Midwest:	Southeast:	Northeast:	International:
Y	Y	Y	Y	Y	Y

OCEANEERING INTERNATIONAL INC

www.oceaneering.com

Industry Group Code: 213112 Ranks within this company's industry group: Sales: 8 Profits: 8

Management:		Sales/Marketing:		Liberal Arts:		Information Systems:		Professionals:		Tech./Scientific:	
Management Trainees:	Y	Marketing Pros.:	Y	Gen. Writing/Editing:		Info. Management:	Y	Finance/Acct.:	Y	Engineers, Electrical:	Y
Experienced Mngmt.:	Y	Retail Sales:		Technical Writing:	Y	Software Dev.:	Y	Law:	Y	Engineers, Other:	Y
International Business:	Y	Commercial/Industrial:	Y	Graphic Arts/Photog.:		Hardware Dev.:		HR/Other:	Y	Health/Lab:	
MBA Grads:	Y	Sales Trainees:		Music:		Consulting/Other:		Training:	Y	Scientists/Research:	
		Advertising Pros.:		Broadcasting:				Health Care:		Petroleum/Chemicals:	Y
				Other:				Consulting:		Math/Other:	

TYPES OF BUSINESS:

Oil & Gas Drilling Support Services
Subsea Construction
Engineered Services & Hardware
Maintenance & Repair Services
Production Systems
Remotely Operated Vehicles
Robotic Systems

BRANDS/DIVISIONS/AFFILIATES:

Oceaneering Intervention Engineering
Grayloc Products
Oceaneering Multiflex
Oceaneering Rotator
Advanced Technologies
Deepwater Technical Solutions

CONTACTS: Note: Officers with more than one job title may be intentionally listed here more than once.

T. Jay Collins, CEO
T. Jay Collins, Pres.
Marvin J. Migura, CFO/Sr. VP
Janet G. Charles, VP-Human Resources
Gregg K. Farris, VP-IT
F. Richard Frisbie, Sr. VP-Deepwater Tech.
George R. Haubenreich, Jr., General Counsel/Sr. VP/Sec.
Stephen E. Bradshaw, VP-Bus. Dev.
Jack Jurkoshek, Dir.-Investor Rel.
W. Cardon Gerner, Chief Acct. Officer/VP
M. Kevin McEvoy, Exec. VP
Kevin Kerins, Sr. VP-Remotely Operated Vehicles
Robert P. Mingoia, Treas./VP
Robert P. Moschetta, VP-Health Safety Environment
John R. Huff, Chmn.
Todd Hoefler, VP-Supply Chain Mgmt.

Phone: 713-329-4500	Fax: 713-329-4951
Toll-Free:	
Address: 11911 FM 529, Houston, TX 77041 US	

GROWTH PLANS/SPECIAL FEATURES:

Oceaneering International, Inc. primarily provides oilfield products and services worldwide to the oil and gas industry. The oil and gas business of the company has five segments: Remotely Operated Vehicles (ROVs), Subsea Products, Subsea Projects, Inspection and Mobile Offshore Production Systems (MOPS). The company uses submersible ROVs to support drilling and construction; pipeline inspection; and subsea production facility operation and maintenance. It designs and builds ROVs, owning a total of 227, one of the largest ROV fleets worldwide. The firm is an industry leader in providing ROV services on deepwater wells, a highly technically demanding operation. Its Subsea Products segment manufactures typically built-to-order items including hydraulic hoses, ROV tooling, control valves, production control equipment and pipeline repair systems. These products are manufactured mainly by the Oceaneering Intervention Engineering; Grayloc Products; Oceaneering Multiflex; and Oceaneering Rotator divisions. The Subsea Projects segment primarily operates in the Gulf of Mexico, offering subsea installation, inspection, maintenance and repair services. The Inspection segment provides nondestructive testing and inspection services, including to the power generation, engineering and petrochemical industries; and it also publishes The Inspection Standard newsletter twice a year, informing customers of technical developments. The MOPS segment consists of two systems: the Ocean Producer, a floating production, storage and offloading system which operates offshore West Africa and Ocean Legend, which operates offshore Western Australia. The company's non-oilfield business is accomplished by its Advanced Technologies unit, which manufactures remotely operated diving vessels used extensively by the U.S. Navy, as well as life-support and robotic systems for use in government space programs. In April 2009, the company opened a Deepwater Technical Solutions facility in Houston.

Employees are offered medical, dental and vision insurance; flexible spending accounts; a 401(k) plan; life insurance; disability coverage; educational assistance and an employee assistance program.

FINANCIALS: Sales and profits are in thousands of dollars—add 000 to get the full amount. 2008 Note: Financial information for 2008 was not available for all companies at press time.

2008 Sales: $1,977,421	2008 Profits: $317,558	U.S. Stock Ticker: OII
2007 Sales: $1,743,080	2007 Profits: $180,374	Int'l Ticker: Int'l Exchange:
2006 Sales: $1,280,198	2006 Profits: $124,494	Employees: 7,900
2005 Sales: $998,543	2005 Profits: $62,680	Fiscal Year Ends: 12/31
2004 Sales: $780,181	2004 Profits: $40,300	Parent Company:

SALARIES/BENEFITS:

Pension Plan:	ESOP Stock Plan:	Profit Sharing:	Top Exec. Salary: $585,000	Bonus: $2,525,000
Savings Plan: Y	Stock Purch. Plan:		Second Exec. Salary: $370,000	Bonus: $1,150,000

OTHER THOUGHTS:

Apparent Women Officers or Directors: 1
Hot Spot for Advancement for Women/Minorities:

LOCATIONS: ("Y" = Yes)

West:	Southwest:	Midwest:	Southeast:	Northeast:	International:
Y	Y		Y	Y	Y

ODYSSEY HEALTHCARE INC

www.odsyhealth.com

Industry Group Code: 6216 Ranks within this company's industry group: Sales: 4 Profits: 4

Management:		Sales/Marketing:		Liberal Arts:		Information Systems:		Professionals:		Tech./Scientific:	
Management Trainees:	Y	Marketing Pros.:	Y	Gen. Writing/Editing:	Y	Info. Management:	Y	Finance/Acct.:	Y	Engineers, Electrical:	
Experienced Mngmt.:	Y	Retail Sales:		Technical Writing:	Y	Software Dev.:		Law:	Y	Engineers, Other:	
International Business:		Commercial/Industrial:		Graphic Arts/Photog.:	Y	Hardware Dev.:		HR/Other:	Y	Health/Lab:	Y
MBA Grads:	Y	Sales Trainees:		Music:		Consulting/Other:		Training:	Y	Scientists/Research:	
		Advertising Pros.:		Broadcasting:				Health Care:	Y	Petroleum/Chemicals:	
				Other:	Y			Consulting:		Math/Other:	

TYPES OF BUSINESS:

Hospice Care Services
Medical Supplies & Equipment

BRANDS/DIVISIONS/AFFILIATES:

Avalon Hospice

CONTACTS: *Note: Officers with more than one job title may be intentionally listed here more than once.*

Robert Lefton, CEO
Craig P. Goguen, COO/Sr. VP
Robert Lefton, Pres.
R. Dirk Allison, CFO/Sr. VP
Brenda A. Belger, Sr. VP-Human Resources
W. Bradley Bickham, General Counsel/Sr. VP/Corp. Sec.
Sally A. Parnell, Sr. VP-Clinical & Regulatory Affairs
Richard R. Burnham, Chmn.

Phone: 214-922-9711	Fax: 214-922-9752
Toll-Free: 888-922-9711	
Address: 717 N. Harwood St., Ste. 1500, Dallas, TX 75201 US	

GROWTH PLANS/SPECIAL FEATURES:

Odyssey HealthCare, Inc. is a leading provider of hospice care in the U.S., with 94 Medicare-certified hospice programs in 29 states and approximately12, 294 patients. Odyssey assigns each of its hospice patients to an interdisciplinary team, composed of a physician, a patient care manager, one or more registered nurses, one or more certified home health aides, a medical social worker, a chaplain, a homemaker and one or more specially trained volunteers. The team assesses the clinical, psychosocial and spiritual needs of the patient and his or her family; develops a plan of care; and delivers, monitors and coordinates that plan of care with the goal of providing appropriate care for the patient and his or her family. Services provided by the company include nursing care; medical social services, physician services, dietary, spiritual and other patient counseling; general inpatient care; medical supplies and equipment; drugs for pain control and symptom management; home health aide services; homemaker services; physical, occupational and speech therapy; respite inpatient care; and family bereavement counseling. Services provided under the Medicare program represented approximately 92.5% of Odyssey's net patient service revenue for 2008. In January 2009, the company acquired Avalon Hospice, a Michigan-based nonprofit organization. Avalon Hospice was subsequently absorbed into the firm.

Employees are offered medical, dental and vision insurance; life insurance; short-term disability coverage; a 401(k) plan; tuition reimbursement; and flexible spending accounts.

FINANCIALS: Sales and profits are in thousands of dollars—add 000 to get the full amount. 2008 Note: Financial information for 2008 was not available for all companies at press time.

2008 Sales: $616,050	2008 Profits: $14,426	U.S. Stock Ticker: ODSY	
2007 Sales: $398,232	2007 Profits: $12,111	Int'l Ticker: Int'l Exchange:	
2006 Sales: $379,218	2006 Profits: $19,729	Employees: 6,013	
2005 Sales: $378,073	2005 Profits: $18,556	Fiscal Year Ends: 12/31	
2004 Sales: $340,180	2004 Profits: $34,996	Parent Company:	

SALARIES/BENEFITS:

Pension Plan:	ESOP Stock Plan:	Profit Sharing:	Top Exec. Salary: $543,000	Bonus: $678,750
Savings Plan: Y	Stock Purch. Plan:		Second Exec. Salary: $321,000	Bonus: $321,000

OTHER THOUGHTS:

Apparent Women Officers or Directors: 2
Hot Spot for Advancement for Women/Minorities: Y

LOCATIONS: ("Y" = Yes)

West:	Southwest:	Midwest:	Southeast:	Northeast:	International:
Y	Y	Y	Y	Y	

OFFICE DEPOT INC

www.officedepot.com

Industry Group Code: 453210 **Ranks within this company's industry group:** Sales: 2 Profits: 2

Management:		Sales/Marketing:		Liberal Arts:		Information Systems:		Professionals:		Tech./Scientific:	
Management Trainees:	Y	Marketing Pros.:	Y	Gen. Writing/Editing:	Y	Info. Management:	Y	Finance/Acct.:	Y	Engineers, Electrical:	
Experienced Mngmt.:	Y	Retail Sales:	Y	Technical Writing:		Software Dev.:	Y	Law:	Y	Engineers, Other:	
International Business:	Y	Commercial/Industrial:	Y	Graphic Arts/Photog.:	Y	Hardware Dev.:		HR/Other:	Y	Health/Lab:	
MBA Grads:	Y	Sales Trainees:	Y	Music:		Consulting/Other:		Training:	Y	Scientists/Research:	
		Advertising Pros.:	Y	Broadcasting:				Health Care:		Petroleum/Chemicals:	
				Other:	Y			Consulting:		Math/Other:	

TYPES OF BUSINESS:

Office Supplies, Retail
Office Design Services
Online Retailing
Copy Services
Direct Marketing
Office Furnishings

BRANDS/DIVISIONS/AFFILIATES:

Break Escapes
Foray
Ativa
Christopher Lowell
Worklife
Netbizz Office Supplies
M.H. Alshaya Co.

CONTACTS: *Note: Officers with more than one job title may be intentionally listed here more than once.*

Steve Odland, CEO
Mike Newman, CFO/Exec. VP
Monica Luechtefeld, Exec. VP-Direct Mktg.
Daisy Vanderlinde, Exec. VP-Human Resources
Kevin Peters, Exec. VP-IT
Elisa D. Garcia C., General Counsel/Corp. Sec./Exec. VP
Monica Luechtefeld, Exec. VP-e-commerce
Chuck Rubin, Pres., North American Retail
Steven M. Schmidt, Pres., North American Bus. Solutions Div.
Steve Odland, Chmn.
Charles E. Brown, Pres., Int'l
Kevin Peters, Exec. VP-Supply Chain

Phone: 561-438-4800	**Fax:**
Toll-Free: 800-463-3768	
Address: 6600 N. Military Rd., Boca Raton, FL 33496 US	

GROWTH PLANS/SPECIAL FEATURES:

Office Depot, Inc. is one of the largest retail office products businesses worldwide, with nearly 1,600 stores in 48 countries. Office Depot operates through three business segments: North American Retail Division, North American Business Solutions Division and International Division. The North American Retail Division sells general office supplies, computer supplies, business machines and office furniture in national brands and its own private brands, which include Office Depot, Foray, Ativa, Break Escapes, Worklife and Christopher Lowell. Most stores also contain a design, print and ship center offering graphic design, printing, reproduction, shipping and other services. Office Depot's North American Business Solutions Division provides nationally branded and private-brand office supplies, technology products, furniture and services through a dedicated sales force in the U.S. and Canada, as well as catalogs and Internet sites. The firm's International Division sells office products and services through direct mail catalogs, contract sales forces, Internet sites and retail stores, using a mix of company-owned operations, joint ventures, licensing and franchise agreements, alliances and other arrangements. The firm announced in December 2008 that it will close 112 stores and six of its 33 distribution centers due to the slow economy. Additionally, it slashed new store openings planned for 2009 to 20 stores. Also in 2008, the company entered a strategic alliance with Netbizz Office Supplies for the sale of office supplies in Singapore. In January 2009, Office Depot signed a franchise agreement with M.H. Alshaya Co. for the marketing of Office Depot-brand products in Saudi Arabia, the United Arab Emirates, Kuwait, Bahrain, Qatar and Oman.

Office Depot offers its employees medical insurance, credit union membership, employee discounts and an employee assistance program. In March 2009, Office Depot was listed as a Top Company for Female Professionals by the National Association for Female Executives (NAFE) for the fifth consecutive year.

FINANCIALS: Sales and profits are in thousands of dollars—add 000 to get the full amount. 2008 Note: Financial information for 2008 was not available for all companies at press time.

2008 Sales: $14,495,544	2008 Profits: $-1,478,938	**U.S. Stock Ticker:** ODP
2007 Sales: $15,527,537	2007 Profits: $395,615	**Int'l Ticker:** Int'l Exchange:
2006 Sales: $15,010,781	2006 Profits: $503,471	**Employees:** 43,000
2005 Sales: $14,278,944	2005 Profits: $273,792	**Fiscal Year Ends:** 12/31
2004 Sales: $13,564,699	2004 Profits: $335,504	**Parent Company:**

SALARIES/BENEFITS:

Pension Plan: Y	ESOP Stock Plan:	Profit Sharing:	Top Exec. Salary: $1,000,000	Bonus: $
Savings Plan:	Stock Purch. Plan: Y		Second Exec. Salary: $625,000	Bonus: $250,000

OTHER THOUGHTS:

Apparent Women Officers or Directors: 7
Hot Spot for Advancement for Women/Minorities: Y

LOCATIONS: ("Y" = Yes)

West:	Southwest:	Midwest:	Southeast:	Northeast:	International:
Y	Y	Y	Y	Y	Y

Note: Financial information, benefits and other data can change quickly and may vary from those stated here.

OIL STATES INTERNATIONAL INC

www.oilstatesintl.com

Industry Group Code: 213112 Ranks within this company's industry group: Sales: 6 Profits: 9

Management:		Sales/Marketing:		Liberal Arts:		Information Systems:		Professionals:		Tech./Scientific:	
Management Trainees:	Y	Marketing Pros.:	Y	Gen. Writing/Editing:		Info. Management:	Y	Finance/Acct.:	Y	Engineers, Electrical:	Y
Experienced Mngmt.:	Y	Retail Sales:		Technical Writing:	Y	Software Dev.:	Y	Law:	Y	Engineers, Other:	Y
International Business:	Y	Commercial/Industrial:	Y	Graphic Arts/Photog.:		Hardware Dev.:		HR/Other:	Y	Health/Lab:	
MBA Grads:	Y	Sales Trainees:		Music:		Consulting/Other:		Training:	Y	Scientists/Research:	
		Advertising Pros.:		Broadcasting:				Health Care:		Petroleum/Chemicals:	Y
				Other:				Consulting:		Math/Other:	

TYPES OF BUSINESS:

Oil & Gas Drilling Support Services
Offshore Products
Well Site Services
Tubular Services
Drilling Services
Catering & Logistics Services
Construction Services
Equipment Rental

BRANDS/DIVISIONS/AFFILIATES:

Oil States Industries Inc.
HWC Energy Services Inc.
PTI Group Inc.

CONTACTS: *Note: Officers with more than one job title may be intentionally listed here more than once.*

Cindy B. Taylor, CEO
Cindy B. Taylor, Pres.
Bradley J. Dodson, CFO/Treas./VP
Lias J. Steen, VP-Human Resources
Robert W. Hampton, Corp. Sec.
Christopher E. Cragg, Sr. VP-Oper.
Robert W. Hampton, Sr. VP-Acct.
Ron R. Green, CEO & Pres., PTI Group Inc.
Howard Hughes, VP-Offshore Products/Pres., Oil States Industries
Lias J. Steen, VP-Legal
Stephen A. Wells, Chmn.

Phone: 713-652-0582	Fax: 713-652-0499
Toll-Free:	
Address: 3 Allen Ctr., 333 Clay St., Ste. 4620, Houston, TX 77002 US	

GROWTH PLANS/SPECIAL FEATURES:

Oil States International, Inc., is a leading provider of specialty products and services to oil and gas drilling/production companies worldwide. Areas of operation include West Africa, the North Sea, the Gulf of Mexico, Central Asia, Canada, South America, Southeast Asia and onshore U.S. It operates in three principal business segments. Its offshore products segment designs and manufactures products for the offshore energy industry, such as flexible bearings and connector products; subsea pipeline products; marine winches, mooring and lifting systems and rig equipment; and blowout prevention stack assembly, integration, testing and repair services. Oil States' tubular services segment offers casing, premium tubing and line pipe, which are purchased from manufacturers and sold to oil/gas companies and drilling contractors. It has also developed an e-commerce portal for pricing, ordering and tracking tubular products, operating under Sooner, Inc. The firm's well site services segment provides worker services, drilling services, rental equipment, remote site accommodations, catering and logistics services and modular building construction services. Subsidiary HWC Energy Services, Inc. provides worldwide well control services, drilling services and rental equipment to the oil and gas industry, while subsidiary PTI Group, Inc. is a supplier of integrated housing, food, site management and logistics support services to remote sites. In recent years, the company acquired the business of Schooner Petroleum Services, Inc., a provider of rental tools and services in Texas, Louisiana, Wyoming and Arkansas, for approximately $66.4 million. In June 2009, the firm's subsidiary, Oil States Industries, Inc., formed a joint venture called Oil States-Uniao S.A. with Uniao Engenharia Fabricacao e Montagem Ltda. to offer deepwater production and subsea pipeline solutions in Brazil.

Employees of the firm receive medical, dental and vision plans; life and AD&D insurance; a 401(k); and a 529 college savings plan.

FINANCIALS: Sales and profits are in thousands of dollars—add 000 to get the full amount. 2008 Note: Financial information for 2008 was not available for all companies at press time.

2008 Sales: $2,948,457	2008 Profits: $222,710	**U.S. Stock Ticker: OIS**
2007 Sales: $2,088,235	2007 Profits: $203,372	**Int'l Ticker:** Int'l Exchange:
2006 Sales: $1,923,357	2006 Profits: $197,634	Employees: 6,983
2005 Sales: $1,531,636	2005 Profits: $121,813	Fiscal Year Ends: 12/31
2004 Sales: $971,012	2004 Profits: $59,362	Parent Company:

SALARIES/BENEFITS:

Pension Plan:	ESOP Stock Plan:	Profit Sharing:	Top Exec. Salary: $474,231	Bonus: $569,077
Savings Plan: Y	Stock Purch. Plan:		Second Exec. Salary: $330,435	Bonus: $330,435

OTHER THOUGHTS:

Apparent Women Officers or Directors: 1
Hot Spot for Advancement for Women/Minorities: Y

LOCATIONS: ("Y" = Yes)

West:	Southwest:	Midwest:	Southeast:	Northeast:	International:
Y	Y	Y	Y		Y

Note: Financial information, benefits and other data can change quickly and may vary from those stated here.

OMNICARE INC

www.omnicare.com

Industry Group Code: 446110 Ranks within this company's industry group: Sales: 4 Profits: 3

Management:		Sales/Marketing:		Liberal Arts:		Information Systems:		Professionals:		Tech./Scientific:	
Management Trainees:	Y	Marketing Pros.:	Y	Gen. Writing/Editing:	Y	Info. Management:	Y	Finance/Acct.:	Y	Engineers, Electrical:	
Experienced Mngmt.:	Y	Retail Sales:		Technical Writing:	Y	Software Dev.:	Y	Law:	Y	Engineers, Other:	
International Business:	Y	Commercial/Industrial:		Graphic Arts/Photog.:		Hardware Dev.:		HR/Other:	Y	Health/Lab:	
MBA Grads:	Y	Sales Trainees:	Y	Music:		Consulting/Other:		Training:	Y	Scientists/Research:	
		Advertising Pros.:	Y	Broadcasting:				Health Care:	Y	Petroleum/Chemicals:	
				Other:				Consulting:		Math/Other:	

TYPES OF BUSINESS:

Specialty Pharmacies
Infusion Therapy
Consulting Services
Pharmaceutical Research
Medical Records Services
Billing Services
Pharmaceutical Distribution
Software Information Systems

BRANDS/DIVISIONS/AFFILIATES:

Omnicare Clinical Research
Advanced Care Scripts, Inc.

CONTACTS: Note: Officers with more than one job title may be intentionally listed here more than once.

Joel F. Gemunder, CEO
Patrick E. Keefe, COO/Exec. VP
Joel F. Gemunder, Pres.
David W. Froesel, Jr., CFO/Sr. VP
Beth A. Kinerk, Sr. VP-Sales & Customer Dev.
Dale B. Evans, VP/CEO-Omnicare Clinical Research
Stephen S. Brown, Sr. VP/CIO
Cheryl D. Hodges, Sr. VP/Sec.
Jeffrey M. Stamps, Sr. VP-Pharmacy Oper.
Tracy Finn, Sr. VP-Strategic Planning & Dev.
Paul W. Baldwin, VP-Public Affairs
Bradley S. Abbott, Controller/Group Exec.-Corp. Financial Svcs.
W. Gary Erwin, Pres., Omnicare Senior Health Outcomes
Donald E. Amorosi, VP-Trade Rel.
D. Michael Laney, VP-Mgmt. Info. Systems
Thomas W. Ludeke, VP
John T. Crotty, Chmn.
Jonathan D. Borman, VP-Strategic Sourcing

Phone: 859-392-3300	Fax:
Toll-Free: 800-990-6664	
Address: 1600 RiverCenter II, 100 E. RiverCenter Blvd., Covington, KY 41011 US	

GROWTH PLANS/SPECIAL FEATURES:

Omnicare, Inc. is a provider of geriatric pharmaceuticals and related geriatric pharmacy services to long-term care institutions. The firm's main business segment, pharmacy services, provides pharmaceutical distribution, related pharmacy consulting, data management services and medical supplies to long-term care facilities. Services include purchasing, repackaging and dispensing pharmaceuticals; computerized medical record keeping; and third-party billing for residents in the institutions. Omnicare also provides consultant pharmacist services, including evaluating monthly patient drug therapy, monitoring the drug distribution system within the nursing facility, assisting in compliance with state and federal regulations and providing proprietary clinical and health management programs. In addition, Omnicare's pharmacy services segment provides ancillary services, such as providing medications and nutrition for intravenous administration and furnishing respiratory therapy services, medical supplies and equipment, clinical care planning, financial software information systems, pharmaceutical informatics services, mail order pharmacy and other pharmacy distribution and patient assistance services for specialty pharmaceuticals. Pharmacy services generated approximately 97% of the firm's 2008 sales. Omnicare's contract research organization services (CRO) segment is a leading international provider of comprehensive product development and research services to client companies in the pharmaceutical, biotechnology, medical device and diagnostics industries, generating approximately 3% of the company's 2008 sales. Subsidiary Omnicare Clinical Research has expertise in various fields including cardiovascular, anti-infectives, oncology, central nervous system and geriatrics areas. In July 2008, Omnicare purchased Advanced Care Scripts Inc., a specialty pharmacy that dispenses oral and injectable medications. In August 2008, Omnicare acquired four pharmacy outlets in Edinburgh, Scotland.

FINANCIALS: Sales and profits are in thousands of dollars—add 000 to get the full amount. 2008 Note: Financial information for 2008 was not available for all companies at press time.

2008 Sales: $6,310,607	2008 Profits: $156,108	**U.S. Stock Ticker:** OCR
2007 Sales: $6,220,010	2007 Profits: $114,056	**Int'l Ticker:** Int'l Exchange:
2006 Sales: $6,492,993	2006 Profits: $183,572	Employees: 17,200
2005 Sales: $5,292,782	2005 Profits: $226,491	Fiscal Year Ends: 12/31
2004 Sales: $4,119,891	2004 Profits: $236,011	Parent Company:

SALARIES/BENEFITS:

Pension Plan:	ESOP Stock Plan:	Profit Sharing:	Top Exec. Salary: $1,816,667	Bonus: $5,125,000
Savings Plan:	Stock Purch. Plan:		Second Exec. Salary: $548,333	Bonus: $1,272,188

OTHER THOUGHTS:

Apparent Women Officers or Directors: 12
Hot Spot for Advancement for Women/Minorities: Y

LOCATIONS: ("Y" = Yes)

West:	Southwest:	Midwest:	Southeast:	Northeast:	International:
Y	Y	Y	Y	Y	Y

Note: Financial information, benefits and other data can change quickly and may vary from those stated here.

OMNICOM GROUP INC

www.omnicomgroup.com

Industry Group Code: 541810 Ranks within this company's industry group: Sales: 1   Profits: 1

Management:		Sales/Marketing:		Liberal Arts:		Information Systems:		Professionals:		Tech./Scientific:
Management Trainees:	Y	Marketing Pros.:	Y	Gen. Writing/Editing:	Y	Info. Management:	Y	Finance/Acct.:	Y	Engineers, Electrical:
Experienced Mngmt.:	Y	Retail Sales:		Technical Writing:		Software Dev.:	Y	Law:	Y	Engineers, Other:
International Business:	Y	Commercial/Industrial:	Y	Graphic Arts/Photog.:	Y	Hardware Dev.:		HR/Other:	Y	Health/Lab:
MBA Grads:	Y	Sales Trainees:		Music:		Consulting/Other:		Training:	Y	Scientists/Research:
		Advertising Pros.:	Y	Broadcasting:				Health Care:		Petroleum/Chemicals:
				Other:				Consulting:	Y	Math/Other:

TYPES OF BUSINESS:

Advertising Services
Public Relations
Market Research
Marketing & Brand Consulting
Interactive & Search Engine Marketing
Media Planning & Buying
Health Care Communications

BRANDS/DIVISIONS/AFFILIATES:

BBDO Worldwide
DDB Worldwide Communications Group Inc
TBWA Worldwide Inc
Agency.com Ltd
Goodby Silverstein & Partners
OMD Worldwide
Alcone Marketing Group
Wolff Olins

CONTACTS: *Note: Officers with more than one job title may be intentionally listed here more than once.*

John D. Wren, CEO
John D. Wren, Pres.
Randall J. Weisenburger, CFO/Exec. VP
Michael J. O'Brien, General Counsel/Sr. VP/Corp. Sec.
Philip J. Angelastro, Sr. VP-Finance/Controller
Asit Mehra, Exec. VP
Bruce Redditt, Exec. VP
Janet Riccio, Exec. VP
Dennis E. Hewitt, Treas.
Bruce Crawford, Chmn.
Michael Birkin, Chmn./CEO-Asia Pacific

Phone: 212-415-3600	Fax: 212-415-3530
Toll-Free:	
Address: 437 Madison Ave., New York, NY 10022 US	

GROWTH PLANS/SPECIAL FEATURES:

Omnicom Group, Inc. is a holding company that, through its subsidiaries, is one of the largest advertising, marketing and corporate communications companies in the world. The firm owns subsidiary agencies that operate in all major markets worldwide. Its agencies provide an extensive range of services, mainly focusing on four fundamental disciplines, including traditional media advertising, customer relationship management, public relations and specialty communications. The company's holdings are managed by the Diversified Agency Services (DAS) division; this sector includes over 100 public relations, marketing, consulting and special communications firms. Omnicom's traditional media advertising is based in three areas: Global advertising brands, such as BBDO Worldwide, DDB Worldwide and TBWA Worldwide; national advertising agencies, including Arnell Group, Goodby, GSD&M, Martin/Williams, Merkley, Zimmerman Advertising and Silverstein Partners; and media services, which offers two full service media companies, OMD Worldwide and PHD Network, and several media specialist companies. Other group activities of note include experiential marketing, mobile marketing, package design, custom printing, reputation consulting and search engine marketing. In 2008, Omnicom laid off 5% of its workforce. In February 2008, the company acquired a majority interest in Shift, a digital consultancy in New Zealand. Also in February 2008, the firm's DAS division acquired California-based marketing firm The Kern Organization (Kern now operates under Rapp Collins Worldwide). In July 2008, Omnicom released G23, a new strategic consultancy solution entirely comprised of the company's female communications experts, to assist clients who desire to form better business relationships with women. In March 2009, the company partnered with Shanghai's Fudan University to release digital:works, a digital marketing executive training program.

FINANCIALS: Sales and profits are in thousands of dollars—add 000 to get the full amount. 2008 Note: Financial information for 2008 was not available for all companies at press time.

2008 Sales: $13,359,900	2008 Profits: $1,000,300	**U.S. Stock Ticker: OMC**
2007 Sales: $12,694,000	2007 Profits: $975,700	**Int'l Ticker:** Int'l Exchange:
2006 Sales: $11,376,900	2006 Profits: $864,000	Employees: 66,500
2005 Sales: $10,481,100	2005 Profits: $790,700	Fiscal Year Ends: 12/31
2004 Sales: $9,747,200	2004 Profits: $723,500	Parent Company:

SALARIES/BENEFITS:

Pension Plan:	ESOP Stock Plan:	Profit Sharing:	Top Exec. Salary: $1,000,000	Bonus: $1,750,000
Savings Plan:	Stock Purch. Plan:		Second Exec. Salary: $975,000	Bonus: $1,325,000

OTHER THOUGHTS:

Apparent Women Officers or Directors: 3
Hot Spot for Advancement for Women/Minorities: Y

LOCATIONS: ("Y" = Yes)

West:	Southwest:	Midwest:	Southeast:	Northeast:	International:
Y	Y	Y	Y	Y	Y

Note: Financial information, benefits and other data can change quickly and may vary from those stated here.

ORACLE CORP

www.oracle.com

Industry Group Code: 511210H Ranks within this company's industry group: Sales: 1 Profits: 1

Management:		Sales/Marketing:		Liberal Arts:		Information Systems:		Professionals:		Tech./Scientific:	
Management Trainees:	Y	Marketing Pros.:	Y	Gen. Writing/Editing:	Y	Info. Management:	Y	Finance/Acct.:	Y	Engineers, Electrical:	Y
Experienced Mngmt.:	Y	Retail Sales:		Technical Writing:	Y	Software Dev.:	Y	Law:	Y	Engineers, Other:	
International Business:	Y	Commercial/Industrial:	Y	Graphic Arts/Photog.:	Y	Hardware Dev.:		HR/Other:	Y	Health/Lab:	
MBA Grads:	Y	Sales Trainees:		Music:		Consulting/Other:	Y	Training:	Y	Scientists/Research:	Y
		Advertising Pros.:	Y	Broadcasting:				Health Care:		Petroleum/Chemicals:	
				Other:	Y			Consulting:		Math/Other:	Y

TYPES OF BUSINESS:

Computer Software-Database Management
e-Business Applications Software
Internet-Based Software
Consulting Services
Human Resources Management Software
CRM Software
Middleware

BRANDS/DIVISIONS/AFFILIATES:

BEA Systems Inc
Global Knowledge Software LLC
Advanced Visual Technology Ltd
Primavera Software Inc
Oracle Insurance
Agile Software Corp
Portal Software Inc
Stellant Inc

CONTACTS: Note: Officers with more than one job title may be intentionally listed here more than once.

Lawrence J. Ellison, CEO
Charles E. Phillips, Jr., Co-Pres.
Jeff Epstein, CFO/Exec. VP
Judith Sim, Chief Mktg. Officer/Sr. VP
Charles Rozwat, Exec. VP-Prod. Dev.
Dorian Daley, General Counsel/Sr. VP/Sec.
Keith Block, Exec. VP-North America
Mary Ann Davidson, Chief Security Officer
Luiz Meisler, Sr. VP-Latin America
Edward Screven, Chief Corp. Architect
Jeffrey O. Henley, Chmn.
Takao Endo, Pres./CEO-Japan

Phone: 650-506-7000	Fax: 650-506-7200
Toll-Free: 800-672-2531	
Address: 500 Oracle Pkwy., Redwood Shores, CA 94065 US	

GROWTH PLANS/SPECIAL FEATURES:

Oracle Corporation is one of the largest enterprise software companies in the world. The firm markets its software directly to corporations rather than dealing in the consumer market. Oracle's products can be categorized into two broad areas: software (representing 80% of revenue) and services. The company's core software business segment is based upon its prepackaged enterprise data management software and Internet applications including Oracle Database, Oracle Fusion Middleware, Oracle Enterprise Manager, Oracle Collaboration Suite, Oracle Developer Suite and Oracle E-Business Suite. Oracle's services business is comprised of Oracle Consulting and Oracle On Demand. Oracle Consulting specializes in the design, implementation, deployment, upgrade and migration of its database technology and applications software. Oracle On Demand offers distributed application services including E-Business Suite On Demand, Technology On Demand and Collaboration Suite On Demand. Oracle Retail Promotion Planning and Optimization is a data mining application for retail analysis, forecasting and planning. Oracle SQL Developer is an upgrade to Oracle's free database development and debugging application, as well as Oracle Management Pack for Linux. Oracle Manufacturing Execution System for Discrete Manufacturing (Oracle MES for Discrete Manufacturing), is an application that lets manufacturers set up Oracle Applications on the shop floor. Subsidiaries include Agile Software Corp, Portal Software Inc and Stellent Inc. In 2008, the company acquired the e-TEST suite products from Emprix; BEA Systems, Inc.; Global Knowledge Software LLC; Advanced Visual Technology Ltd.; and Primavera Software, Inc. In September of the same year, the firm launched Oracle Insurance, a provider of end-to-end software designed to manage aspects of the insurance business such as technical infrastructure and core insurance processing. In April 2009, Oracle agreed to acquire Sun Microsystems for $7.4 billion.

Employees are offered a 401(k) plan; an employee stock purchase plan; an employee assistance program; and health care benefits.

FINANCIALS: Sales and profits are in thousands of dollars—add 000 to get the full amount. 2008 Note: Financial information for 2008 was not available for all companies at press time.

2008 Sales: $22,430,000	2008 Profits: $5,521,000	U.S. Stock Ticker: ORCL
2007 Sales: $17,996,000	2007 Profits: $4,274,000	Int'l Ticker: Int'l Exchange:
2006 Sales: $14,380,000	2006 Profits: $3,381,000	Employees: 86,000
2005 Sales: $11,799,000	2005 Profits: $2,886,000	Fiscal Year Ends: 5/31
2004 Sales: $10,156,000	2004 Profits: $2,681,000	Parent Company:

SALARIES/BENEFITS:

Pension Plan:	ESOP Stock Plan:	Profit Sharing:	Top Exec. Salary: $1,000,000	Bonus: $10,779,000
Savings Plan: Y	Stock Purch. Plan: Y		Second Exec. Salary: $800,000	Bonus: $6,467,000

OTHER THOUGHTS:

Apparent Women Officers or Directors: 5
Hot Spot for Advancement for Women/Minorities: Y

LOCATIONS: ("Y" = Yes)

West:	Southwest:	Midwest:	Southeast:	Northeast:	International:
Y	Y	Y	Y	Y	Y

O'REILLY AUTOMOTIVE INC

www.oreillyauto.com

Industry Group Code: 441310 Ranks within this company's industry group: Sales: 3 Profits: 3

Management:		Sales/Marketing:		Liberal Arts:		Information Systems:		Professionals:		Tech./Scientific:	
Management Trainees:	Y	Marketing Pros.:	Y	Gen. Writing/Editing:	Y	Info. Management:	Y	Finance/Acct.:	Y	Engineers, Electrical:	
Experienced Mngmt.:	Y	Retail Sales:	Y	Technical Writing:		Software Dev.:	Y	Law:	Y	Engineers, Other:	
International Business:		Commercial/Industrial:	Y	Graphic Arts/Photog.:	Y	Hardware Dev.:		HR/Other:	Y	Health/Lab:	
MBA Grads:	Y	Sales Trainees:	Y	Music:		Consulting/Other:		Training:	Y	Scientists/Research:	
		Advertising Pros.:	Y	Broadcasting:				Health Care:		Petroleum/Chemicals:	
				Other:				Consulting:		Math/Other:	

TYPES OF BUSINESS:

Auto Parts, Retail
Tools
Auto Accessories

BRANDS/DIVISIONS/AFFILIATES:

O'Reilly Auto Parts
CSK Auto Corporation
BrakeBest
Checker Auto Parts
Master-Pro
Omnispark
Super Start
Schuck's Auto Supply

CONTACTS: *Note: Officers with more than one job title may be intentionally listed here more than once.*

Greg L. Henslee, CEO/Co-Pres.
Ted F. Wise, COO
Ted F. Wise, Co-Pres.
Tom McFall, CFO
Tony Bartholomew, VP-Sales
Phillip Thompson, VP-Human Resources
Steve Jasinski, VP-Info. Systems
Mike Williams, VP-Advanced Tech.
Mike Swearengin, Sr. VP-Merch.
Phyllis Evans, VP-Store Admin.
Tricia Headley, Corp. Sec./VP
Jeff Shaw, Sr. VP-Store Sales & Oper.
Tom McFall, Exec. VP-Finance
Doug Ruble, VP-Advertising & Mktg.
Alan Fears, VP-Store Acquisitions & Expansion
Greg Johnson, Sr. VP-Dist. Oper.
Barry Sabor, VP-Loss Prevention
David E. O'Reilly, Chmn.
Greg Beck, VP-Purchasing

Phone: 417-862-6708	Fax:
Toll-Free:	
Address: 233 S. Patterson Ave., Springfield, MO 65802 US	

GROWTH PLANS/SPECIAL FEATURES:

O'Reilly Automotive, Inc., founded in 1957, is one of the largest specialty retailers of automotive aftermarket parts, tools, supplies, equipment and accessories in the U.S., selling products to both do-it-yourself (DIY) customers and professional installers. The company operates 3,285 stores in 38 states across the U.S. Stores carry an extensive product line consisting of new and remanufactured automotive hard parts, such as alternators, starters, brake system components, batteries, chassis parts and engine parts; maintenance items, such as oil, antifreeze, fluids, wiper blades, lighting, engine additives and appearance products; accessories, such as floor mats, truck accessories seat covers; and a complete line of auto body paint and related materials, automotive tools and professional service equipment. Store merchandise generally consists of nationally recognized, well-advertised, name-brand products such as AC Delco, Moog, Wagner, Gates Rubber, Federal Mogul, Monroe, Prestone, Quaker State, Pennzoil, Castrol, Valvoline, STP, BWD, Cardone, Wix, Armor All and Turtle Wax. In addition to name-brand products, stores carry a wide variety of high-quality private-label products under the O'Reilly Auto Parts, BestTest, Miles Ahead, Super Start, Ultima and Omnispark name brands. O'Reilly operates 18 distribution centers, each equipped with highly automated material handling equipment that expedites the movement of products to loading areas for shipment to individual stores on a nightly basis. In July 2008, the firm acquired CSK Auto Corporation, a specialty retailer of auto parts, for approximately $1 billion. CSK had 1,342 stores in 22 states at the time of the acquisition, under the Checker Auto Parts, Schuck's Auto Supply, Kragen Auto Parts and Murray's Discount Auto Parts brands. In November 2008, O'Reilly became the official automotive parts retailer of NASCAR.

O'Reilly offers its employees a benefits package that includes medical, dental, vision, pharmacy and life insurance, purchase discounts, a credit union membership and an employee assistance program.

FINANCIALS: Sales and profits are in thousands of dollars—add 000 to get the full amount. 2008 Note: Financial information for 2008 was not available for all companies at press time.

2008 Sales: $3,576,553	2008 Profits: $186,232	**U.S. Stock Ticker: ORLY**
2007 Sales: $2,522,319	2007 Profits: $193,988	**Int'l Ticker:** Int'l Exchange:
2006 Sales: $2,283,222	2006 Profits: $178,085	Employees: 40,735
2005 Sales: $2,045,318	2005 Profits: $164,266	Fiscal Year Ends: 12/31
2004 Sales: $1,721,241	2004 Profits: $139,566	Parent Company:

SALARIES/BENEFITS:

Pension Plan:	ESOP Stock Plan:	Profit Sharing: Y	Top Exec. Salary: $695,413	Bonus: $1,050,000
Savings Plan: Y	Stock Purch. Plan: Y		Second Exec. Salary: $554,034	Bonus: $666,000

OTHER THOUGHTS:

Apparent Women Officers or Directors: 3
Hot Spot for Advancement for Women/Minorities: Y

LOCATIONS: ("Y" = Yes)

West:	Southwest:	Midwest:	Southeast:	Northeast:	International:
Y	Y	Y	Y	Y	

Note: Financial information, benefits and other data can change quickly and may vary from those stated here.

OSHKOSH CORPORATION

www.oshkoshcorporation.com

Industry Group Code: 336120 Ranks within this company's industry group: Sales: 1   Profits: 1

Management:		Sales/Marketing:		Liberal Arts:		Information Systems:		Professionals:		Tech./Scientific:	
Management Trainees:	Y	Marketing Pros.:	Y	Gen. Writing/Editing:	Y	Info. Management:	Y	Finance/Acct.:	Y	Engineers, Electrical:	Y
Experienced Mngmt.:	Y	Retail Sales:		Technical Writing:	Y	Software Dev.:	Y	Law:	Y	Engineers, Other:	Y
International Business:	Y	Commercial/Industrial:	Y	Graphic Arts/Photog.:	Y	Hardware Dev.:	Y	HR/Other:	Y	Health/Lab:	
MBA Grads:	Y	Sales Trainees:		Music:		Consulting/Other:		Training:	Y	Scientists/Research:	
		Advertising Pros.:	Y	Broadcasting:				Health Care:		Petroleum/Chemicals:	
				Other:				Consulting:		Math/Other:	

TYPES OF BUSINESS:

Fire & Emergency Vehicles
Military Trucks
Truck Bodies
Specialty Trucks
Cement Mixers
Refuse Trucks

BRANDS/DIVISIONS/AFFILIATES:

Oshkosh
JLG
Pierce
BAI
JerrDan
Oshkosh Truck Corporation

CONTACTS: Note: Officers with more than one job title may be intentionally listed here more than once.

Robert G. Bohn, CEO
Charles L. Szews, COO
Charles L. Szews, Pres.
David M. Sagehorn, CFO
Ann T. Stawski, VP-Mktg. Comm.
Michael K. Rohrkaste, VP-Human Resources
Michael S. Guzowski, VP-IT
Donald H. Verhoff, Exec. VP-Tech.
Thomas D. Fenner, Exec. VP-Global Mfg. Svcs.
Matthew J. Zolnowski, Chief Admin. Officer/Exec. VP
Bryan J. Blankenfield, General Counsel/Sec./Exec. VP
Mark M. Radue, VP-Bus. Dev.
Joseph H. (Jay) Kimmitt, Exec. VP-Industry Rel. & Gov't Oper.
Patrick N. Davidson, VP-Investor Rel.
Thomas J. Polnaszek, Sr. VP-Finance/Controller
R. Andrew (Andy) Hove, Exec. VP/Pres., Defense
Wilson R. Jones, Exec. VP/Pres., Fire & Emergency
Craig E. Paylor, Exec. VP/Pres., Access Equipment
Michael J. Wuest, Exec. VP/Pres., Commercial
Robert G. Bohn, Chmn.
Gregory L. Fredericksen, Chief Procurement Officer/Sr. VP

Phone: 920-235-9151	Fax: 920-233-9251
Toll-Free:	
Address: 2307 Oregon St., Oshkosh, WI 54902 US	

GROWTH PLANS/SPECIAL FEATURES:

Oshkosh Corporation, formerly Oshkosh Truck Corporation, is a leading designer, manufacturer and marketer of specialty vehicles and vehicle bodies. The company operates in four segments: Access equipment, defense, fire and emergency and commercial. The access equipment segment, through subsidiary JLG, manufactures aerial work platforms, telehandlers, scissor lifts and vertical masts used in construction, agricultural, industrial, institutional and general maintenance applications. JLG markets its products in over 3,500 locations worldwide. The defense segment supplies severe-duty, heavy-payload tactical trucks to the U.S. Department of Defense (DoD). The firm and emergency segment, through subsidiary Pierce, is a leading domestic manufacturer of fire apparatus assembled on custom chassis. It also manufactures fire apparatus assembled on commercially-available chassis, snow removal vehicles and emergency vehicles, including pumpers; aerial and ladder trucks; tankers; light-, medium- and heavy-duty rescue vehicles; rough terrain response vehicles; mobile command and control centers; bomb squad vehicles; and hazardous materials control vehicles. The segment sells aircraft rescue and fire fighting (ARFF) vehicles to domestic and international airports under the Oshkosh and BAI brands. Through its JerrDan subsidiary, the segment also manufactures towing and recovery equipment in the U.S. The commercial segment manufactures rear- and front-discharge concrete mixers; refuse collection vehicles; mobile and stationary compactors and waste transfer units; portable and stationary concrete batch plants; and vehicle components. In February 2008, the company changed its name from Oshkosh Truck Corporation to Oshkosh Corporation. In November 2008, the firm opened a new manufacturing facility in Tianjin, China. In May 2009, Oshkosh agreed to sell its Netherlands-based Geesink Norba Group to Platinum Equity.

Oshkosh offers its employees tuition reimbursement, ongoing training, relocation benefits, a flexible spending account and medical, dental, prescription, vision, life and disability insurance.

FINANCIALS: Sales and profits are in thousands of dollars—add 000 to get the full amount. 2008 Note: Financial information for 2008 was not available for all companies at press time.

2008 Sales: $7,138,300	2008 Profits: $79,300	**U.S. Stock Ticker:** OSK
2007 Sales: $6,307,300	2007 Profits: $268,100	**Int'l Ticker:** Int'l Exchange:
2006 Sales: $3,427,388	2006 Profits: $205,529	Employees: 14,000
2005 Sales: $2,959,900	2005 Profits: $160,205	Fiscal Year Ends: 9/30
2004 Sales: $2,262,305	2004 Profits: $112,806	Parent Company:

SALARIES/BENEFITS:

Pension Plan: Y	ESOP Stock Plan:	Profit Sharing:	Top Exec. Salary: $1,150,000	Bonus: $178,020
Savings Plan: Y	Stock Purch. Plan: Y		Second Exec. Salary: $665,000	Bonus: $82,394

OTHER THOUGHTS:

Apparent Women Officers or Directors: 4
Hot Spot for Advancement for Women/Minorities: Y

LOCATIONS: ("Y" = Yes)

West:	Southwest:	Midwest:	Southeast:	Northeast:	International:
Y	Y	Y	Y	Y	Y

Note: Financial information, benefits and other data can change quickly and may vary from those stated here.

OSI RESTAURANT PARTNERS LLC

www.osirestaurantpartners.com

Industry Group Code: 722110 Ranks within this company's industry group: Sales: 5   Profits: 13

Management:		Sales/Marketing:		Liberal Arts:		Information Systems:		Professionals:		Tech./Scientific:	
Management Trainees:	Y	Marketing Pros.:	Y	Gen. Writing/Editing:	Y	Info. Management:	Y	Finance/Acct.:	Y	Engineers, Electrical:	
Experienced Mngmt.:	Y	Retail Sales:		Technical Writing:		Software Dev.:	Y	Law:	Y	Engineers, Other:	
International Business:	Y	Commercial/Industrial:		Graphic Arts/Photog.:	Y	Hardware Dev.:		HR/Other:	Y	Health/Lab:	
MBA Grads:	Y	Sales Trainees:		Music:		Consulting/Other:		Training:	Y	Scientists/Research:	
		Advertising Pros.:	Y	Broadcasting:				Health Care:		Petroleum/Chemicals:	
				Other:	Y			Consulting:		Math/Other:	

TYPES OF BUSINESS:

Restaurants
Catering
Event Hosting

BRANDS/DIVISIONS/AFFILIATES:

Bain Capital LLC
Catterton Partners
Outback Steakhouse
Bonefish Grill
Carrabba's Italian Grill
Fleming's Prime Steakhouse & Wine Bar
Cheeseburger in Paradise
Roy's

CONTACTS: *Note: Officers with more than one job title may be intentionally listed here more than once.*

A. William Allen, III, CEO
Paul E. Avery, COO
Dirk A. Montgomery, CFO/Sr. VP
Joseph J. Kadow, Chief Corp. & Legal Affairs Officer/Sec./Exec. VP
Richard L. Renninger, Chief Dev. Officer/Exec. VP
Jeff Smith, Pres., Outback Steakhouse
Steven T. Shlemon, Pres., Carrabba's Italian Grill
John W. Cooper, Pres., Bonefish Grill
C. H. (Skip) Fox, Pres., Fleming's Prime Steakhouse & Wine Bar
Michael W. Coble, Pres., Outback Int'l
Irene Wenzel, Chief Purchasing Officer/Sr. VP

Phone: 813-282-1225	Fax:
Toll-Free:	
Address: 2202 N. W. Shore Blvd., 5th Fl., Tampa, FL 33607 US	

GROWTH PLANS/SPECIAL FEATURES:

OSI Restaurant Partners, LLC (OSI), formerly Outback Steakhouse, Inc., owns and operates several casual dining restaurant chains. These restaurants operate under the names Outback Steakhouse (with 978 restaurants worldwide), Carrabba's Italian Grill (238), Bonefish Grill (149), Fleming's Prime Steakhouse and Wine Bar (61), Cheeseburger in Paradise (38), Roy's (26) and Blue Coral Seafood and Spirits (1). OSI operates 1,323 of these 1,491 locations, with the remainder operating under franchise (146) or joint venture (22) agreements. Outback restaurants have an Australian-styled atmosphere that emphasizes quality food in large portions. Carrabba's restaurants have a small, focused menu and a casual, traditional Italian atmosphere. Bonefish is a mid-scale seafood restaurant emphasizing hand-cut fish prepared over a wood-burning grill with original sauces. Fleming's has an upscale contemporary menu, exhibition-style kitchen and an extensive wine list. Cheeseburger in Paradise takes its theme, menu and gift ideas from the Jimmy Buffet song of the same name, including its Key West-style architecture, Tiki bar and famous gourmet cheeseburger. Roy's features an exhibition kitchen and serves primarily Hawaiian-influenced cuisine. Blue Coral Seafood and Spirits features a modern take on fresh seafood and includes an extensive vodka bar. In all of the restaurants, kitchens are uncommonly large and designed for rapid production of a wide variety of food. Servers never cover more than three tables at once, and most restaurants are only open for dinner. Additionally, most locations offer a full liquor service. OSI is 79%-owned by an investor group including Bain Capital LLC and Catterton Partners. In December 2008, the company sold its interest in the Lee Roy Selmon's restaurant chain, which had six locations, to MVP LRS, LLC (a firm controlled by current and former OSI executives) for $4.2 million.

OSI offers its employees medical, dental and prescription coverage; life insurance; an employee assistance program; flexible spending accounts; and adoption assistance.

FINANCIALS: Sales and profits are in thousands of dollars—add 000 to get the full amount. 2008 Note: Financial information for 2008 was not available for all companies at press time.

2008 Sales: $3,962,854	2008 Profits: $-739,409	**U.S. Stock Ticker: Private**
2007 Sales: $4,150,000	2007 Profits: $-22,594	**Int'l Ticker:** Int'l Exchange:
2006 Sales: $3,940,959	2006 Profits: $100,160	Employees: 105,000
2005 Sales: $3,612,717	2005 Profits: $146,746	Fiscal Year Ends: 12/31
2004 Sales: $3,215,989	2004 Profits: $151,571	Parent Company: BAIN CAPITAL LLC

SALARIES/BENEFITS:

Pension Plan:	ESOP Stock Plan:	Profit Sharing:	Top Exec. Salary: $1,060,875	Bonus: $700,177
Savings Plan: Y	Stock Purch. Plan:		Second Exec. Salary: $695,000	Bonus: $1,317,400

OTHER THOUGHTS:

Apparent Women Officers or Directors: 1
Hot Spot for Advancement for Women/Minorities: Y

LOCATIONS: ("Y" = Yes)

West:	Southwest:	Midwest:	Southeast:	Northeast:	International:
Y	Y	Y	Y	Y	Y

OWENS & MINOR INC

www.owens-minor.com

Industry Group Code: 423450 Ranks within this company's industry group: Sales: 2   Profits: 4

Management:		Sales/Marketing:		Liberal Arts:		Information Systems:		Professionals:		Tech./Scientific:	
Management Trainees:	Y	Marketing Pros.:	Y	Gen. Writing/Editing:	Y	Info. Management:	Y	Finance/Acct.:	Y	Engineers, Electrical:	
Experienced Mngmt.:	Y	Retail Sales:		Technical Writing:	Y	Software Dev.:	Y	Law:	Y	Engineers, Other:	
International Business:		Commercial/Industrial:	Y	Graphic Arts/Photog.:	Y	Hardware Dev.:		HR/Other:	Y	Health/Lab:	
MBA Grads:	Y	Sales Trainees:	Y	Music:		Consulting/Other:		Training:	Y	Scientists/Research:	
		Advertising Pros.:	Y	Broadcasting:				Health Care:	Y	Petroleum/Chemicals:	
				Other:				Consulting:		Math/Other:	

TYPES OF BUSINESS:

Distribution-Medical & Surgical Equipment
Supply Chain Management

BRANDS/DIVISIONS/AFFILIATES:

OMSolutions
PANDAC
SurgiTrack
WISDOM Gold
Burrows Company (The)

CONTACTS: *Note: Officers with more than one job title may be intentionally listed here more than once.*

Craig R. Smith, CEO
Craig R. Smith, Pres.
James L. Bierman, CFO/Sr. VP
W. Marshall Simpson, Sr. VP-Sales & Mktg.
Erika T. Davis, Sr. VP-Human Resources
Richard W. Mears, CIO/Sr. VP
Charles C. Colpo, Exec. VP-Admin.
Grace R. den Hartog, General Counsel/Sr. VP/Corp. Sec.
Mark A. Van Sumeren, Sr. VP-Strategic Planning & Bus. Dev.
Hugh F. Gouldthorpe, Jr., VP-Comm. & Quality
Richard F. Bozard, Treas./VP
Olwen B. Cape, Controller/VP
G. Gilmer Minor, III, Chmn.
E. V. Clarke, Exec. VP-Dist.

Phone: 804-723-7000	Fax: 804-723-7100
Toll-Free:	
Address: 9120 Lockwood Blvd., Mechanicsville, VA 23116 US	

GROWTH PLANS/SPECIAL FEATURES:

Owens & Minor, Inc. (OMI), founded in 1882, is a distributor of medical and surgical supplies to the acute-care market and a healthcare supply-chain management company. In its acute-care supply distribution, the company distributes 220,000 finished medical and surgical products produced by over 1,600 suppliers to about 4,500 healthcare provider customers from 55 distribution and service centers nationwide. The firm's primary distribution customers are acute-care hospitals, which account for more than 95% of the company's revenue. Other customers include the U.S. government, for which OMI serves as a vendor for medical and surgical supply distribution services for the U.S. Department of Defense. On a more limited basis, the company serves alternate care providers including clinics, home healthcare organizations, nursing homes, physicians' offices, rehabilitation facilities and surgery centers. The firm typically provides its distribution services under contractual arrangements with terms ranging from 3-5 years. Most of OMI's sales consist of consumable goods such as disposable gloves; dressings; endoscopic products; intravenous products; needles and syringes; sterile procedure trays; surgical products and gowns; urological products; and wound closure products. The company also offers a number of supply chain services, including OMSolutions, comprising OMI's supply chain consulting, customer technology and resource management teams; PANDAC, an operating room-focused inventory management program to help healthcare providers reduce and control suture and endo-mechanical inventory; SurgiTrack, a customizable surgical supply service; and WISDOM Gold, an Internet-based spend management, data normalization and contract management solution. In October 2008, OMI acquired The Burrows Company, an acute-care medical and surgical supplies distributor. In December 2008, the firm agreed to sell assets of its direct-to-consumer diabetes supply business to Liberty Healthcare Group for $63 million.

OMI offers its employees educational assistance; incentive pay; flexible benefit plans; and medical, dental, vision, life and disability insurance.

FINANCIALS: Sales and profits are in thousands of dollars—add 000 to get the full amount. 2008 Note: Financial information for 2008 was not available for all companies at press time.

2008 Sales: $7,243,237	2008 Profits: $93,327	**U.S. Stock Ticker: OMI**	
2007 Sales: $6,800,466	2007 Profits: $72,710	**Int'l Ticker:** Int'l Exchange:	
2006 Sales: $5,533,736	2006 Profits: $48,752	Employees: 5,300	
2005 Sales: $4,822,414	2005 Profits: $64,420	Fiscal Year Ends: 12/31	
2004 Sales: $4,525,105	2004 Profits: $60,500	Parent Company:	

SALARIES/BENEFITS:

Pension Plan:	ESOP Stock Plan:	Profit Sharing:	Top Exec. Salary: $788,077	Bonus: $1,080,000
Savings Plan: Y	Stock Purch. Plan: Y		Second Exec. Salary: $484,615	Bonus: $450,000

OTHER THOUGHTS:

Apparent Women Officers or Directors: 2
Hot Spot for Advancement for Women/Minorities: Y

LOCATIONS: ("Y" = Yes)

West:	Southwest:	Midwest:	Southeast:	Northeast:	International:
Y	Y	Y	Y	Y	

Note: Financial information, benefits and other data can change quickly and may vary from those stated here.

PANTRY INC (THE)

www.thepantry.com

Industry Group Code: 445120 Ranks within this company's industry group: Sales: 1 Profits: 1

Management:		Sales/Marketing:		Liberal Arts:		Information Systems:		Professionals:		Tech./Scientific:	
Management Trainees:		Marketing Pros.:	Y	Gen. Writing/Editing:	Y	Info. Management:	Y	Finance/Acct.:	Y	Engineers, Electrical:	
Experienced Mngmt.:	Y	Retail Sales:	Y	Technical Writing:		Software Dev.:	Y	Law:	Y	Engineers, Other:	
International Business:		Commercial/Industrial:		Graphic Arts/Photog.:	Y	Hardware Dev.:		HR/Other:	Y	Health/Lab:	
MBA Grads:	Y	Sales Trainees:	Y	Music:		Consulting/Other:		Training:	Y	Scientists/Research:	
		Advertising Pros.:	Y	Broadcasting:				Health Care:		Petroleum/Chemicals:	
				Other:	Y			Consulting:		Math/Other:	

TYPES OF BUSINESS:

Convenience Stores
Gas Stations
Fast Food

BRANDS/DIVISIONS/AFFILIATES:

Kangaroo Express

CONTACTS: Note: Officers with more than one job title may be intentionally listed here more than once.

Peter J. Sodini, CEO
Peter J. Sodini, Pres.
Frank G. Paci, CFO
Melissa H. Anderson, Sr. VP-Human Resources
Steven J. Ferreira, Sr. VP-Admin.
Frank G. Paci, Sec.
Brad Williams, VP-Oper.
Frank G. Paci, Sr. VP-Finance
Keith S. Bell, Sr. VP-Fuels
Peter J. Sodini, Chmn.

Phone: 919-774-6700	**Fax:** 919-775-5428
Toll-Free:	
Address: 1801 Douglas Dr., Sanford, NC 27330 US	

GROWTH PLANS/SPECIAL FEATURES:

The Pantry, Inc. is a leading operator of convenience stores in the Southeast U.S., operating 1,679 convenience stores under a variety of brand names including its primary operating banner, Kangaroo Express. The company operates 249 quick service restaurants within 239 of its locations, of which 276 have car wash facilities. Restaurants offer products from nationally branded food franchises including Subway; Quiznos; Hardee's; Krystal; Church's; Dairy Queen; Baskin-Robbins; and Bojangles. In addition, The Pantry offers a variety of proprietary food service programs in about 81 of its quick service restaurants featuring breakfast biscuits, fried chicken, a deli and other hot food offerings. Its stores offer merchandise, gasoline and ancillary products and services. The biggest selling items have historically been tobacco products, which accounted for approximately 31% of 2008 merchandise sales; packaged beverages, 19%; and beer and wine, 16.3%. Merchandise sales in 2008 generated approximately 18.2% of The Pantry's total revenues. Its services revenue is derived from sales of lottery tickets, prepaid products, money orders, public telephones, ATMs and amusement and video gaming service offerings. The Pantry purchases over 50% of its merchandise, including most tobacco and grocery items, from McLane Company, Inc., a subsidiary of Berkshire Hathaway, Inc. The company purchases gasoline from major oil companies and independent refiners and offers a mix of branded and private brand gasoline at its locations based on an evaluation of local market conditions. Approximately 68.4% of the firm's locations that sell gasoline are branded under the BP, CITGO, Chevron, Shell, Texaco or ExxonMobil brand names. Gasoline revenues generated approximately 81.8% of The Pantry's total revenues in 2008. Approximately 33% of the firm's stores are strategically located in coastal or resort areas, while roughly 27% are situated along major interstates and highways. In 2008, The Pantry opened 12 new locations, and closed 23.

FINANCIALS: Sales and profits are in thousands of dollars—add 000 to get the full amount. 2008 Note: Financial information for 2008 was not available for all companies at press time.

2008 Sales: $8,995,626	2008 Profits: $31,783	**U.S. Stock Ticker: PTRY**
2007 Sales: $6,911,163	2007 Profits: $26,732	**Int'l Ticker:** Int'l Exchange:
2006 Sales: $5,961,700	2006 Profits: $89,200	Employees: 14,221
2005 Sales: $4,429,200	2005 Profits: $57,800	Fiscal Year Ends: 9/30
2004 Sales: $3,493,100	2004 Profits: $17,600	Parent Company:

SALARIES/BENEFITS:

Pension Plan:	ESOP Stock Plan:	Profit Sharing:	Top Exec. Salary: $800,000	Bonus: $352,590
Savings Plan:	Stock Purch. Plan:		Second Exec. Salary: $434,769	Bonus: $150,000

OTHER THOUGHTS:

Apparent Women Officers or Directors: 2
Hot Spot for Advancement for Women/Minorities: Y

LOCATIONS: ("Y" = Yes)

West:	Southwest:	Midwest:	Southeast:	Northeast:	International:
		Y	Y	Y	

Note: Financial information, benefits and other data can change quickly and may vary from those stated here.

PARAMETRIC TECHNOLOGY CORP

www.ptc.com

Industry Group Code: 511210N Ranks within this company's industry group: Sales: 2 Profits: 2

Management:		Sales/Marketing:		Liberal Arts:		Information Systems:		Professionals:		Tech./Scientific:	
Management Trainees:	Y	Marketing Pros.:	Y	Gen. Writing/Editing:	Y	Info. Management:	Y	Finance/Acct.:	Y	Engineers, Electrical:	Y
Experienced Mngmt.:	Y	Retail Sales:		Technical Writing:	Y	Software Dev.:	Y	Law:	Y	Engineers, Other:	Y
International Business:	Y	Commercial/Industrial:	Y	Graphic Arts/Photog.:		Hardware Dev.:		HR/Other:	Y	Health/Lab:	
MBA Grads:	Y	Sales Trainees:		Music:		Consulting/Other:		Training:	Y	Scientists/Research:	
		Advertising Pros.:	Y	Broadcasting:				Health Care:		Petroleum/Chemicals:	
				Other:				Consulting:		Math/Other:	

TYPES OF BUSINESS:
Computer Software-Engineering & Manufacturing
Engineering Consulting Services
Enterprise Publishing Software
Product Data Management

BRANDS/DIVISIONS/AFFILIATES:
Pro/ENGINEER
Arbortext, Inc.
Arbortext Advanced Print Publisher
Mathsoft Engineering & Education, Inc.
Mathcad
ITEDO Software LLC
CoCreate Software GmbH
Pro/ENGINEER Manikin

CONTACTS: *Note: Officers with more than one job title may be intentionally listed here more than once.*
C. Richard (Dick) Harrison, CEO
C. Richard (Dick) Harrison, Pres.
Neil F. Moses, CFO/Exec. VP
Paul J. Cunningham, Exec. VP-Worldwide Sales
Steve Horan, CIO/Corp. VP
James E. (Jim) Heppelmann, Chief Prod. Officer/Exec. VP-Software Solutions
Aaron C. von Staats, General Counsel/Sr. VP
Barry F. Cohen, Exec. VP-Strategic Svcs. & Partners
Anita Berryman, Sr. Mgr.-Corp. Comm.
Kristian P. Talvitie, VP-Investor Rel.
Anthony (Tony) DiBona, Exec. VP-Global Maintenance Support
Noel G. Posternak, Chmn.
Paul J. Cunningham, Exec. VP-Dist.

Phone: 781-370-5000	Fax: 781-370-6000
Toll-Free: 877-275-4782	
Address: 140 Kendrick St., Needham, MA 02494 US	

GROWTH PLANS/SPECIAL FEATURES:
Parametric Technology Corp. (PTC) develops, markets and supports product lifecycle management (PLM) and enterprise content management (ECM) software that help companies improve their product development processes. It offers product data management, dynamic publishing solutions, supplier management, digital mockup, enterprise application integration, project management, after-market service, customer needs management and manufacturing planning. PTC's leading product family, Pro/ENGINEER, is a 3D modeling software used by large enterprises including NASA. The Pro/ENGINEER family includes Pro/ENGINEER CAD, CAM and CAE. The firm's Windchill Software enables users to enhance their businesses via the Internet through digital mock-up collaboration, internal library design, product data management tools and cross-application integration. PTC owns Arbortext, Inc., a leader in the dynamic enterprise publishing market, and subsequently released Arbortext Advanced Print Publisher 9.0, designed assist in the production of technical documentation; financial reports; scientific, technical and medical journals; legislation and amendments; marketing brochures; telephone directories; and product catalogs. PTC also owns Mathsoft Engineering & Education, Inc., which creates Mathcad software essential to the PLM process; and ITEDO Software GmbH and ITEDO Software LLC, designers of software which creates technical illustrations. PTC has partnered with many companies in recent years, including Autodesk, Inc., to expand its manufacturing capabilities; International Business Machines Corp. (IBM), to integrate with the IBM Rational Software Development platform and focus on the PLM market in China; and IHS, Inc., to deliver electronic components content to users of PTC Windchill. In November 2008, PTC launched Pro/ENGINEER Manikin, a program than can insert 3D human models into a CAD model to assess human-product interactions, such as ergonomic issues. In December 2008, the company acquired Synapsis Technology, Inc., and plans to integrate Synapsis' technology into Windchill.

Parametric provides its employees with tuition reimbursement; paid time off; medical, dental and vision plans; life insurance; and short- and long-term disability coverage.

FINANCIALS: Sales and profits are in thousands of dollars—add 000 to get the full amount. 2008 Note: Financial information for 2008 was not available for all companies at press time.

2008 Sales: $1,070,330	2008 Profits: $79,702	U.S. Stock Ticker: PMTC
2007 Sales: $941,279	2007 Profits: $143,656	Int'l Ticker: Int'l Exchange:
2006 Sales: $847,983	2006 Profits: $56,804	Employees: 5,087
2005 Sales: $707,975	2005 Profits: $73,187	Fiscal Year Ends: 9/30
2004 Sales: $660,029	2004 Profits: $34,813	Parent Company:

SALARIES/BENEFITS:
Pension Plan:	ESOP Stock Plan:	Profit Sharing:	Top Exec. Salary: $520,000	Bonus: $
Savings Plan: Y	Stock Purch. Plan:		Second Exec. Salary: $487,000	Bonus: $

OTHER THOUGHTS:
Apparent Women Officers or Directors:
Hot Spot for Advancement for Women/Minorities:

LOCATIONS: ("Y" = Yes)
West:	Southwest:	Midwest:	Southeast:	Northeast:	International:
Y	Y	Y	Y	Y	Y

Note: Financial information, benefits and other data can change quickly and may vary from those stated here.

PAREXEL INTERNATIONAL CORP

www.parexel.com

Industry Group Code: 541712 Ranks within this company's industry group: Sales: 3 Profits: 3

Management:		Sales/Marketing:		Liberal Arts:		Information Systems:		Professionals:		Tech./Scientific:	
Management Trainees:	Y	Marketing Pros.:		Gen. Writing/Editing:	Y	Info. Management:	Y	Finance/Acct.:	Y	Engineers, Electrical:	Y
Experienced Mngmt.:	Y	Retail Sales:		Technical Writing:	Y	Software Dev.:	Y	Law:	Y	Engineers, Other:	
International Business:	Y	Commercial/Industrial:	Y	Graphic Arts/Photog.:	Y	Hardware Dev.:		HR/Other:	Y	Health/Lab:	Y
MBA Grads:	Y	Sales Trainees:		Music:		Consulting/Other:	Y	Training:	Y	Scientists/Research:	Y
		Advertising Pros.:		Broadcasting:				Health Care:	Y	Petroleum/Chemicals:	
				Other:				Consulting:	Y	Math/Other:	Y

TYPES OF BUSINESS:

Clinical Trial & Data Management
Biostatistical Analysis & Reporting
Medical Communications Services
Clinical Pharmacology Services
Consulting Services

BRANDS/DIVISIONS/AFFILIATES:

Clinical Research Services
PAREXEL Consulting & Medical Communications Svcs.
Perceptive Informatics, Inc.
Synchron Research
ClinPhone plc
Safe Implementation of Treatments in Stroke

CONTACTS: *Note: Officers with more than one job title may be intentionally listed here more than once.*

Josef H. von Rickenbach, CEO
Mark A. Goldberg, COO
James F. Winschel, Jr., CFO/Sr. VP
Ulf Schneider, Chief Admin. Officer/Sr. VP
Douglas A. Batt, General Counsel/Corp. Sec./Sr. VP
Jill L. Baker, VP-Investor Rel.
Kurt A. Brykman, Pres., PAREXEL Consulting & Medical Comm. Svcs.
Josef H. von Rickenbach, Chmn.

Phone: 781-487-9900	Fax: 781-768-5512
Toll-Free:	
Address: 200 West St., Waltham, MA 02451 US	

GROWTH PLANS/SPECIAL FEATURES:

PAREXEL International is a biopharmaceutical services company providing clinical research, medical communications services, consulting and informatics and advanced technology products and services to the worldwide pharmaceutical, biotechnology and medical device industries. Operating in 71 locations throughout 52 countries, PAREXEL has three business segments: Clinical Research Services (CRS); PAREXEL Consulting and Medical Communications Services (PCMS); and Perceptive Informatics, Inc. PAREXEL's core business, CRS, provides clinical trials management and biostatistics; data management; clinical pharmacology; and related medical advisory, patient recruitment and investigator site services. PCMS provides technical expertise and advice for drug development, regulatory affairs and biopharmaceutical process consulting; offers product launch support, including market development, product development and targeted communications services; identifies alternatives and solutions regarding product development, registration and commercialization; and provides health policy consulting and strategic reimbursement services. Lastly, Perceptive provides information technology designed to improve clients' product development processes, including medical imaging services, IVRS, CTMS, web-based portals, systems integration, and patient diary applications. In March 2008, the company sold a bioanalytical laboratory in Poitiers, France, to a subsidiary of Synchron Research. Also in March 2008, PAREXEL increased its minority stake in clinical pharmacology business of Synchron from 19.5% to 31%. In August 2008, the firm acquired ClinPhone plc, a clinical technology organization. In November 2008, PAREXEL opened an office in Lima, Peru. In December 2008, the company established an alliance with Safe Implementation of Treatments in Stroke (SITS) International to provide PAREXEL clients access to SITS' 800 investigator sites in 40 countries.

FINANCIALS: Sales and profits are in thousands of dollars—add 000 to get the full amount. 2008 Note: Financial information for 2008 was not available for all companies at press time.

2008 Sales: $964,283	2008 Profits: $64,640	**U.S. Stock Ticker: PRXL**
2007 Sales: $741,955	2007 Profits: $37,289	**Int'l Ticker:** Int'l Exchange:
2006 Sales: $614,947	2006 Profits: $23,544	Employees: 9,275
2005 Sales: $544,726	2005 Profits: $-35,177	Fiscal Year Ends: 6/30
2004 Sales: $540,983	2004 Profits: $13,791	Parent Company:

SALARIES/BENEFITS:

Pension Plan:	ESOP Stock Plan:	Profit Sharing:	Top Exec. Salary: $550,000	Bonus: $633,600
Savings Plan:	Stock Purch. Plan:		Second Exec. Salary: $409,679	Bonus: $178,882

OTHER THOUGHTS:

Apparent Women Officers or Directors: 1
Hot Spot for Advancement for Women/Minorities:

LOCATIONS: ("Y" = Yes)

West:	Southwest:	Midwest:	Southeast:	Northeast:	International:
Y				Y	Y

PARSONS BRINCKERHOFF INC

www.pbworld.com

Industry Group Code: 237   Ranks within this company's industry group: Sales: 7   Profits: 6

Management:		Sales/Marketing:		Liberal Arts:		Information Systems:		Professionals:		Tech./Scientific:	
Management Trainees:	Y	Marketing Pros.:	Y	Gen. Writing/Editing:	Y	Info. Management:	Y	Finance/Acct.:	Y	Engineers, Electrical:	Y
Experienced Mngmt.:	Y	Retail Sales:		Technical Writing:	Y	Software Dev.:	Y	Law:	Y	Engineers, Other:	Y
International Business:	Y	Commercial/Industrial:	Y	Graphic Arts/Photog.:	Y	Hardware Dev.:		HR/Other:	Y	Health/Lab:	
MBA Grads:	Y	Sales Trainees:	Y	Music:		Consulting/Other:	Y	Training:	Y	Scientists/Research:	
		Advertising Pros.:		Broadcasting:				Health Care:		Petroleum/Chemicals:	Y
				Other:				Consulting:	Y	Math/Other:	Y

TYPES OF BUSINESS:

Engineering Services
Planning, Design & Construction
Civic Construction Projects
Commercial Construction
Transportation Consulting
Program Management Services
Telecommunications & Environmental Projects

BRANDS/DIVISIONS/AFFILIATES:

Balfour Beatty PLC
PB Aviation, Inc.
PB Farradyne, Inc.
PB Buildings, Inc.
PB Constructors, Inc.
PB Telecommunications, Inc.
Parsons Brinckerhoff Power, Inc.
PB Research Library

CONTACTS: *Note: Officers with more than one job title may be intentionally listed here more than once.*

Keith Hawksworth, CEO
Richard A. Schrader, CFO/Exec. VP
John J. Ryan, Exec. VP/Dir.-Human Resources
Lisa M. Palumbo, General Counsel
Hugh Inglis, Sr. VP-Alltech
Gay Knipper, Dir.-National Program Management, PB Americas
Paul Skoutelas, Market Leader-Transit, PB Americas
James L. Lammie, Chmn.
Patrick Lun, Deputy COO-PB Int'l

Phone: 212-465-5000	Fax: 212-465-5096
Toll-Free:	
Address: 1 Penn Plz., New York, NY 10119 US	

GROWTH PLANS/SPECIAL FEATURES:

Parsons Brinckerhoff, Inc. provides engineering, consulting, and management services to local governments and the transportation, energy, and commercial market sectors. The company also offers construction services, program and project management, and facilities management. Parsons Brinckerhoff has taken on projects for clients such as Bangkok Mass Transit System Corporation and the City of Austin, Texas; and its signature works include the design of New York City's first subway and the reconfiguration of the Fort Washington Way interstate connector in Cincinnati. The company also worked with the Delhi Metro Rail Corporation to build a mass transit system designed as an urban transport system to move over 3 million passengers a day. Other relevant projects have included contracts to build a gas fired power station in Kuwait; to design a web site and communications plan for lower Manhattan, known as lowermanhatten.info; and to design and engineer the Greater Cairo Metro system. Potential clients can view the company's work through the PB Research Library, a body that showcases and publishes the details of important projects. The firm is organized into three divisions: Americas, International and Facilities. The company is employee-owned with 150 offices worldwide. In August 2008, the company entered a joint venture with The Maryland Transportation Authority for inspection and construction management services on an on call-basis. In October 2008, the company was awarded a five-year joint venture contract with The North Texas Tollway Authority for construction management services. In September 2009, the firm agreed to be acquired by U.K.-based construction giant Balfour Beatty PLC.

FINANCIALS: Sales and profits are in thousands of dollars—add 000 to get the full amount. 2008 Note: Financial information for 2008 was not available for all companies at press time.

2008 Sales: $2,343,117	2008 Profits: $73,882	U.S. Stock Ticker: Private	
2007 Sales: $1,853,741	2007 Profits: $62,117	Int'l Ticker: Int'l Exchange:	
2006 Sales: $1,689,964	2006 Profits: $46,386	Employees: 13,010	
2005 Sales: $1,447,756	2005 Profits: $27,160	Fiscal Year Ends: 10/31	
2004 Sales: $1,389,400	2004 Profits: $18,400	Parent Company: BALFOUR BEATTY PLC	

SALARIES/BENEFITS:

Pension Plan:	ESOP Stock Plan:	Profit Sharing:	Top Exec. Salary: $	Bonus: $
Savings Plan:	Stock Purch. Plan:		Second Exec. Salary: $	Bonus: $

OTHER THOUGHTS:

Apparent Women Officers or Directors: 3
Hot Spot for Advancement for Women/Minorities: Y

LOCATIONS: ("Y" = Yes)

West:	Southwest:	Midwest:	Southeast:	Northeast:	International:
Y	Y	Y	Y	Y	Y

PATTERSON COMPANIES INC

www.pattersoncompanies.com

Industry Group Code: 423450 Ranks within this company's industry group: Sales: 4   Profits: 3

Management:		Sales/Marketing:		Liberal Arts:		Information Systems:		Professionals:		Tech./Scientific:	
Management Trainees:	Y	Marketing Pros.:	Y	Gen. Writing/Editing:	Y	Info. Management:	Y	Finance/Acct.:	Y	Engineers, Electrical:	
Experienced Mngmt.:	Y	Retail Sales:		Technical Writing:	Y	Software Dev.:	Y	Law:	Y	Engineers, Other:	
International Business:	Y	Commercial/Industrial:	Y	Graphic Arts/Photog.:	Y	Hardware Dev.:		HR/Other:	Y	Health/Lab:	
MBA Grads:	Y	Sales Trainees:	Y	Music:		Consulting/Other:		Training:	Y	Scientists/Research:	
		Advertising Pros.:	Y	Broadcasting:				Health Care:	Y	Petroleum/Chemicals:	
				Other:				Consulting:		Math/Other:	

TYPES OF BUSINESS:
Dental Products & Related Services
Veterinary Products
Non-Wheelchair Assistive Products

BRANDS/DIVISIONS/AFFILIATES:
Patterson Dental Holdings, Inc.
Direct Dental Supply Co.
Webster Management LP
Patterson Medical Holdings, Inc.
Accu-Bite Dental Products, LLC
Dale Surgical Professional Supply, Inc.
Columbus Serum Company
Mobilis Healthcare Group

CONTACTS: *Note: Officers with more than one job title may be intentionally listed here more than once.*
James W. Wiltz, CEO
James W. Wiltz, Pres.
R. Stephen Armstrong, CFO/Exec. VP
Jerome E. Thygesen, VP-Human Resources
Lynn E. Askew, VP-MIS
Matthew L. Levitt, General Counsel/Sec.
Daniel H. Peckskamp, VP-Oper.
R. Stephen Armstrong, Treas.
George L. Henriques, Pres., Webster Veterinary Supply, Inc.
David P. Sproat, Pres., Patterson Medical
Scott P. Anderson, Pres., Patterson Dental
Peter L. Frechette, Chmn.

Phone: 651-686-1600	Fax: 651-686-9331
Toll-Free: 800-328-5536	
Address: 1031 Mendota Heights Rd., St. Paul, MN 55120 US	

GROWTH PLANS/SPECIAL FEATURES:

Patterson Companies, Inc. is a company engaged in the distribution of products to the dental, veterinary and medical industries. The company operates in three segments: dental supply, veterinary supply and rehabilitation supply. The dental supply segment, Patterson Dental, is one of the largest distributors of dental products in North America. The division provides consumable products, including X-ray film, restorative materials, hand instruments and sterilization products; basic and advanced technology dental equipment; practice management and clinical software; patient education systems; and office forms and stationery. Patterson Dental also offers related services including dental equipment installation; maintenance and repair; dental office design; and equipment financing. The veterinary supply segment, Webster Veterinary, provides products for the diagnosis, treatment and/or prevention of diseases in companion pets and equine animals. Webster's more than 11,000 products are sold by about 235 field sales representatives. The segment also has an agency commission business with several pharmaceutical manufacturers. The rehabilitation supply segment, Patterson Medical, distributes rehabilitation medical supplies and non-wheelchair assistive products. Patterson Medical operates as Sammons Preston Rolyan in North America and Homecraft in international markets. Subsidiaries include Patterson Dental Holdings, Inc.; Direct Dental Supply Co.; Webster Management LP; Patterson Medical Holdings, Inc.; Accu-Bite Dental Products, LLC; and Dale Surgical Professional Supply, Inc. In October 2008, the firm acquired (through Webster Veterinary) Columbus Serum Company, a distributor of companion-pet veterinary equipment, supplies and pharmaceuticals. In December 2008, Patterson Dental acquired Dolphin Imaging Systems, LLC and Dolphin Practice Management, LLC, providers of practice management software and 3D imaging for specialized dental practitioners. In April 2009, Homecraft Rolyan Ltd. acquired Mobilis Healthcare Group, a U.K. distributor of sports medicine, physical therapy and podiatry products. In June 2009, the company acquired the rehabilitation equipment and supplies division of Empi, Rehab Mediequip.

The company offers employee benefits including life, disability, medical, dental and vision insurance.

FINANCIALS: Sales and profits are in thousands of dollars—add 000 to get the full amount. 2008 Note: Financial information for 2008 was not available for all companies at press time.

2008 Sales: $2,998,729	2008 Profits: $224,858	**U.S. Stock Ticker: PDCO**
2007 Sales: $2,798,398	2007 Profits: $208,336	**Int'l Ticker:** Int'l Exchange:
2006 Sales: $2,615,123	2006 Profits: $198,425	Employees: 7,010
2005 Sales: $2,421,457	2005 Profits: $183,698	Fiscal Year Ends: 4/30
2004 Sales: $1,969,349	2004 Profits: $149,465	Parent Company:

SALARIES/BENEFITS:

Pension Plan:	ESOP Stock Plan: Y	Profit Sharing:	Top Exec. Salary: $594,900	Bonus: $
Savings Plan: Y	Stock Purch. Plan: Y		Second Exec. Salary: $289,326	Bonus: $88,481

OTHER THOUGHTS:
Apparent Women Officers or Directors: 1
Hot Spot for Advancement for Women/Minorities:

LOCATIONS: ("Y" = Yes)

West:	Southwest:	Midwest:	Southeast:	Northeast:	International:
Y	Y	Y	Y	Y	Y

PATTERSON-UTI ENERGY INC

www.patenergy.com

Industry Group Code: 213112 Ranks within this company's industry group: Sales: 7 Profits: 7

Management:		Sales/Marketing:		Liberal Arts:		Information Systems:		Professionals:		Tech./Scientific:	
Management Trainees:	Y	Marketing Pros.:	Y	Gen. Writing/Editing:		Info. Management:	Y	Finance/Acct.:	Y	Engineers, Electrical:	Y
Experienced Mngmt.:	Y	Retail Sales:		Technical Writing:	Y	Software Dev.:	Y	Law:	Y	Engineers, Other:	Y
International Business:	Y	Commercial/Industrial:	Y	Graphic Arts/Photog.:		Hardware Dev.:		HR/Other:	Y	Health/Lab:	
MBA Grads:	Y	Sales Trainees:		Music:		Consulting/Other:		Training:	Y	Scientists/Research:	
		Advertising Pros.:		Broadcasting:				Health Care:		Petroleum/Chemicals:	Y
				Other:				Consulting:		Math/Other:	

TYPES OF BUSINESS:

Oil & Gas Services
Onshore Contract Drilling Services
Drilling & Completion Fluid Services
Pressure Pumping Services
Oil & Gas Production

BRANDS/DIVISIONS/AFFILIATES:

TMBR/Sharp Drilling, Inc.

CONTACTS: Note: Officers with more than one job title may be intentionally listed here more than once.

Douglas J. Wall, CEO
Douglas J. Wall, Pres.
John E. Vollmer, III, CFO/Treas.
William L. Moll Jr., General Counsel/Sec.
John E. Vollmer, III, Sr. VP-Corp. Dev.
Greg Pipkin, Chief Acct. Officer
Kenneth N. Berns, Sr. VP
Mark S. Siegel, Chmn.

Phone: 281-765-7100	Fax: 281-765-7175
Toll-Free:	
Address: 450 Gears Rd., Ste. 500, Houston, TX 77067 US	

GROWTH PLANS/SPECIAL FEATURES:

Patterson-UTI Energy, Inc. serves land-based oil and natural gas exploration and production companies. The company operates in Texas, New Mexico, Oklahoma, Arkansas, Louisiana, Mississippi, Colorado, Utah, Wyoming, Montana, North Dakota, South Dakota, Pennsylvania and Western Canada through four business segments: contract drilling; pressure pumping; drilling and completion fluids; and oil and natural gas. The firm operates 350 currently marketable contract drilling rigs, with a maximum drilling depth capacity ranging from 5,000 to 30,000 feet; of these rigs, 281 are mechanical and 69 silicon-controlled rectifier (SCR) electric. Patterson-UTI dug 4,237 wells in 2007, each dug on average in 21 days. It operates 336 trucks and 439 trailers used to transport and support its rigs. Pressure pumping services includes stimulation, which enhances well flow by pumping corrosive acid, nitrogen gas or highly pressurized fracturing fluid into a well; and cementing, which involves inserting a substance between a wellbore and its casing to add support. It operates approximately 344 trucks and three trailers to transport and handle stimulation and cementing materials. Patterson-UTI's drilling fluids cool and lubricate the bit during drilling operations, contain formation pressures to prevent blowout, and remove rock cuttings from the hole; and completion fluids are used to accurately manipulate well pressures as well as meeting other requirements. It owns and operates 20 trucks and 92 trailers and leases another 34 trucks to transport drilling and completion fluids; and owns two mills used to process barite, a material used in drilling fluids. The oil and gas segment operates in Texas, New Mexico, Utah and Mississippi as a working interest owner. Contract drilling provided 82% of the company's 2007 revenue; pressure pumping, 10%; drilling and completion fluids, 6%; and oil and natural gas, 2%. In November 2007, the firm sold the exploration and production portions of the oil and gas segment.

FINANCIALS: Sales and profits are in thousands of dollars—add 000 to get the full amount. 2008 Note: Financial information for 2008 was not available for all companies at press time.

2008 Sales: $2,209,126	2008 Profits: $347,069	**U.S. Stock Ticker: PTEN**
2007 Sales: $2,114,194	2007 Profits: $438,639	**Int'l Ticker:** Int'l Exchange:
2006 Sales: $2,546,586	2006 Profits: $673,254	Employees: 6,600
2005 Sales: $1,740,455	2005 Profits: $372,740	Fiscal Year Ends: 12/31
2004 Sales: $1,000,769	2004 Profits: $94,346	Parent Company:

SALARIES/BENEFITS:

Pension Plan:	ESOP Stock Plan:	Profit Sharing:	Top Exec. Salary: $600,000	Bonus: $1,367,378
Savings Plan: Y	Stock Purch. Plan:		Second Exec. Salary: $350,000	Bonus: $1,823,171

OTHER THOUGHTS:

Apparent Women Officers or Directors:
Hot Spot for Advancement for Women/Minorities:

LOCATIONS: ("Y" = Yes)

West:	Southwest:	Midwest:	Southeast:	Northeast:	International:
Y	Y	Y	Y	Y	Y

Note: Financial information, benefits and other data can change quickly and may vary from those stated here.

PAYCHEX INC

www.paychex.com

Industry Group Code: 518210 Ranks within this company's industry group: Sales: 2   Profits: 2

Management:		Sales/Marketing:		Liberal Arts:		Information Systems:		Professionals:		Tech./Scientific:	
Management Trainees:	Y	Marketing Pros.:	Y	Gen. Writing/Editing:	Y	Info. Management:	Y	Finance/Acct.:	Y	Engineers, Electrical:	
Experienced Mngmt.:	Y	Retail Sales:		Technical Writing:	Y	Software Dev.:	Y	Law:	Y	Engineers, Other:	
International Business:	Y	Commercial/Industrial:	Y	Graphic Arts/Photog.:	Y	Hardware Dev.:		HR/Other:	Y	Health/Lab:	
MBA Grads:	Y	Sales Trainees:	Y	Music:		Consulting/Other:		Training:	Y	Scientists/Research:	
		Advertising Pros.:	Y	Broadcasting:				Health Care:		Petroleum/Chemicals:	
				Other:				Consulting:		Math/Other:	

TYPES OF BUSINESS:

Payroll Processing Services
Payroll & Tax Preparation
Internal Accounting Records
Human Resources Outsourcing
Employee Benefits Outsourcing
Regulatory Compliance
Workers' Compensation Insurance
Online Payroll Services

BRANDS/DIVISIONS/AFFILIATES:

Core Payroll
Major Market Services
Paychex Online

CONTACTS: *Note: Officers with more than one job title may be intentionally listed here more than once.*

Jonathan J. Judge, CEO
Jonathan J. Judge, Pres.
John M. Morphy, CFO/Sr. VP/Corp. Sec.
Walter Turek, Sr. VP-Sales & Mktg.
Martin Stowe, VP-Human Resource Svcs.
Daniel A. Canzano, VP-IT
Stephanie Schaeffer, Chief Legal Officer/VP
Martin Mucci, Sr. VP-Oper.
William G. Kuchta, VP-Organizational Dev.
Laura Saxby Lynch, Dir.-Corp. Comm.
Terri Allen, VP-Investor Rel.
Martin Stowe, VP-Human Resources Svcs.
Michael E. Gioja, VP-Product Mgmt.
Kevin N. Hill, VP-Insurance Oper.
Michael A. McCarthy, VP-Major Market Svcs.
B. Thomas Golisano, Chmn.

Phone: 585-385-6666	**Fax:**
Toll-Free: 800-322-7292	
Address: 911 Panorama Trail S., Rochester, NY 14625-0397 US	

GROWTH PLANS/SPECIAL FEATURES:

Paychex, Inc. provider of comprehensive payroll and integrated human resource and employee benefits outsourcing solutions for small- to medium-sized businesses in the U.S. It serves approximately 572,000 clients through more than 100 offices in the U.S. and serves 1,200 customers in Germany through offices in Hamburg, Berlin, Munich and Dusseldorf. Paychex mainly targets businesses with fewer than 100 employees, with 82% of its customers employing 19 people or less. The company offers services covering payroll processing; payroll tax administration; employee payment; regulatory compliance; human resources; retirement services administration; workers' compensation; health and benefits; and time and attendance solutions. Additionally offering provided by the firm are Major Market Services, which primarily targets companies that have outgrown the Core Payroll service or have more complex needs; and Paychex Online, a secure Internet site with a suite of interactive, always-available self-service products and services, offering employees current and historical time sheets through Paychex Online Reports; and downloadable payroll information through General Ledger Services. The firm's payroll processing services are the foundation of its service portfolio. Its payroll service includes the calculation, preparation, and delivery of employee payroll checks; production of internal accounting records and management reports; preparation of federal, state, and local payroll tax returns; and collection and remittance of clients' payroll obligations. Payroll services are provided through either the core payroll or Major Market Services and are made available to clients via traditional or Internet-based methods.

Employees of Paychex receive medical, vision and dental coverage; life insurance; a prescription drug plan; domestic partner benefits including medical, pharmacy, dental and life insurance; flexible spending accounts; child care and employee assistance programs; tuition reimbursement; The WellPower wellness program; a 401(k) plan; employee stock purchase plan; adoption assistance; employee discounts; a scholarship program; and a referral program.

FINANCIALS: Sales and profits are in thousands of dollars—add 000 to get the full amount. 2008 Note: Financial information for 2008 was not available for all companies at press time.

2008 Sales: $2,066,323	2008 Profits: $576,145	**U.S. Stock Ticker: PAYX**
2007 Sales: $1,886,964	2007 Profits: $515,447	**Int'l Ticker:** Int'l Exchange:
2006 Sales: $1,674,596	2006 Profits: $464,914	Employees: 12,500
2005 Sales: $1,445,143	2005 Profits: $368,849	Fiscal Year Ends: 5/31
2004 Sales: $1,240,093	2004 Profits: $302,950	Parent Company:

SALARIES/BENEFITS:

Pension Plan:	ESOP Stock Plan:	Profit Sharing:	Top Exec. Salary: $908,606	Bonus: $1,030,979
Savings Plan: Y	Stock Purch. Plan: Y		Second Exec. Salary: $411,498	Bonus: $268,362

OTHER THOUGHTS:

Apparent Women Officers or Directors: 6
Hot Spot for Advancement for Women/Minorities: Y

LOCATIONS: ("Y" = Yes)

West:	Southwest:	Midwest:	Southeast:	Northeast:	International:
Y	Y	Y	Y	Y	Y

PEABODY ENERGY CORP

www.peabodyenergy.com

Industry Group Code: 21211 Ranks within this company's industry group: Sales: 1 Profits: 1

Management:		Sales/Marketing:		Liberal Arts:		Information Systems:		Professionals:		Tech./Scientific:	
Management Trainees:	Y	Marketing Pros.:	Y	Gen. Writing/Editing:		Info. Management:	Y	Finance/Acct.:	Y	Engineers, Electrical:	
Experienced Mngmt.:	Y	Retail Sales:		Technical Writing:	Y	Software Dev.:		Law:	Y	Engineers, Other:	Y
International Business:	Y	Commercial/Industrial:	Y	Graphic Arts/Photog.:		Hardware Dev.:		HR/Other:	Y	Health/Lab:	
MBA Grads:	Y	Sales Trainees:		Music:		Consulting/Other:		Training:	Y	Scientists/Research:	
		Advertising Pros.:		Broadcasting:				Health Care:		Petroleum/Chemicals:	Y
				Other:				Consulting:		Math/Other:	

TYPES OF BUSINESS:

Coal Production
Energy Trading & Marketing
Transportation Services
Carbon Capture
Coal Conversion Technologies

BRANDS/DIVISIONS/AFFILIATES:

GreatPoint Energy, Inc.
Peabody-Polo Resources B.V.

CONTACTS: Note: Officers with more than one job title may be intentionally listed here more than once.

Gregory H. Boyce, CEO
Eric Ford, COO/Exec. VP
Richard A. Navarre, Pres./Chief Commercial Officer
Michael C. Crews, CFO/Exec. VP
Lina A. Young, Sr. VP-Mktg. & Commercial Svcs.
George J. Schuller, VP-Tech. & Eng.
Charles Meintjes, Sr. VP-Eng. & Continuous Improvement
Sharon D. Fiehler, Exec. VP-Admin.
Alexander C. Scoch, Chief Legal Officer/Exec. VP
Kemal Williamson, VP-Oper.
Robert L. Reilly, Sr. VP-Bus. Dev.
Vic Svec, Sr. VP-Corp. Comm.
Vic Svec, Sr. VP-Investor Rel.
L. Brent Stottlemyre, Chief Acct. Officer/Controller/Sr. VP
Brian A. Galli, Pres., COALSALES
Paul T. Demzik, Pres., COALTRADE International
Stephen L. Miller, Pres., COALTRADE
Tayeb Tahir, Pres., Peabody China
Gregory H. Boyce, Chmn.
Julian Thornton, Managing Dir.-Australia

Phone: 314-342-3400	Fax: 314-342-7799
Toll-Free:	
Address: 701 Market St., St. Louis, MO 63101 US	

GROWTH PLANS/SPECIAL FEATURES:

Peabody Energy Corp. is a private-sector coal company with operations worldwide. The firm sells approximately 255 million tons of coal annually to a clientele of nearly 330 electricity generating and industrial plants in 21 countries. It shipped 200.4 million tons from 20 U.S. mining operations and 23.9 million tons from 10 Australia operations in 2008. The company has approximately 9.2 billion tons of proven and probable coal reserves. The mining operations consist of three principal operating segments: western U.S. mining, midwestern U.S. mining and Australian mining. In addition to mining operations, the firm markets, brokers and trades coal through a trading and brokerage operations segment. The firm's total tons traded were 192.9 million in 2008. Peabody Energy has international trading locations in London, U.K.; Newcastle, Australia; and Beijing, China. Other energy-related commercial activities include the development of mine-mouth coal-fueled generating plants; the management of vast coal reserve and real estate holdings; the advancement of carbon capture sequestration initiatives in the U.S., China and Australia; and Btu conversion technologies, which are designed to convert coal to natural gas and transportation fuels. During 2008, the company acquired the remaining 15.4% of the Millennium Mine in Queensland, Australia; completed the over $50 million expansion of its Wambo Coal Preparation Facility; acquired a minority interest in GreatPoint Energy, Inc.; and sold its 62.5% interest in the Baralaba Mine in Australia. In May 2009, the firm formed a joint venture, Peabody-Polo Resources B.V., with Polo Resources Limited for the ownership of Polo Resources' Mongolian coal interests. In June 2009, Peabody Energy and Shanxi Lu'an Mining Group Company, Ltd. entered an agreement for the possible joint development and operation of Lu'an Mining's Shaxi Mine in Northwestern China.

FINANCIALS: Sales and profits are in thousands of dollars—add 000 to get the full amount. 2008 Note: Financial information for 2008 was not available for all companies at press time.

2008 Sales: $6,593,400	2008 Profits: $953,500	U.S. Stock Ticker: BTU
2007 Sales: $4,574,712	2007 Profits: $264,285	Int'l Ticker: Int'l Exchange:
2006 Sales: $4,108,396	2006 Profits: $600,697	Employees: 7,200
2005 Sales: $4,644,453	2005 Profits: $422,653	Fiscal Year Ends: 12/31
2004 Sales: $3,631,582	2004 Profits: $175,387	Parent Company:

SALARIES/BENEFITS:

Pension Plan:	ESOP Stock Plan:	Profit Sharing:	Top Exec. Salary: $1,053,750	Bonus: $2,069,375
Savings Plan:	Stock Purch. Plan:		Second Exec. Salary: $730,000	Bonus: $1,116,900

OTHER THOUGHTS:

Apparent Women Officers or Directors: 4
Hot Spot for Advancement for Women/Minorities: Y

LOCATIONS: ("Y" = Yes)

West:	Southwest:	Midwest:	Southeast:	Northeast:	International:
Y		Y			Y

Note: Financial information, benefits and other data can change quickly and may vary from those stated here.

PEPSI BOTTLING GROUP INC

www.pbg.com

Industry Group Code: 3121 Ranks within this company's industry group: Sales: 4 Profits: 3

Management:		Sales/Marketing:		Liberal Arts:		Information Systems:		Professionals:		Tech./Scientific:	
Management Trainees:	Y	Marketing Pros.:	Y	Gen. Writing/Editing:	Y	Info. Management:	Y	Finance/Acct.:	Y	Engineers, Electrical:	
Experienced Mngmt.:	Y	Retail Sales:		Technical Writing:	Y	Software Dev.:	Y	Law:	Y	Engineers, Other:	Y
International Business:	Y	Commercial/Industrial:	Y	Graphic Arts/Photog.:	Y	Hardware Dev.:		HR/Other:	Y	Health/Lab:	
MBA Grads:	Y	Sales Trainees:	Y	Music:		Consulting/Other:		Training:	Y	Scientists/Research:	
		Advertising Pros.:	Y	Broadcasting:				Health Care:		Petroleum/Chemicals:	
				Other:				Consulting:		Math/Other:	

TYPES OF BUSINESS:

Beverages-Soft Drinks Manufacturing
Bottled Water
Iced Tea

BRANDS/DIVISIONS/AFFILIATES:

Mirinda
Pepsi-Cola
Aquafina
Lipton
Mountain Dew
Sobe
Pepsi-Cola Batavia Bottling Corp
Lane Affiliated Companies Inc

CONTACTS: *Note: Officers with more than one job title may be intentionally listed here more than once.*

Eric J. Foss, CEO
Alfred H. Drewes, CFO/Sr. VP
John L. Berisford, Sr. VP/Chief Personnel Officer
Neal A. Bronzo, CIO/Sr. VP
Steven M. Rapp, General Counsel/Sr. VP/Corp. Sec.
Victor L. Crawford, Sr. VP-Global Oper. & System Transformation
Eric Llopis, Sr. VP/Chief Strategy Officer
Thomas M. Lardieri, VP/Controller
Yiannis Petrides, Pres., PBG Europe
Robert C. King, Pres., PBG North America
Brent J. Franks, Pres., PBG Mexico
Eric J. Foss, Chmn.

Phone: 914-767-6000	Fax: 914-767-7761
Toll-Free:	
Address: 1 Pepsi Way, Somers, NY 10589-2201 US	

GROWTH PLANS/SPECIAL FEATURES:

The Pepsi Bottling Group, Inc. (PBG), a 41.7% subsidiary of PepsiCo, Inc., is one of the world's largest manufacturers and distributors of Pepsi-Cola beverages. In certain regions, PBG owns the rights to manufacture, sell and distribute the soft drink products of other companies, such as Dr Pepper and Squirt. In addition, in certain markets, PBG has the right to manufacture, sell and distribute beverages under trademarks which it owns, including Electropura and Garci Crespo. The company has the exclusive right to manufacture, sell and distribute Pepsi-Cola beverages in all or a portion of 41 U.S. states, Washington, D.C., nine Canadian provinces, Spain, Greece, Russia, Turkey and 23 states in Mexico. Principal beverage brands include Pepsi, Diet Pepsi, Mountain Dew, Sierra Mist, Tropicana juice drinks, G2 from Gatorade, Mug Root Beer, 7-UP, Aguas Frescas, Jarritos, Lipton, SoBe, Starbucks Frappuccino, Dole juices and Aquafina bottled water. PBG's sales represent over half of all Pepsi-Cola beverages sold in the U.S. and Canada, and approximately 40% of Pepsi-Cola sales worldwide. Its three largest U.S. brands in terms of volume are Pepsi-Cola, Diet Pepsi and Mountain Dew. Worldwide, the company operates over 100 plants and 545 distribution centers. PBG operates in three reportable segments: U.S. & Canada, representing approximately 76% of annual sales; Europe, representing approximately 14% of annual sales; and Mexico, accounting for approximately 10% of annual sales. In March 2008, the company completed its acquisition of Pepsi-Cola Batavia Bottling Corp. In December 2008, Pepsi Bottling Group completed its acquisition of Lane Affiliated Companies, Inc., a Pepsi bottling company serving parts of Colorado, Arizona and New Mexico. In July 2009, Pepsi Bottling Group, along with fellow Pepsi affiliate PepsiAmericas, Inc., agreed to be wholly acquired by PepsiCo in a transaction valued at approximately $7.8 billion; the acquisition is aimed at consolidating Pepsi's worldwide bottling and distribution operations.

The company offers its employees a 401(k) plan; medical, dental and vision insurance; life and accident insurance; short- and long-term disability insurance; same sex domestic partner coverage; a stock purchase program; and tuition reimbursement.

FINANCIALS: Sales and profits are in thousands of dollars—add 000 to get the full amount. 2008 Note: Financial information for 2008 was not available for all companies at press time.

2008 Sales: $13,796,000	2008 Profits: $162,000	U.S. Stock Ticker: PBG
2007 Sales: $13,591,000	2007 Profits: $532,000	Int'l Ticker: Int'l Exchange:
2006 Sales: $12,730,000	2006 Profits: $522,000	Employees: 66,800
2005 Sales: $11,885,000	2005 Profits: $466,000	Fiscal Year Ends: 12/31
2004 Sales: $10,906,000	2004 Profits: $457,000	Parent Company:

SALARIES/BENEFITS:

Pension Plan:	ESOP Stock Plan:	Profit Sharing:	Top Exec. Salary: $984,615	Bonus: $840,000
Savings Plan: Y	Stock Purch. Plan:		Second Exec. Salary: $754,990	Bonus: $582,176

OTHER THOUGHTS:

Apparent Women Officers or Directors: 4
Hot Spot for Advancement for Women/Minorities: Y

LOCATIONS: ("Y" = Yes)

West:	Southwest:	Midwest:	Southeast:	Northeast:	International:
Y	Y	Y	Y	Y	Y

Note: Financial information, benefits and other data can change quickly and may vary from those stated here.

PEPSICO INC

www.pepsico.com

Industry Group Code: 3121 Ranks within this company's industry group: Sales: 1 Profits: 1

Management:		Sales/Marketing:		Liberal Arts:		Information Systems:		Professionals:		Tech./Scientific:	
Management Trainees:	Y	Marketing Pros.:	Y	Gen. Writing/Editing:	Y	Info. Management:	Y	Finance/Acct.:	Y	Engineers, Electrical:	
Experienced Mngmt.:	Y	Retail Sales:		Technical Writing:	Y	Software Dev.:	Y	Law:	Y	Engineers, Other:	Y
International Business:	Y	Commercial/Industrial:	Y	Graphic Arts/Photog.:	Y	Hardware Dev.:		HR/Other:	Y	Health/Lab:	
MBA Grads:	Y	Sales Trainees:	Y	Music:		Consulting/Other:		Training:	Y	Scientists/Research:	
		Advertising Pros.:	Y	Broadcasting:				Health Care:		Petroleum/Chemicals:	
				Other:	Y			Consulting:		Math/Other:	

TYPES OF BUSINESS:

Soft Drink Manufacturing
Snack Food Manufacturing
Juice & Sports Drink Manufacturing
Cereal Manufacturing
Rice & Pasta Product Manufacturing
Oatmeal Product Manufacturing
Bottled Water Production
Cereal Bar Manufacturing

BRANDS/DIVISIONS/AFFILIATES:

Frito-Lay North America
PepsiCo Beverages North America
PepsiCo International
Quaker Foods North America

CONTACTS: Note: Officers with more than one job title may be intentionally listed here more than once.

Indra K. Nooyi, CEO
Richard Goodman, CFO
Cynthia M. Trudell, Chief Personnel Officer/Sr. VP
Mehmood Khan, Chief Scientific Officer
Larry D. Thompson, General Counsel/Sec./Sr. VP-Gov't Affairs
Wahid Hamid, Sr. VP-Corp. Strategy & Dev.
Julie Hamp, Sr. VP-PepsiCo Comm.
Lionel L. Nowell III, Treas./Sr. VP
Ronald C. Parker, Chief Diversity & Inclusion Officer
Peter A. Bridgman, Controller/Sr. VP
John C. Compton, CEO-PepsiCo Americas Foods
Massimo F. d'Amore, CEO-PepsiCo Americas Beverages
Indra K. Nooyi, Chmn.
Michael D. White, CEO-PepsiCo Int'l
Mitch Adamek, Chief Procurement Officer/Sr. VP

Phone: 914-253-2000	Fax: 914-253-2070
Toll-Free:	
Address: 700 Anderson Hill Rd., Purchase, NY 10577 US	

GROWTH PLANS/SPECIAL FEATURES:

PepsiCo, Inc. is a global manufacturer, marketer and distributer of snack foods and beverages. The company operates in four segments: Frito-Lay North America; PepsiCo Beverages North America; PepsiCo International; and Quaker Foods North America. Frito-Lay North America manufactures or uses contract manufacturers, markets, sells and distributes branded snacks. Brands offered include, but are not limited to, Lay's potato chips, Doritos, Cheetos, Fritos, Ruffles, Quaker Chewy granola bars and SunChips. Approximated 29% of the firm's total net revenue is derived from this division. PepsiCo Beverages North America (PBNA) manufactures, manufactures or uses contract manufacturers, markets and sells a wide variety of brands such as Pepsi, Mountain Dew, Gatorade, Tropicana, Lipton, Sierra Mist and Propel. It also markets ready-to-drink beverages through joint ventures with Unilever and Starbucks. In addition, PBNA licenses the Aquafina water brand to its bottlers and markets the brand. PBNA accounts for approximately 26% of the firm's total net revenue. PepsiCo International manufactures (through consolidated businesses as well as through noncontrolled affiliates) a range of snack foods and beverages for international markets. This division accounts for 40% of total net revenue. Quaker Foods North America (QFNA) manufactures or uses contract manufacturers, markets and sells its line of branded products. QFNA's products include Quaker oatmeal, Aunt Jemima mixes and syrups, Life cereal, Quaker grits, Rice-A-Roni and Pasta Roni. QFNA accounts for approximately 5% of the firm's total net revenue. In October 2008, the company announced plans to cut 3,300 jobs and close six plants. In July 2009, the firm reached an agreement to wholly acquire its two biggest independent bottlers, Pepsi Bottling Group, Inc. and PepsiAmericas, Inc., in a transaction valued at approximately $7.8 billion.

The firm offers employees medical, dental and vision coverage; health and dependent care reimbursement accounts; a wellness program; a pension plan; a stock purchase plan; an employee assistance program; adoption assistance; tuition reimbursement; Ford and GM car discount programs; auto and home insurance programs; and special discounts on cell phones, computers, movie tickets, hotels and resorts and concert tickets.

FINANCIALS: Sales and profits are in thousands of dollars—add 000 to get the full amount. 2008 Note: Financial information for 2008 was not available for all companies at press time.

2008 Sales: $43,251,000	2008 Profits: $6,935,000	**U.S. Stock Ticker:** PEP
2007 Sales: $39,474,000	2007 Profits: $5,658,000	**Int'l Ticker:** Int'l Exchange:
2006 Sales: $35,137,000	2006 Profits: $5,642,000	Employees: 198,000
2005 Sales: $32,562,000	2005 Profits: $4,078,000	Fiscal Year Ends: 12/31
2004 Sales: $29,261,000	2004 Profits: $4,212,000	Parent Company:

SALARIES/BENEFITS:

Pension Plan: Y	ESOP Stock Plan:	Profit Sharing:	Top Exec. Salary: $1,300,000	Bonus: $2,600,000
Savings Plan: Y	Stock Purch. Plan: Y		Second Exec. Salary: $1,000,000	Bonus: $2,289,800

OTHER THOUGHTS:

Apparent Women Officers or Directors: 2
Hot Spot for Advancement for Women/Minorities: Y

LOCATIONS: ("Y" = Yes)

West:	Southwest:	Midwest:	Southeast:	Northeast:	International:
Y	Y	Y	Y	Y	Y

PEROT SYSTEMS CORP

www.perotsystems.com

Industry Group Code: 541513 Ranks within this company's industry group: Sales: 7 Profits: 6

Management:		Sales/Marketing:		Liberal Arts:		Information Systems:		Professionals:		Tech./Scientific:	
Management Trainees:	Y	Marketing Pros.:	Y	Gen. Writing/Editing:	Y	Info. Management:	Y	Finance/Acct.:	Y	Engineers, Electrical:	Y
Experienced Mngmt.:	Y	Retail Sales:		Technical Writing:	Y	Software Dev.:	Y	Law:	Y	Engineers, Other:	
International Business:	Y	Commercial/Industrial:	Y	Graphic Arts/Photog.:	Y	Hardware Dev.:	Y	HR/Other:	Y	Health/Lab:	
MBA Grads:	Y	Sales Trainees:		Music:		Consulting/Other:	Y	Training:	Y	Scientists/Research:	
		Advertising Pros.:	Y	Broadcasting:				Health Care:		Petroleum/Chemicals:	
				Other:	Y			Consulting:	Y	Math/Other:	

TYPES OF BUSINESS:

IT Consulting
Business Process Outsourcing
Management Consulting
Government Services
Infrastructure Services
Systems & Software Development

BRANDS/DIVISIONS/AFFILIATES:

QSS Group Inc
JJWild Inc
Original Solutions Limited

CONTACTS: Note: Officers with more than one job title may be intentionally listed here more than once.

Peter Altabef, CEO
Russell Freeman, COO
Peter Altabef, Pres.
John Harper, CFO
Jeff Renzi, Exec. VP-Mktg. & Sales
Darcy Anderson, Chief People Officer/VP-Corp. Support
Susan Nolan, CIO
Del Williams, General Counsel/VP/Corp. Sec
Raj Asava, Chief Strategy Officer
John King, VP
James Champy, Chmn.-Consulting
Scott Barnes, VP-Infrastructure Solutions
Atul Vohra, Chief Mktg. Officer
Ross Perot, Jr., Chmn.

Phone: 972-577-0000	Fax:
Toll-Free: 888-317-3768	
Address: 2300 W. Plano Pkwy., Plano, TX 75075 US	

GROWTH PLANS/SPECIAL FEATURES:

Perot Systems Corp. is a worldwide provider of information technology (IT) services and business solutions to a broad range of customers. The firm offers integrated solutions designed around specific business objectives, with services including technology outsourcing, business process outsourcing, development and integration of systems and applications, and business and technology consulting services. Services are divided into four primary segments: infrastructure services, applications services, business process services and consulting services. The infrastructure services segment forms multi-year contracts through which it assumes operational responsibility for various aspects of customers' businesses. Perot Systems can take charge of a company's data center management, web hosting and Internet access, desktop solutions, messaging services, network management, program management and security. The applications services segment includes services such as application development and maintenance, including the development and maintenance of custom and packaged application software for customers, and application systems migration and testing, which includes the migration of applications from legacy environments to current technologies, as well as performing quality assurance functions on custom applications. The division also provides other applications services such as application assessment and evaluation, hardware and architecture consulting, systems integration, and web-based services. The business process services segment includes services such as product engineering, claims processing, life insurance policy administration, call center management, payment and settlement management, security, and services to improve the collection of receivables. In addition, this group also provides engineering support and other technical and administrative services to the U.S. government. Consulting services include strategy, enterprise and technology consulting, research and software implementation. The firm's clients include government agencies, healthcare providers, the construction and manufacturing industries and financial services companies. In May 2008, the firm acquired Original Solutions Limited, an IT services company. In September 2009, Perot Systems agreed to be acquired by computer giant Dell.

FINANCIALS: Sales and profits are in thousands of dollars—add 000 to get the full amount. 2008 Note: Financial information for 2008 was not available for all companies at press time.

2008 Sales: $2,779,000	2008 Profits: $117,000	**U.S. Stock Ticker:** PER	
2007 Sales: $2,612,000	2007 Profits: $115,000	**Int'l Ticker:** Int'l Exchange:	
2006 Sales: $2,298,000	2006 Profits: $81,000	Employees: 23,000	
2005 Sales: $1,998,286	2005 Profits: $111,120	Fiscal Year Ends: 12/31	
2004 Sales: $1,773,452	2004 Profits: $94,347	Parent Company:	

SALARIES/BENEFITS:

Pension Plan:	ESOP Stock Plan:	Profit Sharing:	Top Exec. Salary: $670,990	Bonus: $955,000
Savings Plan:	Stock Purch. Plan:		Second Exec. Salary: $572,741	Bonus: $

OTHER THOUGHTS:

Apparent Women Officers or Directors:
Hot Spot for Advancement for Women/Minorities:

LOCATIONS: ("Y" = Yes)

West:	Southwest:	Midwest:	Southeast:	Northeast:	International:
Y	Y	Y	Y	Y	Y

PERRIGO CO

www.perrigo.com

Industry Group Code: 325412 Ranks within this company's industry group: Sales: 17 Profits: 14

Management:		Sales/Marketing:		Liberal Arts:		Information Systems:		Professionals:		Tech./Scientific:	
Management Trainees:	Y	Marketing Pros.:	Y	Gen. Writing/Editing:		Info. Management:	Y	Finance/Acct.:	Y	Engineers, Electrical:	Y
Experienced Mngmt.:	Y	Retail Sales:		Technical Writing:	Y	Software Dev.:	Y	Law:	Y	Engineers, Other:	Y
International Business:	Y	Commercial/Industrial:	Y	Graphic Arts/Photog.:		Hardware Dev.:		HR/Other:	Y	Health/Lab:	Y
MBA Grads:	Y	Sales Trainees:		Music:		Consulting/Other:		Training:	Y	Scientists/Research:	Y
		Advertising Pros.:		Broadcasting:				Health Care:	Y	Petroleum/Chemicals:	Y
				Other:				Consulting:		Math/Other:	Y

TYPES OF BUSINESS:

Generic Prescription Drugs
Over-the-Counter Pharmaceuticals
Nutritional Products
Active Pharmaceutical Ingredients
Consumer Products

BRANDS/DIVISIONS/AFFILIATES:

Chemagis
Neca
Natural Formula
Perrigo New York, Inc.
Perrigo Israel Pharmaceuticals, Ltd.
JB Laboratories
Laboratorios Diba, S.A.
Unico Holdings

CONTACTS: Note: Officers with more than one job title may be intentionally listed here more than once.

Joseph C. Papa, CEO
Joseph C. Papa, Pres.
Judy L. Brown, CFO/Exec. VP
James Tomshack, Sr. VP-Consumer Healthcare Sales
Michael Stewart, Sr. VP-Global Human Resources
Jatin Shah, Chief Scientific Officer/Sr. VP
Thomas M. Farrington, CIO
Todd W. Kingma, General Counsel/Exec. VP/Sec.
John T. Hendrickson, Exec. VP-Global Oper.
Jeffrey R. Needham, Sr. VP-Global Bus. Dev.
Arthur J. Shannon, VP-Corp. Comm.
Arthur J. Shannon, VP-Investor Rel.
Sharon Kochan, Exec. VP-U.S. Generics
Louis Yu, Sr. VP-Global Quality & Compliance
David T. Gibbons, Chmn.
Refael Lebel, Exec. VP/Gen. Mgr.-Perrigo Israel
John T. Hendrickson, Exec. VP-Supply Chain

Phone: 269-673-8451	Fax: 269-673-7534
Toll-Free:	
Address: 515 Eastern Ave., Allegan, MI 49010 US	

GROWTH PLANS/SPECIAL FEATURES:

Perrigo Co. is a global healthcare supplier and one of the world's largest manufacturers of over-the-counter pharmaceutical and nutritional products for the store brand market. The company also develops and manufactures generic prescription drugs, active pharmaceutical ingredients (API) and consumer products. The firm operates through three segments: consumer healthcare, prescription pharmaceuticals and API. The consumer healthcare segment makes a broad line of products including analgesics, cough/cold/allergy/sinus, gastrointestinal, smoking cessation, first aid, vitamin and nutritional supplement products. The pharmaceuticals segment's primary activity is the development, manufacture and sale of generic prescription drug products, generally for the U.S. market. The company currently markets roughly 250 generic prescription products to approximately 110 customers. The API segment, through subsidiary Chemagis, develops, manufactures and markets API for the drug industry and branded pharmaceutical companies. In addition, Perrigo's operations also include the Israel consumer products segment, which consist of cosmetics, toiletries and detergents generally sold under brands such as Careline, Neca and Natural Formula, and the Israel pharmaceutical and diagnostic products segment, which includes the marketing and manufacturing of branded prescription drugs under long-term exclusive licenses and the importation of pharmaceutical, diagnostics and other medical products into Israel based on exclusive agreement with the manufacturers. Perrigo operates through several wholly-owned subsidiaries. In the U.S., these subsidiaries consist primarily of L. Perrigo Co.; Perrigo Co. of South Carolina; and Perrigo New York, Inc. Outside the U.S., the subsidiaries consist primarily of Perrigo Israel Pharmaceuticals, Ltd.; Quimica Y Farmacia S.A. de C.V.; Wrafton Laboratories, Ltd.; and Perrigo U.K., Ltd. In 2008, the company acquired JB Laboratories; the Mexican Manufacturer, Laboratorios Diba, S.A.; and Unico Holdings. In March 2009, the firm received FDA approval to market Sulfacetamide Sodium Topical Suspension, 10%, a topical acne treatment.

FINANCIALS: Sales and profits are in thousands of dollars—add 000 to get the full amount. 2008 Note: Financial information for 2008 was not available for all companies at press time.

2008 Sales: $1,729,921	2008 Profits: $135,773	**U.S. Stock Ticker: PRGO**
2007 Sales: $1,368,351	2007 Profits: $73,797	**Int'l Ticker:** Int'l Exchange:
2006 Sales: $1,366,821	2006 Profits: $71,400	Employees: 7,250
2005 Sales: $1,024,098	2005 Profits: $-325,983	Fiscal Year Ends: 6/30
2004 Sales: $898,204	2004 Profits: $80,567	Parent Company:

SALARIES/BENEFITS:

Pension Plan:	ESOP Stock Plan:	Profit Sharing:	Top Exec. Salary: $775,000	Bonus: $1,658,500
Savings Plan:	Stock Purch. Plan:		Second Exec. Salary: $389,275	Bonus: $487,920

OTHER THOUGHTS:

Apparent Women Officers or Directors: 3
Hot Spot for Advancement for Women/Minorities: Y

LOCATIONS: ("Y" = Yes)

West:	Southwest:	Midwest:	Southeast:	Northeast:	International:
				Y	Y

Note: Financial information, benefits and other data can change quickly and may vary from those stated here.

PETCO ANIMAL SUPPLIES INC

www.petco.com

Industry Group Code: 453910 **Ranks within this company's industry group:** Sales: 2   Profits:

Management:		Sales/Marketing:		Liberal Arts:		Information Systems:		Professionals:		Tech./Scientific:	
Management Trainees:	Y	Marketing Pros.:	Y	Gen. Writing/Editing:	Y	Info. Management:	Y	Finance/Acct.:	Y	Engineers, Electrical:	
Experienced Mngmt.:	Y	Retail Sales:	Y	Technical Writing:		Software Dev.:	Y	Law:	Y	Engineers, Other:	
International Business:		Commercial/Industrial:		Graphic Arts/Photog.:	Y	Hardware Dev.:		HR/Other:	Y	Health/Lab:	
MBA Grads:	Y	Sales Trainees:	Y	Music:		Consulting/Other:		Training:	Y	Scientists/Research:	
		Advertising Pros.:	Y	Broadcasting:				Health Care:		Petroleum/Chemicals:	
				Other:	Y			Consulting:		Math/Other:	

TYPES OF BUSINESS:

Pets & Pet Supplies, Retail
Online Sales
Pet Grooming
Veterinary Services
Obedience Training
Pet Photography

BRANDS/DIVISIONS/AFFILIATES:

Petco Foundation (The)
P.A.L.S.
Think Adoption First
Leonard Green & Partners LP
TPG (Texas Pacific Group)

CONTACTS: *Note: Officers with more than one job title may be intentionally listed here more than once.*

James M. Myers, CEO
Bruce C. Hall, COO
Bruce C. Hall, Pres.
Michael E. Foss, CFO/Exec. VP
Marc Brown, VP-Human Resources
Herman Nell, CIO
David Bolen, Chief Merch. Officer/Exec. VP
Reginald Holden, VP-Procurement
Charlie Piscitello, Chief People Officer/Sr. VP
Brian K. Devine, Chmn.

Phone: 858-453-7845	Fax: 858-677-3489
Toll-Free: 888-824-7257	
Address: 9125 Rehco Rd., San Diego, CA 92121 US	

GROWTH PLANS/SPECIAL FEATURES:

Petco Animal Supplies, Inc. is a leading specialty retailer of premium pet food, supplies and services. The company currently operates over 950 stores and 11 distribution centers in 49 states and Washington, D.C. Petco's superstores carry more than 10,000 products, including premium pet food and treats; small animals, such as fish, birds, reptiles and related supplies; collars and leashes; grooming products; toys; pet carriers; cat furniture; dog houses; vitamins; and veterinary supplies. Most stores also provide a variety of pet services, including professional grooming, veterinary clinics, vaccinations, obedience training and pet photography. Several services are performed in glass-walled stations in order to increase customer awareness and confidence in the services. In light of overpopulation problems, Petco chooses not to sell dogs and cats, though it does support adoption programs such as Petfinder.com through in-store Think Adoption First kiosks in many stores. Petco also operates the P.A.L.S. (Petco Animal Lovers Save) customer loyalty program. P.A.L.S. members receive special benefits and savings through the use of the P.A.L.S. card, which allows Petco to target customers and track shopping habits. In addition to its retail stores, the company operates an e-commerce site, which offers Petco merchandise, pet tips, a community forum, online specials and information about the Petco Foundation, an animal welfare and rights group. The company is owned by Leonard Green & Partners LP and TPG (Texas Pacific Group), two private equity investment firms.

Petco offers its employees health insurance plans, discounted pet insurance, a 401(k) retirement savings plan and merchandise discounts. The company also offers a Management Achievement Program and training programs related to specific types of animals.

FINANCIALS: Sales and profits are in thousands of dollars—add 000 to get the full amount. 2008 Note: Financial information for 2008 was not available for all companies at press time.

2008 Sales: $2,600,000	2008 Profits: $	**U.S. Stock Ticker:** Private	
2007 Sales: $2,400,000	2007 Profits: $	**Int'l Ticker:** Int'l Exchange:	
2006 Sales: $1,996,089	2006 Profits: $75,170	Employees: 21,000	
2005 Sales: $1,812,145	2005 Profits: $82,373	Fiscal Year Ends: 1/31	
2004 Sales: $1,654,138	2004 Profits: $64,713	Parent Company: TPG (TEXAS PACIFIC GROUP)	

SALARIES/BENEFITS:

Pension Plan:	ESOP Stock Plan:	Profit Sharing:	Top Exec. Salary: $	Bonus: $
Savings Plan: Y	Stock Purch. Plan:		Second Exec. Salary: $	Bonus: $

OTHER THOUGHTS:

Apparent Women Officers or Directors:
Hot Spot for Advancement for Women/Minorities:

LOCATIONS: ("Y" = Yes)

West:	Southwest:	Midwest:	Southeast:	Northeast:	International:
Y	Y	Y	Y	Y	

PETSMART INC

www.petsmart.com

Industry Group Code: 453910 Ranks within this company's industry group: Sales: 1   Profits: 1

Management:		Sales/Marketing:		Liberal Arts:		Information Systems:		Professionals:		Tech./Scientific:	
Management Trainees:	Y	Marketing Pros.:	Y	Gen. Writing/Editing:	Y	Info. Management:	Y	Finance/Acct.:	Y	Engineers, Electrical:	
Experienced Mngmt.:	Y	Retail Sales:	Y	Technical Writing:		Software Dev.:	Y	Law:	Y	Engineers, Other:	
International Business:	Y	Commercial/Industrial:		Graphic Arts/Photog.:	Y	Hardware Dev.:		HR/Other:	Y	Health/Lab:	
MBA Grads:	Y	Sales Trainees:	Y	Music:		Consulting/Other:		Training:	Y	Scientists/Research:	
		Advertising Pros.:	Y	Broadcasting:				Health Care:		Petroleum/Chemicals:	
				Other:	Y			Consulting:		Math/Other:	

TYPES OF BUSINESS:

Pets & Pet Supplies, Retail
Online & Catalog Sales
Pet Training
In-Store Adoption Centers
Veterinary Services
Pet Boarding
Pet Grooming

BRANDS/DIVISIONS/AFFILIATES:

Medical Management International, Inc.
Banfield, The Pet Hospital
PetsHotels
PetPerks
PetSmart.com

CONTACTS: Note: Officers with more than one job title may be intentionally listed here more than once.

Robert F. Moran, CEO
Robert F. Moran, Pres.
Lawrence (Chip) Molloy, CFO/Sr. VP
Mary Miller, Chief Mktg. Officer/Sr. VP
David K. Lenhardt, Sr. VP-Human Resources
Donald Beaver, CIO/Sr. VP
Joseph O'Leary, Sr. VP-Merch.
Emily Dickinson, General Counsel/Sr. VP/Sec.
David K. Lenhardt, Sr. VP-Svcs. & Store Oper.
Jaye Perricone, Sr. VP-Real Estate
Philip L. Francis, Chmn.
Joseph O'Leary, Sr. VP-Supply Chain

Phone: 623-580-6100	Fax: 623-395-6517
Toll-Free: 800-738-1385	
Address: 19601 N. 27th Ave., Phoenix, AZ 85027 US	

GROWTH PLANS/SPECIAL FEATURES:

PetSmart, Inc. is a leading operator of superstores specializing in pet food, supplies and services. The company operates more than 1,137 stores in the U.S. and Canada offering an assortment of pet services pet products. PetSmart stores also offer value-added pet services, including grooming, training, boarding and day camp, and the firm operates full-service veterinary hospitals in 741 of its stores. Medical Management International, Inc., an operator of veterinary hospitals, operates 729 of PetSmart's hospitals under the name of Banfield, The Pet Hospital. The remaining hospitals are located in Canada and operated by other third parties. PetSmart offers pet boarding at 152 of its stores through its PetSmart PetsHotels. These PetsHotels offer Doggie Day Camp, which offers climate-controlled daycare for dogs and cats. The company opened or acquired 104 new stores during 2008. Its stores range in size from 19,000 to 27,000 square feet and carry more than 13,000 distinct items, including nationally recognized brand names and a selection of proprietary or private label brands. PetSmart stores sell supplies for dogs, cats, fresh-water tropical fish, birds and other small pets, such as hamsters, gerbils and guinea pigs. Sales of pet food, treats, litter and supplies and pet sales generate approximately 90% of PetSmart's net sales. The company also actively supports pet adoption through its in-store adoption centers. The firm offers a PetPerks loyalty program and sells its products online through PetSmart.com. PetsMart plans to open 40 stores in 2009.

PetSmart offers its employees education assistance, a nurse hotline, store discounts, an employee assistance program, adoption assistance, flexible spending accounts, pet insurance, domestic partner benefits, credit union membership and medical, dental, vision, prescription, life, AD&D and disability insurance.

FINANCIALS: Sales and profits are in thousands of dollars—add 000 to get the full amount. 2008 Note: Financial information for 2008 was not available for all companies at press time.

2008 Sales: $4,672,656	2008 Profits: $258,684	**U.S. Stock Ticker:** PETM
2007 Sales: $4,233,857	2007 Profits: $185,069	**Int'l Ticker:** Int'l Exchange:
2006 Sales: $3,760,499	2006 Profits: $182,490	Employees: 46,000
2005 Sales: $3,363,452	2005 Profits: $171,228	Fiscal Year Ends: 1/31
2004 Sales: $2,996,051	2004 Profits: $139,549	Parent Company:

SALARIES/BENEFITS:

Pension Plan:	ESOP Stock Plan:	Profit Sharing:	Top Exec. Salary: $969,712	Bonus: $360,937
Savings Plan: Y	Stock Purch. Plan: Y		Second Exec. Salary: $745,769	Bonus: $208,187

OTHER THOUGHTS:

Apparent Women Officers or Directors: 5
Hot Spot for Advancement for Women/Minorities: Y

LOCATIONS: ("Y" = Yes)

West:	Southwest:	Midwest:	Southeast:	Northeast:	International:
Y	Y	Y	Y	Y	Y

Note: Financial information, benefits and other data can change quickly and may vary from those stated here.

PFIZER INC

www.pfizer.com

Industry Group Code: 325412 **Ranks within this company's industry group:** Sales: 2 Profits: 2

Management:		Sales/Marketing:		Liberal Arts:		Information Systems:		Professionals:		Tech./Scientific:	
Management Trainees:	Y	Marketing Pros.:	Y	Gen. Writing/Editing:	Y	Info. Management:	Y	Finance/Acct.:	Y	Engineers, Electrical:	Y
Experienced Mngmt.:	Y	Retail Sales:		Technical Writing:	Y	Software Dev.:	Y	Law:	Y	Engineers, Other:	Y
International Business:	Y	Commercial/Industrial:	Y	Graphic Arts/Photog.:	Y	Hardware Dev.:		HR/Other:	Y	Health/Lab:	Y
MBA Grads:	Y	Sales Trainees:	Y	Music:		Consulting/Other:		Training:	Y	Scientists/Research:	Y
		Advertising Pros.:	Y	Broadcasting:				Health Care:	Y	Petroleum/Chemicals:	Y
				Other:				Consulting:		Math/Other:	Y

TYPES OF BUSINESS:

Pharmaceutical Drugs
Prescription Pharmaceuticals
Veterinary Pharmaceuticals

BRANDS/DIVISIONS/AFFILIATES:

Norvasc
Viagra
Zoloft
Revolution/Stronghold
Sutent
Lipitor
Chantix
Rimadyl

CONTACTS: Note: Officers with more than one job title may be intentionally listed here more than once.

Jeffrey B. Kindler, CEO
Frank D'Amelio, CFO
Mary S. McLeod, Sr. VP-Worldwide Human Resources
Martin Mackay, Pres., Pfizer Global R&D
Natale Ricciardi, Pres./Team Leader-Pfizer Global Mfg.
Amy Schulman, General Counsel/Corp. Sec./Sr. VP
William Ringo, Sr. VP-Strategy & Bus. Dev.
Sally Susman, Chief Comm. Officer/Sr. VP
Charles E. Triano, Sr. VP-Investor Rel.
Joe Feckzo, Chief Medical Officer
Corey Goodman, Pres., Biotherapeutics & Bioinnovation Center
Ian Read, Sr. VP/Pres., Worldwide Pharmaceutical Oper.
Jeffrey B. Kindler, Chmn.

Phone: 212-573-2323	Fax:
Toll-Free:	
Address: 235 E. 42nd St., New York, NY 10017 US	

GROWTH PLANS/SPECIAL FEATURES:

Pfizer, Inc. is a research-based, global pharmaceutical company. It discovers, develops, manufactures and markets prescription medicines for humans and animals. The company operates in two segments: pharmaceutical and animal health. The pharmaceutical business is one of the largest in the world, with medicines across 11 therapeutic areas: cardiovascular and metabolic diseases; central nervous system disorders; arthritis and pain; infectious and respiratory diseases; urology; oncology; ophthalmology; and endocrine disorders. Major pharmaceutical products include Lipitor, for the treatment of LDL-cholesterol levels in the blood; Norvasc, for treating hypertension; Zoloft, for the treatment of major depressive disorder and other conditions; and Viagra, a treatment for erectile dysfunction. Pfizer's latest drugs include Chantix, an anti-smoking agent; and Sutent, which kills cancer-infected cells and prevents blood flow from reaching existing tumors. The animal health segment develops and sells products for the prevention and treatment of diseases in livestock/companion animals. Among the products it markets are parasiticides, anti-inflammatories, antibiotics, vaccines, and anti-obesity agents. Brands include Revolution/Stronghold, a parasiticide for dogs and cats; Rimadyl, an arthritis pain medication; and Draxxin, an antibiotic used to treat infections in cattle and swine. In March 2008, the firm agreed to acquire Serenex, Inc. In June 2008, the company acquired Encysive Pharmaceuticals, Inc. In September 2008, Pfizer partnered with Medivation, Inc., to market Dimebon, potential inhibitor of Alzheimer's and Huntington's disease; and bought several European animal product franchises from Schering-Plough Corporation. In January 2009, the company agreed to acquire pharmaceuticals company Wyeth. In March 2009, Pfizer signed licensing agreements with India-based pharmaceutical company Aurobindo Pharma Ltd., expanding its generic medicines market; the firm also partnered with Bausch & Lomb to promote opthamalic pharmaceuticals. Also in March 2009, Pfizer agreed to sell its German insulin plant and assets to MannKind Corporation, and opened a new development plant in Dalian, Liaoning, China.

FINANCIALS: Sales and profits are in thousands of dollars—add 000 to get the full amount. 2008 Note: Financial information for 2008 was not available for all companies at press time.

2008 Sales: $48,296,000	2008 Profits: $8,104,000	**U.S. Stock Ticker: PFE**
2007 Sales: $48,418,000	2007 Profits: $8,144,000	**Int'l Ticker:** Int'l Exchange:
2006 Sales: $48,371,000	2006 Profits: $19,337,000	Employees: 81,800
2005 Sales: $47,405,000	2005 Profits: $8,085,000	Fiscal Year Ends: 12/31
2004 Sales: $48,988,000	2004 Profits: $11,361,000	Parent Company:

SALARIES/BENEFITS:

Pension Plan: Y	ESOP Stock Plan:	Profit Sharing:	Top Exec. Salary: $1,575,000	Bonus: $
Savings Plan: Y	Stock Purch. Plan:		Second Exec. Salary: $1,051,500	Bonus: $

OTHER THOUGHTS:

Apparent Women Officers or Directors: 4
Hot Spot for Advancement for Women/Minorities: Y

LOCATIONS: ("Y" = Yes)

West:	Southwest:	Midwest:	Southeast:	Northeast:	International:
Y	Y	Y	Y	Y	Y

PG&E CORPORATION

www.pgecorp.com

Industry Group Code: 221 Ranks within this company's industry group: Sales: 3 Profits: 2

Management:		Sales/Marketing:		Liberal Arts:		Information Systems:		Professionals:		Tech./Scientific:	
Management Trainees:	Y	Marketing Pros.:	Y	Gen. Writing/Editing:	Y	Info. Management:	Y	Finance/Acct.:	Y	Engineers, Electrical:	Y
Experienced Mngmt.:	Y	Retail Sales:		Technical Writing:	Y	Software Dev.:	Y	Law:	Y	Engineers, Other:	Y
International Business:	Y	Commercial/Industrial:	Y	Graphic Arts/Photog.:	Y	Hardware Dev.:		HR/Other:	Y	Health/Lab:	
MBA Grads:	Y	Sales Trainees:		Music:		Consulting/Other:		Training:	Y	Scientists/Research:	
		Advertising Pros.:	Y	Broadcasting:				Health Care:		Petroleum/Chemicals:	Y
				Other:				Consulting:		Math/Other:	

TYPES OF BUSINESS:

Utilities-Electricity & Natural Gas
Energy Trading
Electricity Generation
Pipelines
Hydroelectric & Nuclear Generation
Natural Gas

BRANDS/DIVISIONS/AFFILIATES:

Pacific Gas and Electric Co

CONTACTS: Note: Officers with more than one job title may be intentionally listed here more than once.

Peter A. Darbee, CEO
John S. Keenan, COO/Sr. VP-Pacific Gas & Electric Co.
Peter A. Darbee, Pres.
Kent M. Harvey, CFO/Sr. VP
John R. Simon, Sr. VP-Human Resources
Patricia Lawicki, CIO/Sr. VP-Pacific Gas & Electric Co.
Edward A. Salas, Sr. VP-Eng., Pacific Gas & Electric Co.
Hyun Park, General Counsel/Sr. VP
Edward A. Salas, Sr. VP-Oper., Pacific Gas & Electric Co.
Rand L. Rosenberg, Sr. VP-Corp. Strategy & Dev.
Nancy E. McFadden, Sr. VP-Public Affairs
Gabriel B. Togneri, VP-Investor Rel.
Stephen J. Cairns, Controller/VP
Dinyar B. Mistry, Chief Risk & Audit Officer/VP
Greg S. Pruett, Sr. VP-Corp. Rel.
Linda Y.H. Cheng, VP-Corp. Governance/Corp. Sec.
Steven L. Kline, VP-Corp. Environmental & Federal Affairs
Peter A. Darbee, Chmn.
Roy M. Kuga, VP-Energy Supply Mgmt., Pacific Gas & Electric Co.

Phone: 415-267-7000	Fax: 415-267-7268
Toll-Free: 800-719-9056	
Address: 1 Market, Spear Tower, Ste. 2400, San Francisco, CA 94105 US	

GROWTH PLANS/SPECIAL FEATURES:

PG&E Corp. is a holding company that markets energy services and products in northern and central California through subsidiary Pacific Gas and Electric Co. The subsidiary is one of the largest electric and natural gas utilities in the U.S., serving roughly 5.1 million electric and 4.2 million natural gas customers. With over 141,000 circuit miles of distribution lines, the company's electricity distribution network extends through most of northern and central California. Pacific owns and operates power plants producing nearly half of the power it sells, including 110 hydroelectric, two nuclear and four fossil fuel facilities. The company's hydroelectric generation system covers 16 counties in northern and central California. It includes over 100 reservoirs; 44 miles of flumes; 170 dams; 184 miles of canals; 56 diversions; 19 miles of pipe; 135 miles of tunnels; and five miles of natural waterways. The company's natural gas operations consist of an integrated transportation, storage and distribution system throughout 40 counties, including most of northern and central California. This system consists of over 40,000 miles of distribution pipelines; over 6,400 miles of backbone and local transmission pipelines; and three storage facilities. Through interconnections with various interstate pipelines, the company receives gas from every major natural gas basin in western North America, including basins in Canada and the southwestern U.S.

The company offers employees supplemental life, medical, dental and vision insurance; health care and dependent care reimbursement accounts; a retirement savings plan; adoption reimbursement; and tuition refund opportunities.

FINANCIALS: Sales and profits are in thousands of dollars—add 000 to get the full amount. 2008 Note: Financial information for 2008 was not available for all companies at press time.

2008 Sales: $14,628,000	2008 Profits: $2,261,000	U.S. Stock Ticker: PCG
2007 Sales: $13,237,000	2007 Profits: $1,006,000	Int'l Ticker: Int'l Exchange:
2006 Sales: $12,539,000	2006 Profits: $2,108,000	Employees: 14,649
2005 Sales: $11,703,000	2005 Profits: $1,970,000	Fiscal Year Ends: 12/31
2004 Sales: $11,080,000	2004 Profits: $7,118,000	Parent Company:

SALARIES/BENEFITS:

Pension Plan: Y	ESOP Stock Plan:	Profit Sharing:	Top Exec. Salary: $1,090,833	Bonus: $273,868
Savings Plan: Y	Stock Purch. Plan:		Second Exec. Salary: $541,457	Bonus: $76,592

OTHER THOUGHTS:

Apparent Women Officers or Directors: 11
Hot Spot for Advancement for Women/Minorities: Y

LOCATIONS: ("Y" = Yes)

West:	Southwest:	Midwest:	Southeast:	Northeast:	International:
Y				Y	

Note: Financial information, benefits and other data can change quickly and may vary from those stated here.

PHARMACEUTICAL PRODUCT DEVELOPMENT INC www.ppdi.com

Industry Group Code: 541712 Ranks within this company's industry group: Sales: 2   Profits: 2

Management:		Sales/Marketing:		Liberal Arts:		Information Systems:		Professionals:		Tech./Scientific:	
Management Trainees:	Y	Marketing Pros.:	Y	Gen. Writing/Editing:		Info. Management:	Y	Finance/Acct.:	Y	Engineers, Electrical:	Y
Experienced Mngmt.:	Y	Retail Sales:		Technical Writing:	Y	Software Dev.:	Y	Law:	Y	Engineers, Other:	
International Business:	Y	Commercial/Industrial:	Y	Graphic Arts/Photog.:	Y	Hardware Dev.:		HR/Other:	Y	Health/Lab:	Y
MBA Grads:	Y	Sales Trainees:		Music:		Consulting/Other:	Y	Training:	Y	Scientists/Research:	Y
		Advertising Pros.:		Broadcasting:				Health Care:	Y	Petroleum/Chemicals:	
				Other:				Consulting:	Y	Math/Other:	

TYPES OF BUSINESS:

Contract Research
Drug Discovery & Development Services
Clinical Data Consulting Services
Medical Marketing & Information Support Services
Drug Development Software
Medical Device Development

BRANDS/DIVISIONS/AFFILIATES:

PPD Discovery Sciences
PPD Development
CSS Informatics
PPD Medical Communications
PPD Virtual
InnoPharm Ltd

CONTACTS: Note: Officers with more than one job title may be intentionally listed here more than once.

Fred N. Eshelman, CEO
William J. Sharbaugh, COO
Daniel Darazsdi, CFO
Christine A. Dingivan, Chief Medical Officer/Exec. VP
B. Judd Hartman, General Counsel/Corp. Sec.
William W. Richardson, Sr. VP-Global Bus. Dev.
Louise Caudle, Dir.-Corp. Comm.
Luke Heagle, Dir.-Investor Rel.
Sue Ann Pentecost, Mgr.-Corp. Comm.
Michael O. Wilkinson, Exec. VP-Global Clinical Dev.
Ernest Mario, Chmn.

Phone: 910-251-0081	Fax: 910-762-5820
Toll-Free:	
Address: 929 N. Front St., Wilmington, NC 28401-3331 US	

GROWTH PLANS/SPECIAL FEATURES:

Pharmaceutical Product Development, Inc. (PPD) provides drug discovery and development services to pharmaceutical and biotechnology companies as well as academic and government organizations. PPD's services are primarily divided into two company segments: Discovery Sciences and Development. Through the combined services of these segments, PPD helps pharmaceutical companies through all stages of clinical testing. The stages of testing can be specifically divided into preclinical, phase I, phase II-IIIb and post-approval. In the preclinical stages of drug testing, PPD provides information concerning the pharmaceutical composition of a new drug, its safety, its formulaic design and how it will be administered to children and adults. During phase I of testing, PPD conducts healthy volunteer clinics, provides data management services and guides companies/laboratories through regulatory affairs. In phase II and III tests, PPD oversees the later stages of product development and government approval, providing project management and clinical monitoring. In the post-approval stage of a drug's development, PPD provides technology and marketing services aimed to maximize the new drug's lifecycle. PPD has experience conducting research and drug development in the areas of antiviral studies, cardiovascular diseases, critical care studies, endocrine/metabolic studies, vaccine development, hematology/oncology studies, immunology studies and ophthalmology studies. The firm conducts regional, national and global studies and research projects through offices in 33 countries worldwide. In June 2008, the company opened an office in Istanbul. In October of the same year, PPD acquired Russia-based independent contract research organization, InnoPharm. In February 2009, the firm agreed to acquire AbC.R.O., Inc., a contract research organization that serves Central and Eastern Europe.

Employees are offered health insurance; life insurance; wellness programs; and a 401(k) savings plan.

FINANCIALS: Sales and profits are in thousands of dollars—add 000 to get the full amount. 2008 Note: Financial information for 2008 was not available for all companies at press time.

2008 Sales: $1,569,901	2008 Profits: $187,519	U.S. Stock Ticker: PPDI
2007 Sales: $1,414,465	2007 Profits: $163,401	Int'l Ticker: Int'l Exchange:
2006 Sales: $1,247,682	2006 Profits: $156,652	Employees: 10,500
2005 Sales: $1,037,090	2005 Profits: $119,897	Fiscal Year Ends: 12/31
2004 Sales: $841,256	2004 Profits: $91,684	Parent Company:

SALARIES/BENEFITS:

Pension Plan:	ESOP Stock Plan:	Profit Sharing:	Top Exec. Salary: $729,167	Bonus: $255,208
Savings Plan: Y	Stock Purch. Plan:		Second Exec. Salary: $366,825	Bonus: $91,706

OTHER THOUGHTS:

Apparent Women Officers or Directors: 4
Hot Spot for Advancement for Women/Minorities: Y

LOCATIONS: ("Y" = Yes)

West:	Southwest:	Midwest:	Southeast:	Northeast:	International:
Y	Y	Y	Y	Y	Y

PITNEY BOWES INC

www.pb.com

Industry Group Code: 333313 Ranks within this company's industry group: Sales: 2 Profits: 1

Management:		Sales/Marketing:		Liberal Arts:		Information Systems:		Professionals:		Tech./Scientific:	
Management Trainees:	Y	Marketing Pros.:	Y	Gen. Writing/Editing:	Y	Info. Management:	Y	Finance/Acct.:	Y	Engineers, Electrical:	Y
Experienced Mngmt.:	Y	Retail Sales:		Technical Writing:	Y	Software Dev.:	Y	Law:	Y	Engineers, Other:	Y
International Business:	Y	Commercial/Industrial:	Y	Graphic Arts/Photog.:	Y	Hardware Dev.:	Y	HR/Other:	Y	Health/Lab:	
MBA Grads:	Y	Sales Trainees:	Y	Music:		Consulting/Other:		Training:	Y	Scientists/Research:	
		Advertising Pros.:	Y	Broadcasting:				Health Care:		Petroleum/Chemicals:	
				Other:				Consulting:		Math/Other:	

TYPES OF BUSINESS:

Business Machines-Mail and Messaging
Business Equipment
Outsourced Services
Mail Logistics Services

BRANDS/DIVISIONS/AFFILIATES:

Pitney Bowes Legal Services
Pitney Bowes Marketing Services
Pitney Bowes Management Services
Pitney Bowes Mail Services
Pitney Bowes Business Insight
Pitney Bowes Software Inc
MapInfo Corp
Pitney Bowes Group 1 Software

CONTACTS: *Note: Officers with more than one job title may be intentionally listed here more than once.*

Murray D. Martin, CEO
Murray D. Martin, Pres.
Michael Monahan, CFO/Exec. VP
Mark Cattini, Pres., Pitney Bowes Mktg. Svcs.
Johnna G. Torsone, Chief Human Resources Officer/Exec. VP
Gregory E. Buoncontri, CIO/Exec. VP
Vicki A. O'Meara, Chief Legal & Compliance Officer/Exec. VP
David C. Dobson, Chief Strategy & Innovation Officer
Juanita T. James, Chief Mktg. & Comm. Officer/VP
Charles F. McBride, VP-Investor Rel.
Steven J. Green, Chief Acct. Officer/VP-Finance
Leslie Abi-Karam, Exec. VP/Pres., Mailing Solutions Mgmt.
Elise R. DeBois, Exec. VP/Pres., Global Financial Svcs.
Amy C. Corn, VP-Chief Governance Officer/Sec.
Helen Shan, VP/Treas.
Murray D. Martin, Chmn.
Patrick Keddy, Exec. VP/Pres., Mailstream Int'l
Neil Metviner, Exec. VP/Pres., Global Mainstream Europe

Phone: 203-356-5000	Fax:
Toll-Free: 800-672-6937	
Address: 1 Elmcroft Rd., Stamford, CT 06926-0700 US	

GROWTH PLANS/SPECIAL FEATURES:

Pitney Bowes, Inc. is a global provider of informed mail and messaging management for corporations and businesses of all sizes. The company conducts business in seven segments. The U.S. Mailing segment includes the U.S. revenue and related expenses from the firm's sale, rental and financing of mail finishing; mail creation; shipping equipment and software; supplies; support; and other professional services. The International Mailing division consists of non-U.S. revenue, expenses and mail-related services. Production Mail focuses on the worldwide sale, financing, support and services of the company's high-speed, production mail systems and sorting equipment. The Software unit consists of the sale and services of non-equipment-based mailing, customer communication and location intelligence software. The Management Services segment involves secure mail services; reprographic, document management services; and litigation support and eDiscovery services. The Mail Services division includes presort mail and cross-border mail services. The Marketing Services division consists of direct marketing services for targeted customers; web-tools for the customization of promotional mail and marketing collateral; and other marketing consulting services. In January 2009, subsidiary, Pitney Bowes Software Inc. created a new business unit composed of Group 1 software and Pitney Bowes Mapinfo called Pitney Bowes Business Insight.

Employees are offered medical, dental and life insurance; short-and long-term disability coverage; travel accident insurance; a stock purchase plan; a 401(k) plan; a college savings plan; and health and dependent care accounts.

FINANCIALS: Sales and profits are in thousands of dollars—add 000 to get the full amount. 2008 Note: Financial information for 2008 was not available for all companies at press time.

2008 Sales: $6,262,305	2008 Profits: $419,793	**U.S. Stock Ticker: PBI**
2007 Sales: $6,129,795	2007 Profits: $366,781	**Int'l Ticker:** Int'l Exchange:
2006 Sales: $5,730,018	2006 Profits: $105,347	Employees: 35,140
2005 Sales: $5,366,936	2005 Profits: $508,611	Fiscal Year Ends: 12/31
2004 Sales: $4,832,304	2004 Profits: $461,996	Parent Company:

SALARIES/BENEFITS:

Pension Plan:	ESOP Stock Plan:	Profit Sharing:	Top Exec. Salary: $941,667	Bonus: $2,109,000
Savings Plan: Y	Stock Purch. Plan: Y		Second Exec. Salary: $808,333	Bonus: $2,802,840

OTHER THOUGHTS:

Apparent Women Officers or Directors: 10
Hot Spot for Advancement for Women/Minorities: Y

LOCATIONS: ("Y" = Yes)

West:	Southwest:	Midwest:	Southeast:	Northeast:	International:
Y	Y	Y	Y	Y	Y

PLEXUS CORP

Industry Group Code: 334419 **Ranks within this company's industry group:** Sales: 3 Profits: 2

Management:		Sales/Marketing:		Liberal Arts:		Information Systems:		Professionals:		Tech./Scientific:	
Management Trainees:	Y	Marketing Pros.:	Y	Gen. Writing/Editing:		Info. Management:	Y	Finance/Acct.:	Y	Engineers, Electrical:	Y
Experienced Mngmt.:	Y	Retail Sales:		Technical Writing:	Y	Software Dev.:	Y	Law:	Y	Engineers, Other:	
International Business:	Y	Commercial/Industrial:	Y	Graphic Arts/Photog.:	Y	Hardware Dev.:	Y	HR/Other:	Y	Health/Lab:	
MBA Grads:	Y	Sales Trainees:		Music:		Consulting/Other:	Y	Training:	Y	Scientists/Research:	
		Advertising Pros.:	Y	Broadcasting:				Health Care:		Petroleum/Chemicals:	
				Other:				Consulting:		Math/Other:	

TYPES OF BUSINESS:

Contract Manufacturing-Diversified Electronics
Hardware & Software Design
Printed Circuit Board Design
Prototyping Services
Material Procurement & Management

BRANDS/DIVISIONS/AFFILIATES:

CONTACTS: *Note: Officers with more than one job title may be intentionally listed here more than once.*

Dean Foate, CEO
Dean Foate, Pres.
Ginger Jones, CFO/VP
Joe Mauthe, VP-Global Human Resources
Tom Czajkowski, CIO/VP
Steve Frisch, Sr. VP-Global Eng. Svcs.
Mike Buseman, Sr. VP-Global Mfg. Oper.
Angelo Ninivaggi, General Counsel/VP/Sec.
Bob Kronser, Chief Strategy Officer
George Setton, Chief Treasury Officer/Corp. Treas.
David A. Clark, Sr. VP-Global Customer Svcs.
Mike Verstegen, Sr. VP-Global Market Dev.
John L. Nussbaum, Chmn.
David A. Clark, VP-Supply Chain

Phone: 920-722-3451	Fax:
Toll-Free:	
Address: 55 Jewelers Park Dr., Neenah, WI 54957-0156 US	

GROWTH PLANS/SPECIAL FEATURES:

Plexus Corp. is a global provider of electronics manufacturing services. The company's customers may outsource all stages of the product realization process, including development and design, materials procurement and management, prototyping and new product introduction, testing, manufacturing configuration, logistics and repair. Additionally, the company provides its customers with fulfillment and logistics services including direct order fulfillment, build to order, configure to order, global logistics management and after-market service and repair. Plexus offers a complete menu of engineering services, including project management, feasibility studies, product conceptualization, specification development for product features and functions, circuit design (such as digital, microprocessor, power, analog, radio frequency, optical and micro-electronics), field programmable gate array design, printed circuit board layout, embedded software design, mechanical design (including thermal analysis, plastic components, sheet metal enclosures, and castings), development of test specifications and product validation testing. Other than certain test equipment and software used for internal operations, the firm does not design or manufacture its own proprietary products, although its product realization services have created complex, high-tech products for large original equipment manufacturers and start-ups. Plexus serves companies from industries including wireline/networking, 44% net sales; medical, 21%; industrial/commercial, 16%; defense/security/aerospace, 10%; and wireless infrastructure, 9%. The company's 10 largest customers accounted for roughly 60% of net sales. Within the top 10 customers, Juniper Networks, Inc. accounts for approximately 20% of sales. As of 2008, Plexus had 19 active facilities throughout 14 locations in Malaysia, Mexico, China, Scotland, and the U.S.

Plexus offers employees medical, dental and vision coverage; a 401(k) plan; complimentary onsite investment and financial planning services; tuition reimbursement; relocation assistance; bonus and success share programs; life insurance; long term disability; an employee assistance program; health and dependant care flexible spending accounts; a scholarship program for children of employees; and various employee discounts.

FINANCIALS: Sales and profits are in thousands of dollars—add 000 to get the full amount. 2008 Note: Financial information for 2008 was not available for all companies at press time.

2008 Sales: $1,841,622	2008 Profits: $84,144	U.S. Stock Ticker: PLXS
2007 Sales: $1,546,264	2007 Profits: $65,718	Int'l Ticker: Int'l Exchange:
2006 Sales: $1,460,557	2006 Profits: $100,025	Employees: 7,900
2005 Sales: $1,228,882	2005 Profits: $-12,417	Fiscal Year Ends: 9/30
2004 Sales: $1,040,858	2004 Profits: $-31,580	Parent Company:

SALARIES/BENEFITS:

Pension Plan:	ESOP Stock Plan:	Profit Sharing:	Top Exec. Salary: $672,981	Bonus: $764,452
Savings Plan: Y	Stock Purch. Plan:		Second Exec. Salary: $302,057	Bonus: $169,418

OTHER THOUGHTS:

Apparent Women Officers or Directors: 1
Hot Spot for Advancement for Women/Minorities:

LOCATIONS: ("Y" = Yes)

West:	Southwest:	Midwest:	Southeast:	Northeast:	International:
Y		Y	Y	Y	Y

POLO RALPH LAUREN CORP

www.polo.com

Industry Group Code: 315 Ranks within this company's industry group: Sales: 1 Profits: 1

Management:		Sales/Marketing:		Liberal Arts:		Information Systems:		Professionals:		Tech./Scientific:	
Management Trainees:	Y	Marketing Pros.:	Y	Gen. Writing/Editing:	Y	Info. Management:	Y	Finance/Acct.:	Y	Engineers, Electrical:	
Experienced Mngmt.:	Y	Retail Sales:	Y	Technical Writing:		Software Dev.:	Y	Law:	Y	Engineers, Other:	
International Business:	Y	Commercial/Industrial:	Y	Graphic Arts/Photog.:	Y	Hardware Dev.:		HR/Other:	Y	Health/Lab:	
MBA Grads:	Y	Sales Trainees:	Y	Music:		Consulting/Other:		Training:	Y	Scientists/Research:	
		Advertising Pros.:	Y	Broadcasting:				Health Care:		Petroleum/Chemicals:	
				Other:	Y			Consulting:		Math/Other:	

TYPES OF BUSINESS:

Men's & Women's Branded Fashions
Apparel Design & Marketing
Accessories
Fragrances
Home Furnishings
Cosmetics
Retail Stores

BRANDS/DIVISIONS/AFFILIATES:

Polo
Ralph Lauren
Club Monaco
Black Label
Chaps
Caban
Rugby
Polo.com

CONTACTS: Note: Officers with more than one job title may be intentionally listed here more than once.

Ralph Lauren, CEO
Roger N. Farah, COO
Roger N. Farah, Pres.
Tracey T. Travis, CFO/Sr. VP-Finance
Mitchell A. Kosh, Sr. VP-Human Resources
Julie Berman, VP-Corp. Comm.
James Hurley, Head-Investor Rel.
Jackwyn L. Nemerov, Exec. VP
Wayne Meichner, COO/Pres., Polo Retail Group
Susie Coulter, Pres., Polo Ralph Lauren Retail Stores
Ralph Lauren, Chmn.
Edouard Roche, Pres., Impact 21 Co., Ltd.

Phone: 212-318-7000	**Fax:** 212-318-7690
Toll-Free: 800-377-7656	
Address: 650 Madison Ave., New York, NY 10022 US	

GROWTH PLANS/SPECIAL FEATURES:

Polo Ralph Lauren Corporation (Polo) designs, markets and distributes premium lifestyle products. Polo licenses the manufacturing of its products to companies worldwide. Capitalizing on the creative force of its founder, Ralph Lauren, the firm's various brand names have become recognizable cultural symbols across the globe. The firm offers four categories of lifestyle products: apparel products (including extensive collections of men's, women's and children's clothing); home products (including bedding and bath products, furniture, fabric, wallpaper, paints, tabletop and giftware); accessories, including footwear, eyewear, jewelry, leather goods, handbags and luggage); and fragrance products (consisting of fragrances and skin care products). The company markets its products through department, specialty, golf and Polo Ralph Lauren stores, as well as via the Internet and mail order catalogs. The firm also offers wholesale products to upscale (and certain mid-tier) department stores, specialty stores and golf/pro shops worldwide. Its brands include Ralph by Ralph Lauren, Glamorous, Romance, Polo, Lauren for Men, Purple Label, Blue Label, Black Label, Lauren Jeans Co., Pink Pony and Polo Sport. It currently operates 163 Ralph Lauren, Caban and Rugby stores (as well as roughly 10,000 shops-within-shops) in North America, Japan, Europe and Latin America. Polo also operates Impact 21 stores in Japan. The company formed Ralph Lauren Media in a joint venture with NBC in order to reach consumers through various media outlets, including the Internet, television, cable and print. Its first initiative was the creation of Polo.com, a web site that brings products and information to consumers in an online magazine format. In 2009, Polo closed eight and opened 16 stores. In February 2009, the firm agreed to acquire direct control of its Southeast Asian retail and wholesale distribution operations from licensee Dickson Concepts International Limited at the beginning of 2010.

FINANCIALS: Sales and profits are in thousands of dollars—add 000 to get the full amount. 2008 Note: Financial information for 2008 was not available for all companies at press time.

2008 Sales: $4,880,100	2008 Profits: $419,800	**U.S. Stock Ticker:** RL
2007 Sales: $4,295,400	2007 Profits: $400,900	**Int'l Ticker:** Int'l Exchange:
2006 Sales: $3,746,300	2006 Profits: $308,000	Employees: 17,000
2005 Sales: $3,305,415	2005 Profits: $190,425	Fiscal Year Ends: 3/31
2004 Sales: $2,380,844	2004 Profits: $170,954	Parent Company:

SALARIES/BENEFITS:

Pension Plan:	ESOP Stock Plan:	Profit Sharing:	Top Exec. Salary: $1,250,000	Bonus: $13,886,364
Savings Plan:	Stock Purch. Plan:		Second Exec. Salary: $900,000	Bonus: $1,980,000

OTHER THOUGHTS:

Apparent Women Officers or Directors: 2
Hot Spot for Advancement for Women/Minorities: Y

LOCATIONS: ("Y" = Yes)

West:	Southwest:	Midwest:	Southeast:	Northeast:	International:
Y	Y	Y	Y	Y	Y

Note: Financial information, benefits and other data can change quickly and may vary from those stated here.

PRAXAIR INC

www.praxair.com

Industry Group Code: 325120 **Ranks within this company's industry group:** Sales: 1 Profits: 1

Management:		Sales/Marketing:		Liberal Arts:		Information Systems:		Professionals:		Tech./Scientific:	
Management Trainees:	Y	Marketing Pros.:	Y	Gen. Writing/Editing:		Info. Management:	Y	Finance/Acct.:	Y	Engineers, Electrical:	Y
Experienced Mngmt.:	Y	Retail Sales:		Technical Writing:	Y	Software Dev.:	Y	Law:	Y	Engineers, Other:	Y
International Business:	Y	Commercial/Industrial:	Y	Graphic Arts/Photog.:		Hardware Dev.:		HR/Other:	Y	Health/Lab:	
MBA Grads:	Y	Sales Trainees:		Music:		Consulting/Other:		Training:	Y	Scientists/Research:	Y
		Advertising Pros.:		Broadcasting:				Health Care:		Petroleum/Chemicals:	Y
				Other:				Consulting:		Math/Other:	

TYPES OF BUSINESS:

Industrial Gases
Atmospheric & Process Gases
Coatings & Powders
On-Site Production Plants
Distribution

BRANDS/DIVISIONS/AFFILIATES:

Praxair Distribution, Inc.
Wilson Welding & Medical Gases
Praxair Surface Technologies, Inc.
Alabama Welding Supply
Fowler Brothers
Service Gas Supply, Inc.

CONTACTS: *Note: Officers with more than one job title may be intentionally listed here more than once.*

Stephen F. Angel, CEO
Stephen F. Angel, Pres.
James S. Sawyer, CFO/Exec. VP
Anne K. Roby, Sr. VP-Global Sales
Sally A. Savoia, VP-Human Resources
Melissa Buckwalter, CIO/VP-Financial Svcs.
Raymond P. Roberge, CTO/VP
James T. Breedlove, General Counsel/Sr. VP/Corp. Sec.
Murray G. Covello, VP-Global Oper. Excellence & Dev.
Sunil Mattoo, VP-Strategic Planning & Mktg.
Nigel D. Muir, VP-Comm. & Public Rel.
Elizabeth T. Hirsch, Dir.-Investor Rel.
Matthew J. White, Controller/VP
James J. Fuchs, Pres., NA Industrial Gases/Praxair Canada
Michael J. Allan, Treas./VP
Domingos H. G. Bulus, Pres., Praxair South America
Joseph S. Cappello, Pres., Praxair Asia
Stephen F. Angel, Chmn.
Eduardo Menezes, Pres., Europe
Dan Yankowski, VP-Global Supply Chain

Phone: 716-879-4077	Fax: 716-879-2040
Toll-Free: 800-772-9247	
Address: 39 Old Ridgebury Rd., Danbury, CT 06810-5113 US	

GROWTH PLANS/SPECIAL FEATURES:

Praxair, Inc. is an industrial gas supplier in North America, South America, Asia and Europe. Praxair's primary products are atmospheric gases, which include oxygen, nitrogen, argon and rare gases, and process gases, which include carbon dioxide, helium, hydrogen, electronic gases, specialty gases and acetylene. The company also designs, engineers, and builds equipment that produces industrial gases for internal use and external sale. Praxair serves approximately 25 industries including aerospace, food and beverages, healthcare, semiconductors, chemicals and refining, as well as others. In 2008, 95% of sales were generated in four regional segments (North America, Europe, South America and Asia) primarily from the sale of industrial gases with the balance generated from the surface technologies segment. Atmospheric gases are the highest volume products produced by Praxair. Using air as its raw material, Praxair produces oxygen, nitrogen and argon through several air separation processes of which cryogenic air separation is the most prevalent. Process gases, including carbon dioxide, hydrogen, carbon monoxide, helium and acetylene are produced by methods other than air separation. Praxair uses three distribution methods for industrial gases: on-site or tonnage; merchant liquid; and packaged or cylinder gases. Through its subsidiary Praxair Surface Technologies, the company supplies wear-resistant and high-temperature corrosion-resistant metallic and ceramic coatings and powders to the aircraft, printing, textile, plastics, primary metals and petrochemical industries. It also manufactures a complete line of electric arc, plasma and high-velocity oxygen fuel spray equipment, as well as arc and flame wire equipment used for the application of wear resistant coatings. In April 2009, subsidiary Praxair Distribution Inc. acquired Alabama Welding Supply in Dolomite, Alabama; Fowler Brothers in Birmingham, Alabama; and Service Gas Supply, Inc. in Midlothian, Texas. In May 2009, subsidiary Praxair Investment Co., Ltd. set up a joint venture with China Petroleum & Chemical Corporation named Praxair-GPC Industrial Gases Co. Ltd.

FINANCIALS: Sales and profits are in thousands of dollars—add 000 to get the full amount. 2008 Note: Financial information for 2008 was not available for all companies at press time.

2008 Sales: $10,796,000	2008 Profits: $1,211,000	**U.S. Stock Ticker: PX**
2007 Sales: $9,402,000	2007 Profits: $1,177,000	**Int'l Ticker:** Int'l Exchange:
2006 Sales: $8,324,000	2006 Profits: $988,000	Employees: 26,936
2005 Sales: $7,656,000	2005 Profits: $726,000	Fiscal Year Ends: 12/31
2004 Sales: $6,594,000	2004 Profits: $697,000	Parent Company:

SALARIES/BENEFITS:

Pension Plan:	ESOP Stock Plan:	Profit Sharing:	Top Exec. Salary: $1,026,250	Bonus: $2,500,000
Savings Plan:	Stock Purch. Plan:		Second Exec. Salary: $576,250	Bonus: $915,360

OTHER THOUGHTS:

Apparent Women Officers or Directors: 3
Hot Spot for Advancement for Women/Minorities: Y

LOCATIONS: ("Y" = Yes)

West:	Southwest:	Midwest:	Southeast:	Northeast:	International:
				Y	Y

Note: Financial information, benefits and other data can change quickly and may vary from those stated here.

PRECISION CASTPARTS CORP

www.precast.com

Industry Group Code: 33351 Ranks within this company's industry group: Sales: 1 Profits: 1

Management:		Sales/Marketing:		Liberal Arts:		Information Systems:		Professionals:		Tech./Scientific:	
Management Trainees:	Y	Marketing Pros.:	Y	Gen. Writing/Editing:		Info. Management:	Y	Finance/Acct.:	Y	Engineers, Electrical:	
Experienced Mngmt.:	Y	Retail Sales:		Technical Writing:	Y	Software Dev.:	Y	Law:	Y	Engineers, Other:	Y
International Business:	Y	Commercial/Industrial:	Y	Graphic Arts/Photog.:	Y	Hardware Dev.:		HR/Other:	Y	Health/Lab:	
MBA Grads:	Y	Sales Trainees:		Music:		Consulting/Other:		Training:	Y	Scientists/Research:	
		Advertising Pros.:		Broadcasting:				Health Care:		Petroleum/Chemicals:	
				Other:				Consulting:		Math/Other:	

TYPES OF BUSINESS:

Machine Parts Manufacturing

BRANDS/DIVISIONS/AFFILIATES:

INCONEL
AEREX
INCOLOY
MULTIPHASE
NIMONIC
MONEL
UDIMET
BRIGHTRAY

CONTACTS: Note: Officers with more than one job title may be intentionally listed here more than once.

Mark Donegan, CEO
Shawn R. Hagel, CFO/Sr. VP
Byron J. Gaddis, CIO/VP
Roger A. Cooke, General Counsel/Sr. VP/Sec.
Kirk G. Pulley, VP-Corp. Dev. & Strategic Planning
Dwight E. Weber, Dir.-Corp. Comm.
Steven C. Blackmore, Treas./VP
Russell S. Pattee, VP/Corp. Controller
John W. Ericksen, Sr. VP-Corp. Training & Organizational Dev.
Steven G. Hackett, Exec. VP
Kevin M. Stein, Exec. VP/Pres., Fastener Prod.
Mark Donegan, Chmn.

Phone: 503-417-4800	Fax: 503-417-4817
Toll-Free:	
Address: 4650 S.W. Macadam Ave., Ste. 440, Portland, OR 97239-4262 US	

GROWTH PLANS/SPECIAL FEATURES:

Precision Castparts Corp. is a worldwide manufacturer of complex metal components and products. The firm specializes in providing investment castings, forgings and fasteners/fastener systems for an array of aerospace and industrial gas turbine (IGT) applications. The company also manufactures nickel alloys, cobalt alloys and product forms for industries such as oil/gas, aerospace, chemical processing and pollution control; investment castings/forgings for armament, medical and general industrial applications; fasteners for automotive and general industrial markets; refiner plates, screen cylinders and other products for the pulp and paper industry; specialty alloys and waxes for the investment casting industry; low-pressure sewer systems; metal-injection-molded and its proprietary ThixoFormed parts for automotive and other markets; gas monitoring systems for the power generation industry; and metalworking tools for the fastener market and other applications. The majority of Precision Castparts Corp.'s sales are derived from the aerospace industry (approximately 53%); sales to power generation companies account for approximately 25% of the firm's sales, while general industrial and other applications account for the remaining 22%. General Electric, the company's biggest client, accounts for roughly 11.8% of its sales. Precision Castparts Corp.'s brands include INCONEL, INCOLOY, AEREX, MULTIPHASE, MONEL, NIMONIC, UDIMET, BRIGHTRAY, MP35N and MP159 and NILO. The firm has approximately 180 manufacturing and administrative facilities worldwide. In October 2008, the company acquired hydraulic and pneumatic fluid fittings supplier Airdrome Holdings, LLC (comprised of Airdrome Precision Components and AF Aerospace Ltd.). In November 2008, Precision Castparts Corp. acquired cold expansion pioneer Fatigue Technology, Inc. In December 2008, the company acquired Hackney Ladish, Inc., a forged pipe fittings manufacturer. In August 2009, the firm agreed to acquire Carlton Forge Works, a seamless rolled ring producer, for approximately $850 million.

FINANCIALS: Sales and profits are in thousands of dollars—add 000 to get the full amount. 2008 Note: Financial information for 2008 was not available for all companies at press time.

2008 Sales: $6,749,800	2008 Profits: $987,300	**U.S. Stock Ticker: PCP**	
2007 Sales: $5,220,800	2007 Profits: $633,100	**Int'l Ticker:** Int'l Exchange:	
2006 Sales: $3,382,100	2006 Profits: $350,600	Employees: 20,611	
2005 Sales: $	2005 Profits: $	Fiscal Year Ends: 3/31	
2004 Sales: $	2004 Profits: $	Parent Company:	

SALARIES/BENEFITS:

Pension Plan:	ESOP Stock Plan:	Profit Sharing:	Top Exec. Salary: $1,275,000	Bonus: $1,689,350
Savings Plan:	Stock Purch. Plan:		Second Exec. Salary: $518,750	Bonus: $734,400

OTHER THOUGHTS:

Apparent Women Officers or Directors:
Hot Spot for Advancement for Women/Minorities:

LOCATIONS: ("Y" = Yes)

West:	Southwest:	Midwest:	Southeast:	Northeast:	International:
Y	Y	Y	Y	Y	Y

Note: Financial information, benefits and other data can change quickly and may vary from those stated here.

PRICESMART INC

www.pricesmart.com

Industry Group Code: 452112 **Ranks within this company's industry group:** Sales: 10 Profits: 8

Management:		Sales/Marketing:		Liberal Arts:		Information Systems:		Professionals:		Tech./Scientific:	
Management Trainees:	Y	Marketing Pros.:	Y	Gen. Writing/Editing:	Y	Info. Management:	Y	Finance/Acct.:	Y	Engineers, Electrical:	
Experienced Mngmt.:	Y	Retail Sales:	Y	Technical Writing:		Software Dev.:	Y	Law:	Y	Engineers, Other:	
International Business:	Y	Commercial/Industrial:		Graphic Arts/Photog.:	Y	Hardware Dev.:		HR/Other:	Y	Health/Lab:	
MBA Grads:	Y	Sales Trainees:	Y	Music:		Consulting/Other:		Training:	Y	Scientists/Research:	
		Advertising Pros.:	Y	Broadcasting:				Health Care:		Petroleum/Chemicals:	
				Other:	Y			Consulting:		Math/Other:	

TYPES OF BUSINESS:

Warehouse Clubs, Retail

BRANDS/DIVISIONS/AFFILIATES:

PSMT Mexico, S.A. de C.V.
Grupo Gigante, S.A.B. de C.V.

CONTACTS: *Note: Officers with more than one job title may be intentionally listed here more than once.*

Robert Price, CEO
William J. Naylon, COO/Exec. VP
Jose Luis Laparte, Pres.
John M. Heffner, CFO/Exec. VP
A. Edward Oats, Exec. VP-IT & Logistics
Thomas D. Martin, Exec. VP-Merch.
Robert M. Gans, General Counsel/Exec. VP/Corp. Sec.
Atul Patel, Sr. VP/Treas.
Brud E. Drachman, Exec. VP-Construction Mgmt.
Jack McGrory, Exec. VP-Real Estate & Dev.
Ernesto Grijalva, Sr. VP-Latin America & Caribbean Legal Affairs
Michael L. McCleary, Sr. VP/Corp. Controller
Robert Price, Chmn.
John D. Hildebrandt, Exec. VP-Central American Oper.

Phone: 858-404-8800	Fax: 858-404-8848
Toll-Free:	
Address: 9740 Scranton Rd., San Diego, CA 92121-1745 US	

GROWTH PLANS/SPECIAL FEATURES:

PriceSmart, Inc. is one of the largest operators of warehouse membership clubs in Central America, the Caribbean and the Philippines. It currently operates 25 warehouse clubs in 11 countries and one U.S. territory, including Aruba, Barbados, the Dominican Republic, El Salvador, Guatemala, Honduras, Jamaica, Nicaragua, Panama, Costa Rica, Trinidad/Tobago and the U.S. Virgin Islands. The firm's operations are managed by subsidiary companies in each of the countries in which it has stores. These subsidiaries typically begin as joint ventures with local businesspeople; the company then purchases the portion it doesn't already own if the stores in the area show promise. These stores provide basic consumer goods, with an emphasis on quality, low prices and efficiency. PriceSmart's merchandise, offered under both brand names and private labels, includes various food items, consumer electronics, appliances, home furnishings, office supplies, apparel, automotive supplies and garden and seasonal goods. About half of its merchandise mix is locally sourced, the rest being sourced in the U.S. The company's stores feature several in-store member services and conveniences, including auto/tire centers, bakeries, banking services, coffee bars, one-hour photo processing, optical centers, pharmacies and rotisserie chicken. A typical store ranges in size from 48,000-72,000 square feet, smaller than U.S. warehouse clubs, and are located in urban areas. The average annual membership fee is $25. In November 2007, PriceSmart sold its 50% interest in PSMT Mexico, S.A. de C.V., its joint venture with Grupo Gigante, S.A.B, de C.V., to Grupo Gigante.

PriceSmart offers its employees medical, dental and vision insurance; life insurance; and short-and long-term disability.

FINANCIALS: Sales and profits are in thousands of dollars—add 000 to get the full amount. 2008 Note: Financial information for 2008 was not available for all companies at press time.

2008 Sales: $1,119,876	2008 Profits: $38,106	U.S. Stock Ticker: PSMT
2007 Sales: $888,801	2007 Profits: $12,926	Int'l Ticker: Int'l Exchange:
2006 Sales: $734,673	2006 Profits: $11,858	Employees: 4,200
2005 Sales: $618,825	2005 Profits: $-42,337	Fiscal Year Ends: 8/31
2004 Sales: $544,191	2004 Profits: $-29,982	Parent Company:

SALARIES/BENEFITS:

Pension Plan:	ESOP Stock Plan:	Profit Sharing:	Top Exec. Salary: $394,000	Bonus: $150,000
Savings Plan:	Stock Purch. Plan:		Second Exec. Salary: $350,000	Bonus: $

OTHER THOUGHTS:

Apparent Women Officers or Directors:
Hot Spot for Advancement for Women/Minorities:

LOCATIONS: ("Y" = Yes)

West:	Southwest:	Midwest:	Southeast:	Northeast:	International:
Y					Y

PRICEWATERHOUSECOOPERS

www.pwcglobal.com

Industry Group Code: 5412 Ranks within this company's industry group: Sales: 1 Profits:

Management:		Sales/Marketing:		Liberal Arts:		Information Systems:		Professionals:		Tech./Scientific:	
Management Trainees:	Y	Marketing Pros.:	Y	Gen. Writing/Editing:	Y	Info. Management:	Y	Finance/Acct.:	Y	Engineers, Electrical:	
Experienced Mngmt.:	Y	Retail Sales:		Technical Writing:	Y	Software Dev.:	Y	Law:	Y	Engineers, Other:	
International Business:	Y	Commercial/Industrial:	Y	Graphic Arts/Photog.:	Y	Hardware Dev.:		HR/Other:	Y	Health/Lab:	
MBA Grads:	Y	Sales Trainees:		Music:		Consulting/Other:	Y	Training:	Y	Scientists/Research:	
		Advertising Pros.:	Y	Broadcasting:				Health Care:		Petroleum/Chemicals:	
				Other:	Y			Consulting:	Y	Math/Other:	

TYPES OF BUSINESS:

Accounting Services
Business Advisory
Corporate Finance Services
Employee Benefits Services
Tax Services
Business Publications

BRANDS/DIVISIONS/AFFILIATES:

PricewaterhouseCoopers, LLP
XPRL
Global VATOnline
Global Best Practices
CFOdirect Network
Comperio

CONTACTS: *Note: Officers with more than one job title may be intentionally listed here more than once.*

Samuel DiPiazza, Jr., CEO
Javier H. Rubinstein, General Counsel
Paul Boorman, Global Oper.
Anthony P. D. Harrington, Global Strategy
Mike Kubena, CEO-PwC Central & Eastern Europe
Donald A. McGovern Jr., VP-Global Assurance Svcs.
Gene Donnelly, Global Managing Partner-Advisory & Tax
Edgardo Pappacena, Global Strategic Sourcing
Dennis M. Nally, Chmn.
Chris Clark, Sr. Partner/CEO-PricewaterhouseCoopers Canada LLP

Phone: 646-471-4000	Fax: 813-286-6000
Toll-Free:	
Address: 300 Madison Ave., Fl. 24, New York, NY 10017 US	

GROWTH PLANS/SPECIAL FEATURES:

PricewaterhouseCoopers (PwC) is a global accounting firm with offices in 150 countries. Locations of PwC offices include Africa, the Americas, Asia/Asia Pacific, Europe and the Middle East. PwC provides accounting and advisory services to a large number of mid-sized and small companies and caters to about 80% of Fortune magazine's Global 500 companies in 22 different industries, which includes aerospace and defense; banking and capital markets; forest, paper and packaging; government/public services; health care; and telecommunications. The firm provides industry-focused services for public and private clients primarily in six areas: audit and assurance; consulting; deals; human resources; and tax. Audit and assurance provides financial statement audits, regulatory and Sarbanes-Oxley compliance and financial accounting while the crisis management sector offers business recovery services with dispute analysis and investigations. Human resource services include employee communications, international assignment solutions and retirement benefits services. The consulting sector is made up of 17,000 consultants in 140 countries. The deals sector specializes in acquisitions and mergers; strategic and valuation advice; and growth and divestments and developing exit strategies. Lastly, the tax sector helps businesses reduce tax risks and improve operating efficiency. PwC also produces a number of publications that provide authoritative information on better business practices and emerging issues facing management and breaking trends in the business world. Online services offered by the company include CFOdirect Network, Comperio, Global Best Practices and XBRL. In recent years, Ambit RSM, a well established financial firm in India, merged its tax practice into PricewaterhouseCoopers'. Operating under the PricewaterhouseCoopers brand, the affiliate now encompasses approximately 4,000 people across different offices in India. In September 2008, the company acquired nearly all of the assets of New Dimension Solutions, Inc., a provider of Enterprise Asset Management consulting services. Details of the transaction were not disclosed.

FINANCIALS: Sales and profits are in thousands of dollars—add 000 to get the full amount. 2008 Note: Financial information for 2008 was not available for all companies at press time.

2008 Sales: $28,185,000	2008 Profits: $	**U.S. Stock Ticker: Private**
2007 Sales: $24,729,000	2007 Profits: $	**Int'l Ticker:** Int'l Exchange:
2006 Sales: $22,000,000	2006 Profits: $	Employees: 155,693
2005 Sales: $20,300,000	2005 Profits: $	Fiscal Year Ends: 6/30
2004 Sales: $16,283,000	2004 Profits: $	Parent Company:

SALARIES/BENEFITS:

Pension Plan: Y	ESOP Stock Plan:	Profit Sharing:	Top Exec. Salary: $	Bonus: $
Savings Plan: Y	Stock Purch. Plan:		Second Exec. Salary: $	Bonus: $

OTHER THOUGHTS:

Apparent Women Officers or Directors: 1
Hot Spot for Advancement for Women/Minorities:

LOCATIONS: ("Y" = Yes)

West:	Southwest:	Midwest:	Southeast:	Northeast:	International:
Y	Y	Y	Y	Y	Y

PRIDE INTERNATIONAL INC

www.prideinternational.com

Industry Group Code: 213111 Ranks within this company's industry group: Sales: 2   Profits: 3

Management:		Sales/Marketing:		Liberal Arts:		Information Systems:		Professionals:		Tech./Scientific:	
Management Trainees:	Y	Marketing Pros.:	Y	Gen. Writing/Editing:		Info. Management:	Y	Finance/Acct.:	Y	Engineers, Electrical:	Y
Experienced Mngmt.:	Y	Retail Sales:		Technical Writing:	Y	Software Dev.:	Y	Law:	Y	Engineers, Other:	Y
International Business:	Y	Commercial/Industrial:	Y	Graphic Arts/Photog.:		Hardware Dev.:		HR/Other:	Y	Health/Lab:	
MBA Grads:	Y	Sales Trainees:		Music:		Consulting/Other:		Training:	Y	Scientists/Research:	
		Advertising Pros.:		Broadcasting:				Health Care:		Petroleum/Chemicals:	Y
				Other:				Consulting:		Math/Other:	

TYPES OF BUSINESS:

Contract Drilling Services
Oil Rig Management Services

BRANDS/DIVISIONS/AFFILIATES:

GP Investments, Ltd.
Ferncliff TIH AS
Blake International LLC

CONTACTS: *Note: Officers with more than one job title may be intentionally listed here more than once.*

Louis A. Raspino, CEO
Rodney W. Eads, COO/Exec. VP
Louis A. Raspino, Pres.
Brian C. Voegele, CFO/Sr. VP
Kevin C. Robert, VP-Mktg.
Lonnie D. Bane, Sr. VP-Human Resources
Jenny M. Rub, CIO/VP
Imran (Ron) Toufeeq, Sr. VP-Eng. & Asset Mgmt.
W. Gregory Looser, Chief Admin. Officer
Brady K. Long, General Counsel/Sec
Imran Toufeeq, Sr. VP-Oper.
Kevin C. Robert, Sr. VP-Bus. Dev.
Jeffrey L. Chastain, VP-Comm.
Jeffrey L. Chastain, VP-Investor Rel.
Steven D. Oldham, Treas./VP
Robert E. Warren, VP-Industry
Leonard Travis, Chief Acct. Officer/VP
Brady K. Long, Chief Compliance Officer
Lonnie D. Bane, Sr. VP-Admin.
David A. B. Brown, Chmn.

Phone: 713-789-1400	Fax: 713-789-1430
Toll-Free:	
Address: 5847 San Felipe St., Ste. 3300, Houston, TX 77057 US	

GROWTH PLANS/SPECIAL FEATURES:

Pride International, Inc. is a leading international provider of offshore contract drilling and related services to oil and natural gas companies worldwide, operating in approximately 15 countries and marine provinces. Pride owns a fleet of 44 rigs, consisting of two deepwater drillships, 12 semisubmersible rigs and 27 jackup rigs, as well as three ultra-deepwater drillships under construction in Korea. Pride's operations are conducted in many of the most active oil and natural gas basins of the world, including South America, the Gulf of Mexico, the Mediterranean Sea, West Africa, the Middle East and Asia Pacific. Pride's customers consist of large multinational oil and natural gas companies, government-owned oil and natural gas companies and independent oil and natural gas producers. The company also provides rig management services, such as technical drilling assistance, personnel, repair and maintenance services and drilling operation management services for a variety of rigs. The company also has management contracts for two deepwater TLP rigs, two deepwater spar rigs and one semisubmersible rig. In May 2008, Pride completed the sale of its platform rig fleet Blake International LLC for $66 million. In August 2008, the firm announced its order for the construction of a fourth advanced-capability, ultra-deepwater drillship expected to be delivered in 2011.

Employees receive a full benefits package that includes medical, vision and dental insurance; a flexible spending account; and an employee assistance program.

FINANCIALS: Sales and profits are in thousands of dollars—add 000 to get the full amount. 2008 Note: Financial information for 2008 was not available for all companies at press time.

2008 Sales: $2,310,400	2008 Profits: $852,100	**U.S. Stock Ticker: PDE**	
2007 Sales: $2,043,800	2007 Profits: $784,300	**Int'l Ticker:** Int'l Exchange:	
2006 Sales: $2,495,400	2006 Profits: $295,300	Employees: 5,700	
2005 Sales: $2,033,300	2005 Profits: $128,300	Fiscal Year Ends: 12/31	
2004 Sales: $1,712,200	2004 Profits: $27,600	Parent Company:	

SALARIES/BENEFITS:

Pension Plan:	ESOP Stock Plan:	Profit Sharing:	Top Exec. Salary: $925,000	Bonus: $1,028,347
Savings Plan: Y	Stock Purch. Plan: Y		Second Exec. Salary: $547,579	Bonus: $428,300

OTHER THOUGHTS:

Apparent Women Officers or Directors: 1
Hot Spot for Advancement for Women/Minorities:

LOCATIONS: ("Y" = Yes)

West:	Southwest:	Midwest:	Southeast:	Northeast:	International:
	Y		Y		Y

Note: Financial information, benefits and other data can change quickly and may vary from those stated here.

PRINCIPAL FINANCIAL GROUP (THE)

www.principal.com

Industry Group Code: 524113 Ranks within this company's industry group: Sales: 4 Profits: 2

Management:		Sales/Marketing:		Liberal Arts:		Information Systems:		Professionals:		Tech./Scientific:	
Management Trainees:	Y	Marketing Pros.:	Y	Gen. Writing/Editing:	Y	Info. Management:	Y	Finance/Acct.:	Y	Engineers, Electrical:	
Experienced Mngmt.:	Y	Retail Sales:		Technical Writing:	Y	Software Dev.:	Y	Law:	Y	Engineers, Other:	
International Business:	Y	Commercial/Industrial:	Y	Graphic Arts/Photog.:	Y	Hardware Dev.:		HR/Other:	Y	Health/Lab:	
MBA Grads:	Y	Sales Trainees:	Y	Music:		Consulting/Other:		Training:	Y	Scientists/Research:	
		Advertising Pros.:	Y	Broadcasting:				Health Care:	Y	Petroleum/Chemicals:	
				Other:	Y			Consulting:		Math/Other:	Y

TYPES OF BUSINESS:

Asset Management
Life Insurance
Health Insurance
Annuities
Disability Insurance
Investment Services
Specialty Benefits Insurance

BRANDS/DIVISIONS/AFFILIATES:

Principal Life Insurance Co.
Principal Financial Services, Inc.
Principal International, Inc.

CONTACTS: Note: Officers with more than one job title may be intentionally listed here more than once.

Larry D. Zimpleman, CEO
Larry D. Zimpleman, Pres.
Terrance Lillis, CFO/Sr. VP
Mary A. O'Keefe, Chief Mktg. Officer/Sr. VP
Ralph C. Eucher, Sr. VP-Human Resources
Gary P. Scholten, CIO/Sr. VP
Karen E. Shaff, General Counsel/Exec. VP
Thomas J. Graf, Sr. VP-Investor Rel.
Greg Elming, Controller/Sr. VP
James P. McCaughan, Pres., Principal Global Investors
Julia M. Lawler, Chief Investment Officer/Sr. VP
Joh E. Aschenbrenner, Pres., Insurance & Financial Svcs.
Ellen Z. Lamale, Chief Risk Officer/Sr. VP
Larry D. Zimpleman, Chmn.

Phone: 515-247-5111	Fax: 515-246-5475
Toll-Free: 800-986-3343	
Address: 711 High St., Des Moines, IA 50392 US	

GROWTH PLANS/SPECIAL FEATURES:

The Principal Financial Group is a leading provider of retirement savings, investment and insurance products and services. It holds a total of $257.7 billion in assets, which it manages for approximately 18.8 million customers throughout the world. The company is organized into four primary business segments: U.S. asset management; global asset management; international asset management and accumulation; and life and health insurance. Its flagship unit is Principal Life Insurance Co., which provides life, health, dental and disability insurance. The firm's U.S. and international operations concentrate on asset accumulation and management, additionally offering individual and group life insurance; group health insurance; and individual and group disability insurance. Principal Financial Group focuses primarily on small and medium sized businesses, which it defines as companies with less than 1,000 employees. The U.S. asset management segment consists of asset management operations, which provide retirement savings and related investment products and services to businesses, their employees and other individuals. The global asset management segment consists of Principal Global Investors and its affiliates, which focus on providing a range of asset management services covering a broad range of asset classes, investment styles and portfolio structures to Principle Financial Group's other segments and third-party institutional clients. The international asset management and accumulation division consists of Principal International, which has operations in Chile, Mexico, Hong Kong, Brazil, India, Indonesia, China, Singapore and Malaysia. The life and health insurance segment offers individual life and disability insurance as well as group health insurance, group dental, group vision, group life and group long-term and short-term disability insurance in the U.S. In August 2009, the company offered a new feature which allows clients with retirement accounts to access their account information through text messages and iGoogle home pages.

Employees are offered medical, dental and vision insurance; flexible spending accounts; disability coverage; life insurance; and banking benefits.

FINANCIALS: Sales and profits are in thousands of dollars—add 000 to get the full amount. 2008 Note: Financial information for 2008 was not available for all companies at press time.

2008 Sales: $9,935,900	2008 Profits: $458,100	U.S. Stock Ticker: PFG
2007 Sales: $10,906,500	2007 Profits: $860,300	Int'l Ticker: Int'l Exchange:
2006 Sales: $9,873,100	2006 Profits: $1,064,300	Employees: 16,234
2005 Sales: $9,041,700	2005 Profits: $919,000	Fiscal Year Ends: 12/31
2004 Sales: $8,320,900	2004 Profits: $825,600	Parent Company:

SALARIES/BENEFITS:

Pension Plan: Y	ESOP Stock Plan:	Profit Sharing:	Top Exec. Salary: $1,000,000	Bonus: $
Savings Plan: Y	Stock Purch. Plan: Y		Second Exec. Salary: $737,475	Bonus: $

OTHER THOUGHTS:

Apparent Women Officers or Directors: 11
Hot Spot for Advancement for Women/Minorities: Y

LOCATIONS: ("Y" = Yes)

West:	Southwest:	Midwest:	Southeast:	Northeast:	International:
Y	Y	Y	Y	Y	Y

Note: Financial information, benefits and other data can change quickly and may vary from those stated here.

PROCTER & GAMBLE CO

Industry Group Code: 3256 Ranks within this company's industry group: Sales: 1   Profits: 1

Management:		Sales/Marketing:		Liberal Arts:		Information Systems:		Professionals:		Tech./Scientific:	
Management Trainees:	Y	Marketing Pros.:	Y	Gen. Writing/Editing:	Y	Info. Management:	Y	Finance/Acct.:	Y	Engineers, Electrical:	
Experienced Mngmt.:	Y	Retail Sales:		Technical Writing:	Y	Software Dev.:	Y	Law:	Y	Engineers, Other:	Y
International Business:	Y	Commercial/Industrial:	Y	Graphic Arts/Photog.:	Y	Hardware Dev.:		HR/Other:	Y	Health/Lab:	Y
MBA Grads:	Y	Sales Trainees:	Y	Music:		Consulting/Other:		Training:	Y	Scientists/Research:	Y
		Advertising Pros.:	Y	Broadcasting:				Health Care:		Petroleum/Chemicals:	Y
				Other:	Y			Consulting:		Math/Other:	

TYPES OF BUSINESS:

Household Products Manufacturing
Pharmaceuticals
Foods & Beverages
Beauty Products
Gastrointestinal Drugs
Musculoskeletal Drugs

BRANDS/DIVISIONS/AFFILIATES:

Cover Girl
Crest
Tide
Pringles
Gillete
Clairol
Zirh
HDS Cosmetics Lab, Inc.

CONTACTS: *Note: Officers with more than one job title may be intentionally listed here more than once.*

Robert A. McDonald, CEO
Robert A. McDonald, Pres.
Jon R. Moeller, CFO
Marc Pritchard, Global Mktg. Officer
Moheet Nagrath, Global Human Resources Officer
Filippo Passerini, CIO/Pres., Global Bus. Svcs.
Bruce Brown, CTO
Steven W. Jemison, Chief Legal Officer/Sec.
Werner Geissler, Vice Chmn.-Global Oper.
Robert L. Fregolle, Jr., Chief Customer Bus. Dev. Officer
Jon Moeller, Treas./VP
Valarie L. Sheppard, Comptroller/VP
Charles V. Bergh, Pres., Personal Care
Mark S. Bertolami, Pres., Duracell
Steven Bishop, Pres., Feminine Care
Alan G. Lafley, Chmn.
Giovanni Ciserani, Pres., Western Europe

Phone: 513-983-1100	Fax: 513-983-9369
Toll-Free:	
Address: 1 Procter & Gamble Plz., Cincinnati, OH 45202 US	

GROWTH PLANS/SPECIAL FEATURES:

Procter & Gamble Co. develops and manufactures a wide range of household goods, including fabric and home care, baby care, feminine care, tissue and towel, beauty care, health care and food and beverage products. Its operations are divided in three segments: beauty, including beauty and grooming products; health and well being, encompassing health care products, snacks and pet care products; and household care, which includes fabric care, home care, baby care and family care. Laundry products generated roughly 17% of 2009 sales in 2009, and the diaper category constituted approximately 11% of sales. The company markets almost 300 brands to more than 5 billion consumers in over 180 countries. These brands include Tide, Crest, Pantene, Tampax, Pringles, Pampers, Jif, Cover Girl, Gillette, Downy, Dawn, Bounty, Charmin and Iams pet food. The firm's products are primarily distributed through food, drug and mass merchandise retail outlets, with Wal-Mart providing roughly 15% of sales. In the U.S., Procter & Gamble operates 36 manufacturing facilities in 21 states. Moreover, it owns and operates 105 facilities in 43 other countries, including Canada, Japan and Western European countries. In November 2008, the firm sold its Folgers Coffee unit to JM Smucker Co. In June 2009, the company acquired the Zirh brand of male grooming products. In August 2009, the company agreed to sell its prescription drug business to Warner Chilcott plc for more than $3 billion. That same month, the company sold its Iams Pet Imaging, LLC subsidiary to AnimalScan, LLC.

FINANCIALS: Sales and profits are in thousands of dollars—add 000 to get the full amount. 2008 Note: Financial information for 2008 was not available for all companies at press time.

			U.S. Stock Ticker: PG
2008 Sales: $81,748,000		2008 Profits: $12,075,000	
2007 Sales: $74,832,000		2007 Profits: $10,340,000	Int'l Ticker: Int'l Exchange:
2006 Sales: $68,222,000		2006 Profits: $8,684,000	Employees: 138,000
2005 Sales: $56,741,000		2005 Profits: $6,923,000	Fiscal Year Ends: 6/30
2004 Sales: $51,407,000		2004 Profits: $6,156,000	Parent Company:

SALARIES/BENEFITS:

Pension Plan:	ESOP Stock Plan:	Profit Sharing:	Top Exec. Salary: $1,800,000	Bonus: $3,100,000
Savings Plan:	Stock Purch. Plan:		Second Exec. Salary: $1,000,000	Bonus: $1,792,134

OTHER THOUGHTS:

Apparent Women Officers or Directors: 11
Hot Spot for Advancement for Women/Minorities: Y

LOCATIONS: ("Y" = Yes)

West:	Southwest:	Midwest:	Southeast:	Northeast:	International:
Y	Y	Y	Y	Y	Y

Note: Financial information, benefits and other data can change quickly and may vary from those stated here.

PROGRESSIVE CORPORATION (THE)

www.progressive.com

Industry Group Code: 524126 Ranks within this company's industry group: Sales: 7 Profits: 7

Management:		Sales/Marketing:		Liberal Arts:		Information Systems:		Professionals:		Tech./Scientific:	
Management Trainees:	Y	Marketing Pros.:	Y	Gen. Writing/Editing:	Y	Info. Management:	Y	Finance/Acct.:	Y	Engineers, Electrical:	
Experienced Mngmt.:	Y	Retail Sales:		Technical Writing:	Y	Software Dev.:	Y	Law:	Y	Engineers, Other:	
International Business:	Y	Commercial/Industrial:		Graphic Arts/Photog.:	Y	Hardware Dev.:		HR/Other:	Y	Health/Lab:	
MBA Grads:	Y	Sales Trainees:	Y	Music:		Consulting/Other:		Training:	Y	Scientists/Research:	
		Advertising Pros.:	Y	Broadcasting:				Health Care:		Petroleum/Chemicals:	
				Other:	Y			Consulting:		Math/Other:	Y

TYPES OF BUSINESS:

Insurance, Direct Property & Casualty
Automobile Insurance
Specialty Insurance

BRANDS/DIVISIONS/AFFILIATES:

ProgressiveResponds.com

CONTACTS: *Note: Officers with more than one job title may be intentionally listed here more than once.*

Glenn M. Renwick, CEO
Glenn M. Renwick, Pres.
Brian Domeck, CFO/VP
Lawrence W. Bloomenkranz, Chief Mktg. Officer
Valerie Krasowski, Chief Human Resources Officer
Raymond M. Voelker, CIO
Charles E. Jarret, Chief Legal Officer/VP/Corp. Sec.
Jeffery W. Basch, Chief Acct. Officer/VP
John P. Sauerland, Pres., Personal Lines Group
John Barbagallo, Pres., Commercial Lines Group
William M. Cody, Chief Investment Officer
Susan Griffith, Pres., Claims Group
Peter B. Lewis, Chmn.

Phone: 440-461-5000	Fax: 800-456-6590
Toll-Free: 800-776-4737	
Address: 6300 Wilson Mills Rd., Mayfield Village, OH 44143 US	

GROWTH PLANS/SPECIAL FEATURES:

The Progressive Corporation, together with its 58 subsidiaries, is one of the largest auto insurers in the U.S. Progressive is divided into three business areas: personal lines, commercial auto and claims. The firm's personal lines segment writes insurance for private passenger automobiles and recreational and other vehicles, including motorcycles, all-terrain vehicles, boats and recreational vehicles. The personal lines business accounted for 87% of total net premiums written in 2008. The commercial auto business writes primary liability and physical damage insurance for automobiles and trucks owned by small businesses and represented 13% of Progressive's total net premiums written in 2008. The firm manages its claims business on a companywide basis through approximately 460 claims offices located throughout the U.S. The company has 54 centers in 41 metropolitan areas across the country, that provide concierge-level claims service. These facilities are designed to provide end-to-end resolution for auto physical damage losses. Customers can choose to bring their vehicles to one of these sites, where they can pick up a rental vehicle. Progressive's representatives will then write the estimate, select a qualified repair shop, arrange the repair and inspect the vehicle once the repairs are complete. Progressive maintains a catastrophe web site, ProgressiveResponds.com, to provide consumers with information about how to stay safe and protect their vehicles and boats before, during and after a catastrophic event. Additionally, the company offers pet insurance and golf cart insurance. In 2009, the firm expanded its coverage to coal haulers.

FINANCIALS: Sales and profits are in thousands of dollars—add 000 to get the full amount. 2008 Note: Financial information for 2008 was not available for all companies at press time.

2008 Sales: $12,840,100	2008 Profits: $-70,000	U.S. Stock Ticker: PGR
2007 Sales: $14,686,800	2007 Profits: $1,182,500	Int'l Ticker: Int'l Exchange:
2006 Sales: $14,786,400	2006 Profits: $1,647,500	Employees: 25,929
2005 Sales: $14,303,400	2005 Profits: $1,393,900	Fiscal Year Ends: 12/31
2004 Sales: $13,782,100	2004 Profits: $1,648,700	Parent Company:

SALARIES/BENEFITS:

Pension Plan:	ESOP Stock Plan:	Profit Sharing:	Top Exec. Salary: $778,846	Bonus: $
Savings Plan: Y	Stock Purch. Plan:		Second Exec. Salary: $424,038	Bonus: $339,231

OTHER THOUGHTS:

Apparent Women Officers or Directors: 5
Hot Spot for Advancement for Women/Minorities: Y

LOCATIONS: ("Y" = Yes)

West:	Southwest:	Midwest:	Southeast:	Northeast:	International:
Y	Y	Y	Y	Y	

Note: Financial information, benefits and other data can change quickly and may vary from those stated here.

PRUDENTIAL FINANCIAL INC

www.prudential.com

Industry Group Code: 524113 **Ranks within this company's industry group:** Sales: 2   Profits: 5

Management:		Sales/Marketing:		Liberal Arts:		Information Systems:		Professionals:		Tech./Scientific:	
Management Trainees:	Y	Marketing Pros.:	Y	Gen. Writing/Editing:	Y	Info. Management:	Y	Finance/Acct.:	Y	Engineers, Electrical:	
Experienced Mngmt.:	Y	Retail Sales:		Technical Writing:	Y	Software Dev.:	Y	Law:	Y	Engineers, Other:	
International Business:	Y	Commercial/Industrial:	Y	Graphic Arts/Photog.:	Y	Hardware Dev.:		HR/Other:	Y	Health/Lab:	
MBA Grads:	Y	Sales Trainees:	Y	Music:		Consulting/Other:		Training:	Y	Scientists/Research:	
		Advertising Pros.:	Y	Broadcasting:				Health Care:	Y	Petroleum/Chemicals:	
				Other:	Y			Consulting:		Math/Other:	Y

TYPES OF BUSINESS:

Insurance-Life
Property & Casualty Insurance
Asset Management, Pension & Benefit Plans
Brokerage Services
Relocation Services

BRANDS/DIVISIONS/AFFILIATES:

Prudential Insurance Company of America (The)
Prudential Real Estate and Relocation Services
Prudential Real Estate Affiliates, Inc.
Yamato Life
Gibraltar Life

CONTACTS: *Note: Officers with more than one job title may be intentionally listed here more than once.*

John Strangfeld, CEO
John Strangfeld, Pres.
Richard J. Carbone, CFO/Exec. VP
Sharon C. Taylor, Sr. VP-Corp. Human Resources
Robert C. Golden, Exec. VP-Systems
Susan L. Blount, General Counsel/Sr. VP
Robert C. Golden, Exec. VP-Oper.
Bob DeFillippo,
Bernard B. Winograd, Exec. VP/COO-U.S. Bus.
Helen M. Galt, Chief Risk Officer/Sr. VP
Margaret M. Foran, Chief Governance Officer/VP/Sec.
John Strangfeld, Chmn.
Edward P. Baird, Exec. VP/COO-Int'l Bus.

Phone: 973-802-6000	Fax: 973-367-6476
Toll-Free: 877-998-7625	
Address: 751 Broad St., Newark, NJ 07102 US	

GROWTH PLANS/SPECIAL FEATURES:

Prudential Financial, Inc. provides insurance, investment management and other financial products and services to individual and institutional customers worldwide. It operates in three divisions: U.S. Retirement Solutions and Investment Management; U.S. Individual Life and Group Insurance; and International Insurance and Investments. The Retirement Solutions and Investment division is composed of three segments: individual annuities, which manufactures and distributes individual variable and fixed annuity products; retirement, which provides retirement investment and income products; and asset management, which provides investment management and advisory services. The Individual Life and Group Insurance division is composed of two segments: individual life, which manufactures and distributes individual variable life, term life and universal life insurance products, and group insurance, which manufactures and distributes group life, long-term and short-term group disability, long-term care and group corporate- and trust-owned life insurance products. This division operates through the Prudential Insurance Company of America, the firm's major subsidiary. The International division operates through two divisions: international insurance, which distributes individual life insurance products in Japan, Korea and other countries outside the U.S., and international investments, which offers proprietary and non-proprietary asset management, investment advice and services to international retail and institutional clients. The firm also operates Prudential Real Estate and Relocation Services, a real estate brokerage and relocation services business. All of the company's operations are divided into either Financial Services Businesses, which are publicly traded on the New York Stock Exchange, or Closed Block Businesses, which represent a former operating division. The company has approximately $580 billion in assets under management. In May 2009, Prudential's Gibraltar Life subsidiary acquired Yamato Life, a Japanese life insurance company.

Prudential offers its employees medical coverage, dental and vision plans; wellness screenings; an employee savings plan; a cash balance plan; tuition assistance; flexible spending accounts; an employee assistance program; and flexible work arrangements.

FINANCIALS: Sales and profits are in thousands of dollars—add 000 to get the full amount. 2008 Note: Financial information for 2008 was not available for all companies at press time.

2008 Sales: $29,275,000	2008 Profits: $-1,073,000	**U.S. Stock Ticker: PRU**
2007 Sales: $34,401,000	2007 Profits: $3,704,000	**Int'l Ticker:** Int'l Exchange:
2006 Sales: $32,268,000	2006 Profits: $3,428,000	Employees: 41,844
2005 Sales: $31,599,000	2005 Profits: $3,540,000	Fiscal Year Ends: 12/31
2004 Sales: $28,096,000	2004 Profits: $2,256,000	Parent Company:

SALARIES/BENEFITS:

Pension Plan: Y	ESOP Stock Plan:	Profit Sharing:	Top Exec. Salary: $970,769	Bonus: $3,300,000
Savings Plan: Y	Stock Purch. Plan:		Second Exec. Salary: $831,731	Bonus: $2,750,000

OTHER THOUGHTS:

Apparent Women Officers or Directors: 5
Hot Spot for Advancement for Women/Minorities: Y

LOCATIONS: ("Y" = Yes)

West:	Southwest:	Midwest:	Southeast:	Northeast:	International:
Y	Y	Y	Y	Y	Y

Note: Financial information, benefits and other data can change quickly and may vary from those stated here.

PSYCHIATRIC SOLUTIONS INC

www.psysolutions.com

Industry Group Code: 622210 Ranks within this company's industry group: Sales: 1 Profits: 1

Management:		Sales/Marketing:		Liberal Arts:		Information Systems:		Professionals:		Tech./Scientific:	
Management Trainees:	Y	Marketing Pros.:	Y	Gen. Writing/Editing:	Y	Info. Management:	Y	Finance/Acct.:	Y	Engineers, Electrical:	
Experienced Mngmt.:	Y	Retail Sales:		Technical Writing:	Y	Software Dev.:		Law:	Y	Engineers, Other:	
International Business:	Y	Commercial/Industrial:		Graphic Arts/Photog.:	Y	Hardware Dev.:		HR/Other:	Y	Health/Lab:	
MBA Grads:	Y	Sales Trainees:		Music:		Consulting/Other:		Training:	Y	Scientists/Research:	
		Advertising Pros.:		Broadcasting:				Health Care:	Y	Petroleum/Chemicals:	
				Other:	Y			Consulting:		Math/Other:	

TYPES OF BUSINESS:

Clinics-Psychiatric
Contract Management Services
Employee Assistance Program Administration

BRANDS/DIVISIONS/AFFILIATES:

United Medical Corporation

CONTACTS: Note: Officers with more than one job title may be intentionally listed here more than once.

Joey A. Jacobs, CEO
Terrance R. (Terry) Bridges, Co-COO
Joey A. Jacobs, Pres.
Brent Turner, Exec. VP-Admin. & Finance
Christopher L. Howard, General Counsel/Sec./Exec. VP
Steven T. Davidson, Chief Dev. Officer
Jack E. Polson, Chief Acct. Officer/Exec. VP
Ron Fincher, Co-COO
Kathy L. Bolmer, Exec. VP-Quality & Compliance
Joey A. Jacobs, Chmn.

Phone: 615-312-5700	Fax: 615-312-5711
Toll-Free:	
Address: 6640 Carothers Pkwy., Ste. 500, Franklin, TN 37067 US	

GROWTH PLANS/SPECIAL FEATURES:

Psychiatric Solutions, Inc. (PSI) primarily offers inpatient behavioral health care services. It operates 88 owned and seven leased inpatient behavioral health care facilities, with almost 10,690 beds, located in 31 states, the U.S. Virgin Islands and Puerto Rico. Forty-four facilities have less than 100 beds and only six have 200 or more. PSI's facilities offer inpatient services for children, adolescents and adults through a combination of acute inpatient behavioral facilities and residential treatment centers (RTCs). Acute inpatient behavioral facilities provide intensive psychiatric care, including 24-hour-a-day skilled nursing observation, daily interventions and oversight by a psychiatrist and intensive, coordinated treatment by a physician-led team of mental health professionals. RTCs provide longer term treatment programs primarily for children and adolescents with long-standing chronic behavioral health problems. RTCs offer physician-led multi-disciplinary treatments that address the patient's medical, psychiatric, social and academic needs. Both of these facilities work closely with others, including psychiatrists, non-psychiatric physicians, emergency rooms, counselors, therapists, social workers, school systems, insurance companies, employee assistance programs (EAPs) and law enforcement and community agencies that interact with individuals who require mental illness or substance abuse treatment. Many of PSI's facilities have mobile assessment teams who travel to prospective clients, assess their condition and determine if they meet established criteria for inpatient care. Those clients not meeting the criteria may qualify for outpatient care or a less intensive level of care provided by the facility. Besides facilities, PSI offers behavioral health care services, primarily contract management, comprising the development, organization and management of behavioral health care programs within hospitals. It also administers EAPs, contracting with employers to assist employees and their dependents with behavioral and other problems. Inpatient facilities generated 90% of 2008 revenue; behavioral services, 10%. In March 2008, PSI acquired five facilities with 400 beds from United Medical Corporation for $120 million.

FINANCIALS: Sales and profits are in thousands of dollars—add 000 to get the full amount. 2008 Note: Financial information for 2008 was not available for all companies at press time.

2008 Sales: $1,765,977	2008 Profits: $104,953	**U.S. Stock Ticker: PSYS**
2007 Sales: $1,460,679	2007 Profits: $76,208	**Int'l Ticker:** Int'l Exchange:
2006 Sales: $1,022,428	2006 Profits: $60,632	Employees: 23,000
2005 Sales: $715,324	2005 Profits: $27,154	Fiscal Year Ends: 12/31
2004 Sales: $470,969	2004 Profits: $16,801	Parent Company:

SALARIES/BENEFITS:

Pension Plan:	ESOP Stock Plan:	Profit Sharing:	Top Exec. Salary: $1,490,384	Bonus: $1,108,000
Savings Plan:	Stock Purch. Plan:		Second Exec. Salary: $456,187	Bonus: $233,567

OTHER THOUGHTS:

Apparent Women Officers or Directors: 1
Hot Spot for Advancement for Women/Minorities:

LOCATIONS: ("Y" = Yes)

West:	Southwest:	Midwest:	Southeast:	Northeast:	International:
Y	Y	Y	Y	Y	Y

Note: Financial information, benefits and other data can change quickly and may vary from those stated here.

PUBLIC STORAGE INC

www.publicstorage.com

Industry Group Code: 531120 Ranks within this company's industry group: Sales: 1   Profits: 1

Management:		Sales/Marketing:		Liberal Arts:		Information Systems:		Professionals:		Tech./Scientific:	
Management Trainees:	Y	Marketing Pros.:	Y	Gen. Writing/Editing:		Info. Management:	Y	Finance/Acct.:	Y	Engineers, Electrical:	
Experienced Mngmt.:	Y	Retail Sales:		Technical Writing:		Software Dev.:		Law:	Y	Engineers, Other:	
International Business:		Commercial/Industrial:		Graphic Arts/Photog.:		Hardware Dev.:		HR/Other:	Y	Health/Lab:	
MBA Grads:	Y	Sales Trainees:		Music:		Consulting/Other:		Training:	Y	Scientists/Research:	
		Advertising Pros.:		Broadcasting:				Health Care:		Petroleum/Chemicals:	
				Other:				Consulting:		Math/Other:	

TYPES OF BUSINESS:

Real Estate Investment Trust
Self-Storage Facilities
Commercial Properties
Transportation Services
Online Storage Reservations

BRANDS/DIVISIONS/AFFILIATES:

PS Business Parks, Inc.
Carson Storage Partners, Ltd.
Del Amo Storage Partners, Ltd.
Connecticut Storage Fund
PS Partners, Ltd.
Van Nuys Storage Partners, Ltd.
Secure Mini-Storage
Shurgard Storage Centers, Inc.

CONTACTS: Note: Officers with more than one job title may be intentionally listed here more than once.

Ronald L. Havner, Jr., CEO
Mark C. Good, COO/Sr. VP
Ronald L. Havner, Jr., Pres./Vice Chmn.
John Reyes, CFO/Sr. VP
Candace N. Krol, Sr. VP-Human Resources
Brian J. Fields, Chief Legal Officer/Sr. VP
John E. Graul, Pres., Self-Storage Oper.
David F. Doll, Pres., Real Estate Div.
B. Wayne Hughes, Chmn.

Phone: 818-244-8080	Fax: 818-553-2388
Toll-Free:	
Address: 701 Western Ave., Ste. 200, Glendale, CA 91201 US	

GROWTH PLANS/SPECIAL FEATURES:

Public Storage, Inc. is a fully integrated, self-administered and self-managed equity real estate investment trust (REIT) that acquires, develops, owns and operates self-storage facilities. It is one of the largest owners and operators of self-storage space in the U.S., with direct and indirect equity investments in over 2,017 self-storage facilities containing approximately 127 million square feet of net rentable space in 38 states and 179 storage facilities in seven Western European nations with nine million square feet of net rentable space. The self-storage facilities consist of three to seven buildings containing 350-750 storages spaces, most of which have between 25 to 400 square feet and an interior height of eight to 12 feet. The company's growth strategy consists of improving the operating performance of its existing traditional self-storage properties; acquiring interests in properties that are owned or operated by others; expanding and repackaging existing real estate facilities; developing properties in selected markets; and participating in the growth of commercial facilities owned primarily by PS Business Parks, Inc. (a publicly traded REIT in which Public Storage holds a 44% interest). Public Storage also controls or has a minority interest in many subsidiary companies, which include Carson Storage Partners, Ltd.; Connecticut Storage Fund; Del Amo Storage Partners, Ltd.; PS Partners, Ltd.; Secure Mini-Storage; and Van Nuys Storage Partners, Ltd.

Employees are offered medical, dental and vision insurance; short-and long-term disability coverage; life insurance; medical and dependent care spending plans; an employee assistance program; and a 401(k) plan.

FINANCIALS: Sales and profits are in thousands of dollars—add 000 to get the full amount. 2008 Note: Financial information for 2008 was not available for all companies at press time.

2008 Sales: $1,745,607	2008 Profits: $935,176	**U.S. Stock Ticker: PSA**
2007 Sales: $1,814,499	2007 Profits: $457,535	**Int'l Ticker:** Int'l Exchange:
2006 Sales: $1,379,066	2006 Profits: $314,026	Employees: 5,200
2005 Sales: $1,059,838	2005 Profits: $456,393	Fiscal Year Ends: 12/31
2004 Sales: $958,157	2004 Profits: $366,213	Parent Company:

SALARIES/BENEFITS:

Pension Plan:	ESOP Stock Plan:	Profit Sharing:	Top Exec. Salary: $952,543	Bonus: $16,000,000
Savings Plan: Y	Stock Purch. Plan:		Second Exec. Salary: $600,000	Bonus: $8,100,000

OTHER THOUGHTS:

Apparent Women Officers or Directors: 1
Hot Spot for Advancement for Women/Minorities:

LOCATIONS: ("Y" = Yes)

West:	Southwest:	Midwest:	Southeast:	Northeast:	International:
Y	Y	Y	Y	Y	

PUBLIX SUPER MARKETS INC

www.publix.com

Industry Group Code: 445110 Ranks within this company's industry group: Sales: 4 Profits: 2

Management:		Sales/Marketing:		Liberal Arts:		Information Systems:		Professionals:		Tech./Scientific:	
Management Trainees:	Y	Marketing Pros.:	Y	Gen. Writing/Editing:	Y	Info. Management:	Y	Finance/Acct.:	Y	Engineers, Electrical:	
Experienced Mngmt.:	Y	Retail Sales:	Y	Technical Writing:		Software Dev.:	Y	Law:	Y	Engineers, Other:	
International Business:		Commercial/Industrial:		Graphic Arts/Photog.:	Y	Hardware Dev.:		HR/Other:	Y	Health/Lab:	
MBA Grads:	Y	Sales Trainees:	Y	Music:		Consulting/Other:		Training:	Y	Scientists/Research:	
		Advertising Pros.:	Y	Broadcasting:				Health Care:		Petroleum/Chemicals:	
				Other:	Y			Consulting:		Math/Other:	

TYPES OF BUSINESS:

Grocery Stores
Dairy, Deli & Bakery Products
Convenience Stores
Liquor Stores
Restaurants

BRANDS/DIVISIONS/AFFILIATES:

Crisper's Restaurants

CONTACTS:
Note: Officers with more than one job title may be intentionally listed here more than once.

William E. Crenshaw, CEO
Randall T. Jones, Sr., Pres.
David P. Phillips, CFO
John Hrabusa, Sr. VP-Human Resources
Laurie S. Zeitlin, CIO/Sr. VP
Mike Smith, VP-Mfg.
John A. Attaway, Jr., General Counsel/Sec./Sr. VP
David P. Phillips, Treas.
G. Gino DiGrazia, VP/Controller
Sandra J. Estrep, VP/Controller
Howard M. Jenkins, Chmn.

Phone: 863-688-1188	Fax: 863-616-9649
Toll-Free: 800-242-1227	
Address: 3300 Publix Corporate Pkwy., Lakeland, FL 33811 US	

GROWTH PLANS/SPECIAL FEATURES:

Publix Super Markets, Inc. is a leading operator of supermarkets, with 1,007 locations in Alabama, Florida, Georgia, South Carolina and Tennessee. The company also operates 10 convenience stores, 84 liquor stores and 41 Crispers restaurants. The firm's supermarkets sell groceries, dairy products, produce, deli foods, bakery items, meat, seafood, housewares and health and beauty care merchandise. Many stores also feature pharmacies, floral departments, photo labs and in-store banking areas. Publix's lines of merchandise include a variety of nationally advertised and private label brands, as well as some unbranded merchandise, such as produce, meat and seafood. In addition to its retail operations, Publix manufactures dairy, bakery and deli products through manufacturing facilities located in Jacksonville, Lakeland and Deerfield Beach, Florida and Lawrenceville and Atlanta, Georgia. The firm is one of the largest employee-owned grocery stores in the U.S. The store recently launched its Publix GreenWise Market brand in Lakeland, Florida which sells all-natural and organic products, combined with conventional products.

Publix offers its employees health, dental and vision coverage; an employee stock ownership plan; holiday bonuses; premium pay for working Sundays; profit sharing; a 401(k) plan; access to a credit union; tuition reimbursement; and an employee assistance plan.

FINANCIALS:
Sales and profits are in thousands of dollars—add 000 to get the full amount. 2008 Note: Financial information for 2008 was not available for all companies at press time.

2008 Sales: $23,929,064	2008 Profits: $1,089,770	**U.S. Stock Ticker: PUSH**
2007 Sales: $23,016,568	2007 Profits: $1,183,925	**Int'l Ticker:** Int'l Exchange:
2006 Sales: $21,654,774	2006 Profits: $1,097,209	Employees: 144,000
2005 Sales: $20,589,130	2005 Profits: $989,156	Fiscal Year Ends: 12/31
2004 Sales: $18,554,486	2004 Profits: $819,383	Parent Company:

SALARIES/BENEFITS:

Pension Plan: Y	ESOP Stock Plan: Y	Profit Sharing: Y	Top Exec. Salary: $754,000	Bonus: $21,166
Savings Plan: Y	Stock Purch. Plan:		Second Exec. Salary: $609,140	Bonus: $17,099

OTHER THOUGHTS:

Apparent Women Officers or Directors: 8
Hot Spot for Advancement for Women/Minorities: Y

LOCATIONS: ("Y" = Yes)

West:	Southwest:	Midwest:	Southeast:	Northeast:	International:
			Y		

QUALCOMM INC

www.qualcomm.com

Industry Group Code: 33441 **Ranks within this company's industry group:** Sales: 2   Profits: 2

Management:		Sales/Marketing:		Liberal Arts:		Information Systems:		Professionals:		Tech./Scientific:	
Management Trainees:	Y	Marketing Pros.:	Y	Gen. Writing/Editing:	Y	Info. Management:	Y	Finance/Acct.:	Y	Engineers, Electrical:	Y
Experienced Mngmt.:	Y	Retail Sales:		Technical Writing:	Y	Software Dev.:	Y	Law:	Y	Engineers, Other:	
International Business:	Y	Commercial/Industrial:	Y	Graphic Arts/Photog.:	Y	Hardware Dev.:	Y	HR/Other:	Y	Health/Lab:	
MBA Grads:	Y	Sales Trainees:		Music:		Consulting/Other:		Training:	Y	Scientists/Research:	Y
		Advertising Pros.:	Y	Broadcasting:				Health Care:		Petroleum/Chemicals:	
				Other:				Consulting:		Math/Other:	Y

TYPES OF BUSINESS:

Telecommunications Equipment
Digital Wireless Communications Products
Integrated Circuits
Mobile Communications Systems
Wireless Software & Services
E-Mail Software
Code Division Multiple Access

BRANDS/DIVISIONS/AFFILIATES:

MediaFLO USA, Inc.
Qualcomm Flarion Technologies, Inc.
Qualcomm MEMS Technologies, Inc.
Firethorn Holdings, LLC
SoftMax, Inc.
Xiam Technologies Limited
Ronda Grupo Consultor, S.L.

CONTACTS: *Note: Officers with more than one job title may be intentionally listed here more than once.*

Paul E. Jacobs, CEO
Len J. Lauer, COO/Exec. VP
Steven R. Altman, Pres.
William E. Keitel, CFO/Exec. VP
William F. Davidson, Jr., Sr. VP-Global Mktg.
Daniel L. Sullivan, Exec. VP-Human Resources
Norm Fjeldheim, CIO/Sr. VP
Roberto Padovani, CTO/Exec. VP
Donald J. Rosenberg, General Counsel/Exec. VP/Corp. Sec.
William Bold, Sr. VP-Gov't Affairs
William F. Davidson, Jr., Sr. VP-Investor Rel.
Margaret L. Johnson, Exec. VP-Americas & India
Derek Aberle, Exec. VP/Pres., Qualcomm Tech. Licensing
Robert Walton, Sr. VP/Pres., Qualcomm Enterprise Svcs.
Paul E. Jacobs, Chmn.
Jing Wang, Exec. VP-Asia Pacific, Middle East & Africa

Phone: 858-587-1121	**Fax:** 858-658-2100
Toll-Free:	
Address: 5775 Morehouse Dr., San Diego, CA 92121 US	

GROWTH PLANS/SPECIAL FEATURES:

Qualcomm, Inc. provides digital wireless communications products, technologies and services. It designs application-specific integrated circuits based on Code Division Multiple Access (CDMA) technology and licenses its technology to domestic and international telecommunications equipment suppliers. CDMA technology is an industry standard for all forms of digital wireless communications networks. The company also produces the e-mail software Eudora and sells Binary Runtime Environment for Wireless (BREW) software to network operators, handset manufacturers and application developers. BREW is an open-standard platform that can interface with many different wireless applications. The firm's wireless business services, which consist of satellite and terrestrial-based two-way data messaging and position reporting, serve transportation companies, private and construction equipment fleets and U.S. government agencies through its government technologies division. Subsidiary Qualcomm MEMS Technologies develops improved graphical systems for handheld devices. Subsidiary MediaFLO USA, Inc. offers services over a nationwide multicast network based on the MediaFLO Media Distribution System (MDS) and Forward Link Only (FLO) technology This network is utilized as a shared resource for wireless operators and partners. Subsidiary Qualcomm Flarion Technologies is a developer and provider of FLASH-OFDM (Orthogonal Frequency Division Multiplexing Access). The firm offers mobile entertainment services via partnerships with a variety of media networks including NBC; CBS; FOX; and MTV. In 2008, the company acquired Xiam Technologies Limited, an Irish wireless content discovery and recommendations discovery provider, and the majority of the assets of Ronda Grupo Consultor, S.L., a provider of fleet management systems in Spain and Portugal. In 2009, the firm acquired the handheld graphics and multimedia assets from Advanced Micro Devices.

Employees are offered medical, dental and vision insurance; dependent and health care reimbursement accounts; tuition reimbursement; adoption assistance; and a wireless device subsidy program.

FINANCIALS: Sales and profits are in thousands of dollars—add 000 to get the full amount. 2008 Note: Financial information for 2008 was not available for all companies at press time.

2008 Sales: $11,142,000	2008 Profits: $3,160,000	**U.S. Stock Ticker: QCOM**
2007 Sales: $8,871,000	2007 Profits: $3,303,000	**Int'l Ticker:** Int'l Exchange:
2006 Sales: $7,526,000	2006 Profits: $2,470,000	Employees: 15,400
2005 Sales: $5,673,000	2005 Profits: $2,143,000	Fiscal Year Ends: 9/30
2004 Sales: $4,880,000	2004 Profits: $1,720,000	Parent Company:

SALARIES/BENEFITS:

Pension Plan:	ESOP Stock Plan:	Profit Sharing:	Top Exec. Salary: $1,112,218	Bonus: $9,100,000
Savings Plan: Y	Stock Purch. Plan: Y		Second Exec. Salary: $817,351	Bonus: $2,909,000

OTHER THOUGHTS:

Apparent Women Officers or Directors: 4
Hot Spot for Advancement for Women/Minorities: Y

LOCATIONS: ("Y" = Yes)

West:	Southwest:	Midwest:	Southeast:	Northeast:	International:
Y	Y	Y	Y	Y	Y

QUANTA SERVICES INC

www.quantaservices.com

Industry Group Code: 237130 Ranks within this company's industry group: Sales: 1   Profits: 1

Management:		Sales/Marketing:		Liberal Arts:		Information Systems:		Professionals:		Tech./Scientific:	
Management Trainees:	Y	Marketing Pros.:	Y	Gen. Writing/Editing:		Info. Management:	Y	Finance/Acct.:	Y	Engineers, Electrical:	Y
Experienced Mngmt.:	Y	Retail Sales:		Technical Writing:	Y	Software Dev.:		Law:	Y	Engineers, Other:	Y
International Business:	Y	Commercial/Industrial:	Y	Graphic Arts/Photog.:		Hardware Dev.:		HR/Other:	Y	Health/Lab:	
MBA Grads:	Y	Sales Trainees:		Music:		Consulting/Other:		Training:	Y	Scientists/Research:	
		Advertising Pros.:		Broadcasting:				Health Care:		Petroleum/Chemicals:	
				Other:				Consulting:		Math/Other:	

TYPES OF BUSINESS:

Construction, Power & Communication Lines
Network Installation & Support Services
Network Design Services
Electric Power Transmission Systems
Gas Pipeline Systems

BRANDS/DIVISIONS/AFFILIATES:

InfraSource Services, Inc.

CONTACTS: *Note: Officers with more than one job title may be intentionally listed here more than once.*

John R. Colson, CEO
James F. O'Neil III, COO
James F. O'Neil III, Pres.
James H. Haddox, CFO
Darren B. Miller, VP-IT
Darren B. Miller, VP-Admin.
Tana L. Pool, General Counsel/VP
Joseph A. Avila, Exec. VP-Strategic Oper. & Progress
Benadetto G. Bosco, Sr. VP-Bus. Dev. & Outsourcing
Derrick A. Jensen, Chief Acct. Officer/Controller
John R. Wilson, Pres., Electric Power & Gas Div.
Kenneth W. Trawick, Pres., Telecommunications & Cable Television Div.
Nicholas Grindstaff, Treas.
John R. Colson, Chmn.

Phone: 713-629-7600	Fax: 713-629-7676
Toll-Free:	
Address: 1360 Post Oak Blvd., Ste. 2100, Houston, TX 77056-3023 US	

GROWTH PLANS/SPECIAL FEATURES:

Quanta Services, Inc. is a specialty contract provider of network services, with operations in all 50 states and parts of Canada. The company designs, installs and maintains networks for the electric power, telecommunications and broadband cable and gas industries. The company lays, repairs and maintains these systems, old or new, servicing electric power transmission lines ranging from 69,000 volts to 765,000 volts. The company also handles control systems for traffic networks and cable and control systems for light rail lines, airports and highways. In 2008, the company's revenues were generated by a variety of customers: 78% was attributable to electric power and gas customers; 14% to telecommunications and cable television customers; and 7% to ancillary services, such as inside electrical wiring, intelligent traffic networks and specialty rock trenching, directional boring and road milling for industrial and commercial customers. Quanta's telecommunications and cable television network services include fiber optic, copper and coaxial cable installation; maintenance for video, data and voice transmission; design, construction and maintenance of digital subscriber line (DSL) networks; leasing point-to-point telecommunications infrastructure through its dark fiber business; and engineering and erection of cellular, digital, personal communication systems (PCS). The company also provides infrastructure construction services for energy and telecommunications sectors through its InfraSource Services brand. Quanta's major clients include AT&T; Pacific Gas & Electric; Puget Sound Energy; and Verizon Communications. In July 2008, Quanta began construction on a 10-megawatt solar energy facility designed to power about 6,400 homes. The company also extended an existing contract from 2013 to 2015, adding $200 million in services for a total value of $950 million.

FINANCIALS: Sales and profits are in thousands of dollars—add 000 to get the full amount. 2008 Note: Financial information for 2008 was not available for all companies at press time.

2008 Sales: $3,780,213	2008 Profits: $176,790	**U.S. Stock Ticker: PWR**
2007 Sales: $2,656,036	2007 Profits: $135,977	**Int'l Ticker:** Int'l Exchange:
2006 Sales: $2,109,632	2006 Profits: $17,483	Employees: 14,751
2005 Sales: $1,858,626	2005 Profits: $29,557	Fiscal Year Ends: 12/31
2004 Sales: $1,626,510	2004 Profits: $-9,194	Parent Company:

SALARIES/BENEFITS:

Pension Plan: Y	ESOP Stock Plan:	Profit Sharing:	Top Exec. Salary: $773,750	Bonus: $916,800
Savings Plan: Y	Stock Purch. Plan:		Second Exec. Salary: $453,750	Bonus: $495,072

OTHER THOUGHTS:

Apparent Women Officers or Directors: 1
Hot Spot for Advancement for Women/Minorities:

LOCATIONS: ("Y" = Yes)

West:	Southwest:	Midwest:	Southeast:	Northeast:	International:
Y	Y	Y	Y	Y	Y

QUEST DIAGNOSTICS INC

www.questdiagnostics.com

Industry Group Code: 6215   Ranks within this company's industry group: Sales: 1   Profits: 1

Management:		Sales/Marketing:		Liberal Arts:		Information Systems:		Professionals:		Tech./Scientific:	
Management Trainees:	Y	Marketing Pros.:		Gen. Writing/Editing:		Info. Management:	Y	Finance/Acct.:	Y	Engineers, Electrical:	
Experienced Mngmt.:	Y	Retail Sales:		Technical Writing:	Y	Software Dev.:	Y	Law:	Y	Engineers, Other:	
International Business:	Y	Commercial/Industrial:	Y	Graphic Arts/Photog.:	Y	Hardware Dev.:		HR/Other:	Y	Health/Lab:	Y
MBA Grads:	Y	Sales Trainees:		Music:		Consulting/Other:		Training:	Y	Scientists/Research:	Y
		Advertising Pros.:		Broadcasting:				Health Care:	Y	Petroleum/Chemicals:	
				Other:				Consulting:		Math/Other:	

TYPES OF BUSINESS:

Services-Testing & Diagnostics
Clinical Laboratory Testing
Clinical Trials Testing
Esoteric Testing Laboratories

BRANDS/DIVISIONS/AFFILIATES:

Cardio CRP
HEPTIMAX
Bio-Intact PTH
Nichols Institute

CONTACTS: Note: Officers with more than one job title may be intentionally listed here more than once.

Surya N. Mohapatra, CEO
Robert A. Hagemann, CFO/Sr. VP
Jon R. Cohen, Chief Medical Officer/Sr. VP
Michael E. Prevoznik, General Counsel/VP-Legal & Compliance
Wayne R. Simmons, VP-Oper.
Laura Park, VP-Comm.
Laura Park, VP-Investor Rel.
Joan E. Miller, Sr. VP-Pathology & Hospital Svcs.
Surya N. Mohapatra, Chmn.

Phone: 201-393-5000	Fax: 201-729-8920
Toll-Free: 800-222-0446	
Address: 3 Giralda Farms, Madison, NJ 07940 US	

GROWTH PLANS/SPECIAL FEATURES:

Quest Diagnostics, Inc. is a U.S. clinical laboratory testing company, offering diagnostic testing and related services to the health care industry.   The firm's operations consist of routine, esoteric and clinical trials testing.   Quest operates through its national network of over 2,000 patient service centers, principal laboratories in more than 30 major metropolitan areas, approximately 150 rapid-response laboratories, outpatient anatomic pathology centers, hospital-based laboratories and esoteric testing laboratories on both coasts.   Routine tests measure various important bodily health parameters.   Tests in this category include blood cholesterol level tests, complete blood cell counts, pap smears, HIV-related tests, urinalyses, pregnancy and prenatal tests and substance-abuse tests.   Esoteric tests require more sophisticated technology and highly skilled personnel.   The firm's tests in this field include Cardio CRP and HEPTIMAX.   Quest's two esoteric testing laboratories, comprising the Nichols Institute, are among the leading esoteric clinical testing laboratories in the world.   Esoteric tests involve endocrinology, genetics, immunology, microbiology, oncology, serology and special chemistry. Clinical trial testing primarily involves assessing the safety and efficacy of new drugs to meet FDA requirements, with services including Bio-Intact PTH.   In May 2009, the company launched the first commercial laboratory test for the H1N1 swine flu virus.   In June of the same year, the firm introduced the EGFR Pathway test, designed to identify genetic mutations in KRAS, NRAS and BRAF genes.

Employees are offered health and dental insurance; a 401(k) plan; an employee stock purchase plan; short- and long-term disability; educational assistance; flexible spending accounts; life insurance; and employee assistance program; credit union membership; veterinary pet care; legal services; auto and homeowners/renters insurance; financial management consulting services; banking services; adoption assistance; and discounted purchase programs.

FINANCIALS: Sales and profits are in thousands of dollars—add 000 to get the full amount. 2008 Note: Financial information for 2008 was not available for all companies at press time.

2008 Sales: $7,249,447	2008 Profits: $581,490	**U.S. Stock Ticker: DGX**
2007 Sales: $6,704,907	2007 Profits: $339,939	**Int'l Ticker:** Int'l Exchange:
2006 Sales: $6,268,659	2006 Profits: $586,421	Employees: 42,800
2005 Sales: $5,456,726	2005 Profits: $546,277	Fiscal Year Ends: 12/31
2004 Sales: $5,066,986	2004 Profits: $499,195	Parent Company:

SALARIES/BENEFITS:

Pension Plan:	ESOP Stock Plan:	Profit Sharing:	Top Exec. Salary: $1,143,868	Bonus: $1,915,693
Savings Plan: Y	Stock Purch. Plan: Y		Second Exec. Salary: $517,713	Bonus: $520,224

OTHER THOUGHTS:

Apparent Women Officers or Directors: 4
Hot Spot for Advancement for Women/Minorities: Y

LOCATIONS: ("Y" = Yes)

West:	Southwest:	Midwest:	Southeast:	Northeast:	International:
Y	Y	Y	Y	Y	Y

Note: Financial information, benefits and other data can change quickly and may vary from those stated here.

QUIKSILVER INC

www.quiksilverinc.com

Industry Group Code: 315211 **Ranks within this company's industry group:** Sales: 1 Profits: 1

Management:		Sales/Marketing:		Liberal Arts:		Information Systems:		Professionals:		Tech./Scientific:	
Management Trainees:	Y	Marketing Pros.:	Y	Gen. Writing/Editing:	Y	Info. Management:	Y	Finance/Acct.:	Y	Engineers, Electrical:	
Experienced Mngmt.:	Y	Retail Sales:	Y	Technical Writing:		Software Dev.:	Y	Law:	Y	Engineers, Other:	
International Business:	Y	Commercial/Industrial:	Y	Graphic Arts/Photog.:	Y	Hardware Dev.:		HR/Other:	Y	Health/Lab:	
MBA Grads:	Y	Sales Trainees:	Y	Music:		Consulting/Other:		Training:	Y	Scientists/Research:	
		Advertising Pros.:	Y	Broadcasting:				Health Care:		Petroleum/Chemicals:	
				Other:	Y			Consulting:		Math/Other:	

TYPES OF BUSINESS:

Sports Apparel & Equipment
Snow & Surf Apparel & Equipment
Accessories
Swimwear
Retail Stores

BRANDS/DIVISIONS/AFFILIATES:

Boardriders Club
Roxy
Look
DC
Roxy Girl
Dynastar
Lange
Kerma

CONTACTS: *Note: Officers with more than one job title may be intentionally listed here more than once.*

Robert B. McKnight, Jr., CEO
Robert B. McKnight, Jr., Pres.
Joseph Scirocco, CFO/Exec. VP
Charles S. Exon, Chief Admin. Officer
Charles S. Exon, General Counsel/Corp. Sec.
Craig Stevenson, Pres., Quiksilver America
Robert B. McKnight, Jr., Chmn.
Pierre Agnes, Pres., Quicksilver Europe

Phone: 714-889-2200	Fax: 714-889-3700
Toll-Free:	
Address: 15202 Graham St., Huntington Beach, CA 92649 US	

GROWTH PLANS/SPECIAL FEATURES:

Quiksilver, Inc. is a globally diversified company that designs, produces, retails and distributes branded apparel, wintersports equipment, footwear, accessories and related products. It operates in three segments: the Americas, which includes the U.S. and Canada; Europe, which includes primarily countries located in Western Europe; and Asia/Pacific, which includes Australia, Japan, New Zealand and Indonesia. The company's brands are focused on different sports within the outdoor market. Quiksilver and Roxy are rooted in the sport of surfing and are leading brands representing the boardriding lifestyle, which includes not only surfing, but also skateboarding and snowboarding. Quiksilver has grown to include shirts, walkshorts, t-shirts, pants, jackets, fleece, pants, snowboardwear, footwear, hats, backpacks, wetsuits, watches, eyewear and other accessories. In addition, the brand has expanded its target market to include boys, toddlers and infants. The Roxy brand includes sportswear, footwear, backpacks, snowboardwear, swimwear, backpacks, snowboard boots, skis, fragrance, beauty care, bedroom furnishings and other accessories for young women. The brand now contains the Teenie Wahine and Roxy Girl brands for girls and infants. DC's reputation is based on its technical shoes made for skateboarding. The firm also developed a portfolio of other brands also inspired by surfing, skateboarding and snowboarding. The wintersports brands include Dynastar, Look, Lange and Kerma, which are focused on equipment for alpine skiing but have extended into areas of wintersports, including snowboarding, freestyle skiing, Nordic skiing and technical outwear. Quiksilver's products are sold in over 90 countries in a wide range of distribution channels, including surf shops, ski shops, snowboard shops, the proprietary Boardriders Club shops, other specialty stores and select department stores. In November 2008, the company sold its Rossignol brand to Chartreuse & Mont Blanc.

FINANCIALS: Sales and profits are in thousands of dollars—add 000 to get the full amount. 2008 Note: Financial information for 2008 was not available for all companies at press time.

2008 Sales: $2,264,636	2008 Profits: $-226,265	U.S. Stock Ticker: ZQK
2007 Sales: $2,047,072	2007 Profits: $-121,119	Int'l Ticker: Int'l Exchange:
2006 Sales: $1,722,150	2006 Profits: $93,016	Employees: 8,400
2005 Sales: $1,780,869	2005 Profits: $107,120	Fiscal Year Ends: 10/31
2004 Sales: $1,266,939	2004 Profits: $81,369	Parent Company:

SALARIES/BENEFITS:

Pension Plan:	ESOP Stock Plan:	Profit Sharing:	Top Exec. Salary: $981,300	Bonus: $660,000
Savings Plan: Y	Stock Purch. Plan:		Second Exec. Salary: $562,500	Bonus: $585,000

OTHER THOUGHTS:

Apparent Women Officers or Directors:
Hot Spot for Advancement for Women/Minorities:

LOCATIONS: ("Y" = Yes)

West:	Southwest:	Midwest:	Southeast:	Northeast:	International:
Y					Y

Note: Financial information, benefits and other data can change quickly and may vary from those stated here.

R R DONNELLEY & SONS CO

www.rrdonelley.com

Industry Group Code: 323 Ranks within this company's industry group: Sales: 1 Profits: 2

Management:		Sales/Marketing:		Liberal Arts:		Information Systems:		Professionals:		Tech./Scientific:	
Management Trainees:	Y	Marketing Pros.:	Y	Gen. Writing/Editing:	Y	Info. Management:	Y	Finance/Acct.:	Y	Engineers, Electrical:	
Experienced Mngmt.:	Y	Retail Sales:		Technical Writing:	Y	Software Dev.:	Y	Law:	Y	Engineers, Other:	
International Business:	Y	Commercial/Industrial:	Y	Graphic Arts/Photog.:	Y	Hardware Dev.:		HR/Other:	Y	Health/Lab:	
MBA Grads:	Y	Sales Trainees:	Y	Music:		Consulting/Other:		Training:	Y	Scientists/Research:	
		Advertising Pros.:		Broadcasting:				Health Care:		Petroleum/Chemicals:	
				Other:	Y			Consulting:		Math/Other:	

TYPES OF BUSINESS:

Commercial Printing
Distributors-Books, Magazines, Catalogs & Direct Mail
Digital Content Management
Creative Services
Logistics Services

BRANDS/DIVISIONS/AFFILIATES:

ECoM
PROSA
Grafikom MIL

CONTACTS: Note: Officers with more than one job title may be intentionally listed here more than once.

Thomas J. Quinlan III, CEO
John R. Paloian, COO
Thomas J. Quinlan III, Pres.
Miles W. McHugh, CFO/Exec. VP
Andrew B. Panega, Sr. VP-Human Resources
Mary Lee Schneider, CTO
Suzanne S. Bettman, General Counsel/Exec. VP/Corp. Sec.
Doug Fitzgerald, Exec. VP-Corp. Comm.
Dave Gardella, VP-Finance
Dan L. Knotts, Group Pres.
Luiz J. Bring, Pres., R R Donnelley Latin America
Mark J. Williams, Sr. VP/Managing Dir.-Int'l Financial Svcs.
Andrew B. Coxhead, Chief Acct. Officer/Controller/Sr. VP
Stephen M. Wolf, Chmn.
Allen Hallis, Pres., R R Donnelley Canada

Phone: 312-326-8000	Fax: 312-326-7706
Toll-Free:	
Address: 111 S. Wacker Dr., Chicago, IL 60606 US	

GROWTH PLANS/SPECIAL FEATURES:

R.R. Donnelley & Sons Co. is a provider of print and related services. The firm markets its services, including business process outsourcing, to customers in the advertising, publishing, healthcare, retail, technology, and financial services industries. R. R. Donnelley operates through two segments: U.S. Print and Related Services and International. The U.S. Print and Related Services division offers products and services such as directories, books, direct mail, forms, labels, financial printing, retail inserts, office products, premedia, magazines, catalogs and logistics services. This segment accounts for approximately 75% of R.R. Donnelley & Sons' revenues. The firm's International segment includes its international printing operations in Asia, Latin America, Canada and Europe; and its business process outsourcing and Global Turnkey Solutions operations. The company's business process outsourcing operations provide statement printing, transactional print and outsourcing services; direct mail; and print management services in Asia, Europe and North America. R.R. Donnelley & Sons' global turnkey solutions group provides outsourcing capabilities such as product configuration; order fulfillment; and customized kitting for technology, medical device and other companies worldwide. This division has operations in North America and Europe. The International segment accounts for roughly 25% of revenues. In December 2008, the firm acquired the assets of the Grafikom MIL facility in Toronto from RSM Richter, Inc. Also In December 2008, the company agreed to build an integrated printing facility in Minnesota. In January 2009, R.R. Donnelley & Sons acquired the assets of Chilean web printing company PROSA from Copesa for approximately $23.5 million. In June 2009, the firm opened a new facility in the Philippines. In August 2009, the company opened a new facility in East Hungary.

R. R. Donnelley offers its employees benefits including life, medical, dental and vision insurance; a 401(k); a stock purchase plan; an assistance program; and a pension plan.

FINANCIALS: Sales and profits are in thousands of dollars—add 000 to get the full amount. 2008 Note: Financial information for 2008 was not available for all companies at press time.

2008 Sales: $11,581,600	2008 Profits: $-189,900	**U.S. Stock Ticker: RRD**
2007 Sales: $11,587,100	2007 Profits: $-48,900	**Int'l Ticker:** Int'l Exchange:
2006 Sales: $9,316,600	2006 Profits: $400,600	Employees: 62,000
2005 Sales: $8,430,200	2005 Profits: $137,100	Fiscal Year Ends: 12/31
2004 Sales: $7,156,400	2004 Profits: $178,300	Parent Company:

SALARIES/BENEFITS:

Pension Plan: Y	ESOP Stock Plan:	Profit Sharing:	Top Exec. Salary: $985,641	Bonus: $
Savings Plan: Y	Stock Purch. Plan: Y		Second Exec. Salary: $700,000	Bonus: $

OTHER THOUGHTS:

Apparent Women Officers or Directors: 1
Hot Spot for Advancement for Women/Minorities:

LOCATIONS: ("Y" = Yes)

West:	Southwest:	Midwest:	Southeast:	Northeast:	International:
Y	Y	Y	Y	Y	Y

Note: Financial information, benefits and other data can change quickly and may vary from those stated here.

RALCORP HOLDINGS INC

www.ralcorp.com

Industry Group Code: 311   Ranks within this company's industry group: Sales: 3   Profits: 4

Management:		Sales/Marketing:		Liberal Arts:		Information Systems:		Professionals:		Tech./Scientific:	
Management Trainees:	Y	Marketing Pros.:	Y	Gen. Writing/Editing:	Y	Info. Management:	Y	Finance/Acct.:	Y	Engineers, Electrical:	
Experienced Mngmt.:	Y	Retail Sales:		Technical Writing:		Software Dev.:		Law:	Y	Engineers, Other:	Y
International Business:	Y	Commercial/Industrial:	Y	Graphic Arts/Photog.:	Y	Hardware Dev.:		HR/Other:	Y	Health/Lab:	
MBA Grads:	Y	Sales Trainees:		Music:		Consulting/Other:		Training:	Y	Scientists/Research:	
		Advertising Pros.:		Broadcasting:				Health Care:		Petroleum/Chemicals:	
				Other:				Consulting:		Math/Other:	

TYPES OF BUSINESS:

Food Processing-Store Brand Products
Crackers & Cookies
Dressings & Sauces
Nuts & Candy
Tomato Processing
Breakfast Cereal

BRANDS/DIVISIONS/AFFILIATES:

Ralston Foods
Bremner, Inc.
Ralcorp Frozen Bakery Products, Inc.
Carriage House Companies, Inc. (The)
Nutcracker Brands, Inc.
Vail Resorts, Inc.
Post Cereals
Honey Bunches of Oats

CONTACTS: *Note: Officers with more than one job title may be intentionally listed here more than once.*

Kevin J. Hunt, Co-CEO/Co-Pres.
David P. Skarie, Co-Pres./Co-CEO/Pres., Ralston Foods
Charles G. Huber, Jr., General Counsel/Sec./VP
Thomas G. Granneman, Controller/VP
Richard R. Koulouris, Pres., Carriage House Companies, Inc./VP
Richard G. Scalise, Pres., Frozen Bakery Prod./VP
Ronald D. Wilkinson, Pres., Ralston Foods/VP
William P. Stiritz, Chmn.

Phone: 314-877-7000	Fax: 314-877-7663
Toll-Free:	
Address: 800 Market St., Ste. 2600, St. Louis, MO 63101 US	

GROWTH PLANS/SPECIAL FEATURES:

Ralcorp Holdings, Inc. manufactures, distributes and markets store brand, or private-label, food products, as well as Post branded cereals. Its business consists of five operating segments: Cereals & Snacks; Crackers & Cookies; Frozen Bakery Products; Dressings, Syrups, Jellies & Sauces; and Snack Nuts & Candy. The cereals & snacks segment includes subsidiary Ralston Foods, a leading manufacturer of private label ready-to-eat and hot cereals, whose products include over 50 varieties that are designed to be comparable to national brands in taste, appearance and nutrition. Ralston also produces snack foods, such as corn-based chips and cereal-based snack mixes. This segment also encompasses the recently-acquired Post line of ready-to-eat cereals, including such brands as Honey Bunches of Oats brand, Pebbles, Post Selects, Spoon Size Shredded Wheat, Post Raisin Bran, Grape-Nuts and Honeycomb. The crackers & cookies segment includes subsidiary Bremner, a manufacturer of private label crackers and cookies, including products such as saltines, grahams, oatmeal cookies, chocolate chip cookies and sandwich crème cookies. The frozen bakery products segment includes the operations of subsidiary Ralcorp Frozen Bakery Products, serving foodservice, in-store bakery, retail and club customers with its products, which include waffles and pancakes, biscuits, rolls, muffins and breads. The dressings, syrups, jellies & sauces segment includes subsidiary Carriage House, which supplies products nationally to grocery retailers, wholesalers, mass merchandisers, drug chains and foodservice customers. The snack nuts & candy segment includes subsidiary Nutcracker, which manufactures products such as peanuts, cashews, mixed nuts, sunflower kernels, chocolate-covered nuts, baking nuts, trail mixes, peanut butter cups and other chocolates and candies. In addition to these operating segments, Ralcorp owns about 19% of Vail Resorts, Inc., a premier mountain resort operator. In August 2008, the firm completed its acquisition of the Post cereals business from Kraft Foods, Inc., in a transaction valued at approximately $2.6 billion.

FINANCIALS: Sales and profits are in thousands of dollars—add 000 to get the full amount. 2008 Note: Financial information for 2008 was not available for all companies at press time.

2008 Sales: $2,824,400	2008 Profits: $167,800	**U.S. Stock Ticker:** RAH
2007 Sales: $2,233,400	2007 Profits: $31,900	**Int'l Ticker:** Int'l Exchange:
2006 Sales: $1,850,200	2006 Profits: $68,300	Employees: 9,000
2005 Sales: $1,675,100	2005 Profits: $71,400	Fiscal Year Ends: 9/30
2004 Sales: $1,558,400	2004 Profits: $65,100	Parent Company:

SALARIES/BENEFITS:

Pension Plan:	ESOP Stock Plan:	Profit Sharing:	Top Exec. Salary: $500,000	Bonus: $550,000
Savings Plan: Y	Stock Purch. Plan:		Second Exec. Salary: $500,000	Bonus: $550,000

OTHER THOUGHTS:

Apparent Women Officers or Directors:
Hot Spot for Advancement for Women/Minorities:

LOCATIONS: ("Y" = Yes)

West:	Southwest:	Midwest:	Southeast:	Northeast:	International:
Y	Y	Y	Y	Y	Y

RAYTHEON CO

www.raytheon.com

Industry Group Code: 33641 **Ranks within this company's industry group:** Sales: 7 Profits: 6

Management:		Sales/Marketing:		Liberal Arts:		Information Systems:		Professionals:		Tech./Scientific:	
Management Trainees:	Y	Marketing Pros.:	Y	Gen. Writing/Editing:	Y	Info. Management:	Y	Finance/Acct.:	Y	Engineers, Electrical:	Y
Experienced Mngmt.:	Y	Retail Sales:		Technical Writing:	Y	Software Dev.:	Y	Law:	Y	Engineers, Other:	Y
International Business:	Y	Commercial/Industrial:	Y	Graphic Arts/Photog.:	Y	Hardware Dev.:	Y	HR/Other:	Y	Health/Lab:	
MBA Grads:	Y	Sales Trainees:		Music:		Consulting/Other:	Y	Training:	Y	Scientists/Research:	Y
		Advertising Pros.:	Y	Broadcasting:				Health Care:		Petroleum/Chemicals:	
				Other:				Consulting:		Math/Other:	Y

TYPES OF BUSINESS:

Aerospace & Defense Technology
Commercial Electronics
Technical Services
Communications & Information Systems
Sensors & Surveillance Equipment
Missile Systems
Space Exploration Devices
Software Engineering

BRANDS/DIVISIONS/AFFILIATES:

Patriot Air & Missile Defense System
Raytheon Systems Limited
Raytheon Australia
Raytheon Canada Limited

CONTACTS: *Note: Officers with more than one job title may be intentionally listed here more than once.*

William H. Swanson, CEO
David C. Wajsgras, CFO/Sr. VP
Keith J. Peden, Sr. VP-Human Resources
Rebecca R. Rhoads, CIO/VP
Mark E. Russell, VP-Tech. & Mission Assurance
Mark E. Russell, VP-Eng.
Jay B. Stephens, General Counsel/Sec./Sr. VP
Richard A. Goglia, VP-Corp. Dev./Treas.
Pamela A. Wickham, VP-Corp. Affairs & Comm.
Michael J. Wood, Chief Acct. Officer/VP
Jon C. Jones, VP/Pres., Space & Airborne Systems
Taylor W. Lawrence, VP/Pres., Missile Systems
Colin Schottlaender, VP/Pres., Network Centric Systems
Daniel L. Smith, VP/Pres., Integrated Defense Systems
William H. Swanson, Chmn.
Thomas M. Culligan, CEO-Raytheon Int'l, Inc./Exec. VP-Bus. Dev.
John D. Harris, II, VP-Contracts & Supply Chain

Phone: 781-522-3000	Fax: 781-522-3001
Toll-Free:	
Address: 870 Winter St., Waltham, MA 02451-1449 US	

GROWTH PLANS/SPECIAL FEATURES:

Raytheon Co. offers aerospace systems, defense and government electronics, IT equipment and technical services. Raytheon operates six segments: Integrated Defense Systems (IDS); Intelligence and Information Systems (IIS); Missile Systems (MS); Network Centric Systems (NCS); Space and Airborne Systems (SAS); and Technical Services (TS). IDS provides integrated space, air, surface, subsurface and homeland security products, including advanced radar and sonar systems; surveillance equipment; sensors; air and missile defense systems, including the Patriot Air & Missile Defense System; and technical services. IIS offers commercial and government customers weather and environmental management; geospatial intelligence; signal and image processing; and ground engineering support. MS produces various missiles, including one anti-satellite system, as well as smart projectiles, missile defense guns and even a microwave-based anti-missile system. NCS develops and produces mission solutions for networking and communications; command and control; battlefield awareness; and transportation management. SAS provides electro-optic/infrared sensors, airborne radars, high-energy lasers, precision guidance systems and space-qualified systems for civil and military applications. Lastly, TS provides technical, scientific and professional services, including training and outsourcing, for defense, federal and commercial customers worldwide. Raytheon's international subsidiaries include Raytheon Systems Limited, which works with IIS, SAS and NCS in the U.K.; Raytheon Australia, which works with IDS and TS in Australia, including managing operations and maintenance for the Canberra Deep Space Communication Complex; and Raytheon Canada Limited, which works with NCS offering air traffic control systems. Its customers include the Department of Homeland Security, all branches of the U.S. military, the National Guard, the F.A.A., the Japanese Defense Agency and the Royal Saudi Air Defense Forces. The U.S. government accounted for 87% of its 2008 sales.

Raytheon employees receive dental, prescription drug and vision care coverage; life and AD&D insurance; short- and long-term disability benefits; paid time off; adoption assistance; educational assistance; and investment services.

FINANCIALS: Sales and profits are in thousands of dollars—add 000 to get the full amount. 2008 Note: Financial information for 2008 was not available for all companies at press time.

2008 Sales: $23,174,000	2008 Profits: $1,672,000	**U.S. Stock Ticker: RTN**
2007 Sales: $21,301,000	2007 Profits: $2,578,000	**Int'l Ticker:** Int'l Exchange:
2006 Sales: $19,707,000	2006 Profits: $1,283,000	Employees: 73,000
2005 Sales: $18,491,000	2005 Profits: $871,000	Fiscal Year Ends: 12/31
2004 Sales: $17,825,000	2004 Profits: $417,000	Parent Company:

SALARIES/BENEFITS:

Pension Plan:	ESOP Stock Plan:	Profit Sharing:	Top Exec. Salary: $1,328,640	Bonus: $3,050,000
Savings Plan: Y	Stock Purch. Plan:		Second Exec. Salary: $789,944	Bonus: $870,000

OTHER THOUGHTS:

Apparent Women Officers or Directors: 4
Hot Spot for Advancement for Women/Minorities: Y

LOCATIONS: ("Y" = Yes)

West:	Southwest:	Midwest:	Southeast:	Northeast:	International:
Y	Y	Y	Y	Y	Y

Note: Financial information, benefits and other data can change quickly and may vary from those stated here.

REGIS CORPORATION

www.regiscorp.com

Industry Group Code: 81211 Ranks within this company's industry group: Sales: 1 Profits: 1

Management:		Sales/Marketing:		Liberal Arts:		Information Systems:		Professionals:		Tech./Scientific:	
Management Trainees:	Y	Marketing Pros.:	Y	Gen. Writing/Editing:	Y	Info. Management:	Y	Finance/Acct.:	Y	Engineers, Electrical:	
Experienced Mngmt.:	Y	Retail Sales:	Y	Technical Writing:		Software Dev.:	Y	Law:	Y	Engineers, Other:	
International Business:	Y	Commercial/Industrial:		Graphic Arts/Photog.:	Y	Hardware Dev.:		HR/Other:	Y	Health/Lab:	
MBA Grads:	Y	Sales Trainees:		Music:		Consulting/Other:		Training:	Y	Scientists/Research:	
		Advertising Pros.:	Y	Broadcasting:				Health Care:		Petroleum/Chemicals:	
				Other:				Consulting:		Math/Other:	

TYPES OF BUSINESS:

Hair Salons
Hair Care Products
Beauty Schools
Hair Restoration Services

BRANDS/DIVISIONS/AFFILIATES:

Regis Salons
MasterCuts
Trade Secret
SmartStyle
SuperCuts
Cameron Capital Investments Inc
Provalliance
Hair Club for Men & Women

CONTACTS: Note: Officers with more than one job title may be intentionally listed here more than once.

Paul D. Finkelstein, CEO
Kris Bergly, COO/Exec. VP
Paul D. Finkelstein, Pres.
Randy L. Pearce, CFO/Sr. Exec. VP
Gordon Nelson, Exec. VP-Mktg., Fashion & Education
Norma Knudsen, Exec. VP-Merch.
Randy L. Pearce, Chief Admin. Officer
Eric A. Bakken, General Counsel/Sr. VP
Bruce Johnson, Exec. VP-Real Estate & Construction
Mark Kartarik, Exec. VP/Pres., Franchise Div.
Andy Cohen, Pres., Regis Salon Div.
C. John Briggs, Sr. VP/Pres., SmartStyle Family Hair Salons
Paul D. Finkelstein, Chmn.
Jackie Lang, Sr. VP/Managing Dir.-Int'l

Phone: 952-947-7777	Fax: 952-947-7600
Toll-Free:	
Address: 7201 Metro Blvd., Edina, MN 55439 US	

GROWTH PLANS/SPECIAL FEATURES:

Regis Corporation is a global owner, operator, franchiser and consolidator of hair and retail product salons. The company owns, franchises or holds ownership interests in over 13,550 worldwide locations. The company's locations consist of 10,745 company-owned and franchise salons, 92 hair restoration centers and 2,714 locations in which the company maintains an ownership interest of less than 100%. The company is organized to manage its operations based on significant lines of business, salons and hair restoration centers. Salon operations are managed based on geographical location, North America and International. The company's North American salon operations comprise 8,110 company-owned salons and 2,163 franchise salons. The company's international operations comprise 472 company-owned salons. The company's worldwide salon locations operate primarily under the trade names of Regis Salons, MasterCuts, Trade Secret, SmartStyle, Supercuts, Cost Cutters and Sassoon. In recent years, the company contributed 51 of its wholly-owned accredited cosmetology schools to Empire Education Group, Inc (EEG) in exchange for a 49% equity interest in EEG. In early 2008, the company merged its continental European franchise salon operations with the operations of the Franck Provost Salon Group in exchange for a 30% equity interest in the newly formed Provalliance entity. The merger with the operations of the Franck Provost Salon Group, created Europe's largest salon operator with approximately 2,300 company-owned and franchise salons as of June 2008. In July 2008, the company announced plans to close up to 160 underperforming company-owned salons. In January 2009, the company sold its Trade Secret retail product division to Premier salons Beauty Inc.

FINANCIALS: Sales and profits are in thousands of dollars—add 000 to get the full amount. 2008 Note: Financial information for 2008 was not available for all companies at press time.

2008 Sales: $2,481,391	2008 Profits: $85,204	**U.S. Stock Ticker: RGS**
2007 Sales: $2,373,338	2007 Profits: $83,170	**Int'l Ticker:** Int'l Exchange:
2006 Sales: $2,430,864	2006 Profits: $109,578	Employees: 59,000
2005 Sales: $2,194,294	2005 Profits: $64,631	Fiscal Year Ends: 6/30
2004 Sales: $1,923,143	2004 Profits: $105,478	Parent Company:

SALARIES/BENEFITS:

Pension Plan:	ESOP Stock Plan:	Profit Sharing:	Top Exec. Salary: $1,141,215	Bonus: $825,000
Savings Plan: Y	Stock Purch. Plan: Y		Second Exec. Salary: $830,955	Bonus: $

OTHER THOUGHTS:

Apparent Women Officers or Directors: 5
Hot Spot for Advancement for Women/Minorities: Y

LOCATIONS: ("Y" = Yes)

West:	Southwest:	Midwest:	Southeast:	Northeast:	International:
Y	Y	Y	Y	Y	Y

RENT-A-CENTER INC

www.rentacenter.com

Industry Group Code: 5322   Ranks within this company's industry group: Sales: 1   Profits: 1

Management:		Sales/Marketing:		Liberal Arts:		Information Systems:		Professionals:		Tech./Scientific:	
Management Trainees:	Y	Marketing Pros.:	Y	Gen. Writing/Editing:	Y	Info. Management:	Y	Finance/Acct.:	Y	Engineers, Electrical:	
Experienced Mngmt.:	Y	Retail Sales:	Y	Technical Writing:		Software Dev.:	Y	Law:	Y	Engineers, Other:	
International Business:	Y	Commercial/Industrial:		Graphic Arts/Photog.:	Y	Hardware Dev.:		HR/Other:	Y	Health/Lab:	
MBA Grads:	Y	Sales Trainees:	Y	Music:		Consulting/Other:		Training:	Y	Scientists/Research:	
		Advertising Pros.:	Y	Broadcasting:				Health Care:		Petroleum/Chemicals:	
				Other:				Consulting:		Math/Other:	

TYPES OF BUSINESS:

Assorted Merchandise, Rental
Retail
Financing

BRANDS/DIVISIONS/AFFILIATES:

Get It Now
Rent-A-Centre
ColorTyme, Inc.
Cash AdvantEdge
Home Choice
RAC Financial Services

CONTACTS: *Note: Officers with more than one job title may be intentionally listed here more than once.*

Mark E. Speese, CEO
Mitchell E. Fadel, COO
Mitchell E. Fadel, Pres.
Robert D. Davis, CFO
Ann L. Davids, Chief Mktg. Officer/Sr. VP-Mktg.
Melvin D. McCall, Sr. VP-Human Resources
Tony F. Fuller, CIO/Sr. VP-IT
Robert W. Rapp, CTO/VP-IT
Dan Glasky, VP-Merch.
Ronald D. DeMoss, General Counsel/Corp. Sec./Exec. VP
Christopher A. Korst, Exec. VP-Oper.
Daniel R. Eichelberger, VP-Bus. Dev.
August E. Whitcomb, VP-Public Affairs
David E. Carpenter, VP-Investor Rel.
Robert D. Davis, Exec. VP-Finance/Treas.
Dwight D. Dumler, Sr. VP-Gov't Affairs
Ricardo Cordon, VP-Tax
David E. West, Exec. VP-Oper. Svcs.
Kent W. Brown, VP-Dev.
Mark E. Speese, Chmn.

Phone: 972-801-1100	Fax: 972-943-0113
Toll-Free: 800-275-2996	
Address: 5501 Headquarters Dr., Plano, TX 75024 US	

GROWTH PLANS/SPECIAL FEATURES:

Rent-A-Center, Inc. operates rent-to-own stores in the U.S., with approximately 3,021 stores in 50 states, Canada and Puerto Rico, including 13 Get It Now stores and 13 Rent-A-Centre and Better Living stores in Canada. The company also operates retail stores, including 35 Get It Now and Home Choice stores in Illinois, Minnesota and Wisconsin. ColorTyme, Inc., a subsidiary of the company, franchises rent-to-own stores, with approximately 218 stores in 33 states under the ColorTyme and Rent-A-Center brand names. The stores provide home electronics, appliances, computers, furniture and assorted accessories including brands such as Sony, Philips and Hitachi home electronics; Whirlpool appliances; Dell, Toshiba and Hewlett-Packard computers; and Ashley, England, Berkshire and Standard furniture. Rent-a-Center offers additional services such as free repair, pick-up and delivery. The company provides rental purchase agreements that allow the customer to obtain ownership of merchandise at the conclusion of a set rental period. Rent-A-Center also offers such financial services as short term and unsecured loans; debit cards; check cashing; and money transfer in 350 of its store locations in 18 states under the trade name Cash AdvantEdge and RAC Financial Services.

FINANCIALS: Sales and profits are in thousands of dollars—add 000 to get the full amount. 2008 Note: Financial information for 2008 was not available for all companies at press time.

2008 Sales: $2,884,172	2008 Profits: $139,624	**U.S. Stock Ticker: RCII**
2007 Sales: $2,906,121	2007 Profits: $76,268	**Int'l Ticker:** Int'l Exchange:
2006 Sales: $2,433,908	2006 Profits: $103,092	Employees: 17,900
2005 Sales: $2,339,107	2005 Profits: $135,738	Fiscal Year Ends: 12/31
2004 Sales: $2,313,255	2004 Profits: $155,855	Parent Company:

SALARIES/BENEFITS:

Pension Plan:	ESOP Stock Plan:	Profit Sharing:	Top Exec. Salary: $800,000	Bonus: $413,000
Savings Plan: Y	Stock Purch. Plan: Y		Second Exec. Salary: $543,000	Bonus: $142,130

OTHER THOUGHTS:

Apparent Women Officers or Directors: 4
Hot Spot for Advancement for Women/Minorities: Y

LOCATIONS: ("Y" = Yes)

West:	Southwest:	Midwest:	Southeast:	Northeast:	International:
Y	Y	Y	Y	Y	Y

Note: Financial information, benefits and other data can change quickly and may vary from those stated here.

RES CARE INC

www.rescare.com

Industry Group Code: 622210 **Ranks within this company's industry group:** Sales: 2   Profits: 2

Management:		Sales/Marketing:		Liberal Arts:		Information Systems:		Professionals:		Tech./Scientific:	
Management Trainees:	Y	Marketing Pros.:	Y	Gen. Writing/Editing:	Y	Info. Management:	Y	Finance/Acct.:	Y	Engineers, Electrical:	
Experienced Mngmt.:	Y	Retail Sales:		Technical Writing:	Y	Software Dev.:		Law:	Y	Engineers, Other:	
International Business:	Y	Commercial/Industrial:		Graphic Arts/Photog.:	Y	Hardware Dev.:		HR/Other:	Y	Health/Lab:	Y
MBA Grads:	Y	Sales Trainees:	Y	Music:		Consulting/Other:		Training:	Y	Scientists/Research:	
		Advertising Pros.:	Y	Broadcasting:				Health Care:	Y	Petroleum/Chemicals:	
				Other:	Y			Consulting:		Math/Other:	

TYPES OF BUSINESS:

Community Services
Job Corps Training Services
Employment Training Services

BRANDS/DIVISIONS/AFFILIATES:

PeopleServe
Select Health Care Services
Care Resources
Friendship Developmental Services
Caregivers Home Health, Inc.
Home Care of Washington

CONTACTS: Note: Officers with more than one job title may be intentionally listed here more than once.

Ralph G. Gronefeld, Jr., CEO
Ralph G. Gronefeld, Jr., Pres.
David W. Miles, CFO
Nina P. Seigle, Chief People Officer
George Watts, CIO
David S. Waskey, General Counsel/Chief Compliance Officer
Richard Tinsley, Chief Dev. Officer
Nel Taylor, Chief Comm. Officer
Derwin A. Wallace, Dir.-Investor Rel.
Patrick G. Kelley, Pres., Community Svcs. Group
Paul G. Dunn, Pres., Arbor E&T
Kelley Abell, Consultant-Gov. Rel.
Michael J. Reibel, Sr. VP-Support Svcs.
Ronald G. Geary, Chmn.

Phone: 502-394-2100	Fax: 502-394-2206

Toll-Free: 800-866-0860

Address: 9901 Linn Station Rd., Louisville, KY 40223-3808 US

GROWTH PLANS/SPECIAL FEATURES:

Res-Care, Inc. provides residential, therapeutic, job training and educational supports. The firm offers these services to adults and youths with intellectual, cognitive and other developmental disabilities; youths who have special educational or support needs, are from disadvantaged backgrounds or have severe emotional disorders; and adults who experience barriers to employment. The firm also offers personal care, meal preparation, housekeeping and transportation to the elderly in their own homes. In addition, Res-Care assists welfare recipients, young people, laid off individuals and those with special barriers to employment to transition into the workforce. The company operates in three segments: community services, job corps training services and employment training services. The community services segment offers programs in 34 states for individual with developmental disabilities designed to encourage greater independence and the development or maintenance of daily living skills. The job corps training services segment operates 17 job corps centers that provide for the educational and vocational skills training, healthcare, employment counseling and other support necessary to enable disadvantaged youths to become responsible working adults. The employment training services segment operates approximately 300 career centers which offer job training and placement programs that assist welfare recipients and disadvantaged job seekers in finding employment and improving their careers prospects. The company provides services in 38 states, Washington, D.C., Puerto Rico, Canada, the U.K., the Netherlands, Germany, Haiti, Bahrain and the United Arab Emirates. In November 2008, Res-Care changed the name of its U.K. operations to PeopleServe. From May 2008 to April 2009, the firm acquired the following companies: Select Health Care Services, a home health care agency in Texas; Caregivers Home Health, Inc., a home personal care provider for seniors; Care Resources, a staffing services firm; Friendship Developmental Services, which serves Californians with intellectual/developmental disabilities; and Home Care of Washington, a personal home services company.

FINANCIALS: Sales and profits are in thousands of dollars—add 000 to get the full amount. 2008 Note: Financial information for 2008 was not available for all companies at press time.

2008 Sales: $1,543,583	2008 Profits: $36,560	**U.S. Stock Ticker: RSCR**
2007 Sales: $1,433,298	2007 Profits: $43,891	**Int'l Ticker:** Int'l Exchange:
2006 Sales: $1,302,118	2006 Profits: $36,696	Employees: 46,400
2005 Sales: $1,046,556	2005 Profits: $21,222	Fiscal Year Ends: 12/31
2004 Sales: $966,185	2004 Profits: $21,507	Parent Company:

SALARIES/BENEFITS:

Pension Plan:	ESOP Stock Plan:	Profit Sharing:	Top Exec. Salary: $440,000	Bonus: $237,160
Savings Plan: Y	Stock Purch. Plan: Y		Second Exec. Salary: $325,000	Bonus: $37,050

OTHER THOUGHTS:

Apparent Women Officers or Directors: 4
Hot Spot for Advancement for Women/Minorities: Y

LOCATIONS: ("Y" = Yes)

West:	Southwest:	Midwest:	Southeast:	Northeast:	International:
Y	Y	Y	Y	Y	Y

Note: Financial information, benefits and other data can change quickly and may vary from those stated here.

RITE AID CORPORATION

www.riteaid.com

Industry Group Code: 446110 **Ranks within this company's industry group:** Sales: 3   Profits: 4

Management:		Sales/Marketing:		Liberal Arts:		Information Systems:		Professionals:		Tech./Scientific:	
Management Trainees:	Y	Marketing Pros.:	Y	Gen. Writing/Editing:	Y	Info. Management:	Y	Finance/Acct.:	Y	Engineers, Electrical:	
Experienced Mngmt.:	Y	Retail Sales:	Y	Technical Writing:		Software Dev.:	Y	Law:	Y	Engineers, Other:	
International Business:		Commercial/Industrial:		Graphic Arts/Photog.:	Y	Hardware Dev.:		HR/Other:	Y	Health/Lab:	
MBA Grads:	Y	Sales Trainees:	Y	Music:		Consulting/Other:		Training:	Y	Scientists/Research:	
		Advertising Pros.:	Y	Broadcasting:				Health Care:	Y	Petroleum/Chemicals:	
				Other:	Y			Consulting:		Math/Other:	

TYPES OF BUSINESS:

Drug Stores
Pharmacy Benefits Management

BRANDS/DIVISIONS/AFFILIATES:

Brooks Eckerd
Rite Aid Health Solutions
MultiCare Express Clinics
Saint Alphonsus Express Care
Rite Aid RX Savings Card
M5 Magnum
Rx Suncare

CONTACTS: *Note: Officers with more than one job title may be intentionally listed here more than once.*

Mary F. Sammons, CEO
John T. Standley, COO
John T. Standley, Pres.
Frank Vitrano, CFO/Sr. Exec. VP
Ken Martindale, Sr. Exec. VP-Mktg. & Logistics
Steve Parsons, Sr. VP-Human Resources
Don P. Davis, CIO/Sr. VP
Ken Martindale, Sr. Exec. VP-Merch.
Frank Vitrano, Chief Admin. Officer
Marc A. Strassler, General Counsel/Exec. VP
Scott Bernard, Sr. VP-Oper.
Christopher Hall, Sr. VP-Strategic Bus. Dev.
Karen Rugen, Sr. VP-Corp. Comm.
Doug Donley, Chief Acct. Officer/Sr. VP
Robert Thompson, Sr. VP-Pharmacy Oper.
Brian Fiala, Exec. VP-Store Oper.
Tony Bellezza, Chief Compliance Officer/Sr. VP
John Learish, Sr. VP-Mktg.
Mary F. Sammons, Chmn.
Wilson A. Lester, Jr., Sr. VP-Supply Chain

Phone: 717-761-2633	Fax: 717-975-5871
Toll-Free: 800-748-3243	
Address: 30 Hunter Ln., Camp Hill, PA 17011 US	

GROWTH PLANS/SPECIAL FEATURES:

Rite Aid Corp. operates nearly 5,000 drug stores in 31 states and Washington, D.C. Rite Aid stores sell prescription drugs, which account for about 67.2% of revenue in fiscal year 2008, and other merchandise such as non-prescription medications; health and beauty aids; personal care items; cosmetics; household items; beverages; convenience foods; greeting cards; and seasonal merchandise. Rite Aid offers roughly 28,000 products, approximately 3,300 of which are under the Rite Aid private brand. Approximately 57% of Rite Aid's stores are freestanding; 49% include a drive-through pharmacy; 42% include one-hour photo shops; and 35% include a GNC store-within-Rite Aid-store. The company's Rite Aid Health Solutions segment provides pharmacy benefit management services to employers, health plans and insurance companies.   In recent years, the company acquired 1,854 Brooks and Eckerd Stores and six distribution centers from The Jean Coutu Group, Inc. The Jean Coutu Group owns approximately 27.6% of Rite Aid common stock. In April 2008, the firm opened its third Saint Alphonsus Express Care in-store clinic in Idaho. In May 2008, the company partnered with MultiCare Health System to open two in-store MultiCare Express Clinics in Washington. In September 2008, Rite Aid introduced the Rite Aid RX Savings Card, a free membership which gives customers discounts on over 10,000 prescriptions and 1,500 over-the counter drugs. In February 2009, the firm agreed to sell five stores in Idaho and seven locations in San Francisco to Walgreens; and launched a privately branded line of Rx Suncare products.

The company offers its employees health, dental and vision coverage; life and AD&D insurance; a 401(k); bereavement leave; flexible spending accounts; a stock purchase plan; and an employee assistance program.

FINANCIALS: Sales and profits are in thousands of dollars—add 000 to get the full amount. 2008 Note: Financial information for 2008 was not available for all companies at press time.

2008 Sales: $24,326,846	2008 Profits: $-1,078,990	**U.S. Stock Ticker:** RAD
2007 Sales: $17,399,383	2007 Profits: $26,826	**Int'l Ticker:** Int'l Exchange:
2006 Sales: $17,163,044	2006 Profits: $1,273,006	Employees: 103,000
2005 Sales: $16,715,598	2005 Profits: $302,478	Fiscal Year Ends: 2/28
2004 Sales: $16,600,449	2004 Profits: $83,311	Parent Company:

SALARIES/BENEFITS:

Pension Plan:	ESOP Stock Plan:	Profit Sharing:	Top Exec. Salary: $1,000,000	Bonus: $
Savings Plan: Y	Stock Purch. Plan: Y		Second Exec. Salary: $504,807	Bonus: $107,119

OTHER THOUGHTS:

Apparent Women Officers or Directors: 5
Hot Spot for Advancement for Women/Minorities: Y

LOCATIONS: ("Y" = Yes)

West:	Southwest:	Midwest:	Southeast:	Northeast:	International:
Y	Y	Y	Y	Y	

Note: Financial information, benefits and other data can change quickly and may vary from those stated here.

RITZ-CARLTON HOTEL COMPANY LLC (THE)   www.ritzcarlton.com

Industry Group Code: 721110 Ranks within this company's industry group: Sales: Profits:

Management:		Sales/Marketing:		Liberal Arts:		Information Systems:		Professionals:		Tech./Scientific:	
Management Trainees:	Y	Marketing Pros.:	Y	Gen. Writing/Editing:	Y	Info. Management:	Y	Finance/Acct.:	Y	Engineers, Electrical:	
Experienced Mngmt.:	Y	Retail Sales:		Technical Writing:		Software Dev.:	Y	Law:	Y	Engineers, Other:	
International Business:	Y	Commercial/Industrial:	Y	Graphic Arts/Photog.:	Y	Hardware Dev.:		HR/Other:	Y	Health/Lab:	
MBA Grads:	Y	Sales Trainees:	Y	Music:		Consulting/Other:		Training:	Y	Scientists/Research:	
		Advertising Pros.:	Y	Broadcasting:				Health Care:		Petroleum/Chemicals:	
				Other:	Y			Consulting:		Math/Other:	

TYPES OF BUSINESS:
Hotels, Luxury
Condominiums
Golf Courses
Spas
Time Share Units

BRANDS/DIVISIONS/AFFILIATES:
Marriott International Inc
Ritz-Carlton Club
Taj Boston
Six Senses
La Prairie
2SPA

CONTACTS: Note: Officers with more than one job title may be intentionally listed here more than once.
Simon F. Cooper, COO
Simon F. Cooper, Pres.
Jim Connelly, CFO
Herve Humler, Pres., Int'l

Phone: 301-547-4700	Fax: 301-547-4723
Toll-Free:	
Address: 4445 Willard Ave., Ste. 800, Chevy Chase, MD 20815 US	

GROWTH PLANS/SPECIAL FEATURES:
The Ritz-Carlton Hotel Co., LLC, a subsidiary of Marriott International, Inc., is one of the world's best-known luxury hotel chains, operating 72 hotels in 24 countries. The firm also maintains 12 international sales offices in various locations including Chicago, New York, Los Angeles, Dubai, Shanghai, Tokyo and London. In an attempt to cater to an upscale clientele base, full-service luxury spas are offered at most of the company's resorts, and plans have been made for additional spas at new or existing hotel locations. Some spas at Ritz-Carlton hotels operate under the brand names Six Senses, La Prairie and 2SPA. Ritz-Carlton also markets its 15 luxury golf courses (many designed by leading names in the golf world such as Greg Norman and Jack Nicklaus) and fitness facilities to both local residents and visitors. The Ritz-Carlton Club is the firm's time share ownership unit, offering a flexible alternative to a second home. This concept features luxury condominiums located at Ritz-Carlton's hotels and resorts worldwide, with features such as marble foyers, walk-in closets, daily housekeeping services, 24-hour room service and access to fitness facilities and spa services. Membership is currently available in locations such as Aspen, St. Thomas, Bachelor Gulch and Jupiter, Florida. The firm plans to expand hotel operations to such locations as Toronto, Canada and Rose Island, Bahamas.

The company offers employees benefits that include medical, dental and vision coverage; domestic partner benefits; leave of absence and bereavement leave; a 401(k) plan; a credit union; an employee stock purchase plan; an employee assistance program; educational assistance program; career development programs; uniforms; and employee discounts on hotel rooms, food and retail items.

FINANCIALS: Sales and profits are in thousands of dollars—add 000 to get the full amount. 2008 Note: Financial information for 2008 was not available for all companies at press time.

2008 Sales: $	2008 Profits: $	**U.S. Stock Ticker: Subsidiary**
2007 Sales: $1,576,000	2007 Profits: $72,000	**Int'l Ticker:** Int'l Exchange:
2006 Sales: $1,423,000	2006 Profits: $	Employees: 38,000
2005 Sales: $	2005 Profits: $	Fiscal Year Ends: 12/31
2004 Sales: $	2004 Profits: $	Parent Company: MARRIOTT INTERNATIONAL INC

SALARIES/BENEFITS:

Pension Plan:	ESOP Stock Plan:	Profit Sharing:	Top Exec. Salary: $	Bonus: $
Savings Plan: Y	Stock Purch. Plan: Y		Second Exec. Salary: $	Bonus: $

OTHER THOUGHTS:
Apparent Women Officers or Directors:
Hot Spot for Advancement for Women/Minorities:

LOCATIONS: ("Y" = Yes)

West:	Southwest:	Midwest:	Southeast:	Northeast:	International:
Y	Y	Y	Y	Y	Y

Note: Financial information, benefits and other data can change quickly and may vary from those stated here.

ROBERT HALF INTERNATIONAL INC

www.rhi.com

Industry Group Code: 561320 Ranks within this company's industry group: Sales: 3   Profits: 1

Management:		Sales/Marketing:		Liberal Arts:		Information Systems:		Professionals:		Tech./Scientific:	
Management Trainees:	Y	Marketing Pros.:	Y	Gen. Writing/Editing:	Y	Info. Management:	Y	Finance/Acct.:	Y	Engineers, Electrical:	
Experienced Mngmt.:	Y	Retail Sales:		Technical Writing:	Y	Software Dev.:	Y	Law:	Y	Engineers, Other:	
International Business:	Y	Commercial/Industrial:	Y	Graphic Arts/Photog.:	Y	Hardware Dev.:		HR/Other:	Y	Health/Lab:	
MBA Grads:	Y	Sales Trainees:	Y	Music:		Consulting/Other:		Training:	Y	Scientists/Research:	
		Advertising Pros.:	Y	Broadcasting:				Health Care:		Petroleum/Chemicals:	
				Other:	Y			Consulting:		Math/Other:	

TYPES OF BUSINESS:

Staffing
Risk Consulting
Internal Audit Services
Litigation Consulting & Forensic Accounting

BRANDS/DIVISIONS/AFFILIATES:

Accountemps
Robert Half Finance & Accounting
Robert Half Management Resources
Robert Half Technology
OfficeTeam
Robert Half Legal
Creative Group (The)
Protiviti Inc

CONTACTS: Note: Officers with more than one job title may be intentionally listed here more than once.

Harold M. Messmer, Jr., CEO
M. Keith Waddell, Pres./Vice Chmn.
M. Keith Waddell, CFO
Elena West, Sr. VP-Mktg.
Michael Buckley, Chief Admin. Officer/Treas./Exec. VP
Steven Karel, General Counsel/Sr. VP/Corp. Sec.
Robert W. Glass, Exec. VP-Corp. Dev.
Reesa M. Staten, VP-Corp. Comm.
Paula Streit, Sr. VP-Operational Finance & Acct.
Paul F. Gentzkow, COO/Pres., Staffing Svcs.
Evelyn Crane-Oliver, VP/Associate General Counsel
Harold M. Messmer, Jr., Chmn.

Phone: 650-234-6000	Fax: 650-234-6999
Toll-Free:	
Address: 2884 Sand Hill Rd., Menlo Park, CA 94025 US	

GROWTH PLANS/SPECIAL FEATURES:

Robert Half International, Inc. (RHI) is a global staffing firm that provides professional staffing and risk consulting services. RHI operates through more than 400 company operated or owned locations in 20 countries around the world, including Europe, Asia, Australia and New Zealand. The company provides temporary, project and full-time workers to firms in areas such as accounting, finance, administrative and legal support, information technology, advertising and marketing. RHI consists of eight staffing divisions: Accountemps for the staffing of accounting and finance professionals; Robert Half Finance and Accounting and Robert Half Management Resources for senior-level accounting and financing professionals; OfficeTeam, a division for highly skilled temporary administrative support; Robert Half Technology for information technology professionals; Robert Half Legal, a staffing sector for attorneys, paralegals and legal support personnel; and the Creative Group for advertising, marketing and web design professionals. Robert Half has increased its focus on providing workers for small to mid-size businesses, and it has a growing number of highly-experienced, older workers on its list. The company's wholly-owned subsidiary, Protiviti, Inc., provides internal audit and risk consulting services by aiding clients in identifying, measuring and managing operational and technology-related risks in areas such as the media, hospitality, communications, energy, financial services, real estate, healthcare, government, education, non-profit, manufacturing, distribution and technology industries. Business risk consultations involve areas such as anti-money laundering, capital projects and construction, energy commodity risks, fraud investigation and forensic accounting. Technology risk consultations provide solutions for security and privacy, continuity, change management, IT assets and application effectiveness. Protiviti's consulting practice includes assistance to firms facing bankruptcy or restructuring.

Employees are offered medical, dental, vision and life insurance; a savings plan; short-and long-term disability coverage; an employee assistance program; and travel accident insurance.

FINANCIALS: Sales and profits are in thousands of dollars—add 000 to get the full amount. 2008 Note: Financial information for 2008 was not available for all companies at press time.

2008 Sales: $4,600,554	2008 Profits: $250,181	U.S. Stock Ticker: RHI
2007 Sales: $4,645,666	2007 Profits: $296,212	Int'l Ticker: Int'l Exchange:
2006 Sales: $4,013,546	2006 Profits: $283,178	Employees: 13,300
2005 Sales: $3,338,439	2005 Profits: $237,870	Fiscal Year Ends: 12/31
2004 Sales: $2,675,696	2004 Profits: $140,604	Parent Company:

SALARIES/BENEFITS:

Pension Plan:	ESOP Stock Plan:	Profit Sharing:	Top Exec. Salary: $525,000	Bonus: $5,708,900
Savings Plan: Y	Stock Purch. Plan:		Second Exec. Salary: $265,000	Bonus: $2,857,979

OTHER THOUGHTS:

Apparent Women Officers or Directors: 4
Hot Spot for Advancement for Women/Minorities: Y

LOCATIONS: ("Y" = Yes)

West:	Southwest:	Midwest:	Southeast:	Northeast:	International:
Y	Y	Y	Y	Y	Y

Note: Financial information, benefits and other data can change quickly and may vary from those stated here.

ROSS STORES INC

www.rossstores.com

Industry Group Code: 448 Ranks within this company's industry group: Sales: 2 Profits: 2

Management:		Sales/Marketing:		Liberal Arts:		Information Systems:		Professionals:		Tech./Scientific:	
Management Trainees:	Y	Marketing Pros.:	Y	Gen. Writing/Editing:	Y	Info. Management:	Y	Finance/Acct.:	Y	Engineers, Electrical:	
Experienced Mngmt.:	Y	Retail Sales:	Y	Technical Writing:		Software Dev.:	Y	Law:	Y	Engineers, Other:	
International Business:	Y	Commercial/Industrial:		Graphic Arts/Photog.:	Y	Hardware Dev.:		HR/Other:	Y	Health/Lab:	
MBA Grads:	Y	Sales Trainees:	Y	Music:		Consulting/Other:		Training:	Y	Scientists/Research:	
		Advertising Pros.:	Y	Broadcasting:				Health Care:		Petroleum/Chemicals:	
				Other:	Y			Consulting:		Math/Other:	

TYPES OF BUSINESS:

Discount Apparel Stores
Home Furnishings

BRANDS/DIVISIONS/AFFILIATES:

dd's DISCOUNTS
Ross Dress for Less

CONTACTS: *Note: Officers with more than one job title may be intentionally listed here more than once.*

Michael A. Balmuth, CEO
Gary Cribb, COO/Exec. VP
Michael Balmuth, Pres.
John G. Call, CFO/Sr. VP
D. Jane Marvin, Sr. VP-Human Resources
Michael K. Kobayashi, CIO/Sr. VP
Lisa Panattoni, Exec. VP-Merch.
Michael B. O'Sullivan, Chief Admin. Officer/Exec. VP
Mark LeHocky, General Counsel/Sr. VP
Ken Caruana, Sr. VP-Strategy, Mktg.-Store Planning & Allocation
Douglas Baker, Sr. VP/Gen. Merch. Mgr.-dd's DISCOUNTS
Art Roth, Sr. VP-Merch. Control
Barbara Rentler, Exec. VP-Merch.
Mary Walter, Sr. VP-Stores
Norman A. Ferber, Chmn.
Michael K. Kobayashi, Sr. VP-Supply Chain

Phone: 925-965-4400	Fax: 925-965-4388
Toll-Free:	
Address: 4440 Rosewood Dr., Pleasanton, CA 94588-3050 US	

GROWTH PLANS/SPECIAL FEATURES:

Ross Stores, Inc. operates 904 off-price retail apparel and home accessories stores in 27 states and Guam, under the Ross Dress for Less brand. The company also operates 52 dd's DISCOUNTS locations in California, Florida, Texas and Arizona. Most of the stores are located in predominantly community and neighborhood strip shopping centers in heavily populated urban and suburban areas. The company's chains target value-conscious women and men age 18-54. Ross offers new, in-season, name-brand and designer apparel, accessories, footwear and home merchandise at savings of 20-60% off department and specialty store regular prices, while dd's DISCOUNTS, targeting lower-income customers, offers similar merchandise, but at savings of up to 70% off department and specialty store prices. The company's stores are supplied by four distribution processing facilities. Ross has combined a network of approximately 7,200 vendors and manufacturers, purchasing the vast majority of its merchandise directly from the manufacturer. By purchasing later in the merchandise buying cycle than department and specialty stores, Ross takes advantage of imbalances between retailers' demand for products and manufacturers' supply of those products. In addition, the company typically does not require that manufacturers provide promotional and markdown allowances, return privileges, split shipments, drop shipments to stores or delayed deliveries of merchandise, further enabling the company to provide significant discounts on in-season merchandise. In 2008, women's accounted for 32% of sales, followed by home accents/bed and bath and men's as the next largest categories, accounting for 23% and 14%, respectively.

Ross offers its employees a merchandise discount, accidental death and dismemberment insurance; long term disability; sick pay; health care spending account; a commuter reimbursement account; and a dependent day care spending account.

FINANCIALS: Sales and profits are in thousands of dollars—add 000 to get the full amount. 2008 Note: Financial information for 2008 was not available for all companies at press time.

2008 Sales: $5,975,212	2008 Profits: $261,051	**U.S. Stock Ticker: ROST**
2007 Sales: $5,570,210	2007 Profits: $241,634	**Int'l Ticker:** Int'l Exchange:
2006 Sales: $4,944,179	2006 Profits: $199,632	Employees: 40,000
2005 Sales: $4,239,990	2005 Profits: $169,902	Fiscal Year Ends: 1/31
2004 Sales: $3,920,583	2004 Profits: $228,102	Parent Company:

SALARIES/BENEFITS:

Pension Plan:	ESOP Stock Plan:	Profit Sharing:	Top Exec. Salary: $1,031,239	Bonus: $1,721,369
Savings Plan: Y	Stock Purch. Plan: Y		Second Exec. Salary: $1,017,614	Bonus: $906,416

OTHER THOUGHTS:

Apparent Women Officers or Directors: 7
Hot Spot for Advancement for Women/Minorities: Y

LOCATIONS: ("Y" = Yes)

West:	Southwest:	Midwest:	Southeast:	Northeast:	International:
Y	Y		Y	Y	Y

Note: Financial information, benefits and other data can change quickly and may vary from those stated here.

ROYAL CARIBBEAN CRUISES LTD

www.royalcaribbean.com

Industry Group Code: 483112 Ranks within this company's industry group: Sales: 2 Profits: 2

Management:		Sales/Marketing:		Liberal Arts:		Information Systems:		Professionals:		Tech./Scientific:	
Management Trainees:	Y	Marketing Pros.:	Y	Gen. Writing/Editing:	Y	Info. Management:	Y	Finance/Acct.:	Y	Engineers, Electrical:	
Experienced Mngmt.:	Y	Retail Sales:		Technical Writing:	Y	Software Dev.:	Y	Law:	Y	Engineers, Other:	Y
International Business:	Y	Commercial/Industrial:	Y	Graphic Arts/Photog.:	Y	Hardware Dev.:		HR/Other:	Y	Health/Lab:	
MBA Grads:	Y	Sales Trainees:	Y	Music:	Y	Consulting/Other:		Training:	Y	Scientists/Research:	
		Advertising Pros.:	Y	Broadcasting:				Health Care:		Petroleum/Chemicals:	
				Other:	Y			Consulting:		Math/Other:	

TYPES OF BUSINESS:

Cruise Line
Rail Tours
Online Travel Services
Academic Tours

BRANDS/DIVISIONS/AFFILIATES:

Royal Caribbean International
Celebrity Cruises
Pullmantur
Azamara Cruises
CDF Croisieres de France
TUI Cruises
Royal Celebrity Tours
Oasis of the Seas

CONTACTS: *Note: Officers with more than one job title may be intentionally listed here more than once.*

Richard D. Fain, CEO
Brian J. Rice, CFO/Exec. VP
Harri U. Kulovaara, Exec. VP-Maritime, Fleet Design
Harri U. Kulovaara, Exec. VP-Maritime, Newbuilt Oper.
Lyan Sierra-Caro, Account Exec.-Corp. Comm.
Craig Milan, Pres., Royal Celebrity Tours
Daniel J. Hanrahan, Pres., Celebrity Cruises & Azamara Cruises
Gonzalo Chico Barbier, Pres., Pullmantur SA
Lisa Bauer, Sr. VP-Hotel Oper.
Richard D. Fain, Chmn.
Adam M. Goldstein, CEO/Pres., Royal Caribbean Int'l

Phone: 305-539-6000	Fax: 305-374-7354
Toll-Free:	
Address: 1050 Caribbean Way, Miami, FL 33132-2096 US	

GROWTH PLANS/SPECIAL FEATURES:

Royal Caribbean Cruises, Ltd. is a global cruise vacation firm serving the contemporary, premium and deluxe cruise markets, including the budget and luxury segments. With 38 ships offering around 78,650 berths, the firm operates five brand names: Royal Caribbean International, Celebrity Cruises, Pullmantur, Azamara Cruises and CDF Croisieres de France. It also has a 50% joint venture investment in TUI Cruises with TUI AG. Royal Caribbean's ships have itineraries that call on approximately 425 destinations worldwide, including Alaska, Australia/New Zealand, the Bahamas, Canada/New England, the Caribbean, Europe, Asia, Hawaii, Mexico, the U.S. Pacific Northwest, the Panama Canal and South America. These ships offer a wide range of activities, services and amenities, including swimming pools, sun decks, salons, gyms, spas, ice skating rinks, rock climbing walls, casinos, lounges, bars, on-board entertainment, retail shopping and movie theaters. Pullmantur, which has substantial operations in Mexico, was negatively impacted by the H1N1 or swine flu out break early in 2009, including being forced to postpone the launch of its new ship, Pacific Dream. The Celebrity Cruises brand targets the higher-end segment of the industry with superior service and facilities and cruises to unusual destinations such as the Arctic, Antarctic and the Galapagos. Azamara Cruises consists of two smaller ships, of about 700 passengers each, that focus on cruises to unique destinations, with an emphasis on on-board lectures and fine dining. Subsidiary Royal Celebrity Tours operates land-tour vacations in several locations, including Alaska, using the world's largest glass-domed train cars; Canada, alongside Rocky Mountaineer Railtours; and Europe. Royal Caribbean will launch a new ship, Oasis of the Seas, one of the world's largest cruise ships, in December 2009. Her sister ship, Allure of the Seas, will follow in 2010.

The firm offers special rates for employees, their families and relatives. For sea-based employees, Royal Caribbean operates on a 14-weeks-on, 14-weeks-off plan.

FINANCIALS: Sales and profits are in thousands of dollars—add 000 to get the full amount. 2008 Note: Financial information for 2008 was not available for all companies at press time.

2008 Sales: $6,532,525	2008 Profits: $573,722	**U.S. Stock Ticker: RCL**
2007 Sales: $6,149,139	2007 Profits: $603,405	**Int'l Ticker:** Int'l Exchange:
2006 Sales: $5,229,584	2006 Profits: $633,922	Employees: 5,050
2005 Sales: $4,903,174	2005 Profits: $715,956	Fiscal Year Ends: 12/31
2004 Sales: $4,555,375	2004 Profits: $474,691	Parent Company:

SALARIES/BENEFITS:

Pension Plan: Y	ESOP Stock Plan:	Profit Sharing:	Top Exec. Salary: $1,000,000	Bonus: $1,440,688
Savings Plan:	Stock Purch. Plan: Y		Second Exec. Salary: $696,346	Bonus: $1,176,322

OTHER THOUGHTS:

Apparent Women Officers or Directors: 4
Hot Spot for Advancement for Women/Minorities: Y

LOCATIONS: ("Y" = Yes)

West:	Southwest:	Midwest:	Southeast:	Northeast:	International:
Y		Y	Y		Y

RRI ENERGY INC

www.rrienergy.com

Industry Group Code: 221 Ranks within this company's industry group: Sales: 7 Profits: 9

Management:		Sales/Marketing:		Liberal Arts:		Information Systems:		Professionals:		Tech./Scientific:	
Management Trainees:	Y	Marketing Pros.:	Y	Gen. Writing/Editing:	Y	Info. Management:	Y	Finance/Acct.:	Y	Engineers, Electrical:	Y
Experienced Mngmt.:	Y	Retail Sales:		Technical Writing:	Y	Software Dev.:	Y	Law:	Y	Engineers, Other:	Y
International Business:		Commercial/Industrial:	Y	Graphic Arts/Photog.:	Y	Hardware Dev.:		HR/Other:	Y	Health/Lab:	
MBA Grads:	Y	Sales Trainees:		Music:		Consulting/Other:		Training:	Y	Scientists/Research:	
		Advertising Pros.:	Y	Broadcasting:				Health Care:		Petroleum/Chemicals:	
				Other:				Consulting:		Math/Other:	

TYPES OF BUSINESS:

Utilities-Electricity
Power Generation
Wholesale Energy Trading & Marketing

BRANDS/DIVISIONS/AFFILIATES:

Reliant Energy Solutions East
Reliant Energy Solutions Northeast

CONTACTS: Note: Officers with more than one job title may be intentionally listed here more than once.

Mark M. Jacobs, CEO
Mark M. Jacobs, Pres.
Rick J. Dobson, CFO/Exec. VP
Karen D. Taylor, Sr. VP-Human Resources/Chief Diversity Officer
Michael L. Jines, Exec. VP/General Counsel/Sec.
David Brast, Sr. VP-Commercial Oper. & Organization
Rogers Herndon, Exec. VP-Strategic Planning & Bus. Dev.
Albert Myres, Sr. VP-Gov't & Public Affairs
Thomas C. Livengood, Controller/Sr. VP
Dave Freysinger, Sr. VP-Generation Oper.
Steven L. Miller, Chmn.

Phone: 713-497-3000	Fax:
Toll-Free:	
Address: 1000 Main St., Houston, TX 77002 US	

GROWTH PLANS/SPECIAL FEATURES:

RRI Energy, Inc., formerly Reliant Energy, Inc., provides electricity and energy services to wholesale customers. The company is one of the largest independent power producers in the U.S., with a power generation capacity of over 14,000 megawatts (MW). The firm operates primarily through a single segment, wholesale energy, which, as of December 2008, owned, had an interest in or leased 36 operating electric power generation facilities. These are located in Pennsylvania, New Jersey, Illinois, Ohio, Mississippi, Florida and California, and run on coal, gas and oil power, including one facility that utilizes circulating fluidized bed (CFB) coal technology. Approximately 48% of the company's plants use gas fuel; 32% use coal; 2% use oil; and 18% use a combination of gas and oil. RRI's commercial operations division sells electricity, generation capacity and ancillary service products to independent power producers; power grids and ISOs (independent system operators; investor-owned utilities; municipalities; cooperatives; banks and trading companies; and other companies that serve end users. In February 2008, the firm agreed to sell its Channelview Cogeneration Plant. In April 2008, the company entered the New York electricity market. In October 2008, RRI completed the sale of its Bighorn Generating Station for approximately $500 million. In December 2008, the company completed the sale of the Northeastern electricity marketing assets of its retail subsidiaries, Reliant Energy Solutions East and Reliant Energy Solutions Northeast, to Hess Corporation. In March 2009, the firm agreed to sell its Texas retail electricity business to NRG Energy, which provides power to about 1.8 million Texas customers. In May 2009, in conjunction with the completion of this sale, the company changed its name to RRI Energy, Inc.

RRI offers its employees medical, dental and vision programs; discount fitness programs; a 401(k) plan; and a profit-sharing plan.

FINANCIALS: Sales and profits are in thousands of dollars—add 000 to get the full amount. 2008 Note: Financial information for 2008 was not available for all companies at press time.

2008 Sales: $12,600,000	2008 Profits: $-739,700	**U.S. Stock Ticker: RRI**
2007 Sales: $11,209,000	2007 Profits: $365,000	**Int'l Ticker:** Int'l Exchange:
2006 Sales: $10,877,000	2006 Profits: $-328,000	Employees: 3,800
2005 Sales: $9,711,995	2005 Profits: $-330,556	Fiscal Year Ends: 12/31
2004 Sales: $8,098,222	2004 Profits: $-29,370	Parent Company:

SALARIES/BENEFITS:

Pension Plan:	ESOP Stock Plan:	Profit Sharing: Y	Top Exec. Salary: $895,000	Bonus: $ 600
Savings Plan: Y	Stock Purch. Plan:		Second Exec. Salary: $655,000	Bonus: $ 600

OTHER THOUGHTS:

Apparent Women Officers or Directors: 2
Hot Spot for Advancement for Women/Minorities: Y

LOCATIONS: ("Y" = Yes)

West:	Southwest:	Midwest:	Southeast:	Northeast:	International:
Y		Y	Y	Y	

SABRE HOLDINGS CORP

www.sabre-holdings.com

Industry Group Code: 5615E **Ranks within this company's industry group:** Sales: 1   Profits:

Management:		Sales/Marketing:		Liberal Arts:		Information Systems:		Professionals:		Tech./Scientific:	
Management Trainees:	Y	Marketing Pros.:	Y	Gen. Writing/Editing:	Y	Info. Management:	Y	Finance/Acct.:	Y	Engineers, Electrical:	Y
Experienced Mngmt.:	Y	Retail Sales:		Technical Writing:	Y	Software Dev.:	Y	Law:	Y	Engineers, Other:	
International Business:	Y	Commercial/Industrial:	Y	Graphic Arts/Photog.:	Y	Hardware Dev.:		HR/Other:	Y	Health/Lab:	
MBA Grads:	Y	Sales Trainees:		Music:		Consulting/Other:		Training:	Y	Scientists/Research:	
		Advertising Pros.:		Broadcasting:				Health Care:		Petroleum/Chemicals:	
				Other:	Y			Consulting:		Math/Other:	

TYPES OF BUSINESS:

Online Travel Reservations
Travel Marketing Solutions
Distribution & Technology Solutions
Consulting Services

BRANDS/DIVISIONS/AFFILIATES:

Silver Lake Partners
Texas Pacific Group
Sabre Travel Network
Travelocity.com LP
LastMinute.com
Sabre Airline Solutions
GetThere.com
E-site Marketing

CONTACTS: *Note: Officers with more than one job title may be intentionally listed here more than once.*

Sam Gilliland, CEO
Jeffery Jackson, CFO/Exec. VP
Paul Rostron, Exec. VP-Human Resources
Sterling Miller, General Counsel/Corp. Sec.
Thomas Klein, Exec. VP/Pres., Sabre Travel Network
Thomas Klein, Pres., Sabre Airline Solutions
Michelle Peluso, Exec. VP/Pres./CEO-Travelocity
Sam Gilliland, Chmn.

Phone: 682-605-1000	Fax:
Toll-Free:	
Address: 3150 Sabre Dr., Southlake, TX 76092 US	

GROWTH PLANS/SPECIAL FEATURES:

Sabre Holdings Corp., an entity owned by private equity giants Silver Lake Partners and Texas Pacific Group, is a provider of travel commerce. It offers a broad portfolio of travel marketing, distribution and technology solutions. The company operates in three segments: Travelocity, Sabre Travel Network and Sabre Airline Solutions. The Travelocity segment markets and distributes travel-related products and services directly to individuals, including leisure travelers and business travelers, through the Travelocity.com, LastMinute.com and Zuji.com web sites and contact centers. Travelers can access offerings, pricing and information about airlines, hotels, car rental companies, cruise lines, vacation and last-minute travel packages and other travel-related services. It also provides content and functionality to, and markets and sells products and services through private-label web sites for, suppliers, distribution partners and travel agencies. The Travelocity Business online corporate travel agency provides business travelers the offerings of the GetThere products. The Sabre Travel Network segment markets and distributes travel-related products and services for the travel supplier participants through the online and offline travel agency and corporate channels. Users of the Sabre system can access information about, book reservations for and purchase a variety of travel offerings, including airline trips, hotel stays, car rentals, cruises and tour packages. The division provides travel agencies with office automation tools and enables them to provide services via the Internet. In addition, Sabre Travel provides marketing information to suppliers and reservation management and technology services to hotel properties. The Sabre Airline Solutions segment provides passenger management solutions; software products and related services; and consulting services, which range from one time to extended engagements. It offers airline reservations, inventory and check-in hosting solutions. In December 2008, the firm acquired, the London based, EB2 International Limited. In September 2008, Sabre acquired Flight Explorer, a provider of commercial aircraft situation display solutions.

FINANCIALS: Sales and profits are in thousands of dollars—add 000 to get the full amount. 2008 Note: Financial information for 2008 was not available for all companies at press time.

2008 Sales: $3,000,000	2008 Profits: $	**U.S. Stock Ticker:** Private
2007 Sales: $3,000,000	2007 Profits: $	**Int'l Ticker:** Int'l Exchange:
2006 Sales: $2,823,797	2006 Profits: $155,638	Employees: 9,000
2005 Sales: $2,521,255	2005 Profits: $172,152	Fiscal Year Ends: 12/31
2004 Sales: $2,130,971	2004 Profits: $190,419	Parent Company: SILVER LAKE PARTNERS

SALARIES/BENEFITS:

Pension Plan:	ESOP Stock Plan:	Profit Sharing:	Top Exec. Salary: $	Bonus: $
Savings Plan: Y	Stock Purch. Plan:		Second Exec. Salary: $	Bonus: $

OTHER THOUGHTS:

Apparent Women Officers or Directors: 1
Hot Spot for Advancement for Women/Minorities: Y

LOCATIONS: ("Y" = Yes)

West:	Southwest:	Midwest:	Southeast:	Northeast:	International:
	Y				Y

SAFECO INSURANCE COMPANY OF AMERICA
www.safeco.com

Industry Group Code: 524126 Ranks within this company's industry group: Sales: Profits:

Management:		Sales/Marketing:		Liberal Arts:		Information Systems:		Professionals:		Tech./Scientific:	
Management Trainees:	Y	Marketing Pros.:	Y	Gen. Writing/Editing:	Y	Info. Management:	Y	Finance/Acct.:	Y	Engineers, Electrical:	
Experienced Mngmt.:	Y	Retail Sales:		Technical Writing:	Y	Software Dev.:	Y	Law:	Y	Engineers, Other:	
International Business:	Y	Commercial/Industrial:	Y	Graphic Arts/Photog.:	Y	Hardware Dev.:		HR/Other:	Y	Health/Lab:	
MBA Grads:	Y	Sales Trainees:	Y	Music:		Consulting/Other:		Training:	Y	Scientists/Research:	
		Advertising Pros.:	Y	Broadcasting:				Health Care:		Petroleum/Chemicals:	
				Other:	Y			Consulting:		Math/Other:	

TYPES OF BUSINESS:
Direct Property & Casualty Insurance
Personal Insurance

BRANDS/DIVISIONS/AFFILIATES:
Liberty Mutual Insurance Co.

CONTACTS: Note: Officers with more than one job title may be intentionally listed here more than once.
Matthew D. Nickerson, COO/Exec. VP
Michael Hughes, Pres.
Loralie Levenhagen, Assistant VP/Mgr.-Human Resources
Christopher G. Cunniff, Mgr.-Prod.
Donald J. DeShaw, General Counsel/VP-Corp. Legal
David M. Monfried, Sr. VP-Corp. Comm.
Kris L. Hill, Sr. VP/Mgr.-Finance
Gary R. Gregg, Pres., Liberty Mutual Agency Markets
Jeffrey G. Kuss, Sr. VP/Mgr.-Claims
Christopher G. Cunniff, Sr. VP/Mgr.-Underwriting & Actuarial

Phone: 206-545-5000	Fax: 206-545-5995
Toll-Free:	
Address: 1001 Fourth Avenue, Safeco Plz., Seattle, WA 98154 US	

GROWTH PLANS/SPECIAL FEATURES:
Safeco Insurance Company of America, formerly Safeco Corp., is a provider of property and casualty insurance to homeowners and drivers. The firm's personal insurance services include auto, homeowners, condo, rental, and specialty insurance products for individuals. Specialty insurance includes umbrella, classic car, motorcycle, recreational vehicle and boat owners' insurance coverage for individuals. The personal insurance division also offers individual surety bonds. The firm's business insurance operations are handled by Safeco's sister companies, such as Liberty Northwest, Colorado Casualty, America First Insurance, Golden Eagle Insurance and Peerless Insurance. These firms provide business-owner policies, surety bonds, commercial auto, commercial multi-peril, workers' compensation, commercial property and general liability policies for small- and mid-sized businesses. In September 2008, the firm was acquired by Liberty Mutual for $6.2 billion. The company became Safeco Insurance Company of America, a subsidiary of Liberty Mutual.

FINANCIALS: Sales and profits are in thousands of dollars—add 000 to get the full amount. 2008 Note: Financial information for 2008 was not available for all companies at press time.

2008 Sales: $	2008 Profits: $	U.S. Stock Ticker: Subsidiary
2007 Sales: $6,208,800	2007 Profits: $707,800	Int'l Ticker: Int'l Exchange:
2006 Sales: $6,289,900	2006 Profits: $880,000	Employees: 7,000
2005 Sales: $6,350,900	2005 Profits: $691,100	Fiscal Year Ends: 12/31
2004 Sales: $6,195,400	2004 Profits: $562,400	Parent Company: LIBERTY MUTUAL GROUP INC

SALARIES/BENEFITS:

Pension Plan:	ESOP Stock Plan:	Profit Sharing:	Top Exec. Salary: $	Bonus: $1,250,000
Savings Plan:	Stock Purch. Plan:		Second Exec. Salary: $	Bonus: $

OTHER THOUGHTS:
Apparent Women Officers or Directors: 2
Hot Spot for Advancement for Women/Minorities: Y

LOCATIONS: ("Y" = Yes)

West:	Southwest:	Midwest:	Southeast:	Northeast:	International:
Y	Y	Y	Y	Y	

Note: Financial information, benefits and other data can change quickly and may vary from those stated here.

SAFEWAY INC

www.safeway.com

Industry Group Code: 445110 Ranks within this company's industry group: Sales: 2   Profits: 3

Management:		Sales/Marketing:		Liberal Arts:		Information Systems:		Professionals:		Tech./Scientific:	
Management Trainees:	Y	Marketing Pros.:	Y	Gen. Writing/Editing:	Y	Info. Management:	Y	Finance/Acct.:	Y	Engineers, Electrical:	
Experienced Mngmt.:	Y	Retail Sales:	Y	Technical Writing:		Software Dev.:	Y	Law:	Y	Engineers, Other:	
International Business:	Y	Commercial/Industrial:		Graphic Arts/Photog.:	Y	Hardware Dev.:		HR/Other:	Y	Health/Lab:	
MBA Grads:	Y	Sales Trainees:	Y	Music:		Consulting/Other:		Training:	Y	Scientists/Research:	
		Advertising Pros.:	Y	Broadcasting:				Health Care:		Petroleum/Chemicals:	
				Other:	Y			Consulting:		Math/Other:	

TYPES OF BUSINESS:

Grocery Stores
Food Processing & Packaging
Online Grocery Sales & Home Delivery
Pharmacies
Gift Cards & Payment Processing Technology

BRANDS/DIVISIONS/AFFILIATES:

Carr-Gottstein Foods Co
Randall's Food Markets Inc.
Vons Companies Inc. (The)
Canada Safeway Limited
GroceryWorks
Safeway SELECT
Casa Ley, S.A. de C.V.
Blackhawk Network

CONTACTS: *Note: Officers with more than one job title may be intentionally listed here more than once.*

Steven A. Burd, CEO
Steven A. Burd, Pres.
Robert L. Edwards, CFO/Exec. VP
Diane M. Deitz, Chief Mktg. Officer
Russell M. Jackson, Sr. VP-Human Resources
David T. Ching, CIO/Sr. VP
Donald P. Wright, Sr. VP-Real Estate & Eng.
Larree M. Renda, Chief Strategist & Admin. Officer/Exec. VP
Robert A. Gordon, General Counsel/Sr. VP
Bruce L. Everette, Exec. VP-Retail Oper.
David R. Stern, Sr. VP-Bus. Dev. & Planning
Melissa C. Plaisance, Sr. VP-Finance & Investor Rel.
David F. Bond, Sr. VP-Finance & Control/Chief Acct. Officer
Thomas L. Schwilke, Pres., Randall's Food & Drugs
Kenneth M. Shachmut, Sr. VP-Reengineering & Strategic Initiatives
Donald Keprta, Pres., Dominic's Finer Foods, LLC
Thomas C. Keller, Pres., The Vons Companies, Inc.
Steven A. Burd, Chmn.
Jerry Tidwell, Sr. VP-Supply Oper.

Phone: 925-467-3000	Fax: 925-467-3323
Toll-Free: 877-723-3929	
Address: 5918 Stoneridge Mall Rd., Pleasanton, CA 94588 US	

GROWTH PLANS/SPECIAL FEATURES:

Safeway, Inc., originally incorporated as SSI Holdings Corporations and then Safeway Stores, is one of the largest food retailers in North America, operating 1,739 stores located principally in California, Oregon, Washington, Alaska, Colorado, Arizona, Texas, the Chicago metropolitan area and the Mid-Atlantic region. The company's Canadian retail operations are located principally in British Columbia, Alberta and Saskatchewan. These stores operate regionally under the names Safeway, Carrs, Genuardi's, Pavilions, Tom Thumb, Dominick's, Randall's and Vons, which each offer a wide selection of both food and general merchandise and feature a variety of special departments such as bakery, delicatessen, pharmacy and floral departments. In addition, the company offers online grocery shopping and home delivery through its wholly-owned subsidiary, GroceryWorks. Safeway has developed a line of hundreds of Safeway SELECT brand products, ranging from packaged foods to laundry detergent, and offers an additional 2,500 corporate-brand products under the Safeway and subsidiary labels. The company recently expanded its O Organics line of certified organic foods and beverages to over 300 exclusive products. Safeway operates 32 processing plants and 17 distribution/warehousing centers in the U.S. and Canada. Safeway also owns a 49% interest in Casa Ley, S.A. de C.V., which operates over 146 general merchandise and food stores in Mexico. Beyond these operations, the firm manages its Blackhawk Network subsidiary, which is one of the largest providers of third-party prepaid gift cards in the country with a gift card offering of more than 100 brands from retailers such as Barnes & Noble Booksellers, Best Buy, Pizza Hut and Starbucks Coffee.

Safeway offers its employees medical, prescription drug, vision and dental coverage; an employee assistance plan; flexible spending accounts; life insurance; short- and long-term disability; a retirement plan; and a 401(k) plan.

FINANCIALS: Sales and profits are in thousands of dollars—add 000 to get the full amount. 2008 Note: Financial information for 2008 was not available for all companies at press time.

2008 Sales: $44,104,000	2008 Profits: $965,300	**U.S. Stock Ticker: SWY**	
2007 Sales: $42,286,000	2007 Profits: $888,400	**Int'l Ticker:** Int'l Exchange:	
2006 Sales: $40,185,000	2006 Profits: $870,600	Employees: 197,000	
2005 Sales: $38,416,000	2005 Profits: $561,100	Fiscal Year Ends: 12/31	
2004 Sales: $35,822,900	2004 Profits: $560,200	Parent Company:	

SALARIES/BENEFITS:

Pension Plan: Y	ESOP Stock Plan:	Profit Sharing:	Top Exec. Salary: $1,467,442	Bonus: $399,944
Savings Plan: Y	Stock Purch. Plan: Y		Second Exec. Salary: $678,999	Bonus: $227,641

OTHER THOUGHTS:

Apparent Women Officers or Directors: 5
Hot Spot for Advancement for Women/Minorities: Y

LOCATIONS: ("Y" = Yes)

West:	Southwest:	Midwest:	Southeast:	Northeast:	International:
Y	Y	Y		Y	Y

Note: Financial information, benefits and other data can change quickly and may vary from those stated here.

SAIC INC

Industry Group Code: 541513 **Ranks within this company's industry group:** Sales: 4 Profits: 4

Management:		Sales/Marketing:		Liberal Arts:		Information Systems:		Professionals:		Tech./Scientific:	
Management Trainees:	Y	Marketing Pros.:	Y	Gen. Writing/Editing:	Y	Info. Management:	Y	Finance/Acct.:	Y	Engineers, Electrical:	Y
Experienced Mngmt.:	Y	Retail Sales:		Technical Writing:	Y	Software Dev.:	Y	Law:	Y	Engineers, Other:	Y
International Business:	Y	Commercial/Industrial:	Y	Graphic Arts/Photog.:	Y	Hardware Dev.:	Y	HR/Other:	Y	Health/Lab:	
MBA Grads:	Y	Sales Trainees:		Music:		Consulting/Other:	Y	Training:	Y	Scientists/Research:	Y
		Advertising Pros.:		Broadcasting:				Health Care:		Petroleum/Chemicals:	
				Other:	Y			Consulting:	Y	Math/Other:	

TYPES OF BUSINESS:

Systems Integration Services
Consulting Services
Research & Development
Software Development
Venture Capital
Engineering

BRANDS/DIVISIONS/AFFILIATES:

Icon Systems, Inc.
SM Consulting, Inc.

CONTACTS: Note: Officers with more than one job title may be intentionally listed here more than once.

Kenneth C. (Ken) Dahlberg, CEO
Lawrence B. Prior, III, COO
Mark W. Sopp, CFO/Exec. VP
Brian F. Keenan, Exec. VP-Human Resources
Charles F. Koontz, Pres., IT & Network Solutions Group
Amy E. Alving, CTO
Joseph W. Craver, III, Pres., Prod. Solutions Group
Douglas E. Scott, General Counsel/Exec. VP/Corp. Sec.
Greg Henson, Sr. VP/Dir.-Bus. Dev.
Arnold L. Punaro, Exec. VP
Joseph P. Walkush, Exec. VP-Strategic Initiatives
Deborah H. Alderson, Pres., Defense Solutions Group
K. Stuart Shea, Pres., Intelligence, Security & Tech. Group
Kenneth C. (Ken) Dahlberg, Chmn.
Donald H. Foley, Exec. VP-Special Int'l Assignment
Joseph W. Craver, III, Pres., Logistics & Infrastructure Group

Phone: 858-826-6000	Fax:
Toll-Free:	
Address: 10260 Campus Point Dr., San Diego, CA 92121 US	

GROWTH PLANS/SPECIAL FEATURES:

SAIC, Inc., formerly Science Applications International Corporation, provides scientific, engineering, systems integration and technical services for all branches of the U.S. military, agencies of the U.S. Department of Defense (DoD), the intelligence community, the U.S. Department of Homeland Security (DHS), other U.S. government agencies, foreign governments and customers in selected commercial markets. SAIC offers products and solutions in three segments: government, commercial and corporate. The government segment, which generated 94% of the firm's revenues in 2008, offers services and solutions in the areas of defense; intelligence; homeland security; logistics and product support; systems engineering and integration; and research and development. SAIC's commercial segment, which generated 6% of its revenue in 2008, primarily targets commercial customers worldwide in selected industry markets, which currently include oil and gas; utilities; and life sciences. While the commercial segment provides a number of IT systems integration and advanced technical services, the focused offerings include applications and IT infrastructure management; data lifecycle management; and business transformation services. During 2008, SAIC disposed of its 55% interest in AMSEC LLC, a provider of maintenance engineering and technical support services to the U.S. Navy and marine industry customers, in exchange for the acquisition of certain divisions and subsidiaries of AMSEC. In April 2008, the company acquired Icon Systems, Inc., a designer, developer and producer of laser-based systems and products for military training and testing. In May 2008, SAIC acquired SM Consulting, Inc., a provider or language, intelligence, IT, management consulting, business process outsourcing, training and logistics to federal, state and local governments and private industry.

SAIC offers its employees education assistance, access to SAIC University, a commuting program, an employee assistance plan, backup childcare, onsite fitness centers, domestic partner benefits and medical, dental, vision, life, accident and disability insurance.

FINANCIALS: Sales and profits are in thousands of dollars—add 000 to get the full amount. 2008 Note: Financial information for 2008 was not available for all companies at press time.

2008 Sales: $8,926,000	2008 Profits: $416,000	**U.S. Stock Ticker:** SAI
2007 Sales: $8,060,000	2007 Profits: $390,000	**Int'l Ticker:** Int'l Exchange:
2006 Sales: $7,518,000	2006 Profits: $927,000	Employees: 45,400
2005 Sales: $6,910,000	2005 Profits: $409,000	Fiscal Year Ends: 1/31
2004 Sales: $6,720,000	2004 Profits: $351,000	Parent Company:

SALARIES/BENEFITS:

Pension Plan:	ESOP Stock Plan:	Profit Sharing:	Top Exec. Salary: $1,000,000	Bonus: $1,050,000
Savings Plan: Y	Stock Purch. Plan:		Second Exec. Salary: $519,231	Bonus: $485,000

OTHER THOUGHTS:

Apparent Women Officers or Directors: 5
Hot Spot for Advancement for Women/Minorities: Y

LOCATIONS: ("Y" = Yes)

West:	Southwest:	Midwest:	Southeast:	Northeast:	International:
Y	Y	Y	Y	Y	Y

SAM'S CLUB
www.samsclub.com

Industry Group Code: 452112 Ranks within this company's industry group: Sales: 4   Profits: 3

Management:		Sales/Marketing:		Liberal Arts:		Information Systems:		Professionals:		Tech./Scientific:	
Management Trainees:	Y	Marketing Pros.:	Y	Gen. Writing/Editing:	Y	Info. Management:	Y	Finance/Acct.:	Y	Engineers, Electrical:	
Experienced Mngmt.:	Y	Retail Sales:	Y	Technical Writing:		Software Dev.:	Y	Law:	Y	Engineers, Other:	
International Business:	Y	Commercial/Industrial:		Graphic Arts/Photog.:	Y	Hardware Dev.:		HR/Other:	Y	Health/Lab:	
MBA Grads:	Y	Sales Trainees:	Y	Music:		Consulting/Other:		Training:	Y	Scientists/Research:	
		Advertising Pros.:	Y	Broadcasting:				Health Care:		Petroleum/Chemicals:	
				Other:	Y			Consulting:		Math/Other:	

TYPES OF BUSINESS:
Warehouse Clubs, Retail

BRANDS/DIVISIONS/AFFILIATES:
Wal-Mart Stores Inc
Member's Mark
Bakers & Chefs
Business Membership
Advantage Membership
Plus Membership Card
Sam's Cafe

CONTACTS: *Note: Officers with more than one job title may be intentionally listed here more than once.*
Brian C. Cornell, CEO
Brian C. Cornell, Pres.
Cindy Davis, Exec. VP-Mktg. & Membership
Sharon Orlopp, Sr. VP-Sam's Club People Div.
Linda Hefner, Chief Merch. Officer/Exec. VP
Whitney Head, General Counsel
Ignacio Perez Lizaur, Exec. VP-Oper.
Cindy Davis, Exec. VP-E-Commerce
Susan Koehler, Media Contact

Phone: 479-277-7000	Fax:
Toll-Free: 800-331-0085	
Address: 608 S.W. 8th St., Bentonville, AR 72716-0745 US	

GROWTH PLANS/SPECIAL FEATURES:
Sam's Club, a subsidiary of Wal-Mart Stores, Inc. and one of the nation's largest members-only warehouse clubs, operates 602 stores in the U.S. with over 47 million members. Additionally, Wal-Mart's International division operates 110 Sam's Clubs in Brazil, Canada, China, Mexico and Puerto Rico. Sam's offers discounted prices on more than 4,000 items, including appliances and electronics, office supplies, fresh food, clothing, optical and pharmacy services, home furnishings, books, batteries and auto supplies. It also sells selected private-label items under the Member's Mark, Bakers & Chefs and Sam's Club brands. Most locations also offer photo processing, pharmaceuticals, optical departments, gasoline stations and fresh departments, including bakery, meat, produce, floral and Sam's Cafe. Sam's requires a customer to become a member, providing two options: Business Membership or Advantage Membership. Both member groups pay an annual fee. Business members include anyone who holds a valid city/state business or tax permit or anyone who holds a professional license. Everyone else can purchase an Advantage Membership. In addition, Sam's offers a PLUS Membership Card, which offers extra benefits on either level. In addition to merchandise discounts, Sam's offers its members discounted services that include various types of insurance, a travel club, an auto purchase program, discount credit card processing, software training, mail-order pharmacy services, Internet access and long-distance services. Sam's Club stores, averaging 72,000-190,000 square feet, are designed to resemble a warehouse, with merchandise displayed on shipping pallets or in large freezer/cooler units. In 2008, sundries, such as alcohol and tobacco, generated the largest share (37%) of Sam's sales, followed by food (30%); hardgoods, such as electronics and furniture (16%); services, including fuel (12%); and softgoods, such as apparel and small appliances (5%).

Sam's Club offers its employees medical, dental and life insurance; merchandise discounts; education assistance; GED reimbursement; and scholarships.

FINANCIALS: Sales and profits are in thousands of dollars—add 000 to get the full amount. 2008 Note: Financial information for 2008 was not available for all companies at press time.
2008 Sales: $44,357,000	2008 Profits: $1,618,000	**U.S. Stock Ticker: Subsidiary**
2007 Sales: $41,582,000	2007 Profits: $1,480,000	**Int'l Ticker:** Int'l Exchange:
2006 Sales: $39,798,000	2006 Profits: $	Employees: 220,000
2005 Sales: $37,100,000	2005 Profits: $1,280,000	Fiscal Year Ends: 1/31
2004 Sales: $34,537,000	2004 Profits: $1,126,000	Parent Company: WAL-MART STORES INC

SALARIES/BENEFITS:
Pension Plan:	ESOP Stock Plan: Y	Profit Sharing:	Top Exec. Salary: $	Bonus: $
Savings Plan: Y	Stock Purch. Plan:		Second Exec. Salary: $	Bonus: $

OTHER THOUGHTS:
Apparent Women Officers or Directors: 4
Hot Spot for Advancement for Women/Minorities: Y

LOCATIONS: ("Y" = Yes)					
West:	Southwest:	Midwest:	Southeast:	Northeast:	International:
Y	Y	Y	Y	Y	Y

SAPIENT CORPORATION

www.sapient.com

Industry Group Code: 541513 **Ranks within this company's industry group:** Sales: 11 Profits: 9

Management:		Sales/Marketing:		Liberal Arts:		Information Systems:		Professionals:		Tech./Scientific:	
Management Trainees:	Y	Marketing Pros.:	Y	Gen. Writing/Editing:	Y	Info. Management:	Y	Finance/Acct.:	Y	Engineers, Electrical:	Y
Experienced Mngmt.:	Y	Retail Sales:		Technical Writing:	Y	Software Dev.:	Y	Law:	Y	Engineers, Other:	
International Business:	Y	Commercial/Industrial:	Y	Graphic Arts/Photog.:	Y	Hardware Dev.:	Y	HR/Other:	Y	Health/Lab:	
MBA Grads:	Y	Sales Trainees:		Music:		Consulting/Other:	Y	Training:	Y	Scientists/Research:	
		Advertising Pros.:		Broadcasting:				Health Care:		Petroleum/Chemicals:	
				Other:	Y			Consulting:	Y	Math/Other:	

TYPES OF BUSINESS:

Information Technology Consulting
Internet Strategy Consulting

BRANDS/DIVISIONS/AFFILIATES:

Sapient Interactive
Sapient Consulting

CONTACTS: Note: Officers with more than one job title may be intentionally listed here more than once.

Alan Herrick, CEO
Preston B. Bradford, COO/Sr. VP
Alan Herrick, Pres.
Joe Tibbetts, CFO/Sr. VP
Preston B. Bradford, Chief Admin. Officer
Jane E. Owens, General Counsel/Sr. VP/Sec.
Gaston Legorburu, Sr. VP/Chief Creative Officer
Alan Wexler, Sr. VP/Lead-North America
Darius W. Gaskins, Jr., Chmn.
Christian Oversohl, Sr. VP/European Lead

Phone: 617-621-0200	**Fax:** 617-621-1300
Toll-Free:	
Address: 131 Dartmouth St., 3rd Fl., Boston, MA 02116 US	

GROWTH PLANS/SPECIAL FEATURES:

Sapient Corp. is a business consulting and technology services firm that designs and manages information technology to improve business performance for clients in the U.S. and abroad. Sapient has offices in the U.S., Canada, the U.K., Germany, the Netherlands, Switzerland, Sweden and India. The firm operates through two primary areas of focus: Sapient Interactive and Sapient Consulting. Sapient Interactive, a leading global interactive marketing agency, provides interactive (online or Internet-based) marketing and creative services; web site and interactive development; media planning and buying; strategic planning and market analytics; and marketing technologies. Sapient Consulting works with clients across four primary service areas: business and IT strategy; business applications; business intelligence; and outsourcing. Additionally, the consulting business specializes in trading and risk management services that help leading capital markets and energy firms improve the performance of their trading operations via a comprehensive set of services and solutions. Sapient works on both long and short-term consulting projects. Sapient operates through a proprietary Global Distributed Delivery (GDD) model, which allows associates in widely disparate locations to work together efficiently. Clients consist of companies within the following industries: technology, communications, energy and utilities, financial services, media and entertainment, automotive, transportation, health care and life sciences, education, consumer/retail products, travel and hospitality. The firm also provides services to federal, state and local government clients within the U.S. and to provincial and other governmental entities in Canada and Europe. Clients include AT&T; Bank of America; Capital One; Motorola; the Royal Bank of Canada; the U.S. Navy; and Wal-Mart. In August 2008, Sapient acquired London-based Derivatives Consulting Group Limited, provider of derivatives consulting and outsourcing services to investment banks, hedge funds, asset managers and commercial banking clients.

Sapient offers its employees education assistance, dependent care assistance, employee assistance programs, life insurance and flexible health and dental care.

FINANCIALS: Sales and profits are in thousands of dollars—add 000 to get the full amount. 2008 Note: Financial information for 2008 was not available for all companies at press time.

2008 Sales: $687,488	2008 Profits: $62,476	**U.S. Stock Ticker:** SAPE	
2007 Sales: $565,989	2007 Profits: $15,216	**Int'l Ticker:** Int'l Exchange:	
2006 Sales: $421,643	2006 Profits: $3,136	Employees: 6,360	
2005 Sales: $327,098	2005 Profits: $26,399	Fiscal Year Ends: 12/31	
2004 Sales: $260,254	2004 Profits: $31,302	Parent Company:	

SALARIES/BENEFITS:

Pension Plan:	ESOP Stock Plan:	Profit Sharing:	Top Exec. Salary: $531,250	Bonus: $416,500
Savings Plan: Y	Stock Purch. Plan:		Second Exec. Salary: $353,122	Bonus: $204,413

OTHER THOUGHTS:

Apparent Women Officers or Directors: 1
Hot Spot for Advancement for Women/Minorities:

LOCATIONS: ("Y" = Yes)

West:	Southwest:	Midwest:	Southeast:	Northeast:	International:
Y	Y	Y	Y	Y	Y

Note: Financial information, benefits and other data can change quickly and may vary from those stated here.

SARA LEE CORP   www.saralee.com

Industry Group Code: 3118 Ranks within this company's industry group: Sales: 1   Profits: 1

Management:		Sales/Marketing:		Liberal Arts:		Information Systems:		Professionals:		Tech./Scientific:	
Management Trainees:	Y	Marketing Pros.:	Y	Gen. Writing/Editing:	Y	Info. Management:	Y	Finance/Acct.:	Y	Engineers, Electrical:	
Experienced Mngmt.:	Y	Retail Sales:		Technical Writing:	Y	Software Dev.:	Y	Law:	Y	Engineers, Other:	Y
International Business:	Y	Commercial/Industrial:	Y	Graphic Arts/Photog.:	Y	Hardware Dev.:		HR/Other:	Y	Health/Lab:	
MBA Grads:	Y	Sales Trainees:	Y	Music:		Consulting/Other:		Training:	Y	Scientists/Research:	
		Advertising Pros.:	Y	Broadcasting:				Health Care:		Petroleum/Chemicals:	
				Other:				Consulting:		Math/Other:	

TYPES OF BUSINESS:

Food & Beverage, Manufacturing
Household Products
Bakery Products
Processed Meats
Coffee & Tea
Foodservice Distribution
Apparel

BRANDS/DIVISIONS/AFFILIATES:

Ball Park
Hillshire Farm
Jimmy Dean
State Fair
Maison du Cafe
Superior
Hanesbrands Inc
Kiwi

CONTACTS: *Note: Officers with more than one job title may be intentionally listed here more than once.*

Brenda C. Barnes, CEO
Christopher J. Fraleigh, COO/Exec. VP
L. M. de Kool, CFO
Stephen J. Cerrone, Exec. VP-Human Resources
L. M. de Kool, Chief Admin. Officer/Exec. VP
Margaret M. Foran, General Counsel/Exec. VP/Corp. Sec.
B. Thomas Hansson, Sr. VP-Strategic Planning & Corp. Dev.
Frank van Oers, Exec. VP/CEO-Coffee & Tea, Sara Lee Int'l
James W. Nolan, Exec. VP/CEO-Sara Lee Fresh Bakery
Brenda C. Barnes, Chmn.
Vincent Janssen, Exec. VP/CEO-Household & Body, Sara Lee Int'l

Phone: 630-598-6000	Fax: 630-598-8482
Toll-Free:	
Address: 3500 Lacey Rd., Downers Grove, IL 60515-5424 US	

GROWTH PLANS/SPECIAL FEATURES:

Sara Lee Corp. manufactures and markets brand-name food products worldwide. The company is divided into six operating segments: North American retail meats, accounting for 18.3% of sales, North American retail bakery, 16.5%; foodservice, 16.8%; international beverage, 24.1%; international bakery, 7%; and household and body care, 17.3%. These in turn are organized into: international, food and beverage, and foodservice. The Sara Lee Food and Beverage subsidiary manufactures packaged meat products under the names Ball Park, Best's Kosher, Hillshire Farm and Jimmy Dean, and the Sara Lee Bakery Group produces specialty breads, fresh and frozen pies, pound cakes, cheesecakes and Danishes in North America. Sara Lee Foodservice oversees the bakery, coffee and meats foodservice business in North America. Sara Lee International manages the firm's worldwide coffee and tea operations (including the Superior tea and Maison du Cafe brands), its household products segment and the direct-selling operations, which distributes a range of products including cosmetics, jewelry, nutritional supplements and household products, such as Endust furniture cleaner, Kiwi shoe care products and Ambi Pure air fresheners, through a network of independent sales representatives. Sara Lee's apparel business, Hanesbrands, Inc., includes well known brands such as Hanes, Playtex, Barely There, Wonder Bra and Champion. Roughly 48% of sales are derived outside of the U.S. In 2008, the company sold its 49.9% stake in the Qualtia Alimentos meats business in Mexico to Xignux, its joint venture partner. Also in 2008, the firm agreed to acquire the Café Moka coffee business in Sao Paulo, Brazil.

Employees are offered medical, dental and vision insurance; adoption, parenting, eldercare and child care assistance; a 401(k) plan; legal and financial information services; health club subsidies; and employee discounts on company products.

FINANCIALS: Sales and profits are in thousands of dollars—add 000 to get the full amount. 2008 Note: Financial information for 2008 was not available for all companies at press time.

2008 Sales: $13,212,000	2008 Profits: $-79,000	**U.S. Stock Ticker: SLE**
2007 Sales: $11,983,000	2007 Profits: $504,000	**Int'l Ticker:** Int'l Exchange:
2006 Sales: $11,175,000	2006 Profits: $555,000	Employees: 41,000
2005 Sales: $11,346,000	2005 Profits: $719,000	Fiscal Year Ends: 6/30
2004 Sales: $15,892,000	2004 Profits: $1,272,000	Parent Company:

SALARIES/BENEFITS:

Pension Plan:	ESOP Stock Plan:	Profit Sharing:	Top Exec. Salary: $1,000,000	Bonus: $1,993,597
Savings Plan: Y	Stock Purch. Plan:		Second Exec. Salary: $802,750	Bonus: $1,204,832

OTHER THOUGHTS:

Apparent Women Officers or Directors: 4
Hot Spot for Advancement for Women/Minorities: Y

LOCATIONS: ("Y" = Yes)

West:	Southwest:	Midwest:	Southeast:	Northeast:	International:
Y	Y	Y	Y	Y	Y

SAS INSTITUTE INC

www.sas.com

Industry Group Code: 511210H Ranks within this company's industry group: Sales: 2   Profits:

Management:		Sales/Marketing:		Liberal Arts:		Information Systems:		Professionals:		Tech./Scientific:	
Management Trainees:	Y	Marketing Pros.:	Y	Gen. Writing/Editing:	Y	Info. Management:	Y	Finance/Acct.:	Y	Engineers, Electrical:	Y
Experienced Mngmt.:	Y	Retail Sales:		Technical Writing:	Y	Software Dev.:	Y	Law:	Y	Engineers, Other:	
International Business:	Y	Commercial/Industrial:	Y	Graphic Arts/Photog.:	Y	Hardware Dev.:		HR/Other:	Y	Health/Lab:	
MBA Grads:	Y	Sales Trainees:		Music:		Consulting/Other:	Y	Training:	Y	Scientists/Research:	Y
		Advertising Pros.:	Y	Broadcasting:				Health Care:		Petroleum/Chemicals:	
				Other:	Y			Consulting:	Y	Math/Other:	Y

TYPES OF BUSINESS:

Software-Statistical Analysis
Business Intelligence Software
Data Warehousing
Online Bookstore

BRANDS/DIVISIONS/AFFILIATES:

SAS9
SAS Enterprise BI Server
DataFlux
SAS Revenue Optimization
SAS Promotion Optimization
SAS Enterprise Intelligence Platform

CONTACTS: *Note: Officers with more than one job title may be intentionally listed here more than once.*

James Goodnight, CEO
James Goodnight, Pres.
Don Parker, CFO/Sr. VP
Jim Davis, Chief Mktg. Officer/Sr. VP
Jennifer Mann, VP-Human Resources
Suzanne Gordon, CIO/VP-IT
Keith Collins, CTO/Sr. VP
John Sall, Exec. VP
James Goodnight, Chmn.
Mikael Hagstrom, Exec. VP-EMEA & APAC

Phone: 919-677-8000	Fax: 919-677-4444
Toll-Free: 800-727-0025	
Address: 100 SAS Campus Dr., Cary, NC 27513-2414 US	

GROWTH PLANS/SPECIAL FEATURES:

SAS Institute, Inc. provides statistical analysis software. The company's products are designed to extract, manage and analyze large volumes of data, often assisting in financial reporting and credit analysis. Individual contracts can be tailored to specific global and local industries, such as banking, manufacturing and government. SAS's top products are SAS9 and SAS Enterprise BI Server. The SAS9 platform is centered on providing extensive data management and analytics integration. It also features predictive applications, a highly adaptable interface and unique grid computing capabilities. SAS Enterprise BI Server is an enhanced reporting and analysis system for the organization and reporting of business intelligence. SAS also provides data warehousing services for large amounts of data, as well as consulting, training and technical support through its SAS Services unit. The company's DataFlux subsidiary helps it deliver quality capabilities in SAS Data Integration solutions. In addition, the firm operates an online bookstore offering a library of SAS-produced books, documentation and training materials. SAS serves more than 45,000 business, government and university sites in 111 different countries, including 91 of the top 100 companies on the Fortune Global 500 list. Some of the firm's more prominent clients are Hewlett Packard; Brooks Brothers; the U.S. Department of Defense; Staples, Subway; and Allstate Financial. In March 2008, the firm acquired Teragram, a natural language processing and linguistic technology company. In August 2008, the company acquired IDeaS Revenue Optimization, which provides revenue management software for the hospitality industry.

The SAS headquarters features on-site childcare centers, an eldercare information and referral program, an employee health care center, wellness programs and a 58,000 square foot recreation and fitness center. The firm has been listed in Fortune's Top 100 Companies to Work For in America for 11 consecutive years.

FINANCIALS: Sales and profits are in thousands of dollars—add 000 to get the full amount. 2008 Note: Financial information for 2008 was not available for all companies at press time.

2008 Sales: $2,260,000	2008 Profits: $	U.S. Stock Ticker: Private
2007 Sales: $2,150,000	2007 Profits: $	Int'l Ticker: Int'l Exchange:
2006 Sales: $1,900,000	2006 Profits: $	Employees: 11,139
2005 Sales: $1,680,000	2005 Profits: $	Fiscal Year Ends: 12/31
2004 Sales: $1,530,000	2004 Profits: $	Parent Company:

SALARIES/BENEFITS:

Pension Plan:	ESOP Stock Plan:	Profit Sharing: Y	Top Exec. Salary: $	Bonus: $
Savings Plan: Y	Stock Purch. Plan:		Second Exec. Salary: $	Bonus: $

OTHER THOUGHTS:

Apparent Women Officers or Directors: 2
Hot Spot for Advancement for Women/Minorities: Y

LOCATIONS: ("Y" = Yes)

West:	Southwest:	Midwest:	Southeast:	Northeast:	International:
Y	Y	Y	Y	Y	Y

SCANA CORPORATION

Industry Group Code: 221   Ranks within this company's industry group: Sales: 11   Profits: 8

Management:		Sales/Marketing:		Liberal Arts:		Information Systems:		Professionals:		Tech./Scientific:	
Management Trainees:	Y	Marketing Pros.:	Y	Gen. Writing/Editing:	Y	Info. Management:	Y	Finance/Acct.:	Y	Engineers, Electrical:	Y
Experienced Mngmt.:	Y	Retail Sales:		Technical Writing:	Y	Software Dev.:	Y	Law:	Y	Engineers, Other:	Y
International Business:		Commercial/Industrial:	Y	Graphic Arts/Photog.:	Y	Hardware Dev.:		HR/Other:	Y	Health/Lab:	
MBA Grads:	Y	Sales Trainees:		Music:		Consulting/Other:		Training:	Y	Scientists/Research:	
		Advertising Pros.:	Y	Broadcasting:				Health Care:		Petroleum/Chemicals:	Y
				Other:				Consulting:		Math/Other:	

TYPES OF BUSINESS:

Electricity & Natural Gas
Telecommunications Services
Ethernet Services & Data Center Facilities
Communications Towers Management
Management & Maintenance Services
Service Contracts
Risk Management Services

BRANDS/DIVISIONS/AFFILIATES:

South Carolina Electric & Gas Co.
South Carolina Generating Co., Inc.
South Carolina Fuel Co., Inc.
Public Service Co. of North Carolina, Inc.
Carolina Gas Transmission Corp.
SCANA Communications, Inc.
SCANA Energy Marketing, Inc.
ServiceCare, Inc.

CONTACTS: *Note: Officers with more than one job title may be intentionally listed here more than once.*

William B. Timmerman, CEO
William B. Timmerman, Pres.
Jimmy Addison, CFO/Sr. VP
George J. Bullwinkel, Jr., Pres./COO-Scana Energy Mktg.
Joseph C. Bouknight, Sr. VP-Human Resources
Francis P. Mood, Jr., General Counsel/Sr. VP
Mark R. Cannon, Treas./Risk Mgmt. Officer
Kevin B. Marsh, Pres./COO-South Carolina Electric & Gas Co.
Charles McFadden, Sr. VP-Gov't Affairs & Economic Dev.
Paul V. Fant, Pres./COO-Carolina Gas Transmission
Gina S. Champion, Corp. Sec./Associate General Counsel
William B. Timmerman, Chmn.
Sarena D. Burch, Sr. VP-Fuel Procurement & Asset Mgmt.

Phone: 803-217-9000	Fax: 803-217-8119
Toll-Free: 800-763-5891	
Address: 1426 Main St., Columbia, SC 29201 US	

GROWTH PLANS/SPECIAL FEATURES:

SCANA Corp. is an energy-based holding company that operates through wholly-owned subsidiaries. South Carolina Electric & Gas Company (SCE&G) generates and sells electricity to retail and wholesale customers, and purchases, sells and transports natural gas to retail customers. South Carolina Generating Company, Inc. owns and operates Williams Station and sells electricity solely to SCE&G. South Carolina Fuel Company, Inc. owns and provides financing for SCE&G's nuclear fuel, fossil fuel and emission allowances. Public Service Company of North Carolina, Inc. purchases, sells and transports natural gas to retail customers. Carolina Gas Transmission Corp. (CGTC) transports natural gas in southeastern Georgia and South Carolina. SCANA Communications, Inc. (SCI) provides fiber optic communications, ethernet services and data center facilities through a 500-mile fiber optic telecommunications network. SCI also builds, manages and leases communications towers in South Carolina, North Carolina and Georgia. SCANA Energy Marketing, Inc. (SEMI) markets natural gas, primarily in the southeast, and provides energy-related risk management services. Through its SCANA Energy division, SEMI markets natural gas in Georgia's retail natural gas market. ServiceCare, Inc. provides service contracts on home appliances and heating and air conditioning units. SCANA Services, Inc. provides administrative, management and other services to the subsidiaries and business units within SCANA. These are the firm's 10 primary subsidiaries, in addition to which the firm also owns three smaller energy-related companies. All together, SCANA's electric service area extends into 24 counties covering roughly 16,000 square miles and serving 649,600 customers. The company's natural gas operations own liquefied natural gas liquefaction and storage facilities and transports natural gas to over one million customers. In 2008, SCE&G and Santee Cooper, a state-owned electric and water utility in South Carolina, joined together to construct two nuclear electric-generating units.

The company offers its employees medical, dental and vision insurance; a retirement plan; and a 401(k) plan.

FINANCIALS: Sales and profits are in thousands of dollars—add 000 to get the full amount. 2008 Note: Financial information for 2008 was not available for all companies at press time.

2008 Sales: $5,319,000	2008 Profits: $346,000	U.S. Stock Ticker: SCG
2007 Sales: $4,621,000	2007 Profits: $320,000	Int'l Ticker: Int'l Exchange:
2006 Sales: $4,563,000	2006 Profits: $310,000	Employees: 5,786
2005 Sales: $4,777,000	2005 Profits: $320,000	Fiscal Year Ends: 12/31
2004 Sales: $3,885,000	2004 Profits: $257,000	Parent Company:

SALARIES/BENEFITS:

Pension Plan: Y	ESOP Stock Plan:	Profit Sharing:	Top Exec. Salary: $1,094,985	Bonus: $653,905
Savings Plan: Y	Stock Purch. Plan:		Second Exec. Salary: $577,692	Bonus: $263,500

OTHER THOUGHTS:

Apparent Women Officers or Directors: 5
Hot Spot for Advancement for Women/Minorities: Y

LOCATIONS: ("Y" = Yes)

West:	Southwest:	Midwest:	Southeast:	Northeast:	International:
			Y	Y	

SCHERING-PLOUGH CORP

www.schering-plough.com

Industry Group Code: 325412 Ranks within this company's industry group: Sales: 7 Profits: 9

Management:		Sales/Marketing:		Liberal Arts:		Information Systems:		Professionals:		Tech./Scientific:	
Management Trainees:	Y	Marketing Pros.:	Y	Gen. Writing/Editing:	Y	Info. Management:	Y	Finance/Acct.:	Y	Engineers, Electrical:	Y
Experienced Mngmt.:	Y	Retail Sales:		Technical Writing:	Y	Software Dev.:	Y	Law:	Y	Engineers, Other:	Y
International Business:	Y	Commercial/Industrial:	Y	Graphic Arts/Photog.:	Y	Hardware Dev.:		HR/Other:	Y	Health/Lab:	Y
MBA Grads:	Y	Sales Trainees:	Y	Music:		Consulting/Other:		Training:	Y	Scientists/Research:	Y
		Advertising Pros.:	Y	Broadcasting:				Health Care:	Y	Petroleum/Chemicals:	Y
				Other:				Consulting:		Math/Other:	Y

TYPES OF BUSINESS:

Drugs-Diversified
Anti-Infective & Anti-Cancer Drugs
Dermatologicals
Cardiovascular Drugs
Animal Health Products
Over-the-Counter Drugs
Foot & Sun Care Products

BRANDS/DIVISIONS/AFFILIATES:

Bovilis/Vista
HOMEAGAIN
Dr. Scholl's
Coppertone
Nuflor
Livial
Vytorin
Lotrimin

CONTACTS: *Note: Officers with more than one job title may be intentionally listed here more than once.*

Fred Hassan, CEO
Robert J. Bertolini, CFO/Exec. VP
C. Ron Cheeley, Sr. VP-Global Human Resources
Thomas P. Koestler, Exec. VP/Pres., Schering-Plough Research Institute
Thomas Sabatino, Jr., General Counsel/Exec. VP
Janet M. Barth, VP-Investor Rel.
Steven H. Koehler, Chief Acct. Officer/Controller/VP
Richard S. Bowles III, Sr. VP-Global Quality Oper.
Carrie S. Cox, Exec. VP/Pres., Global Pharmaceuticals
Lori Queisser, Sr. VP-Global Compliance & Bus. Practices
Brent Saunders, Sr. VP/Pres., Consumer Health Care
Fred Hassan, Chmn.
Ian McInnes, Sr. VP/Pres., Global Supply Chain

Phone: 908-298-4000	Fax: 908-298-7653
Toll-Free:	
Address: 2000 Galloping Hill Rd., Kenilworth, NJ 07033 US	

GROWTH PLANS/SPECIAL FEATURES:

Schering-Plough Corp. is a science-centered global heath care company. The company operates in three segments: human prescription pharmaceuticals, animal health and consumer health care. The human prescription pharmaceuticals segment discovers, develops, manufactures and markets human pharmaceutical products. Within the segment, the firm has a broad range of research projects and marketed products in six therapeutic areas: cardiovascular, central nervous system, immunology and infectious disease, oncology, respiratory and women's health. Marketed products include Vytorin, a cholesterol-lowering tablet; Remeron, an antidepressant; Livial, a menopausal therapy; and Temodar capsules for certain types of brain tumors including newly diagnosed glioblastoma multiforme. The animal health segment discovers, develops, manufactures and markets animal health products, including vaccines. Principal marketed products in this segment include Nuflor fish, bovine and swine antibiotics; Bovilis/Vista vaccine lines for infectious diseases in cattle; Innovax ND-SB vaccine for poultry; Otomax, a canine ear treatment; and HOMEAGAIN, which identifies pet cats and dogs and makes them easier to recover if lost. The consumer health care segment develops, manufactures and markets various over-the-counter, foot care and sun care products. Principal products in this division include Claritin non-sedating antihistamines; Dr. Scholl's foot care products; Lotrimin topical antifungal products; and Coppertone sun care lotions, sprays, dry oils, lip protection products and sunless tanning products. Throughout 2008, the firm continued the integration of its 2007 acquisition, Organon BioSciences, into its operations. In February 2008, the company partnered with OraSure Technologies, Inc., to develop a rapid oral hepatitis C test. In April 2008, Schering-Plough agreed to sell a combined 12 European animal product franchises to Virbac, S.A., and Pfizer Animal Health. In August 2008, the firm founded Shanghai Schering-Plough Pharmaceutical Co. Ltd., to expand its Chinese allergy and skincare product market. In August 2009, the firm approved a merger agreement with Merck & Co.

FINANCIALS: Sales and profits are in thousands of dollars—add 000 to get the full amount. 2008 Note: Financial information for 2008 was not available for all companies at press time.

2008 Sales: $18,502,000	2008 Profits: $1,903,000	**U.S. Stock Ticker: SGP**
2007 Sales: $12,690,000	2007 Profits: $-1,473,000	**Int'l Ticker:** Int'l Exchange:
2006 Sales: $10,594,000	2006 Profits: $1,143,000	Employees: 51,000
2005 Sales: $9,508,000	2005 Profits: $269,000	Fiscal Year Ends: 12/31
2004 Sales: $8,272,000	2004 Profits: $-947,000	Parent Company:

SALARIES/BENEFITS:

Pension Plan:	ESOP Stock Plan:	Profit Sharing:	Top Exec. Salary: $1,720,250	Bonus: $3,387,150
Savings Plan:	Stock Purch. Plan: Y		Second Exec. Salary: $1,089,000	Bonus: $1,146,080

OTHER THOUGHTS:

Apparent Women Officers or Directors: 8
Hot Spot for Advancement for Women/Minorities: Y

LOCATIONS: ("Y" = Yes)

West:	Southwest:	Midwest:	Southeast:	Northeast:	International:
Y	Y	Y	Y	Y	Y

SCHLUMBERGER LIMITED

www.slb.com

Industry Group Code: 213112 Ranks within this company's industry group: Sales: 1 Profits: 1

Management:		Sales/Marketing:		Liberal Arts:		Information Systems:		Professionals:		Tech./Scientific:	
Management Trainees:	Y	Marketing Pros.:	Y	Gen. Writing/Editing:	Y	Info. Management:	Y	Finance/Acct.:	Y	Engineers, Electrical:	Y
Experienced Mngmt.:	Y	Retail Sales:		Technical Writing:	Y	Software Dev.:	Y	Law:	Y	Engineers, Other:	Y
International Business:	Y	Commercial/Industrial:	Y	Graphic Arts/Photog.:	Y	Hardware Dev.:		HR/Other:	Y	Health/Lab:	
MBA Grads:	Y	Sales Trainees:		Music:		Consulting/Other:		Training:	Y	Scientists/Research:	Y
		Advertising Pros.:	Y	Broadcasting:				Health Care:		Petroleum/Chemicals:	Y
				Other:				Consulting:		Math/Other:	Y

TYPES OF BUSINESS:

Oil & Gas Drilling Support Services
Seismic Services
Reservoir Imaging
Data & IT Consulting Services
Outsourcing
Stimulation Services

BRANDS/DIVISIONS/AFFILIATES:

Schlumberger Oilfield Services
WesternGeco
Framo Engineering
M-I Drilling Fluids
Extreme Engineering Limited
Saxon Energy Services Inc

CONTACTS:
Note: Officers with more than one job title may be intentionally listed here more than once.

Andrew Gould, CEO
Simon Ayat, CFO/Exec. VP
Ashok Belani, CTO
Satish Pai, VP-Oper., Oilfield Svcs.
Malcolm Theobald, VP-Investor Rel.
Chakib Sbiti, Exec. VP-Oilfield Svcs.
Dalton Boutte, Pres., WesternGeco
Imran Kizilbash, Pres., Reservoir Characterization Group
Doug Pferdehirt, Pres., Reservoir Product Group
Andrew Gould, Chmn.

Phone: 713-513-2000	Fax: 281-285-8548
Toll-Free:	
Address: 5599 San Felipe St., Fl. 17, Houston, TX 77056 US	

GROWTH PLANS/SPECIAL FEATURES:

Schlumberger, Ltd. (SLB) is a leading oil field service company offering technology, project management and information solutions for customers in the international oil and gas industry. Schlumberger operates in 80 countries throughout North America, Latin America, Europe, Africa, the Middle East and Asia in 31 oilfield service GeoMarket regions and 20 research and engineering facilities. The SLB Oilfield Services segment is divided into eight technology-based service lines, which include wireline, drilling and measurements, well testing, well services, completions, artificial lift, data and consulting services and SLB information solutions. The overall purpose of the Oilfield Services sector is to provide proper exploration with production services and technologies throughout the entire life cycle of a reservoir. Another SLB service is its Integrated Project Management (IPM) line, which provides consulting, project management and engineering services for well construction using SLB technology. The company owns 40% of M-I Drilling Fluids along with Smith International, which offers drilling and completion fluids to stabilize rock and minimize formation damage. In addition, the firm owns a majority stake in Framo Engineering, a Norwegian-based company that provides multiphase booster pumps, flow metering equipment and swivel stack systems. Another subsidiary of SLB, WesternGeco, offers worldwide marine and seismic reservoir imaging, data processing centers and a multi-client seismic library for monitoring and development services. Additional services include 3-D, time-lapse and multicomponent surveys for delineating prospects and reservoir management. In June 2008, SLB acquired Extreme Engineering Limited, a supplier of unmanned measurement-while-drilling (MWD) systems. Also during 2008, in partnership with U.S. private equity firm First Reserve, the company acquired Saxon Energy Services, Inc., a Canadian provider of oil field equipment and services.

FINANCIALS:
Sales and profits are in thousands of dollars—add 000 to get the full amount. 2008 Note: Financial information for 2008 was not available for all companies at press time.

2008 Sales: $27,163,000	2008 Profits: $5,435,000	**U.S. Stock Ticker: SLB**
2007 Sales: $23,277,000	2007 Profits: $5,177,000	**Int'l Ticker:** Int'l Exchange:
2006 Sales: $19,230,000	2006 Profits: $3,710,000	Employees: 87,000
2005 Sales: $14,309,000	2005 Profits: $2,207,000	Fiscal Year Ends: 12/31
2004 Sales: $11,480,200	2004 Profits: $1,223,900	Parent Company:

SALARIES/BENEFITS:

Pension Plan: Y	ESOP Stock Plan:	Profit Sharing:	Top Exec. Salary: $2,500,000	Bonus: $1,125,000
Savings Plan: Y	Stock Purch. Plan: Y		Second Exec. Salary: $1,032,478	Bonus: $443,953

OTHER THOUGHTS:

Apparent Women Officers or Directors:
Hot Spot for Advancement for Women/Minorities:

LOCATIONS: ("Y" = Yes)

West:	Southwest:	Midwest:	Southeast:	Northeast:	International:
Y	Y	Y		Y	Y

Note: Financial information, benefits and other data can change quickly and may vary from those stated here.

SCIENTIFIC GAMES CORPORATION

www.scientificgames.com

Industry Group Code: 329999 Ranks within this company's industry group: Sales: 1 Profits: 1

Management:		Sales/Marketing:		Liberal Arts:		Information Systems:		Professionals:		Tech./Scientific:	
Management Trainees:	Y	Marketing Pros.:	Y	Gen. Writing/Editing:	Y	Info. Management:	Y	Finance/Acct.:	Y	Engineers, Electrical:	Y
Experienced Mngmt.:	Y	Retail Sales:		Technical Writing:	Y	Software Dev.:	Y	Law:	Y	Engineers, Other:	Y
International Business:	Y	Commercial/Industrial:	Y	Graphic Arts/Photog.:	Y	Hardware Dev.:		HR/Other:	Y	Health/Lab:	
MBA Grads:	Y	Sales Trainees:		Music:		Consulting/Other:		Training:	Y	Scientists/Research:	
		Advertising Pros.:	Y	Broadcasting:				Health Care:		Petroleum/Chemicals:	
				Other:	Y			Consulting:		Math/Other:	

TYPES OF BUSINESS:

Gambling Equipment-Computer-Based Lottery Systems
Pari-Mutuel Wagering Systems
Satellite Broadcasting Services
Telecommunications Products
Off-Track Betting Facilities Management
Lottery Services
Race Simulcasting
Prepaid Phone Cards

BRANDS/DIVISIONS/AFFILIATES:

Global Draw Limited (The)
Scientific Games Racing LLC
Games Media Limited
Scientific Games China

CONTACTS: Note: Officers with more than one job title may be intentionally listed here more than once.

Joseph R. Wright, CEO
Michael R. Chambrello, COO
Michael R. Chambrello, Pres.
Jeff S. Lipkin, CFO/VP
Ira H. Raphaelson, General Counsel/Corp. Sec./VP
David Pye, VP-Corp. Dev.
Stephen L. Gibbs, Chief Acct. Officer/VP
Robert C. Becker, Treas./VP
Larry A. Potts, Chief Compliance Officer/Corp. Dir.-Security/VP
Brooks Pierce, VP/Pres., Racing & Sports
Steven M. Saferin, Chief Creative Officer/VP
A. Lorne Weil, Chmn.
Yan Xuan, Pres., Greater China

Phone: 212-754-2233	Fax: 212-754-2372
Toll-Free: 800-367-9345	
Address: 750 Lexington Ave. 25th Fl., New York, NY 10022 US	

GROWTH PLANS/SPECIAL FEATURES:

Scientific Games Corp. is a leading supplier of technology-based products, systems and services to gaming markets worldwide, including 40 of the 42 U.S. jurisdictions that currently sell lottery tickets and over 60 countries. Scientific Games operates in three business segments: Printed Products Group, Lottery Systems Group and Diversified Gaming Group. The Printed Products Group is composed of its instant lottery ticket business and its prepaid phone card business, providing lotteries with some of the world's most popular entertainment brands, including Major League Baseball, NASCAR, National Basketball Association, Wheel-of-Fortune, Monopoly, World Poker Tour and Deal or No Deal. The Lottery Systems Group provides software, equipment and data communication services to government-sponsored and privately-operated lotteries in the U.S. and abroad. This segment includes daily numbers, cash games and jackpot games, as well as online alternatives such as instant win, probability, sports and word games. The Diversified Gaming Group provides services and systems to private and public operators in the wide area gaming markets and the wagering industry, with products including fixed odds betting terminals; video lottery terminals; monitor games; wagering systems for the racing industry; sports betting systems and services; and Amusement With Prize and Skill With Prize terminals. Business units within the Diversified Gaming Group include The Global Draw Limited, Scientific Games Racing LLC and Games Media Limited. In January 2009, the company's China-based wholly-owned subsidiary, Scientific Games China, began production of instant lottery tickets with China Sports Lottery Printing, Ltd. The joint venture is the first state of the art instant ticket provider in China.

FINANCIALS: Sales and profits are in thousands of dollars—add 000 to get the full amount. 2008 Note: Financial information for 2008 was not available for all companies at press time.

2008 Sales: $1,118,829	2008 Profits: $8,488	**U.S. Stock Ticker: SGMS**	
2007 Sales: $1,046,704	2007 Profits: $65,367	**Int'l Ticker:** Int'l Exchange:	
2006 Sales: $897,230	2006 Profits: $66,761	Employees: 4,900	
2005 Sales: $781,683	2005 Profits: $75,319	Fiscal Year Ends: 12/31	
2004 Sales: $725,495	2004 Profits: $65,742	Parent Company:	

SALARIES/BENEFITS:

Pension Plan:	ESOP Stock Plan:	Profit Sharing:	Top Exec. Salary: $1,606,367	Bonus: $566,667
Savings Plan: Y	Stock Purch. Plan: Y		Second Exec. Salary: $915,630	Bonus: $486,396

OTHER THOUGHTS:

Apparent Women Officers or Directors: 1
Hot Spot for Advancement for Women/Minorities:

LOCATIONS: ("Y" = Yes)

West:	Southwest:	Midwest:	Southeast:	Northeast:	International:
Y	Y	Y	Y	Y	Y

SCOTTS MIRACLE GROW CO

www.scotts.com

Industry Group Code: 11511 Ranks within this company's industry group: Sales: 2 Profits: 2

Management:		Sales/Marketing:		Liberal Arts:		Information Systems:		Professionals:		Tech./Scientific:	
Management Trainees:	Y	Marketing Pros.:	Y	Gen. Writing/Editing:	Y	Info. Management:	Y	Finance/Acct.:	Y	Engineers, Electrical:	
Experienced Mngmt.:	Y	Retail Sales:	Y	Technical Writing:	Y	Software Dev.:		Law:	Y	Engineers, Other:	Y
International Business:	Y	Commercial/Industrial:	Y	Graphic Arts/Photog.:	Y	Hardware Dev.:		HR/Other:	Y	Health/Lab:	
MBA Grads:	Y	Sales Trainees:	Y	Music:		Consulting/Other:		Training:	Y	Scientists/Research:	Y
		Advertising Pros.:	Y	Broadcasting:				Health Care:		Petroleum/Chemicals:	Y
				Other:				Consulting:		Math/Other:	

TYPES OF BUSINESS:

Horticulture & Turf Products Manufacturer
Fertilizers
Herbicides
Plant Foods
Lawn Services
Outdoor & Garden Products
Plants & Seeds
Mowers & Tractors

BRANDS/DIVISIONS/AFFILIATES:

Turf Builder
Miracle-Gro
Osmocote
Ortho
Weedol
EverGreen
Scotts LawnService
Smith & Hawken

CONTACTS: *Note: Officers with more than one job title may be intentionally listed here more than once.*

Jim Hagedorn, CEO
Mark Baker, COO
Mark Baker, Pres.
Dave Evans, CFO/Exec. VP
Claude Lopez, Chief Mktg. Officer
Denise Stump, Exec. VP-Global Human Resources
Jeff Garascia, Sr. VP-R&D
Mike Lukemire, Sr. VP-Global Tech.
Vince Brockman, General Counsel/Exec. VP
Mike Lukemire, Sr. VP-Oper.
Richard Shank, Chief Environmental Officer/Sr. VP-Gov't Affairs
Barry Sanders, Sr. VP-North America
Michel Gasnier, Sr. VP/CFO-Int'l Oper.
Jim King, Sr. VP-Corp. Affairs
Jim Hagedorn, Chmn.
Claude Lopez, Exec. VP-Int'l
Dave Swihart, Sr. VP-Global Supply Chain

Phone: 937-644-0011	Fax: 937-578-5754
Toll-Free: 888-270-3714	
Address: 14111 Scottslawn Rd., Marysville, OH 43041 US	

GROWTH PLANS/SPECIAL FEATURES:

The Scotts Miracle-Gro Company (SMG) is a marketer of do-it-yourself lawn, garden and home protection products in North America and Europe. Its products include consumer fertilizers, plant foods, soils and mulches, pest controls, grass seed and bird food. The company's principal brands in North America are Scotts, Miracle-Gro, and Ortho. International consumer brands include Miracle-Gro, Evergreen, Fertiligene, Celaflor, KB, Substral, Levington and Weedol. SMG operates through the following business segments: Global Consumer; Global Professional, Scotts LawnService; and Corporate & Other. The Global Consumer segment sells products in the following categories: Lawns, including lawn fertilizer, crabgrass control, weed control or pest control; Gardens, which offers a complete line of plant foods marketed under the Miracle-Gro brand name; Growing Media, which includes potting mix, garden soils, topsoil and manures; Grass Seed products for both the consumer and the professional user; Wild Bird Food, which includes products under the Morning Song and Scotts brands; and Controls, which includes a broad line of weed control, indoor and outdoor pest control and plant disease control products. The Global Professional segment sells professional products to commercial nurseries, greenhouses, and specialty crop growers worldwide and includes control release fertilizers, plant protection products, wetting agents, growing media, and grass seed. Brand names under this segment include Osmocote, Sierrablen Plus, and Scotts Turfseed. The Scotts LawnService segment provides residential lawn care, lawn aeration, tree and shrub care and external pest control services in the U.S. The Corporate and Other segment includes the Smith & Hawken brand of lifestyle products such as high-end outdoor furniture, pottery, garden tools, gardening containers and live goods.

Employees are offered medical, dental and vision benefits; fitness club reimbursements; flexible spending accounts; business travel accident insurance; disability programs; adoption assistance; an employee assistance program; and mental health and substance abuse benefits.

FINANCIALS: Sales and profits are in thousands of dollars—add 000 to get the full amount. 2008 Note: Financial information for 2008 was not available for all companies at press time.

2008 Sales: $2,981,800	2008 Profits: $-10,900	**U.S. Stock Ticker: SMG**
2007 Sales: $2,871,800	2007 Profits: $113,400	**Int'l Ticker:** Int'l Exchange:
2006 Sales: $2,697,100	2006 Profits: $132,700	Employees: 5,303
2005 Sales: $2,369,300	2005 Profits: $100,600	Fiscal Year Ends: 9/30
2004 Sales: $2,106,500	2004 Profits: $100,900	Parent Company:

SALARIES/BENEFITS:

Pension Plan:	ESOP Stock Plan:	Profit Sharing:	Top Exec. Salary: $600,000	Bonus: $293,340
Savings Plan: Y	Stock Purch. Plan: Y		Second Exec. Salary: $420,802	Bonus: $154,395

OTHER THOUGHTS:

Apparent Women Officers or Directors: 5
Hot Spot for Advancement for Women/Minorities: Y

LOCATIONS: ("Y" = Yes)

West:	Southwest:	Midwest:	Southeast:	Northeast:	International:
Y	Y	Y	Y	Y	Y

SEACOR HOLDINGS INC

www.seacorholdings.com

Industry Group Code: 483111 Ranks within this company's industry group: Sales: 1   Profits: 1

Management:		Sales/Marketing:		Liberal Arts:		Information Systems:		Professionals:		Tech./Scientific:	
Management Trainees:	Y	Marketing Pros.:	Y	Gen. Writing/Editing:	Y	Info. Management:	Y	Finance/Acct.:	Y	Engineers, Electrical:	Y
Experienced Mngmt.:	Y	Retail Sales:		Technical Writing:	Y	Software Dev.:	Y	Law:	Y	Engineers, Other:	Y
International Business:	Y	Commercial/Industrial:	Y	Graphic Arts/Photog.:		Hardware Dev.:		HR/Other:	Y	Health/Lab:	
MBA Grads:	Y	Sales Trainees:		Music:		Consulting/Other:		Training:	Y	Scientists/Research:	
		Advertising Pros.:		Broadcasting:				Health Care:		Petroleum/Chemicals:	Y
				Other:				Consulting:		Math/Other:	

TYPES OF BUSINESS:
Offshore Oil Platform Logistics
Inland Shipping
Aviation Services
Environmental Services
Maritime Communications
Helicopter Services

BRANDS/DIVISIONS/AFFILIATES:
V&A Commodity Traders, Inc.
EraMed LLC
National Response Corp.
SCF Marine Inc.
O'Brien Response Management, Inc.
Era Helicopters LLC
Seabulk Towing

CONTACTS: *Note: Officers with more than one job title may be intentionally listed here more than once.*
Charles Fabrikant, CEO
Charles Fabrikant, Pres.
Richard Ryan, CFO/Sr. VP
Paul Robinson, General Counsel/Sr. VP/Corp. Sec.
Dick Fagerstal, Sr. VP-Corp. Dev./Treas.
Molly Hottinger, VP-Corp. Comm.
Molly Hottinger, VP-Investor Rel.
Matthew Cenac, Chief Acct. Officer/VP
John Gellert, Sr. VP-Offshore Marine Svcs.
James Cowderoy, Sr. VP
Randall Blank, Sr. VP/Pres./CEO-Environmental Svcs.
Alice Gran, Sr. VP-Legal Affairs
Charles Fabrikant, Chmn.

Phone: 954-523-2200	Fax: 212-582-8522
Toll-Free:	
Address: 2200 Eller Dr., Ft. Lauderdale, FL 33316 US	

GROWTH PLANS/SPECIAL FEATURES:
SEACOR Holdings, Inc. is in the business of owning, operating, investing in, marketing and remarketing equipment primarily in the offshore oil and gas and inland transportation industries, as well as providing oil spill response and environmental remediation services. The company's operations are divided into six business segments. The firm's principal business segment, offshore marine services, operates a diversified fleet of offshore support vessels primarily servicing offshore oil and gas exploration, development and production facilities worldwide. The marine transportation services segment operates a fleet of eight U.S.-flag tankers providing marine transportation services for petroleum products, petrochemicals and chemicals moving in the U.S. domestic or coastwise trade. The inland river services division, trading under the name SCF Marine, Inc., operates a fleet of 1,096 dry cargo vessels, which carry ore, grain, coal, aggregate, steel, scrap and fertilizers on the U.S rivers and their tributaries and the Gulf Intracoastal Waterways. The aviation services segment operates 176 helicopters primarily servicing the offshore oil and gas markets in the Gulf of Mexico and Alaska. The company's wholly-owned subsidiary, Era Helicopters LLC, supports energy and environmental operations in these areas. EraMed LLC provides medical and Life Flight services. The firm's harbor and offshore towing services subsidiary, Seabulk Towing, is one of the leading tugboat operators in the U.S. Finally, the environmental services group, which comprises various subsidiaries including National Response Corporation and O'Brien Response Management, Inc. among others, provides emergency preparedness services and response services such as management of industrial fires, hazardous materials releases and oil spills. In May 2009, the company acquired V&A Commodity Traders, Inc., a sugar trading business.

FINANCIALS: Sales and profits are in thousands of dollars—add 000 to get the full amount. 2008 Note: Financial information for 2008 was not available for all companies at press time.

2008 Sales: $1,655,956	2008 Profits: $223,688	**U.S. Stock Ticker: CKH**	
2007 Sales: $1,359,230	2007 Profits: $241,648	**Int'l Ticker:** Int'l Exchange:	
2006 Sales: $1,323,445	2006 Profits: $234,394	Employees: 5,316	
2005 Sales: $972,004	2005 Profits: $170,709	Fiscal Year Ends: 12/31	
2004 Sales: $491,860	2004 Profits: $19,889	Parent Company:	

SALARIES/BENEFITS:
Pension Plan:	ESOP Stock Plan:	Profit Sharing:	Top Exec. Salary: $700,000	Bonus: $3,500,000
Savings Plan: Y	Stock Purch. Plan: Y		Second Exec. Salary: $375,000	Bonus: $965,000

OTHER THOUGHTS:
Apparent Women Officers or Directors: 3
Hot Spot for Advancement for Women/Minorities: Y

LOCATIONS: ("Y" = Yes)
West:	Southwest:	Midwest:	Southeast:	Northeast:	International:
Y	Y	Y	Y	Y	Y

Note: Financial information, benefits and other data can change quickly and may vary from those stated here.

SELECT MEDICAL

www.selectmedicalcorp.com

Industry Group Code: 622110 **Ranks within this company's industry group:** Sales: 9   Profits: 7

Management:		Sales/Marketing:		Liberal Arts:		Information Systems:		Professionals:		Tech./Scientific:	
Management Trainees:	Y	Marketing Pros.:	Y	Gen. Writing/Editing:	Y	Info. Management:	Y	Finance/Acct.:	Y	Engineers, Electrical:	
Experienced Mngmt.:	Y	Retail Sales:		Technical Writing:	Y	Software Dev.:	Y	Law:	Y	Engineers, Other:	
International Business:	Y	Commercial/Industrial:		Graphic Arts/Photog.:	Y	Hardware Dev.:		HR/Other:	Y	Health/Lab:	Y
MBA Grads:	Y	Sales Trainees:		Music:		Consulting/Other:		Training:	Y	Scientists/Research:	
		Advertising Pros.:	Y	Broadcasting:				Health Care:	Y	Petroleum/Chemicals:	
				Other:	Y			Consulting:		Math/Other:	

TYPES OF BUSINESS:

Specialty Acute Care Hospitals
Long-Term Acute Care
Outpatient Rehabilitation Clinics
Contract Therapy Services
Medical Equipment Distribution

BRANDS/DIVISIONS/AFFILIATES:

Kessler Institute for Rehabilitation
Kentucky Orthopedic Rehab Team
NovaCare Rehabilitation
Select Physical Therapy
Kessler Rehabilitation Centers

CONTACTS: *Note: Officers with more than one job title may be intentionally listed here more than once.*

Robert A. Ortenzio, CEO
Patricia A. Rice, COO
Patricia A. Rice, Pres.
Martin F. Jackson, CFO/Exec. VP
S. Frank Fritsch, Chief Human Resources Officer/Exec. VP
James J. Talalai, CIO/Exec. VP
Michael E. Tarvin, Chief Legal Officer/Exec. VP/Corp. Sec.
David W. Cross, Chief Dev. Officer/Exec. VP
Scott A. Romberger, Chief Acct. Officer/Controller/Sr. VP
Robert G. Breighner, Jr., VP-Compliance & Audit Svcs.
Robert G. Breighner, Jr., Corp. Compliance Officer
Rocco A. Ortenzio, Exec. Chmn.

Phone: 717-972-1100	Fax: 717-972-1042
Toll-Free:	

Address: 4716 Old Gettysburg Rd., Mechanicsburg, PA 17055 US

GROWTH PLANS/SPECIAL FEATURES:

Select Medical Corporation operates specialty acute care hospitals for long-term stay patients in the U.S. The firm operates 948 outpatient rehabilitation clinics and 92 long-term acute care hospitals across the country. The company also provides medical rehabilitation services on a contract basis at assisted living centers, nursing homes, hospitals, schools, senior care centers and worksites. The firm's business is divided between specialty hospitals and outpatient rehabilitation. The company's hospitals treat patients with serious, often complex medical conditions, such as respiratory failure; neuromuscular disorders; cardiac disorders; non-healing wounds; renal disorders; and cancer. Kessler Institute for Rehabilitation, one of Select Medical's most well known hospitals, specializes in treating amputee, spinal cord, stroke and traumatic brain injuries. The majority of Select Medical's specialty hospitals are located in leased space within a host general hospital. The firm's outpatient rehabilitation segment is designed to help patients minimize physical and cognitive impairments and maximize functional ability. Services at its clinics include physical, occupational and speech rehabilitation programs; work injury prevention and management; sports performance; women's health; vestibular rehabilitation; and athletic training services. This segment operates through brand names such as Kentucky Orthopedic Rehab Team, NovaCare Rehabilitation, Select Physical Therapy and Kessler Rehabilitation Centers.

Select Medical's employee benefits include life, health, dental, vision and prescription insurance; a 401(k); personal and family medical leave; short and long-term disability coverage; continuing education; and tuition reimbursement.

FINANCIALS: Sales and profits are in thousands of dollars—add 000 to get the full amount. 2008 Note: Financial information for 2008 was not available for all companies at press time.

2008 Sales: $2,153,362	2008 Profits: $43,373	**U.S. Stock Ticker: Private**	
2007 Sales: $1,991,666	2007 Profits: $55,145	**Int'l Ticker:**	Int'l Exchange:
2006 Sales: $1,851,498	2006 Profits: $94,879	Employees: 21,300	
2005 Sales: $1,580,706	2005 Profits: $85,575	Fiscal Year Ends: 12/31	
2004 Sales: $1,601,524	2004 Profits: $118,184	Parent Company:	

SALARIES/BENEFITS:

Pension Plan:	ESOP Stock Plan:	Profit Sharing:	Top Exec. Salary: $	Bonus: $640,000
Savings Plan: Y	Stock Purch. Plan:		Second Exec. Salary: $	Bonus: $

OTHER THOUGHTS:

Apparent Women Officers or Directors: 1
Hot Spot for Advancement for Women/Minorities:

LOCATIONS: ("Y" = Yes)

West:	Southwest:	Midwest:	Southeast:	Northeast:	International:
Y	Y	Y	Y	Y	

Note: Financial information, benefits and other data can change quickly and may vary from those stated here.

SEMPRA ENERGY

www.sempra.com

Industry Group Code: 221 Ranks within this company's industry group: Sales: 8 Profits: 6

Management:		Sales/Marketing:		Liberal Arts:		Information Systems:		Professionals:		Tech./Scientific:	
Management Trainees:	Y	Marketing Pros.:	Y	Gen. Writing/Editing:	Y	Info. Management:	Y	Finance/Acct.:	Y	Engineers, Electrical:	Y
Experienced Mngmt.:	Y	Retail Sales:		Technical Writing:	Y	Software Dev.:	Y	Law:	Y	Engineers, Other:	Y
International Business:	Y	Commercial/Industrial:	Y	Graphic Arts/Photog.:	Y	Hardware Dev.:		HR/Other:	Y	Health/Lab:	
MBA Grads:	Y	Sales Trainees:		Music:		Consulting/Other:		Training:	Y	Scientists/Research:	
		Advertising Pros.:	Y	Broadcasting:				Health Care:		Petroleum/Chemicals:	Y
				Other:				Consulting:		Math/Other:	

TYPES OF BUSINESS:

Utilities-Electricity & Natural Gas
Energy Management
Energy Marketing
Power Generation-Natural Gas Plants
LNG Pipelines, Storage & Terminals
Commodities Marketing
Power Generation-Solar Power Plants

BRANDS/DIVISIONS/AFFILIATES:

Southern California Gas Company
San Diego Gas & Electric Company
Sempra Generation
Sempra Commodities
Sempra Pipeline & Storage
Sempra LNG
EnergySouth, Inc.

CONTACTS: Note: Officers with more than one job title may be intentionally listed here more than once.

Donald E. Felsinger, CEO
Neal E. Schmale, COO
Neal E. Schmale, Pres.
Mark A. Snell, CFO/Exec. VP
G. Joyce Rowland, Sr. VP-Human Resources
Javade Chaudhri, General Counsel/Exec. VP
Monica Haas, VP-Corp. Planning
Steven D. Davis, VP-Comm. & Community Partnerships
Jeff Martin, VP-Investor Rel.
Joseph A. Householder, Chief Acct. Officer/Controller/Sr. VP
Jessie J. Knight, Jr., Exec. VP-External Affairs
Amy Chiu, VP-Audit Svcs.
Erbin B. Keith, Chief Compliance Officer/VP-Regulatory Affairs
Richard A. Vaccari, VP-Mergers & Acquisitions
Donald E. Felsinger, Chmn.

Phone: 619-696-2000	Fax: 619-696-2374
Toll-Free: 877-736-7729	
Address: 101 Ash St., San Diego, CA 92101-3017 US	

GROWTH PLANS/SPECIAL FEATURES:

Sempra Energy provides electric, natural gas and other energy products and services mainly in California and internationally. The company operates through two main branches: Sempra Utilities and Sempra Global. Sempra Utilities includes the Southern California Gas Co., a natural gas distribution utility that supplies natural gas to a population of 20.5 million in a 20,000-square-mile service territory in southern and central California. The other segment of Sempra Utilities is San Diego Gas and Electric (SDG&E), which provides electricity distribution and transmission and natural gas distribution services to more than 3 million customers across 4,100 square miles in southern Orange County and San Diego, California. The Sempra Global is primarily composed of subsidiaries not subject to California utility regulations, including Sempra Commodities; Sempra Generation; Sempra Pipelines and Storage; and Sempra LNG. Sempra Generation develops, owns and operates electric power plants in the U.S. and Mexico, including the largest thin-film solar power facility in North America. Sempra Commodities is a joint venture with the Royal Bank of Scotland that markets and trades financial and physical commodity products, including natural gas, oil, power, coal, metals, plastics, steel, green credits and agricultural products. Sempra Pipeline and Storage develops and operates natural gas pipelines and storage facilities in Mexico and the U.S. Sempra LNG develops liquefied natural gas (LNG) receipt terminals in North America. In April 2008, Sempra formed a joint venture with the Royal Bank of Scotland. In October 2008, the firm acquired EnergySouth, Inc. for $510 million. In December 2008, Sempra completed the construction of a 10-megawatt photovoltaic power generation facility in Nevada. In July 2009, the company's new LNG terminal in Louisiana became operational.

Sempra offers its employees medical, dental and vision care; tuition reimbursement; an employee assistance program; a health club membership subsidy; volunteer/giving incentive programs; and a mass-transit/parking subsidy.

FINANCIALS: Sales and profits are in thousands of dollars—add 000 to get the full amount. 2008 Note: Financial information for 2008 was not available for all companies at press time.

2008 Sales: $10,758,000	2008 Profits: $1,113,000	**U.S. Stock Ticker: SRE**
2007 Sales: $11,438,000	2007 Profits: $1,099,000	**Int'l Ticker:** Int'l Exchange:
2006 Sales: $11,761,000	2006 Profits: $1,406,000	Employees: 13,673
2005 Sales: $11,512,000	2005 Profits: $920,000	Fiscal Year Ends: 12/31
2004 Sales: $9,234,000	2004 Profits: $895,000	Parent Company:

SALARIES/BENEFITS:

Pension Plan: Y	ESOP Stock Plan:	Profit Sharing:	Top Exec. Salary: $1,143,957	Bonus: $2,530,000
Savings Plan: Y	Stock Purch. Plan:		Second Exec. Salary: $808,812	Bonus: $1,295,700

OTHER THOUGHTS:

Apparent Women Officers or Directors: 4
Hot Spot for Advancement for Women/Minorities: Y

LOCATIONS: ("Y" = Yes)

West:	Southwest:	Midwest:	Southeast:	Northeast:	International:
Y	Y		Y		Y

Note: Financial information, benefits and other data can change quickly and may vary from those stated here.

SENSIENT TECHNOLOGIES CORPORATION
www.sensient-tech.com

Industry Group Code: 325 Ranks within this company's industry group: Sales: 4 Profits: 3

Management:		Sales/Marketing:		Liberal Arts:		Information Systems:		Professionals:		Tech./Scientific:	
Management Trainees:	Y	Marketing Pros.:	Y	Gen. Writing/Editing:	Y	Info. Management:	Y	Finance/Acct.:	Y	Engineers, Electrical:	
Experienced Mngmt.:	Y	Retail Sales:		Technical Writing:	Y	Software Dev.:	Y	Law:	Y	Engineers, Other:	Y
International Business:	Y	Commercial/Industrial:	Y	Graphic Arts/Photog.:	Y	Hardware Dev.:		HR/Other:	Y	Health/Lab:	
MBA Grads:	Y	Sales Trainees:		Music:		Consulting/Other:		Training:	Y	Scientists/Research:	Y
		Advertising Pros.:		Broadcasting:				Health Care:		Petroleum/Chemicals:	Y
				Other:				Consulting:		Math/Other:	

TYPES OF BUSINESS:
Flavor, Fragrance & Color Chemicals
Inks & Pigments
Pharmaceutical & Cosmetic Ingredients
Specialty Chemicals
Dehydrated Vegetables

BRANDS/DIVISIONS/AFFILIATES:
Sensient Food Colors
Sensient Pharmaceutical Technologies
Sensient Imaging Technologies
Sensient Cosmetic Technologies
Sensient Flavors
Sensient Dehydrated Flavors Company
Sensient Fragrances

CONTACTS: *Note: Officers with more than one job title may be intentionally listed here more than once.*
Kenneth P. Manning, CEO
Neil G. Cracknell, COO
Neil G. Cracknell, Pres.
Richard F. Hobbs, CFO/ Sr. VP
Douglas S. Pepper, VP-Admin.
John L. Hammond, General Counsel/Sec./VP
Stephen J. Rolfs, Chief Acct. Officer/Controller/VP
Peter Bradley, Pres., Color Group
John F. Collopy, Treas./VP
Kenneth P. Manning, Chmn.
Robert Wilkins, Pres., Asia Pacific

Phone: 414-271-6755	Fax: 414-347-3785
Toll-Free: 800-558-9892	
Address: 777 E. Wisconsin Ave., Milwaukee, WI 53202-5304 US	

GROWTH PLANS/SPECIAL FEATURES:

Sensient Technologies Corporation, incorporated in 1882, manufactures and markets fragrances, flavors and colors worldwide. Its operations include producing specialty food and beverage systems; cosmetic and pharmaceutical ingredient systems; and inkjet and specialty inks and colors. The company's customers include major international manufacturers representing some of the world's best-known brands. Sensient is composed of two segments: Flavors & Fragrances Group and Color Group. The Flavors & Fragrances Group manufactures and markets flavor and fragrance systems for food, beverage, household and personal care products. Dehydrated flavors generated 27% of this segment's 2008 revenue; dairy flavors, 21%; savory flavors, 19%; beverage flavors, 9%; confectionary & bakery flavors, 5%; all other flavors, 9%; and all fragrances combined, 10%. Group subsidiaries include Sensient Dehydrated Flavors, Sensient Flavors and Sensient Fragrances. The Color group manufactures and markets natural and synthetic colors, including those for textiles and papers. Food and beverage colors generated 58% of this segment's 2008 revenue; cosmetics, 22%; inkjet & specialty inks and colors, 10%; pharmaceuticals, 4%; and other technical colors, 6%. Trade names within the group include Sensient Food Colors, Sensient Pharmaceutical Technologies, Sensient Cosmetic Technologies and Sensient Imaging Technologies. Headquartered in Australia, the Asia Pacific Group markets the full line of products for Pacific Rim countries, as well as specialty products designed to appeal to local preferences. It maintains manufacturing facilities in Australia, New Zealand and the Philippines. Sensient has 70 offices located across 30 countries, and 59% of its revenue is generated outside the U.S.

FINANCIALS: Sales and profits are in thousands of dollars—add 000 to get the full amount. 2008 Note: Financial information for 2008 was not available for all companies at press time.

2008 Sales: $1,252,620	2008 Profits: $90,861	**U.S. Stock Ticker:** SXT
2007 Sales: $1,184,778	2007 Profits: $77,786	**Int'l Ticker:** Int'l Exchange:
2006 Sales: $1,098,774	2006 Profits: $66,425	Employees: 3,613
2005 Sales: $1,023,930	2005 Profits: $44,195	Fiscal Year Ends: 12/31
2004 Sales: $1,047,133	2004 Profits: $73,918	Parent Company:

SALARIES/BENEFITS:

Pension Plan:	ESOP Stock Plan:	Profit Sharing:	Top Exec. Salary: $878,500	Bonus: $1,493,450
Savings Plan:	Stock Purch. Plan:		Second Exec. Salary: $428,000	Bonus: $556,400

OTHER THOUGHTS:
Apparent Women Officers or Directors: 2
Hot Spot for Advancement for Women/Minorities: Y

LOCATIONS: ("Y" = Yes)

West:	Southwest:	Midwest:	Southeast:	Northeast:	International:
Y		Y		Y	Y

SHAW GROUP INC (THE)

www.shawgrp.com

Industry Group Code: 237 Ranks within this company's industry group: Sales: 4 Profits: 5

Management:		Sales/Marketing:		Liberal Arts:		Information Systems:		Professionals:		Tech./Scientific:	
Management Trainees:	Y	Marketing Pros.:	Y	Gen. Writing/Editing:		Info. Management:	Y	Finance/Acct.:	Y	Engineers, Electrical:	Y
Experienced Mngmt.:	Y	Retail Sales:		Technical Writing:	Y	Software Dev.:		Law:	Y	Engineers, Other:	Y
International Business:	Y	Commercial/Industrial:	Y	Graphic Arts/Photog.:	Y	Hardware Dev.:		HR/Other:	Y	Health/Lab:	
MBA Grads:	Y	Sales Trainees:		Music:		Consulting/Other:		Training:	Y	Scientists/Research:	
		Advertising Pros.:		Broadcasting:				Health Care:		Petroleum/Chemicals:	
				Other:				Consulting:		Math/Other:	

TYPES OF BUSINESS:

Pipe Manufacturing
Construction & Engineering
Consulting Services
Environmental Services
Facilities Management
Power Plant Construction
Nuclear Power Plant Construction

BRANDS/DIVISIONS/AFFILIATES:

Westinghouse Electric Company, L.L.C
Ezeflow, Inc.
Shaw Capital, Inc.

CONTACTS: Note: Officers with more than one job title may be intentionally listed here more than once.

James M. Bernhard, Jr., CEO
Gary P. Graphia, COO/Exec. VP
James M. Bernhard, Jr., Pres.
Brian K. Ferraioli, CFO/Exec. VP
David L. Chapman Sr., Pres., Fabrication & Mfg. Group
Dirk J. Wild, Sr. VP-Admin.
Cliff S. Rankin, General Counsel/Corp. Sec.
Michael J. Kershaw, Sr. VP/Chief Acct. Officer
Robert L. Belk, Exec. VP
Louis J. Pucher, Pres., Energy & Chemicals Group
George P. Bevan, Pres., Environmental & Infrastructure Group
David P. Barry, Pres., Nuclear Div.
James M. Bernhard, Jr., Chmn.
Ronald W. Oakley, Managing Dir.-Europe

Phone: 225-932-2500	Fax: 225-987-3328
Toll-Free:	
Address: 4171 Essen Ln., Baton Rouge, LA 70809 US	

GROWTH PLANS/SPECIAL FEATURES:

The Shaw Group, Inc. is a construction and engineering contractor firm. It is involved in engineering; technology; construction; fabrication; and environmental and industrial services. The company operates in six segments: power; energy & chemicals (E&C); environmental & infrastructure (E&I); power maintenance; fabrication & manufacturing (F&M); and project development, finance and investments (PDF&I). The power segment provides a range of project-related services, primarily to the global fossil and nuclear power generation industries. The E&C division's offerings include design, engineering, construction, procurement, technology and consulting services, primarily to the oil and gas, refinery, petrochemical and chemical industries. The E&I segment designs and executes remediation solutions involving contaminants in soil, air and water. It also provides project/facilities management for non-environmental construction, watershed restoration, emergency response services, program management and solutions to support and enhance domestic and global land, water and air transportation systems. The maintenance segment performs routine and outage/turnaround maintenance, engineering, construction, recovery and specialty services. The power maintenance sector' services include fossil/nuclear maintenance and turbine generator repair. The F&M segment supplies fabricated piping systems. The PDF&I segment is operated by Shaw Group's wholly-owned subsidiary, Shaw Capital, Inc.; this sector handles the evaluation of energy, chemical, infrastructural and environmental investments. The company's customer base includes multinational oil companies and industrial corporations; regulated utilities; independent and merchant power producers; government agencies; and other equipment manufacturers. Shaw recently acquired Ezeflow, Inc., a manufacturer of pipe fittings. In June 2008, the firm agreed to sell the assets of Shaw Energy Delivery Services, Inc., to Pike Electric, Inc., for approximately $24 million. In August 2008, Shaw Group partnered with Westinghouse Electric Company, L.L.C., to build a new fabrication plant in Lake Charles, Louisiana.

FINANCIALS: Sales and profits are in thousands of dollars—add 000 to get the full amount. 2008 Note: Financial information for 2008 was not available for all companies at press time.

2008 Sales: $6,998,011	2008 Profits: $140,717	U.S. Stock Ticker: SGR	
2007 Sales: $5,723,712	2007 Profits: $-19,000	Int'l Ticker:	Int'l Exchange:
2006 Sales: $4,775,649	2006 Profits: $50,226	Employees: 26,000	
2005 Sales: $3,267,702	2005 Profits: $15,671	Fiscal Year Ends: 8/31	
2004 Sales: $3,014,709	2004 Profits: $-33,075	Parent Company:	

SALARIES/BENEFITS:

Pension Plan:	ESOP Stock Plan:	Profit Sharing:	Top Exec. Salary: $1,735,386	Bonus: $264,000
Savings Plan: Y	Stock Purch. Plan:		Second Exec. Salary: $603,891	Bonus: $135,400

OTHER THOUGHTS:

Apparent Women Officers or Directors:
Hot Spot for Advancement for Women/Minorities:

LOCATIONS: ("Y" = Yes)

West:	Southwest:	Midwest:	Southeast:	Northeast:	International:
Y	Y	Y	Y	Y	Y

Note: Financial information, benefits and other data can change quickly and may vary from those stated here.

SHELL OIL CO

www.shell.us

Industry Group Code: 211111 Ranks within this company's industry group: Sales: 4 Profits:

Management:		Sales/Marketing:		Liberal Arts:		Information Systems:		Professionals:		Tech./Scientific:	
Management Trainees:	Y	Marketing Pros.:		Gen. Writing/Editing:	Y	Info. Management:	Y	Finance/Acct.:	Y	Engineers, Electrical:	Y
Experienced Mngmt.:	Y	Retail Sales:		Technical Writing:	Y	Software Dev.:	Y	Law:	Y	Engineers, Other:	Y
International Business:	Y	Commercial/Industrial:		Graphic Arts/Photog.:	Y	Hardware Dev.:		HR/Other:	Y	Health/Lab:	
MBA Grads:	Y	Sales Trainees:		Music:		Consulting/Other:		Training:	Y	Scientists/Research:	Y
		Advertising Pros.:	Y	Broadcasting:				Health Care:		Petroleum/Chemicals:	Y
				Other:				Consulting:		Math/Other:	Y

TYPES OF BUSINESS:

Oil & Gas Exploration & Production
Chemicals
Power Generation
Nanocomposites
Nanocatalysts
Refineries
Pipelines & Shipping
Hydrogen Storage Technology

BRANDS/DIVISIONS/AFFILIATES:

Shell Oil Products US
Shell Chemicals Limited
Shell Gas and Power
Shell Exploration and Production
Royal Dutch Shell (Shell Group)
Motiva Enterprises LLC
Perdido Development

CONTACTS: Note: Officers with more than one job title may be intentionally listed here more than once.

Marvin E. Odum, Pres.
William C. (Bill) Lowrey, General Counsel/Sr. VP/Corp. Sec.
Allen Kirkley, VP-Strategy & Portfolio
Curtis R. Frasier, Exec. VP-Americas Shell Gas & Power
Marvin E. Odum, Exec. VP-Shell Exploration & Production, Americas
Mark Quartermain, Pres., Shell Energy North America (US) L.P.

Phone: 713-241-6161	Fax: 713-241-4044
Toll-Free:	
Address: 1 Shell Plz., 910 Louisiana St., Houston, TX 77002 US	

GROWTH PLANS/SPECIAL FEATURES:

Shell Oil Company, an affiliate of the Shell Group, is a chemical, oil and natural gas producer in the U.S., with operations in all 50 states. Shell Oil has a number of division and operations, including Shell Oil Products U.S., Motiva Enterprises, Shell Chemicals, Shell Gas and Power, Shell Exploration and Production (SEPCo) and others. These companies discover, develop, manufacture, transport and market crude oil, natural gas and chemical products. Specifically, Shell Oil Products has four refineries which produce a total of 753,000 barrels of oil per day, as well as a network of approximately 6,000 branded gasoline stations in the western U.S. Shell Oil Products also maintains 50% ownership of Motiva Enterprises LLC, with whom the firm refines and ships gasoline to approximately 7,900 Shell-branded stations in the eastern and southern U.S. Shell Chemicals is involved in manufacturing chemicals, including ethylene and propylene, for use in cars, computers, packaging and paints. SEPCo explores and develops natural gas in the U.S, with interests in five states and the Gulf of Mexico. Shell Oil's Gas and Power business is involved in power generation, gas pipeline transmission, receiving terminals, liquefied natural gas (LNG), shipping and coal gasification. Other divisions include Shell Hydrogen, focused on the development of hydrogen and fuel cell technologies from regional bases in Houston and Tokyo; and Shell Renewables, which invests heavily in wind and solar power research. During 2008, the firm began work on its Perdido Development project, currently the world's deepest offshore well at 9,365 feet below the water's surface. In December 2008, subsidiary Shell Energy North America acquired the assets of Enspire Energy LLC, a Virginia-based energy marketing firm. In March 2009, the company launched a new nitrogen-enriched gasoline for automotive use, formulated to remove carbon deposits and remain stable at the high operating temperatures common in modern engines.

FINANCIALS: Sales and profits are in thousands of dollars—add 000 to get the full amount. 2008 Note: Financial information for 2008 was not available for all companies at press time.

2008 Sales: $100,818,000	2008 Profits: $	**U.S. Stock Ticker: Subsidiary**
2007 Sales: $87,548,000	2007 Profits: $	**Int'l Ticker:** Int'l Exchange:
2006 Sales: $80,974,000	2006 Profits: $	Employees: 24,000
2005 Sales: $70,000,000	2005 Profits: $	Fiscal Year Ends: 12/31
2004 Sales: $60,000,000	2004 Profits: $	Parent Company: ROYAL DUTCH SHELL (SHELL GROUP)

SALARIES/BENEFITS:

Pension Plan:	ESOP Stock Plan:	Profit Sharing:	Top Exec. Salary: $	Bonus: $
Savings Plan: Y	Stock Purch. Plan:		Second Exec. Salary: $	Bonus: $

OTHER THOUGHTS:

Apparent Women Officers or Directors:
Hot Spot for Advancement for Women/Minorities:

LOCATIONS: ("Y" = Yes)

West:	Southwest:	Midwest:	Southeast:	Northeast:	International:
Y	Y	Y	Y	Y	Y

SHERWIN WILLIAMS COMPANY (THE)

www.sherwin-williams.com

Industry Group Code: 444120 Ranks within this company's industry group: Sales: 1 Profits: 1

Management:		Sales/Marketing:		Liberal Arts:		Information Systems:		Professionals:		Tech./Scientific:	
Management Trainees:	Y	Marketing Pros.:	Y	Gen. Writing/Editing:	Y	Info. Management:	Y	Finance/Acct.:	Y	Engineers, Electrical:	
Experienced Mngmt.:	Y	Retail Sales:	Y	Technical Writing:	Y	Software Dev.:	Y	Law:	Y	Engineers, Other:	
International Business:	Y	Commercial/Industrial:	Y	Graphic Arts/Photog.:	Y	Hardware Dev.:		HR/Other:	Y	Health/Lab:	
MBA Grads:	Y	Sales Trainees:	Y	Music:		Consulting/Other:		Training:	Y	Scientists/Research:	Y
		Advertising Pros.:	Y	Broadcasting:				Health Care:		Petroleum/Chemicals:	Y
				Other:				Consulting:		Math/Other:	

TYPES OF BUSINESS:

Paints & Coatings Manufacturing
Retail Paint Stores
Wall Coverings
Automotive Finishing Products
Design Consulting

BRANDS/DIVISIONS/AFFILIATES:

Duron Inc
Martin-Senour
Dutch Boy
Thompson's
Becker Powder Coatings, Inc
Flex Recubrimientos, Acabados Automotrices
Waterbased Acrolon 100
Polylon HP Polyurethane

CONTACTS: Note: Officers with more than one job title may be intentionally listed here more than once.

Christopher M. Connor, CEO
John G. Morikis, COO
John G. Morikis, Pres.
Sean P. Hennessy, CFO/Sr. VP-Finance
Thomas E. Hopkins, Sr. VP-Human Resources
Richard M. Weaver, VP-Admin.
Louis E. Stellato, General Counsel/Sec./Sr. VP
Timothy A. Knight, Sr. VP-Corp. Planning & Dev.
Robert J. Wells, VP-Corp. Comm. & Public Affairs
Cynthia D. Brogran, Treas./VP
Joel D. Baxter, Pres./Gen Mgr.-Paint & Coatings Div.
George E. Heath, Pres., Global Finishes Group
Thomas W. Seitz, Sr. VP-Strategic Excellence Initiatives
Steven J. Oberfeld, Pres., Paint Stores Group
Christopher M. Connor, Chmn.

Phone: 216-566-2200	Fax: 216-566-2947
Toll-Free: 800-474-3794	
Address: 101 Prospect Ave. NW, Cleveland, OH 44115-1075 US	

GROWTH PLANS/SPECIAL FEATURES:

The Sherwin-Williams Company is one of the largest international manufacturers, distributors and retailers of paint and related products to professional, industrial, commercial and retail customers. The company operates in three segments: paint stores group, consumer group and global finishes group. The paint stores group consists of 3,346 company-operated stores, which sell Sherwin-Williams brand architectural paint and coating and other associated products and brands. Several subsidiaries operate under this division, including Duron, Inc., a Maryland paint producer. In the last year, this segment opened over 100 new stores. It has operations in the U.S., Canada, Puerto Rico, Jamaica, Trinidad and Tobago and the Virgin Islands. This division also sells industrial products, marine products and finishes for original equipment manufacturers (OEM). The consumer group produces and distributes paint, coatings and related products to third-party customers and to the paint stores group (which represented 56% of the consumer group's sales in 2008). The global finishes group, through 541 branches, manufactures, licenses, distributes and sells paints and coatings, industrial and marine products, automotive finishes, refinish products and OEM coatings. In all three segments, the company's varnish, applicators, paint, finishes and coatings are marketed under various name brands, including several private labels such as Sherwin-Williams, Pratt and Lambert, Martin-Senour, Dutch Boy, Thompson's, Minwax and Krylon. Additionally, the firm sells wallpaper and flooring such as Shaw carpet. In 2008, the company along with Marine Coatings, introduced Waterbased Acrolon 100, an environmentally friendly Acrylic Polyurethane and Polylon HP Polyurethane, a low VOC polyester-aliphatic urethane coating.

Employees are offered medical, vision and dental insurance; a pension plan; a 401(k) plan; a stock purchase plan; tuition aid; adoption assistance; an employee discount program; short- and long-term disability coverage; and life insurance.

FINANCIALS: Sales and profits are in thousands of dollars—add 000 to get the full amount. 2008 Note: Financial information for 2008 was not available for all companies at press time.

2008 Sales: $7,980,000	2008 Profits: $477,000	**U.S. Stock Ticker: SHW**
2007 Sales: $8,005,000	2007 Profits: $616,000	**Int'l Ticker:** Int'l Exchange:
2006 Sales: $7,810,000	2006 Profits: $576,000	Employees: 30,677
2005 Sales: $7,191,000	2005 Profits: $463,000	Fiscal Year Ends: 12/31
2004 Sales: $6,113,789	2004 Profits: $393,254	Parent Company:

SALARIES/BENEFITS:

Pension Plan: Y	ESOP Stock Plan:	Profit Sharing:	Top Exec. Salary: $1,214,590	Bonus: $
Savings Plan: Y	Stock Purch. Plan: Y		Second Exec. Salary: $701,295	Bonus: $

OTHER THOUGHTS:

Apparent Women Officers or Directors: 3
Hot Spot for Advancement for Women/Minorities: Y

LOCATIONS: ("Y" = Yes)

West:	Southwest:	Midwest:	Southeast:	Northeast:	International:
Y	Y	Y	Y	Y	Y

SIGMA-ALDRICH CORP

www.sigmaaldrich.com

Industry Group Code: 325 Ranks within this company's industry group: Sales: 3 Profits: 2

Management:		Sales/Marketing:		Liberal Arts:		Information Systems:		Professionals:		Tech./Scientific:	
Management Trainees:	Y	Marketing Pros.:	Y	Gen. Writing/Editing:		Info. Management:	Y	Finance/Acct.:	Y	Engineers, Electrical:	Y
Experienced Mngmt.:	Y	Retail Sales:		Technical Writing:	Y	Software Dev.:	Y	Law:	Y	Engineers, Other:	Y
International Business:	Y	Commercial/Industrial:	Y	Graphic Arts/Photog.:		Hardware Dev.:		HR/Other:	Y	Health/Lab:	
MBA Grads:	Y	Sales Trainees:		Music:		Consulting/Other:		Training:	Y	Scientists/Research:	Y
		Advertising Pros.:		Broadcasting:				Health Care:		Petroleum/Chemicals:	Y
				Other:				Consulting:		Math/Other:	

TYPES OF BUSINESS:

Chemicals Manufacturing
Biotechnology Equipment
Pharmaceutical Ingredients
Fine Chemicals
Chromatography Products

BRANDS/DIVISIONS/AFFILIATES:

Research Essentials
Research Specialties
Research Biotech
SAFC
Seppro
Sigma-Aldrich Quimica Ltda

CONTACTS: *Note: Officers with more than one job title may be intentionally listed here more than once.*

Jai Nagarkatti, CEO
Jai Nagarkatti, Pres.
Rakesh Sachdev, CFO/VP
Gerrit van den Dool, VP-Sales
Doug Rau, VP-Human Resources
Carl Turza, CIO
Rakesh Sachdev, Sec.
Karen Miller, VP-Strategy & Corp. Dev.
Kirk Richter, Treas.
Gilles Cottier, Pres., SAFC
Frank Wicks, Pres., Research Specialties & Essentials
David Smoller, Pres., Research Biotech
Steve Walton, VP-Quality & Safety
Jai Nagarkatti, Chmn.
Dave Julien, Pres., Supply Chain

Phone: 314-771-5765	Fax: 314-771-5757
Toll-Free:	
Address: 3050 Spruce St., St. Louis, MO 63103 US	

GROWTH PLANS/SPECIAL FEATURES:

Sigma-Aldrich Corp. is a life science and technology company that develops, manufactures, purchases and distributes a broad range of biochemicals and organic chemicals. The company offers roughly 100,000 chemicals (including 46,000 chemicals manufactured in-house) and 30,000 equipment products used for scientific and genomic research; biotechnology; pharmaceutical development; disease diagnosis; and pharmaceutical and high technology manufacturing. Sigma-Aldrich is structured into four units: Research essentials, research specialties, research biotech and SAFC, a fine chemicals unit. The research essentials unit sells biological buffers; cell culture reagents; biochemicals; chemicals; solvents; and other reagents and kits. The research specialties unit provides organic chemicals, biochemicals, analytical reagents, chromatography consumables, reference materials and high-purity products. The research biotech unit supplies immunochemical, molecular biology, cell signaling and neuroscience biochemicals and kits used in biotechnology, genomic, proteomic and other life science research applications. The SAFC unit offers large-scale organic chemicals and biochemicals used in development and production by pharmaceutical, biotechnology, industrial and diagnostic companies. The company operates in 37 countries, selling its products in nearly 160 countries and servicing over 1 million customers. Customers include commercial laboratories; pharmaceutical and industrial companies; universities; diagnostics, chemical and biotechnology companies and hospitals; non-profit organizations; and governmental institutions. In January 2009, the firm acquired the Seppro affinity depletion technology and 700 avian-derived antibodies from GenWay Biotech, Inc. Also in 2009, Sigma-Aldrich acquired Sigal Ltda, its Chilean distributor and established Sigma-Aldrich Quimica Ltda.

FINANCIALS: Sales and profits are in thousands of dollars—add 000 to get the full amount. 2008 Note: Financial information for 2008 was not available for all companies at press time.

2008 Sales: $2,200,700	2008 Profits: $341,500	**U.S. Stock Ticker: SIAL**
2007 Sales: $2,038,700	2007 Profits: $311,100	**Int'l Ticker:** Int'l Exchange:
2006 Sales: $1,797,500	2006 Profits: $276,800	Employees: 7,925
2005 Sales: $1,666,500	2005 Profits: $258,300	Fiscal Year Ends: 12/31
2004 Sales: $1,409,200	2004 Profits: $232,900	Parent Company:

SALARIES/BENEFITS:

Pension Plan: Y	ESOP Stock Plan:	Profit Sharing:	Top Exec. Salary: $750,000	Bonus: $356,625
Savings Plan: Y	Stock Purch. Plan:		Second Exec. Salary: $394,167	Bonus: $124,951

OTHER THOUGHTS:

Apparent Women Officers or Directors: 2
Hot Spot for Advancement for Women/Minorities: Y

LOCATIONS: ("Y" = Yes)

West:	Southwest:	Midwest:	Southeast:	Northeast:	International:
Y	Y	Y	Y	Y	Y

SISTERS OF MERCY HEALTH SYSTEMS

www.mercy.net

Industry Group Code: 622110 **Ranks within this company's industry group:** Sales: 8 Profits: 6

Management:		Sales/Marketing:		Liberal Arts:		Information Systems:		Professionals:		Tech./Scientific:	
Management Trainees:	Y	Marketing Pros.:	Y	Gen. Writing/Editing:	Y	Info. Management:	Y	Finance/Acct.:	Y	Engineers, Electrical:	
Experienced Mngmt.:	Y	Retail Sales:		Technical Writing:	Y	Software Dev.:	Y	Law:	Y	Engineers, Other:	
International Business:	Y	Commercial/Industrial:		Graphic Arts/Photog.:	Y	Hardware Dev.:		HR/Other:	Y	Health/Lab:	Y
MBA Grads:	Y	Sales Trainees:		Music:		Consulting/Other:		Training:	Y	Scientists/Research:	
		Advertising Pros.:	Y	Broadcasting:				Health Care:	Y	Petroleum/Chemicals:	
				Other:	Y			Consulting:		Math/Other:	

TYPES OF BUSINESS:

Hospitals-General
Outpatient Care
Health Classes
Long-Term Care
Community Service & Outreach

BRANDS/DIVISIONS/AFFILIATES:

Mercy Health Plans
Sisters of Mercy-St. Louis Regional Community
Mercy Ministries of Laredo

CONTACTS: Note: Officers with more than one job title may be intentionally listed here more than once.

Lynn Britton, CEO
Mike McCurry, COO/Exec. VP
Lynn Britton, Pres.
Randy Combs, CFO/Sr. VP
Judy Akins, VP-Mktg.
Anthony Kinslow, VP-Human Resources
Will Showalter, CIO/VP
Philip Wheeler, General Counsel/Sr. VP
Barb Meyer, VP-Comm.
James R. Jaacks, Exec. VP-Finance
Vance Moore, VP-Resource Optimization/Pres., ROi
Myra K. Aubuchon, Sr. VP
Jolene Goedken, Sr. VP-Medical Svcs.
Glenn Mitchell, Chief Medical Officer/VP
Ronald B. Ashworth, Chmn.

Phone: 314-579-6100	Fax: 314-628-3723
Toll-Free:	
Address: 14528 S. Outer Forty, Ste. 100, Chesterfield, MO 63017 US	

GROWTH PLANS/SPECIAL FEATURES:

Sisters of Mercy Health Systems (Mercy), established in 1986, is one of the largest Catholic health care systems in the U.S. It is sponsored by the St. Louis Regional Community of the Sisters of Mercy religious order. It operates outpatient clinics, physician practices, hospitals, managed health plans and community outreach programs in seven states: Arkansas, Kansas, Louisiana, Mississippi, Missouri, Oklahoma and Texas. The organization's members include a heart hospital, outpatient care facilities, skilled nursing services providers, long-term residential care facilities, stand-alone clinics and over 4,000 licensed beds in 18 acute care hospitals. It runs Mercy Health Plans, an HMO and third-party administrator in communities served by Mercy. The group also operates an active advocacy program for issues of social justice, especially in the field of health care, providing participants with updates on issues of concern and the means of contacting elected officials. Mercy offers a variety of free or inexpensive classes at its hospitals, including a healing-through-the-arts program, babysitter skills training, massage classes, infant care and CPR/first aid classes, as well as substance abuse and terminal illness support groups. With outreach programs in Louisiana, Texas, Mississippi and Belize, Mercy allocates money for subsidized care, community outreach ministries and charity care. It also operates Mercy Ministries of Laredo, an outpatient program that provides services primarily for women, children and the poor, with 14 sites in the Laredo, Texas area. Services include women's and children's health programs, health education, a diabetes center, a domestic violence shelter, and medication assistance and nutritional assistance programs. In April 2008, the company broke ground on a new data center in Washington, Missouri, scheduled to open in 2010. In May 2009, Mercy announced that it was in talks with Catholic Health Initiatives to acquire sponsorship of St. John's Regional Medical Center in Joplin, Missouri.

FINANCIALS: Sales and profits are in thousands of dollars—add 000 to get the full amount. 2008 Note: Financial information for 2008 was not available for all companies at press time.

2008 Sales: $3,747,805	2008 Profits: $54,900	**U.S. Stock Ticker: Nonprofit**
2007 Sales: $3,653,898	2007 Profits: $67,667	**Int'l Ticker:** Int'l Exchange:
2006 Sales: $3,574,416	2006 Profits: $45,708	Employees: 36,818
2005 Sales: $3,246,696	2005 Profits: $55,460	Fiscal Year Ends: 6/30
2004 Sales: $3,012,669	2004 Profits: $97,731	Parent Company:

SALARIES/BENEFITS:

Pension Plan:	ESOP Stock Plan:	Profit Sharing:	Top Exec. Salary: $	Bonus: $
Savings Plan:	Stock Purch. Plan:		Second Exec. Salary: $	Bonus: $

OTHER THOUGHTS:

Apparent Women Officers or Directors: 6
Hot Spot for Advancement for Women/Minorities: Y

LOCATIONS: ("Y" = Yes)

West:	Southwest:	Midwest:	Southeast:	Northeast:	International:
	Y	Y	Y		Y

Note: Financial information, benefits and other data can change quickly and may vary from those stated here.

SMITH INTERNATIONAL INC

www.smith.com

Industry Group Code: 213112 Ranks within this company's industry group: Sales: 3 Profits: 6

Management:		Sales/Marketing:		Liberal Arts:		Information Systems:		Professionals:		Tech./Scientific:	
Management Trainees:	Y	Marketing Pros.:	Y	Gen. Writing/Editing:		Info. Management:	Y	Finance/Acct.:	Y	Engineers, Electrical:	Y
Experienced Mngmt.:	Y	Retail Sales:		Technical Writing:	Y	Software Dev.:	Y	Law:	Y	Engineers, Other:	Y
International Business:	Y	Commercial/Industrial:	Y	Graphic Arts/Photog.:		Hardware Dev.:		HR/Other:	Y	Health/Lab:	
MBA Grads:	Y	Sales Trainees:		Music:		Consulting/Other:		Training:	Y	Scientists/Research:	
		Advertising Pros.:	Y	Broadcasting:				Health Care:		Petroleum/Chemicals:	Y
				Other:				Consulting:		Math/Other:	

TYPES OF BUSINESS:

Oil & Gas Drilling Support Services
Waste Management Services
Drilling Equipment
Supply Chain Services

BRANDS/DIVISIONS/AFFILIATES:

M-I SWACO
Smith Technologies
Smith Services
Wilson
W-H Energy Services, Inc.
Smith Bits
Applied Technologies
Neyrfor

CONTACTS: *Note: Officers with more than one job title may be intentionally listed here more than once.*

John Yearwood, CEO
John Yearwood, COO
John Yearwood, Pres.
Margaret K. Dorman, CFO/Sr. VP/Treas.
Malcolm W. Anderson, Sr. VP-Human Resources
Richard E. Chandler, Jr., General Counsel/Sr. VP/Corp. Sec.
Peter J. Pintar, VP-Corp. Strategy & Bus. Dev.
Geraldine Wilde, VP-Taxes/Asst. Treas.
Bryan L. Dudman, Exec. VP/Pres., Smith Drilling & Evaluation
Christopher I.S. Rivers, CEO/Pres., M-I SWACO
John J. Kennedy, Pres./CEO-Wilson
Michael D. Pearce, Exec. VP/Pres., Smith Technologies
Douglas L. Rock, Chmn.

Phone: 281-443-3370	Fax: 281-233-5996
Toll-Free: 800-877-6484	
Address: P.O. Box 60068, Houston, TX 77205-0068 US	

GROWTH PLANS/SPECIAL FEATURES:

Smith International, Inc. is a leading worldwide supplier of premium products and services to the oil and gas exploration and production industry. The company operates through two segments: Oilfield services and distribution. The company's oilfield products and services segment consists of M-I SWACO, Smith Technologies and Smith Services. M-I SWACO, a 60% owned joint-venture, provides drilling and completion fluid systems, solids-control and separation equipment, engineering and technical services, waste management and oil field production chemicals. Key products include the MUD D-GASSER and SUPER CHOKE pressure controllers. Smith Technologies designs, manufactures and sells three-cone and diamond drill bits, turbines and borehole enlargement tools. These products, as well as well planning software and specialty services, are provided by the individual operating units Smith Bits, Applied Technologies and Nyrfor. Smith Services manufactures and markets products and services for drilling, workover, well completion and well re-entry operations. It sells and rents impact drilling tools such as Hydra-Jar and Accelerator, as well as selling drill collars, subs, stabilizers, kellys and the Hevi-Wate DrillPipe. Smith Services also provides complete fishing, remedial and thru-tubing services. Smith International's distribution segment consists of the Wilson supply chain management company. The company markets pipe, valves and fittings as well as mill, safety and other maintenance products to energy and industrial markets. The firm recently completed the acquisition of W-H Energy Services, Inc., a Texas-based drilling a completion technology company.

Smith International offers its employees medical and dental coverage; life and AD&D insurance; paid time off; a 401(k) plan; educational assistance; dependent scholarships; and an employee assistance program.

FINANCIALS: Sales and profits are in thousands of dollars—add 000 to get the full amount. 2008 Note: Financial information for 2008 was not available for all companies at press time.

2008 Sales: $10,770,838	2008 Profits: $767,284	U.S. Stock Ticker: SII
2007 Sales: $8,764,330	2007 Profits: $647,051	Int'l Ticker: Int'l Exchange:
2006 Sales: $7,333,559	2006 Profits: $502,006	Employees: 25,709
2005 Sales: $5,579,003	2005 Profits: $302,305	Fiscal Year Ends: 12/31
2004 Sales: $4,419,015	2004 Profits: $182,451	Parent Company:

SALARIES/BENEFITS:

Pension Plan: Y	ESOP Stock Plan:	Profit Sharing:	Top Exec. Salary: $1,347,115	Bonus: $1,341,600
Savings Plan: Y	Stock Purch. Plan:		Second Exec. Salary: $631,092	Bonus: $220,513

OTHER THOUGHTS:

Apparent Women Officers or Directors: 3
Hot Spot for Advancement for Women/Minorities: Y

LOCATIONS: ("Y" = Yes)

West:	Southwest:	Midwest:	Southeast:	Northeast:	International:
Y	Y	Y	Y	Y	Y

SMITHFIELD FOODS INC

www.smithfieldfoods.com

Industry Group Code: 311612 Ranks within this company's industry group: Sales: 1 Profits: 1

Management:		Sales/Marketing:		Liberal Arts:		Information Systems:		Professionals:		Tech./Scientific:	
Management Trainees:	Y	Marketing Pros.:	Y	Gen. Writing/Editing:	Y	Info. Management:	Y	Finance/Acct.:	Y	Engineers, Electrical:	
Experienced Mngmt.:	Y	Retail Sales:		Technical Writing:		Software Dev.:		Law:	Y	Engineers, Other:	
International Business:	Y	Commercial/Industrial:	Y	Graphic Arts/Photog.:	Y	Hardware Dev.:		HR/Other:	Y	Health/Lab:	
MBA Grads:	Y	Sales Trainees:	Y	Music:		Consulting/Other:		Training:	Y	Scientists/Research:	
		Advertising Pros.:	Y	Broadcasting:				Health Care:		Petroleum/Chemicals:	
				Other:				Consulting:		Math/Other:	

TYPES OF BUSINESS:

Meat Processing, Pork
Hog Production
Beef Production
Turkey Production and Processing

BRANDS/DIVISIONS/AFFILIATES:

Premium Standard Firms Inc
Smithfield Premium Genetics
Butterball LLC
Campofrio Food Group

CONTACTS: *Note: Officers with more than one job title may be intentionally listed here more than once.*

C. Larry Pope, CEO
George H. Richter, COO/Pres.
C. Larry Pope, Pres.
Robert W. Manly, IV, CFO/Exec. VP
Joseph W. Luter, IV, Exec. VP-Mktg. & Sales
Mansour T. Zadeh, CIO
Henry L. Morris, Sr. Corp. VP-Eng.
Michael H. Cole, Chief Legal Officer/VP/Sec.
Henry L. Morris, Sr. Corp. VP-Oper.
Jerry Hostetter, VP-Corp. Comm.
Jerry Hostetter, VP-Investor Rel.
Carey J. Dubois, VP-Finance
Richard J.M. Poulson, Exec. VP-Mergers & Acquisitions
Jeffrey A. Deel, Corp. Controller/VP
Michael D. Flemming, Sr. Counsel/VP
Dennis H. Treacy, VP-Environmental & Corp. Affairs
Joseph W. Luter, III, Chmn.
Jeffrey M. Luckman, VP-Livestock Procurement

Phone: 757-365-3000	**Fax:** 757-365-3017
Toll-Free: 888-366-6767	
Address: 200 Commerce St., Smithfield, VA 23430 US	

GROWTH PLANS/SPECIAL FEATURES:

Smithfield Foods, Inc. is a hog producer, processor and supplier of pork and turkey products. The firms companies and joint ventures offer over 50 brands of pork and turkey items and more than 200 gourmet foods. Brands offered include Smithfield, Butterball, Farmland, John Morrell, Armour and Eckrich, among others. It operates in four segments: pork, international, hog production, other and corporate. The pork segment produces a variety of fresh pork and packaged meat products in the U.S. and markets them in the U.S. and internationally. In 2008, the division processed 31 million hogs and sold approximately 4 billion pounds of fresh pork and nearly 3.1 billion pounds of packaged meat products. The international segment includes the company's international meat processing operations that produce a wide variety of fresh and packaged meats products. In 2008, packaged meats proved to be the largest source of revenue for the international division with 41% of sales; fresh pork made up 19%; and other meat products (which include poultry, beef, by-products and rendering) made up 40%. The hog producing segment operates numerous hog production facilities with roughly 1.1 million sows producing approximately 19.4 million market hogs annually. The segment also owns certain genetic lines of specialized breeding stock that are marketed using the name Smithfield Premium Genetics. The other segment is comprised of the turkey production and hatchery operations; and the 49% interests in Butterball, LLC. The corporate segment is comprised of firm operations not related to the other segments. In December 2008, the firm completed a merger between Campofrio Alimentacion S.A. and Group Smithfield Holdings S.L. The newly formed company is called Campofrio Food Group. In October 2008, the company sold Smithfield Beef Group, Inc. to JBS S.A. for approximately $565 million. The sale included its beef processing and cattle feeding operations, as well as Five Rivers Ranch Cattle Feeding LLC.

FINANCIALS: Sales and profits are in thousands of dollars—add 000 to get the full amount. 2008 Note: Financial information for 2008 was not available for all companies at press time.

2008 Sales: $11,351,200	2008 Profits: $128,900	**U.S. Stock Ticker:** SFD
2007 Sales: $9,359,300	2007 Profits: $166,800	**Int'l Ticker:** Int'l Exchange:
2006 Sales: $8,828,100	2006 Profits: $172,700	Employees: 52,400
2005 Sales: $11,248,400	2005 Profits: $296,200	Fiscal Year Ends: 4/30
2004 Sales: $9,178,200	2004 Profits: $227,100	Parent Company:

SALARIES/BENEFITS:

Pension Plan: Y	ESOP Stock Plan:	Profit Sharing:	Top Exec. Salary: $1,100,000	Bonus: $
Savings Plan: Y	Stock Purch. Plan:		Second Exec. Salary: $800,000	Bonus: $1,500,000

OTHER THOUGHTS:

Apparent Women Officers or Directors:
Hot Spot for Advancement for Women/Minorities:

LOCATIONS: ("Y" = Yes)

West:	Southwest:	Midwest:	Southeast:	Northeast:	International:
	Y	Y	Y	Y	Y

Note: Financial information, benefits and other data can change quickly and may vary from those stated here.

SOUTHERN CALIFORNIA EDISON COMPANY

www.sce.com

Industry Group Code: 2211   Ranks within this company's industry group: Sales: Profits:

Management:		Sales/Marketing:		Liberal Arts:		Information Systems:		Professionals:		Tech./Scientific:	
Management Trainees:	Y	Marketing Pros.:	Y	Gen. Writing/Editing:	Y	Info. Management:	Y	Finance/Acct.:	Y	Engineers, Electrical:	Y
Experienced Mngmt.:	Y	Retail Sales:		Technical Writing:	Y	Software Dev.:	Y	Law:	Y	Engineers, Other:	Y
International Business:		Commercial/Industrial:	Y	Graphic Arts/Photog.:	Y	Hardware Dev.:		HR/Other:	Y	Health/Lab:	
MBA Grads:	Y	Sales Trainees:		Music:		Consulting/Other:		Training:	Y	Scientists/Research:	
		Advertising Pros.:		Broadcasting:				Health Care:		Petroleum/Chemicals:	
				Other:				Consulting:		Math/Other:	

TYPES OF BUSINESS:

Electric Utility
Nuclear Generation
Hydroelectric Generation

BRANDS/DIVISIONS/AFFILIATES:

Edison International

CONTACTS:
Note: Officers with more than one job title may be intentionally listed here more than once.

Alan J. Fohrer, CEO
John Fielder, Pres.
Thomas Noonan, CFO/Sr. VP
Mahvash Yazdi, CIO/Sr. VP-Bus. Integration
Stephen E. Pickett, General Counsel/Sr. VP
Cecil R. House, Sr. VP-Oper. Support/Chief Procurement Officer
Barbara J. Parsky, Sr. VP-Corp. Comm.
Linda G. Sullivan, Controller/VP
Richard M. Rosenblum, Sr. VP-Generation
Ronald Litzinger, Sr. VP-Transmission & Distribution
Lynda L. Ziegler, Sr. VP-Customer Service
Polly L. Gault, Sr. VP-Public Affairs
Alan J. Fohrer, Chmn.
Pedro J. Pizarro, VP-Power Procurement

Phone: 626-302-1212	**Fax:** 626-302-2517
Toll-Free: 800-655-4555	
Address: 2244 Walnut Grove Ave., Rosemead, CA 91770 US	

GROWTH PLANS/SPECIAL FEATURES:

Southern California Edison Company (SCE) is one of the largest electric utilities in the U.S. The firm is the largest subsidiary of Edison International, an electric power generator, distributor and investor in infrastructure and renewable energy projects. SCE serves more than 13 million individuals in 430 cities and communities in a 50,000-square-mile service area within central, coastal and southern California, excluding Los Angeles. The firm operates the following generating facilities: a 78.21% interest in San Onofre Units 2 and 3, pressurized water nuclear units with 1,690 MW capacity; the natural-gas fueled Mountainview plant, 1,050 MW capacity; 36 hydroelectric plants located in surrounding mountain passes, 1,179 MW; a 15.8% interest in Palo Verde, 601 MW; a 48% in Units 4 and 5 at Four Corners Generating Station, 720 MW; and other smaller generating facilities. It has a total capacity of 42% nuclear, 22% hydroelectric, 23% natural gas, 13% coal and less than 1% diesel, with power generation in California, Nevada, Arizona and New Mexico. SCE's transmission network consists of approximately 12,000 circuit miles of lines and 858 substations, while its distribution network consists of approximately 60,000 circuit miles of overhead lines, 39,000 miles of underground lines, 1.5 million poles and 588 distribution substations. In 2007, revenue was generated from the following customers: 41% commercial customers, 37% residential customers, 4% resale sales, 7% industrial customers, 5% other electric revenue, 5% public authorities, and 1% agricultural and other customers.

Employee benefits include medical, dental, and vision benefits; 401(k) with company match; employee assistance program; retirement pension plan; and educational reimbursements.

FINANCIALS:
Sales and profits are in thousands of dollars—add 000 to get the full amount. 2008 Note: Financial information for 2008 was not available for all companies at press time.

2008 Sales: $	2008 Profits: $	**U.S. Stock Ticker:** Subsidiary
2007 Sales: $10,478,000	2007 Profits: $	**Int'l Ticker:** Int'l Exchange:
2006 Sales: $10,312,000	2006 Profits: $827,000	Employees:
2005 Sales: $9,500,000	2005 Profits: $749,000	Fiscal Year Ends: 12/31
2004 Sales: $8,448,000	2004 Profits: $921,000	Parent Company: EDISON INTERNATIONAL

SALARIES/BENEFITS:

Pension Plan: Y	ESOP Stock Plan:	Profit Sharing:	Top Exec. Salary: $	Bonus: $1,936,000
Savings Plan: Y	Stock Purch. Plan:		Second Exec. Salary: $	Bonus: $

OTHER THOUGHTS:

Apparent Women Officers or Directors: 4
Hot Spot for Advancement for Women/Minorities: Y

LOCATIONS: ("Y" = Yes)

West:	Southwest:	Midwest:	Southeast:	Northeast:	International:
Y	Y				

SOUTHERN COMPANY (THE)

www.southerncompany.com

Industry Group Code: 2211 Ranks within this company's industry group: Sales: 1 Profits: 1

Management:		Sales/Marketing:		Liberal Arts:		Information Systems:		Professionals:		Tech./Scientific:	
Management Trainees:	Y	Marketing Pros.:	Y	Gen. Writing/Editing:	Y	Info. Management:	Y	Finance/Acct.:	Y	Engineers, Electrical:	Y
Experienced Mngmt.:	Y	Retail Sales:		Technical Writing:	Y	Software Dev.:	Y	Law:	Y	Engineers, Other:	Y
International Business:		Commercial/Industrial:	Y	Graphic Arts/Photog.:	Y	Hardware Dev.:		HR/Other:	Y	Health/Lab:	
MBA Grads:	Y	Sales Trainees:		Music:		Consulting/Other:		Training:	Y	Scientists/Research:	
		Advertising Pros.:	Y	Broadcasting:				Health Care:		Petroleum/Chemicals:	Y
				Other:				Consulting:		Math/Other:	

TYPES OF BUSINESS:

Utilities-Electricity & Natural Gas
Wireless Communications Services
Fiber Optic Solutions
Nuclear Power Operating Services
Consulting Services

BRANDS/DIVISIONS/AFFILIATES:

Alabama Power Company
Georgia Power Company
Mississippi Power Company
Gulf Power Company
Southern Power
SEGCO
Southern Nuclear
SouthernLINC Wireless

CONTACTS: *Note: Officers with more than one job title may be intentionally listed here more than once.*

David M. Ratcliffe, CEO
Thomas A. Fanning, COO/Exec. VP
David M. Ratcliffe, Pres.
W. Paul Bowers, CFO/Exec. VP
G. Edison Holland, Jr., General Counsel/Exec. VP/Corp. Sec.
Michael D. Garrett, Exec. VP/CEO/Pres., Georgia Power
C. Alan Martin, Exec. VP/CEO/Pres., Southern Company Svcs.
Charles D. McCrary, Exec. VP/CEO/Pres., Alabama Power
James H. (Jim) Miller, III, CEO/Pres., Southern Nuclear
David M. Ratcliffe, Chmn.

Phone: 404-506-5000	Fax: 404-506-0455
Toll-Free:	
Address: 30 Ivan Allen Jr. Blvd. N.W., Atlanta, GA 30308 US	

GROWTH PLANS/SPECIAL FEATURES:

The Southern Company, through its subsidiaries, is a producer and distributor of electricity in the U.S. Its four main subsidiaries (Alabama Power Company; Georgia Power Company; Mississippi Power Company; and Gulf Power Company) have a combined service territory of 120,000 square miles. It also owns Southern Power, which constructs, acquires and manages power generation assets as well as selling electricity wholesale. Southern Power currently owns almost 5,400 megawatts (MW) of generating capacity, through a total of six power plants, and serves 75 utilities, electric cooperatives and municipalities across six states. Alabama Power and Georgia Power each own 50% of SEGCO, which operates a power generation plant and 230,000 miles of transmission lines in Alabama, supplying electricity to both Alabama and Georgia. Combined, the company's utility subsidiaries have a generating capacity of roughly 42,000 MW and serve more than 4.4 million residential, commercial and industrial electricity customers in the southeastern U.S. through approximately 27,000 miles of transmission lines. Its sources of generation consist of 68% coal; 16% oil and gas; 15% nuclear; and 1% hydro. The firm also owns Southern Nuclear, which operates the company's three nuclear power plants; SouthernLINC Wireless, which provides communications services; and Southern Telecom, which is a wholesaler of fiber optics. In December 2008, Southern Power announced plans to build an electric generating plant in North Carolina, with construction expected to begin in 2010 and be completed by 2012.

The Southern Company offers its employees tuition reimbursement, credit union membership, a U.S. savings bond program, financial planning services, an employee assistance program, flexible spending accounts and medical, prescription, business travel, disability and life insurance.

FINANCIALS: Sales and profits are in thousands of dollars—add 000 to get the full amount. 2008 Note: Financial information for 2008 was not available for all companies at press time.

2008 Sales: $17,127,000	2008 Profits: $1,742,000	**U.S. Stock Ticker: SO**
2007 Sales: $15,353,000	2007 Profits: $1,734,000	**Int'l Ticker:** Int'l Exchange:
2006 Sales: $14,356,000	2006 Profits: $1,573,000	Employees: 27,276
2005 Sales: $13,554,000	2005 Profits: $1,591,000	Fiscal Year Ends: 12/31
2004 Sales: $11,729,000	2004 Profits: $1,532,000	Parent Company:

SALARIES/BENEFITS:

Pension Plan: Y	ESOP Stock Plan:	Profit Sharing:	Top Exec. Salary: $1,118,090	Bonus: $5,267,878
Savings Plan: Y	Stock Purch. Plan:		Second Exec. Salary: $679,641	Bonus: $1,283,734

OTHER THOUGHTS:

Apparent Women Officers or Directors: 3
Hot Spot for Advancement for Women/Minorities: Y

LOCATIONS: ("Y" = Yes)

West:	Southwest:	Midwest:	Southeast:	Northeast:	International:
			Y		

SOUTHWEST AIRLINES CO

www.southwest.com

Industry Group Code: 481111　Ranks within this company's industry group: Sales: 1　Profits: 1

Management:		Sales/Marketing:		Liberal Arts:		Information Systems:		Professionals:		Tech./Scientific:	
Management Trainees:	Y	Marketing Pros.:	Y	Gen. Writing/Editing:	Y	Info. Management:	Y	Finance/Acct.:	Y	Engineers, Electrical:	Y
Experienced Mngmt.:	Y	Retail Sales:		Technical Writing:	Y	Software Dev.:	Y	Law:	Y	Engineers, Other:	Y
International Business:		Commercial/Industrial:		Graphic Arts/Photog.:	Y	Hardware Dev.:		HR/Other:	Y	Health/Lab:	
MBA Grads:	Y	Sales Trainees:	Y	Music:		Consulting/Other:		Training:	Y	Scientists/Research:	
		Advertising Pros.:	Y	Broadcasting:				Health Care:	Y	Petroleum/Chemicals:	
				Other:	Y			Consulting:		Math/Other:	

TYPES OF BUSINESS:

Airline-Domestic
Air Freight

BRANDS/DIVISIONS/AFFILIATES:

CONTACTS: *Note: Officers with more than one job title may be intentionally listed here more than once.*

Gary C. Kelly, CEO
Michael G. Van De Ven, COO/Exec. VP
Gary Kelly, Pres.
Laura H. Wright, CFO
Dave Ridley, Sr. VP-Mktg. & Revenue Mgmt.
Jeff Lamb, Chief People Officer
Jan Marshall, CIO
Bob Young, CTO/VP-Tech
Jim Sokol, VP-Eng. & Maintenance
Jeff Lamb, Sr. VP-Admin.
Deborah Ackerman, General Counsel/VP
Greg Wells, Sr. VP-Oper.
Robert E. Jordan, Exec. VP-Strategy & Planning
Ginger C. Hardage, Sr. VP-Corp. Comm. & Culture
Laura H. Wright, Sr. VP-Finance
Daryl Krause, Sr. VP-Customer Service
Ron Ricks, Exec. VP-Corp. Svcs./Sec.
Mike Hafner, VP-Inflight Svcs.
Ellen Torbert, VP-Reservations
Gary C. Kelly, Chmn.
Ray Sears, VP-Purchasing

Phone: 214-792-4000	**Fax:** 214-792-5015
Toll-Free: 800-435-9792	
Address: 2702 Love Field Dr., Dallas, TX 75235 US	

GROWTH PLANS/SPECIAL FEATURES:

Southwest Airlines Co. is a low-fare domestic airline that provides short haul, high-frequency airline services. Southwest is one of the four largest carriers in the U.S. based on number of domestic passengers. The firm operates 537 Boeing 737 planes, serving 64 cities in 32 states throughout the U.S. The firm serves 438 nonstop city pairs, and operates approximately 3,200 flights daily. Its busiest routes include those to Las Vegas, Phoenix, Baltimore, Houston, Chicago and Dallas. Using only one type of airplane simplifies the company's scheduling, maintenance, flight operations and training activities. Southwest also utilizes a very simple fare structure that features unlimited, low-cost coach fares. The firm employs a point-to-point route system which provides for more direct nonstop flights that minimize connections, delays and total trip time. Southwest primarily flies to many conveniently located secondary or downtown airports such as Dallas Love Field, Houston Hobby, Chicago Midway, Baltimore-Washington International, Burbank, Manchester, Oakland, Providence, and Long Island Islip airports, which are typically less congested than other airlines' hub airports. The airline flies its planes an average of seven flights totaling 12 hours daily. Southwest focuses principally on point-to-point service, which allows for more direct nonstop routing, thereby minimizing connections, delays, and total trip time. As a result, approximately 78% of Southwest's Customers fly nonstop. The company made a profit for 30 straight years.

Employees of the firm are offered medical, dental, vision and life insurance; health and dependent care spending accounts; adoption assistance; an employee assistance program; a 401(k) plan; a profit sharing plan; an employee stock purchase plan; free flights Southwest Airlines and discounted flights with other carriers; the Buddy Pass Program; various travel related discounts; access to the University for People; the Manager in Training Program (MIT); and personal development and leadership training.

FINANCIALS: Sales and profits are in thousands of dollars—add 000 to get the full amount. 2008 Note: Financial information for 2008 was not available for all companies at press time.

2008 Sales: $11,023,000	2008 Profits: $178,000	**U.S. Stock Ticker:** LUV
2007 Sales: $9,860,000	2007 Profits: $645,000	**Int'l Ticker:**　Int'l Exchange:
2006 Sales: $9,086,000	2006 Profits: $499,000	Employees: 35,499
2005 Sales: $7,584,000	2005 Profits: $484,000	Fiscal Year Ends: 12/31
2004 Sales: $6,530,000	2004 Profits: $215,000	Parent Company:

SALARIES/BENEFITS:

Pension Plan:	ESOP Stock Plan:	Profit Sharing: Y	Top Exec. Salary: $441,121	Bonus: $462,000
Savings Plan: Y	Stock Purch. Plan: Y		Second Exec. Salary: $346,375	Bonus: $340,000

OTHER THOUGHTS:

Apparent Women Officers or Directors: 11
Hot Spot for Advancement for Women/Minorities: Y

LOCATIONS: ("Y" = Yes)

West:	Southwest:	Midwest:	Southeast:	Northeast:	International:
	Y	Y		Y	

Note: Financial information, benefits and other data can change quickly and may vary from those stated here.

SRA INTERNATIONAL INC

www.sra.com

Industry Group Code: 541513 Ranks within this company's industry group: Sales: 8 Profits: 8

Management:		Sales/Marketing:		Liberal Arts:		Information Systems:		Professionals:		Tech./Scientific:	
Management Trainees:	Y	Marketing Pros.:	Y	Gen. Writing/Editing:	Y	Info. Management:	Y	Finance/Acct.:	Y	Engineers, Electrical:	Y
Experienced Mngmt.:	Y	Retail Sales:		Technical Writing:	Y	Software Dev.:	Y	Law:	Y	Engineers, Other:	
International Business:		Commercial/Industrial:	Y	Graphic Arts/Photog.:	Y	Hardware Dev.:	Y	HR/Other:	Y	Health/Lab:	
MBA Grads:	Y	Sales Trainees:		Music:		Consulting/Other:	Y	Training:	Y	Scientists/Research:	
		Advertising Pros.:	Y	Broadcasting:				Health Care:		Petroleum/Chemicals:	
				Other:	Y			Consulting:	Y	Math/Other:	Y

TYPES OF BUSINESS:

Technology Consulting
Strategic Consulting
Systems Design
Systems Integration
Managed Services
Outsourcing

BRANDS/DIVISIONS/AFFILIATES:

RABA Technologies, LLC
NetOwl
ORIONMagic
Era Systems Corporation
Interface & Control Systems, Inc.

CONTACTS: Note: Officers with more than one job title may be intentionally listed here more than once.

Stanton D. Sloane, CEO
Timothy J. Atkin, COO/Exec. VP
Stanton D. Sloane, Pres.
Melissa Burgum, Acting CFO
Jeffrey Rydant, Sr. VP-Mktg. & Sales
Mary E. Good, Sr. VP-Human Resources
Brian Michl, CIO/VP
David L. Matthews, Sr. VP-Tech. Oper.
Mark D. Schultz, General Counsel
Michael M. Fox, Sr. VP-Strategic Dev.
Sheila S. Blackwell, VP-Comm. & Public Affairs
David Keefer, Dir.-Investor Rel.
Judith K. Sakowitz, Quality Systems Officer/VP
Stewart Simonson, VP-Gov't Affairs
Patrick Burke, Sr. VP-National Security Sector
Max N. Hall, Sr. VP-Civil Sector
Ernst Volgenau, Chmn.

Phone: 703-803-1500	Fax: 703-803-1509
Toll-Free:	
Address: 4300 Fair Lakes Ct., Fairfax, VA 22033 US	

GROWTH PLANS/SPECIAL FEATURES:

SRA International, Inc. provides technology and strategic consulting services and solutions to a broad range of clients involved in national security; civil government; and health care and public health. Its largest market is national security, in which the firm services the Department of Defense, the National Guard, the Department of Homeland Security, the CIA and FBI and various other federal agencies with homeland security missions. The company's services across all sectors include strategic consulting; systems design, development and integration; outsourcing and managed services; contingency and disaster response planning; information assurance; business intelligence; privacy protection; enterprise architecture; infrastructure management; and wireless integration. Currently, SRA serves over 300 government clients on over 900 active engagements. The firm uses proprietary NetOwl text mining software tools and ORIONMagic knowledge management software to improve a client's method of managing, exploiting and analyzing large amounts of data. In July 2008, the company acquired Era Systems Corporation and Interface & Control Systems, Inc. In September of the same year, SRA sold Constella Futures LLC.

Employees are offered medical, vision and dental insurance; a 401(k) plan; life insurance; disability coverage; health and dependent care flexible spending programs; a stock purchase program; educational assistance; commuter expense reimbursement; college savings plans; and financial planning assistance.

FINANCIALS: Sales and profits are in thousands of dollars—add 000 to get the full amount. 2008 Note: Financial information for 2008 was not available for all companies at press time.

2008 Sales: $1,506,933	2008 Profits: $73,264	U.S. Stock Ticker: SRX
2007 Sales: $1,268,872	2007 Profits: $63,430	Int'l Ticker: Int'l Exchange:
2006 Sales: $1,179,267	2006 Profits: $62,520	Employees: 6,977
2005 Sales: $881,770	2005 Profits: $57,723	Fiscal Year Ends: 6/30
2004 Sales: $615,802	2004 Profits: $38,937	Parent Company:

SALARIES/BENEFITS:

Pension Plan:	ESOP Stock Plan:	Profit Sharing:	Top Exec. Salary: $650,000	Bonus: $450,812
Savings Plan: Y	Stock Purch. Plan: Y		Second Exec. Salary: $325,000	Bonus: $267,518

OTHER THOUGHTS:

Apparent Women Officers or Directors: 5
Hot Spot for Advancement for Women/Minorities: Y

LOCATIONS: ("Y" = Yes)

West:	Southwest:	Midwest:	Southeast:	Northeast:	International:
Y	Y	Y	Y	Y	

ST JUDE MEDICAL INC

www.sjm.com

Industry Group Code: 33911 **Ranks within this company's industry group:** Sales: 7   Profits: 8

Management:		Sales/Marketing:		Liberal Arts:		Information Systems:		Professionals:		Tech./Scientific:	
Management Trainees:	Y	Marketing Pros.:	Y	Gen. Writing/Editing:	Y	Info. Management:	Y	Finance/Acct.:	Y	Engineers, Electrical:	Y
Experienced Mngmt.:	Y	Retail Sales:		Technical Writing:	Y	Software Dev.:	Y	Law:	Y	Engineers, Other:	Y
International Business:	Y	Commercial/Industrial:	Y	Graphic Arts/Photog.:	Y	Hardware Dev.:		HR/Other:	Y	Health/Lab:	Y
MBA Grads:	Y	Sales Trainees:	Y	Music:		Consulting/Other:		Training:	Y	Scientists/Research:	Y
		Advertising Pros.:	Y	Broadcasting:				Health Care:	Y	Petroleum/Chemicals:	
				Other:				Consulting:		Math/Other:	

TYPES OF BUSINESS:

Cardiovascular Medical Devices
Cardiac Rhythm Management Devices
Cardiac Surgery Devices
Cardiology Devices
Atrial Fibrillation Devices

BRANDS/DIVISIONS/AFFILIATES:

Radi Medical AB
Victory
MediGuide, Inc.
EP MedSystems, Inc.

CONTACTS: *Note: Officers with more than one job title may be intentionally listed here more than once.*

Daniel J. Starks, CEO
Daniel J. Starks, Pres.
John C. Heinmiller, CFO/Exec. VP
Paul Bae, VP-Human Resources
Mark D. Carlson, Chief Medical Officer
Thomas R. Northenscold, CIO/VP-IT
Thomas R. Northenscold, VP-Admin.
Pamela S. Krop, General Counsel/VP/Sec.
Angela D. Craig, VP-Corp. Rel.
Jane J. Song, Pres., Atrial Fibrillation Div.
Christopher G. Chavez, Pres., Neuromodulation Div.
Eric S. Fain, Pres., Cardiac Rhythm Mgmt. Div.
Frank J. Callaghan, Pres., Cardiovascular Div.
Daniel J. Starks, Chmn.
Denis M. Gestin, Pres., Int'l Div.

Phone: 651-483-2000	Fax: 651-482-8318
Toll-Free: 800-328-9634	
Address: 1 Lillehei Plz., St. Paul, MN 55117 US	

GROWTH PLANS/SPECIAL FEATURES:

St. Jude Medical, Inc. is a developer, manufacturer and distributor of cardiovascular medical devices and implantable neuromodulation devices. The company operates in four segments: cardiac rhythm management, whose products include tachycardia implantable cardioverter defribrillator systems and bradycardia pacemaker systems; cardiovascular, whose products include vascular closure devices, heart valves and valve repair products; neuromodulation systems, whose products include neurostimulation devices; and atrial fibrillation, whose products include electrophysiology introducers/catheters, advanced cardiac mapping/navigation systems and ablation systems. St. Jude's Neuromodulation Division focuses its efforts on the related therapy areas. Neuromodulation is the delivery of very small, precise doses of electric current or drugs directly to nerve sites and is aimed at treating patients suffering from chronic pain or other disabling nervous system disorders. The firm markets and sells its products through a direct sales force and independent distributors. The principal geographic markets for its products are the U.S., Europe, Japan and the Asia-Pacific region. St. Jude also sells products in Canada and Latin America. The cardiac rhythm management products generate approximately 61.9% of St. Jude Medical's revenues. In July 2008, the company acquired EP MedSystems, Inc., which develops, manufactures and markets products for cardiac rhythm management. In November 2008, the firm launched its Victory pacemaker series in Japan. In December 2008, St. Jude Medical acquired two companies: Radi Medical AB, a marketer of cardiovascular medical devices, and Israeli cardiology navigation technology provider MediGuide, Inc.

The company offers its employees benefits including medical, dental and vision coverage; flexible spending accounts; access to a credit union; life and disability insurance; a physical fitness program; a matching gift program; and tuition reimbursement.

FINANCIALS: Sales and profits are in thousands of dollars—add 000 to get the full amount. 2008 Note: Financial information for 2008 was not available for all companies at press time.

2008 Sales: $4,363,251	2008 Profits: $384,327	**U.S. Stock Ticker: STJ**
2007 Sales: $3,779,277	2007 Profits: $559,038	**Int'l Ticker:** Int'l Exchange:
2006 Sales: $3,302,447	2006 Profits: $548,251	Employees: 14,000
2005 Sales: $2,915,280	2005 Profits: $393,490	Fiscal Year Ends: 12/31
2004 Sales: $2,294,173	2004 Profits: $409,934	Parent Company:

SALARIES/BENEFITS:

Pension Plan:	ESOP Stock Plan:	Profit Sharing: Y	Top Exec. Salary: $993,750	Bonus: $1,365,413
Savings Plan: Y	Stock Purch. Plan: Y		Second Exec. Salary: $652,308	Bonus: $746,892

OTHER THOUGHTS:

Apparent Women Officers or Directors: 4
Hot Spot for Advancement for Women/Minorities: Y

LOCATIONS: ("Y" = Yes)

West:	Southwest:	Midwest:	Southeast:	Northeast:	International:
Y	Y	Y	Y	Y	Y

STAPLES INC

www.staples.com

Industry Group Code: 453210 **Ranks within this company's industry group:** Sales: 1 Profits: 1

Management:		Sales/Marketing:		Liberal Arts:		Information Systems:		Professionals:		Tech./Scientific:	
Management Trainees:	Y	Marketing Pros.:	Y	Gen. Writing/Editing:	Y	Info. Management:	Y	Finance/Acct.:	Y	Engineers, Electrical:	
Experienced Mngmt.:	Y	Retail Sales:	Y	Technical Writing:		Software Dev.:	Y	Law:	Y	Engineers, Other:	
International Business:	Y	Commercial/Industrial:	Y	Graphic Arts/Photog.:	Y	Hardware Dev.:		HR/Other:	Y	Health/Lab:	
MBA Grads:	Y	Sales Trainees:	Y	Music:		Consulting/Other:		Training:	Y	Scientists/Research:	
		Advertising Pros.:	Y	Broadcasting:				Health Care:		Petroleum/Chemicals:	
				Other:	Y			Consulting:		Math/Other:	

TYPES OF BUSINESS:

Office Supplies, Retail
Contract Stationery Services
Online & Catalog Sales
Catalogs
Office Furniture

BRANDS/DIVISIONS/AFFILIATES:

Quill Corp.
Staples Business Delivery
Staples National Advantage
Staples Business Advantage

CONTACTS: *Note: Officers with more than one job title may be intentionally listed here more than once.*

Ronald L. Sargent, CEO
Michael Miles, COO
Michael Miles, Pres.
John J. Mahoney, CFO
Jevin Eagle, Head-Merch.
Kristin A. Campbell, General Counsel/Sr. VP/Sec.
Christine T. Komola, Corp. Controller/Sr. VP
Joseph G. Doody, Pres., North American Delivery
Demos Parneros, Pres., U.S. Retail
Ronald L. Sargent, Chmn.

Phone: 508-253-5000	Fax: 508-253-8989
Toll-Free: 800-378-2753	
Address: 500 Staples Dr., Framingham, MA 01702 US	

GROWTH PLANS/SPECIAL FEATURES:

Staples Inc. markets office supply products through three sales channels: North American retail, North American delivery and international operations. The North American retail segment, consisting of 1,835 stores throughout the U.S. and Canada at the end of fiscal 2008, generates the majority of the firm's sales and profits. The North American retail stores are located in 47 states, Washington, D.C., 10 Canadian provinces and two Canadian territories in both major metropolitan markets and smaller markets. The company also markets its products via catalogues and the Internet. A typical superstore carries over 1,000 Staples-brand and 7,000 brand-name products, including ink and toner; paper; small business machines; computers; and peripherals, as well as a copy center and a business technology center. The North American delivery segment comprises three business units: Staples business delivery, Quill Corp. and the contract business. The Staples business delivery segment operations consist of the combined direct mail catalog and Internet sales both in the U.S. and Canada, and it is tailored primarily to the needs of small and medium-sized businesses. Quill Corp., a direct mail catalog and Internet distributor, supplies business products to more than 1 million small to medium-sized businesses in the U.S. Staples National Advantage and Staples Business Advantage, the firm's contract stationery operations, focus primarily on serving medium to large businesses. The international operations division handles all retail stores, catalog and Internet businesses operating in 27 countries in Europe, South America and Asia and comprises the firm's 58.79% interest in Corporate Express Australia Limited. The company also markets its products via catalogues and the Internet. In July 2008, Staples acquired Corporate Express N.V.

The company offers its employees medical, dental and vision insurance; life and disability insurance; a 401(k) plan; an employee stock purchase plan; domestic partner benefits; homeowners, auto, legal and pet insurance; tuition reimbursement; and shopping discounts.

FINANCIALS: Sales and profits are in thousands of dollars—add 000 to get the full amount. 2008 Note: Financial information for 2008 was not available for all companies at press time.

2008 Sales: $19,372,682	2008 Profits: $995,670	**U.S. Stock Ticker:** SPLS
2007 Sales: $18,160,789	2007 Profits: $973,677	**Int'l Ticker:** Int'l Exchange:
2006 Sales: $16,078,852	2006 Profits: $834,409	Employees: 91,125
2005 Sales: $14,448,378	2005 Profits: $708,388	Fiscal Year Ends: 1/31
2004 Sales: $13,181,222	2004 Profits: $490,211	Parent Company:

SALARIES/BENEFITS:

Pension Plan:	ESOP Stock Plan:	Profit Sharing:	Top Exec. Salary: $1,112,000	Bonus: $
Savings Plan: Y	Stock Purch. Plan: Y		Second Exec. Salary: $673,400	Bonus: $

OTHER THOUGHTS:

Apparent Women Officers or Directors: 3
Hot Spot for Advancement for Women/Minorities: Y

LOCATIONS: ("Y" = Yes)

West:	Southwest:	Midwest:	Southeast:	Northeast:	International:
Y	Y	Y	Y	Y	Y

Note: Financial information, benefits and other data can change quickly and may vary from those stated here.

STARTEK INC

www.startek.com

Industry Group Code: 561 **Ranks within this company's industry group:** Sales: 1 Profits: 1

Management:		Sales/Marketing:		Liberal Arts:		Information Systems:		Professionals:		Tech./Scientific:	
Management Trainees:	Y	Marketing Pros.:	Y	Gen. Writing/Editing:	Y	Info. Management:	Y	Finance/Acct.:	Y	Engineers, Electrical:	
Experienced Mngmt.:	Y	Retail Sales:		Technical Writing:	Y	Software Dev.:	Y	Law:	Y	Engineers, Other:	
International Business:	Y	Commercial/Industrial:	Y	Graphic Arts/Photog.:	Y	Hardware Dev.:		HR/Other:	Y	Health/Lab:	
MBA Grads:	Y	Sales Trainees:		Music:		Consulting/Other:		Training:	Y	Scientists/Research:	
		Advertising Pros.:		Broadcasting:				Health Care:		Petroleum/Chemicals:	
				Other:				Consulting:		Math/Other:	

TYPES OF BUSINESS:

Outsourcing-Supply Chain Management
Business Process Management
Telecommunications Services
Internet Domain Name Licensing

BRANDS/DIVISIONS/AFFILIATES:

StarTek Connect

CONTACTS: *Note: Officers with more than one job title may be intentionally listed here more than once.*

A. Laurence Jones, CEO
A. Laurence Jones, Pres.
David Durham, CFO
Mary Beth Loesch, Sr. VP-Mktg.
Susan Morse, Sr. VP-Human Resources
Doug Pontious, CIO
Michael Stefanoudakis, General Counsel/Corp. Sec.
Chad Thorpe, Sr. VP-Oper.
Mary Beth Loesch, Sr. VP-Bus. Dev.
David Durham, Treas.
Faye Victora, VP-@Home Oper.
Bret Milne, Regional VP-Oper.
Lana Little, VP-Process Improvement & Support Svcs.
Ed Zschau, Chmn.

Phone: 303-262-4500	Fax: 303-388-9970
Toll-Free: 800-541-1130	
Address: 44 Cook St., Ste. 400, Denver, CO 80206 US	

GROWTH PLANS/SPECIAL FEATURES:

StarTek, Inc. provides business process management services to the communications industry. Its offerings include provision management, customer care, receivables management, wireless telephone activations, high-end technical support and wireline telephone number portability services. The company provides these services through 22 operational facilities in the U.S., the Philippines and Canada. StarTek operates in three segments that are based on these geographic regions. The firm's business process optimization services include large scale project implementation, distributed resource planning and extended training and quality assurance, which ultimately lowers operational costs, improves quality and adds value to client companies. Current technologies of the company include virtual queuing; hosted IT infrastructure and application services; eWorkforce management; IP-PBX; quality assurance monitoring; and disposition tolls. In addition, StarTek offers a communications package that provides software, infrastructure and service through Telephony via TDM (Time Division Multiplexing); Telephony via VoIP (Voice Over Internet Protocol); Unified e-Mail; IVR (Interactive Voice Response); CTI (Computer Telephony Integration); and StarTek Connect, which allows end-to-end integrated, real time reporting. In April 2008, the company announced plans to open a new customer care center in Jonesboro, Arkansas. In January 2009, the firm opened its Makati facility, officially beginning operations in the Philippines.

The firm offers its employees life, health, dental and vision insurance; an employee assistance program; flexible vacation time; a 401(K); and bereavement and military leave.

FINANCIALS: Sales and profits are in thousands of dollars—add 000 to get the full amount. 2008 Note: Financial information for 2008 was not available for all companies at press time.

2008 Sales: $272,890	2008 Profits: $-9,901	**U.S. Stock Ticker: SRT**
2007 Sales: $245,304	2007 Profits: $-2,831	**Int'l Ticker:** Int'l Exchange:
2006 Sales: $237,612	2006 Profits: $5,764	Employees: 9,500
2005 Sales: $216,371	2005 Profits: $12,860	Fiscal Year Ends: 12/31
2004 Sales: $221,906	2004 Profits: $20,976	Parent Company:

SALARIES/BENEFITS:

Pension Plan:	ESOP Stock Plan:	Profit Sharing:	Top Exec. Salary: $463,500	Bonus: $157,244
Savings Plan: Y	Stock Purch. Plan:		Second Exec. Salary: $323,750	Bonus: $65,936

OTHER THOUGHTS:

Apparent Women Officers or Directors: 4
Hot Spot for Advancement for Women/Minorities: Y

LOCATIONS: ("Y" = Yes)

West:	Southwest:	Midwest:	Southeast:	Northeast:	International:
Y	Y	Y	Y	Y	Y

STARWOOD HOTELS & RESORTS WORLDWIDE INC

www.starwoodhotels.com

Industry Group Code: 721110 Ranks within this company's industry group: Sales: 3 Profits: 2

Management:		Sales/Marketing:		Liberal Arts:		Information Systems:		Professionals:		Tech./Scientific:	
Management Trainees:	Y	Marketing Pros.:	Y	Gen. Writing/Editing:	Y	Info. Management:	Y	Finance/Acct.:	Y	Engineers, Electrical:	
Experienced Mngmt.:	Y	Retail Sales:		Technical Writing:		Software Dev.:	Y	Law:	Y	Engineers, Other:	
International Business:	Y	Commercial/Industrial:	Y	Graphic Arts/Photog.:	Y	Hardware Dev.:		HR/Other:	Y	Health/Lab:	
MBA Grads:	Y	Sales Trainees:	Y	Music:		Consulting/Other:		Training:	Y	Scientists/Research:	
		Advertising Pros.:	Y	Broadcasting:				Health Care:		Petroleum/Chemicals:	
				Other:	Y			Consulting:		Math/Other:	

TYPES OF BUSINESS:

Hotels & Resorts
Financial Services
Hotel Management & Franchising
Spa Services
Online Auction Web Site
Preferred Guest Club

BRANDS/DIVISIONS/AFFILIATES:

Sheraton
W
Four Points
Westin
Le Meridien
St. Regis
Luxury Collection
Aloft

CONTACTS: Note: Officers with more than one job title may be intentionally listed here more than once.

Frits van Paasschen, CEO
Frits van Paasschen, Pres.
Vasant M. Prabhu, CFO/Exec. VP
Christie Hicks, Sr. VP-Global Sales
Jeffrey M. Cava, Exec. VP/Chief Human Resources Officer
Phil McAveety, Exec. VP/Chief Brand Officer
Kenneth S. Siegel, Chief Admin. Officer
Kenneth S. Siegel, General Counsel
Simon Turner, Pres., Global Dev.
Alan Schnaid, Controller/Sr. VP
Roeland Vos, Pres., EMEA Div.
Lynne Dougherty, Sr. VP-Owner Rel. & Franchise
Miguel Ko, Pres., Asia-Pacific
Bruce W. Duncan, Chmn.
Osvaldo V. Librizzi, Pres., Latin America

Phone: 914-640-8100	Fax: 914-640-8310
Toll-Free:	
Address: 1111 Westchester Ave., White Plains, NY 10604 US	

GROWTH PLANS/SPECIAL FEATURES:

Starwood Hotels & Resorts Worldwide, Inc. manages the global operation of hotels and resorts, primarily in the luxury and upscale segments of the industry. It owns, leases, manages or franchises approximately 942 hotels containing about 285,000 rooms in roughly 100 countries. The company's hotel brand names include St. Regis, The Luxury Collection, W, Westin, Le Meridien, Sheraton, Four Points, Aloft and Element. The firm's earnings are derived mainly from its hotel and leisure operations; the receipt of franchise fees; and the development, ownership and operation of vacation ownership resorts. Additionally, Starwood provides financing to customers who purchase interests in resorts. The firm's frequent guest loyalty program, Starwood Preferred Guest, boasts over 47 million members and is unique in the hotel industry for its lack of capacity controls and blackout dates. Starwood's property portfolio includes the St. Regis in New York, New York; The Phoenician in Scottsdale, Arizona; the Hotel Gritti Palace in Venice, Italy; and the St. Regis in Beijing, China. From 2008 through 2012, Starwood plans the construction of a number of new hotels, at least half of which will be in countries such as China, India and Qatar. In September 2008, the company announced the opening of the St. Regis Bali Resort. The firm also plans to open approximately 70 Aloft hotels between 2009 and 2011, with new locations under development in North America, Europe, the Middle East, India, Thailand and China. The Aloft brand of select-service hotels opened its first location in 2008, and currently has 26 operational hotels, including an international hotel in Beijing, which opened in November 2008.

The company offers its employees medical, dental and vision insurance; a 401(k) plan; life and disability insurance; an employee stock purchase plan; an employee assistance program; and domestic partner benefits.

FINANCIALS: Sales and profits are in thousands of dollars—add 000 to get the full amount. 2008 Note: Financial information for 2008 was not available for all companies at press time.

2008 Sales: $5,907,000	2008 Profits: $329,000	U.S. Stock Ticker: HOT
2007 Sales: $6,153,000	2007 Profits: $542,000	Int'l Ticker: Int'l Exchange:
2006 Sales: $5,979,000	2006 Profits: $1,043,000	Employees: 145,000
2005 Sales: $5,977,000	2005 Profits: $422,000	Fiscal Year Ends: 12/31
2004 Sales: $5,368,000	2004 Profits: $395,000	Parent Company:

SALARIES/BENEFITS:

Pension Plan:	ESOP Stock Plan:	Profit Sharing:	Top Exec. Salary: $1,000,000	Bonus: $1,365,000
Savings Plan: Y	Stock Purch. Plan:		Second Exec. Salary: $638,054	Bonus: $437,249

OTHER THOUGHTS:

Apparent Women Officers or Directors: 8
Hot Spot for Advancement for Women/Minorities: Y

LOCATIONS: ("Y" = Yes)

West:	Southwest:	Midwest:	Southeast:	Northeast:	International:
Y	Y	Y	Y	Y	Y

Note: Financial information, benefits and other data can change quickly and may vary from those stated here.

STERIS CORP

www.steris.com

Industry Group Code: 33911 **Ranks within this company's industry group:** Sales: 13 Profits: 13

Management:		Sales/Marketing:		Liberal Arts:		Information Systems:		Professionals:		Tech./Scientific:	
Management Trainees:	Y	Marketing Pros.:		Gen. Writing/Editing:		Info. Management:	Y	Finance/Acct.:	Y	Engineers, Electrical:	Y
Experienced Mngmt.:	Y	Retail Sales:		Technical Writing:	Y	Software Dev.:	Y	Law:	Y	Engineers, Other:	Y
International Business:	Y	Commercial/Industrial:	Y	Graphic Arts/Photog.:	Y	Hardware Dev.:		HR/Other:	Y	Health/Lab:	Y
MBA Grads:	Y	Sales Trainees:		Music:		Consulting/Other:		Training:	Y	Scientists/Research:	Y
		Advertising Pros.:	Y	Broadcasting:				Health Care:	Y	Petroleum/Chemicals:	
				Other:				Consulting:		Math/Other:	

TYPES OF BUSINESS:

Healthcare Products & Related Services
Life Sciences Products
Sterilization Services

BRANDS/DIVISIONS/AFFILIATES:

STERIS Isomedix Services
STERIS SYSTEM 1
Finn-Aqua
Amsco
STERIS 5085 SRT (The)
STERIS 5085 (The)
Reliance Vision Single-Chamber Washer/Disinfector
STERIS 4085 (The)

CONTACTS: *Note: Officers with more than one job title may be intentionally listed here more than once.*

Walter M. Rosebrough Jr., CEO
Walter M. Rosebrough Jr., Pres.
Michael J. Tokich, CFO/Sr. VP
Peter A. Burke, CTO/Sr. VP
Gerard J. Reis, Sr. VP/Group Pres., Admin. & Gov't
Mark D. McGinley, General Counsel/Sr. VP/Sec.
Stephen Norton, Dir.-Corp. Comm.
William L. Aamoth, Corp. Treas./VP
Timothy L. Chapman, Sr. VP/Pres., Healthcare
Robert E. Moss, Pres., Steris Isomedix Svcs.
R. Gregoire Blackmore, Sr. VP/Pres., Life Sciences
John P. Wareham, Chmn.

Phone: 440-354-2600	Fax: 440-392-8972
Toll-Free: 800-548-4873	
Address: 5960 Heisley Rd., Mentor, OH 44060 US	

GROWTH PLANS/SPECIAL FEATURES:

Steris Corp. provides infection prevention and surgical products/services to the healthcare, pharmaceutical and research markets. The company offers capital products such as sterilizers and surgical tables; consumable products such as detergents and skin care products; bulk sterilization of single-use medical devices; and services, such as equipment installation and maintenance. The firm operates in four segments: healthcare, life sciences, STERIS Isomedix Services and corporate/other. The healthcare segment, which accounts for about 71.7% of the firm's revenues, manufactures and sells capital equipment and accessories used in surgical and critical environments; emergency departments; gastrointestinal and sterile processing environments; and in infection control processes. This segment also provides various equipment maintenance programs and repair services to support effective operation of health care equipment. The health care segment includes products such as the company's STERIS SYSTEM 1, a complete system for sterile processing at or near the site of patient care. The life sciences segment, responsible for roughly 16.7% of revenues, provides decontamination and sterilization technologies, products and services to pharmaceutical manufacturers and research facilities. Systems and products offered include brand names such as Finn-Aqua and Amsco sterilizers; Reliance washers; and consumable products for contamination prevention, surface cleaning and sterility assurance. STERIS Isomedix Services, which contributes about 11.0% of revenues, performs sterilization services on a contract basis through 20 facilities in North America, where Steris sterilizes medical devices and other products in bulk. The corporate/other segment houses the defense and industrial division; which accounts for approximately 1% of the company's revenues. In March 2009, the firm agreed to collaborate with GE Healthcare, thereby allowing Steris products to be carried on GE's interventional suites. In March and June 2009, the firm launched five new products: The Reliance Vision Single-Chamber Washer/Disinfector; The STERIS 4085, 5085 and 5085 SRT Surgical Tables; and the Reliance 680PG Pharmaceutical Grade Washer.

FINANCIALS: Sales and profits are in thousands of dollars—add 000 to get the full amount. 2008 Note: Financial information for 2008 was not available for all companies at press time.

2008 Sales: $1,265,090	2008 Profits: $77,106	**U.S. Stock Ticker:** STE
2007 Sales: $1,197,407	2007 Profits: $82,155	**Int'l Ticker:** Int'l Exchange:
2006 Sales: $1,160,285	2006 Profits: $70,289	Employees: 5,000
2005 Sales: $1,081,674	2005 Profits: $85,980	Fiscal Year Ends: 3/31
2004 Sales: $1,031,908	2004 Profits: $94,243	Parent Company:

SALARIES/BENEFITS:

Pension Plan:	ESOP Stock Plan:	Profit Sharing:	Top Exec. Salary: $745,593	Bonus: $1,265,250
Savings Plan: Y	Stock Purch. Plan:		Second Exec. Salary: $316,845	Bonus: $141,445

OTHER THOUGHTS:

Apparent Women Officers or Directors: 2
Hot Spot for Advancement for Women/Minorities: Y

LOCATIONS: ("Y" = Yes)

West:	Southwest:	Midwest:	Southeast:	Northeast:	International:
Y	Y	Y	Y	Y	Y

STIFEL FINANCIAL CORP

www.stifel.com

Industry Group Code: 523110 Ranks within this company's industry group: Sales: 2 Profits: 2

Management:		Sales/Marketing:		Liberal Arts:		Information Systems:		Professionals:		Tech./Scientific:	
Management Trainees:	Y	Marketing Pros.:	Y	Gen. Writing/Editing:	Y	Info. Management:	Y	Finance/Acct.:	Y	Engineers, Electrical:	
Experienced Mngmt.:	Y	Retail Sales:		Technical Writing:		Software Dev.:	Y	Law:	Y	Engineers, Other:	
International Business:	Y	Commercial/Industrial:		Graphic Arts/Photog.:		Hardware Dev.:		HR/Other:	Y	Health/Lab:	
MBA Grads:	Y	Sales Trainees:		Music:		Consulting/Other:		Training:	Y	Scientists/Research:	
		Advertising Pros.:		Broadcasting:				Health Care:		Petroleum/Chemicals:	
				Other:				Consulting:		Math/Other:	

TYPES OF BUSINESS:

Stock Brokerage/Investment Banking
Underwriting
Broker-Dealer
Investment Advisory Services
Research
Insurance
Annuities

BRANDS/DIVISIONS/AFFILIATES:

Stifel Nicolaus & Company, Inc.
Century Securities Associates, Inc.
Stifel Nicolaus Ltd.
Stifel Bank & Trust

CONTACTS: Note: Officers with more than one job title may be intentionally listed here more than once.

Ronald J. Kruszewski, CEO
Ronald J. Kruszewski, Pres.
James M. Zemlyak, CFO/Sr. VP
David M. Minnick, General Counsel/Sr. VP/Corp. Sec.
James M. Zemlyak, Treas.
Thomas P. Mulroy, Exec. VP/Dir.-Equity Markets, Stifel Nicolaus
Richard J. Himelfarb, Dir.-Investment Banking, Stifel Nicolaus
James M. Zemlyak, CFO/Co-COO, Stifel Nicolaus
Scott B. McCuaig, Pres./Co-COO-Stifel Nicolaus
Ronald J. Kruszewski, Chmn.

Phone: 314-342-2000	**Fax:** 314-342-2151
Toll-Free:	
Address: 501 N. Broadway, St. Louis, MO 63102-2188 US	

GROWTH PLANS/SPECIAL FEATURES:

Stifel Financial Corp. is a financial services holding company. Its principal subsidiary is Stifel Nicolaus & Company, Inc., a full service retail and institutional brokerage and investment banking firm. Other subsidiaries include Century Securities Associates, Inc. (CSA), an independent contractor broker-dealer firm; Stifel Nicolaus Limited, the company's international subsidiary; and Stifel Bank & Trust, a retail and commercial bank. The Stifel group of companies provides research, brokerage, trading, investment banking, investment advisory, insurance, annuities and related financial services to customers throughout the U.S. and internationally. The firm operates in the following business segments: Private Client Group, Equity Capital Markets, Fixed Income Capital Markets, Stifel Bank and Other. The Private Client segment provides securities transaction, brokerage and investment services to clients through the consolidated Stifel Nicolaus branch system and through CSA, which has affiliations with approximately 197 independent contractors in 33 states. The Equity Capital Markets segment includes research, institutional sales and trading, investment banking and syndicate. The Fixed Income Capital Markets segment includes public finance; institutional sales and competitive underwriting; and trading. The Stifel Bank segment offers retail and commercial banking services to private and corporate clients in the St. Louis area. The Other segment includes revenues and expenses associated with the clearing of transactions by Stifel Nicolaus for another non-affiliated independent introducing broker-dealer, along with certain overhead costs. The company operates 194 offices in 35 states and Washington D.C. through Stifel Nicolaus & Company, Inc and three European offices through Stifel Nicolaus Limited.

The company offers its employees medical and dental insurance; life and AD&D insurance; life insurance; long-term disability insurance; personal accident and travel accident insurance; an employee assistance plan; a profit sharing and 401(k) plan; an employee stock ownership plan; and tuition assistance.

FINANCIALS: Sales and profits are in thousands of dollars—add 000 to get the full amount. 2008 Note: Financial information for 2008 was not available for all companies at press time.

2008 Sales: $888,847	2008 Profits: $55,502	**U.S. Stock Ticker:** SF
2007 Sales: $793,090	2007 Profits: $32,170	**Int'l Ticker:** Int'l Exchange:
2006 Sales: $471,388	2006 Profits: $15,431	Employees: 3,371
2005 Sales: $270,010	2005 Profits: $19,644	Fiscal Year Ends: 12/31
2004 Sales: $246,823	2004 Profits: $23,148	Parent Company:

SALARIES/BENEFITS:

Pension Plan:	ESOP Stock Plan: Y	Profit Sharing: Y	Top Exec. Salary: $250,000	Bonus: $910,000
Savings Plan: Y	Stock Purch. Plan:		Second Exec. Salary: $200,000	Bonus: $2,720,000

OTHER THOUGHTS:

Apparent Women Officers or Directors:
Hot Spot for Advancement for Women/Minorities:

LOCATIONS: ("Y" = Yes)

West:	Southwest:	Midwest:	Southeast:	Northeast:	International:
Y	Y	Y	Y	Y	Y

Note: Financial information, benefits and other data can change quickly and may vary from those stated here.

STRYKER CORP

www.stryker.com

Industry Group Code: 33911 **Ranks within this company's industry group:** Sales: 6 Profits: 4

Management:		Sales/Marketing:		Liberal Arts:		Information Systems:		Professionals:		Tech./Scientific:	
Management Trainees:	Y	Marketing Pros.:	Y	Gen. Writing/Editing:	Y	Info. Management:	Y	Finance/Acct.:	Y	Engineers, Electrical:	
Experienced Mngmt.:	Y	Retail Sales:		Technical Writing:	Y	Software Dev.:	Y	Law:	Y	Engineers, Other:	Y
International Business:	Y	Commercial/Industrial:	Y	Graphic Arts/Photog.:	Y	Hardware Dev.:		HR/Other:	Y	Health/Lab:	Y
MBA Grads:	Y	Sales Trainees:		Music:		Consulting/Other:		Training:	Y	Scientists/Research:	Y
		Advertising Pros.:	Y	Broadcasting:				Health Care:	Y	Petroleum/Chemicals:	
				Other:				Consulting:		Math/Other:	

TYPES OF BUSINESS:

Equipment-Orthopedic Implants
Powered Surgical Instruments
Endoscopic Systems
Patient Care & Handling Equipment
Imaging Software

BRANDS/DIVISIONS/AFFILIATES:

Stryker Orthopaedics
Stryker Osteosynthesis
Stryker Spine
Stryker Biotech
Stryker Instruments
Stryker Endoscopy
Stryker Medical

CONTACTS: *Note: Officers with more than one job title may be intentionally listed here more than once.*

Stephen P. MacMillan, CEO
Stephen P. MacMillan, Pres.
Curt R. Hartman, CFO/VP
Michael W. Rude, VP-Human Resources
Curtis E. Hall, General Counsel/VP
James E. Kemler, VP/Group Pres., Dev.
J. Patrick Anderson, VP-Corp. Affairs
Katherine A. Owen, VP-Investor Rel. & Strategy
Jeanne M. Blondia, Treas./VP
Edward B. Lipes, Exec. VP
Lonny Carpenter, Group Pres., Stryker Instruments & Stryker Medical
Tim Scannell, Group Pres., Stryker Spine & Stryker Endoscopy
James E. Kemler, Group Pres., Stryker Biotech & Osteosynthesis
John W. Brown, Chmn.
Andrew G. Fox-Smith, Group Pres., Int'l

Phone: 269-385-2600	Fax: 269-385-1062
Toll-Free:	
Address: 2825 Airview Blvd., Kalamazoo, MI 49002 US	

GROWTH PLANS/SPECIAL FEATURES:

Stryker Corp. develops, manufactures and markets specialty surgical and medical products for the global market. These products include orthopedic implants, patient care and handling equipment, powered surgical instruments and endoscopic systems. The firm's products are produced by two segments: Orthopedic Implants (which generated approximately 59% of Stryker's 2008 sales) and MedSurg equipment (the remaining 41%). The Orthopedic Implant segment's products include reconstructive implants for knee, hip, elbow, shoulder and other joint surgeries; nailing, plating and external fixation systems to mend trauma injuries; spine implants; micro implants for craniomaxillofacial and hand surgery; bone cement; and osteobiologic products, including OP-1, which induces bone formation through a combination of a recombinant human protein, called either bone morphogenetic protein-7 (BMP7) or osteogenic protein-1 (OP-1), and a bioresorbable collagen matrix. Other osteobiologic products include BoneSource BVF, a bone substitute. Bone implants are typically made from cobalt chromium, titanium alloys, ceramics or ultrahigh molecular weight polyethylene. This segment's products are designed and manufactured by subsidiaries Stryker Orthopaedics, Stryker Osteosynthesis, Stryker Spine and Stryker Biotech. The MedSurg Equipment segment includes powered surgical instruments (including bone saws, drills and rasps), surgical navigation systems (including navigation software), hospital beds and stretchers, endoscopic products, emergency medical equipment and medical video imaging equipment. These devices are produced by Stryker Instruments, Stryker Endoscopy and Stryker Medical. The company maintains administrative, sales, warehousing and distribution sites in 41 countries in Europe, Asia, Africa and the Americas, as well as exporting products to numerous international destinations. Geographically, domestic operations generated the larger share (64%) of 2008 sales, with international activities producing the remainder (36%).

Employees of Stryker receive benefits including medical, dental, vision, prescription, disability and life insurance; flexible spending accounts; an employee assistance program; onsite fitness centers and cafeterias; tuition reimbursement; adoption assistance; and paid vacations, holidays and maternity leave.

FINANCIALS: Sales and profits are in thousands of dollars—add 000 to get the full amount. 2008 Note: Financial information for 2008 was not available for all companies at press time.

2008 Sales: $6,718,200	2008 Profits: $1,147,800	**U.S. Stock Ticker: SYK**
2007 Sales: $6,000,500	2007 Profits: $1,017,400	**Int'l Ticker:** Int'l Exchange:
2006 Sales: $5,147,200	2006 Profits: $777,700	Employees: 17,694
2005 Sales: $4,871,500	2005 Profits: $643,600	Fiscal Year Ends: 12/31
2004 Sales: $4,262,300	2004 Profits: $440,000	Parent Company:

SALARIES/BENEFITS:

Pension Plan:	ESOP Stock Plan:	Profit Sharing:	Top Exec. Salary: $1,200,000	Bonus: $617,280
Savings Plan: Y	Stock Purch. Plan: Y		Second Exec. Salary: $545,000	Bonus: $369,471

OTHER THOUGHTS:

Apparent Women Officers or Directors: 6
Hot Spot for Advancement for Women/Minorities: Y

LOCATIONS: ("Y" = Yes)

West:	Southwest:	Midwest:	Southeast:	Northeast:	International:
Y	Y	Y	Y	Y	Y

SUN HEALTHCARE GROUP

www.sunpsychiatrichospital.com

Industry Group Code: 623110 Ranks within this company's industry group: Sales: 3 Profits: 1

Management:		Sales/Marketing:		Liberal Arts:		Information Systems:		Professionals:		Tech./Scientific:	
Management Trainees:	Y	Marketing Pros.:	Y	Gen. Writing/Editing:	Y	Info. Management:	Y	Finance/Acct.:	Y	Engineers, Electrical:	
Experienced Mngmt.:	Y	Retail Sales:		Technical Writing:	Y	Software Dev.:		Law:	Y	Engineers, Other:	
International Business:		Commercial/Industrial:		Graphic Arts/Photog.:	Y	Hardware Dev.:		HR/Other:	Y	Health/Lab:	
MBA Grads:	Y	Sales Trainees:		Music:		Consulting/Other:		Training:	Y	Scientists/Research:	
		Advertising Pros.:	Y	Broadcasting:				Health Care:	Y	Petroleum/Chemicals:	
				Other:	Y			Consulting:		Math/Other:	

TYPES OF BUSINESS:

Long-Term Care
Sub-Acute Care
Assisted Living Services
Temporary Medical Staffing
Mobile Radiology
Medical Laboratory Services
Home Health Care Services
Physical Therapy

BRANDS/DIVISIONS/AFFILIATES:

SunDance Rehabilitation Corp.
CareerStaff Unlimited, Inc.
SunPlus Home Health Services
Harborside Healthcare Corporation
Twilight Wish Foundation
SolAmor Hospice Corporation
Holisticare Hospice, LLC
SunBridge Healthcare Corp.

CONTACTS: Note: Officers with more than one job title may be intentionally listed here more than once.

Richard K. Matros, CEO
L. Bryan Shaul, CFO/Exec. VP
Cindy Chrispell, Sr. VP-Human Resources
Michael Newman, General Counsel/Exec. VP
Jeffrey M. Kreger, VP/Corp. Controller
Michael Montevideo, VP/Treas.
Chauncey J. Hunker, Sr. VP/Corp. Compliance Officer/Chief Risk Officer
Sue Gwyn, Pres., SunDance Rehabilitation Corp.
Richard Peranton, Pres., CareerStaff Unlimited
Richard K. Matros, Chmn.

Phone: 949-255-7100	Fax:
Toll-Free: 800-729-6600	
Address: 18831 Von Karman, Ste. 400, Irvine, CA 92612 US	

GROWTH PLANS/SPECIAL FEATURES:

Sun Healthcare Group, Inc., through its subsidiaries, is a nationwide provider of long-term, sub-acute and related specialty healthcare services primarily to the senior population in the U.S. The firm operates in three principal business segments: inpatient services, rehabilitation therapy services and medical staffing services. Its core business is providing inpatient services, primarily through approximately 184 skilled nursing facilities, 15 assisted and independent living facilities and eight mental health facilities with 23,345 licensed beds located in 25 states. These facilities provide inpatient skilled nursing and custodial services including therapeutic rehabilitation; housekeeping; daily nursing; social services; and dietary and administrative services for individuals requiring certain assistance for activities in daily living. Specialized care is available for patients with Alzheimer's disease. The firm's rehabilitation services are provided at approximately 445 facilities in 33 states through SunDance Rehabilitation Corporation. These services include physical therapy, speech pathology and occupational therapy. Sun Healthcare's medical staffing services, through CareerStaff Unlimited, Inc., operates in 37 states and provides licensed therapists skilled in physical, occupational and speech therapy; the subsidiary also provides nurses, pharmacists, pharmacist technicians, medical imaging technicians, physicians and related medical personnel. CareerStaff customers include hospitals, skilled nursing facilities, schools and prisons. Subsidiary SunBridge Healthcare Corp. provides long-term residential skilled care and healthcare services; short-term care; and rehabilitation in over 200 locations across the U.S. In recent years, Sun Healthcare acquired Harborside Healthcare Corporation, a private healthcare company operating 73 skilled nursing facilities, one assisted living facility and one independent living facility, for $349.4 million. In February 2008, the firm announced a partnership with the Twilight Wish Foundation, a non-profit organization which helps seniors realize some of their wishes. In September 2008, the firm's hospice subsidiary, SolAmor Hospice Corporation, acquired New Jersey-based Holisticare Hospice, LLC, for $7.7 million. SolAmor Hospice now offers its services in six states.

FINANCIALS: Sales and profits are in thousands of dollars—add 000 to get the full amount. 2008 Note: Financial information for 2008 was not available for all companies at press time.

2008 Sales: $1,824,184	2008 Profits: $109,287	**U.S. Stock Ticker:** SUNH
2007 Sales: $1,587,307	2007 Profits: $57,510	**Int'l Ticker:** Int'l Exchange:
2006 Sales: $1,004,897	2006 Profits: $27,118	Employees: 29,845
2005 Sales: $765,782	2005 Profits: $24,761	Fiscal Year Ends: 12/31
2004 Sales: $700,863	2004 Profits: $-18,627	Parent Company:

SALARIES/BENEFITS:

Pension Plan:	ESOP Stock Plan:	Profit Sharing:	Top Exec. Salary: $870,833	Bonus: $511,875
Savings Plan: Y	Stock Purch. Plan:		Second Exec. Salary: $588,459	Bonus: $292,500

OTHER THOUGHTS:

Apparent Women Officers or Directors: 3
Hot Spot for Advancement for Women/Minorities: Y

LOCATIONS: ("Y" = Yes)

West:	Southwest:	Midwest:	Southeast:	Northeast:	International:
Y	Y	Y	Y	Y	

Note: Financial information, benefits and other data can change quickly and may vary from those stated here.

SUNGARD DATA SYSTEMS INC

www.sungard.com

Industry Group Code: 511210 **Ranks within this company's industry group:** Sales: 1 Profits: 2

Management:		Sales/Marketing:		Liberal Arts:		Information Systems:		Professionals:		Tech./Scientific:	
Management Trainees:	Y	Marketing Pros.:	Y	Gen. Writing/Editing:	Y	Info. Management:	Y	Finance/Acct.:	Y	Engineers, Electrical:	Y
Experienced Mngmt.:	Y	Retail Sales:		Technical Writing:	Y	Software Dev.:	Y	Law:	Y	Engineers, Other:	
International Business:	Y	Commercial/Industrial:	Y	Graphic Arts/Photog.:	Y	Hardware Dev.:		HR/Other:	Y	Health/Lab:	
MBA Grads:	Y	Sales Trainees:		Music:		Consulting/Other:	Y	Training:	Y	Scientists/Research:	
		Advertising Pros.:	Y	Broadcasting:				Health Care:		Petroleum/Chemicals:	
				Other:				Consulting:		Math/Other:	

TYPES OF BUSINESS:

Outsourced Information Processing & Services
Workflow Management Systems
Data Protection
Financial Services Software
Education Software
Administrative Software

BRANDS/DIVISIONS/AFFILIATES:

ICE Risk Solution
Performance Pathways, Inc.
Genix Systems AG
GL Trade

CONTACTS: *Note: Officers with more than one job title may be intentionally listed here more than once.*

Cristobal Conde, CEO
Cristobal Conde, Pres.
Michale J. Ruane, CFO
Brian Robins, Sr. VP-Mktg./Chief Mktg. Officer
Kathleen Asser Weslock, Chief Human Resources Officer/Sr. VP
Victoria E. Silbey, General Counsel/VP-Legal
Richard C. Tarbox, Sr. VP-Corp. Dev.
Suzanne DeFruscio, VP-Corp. Comm.
Michale J. Ruane, Sr. VP-Finance
Jim Ashton, Div. CEO-Financial Systems
Harold Finders, Div. CEO-Financial Systems
Eric Berg, Group CEO-Availability Svcs.
Ron Lang, CEO-Higher Education
James L. Mann, Chmn.

Phone: 484-582-2000	Fax:
Toll-Free: 800-825-2518	
Address: 680 E. Swedesford Rd., Wayne, PA 19087-1586 US	

GROWTH PLANS/SPECIAL FEATURES:

SunGard Data Systems, Inc. is a leading global provider of integrated software and information technology services for financial services companies, higher education and the public sector. The firm serves more than 25,000 clients in over 70 countries. SunGard is organized into four business segments: Financial Systems, Higher Education, Public Sector and Availability Services. SunGard Financial Systems serves financial services companies specializing in alternative investments; banking; benefit administration; brokerage and clearance; capital markets and investment banking; energy trading and risk management; institutional asset management; insurance; trading; treasury management; and wealth management. The Higher Education segment provides specialized enterprise resource planning and administrative software to over 1,600 higher education institutions. SunGard Public Sector serves school districts, nonprofit organizations and local, state and federal government agencies, with solutions for accounting; human resources; payroll; utility billing; land management; public safety and criminal justice; and grant and project management. The Availability Services segment provides solutions to information-dependent companies across virtually all industries protecting against breaches of security; network or hardware failures; data loss; power failure; and extreme events, such as natural disaster and terrorism. In October 2008, Sungard acquired a majority interest in GL Trade, a Paris-based developer of financial software. In March 2009, the company acquired Performance Pathways, Inc., which creates software geared towards K-12 educational environments. In April 2009, the firm acquired Genix Systems AG, a Zurich, Switzerland-based entity which serves private banking information needs. In May 2009, the company acquired ICE Risk Solution from InterContinental Exchange, which evaluates risk across multiple trading venues.

Sungard offers its employees medical, dental and vision insurance; an employee assistance program; a flexible compensation plan; short- and long-term disability; life and AD&D insurance; a retirement savings plan; a college tuition savings plan; tuition reimbursement; and adoption assistance.

FINANCIALS: Sales and profits are in thousands of dollars—add 000 to get the full amount. 2008 Note: Financial information for 2008 was not available for all companies at press time.

2008 Sales: $5,596,000	2008 Profits: $470,000	**U.S. Stock Ticker:** Private
2007 Sales: $4,901,000	2007 Profits: $-60,000	**Int'l Ticker:** Int'l Exchange:
2006 Sales: $4,323,000	2006 Profits: $-118,000	Employees: 20,000
2005 Sales: $4,002,000	2005 Profits: $117,000	Fiscal Year Ends: 12/31
2004 Sales: $3,555,900	2004 Profits: $453,600	Parent Company:

SALARIES/BENEFITS:

Pension Plan:	ESOP Stock Plan:	Profit Sharing:	Top Exec. Salary: $	Bonus: $1,517,972
Savings Plan: Y	Stock Purch. Plan:		Second Exec. Salary: $	Bonus: $

OTHER THOUGHTS:

Apparent Women Officers or Directors: 3
Hot Spot for Advancement for Women/Minorities: Y

LOCATIONS: ("Y" = Yes)

West:	Southwest:	Midwest:	Southeast:	Northeast:	International:
Y	Y	Y	Y	Y	Y

SUNOCO INC

www.sunocoinc.com

Industry Group Code: 324110 Ranks within this company's industry group: Sales: 3   Profits: 1

Management:		Sales/Marketing:		Liberal Arts:		Information Systems:		Professionals:		Tech./Scientific:	
Management Trainees:	Y	Marketing Pros.:	Y	Gen. Writing/Editing:	Y	Info. Management:	Y	Finance/Acct.:	Y	Engineers, Electrical:	Y
Experienced Mngmt.:	Y	Retail Sales:		Technical Writing:	Y	Software Dev.:	Y	Law:	Y	Engineers, Other:	Y
International Business:	Y	Commercial/Industrial:	Y	Graphic Arts/Photog.:	Y	Hardware Dev.:		HR/Other:	Y	Health/Lab:	
MBA Grads:	Y	Sales Trainees:		Music:		Consulting/Other:		Training:	Y	Scientists/Research:	
		Advertising Pros.:		Broadcasting:				Health Care:		Petroleum/Chemicals:	Y
				Other:				Consulting:		Math/Other:	

TYPES OF BUSINESS:

Petroleum Refiner & Chemicals Manufacturer
Petrochemicals & Lubricants
Coke Manufacturing

BRANDS/DIVISIONS/AFFILIATES:

SunCoke Energy, Inc.
Sunoco Logistic Partners L.P.
Gateway Energy and Coke Company
Sunoco Chemicals

CONTACTS: *Note: Officers with more than one job title may be intentionally listed here more than once.*

Lynn L. Elsenhans, CEO
Lynn L. Elsenhans, Pres.
Terence P. Delaney, Interim CFO
Robert W. Owens, Sr. VP-Mktg.
Dennis Zeleny, Chief Human Resources Officer/Sr. VP
Michael S. Kuritzkes, General Counsel/Sr. VP
Bruce G. Fischer, Sr. VP-Strategy & Portfolio
Joseph P. Krott, Comptroller
Michael J. Thomson, Pres., SunCoke Energy, Inc.
Vincent J. Kelley, Sr. VP-Refining & Supply
Ann C. Mule, Chief Governance Officer/Corp. Sec.
Bruce D. Rubin, VP-Chemicals
Lynn L. Elsenhans, Chmn.

Phone: 215-977-3000	Fax: 215-977-3409
Toll-Free: 800-786-6261	
Address: 1735 Market St., Ste. LL, Philadelphia, PA 19103-7583 US	

GROWTH PLANS/SPECIAL FEATURES:

Sunoco, Inc., through its subsidiaries, is principally a petroleum refiner and chemicals manufacturer with interests in logistics and cokemaking. Sunoco operates five segments: Refining and supply, retail marketing, chemicals, logistics and coke. Additionally, the firm has a holding company and a professional services group. The holding company is a non-operating parent company and the professional services group consists of a number of staff functions including finance, risk management, human resources, information systems and engineering services. The refining and supply business manufactures petroleum products, including gasoline, middle distillates and residual fuel oil; commodity petrochemicals including olefins and their derivatives; and aromatics and their derivates. The retail marketing business consists of the retail sale of gasoline and middle distillates and the operation of convenience stores in 26 states. The chemicals segment, operating through Sunoco Chemicals, manufactures, distributes and markets commodity and intermediate petrochemicals. The logistics division, including Sunoco Logistic Partners L.P., operates refined product and crude oil pipelines and terminals and conducts crude oil acquisition and marketing activities. The coke segment operates metallurgical coke plants and metallurgical coal mines through SunCoke Energy, Inc. Sunoco also owns and operates facilities in Pennsylvania and Ohio, which produce phenol and acetone; and in West Virginia, which produce polypropylene. The firm operates five refineries and markets gasoline, middle distillates and other convenience store merchandise through 4,720 retail outlets. In April 2009, the firm agreed to sell its refinery in Tulsa, Oklahoma to Holly Corporation for approximately $65 million. In March 2009, Sunoco announced plans to reduce its workforce by 20% or approximately 750 positions throughout 2009. In January 2009, Sunoco announced plans to close its polypropylene plant in Bayport, Texas.

The company offers employees medical and dental insurance; an employee assistance program; a 401(k) plan; flexible spending accounts; and an educational assistance plan.

FINANCIALS: Sales and profits are in thousands of dollars—add 000 to get the full amount. 2008 Note: Financial information for 2008 was not available for all companies at press time.

2008 Sales: $54,052,000	2008 Profits: $776,000	**U.S. Stock Ticker:** SUN
2007 Sales: $44,470,000	2007 Profits: $891,000	**Int'l Ticker:** Int'l Exchange:
2006 Sales: $38,636,000	2006 Profits: $979,000	Employees: 13,700
2005 Sales: $33,754,000	2005 Profits: $974,000	Fiscal Year Ends: 12/31
2004 Sales: $25,468,000	2004 Profits: $605,000	Parent Company:

SALARIES/BENEFITS:

Pension Plan:	ESOP Stock Plan:	Profit Sharing:	Top Exec. Salary: $758,308	Bonus: $1,169,836
Savings Plan: Y	Stock Purch. Plan:		Second Exec. Salary: $523,962	Bonus: $509,461

OTHER THOUGHTS:

Apparent Women Officers or Directors: 2
Hot Spot for Advancement for Women/Minorities: Y

LOCATIONS: ("Y" = Yes)

West:	Southwest:	Midwest:	Southeast:	Northeast:	International:
Y	Y	Y	Y	Y	Y

SUNRISE SENIOR LIVING   www.sunriseseniorliving.com

Industry Group Code: 623110 Ranks within this company's industry group: Sales: 4   Profits: 5

Management:		Sales/Marketing:		Liberal Arts:		Information Systems:		Professionals:		Tech./Scientific:	
Management Trainees:	Y	Marketing Pros.:	Y	Gen. Writing/Editing:	Y	Info. Management:	Y	Finance/Acct.:	Y	Engineers, Electrical:	
Experienced Mngmt.:	Y	Retail Sales:		Technical Writing:	Y	Software Dev.:		Law:	Y	Engineers, Other:	
International Business:	Y	Commercial/Industrial:		Graphic Arts/Photog.:	Y	Hardware Dev.:		HR/Other:	Y	Health/Lab:	
MBA Grads:	Y	Sales Trainees:		Music:		Consulting/Other:		Training:	Y	Scientists/Research:	
		Advertising Pros.:	Y	Broadcasting:				Health Care:	Y	Petroleum/Chemicals:	
				Other:	Y			Consulting:		Math/Other:	

TYPES OF BUSINESS:

Long-Term Health Care
Assisted Living Centers
Independent Living Centers
Nursing Homes

BRANDS/DIVISIONS/AFFILIATES:

Sunrise Assisted Living
Aston Gardens
Trinity Hospice, Inc.

CONTACTS: *Note: Officers with more than one job title may be intentionally listed here more than once.*

Mark S. Ordan, CEO
Julie A. Pangelinan, CFO
Kurt Conway, Sr. VP-Mktg. & Sales
Jeffery M. Jasnoff, Sr. VP-Human Resources
Daniel Schwartz, Sr. VP-North American Oper.
Meghan Lublin, Sr. Dir.-Investor Comm.
Julie A. Pangelinan, Treas.
Teresa M. Klaassen, Chief Cultural Officer/Exec. VP
Greg Neeb, Chief Investment Officer
Paul J. Klaassen, Chmn.
Tiffany L. Tomasso, Head-European Oper.

Phone: 703-273-7500	**Fax:** 703-744-1601
Toll-Free: 888-434-4648	
Address: 7902 Westpark Dr., McLean, VA 22102 US	

GROWTH PLANS/SPECIAL FEATURES:

Sunrise Senior Living is an international provider of senior living services. The firm operates approximately 435 senior living communities in the U.S., the U.K., Germany and Canada, with a resident capacity of approximately 54,340. The company also has 26 more communities under construction. Sunrise Senior Living offers services tailored to the unique needs of each of its residents, typically in apartment-like assisted living environments. Upon move-in, Sunrise assists the resident in developing an individualized service plan, including selection of resident accommodations and the appropriate level of care. The services provided range from basic care, consisting of assistance with activities of daily living; to reminiscence care, which consists of programs and services to help cognitively impaired residents, including residents with Alzheimer's disease. The firm targets sites for development located in major metropolitan areas and their surrounding suburban communities, considering factors such as population, age demographics and estimated level of market demand. The company often revitalizes existing senior living centers and operates the home for a third-party owner. It owns or has interest in approximately 260 of the properties where it maintains services. In 2008, the firm opened a total of 19 facilities with a combined occupant capacity of 26,000.

Sunrise offers employees flexible spending accounts; a scholarship program; tuition assistance; a meal discount program; health, dental, vision and life insurance; and a 401(k).

FINANCIALS: Sales and profits are in thousands of dollars—add 000 to get the full amount. 2008 Note: Financial information for 2008 was not available for all companies at press time.

2008 Sales: $1,701,643	2008 Profits: $-439,179	**U.S. Stock Ticker: SRZ**
2007 Sales: $1,583,241	2007 Profits: $-70,275	**Int'l Ticker:** Int'l Exchange:
2006 Sales: $1,628,605	2006 Profits: $15,284	Employees: 37,800
2005 Sales: $1,509,438	2005 Profits: $87,089	Fiscal Year Ends: 12/31
2004 Sales: $1,446,471	2004 Profits: $50,687	Parent Company:

SALARIES/BENEFITS:

Pension Plan:	ESOP Stock Plan:	Profit Sharing:	Top Exec. Salary: $650,000	Bonus: $
Savings Plan: Y	Stock Purch. Plan: Y		Second Exec. Salary: $500,000	Bonus: $

OTHER THOUGHTS:

Apparent Women Officers or Directors: 4
Hot Spot for Advancement for Women/Minorities: Y

LOCATIONS: ("Y" = Yes)

West:	Southwest:	Midwest:	Southeast:	Northeast:	International:
Y	Y	Y	Y	Y	Y

SUPERVALU INC

www.supervalu.com

Industry Group Code: 445110 **Ranks within this company's industry group:** Sales: 3 Profits: 4

Management:		Sales/Marketing:		Liberal Arts:		Information Systems:		Professionals:		Tech./Scientific:	
Management Trainees:	Y	Marketing Pros.:	Y	Gen. Writing/Editing:	Y	Info. Management:	Y	Finance/Acct.:	Y	Engineers, Electrical:	
Experienced Mngmt.:	Y	Retail Sales:	Y	Technical Writing:		Software Dev.:	Y	Law:	Y	Engineers, Other:	
International Business:		Commercial/Industrial:		Graphic Arts/Photog.:	Y	Hardware Dev.:		HR/Other:	Y	Health/Lab:	
MBA Grads:	Y	Sales Trainees:	Y	Music:		Consulting/Other:		Training:	Y	Scientists/Research:	
		Advertising Pros.:	Y	Broadcasting:				Health Care:		Petroleum/Chemicals:	
				Other:	Y			Consulting:		Math/Other:	

TYPES OF BUSINESS:

Grocery Stores
Food Distribution & Logistics
Natural & Organic Foods

BRANDS/DIVISIONS/AFFILIATES:

Albertsons
Save-A-Lot
Shaw's Supermarkets
Jewel-Osco
Acme Markets
Sunflower Market
Club Foods
Farm Fresh

CONTACTS: *Note: Officers with more than one job title may be intentionally listed here more than once.*

Craig R. Herkert, CEO
Michael L. Jackson, COO
Michael L. Jackson, Pres.
Pamela K. Knous, CFO/Exec. VP
Duncan Mac Naughton, Exec. VP-Mktg.
Dave Pylipow, Sr. VP-Human Resources
Duncan Mac Naughton, Exec. VP-Merch.
David Boehnen, Exec. VP-Legal, Real Estate & Gov't Affairs
David Boehnen, Exec. VP-Corp. Dev.
Sherry Smith, Sr. VP-Finance
Pete Van Helden, Exec. VP-Retail
Jeffrey Noddle, Chmn.
Janel Haugarth, Exec VP/Pres./COO-Supply Chain Svcs.

Phone: 952-828-4000	Fax: 952-828-8955
Toll-Free:	
Address: 11840 Valley View Rd., Eden Prairie, MN 55344 US	

GROWTH PLANS/SPECIAL FEATURES:

Supervalu, Inc. is a supermarket retailer and food distributor. Supervalu conducts its retail operations under three retail food store formats: combination stores, food stores and limited assortment food stores. The company operates approximately 2,418 stores under the following banners: Albertson's, Shaw's Supermarkets, Jewel-Osco, Acme Markets, Shoppers Food & Pharmacy, Cub Foods, Farm Fresh, Lucky, Shop 'n Save, Scott's, Star Markets, Bristol Farms, bigg's, Hornbacher's, Sunflower Market and Save-A-Lot. Supervalu's roughly 874 combination stores combine a grocery and a drug store under one roof, most often including a complete grocery offering, prescription drugs and expanded sections of cosmetics and general merchandise, in addition to specialty departments such as service seafood and meat, bakery, service delicatessen, liquor, floral and in-store banks. Typical combination stores carry about 50,000 items and average approximately 60,000 square feet. Supervalu's food stores focus primarily on food departments and include many of the same product and service offerings as combination stores, but on a more limited basis and without a pharmacy. Typical food stores carry about 40,000 items and average approximately 40,000 square feet. Supervalu operates 369 limited assortment stores, including 316 under the Save-A-Lot banner. The company licenses 866 Save-A-Lot stores to independent operators. Supervalu also operates approximately 131 fuel centers and 23 distribution centers. Save-A-Lot stores are typically 15,000 square feet in size, stocking approximately 1,400 high volume food items generally in a single size for each product sold, as well as a limited offering of general merchandise items. At a Save-A-Lot store, the majority of the food products offered for sale are custom branded products. In 2009, the company added 44 new stores and closed 97.

Supervalu offers its employees medical, dental and life insurance; short- and long-term disability; a 401(k) plan; profit sharing; tuition reimbursement; flexible spending accounts; employee assistance programs; and adoption assistance.

FINANCIALS: Sales and profits are in thousands of dollars—add 000 to get the full amount. 2008 Note: Financial information for 2008 was not available for all companies at press time.

2008 Sales: $44,048,000	2008 Profits: $593,000	**U.S. Stock Ticker:** SVU
2007 Sales: $37,406,000	2007 Profits: $452,000	**Int'l Ticker:** **Int'l Exchange:**
2006 Sales: $19,863,599	2006 Profits: $206,169	**Employees:** 178,000
2005 Sales: $19,543,240	2005 Profits: $385,823	**Fiscal Year Ends:** 2/28
2004 Sales: $20,209,700	2004 Profits: $280,100	**Parent Company:**

SALARIES/BENEFITS:

Pension Plan:	ESOP Stock Plan:	Profit Sharing: Y	Top Exec. Salary: $1,163,844	Bonus: $
Savings Plan: Y	Stock Purch. Plan:		Second Exec. Salary: $662,828	Bonus: $454,900

OTHER THOUGHTS:

Apparent Women Officers or Directors: 6
Hot Spot for Advancement for Women/Minorities: Y

LOCATIONS: ("Y" = Yes)

West:	Southwest:	Midwest:	Southeast:	Northeast:	International:
Y	Y	Y	Y	Y	

Note: Financial information, benefits and other data can change quickly and may vary from those stated here.

SYKES ENTERPRISES INC

www.sykes.com

Industry Group Code: 56142 Ranks within this company's industry group: Sales: 3 Profits: 2

Management:		Sales/Marketing:		Liberal Arts:		Information Systems:		Professionals:		Tech./Scientific:	
Management Trainees:	Y	Marketing Pros.:	Y	Gen. Writing/Editing:	Y	Info. Management:	Y	Finance/Acct.:	Y	Engineers, Electrical:	
Experienced Mngmt.:	Y	Retail Sales:		Technical Writing:	Y	Software Dev.:	Y	Law:	Y	Engineers, Other:	
International Business:	Y	Commercial/Industrial:	Y	Graphic Arts/Photog.:		Hardware Dev.:		HR/Other:	Y	Health/Lab:	
MBA Grads:	Y	Sales Trainees:		Music:		Consulting/Other:		Training:	Y	Scientists/Research:	
		Advertising Pros.:		Broadcasting:				Health Care:		Petroleum/Chemicals:	
				Other:				Consulting:		Math/Other:	

TYPES OF BUSINESS:

Consulting-Technical Support
Outsourcing Services
Staffing Services

BRANDS/DIVISIONS/AFFILIATES:

Contact Center Services
TeleHealth Services

CONTACTS: Note: Officers with more than one job title may be intentionally listed here more than once.

Charles E. Sykes, CEO
Charles E. Sykes, Pres.
W. Michael Kipphut, CFO/Sr. VP
Lawrence R. Zingale, Sr. VP-Global Sales & Client Mgmt.
Jenna R. Nelson, Sr. VP-Human Resources
David L. Pearson, CIO/Sr. VP
James T. Holder, General Counsel/Sr. VP/Corp. Sec.
James C. Hobby, Sr. VP-Global Oper.
Daniel L.Hernandez, Sr. VP-Global Strategy
Subhaash Kumar, VP-Investor Rel.
William N. Rocktoff, Controller/VP
Paul L. Whiting, Chmn.

Phone: 813-274-1000	Fax: 813-273-0148
Toll-Free:	
Address: 400 N. Ashley Dr., Tampa, FL 33602 US	

GROWTH PLANS/SPECIAL FEATURES:

Sykes Enterprises, Inc. provides outsourced customer contact management solutions and services in the business process outsourcing arena. Clients range from Fortune 100 companies to medium-sized businesses and public institutions in the communications, consumer technology, financial services, healthcare, transportation and leisure industries. The company operates within the U.S., Canada, Latin America, India, the Asia Pacific Rim, Europe, the Middle East and Africa. Sykes provides support via phone, e-mail, web and chat interfaces through global network customer support centers, which provide support capabilities in more than 30 languages. The company offers services in three areas: Outsourced customer contact management services, fulfillment services and enterprise support services. Outsourced customer care management services operate in 20 countries in 47 contact management centers and provides customer care by processing product information requests, activating customer accounts, resolving complaints, warranty management, billing inquiries, technical support, communications services, communications equipment, Internet access technology and portal usage. This sector also offers support in acquisitions, which are primarily focused on inbound up-selling/cross-selling of each client's products and services. The fulfillment services segment is integrated with customer care and technical support services and involves multilingual sales order processing via the Internet and phone; payment processing; inventory control; product delivery; and product returns handling. The enterprise support segment offers services in technical staffing and solutions for outsourced corporate health desks. The company's Contact Center Services division handles customer service, billing and complex technical support problems of companies in such industries as broadband, wireless, managed telecom services, consumer electronics, high-tech, card services and retail banking. Its TeleHealth Services division develops programs including chronic care, symptom management, health information services, wellness and prevention services and behavioral health services.

FINANCIALS: Sales and profits are in thousands of dollars—add 000 to get the full amount. 2008 Note: Financial information for 2008 was not available for all companies at press time.

2008 Sales: $819,190	2008 Profits: $60,561	U.S. Stock Ticker: SYKE
2007 Sales: $710,120	2007 Profits: $39,859	Int'l Ticker: Int'l Exchange:
2006 Sales: $574,223	2006 Profits: $42,323	Employees: 32,940
2005 Sales: $494,918	2005 Profits: $23,408	Fiscal Year Ends: 12/31
2004 Sales: $466,713	2004 Profits: $10,814	Parent Company:

SALARIES/BENEFITS:

Pension Plan:	ESOP Stock Plan:	Profit Sharing:	Top Exec. Salary: $500,000	Bonus: $473,797
Savings Plan: Y	Stock Purch. Plan:		Second Exec. Salary: $374,558	Bonus: $295,780

OTHER THOUGHTS:

Apparent Women Officers or Directors: 2
Hot Spot for Advancement for Women/Minorities: Y

LOCATIONS: ("Y" = Yes)

West:	Southwest:	Midwest:	Southeast:	Northeast:	International:
Y	Y	Y	Y	Y	Y

Note: Financial information, benefits and other data can change quickly and may vary from those stated here.

SYMANTEC CORP

www.symantec.com

Industry Group Code: 511210E Ranks within this company's industry group: Sales: 1 Profits: 1

Management:		Sales/Marketing:		Liberal Arts:		Information Systems:		Professionals:		Tech./Scientific:	
Management Trainees:	Y	Marketing Pros.:	Y	Gen. Writing/Editing:	Y	Info. Management:	Y	Finance/Acct.:	Y	Engineers, Electrical:	Y
Experienced Mngmt.:	Y	Retail Sales:		Technical Writing:	Y	Software Dev.:	Y	Law:	Y	Engineers, Other:	
International Business:	Y	Commercial/Industrial:	Y	Graphic Arts/Photog.:	Y	Hardware Dev.:		HR/Other:	Y	Health/Lab:	
MBA Grads:	Y	Sales Trainees:		Music:		Consulting/Other:	Y	Training:	Y	Scientists/Research:	
		Advertising Pros.:	Y	Broadcasting:				Health Care:		Petroleum/Chemicals:	
				Other:				Consulting:		Math/Other:	Y

TYPES OF BUSINESS:

Software-Security
Remote Management Products
IT Consulting Services

BRANDS/DIVISIONS/AFFILIATES:

nSuite Technologies, Inc.
LiveUpdate
Norton AntiVirus
Norton Internet Security
AppStream, Inc.
SwapDrive, Inc.
Transparent Logic Technologies
MessageLabs

CONTACTS: *Note: Officers with more than one job title may be intentionally listed here more than once.*

John W. Thompson, CEO
Enrique T. Salem, COO
James Beer, CFO/Exec. VP
Carine Clark, Sr. VP-Mktg.
Rebecca Ranninger, Chief Human Resources Officer/Exec. VP
David Thompson, CIO/Exec. VP
Mark Bregman, CTO/Exec. VP
Scott Taylor, General Counsel/Exec. VP/Sec.
Greg Hughes, Chief Strategy Officer
David Thompson, Pres., IT & Services Group
Janice Chaffin, Pres., Consumer Bus. Unit
Brad Kingsbury, Sr. VP-Endpoint Security & Mgmt.
Francis deSouza, Sr. VP-Info. Risk Mgmt. Group
John W. Thompson, Chmn.
John Brigden, Sr. VP-EMEA

Phone: 408-517-8000	Fax: 408-517-8186
Toll-Free:	
Address: 20330 Stevens Creek Blvd., Cupertino, CA 95014 US	

GROWTH PLANS/SPECIAL FEATURES:

Symantec Corp. provides a range of software, appliances and services designed to secure and manage information technology (IT) infrastructure. The company provides customers worldwide with software and services that protect, manage and control information risks related to security, data protection, storage, compliance, and systems management. The firm has five operating segments: consumer products; security and compliance; storage and server management; services; and other. The consumer products segment delivers Internet security, PC tuneup and backup products. The company's Norton brand provides protection for Windows and Macintosh platforms. Primary consumer products include Norton Antivirus and Norton Internet Security, which helps defend home and home office users by blocking online identity theft, detecting and eliminating spyware and protecting against hackers from entering a user's system. The security and compliance segment provides solutions for compliance and security management, endpoint security, messaging management and data protection management software solutions that allow customers to secure, provision, backup and remotely access laptops, PCs, mobile devices and servers. The storage and server management segment provides storage and server management, data protection, and application performance services that manage IT risk on an ongoing basis. The other segment includes sunset products and products nearing the end of their life cycle. During 2008, the firm acquired nSuite Technologies, Inc., a provider of connection broker technology; AppStream, Inc., a provider of endpoint virtualization software; SwapDrive, Inc., a provider of online storage products; MessageLabs, provider of online messaging, PC Tools, provider of security software; and Transparent Logic Technologies, provider of business automation products. In February 2008, Symantec formed the joint venture Huawei-Symantec, Inc. with a subsidiary of Huawei Technologies Co., Ltd. The joint venture operates in Chengdu, China.

The company offers employees medical, dental and vision insurance; a 401(k) plan; stock options; life and dismemberment insurance; tuition reimbursement; and an employee assistance program.

FINANCIALS: Sales and profits are in thousands of dollars—add 000 to get the full amount. 2008 Note: Financial information for 2008 was not available for all companies at press time.

2008 Sales: $5,874,419	2008 Profits: $463,850	**U.S. Stock Ticker: SYMC**
2007 Sales: $5,199,370	2007 Profits: $404,380	**Int'l Ticker:** Int'l Exchange:
2006 Sales: $4,143,392	2006 Profits: $156,852	Employees: 17,400
2005 Sales: $2,582,849	2005 Profits: $536,159	Fiscal Year Ends: 3/31
2004 Sales: $1,870,129	2004 Profits: $370,619	Parent Company:

SALARIES/BENEFITS:

Pension Plan:	ESOP Stock Plan:	Profit Sharing:	Top Exec. Salary: $800,000	Bonus: $2,430,000
Savings Plan: Y	Stock Purch. Plan: Y		Second Exec. Salary: $660,000	Bonus: $1,079,700

OTHER THOUGHTS:

Apparent Women Officers or Directors: 3
Hot Spot for Advancement for Women/Minorities: Y

LOCATIONS: ("Y" = Yes)

West:	Southwest:	Midwest:	Southeast:	Northeast:	International:
Y	Y	Y	Y	Y	Y

Note: Financial information, benefits and other data can change quickly and may vary from those stated here.

SYNOPSYS INC

www.synopsys.com

Industry Group Code: 511210N Ranks within this company's industry group: Sales: 1 Profits: 1

Management:		Sales/Marketing:		Liberal Arts:		Information Systems:		Professionals:		Tech./Scientific:	
Management Trainees:	Y	Marketing Pros.:	Y	Gen. Writing/Editing:	Y	Info. Management:	Y	Finance/Acct.:	Y	Engineers, Electrical:	Y
Experienced Mngmt.:	Y	Retail Sales:		Technical Writing:	Y	Software Dev.:	Y	Law:	Y	Engineers, Other:	
International Business:	Y	Commercial/Industrial:	Y	Graphic Arts/Photog.:		Hardware Dev.:		HR/Other:	Y	Health/Lab:	
MBA Grads:	Y	Sales Trainees:		Music:		Consulting/Other:		Training:	Y	Scientists/Research:	
		Advertising Pros.:	Y	Broadcasting:				Health Care:		Petroleum/Chemicals:	
				Other:				Consulting:		Math/Other:	

TYPES OF BUSINESS:

Computer Software-Electronic Design Automation
Consulting & Support Services

BRANDS/DIVISIONS/AFFILIATES:

Galaxy Design Platform
Discovery Verification Platform
ArchPro Design Automation, Inc.
Sandwork Design
MOSAID Technologies Incorporated
Synplicity Inc
CHIPit

CONTACTS: *Note: Officers with more than one job title may be intentionally listed here more than once.*

Aart de Geus, CEO
Chi-Foon Chan, COO
Chi-Foon Chan, Pres.
Brian Beattie, CFO
John Chilton, Sr. VP-Mktg.
Jan Collinson, Sr. VP-Human Resources & Facilities
Brian Cabrera, General Counsel/VP/Corp. Sec.
John Chilton, Sr. VP-Strategic Dev.
Deirdre Hanford, Sr. VP-Global Tech. Svcs.
Antun Domic, Sr. VP/Gen. Mgr.-Implementation Group
Manoj Gandhi, Sr. VP/Gen. Mgr.-Verification Group
Howard Ko, Sr. VP/Gen. Mgr.-Silicon Engineering Group
Aart de Geus, Chmn.
Joe Logan, Sr. VP-Worldwide Sales

Phone: 650-584-5000	Fax:
Toll-Free: 800-541-7737	
Address: 700 E. Middlefield Rd., Mountain View, CA 94043 US	

GROWTH PLANS/SPECIAL FEATURES:

Synopsys, Inc. is a supplier of electronic design automation (EDA) software and related services for semiconductor design companies. The firm offers semiconductor design and verification software platforms and integrated circuit (IC) manufacturing software products to the global electronics market, enabling the development and production of complex systems-on-chips (SoCs). Additionally, Synopsys provides intellectual property (IP), system-level design hardware and software products and design. Finally, the company provides software and services that help customers prepare and optimize their designs for manufacturing. The firm's products offer customers the opportunity to design ICs that are optimized for speed, area, power consumption and production cost, while reducing overall design time. Products offered are categorized into five groupings. The Galaxy Design Platform, which provides customers with many diverse common design requirements in a single application; the Discovery Verification Platform, which combines simulation and verification products and design-for-verification methodologies to provide a consistent control environment; IP and Systems-Level Solutions group, which responds to the portfolio demands of designers seeking solutions to reduce their risk and time-to-market; the Manufacturing Solutions group, which addresses the mask-making and yield enhancement of very small geometry IC, as well as very high-level modeling of physical effects within the ICs; and lastly, the Professional Services group, which provides consulting and design services covering all critical phases of the SoC development process. In addition, Synopsys provides consulting services to assist customers with their IC designs, as well as training and support services. The firm has licensed products to most of the world's leading semiconductor, computer, communications and electronics companies. In 2008, the firm acquired Synplicity, Inc. as well as the CHIPit business of ProDesigns.

Employees are offered medical, dental and vision coverage; an employee assistance program; educational assistance; adoption benefits; shopping discounts; flexible spending accounts; a wellness program; and telecommuting options.

FINANCIALS: Sales and profits are in thousands of dollars—add 000 to get the full amount. 2008 Note: Financial information for 2008 was not available for all companies at press time.

2008 Sales: $1,336,951	2008 Profits: $189,978	**U.S. Stock Ticker: SNPS**
2007 Sales: $1,212,469	2007 Profits: $130,491	**Int'l Ticker:** Int'l Exchange:
2006 Sales: $1,095,560	2006 Profits: $24,742	Employees: 5,691
2005 Sales: $991,931	2005 Profits: $-17,114	Fiscal Year Ends: 10/31
2004 Sales: $1,092,104	2004 Profits: $74,337	Parent Company:

SALARIES/BENEFITS:

Pension Plan:	ESOP Stock Plan:	Profit Sharing:	Top Exec. Salary: $500,000	Bonus: $1,415,800
Savings Plan: Y	Stock Purch. Plan: Y		Second Exec. Salary: $450,000	Bonus: $902,600

OTHER THOUGHTS:

Apparent Women Officers or Directors: 2
Hot Spot for Advancement for Women/Minorities: Y

LOCATIONS: ("Y" = Yes)

West:	Southwest:	Midwest:	Southeast:	Northeast:	International:
Y	Y	Y	Y	Y	Y

SYNTEL INC

www.syntelinc.com

Industry Group Code: 541513 **Ranks within this company's industry group:** Sales: 12 Profits: 7

Management:		Sales/Marketing:		Liberal Arts:		Information Systems:		Professionals:		Tech./Scientific:	
Management Trainees:	Y	Marketing Pros.:	Y	Gen. Writing/Editing:	Y	Info. Management:	Y	Finance/Acct.:	Y	Engineers, Electrical:	Y
Experienced Mngmt.:	Y	Retail Sales:		Technical Writing:	Y	Software Dev.:	Y	Law:	Y	Engineers, Other:	
International Business:	Y	Commercial/Industrial:	Y	Graphic Arts/Photog.:	Y	Hardware Dev.:	Y	HR/Other:	Y	Health/Lab:	
MBA Grads:	Y	Sales Trainees:		Music:		Consulting/Other:	Y	Training:	Y	Scientists/Research:	
		Advertising Pros.:		Broadcasting:				Health Care:		Petroleum/Chemicals:	
				Other:	Y			Consulting:	Y	Math/Other:	

TYPES OF BUSINESS:

IT Consulting
Outsourcing Services
e-Business Solutions
Application Development & Management

BRANDS/DIVISIONS/AFFILIATES:

TeamSourcing
Identeon
Syntelovation

CONTACTS: *Note: Officers with more than one job title may be intentionally listed here more than once.*

Keshav Murugesh, CEO
Keshav Murugesh, Pres.
Arvind Godbole, CFO
Lakshmanan Chidambaram, VP-Sales
Srikanth Karra, VP-Global Human Resources
Arvind Godbole, Chief Info. Security Officer
Daniel Moore, Chief Admin. Officer
Daniel Moore, General Counsel
Neerja Sethi, VP-Corp. Affairs
R. Ramdas, Sr. VP-Corp. Svcs.
Anil Jain, Sr. VP-Insurance Verital
Bharat Desai, Chmn.
Amit Chatterjee, Head-Europe

Phone: 248-619-2800	Fax: 248-619-2888
Toll-Free:	
Address: 525 E. Big Beaver Rd., 3rd. Fl., Troy, MI 48083 US	

GROWTH PLANS/SPECIAL FEATURES:

Syntel, Inc. delivers flexible, custom information technology (IT) and business process outsourcing (BPO) services to its Global 2000 companies and government entities. The firm caters to 109 customers in the U.S., Europe and Southeast Asia; these clients include Chrysler, FedEx and AIG. Services are divided into four segments: Applications Outsourcing, e-Business, Knowledge Process Outsourcing (KPO) and TeamSourcing. The Applications Outsourcing division outsources services for ongoing management, development and maintenance of business applications; this division contributes 67% of consolidated revenues. The e-Business unit provides customized technology services in web solutions (including architecture, web-enablement of legacy applications and portal development), customer relationship management services and maintains alliances with major IT application software infrastructure providers (such as IBM, Oracle and AB Initio); this division accounts for 11% of revenues. The KPO division focuses on transaction processing, loan servicing, retirement processing and collections; operating through the use of Identeon, which assists in strategic assessments of business processes, this business unit accounts for 20% of revenue. TeamSourcing provides professional IT consulting services including systems specification, design, development, implementation and maintenance of applications involving diverse computer hardware, software and networking technologies; it accounts for 2% of total revenues. Syntel holds strategic partnerships with over 25 technology companies, including IBM, Hewlett-Packard, Citrix, BEA Systems and Oracle. The company recently launched Syntelovation, a unit created to develop, collect and evaluate new business innovations. In January 2009, Syntel partnered with ArtinSoft, an automated software migration company, to create a joint migration platform for customers. In March 2009, the firm agreed to partner with Global Analytics, a risk management company, to offer clients bankcard fraud protection.

FINANCIALS: Sales and profits are in thousands of dollars—add 000 to get the full amount. 2008 Note: Financial information for 2008 was not available for all companies at press time.

2008 Sales: $410,426	2008 Profits: $86,681	**U.S. Stock Ticker:** SYNT
2007 Sales: $337,673	2007 Profits: $62,860	**Int'l Ticker:** Int'l Exchange:
2006 Sales: $270,229	2006 Profits: $50,916	Employees: 12,363
2005 Sales: $226,189	2005 Profits: $30,321	Fiscal Year Ends: 12/31
2004 Sales: $186,573	2004 Profits: $40,974	Parent Company:

SALARIES/BENEFITS:

Pension Plan:	ESOP Stock Plan:	Profit Sharing:	Top Exec. Salary: $310,762	Bonus: $231,378
Savings Plan: Y	Stock Purch. Plan: Y		Second Exec. Salary: $300,000	Bonus: $

OTHER THOUGHTS:

Apparent Women Officers or Directors:
Hot Spot for Advancement for Women/Minorities:

LOCATIONS: ("Y" = Yes)

West:	Southwest:	Midwest:	Southeast:	Northeast:	International:
Y	Y	Y		Y	Y

Note: Financial information, benefits and other data can change quickly and may vary from those stated here.

SYSCO CORP

www.sysco.com

Industry Group Code: 4244 Ranks within this company's industry group: Sales: 1 Profits: 1

Management:		Sales/Marketing:		Liberal Arts:		Information Systems:		Professionals:		Tech./Scientific:	
Management Trainees:	Y	Marketing Pros.:	Y	Gen. Writing/Editing:	Y	Info. Management:	Y	Finance/Acct.:	Y	Engineers, Electrical:	
Experienced Mngmt.:	Y	Retail Sales:		Technical Writing:		Software Dev.:	Y	Law:	Y	Engineers, Other:	
International Business:	Y	Commercial/Industrial:	Y	Graphic Arts/Photog.:	Y	Hardware Dev.:		HR/Other:	Y	Health/Lab:	
MBA Grads:	Y	Sales Trainees:	Y	Music:		Consulting/Other:		Training:	Y	Scientists/Research:	
		Advertising Pros.:	Y	Broadcasting:				Health Care:		Petroleum/Chemicals:	
				Other:				Consulting:		Math/Other:	

TYPES OF BUSINESS:

Food-Wholesale Distribution
Restaurant Supplies Distribution
Medical & Surgical Supplies Distribution
Cleaning Supplies Distribution

BRANDS/DIVISIONS/AFFILIATES:

SYGMA Network
Baugh Supply Chain Cooperative
SYSCO NaturalA
SYSCO Reliance
SYSCO Imperial
SYSCO Classic
SYSCO Supreme
Pallas Foods Limited

CONTACTS: *Note: Officers with more than one job title may be intentionally listed here more than once.*

William J. DeLaney, III, CEO
Kenneth F. Spitler, COO
Kenneth F. Spitler, Pres.
William J. DeLaney, III, CFO
Larry G. Pulliam, Exec. VP-Sales
Evelyn J. Pulliam, VP-Human Resources
Lucas Wagenaar, VP-IT
John T. McIntyre, VP-Merch.
Michael C. Nichols, General Counsel/Sr. VP/Corp. Sec.
Jeanne-Mey Sun, VP-Strategy
Mark A. Palmer, VP-Corp. Comm.
Neil A. Russell, VP-Investor Rel.
Kirk G. Drummond, Sr. VP-Finance/Treas.
William B. Day, Sr. VP-Supply Chain
Twila M. Day, CIO/VP
Albert L. Gaylor, VP-Industry Rel. & Diversity
G. Mitchell Elmer, Chief Acct. Officer/Controller/Sr. VP
Manuel A. Fernandez, Chmn.
G. Kent Humphries, Sr. VP-Canadian Food Service Oper.
Larry G. Pulliam, Exec. VP-Global Supply Chain

Phone: 281-584-1390	Fax: 281-584-2721
Toll-Free:	
Address: 1390 Enclave Pkwy., Houston, TX 77077-2099 US	

GROWTH PLANS/SPECIAL FEATURES:

SYSCO Corp., through its subsidiaries, is one of the largest distributors of food and food-related products to the foodservice industry in North America. The firm provides products and services to more than 400,000 customers, including restaurants, healthcare companies, educational facilities and lodging establishments. Restaurants account for approximately 63% of the company's sales; hospitals and nursing homes account for 10%; 5% are derived from schools and colleges; hotels and motels sales account for 6%; and 16% are derived from other sources. SYSCO distributes a wide variety of frozen and imported foods; fresh meats and seafood; dairy items; fresh produce; and nonfood items, including tableware, restaurant/kitchen equipment, medical/surgical supplies and cleaning supplies. Subsidiary SYGMA Network specializes in serving chain restaurants, especially Wendy's International, which accounts for 5% of SYSCO's sales and 34% of SYGMA's sales. Subsidiary Baugh Supply Chain Cooperative, Inc., covers the purchasing and marketing of SYSCO-brand merchandise, as well as private-label and national-brand merchandise. The firm operates 180 distribution facilities throughout the U.S. and Canada, with a fleet of approximately 9,100 delivery trucks; approximately 87% of these vehicles are owned. SYSCO's brands include SYSCO NaturalA, its produce line; SYSCO Reliance low-cost food items; SYSCO Classic, featuring higher quality foods; and SYSCO Imperial and SYSCO Supreme, both of which offer the company's highest quality and most expensive products. In March 2009, the firm acquired Pallas Foods Limited, an Irish foodservice distributor of over 7,000 products to approximately 6,000 customers.

SYSCO offers its employees life, disability, medical, dental and vision insurance; annual performance incentives; an assistance program; tuition assistance; a retirement plan; a stock purchase plan; matching charity gifts; a 401(k); and product discounts.

FINANCIALS: Sales and profits are in thousands of dollars—add 000 to get the full amount. 2008 Note: Financial information for 2008 was not available for all companies at press time.

2008 Sales: $37,522,111	2008 Profits: $1,106,151	**U.S. Stock Ticker:** SYY	
2007 Sales: $35,042,075	2007 Profits: $1,001,076	**Int'l Ticker:**	Int'l Exchange:
2006 Sales: $32,628,438	2006 Profits: $855,325	Employees: 47,000	
2005 Sales: $30,281,914	2005 Profits: $961,457	Fiscal Year Ends: 6/30	
2004 Sales: $29,335,403	2004 Profits: $907,214	Parent Company:	

SALARIES/BENEFITS:

Pension Plan: Y	ESOP Stock Plan:	Profit Sharing:	Top Exec. Salary: $1,146,500	Bonus: $7,048,400
Savings Plan: Y	Stock Purch. Plan: Y		Second Exec. Salary: $690,000	Bonus: $2,698,836

OTHER THOUGHTS:

Apparent Women Officers or Directors: 8
Hot Spot for Advancement for Women/Minorities: Y

LOCATIONS: ("Y" = Yes)

West:	Southwest:	Midwest:	Southeast:	Northeast:	International:
Y	Y	Y	Y	Y	Y

TARGET CORPORATION

www.target.com

Industry Group Code: 452112 Ranks within this company's industry group: Sales: 3 Profits: 2

Management:		Sales/Marketing:		Liberal Arts:		Information Systems:		Professionals:		Tech./Scientific:	
Management Trainees:	Y	Marketing Pros.:	Y	Gen. Writing/Editing:	Y	Info. Management:	Y	Finance/Acct.:	Y	Engineers, Electrical:	
Experienced Mngmt.:	Y	Retail Sales:	Y	Technical Writing:		Software Dev.:	Y	Law:	Y	Engineers, Other:	
International Business:	Y	Commercial/Industrial:		Graphic Arts/Photog.:	Y	Hardware Dev.:		HR/Other:	Y	Health/Lab:	
MBA Grads:	Y	Sales Trainees:	Y	Music:		Consulting/Other:		Training:	Y	Scientists/Research:	
		Advertising Pros.:	Y	Broadcasting:				Health Care:		Petroleum/Chemicals:	
				Other:	Y			Consulting:		Math/Other:	

TYPES OF BUSINESS:
Discount Department Stores
Online Sales
Catalog Sales
Groceries
Credit Cards

BRANDS/DIVISIONS/AFFILIATES:
SuperTarget
Target.com
Market Pantry
Archer Farms
Merona
Xhilaration
Choxie
Target Card

CONTACTS: *Note: Officers with more than one job title may be intentionally listed here more than once.*
Gregg W. Steinhafel, CEO
Gregg W. Steinhafel, Pres.
Douglas A. Scovanner, CFO/Exec. VP
Michael R. Francis, Chief Mktg. Officer/Exec. VP
Jodeen A. Kozlak, Exec. VP-Human Resources
Beth M. Jacob, CIO/Sr. VP-Tech. Svcs.
Janet M. Schalk, Sr. VP-Tech. Svcs.
Kathryn A. Tesija, Exec. VP-Merch.
Timothy R. Baer, General Counsel/Corp. Sec./Exec. VP
Ellen Tansey, Exec. VP-Global Oper. & Target Sourcing Svcs.
John D. Griffith, Exec. VP-Property Dev.
Steve Eastman, Pres., Target.com
Susan D. Kahn, VP-Comm.
Susan D. Kahn, VP-Investor Rel.
Jane P. Windmeier, Sr. VP-Finance
Troy H. Risch, Exec. VP-Stores
Terrence J. Scully, Pres., Target Financial Svcs.
Stacia J. Anderson, Pres., Target Sourcing Svcs.
Carmela Batacchi, Sr. VP-Target Sourcing Svcs., Regions II & III
Gregg W. Steinhafel, Chmn.
Lalit Ahuja, Managing Dir. & Pres., Target India
Mitchell L. Stover, Sr. VP-Dist.

Phone: 612-304-6073	Fax: 612-696-3731
Toll-Free:	
Address: 1000 Nicollet Mall, Minneapolis, MN 55403 US	

GROWTH PLANS/SPECIAL FEATURES:
Target Corporation operates large-format general merchandise and food discount stores in the U.S., which include Target and SuperTarget stores. The firm operates in two segments: retail operations and credit cards. The company operates 1,719 stores in 49 states, as well as 34 distribution centers. Target also owns approximately 241 SuperTarget stores, which combine grocery and general merchandise in a single format. SuperTarget stores feature coffee bars, bakeries, banking areas, pharmacies and photo services. The company operates three stores in India as well. Target carries brands such as Playwonder; Room Essentials; Archer Farms; Durabuilt; Embark; Garden Place; Boots & Barkley; Choxie; Circo; Gilligan & O'Malley; Kaori; and Sutton and Dodge. In addition, Target sells merchandise under its own private-label brands, including Target brand, Market Pantry, Archer Farms, Merona, Xhilaration, Choxie, Trutech and Target Limited Edition. Target stores derive the largest percentage of sales from consumables and commodities (approximately 37%); electronics, sporting goods, toys and entertainment items account for 22%; home furniture and décor for 21%; and apparel and accessories for 20%. The company's branded proprietary credit card products, called REDcards, provide discounts in an attempt to gain customer loyalty. REDcards are sold under the Target Visa and Target Card names. Target also sells merchandise via its e-commerce site, Target.com. In July 2009, the firm opened 23 new stores in 15 states; two of these are SuperTargets.

Target offers employees benefits including life and disability insurance; medical, dental and prescription drug coverage; a 401(k); educational loans; tuition reimbursement; home loans; home buyer's, childcare, tax preparation and adoption assistance; and several discount plans.

FINANCIALS: Sales and profits are in thousands of dollars—add 000 to get the full amount. 2008 Note: Financial information for 2008 was not available for all companies at press time.

2008 Sales: $63,367,000	2008 Profits: $2,849,000	**U.S. Stock Ticker:** TGT	
2007 Sales: $59,490,000	2007 Profits: $2,787,000	**Int'l Ticker:**	**Int'l Exchange:**
2006 Sales: $52,620,000	2006 Profits: $2,408,000	Employees: 351,000	
2005 Sales: $46,839,000	2005 Profits: $3,198,000	Fiscal Year Ends: 1/31	
2004 Sales: $42,025,000	2004 Profits: $1,809,000	Parent Company:	

SALARIES/BENEFITS:

Pension Plan:	ESOP Stock Plan:	Profit Sharing:	Top Exec. Salary: $1,345,769	Bonus: $447,680
Savings Plan: Y	Stock Purch. Plan: Y		Second Exec. Salary: $972,115	Bonus: $270,203

OTHER THOUGHTS:
Apparent Women Officers or Directors: 19
Hot Spot for Advancement for Women/Minorities: Y

LOCATIONS: ("Y" = Yes)

West:	Southwest:	Midwest:	Southeast:	Northeast:	International:
Y	Y	Y	Y	Y	Y

Note: Financial information, benefits and other data can change quickly and may vary from those stated here.

TBC CORPORATION

www.tbccorp.com

Industry Group Code: 441320 Ranks within this company's industry group: Sales: Profits:

Management:		Sales/Marketing:		Liberal Arts:		Information Systems:		Professionals:		Tech./Scientific:	
Management Trainees:	Y	Marketing Pros.:	Y	Gen. Writing/Editing:	Y	Info. Management:	Y	Finance/Acct.:	Y	Engineers, Electrical:	
Experienced Mngmt.:	Y	Retail Sales:	Y	Technical Writing:		Software Dev.:	Y	Law:	Y	Engineers, Other:	
International Business:	Y	Commercial/Industrial:	Y	Graphic Arts/Photog.:	Y	Hardware Dev.:		HR/Other:	Y	Health/Lab:	
MBA Grads:	Y	Sales Trainees:	Y	Music:		Consulting/Other:		Training:	Y	Scientists/Research:	
		Advertising Pros.:	Y	Broadcasting:				Health Care:		Petroleum/Chemicals:	
				Other:				Consulting:		Math/Other:	

TYPES OF BUSINESS:

Tire Stores
Wholesale Tire Distribution

BRANDS/DIVISIONS/AFFILIATES:

Sumitomo Corporation
Tire Kingdom, Inc.
Cordovan
Big O Tires, Inc.
Sigma
National Tire & Battery
Carroll Tire Company
Treadways

CONTACTS: *Note: Officers with more than one job title may be intentionally listed here more than once.*

Lawrence C. Day, CEO
Lawrence C. Day, Pres.
Timothy J. Miller, CFO
Orland M. Wolford, Pres./CEO-TBC Retail Group
Peter Wellman, CIO/Sr. VP
Susan D. Hendee, General Counsel/Corp. Sec.
Timothy J. Miller, Treas./Exec. VP
Gary M. Paulsen, Pres., TBC Private Brands
Eric R. Olsen, Pres./CEO-TBC Wholesale Group
N. Willian Inhken, Exec. VP/COO-Tire Kingdom Group
Kevin A. Kormondy, Exec. VP/COO-Big O Tires
Lawrence C. Day, Chmn.
J. Glen Gravatt, Pres., Purchasing & Dist. Div.

Phone: 561-227-0955	Fax:
Toll-Free:	
Address: 7111 Fairway Dr., Ste. 201, Palm Beach Gardens, FL 33418 US	

GROWTH PLANS/SPECIAL FEATURES:

TBC Corporation markets and distributes replacement automobile tires through wholesale and retail operations. The wholesale segment of TBC's business markets and distributes its proprietary brands of tires, as well as other tires and related products, to regional tire chains and distributors serving independent tire dealers covering the U.S., Canada and Mexico. The company also markets directly to independent tire dealers in the U.S. through its 38 Carroll Tire wholesale distribution centers. Tires marketed under the company's proprietary brands Multi-Mile, Cordovan, Sigma and Vanderbilt are manufactured and marketed through subsidiary TBC Private Brands. TBC Private Brands specializes in passenger, commercial, farm and specialty tires. The Treadways subsidiary provides high performance, passenger, light and medium truck, farm and industrial tires under the Sumitomo, Eldorado, Telstar, Laramie and Jetzon brands. The retail segment of the company's business consists of both the franchised retail tire business conducted by the company's Big O Tires, Inc. subsidiary and the company-owned stores operated through TBC Retail Group, which maintains stores under the brands Tire Kingdom, National Tire and Battery and Merchant's Tire and Auto Centers. Tire Kingdom International sells wholesale tires in domestic and international markets. TBC is owned by the Sumitomo Corporation, one of Japan's largest integrated trading and investment business organizations.

FINANCIALS: Sales and profits are in thousands of dollars—add 000 to get the full amount. 2008 Note: Financial information for 2008 was not available for all companies at press time.

2008 Sales: $	2008 Profits: $	**U.S. Stock Ticker: Subsidiary**	
2007 Sales: $1,779,400	2007 Profits: $	**Int'l Ticker:** Int'l Exchange:	
2006 Sales: $	2006 Profits: $	Employees: 9,500	
2005 Sales: $	2005 Profits: $	Fiscal Year Ends: 12/31	
2004 Sales: $1,855,418	2004 Profits: $37,598	Parent Company: SUMITOMO CORPORATION	

SALARIES/BENEFITS:

Pension Plan:	ESOP Stock Plan:	Profit Sharing:	Top Exec. Salary: $	Bonus: $
Savings Plan:	Stock Purch. Plan:		Second Exec. Salary: $	Bonus: $

OTHER THOUGHTS:

Apparent Women Officers or Directors: 1
Hot Spot for Advancement for Women/Minorities:

LOCATIONS: ("Y" = Yes)

West:	Southwest:	Midwest:	Southeast:	Northeast:	International:
Y	Y		Y		

Note: Financial information, benefits and other data can change quickly and may vary from those stated here.

TEAM INC
www.teamindustrialservices.com

Industry Group Code: 213112 Ranks within this company's industry group: Sales: 10 Profits: 10

Management:		Sales/Marketing:		Liberal Arts:		Information Systems:		Professionals:		Tech./Scientific:	
Management Trainees:	Y	Marketing Pros.:	Y	Gen. Writing/Editing:		Info. Management:	Y	Finance/Acct.:	Y	Engineers, Electrical:	
Experienced Mngmt.:	Y	Retail Sales:		Technical Writing:	Y	Software Dev.:		Law:	Y	Engineers, Other:	Y
International Business:	Y	Commercial/Industrial:	Y	Graphic Arts/Photog.:		Hardware Dev.:		HR/Other:	Y	Health/Lab:	
MBA Grads:	Y	Sales Trainees:		Music:		Consulting/Other:		Training:	Y	Scientists/Research:	
		Advertising Pros.:		Broadcasting:				Health Care:		Petroleum/Chemicals:	
				Other:				Consulting:		Math/Other:	

TYPES OF BUSINESS:
Piping System Maintenance & Construction Services

BRANDS/DIVISIONS/AFFILIATES:
Team Industrial Services, Inc.
Team Industrial Services International, Inc.
Team Industrial Services Asia (PTE) Ltd.
TISI Canada, Inc.

CONTACTS: *Note: Officers with more than one job title may be intentionally listed here more than once.*
Philip J. Hawk, CEO
Ted W. Owen, CFO/Sr. VP
John P. Kearns, Sr. VP-Eng.
John P. Kearns, Sr. VP-Mfg.
Andre C. (Butch) Bouchard, Sr. VP-Admin.
Andre C. (Butch) Bouchard, General Counsel/Sec.
Pete W. Wallace, Sr. VP-Bus. Dev. & Commercial Support
David C. Palmore, Sr. VP-TMS Div.
Art Victorson, Sr. VP-TCM Div.
Philip J. Hawk, Chmn.

Phone: 281-331-6154	Fax:
Toll-Free: 800-662-8326	
Address: 200 Hermann Dr., Alvin, TX 77511 US	

GROWTH PLANS/SPECIAL FEATURES:
Team, Inc. is a provider of specialty maintenance and construction services related primarily to the maintenance of high temperature and high pressure piping systems utilized in heavy industries. The company's offerings encompass a range of services, including leak repair, hot tapping, fugitive emissions control, field machining, technical bolting, field valve repair, non-destructive testing and field heat treating. Team's services are available 24-hour-a-day, seven-days-a-week, and are marketed to companies in a broad range of industries, including petrochemicals, refining, power, pipeline, pulp and paper, steel, shipbuilding, original equipment manufacturers (OEMs), municipalities and large engineering and construction firms. Team's leak repair services consist of on-stream repairs of leaks in pipes, valves, flanges and other parts of piping systems and related equipment, utilizing both standard and custom-designed clamps and enclosures for piping systems. The company's hot tapping services involve utilizing special equipment to cut a hole in a pressurized pipeline so that a new branch pipe can be connected onto the existing pipeline without interrupting operations. Emissions control services are focused on fugitive volatile organic chemical leaks, and include identification, monitoring, data management and reporting services primarily for the chemical, refining and natural gas processing industries. Field machining services include flange facing, pipe cutting, line boring, journal turning, drilling and milling, while technical bolting services help to maintain leak-free connections. Field valve services encompass on-site repairs for a variety of valves, as well as diagnostics and repair for specialty valve actuators. The company maintains over 100 locations throughout the U.S., and well as international locations serving markets such as Canada, Aruba, Belgium, Singapore, the Netherlands, Trinidad and Venezuela. About 70% of the firm's revenues are generated by business in the U.S., while Canada accounts for approximately 23% and Europe accounts for 5%, with other foreign locations accounting for the remaining 2%.

FINANCIALS: Sales and profits are in thousands of dollars—add 000 to get the full amount. 2008 Note: Financial information for 2008 was not available for all companies at press time.

2008 Sales: $478,475	2008 Profits: $23,623	U.S. Stock Ticker: TISI
2007 Sales: $318,348	2007 Profits: $15,515	Int'l Ticker: Int'l Exchange:
2006 Sales: $259,838	2006 Profits: $10,636	Employees: 3,400
2005 Sales: $	2005 Profits: $	Fiscal Year Ends: 5/31
2004 Sales: $	2004 Profits: $	Parent Company:

SALARIES/BENEFITS:
Pension Plan:	ESOP Stock Plan:	Profit Sharing:	Top Exec. Salary: $550,000	Bonus: $220,000
Savings Plan: Y	Stock Purch. Plan:		Second Exec. Salary: $273,075	Bonus: $152,000

OTHER THOUGHTS:
Apparent Women Officers or Directors:
Hot Spot for Advancement for Women/Minorities:

LOCATIONS: ("Y" = Yes)
West:	Southwest:	Midwest:	Southeast:	Northeast:	International:
Y	Y	Y	Y	Y	Y

TECH DATA CORP

www.techdata.com

Industry Group Code: 423430 Ranks within this company's industry group: Sales: 2   Profits: 2

Management:		Sales/Marketing:		Liberal Arts:		Information Systems:		Professionals:		Tech./Scientific:	
Management Trainees:	Y	Marketing Pros.:	Y	Gen. Writing/Editing:	Y	Info. Management:	Y	Finance/Acct.:	Y	Engineers, Electrical:	
Experienced Mngmt.:	Y	Retail Sales:		Technical Writing:	Y	Software Dev.:	Y	Law:	Y	Engineers, Other:	
International Business:	Y	Commercial/Industrial:	Y	Graphic Arts/Photog.:	Y	Hardware Dev.:		HR/Other:	Y	Health/Lab:	
MBA Grads:	Y	Sales Trainees:	Y	Music:		Consulting/Other:		Training:	Y	Scientists/Research:	
		Advertising Pros.:	Y	Broadcasting:				Health Care:		Petroleum/Chemicals:	
				Other:				Consulting:		Math/Other:	

TYPES OF BUSINESS:

Computer & Software Products, Distribution
Training
Assembly Services

BRANDS/DIVISIONS/AFFILIATES:

Tech Data Germany AG
Globelle Corp
Scribona AB

CONTACTS: *Note: Officers with more than one job title may be intentionally listed here more than once.*

Robert M. Dutkowsky, CEO
Jeffery P. Howells, CFO/Exec. VP
Joseph A. Osbourn, Worldwide CIO/Exec. VP
David R. Vetter, General Counsel/Sr. VP/Sec.
Charles V. Dannewitz, Treas./Sr. VP-Tax
Kenneth Lamneck, Pres., Americas
Joseph B. Trepani, Controller/Sr. VP
Steven A. Raymund, Chmn.
Nestor Cano, Pres., Europe

Phone: 727-539-7429	Fax:
Toll-Free: 800-237-8931	
Address: 5350 Tech Data Dr., Clearwater, FL 33760 US	

GROWTH PLANS/SPECIAL FEATURES:

Tech Data Corp. is a worldwide distributor of information technology (IT) products, logistics management and other value-added services. The company serves more than 100,000 value-added resellers (VARs), direct marketers, retailers and corporate resellers in more than 100 countries throughout North America, Latin America and Europe. It offers a variety of products from manufacturers and publishers such as Acer, Adobe, American Power, Apple, Autodesk, Canon, Cisco Systems, Epson, Fujitsu-Siemens, Hewlett-Packard, IBM, Intel, Kingston, Lexmark, Lenovo, Microsoft, Nortel Networks, Samsung, Sony, Symantec, Toshiba, Western Digital and Xerox. Products are typically purchased directly from manufacturers or software publishers on a non-exclusive basis, and then shipped to customers from one of Tech Data's 24 regionally located logistics centers. The company's vendor agreements do not restrict it from selling similar products manufactured by competitors, nor do they require it to sell a specified quantity of product. The firm also provides resellers with extensive pre- and post-sale training, service and support, as well as configuration and assembly services and e-commerce tools. Tech Data provides products and services to the online reseller channel and does business with thousands of resellers via its web site. The firm's entire electronic catalog is available online, and its electronic software distribution initiative allows resellers and vendors to easily access software titles directly from a secure location on the web site. The company owns Tech Data Germany AG, a European IT distributor, and Globelle Corp., a Canadian IT distributor. In May 2008, Tech Data announced its acquisition of certain assets of Scribona AB, a European IT distribution company with operations in Sweden, Finland and Norway, for approximately $83 million.

Tech Data offers its employees medical, dental and life insurance; short- and long-term disability insurance; tuition reimbursement; a 401(k) plan; and a discount stock purchase program.

FINANCIALS: Sales and profits are in thousands of dollars—add 000 to get the full amount. 2008 Note: Financial information for 2008 was not available for all companies at press time.

2008 Sales: $23,423,078	2008 Profits: $108,269	**U.S. Stock Ticker: TECD**
2007 Sales: $21,440,445	2007 Profits: $-96,981	**Int'l Ticker:** Int'l Exchange:
2006 Sales: $20,482,851	2006 Profits: $26,586	Employees: 8,000
2005 Sales: $19,730,917	2005 Profits: $162,460	Fiscal Year Ends: 1/31
2004 Sales: $17,358,525	2004 Profits: $104,147	Parent Company:

SALARIES/BENEFITS:

Pension Plan:	ESOP Stock Plan:	Profit Sharing:	Top Exec. Salary: $916,154	Bonus: $1,590,000
Savings Plan: Y	Stock Purch. Plan: Y		Second Exec. Salary: $667,455	Bonus: $954,800

OTHER THOUGHTS:

Apparent Women Officers or Directors:
Hot Spot for Advancement for Women/Minorities:

LOCATIONS: ("Y" = Yes)

West:	Southwest:	Midwest:	Southeast:	Northeast:	International:
Y	Y	Y	Y	Y	Y

Note: Financial information, benefits and other data can change quickly and may vary from those stated here.

TEKTRONIX INC

Industry Group Code: 3345 Ranks within this company's industry group: Sales: Profits:

Management:		Sales/Marketing:		Liberal Arts:		Information Systems:		Professionals:		Tech./Scientific:	
Management Trainees:	Y	Marketing Pros.:	Y	Gen. Writing/Editing:		Info. Management:	Y	Finance/Acct.:	Y	Engineers, Electrical:	Y
Experienced Mngmt.:	Y	Retail Sales:		Technical Writing:	Y	Software Dev.:	Y	Law:	Y	Engineers, Other:	Y
International Business:	Y	Commercial/Industrial:	Y	Graphic Arts/Photog.:	Y	Hardware Dev.:	Y	HR/Other:	Y	Health/Lab:	
MBA Grads:	Y	Sales Trainees:		Music:		Consulting/Other:		Training:	Y	Scientists/Research:	Y
		Advertising Pros.:	Y	Broadcasting:				Health Care:		Petroleum/Chemicals:	
				Other:				Consulting:		Math/Other:	Y

TYPES OF BUSINESS:

Test & Measurement Equipment
Support Services
Oscilloscopes
Logic analyzers
Video test equipment
Communications test equipment

BRANDS/DIVISIONS/AFFILIATES:

MAXTEK
TEKTRONIX
Danaher Corp
Arantech

CONTACTS: *Note: Officers with more than one job title may be intentionally listed here more than once.*

James A. Lico, CEO
James A. Lico, Pres.
Chuck McLaughlin, CFO
Robert W. Blaskowsky, CIO/VP
Neil Huddlestone, Pres., Tektronix China
Fuki Yoneyama, Pres., Japan Region/VP-Japan Sales

Phone: 503-627-7111	Fax: 503-627-6108
Toll-Free: 800-835-9433	
Address: 14200 SW Karl Braun Dr., Beaverton, OR 97077 US	

GROWTH PLANS/SPECIAL FEATURES:

Tektronix, Inc. develops, manufactures and markets test, measurement and monitoring products to a wide variety of customers in the computing, communications semiconductors, education, computer, military/aerospace, research and consumer electronics industries. The company provides general purpose testing products and video test, measurement and monitoring products, which includes oscilloscopes, logic analyzers, signal sources and spectrum analyzers. Additional video products include waveform monitors, video signal generators, compressed digital video test products and other test and measurement for video equipment manufacturers, content developers and traditional television broadcasters. The general testing products are designed to capture, display and analyze streams of electrical data, while video products ensure the delivery of the best possible video experience to the viewer. The firm also offers telecommunications network management and network diagnostics products. Network management products consist of network monitoring systems that actively test networks and provide troubleshooting, provisioning and automated service quality monitoring. The firm's products are sold under the TEKTRONIX and MAXTEK brand names. The company is a subsidiary of Danaher Corporation, a designer and manufacturer of a variety of professional, medical, industrial and consumer products. In April 2009, the company acquired Arantech, an Ireland-based provider of Customer Experience Management (CEM) solutions.

Employees are offered medical and dental insurance; disability coverage; life insurance; and retirement plans.

FINANCIALS: Sales and profits are in thousands of dollars—add 000 to get the full amount. 2008 Note: Financial information for 2008 was not available for all companies at press time.

2008 Sales: $	2008 Profits: $	**U.S. Stock Ticker: Subsidiary**
2007 Sales: $1,105,172	2007 Profits: $90,408	**Int'l Ticker:** Int'l Exchange:
2006 Sales: $1,039,870	2006 Profits: $92,355	Employees: 4,400
2005 Sales: $1,034,654	2005 Profits: $81,596	Fiscal Year Ends: 12/31
2004 Sales: $920,620	2004 Profits: $116,095	Parent Company: DANAHER CORP

SALARIES/BENEFITS:

Pension Plan:	ESOP Stock Plan:	Profit Sharing:	Top Exec. Salary: $	Bonus: $472,900
Savings Plan:	Stock Purch. Plan:		Second Exec. Salary: $	Bonus: $

OTHER THOUGHTS:

Apparent Women Officers or Directors:
Hot Spot for Advancement for Women/Minorities:

LOCATIONS: ("Y" = Yes)

West:	Southwest:	Midwest:	Southeast:	Northeast:	International:
Y	Y			Y	Y

TELEDYNE TECHNOLOGIES INCORPORATED   www.teledyne.com

Industry Group Code: 33641 Ranks within this company's industry group: Sales: 8   Profits: 7

Management:		Sales/Marketing:		Liberal Arts:		Information Systems:		Professionals:		Tech./Scientific:	
Management Trainees:	Y	Marketing Pros.:	Y	Gen. Writing/Editing:		Info. Management:	Y	Finance/Acct.:	Y	Engineers, Electrical:	Y
Experienced Mngmt.:	Y	Retail Sales:		Technical Writing:	Y	Software Dev.:	Y	Law:	Y	Engineers, Other:	Y
International Business:	Y	Commercial/Industrial:	Y	Graphic Arts/Photog.:	Y	Hardware Dev.:	Y	HR/Other:	Y	Health/Lab:	
MBA Grads:	Y	Sales Trainees:		Music:		Consulting/Other:		Training:	Y	Scientists/Research:	Y
		Advertising Pros.:	Y	Broadcasting:				Health Care:		Petroleum/Chemicals:	
				Other:				Consulting:		Math/Other:	Y

TYPES OF BUSINESS:

Electronics & Communications Products
Systems Engineering Solutions
Aerospace Engines & Components
Energy Systems

BRANDS/DIVISIONS/AFFILIATES:

Teledyne Isco Inc
Teledyne Brown Engineering
Teledyne Tekmar Co
Teledyne Solutions Inc
Teledyne Energy Systems Inc
Cormon Limited
Teledyne Odom Hydrographic, Inc.
Teledyne Controls

CONTACTS: *Note: Officers with more than one job title may be intentionally listed here more than once.*

Robert Mehrabian, CEO
Robert Mehrabian, Pres.
Dale A. Schnittjer, CFO/Sr. VP
Robyn E. McGowan, VP-Human Resources
Robert W. Steenberge, CTO/VP
Robyn E. McGowan, VP-Admin.
John T. Kuelbs, General Counsel/Exec. VP/Sec.
Jason VanWees, VP-Corp. Dev.
Jason VanWees, VP-Investor Rel.
Susan L. Main, Controller/VP
Ivars R. Blukis, Chief Bus. Risk Assurance Officer
Aldo Pichelli, COO/Pres., Electronics & Comm. Segment
Stephen F. Blackwood, Treas./VP
Rex Geveden, Pres., Teledyne Brown Eng.
Robert Mehrabian, Chmn.

Phone: 805-373-4545	Fax: 805-373-4775
Toll-Free:	
Address: 1049 Camino Dos Rios, Thousand Oaks, CA 91360 US	

GROWTH PLANS/SPECIAL FEATURES:

Teledyne Technologies, Inc. through its subsidiaries, provides electronic components, instruments and communications products including defense electronics, monitoring and control instrumentation for marine, environmental and industrial applications; data acquisition and communications equipment for airlines and business aircraft and components; and subsystems for wireless and satellite communications. The company also provides systems engineering and information technology services for defense, space and environmental applications, and manufactures general aviation engines and components, supply energy generation, energy storage and small propulsion products. The firm operates in four segments: electronics and communications, responsible for 68% of revenue in 2008; engineered systems, which accounted for 19% of revenue; aerospace engines and components, which generated 9%; and energy and power systems, which accounted for 4%. Subsidiaries include Teledyne Isco, Inc., a producer of water quality monitoring products such as wastewater samplers and open channel flow meters; Teledyne Brown Engineering, a full-service missile defense contractor; Teledyne Solutions, Inc., a missile defense systems engineering contractor for the U.S. Army; Teledyne Energy Systems, Inc., a provider of Teledyne Titan hydrogen gas generators and thermoelectric and fuel cell-based power sources; and Teledyne Tekmar Co., a manufacturer of instruments that automate the preparation and concentrations of drinking water and wastewater. In October 2008, another subsidiary, Teledyne Limited, acquired Cormon Limited and Cormon Technology Limited, which manufacture flow integrity monitoring systems and corrosion sensors. In December of the same year, through subsidiary, Teledyne RD Instruments, Inc., the company acquired Odom Hydrographic Systems, Inc., a Louisiana based designer of hydrographic surveying instruments, which was subsequently named Teledyne Odom Hydrographic, Inc. Also in December 2008, the firm acquired the assets of Demo Systems LLC, a manufacturer of aircraft data loading equipment and data distribution software, which was renamed to Teledyne Controls.

FINANCIALS: Sales and profits are in thousands of dollars—add 000 to get the full amount. 2008 Note: Financial information for 2008 was not available for all companies at press time.

2008 Sales: $1,893,000	2008 Profits: $111,300	**U.S. Stock Ticker: TDY**
2007 Sales: $1,622,300	2007 Profits: $98,500	**Int'l Ticker:** Int'l Exchange:
2006 Sales: $1,433,200	2006 Profits: $80,300	Employees: 8,800
2005 Sales: $1,206,500	2005 Profits: $64,200	Fiscal Year Ends: 12/31
2004 Sales: $1,016,600	2004 Profits: $41,700	Parent Company:

SALARIES/BENEFITS:

Pension Plan: Y	ESOP Stock Plan: Y	Profit Sharing:	Top Exec. Salary: $814,615	Bonus: $2,213,254
Savings Plan: Y	Stock Purch. Plan:		Second Exec. Salary: $419,840	Bonus: $869,029

OTHER THOUGHTS:

Apparent Women Officers or Directors: 4
Hot Spot for Advancement for Women/Minorities: Y

LOCATIONS: ("Y" = Yes)

West:	Southwest:	Midwest:	Southeast:	Northeast:	International:
Y	Y	Y	Y	Y	Y

TELEPHONE AND DATA SYSTEMS INC (TDS)

www.teldta.com

Industry Group Code: 517110 Ranks within this company's industry group: Sales: 10 Profits: 7

Management:		Sales/Marketing:		Liberal Arts:		Information Systems:		Professionals:		Tech./Scientific:	
Management Trainees:	Y	Marketing Pros.:	Y	Gen. Writing/Editing:	Y	Info. Management:	Y	Finance/Acct.:	Y	Engineers, Electrical:	Y
Experienced Mngmt.:	Y	Retail Sales:		Technical Writing:	Y	Software Dev.:	Y	Law:	Y	Engineers, Other:	Y
International Business:		Commercial/Industrial:	Y	Graphic Arts/Photog.:	Y	Hardware Dev.:		HR/Other:	Y	Health/Lab:	
MBA Grads:	Y	Sales Trainees:	Y	Music:		Consulting/Other:		Training:	Y	Scientists/Research:	
		Advertising Pros.:	Y	Broadcasting:				Health Care:		Petroleum/Chemicals:	
				Other:				Consulting:		Math/Other:	

TYPES OF BUSINESS:

Local Telephone Service
Cellular Telephone Services
Internet Access
Printing Services
Long-Distance Telephone Service
Data Networks

BRANDS/DIVISIONS/AFFILIATES:

US Cellular
TDS Telecom
TDS Metrocom
Suttle Straus Inc

CONTACTS: Note: Officers with more than one job title may be intentionally listed here more than once.

LeRoy T. Carlson, Jr., CEO
LeRoy T. Carlson, Jr., Pres.
Kenneth R. Meyers, CFO/Exec. VP
C. Theodore Herbert, VP-Human Resources
Kurt Thaus, CIO/Sr. VP
Joseph R. Hanley, VP-Tech. Planning & Svcs.
Kevin C. Gallagher, VP/Corp. Sec.
Scott H. Williamson, Sr. VP-Corp. Dev. & Acquisitions
Mark A. Steinkrauss, VP-Corp. Rel.
Ljubica A. Petrich, Sr. VP/Corp. Controller
Frieda E. Ireland, VP-Internal Audit
Kenneth M. Kotylo, VP-Corp. Dev. & Acquisitions
Peter L. Sereda, VP/Treas.
James Twesme, VP-Corp. Finance
Walter C. D. Carlson, Chmn.

Phone: 312-630-1900	Fax: 312-630-1908
Toll-Free:	
Address: 30 N. LaSalle St., Ste. 4000, Chicago, IL 60602 US	

GROWTH PLANS/SPECIAL FEATURES:

Telephone and Data Systems, Inc. (TDS), a Fortune 500 company, is a diversified telecommunications service company with wireless telephone and wireline telephone operations. It has approximately 7.4 million customers in 36 states. TDS has three subsidiary companies through which it operates: U.S. Cellular (USM), which generates the majority of revenues; TDS Telecommunications Corporation (TDS Telecom); and Suttle-Strauss. The firm owns approximately 82% of USM, which is the nation's sixth-largest wireless telecommunications provider, with more than 5 million customers in four major regions of the U.S. TDS conducts substantially all its wireless operations through USM. TDS conducts its wireline telephone operations through wholly-owned subsidiary TDS Telecom. This branch offers local, long-distance, broadband and entertainment solutions. TDS Telecom serves rural and suburban communities in 30 states through its incumbent local exchange carrier (ILEC) business and its competitive local exchange carrier (CLEC) business, which operates under the brand TDS Metrocom. TDS Metrocom provides telecommunications services in a five-state footprint in the Midwest. Majority-owned subsidiary (80%) Suttle-Straus is a full-service printing and communications company that offers customers a wide range of services.

Employees are offered health insurance; flexible spending accounts; a pension plan; a 401(k) plan; a stock purchase plan; employee assistance and wellness programs; and product and entertainment discounts.

FINANCIALS: Sales and profits are in thousands of dollars—add 000 to get the full amount. 2008 Note: Financial information for 2008 was not available for all companies at press time.

2008 Sales: $5,092,000	2008 Profits: $93,500	U.S. Stock Ticker: TDS
2007 Sales: $4,829,000	2007 Profits: $386,100	Int'l Ticker: Int'l Exchange:
2006 Sales: $4,364,500	2006 Profits: $161,800	Employees: 12,500
2005 Sales: $3,953,000	2005 Profits: $647,700	Fiscal Year Ends: 12/31
2004 Sales: $3,720,400	2004 Profits: $49,000	Parent Company:

SALARIES/BENEFITS:

Pension Plan: Y	ESOP Stock Plan:	Profit Sharing:	Top Exec. Salary: $1,275,000	Bonus: $950,000
Savings Plan: Y	Stock Purch. Plan: Y		Second Exec. Salary: $855,000	Bonus: $675,000

OTHER THOUGHTS:

Apparent Women Officers or Directors: 4
Hot Spot for Advancement for Women/Minorities: Y

LOCATIONS: ("Y" = Yes)

West:	Southwest:	Midwest:	Southeast:	Northeast:	International:
Y	Y	Y	Y	Y	

TELETECH HOLDINGS INC

www.teletech.com

Industry Group Code: 56142 **Ranks within this company's industry group:** Sales: 2 Profits: 1

Management:		Sales/Marketing:		Liberal Arts:		Information Systems:		Professionals:		Tech./Scientific:	
Management Trainees:	Y	Marketing Pros.:	Y	Gen. Writing/Editing:	Y	Info. Management:	Y	Finance/Acct.:	Y	Engineers, Electrical:	
Experienced Mngmt.:	Y	Retail Sales:		Technical Writing:		Software Dev.:	Y	Law:	Y	Engineers, Other:	
International Business:	Y	Commercial/Industrial:	Y	Graphic Arts/Photog.:		Hardware Dev.:		HR/Other:	Y	Health/Lab:	
MBA Grads:	Y	Sales Trainees:		Music:		Consulting/Other:		Training:	Y	Scientists/Research:	
		Advertising Pros.:	Y	Broadcasting:				Health Care:		Petroleum/Chemicals:	
				Other:				Consulting:		Math/Other:	

TYPES OF BUSINESS:

Call Centers
Database & Direct Marketing Services
Outsourced Customer Service
Customer Retention Services
Consulting

BRANDS/DIVISIONS/AFFILIATES:

Percepta
Ford Motor Co

CONTACTS: *Note: Officers with more than one job title may be intentionally listed here more than once.*

Kenneth Tuchman, CEO
John Troka, Interim CFO
Mike Jossi, Exec. VP-Global Human Capital
Carol Kline, CIO/Exec. VP
Alan Schuzman, General Counsel/Exec. VP/Corp. Sec.
Karen Breen, VP-Investor Rel.
Karen Breen, Treas.
James Barlett, Vice Chmn.
Gregory G. Hopkins, Exec. VP-Global Accounts
Kenneth Tuchman, Chmn.

Phone: 303-397-8100	Fax: 303-397-8199
Toll-Free: 800-835-3832	
Address: 9197 S. Peoria St., Englewood, CO 80112-5833 US	

GROWTH PLANS/SPECIAL FEATURES:

TeleTech Holdings, Inc. provides outsourced customer management services to a significant number of Global 1000 companies. The firm focuses on large global corporations in the automotive, communications and media, financial services, government, health care, logistics, retail, technology and travel industries. TeleTech has 86 office locations in 17 countries, and about 60% of the firm's revenue is generated outside the U.S. With service offered in up to 29 languages daily, TeleTech's customer management services business provides outsourced customer support and marketing services via call centers throughout the world. This business is divided into North American customer care, serving the U.S. and Canada, and international customer care. The customer management services business manages telephone, e-mail, automated/interactive voice response and web-based customer interactions. Services include customer acquisition, provisioning, support, development and other customer-related programs. Within this segment is subsidiary Percepta, a joint venture with Ford Motor Company, which provides customer management services to Ford customers. TeleTech's database marketing and consulting business provides outsourced database management, direct marketing and related customer retention services for automotive dealerships and manufacturers in North America.

Employees are offered medical, dental and vision insurance; life insurance; disability coverage; a 401(k) plan; and tuition reimbursement.

FINANCIALS: Sales and profits are in thousands of dollars—add 000 to get the full amount. 2008 Note: Financial information for 2008 was not available for all companies at press time.

2008 Sales: $1,400,147	2008 Profits: $73,747	**U.S. Stock Ticker:** TTEC
2007 Sales: $1,369,632	2007 Profits: $53,103	**Int'l Ticker:** Int'l Exchange:
2006 Sales: $1,210,753	2006 Profits: $50,981	Employees: 55,000
2005 Sales: $1,085,903	2005 Profits: $26,286	Fiscal Year Ends: 12/31
2004 Sales: $1,052,690	2004 Profits: $24,003	Parent Company:

SALARIES/BENEFITS:

Pension Plan:	ESOP Stock Plan:	Profit Sharing:	Top Exec. Salary: $350,000	Bonus: $
Savings Plan: Y	Stock Purch. Plan:		Second Exec. Salary: $350,000	Bonus: $

OTHER THOUGHTS:

Apparent Women Officers or Directors: 4
Hot Spot for Advancement for Women/Minorities: Y

LOCATIONS: ("Y" = Yes)

West:	Southwest:	Midwest:	Southeast:	Northeast:	International:
Y	Y	Y	Y	Y	Y

TESORO CORP

www.tsocorp.com

Industry Group Code: 324110 **Ranks within this company's industry group:** Sales: 4 Profits: 2

Management:		Sales/Marketing:		Liberal Arts:		Information Systems:		Professionals:		Tech./Scientific:	
Management Trainees:	Y	Marketing Pros.:	Y	Gen. Writing/Editing:	Y	Info. Management:	Y	Finance/Acct.:	Y	Engineers, Electrical:	Y
Experienced Mngmt.:	Y	Retail Sales:		Technical Writing:	Y	Software Dev.:	Y	Law:	Y	Engineers, Other:	Y
International Business:	Y	Commercial/Industrial:	Y	Graphic Arts/Photog.:	Y	Hardware Dev.:		HR/Other:	Y	Health/Lab:	
MBA Grads:	Y	Sales Trainees:		Music:		Consulting/Other:		Training:	Y	Scientists/Research:	
		Advertising Pros.:		Broadcasting:				Health Care:		Petroleum/Chemicals:	Y
				Other:				Consulting:		Math/Other:	

TYPES OF BUSINESS:

Petroleum Refining
Gas Stations
Aviation & Heavy Fuels

BRANDS/DIVISIONS/AFFILIATES:

Mirastar
Tesoro Alaska

CONTACTS: *Note: Officers with more than one job title may be intentionally listed here more than once.*

Bruce A. Smith, CEO
Everett Lewis, COO/Exec. VP
Bruce A. Smith, Pres.
Gregory A. Wright, CFO/Exec. VP
Claude P. Moreau, Sr. VP-Mktg.
Otto C. Schwethelm, Sr. VP-IT
Susan A. Lerette, Sr. VP-Admin.
Charles S. Parrish, General Counsel/Sr. VP/Sec.
William J. Finnerty, Exec. VP-Strategy & Corp. Dev.
C.A. Flagg, Sr. VP-System Optimization
G. Scott Spendlove, Sr. VP-Risk Mgmt.
Dan Porter, Sr. VP-Refining
Arlen Glenewinkel Jr., VP-Admin.
Bruce A. Smith, Chmn.
Joseph G. McCoy, Sr. VP-Supply & Training

Phone: 210-828-8484	Fax: 210-828-8600
Toll-Free: 800-837-6768	
Address: 300 Concord Plaza Dr., San Antonio, TX 78216 US	

GROWTH PLANS/SPECIAL FEATURES:

Tesoro Corp. formerly known as Tesoro Petroleum Corp., is a U.S. independent petroleum refiner. The company operates in two segments: refining and marketing and distribution. Through the refining segment, the firm owns and operates seven petroleum refineries located in California, Alaska, Washington, Hawaii, North Dakota and Utah and sells refined products to a wide variety of customers in the western and mid-continental U.S. Tesoro's refineries produce a high proportion of its refined product sales volumes, and the company purchases the remainder from its other refiners and suppliers. The firm's seven refineries have a combined crude oil capacity of 665,000 barrels per day. Tesoro operates some of the largest refineries in Hawaii, Utah, northern California and Alaska, in addition to the only refinery in North Dakota. Through the marketing and distribution segment, the company sells refined products including gasoline and gasoline blendstocks, jet fuel, diesel fuel, heavy fuel oils and residual products in both the bulk and wholesale markets. The majority of its wholesale volumes are sold in 15 states to independent unbranded distributors that sell refined products through the firm's owned and third-party terminals. Tesoro's bulk volumes are primarily sold to independent and other oil companies; electric power producers; railroads; airlines; and marine and industrial end-users, which are distributed by pipelines, ships, railcars and trucks. In addition, the company sells refined products that it manufactures, purchases or receives on exchange from third parties. Tesoro's retail marketing operations include about 879 branded retail locations in the western U.S., Alaska and Hawaii, including Tesoro, Tesoro Alaska, Shell, USA Gasoline and 34 Mirastar-brand stations at Wal-Mart locations in the western U.S. Roughly 389 of these locations are company-operated.

Tesoro offers its employees health coverage; life and AD&D insurance; a savings plan; flexible spending accounts; education assistance; long-term disability; and long-term care insurance.

FINANCIALS: Sales and profits are in thousands of dollars—add 000 to get the full amount. 2008 Note: Financial information for 2008 was not available for all companies at press time.

2008 Sales: $23,309,000	2008 Profits: $278,000	**U.S. Stock Ticker:** TSO
2007 Sales: $21,915,000	2007 Profits: $566,000	**Int'l Ticker:** Int'l Exchange:
2006 Sales: $18,104,000	2006 Profits: $801,000	Employees: 5,620
2005 Sales: $16,581,000	2005 Profits: $507,000	Fiscal Year Ends: 12/31
2004 Sales: $12,262,200	2004 Profits: $327,900	Parent Company:

SALARIES/BENEFITS:

Pension Plan:	ESOP Stock Plan:	Profit Sharing:	Top Exec. Salary: $1,298,634	Bonus: $
Savings Plan: Y	Stock Purch. Plan:		Second Exec. Salary: $776,686	Bonus: $

OTHER THOUGHTS:

Apparent Women Officers or Directors: 2
Hot Spot for Advancement for Women/Minorities: Y

LOCATIONS: ("Y" = Yes)

West:	Southwest:	Midwest:	Southeast:	Northeast:	International:
Y	Y	Y			Y

THERMO FISHER SCIENTIFIC INC

www.thermofisher.com

Industry Group Code: 423450 Ranks within this company's industry group: Sales: 1   Profits: 1

Management:		Sales/Marketing:		Liberal Arts:		Information Systems:		Professionals:		Tech./Scientific:	
Management Trainees:	Y	Marketing Pros.:	Y	Gen. Writing/Editing:		Info. Management:	Y	Finance/Acct.:	Y	Engineers, Electrical:	
Experienced Mngmt.:	Y	Retail Sales:		Technical Writing:	Y	Software Dev.:	Y	Law:	Y	Engineers, Other:	
International Business:	Y	Commercial/Industrial:	Y	Graphic Arts/Photog.:	Y	Hardware Dev.:		HR/Other:	Y	Health/Lab:	
MBA Grads:	Y	Sales Trainees:		Music:		Consulting/Other:		Training:	Y	Scientists/Research:	
		Advertising Pros.:		Broadcasting:				Health Care:		Petroleum/Chemicals:	
				Other:				Consulting:		Math/Other:	

TYPES OF BUSINESS:

Laboratory Equipment & Supplies Distribution
Contract Manufacturing
Equipment Calibration & Repair
Clinical Trial Services
Laboratory Workstations
Clinical Consumables
Diagnostic Reagents
Custom Chemical Synthesis

BRANDS/DIVISIONS/AFFILIATES:

Biolab
LTQ Velos
Heraeus
M-PULSe
Affinity BioReagants
FIBERLite
Open Biosystems, Inc.

CONTACTS:
Note: Officers with more than one job title may be intentionally listed here more than once.

Marijn E. Dekkers, CEO
Marc N. Casper, COO/Exec. VP
Marijn E. Dekkers, Pres.
Peter M. Wilver, CFO/Sr. VP
Stephen G. Sheehan, Sr. VP-Human Resources
Seth H. Hoogasian, General Counsel/Sec./Sr. VP
Peter E. Hornstra, Chief Acct. Officer/VP
Alan J. Malus, Sr. VP
Gregory J. Herrema, Sr. VP
Yuh-Geng Tsay, Sr. VP
Jim Manzi, Chmn.

Phone: 781-622-1000	**Fax:** 781-622-1207
Toll-Free: 800-678-5599	
Address: 81 Wyman St., Waltham, MA 02454 US	

GROWTH PLANS/SPECIAL FEATURES:

Thermo Fisher Scientific Inc. is a distributor of products and services principally to the scientific-research and clinical laboratory markets. The firm serves over 350,000 customers including biotechnology and pharmaceutical companies; colleges and universities; medical-research institutions; hospitals; reference, quality control, process-control and research and development labs in various industries; and government agencies. Thermo Fisher offers an array of products, including analytical instruments; automation and robotics; life science research supplies; chemicals; disposable laboratory supplies; diagnostic supplies; laboratory equipment; furniture; software; and custom products. The company's services include asset management, instrument standards compliance services, education, technical support and professional assistance. In 2008, the firm acquired the Analytical Technologies and Environment Instrumentation divisions of Chemito Technologies Pvt. Ltd, the leading analytical instrument provider in India; Open Biosystems Inc., a provider of RNA Interference, gene expression and protein detection products for life science research and drug discovery; Affinity BioReagents, a provider of antibodies, peptides, proteins and other reagents for research; and FIBERLite, the world's leading supplier of carbon fiber centrifuge rotors. In December 2008, Thermo Fisher opened a new clinical services facility in India in order to establish a more significant presence in that market. In April 2009, the company acquired Biolab, an Australian provider of analytical equipment and the scientific and medical division of Alesco Corp., Ltd., for $120 million, in addition to a handful of other company acquisitions.

ThermoFisher offers its employees comprehensive benefits, paid time off, tuition reimbursement, retirement plans and employee recognition awards.

FINANCIALS:
Sales and profits are in thousands of dollars—add 000 to get the full amount. 2008 Note: Financial information for 2008 was not available for all companies at press time.

2008 Sales: $10,498,000	2008 Profits: $994,200	**U.S. Stock Ticker:** TMO
2007 Sales: $9,746,400	2007 Profits: $761,100	**Int'l Ticker:** Int'l Exchange:
2006 Sales: $3,791,617	2006 Profits: $168,935	Employees: 34,500
2005 Sales: $2,633,027	2005 Profits: $223,218	Fiscal Year Ends: 12/31
2004 Sales: $2,205,995	2004 Profits: $361,837	Parent Company: THERMO ELECTRON CORP

SALARIES/BENEFITS:

Pension Plan:	ESOP Stock Plan:	Profit Sharing:	Top Exec. Salary: $1,163,750	Bonus: $1,865,643
Savings Plan: Y	Stock Purch. Plan:		Second Exec. Salary: $701,250	Bonus: $823,266

OTHER THOUGHTS:

Apparent Women Officers or Directors: 2
Hot Spot for Advancement for Women/Minorities: Y

LOCATIONS: ("Y" = Yes)

West:	Southwest:	Midwest:	Southeast:	Northeast:	International:
Y		Y	Y	Y	Y

TIFFANY & CO

www.tiffany.com

Industry Group Code: 448310 **Ranks within this company's industry group:** Sales: 1 Profits: 1

Management:		Sales/Marketing:		Liberal Arts:		Information Systems:		Professionals:		Tech./Scientific:	
Management Trainees:	Y	Marketing Pros.:	Y	Gen. Writing/Editing:	Y	Info. Management:	Y	Finance/Acct.:	Y	Engineers, Electrical:	
Experienced Mngmt.:	Y	Retail Sales:	Y	Technical Writing:		Software Dev.:	Y	Law:	Y	Engineers, Other:	
International Business:	Y	Commercial/Industrial:		Graphic Arts/Photog.:	Y	Hardware Dev.:		HR/Other:	Y	Health/Lab:	
MBA Grads:	Y	Sales Trainees:	Y	Music:		Consulting/Other:		Training:	Y	Scientists/Research:	
		Advertising Pros.:	Y	Broadcasting:				Health Care:		Petroleum/Chemicals:	
				Other:	Y			Consulting:		Math/Other:	

TYPES OF BUSINESS:

Jewelry & Other Luxury Items, Retail
Catalog & Online Sales
Jewelry
Fragrance
Timepieces
Stationery
Home Décor

BRANDS/DIVISIONS/AFFILIATES:

Tiffany and Company
Tiffany & Co. Japan, Inc.
Mitsukoshi Ltd.
Iridesse, Inc.
Little Switzerland
NXP Corporation

CONTACTS: Note: Officers with more than one job title may be intentionally listed here more than once.

Michael J. Kowalski, CEO
James E. Quinn, Pres.
James N. Fernandez, CFO/Exec. VP
Caroline D. Naggiar, Chief Mktg. Officer
Victoria Berger-Gross, Sr. VP-Global Human Resources
Pamela H. Cloud, Sr. VP-Merch.
Patrick B. Dorsey, General Counsel/Sec./Sr. VP
John S. Petterson, Sr. VP-Oper.
Patrick F. McGuiness, Sr. VP-Finance
Beth O. Canavan, Exec. VP
Jon M. King, Exec. VP
Henry Iglesias, Controller/VP
Michael J. Kowalski, Chmn.

Phone: 212-755-8000	Fax: 212-605-4465
Toll-Free:	
Address: 727 Fifth Ave., New York, NY 10022 US	

GROWTH PLANS/SPECIAL FEATURES:

Tiffany & Co. is a holding company that operates through its principle subsidiary, Tiffany and Company, founded in 1837, a retail firm mainly selling jewelry, but also selling timepieces, sterling silver goods, china, crystal, stationery, fragrances and personal accessories. Its products are sold through U.S. and international Tiffany & Co. stores; as well as through direct marketing, including business-to-business, mail-order, Internet and wholesale sales. The firm operates approximately 67 branch stores in the U.S.; 10 stores divided between Canada, Central and South America; 57 stores in Japan; 39 in other Asia-Pacific regions; and 24 in Europe. In 2008, 87% of net sales were attributed to Tiffany & CO. jewelry, the remaining 13% of sales came from all other brand products. Tiffany & Co. Japan, Inc. has a partnership with Mitsukoshi Ltd., operating 18 Mitsukoshi department stores and other retail locations in Japan. The typical store has traditionally measured less than 10,000 square feet; however the company has switched to a smaller store format and plans to begin opening 5-7 new 5,000 square-foot Tiffany & Co. branch stores each year. The firm opened several new stores in the U.S. in 2008, and it is planning to open 8-12 stores in 2009. In September 2008, the company opened a 1,670-square-foot boutique in Berlin, Germany. In March 2009, the firm announced plans to open a new store in Amsterdam, the Netherlands. In August 2009, the company announced plans to open a store in Chadstone, Australia.

FINANCIALS: Sales and profits are in thousands of dollars—add 000 to get the full amount. 2008 Note: Financial information for 2008 was not available for all companies at press time.

2008 Sales: $2,938,771	2008 Profits: $323,478	**U.S. Stock Ticker: TIF**	
2007 Sales: $2,560,734	2007 Profits: $272,897	**Int'l Ticker:** Int'l Exchange:	
2006 Sales: $2,312,792	2006 Profits: $254,655	Employees: 9,000	
2005 Sales: $2,204,831	2005 Profits: $304,299	Fiscal Year Ends: 1/31	
2004 Sales: $2,000,045	2004 Profits: $215,517	Parent Company:	

SALARIES/BENEFITS:

Pension Plan:	ESOP Stock Plan:	Profit Sharing:	Top Exec. Salary: $1,037,975	Bonus: $
Savings Plan:	Stock Purch. Plan:		Second Exec. Salary: $766,398	Bonus: $

OTHER THOUGHTS:

Apparent Women Officers or Directors: 6
Hot Spot for Advancement for Women/Minorities: Y

LOCATIONS: ("Y" = Yes)

West:	Southwest:	Midwest:	Southeast:	Northeast:	International:
				Y	

TIME WARNER INC

www.timewarner.com

Industry Group Code: 517110 Ranks within this company's industry group: Sales: 3 Profits: 12

Management:		Sales/Marketing:		Liberal Arts:		Information Systems:		Professionals:		Tech./Scientific:	
Management Trainees:	Y	Marketing Pros.:	Y	Gen. Writing/Editing:	Y	Info. Management:	Y	Finance/Acct.:	Y	Engineers, Electrical:	Y
Experienced Mngmt.:	Y	Retail Sales:		Technical Writing:	Y	Software Dev.:	Y	Law:	Y	Engineers, Other:	Y
International Business:	Y	Commercial/Industrial:	Y	Graphic Arts/Photog.:	Y	Hardware Dev.:		HR/Other:	Y	Health/Lab:	
MBA Grads:	Y	Sales Trainees:		Music:	Y	Consulting/Other:		Training:	Y	Scientists/Research:	
		Advertising Pros.:	Y	Broadcasting:	Y			Health Care:		Petroleum/Chemicals:	
				Other:	Y			Consulting:		Math/Other:	

TYPES OF BUSINESS:
Cable TV Networks
Television Production
Cable TV Service
Magazine Publishing
Entertainment Investments
Film Production

BRANDS/DIVISIONS/AFFILIATES:
Home Box Office, Inc.
Time Warner Cable Inc
Warner Bros Entertainment Inc
Time Inc
New Line Cinema
Turner Broadcasting System, Inc.
Central European Media Company
AOL LLC

CONTACTS: *Note: Officers with more than one job title may be intentionally listed here more than once.*
Jeffrey L. Bewkes, CEO
Jeffrey L. Bewkes, Pres.
John K. Martin, CFO/Exec. VP
Patricia Fili-Krushel, Exec. VP-Admin.
Paul T. Cappuccio, General Counsel/Exec. VP
Edward I. Adler, Exec. VP-Corp. Comm.
James Burtson, Sr. VP-Investor Rel.
Carol Melton, Exec. VP-Global Public Policy
Olaf Olafsson, Exec. VP
Richard Parsons, Chmn.

Phone: 212-484-8000	Fax:
Toll-Free:	
Address: 1 Time Warner Ctr., New York, NY 10019 US	

GROWTH PLANS/SPECIAL FEATURES:
Time Warner, Inc. is a global media and entertainment company. The firm operates in four segments: networks, filmed entertainment, publishing and AOL LLC. The networks segment consists principally of domestic and international basic cable networks and pay television programming services. This division includes basic cable networks owned by subsidiary Turner Broadcasting System, Inc. (TBS) and pay television programming, such as the HBO and Cinemax channels, operated by Home Box Office, Inc. The segment also produces original programming such as Sex and the City, The Sopranos, Entourage, Rome and True Blood. The filmed entertainment segment, operated principally through subsidiary Warner Bros. Entertainment Group, produces and distributes theatrical motion pictures, television shows, animation and other programming, distributes home video product, and licenses rights to the company's feature films, television programming and characters. Time Warner's publishing business consists principally of magazine publishing and related web sites as well as a number of direct-marketing and direct-selling businesses. Time, Inc. publishes 23 magazines in the U.S., including People, Sports Illustrated, Time, InStyle, Real Simple, Southern Living and Fortune, and over 90 magazines outside the U.S., primarily through IPC Media in the U.K. and Grupo Editorial Expansion in Mexico. AOL LLC is a digital content and Internet access provider that offers publishing, advertising and social media products. In March 2009, Time Warner completed the spin-off of cable television provider Time Warner Cable, Inc. In May 2009, the company acquired a 31% interest in Central European Media Company. That same month, the company announced plans to spin off AOL, making it an independent, publicly traded company.

Employees of the firm are offered healthcare packages for families and domestic partners; disability, life and long-term care benefits; an employee assistance program; reimbursement for wellness activities; onsite fitness center and health services; onsite child care options; and career development programs.

FINANCIALS: Sales and profits are in thousands of dollars—add 000 to get the full amount. 2008 Note: Financial information for 2008 was not available for all companies at press time.
2008 Sales: $46,984,000	2008 Profits: $-13,402,000	U.S. Stock Ticker: TWX
2007 Sales: $46,482,000	2007 Profits: $4,387,000	Int'l Ticker: Int'l Exchange:
2006 Sales: $43,690,000	2006 Profits: $6,552,000	Employees: 87,000
2005 Sales: $42,401,000	2005 Profits: $2,671,000	Fiscal Year Ends: 12/31
2004 Sales: $40,993,000	2004 Profits: $3,108,000	Parent Company:

SALARIES/BENEFITS:
Pension Plan:	ESOP Stock Plan:	Profit Sharing:	Top Exec. Salary: $1,750,000	Bonus: $7,600,000
Savings Plan:	Stock Purch. Plan:		Second Exec. Salary: $1,500,000	Bonus: $2,600,000

OTHER THOUGHTS:
Apparent Women Officers or Directors: 4
Hot Spot for Advancement for Women/Minorities: Y

LOCATIONS: ("Y" = Yes)
West:	Southwest:	Midwest:	Southeast:	Northeast:	International:
Y	Y	Y	Y	Y	Y

TJX COMPANIES INC (THE)

Industry Group Code: 448 Ranks within this company's industry group: Sales: 1 Profits: 1

Management:		Sales/Marketing:		Liberal Arts:		Information Systems:		Professionals:		Tech./Scientific:	
Management Trainees:	Y	Marketing Pros.:	Y	Gen. Writing/Editing:	Y	Info. Management:	Y	Finance/Acct.:	Y	Engineers, Electrical:	
Experienced Mngmt.:	Y	Retail Sales:	Y	Technical Writing:		Software Dev.:	Y	Law:	Y	Engineers, Other:	
International Business:	Y	Commercial/Industrial:		Graphic Arts/Photog.:	Y	Hardware Dev.:		HR/Other:	Y	Health/Lab:	
MBA Grads:	Y	Sales Trainees:	Y	Music:		Consulting/Other:		Training:	Y	Scientists/Research:	
		Advertising Pros.:	Y	Broadcasting:				Health Care:		Petroleum/Chemicals:	
				Other:	Y			Consulting:		Math/Other:	

TYPES OF BUSINESS:

Discount Apparel Stores
Domestics
Footwear
Jewelry
Home Furnishings
Accessories

BRANDS/DIVISIONS/AFFILIATES:

T.J. Maxx
Marshalls
HomeGoods
A.J. Wright
Winners
T.K. Maxx
HomeSense

CONTACTS:
Note: Officers with more than one job title may be intentionally listed here more than once.

Carol Meyrowitz, CEO
Carol Meyrowitz, Pres.
Jeffrey G. Naylor, CFO
John Gilbert, Chief Mktg. Officer/Exec. VP
Jeffrey G. Naylor, Chief Admin. Officer
Jeffrey G. Naylor, Chief Bus. Dev. Officer
Ernie Herman, Sr. Exec. VP/Pres., The Marmaxx Group
Arnold S. Barron, Sr. Exec. VP/Group Pres.
Donald G. Campbell, Vice Chmn.
Jerome R. Rossi, Sr. Exec. VP/Group Pres.
Bernard Cammarata, Chmn.
Paul Sweetenham, Sr. Exec. VP/Group Pres., Europe

Phone: 508-390-1000	Fax: 508-390-2828
Toll-Free:	
Address: 770 Cochituate Rd., Framingham, MA 01701 US	

GROWTH PLANS/SPECIAL FEATURES:

The TJX Companies, Inc. is a low-price apparel and home fashions retailer, operating over 2,600 stores through eight businesses including T.J. Maxx, Marshalls, HomeGoods, A.J. Wrights and Bob's Stores in the U.S.; Winners and HomeSense in Canada; and T.K. Maxx in Europe. TJX's 1,680 T.J. Maxx stores and Marshalls stores offer brand-name family apparel, giftware, domestics and accessories in 42 states across the U.S. and 14 in Puerto Rico. The chains are similar, although Marshalls features a full-line shoe department and a larger men's department while T.J. Maxx now carries an extended line of jewelry and accessories. TJX also operates 318 HomeGoods stores, which sell low-priced home fashions. The chain offers a broad array of giftware, accent furniture, lamps, rugs, accessories and seasonal merchandise. The company also combines HomeGoods stores with a T.J. Maxx or a Marshalls store under the names T.J. Maxx 'N More and Marshalls Mega-Store. TJX's 135 A.J. Wright stores, catering to moderate-income customers, provide low-price family apparel and home fashions. TJX also operates the 202 store Winners chain, patterned after T.J. Maxx, in Canada. The firm's 235 T.K. Maxx stores in Europe resemble its domestic stores, although with a slight name change. The stores sell much of its merchandise off-price, which means that the company purchases its inventory on an opportunistic basis, doing business with over 10,000 vendors worldwide. The 34 Bob's Stores were sold to private equity firms Versa Capital Management and Crystal Capital in August 2008.

The company offers its employees medical, dental, vision, disability and life insurance; a 401(k) plan; a profit sharing plan; auto and home insurance; a college savings program; store discounts; a mortgage discount program; a tuition assistance program; and long term care insurance. Corporate employees have access to basketball courts, fitness classes and indoor golf driving ranges.

FINANCIALS: Sales and profits are in thousands of dollars—add 000 to get the full amount. 2008 Note: Financial information for 2008 was not available for all companies at press time.

2008 Sales: $18,336,726	2008 Profits: $771,750	**U.S. Stock Ticker:** TJX
2007 Sales: $14,104,013	2007 Profits: $738,039	**Int'l Ticker:** Int'l Exchange:
2006 Sales: $15,955,943	2006 Profits: $689,834	Employees: 133,000
2005 Sales: $14,860,746	2005 Profits: $610,217	Fiscal Year Ends: 1/31
2004 Sales: $13,327,938	2004 Profits: $609,412	Parent Company:

SALARIES/BENEFITS:

Pension Plan:	ESOP Stock Plan:	Profit Sharing:	Top Exec. Salary: $1,503,366	Bonus: $2,258,393
Savings Plan: Y	Stock Purch. Plan:		Second Exec. Salary: $773,558	Bonus: $985,209

OTHER THOUGHTS:

Apparent Women Officers or Directors: 3
Hot Spot for Advancement for Women/Minorities: Y

LOCATIONS: ("Y" = Yes)

West:	Southwest:	Midwest:	Southeast:	Northeast:	International:
Y	Y	Y	Y	Y	Y

Note: Financial information, benefits and other data can change quickly and may vary from those stated here.

T-MOBILE USA

www.t-mobile.com

Industry Group Code: 5172 Ranks within this company's industry group: Sales: 2 Profits: 1

Management:		Sales/Marketing:		Liberal Arts:		Information Systems:		Professionals:		Tech./Scientific:	
Management Trainees:	Y	Marketing Pros.:	Y	Gen. Writing/Editing:	Y	Info. Management:	Y	Finance/Acct.:	Y	Engineers, Electrical:	Y
Experienced Mngmt.:	Y	Retail Sales:	Y	Technical Writing:	Y	Software Dev.:	Y	Law:	Y	Engineers, Other:	Y
International Business:	Y	Commercial/Industrial:	Y	Graphic Arts/Photog.:	Y	Hardware Dev.:		HR/Other:	Y	Health/Lab:	
MBA Grads:	Y	Sales Trainees:	Y	Music:		Consulting/Other:		Training:	Y	Scientists/Research:	
		Advertising Pros.:	Y	Broadcasting:				Health Care:		Petroleum/Chemicals:	
				Other:	Y			Consulting:		Math/Other:	

TYPES OF BUSINESS:

PCS Cellular Telephone Service
Wireless Internet Services

BRANDS/DIVISIONS/AFFILIATES:

Deutsche Telekom AG
T-Mobile International AG
T-Mobile HotSpot
SunCom Wireless Holdings, Inc.
T-Mobile webConnect USB Laptop Stick

CONTACTS: *Note: Officers with more than one job title may be intentionally listed here more than once.*

Robert Dotson, CEO
Susan Nokes, COO/Chief Customer Officer
Robert P. Dotson, Pres.
Brian Kirkpatrick, CFO/Exec. VP
Denny Post, Chief Mktg. Officer/Sr. VP
Larry Myers, Chief People Officer/Sr. VP
Rob Strickland, CIO/Sr. VP
Cole Brodman, CTO/Chief Innovation Officer
Neville Ray, Sr. VP-Eng. Oper.
Dave Miller, General Counsel/Sr. VP
John Birrer, Sr. VP-Customer Service
John W. Stanton, Chmn.

Phone: 425-378-4000	**Fax:** 425-378-4040
Toll-Free: 800-318-9270	
Address: 12920 SE 38th St., Bellevue, WA 98006 US	

GROWTH PLANS/SPECIAL FEATURES:

T-Mobile USA (T-Mobile) is a national provider of wireless voice, messaging and data services. The company is the U.S. operating entity of T-Mobile International AG & Co., the mobile communications subsidiary of Deutsche Telekom AG & Co. K.G. T-Mobile uses GSM (global system for mobile communications) technology and is a member of the North American GSM Alliance, a group of U.S. and Canadian digital wireless carriers that provide seamless GSM wireless communications for its members in North America and internationally. The firm's nationwide rate plans offer complimentary long distance and digital GSM roaming, providing service to more than 268 million customers in the U.S. who are also able to connect to GSM networks in over 150 countries around the world. The company offers wireless Internet service to phones through its T-Mobile Internet program and high-speed wireless access through its T-Mobile HotSpot service. HotSpot locations can be found at airports, airline clubs and lounges of American Airlines, Delta Air Lines and United Airlines; Borders Books and Music; Kinko's; and Starbucks coffeehouses. With more than 10,000 locations, the T-Mobile HotSpot network is the largest public Wi-Fi network in the U.S. In March 2009, the firm launched the T-Mobile webConnect USB Laptop Stick. The laptop stick enables customers to connect to the Internet when a HotSpot is not available. In February 2008, the firm acquired SunCom Wireless. Through the acquisition, T-Mobile gained approximately 1.1 million customers in North Carolina, South Carolina, Tennessee, Georgia, Puerto Rico and the U.S. Virgin Islands.

The firm offers employees medical, dental and vision coverage; a performance recognition program; a phone and service discount program; an employee referral program; a wellness program; flexible spending accounts; an employee assistance and work/balance program; educational assistance; childcare subsidy; life and disability insurance; and a 401(k) plan.

FINANCIALS: Sales and profits are in thousands of dollars—add 000 to get the full amount. 2008 Note: Financial information for 2008 was not available for all companies at press time.

2008 Sales: $21,885,000	2008 Profits: $6,123,000	**U.S. Stock Ticker:** Subsidiary
2007 Sales: $19,288,000	2007 Profits: $5,350,000	**Int'l Ticker:** Int'l Exchange:
2006 Sales: $17,138,000	2006 Profits: $4,712,000	Employees: 37,500
2005 Sales: $14,806,000	2005 Profits: $	Fiscal Year Ends: 12/31
2004 Sales: $11,679,000	2004 Profits: $	Parent Company: DEUTSCHE TELEKOM AG

SALARIES/BENEFITS:

Pension Plan:	ESOP Stock Plan:	Profit Sharing:	Top Exec. Salary: $	Bonus: $1,000,000
Savings Plan: Y	Stock Purch. Plan:		Second Exec. Salary: $	Bonus: $

OTHER THOUGHTS:

Apparent Women Officers or Directors: 1
Hot Spot for Advancement for Women/Minorities:

LOCATIONS: ("Y" = Yes)

West:	Southwest:	Midwest:	Southeast:	Northeast:	International:
Y	Y	Y	Y	Y	

Note: Financial information, benefits and other data can change quickly and may vary from those stated here.

TOTAL SYSTEM SERVICES INC (TSYS)

www.tsys.com

Industry Group Code: 522320 Ranks within this company's industry group: Sales: 4 Profits: 1

Management:		Sales/Marketing:		Liberal Arts:		Information Systems:		Professionals:		Tech./Scientific:	
Management Trainees:	Y	Marketing Pros.:	Y	Gen. Writing/Editing:	Y	Info. Management:	Y	Finance/Acct.:	Y	Engineers, Electrical:	
Experienced Mngmt.:	Y	Retail Sales:		Technical Writing:		Software Dev.:	Y	Law:	Y	Engineers, Other:	
International Business:	Y	Commercial/Industrial:	Y	Graphic Arts/Photog.:	Y	Hardware Dev.:		HR/Other:	Y	Health/Lab:	
MBA Grads:	Y	Sales Trainees:	Y	Music:		Consulting/Other:		Training:	Y	Scientists/Research:	
		Advertising Pros.:	Y	Broadcasting:				Health Care:		Petroleum/Chemicals:	
				Other:				Consulting:		Math/Other:	

TYPES OF BUSINESS:

Credit Card Processing
Risk Management Tools
Direct Mail Services
Fraud Detection
Printing Services
Debt Collection Services
Reward Programs
Staffing Services

BRANDS/DIVISIONS/AFFILIATES:

Synovus Financial Corp.
Columbus Depot Equipment Company
Columbus Productions
TSYS Canada Inc
TSYS Total Debt Management Inc
TSYS Technology Center Inc
UnionPay Data Co Ltd
TSYS Okinawa Data Center

CONTACTS: Note: Officers with more than one job title may be intentionally listed here more than once.

Philip W. Tomlinson, CEO
M. Troy Woods, COO
M. Troy Woods, Pres.
James B. Lipham, CFO/Sr. Exec. VP
Gaylon M. Jowers, Jr., Exec. VP-Sales
Suzanne Kump, Group Exec.-Human Resources
Kenneth L. Tye, CIO/Sr. Exec. VP
Stephen W. Humber, CTO/Exec. VP
Connie C. Dudley, Exec. VP-Prod. & Client Dev.
Ryland L. Harrelson, Exec. VP-Admin. Svcs.
G. Sanders Griffith, III, General Counsel/Sr. Exec. VP/Sec.
Gaylon M. Jowers, Jr., Exec. VP-Strategy & Emerging Markets
Virginia A. Holeman, Group Exec.-Corp Comm.
Dorenda K. Weaver, Chief Acct. Officer/Exec. VP
William A. Pruett, Chief Customer Officer/Sr. Exec. VP
Colleen W. Kynard, Exec. VP-Customer Care
Jim Cosgrove, Treas.
Kelly Knutson, Exec. VP-Global Svcs.
Philip W. Tomlinson, Chmn.
David Duncan, Group Exec.-China & Southeast Asia

Phone: 706-649-2310	Fax: 706-644-8065
Toll-Free:	
Address: 1600 1st Ave., Columbus, GA 31901 US	

GROWTH PLANS/SPECIAL FEATURES:

Total System Services (TSYS) is one of the world's largest electronic payment processors of consumer credit, debit, commercial, stored-value, chip and retail cards. Its majority owner, Synovus Financial Corp., has an 81% stake in the firm. TSYS serves 300 clients throughout the U.S., Canada, Mexico, Honduras, the Caribbean and Europe. The company also offers value-added products and services, including risk management tools and techniques like credit evaluation, fraud detection and prevention and behavior analysis tools, as well as revenue enhancement tools, such as loyalty programs and bonus rewards. TSYS's operations are divided into three segments: North America Services, accounting for 68.7% of 2008 revenues; Global Services, accounting for 16.2%; and Merchant Services, accounting for 15.2%. The firm's subsidiaries include Columbus Depot Equipment Company, which sells and leases computer-related equipment; Columbus Productions, which provides full-service commercial printing and related services; TSYS Acquiring Solutions, a supplier of acquiring solutions, related systems and integrated support services; TSYS Canada, Inc., which provides programming support and assistance with conversion of card portfolios to TS2; and TSYS Total Debt Management, Inc., which provides debt collection and bankruptcy management services. TSYS Technology Center, Inc. provides flexible staffing solutions to help TSYS address its implementation and development pipeline of clients and prospective clients. The company also owns an equity interest in a joint venture company called Total System Services de Mexico, as well as a 45% interest in China UnionPay Data Co., Ltd. In 2008, the firm opened a new sales office in Warsaw, Poland and a data center, called TSYS Okinawa Data Center (TODC) in Nago City, Okinawa, Japan.

Employees are offered medical, dental and vision insurance; flexible spending accounts; long-term disability coverage; discounted banking services; a pension plan: a 401(k) plan; a profit sharing plan; and a stock purchase plan.

FINANCIALS: Sales and profits are in thousands of dollars—add 000 to get the full amount. 2008 Note: Financial information for 2008 was not available for all companies at press time.

2008 Sales: $1,938,608	2008 Profits: $250,100	U.S. Stock Ticker: TSS
2007 Sales: $1,805,836	2007 Profits: $237,443	Int'l Ticker: Int'l Exchange:
2006 Sales: $1,787,171	2006 Profits: $249,163	Employees: 8,110
2005 Sales: $1,602,931	2005 Profits: $194,520	Fiscal Year Ends: 12/31
2004 Sales: $1,187,008	2004 Profits: $150,558	Parent Company:

SALARIES/BENEFITS:

Pension Plan: Y	ESOP Stock Plan:	Profit Sharing: Y	Top Exec. Salary: $827,774	Bonus: $206,943
Savings Plan: Y	Stock Purch. Plan: Y		Second Exec. Salary: $610,018	Bonus: $152,504

OTHER THOUGHTS:

Apparent Women Officers or Directors: 7
Hot Spot for Advancement for Women/Minorities: Y

LOCATIONS: ("Y" = Yes)

West:	Southwest:	Midwest:	Southeast:	Northeast:	International:
Y	Y	Y	Y	Y	Y

Note: Financial information, benefits and other data can change quickly and may vary from those stated here.

TOWERS PERRIN

www.towersperrin.com

Industry Group Code: 541612　Ranks within this company's industry group: Sales: 3　Profits:

Management:		Sales/Marketing:		Liberal Arts:		Information Systems:		Professionals:		Tech./Scientific:	
Management Trainees:	Y	Marketing Pros.:	Y	Gen. Writing/Editing:	Y	Info. Management:	Y	Finance/Acct.:	Y	Engineers, Electrical:	
Experienced Mngmt.:	Y	Retail Sales:		Technical Writing:	Y	Software Dev.:	Y	Law:	Y	Engineers, Other:	
International Business:	Y	Commercial/Industrial:	Y	Graphic Arts/Photog.:	Y	Hardware Dev.:		HR/Other:	Y	Health/Lab:	
MBA Grads:	Y	Sales Trainees:		Music:		Consulting/Other:	Y	Training:	Y	Scientists/Research:	
		Advertising Pros.:	Y	Broadcasting:				Health Care:		Petroleum/Chemicals:	
				Other:	Y			Consulting:	Y	Math/Other:	

TYPES OF BUSINESS:

Human Resources Consulting
Benefit Plan & Compensation Consulting
Actuarial & Management Consulting
Reinsurance Consulting
Human Resources Outsourcing
Human Resources Consulting

BRANDS/DIVISIONS/AFFILIATES:

Tillinghast
Towers Perrin Reinsurance
ExcellerateHRO
Watson Wyatt Worldwide
Towers Watson & Co.

CONTACTS: *Note: Officers with more than one job title may be intentionally listed here more than once.*

Mark Mactas, CEO
Bob Hogan, CFO
Tony Candito, Chief Admin. Officer
Kevin Young, General Counsel/Sec.
Tricia Guinn, Managing Dir.-Risk & Financial Svcs.
James K. Foreman, Managing Dir.-Human Capital Group
Don Lowman, Managing Dir.-Human Capital Group
Mark Mactas, Chmn.

Phone: 203-326-5400	Fax: 203-326-5499
Toll-Free:	
Address: 1 Stamford Plz., 263 Tresser Blvd., Stamford, CT 06901-3226 US	

GROWTH PLANS/SPECIAL FEATURES:

Towers Perrin provides human resources, benefit plan and compensation consultation. The firm operates out of more than 90 offices in 26 countries. The firm has worked with three-quarters of the world's 500 largest companies and three-quarters of the Fortune 1000 U.S. companies. Towers Perrin's services include third-party administration for retirement, health and welfare plans and compensation administration; human resources consulting, including communication training; employee hiring research; and rewards and performance management. The company is divided into three sections: HR services, reinsurance and the subsidiary Tillinghast. The HR services business provides international human resources consulting and related services. Services include assistance with employee benefits, compensation, and communication and change management. Towers Perrin's reinsurance business provides intermediary services and consulting expertise for reinsurance through a blend of risk transfer vehicles. The firm helps with reinsurance strategy and program review; claims management and program administration; catastrophe exposure management; contract negotiation and placement; and market security issues. Tillinghast provides global actuarial and management consulting to insurance and financial services companies and advises other organizations on risk financing and self-insurance including mergers, acquisitions and restructuring; financial and regulatory reporting; risk, capital and value management; products, markets and distribution; and financial modeling software solutions. In January 2008, the firm launched a new reinsurance business in France, expanding its European market.

FINANCIALS: Sales and profits are in thousands of dollars—add 000 to get the full amount. 2008 Note: Financial information for 2008 was not available for all companies at press time.

2008 Sales: $2,500,000	2008 Profits: $	U.S. Stock Ticker: Private
2007 Sales: $2,300,000	2007 Profits: $	Int'l Ticker:　　Int'l Exchange:
2006 Sales: $2,200,000	2006 Profits: $	Employees: 6,500
2005 Sales: $2,000,000	2005 Profits: $	Fiscal Year Ends: 12/31
2004 Sales: $1,700,000	2004 Profits: $	Parent Company:

SALARIES/BENEFITS:

Pension Plan: Y	ESOP Stock Plan:	Profit Sharing:	Top Exec. Salary: $	Bonus: $
Savings Plan:	Stock Purch. Plan:		Second Exec. Salary: $	Bonus: $

OTHER THOUGHTS:

Apparent Women Officers or Directors: 1
Hot Spot for Advancement for Women/Minorities:

LOCATIONS: ("Y" = Yes)

West:	Southwest:	Midwest:	Southeast:	Northeast:	International:
Y	Y	Y	Y	Y	Y

TRANSOCEAN INC

www.deepwater.com

Industry Group Code: 211111 Ranks within this company's industry group: Sales: 10   Profits: 10

Management:		Sales/Marketing:		Liberal Arts:		Information Systems:		Professionals:		Tech./Scientific:	
Management Trainees:	Y	Marketing Pros.:	Y	Gen. Writing/Editing:		Info. Management:	Y	Finance/Acct.:	Y	Engineers, Electrical:	Y
Experienced Mngmt.:	Y	Retail Sales:		Technical Writing:	Y	Software Dev.:		Law:	Y	Engineers, Other:	Y
International Business:	Y	Commercial/Industrial:	Y	Graphic Arts/Photog.:		Hardware Dev.:		HR/Other:	Y	Health/Lab:	
MBA Grads:	Y	Sales Trainees:		Music:		Consulting/Other:		Training:	Y	Scientists/Research:	
		Advertising Pros.:		Broadcasting:				Health Care:		Petroleum/Chemicals:	Y
				Other:				Consulting:		Math/Other:	

TYPES OF BUSINESS:

Oil & Gas Exploration & Production
Mobile Offshore Production Units
Offshore Drilling & Production
Drilling Management Services
Dual-Activity Drilling
High-Specification Drillships

BRANDS/DIVISIONS/AFFILIATES:

Applied Drilling Technology Inc.
ADT International
Transocean Inc.

CONTACTS: Note: Officers with more than one job title may be intentionally listed here more than once.

Robert L. Long, CEO
Steven L. Newman, COO
Steven L. Newman, Pres.
Ricardo H. Rosa, CFO/Sr. VP
Terry B. Bonno, Sr. VP-Mktg.
Sherry Richard, Sr. VP-Human Resources & IT
John L. Truschinger, CIO/VP
N. Pharr Smith, VP-Eng. & Tech. Svcs.
Eric B. Brown, General Counsel/Sr. VP
Ihab Toma, Sr. VP-Planning & Mktg.
Gregory S. Panagos, VP-Comm.
Gregory S. Panagos, VP-Investor Rel.
John H. Briscoe, Controller/VP
Adrian P. Rose, VP-Quality, Health, Safety & Environment
Arnaud A.Y. Bobillier, Exec. VP-Assets
David A. Tonnel, Sr. VP-Europe & Africa Unit
Rob Saltiel, Exec. VP-Performance
Robert E. Rose, Chmn.
Deepak C. Munganahalli, VP-Asia & Pacific Unit

GROWTH PLANS/SPECIAL FEATURES:

Transocean, Ltd., together with its subsidiaries, is a leading international provider of deepwater and harsh environment offshore contract drilling services for oil and gas wells. The company owns, partially owns or operates 133 mobile offshore drilling units, consisting of 39 high-specification floaters (ultra-deepwater, deepwater and harsh environment semisubmersibles and drillships); 26 midwater floaters; 10 high-specification jackups; 55 standard jackups; and three other rigs. These units operate worldwide, with 19 units in the Asia Pacific and Southeast Asia, 14 units in India, 13 units in the U.S. Gulf of Mexico, 18 units in the U.K.'s North Sea, 10 units in Nigeria, 11 units in Egypt, 11 units in Brazil, 11 units in Angola, seven units in other West African countries, six units in the Middle East, five units in Norway, two units in Trinidad and Tobago, two units in Australia, two units in Italy, and one unit each in Russia, Libya, the Caspian Sea and Canada. The company also has 10 ultra-deepwater floaters under construction or contracted for construction. The firm contracts its drilling rigs, related equipment and work crews primarily on a dayrate basis to drill oil and gas wells. Transocean also provides oil and gas drilling management services, drilling engineering and drilling project management services through Applied Drilling Technology, Inc., a wholly-owned subsidiary, and ADT International, a division of one of its U.K. subsidiaries. In February 2008, the firm agreed to sell three jackup drilling rigs to Hercules Offshore, Inc. In July 2008, the company agreed to sell its GSF Arctic II and GSF Arctic IV semisubmersible rigs. In December 2008, Transocean, Inc. changed its place of incorporation from the Cayman Islands to Switzerland through a merger with Swiss subsidiary Transocean, Ltd., whose name the company retained.

Phone: 41-22-930-9000	**Fax:**

Toll-Free:

Address: Chemin de Blandonnet 2, Vernier, CH-1214 Switzerland

FINANCIALS: Sales and profits are in thousands of dollars—add 000 to get the full amount. 2008 Note: Financial information for 2008 was not available for all companies at press time.

2008 Sales: $12,674,000	2008 Profits: $4,202	**U.S. Stock Ticker: RIG**
2007 Sales: $6,377,000	2007 Profits: $3,131,000	**Int'l Ticker:** Int'l Exchange:
2006 Sales: $3,882,000	2006 Profits: $1,385,000	Employees: 21,600
2005 Sales: $2,891,700	2005 Profits: $715,600	Fiscal Year Ends: 12/31
2004 Sales: $2,613,900	2004 Profits: $152,200	Parent Company:

SALARIES/BENEFITS:

Pension Plan:	ESOP Stock Plan:	Profit Sharing:	Top Exec. Salary: $1,051,042	Bonus: $918,611
Savings Plan:	Stock Purch. Plan:		Second Exec. Salary: $544,583	Bonus: $350,438

OTHER THOUGHTS:

Apparent Women Officers or Directors: 2
Hot Spot for Advancement for Women/Minorities: Y

LOCATIONS: ("Y" = Yes)

West:	Southwest:	Midwest:	Southeast:	Northeast:	International:
	Y				Y

TRAVELERS COMPANIES INC (THE)   www.travelers.com

Industry Group Code: 524126 **Ranks within this company's industry group:** Sales: 3 Profits: 2

Management:		Sales/Marketing:		Liberal Arts:		Information Systems:		Professionals:		Tech./Scientific:	
Management Trainees:	Y	Marketing Pros.:	Y	Gen. Writing/Editing:	Y	Info. Management:	Y	Finance/Acct.:	Y	Engineers, Electrical:	
Experienced Mngmt.:	Y	Retail Sales:		Technical Writing:	Y	Software Dev.:	Y	Law:	Y	Engineers, Other:	
International Business:	Y	Commercial/Industrial:	Y	Graphic Arts/Photog.:	Y	Hardware Dev.:		HR/Other:	Y	Health/Lab:	
MBA Grads:	Y	Sales Trainees:	Y	Music:		Consulting/Other:		Training:	Y	Scientists/Research:	
		Advertising Pros.:	Y	Broadcasting:				Health Care:		Petroleum/Chemicals:	
				Other:	Y			Consulting:		Math/Other:	Y

TYPES OF BUSINESS:

Direct Property & Casualty Insurance
Reinsurance
Automobile & Homeowners' Insurance
General Liability & Commercial Multi-Peril Insurance
Marine Insurance
Risk Management Services

BRANDS/DIVISIONS/AFFILIATES:

St. Paul Companies Inc.
St. Paul Fire and Marine Insurance Company
Unionamerica Holdings Limited
AgentU
Lloyd's

CONTACTS: *Note: Officers with more than one job title may be intentionally listed here more than once.*

Jay S. Fishman, CEO
Brian W. MacLean, COO
Brian W. MacLean, Pres.
Jay S. Benet, CFO
Anne MacDonald, Chief Mktg. Officer/Exec. VP
John P. Clifford, Jr., Exec. VP-Human Resources
William Bloom, CIO/Exec. VP-Insurance Oper.
Andy F. Bessette, Chief Admin. Officer/Exec. VP
Kenneth F. Spence III, General Counsel/Exec. VP
Samuel Liss, Exec. VP-Strategic Dev.
Gabriella Nawi, Sr. VP-Investor Rel.
Maria Olivo, Treas./Exec. VP
William H. Heyman, Chief Investment Officer
John J. Albano, Exec. VP-Bus. Insurance
Alan D. Schnitzer, Chief Legal Officer
Joan Kois Woodward, Exec. VP-Public Policy
Jay S. Fishman, Chmn.

Phone: 917-778-6000	Fax: 917-778-7007
Toll-Free: 800-328-2189	
Address: 485 Lexington Ave., New York, NY 10017-2630 US	

GROWTH PLANS/SPECIAL FEATURES:

The Travelers Companies, Inc., formerly St. Paul Travelers Companies, Inc., is a holding company principally engaged in providing commercial and personal property and casualty insurance products and services to businesses, government units, associations and individuals. The company operates in three segments: business insurance; financial, professional and international insurance; and personal insurance. The business insurance segment offers a broad array of property and casualty insurance and insurance-related services primarily in the U.S. The division is organized in six groups: select accounts, commercial accounts, national accounts, industry-focused underwriting, target risk underwriting and specialized distribution. These groups provide a wide array of insurance coverage, including commercial multi-peril, property, general liability, commercial auto, workers' compensation and marine, as well as providing risk management, claims handling, reinsurance, healthcare and other services. The business insurance group also includes the Specialty Liability Group, which manages the company's asbestos and environmental liabilities. The financial, professional and international insurance segment includes surety and financial liability coverages, which require a primarily credit-based underwriting process, as well as property and casualty products marketed on an international basis. This division operates through two groups: bond and financial products, which provides bond and insurance products and risk management services; and International, which offers specialized insurance and risk management services marketed in the U.K., Ireland and Canada and on a wider international basis through Lloyd's. The personal insurance segment writes virtually all types of property and casualty insurance covering personal risks. The primary coverages in this segment are automobile and homeowners insurance. In October 2008, St. Paul Fire and Marine Insurance Company, a wholly-owned subsidiary of the company, agreed to sell Unionamerica Holdings Limited, which is involved in direct insurance and reinsurance, to Royston Run-Off Limited. In July 2009, the company launched AgentU, intended as an insurance agent education tool.

FINANCIALS: Sales and profits are in thousands of dollars—add 000 to get the full amount. 2008 Note: Financial information for 2008 was not available for all companies at press time.

2008 Sales: $24,477,000	2008 Profits: $2,924,000	**U.S. Stock Ticker:** TRV
2007 Sales: $26,017,000	2007 Profits: $4,601,000	**Int'l Ticker:** **Int'l Exchange:**
2006 Sales: $25,090,000	2006 Profits: $4,208,000	Employees: 33,000
2005 Sales: $24,365,000	2005 Profits: $1,622,000	Fiscal Year Ends: 12/31
2004 Sales: $22,544,000	2004 Profits: $955,000	Parent Company:

SALARIES/BENEFITS:

Pension Plan: Y	ESOP Stock Plan:	Profit Sharing:	Top Exec. Salary: $1,000,000	Bonus: $5,000,000
Savings Plan: Y	Stock Purch. Plan:		Second Exec. Salary: $700,000	Bonus: $2,500,000

OTHER THOUGHTS:

Apparent Women Officers or Directors: 6
Hot Spot for Advancement for Women/Minorities: Y

LOCATIONS: ("Y" = Yes)

West:	Southwest:	Midwest:	Southeast:	Northeast:	International:
Y	Y	Y	Y	Y	Y

Note: Financial information, benefits and other data can change quickly and may vary from those stated here.

TREEHOUSE FOODS INC

www.treehousefoods.com

Industry Group Code: 311 Ranks within this company's industry group: Sales: 5 Profits: 5

Management:		Sales/Marketing:		Liberal Arts:		Information Systems:		Professionals:		Tech./Scientific:	
Management Trainees:	Y	Marketing Pros.:	Y	Gen. Writing/Editing:		Info. Management:	Y	Finance/Acct.:	Y	Engineers, Electrical:	
Experienced Mngmt.:	Y	Retail Sales:		Technical Writing:		Software Dev.:		Law:	Y	Engineers, Other:	Y
International Business:		Commercial/Industrial:	Y	Graphic Arts/Photog.:	Y	Hardware Dev.:		HR/Other:	Y	Health/Lab:	
MBA Grads:	Y	Sales Trainees:		Music:		Consulting/Other:		Training:	Y	Scientists/Research:	
		Advertising Pros.:		Broadcasting:				Health Care:		Petroleum/Chemicals:	
				Other:				Consulting:		Math/Other:	

TYPES OF BUSINESS:
Food Manufacturing & Distribution
Food Manufacturing & Distribution

BRANDS/DIVISIONS/AFFILIATES:
Bay Valley Foods LLC
E. D. Smith Valley Foods LTD

CONTACTS: Note: Officers with more than one job title may be intentionally listed here more than once.
Sam K. Reed, CEO
David B. Vermylen, COO
David B. Vermylen, Pres.
Dennis F. Riordan, CFO/Sr. VP
Thomas E. O'Neill, Chief Admin. Officer/Sr. VP
Thomas E. O'Neill, General Counsel
Erik T. Kahler, Sr. VP-Corp. Dev.
Sharon M. Flanagan, Sr. VP-Strategy
Harry J. Walsh, Pres., Bay Valley Foods LLC
Alan T. Gambrel, Chief Admin. Officer-Bay Valley Foods LLC
Danny J. Coning, Sr. VP-Supply Chain

Phone: 708-483-1300	Fax:
Toll-Free:	
Address: 2 Westbrook Corporate Ctr. Ste. 1070, Westchester, IL 60154 US	

GROWTH PLANS/SPECIAL FEATURES:
TreeHouse Foods Inc. is a food manufacturer servicing primarily the retail grocery and foodservice distribution industry. The firm operates in the U.S. through its wholly-owned subsidiary, Bay Valley Foods LLC; and in Canada through Bay Valley Foods' wholly-owned subsidiary, E.D. Smith Valley Foods LTD. The company's products include salad dressings and sauces; non-dairy powdered coffee creamer; Mexican sauces; pickles; private label soup; jams and pie fillings; salad dressings and sauces; and infant foods. The firm manufactures these products under private labels to retailers such as mass merchandisers and supermarkets; these are resold under either the retailers' own or controlled brand names. TreeHouse Foods also markets its products to the foodservice industry, including foodservice distributors and national restaurant operators, under its own labels and brands; sells to industrial customers who use the firm's products as ingredients in other products or repackage them in portion control packages; and sells items under its own brands, primarily on a regional basis to retail customers. The company operates in three segments: North American Retail Grocery; Food Away From Home; and Industrial and Export. The North American Retail Grocery division sells branded and private label products to customers within the United States and Canada under brand names such as San Antonio Farms, Farman's, Nalley's, Nature's Goodness, Peter Piper, Second Nature and Steinfeld. The Food Away From Home segment sells products such as pickles, salsas, non-dairy powdered creamers, aseptic and refrigerated products to the U.S. and Canadian food service industry. TreeHouse Foods' Industrial and Export group offers co-pack business and non-dairy powdered creamers for use in industrial applications. In May 2009, the company's subsidiary Bay Valley Foods reopened its New Hampton, Iowa plant.

FINANCIALS: Sales and profits are in thousands of dollars—add 000 to get the full amount. 2008 Note: Financial information for 2008 was not available for all companies at press time.

2008 Sales: $1,500,650	2008 Profits: $28,224	U.S. Stock Ticker: THS
2007 Sales: $1,157,902	2007 Profits: $41,622	Int'l Ticker: Int'l Exchange:
2006 Sales: $939,396	2006 Profits: $44,856	Employees: 3,300
2005 Sales: $	2005 Profits: $	Fiscal Year Ends: 12/31
2004 Sales: $	2004 Profits: $	Parent Company:

SALARIES/BENEFITS:

Pension Plan:	ESOP Stock Plan:	Profit Sharing:	Top Exec. Salary: $827,250	Bonus: $1,045,306
Savings Plan:	Stock Purch. Plan:		Second Exec. Salary: $551,833	Bonus: $557,832

OTHER THOUGHTS:
Apparent Women Officers or Directors: 3
Hot Spot for Advancement for Women/Minorities: Y

LOCATIONS: ("Y" = Yes)

West:	Southwest:	Midwest:	Southeast:	Northeast:	International:
		Y			

TW TELECOM INC

www.twtelecom.com

Industry Group Code: 517110 **Ranks within this company's industry group:** Sales: 13 Profits: 8

Management:		Sales/Marketing:		Liberal Arts:		Information Systems:		Professionals:		Tech./Scientific:	
Management Trainees:	Y	Marketing Pros.:	Y	Gen. Writing/Editing:	Y	Info. Management:	Y	Finance/Acct.:	Y	Engineers, Electrical:	Y
Experienced Mngmt.:	Y	Retail Sales:		Technical Writing:	Y	Software Dev.:	Y	Law:	Y	Engineers, Other:	
International Business:		Commercial/Industrial:	Y	Graphic Arts/Photog.:	Y	Hardware Dev.:		HR/Other:	Y	Health/Lab:	
MBA Grads:	Y	Sales Trainees:		Music:		Consulting/Other:		Training:	Y	Scientists/Research:	
		Advertising Pros.:	Y	Broadcasting:				Health Care:		Petroleum/Chemicals:	
				Other:				Consulting:		Math/Other:	

TYPES OF BUSINESS:

Voice & Data Networking Solutions
Ethernet Services
Internet Access

BRANDS/DIVISIONS/AFFILIATES:

Xspedius Communications LLC
Time Warner Telecom, Inc.

CONTACTS: *Note: Officers with more than one job title may be intentionally listed here more than once.*

Larissa Herda, CEO
John Blount, COO
Larissa Herda, Pres.
Mark A. Peters, CFO/Exec. VP
Graham Taylor, Sr. VP-Mktg. & Sales
Steve Hardardt, Sr. VP-Human Resources
Harold W. Teets, Sr. VP-IT & Network Tech.
Steve Hardardt, Sr. VP-Bus. Admin.
Paul B. Jones, General Counsel/Exec. VP
Mark Willency, Sr. VP-Corp. Oper.
Michael A. Rouleau, Sr. VP-Bus. Dev. & Strategy
Bob Meldrum, VP-Corp. Comm.
Carole Curtin, VP-Investor Rel.
Jill R. Stuart, Sr. VP-Finance & Acct./Chief Acct. Officer
Robert W. Gaskins, Sr. VP-Corp. Dev. & Strategy
Larissa Herda, Chmn.

GROWTH PLANS/SPECIAL FEATURES:

TW Telecom (TW), formerly known as Time Warner Telecom, Inc., is a provider of managed network services, including Ethernet and data networking, Internet access, local and long distance voice, virtual private network (VPN), voice over Internet protocol (VoIP) and network security services, to a broad range of business customers and organizations throughout the U.S. Through its subsidiaries, including Xspedius, the company provides data, Internet access and local and long distance voice services and operates in 75 metropolitan areas in 30 states and D.C. over its 27,000 route-mile network of fiber-optic cable, directly connecting 9,700 building served directly by its facilities. The firm's customers are principally long-distance carriers, Internet service providers, incumbent local exchange carriers, competitive local exchange carriers, wireless communications companies, governmental entities and telecommunications-intensive enterprise organizations in the distribution, health care, finance, service and manufacturing industries. In July 2008, the firm changed its name to TW Telecom. In March 2009, TW announced the expansion of its Portland, Oregon network into the Tualatin and Lake Oswego business districts.

The company offers its employees medical, vision and dental insurance; life and disability insurance; flexible spending accounts; a 401(k) plan; an employee assistance program; and a stock option plan.

Phone: 303-566-1000	Fax:
Toll-Free:	
Address: 10475 Park Meadows Dr., Littleton, CO 80124 US	

FINANCIALS: Sales and profits are in thousands of dollars—add 000 to get the full amount. 2008 Note: Financial information for 2008 was not available for all companies at press time.

2008 Sales: $1,159,019	2008 Profits: $8,525	**U.S. Stock Ticker:** TWTC	
2007 Sales: $1,083,679	2007 Profits: $-40,269	**Int'l Ticker:** Int'l Exchange:	
2006 Sales: $812,375	2006 Profits: $-98,819	Employees: 2,844	
2005 Sales: $708,727	2005 Profits: $-108,064	Fiscal Year Ends: 12/31	
2004 Sales: $653,087	2004 Profits: $-133,037	Parent Company:	

SALARIES/BENEFITS:

Pension Plan:	ESOP Stock Plan:	Profit Sharing:	Top Exec. Salary: $850,000	Bonus: $1,600,000
Savings Plan: Y	Stock Purch. Plan: Y		Second Exec. Salary: $492,660	Bonus: $541,926

OTHER THOUGHTS:

Apparent Women Officers or Directors: 3
Hot Spot for Advancement for Women/Minorities: Y

LOCATIONS: ("Y" = Yes)

West:	Southwest:	Midwest:	Southeast:	Northeast:	International:
Y	Y	Y	Y	Y	

TYSON FOODS INC

www.tyson.com

Industry Group Code: 311615 Ranks within this company's industry group: Sales: 1 Profits: 1

Management:		Sales/Marketing:		Liberal Arts:		Information Systems:		Professionals:		Tech./Scientific:	
Management Trainees:	Y	Marketing Pros.:	Y	Gen. Writing/Editing:	Y	Info. Management:	Y	Finance/Acct.:	Y	Engineers, Electrical:	
Experienced Mngmt.:	Y	Retail Sales:		Technical Writing:		Software Dev.:		Law:	Y	Engineers, Other:	
International Business:	Y	Commercial/Industrial:	Y	Graphic Arts/Photog.:	Y	Hardware Dev.:		HR/Other:	Y	Health/Lab:	
MBA Grads:	Y	Sales Trainees:	Y	Music:		Consulting/Other:		Training:	Y	Scientists/Research:	
		Advertising Pros.:	Y	Broadcasting:				Health Care:		Petroleum/Chemicals:	
				Other:				Consulting:		Math/Other:	

TYPES OF BUSINESS:

Poultry Processing
Beef & Pork Products
Ethnic Foods
Soups & Sauces
Frozen & Refrigerated Food

BRANDS/DIVISIONS/AFFILIATES:

Cobb-Vantress, Inc.
Tyson de Mexico
Godrej Tyson Foods
Tyson Dalong
Jiangsu-Tyson
Cactus Argentina
Lakeside Farm Industries

CONTACTS: Note: Officers with more than one job title may be intentionally listed here more than once.

Leland Tollett, Interim CEO
Dennis Leatherby, CFO/Exec. VP
Kenneth Kimbro, Chief Human Resources Officer/Sr. VP
Howell P. Carper, VP-R&D
Gary Cooper, CIO
Howell P. Carper, VP-Tech. Svcs.
David L. Van Bebber, General Counsel/Exec. VP
Ruth A. Wisener, VP-Investor Rel.
Craig J. Hart, Chief Acct. Officer/Controller/Sr. VP
James Lochner, Sr. VP-Fresh Meats & Margin Optimization
Donnie D. King, VP-Refrigerated & Deli
Bernard Leonard, VP-Food Service
Donnie Smith, VP-Consumer Prod.
John Tyson, Chmn.
Richard A. Greubal, Jr., Pres., Int'l
Howell P. Carper, VP-Logistics

Phone: 479-290-4000	Fax: 501-290-4061
Toll-Free: 800-643-3410	
Address: 2200 Don Tyson Pkwy., Springdale, AR 72762 US	

GROWTH PLANS/SPECIAL FEATURES:

Tyson Foods, Inc. is a producer, distributor and marketer of chicken, beef, pork, prepared foods and related products. The company operates in four segments: chicken, beef, pork and prepared foods. The chicken operations include breeding and raising chickens, as well as processing live chickens into fresh, frozen and value-added chicken products. The beef operations include processing live cattle and fabricating dressed beef carcasses into primal and sub-primal meat cuts and case-ready products. This segment also includes sales from allied products, such as hides and variety meats. The pork operations include processing live market hogs and fabricating pork carcasses into primal and sub-primal cuts and case-ready products. This segment also includes the live swine group and related allied product processing activities. Prepared food operations include the manufacture and marketing of frozen and refrigerated food products. Products include pepperoni, bacon, beef and pork pizza toppings, pizza crusts, flour and corn tortilla products, appetizers, prepared meals, ethnic foods, soups, sauces, side dishes, meat dishes and processed meats. Products are marketed domestically to food retailers, foodservice distributors, restaurant operators and noncommercial foodservice establishments such as schools, hotel chains, healthcare facilities, the military and other food processors, as well as to international markets. The firm's international operations] include a Mexican poultry production subsidiary; a majority interest in a poultry processing business in India; a chicken breeding stock subsidiary, Cobb-Vantress, Inc.; a majority interest in a beef operation in Argentina; and a majority interest in a chicken further processing facility and a chicken breeding company in China. In June 2008, the firm announced plans to sell Lakeside Farm Industries, its Canadian beef operation. In October 2008, the company purchased three poultry companies in Brazil.

Tyson offers its employees health, dental, vision and life insurance, stock purchase plans, retirement savings plans, a credit union and product discounts.

FINANCIALS: Sales and profits are in thousands of dollars—add 000 to get the full amount. 2008 Note: Financial information for 2008 was not available for all companies at press time.

2008 Sales: $26,862,000	2008 Profits: $86,000	U.S. Stock Ticker: TSN
2007 Sales: $25,729,000	2007 Profits: $268,000	Int'l Ticker: Int'l Exchange:
2006 Sales: $24,589,000	2006 Profits: $-196,000	Employees: 107,000
2005 Sales: $26,014,000	2005 Profits: $372,000	Fiscal Year Ends: 9/30
2004 Sales: $26,441,000	2004 Profits: $403,000	Parent Company:

SALARIES/BENEFITS:

Pension Plan: Y	ESOP Stock Plan:	Profit Sharing:	Top Exec. Salary: $1,251,204	Bonus: $
Savings Plan:	Stock Purch. Plan: Y		Second Exec. Salary: $583,673	Bonus: $92,666

OTHER THOUGHTS:

Apparent Women Officers or Directors: 2
Hot Spot for Advancement for Women/Minorities: Y

LOCATIONS: ("Y" = Yes)

West:	Southwest:	Midwest:	Southeast:	Northeast:	International:
Y	Y	Y	Y	Y	Y

UNITED NATURAL FOODS INC

www.unfi.com

Industry Group Code: 4244 **Ranks within this company's industry group:** Sales: 3   Profits: 3

Management:		Sales/Marketing:		Liberal Arts:		Information Systems:		Professionals:		Tech./Scientific:	
Management Trainees:	Y	Marketing Pros.:	Y	Gen. Writing/Editing:	Y	Info. Management:	Y	Finance/Acct.:	Y	Engineers, Electrical:	
Experienced Mngmt.:	Y	Retail Sales:		Technical Writing:		Software Dev.:	Y	Law:	Y	Engineers, Other:	
International Business:		Commercial/Industrial:	Y	Graphic Arts/Photog.:	Y	Hardware Dev.:		HR/Other:	Y	Health/Lab:	
MBA Grads:	Y	Sales Trainees:	Y	Music:		Consulting/Other:		Training:	Y	Scientists/Research:	
		Advertising Pros.:		Broadcasting:				Health Care:		Petroleum/Chemicals:	
				Other:				Consulting:		Math/Other:	

TYPES OF BUSINESS:

Food Distribution
Natural & Organic Foods Distribution
Nutritional Supplements Distribution
Personal Care Products Distribution
Retail Stores

BRANDS/DIVISIONS/AFFILIATES:

Natural Retail Group, Inc.
Woodstock Farms
Albert's Organics
Blooming Prairie
Roots & Fruits Cooperative Produce
Harvest Bay
Organic Baby
Rising Moon Organics

CONTACTS: *Note: Officers with more than one job title may be intentionally listed here more than once.*

Steven L. Spinner, CEO
Steven L. Spinner, Pres.
Mark E. Shamber, CFO/VP
Daniel V. Atwood, Chief Mktg. Officer/Pres., United Natural Brands
Carl F. Koch III, Chief Human Resources Officer/VP
John Stern, CIO
Joseph J. Traficanti, General Counsel/Sr. VP/Chief Compliance Officer
Mark E. Shamber, Treas.
David A. Matthews, Pres., Eastern Region
Thomas A. Dziki, VP-Sustainable Dev.
Kurt Luttecke, Pres., Western Region
Michael S. Funk, Chmn.
Michael D. Beaudry, Sr. VP-Dist.

Phone: 860-779-2800	Fax:
Toll-Free: 800-877-8898	
Address: 260 Lake Rd., Dayville, CT 06241 US	

GROWTH PLANS/SPECIAL FEATURES:

United Natural Foods, Inc. (UNFI) is a national distributor of natural and organic foods and related products. The company, which is a Certified Organic Distributor, carries more than 60,000 natural and organic products; these are sold under regional brand, national brand, private and master distribution labels. The firm offers six types of products: grocery and general merchandise; personal care items; produce; nutritional supplements; perishables and frozen foods; and bulk and food service products. UNFI serves over 17,000 customers, including supernatural chains (large chains of natural foods supermarkets), independently owned natural products retailers and conventional supermarkets located across the U.S. The company also distributes through the food service, international and buying club channels. The company has been the primary distributor to one of the largest natural foods chain in the U.S., Whole Foods Market, Inc., for more than 10 years. UNFI is also the primary distributor for another major organic chain, Wild Oats Market, which is owned by Whole Foods. The company's operations comprise three principal divisions: wholesale, which includes its distribution business; retail, which consists of UNFI's 13 owned and managed retail stores (through subsidiary Natural Retail Group, Inc.); and manufacturing, which is comprised of its subsidiary, Woodstock Farms, and its branded product lines. Woodstock Farms is an importer, processor, packager, and wholesale distributors of natural and organic products; trail mixes; nuts; seeds; dried fruit; and confections. Distribution members of UNFI include Albert's Organics; Northeast Cooperatives; Blooming Prairie; Mountain People's Warehouse; and Roots & Fruits Cooperative Produce. UNFI has a number of company-owned brands including Woodstock Farms, Rising Moon Organics, Harvest Bay and Organic Baby. In June 2009, Hershey Imports Co. agreed to change its name to Woodstock Farms, reflecting UNFI's main brand.

UNFI offers employees medical, dental, life and disability insurance; profit sharing; a 401(k); and an assistance program.

FINANCIALS: Sales and profits are in thousands of dollars—add 000 to get the full amount. 2008 Note: Financial information for 2008 was not available for all companies at press time.

2008 Sales: $3,365,857	2008 Profits: $48,479	**U.S. Stock Ticker: UNFI**
2007 Sales: $2,754,280	2007 Profits: $50,153	**Int'l Ticker:** Int'l Exchange:
2006 Sales: $2,433,594	2006 Profits: $43,277	Employees: 6,300
2005 Sales: $2,059,568	2005 Profits: $41,572	Fiscal Year Ends: 7/31
2004 Sales: $1,669,952	2004 Profits: $31,986	Parent Company:

SALARIES/BENEFITS:

Pension Plan:	ESOP Stock Plan:	Profit Sharing: Y	Top Exec. Salary: $713,462	Bonus: $
Savings Plan: Y	Stock Purch. Plan:		Second Exec. Salary: $484,135	Bonus: $

OTHER THOUGHTS:

Apparent Women Officers or Directors: 1
Hot Spot for Advancement for Women/Minorities:

LOCATIONS: ("Y" = Yes)

West:	Southwest:	Midwest:	Southeast:	Northeast:	International:
Y		Y	Y	Y	

Note: Financial information, benefits and other data can change quickly and may vary from those stated here.

UNITED PARCEL SERVICE INC (UPS)

www.ups.com

Industry Group Code: 4921 Ranks within this company's industry group: Sales: 1   Profits: 1

Management:		Sales/Marketing:		Liberal Arts:		Information Systems:		Professionals:		Tech./Scientific:	
Management Trainees:	Y	Marketing Pros.:	Y	Gen. Writing/Editing:	Y	Info. Management:	Y	Finance/Acct.:	Y	Engineers, Electrical:	Y
Experienced Mngmt.:	Y	Retail Sales:		Technical Writing:	Y	Software Dev.:	Y	Law:	Y	Engineers, Other:	
International Business:	Y	Commercial/Industrial:	Y	Graphic Arts/Photog.:	Y	Hardware Dev.:		HR/Other:	Y	Health/Lab:	
MBA Grads:	Y	Sales Trainees:		Music:		Consulting/Other:		Training:	Y	Scientists/Research:	
		Advertising Pros.:	Y	Broadcasting:				Health Care:		Petroleum/Chemicals:	
				Other:	Y			Consulting:		Math/Other:	Y

TYPES OF BUSINESS:

Express Delivery Service
Logistics Services
Supply Chain Services
International Products & Services
Ground & Air Delivery Services
Visibility & Technology Services

BRANDS/DIVISIONS/AFFILIATES:

UPS Freight
UPS Supply Chain Solutions
UPS WorldShip
Quantum View
UPS Next Day Air
UPS Hundredweight Services
Flex Global View
UPS Billing Analysis Tool

CONTACTS: *Note: Officers with more than one job title may be intentionally listed here more than once.*

D. Scott Davis, CEO
David Abney, COO
Kurt Kuehn, CFO
Alan Gershenhorn, Sr. VP-Worldwide Sales & Mktg.
Allen E. Hill, Sr. VP-Human Resources
David Barnes, CIO/Sr. VP
Bob Stoffel, Sr. VP-Eng.
Teri P. McClure, General Counsel/Sr. VP-Legal/Corp. Sec.
Bob Stoffel, Sr. VP-Strategy
Christine M. Owens, Sr. VP-Comm. & Brand Mgmt.
John McDevitt, Sr. VP-Global Transportation Svcs.
David Abney, Pres., UPS Airlines
Jim Winestock, Sr. VP-US Oper.
D. Scott Davis, Chmn.
Daniel J. Brutto, Pres., UPS Int'l
Bob Stoffel, Sr. VP-Supply Chain

Phone: 404-828-6000	**Fax:** 404-828-6562
Toll-Free: 800-874-5877	
Address: 55 Glenlake Pkwy., NE, Atlanta, GA 30328 US	

GROWTH PLANS/SPECIAL FEATURES:

United Parcel Service, Inc. (UPS) is a package delivery company and a global provider of supply chain management. It delivers packages each business day for 1.8 million shipping customers to 6.1 million consignees in over 200 countries. The company delivers an average of 15.75 million pieces per day worldwide. In addition, the supply chain solutions capabilities are available in over 200 countries. The firm is also a major provider of less-than-truckload transportation services. Offerings include domestic and international package products and services; supply chain and freight services; and visibility and technology solutions. The U.S. domestic package products and services business delivers packages traveling by ground or air transportation. In addition to the standard ground delivery products, UPS Hundredweight Services offers guaranteed, time-definite service to customers sending multiple packages shipments. UPS Next Day Air offers guaranteed next business day delivery by 10:30 am to 75% of the U.S. population and delivery by noon to areas covering an additional 15% of the population. International services include guaranteed early morning, morning and noon delivery to major cities around the world, as well as scheduled day-definite air and ground services. Supply chain and freight segment consists of its forwarding and logistics capabilities as well as its freight business unit. This division focuses on a broad range of transportation solutions to customers worldwide, including air, ocean and ground freight, as well as customs brokerage, and trade and materials management. In March 2008, the firm agreed to acquire Trans Courier Services in Romania.

The company offers its employees medical, dental and vision insurance; a prescription drug program; life insurance; a 401(k) plan; a defined benefit pension plan; an employee stock purchase plan; health, child and elder care spending accounts; adoption assistance; an employee assistance program; an employee discount program; and education assistance.

FINANCIALS: Sales and profits are in thousands of dollars—add 000 to get the full amount. 2008 Note: Financial information for 2008 was not available for all companies at press time.

2008 Sales: $51,486,000	2008 Profits: $3,003,000	**U.S. Stock Ticker:** UPS
2007 Sales: $49,700,000	2007 Profits: $382,000	**Int'l Ticker:** Int'l Exchange:
2006 Sales: $47,547,000	2006 Profits: $4,202,000	Employees: 426,000
2005 Sales: $42,581,000	2005 Profits: $3,870,000	Fiscal Year Ends: 12/31
2004 Sales: $36,582,000	2004 Profits: $3,333,000	Parent Company:

SALARIES/BENEFITS:

Pension Plan: Y	ESOP Stock Plan:	Profit Sharing:	Top Exec. Salary: $960,000	Bonus: $176,844
Savings Plan: Y	Stock Purch. Plan: Y		Second Exec. Salary: $440,000	Bonus: $88,800

OTHER THOUGHTS:

Apparent Women Officers or Directors: 4
Hot Spot for Advancement for Women/Minorities: Y

LOCATIONS: ("Y" = Yes)

West:	Southwest:	Midwest:	Southeast:	Northeast:	International:
Y	Y	Y	Y	Y	Y

UNITED STATES CELLULAR CORP

www.uscc.com

Industry Group Code: 5172 Ranks within this company's industry group: Sales: 3 Profits: 3

Management:		Sales/Marketing:		Liberal Arts:		Information Systems:		Professionals:		Tech./Scientific:	
Management Trainees:	Y	Marketing Pros.:	Y	Gen. Writing/Editing:	Y	Info. Management:	Y	Finance/Acct.:	Y	Engineers, Electrical:	Y
Experienced Mngmt.:	Y	Retail Sales:	Y	Technical Writing:	Y	Software Dev.:	Y	Law:	Y	Engineers, Other:	Y
International Business:		Commercial/Industrial:	Y	Graphic Arts/Photog.:	Y	Hardware Dev.:		HR/Other:	Y	Health/Lab:	
MBA Grads:	Y	Sales Trainees:	Y	Music:		Consulting/Other:		Training:	Y	Scientists/Research:	
		Advertising Pros.:	Y	Broadcasting:				Health Care:		Petroleum/Chemicals:	
				Other:				Consulting:		Math/Other:	

TYPES OF BUSINESS:

Cellular Telephone Service
PCS Service

BRANDS/DIVISIONS/AFFILIATES:

Telephone and Data Systems Inc
easyedge
Qualcomm Inc.
Mobile Broadband

CONTACTS: *Note: Officers with more than one job title may be intentionally listed here more than once.*

John E. Rooney, CEO
Jay M. Ellison, COO/Exec. VP
John E. Rooney, Pres.
Steven T. Campbell, CFO/Exec. VP-Finance/Treas.
Alan D. Ferber, VP-Sales Oper./Chief Mktg. Officer
Jeffrey J. Childs, Chief Human Resources Officer/Sr. VP
John M. Cregier, VP-IT Delivery
Michael S. Irizarry, CTO/Exec. VP
John C. Gockley, VP-Legal & Regulatory Affairs
Kevin R. Lowell, VP-National Network Oper.
Karen C. Ehlers, VP-Public Affairs & Comm.
Thomas S. (Tom) Weber, VP-Financial Strategy
Rochelle J. Boersma, VP-Midwest Oper.
Thomas P. Catani, VP-East Oper.
Nick B. Wright, VP-West Oper.
Katherine L. Hust, VP-Central Oper.
LeRoy T. Carlson, Jr., Chmn.

Phone: 773-399-8900	Fax: 773-399-7054
Toll-Free: 888-944-9400	
Address: 8410 W. Bryn Mawr Ave., Ste. 700, Chicago, IL 60631 US	

GROWTH PLANS/SPECIAL FEATURES:

United States Cellular Corporation (U.S. Cellular), a majority-owned subsidiary of Telephone and Data Systems, Inc., is a leading wireless service provider in the U.S., serving roughly 6.2 million customers in 26 states. The company owns interests in 239 consolidated wireless markets that cover portions of 34 states and a total population of roughly 83 million. U.S. Cellular operates approximately 6,900 cell sites and over 400 retail stores. The company's ownership interests in wireless licenses include both consolidated and investment interests in cellular licenses covering metropolitan statistical areas and rural service areas; digital PCS (personal communication service) licenses; advanced wireless service licenses; and 700 megahertz (MHz) licenses. It manages the operations of all but two of the licenses in which it owns a controlling interest. U.S. Cellular also manages the operations of additional licenses in which it does not own a controlling interest. Additionally, the company offers a range of wireless handset devices, laptop cards and such accessories as carrying cases, hands-free devices, memory cards, batteries and battery chargers. The company's easyedge brand of enhanced data services uses a binary runtime environment for wireless (BREW) technology, licensed from Qualcomm, and adds limited computer-like functionality to handsets, enabling applications to be downloaded over-the-air directly to the customer's wireless device. These enhanced data services include downloading news, weather, sports information, games, ring tones and other services. Telephone and Data Systems owns approximately 82% of the company. In October 2008, U.S. Cellular announced that it had launched Mobile Broadband, a service to increase the speed at which cell phones access data through EVDO (Evolution-Data Optimized, also called 3G) technology.

U.S. Cellular offers its employees an associate scholar program; a PC purchase program; flexible hours; adoption assistance; a flexible spending account; and medical, dental, vision, life and disability insurance.

FINANCIALS: Sales and profits are in thousands of dollars—add 000 to get the full amount. 2008 Note: Financial information for 2008 was not available for all companies at press time.

2008 Sales: $4,243,185	2008 Profits: $32,990	**U.S. Stock Ticker: USM**
2007 Sales: $3,946,264	2007 Profits: $314,734	**Int'l Ticker:** Int'l Exchange:
2006 Sales: $3,473,155	2006 Profits: $179,490	Employees: 8,470
2005 Sales: $3,030,765	2005 Profits: $154,951	Fiscal Year Ends: 12/31
2004 Sales: $2,808,201	2004 Profits: $109,516	Parent Company: TELEPHONE AND DATA SYSTEMS INC (TDS)

SALARIES/BENEFITS:

Pension Plan: Y	ESOP Stock Plan:	Profit Sharing:	Top Exec. Salary: $855,000	Bonus: $675,000
Savings Plan: Y	Stock Purch. Plan: Y		Second Exec. Salary: $542,244	Bonus: $401,000

OTHER THOUGHTS:

Apparent Women Officers or Directors: 4
Hot Spot for Advancement for Women/Minorities: Y

LOCATIONS: ("Y" = Yes)

West:	Southwest:	Midwest:	Southeast:	Northeast:	International:
Y	Y	Y	Y	Y	

UNITED TECHNOLOGIES CORPORATION

www.utc.com

Industry Group Code: 33641 **Ranks within this company's industry group:** Sales: 2 Profits: 1

Management:		Sales/Marketing:		Liberal Arts:		Information Systems:		Professionals:		Tech./Scientific:	
Management Trainees:	Y	Marketing Pros.:	Y	Gen. Writing/Editing:	Y	Info. Management:	Y	Finance/Acct.:	Y	Engineers, Electrical:	Y
Experienced Mngmt.:	Y	Retail Sales:		Technical Writing:	Y	Software Dev.:	Y	Law:	Y	Engineers, Other:	Y
International Business:	Y	Commercial/Industrial:	Y	Graphic Arts/Photog.:	Y	Hardware Dev.:	Y	HR/Other:	Y	Health/Lab:	
MBA Grads:	Y	Sales Trainees:		Music:		Consulting/Other:	Y	Training:	Y	Scientists/Research:	Y
		Advertising Pros.:	Y	Broadcasting:				Health Care:		Petroleum/Chemicals:	
				Other:				Consulting:		Math/Other:	Y

TYPES OF BUSINESS:

Aerospace Technology
Elevator & Escalator Systems
HVAC Systems
Fuel Cells & Power Generation
Industrial Systems
Aircraft Parts & Maintenance
Flight Systems
Security Products & Services

BRANDS/DIVISIONS/AFFILIATES:

Otis Elevator Company
Carrier Corp.
Sikorsky
Pratt & Whitney
Hamilton Sundstrand
UTC Fire and Security
UTC Power
Architectural Energy Corp

CONTACTS: Note: Officers with more than one job title may be intentionally listed here more than once.

Louis R. Chenevert, CEO
Louis R. Chenevert, Pres.
Gregory J. Hayes, CFO/Sr. VP
J. Thomas Bowler, Jr., Sr. VP-Human Resources & Organization
J. Michael McQuade, Sr. VP-Science & Tech.
John Doucette, CIO/VP
Charles D. Gill, General Counsel/Sr. VP
Jothi Purushotaman, VP-Oper.
James E. Geisler, VP-Corp. Strategy & Planning
Nancy T. Lintner, VP-Corp. Comm.
Ari Bousbib, Corp. Exec. VP/Pres., Commercial Companies
William M. Brown, Pres., UTC Fire & Security
Geraud Darnis, Pres., Carrier
Didier Michaud-Daniel, Pres., Otis
George David, Chmn.

Phone: 860-728-7000	**Fax:** 860-728-7028
Toll-Free:	
Address: 1 Financial Plz., Hartford, CT 06101 US	

GROWTH PLANS/SPECIAL FEATURES:

United Technologies Corporation (UTC) provides high-technology products and services to the building systems and aerospace industries worldwide. The company operates through seven companies: Carrier Corp., Hamilton Sundstrand, Otis Elevator Company, Pratt & Whitney, Sikorsky, UTC Fire & Security and UTC Power. Carrier manufactures commercial and residential heating, ventilation and air conditioning (HVAC) systems and equipment. It also produces, sells, services and provides components for commercial and transport refrigeration equipment. Hamilton Sundstrand serves commercial, military, regional and corporate aviation, as well as space and undersea applications. Its products include power generation management and distribution systems; flight systems, engine control systems, environmental control systems, fire protection and detection systems, auxiliary power units and propeller systems. Otis is one of the world's largest elevator and escalator manufacturing, installation and maintenance companies. Otis designs, manufactures, sells and installs a wide range of passenger and freight elevators for low-, medium- and high-speed applications, as well as a broad line of escalators and moving walkways. Pratt & Whitney produces and services commercial, general aviation and military aircraft engines. It also handles rocket engine production for commercial and government space applications. Sikorsky is a world leader in helicopters manufacturing and design, whose customers include the U.S. military and 40 other countries. UTC Fire & Security operates in the electronic security industry and the fire safety industry. UTC Power develops and markets distributed generation power systems and fuel cell power plants for stationary, transportation, space and defense applications. UTC Power recently acquired Architectural Energy Corp, a private energy engineering firm working to optimize the environmental performance of buildings.

FINANCIALS: Sales and profits are in thousands of dollars—add 000 to get the full amount. 2008 Note: Financial information for 2008 was not available for all companies at press time.

2008 Sales: $58,681,000	2008 Profits: $4,689,000	**U.S. Stock Ticker:** UTX
2007 Sales: $54,759,000	2007 Profits: $4,224,000	**Int'l Ticker:** Int'l Exchange:
2006 Sales: $47,829,000	2006 Profits: $3,732,000	Employees: 223,100
2005 Sales: $42,725,000	2005 Profits: $3,069,000	Fiscal Year Ends: 12/31
2004 Sales: $37,445,000	2004 Profits: $2,788,000	Parent Company:

SALARIES/BENEFITS:

Pension Plan:	ESOP Stock Plan:	Profit Sharing:	Top Exec. Salary: $1,318,974	Bonus: $4,294,844
Savings Plan:	Stock Purch. Plan:		Second Exec. Salary: $1,262,500	Bonus: $6,468,768

OTHER THOUGHTS:

Apparent Women Officers or Directors: 2
Hot Spot for Advancement for Women/Minorities: Y

LOCATIONS: ("Y" = Yes)

West:	Southwest:	Midwest:	Southeast:	Northeast:	International:
Y	Y	Y	Y	Y	Y

Note: Financial information, benefits and other data can change quickly and may vary from those stated here.

UNITEDHEALTH GROUP INC

www.unitedhealthgroup.com

Industry Group Code: 524114 Ranks within this company's industry group: Sales: 1 Profits: 1

Management:		Sales/Marketing:		Liberal Arts:		Information Systems:		Professionals:		Tech./Scientific:	
Management Trainees:	Y	Marketing Pros.:	Y	Gen. Writing/Editing:	Y	Info. Management:	Y	Finance/Acct.:	Y	Engineers, Electrical:	
Experienced Mngmt.:	Y	Retail Sales:		Technical Writing:	Y	Software Dev.:	Y	Law:	Y	Engineers, Other:	
International Business:	Y	Commercial/Industrial:	Y	Graphic Arts/Photog.:	Y	Hardware Dev.:		HR/Other:	Y	Health/Lab:	
MBA Grads:	Y	Sales Trainees:		Music:		Consulting/Other:		Training:	Y	Scientists/Research:	
		Advertising Pros.:	Y	Broadcasting:				Health Care:	Y	Petroleum/Chemicals:	
				Other:	Y			Consulting:		Math/Other:	

TYPES OF BUSINESS:

Medical Insurance
Wellness Plans
Dental & Vision Insurance

BRANDS/DIVISIONS/AFFILIATES:

Sierra Health Services, Inc
Unison Health Plans
Mid Atlantic Medical Services, Inc.
Dental Benefits Providers
Pacificare Health Systems, Inc.
Golden Rule Insurance Company
Americhoice Corporation
UnitedHealthcare National Accounts

CONTACTS: Note: Officers with more than one job title may be intentionally listed here more than once.

Stephen J. Hemsley, CEO
Stephen J. Hemsley, Pres.
G. Mike Mikan, CFO/Exec. VP
Lori Sweere, Exec. VP-Human Capital
Don Nathan, Chief Comm. Officer/Sr. VP
Gail K. Boudreaux, Exec. VP/Pres., UnitedHealthcare
William A. Munsell, Exec. VP/Pres., Enterprise Services Group
Larry C. Renfro, Exec. VP/CEO-Ovations
Simon Stevens, Exec. VP/Pres., Global Health
Richard T. Burke, Chmn.

Phone: 952-936-1300	Fax: 952-936-1819
Toll-Free: 800-328-5979	
Address: 9900 Bren Rd. E., Minnetonka, MN 55343 US	

GROWTH PLANS/SPECIAL FEATURES:

UnitedHealth Group, Inc. is a diversified health and well-being company, serving more than 70 million Americans. The company provides individuals with access to healthcare services and resources through more than 580,000 physicians and other care providers and 4,900 hospitals across the U.S. The company has four operating segments: Health Care Services; OptumHealth; Ingenix; and Prescription Solutions. The Health Care Services segment, which includes UnitedHealthcare, Ovations and AmeriChoice, provides consumer-oriented health benefit plans and services for large national employers, public sector employers, mid-sized employers, small businesses and individuals nationwide; health and well-being services for individuals age 50 and older; and network-based health services for beneficiaries of government-sponsored health care programs. The OptumHealth segment is engaged in care solutions, behavioral solutions, specialty benefits and financial services in fields such as dental, vision, disability, therapy and stop-loss coverage. The Ingenix segment offers database and data management services; software products; publications; consulting and actuarial services; business process outsourcing services; pharmaceutical data consulting and research; and pharmaceutical development services nationwide and internationally. Ingenix's customers include more than 6,000 hospitals; 240,000 physicians; 1,500 payers and intermediaries; 260 Fortune 500 companies; 250 government entities; and 300 life sciences companies. The Prescription Solutions segment offers a comprehensive suite of integrated pharmacy benefit management (PBM) services to approximately 10 million people, through about 60,000 retail network pharmacies and two mail service facilities. UnitedHealth's recent acquisitions include Sierra Health Services, Inc.; Unison Health Plans (Unison), a provider of government-sponsored health plan coverage; Fiserv, Inc.'s health-related business; a minority stake in Sedgwick Claims Management Services, Inc.; and AIM Healthcare Services, Inc., a provider of payment accuracy solutions to health care payer and hospital clients.

The company offers its employees medical, vision and dental insurance; flexible spending accounts; life and AD&D insurance; an employee assistance program; adoption assistance; and tuition reimbursement.

FINANCIALS: Sales and profits are in thousands of dollars—add 000 to get the full amount. 2008 Note: Financial information for 2008 was not available for all companies at press time.

2008 Sales: $81,186,000	2008 Profits: $2,977,000	**U.S. Stock Ticker:** UNH
2007 Sales: $75,431,000	2007 Profits: $4,654,000	**Int'l Ticker:** Int'l Exchange:
2006 Sales: $71,542,000	2006 Profits: $4,159,000	Employees: 75,000
2005 Sales: $46,425,000	2005 Profits: $3,083,000	Fiscal Year Ends: 12/31
2004 Sales: $38,217,000	2004 Profits: $2,411,000	Parent Company:

SALARIES/BENEFITS:

Pension Plan:	ESOP Stock Plan:	Profit Sharing:	Top Exec. Salary: $1,300,000	Bonus: $1,822,019
Savings Plan: Y	Stock Purch. Plan: Y		Second Exec. Salary: $692,115	Bonus: $2,000,000

OTHER THOUGHTS:

Apparent Women Officers or Directors: 4
Hot Spot for Advancement for Women/Minorities: Y

LOCATIONS: ("Y" = Yes)

West:	Southwest:	Midwest:	Southeast:	Northeast:	International:
Y	Y	Y	Y	Y	Y

Note: Financial information, benefits and other data can change quickly and may vary from those stated here.

UNIVERSAL HEALTH SERVICES INC

www.uhsinc.com

Industry Group Code: 6214 Ranks within this company's industry group: Sales: 2 Profits: 2

Management:		Sales/Marketing:		Liberal Arts:		Information Systems:		Professionals:		Tech./Scientific:	
Management Trainees:	Y	Marketing Pros.:	Y	Gen. Writing/Editing:		Info. Management:	Y	Finance/Acct.:	Y	Engineers, Electrical:	
Experienced Mngmt.:	Y	Retail Sales:		Technical Writing:	Y	Software Dev.:	Y	Law:	Y	Engineers, Other:	
International Business:	Y	Commercial/Industrial:		Graphic Arts/Photog.:		Hardware Dev.:		HR/Other:	Y	Health/Lab:	Y
MBA Grads:	Y	Sales Trainees:		Music:		Consulting/Other:		Training:	Y	Scientists/Research:	
		Advertising Pros.:		Broadcasting:				Health Care:	Y	Petroleum/Chemicals:	
				Other:				Consulting:		Math/Other:	

TYPES OF BUSINESS:

Acute Care Hospitals
Radiation Oncology Centers
Behavioral Health Hospitals
Surgical Hospitals

BRANDS/DIVISIONS/AFFILIATES:

SummitRidge Hospital
Central Florida Behavioral Hospital

CONTACTS: Note: Officers with more than one job title may be intentionally listed here more than once.

Alan B. Miller, CEO
Marc D. Miller, Pres.
Steve G. Filton, CFO/Sr. VP/Sec.
Paul Yakulis, VP-Human Resources
Michael S. Nelson, VP-Info. Svcs.
Matthew D. Klein, General Counsel/VP
Richard C. Wright, VP-Dev.
Cheryl K. Ramagano, Treas./VP
Charles F. Boyle, Controller/VP
Michael Marquez, Sr. VP
Debra K. Osteen, Sr. VP
David E. Bussone, Sr. VP
Alan B. Miller, Chmn.

Phone: 610-768-3300	Fax: 610-992-4545
Toll-Free:	
Address: 367 S. Gulph Rd., King of Prussia, PA 19406 US	

GROWTH PLANS/SPECIAL FEATURES:

Universal Health Services, Inc. (UHS) owns and operates, through its subsidiaries, acute care hospitals, behavioral health centers, surgical hospitals, ambulatory surgery centers and radiation oncology centers. UHS has 26 acute care hospitals and 101 behavioral health centers located in 32 states, Washington, D.C. and Puerto Rico. As part of its ambulatory treatment centers division, the firm manages or partially/wholly owns nine surgical hospitals and surgery and radiation oncology centers located in six states and Puerto Rico. UHS hospitals provide general surgery, pharmaceutical services, internal medicine, pediatric services, obstetrics, emergency room care, radiology, oncology, diagnostic care, coronary care and behavioral health services. The company also provides non-medical services to its facilities, including a variety of management services such as central purchasing; facilities planning; administrative personnel management; finance and control systems; information services; physician recruitment services; marketing; and public relations. Acute care hospitals, surgery centers, surgical hospitals and radiation oncology centers make up approximately 74% of the firm's revenue, with behavioral health care facilities accounting for roughly 25%. In September 2008, UHS agreed to sell a 125-bed acute care hospital in Pennsylvania, Central Montgomery Medical Center, to Abington Memorial Hospital. Also in September 2008, the firm acquired SummitRidge Hospital, a 76-bed behavioral health hospital in Georgia; and completed renovations on the 120-bed Central Florida Behavioral Hospital.

The company offers its employees medical, dental and vision coverage; life, AD&D and disability insurance; paid time off; a 401(k) plan; an employee stock purchase plan; and flexible spending accounts.

FINANCIALS: Sales and profits are in thousands of dollars—add 000 to get the full amount. 2008 Note: Financial information for 2008 was not available for all companies at press time.

2008 Sales: $5,022,417	2008 Profits: $192,941	**U.S. Stock Ticker: UHS**
2007 Sales: $4,751,005	2007 Profits: $170,387	**Int'l Ticker:** Int'l Exchange:
2006 Sales: $4,191,300	2006 Profits: $259,458	Employees: 39,500
2005 Sales: $3,935,480	2005 Profits: $240,845	Fiscal Year Ends: 12/31
2004 Sales: $3,637,490	2004 Profits: $169,492	Parent Company:

SALARIES/BENEFITS:

Pension Plan:	ESOP Stock Plan:	Profit Sharing:	Top Exec. Salary: $1,350,052	Bonus: $3,375,130
Savings Plan: Y	Stock Purch. Plan: Y		Second Exec. Salary: $471,643	Bonus: $468,500

OTHER THOUGHTS:

Apparent Women Officers or Directors: 9
Hot Spot for Advancement for Women/Minorities: Y

LOCATIONS: ("Y" = Yes)

West:	Southwest:	Midwest:	Southeast:	Northeast:	International:
Y	Y	Y	Y	Y	

Note: Financial information, benefits and other data can change quickly and may vary from those stated here.

UNIVISION COMMUNICATIONS INC

www.univision.com

Industry Group Code: 515120 Ranks within this company's industry group: Sales: Profits:

Management:		Sales/Marketing:		Liberal Arts:		Information Systems:		Professionals:		Tech./Scientific:	
Management Trainees:	Y	Marketing Pros.:	Y	Gen. Writing/Editing:	Y	Info. Management:	Y	Finance/Acct.:	Y	Engineers, Electrical:	Y
Experienced Mngmt.:	Y	Retail Sales:		Technical Writing:		Software Dev.:	Y	Law:	Y	Engineers, Other:	
International Business:	Y	Commercial/Industrial:	Y	Graphic Arts/Photog.:	Y	Hardware Dev.:		HR/Other:	Y	Health/Lab:	
MBA Grads:	Y	Sales Trainees:		Music:	Y	Consulting/Other:		Training:	Y	Scientists/Research:	
		Advertising Pros.:	Y	Broadcasting:	Y			Health Care:		Petroleum/Chemicals:	
				Other:	Y			Consulting:		Math/Other:	

TYPES OF BUSINESS:

Spanish Television Broadcasting
Cable Television Programming
Online Portal
Radio Broadcasting

BRANDS/DIVISIONS/AFFILIATES:

Univision Television Group
Galavision
TeleFutura
Univision Interactive Media
Univision Radio, Inc.
Broadcasting Media Partners, Inc.

CONTACTS: Note: Officers with more than one job title may be intentionally listed here more than once.

Joe Uva, CEO
Ray Rodriguez, COO
Ray Rodriguez, Pres.
Andrew W. Hobson, CFO/Sr. Exec. VP
C. Douglas Kranwinkle, General Counsel/Exec. VP
Cesar Conde, Chief Strategic Officer
Peter H. Lori, Chief Acct. Officer/Controller/Sr. VP
Haim Saban, Chmn.

Phone: 212-455-5200	Fax: 212-867-6710
Toll-Free:	
Address: 605 3rd Ave., 12th Fl., New York, NY 10158 US	

GROWTH PLANS/SPECIAL FEATURES:

Univision Communications, Inc. is the leading Spanish-language media company in the U.S. The company currently operates in three business segments: television, radio and interactive media. The television segment, which accounts for approximately 77% of net revenues, consists of the Univision, TeleFutura and the Galavision cable television networks. Univision's radio segment, which accounts for roughly 21% of revenues, is operated through Univision Radio, Inc., an owner of 67 radio stations in 16 of the top 25 U.S. Hispanic markets and five stations in Puerto Rico. The Interactive media division, which is operated by Univision Interactive Media, consists of univision.com, a web portal with an annual average of 3 billion hits; and Univision Movil, a Spanish-language suite of mobile offerings. This segment accounts for the remaining 2% of the firm's revenues. Each of these three segments represents the largest Spanish-language media application in their respective fields within the U.S. The firm is able to reach 96% of all U.S. Hispanic households via its nationwide Univision broadcast and cable channels. TeleFutura is the company's 24-hour Spanish-language broadcast television network, reaching 85% of U.S. Hispanic households. TeleFutura Television Group is the owner and operator of 18 full-power and 1425elow-power Spanish-language stations. The company's Galavision network is the leading Spanish-language cable television network, which covers approximately 82% of U.S. Hispanic cable households. Broadcast is supported by the Univision Television Group, which owns and operates 20 full-power and 9 low-power Univision Network stations. In recent years, Broadcasting Media Partners, Inc., a consortium of private-equity investors, acquired Univision and all of its subsidiaries. In January 2009, Univision Online was renamed Univision Interactive Media and will offer Univision Movil, a Spanish-language suite of mobile offerings. In April 2009, the company launched Univision Interactive Self-Service, a display advertising platform aimed at marketers seeking to reach a large web-based audience.

FINANCIALS: Sales and profits are in thousands of dollars—add 000 to get the full amount. 2008 Note: Financial information for 2008 was not available for all companies at press time.

2008 Sales: $	2008 Profits: $	U.S. Stock Ticker: Subsidiary
2007 Sales: $2,196,000	2007 Profits: $-314,900	Int'l Ticker: Int'l Exchange:
2006 Sales: $2,166,652	2006 Profits: $349,174	Employees: 4,000
2005 Sales: $1,952,531	2005 Profits: $187,179	Fiscal Year Ends: 12/31
2004 Sales: $1,786,935	2004 Profits: $255,883	Parent Company: BROADCASTING MEDIA PARTNERS, INC

SALARIES/BENEFITS:

Pension Plan:	ESOP Stock Plan:	Profit Sharing:	Top Exec. Salary: $	Bonus: $
Savings Plan:	Stock Purch. Plan:		Second Exec. Salary: $	Bonus: $

OTHER THOUGHTS:

Apparent Women Officers or Directors: 1
Hot Spot for Advancement for Women/Minorities:

LOCATIONS: ("Y" = Yes)

West:	Southwest:	Midwest:	Southeast:	Northeast:	International:
Y	Y	Y	Y	Y	Y

URS CORPORATION

www.urscorp.com

Industry Group Code: 541330 Ranks within this company's industry group: Sales: 1   Profits: 2

Management:		Sales/Marketing:		Liberal Arts:		Information Systems:		Professionals:		Tech./Scientific:	
Management Trainees:	Y	Marketing Pros.:	Y	Gen. Writing/Editing:	Y	Info. Management:	Y	Finance/Acct.:	Y	Engineers, Electrical:	Y
Experienced Mngmt.:	Y	Retail Sales:		Technical Writing:	Y	Software Dev.:	Y	Law:	Y	Engineers, Other:	Y
International Business:	Y	Commercial/Industrial:	Y	Graphic Arts/Photog.:	Y	Hardware Dev.:		HR/Other:	Y	Health/Lab:	
MBA Grads:	Y	Sales Trainees:		Music:		Consulting/Other:	Y	Training:	Y	Scientists/Research:	
		Advertising Pros.:		Broadcasting:				Health Care:		Petroleum/Chemicals:	
				Other:				Consulting:	Y	Math/Other:	

TYPES OF BUSINESS:

Engineering Design Services
Systems Engineering & Technical Assistance
Operations & Maintenance Services
Construction

BRANDS/DIVISIONS/AFFILIATES:

EG&G Division
URS Division
Washington Division

CONTACTS: *Note: Officers with more than one job title may be intentionally listed here more than once.*

Martin M. Koffel, CEO
Martin M. Koffel, Pres.
H. Thomas Hicks, CFO/VP-Finance
Joseph Masters, General Counsel/Sec.
Thomas W. Bishop, VP-Strategy/Sr. VP-Construction Svcs.
Susan B. Kilgannon, VP-Comm.
Reed N. Brimhall, Chief Acct. Officer/Controller/VP
Thomas H. Zarges, Pres., Washington Div.
Gary V. Jandegian, VP/Pres., URS Div.
Randall A. Wotring, VP/Pres., EG&G Div.
Martin M. Koffel, Chmn.

Phone: 415-774-2700	Fax: 415-398-1905
Toll-Free:	
Address: 600 Montgomery St., Fl. 26, San Francisco, CA 94111 US	

GROWTH PLANS/SPECIAL FEATURES:

URS Corp. is a worldwide engineering design services firm and a U.S. federal government contractor for systems engineering, technical assistance, operations and maintenance services. The company focuses primarily on providing fee-based professional and technical services in the engineering and construction services and defense markets. The firm operates in three divisions: URS, EG&G and the Washington division. The URS division provides professional planning and design; program management; construction management; and operations and maintenance services to various government agencies and departments in the U.S. and internationally, as well as to private industry clients. The EG&G division provides planning; systems engineering and technical assistance; operations and maintenance; and program management services to various U.S. governmental agencies, including the Departments of Defense and Homeland Security. The Washington division builds transportation infrastructure, including airports, mass transit systems and tolls roads. The unit also performs intricate tasks such as nuclear waste disposal, mining, engineering and facility management. The company has a network of offices and job sites across the U.S. and in more than 30 foreign countries in the Americas, Europe, the Middle East and Asia-Pacific. The federal government accounted for 35% of the company's revenues in 2008, while industrial and commercial, power and infrastructure projects accounted for 29%, 19% and 17%, respectively. In June 2009, the company sold its stake in the German mining and power joint venture MIBRAG.

URS offers its employees medical, vision and dental insurance; a 401(k) plan; an employee stock purchase plan; short- and long-term insurance; life and AD&D insurance; an employee assistance program; flexible spending accounts; and tuition reimbursement.

FINANCIALS: Sales and profits are in thousands of dollars—add 000 to get the full amount. 2008 Note: Financial information for 2008 was not available for all companies at press time.

2008 Sales: $10,086,289	2008 Profits: $219,791	**U.S. Stock Ticker:** URS
2007 Sales: $5,383,007	2007 Profits: $132,243	**Int'l Ticker:** Int'l Exchange:
2006 Sales: $4,222,869	2006 Profits: $113,012	Employees: 50,000
2005 Sales: $3,890,282	2005 Profits: $82,475	Fiscal Year Ends: 12/31
2004 Sales: $3,381,963	2004 Profits: $61,704	Parent Company:

SALARIES/BENEFITS:

Pension Plan: Y	ESOP Stock Plan:	Profit Sharing:	Top Exec. Salary: $1,019,232	Bonus: $2,500,003
Savings Plan: Y	Stock Purch. Plan: Y		Second Exec. Salary: $713,462	Bonus: $1,047,122

OTHER THOUGHTS:

Apparent Women Officers or Directors: 2
Hot Spot for Advancement for Women/Minorities: Y

LOCATIONS: ("Y" = Yes)

West:	Southwest:	Midwest:	Southeast:	Northeast:	International:
Y	Y	Y	Y	Y	Y

USAA

www.usaa.com

Industry Group Code: 524126 **Ranks within this company's industry group:** Sales: 6   Profits: 5

Management:		Sales/Marketing:		Liberal Arts:		Information Systems:		Professionals:		Tech./Scientific:	
Management Trainees:	Y	Marketing Pros.:	Y	Gen. Writing/Editing:	Y	Info. Management:	Y	Finance/Acct.:	Y	Engineers, Electrical:	
Experienced Mngmt.:	Y	Retail Sales:		Technical Writing:	Y	Software Dev.:	Y	Law:	Y	Engineers, Other:	
International Business:	Y	Commercial/Industrial:		Graphic Arts/Photog.:	Y	Hardware Dev.:		HR/Other:	Y	Health/Lab:	
MBA Grads:	Y	Sales Trainees:	Y	Music:		Consulting/Other:		Training:	Y	Scientists/Research:	
		Advertising Pros.:	Y	Broadcasting:				Health Care:		Petroleum/Chemicals:	
				Other:	Y			Consulting:		Math/Other:	Y

TYPES OF BUSINESS:

Insurance, Direct Property & Casualty
Banking
Life Insurance
Real Estate Development
Discount Brokerage
Investment Management
Mutual Funds

BRANDS/DIVISIONS/AFFILIATES:

USAA Investment Management Company
USAA Alliance Services
USAA Educational Foundation

CONTACTS: *Note: Officers with more than one job title may be intentionally listed here more than once.*

Josue (Joe) Robles, Jr., CEO
Josue (Joe) Robles, Jr., Pres.
Kristi A. Matus, CFO/Exec. VP
Roger V. Chacko, Chief Mktg. Officer/Exec. VP
Elizabeth D. Conklyn, Exec. VP-People Svcs.
Steven A. Bennett, General Counsel/Corp. Sec/Exec. VP
Wayne Peacock, Exec. VP-Enterprise Bus. Oper.
Wendi E. Strong, Exec. VP-Corp. Comm.
F. David Bohne, Pres., USAA Fed. Savings Bank
Stuart Parker, Pres., USAA Property & Casualty Insurance Group
Christopher W. Claus, Pres., USAA Financial Svcs. Group
John H. Moellering, Chmn.

Phone: 210-498-2211	**Fax:** 210-498-9940
Toll-Free: 800-531-8722	
Address: 9800 Fredericksburg Rd., San Antonio, TX 78288 US	

GROWTH PLANS/SPECIAL FEATURES:

USAA (United Services Automobile Association) is a mutual insurance company that serves 7.2 million members, comprising exclusively U.S. military personnel and their families. It owns and manages over $119 billion in assets from offices in Texas, Colorado, Arizona, Virginia, Colorado, Florida and California; and international offices in London and Frankfurt. USAA offers more than 150 financial services and products, primarily automobile, homeowner's and renter's insurance as well as automobile, mortgage and home equity loans. The company also manages checking accounts, savings accounts, credit cards and personal loans for its military customers. Customers also have access to mutual funds and brokerage services through USAA Investment Management Company. Members can access their accounts and conduct investing, banking and insurance business online. Additionally, subsidiary USAA Alliance Services, LLC has formed a series of partnerships to provide members with discounts on home security, travel services and insurance, floral services, car rentals and diamond and fine jewelry. The firm's USAA Educational Foundation division, a nonprofit entity, provides consumer education to the general public on topics including personal finance, safety and quality of life. During 2008, USAA expanded its membership eligibility to include military retirees, regardless of when they retired; military personnel who were honorably discharged on or after Jan. 1, 1996; and widows or widowers of military personnel killed in action while eligible.

USAA employee's benefits include educational assistance, flextime, flexible spending accounts, wellness benefits and blood pressure screenings. Company employees called to active military duty receive their accustomed pay for four weeks, and pay differential for up to two years after deployment. USAA employees are eligible to receive benefits, holiday bonuses and corporate performance bonuses during the time they are deployed. Women account for 62% of USAA's employees.

FINANCIALS: Sales and profits are in thousands of dollars—add 000 to get the full amount. 2008 Note: Financial information for 2008 was not available for all companies at press time.

2008 Sales: $12,912,000	2008 Profits: $423,000	**U.S. Stock Ticker: Mutual Company**
2007 Sales: $14,417,900	2007 Profits: $1,855,500	**Int'l Ticker:** Int'l Exchange:
2006 Sales: $13,416,000	2006 Profits: $2,330,000	Employees: 21,900
2005 Sales: $11,980,000	2005 Profits: $1,388,000	Fiscal Year Ends: 12/31
2004 Sales: $11,273,000	2004 Profits: $1,597,000	Parent Company:

SALARIES/BENEFITS:

Pension Plan: Y	ESOP Stock Plan:	Profit Sharing:	Top Exec. Salary: $	Bonus: $
Savings Plan: Y	Stock Purch. Plan:		Second Exec. Salary: $	Bonus: $

OTHER THOUGHTS:

Apparent Women Officers or Directors: 4
Hot Spot for Advancement for Women/Minorities: Y

LOCATIONS: ("Y" = Yes)

West:	Southwest:	Midwest:	Southeast:	Northeast:	International:
Y	Y		Y	Y	Y

VALERO ENERGY CORP

www.valero.com

Industry Group Code: 324110 **Ranks within this company's industry group:** Sales: 1 Profits: 3

Management:		Sales/Marketing:		Liberal Arts:		Information Systems:		Professionals:		Tech./Scientific:	
Management Trainees:	Y	Marketing Pros.:	Y	Gen. Writing/Editing:	Y	Info. Management:	Y	Finance/Acct.:	Y	Engineers, Electrical:	Y
Experienced Mngmt.:	Y	Retail Sales:	Y	Technical Writing:	Y	Software Dev.:	Y	Law:	Y	Engineers, Other:	Y
International Business:	Y	Commercial/Industrial:	Y	Graphic Arts/Photog.:	Y	Hardware Dev.:		HR/Other:	Y	Health/Lab:	
MBA Grads:	Y	Sales Trainees:	Y	Music:		Consulting/Other:		Training:	Y	Scientists/Research:	
		Advertising Pros.:	Y	Broadcasting:				Health Care:		Petroleum/Chemicals:	Y
				Other:				Consulting:		Math/Other:	

TYPES OF BUSINESS:
Petroleum Refineries & Retail Marketing
Convenience Stores
Home Heating Fuels
Wholesale Fuel Marketing
Asphalt
Marine Transportation
Ethanol Production

BRANDS/DIVISIONS/AFFILIATES:
Diamond Shamrock
Corner Store
Stop N Go

CONTACTS: *Note: Officers with more than one job title may be intentionally listed here more than once.*
William R. Klesse, CEO
Richard J. Marcogliese, COO/Exec. VP
William R. Klesse, Pres.
Michael S. Ciskowski, CFO/Exec. VP
Joseph W. Gorder, Exec. VP-Mktg.
Mike Crownover, Sr. VP-Human Resources
Hal Zesch, CIO/Sr. VP
Kim Bowers, General Counsel/Exec. VP
S. Eugene Edwards, Exec. VP-Corp. Dev. & Strategic Planning
Eric Fisher, VP-Corp. Comm.
Eric Fisher, VP-Investor Comm.
Donna Titzman, Treas./VP
Gary Arthur, Jr., Sr. VP-Retail Mktg.
Jay D. Browning, Sec./Sr. VP-Corp. Law
Clay Killinger, Sr. VP/Controller
Steve Gilbert, Assistant Sec./Disclosure & Compliance Officer
William R. Klesse, Chmn.
Joseph W. Gorder, Exec. VP-Supply

Phone: 210-345-2000	Fax: 210-345-2646
Toll-Free: 800-531-7911	
Address: 1 Valero Way, San Antonio, TX 78249 US	

GROWTH PLANS/SPECIAL FEATURES:
Valero Energy Corporation is a refiner and retailer of gasoline and other oil related products. Valero owns and operates 16 refineries located in the U.S., Canada and Aruba that produce refined products such as conventional gasolines, distillates, jet fuel, asphalt, petrochemicals and lubricants; and a slate of premium products including low-sulfur/ultra-low-sulfur diesel fuel and oxygenates (liquid hydrocarbon compounds containing oxygen). The firm markets branded and unbranded refined products on a wholesale basis in the U.S. and Canada through an extensive bulk and rack marketing network. Valero also sells refined products through a network of about 5,800 retail and wholesale branded outlets in the U.S., Canada and Aruba. The company's business is organized into two reportable segments: refining and retail. The refining segment offers refining and transportation operations; wholesale marketing; and product supply. The segment has a total throughput capacity of approximately 3.0 million barrels per day. Valero's retail segment sells transportation fuels at retail stores and unattended, self-service cardlocks; convenience store merchandise in retail stores; and home heating oil to residential customers. The segment is separated into two groups: Retail-U.S., which owns or leases over 1,000 stores under the names Corner Store and Stop N Go and sells transportation fuel under the Valero and Diamond Shamrock brands; and Retail-Canada, which owns or leases 412 retail stores, distributes gasoline to 453 dealers/jobbers and sells transportation fuels under the Ultramar brand through a network of 920 outlets. In recent years, Valero sold its Lima, Ohio refinery to Husky Energy, Inc., for $1.9 billion. In early 2009, the firm agreed to acquire most of the ethanol production assets of bankrupt VeraSun, which will give Valero 780 million gallons of ethanol capacity yearly. In August 2009, the company agreed to indefinitely close its Aruba refinery plant.

FINANCIALS: Sales and profits are in thousands of dollars—add 000 to get the full amount. 2008 Note: Financial information for 2008 was not available for all companies at press time.

2008 Sales: $119,114,000	2008 Profits: $-1,131,000	**U.S. Stock Ticker:** VLO
2007 Sales: $95,327,000	2007 Profits: $5,234,000	**Int'l Ticker:** Int'l Exchange:
2006 Sales: $87,640,000	2006 Profits: $5,463,000	Employees: 21,765
2005 Sales: $80,616,000	2005 Profits: $3,590,000	Fiscal Year Ends: 12/31
2004 Sales: $54,589,000	2004 Profits: $	Parent Company:

SALARIES/BENEFITS:
Pension Plan:	ESOP Stock Plan:	Profit Sharing:	Top Exec. Salary: $1,500,000	Bonus: $705,510
Savings Plan:	Stock Purch. Plan:		Second Exec. Salary: $855,000	Bonus: $627,707

OTHER THOUGHTS:
Apparent Women Officers or Directors: 3
Hot Spot for Advancement for Women/Minorities: Y

LOCATIONS: ("Y" = Yes)
West:	Southwest:	Midwest:	Southeast:	Northeast:	International:
Y	Y	Y	Y	Y	Y

Note: Financial information, benefits and other data can change quickly and may vary from those stated here.

VALSPAR CORPORATION (THE)

www.valspar.com

Industry Group Code: 325510 Ranks within this company's industry group: Sales: 1   Profits: 1

Management:		Sales/Marketing:		Liberal Arts:		Information Systems:		Professionals:		Tech./Scientific:	
Management Trainees:	Y	Marketing Pros.:	Y	Gen. Writing/Editing:	Y	Info. Management:	Y	Finance/Acct.:	Y	Engineers, Electrical:	
Experienced Mngmt.:	Y	Retail Sales:		Technical Writing:	Y	Software Dev.:	Y	Law:	Y	Engineers, Other:	Y
International Business:	Y	Commercial/Industrial:	Y	Graphic Arts/Photog.:	Y	Hardware Dev.:		HR/Other:	Y	Health/Lab:	
MBA Grads:	Y	Sales Trainees:		Music:		Consulting/Other:		Training:	Y	Scientists/Research:	Y
		Advertising Pros.:	Y	Broadcasting:				Health Care:		Petroleum/Chemicals:	Y
				Other:				Consulting:		Math/Other:	

TYPES OF BUSINESS:

Coatings & Paints
Packaging Products
Specialty Polymers
General Industrial, Coil & Wood Products
Colorants & Gelcoats
Furniture Protection Plans

BRANDS/DIVISIONS/AFFILIATES:

Valspar Refinish
De Beer
House of Kolor
Teknos Nova Coil TNC Oy
Tekno S.A.
Huarun Paints
H.B. Fuller
Aries Coil Coatings S.A. de C.V.

CONTACTS: *Note: Officers with more than one job title may be intentionally listed here more than once.*

William L. Mansfield, CEO
Gary E. Hendrickson, COO
Gary E. Hendrickson, Pres.
Lori A. Walker, CFO/Sr. VP
Anthony L. Blaine, Sr. VP-Human Resources
Rolf Engh, General Counsel/Exec. VP/Sec.
Tyler N. Treat, Investor Rel.
Steven L. Erdahl, Exec. VP
Paul C. Reyelts, Exec. VP
Howard C. Heckes, Sr. VP-Global Architectural
William L. Mansfield, Chmn.

Phone: 612-851-7000	**Fax:** 612-851-7408
Toll-Free:	
Address: 901 3rd Ave. S., Minneapolis, MN 55415-1211 US	

GROWTH PLANS/SPECIAL FEATURES:

The Valspar Corporation is a global provider of paints, coatings and related products. The company operates in two segments, coatings and paints. The coatings segment includes a range of decorative and protective coatings for metal, wood, plastic and glass, primarily sold to original equipment manufacturers (OEM). Products within this segment include primers, top coats, varnishes, inks, sprays, stains, fillers and other coatings used in manufacturing industries such as building products, appliances, furniture, transportation, agricultural and construction equipment, metal packaging and metal fabrication. This segment includes the firm's packaging product line and three industrial product lines: general industrial, coil and wood. The packaging product line includes coatings for the interior and exterior of metal packaging containers, principally food containers and beverage cans. The firm also produces coatings for aerosol and paint cans; bottle crowns for glass; plastic packaging; and bottle closures. The coil coatings unit includes the firm's subsidiaries Teknos Nova Coil TNC Oy, in Finland; Tekno S.A., in Brazil; and Aries Coil Coatings S.A. de C.V., in Mexico. The wood coatings unit includes an 86% interest in Huarun Paints. The industrial coatings unit includes H.B. Fuller, a U.K.-based powder coatings business. The paints segment offers interior and exterior paints; stains; primers; varnishes; high performance floor paints; and specialty decorative products. This segment also markets automotive refinish paints and aerosol spray paints under brand names Valspar Refinish, De Beer and House of Kolor. In addition to these product lines, Valspar makes and sells specialty polymers, colorants, gelcoats and furniture protection plans. The company's gelcoats and related products are sold to boat manufacturers, shower and tub manufacturers and others. During 2008, the company acquired the outstanding shares of Tekno S.A. and Aries Coil Coatings S.A. de C.V.

Valspar offers employees medical, dental and life insurance; education assistance; and an employee assistance program.

FINANCIALS: Sales and profits are in thousands of dollars—add 000 to get the full amount. 2008 Note: Financial information for 2008 was not available for all companies at press time.

2008 Sales: $3,482,378	2008 Profits: $150,766	**U.S. Stock Ticker: VAL**	
2007 Sales: $3,249,287	2007 Profits: $172,115	**Int'l Ticker:** Int'l Exchange:	
2006 Sales: $2,978,062	2006 Profits: $175,252	Employees: 9,400	
2005 Sales: $2,713,950	2005 Profits: $147,618	Fiscal Year Ends: 10/31	
2004 Sales: $2,440,692	2004 Profits: $142,836	Parent Company:	

SALARIES/BENEFITS:

Pension Plan:	ESOP Stock Plan:	Profit Sharing:	Top Exec. Salary: $911,346	Bonus: $1,197,099
Savings Plan:	Stock Purch. Plan:		Second Exec. Salary: $566,896	Bonus: $633,011

OTHER THOUGHTS:

Apparent Women Officers or Directors: 2
Hot Spot for Advancement for Women/Minorities: Y

LOCATIONS: ("Y" = Yes)

West:	Southwest:	Midwest:	Southeast:	Northeast:	International:
Y	Y	Y	Y	Y	Y

VARIAN MEDICAL SYSTEMS INC

www.varian.com

Industry Group Code: 33911 Ranks within this company's industry group: Sales: 11 Profits: 10

Management:		Sales/Marketing:		Liberal Arts:		Information Systems:		Professionals:		Tech./Scientific:	
Management Trainees:		Marketing Pros.:	Y	Gen. Writing/Editing:	Y	Info. Management:	Y	Finance/Acct.:	Y	Engineers, Electrical:	Y
Experienced Mngmt.:	Y	Retail Sales:		Technical Writing:	Y	Software Dev.:	Y	Law:	Y	Engineers, Other:	Y
International Business:	Y	Commercial/Industrial:	Y	Graphic Arts/Photog.:	Y	Hardware Dev.:	Y	HR/Other:	Y	Health/Lab:	Y
MBA Grads:	Y	Sales Trainees:		Music:		Consulting/Other:		Training:	Y	Scientists/Research:	Y
		Advertising Pros.:	Y	Broadcasting:				Health Care:	Y	Petroleum/Chemicals:	
				Other:				Consulting:		Math/Other:	Y

TYPES OF BUSINESS:

Radiation Oncology Systems
X-Ray Equipment
Software Systems
Security & Inspection Products

BRANDS/DIVISIONS/AFFILIATES:

RapidArc
Ginzton Technology Center
Varian Particle Therapy
Linatron
Research Instruments
IKOEmed
IKOEtech

CONTACTS: *Note: Officers with more than one job title may be intentionally listed here more than once.*

Timothy E. Guertin, CEO
Timothy E. Guertin, Pres.
Elisha W. Finney, CFO/Sr. VP
Wendy S. Reitherman, VP-Human Resources
Jessica Denecour, CIO/VP
John W. Kuo, General Counsel/VP/Corp. Sec.
J. A. Thorson, VP-Bus. Dev. & Finance
Spencer R. Sias, VP-Corp. Comm.
Spencer R. Sias, VP-Investor Rel.
Tai-Yun Chen, VP-Finance/Controller
Lester Boeh, VP-Emerging Bus.
Robert H. Kluge, VP/Pres., X-Ray Prod.
Dow R. Wilson, Exec. VP/Pres., Oncology Systems
George A. Zdasiuk, VP/CTO-Ginzton Tech. Center
Richard M. Levy, Chmn.

Phone: 650-493-4000	**Fax:**
Toll-Free: 800-544-4636	
Address: 3100 Hansen Way, Palo Alto, CA 94304 US	

GROWTH PLANS/SPECIAL FEATURES:

Varian Medical Systems, Inc. designs, manufactures, sells and services equipment and software products for treating cancer with radiotherapy, stereotactic radiosurgery and brachytherapy. The firm operates in three segments: oncology systems, X-ray products and other. The oncology systems segment provides software and hardware for treating cancer with radiation, including linear accelerators; brachytherapy afterloaders; treatment simulation and verification equipment and accessories; and information management, treatment planning and image processing software. The RapidArc radiotherapy planning and treatment delivery products, which were recently developed, delivers image-guided, intensity-modulated radiation therapy (IMRT) 2-8 times faster than conventional IMRT. The X-ray products segment manufactures and sells X-ray imaging components and subsystems, namely X-ray tubes for use in a range of applications including computed tomography (CT) scanning; radioscopic/fluoroscopic imaging; mammography; special procedures; industrial applications; and flat panel detectors for digital X-ray image capture, which is an alternative to image intensifier tubes for fluoroscopy and X-ray film for radiography. The other segment includes the security and inspection products business, which provides Linatron X-ray accelerators to original equipment manufacturers; the Varian Particle Therapy business, which designs and manufactures products and systems for delivering proton therapy; and technologies developed by the Ginzton Technology Center, including digital X-ray imaging technology; volumetric and functional imaging; improved X-ray sources; and technology for security and cargo screening applications. In January 2008, the firm received FDA 510(k) clearance for its RapidArc radiotherapy technology. In May 2008, the company opened a new security and inspections product factory in Las Vegas, Nevada. In early 2009, Varian sold Research Instruments, a scientific instrument component and system manufacturer. Also in 2009, the company acquired certain assets of IKOEmed and IKOEtech, suppliers of software to the radiotherapy and radiosurgery segments.

Varian offers employees medical, dental and vision plans; educational reimbursement; an employee assistance program; and a stock purchase plan.

FINANCIALS: Sales and profits are in thousands of dollars—add 000 to get the full amount. 2008 Note: Financial information for 2008 was not available for all companies at press time.

2008 Sales: $2,069,700	2008 Profits: $279,500	**U.S. Stock Ticker: VAR**
2007 Sales: $1,776,600	2007 Profits: $239,500	**Int'l Ticker:** Int'l Exchange:
2006 Sales: $1,597,800	2006 Profits: $245,100	Employees: 4,900
2005 Sales: $1,382,600	2005 Profits: $206,600	Fiscal Year Ends: 8/31
2004 Sales: $1,235,523	2004 Profits: $167,700	Parent Company:

SALARIES/BENEFITS:

Pension Plan: Y	ESOP Stock Plan:	Profit Sharing:	Top Exec. Salary: $825,594	Bonus: $1,675,731
Savings Plan: Y	Stock Purch. Plan: Y		Second Exec. Salary: $574,632	Bonus: $319,992

OTHER THOUGHTS:

Apparent Women Officers or Directors: 5
Hot Spot for Advancement for Women/Minorities: Y

LOCATIONS: ("Y" = Yes)

West:	Southwest:	Midwest:	Southeast:	Northeast:	International:
Y		Y	Y	Y	Y

Note: Financial information, benefits and other data can change quickly and may vary from those stated here.

VCA ANTECH INC

www.vcaantech.com

Industry Group Code: 541940 **Ranks within this company's industry group:** Sales: 1 Profits: 1

Management:		Sales/Marketing:		Liberal Arts:		Information Systems:		Professionals:		Tech./Scientific:	
Management Trainees:	Y	Marketing Pros.:	Y	Gen. Writing/Editing:	Y	Info. Management:	Y	Finance/Acct.:	Y	Engineers, Electrical:	
Experienced Mngmt.:	Y	Retail Sales:		Technical Writing:	Y	Software Dev.:	Y	Law:	Y	Engineers, Other:	
International Business:		Commercial/Industrial:		Graphic Arts/Photog.:	Y	Hardware Dev.:		HR/Other:	Y	Health/Lab:	Y
MBA Grads:	Y	Sales Trainees:		Music:		Consulting/Other:		Training:	Y	Scientists/Research:	
		Advertising Pros.:		Broadcasting:				Health Care:	Y	Petroleum/Chemicals:	
				Other:				Consulting:		Math/Other:	

TYPES OF BUSINESS:

Animal Health Care Services
Veterinary Diagnostic Laboratories
Full-Service Animal Hospitals
Veterinary Equipment
Ultrasound Imaging

BRANDS/DIVISIONS/AFFILIATES:

Antech Diagnostics
VCA Animal Hospitals
Elkin Medical Systems, Inc.

CONTACTS: *Note: Officers with more than one job title may be intentionally listed here more than once.*

Robert Antin, CEO
Arthur J. Antin, COO/Sr. VP
Robert Antin, Pres.
Tomas W. Fuller, CFO
Josh Drake, Pres., Laboratory Div., Antech Diagnostics
Tomas W. Fuller, Corp. Sec./VP
Neil Tauber, Sr. VP-Dev.
Dawn R. Olsen, Principal Acct. Officer/Controller/VP
Robert Antin, Chmn.

Phone: 310-571-6500	Fax: 310-571-6700
Toll-Free: 800-966-1822	
Address: 12401 W. Olympic Blvd., Los Angeles, CA 90064-1022 US	

GROWTH PLANS/SPECIAL FEATURES:

VCA Antech, Inc. (VCA) provides animal health care services and operates one of the largest networks of veterinary diagnostic laboratories and freestanding, full-service animal hospitals in the U.S. The firm's veterinary diagnostic laboratories, run by the Antech Diagnostics division, provides 300 different testing services as well as consulting services to veterinarians, who use these services in the detection, diagnosis, evaluation, monitoring, treatment and prevention of diseases and other conditions. The division operates 44 laboratories. Services rendered in major metropolitan areas accounted for 74% of laboratory revenue for 2008. The laboratories provide testing daily to over 17,000 animal hospitals and zoos in all 50 states, as well as government agencies, and it offers clients access to results online through Zoasis.com. The VCA Animal Hospitals division operates 471 animal hospitals in 39 states, offering a full range of general medical and surgical services for animals, as well as specialized treatments including advanced diagnostic services, internal medicine, oncology, ophthalmology, dermatology and cardiology. The division, which has most of its hospitals located in California, Florida and Illinois, is supported by 1,700 veterinarians. VCA animal hospitals typically have three to five full-time veterinarians on staff, and are open 10-15 hours per day, six or seven days a week. Subsidiary Sound Technologies, Inc., the company's medical technology segment, sells medical imaging, primarily ultrasound and digital radiography, equipment and related software and services. In July 2009, the company acquired Eklin Medical Systems, Inc., a supplier of digital radiology, ultrasound and practice management software for the veterinary industry.

VCA offers its employees health, life, dental and vision insurance; tuition reimbursement; disability coverage; and veterinary care discounts.

FINANCIALS: Sales and profits are in thousands of dollars—add 000 to get the full amount. 2008 Note: Financial information for 2008 was not available for all companies at press time.

2008 Sales: $1,277,470	2008 Profits: $132,984	U.S. Stock Ticker: WOOF
2007 Sales: $1,156,145	2007 Profits: $121,012	Int'l Ticker: Int'l Exchange:
2006 Sales: $983,313	2006 Profits: $105,529	Employees: 9,000
2005 Sales: $839,666	2005 Profits: $67,816	Fiscal Year Ends: 12/31
2004 Sales: $674,089	2004 Profits: $63,572	Parent Company:

SALARIES/BENEFITS:

Pension Plan:	ESOP Stock Plan:	Profit Sharing:	Top Exec. Salary: $867,951	Bonus: $892,321
Savings Plan: Y	Stock Purch. Plan:		Second Exec. Salary: $552,332	Bonus: $511,059

OTHER THOUGHTS:

Apparent Women Officers or Directors: 1
Hot Spot for Advancement for Women/Minorities:

LOCATIONS: ("Y" = Yes)

West:	Southwest:	Midwest:	Southeast:	Northeast:	International:
Y	Y	Y	Y	Y	

Note: Financial information, benefits and other data can change quickly and may vary from those stated here.

VERISIGN INC

www.verisign.com

Industry Group Code: 511210E Ranks within this company's industry group: Sales: 3 Profits: 3

Management:		Sales/Marketing:		Liberal Arts:		Information Systems:		Professionals:		Tech./Scientific:	
Management Trainees:	Y	Marketing Pros.:	Y	Gen. Writing/Editing:	Y	Info. Management:	Y	Finance/Acct.:	Y	Engineers, Electrical:	Y
Experienced Mngmt.:	Y	Retail Sales:		Technical Writing:	Y	Software Dev.:	Y	Law:	Y	Engineers, Other:	
International Business:	Y	Commercial/Industrial:	Y	Graphic Arts/Photog.:	Y	Hardware Dev.:		HR/Other:	Y	Health/Lab:	
MBA Grads:	Y	Sales Trainees:		Music:		Consulting/Other:	Y	Training:	Y	Scientists/Research:	
		Advertising Pros.:	Y	Broadcasting:				Health Care:		Petroleum/Chemicals:	
				Other:				Consulting:		Math/Other:	

TYPES OF BUSINESS:

Software-Security
Telecommunications Services
Network & e-Mail Security
Managed Security Services
Digital Brand Management
Wireless Content Services
Wireless & Wireline Billing Services
Domain Name Registration

BRANDS/DIVISIONS/AFFILIATES:

SSL

CONTACTS: Note: Officers with more than one job title may be intentionally listed here more than once.

Jim Bidzos, Interim CEO
Mark D. McLaughlin, COO
Mark D. McLaughlin, Pres.
Brian G. Robins, Acting CFO/Sr. VP
Anne-Marie Law, Sr. VP-Global Human Resources
Kenneth J. Silva, CTO/Sr. VP
Grant L. Clark, Chief Admin. Officer/Sr. VP
Richard H. Goshorn, General Counsel/Sr. VP/Corp. Sec.
Kevin A. Werner, Sr. VP-Corp. Dev. & Strategy
Russell S. Lewis, Sr. VP-Strategic Dev.
D. James Bidzos, Chmn.
Teruhide Hashimoto, Pres./CEO-VeriSign Japan

Phone: 650-961-7500	Fax: 650-961-7300
Toll-Free:	
Address: 487 E. Middlefield Rd., Mountain View, CA 94043 US	

GROWTH PLANS/SPECIAL FEATURES:

VeriSign, Inc. operates infrastructure services that enable and protect billions of interactions every day across worldwide voice, video and data networks. It offers a variety of Internet and communications-related service that are marketed through web site sales, direct field sales, channel sales, telesales and member organizations in its global affiliate network. The company operates in two segments: the Internet services group and the communications services group. The Internet services group consists of the information/security and Naming services business. The information/security services business provides products and services that protect online and network interactions, enabling companies to manage reputational, operational and compliance risks. Offerings include SSL certificate services, which enable enterprises and Internet merchants to implement secure networks and web sites that utilize SSL protocol; identity and authentication services, which include the Managed PKI service, the Unified Authentication services and the VeriSign Identity Protection service; and real-time publisher services, which allow organizations to obtain access to and organize large amounts of constantly updated content and distribute it to enterprises, web-portal developers, application developers and consumers. The Naming services business is the authoritative directory provider of all .com, .net, .cc and .tv domain names. In April 2008, the company sold its Self-Care and Analytics business unit to Globys, Inc., provider of online analytic solutions, for an undisclosed amount. In May 2008, VeriSign released its Broadband Content Services assets, which have been reclaimed by the company's former acquisition, Kontiki, Inc. In June 2008, the firm extended its infrastructure, opening new Internet sites in Belgium, Paris, France and Brussels. In October 2008, VeriSign sold its minority share of a joint venture with News Corporation to that company for approximately $200 million. In March 2009, the company agreed to sell its Communication Services Group to TNS, Inc., a global communications company, for $230 million cash.

FINANCIALS: Sales and profits are in thousands of dollars—add 000 to get the full amount. 2008 Note: Financial information for 2008 was not available for all companies at press time.

2008 Sales: $961,735	2008 Profits: $-374,692	**U.S. Stock Ticker:** VRSN	
2007 Sales: $847,457	2007 Profits: $-149,328	**Int'l Ticker:** Int'l Exchange:	
2006 Sales: $982,734	2006 Profits: $382,930	Employees: 3,297	
2005 Sales: $1,612,574	2005 Profits: $428,978	Fiscal Year Ends: 12/31	
2004 Sales: $1,120,595	2004 Profits: $152,820	Parent Company:	

SALARIES/BENEFITS:

Pension Plan:	ESOP Stock Plan:	Profit Sharing:	Top Exec. Salary: $475,458	Bonus: $
Savings Plan:	Stock Purch. Plan:		Second Exec. Salary: $415,385	Bonus: $

OTHER THOUGHTS:

Apparent Women Officers or Directors: 2
Hot Spot for Advancement for Women/Minorities: Y

LOCATIONS: ("Y" = Yes)

West:	Southwest:	Midwest:	Southeast:	Northeast:	International:
Y	Y	Y	Y	Y	Y

VERIZON COMMUNICATIONS

www22.verizon.com

Industry Group Code: 517110 **Ranks within this company's industry group:** Sales: 2 Profits: 2

Management:		Sales/Marketing:		Liberal Arts:		Information Systems:		Professionals:		Tech./Scientific:	
Management Trainees:	Y	Marketing Pros.:	Y	Gen. Writing/Editing:	Y	Info. Management:	Y	Finance/Acct.:	Y	Engineers, Electrical:	Y
Experienced Mngmt.:	Y	Retail Sales:	Y	Technical Writing:	Y	Software Dev.:	Y	Law:	Y	Engineers, Other:	Y
International Business:	Y	Commercial/Industrial:	Y	Graphic Arts/Photog.:	Y	Hardware Dev.:		HR/Other:	Y	Health/Lab:	
MBA Grads:	Y	Sales Trainees:	Y	Music:		Consulting/Other:		Training:	Y	Scientists/Research:	
		Advertising Pros.:	Y	Broadcasting:				Health Care:		Petroleum/Chemicals:	
				Other:	Y			Consulting:		Math/Other:	

TYPES OF BUSINESS:

Local Telephone Service
Telecommunications Services
Wireless Services
Long-Distance Services
High-Speed Internet Access
Video-on-Demand Services
e-Commerce & Online Services

BRANDS/DIVISIONS/AFFILIATES:

Verizon Wireless
Verizon Business
Verizon Telecom
Alltel Corporation
Rural Cellular Corporation

CONTACTS: *Note: Officers with more than one job title may be intentionally listed here more than once.*

Ivan G. Seidenberg, CEO
Dennis F. Strigl, COO
Dennis F. Strigl, Pres.
John F. Killian, CFO/Exec. VP
John G. Stratton, Chief Mktg. Officer/Exec. VP
Marc C. Reed, Exec. VP-Human Resources
Shaygan Kheradpir, CIO/Exec. VP
Richard J. Lynch, CTO/Exec. VP
Randal S. Milch, General Counsel/Exec. VP
John W. Diercksen, Exec. VP-Strategy, Dev. & Planning
Thomas J. Tauke, Exec. VP-Public Affairs, Policy & Comm.
Ronald H. Lataille, Sr. VP-Investor Rel.
Robert J. Barish, Controller/Sr. VP
Lowell C. McAdam, Exec. VP/Pres. & CEO-Verizon Wireless
Francis J. Shammo, Pres., Verizon Bus.
Marianne Drost, Sr. VP/Corp. Sec.
Catherine T. Webster, Sr. VP/Treas.
Ivan G. Seidenberg, Chmn.

Phone: 212-395-1000	Fax: 212-571-1897
Toll-Free: 800-621-9900	
Address: 140 West St., New York, NY 10007 US	

GROWTH PLANS/SPECIAL FEATURES:

Verizon Communications, Inc. and its subsidiaries form one of the world's largest providers of communications services. It operates in two segments: wireline and domestic wireless. The wireline segment, operating in 150 countries, comprises two units: Verizon Telecom and Verizon Business. Verizon Telecom provides voice, video and data services to residential and small business customers in 28 states and Washington, D.C. It is organized in three marketing units: mass markets, offering services to residential and small businesses; wholesale, offerings long distance and local exchange network facilities for resale to interexchange carriers, competitive local exchange carriers, wireless carriers and Internet identification; and other, whose offerings include operator services, public telephone and dial around services. Verizon Business provides voice, data, Internet communications, next-generation Internet protocol (IP) networking and IT products and service to medium and large businesses and government customers, both domestically and internationally. It is organized in three units: enterprise business; wholesale; and international & other. The domestic wireless segment's products and services include wireless voice, data products and other value added services and equipment sales across the U.S. The division includes Verizon Wireless, in which Verizon holds a 55% controlling interest, with Vodafone controlling the rest. Verizon Wireless operations encompass over 30 countries in the Americas, Europe and Asia Pacific. Verizon's Internet growth strategy is centered on FiOS, delivering a choice of TV via IP, VoIP phone service and Internet access at speeds up to 50 Mbps. By October 2008, 2.2 million customers were subscribing to FiOS services. In August 2008, Verizon Wireless acquired Rural Cellular Corporation (operating as Unicel) for $2.66 billion. In January 2009, Verizon Wireless acquired Alltel Corporation from Atlantis Holdings LLC for $5.9 billion and $22.2 billion in debt acquisition.

FINANCIALS: Sales and profits are in thousands of dollars—add 000 to get the full amount. 2008 Note: Financial information for 2008 was not available for all companies at press time.

2008 Sales: $97,354,000	2008 Profits: $6,428,000	**U.S. Stock Ticker:** VZ
2007 Sales: $93,469,000	2007 Profits: $5,521,000	**Int'l Ticker:** Int'l Exchange:
2006 Sales: $88,182,000	2006 Profits: $6,197,000	Employees: 223,900
2005 Sales: $69,518,000	2005 Profits: $7,397,000	Fiscal Year Ends: 12/31
2004 Sales: $65,751,000	2004 Profits: $7,831,000	Parent Company:

SALARIES/BENEFITS:

Pension Plan:	ESOP Stock Plan:	Profit Sharing:	Top Exec. Salary: $2,100,000	Bonus: $3,740,625
Savings Plan: Y	Stock Purch. Plan:		Second Exec. Salary: $1,319,231	Bonus: $1,888,125

OTHER THOUGHTS:

Apparent Women Officers or Directors: 6
Hot Spot for Advancement for Women/Minorities: Y

LOCATIONS: ("Y" = Yes)

West:	Southwest:	Midwest:	Southeast:	Northeast:	International:
Y	Y	Y	Y	Y	Y

VIACOM INC

www.viacom.com

Industry Group Code: 515210 **Ranks within this company's industry group:** Sales: 2 Profits: 2

Management:		Sales/Marketing:		Liberal Arts:		Information Systems:		Professionals:		Tech./Scientific:	
Management Trainees:	Y	Marketing Pros.:	Y	Gen. Writing/Editing:	Y	Info. Management:	Y	Finance/Acct.:	Y	Engineers, Electrical:	Y
Experienced Mngmt.:	Y	Retail Sales:		Technical Writing:		Software Dev.:	Y	Law:	Y	Engineers, Other:	
International Business:	Y	Commercial/Industrial:	Y	Graphic Arts/Photog.:	Y	Hardware Dev.:		HR/Other:	Y	Health/Lab:	
MBA Grads:	Y	Sales Trainees:		Music:	Y	Consulting/Other:		Training:	Y	Scientists/Research:	
		Advertising Pros.:	Y	Broadcasting:	Y			Health Care:		Petroleum/Chemicals:	
				Other:	Y			Consulting:		Math/Other:	

TYPES OF BUSINESS:

Cable TV Networks
Television Production/Syndication
Film Production
Online Media
Video Distribution
Video Games

BRANDS/DIVISIONS/AFFILIATES:

National Amusement, Inc.
MTV Networks
Nickelodeon
Comedy Central
CMT: Country Music Television
Paramount Pictures Corp
United Paramount Network (UPN)
DreamWorks SKG

CONTACTS: Note: Officers with more than one job title may be intentionally listed here more than once.

Philippe Dauman, CEO
Philippe P. Dauman, Pres.
Thomas E. Dooley, CFO
Denise White, Exec. VP-Human Resources & Admin.
Thomas E. Dooley, Chief Admin. Officer/Sr. Exec. VP
Michael D. Fricklas, General Counsel/Sec./Exec. VP
Wade Davis, Sr. VP-Strategy, Mergers & Acquisitions
Carl D. Folta, Exec. VP-Corp. Comm.
James Bombassei, Sr. VP-Investor Rel.
Jacques Tortoroli, Chief Acct. Officer/Corp. Controller/Sr. VP
Brad Grey, Chmn./CEO-Paramount Motion Picture Group
Debra Lee, CEO/Pres., BET Networks
Judy McGrath, Chmn./CEO-MTV Networks
DeDe Lea, Exec. VP-Gov't Affairs
Sumner M. Redstone, Exec. Chmn.

Phone: 212-258-6000	Fax: 212-258-6464
Toll-Free: 800-516-4399	
Address: 1515 Broadway, New York, NY 10036 US	

GROWTH PLANS/SPECIAL FEATURES:

Viacom, Inc., spun off from now CBS Corp. (formerly Viacom, Inc.), is an international media conglomerate. National Amusement, Inc., owned by the Redstone family, owns 73% of Viacom. Viacom is composed of two segments: Media Networks, which includes MTV Networks and BET Networks, and Filmed Entertainment. Through a combination of original and acquired programming and other entertainment content, the Media Networks brands are focused on providing content that appeals to key demographics attractive to advertisers across multiple distribution platforms, including cable television, satellite, mobile and digital media assets. Media Networks operates more than 135 television networks and accounted for 60% of the firm's 2007 revenues. The Filmed Entertainment segment produces, finances and distributes motion pictures and other entertainment content through its well-known group of brands including Paramount Pictures Corp. Revenues from the Filmed Entertainment segment are generated primarily from feature film production and distribution, including exhibition of motion pictures in theatrical release, sale of home entertainment product, and distribution to pay and basic cable television, broadcast television, syndicated television and digital media. This division accounted for 40% of 2007 revenues. The company's online gaming communication and community platform include Xfire, Inc.; Atom Entertainment, Inc., an online game, short film and animation destination; and Harmonix Music Systems, Inc., popular videogame title Guitar Hero developer. Viacom also owns DreamWorks, which produces movies and television programming and markets these properties for home entertainment. Other Paramount companies include Paramount Vantage, Paramount Classics, MTV Films and Nickelodeon Movies.

FINANCIALS: Sales and profits are in thousands of dollars—add 000 to get the full amount. 2008 Note: Financial information for 2008 was not available for all companies at press time.

2008 Sales: $14,625,000	2008 Profits: $1,251,000	U.S. Stock Ticker: VIA
2007 Sales: $13,423,100	2007 Profits: $1,838,100	Int'l Ticker: Int'l Exchange:
2006 Sales: $11,361,100	2006 Profits: $1,592,100	Employees: 11,500
2005 Sales: $9,609,600	2005 Profits: $1,256,900	Fiscal Year Ends: 12/31
2004 Sales: $8,132,200	2004 Profits: $293,700	Parent Company:

SALARIES/BENEFITS:

Pension Plan: Y	ESOP Stock Plan:	Profit Sharing:	Top Exec. Salary: $2,500,000	Bonus: $7,885,000
Savings Plan: Y	Stock Purch. Plan:		Second Exec. Salary: $2,000,000	Bonus: $6,308,000

OTHER THOUGHTS:

Apparent Women Officers or Directors: 6
Hot Spot for Advancement for Women/Minorities: Y

LOCATIONS: ("Y" = Yes)

West:	Southwest:	Midwest:	Southeast:	Northeast:	International:
Y		Y		Y	Y

Note: Financial information, benefits and other data can change quickly and may vary from those stated here.

VICTORIAS SECRET

www.victoriassecret.com

Industry Group Code: 448120 Ranks within this company's industry group: Sales: 2 Profits:

Management:		Sales/Marketing:		Liberal Arts:		Information Systems:		Professionals:		Tech./Scientific:	
Management Trainees:	Y	Marketing Pros.:	Y	Gen. Writing/Editing:	Y	Info. Management:	Y	Finance/Acct.:	Y	Engineers, Electrical:	
Experienced Mngmt.:	Y	Retail Sales:	Y	Technical Writing:		Software Dev.:	Y	Law:	Y	Engineers, Other:	
International Business:	Y	Commercial/Industrial:	Y	Graphic Arts/Photog.:	Y	Hardware Dev.:		HR/Other:	Y	Health/Lab:	
MBA Grads:	Y	Sales Trainees:	Y	Music:		Consulting/Other:		Training:	Y	Scientists/Research:	
		Advertising Pros.:	Y	Broadcasting:				Health Care:		Petroleum/Chemicals:	
				Other:	Y			Consulting:		Math/Other:	

TYPES OF BUSINESS:

Intimate Apparel-Women's, Retail
Cosmetics
Fragrances
Personal Care Products
Online Sales
Catalogs
Candles
Professional Apparel

BRANDS/DIVISIONS/AFFILIATES:

PINK
Victoria's Secret Direct
Victoria's Secret Beauty
Angels
IPEX
Collegiate Collection
La Senza

CONTACTS: *Note: Officers with more than one job title may be intentionally listed here more than once.*

Sharen Jester Turney, CEO
Leonard A. Schlesinger, COO/Group Pres., Beauty & Personal Care
Sharen Jester Turney, Pres.
Stuart Burgdoerfer, CFO/Exec. VP
Jane L. Ramsey, Exec. VP-Human Resources
Martyn R. Redgrave, Chief Admin. Officer/Exec. VP
Deborah I. Fine, CEO-PINK
Lexlie H. Wexner, Chmn.

Phone: 614-415-7000	Fax: 614-415-7278
Toll-Free:	
Address: 4 Limited Pkwy. E, Reynoldsburg, OH 43068 US	

GROWTH PLANS/SPECIAL FEATURES:

Victoria's Secret, a wholly-owned subsidiary of Limited Brands, Inc., purchases, distributes and sells lingerie, personal care products and women's apparel through over 1,000 retail stores, the Internet and direct mail channels. Victoria's Secret is a leading specialty retailer of women's intimate apparel, hosiery and related products. The stores offer branded merchandise such as IPEX, PINK and Angel. The firm also owns eight PINK stores in the U.S. which sell intimate apparel, denim, casual apparel and body products targeted to young women ages 13-25. Victoria's Secret Beauty offers a complete line of fragrance, cosmetics and body products for skin and hair. In addition to its retail stores, the company operates Victoria's Secret Direct, which consists of the famous Victoria's Secret Catalog and an e-commerce site, VictoriaSecret.com. The firm's widely distributed catalog offers women's fashion apparel, lingerie, swimwear and footwear through its over 390 million annually distributed copies. Street apparel such as dresses, pants, skirts, shorts, tops and shoes are available from the catalog and online, but not in stores. Once each year, Victoria's Secret conducts a televised fashion show featuring some of the world's top models and performances by pop stars such as Justin Timberlake and Seal. In 2008, the company's PINK line partnered with 33 U.S. colleges and universities to make cross-branded casual apparel featuring school colors, names and mascots in a line called the Collegiate Collection. The Victoria's Secret group also includes the operations of La Senza, a Canadian lingerie store chain acquired by Limited Brands in 2007.

The company offers its employees merchandise discounts, education assistance, school loans, adoption assistance, bonus programs and an annual retirement contribution.

FINANCIALS: Sales and profits are in thousands of dollars—add 000 to get the full amount. 2008 Note: Financial information for 2008 was not available for all companies at press time.

2008 Sales: $5,601,046	2008 Profits: $	**U.S. Stock Ticker: Subsidiary**	
2007 Sales: $5,606,993	2007 Profits: $	**Int'l Ticker:** Int'l Exchange:	
2006 Sales: $5,138,741	2006 Profits: $	Employees: 45,000	
2005 Sales: $6,401,000	2005 Profits: $	Fiscal Year Ends: 1/31	
2004 Sales: $5,751,000	2004 Profits: $	Parent Company: LIMITED BRANDS INC	

SALARIES/BENEFITS:

Pension Plan:	ESOP Stock Plan:	Profit Sharing:	Top Exec. Salary: $	Bonus: $758,880
Savings Plan: Y	Stock Purch. Plan:		Second Exec. Salary: $	Bonus: $

OTHER THOUGHTS:

Apparent Women Officers or Directors: 6
Hot Spot for Advancement for Women/Minorities: Y

LOCATIONS: ("Y" = Yes)

West:	Southwest:	Midwest:	Southeast:	Northeast:	International:
Y	Y	Y	Y	Y	Y

VISA INC

www.visa.com

Industry Group Code: 522210 **Ranks within this company's industry group:** Sales: 1 Profits: 1

Management:		Sales/Marketing:		Liberal Arts:		Information Systems:		Professionals:		Tech./Scientific:	
Management Trainees:	Y	Marketing Pros.:	Y	Gen. Writing/Editing:	Y	Info. Management:	Y	Finance/Acct.:	Y	Engineers, Electrical:	
Experienced Mngmt.:	Y	Retail Sales:		Technical Writing:		Software Dev.:	Y	Law:	Y	Engineers, Other:	
International Business:	Y	Commercial/Industrial:	Y	Graphic Arts/Photog.:	Y	Hardware Dev.:		HR/Other:	Y	Health/Lab:	
MBA Grads:	Y	Sales Trainees:		Music:		Consulting/Other:		Training:	Y	Scientists/Research:	
		Advertising Pros.:	Y	Broadcasting:				Health Care:		Petroleum/Chemicals:	
				Other:	Y			Consulting:		Math/Other:	

TYPES OF BUSINESS:

Credit Cards
Debit Cards

BRANDS/DIVISIONS/AFFILIATES:

Visa Direct
Visa Giro
Visa U.S.A., Inc.
Visa Canada Association
Visa International Service Association
Inovant LLC
Visa International
Syncada

CONTACTS: *Note: Officers with more than one job title may be intentionally listed here more than once.*

Joseph W. Saunders, CEO
John Partridge, COO
John C. Morris, Pres.
Byron H. Pollitt, CFO
Antonio Lucio, Chief Mktg. Officer
Rick Leweke, Head-Human Resources
Michael L. Dreyer, CIO
Josh Floum, General Counsel/Corp. Sec.
Keith Hunter, Head-Oper.
Oliver Jenkyn, Head-Strategy & Corp. Dev.
Doug Michelman, Head-Corp. Rel.
Jack Carsky, Head-Investor Rel.
Tim Wilson, Head-Canada
Elizabeth Buse, Head-Product
Ellen Richey, Head-Enterprise Risk
Eduardo Erana, Pres., Latin America & Caribbean
Joseph Saunders, Chmn.
David Lee, Pres., Asia Pacific

Phone: 415-932-2100	Fax:
Toll-Free:	
Address: P.O. Box 8999, San Francisco, CA 94128-8999 US	

GROWTH PLANS/SPECIAL FEATURES:

Visa Inc., formerly Visa International, operates one of the largest consumer payment systems in the world, with approximately 1.7 billion Visa cards in use and money transfer operations in over 170 countries. Visa's payment platforms include credit, debit, prepaid and personal consumption expenditure. In 2008, Visa sales volume across these platforms grew to over $4.3 trillion. The company operates through regional organizations covering Europe; Central and Eastern Europe, the Middle East and Africa (CEMEA); the U.S.; Latin America and the Caribbean; Canada; and the Asia Pacific region. Through the Visa brand, the firm's products include credit, debit and prepaid cards; Internet payment systems; traveler's checks and fund transfers; and programs and benefits for commercial and governmental enterprises. Visa offers several types of credit card for individuals and for commercial and governmental offices, with various benefits and credit limits. The company has 16, 300 financial institution customers, 28 million merchant outlets and 1.4 million ATMs. Visa has partnerships with several leading industry companies and charities, including Delta, Marriott, Le Meridien, USAID and GlobalGiving. To facilitate its transactions, Visa also has partnerships with various Internet and payment-processing companies, including Oasis Technology; VeriSign, Inc.; Trintech Group PCC; WAY Systems; Worlds.com Inc.; and Yahoo, Inc. The company does not issue cards, set fees or determine the interest rates consumers will be charged. The firm earns revenues by charging banks to issue Visa-branded cards and merchants to accept Visa-branded cards. Subsidiaries of the company include Visa Canada Association; Visa U.S.A., Inc.; Visa International Service Association; and Inovant LLC. Visa Europe remains a membership association and is a licensee of, and owns a minority interest in Visa, Inc. In July 2009, the company formed Syncada, a joint venture with U.S. bank that provides business to business network services for governments and corporations.

FINANCIALS: Sales and profits are in thousands of dollars—add 000 to get the full amount. 2008 Note: Financial information for 2008 was not available for all companies at press time.

2008 Sales: $6,263,000	2008 Profits: $804,000	U.S. Stock Ticker: V	
2007 Sales: $3,589,796	2007 Profits: $-1,076,095	Int'l Ticker:	Int'l Exchange:
2006 Sales: $2,948,126	2006 Profits: $454,561	Employees: 5,765	
2005 Sales: $1,162,316	2005 Profits: $83,200	Fiscal Year Ends: 9/30	
2004 Sales: $1,427,002	2004 Profits: $32,289	Parent Company:	

SALARIES/BENEFITS:

Pension Plan: Y	ESOP Stock Plan:	Profit Sharing:	Top Exec. Salary: $950,009	Bonus: $4,668,241
Savings Plan: Y	Stock Purch. Plan:		Second Exec. Salary: $750,029	Bonus: $2,150,000

OTHER THOUGHTS:

Apparent Women Officers or Directors: 6
Hot Spot for Advancement for Women/Minorities: Y

LOCATIONS: ("Y" = Yes)

West:	Southwest:	Midwest:	Southeast:	Northeast:	International:
Y	Y	Y	Y	Y	Y

Note: Financial information, benefits and other data can change quickly and may vary from those stated here.

VOLT INFORMATION SCIENCES INC

www.volt.com

Industry Group Code: 561320 Ranks within this company's industry group: Sales: 4 Profits: 3

Management:		Sales/Marketing:		Liberal Arts:		Information Systems:		Professionals:		Tech./Scientific:	
Management Trainees:	Y	Marketing Pros.:	Y	Gen. Writing/Editing:	Y	Info. Management:	Y	Finance/Acct.:	Y	Engineers, Electrical:	
Experienced Mngmt.:	Y	Retail Sales:		Technical Writing:	Y	Software Dev.:	Y	Law:	Y	Engineers, Other:	
International Business:	Y	Commercial/Industrial:	Y	Graphic Arts/Photog.:	Y	Hardware Dev.:		HR/Other:	Y	Health/Lab:	
MBA Grads:	Y	Sales Trainees:	Y	Music:		Consulting/Other:		Training:	Y	Scientists/Research:	
		Advertising Pros.:	Y	Broadcasting:				Health Care:		Petroleum/Chemicals:	
				Other:	Y			Consulting:		Math/Other:	

TYPES OF BUSINESS:

Temporary Staffing Services
Telecommunications Services
Information Services
Directory Publishing
Computer Systems

BRANDS/DIVISIONS/AFFILIATES:

Volt Human Resources
Volt Services Group
Volt Europe
LSSi Data
VoltDelta Resources LLC
VoltDelta International
Volt Consulting-Managed Services Programs

CONTACTS: *Note: Officers with more than one job title may be intentionally listed here more than once.*

Steven A. Shaw, CEO
Steven A. Shaw, COO
Steven A. Shaw, Pres.
Jack Eagan, CFO/Sr. VP
Louise Ross, VP-Human Resources
Howard B. Weinreich, General Counsel/Sr. VP
Ludwig M. Guarino, Treas./Sr. VP
Jerome Shaw, Exec. VP/Sec.
Thomas Daley, Sr. VP
Daniel G. Hallihan, VP-Acct. Oper.
Ronald Kochman, VP

Phone: 212-704-2400	Fax: 212-704-2413
Toll-Free:	
Address: 1600 Stewart Ave. 4th Fl., Westbury, NY 11590 US	

GROWTH PLANS/SPECIAL FEATURES:

Volt Information Sciences, Inc., provides staffing and telecommunications services as well as computer systems to businesses in the U.S., Canada, the U.K., Latin America and the Asia-Pacific region. Volt Services Group, Volt Europe and Volt Human Resources provide employee staffing and professional services through over 300 branches and on-site client offices. The company's staffing services include managed staffing, temporary personnel employment and direct hire placement; information technology solutions such as consulting, project management and software and web development; and e-procurement solutions. The firm's telecommunications services segment provides design, engineering, installation, maintenance and removal of telecommunications equipment for outside plant and central offices of cable companies and government entities. In addition, it provides detailed engineering services for wireless telecommunications providers and wireless infrastructure suppliers. The computer systems segment provides information and other operator services; it also designs, develops, sells, leases and maintains computer-based directory assistance outsourcing to wireline and wireless telecommunications companies. This segment operates through VoltDelta Resources, LLC and its subsidiary Volt Delta International; LSSiDATA, as well as the Maintech computer maintenance division. Volt Information Sciences also provides printing services and telephone directory publishing in Uruguay. In September 2008, the firm sold its directory systems and its directory publishing operations to Yellow Pages Group for $179 million. In July 2009, the company launched Volt Consulting-Managed Services Programs, created to provide customers with human capital supply chain management services.

Volt employee benefits include health, dental and vision coverage; life insurance; disability plans; flexible spending accounts; training programs; referral bonuses; and reward programs.

FINANCIALS: Sales and profits are in thousands of dollars—add 000 to get the full amount. 2008 Note: Financial information for 2008 was not available for all companies at press time.

2008 Sales: $2,427,318	2008 Profits: $-40,648	**U.S. Stock Ticker: VOL**
2007 Sales: $2,353,082	2007 Profits: $39,332	**Int'l Ticker:** Int'l Exchange:
2006 Sales: $2,338,453	2006 Profits: $30,650	Employees: 42,000
2005 Sales: $2,177,619	2005 Profits: $17,040	Fiscal Year Ends: 10/31
2004 Sales: $1,924,777	2004 Profits: $33,716	Parent Company:

SALARIES/BENEFITS:

Pension Plan:	ESOP Stock Plan:	Profit Sharing:	Top Exec. Salary: $576,538	Bonus: $
Savings Plan: Y	Stock Purch. Plan:		Second Exec. Salary: $547,600	Bonus: $

OTHER THOUGHTS:

Apparent Women Officers or Directors: 2
Hot Spot for Advancement for Women/Minorities: Y

LOCATIONS: ("Y" = Yes)

West:	Southwest:	Midwest:	Southeast:	Northeast:	International:
Y				Y	Y

W R BERKLEY CORPORATION

www.wrberkley.com

Industry Group Code: 524126 Ranks within this company's industry group: Sales: 8 Profits: 6

Management:		Sales/Marketing:		Liberal Arts:		Information Systems:		Professionals:		Tech./Scientific:	
Management Trainees:	Y	Marketing Pros.:	Y	Gen. Writing/Editing:	Y	Info. Management:	Y	Finance/Acct.:	Y	Engineers, Electrical:	
Experienced Mngmt.:	Y	Retail Sales:		Technical Writing:	Y	Software Dev.:	Y	Law:	Y	Engineers, Other:	
International Business:	Y	Commercial/Industrial:	Y	Graphic Arts/Photog.:	Y	Hardware Dev.:		HR/Other:	Y	Health/Lab:	
MBA Grads:	Y	Sales Trainees:	Y	Music:		Consulting/Other:		Training:	Y	Scientists/Research:	
		Advertising Pros.:	Y	Broadcasting:				Health Care:		Petroleum/Chemicals:	
				Other:	Y			Consulting:		Math/Other:	Y

TYPES OF BUSINESS:

Insurance, Direct Property & Casualty
Reinsurance
Regional Insurance
Specialty Insurance
Risk Management
Liability Insurance

BRANDS/DIVISIONS/AFFILIATES:

Admiral Insurance Company
Signet Star Re LLC
Berkley Agribusiness Risk Specialists
Berkley Underwriting Managers Canada Ltd
Continental Western Group LLC
Berkley Asset Protection Underwriters LLC
FinSecure LLC
Carolina Casualty Insurance Group LLC

CONTACTS: Note: Officers with more than one job title may be intentionally listed here more than once.

William R. Berkley, CEO
Eugene G. Ballard, CFO/Sr. VP
Joseph M. Pennachio, VP-Human Resources
Kevin H. Ebers, Sr. VP-IT
Ira S. Lederman, General Counsel/Sr. VP/Corp. Sec.
Robert P. Cole, Sr. VP-Regional Oper.
Karen A. Horvath, VP-External Financial Comm.
Richard M. Baio, Treas./VP
W. Robert Berkley, Jr., Exec. VP
Robert W. Gosselink, Sr. VP-Insurance Risk Mgmt.
Clement P. Patafio, Corp. Controller/VP
James G. Shiel, Sr. VP-Investments
William R. Berkley, Chmn.
Steven W. Taylor, Sr. VP-Int'l Oper.
Robert C. Hewitt, Sr. VP-Excess & Surplus Lines

Phone: 203-629-3000	Fax: 203-629-3073
Toll-Free:	
Address: 475 Steamboat Rd., Greenwich, CT 06830 US	

GROWTH PLANS/SPECIAL FEATURES:

W.R. Berkley Corporation is one of the largest insurance holding companies in the U.S. The firm operates in five segments of the property casualty insurance business: regional property/casualty insurance; reinsurance; specialty lines of insurance; international operations; and alternative markets. Berkley's regional subsidiaries provide commercial lines coverage for small and mid-sized business firms and governmental entities in 45 states and the District of Columbia. The reinsurance unit operates through six divisions, including Signet Star Re, LLC. These groups underwrite property casualty reinsurance on both a facultative and a treaty basis. The specialty insurance unit's services include general, professional, product, excess and umbrella liability, workers' compensation and property coverages. Admiral Insurance Company is the largest of W.R. Berkley's specialty insurance subsidiaries. W.R. Berkley's international operations are conducted in Canada, Europe, South America, Australia and Hong Kong. The company's alternative market operations specialize in developing and administering self-insurance programs and other alternative risk transfer mechanisms. The segment's primary line of business is workers' compensation, though it also offers hospital professional liability and medical stop loss insurance. In total, the company's five segments conduct business through 34 units. In 2008, the company formed Berkley Asset Protection Underwriters LLC, which offers coverage for fine arts, jewelers block and fidelity and crime; FinSecure LLC, which offers integrated property and liability insurance for financial institutions and financial services companies; and Berkley Underwriting Managers Canada, Ltd., which provides specialty casualty commercial insurance products such as products liability and general liability in Canada. In 2009, W.R. Berkley formed Berkley Agribusiness Risk Specialists (as a division of Continental Western Group, LLC) to provide property and casualty insurance products to mid-sized and larger commercial agribusiness customers; and Gemini Transportation Underwriters (as a division of Carolina Casualty Insurance Group, LLC) to offer underwriting transportation excess liability insurance.

FINANCIALS: Sales and profits are in thousands of dollars—add 000 to get the full amount. 2008 Note: Financial information for 2008 was not available for all companies at press time.

2008 Sales: $4,033,899	2008 Profits: $281,141	U.S. Stock Ticker: WRB	
2007 Sales: $4,575,989	2007 Profits: $743,646	Int'l Ticker: Int'l Exchange:	
2006 Sales: $4,818,993	2006 Profits: $699,518	Employees: 5,768	
2005 Sales: $4,996,839	2005 Profits: $544,892	Fiscal Year Ends: 12/31	
2004 Sales: $4,512,235	2004 Profits: $438,105	Parent Company:	

SALARIES/BENEFITS:

Pension Plan:	ESOP Stock Plan:	Profit Sharing:	Top Exec. Salary: $1,000,000	Bonus: $8,880,600
Savings Plan:	Stock Purch. Plan:		Second Exec. Salary: $700,000	Bonus: $1,832,025

OTHER THOUGHTS:

Apparent Women Officers or Directors: 7
Hot Spot for Advancement for Women/Minorities: Y

LOCATIONS: ("Y" = Yes)

West:	Southwest:	Midwest:	Southeast:	Northeast:	International:
Y	Y	Y	Y	Y	Y

Note: Financial information, benefits and other data can change quickly and may vary from those stated here.

WABTEC CORP

www.wabtec.com

Industry Group Code: 336510 **Ranks within this company's industry group:** Sales: 1 Profits: 1

Management:		Sales/Marketing:		Liberal Arts:		Information Systems:		Professionals:		Tech./Scientific:	
Management Trainees:	Y	Marketing Pros.:	Y	Gen. Writing/Editing:		Info. Management:	Y	Finance/Acct.:	Y	Engineers, Electrical:	Y
Experienced Mngmt.:	Y	Retail Sales:		Technical Writing:	Y	Software Dev.:	Y	Law:	Y	Engineers, Other:	Y
International Business:	Y	Commercial/Industrial:	Y	Graphic Arts/Photog.:	Y	Hardware Dev.:	Y	HR/Other:	Y	Health/Lab:	
MBA Grads:	Y	Sales Trainees:		Music:		Consulting/Other:		Training:	Y	Scientists/Research:	
		Advertising Pros.:		Broadcasting:				Health Care:		Petroleum/Chemicals:	
				Other:				Consulting:		Math/Other:	

TYPES OF BUSINESS:

Railroad Equipment Manufacturing

BRANDS/DIVISIONS/AFFILIATES:

Standard Car Truck
Beijing Wabtec Huaxia Technology Company, Ltd.
CNR Wabtec Railway Brake Technology Company, Ltd.
Wabtec Passenger Transit
Wabtec Australia Pty Ltd
Wabtec de Mexico
Wabtec Foundry
Wabtec Global Services

CONTACTS: *Note: Officers with more than one job title may be intentionally listed here more than once.*

Albert J. Neupayer, CEO
Albert J. Neupayer, Pres.
Alvaro Garcia-Tunon, CFO/Sr. VP
Scott E. Wahlstrom, VP-Human Resources
Alvaro Garcia-Tunon, Corp. Sec.
R. Mark Cox, Corp. Dev.
Timothy R. Wesley, VP-Corp. Comm.
Timothy R. Wesley, VP-Investor Rel.
Patrick D. Dugan, Controller/VP
Raymond T. Betler, VP
Charles F. Kovac, VP
Richard A. Mathes, VP
William E. Kassling, Chmn.
Robert L. Witt, VP-Int'l

Phone: 412-825-1000	Fax: 412-825-1019
Toll-Free:	
Address: 1001 Air Brake Ave., Wilmerding, PA 15148 US	

GROWTH PLANS/SPECIAL FEATURES:

Westinghouse Air Brake Technologies Corporation, doing business as Wabtec Corp., is a provider of technology-based equipment and services for the global rail industry. It develops products suck as railway braking equipment; freight car truck components; draft gears; air compressors; railway electronics; brake shoes and pads; rail and bus door assemblies; accessibility lifts and ramps; heat exchangers and cooling products; and commuter and switcher locomotives. The company operates into two business segment: the Freight Group and the Transit Group. The Freight Group, accounting for 49% of sales, manufactures and services components for new existing freight cars and locomotives, builds new switcher locomotives and rebuilds freight locomotives. Its customers are traded railroads; leasing companies; and manufacturers of locomotives and freight cars. The Transit Group, accounting for 51% of the company's sales, produces components for new and existing transit vehicles, typically subway cars and buses, builds new commuter locomotives and refurbishes subway cars. Customers include transit authorities; leasing companies; and manufacturers of subway cars and busses. The company owns 1,500 active patents worldwide and over 600 U.S. patents. Wabtec has around 50 manufacturing plants and operations in the U.S., Canada, Mexico, Europe, Asia, Australia and South America. Customers outside the U.S. accounted for 41% of sales in 2008. In December 2008, the company acquired Standard Car Truck, an Illinois-based provider of rail equipment for approximately $300 million. Also in 2008, Wabtec formed Beijing Wabtec Huaxia Technology Company, Ltd., a joint venture with Beijing Huaxia United Friendship New Technology of Electrification Development Co., Ltd., for the purpose of bringing its friction products to the rail market in China. In April 2009, the firm formed a joint venture with Shenyang Locomotive and Rolling Stock Railways Brakes., Ltd. The joint venture, CNR Wabtec Railway Brake Technology Company, Ltd. will produce brake equipment for the Chinese market.

FINANCIALS: Sales and profits are in thousands of dollars—add 000 to get the full amount. 2008 Note: Financial information for 2008 was not available for all companies at press time.

		U.S. Stock Ticker: WAB
2008 Sales: $1,575,000	2008 Profits: $130,550	Int'l Ticker: Int'l Exchange:
2007 Sales: $	2007 Profits: $	Employees: 5,000
2006 Sales: $	2006 Profits: $	Fiscal Year Ends: 12/31
2005 Sales: $	2005 Profits: $	Parent Company:
2004 Sales: $	2004 Profits: $	

SALARIES/BENEFITS:

Pension Plan:	ESOP Stock Plan:	Profit Sharing:	Top Exec. Salary: $758,704	Bonus: $710,881
Savings Plan:	Stock Purch. Plan:		Second Exec. Salary: $343,512	Bonus: $273,788

OTHER THOUGHTS:

Apparent Women Officers or Directors: 1
Hot Spot for Advancement for Women/Minorities:

LOCATIONS: ("Y" = Yes)

West:	Southwest:	Midwest:	Southeast:	Northeast:	International:
Y	Y	Y	Y	Y	Y

WALGREEN CO

www.walgreens.com

Industry Group Code: 446110 Ranks within this company's industry group: Sales: 2 Profits: 2

Management:		Sales/Marketing:		Liberal Arts:		Information Systems:		Professionals:		Tech./Scientific:	
Management Trainees:	Y	Marketing Pros.:	Y	Gen. Writing/Editing:	Y	Info. Management:	Y	Finance/Acct.:	Y	Engineers, Electrical:	
Experienced Mngmt.:	Y	Retail Sales:	Y	Technical Writing:		Software Dev.:	Y	Law:	Y	Engineers, Other:	
International Business:	Y	Commercial/Industrial:		Graphic Arts/Photog.:	Y	Hardware Dev.:		HR/Other:	Y	Health/Lab:	
MBA Grads:	Y	Sales Trainees:	Y	Music:		Consulting/Other:		Training:	Y	Scientists/Research:	
		Advertising Pros.:	Y	Broadcasting:				Health Care:	Y	Petroleum/Chemicals:	
				Other:	Y			Consulting:		Math/Other:	

TYPES OF BUSINESS:

Drug Stores
Mail-Order Pharmacy Services
Pharmacy Benefit Management
Health Care Center Management
Online Pharmacy Services
Photo Printing Services
Specialty Pharmacy Services
Home Infusion Services

BRANDS/DIVISIONS/AFFILIATES:

Walgreen's Health Services
I-trax, Inc.
Take Care Health Systems LLC
Whole Health Management
CuraScript Infusion Pharmacy, Inc.
Option Care, Inc.

CONTACTS: *Note: Officers with more than one job title may be intentionally listed here more than once.*

Gregory D. Wasson, CEO
Gregory D. Wasson, Pres.
Wade D. Miquelon, CFO/Exec. VP
Jeffrey J. Zavada, Chief Sales Officer/VP
Dana I. Green, General Counsel/Sr. VP/Corp. Sec.
Mark A. Wagner, Exec. VP-Oper. & Community Mgmt.
Sona Chawla, Sr. VP-e-commerce
Stanley B. Blaylock, Sr. VP/Pres., Walgreens Health Services
Hal F. Rosenbluth, Sr. VP/Pres., Walgreens Health & Wellness
Kermit R. Crawford, Sr. VP-Pharmacy
George J. Reidl, Sr. VP-Pharmacy Innovation & Purchasing
Alan McNally, Chmn.
J. Randolph Lewis, Sr. VP-Supply Chain Mgmt.

Phone: 847-940-2500	**Fax:** 847-914-2804
Toll-Free: 800-925-4733	
Address: 200 Wilmot Rd., Deerfield, IL 60015 US	

GROWTH PLANS/SPECIAL FEATURES:

Walgreen Co. operates one of the largest chains of U.S. drug stores based on sales. The company has 7,361 drugstores in all 50 U.S. states, Washington, D.C., Guam and Puerto Rico; 15 full-service distribution centers; and two prescription mail service facilities. Stores offer prescription and non-prescription drugs, as well as general merchandise. To coordinate its operations, the firm uses Intercom Plus, a proprietary computer system for filling prescriptions, linking all stores into a single network. A large percentage of the company's stores have drive-through pharmacies, and most stores offer one-hour photo processing. The firm also accepts prescription refill orders online through its web site. Prescription sales account for approximately 64.9% of total sales and continue to increase each year. The company also operates Walgreens Health Services, a benefit management, mail service, home care and specialty pharmacy services business. A new growth strategy is Walgreen's plan to provide health clinics within the premises of major employers. In May 2008, the company acquired I-trax, Inc. and Whole Health Management, two leaders in this field, and established a new division by combining these businesses with its Take Care Health unit. The company operates more than 680 health and wellness clinics in stores and on employer worksites, and plans to expand this division to 800 sites by the end of fiscal 2009. Other recent acquisitions by Walgreen include: 20 drugstores in Puerto Rico from Farmacias El Amal; CuraScript Infusion Pharmacy, Inc., a provider of infusion services; McKesson Corporation's specialty pharmacy business; 12 Rite Aid locations in San Francisco and Idaho; the home infusion operations of Air Products Healthcare; and 31 Drug Fair stores in New Jersey. The firm recently announced plans to slow its rapid growth, aiming for a 3% increase in stores by fiscal 2011.

FINANCIALS: Sales and profits are in thousands of dollars—add 000 to get the full amount. 2008 Note: Financial information for 2008 was not available for all companies at press time.

2008 Sales: $59,034,000	2008 Profits: $2,157,000	**U.S. Stock Ticker: WAG**
2007 Sales: $53,762,000	2007 Profits: $2,041,300	**Int'l Ticker:** Int'l Exchange:
2006 Sales: $47,409,000	2006 Profits: $1,750,600	Employees: 237,000
2005 Sales: $42,201,600	2005 Profits: $1,559,500	Fiscal Year Ends: 8/31
2004 Sales: $37,508,200	2004 Profits: $1,360,200	Parent Company:

SALARIES/BENEFITS:

Pension Plan:	ESOP Stock Plan:	Profit Sharing:	Top Exec. Salary: $1,200,000	Bonus: $1,356,307
Savings Plan: Y	Stock Purch. Plan: Y		Second Exec. Salary: $750,000	Bonus: $649,538

OTHER THOUGHTS:

Apparent Women Officers or Directors: 2
Hot Spot for Advancement for Women/Minorities: Y

LOCATIONS: ("Y" = Yes)

West:	Southwest:	Midwest:	Southeast:	Northeast:	International:
Y	Y	Y	Y	Y	Y

Note: Financial information, benefits and other data can change quickly and may vary from those stated here.

WAL-MART STORES INC

www.walmartstores.com

Industry Group Code: 452112 Ranks within this company's industry group: Sales: 1 Profits: 1

Management:		Sales/Marketing:		Liberal Arts:		Information Systems:		Professionals:		Tech./Scientific:	
Management Trainees:	Y	Marketing Pros.:	Y	Gen. Writing/Editing:	Y	Info. Management:	Y	Finance/Acct.:	Y	Engineers, Electrical:	
Experienced Mngmt.:	Y	Retail Sales:	Y	Technical Writing:		Software Dev.:	Y	Law:	Y	Engineers, Other:	
International Business:	Y	Commercial/Industrial:		Graphic Arts/Photog.:	Y	Hardware Dev.:		HR/Other:	Y	Health/Lab:	
MBA Grads:	Y	Sales Trainees:	Y	Music:		Consulting/Other:		Training:	Y	Scientists/Research:	
		Advertising Pros.:	Y	Broadcasting:	Y			Health Care:		Petroleum/Chemicals:	
				Other:	Y			Consulting:		Math/Other:	

TYPES OF BUSINESS:

Discount Department Stores
Supermarkets
Warehouse Membership Clubs
Online Sales
Pharmacies
Vision Centers
Auto Repair Centers

BRANDS/DIVISIONS/AFFILIATES:

SAM'S CLUB
Wal-Mart Supercenter
Marketside Neighborhood Market
Best Price

CONTACTS: *Note: Officers with more than one job title may be intentionally listed here more than once.*

Michael T. Duke, CEO
William Simon, COO/Exec. VP-Wal-Mart U.S.
Michael T. Duke, Pres.
Thomas M. Schoewe, CFO/Exec. VP
Stephen Quinn, Chief Mktg. Officer/Exec. VP
M. Susan Chambers, Exec. VP-People
Rollin L. Ford, CIO/Exec. VP
John E. Fleming, Chief Merch. Officer/Exec. VP
Thomas A. Mars, Chief Admin. Officer/Exec. VP
Jeffrey J. Gearhart, General Counsel/Exec. VP
Ignacio Perez Lizuar, Exec. VP-Oper., Sam's Club
John T. Westling, Exec. VP-Replenishment, Pricing & Planning
Leslie A. Dach, Exec. VP-Corp. Affairs & Gov't Rel.
Mike Beckstead, Dir.-Investor Rel.
Charles M. Holley, Jr., Exec. VP-Finance/Treas.
Eduardo Castro-Wright, Vice Chmn.
Thomas D. Hyde, Corp. Sec./Exec. VP-Legal, Compliance & Ethics
Brian Cornell, Pres./CEO-Sam's Club
Stephen P. Whaley, Sr. VP/Controller
S. Robson Walton, Chmn.
C. Douglas McMillon, Pres./CEO-Wal-Mart Int'l
Johnnie C. Dobbs, Exec. VP-Logistics & Supply Chain

Phone: 479-273-4000	Fax:
Toll-Free: 800-925-6278	
Address: 702 SW 8th St., Bentonville, AR 72716 US	

GROWTH PLANS/SPECIAL FEATURES:

Wal-Mart Stores, Inc., one of the world's largest retailers, operates through a massive base of Wal-Mart stores, Wal-Mart Supercenters, Sam's Clubs, Marketside, Neighborhood Markets and WalMart.com. The company operates in three business segments: Wal-Mart Stores, representing 63.7% of net sales for 2009; Sam's Club, generating 11.7% for 2009; and International, accounting for 24.6% of net sales during 2009. The company serves over 200 million customers annually through 7,953 stores, with 3,685 of its stores located internationally. Wal-Mart offers a wide variety of discount merchandise in six merchandise units, including family apparel; entertainment, such as electronics, toys and photo-processing services; hardlines, which consists of fabrics, books, hardware, sporting goods and seasonal merchandise; health and wellness, including pharmacy and optical services; and home, including home furnishings, housewares and small appliances. Wal-Mart Supercenters, located in 48 states, are larger stores that combine a full-line supermarket with a discount department store. Sam's Club is a members-only warehouse club that sells merchandise at warehouse prices to consumers and small businesses. The International segment consists of wholly-owned subsidiaries in Argentina, Brazil, Canada, Japan, Puerto Rico and the U.K.; majority-owned subsidiaries in Central America, Chile and Mexico; joint ventures in India and China; and minority-owned subsidiaries in China. The company plans to open about 150 new stores during the fiscal year ending January 31, 2010, after opening 191 the previous year. New stores will focus on small formats, including the Marketside neighborhood market. The company will also concentrate on remodeling existing stores. Wal-Mart is expanding into India through a joint venture, opening several Best Price wholesale distribution centers. In June 2008, the firm agreed to sell Gazeley Limited Group. Also in 2008, subsidiary The Seiyu, Ltd., announced plans to close 23 stores, and Wal-Mart Stores acquired 58.2% of Distribucion Y Servicio D&S S.A., a Chile-based retail chain.

FINANCIALS: Sales and profits are in thousands of dollars—add 000 to get the full amount. 2008 Note: Financial information for 2008 was not available for all companies at press time.

2008 Sales: $374,526,000	2008 Profits: $12,731,000	**U.S. Stock Ticker: WMT**
2007 Sales: $344,992,000	2007 Profits: $11,284,000	**Int'l Ticker:** Int'l Exchange:
2006 Sales: $308,945,000	2006 Profits: $11,231,000	Employees: 2,100,000
2005 Sales: $281,488,000	2005 Profits: $10,267,000	Fiscal Year Ends: 1/31
2004 Sales: $256,329,000	2004 Profits: $9,054,000	Parent Company:

SALARIES/BENEFITS:

Pension Plan:	ESOP Stock Plan:	Profit Sharing: Y	Top Exec. Salary: $1,456,000	Bonus: $5,824,000
Savings Plan: Y	Stock Purch. Plan: Y		Second Exec. Salary: $1,040,000	Bonus: $4,166,624

OTHER THOUGHTS:

Apparent Women Officers or Directors: 8
Hot Spot for Advancement for Women/Minorities: Y

LOCATIONS: ("Y" = Yes)

West:	Southwest:	Midwest:	Southeast:	Northeast:	International:
Y	Y	Y	Y	Y	Y

Note: Financial information, benefits and other data can change quickly and may vary from those stated here.

WALT DISNEY COMPANY (THE)

corporate.disney.go.com

Industry Group Code: 515210 Ranks within this company's industry group: Sales: 1   Profits: 1

Management:		Sales/Marketing:		Liberal Arts:		Information Systems:		Professionals:		Tech./Scientific:	
Management Trainees:	Y	Marketing Pros.:	Y	Gen. Writing/Editing:	Y	Info. Management:	Y	Finance/Acct.:	Y	Engineers, Electrical:	Y
Experienced Mngmt.:	Y	Retail Sales:		Technical Writing:		Software Dev.:	Y	Law:	Y	Engineers, Other:	
International Business:	Y	Commercial/Industrial:	Y	Graphic Arts/Photog.:	Y	Hardware Dev.:		HR/Other:	Y	Health/Lab:	
MBA Grads:	Y	Sales Trainees:	Y	Music:	Y	Consulting/Other:		Training:	Y	Scientists/Research:	
		Advertising Pros.:	Y	Broadcasting:	Y			Health Care:		Petroleum/Chemicals:	
				Other:	Y			Consulting:		Math/Other:	

TYPES OF BUSINESS:

Cable TV Networks, Broadcasting & Entertainment
Filmed Entertainment
Merchandising
Television Networks
Music & Book Publishing
Online Entertainment Programs
Theme Parks, Resorts & Cruise Lines

BRANDS/DIVISIONS/AFFILIATES:

Walt Disney Parks & Resorts
ESPN Inc
ABC Inc
Walt Disney Studios (The)
Walt Disney World Resort
Miramax Film Corp
Walt Disney Pictures
ABC Entertainment Group

CONTACTS: *Note: Officers with more than one job title may be intentionally listed here more than once.*

Robert A. Iger, CEO
Robert A. Iger, Pres.
Thomas O. Staggs, CFO/Sr. Exec. VP
Dennis W. Shuler, Chief Human Resources Officer/Exec. VP
Kevin Mayer, Exec. VP-Tech. Group
Alan Braverman, General Counsel/Sr. Exec. VP/Corp. Sec.
Kevin Mayer, Exec. VP-Corp. Strategy & Bus. Dev.
Zenia Mucha, Exec. VP-Corp. Comm.
Christine M. McCarthy, Exec. VP-Corp. Finance & Real Estate/Treas.
Ronald L. Iden, Sr. VP-Security
Preston Padden, Exec. VP-Worldwide Gov't Rel.
Brent Woodford, Sr. VP-Planning & Control
Richard Cook, Chmn.-The Walt Disney Studios
John E. Pepper, Jr., Chmn.
Diego Lerner, Pres., EMEA

Phone: 818-560-1000	Fax: 818-560-1930
Toll-Free:	
Address: 500 S. Buena Vista St., Burbank, CA 91521 US	

GROWTH PLANS/SPECIAL FEATURES:

The Walt Disney Company is an international entertainment company operating in four major business segments: media networks; studio entertainment; consumer products; and parks and resorts. The media networks segment, which operates ABC Television Network, is involved in domestic broadcast television networks and stations; cable/satellite networks; international broadcast operations; television production and distribution; domestic broadcast radio networks and stations; and Internet operations. The company also owns interest in and/or operates many cable networks, including ESPN, ABC Family, the History Channel and A&E. The studio entertainment segment produces and acquires live action and animated motion pictures, direct-to-video programming, musical recordings and live stage plays. The consumer products segment designs, promotes and sells merchandise based on the firm's intellectual property. The parks and resorts segment owns/operates Florida's Walt Disney World Resort and the Disney Cruise Line; the Disneyland resort in California; ESPN Zone facilities in several states; and the Disney Vacation Club. It also holds interest in the Disneyland Resort Paris and Hong Kong Disneyland, and licenses the Tokyo Disney Resort in Japan. The Walt Disney World Resort includes Magic Kingdom, Epcot, Disney's Hollywood Studios and Disney's Animal Kingdom. It also owns/operates hotels, the Wide World of Sports complex and more. The firm operates eight ESPN Zones, located in California, Georgia, Maryland, Illinois, Colorado, Nevada, New York and Washington, D.C. In December 2008, the company signed a joint venture agreement with Russian firm Media-One Holdings Limited to launch a Disney-branded television channel in Russia. That same month, Disney acquired all outstanding shares of Jetix Europe. In January 2009, the company combined the operations of its ABC Entertainment and ABC Studios subsidiaries, which now operate as ABC Entertainment Group. In March 2009, Disney's media networks division and YouTube agreed to launch ad-supported channels which will show clips from the Disney/ABC Television Group and ESPN. In August 2009, Disney agreed to acquire comic book publisher Marvel Entertainment for $4 billion.

FINANCIALS: Sales and profits are in thousands of dollars—add 000 to get the full amount. 2008 Note: Financial information for 2008 was not available for all companies at press time.

2008 Sales: $37,843,000	2008 Profits: $4,427,000	**U.S. Stock Ticker: DIS**
2007 Sales: $35,510,000	2007 Profits: $4,687,000	**Int'l Ticker:** Int'l Exchange:
2006 Sales: $33,747,000	2006 Profits: $3,374,000	Employees: 150,000
2005 Sales: $31,374,000	2005 Profits: $2,533,000	Fiscal Year Ends: 9/30
2004 Sales: $30,752,000	2004 Profits: $2,345,000	Parent Company:

SALARIES/BENEFITS:

Pension Plan: Y	ESOP Stock Plan:	Profit Sharing:	Top Exec. Salary: $2,000,000	Bonus: $13,945,493
Savings Plan: Y	Stock Purch. Plan:		Second Exec. Salary: $1,187,019	Bonus: $4,100,000

OTHER THOUGHTS:

Apparent Women Officers or Directors: 6
Hot Spot for Advancement for Women/Minorities: Y

LOCATIONS: ("Y" = Yes)

West:	Southwest:	Midwest:	Southeast:	Northeast:	International:
Y	Y	Y	Y	Y	Y

Note: Financial information, benefits and other data can change quickly and may vary from those stated here.

WASTE MANAGEMENT INC

www.wm.com

Industry Group Code: 562 Ranks within this company's industry group: Sales: 1 Profits: 1

Management:		Sales/Marketing:		Liberal Arts:		Information Systems:		Professionals:		Tech./Scientific:	
Management Trainees:	Y	Marketing Pros.:	Y	Gen. Writing/Editing:	Y	Info. Management:	Y	Finance/Acct.:	Y	Engineers, Electrical:	
Experienced Mngmt.:	Y	Retail Sales:		Technical Writing:	Y	Software Dev.:	Y	Law:	Y	Engineers, Other:	Y
International Business:		Commercial/Industrial:	Y	Graphic Arts/Photog.:	Y	Hardware Dev.:		HR/Other:	Y	Health/Lab:	
MBA Grads:	Y	Sales Trainees:	Y	Music:		Consulting/Other:		Training:	Y	Scientists/Research:	
		Advertising Pros.:	Y	Broadcasting:				Health Care:		Petroleum/Chemicals:	
				Other:				Consulting:		Math/Other:	

TYPES OF BUSINESS:

Waste Disposal
Recycling Services
Landfill Operation
Hazardous Waste Management
Transfer Stations
Recycled Commodity Trading
Medical Waste Disposal
Waste Methane Generation

BRANDS/DIVISIONS/AFFILIATES:

Recycle America Alliance
TOSS
Bio-In-A-Box
BioSite
Wheelbrator
Think Green
H.T.R., Inc.
Earth Protection Services, Inc.

CONTACTS: *Note: Officers with more than one job title may be intentionally listed here more than once.*

David P. Steiner, CEO
Lawrence O'Donnell, III, COO
Lawrence O'Donnell, III, Pres.
Robert G. Simpson, CFO/Sr. VP
David Aardsma, Sr. VP-Mktg. & Sales
Michael (Jay) Romans, Sr. VP-People
Lynn M. Caddell, CIO/Sr. VP
Rick L. Wittenbraker, General Counsel/Chief Compliance Officer/Sr. VP
Barry H. Caldwell, Sr. VP-Gov't Affairs & Corp. Comm.
Cherie C. Rice, VP-Finance/Treas.
Patrick J. DeRueda, Pres., Waste Management Recycle America
Mark A. Weidman, Pres., Wheelabrator Technologies Inc.
Jay Romans, Sr. VP-People
Jeff Harris, Sr. VP-Midwestern Group
John (Jack) Pope, Chmn.

Phone: 713-512-6200	Fax: 713-512-6299
Toll-Free:	
Address: 1001 Fannin St., Ste. 4000, Houston, TX 77002 US	

GROWTH PLANS/SPECIAL FEATURES:

Waste Management, Inc. provides comprehensive waste management services to municipal, commercial, industrial and residential customers throughout North America. The company utilizes a number of transfer stations when it is not economical to transport solid waste generated from urban markets directly to landfills. Within these transfer stations, waste is consolidated, compacted and loaded onto long-haul trailers for transport to landfills. Waste Management is the nation's largest collector of recyclables from businesses and households, collecting recyclable materials through subsidiary Recycle America Alliance and depositing them at about a hundred local materials recovery facilities. The firm recycles several different materials, including plastics, rubber, electronics and commodities. The company also has a pulp and paper trading group that reduces paper's overall long-term commodity price exposure. The firm operates about 267 solid waste landfills and six secure hazardous waste landfills. Waste Management's hazardous waste management services include geosynthetic manufacturing, radioactive waste services and landfill liner installation. The company has developed TOSS, Bio-In-A-Box and BioSite, bioremediation systems for materials contaminated with petrochemicals, pesticides, explosives or hazardous organics. Through the subsidiary Wheelbrator, the company operates 16 waste-to-energy facilities, which produce electricity through burning solid waste at high temperatures. Additionally, Waste Management promotes environmental initiatives such as Keep America Beautiful, Habitat for Humanity, Red Cross/FEMA, Wildlife Habitat Council, as well as Waste Management's own Think Green. In 2009, the company opened new green facilities in Oregon, California and Michigan. In March 2009, the firm acquired H.T.R., Inc. and Earth Protection Services, Inc. in order to expand the fluorescent lamp recycling program WM LampTracker.

Waste Management offers its employees medical, dental, vision and prescription drug coverage; life and AD&D insurance; family assistance programs; flexible spending accounts; adoption assistance; education savings accounts; scholarships; a 401(k) plan; legal services; an employee stock purchase plan; and tuition reimbursement.

FINANCIALS: Sales and profits are in thousands of dollars—add 000 to get the full amount. 2008 Note: Financial information for 2008 was not available for all companies at press time.

2008 Sales: $13,388,000	2008 Profits: $1,087,000	**U.S. Stock Ticker: WM**
2007 Sales: $13,310,000	2007 Profits: $1,163,000	**Int'l Ticker:** Int'l Exchange:
2006 Sales: $13,363,000	2006 Profits: $1,149,000	Employees: 45,900
2005 Sales: $13,074,000	2005 Profits: $1,182,000	Fiscal Year Ends: 12/31
2004 Sales: $12,516,000	2004 Profits: $939,000	Parent Company:

SALARIES/BENEFITS:

Pension Plan:	ESOP Stock Plan:	Profit Sharing:	Top Exec. Salary: $1,066,049	Bonus: $1,050,895
Savings Plan: Y	Stock Purch. Plan: Y		Second Exec. Salary: $768,754	Bonus: $659,102

OTHER THOUGHTS:

Apparent Women Officers or Directors: 2
Hot Spot for Advancement for Women/Minorities: Y

LOCATIONS: ("Y" = Yes)

West:	Southwest:	Midwest:	Southeast:	Northeast:	International:
Y	Y	Y	Y	Y	

WATERS CORP

www.waters.com

Industry Group Code: 33911 **Ranks within this company's industry group:** Sales: 14 Profits: 9

Management:		Sales/Marketing:		Liberal Arts:		Information Systems:		Professionals:		Tech./Scientific:	
Management Trainees:	Y	Marketing Pros.:	Y	Gen. Writing/Editing:		Info. Management:	Y	Finance/Acct.:	Y	Engineers, Electrical:	Y
Experienced Mngmt.:	Y	Retail Sales:		Technical Writing:	Y	Software Dev.:	Y	Law:	Y	Engineers, Other:	Y
International Business:	Y	Commercial/Industrial:	Y	Graphic Arts/Photog.:	Y	Hardware Dev.:		HR/Other:	Y	Health/Lab:	Y
MBA Grads:	Y	Sales Trainees:		Music:		Consulting/Other:		Training:	Y	Scientists/Research:	Y
		Advertising Pros.:	Y	Broadcasting:				Health Care:		Petroleum/Chemicals:	
				Other:				Consulting:		Math/Other:	

TYPES OF BUSINESS:

Equipment-Liquid Chromatography Instruments
Mass Spectrometry Systems
Thermal Analyzers
Rheometry Equipment
Software Development
Food Safety Technology

BRANDS/DIVISIONS/AFFILIATES:

Waters Division
Alliance
TA Instruments, Inc.
Waters Xevo TQ MS System (The)
TRIZAIC UPLC System (The)
Analytical Products Group, Inc.
VTI Corporation
NuGenesis Scientific Data Management System

CONTACTS: Note: Officers with more than one job title may be intentionally listed here more than once.

Douglas A. Berthiaume, CEO
Douglas A. Berthiaume, Pres.
John Ornell, CFO
Elizabeth B. Rae, VP-Human Resources
John Ornell, VP-Admin.
Mark T. Beaudouin, General Counsel/VP/Corp. Sec.
Jeff Tarmy, Mgr.-Corp. Comm.
Gene Cassis, VP-Investor Rel.
John Ornell, VP-Finance
Arthur G. Caputo, Exec. VP/Pres., Waters Div.
Terrence P. Kelly, Pres., TA Instruments, Inc.
Douglas A. Berthiaume, Chmn.

Phone: 508-482-2000	Fax: 508-872-1990
Toll-Free: 800-252-4752	
Address: 34 Maple St., Milford, MA 01757 US	

GROWTH PLANS/SPECIAL FEATURES:

Waters Corporation designs, manufactures and markets analytical instruments. The firm operates in two segments: the Waters division and TA Instruments, Inc. The Waters division offers high-performance liquid chromatography (HPLC) and mass spectrometry instrument systems and associated service and support products, including chromatography columns and laboratory informatics software. HPLC equipment detects, identifies, monitors and measures the chemical, physical and biological composition of materials. Waters Corp.'s liquid chromatography instruments allow for different degrees of automation, from component-configured systems to its fully-automated Alliance systems. Mass spectrometry is an analytical technique that identifies unknown compounds and quantifies known materials. These instruments are used primarily in conjunction with the firm's HPLC products by a wide array of industries, particularly the life sciences pharmaceutical, biomedical, clinical and environmental market segments. The firm's mass spectrometer products include the Waters Xevo TQ MS System, TRIZAIC UPLC System; Waters SYNAPT G2 System; and YNAPT High Definition MS. Through its TA Instruments division, the company designs, manufactures, services and sells thermal analysis instruments that measure the physical characteristics of materials as a function of temperature. In addition to thermal analyzers, TA Instruments produces rheometry instruments, which complement thermal analyzers by characterizing materials' viscosities and fluid behavior. TA Instruments is also a developer and supplier of software-based products that interface with the company's instruments. The thermal analytic and rheometry instruments are used by material testing laboratories for the development and production of materials used in plastics, automobiles, electronics and chemicals. In July 2008, the firm acquired the assets of VTI Corporation for $3 million. In December 2008, the company acquired the assets of Analytical Products Group, Inc. In March 2009, Waters Corp. and LabVantage Solutions, Inc., partnered to integrate the firm's NuGenesis Scientific Data Management System and Empower 2 chromatography data software solutions with LabVantage Solutions' SAPPHIRE Laboratory Information Management Suite.

FINANCIALS: Sales and profits are in thousands of dollars—add 000 to get the full amount. 2008 Note: Financial information for 2008 was not available for all companies at press time.

2008 Sales: $1,139,886	2008 Profits: $322,479	**U.S. Stock Ticker: WAT**	
2007 Sales: $1,087,592	2007 Profits: $268,072	**Int'l Ticker:** Int'l Exchange:	
2006 Sales: $922,532	2006 Profits: $222,200	Employees: 5,033	
2005 Sales: $1,158,236	2005 Profits: $201,975	Fiscal Year Ends: 12/31	
2004 Sales: $1,104,536	2004 Profits: $224,053	Parent Company:	

SALARIES/BENEFITS:

Pension Plan: Y	ESOP Stock Plan:	Profit Sharing:	Top Exec. Salary: $735,000	Bonus: $1,470,000
Savings Plan:	Stock Purch. Plan: Y		Second Exec. Salary: $450,000	Bonus: $810,000

OTHER THOUGHTS:

Apparent Women Officers or Directors: 3
Hot Spot for Advancement for Women/Minorities: Y

LOCATIONS: ("Y" = Yes)

West:	Southwest:	Midwest:	Southeast:	Northeast:	International:
Y	Y	Y	Y	Y	Y

Note: Financial information, benefits and other data can change quickly and may vary from those stated here.

WATSON PHARMACEUTICALS INC

www.watson.com

Industry Group Code: 325412 Ranks within this company's industry group: Sales: 14   Profits: 12

Management:		Sales/Marketing:		Liberal Arts:		Information Systems:		Professionals:		Tech./Scientific:	
Management Trainees:	Y	Marketing Pros.:	Y	Gen. Writing/Editing:	Y	Info. Management:	Y	Finance/Acct.:	Y	Engineers, Electrical:	Y
Experienced Mngmt.:	Y	Retail Sales:		Technical Writing:	Y	Software Dev.:	Y	Law:	Y	Engineers, Other:	Y
International Business:	Y	Commercial/Industrial:	Y	Graphic Arts/Photog.:	Y	Hardware Dev.:		HR/Other:	Y	Health/Lab:	Y
MBA Grads:	Y	Sales Trainees:		Music:		Consulting/Other:		Training:	Y	Scientists/Research:	Y
		Advertising Pros.:		Broadcasting:				Health Care:	Y	Petroleum/Chemicals:	Y
				Other:				Consulting:		Math/Other:	Y

TYPES OF BUSINESS:

Generic Pharmaceuticals
Branded Drugs
Urology Drugs
Anti-Hypertensive Drugs
Nephrology Drugs
Anti-Inflammatory Drugs
Oral Contraceptive Drugs
Pain Management Drugs

BRANDS/DIVISIONS/AFFILIATES:

Watson Laboratories
Anda
Anda Pharmaceuticals
Andrx Corp.
Trelstar Depot
Valmed
Gelnique
Arrow Group

CONTACTS: Note: Officers with more than one job title may be intentionally listed here more than once.

Paul M. Bisaro, CEO
Paul M. Bisaro, Pres.
Mark Durand, CFO/Sr. VP
Clare Carmichael, Sr. VP-Human Resources
Charles D. Ebert, Sr. VP-R&D
Thomas R. Giordano, CIO/Sr. VP
David A. Buchen, General Counsel/Sr. VP/Sec.
Patricia L. Eisenhauer, VP-Corp. Comm.
Patricia L. Eisenhauer, VP-Investor Rel.
Edward F. Heimers, Jr., Exec. VP/Pres., Brand Division
Albert Paonessa III, Exec. VP/COO-Anda, Inc.
Gordon Munro, Sr. VP-Quality Assurance
Thomas R. Russillo, Exec. VP/Pres., U.S. Generics Division
Andrew L. Turner, Chmn.

Phone: 951-493-5300	Fax:
Toll-Free:	
Address: 311 Bonnie Cir., Corona, CA 92880 US	

GROWTH PLANS/SPECIAL FEATURES:

Watson Pharmaceuticals, Inc. develops, manufactures, markets, sells and distributes over 27 branded and over 150 generic pharmaceutical products. The firm operates through three segments: generic, brand and distribution. The generic segment includes pharmaceutical products that are therapeutically equivalent to proprietary products. These generic products address the therapeutic areas of antibiotics, anti-inflammatories, depression, hypertension, oral contraceptives, pain management and smoking cessation. Generic products accounted for roughly 60% of net revenues in 2008. The brand segment develops, manufactures, markets, sells and distributes products primarily through two core areas: specialty products and nephrology. The specialty products include urology and a number of non-promoted products. The nephrology product line concerns products for the treatment of iron deficiency anemia. Brands include Trelstar Depot and Trelstar LA, treatments for advanced prostate cancer; Gelnique, a treatment for overactive bladder symptoms; Rapaflo, a treatment for symptoms of benign prostatic hyperplasia; and Ferrlecit and INFeD, iron replacement therapies for patients with iron deficiency anemia. The company markets its brand products through 380 sales professionals. Brand products accounted for roughly 18% of total revenue in 2008. The distribution segment distributes generic products and select brand products to independent pharmacies, pharmacy chains, pharmacy buying groups, alternative care facilities, including long-term care pharmacies, and physicians' offices in the U.S. The company's distribution business subsidiaries include Anda, Anda Pharmaceuticals and Valmed. In November 2008, the company agreed to acquire a portfolio of generic pharmaceutical products conditional to the merger of Teva Pharmaceutical Industries, Ltd., and Barr Pharmaceuticals, Inc. In June 2009, Watson announced that it would acquire London-based Arrow Group for approximately $1.75 billion.

The company offers employees medical, dental and vision insurance; a 401(k) plan; life and AD&D insurance; domestic partner coverage; flexible spending accounts; business travel accident insurance; short- and long-term disability; pet insurance; and tuition reimbursement.

FINANCIALS: Sales and profits are in thousands of dollars—add 000 to get the full amount. 2008 Note: Financial information for 2008 was not available for all companies at press time.

2008 Sales: $2,535,501	2008 Profits: $238,379	U.S. Stock Ticker: WPI	
2007 Sales: $2,496,651	2007 Profits: $141,030	Int'l Ticker:	Int'l Exchange:
2006 Sales: $1,979,244	2006 Profits: $-445,005	Employees: 5,070	
2005 Sales: $1,646,203	2005 Profits: $138,557	Fiscal Year Ends: 12/31	
2004 Sales: $1,640,551	2004 Profits: $150,018	Parent Company:	

SALARIES/BENEFITS:

Pension Plan:	ESOP Stock Plan:	Profit Sharing:	Top Exec. Salary: $1,000,000	Bonus: $997,200
Savings Plan: Y	Stock Purch. Plan:		Second Exec. Salary: $790,608	Bonus: $430,486

OTHER THOUGHTS:

Apparent Women Officers or Directors: 2
Hot Spot for Advancement for Women/Minorities: Y

LOCATIONS: ("Y" = Yes)

West:	Southwest:	Midwest:	Southeast:	Northeast:	International:
Y		Y	Y	Y	

WATSON WYATT WORLDWIDE INC

www.watsonwyatt.com

Industry Group Code: 541612 Ranks within this company's industry group: Sales: 4 Profits: 2

Management:		Sales/Marketing:		Liberal Arts:		Information Systems:		Professionals:		Tech./Scientific:	
Management Trainees:	Y	Marketing Pros.:	Y	Gen. Writing/Editing:	Y	Info. Management:	Y	Finance/Acct.:	Y	Engineers, Electrical:	
Experienced Mngmt.:	Y	Retail Sales:		Technical Writing:	Y	Software Dev.:	Y	Law:	Y	Engineers, Other:	
International Business:	Y	Commercial/Industrial:	Y	Graphic Arts/Photog.:	Y	Hardware Dev.:		HR/Other:	Y	Health/Lab:	
MBA Grads:	Y	Sales Trainees:		Music:		Consulting/Other:	Y	Training:	Y	Scientists/Research:	
		Advertising Pros.:	Y	Broadcasting:				Health Care:		Petroleum/Chemicals:	
				Other:	Y			Consulting:	Y	Math/Other:	

TYPES OF BUSINESS:

Human Resources Consulting
Compensation Consulting
Benefit Plan Consulting
Technology Services

BRANDS/DIVISIONS/AFFILIATES:

Watson Wyatt & Company Holdings
Watson Wyatt Brans & Co.
Towers Perrin
Towers Watson & Co.

CONTACTS: *Note: Officers with more than one job title may be intentionally listed here more than once.*

John J. Haley, CEO
John J. Haley, Pres.
Roger Millay, CFO/VP
Robert J. McKee, VP/Global Dir.-Mktg.
Stephen E. Mele, Chief Human Resources Officer/VP
Jeffrey J. Held, CIO/VP
Walter W. Bardenwerper, General Counsel/VP/Corp. Sec.
David M. E. Dow, VP/Global Practice Dir.-Tech, & Admin. Solutions
Roger C. Urwin, Practice Dir.-Investment Consulting
Gene H. Wickes, VP/Dir.-Global Benefits Practice
Philip G. H. Brook, VP/Global Practice Dir.-Insurance & Financial Svcs
John J. Haley, Chmn.
Chandrasekhar Ramamurthy, VP/Regional Mgr.-Europe

Phone: 703-258-8000	**Fax:** 703-258-7495
Toll-Free:	
Address: 901 N. Glebe Rd., Arlington, VA 22203 US	

GROWTH PLANS/SPECIAL FEATURES:

Watson Wyatt Worldwide, Inc. (WW), formerly Watson Wyatt & Company Holdings, along with its subsidiaries, is a global consulting firm focused on providing human capital and financial management consulting services. The company operates through roughly 96 offices in 30 countries, and divides its operations into five groups: benefits; technology and administration; human capital; investment consulting; and insurance and financial services. WW's benefits group, which generates over 50% of its revenues, provides benefit program design and management; funding and risk management strategies; expatriate and international human resource strategies; strategic workforce planning; and compliance and governance. Services of the technology and administration solutions group include web-based applications and outsourcing systems for health, welfare, pension and compensation administration; call center strategy, design and tools; and strategic human resources technology. WW's human capital group offers advice concerning compensation plans, including broad-based and executive compensation, stock and other long-term incentive programs; strategies to align workforce performance with business objectives; organization effectiveness consulting, including talent management; strategies for attracting, retaining and motivating employees; and data services. The investment consulting group provides investment consulting services to pension plans and other institutional funds; input on governance and regulatory issues; analysis of asset allocation and investment strategies; investment structure analysis; selection and evaluation of managers; and performance monitoring. WW's insurance and financial services group provides independent actuarial and strategic advice; assessment and advice regarding financial condition and risk management; and financial modeling software tools for product design, pricing, planning, projections, reporting, valuations and risk management. In June 2008, the firm acquired Marcu & Asociados, an Argentinean consulting firm. In December 2008, the company acquired SMART Human Resource Vietnam Company Limited. In June 2009, the firm announced plans to merge with Towers Perrin. The new company will be called Towers Watson & Co., and will have 14,000 employees and $3.2 billion in annual revenues.

FINANCIALS: Sales and profits are in thousands of dollars—add 000 to get the full amount. 2008 Note: Financial information for 2008 was not available for all companies at press time.

2008 Sales: $1,760,055	2008 Profits: $155,441	**U.S. Stock Ticker:** WW
2007 Sales: $1,486,523	2007 Profits: $116,275	**Int'l Ticker:** Int'l Exchange:
2006 Sales: $1,271,811	2006 Profits: $87,191	Employees: 7,700
2005 Sales: $737,421	2005 Profits: $52,162	Fiscal Year Ends: 6/30
2004 Sales: $702,005	2004 Profits: $50,593	Parent Company:

SALARIES/BENEFITS:

Pension Plan: Y	ESOP Stock Plan:	Profit Sharing:	Top Exec. Salary: $865,000	Bonus: $1,300,000
Savings Plan: Y	Stock Purch. Plan: Y		Second Exec. Salary: $546,250	Bonus: $465,000

OTHER THOUGHTS:

Apparent Women Officers or Directors: 1
Hot Spot for Advancement for Women/Minorities:

LOCATIONS: ("Y" = Yes)

West:	Southwest:	Midwest:	Southeast:	Northeast:	International:
Y	Y	Y	Y	Y	Y

WEATHERFORD INTERNATIONAL LTD

www.weatherford.com

Industry Group Code: 213112 Ranks within this company's industry group: Sales: 4 Profits: 5

Management:		Sales/Marketing:		Liberal Arts:		Information Systems:		Professionals:		Tech./Scientific:	
Management Trainees:	Y	Marketing Pros.:	Y	Gen. Writing/Editing:		Info. Management:	Y	Finance/Acct.:	Y	Engineers, Electrical:	Y
Experienced Mngmt.:	Y	Retail Sales:		Technical Writing:	Y	Software Dev.:	Y	Law:	Y	Engineers, Other:	Y
International Business:	Y	Commercial/Industrial:	Y	Graphic Arts/Photog.:		Hardware Dev.:		HR/Other:	Y	Health/Lab:	
MBA Grads:	Y	Sales Trainees:		Music:		Consulting/Other:		Training:	Y	Scientists/Research:	
		Advertising Pros.:		Broadcasting:				Health Care:		Petroleum/Chemicals:	Y
				Other:				Consulting:		Math/Other:	

TYPES OF BUSINESS:

Oil & Gas Drilling Support Services
Artificial Lift Systems
Completion Systems
Research & Development

BRANDS/DIVISIONS/AFFILIATES:

International Logging Inc

CONTACTS: *Note: Officers with more than one job title may be intentionally listed here more than once.*

Bernard J. Duroc-Danner, CEO
Bernard J. Duroc-Danner, Pres.
Andrew P. Becnel, CFO/Sr. VP
Wolfgang Puennel, VP-Global Mktg.
Stuart E. Ferguson, CTO
Stuart E. Ferguson, Sr. VP-Prod.
Burt M. Martin, General Counsel/Sr. VP/Sec.
M. Jessica Abarca, Chief Acct. Officer/VP-Acct.
Keith R. Morley, Sr. VP-Well Construction & Oper. Support
Stuart E. Ferguson, Sr. VP-Reservoir
M. David Colley, VP-Artificial Lift Global Bus. Unit
James M. Hudgins, VP-Tax
Bernard J. Duroc-Danner, Chmn.
Kyle Chapman, Regional Mgr.-Prod. & Svc. Line, Latin America

Phone: 41-22-816-1500	Fax:
Toll-Free:	
Address: 4-6 Rue Jean-Francois Bartholoni, Geneva, 1204 Switzerland	

GROWTH PLANS/SPECIAL FEATURES:

Weatherford International, Inc. provides equipment and services for the oil and natural gas industry. The firm operates throughout the U.S. and in over 100 countries around the world, with more than 800 service, sales and manufacturing locations. The company offers oil/natural gas well drilling, evaluation, completion, production, intervention and industrial products/services. Weatherford International's drilling offerings include controlled pressure drilling systems; well installation services; cementing products; and measurement-while-drilling systems. With regard to evaluation, the company provides testing, data, geoscience, cased-hole and open-hole services; surface logging systems; and microseismic monitoring. The firm's completion system activities include hydraulic intelligent, open-hole, cased-hole and expandable completion systems, as well as intelligent well, liner, packer and flow control systems. The firm's artificial lift system activities provide all forms of artificial lift primarily used for the production of oil. This operation also provides production optimization services and automation and monitoring of well head production. Weatherford's intervention services are intended to extend the production capacity of oil and natural gas wells; these include fishing services, multilateral systems, casing exit systems and thru-tubing packers. The firm's industrial operations focus primarily on pumping technologies, including multiplex pumps, horizontal surface pumping units and progressing cavity pumps. These are used in a variety of applications related to industries such as pulp and paper; oil and gas; poultry and dairy; petrochemical; and automotives and aircrafts. In August 2008, the firm acquired International Logging, Inc., a provider of surface logging and formation evaluation and drilling related services at the well site. In February 2009, Weatherford International moved its corporate headquarters from the U.S. to Switzerland. In July 2009, the company acquired the Oil Field Services unit of TNK-BP, a Russian oil firm.

FINANCIALS: Sales and profits are in thousands of dollars—add 000 to get the full amount. 2008 Note: Financial information for 2008 was not available for all companies at press time.

2008 Sales: $9,600,564	2008 Profits: $1,353,903	**U.S. Stock Ticker: WFT**
2007 Sales: $7,832,062	2007 Profits: $1,070,606	**Int'l Ticker:** Int'l Exchange:
2006 Sales: $6,578,928	2006 Profits: $896,369	Employees: 47,000
2005 Sales: $4,333,227	2005 Profits: $467,420	Fiscal Year Ends: 12/31
2004 Sales: $3,131,774	2004 Profits: $330,146	Parent Company:

SALARIES/BENEFITS:

Pension Plan:	ESOP Stock Plan:	Profit Sharing:	Top Exec. Salary: $1,497,909	Bonus: $3,000,000
Savings Plan:	Stock Purch. Plan:		Second Exec. Salary: $623,265	Bonus: $525,000

OTHER THOUGHTS:

Apparent Women Officers or Directors: 1
Hot Spot for Advancement for Women/Minorities:

LOCATIONS: ("Y" = Yes)

West:	Southwest:	Midwest:	Southeast:	Northeast:	International:
Y	Y	Y	Y	Y	Y

WEIGHT WATCHERS INTERNATIONAL INC
www.weightwatchers.com

Industry Group Code: 446199 Ranks within this company's industry group: Sales: 1 Profits: 1

Management:		Sales/Marketing:		Liberal Arts:		Information Systems:		Professionals:		Tech./Scientific:	
Management Trainees:	Y	Marketing Pros.:	Y	Gen. Writing/Editing:	Y	Info. Management:	Y	Finance/Acct.:	Y	Engineers, Electrical:	
Experienced Mngmt.:	Y	Retail Sales:		Technical Writing:		Software Dev.:	Y	Law:	Y	Engineers, Other:	
International Business:	Y	Commercial/Industrial:		Graphic Arts/Photog.:	Y	Hardware Dev.:		HR/Other:	Y	Health/Lab:	
MBA Grads:	Y	Sales Trainees:	Y	Music:		Consulting/Other:		Training:	Y	Scientists/Research:	
		Advertising Pros.:	Y	Broadcasting:				Health Care:	Y	Petroleum/Chemicals:	
				Other:	Y			Consulting:		Math/Other:	

TYPES OF BUSINESS:
Weight Management Programs
Franchising
Branded Diet Products

BRANDS/DIVISIONS/AFFILIATES:
Flex Plan
Core Plan
Weight Watchers Online
Weight Watchers eTools

CONTACTS:
Note: Officers with more than one job title may be intentionally listed here more than once.
David P. Kirchhoff, CEO
Thilo Semmelbauer, COO
David P. Kirchhoff, Pres.
Ann M. Sardini, CFO/VP
Jeffrey A. Fiarman, General Counsel/Sec./Exec. VP
Kevin Eberly, VP-North American Oper.
Michael Basone, Pres., WeightWatchers.com
Raymond Debbane, Chmn.
Melanie Stack Stubbing, Pres., Int'l

Phone: 212-589-2700	Fax: 212-589-2601
Toll-Free:	
Address: 11 Madison Ave., 17th Fl., New York, NY 10010 US	

GROWTH PLANS/SPECIAL FEATURES:
Weight Watchers International, Inc. is a global weight management services provider, operating globally through a network of company-owned and franchise operations. It offers two main services: weight management plans and meetings. The plans consist of Flex Plans and Core Plans. The Flex Plan offers customers a list of foods graded on a POINTS scale, which takes into consideration calories, fat and dietary fiber. This plan allows the dieter to eat any food from the list up to a weekly POINTS total. The Core Plan offers the dieter a list of low calorie density core foods which they can eat freely, without limit; and allows the dieter to eat certain non-core foods up to a POINTS limit. Weight Watchers' one hour long weekly meetings promote weight loss through diet, exercise, behavior modification and group support. Each week, 1.4 million people attend 50,000 meetings worldwide. These are run by 16,000 classroom leaders, all of whom have participated in the company's weight loss program. During 2008, franchised operations drew in more than 12 million people, representing 18% of the company's total attendance. Besides services, the firm offers various products primarily sold at Weight Watchers meetings and to franchises; these products include bars, snacks, cookbooks, POINTS value guides and Weight Watchers magazines. Product sales generated 22% of the firm's 2008 revenue. The company's web site offers two subscription weight management products to consumers: Weight Watchers Online and Weight Watchers eTools. Weight Watchers Online provides interactive and personalized resources that allow users to follow the company's weight management plans via the Internet. Weight Watchers eTools is the Internet weight management companion for Weight Watchers meetings members who want to interactively manage the day-to-day aspects of their weight management plans on the Internet.

FINANCIALS:
Sales and profits are in thousands of dollars—add 000 to get the full amount. 2008 Note: Financial information for 2008 was not available for all companies at press time.

2008 Sales: $1,535,812	2008 Profits: $204,331	**U.S. Stock Ticker: WTW**
2007 Sales: $1,467,167	2007 Profits: $201,180	**Int'l Ticker:** Int'l Exchange:
2006 Sales: $1,233,300	2006 Profits: $209,800	Employees: 52,000
2005 Sales: $1,151,300	2005 Profits: $174,400	Fiscal Year Ends: 12/31
2004 Sales: $1,024,900	2004 Profits: $183,100	Parent Company:

SALARIES/BENEFITS:

Pension Plan:	ESOP Stock Plan:	Profit Sharing:	Top Exec. Salary: $643,558	Bonus: $215,902
Savings Plan:	Stock Purch. Plan:		Second Exec. Salary: $406,865	Bonus: $147,632

OTHER THOUGHTS:
Apparent Women Officers or Directors: 2
Hot Spot for Advancement for Women/Minorities: Y

LOCATIONS: ("Y" = Yes)

West:	Southwest:	Midwest:	Southeast:	Northeast:	International:
Y	Y	Y	Y	Y	Y

Note: Financial information, benefits and other data can change quickly and may vary from those stated here.

WELLPOINT INC

www.wellpoint.com

Industry Group Code: 524114 Ranks within this company's industry group: Sales: 2 Profits: 2

Management:		Sales/Marketing:		Liberal Arts:		Information Systems:		Professionals:		Tech./Scientific:	
Management Trainees:	Y	Marketing Pros.:	Y	Gen. Writing/Editing:	Y	Info. Management:	Y	Finance/Acct.:	Y	Engineers, Electrical:	
Experienced Mngmt.:	Y	Retail Sales:		Technical Writing:	Y	Software Dev.:	Y	Law:	Y	Engineers, Other:	
International Business:		Commercial/Industrial:	Y	Graphic Arts/Photog.:	Y	Hardware Dev.:		HR/Other:	Y	Health/Lab:	
MBA Grads:	Y	Sales Trainees:		Music:		Consulting/Other:		Training:	Y	Scientists/Research:	
		Advertising Pros.:	Y	Broadcasting:				Health Care:	Y	Petroleum/Chemicals:	
				Other:	Y			Consulting:		Math/Other:	

TYPES OF BUSINESS:

Health Insurance
Health Maintenance Organizations (HMOs)
Point-of-Service Plans
Dental Plans
Actuarial Services
Managed Care Services

BRANDS/DIVISIONS/AFFILIATES:

WellChoice, Inc.
Unicare
Blue Cross of California
Blue Cross and Blue Shield of Georgia, Inc.
Decare International
DeCare Dental
Resolution Health, Inc.
Anthem Blue Cross Blue Shield

CONTACTS: Note: Officers with more than one job title may be intentionally listed here more than once.

Angela F. Braly, CEO
Angela F. Braly, Pres.
Wayne S. DeVeydt, CFO/Exec. VP
Randy L. Brown, Exec. VP/Chief Human Resources Officer
Lori Beer, CIO/Exec. VP
John Cannon, General Counsel/Exec. VP/Sec.
Brad M. Fluegel, Chief Strategy Officer/Exec. VP
Brad M. Fluegel, Chief External Affairs Officer
Sean Meenan, Dir.-Investor Rel.
Martin Miller, Chief Acct. Officer/Sr. VP
Ken Goulet, Pres./CEO-Commercial Bus. Unit
Dijuana Lewi, Pres./CEO-Wellpoint Comprehensive Health Solutions
Randall J. Lewis, Exec. VP-Internal Audit & Chief Compliance Officer
Samuel R. Nussbaum, Chief Medical Officer/Exec. VP
Larry C. Glasscock, Chmn.

Phone: 317-532-6000	Fax: 317-488-6200
Toll-Free:	
Address: 120 Monument Cir., Indianapolis, IN 46204 US	

GROWTH PLANS/SPECIAL FEATURES:

WellPoint, Inc. is a health benefits company, serving more than 34 million medical members. The company is an independent licensee of the Blue Cross and Blue Shield Association, an association of independent health benefit plans, and also serves customers as Unicare. The firm offers network-based managed care plans to the large and small employer, individual, Medicaid and senior markets. The managed care plans include preferred provider organizations, health maintenance organizations, point-of-service plans, traditional indemnity plans and other hybrid plans including consumer-driven health plans, hospital only and limited benefit products. In addition, WellPoint provides managed care services to self-funded customers, including claims processing, underwriting, stop loss insurance, actuarial services, provider network access, medical cost management and other administrative services. The company also provides specialty and other products and services including life and disability insurance benefits; dental; vision; behavioral health benefit services; long-term care insurance; and flexible spending accounts. The firm markets its products through a network of independent agents and brokers and through its in-house sales force. Subsidiaries include Blue Cross of California and Blue Cross Blue Shield of Georgia, as well as non-Blue Cross subsidiaries such as Healthlink, PrecisionRx, WellPoint Behavioral Health, WellPoint Dental Services and WellPoint Workers' Compensation Managed Care Services. In June 2008, the company launched the Maternity Depression Program, aimed at providing new mothers with depression screenings, education and support in order to help them receive behavioral health treatment post-pregnancy. In April 2009, the firm ageed to sell its pharmacy benefits management unit to Express Scripts for $4.7 billion.

WellPoint offers employees tuition assistance; a 401(k) plan; an employee stock purchase plan; retiree medical spending accounts; life insurance; medical, dental and vision coverage; and flexible spending accounts.

FINANCIALS: Sales and profits are in thousands of dollars—add 000 to get the full amount. 2008 Note: Financial information for 2008 was not available for all companies at press time.

2008 Sales: $61,251,000	2008 Profits: $2,491,000	U.S. Stock Ticker: WLP
2007 Sales: $61,134,300	2007 Profits: $3,345,400	Int'l Ticker: Int'l Exchange:
2006 Sales: $57,038,800	2006 Profits: $3,094,900	Employees: 42,900
2005 Sales: $44,541,300	2005 Profits: $2,463,800	Fiscal Year Ends: 12/31
2004 Sales: $20,707,900	2004 Profits: $960,100	Parent Company:

SALARIES/BENEFITS:

Pension Plan:	ESOP Stock Plan:	Profit Sharing:	Top Exec. Salary: $1,135,538	Bonus: $73,810
Savings Plan: Y	Stock Purch. Plan: Y		Second Exec. Salary: $648,769	Bonus: $27,573

OTHER THOUGHTS:

Apparent Women Officers or Directors: 8
Hot Spot for Advancement for Women/Minorities: Y

LOCATIONS: ("Y" = Yes)

West:	Southwest:	Midwest:	Southeast:	Northeast:	International:
Y	Y	Y	Y	Y	

WELLS FARGO & CO

www.wellsfargo.com

Industry Group Code: 522110 Ranks within this company's industry group: Sales: 3 Profits: 3

Management:		Sales/Marketing:		Liberal Arts:		Information Systems:		Professionals:		Tech./Scientific:	
Management Trainees:	Y	Marketing Pros.:	Y	Gen. Writing/Editing:	Y	Info. Management:	Y	Finance/Acct.:	Y	Engineers, Electrical:	
Experienced Mngmt.:	Y	Retail Sales:		Technical Writing:		Software Dev.:	Y	Law:	Y	Engineers, Other:	
International Business:	Y	Commercial/Industrial:	Y	Graphic Arts/Photog.:	Y	Hardware Dev.:		HR/Other:	Y	Health/Lab:	
MBA Grads:	Y	Sales Trainees:		Music:		Consulting/Other:		Training:	Y	Scientists/Research:	
		Advertising Pros.:	Y	Broadcasting:				Health Care:		Petroleum/Chemicals:	
				Other:	Y			Consulting:		Math/Other:	

TYPES OF BUSINESS:

Banking
Credit & Debit Cards
Personal Trust Accounts Management
Mutual Fund Administration
Mortgages
Insurance Services
Investment Banking
Asset Management

BRANDS/DIVISIONS/AFFILIATES:

Wachovia Corp.
HD Vest, Inc.
Wells Fargo Insurance Services
Wells Capital Management
Wachovia Corporation
GE Healthcare Financial Services
BridgeStreet Consulting Group
EMAR Group (The)

CONTACTS: Note: Officers with more than one job title may be intentionally listed here more than once.

John G. Stumpf, CEO
John G. Stumpf, Pres.
Howard I. Atkins, CFO/Sr. Exec. VP
Julie M. White, Exec. VP/Dir.-Human Resources
Avid Modjtabai, Exec. VP-Tech.
James M. Strother, General Counsel/Exec. VP-Law & Gov't Rel.
Avid Modjtabai, Exec. VP-Oper.
Richard D. Levy, Exec. VP/Controller
Mark C. Oman, Sr. VP-Home & Consumer Finance
David A. Hoyt, Sr. Exec. VP-Wholesale Banking
Michael J. Loughlin, Chief Credit Officer/Exec. VP
David M. Carroll, Sr. Exec. VP-Wealth, Brokerage & Retirement Svcs.
Richard M. Kovacevich, Chmn.

Phone:	Fax:
Toll-Free: 888-662-7865	
Address: 420 Montgomery St., San Francisco, CA 94104 US	

GROWTH PLANS/SPECIAL FEATURES:

Wells Fargo & Co. is a financial services company that provides retail, commercial and corporate banking. Services include wholesale banking, mortgage banking, consumer finance, equipment leasing, agricultural finance, securities brokerage and investment banking, insurance agency and brokerage services, data processing services, trust services, investment consulting, mortgage-backed securities servicing and venture capital investment. The firm has three business segments: Community Banking; Wholesale Banking; and Wealth, Brokerage and Retirement. The Community Banking group offers diversified financial products and services to consumers and small businesses, including investment, insurance and trust services and mortgage and home equity loans. The Wholesale Banking group serves businesses with more than $10 million dollars in annual revenue. These services include middle market banking, treasury management, asset-based lending, insurance brokerage, correspondent banking, trade services, specialized lending, investment banking, equity trading, fixed-income sales and trading, equipment finance, corporate trust, investment banking, capital markets and asset management. Wealth, Brokerage and Retirement provides financial advisory services, such as financial planning, private banking, credit, investment management, trust and estate services and business succession planning services, to high-net-worth clients. During 2008, the company's activities included the formation of a joint venture with Bank of America; and the acquisition of the Farmers State Bank of Fort Morgan; Transcap Associates, Inc.; Flatiron Credit Company, Inc.; the EMAR Group; and Century Bancshares. In December 2008, Wells Fargo acquired Wachovia Corp. The combined company has approximately $1.3 trillion in assets, 280,000 employees, 70 million customers and 11,000 offices in 39 states. Wells Fargo's 2009 acquisitions included BridgeStreet Consulting Group; the assets of North Coast Surety Insurance Services and North Coast Surety Technologies; and loan and lease receivables from GE Healthcare Financial Services-Equipment Finance.

Wells Fargo offers its employees tuition reimbursement, adoption assistance, commuter benefits, gift matching, free checking and savings accounts and scholarships for dependent children.

FINANCIALS: Sales and profits are in thousands of dollars—add 000 to get the full amount. 2008 Note: Financial information for 2008 was not available for all companies at press time.

2008 Sales: $51,652,000	2008 Profits: $2,655,000	**U.S. Stock Ticker:** WFC
2007 Sales: $53,593,000	2007 Profits: $8,057,000	**Int'l Ticker:** Int'l Exchange:
2006 Sales: $47,998,000	2006 Profits: $8,482,000	Employees: 281,000
2005 Sales: $40,527,000	2005 Profits: $7,671,000	Fiscal Year Ends: 12/31
2004 Sales: $33,876,000	2004 Profits: $7,014,000	Parent Company:

SALARIES/BENEFITS:

Pension Plan:	ESOP Stock Plan:	Profit Sharing:	Top Exec. Salary: $992,955	Bonus: $
Savings Plan: Y	Stock Purch. Plan:		Second Exec. Salary: $878,920	Bonus: $

OTHER THOUGHTS:

Apparent Women Officers or Directors: 7
Hot Spot for Advancement for Women/Minorities: Y

LOCATIONS: ("Y" = Yes)

West:	Southwest:	Midwest:	Southeast:	Northeast:	International:
Y	Y	Y	Y	Y	Y

Note: Financial information, benefits and other data can change quickly and may vary from those stated here.

WENDY'S/ARBY'S GROUP INC

www.wendysarbys.com

Industry Group Code: 722110 Ranks within this company's industry group: Sales: 9 Profits: 12

Management:		Sales/Marketing:		Liberal Arts:		Information Systems:		Professionals:		Tech./Scientific:	
Management Trainees:	Y	Marketing Pros.:	Y	Gen. Writing/Editing:	Y	Info. Management:	Y	Finance/Acct.:	Y	Engineers, Electrical:	
Experienced Mngmt.:	Y	Retail Sales:		Technical Writing:		Software Dev.:	Y	Law:	Y	Engineers, Other:	
International Business:	Y	Commercial/Industrial:		Graphic Arts/Photog.:	Y	Hardware Dev.:		HR/Other:	Y	Health/Lab:	
MBA Grads:	Y	Sales Trainees:	Y	Music:		Consulting/Other:		Training:	Y	Scientists/Research:	
		Advertising Pros.:	Y	Broadcasting:				Health Care:		Petroleum/Chemicals:	
				Other:	Y			Consulting:		Math/Other:	

TYPES OF BUSINESS:

Fast Food Restaurants
Franchising
Asset Management
Bakeries

BRANDS/DIVISIONS/AFFILIATES:

Arby's
Wendy's
T.J. Cinnamons
Triarc Companies, Inc.

CONTACTS: *Note: Officers with more than one job title may be intentionally listed here more than once.*

Roland C. Smith, CEO
Roland C. Smith, Pres.
Stephen E. Hare, CFO/Sr. VP
Sharron L. Barton, Sr. VP/Chief Admin. Officer
Nils H. Okeson, General Counsel/Sr. VP/Corp. Sec.
Kay Sharpton, VP-Strategic Planning
John D. Barker, Sr. VP/Chief Comm. Officer
Kay Sharpton, VP-Investor Rel.
Steven B. Graham, Chief Acct. Officer/Sr. VP
Thomas A. Garrett, Chmn./CEO-Arby's Restaurant Group, Inc.
J. David Karam, Pres., Wendy's Int'l Inc.
Nelson Peltz, Chmn.

Phone: 678-514-4500	Fax:
Toll-Free: 888-514-0924	
Address: 1155 Perimeter Center West, Atlanta, GA 30338 US	

GROWTH PLANS/SPECIAL FEATURES:

Wendy's/Arby's Group, Inc. was formed by the September 2008 merger of Triarc Companies, Inc. and Wendy's International, Inc. It is the owner and operator of over 10,000 restaurants, including 3,750 Arby's restaurants. Of these restaurants, 1,175 are company-owned and approximately 2,560 are franchised locations. Arby's is one of the largest restaurant franchising systems specializing in the roast beef sandwich segment. Other Arby's products include Market Fresh sandwiches, Jamocha shakes, wraps and salads. The company also owns the T.J. Cinnamons concept, which consists of gourmet cinnamon rolls, gourmet coffees and other related products. Of the total number of T.J. Cinnamons outlets, more than 140 are multi-braded with domestic Arby's restaurants. There are 6,600 Wendy's restaurants in operation across the U.S. and in 21 international markets. Only 1,400 are operated by the company, while 5,200 are operated by franchisees. Each Wendy's restaurant offers a standard menu featuring hamburgers and chicken breast sandwiches, prepared to order with the customer's choice of condiments, as well as chicken nuggets, chili, baked potatoes, french-fries, salads, desserts, soft drinks and children's meals. Company subsidiary The New Bakery Co., Inc., supplies buns for Wendy's operated by the company and restaurants operated by franchisees, as well as some third parties. In September 2008, Triarc Companies, Inc. and Wendy's International, Inc. completed their merger transaction and began conducting business under the Wendy's/Arby's Group, Inc. name.

FINANCIALS: Sales and profits are in thousands of dollars—add 000 to get the full amount. 2008 Note: Financial information for 2008 was not available for all companies at press time.

2008 Sales: $1,662,291	2008 Profits: $-479,741	**U.S. Stock Ticker: WEN**	
2007 Sales: $1,113,436	2007 Profits: $16,081	**Int'l Ticker:** Int'l Exchange:	
2006 Sales: $1,073,271	2006 Profits: $-10,932	Employees: 70,000	
2005 Sales: $570,800	2005 Profits: $-55,600	Fiscal Year Ends: 12/31	
2004 Sales: $205,600	2004 Profits: $13,941	Parent Company:	

SALARIES/BENEFITS:

Pension Plan:	ESOP Stock Plan:	Profit Sharing:	Top Exec. Salary: $1,000,000	Bonus: $500,000
Savings Plan: Y	Stock Purch. Plan:		Second Exec. Salary: $800,000	Bonus: $250,000

OTHER THOUGHTS:

Apparent Women Officers or Directors: 2
Hot Spot for Advancement for Women/Minorities: Y

LOCATIONS: ("Y" = Yes)

West:	Southwest:	Midwest:	Southeast:	Northeast:	International:
Y	Y	Y	Y	Y	Y

Note: Financial information, benefits and other data can change quickly and may vary from those stated here.

WEST CORPORATION

www.west.com

Industry Group Code: 56142 Ranks within this company's industry group: Sales: 1 Profits: 3

Management:		Sales/Marketing:		Liberal Arts:		Information Systems:		Professionals:		Tech./Scientific:	
Management Trainees:	Y	Marketing Pros.:	Y	Gen. Writing/Editing:	Y	Info. Management:	Y	Finance/Acct.:	Y	Engineers, Electrical:	
Experienced Mngmt.:	Y	Retail Sales:		Technical Writing:		Software Dev.:	Y	Law:	Y	Engineers, Other:	
International Business:	Y	Commercial/Industrial:	Y	Graphic Arts/Photog.:		Hardware Dev.:		HR/Other:	Y	Health/Lab:	
MBA Grads:	Y	Sales Trainees:		Music:		Consulting/Other:		Training:	Y	Scientists/Research:	
		Advertising Pros.:		Broadcasting:				Health Care:		Petroleum/Chemicals:	
				Other:				Consulting:		Math/Other:	

TYPES OF BUSINESS:

Call Centers
Voice Transaction Services
Business Process Outsourcing
Conferencing Communications
Receivables Management

BRANDS/DIVISIONS/AFFILIATES:

West Business Services
Intrado, Inc.
InterCall, Inc.
Omnium Worldwide, Inc
IntelliCast
SmartSell

CONTACTS: *Note: Officers with more than one job title may be intentionally listed here more than once.*

Thomas B. Barker, CEO
Nancee S. Berger, COO
Nancee S. Berger, Pres.
Paul M. Mendlik, CFO
Mike Sturgeon, Exec. VP-Sales & Mktg.
Mark Lavin, Chief Admin. Officer/Exec. VP
Dave Mussman, General Counsel/Sec./Exec. VP
Dave Treinen, Exec. VP-Corp. Dev. & Planning.
Steven M. Stangl, Pres., West Comm. Svcs.
Paul M. Mendlik, Treas./Exec. VP-Finance
Skip Hanson, Pres., West Telemarketing Corp.
George Heinrichs, Pres., Intrado, Inc.
Pam Mortenson, Pres., West Interactive Corp.
John Sanley, Pres., West Business Services Corp.
Thomas B. Barker, Chmn.

Phone: 402-963-1200	**Fax:** 402-963-1602
Toll-Free: 800-232-0900	
Address: 11808 Miracle Hills Dr., Omaha, NE 68154 US	

GROWTH PLANS/SPECIAL FEATURES:

West Corporation provides business process outsourcing services to many of the world's largest companies, organizations and government agencies. The firm provides a broad portfolio of voice transaction services, delivered through three segments: communication services, conferencing services and receivables management. Communication services operates through agent and automated services and offers customer acquisition, retention and care; direct response; upselling and cross-selling through SmartSell solution; business-to-business sales through West Business Services; and public safety and security through subsidiary Intrado, Inc. West's conferencing services include an integrated suite of audio, video, event and web conferencing services, including reservationless, operator-assisted conferencing. Operating through subsidiary InterCall, Inc., the firm has conferencing service facilities in the U.S., the U.K., Canada, Singapore, Australia, Hong Kong, Japan and New Zealand. The company's receivables management operations include first-party, contingent/third-party, governmental and commercial collections; revenue cycle management; debt purchasing; and collection/recovery solutions. The division caters to the financial services, insurance, healthcare and communications industries. In 2008, West's operations managed and processed more than 16.5 billion telephony minutes, over 49 million conference calls and more than 240 million 911 calls. In recent years, the firm acquired Omnium Worldwide, Inc., a provider of revenue cycle management solutions. In May 2008, the company announced plans to purchase Genesys, a leading global multimedia collaboration service provider, for approximately $345 million. In November 2008, West Corporation agreed to acquire the Command Systems division of IPC Systems, Inc., and incorporate it into its Intrado subsidiary.

West employees are offered comprehensive medical benefits; vision and dental plans; a 401K plan; disability and life insurance; a college savings plan; and the West Scholarship Program.

FINANCIALS: Sales and profits are in thousands of dollars—add 000 to get the full amount. 2008 Note: Financial information for 2008 was not available for all companies at press time.

2008 Sales: $2,247,434	2008 Profits: $19,507	**U.S. Stock Ticker:** WSTC
2007 Sales: $2,099,492	2007 Profits: $5,382	**Int'l Ticker:** Int'l Exchange:
2006 Sales: $1,856,038	2006 Profits: $68,763	Employees: 46,500
2005 Sales: $1,523,923	2005 Profits: $150,349	Fiscal Year Ends: 12/31
2004 Sales: $1,217,383	2004 Profits: $113,171	Parent Company:

SALARIES/BENEFITS:

Pension Plan:	ESOP Stock Plan:	Profit Sharing:	Top Exec. Salary: $897,500	Bonus: $1,291,800
Savings Plan: Y	Stock Purch. Plan:		Second Exec. Salary: $598,077	Bonus: $738,135

OTHER THOUGHTS:

Apparent Women Officers or Directors: 2
Hot Spot for Advancement for Women/Minorities: Y

LOCATIONS: ("Y" = Yes)

West:	Southwest:	Midwest:	Southeast:	Northeast:	International:
Y	Y	Y	Y	Y	Y

WEST PHARMACEUTICAL SERVICES INC   www.westpharma.com

Industry Group Code: 3222   Ranks within this company's industry group: Sales: 1   Profits: 1

Management:		Sales/Marketing:		Liberal Arts:		Information Systems:		Professionals:		Tech./Scientific:	
Management Trainees:	Y	Marketing Pros.:	Y	Gen. Writing/Editing:		Info. Management:	Y	Finance/Acct.:	Y	Engineers, Electrical:	
Experienced Mngmt.:	Y	Retail Sales:		Technical Writing:	Y	Software Dev.:	Y	Law:	Y	Engineers, Other:	Y
International Business:	Y	Commercial/Industrial:	Y	Graphic Arts/Photog.:	Y	Hardware Dev.:		HR/Other:	Y	Health/Lab:	Y
MBA Grads:	Y	Sales Trainees:		Music:		Consulting/Other:		Training:	Y	Scientists/Research:	Y
		Advertising Pros.:	Y	Broadcasting:				Health Care:	Y	Petroleum/Chemicals:	
				Other:				Consulting:		Math/Other:	

TYPES OF BUSINESS:

Injectable Drug Delivery Systems Components
Plastic Packaging Systems Components
Elastomer & Metal Components

BRANDS/DIVISIONS/AFFILIATES:

Medimop Medical Projects, Ltd.
West Analytical Services

CONTACTS: *Note: Officers with more than one job title may be intentionally listed here more than once.*

Donald E. Morel, Jr., CEO
Matthew T. Mullarkey, COO
Steven A. Ellers, Pres.
William J. Federici, CFO/VP
Richard D. Luzzi, VP-Human Resources
Michael A. Anderson, Treas./VP
Robert S. Hargesheimer, Pres., Tech Group
Donald A. McMillan, Pres., Americas-Pharmaceutical Systems Div.
Joseph E. Abbott, VP/Corp. Controller
Donald E. Morel, Jr., Chmn.
Robert J. Keating, Pres., Europe & Asia Pacific-Pharmaceutical Div.

Phone: 610-594-2900	Fax: 610-594-3000
Toll-Free:	
Address: 101 Gordon Dr., Lionville, PA 19341 US	

GROWTH PLANS/SPECIAL FEATURES:

West Pharmaceutical Services, Inc. manufactures components and systems for injectable drug delivery and plastic packaging and markets delivery system components for the healthcare, personal care and consumer products industries. The company's products include stoppers and seals for vials; components used in syringes; intravenous delivery systems; and blood collection systems. The firm operates in two segments: pharmaceutical systems and tech group. The pharmaceutical systems segment designs, manufactures and sells pharmaceutical packaging components and a variety of plastic, elastomer and metal components used in parenteral drug delivery. Products include elastomeric stoppers and discs; secondary closures for pharmaceutical vials; blood collection systems components; and more. Operating under this segment, Medimop Medical Projects, Ltd. provides transfer, mixing and administration systems for injectable pharmaceuticals. The firm also offers contract analytical laboratory services with support from West Analytical Services. The tech group segment is a global custom injection molder, offering contract manufacturing solutions for the healthcare and consumer industries. This segment has manufacturing operations in the U.S., Puerto Rico and Ireland. It designs and manufactures unique components for surgical, ophthalmic, diagnostic and drug delivery systems such as contact lens storage kits, pill dispensers and disposable blood collection systems and components. The Tech Group segment also has expertise in product design and development, including in-house mold design and construction, an engineering center for developmental and prototype tooling, process design and validation and high-speed automated assemblies. Technologies include multi-component molding, in-mold labeling, ultrasonic welding and clean room molding and device assembly.

The company offers employees medical, dental, life and disability coverage; a retirement plan; a stock purchase plan; an employee assistance program; education assistance; a scholarship program; and flexible spending accounts.

FINANCIALS: Sales and profits are in thousands of dollars—add 000 to get the full amount. 2008 Note: Financial information for 2008 was not available for all companies at press time.

2008 Sales: $1,051,100	2008 Profits: $86,000	U.S. Stock Ticker: WST
2007 Sales: $1,020,100	2007 Profits: $70,700	Int'l Ticker: Int'l Exchange:
2006 Sales: $913,300	2006 Profits: $67,100	Employees: 6,300
2005 Sales: $699,700	2005 Profits: $45,600	Fiscal Year Ends: 12/31
2004 Sales: $541,600	2004 Profits: $19,400	Parent Company:

SALARIES/BENEFITS:

Pension Plan: Y	ESOP Stock Plan:	Profit Sharing:	Top Exec. Salary: $811,180	Bonus: $653,400
Savings Plan: Y	Stock Purch. Plan:		Second Exec. Salary: $492,794	Bonus: $298,723

OTHER THOUGHTS:

Apparent Women Officers or Directors:
Hot Spot for Advancement for Women/Minorities:

LOCATIONS: ("Y" = Yes)

West:	Southwest:	Midwest:	Southeast:	Northeast:	International:
	Y	Y	Y	Y	Y

WESTERN DIGITAL CORP

www.westerndigital.com

Industry Group Code: 334112 Ranks within this company's industry group: Sales: 2 Profits: 2

Management:		Sales/Marketing:		Liberal Arts:		Information Systems:		Professionals:		Tech./Scientific:	
Management Trainees:	Y	Marketing Pros.:	Y	Gen. Writing/Editing:		Info. Management:	Y	Finance/Acct.:	Y	Engineers, Electrical:	Y
Experienced Mngmt.:	Y	Retail Sales:		Technical Writing:	Y	Software Dev.:	Y	Law:	Y	Engineers, Other:	
International Business:	Y	Commercial/Industrial:	Y	Graphic Arts/Photog.:	Y	Hardware Dev.:	Y	HR/Other:	Y	Health/Lab:	
MBA Grads:	Y	Sales Trainees:		Music:		Consulting/Other:		Training:	Y	Scientists/Research:	Y
		Advertising Pros.:	Y	Broadcasting:				Health Care:		Petroleum/Chemicals:	
				Other:				Consulting:		Math/Other:	Y

TYPES OF BUSINESS:

Data Storage Hardware
Hard Drives

BRANDS/DIVISIONS/AFFILIATES:

Komag Inc.
Caviar
Raptor
Scorpio
VelociRaptor
My Passport
My Book
GreenPower

CONTACTS: Note: Officers with more than one job title may be intentionally listed here more than once.

John F. Coyne, CEO
John F. Coyne, Pres.
Timothy M. Leyden, CFO/Exec. VP
Hossein M. Moghadam, CTO/Sr. VP
Raymond M. Bukaty, Sr. VP-Admin.
Raymond M. Bukaty, General Counsel/Corp. Sec.
Thomas E. Pardun, Chmn.

Phone: 949-672-7000	Fax: 949-672-5490
Toll-Free:	
Address: 20511 Lake Forest Dr., Lake Forest, CA 92630-7741 US	

GROWTH PLANS/SPECIAL FEATURES:

Western Digital Corporation is a leader in the data storage industry through hard drive manufacturing for desktop and notebook computers; enterprise applications such as servers, workstations, network attached storage, storage area networks and video surveillance equipment; and consumer electronic devices such as digital video recorders (DVRs) and satellite and cable set-top boxes. In addition, the company's hard disk drives are used in external hard disk drive products that feature high-speed buses such as FireWire, Universal Serial Bus 2.0 (USB), external Serial Advanced Technology Attachment (SATA) and Ethernet. A range of hard drives are available, including desktop hard drive, mobile hard drive and enterprise hard drive products, which the company markets under the WD Caviar, WD Raptor, WD VelociRaptor, WD Scorpio, WD Elements, My Passport, My Book, My DVR Expander and GreenPower brands. The firm also offers a line of hard drives, under the WD AV brand, designed for use in DVRs, STBs, karaoke systems, multi-function printers and gaming systems. The company's hard drives include .5-inch and 2.5-inch form factor drives, having capacities ranging from 40 gigabytes to 1 terabyte; nominal rotation speeds of 5,400, 7,200 and 10,000 revolutions per minute; and offer interfaces including both Enhanced Integrated Drive Electronics (EIDE) and SATA. Recently introduced hard drives include the GreenPower drives, designed to consume substantially less power than standard drives. Late in 2007, the firm announced its hard drive density achievement of 520 Gb/in2, the hard drive industry's highest demonstrated density using continuous media. The company has manufacturing operations in Malaysia, Thailand and California. In September 2007, the firm's wholly-owned subsidiary, State M Corporation, completed the acquisition of Komag, Inc., a manufacturer of data-recording rotating disks.

Western Digital employees receive health care benefits, dependent care and educational reimbursements and an employee assistance program.

FINANCIALS: Sales and profits are in thousands of dollars—add 000 to get the full amount. 2008 Note: Financial information for 2008 was not available for all companies at press time.

2008 Sales: $8,074,000	2008 Profits: $867,000	**U.S. Stock Ticker:** WDC	
2007 Sales: $5,468,000	2007 Profits: $564,000	**Int'l Ticker:** Int'l Exchange:	
2006 Sales: $4,341,300	2006 Profits: $395,900	Employees: 45,991	
2005 Sales: $3,638,800	2005 Profits: $198,400	Fiscal Year Ends: 6/30	
2004 Sales: $2,046,700	2004 Profits: $151,300	Parent Company:	

SALARIES/BENEFITS:

Pension Plan:	ESOP Stock Plan:	Profit Sharing: Y	Top Exec. Salary: $800,000	Bonus: $135,000
Savings Plan: Y	Stock Purch. Plan:		Second Exec. Salary: $442,904	Bonus: $84,375

OTHER THOUGHTS:

Apparent Women Officers or Directors: 1
Hot Spot for Advancement for Women/Minorities:

LOCATIONS: ("Y" = Yes)

West:	Southwest:	Midwest:	Southeast:	Northeast:	International:
Y					Y

Note: Financial information, benefits and other data can change quickly and may vary from those stated here.

WHOLE FOODS MARKET INC

www.wholefoodsmarket.com

Industry Group Code: 445110 Ranks within this company's industry group: Sales: 7 Profits: 5

Management:		Sales/Marketing:		Liberal Arts:		Information Systems:		Professionals:		Tech./Scientific:	
Management Trainees:	Y	Marketing Pros.:	Y	Gen. Writing/Editing:	Y	Info. Management:	Y	Finance/Acct.:	Y	Engineers, Electrical:	
Experienced Mngmt.:	Y	Retail Sales:	Y	Technical Writing:		Software Dev.:	Y	Law:	Y	Engineers, Other:	
International Business:	Y	Commercial/Industrial:		Graphic Arts/Photog.:	Y	Hardware Dev.:		HR/Other:	Y	Health/Lab:	
MBA Grads:	Y	Sales Trainees:	Y	Music:		Consulting/Other:		Training:	Y	Scientists/Research:	
		Advertising Pros.:	Y	Broadcasting:				Health Care:		Petroleum/Chemicals:	
				Other:	Y			Consulting:		Math/Other:	

TYPES OF BUSINESS:

Natural Foods Grocery Stores
Nutritional Supplements
Seafood Processing
Coffee Roasting

BRANDS/DIVISIONS/AFFILIATES:

365 Organic Everyday Value
365 Everyday Value
Whole Kitchen
Whole Pantry
Allegro Coffee Company
Pigeon Cove
Select Fish
Wild Oats Markets, Inc.

CONTACTS: Note: Officers with more than one job title may be intentionally listed here more than once.

John P. Mackey, CEO
Walter Robb, Co-COO/Co-Pres.
A. C. Gallo, Co-Pres./Co-COO
Glenda Chamberlain, CFO/Exec. VP
Michael Besancon, Sr. Global VP-Mktg.
Mike Clifford, CIO/VP
Roberta Lang, General Counsel/Global VP-Legal Affairs
Jim Sud, Exec. VP-Growth & Bus. Dev.
Margaret Wittenberg, Global VP-Public Affairs & Quality Standards
Cindy McCann, Global VP-Investor Rel.
Sam Ferguson, Global VP-Acct./Controller
Mark Ehrnstein, Global VP-Team Member Svcs.
Bart Beilman, Global VP-Dist.
Lee Matecko, Global VP-Construction & Store Dev.
Brian O'Connell, Global VP-Oper. Finance
John P. Mackey, Chmn.
Michael Besancon, Sr. Global VP-Purchasing & Dist.

Phone: 512-477-4455	Fax: 512-482-7000
Toll-Free:	
Address: 550 Bowie St., Austin, TX 78703 US	

GROWTH PLANS/SPECIAL FEATURES:

Whole Foods Market, Inc., owns and operates a chain of natural organic food supermarkets in the U.S. and internationally. The firm's stores generally feature foods made from natural ingredients and free of chemical additives. The company's merchandise line of over 1,500 items includes organically grown and high-grade commercial produce; grocery products; environmentally safe household items; hormone- and antibiotic-free meats; bulk foods; fresh bakery goods; soups, salads, entrees and sandwiches; vitamins; cosmetics; and miscellaneous items. Merchandise is also sold through four private-label brands: 365 Everyday Value; 365 Organic Everyday Value; and Whole Kitchen and Whole Pantry, which are chef quality, all natural foods. The company owns about 264 store locations in 38 states and Washington, D.C., as well as five stores in the U.K. and six stores in Canada. Its stores are supplemented by regional distribution centers, bakeries, commissary kitchens, seafood-processing facilities, produce procurement centers and a coffee roasting operation. The company operates a web site that offers features such as online recipes, health information and environmental issue information. The firm's subsidiaries include Allegro Coffee Company; Pigeon Cove and Select Fish, both seafood processing facilities; and Produce Field Inspection Office. In recent years, Whole Foods acquired Wild Oats Markets, Inc., an owner of 109 natural grocery stores, for $565 million. In 2008, Whole Foods opened stores in Oregon, Connecticut and Massachusetts. From fiscal 2009 through 2012, the company plans 70 store openings, including 15 relocations. Eight new markets will be entered for the first time. In late 2008, the firm received an equity injection of $425 million from the sale of preferred shares.

Whole Foods has been named one of the 100 Best Companies to Work For in America by Fortune Magazine for 12 consecutive years. Employees are offered benefits including medical, dental and vision insurance; a personal wellness account; gain sharing; and stock purchase/option plans.

FINANCIALS: Sales and profits are in thousands of dollars—add 000 to get the full amount. 2008 Note: Financial information for 2008 was not available for all companies at press time.

2008 Sales: $7,953,912	2008 Profits: $114,524	**U.S. Stock Ticker: WFMI**
2007 Sales: $6,591,773	2007 Profits: $182,740	**Int'l Ticker:** Int'l Exchange:
2006 Sales: $5,607,376	2006 Profits: $203,828	Employees: 54,000
2005 Sales: $4,701,289	2005 Profits: $136,351	Fiscal Year Ends: 9/30
2004 Sales: $3,864,950	2004 Profits: $137,113	Parent Company:

SALARIES/BENEFITS:

Pension Plan: Y	ESOP Stock Plan:	Profit Sharing: Y	Top Exec. Salary: $406,650	Bonus: $553,233
Savings Plan: Y	Stock Purch. Plan: Y		Second Exec. Salary: $394,960	Bonus: $560,388

OTHER THOUGHTS:

Apparent Women Officers or Directors: 8
Hot Spot for Advancement for Women/Minorities: Y

LOCATIONS: ("Y" = Yes)

West:	Southwest:	Midwest:	Southeast:	Northeast:	International:
Y	Y	Y	Y	Y	Y

WILLIAMS COMPANIES INC (THE)

www.williams.com

Industry Group Code: 211111 Ranks within this company's industry group: Sales: 12 Profits: 7

Management:		Sales/Marketing:		Liberal Arts:		Information Systems:		Professionals:		Tech./Scientific:	
Management Trainees:	Y	Marketing Pros.:	Y	Gen. Writing/Editing:		Info. Management:	Y	Finance/Acct.:	Y	Engineers, Electrical:	Y
Experienced Mngmt.:	Y	Retail Sales:		Technical Writing:	Y	Software Dev.:	Y	Law:	Y	Engineers, Other:	Y
International Business:	Y	Commercial/Industrial:	Y	Graphic Arts/Photog.:		Hardware Dev.:		HR/Other:	Y	Health/Lab:	
MBA Grads:	Y	Sales Trainees:		Music:		Consulting/Other:		Training:	Y	Scientists/Research:	
		Advertising Pros.:		Broadcasting:				Health Care:		Petroleum/Chemicals:	Y
				Other:				Consulting:		Math/Other:	

TYPES OF BUSINESS:

Gas Exploration & Production
Natural Gas Transportation
Pipelines
Wholesale Power

BRANDS/DIVISIONS/AFFILIATES:

Williams Production Co LLC
Williams Production RMT Co.
Williams Gas Pipeline Co LLC
Williams Field Services Group LLC
Laurel Mountain Midstream LLC
Williams Partners L.P.
Williams Power Co Inc
Transco

CONTACTS: Note: Officers with more than one job title may be intentionally listed here more than once.

Steven J. Malcomb, CEO
Steven J. Malcomb, Pres.
Don R. Chappel, CFO/Sr. VP
Ralph A. Hill, Pres., Prod.
Robyn L. Ewing, Chief Admin. Officer/Sr. VP-Admin.
James J. Bender, General Counsel/Sr. VP
Robyn L. Ewing, Sr. VP-Strategic Svcs.
Alan Armstrong, Pres., Midstream Gathering & Processing
Ralph A. Hill, Pres., Exploration
Phillip D. Wright, Pres., Gas Pipeline
Steven J. Malcolm, Chmn.

Phone: 918-573-2000	Fax: 918-573-6714
Toll-Free: 800-945-5426	
Address: 1 Williams Ctr., Tulsa, OK 74172 US	

GROWTH PLANS/SPECIAL FEATURES:

The Williams Companies, Inc., finds, produces, gathers, processes and transports natural gas. The firm operates in five segments: exploration and production; gas pipeline; midstream gas and liquids; gas marketing services; and other. The exploration and production segment produces, develops and manages natural gas reserves primarily located in the Rocky Mountain and Mid-Continent regions of the U.S. It is operated through subsidiaries such as Williams Production RMT Company and Williams Production Company LLC. The gas pipeline segment includes natural gas pipelines and pipeline joint venture investments organized under subsidiary Williams Gas Pipeline Co., LLC. The midstream and gas liquids segment includes its natural gas gathering, treating and processing business; it is comprised of several subsidiaries, including Williams Natural Gas Liquids, Inc.; Williams Field Services Group LLC; and Williams Partners L.P. The gas marketing services segment manages the firm's natural gas commodity risk through purchases, sales and other related transactions through subsidiary Williams Gas Marketing, Inc. The other segment primarily consists of corporate operations. The division includes the company's interest in Longhorn Partners Pipeline, L.P. Williams operates over 15,000 miles of interstate natural gas pipeline and has three interstate natural gas pipelines, including the Transco system. The company owns holdings in several production basins, including the Piceance Basin in Colorado, the San Juan Basin in New Mexico, the Powder River Basin in Wyoming and the Arkoma Basin in Arkansas and Oklahoma. In September 2008, the firm acquired certain assets of the Barnett Shale region from Aspect Abundant Shale LP for $147 million. In June 2009, Williams and Atlas Pipeline Partners L.P. formed joint venture Laurel Mountain Midstream LLC. In April 2009, the company agreed to build a new pipeline in Alberta, Canada. In August 2009, the firm agreed to buy 21,800 additional acres in the Piceance Valley for $258 million.

FINANCIALS: Sales and profits are in thousands of dollars—add 000 to get the full amount. 2008 Note: Financial information for 2008 was not available for all companies at press time.

2008 Sales: $12,352,000	2008 Profits: $1,418,000	U.S. Stock Ticker: WMB
2007 Sales: $10,555,800	2007 Profits: $990,000	Int'l Ticker: Int'l Exchange:
2006 Sales: $9,376,000	2006 Profits: $309,000	Employees: 4,704
2005 Sales: $12,583,600	2005 Profits: $317,400	Fiscal Year Ends: 12/31
2004 Sales: $12,461,300	2004 Profits: $93,200	Parent Company:

SALARIES/BENEFITS:

Pension Plan: Y	ESOP Stock Plan:	Profit Sharing:	Top Exec. Salary: $1,094,231	Bonus: $2,000,000
Savings Plan: Y	Stock Purch. Plan:		Second Exec. Salary: $597,115	Bonus: $780,008

OTHER THOUGHTS:

Apparent Women Officers or Directors: 4
Hot Spot for Advancement for Women/Minorities: Y

LOCATIONS: ("Y" = Yes)

West:	Southwest:	Midwest:	Southeast:	Northeast:	International:
Y	Y	Y	Y	Y	Y

WW GRAINGER INC

www.grainger.com

Industry Group Code: 4238 **Ranks within this company's industry group:** Sales: 1 Profits: 1

Management:		Sales/Marketing:		Liberal Arts:		Information Systems:		Professionals:		Tech./Scientific:	
Management Trainees:	Y	Marketing Pros.:	Y	Gen. Writing/Editing:	Y	Info. Management:	Y	Finance/Acct.:	Y	Engineers, Electrical:	
Experienced Mngmt.:	Y	Retail Sales:		Technical Writing:	Y	Software Dev.:	Y	Law:	Y	Engineers, Other:	
International Business:	Y	Commercial/Industrial:	Y	Graphic Arts/Photog.:	Y	Hardware Dev.:		HR/Other:	Y	Health/Lab:	
MBA Grads:	Y	Sales Trainees:	Y	Music:		Consulting/Other:		Training:	Y	Scientists/Research:	
		Advertising Pros.:	Y	Broadcasting:				Health Care:		Petroleum/Chemicals:	
				Other:				Consulting:		Math/Other:	

TYPES OF BUSINESS:

Industrial Equipment & Products-Wholesale
Maintenance & Repair Products
Online Sales
Safety Products
Logistics Services
Outsourcing

BRANDS/DIVISIONS/AFFILIATES:

Acklands-Grainger, Inc.
Lab Safety Supply, Inc.
Grainger Industrial Supply
Grainger, S.A. de C.V.
Grainger Caribe, Inc.
Grainger China LLC
DAYTON
SPEEDAIRE

CONTACTS: Note: Officers with more than one job title may be intentionally listed here more than once.

James T. Ryan, CEO
James T. Ryan, COO
James T. Ryan, Pres.
Ronald L. Jadin, CFO/Sr. VP
John L. Howard, General Counsel/Sr. VP
Ernest Duplessis, VP-Internal & External Comm.
Laura Brown, VP-Investor Rel.
Gregory S. Irving, Principal Acct. Officer/VP/Controller
Michael A. Pulick, Sr. VP/Pres., Grainger Industrial Supply
Larry J. Loizzo, VP-Specialty Brands/Pres., Lab Safety Supply, Inc.
C. L. Kogl, Corp. Sec.
Y.C. Chen, Int'l Advisor
James T. Ryan, Chmn.
Court Carruthers, Pres., Acklands-Grainger & Grainger S.A. de C.V
D.G. Macpherson, Sr. VP-Global Supply Chain Function

Phone: 847-535-1000	Fax: 847-535-0878
Toll-Free:	
Address: 100 Grainger Pkwy., Lake Forest, IL 60045-5201 US	

GROWTH PLANS/SPECIAL FEATURES:

W. W. Grainger, Inc. (Grainger) offers maintenance, repair and operating (MRO) products, services and information products to approximately 1.8 million businesses and institutions. The company is divided into three segments: Grainger Branch-based, Acklands-Grainger Branch-based (Acklands-Grainger) and Lab Safety Supply, Inc. (Lab Safety). The Grainger Branch-based businesses serve the MRO needs of North American businesses through 437 locations in all 50 states, catalogs and the Internet. This segment includes Grainger Industrial Supply; Grainger Panama S.A. in Panama; Grainger, S.A. de C.V. in Mexico; Grainger Caribe, Inc., in Puerto Rico; and Grainger China LLC in China. Grainger Industrial Supply serves outsourcing customers on-site business process reengineering, inventory and tool crib management, purchasing management and information management. Acklands-Grainger is one of Canada's leading broad-line distributors of industrial and safety supplies. It serves customers through 154 branches and five distribution centers across Canada. Lab Safety is a direct marketer of safety and other industrial products to businesses in Canada and the U.S., primarily reaching its customers through the distribution of multiple branded catalogs and other marketing materials distributed throughout the year to targeted markets. Lab Safety provides access to approximately 258,000 products through its targeted catalogs and distributes its products from two distribution centers. The company's registered trademarks include DAYTON, SPEEDAIRE, AIR HANDLER, DEM-KOTE, WESTWARD, CONDOR and LUMAPRO. In June 2008, Acklands-Grainger acquired Excel Industriel, a distributor of MRO supplies. In July 2008, Lab Safety acquired Highsmith, Inc., a library equipment, furniture and supplies marketer. In June 2009, Grainger agreed to acquire all remaining interest in joint venture Asia Pacific Brands India Private Ltd., an Indian industrial and electrical wholesale distributor; and agreed to purchase 53% ownership of Japanese MRO firm MonotaRO.

Employee benefits at Grainger include health, dental and vision insurance; an assistance program; adoption benefits; and a 3-for-1 matching charitable gifts program.

FINANCIALS: Sales and profits are in thousands of dollars—add 000 to get the full amount. 2008 Note: Financial information for 2008 was not available for all companies at press time.

2008 Sales: $6,850,032	2008 Profits: $475,355	**U.S. Stock Ticker:** GWW
2007 Sales: $6,418,014	2007 Profits: $420,120	**Int'l Ticker:** Int'l Exchange:
2006 Sales: $5,883,654	2006 Profits: $383,399	Employees: 18,334
2005 Sales: $5,526,636	2005 Profits: $346,324	Fiscal Year Ends: 12/31
2004 Sales: $5,049,800	2004 Profits: $286,900	Parent Company:

SALARIES/BENEFITS:

Pension Plan: Y	ESOP Stock Plan:	Profit Sharing: Y	Top Exec. Salary: $1,012,500	Bonus: $716,850
Savings Plan:	Stock Purch. Plan:		Second Exec. Salary: $787,508	Bonus: $631,125

OTHER THOUGHTS:

Apparent Women Officers or Directors: 2
Hot Spot for Advancement for Women/Minorities: Y

LOCATIONS: ("Y" = Yes)

West:	Southwest:	Midwest:	Southeast:	Northeast:	International:
Y	Y	Y	Y	Y	Y

Note: Financial information, benefits and other data can change quickly and may vary from those stated here.

WYETH

Industry Group Code: 325412 Ranks within this company's industry group: Sales: 5 Profits: 5

Management:		Sales/Marketing:		Liberal Arts:		Information Systems:		Professionals:		Tech./Scientific:	
Management Trainees:	Y	Marketing Pros.:	Y	Gen. Writing/Editing:	Y	Info. Management:	Y	Finance/Acct.:	Y	Engineers, Electrical:	Y
Experienced Mngmt.:	Y	Retail Sales:		Technical Writing:	Y	Software Dev.:	Y	Law:	Y	Engineers, Other:	Y
International Business:	Y	Commercial/Industrial:	Y	Graphic Arts/Photog.:	Y	Hardware Dev.:		HR/Other:	Y	Health/Lab:	Y
MBA Grads:	Y	Sales Trainees:	Y	Music:		Consulting/Other:		Training:	Y	Scientists/Research:	Y
		Advertising Pros.:	Y	Broadcasting:				Health Care:	Y	Petroleum/Chemicals:	Y
				Other:				Consulting:		Math/Other:	Y

TYPES OF BUSINESS:

Drugs-Diversified
Wholesale Pharmaceuticals
Animal Health Care Products
Biologicals
Vaccines
Over-the-Counter Drugs
Women's Health Care Products
Nutritional Supplements

BRANDS/DIVISIONS/AFFILIATES:

Chap Stick
Premarin
Dimetapp
Advil
Robitussin
Preparation H
Thiakis Limited
Fort Dodge Animal Health

CONTACTS: *Note: Officers with more than one job title may be intentionally listed here more than once.*

Bernard Poussot, CEO
Bernard Poussot, Pres.
Gregory Norden, CFO/Sr. VP
Denise Peppard, Sr. VP-Human Resources
Jeffrey E. Keisling, CIO/VP-Corp. Info. Svcs.
Lawrence V. Stein, General Counsel/Sr. VP
Thomas Hofstaetter, Sr. VP-Corp. Bus. Dev.
Timothy P. Cost, Sr. VP-Corp. Affairs
Justin R. Victoria, VP-Investor Rel.
Mary K. Wold, Sr. VP-Finance
Mikael Dolsten, Sr. VP
Joseph M. Mahady, Sr. VP
Leo C. Jardot, VP-Gov't Rel.
Andrew F. Davidson, VP-Internal Audit
Bernard Poussot, Chmn.

Phone: 973-660-5000	Fax: 973-660-7026
Toll-Free:	
Address: 5 Giralda Farms, Madison, NJ 07940 US	

GROWTH PLANS/SPECIAL FEATURES:

Wyeth is a global leader in pharmaceuticals, consumer health care products and animal health care products. The firm discovers, develops, manufactures, distributes and sells a diversified line of products arising from three divisions: Wyeth Pharmaceuticals, Wyeth Consumer Health care and Fort Dodge Animal Health. The pharmaceuticals segment is itself divided into women's health care, neuroscience, vaccines and infectious disease, musculoskeletal, internal medicine, hemophilia and immunology and oncology. The division sells branded and generic pharmaceuticals, biological and nutraceutical products as well as animal biological products and pharmaceuticals. Its branded products include Advil, Dimetapp, Premarin, Prempro, Premphase, Triphasil, Ativan, Effexor, Altace, Inderal, Zoton, Protonix and Enbrel. The consumer health care segment's products include analgesics, cough/cold/allergy remedies, nutritional supplements, lip balm and hemorrhoidal, antacid, asthma and other relief items sold over-the-counter. The segment's well-known over-the-counter products include Advil, cold medicines Robitussin and Dimetapp and nutritional supplement Centrum, as well as Chap Stick, Caltrate, Preparation H and Solgar. The company's animal health care products include vaccines, pharmaceuticals, endectocides (dewormers that control both internal and external parasites) and growth implants under the brand names LymeVax, Duramune and Fel-O-Vax. In December 2008, Wyeth acquired Thiakis Limited, a U.K.-based private biotechnology company for approximately $30 million. In January 2009, the firm announced its agreement to be acquired by Pfizer for $68 billion.

Employees are offered a pension plan; a 401(k) plan; child care subsidies; and educational assistance.

FINANCIALS: Sales and profits are in thousands of dollars—add 000 to get the full amount. 2008 Note: Financial information for 2008 was not available for all companies at press time.

2008 Sales: $22,833,908	2008 Profits: $4,417,833	**U.S. Stock Ticker: WYE**
2007 Sales: $22,399,798	2007 Profits: $4,615,960	Int'l Ticker: Int'l Exchange:
2006 Sales: $20,350,655	2006 Profits: $4,196,706	Employees: 47,426
2005 Sales: $18,755,790	2005 Profits: $3,656,298	Fiscal Year Ends: 12/31
2004 Sales: $17,358,028	2004 Profits: $1,233,997	Parent Company:

SALARIES/BENEFITS:

Pension Plan: Y	ESOP Stock Plan:	Profit Sharing:	Top Exec. Salary: $1,450,000	Bonus: $2,750,000
Savings Plan: Y	Stock Purch. Plan:		Second Exec. Salary: $925,000	Bonus: $1,341,000

OTHER THOUGHTS:

Apparent Women Officers or Directors: 5
Hot Spot for Advancement for Women/Minorities: Y

LOCATIONS: ("Y" = Yes)

West:	Southwest:	Midwest:	Southeast:	Northeast:	International:
Y	Y	Y	Y	Y	Y

Note: Financial information, benefits and other data can change quickly and may vary from those stated here.

WYNDHAM WORLDWIDE

www.wyndhamworldwide.com

Industry Group Code: 721110 Ranks within this company's industry group: Sales: 4   Profits: 4

Management:		Sales/Marketing:		Liberal Arts:		Information Systems:		Professionals:		Tech./Scientific:	
Management Trainees:	Y	Marketing Pros.:	Y	Gen. Writing/Editing:	Y	Info. Management:	Y	Finance/Acct.:	Y	Engineers, Electrical:	
Experienced Mngmt.:	Y	Retail Sales:		Technical Writing:		Software Dev.:	Y	Law:	Y	Engineers, Other:	
International Business:	Y	Commercial/Industrial:	Y	Graphic Arts/Photog.:	Y	Hardware Dev.:		HR/Other:	Y	Health/Lab:	
MBA Grads:	Y	Sales Trainees:	Y	Music:		Consulting/Other:		Training:	Y	Scientists/Research:	
		Advertising Pros.:	Y	Broadcasting:				Health Care:		Petroleum/Chemicals:	
				Other:	Y			Consulting:		Math/Other:	

TYPES OF BUSINESS:

Hotels, Motels & Resorts
Property Management
Hotel Development
Vacation Property Exchange and Rental
Timeshare Resorts
Franchising
Vacation Ownership

BRANDS/DIVISIONS/AFFILIATES:

Wyndham Hotels
Wingate Inns
Ramada
Days Inn
Super 8
Howard Johnson
AmeriHost
Trendwest

CONTACTS: Note: Officers with more than one job title may be intentionally listed here more than once.

Stephen P. Holmes, CEO
Virginia M. Wilson, CFO/Exec. VP
Betsy O'Rourke, Sr. VP-Mktg.
Mary R. Falvey, Exec. VP/Chief Human Resources Officer
Scott G. McLester, General Counsel/Exec. VP
Betsy O'Rourke, Sr. VP-Comm.
Nicola Rossi, Sr. VP/Chief Acct. Officer
Franz S. Hanning, Pres./CEO-Wyndham Vacation Ownership
Steven A. Rudnitsky, Pres./CEO-Wyndham Hotel Group
Geoff Ballotti, Pres./CEO-Group RCI
Tom Anderson, Exec. VP/Chief Real Estate Dev. Officer
Stephen P. Holmes, Chmn.

Phone: 973-428-9700	Fax:
Toll-Free:	
Address: 7 Sylvan Way, Parsippany, NJ 07054 US	

GROWTH PLANS/SPECIAL FEATURES:

Wyndham Worldwide (WW) is a hospitality company offering individual consumers and business customers an array of hospitality products and services as well as various accommodation alternatives and price ranges through its portfolio of world-renowned brands. The company encompasses nearly 6,500 hotels representing approximately 550,000 rooms on six continents. Wyndham Hotel Group offers the TripRewards loyalty program. Group RCI, the firm's vacation exchange business, offers its 3.6 million members access for specified periods to 67,000 vacation properties in 100 countries around the world. WW also offers Wyndham Vacation Ownership, which includes marketing and sales of vacation ownership interests, consumer financing in conjunction with the purchase of vacation ownership interests, property management services to property owners' associations and development and acquisition of vacation ownership resorts. Wyndham Vacation has approximately 145 vacation ownership resorts in U.S., Canada, Mexico, the Caribbean and the South Pacific representing over 800,000 owners of vacation ownership interests. WW's extensive portfolio of brands includes AmeriHost Inn; Baymont Inn & Suites; Days Inn; Howard Johnson; Ramada; Super 8; Travelodge; Wingate Inn; Wyndham Hotels and Resorts; Wyndham Vacation Resorts; Chez Nous; Cuendet; Novasol; RCI; Ski Life; Dansk Familiefierie; French Life; Country Cottages; Country Holidays; and Country Manors. The firm also holds 30% interest in CHI Limited; this joint venture provides management services to luxury and upscale hotels in Europe, the Middle East and Africa. The firm provided management services to 14 hotels, as of 2007, many of which were re-branded as a Wyndham brand in early 2008. In 2007, WW unveiled The Blue Harmony Spa and Fitness Experience for its Wyndham hotels and timeshare resorts. In July 2008, the company acquired the Microtel Inns & Suites and Hawthorn Suites brands.

FINANCIALS: Sales and profits are in thousands of dollars—add 000 to get the full amount. 2008 Note: Financial information for 2008 was not available for all companies at press time.

2008 Sales: $4,281,000	2008 Profits: $-1,074,000	U.S. Stock Ticker: WYN	
2007 Sales: $4,360,000	2007 Profits: $403,000	Int'l Ticker: Int'l Exchange:	
2006 Sales: $3,842,000	2006 Profits: $287,000	Employees: 27,000	
2005 Sales: $3,471,000	2005 Profits: $431,000	Fiscal Year Ends: 12/31	
2004 Sales: $3,014,000	2004 Profits: $349,000	Parent Company:	

SALARIES/BENEFITS:

Pension Plan:	ESOP Stock Plan:	Profit Sharing:	Top Exec. Salary: $1,076,355	Bonus: $
Savings Plan: Y	Stock Purch. Plan:		Second Exec. Salary: $599,470	Bonus: $2,462,000

OTHER THOUGHTS:

Apparent Women Officers or Directors: 4
Hot Spot for Advancement for Women/Minorities: Y

LOCATIONS: ("Y" = Yes)

West:	Southwest:	Midwest:	Southeast:	Northeast:	International:
Y	Y	Y	Y	Y	Y

Note: Financial information, benefits and other data can change quickly and may vary from those stated here.

WYNN RESORTS LIMITED

www.wynnresorts.com

Industry Group Code: 721120 Ranks within this company's industry group: Sales: 4 Profits: 1

Management:		Sales/Marketing:		Liberal Arts:		Information Systems:		Professionals:		Tech./Scientific:	
Management Trainees:	Y	Marketing Pros.:	Y	Gen. Writing/Editing:	Y	Info. Management:	Y	Finance/Acct.:	Y	Engineers, Electrical:	
Experienced Mngmt.:	Y	Retail Sales:		Technical Writing:		Software Dev.:	Y	Law:	Y	Engineers, Other:	
International Business:	Y	Commercial/Industrial:	Y	Graphic Arts/Photog.:	Y	Hardware Dev.:		HR/Other:	Y	Health/Lab:	
MBA Grads:	Y	Sales Trainees:	Y	Music:	Y	Consulting/Other:		Training:	Y	Scientists/Research:	
		Advertising Pros.:	Y	Broadcasting:				Health Care:		Petroleum/Chemicals:	
				Other:	Y			Consulting:		Math/Other:	

TYPES OF BUSINESS:
Hotel Casinos

BRANDS/DIVISIONS/AFFILIATES:
Wynn Las Vegas, LLC
Wynn Resorts (Macau), S.A.
Encore Suites at Wynn Las Vegas
Encore Suites at Wynn Macau

CONTACTS: *Note: Officers with more than one job title may be intentionally listed here more than once.*
Stephen A. Wynn, CEO
Marc D. Schorr, COO
Matt Maddox, CFO
Linda Chen, Pres., Wynn Int'l Mktg., Ltd.
John Strzemp, Chief Admin. Officer/Exec. VP
Kim Sinatra, General Counsel/Sec./Sr. VP
Matt Maddox, Treas.
Andrew Pascal, Pres., Wynn Las Vegas, LLC
David R. Sisk, Exec. VP/CFO-Wynn Las Vegas, LLC
Scott Peterson, CFO-Wynn Resorts (Macau), S.A.
Kazuo Okada, Vice Chmn.
Stephen A. Wynn, Chmn.
Ian M. Coughlan, Pres., Wynn Resorts (Macau), S.A.

Phone: 702-770-7555	Fax:
Toll-Free:	
Address: 3131 Las Vegas Blvd. S., Las Vegas, NV 89109 US	

GROWTH PLANS/SPECIAL FEATURES:
Wynn Resorts Limited is a leading developer, owner and operator of destination casino resorts. It owns and operates three destination casino resorts: The Wynn Las Vegas on the Strip in Las Vegas, Nevada; Encore Suites, adjacent to Wynn Las Vegas; and the Wynn Macau in the Macau Special Administrative Region of China. The firm is currently constructing Encore at Wynn Macau, an extension of Wynn Macao. Wynn Las Vegas offers 2,716 rooms and suites. The approximately 111,000-square-foot casino features 135 table games, a baccarat salon, private VIP gaming rooms, a poker room, approximately 1,935 slot machines, and a race and sports book. The resort's 22 food and beverage outlets feature six fine dining restaurants, including three that have been awarded Michelin stars. Other amenities include two nightclubs; a spa and salon; a Ferrari and Maserati automobile dealership; wedding chapels; an 18-hole golf course; approximately 223,000 square feet of meeting space; and an approximately 74,000-square-foot retail promenade featuring boutiques from Alexander McQueen, Cartier, Chanel, Louis Vuitton and Vertu. Wynn Las Vegas also has a showroom, The Le Reve Theater. The Wynn Macau features approximately 600 hotel rooms and suites; 370 table games, 1,250 slot machines and a poker room; five restaurants; a spa and salon; lounges; meeting facilities; and approximately 46,000 square feet of retail space. The new 2,034-suite Encore resort opened in December 2008, next door to the Wynn Las Vegas, at an investment of $2.3 billion. It includes an approximately 72,000-square-foot casino with 95 table games, a baccarat salon, 835 slot machines and a sports book. Encore also features 12 food and beverage outlets; a night club; a spa and salon; meeting space; and upscale retail outlets, as well as The Encore Theater. Long term, the firm hopes to develop a 1.5 million square foot convention center and a total of 10,000 rooms in its Las Vegas complex.

Wynn Resorts offers its employees financial assistance with continuing education, an employee assistance program, health and life insurance and assistance in preparing for the U.S. Citizenship test.

FINANCIALS: Sales and profits are in thousands of dollars—add 000 to get the full amount. 2008 Note: Financial information for 2008 was not available for all companies at press time.

2008 Sales: $2,987,324	2008 Profits: $210,206	U.S. Stock Ticker: WYNN
2007 Sales: $2,687,519	2007 Profits: $258,148	Int'l Ticker: Int'l Exchange:
2006 Sales: $1,432,257	2006 Profits: $628,728	Employees: 20,600
2005 Sales: $721,981	2005 Profits: $-90,836	Fiscal Year Ends: 12/31
2004 Sales: $ 195	2004 Profits: $-204,171	Parent Company:

SALARIES/BENEFITS:
Pension Plan:	ESOP Stock Plan:	Profit Sharing:	Top Exec. Salary: $3,250,000	Bonus: $4,062,500
Savings Plan: Y	Stock Purch. Plan:		Second Exec. Salary: $1,947,115	Bonus: $2,000,000

OTHER THOUGHTS:
Apparent Women Officers or Directors: 4
Hot Spot for Advancement for Women/Minorities: Y

LOCATIONS: ("Y" = Yes)
West:	Southwest:	Midwest:	Southeast:	Northeast:	International:
Y					Y

XEROX CORP

www.xerox.com

Industry Group Code: 333313 **Ranks within this company's industry group:** Sales: 1   Profits: 2

Management:		Sales/Marketing:		Liberal Arts:		Information Systems:		Professionals:		Tech./Scientific:	
Management Trainees:	Y	Marketing Pros.:	Y	Gen. Writing/Editing:	Y	Info. Management:	Y	Finance/Acct.:	Y	Engineers, Electrical:	Y
Experienced Mngmt.:	Y	Retail Sales:		Technical Writing:	Y	Software Dev.:	Y	Law:	Y	Engineers, Other:	Y
International Business:	Y	Commercial/Industrial:	Y	Graphic Arts/Photog.:	Y	Hardware Dev.:	Y	HR/Other:	Y	Health/Lab:	
MBA Grads:	Y	Sales Trainees:	Y	Music:		Consulting/Other:		Training:	Y	Scientists/Research:	Y
		Advertising Pros.:	Y	Broadcasting:				Health Care:		Petroleum/Chemicals:	
				Other:				Consulting:		Math/Other:	

TYPES OF BUSINESS:

Business Machines-Copiers, Printers & Scanners
Managed Print Services Outsourcing
Software
Multipurpose Office Machines
Consulting Services
Desktop Printers

BRANDS/DIVISIONS/AFFILIATES:

Fuji Xerox
DocuColor
CopyCentre
Xerox Canada Inc
Palo Alto Research Center
Global Imaging Systems Inc
Advectis Inc
Image Quest Inc

CONTACTS: *Note: Officers with more than one job title may be intentionally listed here more than once.*

Ursula M. Burns, CEO
Ursula M. Burns, Pres.
Lawrence A. Zimmerman, CFO/Corp. Exec. VP
Michael C. Mac Donald, Sr. VP/Pres., Mktg. Oper.
Patricia M. Nazemetz, Chief Human Resources & Ethics Officer/VP
John McDermott, CIO/VP
Sophie V. Vandebroek, CTO/VP/Pres., Xerox Innovation Group
Anthony M. Federico, Chief Engineer
Don Liu, General Counsel/Sr. VP/Sec.
James A. Firestone, Corp. Exec. VP-Corporate Oper.
Eric Armour, Corp. VP-Strategy
James H. Lesko, VP-Investor Rel.
Gary R. Kabureck, Chief Acct. Officer/VP
John M. Kelly, Corp. VP-Xerox Global Services North America
Jean-Noel Machon, Sr. VP/Pres., Developing Markets Oper.
Jule Limoli, Pres., North American Agent Oper.
Rick Dastin, Pres., Xerox Office Group
Anne M. Mulcahy, Chmn.
Eric Armour, Pres., Global Bus. & Strategic Mktg. Group

Phone: 203-968-3000	**Fax:** 203-968-3944
Toll-Free:	
Address: 45 Glober Ave., P.O. Box 4505, Norwalk, CT 06856 US	

GROWTH PLANS/SPECIAL FEATURES:

Xerox Corp. is a technology and services company operating in the global document market. It operates in four segments: Production, Office, Developing Markets Operations (DMO) and Services/Paper/Other. The Production segment manufactures high-end digital monochrome and color systems designed for customers in the graphic communications industry and for large enterprises. These products enable digital on-demand printing, digital full-color printing and enterprise printing. The division offers a complete family of monochrome production systems from 65-288 pages per minute (ppm) and color production systems from 40-110 ppm. Additionally, it offers a variety of pre-press and post-press options, as well as workflow software. The Office segment's systems and services, which offer monochrome devices at speeds up to 95 ppm and color devices up to 60 ppm, include the family of CopyCentre, WorkCentre and WorkCentre Pro digital multifunction systems; DocuColor printer/copiers; color laser, LED (light emitting diode), solid ink and monochrome laser desktop printers; digital copiers; and light-lens copiers and facsimile products. The DMO segment includes the marketing, sales and servicing of Xerox products, supplies and services around the world. The Services/Paper/Other segment primarily includes revenue from paper sales, value-added services and wide-format systems. This unit includes managed print services, an outsourcing service where Xerox assumes complete ownership and/or operation of a client company's desktop printers, copiers and similar machines, with a goal of saving the client up to 30% in yearly costs. Xerox received about 20% of its 2008 revenues from managed print services. Fuji Xerox, an unconsolidated entity of which Xerox owns 25%, develops, manufactures and distributes document management system, supplies and services. In 2007, Xerox acquired Global Imaging Systems, Inc. for $1.46 billion. In 2008, Global Imaging Systems acquired Precision Copier Service, Inc.; Saxon Business Systems; and Sierra Office Solutions. In 2009, the subsidiary completed its acquisition of ComDoc, a dealer of document management systems.

The company offers its employees medical and dental insurance; an employee assistance program; and tuition reimbursement.

FINANCIALS: Sales and profits are in thousands of dollars—add 000 to get the full amount. 2008 Note: Financial information for 2008 was not available for all companies at press time.

2008 Sales: $17,608,000	2008 Profits: $230,000	**U.S. Stock Ticker:** XRX
2007 Sales: $17,228,000	2007 Profits: $1,135,000	**Int'l Ticker:** Int'l Exchange:
2006 Sales: $15,895,000	2006 Profits: $1,210,000	Employees: 57,100
2005 Sales: $15,701,000	2005 Profits: $978,000	Fiscal Year Ends: 12/31
2004 Sales: $15,722,000	2004 Profits: $859,000	Parent Company:

SALARIES/BENEFITS:

Pension Plan:	ESOP Stock Plan:	Profit Sharing:	Top Exec. Salary: $1,320,000	Bonus: $990,000
Savings Plan: Y	Stock Purch. Plan:		Second Exec. Salary: $887,500	Bonus: $554,688

OTHER THOUGHTS:

Apparent Women Officers or Directors: 6
Hot Spot for Advancement for Women/Minorities: Y

LOCATIONS: ("Y" = Yes)

West:	Southwest:	Midwest:	Southeast:	Northeast:	International:
Y	Y	Y	Y	Y	Y

Note: Financial information, benefits and other data can change quickly and may vary from those stated here.

YAHOO! INC

www.yahoo.com

Industry Group Code: 519130 Ranks within this company's industry group: Sales: 2   Profits: 2

Management:		Sales/Marketing:		Liberal Arts:		Information Systems:		Professionals:		Tech./Scientific:	
Management Trainees:	Y	Marketing Pros.:	Y	Gen. Writing/Editing:	Y	Info. Management:	Y	Finance/Acct.:	Y	Engineers, Electrical:	Y
Experienced Mngmt.:	Y	Retail Sales:		Technical Writing:	Y	Software Dev.:	Y	Law:	Y	Engineers, Other:	
International Business:	Y	Commercial/Industrial:	Y	Graphic Arts/Photog.:	Y	Hardware Dev.:	Y	HR/Other:	Y	Health/Lab:	
MBA Grads:	Y	Sales Trainees:		Music:		Consulting/Other:		Training:	Y	Scientists/Research:	
		Advertising Pros.:	Y	Broadcasting:				Health Care:		Petroleum/Chemicals:	
				Other:	Y			Consulting:		Math/Other:	

TYPES OF BUSINESS:

Online Portal-Search Engine
Broadcast Media
Job Placement Services
Paid Positioning Services
Advertising Services
Online Business & Consumer Information
Search Technology Licensing
E-Commerce

BRANDS/DIVISIONS/AFFILIATES:

Yahoo.com
Yahoo! Mail
Yahoo! Messenger
Yahoo! Distribution of Hadoop
Yahoo! News
HotJobs.com, Ltd.
Yahoo! Finance
Yahoo! Sports

CONTACTS: *Note: Officers with more than one job title may be intentionally listed here more than once.*

Carol Bartz, CEO
Timothy R. Morse, CFO/Exec. VP
Elisa Steele, Chief Mktg. Officer/Exec. VP
David Windley, Chief Human Resources Officer/Exec. VP
Aristotle Balogh, CTO
Aristotle Balogh, Exec. VP-Prod.
David Dibble, Exec. VP-Svc. Eng.
Michael J. Callahan, General Counsel/Exec. VP/Sec.
David Dibble, Exec. VP-Oper.
Eric C. Brown, Sr. VP-Global Comm.
Michael A. Murray, Sr. VP-Finance/Chief Acct. Officer
Penny Baldwin, Sr. VP-Global Integrated Mktg. & Brand Mgmt.
Hilary Schneider, Exec. VP-North America
Jeff Russakow, Exec. VP-Customer Advocacy
Joanne K. Bradford, Sr. VP-U.S. Revenue & Market Dev.
Roy J. Bostock, Chmn.
Rich Riley, Sr. VP-Europe & Canada

Phone: 408-349-3300	Fax: 408-349-3301
Toll-Free:	
Address: 701 First Ave., Sunnyvale, CA 94089 US	

GROWTH PLANS/SPECIAL FEATURES:

Yahoo!, Inc. is a provider of online products and services to consumers and businesses worldwide. For users, the company's offerings fall into six categories: Front Doors, such as Yahoo! Front Page and Yahoo! Toolbar; Search through Yahoo! Search, Yahoo! Yellow Pages, Yahoo! Maps and Yahoo! Local; Communications through Yahoo! Mail, Zimbra Mail, and Yahoo! Messenger; Communities such as Yahoo! Groups and Yahoo! Answers; Audience, including Yahoo! News, Yahoo! Finance and Yahoo! Sports; and Connected Life through Yahoo! Mobile and Yahoo! Connected TV. The majority of these offerings are available in over 30 languages. For advertisers and publishers, Yahoo! provides a range of marketing solutions and tools that enable businesses to reach users who visit Yahoo! Properties and its Affiliate sites. For developers, Yahoo provides an innovative and easily accessible array of Web Services and Application Programming Interfaces (APIs), technical resources, tools, and channels to market. Yahoo! is present in over 30 markets in Europe, Latin America, Asia Pacific and North America. The company has entered into relationships with business partners that offer content, technology and distribution capabilities, which permit the company to bring Yahoo!-branded, targeted media products to the market more quickly. The company also operates HotJobs.com, Ltd., a leading Internet job placement and recruiting company. In June 2009, the firm released Yahoo! Distribution of Hadoop, a distributed file program that allows for the processing of massive amounts of data, and released Yahoo! Mobile experience in nine additional countries. In July 2009, Yahoo! launched Search Pad beta, a program that aids those doing extensive online research by capturing, organizing, saving and sharing information during searches. Also in July 2009, the firm and Microsoft Corp. agreed to a deal by which Microsoft's Bing search engine will replace the Yahoo! Search Engine on all Yahoo! web pages, while Yahoo! will handle all of the search advertising for both firms.

FINANCIALS: Sales and profits are in thousands of dollars—add 000 to get the full amount. 2008 Note: Financial information for 2008 was not available for all companies at press time.

2008 Sales: $7,208,502	2008 Profits: $424,298	**U.S. Stock Ticker: YHOO**
2007 Sales: $6,969,274	2007 Profits: $660,000	**Int'l Ticker:** Int'l Exchange:
2006 Sales: $6,425,679	2006 Profits: $751,391	Employees: 13,600
2005 Sales: $5,257,668	2005 Profits: $1,896,230	Fiscal Year Ends: 12/31
2004 Sales: $3,575,000	2004 Profits: $839,553	Parent Company:

SALARIES/BENEFITS:

Pension Plan:	ESOP Stock Plan:	Profit Sharing:	Top Exec. Salary: $815,000	Bonus: $611,250
Savings Plan: Y	Stock Purch. Plan: Y		Second Exec. Salary: $487,500	Bonus: $250,000

OTHER THOUGHTS:

Apparent Women Officers or Directors: 6
Hot Spot for Advancement for Women/Minorities: Y

LOCATIONS: ("Y" = Yes)

West:	Southwest:	Midwest:	Southeast:	Northeast:	International:
Y					Y

YUM! BRANDS INC

www.yum.com

Industry Group Code: 722110 **Ranks within this company's industry group:** Sales: 2 Profits: 2

Management:		Sales/Marketing:		Liberal Arts:		Information Systems:		Professionals:		Tech./Scientific:	
Management Trainees:	Y	Marketing Pros.:	Y	Gen. Writing/Editing:	Y	Info. Management:	Y	Finance/Acct.:	Y	Engineers, Electrical:	
Experienced Mngmt.:	Y	Retail Sales:		Technical Writing:		Software Dev.:	Y	Law:	Y	Engineers, Other:	
International Business:	Y	Commercial/Industrial:		Graphic Arts/Photog.:	Y	Hardware Dev.:		HR/Other:	Y	Health/Lab:	
MBA Grads:	Y	Sales Trainees:		Music:		Consulting/Other:		Training:	Y	Scientists/Research:	
		Advertising Pros.:	Y	Broadcasting:				Health Care:		Petroleum/Chemicals:	
				Other:	Y			Consulting:		Math/Other:	

TYPES OF BUSINESS:

Fast Food Restaurants

BRANDS/DIVISIONS/AFFILIATES:

Pizza Hut
KFC
Taco Bell
Long John Silver's
A&W All-American Food
Yum! Restaurants International
Yum! China
Internacional Restaurantes do Brasil

CONTACTS: *Note: Officers with more than one job title may be intentionally listed here more than once.*

David C. Novak, CEO
Emil J. Brolick, COO
David C. Novak, Pres.
Richard T. Carucci, CFO
Anne P. Byerlein, Chief People Officer
Christian L. Campbell, General Counsel/Sr. VP/Sec.
Emil J. Brolick, Chief Dev. Officer
Jonathan D. Blum, Chief Public Affairs Officer
Timothy P. Jerzyk, Sr. VP-Investor Rel./Treas.
Ted F. Knopf, Sr. VP-Finance/Corp. Controller
Scott O. Bergren, Pres./Chief Concept Officer-Pizza Hut
Roger Eaton, Pres./Chief Concept Officer-KFC
Greg Creed, Pres./Chief Concept Officer-Taco Bell
Jing-Shyh S. Su, Pres., Yum! China Div.
David C. Novak, Chmn.
Graham D. Allan, Pres., Yum Restaurants Int'l

Phone: 502-874-8300	Fax: 502-874-8790
Toll-Free:	
Address: 1441 Gardiner Ln., Louisville, KY 40213 US	

GROWTH PLANS/SPECIAL FEATURES:

Yum! Brands, Inc., is a fast-food restaurant company with over 36,000 restaurants in more than 110 countries and territories. The firm is divided into six operating companies, organized around five restaurant chains: KFC, Pizza Hut, Taco Bell, A&W and Long John Silver's. Through these concepts, the company develops, operates, franchises and licenses a system of restaurants that operate, package and sell a menu of competitively priced food items. The restaurants are operated by the company, independent third-party franchisees, or by affiliates in which it owns a non-controlling equity interest. In all five chains, customers are offered dine in and carry out options; all but Pizza Hut offer drive-through options at certain locations. Yum! Brand's International Division comprises roughly 13,000 restaurants, which are primarily KFCs and Pizza Huts. The China Division has approximately 3,600 restaurants which are predominantly KFCs. Mainland China is the company's biggest market for new company restaurant development. KFC, Pizza Hut, Taco Bell and Long John Silver's are global leaders, respectively, in the chicken, pizza, Mexican-style and seafood fast-food segments. The company firm also utilizes multi-branding, where at least two of its restaurants are operated as a single unit. Yum! Brands owns approximately 4,958 multibranded locations worldwide, of which 4,629 are in the U.S. In August 2008, Yum! Brand's Brazilian Pizza Hut franchise, Internacional Restaurantes do Brasil, sold 60% of its shares to Brazil Fast Food Corp. In March 2009, Yum! Brands opened a new KFC-Taco Bell restaurant in Massachusetts. The location was designed to reduce CO_2 emissions; use 30 percent less energy and water than a conventional building; and lessen the amount of waste being sent to landfills and incinerators.

Yum! offers its employees benefits including life, disability, medical, dental, vision and hearing insurance; flexible spending accounts; an assistance program; discount programs; and tuition reimbursement.

FINANCIALS: Sales and profits are in thousands of dollars—add 000 to get the full amount. 2008 Note: Financial information for 2008 was not available for all companies at press time.

2008 Sales: $11,279,000	2008 Profits: $964,000	**U.S. Stock Ticker:** YUM
2007 Sales: $10,416,000	2007 Profits: $909,000	**Int'l Ticker:** Int'l Exchange:
2006 Sales: $9,561,000	2006 Profits: $824,000	Employees: 336,000
2005 Sales: $9,349,000	2005 Profits: $762,000	Fiscal Year Ends: 12/31
2004 Sales: $9,011,000	2004 Profits: $740,000	Parent Company:

SALARIES/BENEFITS:

Pension Plan:	ESOP Stock Plan:	Profit Sharing:	Top Exec. Salary: $1,393,846	Bonus: $4,057,200
Savings Plan: Y	Stock Purch. Plan: Y		Second Exec. Salary: $769,231	Bonus: $1,609,598

OTHER THOUGHTS:

Apparent Women Officers or Directors: 3
Hot Spot for Advancement for Women/Minorities: Y

LOCATIONS: ("Y" = Yes)

West:	Southwest:	Midwest:	Southeast:	Northeast:	International:
Y	Y	Y	Y	Y	Y

Note: Financial information, benefits and other data can change quickly and may vary from those stated here.

ZIMMER HOLDINGS INC

www.zimmer.com

Industry Group Code: 33911 Ranks within this company's industry group: Sales: 8 Profits: 6

Management:		Sales/Marketing:		Liberal Arts:		Information Systems:		Professionals:		Tech./Scientific:	
Management Trainees:	Y	Marketing Pros.:	Y	Gen. Writing/Editing:	Y	Info. Management:	Y	Finance/Acct.:	Y	Engineers, Electrical:	
Experienced Mngmt.:	Y	Retail Sales:		Technical Writing:	Y	Software Dev.:	Y	Law:	Y	Engineers, Other:	Y
International Business:	Y	Commercial/Industrial:	Y	Graphic Arts/Photog.:	Y	Hardware Dev.:		HR/Other:	Y	Health/Lab:	Y
MBA Grads:	Y	Sales Trainees:	Y	Music:		Consulting/Other:		Training:	Y	Scientists/Research:	
		Advertising Pros.:	Y	Broadcasting:				Health Care:	Y	Petroleum/Chemicals:	
				Other:				Consulting:		Math/Other:	

TYPES OF BUSINESS:

Orthopedic Supplies
Orthopedic Reconstructive Implants
Dental Implants
Spinal Surgery Products
Trauma Management Products
Orthopedic Surgical Products
Orthobiological Products
Healthcare Consulting

BRANDS/DIVISIONS/AFFILIATES:

NexGen
VerSys
Anatomical Shoulder
Tapered Screw-Vent
Puros
CopiOs
Pulsavac Plus
Abbott Spine

CONTACTS: Note: Officers with more than one job title may be intentionally listed here more than once.

David C. Dvorak, CEO
David C. Dvorak, Pres.
James T. Crines, CFO/Exec. VP-Finance
David Weidenbenner, Sr. VP-Global Mktg.
Renee Rogers, VP-Global Human Resources
Cheryl R. Blanchard, Sr. VP-R&D/Chief Scientific Officer
Chad F. Phipps, General Counsel/Sec./Sr. VP
Richard C. Stair, Sr. VP-Global Oper.
Paul G. Blair, VP-Investor Rel.
Derek Davis, VP-Finance/Corp. Controller/Chief Acct. Officer
Jeffery A. McCaulley, Pres., Zimmer Reconstructive
Jon E. Kramer, Pres., U.S. Sales
Stephen H. L. Ooi, Pres., Asia Pacific
Laura O'Donnell, Chief Compliance Officer
John L. McGoldrick, Chmn.
Bruno A. Melzi, Chmn.-EMEA
Richard C. Stair, Sr. VP-Logistics

Phone: 574-267-6131	Fax:
Toll-Free: 800-613-6131	
Address: 345 E. Main St., Warsaw, IN 46580 US	

GROWTH PLANS/SPECIAL FEATURES:

Zimmer Holdings, Inc., founded in 1927, primarily designs, develops, manufactures and markets implants and related surgical products. Zimmer's main products comprise orthopedic reconstructive implants, spine products, trauma products and orthopedic surgical products. Orthopedic reconstructive implants include: knee replacement products, including NexGen and Natural-Knee II; hip implants, VerSys and Fitmore; extremity implants, Anatomical Shoulder and Coonrad/Morrey Total Elbow; dental reconstructive implants, Tapered Screw-Vent tooth implants; dental restorative products, Zimmer Hex-Lock abutments; and dental regenerative products, Puros allograft materials. Spine products cover stabilization equipment for spinal surgery, implants for correcting spinal deformations (including scoliosis) and CopiOs bone void filler. Trauma products are used primarily to reattach or stabilize damaged bone or tissue to support the body's natural healing process. Specific products include Zimmer Universal Locking System plates and the Zimmer Intertrochanteric/Subtrochanteric (ITST) Nailing System, a hip fracture treatment. Lastly, orthopedic surgical products include the Pulsavac Plus wound cleaning and debridement (dead tissue removal) system and the Automatic Tourniquet System (ATS). Besides the above-mentioned products, Zimmer develops orthobiological materials, including tissue regeneration products, and it also provides hospital-focused consulting services to help member institutions design, implement and manage orthopedic programs. Its primary customers include musculoskeletal surgeons, neurosurgeons, oral surgeons, dentists, hospitals, distributors, healthcare dealers and healthcare purchasing organizations or buying groups. Zimmer has operations in over 25 countries and markets its products in 100 countries. The Americas generated the majority (57%) of 2008 net sales, followed by Europe (29%) and Asia-Pacific (14%). In October 2008, the firm acquired Abbott Spine from Abbott Laboratories for $360 million, improving not only its spinal product line-up but also its spine-related research and development capabilities.

Zimmer offers its employees medical, dental and vision care plans; life and AD&D insurance; flexible spending accounts; disability income protection plans; an employee stock purchase plan; paid time off; and tuition reimbursement.

FINANCIALS: Sales and profits are in thousands of dollars—add 000 to get the full amount. 2008 Note: Financial information for 2008 was not available for all companies at press time.

2008 Sales: $4,121,100	2008 Profits: $848,600	U.S. Stock Ticker: ZMH
2007 Sales: $3,897,500	2007 Profits: $773,200	Int'l Ticker: Int'l Exchange:
2006 Sales: $3,495,400	2006 Profits: $834,500	Employees: 8,500
2005 Sales: $3,286,100	2005 Profits: $732,500	Fiscal Year Ends: 12/31
2004 Sales: $2,980,900	2004 Profits: $541,800	Parent Company:

SALARIES/BENEFITS:

Pension Plan:	ESOP Stock Plan:	Profit Sharing:	Top Exec. Salary: $742,308	Bonus: $691,350
Savings Plan: Y	Stock Purch. Plan:		Second Exec. Salary: $586,114	Bonus: $301,731

OTHER THOUGHTS:

Apparent Women Officers or Directors: 4
Hot Spot for Advancement for Women/Minorities: Y

LOCATIONS: ("Y" = Yes)

West:	Southwest:	Midwest:	Southeast:	Northeast:	International:
Y	Y	Y	Y	Y	Y

Note: Financial information, benefits and other data can change quickly and may vary from those stated here.

ADDITIONAL INDEXES

CONTENTS:

INDEX OF FIRMS NOTED AS HOT SPOTS FOR ADVANCEMENT FOR WOMEN & MINORITIES

3M COMPANY
7-ELEVEN INC
ABBOTT LABORATORIES
ABM INDUSTRIES INC
ACCENTURE LTD
ACTIVISION BLIZZARD INC
ACXIOM CORP
ADC TELECOMMUNICATIONS INC
ADESA INC
ADOBE SYSTEMS INC
ADVANCE AUTO PARTS INC
AECOM TECHNOLOGY
CORPORATION
AES CORPORATION (THE)
AETNA INC
AFFILIATED COMPUTER SERVICES
INC
AFLAC INC
AGILENT TECHNOLOGIES INC
AIR PRODUCTS & CHEMICALS INC
ALLERGAN INC
ALLSTATE CORPORATION (THE)
ALTRIA GROUP INC
AMAZON.COM INC
AMEDISYS INC
AMERICAN ELECTRIC POWER
COMPANY INC (AEP)
AMERISOURCEBERGEN CORP
AMGEN INC
ANADARKO PETROLEUM
CORPORATION
ANNTAYLOR STORES CORP
APACHE CORP
APOLLO GROUP INC
ARCHER DANIELS MIDLAND CO
ARROW ELECTRONICS INC
ARTHUR J GALLAGHER & CO
ASCENSION HEALTH
AT&T INC
AUTOMATIC DATA PROCESSING INC
AUTOZONE INC
AVERY DENNISON CORP
AVIS BUDGET GROUP INC
AVNET INC
AVON PRODUCTS INC
AXA FINANCIAL INC
BAKER HUGHES INC
BALTIMORE GAS AND ELECTRIC
COMPANY
BANK OF AMERICA CORP
BARNES & NOBLE INC
BASS PRO SHOPS INC
BAXTER INTERNATIONAL INC
BEBE STORES INC
BECHTEL GROUP INC
BECKMAN COULTER INC
BECTON DICKINSON & CO
BED BATH & BEYOND INC

BERKSHIRE HATHAWAY INC
BEST BUY CO INC
BIO RAD LABORATORIES INC
BJ'S WHOLESALE CLUB INC
BLACK & DECKER CORP
BLACKROCK INC
BLOOMBERG LP
BOEING COMPANY (THE)
BOSTON SCIENTIFIC CORP
BRINKER INTERNATIONAL INC
BROWN & BROWN INC
BUCKLE INC (THE)
BUFFALO WILD WINGS INC
BURGER KING HOLDINGS INC
CABLEVISION SYSTEMS CORP
CACI INTERNATIONAL INC
CARDINAL HEALTH INC
CARGILL INC
CARMAX GROUP
CARNIVAL CORPORATION
CATERPILLAR INC
CATHOLIC HEALTH INITIATIVES
CDW CORPORATION
CELLCO PARTNERSHIP (VERIZON
WIRELESS)
CH ROBINSON WORLDWIDE INC
CH2M HILL COMPANIES LTD
CHARLOTTE RUSSE HOLDING
CHARMING SHOPPES INC
CHEMED CORPORATION
CHEVRON CORPORATION
CHEVRON PHILLIPS CHEMICAL
COMPANY LLC
CHICO'S FAS INC
CHRISTOPHER & BANKS CORP
CHUBB CORPORATION (THE)
CIBER INC
CIGNA CORP
CISCO SYSTEMS INC
CLUBCORP INC
COACH INC
COCA-COLA COMPANY (THE)
COCA-COLA ENTERPRISES INC
COLDWATER CREEK INC
COLGATE PALMOLIVE CO
COMCAST CORP
COMMUNITY HEALTH SYSTEMS INC
CONAGRA FOODS INC
CONOCOPHILLIPS COMPANY
CONSOL ENERGY INC
CONSOLIDATED EDISON INC
COOPER COMPANIES INC
COSTCO WHOLESALE CORP
COVANCE INC
COVENTRY HEALTH CARE INC
COX COMMUNICATIONS INC
CR BARD INC
CRACKER BARREL OLD COUNTRY
STORE INC
CUMMINS INC
CVS CAREMARK CORPORATION
DARDEN RESTAURANTS INC
DAVITA INC
DEAN FOODS CO
DEERE & CO

DENNY'S CORPORATION
DEVON ENERGY CORPORATION
DEVRY INC
DICK'S SPORTING GOODS INC
DIEBOLD INC
DINEEQUITY INC
DOLLAR GENERAL CORPORATION
DOLLAR THRIFTY AUTOMOTIVE
GROUP INC
DRESS BARN INC (THE)
DTE ENERGY COMPANY
DUKE ENERGY CORP
E I DU PONT DE NEMOURS & CO
(DUPONT)
EATON CORP
EBAY INC
EDISON INTERNATIONAL
ELECTRONIC ARTS INC
ELI LILLY & COMPANY
EMBARQ CORP
EMC CORP
EMERITUS CORP
EMERSON ELECTRIC CO
ENTERGY CORP
ENTERPRISE RENT-A-CAR
ESTEE LAUDER COMPANIES INC
(THE)
EXELON CORPORATION
EXPRESS SCRIPTS INC
EXXON MOBIL CORPORATION
(EXXONMOBIL)
FAMILY DOLLAR STORES INC
FEDEX CORPORATION
FINISH LINE INC (THE)
FIRST ADVANTAGE CORPORATION
FIRSTENERGY CORP
FLUOR CORP
FOREST LABORATORIES INC
FORTUNE BRANDS INC
FOSSIL INC
FOSTER WHEELER AG
FPL GROUP INC
FRONTIER COMMUNICATIONS
CORPORATION
FTI CONSULTING INC
GENENTECH INC
GENERAL DYNAMICS CORP
GENERAL ELECTRIC CO (GE)
GENERAL MILLS INC
GENESCO INC
GENWORTH FINANCIAL INC
GILEAD SCIENCES INC
GLOBAL HYATT CORPORATION
GLOBAL PAYMENTS INC
GOLDMAN SACHS GROUP INC
GOOGLE INC
GRANT THORNTON LLP
GUESS? INC
HALLIBURTON COMPANY
HARRAH'S ENTERTAINMENT INC
HARRIS CORPORATION
HARTFORD FINANCIAL SERVICES
GROUP INC (THE)
HAWAIIAN ELECTRIC INDUSTRIES
INC

HCA INC
HE BUTT GROCERY COMPANY (HEB)
HEALTH CARE SERVICE CORPORATION
HEALTH FITNESS CORP
HEALTH MANAGEMENT ASSOCIATES INC
HEALTH NET INC
HEALTHWAYS INC
HENRY SCHEIN INC
HERTZ GLOBAL HOLDINGS INC
HESS CORPORATION
HEWITT ASSOCIATES
HILTON HOTELS CORP
HOME DEPOT INC
HONEYWELL INTERNATIONAL INC
HUMANA INC
IAC/INTERACTIVECORP
IBM GLOBAL SERVICES
ICT GROUP INC
IDEXX LABORATORIES INC
IGATE CORPORATION
IMS HEALTH INC
INGRAM MICRO INC
INTEL CORP
INTERNATIONAL BUSINESS MACHINES CORP (IBM)
INTUIT INC
J C PENNEY COMPANY INC
JABIL CIRCUIT INC
JACK IN THE BOX INC
JACOBS ENGINEERING GROUP INC
JETBLUE AIRWAYS CORPORATION
JM SMUCKER CO
JOHNSON & JOHNSON
JOHNSON CONTROLS INC
JP MORGAN CHASE & CO INC
JUNIPER NETWORKS INC
KAISER PERMANENTE
KELLOGG CO
KELLY SERVICES INC
KENDLE INTERNATIONAL INC
KIMBERLY-CLARK CORP
KINDRED HEALTHCARE INC
KOHL'S CORP
KPMG LLP
KRAFT FOODS INC
KROGER CO (THE)
L-3 COMMUNICATIONS HOLDINGS INC
LABORATORY CORP OF AMERICA HOLDINGS
LEVEL 3 COMMUNICATIONS INC
LEXMARK INTERNATIONAL INC
LIBERTY GLOBAL INC
LIBERTY MUTUAL GROUP INC
LIMITED BRANDS INC
LINCOLN NATIONAL CORPORATION
LOCKHEED MARTIN CORP
LODGIAN INC
LOEWS CORPORATION
LOWE'S COMPANIES INC
MACY'S INC
MANPOWER INC
MARRIOTT INTERNATIONAL INC

MARSH & MCLENNAN COMPANIES INC
MARY KAY INC
MASSEY ENERGY COMPANY
MATTEL INC
MAYO FOUNDATION FOR MEDICAL EDUCATION AND RESEARCH
MCDERMOTT INTERNATIONAL INC
MCDONALD'S CORP
MCKESSON CORPORATION
MEDCO HEALTH SOLUTIONS
MEDTRONIC INC
MERCER INC
MERCK & CO INC
METHODIST HEALTH CARE SYSTEM
METLIFE INC
MGM MIRAGE
MICROCHIP TECHNOLOGY INC
MICRON TECHNOLOGY INC
MICROSOFT CORP
MILLIPORE CORP
MONSANTO CO
MURPHY OIL CORPORATION
MYLAN INC
NETAPP INC
NEWS CORP
NII HOLDINGS INC
NIKE INC
NOBLE CORPORATION
NORTHROP GRUMMAN CORP
NRG ENERGY INC
OCCIDENTAL PETROLEUM CORP
ODYSSEY HEALTHCARE INC
OFFICE DEPOT INC
OIL STATES INTERNATIONAL INC
OMNICARE INC
OMNICOM GROUP INC
ORACLE CORP
O'REILLY AUTOMOTIVE INC
OSHKOSH CORPORATION
OSI RESTAURANT PARTNERS LLC
OWENS & MINOR INC
PANTRY INC (THE)
PARSONS BRINCKERHOFF INC
PAYCHEX INC
PEABODY ENERGY CORP
PEPSI BOTTLING GROUP INC
PEPSICO INC
PERRIGO CO
PETSMART INC
PFIZER INC
PG&E CORPORATION
PHARMACEUTICAL PRODUCT DEVELOPMENT INC
PITNEY BOWES INC
POLO RALPH LAUREN CORP
PRAXAIR INC
PRINCIPAL FINANCIAL GROUP (THE)
PROCTER & GAMBLE CO
PROGRESSIVE CORPORATION (THE)
PRUDENTIAL FINANCIAL INC
PUBLIX SUPER MARKETS INC
QUALCOMM INC
QUEST DIAGNOSTICS INC
RAYTHEON CO

REGIS CORPORATION
RENT-A-CENTER INC
RES CARE INC
RITE AID CORPORATION
ROBERT HALF INTERNATIONAL INC
ROSS STORES INC
ROYAL CARIBBEAN CRUISES LTD
RRI ENERGY INC
SABRE HOLDINGS CORP
SAFECO INSURANCE COMPANY OF AMERICA
SAFEWAY INC
SAIC INC
SAM'S CLUB
SARA LEE CORP
SAS INSTITUTE INC
SCANA CORPORATION
SCHERING-PLOUGH CORP
SCOTTS MIRACLE GROW CO
SEACOR HOLDINGS INC
SEMPRA ENERGY
SENSIENT TECHNOLOGIES CORPORATION
SHERWIN WILLIAMS COMPANY (THE)
SIGMA-ALDRICH CORP
SISTERS OF MERCY HEALTH SYSTEMS
SMITH INTERNATIONAL INC
SOUTHERN CALIFORNIA EDISON COMPANY
SOUTHERN COMPANY (THE)
SOUTHWEST AIRLINES CO
SRA INTERNATIONAL INC
ST JUDE MEDICAL INC
STAPLES INC
STARTEK INC
STARWOOD HOTELS & RESORTS WORLDWIDE INC
STERIS CORP
STRYKER CORP
SUN HEALTHCARE GROUP
SUNGARD DATA SYSTEMS INC
SUNOCO INC
SUNRISE SENIOR LIVING
SUPERVALU INC
SYKES ENTERPRISES INC
SYMANTEC CORP
SYNOPSYS INC
SYSCO CORP
TARGET CORPORATION
TELEDYNE TECHNOLOGIES INCORPORATED
TELEPHONE AND DATA SYSTEMS INC (TDS)
TELETECH HOLDINGS INC
TESORO CORP
THERMO FISHER SCIENTIFIC INC
TIFFANY & CO
TIME WARNER INC
TJX COMPANIES INC (THE)
TOTAL SYSTEM SERVICES INC (TSYS)
TRANSOCEAN INC
TRAVELERS COMPANIES INC (THE)

TREEHOUSE FOODS INC
TW TELECOM INC
TYSON FOODS INC
UNITED PARCEL SERVICE INC (UPS)
UNITED STATES CELLULAR CORP
UNITED TECHNOLOGIES
CORPORATION
UNITEDHEALTH GROUP INC
UNIVERSAL HEALTH SERVICES INC
URS CORPORATION
USAA
VALERO ENERGY CORP
VALSPAR CORPORATION (THE)
VARIAN MEDICAL SYSTEMS INC
VERISIGN INC
VERIZON COMMUNICATIONS
VIACOM INC
VICTORIAS SECRET
VISA INC
VOLT INFORMATION SCIENCES INC
W R BERKLEY CORPORATION
WALGREEN CO
WAL-MART STORES INC
WALT DISNEY COMPANY (THE)
WASTE MANAGEMENT INC
WATERS CORP
WATSON PHARMACEUTICALS INC
WEIGHT WATCHERS
INTERNATIONAL INC
WELLPOINT INC
WELLS FARGO & CO
WENDY'S/ARBY'S GROUP INC
WEST CORPORATION
WHOLE FOODS MARKET INC
WILLIAMS COMPANIES INC (THE)
WW GRAINGER INC
WYETH
WYNDHAM WORLDWIDE
WYNN RESORTS LIMITED
XEROX CORP
YAHOO! INC
YUM! BRANDS INC
ZIMMER HOLDINGS INC

INDEX OF SUBSIDIARIES, BRAND NAMES AND AFFILIATIONS

Brand or subsidiary, followed by the name of the related corporation

INDEX OF SUBSIDIARIES, BRAND NAMES AND AFFILIATIONS, CONT.

INDEX OF SUBSIDIARIES, BRAND NAMES AND AFFILIATIONS, CONT.

INDEX OF SUBSIDIARIES, BRAND NAMES AND AFFILIATIONS, CONT.

INDEX OF SUBSIDIARIES, BRAND NAMES AND AFFILIATIONS, CONT.

INDEX OF SUBSIDIARIES, BRAND NAMES AND AFFILIATIONS, CONT.

INDEX OF SUBSIDIARIES, BRAND NAMES AND AFFILIATIONS, CONT.

INDEX OF SUBSIDIARIES, BRAND NAMES AND AFFILIATIONS, CONT.

Diamond Offshore Drilling, Inc.; **LOEWS CORPORATION**
Diamond Shamrock; **VALERO ENERGY CORP**
DIANON Systems, Inc.; **LABORATORY CORP OF AMERICA HOLDINGS**
Digital Signal Controllers; **MICROCHIP TECHNOLOGY INC**
Dimensions International; **HONEYWELL INTERNATIONAL INC**
Dimetapp; **WYETH**
Direct Dental Supply Co.; **PATTERSON COMPANIES INC**
Direct2You; **AETNA INC**
Direct-Q 3; **MILLIPORE CORP**
DIRECTV Latin America; **DIRECTV GROUP INC (THE)**
DIRECTV U.S.; **DIRECTV GROUP INC (THE)**
Discovery Verification Platform; **SYNOPSYS INC**
Disney Classics; **MATTEL INC**
Dixie Pipeline Company; **ENTERPRISE PRODUCTS PARTNERS LP**
Dixie Terminals and Storage Company; **ENTERPRISE PRODUCTS PARTNERS LP**
DM Label Group; **AVERY DENNISON CORP**
DMJM Aviation; **AECOM TECHNOLOGY CORPORATION**
Dockers; **GENESCO INC**
Docpharma; **MYLAN INC**
DocuColor; **XEROX CORP**
Document Sciences Corporation; **EMC CORP**
Dogwood Canyon; **BASS PRO SHOPS INC**
Dolefil; **DOLE FOOD COMPANY INC**
DolEx; **GLOBAL PAYMENTS INC**
Dollar Rent A Car, Inc.; **DOLLAR THRIFTY AUTOMOTIVE GROUP INC**
Dollar Thrifty Funding Corp.; **DOLLAR THRIFTY AUTOMOTIVE GROUP INC**
DollarsDirect.com.au; **CASH AMERICA INTERNATIONAL INC**
Domain; **MARY KAY INC**
Donnelley Marketing; **INFOGROUP INC**
Dow Chemical Company (The); **EXXONMOBIL CHEMICAL**
Dow Jones & Co Inc; **NEWS CORP**
Dr. Scholl's; **SCHERING-PLOUGH CORP**
Dragon Development Corp.; **CACI INTERNATIONAL INC**
DreamWorks SKG; **VIACOM INC**
Dress Barn Woman; **DRESS BARN INC (THE)**
dsPIC; **MICROCHIP TECHNOLOGY INC**

DSX1/3; **ADC TELECOMMUNICATIONS INC**
DTE Biomass Energy; **DTE ENERGY COMPANY**
DTE Coal Services; **DTE ENERGY COMPANY**
DTE Energy Services; **DTE ENERGY COMPANY**
DTG Operations, Inc.; **DOLLAR THRIFTY AUTOMOTIVE GROUP INC**
Dual Core; **INTEL CORP**
Duckworth Flavors; **CARGILL INC**
Duke Energy Generation Services; **DUKE ENERGY CORP**
Duke Energy International, LLC; **DUKE ENERGY CORP**
Dunn's; **CABELA'S INC**
Duron Inc; **SHERWIN WILLIAMS COMPANY (THE)**
Dustbuster; **BLACK & DECKER CORP**
Dutch Boy; **SHERWIN WILLIAMS COMPANY (THE)**
Dynastar; **QUIKSILVER INC**
Dysphagia @ Home; **AMEDISYS INC**
E! Channel; **COMCAST CORP**
E. D. Smith Valley Foods LTD; **TREEHOUSE FOODS INC**
EA Casual Entertainment; **ELECTRONIC ARTS INC**
EA Games; **ELECTRONIC ARTS INC**
EA Sports; **ELECTRONIC ARTS INC**
EA-6B; **NORTHROP GRUMMAN CORP**
Early Stage; **KENDLE INTERNATIONAL INC**
Earth Protection Services, Inc.; **WASTE MANAGEMENT INC**
Earth Tech Inc; **AECOM TECHNOLOGY CORPORATION**
Easy Dental; **HENRY SCHEIN INC**
easyedge; **UNITED STATES CELLULAR CORP**
Easywell; **HALLIBURTON COMPANY**
EB Games; **GAMESTOP CORP**
eBay Express; **EBAY INC**
EBGames.com; **GAMESTOP CORP**
ECoM; **R R DONNELLEY & SONS CO**
Edge Wireless; **AT&T INC**
Edison Capital; **EDISON INTERNATIONAL**
Edison International; **SOUTHERN CALIFORNIA EDISON COMPANY**
Edison Mission Energy; **EDISON INTERNATIONAL**
Edwards and Kelcey; **JACOBS ENGINEERING GROUP INC**
EEPROM; **MICROCHIP TECHNOLOGY INC**
EG&G Division; **URS CORPORATION**
Eggo; **KELLOGG CO**

eKendleCollege; **KENDLE INTERNATIONAL INC**
Elan; **MANPOWER INC**
Electronic Vault Attendant Elite; **DIEBOLD INC**
Element Agency (The); **FTI CONSULTING INC**
Elfa; **CONTAINER STORE (THE)**
Elige; **MARY KAY INC**
Elite Protection Services; **ABM INDUSTRIES INC**
Elkin Medical Systems, Inc.; **VCA ANTECH INC**
EMAR Group (The); **WELLS FARGO & CO**
Embassy Suits; **HILTON HOTELS CORP**
Embrace; **MARY KAY INC**
EMEND; **MERCK & CO INC**
Emerald Renewable Energy LLC; **CARGILL INC**
Emhart Teknologies; **BLACK & DECKER CORP**
EMPOWERED Health Coaching; **HEALTH FITNESS CORP**
Empowr; **GENERAL CABLE CORP**
Emtriva; **GILEAD SCIENCES INC**
Enbrel; **AMGEN INC**
EnCana Corporation; **ENTERPRISE PRODUCTS PARTNERS LP**
Encompass; **ALLSTATE CORPORATION (THE)**
Encore Suites at Wynn Las Vegas; **WYNN RESORTS LIMITED**
Encore Suites at Wynn Macau; **WYNN RESORTS LIMITED**
EndoVive; **BOSTON SCIENTIFIC CORP**
EnergySouth, Inc.; **SEMPRA ENERGY**
Enlightened; **BAXTER INTERNATIONAL INC**
Enraf Holdings B.V.; **HONEYWELL INTERNATIONAL INC**
Ensure; **ABBOTT LABORATORIES**
Entergy Arkansas, Inc.; **ENTERGY CORP**
Entergy Gulf States Louisiana, LLC; **ENTERGY CORP**
Entergy Louisiana LLC; **ENTERGY CORP**
Entergy Mississipi, Inc.; **ENTERGY CORP**
Entergy New Orleans, Inc.; **ENTERGY CORP**
Entergy Nuclear, Inc.; **ENTERGY CORP**
Entergy Texas, Inc.; **ENTERGY CORP**
Enterprise Car Sales; **ENTERPRISE RENT-A-CAR**
Enterprise Fleet Services; **ENTERPRISE RENT-A-CAR**
Enterprise Rent-a-Car; **ENTERPRISE RENT-A-CAR**

INDEX OF SUBSIDIARIES, BRAND NAMES AND AFFILIATIONS, CONT.

Enterprise Rent-a-Truck; **ENTERPRISE RENT-A-CAR**
Entrepreneur of the Year Award; **ERNST & YOUNG LLP**
EP MedSystems, Inc.; **ST JUDE MEDICAL INC**
EPOGEN; **AMGEN INC**
ePRISM; **MERCER INC**
EPROM Memory; **MICROCHIP TECHNOLOGY INC**
Epsilon; **ALLIANCE DATA SYSTEMS CORPORATION**
Era Helicopters LLC; **SEACOR HOLDINGS INC**
Era Systems Corporation; **SRA INTERNATIONAL INC**
EraMed LLC; **SEACOR HOLDINGS INC**
Ernst & Young International; **ERNST & YOUNG LLP**
Ernst & Young Online; **ERNST & YOUNG LLP**
E-Series; **JUNIPER NETWORKS INC**
E-site Marketing; **SABRE HOLDINGS CORP**
Esoterix; **LABORATORY CORP OF AMERICA HOLDINGS**
ESPN Inc; **WALT DISNEY COMPANY (THE)**
Eteq Components Pte Ltd; **ARROW ELECTRONICS INC**
Ethicon Inc; **JOHNSON & JOHNSON**
Eurequat SA; **INGRAM MICRO INC**
Europa Apotheek Venlo; **MEDCO HEALTH SOLUTIONS**
Ever; **AFLAC INC**
EverGreen; **SCOTTS MIRACLE GROW CO**
Evian; **COCA-COLA COMPANY (THE)**
Evite; **IAC/INTERACTIVECORP**
EXACT; **HENRY SCHEIN INC**
Excalibur; **MGM MIRAGE**
Excel Tech Inc; **ARROW ELECTRONICS INC**
ExcellerateHRO; **TOWERS PERRIN**
Excite.com; **IAC/INTERACTIVECORP**
ExecuStay; **MARRIOTT INTERNATIONAL INC**
Executive Choice; **BJ'S WHOLESALE CLUB INC**
Executive Risk Indemnity, Inc; **CHUBB CORPORATION (THE)**
Exelon Business Services Company; **EXELON CORPORATION**
Exelon Generation Company LLC; **EXELON CORPORATION**
Experian Group; **EXPERIAN AMERICAS**
Experian Information Solutions, Inc.; **EXPERIAN AMERICAS**
EXPO Design Centers; **HOME DEPOT INC**

Extreme Engineering Limited; **SCHLUMBERGER LIMITED**
Exxon Mobil Corporation (ExxonMobil); **EXXONMOBIL CHEMICAL**
Exxon Neftegas Limited; **EXXON MOBIL CORPORATION (EXXONMOBIL)**
ExxonMobil Chemical; **EXXON MOBIL CORPORATION (EXXONMOBIL)**
Ezeflow, Inc.; **SHAW GROUP INC (THE)**
F/A-18; **NORTHROP GRUMMAN CORP**
F-35; **NORTHROP GRUMMAN CORP**
Faber Maunsell; **AECOM TECHNOLOGY CORPORATION**
Fabric.com; **AMAZON.COM INC**
Fairfield Inn; **MARRIOTT INTERNATIONAL INC**
Fandango Inc; **COMCAST CORP**
Fandango Inc; **COMCAST CORP**
Fanor; **DEVRY INC**
Farm Fresh; **SUPERVALU INC**
Fashion Bug; **CHARMING SHOPPES INC**
Fasson; **AVERY DENNISON CORP**
Fast Search & Transfer ASA; **MICROSOFT CORP**
FD Kinesis; **FTI CONSULTING INC**
FDS Bank; **MACY'S INC**
Federal Insurance Company; **CHUBB CORPORATION (THE)**
Federated Department Stores, Inc.; **MACY'S INC**
FedEx Custom Critical Inc; **FEDEX CORPORATION**
FedEx Express Corp; **FEDEX CORPORATION**
FedEx Freight Corp; **FEDEX CORPORATION**
FedEx Ground Package System Inc; **FEDEX CORPORATION**
FedEx Home Delivery; **FEDEX CORPORATION**
FedEx Kinkos Office And Print Services Inc; **FEDEX CORPORATION**
Fedex Supply Chain Services Inc; **FEDEX CORPORATION**
FedEx Trade Networks Inc; **FEDEX CORPORATION**
Fentora; **CEPHALON INC**
Ferncliff TIH AS; **PRIDE INTERNATIONAL INC**
Fiber Guide Raceway; **ADC TELECOMMUNICATIONS INC**
FIBERLite; **THERMO FISHER SCIENTIFIC INC**
Fictionwise; **BARNES & NOBLE INC**
Fifty-Four by Fossil; **FOSSIL INC**
Figi's; **CHARMING SHOPPES INC**
Financiere Burgienne; **3M COMPANY**
Finish Line; **FINISH LINE INC (THE)**

Finish Line Man Alive, Inc. (The); **FINISH LINE INC (THE)**
Finn-Aqua; **STERIS CORP**
FinSecure LLC; **W R BERKLEY CORPORATION**
Firestone Country Club; **CLUBCORP INC**
Firethorn Holdings, LLC; **QUALCOMM INC**
First American Corp; **FIRST ADVANTAGE CORPORATION**
First Data Loyalty Solution; **FIRST DATA CORP**
First Merchant Solutions; **FIRST DATA CORP**
Fisher-Price; **MATTEL INC**
Fitigues; **CHICO'S FAS INC**
Flamingo; **HARRAH'S ENTERTAINMENT INC**
Flash; **MICROCHIP TECHNOLOGY INC**
FleetBoston; **BANK OF AMERICA CORP**
Fleming's Prime Steakhouse & Wine Bar; **OSI RESTAURANT PARTNERS LLC**
Flex Global View; **UNITED PARCEL SERVICE INC (UPS)**
Flex Plan; **WEIGHT WATCHERS INTERNATIONAL INC**
Flex Recubrimientos, Acabados Automotrices; **SHERWIN WILLIAMS COMPANY (THE)**
FlexRig3; **HELMERICH & PAYNE INC**
FlexRig4; **HELMERICH & PAYNE INC**
FlexRigs; **HELMERICH & PAYNE INC**
FlexVol; **NETAPP INC**
Flint Hills Resources; **KOCH INDUSTRIES INC**
Florida Power & Light Company; **FPL GROUP INC**
Fluor Canada; **FLUOR CORP**
Fluor Construction Company; **FLUOR CORP**
FOCALIN; **CELGENE CORP**
FOCALIN XR; **CELGENE CORP**
Focus Europe, S.r.l.; **GUESS? INC**
Folgers; **JM SMUCKER CO**
Foray; **OFFICE DEPOT INC**
Ford Motor Co; **TELETECH HOLDINGS INC**
Forest Laboratories Europe; **FOREST LABORATORIES INC**
Forest Pharmaceuticals, Inc.; **FOREST LABORATORIES INC**
Forest Research Institute; **FOREST LABORATORIES INC**
Fort Dodge Animal Health; **WYETH**
Fosamax; **MERCK & CO INC**
Fossil; **FOSSIL INC**
Foster Wheeler Constructors; **FOSTER WHEELER AG**

INDEX OF SUBSIDIARIES, BRAND NAMES AND AFFILIATIONS, CONT.

INDEX OF SUBSIDIARIES, BRAND NAMES AND AFFILIATIONS, CONT.

GP Investments, Ltd.; **PRIDE INTERNATIONAL INC**
Grafikom MIL; **R R DONNELLEY & SONS CO**
Grainger Caribe, Inc.; **WW GRAINGER INC**
Grainger China LLC; **WW GRAINGER INC**
Grainger Industrial Supply; **WW GRAINGER INC**
Grainger, S.A. de C.V.; **WW GRAINGER INC**
Grand Hyatt; **GLOBAL HYATT CORPORATION**
Grant Prideco Inc; **NATIONAL OILWELL VARCO INC**
Grant Thornton International; **GRANT THORNTON LLP**
Grayloc Products; **OCEANEERING INTERNATIONAL INC**
GreatPoint Energy, Inc.; **PEABODY ENERGY CORP**
Greenhouse Gas Services, LLC; **AES CORPORATION (THE)**
GreenPower; **WESTERN DIGITAL CORP**
GroceryWorks; **SAFEWAY INC**
Grupo Gigante, S.A.B. de C.V.; **PRICESMART INC**
Grupo Multivoice; **AFFILIATED COMPUTER SERVICES INC**
GS Capital Partners; **ARAMARK CORPORATION**
GSW Worldwide; **INVENTIV HEALTH INC**
GUESS by MARCIANO; **GUESS? INC**
Guess? Jeans; **GUESS? INC**
Guitar Hero; **ACTIVISION BLIZZARD INC**
Gulf Power Company; **SOUTHERN COMPANY (THE)**
Gulfstream Aerospace; **GENERAL DYNAMICS CORP**
Guy Carpenter & Company, LLC; **MARSH & MCLENNAN COMPANIES INC**
GVN Services; **FRONTIER COMMUNICATIONS CORPORATION**
H.B. Fuller; **VALSPAR CORPORATION (THE)**
H.T.R., Inc.; **WASTE MANAGEMENT INC**
Hair Club for Men & Women; **REGIS CORPORATION**
Hamilton Sundstrand; **UNITED TECHNOLOGIES CORPORATION**
Hampshire Company Inc; **MICROCHIP TECHNOLOGY INC**
Hampton Inn; **HILTON HOTELS CORP**
Hanesbrands Inc; **SARA LEE CORP**

Harbor Breeze; **LOWE'S COMPANIES INC**
Harborside Healthcare Corporation; **SUN HEALTHCARE GROUP**
Harmon Stores, Inc.; **BED BATH & BEYOND INC**
HarperCollins Publishers Inc; **NEWS CORP**
Harrah's Operating Company Inc; **HARRAH'S ENTERTAINMENT INC**
Harris Stratex; **HARRIS CORPORATION**
Hartford International Management Services Company; **HARTFORD FINANCIAL SERVICES GROUP INC (THE)**
Hartford Investment Financial Services, LLC; **HARTFORD FINANCIAL SERVICES GROUP INC (THE)**
Hartford Life and Accident; **HARTFORD FINANCIAL SERVICES GROUP INC (THE)**
Hartford Life and Annuity; **HARTFORD FINANCIAL SERVICES GROUP INC (THE)**
Hartford Life Group Insurance Company; **HARTFORD FINANCIAL SERVICES GROUP INC (THE)**
Hartford Mutual Funds, Inc. (The); **HARTFORD FINANCIAL SERVICES GROUP INC (THE)**
Hartford Wolf Pack; **CABLEVISION SYSTEMS CORP**
Harvest Bay; **UNITED NATURAL FOODS INC**
Harvest Energy Technology Inc; **AIR PRODUCTS & CHEMICALS INC**
HAS Systems Pty Limited; **L-3 COMMUNICATIONS HOLDINGS INC**
Hat World Corporation; **GENESCO INC**
Haven Behavioral Healthcare; **ASCENSION HEALTH**
Hawaiian Electric Company; **HAWAIIAN ELECTRIC INDUSTRIES INC**
Hawaiian Electric Light Company; **HAWAIIAN ELECTRIC INDUSTRIES INC**
HCR Manor Care; **MANOR CARE INC**
HD Vest, Inc.; **WELLS FARGO & CO**
HDS Cosmetics Lab, Inc.; **PROCTER & GAMBLE CO**
Health Services Research Network; **IMS HEALTH INC**
HealthAmerica; **COVENTRY HEALTH CARE INC**
HealthAssurance; **COVENTRY HEALTH CARE INC**
Healthy Choice; **CONAGRA FOODS INC**
Heart @ Home; **AMEDISYS INC**
Heartland; **MANOR CARE INC**

H-E-B; **HE BUTT GROCERY COMPANY (HEB)**
H-E-B Insurance Agency; **HE BUTT GROCERY COMPANY (HEB)**
H-E-B plus!; **HE BUTT GROCERY COMPANY (HEB)**
H-E-B Wireless; **HE BUTT GROCERY COMPANY (HEB)**
HEI Diversified; **HAWAIIAN ELECTRIC INDUSTRIES INC**
Hemenway's Seafood Grille & Oyster Bar; **DARDEN RESTAURANTS INC**
Hennessy Industries; **DANAHER CORP**
Hepsera; **GILEAD SCIENCES INC**
HeptaCon; **HEWITT ASSOCIATES**
HEPTIMAX; **QUEST DIAGNOSTICS INC**
Heraeus; **THERMO FISHER SCIENTIFIC INC**
Herceptin; **GENENTECH INC**
Hershey's; **DEAN FOODS CO**
Hertz Car Sales; **HERTZ GLOBAL HOLDINGS INC**
Hertz Equipment Rental Corp.; **HERTZ GLOBAL HOLDINGS INC**
Hertz Leasing; **HERTZ GLOBAL HOLDINGS INC**
Hertz Local Edition; **HERTZ GLOBAL HOLDINGS INC**
Hertz Rent A Car; **HERTZ GLOBAL HOLDINGS INC**
HFC Fitness Programs; **HEALTH FITNESS CORP**
HFC Wellness Programs; **HEALTH FITNESS CORP**
Hhonors; **HILTON HOTELS CORP**
Hibbett Sports; **HIBBETT SPORTS INC**
Hibbett Team Sales, Inc.; **HIBBETT SPORTS INC**
HighMount Exploration & Production, LLC; **LOEWS CORPORATION**
HI-LITER; **AVERY DENNISON CORP**
Hill's Pet Nutrition; **COLGATE PALMOLIVE CO**
Hillshire Farm; **SARA LEE CORP**
Hilton Garden Vacations Company LLC; **HILTON HOTELS CORP**
Hilton Group plc; **HILTON HOTELS CORP**
Hilton Group plc; **LODGIAN INC**
HIS; **IMS HEALTH INC**
Holiday Inn; **LODGIAN INC**
Holisticare Hospice, LLC; **SUN HEALTHCARE GROUP**
Holland America Line; **CARNIVAL CORPORATION**
Home & More; **BED BATH & BEYOND INC**
Home Box Office, Inc.; **TIME WARNER INC**
Home Care of Washington; **RES CARE INC**

INDEX OF SUBSIDIARIES, BRAND NAMES AND AFFILIATIONS, CONT.

INDEX OF SUBSIDIARIES, BRAND NAMES AND AFFILIATIONS, CONT.

International Dairy Queen; **BERKSHIRE HATHAWAY INC**
International Delight; **DEAN FOODS CO**
International Direct Connect; **NII HOLDINGS INC**
International House of Pancakes; **DINEEQUITY INC**
International Logging Inc; **WEATHERFORD INTERNATIONAL LTD**
International Resources Group Ltd.; **L-3 COMMUNICATIONS HOLDINGS INC**
Internet Security Systems Inc; **INTERNATIONAL BUSINESS MACHINES CORP (IBM)**
InterQual; **MCKESSON CORPORATION**
Intertrade A F AG; **INGRAM MICRO INC**
Interventional Spine; **ASCENSION HEALTH**
Intervoice, Inc.; **CONVERGYS CORPORATION**
Intrado, Inc.; **WEST CORPORATION**
Intuit Real Estate Solutions; **INTUIT INC**
inVentiv Clinical Services; **INVENTIV HEALTH INC**
inVentiv Commercial Services; **INVENTIV HEALTH INC**
inVentiv Communications; **INVENTIV HEALTH INC**
inVentiv Patient Outcomes; **INVENTIV HEALTH INC**
INVISTA; **KOCH INDUSTRIES INC**
Inwood Laboratories; **FOREST LABORATORIES INC**
Iomega Corp; **EMC CORP**
IPEX; **VICTORIAS SECRET**
iPhone; **APPLE INC**
iPod; **APPLE INC**
Iridesse, Inc.; **TIFFANY & CO**
Irish Spring; **COLGATE PALMOLIVE CO**
Irving Weber Associates, Inc.; **BROWN & BROWN INC**
iScript; **BIO RAD LABORATORIES INC**
Isotec, Inc.; **GENERAL CABLE CORP**
Isto Technologies; **ASCENSION HEALTH**
It's Your Life Wellsite; **HEALTH NET INC**
Iteamic Pvt. Ltd.; **CIBER INC**
ITEDO Software LLC; **PARAMETRIC TECHNOLOGY CORP**
I-trax, Inc.; **WALGREEN CO**
J. Ray McDermott, S.A.; **MCDERMOTT INTERNATIONAL INC**
J.D. Edwards; **DELOITTE CONSULTING LLP**
J.P. Morgan Partners; **ARAMARK CORPORATION**

J.P. Morgan Securities; **JP MORGAN CHASE & CO INC**
J2MSoft Inc; **ELECTRONIC ARTS INC**
Jabber, Inc.; **CISCO SYSTEMS INC**
JAC; **AVERY DENNISON CORP**
Jack in the Box; **JACK IN THE BOX INC**
Jack in the Box Foundation; **JACK IN THE BOX INC**
Jackfish; **DEVON ENERGY CORPORATION**
Jack's Ultimate Salads; **JACK IN THE BOX INC**
Jackson Products, Inc.; **KIMBERLY-CLARK CORP**
Jacobs; **KRAFT FOODS INC**
Jacobs Chuck Manufacturing Company; **DANAHER CORP**
Jacobs Technology, Inc.; **JACOBS ENGINEERING GROUP INC**
Jacobs Vehicle Systems; **DANAHER CORP**
James Webb Space Telescope; **NORTHROP GRUMMAN CORP**
Jamilco; **COACH INC**
Japanese Practice; **KPMG LLP**
JB Laboratories; **PERRIGO CO**
JCPenney Custom Decorating; **J C PENNEY COMPANY INC**
JCPenney Optical Services; **J C PENNEY COMPANY INC**
JCPenney Portraits; **J C PENNEY COMPANY INC**
JCPenney Salon; **J C PENNEY COMPANY INC**
jcpenney.com; **J C PENNEY COMPANY INC**
Jefferson Wells; **MANPOWER INC**
Jell-O; **KRAFT FOODS INC**
JerrDan; **OSHKOSH CORPORATION**
Jersey Central Power & Light Co.; **FIRSTENERGY CORP**
JET; **CONOCOPHILLIPS COMPANY**
Jet Aviation; **GENERAL DYNAMICS CORP**
Jewel-Osco; **SUPERVALU INC**
Jiangsu-Tyson; **TYSON FOODS INC**
Jif; **JM SMUCKER CO**
Jimmy Dean; **SARA LEE CORP**
JJWild Inc; **PEROT SYSTEMS CORP**
JLG; **OSHKOSH CORPORATION**
John Deere; **DEERE & CO**
John Middleton Co; **ALTRIA GROUP INC**
Johnson Controls (Wuhu) Automotive Interiors; **JOHNSON CONTROLS INC**
Johnson Controls-Saft Advanced Power Solutions; **JOHNSON CONTROLS INC**
Johnston & Murphy; **GENESCO INC**
Jonah Gas Gathering Company; **ENTERPRISE PRODUCTS PARTNERS LP**

Journey; **MARY KAY INC**
Journeymen Select; **GEORGIA GULF CORPORATION**
Journeys; **GENESCO INC**
Journeys Kidz; **GENESCO INC**
JP Fruit Distributors Ltd.; **DOLE FOOD COMPANY INC**
JP Morgan Commodities Canada Corp.; **JP MORGAN CHASE & CO INC**
JPMorgan Chase Vastera Inc; **JP MORGAN CHASE & CO INC**
JPMorgan Partners; **JP MORGAN CHASE & CO INC**
J-Series; **JUNIPER NETWORKS INC**
Jubail Chevron Phillips Company; **CHEVRON PHILLIPS CHEMICAL COMPANY LLC**
Jumbo Jack; **JACK IN THE BOX INC**
JumpStart; **HEALTH FITNESS CORP**
JUNOS; **JUNIPER NETWORKS INC**
Jupiter Telecommunications Co., Ltd.; **LIBERTY GLOBAL INC**
K&G; **MEN'S WEARHOUSE INC (THE)**
Kaiser Foundation Health Plan, Inc.; **KAISER PERMANENTE**
Kaiser Foundation Hospitals; **KAISER PERMANENTE**
Kaiser Permanente Healthcare Institute; **KAISER PERMANENTE**
Kangaroo Express; **PANTRY INC (THE)**
KB Industries; **CAMERON INTERNATIONAL CORPORATION**
Keebler; **KELLOGG CO**
Keller Graduate School of Management; **DEVRY INC**
Kellogg Snacks Division; **KELLOGG CO**
Kelly Financial Resources; **KELLY SERVICES INC**
Kelly Office Services; **KELLY SERVICES INC**
Kelly Scientific Resources; **KELLY SERVICES INC**
Kelly's Sales & Leasing; **AARON'S INC**
KellyConnect; **KELLY SERVICES INC**
KellyDirect; **KELLY SERVICES INC**
Kentucky Orthopedic Rehab Team; **SELECT MEDICAL**
Kentucky Power; **AMERICAN ELECTRIC POWER COMPANY INC (AEP)**
Kerma; **QUIKSILVER INC**
Kern River Gas Transmission Company; **MIDAMERICAN ENERGY HOLDINGS CO**
Kerr-McGee Corporation; **ANADARKO PETROLEUM CORPORATION**
Kessler Institute for Rehabilitation; **SELECT MEDICAL**
Kessler Rehabilitation Centers; **SELECT MEDICAL**

INDEX OF SUBSIDIARIES, BRAND NAMES AND AFFILIATIONS, CONT.

INDEX OF SUBSIDIARIES, BRAND NAMES AND AFFILIATIONS, CONT.

INDEX OF SUBSIDIARIES, BRAND NAMES AND AFFILIATIONS, CONT.

INDEX OF SUBSIDIARIES, BRAND NAMES AND AFFILIATIONS, CONT.

INDEX OF SUBSIDIARIES, BRAND NAMES AND AFFILIATIONS, CONT.

INDEX OF SUBSIDIARIES, BRAND NAMES AND AFFILIATIONS, CONT.

INDEX OF SUBSIDIARIES, BRAND NAMES AND AFFILIATIONS, CONT.

Pure Digital Technologies, Inc.; **CISCO SYSTEMS INC**
Pure Networks; **CISCO SYSTEMS INC**
Puros; **ZIMMER HOLDINGS INC**
Putnam LLC; **MARSH & MCLENNAN COMPANIES INC**
PxMax; **EXXONMOBIL CHEMICAL**
Pyxis; **CARDINAL HEALTH INC**
Pyxis Infant Care Verification; **CARDINAL HEALTH INC**
Pyxsis MedStation 4000; **CARDINAL HEALTH INC**
Q*VIEW; **COGNIZANT TECHNOLOGY SOLUTIONS CORP**
Qdoba Mexican Grill; **JACK IN THE BOX INC**
Qdoba Restaurant Corporation; **JACK IN THE BOX INC**
QFC; **KROGER CO (THE)**
QSS Group Inc; **PEROT SYSTEMS CORP**
Quaker Foods North America; **PEPSICO INC**
Qualcomm Flarion Technologies, Inc.; **QUALCOMM INC**
Qualcomm Inc.; **UNITED STATES CELLULAR CORP**
Qualcomm MEMS Technologies, Inc.; **QUALCOMM INC**
Qualcomm, Inc.; **ADVANCED MICRO DEVICES INC (AMD)**
Quality Home Care, Inc.; **CAPITAL SENIOR LIVING CORP**
Quamut.com; **BARNES & NOBLE INC**
Quantum View; **UNITED PARCEL SERVICE INC (UPS)**
Quellos Group LLC; **BLACKROCK INC**
Quest Technologies Inc; **3M COMPANY**
Question Mark; **GUESS? INC**
Quick Stuff; **JACK IN THE BOX INC**
QuickBooks; **INTUIT INC**
QuickBooks Payroll; **INTUIT INC**
Quicken; **INTUIT INC**
Quicken.com; **INTUIT INC**
QuickQuid.co.uk; **CASH AMERICA INTERNATIONAL INC**
Quik Stop; **KROGER CO (THE)**
Quill Corp.; **STAPLES INC**
Quinetix LLC; **ACXIOM CORP**
Quorum Health Resources, LLC (QHR); **COMMUNITY HEALTH SYSTEMS INC**
Quotient Engineering, Inc.; **FOSTER WHEELER AG**
RABA Technologies, LLC; **SRA INTERNATIONAL INC**
RAC Financial Services; **RENT-A-CENTER INC**
Rachel's Organic; **DEAN FOODS CO**
Radi Medical AB; **ST JUDE MEDICAL INC**

Rainbow Media Holdings LLC; **CABLEVISION SYSTEMS CORP**
Ralcorp Frozen Bakery Products, Inc.; **RALCORP HOLDINGS INC**
Ralph Lauren; **POLO RALPH LAUREN CORP**
Ralph's; **KROGER CO (THE)**
Ralston Foods; **RALCORP HOLDINGS INC**
Ramada; **WYNDHAM WORLDWIDE**
Ramcell; **CELLCO PARTNERSHIP (VERIZON WIRELESS)**
Randall's Food Markets Inc.; **SAFEWAY INC**
Ranexa; **GILEAD SCIENCES INC**
RapidArc; **VARIAN MEDICAL SYSTEMS INC**
Raptor; **WESTERN DIGITAL CORP**
Rational Software Corp; **INTERNATIONAL BUSINESS MACHINES CORP (IBM)**
RationalMed; **MEDCO HEALTH SOLUTIONS**
Raytheon Australia; **RAYTHEON CO**
Raytheon Canada Limited; **RAYTHEON CO**
Raytheon Systems Limited; **RAYTHEON CO**
RealLife HR; **HEWITT ASSOCIATES**
Recombinant Capital Inc; **DELOITTE & TOUCHE USA LLP**
Reconnex; **MCAFEE INC**
Recycle America Alliance; **WASTE MANAGEMENT INC**
Red Bluff; **NRG ENERGY INC**
Red Flag Rules; **EXPERIAN AMERICAS**
Red Lobster; **DARDEN RESTAURANTS INC**
RedHead; **BASS PRO SHOPS INC**
Refuge; **CHARLOTTE RUSSE HOLDING**
Regis Salons; **REGIS CORPORATION**
Registry Power Cleaner; **MCAFEE INC**
Rehab @ Home; **AMEDISYS INC**
Reliabilt; **LOWE'S COMPANIES INC**
Reliance Vision Single-Chamber Washer/Disinfector; **STERIS CORP**
Reliant Energy Solutions East; **RRI ENERGY INC**
Reliant Energy Solutions Northeast; **RRI ENERGY INC**
Relic; **FOSSIL INC**
Renaissance Hotels, Resorts and ClubSport; **MARRIOTT INTERNATIONAL INC**
Renal; **BAXTER INTERNATIONAL INC**
RenalSoft HD; **BAXTER INTERNATIONAL INC**
Renessen Feed & Processing; **CARGILL INC**

Renewable Hawaii, Inc.; **HAWAIIAN ELECTRIC INDUSTRIES INC**
Rent.com; **EBAY INC**
Rent-A-Centre; **RENT-A-CENTER INC**
Rental Car Finance Corp.; **DOLLAR THRIFTY AUTOMOTIVE GROUP INC**
Research Biotech; **SIGMA-ALDRICH CORP**
Research Essentials; **SIGMA-ALDRICH CORP**
Research Institute for Safety; **LIBERTY MUTUAL GROUP INC**
Research Instruments; **VARIAN MEDICAL SYSTEMS INC**
Research Specialties; **SIGMA-ALDRICH CORP**
Residence Inn by Marriott; **LODGIAN INC**
Resolution Health, Inc.; **WELLPOINT INC**
Respiratory Healthways; **HEALTHWAYS INC**
Restasis; **ALLERGAN INC**
Restore Medical Inc; **MEDTRONIC INC**
REVLIMID; **CELGENE CORP**
Revolution/Stronghold; **PFIZER INC**
RF Worx; **ADC TELECOMMUNICATIONS INC**
Rice Krispies; **KELLOGG CO**
Right Management; **MANPOWER INC**
Rimadyl; **PFIZER INC**
Ringtail; **FTI CONSULTING INC**
Rintekno; **JACOBS ENGINEERING GROUP INC**
Rio; **HARRAH'S ENTERTAINMENT INC**
Rising Moon Organics; **UNITED NATURAL FOODS INC**
RITALIN; **CELGENE CORP**
Rite Aid Health Solutions; **RITE AID CORPORATION**
Rite Aid RX Savings Card; **RITE AID CORPORATION**
Rituxan; **GENENTECH INC**
Ritz-Carlton (The); **MARRIOTT INTERNATIONAL INC**
Ritz-Carlton Club; **RITZ-CARLTON HOTEL COMPANY LLC (THE)**
RLM Systems, Ltd.; **LOCKHEED MARTIN CORP**
RMBC; **IMS HEALTH INC**
Robert Half Finance & Accounting; **ROBERT HALF INTERNATIONAL INC**
Robert Half Legal; **ROBERT HALF INTERNATIONAL INC**
Robert Half Management Resources; **ROBERT HALF INTERNATIONAL INC**
Robert Half Technology; **ROBERT HALF INTERNATIONAL INC**

INDEX OF SUBSIDIARIES, BRAND NAMES AND AFFILIATIONS, CONT.

INDEX OF SUBSIDIARIES, BRAND NAMES AND AFFILIATIONS, CONT.

INDEX OF SUBSIDIARIES, BRAND NAMES AND AFFILIATIONS, CONT.

INDEX OF SUBSIDIARIES, BRAND NAMES AND AFFILIATIONS, CONT.

INDEX OF SUBSIDIARIES, BRAND NAMES AND AFFILIATIONS, CONT.

INDEX OF SUBSIDIARIES, BRAND NAMES AND AFFILIATIONS, CONT.

W; **STARWOOD HOTELS & RESORTS WORLDWIDE INC**
W. R. Reed & Co.; **BROWN & BROWN INC**
Wabtec Australia Pty Ltd; **WABTEC CORP**
Wabtec de Mexico; **WABTEC CORP**
Wabtec Foundry; **WABTEC CORP**
Wabtec Global Services; **WABTEC CORP**
Wabtec Passenger Transit; **WABTEC CORP**
Wachovia Corp.; **WELLS FARGO & CO**
Wachovia Corporation; **WELLS FARGO & CO**
Wade & Assoicates, Inc.; **CH2M HILL COMPANIES LTD**
Waldorf=Astoria Collection; **HILTON HOTELS CORP**
Walgreen's Health Services; **WALGREEN CO**
Wal-Mart Stores Inc; **SAM'S CLUB**
Wal-Mart Supercenter; **WAL-MART STORES INC**
Walt Disney Parks & Resorts; **WALT DISNEY COMPANY (THE)**
Walt Disney Pictures; **WALT DISNEY COMPANY (THE)**
Walt Disney Studios (The); **WALT DISNEY COMPANY (THE)**
Walt Disney World Resort; **WALT DISNEY COMPANY (THE)**
Walter Karl; **INFOGROUP INC**
Warburg Pincus LLC; **ARAMARK CORPORATION**
Warner Bros Entertainment Inc; **TIME WARNER INC**
Washington Division; **URS CORPORATION**
Washington Mutual (WAMU); **JP MORGAN CHASE & CO INC**
Waterbased Acrolon 100; **SHERWIN WILLIAMS COMPANY (THE)**
Waters Division; **WATERS CORP**
Waters Xevo TQ MS System (The); **WATERS CORP**
Watson Laboratories; **WATSON PHARMACEUTICALS INC**
Watson Wyatt & Company Holdings; **WATSON WYATT WORLDWIDE INC**
Watson Wyatt Brans & Co.; **WATSON WYATT WORLDWIDE INC**
Watson Wyatt Worldwide; **TOWERS PERRIN**
Watts Brothers; **CONAGRA FOODS INC**
Wayport, Inc.; **AT&T INC**
Wayzata Investment Partners LLC; **NRG ENERGY INC**
Webex Communications Inc; **CISCO SYSTEMS INC**
Webster Management LP; **PATTERSON COMPANIES INC**

Weedol; **SCOTTS MIRACLE GROW CO**
Weight Watchers eTools; **WEIGHT WATCHERS INTERNATIONAL INC**
Weight Watchers Online; **WEIGHT WATCHERS INTERNATIONAL INC**
Weill Medical College of Cornell University; **METHODIST HEALTH CARE SYSTEM**
WellChoice, Inc.; **WELLPOINT INC**
WellDynamics; **HALLIBURTON COMPANY**
WellPath; **COVENTRY HEALTH CARE INC**
Wells Capital Management; **WELLS FARGO & CO**
Wells Fargo Insurance Services; **WELLS FARGO & CO**
Wendy's; **WENDY'S/ARBY'S GROUP INC**
West Analytical Services; **WEST PHARMACEUTICAL SERVICES INC**
West Business Services; **WEST CORPORATION**
West Coast Hitech L.P.; **ADVANCED MICRO DEVICES INC (AMD)**
Western Auto; **ADVANCE AUTO PARTS INC**
Western Gas Resources, Inc.; **ANADARKO PETROLEUM CORPORATION**
Western International University, Inc.; **APOLLO GROUP INC**
WesternGeco; **SCHLUMBERGER LIMITED**
Westin; **STARWOOD HOTELS & RESORTS WORLDWIDE INC**
Westinghouse Electric Company, L.L.C; **SHAW GROUP INC (THE)**
Westport, Ltd.; **DRESS BARN INC (THE)**
Wexford Group International; **CACI INTERNATIONAL INC**
W-H Energy Services, Inc.; **SMITH INTERNATIONAL INC**
Wheelbrator; **WASTE MANAGEMENT INC**
White Barn Candle Company; **LIMITED BRANDS INC**
White Hen Pantry, Inc.; **7-ELEVEN INC**
White House/Black Market; **CHICO'S FAS INC**
White River Fly Shops; **BASS PRO SHOPS INC**
WhiteWave Foods Company; **DEAN FOODS CO**
Whole Health Management; **WALGREEN CO**
Whole Kitchen; **WHOLE FOODS MARKET INC**
Whole Pantry; **WHOLE FOODS MARKET INC**

Whopper; **BURGER KING HOLDINGS INC**
Wide Area Workflow; **CACI INTERNATIONAL INC**
Wild Flatbreads; **BUFFALO WILD WINGS INC**
Wild Oats Markets, Inc.; **WHOLE FOODS MARKET INC**
Wild Wings; **CABELA'S INC**
Williams Field Services Group LLC; **WILLIAMS COMPANIES INC (THE)**
Williams Gas Pipeline Co LLC; **WILLIAMS COMPANIES INC (THE)**
Williams Partners L.P.; **WILLIAMS COMPANIES INC (THE)**
Williams Power Co Inc; **WILLIAMS COMPANIES INC (THE)**
Williams Production Co LLC; **WILLIAMS COMPANIES INC (THE)**
Williams Production RMT Co.; **WILLIAMS COMPANIES INC (THE)**
Williamson Memorial Hospital; **HEALTH MANAGEMENT ASSOCIATES INC**
Willis; **CAMERON INTERNATIONAL CORPORATION**
Wilmar International Limited; **ARCHER DANIELS MIDLAND CO**
Wilson; **SMITH INTERNATIONAL INC**
Wilson Welding & Medical Gases; **PRAXAIR INC**
Wind River Systems, Inc.; **INTEL CORP**
Windows 7; **MICROSOFT CORP**
Wingate Inns; **WYNDHAM WORLDWIDE**
Winners; **TJX COMPANIES INC (THE)**
WISDOM Gold; **OWENS & MINOR INC**
Wm Wrigley Jr Company; **MARS INC**
Wolff Olins; **OMNICOM GROUP INC**
Woodstock Farms; **UNITED NATURAL FOODS INC**
Worklife; **OFFICE DEPOT INC**
World of Warcraft; **ACTIVISION BLIZZARD INC**
World Ovens Bakery; **7-ELEVEN INC**
World's Foremost Bank; **CABELA'S INC**
Worthington; **J C PENNEY COMPANY INC**
Wyndham Hotels; **WYNDHAM WORLDWIDE**
Wyndham Worldwide; **LODGIAN INC**
Wynn Las Vegas, LLC; **WYNN RESORTS LIMITED**
Wynn Resorts (Macau), S.A.; **WYNN RESORTS LIMITED**
Xbox; **MICROSOFT CORP**
Xcelicor, Inc.; **DELOITTE CONSULTING LLP**
Xerox Canada Inc; **XEROX CORP**
Xhilaration; **TARGET CORPORATION**

INDEX OF SUBSIDIARIES, BRAND NAMES AND AFFILIATIONS, CONT.

INDEX BY COMPANIES FOR SPECIFIC TYPES OF JOB SEEKERS

Indexed by the following categories:	
Information Systems	**648**
Liberal Arts	**655**
Management	**666**
Professionals	**679**
Sales/Marketing	**695**
Technical/Scientific	**707**

Information Systems

Consulting/Other
ACCENTURE LTD
ADOBE SYSTEMS INC
AECOM TECHNOLOGY CORPORATION
AFFILIATED COMPUTER SERVICES INC
AGILENT TECHNOLOGIES INC
APPLE INC
AUTOMATIC DATA PROCESSING INC
BDO SEIDMAN LLP
BECHTEL GROUP INC
BENCHMARK ELECTRONICS INC
BOEING COMPANY (THE)
BOOZ ALLEN HAMILTON
CACI INTERNATIONAL INC
CH2M HILL COMPANIES LTD
CIBER INC
CISCO SYSTEMS INC
COGNIZANT TECHNOLOGY SOLUTIONS CORP
COVANCE INC
DELOITTE & TOUCHE USA LLP
DELOITTE CONSULTING LLP
DIEBOLD INC
ERNST & YOUNG LLP
FLUOR CORP
FOSTER WHEELER AG
FTI CONSULTING INC
GENERAL DYNAMICS CORP
GRANT THORNTON LLP
HARRIS CORPORATION
HEWITT ASSOCIATES
HONEYWELL INTERNATIONAL INC

IBM GLOBAL SERVICES
IGATE CORPORATION
INTEL CORP
INTERNATIONAL BUSINESS MACHINES CORP (IBM)
INVENTIV HEALTH INC
JACOBS ENGINEERING GROUP INC
KEANE INC
KENDLE INTERNATIONAL INC
KPMG LLP
L-3 COMMUNICATIONS HOLDINGS INC
LOCKHEED MARTIN CORP
MCAFEE INC
MCDERMOTT INTERNATIONAL INC
MCKESSON CORPORATION
MCKINSEY & COMPANY INC
MERCER INC
MICROSOFT CORP
NORTHROP GRUMMAN CORP
ORACLE CORP
PAREXEL INTERNATIONAL CORP
PARSONS BRINCKERHOFF INC
PEROT SYSTEMS CORP
PHARMACEUTICAL PRODUCT DEVELOPMENT INC
PLEXUS CORP
PRICEWATERHOUSECOOPERS
RAYTHEON CO
SAIC INC
SAPIENT CORPORATION
SAS INSTITUTE INC
SRA INTERNATIONAL INC
SUNGARD DATA SYSTEMS INC
SYMANTEC CORP
SYNTEL INC
TOWERS PERRIN
UNITED TECHNOLOGIES CORPORATION
URS CORPORATION
VERISIGN INC
WATSON WYATT WORLDWIDE INC

Hardware Development
ACCENTURE LTD
ADC TELECOMMUNICATIONS INC
ADVANCED MICRO DEVICES INC (AMD)
AFFILIATED COMPUTER SERVICES INC
AGILENT TECHNOLOGIES INC

AMERICAN POWER CONVERSION (APC)
ANALOG DEVICES INC
APPLE INC
BECKMAN COULTER INC
BENCHMARK ELECTRONICS INC
BLACK & DECKER CORP
BLOOMBERG LP
BOEING COMPANY (THE)
BROADCOM CORP
BUCYRUS INTERNATIONAL INC
CACI INTERNATIONAL INC
CAMERON INTERNATIONAL CORPORATION
CATERPILLAR INC
CIBER INC
CISCO SYSTEMS INC
COGNIZANT TECHNOLOGY SOLUTIONS CORP
CTS CORP
CUBIC CORP
CUMMINS INC
DANAHER CORP
DEERE & CO
DIEBOLD INC
DIRECTV GROUP INC (THE)
EMC CORP
EMERSON ELECTRIC CO
GENERAL DYNAMICS CORP
GOOGLE INC
HARRIS CORPORATION
HONEYWELL INTERNATIONAL INC
IBM GLOBAL SERVICES
IGATE CORPORATION
INTEL CORP
INTERNATIONAL BUSINESS MACHINES CORP (IBM)
JABIL CIRCUIT INC
JOHNSON CONTROLS INC
JUNIPER NETWORKS INC
KEANE INC
L-3 COMMUNICATIONS HOLDINGS INC
LEVEL 3 COMMUNICATIONS INC
LEXMARK INTERNATIONAL INC
LOCKHEED MARTIN CORP
MAXIM INTEGRATED PRODUCTS INC
MEDTRONIC INC
MICROCHIP TECHNOLOGY INC
MICRON TECHNOLOGY INC

MILLIPORE CORP	ALLIANCE DATA SYSTEMS CORPORATION	BLACK & DECKER CORP
NETAPP INC	ALLSTATE CORPORATION (THE)	BLACKROCK INC
NORTHROP GRUMMAN CORP	ALTRIA GROUP INC	BLOOMBERG LP
OSHKOSH CORPORATION	AMAZON.COM INC	BOEING COMPANY (THE)
PEROT SYSTEMS CORP	AMEDISYS INC	BOOZ ALLEN HAMILTON
PITNEY BOWES INC	AMERICAN ELECTRIC POWER COMPANY INC (AEP)	BOSTON SCIENTIFIC CORP
PLEXUS CORP		BRINKER INTERNATIONAL INC
QUALCOMM INC	AMERICAN POWER CONVERSION (APC)	BRINKS COMPANY (THE)
RAYTHEON CO		BROADCOM CORP
SAIC INC	AMERISOURCEBERGEN CORP	BROWN & BROWN INC
SAPIENT CORPORATION	AMGEN INC	BUCKLE INC (THE)
SRA INTERNATIONAL INC	ANADARKO PETROLEUM CORPORATION	BUCYRUS INTERNATIONAL INC
SYNTEL INC		BUFFALO WILD WINGS INC
TEKTRONIX INC	ANALOG DEVICES INC	BUNGE LTD
TELEDYNE TECHNOLOGIES INCORPORATED	ANNTAYLOR STORES CORP	BURGER KING HOLDINGS INC
	APACHE CORP	CABELA'S INC
UNITED TECHNOLOGIES CORPORATION	APOLLO GROUP INC	CABLEVISION SYSTEMS CORP
	APPLE INC	CACI INTERNATIONAL INC
VARIAN MEDICAL SYSTEMS INC	ARAMARK CORPORATION	CAMERON INTERNATIONAL CORPORATION
WABTEC CORP	ARCHER DANIELS MIDLAND CO	
WESTERN DIGITAL CORP	ARROW ELECTRONICS INC	CAPITAL SENIOR LIVING CORP
XEROX CORP	ARTHUR J GALLAGHER & CO	CARDINAL HEALTH INC
YAHOO! INC	ASCENSION HEALTH	CARGILL INC
	AT&T INC	CARMAX GROUP
Information Management	AUTOMATIC DATA PROCESSING INC	CARNIVAL CORPORATION
3M COMPANY		CASH AMERICA INTERNATIONAL INC
7-ELEVEN INC	AUTOZONE INC	
AARON'S INC	AVERY DENNISON CORP	CATERPILLAR INC
ABBOTT LABORATORIES	AVIS BUDGET GROUP INC	CATHOLIC HEALTH INITIATIVES
ABM INDUSTRIES INC	AVNET INC	CDW CORPORATION
ACADEMY SPORTS & OUTDOORS LTD	AVON PRODUCTS INC	CELGENE CORP
	AXA FINANCIAL INC	CELLCO PARTNERSHIP (VERIZON WIRELESS)
ACCENTURE LTD	BAKER HUGHES INC	
ACTIVISION BLIZZARD INC	BALTIMORE GAS AND ELECTRIC COMPANY	CEPHALON INC
ACXIOM CORP		CH ROBINSON WORLDWIDE INC
ADC TELECOMMUNICATIONS INC	BANK OF AMERICA CORP	CH2M HILL COMPANIES LTD
ADESA INC	BARNES & NOBLE INC	CHARLOTTE RUSSE HOLDING
ADOBE SYSTEMS INC	BASS PRO SHOPS INC	CHARMING SHOPPES INC
ADVANCE AUTO PARTS INC	BAXTER INTERNATIONAL INC	CHEMED CORPORATION
ADVANCED MICRO DEVICES INC (AMD)	BDO SEIDMAN LLP	CHEVRON CORPORATION
	BEBE STORES INC	CHEVRON PHILLIPS CHEMICAL COMPANY LLC
AECOM TECHNOLOGY CORPORATION	BECHTEL GROUP INC	
	BECKMAN COULTER INC	CHICO'S FAS INC
AES CORPORATION (THE)	BECTON DICKINSON & CO	CHIPOTLE MEXICAN GRILL INC
AETNA INC	BED BATH & BEYOND INC	CHRISTOPHER & BANKS CORP
AFFILIATED COMPUTER SERVICES INC	BENCHMARK ELECTRONICS INC	CHS INC
	BERKSHIRE HATHAWAY INC	CHUBB CORPORATION (THE)
AFLAC INC	BEST BUY CO INC	CIBER INC
AGILENT TECHNOLOGIES INC	BIO RAD LABORATORIES INC	CIGNA CORP
AIR PRODUCTS & CHEMICALS INC	BJ'S WHOLESALE CLUB INC	CINTAS CORP
ALLERGAN INC		CISCO SYSTEMS INC

CLUBCORP INC	E I DU PONT DE NEMOURS & CO (DUPONT)	GILEAD SCIENCES INC
COACH INC	EATON CORP	GLOBAL HYATT CORPORATION
COCA-COLA COMPANY (THE)	EBAY INC	GLOBAL PAYMENTS INC
COCA-COLA ENTERPRISES INC	EDISON INTERNATIONAL	GOLDMAN SACHS GROUP INC
COGNIZANT TECHNOLOGY SOLUTIONS CORP	ELECTRONIC ARTS INC	GOOGLE INC
COLDWATER CREEK INC	ELI LILLY & COMPANY	GRANT THORNTON LLP
COLGATE PALMOLIVE CO	EMBARQ CORP	GUESS? INC
COMCAST CORP	EMC CORP	HALLIBURTON COMPANY
COMMUNITY HEALTH SYSTEMS INC	EMERITUS CORP	HARRAH'S ENTERTAINMENT INC
CONAGRA FOODS INC	EMERSON ELECTRIC CO	HARRIS CORPORATION
CONOCOPHILLIPS COMPANY	ENTERGY CORP	HARTFORD FINANCIAL SERVICES GROUP INC (THE)
CONSOL ENERGY INC	ENTERPRISE PRODUCTS PARTNERS LP	HAWAIIAN ELECTRIC INDUSTRIES INC
CONSOLIDATED EDISON INC	ENTERPRISE RENT-A-CAR	HCA INC
CONTAINER STORE (THE)	ERNST & YOUNG LLP	HE BUTT GROCERY COMPANY (HEB)
CONVERGYS CORPORATION	ESTEE LAUDER COMPANIES INC (THE)	HEALTH CARE SERVICE CORPORATION
COOPER COMPANIES INC	EXELON CORPORATION	
COSTCO WHOLESALE CORP	EXPERIAN AMERICAS	HEALTH FITNESS CORP
COVANCE INC	EXPRESS SCRIPTS INC	HEALTH MANAGEMENT ASSOCIATES INC
COVENTRY HEALTH CARE INC	EXXON MOBIL CORPORATION (EXXONMOBIL)	HEALTH NET INC
COX COMMUNICATIONS INC	EXXONMOBIL CHEMICAL	HEALTHWAYS INC
CR BARD INC	FAMILY DOLLAR STORES INC	HELMERICH & PAYNE INC
CRACKER BARREL OLD COUNTRY STORE INC	FEDEX CORPORATION	HENRY SCHEIN INC
CTS CORP	FINISH LINE INC (THE)	HERTZ GLOBAL HOLDINGS INC
CUBIC CORP	FIRST ADVANTAGE CORPORATION	HESS CORPORATION
CUMMINS INC	FIRST DATA CORP	HEWITT ASSOCIATES
CVS CAREMARK CORPORATION	FIRSTENERGY CORP	HIBBETT SPORTS INC
DANAHER CORP	FLUOR CORP	HILTON HOTELS CORP
DARDEN RESTAURANTS INC	FOREST LABORATORIES INC	HOME DEPOT INC
DAVITA INC	FORTUNE BRANDS INC	HONEYWELL INTERNATIONAL INC
DEAN FOODS CO	FOSSIL INC	HUMANA INC
DEERE & CO	FOSTER WHEELER AG	IAC/INTERACTIVECORP
DELOITTE & TOUCHE USA LLP	FOX ENTERTAINMENT GROUP INC	IBM GLOBAL SERVICES
DELOITTE CONSULTING LLP	FPL GROUP INC	ICT GROUP INC
DENNY'S CORPORATION	FRED'S INC	IDEXX LABORATORIES INC
DEVON ENERGY CORPORATION	FRONTIER COMMUNICATIONS CORPORATION	IGATE CORPORATION
DEVRY INC		IMS HEALTH INC
DIAMOND OFFSHORE DRILLING INC	FTI CONSULTING INC	INFOGROUP INC
DICK'S SPORTING GOODS INC	GAMESTOP CORP	INGRAM MICRO INC
DIEBOLD INC	GENENTECH INC	INTEL CORP
DINEEQUITY INC	GENERAL CABLE CORP	INTERNATIONAL BUSINESS MACHINES CORP (IBM)
DIRECTV GROUP INC (THE)	GENERAL DYNAMICS CORP	
DOLE FOOD COMPANY INC	GENERAL ELECTRIC CO (GE)	INTUIT INC
DOLLAR GENERAL CORPORATION	GENERAL MILLS INC	INVENTIV HEALTH INC
DOLLAR THRIFTY AUTOMOTIVE GROUP INC	GENESCO INC	J C PENNEY COMPANY INC
DRESS BARN INC (THE)	GENWORTH FINANCIAL INC	JABIL CIRCUIT INC
DTE ENERGY COMPANY	GEO GROUP INC	JACK IN THE BOX INC
DUKE ENERGY CORP	GEORGIA GULF CORPORATION	JACOBS ENGINEERING GROUP INC
DYCOM INDUSTRIES INC		

JETBLUE AIRWAYS CORPORATION	MCDERMOTT INTERNATIONAL INC	PAYCHEX INC
JM SMUCKER CO	MCDONALD'S CORP	PEABODY ENERGY CORP
JOHNSON & JOHNSON	MCKESSON CORPORATION	PEPSI BOTTLING GROUP INC
JOHNSON CONTROLS INC	MCKINSEY & COMPANY INC	PEPSICO INC
JP MORGAN CHASE & CO INC	MEDCO HEALTH SOLUTIONS	PEROT SYSTEMS CORP
JUNIPER NETWORKS INC	MEDTRONIC INC	PERRIGO CO
KAISER PERMANENTE	MEIJER INC	PETCO ANIMAL SUPPLIES INC
KEANE INC	MEN'S WEARHOUSE INC (THE)	PETSMART INC
KELLOGG CO	MERCER INC	PFIZER INC
KELLY SERVICES INC	MERCK & CO INC	PG&E CORPORATION
KENDLE INTERNATIONAL INC	METHODIST HEALTH CARE SYSTEM	PHARMACEUTICAL PRODUCT DEVELOPMENT INC
KIMBERLY-CLARK CORP	METLIFE INC	PITNEY BOWES INC
KINDRED HEALTHCARE INC	MGM MIRAGE	PLEXUS CORP
KOCH INDUSTRIES INC	MICROCHIP TECHNOLOGY INC	POLO RALPH LAUREN CORP
KOHL'S CORP	MICRON TECHNOLOGY INC	PRAXAIR INC
KPMG LLP	MICROSOFT CORP	PRECISION CASTPARTS CORP
KRAFT FOODS INC	MIDAMERICAN ENERGY HOLDINGS CO	PRICESMART INC
KROGER CO (THE)		PRICEWATERHOUSECOOPERS
L-3 COMMUNICATIONS HOLDINGS INC	MILLIPORE CORP	PRIDE INTERNATIONAL INC
LABORATORY CORP OF AMERICA HOLDINGS	MONRO MUFFLER BRAKE INC	PRINCIPAL FINANCIAL GROUP (THE)
	MONSANTO CO	
LAS VEGAS SANDS CORP (THE VENETIAN)	MURPHY OIL CORPORATION	PROCTER & GAMBLE CO
	MYLAN INC	PROGRESSIVE CORPORATION (THE)
LEVEL 3 COMMUNICATIONS INC	NATIONAL OILWELL VARCO INC	
LEXMARK INTERNATIONAL INC	NETAPP INC	PRUDENTIAL FINANCIAL INC
LIBERTY GLOBAL INC	NEWS CORP	PSYCHIATRIC SOLUTIONS INC
LIBERTY MUTUAL GROUP INC	NII HOLDINGS INC	PUBLIC STORAGE INC
LIMITED BRANDS INC	NIKE INC	PUBLIX SUPER MARKETS INC
LINCARE HOLDINGS INC	NOBLE CORPORATION	QUALCOMM INC
LINCOLN NATIONAL CORPORATION	NORTHROP GRUMMAN CORP	QUANTA SERVICES INC
LKQ CORP	NRG ENERGY INC	QUEST DIAGNOSTICS INC
LOCKHEED MARTIN CORP	OCCIDENTAL PETROLEUM CORP	QUIKSILVER INC
LODGIAN INC	OCEANEERING INTERNATIONAL INC	R R DONNELLEY & SONS CO
LOEWS CORPORATION		RALCORP HOLDINGS INC
LOWE'S COMPANIES INC	ODYSSEY HEALTHCARE INC	RAYTHEON CO
MACY'S INC	OFFICE DEPOT INC	REGIS CORPORATION
MANOR CARE INC	OIL STATES INTERNATIONAL INC	RENT-A-CENTER INC
MANPOWER INC	OMNICARE INC	RES CARE INC
MARRIOTT INTERNATIONAL INC	OMNICOM GROUP INC	RITE AID CORPORATION
MARS INC	ORACLE CORP	RITZ-CARLTON HOTEL COMPANY LLC (THE)
MARSH & MCLENNAN COMPANIES INC	O'REILLY AUTOMOTIVE INC	
	OSHKOSH CORPORATION	ROBERT HALF INTERNATIONAL INC
MARY KAY INC	OSI RESTAURANT PARTNERS LLC	ROSS STORES INC
MASSEY ENERGY COMPANY	OWENS & MINOR INC	ROYAL CARIBBEAN CRUISES LTD
MATTEL INC	PANTRY INC (THE)	RRI ENERGY INC
MAXIM INTEGRATED PRODUCTS INC	PARAMETRIC TECHNOLOGY CORP	SABRE HOLDINGS CORP
	PAREXEL INTERNATIONAL CORP	SAFECO INSURANCE COMPANY OF AMERICA
MAYO FOUNDATION FOR MEDICAL EDUCATION AND RESEARCH	PARSONS BRINCKERHOFF INC	
	PATTERSON COMPANIES INC	SAFEWAY INC
MCAFEE INC	PATTERSON-UTI ENERGY INC	SAIC INC

SAM'S CLUB
SAPIENT CORPORATION
SARA LEE CORP
SAS INSTITUTE INC
SCANA CORPORATION
SCHERING-PLOUGH CORP
SCHLUMBERGER LIMITED
SCIENTIFIC GAMES CORPORATION
SCOTTS MIRACLE GROW CO
SEACOR HOLDINGS INC
SELECT MEDICAL
SEMPRA ENERGY
SENSIENT TECHNOLOGIES CORPORATION
SHAW GROUP INC (THE)
SHELL OIL CO
SHERWIN WILLIAMS COMPANY (THE)
SIGMA-ALDRICH CORP
SISTERS OF MERCY HEALTH SYSTEMS
SMITH INTERNATIONAL INC
SMITHFIELD FOODS INC
SOUTHERN CALIFORNIA EDISON COMPANY
SOUTHERN COMPANY (THE)
SOUTHWEST AIRLINES CO
SRA INTERNATIONAL INC
ST JUDE MEDICAL INC
STAPLES INC
STARTEK INC
STARWOOD HOTELS & RESORTS WORLDWIDE INC
STERIS CORP
STIFEL FINANCIAL CORP
STRYKER CORP
SUN HEALTHCARE GROUP
SUNGARD DATA SYSTEMS INC
SUNOCO INC
SUNRISE SENIOR LIVING
SUPERVALU INC
SYKES ENTERPRISES INC
SYMANTEC CORP
SYNOPSYS INC
SYNTEL INC
SYSCO CORP
TARGET CORPORATION
TBC CORPORATION
TEAM INC
TECH DATA CORP
TEKTRONIX INC

TELEDYNE TECHNOLOGIES INCORPORATED
TELEPHONE AND DATA SYSTEMS INC (TDS)
TELETECH HOLDINGS INC
TESORO CORP
THERMO FISHER SCIENTIFIC INC
TIFFANY & CO
TIME WARNER INC
TJX COMPANIES INC (THE)
T-MOBILE USA
TOTAL SYSTEM SERVICES INC (TSYS)
TOWERS PERRIN
TRANSOCEAN INC
TRAVELERS COMPANIES INC (THE)
TREEHOUSE FOODS INC
TW TELECOM INC
TYSON FOODS INC
UNITED NATURAL FOODS INC
UNITED PARCEL SERVICE INC (UPS)
UNITED STATES CELLULAR CORP
UNITED TECHNOLOGIES CORPORATION
UNITEDHEALTH GROUP INC
UNIVERSAL HEALTH SERVICES INC
UNIVISION COMMUNICATIONS INC
URS CORPORATION
USAA
VALERO ENERGY CORP
VALSPAR CORPORATION (THE)
VARIAN MEDICAL SYSTEMS INC
VCA ANTECH INC
VERISIGN INC
VERIZON COMMUNICATIONS
VIACOM INC
VICTORIAS SECRET
VISA INC
VOLT INFORMATION SCIENCES INC
W R BERKLEY CORPORATION
WABTEC CORP
WALGREEN CO
WAL-MART STORES INC
WALT DISNEY COMPANY (THE)
WASTE MANAGEMENT INC
WATERS CORP
WATSON PHARMACEUTICALS INC
WATSON WYATT WORLDWIDE INC
WEATHERFORD INTERNATIONAL LTD

WEIGHT WATCHERS INTERNATIONAL INC
WELLPOINT INC
WELLS FARGO & CO
WENDY'S/ARBY'S GROUP INC
WEST CORPORATION
WEST PHARMACEUTICAL SERVICES INC
WESTERN DIGITAL CORP
WHOLE FOODS MARKET INC
WILLIAMS COMPANIES INC (THE)
WW GRAINGER INC
WYETH
WYNDHAM WORLDWIDE
WYNN RESORTS LIMITED
XEROX CORP
YAHOO! INC
YUM! BRANDS INC
ZIMMER HOLDINGS INC

Software Development
3M COMPANY
7-ELEVEN INC
AARON'S INC
ABBOTT LABORATORIES
ACADEMY SPORTS & OUTDOORS LTD
ACCENTURE LTD
ACTIVISION BLIZZARD INC
ACXIOM CORP
ADC TELECOMMUNICATIONS INC
ADOBE SYSTEMS INC
ADVANCE AUTO PARTS INC
ADVANCED MICRO DEVICES INC (AMD)
AECOM TECHNOLOGY CORPORATION
AES CORPORATION (THE)
AETNA INC
AFFILIATED COMPUTER SERVICES INC
AFLAC INC
AGILENT TECHNOLOGIES INC
AIR PRODUCTS & CHEMICALS INC
ALLERGAN INC
ALLIANCE DATA SYSTEMS CORPORATION
ALLSTATE CORPORATION (THE)
ALTRIA GROUP INC
AMAZON.COM INC
AMERICAN ELECTRIC POWER COMPANY INC (AEP)

AMERICAN POWER CONVERSION (APC)	BROWN & BROWN INC	CONVERGYS CORPORATION
AMERISOURCEBERGEN CORP	BUCKLE INC (THE)	COOPER COMPANIES INC
AMGEN INC	BUFFALO WILD WINGS INC	COSTCO WHOLESALE CORP
ANADARKO PETROLEUM CORPORATION	BURGER KING HOLDINGS INC	COVANCE INC
ANALOG DEVICES INC	CABELA'S INC	COVENTRY HEALTH CARE INC
ANNTAYLOR STORES CORP	CABLEVISION SYSTEMS CORP	COX COMMUNICATIONS INC
APACHE CORP	CACI INTERNATIONAL INC	CR BARD INC
APOLLO GROUP INC	CAMERON INTERNATIONAL CORPORATION	CRACKER BARREL OLD COUNTRY STORE INC
APPLE INC	CARDINAL HEALTH INC	CTS CORP
ARAMARK CORPORATION	CARGILL INC	CUBIC CORP
ARCHER DANIELS MIDLAND CO	CARMAX GROUP	CUMMINS INC
ARROW ELECTRONICS INC	CARNIVAL CORPORATION	CVS CAREMARK CORPORATION
ARTHUR J GALLAGHER & CO	CASH AMERICA INTERNATIONAL INC	DANAHER CORP
ASCENSION HEALTH	CATERPILLAR INC	DARDEN RESTAURANTS INC
AT&T INC	CATHOLIC HEALTH INITIATIVES	DAVITA INC
AUTOMATIC DATA PROCESSING INC	CDW CORPORATION	DEERE & CO
AUTOZONE INC	CELGENE CORP	DELOITTE & TOUCHE USA LLP
AVERY DENNISON CORP	CELLCO PARTNERSHIP (VERIZON WIRELESS)	DELOITTE CONSULTING LLP
AVIS BUDGET GROUP INC	CEPHALON INC	DENNY'S CORPORATION
AVON PRODUCTS INC	CH ROBINSON WORLDWIDE INC	DEVON ENERGY CORPORATION
AXA FINANCIAL INC	CH2M HILL COMPANIES LTD	DEVRY INC
BAKER HUGHES INC	CHARLOTTE RUSSE HOLDING	DIAMOND OFFSHORE DRILLING INC
BALTIMORE GAS AND ELECTRIC COMPANY	CHARMING SHOPPES INC	DICK'S SPORTING GOODS INC
BANK OF AMERICA CORP	CHEVRON CORPORATION	DIEBOLD INC
BARNES & NOBLE INC	CHEVRON PHILLIPS CHEMICAL COMPANY LLC	DINEEQUITY INC
BASS PRO SHOPS INC	CHICO'S FAS INC	DIRECTV GROUP INC (THE)
BAXTER INTERNATIONAL INC	CHIPOTLE MEXICAN GRILL INC	DOLE FOOD COMPANY INC
BDO SEIDMAN LLP	CHRISTOPHER & BANKS CORP	DOLLAR GENERAL CORPORATION
BEBE STORES INC	CHUBB CORPORATION (THE)	DOLLAR THRIFTY AUTOMOTIVE GROUP INC
BECHTEL GROUP INC	CIBER INC	DRESS BARN INC (THE)
BECKMAN COULTER INC	CIGNA CORP	DTE ENERGY COMPANY
BECTON DICKINSON & CO	CINTAS CORP	DUKE ENERGY CORP
BED BATH & BEYOND INC	CISCO SYSTEMS INC	E I DU PONT DE NEMOURS & CO (DUPONT)
BENCHMARK ELECTRONICS INC	CLUBCORP INC	EATON CORP
BERKSHIRE HATHAWAY INC	COACH INC	EBAY INC
BEST BUY CO INC	COCA-COLA COMPANY (THE)	EDISON INTERNATIONAL
BIO RAD LABORATORIES INC	COCA-COLA ENTERPRISES INC	ELECTRONIC ARTS INC
BJ'S WHOLESALE CLUB INC	COGNIZANT TECHNOLOGY SOLUTIONS CORP	ELI LILLY & COMPANY
BLACK & DECKER CORP	COLDWATER CREEK INC	EMBARQ CORP
BLACKROCK INC	COLGATE PALMOLIVE CO	EMC CORP
BLOOMBERG LP	COMCAST CORP	EMERSON ELECTRIC CO
BOEING COMPANY (THE)	COMMUNITY HEALTH SYSTEMS INC	ENTERGY CORP
BOOZ ALLEN HAMILTON	CONAGRA FOODS INC	ENTERPRISE PRODUCTS PARTNERS LP
BOSTON SCIENTIFIC CORP	CONOCOPHILLIPS COMPANY	ENTERPRISE RENT-A-CAR
BRINKER INTERNATIONAL INC	CONSOLIDATED EDISON INC	ERNST & YOUNG LLP
BRINKS COMPANY (THE)	CONTAINER STORE (THE)	ESTEE LAUDER COMPANIES INC (THE)
BROADCOM CORP		

EXELON CORPORATION	HEALTH MANAGEMENT ASSOCIATES INC	LAS VEGAS SANDS CORP (THE VENETIAN)
EXPERIAN AMERICAS	HEALTH NET INC	LEVEL 3 COMMUNICATIONS INC
EXPRESS SCRIPTS INC	HEALTHWAYS INC	LEXMARK INTERNATIONAL INC
EXXON MOBIL CORPORATION (EXXONMOBIL)	HENRY SCHEIN INC	LIBERTY GLOBAL INC
EXXONMOBIL CHEMICAL	HERTZ GLOBAL HOLDINGS INC	LIBERTY MUTUAL GROUP INC
FAMILY DOLLAR STORES INC	HESS CORPORATION	LIMITED BRANDS INC
FEDEX CORPORATION	HEWITT ASSOCIATES	LINCOLN NATIONAL CORPORATION
FINISH LINE INC (THE)	HIBBETT SPORTS INC	LOCKHEED MARTIN CORP
FIRST ADVANTAGE CORPORATION	HILTON HOTELS CORP	LOEWS CORPORATION
FIRST DATA CORP	HOME DEPOT INC	LOWE'S COMPANIES INC
FIRSTENERGY CORP	HONEYWELL INTERNATIONAL INC	MACY'S INC
FLUOR CORP	HUMANA INC	MANPOWER INC
FOREST LABORATORIES INC	IAC/INTERACTIVECORP	MARRIOTT INTERNATIONAL INC
FORTUNE BRANDS INC	IBM GLOBAL SERVICES	MARS INC
FOSSIL INC	ICT GROUP INC	MARSH & MCLENNAN COMPANIES INC
FOSTER WHEELER AG	IDEXX LABORATORIES INC	MARY KAY INC
FOX ENTERTAINMENT GROUP INC	IGATE CORPORATION	MATTEL INC
FPL GROUP INC	IMS HEALTH INC	MAXIM INTEGRATED PRODUCTS INC
FRED'S INC	INFOGROUP INC	MAYO FOUNDATION FOR MEDICAL EDUCATION AND RESEARCH
FRONTIER COMMUNICATIONS CORPORATION	INGRAM MICRO INC	
	INTEL CORP	MCAFEE INC
FTI CONSULTING INC	INTERNATIONAL BUSINESS MACHINES CORP (IBM)	MCDERMOTT INTERNATIONAL INC
GAMESTOP CORP		MCDONALD'S CORP
GENENTECH INC	INTUIT INC	MCKESSON CORPORATION
GENERAL DYNAMICS CORP	INVENTIV HEALTH INC	MCKINSEY & COMPANY INC
GENERAL ELECTRIC CO (GE)	J C PENNEY COMPANY INC	MEDCO HEALTH SOLUTIONS
GENERAL MILLS INC	JABIL CIRCUIT INC	MEDTRONIC INC
GENESCO INC	JACK IN THE BOX INC	MEIJER INC
GENWORTH FINANCIAL INC	JACOBS ENGINEERING GROUP INC	MEN'S WEARHOUSE INC (THE)
GEO GROUP INC	JETBLUE AIRWAYS CORPORATION	MERCER INC
GEORGIA GULF CORPORATION	JOHNSON & JOHNSON	MERCK & CO INC
GILEAD SCIENCES INC	JOHNSON CONTROLS INC	METHODIST HEALTH CARE SYSTEM
GLOBAL HYATT CORPORATION	JP MORGAN CHASE & CO INC	
GLOBAL PAYMENTS INC	JUNIPER NETWORKS INC	METLIFE INC
GOLDMAN SACHS GROUP INC	KAISER PERMANENTE	MGM MIRAGE
GOOGLE INC	KEANE INC	MICROCHIP TECHNOLOGY INC
GRANT THORNTON LLP	KELLOGG CO	MICRON TECHNOLOGY INC
GUESS? INC	KELLY SERVICES INC	MICROSOFT CORP
HALLIBURTON COMPANY	KENDLE INTERNATIONAL INC	MIDAMERICAN ENERGY HOLDINGS CO
HARRAH'S ENTERTAINMENT INC	KIMBERLY-CLARK CORP	
HARRIS CORPORATION	KINDRED HEALTHCARE INC	MILLIPORE CORP
HARTFORD FINANCIAL SERVICES GROUP INC (THE)	KOCH INDUSTRIES INC	MONRO MUFFLER BRAKE INC
	KOHL'S CORP	MONSANTO CO
HAWAIIAN ELECTRIC INDUSTRIES INC	KPMG LLP	MYLAN INC
	KRAFT FOODS INC	NATIONAL OILWELL VARCO INC
HCA INC	KROGER CO (THE)	NETAPP INC
HE BUTT GROCERY COMPANY (HEB)	L-3 COMMUNICATIONS HOLDINGS INC	NEWS CORP
		NII HOLDINGS INC
HEALTH CARE SERVICE CORPORATION	LABORATORY CORP OF AMERICA HOLDINGS	

NIKE INC	R R DONNELLEY & SONS CO	SYKES ENTERPRISES INC
NOBLE CORPORATION	RAYTHEON CO	SYMANTEC CORP
NORTHROP GRUMMAN CORP	REGIS CORPORATION	SYNOPSYS INC
NRG ENERGY INC	RENT-A-CENTER INC	SYNTEL INC
OCCIDENTAL PETROLEUM CORP	RITE AID CORPORATION	SYSCO CORP
OCEANEERING INTERNATIONAL INC	RITZ-CARLTON HOTEL COMPANY LLC (THE)	TARGET CORPORATION
OFFICE DEPOT INC	ROBERT HALF INTERNATIONAL INC	TBC CORPORATION
OIL STATES INTERNATIONAL INC	ROSS STORES INC	TECH DATA CORP
OMNICARE INC	ROYAL CARIBBEAN CRUISES LTD	TEKTRONIX INC
OMNICOM GROUP INC	RRI ENERGY INC	TELEDYNE TECHNOLOGIES INCORPORATED
ORACLE CORP	SABRE HOLDINGS CORP	TELEPHONE AND DATA SYSTEMS INC (TDS)
O'REILLY AUTOMOTIVE INC	SAFECO INSURANCE COMPANY OF AMERICA	
OSHKOSH CORPORATION	SAFEWAY INC	TELETECH HOLDINGS INC
OSI RESTAURANT PARTNERS LLC	SAIC INC	TESORO CORP
OWENS & MINOR INC	SAM'S CLUB	THERMO FISHER SCIENTIFIC INC
PANTRY INC (THE)	SAPIENT CORPORATION	TIFFANY & CO
PARAMETRIC TECHNOLOGY CORP	SARA LEE CORP	TIME WARNER INC
PAREXEL INTERNATIONAL CORP	SAS INSTITUTE INC	TJX COMPANIES INC (THE)
PARSONS BRINCKERHOFF INC	SCANA CORPORATION	T-MOBILE USA
PATTERSON COMPANIES INC	SCHERING-PLOUGH CORP	TOTAL SYSTEM SERVICES INC (TSYS)
PATTERSON-UTI ENERGY INC	SCHLUMBERGER LIMITED	
PAYCHEX INC	SCIENTIFIC GAMES CORPORATION	TOWERS PERRIN
PEPSI BOTTLING GROUP INC	SEACOR HOLDINGS INC	TRAVELERS COMPANIES INC (THE)
PEPSICO INC	SELECT MEDICAL	TW TELECOM INC
PEROT SYSTEMS CORP	SEMPRA ENERGY	UNITED NATURAL FOODS INC
PERRIGO CO	SENSIENT TECHNOLOGIES CORPORATION	UNITED PARCEL SERVICE INC (UPS)
PETCO ANIMAL SUPPLIES INC		
PETSMART INC	SHELL OIL CO	UNITED STATES CELLULAR CORP
PFIZER INC	SHERWIN WILLIAMS COMPANY (THE)	UNITED TECHNOLOGIES CORPORATION
PG&E CORPORATION		
PHARMACEUTICAL PRODUCT DEVELOPMENT INC	SIGMA-ALDRICH CORP	UNITEDHEALTH GROUP INC
	SISTERS OF MERCY HEALTH SYSTEMS	UNIVERSAL HEALTH SERVICES INC
PITNEY BOWES INC		UNIVISION COMMUNICATIONS INC
PLEXUS CORP	SMITH INTERNATIONAL INC	URS CORPORATION
POLO RALPH LAUREN CORP	SOUTHERN CALIFORNIA EDISON COMPANY	USAA
PRAXAIR INC		VALERO ENERGY CORP
PRECISION CASTPARTS CORP	SOUTHERN COMPANY (THE)	VALSPAR CORPORATION (THE)
PRICESMART INC	SOUTHWEST AIRLINES CO	VARIAN MEDICAL SYSTEMS INC
PRICEWATERHOUSECOOPERS	SRA INTERNATIONAL INC	VCA ANTECH INC
PRIDE INTERNATIONAL INC	ST JUDE MEDICAL INC	VERISIGN INC
PRINCIPAL FINANCIAL GROUP (THE)	STAPLES INC	VERIZON COMMUNICATIONS
	STARTEK INC	VIACOM INC
PROCTER & GAMBLE CO	STARWOOD HOTELS & RESORTS WORLDWIDE INC	VICTORIAS SECRET
PROGRESSIVE CORPORATION (THE)		VISA INC
	STERIS CORP	VOLT INFORMATION SCIENCES INC
PRUDENTIAL FINANCIAL INC	STIFEL FINANCIAL CORP	W R BERKLEY CORPORATION
PUBLIX SUPER MARKETS INC	STRYKER CORP	WABTEC CORP
QUALCOMM INC	SUNGARD DATA SYSTEMS INC	WALGREEN CO
QUEST DIAGNOSTICS INC	SUNOCO INC	WAL-MART STORES INC
QUIKSILVER INC	SUPERVALU INC	WALT DISNEY COMPANY (THE)

WASTE MANAGEMENT INC	ACTIVISION BLIZZARD INC	BEBE STORES INC
WATERS CORP	ACXIOM CORP	BECHTEL GROUP INC
WATSON PHARMACEUTICALS INC	ADESA INC	BECKMAN COULTER INC
WATSON WYATT WORLDWIDE INC	ADOBE SYSTEMS INC	BECTON DICKINSON & CO
WEATHERFORD INTERNATIONAL LTD	ADVANCE AUTO PARTS INC	BED BATH & BEYOND INC
WEIGHT WATCHERS INTERNATIONAL INC	AES CORPORATION (THE)	BERKSHIRE HATHAWAY INC
WELLPOINT INC	AETNA INC	BEST BUY CO INC
WELLS FARGO & CO	AFFILIATED COMPUTER SERVICES INC	BIO RAD LABORATORIES INC
WENDY'S/ARBY'S GROUP INC	AFLAC INC	BJ'S WHOLESALE CLUB INC
WEST CORPORATION	AGILENT TECHNOLOGIES INC	BLACK & DECKER CORP
WEST PHARMACEUTICAL SERVICES INC	AIR PRODUCTS & CHEMICALS INC	BLACKROCK INC
WESTERN DIGITAL CORP	ALLERGAN INC	BLOOMBERG LP
WHOLE FOODS MARKET INC	ALLIANCE DATA SYSTEMS CORPORATION	BOEING COMPANY (THE)
WILLIAMS COMPANIES INC (THE)	ALLSTATE CORPORATION (THE)	BOOZ ALLEN HAMILTON
WW GRAINGER INC	ALTRIA GROUP INC	BOSTON SCIENTIFIC CORP
WYETH	AMAZON.COM INC	BRINKER INTERNATIONAL INC
WYNDHAM WORLDWIDE	AMEDISYS INC	BRINKS COMPANY (THE)
WYNN RESORTS LIMITED	AMERICAN ELECTRIC POWER COMPANY INC (AEP)	BROWN & BROWN INC
XEROX CORP	AMERICAN POWER CONVERSION (APC)	BUCKLE INC (THE)
YAHOO! INC		BUFFALO WILD WINGS INC
YUM! BRANDS INC	AMERISOURCEBERGEN CORP	BURGER KING HOLDINGS INC
ZIMMER HOLDINGS INC	AMGEN INC	CABELA'S INC
	ANADARKO PETROLEUM CORPORATION	CABLEVISION SYSTEMS CORP
	ANNTAYLOR STORES CORP	CACI INTERNATIONAL INC

Liberal Arts

Broadcasting
CABLEVISION SYSTEMS CORP
COMCAST CORP
COX COMMUNICATIONS INC
DIRECTV GROUP INC (THE)
FOX ENTERTAINMENT GROUP INC
IAC/INTERACTIVECORP
NEWS CORP
TIME WARNER INC
UNIVISION COMMUNICATIONS INC
VIACOM INC
WAL-MART STORES INC
WALT DISNEY COMPANY (THE)

General Writing
3M COMPANY
7-ELEVEN INC
AARON'S INC
ABBOTT LABORATORIES
ABM INDUSTRIES INC
ACADEMY SPORTS & OUTDOORS LTD
ACCENTURE LTD

APACHE CORP
APOLLO GROUP INC
APPLE INC
ARAMARK CORPORATION
ARCHER DANIELS MIDLAND CO
ARROW ELECTRONICS INC
ARTHUR J GALLAGHER & CO
ASCENSION HEALTH
AT&T INC
AUTOMATIC DATA PROCESSING INC
AUTOZONE INC
AVERY DENNISON CORP
AVIS BUDGET GROUP INC
AVON PRODUCTS INC
AXA FINANCIAL INC
BAKER HUGHES INC
BALTIMORE GAS AND ELECTRIC COMPANY
BANK OF AMERICA CORP
BARNES & NOBLE INC
BASS PRO SHOPS INC
BAXTER INTERNATIONAL INC
BDO SEIDMAN LLP

CAPITAL SENIOR LIVING CORP
CARDINAL HEALTH INC
CARGILL INC
CARMAX GROUP
CARNIVAL CORPORATION
CASH AMERICA INTERNATIONAL INC
CATERPILLAR INC
CATHOLIC HEALTH INITIATIVES
CDW CORPORATION
CELLCO PARTNERSHIP (VERIZON WIRELESS)
CH ROBINSON WORLDWIDE INC
CH2M HILL COMPANIES LTD
CHARLOTTE RUSSE HOLDING
CHARMING SHOPPES INC
CHEMED CORPORATION
CHEVRON CORPORATION
CHEVRON PHILLIPS CHEMICAL COMPANY LLC
CHICO'S FAS INC
CHIPOTLE MEXICAN GRILL INC
CHRISTOPHER & BANKS CORP
CHS INC
CHUBB CORPORATION (THE)
CIBER INC
CIGNA CORP

CINTAS CORP	ELI LILLY & COMPANY	INC
CISCO SYSTEMS INC	EMBARQ CORP	HCA INC
CLUBCORP INC	EMERITUS CORP	HE BUTT GROCERY COMPANY (HEB)
COACH INC	ENTERGY CORP	
COCA-COLA COMPANY (THE)	ENTERPRISE RENT-A-CAR	HEALTH CARE SERVICE CORPORATION
COCA-COLA ENTERPRISES INC	ERNST & YOUNG LLP	
COGNIZANT TECHNOLOGY SOLUTIONS CORP	ESTEE LAUDER COMPANIES INC (THE)	HEALTH FITNESS CORP
		HEALTH MANAGEMENT ASSOCIATES INC
COLDWATER CREEK INC	EXELON CORPORATION	
COLGATE PALMOLIVE CO	EXPERIAN AMERICAS	HEALTH NET INC
COMCAST CORP	EXPRESS SCRIPTS INC	HEALTHWAYS INC
COMMUNITY HEALTH SYSTEMS INC	EXXON MOBIL CORPORATION (EXXONMOBIL)	HENRY SCHEIN INC
		HERTZ GLOBAL HOLDINGS INC
CONAGRA FOODS INC		HEWITT ASSOCIATES
CONOCOPHILLIPS COMPANY	EXXONMOBIL CHEMICAL	HIBBETT SPORTS INC
CONSOLIDATED EDISON INC	FAMILY DOLLAR STORES INC	HILTON HOTELS CORP
CONTAINER STORE (THE)	FEDEX CORPORATION	HOME DEPOT INC
CONVERGYS CORPORATION	FINISH LINE INC (THE)	HONEYWELL INTERNATIONAL INC
COSTCO WHOLESALE CORP	FIRST ADVANTAGE CORPORATION	HUMANA INC
COVENTRY HEALTH CARE INC	FIRST DATA CORP	IAC/INTERACTIVECORP
COX COMMUNICATIONS INC	FIRSTENERGY CORP	IBM GLOBAL SERVICES
CR BARD INC	FLUOR CORP	ICT GROUP INC
CRACKER BARREL OLD COUNTRY STORE INC	FOREST LABORATORIES INC	IGATE CORPORATION
	FORTUNE BRANDS INC	IMS HEALTH INC
CUMMINS INC	FOSSIL INC	INFOGROUP INC
CVS CAREMARK CORPORATION	FOSTER WHEELER AG	INGRAM MICRO INC
DANAHER CORP	FOX ENTERTAINMENT GROUP INC	INTEL CORP
DARDEN RESTAURANTS INC	FPL GROUP INC	INTERNATIONAL BUSINESS MACHINES CORP (IBM)
DAVITA INC	FRED'S INC	
DEAN FOODS CO	FRONTIER COMMUNICATIONS CORPORATION	INTUIT INC
DEERE & CO		INVENTIV HEALTH INC
DELOITTE & TOUCHE USA LLP	FTI CONSULTING INC	J C PENNEY COMPANY INC
DELOITTE CONSULTING LLP	GAMESTOP CORP	JACK IN THE BOX INC
DENNY'S CORPORATION	GENENTECH INC	JACOBS ENGINEERING GROUP INC
DEVON ENERGY CORPORATION	GENERAL DYNAMICS CORP	JETBLUE AIRWAYS CORPORATION
DEVRY INC	GENERAL ELECTRIC CO (GE)	JM SMUCKER CO
DICK'S SPORTING GOODS INC	GENERAL MILLS INC	JOHNSON & JOHNSON
DIEBOLD INC	GENESCO INC	JOHNSON CONTROLS INC
DINEEQUITY INC	GENWORTH FINANCIAL INC	JP MORGAN CHASE & CO INC
DIRECTV GROUP INC (THE)	GEO GROUP INC	JUNIPER NETWORKS INC
DOLE FOOD COMPANY INC	GLOBAL HYATT CORPORATION	KAISER PERMANENTE
DOLLAR GENERAL CORPORATION	GLOBAL PAYMENTS INC	KEANE INC
DOLLAR THRIFTY AUTOMOTIVE GROUP INC	GOLDMAN SACHS GROUP INC	KELLOGG CO
	GOOGLE INC	KELLY SERVICES INC
DRESS BARN INC (THE)	GRANT THORNTON LLP	KIMBERLY-CLARK CORP
DTE ENERGY COMPANY	GUESS? INC	KINDRED HEALTHCARE INC
DUKE ENERGY CORP	HALLIBURTON COMPANY	KOCH INDUSTRIES INC
E I DU PONT DE NEMOURS & CO (DUPONT)	HARRAH'S ENTERTAINMENT INC	KOHL'S CORP
	HARRIS CORPORATION	KPMG LLP
EBAY INC	HARTFORD FINANCIAL SERVICES GROUP INC (THE)	KRAFT FOODS INC
EDISON INTERNATIONAL		KROGER CO (THE)
ELECTRONIC ARTS INC	HAWAIIAN ELECTRIC INDUSTRIES	

LABORATORY CORP OF AMERICA HOLDINGS	NRG ENERGY INC	SABRE HOLDINGS CORP
LAS VEGAS SANDS CORP (THE VENETIAN)	OCCIDENTAL PETROLEUM CORP	SAFECO INSURANCE COMPANY OF AMERICA
LEVEL 3 COMMUNICATIONS INC	ODYSSEY HEALTHCARE INC	SAFEWAY INC
LEXMARK INTERNATIONAL INC	OFFICE DEPOT INC	SAIC INC
LIBERTY GLOBAL INC	OMNICARE INC	SAM'S CLUB
LIBERTY MUTUAL GROUP INC	OMNICOM GROUP INC	SAPIENT CORPORATION
LIMITED BRANDS INC	ORACLE CORP	SARA LEE CORP
LINCARE HOLDINGS INC	O'REILLY AUTOMOTIVE INC	SAS INSTITUTE INC
LINCOLN NATIONAL CORPORATION	OSHKOSH CORPORATION	SCANA CORPORATION
LOCKHEED MARTIN CORP	OSI RESTAURANT PARTNERS LLC	SCHERING-PLOUGH CORP
LODGIAN INC	OWENS & MINOR INC	SCHLUMBERGER LIMITED
LOEWS CORPORATION	PANTRY INC (THE)	SCIENTIFIC GAMES CORPORATION
LOWE'S COMPANIES INC	PARAMETRIC TECHNOLOGY CORP	SCOTTS MIRACLE GROW CO
MACY'S INC	PAREXEL INTERNATIONAL CORP	SEACOR HOLDINGS INC
MANOR CARE INC	PARSONS BRINCKERHOFF INC	SELECT MEDICAL
MANPOWER INC	PATTERSON COMPANIES INC	SEMPRA ENERGY
MARRIOTT INTERNATIONAL INC	PAYCHEX INC	SENSIENT TECHNOLOGIES CORPORATION
MARS INC	PEPSI BOTTLING GROUP INC	SHELL OIL CO
MARSH & MCLENNAN COMPANIES INC	PEPSICO INC	SHERWIN WILLIAMS COMPANY (THE)
MARY KAY INC	PEROT SYSTEMS CORP	SISTERS OF MERCY HEALTH SYSTEMS
MATTEL INC	PETCO ANIMAL SUPPLIES INC	
MAYO FOUNDATION FOR MEDICAL EDUCATION AND RESEARCH	PETSMART INC	SMITHFIELD FOODS INC
MCAFEE INC	PFIZER INC	SOUTHERN CALIFORNIA EDISON COMPANY
MCDERMOTT INTERNATIONAL INC	PG&E CORPORATION	
MCDONALD'S CORP	PITNEY BOWES INC	SOUTHERN COMPANY (THE)
MCKESSON CORPORATION	POLO RALPH LAUREN CORP	SOUTHWEST AIRLINES CO
MCKINSEY & COMPANY INC	PRICESMART INC	SRA INTERNATIONAL INC
MEDCO HEALTH SOLUTIONS	PRICEWATERHOUSECOOPERS	ST JUDE MEDICAL INC
MEDTRONIC INC	PRINCIPAL FINANCIAL GROUP (THE)	STAPLES INC
MEIJER INC		STARTEK INC
MEN'S WEARHOUSE INC (THE)	PROCTER & GAMBLE CO	STARWOOD HOTELS & RESORTS WORLDWIDE INC
MERCER INC	PROGRESSIVE CORPORATION (THE)	
MERCK & CO INC	PRUDENTIAL FINANCIAL INC	STIFEL FINANCIAL CORP
METHODIST HEALTH CARE SYSTEM	PSYCHIATRIC SOLUTIONS INC	STRYKER CORP
	PUBLIX SUPER MARKETS INC	SUN HEALTHCARE GROUP
METLIFE INC	QUALCOMM INC	SUNGARD DATA SYSTEMS INC
MGM MIRAGE	QUIKSILVER INC	SUNOCO INC
MICROSOFT CORP	R R DONNELLEY & SONS CO	SUNRISE SENIOR LIVING
MIDAMERICAN ENERGY HOLDINGS CO	RALCORP HOLDINGS INC	SUPERVALU INC
	RAYTHEON CO	SYKES ENTERPRISES INC
MONRO MUFFLER BRAKE INC	REGIS CORPORATION	SYMANTEC CORP
MONSANTO CO	RENT-A-CENTER INC	SYNOPSYS INC
NETAPP INC	RES CARE INC	SYNTEL INC
NEWS CORP	RITE AID CORPORATION	SYSCO CORP
NII HOLDINGS INC	RITZ-CARLTON HOTEL COMPANY LLC (THE)	TARGET CORPORATION
NIKE INC		TBC CORPORATION
NORTHROP GRUMMAN CORP	ROBERT HALF INTERNATIONAL INC	TECH DATA CORP
	ROSS STORES INC	TELEPHONE AND DATA SYSTEMS INC (TDS)
	ROYAL CARIBBEAN CRUISES LTD	
	RRI ENERGY INC	

TELETECH HOLDINGS INC	YAHOO! INC	INC
TESORO CORP	YUM! BRANDS INC	AUTOZONE INC
TIFFANY & CO	ZIMMER HOLDINGS INC	AVERY DENNISON CORP
TIME WARNER INC		AVIS BUDGET GROUP INC
TJX COMPANIES INC (THE)	**Graphic Arts**	AVNET INC
T-MOBILE USA	3M COMPANY	AVON PRODUCTS INC
TOTAL SYSTEM SERVICES INC (TSYS)	7-ELEVEN INC	AXA FINANCIAL INC
TOWERS PERRIN	AARON'S INC	BAKER HUGHES INC
TRAVELERS COMPANIES INC (THE)	ABBOTT LABORATORIES	BALTIMORE GAS AND ELECTRIC COMPANY
TW TELECOM INC	ACADEMY SPORTS & OUTDOORS LTD	BANK OF AMERICA CORP
TYSON FOODS INC	ACCENTURE LTD	BARNES & NOBLE INC
UNITED NATURAL FOODS INC	ACTIVISION BLIZZARD INC	BASS PRO SHOPS INC
UNITED PARCEL SERVICE INC (UPS)	ADC TELECOMMUNICATIONS INC	BAXTER INTERNATIONAL INC
UNITED STATES CELLULAR CORP	ADOBE SYSTEMS INC	BDO SEIDMAN LLP
UNITED TECHNOLOGIES CORPORATION	ADVANCE AUTO PARTS INC	BEBE STORES INC
UNITEDHEALTH GROUP INC	ADVANCED MICRO DEVICES INC (AMD)	BECHTEL GROUP INC
UNIVISION COMMUNICATIONS INC	AECOM TECHNOLOGY CORPORATION	BECKMAN COULTER INC
URS CORPORATION	AES CORPORATION (THE)	BECTON DICKINSON & CO
USAA	AETNA INC	BED BATH & BEYOND INC
VALERO ENERGY CORP	AFFILIATED COMPUTER SERVICES INC	BENCHMARK ELECTRONICS INC
VALSPAR CORPORATION (THE)	AFLAC INC	BERKSHIRE HATHAWAY INC
VARIAN MEDICAL SYSTEMS INC	AGILENT TECHNOLOGIES INC	BEST BUY CO INC
VCA ANTECH INC	ALLERGAN INC	BIO RAD LABORATORIES INC
VERISIGN INC	ALLIANCE DATA SYSTEMS CORPORATION	BJ'S WHOLESALE CLUB INC
VERIZON COMMUNICATIONS	ALLSTATE CORPORATION (THE)	BLACK & DECKER CORP
VIACOM INC	ALTRIA GROUP INC	BLOOMBERG LP
VICTORIAS SECRET	AMAZON.COM INC	BOEING COMPANY (THE)
VISA INC	AMEDISYS INC	BOOZ ALLEN HAMILTON
VOLT INFORMATION SCIENCES INC	AMERICAN ELECTRIC POWER COMPANY INC (AEP)	BOSTON SCIENTIFIC CORP
W R BERKLEY CORPORATION	AMERICAN POWER CONVERSION (APC)	BRINKER INTERNATIONAL INC
WALGREEN CO	AMERISOURCEBERGEN CORP	BRINKS COMPANY (THE)
WAL-MART STORES INC	AMGEN INC	BROADCOM CORP
WALT DISNEY COMPANY (THE)	ANADARKO PETROLEUM CORPORATION	BROWN & BROWN INC
WASTE MANAGEMENT INC	ANALOG DEVICES INC	BUCKLE INC (THE)
WATSON PHARMACEUTICALS INC	ANNTAYLOR STORES CORP	BUCYRUS INTERNATIONAL INC
WATSON WYATT WORLDWIDE INC	APOLLO GROUP INC	BUFFALO WILD WINGS INC
WEIGHT WATCHERS INTERNATIONAL INC	APPLE INC	BUNGE LTD
WELLPOINT INC	ARAMARK CORPORATION	BURGER KING HOLDINGS INC
WELLS FARGO & CO	ARCHER DANIELS MIDLAND CO	CABELA'S INC
WENDY'S/ARBY'S GROUP INC	ARROW ELECTRONICS INC	CABLEVISION SYSTEMS CORP
WEST CORPORATION	ARTHUR J GALLAGHER & CO	CACI INTERNATIONAL INC
WHOLE FOODS MARKET INC	ASCENSION HEALTH	CAMERON INTERNATIONAL CORPORATION
WW GRAINGER INC	AT&T INC	CAPITAL SENIOR LIVING CORP
WYETH	AUTOMATIC DATA PROCESSING	CARDINAL HEALTH INC
WYNDHAM WORLDWIDE		CARGILL INC
WYNN RESORTS LIMITED		CARMAX GROUP
XEROX CORP		CARNIVAL CORPORATION
		CASH AMERICA INTERNATIONAL INC

CATERPILLAR INC	DEERE & CO	CORPORATION
CATHOLIC HEALTH INITIATIVES	DELOITTE & TOUCHE USA LLP	FTI CONSULTING INC
CDW CORPORATION	DELOITTE CONSULTING LLP	GAMESTOP CORP
CELGENE CORP	DENNY'S CORPORATION	GENENTECH INC
CELLCO PARTNERSHIP (VERIZON WIRELESS)	DEVRY INC	GENERAL CABLE CORP
CEPHALON INC	DICK'S SPORTING GOODS INC	GENERAL DYNAMICS CORP
CH2M HILL COMPANIES LTD	DIEBOLD INC	GENERAL ELECTRIC CO (GE)
CHARLOTTE RUSSE HOLDING	DINEEQUITY INC	GENERAL MILLS INC
CHARMING SHOPPES INC	DIRECTV GROUP INC (THE)	GENESCO INC
CHEMED CORPORATION	DOLE FOOD COMPANY INC	GENWORTH FINANCIAL INC
CHEVRON CORPORATION	DOLLAR GENERAL CORPORATION	GILEAD SCIENCES INC
CHICO'S FAS INC	DOLLAR THRIFTY AUTOMOTIVE GROUP INC	GLOBAL HYATT CORPORATION
CHIPOTLE MEXICAN GRILL INC	DRESS BARN INC (THE)	GLOBAL PAYMENTS INC
CHRISTOPHER & BANKS CORP	DTE ENERGY COMPANY	GOLDMAN SACHS GROUP INC
CHS INC	DUKE ENERGY CORP	GOOGLE INC
CHUBB CORPORATION (THE)	DYCOM INDUSTRIES INC	GRANT THORNTON LLP
CIBER INC	EATON CORP	GUESS? INC
CIGNA CORP	EBAY INC	HALLIBURTON COMPANY
CINTAS CORP	EDISON INTERNATIONAL	HARRAH'S ENTERTAINMENT INC
CISCO SYSTEMS INC	ELECTRONIC ARTS INC	HARRIS CORPORATION
CLUBCORP INC	ELI LILLY & COMPANY	HARTFORD FINANCIAL SERVICES GROUP INC (THE)
COACH INC	EMBARQ CORP	HAWAIIAN ELECTRIC INDUSTRIES INC
COCA-COLA COMPANY (THE)	EMC CORP	HCA INC
COCA-COLA ENTERPRISES INC	EMERITUS CORP	HE BUTT GROCERY COMPANY (HEB)
COGNIZANT TECHNOLOGY SOLUTIONS CORP	EMERSON ELECTRIC CO	HEALTH CARE SERVICE CORPORATION
COLDWATER CREEK INC	ENTERGY CORP	
COLGATE PALMOLIVE CO	ENTERPRISE RENT-A-CAR	HEALTH FITNESS CORP
COMCAST CORP	ERNST & YOUNG LLP	HEALTH MANAGEMENT ASSOCIATES INC
COMMUNITY HEALTH SYSTEMS INC	ESTEE LAUDER COMPANIES INC (THE)	HEALTH NET INC
CONAGRA FOODS INC	EXELON CORPORATION	HEALTHWAYS INC
CONOCOPHILLIPS COMPANY	EXPERIAN AMERICAS	HENRY SCHEIN INC
CONSOLIDATED EDISON INC	EXPRESS SCRIPTS INC	HERTZ GLOBAL HOLDINGS INC
CONTAINER STORE (THE)	EXXON MOBIL CORPORATION (EXXONMOBIL)	HEWITT ASSOCIATES
CONVERGYS CORPORATION		HIBBETT SPORTS INC
COOPER COMPANIES INC	FAMILY DOLLAR STORES INC	HILTON HOTELS CORP
COSTCO WHOLESALE CORP	FEDEX CORPORATION	HOME DEPOT INC
COVANCE INC	FINISH LINE INC (THE)	HONEYWELL INTERNATIONAL INC
COVENTRY HEALTH CARE INC	FIRST ADVANTAGE CORPORATION	HUMANA INC
COX COMMUNICATIONS INC	FIRST DATA CORP	IAC/INTERACTIVECORP
CR BARD INC	FIRSTENERGY CORP	IBM GLOBAL SERVICES
CRACKER BARREL OLD COUNTRY STORE INC	FLUOR CORP	ICT GROUP INC
	FOREST LABORATORIES INC	IGATE CORPORATION
CTS CORP	FORTUNE BRANDS INC	IMS HEALTH INC
CUBIC CORP	FOSSIL INC	INFOGROUP INC
CUMMINS INC	FOSTER WHEELER AG	INGRAM MICRO INC
CVS CAREMARK CORPORATION	FOX ENTERTAINMENT GROUP INC	INTEL CORP
DANAHER CORP	FPL GROUP INC	INTERNATIONAL BUSINESS
DARDEN RESTAURANTS INC	FRED'S INC	
DEAN FOODS CO	FRONTIER COMMUNICATIONS	

MACHINES CORP (IBM)	MAXIM INTEGRATED PRODUCTS INC	PG&E CORPORATION
INTUIT INC	MAYO FOUNDATION FOR MEDICAL EDUCATION AND RESEARCH	PHARMACEUTICAL PRODUCT DEVELOPMENT INC
INVENTIV HEALTH INC	MCAFEE INC	PITNEY BOWES INC
J C PENNEY COMPANY INC	MCDERMOTT INTERNATIONAL INC	PLEXUS CORP
JABIL CIRCUIT INC	MCDONALD'S CORP	POLO RALPH LAUREN CORP
JACK IN THE BOX INC	MCKESSON CORPORATION	PRECISION CASTPARTS CORP
JACOBS ENGINEERING GROUP INC	MCKINSEY & COMPANY INC	PRICESMART INC
JETBLUE AIRWAYS CORPORATION	MEDCO HEALTH SOLUTIONS	PRICEWATERHOUSECOOPERS
JM SMUCKER CO	MEDTRONIC INC	PRINCIPAL FINANCIAL GROUP (THE)
JOHNSON & JOHNSON	MEIJER INC	PROCTER & GAMBLE CO
JOHNSON CONTROLS INC	MEN'S WEARHOUSE INC (THE)	PROGRESSIVE CORPORATION (THE)
JP MORGAN CHASE & CO INC	MERCER INC	PRUDENTIAL FINANCIAL INC
JUNIPER NETWORKS INC	MERCK & CO INC	PSYCHIATRIC SOLUTIONS INC
KAISER PERMANENTE	METHODIST HEALTH CARE SYSTEM	PUBLIX SUPER MARKETS INC
KEANE INC	METLIFE INC	QUALCOMM INC
KELLOGG CO	MGM MIRAGE	QUEST DIAGNOSTICS INC
KELLY SERVICES INC	MICROCHIP TECHNOLOGY INC	QUIKSILVER INC
KENDLE INTERNATIONAL INC	MICRON TECHNOLOGY INC	R R DONNELLEY & SONS CO
KIMBERLY-CLARK CORP	MICROSOFT CORP	RALCORP HOLDINGS INC
KINDRED HEALTHCARE INC	MIDAMERICAN ENERGY HOLDINGS CO	RAYTHEON CO
KOCH INDUSTRIES INC	MILLIPORE CORP	REGIS CORPORATION
KOHL'S CORP	MONRO MUFFLER BRAKE INC	RENT-A-CENTER INC
KPMG LLP	MONSANTO CO	RES CARE INC
KRAFT FOODS INC	NEWS CORP	RITE AID CORPORATION
KROGER CO (THE)	NII HOLDINGS INC	RITZ-CARLTON HOTEL COMPANY LLC (THE)
L-3 COMMUNICATIONS HOLDINGS INC	NIKE INC	ROBERT HALF INTERNATIONAL INC
LABORATORY CORP OF AMERICA HOLDINGS	NORTHROP GRUMMAN CORP	ROSS STORES INC
LAS VEGAS SANDS CORP (THE VENETIAN)	NRG ENERGY INC	ROYAL CARIBBEAN CRUISES LTD
LEVEL 3 COMMUNICATIONS INC	ODYSSEY HEALTHCARE INC	RRI ENERGY INC
LEXMARK INTERNATIONAL INC	OFFICE DEPOT INC	SABRE HOLDINGS CORP
LIBERTY GLOBAL INC	OMNICOM GROUP INC	SAFECO INSURANCE COMPANY OF AMERICA
LIBERTY MUTUAL GROUP INC	ORACLE CORP	SAFEWAY INC
LIMITED BRANDS INC	O'REILLY AUTOMOTIVE INC	SAIC INC
LINCARE HOLDINGS INC	OSHKOSH CORPORATION	SAM'S CLUB
LINCOLN NATIONAL CORPORATION	OSI RESTAURANT PARTNERS LLC	SAPIENT CORPORATION
LOCKHEED MARTIN CORP	OWENS & MINOR INC	SARA LEE CORP
LODGIAN INC	PANTRY INC (THE)	SAS INSTITUTE INC
LOEWS CORPORATION	PAREXEL INTERNATIONAL CORP	SCANA CORPORATION
LOWE'S COMPANIES INC	PARSONS BRINCKERHOFF INC	SCHERING-PLOUGH CORP
MACY'S INC	PATTERSON COMPANIES INC	SCHLUMBERGER LIMITED
MANOR CARE INC	PAYCHEX INC	SCIENTIFIC GAMES CORPORATION
MANPOWER INC	PEPSI BOTTLING GROUP INC	SCOTTS MIRACLE GROW CO
MARRIOTT INTERNATIONAL INC	PEPSICO INC	SELECT MEDICAL
MARS INC	PEROT SYSTEMS CORP	SEMPRA ENERGY
MARSH & MCLENNAN COMPANIES INC	PETCO ANIMAL SUPPLIES INC	SENSIENT TECHNOLOGIES CORPORATION
MARY KAY INC	PETSMART INC	
MATTEL INC	PFIZER INC	

SHAW GROUP INC (THE)
SHELL OIL CO
SHERWIN WILLIAMS COMPANY (THE)
SISTERS OF MERCY HEALTH SYSTEMS
SMITHFIELD FOODS INC
SOUTHERN CALIFORNIA EDISON COMPANY
SOUTHERN COMPANY (THE)
SOUTHWEST AIRLINES CO
SRA INTERNATIONAL INC
ST JUDE MEDICAL INC
STAPLES INC
STARTEK INC
STARWOOD HOTELS & RESORTS WORLDWIDE INC
STERIS CORP
STRYKER CORP
SUN HEALTHCARE GROUP
SUNGARD DATA SYSTEMS INC
SUNOCO INC
SUNRISE SENIOR LIVING
SUPERVALU INC
SYMANTEC CORP
SYNTEL INC
SYSCO CORP
TARGET CORPORATION
TBC CORPORATION
TECH DATA CORP
TEKTRONIX INC
TELEDYNE TECHNOLOGIES INCORPORATED
TELEPHONE AND DATA SYSTEMS INC (TDS)
TESORO CORP
THERMO FISHER SCIENTIFIC INC
TIFFANY & CO
TIME WARNER INC
TJX COMPANIES INC (THE)
T-MOBILE USA
TOTAL SYSTEM SERVICES INC (TSYS)
TOWERS PERRIN
TRAVELERS COMPANIES INC (THE)
TREEHOUSE FOODS INC
TW TELECOM INC
TYSON FOODS INC
UNITED NATURAL FOODS INC
UNITED PARCEL SERVICE INC (UPS)
UNITED STATES CELLULAR CORP

UNITED TECHNOLOGIES CORPORATION
UNITEDHEALTH GROUP INC
UNIVISION COMMUNICATIONS INC
URS CORPORATION
USAA
VALERO ENERGY CORP
VALSPAR CORPORATION (THE)
VARIAN MEDICAL SYSTEMS INC
VCA ANTECH INC
VERISIGN INC
VERIZON COMMUNICATIONS
VIACOM INC
VICTORIAS SECRET
VISA INC
VOLT INFORMATION SCIENCES INC
W R BERKLEY CORPORATION
WABTEC CORP
WALGREEN CO
WAL-MART STORES INC
WALT DISNEY COMPANY (THE)
WASTE MANAGEMENT INC
WATERS CORP
WATSON PHARMACEUTICALS INC
WATSON WYATT WORLDWIDE INC
WEIGHT WATCHERS INTERNATIONAL INC
WELLPOINT INC
WELLS FARGO & CO
WENDY'S/ARBY'S GROUP INC
WEST PHARMACEUTICAL SERVICES INC
WESTERN DIGITAL CORP
WHOLE FOODS MARKET INC
WW GRAINGER INC
WYETH
WYNDHAM WORLDWIDE
WYNN RESORTS LIMITED
XEROX CORP
YAHOO! INC
YUM! BRANDS INC
ZIMMER HOLDINGS INC

Music
ACTIVISION BLIZZARD INC
APPLE INC
CARNIVAL CORPORATION
ELECTRONIC ARTS INC
FOX ENTERTAINMENT GROUP INC
HARRAH'S ENTERTAINMENT INC
LAS VEGAS SANDS CORP (THE

VENETIAN)
MGM MIRAGE
MICROSOFT CORP
NEWS CORP
ROYAL CARIBBEAN CRUISES LTD
TIME WARNER INC
UNIVISION COMMUNICATIONS INC
VIACOM INC
WALT DISNEY COMPANY (THE)
WYNN RESORTS LIMITED

Other
3M COMPANY
7-ELEVEN INC
ACADEMY SPORTS & OUTDOORS LTD
ACCENTURE LTD
ACTIVISION BLIZZARD INC
ADOBE SYSTEMS INC
AETNA INC
AFFILIATED COMPUTER SERVICES INC
AFLAC INC
ALLSTATE CORPORATION (THE)
AMAZON.COM INC
ANNTAYLOR STORES CORP
APOLLO GROUP INC
APPLE INC
ASCENSION HEALTH
AT&T INC
AVERY DENNISON CORP
AVIS BUDGET GROUP INC
AVON PRODUCTS INC
AXA FINANCIAL INC
BANK OF AMERICA CORP
BARNES & NOBLE INC
BDO SEIDMAN LLP
BEBE STORES INC
BERKSHIRE HATHAWAY INC
BEST BUY CO INC
BJ'S WHOLESALE CLUB INC
BLACK & DECKER CORP
BLOOMBERG LP
BOEING COMPANY (THE)
BOOZ ALLEN HAMILTON
BRINKER INTERNATIONAL INC
BROWN & BROWN INC
BUCKLE INC (THE)
BUFFALO WILD WINGS INC
BURGER KING HOLDINGS INC

CABELA'S INC	EXPERIAN AMERICAS	KPMG LLP
CABLEVISION SYSTEMS CORP	FAMILY DOLLAR STORES INC	KROGER CO (THE)
CAPITAL SENIOR LIVING CORP	FEDEX CORPORATION	LAS VEGAS SANDS CORP (THE VENETIAN)
CARNIVAL CORPORATION	FINISH LINE INC (THE)	
CATHOLIC HEALTH INITIATIVES	FOSSIL INC	LIBERTY MUTUAL GROUP INC
CELLCO PARTNERSHIP (VERIZON WIRELESS)	FOX ENTERTAINMENT GROUP INC	LIMITED BRANDS INC
	FRED'S INC	LINCOLN NATIONAL CORPORATION
CHARLOTTE RUSSE HOLDING	FTI CONSULTING INC	LOEWS CORPORATION
CHARMING SHOPPES INC	GAMESTOP CORP	LOWE'S COMPANIES INC
CHEMED CORPORATION	GENERAL ELECTRIC CO (GE)	MACY'S INC
CHICO'S FAS INC	GENESCO INC	MANOR CARE INC
CHIPOTLE MEXICAN GRILL INC	GENWORTH FINANCIAL INC	MANPOWER INC
CHRISTOPHER & BANKS CORP	GLOBAL HYATT CORPORATION	MARRIOTT INTERNATIONAL INC
CHUBB CORPORATION (THE)	GOLDMAN SACHS GROUP INC	MARSH & MCLENNAN COMPANIES INC
CIGNA CORP	GOOGLE INC	
CLUBCORP INC	GRANT THORNTON LLP	MARY KAY INC
COACH INC	GUESS? INC	MATTEL INC
COCA-COLA COMPANY (THE)	HARRAH'S ENTERTAINMENT INC	MAYO FOUNDATION FOR MEDICAL EDUCATION AND RESEARCH
COGNIZANT TECHNOLOGY SOLUTIONS CORP	HARTFORD FINANCIAL SERVICES GROUP INC (THE)	
		MCDONALD'S CORP
COLDWATER CREEK INC	HCA INC	MCKINSEY & COMPANY INC
COLGATE PALMOLIVE CO	HE BUTT GROCERY COMPANY (HEB)	MEIJER INC
COMCAST CORP		MEN'S WEARHOUSE INC (THE)
COMMUNITY HEALTH SYSTEMS INC	HEALTH CARE SERVICE CORPORATION	MERCER INC
CONTAINER STORE (THE)		METHODIST HEALTH CARE SYSTEM
COSTCO WHOLESALE CORP	HEALTH FITNESS CORP	
COVENTRY HEALTH CARE INC	HEALTH MANAGEMENT ASSOCIATES INC	METLIFE INC
COX COMMUNICATIONS INC		MGM MIRAGE
CRACKER BARREL OLD COUNTRY STORE INC	HEALTH NET INC	MICROSOFT CORP
	HERTZ GLOBAL HOLDINGS INC	NEWS CORP
CVS CAREMARK CORPORATION	HEWITT ASSOCIATES	NIKE INC
DARDEN RESTAURANTS INC	HILTON HOTELS CORP	ODYSSEY HEALTHCARE INC
DELOITTE & TOUCHE USA LLP	HOME DEPOT INC	OFFICE DEPOT INC
DELOITTE CONSULTING LLP	HUMANA INC	ORACLE CORP
DENNY'S CORPORATION	IAC/INTERACTIVECORP	OSI RESTAURANT PARTNERS LLC
DEVRY INC	IBM GLOBAL SERVICES	PANTRY INC (THE)
DICK'S SPORTING GOODS INC	IMS HEALTH INC	PEPSICO INC
DIEBOLD INC	INTEL CORP	PEROT SYSTEMS CORP
DINEEQUITY INC	INTERNATIONAL BUSINESS MACHINES CORP (IBM)	PETCO ANIMAL SUPPLIES INC
DIRECTV GROUP INC (THE)		PETSMART INC
DOLLAR GENERAL CORPORATION	INVENTIV HEALTH INC	POLO RALPH LAUREN CORP
DOLLAR THRIFTY AUTOMOTIVE GROUP INC	J C PENNEY COMPANY INC	PRICESMART INC
	JACK IN THE BOX INC	PRICEWATERHOUSECOOPERS
DRESS BARN INC (THE)	JETBLUE AIRWAYS CORPORATION	PRINCIPAL FINANCIAL GROUP (THE)
EBAY INC	JP MORGAN CHASE & CO INC	
ELECTRONIC ARTS INC	KAISER PERMANENTE	PROCTER & GAMBLE CO
EMERITUS CORP	KEANE INC	PROGRESSIVE CORPORATION (THE)
ENTERPRISE RENT-A-CAR	KELLY SERVICES INC	
ERNST & YOUNG LLP	KIMBERLY-CLARK CORP	PRUDENTIAL FINANCIAL INC
ESTEE LAUDER COMPANIES INC (THE)	KINDRED HEALTHCARE INC	PSYCHIATRIC SOLUTIONS INC
	KOHL'S CORP	PUBLIX SUPER MARKETS INC

QUIKSILVER INC	WATSON WYATT WORLDWIDE INC	AUTOMATIC DATA PROCESSING INC
R R DONNELLEY & SONS CO	WEIGHT WATCHERS INTERNATIONAL INC	AVERY DENNISON CORP
RES CARE INC	WELLPOINT INC	AVNET INC
RITE AID CORPORATION	WELLS FARGO & CO	BAKER HUGHES INC
RITZ-CARLTON HOTEL COMPANY LLC (THE)	WENDY'S/ARBY'S GROUP INC	BALTIMORE GAS AND ELECTRIC COMPANY
ROBERT HALF INTERNATIONAL INC	WHOLE FOODS MARKET INC	BAXTER INTERNATIONAL INC
ROSS STORES INC	WYNDHAM WORLDWIDE	BDO SEIDMAN LLP
ROYAL CARIBBEAN CRUISES LTD	WYNN RESORTS LIMITED	BECHTEL GROUP INC
SABRE HOLDINGS CORP	YAHOO! INC	BECKMAN COULTER INC
SAFECO INSURANCE COMPANY OF AMERICA	YUM! BRANDS INC	BECTON DICKINSON & CO
SAFEWAY INC		BENCHMARK ELECTRONICS INC
SAIC INC	**Technical Writing**	BERKSHIRE HATHAWAY INC
SAM'S CLUB	3M COMPANY	BIO RAD LABORATORIES INC
SAPIENT CORPORATION	ABBOTT LABORATORIES	BLACK & DECKER CORP
SAS INSTITUTE INC	ACCENTURE LTD	BLOOMBERG LP
SCIENTIFIC GAMES CORPORATION	ACTIVISION BLIZZARD INC	BOEING COMPANY (THE)
SELECT MEDICAL	ACXIOM CORP	BOOZ ALLEN HAMILTON
SISTERS OF MERCY HEALTH SYSTEMS	ADC TELECOMMUNICATIONS INC	BOSTON SCIENTIFIC CORP
SOUTHWEST AIRLINES CO	ADOBE SYSTEMS INC	BROADCOM CORP
SRA INTERNATIONAL INC	ADVANCED MICRO DEVICES INC (AMD)	BROWN & BROWN INC
STAPLES INC	AECOM TECHNOLOGY CORPORATION	BUCYRUS INTERNATIONAL INC
STARWOOD HOTELS & RESORTS WORLDWIDE INC	AES CORPORATION (THE)	CABLEVISION SYSTEMS CORP
SUN HEALTHCARE GROUP	AETNA INC	CACI INTERNATIONAL INC
SUNRISE SENIOR LIVING	AFFILIATED COMPUTER SERVICES INC	CAMERON INTERNATIONAL CORPORATION
SUPERVALU INC	AFLAC INC	CAPITAL SENIOR LIVING CORP
SYNTEL INC	AGILENT TECHNOLOGIES INC	CARDINAL HEALTH INC
TARGET CORPORATION	AIR PRODUCTS & CHEMICALS INC	CARGILL INC
TIFFANY & CO	ALLERGAN INC	CARNIVAL CORPORATION
TIME WARNER INC	ALLSTATE CORPORATION (THE)	CATERPILLAR INC
TJX COMPANIES INC (THE)	AMAZON.COM INC	CATHOLIC HEALTH INITIATIVES
T-MOBILE USA	AMEDISYS INC	CDW CORPORATION
TOWERS PERRIN	AMERICAN ELECTRIC POWER COMPANY INC (AEP)	CELGENE CORP
TRAVELERS COMPANIES INC (THE)	AMERICAN POWER CONVERSION (APC)	CELLCO PARTNERSHIP (VERIZON WIRELESS)
UNITED PARCEL SERVICE INC (UPS)	AMERISOURCEBERGEN CORP	CEPHALON INC
UNITEDHEALTH GROUP INC	AMGEN INC	CH ROBINSON WORLDWIDE INC
UNIVISION COMMUNICATIONS INC	ANADARKO PETROLEUM CORPORATION	CH2M HILL COMPANIES LTD
USAA	ANALOG DEVICES INC	CHEMED CORPORATION
VERIZON COMMUNICATIONS	APACHE CORP	CHEVRON CORPORATION
VIACOM INC	APPLE INC	CHEVRON PHILLIPS CHEMICAL COMPANY LLC
VICTORIAS SECRET	ARAMARK CORPORATION	CHUBB CORPORATION (THE)
VISA INC	ARCHER DANIELS MIDLAND CO	CIBER INC
VOLT INFORMATION SCIENCES INC	ARROW ELECTRONICS INC	CIGNA CORP
W R BERKLEY CORPORATION	ARTHUR J GALLAGHER & CO	CISCO SYSTEMS INC
WALGREEN CO	ASCENSION HEALTH	COCA-COLA COMPANY (THE)
WAL-MART STORES INC	AT&T INC	COCA-COLA ENTERPRISES INC
WALT DISNEY COMPANY (THE)		COGNIZANT TECHNOLOGY

SOLUTIONS CORP	FEDEX CORPORATION	JABIL CIRCUIT INC
COLGATE PALMOLIVE CO	FIRST ADVANTAGE CORPORATION	JACOBS ENGINEERING GROUP INC
COMCAST CORP	FIRSTENERGY CORP	JETBLUE AIRWAYS CORPORATION
COMMUNITY HEALTH SYSTEMS INC	FLUOR CORP	JOHNSON & JOHNSON
CONAGRA FOODS INC	FOREST LABORATORIES INC	JOHNSON CONTROLS INC
CONOCOPHILLIPS COMPANY	FORTUNE BRANDS INC	JUNIPER NETWORKS INC
CONSOL ENERGY INC	FOSSIL INC	KAISER PERMANENTE
CONSOLIDATED EDISON INC	FOSTER WHEELER AG	KEANE INC
COOPER COMPANIES INC	FPL GROUP INC	KELLOGG CO
COVANCE INC	FRONTIER COMMUNICATIONS CORPORATION	KELLY SERVICES INC
COVENTRY HEALTH CARE INC	FTI CONSULTING INC	KENDLE INTERNATIONAL INC
COX COMMUNICATIONS INC	GENENTECH INC	KINDRED HEALTHCARE INC
CR BARD INC	GENERAL CABLE CORP	KOCH INDUSTRIES INC
CTS CORP	GENERAL DYNAMICS CORP	KPMG LLP
CUBIC CORP	GENERAL ELECTRIC CO (GE)	KRAFT FOODS INC
CUMMINS INC	GENERAL MILLS INC	L-3 COMMUNICATIONS HOLDINGS INC
DANAHER CORP	GENWORTH FINANCIAL INC	LABORATORY CORP OF AMERICA HOLDINGS
DAVITA INC	GEORGIA GULF CORPORATION	
DEERE & CO	GILEAD SCIENCES INC	LEVEL 3 COMMUNICATIONS INC
DELOITTE & TOUCHE USA LLP	GOOGLE INC	LEXMARK INTERNATIONAL INC
DELOITTE CONSULTING LLP	GRANT THORNTON LLP	LIBERTY GLOBAL INC
DEVON ENERGY CORPORATION	HALLIBURTON COMPANY	LIBERTY MUTUAL GROUP INC
DIAMOND OFFSHORE DRILLING INC	HARRIS CORPORATION	LINCARE HOLDINGS INC
DIEBOLD INC	HARTFORD FINANCIAL SERVICES GROUP INC (THE)	LINCOLN NATIONAL CORPORATION
DIRECTV GROUP INC (THE)		LKQ CORP
DTE ENERGY COMPANY	HAWAIIAN ELECTRIC INDUSTRIES INC	LOCKHEED MARTIN CORP
DUKE ENERGY CORP		LOEWS CORPORATION
DYCOM INDUSTRIES INC	HCA INC	MANOR CARE INC
E I DU PONT DE NEMOURS & CO (DUPONT)	HEALTH CARE SERVICE CORPORATION	MANPOWER INC
EATON CORP	HEALTH MANAGEMENT ASSOCIATES INC	MARS INC
EBAY INC		MARSH & MCLENNAN COMPANIES INC
EDISON INTERNATIONAL	HEALTH NET INC	
ELECTRONIC ARTS INC	HEALTHWAYS INC	MASSEY ENERGY COMPANY
ELI LILLY & COMPANY	HELMERICH & PAYNE INC	MATTEL INC
EMBARQ CORP	HENRY SCHEIN INC	MAXIM INTEGRATED PRODUCTS INC
EMC CORP	HESS CORPORATION	
EMERITUS CORP	HEWITT ASSOCIATES	MAYO FOUNDATION FOR MEDICAL EDUCATION AND RESEARCH
EMERSON ELECTRIC CO	HONEYWELL INTERNATIONAL INC	
ENTERGY CORP	HUMANA INC	MCAFEE INC
ENTERPRISE PRODUCTS PARTNERS LP	IBM GLOBAL SERVICES	MCDERMOTT INTERNATIONAL INC
	IDEXX LABORATORIES INC	MCKESSON CORPORATION
ERNST & YOUNG LLP	IGATE CORPORATION	MCKINSEY & COMPANY INC
ESTEE LAUDER COMPANIES INC (THE)	IMS HEALTH INC	MEDCO HEALTH SOLUTIONS
	INGRAM MICRO INC	MEDTRONIC INC
EXELON CORPORATION	INTEL CORP	MERCER INC
EXPERIAN AMERICAS	INTERNATIONAL BUSINESS MACHINES CORP (IBM)	MERCK & CO INC
EXPRESS SCRIPTS INC		METHODIST HEALTH CARE SYSTEM
EXXON MOBIL CORPORATION (EXXONMOBIL)	INTUIT INC	
	INVENTIV HEALTH INC	METLIFE INC
EXXONMOBIL CHEMICAL		MICROCHIP TECHNOLOGY INC

MICRON TECHNOLOGY INC	PSYCHIATRIC SOLUTIONS INC	SYNTEL INC
MICROSOFT CORP	QUALCOMM INC	TEAM INC
MIDAMERICAN ENERGY HOLDINGS CO	QUANTA SERVICES INC	TECH DATA CORP
MILLIPORE CORP	QUEST DIAGNOSTICS INC	TEKTRONIX INC
MONRO MUFFLER BRAKE INC	R R DONNELLEY & SONS CO	TELEDYNE TECHNOLOGIES INCORPORATED
MONSANTO CO	RAYTHEON CO	TELEPHONE AND DATA SYSTEMS INC (TDS)
MURPHY OIL CORPORATION	RES CARE INC	TESORO CORP
MYLAN INC	ROBERT HALF INTERNATIONAL INC	THERMO FISHER SCIENTIFIC INC
NATIONAL OILWELL VARCO INC	ROYAL CARIBBEAN CRUISES LTD	TIME WARNER INC
NETAPP INC	RRI ENERGY INC	T-MOBILE USA
NII HOLDINGS INC	SABRE HOLDINGS CORP	TOWERS PERRIN
NOBLE CORPORATION	SAFECO INSURANCE COMPANY OF AMERICA	TRANSOCEAN INC
NORTHROP GRUMMAN CORP	SAIC INC	TRAVELERS COMPANIES INC (THE)
NRG ENERGY INC	SAPIENT CORPORATION	TW TELECOM INC
OCCIDENTAL PETROLEUM CORP	SARA LEE CORP	UNITED PARCEL SERVICE INC (UPS)
OCEANEERING INTERNATIONAL INC	SAS INSTITUTE INC	UNITED STATES CELLULAR CORP
ODYSSEY HEALTHCARE INC	SCANA CORPORATION	UNITED TECHNOLOGIES CORPORATION
OIL STATES INTERNATIONAL INC	SCHERING-PLOUGH CORP	UNITEDHEALTH GROUP INC
OMNICARE INC	SCHLUMBERGER LIMITED	UNIVERSAL HEALTH SERVICES INC
ORACLE CORP	SCIENTIFIC GAMES CORPORATION	URS CORPORATION
OSHKOSH CORPORATION	SCOTTS MIRACLE GROW CO	USAA
OWENS & MINOR INC	SEACOR HOLDINGS INC	VALERO ENERGY CORP
PARAMETRIC TECHNOLOGY CORP	SELECT MEDICAL	VALSPAR CORPORATION (THE)
PAREXEL INTERNATIONAL CORP	SEMPRA ENERGY	VARIAN MEDICAL SYSTEMS INC
PARSONS BRINCKERHOFF INC	SENSIENT TECHNOLOGIES CORPORATION	VCA ANTECH INC
PATTERSON COMPANIES INC	SHAW GROUP INC (THE)	VERISIGN INC
PATTERSON-UTI ENERGY INC	SHELL OIL CO	VERIZON COMMUNICATIONS
PAYCHEX INC	SHERWIN WILLIAMS COMPANY (THE)	VOLT INFORMATION SCIENCES INC
PEABODY ENERGY CORP	SIGMA-ALDRICH CORP	W R BERKLEY CORPORATION
PEPSI BOTTLING GROUP INC	SISTERS OF MERCY HEALTH SYSTEMS	WABTEC CORP
PEPSICO INC	SMITH INTERNATIONAL INC	WASTE MANAGEMENT INC
PEROT SYSTEMS CORP	SOUTHERN CALIFORNIA EDISON COMPANY	WATERS CORP
PERRIGO CO	SOUTHERN COMPANY (THE)	WATSON PHARMACEUTICALS INC
PFIZER INC	SOUTHWEST AIRLINES CO	WATSON WYATT WORLDWIDE INC
PG&E CORPORATION	SRA INTERNATIONAL INC	WEATHERFORD INTERNATIONAL LTD
PHARMACEUTICAL PRODUCT DEVELOPMENT INC	ST JUDE MEDICAL INC	WELLPOINT INC
PITNEY BOWES INC	STARTEK INC	WEST PHARMACEUTICAL SERVICES INC
PLEXUS CORP	STERIS CORP	WESTERN DIGITAL CORP
PRAXAIR INC	STRYKER CORP	WILLIAMS COMPANIES INC (THE)
PRECISION CASTPARTS CORP	SUN HEALTHCARE GROUP	WW GRAINGER INC
PRICEWATERHOUSECOOPERS	SUNGARD DATA SYSTEMS INC	WYETH
PRIDE INTERNATIONAL INC	SUNOCO INC	XEROX CORP
PRINCIPAL FINANCIAL GROUP (THE)	SUNRISE SENIOR LIVING	YAHOO! INC
PROCTER & GAMBLE CO	SYKES ENTERPRISES INC	ZIMMER HOLDINGS INC
PROGRESSIVE CORPORATION (THE)	SYMANTEC CORP	
PRUDENTIAL FINANCIAL INC	SYNOPSYS INC	

Management

Experienced Management
3M COMPANY
7-ELEVEN INC
AARON'S INC
ABBOTT LABORATORIES
ABM INDUSTRIES INC
ACADEMY SPORTS & OUTDOORS LTD
ACCENTURE LTD
ACTIVISION BLIZZARD INC
ACXIOM CORP
ADC TELECOMMUNICATIONS INC
ADESA INC
ADOBE SYSTEMS INC
ADVANCE AUTO PARTS INC
ADVANCED MICRO DEVICES INC (AMD)
AECOM TECHNOLOGY CORPORATION
AES CORPORATION (THE)
AETNA INC
AFFILIATED COMPUTER SERVICES INC
AFLAC INC
AGILENT TECHNOLOGIES INC
AIR PRODUCTS & CHEMICALS INC
ALLERGAN INC
ALLIANCE DATA SYSTEMS CORPORATION
ALLSTATE CORPORATION (THE)
ALTRIA GROUP INC
AMAZON.COM INC
AMEDISYS INC
AMERICAN ELECTRIC POWER COMPANY INC (AEP)
AMERICAN POWER CONVERSION (APC)
AMERISOURCEBERGEN CORP
AMGEN INC
ANADARKO PETROLEUM CORPORATION
ANALOG DEVICES INC
ANNTAYLOR STORES CORP
APACHE CORP
APOLLO GROUP INC
APPLE INC
ARAMARK CORPORATION
ARCHER DANIELS MIDLAND CO
ARROW ELECTRONICS INC
ARTHUR J GALLAGHER & CO

ASCENSION HEALTH
AT&T INC
AUTOMATIC DATA PROCESSING INC
AUTOZONE INC
AVERY DENNISON CORP
AVIS BUDGET GROUP INC
AVNET INC
AVON PRODUCTS INC
AXA FINANCIAL INC
BAKER HUGHES INC
BALTIMORE GAS AND ELECTRIC COMPANY
BANK OF AMERICA CORP
BARNES & NOBLE INC
BASS PRO SHOPS INC
BAXTER INTERNATIONAL INC
BDO SEIDMAN LLP
BEBE STORES INC
BECHTEL GROUP INC
BECKMAN COULTER INC
BECTON DICKINSON & CO
BED BATH & BEYOND INC
BENCHMARK ELECTRONICS INC
BERKSHIRE HATHAWAY INC
BEST BUY CO INC
BIO RAD LABORATORIES INC
BJ'S WHOLESALE CLUB INC
BLACK & DECKER CORP
BLACKROCK INC
BLOOMBERG LP
BOEING COMPANY (THE)
BOOZ ALLEN HAMILTON
BOSTON SCIENTIFIC CORP
BRINKER INTERNATIONAL INC
BRINKS COMPANY (THE)
BROADCOM CORP
BROWN & BROWN INC
BUCKLE INC (THE)
BUCYRUS INTERNATIONAL INC
BUFFALO WILD WINGS INC
BUNGE LTD
BURGER KING HOLDINGS INC
CABELA'S INC
CABLEVISION SYSTEMS CORP
CACI INTERNATIONAL INC
CAMERON INTERNATIONAL CORPORATION
CAPITAL SENIOR LIVING CORP
CARDINAL HEALTH INC
CARGILL INC

CARMAX GROUP
CARNIVAL CORPORATION
CASH AMERICA INTERNATIONAL INC
CATERPILLAR INC
CATHOLIC HEALTH INITIATIVES
CDW CORPORATION
CELGENE CORP
CELLCO PARTNERSHIP (VERIZON WIRELESS)
CEPHALON INC
CH ROBINSON WORLDWIDE INC
CH2M HILL COMPANIES LTD
CHARLOTTE RUSSE HOLDING
CHARMING SHOPPES INC
CHEMED CORPORATION
CHEVRON CORPORATION
CHEVRON PHILLIPS CHEMICAL COMPANY LLC
CHICO'S FAS INC
CHIPOTLE MEXICAN GRILL INC
CHRISTOPHER & BANKS CORP
CHS INC
CHUBB CORPORATION (THE)
CIBER INC
CIGNA CORP
CINTAS CORP
CISCO SYSTEMS INC
CLUBCORP INC
COACH INC
COCA-COLA COMPANY (THE)
COCA-COLA ENTERPRISES INC
COGNIZANT TECHNOLOGY SOLUTIONS CORP
COLDWATER CREEK INC
COLGATE PALMOLIVE CO
COMCAST CORP
COMMUNITY HEALTH SYSTEMS INC
CONAGRA FOODS INC
CONOCOPHILLIPS COMPANY
CONSOL ENERGY INC
CONSOLIDATED EDISON INC
CONTAINER STORE (THE)
CONVERGYS CORPORATION
COOPER COMPANIES INC
COSTCO WHOLESALE CORP
COVANCE INC
COVENTRY HEALTH CARE INC
COX COMMUNICATIONS INC
CR BARD INC
CRACKER BARREL OLD COUNTRY

STORE INC	EXXONMOBIL CHEMICAL	HEALTHWAYS INC
CTS CORP	FAMILY DOLLAR STORES INC	HELMERICH & PAYNE INC
CUBIC CORP	FEDEX CORPORATION	HENRY SCHEIN INC
CUMMINS INC	FINISH LINE INC (THE)	HERTZ GLOBAL HOLDINGS INC
CVS CAREMARK CORPORATION	FIRST ADVANTAGE CORPORATION	HESS CORPORATION
DANAHER CORP	FIRST DATA CORP	HEWITT ASSOCIATES
DARDEN RESTAURANTS INC	FIRSTENERGY CORP	HIBBETT SPORTS INC
DAVITA INC	FLUOR CORP	HILTON HOTELS CORP
DEAN FOODS CO	FOREST LABORATORIES INC	HOME DEPOT INC
DEERE & CO	FORTUNE BRANDS INC	HONEYWELL INTERNATIONAL INC
DELOITTE & TOUCHE USA LLP	FOSSIL INC	HUMANA INC
DELOITTE CONSULTING LLP	FOSTER WHEELER AG	IAC/INTERACTIVECORP
DENNY'S CORPORATION	FOX ENTERTAINMENT GROUP INC	IBM GLOBAL SERVICES
DEVON ENERGY CORPORATION	FPL GROUP INC	ICT GROUP INC
DEVRY INC	FRED'S INC	IDEXX LABORATORIES INC
DIAMOND OFFSHORE DRILLING INC	FRONTIER COMMUNICATIONS CORPORATION	IGATE CORPORATION
DICK'S SPORTING GOODS INC		IMS HEALTH INC
DIEBOLD INC	FTI CONSULTING INC	INFOGROUP INC
DINEEQUITY INC	GAMESTOP CORP	INGRAM MICRO INC
DIRECTV GROUP INC (THE)	GENENTECH INC	INTEL CORP
DOLE FOOD COMPANY INC	GENERAL CABLE CORP	INTERNATIONAL BUSINESS MACHINES CORP (IBM)
DOLLAR GENERAL CORPORATION	GENERAL DYNAMICS CORP	
DOLLAR THRIFTY AUTOMOTIVE GROUP INC	GENERAL ELECTRIC CO (GE)	INTUIT INC
	GENERAL MILLS INC	INVENTIV HEALTH INC
DRESS BARN INC (THE)	GENESCO INC	J C PENNEY COMPANY INC
DTE ENERGY COMPANY	GENWORTH FINANCIAL INC	JABIL CIRCUIT INC
DUKE ENERGY CORP	GEO GROUP INC	JACK IN THE BOX INC
DYCOM INDUSTRIES INC	GEORGIA GULF CORPORATION	JACOBS ENGINEERING GROUP INC
E I DU PONT DE NEMOURS & CO (DUPONT)	GILEAD SCIENCES INC	JETBLUE AIRWAYS CORPORATION
	GLOBAL HYATT CORPORATION	JM SMUCKER CO
EATON CORP	GLOBAL PAYMENTS INC	JOHNSON & JOHNSON
EBAY INC	GOLDMAN SACHS GROUP INC	JOHNSON CONTROLS INC
EDISON INTERNATIONAL	GOOGLE INC	JP MORGAN CHASE & CO INC
ELECTRONIC ARTS INC	GRANT THORNTON LLP	JUNIPER NETWORKS INC
ELI LILLY & COMPANY	GUESS? INC	KAISER PERMANENTE
EMBARQ CORP	HALLIBURTON COMPANY	KEANE INC
EMC CORP	HARRAH'S ENTERTAINMENT INC	KELLOGG CO
EMERITUS CORP	HARRIS CORPORATION	KELLY SERVICES INC
EMERSON ELECTRIC CO	HARTFORD FINANCIAL SERVICES GROUP INC (THE)	KENDLE INTERNATIONAL INC
ENTERGY CORP		KIMBERLY-CLARK CORP
ENTERPRISE PRODUCTS PARTNERS LP	HAWAIIAN ELECTRIC INDUSTRIES INC	KINDRED HEALTHCARE INC
		KOCH INDUSTRIES INC
ENTERPRISE RENT-A-CAR	HCA INC	KOHL'S CORP
ERNST & YOUNG LLP	HE BUTT GROCERY COMPANY (HEB)	KPMG LLP
ESTEE LAUDER COMPANIES INC (THE)		KRAFT FOODS INC
	HEALTH CARE SERVICE CORPORATION	KROGER CO (THE)
EXELON CORPORATION		L-3 COMMUNICATIONS HOLDINGS INC
EXPERIAN AMERICAS	HEALTH FITNESS CORP	
EXPRESS SCRIPTS INC	HEALTH MANAGEMENT ASSOCIATES INC	LABORATORY CORP OF AMERICA HOLDINGS
EXXON MOBIL CORPORATION (EXXONMOBIL)		
	HEALTH NET INC	LAS VEGAS SANDS CORP (THE

VENETIAN)	MYLAN INC	PROGRESSIVE CORPORATION (THE)
LEVEL 3 COMMUNICATIONS INC	NATIONAL OILWELL VARCO INC	PRUDENTIAL FINANCIAL INC
LEXMARK INTERNATIONAL INC	NETAPP INC	PSYCHIATRIC SOLUTIONS INC
LIBERTY GLOBAL INC	NEWS CORP	PUBLIC STORAGE INC
LIBERTY MUTUAL GROUP INC	NII HOLDINGS INC	PUBLIX SUPER MARKETS INC
LIMITED BRANDS INC	NIKE INC	QUALCOMM INC
LINCARE HOLDINGS INC	NOBLE CORPORATION	QUANTA SERVICES INC
LINCOLN NATIONAL CORPORATION	NORTHROP GRUMMAN CORP	QUEST DIAGNOSTICS INC
LKQ CORP	NRG ENERGY INC	QUIKSILVER INC
LOCKHEED MARTIN CORP	OCCIDENTAL PETROLEUM CORP	R R DONNELLEY & SONS CO
LODGIAN INC	OCEANEERING INTERNATIONAL INC	RALCORP HOLDINGS INC
LOEWS CORPORATION	ODYSSEY HEALTHCARE INC	RAYTHEON CO
LOWE'S COMPANIES INC	OFFICE DEPOT INC	REGIS CORPORATION
MACY'S INC	OIL STATES INTERNATIONAL INC	RENT-A-CENTER INC
MANOR CARE INC	OMNICARE INC	RES CARE INC
MANPOWER INC	OMNICOM GROUP INC	RITE AID CORPORATION
MARRIOTT INTERNATIONAL INC	ORACLE CORP	RITZ-CARLTON HOTEL COMPANY LLC (THE)
MARS INC	O'REILLY AUTOMOTIVE INC	ROBERT HALF INTERNATIONAL INC
MARSH & MCLENNAN COMPANIES INC	OSHKOSH CORPORATION	ROSS STORES INC
MARY KAY INC	OSI RESTAURANT PARTNERS LLC	ROYAL CARIBBEAN CRUISES LTD
MASSEY ENERGY COMPANY	OWENS & MINOR INC	RRI ENERGY INC
MATTEL INC	PANTRY INC (THE)	SABRE HOLDINGS CORP
MAXIM INTEGRATED PRODUCTS INC	PARAMETRIC TECHNOLOGY CORP	SAFECO INSURANCE COMPANY OF AMERICA
MAYO FOUNDATION FOR MEDICAL EDUCATION AND RESEARCH	PAREXEL INTERNATIONAL CORP	SAFEWAY INC
	PARSONS BRINCKERHOFF INC	SAIC INC
MCAFEE INC	PATTERSON COMPANIES INC	SAM'S CLUB
MCDERMOTT INTERNATIONAL INC	PATTERSON-UTI ENERGY INC	SAPIENT CORPORATION
MCDONALD'S CORP	PAYCHEX INC	SARA LEE CORP
MCKESSON CORPORATION	PEABODY ENERGY CORP	SAS INSTITUTE INC
MCKINSEY & COMPANY INC	PEPSI BOTTLING GROUP INC	SCANA CORPORATION
MEDCO HEALTH SOLUTIONS	PEPSICO INC	SCHERING-PLOUGH CORP
MEDTRONIC INC	PEROT SYSTEMS CORP	SCHLUMBERGER LIMITED
MEIJER INC	PERRIGO CO	SCIENTIFIC GAMES CORPORATION
MEN'S WEARHOUSE INC (THE)	PETCO ANIMAL SUPPLIES INC	SCOTTS MIRACLE GROW CO
MERCER INC	PETSMART INC	SEACOR HOLDINGS INC
MERCK & CO INC	PFIZER INC	SELECT MEDICAL
METHODIST HEALTH CARE SYSTEM	PG&E CORPORATION	SEMPRA ENERGY
METLIFE INC	PHARMACEUTICAL PRODUCT DEVELOPMENT INC	SENSIENT TECHNOLOGIES CORPORATION
MGM MIRAGE	PITNEY BOWES INC	SHAW GROUP INC (THE)
MICROCHIP TECHNOLOGY INC	PLEXUS CORP	SHELL OIL CO
MICRON TECHNOLOGY INC	POLO RALPH LAUREN CORP	SHERWIN WILLIAMS COMPANY (THE)
MICROSOFT CORP	PRAXAIR INC	
MIDAMERICAN ENERGY HOLDINGS CO	PRECISION CASTPARTS CORP	SIGMA-ALDRICH CORP
MILLIPORE CORP	PRICESMART INC	SISTERS OF MERCY HEALTH SYSTEMS
MONRO MUFFLER BRAKE INC	PRICEWATERHOUSECOOPERS	
MONSANTO CO	PRIDE INTERNATIONAL INC	SMITH INTERNATIONAL INC
MURPHY OIL CORPORATION	PRINCIPAL FINANCIAL GROUP (THE)	SMITHFIELD FOODS INC
	PROCTER & GAMBLE CO	

SOUTHERN CALIFORNIA EDISON COMPANY	UNITED TECHNOLOGIES CORPORATION	AARON'S INC
SOUTHERN COMPANY (THE)	UNITEDHEALTH GROUP INC	ABBOTT LABORATORIES
SOUTHWEST AIRLINES CO	UNIVERSAL HEALTH SERVICES INC	ABM INDUSTRIES INC
SRA INTERNATIONAL INC	UNIVISION COMMUNICATIONS INC	ACCENTURE LTD
ST JUDE MEDICAL INC	URS CORPORATION	ACTIVISION BLIZZARD INC
STAPLES INC	USAA	ACXIOM CORP
STARTEK INC	VALERO ENERGY CORP	ADC TELECOMMUNICATIONS INC
STARWOOD HOTELS & RESORTS WORLDWIDE INC	VALSPAR CORPORATION (THE)	ADESA INC
STERIS CORP	VARIAN MEDICAL SYSTEMS INC	ADOBE SYSTEMS INC
STIFEL FINANCIAL CORP	VCA ANTECH INC	ADVANCE AUTO PARTS INC
STRYKER CORP	VERISIGN INC	ADVANCED MICRO DEVICES INC (AMD)
SUN HEALTHCARE GROUP	VERIZON COMMUNICATIONS	AECOM TECHNOLOGY CORPORATION
SUNGARD DATA SYSTEMS INC	VIACOM INC	
SUNOCO INC	VICTORIAS SECRET	AES CORPORATION (THE)
SUNRISE SENIOR LIVING	VISA INC	AFFILIATED COMPUTER SERVICES INC
SUPERVALU INC	VOLT INFORMATION SCIENCES INC	
SYKES ENTERPRISES INC	W R BERKLEY CORPORATION	AFLAC INC
SYMANTEC CORP	WABTEC CORP	AGILENT TECHNOLOGIES INC
SYNOPSYS INC	WALGREEN CO	AIR PRODUCTS & CHEMICALS INC
SYNTEL INC	WAL-MART STORES INC	ALLERGAN INC
SYSCO CORP	WALT DISNEY COMPANY (THE)	ALLIANCE DATA SYSTEMS CORPORATION
TARGET CORPORATION	WASTE MANAGEMENT INC	
TBC CORPORATION	WATERS CORP	ALLSTATE CORPORATION (THE)
TEAM INC	WATSON PHARMACEUTICALS INC	ALTRIA GROUP INC
TECH DATA CORP	WATSON WYATT WORLDWIDE INC	AMAZON.COM INC
TEKTRONIX INC	WEATHERFORD INTERNATIONAL LTD	AMERICAN ELECTRIC POWER COMPANY INC (AEP)
TELEDYNE TECHNOLOGIES INCORPORATED	WEIGHT WATCHERS INTERNATIONAL INC	AMERICAN POWER CONVERSION (APC)
TELEPHONE AND DATA SYSTEMS INC (TDS)	WELLPOINT INC	AMERISOURCEBERGEN CORP
TELETECH HOLDINGS INC	WELLS FARGO & CO	AMGEN INC
TESORO CORP	WENDY'S/ARBY'S GROUP INC	ANADARKO PETROLEUM CORPORATION
THERMO FISHER SCIENTIFIC INC	WEST CORPORATION	
TIFFANY & CO	WEST PHARMACEUTICAL SERVICES INC	ANALOG DEVICES INC
TIME WARNER INC		ANNTAYLOR STORES CORP
TJX COMPANIES INC (THE)	WESTERN DIGITAL CORP	APACHE CORP
T-MOBILE USA	WHOLE FOODS MARKET INC	APOLLO GROUP INC
TOTAL SYSTEM SERVICES INC (TSYS)	WILLIAMS COMPANIES INC (THE)	APPLE INC
TOWERS PERRIN	WW GRAINGER INC	ARAMARK CORPORATION
TRANSOCEAN INC	WYETH	ARCHER DANIELS MIDLAND CO
TRAVELERS COMPANIES INC (THE)	WYNDHAM WORLDWIDE	ARROW ELECTRONICS INC
TREEHOUSE FOODS INC	WYNN RESORTS LIMITED	ARTHUR J GALLAGHER & CO
TW TELECOM INC	XEROX CORP	AT&T INC
TYSON FOODS INC	YAHOO! INC	AUTOMATIC DATA PROCESSING INC
UNITED NATURAL FOODS INC	YUM! BRANDS INC	
UNITED PARCEL SERVICE INC (UPS)	ZIMMER HOLDINGS INC	AUTOZONE INC
		AVERY DENNISON CORP
UNITED STATES CELLULAR CORP		AVIS BUDGET GROUP INC

International Business
3M COMPANY
7-ELEVEN INC

AVNET INC
AVON PRODUCTS INC
AXA FINANCIAL INC

BAKER HUGHES INC	CIGNA CORP	ENTERGY CORP
BANK OF AMERICA CORP	CINTAS CORP	ENTERPRISE RENT-A-CAR
BASS PRO SHOPS INC	CISCO SYSTEMS INC	ERNST & YOUNG LLP
BAXTER INTERNATIONAL INC	CLUBCORP INC	ESTEE LAUDER COMPANIES INC (THE)
BDO SEIDMAN LLP	COACH INC	EXPRESS SCRIPTS INC
BEBE STORES INC	COCA-COLA COMPANY (THE)	EXXON MOBIL CORPORATION (EXXONMOBIL)
BECHTEL GROUP INC	COCA-COLA ENTERPRISES INC	EXXONMOBIL CHEMICAL
BECKMAN COULTER INC	COGNIZANT TECHNOLOGY SOLUTIONS CORP	FEDEX CORPORATION
BECTON DICKINSON & CO	COLGATE PALMOLIVE CO	FIRST ADVANTAGE CORPORATION
BED BATH & BEYOND INC	COMCAST CORP	FIRST DATA CORP
BENCHMARK ELECTRONICS INC	CONAGRA FOODS INC	FLUOR CORP
BERKSHIRE HATHAWAY INC	CONOCOPHILLIPS COMPANY	FOREST LABORATORIES INC
BEST BUY CO INC	CONSOL ENERGY INC	FORTUNE BRANDS INC
BIO RAD LABORATORIES INC	CONSOLIDATED EDISON INC	FOSSIL INC
BLACK & DECKER CORP	CONVERGYS CORPORATION	FOSTER WHEELER AG
BLACKROCK INC	COOPER COMPANIES INC	FOX ENTERTAINMENT GROUP INC
BLOOMBERG LP	COSTCO WHOLESALE CORP	FTI CONSULTING INC
BOEING COMPANY (THE)	COVANCE INC	GAMESTOP CORP
BOOZ ALLEN HAMILTON	COX COMMUNICATIONS INC	GENENTECH INC
BOSTON SCIENTIFIC CORP	CR BARD INC	GENERAL CABLE CORP
BRINKER INTERNATIONAL INC	CTS CORP	GENERAL DYNAMICS CORP
BRINKS COMPANY (THE)	CUBIC CORP	GENERAL ELECTRIC CO (GE)
BROADCOM CORP	CUMMINS INC	GENERAL MILLS INC
BROWN & BROWN INC	DANAHER CORP	GENESCO INC
BUNGE LTD	DARDEN RESTAURANTS INC	GENWORTH FINANCIAL INC
BURGER KING HOLDINGS INC	DEAN FOODS CO	GEO GROUP INC
CABELA'S INC	DEERE & CO	GEORGIA GULF CORPORATION
CACI INTERNATIONAL INC	DELOITTE & TOUCHE USA LLP	GILEAD SCIENCES INC
CAMERON INTERNATIONAL CORPORATION	DELOITTE CONSULTING LLP	GLOBAL HYATT CORPORATION
CARDINAL HEALTH INC	DENNY'S CORPORATION	GLOBAL PAYMENTS INC
CARGILL INC	DEVON ENERGY CORPORATION	GOLDMAN SACHS GROUP INC
CARNIVAL CORPORATION	DEVRY INC	GOOGLE INC
CASH AMERICA INTERNATIONAL INC	DIAMOND OFFSHORE DRILLING INC	GUESS? INC
CATERPILLAR INC	DIEBOLD INC	HALLIBURTON COMPANY
CDW CORPORATION	DINEEQUITY INC	HARRAH'S ENTERTAINMENT INC
CELGENE CORP	DIRECTV GROUP INC (THE)	HARRIS CORPORATION
CEPHALON INC	DOLE FOOD COMPANY INC	HARTFORD FINANCIAL SERVICES GROUP INC (THE)
CH ROBINSON WORLDWIDE INC	DOLLAR THRIFTY AUTOMOTIVE GROUP INC	HCA INC
CH2M HILL COMPANIES LTD	DUKE ENERGY CORP	HE BUTT GROCERY COMPANY (HEB)
CHARLOTTE RUSSE HOLDING	E I DU PONT DE NEMOURS & CO (DUPONT)	HEALTH FITNESS CORP
CHARMING SHOPPES INC	EATON CORP	HEALTHWAYS INC
CHEMED CORPORATION	EBAY INC	HELMERICH & PAYNE INC
CHEVRON CORPORATION	EDISON INTERNATIONAL	HENRY SCHEIN INC
CHEVRON PHILLIPS CHEMICAL COMPANY LLC	ELECTRONIC ARTS INC	HERTZ GLOBAL HOLDINGS INC
CHICO'S FAS INC	ELI LILLY & COMPANY	HESS CORPORATION
CHIPOTLE MEXICAN GRILL INC	EMC CORP	HEWITT ASSOCIATES
CHUBB CORPORATION (THE)	EMERITUS CORP	HILTON HOTELS CORP
CIBER INC	EMERSON ELECTRIC CO	

HOME DEPOT INC	MANPOWER INC	PATTERSON-UTI ENERGY INC
HONEYWELL INTERNATIONAL INC	MARRIOTT INTERNATIONAL INC	PAYCHEX INC
HUMANA INC	MARS INC	PEABODY ENERGY CORP
IAC/INTERACTIVECORP	MARSH & MCLENNAN COMPANIES INC	PEPSI BOTTLING GROUP INC
IBM GLOBAL SERVICES	MARY KAY INC	PEPSICO INC
ICT GROUP INC	MATTEL INC	PEROT SYSTEMS CORP
IDEXX LABORATORIES INC	MAXIM INTEGRATED PRODUCTS INC	PERRIGO CO
IGATE CORPORATION	MCAFEE INC	PETSMART INC
IMS HEALTH INC	MCDERMOTT INTERNATIONAL INC	PFIZER INC
INFOGROUP INC	MCDONALD'S CORP	PG&E CORPORATION
INGRAM MICRO INC	MCKESSON CORPORATION	PHARMACEUTICAL PRODUCT DEVELOPMENT INC
INTEL CORP	MCKINSEY & COMPANY INC	PITNEY BOWES INC
INTERNATIONAL BUSINESS MACHINES CORP (IBM)	MEDTRONIC INC	PLEXUS CORP
INTUIT INC	MEN'S WEARHOUSE INC (THE)	POLO RALPH LAUREN CORP
INVENTIV HEALTH INC	MERCER INC	PRAXAIR INC
J C PENNEY COMPANY INC	MERCK & CO INC	PRECISION CASTPARTS CORP
JABIL CIRCUIT INC	METLIFE INC	PRICESMART INC
JACOBS ENGINEERING GROUP INC	MGM MIRAGE	PRICEWATERHOUSECOOPERS
JETBLUE AIRWAYS CORPORATION	MICROCHIP TECHNOLOGY INC	PRIDE INTERNATIONAL INC
JM SMUCKER CO	MICRON TECHNOLOGY INC	PRINCIPAL FINANCIAL GROUP (THE)
JOHNSON & JOHNSON	MICROSOFT CORP	PROCTER & GAMBLE CO
JOHNSON CONTROLS INC	MIDAMERICAN ENERGY HOLDINGS CO	PROGRESSIVE CORPORATION (THE)
JP MORGAN CHASE & CO INC	MILLIPORE CORP	PRUDENTIAL FINANCIAL INC
JUNIPER NETWORKS INC	MONSANTO CO	PSYCHIATRIC SOLUTIONS INC
KEANE INC	MURPHY OIL CORPORATION	QUALCOMM INC
KELLOGG CO	MYLAN INC	QUANTA SERVICES INC
KELLY SERVICES INC	NATIONAL OILWELL VARCO INC	QUEST DIAGNOSTICS INC
KENDLE INTERNATIONAL INC	NETAPP INC	QUIKSILVER INC
KIMBERLY-CLARK CORP	NEWS CORP	R R DONNELLEY & SONS CO
KOCH INDUSTRIES INC	NII HOLDINGS INC	RALCORP HOLDINGS INC
KPMG LLP	NIKE INC	RAYTHEON CO
KRAFT FOODS INC	NOBLE CORPORATION	REGIS CORPORATION
L-3 COMMUNICATIONS HOLDINGS INC	NORTHROP GRUMMAN CORP	RENT-A-CENTER INC
LABORATORY CORP OF AMERICA HOLDINGS	NRG ENERGY INC	RES CARE INC
LAS VEGAS SANDS CORP (THE VENETIAN)	OCCIDENTAL PETROLEUM CORP	RITZ-CARLTON HOTEL COMPANY LLC (THE)
	OCEANEERING INTERNATIONAL INC	
LEVEL 3 COMMUNICATIONS INC	OFFICE DEPOT INC	ROBERT HALF INTERNATIONAL INC
LEXMARK INTERNATIONAL INC	OIL STATES INTERNATIONAL INC	ROSS STORES INC
LIBERTY GLOBAL INC	OMNICARE INC	ROYAL CARIBBEAN CRUISES LTD
LIBERTY MUTUAL GROUP INC	OMNICOM GROUP INC	SABRE HOLDINGS CORP
LIMITED BRANDS INC	ORACLE CORP	SAFECO INSURANCE COMPANY OF AMERICA
LINCOLN NATIONAL CORPORATION	OSHKOSH CORPORATION	
LOCKHEED MARTIN CORP	OSI RESTAURANT PARTNERS LLC	SAFEWAY INC
LODGIAN INC	PARAMETRIC TECHNOLOGY CORP	SAIC INC
LOEWS CORPORATION	PAREXEL INTERNATIONAL CORP	SAM'S CLUB
LOWE'S COMPANIES INC	PARSONS BRINCKERHOFF INC	SAPIENT CORPORATION
MACY'S INC	PARSONS BRINCKERHOFF INC	SARA LEE CORP
MANOR CARE INC	PATTERSON COMPANIES INC	SAS INSTITUTE INC

SCHERING-PLOUGH CORP	TRANSOCEAN INC	**Management Trainees**
SCHLUMBERGER LIMITED	TRAVELERS COMPANIES INC (THE)	3M COMPANY
SCIENTIFIC GAMES CORPORATION	TYSON FOODS INC	7-ELEVEN INC
SCOTTS MIRACLE GROW CO	UNITED PARCEL SERVICE INC (UPS)	AARON'S INC
SEACOR HOLDINGS INC		ABBOTT LABORATORIES
SELECT MEDICAL	UNITED TECHNOLOGIES CORPORATION	ABM INDUSTRIES INC
SEMPRA ENERGY		ACADEMY SPORTS & OUTDOORS LTD
SENSIENT TECHNOLOGIES CORPORATION	UNITEDHEALTH GROUP INC	
	UNIVERSAL HEALTH SERVICES INC	ACCENTURE LTD
SHAW GROUP INC (THE)	UNIVISION COMMUNICATIONS INC	ACTIVISION BLIZZARD INC
SHELL OIL CO	URS CORPORATION	ACXIOM CORP
SHERWIN WILLIAMS COMPANY (THE)	USAA	ADC TELECOMMUNICATIONS INC
	VALERO ENERGY CORP	ADESA INC
SIGMA-ALDRICH CORP	VALSPAR CORPORATION (THE)	ADOBE SYSTEMS INC
SISTERS OF MERCY HEALTH SYSTEMS	VARIAN MEDICAL SYSTEMS INC	ADVANCE AUTO PARTS INC
	VERISIGN INC	ADVANCED MICRO DEVICES INC (AMD)
SMITH INTERNATIONAL INC	VERIZON COMMUNICATIONS	
SMITHFIELD FOODS INC	VIACOM INC	AECOM TECHNOLOGY CORPORATION
ST JUDE MEDICAL INC	VICTORIAS SECRET	
STAPLES INC	VISA INC	AES CORPORATION (THE)
STARTEK INC	VOLT INFORMATION SCIENCES INC	AETNA INC
STARWOOD HOTELS & RESORTS WORLDWIDE INC	W R BERKLEY CORPORATION	AFFILIATED COMPUTER SERVICES INC
	WABTEC CORP	
STERIS CORP	WALGREEN CO	AFLAC INC
STIFEL FINANCIAL CORP	WAL-MART STORES INC	AGILENT TECHNOLOGIES INC
STRYKER CORP	WALT DISNEY COMPANY (THE)	AIR PRODUCTS & CHEMICALS INC
SUNGARD DATA SYSTEMS INC	WATERS CORP	ALLERGAN INC
SUNOCO INC	WATSON PHARMACEUTICALS INC	ALLIANCE DATA SYSTEMS CORPORATION
SUNRISE SENIOR LIVING	WATSON WYATT WORLDWIDE INC	
SYKES ENTERPRISES INC	WEATHERFORD INTERNATIONAL LTD	ALLSTATE CORPORATION (THE)
SYMANTEC CORP		ALTRIA GROUP INC
SYNOPSYS INC	WEIGHT WATCHERS INTERNATIONAL INC	AMAZON.COM INC
SYNTEL INC		AMEDISYS INC
SYSCO CORP	WELLS FARGO & CO	AMERICAN ELECTRIC POWER COMPANY INC (AEP)
TARGET CORPORATION	WENDY'S/ARBY'S GROUP INC	
TBC CORPORATION	WEST CORPORATION	AMERICAN POWER CONVERSION (APC)
TEAM INC	WEST PHARMACEUTICAL SERVICES INC	
TECH DATA CORP		AMERISOURCEBERGEN CORP
TEKTRONIX INC	WESTERN DIGITAL CORP	AMGEN INC
TELEDYNE TECHNOLOGIES INCORPORATED	WHOLE FOODS MARKET INC	ANADARKO PETROLEUM CORPORATION
	WILLIAMS COMPANIES INC (THE)	
TELETECH HOLDINGS INC	WW GRAINGER INC	ANALOG DEVICES INC
TESORO CORP	WYETH	ANNTAYLOR STORES CORP
THERMO FISHER SCIENTIFIC INC	WYNDHAM WORLDWIDE	APACHE CORP
TIFFANY & CO	WYNN RESORTS LIMITED	APOLLO GROUP INC
TIME WARNER INC	XEROX CORP	APPLE INC
TJX COMPANIES INC (THE)	YAHOO! INC	ARAMARK CORPORATION
T-MOBILE USA	YUM! BRANDS INC	ARCHER DANIELS MIDLAND CO
TOTAL SYSTEM SERVICES INC (TSYS)	ZIMMER HOLDINGS INC	ARROW ELECTRONICS INC
		ARTHUR J GALLAGHER & CO
TOWERS PERRIN		ASCENSION HEALTH
		AT&T INC

AUTOMATIC DATA PROCESSING INC	CASH AMERICA INTERNATIONAL INC	CUBIC CORP
AUTOZONE INC	CATERPILLAR INC	CUMMINS INC
AVERY DENNISON CORP	CATHOLIC HEALTH INITIATIVES	CVS CAREMARK CORPORATION
AVIS BUDGET GROUP INC	CDW CORPORATION	DANAHER CORP
AVNET INC	CELGENE CORP	DARDEN RESTAURANTS INC
AVON PRODUCTS INC	CELLCO PARTNERSHIP (VERIZON WIRELESS)	DAVITA INC
AXA FINANCIAL INC		DEAN FOODS CO
BAKER HUGHES INC	CEPHALON INC	DEERE & CO
BALTIMORE GAS AND ELECTRIC COMPANY	CH ROBINSON WORLDWIDE INC	DELOITTE & TOUCHE USA LLP
	CH2M HILL COMPANIES LTD	DELOITTE CONSULTING LLP
BANK OF AMERICA CORP	CHARLOTTE RUSSE HOLDING	DENNY'S CORPORATION
BARNES & NOBLE INC	CHARMING SHOPPES INC	DEVON ENERGY CORPORATION
BASS PRO SHOPS INC	CHEMED CORPORATION	DEVRY INC
BAXTER INTERNATIONAL INC	CHEVRON CORPORATION	DIAMOND OFFSHORE DRILLING INC
BDO SEIDMAN LLP	CHEVRON PHILLIPS CHEMICAL COMPANY LLC	DICK'S SPORTING GOODS INC
BEBE STORES INC		DIEBOLD INC
BECHTEL GROUP INC	CHICO'S FAS INC	DINEEQUITY INC
BECKMAN COULTER INC	CHIPOTLE MEXICAN GRILL INC	DIRECTV GROUP INC (THE)
BECTON DICKINSON & CO	CHRISTOPHER & BANKS CORP	DOLE FOOD COMPANY INC
BED BATH & BEYOND INC	CHS INC	DOLLAR GENERAL CORPORATION
BENCHMARK ELECTRONICS INC	CHUBB CORPORATION (THE)	DOLLAR THRIFTY AUTOMOTIVE GROUP INC
BERKSHIRE HATHAWAY INC	CIBER INC	
BEST BUY CO INC	CIGNA CORP	DRESS BARN INC (THE)
BIO RAD LABORATORIES INC	CINTAS CORP	DTE ENERGY COMPANY
BJ'S WHOLESALE CLUB INC	CISCO SYSTEMS INC	DUKE ENERGY CORP
BLACK & DECKER CORP	CLUBCORP INC	DYCOM INDUSTRIES INC
BLACKROCK INC	COACH INC	E I DU PONT DE NEMOURS & CO (DUPONT)
BLOOMBERG LP	COCA-COLA COMPANY (THE)	
BOEING COMPANY (THE)	COCA-COLA ENTERPRISES INC	EATON CORP
BOOZ ALLEN HAMILTON	COGNIZANT TECHNOLOGY SOLUTIONS CORP	EBAY INC
BOSTON SCIENTIFIC CORP		EDISON INTERNATIONAL
BRINKER INTERNATIONAL INC	COLDWATER CREEK INC	ELECTRONIC ARTS INC
BRINKS COMPANY (THE)	COLGATE PALMOLIVE CO	ELI LILLY & COMPANY
BROADCOM CORP	COMCAST CORP	EMBARQ CORP
BROWN & BROWN INC	COMMUNITY HEALTH SYSTEMS INC	EMC CORP
BUCKLE INC (THE)	CONAGRA FOODS INC	EMERITUS CORP
BUCYRUS INTERNATIONAL INC	CONOCOPHILLIPS COMPANY	EMERSON ELECTRIC CO
BUFFALO WILD WINGS INC	CONSOL ENERGY INC	ENTERGY CORP
BUNGE LTD	CONSOLIDATED EDISON INC	ENTERPRISE PRODUCTS PARTNERS LP
BURGER KING HOLDINGS INC	CONTAINER STORE (THE)	
CABELA'S INC	CONVERGYS CORPORATION	ENTERPRISE RENT-A-CAR
CABLEVISION SYSTEMS CORP	COOPER COMPANIES INC	ERNST & YOUNG LLP
CACI INTERNATIONAL INC	COSTCO WHOLESALE CORP	ESTEE LAUDER COMPANIES INC (THE)
CAMERON INTERNATIONAL CORPORATION	COVANCE INC	
	COVENTRY HEALTH CARE INC	EXELON CORPORATION
CAPITAL SENIOR LIVING CORP	COX COMMUNICATIONS INC	EXPERIAN AMERICAS
CARDINAL HEALTH INC	CR BARD INC	EXPRESS SCRIPTS INC
CARGILL INC	CRACKER BARREL OLD COUNTRY STORE INC	EXXON MOBIL CORPORATION (EXXONMOBIL)
CARMAX GROUP		
CARNIVAL CORPORATION	CTS CORP	EXXONMOBIL CHEMICAL
		FAMILY DOLLAR STORES INC

FEDEX CORPORATION	HENRY SCHEIN INC	LEXMARK INTERNATIONAL INC
FINISH LINE INC (THE)	HERTZ GLOBAL HOLDINGS INC	LIBERTY GLOBAL INC
FIRST ADVANTAGE CORPORATION	HESS CORPORATION	LIBERTY MUTUAL GROUP INC
FIRST DATA CORP	HEWITT ASSOCIATES	LIMITED BRANDS INC
FIRSTENERGY CORP	HIBBETT SPORTS INC	LINCARE HOLDINGS INC
FLUOR CORP	HILTON HOTELS CORP	LINCOLN NATIONAL CORPORATION
FOREST LABORATORIES INC	HOME DEPOT INC	LKQ CORP
FORTUNE BRANDS INC	HONEYWELL INTERNATIONAL INC	LOCKHEED MARTIN CORP
FOSSIL INC	HUMANA INC	LODGIAN INC
FOSTER WHEELER AG	IAC/INTERACTIVECORP	LOEWS CORPORATION
FOX ENTERTAINMENT GROUP INC	IBM GLOBAL SERVICES	LOWE'S COMPANIES INC
FPL GROUP INC	ICT GROUP INC	MACY'S INC
FRED'S INC	IDEXX LABORATORIES INC	MANOR CARE INC
FRONTIER COMMUNICATIONS CORPORATION	IGATE CORPORATION	MANPOWER INC
FTI CONSULTING INC	IMS HEALTH INC	MARRIOTT INTERNATIONAL INC
GAMESTOP CORP	INFOGROUP INC	MARS INC
GENENTECH INC	INGRAM MICRO INC	MARSH & MCLENNAN COMPANIES INC
GENERAL CABLE CORP	INTEL CORP	MARY KAY INC
GENERAL DYNAMICS CORP	INTERNATIONAL BUSINESS MACHINES CORP (IBM)	MASSEY ENERGY COMPANY
GENERAL ELECTRIC CO (GE)	INTUIT INC	MATTEL INC
GENERAL MILLS INC	INVENTIV HEALTH INC	MAXIM INTEGRATED PRODUCTS INC
GENESCO INC	J C PENNEY COMPANY INC	MAYO FOUNDATION FOR MEDICAL EDUCATION AND RESEARCH
GENWORTH FINANCIAL INC	JABIL CIRCUIT INC	MCAFEE INC
GEO GROUP INC	JACK IN THE BOX INC	MCDERMOTT INTERNATIONAL INC
GEORGIA GULF CORPORATION	JACOBS ENGINEERING GROUP INC	MCDONALD'S CORP
GILEAD SCIENCES INC	JETBLUE AIRWAYS CORPORATION	MCKESSON CORPORATION
GLOBAL HYATT CORPORATION	JM SMUCKER CO	MCKINSEY & COMPANY INC
GLOBAL PAYMENTS INC	JOHNSON & JOHNSON	MEDCO HEALTH SOLUTIONS
GOLDMAN SACHS GROUP INC	JOHNSON CONTROLS INC	MEDTRONIC INC
GOOGLE INC	JP MORGAN CHASE & CO INC	MEIJER INC
GRANT THORNTON LLP	JUNIPER NETWORKS INC	MEN'S WEARHOUSE INC (THE)
GUESS? INC	KAISER PERMANENTE	MERCER INC
HALLIBURTON COMPANY	KEANE INC	MERCK & CO INC
HARRAH'S ENTERTAINMENT INC	KELLOGG CO	METHODIST HEALTH CARE SYSTEM
HARRIS CORPORATION	KELLY SERVICES INC	METLIFE INC
HARTFORD FINANCIAL SERVICES GROUP INC (THE)	KENDLE INTERNATIONAL INC	MGM MIRAGE
HAWAIIAN ELECTRIC INDUSTRIES INC	KIMBERLY-CLARK CORP	MICROCHIP TECHNOLOGY INC
	KINDRED HEALTHCARE INC	MICRON TECHNOLOGY INC
HCA INC	KOCH INDUSTRIES INC	MICROSOFT CORP
HE BUTT GROCERY COMPANY (HEB)	KOHL'S CORP	MIDAMERICAN ENERGY HOLDINGS CO
HEALTH CARE SERVICE CORPORATION	KPMG LLP	MILLIPORE CORP
	KRAFT FOODS INC	MONRO MUFFLER BRAKE INC
HEALTH FITNESS CORP	KROGER CO (THE)	MONSANTO CO
HEALTH MANAGEMENT ASSOCIATES INC	L-3 COMMUNICATIONS HOLDINGS INC	MURPHY OIL CORPORATION
HEALTH NET INC	LABORATORY CORP OF AMERICA HOLDINGS	MYLAN INC
HEALTHWAYS INC	LAS VEGAS SANDS CORP (THE VENETIAN)	NATIONAL OILWELL VARCO INC
HELMERICH & PAYNE INC	LEVEL 3 COMMUNICATIONS INC	

NETAPP INC	PRUDENTIAL FINANCIAL INC	SOUTHERN COMPANY (THE)
NEWS CORP	PSYCHIATRIC SOLUTIONS INC	SOUTHWEST AIRLINES CO
NII HOLDINGS INC	PUBLIC STORAGE INC	SRA INTERNATIONAL INC
NIKE INC	PUBLIX SUPER MARKETS INC	ST JUDE MEDICAL INC
NOBLE CORPORATION	QUALCOMM INC	STAPLES INC
NORTHROP GRUMMAN CORP	QUANTA SERVICES INC	STARTEK INC
NRG ENERGY INC	QUEST DIAGNOSTICS INC	STARWOOD HOTELS & RESORTS WORLDWIDE INC
OCCIDENTAL PETROLEUM CORP	QUIKSILVER INC	STERIS CORP
OCEANEERING INTERNATIONAL INC	R R DONNELLEY & SONS CO	STIFEL FINANCIAL CORP
ODYSSEY HEALTHCARE INC	RALCORP HOLDINGS INC	STRYKER CORP
OFFICE DEPOT INC	RAYTHEON CO	SUN HEALTHCARE GROUP
OIL STATES INTERNATIONAL INC	REGIS CORPORATION	SUNGARD DATA SYSTEMS INC
OMNICARE INC	RENT-A-CENTER INC	SUNOCO INC
OMNICOM GROUP INC	RES CARE INC	SUNRISE SENIOR LIVING
ORACLE CORP	RITE AID CORPORATION	SUPERVALU INC
O'REILLY AUTOMOTIVE INC	RITZ-CARLTON HOTEL COMPANY LLC (THE)	SYKES ENTERPRISES INC
OSHKOSH CORPORATION	ROBERT HALF INTERNATIONAL INC	SYMANTEC CORP
OSI RESTAURANT PARTNERS LLC	ROSS STORES INC	SYNOPSYS INC
OWENS & MINOR INC	ROYAL CARIBBEAN CRUISES LTD	SYNTEL INC
PANTRY INC (THE)	RRI ENERGY INC	SYSCO CORP
PARAMETRIC TECHNOLOGY CORP	SABRE HOLDINGS CORP	TARGET CORPORATION
PAREXEL INTERNATIONAL CORP	SAFECO INSURANCE COMPANY OF AMERICA	TBC CORPORATION
PARSONS BRINCKERHOFF INC	SAFEWAY INC	TEAM INC
PATTERSON COMPANIES INC	SAIC INC	TECH DATA CORP
PATTERSON-UTI ENERGY INC	SAM'S CLUB	TEKTRONIX INC
PAYCHEX INC	SAPIENT CORPORATION	TELEDYNE TECHNOLOGIES INCORPORATED
PEABODY ENERGY CORP	SARA LEE CORP	TELEPHONE AND DATA SYSTEMS INC (TDS)
PEPSI BOTTLING GROUP INC	SAS INSTITUTE INC	TELETECH HOLDINGS INC
PEPSICO INC	SCANA CORPORATION	TESORO CORP
PEROT SYSTEMS CORP	SCHERING-PLOUGH CORP	THERMO FISHER SCIENTIFIC INC
PERRIGO CO	SCHLUMBERGER LIMITED	TIFFANY & CO
PETCO ANIMAL SUPPLIES INC	SCIENTIFIC GAMES CORPORATION	TIME WARNER INC
PETSMART INC	SCOTTS MIRACLE GROW CO	TJX COMPANIES INC (THE)
PFIZER INC	SEACOR HOLDINGS INC	T-MOBILE USA
PG&E CORPORATION	SELECT MEDICAL	TOTAL SYSTEM SERVICES INC (TSYS)
PHARMACEUTICAL PRODUCT DEVELOPMENT INC	SEMPRA ENERGY	TOWERS PERRIN
PITNEY BOWES INC	SENSIENT TECHNOLOGIES CORPORATION	TRANSOCEAN INC
PLEXUS CORP	SHAW GROUP INC (THE)	TRAVELERS COMPANIES INC (THE)
POLO RALPH LAUREN CORP	SHELL OIL CO	TREEHOUSE FOODS INC
PRAXAIR INC	SHERWIN WILLIAMS COMPANY (THE)	TW TELECOM INC
PRECISION CASTPARTS CORP	SIGMA-ALDRICH CORP	TYSON FOODS INC
PRICESMART INC	SISTERS OF MERCY HEALTH SYSTEMS	UNITED NATURAL FOODS INC
PRICEWATERHOUSECOOPERS	SMITH INTERNATIONAL INC	UNITED PARCEL SERVICE INC (UPS)
PRIDE INTERNATIONAL INC	SMITHFIELD FOODS INC	UNITED STATES CELLULAR CORP
PRINCIPAL FINANCIAL GROUP (THE)	SOUTHERN CALIFORNIA EDISON COMPANY	UNITED TECHNOLOGIES CORPORATION
PROCTER & GAMBLE CO		
PROGRESSIVE CORPORATION (THE)		

UNITEDHEALTH GROUP INC	ABM INDUSTRIES INC	AVNET INC
UNIVERSAL HEALTH SERVICES INC	ACADEMY SPORTS & OUTDOORS LTD	AVON PRODUCTS INC
UNIVISION COMMUNICATIONS INC	ACCENTURE LTD	AXA FINANCIAL INC
URS CORPORATION	ACTIVISION BLIZZARD INC	BAKER HUGHES INC
USAA	ACXIOM CORP	BALTIMORE GAS AND ELECTRIC COMPANY
VALERO ENERGY CORP	ADC TELECOMMUNICATIONS INC	BANK OF AMERICA CORP
VALSPAR CORPORATION (THE)	ADESA INC	BARNES & NOBLE INC
VARIAN MEDICAL SYSTEMS INC	ADOBE SYSTEMS INC	BASS PRO SHOPS INC
VCA ANTECH INC	ADVANCE AUTO PARTS INC	BAXTER INTERNATIONAL INC
VERISIGN INC	ADVANCED MICRO DEVICES INC (AMD)	BDO SEIDMAN LLP
VERIZON COMMUNICATIONS	AECOM TECHNOLOGY CORPORATION	BEBE STORES INC
VIACOM INC	AES CORPORATION (THE)	BECHTEL GROUP INC
VICTORIAS SECRET	AETNA INC	BECKMAN COULTER INC
VISA INC	AFFILIATED COMPUTER SERVICES INC	BECTON DICKINSON & CO
VOLT INFORMATION SCIENCES INC	AFLAC INC	BED BATH & BEYOND INC
W R BERKLEY CORPORATION	AGILENT TECHNOLOGIES INC	BENCHMARK ELECTRONICS INC
WABTEC CORP	AIR PRODUCTS & CHEMICALS INC	BERKSHIRE HATHAWAY INC
WALGREEN CO	ALLERGAN INC	BEST BUY CO INC
WAL-MART STORES INC	ALLIANCE DATA SYSTEMS CORPORATION	BIO RAD LABORATORIES INC
WALT DISNEY COMPANY (THE)	ALLSTATE CORPORATION (THE)	BJ'S WHOLESALE CLUB INC
WASTE MANAGEMENT INC	ALTRIA GROUP INC	BLACK & DECKER CORP
WATERS CORP	AMAZON.COM INC	BLACKROCK INC
WATSON PHARMACEUTICALS INC	AMEDISYS INC	BLOOMBERG LP
WATSON WYATT WORLDWIDE INC	AMERICAN ELECTRIC POWER COMPANY INC (AEP)	BOEING COMPANY (THE)
WEATHERFORD INTERNATIONAL LTD	AMERICAN POWER CONVERSION (APC)	BOOZ ALLEN HAMILTON
WEIGHT WATCHERS INTERNATIONAL INC	AMERISOURCEBERGEN CORP	BOSTON SCIENTIFIC CORP
WELLPOINT INC	AMGEN INC	BRINKER INTERNATIONAL INC
WELLS FARGO & CO	ANADARKO PETROLEUM CORPORATION	BRINKS COMPANY (THE)
WENDY'S/ARBY'S GROUP INC	ANALOG DEVICES INC	BROADCOM CORP
WEST CORPORATION	ANNTAYLOR STORES CORP	BROWN & BROWN INC
WEST PHARMACEUTICAL SERVICES INC	APACHE CORP	BUCKLE INC (THE)
WESTERN DIGITAL CORP	APOLLO GROUP INC	BUCYRUS INTERNATIONAL INC
WHOLE FOODS MARKET INC	APPLE INC	BUFFALO WILD WINGS INC
WILLIAMS COMPANIES INC (THE)	ARAMARK CORPORATION	BUNGE LTD
WW GRAINGER INC	ARCHER DANIELS MIDLAND CO	BURGER KING HOLDINGS INC
WYETH	ARROW ELECTRONICS INC	CABELA'S INC
WYNDHAM WORLDWIDE	ARTHUR J GALLAGHER & CO	CABLEVISION SYSTEMS CORP
WYNN RESORTS LIMITED	ASCENSION HEALTH	CACI INTERNATIONAL INC
XEROX CORP	AT&T INC	CAMERON INTERNATIONAL CORPORATION
YAHOO! INC	AUTOMATIC DATA PROCESSING INC	CAPITAL SENIOR LIVING CORP
YUM! BRANDS INC	AUTOZONE INC	CARDINAL HEALTH INC
ZIMMER HOLDINGS INC	AVERY DENNISON CORP	CARGILL INC
	AVIS BUDGET GROUP INC	CARMAX GROUP

MBA Graduates
3M COMPANY
7-ELEVEN INC
AARON'S INC
ABBOTT LABORATORIES

CARNIVAL CORPORATION
CASH AMERICA INTERNATIONAL INC
CATERPILLAR INC
CATHOLIC HEALTH INITIATIVES
CDW CORPORATION

CELGENE CORP	DAVITA INC	FLUOR CORP
CELLCO PARTNERSHIP (VERIZON WIRELESS)	DEAN FOODS CO	FOREST LABORATORIES INC
CEPHALON INC	DEERE & CO	FORTUNE BRANDS INC
CH ROBINSON WORLDWIDE INC	DELOITTE & TOUCHE USA LLP	FOSSIL INC
CH2M HILL COMPANIES LTD	DELOITTE CONSULTING LLP	FOSTER WHEELER AG
CHARLOTTE RUSSE HOLDING	DENNY'S CORPORATION	FOX ENTERTAINMENT GROUP INC
CHARMING SHOPPES INC	DEVON ENERGY CORPORATION	FPL GROUP INC
CHEMED CORPORATION	DEVRY INC	FRED'S INC
CHEVRON CORPORATION	DIAMOND OFFSHORE DRILLING INC	FRONTIER COMMUNICATIONS CORPORATION
CHEVRON PHILLIPS CHEMICAL COMPANY LLC	DICK'S SPORTING GOODS INC	FTI CONSULTING INC
CHICO'S FAS INC	DIEBOLD INC	GAMESTOP CORP
CHIPOTLE MEXICAN GRILL INC	DINEEQUITY INC	GENENTECH INC
CHRISTOPHER & BANKS CORP	DIRECTV GROUP INC (THE)	GENERAL CABLE CORP
CHS INC	DOLE FOOD COMPANY INC	GENERAL DYNAMICS CORP
CHUBB CORPORATION (THE)	DOLLAR GENERAL CORPORATION	GENERAL ELECTRIC CO (GE)
CIBER INC	DOLLAR THRIFTY AUTOMOTIVE GROUP INC	GENERAL MILLS INC
CIGNA CORP	DRESS BARN INC (THE)	GENESCO INC
CINTAS CORP	DTE ENERGY COMPANY	GENWORTH FINANCIAL INC
CISCO SYSTEMS INC	DUKE ENERGY CORP	GEO GROUP INC
CLUBCORP INC	DYCOM INDUSTRIES INC	GEORGIA GULF CORPORATION
COACH INC	E I DU PONT DE NEMOURS & CO (DUPONT)	GILEAD SCIENCES INC
COCA-COLA COMPANY (THE)	EATON CORP	GLOBAL HYATT CORPORATION
COCA-COLA ENTERPRISES INC	EBAY INC	GLOBAL PAYMENTS INC
COGNIZANT TECHNOLOGY SOLUTIONS CORP	EDISON INTERNATIONAL	GOLDMAN SACHS GROUP INC
COLDWATER CREEK INC	ELECTRONIC ARTS INC	GOOGLE INC
COLGATE PALMOLIVE CO	ELI LILLY & COMPANY	GRANT THORNTON LLP
COMCAST CORP	EMBARQ CORP	GUESS? INC
COMMUNITY HEALTH SYSTEMS INC	EMC CORP	HALLIBURTON COMPANY
CONAGRA FOODS INC	EMERITUS CORP	HARRAH'S ENTERTAINMENT INC
CONOCOPHILLIPS COMPANY	EMERSON ELECTRIC CO	HARRIS CORPORATION
CONSOL ENERGY INC	ENTERGY CORP	HARTFORD FINANCIAL SERVICES GROUP INC (THE)
CONSOLIDATED EDISON INC	ENTERPRISE PRODUCTS PARTNERS LP	HAWAIIAN ELECTRIC INDUSTRIES INC
CONTAINER STORE (THE)	ENTERPRISE RENT-A-CAR	HCA INC
CONVERGYS CORPORATION	ERNST & YOUNG LLP	HE BUTT GROCERY COMPANY (HEB)
COOPER COMPANIES INC	ESTEE LAUDER COMPANIES INC (THE)	HEALTH CARE SERVICE CORPORATION
COSTCO WHOLESALE CORP	EXELON CORPORATION	HEALTH FITNESS CORP
COVANCE INC	EXPERIAN AMERICAS	HEALTH MANAGEMENT ASSOCIATES INC
COVENTRY HEALTH CARE INC	EXPRESS SCRIPTS INC	HEALTH NET INC
COX COMMUNICATIONS INC	EXXON MOBIL CORPORATION (EXXONMOBIL)	HEALTHWAYS INC
CR BARD INC	EXXONMOBIL CHEMICAL	HELMERICH & PAYNE INC
CRACKER BARREL OLD COUNTRY STORE INC	FAMILY DOLLAR STORES INC	HENRY SCHEIN INC
CTS CORP	FEDEX CORPORATION	HERTZ GLOBAL HOLDINGS INC
CUBIC CORP	FINISH LINE INC (THE)	HESS CORPORATION
CUMMINS INC	FIRST ADVANTAGE CORPORATION	HEWITT ASSOCIATES
CVS CAREMARK CORPORATION	FIRST DATA CORP	HIBBETT SPORTS INC
DANAHER CORP	FIRSTENERGY CORP	
DARDEN RESTAURANTS INC		

HILTON HOTELS CORP	LINCOLN NATIONAL CORPORATION	NORTHROP GRUMMAN CORP
HOME DEPOT INC	LKQ CORP	NRG ENERGY INC
HONEYWELL INTERNATIONAL INC	LOCKHEED MARTIN CORP	OCCIDENTAL PETROLEUM CORP
HUMANA INC	LODGIAN INC	OCEANEERING INTERNATIONAL INC
IAC/INTERACTIVECORP	LOEWS CORPORATION	ODYSSEY HEALTHCARE INC
IBM GLOBAL SERVICES	LOWE'S COMPANIES INC	OFFICE DEPOT INC
ICT GROUP INC	MACY'S INC	OIL STATES INTERNATIONAL INC
IDEXX LABORATORIES INC	MANOR CARE INC	OMNICARE INC
IGATE CORPORATION	MANPOWER INC	OMNICOM GROUP INC
IMS HEALTH INC	MARRIOTT INTERNATIONAL INC	ORACLE CORP
INFOGROUP INC	MARS INC	O'REILLY AUTOMOTIVE INC
INGRAM MICRO INC	MARSH & MCLENNAN COMPANIES INC	OSHKOSH CORPORATION
INTEL CORP	MARY KAY INC	OSI RESTAURANT PARTNERS LLC
INTERNATIONAL BUSINESS MACHINES CORP (IBM)	MASSEY ENERGY COMPANY	OWENS & MINOR INC
INTUIT INC	MATTEL INC	PANTRY INC (THE)
INVENTIV HEALTH INC	MAXIM INTEGRATED PRODUCTS INC	PARAMETRIC TECHNOLOGY CORP
J C PENNEY COMPANY INC	MAYO FOUNDATION FOR MEDICAL EDUCATION AND RESEARCH	PAREXEL INTERNATIONAL CORP
JABIL CIRCUIT INC		PARSONS BRINCKERHOFF INC
JACK IN THE BOX INC	MCAFEE INC	PATTERSON COMPANIES INC
JACOBS ENGINEERING GROUP INC	MCDERMOTT INTERNATIONAL INC	PATTERSON-UTI ENERGY INC
JETBLUE AIRWAYS CORPORATION	MCDONALD'S CORP	PAYCHEX INC
JM SMUCKER CO	MCKESSON CORPORATION	PEABODY ENERGY CORP
JOHNSON & JOHNSON	MCKINSEY & COMPANY INC	PEPSI BOTTLING GROUP INC
JOHNSON CONTROLS INC	MEDCO HEALTH SOLUTIONS	PEPSICO INC
JP MORGAN CHASE & CO INC	MEDTRONIC INC	PEROT SYSTEMS CORP
JUNIPER NETWORKS INC	MEIJER INC	PERRIGO CO
KAISER PERMANENTE	MEN'S WEARHOUSE INC (THE)	PETCO ANIMAL SUPPLIES INC
KEANE INC	MERCER INC	PETSMART INC
KELLOGG CO	MERCK & CO INC	PFIZER INC
KELLY SERVICES INC	METHODIST HEALTH CARE SYSTEM	PG&E CORPORATION
KENDLE INTERNATIONAL INC		PHARMACEUTICAL PRODUCT DEVELOPMENT INC
KIMBERLY-CLARK CORP	METLIFE INC	PITNEY BOWES INC
KINDRED HEALTHCARE INC	MGM MIRAGE	PLEXUS CORP
KOCH INDUSTRIES INC	MICROCHIP TECHNOLOGY INC	POLO RALPH LAUREN CORP
KOHL'S CORP	MICRON TECHNOLOGY INC	PRAXAIR INC
KPMG LLP	MICROSOFT CORP	PRECISION CASTPARTS CORP
KRAFT FOODS INC	MIDAMERICAN ENERGY HOLDINGS CO	PRICESMART INC
KROGER CO (THE)	MILLIPORE CORP	PRICEWATERHOUSECOOPERS
L-3 COMMUNICATIONS HOLDINGS INC	MONRO MUFFLER BRAKE INC	PRIDE INTERNATIONAL INC
LABORATORY CORP OF AMERICA HOLDINGS	MONSANTO CO	PRINCIPAL FINANCIAL GROUP (THE)
	MURPHY OIL CORPORATION	PROCTER & GAMBLE CO
LAS VEGAS SANDS CORP (THE VENETIAN)	MYLAN INC	PROGRESSIVE CORPORATION (THE)
LEVEL 3 COMMUNICATIONS INC	NATIONAL OILWELL VARCO INC	
LEXMARK INTERNATIONAL INC	NETAPP INC	PRUDENTIAL FINANCIAL INC
LIBERTY GLOBAL INC	NEWS CORP	PSYCHIATRIC SOLUTIONS INC
LIBERTY MUTUAL GROUP INC	NII HOLDINGS INC	PUBLIC STORAGE INC
LIMITED BRANDS INC	NIKE INC	PUBLIX SUPER MARKETS INC
LINCARE HOLDINGS INC	NOBLE CORPORATION	QUALCOMM INC

QUANTA SERVICES INC	STARTEK INC	VALERO ENERGY CORP
QUEST DIAGNOSTICS INC	STARWOOD HOTELS & RESORTS WORLDWIDE INC	VALSPAR CORPORATION (THE)
QUIKSILVER INC		VARIAN MEDICAL SYSTEMS INC
R R DONNELLEY & SONS CO	STERIS CORP	VCA ANTECH INC
RALCORP HOLDINGS INC	STIFEL FINANCIAL CORP	VERISIGN INC
RAYTHEON CO	STRYKER CORP	VERIZON COMMUNICATIONS
REGIS CORPORATION	SUN HEALTHCARE GROUP	VIACOM INC
RENT-A-CENTER INC	SUNGARD DATA SYSTEMS INC	VICTORIAS SECRET
RES CARE INC	SUNOCO INC	VISA INC
RITE AID CORPORATION	SUNRISE SENIOR LIVING	VOLT INFORMATION SCIENCES INC
RITZ-CARLTON HOTEL COMPANY LLC (THE)	SUPERVALU INC	W R BERKLEY CORPORATION
ROBERT HALF INTERNATIONAL INC	SYKES ENTERPRISES INC	WABTEC CORP
ROSS STORES INC	SYMANTEC CORP	WALGREEN CO
ROYAL CARIBBEAN CRUISES LTD	SYNOPSYS INC	WAL-MART STORES INC
RRI ENERGY INC	SYNTEL INC	WALT DISNEY COMPANY (THE)
SABRE HOLDINGS CORP	SYSCO CORP	WASTE MANAGEMENT INC
SAFECO INSURANCE COMPANY OF AMERICA	TARGET CORPORATION	WATERS CORP
SAFEWAY INC	TBC CORPORATION	WATSON PHARMACEUTICALS INC
SAIC INC	TEAM INC	WATSON WYATT WORLDWIDE INC
SAM'S CLUB	TECH DATA CORP	WEATHERFORD INTERNATIONAL LTD
SAPIENT CORPORATION	TEKTRONIX INC	
SARA LEE CORP	TELEDYNE TECHNOLOGIES INCORPORATED	WEIGHT WATCHERS INTERNATIONAL INC
SAS INSTITUTE INC	TELEPHONE AND DATA SYSTEMS INC (TDS)	WELLPOINT INC
SCANA CORPORATION		WELLS FARGO & CO
SCHERING-PLOUGH CORP	TELETECH HOLDINGS INC	WENDY'S/ARBY'S GROUP INC
SCHLUMBERGER LIMITED	TESORO CORP	WEST CORPORATION
SCIENTIFIC GAMES CORPORATION	THERMO FISHER SCIENTIFIC INC	WEST PHARMACEUTICAL SERVICES INC
SCOTTS MIRACLE GROW CO	TIFFANY & CO	
SEACOR HOLDINGS INC	TIME WARNER INC	WESTERN DIGITAL CORP
SELECT MEDICAL	TJX COMPANIES INC (THE)	WHOLE FOODS MARKET INC
SEMPRA ENERGY	T-MOBILE USA	WILLIAMS COMPANIES INC (THE)
SENSIENT TECHNOLOGIES CORPORATION	TOTAL SYSTEM SERVICES INC (TSYS)	WW GRAINGER INC
SHAW GROUP INC (THE)	TOWERS PERRIN	WYETH
SHELL OIL CO	TRANSOCEAN INC	WYNDHAM WORLDWIDE
SHERWIN WILLIAMS COMPANY (THE)	TRAVELERS COMPANIES INC (THE)	WYNN RESORTS LIMITED
	TREEHOUSE FOODS INC	XEROX CORP
SIGMA-ALDRICH CORP	TW TELECOM INC	YAHOO! INC
SISTERS OF MERCY HEALTH SYSTEMS	TYSON FOODS INC	YUM! BRANDS INC
SMITH INTERNATIONAL INC	UNITED NATURAL FOODS INC	ZIMMER HOLDINGS INC
SMITHFIELD FOODS INC	UNITED PARCEL SERVICE INC (UPS)	
SOUTHERN CALIFORNIA EDISON COMPANY	UNITED STATES CELLULAR CORP	
SOUTHERN COMPANY (THE)	UNITED TECHNOLOGIES CORPORATION	
SOUTHWEST AIRLINES CO	UNITEDHEALTH GROUP INC	
SRA INTERNATIONAL INC	UNIVERSAL HEALTH SERVICES INC	
ST JUDE MEDICAL INC	UNIVISION COMMUNICATIONS INC	
STAPLES INC	URS CORPORATION	
	USAA	

Professionals

Consulting
ACCENTURE LTD
AECOM TECHNOLOGY CORPORATION
AFFILIATED COMPUTER SERVICES INC
BDO SEIDMAN LLP
BECHTEL GROUP INC

BOOZ ALLEN HAMILTON	ABM INDUSTRIES INC	AVNET INC
CACI INTERNATIONAL INC	ACADEMY SPORTS & OUTDOORS LTD	AVON PRODUCTS INC
CH2M HILL COMPANIES LTD	ACCENTURE LTD	AXA FINANCIAL INC
CIBER INC	ACTIVISION BLIZZARD INC	BAKER HUGHES INC
COGNIZANT TECHNOLOGY SOLUTIONS CORP	ACXIOM CORP	BALTIMORE GAS AND ELECTRIC COMPANY
COVANCE INC	ADC TELECOMMUNICATIONS INC	BANK OF AMERICA CORP
DELOITTE & TOUCHE USA LLP	ADESA INC	BARNES & NOBLE INC
DELOITTE CONSULTING LLP	ADOBE SYSTEMS INC	BASS PRO SHOPS INC
ERNST & YOUNG LLP	ADVANCE AUTO PARTS INC	BAXTER INTERNATIONAL INC
FLUOR CORP	ADVANCED MICRO DEVICES INC (AMD)	BDO SEIDMAN LLP
FOSTER WHEELER AG		BEBE STORES INC
FTI CONSULTING INC	AECOM TECHNOLOGY CORPORATION	BECHTEL GROUP INC
GRANT THORNTON LLP	AES CORPORATION (THE)	BECKMAN COULTER INC
HEWITT ASSOCIATES	AETNA INC	BECTON DICKINSON & CO
IBM GLOBAL SERVICES	AFFILIATED COMPUTER SERVICES INC	BED BATH & BEYOND INC
ICT GROUP INC		BENCHMARK ELECTRONICS INC
IGATE CORPORATION	AFLAC INC	BERKSHIRE HATHAWAY INC
IMS HEALTH INC	AGILENT TECHNOLOGIES INC	BEST BUY CO INC
INTERNATIONAL BUSINESS MACHINES CORP (IBM)	AIR PRODUCTS & CHEMICALS INC	BIO RAD LABORATORIES INC
	ALLERGAN INC	BJ'S WHOLESALE CLUB INC
INVENTIV HEALTH INC	ALLIANCE DATA SYSTEMS CORPORATION	BLACK & DECKER CORP
JACOBS ENGINEERING GROUP INC		BLACKROCK INC
KEANE INC	ALLSTATE CORPORATION (THE)	BLOOMBERG LP
KPMG LLP	ALTRIA GROUP INC	BOEING COMPANY (THE)
MARSH & MCLENNAN COMPANIES INC	AMAZON.COM INC	BOOZ ALLEN HAMILTON
	AMEDISYS INC	BOSTON SCIENTIFIC CORP
MCDERMOTT INTERNATIONAL INC	AMERICAN ELECTRIC POWER COMPANY INC (AEP)	BRINKER INTERNATIONAL INC
MCKINSEY & COMPANY INC		BRINKS COMPANY (THE)
MERCER INC	AMERICAN POWER CONVERSION (APC)	BROADCOM CORP
OMNICOM GROUP INC		BROWN & BROWN INC
PAREXEL INTERNATIONAL CORP	AMERISOURCEBERGEN CORP	BUCKLE INC (THE)
PARSONS BRINCKERHOFF INC	AMGEN INC	BUCYRUS INTERNATIONAL INC
PEROT SYSTEMS CORP	ANADARKO PETROLEUM CORPORATION	BUFFALO WILD WINGS INC
PHARMACEUTICAL PRODUCT DEVELOPMENT INC		BUNGE LTD
	ANALOG DEVICES INC	BURGER KING HOLDINGS INC
PRICEWATERHOUSECOOPERS	ANNTAYLOR STORES CORP	CABELA'S INC
SAIC INC	APACHE CORP	CABLEVISION SYSTEMS CORP
SAPIENT CORPORATION	APOLLO GROUP INC	CACI INTERNATIONAL INC
SAS INSTITUTE INC	APPLE INC	CAMERON INTERNATIONAL CORPORATION
SRA INTERNATIONAL INC	ARAMARK CORPORATION	
SYNTEL INC	ARCHER DANIELS MIDLAND CO	CAPITAL SENIOR LIVING CORP
TOWERS PERRIN	ARROW ELECTRONICS INC	CARDINAL HEALTH INC
URS CORPORATION	ARTHUR J GALLAGHER & CO	CARGILL INC
WATSON WYATT WORLDWIDE INC	ASCENSION HEALTH	CARMAX GROUP
	AT&T INC	CARNIVAL CORPORATION
	AUTOMATIC DATA PROCESSING INC	CASH AMERICA INTERNATIONAL INC
Finance/Accounting		
3M COMPANY	AUTOZONE INC	CATERPILLAR INC
7-ELEVEN INC	AVERY DENNISON CORP	CATHOLIC HEALTH INITIATIVES
AARON'S INC	AVIS BUDGET GROUP INC	CDW CORPORATION
ABBOTT LABORATORIES		

CELGENE CORP	DAVITA INC	FLUOR CORP
CELLCO PARTNERSHIP (VERIZON WIRELESS)	DEAN FOODS CO	FOREST LABORATORIES INC
CEPHALON INC	DEERE & CO	FORTUNE BRANDS INC
CH ROBINSON WORLDWIDE INC	DELOITTE & TOUCHE USA LLP	FOSSIL INC
CH2M HILL COMPANIES LTD	DELOITTE CONSULTING LLP	FOSTER WHEELER AG
CHARLOTTE RUSSE HOLDING	DENNY'S CORPORATION	FOX ENTERTAINMENT GROUP INC
CHARMING SHOPPES INC	DEVON ENERGY CORPORATION	FPL GROUP INC
CHEMED CORPORATION	DEVRY INC	FRED'S INC
CHEVRON CORPORATION	DIAMOND OFFSHORE DRILLING INC	FRONTIER COMMUNICATIONS CORPORATION
CHEVRON PHILLIPS CHEMICAL COMPANY LLC	DICK'S SPORTING GOODS INC	FTI CONSULTING INC
CHICO'S FAS INC	DIEBOLD INC	GAMESTOP CORP
CHIPOTLE MEXICAN GRILL INC	DINEEQUITY INC	GENENTECH INC
CHRISTOPHER & BANKS CORP	DIRECTV GROUP INC (THE)	GENERAL CABLE CORP
CHS INC	DOLE FOOD COMPANY INC	GENERAL DYNAMICS CORP
CHUBB CORPORATION (THE)	DOLLAR GENERAL CORPORATION	GENERAL ELECTRIC CO (GE)
CIBER INC	DOLLAR THRIFTY AUTOMOTIVE GROUP INC	GENERAL MILLS INC
CIGNA CORP	DRESS BARN INC (THE)	GENESCO INC
CINTAS CORP	DTE ENERGY COMPANY	GENWORTH FINANCIAL INC
CISCO SYSTEMS INC	DUKE ENERGY CORP	GEO GROUP INC
CLUBCORP INC	DYCOM INDUSTRIES INC	GEORGIA GULF CORPORATION
COACH INC	E I DU PONT DE NEMOURS & CO (DUPONT)	GILEAD SCIENCES INC
COCA-COLA COMPANY (THE)	EATON CORP	GLOBAL HYATT CORPORATION
COCA-COLA ENTERPRISES INC	EBAY INC	GLOBAL PAYMENTS INC
COGNIZANT TECHNOLOGY SOLUTIONS CORP	EDISON INTERNATIONAL	GOLDMAN SACHS GROUP INC
COLDWATER CREEK INC	ELECTRONIC ARTS INC	GOOGLE INC
COLGATE PALMOLIVE CO	ELI LILLY & COMPANY	GRANT THORNTON LLP
COMCAST CORP	EMBARQ CORP	GUESS? INC
COMMUNITY HEALTH SYSTEMS INC	EMC CORP	HALLIBURTON COMPANY
CONAGRA FOODS INC	EMERITUS CORP	HARRAH'S ENTERTAINMENT INC
CONOCOPHILLIPS COMPANY	EMERSON ELECTRIC CO	HARRIS CORPORATION
CONSOL ENERGY INC	ENTERGY CORP	HARTFORD FINANCIAL SERVICES GROUP INC (THE)
CONSOLIDATED EDISON INC	ENTERPRISE PRODUCTS PARTNERS LP	HAWAIIAN ELECTRIC INDUSTRIES INC
CONTAINER STORE (THE)	ENTERPRISE RENT-A-CAR	HCA INC
CONVERGYS CORPORATION	ERNST & YOUNG LLP	HE BUTT GROCERY COMPANY (HEB)
COOPER COMPANIES INC	ESTEE LAUDER COMPANIES INC (THE)	HEALTH CARE SERVICE CORPORATION
COSTCO WHOLESALE CORP	EXELON CORPORATION	HEALTH FITNESS CORP
COVANCE INC	EXPERIAN AMERICAS	HEALTH MANAGEMENT ASSOCIATES INC
COVENTRY HEALTH CARE INC	EXPRESS SCRIPTS INC	HEALTH NET INC
COX COMMUNICATIONS INC	EXXON MOBIL CORPORATION (EXXONMOBIL)	HEALTHWAYS INC
CR BARD INC	EXXONMOBIL CHEMICAL	HELMERICH & PAYNE INC
CRACKER BARREL OLD COUNTRY STORE INC	FAMILY DOLLAR STORES INC	HENRY SCHEIN INC
CTS CORP	FEDEX CORPORATION	HERTZ GLOBAL HOLDINGS INC
CUBIC CORP	FINISH LINE INC (THE)	HESS CORPORATION
CUMMINS INC	FIRST ADVANTAGE CORPORATION	HEWITT ASSOCIATES
CVS CAREMARK CORPORATION	FIRST DATA CORP	HIBBETT SPORTS INC
DANAHER CORP	FIRSTENERGY CORP	
DARDEN RESTAURANTS INC		

HILTON HOTELS CORP	LINCOLN NATIONAL CORPORATION	NORTHROP GRUMMAN CORP
HOME DEPOT INC	LKQ CORP	NRG ENERGY INC
HONEYWELL INTERNATIONAL INC	LOCKHEED MARTIN CORP	OCCIDENTAL PETROLEUM CORP
HUMANA INC	LODGIAN INC	OCEANEERING INTERNATIONAL INC
IAC/INTERACTIVECORP	LOEWS CORPORATION	
IBM GLOBAL SERVICES	LOWE'S COMPANIES INC	ODYSSEY HEALTHCARE INC
ICT GROUP INC	MACY'S INC	OFFICE DEPOT INC
IDEXX LABORATORIES INC	MANOR CARE INC	OIL STATES INTERNATIONAL INC
IGATE CORPORATION	MANPOWER INC	OMNICARE INC
IMS HEALTH INC	MARRIOTT INTERNATIONAL INC	OMNICOM GROUP INC
INFOGROUP INC	MARS INC	ORACLE CORP
INGRAM MICRO INC	MARSH & MCLENNAN COMPANIES INC	O'REILLY AUTOMOTIVE INC
INTEL CORP		OSHKOSH CORPORATION
INTERNATIONAL BUSINESS MACHINES CORP (IBM)	MARY KAY INC	OSI RESTAURANT PARTNERS LLC
	MASSEY ENERGY COMPANY	OWENS & MINOR INC
INTUIT INC	MATTEL INC	PANTRY INC (THE)
INVENTIV HEALTH INC	MAXIM INTEGRATED PRODUCTS INC	PARAMETRIC TECHNOLOGY CORP
J C PENNEY COMPANY INC		PAREXEL INTERNATIONAL CORP
JABIL CIRCUIT INC	MAYO FOUNDATION FOR MEDICAL EDUCATION AND RESEARCH	PARSONS BRINCKERHOFF INC
JACK IN THE BOX INC		PATTERSON COMPANIES INC
JACOBS ENGINEERING GROUP INC	MCAFEE INC	PATTERSON-UTI ENERGY INC
JETBLUE AIRWAYS CORPORATION	MCDERMOTT INTERNATIONAL INC	PAYCHEX INC
JM SMUCKER CO	MCDONALD'S CORP	PEABODY ENERGY CORP
JOHNSON & JOHNSON	MCKESSON CORPORATION	PEPSI BOTTLING GROUP INC
JOHNSON CONTROLS INC	MCKINSEY & COMPANY INC	PEPSICO INC
JP MORGAN CHASE & CO INC	MEDCO HEALTH SOLUTIONS	PEROT SYSTEMS CORP
JUNIPER NETWORKS INC	MEDTRONIC INC	PERRIGO CO
KAISER PERMANENTE	MEIJER INC	PETCO ANIMAL SUPPLIES INC
KEANE INC	MEN'S WEARHOUSE INC (THE)	PETSMART INC
KELLOGG CO	MERCER INC	PFIZER INC
KELLY SERVICES INC	MERCK & CO INC	PG&E CORPORATION
KENDLE INTERNATIONAL INC	METHODIST HEALTH CARE SYSTEM	PHARMACEUTICAL PRODUCT DEVELOPMENT INC
KIMBERLY-CLARK CORP		
KINDRED HEALTHCARE INC	METLIFE INC	PITNEY BOWES INC
KOCH INDUSTRIES INC	MGM MIRAGE	PLEXUS CORP
KOHL'S CORP	MICROCHIP TECHNOLOGY INC	POLO RALPH LAUREN CORP
KPMG LLP	MICRON TECHNOLOGY INC	PRAXAIR INC
KRAFT FOODS INC	MICROSOFT CORP	PRECISION CASTPARTS CORP
KROGER CO (THE)	MIDAMERICAN ENERGY HOLDINGS CO	PRICESMART INC
L-3 COMMUNICATIONS HOLDINGS INC		PRICEWATERHOUSECOOPERS
	MILLIPORE CORP	PRIDE INTERNATIONAL INC
LABORATORY CORP OF AMERICA HOLDINGS	MONRO MUFFLER BRAKE INC	PRINCIPAL FINANCIAL GROUP (THE)
	MONSANTO CO	
LAS VEGAS SANDS CORP (THE VENETIAN)	MURPHY OIL CORPORATION	PROCTER & GAMBLE CO
	MYLAN INC	PROGRESSIVE CORPORATION (THE)
LEVEL 3 COMMUNICATIONS INC	NATIONAL OILWELL VARCO INC	
LEXMARK INTERNATIONAL INC	NETAPP INC	PRUDENTIAL FINANCIAL INC
LIBERTY GLOBAL INC	NEWS CORP	PSYCHIATRIC SOLUTIONS INC
LIBERTY MUTUAL GROUP INC	NII HOLDINGS INC	PUBLIC STORAGE INC
LIMITED BRANDS INC	NIKE INC	PUBLIX SUPER MARKETS INC
LINCARE HOLDINGS INC	NOBLE CORPORATION	QUALCOMM INC

QUANTA SERVICES INC	STARTEK INC	VALERO ENERGY CORP
QUEST DIAGNOSTICS INC	STARWOOD HOTELS & RESORTS WORLDWIDE INC	VALSPAR CORPORATION (THE)
QUIKSILVER INC		VARIAN MEDICAL SYSTEMS INC
R R DONNELLEY & SONS CO	STERIS CORP	VCA ANTECH INC
RALCORP HOLDINGS INC	STIFEL FINANCIAL CORP	VERISIGN INC
RAYTHEON CO	STRYKER CORP	VERIZON COMMUNICATIONS
REGIS CORPORATION	SUN HEALTHCARE GROUP	VIACOM INC
RENT-A-CENTER INC	SUNGARD DATA SYSTEMS INC	VICTORIAS SECRET
RES CARE INC	SUNOCO INC	VISA INC
RITE AID CORPORATION	SUNRISE SENIOR LIVING	VOLT INFORMATION SCIENCES INC
RITZ-CARLTON HOTEL COMPANY LLC (THE)	SUPERVALU INC	W R BERKLEY CORPORATION
ROBERT HALF INTERNATIONAL INC	SYKES ENTERPRISES INC	WABTEC CORP
ROSS STORES INC	SYMANTEC CORP	WALGREEN CO
ROYAL CARIBBEAN CRUISES LTD	SYNOPSYS INC	WAL-MART STORES INC
RRI ENERGY INC	SYNTEL INC	WALT DISNEY COMPANY (THE)
SABRE HOLDINGS CORP	SYSCO CORP	WASTE MANAGEMENT INC
SAFECO INSURANCE COMPANY OF AMERICA	TARGET CORPORATION	WATERS CORP
	TBC CORPORATION	WATSON PHARMACEUTICALS INC
SAFEWAY INC	TEAM INC	WATSON WYATT WORLDWIDE INC
SAIC INC	TECH DATA CORP	WEATHERFORD INTERNATIONAL LTD
SAM'S CLUB	TEKTRONIX INC	
SAPIENT CORPORATION	TELEDYNE TECHNOLOGIES INCORPORATED	WEIGHT WATCHERS INTERNATIONAL INC
SARA LEE CORP	TELEPHONE AND DATA SYSTEMS INC (TDS)	WELLPOINT INC
SAS INSTITUTE INC		WELLS FARGO & CO
SCANA CORPORATION	TELETECH HOLDINGS INC	WENDY'S/ARBY'S GROUP INC
SCHERING-PLOUGH CORP	TESORO CORP	WEST CORPORATION
SCHLUMBERGER LIMITED	THERMO FISHER SCIENTIFIC INC	WEST PHARMACEUTICAL SERVICES INC
SCIENTIFIC GAMES CORPORATION	TIFFANY & CO	
SCOTTS MIRACLE GROW CO	TIME WARNER INC	WESTERN DIGITAL CORP
SEACOR HOLDINGS INC	TJX COMPANIES INC (THE)	WHOLE FOODS MARKET INC
SELECT MEDICAL	T-MOBILE USA	WILLIAMS COMPANIES INC (THE)
SEMPRA ENERGY	TOTAL SYSTEM SERVICES INC (TSYS)	WW GRAINGER INC
SENSIENT TECHNOLOGIES CORPORATION		WYETH
	TOWERS PERRIN	WYNDHAM WORLDWIDE
SHAW GROUP INC (THE)	TRANSOCEAN INC	WYNN RESORTS LIMITED
SHELL OIL CO	TRAVELERS COMPANIES INC (THE)	XEROX CORP
SHERWIN WILLIAMS COMPANY (THE)	TREEHOUSE FOODS INC	YAHOO! INC
	TW TELECOM INC	YUM! BRANDS INC
SIGMA-ALDRICH CORP	TYSON FOODS INC	ZIMMER HOLDINGS INC
SISTERS OF MERCY HEALTH SYSTEMS	UNITED NATURAL FOODS INC	
SMITH INTERNATIONAL INC	UNITED PARCEL SERVICE INC (UPS)	
SMITHFIELD FOODS INC	UNITED STATES CELLULAR CORP	
SOUTHERN CALIFORNIA EDISON COMPANY	UNITED TECHNOLOGIES CORPORATION	

Health Care	
3M COMPANY
ABBOTT LABORATORIES
AETNA INC
AFLAC INC
ALLERGAN INC
AMEDISYS INC
AMGEN INC
ASCENSION HEALTH
BAXTER INTERNATIONAL INC

SOUTHERN COMPANY (THE)	UNITEDHEALTH GROUP INC
SOUTHWEST AIRLINES CO	UNIVERSAL HEALTH SERVICES INC
SRA INTERNATIONAL INC	UNIVISION COMMUNICATIONS INC
ST JUDE MEDICAL INC	URS CORPORATION
STAPLES INC	USAA

BECKMAN COULTER INC	MEDTRONIC INC	ABM INDUSTRIES INC
BECTON DICKINSON & CO	MERCK & CO INC	ACADEMY SPORTS & OUTDOORS LTD
BIO RAD LABORATORIES INC	METHODIST HEALTH CARE SYSTEM	ACCENTURE LTD
BOSTON SCIENTIFIC CORP	METLIFE INC	ACTIVISION BLIZZARD INC
CAPITAL SENIOR LIVING CORP	MYLAN INC	ACXIOM CORP
CATHOLIC HEALTH INITIATIVES	ODYSSEY HEALTHCARE INC	ADC TELECOMMUNICATIONS INC
CELGENE CORP	OMNICARE INC	ADESA INC
CEPHALON INC	OWENS & MINOR INC	ADOBE SYSTEMS INC
CHEMED CORPORATION	PAREXEL INTERNATIONAL CORP	ADVANCE AUTO PARTS INC
CIGNA CORP	PATTERSON COMPANIES INC	ADVANCED MICRO DEVICES INC (AMD)
COMMUNITY HEALTH SYSTEMS INC	PERRIGO CO	AECOM TECHNOLOGY CORPORATION
COOPER COMPANIES INC	PFIZER INC	AES CORPORATION (THE)
COVANCE INC	PHARMACEUTICAL PRODUCT DEVELOPMENT INC	AETNA INC
COVENTRY HEALTH CARE INC	PRINCIPAL FINANCIAL GROUP (THE)	AFFILIATED COMPUTER SERVICES INC
CR BARD INC	PRUDENTIAL FINANCIAL INC	AFLAC INC
CVS CAREMARK CORPORATION	PSYCHIATRIC SOLUTIONS INC	AGILENT TECHNOLOGIES INC
DAVITA INC	QUEST DIAGNOSTICS INC	AIR PRODUCTS & CHEMICALS INC
ELI LILLY & COMPANY	RES CARE INC	ALLERGAN INC
EMERITUS CORP	RITE AID CORPORATION	ALLIANCE DATA SYSTEMS CORPORATION
EXPRESS SCRIPTS INC	SCHERING-PLOUGH CORP	ALLSTATE CORPORATION (THE)
FOREST LABORATORIES INC	SELECT MEDICAL	ALTRIA GROUP INC
GENENTECH INC	SISTERS OF MERCY HEALTH SYSTEMS	AMAZON.COM INC
GENWORTH FINANCIAL INC	SOUTHWEST AIRLINES CO	AMEDISYS INC
GILEAD SCIENCES INC	ST JUDE MEDICAL INC	AMERICAN ELECTRIC POWER COMPANY INC (AEP)
HARTFORD FINANCIAL SERVICES GROUP INC (THE)	STERIS CORP	AMERICAN POWER CONVERSION (APC)
HCA INC	STRYKER CORP	AMERISOURCEBERGEN CORP
HEALTH CARE SERVICE CORPORATION	SUN HEALTHCARE GROUP	AMGEN INC
HEALTH MANAGEMENT ASSOCIATES INC	SUNRISE SENIOR LIVING	ANADARKO PETROLEUM CORPORATION
HEALTH NET INC	UNITEDHEALTH GROUP INC	ANALOG DEVICES INC
HEALTHWAYS INC	UNIVERSAL HEALTH SERVICES INC	ANNTAYLOR STORES CORP
HENRY SCHEIN INC	VARIAN MEDICAL SYSTEMS INC	APACHE CORP
HUMANA INC	VCA ANTECH INC	APOLLO GROUP INC
IDEXX LABORATORIES INC	WALGREEN CO	APPLE INC
IMS HEALTH INC	WATSON PHARMACEUTICALS INC	ARAMARK CORPORATION
INVENTIV HEALTH INC	WEIGHT WATCHERS INTERNATIONAL INC	ARCHER DANIELS MIDLAND CO
JETBLUE AIRWAYS CORPORATION	WELLPOINT INC	ARROW ELECTRONICS INC
JOHNSON & JOHNSON	WEST PHARMACEUTICAL SERVICES INC	ARTHUR J GALLAGHER & CO
KAISER PERMANENTE	WYETH	ASCENSION HEALTH
KENDLE INTERNATIONAL INC	ZIMMER HOLDINGS INC	AT&T INC
KINDRED HEALTHCARE INC		AUTOMATIC DATA PROCESSING INC
LABORATORY CORP OF AMERICA HOLDINGS	**Human Resources/Other**	AUTOZONE INC
LINCARE HOLDINGS INC	3M COMPANY	AVERY DENNISON CORP
LINCOLN NATIONAL CORPORATION	7-ELEVEN INC	AVIS BUDGET GROUP INC
MANOR CARE INC	AARON'S INC	
MAYO FOUNDATION FOR MEDICAL EDUCATION AND RESEARCH	ABBOTT LABORATORIES	
MEDCO HEALTH SOLUTIONS		

AVNET INC	CELGENE CORP	DAVITA INC
AVON PRODUCTS INC	CELLCO PARTNERSHIP (VERIZON WIRELESS)	DEAN FOODS CO
AXA FINANCIAL INC		DEERE & CO
BAKER HUGHES INC	CEPHALON INC	DELOITTE & TOUCHE USA LLP
BALTIMORE GAS AND ELECTRIC COMPANY	CH ROBINSON WORLDWIDE INC	DELOITTE CONSULTING LLP
	CH2M HILL COMPANIES LTD	DENNY'S CORPORATION
BANK OF AMERICA CORP	CHARLOTTE RUSSE HOLDING	DEVON ENERGY CORPORATION
BARNES & NOBLE INC	CHARMING SHOPPES INC	DEVRY INC
BASS PRO SHOPS INC	CHEMED CORPORATION	DIAMOND OFFSHORE DRILLING INC
BAXTER INTERNATIONAL INC	CHEVRON CORPORATION	DICK'S SPORTING GOODS INC
BDO SEIDMAN LLP	CHEVRON PHILLIPS CHEMICAL COMPANY LLC	DIEBOLD INC
BEBE STORES INC		DINEEQUITY INC
BECHTEL GROUP INC	CHICO'S FAS INC	DIRECTV GROUP INC (THE)
BECKMAN COULTER INC	CHIPOTLE MEXICAN GRILL INC	DOLE FOOD COMPANY INC
BECTON DICKINSON & CO	CHRISTOPHER & BANKS CORP	DOLLAR GENERAL CORPORATION
BED BATH & BEYOND INC	CHS INC	DOLLAR THRIFTY AUTOMOTIVE GROUP INC
BENCHMARK ELECTRONICS INC	CHUBB CORPORATION (THE)	
BERKSHIRE HATHAWAY INC	CIBER INC	DRESS BARN INC (THE)
BEST BUY CO INC	CIGNA CORP	DTE ENERGY COMPANY
BIO RAD LABORATORIES INC	CINTAS CORP	DUKE ENERGY CORP
BJ'S WHOLESALE CLUB INC	CISCO SYSTEMS INC	DYCOM INDUSTRIES INC
BLACK & DECKER CORP	CLUBCORP INC	E I DU PONT DE NEMOURS & CO (DUPONT)
BLACKROCK INC	COACH INC	
BLOOMBERG LP	COCA-COLA COMPANY (THE)	EATON CORP
BOEING COMPANY (THE)	COCA-COLA ENTERPRISES INC	EBAY INC
BOOZ ALLEN HAMILTON	COGNIZANT TECHNOLOGY SOLUTIONS CORP	EDISON INTERNATIONAL
BOSTON SCIENTIFIC CORP		ELECTRONIC ARTS INC
BRINKER INTERNATIONAL INC	COLDWATER CREEK INC	ELI LILLY & COMPANY
BRINKS COMPANY (THE)	COLGATE PALMOLIVE CO	EMBARQ CORP
BROADCOM CORP	COMCAST CORP	EMC CORP
BROWN & BROWN INC	COMMUNITY HEALTH SYSTEMS INC	EMERITUS CORP
BUCKLE INC (THE)	CONAGRA FOODS INC	EMERSON ELECTRIC CO
BUCYRUS INTERNATIONAL INC	CONOCOPHILLIPS COMPANY	ENTERGY CORP
BUFFALO WILD WINGS INC	CONSOL ENERGY INC	ENTERPRISE PRODUCTS PARTNERS LP
BUNGE LTD	CONSOLIDATED EDISON INC	
BURGER KING HOLDINGS INC	CONTAINER STORE (THE)	ENTERPRISE RENT-A-CAR
CABELA'S INC	CONVERGYS CORPORATION	ERNST & YOUNG LLP
CABLEVISION SYSTEMS CORP	COOPER COMPANIES INC	ESTEE LAUDER COMPANIES INC (THE)
CACI INTERNATIONAL INC	COSTCO WHOLESALE CORP	
CAMERON INTERNATIONAL CORPORATION	COVANCE INC	EXELON CORPORATION
	COVENTRY HEALTH CARE INC	EXPERIAN AMERICAS
CAPITAL SENIOR LIVING CORP	COX COMMUNICATIONS INC	EXPRESS SCRIPTS INC
CARDINAL HEALTH INC	CR BARD INC	EXXON MOBIL CORPORATION (EXXONMOBIL)
CARGILL INC	CRACKER BARREL OLD COUNTRY STORE INC	
CARMAX GROUP		EXXONMOBIL CHEMICAL
CARNIVAL CORPORATION	CTS CORP	FAMILY DOLLAR STORES INC
CASH AMERICA INTERNATIONAL INC	CUBIC CORP	FEDEX CORPORATION
	CUMMINS INC	FINISH LINE INC (THE)
CATERPILLAR INC	CVS CAREMARK CORPORATION	FIRST ADVANTAGE CORPORATION
CATHOLIC HEALTH INITIATIVES	DANAHER CORP	FIRST DATA CORP
CDW CORPORATION	DARDEN RESTAURANTS INC	FIRSTENERGY CORP

FLUOR CORP	HILTON HOTELS CORP	LINCOLN NATIONAL CORPORATION
FOREST LABORATORIES INC	HOME DEPOT INC	LKQ CORP
FORTUNE BRANDS INC	HONEYWELL INTERNATIONAL INC	LOCKHEED MARTIN CORP
FOSSIL INC	HUMANA INC	LODGIAN INC
FOSTER WHEELER AG	IAC/INTERACTIVECORP	LOEWS CORPORATION
FOX ENTERTAINMENT GROUP INC	IBM GLOBAL SERVICES	LOWE'S COMPANIES INC
FPL GROUP INC	ICT GROUP INC	MACY'S INC
FRED'S INC	IDEXX LABORATORIES INC	MANOR CARE INC
FRONTIER COMMUNICATIONS CORPORATION	IGATE CORPORATION	MANPOWER INC
FTI CONSULTING INC	IMS HEALTH INC	MARRIOTT INTERNATIONAL INC
GAMESTOP CORP	INFOGROUP INC	MARS INC
GENENTECH INC	INGRAM MICRO INC	MARSH & MCLENNAN COMPANIES INC
GENERAL CABLE CORP	INTEL CORP	MARY KAY INC
GENERAL DYNAMICS CORP	INTERNATIONAL BUSINESS MACHINES CORP (IBM)	MASSEY ENERGY COMPANY
GENERAL ELECTRIC CO (GE)	INTUIT INC	MATTEL INC
GENERAL MILLS INC	INVENTIV HEALTH INC	MAXIM INTEGRATED PRODUCTS INC
GENESCO INC	J C PENNEY COMPANY INC	
GENWORTH FINANCIAL INC	JABIL CIRCUIT INC	MAYO FOUNDATION FOR MEDICAL EDUCATION AND RESEARCH
GEO GROUP INC	JACK IN THE BOX INC	
GEORGIA GULF CORPORATION	JACOBS ENGINEERING GROUP INC	MCAFEE INC
GILEAD SCIENCES INC	JETBLUE AIRWAYS CORPORATION	MCDERMOTT INTERNATIONAL INC
GLOBAL HYATT CORPORATION	JM SMUCKER CO	MCDONALD'S CORP
GLOBAL PAYMENTS INC	JOHNSON & JOHNSON	MCKESSON CORPORATION
GOLDMAN SACHS GROUP INC	JOHNSON CONTROLS INC	MCKINSEY & COMPANY INC
GOOGLE INC	JP MORGAN CHASE & CO INC	MEDCO HEALTH SOLUTIONS
GRANT THORNTON LLP	JUNIPER NETWORKS INC	MEDTRONIC INC
GUESS? INC	KAISER PERMANENTE	MEIJER INC
HALLIBURTON COMPANY	KEANE INC	MEN'S WEARHOUSE INC (THE)
HARRAH'S ENTERTAINMENT INC	KELLOGG CO	MERCER INC
HARRIS CORPORATION	KELLY SERVICES INC	MERCK & CO INC
HARTFORD FINANCIAL SERVICES GROUP INC (THE)	KENDLE INTERNATIONAL INC	METHODIST HEALTH CARE SYSTEM
HAWAIIAN ELECTRIC INDUSTRIES INC	KIMBERLY-CLARK CORP	METLIFE INC
	KINDRED HEALTHCARE INC	MGM MIRAGE
HCA INC	KOCH INDUSTRIES INC	MICROCHIP TECHNOLOGY INC
HE BUTT GROCERY COMPANY (HEB)	KOHL'S CORP	MICRON TECHNOLOGY INC
	KPMG LLP	MICROSOFT CORP
HEALTH CARE SERVICE CORPORATION	KRAFT FOODS INC	MIDAMERICAN ENERGY HOLDINGS CO
	KROGER CO (THE)	
HEALTH FITNESS CORP	L-3 COMMUNICATIONS HOLDINGS INC	MILLIPORE CORP
HEALTH MANAGEMENT ASSOCIATES INC		MONRO MUFFLER BRAKE INC
	LABORATORY CORP OF AMERICA HOLDINGS	MONSANTO CO
HEALTH NET INC		MURPHY OIL CORPORATION
HEALTHWAYS INC	LAS VEGAS SANDS CORP (THE VENETIAN)	MYLAN INC
HELMERICH & PAYNE INC		NATIONAL OILWELL VARCO INC
HENRY SCHEIN INC	LEVEL 3 COMMUNICATIONS INC	NETAPP INC
HERTZ GLOBAL HOLDINGS INC	LEXMARK INTERNATIONAL INC	NEWS CORP
HESS CORPORATION	LIBERTY GLOBAL INC	NII HOLDINGS INC
HEWITT ASSOCIATES	LIBERTY MUTUAL GROUP INC	NIKE INC
HIBBETT SPORTS INC	LIMITED BRANDS INC	NOBLE CORPORATION
	LINCARE HOLDINGS INC	

NORTHROP GRUMMAN CORP	QUANTA SERVICES INC	STARTEK INC
NRG ENERGY INC	QUEST DIAGNOSTICS INC	STARWOOD HOTELS & RESORTS WORLDWIDE INC
OCCIDENTAL PETROLEUM CORP	QUIKSILVER INC	STERIS CORP
OCEANEERING INTERNATIONAL INC	R R DONNELLEY & SONS CO	STIFEL FINANCIAL CORP
ODYSSEY HEALTHCARE INC	RALCORP HOLDINGS INC	STRYKER CORP
OFFICE DEPOT INC	RAYTHEON CO	SUN HEALTHCARE GROUP
OIL STATES INTERNATIONAL INC	REGIS CORPORATION	SUNGARD DATA SYSTEMS INC
OMNICARE INC	RENT-A-CENTER INC	SUNOCO INC
OMNICOM GROUP INC	RES CARE INC	SUNRISE SENIOR LIVING
ORACLE CORP	RITE AID CORPORATION	SUPERVALU INC
O'REILLY AUTOMOTIVE INC	RITZ-CARLTON HOTEL COMPANY LLC (THE)	SYKES ENTERPRISES INC
OSHKOSH CORPORATION	ROBERT HALF INTERNATIONAL INC	SYMANTEC CORP
OSI RESTAURANT PARTNERS LLC	ROSS STORES INC	SYNOPSYS INC
OWENS & MINOR INC	ROYAL CARIBBEAN CRUISES LTD	SYNTEL INC
PANTRY INC (THE)	RRI ENERGY INC	SYSCO CORP
PARAMETRIC TECHNOLOGY CORP	SABRE HOLDINGS CORP	TARGET CORPORATION
PAREXEL INTERNATIONAL CORP	SAFECO INSURANCE COMPANY OF AMERICA	TBC CORPORATION
PARSONS BRINCKERHOFF INC	SAFEWAY INC	TEAM INC
PATTERSON COMPANIES INC	SAIC INC	TECH DATA CORP
PATTERSON-UTI ENERGY INC	SAM'S CLUB	TEKTRONIX INC
PAYCHEX INC	SAPIENT CORPORATION	TELEDYNE TECHNOLOGIES INCORPORATED
PEABODY ENERGY CORP	SARA LEE CORP	TELEPHONE AND DATA SYSTEMS INC (TDS)
PEPSI BOTTLING GROUP INC	SAS INSTITUTE INC	
PEPSICO INC	SCANA CORPORATION	TELETECH HOLDINGS INC
PEROT SYSTEMS CORP	SCHERING-PLOUGH CORP	TESORO CORP
PERRIGO CO	SCHLUMBERGER LIMITED	THERMO FISHER SCIENTIFIC INC
PETCO ANIMAL SUPPLIES INC	SCIENTIFIC GAMES CORPORATION	TIFFANY & CO
PETSMART INC	SCOTTS MIRACLE GROW CO	TIME WARNER INC
PFIZER INC	SEACOR HOLDINGS INC	TJX COMPANIES INC (THE)
PG&E CORPORATION	SELECT MEDICAL	T-MOBILE USA
PHARMACEUTICAL PRODUCT DEVELOPMENT INC	SEMPRA ENERGY	TOTAL SYSTEM SERVICES INC (TSYS)
PITNEY BOWES INC	SENSIENT TECHNOLOGIES CORPORATION	TOWERS PERRIN
PLEXUS CORP	SHAW GROUP INC (THE)	TRANSOCEAN INC
POLO RALPH LAUREN CORP	SHELL OIL CO	TRAVELERS COMPANIES INC (THE)
PRAXAIR INC	SHERWIN WILLIAMS COMPANY (THE)	TREEHOUSE FOODS INC
PRECISION CASTPARTS CORP		TW TELECOM INC
PRICESMART INC	SIGMA-ALDRICH CORP	TYSON FOODS INC
PRICEWATERHOUSECOOPERS	SISTERS OF MERCY HEALTH SYSTEMS	UNITED NATURAL FOODS INC
PRIDE INTERNATIONAL INC	SMITH INTERNATIONAL INC	UNITED PARCEL SERVICE INC (UPS)
PRINCIPAL FINANCIAL GROUP (THE)	SMITHFIELD FOODS INC	
PROCTER & GAMBLE CO	SOUTHERN CALIFORNIA EDISON COMPANY	UNITED STATES CELLULAR CORP
PROGRESSIVE CORPORATION (THE)		UNITED TECHNOLOGIES CORPORATION
PRUDENTIAL FINANCIAL INC	SOUTHERN COMPANY (THE)	UNITEDHEALTH GROUP INC
PSYCHIATRIC SOLUTIONS INC	SOUTHWEST AIRLINES CO	UNIVERSAL HEALTH SERVICES INC
PUBLIC STORAGE INC	SRA INTERNATIONAL INC	UNIVISION COMMUNICATIONS INC
PUBLIX SUPER MARKETS INC	ST JUDE MEDICAL INC	URS CORPORATION
QUALCOMM INC	STAPLES INC	USAA

VALERO ENERGY CORP	ACXIOM CORP	COMPANY
VALSPAR CORPORATION (THE)	ADC TELECOMMUNICATIONS INC	BANK OF AMERICA CORP
VARIAN MEDICAL SYSTEMS INC	ADESA INC	BARNES & NOBLE INC
VCA ANTECH INC	ADOBE SYSTEMS INC	BASS PRO SHOPS INC
VERISIGN INC	ADVANCE AUTO PARTS INC	BAXTER INTERNATIONAL INC
VERIZON COMMUNICATIONS	ADVANCED MICRO DEVICES INC (AMD)	BDO SEIDMAN LLP
VIACOM INC	AECOM TECHNOLOGY CORPORATION	BEBE STORES INC
VICTORIAS SECRET		BECHTEL GROUP INC
VISA INC	AES CORPORATION (THE)	BECKMAN COULTER INC
VOLT INFORMATION SCIENCES INC	AETNA INC	BECTON DICKINSON & CO
W R BERKLEY CORPORATION	AFFILIATED COMPUTER SERVICES INC	BED BATH & BEYOND INC
WABTEC CORP		BENCHMARK ELECTRONICS INC
WALGREEN CO	AFLAC INC	BERKSHIRE HATHAWAY INC
WAL-MART STORES INC	AGILENT TECHNOLOGIES INC	BEST BUY CO INC
WALT DISNEY COMPANY (THE)	AIR PRODUCTS & CHEMICALS INC	BIO RAD LABORATORIES INC
WASTE MANAGEMENT INC	ALLERGAN INC	BJ'S WHOLESALE CLUB INC
WATERS CORP	ALLIANCE DATA SYSTEMS CORPORATION	BLACK & DECKER CORP
WATSON PHARMACEUTICALS INC		BLACKROCK INC
WATSON WYATT WORLDWIDE INC	ALLSTATE CORPORATION (THE)	BLOOMBERG LP
WEATHERFORD INTERNATIONAL LTD	ALTRIA GROUP INC	BOEING COMPANY (THE)
	AMAZON.COM INC	BOOZ ALLEN HAMILTON
WEIGHT WATCHERS INTERNATIONAL INC	AMEDISYS INC	BOSTON SCIENTIFIC CORP
	AMERICAN ELECTRIC POWER COMPANY INC (AEP)	BRINKER INTERNATIONAL INC
WELLPOINT INC		BRINKS COMPANY (THE)
WELLS FARGO & CO	AMERICAN POWER CONVERSION (APC)	BROADCOM CORP
WENDY'S/ARBY'S GROUP INC		BROWN & BROWN INC
WEST CORPORATION	AMERISOURCEBERGEN CORP	BUCKLE INC (THE)
WEST PHARMACEUTICAL SERVICES INC	AMGEN INC	BUCYRUS INTERNATIONAL INC
	ANADARKO PETROLEUM CORPORATION	BUFFALO WILD WINGS INC
WESTERN DIGITAL CORP		BUNGE LTD
WHOLE FOODS MARKET INC	ANALOG DEVICES INC	BURGER KING HOLDINGS INC
WILLIAMS COMPANIES INC (THE)	ANNTAYLOR STORES CORP	CABELA'S INC
WW GRAINGER INC	APACHE CORP	CABLEVISION SYSTEMS CORP
WYETH	APOLLO GROUP INC	CACI INTERNATIONAL INC
WYNDHAM WORLDWIDE	APPLE INC	CAMERON INTERNATIONAL CORPORATION
WYNN RESORTS LIMITED	ARAMARK CORPORATION	
XEROX CORP	ARCHER DANIELS MIDLAND CO	CAPITAL SENIOR LIVING CORP
YAHOO! INC	ARROW ELECTRONICS INC	CARDINAL HEALTH INC
YUM! BRANDS INC	ARTHUR J GALLAGHER & CO	CARGILL INC
ZIMMER HOLDINGS INC	ASCENSION HEALTH	CARMAX GROUP
	AT&T INC	CARNIVAL CORPORATION
	AUTOMATIC DATA PROCESSING INC	CASH AMERICA INTERNATIONAL INC
Law		
3M COMPANY	AUTOZONE INC	CATERPILLAR INC
7-ELEVEN INC	AVERY DENNISON CORP	CATHOLIC HEALTH INITIATIVES
AARON'S INC	AVIS BUDGET GROUP INC	CDW CORPORATION
ABBOTT LABORATORIES	AVNET INC	CELGENE CORP
ABM INDUSTRIES INC	AVON PRODUCTS INC	CELLCO PARTNERSHIP (VERIZON WIRELESS)
ACADEMY SPORTS & OUTDOORS LTD	AXA FINANCIAL INC	
	BAKER HUGHES INC	CEPHALON INC
ACCENTURE LTD	BALTIMORE GAS AND ELECTRIC	CH ROBINSON WORLDWIDE INC
ACTIVISION BLIZZARD INC		

CH2M HILL COMPANIES LTD	DENNY'S CORPORATION	FOX ENTERTAINMENT GROUP INC
CHARLOTTE RUSSE HOLDING	DEVON ENERGY CORPORATION	FPL GROUP INC
CHARMING SHOPPES INC	DEVRY INC	FRED'S INC
CHEMED CORPORATION	DIAMOND OFFSHORE DRILLING INC	FRONTIER COMMUNICATIONS CORPORATION
CHEVRON CORPORATION	DICK'S SPORTING GOODS INC	
CHEVRON PHILLIPS CHEMICAL COMPANY LLC	DIEBOLD INC	FTI CONSULTING INC
	DINEEQUITY INC	GAMESTOP CORP
CHICO'S FAS INC	DIRECTV GROUP INC (THE)	GENENTECH INC
CHIPOTLE MEXICAN GRILL INC	DOLE FOOD COMPANY INC	GENERAL CABLE CORP
CHRISTOPHER & BANKS CORP	DOLLAR GENERAL CORPORATION	GENERAL DYNAMICS CORP
CHS INC	DOLLAR THRIFTY AUTOMOTIVE GROUP INC	GENERAL ELECTRIC CO (GE)
CHUBB CORPORATION (THE)		GENERAL MILLS INC
CIBER INC	DRESS BARN INC (THE)	GENESCO INC
CIGNA CORP	DTE ENERGY COMPANY	GENWORTH FINANCIAL INC
CINTAS CORP	DUKE ENERGY CORP	GEO GROUP INC
CISCO SYSTEMS INC	DYCOM INDUSTRIES INC	GEORGIA GULF CORPORATION
CLUBCORP INC	E I DU PONT DE NEMOURS & CO (DUPONT)	GILEAD SCIENCES INC
COACH INC		GLOBAL HYATT CORPORATION
COCA-COLA COMPANY (THE)	EATON CORP	GLOBAL PAYMENTS INC
COCA-COLA ENTERPRISES INC	EBAY INC	GOLDMAN SACHS GROUP INC
COGNIZANT TECHNOLOGY SOLUTIONS CORP	EDISON INTERNATIONAL	GOOGLE INC
	ELECTRONIC ARTS INC	GRANT THORNTON LLP
COLDWATER CREEK INC	ELI LILLY & COMPANY	GUESS? INC
COLGATE PALMOLIVE CO	EMBARQ CORP	HALLIBURTON COMPANY
COMCAST CORP	EMC CORP	HARRAH'S ENTERTAINMENT INC
COMMUNITY HEALTH SYSTEMS INC	EMERITUS CORP	HARRIS CORPORATION
CONAGRA FOODS INC	EMERSON ELECTRIC CO	HARTFORD FINANCIAL SERVICES GROUP INC (THE)
CONOCOPHILLIPS COMPANY	ENTERGY CORP	
CONSOL ENERGY INC	ENTERPRISE PRODUCTS PARTNERS LP	HAWAIIAN ELECTRIC INDUSTRIES INC
CONSOLIDATED EDISON INC		
CONTAINER STORE (THE)	ENTERPRISE RENT-A-CAR	HCA INC
CONVERGYS CORPORATION	ERNST & YOUNG LLP	HE BUTT GROCERY COMPANY (HEB)
COOPER COMPANIES INC	ESTEE LAUDER COMPANIES INC (THE)	
COSTCO WHOLESALE CORP		HEALTH CARE SERVICE CORPORATION
COVANCE INC	EXELON CORPORATION	
COVENTRY HEALTH CARE INC	EXPERIAN AMERICAS	HEALTH FITNESS CORP
COX COMMUNICATIONS INC	EXPRESS SCRIPTS INC	HEALTH MANAGEMENT ASSOCIATES INC
CR BARD INC	EXXON MOBIL CORPORATION (EXXONMOBIL)	
CRACKER BARREL OLD COUNTRY STORE INC		HEALTH NET INC
	EXXONMOBIL CHEMICAL	HEALTHWAYS INC
CTS CORP	FAMILY DOLLAR STORES INC	HELMERICH & PAYNE INC
CUBIC CORP	FEDEX CORPORATION	HENRY SCHEIN INC
CUMMINS INC	FINISH LINE INC (THE)	HERTZ GLOBAL HOLDINGS INC
CVS CAREMARK CORPORATION	FIRST ADVANTAGE CORPORATION	HESS CORPORATION
DANAHER CORP	FIRST DATA CORP	HEWITT ASSOCIATES
DARDEN RESTAURANTS INC	FIRSTENERGY CORP	HIBBETT SPORTS INC
DAVITA INC	FLUOR CORP	HILTON HOTELS CORP
DEAN FOODS CO	FOREST LABORATORIES INC	HOME DEPOT INC
DEERE & CO	FORTUNE BRANDS INC	HONEYWELL INTERNATIONAL INC
DELOITTE & TOUCHE USA LLP	FOSSIL INC	HUMANA INC
DELOITTE CONSULTING LLP	FOSTER WHEELER AG	IAC/INTERACTIVECORP

IBM GLOBAL SERVICES	LOWE'S COMPANIES INC	ODYSSEY HEALTHCARE INC
ICT GROUP INC	MACY'S INC	OFFICE DEPOT INC
IDEXX LABORATORIES INC	MANOR CARE INC	OIL STATES INTERNATIONAL INC
IGATE CORPORATION	MANPOWER INC	OMNICARE INC
IMS HEALTH INC	MARRIOTT INTERNATIONAL INC	OMNICOM GROUP INC
INFOGROUP INC	MARS INC	ORACLE CORP
INGRAM MICRO INC	MARSH & MCLENNAN COMPANIES INC	O'REILLY AUTOMOTIVE INC
INTEL CORP		OSHKOSH CORPORATION
INTERNATIONAL BUSINESS MACHINES CORP (IBM)	MARY KAY INC	OSI RESTAURANT PARTNERS LLC
	MASSEY ENERGY COMPANY	OWENS & MINOR INC
INTUIT INC	MATTEL INC	PANTRY INC (THE)
INVENTIV HEALTH INC	MAXIM INTEGRATED PRODUCTS INC	PARAMETRIC TECHNOLOGY CORP
J C PENNEY COMPANY INC		PAREXEL INTERNATIONAL CORP
JABIL CIRCUIT INC	MAYO FOUNDATION FOR MEDICAL EDUCATION AND RESEARCH	PARSONS BRINCKERHOFF INC
JACK IN THE BOX INC		PATTERSON COMPANIES INC
JACOBS ENGINEERING GROUP INC	MCAFEE INC	PATTERSON-UTI ENERGY INC
JETBLUE AIRWAYS CORPORATION	MCDERMOTT INTERNATIONAL INC	PAYCHEX INC
JM SMUCKER CO	MCDONALD'S CORP	PEABODY ENERGY CORP
JOHNSON & JOHNSON	MCKESSON CORPORATION	PEPSI BOTTLING GROUP INC
JOHNSON CONTROLS INC	MCKINSEY & COMPANY INC	PEPSICO INC
JP MORGAN CHASE & CO INC	MEDCO HEALTH SOLUTIONS	PEROT SYSTEMS CORP
JUNIPER NETWORKS INC	MEDTRONIC INC	PERRIGO CO
KAISER PERMANENTE	MEIJER INC	PETCO ANIMAL SUPPLIES INC
KEANE INC	MEN'S WEARHOUSE INC (THE)	PETSMART INC
KELLOGG CO	MERCER INC	PFIZER INC
KELLY SERVICES INC	MERCK & CO INC	PG&E CORPORATION
KENDLE INTERNATIONAL INC	METHODIST HEALTH CARE SYSTEM	PHARMACEUTICAL PRODUCT DEVELOPMENT INC
KIMBERLY-CLARK CORP		
KINDRED HEALTHCARE INC	METLIFE INC	PITNEY BOWES INC
KOCH INDUSTRIES INC	MGM MIRAGE	PLEXUS CORP
KOHL'S CORP	MICROCHIP TECHNOLOGY INC	POLO RALPH LAUREN CORP
KPMG LLP	MICRON TECHNOLOGY INC	PRAXAIR INC
KRAFT FOODS INC	MICROSOFT CORP	PRECISION CASTPARTS CORP
KROGER CO (THE)	MIDAMERICAN ENERGY HOLDINGS CO	PRICESMART INC
L-3 COMMUNICATIONS HOLDINGS INC		PRICEWATERHOUSECOOPERS
	MILLIPORE CORP	PRIDE INTERNATIONAL INC
LABORATORY CORP OF AMERICA HOLDINGS	MONRO MUFFLER BRAKE INC	PRINCIPAL FINANCIAL GROUP (THE)
	MONSANTO CO	
LAS VEGAS SANDS CORP (THE VENETIAN)	MURPHY OIL CORPORATION	PROCTER & GAMBLE CO
	MYLAN INC	PROGRESSIVE CORPORATION (THE)
LEVEL 3 COMMUNICATIONS INC	NATIONAL OILWELL VARCO INC	
LEXMARK INTERNATIONAL INC	NETAPP INC	PRUDENTIAL FINANCIAL INC
LIBERTY GLOBAL INC	NEWS CORP	PSYCHIATRIC SOLUTIONS INC
LIBERTY MUTUAL GROUP INC	NII HOLDINGS INC	PUBLIC STORAGE INC
LIMITED BRANDS INC	NIKE INC	PUBLIX SUPER MARKETS INC
LINCARE HOLDINGS INC	NOBLE CORPORATION	QUALCOMM INC
LINCOLN NATIONAL CORPORATION	NORTHROP GRUMMAN CORP	QUANTA SERVICES INC
LKQ CORP	NRG ENERGY INC	QUEST DIAGNOSTICS INC
LOCKHEED MARTIN CORP	OCCIDENTAL PETROLEUM CORP	QUIKSILVER INC
LODGIAN INC	OCEANEERING INTERNATIONAL INC	R R DONNELLEY & SONS CO
LOEWS CORPORATION		RALCORP HOLDINGS INC

RAYTHEON CO	SUN HEALTHCARE GROUP	VIACOM INC
REGIS CORPORATION	SUNGARD DATA SYSTEMS INC	VICTORIAS SECRET
RENT-A-CENTER INC	SUNOCO INC	VISA INC
RES CARE INC	SUNRISE SENIOR LIVING	VOLT INFORMATION SCIENCES INC
RITE AID CORPORATION	SUPERVALU INC	W R BERKLEY CORPORATION
RITZ-CARLTON HOTEL COMPANY LLC (THE)	SYKES ENTERPRISES INC	WABTEC CORP
ROBERT HALF INTERNATIONAL INC	SYMANTEC CORP	WALGREEN CO
ROSS STORES INC	SYNOPSYS INC	WAL-MART STORES INC
ROYAL CARIBBEAN CRUISES LTD	SYNTEL INC	WALT DISNEY COMPANY (THE)
RRI ENERGY INC	SYSCO CORP	WASTE MANAGEMENT INC
SABRE HOLDINGS CORP	TARGET CORPORATION	WATERS CORP
SAFECO INSURANCE COMPANY OF AMERICA	TBC CORPORATION	WATSON PHARMACEUTICALS INC
SAFEWAY INC	TEAM INC	WATSON WYATT WORLDWIDE INC
SAIC INC	TECH DATA CORP	WEATHERFORD INTERNATIONAL LTD
SAM'S CLUB	TEKTRONIX INC	WEIGHT WATCHERS INTERNATIONAL INC
SAPIENT CORPORATION	TELEDYNE TECHNOLOGIES INCORPORATED	WELLPOINT INC
SARA LEE CORP	TELEPHONE AND DATA SYSTEMS INC (TDS)	WELLS FARGO & CO
SAS INSTITUTE INC	TELETECH HOLDINGS INC	WENDY'S/ARBY'S GROUP INC
SCANA CORPORATION	TESORO CORP	WEST CORPORATION
SCHERING-PLOUGH CORP	THERMO FISHER SCIENTIFIC INC	WEST PHARMACEUTICAL SERVICES INC
SCHLUMBERGER LIMITED	TIFFANY & CO	WESTERN DIGITAL CORP
SCIENTIFIC GAMES CORPORATION	TIME WARNER INC	WHOLE FOODS MARKET INC
SCOTTS MIRACLE GROW CO	TJX COMPANIES INC (THE)	WILLIAMS COMPANIES INC (THE)
SEACOR HOLDINGS INC	T-MOBILE USA	WW GRAINGER INC
SELECT MEDICAL	TOTAL SYSTEM SERVICES INC (TSYS)	WYETH
SEMPRA ENERGY	TOWERS PERRIN	WYNDHAM WORLDWIDE
SENSIENT TECHNOLOGIES CORPORATION	TRANSOCEAN INC	WYNN RESORTS LIMITED
SHAW GROUP INC (THE)	TRAVELERS COMPANIES INC (THE)	XEROX CORP
SHELL OIL CO	TREEHOUSE FOODS INC	YAHOO! INC
SHERWIN WILLIAMS COMPANY (THE)	TW TELECOM INC	YUM! BRANDS INC
SIGMA-ALDRICH CORP	TYSON FOODS INC	ZIMMER HOLDINGS INC
SISTERS OF MERCY HEALTH SYSTEMS	UNITED NATURAL FOODS INC	
SMITH INTERNATIONAL INC	UNITED PARCEL SERVICE INC (UPS)	**Training**
SMITHFIELD FOODS INC	UNITED STATES CELLULAR CORP	3M COMPANY
SOUTHERN CALIFORNIA EDISON COMPANY	UNITED TECHNOLOGIES CORPORATION	7-ELEVEN INC
SOUTHERN COMPANY (THE)	UNITEDHEALTH GROUP INC	AARON'S INC
SOUTHWEST AIRLINES CO	UNIVERSAL HEALTH SERVICES INC	ABBOTT LABORATORIES
SRA INTERNATIONAL INC	UNIVISION COMMUNICATIONS INC	ABM INDUSTRIES INC
ST JUDE MEDICAL INC	URS CORPORATION	ACADEMY SPORTS & OUTDOORS LTD
STAPLES INC	USAA	ACCENTURE LTD
STARTEK INC	VALERO ENERGY CORP	ACTIVISION BLIZZARD INC
STARWOOD HOTELS & RESORTS WORLDWIDE INC	VALSPAR CORPORATION (THE)	ACXIOM CORP
STERIS CORP	VARIAN MEDICAL SYSTEMS INC	ADC TELECOMMUNICATIONS INC
STIFEL FINANCIAL CORP	VCA ANTECH INC	ADESA INC
STRYKER CORP	VERISIGN INC	ADOBE SYSTEMS INC
	VERIZON COMMUNICATIONS	ADVANCE AUTO PARTS INC
		ADVANCED MICRO DEVICES INC

(AMD)	BEBE STORES INC	COMPANY LLC
AECOM TECHNOLOGY CORPORATION	BECHTEL GROUP INC	CHICO'S FAS INC
AES CORPORATION (THE)	BECKMAN COULTER INC	CHIPOTLE MEXICAN GRILL INC
AETNA INC	BECTON DICKINSON & CO	CHRISTOPHER & BANKS CORP
AFFILIATED COMPUTER SERVICES INC	BED BATH & BEYOND INC	CHS INC
AFLAC INC	BENCHMARK ELECTRONICS INC	CHUBB CORPORATION (THE)
AGILENT TECHNOLOGIES INC	BERKSHIRE HATHAWAY INC	CIBER INC
AIR PRODUCTS & CHEMICALS INC	BEST BUY CO INC	CIGNA CORP
ALLERGAN INC	BIO RAD LABORATORIES INC	CINTAS CORP
ALLIANCE DATA SYSTEMS CORPORATION	BJ'S WHOLESALE CLUB INC	CISCO SYSTEMS INC
ALLSTATE CORPORATION (THE)	BLACK & DECKER CORP	CLUBCORP INC
ALTRIA GROUP INC	BLACKROCK INC	COACH INC
AMAZON.COM INC	BLOOMBERG LP	COCA-COLA COMPANY (THE)
AMEDISYS INC	BOEING COMPANY (THE)	COCA-COLA ENTERPRISES INC
AMERICAN ELECTRIC POWER COMPANY INC (AEP)	BOOZ ALLEN HAMILTON	COGNIZANT TECHNOLOGY SOLUTIONS CORP
AMERICAN POWER CONVERSION (APC)	BOSTON SCIENTIFIC CORP	COLDWATER CREEK INC
	BRINKER INTERNATIONAL INC	COLGATE PALMOLIVE CO
AMERISOURCEBERGEN CORP	BRINKS COMPANY (THE)	COMCAST CORP
AMGEN INC	BROADCOM CORP	COMMUNITY HEALTH SYSTEMS INC
ANADARKO PETROLEUM CORPORATION	BROWN & BROWN INC	CONAGRA FOODS INC
	BUCKLE INC (THE)	CONOCOPHILLIPS COMPANY
ANALOG DEVICES INC	BUCYRUS INTERNATIONAL INC	CONSOL ENERGY INC
ANNTAYLOR STORES CORP	BUFFALO WILD WINGS INC	CONSOLIDATED EDISON INC
APACHE CORP	BUNGE LTD	CONTAINER STORE (THE)
APOLLO GROUP INC	BURGER KING HOLDINGS INC	CONVERGYS CORPORATION
APPLE INC	CABELA'S INC	COOPER COMPANIES INC
ARAMARK CORPORATION	CABLEVISION SYSTEMS CORP	COSTCO WHOLESALE CORP
ARCHER DANIELS MIDLAND CO	CACI INTERNATIONAL INC	COVANCE INC
ARROW ELECTRONICS INC	CAMERON INTERNATIONAL CORPORATION	COVENTRY HEALTH CARE INC
ARTHUR J GALLAGHER & CO		COX COMMUNICATIONS INC
ASCENSION HEALTH	CAPITAL SENIOR LIVING CORP	CR BARD INC
AT&T INC	CARDINAL HEALTH INC	CRACKER BARREL OLD COUNTRY STORE INC
AUTOMATIC DATA PROCESSING INC	CARGILL INC	
	CARMAX GROUP	CTS CORP
AUTOZONE INC	CARNIVAL CORPORATION	CUBIC CORP
AVERY DENNISON CORP	CASH AMERICA INTERNATIONAL INC	CUMMINS INC
AVIS BUDGET GROUP INC		CVS CAREMARK CORPORATION
AVNET INC	CATERPILLAR INC	DANAHER CORP
AVON PRODUCTS INC	CATHOLIC HEALTH INITIATIVES	DARDEN RESTAURANTS INC
AXA FINANCIAL INC	CDW CORPORATION	DAVITA INC
BAKER HUGHES INC	CELGENE CORP	DEAN FOODS CO
BALTIMORE GAS AND ELECTRIC COMPANY	CELLCO PARTNERSHIP (VERIZON WIRELESS)	DEERE & CO
		DELOITTE & TOUCHE USA LLP
BANK OF AMERICA CORP	CEPHALON INC	DELOITTE CONSULTING LLP
BARNES & NOBLE INC	CH ROBINSON WORLDWIDE INC	DENNY'S CORPORATION
BASS PRO SHOPS INC	CH2M HILL COMPANIES LTD	DEVON ENERGY CORPORATION
BAXTER INTERNATIONAL INC	CHARLOTTE RUSSE HOLDING	DEVRY INC
BDO SEIDMAN LLP	CHARMING SHOPPES INC	DIAMOND OFFSHORE DRILLING INC
	CHEMED CORPORATION	DICK'S SPORTING GOODS INC
	CHEVRON CORPORATION	DIEBOLD INC
	CHEVRON PHILLIPS CHEMICAL	

DINEEQUITY INC	GAMESTOP CORP	INGRAM MICRO INC
DIRECTV GROUP INC (THE)	GENENTECH INC	INTEL CORP
DOLE FOOD COMPANY INC	GENERAL CABLE CORP	INTERNATIONAL BUSINESS MACHINES CORP (IBM)
DOLLAR GENERAL CORPORATION	GENERAL DYNAMICS CORP	INTUIT INC
DOLLAR THRIFTY AUTOMOTIVE GROUP INC	GENERAL ELECTRIC CO (GE)	INVENTIV HEALTH INC
DRESS BARN INC (THE)	GENERAL MILLS INC	J C PENNEY COMPANY INC
DTE ENERGY COMPANY	GENESCO INC	JABIL CIRCUIT INC
DUKE ENERGY CORP	GENWORTH FINANCIAL INC	JACK IN THE BOX INC
DYCOM INDUSTRIES INC	GEO GROUP INC	JACOBS ENGINEERING GROUP INC
E I DU PONT DE NEMOURS & CO (DUPONT)	GEORGIA GULF CORPORATION	JETBLUE AIRWAYS CORPORATION
EATON CORP	GILEAD SCIENCES INC	JM SMUCKER CO
EBAY INC	GLOBAL HYATT CORPORATION	JOHNSON & JOHNSON
EDISON INTERNATIONAL	GLOBAL PAYMENTS INC	JOHNSON CONTROLS INC
ELECTRONIC ARTS INC	GOLDMAN SACHS GROUP INC	JP MORGAN CHASE & CO INC
ELI LILLY & COMPANY	GOOGLE INC	JUNIPER NETWORKS INC
EMBARQ CORP	GRANT THORNTON LLP	KAISER PERMANENTE
EMC CORP	GUESS? INC	KEANE INC
EMERITUS CORP	HALLIBURTON COMPANY	KELLOGG CO
EMERSON ELECTRIC CO	HARRAH'S ENTERTAINMENT INC	KELLY SERVICES INC
ENTERGY CORP	HARRIS CORPORATION	KENDLE INTERNATIONAL INC
ENTERPRISE PRODUCTS PARTNERS LP	HARTFORD FINANCIAL SERVICES GROUP INC (THE)	KIMBERLY-CLARK CORP
ENTERPRISE RENT-A-CAR	HAWAIIAN ELECTRIC INDUSTRIES INC	KINDRED HEALTHCARE INC
ERNST & YOUNG LLP	HCA INC	KOCH INDUSTRIES INC
ESTEE LAUDER COMPANIES INC (THE)	HE BUTT GROCERY COMPANY (HEB)	KOHL'S CORP
EXELON CORPORATION	HEALTH CARE SERVICE CORPORATION	KPMG LLP
EXPERIAN AMERICAS	HEALTH FITNESS CORP	KRAFT FOODS INC
EXPRESS SCRIPTS INC	HEALTH MANAGEMENT ASSOCIATES INC	KROGER CO (THE)
EXXON MOBIL CORPORATION (EXXONMOBIL)	HEALTH NET INC	L-3 COMMUNICATIONS HOLDINGS INC
EXXONMOBIL CHEMICAL	HEALTHWAYS INC	LABORATORY CORP OF AMERICA HOLDINGS
FAMILY DOLLAR STORES INC	HELMERICH & PAYNE INC	LAS VEGAS SANDS CORP (THE VENETIAN)
FEDEX CORPORATION	HENRY SCHEIN INC	LEVEL 3 COMMUNICATIONS INC
FINISH LINE INC (THE)	HERTZ GLOBAL HOLDINGS INC	LEXMARK INTERNATIONAL INC
FIRST ADVANTAGE CORPORATION	HESS CORPORATION	LIBERTY GLOBAL INC
FIRST DATA CORP	HEWITT ASSOCIATES	LIBERTY MUTUAL GROUP INC
FIRSTENERGY CORP	HIBBETT SPORTS INC	LIMITED BRANDS INC
FLUOR CORP	HILTON HOTELS CORP	LINCARE HOLDINGS INC
FOREST LABORATORIES INC	HOME DEPOT INC	LINCOLN NATIONAL CORPORATION
FORTUNE BRANDS INC	HONEYWELL INTERNATIONAL INC	LKQ CORP
FOSSIL INC	HUMANA INC	LOCKHEED MARTIN CORP
FOSTER WHEELER AG	IAC/INTERACTIVECORP	LODGIAN INC
FOX ENTERTAINMENT GROUP INC	IBM GLOBAL SERVICES	LOEWS CORPORATION
FPL GROUP INC	ICT GROUP INC	LOWE'S COMPANIES INC
FRED'S INC	IDEXX LABORATORIES INC	MACY'S INC
FRONTIER COMMUNICATIONS CORPORATION	IGATE CORPORATION	MANOR CARE INC
	IMS HEALTH INC	MANPOWER INC
FTI CONSULTING INC	INFOGROUP INC	MARRIOTT INTERNATIONAL INC
		MARS INC

MARSH & MCLENNAN COMPANIES INC	O'REILLY AUTOMOTIVE INC	LLC (THE)
MARY KAY INC	OSHKOSH CORPORATION	ROBERT HALF INTERNATIONAL INC
MASSEY ENERGY COMPANY	OSI RESTAURANT PARTNERS LLC	ROSS STORES INC
MATTEL INC	OWENS & MINOR INC	ROYAL CARIBBEAN CRUISES LTD
MAXIM INTEGRATED PRODUCTS INC	PANTRY INC (THE)	RRI ENERGY INC
MAYO FOUNDATION FOR MEDICAL EDUCATION AND RESEARCH	PARAMETRIC TECHNOLOGY CORP	SABRE HOLDINGS CORP
	PAREXEL INTERNATIONAL CORP	SAFECO INSURANCE COMPANY OF AMERICA
MCAFEE INC	PARSONS BRINCKERHOFF INC	SAFEWAY INC
MCDERMOTT INTERNATIONAL INC	PATTERSON COMPANIES INC	SAIC INC
MCDONALD'S CORP	PATTERSON-UTI ENERGY INC	SAM'S CLUB
MCKESSON CORPORATION	PAYCHEX INC	SAPIENT CORPORATION
MCKINSEY & COMPANY INC	PEABODY ENERGY CORP	SARA LEE CORP
MEDCO HEALTH SOLUTIONS	PEPSI BOTTLING GROUP INC	SAS INSTITUTE INC
MEDTRONIC INC	PEPSICO INC	SCANA CORPORATION
MEIJER INC	PEROT SYSTEMS CORP	SCHERING-PLOUGH CORP
MEN'S WEARHOUSE INC (THE)	PERRIGO CO	SCHLUMBERGER LIMITED
MERCER INC	PETCO ANIMAL SUPPLIES INC	SCIENTIFIC GAMES CORPORATION
MERCK & CO INC	PETSMART INC	SCOTTS MIRACLE GROW CO
METHODIST HEALTH CARE SYSTEM	PFIZER INC	SEACOR HOLDINGS INC
	PG&E CORPORATION	SELECT MEDICAL
METLIFE INC	PHARMACEUTICAL PRODUCT DEVELOPMENT INC	SEMPRA ENERGY
MGM MIRAGE	PITNEY BOWES INC	SENSIENT TECHNOLOGIES CORPORATION
MICROCHIP TECHNOLOGY INC	PLEXUS CORP	
MICRON TECHNOLOGY INC	POLO RALPH LAUREN CORP	SHAW GROUP INC (THE)
MICROSOFT CORP	PRAXAIR INC	SHELL OIL CO
MIDAMERICAN ENERGY HOLDINGS CO	PRECISION CASTPARTS CORP	SHERWIN WILLIAMS COMPANY (THE)
	PRICESMART INC	SIGMA-ALDRICH CORP
MILLIPORE CORP	PRICEWATERHOUSECOOPERS	SISTERS OF MERCY HEALTH SYSTEMS
MONRO MUFFLER BRAKE INC	PRIDE INTERNATIONAL INC	
MONSANTO CO	PRINCIPAL FINANCIAL GROUP (THE)	SMITH INTERNATIONAL INC
MURPHY OIL CORPORATION		SMITHFIELD FOODS INC
MYLAN INC	PROCTER & GAMBLE CO	SOUTHERN CALIFORNIA EDISON COMPANY
NATIONAL OILWELL VARCO INC	PROGRESSIVE CORPORATION (THE)	
NETAPP INC		SOUTHERN COMPANY (THE)
NEWS CORP	PRUDENTIAL FINANCIAL INC	SOUTHWEST AIRLINES CO
NII HOLDINGS INC	PSYCHIATRIC SOLUTIONS INC	SRA INTERNATIONAL INC
NIKE INC	PUBLIC STORAGE INC	ST JUDE MEDICAL INC
NOBLE CORPORATION	PUBLIX SUPER MARKETS INC	STAPLES INC
NORTHROP GRUMMAN CORP	QUALCOMM INC	STARTEK INC
NRG ENERGY INC	QUANTA SERVICES INC	STARWOOD HOTELS & RESORTS WORLDWIDE INC
OCCIDENTAL PETROLEUM CORP	QUEST DIAGNOSTICS INC	
OCEANEERING INTERNATIONAL INC	QUIKSILVER INC	STERIS CORP
	R R DONNELLEY & SONS CO	STIFEL FINANCIAL CORP
ODYSSEY HEALTHCARE INC	RALCORP HOLDINGS INC	STRYKER CORP
OFFICE DEPOT INC	RAYTHEON CO	SUN HEALTHCARE GROUP
OIL STATES INTERNATIONAL INC	REGIS CORPORATION	SUNGARD DATA SYSTEMS INC
OMNICARE INC	RENT-A-CENTER INC	SUNOCO INC
OMNICOM GROUP INC	RES CARE INC	SUNRISE SENIOR LIVING
ORACLE CORP	RITE AID CORPORATION	SUPERVALU INC
	RITZ-CARLTON HOTEL COMPANY	

SYKES ENTERPRISES INC

SYMANTEC CORP

SYNOPSYS INC

SYNTEL INC

SYSCO CORP

TARGET CORPORATION

TBC CORPORATION

TEAM INC

TECH DATA CORP

TEKTRONIX INC

TELEDYNE TECHNOLOGIES INCORPORATED

TELEPHONE AND DATA SYSTEMS INC (TDS)

TELETECH HOLDINGS INC

TESORO CORP

THERMO FISHER SCIENTIFIC INC

TIFFANY & CO

TIME WARNER INC

TJX COMPANIES INC (THE)

T-MOBILE USA

TOTAL SYSTEM SERVICES INC (TSYS)

TOWERS PERRIN

TRANSOCEAN INC

TRAVELERS COMPANIES INC (THE)

TREEHOUSE FOODS INC

TW TELECOM INC

TYSON FOODS INC

UNITED NATURAL FOODS INC

UNITED PARCEL SERVICE INC (UPS)

UNITED STATES CELLULAR CORP

UNITED TECHNOLOGIES CORPORATION

UNITEDHEALTH GROUP INC

UNIVERSAL HEALTH SERVICES INC

UNIVISION COMMUNICATIONS INC

URS CORPORATION

USAA

VALERO ENERGY CORP

VALSPAR CORPORATION (THE)

VARIAN MEDICAL SYSTEMS INC

VCA ANTECH INC

VERISIGN INC

VERIZON COMMUNICATIONS

VIACOM INC

VICTORIAS SECRET

VISA INC

VOLT INFORMATION SCIENCES INC

W R BERKLEY CORPORATION

WABTEC CORP

WALGREEN CO

WAL-MART STORES INC

WALT DISNEY COMPANY (THE)

WASTE MANAGEMENT INC

WATERS CORP

WATSON PHARMACEUTICALS INC

WATSON WYATT WORLDWIDE INC

WEATHERFORD INTERNATIONAL LTD

WEIGHT WATCHERS INTERNATIONAL INC

WELLPOINT INC

WELLS FARGO & CO

WENDY'S/ARBY'S GROUP INC

WEST CORPORATION

WEST PHARMACEUTICAL SERVICES INC

WESTERN DIGITAL CORP

WHOLE FOODS MARKET INC

WILLIAMS COMPANIES INC (THE)

WW GRAINGER INC

WYETH

WYNDHAM WORLDWIDE

WYNN RESORTS LIMITED

XEROX CORP

YAHOO! INC

YUM! BRANDS INC

ZIMMER HOLDINGS INC

Sales/Marketing

Advertising Professionals
3M COMPANY
7-ELEVEN INC
AARON'S INC
ABBOTT LABORATORIES
ABM INDUSTRIES INC
ACADEMY SPORTS & OUTDOORS LTD
ACCENTURE LTD
ACTIVISION BLIZZARD INC
ADC TELECOMMUNICATIONS INC
ADOBE SYSTEMS INC
ADVANCE AUTO PARTS INC
ADVANCED MICRO DEVICES INC (AMD)
AES CORPORATION (THE)
AETNA INC
AFLAC INC
AGILENT TECHNOLOGIES INC

ALLERGAN INC

ALLIANCE DATA SYSTEMS CORPORATION

ALLSTATE CORPORATION (THE)

ALTRIA GROUP INC

AMAZON.COM INC

AMERICAN ELECTRIC POWER COMPANY INC (AEP)

AMERICAN POWER CONVERSION (APC)

AMERISOURCEBERGEN CORP

ANALOG DEVICES INC

ANNTAYLOR STORES CORP

APOLLO GROUP INC

APPLE INC

ARAMARK CORPORATION

ARCHER DANIELS MIDLAND CO

ARROW ELECTRONICS INC

ARTHUR J GALLAGHER & CO

ASCENSION HEALTH

AT&T INC

AUTOMATIC DATA PROCESSING INC

AUTOZONE INC

AVERY DENNISON CORP

AVIS BUDGET GROUP INC

AVON PRODUCTS INC

AXA FINANCIAL INC

BALTIMORE GAS AND ELECTRIC COMPANY

BANK OF AMERICA CORP

BARNES & NOBLE INC

BASS PRO SHOPS INC

BAXTER INTERNATIONAL INC

BDO SEIDMAN LLP

BEBE STORES INC

BECKMAN COULTER INC

BECTON DICKINSON & CO

BED BATH & BEYOND INC

BENCHMARK ELECTRONICS INC

BERKSHIRE HATHAWAY INC

BEST BUY CO INC

BIO RAD LABORATORIES INC

BJ'S WHOLESALE CLUB INC

BLACK & DECKER CORP

BLOOMBERG LP

BOEING COMPANY (THE)

BOOZ ALLEN HAMILTON

BOSTON SCIENTIFIC CORP

BRINKER INTERNATIONAL INC

BRINKS COMPANY (THE)

BROADCOM CORP	CVS CAREMARK CORPORATION	CORPORATION
BROWN & BROWN INC	DANAHER CORP	GAMESTOP CORP
BUCKLE INC (THE)	DARDEN RESTAURANTS INC	GENENTECH INC
BUFFALO WILD WINGS INC	DEAN FOODS CO	GENERAL DYNAMICS CORP
BURGER KING HOLDINGS INC	DEERE & CO	GENERAL ELECTRIC CO (GE)
CABELA'S INC	DELOITTE & TOUCHE USA LLP	GENERAL MILLS INC
CABLEVISION SYSTEMS CORP	DELOITTE CONSULTING LLP	GENESCO INC
CAPITAL SENIOR LIVING CORP	DENNY'S CORPORATION	GENWORTH FINANCIAL INC
CARDINAL HEALTH INC	DEVRY INC	GLOBAL HYATT CORPORATION
CARGILL INC	DICK'S SPORTING GOODS INC	GLOBAL PAYMENTS INC
CARMAX GROUP	DIEBOLD INC	GOLDMAN SACHS GROUP INC
CARNIVAL CORPORATION	DINEEQUITY INC	GOOGLE INC
CASH AMERICA INTERNATIONAL INC	DIRECTV GROUP INC (THE)	GRANT THORNTON LLP
CATERPILLAR INC	DOLE FOOD COMPANY INC	GUESS? INC
CATHOLIC HEALTH INITIATIVES	DOLLAR GENERAL CORPORATION	HALLIBURTON COMPANY
CDW CORPORATION	DOLLAR THRIFTY AUTOMOTIVE GROUP INC	HARRAH'S ENTERTAINMENT INC
CELLCO PARTNERSHIP (VERIZON WIRELESS)	DRESS BARN INC (THE)	HARRIS CORPORATION
CH ROBINSON WORLDWIDE INC	DTE ENERGY COMPANY	HARTFORD FINANCIAL SERVICES GROUP INC (THE)
CHARLOTTE RUSSE HOLDING	DUKE ENERGY CORP	HAWAIIAN ELECTRIC INDUSTRIES INC
CHARMING SHOPPES INC	EATON CORP	HCA INC
CHEVRON CORPORATION	EBAY INC	HE BUTT GROCERY COMPANY (HEB)
CHICO'S FAS INC	EDISON INTERNATIONAL	HEALTH FITNESS CORP
CHIPOTLE MEXICAN GRILL INC	ELECTRONIC ARTS INC	HEALTH MANAGEMENT ASSOCIATES INC
CHRISTOPHER & BANKS CORP	ELI LILLY & COMPANY	HEALTH NET INC
CHUBB CORPORATION (THE)	EMBARQ CORP	HEALTHWAYS INC
CIGNA CORP	EMC CORP	HENRY SCHEIN INC
CINTAS CORP	EMERITUS CORP	HERTZ GLOBAL HOLDINGS INC
CISCO SYSTEMS INC	EMERSON ELECTRIC CO	HEWITT ASSOCIATES
COACH INC	ENTERGY CORP	HIBBETT SPORTS INC
COCA-COLA COMPANY (THE)	ENTERPRISE RENT-A-CAR	HILTON HOTELS CORP
COCA-COLA ENTERPRISES INC	ERNST & YOUNG LLP	HOME DEPOT INC
COLDWATER CREEK INC	ESTEE LAUDER COMPANIES INC (THE)	HONEYWELL INTERNATIONAL INC
COLGATE PALMOLIVE CO	EXELON CORPORATION	HUMANA INC
COMCAST CORP	EXPERIAN AMERICAS	IAC/INTERACTIVECORP
COMMUNITY HEALTH SYSTEMS INC	EXPRESS SCRIPTS INC	IBM GLOBAL SERVICES
CONAGRA FOODS INC	EXXON MOBIL CORPORATION (EXXONMOBIL)	IMS HEALTH INC
CONOCOPHILLIPS COMPANY	FAMILY DOLLAR STORES INC	INFOGROUP INC
CONSOLIDATED EDISON INC	FEDEX CORPORATION	INGRAM MICRO INC
CONTAINER STORE (THE)	FINISH LINE INC (THE)	INTEL CORP
CONVERGYS CORPORATION	FIRST DATA CORP	INTERNATIONAL BUSINESS MACHINES CORP (IBM)
COOPER COMPANIES INC	FIRSTENERGY CORP	INTUIT INC
COSTCO WHOLESALE CORP	FLUOR CORP	J C PENNEY COMPANY INC
COVANCE INC	FORTUNE BRANDS INC	JABIL CIRCUIT INC
COVENTRY HEALTH CARE INC	FOSSIL INC	JACK IN THE BOX INC
COX COMMUNICATIONS INC	FOX ENTERTAINMENT GROUP INC	JETBLUE AIRWAYS CORPORATION
CR BARD INC	FPL GROUP INC	JM SMUCKER CO
CRACKER BARREL OLD COUNTRY STORE INC	FRED'S INC	
CUMMINS INC	FRONTIER COMMUNICATIONS	

JOHNSON & JOHNSON	MERCK & CO INC	RENT-A-CENTER INC
JOHNSON CONTROLS INC	METHODIST HEALTH CARE SYSTEM	RES CARE INC
JP MORGAN CHASE & CO INC	METLIFE INC	RITE AID CORPORATION
JUNIPER NETWORKS INC	MGM MIRAGE	RITZ-CARLTON HOTEL COMPANY LLC (THE)
KAISER PERMANENTE	MICROCHIP TECHNOLOGY INC	ROBERT HALF INTERNATIONAL INC
KEANE INC	MICRON TECHNOLOGY INC	ROSS STORES INC
KELLOGG CO	MICROSOFT CORP	ROYAL CARIBBEAN CRUISES LTD
KELLY SERVICES INC	MILLIPORE CORP	RRI ENERGY INC
KIMBERLY-CLARK CORP	MONRO MUFFLER BRAKE INC	SAFECO INSURANCE COMPANY OF AMERICA
KINDRED HEALTHCARE INC	MONSANTO CO	SAFEWAY INC
KOHL'S CORP	NETAPP INC	SAM'S CLUB
KPMG LLP	NEWS CORP	SARA LEE CORP
KRAFT FOODS INC	NII HOLDINGS INC	SAS INSTITUTE INC
KROGER CO (THE)	NIKE INC	SCANA CORPORATION
L-3 COMMUNICATIONS HOLDINGS INC	NORTHROP GRUMMAN CORP	SCHERING-PLOUGH CORP
LAS VEGAS SANDS CORP (THE VENETIAN)	OFFICE DEPOT INC	SCHLUMBERGER LIMITED
LEVEL 3 COMMUNICATIONS INC	OMNICARE INC	SCIENTIFIC GAMES CORPORATION
LEXMARK INTERNATIONAL INC	OMNICOM GROUP INC	SCOTTS MIRACLE GROW CO
LIBERTY GLOBAL INC	ORACLE CORP	SELECT MEDICAL
LIBERTY MUTUAL GROUP INC	O'REILLY AUTOMOTIVE INC	SEMPRA ENERGY
LIMITED BRANDS INC	OSHKOSH CORPORATION	SHELL OIL CO
LINCOLN NATIONAL CORPORATION	OSI RESTAURANT PARTNERS LLC	SHERWIN WILLIAMS COMPANY (THE)
LOCKHEED MARTIN CORP	OWENS & MINOR INC	SISTERS OF MERCY HEALTH SYSTEMS
LODGIAN INC	PANTRY INC (THE)	SMITH INTERNATIONAL INC
LOEWS CORPORATION	PARAMETRIC TECHNOLOGY CORP	SMITHFIELD FOODS INC
LOWE'S COMPANIES INC	PATTERSON COMPANIES INC	SOUTHERN COMPANY (THE)
MACY'S INC	PAYCHEX INC	SOUTHWEST AIRLINES CO
MANOR CARE INC	PEPSI BOTTLING GROUP INC	SRA INTERNATIONAL INC
MANPOWER INC	PEPSICO INC	ST JUDE MEDICAL INC
MARRIOTT INTERNATIONAL INC	PEROT SYSTEMS CORP	STAPLES INC
MARS INC	PETCO ANIMAL SUPPLIES INC	STARWOOD HOTELS & RESORTS WORLDWIDE INC
MARSH & MCLENNAN COMPANIES INC	PETSMART INC	STERIS CORP
MARY KAY INC	PFIZER INC	STRYKER CORP
MATTEL INC	PG&E CORPORATION	SUN HEALTHCARE GROUP
MAXIM INTEGRATED PRODUCTS INC	PITNEY BOWES INC	SUNGARD DATA SYSTEMS INC
MAYO FOUNDATION FOR MEDICAL EDUCATION AND RESEARCH	PLEXUS CORP	SUNRISE SENIOR LIVING
MCAFEE INC	POLO RALPH LAUREN CORP	SUPERVALU INC
MCDERMOTT INTERNATIONAL INC	PRICESMART INC	SYMANTEC CORP
MCDONALD'S CORP	PRICEWATERHOUSECOOPERS	SYNOPSYS INC
MCKESSON CORPORATION	PRINCIPAL FINANCIAL GROUP (THE)	SYSCO CORP
MCKINSEY & COMPANY INC	PROCTER & GAMBLE CO	TARGET CORPORATION
MEDCO HEALTH SOLUTIONS	PROGRESSIVE CORPORATION (THE)	TBC CORPORATION
MEDTRONIC INC	PRUDENTIAL FINANCIAL INC	TECH DATA CORP
MEIJER INC	PUBLIX SUPER MARKETS INC	TEKTRONIX INC
MEN'S WEARHOUSE INC (THE)	QUALCOMM INC	TELEDYNE TECHNOLOGIES INCORPORATED
MERCER INC	QUIKSILVER INC	
	RAYTHEON CO	
	REGIS CORPORATION	

TELEPHONE AND DATA SYSTEMS INC (TDS)

TELETECH HOLDINGS INC

TIFFANY & CO

TIME WARNER INC

TJX COMPANIES INC (THE)

T-MOBILE USA

TOTAL SYSTEM SERVICES INC (TSYS)

TOWERS PERRIN

TRAVELERS COMPANIES INC (THE)

TW TELECOM INC

TYSON FOODS INC

UNITED PARCEL SERVICE INC (UPS)

UNITED STATES CELLULAR CORP

UNITED TECHNOLOGIES CORPORATION

UNITEDHEALTH GROUP INC

UNIVISION COMMUNICATIONS INC

USAA

VALERO ENERGY CORP

VALSPAR CORPORATION (THE)

VARIAN MEDICAL SYSTEMS INC

VERISIGN INC

VERIZON COMMUNICATIONS

VIACOM INC

VICTORIAS SECRET

VISA INC

VOLT INFORMATION SCIENCES INC

W R BERKLEY CORPORATION

WALGREEN CO

WAL-MART STORES INC

WALT DISNEY COMPANY (THE)

WASTE MANAGEMENT INC

WATERS CORP

WATSON WYATT WORLDWIDE INC

WEIGHT WATCHERS INTERNATIONAL INC

WELLPOINT INC

WELLS FARGO & CO

WENDY'S/ARBY'S GROUP INC

WEST PHARMACEUTICAL SERVICES INC

WESTERN DIGITAL CORP

WHOLE FOODS MARKET INC

WW GRAINGER INC

WYETH

WYNDHAM WORLDWIDE

WYNN RESORTS LIMITED

XEROX CORP

YAHOO! INC

YUM! BRANDS INC

ZIMMER HOLDINGS INC

Commercial/Industrial

3M COMPANY

ABBOTT LABORATORIES

ABM INDUSTRIES INC

ACCENTURE LTD

ACXIOM CORP

ADC TELECOMMUNICATIONS INC

ADESA INC

ADOBE SYSTEMS INC

ADVANCE AUTO PARTS INC

ADVANCED MICRO DEVICES INC (AMD)

AECOM TECHNOLOGY CORPORATION

AES CORPORATION (THE)

AETNA INC

AFFILIATED COMPUTER SERVICES INC

AFLAC INC

AGILENT TECHNOLOGIES INC

AIR PRODUCTS & CHEMICALS INC

ALLERGAN INC

ALLIANCE DATA SYSTEMS CORPORATION

ALLSTATE CORPORATION (THE)

ALTRIA GROUP INC

AMEDISYS INC

AMERICAN ELECTRIC POWER COMPANY INC (AEP)

AMERICAN POWER CONVERSION (APC)

AMERISOURCEBERGEN CORP

AMGEN INC

ANALOG DEVICES INC

APPLE INC

ARAMARK CORPORATION

ARCHER DANIELS MIDLAND CO

ARROW ELECTRONICS INC

ARTHUR J GALLAGHER & CO

AT&T INC

AUTOMATIC DATA PROCESSING INC

AUTOZONE INC

AVERY DENNISON CORP

AVIS BUDGET GROUP INC

AVNET INC

AXA FINANCIAL INC

BAKER HUGHES INC

BALTIMORE GAS AND ELECTRIC COMPANY

BANK OF AMERICA CORP

BAXTER INTERNATIONAL INC

BDO SEIDMAN LLP

BECHTEL GROUP INC

BECKMAN COULTER INC

BECTON DICKINSON & CO

BED BATH & BEYOND INC

BENCHMARK ELECTRONICS INC

BERKSHIRE HATHAWAY INC

BEST BUY CO INC

BIO RAD LABORATORIES INC

BLACK & DECKER CORP

BLOOMBERG LP

BOEING COMPANY (THE)

BOOZ ALLEN HAMILTON

BOSTON SCIENTIFIC CORP

BRINKS COMPANY (THE)

BROADCOM CORP

BROWN & BROWN INC

BUCYRUS INTERNATIONAL INC

BUNGE LTD

CABLEVISION SYSTEMS CORP

CACI INTERNATIONAL INC

CAMERON INTERNATIONAL CORPORATION

CARDINAL HEALTH INC

CARGILL INC

CARMAX GROUP

CARNIVAL CORPORATION

CASH AMERICA INTERNATIONAL INC

CATERPILLAR INC

CDW CORPORATION

CELGENE CORP

CELLCO PARTNERSHIP (VERIZON WIRELESS)

CEPHALON INC

CH ROBINSON WORLDWIDE INC

CH2M HILL COMPANIES LTD

CHEMED CORPORATION

CHEVRON CORPORATION

CHEVRON PHILLIPS CHEMICAL COMPANY LLC

CHS INC

CHUBB CORPORATION (THE)

CIBER INC

CIGNA CORP

CINTAS CORP

CISCO SYSTEMS INC

CLUBCORP INC	(THE)	HEWITT ASSOCIATES
COACH INC	EXELON CORPORATION	HILTON HOTELS CORP
COCA-COLA COMPANY (THE)	EXPERIAN AMERICAS	HOME DEPOT INC
COCA-COLA ENTERPRISES INC	EXPRESS SCRIPTS INC	HONEYWELL INTERNATIONAL INC
COGNIZANT TECHNOLOGY SOLUTIONS CORP	EXXON MOBIL CORPORATION (EXXONMOBIL)	HUMANA INC
COLGATE PALMOLIVE CO	EXXONMOBIL CHEMICAL	IAC/INTERACTIVECORP
COMCAST CORP	FEDEX CORPORATION	IBM GLOBAL SERVICES
CONAGRA FOODS INC	FIRST ADVANTAGE CORPORATION	ICT GROUP INC
CONOCOPHILLIPS COMPANY	FIRST DATA CORP	IDEXX LABORATORIES INC
CONSOL ENERGY INC	FIRSTENERGY CORP	IGATE CORPORATION
CONSOLIDATED EDISON INC	FLUOR CORP	IMS HEALTH INC
CONTAINER STORE (THE)	FOREST LABORATORIES INC	INFOGROUP INC
CONVERGYS CORPORATION	FORTUNE BRANDS INC	INGRAM MICRO INC
COOPER COMPANIES INC	FOSSIL INC	INTEL CORP
COVANCE INC	FOSTER WHEELER AG	INTERNATIONAL BUSINESS MACHINES CORP (IBM)
COVENTRY HEALTH CARE INC	FOX ENTERTAINMENT GROUP INC	INTUIT INC
COX COMMUNICATIONS INC	FPL GROUP INC	INVENTIV HEALTH INC
CR BARD INC	FRONTIER COMMUNICATIONS CORPORATION	JABIL CIRCUIT INC
CTS CORP	FTI CONSULTING INC	JACOBS ENGINEERING GROUP INC
CUBIC CORP	GENENTECH INC	JM SMUCKER CO
CUMMINS INC	GENERAL CABLE CORP	JOHNSON & JOHNSON
DANAHER CORP	GENERAL DYNAMICS CORP	JOHNSON CONTROLS INC
DAVITA INC	GENERAL ELECTRIC CO (GE)	JP MORGAN CHASE & CO INC
DEAN FOODS CO	GENERAL MILLS INC	JUNIPER NETWORKS INC
DEERE & CO	GENESCO INC	KAISER PERMANENTE
DELOITTE & TOUCHE USA LLP	GENWORTH FINANCIAL INC	KEANE INC
DELOITTE CONSULTING LLP	GEO GROUP INC	KELLOGG CO
DIAMOND OFFSHORE DRILLING INC	GEORGIA GULF CORPORATION	KELLY SERVICES INC
DIEBOLD INC	GILEAD SCIENCES INC	KENDLE INTERNATIONAL INC
DOLE FOOD COMPANY INC	GLOBAL HYATT CORPORATION	KIMBERLY-CLARK CORP
DOLLAR THRIFTY AUTOMOTIVE GROUP INC	GLOBAL PAYMENTS INC	KOCH INDUSTRIES INC
DTE ENERGY COMPANY	GOLDMAN SACHS GROUP INC	KPMG LLP
DUKE ENERGY CORP	GOOGLE INC	KRAFT FOODS INC
DYCOM INDUSTRIES INC	GRANT THORNTON LLP	L-3 COMMUNICATIONS HOLDINGS INC
E I DU PONT DE NEMOURS & CO (DUPONT)	HALLIBURTON COMPANY	LABORATORY CORP OF AMERICA HOLDINGS
	HARRAH'S ENTERTAINMENT INC	
EATON CORP	HARRIS CORPORATION	LAS VEGAS SANDS CORP (THE VENETIAN)
EDISON INTERNATIONAL	HARTFORD FINANCIAL SERVICES GROUP INC (THE)	LEVEL 3 COMMUNICATIONS INC
ELECTRONIC ARTS INC		LEXMARK INTERNATIONAL INC
ELI LILLY & COMPANY	HAWAIIAN ELECTRIC INDUSTRIES INC	LIBERTY GLOBAL INC
EMBARQ CORP		LIBERTY MUTUAL GROUP INC
EMC CORP	HEALTH CARE SERVICE CORPORATION	LINCARE HOLDINGS INC
EMERSON ELECTRIC CO		LINCOLN NATIONAL CORPORATION
ENTERGY CORP	HEALTH FITNESS CORP	LKQ CORP
ENTERPRISE PRODUCTS PARTNERS LP	HEALTH NET INC	
	HEALTHWAYS INC	LOCKHEED MARTIN CORP
ENTERPRISE RENT-A-CAR	HELMERICH & PAYNE INC	LODGIAN INC
ERNST & YOUNG LLP	HENRY SCHEIN INC	LOEWS CORPORATION
ESTEE LAUDER COMPANIES INC	HERTZ GLOBAL HOLDINGS INC	LOWE'S COMPANIES INC

MANPOWER INC	PEABODY ENERGY CORP	SIGMA-ALDRICH CORP
MARRIOTT INTERNATIONAL INC	PEPSI BOTTLING GROUP INC	SMITH INTERNATIONAL INC
MARS INC	PEPSICO INC	SMITHFIELD FOODS INC
MARSH & MCLENNAN COMPANIES INC	PEROT SYSTEMS CORP	SOUTHERN CALIFORNIA EDISON COMPANY
MASSEY ENERGY COMPANY	PERRIGO CO	SOUTHERN COMPANY (THE)
MATTEL INC	PFIZER INC	SRA INTERNATIONAL INC
MAXIM INTEGRATED PRODUCTS INC	PG&E CORPORATION	ST JUDE MEDICAL INC
MCAFEE INC	PHARMACEUTICAL PRODUCT DEVELOPMENT INC	STAPLES INC
MCDERMOTT INTERNATIONAL INC	PITNEY BOWES INC	STARTEK INC
MCKESSON CORPORATION	PLEXUS CORP	STARWOOD HOTELS & RESORTS WORLDWIDE INC
MCKINSEY & COMPANY INC	POLO RALPH LAUREN CORP	STERIS CORP
MEDCO HEALTH SOLUTIONS	PRAXAIR INC	STRYKER CORP
MEDTRONIC INC	PRECISION CASTPARTS CORP	SUNGARD DATA SYSTEMS INC
MERCER INC	PRICEWATERHOUSECOOPERS	SUNOCO INC
MERCK & CO INC	PRIDE INTERNATIONAL INC	SYKES ENTERPRISES INC
METLIFE INC	PRINCIPAL FINANCIAL GROUP (THE)	SYMANTEC CORP
MGM MIRAGE	PROCTER & GAMBLE CO	SYNOPSYS INC
MICROCHIP TECHNOLOGY INC	PRUDENTIAL FINANCIAL INC	SYNTEL INC
MICRON TECHNOLOGY INC	QUALCOMM INC	SYSCO CORP
MICROSOFT CORP	QUANTA SERVICES INC	TBC CORPORATION
MIDAMERICAN ENERGY HOLDINGS CO	QUEST DIAGNOSTICS INC	TEAM INC
MILLIPORE CORP	QUIKSILVER INC	TECH DATA CORP
MONSANTO CO	R R DONNELLEY & SONS CO	TEKTRONIX INC
MURPHY OIL CORPORATION	RALCORP HOLDINGS INC	TELEDYNE TECHNOLOGIES INCORPORATED
MYLAN INC	RAYTHEON CO	TELEPHONE AND DATA SYSTEMS INC (TDS)
NATIONAL OILWELL VARCO INC	RITZ-CARLTON HOTEL COMPANY LLC (THE)	TELETECH HOLDINGS INC
NETAPP INC	ROBERT HALF INTERNATIONAL INC	TESORO CORP
NEWS CORP	ROYAL CARIBBEAN CRUISES LTD	THERMO FISHER SCIENTIFIC INC
NII HOLDINGS INC	RRI ENERGY INC	TIME WARNER INC
NIKE INC	SABRE HOLDINGS CORP	T-MOBILE USA
NOBLE CORPORATION	SAFECO INSURANCE COMPANY OF AMERICA	TOTAL SYSTEM SERVICES INC (TSYS)
NORTHROP GRUMMAN CORP	SAIC INC	TOWERS PERRIN
NRG ENERGY INC	SAPIENT CORPORATION	TRANSOCEAN INC
OCEANEERING INTERNATIONAL INC	SARA LEE CORP	TRAVELERS COMPANIES INC (THE)
OFFICE DEPOT INC	SAS INSTITUTE INC	TREEHOUSE FOODS INC
OIL STATES INTERNATIONAL INC	SCANA CORPORATION	TW TELECOM INC
OMNICOM GROUP INC	SCHERING-PLOUGH CORP	TYSON FOODS INC
ORACLE CORP	SCHLUMBERGER LIMITED	UNITED NATURAL FOODS INC
O'REILLY AUTOMOTIVE INC	SCIENTIFIC GAMES CORPORATION	UNITED PARCEL SERVICE INC (UPS)
OSHKOSH CORPORATION	SCOTTS MIRACLE GROW CO	
OWENS & MINOR INC	SEACOR HOLDINGS INC	UNITED STATES CELLULAR CORP
PARAMETRIC TECHNOLOGY CORP	SEMPRA ENERGY	UNITED TECHNOLOGIES CORPORATION
PAREXEL INTERNATIONAL CORP	SENSIENT TECHNOLOGIES CORPORATION	UNITEDHEALTH GROUP INC
PARSONS BRINCKERHOFF INC	SHAW GROUP INC (THE)	UNIVISION COMMUNICATIONS INC
PATTERSON COMPANIES INC	SHERWIN WILLIAMS COMPANY (THE)	URS CORPORATION
PATTERSON-UTI ENERGY INC		VALERO ENERGY CORP
PAYCHEX INC		

VALSPAR CORPORATION (THE)	AETNA INC	BENCHMARK ELECTRONICS INC
VARIAN MEDICAL SYSTEMS INC	AFFILIATED COMPUTER SERVICES INC	BERKSHIRE HATHAWAY INC
VERISIGN INC	AFLAC INC	BEST BUY CO INC
VERIZON COMMUNICATIONS	AGILENT TECHNOLOGIES INC	BIO RAD LABORATORIES INC
VIACOM INC	AIR PRODUCTS & CHEMICALS INC	BJ'S WHOLESALE CLUB INC
VISA INC	ALLERGAN INC	BLACK & DECKER CORP
VOLT INFORMATION SCIENCES INC	ALLIANCE DATA SYSTEMS CORPORATION	BLACKROCK INC
W R BERKLEY CORPORATION	ALLSTATE CORPORATION (THE)	BLOOMBERG LP
WABTEC CORP	ALTRIA GROUP INC	BOEING COMPANY (THE)
WALT DISNEY COMPANY (THE)	AMAZON.COM INC	BOOZ ALLEN HAMILTON
WASTE MANAGEMENT INC	AMEDISYS INC	BOSTON SCIENTIFIC CORP
WATERS CORP	AMERICAN ELECTRIC POWER COMPANY INC (AEP)	BRINKER INTERNATIONAL INC
WATSON PHARMACEUTICALS INC		BRINKS COMPANY (THE)
WATSON WYATT WORLDWIDE INC	AMERICAN POWER CONVERSION (APC)	BROADCOM CORP
WEATHERFORD INTERNATIONAL LTD	AMERISOURCEBERGEN CORP	BROWN & BROWN INC
	AMGEN INC	BUCKLE INC (THE)
WELLPOINT INC	ANADARKO PETROLEUM CORPORATION	BUCYRUS INTERNATIONAL INC
WELLS FARGO & CO		BUFFALO WILD WINGS INC
WEST CORPORATION	ANALOG DEVICES INC	BUNGE LTD
WEST PHARMACEUTICAL SERVICES INC	ANNTAYLOR STORES CORP	BURGER KING HOLDINGS INC
	APACHE CORP	CABELA'S INC
WESTERN DIGITAL CORP	APOLLO GROUP INC	CABLEVISION SYSTEMS CORP
WILLIAMS COMPANIES INC (THE)	APPLE INC	CACI INTERNATIONAL INC
WW GRAINGER INC	ARAMARK CORPORATION	CAMERON INTERNATIONAL CORPORATION
WYETH	ARCHER DANIELS MIDLAND CO	
WYNDHAM WORLDWIDE	ARROW ELECTRONICS INC	CAPITAL SENIOR LIVING CORP
WYNN RESORTS LIMITED	ARTHUR J GALLAGHER & CO	CARDINAL HEALTH INC
XEROX CORP	AT&T INC	CARGILL INC
YAHOO! INC	AUTOMATIC DATA PROCESSING INC	CARMAX GROUP
ZIMMER HOLDINGS INC		CARNIVAL CORPORATION
	AUTOZONE INC	CASH AMERICA INTERNATIONAL INC
	AVERY DENNISON CORP	
Marketing Professionals	AVIS BUDGET GROUP INC	CATERPILLAR INC
3M COMPANY	AVNET INC	CATHOLIC HEALTH INITIATIVES
7-ELEVEN INC	AVON PRODUCTS INC	CDW CORPORATION
AARON'S INC	AXA FINANCIAL INC	CELGENE CORP
ABBOTT LABORATORIES	BAKER HUGHES INC	CELLCO PARTNERSHIP (VERIZON WIRELESS)
ABM INDUSTRIES INC	BALTIMORE GAS AND ELECTRIC COMPANY	
ACADEMY SPORTS & OUTDOORS LTD		CEPHALON INC
	BANK OF AMERICA CORP	CH ROBINSON WORLDWIDE INC
ACCENTURE LTD	BARNES & NOBLE INC	CH2M HILL COMPANIES LTD
ACTIVISION BLIZZARD INC	BASS PRO SHOPS INC	CHARLOTTE RUSSE HOLDING
ACXIOM CORP	BAXTER INTERNATIONAL INC	CHARMING SHOPPES INC
ADC TELECOMMUNICATIONS INC	BDO SEIDMAN LLP	CHEMED CORPORATION
ADESA INC	BEBE STORES INC	CHEVRON CORPORATION
ADOBE SYSTEMS INC	BECHTEL GROUP INC	CHEVRON PHILLIPS CHEMICAL COMPANY LLC
ADVANCE AUTO PARTS INC	BECKMAN COULTER INC	
ADVANCED MICRO DEVICES INC (AMD)	BECTON DICKINSON & CO	CHICO'S FAS INC
	BED BATH & BEYOND INC	CHIPOTLE MEXICAN GRILL INC
AECOM TECHNOLOGY CORPORATION		CHRISTOPHER & BANKS CORP
AES CORPORATION (THE)		CHS INC

CHUBB CORPORATION (THE)	GROUP INC	GENERAL MILLS INC
CIBER INC	DRESS BARN INC (THE)	GENESCO INC
CIGNA CORP	DTE ENERGY COMPANY	GENWORTH FINANCIAL INC
CINTAS CORP	DUKE ENERGY CORP	GEO GROUP INC
CISCO SYSTEMS INC	DYCOM INDUSTRIES INC	GEORGIA GULF CORPORATION
CLUBCORP INC	E I DU PONT DE NEMOURS & CO (DUPONT)	GILEAD SCIENCES INC
COACH INC	EATON CORP	GLOBAL HYATT CORPORATION
COCA-COLA COMPANY (THE)	EBAY INC	GLOBAL PAYMENTS INC
COCA-COLA ENTERPRISES INC	EDISON INTERNATIONAL	GOLDMAN SACHS GROUP INC
COGNIZANT TECHNOLOGY SOLUTIONS CORP	ELECTRONIC ARTS INC	GOOGLE INC
COLDWATER CREEK INC	ELI LILLY & COMPANY	GRANT THORNTON LLP
COLGATE PALMOLIVE CO	EMBARQ CORP	GUESS? INC
COMCAST CORP	EMC CORP	HALLIBURTON COMPANY
COMMUNITY HEALTH SYSTEMS INC	EMERITUS CORP	HARRAH'S ENTERTAINMENT INC
CONAGRA FOODS INC	EMERSON ELECTRIC CO	HARRIS CORPORATION
CONOCOPHILLIPS COMPANY	ENTERGY CORP	HARTFORD FINANCIAL SERVICES GROUP INC (THE)
CONSOL ENERGY INC	ENTERPRISE PRODUCTS PARTNERS LP	HAWAIIAN ELECTRIC INDUSTRIES INC
CONSOLIDATED EDISON INC	ENTERPRISE RENT-A-CAR	HCA INC
CONTAINER STORE (THE)	ERNST & YOUNG LLP	HE BUTT GROCERY COMPANY (HEB)
CONVERGYS CORPORATION	ESTEE LAUDER COMPANIES INC (THE)	HEALTH CARE SERVICE CORPORATION
COOPER COMPANIES INC	EXELON CORPORATION	
COSTCO WHOLESALE CORP	EXPERIAN AMERICAS	HEALTH FITNESS CORP
COVANCE INC	EXPRESS SCRIPTS INC	HEALTH MANAGEMENT ASSOCIATES INC
COVENTRY HEALTH CARE INC	EXXON MOBIL CORPORATION (EXXONMOBIL)	HEALTH NET INC
COX COMMUNICATIONS INC	EXXONMOBIL CHEMICAL	HEALTHWAYS INC
CR BARD INC	FAMILY DOLLAR STORES INC	HELMERICH & PAYNE INC
CRACKER BARREL OLD COUNTRY STORE INC	FEDEX CORPORATION	HENRY SCHEIN INC
CTS CORP	FINISH LINE INC (THE)	HERTZ GLOBAL HOLDINGS INC
CUBIC CORP	FIRST ADVANTAGE CORPORATION	HESS CORPORATION
CUMMINS INC	FIRST DATA CORP	HEWITT ASSOCIATES
CVS CAREMARK CORPORATION	FIRSTENERGY CORP	HIBBETT SPORTS INC
DANAHER CORP	FLUOR CORP	HILTON HOTELS CORP
DARDEN RESTAURANTS INC	FOREST LABORATORIES INC	HOME DEPOT INC
DAVITA INC	FORTUNE BRANDS INC	HONEYWELL INTERNATIONAL INC
DEAN FOODS CO	FOSSIL INC	HUMANA INC
DEERE & CO	FOSTER WHEELER AG	IAC/INTERACTIVECORP
DELOITTE & TOUCHE USA LLP	FOX ENTERTAINMENT GROUP INC	IBM GLOBAL SERVICES
DELOITTE CONSULTING LLP	FPL GROUP INC	ICT GROUP INC
DENNY'S CORPORATION	FRED'S INC	IDEXX LABORATORIES INC
DEVON ENERGY CORPORATION	FRONTIER COMMUNICATIONS CORPORATION	IGATE CORPORATION
DEVRY INC		IMS HEALTH INC
DIAMOND OFFSHORE DRILLING INC	FTI CONSULTING INC	INFOGROUP INC
DICK'S SPORTING GOODS INC	GAMESTOP CORP	INGRAM MICRO INC
DIEBOLD INC	GENENTECH INC	INTEL CORP
DINEEQUITY INC	GENERAL CABLE CORP	INTERNATIONAL BUSINESS MACHINES CORP (IBM)
DIRECTV GROUP INC (THE)	GENERAL DYNAMICS CORP	
DOLE FOOD COMPANY INC	GENERAL ELECTRIC CO (GE)	INTUIT INC
DOLLAR GENERAL CORPORATION		
DOLLAR THRIFTY AUTOMOTIVE		

INVENTIV HEALTH INC	MAXIM INTEGRATED PRODUCTS INC	PARSONS BRINCKERHOFF INC
J C PENNEY COMPANY INC	MAYO FOUNDATION FOR MEDICAL EDUCATION AND RESEARCH	PATTERSON COMPANIES INC
JABIL CIRCUIT INC		PATTERSON-UTI ENERGY INC
JACK IN THE BOX INC	MCAFEE INC	PAYCHEX INC
JACOBS ENGINEERING GROUP INC	MCDERMOTT INTERNATIONAL INC	PEABODY ENERGY CORP
JETBLUE AIRWAYS CORPORATION	MCDONALD'S CORP	PEPSI BOTTLING GROUP INC
JM SMUCKER CO	MCKESSON CORPORATION	PEPSICO INC
JOHNSON & JOHNSON	MCKINSEY & COMPANY INC	PEROT SYSTEMS CORP
JOHNSON CONTROLS INC	MEDCO HEALTH SOLUTIONS	PERRIGO CO
JP MORGAN CHASE & CO INC	MEDTRONIC INC	PETCO ANIMAL SUPPLIES INC
JUNIPER NETWORKS INC	MEIJER INC	PETSMART INC
KAISER PERMANENTE	MEN'S WEARHOUSE INC (THE)	PFIZER INC
KEANE INC	MERCER INC	PG&E CORPORATION
KELLOGG CO	MERCK & CO INC	PHARMACEUTICAL PRODUCT DEVELOPMENT INC
KELLY SERVICES INC	METLIFE INC	
KENDLE INTERNATIONAL INC	MGM MIRAGE	PITNEY BOWES INC
KIMBERLY-CLARK CORP	MICROCHIP TECHNOLOGY INC	PLEXUS CORP
KINDRED HEALTHCARE INC	MICRON TECHNOLOGY INC	POLO RALPH LAUREN CORP
KOCH INDUSTRIES INC	MICROSOFT CORP	PRAXAIR INC
KOHL'S CORP	MIDAMERICAN ENERGY HOLDINGS CO	PRECISION CASTPARTS CORP
KPMG LLP		PRICESMART INC
KRAFT FOODS INC	MILLIPORE CORP	PRICEWATERHOUSECOOPERS
KROGER CO (THE)	MONRO MUFFLER BRAKE INC	PRIDE INTERNATIONAL INC
L-3 COMMUNICATIONS HOLDINGS INC	MONSANTO CO	PRINCIPAL FINANCIAL GROUP (THE)
	MURPHY OIL CORPORATION	
LABORATORY CORP OF AMERICA HOLDINGS	MYLAN INC	PROCTER & GAMBLE CO
	NATIONAL OILWELL VARCO INC	PROGRESSIVE CORPORATION (THE)
LAS VEGAS SANDS CORP (THE VENETIAN)	NETAPP INC	
	NEWS CORP	PRUDENTIAL FINANCIAL INC
LEVEL 3 COMMUNICATIONS INC	NII HOLDINGS INC	PSYCHIATRIC SOLUTIONS INC
LEXMARK INTERNATIONAL INC	NIKE INC	PUBLIC STORAGE INC
LIBERTY GLOBAL INC	NOBLE CORPORATION	PUBLIX SUPER MARKETS INC
LIBERTY MUTUAL GROUP INC	NORTHROP GRUMMAN CORP	QUALCOMM INC
LIMITED BRANDS INC	NRG ENERGY INC	QUANTA SERVICES INC
LINCARE HOLDINGS INC	OCCIDENTAL PETROLEUM CORP	QUEST DIAGNOSTICS INC
LINCOLN NATIONAL CORPORATION	OCEANEERING INTERNATIONAL INC	QUIKSILVER INC
LKQ CORP		R R DONNELLEY & SONS CO
LOCKHEED MARTIN CORP	ODYSSEY HEALTHCARE INC	RALCORP HOLDINGS INC
LODGIAN INC	OFFICE DEPOT INC	RAYTHEON CO
LOEWS CORPORATION	OIL STATES INTERNATIONAL INC	REGIS CORPORATION
LOWE'S COMPANIES INC	OMNICARE INC	RENT-A-CENTER INC
MACY'S INC	OMNICOM GROUP INC	RES CARE INC
MANOR CARE INC	ORACLE CORP	RITE AID CORPORATION
MANPOWER INC	O'REILLY AUTOMOTIVE INC	RITZ-CARLTON HOTEL COMPANY LLC (THE)
MARRIOTT INTERNATIONAL INC	OSHKOSH CORPORATION	
MARS INC	OSI RESTAURANT PARTNERS LLC	ROBERT HALF INTERNATIONAL INC
MARSH & MCLENNAN COMPANIES INC	OWENS & MINOR INC	ROSS STORES INC
	PANTRY INC (THE)	ROYAL CARIBBEAN CRUISES LTD
MARY KAY INC	PARAMETRIC TECHNOLOGY CORP	RRI ENERGY INC
MASSEY ENERGY COMPANY	PAREXEL INTERNATIONAL CORP	SABRE HOLDINGS CORP
MATTEL INC		SAFECO INSURANCE COMPANY OF

AMERICA	TEAM INC	WATSON WYATT WORLDWIDE INC
SAFEWAY INC	TECH DATA CORP	WEATHERFORD INTERNATIONAL LTD
SAIC INC	TEKTRONIX INC	WEIGHT WATCHERS INTERNATIONAL INC
SAM'S CLUB	TELEDYNE TECHNOLOGIES INCORPORATED	WELLPOINT INC
SAPIENT CORPORATION	TELEPHONE AND DATA SYSTEMS INC (TDS)	WELLS FARGO & CO
SARA LEE CORP	TELETECH HOLDINGS INC	WENDY'S/ARBY'S GROUP INC
SAS INSTITUTE INC	TESORO CORP	WEST CORPORATION
SCANA CORPORATION	THERMO FISHER SCIENTIFIC INC	WEST PHARMACEUTICAL SERVICES INC
SCHERING-PLOUGH CORP	TIFFANY & CO	WESTERN DIGITAL CORP
SCHLUMBERGER LIMITED	TIME WARNER INC	WHOLE FOODS MARKET INC
SCIENTIFIC GAMES CORPORATION	TJX COMPANIES INC (THE)	WILLIAMS COMPANIES INC (THE)
SCOTTS MIRACLE GROW CO	T-MOBILE USA	WW GRAINGER INC
SEACOR HOLDINGS INC	TOTAL SYSTEM SERVICES INC (TSYS)	WYETH
SELECT MEDICAL	TOWERS PERRIN	WYNDHAM WORLDWIDE
SEMPRA ENERGY	TRANSOCEAN INC	WYNN RESORTS LIMITED
SENSIENT TECHNOLOGIES CORPORATION	TRAVELERS COMPANIES INC (THE)	XEROX CORP
SHAW GROUP INC (THE)	TREEHOUSE FOODS INC	YAHOO! INC
SHELL OIL CO	TW TELECOM INC	YUM! BRANDS INC
SHERWIN WILLIAMS COMPANY (THE)	TYSON FOODS INC	ZIMMER HOLDINGS INC
SIGMA-ALDRICH CORP	UNITED NATURAL FOODS INC	
SISTERS OF MERCY HEALTH SYSTEMS	UNITED PARCEL SERVICE INC (UPS)	**Retail Sales**
SMITH INTERNATIONAL INC	UNITED STATES CELLULAR CORP	7-ELEVEN INC
SMITHFIELD FOODS INC	UNITED TECHNOLOGIES CORPORATION	AARON'S INC
SOUTHERN CALIFORNIA EDISON COMPANY	UNITEDHEALTH GROUP INC	ACADEMY SPORTS & OUTDOORS LTD
SOUTHERN COMPANY (THE)	UNIVERSAL HEALTH SERVICES INC	ADVANCE AUTO PARTS INC
SOUTHWEST AIRLINES CO	UNIVISION COMMUNICATIONS INC	AMAZON.COM INC
SRA INTERNATIONAL INC	URS CORPORATION	ANNTAYLOR STORES CORP
ST JUDE MEDICAL INC	USAA	APPLE INC
STAPLES INC	VALERO ENERGY CORP	AT&T INC
STARTEK INC	VALSPAR CORPORATION (THE)	AUTOZONE INC
STARWOOD HOTELS & RESORTS WORLDWIDE INC	VARIAN MEDICAL SYSTEMS INC	AVIS BUDGET GROUP INC
STERIS CORP	VCA ANTECH INC	AVON PRODUCTS INC
STIFEL FINANCIAL CORP	VERISIGN INC	BARNES & NOBLE INC
STRYKER CORP	VERIZON COMMUNICATIONS	BASS PRO SHOPS INC
SUN HEALTHCARE GROUP	VIACOM INC	BEBE STORES INC
SUNGARD DATA SYSTEMS INC	VICTORIAS SECRET	BED BATH & BEYOND INC
SUNOCO INC	VISA INC	BERKSHIRE HATHAWAY INC
SUNRISE SENIOR LIVING	VOLT INFORMATION SCIENCES INC	BEST BUY CO INC
SUPERVALU INC	W R BERKLEY CORPORATION	BJ'S WHOLESALE CLUB INC
SYKES ENTERPRISES INC	WABTEC CORP	BUCKLE INC (THE)
SYMANTEC CORP	WALGREEN CO	CABELA'S INC
SYNOPSYS INC	WAL-MART STORES INC	CARMAX GROUP
SYNTEL INC	WALT DISNEY COMPANY (THE)	CASH AMERICA INTERNATIONAL INC
SYSCO CORP	WASTE MANAGEMENT INC	CELLCO PARTNERSHIP (VERIZON WIRELESS)
TARGET CORPORATION	WATERS CORP	CHARLOTTE RUSSE HOLDING
TBC CORPORATION	WATSON PHARMACEUTICALS INC	

CHARMING SHOPPES INC	SAFEWAY INC	AXA FINANCIAL INC
CHICO'S FAS INC	SAM'S CLUB	BARNES & NOBLE INC
CHRISTOPHER & BANKS CORP	SCOTTS MIRACLE GROW CO	BASS PRO SHOPS INC
COACH INC	SHERWIN WILLIAMS COMPANY (THE)	BAXTER INTERNATIONAL INC
COLDWATER CREEK INC		BEBE STORES INC
CONTAINER STORE (THE)	STAPLES INC	BECHTEL GROUP INC
COSTCO WHOLESALE CORP	SUPERVALU INC	BED BATH & BEYOND INC
CVS CAREMARK CORPORATION	TARGET CORPORATION	BERKSHIRE HATHAWAY INC
DICK'S SPORTING GOODS INC	TBC CORPORATION	BEST BUY CO INC
DOLLAR GENERAL CORPORATION	TIFFANY & CO	BJ'S WHOLESALE CLUB INC
DOLLAR THRIFTY AUTOMOTIVE GROUP INC	TJX COMPANIES INC (THE)	BLACK & DECKER CORP
	T-MOBILE USA	BLOOMBERG LP
DRESS BARN INC (THE)	UNITED STATES CELLULAR CORP	BRINKS COMPANY (THE)
ENTERPRISE RENT-A-CAR	VALERO ENERGY CORP	BUCKLE INC (THE)
ESTEE LAUDER COMPANIES INC (THE)	VERIZON COMMUNICATIONS	CABELA'S INC
FAMILY DOLLAR STORES INC	VICTORIAS SECRET	CABLEVISION SYSTEMS CORP
FINISH LINE INC (THE)	WALGREEN CO	CARDINAL HEALTH INC
FOSSIL INC	WAL-MART STORES INC	CARMAX GROUP
FRED'S INC	WHOLE FOODS MARKET INC	CARNIVAL CORPORATION
GAMESTOP CORP		CASH AMERICA INTERNATIONAL INC
GENESCO INC	**Sales Trainees**	CDW CORPORATION
GUESS? INC	3M COMPANY	CELLCO PARTNERSHIP (VERIZON WIRELESS)
HE BUTT GROCERY COMPANY (HEB)	7-ELEVEN INC	CHARLOTTE RUSSE HOLDING
HERTZ GLOBAL HOLDINGS INC	AARON'S INC	CHARMING SHOPPES INC
HIBBETT SPORTS INC	ABBOTT LABORATORIES	CHEMED CORPORATION
HOME DEPOT INC	ABM INDUSTRIES INC	CHEVRON CORPORATION
J C PENNEY COMPANY INC	ACADEMY SPORTS & OUTDOORS LTD	CHICO'S FAS INC
KOHL'S CORP	ADESA INC	CHRISTOPHER & BANKS CORP
KROGER CO (THE)	ADOBE SYSTEMS INC	CHUBB CORPORATION (THE)
LIMITED BRANDS INC	ADVANCE AUTO PARTS INC	CINTAS CORP
LOWE'S COMPANIES INC	AETNA INC	CISCO SYSTEMS INC
MACY'S INC	AFLAC INC	COACH INC
MARY KAY INC	ALLSTATE CORPORATION (THE)	COCA-COLA COMPANY (THE)
MEIJER INC	ALTRIA GROUP INC	COCA-COLA ENTERPRISES INC
MEN'S WEARHOUSE INC (THE)	AMAZON.COM INC	COLDWATER CREEK INC
NIKE INC	AMERICAN POWER CONVERSION (APC)	COLGATE PALMOLIVE CO
OFFICE DEPOT INC	AMERISOURCEBERGEN CORP	COMCAST CORP
O'REILLY AUTOMOTIVE INC	AMGEN INC	CONOCOPHILLIPS COMPANY
PANTRY INC (THE)	ANNTAYLOR STORES CORP	CONTAINER STORE (THE)
PETCO ANIMAL SUPPLIES INC	APPLE INC	COSTCO WHOLESALE CORP
PETSMART INC	ARAMARK CORPORATION	COX COMMUNICATIONS INC
POLO RALPH LAUREN CORP	ARROW ELECTRONICS INC	CRACKER BARREL OLD COUNTRY STORE INC
PRICESMART INC	AT&T INC	CVS CAREMARK CORPORATION
PUBLIX SUPER MARKETS INC	AUTOMATIC DATA PROCESSING INC	DANAHER CORP
QUIKSILVER INC	AUTOZONE INC	DEAN FOODS CO
REGIS CORPORATION	AVERY DENNISON CORP	DICK'S SPORTING GOODS INC
RENT-A-CENTER INC	AVIS BUDGET GROUP INC	DIEBOLD INC
RITE AID CORPORATION	AVON PRODUCTS INC	DIRECTV GROUP INC (THE)
ROSS STORES INC		

DOLE FOOD COMPANY INC	JUNIPER NETWORKS INC	QUIKSILVER INC
DOLLAR GENERAL CORPORATION	KELLOGG CO	R R DONNELLEY & SONS CO
DOLLAR THRIFTY AUTOMOTIVE GROUP INC	KELLY SERVICES INC	RENT-A-CENTER INC
DRESS BARN INC (THE)	KIMBERLY-CLARK CORP	RITE AID CORPORATION
ELECTRONIC ARTS INC	KOHL'S CORP	RITZ-CARLTON HOTEL COMPANY LLC (THE)
ELI LILLY & COMPANY	KRAFT FOODS INC	ROBERT HALF INTERNATIONAL INC
EMBARQ CORP	KROGER CO (THE)	ROSS STORES INC
ENTERPRISE RENT-A-CAR	LAS VEGAS SANDS CORP (THE VENETIAN)	ROYAL CARIBBEAN CRUISES LTD
ESTEE LAUDER COMPANIES INC (THE)	LEXMARK INTERNATIONAL INC	SAFECO INSURANCE COMPANY OF AMERICA
EXPERIAN AMERICAS	LIMITED BRANDS INC	SAFEWAY INC
EXXON MOBIL CORPORATION (EXXONMOBIL)	LINCOLN NATIONAL CORPORATION	SAM'S CLUB
FAMILY DOLLAR STORES INC	LOEWS CORPORATION	SARA LEE CORP
FEDEX CORPORATION	LOWE'S COMPANIES INC	SCHERING-PLOUGH CORP
FINISH LINE INC (THE)	MACY'S INC	SCOTTS MIRACLE GROW CO
FIRST ADVANTAGE CORPORATION	MANPOWER INC	SHERWIN WILLIAMS COMPANY (THE)
FIRST DATA CORP	MARRIOTT INTERNATIONAL INC	SMITHFIELD FOODS INC
FLUOR CORP	MARS INC	SOUTHWEST AIRLINES CO
FORTUNE BRANDS INC	MARY KAY INC	ST JUDE MEDICAL INC
FOSSIL INC	MCKESSON CORPORATION	STAPLES INC
FOSTER WHEELER AG	MEDTRONIC INC	STARWOOD HOTELS & RESORTS WORLDWIDE INC
FRED'S INC	MEIJER INC	SUPERVALU INC
GAMESTOP CORP	MEN'S WEARHOUSE INC (THE)	SYSCO CORP
GENENTECH INC	MERCK & CO INC	TARGET CORPORATION
GENERAL MILLS INC	METLIFE INC	TBC CORPORATION
GENESCO INC	MGM MIRAGE	TECH DATA CORP
GENWORTH FINANCIAL INC	MONSANTO CO	TELEPHONE AND DATA SYSTEMS INC (TDS)
GLOBAL HYATT CORPORATION	NIKE INC	TIFFANY & CO
GLOBAL PAYMENTS INC	OFFICE DEPOT INC	TJX COMPANIES INC (THE)
GUESS? INC	OMNICARE INC	T-MOBILE USA
HARRAH'S ENTERTAINMENT INC	O'REILLY AUTOMOTIVE INC	TOTAL SYSTEM SERVICES INC (TSYS)
HARTFORD FINANCIAL SERVICES GROUP INC (THE)	OWENS & MINOR INC	TRAVELERS COMPANIES INC (THE)
HE BUTT GROCERY COMPANY (HEB)	PANTRY INC (THE)	TYSON FOODS INC
HEALTH FITNESS CORP	PARSONS BRINCKERHOFF INC	UNITED NATURAL FOODS INC
HENRY SCHEIN INC	PATTERSON COMPANIES INC	UNITED STATES CELLULAR CORP
HERTZ GLOBAL HOLDINGS INC	PAYCHEX INC	USAA
HIBBETT SPORTS INC	PEPSI BOTTLING GROUP INC	VALERO ENERGY CORP
HILTON HOTELS CORP	PEPSICO INC	VERIZON COMMUNICATIONS
HOME DEPOT INC	PETCO ANIMAL SUPPLIES INC	VICTORIAS SECRET
INFOGROUP INC	PETSMART INC	VOLT INFORMATION SCIENCES INC
INGRAM MICRO INC	PFIZER INC	W R BERKLEY CORPORATION
INTERNATIONAL BUSINESS MACHINES CORP (IBM)	PITNEY BOWES INC	WALGREEN CO
J C PENNEY COMPANY INC	POLO RALPH LAUREN CORP	WAL-MART STORES INC
JACOBS ENGINEERING GROUP INC	PRICESMART INC	WALT DISNEY COMPANY (THE)
JM SMUCKER CO	PRINCIPAL FINANCIAL GROUP (THE)	WASTE MANAGEMENT INC
JOHNSON & JOHNSON	PROCTER & GAMBLE CO	WEIGHT WATCHERS INTERNATIONAL INC
	PROGRESSIVE CORPORATION (THE)	
	PRUDENTIAL FINANCIAL INC	
	PUBLIX SUPER MARKETS INC	

WENDY'S/ARBY'S GROUP INC	BLACK & DECKER CORP	(EXXONMOBIL)
WHOLE FOODS MARKET INC	BLOOMBERG LP	EXXONMOBIL CHEMICAL
WW GRAINGER INC	BOEING COMPANY (THE)	FEDEX CORPORATION
WYETH	BROADCOM CORP	FIRSTENERGY CORP
WYNDHAM WORLDWIDE	BUCYRUS INTERNATIONAL INC	FLUOR CORP
WYNN RESORTS LIMITED	CABLEVISION SYSTEMS CORP	FOREST LABORATORIES INC
XEROX CORP	CACI INTERNATIONAL INC	FOSSIL INC
ZIMMER HOLDINGS INC	CAMERON INTERNATIONAL CORPORATION	FOSTER WHEELER AG

Technical/Scientific

Engineers, Electrical	CATERPILLAR INC	FOX ENTERTAINMENT GROUP INC
3M COMPANY	CELGENE CORP	FPL GROUP INC
ABBOTT LABORATORIES	CELLCO PARTNERSHIP (VERIZON WIRELESS)	FRONTIER COMMUNICATIONS CORPORATION
ACCENTURE LTD	CEPHALON INC	GENENTECH INC
ACTIVISION BLIZZARD INC	CH2M HILL COMPANIES LTD	GENERAL CABLE CORP
ACXIOM CORP	CHEVRON CORPORATION	GENERAL DYNAMICS CORP
ADC TELECOMMUNICATIONS INC	CHEVRON PHILLIPS CHEMICAL COMPANY LLC	GENERAL ELECTRIC CO (GE)
ADOBE SYSTEMS INC	CIBER INC	GILEAD SCIENCES INC
ADVANCED MICRO DEVICES INC (AMD)	CISCO SYSTEMS INC	GOOGLE INC
AECOM TECHNOLOGY CORPORATION	COGNIZANT TECHNOLOGY SOLUTIONS CORP	HALLIBURTON COMPANY
AES CORPORATION (THE)	COMCAST CORP	HARRIS CORPORATION
AFFILIATED COMPUTER SERVICES INC	CONOCOPHILLIPS COMPANY	HAWAIIAN ELECTRIC INDUSTRIES INC
AGILENT TECHNOLOGIES INC	CONSOLIDATED EDISON INC	HELMERICH & PAYNE INC
AIR PRODUCTS & CHEMICALS INC	COX COMMUNICATIONS INC	HESS CORPORATION
ALLERGAN INC	CTS CORP	HONEYWELL INTERNATIONAL INC
AMERICAN ELECTRIC POWER COMPANY INC (AEP)	CUBIC CORP	IAC/INTERACTIVECORP
AMERICAN POWER CONVERSION (APC)	CUMMINS INC	IBM GLOBAL SERVICES
AMGEN INC	DANAHER CORP	IDEXX LABORATORIES INC
ANADARKO PETROLEUM CORPORATION	DEERE & CO	IGATE CORPORATION
ANALOG DEVICES INC	DEVON ENERGY CORPORATION	IMS HEALTH INC
APACHE CORP	DIAMOND OFFSHORE DRILLING INC	INTEL CORP
APPLE INC	DIEBOLD INC	INTERNATIONAL BUSINESS MACHINES CORP (IBM)
AT&T INC	DIRECTV GROUP INC (THE)	INTUIT INC
AUTOMATIC DATA PROCESSING INC	DTE ENERGY COMPANY	JABIL CIRCUIT INC
BAKER HUGHES INC	DUKE ENERGY CORP	JACOBS ENGINEERING GROUP INC
BALTIMORE GAS AND ELECTRIC COMPANY	DYCOM INDUSTRIES INC	JETBLUE AIRWAYS CORPORATION
BAXTER INTERNATIONAL INC	E I DU PONT DE NEMOURS & CO (DUPONT)	JOHNSON & JOHNSON
BECHTEL GROUP INC	EATON CORP	JOHNSON CONTROLS INC
BECKMAN COULTER INC	EBAY INC	JUNIPER NETWORKS INC
BECTON DICKINSON & CO	EDISON INTERNATIONAL	KEANE INC
BENCHMARK ELECTRONICS INC	ELECTRONIC ARTS INC	KENDLE INTERNATIONAL INC
BERKSHIRE HATHAWAY INC	ELI LILLY & COMPANY	KOCH INDUSTRIES INC
BIO RAD LABORATORIES INC	EMBARQ CORP	L-3 COMMUNICATIONS HOLDINGS INC
	EMC CORP	LEVEL 3 COMMUNICATIONS INC
	EMERSON ELECTRIC CO	LEXMARK INTERNATIONAL INC
	ENTERGY CORP	LIBERTY GLOBAL INC
	EXELON CORPORATION	LOCKHEED MARTIN CORP
	EXXON MOBIL CORPORATION	MATTEL INC
		MAXIM INTEGRATED PRODUCTS

INC	SCIENTIFIC GAMES CORPORATION	YAHOO! INC
MCAFEE INC	SEACOR HOLDINGS INC	
MCDERMOTT INTERNATIONAL INC	SEMPRA ENERGY	**Engineers, Other**
MEDTRONIC INC	SHAW GROUP INC (THE)	3M COMPANY
MERCK & CO INC	SHELL OIL CO	ABBOTT LABORATORIES
MICROCHIP TECHNOLOGY INC	SIGMA-ALDRICH CORP	ACCENTURE LTD
MICRON TECHNOLOGY INC	SMITH INTERNATIONAL INC	AECOM TECHNOLOGY CORPORATION
MICROSOFT CORP	SOUTHERN CALIFORNIA EDISON COMPANY	AES CORPORATION (THE)
MIDAMERICAN ENERGY HOLDINGS CO	SOUTHERN COMPANY (THE)	AIR PRODUCTS & CHEMICALS INC
MILLIPORE CORP	SOUTHWEST AIRLINES CO	ALLERGAN INC
MURPHY OIL CORPORATION	SRA INTERNATIONAL INC	AMERICAN ELECTRIC POWER COMPANY INC (AEP)
MYLAN INC	ST JUDE MEDICAL INC	AMERICAN POWER CONVERSION (APC)
NATIONAL OILWELL VARCO INC	STERIS CORP	
NETAPP INC	SUNGARD DATA SYSTEMS INC	AMGEN INC
NEWS CORP	SUNOCO INC	ANADARKO PETROLEUM CORPORATION
NII HOLDINGS INC	SYMANTEC CORP	APACHE CORP
NOBLE CORPORATION	SYNOPSYS INC	ARCHER DANIELS MIDLAND CO
NORTHROP GRUMMAN CORP	SYNTEL INC	AT&T INC
NRG ENERGY INC	TEKTRONIX INC	AVERY DENNISON CORP
OCCIDENTAL PETROLEUM CORP	TELEDYNE TECHNOLOGIES INCORPORATED	BAKER HUGHES INC
OCEANEERING INTERNATIONAL INC	TELEPHONE AND DATA SYSTEMS INC (TDS)	BALTIMORE GAS AND ELECTRIC COMPANY
OIL STATES INTERNATIONAL INC	TESORO CORP	BAXTER INTERNATIONAL INC
ORACLE CORP	TIME WARNER INC	BECHTEL GROUP INC
OSHKOSH CORPORATION	T-MOBILE USA	BECKMAN COULTER INC
PARAMETRIC TECHNOLOGY CORP	TRANSOCEAN INC	BECTON DICKINSON & CO
PAREXEL INTERNATIONAL CORP	TW TELECOM INC	BENCHMARK ELECTRONICS INC
PARSONS BRINCKERHOFF INC	UNITED PARCEL SERVICE INC (UPS)	BIO RAD LABORATORIES INC
PATTERSON-UTI ENERGY INC	UNITED STATES CELLULAR CORP	BLACK & DECKER CORP
PEROT SYSTEMS CORP	UNITED TECHNOLOGIES CORPORATION	BOEING COMPANY (THE)
PERRIGO CO		BOSTON SCIENTIFIC CORP
PFIZER INC	UNIVISION COMMUNICATIONS INC	BUCYRUS INTERNATIONAL INC
PG&E CORPORATION	URS CORPORATION	BUNGE LTD
PHARMACEUTICAL PRODUCT DEVELOPMENT INC	VALERO ENERGY CORP	CABLEVISION SYSTEMS CORP
PITNEY BOWES INC	VARIAN MEDICAL SYSTEMS INC	CAMERON INTERNATIONAL CORPORATION
PLEXUS CORP	VERISIGN INC	
PRAXAIR INC	VERIZON COMMUNICATIONS	CARGILL INC
PRIDE INTERNATIONAL INC	VIACOM INC	CARNIVAL CORPORATION
QUALCOMM INC	WABTEC CORP	CATERPILLAR INC
QUANTA SERVICES INC	WALT DISNEY COMPANY (THE)	CELGENE CORP
RAYTHEON CO	WATERS CORP	CELLCO PARTNERSHIP (VERIZON WIRELESS)
RRI ENERGY INC	WATSON PHARMACEUTICALS INC	
SABRE HOLDINGS CORP	WEATHERFORD INTERNATIONAL LTD	CEPHALON INC
SAIC INC		CH2M HILL COMPANIES LTD
SAPIENT CORPORATION	WESTERN DIGITAL CORP	CHEVRON CORPORATION
SAS INSTITUTE INC	WILLIAMS COMPANIES INC (THE)	CHEVRON PHILLIPS CHEMICAL COMPANY LLC
SCANA CORPORATION	WYETH	
SCHERING-PLOUGH CORP	XEROX CORP	COCA-COLA COMPANY (THE)
SCHLUMBERGER LIMITED		COCA-COLA ENTERPRISES INC

COLGATE PALMOLIVE CO	HAWAIIAN ELECTRIC INDUSTRIES INC	PRAXAIR INC
COMCAST CORP	HELMERICH & PAYNE INC	PRECISION CASTPARTS CORP
CONAGRA FOODS INC	HESS CORPORATION	PRIDE INTERNATIONAL INC
CONOCOPHILLIPS COMPANY	HONEYWELL INTERNATIONAL INC	PROCTER & GAMBLE CO
CONSOL ENERGY INC	IBM GLOBAL SERVICES	QUANTA SERVICES INC
CONSOLIDATED EDISON INC	IDEXX LABORATORIES INC	RALCORP HOLDINGS INC
COOPER COMPANIES INC	INTERNATIONAL BUSINESS MACHINES CORP (IBM)	RAYTHEON CO
COX COMMUNICATIONS INC		ROYAL CARIBBEAN CRUISES LTD
CR BARD INC	JACOBS ENGINEERING GROUP INC	RRI ENERGY INC
CUBIC CORP	JETBLUE AIRWAYS CORPORATION	SAIC INC
CUMMINS INC	JM SMUCKER CO	SARA LEE CORP
DANAHER CORP	JOHNSON & JOHNSON	SCANA CORPORATION
DEAN FOODS CO	JOHNSON CONTROLS INC	SCHERING-PLOUGH CORP
DEERE & CO	KELLOGG CO	SCHLUMBERGER LIMITED
DEVON ENERGY CORPORATION	KENDLE INTERNATIONAL INC	SCIENTIFIC GAMES CORPORATION
DIAMOND OFFSHORE DRILLING INC	KOCH INDUSTRIES INC	SCOTTS MIRACLE GROW CO
DIRECTV GROUP INC (THE)	KRAFT FOODS INC	SEACOR HOLDINGS INC
DTE ENERGY COMPANY	LEVEL 3 COMMUNICATIONS INC	SEMPRA ENERGY
DUKE ENERGY CORP	LIBERTY GLOBAL INC	SENSIENT TECHNOLOGIES CORPORATION
DYCOM INDUSTRIES INC	LKQ CORP	
E I DU PONT DE NEMOURS & CO (DUPONT)	LOCKHEED MARTIN CORP	SHAW GROUP INC (THE)
	MARS INC	SHELL OIL CO
EATON CORP	MASSEY ENERGY COMPANY	SIGMA-ALDRICH CORP
EDISON INTERNATIONAL	MEDTRONIC INC	SMITH INTERNATIONAL INC
ELI LILLY & COMPANY	MERCK & CO INC	SOUTHERN CALIFORNIA EDISON COMPANY
EMBARQ CORP	MIDAMERICAN ENERGY HOLDINGS CO	
EMERSON ELECTRIC CO		SOUTHERN COMPANY (THE)
ENTERGY CORP	MONSANTO CO	SOUTHWEST AIRLINES CO
ENTERPRISE PRODUCTS PARTNERS LP	MURPHY OIL CORPORATION	ST JUDE MEDICAL INC
	MYLAN INC	STERIS CORP
ESTEE LAUDER COMPANIES INC (THE)	NATIONAL OILWELL VARCO INC	STRYKER CORP
	NII HOLDINGS INC	SUNOCO INC
EXELON CORPORATION	NOBLE CORPORATION	TEAM INC
EXXON MOBIL CORPORATION (EXXONMOBIL)	NORTHROP GRUMMAN CORP	TEKTRONIX INC
	NRG ENERGY INC	TELEDYNE TECHNOLOGIES INCORPORATED
EXXONMOBIL CHEMICAL	OCCIDENTAL PETROLEUM CORP	
FIRSTENERGY CORP	OCEANEERING INTERNATIONAL INC	TELEPHONE AND DATA SYSTEMS INC (TDS)
FLUOR CORP		
FOREST LABORATORIES INC	OIL STATES INTERNATIONAL INC	TESORO CORP
FORTUNE BRANDS INC	OSHKOSH CORPORATION	TIME WARNER INC
FOSTER WHEELER AG	PARAMETRIC TECHNOLOGY CORP	T-MOBILE USA
FPL GROUP INC	PARSONS BRINCKERHOFF INC	TRANSOCEAN INC
FRONTIER COMMUNICATIONS CORPORATION	PATTERSON-UTI ENERGY INC	TREEHOUSE FOODS INC
	PEABODY ENERGY CORP	UNITED STATES CELLULAR CORP
GENENTECH INC	PEPSI BOTTLING GROUP INC	UNITED TECHNOLOGIES CORPORATION
GENERAL CABLE CORP	PEPSICO INC	
GENERAL DYNAMICS CORP	PERRIGO CO	URS CORPORATION
GENERAL MILLS INC	PFIZER INC	VALERO ENERGY CORP
GEORGIA GULF CORPORATION	PG&E CORPORATION	VALSPAR CORPORATION (THE)
GILEAD SCIENCES INC	PITNEY BOWES INC	VARIAN MEDICAL SYSTEMS INC
HALLIBURTON COMPANY		VERIZON COMMUNICATIONS

WABTEC CORP
WASTE MANAGEMENT INC
WATERS CORP
WATSON PHARMACEUTICALS INC
WEATHERFORD INTERNATIONAL LTD
WEST PHARMACEUTICAL SERVICES INC
WILLIAMS COMPANIES INC (THE)
WYETH
XEROX CORP
ZIMMER HOLDINGS INC

Health/Laboratory
3M COMPANY
ABBOTT LABORATORIES
ALLERGAN INC
AMEDISYS INC
AMGEN INC
ASCENSION HEALTH
BAXTER INTERNATIONAL INC
BECKMAN COULTER INC
BECTON DICKINSON & CO
BIO RAD LABORATORIES INC
BOSTON SCIENTIFIC CORP
CATHOLIC HEALTH INITIATIVES
CELGENE CORP
CEPHALON INC
CHEMED CORPORATION
COLGATE PALMOLIVE CO
COMMUNITY HEALTH SYSTEMS INC
COOPER COMPANIES INC
COVANCE INC
CR BARD INC
DAVITA INC
E I DU PONT DE NEMOURS & CO (DUPONT)
ELI LILLY & COMPANY
FOREST LABORATORIES INC
GENENTECH INC
GILEAD SCIENCES INC
HCA INC
HEALTH MANAGEMENT ASSOCIATES INC
HEALTHWAYS INC
IDEXX LABORATORIES INC
IMS HEALTH INC
JOHNSON & JOHNSON
KAISER PERMANENTE
KENDLE INTERNATIONAL INC
KINDRED HEALTHCARE INC

LABORATORY CORP OF AMERICA HOLDINGS
LINCARE HOLDINGS INC
MAYO FOUNDATION FOR MEDICAL EDUCATION AND RESEARCH
MEDTRONIC INC
MERCK & CO INC
METHODIST HEALTH CARE SYSTEM
MILLIPORE CORP
MYLAN INC
ODYSSEY HEALTHCARE INC
PAREXEL INTERNATIONAL CORP
PERRIGO CO
PFIZER INC
PHARMACEUTICAL PRODUCT DEVELOPMENT INC
PROCTER & GAMBLE CO
QUEST DIAGNOSTICS INC
RES CARE INC
SCHERING-PLOUGH CORP
SELECT MEDICAL
SISTERS OF MERCY HEALTH SYSTEMS
ST JUDE MEDICAL INC
STERIS CORP
STRYKER CORP
UNIVERSAL HEALTH SERVICES INC
VARIAN MEDICAL SYSTEMS INC
VCA ANTECH INC
WATERS CORP
WATSON PHARMACEUTICALS INC
WEST PHARMACEUTICAL SERVICES INC
WYETH
ZIMMER HOLDINGS INC

Math/Other
3M COMPANY
ABBOTT LABORATORIES
ADVANCED MICRO DEVICES INC (AMD)
AGILENT TECHNOLOGIES INC
ALLERGAN INC
ALLSTATE CORPORATION (THE)
AMGEN INC
ANALOG DEVICES INC
APPLE INC
AXA FINANCIAL INC
BECHTEL GROUP INC
BECKMAN COULTER INC
BERKSHIRE HATHAWAY INC

BOEING COMPANY (THE)
BOOZ ALLEN HAMILTON
CELGENE CORP
CEPHALON INC
CHEVRON CORPORATION
CHUBB CORPORATION (THE)
CISCO SYSTEMS INC
CONOCOPHILLIPS COMPANY
DELOITTE CONSULTING LLP
DIEBOLD INC
ELI LILLY & COMPANY
EMC CORP
EMERSON ELECTRIC CO
EXPERIAN AMERICAS
EXXON MOBIL CORPORATION (EXXONMOBIL)
FEDEX CORPORATION
FLUOR CORP
FOREST LABORATORIES INC
FOSTER WHEELER AG
GENENTECH INC
GENERAL DYNAMICS CORP
GENERAL ELECTRIC CO (GE)
GENWORTH FINANCIAL INC
GILEAD SCIENCES INC
GOLDMAN SACHS GROUP INC
HARRIS CORPORATION
HARTFORD FINANCIAL SERVICES GROUP INC (THE)
HONEYWELL INTERNATIONAL INC
INTEL CORP
INTERNATIONAL BUSINESS MACHINES CORP (IBM)
JOHNSON & JOHNSON
JOHNSON CONTROLS INC
JUNIPER NETWORKS INC
KENDLE INTERNATIONAL INC
L-3 COMMUNICATIONS HOLDINGS INC
LINCOLN NATIONAL CORPORATION
LOCKHEED MARTIN CORP
LOEWS CORPORATION
MCKINSEY & COMPANY INC
MEDTRONIC INC
MERCK & CO INC
METLIFE INC
MICROSOFT CORP
MILLIPORE CORP
MONSANTO CO
MYLAN INC
NORTHROP GRUMMAN CORP

ORACLE CORP	COMPANY LLC	PARSONS BRINCKERHOFF INC
PAREXEL INTERNATIONAL CORP	COLGATE PALMOLIVE CO	PATTERSON-UTI ENERGY INC
PARSONS BRINCKERHOFF INC	CONOCOPHILLIPS COMPANY	PEABODY ENERGY CORP
PERRIGO CO	CONSOL ENERGY INC	PERRIGO CO
PFIZER INC	CONSOLIDATED EDISON INC	PFIZER INC
PRINCIPAL FINANCIAL GROUP (THE)	DEVON ENERGY CORPORATION	PG&E CORPORATION
PROGRESSIVE CORPORATION (THE)	DIAMOND OFFSHORE DRILLING INC	PRAXAIR INC
	DTE ENERGY COMPANY	PRIDE INTERNATIONAL INC
PRUDENTIAL FINANCIAL INC	DUKE ENERGY CORP	PROCTER & GAMBLE CO
QUALCOMM INC	E I DU PONT DE NEMOURS & CO (DUPONT)	SCANA CORPORATION
RAYTHEON CO		SCHERING-PLOUGH CORP
SAS INSTITUTE INC	EDISON INTERNATIONAL	SCHLUMBERGER LIMITED
SCHERING-PLOUGH CORP	ELI LILLY & COMPANY	SCOTTS MIRACLE GROW CO
SCHLUMBERGER LIMITED	ENTERPRISE PRODUCTS PARTNERS LP	SEACOR HOLDINGS INC
SHELL OIL CO		SEMPRA ENERGY
SRA INTERNATIONAL INC	ESTEE LAUDER COMPANIES INC (THE)	SENSIENT TECHNOLOGIES CORPORATION
SYMANTEC CORP		
TEKTRONIX INC	EXELON CORPORATION	SHELL OIL CO
TELEDYNE TECHNOLOGIES INCORPORATED	EXXON MOBIL CORPORATION (EXXONMOBIL)	SHERWIN WILLIAMS COMPANY (THE)
TRAVELERS COMPANIES INC (THE)	EXXONMOBIL CHEMICAL	SIGMA-ALDRICH CORP
UNITED PARCEL SERVICE INC (UPS)	FIRSTENERGY CORP	SMITH INTERNATIONAL INC
	FLUOR CORP	SOUTHERN COMPANY (THE)
UNITED TECHNOLOGIES CORPORATION	FOREST LABORATORIES INC	SUNOCO INC
	FOSTER WHEELER AG	TESORO CORP
USAA	FPL GROUP INC	TRANSOCEAN INC
VARIAN MEDICAL SYSTEMS INC	GENENTECH INC	VALERO ENERGY CORP
W R BERKLEY CORPORATION	GEORGIA GULF CORPORATION	VALSPAR CORPORATION (THE)
WATSON PHARMACEUTICALS INC	GILEAD SCIENCES INC	WATSON PHARMACEUTICALS INC
WESTERN DIGITAL CORP	HALLIBURTON COMPANY	WEATHERFORD INTERNATIONAL LTD
WYETH	HELMERICH & PAYNE INC	
	HESS CORPORATION	WILLIAMS COMPANIES INC (THE)
	JACOBS ENGINEERING GROUP INC	WYETH
Petroleum/Chemicals	JOHNSON & JOHNSON	
ABBOTT LABORATORIES	KENDLE INTERNATIONAL INC	
AIR PRODUCTS & CHEMICALS INC	KOCH INDUSTRIES INC	**Scientists/Research**
ALLERGAN INC	LINCARE HOLDINGS INC	3M COMPANY
AMGEN INC	MARY KAY INC	ABBOTT LABORATORIES
ANADARKO PETROLEUM CORPORATION	MASSEY ENERGY COMPANY	ADC TELECOMMUNICATIONS INC
	MERCK & CO INC	ADVANCED MICRO DEVICES INC (AMD)
APACHE CORP	MIDAMERICAN ENERGY HOLDINGS CO	
ARCHER DANIELS MIDLAND CO		AGILENT TECHNOLOGIES INC
AVON PRODUCTS INC	MONSANTO CO	AIR PRODUCTS & CHEMICALS INC
BAKER HUGHES INC	MURPHY OIL CORPORATION	ALLERGAN INC
BALTIMORE GAS AND ELECTRIC COMPANY	MYLAN INC	AMGEN INC
	NATIONAL OILWELL VARCO INC	ANALOG DEVICES INC
BECHTEL GROUP INC	NOBLE CORPORATION	APPLE INC
CARGILL INC	OCCIDENTAL PETROLEUM CORP	ARCHER DANIELS MIDLAND CO
CELGENE CORP	OCEANEERING INTERNATIONAL INC	BAXTER INTERNATIONAL INC
CEPHALON INC		BECKMAN COULTER INC
CHEVRON CORPORATION	OIL STATES INTERNATIONAL INC	BECTON DICKINSON & CO
CHEVRON PHILLIPS CHEMICAL		BIO RAD LABORATORIES INC

BOEING COMPANY (THE)	MICROCHIP TECHNOLOGY INC
BOSTON SCIENTIFIC CORP	MICRON TECHNOLOGY INC
BUNGE LTD	MICROSOFT CORP
CARGILL INC	MILLIPORE CORP
CELGENE CORP	MONSANTO CO
CEPHALON INC	MYLAN INC
CHEVRON CORPORATION	NORTHROP GRUMMAN CORP
CHEVRON PHILLIPS CHEMICAL COMPANY LLC	ORACLE CORP
CISCO SYSTEMS INC	PAREXEL INTERNATIONAL CORP
COLGATE PALMOLIVE CO	PERRIGO CO
CONOCOPHILLIPS COMPANY	PFIZER INC
COVANCE INC	PHARMACEUTICAL PRODUCT DEVELOPMENT INC
CR BARD INC	PRAXAIR INC
CUBIC CORP	PROCTER & GAMBLE CO
DAVITA INC	QUALCOMM INC
DIEBOLD INC	QUEST DIAGNOSTICS INC
E I DU PONT DE NEMOURS & CO (DUPONT)	RAYTHEON CO
EATON CORP	SAIC INC
ELI LILLY & COMPANY	SAS INSTITUTE INC
EMC CORP	SCHERING-PLOUGH CORP
EMERSON ELECTRIC CO	SCHLUMBERGER LIMITED
ESTEE LAUDER COMPANIES INC (THE)	SCOTTS MIRACLE GROW CO
EXXON MOBIL CORPORATION (EXXONMOBIL)	SENSIENT TECHNOLOGIES CORPORATION
EXXONMOBIL CHEMICAL	SHELL OIL CO
FOREST LABORATORIES INC	SHERWIN WILLIAMS COMPANY (THE)
GENENTECH INC	SIGMA-ALDRICH CORP
GENERAL DYNAMICS CORP	ST JUDE MEDICAL INC
GENERAL ELECTRIC CO (GE)	STERIS CORP
GEORGIA GULF CORPORATION	STRYKER CORP
GILEAD SCIENCES INC	TEKTRONIX INC
HALLIBURTON COMPANY	TELEDYNE TECHNOLOGIES INCORPORATED
HARRIS CORPORATION	UNITED TECHNOLOGIES CORPORATION
HONEYWELL INTERNATIONAL INC	VALSPAR CORPORATION (THE)
IDEXX LABORATORIES INC	VARIAN MEDICAL SYSTEMS INC
INTEL CORP	WATERS CORP
INTERNATIONAL BUSINESS MACHINES CORP (IBM)	WATSON PHARMACEUTICALS INC
JOHNSON & JOHNSON	WEST PHARMACEUTICAL SERVICES INC
JOHNSON CONTROLS INC	WESTERN DIGITAL CORP
JUNIPER NETWORKS INC	WYETH
KENDLE INTERNATIONAL INC	XEROX CORP
LABORATORY CORP OF AMERICA HOLDINGS	
LOCKHEED MARTIN CORP	
MAXIM INTEGRATED PRODUCTS INC	
MEDTRONIC INC	
MERCK & CO INC	